P9-EEK-468

FOR REFERENCE

Do Not Take From This Room

Short Story Criticism

Guide to Gale Literary Criticism Series

For criticism on	Consult these Gale series
Authors now living or who died after December 31, 1959	*CONTEMPORARY LITERARY CRITICISM (CLC)*
Authors who died between 1900 and 1959	*TWENTIETH-CENTURY LITERARY CRITICISM (TCLC)*
Authors who died between 1800 and 1899	*NINETEENTH-CENTURY LITERATURE CRITICISM (NCLC)*
Authors who died between 1400 and 1799	*LITERATURE CRITICISM FROM 1400 TO 1800 (LC)* *SHAKESPEAREAN CRITICISM (SC)*
Authors who died before 1400	*CLASSICAL AND MEDIEVAL LITERATURE CRITICISM (CMLC)*
Black writers of the past two hundred years	*BLACK LITERATURE CRITICISM (BLC)*
Authors of books for children and young adults	*CHILDREN'S LITERATURE REVIEW (CLR)*
Dramatists	*DRAMA CRITICISM (DC)*
Hispanic writers of the late nineteenth and twentieth centuries	*HISPANIC LITERATURE CRITICISM (HLC)*
Native North American writers and orators of the eighteenth, nineteenth, and twentieth centuries	*NATIVE NORTH AMERICAN LITERATURE (NNAL)*
Poets	*POETRY CRITICISM (PC)*
Short story writers	*SHORT STORY CRITICISM (SSC)*
Major authors from the Renaissance to the present	*WORLD LITERATURE CRITICISM, 1500 TO THE PRESENT (WLC)*

ISSN 0895-9493

Volume 18

Short Story Criticism

Excerpts from Criticism of the Works of Short Fiction Writers

Drew Kalasky, Editor

Margaret Haerens
Jeff Hill
Jane Kelly Kosek
Thomas Ligotti
Christine Slovey
Lawrence J. Trudeau
Associate Editors

Gale Research Inc.

An International Thomson Publishing Company

Riverside Community College
Library
4800 Magnolia Avenue
Riverside, California 92506

JUL '95

Changing the Way the World Learns

NEW YORK • LONDON • BONN • BOSTON • DETROIT • MADRID
MELBOURNE • MEXICO CITY • PARIS • SINGAPORE • TOKYO
TORONTO • WASHINGTON • ALBANY NY • BELMONT CA • CINCINNATI OH

REF PN 3373 .S386 v.18

Short story criticism

STAFF

Drew Kalasky, *Editor*

Margaret Haerens, Jeff Hill, Jane Kelly Kosek, Thomas Ligotti,
Christine Slovey, Lawrence J. Trudeau,
Associate Editors

Martha Bommarito, Debra A. Wells, *Assistant Editors*

Marlene H. Lasky, *Permissions Manager*
Margaret A. Chamberlain, Linda M. Pugliese, *Permissions Specialists*

Susan Brohman, Diane Cooper, Maria Franklin, Arlene Johnson, Michele Lonoconus, Maureen Puhl,
Shalice Shah, Kimberly F. Smilay, Barbara A. Wallace, *Permissions Associates*

Edna Hedblad, Margaret McAvoy-Amato, Tyra Y. Phillips, Lori Schoenenberger, *Permissions Assistants*

Victoria B. Cariappa, *Research Manager*
Maria E. Bryson, Eva M. Felts, Mary Beth McElmeel, Tamara C. Nott, Michele P. Pica,
Tracie A. Richardson, Norma Sawaya, Amy T. Steel, *Research Associates*

Alicia Noel Biggers, Melissa E. Brown, Julia C. Daniel, Michele McRobert,
Phyllis N. Shepherd, *Research Assistants*

Mary Beth Trimper, *Production Director*
Mary Kelley, *Production Associate*

Barbara J. Yarrow, *Graphic Services Supervisor*
Sherrell Hobbs, *Macintosh Artist*
Willie F. Mathis, *Camera Operator*
Pamela Hayes, *Photography Coordinator*

Jeff Hill, Drew Kalasky, Jane Kelly Kosek, Michael L. LaBlanc,
Christine Slovey, Lawrence J. Trudeau, *Desktop Typesetters*

Since this page cannot legibly accommodate all copyright notices, the acknowledgments constitute an extension of the copyright notice.

While every effort has been made to ensure the reliability of the information presented in this publication, Gale Research Inc. neither guarantees the accuracy of the data contained herein nor assumes any responsibility for errors, omissions or discrepancies. Gale accepts no payment for listing, and inclusion in the publication of any organization, agency, institution, publication, service, or individual does not imply endorsement of the editors or publisher. Errors brought to the attention of the publisher and verified to the satisfaction of the publisher will be corrected in future editions.

The paper used in this publication meets the minimum requirements of American National Standard for Information Sciences—Permanence Paper for Printed Library Materials, ANSI Z39.48-1984. ∞™

This publication is a creative work fully protected by all applicable copyright laws, as well as by misappropriation, trade secret, unfair competition, and other applicable laws. The authors and editors of this work have added value to the underlying factual material herein through one or more of the following: unique and original selection, coordination, expression, arrangement, and classification of the information.

All rights to this publication will be vigorously defended.

Copyright © 1995
Gale Research Inc.
835 Penobscot Building
Detroit, MI 48226-4094

All rights reserved including the right of reproduction in whole or in part in any form.

Library of Congress Catalog Card Number 88-641014
ISBN 0-8103-9282-8
ISSN 0895-9493

Printed in the United States of America
10 9 8 7 6 5 4 3 2 1

Contents

Preface   vii

Acknowledgments   xi

Charles Baudelaire 1821-1867 1

Mikhail Bulgakov 1891-1940.. 68

Daphne du Maurier 1907-1989 124

Hamlin Garland 1860-1940 140

Henry Lawson 1867-1922 196

Gordon Lish 1934-.. 265

Robert Musil 1880-1942 287

Gérard de Nerval 1808-1855.. 327

Ruth Suckow 1892-1960 388

Appendix: Select Bibliography of General Sources on Short Fiction   427

Literary Criticism Series Cumulative Author Index   433

SSC Cumulative Nationality Index   505

SSC Cumulative Title Index   507

Preface

A Comprehensive Information Source
on World Short Fiction

S hort Story Criticism (SSC) presents significant passages from criticism of the world's greatest short story writers and provides supplementary biographical and bibliographical materials to guide the interested reader to a greater understanding of the authors of short fiction. This series was developed in response to suggestions from librarians serving high school, college, and public library patrons, who had noted a considerable number of requests for critical material on short story writers. Although major short story writers are covered in such Gale series as *Contemporary Literary Criticism (CLC), Twentieth-Century Literary Criticism (TCLC), Nineteenth-Century Literature Criticism (NCLC),* and *Literature Criticism from 1400 to 1800 (LC),* librarians perceived the need for a series devoted solely to writers of the short story genre.

Coverage

SSC is designed to serve as an introduction to major short story writers of all eras and nationalities. Since these authors have inspired a great deal of relevant critical material, *SSC* is necessarily selective, and the editors have chosen the most important published criticism to aid readers and students in their research.

Approximately eight to ten authors are included in each volume, and each entry presents a historical survey of the critical response to that author's work. The length of an entry is intended to reflect the amount of critical attention the author has received from critics writing in English and from foreign critics in translation. Every attempt has been made to identify and include excerpts from the most significant essays on each author's work. In order to provide these important critical pieces, the editors sometimes reprint essays that have appeared elsewhere in Gale's Literary Criticism Series. Such duplication, however, never exceeds twenty percent of an *SSC* volume.

Organization

An *SSC* author entry consists of the following elements:

- The **Author Heading** cites the name under which the author most commonly wrote, followed by birth and death dates. If the author wrote consistently under a pseudonym, the pseudonym will be listed in the author heading and the author's actual name given in parentheses on the first line of the biographical and critical introduction.

- The **Biographical and Critical Introduction** contains background information designed to introduce a reader to the author and the critical debates surrounding his or her work.

- A **Portrait of the Author** is included when available. Many entries also contain illustrations of materials pertinent to an author's career, including holographs of manuscript pages, title pages, dust jackets, letters, or representations of important people, places, and events in the author's life.

- The list of **Principal Works** is chronological by date of first publication and lists the most important works by the author. The first section comprises short story collections, novellas, and novella collections. The second section gives information on other major works by the author. For foreign authors, the editors have provided original foreign-language publication information and have selected what are considered the best and most complete English-language editions of their works.

- **Criticism** is arranged chronologically in each author entry to provide a useful perspective on changes in critical evaluation over the years. All short story, novella, and collection titles by the author featured in the entry are printed in boldface type to enable a reader to ascertain without difficulty the works discussed. Also for purposes of easier identification, the critic's name and the publication date of the essay are given at the beginning of each piece of criticism. Unsigned criticism is preceded by the title of the journal in which it appeared.

- Critical essays are prefaced with **Explanatory Notes** as an additional aid to students and readers using *SSC*. An explanatory note may provide useful information of several types, including: the reputation of the critic, the intent or scope of the critical essay, and the orientation of the criticism (biographical, psychoanalytic, structuralist, etc.).

- A complete **Bibliographical Citation,** designed to help the interested reader locate the original essay or book, precedes each piece of criticism.

- The **Further Reading List** appearing at the end of each author entry suggests additional materials on the author. In some cases it includes essays for which the editors could not obtain reprint rights. Boxed material following the further reading list provides references to other biographical and critical sources on the author in series published by Gale.

Beginning with volume six, *SSC* contains two additional features designed to enhance the reader's understanding of short fiction writers and their works:

- Each *SSC* entry now includes, when available, **Comments by the Author** that illuminate his or her own works or the short story genre in general. These statements are set within boxes or bold rules to distinguish them from the criticism.

- A **Select Bibliography of General Sources on Short Fiction** is included as an appendix. This listing of materials for further research provides readers with a selection of the best available general studies of the short story genre.

Other Features

A **Cumulative Author Index** lists all the authors who have appeared in *SSC, CLC, TCLC, NCLC, LC,* and *Classical and Medieval Literature Criticism (CMLC),* as well as cross-references to other Gale series. Users will welcome this cumulated index as a useful tool for locating an author within the Literary Criticism Series.

A **Cumulative Nationality Index** lists all authors featured in *SSC* by nationality, followed by the number of the *SSC* volume in which their entry appears.

A **Cumulative Title Index** lists in alphabetical order all short story, novella, and collection titles contained in the *SSC* series. Titles of short story collections, separately published novellas, and novella collections are printed in italics, while titles of individual short stories are printed in roman type with quotation marks.

Each title is followed by the author's name and corresponding volume and page numbers where commentary on the work is located. English-language translations of original foreign-language titles are cross-referenced to the foreign titles so that all references to discussion of a work are combined in one listing.

Citing *Short Story Criticism*

When writing papers, students who quote directly from any volume in the Literary Criticism Series may use the following general forms to footnote reprinted criticism. The first example pertains to material drawn from periodicals, the second to material reprinted from books:

[1]Henry James, Jr., "Honoré de Balzac," *The Galaxy 20* (December 1875), 814-36; excerpted and reprinted in *Short Story Criticism,* Vol. 5, ed. Thomas Votteler (Detroit: Gale Research, 1990), pp. 8-11.

[2]F. R. Leavis, *D. H. Lawrence: Novelist* (Alfred A. Knopf, 1956); excerpted and reprinted in *Short Story Criticism,* Vol. 4, ed. Thomas Votteler (Detroit: Gale Research, 1990), pp. 202-06.

Comments

Readers who wish to suggest authors to appear in future volumes, or who have other suggestions, are invited to contact the editors by writing to Gale Research Inc., Literary Criticism Division, 835 Penobscot Building, Detroit, MI 48226-4094.

Acknowledgments

The editors wish to thank the copyright holders of the excerpted criticism included in this volume and the permissions managers of many book and magazine publishing companies for assisting us in securing reprint rights. We are also grateful to the staffs of the Detroit Public Library, the Library of Congress, the University of Detroit Mercy Library, Wayne State University Purdy/Kresge Library Complex, and the University of Michigan Libraries for making their resources available to us. Following is a list of the copyright holders who have granted us permission to reprint material in this volume of *SSC*. Every effort has been made to trace copyright, but if omissions have been made, please let us know.

EXCERPTS IN *SSC*, VOLUME 18, WERE REPRINTED FROM THE FOLLOWING PERIODICALS:

American Literature, v. XXVI, November, 1954. Copyright 1954, renewed 1982 Duke University Press, Durham, NC. Reprinted by permission of the publisher.—*Australian Literary Studies,* v. 9, May, 1980 for "Narrative Technique in Lawson" by D. R. Jarvis; v. 11, October, 1983 for " 'The Loaded Dog': A Celebration" by Ken Stewart. Both reprinted by permission of the respective authors.—*Brigham Young University Studies,* v. VII, Autumn, 1965. Reprinted by permission of the publisher.—*L'esprit créateur,* v. XXVIII, Spring, 1988. Copyright © 1988 by *L'esprit créateur.* Reprinted by permission of the publisher.—*Literature and Medicine,* v. 7, 1988. Copyright © 1988 by The Johns Hopkins University Press. Reprinted by permission of the publisher.—*Meanjin,* v. XXVII, March, 1968 for " 'The Drover's Wife' Writ Large: One Measure of Lawson's Achievement" by Brian Matthews. Reprinted by permission of the author./ v. XXIV, 1965. Reprinted by permission of Irvington Publishers.—*The Michigan Academician,* v. XXIV, Winter, 1992. Copyright © The Michigan Academy of Science, Arts, and Letters, 1992. Reprinted by permission of the publisher.—*MidAmerica,* v. IX, 1982 for "Hamlin Garland: Realist of Old Age" by Leland Krauth. Copyright 1982 by The Society for the Study of Midwestern Literature. Reprinted by permission of the publisher and the author.—*Modern Austrian Literature,* v. 17, 1984. © copyright International Arthur Schnitzler Association 1984. Reprinted by permission of the publisher.—*Monatshefte,* v. 64, Summer, 1972; v. 79, Summer, 1987. Copyright © 1972, 1987 by the Board of Regents of the University of Wisconsin System. Both reprinted by permission of The University of Wisconsin Press.—*New Statesman,* v. 89, June 20, 1975. © 1975 The Statesman & Nation Publishing Co. Ltd. Reprinted by permission of the publisher.—*New York Herald Tribune Books,* October 3, 1926; August 16, 1931. Copyright 1926, renewed 1953, copyright 1931, renewed 1959 New York Herald Tribune Inc. All rights reserved. Both reprinted by permission.—*The New York Review of Books,* v. XI, July 11, 1968. Copyright © 1968 Nyrev, Inc. Reprinted with permission from *The New York Review of Books.*—*The New York Times Book Review,* July 28, 1968; October 17, 1971. Copyright © 1968, 1971 by The New York Times Company. Both reprinted by permission of the publisher./ October 14, 1923; August 23, 1931; January 6, 1952; March 8, 1953; February 9, 1958; October 25, 1959. Copyright 1923, renewed 1951, copyright 1931, renewed 1960, copyright 1952, renewed 1980, copyright 1953, renewed 1981, copyright © 1958, renewed 1986, copyright © 1959, renewed 1987, by The New York Times Company. All reprinted by permission of the publisher.—*Nineteenth-Century French Studies,* v. XII, Fall-Winter, 1983; v. XII, Fall-Winter, 1983-84 XIV; Fall-Winter, 1985-86. © 1983, 1984, 1986 by T. H. Goetz. All reprinted by permission of the publisher.—*Nottingham French Studies,* v. 20, May, 1981. Reprinted by permission of the publisher.—*Orbis Litterarum,* v. 25, 1970. Reprinted by permission of the publisher.—*The Palimpsest,* v. XXXV, February, 1954. Copyright 1954, renewed 1982 by The State Historical Society of Iowa. Reprinted by permission of the publisher.—*Paragraph,* v. 4, October, 1984.—*Russian Literature Triquarterly,* n. 15, 1978. © 1978 by Ardis Publishers. Reprinted by permission of the publisher.—*The Russian Review,* v. 52, January, 1993. Copyright 1972 by The Russian Review, Inc. Reprinted by permission of the publisher.—*Slavic and East-European Journal,* v. 33, Fall, 1989. © 1989 by AATSEEL of the U.S., Inc. Reprinted by permission of the publisher.—*Slavic Review,* v. 51, Fall, 1992 for "The Social and Political Context of Bulgakov's 'The Fatal Eggs'" by Edythe C. Haber. Copyright © 1992 by the American Association for the Advancement of Slavic Studies, Inc. Reprinted by permission of the publisher and the author.—*The South Dakota Review,* v. 10, Winter, 1972-73. ©

1973, University of South Dakota. Reprinted by permission of the publisher.—*Southerly,* v. 37, March, 1977 for "Narrative Technique in Lawson's Joe Wilson Stories" by John Maddocks. Copyright 1977 by the author. Reprinted by permission of the publisher and the author.—*Studies in Short Fiction,* v. XI, Spring, 1974. Copyright 1974 by Newberry College. Reprinted by permission of the publisher.—*Texas Studies in Literature and Language,* v. XII, Spring, 1970 for "Intimacy and Distance in Baudelaire's Prose-Poems" by Renée Riese Hubert. Copyright © 1970 by the University of Texas Press. Reprinted by permission of the publisher and the author.—*Western American Literature,* v. XV, November, 1980; v. XXI, August, 1986. Copyright 1980, 1986 by the Western Literature Association. Both reprinted by permission of the publisher.

COPYRIGHTED EXCERPTS IN *SSC,* VOLUME 18, WERE REPRINTED FROM THE FOLLOWING BOOKS:

Bangerter, Lowell A. From *Robert Musil.* Continuum, 1989. Copyright © 1988 by Lowell A. Bangerter. All rights reserved. Reprinted by permission of the publisher.—Barnes, John. From an introduction to *The Penguin Henry Lawson: Short Stories.* Edited by John Barnes. Penguin Books, 1986. Introduction copyright © John Barnes, 1986. All rights reserved. Reprinted by permission of Penguin Books Australia Limited.—Bledsoe, Thomas A. From an introduction to *Main-Travelled Roads: Six Mississippi Valley Stories.* By Hamlin Garland, edited by Thomas A. Bledsoe. Rinehart & Co., Inc., 1954. Introduction copyright, 1954, by Thomas A. Bledsoe. Renewed 1982 by Elizabeth Bledsoe. Reprinted by permission of Holt, Rinehart and Winston, Inc.—Chambers, Ross. From *Story and Situation: Narrative Seduction and the Power of Fiction.* University of Minnesota Press, 1984. Copyright © 1984 by the University of Minnesota Press. All rights reserved. Reprinted by permission of the publisher.—Davis, Jack L. From "Hamlin Garland's Indians and the Quality of Civilized Life," in *The Critical Reception of Hamlin Garland: 1891-1978.* Charles L. P. Silet, Robert E. Welch, Richard Boudreau, eds. The Whitston Publishing Company, 1985. Copyright 1985 Charles L. P. Silet, Robert E. Welch and Richard Boudreau, editors. Reprinted by permission of the author.—Folsom, James K. From *The American Western Novel.* NCUP, Inc. (Formerly New College & University Press), 1966. Copyright © 1966 by New College and University Press, Inc. All rights reserved. Reprinted by permission of the publisher.—Forster, Margaret. From *Daphne du Maurier: The Secret Life of the Renowned Storyteller.* Doubleday, 1993. Copyright © 1993 by Margaret Forster. All rights reserved. Used by permission of Doubleday, a division of Bantam Doubleday Dell Publishing Group, Inc.—Hamblen, Abigail Ann. From *Ruth Suckow.* Boise State University, 1978. Copyright 1978 by the Boise State University Western Writers Series. All rights reserved. Reprinted by permission of the publisher and the author.—Heseltine, Harry. From *The Uncertain Self: Essays in Australian Literature and Criticism.* Oxford University Press, Melbourne, 1986. Copyright © 1986 Harry Heseltine. Reprinted by permission of Oxford University Press, Inc.—Hiddleston, J. A. From *Baudelaire and "Le spleen de Paris."* Oxford at the Clarendon Press, 1987. © J. A. Hiddleston 1987. All rights reserved. Reprinted by permission of Oxford University Press.—Kaplan, Edward K. From *Baudelaire's Prose Poems: The Esthetic, the Ethical, and the Religious in the Parisian Prowler.* University of Georgia Press, 1990. © 1990 by the University of Georgia Press. All rights reserved. Reprinted by permission of the publisher.—Kelly, Richard. From *Daphne du Maurier.* Twayne, 1987. Copyright © 1987 by G. K. Hall & Co. All rights reserved. Reprinted with the permission of Twayne Publishers, an imprint of Macmillan Publishing Company.—Kermode, Frank. From a preface to *Five Women.* By Robert Musil, translated by Eithne Wilkins and Ernest Kaiser. Delacorte Press, 1966. Copyright © 1966 by Dell Publishing Co., Inc. All rights reserved. Reprinted by permission of Delacorte Press, a division of Bantam Doubleday Dell Publishing Group, Inc.—Kissane, Leedice McAnelly. From *Ruth Suckow.* Twayne, 1969. Copyright © 1969 by Twayne Publishers, Inc. Reprinted with the permission of Twayne Publishers, Inc., an imprint of Macmillan Publishing Company.—Knapp, Bettina L. From *Gérard de Nerval: The Mystic's Dilemma.* University of Alabama Press, 1980. Copyright © 1980 by The University of Alabama Press. All rights reserved. Reprinted by permission of the publisher.—Knight, Grant C. From *The Critical Period in American Literature.* University of North Carolina Press, 1951. Copyright, 1951, by The University of North Carolina Press. Renewed 1979 by Ruth E. Knight. Reprinted by permission of the publisher.—Lokke, Kari. From *Gérard de Nerval: The Poet as Social Visionary.* French Forum, 1987. Copyright © 1987 by French Forum Publishers, Incorporated, P. O. Box 5108, Lexington, Kentucky 40505. All rights reserved. Reprinted by permission of the publisher.—MacLennan, George. From *Lucid Interval: Subjective Writing and Madness in History.* Fairleigh Dickinson University Press, 1992. © George MacLennan 1992. All rights reserved. Reprinted by permission of the publisher.—Mann, Cecil. From an introduction to *The Stories of Henry Lawson, first series.* Edited by Cecil Mann. Angus and Robertson, 1964, renewed 1992. Copyright. Reprinted by permission of the publisher.—Matthews, Brian. From "Eve Exonerated: Henry Lawson's Unfinished Love Stories," in *Who Is She?* Edited by Shirley Walker. St. Martin's Press, 1983. © University of Queensland Press St. Lucia, Queensland 1983. All rights reserved. Reprinted by permission of University of Queensland Press. In the U.S. with permission of St. Martin's Press, Incorporated.—Monroe, Jonathan. From *A Poverty of Objects: The Prose Poem and the Politics of Genre.* Cornell, 1987. Copyright © 1987 by Cornell University. All rights reserved. Used by permission of the publisher, Cornell University Press.—Noakes, Susan. From *Timely Reading: Between Exegesis and Interpretation.* Cornell, 1988. Copyright © 1988 by Cornell University. All rights reserved. Used by permission of the publisher, Cornell University Press.—Omrcanin, Margaret Stewart. From *Ruth Suckow: A Critical Study of Her Fiction.* Dorrance & Company, 1972. Copyright © 1972 by Margaret Stewart Omrcanin. All rights reserved. Reprinted by permission of the publisher.—Paulson, Ronald M. From "Myth and Fairy Tale in Robert Musil's 'Griga'," in *Turn of the Century: German Literature and Art, 1890-1915.* Edited by Gerald Chapple and Hans H. Schulte. Bouvier Verlag, 1981. © Bouvier Verlag Herbert Grundmann, Bonn 1981. Reprinted by permission of the publisher.—Peters, Frederick G. From *Robert Musil, Master of the Hovering Life: A Study of the Major Fiction.* Columbia University Press, 1978. Copyright © 1978 Columbia University Press, New York. All rights reserved. Reprinted with the permission of the publisher.—Pike, Burton. From *Robert Musil: An Introduction to His Work.* Cornell, 1961. © 1961 by Cornell University. Renewed 1961 Burton Pike. Used by permission of the publisher, Cornell University Press.—Proffer, Ellendea, and Carl R. Proffer. From an introduction to *Diaboliad and Other Stories.* By Mikhail Bulgakov, edited by Ellendea Proffer and Carl R. Proffer, translated by Carl R. Proffer. Copyright © 1972 by Indiana University Press. All rights reserved. Reprinted by permission of the author.—Proffer, Ellendea. From *Bulgakov: Life and Work.* Ardis Publishers, 1984. Copyright © 1984 by Ellendea Proffer. All rights reserved. Reprinted by permission of the publisher.—Roderick, Colin. From *Henry Lawson: Poet and Short Story Writer.* Angus and Robertson, 1966. Copyright 1966 Colin Roderick. Reprinted by permission of the publisher.—Taylor, Walter Fuller. From *The Economic Novel in America.* University of North Carolina Press, 1942. Copyright 1942, by The University of North Carolina Press. Reprinted by permission of the publisher.—Van Doren, Carl. From *Contemporary American Novelists: 1900-1920.* The Macmillan Company, 1922. Copyright 1922 by Macmillan Publishing Company. Renewed 1949 by Carl Van Doren. All rights reserved. Reprinted by permission of the Literary Estate of Carl Van Doren.—Wright, A. Colin. From *Mikhail Bulgakov: Life and Interpretations.* University of Toronto Press, 1978. © University of Toronto Press 1978. Reprinted by permission of University of Toronto Press Incorporated.—Wright, Barbara. From an introduction to *Baudelaire: "La Fanfarlo" and "Le spleen de Paris."* By Barbara Wright and David H. T. Scott. Grant & Cutler Ltd., 1984. © Grant & Cutler Ltd 1984. Reprinted by permission of the publisher.

PHOTOGRAPHS AND ILLUSTRATIONS APPEARING IN *SSC*, VOLUME 18, WERE RECEIVED FROM THE FOLLOWING SOURCES:

Photograph by Charles Schlaks, Jr.: **p. 68**; Bequest of H. W. L. Dana, Harvard Theatre Collection: **p. 79**; Photograph by H & B Graeme, Fowey, England: **p. 124**; Popperfoto: **p. 131**; The Granger Collection, New York: **pp. 140, 287**; Culver Pictures: **p. 188**; Photograph by Bill Haywood: **p. 265**; Cover of What I Know So Far by Gordon Lish. Holt, Rinehart & Winston, 1984. Reprinted by permission of Henry Holt and Company, Inc. Photograph by S. Beckett: **p. 272**; Courtesy of Gordon Lish: **p. 279**; Photograph by Staub: **p. 298**; Briefe Nach Prag: **p. 311**; New York Public Library: **p. 327**; Photograph by James Villas: **p. 351**; University of Iowa Libraries: **p. 408**.

Charles Baudelaire
1821-1867

French poet, critic, translator, novella and short fiction writer, diarist, and dramatist.

INTRODUCTION

Regarded among the world's greatest lyric poets, Baudelaire is the author of *Les fleurs du mal* (*The Flowers of Evil*), a highly influential work esteemed both for its technical artistry and as the first collection of poems to depict human life from a distinctly modern perspective. Baudelaire's view of contemporary life also informs his pioneering achievement in the prose poem genre, *Petits poèmes en prose: Le spleen de Paris,* a collection of short fictional sketches possessing characteristics often associated with poetry: concision, emphasis of images over plot, and heightened attention to word choice, phrasing, and cadence. Baudelaire's only other fictional composition, the novella *La Fanfarlo,* revolves around the artistic aspirations and amorous entanglements of a young Parisian writer and is prized for its autobiographical content and elucidation of Baudelaire's aesthetic theories.

Biographical Information

Baudelaire was born in Paris to financially secure parents. His father, who was thirty-four years older than his mother, died when Baudelaire was six years old. Afterward Baudelaire grew very close to his mother, and he later remembered their relationship as "ideal, romantic . . . as if I were courting her." When Madame Baudelaire married Jacques Aupick in 1928, Baudelaire became deeply resentful. Initially he had excelled in school, but as he grew older he increasingly neglected his studies in favor of a dissipated, rebellious lifestyle. In 1841 the Aupicks sent him on a trip to India in hopes that his experiences abroad would reform him. During his travels he began writing poetry and composed the first poems that would be included in *The Flowers of Evil.* When Baudelaire returned to Paris in 1842, he received a large inheritance and began to live as a highly self-conscious dandy. In Baudelaire's view, the dandy was one who glorified the ego as the ultimate spiritual and creative power—a heroic individualist revolting against society. At this time, Baudelaire fell in love with Jeanne Duval, whom many scholars believe inspired not only the "Black Venus" cycle of love poems in *The Flowers of Evil* but also the titular character of *La Fanfarlo.* In 1844 Baudelaire's mother obtained a court order blocking his inheritance, and thereafter he supported himself by his writing, much of it art criticism. Published in 1857, *The Flowers of Evil* shocked readers with its depictions of sexual perversion, physical and psychological morbidity, and moral corruption. Not only was the work a critical and popular failure during Baude-

laire's lifetime, he and his publisher were consequently prosecuted and convicted of offenses against religion and public morality. Several years later Baudelaire attempted to reestablish his reputation and deteriorating financial situation by traveling to Belgium on a lecture tour. The tour was unsuccessful, and in 1866 he returned to Paris, where he suffered a debilitating stroke. Having recently reconciled with his mother, he remained in her care until his death in 1867.

Major Works of Short Fiction

Petits poèmes en prose comprises fifty prose poems; Baudelaire projected the collection to contain one hundred pieces but his vision of the work was never realized. The prose poems tend to present a disheartening picture of the world inhabited by Parisian underclasses and low-life; a broader underlying theme is the fragmented, alienating quality of modern life, especially as manifested in human relationships. For example, "Les yeux des pauvres" ("The Eyes of the Poor") depicts an impoverished family on the street gazing in the window of an expensive restaurant in which a couple sits discussing their opinions

1

about the people outside. The social and economic disparity between the two diners and the poor is apparent, but the reader also becomes cognizant of a basic incompatibility between the diners, as evidenced in the personal convictions and outlooks on life that surface in their dialogue. The prose poem "Le désespoir de la vieille" ("The Old Woman's Despair") describes an elderly woman who stops to admire a baby but is rebuked when the child begins to cry. Here the reader senses an inherent inability of humans to establish community. In "Le mauvais vitrier" ("The Bad Glazier") a deluded man smashes the transparent panes carried by a window maker in the belief that the world, seen through colorful tinted windows, would be a more happy place. In the novella *La Fanfarlo,* a young aesthete named Samuel Cramer—in whom many commentators have observed a strong similarity with Baudelaire—fancies himself to be a gigolo and a very talented poet. As a result of his egotism as well as his love for a married woman whose husband left her for the dancer La Fanfarlo, Cramer accepts the challenge of seducing La Fanfarlo away from the unfaithful husband. By the conclusion of the story, Cramer is revealed to have neither true commitment to his art nor the upper hand in his personal relationships.

Critical Response

Considered the earliest significant collection of prose poetry in French literature, *Petits poèmes en prose* deviates sharply from traditional poetry in its subject matter. Here Baudelaire portrays marginal and loveless lives in prosaic, urban terms, rejecting more elevated themes and language. While critics such as Jonathan Monroe and Edward K. Kaplan have insisted that the prose poems are concerned with ethics and social injustice, J. A. Hiddleston avers that in this collection Baudelaire depicts the world as absurd and lacking moral order. Commenting on *La Fanfarlo,* some scholars have speculated that Baudelaire feared that he was like the protagonist Cramer, an arrogant, self-absorbed, affectatious artist with unproven talent. Critics agree that in *La Fanfarlo* Baudelaire expresses contempt for the character of Cramer, a man with an overactive imagination and an inclination toward extreme romanticism, and *La Fanfarlo* is generally considered a reproof to the moralizing stories by Romantic writers in France, who had done little to legitimize the short story as a genre. According to historians of French literature, *La Fanfarlo* and works by Gérard de Nerval and Gustave Flaubert precipitated the modern short story, and, consequently, accomplished writers in the second half of the nineteenth century began to specialize in short fiction.

PRINCIPAL WORKS

Short Fiction

La Fanfarlo 1847
Petits poèmes en prose: Le spleen de Paris 1869

Other Major Works

Histoires extraordinaires [translator; from the short stories of Edgar Allan Poe] (short stories) 1856
Les épaves (poetry) 1857
Les fleurs du mal [*The Flowers of Evil*] (poetry) 1857
Nouvelles histoires extraordinaires [translator; from the short stories of Edgar Allan Poe] (short stories) 1857
Aventures d'Arthur Pym [translator; from the novel *The Narrative of Arthur Gordon Pym* by Edgar Allan Poe] (novel) 1858
Les paradis artificiels: Opium et haschisch [*Artificial Paradises: On Hashish and Wine as a Means of Expanding Individuality*] (autobiography and poetry) 1860
Curiosités esthétiques (criticism) 1868
L'art romantique (criticism) 1869
†*Journaux intimes* [*Intimate Journals*] (diaries) 1887
Lettres: 1841-1866 (letters) 1905
Oeuvres complètes de Charles Baudelaire. 19 vols. (poetry, criticism, essays, novella, letters, journals, autobiography, and translations) 1922-63
The Letters of Charles Baudelaire (letters) 1927
Baudelaire on Poe (criticism) 1952
The Mirror of Art: Critical Studies (criticism) 1955
Baudelaire as a Literary Critic (criticism) 1964
Art in Paris, 1845-1862: Salons and Other Exhibitions Reviewed by Charles Baudelaire (criticism) 1965
Selected Writings on Art and Artists (criticism) 1986

*Includes Baudelaire's translation of Thomas De Quincey's *Confessions of an English Opium Eater.*

†Includes the diaries "Fusées" ("Skyrockets") and "Mon coeur mis á nu" ("My Heart Laid Bare").

CRITICISM

Charles Baudelaire (letter date 1862)

SOURCE: "To Arsène Houssaye," in *Paris Spleen, 1869,* translated by Louise Varèse, New Directions, 1947, pp. ix-x.

[*Below, Baudelaire describes his prose poems to Arsène Houssaye, editor of* La Presse, *who published twenty of his pieces in late 1862.*]

My dear friend, I send you a little work of which no one can say, without doing it an injustice, that it has neither head nor tail, since, on the contrary, everything in it is both head and tail, alternately and reciprocally. I beg you to consider how admirably convenient this combination is for àll of us, for you, for me, and for the reader. We can cut wherever we please, I my dreaming, you your manuscript, the reader his reading; for I do not keep the reader's restive mind hanging in suspense on the threads of an interminable and superfluous plot. Take away one vertebra and the two ends of this tortuous fantasy come together again without pain. Chop it into numerous pieces and you will see that each one can get along alone. In the hope that there is enough life in some of these segments to please and to amuse you, I take the liberty of dedicating the whole serpent to you.

I have a little confession to make. It was while running through, for the twentieth time at least, the pages of the famous *Gaspard de la Nuit* of Aloysius Bertrand (has not a book known to you, to me, and to a few of our friends the right to be called famous?) that the idea came to me of attempting something in the same vein, and of applying to the description of our more abstract modern life the same method he used in depicting the old days, so strangely picturesque.

Which one of us, in his moments of ambition, has not dreamed of the miracle of a poetic prose, musical, without rhythm and without rhyme, supple enough and rugged enough to adapt itself to the lyrical impulses of the soul, the undulations of reverie, the jibes of conscience?

It was, above all, out of my exploration of huge cities, out of the medley of their innumerable interrelations, that this haunting ideal was born. You yourself, dear friend, have you not tried to translate in a song the *Glazier's* strident cry, and to express in lyric prose all the dismal suggestions this cry sends up through the fog of the street to the highest garrets?

To tell the truth, however, I am afraid that my envy has not been propitious. From the very beginning I perceived that I was not only far from my mysterious and brilliant model, but was, indeed, doing something (if it can be called *something*) singularly different, an accident which any one else would glory in, no doubt, but which can only deeply humiliate a mind convinced that the greatest honor for a poet is to succeed in doing exactly what he set out to do.

Yours most affectionately,

C.B.

Renée Riese Hubert (essay date 1970)

SOURCE: "Contexts of Twilight in Baudelaire's 'Petits poèmes en prose,'" in *Orbis Litterarum,* Vol. 25, 1970, pp. 352-60.

[*Hubert is a German-born poet and educator specializing in contemporary art and literature. In the following essay, she examines the symbolic uses of light, darkness, and color in* Petits poèmes en prose.]

Even if its effect and function seem more limited than in *Les Fleurs du mal,* even if it never suggests spiritual aspiration as in "Bénédiction", light is present in most of the *Petits poèmes en prose.* Nothing offers escape, in **"Le Fou et la Vénus"**, from the dazzling sun whose watchful eye never blinks. Overpowered by this force, nature voices no protest; not even the murmur of waters can disturb the silence. But muteness does not imply the reduction of nature to an object. The word ecstasy ("L'extase universelle des choses") refers to sensuous pleasure while expressing a feeling of admiration, as well as an expansion upward, echoed by such terms as *rivaliser, croissant, crescendo.* As a result, the silence, comparable to meditation, is compensated for by visual effects. As every particle of nature sparkles and produces heat, light fills the world with visible elements, generating enough power and energy to make even the fragrance of flowers perceivable. What relation does this setting, where every flower expresses an erotic vitality, bear to the scene between Venus and the fool? Does the goddess of love encourage those who look up to her or pay her homage? Surrounded by sensuous lights, Venus remains cold to the entreaties of the fool. Her marble eyes, peering into the distance, contrast with the fiery glance of the sun, as the bent posture of the teary-eyed fool contrasts with the upward drive of nature. For the solitary fool who remains estranged, the sun creates but an inhuman illusion.

The same omnipresent sun prevails in the tropical setting of **"La Belle Dorothée"** where sand and sea become but dazzling reflections. As in **"Le Fou et la Vénus"** its luminosity, its erotic temptations appear all-pervading. However, it suffices to oppose the initial sentences: "Quelle admirable jour-née!" of **"Le Fou et la Vénus"** to "Le Soleil accable la ville de sa lumière droite et terrible" of **"La Belle Dorothée"**, to note that nature is no longer characterized by fertility, by an upward motion, but by a downward gesture, a sort of capitulation: "une sieste qui est une espèce de mort savoureuse". As the sun crushes the world by light and weight rather than heat, man submits to this hostile force, the vertical sun rays that act like daggers. But Dorothée asserts herself against the mighty sun. She becomes a rival of the star by wandering alone through the streets, by maintaining her upright posture while others take a siesta. In spite of her black skin Dorothée becomes a focal point of luminosity: "faisant sur la lumière une tache éclatante et noire". This radiant blackness is stressed a second time: her leg bared by the wind is "luisante et superbe". To the strong color and light of her skin, Dorothée adds those of her clothes: a brilliant pink dress, a red sunshade. Dorothée, who has left her cozy, well-adorned boudoir, triumphs symbolically in a world where man dares not withstand sunlight. A former slave, she asserts her freedom at the very moment when she consents to make love. Not only does she become stronger and more beautiful than everyone else on her tropical island, but she reasserts her superiority over sophisticated Parisians. Like the sun, she creates reflections of her power around her: "Elle apercevait au loin dans l'escape un miroir reflétant sa démarche et sa beauté". Within Dorothée, at once proud and nonchalant, the contrasts that divorce mankind from the sun harmoniously unite.

In **"Le Tir et le cimetière"**, even less than in **"Le Fou et la Vénus"** and in **"La Belle Dorothée"**, does brilliant sunshine espouse the human cause. Near the cemetery the sun attains its greatest intensity, rolling like a drunk person on the flowerbeds to the accompaniment of explosions from a nearby shooting stand. The vitality and richness (cf. *magnifiques, riches, engraissées*) of grass, sun and flowers banishes the sadness and even the very silence of the tombs. Yet the heat and light, which permeate the earth, arouse the voice of death, which denounces the futility and nothingness of life: "Si vous saviez . . . combien tout est néant, excepté la Mort". Although the illuminating qualities of light have momentarily created the illusion that the powers of life are enhanced, the overwhelming presence of the sun remains alien once more to human sensitivity and communication.

The sunlight in the three preceding poems manifests its power by an excess of its natural qualities, whereas the moon in **"Les Bienfaits de la lune"** suggests a world of dream and legend upon which reality barely encroaches. Metamorphosed into a goddess, it can, through its powers of expansion, fill any room. Its permeating quality, expressed by analogies with the sea, and its poisonous nature, manifested by phosphorescence, a combination of a greenish color and a shining light which darkness can hardly overcome, explain its powers of seduction. The moon goddess stares at a child, resting at first in her cradle; then crossing the window, she stoops over the baby girl and grips her by the neck. In a threatening cradle song she predicts that the little girl, unable to resist, will become just like the goddess: "Tu seras belle à ma manière. Tu aimeras ce que j'aime et ce qui m'aime". Indeed, whereas at first, the moon merely colored the child's face with its green colors and opened widely her eyes in bewilderment, towards the end the child is so fully impregnated by the moon's characteristics that the poet can seek the goddess' reflection in her: "Cherchant dans toute ta personne le reflet de la redoutable Divinité". The strong sunlight merely remained indifferent to human endeavors; the moon, a far more dangerous force, bewitches even the innocent by means of its supernatural, not to say diabolical powers.

In **"Les Yeux des pauvres"** the scene takes place in a café into which no natural light ever penetrates. Gas lighting, by bringing out the whiteness of the table cloth and heightening the reflection of the mirrors, intensifies the effects of bad taste. However, to the poor, who watch from the sidewalk, this repulsive world takes on the dimensions of the marvelous. Their eyes, described by the poet's heartless mistress as "ouverts comme des portes cochères", characterize their receptivity, so different from the aggressive pretensions of the light. In the gas light, so destructive of dream and illusion, objects display themselves with ostentation, but never harmonize. Thus the café represents a stage in the poet's discovery of his mistress' inhumanity.

In **"Le Vieux Saltimbanque"** and **"Les Veuves"** Baudelaire expresses man's desire for joy and festivity, his escape from reality, by repeated explosions of sound and light. In the former text, the swiftly turning skirts of beautiful dancers sparkle in the light. By linking the following paradoxical terms: "Tout n'était que lumière, poussière, cris, joie, tumulte", Baudelaire implicitly condemns these circus performers and spectators, as opposed to the saltimbanque who dwells in a mysterious, deep darkness upheld by silence and feeble candlelight. The crowd, as already indicated by the juxtaposition of the three verbs in the initial sentence: "Partout s'étalait, se répandait, s'ébaudissait", has the expanding quality associated with light; the old Saltimbanque, in contrast, seems (like the bent-down fool) restricted to a limited space. To the *partout* of the pleasure-seekers Baudelaire opposes the *ici* of the saltimbanque. Like the family of **"Les Yeux des pauvres"** his meaningful glance reveals the shallowness of the world clad in light.

The contrast between a crowd, which is only too visible and audible, and a solitary, self-effacing human being occurs also in **"Les Veuves"** where the widows' black dresses differ from the glittering manifestations of apparent joy and wealth. Yet their glance ("yeux caves et ternes") can contain this large, motley, somewhat hellish world which Baudelaire refers to as "l'étincelante fournaise". The spiritual greatness of one of these widows becomes outwardly manifest when the very blackness of her attire appears radiant. Twice the term *éclatant* is applied to the widow in order to suggest the revelation she brings to the poet. By her sadness and dignity, by the darkness and luminosity of her appearance, she becomes the creator of a new form of harmony more powerful than that of the "étincelante fournaise" and the orchestra. In **"Le Vieux Saltimbanque"** and **"Les Veuves"** light created by man embodies his ostentation and lack of depth, darkness becomes the sign of spiritual values.

In other poems, Baudelaire tends not only to dissociate light from spiritual illumination, but also from moral values. In **"Le *Confitéor* de l'artiste"** harmony, a state which defies explanation or analysis, characterizes at first the relationship between the poet and the world. As man embraces the outer world, the dusk of autumnal days penetrates his inner universe. The pulse of time does not beat, the past and the present merge into a single sensation of unbearable intensity. Then the poet's sensations revert from pleasure to pain, from peace to tension; he asserts himself against nature, which assumes more and more the cold beauty of Venus. What burdens him is the very purity and transparence of the sky, this absolute blueness which assumes, as the sun in **"La Belle Dorothée"**, the characteristics of cruelty and indifference. To this attitude **"L'Etranger"** who finds comfort in an affinity with the clouds, provides a corollary. He opts for the veiled, the imprecise, the mysterious so different from the sharpness of the clear sunlight or azure. Yet how can we explain, in the same context, **"A Chacun sa chimère"**, which evokes the spleen descending upon the poet through an all-pervading atmosphere of grayness? No flower, vegetation, or path will throw a speck of light or reflection onto the gray cupola, the outlines of which are mysteriously re-echoed by every man who advances with a sack on his back. From the sky and the procession, representing the spleen which envelops the poet's soul, there is no escape. In **"A**

Chacun sa chimère", the grayness or lack of light evokes an undivided world without opposition, whereas in the texts where light emerges appear contrasts, conflicts or tensions. In order to assert the stranger's loneliness and his opting for, not the sky, but the clouds, the poet chose the dialogue form. In **"La Belle Dorothée"** the opposition between light and darkness constitutes the basis of a dramatic conflict. In **"Le Vieux Saltimbanque"** it stresses an irretrievable division.

"Anywhere out of the world" includes, however, both the spleen and the tension arising from changes in luminosity. The poet proposes voyages, new domains to his blasé soul, until the very limits of imagination have been reached. In the polar regions where the sun throws oblique rays falling into sheaves, light and darkness alternate with agonizing slowness. While **"A Chacun sa chimère"** evokes, through an absence of light, the poet's succumbing to spleen, **"Anywhere out of the world"**, by a succession of light and obscurity, suggests the difficulty of overcoming this state. Still, this prolonged monotonous state moves towards a climax equivalent to damnation, an intensification of the previous light sequences against which the poet (as in *"Confitéor de l'artiste"*) reacts by an inner violence.

"Le Crépuscule du soir" shows the poet, gradually succumbing to peace as the day ebbs. The first suggestions of light, "Les couleurs tendres et indécises du crépuscule" and "les nues transparentes du soir", pointing towards a diminished harshness, lend to dusk the mysterious, indefinite qualities that **"L'Etranger"** is seeking in the clouds. Twilight produces a soothing effect by obliterating the struggle and anguish that the city at daytime creates in the poet, but spurs some people to violence or even to mania. Such distinctions lie in the very nature of twilight, its basic duality at once peaceful and stormy—as revealed by such expressions as: "l'harmonie de l'enfer", "lugubre harmonie". The approaching darkness frees not only the poet from the sorrows of work and the oppressions of reality, it creates an inner festivity, an imaginary spectacle, represented by the dying redness of day and the appearance of the first city lights. The sky, belonging at once to dream and reality, assumes erotic qualities as it simulates the dark skirt of a dancer which is sown with sparkling stars. Between the expanses of the sky and the walls of the mind no basic distinction remains: the same lights and colors shine within a pervading darkness. Bright lights, as we stated earlier, are usually dissociated from spiritual illumination. Twilight, not only in **"Le Crépuscule du soir"**, but also in **"Les Vocations"**, coincides with a form of self-knowledge, of religious contemplation.

The juxtaposition of the two rooms in **"La Chambre double"**, translating again the poet's desire for escape, seems at first related to the alternation of *ténèbres* and *aurores boréales* of **"N'importe où hors du monde"**. However, into the first, the timeless room, no sunlight penetrates. Indefiniteness characterizes its blue and pink shades, imitating those of sky and clouds: "C'est quelque chose de crépusculaire, de bleuâtre et de rosâtre". In this room

more and more endowed with the subdued, dissolving qualities of dusk, the poet's dreams encounter no obstacles. The word *harmonie* stresses the blending of two elements: "Ici tout a la suffisante clarté et la délicieuse obscurité de l'harmonie". The lack of a precise source of light is crystallized in the word *éclipse*. The eventual emergence of the Idol with her eyes, at once luminous and dark, "ces toiles noires" consumates this state of well-being where the poet's mind no longer seeks to assert itself. In the context of twilight this prose-poem comes close to **"Crépuscule du soir"**, where the effects of a mellowing light, unadulterated by shade, matters more than references to time or timelessness.

The contemplation of a port scene where the lighthouse constitutes the main but not sole source of light, provides a similar peace to the poet's tired mind. The motion of clouds, an animated force in the vast sky, is echoed through the sea. Both movements exist independently and as reflections of each other. Clouds and sea, which bring into the great expanse a rhythmical sequence of movement and color, meet the glittering vibrations of the beams projected from the lighthouse. The beams, an independent entity, constitute also an extension of the harmonious movement of sea and sky. Epitomizing light, color and movement, they represent the essence of an ordered beauty which constantly recreates itself according to its own laws. Their encounter, transformation and concentration in the eye, is suggested by the word *prisme*. Thereby the phenomena of the outer world reach the poet's mind of which they are a reflection. This prism of understanding, reverberating the unending movement of ships in the harbor, indicates once more the inseparability and simultaneity of light and color vibrations. As in **"La Chambre double"**, peaceful contemplation, lack of suffering stem from lights, of a complex or compound nature, where the corresponding elements blend and recreate effects.

In both **"L'Invitation au voyage"** and **"Un Hémisphère dans une chevelure"** the poet reaches out for an absent or imaginary world. In the former, similar to the first part of **"La Chambre double"**, a mysterious order unthreatened by time or other interference propagates an atmosphere of peace. It stems from an equilibrium of spiritual and sensuous terms crystallized in such expressions as "l'infini des sensations" and "âmes raffinées" and brings out the similarity between the ideal land and the woman, mysterious, secret, yet tangible. The correspondence of soul and body, landscape and woman, intimacy and vastness, fantasy and simplicity, simulates not the recapturing of a natural land, but of a painting: "Verrons-nous jamais, passerons-nous jamais dans ce tableau qu'a peint mon esprit, ce tableau qui te ressemble?" In this silent painting, light, color and motion, first clad in a mysterious mist with subdued clearness, will become inseparable as in **"Le Port"**. Later, when the poet evokes an interior, rich in painterly qualities, words referring to light abound. From "les soleils couchants" (the plural stresses again the reference to paintings) emanates a light in evolution gradually suffused by darkness which endows the objects in the room with picture-like attributes: *panneaux, cuirs* *dorés, peintures béates, tamisés par de belles étoffes, ces hautes fenêtres ouvragées, meubles vastes et curieux, les miroirs.* Every object is at once a receiver and a generator of light, blending its luminosity with that of others, producing thus a filtration which purifies or elevates spiritually. After the misty atmosphere of the beginning, followed by reflections which transform the evening sun into a work of art, the universe mirrors its infinite sky and sea in the limpidity of the woman's soul. In **"Le Port"** the interrelation of motion and light as well as the various constituents of the landscape, decomposed and recomposed, attain a unity which parallels that of the room in **"L'Invitation au voyage"**. The limpidity or purity suggested in the final paragraph consumates not only the invitation to the imaginary land, but makes all sources of light obsolete and stresses, more than any of the previous poems, an inner experience with an inner landscape and an inner light.

Visual elements play a less significant role in **"Un hémisphère dans une chevelure"** for the woman's hair becomes a mysterious container of different sensations: "Tout ce que je vois! tout ce que je sens! tout ce que j'entends dans tes cheveux!" As intertwined visual, auditory, and olfactory memories recur, the very hair of the woman reflects alternately the immensity of the ocean or sky and the warmth of a hearth until the culminating image: "dans la nuit de ta chevelure, je vois resplendir l'infini de l'azur tropical". The very blackness of the woman's hair, simulating the walls of a boudoir, evokes the infinite, spacious luminosity of the skies. The mysterious azure reborn from an instantaneous sensation, the scent of the dark hair, constitute the threshold to the pure, lasting light of dream, so far removed from the aggressive sunlight, a dramatic condensation of reality.

Thus we may conclude that the solitary strength of the outer light is less beneficial than the atonement of dusk, its mystery, its harmonious blending with other sensations and that dusk in its turn is less propitious than the inner light, divorced from the world of reality. **"Les Fenêtres"** summarizes these very ideas. Looking through an open window with the help of sunlight does not permit the artist to discover or attain life, its truth, its suffering. Looking through a closed window dimly lit by a candle reveals an unsuspected depth which the direct light entering upon an open space fails to show. This rich vision, like the widow's eyes, like the Dutch interiors, contains at once darkness and light: "plus ténébreux, plus éblouissant qu'une fenêtre", "dans ce trou noir ou lumineux". A penetration into a world not solely revealed from a unilateral, outside source must be attained through aesthetic distance. In **"Le Mauvais Vitrier"** the perfect panes are unrevealing until the poet breaks the glass, until he creates, be it by means of destruction, a rainbow of color and light. And alone the dim panes in **"Les Fenêtres"** stir him to creativity and to communion with others. Baudelaire, the symbolist, the modern poet, sought the challenge of retrieving distant elements from darkness rather than admiring the luminous contours offered by the skies.

Renée Riese Hubert (essay date 1970)

SOURCE: "Intimacy and Distance in Baudelaire's Prose-Poems," in *Texas Studies in Literature and Language,* Vol. XII, No. 1, Spring, 1970, pp. 241-47.

[In the following essay, Hubert finds that Baudelaire's prose poems present true intimacy as virtually unattainable.]

In his *Poesie in prosaischer Welt,* Fritz Nies claims that some typical Baudelairean themes, such as love, do not fully belong to the world of the *Petits poèmes en prose.* To be sure, Baudelaire, by emphasizing the contemporary scene either in its everyday aspects or viewed as a satanic city haunted by humble but disturbing creatures, recasts, as it were, the traditional lyrical themes. Nonetheless, love is present, in all its diversity, from the mysterious charm of a beautiful woman in **"Un hémisphère dans une chevelure"** and **"La Belle Dorothée,"** or woman's paradoxical nature in **"Laquelle est la vraie?"** and **"Le Désir de peindre"** to man's unrequited love in **"Le Fou et la Vénus"** and **"Les Yeux des pauvres,"** or even imaginary love inspired by dream in **"Les Projets"** and **"L'Invitation au voyage."** The opposition between spleen and ideal, suffering and dream, mystery and discovery, is usually expressed within each prose-poem rather than suggested by contrasting series of poems as in *Les Fleurs du mal.* Thus conflict and tension become dominant. **"Un Cheval de race"** begins with the contradictory statement: "Elle est bien laide. Elle est délicieuse pourtant." In **"Laquelle est la vraie?"** to the poet's claim: "J'ai connu une certaine Bénédicta, qui remplissait l'atmosphère d'idéal . . ." the woman opposes her verdict: "C'est moi, la vraie Bénédicta! C'est moi, une fameuse canaille!" Woman, an ambivalent creature, will inspire a mixture of hatred and love, of disappointment and hope, of cruelty and affection. Repeatedly Baudelaire addresses as "mon ange" or "ma très chère" women whom he detests, curses, or threatens. In **"L'Horloge"** he hopes to escape the tyranny of time by looking in the eyes of Féline. But the poet's wish that in one glance he might arrest time and affirm an intimate relationship cannot be granted. Féline with her adorable eyes becomes a remote "Madame" when the poet shows his ironic attitude toward the madrigal he has just devoted to her. A similar desire for intimacy, to be sealed by a meaningful glance, marks **"Les Yeux des pauvres."** Next to the poet sits a woman with whom he had exchanged a pledge: "Nous nous étions bien promis que toutes nos pensées nous seraient communes à l'un et à l'autre et que nos deux âmes désormais n'en feraient plus qu'une." By looking into the eyes of the three poor people the poet feels the kind of mysterious solidarity he hopes to attain with his mistress. In her dangerous green eyes he discovers that she does not share his warm feelings for the deprived family, whose very presence in the cafe she finds objectionable. Her unvoiced comment, which does not directly concern the lovers' relationship, actually seals their separation. **"Le galant tireur"** describes his wife as "chère," "Délicieuse," and "exécrable." Her merciless laughter at his failure to hit a target at a fair spurs him to success. He kills "ce monstre-là," an impertinent doll in which he sees a symbol of man's perennial enemy, Time, as well as the very image of his wife. The first shots directed against time with a capital *T* were aimed too high and pierced the ceiling. But, when the marksman closes his eyes, an inner vision or hostile awareness frees him from the immediate source of boredom and separates him from the woman, who is thus reduced to the state of victim and onlooker.

In the texts discussed so far, the poet's conflicting attitudes, born from woman's paradoxical nature, ultimately bring about a detachment, a greater distance rather than a renewed promise of intimacy. It would seem, however, that when the poet in **"Le Désir de peindre"** tries to recreate the absent, beautiful woman within his own universe no tensions could possibly arise. Nevertheless, her dangerous, dark features emerge. Her eyes flash like fiery warnings preceding a storm, illuminating a dark abyss. A remark concerning his critical method, taken from the *Curiosités esthétiques*—"Il m'arrivera souvent d'apprécìer un tableau uniquement par la somme d'idées ou de rêveries qu'il apportera dans mon esprit"—sheds light on **"Le Désir de peindre,"** for the woman's physical appearance is alluded to only in regard to the effect she produces. Her mysterious beauty bears no relationship to any terrestrial scene. Not even a black sun, radiating a heretofore unseen light, offers an equivalent. The woman whose very eyes possess the power of lightning and storm resembles a moon covered with volcanic peaks. Her allure pertains less to the poet's earthly attachments than to his aspiration toward the unknown. She is not merely an absent beauty who by her very distance in space intensifies the poet's desire. A modern muse who refuses to whisper soothing verse into the poet's ear, she conquers him by her determination and her predatory passion. Desire and suffering become more necessary than intimacy to artistic inspiration.

The three dreams evoked in **"Les Projets,"** which have little to do with everyday experience or memory, barely refer to the paradoxical nature of women. As the poet wanders through a big deserted park, then along a street with shop windows, and finally along an alley, he daydreams. The first imaginary woman whom the poet pursues in his quest for beauty assumes the air of a princess. Dressed in a ritual costume, she steps down the marble staircase in the midst of a vast lawn. She remains remote, as if she belonged to the world of fairytales or painting. This pompous vision, where every detail is foreseen, soon bores the poet. He sets eyes on a tropical landscape represented in an engraving, which enables him to imagine a richer, more sensuous dwelling. And the poet hopes to enjoy a greater intimacy with a second, but equally imaginary, woman than that bestowed by the ceremonious princess. The nearby seawaves will rock the lovers in their little wooden hut, surrounded by brightly colored, scented trees. In spite of the repeated *chez nous, autour de nous,* as well as *notre petit domaine* (as opposed to the *grande pelouse* and the *grand parc* of the first paragraph), the attainment of this happiness remains out of reach. The poet attempts to focus his attention on this woman. But his mind wanders on—"plus loin," "derrière notre petit

domaine," "au-delà de la chambre éclairée," "au-delà de la varangue"—until he realizes that all this was a mere decor. He wonders why he has strayed so far, as he passes an inn glowing with an intimacy belonging to everyday existence: "un grand feu, des faïences voyantes, un souper passable, un vin rude, et un lit très large." A feminine presence is missing in this cozy setting, which, by its very existence, evokes the fulfillment of a promise and suggests, as do all the settings in this poem, the security of peace. Thus the growing intimacy of the decor veils the increasing distance from the woman or, rather, the remoteness of the poet's encounter with her.

As **"La Belle Dorothée"** does not belong to this distant world of dream or desire, a form of intimacy could emerge from this poem. Dorothée walks in the bright sunlight, swaying from her hips, her earrings dangling, her tight dress revealing the curves of her body. She is undoubtedly on her way to a tryst. But let us not mistake the meaning of such a possible meeting. Dorothée, like so many other women of the *Petits poèmes en prose,* possesses antithetical attributes: "tête délicate," "énorme chevelure," "torse mince," "hanches larges," "lourdes pendeloques," "mignonnes oreilles," "visage sombre," "fard sanglant." Above all, she is both "triomphant" and "paresseux." She gives way to her indolence when, in her boudoir, she relaxes under the coolness of a fan or looks in the mirror. Now, in the dazzling sunlight, the more active side of her personality takes the upper hand. Under the heat of the daggerlike beams, nature, bereft of energy, seems to languish. Against this prostration, Dorothée scores her first triumph; she walks, "Forte et fière comme le soleil" in the deserted streets, creating a dark shadow in the azure. When the wind bares her legs, she becomes a statue who needs no admirers: ". . . elle apercevait au loin dans l'espace un miroir reflétant sa démarche et sa beauté." When she does meet with the officer, she will assert her freedom, as though aware of the superiority of her natural beauty over the pale, artificial world of Paris. Although Dorothée is undoubtedly a prostitute, her self-sufficient beauty triumphs in all its majesty. The reflection of her beauty in the distance, rather than her feminine attractions, constitutes the highpoint of the poem.

"Laisse-moi respirer longtemps, longtemps, l'odeur de tes cheveux, y plonger tout mon visage." The very beginning of **"Un Hémisphère dans une chevelure"** promises an intimate relationship between the poet and a woman. Contact through sight, smell, and touch provides a blissful state that the poet wishes to prolong. As he caresses the woman's hair, his memories awaken. He repeats in imagination voyages through sea and landscapes. Houses, people, songs, scent, flowers make up this dreamlike universe that has become as close as the locks the poet touches. The woman thus plays the role of an intermediary who reinvigorates the poet by kindling his memory and imagination. Time and space are abolished, thus allowing the poet to experience a state of intensity as though he were truly intoxicated by opium under the tropics. The woman, sensed merely as an ocean of black hair, repeatedly recedes in the background whenever the vision of beautiful lands becomes immediate.

Does this mediator between everyday existence and dream participate—be it for one brief moment—in the poet's experience? Does she share his sensations, feelings, or ideas? "Si tu pouvais savoir tout ce que je vois! tout ce que je sens! tout ce que j'entends dans tes cheveux!" Does this statement express merely the poet's gratitude, or also his awareness that the woman cannot take the trip from sensation to imagination with him? Although the final sentence has striking overtones in which the spiritual assets of memory are barely stressed—"Quand je mordille tes cheveux élastiques et rebelles, il me semble que je mange des souvenirs"—it confirms the separateness of the poet and the woman by the very absence of the pronoun *nous* and by the use of the indefinite article before *souvenirs*.

Does the same distance separate the poet and the woman in the verse poem where the word *nous* is equally absent? A comparison of the opening sentences of the two versions immediately brings out important differences: "O toison moutonnant jusque sur l'encolure" and "Laisse-moi respirer longtemps." The poet, merely by addressing the latter words to the woman, by begging her consent, grants her a willful existence beyond the presence of her hair. In **"La Chevelure"** the invocation expresses an immediacy, an expectancy that makes her wishes in the matter superfluous. Her hair and the sea are not merely associated; they are metaphorically interwoven. Warmth, fertility, and indolence characterize a passionate state belonging to both the tropical landscape and the woman, while the sea opens her arms in an erotic gesture. The poet's imaginary voyage, indistinguishable from the movement of the sea, becomes a poetic trance where the very fusion of woman and journey makes distance irrelevant.

In **"L'Invitation au voyage"** the hope for a common journey binds from the beginning the poet to the woman. "Il est un pays superbe, un vrai pays de Cocagne, dit-on." The last two words indicate that the land exists only according to a still unproven legend. It is a land where nature is transformed into art, where reign harmony, order, peace, a land without the threat of contradictions and the sorrows of fragmentation. It represents not only an artistic dream, but also the very image of the beloved—in other words, the chosen land where ideal love would find a haven. Baudelaire first addresses the woman as "une vieille amie," later as "mon cher ange"; at first, he uses "vous," later the familiar "tu." He mentions first the resemblance between the girl and the land, then he states an identity: "ces parfums, ces fleurs miraculeuses, c'est toi." Has he thus moved closer to fulfillment? Not really. More than in the verse poem, Baudelaire suggests an invitation rather than an attainment. Repeatedly he interjects questions, moments of doubt: "Vivrons-nous jamais, passerons-nous jamais dans ce tableau?" In the verse poem the songlike qualities of the verse so transport the reader that he barely wonders whether or not the dream has become true. Moreover, the resemblance between the woman and the imaginary land is not only stated, but evoked—for instance, in a comparison between her eyes and the sky:

> Les soleils mouillés
> De ces ciels brouillés
> Pour mon esprit ont les charmes
>
> Si mystérieux
> De tes traîtres yeux
> Brillant à travers leurs larmes.

The room, a mysterious series of correspondences between reflections and perfumes, becomes not merely an ideal interior, but a home for the poet and the beloved. In the final stanza—written in the present indicative instead of the conditional—the poet shows a perfectly visible scene to his mistress:

> Vois sur ces canaux
> Dormir ces vaisseaux.

At sunset, when the world sinks into a gentle sleep and dream, the beloved does not need persuasion or encouragement as in the prose-poem. In the latter, the poet has extended the barriers of the world and its movements in order to tell the woman that her soul mirrors the infinite sea and the deep sky. In the verse poem, the motionless boats in the port under the evening sun enclose the lovers in an intimacy where all dreams and desires can find fulfillment.

Whether motivated by love, hatred, or ambivalence, in the *Petits poèmes en prose* all attempts to establish satisfying human relationships are threatened by failure. Yet the poet evokes a harmonious relation and an intimacy with the outer world—be it only temporarily—in such poems as **"Le Gâteau," "Le Crépuscule du soir," "Le Confitéor de l'artiste,"** and **"La Chambre double."** These texts, when compared with poems devoted to women, contain a great number of sensuous, almost erotic terms: "Grand délice que celui de noyer son regard dans l'immensité du ciel et de la mer! Solitude, silence, incomparable chasteté de l'azur!" And does the poet often say to a woman such words as he addresses to dusk? " . . . comme vous . . . êtes doux et tendre!" In most cases an ephemeral harmony or intimacy is followed by a reversal where the poet becomes, as in poems that deal with love, the victim, spectator, or performer of a violent action. No basic distinction exists, according to **"L'Etranger,"** between man's love for man, for the world, for beauty. The duel that the artist has to fight against nature, seen as a bewitching woman, in **"Le Confitéor de l'artiste,"** belongs in the same world as his attack on "la petite maîtresse," who barely disguises her true nature, that of a savage woman. In **"Le Fou et la Vénus"** the goddess' coldness and beauty inflict even greater suffering, since the fool is surrounded by a sunny, sensuous landscape where every flower quivers with excitement. In this expansive universe no doors separate man from the outer world, dream from reality. A reality that lies within easy reach may lead to the temptation of the infinite; relationships that promise an obvious kinship may be metamorphosed through an act of revolt. Baudelaire is never the chronicler of obvious feelings. He refuses to accept the romantic and usually sterile familiarity with the self until he has uncovered kindred souls in an everchanging world.

In **"Les Fenêtres,"** the poet observes a woman at a window. Belonging to the same family as **"Les Veuves,"** she evokes in the poet a mysterious bond unsullied by any sign or gesture. He feels the urge to decipher the enigma, to recreate the woman's life, "Je me couche, fier d'avoir vécu et souffert dans d'autres que moi-même." Here, through suffering, the poet achieves an understanding that love has not provided and that he prefaces with an aesthetic credo: "Celui qui regarde du dehors à travers une fenêtre ouverte ne voit jamais autant de chose que celui qui regarde une fenêtre fermée." Thus communication, related to distance, leads the poet to a deeper probing.

Long before the Surrealists, Baudelaire aspired to the spiritual fusion of the lovers, an intimacy that in his universe is irrevocably associated with distance.

John Jeremy (essay date 1981)

SOURCE: "Samuel Cramer—Eclectic or Individualist?," in *Nottingham French Studies,* Vol. 20, No. 1, May, 1981, pp. 10-21.

[*In the following essay, Jeremy maintains that the protagonist of* La Fanfarlo *is a writer who lacks the intense focus and aesthetic vision of an artistic genius, and therefore represents Baudelaire's fear about himself.*]

Baudelaire criticism has long been familiar with the idea of Samuel Cramer as the poet's *alter ego* and of a Baudelaire who treats his fictional counterpart with indulgent irony—"un Baudelaire dont Baudelaire se détache" as Ferran calls him [in *L'esthéstique de Baudelaire,* 1933]— in order to mock and no doubt also to exorcize his own weaknesses, and to examine, within the secure boundaries of fictional invention, the complexities of his own nature. [In "Baudelaire and Samuel Cramer", *Australian Journal of French Studies* 6, nos. 2-3] C. A. Hackett goes further. "Above all, it seems that he needed, at this moment in his career, to exhibit all his talents, to test, examine and analyse himself"; and he draws attention to the ambiguity in the character of Samuel and to Baudelaire's ambivalent relationship with his hero, varying as it does between close identification and ironic distance. Jean Prévost is convinced that the *nouvelle* expresses Baudelaire's anxiety that he may "manquer sa carrière" [*Baudelaire,* 1953]; and if we accept Claude Pichois's date [offered in Pinchois's edition of Baudelaire's *Oeuvres complètes*] for the composition—or, at any rate, the completion—of *La Fanfarlo,* then we may suppose it to be roughly contemporary with the *Conseils aux Jeunes Littérateurs* (published 15th April 1846) and we may assume that Baudelaire's rather brisk advice in these pages about the importance of cultivating the will and refusing to accept the existence of *le guignon* is directed equally at himself: "la littérature", says the poet-journalist in 1846, "est avant tout un remplissage de colonnes".

Baudelaire presents Samuel's story as a cautionary tale, a warning to himself of the dangers into which he may be led by his own paradoxical nature and his laziness. In the opening paragraphs Baudelaire introduces Samuel to the reader in the present tense, although there is no suggestion that this is a *Rahmenerzählung* or that the events to be narrated have already occurred. It seems that the choice of this tense is to provide Baudelaire with a distancing device whereby he can offer his hero to the reader's gaze as an object for analysis before the story begins, as a complex phenomenon to be illustrated in the events which follow. This effect of separation from the narrative as such is strengthened by his addressing the reader directly: "ajoutez à cette double origine [a German father and a Chilean mother] une éducation française et une civilisation littéraire, vous serez moins surpris,—sinon satisfait et édifié,—des complications bizarres de ce caractère". At the end of *La Fanfarlo* and at certain moments during the narrative Baudelaire once again slips into the present tense, for similar effect.

The poet makes it clear that Samuel is already an anachronism, "l'un des derniers romantiques que possède la France"; his "folies romantiques" were written "dans le bon temps du romantisme". For Ferran, he is "un fantôme de jeunesse qui se transforme peu à peu et devient le poète-type de 1840". [Samuel's verse collection] *Les Orfraies* is described by Baudelaire as "un recueil de sonnets, comme nous en avons tous fait et tous lu, dans le temps où nous avions le jugement si court et les cheveux si longs". By emphasizing that his young hero is also a grotesque survivor from another age—and by presenting this survivor to the reader as a typical contemporary phenonemon—"dans le monde actuel, ce genre de caractère est plus fréquent qu'on ne le pense"—the poet is enabled to pose sharply the question of Baudelaire-Cramer's future and that of a whole generation. This is the problem that is to the forefront of the *Salons* of 1845 and 1846 in the famous plea for modernity and a new Romanticism. Baudelaire is at this moment in his life attempting to create for himself an aesthetic based on the visual arts; and it is no accident that as *La Fanfarlo* develops it becomes more and more the story of a man's relationship with a woman whom he treats as though she were a work of art.

At this moment in Baudelaire's life his heroes are above all Balzac and Delacroix. Balzac directly influenced *La Fanfarlo,* as Prévost has shown, and Delacroix is the object of a sustained eulogy in the *Salon de 1846.* To the young poet these are the great individualists of the age by virtue of the strength and primacy of their inner vision. When Samuel Cramer speaks derisively of Scott to Mme de Cosmelly he contrasts the "ennuyeux écrivain" with "nos bons romanciers français" in whose works "la passion et la morale l'emportent toujours sur la description matérielle des objets". Delacroix, the hero of the *Salon de 1846,* is there described as "toujours respectueux de son idéal".

Moreover, the *nouvelle* reveals a Baudelaire who is as hypersensitive to the dangers of the *poncif* for the creative artist as he is in the *Salon de 1845.* In *La Fanfarlo,* cliché everywhere threatens: *Les Orfraies* themselves, the Romantic storm which rages at the climax of the story, the final drearily predictable defeat of the enslaved poet all testify to the fact that behind the obvious irony Baudelaire is concerned with the question of artistic integrity. Indeed, Samuel's "faculté comédienne" puts the matter firmly in the centre of things.

If we can accept that the poet is laying his own ghost (and that of a generation) and measuring his potential against the gigantic achievement of his two heroes, then the detailed presentation of Samuel and his predicament may help us to understand Baudelaire's precise anxieties and aspirations at this period. What details of the self-portrait does he cause to emerge most clearly? He emphasizes Samuel's heredity and his abnormal psychological make-up in order to explain why his hero allows himself to become the dupe of two women. Both women are, in their different ways, strong and integrated personalities compared with Samuel. Mme de Cosmelly is allowed to tell her story at length, and she does so with the impressive straightforwardness of a normally virtuous and by now experienced woman. La Fanfarlo, through Baudelaire's powerful evocation of her and her surroundings, is an equally dominant figure in the later part of the story. There is, of course, a ready psychological explanation of the two relationships in Baudelaire's famous sado-masochism, of which there are many hints scattered throughout the narrative, and no doubt this aspect is important: his own drawing shows the figure of La Fanfarlo dominating the tiny, impassive head bearing his own features. But this is not the whole explanation. The tyranny La Fanfarlo exercises over him, finally annihilating him as a creative being—he is forced to experience "toutes les horreurs de ce mariage vicieux qu'on nomme le concubinage" and becomes a *littérateur* whose mistress is angling for honours on his behalf—springs from the fact that he is unable to leave her because for the first time in his life he feels genuine passion: "quant à lui, il a été puni par où il avait péché. Il avait souvent singé la passion; il fut contraint de la connaître"; and this passion, at the moment when it came into being, was an aesthetic phenomenon, "moins une affaire des sens que du raisonnement", "surtout l'appétit et l'admiration du beau". The identification of woman with "le beau" is commonplace in *Les Fleurs du Mal,* but here Baudelaire evokes explicitly the destructive power of Beauty (symbolized by Woman) for the artist who is irresistibly drawn to pursue it. This survivor in a post-Romantic world, who has not yet discovered a new orientation, is aroused, then enslaved and destroyed by his uncritical pursuit of Beauty; he is, in Diderot's terms (which Baudelaire borrows to explain Samuel's character) "crédule"; he sees too many possibilities in every circumstance (unlike the "incrédule" Mme de Cosmelly, who lives in a closed world of enduring rules and immediate self-interest); he is the moth dazzled by the candle or the poet/sun tempted by all experience: "il se jetait dans toutes les flammes et entrait par toutes les fenêtres".

The artist cannot but pursue the Beautiful; but, as an artist in an age of individualism, he is forced to pursue it without the supporting and controlling influence of tradition. "Il est vrai que la grande tradition s'est perdue, et que la nouvelle n'est pas faite" (*Salon de 1846*). Even the guarantee that he has attained his ideal is purely subjective, since the absolute *beau idéal* has been dethroned. In Baudelaire's new romanticism, as he says in the same *Salon,* "il y a autant de beautés qu'il y a de manières habituelles de chercher le bonheur". Under the circumstances, individualism can be either a magnificent victory of the artist over his subject-matter, or a miserable defeat.

This problem is dealt with directly in the art criticism of this period in Baudelaire's life. The main preoccupation of the two *Salons* is the need for contemporary painters to find a way of expressing their own "tempérament"; mere observance of academic rules (the following of a dead tradition), even technical brilliance on its own, leads to lifelessness. Baudelaire describes a painting by Baron in the *Salon de 1845* as "le rococo du romantisme"—the painter at the tail-end of a tradition that has lost its vigour and authority—just as Samuel Cramer's *Les Orfraies* are the standard poetic product of 1840. Any artist at this moment in history, including Baudelaire himself, must wrench himself free of this imitative sterility and embrace modernity, but "pour courir sur les toits, il faut avoir le pied solide et l'œil illuminé par la lumière intérieure" [Baudelaire, "Eugène Delacroix"]. The hero of the modern movement, Delacroix, is able to "courir sur les toits", first because he is a master of the technical aspects of his craft, but more particularly because he possesses "tempérament", because he can dominate his subject-matter: "Delacroix part donc de ce principe, qu'un tableau doit avant tout reproduire la pensée intime de l'artiste, qui domine le modèle, comme le créateur la création". For weaker souls, left without the support of a strong and living tradition, the risk is that they will be defeated by their subject-matter: they painstakingly copy the external details of nature or make an elaborate display of technical skill.

What both Samuel (from one point of view) and Horace Vernet ("nulle passion et une mémoire d'almanach") represent for Baudelaire is the perils of individualism for all but the genius. And yet individualism, in this post-Romantic world, is the inescapable fate of every artist. Baudelaire deals with the subject explicitly in the section of the *Salon de 1846* called "Des écoles et des ouvriers". Only the genius, says Baudelaire, has the power and originality to create a new style or impose a fresh vision, and the disappearance of the "écoles" means that lesser men must do without the instruction and leadership that could have given to their talents some of the masters' authority: "la division des efforts et le fractionnement de la volonté humaine ont amené cette faiblesse, ce doute et cette pauvreté d'invention".

"Ce doute et cette pauvreté d'invention"—these are the weaknesses which, according to the *Salon de 1846,* result from one kind of individualism, namely eclecticism. Samuel Cramer, the eclectic par excellence, is analysed in similar terms. Doubt, in his case, expresses itself as a willingness to pursue any inspiration, and this very "crédulité" engenders his "impuissance", the inability to bring any project to a successful conclusion. And so the eclectic's curse, that "impartialité" which Baudelaire adduces in the 1846 *Salon* as the reason for creative weakness, is at the heart also of Samuel's character, which is, we are told, that of a "comédien". His ability, like that of the actor, to feel at home in any role, implies the lack of a distinct personality independent of role-playing—indeed, even when he finally falls in love, we remember, "Samuel s'arrêta avec respect,—ou feignit de s'arrêter avec respect; car, avec ce diable d'homme, le grand problème est toujours de savoir où le comédien commence". The most striking example of his eclecticism is one on which Baudelaire dwells at length, a kind of psychological plagiarism: "après une lecture passionnée d'un beau livre, sa conclusion involontaire était: voilà qui est assez beau pour être de moi!—et de là à penser: c'est donc de moi,—il n'y a que l'espace d'un tiret".

Eclecticism makes ultimately impossible that expression of "tempérament" which Baudelaire proclaims in the Salons to be the only salvation for an artist in an individualistic age. In 1845 he makes frequent use of the word *naïveté* to describe this spontaneous and sincere expression of the artist's nature: it is seen as the only possible alternative in an individualistic world to pedantic academicism. By 1846 the concept of *naïveté* has widened to include technical skill, "la science du métier", but it is still above all "la domination du tempérament dans la manière" [Baudelaire, "Des écoles et des ouvriers"]: the artist can produce great work only if he allows his "tempérament" to express itself independently of academic tradition, with even technical virtuosity kept under firm control. But this form of extreme individualism is rare, as Baudelaire confesses; it is "un privilège divin dont presque tous sont privés". Only Delacroix, among the artists discussed in 1846, truly possesses it. Unless, therefore, the artist is a great master, by virtue of the "fatalité de son organisation"—if, like Samuel Cramer, he is only a "demi-grand homme"—then he is bound to be, in an age without tradition, an eclectic, the other form of extreme individualist: in place of "une école, c'est-à-dire l'impossibilité du doute" we have "une vaste population de médiocrités, singes de races diverses et croisées, nation flottante de métis qui passent chaque jour d'un pays dans un autre, emportent de chacun les usages qui leur conviennent, et cherchent à se faire un caractère par un système d'emprunts contradictoires".

How is the artist to know whether he is genius or eclectic, whether his "tempérament" is his own, or borrowed? The question is not as absurd as it sounds and it brings us close to Baudelaire's deepest anxiety in *La Fanfarlo*. Samuel Cramer checks on the genuineness of his own emotions by observing his physical reactions in the mirror or by exaggerating his expression of these emotions; and although this is not the *gnôti séauton* of the *Salon de 1846* (an indispensable ingredient of Delacroix's "grands poèmes naïvement conçus"), Baudelaire does make a point of warning us that Samuel could also experience genuine deep feeling and that "en dépit de cette faculté comédienne [il] restait profondément original". He is at one and the same time eclectic and original, he has no "tempérament" except that appropriate to the role he may be playing, and yet "il était toujours le doux, le fantasque, le

paresseux, le terrible, le savant, l'ignorant, le débraillé, le coquet Samuel Cramer, la romantique Manuela de Monteverde". Samuel has somehow to fit both roles so that he may represent what Baudelaire approves of in himself and what he wishes to reject. The fictional *alter ego,* by a failure of will, takes a wrong turning and is defeated as a man and as a poet; Baudelaire in real life must not make the same mistake.

The Delacroix figures, the true "génies" possessed of "naïveté" and able to ride the storm of individualism, are characterized by unity and concentration. Baudelaire is obsessed with unity in the critical writings of the 1840s, and not merely in its aesthetic manifestations. In the *Salon de 1846* questions of social and political unity are made the launching-pad for his argument: republicanism, whether in art or politics ("les singes sont les républicains de l'art"), is destructive of sustained achievement; moreover, his sense of the interpenetration of the various elements in society leads him to hope that the bourgeois will recognize that he too needs art in order to re-establish his inner equilibrium, to find unity in his daily life. The long and expert analysis of the nature and role of colour in painting asserts that one of its main functions is to give a picture of harmony or unity. The artist, in pursuit of his unique vision of beauty, will nonetheless be linked with every other such individual pursuit; his vision is only a variant of the absolute, it is "le beau exprimé par le sentiment, la passion et la rêverie de chacun, c'est-à-dire la variété dans l'unité, ou les faces diverses de l'absolu". The approach of the critic, hoping to elucidate the artist's work, must be equally concentrated—"partiale, passionnée, politique". Throughout the *Salon de 1846* unity and concentration are indispensable conditions of understanding and achievement.

In *La Fanfarlo,* Samuel Cramer, as we have seen, lacks this concentration; he has the fragmented consciousness of the actor. There are about him also suggestions of sexlessness, another symbol of energy that has not been properly focused; he is the "dieu de l'impuissance,—dieu moderne et hermaphrodite": he even signs his poems with a feminine pseudonym. The most striking symbol of his lack of unity is however his mixed blood: he is "le produit contradictoire d'un blême Allemand et d'une brune Chilienne". This mixture of North and South, Old World and New, introvert and sensualist, Christian and pagan, is insisted on at several important points in the story: when Samuel leaves his room to begin his overtures to Mme de Cosmelly he blows out two candles, one standing on a volume of Swedenborg, the other on a "livre honteux". Baudelaire's eulogy of the dance—the moment in the story where Samuel finally submits to the emotional domination of La Fanfarlo—asserts that "certaines organisations païennes" have always understood that dancing is the supreme art, but "Fanfarlo la catholique" can bring to it also "tout l'art des divinités plus modernes": "elle fut à la fois un caprice de Shakespeare et une bouffonnerie italienne". She reminds us at this moment of the "Rêve d'Eschyle éclos au climat des autans". Both La Fanfarlo and Samuel have therefore a kind of universal personality, but whereas in his case it is and remains polarized, "contradictoire", the dancer fuses the contrary elements in a higher and more potent unity, which acts as a sort of focused mirror-image for Samuel and draws him irresistibly on. He sees himself in an integrated and concentrated form, the eclectic who is also the genius.

La Fanfarlo herself is equally expert in every role she dances; she is "tour à tour décente, féerique, folle, enjouée"; but her expertise in so many parts does not—as is the case with Samuel—detract from the force and concentration of her personality. Her costumes and trappings are to her a "professional pose, not an attitude to life" says Sheila Booth in an unpublished thesis on "The art of Baudelaire's *La Fanfarlo*". The dancer's reactions to Samuel, despite the fact that she finds him "bizarre", are always immediate and unambiguous; she has no doubts, unlike the eclectic artist; her room, so evocative of pleasure for Samuel, is a harmonious extension of her personality. Samuel is enraptured to find that her tastes in food, as in furnishing, are identical with his, and "cette similitude de goûts les lia vivement". But although Samuel has experienced love for the first and only time in his life as a result of a unique appeal to both sides of his conflicting personality, he remains enslaved purely because of La Fanfarlo's capacity to enchant his senses, which is only one aspect of her appeal. Significantly, as they are about to make love, a Romantic "northern" storm rages outside, in contrast to the warm and intimate delights of her room; the Chattertons and Savages of the rue St-Jacques, evoked by Baudelaire in a delightful spirit of mockery (both of himself and of a certain romantic tradition), toil away in their garrets as Samuel by contrast decides on a short cut to happiness, pausing only (like Rastignac) to enjoy a sensation of victory over "la ville maudite". The two sides of Samuel's personality have here come apart and the idealistic half has been left "outside". Unity and concentration have disappeared. We find these two contrasting aspects described in the *Choix de maximes consolantes sur l'amour* of 1846: "Homme du Nord, ardent navigateur perdu dans les brouillards, chercheur d'aurores boréales plus belles que le soleil, infatigable soifier d'idéal, aimez les femmes froides . . . Homme du Midi, à qui la nature claire ne peut pas donner le goût des secrets et des mystères,—homme frivole,—de Bordeaux, de Marseille ou d'Italie,—que les femmes ardentes vous suffisent". Samuel has abandoned the impassioned search of the "homme du Nord" to the Chattertons and the Savages, he has relapsed into the state of an "homme frivole"—"abaissant son regard sur les diverses félicités qu'il avait à côté de lui, il se hâta d'en jouir". For Samuel, and for the kind of universal genius Baudelaire is postulating in this union of "North" and "South", this relapse represents allegorically the failure of eclecticism to "courir sur les toits". Samuel's pursuit of beauty ultimately lacks integrity and strenuousness; he is once again "l'homme des belles oeuvres ratées", the mere eclectic whom Baudelaire fears to recognize in himself and whom he is concerned in *La Fanfarlo* to exorcize. The Delacroix of literature, the Balzac of poetry must be able, without abandoning any aspect of his genius, to concentrate and exert it in the direction of creativity.

What Samuel lacks, in Baudelaire's terms, is *volonté,* a concept that will remain for Baudelaire all his life a central preoccupation. In the *Conseils aux jeunes littérateurs, volonté* already occupies an important place: through a complicated image of moving circumferences Baudelaire here asserts the identification of "liberté" and "fatalité" and the capacity of the artist to defy circumstances and to deny the existence of "le guignon" by the exercise of his will. And we have already noticed at the end of the *Salon de 1846* that one of the consequences of individualism in the modern world is a "fractionnement de la volonté humaine".

Without will-power to concentrate and direct the different and often warring elements of the artistic personality bereft of a controlling tradition, the energetic self-expression characteristic of "naïveté" is not possible. The eclectic or doubter lacks "volonté"; Samuel allows his vision of beauty to dwindle and himself to become the passive victim of one aspect (the sensual) of what was originally a complex phenomenon, in pursuit of which his whole personality was at first energetically engaged. And this initial commitment (or inspiration) is itself as important to major artistic achievement as is the will. The two together represent the problem that is at the core of *La Fanfarlo* and of the art criticism of the 1840s, namely the relationship between the artist and his material or model and the parallel relationship between the work of art and the spectator. In any age of individualism, when tradition has disappeared, this relationship between artist and material and between work of art and spectator—an infinite number of private channels for the communication of intense experience—becomes the only absolute, the only guarantee of artistic success. The sudden awareness of "l'unité profonde", that awareness "qui vous saisit l'âme", the tremor of intense excitement that Baudelaire will later attribute to the action of the imagination (whether felt by the artist for his material or by the spectator for the finished work) can alone prove the existence of "génie".

A footnote to the discussion of Horace Vernet in the *Salon de 1846* explains, with a quotation from Hoffmann, that "la véritable mémoire", as opposed to Vernet's pedantic "mémoire d'almanach", consists in "une imagination très vive facile à s'émouvoir, et par conséquent susceptible d'évoquer à l'appui de chaque sensation les scènes du passé, en les douant, comme par enchantement, de la vie et du caractère propres à chacune d'elles". This form of memory has a specific function in the process of enjoying as well as creating a work of art. In the same *Salon* Baudelaire makes his famous statement that a painting in which colour has been properly handled, to create unity or "melody", will make an impact even if viewed from so far away that the subject of the painting is not clear: "S'il est mélodieux, il a déjà un sens, et il a déjà pris sa place dans le répertoire des souvenirs". Memory seems, therefore, to be the instantaneous recording by the imagination of an experience significant enough to make the recording mechanism work; the experience is recorded and perpetuated precisely because it stands apart from the fragmentary nature of most experience. The mechanism is the same for the artist confronted with nature or with his model and for the spectator observing the painting which the artist has made from this confrontation. Of Delacroix's work Baudelaire says: "cette peinture, qui procède surtout du souvenir, parle surtout au souvenir".

In the section of the same *Salon* called "De l'idéal et du modèle" Baudelaire discusses the artist's attitude to his model or subject-matter. He objects to the "idéalisation" of the model (in the traditional academic sense) because such a process is based on abstraction; equally, the opposite process, the slavish imitation of the model, blunts the impact of a painting because of its inclusion of irrelevant detail. The artist's job is rather to convey his own experience of the model in its full intensity, so that the experience may be shared by the spectator, and he does this by revealing nature's unconscious intentions in the model: "Il ne s'agit pas pour lui de copier mais d'interpréter dans une langue plus simple et plus lumineuse". This revelation is based on the artist's understanding of the innate harmony created by the constituent parts of his model: if every part seems inevitably implied by every other, then the model's essential personality is expressed: "Telle main veut tel pied; chaque épiderme engendre son poil. Chaque individu a donc son idéal". In this way the model remains itself, but through the agency of the artist—who is gifted, like the *comédien,* with a unique capacity to understand the personality of others, the nature of the *non-moi*—it becomes more intensely itself, it is "l'individu redressé par l'individu".

This is the process which we see in action in *La Fanfarlo* in the famous episode of "le rouge". By calling for the Columbine costume and the rouge in order to restore the completeness and intensity of his original feelings for La Fanfarlo, Samuel is recognizing that "chaque individu a . . . son idéal", he is "revealing" the quintessential La Fanfarlo (quintessential as far as he is concerned). Baudelaire prepares us carefully for this moment: "Quel est l'homme qui ne voudrait, même au prix de la moitié de ses jours, voir son rêve, son vrai rêve poser sans voile devant lui . . . ?" But his idol without clothes would be for Samuel too entirely herself—she would not be his creation, i.e. a self given meaning by the capacity of the artist to reveal that meaning. In restoring her to the appearance that she had at the moment when he was emotionally aroused by her, Samuel restores the primacy of his emotional reaction ("idéal") over her independent existence ("modèle"): he controls the real world, conferring beauty and significance upon it by the fusion of his capacity to feel and visualize intensely ("souvenir") with the exercise of his "volonté". In calling for the Columbine costume and the rouge in order to complete his personal vision of La Fanfarlo as he recalls her from his first experience of her, Samuel is making use of memory in the same way as the painter: the model makes an impact because of its capacity to be memorable to the artist; it is memorable in this way only because the artist is viewing it as "revealed" by his own inner vision; it is restored on the canvas—or in La Fanfarlo's room— because the artist has the unique power to restore and recreate his original vision.

There are other striking examples in the *nouvelle* of this faculty in action: it appears as possessiveness, containing

also a hint of sadism, in the episode where Mme de Cosmelly is moved to tears and Samuel treats these as if they were his own poems: "le brutal et hypocrite comédien était fier de ces belles larmes; il les considérait comme son oeuvre et sa propriété littéraire"; and again, when he recreates the attraction she used to have for him as a girl, he does so by a gradual and conscious process of "recognition": "à force de la regarder et pour ainsi dire de la reconnaître, il avait retrouvé un à un tous les menus souvenirs qui se rattachaient à elle dans son imagination, il s'était raconté à lui-même, détail par détail, tout ce jeune roman qui, depuis, s'était perdu dans les préoccupations de sa vie et le dédale de ses passions". Samuel also makes use of the same phenomenon to help him in his attempts to seduce Mme de Cosmelly by carefully evoking the details and atmosphere of their childhood happiness near Lyon. But the most notable example is perhaps his long exposition of his theory of passion—on the face of it no more than the suitably conventional Romantic belief that all dreams must remain unfulfilled; but behind Baudelaire's irony at Samuel's (and his own) expense is as usual the serious voice of warning: every "rêve", he says, "quelque idéal qu'il soit", must end with "un poupard glouton suspendu au sein". At the very moment of ecstasy a voice whispers of the day when "l'idole" will have become an "objet". Man is then like a happy traveller in a beautiful landscape who finds that it has suddenly become a "désert d'ennui". But, says Samuel, there is an escape from this desert, which is a purely mental phenomenon created by the insistent, disillusioned voice of Reason. The escape is through hope, or optimism—the tone of the *Conseils aux jeunes littérateurs*— and for Mme de Cosmelly, he implies, it is through transferring her affections to him: "A ce funèbre avertissement, [the voice of Reason] toutes les âmes loyales s'écrieraient: Seigneur, enlevez-moi d'ici avec mon rêve, intact et pur: je veux rendre à la nature ma passion avec toute sa virginité, et porter ailleurs ma couronne inflétrie". The process involved here is none other than the preservation of the ideal in its original integrity, while the "modèle" that awakened it is rejected for another that can sustain it in its original form.

It is his failure to observe his own rule that brings Samuel to disaster. When his "rêve" no longer finds a perfect correspondence in his "modèle", La Fanfarlo, and he is often "seul dans son paradis, nul ne pouvant l'habiter avec lui", he does not carry his vision elsewhere and impose it once again on the real world, he remains bewitched by "ce contentement savoureux, cette rêverie sensuelle, qui vaut peut-être mieux que l'amour comme l'entend le vulgaire". But this "entente profonde de la vie sensuelle" is no longer aesthetic excitement, it is an aspect of "paresse" and fatal to creativity. One side of Samuel's personality, symbolized by his "Southern" sensuality, has been enslaved, and the other makes no protest. His "volonté" has been silenced; his punishment will be to find himself ultimately chained to a vision with "un poupard glouton suspendu au sein".

The interest of *La Fanfarlo* for Baudelaire's aesthetic theories can be seen as twofold: it illustrates his tendency, even at this early stage in his career, to see aesthetic, moral, psychological—even political—problems as inseparable; and it shows that his developing ideas about "l'idéal" and "le souvenir", however dependent in detail on Stendhal or Diderot or Delacroix's conversations with him (and on a longstanding aesthetic tradition) are enmeshed in his private anxieties about the extent and nature of his own talent and of the position of that talent in the world of contemporary literature. Samuel's "impuissance", when put to the test, may be compared to that failure of creative power which is the subject of so many of the *spleen* poems—indeed, the "royal solitaire" who is "seul dans son paradis" reminds us of "le roi d'un pays pluvieux, / Riche, mais impuissant, jeune et pourtant très vieux" and of *La Vie antérieure* with its "secret douloureux qui me faisait languir". Samuel's ultimate fate is less desolate, more matter-of-fact, perhaps more appalling: "La Fanfarlo veut que son amant soit de l'Institut et elle intrigue au ministère pour qu'il ait la croix". However autobiographical *La Fanfarlo* may be, this final vision of a Cramer-Baudelaire contentedly and unconsciously degraded both as man and poet looks forward to a future that never happened. But Baudelaire has given himself the warning: if he is to become the Delacroix of poetry, to "courir sur les toits", he must avoid Samuel's "matérialisme", his idleness, his flagging will. "Il faut vouloir rêver et savoir rêver. Évocation de l'inspiration. Art magique. Se mettre tout de suite à écrire. Je raisonne trop."

J. A. Hiddleston (essay date 1983-84)

SOURCE: "Baudelaire and the Poetry of Prose," *Nineteenth-Century French Studies*, Vol. XII, Nos. 1 & 2, Fall-Winter, 1983-84, pp. 124-27.

[*Hiddleston is the author of* Baudelaire and "Le spleen de Paris" *(1987). In the following essay, he contends that Baudelaire's prose poems are poetical though they lack qualities traditionally associated with poetry, such as compact form and elevated language, sentiments, and subjects.*]

It is clear from the references to the *Petits Poèmes en prose* in his correspondence that Baudelaire intended them to complement *Les Fleurs du mal* and to provide a kind of companion volume. In 1862 he talks of the two works as "se faisant pendant réciproquement," and as late as 1866 he writes of the prose poems as being "encore *Les Fleurs du mal*, mais avec beaucoup plus de liberté, et de détail, et de raillerie" [Baudelaire, *Correspondance*, Pléiade edition, 1973]. In order to give expression to "toute l'amertume et toute la mauvaise humeur dont je suis plein," he constantly places the emphasis upon an intensification of that clash of opposites—Spleen/Ideal, God/Satan, "extase de la vie"/"horreur de la vie"—which characterizes *Les Fleurs du mal*. He will associate "l'effrayant avec le bouffon, et même la tendresse avec la haine." But the differences between the two volumes are more numerous and more profound than this intensification of ironic stridency and disharmony, firstly because, in spite of his

constant fear of producing a mere plaquette, Baudelaire seems to have come to a different conception of what constitutes a collection of poetry. In *Les Fleurs du mal* the role of art is to record a spiritual journey, showing the dilemma of modern man, a prey to the tyranny of modern civilisation and, more particularly, to his own irremediably fallen nature. Because of its comprehensive view of the passions and human nature, *Les Fleurs du mal* presents a kind of synthesis of experience from the standpoint of an austere, unorthodox, vacillating and restricted Christianity. Although Baudelaire is at pains elsewhere to point to the simultaneous pull of the contradictory elements in man, and although the poems were clearly not written in the order in which they appear in the collection, by arranging them in that order he has given the impression of a development and a synthesis. [In *Baudelaire and Freud,* 1977] Leo Bersani has cast some doubt upon the validity of the "architecture" of *Les Fleurs du mal,* since "what is begun and what is ended is an experiment that might have resulted in a universe of meaning in which beginnings and endings would be irrelevant." There may well be much merit in such a view which stresses the relative and contingent aspects of Baudelaire's outlook and poetic experience. It remains that in *Les Fleurs du mal* the poet has made an act of faith in the power of the intellect to bring order into and synthesize the anarchy of experience from birth to death.

However, when we turn from *Les Fleurs du mal* to *Petits Poèmes en prose,* we find no such effort towards unity. We pass from synthesis to fragmentation, contradiction and uncertainty. In this respect the prose poems appear more disillusioned and pessimistic, since what remains after our reading of the fifty pieces is an impression of perpetual clash and of sentimental and moral anarchy. Fragmentation, discontinuity, external and internal chaos are the essential elements of this work, itself only a fragment, which is meant to depict the disharmony of modern man both by its content and by its form. Baudelaire's claim to Vigny that *Les Fleurs du mal* is not a mere album of poems but that it has a beginning and an end contrasts sharply with the "Dédicace" to Houssaye for the twenty poems published in *La Presse* in August and September 1862, in which he permits the director of the review to publish the poems in any order and to omit whichever ones he pleases:

> Mon cher ami, je vous envoie un petit ouvrage dont on ne pourrait pas dire, sans injustice, qu'il n'a ni queue ni tête, puisque tout, au contraire, y est à la fois tête et queue, alternativement et réciproquement. Considérez, je vous prie, quelles admirables commodités cette combinaison nous offre à tous, à vous, à moi et au lecteur. Nous pouvons couper où nous voulons, moi ma rêverie, vous le manuscrit, le lecteur sa lecture; car je ne suspends pas la volonté rétive de celui-ci au fil interminable d'une intrigue superflue.

There being no "plot," the dislocation of the "petit ouvrage" would appear to be intentional and there is no attempt to group the poems according to theme or "genre," or to give the impression of a development or intensification. Of course, we have no clear idea how Baudelaire would have arranged the collection if he had completed it, bringing the number of poems possibly up to one hundred, the same as in the first edition of *Les Fleurs du mal*. The divisions—"Choses parisiennes," "Onéirocritie," "Symboles et moralités"—which can be found in the "Listes de projets" may correspond to those which he intended for the completed collection or they may simply have been for his own guidance. But as late as January 1866 when all but eight of the prose poems have been published, his intention still appears to be to produce a work in which the order would be random, as his letter to Sainte-Beuve indicates: "j'ai l'espoir de pouvoir montrer, un de ces jours, un nouveau Joseph Delorme accrochant sa pensée *rapsodique* à chaque accident de sa flânerie et tirant de chaque objet une morale désagréable" (my italics). At all events the collection as we have it provides an excellent example of the decadent style as defined by Bourget in his study on Baudelaire in *Essais de psychologie contemporaine*: "celui où l'unité du livre se décompose pour laisser la place à l'indépendance de la page . . ." Indeed the *Petits Poèmes en prose* with their uncertain, hybrid and varied genre, and their emphasis upon fragmentation and discontinuity show many of the formal characteristics of decadent literature. The result is a complete lack of tension in comparison with *Les Fleurs du mal*. The sudden changes in tone and theme conform to no pattern, and the poet appears buffeted from one mood to another in a world that seems devoid of any transcendence or hope of transcendence or of any synthesizing factor.

A second difference is that in *Petits Poèmes en prose* the artist is increasingly identified with the fool, the buffoon and the saltimbanque, as in **"Le Fou et la Vénus," "Le Vieux Saltimbanque"** and **"Une Mort héroique,"** whereas in *Les Fleurs du mal* the references are few and of little thematic consequence. The shift reflects possibly a sense of failure on the poet's part, a feeling of social defeat accentuated by increasing fears about the waning of his creative powers after 1861. Charles Mauron in *Le Dernier Baudelaire* has identified the triumph of the social self over the creative artist, to which may be added doubts about the nature and function of art and an inability to believe in the reality of higher truths and values than those degraded ones which constitute the reigning ideology. The fascinating paradox of **"Une Mort héroique"** is that the buffoon Fancioulle excels in the "drames féeriques dont l'objet est de représenter symboliquement le mystère de la vie," and that he is able to introduce the divine and the supernatural "jusque dans les plus extravagantes bouffonneries." We witness accordingly the curious double role of the artist which is at the same time to entertain as fool and to represent the mystery of life as do the greatest creators such as Hugo and Delacroix. However, although the intoxication of art is more suited than any other to veiling the terrors of the abyss, the artist is still only a buffoon, his art merely a "drame féerique" and the veiling of the abyss an illusion. Art is indeed fundamentally lacking in seriousness, even when it claims or is thought to represent the mystery of life; it is a lie, a Pascalian "divertissement" concealing

from men the realities of their condition, and in the person of the cruel prince there is embodied a revolt against the naivety of the childlike buffoon-artist and also by implication against what Proust in another, disillusioned, context called the "magie illusoire de la littérature." As a result there is a constant degrading of many of the ideals put forward, admittedly not always unequivocally, in *Les Fleurs du mal*. In particular women, love and any notion of some possible communion between lovers are shown as aberrations. Women are selfish, savage, vulgar, cruel, that is when they are not mad or widows. Mothers are callous and devoid of maternal feeling. The voice of the poet's mistress, of his "folle petite bien-aimée," is raucous, hysterical, roughened by cheap spirits and prone to violent language, as is her fist to violent action. Even physical love is not seen as some search for the absolute in sensation, but as something resembling a surgical operation. In **"Les Tentations"** Eros is portrayed as having hanging from his belt phials of sinister liquids, gleaming knives and surgical instruments, and in **"Mademoiselle Bistouri"** Baudelaire's good-hearted whore, a vast sophistication of the romantic version, is out of her mind and professes a bizarre taste for doctors and surgeons, especially those with blood-stained aprons.

Finally, the language and the style of the prose poems have little of the refinement and nobility of *Les Fleurs du mal*: there is reference to spit, soot, excrement, rats, concubines, soup, kitchen utensils, hen-pecked husbands, "volailles piaillantes," "canaille" broken teeth and blacked eyes. Critics have noted that Baudelaire seems carefully to have sought "les cadences impaires et les harmonies rompues" [Daniel-Rops, in a 1934 edition of *Petits poèmes en prose*] and have detected even in the prose versions of the *Fleurs* a deliberate prosaic quality and neutrality of tone. The playing down of metaphor and suggestiveness, the frequency of dialogue, the emphasis upon time and narration as opposed to evocation and on truisms and clichés, such as "tuer le temps," "voir la vie en beau," "le crépuscule excite les fous," the deliberately exhausted puns (the devil admits to being "bon diable," the cruel prince who brings about the death of Fancioulle was trying out "une expérience physiologique d'un intérêt *capital*") all contribute to the creation of a predominantly prosaic style.

For these reasons and many more, it can be said that Baudelaire achieved in the prose poems something other than his comments in the *Correspondance* would indicate, something rather different from a companion volume to *Les Fleurs du mal*. Indeed there seems to be a discrepancy between intention and achievement, and one suspects not only that his conception of the prose poem evolved considerably from his first experiments in the 1840s, but also that he was not always totally in command of what he was doing and was not always sure of the direction he wished to take. It may well be that the difficulty of composition which he repeatedly mentions in his letters can in part be attributed to this uncertainty. It is clear from a letter of February 1861 and from the "Dédicace" that the point of departure for the prose poems was Aloysius Bertrand's *Gaspard de la nuit*. Baudelaire's original intention was to create something analogous and to apply to the description of modern life, or rather "d'*une* vie moderne et plus abstraite, le procédé qu'il avait appliqué à la peinture de la vie ancienne." In the event he is aware "que je faisais quelque chose . . . de singulièrement différent," calling his creation an accident "qui ne peut qu'humilier profondément un esprit qui regarde comme le plus grand honneur du poète d'accomplir *juste* ce qu'il a projeté de faire." Even when allowance is made for false modesty and a playful irony towards Bertrand, the sense of an aesthetic accident is not entirely dispelled. If anything it is strengthened when we compare his intention of creating

> une prose poétique, musicale sans rythme et sans rime, assez souple et assez heurtée pour s'adapter aux mouvements lyriques de l'âme, aux ondulations de la rêverie, aux soubresauts de la conscience . . .

with what he actually achieves in the prose poems, where the emphasis falls increasingly upon disharmony rather than on the moments of lyricism, which in any case often appear to restrain or cut short a promised effusion.

The *Petits Poèmes en prose* with their uncertain, hybrid and varied genre, and their emphasis upon fragmentation and discontinuity show many of the formal characteristics of decadent literature. The result is a complete lack of tension in comparison with *Les Fleurs du mal*.

—*J. A. Hiddleston*

What Baudelaire actually did achieve in the *Petits Poèmes en prose* is a puzzle to critics, as it was perhaps to the poet himself. Totally different from Bertrand and certainly from Chateaubriand and Flaubert with their rising and falling cadences, their swelling and expansive ternary sentences and the undulations of their reverie, Baudelaire has no real predecessors in the genre, nor has he any worthy followers. The prose poem in Rimbaud and Char for example, moves towards greater compression, the sudden illumination from the extraordinary image, the disruption of grammar, syntax and logical development, the short circuiting of meaning, whereas Baudelaire stresses the prosaic quality of his prose poems, so many of which are anecdotes, narrations of one kind or another, to such an extent that we wonder wherein lies the poetic element of many of the pieces. Why call them poems at all? Has Baudelaire perhaps failed in the impossible task of squaring the circle and making poetry out of the most naked and uncompromising prose?

Poe is of course relevant to a discussion of Baudelaire's prose poems, not only because **"Le Mauvais Vitrier"** for example shows something of Poe's imp of the perverse, but because Baudelaire was fascinated by Poe's short stories and admired them greatly. He liked them for their grotesque, macabre and morbid subject matter, concentrating on the horrors and infirmities of the mind; but he also liked them for their shortness for the same reasons no doubt as he preferred short poems to epic poems—not just because he was a "paresseux nerveux" temperamentally incapable of the prolonged piece, but because he thought the epic did not produce "cette excitation, . . . cet *enlèvement* de l'âme," and could not have unity and totality of effect, even though it might have unity of composition. Long poems are "la ressource de ceux qui sont incapables d'en faire de courts." Similarly, he prefers the short story to the novel because it has the immense advantage over the novel of vast proportions that its brevity adds to the intensity of effect. Like the short poem it produces the same unity of impression and totality of effect. Baudelaire's prose poems themselves and the use of the adjective *petits* in the title reflect this aesthetic conviction that the poetic quality is related to the shortness of the pieces, though not in any mechanical way as suggested by Suzanne Bernard in her admirable *Le Poème en prose de Baudelaire à nos jours*. If this were the case, the eleven lines of the "boutade" **"Le Miroir"** would be more "poetic" than the one hundred and thirty-one lines of **"Mademoiselle Bistouri"** or the one hundred and sixty lines of **"Une Mort héroique,"** which is clearly not so. Suzanne Bernard's criterion however contains the germ of the truth. The criterion of poetic excellence should not be the brevity, but the concentration and intensity of the piece, which with only the appearance of a paradox gives us a feeling of expansion, of a kind of "psychedelic" multiplicity, not unlike the sudden illumination in Rimbaud, but on the level of subject matter rather than image. As after reading **"Mademoiselle Bistouri"** or **"Une Mort héroique"** we ponder the link between love and surgery, between prostitution and innocence, between madness and kindness, or as we ponder the identity of the cruel prince and the mime, and the links between art, buffoonery, violence and death, these stories fascinate us with a meaning or meanings which go far beyond their literal sense. They have something of the elliptic allegories of, say, Kafka, and before such stories and narrations we can adopt the same criterion as Baudelaire himself for judging the excellence of a painting:

> Il m'arrivera souvent d'apprécier un tableau uniquement par la somme d'idées ou de rêveries qu'il apportera dans mon esprit.

Such pieces might be said to be as successful poetically as "La Chevelure" or "Parfum exotique," since the story they relate has a power and a "rayonnement" analogous to those of the images in Baudelaire's finest verse poems.

A second criterion of poetic excellence might be thought to be the extent to which the poet creates a violent and surreal world. It has been too often affirmed that *Petits Poèmes en prose* are marked by a realism of detail and description which provides a compelling evocation of the life of the modern capital. But very few of the poems are in fact descriptions of the real world and nothing more, and they tend to be among the least interesting in the collection, for example **"Le Désespoir de la vieille"** and **"Le Chien et le flacon."** Several are placed resolutely within a fantasy or dream world, such as **"Les Dons des fées," "Les Tentations," "Chacun sa chimère," "L'Invitation au voyage," "Un Hémisphère dans une chevelure."** But among the most compelling are those where Baudelaire mingles and fuses the real with the imaginary, so that the poems take on the properties of an hallucination in which "la profondeur de la vie" is revealed at its most intense and most disturbing. They are similar to such poems from *Les Fleurs du mal* as "Les Sept Vieillars" where the poet's baleful vision of the seven old men becomes an incomprehensible and nightmarish hallucination:

Vainement ma raison voulait prendre la barre;
La tempête en jouant déroutait ses efforts,
Et mon âme dansait, dansait, vieille gabarre
Sans mâts, sur une mer monstrueuse et sans bords!

On the very simplest level, for example, **"Les Veuves"** is almost a list of the various kinds of widow that one can see in the streets and gardens of Paris, until the evocation of the central figure, "un être dont la noblesse faisait un éclatant contraste avec toute la trivialité environnante." He describes her as "une femme grande, majestueuse, et si noble dans tout son air, que je n'ai pas souvenir d'avoir vu sa pareille. . . ." He describes her "parfum de hautaine vertu," and sad and gaunt face, until the figure becomes so detached from the base and trivial surroundings that it becomes a "Singulière vision" standing above the rest of humanity and endowed with a heightened significance. The moment in which the poet catches sight of her, as in "A une passante," seems to stand outside time, and this heightening of reality transforms the widow from a "chose vue" into an allegorical figure of loneliness and disproportion.

Often the passage from the real to the surreal in the prose poems is brought about through the heightening and intensification of the power and vitality of a street scene, as for example in the "explosion" of the New Year in **"Un Plaisant"**:

C'était l'explosion du nouvel an: chaos de boue et de neige, traversé de mille carosses, étincelant de joujoux et de bonbons, grouillant de cupidités et de désespoirs, délire officiel d'une grande ville fait pour troubler le cerveau du solitaire le plus fort.

At the beginning of this anecdote we are plunged into a real world which threatens to return to chaos and where men appear to have gone mad. Similarly, but more acutely, in **"Le Vieux Saltimbanque"** we have the evocation of the vitality and stridency of the fair: "Partout s'étalait, se répandait, s'ébaudissait le peuple en vacances." There are the "baraques" which "piaillaient, beuglaient, hurlaient." "C'était un mélange de cris, de détonations de cuivre et d'explosions de fusées." We are told that "Tout n'était que lumière, poussière, cris, joie, tumulte." In this "real" world the mind is bombarded with many new and unusual happenings and sensations of all kinds, so that it takes on the terrifying unreality of a nightmare in which reason has lost its grip and is numbed and bewildered by the assault upon the senses. Against such a reality which has returned to chaos and is engulfed in madness, the figure of the Saltimbanque stands out with greater poignancy, like Awareness itself isolated amidst the unthinking absurdity and primitive clamour of the passions and the senses.

There are other transitions from the real to the surreal which are apparently more calm, as for example in **"Le Crépuscule du soir"**:

Le jour tombe. Un grand apaisement se fait dans les pauvres esprits fatigués du labeur de la journée; et leurs pensées prennent maintenant les couleurs tendres et indécises du crépuscule.

Cependant du haut de la montagne arrive à mon balcon, à travers les nues transparentes du soir, un grand hurlement, composé d'une foule de cris discordants, que l'espace transforme en une lugubre harmonie, comme celle de la marée qui monte ou d'une tempête qui s'éveille.

The references to the peace of evening, to the mountain top and the transparent clouds prepare us for the relaxation and the *vague-à-l'âme* of a Lamartinian meditation, but gradually we find ourselves in another world where the complaint of the wretched is made audible, and where a "lugubre harmonie" is made out of what is discordant, a harmony which threatens to return to an even greater chaos than before, like the uneasy peace before the unleashing of a storm. We start in one mode of perception and end in another, where the abstract is made concrete and where harmony and discordance appear momentarily at least reconciled.

Such an example might be said to be half way between the discordant clamour and the outburst of vitality we have witnessed in the fair or the Paris street scene and that silent orgy of light and energy which is to be found in **"Le Fou et la Vénus."** We start in a real park, but immediately the heightened presence of light and indeed of all things gives to it the intensity it can have only in certain dreams or states of hallucination, when a sense of menace is present together with one of tranquillity:

Quelle admirable journée! Le vaste parc se pâme sous l'oeil brûlant du soleil, comme la jeunesse sous la domination de l'Amour.

L'extase universelle des choses ne s'exprime par aucun bruit; les eaux ellesmêmes sont comme endormies. Bien différentes des fêtes humaines, c'est ici une orgie silencieuse.

On dirait qu'une lumière toujours croissante fait de plus en plus étinceler les objets; que les fleurs excitées brûlent du désir de rivaliser avec l'azur du ciel par l'énergie de leurs couleurs, et que la chaleur, rendant visibles les parfums, les fait monter vers l'astre comme des fumées.

It is as if nature itself here had taken on the same fascinating quality and were endowed with the same intense presence as the visions of **"La Chambre double"** and *Les Paradis artificiels,* as if it had a life and a being of its own totally independent of human thought and action, and this feeling is made all the more powerful by the detachment of the figure of the Fool absorbed in his worship of the implacable and immortal goddess Venus. Such a hyperbolic description with its increasing intensity is at once ecstatic and disquieting, in much the same way as Hugo's descriptions fill us with fear before a numinous world where "tout est plein d'âmes."

Once again, as in **"Le Vieux Saltimbanque,"** we feel the rational mind slowly losing its grip as the surreal invades the real. Such a vision with its suggestion of the elevation of all things towards the light and the spiritual world threatens to degenerate into a nightmare and instead of a beatific vision we have a terrifying glimpse, albeit momentary, of the horrific orgy of the natural world described by Sartre in *La Nausée,* of the hellish otherness of things which threaten to violate and engulf the mind. A similar disquiet at the exuberance of nature is evident in **"Le Tir et le cimetière"** where "le soleil ivre se vautrait tout de son long sur un tapis de fleurs magnifiques engraissées par la destruction." It is rendered all the more threatening by the parallel which is established between the clamour of nature and that of the unthinking public at the firing range.

In this connection it is instructive to notice the frequency and the particular use of the word "explosion" in some of the prose poems, signifying not so much an outburst of creative activity as the subjection of the poet to a sensory experience in which the controlling factors of reason and awareness and lost: in **"Un Plaisant,"** "C'était l'explosion du nouvel an"; in **"Le Désir de peindre"** there is an "explosion dans les ténèbres" in the eye of his mistress, and in **"Une Mort héroique"** the admiring crowd breaks out into "explosions de la joie et de l'admiration" which have the power and energy of continuous thunder. In all these explosions there is some threat which is more or less explicit, even in those which seem to reach a reconciliation between violence and tranquillity. In **"Le Désir de peindre"** for example we are given a sense of calm by the comparison of the light in his mistress's eyes with that of the moon, until we are told that it is not the white moon of idylls, but the moon which has been "arrachée du ciel, vaincue et révoltée, que les Sorcières thessaliennes contraignent durement à danser sur l'herbe terrifiée." The sense of calm is soon dispersed by the suggestion of some kind of cosmic disaster in which the world is given over to the forces of chaos and unreason.

Closely linked with these violent outbursts are those pieces which describe "les soubresauts de la conscience," these sudden changes of mood or feeling which always move in *Petits Poèmes en prose* from the serene, ecstatic and ideal towards anguish, torment and a debased reality. One thinks immediately of such pieces as **"La Chambre double,"** **"Le Confitéor de l'artiste"** and **"Le Gâteau,"** where the movement from one extreme to its opposite creates the impression of chaotic discontinuity. In **"Le Confitéor . . ."** the movement is all the more intense and striking for being unmotivated. No reason is given for the change from a serene contemplation of sea and sky, in which the poet identifies himself in a quasi-pantheistic fashion with the immensity of nature, to the violent and anguished outcry that "maintenant la profondeur du ciel me consterne; sa limpidité m'exaspère. L'insensibilité de la mer, l'immuabilité du spectacle, me révoltent." The fault is not as in **"La Chambre double"** with the intrusion of an importunate and philistine outside world: the fault lies within the poet himself whose nerves seem unable to tolerate the tension of the aesthetic experience. It is important to stress that in these "soubresauts de la conscience" the movement is always from ideal to spleen; the curve of the pieces never goes in the opposite direction, which again contributes to the poet's doubts about the status of art and of the artist, creating ultimately as in **"Chacun sa Chimère"** a sense of lassitude, despair and ultimately of indifference.

There are many forms of humour in the prose poems which would merit a sympathetic and detailed study. They range from the wilfully debilitated to the most original, to what André Breton called black humour, that extreme exaggeration of "le rire en pleurs." There are several examples of it in the collection, all related in one way or another to an outburst of violence, whether it be the controlled violence of the man in **"Le Galant Tireur"** who imagines the doll at the firing range is his wife, or that of the "désabusé" rake of **"Portraits de maîtresses"** who alludes in impeccable good taste and understatement to his murder of his mistress by drowning because she was too perfect, or that of the poet who instead of giving alms to the man who asks for help proceeds to beat him up. The best and most notorious example is without doubt **"Le Mauvais Vitrier"** which is also among the most perfect of the collection. From his sixth-floor garret the poet sees a poor "vitrier" whose piercing and discordant cry rises up to him through the muggy Paris atmosphere. He calls him up, and then gruffly dismisses him for not having rose coloured panes through which to see "la vie en beau." When the man goes back down to the street, the poet throws a flower-pot down at him, smashing all his panes and depriving him and his family of the proceeds of a day's labour.

Much has been written about this poem, which can be difficult to explain to those who prefer a literature of "bons sentiments." Perhaps it reflects Baudelaire's desire to mystify and his "plaisir aristocratique de déplaire," but what is significant and blackly humorous is the sudden change from contemplation and lethargy on the part of the poet to violent, hysterical and apparently unmotivated action. The cruelty stems from exasperation with the imperfect world of men and things taken to the extreme of a nightmarish paroxysm. In such moments, as in the painting of Goya whom he admired, and as in the poems of Lautréamont whom he prefigures, it is as if the poet took the side of the dark, ugly and arbitrary powers which seem to govern our world, and thereby he gives us a deeper insight into our condition, showing at the same time the inadequacies of a facile and unthinking humanism.

It is not clear from his writings on the essence of laughter and on French and foreign caricaturists how Baudelaire would have classified the kind of black humour he uses in **"Le Mauvais Vitrier."** On the one hand it has in an exaggerated form something of the diabolical laughter of Melmoth and the accompanying sense of original sin; on the other hand, paradoxically, it seems to have the violence, the "vertige de l'hyperbole" and "quelque chose de terrible et d'irrésistible" which Baudelaire recognises as the distinctive signs of the grotesque and the "comique absolu," though of course it has none of that essential sense of joy and innocence which distinguishes the latter from the "rire significatif." At all events violence, hallucination and chaos are all associated by Baudelaire with certain kinds of humour and caricature, and are all powerful ingredients of *Petits Poèmes en prose,* pointing to a world where order and reason have been replaced by anarchy, both in the moral and physical sphere; for in these prose poems men are not fundamentally rational creatures; they act without premeditation or against their own best interests; they light cigars beside barrels of gunpowder to tempt destiny; they boast of unworthy actions they have not committed and refuse to do a small service for a friend, yet they readily help the unworthy; they throw chickens at maîtres d'hôtel at the time of the full moon; they fall in love with those with whom they have nothing in common and kill their favourite buffoon or perfect mistress, to such an extent that one would be apt to attribute to Baudelaire the invention of the gratuitous act long before Gide thought of it. At the heart of human actions and emotions there is moral anarchy. In **"Les Tentations"** for example, the poet in his high-mindedness rejects in his dream the blandishments of Eros, Plutus and Fame, but in his waking life he ironically implores them to return so that he can succumb to them. Similarly, in **"Le Joueur généreux"** he rejects the devil's offer in return for his soul to be free from ennui; any wish will be granted. But the offer is rejected not out of any strength of mind or character, but out of suspicion and distrust and an inability to believe in his good fortune, and the poet finds himself praying to God to make the devil keep his word, a sure sign of moral, spiritual and theological chaos. Indeed all the prayers in the collection are, to say the least, unorthodox. In **"A une heure du matin"** in a prayer which is reminiscent of the Pharisee's prayer in Luke the poet asks God to grant him the power to produce some fine verses to prove to himself that he is not inferior to those whom he despises, a prayer which is hardly informed by Christian humility and charity; and the prayer at the end of **"Mademoiselle Bistouri"** which pleads in favour of such innocent monsters, is as much a challenge to the existence of divine providence and order, as an indication of submission and belief in its reality. The prayer borders on the blasphemous and points to a moral anarchy at the heart of the universe, elements of which are to be found in for example **"Les Dons des Fées"** where various gifts and talents are given to the most unsuitable

people: the gift of money and riches to one who is already rich and has no sense of charity; the love of the beautiful and poetry to a "sombre gueux" with no means of exploiting it; the gift of pleasing to those incapable of understanding its value.

However, it may be justly asked why the violent, the gratuitous and the chaotic should be equated with the poetic. It seems that what Baudelaire achieved in many of *Petits Poèmes en prose* and may well have had in mind as a partially conceived intention was a kind of poetry of disharmony, an intoxication not with things having "l'expansion des choses infinies," but with what may be called an "ivresse de l'absurde," an ecstasy made not of a spiritual elevation in which all things flow together "Dans une ténébreuse et profonde unité, / Vaste comme la nuit et comme la clarté," but as Malraux said in a different context "une extase vers le bas," an ecstasy at the horrific and gratuitous presence of things and events, which refuse to submit to the analyses and categories of the mind and which seem to escape from the domain of prose and logical discourse. The highest flights of lyricism in *Les Fleurs du mal* point to another order of things, a vision of the one where contradiction is overcome, where time and separation no longer prevail, and where analysis is replaced by the perceptions of a superior faculty. The "lyricism" of many of the *Petits Poèmes en prose* is at the opposite pole, describing an ecstasis before the irrational in which mere juxtaposition has stunned and paralysed the mind into a sense of infernal timelessness.

Barbara Wright (essay date 1984)

SOURCE: An introduction to *La Fanfarlo,* in *Baudelaire: "La Fanfarlo" and "Le spleen de Paris"* by Barbara Wright and David H. T. Scott, Grant & Cutler Ltd., 1984, pp. 9-33.

[*Wright is an educator specializing in French literature. In the following essay on* La Fanfarlo, *she discusses the structure of the novella and assesses the relationship between the narrator and the story told.*]

Ambivalence surrounds virtually everything concerned with *La Fanfarlo.* First published in January 1847 in the periodical *Bulletin de la Société des gens de lettres,* the precise date of its composition is the source of disagreement among scholars. It was probably written some time between 1843 and the end of 1846.

The autobiographical links, likewise, are tantalisingly elusive. If Asselineau and Gautier were among the first of many authoritative commentators to reach unanimity on the striking resemblance, physical and otherwise, between Samuel Cramer and Baudelaire himself, the parallelism with Emile Deroy (1820-46) is none the less significant. Deroy's early portrait of Baudelaire is probably the best visual representation available of the quasi-fictitious Samuel Cramer. Furthermore, since Baudelaire did not become acquainted with Delacroix until March 1846, Emile

Deroy is now thought to have been Baudelaire's aesthetic mentor in the period leading up to *Le Salon de 1845*; his possible influence on the artistic views expressed by Samuel Cramer is therefore far from negligible.

In 1842, Baudelaire first met Jeanne Duval, then an actress at the Théâtre de la Porte Saint-Antoine. She may thus be one of the possible sources of inspiration for the dancer in *La Fanfarlo*. So too may Marie Daubrun, an actress at the Théâtre Montmartre from autumn 1845, whose influence in this connection has been explored by Claude Pichois [in his editions of Baudelaire's *La Fanfarlo* and *Oeuvres complètes* and in an essay in *Mercure de France,* décembre, 1956]. Recent researches have shown, however, that Baudelaire may have written *La Fanfarlo,* along with *Choix de maximes consolantes sur l'amour* (1846), at least partially as a tongue-in-cheek homage to Félicité Baudelaire. Félicité Baudelaire was the wife of Baudelaire's half-brother, Alphonse, from whom he sought vengeance for having been 'betrayed' on several counts: having at first got on well with his half-brother, Baudelaire subsequently held the latter responsible for collusion with his hated stepfather, General Aupick, in having him sent abroad on a long journey (1841-42); for divulging confidences about his incipient syphilis; and for contributing towards his disinheritance. In the two years after attaining his majority, Baudelaire had spent about half the money bequeathed to him by his father. His family, seeking to have the balance held in trust for him, proceeded to have a 'conseil judiciaire' appointed in September 1844, with Maître Ancelle as the lawyer in charge. Baudelaire was humiliated by this experience, which, in the view of Michel Butor [*Histoire extraordinaire: essai sur un rêve de Baudelaire,* 1961], morally, at least, emasculated him. In 1845, having left everything to Jeanne Duval, Baudelaire attempted suicide.

Neither the author's name, nor even the title of the novella, is free of deliberate ambiguity. When published in 1847, *La Fanfarlo* was signed by Charles Defayis, 'Defayis' being the maiden name of Baudelaire's mother. And the title? Despite many suggestions, it still retains all the mystery of a conundrum. There are possible associations with a polka-dancer of the time, called Fanfarnou; or, more simply still, the name may derive from the substantive 'fanfare'; but what is perhaps most fascinating of all is the sound of the name, combining the feminine ending 'a' with the masculine ending 'o'. Typically, too, the title of the novella is not clarified until the tale is well advanced, a technique which Baudelaire will later use in the prose poem, **'Un Cheval de race'**.

As Baudelaire himself said in relation to E. T. A. Hoffmann, Samuel Cramer, the protagonist in *La Fanfarlo,* is 'atteint d'un dualisme chronique'. This dual nature is highlighted, from the outset, by the fact that Samuel Cramer once wrote under a feminine pseudonym, Manuela de Monteverde, as Mérimée had done in *Le Théâtre de Clara Gazul.* Even though these names may be seen to have emanated from a single source, they nevertheless point to a fundamental duality within the protagonist.

However, this duality, this ambivalence, is, for the most part, a reflection of Baudelaire's conscious and deliberate intention: it is at the core of his early dramatic work, *Idéolus* (started in 1843, in association with Ernest Prarond), the plot of which has many parallels with **La Fanfarlo**. In a manner less impish than Gide's subsequent refusal to be pinned down to any one specific attitude if that were necessarily to preclude its opposite, Baudelaire's work involves a series of swings of the pendulum, encompassing, at one and the same time, attitudes and expressions which might often be seen as mutually exclusive. This is mirrored in his use of form, where he builds up patterns and expectations and then introduces shock tactics, concluding with some quite unexpected turn, after what might have been thought to prefigure a harmonious resolution of suspense.

Duality pervades *La Fanfarlo,* in which, thematically and structurally, the binary movement is predominant. For the purposes of this brief study, two sets of polar opposites will be distinguished, as areas of possible emphasis in further work on the subject, rather than as neat categories:

> 1. Duality within the double narrative sequence, the first sequence being that in which the protagonist, Samuel Cramer, presented as a latter-day knight-errant, ends by setting out on a mission for his *belle dame sans merci,* Mme de Cosmelly; the second sequence being that in which Samuel Cramer, in seeking to woo the dancer, La Fanfarlo, away from Mme de Cosmelly's husband, succeeds in falling in love with her himself, thus getting caught in a trap of his own making, since it was with the ulterior motive of obtaining a 'reward' from Mme de Cosmelly that Samuel Cramer had embarked on the venture in the first place.

> 2. Duality inherent in the narrator's attitude towards his discourse.

Between the first and second narrative sequences, there is a relationship of call and echo which heightens the effect of their juxtaposition, allowing for ironic interplay between the two, coupled with constant shifts in the point of view of the narrator.

The first narrative sequence involves an overt parody of first-generation Romanticism, while adopting many of the stances of Balzac as omniscient narrator and of Stendhal as ironic deflator.

Four encounters, in all, are involved in the development of Samuel Cramer's relationship with Mme de Cosmelly. From his studious attic, his typically elevated 'prison romantique' ('du haut de sa solitude'), Samuel had seen and admired Mme de Cosmelly, whom he remembered from his provincial days in Lyon. Leaving his bedside reading, which included some Swedenborg (often hailed as the 'link' between Balzac's 'langage des fleurs' and Baudelaire's later development of the aesthetics of 'correspondances'), Samuel attired himself elegantly, as Rastignac might have done before him, and set out to contrive an encounter with Mme de Cosmelly. This meeting takes place on neutral ground, in a public park. By contrast, in the second narrative sequence, Samuel will seek out La Fanfarlo in the intimacy of her back-stage dressing-room and, later, in her private apartment. With Mme de Cosmelly, he never progresses beyond the bench in the Luxembourg Gardens.

The first encounter with Mme de Cosmelly serves, therefore, to establish identity. Samuel, recalling how they had grown up together in Lyon, assembles 'tout ce jeune roman' which, in the hands of a more conventional author, might have been the pretext for the development of a subplot of some sort. Mme de Cosmelly, in consultation with her maid-servant, recognizes Samuel. This establishment of identities is again in contrast with the necessarily more oblique way in which Samuel will make himself known to the dancer, La Fanfarlo, by writing reviews of her performances in terms so scathing that her professional reputation requires her to find out more about one who is ostensibly so hostile towards her.

The second encounter is contrived by Mme de Cosmelly, who adopts the fairly standard ploy of leaving her book and her handkerchief on the bench, thus affording Samuel the pretext of returning these to her. Later, he will seek to develop his relationship with Mme de Cosmelly by offering her his collection of sonnets and by responding to her reaction to his work which we, as readers, know only indirectly. Again, in the intermediary section between the two principal narrative sequences, we learn how Samuel will offer sonnets to both Mme de Cosmelly and La Fanfarlo, confusing, ironically, the addressees.

The development takes place through oblique means in both narrative sequences. In the course of the second encounter with Mme de Cosmelly, Samuel launches into an attack on Walter Scott, the author of the novel left behind by Mme de Cosmelly. In his *Conseils aux jeunes littérateurs* (1846), Baudelaire distinguishes, in criticism, between two methods of slating: 'éreintage . . . par la ligne courbe, et par la ligne droite, qui est le plus court chemin'. Both the narrative sequences in **La Fanfarlo** contain such 'éreintage': the target is Scott, in the first instance (a sally not without its boomerang effect on his disciple, Balzac); in the second, it is La Fanfarlo herself. In terms of plot, the effect of both is similar, in that a pretext has been found for entering into a more personal phase in the separate relationships. There is, however, this difference that the 'writing', in the second narrative sequence, is unashamedly journalistic, whereas in the first it is pretentiously literary, with Samuel undertaking to offer Mme de Cosmelly his collection of sonnets, *Les Orfraies,* on the following day, the occasion of their third encounter.

The fourth and final encounter with Mme de Cosmelly centres, primarily, on her reaction to *Les Orfraies*. In Samuel's work, she criticizes many of the devices which were not merely characteristic of the period, but which will reappear in the second narrative sequence, in the context of La Fanfarlo. By contrast with Mme de Cosmelly, who, in the first narrative sequence, had been de-

Baudelaire's sketch of his mistress, Jeanne Duval. Duval is widely believed to be the model for the character La Fanfarlo in Baudelaire's novella of the same name.

scribed in only the vaguest of terms ('ses traits . . . avaient la grâce profonde et décente de l'honnête femme'), La Fanfarlo is described with all the hyperbole so castigated earlier on. Yet, conversely, the force of this hyperbole is undercut, in terms of its ironic impact, by virtue of Mme de Cosmelly's previous condemnation. In language which is often 'mystique', as well as sensuous and exotic, La Fanfarlo, projected as the Dancer, is evoked in terms reminiscent of both 'des créatures bizarres' and 'des sultanes de bas lieu'. The scene in which, anticipating the ballet-dancers of Degas by over twenty years, La Fanfarlo, is leaning over to lace up her boots, is suggestive of a geometrical pattern, pin-pointed in terms both mathematical and anatomical: 'Tranchée perpendiculairement à l'endroit le plus large, cette jambe eût donné une espèce de triangle dont le sommet eût été sur le tibia, et dont la ligne arrondie du mollet eût fourni la base convexe'. Again, in her bent posture, 'sa tête, inclinée vers son pied . . . laissait deviner l'ornière des omoplates'. All of this constitutes an ironic echo of Mme de Cosmelly's earlier rejection of Samuel's 'descriptions d'anatomie'. Furthermore, Mme de Cosmelly deplores the poet's adulation of the feet and hands of his mistress when, according to strict bourgeois ethics, a woman should be knitting socks and mittens for her children's feet and hands; in the second narrative sequence, the narrator, with ironical detachment, gives an account of Samuel's behaviour when first received in the home of La Fanfarlo: 'Notre homme exprimait son admiration par des baisers muets qu'il lui appliquait avec ferveur sur les pieds et les mains'.

The observations by Mme de Cosmelly provoke a torrent of Romantic outpouring on the part of Samuel, punctuated at four points: the first, where Mme de Cosmelly seeks to deflect his attention to the springtime flowers in the park; the second, where she is unable to get in a word edgeways; the third, where Samuel is cut short by the realization of the hurt being caused to her by his rhetorical monologue; and the fourth, where she weeps and her tears lead to a double misunderstanding, with role-playing involved on both sides (her 'candide désolation' ironically underscoring the 'mission' with which she will shortly proceed to charge her gallant knight-errant, and his hypocritical pride at having been able to move her to tears, as he thought, seeing in the emotion of the percipient 'son œuvre et sa propriété littéraire'). The four set pieces, thus punctuated, are essentially displays of 'jargon romantique' and are followed by a fifth, in the hypocritically didactic vein characterized by the term 'patois séminariste'. Together, they form a marked contrast with the 'Qui, Madame', uttered by Samuel to La Fanfarlo in the second narrative sequence; his earlier outpourings to Mme de Cosmelly are here recalled in terms of one who had 'bavardé comme une pie romantique'.

It is, perhaps, not without significance that Baudelaire who, in the last analysis, is remembered primarily for his outstanding achievement in verse poetry, chose to have Samuel 'mettre en prose et . . . déclamer quelques mauvaises stances composées dans sa première manière'. His attempts seem deliberately pedestrian and contrast with the more poetic prose contained in parts of the second narrative sequence. In general terms, it is agreed that verse pre-dates prose in the creative imagination of Baudelaire; but equally it is clear that, from the outset of his literary career, he was concerned to make a distinction between these two forms. Overt reference to an alexandrine, in *La Fanfarlo,* would seem to be rejected, as though for fear of making the writing seem that much more suspect as prose. In the second narrative sequence, there is an instance where the poetry reworked has been variously identified as that of Ernest Prarond or of Baudelaire himself, and where the original alexandrine would appear to have been wilfully distorted, metrically, as well as in terms of semantic context:

> Le ruisseau, lit funèbre où s'en vont les dégoûts
> (Original)
> Le ruisseau, lit funèbre où s'en vont les billets doux
> (*La Fanfarlo*)

The change, by Baudelaire, from 'dégoûts' to 'billets doux', is also indicative of his overall concern with ironic deflation in *La Fanfarlo*. Born into and yet reacting against the tradition of luxuriously poetic prose, as evolved by Rousseau and Chateaubriand, the future author of *Le Spleen de Paris* was already wanting to mark his originality in this art-form in which he was so clearly indebted to his precursors.

Again, in these passages declaimed by Samuel, 'à qui la phrase et la période étaient venues', some of the central themes of *Les Fleurs du Mal* are paralleled—ironically. There is, for example, an analogy with the poet of 'Bénédiction' in the following imprecation ('Bénédiction' was first published in 1857, but the date of its original composition may go back to the period 1844-46): 'Malheur, trois fois malheur aux pères infirmes qui nous ont faits rachitiques et mal venus, prédestinés que nous sommes à n'enfanter que des morts-nés!' This is a reminder of the self-pitying introverts following in the wake of Chateaubriand's René and victims of the so-called 'mal du siècle'. Samuel differentiates his fellow-poets from ordinary mortals in the following terms: 'Ils vivent pour vivre, et nous, hélas! nous vivons pour savoir'. And yet the secret of Samuel's relative success in the second narrative sequence was precisely due to the fact that 'l'amour était chez lui moins une affaire des sens que du raisonnement'.

The first narrative sequence concludes with Mme de Cosmelly's account, in terms reminiscent of Balzac's *Etudes de femme* and *Physiologie du mariage,* or, indeed, Baudelaire's own *Choix de maximes consolantes sur l'amour,* of how, since they had moved to Paris from the provinces, she had lost the love of her husband to a dancer, here named, for the first time, as La Fanfarlo. This 'douleur de province' is simply told as 'une histoire banale, l'histoire de toutes les malheureuses,—un roman de province!' At the end of it all, thanks to the intervention of Samuel, whose eyes, it will be remembered, were 'brillants comme des gouttes de café', the reconciliation scene between husband and wife takes place after Mme de Cosmelly has prepared 'le meilleur thé du monde, dans une théière bien modeste et bien fêlée'. Interestingly, however, when Mme de Cosmelly has recourse to artifice in order to try to regain her husband's affection (and before she has met Samuel again in Paris), she tarts herself up, 'la mort dans le cœur', in a way which prefigures the 'accoutrement fantasque' of La Fanfarlo: 'Moi, la chaste épouse qu'il était allé chercher au fond d'un pauvre château, j'ai paradé devant lui avec des robes de fille'. La Fanfarlo's dancing costumes, made of 'étoffes . . . pailletées', are, to a small extent, anticipated in Mme de Cosmelly's admission to Samuel: 'J'ai pailleté mon désespoir avec des sourires étincelants. Hélas! il n'a rien vu'. And, more obviously, the next remark by Mme de Cosmelly prefigures Samuel's almost hysterical request, in the seduction scene, that La Fanfarlo's Columbine costume be fetched, calling after her servant, Flore: 'Eh! n'oubliez pas le rouge!': 'J'ai mis du rouge, Monsieur, j'ai mis du rouge!'. All to no avail, it would appear.

Between the two narrative sequences, there is thus continuity, cross-referencing and irony. Nowhere is this more evident than in the role-playing of all the protagonists, notably Samuel Cramer himself. Frequently characterized as a 'comédien', his play-acting in the first narrative sequence is mostly hypocritical. In the second, this is not so often the case, since he is described in less deprecatory terms. Endowed with some sense of originality (for La Fanfarlo, at any rate, he had 'l'attrait de la nouveauté'), he takes on what Nathaniel Wing [in 'The Poetics of Irony in Baudelaire's *La Fanfarlo*', *Neophilologus* LIX, No. 2 (April 1975)] has called 'the capacity to astonish': '. . . avec ce diable d'homme, le grand problème est toujours de savoir où le comédien commence'. This time, at least, Samuel was not 'ridicule'.

It is in this more positive projection (with La Fanfarlo's art as a pendant to that of Samuel) that, despite continuing elements of irony, the couple here become 'le poète et la danseuse'. Furthermore, far from the affected 'dandysme', which first offended Mme de Cosmelly in the gradual detachment of her husband, Samuel actually takes on the lifestyle of the *dandy* in the second narrative sequence, in terms which prefigure Baudelaire's later adumbrations on the subject in *Le Peintre de la vie moderne* (1863). He conducts his sensual life in the company of La Fanfarlo with the control of an actor or a poet. In short, the central difference in tone between the two narrative sequences is that, whereas, in the first, the predominant emphasis is on the parody of first-generation Romanticism, in the style of Gautier's *Les Jeunes-France,* in the second, there are elements of a continuing Romanticism which will pave the way for the later 'modernité' of Baudelaire, again as characterized in *Le Peintre de la vie moderne*: 'la beauté passagère, fugace, de la vie présente'.

Typically, of course, Baudelaire will not be content to take comfort in the predictable swing of this binary movement from the first narrative sequence to the second, with all the sub-sets of call and echo subsumed in that structure. He will end the novella with a *pointe,* intended to disturb, if not to assault the reader, as he will do in some of the later prose poems. 'Intelligence malhonnête', he concludes, adding a throw-away line which is, in fact, a punch-line, '—comme dit cet honnête M. Nisard'. In order to savour this *boutade* to the full, the reader needs to know that Désiré Nisard was a critic hostile to Romanticism and much scorned by Baudelaire, Gautier and others. So, this pungent last phrase of **La Fanfarlo** was in the nature of an 'in-joke'. The very fact that, in order to understand it, we need the benefit of critical apparatus, not merely to enrich but to ensure our comprehension of the ironic antiphrasis contained in 'cet honnête M. Nisard', serves to accentuate the distinction between the 'modern', in the sense of the ephemeral (as here) and elements of 'modernité', fleetingly beautiful and nevertheless lasting in their transience (as in certain parts of the second narrative sequence). Structurally, however, this ambiguous end anticipates analogous types of closure in **Le Spleen de Paris**. Also, as has been pointed out very pertinently by Nathaniel Wing, it implicates the reader, since 'it clearly sets up an uneasy alignment of the reader's views with a critic hostile to Romanticism'. The reader is left to pirouette in a state of uncertainty and ambiguity.

In the sense that the central duality, inherent in the double narrative sequence of **La Fanfarlo,** represents the deflation of the ideal by the real and, conversely, the defiant disdain of the world by the *dandy* whose ideal is encapsulated in the phrase, 'vivre et dormir devant un miroir', Baudelaire's novella has rightly been seen as exemplifying many of the themes of Romantic Irony. This irony in

Samuel Cramer's relationship to external reality has a parallel in Baudelaire's relationship to his novella. Baudelaire uses a narrator, or pseudo-author to tell the tale. This narrator is, however, no passive mouth-piece: by means of his constantly shifting view, the dynamic of life is introduced into what would otherwise have been the simple recounting of a story and, in consequence, a further dimension is introduced into the work. Constantly distancing himself, in almost prophylactic self-irony, from 'le pauvre Samuel', the narrator will, at times, intervene to address the reader directly as 'vous'. At the beginning of the second paragraph of the novella, such reader-involvement is actively sought: 'Comment vous mettre au fait, et vous faire voir bien clair dans cette nature ténébreuse . . . ?' This narrative mode is picked up again later, when the pseudo-author mockingly warns the reader not to be taken in by Samuel, with the admonition '. . . gardez-vous de croire qu'il fût incapable de connaître les sentiments vrais'. Elsewhere, the narrator will intervene to express his agreement with the protagonist: 'Cramer haïssait profondément, et il avait, *selon moi*, parfaitement raison, les grandes lignes droites en matière d'appartements' (italics mine). Generally, however, the distinction between 'je' and 'il' is clearly evident. Furthermore, this 'je' is at times extended into the plural form, to give a presentation of Samuel as 'l'homme le plus faux . . . de nos amis', where the first-person plural has less of a distancing function than in the quasi-Stendhalian use of such locutions as 'notre homme', 'notre poète', 'notre jeune roué'. We are all implicated (protagonist, narrator, author and reader), when the role of 'nous' widens out from the specific to the general, as in the use of 'nous' when applied to the non-achievement of Samuel in *Les Orfraies,* 'recueil de sonnets, comme nous en avons tous fait et tous lu'. Yet, such authorial intrusions, intended to connote a critical attitude and a clearer sense of focus, are in no sense as rigorously objective as might at first appear, since the attitude of the narrator is coloured by his realization of the limitations of the protagonist. Ever conscious of the victim's confident unawareness, the ironical observer is never completely detached.

Just as, in the relationship between the first and the second narrative sequences, it was possible to establish a pattern of call and echo, a similar interplay may be detected between the narrative and the general discourse of the narrator. No doubt the most celebrated exemplification of this duality is the contrast between the narrator's initial description of Samuel and the ironically undercutting effect of the later descriptions of Samuel from the point of view of La Fanfarlo: from being 'pur et noble', Samuel's forehead now appears 'trop haut'; the nose, which was earlier described as 'taquin et railleur', has been diminished to become a 'nez de priseur'; above all, the 'chevelure prétentieusement raphaélesque' is now simply undisciplined ('cheveux en forêt vierge'). The regression, as C. A. Hackett suggests [in 'Baudelaire and Samuel Cramer', *Australian Journal of French Studies* VI, Nos. 2-3 (1969)], is further accentuated by the fact that the second of the two portraits has only three of the six features mentioned in the first one. Finally, the last nail in the coffin comes when La Fanfarlo, *despite* these features, which Samuel had no doubt seen as his glory, 'le trouva *presque* bien' (italics mine). The puncturing effect of this 'presque' (echoing two earlier though somewhat less devastating uses of the same effect) may be compared with a similar technique adopted by Flaubert in *Madame Bovary,* where the coach 'ressembla *presque* à un tilbury' (italics mine). The ironical presentation of a superficially flattering portrait is thus further heightened, to the power of two, on its second appearance: the initial portrait had, after all, introduced the reader to Samuel, in terms of 'cette moitié de génie dont le ciel l'a doué', notable among all the 'demi-grands hommes' in Paris at the time.

A further instance of such regression in repetition may be seen in the 'doublet' of Samuel, as he emerges from meeting Mme de Cosmelly again in the Luxembourg Gardens and the subsequent account of how he fared later in life. Having launched on his tirade against Walter Scott, 'l'ennuyeux écrivain', Samuel is ironically typed as belonging to 'la classe des gens *absorbants*': we are told that travelling salesmen are to 'poètes *absorbants*' as 'la réclame' is to 'la prédication', with this difference, that 'le vice de ces derniers est tout à fait désintéressé'. Of the four 'livres de science' eventually written by Samuel, his volume on the four Evangelists takes up the theme of 'la prédication', while another, 'un mémoire sur un nouveau système d'annonces', echoes 'la réclame'.

Call and echo between the narrator's discourse and the narrative sequence, as such, are manifest in the account by Mme de Cosmelly of the favourable reports which attracted her to her future husband ('on citait de lui les traits les plus beaux: un bras cassé en duel pour un ami un peu poltron qui lui avait confié l'honneur de sa sœur, des sommes énormes prêtées à d'anciens camarades sans fortune') and the ironical prefiguration of this in the narrator's description of the unpredictability of Samuel's behaviour: 'Il eût vendu ses chemises pour un homme qu'il connaissait à peine . . . Il se fût battu en duel pour un auteur ou un artiste mort depuis deux siècles'. Again, the narrator's initial account of Samuel in terms of a 'dieu moderne et hermaphrodite' is echoed in the androgynous description of La Fanfarlo's leg. Like Samuel, she too has long hair. Similarly, the presentation of La Fanfarlo as 'tour à tour décente, féerique, folle, enjouée' constitutes a union of incompatibles directly comparable to that indicated, at the outset, by the narrator in relation to Samuel.

All of these repetitions, ranging from internal contradictions (as in the case of the alternative descriptions of Samuel) to variations on a theme (as in the androgynous parallels between Samuel and the Dancer), indicate a double level in the structure of *La Fanfarlo,* one of which relates to the world inside the double narrative sequence and the other to the world outside, the world of the narrator. For the reader, placed at a third point, outside this double helix, the effect of such conscious reordering of existing elements is essentially two-fold: firstly, these subtle changes of focus can produce rapier-like thrusts of irony, mirroring the non-achievement of the protagonist

in both art and life; secondly, by the identification of certain constant elements, coupled with an awareness of the inherent paradox and contradiction endemic to human affairs, the reader becomes conscious of a harmony of opposites, between identification (static) and contradiction (dynamic), which lies at the heart of artistic illusion as presented by Baudelaire. Of the many literary avatars mentioned specifically in *La Fanfarlo*, perhaps Sterne and Diderot are the most significant in this connection. Coming after Sterne's anti-autobiography, *Tristram Shandy* (1760-67) and Diderot's anti-novel, *Jacques le fataliste* (1773), there is a case for viewing Baudelaire's *La Fanfarlo* as an anti-novella, at the end of what Albert George has described [in *Short Fiction in France: 1800-1850,* 1964] as the 'seed time of short narrative' in French literature.

Indeed, *La Fanfarlo* subsumes a hidden roll-call of such literary avatars, each placed to produce maximum effect. Plagiarism is, of course, a noteworthy characteristic of Samuel: 'après une lecture passionnée d'un beau livre, sa conclusion involontaire était: voilà qui est assez beau pour être de moi! et de là à penser: c'est donc de moi,—il n'y a que l'espace d'un tiret'. But plagiarism, coupled with irony, can provide the pretext for conscious innovation. Delacroix, in *Le Salon de 1846,* is, after all, portrayed as 'un des rares hommes qui restent originaux après avoir puisé à toutes les vraies sources'. Later, in *Le Salon de 1859,* Baudelaire will declare: 'l'imitation est le vertige des esprits souples et brillants, et souvent même une preuve de supériorité'.

By common agreement [among critics], Balzac is the major source of literary inspiration in *La Fanfarlo*: 'C'est Balzac traduit en Baudelaire par Baudelaire' [Yves Florenne, in his edition of *La Fanfarlo,* 1969]. The debt to *La Fille aux yeux d'or* is indicated by Baudelaire in a footnote and the thematic resemblance to *Béatrix* is virtually textual. Beyond the multiple superficial parallels between a Rubempré or a Rastignac and Samuel Cramer in this 'terrible vie parisienne' (where even Mme de Cosmelly's address, 'dans une des rues les plus aristocratiques du faubourg Saint-Germain' shows the Balzacian imprint), themes are echoed, not merely to show the connection, but also to indicate points of difference. The most thinly-veiled quotation without quotation-marks in *La Fanfarlo* is the reference to Rastignac's 'coup d'oeil de vainqueur sur la ville maudite' at the end of *Le Père Goriot,* but with the ironical difference that Samuel does not muse over his triumph from a distance, but hastens to enjoy 'les diverses félicités qu'il avait à côté de lui'. Baudelaire rushes to the end of his narrative in a temporal acceleration which is not without counterpart in the world of Balzac. Conversely, however, as Jean Prévost [*Baudelaire: Essai sur l'inspiration et la création poétiques,* 1953] and Claude Pichois [in his edition of *La Fanfarlo*] have indicated, Baudelaire leaves obvious gaps in his narrative, notably in relation to the breaking-off of the liaison between La Fanfarlo and M. de Cosmelly, which Balzac would not have omitted. Likewise, Baudelaire does little to inform the reader about the material and financial situation of the Cosmelly couple or about how Samuel came to have his newspaper articles published, whereas Balzac would have revelled in such details. Indeed, from many points of view, *La Fanfarlo* could be said to represent a reversal of Balzacian values, in the sense that this arrival of a provincial young man in Paris ends in a bourgeois degradation of a kind which anticipates Flaubert as much as it echoes Balzac.

It would be tedious, and beyond the terms of reference of this short study, to go into all the literary quotations contained in *La Fanfarlo,* from Marivaux, Laclos, Hoffmann, Musset, Pétrus Borel and Gautier, to the tradition of *Tartuffe,* with its repercussions on the theme of hypocrisy as treated by Stendhal. Virtually all of these echoes have been adopted and adapted by Baudelaire, with open-ended irony. Just as the identification of La Fanfarlo proceeds through metamorphoses in various national cultures, so Samuel is situated among his literary precursors in autobiographical or semi-autobiographical fiction. Imitation can give rise to parody, as happened with the gradual deflation of the stereotype of ill-fated Romantic genius. In Mme de Cosmelly, we have 'la discrète et vertueuse épouse' of the nineteenth-century personal novel. The difficulties involved in the attainment of Samuel's original ambition are almost visualized in the phrase which tells us that she was 'plus escarpée qu'elle n'en avait l'air', suggesting the hard climb up from the typically Romantic 'abîme'. She sees that she may have lost her husband's love by showing him 'trop d'amour', a theme common in the personal novel since *La Princesse de Clèves,* though here used by Baudelaire with ironic effect. Whatever Samuel's intentions may be, Mme de Cosmelly, as the reader can easily see, in advance of Samuel, will want to maintain their relationship on a footing of 'amitié' and 'choses platoniques'. For his part, Samuel presents a parodying pastiche of his counterparts in the tradition of the personal novel, in that he is a conscious victim of paralyzing self-analysis and of his own 'impuissance'.

The reworking of these literary themes constitutes a homage to a collective tradition and a flouting of this same tradition as an anachronistic irrelevance. Nowhere is this more evident than in the passage where the narrator feigns withdrawal from the narrative and, inspired by a quotation from Diderot, taunts the reader with being too incredulous, seeking for verisimilitude where it is clear that intrigue, as such, is of quite secondary importance.

From the macrocontext to the microcontext, the same holds true, in relation to fossilized phrases, maxims and clichés. The impudent epigraph, *Aura sacra fames* (in a foreign language, like 'Any where out of the world' in *Le Spleen de Paris*), signifies, ostensibly, the cursed lust for gold. In context, however, it is cheeky in the extreme, since it indicates that the gratuitous gesture of literary creativity has degenerated, in the case of Samuel, into the money-making cultivation of functional practical writing on unmentionable subjects. Even the celebrated condemnation, 'dans le temps où nous avions le jugement si court et les cheveux si longs', has now been shown to have its origin in a popular proverb, 'La femme est un animal à cheveux

longs et à idées courtes', although its full ironical force in Baudelaire's novella comes from its contextual situation.

Maxims are half-hidden in *La Fanfarlo,* to an extent which only emerges fully after a parallel reading of the approximately contemporaneous *Choix de maximes consolantes sur l'amour* (1846), and in the light of Balzac's *Physiologie du mariage* (1829) and some of the later prose poems, such as '**Portraits de maîtresses**'. La Fanfarlo, for instance, is described as 'une danseuse aussi bête que belle', in a doublet of the maxim, 'La bêtise est souvent l'ornement de la beauté'. Again, the agoraphobic 'calèche basse et bien fermée', which transports Samuel and La Fanfarlo to her house, where the small, low-ceilinged bedroom provides an idyllic 'réduit amoureux', is subsumed in a maxim-like generalization: 'Les sentiments intimes ne se recueillent à loisir que dans un espace très étroit'. Conversely, the national stereotypes (with shades of Montesquieu, Mme de Staël and Stendhal), of which Samuel is presented as being 'le produit contradictoire', emerge clearly, in the *Choix de maximes consolantes sur l'amour,* as the 'Homme du Nord', enjoined to love 'femmes froides' and the 'Homme du Midi', more suited to 'les femmes ardentes'.

The element of duality already indicated in relation to the double narrative sequence and, subsequently, in relation to the ambiguity inherent in the narrator's discourse and the narrative as an entity in itself, is most evident of all in the two dimensions which may be perceived in Baudelaire's use of language in *La Fanfarlo*: the outward form of the language, on the one hand and, on the other, the inner meaning which it subtends. Sometimes this 'double register' is conveyed by syntactical devices, such as the use of an adjective in anteposition, forming part of a chiasmus designed to produce a subtle contrast: 'féconde en desseins difficiles et en risibles avortements'. Elsewhere, irony is expressed obliquely, but all the more effectively, through the medium of imagery: parodying the analogous collection of sonnets by Rubempré in *Illusions perdues* (*Les Marguerites*) and Baudelaire's own projected antecedents to *Les Fleurs du Mal* (*Les Lesbiennes,* later to become *Les Limbes*), Samuel entitles his collection *Les Orfraies,* referring, in the osprey, to a species of birds of prey, 'vilains oiseaux'; the osprey here represents a negative form of bird or 'anti-oiseau' [see Michael Riffaterre, *La production du texte,* 1979] and the abortive inspiration thus suggested is further reinforced by the juxtaposition with a correspondingly negative term, 'mort-nés', in this context of non-achievement.

By far the most effective device for the ironizing of empty rhetoric is, however, as Michael Riffaterre has pertinently pointed out [in *Essais de stylistique structurale,* 1971], Baudelaire's use of the cliché. Here, the 'double register' works quite devastatingly to show identity, in the shape of a well-worn cliché, coupled with contrast, in the sudden change or adaptation of one of the terms of the cliché. One of the examples selected by Michael Riffaterre for analysis in this connection is the hyperbolic reference to Samuel's 'voix tonnante', in calling after Flore not to forget La Fanfarlo's rouge, when fetching her costume.

This fossilized cliché takes its effect from the incongruity of an excessively booming voice in the restricted confines of the dancer's small and low bedroom. Here, then, it is the context which renews the impact of the cliché. Elsewhere, the simple addition of 'romantique' to the well-worn expression, 'bavarder comme une pie', produces the requisite shock. The combination of cliché and metaphor is evident in the phrase, 'autres linges sales de la vie privée'. Most frequently, however, it is the ironical intrusion of a phrase, hardened by use, into a context in which it would normally be considered alien, which constitutes the central innovative effect of Baudelaire's use of the cliché. Thus, the juxtaposition of 'paroles mielleuses' and the deflatory 'etc.' permits of a widening of the semantic field.

If, then, we take the reworking of a proverb (e.g. 'dans le temps où nous avions le jugement si court et les cheveux si longs'), a self-quotation, or a direct quotation (as already discussed in relation to Balzac and others), this 'double register', at the level of the microcontext, may be seen to produce an effect analogous to the principle of juxtaposition and discontinuity already established at the level of the macrocontext. 'Il faut remarquer', writes Baudelaire, in *De l'essence du rire,* 'que chaque terme de chaque classification peut se compléter et se nuancer par l'adjonction d'un terme d'une autre, comme la loi grammaticale nous enseigne à modifier le substantif par l'adjectif'. One final example may serve to illustrate this point. 'Il n'est pas de rêve', Samuel tells Mme de Cosmelly, 'quelque idéal qu'il soit, qu'on ne retrouve avec un poupard glouton suspendu au sein'. This image is one which involves cross-referencing within **La Fanfarlo** (Samuel thinks of pregnancy as 'une maladie d'araignée', where the spider connotes imprisonment as well as enlargement) and self-quotation. It also, as Michael Riffaterre has pointed out [in *La production du texte*], constitutes a binary combination of polar opposites, in that 'poupard glouton' suggests a negative version of the stereotype of motherhood. The Romantic irony of the entire novella may be seen, in concentrated form, in the functioning of this combination of contradictory elements, rendered dynamic, not by any notation of external reality, nor yet again by any injection of strength from the plot (from which it is, strictly speaking, extraneous), but simply by its negativity, suggesting much of the rich, ironic potential of the authorial persona of Baudelaire.

In the light of the multiple dualities already discussed, the three apparently self-contained sections in the second narrative sequence would need to be up-graded from the status of digressions, which 'ruined the economy of the tale', in the words of Albert George, to a position of prime importance in any assessment of the originality and achievement of Baudelaire in **La Fanfarlo**. These three sections, on dance, the culinary arts and architecture respectively, constitute a mosaic-type pattern.

These ostensibly parenthetical passages contribute to the narrative obliquely, as Nathaniel Wing has shown with great subtlety. They do so on two levels. Firstly, Samuel, in his seduction of La Fanfarlo, was able to cultivate the detachment necessary to the Dandy and the true Artist. La Fanfarlo, for her part, transcends physical attractiveness and appeals to Samuel through a multiplicity of identities and aesthetic values, in the history of pantomime and the *commedia dell'arte* (Colombine, Zéphyrine etc.). 'Un battement perpétuel', in the words of Jean Starobinski, 'enlève le corps dans une signification fictive et le renvoie de cette signification à la présence physique littérale' [*Portrait de l'artiste en saltimbanque,* 1970]. The Dancer is identified in the context of her culture ('un caprice de Shakespeare et une bouffonnerie italienne'), just as the Poet is situated in the context of his literary tradition. As Nathaniel Wing has put it, 'the consonance of the lovers' sentiments is only possible because they have renounced the *myth of presence*'. La Fanfarlo prefigures the section 'La Femme' in *Le Peintre de la vie moderne,* in that, amid the magic, glitter and fantasy of the theatre, 'la femme et . . . la robe' constitute 'une toilette indivisible'. Her make-up (a further prefiguration of 'Eloge du maquillage') combines with her spangled costume to form part of her attraction for Samuel, just as the connivance of the glance, in 'a une passante', is inseparable from the swirl of the dress. Furthermore, her aesthetic control of movement and form is comparable to the blend of 'volupté' and 'connaissance', so central to artistic achievement, in the view of Baudelaire. The reference to the 'grands peuples voluptueux et savants', in the context of architecture, is thus in keeping with the combination of passion and order in the sequence as a whole. The culinary arts, we are told, require a vigorous understanding of the chemical properties of matter, consciously selected with a view to inducing a sense of well-being or voluptuousness. La Fanfarlo has so far transcended mastery of technique as a ballet-dancer that she has become 'sublime dans son art, autant comédienne par les jambes que danseuse par les yeux'. When once she loses this domination, the charm is broken: La Fanfarlo becomes a high-class tart ('une espèce de lorette ministérielle') and gets fat. 'La femme est le contraire du Dandy', Baudelaire will comment later, in *Mon Cœur mis à nu.* 'Donc elle doit faire horreur'. A similar fate awaits Samuel when he becomes the victim of his own passion, loses his sense of artistic detachment and drops, in consequence, from the status of Poet-Dandy: 'Il avait souvent singé la passion; il fut contraint de la connaître; . . . ce fut . . . l'amour maladif des courtisanes'. Baudelaire's interest in dance anticipates subsequent developments in the work of Mallarmé and Valéry, coupled with manifestations of the Salome figure in the work of Flaubert, Gustave Moreau, Huysmans and Wilde.

The second level on which these parenthetical passages advance the narrative obliquely lies in the extent to which La Fanfarlo, the Dancer, may be seen as a disguised self-projection of Samuel, the Poet. Not only does she present an emblem with a double aspect (aesthetic, as well as physical; controlled, as well as seductive); she also presents a manifestation of the age-old distinction between self and anti-self, face and mask, which was to be of such fascination for the mirror-contemplating Samuel. Musset's Fantasio embodies just such a disguised self-representation. In the case of Baudelaire, however, the effect is almost one of *mise en abyme* in that Samuel, already semi-autobiographical, here gives a projection of the Dancer as the consummate artist he himself vainly hopes to become, a projection given heightened irony by the narrator's distinctly anti-establishment thrusts in the closing paragraphs of the novella. In the transition from mythological goddesses to a real ballerina; in the metamorphosis of a genre scene to 'ce ravissant taudis, qui tenait à la fois du mauvais lieu et du sanctuaire', with echoes, besides, of Delacroix's *Femmes d'Alger,* as described by Baudelaire in *Le Salon de 1846;* in the shift of emphasis from a non-genius, an anti-hero, to an ideal of beauty explicable in terms of 'modernité', or the encapsulation of the ephemeral; in all of these ways, Baudelaire is introducing a new dimension into his novella and is producing an effect which is strikingly original. Far from giving a direct narrative account of the relationship between the Poet and the Dancer, he suggests this evolution obliquely through a discussion of the consonance of their views (corresponding closely, of course, with his own). The parallel sets develop in almost geometrical progression, with the truffle acting as an intensifier: 'la truffe . . . a l'effet de plusieurs zéros après un chiffre'.

The Poet/Dancer sequence of *La Fanfarlo* is written in poetic prose. It aims at combining the unexpected and the predictable in a metrical prose best typified by the description of the Dancer's movements, 'pleins d'une cadence précise'. In general terms, however, rhythm is seen by Baudelaire as incompatible with prose writing, 'un obstacle insurmontable à ce développement minutieux de pensées et d'expressions qui a pour objet la *vérité*'. These aesthetic considerations may well have been a major factor in the non-fulfilment of Baudelaire's early ambition, as expressed by him in a letter to his mother in 1847, to become a successful novelist, and repeated in 1858, after the publication of *Les Fleurs du Mal.* The 'multitude de tons', which he admired in relation to Poe's short stories, coupled with the unity of effect which he saw as ideal for that art form, were well exemplified by Baudelaire in *La Fanfarlo.* But this work is an anti-novella in a context more particularized than that of literary history: it did nothing to discourage Baudelaire from including *contes* in *Le Spleen de Paris;* yet, by his evident lack of interest in plot and sequential analysis, it may well have convinced the poet that his qualities were not those which he deemed appropriate for a successful novelist. On the other hand, the sequences in the novella which, superficially, appear to be only tangential to the story-line, are those in which Baudelaire's achievement is most noteworthy, in terms of suggestive art. The 'entente profonde', between the Poet and the Dancer, is expressed 'dans chaque regard et dans chaque parole', a typically Baudelairean communion of 'l'esprit' and 'les sens'. Their conversation is characterized as being 'tantôt brutale comme un chiffre, tantôt délicate et parfumée comme une fleur ou un sachet', a combination of the precise and the subtly evocative. Perhaps the most lasting impression of *La Fanfarlo* is just such a tension between the message and the medium through which it is conveyed. All the various dualities then converge in the ultimate communion between the author, in his multiple transformations, and the reader,

whose response is actively sought. Where such a symbiosis can be achieved, the highest value of creative art, as posited by Baudelaire, has been attained.

The poetry of Baudelaire's prose poems:

Baudelaire believed that prose could be made quite as poetical as verse or even more so, for a prose that could preserve the rhythm of poetry without its monotony, and the melody of poetry without rhythm, might become in the hands of the master even more effective than verse. I do not know whether this is really true. I am inclined to think that it is; but I do not feel sufficiently learned in certain matters related to the question to venture a definite opinion. Enough to say that Baudelaire thought it possible, and he tried to make a new kind of prose; and the book containing these attempts entitled *Little Poems in Prose* is a wonderful treasure. But Baudelaire did not say anything very extravagant in its preface. He only expressed the conviction that a poetical prose might be used with good effects for certain particular subjects,—dreams, reveries, the thoughts that men think in solitude, when the life of the world is not about them to disturb their meditations; his prose essays are all reveries, dreams, fantasies. . . .

[*Little Poems in Prose*] has the qualities of poetry, although not poetry; it has the same resonance, the same groupings of vowel sounds, the same alliteration, the same cadences. It is very strange, and it is also really beautiful. Probably Baudelaire's poetical prose is the most perfect attempt of the kind ever made; and there is a good deal of it. But being a very great artist, he saw, as I have told you before, that this kind of prose is suitable only for reveries, dreams, philosophical fancies.

    Lafcadio Hearn, "Baudelaire," in Talks to
              Writers, *1927.*

Vivien L. Rubin (essay date 1985-86)

SOURCE: "Two Prose Poems by Baudelaire: 'Le vieux saltimbanque' and 'Une mort héroïque,'" in *Nineteenth-Century French Studies,* Vol. XIV, Nos. 1 & 2, Fall-Winter, 1985-86, pp. 51-60.

[*In the following essay, Rubin suggests that in the prose poems "Le vieux saltimbanque" and "Une mort héroique" Baudelaire defends the role of the artist and the power of art.*]

In **"Le Vieux Saltimbanque"** and **"Une Mort héroique,"** we read of the failure or death of two clown figures whom Baudelaire proposes as symbols of the poet. Two critics in particular, Jean Starobinski and Ross Chambers, have written illuminating essays on the idea of the poet as actor and clown in Baudelaire and, along with other commentators, they both see these poems as expressing the failure of the artist and, as Starobinski puts it [in "Sur quelques répondants allégoriques du poète," *Revue d'histoire lit-teraire de la France,* 67 (avril-juin 1967)], "la conscience de la mort et l'impuissance de l'art." Chambers, for his part, asserts [in "L'art sublime du comédien," *Saggie e ricerche di Letteratura Francesa* 11 (1971)] that the function of Baudelaire's "comédiens" is to show that "tout artiste, même le plus accompli, est voué à la catastrophe du sifflet." Without denying the pessimism evident here, I should like to propose a shift in perspective, and to suggest that in these two poems Baudelaire in fact defends, with however devious a tenacity, the validity of the role of the artist and affirms once again the power of art, even in the face of suffering and death.

The setting for **"Le Vieux Saltimbanque"** is a fairground on a public holiday and the narrator recounts how, as he was inspecting the stalls, his attention was caught by the sight of the miserable stand of a wretched *saltimbanque* at the very end of the line of booths. The *saltimbanque* is clearly an outcast, a pariah, and so is bound to arouse, if not the sympathy, at least the curiosity of the poet-narrator. And indeed the narrator is profoundly moved by the sight of the decrepit figure and by the speaking, albeit enigmatic, look that he bends on the crowd. The narrator has just made up his mind to make a discreet donation when he is swept away by a sudden rush of people. Looking back and trying to understand the reason for the emotion that had overcome him, he tells himself: "Je viens de voir l'image du vieil homme de lettres qui a survécu à la génération dont il fut le brillant amuseur; du vieux poète sans amis, sans famille, sans enfants, dégradé par sa misère et par l'ingratitude publique, et dans la baraque de qui le monde oublieux ne veut plus entrer!"

[In his edition of Baudelaire's **Petits poèmes en prose**] Henri Lemaître has commented that the fair is given a special dimension through the use of such expressions as "ces solennités," "ces époques solennelles," "ce jubilé populaire." The nature of this solemn occasion, however, is particularly significant, for it represents, on one level, a ritual celebration through which the power of art is made manifest. When the narrator recalls the smell of frying, it is to comment that it was "comme l'encens de cette fête," while performers are compared to princesses, to fairies, to gods. These performers, who are themselves metamorphosed by the power of their art, in turn transform. And although the power of art is not limitless—it is only an "armistice," after all, that is concluded with "les puissances malfaisantes de la vie"—yet, under its spell, pain and toil are forgotten and innocence is come again: "il me semble que le peuple oublie tout, la douleur et le travail; il devient pareil aux enfants."

Alas, the miserable *saltimbanque* has quite lost the alchemist's touch. In the rest of the fair, all is light, agility, horizontality—conditions that define what Henri Leyreloup calls the "réalité antérieure où l'art était possible" ["Baudelaire, Portrait du poète en saltimbanque," *Revue de Pacifique* 2 (1976)]. But the *saltimbanque* himself is the image of physical decrepitude, immobility, silence, while the two smoking, guttering candles that light up his repulsive booth complete the image of the fall from grace,

of exile to the outer darkness. Excluded from participation in the fair as either magical performer or enthralled spectator, he is doubly excluded from the realm of art and the ideal, where the dross of everyday life falls away and man and his surroundings become, however fleetingly, transfigured.

But if the fair represents, among other things, "la fête de l'art," as Chambers puts it, it is not surprising, given Baudelaire's constant sense of opposition, that it also has negative aspects. Hannelore Zaubitzer's suggestion that the fair represents the vanity of mortal fame seems inadequate, for if on one level the fair represents the transforming power of art, on another it represents a debased art, a tainted ideal and the world of the prostituted artist [Zaubitzer, "Clownmetaphern bei Baudelaire, Mallarmé und Michaux," *Die Neueren Sprachen* 15 (1966)]. Understood in this way, the all-pervading smell of frying takes on a more strongly ironic tone, and the "frenetic" explosion of vitality gives us a painful sense of the crude, undisciplined dissipation of animal spirits. We become aware of the emphasis on excess, almost on distortion, on the material and the physical: the performers "piaillaient, beuglaient, hurlaient," "les queues-rouges et les Jocrisses convulsaient les traits de leurs visages basanés, racornis par le vent, la pluie et le soleil," "les Hercules, fiers de l'énormité de leurs membres, sans front et sans crâne, comme les orangoutangs, se prélassaient majestueusement. . . ." Here, the performers, far from incarnating the ideal, resemble more closely animals in a menagerie. The theme of the prostitution of the artist is thus already prepared well before the closing lines: we see the *saltimbanque* excluded from a celebration in which we are uncomfortably aware of quite unspiritualized matter, of false glitter, of plebeian smells. And this is the fair in which he himself had been wont to hawk his wares.

The fair is, indeed, in some respects painfully like the market place. Certainly, the situation here is not that evoked in, for instance, "La Muse vénale," where the poet's muse, "saltimbanque à jeun," is forced to "étaler (ses) appas / Et (son) rire trempé de pleurs qu'on ne voit pas." In the fair, there is no suggestion of exploitation but rather one of beneficent reciprocity, with both performers and public "également joyeux." Yet the idea of buying and selling, already to some extent inseparable from the idea of the fair, is stressed by the narrator when he comments, "les uns dépensaient, les autres gagnaient," and again, "partout la joie, le gain, la débauche"—thus underlining the commercial element in the exchange between performer and public. And this sense of the fair as the world of the prostituted artist is reinforced when the narrator explains to himself the reasons for his emotion at the sight of the old man. For when the narrator compares the *saltimbanque* to a "vieil homme de lettres," he insists on the analogy in somewhat denigrating terms, identifying the showman as he does with a mere "brillant amuseur." Similarly, comparing the showman to an old, friendless poet with the words "dans la baraque de qui le monde oublieux ne veut plus entrer," he suggests the venality of the poet figure and stresses the showman-charlatan element of the poet that the old *saltimbanque* brings to mind.

Even the suggestion of a brilliant past for the poet-show-man reinforces our sense of the somewhat pejorative nuances of the image. We need only remember Baude-laire's comment in the article on Gautier: "Pour devenir tout à fait populaire, ne faut-il pas mériter de l'être, c'est-à-dire, ne faut-il pas, par un petit côté secret, un presque rien qui fait tache, se montrer un peu populacier?" In **"Le Vieux Saltimbanque,"** the old showman is endowed with a significance beyond his immediate presence, but the images of writer and poet that he conjures up in the mind of the narrator are proportionately reduced in dignity and virtue and represent compromised, flawed figures.

If Baudelaire reduced the poet to hawker and showman, rather than simply elevating the *saltimbanque* to the dig-nity of poet, as did Banville for example, it is not merely to dramatize the unhappy lot of the poet-*saltimbanque* victim, but to comment on the nature of the fate that has overtaken him. Baudelaire stresses the physical decrepi-tude of the old man, "voûté, caduc, décrépit, une ruine d'homme." But it is not simply age that has defeated the *saltimbanque,* nor is it just the fickleness of the public: the fate of the old showman is that which overcomes the artist who has trod not the austere paths of Art, but the glittering road to Success. He symbolizes the poet whose dependence on his public results in artistic death when the public's approval is withdrawn—for then there is nothing left for him and he is simply a broken old man. More horrifying for the narrator, and for Baudelaire, than the poverty of this figure, or his loss of popularity, is surely his loss of will that, we can only feel, results at least in part from the loss of his public. The narrator describes the immobility, the inertness of the showman as he leans against one of the poles of his hut. Contrary to Starobinski's belief that "Il continue à s'offrir en specta-cle, dans le fol espoir de trouver un public à qui se pros-tituer," the narrator is explicit that the showman stood at the very edge of the fairground, "comme si, honteux, il s'était exilé lui-même." He insists, "il avait renoncé, il avait abdiqué. Sa destinée était faite." For the poet of the *Journaux intimes,* who reminds himself:

> Plus on veut, mieux on veut.
> Plus on travaille et plus on veut travailler. Plus on
>   produit, plus on devient fécond,

the "failure" of this figure lies especially in this abdica-tion. The fate of the old *saltimbanque* is poignant because he is reduced to repellant poverty; it is tragic because, having lost his will and so necessarily his power to act— but not his consciousness of exclusion—he can no longer, through his art, attain those moments of ideal vision that constitute a truce with "les puissances malfaisantes de la vie."

In this, as in other of the prose poems, the narrator's is an essential voice. [In *La dernier Baudelaire,* 1966] Charles Mauron has shown that the narrator in the **Petits Poèmes en Prose** is often attracted to, but then refuses contact with, a character who has caught his attention. In this case, the feelings aroused are stronger than usual, as Star-obinski has observed, but his movement of withdrawal is decisive. The narrator has tears in his eyes, but we are told explicitly that they do not fall, and although he feels the hand of hysteria at his throat, he preserves his role of observer, for he is carried away by the crowd before he has performed the action that would have associated him, however tenuously, more directly with the fallen *saltim-banque.* The distance that the narrator puts between him-self and the *saltimbanque* is of course a symbolic dis-tance and this symbolic distance is reinforced by the very precise and yet strikingly limited explanation that, we saw, he gives of the "vision" that he had just seen. Starobinski merely comments that Baudelaire explains the sense of the vision rather narrowly, "de façon nette mais un peu étroite," and does not speculate on possible reasons for this. Chambers, on the other hand, specifically rejects the possibility that these identifications have any limiting force: "On peut prétendre sans doute que ce saltimbanque n'avait jamais été qu'un mauvais artiste, un 'brillant amuseur' . . . ; mais ce serait se méprendre sur l'intention de Baudelaire." Yet the narrator's explanation, which can be felt to be narrow, but which includes two separate images and takes five lines of text, is detailed and specif-ic, and enables the narrator, after the initial shock of sympathetic recognition, to separate himself from the showman. After an initial moment of horrified recogni-tion of weaknesses and failures that fill him with panic and fear, the narrator, melting back into the brilliance and activity of the crowd, clearly reasserts his difference: he proposes the *saltimbanque* as a figure of failure and de-feat and refuses to identify with him.

In **"Une Mort héroique,"** it is the brilliant buffoon, Fan-cioulle, who represents the creative artist: actor of con-summate skill, he demonstrates the power of art to create an ideal world more compelling than reality. In the poem, the artist-poet figure confronts three different publics: the unpromising audience, "blasé, frivole," of the court, the powerful Prince, his master, and finally the narrator him-self. Again, one of the themes will be that of the relation-ship between the artist and his public. And, once again, the artist is not an independent agent: he is one whose job it is, like that of the buffoon in *Le Fou et la Vénus,* to "faire rire (le roi) quand l'Ennui et le Remords (l')obsèdent." In this case, the buffoon is represented as having made, apparently futile, efforts to free himself from dependence, by joining in a conspiracy against the tyran-nical Prince. Starobinski, for one, understands Baudelaire as condemning Fancioulle for this revolt: "Il s'agit d'une transgression de l'ordre établi," declares Starobinski, be-fore continuing, "Cet ordre établi fût-il injuste et despo-tique, la transgression prend valeur de sacrilège car elle ne s'élève pas seulement contre l'autorité, mais contre l'amitié." But Baudelaire's comment in *Mon Cœur mis à nu*: "de la vraie grandeur des parias," reminds us that for Baudelaire, Fancioulle's error is more likely to have been that, by identifying himself with the disaffected nobles, he was in effect attempting to escape from the isolation of the pariah, which Baudelaire saw as one of the "titres de gloire" of the *comédien.* Is the buffoon guilty of treason against friendship, as Starobinski suggests? When we are told, in an opening that is saturated with irony, that Fan-cioulle was "presque un des amis du Prince," this too is surely to be taken ironically. As we read on, it becomes apparent that friendship is not a relationship that could, in any degree, have interested the Prince. But, by entering the conspiracy, Fancioulle was endeavoring to reject the ambiguous, marginal nature of his connections with society. One result is that, when he attempts to enter more completely into society, he becomes liable to its laws, and he is condemned: "Les seigneurs en question furent arrêtés, ainsi que Fancioulle, et voués à une mort certaine."

The act of rebellion, although it seems at first to deliver Fancioulle more completely into the hands of the Prince, in fact effectively releases him from bondage. Paradoxically, it is the certainty of death which frees the mime. For, contrary to Starobinski's belief that the Prince "promet à Fancioulle la vie sauve à la condition que celui-ci joue à la perfection" (*Portrait de l'artiste en saltimbanque,* 1970) one of his principal and best roles, nothing is less certain. The narrator specifically notes that he himself was not misled by the rumors of clemency that had started to circulate and that he had surmised that the Prince had wanted to see what effect a sentence of death would have on the artist's performance: "De la part d'un homme aussi naturellement et volontairement excentrique, tout était possible, même la vertu, même la clémence. . . . Mais pour ceux qui, comme moi, avaient pu pénétrer plus avant dans les profondeurs de cette âme curieuse et malade, il était infiniment plus probable que le Prince voulait juger de la valeur des talents scéniques d'un homme condamné à mort." In my view, Chambers also forces the text and in doing so oversimplifies the dilemma proposed by Baudelaire when, arguing along the same lines as Starobinski, he writes: "Seulement, l'art vrai est peut-être ce qui nous sauve de la mort? C'est ce que l'expérience du prince, imposant à Fancioulle de mériter le pardon par l'excellence de son jeu, va tenter de découvrir" ("L'Art sublime du comédien," *Saggie e ricerche di letteratura Francesa* 11, 1971) The difference in readings is an important one: buoyed by the hope of pardon, a disciplined, or even a merely desperate, artist might be able, after all, to rise to the occasion. But faced with the certainty of death, will despair and loss of will immobilize the actor, as it immobilizes the old *saltimbanque?* Fancioulle, on the day of the final performance, knowing that he is about to pay the supreme penalty, owes the Prince nothing and has nothing further to hope or to fear from him. The paradox is that Fancioulle is now in an ideal situation for an artist in that he has a public, but his relationship with it is not in any degree degrading, since he is neither asking nor receiving anything from it (except its appreciative participation) in return for his performance. Fancioulle is seen by the narrator in terms of the martyred, and so by definition, the now innocent artist. Far from acting well in order to earn his reprieve, and thereby falling to an even greater degree into the power of the Prince, the mime has not now recovered, but has at last achieved, freedom. It is this, no doubt, which enables him to give a performance such as, the narrator implies, Fancioulle had never before given: "Fancioulle fut ce soir-là une parfaite idéalisation qu'il était impossible de ne nas supposer vivante, possible, réelle."

Two opposing aesthetic principles confront each other in the persons of Fancioulle and the Prince. On the one hand, the sustained efforts of the actor result in a superb act of creation; on the other, a moment's "inspiration" results in an act of destruction. When we remember Baudelaire's comments on the need for sustained creative effort, it might seem perverse of him to choose the art of mime to represent the power of art if, that is, we accepted Starobinski's comment that "la décision du Prince est d'improvisation, *comme l'art de Fancioulle*" (*Portrait,* my emphasis). In fact, the improvisory nature of the Prince's art establishes another distinction between the two, for although in the art of mime improvisation plays a part, it is a limited part—certainly this is true of the pantomimes which Baudelaire would have seen in the mid-nineteenth century. It depends, rather, on experience, on a repertoire of gestures and developments, rehearsed, modified, refined, and then applied to a stock range of situations. In **"Une Mort héroique,"** moreover, the narrator is explicit that Fancioulle was performing in one of his most well-known roles. Again, as Chambers reminds us, the actor represents the artist who has understood that inspiration "n'est que la récompense de l'exercice quotidien" (*Les Martyrs ridicules*). The achievement of such an artist is not the absurdly impossible one of preserving either himself or us from death. The immortality which poets bestow is never a fleshly one. The achievement of such an artist is that he is able to create both for himself and for others that expansion of the spirit, that state of "enivrement" which Baudelaire so often extolled and which has the power to lift us for a while out of time and the contingent: "Fancioulle me prouvait, d'une manière péremptoire, irréfutable, que l'ivresse de l'art est plus apte que tout autre à voiler les terreurs du gouffre; que le génie peut jouer la comédie au bord de la tombe avec une joie qui l'empêche de voir la tombe, perdu comme il est dans un paradis excluant toute idée de tombe et de destruction."

But the fact that Baudelaire specifies that Fancioulle was a mime actor who excelled above all "dans les rôles muets ou peu chargés de paroles," has another, more profound significance. For when Fancioulle gives his unparalleled performance, he is not interpreting another's text: he himself is the poet, the creator and, extraordinary feat, he himself becomes the work of art that he creates: "Fancioulle fut, ce soir-là, une parfaite idéalisation, qu'il était impossible de ne pas supposer vivante, possible, réelle." Having at first attemped to identify too closely with society, Fancioulle now tips the balance in the other direction and succumbs to the temptation that stands at the other pole to the one which had destroyed the old showman in **"Le Vieux Saltimbanque"**: leaving the real world, Fancioulle now identifies too completely with art. Total identification with art is inevitably the end of life. And when the real world, in the form of the whistle, interrupts and so destroys the creation with which he has identified, which he himself incarnates, he is himself necessarily also destroyed, for he and his creation are one and the same.

Opposed to Fancioulle is that other artist, the Prince himself. "Amoureux passionné des beaux-arts," "véritable artiste lui-même," the Prince is at once the incarnation of

The torment of Baudelaire's life:

Gaëtan Picon remarked that in the Nadar photograph of 1862 the 41-year-old Baudelaire looked as if he were a hundred (Baudelaire himself, in one of the *Spleen* poems, made it a thousand). The face, above all the eyes with their look at once haunted and hunted, confirm the sentiment of overwhelming weariness expressed two years previously in a letter to his mother: 'Oh how weary I am, how weary I've been for many years already, of this need to live twenty-four hours every day!' He also wrote to his mother, in ghostly retrospect, as if he were the true author of the *Mémoires d'outre-tombe*: 'I gaze back over all the dead years, the horrible dead years.' The photograph, too, suggests something of the ghost, akin to the spectral presences-absences that populate the street poems in the 'Tableaux parisiens' section of *Les Fleurs du mal* (the title for the collection as a whole was originally to have been *Les Limbes*).

Though death-haunted, this is also the face of a life lived in relation to an age, stamped with the nervous intensity of modernity's rhythms and pressures. Verlaine captured the relation perfectly: 'The profound originality of Charles Baudelaire is . . . to represent modern man, powerfully and in his essence . . . modern man, with his sharpened, vibrant senses, his painfully subtle mind, his brain saturated with tobacco, his blood burnt with alcohol.'

Christopher Prendergast, "Horrible Dead Years,"
in London Review of Books, *March 24, 1994.*

Ennui and its victim. He has his own art, we are told, "(l'art) de terrifier les cœurs et d'engourdir les esprits," the very art of Ennui itself. At the same time, Ennui is his greatest enemy and he has recourse to perverse stratagems to ward it off. He is to be numbered with those who seek to reach "d'un seul coup" intense aesthetic and spiritual pleasure. When the Prince is frustrated in his expectations and sees that, contrary to all reason, Fancioulle, taking his audience with him, is able to enter a world from which all thought of death is banished, he is not, as eternal victim of Ennui, able to enter fully into that world with the rest. On the other hand, he does not remain a mere spectator. Artist that he is, he has an "inspiration" and orders his page to blow a whistle. Ceasing to be a spectator, he adds his own inimitable touch to the scenario, as a result of which the creative artist's vision and the artist himself are destroyed.

Fancioulle dies, but in my view it is a mistake to believe that the narrator's affirmation of the power of art is mere irony and that it is negated by the death of the mime. The death of the mime was never in doubt and, within the fiction, he is already dead when the narrator recalls the power of the actor's last performance and describes the "indestructible" halo above the actor's head. If art were not powerful indeed, Fancioulle would not die as he does. As it is, he dies, not as a conspirator, but as an actor; he dies not the degraded death of a forgotten *saltimbanque* whom the Muses have abandoned, but the heroic death of the supreme artist. Nor does the death of the artist negate the affirmation that art which springs from our yearning for beauty and which is the result of a constant striving for perfection can perform an amazing feat: by creating intense emotion it can bring such intoxication and joy that it banishes for a moment the thought of death in the very presence of death itself. And even if, as we saw in **"Le Vieux Saltimbanque,"** the intoxication of art is transitory, yet it can be renewed. Fancioulle's performance lives on in the memory of the narrator and still retains its power to move to tears. The nature and the cause of the emotion felt by the narrator in this poem are not the same as for that which he experienced in **"Le Vieux Saltimbanque,"** for it is at the climax of the poem, when he is recalling not the death, but the supreme achievement of the actor, that he writes: "des larmes d'une émotion toujours présente me montent aux yeux pendant que je cherche à vous décrire cette inoubliable soirée."

Once again, associated with the narrator's ability to identify with the other, is the affirmation of his difference. At the time of the performance, he preserves his detachment sufficiently to observe actor and Prince alike. And although his eyes are filling with tears, we are told, as he recalls that unforgettable evening, the characteristically deliberate tone, the ironic style and punning conceits are expressions of the symbolic distance that separates the narrator from the symbolic events which he records. The narrator was not the old showman, nor is he either Fancioulle or the Prince.

These two poems may be seen in part as *exempla* in which Baudelaire exposes not so much the failure of art as the failings of the artist. They are also brilliant illustrations of the affirmation that the "poète actif et fécond" can "à sa guise être lui-même et autrui" (**"Les Foules"**). In both, the narrator is an essential element: unlike the old showman or Fancioulle or the Prince, he has succeeded in maintaining that precarious equilibrium that, it seems, is a necessary condition of art in life and of the artist in the world. It is the narrator who holds in balance the Baudelairian polarities of intoxication as opposed to continual self-awareness, of "prostitution" and "concentration," of "surnaturalisme" and "ironie." The narrator identifies imaginatively with figures who represent temptations and dangers that beset the artist, but he also demonstrates conclusively that he himself has not succumbed, nor suffered their fate.

Moreover, Baudelaire here affirms the continuity of art, regardless of the fate of the individual. The old showman has lost all creative powers but the fair continues and performers and spectators alike can depend upon its regular return. Fancioulle achieves immortality, moving from the "memory" of the narrator into the text of the poem. The narrator, himself a poet figure, is perceived as having transformed his consciousness of the frailties of man, of the poignant, even tragic aspects of the artist's condition and, yes, even of the limitations of art, into poetry. Baude-laire, through the narrator, rejects inertia and despair and affirms the possibility of life *and* art, by the very act of composing these meditations on the role of art and the condition of the artist and *by being seen to record,* "ma plume tremble," this time in more enduring form, the affirmation of the power of art that Fancioulle's perfor-mance represented.

J. A. Hiddleston (essay date 1987)

SOURCE: "'Une morale désagréable,'" in *Baudelaire and "Le spleen de Paris,"* Oxford at the Clarendon Press, 1987, pp. 33-61.

[*In the following excerpt, Hiddleston argues that* Le spleen de Paris *is a pessimistic work refuting the presence of moral order and divine providence in the world.*]

It was Baudelaire's stated intention in *Le spleen de Paris* to emphasize the random and accidental aspects of his thought and inspiration and to draw, or to give the im-pression of drawing, from his observation of Paris street scenes through the disillusioned eyes of a man afflicted by the ennui of a vast modern capital, an unpleasant moral lesson. His intention . . . was to show another Joseph Delorme, without the languor and the elegant melancholy, but with the added qualities of irony, bitterness, and modernity, 'accrochant sa pensée rapsodique à chaque accident de sa flânerie et tirant de chaque objet une mo-rale désagréable' [Baudelaire, *Correspondance,* edited by Claude Pinchois, 1973], an intention which, though enun-ciated as late as 1866, becomes increasingly obvious in the various alternative titles he envisaged for the collec-tion: *Poèmes nocturnes, La Lueur et la fumée, Le Prome-neur solitaire, Le Rôdeur parisien, Le Flâneur des deux rives.* There is, consequently, in many of the prose po-ems, which bear witness to that fascination with crowds and urban life which Baudelaire admired in Hugo, Poe, and Constantin Guys, a strong sense of the fortuitous or accidental, the feeling that the poet just happens to be there and, by a chance turn of his random wandering through the capital, is vouchsafed, in the observation of an apparently trivial occurrence, a glimpse into a more significant and deeper reality. It is as if, through the en-counter with the trivial, some secret truth is revealed, so that if the poet often appears in the role of a voyeur, his voyeurism is not limited to the petty trivialities which normally remain unnoticed, but gives on to a deeper un-derstanding of things. It is a voyeurism which might be thought of as the moral equivalent of that most poetic of all faculties, 'voyance'. Since 'la vie parisienne est fé-conde en sujets poétiques et merveilleux', and since 'le merveilleux nous enveloppe et nous abreuve comme l'atmosphère' [*Oeuvres complètes*], the result is that the 'choses vues' tend to take on the power and significance of symbolic or allegorical figures. One of the finest ex-amples is '**Les Veuves**' which, on the very simplest level, appears little more than a list of the various types of widow that can be seen in the streets or gardens of Paris, until

the evocation of the central figure, 'un être dont la no-blesse faisait un éclatant contraste avec toute la trivialité environnante'. He describes the 'parfum de hautaine ver-tu' and the sad, gaunt face of this 'femme grande, majes-tueuse, et si noble dans tout son air, que je n'ai pas sou-venir d'avoir vu sa pareille . . . ' until the figure becomes so detached from the base and ignoble surroundings that it becomes a 'Singulière vision' standing above the rest of humanity and endowed with a heightened significance. The moment in which the poet catches sight of her seems, as in 'A une passante', to stand outside time, and this heightening of reality transforms the widow from a 'chose vue' into an allegorical figure of loneliness and dispro-portion. Or take the mountebank in '**Le Vieux Saltim-banque**' who is not just a sad old man whose act has ceased to draw the public; he has become the incarnation of the once successful writer whose message is no longer acceptable or of interest to a public bent on the most strident and mindless 'divertissements'.

But not all such 'choses vues' are as successful. There can, as in '**Un plaisant**,' be a gap which is difficult to overcome between the description, in this case the splen-didly vigorous and chaotic 'explosion' of the New Year, and the moral significance which the poet wishes to at-tach to it. The 'beau monsieur' who wishes the donkey a happy new year in the middle of the street somehow fails to be elevated to a representative figure of the spirit of France. Whereas the correlation between the mountebank and the poet was immediately perceptible and rich in possible associations and resonances, that between the 'magnifique imbécile' and 'tout l'esprit de la France' seems poor, and indeed seems to detract from the vivid street scene, a veritable 'croquis parisien' worthy of Con-stantin Guys, having such an immediate appeal to the reader's imagination and memory as to be able to stand on its own without its spurious and redundant crutches. The moral lesson—that France is composed of vain and useless imbeciles who scoff at the humble and useful who are themselves driven by gross, barbarous, and cruel task-masters—is unlikely to impress itself on the mind as a great and profound truth. Perhaps because the gesture of the fine gentleman bowing before the donkey is too bi-zarre and extravagant, and because 'l'esprit de la France' is too vague and general as a concept, '**Un plaisant**' re-mains an anecdote, and we are uncomfortably aware of the poet striving to graft on to this 'accident de sa flâne-rie' a disagreeable message, which does not manage to rise much above the snide or gratuitously cynical remark.

The impact of a piece such as '**Le Désespoir de la vie-ille**', which relates the despair of an old woman who smilingly approaches a baby and is rebuffed by vigorous infant squallings, may at first seem exceedingly meagre and banal, until we glimpse behind it the literary or cul-tural commonplace which it upsets. It is a banality to link infancy to old age, and the poem obediently shows us the old woman and the infant, defenceless and frail, without teeth and without hair. There is in the commonplace a sense of recurrence which is not without comfort, a sense of a return not only to innocence when the aged have been removed from action, but also perhaps a sense of a return to origins and a circular view of time in which there is a suggestion of the identity of beginning and end. It is this veiled presence of a cultural commonplace together with the strongly visual properties of the piece which no doubt prompted René Jasinski to describe it [in *A travers le XIXe siècle,* 1975] as a 'scène familière, qui confine au tableau de genre', and it could well be this also which caused the organizers of the Baudelaire exhibition at the Bibliothèque Nationale in 1957—unconvincingly according to Kopp [in his edition of *Petits poèms en prose,* 1969]—to state that the Daumier drawing 'La Vieille Femme et l'enfant' was 'en rapport' with Baudelaire's prose poem. But the organizers were right, only it is a relationship of contrast rather than similarity, since Daumier's drawing shows a serene old woman looking thoughtfully into the face of a placid baby. Baudelaire panders to the *poncif* in the first part of the poem, whose force and 'rayonnement' stem from the sudden 'soubresaut' caused in the mind of the reader who is expecting a reassuring moral message, but is left with a 'morale désagréable' and a poignant sense of solitude and despair.

Commonplaces, platitudes, and 'idées reçues', which fascinated Baudelaire every bit as much as Flaubert, abound in the prose poems, where they serve the purpose of pointing an unpleasant moral lesson in a wilfully prosaic and debilitated style. Superficially and taken out of context, nothing could appear more pedestrian than such statements as 'le crépuscule excite les fous', 'il ne faut pas manger tout son bien en un jour', 'il y a si peu d'amusements qui ne soient pas coupables', 'la pensée est incommunicable' [see **'Le Crépuscule du soir'**, **'La Femme sauvage et la petite-maîtresse'**, **'Le Joujou du pauvre'**, and **'Les Yeux des pauvres'**, respectively]. At first glance, they appear to have the same deflating and prosaic effect as when the poet reminds us in **'Le Chien et le flacon'**, with the studied uncertainty of the man of taste who wishes to appear ignorant of such lowly matters, that the wagging of a dog's tail is a sign corresponding to smiling or laughing in human beings. But the function of such platitudes is sometimes more complex than may at first appear. For example, the irony of 'il ne faut pas manger tout son bien en un jour' in **'Le Femme sauvage et la petite-maîtresse'** springs not just from the discrepancy between the mock reasonableness of the husband and the frenzied appetite of the savage wife devouring live rabbits and chickens; it points rather to a total rift between the accepted wisdom of conventional morality and the realities of human nature and passion which they are not able to modify or control. It uncovers the savagery which hides behind the front of decency and reasonableness, with the implication that civilized behaviour is nothing more than controlled rapacity.

On other occasions Baudelaire shows his impatience and distaste for the kind of platitudes which stem from a lax, superficial and sentimental humanitarianism. In **'Les Yeux des pauvres'**, for example, he ironically quotes the platitude, put forward by such excellent moralists as the writers of popular songs, affirming that 'le plaisir rend l'âme bonne et amollit le coeur', which goes blatantly counter to the events of the anecdote and, of course, to Baude-

laire's own view of the corrupting power of pleasure. The irony is clear, since the poet's mistress, far from being moved by the sight of the poor man and his children staring at them as they enjoy the pleasure of the brightly lit new café, finds them insufferable and asks that they be sent away. But even so, the reader cannot find refuge or solace in a sceptical view of human nature, for the irony extends to the poet himself, who confesses that his heart has been moved; he has been 'attendri par cette famille d'yeux', an expression which indicates at one and the same time concern for the poor, an embarrassed self-consciousness, and a humorous detachment which appears to deny the sympathetic *élan*. Though he is ashamed 'de nos verres et de nos carafes, plus grands que notre soif', his attitude towards the family of eyes remains ambivalent; he sympathizes with their feeling of exclusion and is moved by the wonder of the youngest, whose eyes were 'trop fascinés pour exprimer autre chose qu'une joie stupide et profonde', and yet, at the same time, he is aware of the vulgarity of the place, the décor of which, with its Hebes and Ganymedes, expresses 'toute l'histoire et toute la mythologie mises au service de la goinfrerie'. His attitude is, to say the least, complex, being composed of irritation with his mistress, distaste for his surroundings, pity for the poor, which in turn is mingled with embarrassment and the aristocratic aloofness of the dandy who is aware that all men, even the poor, belong to fallen humanity, and are equally likely to be corrupted by pleasure. Towards the end of the poem the poet turns his gaze towards his mistress in the hope of seeing his thoughts reflected in her eyes, but with typical imperturbability she asks him to get the waiter to move the man and his children away, and the poet concludes with the grating cliché: 'Tant il est difficile de s'entendre, mon cher ange, et tant la pensée est incommunicable, même entre gens qui s'aiment'. Without the ironic repetition of 'tant' and the reference to his exasperating mistress as 'mon cher ange', the sentence is the kind of unadorned 'idée reçue' which the poet's mistress would appreciate and possibly utter in moments of feeling misunderstood. But irony is apparent also, since the platitude is raised to the dignity of an article of faith—at least implicitly—by those very people who are so lacking in awareness as to be insensitive to the thoughts, needs, and feelings of other people, by those, in short, who have never made a sustained effort to communicate with other people and who, through lack of imagination, are unable to get out of themselves. The 'idée reçue' belongs to the collective wisdom of those who have never thought beyond themselves and whose unassailable self-sufficiency has shielded them from the real problems of being a human being and, above all, from the awareness of that fundamental void which constitutes our inner loneliness.

At the same time the platitude is appropriated by the poet who has lived out these realities to the full and has sought in vain the Romantic ideal of a spiritual union with the loved one, and whose idealism, like that of Constant's Adolphe or of Nerval, has been misdirected into the fatal and pathetic confusion of love and religion, seen as the ultimate resolution of the contradictions and divisions which beset human beings.

In the light of this, the attitude of the poet towards the poor becomes clear. Just as he has misdirected his idealism into love, erroneously seeing mystery and the promise of happiness in her eyes, 'habités par le Caprice et inspirés par la Lune', so also have the poor mistaken the ostentatious vulgarity of the palace of gluttony as a manifestation of beauty. Both are mistaken, and both are outcasts. In the poor the poet sees a mirror image of himself, but with his illusions still intact; hence the ambivalence of his attitude, made of both sympathy and impatience, endowing the poem with the same moral uncertainty as we find in **'Une mort héroique'** and **'Le Mauvais Vitrier'**.

However, there are statements of truth which are even more discreet and whose irony is so delicate as to have a similar effect to the one intended by Flaubert, that the reader does not know 'si on se fout de lui, oui ou non' [*Correspondance*]. For example, the opening sentence of **'Le Joujou du pauvre'** might, on first reading, appear perfectly innocent and banal: 'Je veux donner l'idée d'un divertissement innocent. Il y a si peu d'amusements qui ne soient pas coupables!' An uninitiated reader coming upon the piece for the first time in an anthology, or separated from the rest of Baudelaire's work, might well take the statement about amusements at face value and expect to be told of some harmless pastime by some middle-aged author with a benignly tolerant view of human nature. But the reader who has been alerted to Baudelaire's Jansenistic view of the passions, and who has picked up a remote resonance from Pascal's famous passage on 'divertissement', will immediately recognize the irony concealed in the exclamation mark and in the falsely regretful intensifying 'si peu d'amusements'. The author, and his reader, seem to sigh as if dismissing with resignation and regret another little temptation to which they would gladly have given in.

But clearly the full irony of these sentences can only emerge when we learn the true nature of the innocent diversion which takes the form of an experiment. The reader is invited to fill his pockets, before going out to idle in the streets, with all sorts of 'petites inventions à un sol' and to distribute them to the poor children who cross his way. Nothing could appear more innocent; indeed, the action appears charitable, since the children, all agog, are unable to believe in their good fortune. But then we are told that they snatch at the present and run away 'comme font les chats qui vont manger loin de vous le morceau que vous leur avez donné, ayant appris à se défier de l'homme'. The violence of the gesture, the furtive flight away from any companions to play with the toy in solitude as an animal will eat its prey, all point to a natural, spontaneous, primitive animality in children, closer to fallen nature than to redeemed humanity. By concentrating on the scene with the rat, dwelling on the idea of the innocent 'divertissement', and by omitting the long introduction to the much earlier *Morale du joujou* on which the prose poem is based and which deals with the way toys reflect and develop the child's innate aesthetic sense, Baudelaire has, as Zimmerman has suggested [in his edition of **Petits poèmes en prose**], made the two pieces

irreconcilable, and instead of a 'morale agréable' which would see children in a favourable light, he has drawn an unpleasant moral which emphasizes their animality and their greater proximity to original sin.

In the light of all this, what are we to make of the innocent pastime? What innocence can there be in an experiment which rejoices in revealing the baseness and animality of mankind? It reveals the guilty nature of man, from which the poet-narrator is not immune, since he provokes such reactions, and rejoices and finds pleasure in the spectacle of evil. The innocent pastime is, in fact, as guilty as the mad cackle of the villain in melodrama which Baudelaire mentions in *De l'essence du rire,* since it measures the distance that man has fallen from perfection.

Similarly, one suspects that there is more than a little pulling of the reader's leg in the words whispered in the disturbing **'Assommons les pauvres!'** by the poet's demon of action who bears some resemblance to the imp of the perverse and to the 'démons malicieux' of **'Le Mauvais Vitrier'**. 'Celui-là seul est l'égal d'un autre, qui le prouve, et celui-là seul est digne de la liberté, qui sait la conquérir' appears less as some kind of liberating maxim, which some commentators have suggested, than as a political doctrine reduced to the status of an 'idée reçue' and endowed with the punch and the brutality of a slogan. One would need to subscribe to the social and economic views of the self-made man or to believe that Baudelaire was some kind of precursor of Nietzsche not to suspect some trace of irony in the passage, though it is true that the anarchist Camille Pissarro appears to have taken it uncritically when he used it as an epigraph to his drawing 'Le Mendiant' in *Turpitudes sociales*. The beggar is seen holding out his hat for alms, his back turned to a shop window stocked with rich food: which prompts the comment from Pissarro in a letter: 'ce parias [*sic*] n'a pas l'énergie de prendre de force les plantureuses victuailles exposées a [*sic*] la vitrine derrière lui, il aime mieux mourrir [*sic*] de faim! étrange!!' Pissarro seems, like some other commentators since, to have fallen into the trap of taking seriously the injunction to beat up the poor to increase their self-reliance, instead of interpreting the piece, like 'Le Reniement de saint Pierre', as an ironical denunciation of the inhumanity of modern society, in which only the strongest and most fortunate can survive, and where it is futile to expect charity. It may well be that, in spite of his view that Proudhon was merely 'un *bon bougre*' and not a dandy, Baudelaire continued to be marked by his social views right down to the time of writing **'Assommons les pauvres!'** and that Proudhon's 'mutualisme' is the hidden intertext behind the suppressed last sentence of the manuscript of the poem, 'Qu'en distu, Citoyen Proudhon?'; but from there it is a long way to go to claim, as Dolf Oehler does, that the poem should be read as an incitement to class struggle and revolutionary violence. As Wolfgang Drost says, 'The irony which to such a high degree pervades **"Assommons les pauvres!"** gives a key to his attitude towards Revolution, an attitude which is one of considerable detachment', ['Baudelaire between Marx, Sade, and Satan,' in *Baudelaire, Mallarmé,*

Valéry: New Essays in Honour of Lloyd Austin, 1982].
Whatever the exact nature of Baudelaire's political views
in 1848 and 1866, I'd suggest that the poem can no more
be read as a plea for violence than 'Le Reniement de saint
Pierre' can be said to show his scorn for those for whom
'l'action n'est pas la soeur du rêve' [Lois Boe Hyslop,
French Studies XXX, No. 3]. Interpretations of these
poems which do not take sufficient account of the poet's
irony and his desire to mystify run the grave risk of being
naïvely literal. The convulsive violence of the piece, and
the picture of the beggar holding out his hat for alms
'avec un de ces regards inoubliables qui culbuteraient les
trônes, si l'esprit remuait la matière', like that of Christ
'monté sur une douce ânesse', seem to indicate that the
key to both pieces should be found not 'dans l'intertexte
de Proudhon', but in a veiled and ironic reference to that
part of the Sermon on the Mount which proclaims the
blessedness of the meek, 'for they shall inherit the earth'.

Baudelaire's use of the popular saying is clearly linked to
his preoccupation with the commonplace and the 'idée
reçue'. Sometimes the saying is merely incidental, its
function being simply to produce a clash of linguistic
register, as, for example, with 'chercher midi à quatorze
heures' in **'La Fausse Monnaie'**. Sometimes the saying
lies hidden below the surface of the text, as with 'la corde
du pendu' in **'La Corde'** and 'les auréoles changent souvent de tête' in **'Perte d'auréole'**; and at other times
Baudelaire will revitalize expressions such as 'la vie en
beau', 'marchand de nuages', and 'tuer le temps', in order to give an insight into the complex situation of the
poet and his relationship to his art, showing his ability to
exploit the secret depths, the 'profondeur immense de
pensée dans les locutions vulgaires, trous creusés par des
générations de fourmis' [*Oeuvres complètes*]. Even as
early as in 1857 in **'L'Invitation au voyage'**, a more
conventionally 'lyrical' poem in which Baudelaire still
seems uncertain about what he wished to achieve in the
genre, the popular saying or expression has a role to play,
its function in the exclamation 'Moi, j'ai trouvé ma *tulipe
noire* et mon *dablia bleu*!' being able to provide an ironic
'soubresaut' by juxtaposing the researches of the alche-
mists of horticulture and the poet's discovery of the geographical counterpart to the soul of his mistress, with the
result that the reader hesitates in his interpretation and
reaction between dignifying the search for an unusual
flower and degrading the spiritual quest of the poet. Is the
poet's dream of the perfect correspondence between his
mistress and an ideal country as gratuitous and trivial as
the search for an unnatural tulip or dahlia, or can the
search for the unnatural flower be seen as another manifestation of man's search for the impossible, a spiritual
quest revealing the superiority of the mind and of art over
nature? It is no doubt because it provides him with such
fruitful ambiguities that Baudelaire finds 'rien de plus
beau que le lieu commun' [*Correspondance*] and that he
uses it with increasing frequency in the prose poems of
the sixties.

In **'Le Tir et le cimetière'** he plays with the popular
expression 'mettre dans le but', giving it a double meaning, both to hit the mark and die, by alluding to the dead

as those who 'depuis longtemps ont mis dans le But, dans
le seul vrai but de la détestable vie'. Zimmerman has
suggested a parallel between the prose poem and 'La Mort
des artistes' whose first quatrain reads as follows:

> Combien faut-il de fois secouer mes grelots
> Et baiser ton front bas, morne caricature?
> Pour piquer dans le but, de mystique nature,
> Combien, ô mon carquois, perdre de javelots?

But the 'but' of the sonnet is the elusive image of poetic
beauty and the figure is dignified by the comparison of
the poet to a hunter with his bow and arrows, with the
result that any sense of a discrepancy between tenor and
vehicle, and any consequent dissonance, is rapidly muted;
whereas in the prose poem the effect of the figure is doubly
discordant because of the macabrely comic intrusion of a
popular expression into the prosopopeia of the dead ('Maudites soient vos cibles [. . .] Maudites soient vos ambitions, maudits soient vos calculs', etc.), and the grim
appropriateness of human beings practising shooting and
the art of killing beside the sanctuary of death (cf. 'Un
cabaret folâtre'). Furthermore, the play upon words operates a curious reversal of the figure, and with it a whole
associated vocabulary which deals with men's aims and
the achievement of their ends of happiness and freedom—
so that 'mettre dans le But' ceases to mean to practise the
art of shooting or achieving one's ambitions, but rather to
aim at killing oneself, to bring about one's own death as
the only aim in life. The idea that death ends everything
and is the only meaning of life is a banality; but the idea,
stemming from the renovation of the figure, that death is
the sole purpose of life which all men are enthusiastically
pursuing even when they think themselves free and defending or enhancing their lives, reaches greater depths of
originality and gloom. And indeed the figure seems to
carry further, moral and social, overtones with the implication that by shooting at the range and by studying the
art of killing the activities of men involve a positive
hostility towards others, so that the negative image of the
human condition is doubled by an equally negative image
of society.

'Chacun sa chimère' has the overtones and the form of
a proverb or popular saying such as 'chacun son goût', or
'chacun son beau'. It also has something of the captions
which great caricaturists like Daumier or Goya used for
their drawings, and indeed it has been very convincingly
suggested that in writing this piece Baudelaire had in mind
the *capricho* by Goya entitled 'Tu que no puedes', which
depicts Spaniards carrying on their backs asses with faint-
ly human expressions. As Jean Prévost has pointed out
[in *Baudelaire,* 1953], the moral message is clear and
simple: Spain is groaning under the oppression of fools.
Prévost is also right to say that in this poem Baudelaire
'entrevoit devant ce dessin une vérité humaine et immense:
chacun de nous porte sa Chimère, sans même la voir',
though it is a pity that his analysis of the figure stops at
this point. Baudelaire's insight implies that men are totally in the grip of a huge 'chimère' of which they know
nothing and which drives them along independently of
their will. Whereas Vigny's poem 'Les Destinées', to

which **'Chacun sa chimère'** has been compared, sees men in the grip of fate and of predestination, Baudelaire makes of the chimera something resembling the dictates of the unconscious mind. Furthermore, it is clear that there is nowhere to go in this bleak and desolate landscape which has been compared to Dante's limbo, and that there can be no possible realization of the vain ideals which push men along and give unfailing hope to those who have 'la physionomie résignée de ceux qui sont condamnés à es-pérer toujours'. Baudelaire's view of mankind in this prose poem is similar to Beckett's in *Waiting for Godot* or to Gisors's in *La Condition humaine,* where it is stated that 'sans doute, au plus profond, Gisors était-il espoir comme il était angoisse, espoir de rien, attente'. The moral of the piece is made even more melancholy in the final para-graph in which the poet seeks in vain to understand the mystery of this nightmarish vision, but stops short, over-whelmed by indifference which weighs on him even more heavily than the 'Chimères' on their victims. The moral is more pessimistic and unpleasant than in **'L'Invitation au voyage'** where it is proclaimed triumphantly and with only the merest suspicion of irony that 'chaque homme porte en lui sa dose d'opium naturel'; men are deluded and their lives are dictated by chimeras which give them hope in a hopeless world; without such illusions and false hope, man is perhaps free, but it is a freedom to do and to believe in nothing.

Baudelaire's use of the expression 'tuer le temps' in **'Le Galant Tireur'** has been very ingeniously, and somewhat punningly, analysed by Barbara Johnson [in *Défigura-tions du langage poétique,* 1978] in order, primarily, to show the mechanics of figural language. I should like to add some comments which might help to elucidate the poem within the specific context of the poet's preoccupa-tion with a 'morale désagréable'. It would be useful to quote the whole of the poem.

Comme la voiture traversait le bois, il la fit arrêter dans le voisinage d'un tir, disant qu'il lui serait agréable de tirer quelques balles pour *tuer* le Temps. Tuer ce monstre-là, n'est-ce pas l'occupation la plus ordinaire et la plus légitime de chacun?—Et il offrit galamment la main à sa chère, délicieuse et exécrable femme, à cette mystérieuse femme à laquelle il doit tant de plaisirs, tant de douleurs, et peut-être aussi une grande partie de son génie.

Plusieurs balles frappèrent loin du but proposé; l'une d'elles s'enfonça même dans le plafond; et comme la charmante créature riait follement, se moquant de la maladresse de son époux, celui-ci se tourna brusquement vers elle, et lui dit: 'Observez cette poupée, là-bas, à droite, qui porte le nez en l'air et qui a la mine si hautaine. Eh bien! cher ange, *je me figure que c'est vous.*' Et il ferma les yeux et il lâcha la détente. La poupée fut nettement décapitée.

Alors s'inclinant vers sa chère, sa délicieuse, son exécrable femme, son inévitable et impitoyable Muse, et lui baisant respectueusement la main, il ajouta: 'Ah! mon cher ange, combien je vous remercie de mon adresse!'

As Barbara Johnson says, the two figures of killing Time and decapitating the doll are closely related. In everyday existence one kills time in order to escape from boredom and, as the poem wryly indicates, what could be more natural or legitimate? But Baudelaire italicizes *kill* and capitalizes Time to renovate and resuscitate a dead met-aphor which has itself been killed by time and usage (Johnson), and to indicate also that the desire to kill time stems not so much from the common boredom which affects all men and which is no doubt the principal *raison d'être* of firing ranges, but from the apprehension that time is the enemy of man, that it is the stuff of our im-perfection, making it impossible for us ever to achieve that god-like completion and unity of being to which we aspire, and perpetually reminding us that our state is one of dispersion, fragmentation, and becoming. To kill Time we would need more than a firing range, we would need a fundamental transformation of the relationship of con-sciousness with the world resulting in the impossible syn-thesis of 'en-soi' and 'pour-soi' which Sartre speculates on in *L'Être et le néant*; but the figure is appropriate because the violence involved in the anecdote hints at a kind of paroxysm of frustration as the bullets are fired 'loin du but proposé'. The implication would seem to be that, though he cannot kill time with a capital T, for his wife, who cannot understand his intentions and who finds his antics amusing, time with a small t is effectively killed. At this point the poet substitutes mentally his wife for the doll and there ensues a ritual killing in effigy which gives an extremely macabre tone to what was at first an inno-cent firing range. The killing in effigy exemplifies the relationship between love and violence which Baudelaire treats elsewhere in **'Mademoiselle Bistouri'**, **'Les Ten-tations'**, and 'A celle qui est trop gaie', and critics have suggested convincingly that there may be a link between **'Le Galant Tireur'** and the anecdote of the hunter in *Journaux intimes* dealing with the 'liaison intime de la férocité et de l'amour'. But more than that, the shooting in effigy points to the problematical relationship between the poet and art, symbolized by his wife as muse. She is both execrable and delightful. He owes to her a great deal of his genius, not so much because she elevates his thoughts towards higher things, but because the discrepancy be-tween her physical attractions, and the accompanying associations which they give rise to, and her spiritual and intellectual nullity so irritates him that, shutting his eyes as if inspired, he aims correctly and decapitates the doll. This bitter little piece can be seen as a symbol of artistic creation in which the poet's muse inspires him to perfec-tion, but only through a ritual whereby he imagines he is killing the very thing which inspires him. The opposites of creation and destruction are overcome in an ironic paradox in which the poet's spurious romantic angel causes a kind of 'salut à rebours' by projecting him into a hell of incompatibility, irritation, and violence. The bullet hits its mark, and at the same time the imperfections of the muse are transformed in the perfection of the poet's skill. The moral lesson is doubly paradoxical; the conscious attempt to kill Time is a vain frenzy, and what would a poet do without a muse to inspire him but fall prey to Time and ennui which cannot be killed? But to kill the wife-muse fictitiously is to accede to the 'ivresse de l'art' which at least momentarily gives the illusion of having killed Time and, at the same time, renders the muse's imperfection an instrument of artistic perfection.

The poem is clearly closely linked to **'Portraits de maîtresses'** by the use of the expression 'tuer le temps', by the killing (this time real) of the mistress, and by the contradictions in the notion of perfection. The poem involves the reminiscences of four middle-aged dandies of the extraordinary mistresses they had known. The most bizarre and interesting story is that of the fourth dandy who tells how he had to get rid of his mistress for the paradoxical reason that she was perfect; 'incapable de commettre une erreur de sentiment ou de calcul', she had 'une sérénité désolante de caractère; un dévouement sans comédie et sans emphase; une douceur sans faiblesse; une énergie sans violence'. With a cold and invincible will, she had barred the way to all his caprices, so that in his frustration he admired her with a heart full of hatred, in the end drowning her one evening in a pond in a lonely wood. The story momentarily intrigues and surprises the cynical companions until, at last, new bottles are brought and they resume their drinking 'pour tuer le Temps qui a la vie si dure, et accélérer la Vie qui coule si lentement'. The contrasts between the dead-pan narration of the remorseless drowning (euphemistically referred to as 'une action rigoureuse') and their normal drinking habits, and secondly, between the ease with which she is disposed of as if by magic and the 'grands moyens' of alcoholic poisoning which have to be used to kill the much more resilient Time, are, of course, highly amusing and ironic, and there is something positively grating and sick in the use of the popular saying within the context of a real killing which is accepted so readily. The saying maintains its triteness which is pushed to the point of vulgarity and bad taste, and at the same time the reader, shocked at the author's evident 'plaisir aristocratique de déplaire' [*Oeuvres complètes*], is aware of its many wider resonances and subtleties. As in **'Le Galant Tireur'** the popular saying is revitalized, with the result that a real killing replaces the metaphorical killing of time in order precisely to kill Time and deliver from ennui; for, as Robert Kopp says in his edition, 'la raison de l'assassinat disparaît, elle devient métaphysique', since it is based upon the absolute incompatibility between moral beauty and life, or, as Baudelaire himself puts it in the *Salon of 1846*: 'Les poètes, les artistes et toute la race humaine seraient bien malheureux, si l'idéal, cette absurdité, cette impossibilitié, était trouvé. Qu'est-ce que chacun ferait désormais de son pauvre *moi*,—de sa ligne brisée?' The moral of the two pieces taken together is that we need imperfection in order to aspire towards a perfection which will remain perfect provided it is never realized. In their contrasting and opposite ways the two stories go to the heart of Baudelaire's aesthetics and, implicitly, of his strangely incomplete and agnostic Christianity, since they depict men with aspirations to which nothing in this world can correspond and which nothing can fulfil.

Baudelaire's use of the aphorism and of the moral maxim is even more subtle and complex than his use of the commonplace and popular saying. He seems to have been intrigued by the possibilities of the genre from a very early stage in his career, and a brief survey of his practice in other writings would help to elucidate its various functions in the prose poems. The *Choix de maximes consolantes sur l'amour,* which he sent as a rather cruel joke to the bewildered and prudish wife of his half-brother Alphonse, is a useful starting-point. Its opening sentence, 'Quiconque écrit des maximes aime charger son caractère;—les jeunes se griment,—les vieux s'adonisent', provides, assuredly, an arresting 'entrée en matière', not so much for its pithiness or sententiousness, as for its manifest unreliability. A maxim which calls in question the motives of creators of maxims (who, according to a more orthodox view, might be thought to have a greater degree of self-knowledge than most men), does not attract immediate confidence and belief, having something of the self-defeating qualities of the notice which states that 'all notices on this board are false'. The reader is left wondering whether such a maxim has not itself been contaminated by the inauthenticity of its progenitor which it unashamedly proclaims, so that the maxim and the ensuing piece it presides over appear, as they were no doubt intended to, as a kind of 'spoof' designed to amuse, and possibly to mystify, the reader by a display of literary pyrotechnics. The undisguised pastiche of Stendhal's *De l'amour,* and, above all, the flippant and ironic tone evident in the inflated sententiousness of the 'maximes particulières sur des questions délicates' and in the 'patois séminariste', dealing with the problem of freedom in theology and in love, enable the young Baudelaire, as in *La Fanfarlo,* to put forward some of his principal ideas concerning physiognomy, Nature, the union of opposites, moral and physical beauty and ugliness in women, and to detach himself at the same time and take no responsibility for them. Nathaniel Wing's very pertinent remarks on *La Fanfarlo* ["The Poetics of Irony in Baudelaire's *La Fanfarlo,*" *Neophilologus* LIX, No. 2 (April 1975)] are also relevant to the *Choix de maximes*; for what is at issue is style as well as thematic substance, the somewhat oblique criticism falling not just upon a certain Romantic bric-à-brac, but on Romantic rhetoric as well. Consequently, the sententious utterances of the piece appear both as commonplaces which are to be condemned for their banality, and as truths rendered problematic by the self-conscious posturing of a young writer both claiming and rejecting, in default of a style of his own, a wisdom beyond the reach, and possibly even the conviction, of his years.

At the opposite pole to this decidedly ambivalent attitude, and as evidence of the poet's enduring preoccupation with binary opposites, we find in the section of the *Journaux intimes* entitled 'Hygiène' the grave injunctions and moral principles which he strives to adopt in order to improve the conduct of his life and to make it more purposeful and creative: 'Plus on travaille, mieux on travaille, et plus on veut travailler. Plus on produit, plus on devient fécond.' Or take the following rule which is also a 'cri du coeur': 'Faire tous les matins ma *prière à Dieu, réservoir de toute force et de toute justice, à mon père, à Mariette et à Poe,* comme intercesseurs'. This belief in the almost magical power of prayer is also present in a maxim which, were it not for the poignant circumstances, might be thought to be invalidated by the solemnity and the unsophistication of a 'bon sentiment', unworthy of the great poet: 'L'homme qui fait sa prière le soir est un capitaine qui pose des sentinelles. Il peut dormir.' His aim in these private notations is to establish a 'sagesse abrégée' based on the triple foundation of 'Toilette, prière, travail', in order to correct the anarchy of his life and to pinpoint some uncertainties in the midst of doubt and chaos. It is ironic that in striving for regeneration he should use the same turn of phrase as he used, damningly, to praise the moral and psychological over-simplifications of Hugo whom he pictured 'appuyé sur une sagesse abrégée, faite de quelques axiomes irréfutables', in much the same way as the characters of *Les Misérables* were to appear to him all of a piece, reduced to one or two invariable character traits.

Commonplaces, platitudes, and 'idées reçues', which fascinated Baudelaire every bit as much as Flaubert, abound in the prose poems, where they serve the purpose of pointing an unpleasant moral lesson in a wilfully prosaic and debilitated style.

—J. A. Hiddleston

However, the flippancy of the 'maximes consolantes', which seem to indicate some doubts about the validity of writing maxims, and the simple moral injunctions of 'Hygiène' did not prevent Baudelaire from taking the genre seriously and from being an excellent practitioner of it, as other parts of the *Journaux intimes* testify. But what is not altogether clear is the status of the various maxims and sentences in the *Journaux*. It is most likely that the ones we find in 'Mon Coeur mis à nu' would have lost much of their sententiousness and their fragmentary appearance within the elaboration of the autobiography itself, in much the same way as Pascal's *Pensées* would have been transformed in the completed apology. The famous 'De la vaporisation et de la centralisation du *Moi*. Tout est là' (is it a maxim or merely a note?) might well have lost some of its mystery, which has prompted so much ingenious interpretation, once inserted into a particular context, biographical, psychological, aesthetic, or moral. And what are we to make of the 'fusée' enigmatically couched in the form of a question: 'Se livrer à Satan, qu'est-ce que c'est?' Would Baudelaire have published it along with other similar mind-expanding utterances and maxims, would it have become part of a chapter on his own life and his view of the senses, or would it have become an exploration of the moral and theological meaninglessness of the notion of giving oneself knowingly to the Devil? Whatever the many possible answers to such speculations may be, what is clear is the wide variety of the genre to be found in the *Journaux* and the

section entitled 'Aphorismes' in the two-volume Pléiade *Oeuvres complètes*. They range from the highly serious utterances on psychology, aesthetics, and theology to such frivolous 'boutades' as 'Si un poète demandait à l'État le droit d'avoir quelques bourgeois dans son écurie, on serait fort étonné, tandis que si un bourgeois demandait du poète rôti, on le trouverait tout naturel.' The humour arises here not least from the incongruity of the perfect balance of the form and the triviality of the content. One can find strident vulgarities about women alongside bizarre definitions such as the one recorded in Asselineau's *carnet* to the effect that 'Un chat est un vampire sucré', enhanced in surreality by the alternative reading 'vampire sacré', which seems to forbid one to speculate in public about the kind of fantasy which can produce such exquisitely decadent thoughts about the domestic cat.

However, it is in **Le spleen de Paris** that we find the highest incidence of maxims and commonplaces in Baudelaire's works—predictably, at least at first sight, since such utterances would appear to belong primarily to the domain of prose and to be out of place in lyric poetry; and indeed, if we discount such metaphors as 'La Haine est un ivrogne au fond d'une taverne' in 'Le Tonneau de la Haine', *Les Fleurs du Mal* provides few examples of sententiousness. Some of the prose poems amalgamate and elaborate notations from the *Journaux intimes*. For example, the famous comments on love, religion, art, and prostitution—'L'amour, c'est le goût de la prostitution. [. . .] Qu'est-ce que l'art? Prostitution.' 'L'être le plus prostitué, c'est l'être par excellence, c'est Dieu'—are fused and developed in **'Les Foules'**, culminating in the splendid 'fusée' and article of faith: 'Ce que les hommes nomment amour est bien petit, bien restreint et bien faible, comparé à cette ineffable orgie, à cette sainte prostitution de l'âme qui se donne tout entière, poésie et charité, à l'imprévu qui se montre, à l'inconnu qui passe.' And the bizarre comparison of love to surgery, 'Il y a dans l'acte de l'amour une grande ressemblance avec la torture, ou avec une opération chirurgicale', which is suggested in **'Les Tentations'**, where Eros appears with sinister phials and surgical instruments hanging from the snake which serves as a living belt round his middle, is exemplified and dramatized in **'Mademoiselle Bistouri'**, which also takes up the theme of prostitution. The sententiousness disappears in the anecdote, which sets the abstractions of the maxim in a real person and a real place. And this concretization of an arresting though somewhat cryptic maxim, paradoxically, has the effect of an increase of suggestiveness, as the reader is led to reflect not just on the sadomasochistic elements already present in the original sentence and the reversal of the usual associations of love with pleasure and tenderness, but on the implication that the paradox of love, involving, as it would seem, both tenderness and cruelty, could not be lived out by any sane person, and that sensuality and intellect must be totally dissociated before one can enter what Proust called 'le monde inhumain du plaisir', that domain of the perverse ot of the 'monstres innocents' who are out of their minds.

Baudelaire's interest in the great 'moralistes' of the past is witnessed in the frequent mention in his works and correspondence of Bossuet, Buffon, Chamfort, Fénelon,

Joubert, La Bruyère, La Fontaine, Pascal, and Vauvenargues; but it is significant that it is in the prose poems that he makes the most specific references and quotes, or rather misquotes, them. Buffon has a glancing reference in **'Les Bons Chiens'**, Vauvenargues's 'Sur les misères cachées' is present in the introduction to **'Les Veuves'**, and La Bruyère and Pascal figure directly in **'Le Solitude'**, whose first sentence, 'Un gazetier philanthrope me dit que la solitude est mauvaise pour l'homme', contains, possibly, a muffled echo of le père Souël's words at the end of *René*: 'La solitude est mauvaise à celui qui n'y vit pas avec Dieu.' Such references have, no doubt, the familiar function of giving authority to the speculations of a learned, but still relatively unknown, writer, and the misquotations from La Bruyère and Pascal could be explained by a desire for concision and terseness within the necessary economy of the 'petit poème en prose', though it should be noted that Baudelaire took the misquotation from La Bruyère from Poe's *The Man of the Crowd*. But one wonders why he should add to the misquotation of the passage in the *Pensées* concerning man's inability to remain within the four walls of his room 'dit un autre sage, Pascal, je crois', and how to interpret the patronizing and falsely uncertain attribution of what is, after all, one of Pascal's most famous thoughts, a commonplace recognizable by any schoolboy; unless Baudelaire wishes both to embrace and to play down the wisdom of the great man and, in a collection which praises the virtues of both solitude and of the 'bain de multitude', to cast doubt upon the validity of such acknowledged truths which, before the complexities of real life, appear as glib and facile as an 'idée reçue'.

Such uncertainties are of course deliberate and intended to mystify the reader, or at least some readers. One of the most interesting examples is **'La Corde'**, where the narrator remains deluded even at the end of his narration, which is supposed to record the circumstances in which he lost his illusions. In this highly complex and bitter piece Baudelaire's comment about the makers of maxims in the *Choix de maximes* . . . seems very appropriate; for the narrator's recourse to such resounding truths as 'Les illusions sont aussi innombrables peutêtre que les rapports des hommes entre eux', 'Il est aussi difficile de supposer une mère sans amour maternel qu'une lumière sans chaleur', and 'Les douleurs les plus terribles sont les douleurs muettes', is accompanied by a pomposity of tone betraying a desire to 'se grimer' and to appear full of experience and sagacity. Many critics have followed the narrator in the belief that the story shows that even so fundamental an instinct as maternal love can be corrupted by the love of money, and nothing more. But such an interpretation smacks of the 'idée reçue' and is, in any case, . . . rendered suspect by the narrator's self-satisfaction, glibness, and insensitivity to the real needs and feelings of the boy, whom he treats more as an object than as a human being. It is Baudelaire's skilful use of maxims and commonplaces which helps to direct the reader's attention away from the superficial meaning of the poem about the nature of mother love towards its deeper implications about the nature and validity of art itself.

The prose poems abound in maxims of Baudelaire's own coining which would not have disgraced his great predecessors in the seventeenth and eighteenth centuries. Among his greatest 'trouvailles' are what I should like to call his 'aphorismes-abîmes' which either introduce or conclude a poem, and form its substance. I am thinking of such statements as 'L'étude du beau est un duel où l'artiste crie de frayeur avant d'être vaincu', the one concerning 'sainte prostitution', or 'Cette vie est un hôpital où chaque malade est possédé du désir de changer de lit'. Such aphorisms contain a great depth of philosophical, artistic, or moral truth and have the power to impress themselves on the memory and fascinate the mind with their many ramifications. Take, for example, the statement which concludes and sums up **'La Fausse Monnaie'**: 'le plus irréparable des vices est de faire le mal par bêtise'. The anecdote concerns a friend of the poet who astonishes a grateful beggar by the generous gift of a coin of unexpected value. But the coin is false and the poet eventually understands that his friend 'avait voulu faire à la fois la charité et une bonne affaire; gagner quarante sols et le coeur de Dieu; emporter le paradis économiquement; enfin attraper gratis un brevet d'homme charitable', and the poet concludes the piece with the statement that the most irreparable of vices is to do evil out of stupidity. At first sight the statement might appear to go counter to common sense which would tend to excuse an evil act if the intention was not evil. Most people would wish to distinguish subjective from objective guilt, and would accept that stupidity would be a mitigating factor, since it involves a degree of innocence and inability to assess the evil and its consequences. The anecdote, which has the appearance of an amusing real experience, gives on to a profound view of human nature, since the poet's stupid friend appears beyond redemption, having no awareness or knowledge of his evil. The curse upon Adam and Eve, as they were driven from the garden of Eden, was that they would be like gods knowing good and evil, and this knowledge, as Pascal reminds us, is both our grandeur and our 'misère', since, though it cuts us off from paradise, it gives us the means of a possible salvation, the spiritual life which might bring us back to God. Baudelaire was of course well aware of Pascal's lesson, which no doubt presided over his impatience with the pastoral innocence of George Sand's creations and his admiration for Madame de Merteuil in *Les Liaisons dangereuses*. He was well aware that 'la conscience dans le Mal' is the sign and proof of our humanity. The 'étourderie' of the poet's friend is worse than culpable; it makes of him a sub-man, a curious hybrid creature, a moral and metaphysical accident, deprived at once of the innocence of man before the Fall and of the intelligence which would explain his presence in time and the fallen world, and dignify him as a man. He is a kind of monster at large in a limbo between a paradise he does not know he has lost and a hell which he fails to recognize. The vice is irreparable because unconscious, and Baudelaire's condemnation of the man is final.

It is interesting that the poet should entertain the passing thought that his friend's action might be excused by a desire to see which of many possible outcomes might result from giving to the beggar apparently so large a sum. Would it lead to prison, or to the foundation of a great fortune? Such curiosity would relate the friend to Gide's curious waiter in *Prométhé mal enchaîné* whose fascination with bizarre situations leads him to set at the same table people who appear totally different or incompatible. Spurred on by such an idea, the poet's imagination 'allait son train, prêtant des ailes à l'esprit de mon ami et tirant toutes les déductions possibles de toutes les hypothèses possibles'. It is easy to see how such an idea would explain his friend's action, but it is hard to see how it would justify it. A passage from *L'École païenne* of 1852 which, as Kopp has pointed out, contains the germ of the prose poem, is illuminating in this context:

Le goût immodéré de la forme pousse à des désordres monstrueux et inconnus. Absorbées par la passion féroce du beau, du drôle, du joli, du pittoresque, car il y a des degrés, les notions du juste et du vrai disparaissent. La passion frénétique de l'art est un chancre qui dévore le reste; et, comme l'absence nette du juste et du vrai dans l'art équivaut à l'absence d'art, l'homme entier s'évanouit; la spécialisation excessive d'une faculté aboutit au néant. [. . .] La folie de l'art est égale à l'abus de l'esprit. La création d'une de ces deux suprématies engendre la sottise, la dureté du coeur et une immensité d'orgueil et d'égoïsme. Je me rappelle avoir entendu dire à un artiste farceur qui avait reçu une pièce de monnaie fausse: Je la garde pour un pauvre. Le misérable prenait un infernal plaisir à voler le pauvre et à jouir en même temps des bénéfices d'une réputation de charité.

The passage establishes a parallel between the art for art's sake school and the spurious generosity of the 'artiste farceur'. Just as the art for art's sake writers are forgetful of the notions of justice and truth in their search for what is beautiful, picturesque, or strange, so also is the 'farceur' forgetful of his own basic humanity and that of the poor man. While suppressing the analogy with the artists of the pagan school, Baudelaire in **'La Fausse Monnaie'** has kept an element of the original analogy which is its psychological and moral interest. The friend's need for newness and *drôlerie* is put forward as a possible explanation of his conduct, only to be dismissed and replaced by the explanation that he was seeking a cheap way to heaven and that he has committed the act out of sheer stupidity alone. The moral message is thus all the stronger for being undiluted, although one should point out that the poet's attitude towards sententiousness is not without ambiguity, as is evidenced in the way his naïvely proffered 'bon sentiment'—'après le plaisir d'être étonné, il n'en est pas de plus grand que celui de causer une surprise'—is appropriated by his fraudulently generous friend.

The second 'aphorisme-abîme' I should like to discuss is one which is not entirely original. As Margaret Gilman has pointed out [in 'Baudelaire and Emerson', *Romantic Review* XXXIV, No. 3 (October 1943)], the arresting opening sentence of **'Any where out of this world'**, 'Cette vie est un hôpital où chaque malade est possédé du désir de changer de lit', appears to have been directly inspired

by Emerson's statement in the final chapter of *The Conduct of Life* that 'Like sick men in hospitals, we change only from bed to bed'. Baudelaire's interest in Emerson is well known, and it is generally agreed that we are undoubtedly in the presence here of a more or less certain source. However, there can, I think, be no question of his deliberately misquoting Emerson as he had with La Bruyère and Pascal in order to create an ambiguous tone. Even although the Emerson sentence does not appear in Baudelaire's list from *The Conduct of Life,* it is very unlikely that in the prose poem he was quoting from memory. What he has done is to improve on Emerson's idea and to give it a power and, above all, a universality and a permanence which are absent in the original. Emerson's comparison of our actions to those of sick men in hospitals changing beds appears weak when set against Baudelaire's metaphor in which life is said to be a hospital, thus emphasizing the permanence of the state and increasing the pessimism which informs what has now become a striking maxim.

Once again we find ourselves in presence of a maxim which contains a whole philosophy, an 'aphorisme-abîme'. Nothing could be further from the attitude of some eighteenth-century rationalists who would affirm after Voltaire in one of his more confident moods that 'L'homme paraît être à sa place dans la nature', and that, consequently, there is a kind of 'correspondance' between man's desire for order and rationality and the order of the universe. According to such a view, to affirm that somehow man and the world are not compatible or that they were not 'made' for each other, would be as foolish as to suggest that the fish is not at home in the water. The preoccupation of the Romantics with Plato and certain aspects of Christianity was responsible for the decline, at least among writers, in such a belief, which was replaced by an attitude which emphasized the discrepancy between man and his world and which lived out a sense of a tragic distance between them, which Voltaire certainly knew, but did not choose to celebrate or to magnify. Indeed, for some writers the more a man felt separated not just from society, but from the world, the greater the sense of exile and the greater his superiority. The superior man is not he in whom the faculties work together to produce balance, happiness, and sanity, but rather he whose sense of exile, imbalance, and inner turmoil cause him to embrace madness as opposed to sanity, and alienation and illness as opposed to integration and health. Hence the prestige of the Werthers and Renés, and of the 'femme fatale' and her male counterpart. It is clear that Baudelaire's maxim participates in such a view, but with none of the languid yearning and elegant other-worldliness of René. The illness which is life is no longer the affliction of a spiritual élite, but of all mankind, and the idealism and the elegance have been replaced by a realism which sees life as a hospital in which all mankind, though incurably ill, is possessed of the foolish notion that one might be cured by changing position. And, of course, the figure of a hospital leads the mind to the immediate paradox that the only cure for life is death. The normal associations of life—health, abundance, happiness, fulfilment, hope, renewal—are all illusory. 'Vivre est un mal'; life is illness, restriction, imprisonment, stunting, negation, with not even the notion of a window, as in Mallarmé's poem ['Les Fenêtres'], to give some sense of hope; and the cure lies in extinction.

Baudelaire's often ironic remodelling of the popular saying is such as to deprive it of any reassuring qualities it may have had, and to point to an unstable and chaotic world where there is little in the way of certainty in human values, actions, or motives. Similarly, his own, on occasion, highly original maxims and aphorisms bear witness to his desire to avoid a literature of 'bons sentiments', such as he detested in George Sand and in Victor Hugo's novels; and, like the popular saying, they articulate not stable truths and essences, but the sudden, and often provisional and contradictory illuminations of the 'pensée rapsodique'. Thus, in order to give expression to his 'morale désagréable', he deliberately cultivates paradox and statements which, at first sight at least, go counter to common sense and experience. They often have a palpably refutable quality until the mind of the reader, fascinated by their explosive force, comes to an understanding of a wider and deeper reality. By juxtaposing two contradictory areas of experience, such maxims have a power to inflame the mind in the same way as the most daring and successful similes and metaphors, and they take on some of the dynamite and the brilliance of the 'fusée'. There is something profoundly shocking, causing a violent 'soubresaut de la conscience', in these 'comparaisons énormes' where life is compared to a hospital, and poetic creation to a prostitution which is said to be holy. It is precisely the widening of the gap between tenor and vehicle, and the stridency of the juxtaposition which create an emotional charge which is more violent and jarring than anything produced in *Les Fleurs du Mal,* where, of course, the regular metres and the harmony of rhyme and rhythm domesticate the inherent wildness of some of the images. It was perhaps because of this aspect of Baudelaire's maxims and commonplaces that André Breton thought him 'surréaliste dans la morale' ['Premier Manifeste', *Les Manifestes du Surréalisme*]. On the most superficial level, one can interpret their high incidence and wide variety in the prose poems as proof of Baudelaire's desire to mingle the genres and to create a new art form by adding to the 'ondulations de la rêverie' the 'soubresauts' of the most uncompromising prose. But their concision, suggestiveness, irony, paradoxicality, and intellectual radiance which give them the power of the most successful poetic images, together with the number of ideas and reveries they arouse in the mind of the reader bear witness to the fulfilment of his desire to be 'toujours poète, même en prose'.

The moral lesson which Baudelaire draws in the prose poems is predominantly pessimistic, and the world he evokes is one in which order and reason have been replaced by anarchy in both the moral and the physical spheres; for in these poems men are not fundamentally rational creatures; they act without premeditation, or against their own best interests; they light cigars beside barrels of gunpowder to tempt destiny; they boast of unworthy actions they have not committed and refuse to

do a small service for a friend, yet they readily help the unworthy; they throw chickens at *maîtres d'hôtel* at the time of the full moon. They fall in love with those with whom they have nothing in common and kill their favourite buffoon or perfect mistress, to such an extent that one would be apt to attribute to Baudelaire the invention of the gratuitous act long before Gide thought of it. It may well be that the function of gratuitous acts in Baudelaire's own life is, as Sartre would have it, a means whereby the dandy tries to 'transformer [. . .] sa vie en destin' [Jean-Paul Sartre, *Baudelaire,* 1947] and to make himself the victim rather than the perpetrator of events. Such mysteries can be left to the competence of psychoanalysts, since, if one examines the universe which is created in and by the poems themselves, one will see clearly that their function is to show the moral anarchy which lies at the heart of all human actions and emotions. In **'Les Tentations'**, for example, the poet in his high-mindedness rejects in his dream the blandishments of Eros, Plutus, and Fame, but in his waking life he ironically implores them to return so that he can succumb to them. Similarly, in **'Le Joueur généreux'** he rejects the Devil's offer that, in return for his soul, he should be free from ennui; any wish will be granted. But the offer is rejected not out of any strength of mind or character, but out of suspicion, distrust, and an inability to believe in his good fortune; and the poet finds himself praying to God to make the Devil keep his word, a sure sign of moral, spiritual, and theological chaos. Indeed, all the prayers in the collection are, to say the least, unorthodox. In **'A une heure du matin'** the poet prays to God to grant him the power to produce some fine verses to prove to himself that he is not inferior to those whom he despises, a prayer which is hardly informed by Christian humility and charity. Indeed, it has more than a trace of the Pharisee's prayer in Luke: 'God, I thank thee, that I am not as other men are, extortioners, unjust, adulterers, or even as this publican'— which is refused in favour of that of the humble and truly repentant publican. It is not at all difficult to accept with Zimmerman that the prayer is not authentic, since there is a contradiction in praying to God for confirmation that one is superior to those one scorns, and Zimmerman goes on to quote Georges Blin's excellent *Le Sadisme de Baudelaire* which he thinks casts light on **'A une heure du matin'**: 'Ce que Baudelaire souhaite [. . .] c'est un Dieu que l'on puisse prier sans avoir besoin de se sacrifier à lui, et même, à la limite, sans qu'il soit nécessaire de croire en son existence.' However much this statement illuminates Baudelaire's attitude to prayer in general, it does not perhaps fully account for the complexities of this particular instance. It would be useful to quote the prayer in full:

> Âmes de ceux que j'ai aimés, âmes de ceux que j'ai chantés, fortifiez-moi, soutenez-moi, éloignez de moi le mensonge et les vapeurs corruptrices du monde, et vous, Seigneur mon Dieu! accordez-moi la grâce de produire quelques beaux vers qui me prouvent à moi-même que je ne suis pas le dernier des hommes, que je ne suis pas inférieur à ceux que je méprise!

The similarities with, and the differences from, the Pharisee's prayer are immediately obvious. The Pharisee's is one of profound self-satisfaction, whereas the poet's comes from the depths of despair and self-hatred. Henri Lemaître, wrongly according to Zimmerman, judges the prayer to be authentic by placing it in the context of Baudelaire's views on the redemptive power of art which are evident in 'Bénédiction' and have influenced so much of modern poetry right down to Eliot. But Zimmerman and Lemaître are not very far apart, and their disagreement can be overcome and resolved if the analysis of the poem is carried one step further. The prayer starts as an apparently genuine cry 'de profundis' after one of the poet's habitual 'examens de conscience', and is reminiscent of the one already quoted from 'Hygiène' in which he resolves to pray every morning to God, with his old family maid and Poe as intercessors, to give him strength to fulfil his duty. But what gives the prayer its force, and also makes it typical of the prose poems, is the sudden 'soubresaut' at the end in which he wishes to be superior to those he despises. The noble plea to God and intercessors to lift him out of his distress through the grace of artistic creation contrasts brutally with the narrow outlook which disrupts and subverts the prayer at the end and calls in doubt not only the authenticity of the spiritual exercise itself, but also, most palpably, the ideal which in *Les Fleurs du Mal* survived all the other disasters, the redemptive power of art. The final irony makes our reading of the piece, to say the least, problematic, since it calls in question the 'examen de conscience' which the poem is meant to celebrate, and yet by a curious detour the prose poem itself might be taken as an example of the kind of artistic creation which precisely proves the poet's superiority, though plainly it is not in the 'beaux vers' the prayer asks for. Indeed, the piece is written in the most wilfully prosaic style, and the poet's apparent inability to create even a few lines of fine verse indicates that he is damned to remain with the banal vulgarities he despises, without the consolation of a glimpse into a higher reality which might be accorded by a lyrical outburst, however brief. The 'morale désagréable' which emerges casts doubt upon that superiority which, even if attained, would be seen as morally indefensible, and we are left with the uncomfortable picture of the poet trapped within a hell of imperfection in which the light of 'la conscience dans le Mal' shines much more dimly than in 'L'Irrémédiable', since it illumines less a means of salvation than the satanic pride and arrogance which damned Lucifer himself. If Satan could pray, his prayer might not differ much from this one which is uttered in the depths of the night.

The sense of moral uncertainty is strong in **'Mademoiselle Bistouri'** which also ends with a prayer which is ambiguous. The story, whose macabre content fixes on the fantasies of a deranged mind presenting an obvious parallel with Poe, concerns the poet's encounter during his promenade in Paris with a bizarre lady of pleasure, who presents a vast sophistication of the Romantic commonplace of the good-hearted whore. She insists in spite of his irritated protests that he must be a doctor until, succumbing to his sense of mystery and his love of the bizarre, he accompanies her to her lodging where she regales him with mulled wine and cigars in front of a brightly burning fire. It is then that gradually he learns of her curious obsession with sex and surgery, which gives her her nickname and which leads her

to fantasize that her favourite *interne* should visit her 'avec sa trousse et son tablier, même avec un peu de sang dessus'. Like the poet, the reader is unable to explain the mystery of motive and to reconcile the coexistence in the same person of so much gentleness and such a violent and sick imagination. Her tenderness is evident in her actions and in her speech, and her innocence emerges from her astonishment that one of the doctors had been so cruel as to denounce to the government those wounded insurrectionists whom he had treated at the hospital: 'Comment est-ce possible qu'un si bel homme ait si peu de cœur?' The question is reminiscent of the angel of pity's tremulous half-question half-statement to Satan in Vigny's 'Eloa': 'Puisque vous êtes beau, vous êtes bon, sans doute', as if beauty, truth, and goodness were indissoluble. But Mademoiselle Bistouri's question has wider implications, bristling with paradoxes which concern both the doctor and herself. How indeed can a man whose life is dedicated to healing hand over the patient he has cared for to his executioners? Is it mere heartlessness, made possible by a complete disjoining of professional and humanitarian conscience from the sense of social duty which, in turn, is based upon a certain, reactionary, notion of what society should be like? How can two such conflicting values coexist in the same man? Baudelaire does not explore these problems, which he is content to raise here in the context of the medical profession, and he leaves the reader to speculate on possible explanations. But what is even more interesting is that the question bends back on Mademoiselle Bistouri herself. How can such a gentle person be so preoccupied with surgery and its attendant physical violence? Her admiration for one of the doctors—'En voilà un homme qui aime couper, tailler et rogner!'—is expressed in terms one might expect from an enthusiastic and dedicated sadist. How are we to understand the links between madness and kindness, between prostitution and innocence, between sex and surgery? The implication is of course that in eroticism one partner appears to 'operate' upon the other, the resulting 'sadism' of which has been analysed in their various very differing ways by Sade, Laclos, Malraux, and Sartre, to name but a few. We have already drawn attention to the famous scene at Monjouvain in which Proust shows how the very sensitive can enter the inhuman world of pleasure only by putting themselves imaginatively into the skin of evil people; so that the tension between the inhuman violence of sex and the sensitivity of the 'âme tendre' is temporarily overcome by the suppression of the sensibility. The solution of this conflict in **'Mademoiselle Bistouri'** is more radical and permanent, since it is provided by her insanity, the loss of reason enabling her gentleness and her erotic and sado-masochistic fantasies to coexist. 'Peux-tu te souvenir de l'époque et de l'occasion où est née en toi cette passion si particulière?' asks the poet whose tone has switched from detached curiosity and surly impatience to pity; but she has no recollection, and we are left to speculate on the possible trauma which could have produced such an innocent monster.

Like the prayer in **'A une heure du matin',** the one which ends **'Mademoiselle Bistouri'** is ambiguous, being both a cry of distress and a veiled indictment of the justice of an omniscient God:

La vie fourmille de monstres innocents.—Seigneur, mon Dieu! vous, le Créateur, vous, le Maître; vous qui avez fait la Loi et la Liberté; vous, le souverain qui laissez faire, vous, le juge qui pardonnez; vous qui êtes plein de motifs et de causes, et qui avez peut-être mis dans mon esprit le goût de l'horreur pour convertir mon cœur, comme la guérison au bout d'une lame; Seigneur, ayez pitié, ayez pitié des fous et des folles! O Créateur! peut-il exister des monstres aux yeux de Celui-là seul qui sait pourquoi ils existent, comment ils *se sont faits* et comment ils auraient pu *ne pas se faire*?

The prayer is curiously problematic not just for the hidden challenge to God's goodness implicit in the affirmation of her innocence, but because of the mixture of register in the vocabulary and style. The serious apostrophe to God the Creator appears somewhat diminished by the use of the expression 'le Maître' which has colloquial overtones, and even more by the addition of the phrases about the God who has made Law and Liberty and who is full of motives and causes. These phrases seem to be in contradiction with each other, since Liberty, with its ironical capital L, seems hardly compatible with the motives and causes which, perhaps unknown to us, direct our actions according to God's inscrutable plan ('qui avez peut-être mis dans mon esprit le goût de l'horreur pour convertir mon cœur'). What freedom can the 'monstre innocent' who is Mademoiselle Bistouri enjoy in her madness? What Law has she transgressed to merit such a punishment? The poet seems to be stating categorically that God knows why such monsters exist, how they have made themselves like that, and how they could have chosen not to have made themselves like that, drawing attention to their freedom of choice by italicizing the verbs, as if men were responsible for their lives and destinies. But the story has posited the innocence of the girl, who, in any case, has no recollection of how and why her strange obsession began, so that if she is being punished it is without knowledge of her sin or of the Law that is punishing her. Madness, which Baudelaire greatly feared towards the end of his life as his malady progressed ('Maintenant j'ai toujours le vertige, et aujourd'hui 23 janvier 1862, j'ai subi un singulier avertissement, j'ai senti passer sur moi *le vent de l'aile de l'imbécillité*'), is the ultimate scandal, since it places the chaos of the world within man himself and at the same time, worse than stupidity, which after all may be temporary or sporadic, extinguishes the only light which lends human beings any dignity. The prayer which seems to plead in favour of innocent monsters is as much a challenge to the existence of divine providence and order, as an indication of submission and belief in their reality; it borders on the blasphemous, and like, for example, the much less sombre **'Les Dons des fées'**, where various gifts are given to the most unsuitable people (the gift of money and riches to one who is already rich and has no sense of charity, the love of the beautiful and poetry to a 'sombre gueux' with no means of exploiting it, the priceless gift of pleasing to those incapable of understanding its value), it points not to providence but to a moral anarchy at the heart of the universe.

Baudelaire and women:

[Passionate] clinging to his maternal apron-strings crippled Baudelaire's sexuality. Contempt made him, it seems, impotent: in his poetry he is left, supremely, a voyeur. The ideals of mutual or procreative love held no allure for him: he felt only a sado-masochistic struggle 'in which one of the players must lose their self-control' [Joanna Richardson, *Baudelaire*, 1994]. Hence his long devotion to the octoroon Jeanne Duval, the *démon sans pitié* who bled him dry and damned him black; hence his long devotion to Apollonie Sabatier, the untouchable *Vénus blanche* and redeeming Madonna. Beneath the contempt was an even deeper fear: no great poet has written more powerfully of women as agents of men's destruction. In 'Un Voyage à Cythère', for example, he finds nothing standing on Venus's island except 'un gibet symbolique ou pendait mon image'. Those flashes of nightmare vision were what made Baudelaire scandalously original and brought Sainte-Beauve's patronising but prophetic comment that

you must have suffered greatly, my dear child . . . this particular sadness which rises from your pages, this sadness in which I recognise the final symptom of a sick generation . . . is also what will be esteemed in you.

Rupert Christiansen, "The Sadness of a Sick Generation," The Spectator, *March 26, 1994.*

Jonathan Monroe (essay date 1987)

SOURCE: "Baudelaire's Poor: The *Petitis poèmes en prose* and the Social Reinscription of the Lyric," in *A Poverty of Objects: The Prose Poem and the Politics of Genre,* Cornell, 1987, pp. 93-124.

[*Monroe is an American educator and critic. In the following excerpt, he maintains that economic and social concerns motivated Baudelaire's use of the prose poem.*]

The principal force behind the modern prose poem was a writer already accomplished, before coming to the genre, not only in the verse lyric but in critical prose as well. Clearly, this combination is significant both for the genre's emergence and for its subsequent development. As his own commitment to critical activities indicates, Baudelaire was acutely aware of the importance of the question of the relationship between author and reader and of the de facto impotence of a work of art without an audience. Yet however much Baudelaire was, as Walter Benjamin has said, his own impresario, he remained badly placed on the literary market during his lifetime. Although it was possible for such novelists as Eugène Sue and Alexandre Dumas to earn fortunes through their writing, by the mid-

1850s conditions for the reception of lyric poetry were already considerably less favorable.

Although poets have long since grown all too accustomed to an extremely limited audience, the rapidly growing size of the reading public in the mid-nineteenth century, evidenced by the success of the serial novel (or *roman feuilleton*), must have held out prospects to the poet which seemed continually to be snatched from his hand by the writer of prose. Seeing the success of a writer such as Victor Hugo, for whom he had great respect, Baudelaire was far from averse to taking advantage of the possibilities. In the *Salon of 1848* he writes, already with some irony: " . . . the bourgeois . . . is quite respectable; you've got to please those at whose expense you want to live." Baudelaire's attitude toward the bourgeois public—his brother, the "hypocrite reader"—was one of growing disdain over the years, a consequence perhaps in part of his having tried and failed to gain the broad audience he desired. Although the achievement of a collection such as Baudelaire's *Petits poèmes en prose* (*Le spleen de Paris*) is not, of course, reducible in any way to a mere function of his economic situation as a writer/producer in "the age of high capitalism," Baudelaire's correspondence indicates clearly the extent to which his efforts in the genre are bound up with financial concerns and market strategy. The contract Baudelaire signed on January 13, 1863, giving Pierre-Jules Hetzel the rights to reprint the *Fleurs du mal* and to publish the *Petits poèmes en prose* for the first time in their entirety brought Baudelaire 600 francs in advance for each of the two works, a total of only 1,200 francs. In a letter to Hetzel two months later (March 20, 1863) referring to the "great importance" he attributed to the unfinished prose collection, Baudelaire writes: "I believe that, thanks to my nerves, I won't be ready before the 10th or 15th of April. But I can guarantee you a *singular book that will be easy to sell*" (*un* livre singulier et facile à vendre).

In a previous letter to Madame Aupick dated March 29, 1862, Baudelaire's impatience at not having finished the collection is again expressed in financial terms: "The *Poèmes en prose* will also go to *La Presse*. A thousand francs! but, alas! it's not FINISHED." Since in the twentieth century most "serious" poets have become accustomed to publishing the bulk of their work prior to book publication in so-called little magazines with only minimal circulation, it is worth recalling the important role in the history of printed media played by the journal that was destined to be the first to publish texts later collected in the *Petits poèmes en prose*. *La presse*, which published the first twenty of Baudelaire's prose poems over the course of three issues (August 26, August 27, and September 24, 1862), was not merely or even primarily a literary journal but, rather, a daily newspaper founded in 1836 by Emile de Girardin and Moïse Millaud. As Richard Terdiman has pointed out in his illuminating discussion of the rise of newspaper culture in nineteenth-century France, *La presse* was at the vanguard of the discursive/publishing innovations that led to the deliberate depoliticization and commercialization of the daily newspaper and its establishment as "an authentic *mass* medium," [*Discourse/Counter-*

Discourse]. Seen in the context of Baudelaire's literary production, the circulation figures Terdiman has assembled reveal to what extent the period that immediately concerns us here, that of Baudelaire's work in the prose poem, was a period as well of an unprecedented massification of the written word. By July 1863, roughly a year after *La presse* published Baudelaire's first prose poems—including the celebrated preface to Arsène Houssaye, the daily's literary editor—the circulation of another Millaud daily, *Le petit journal,* had attained a circulation of 38,000. By 1869, the year of the first publication of the *Petits poèmes en prose* in its entirety (following Baudelaire's death two years earlier), the circulation of *Le petit journal* had jumped to more than 300,000, a figure over five times that of all Paris papers in 1830.

Although Baudelaire initially entertained hopes that the prose poetry of *Le spleen de Paris* would find a broader public than did the verse poetry of *Fleurs du mal,* it soon became clear that prose poetry could not compete with the novel either. In the same letter to Madame Aupick, Baudelaire goes on to speak admiringly of Flaubert's "next novel" and the coming publication of Hugo's *Misérables* in ten volumes as "one more reason" for his *Petits poèmes en prose* not to be rushed onto the marketplace. A letter to Auguste Poulet-Malassis of December 13, 1862, confirms Baudelaire's suspicion that the competition would be too great: "As for *Salammbô*, great, great success. One two thousand volume edition bought up in two days." If the *Petits poèmes en prose* had been completed, with all of the one hundred prose poems Baudelaire had planned for it, it would itself have approximated a medium-length novel more closely than the fifty-poem collection that has been left to us. In the end, although the collection remained unfinished, Baudelaire continued to hope against hope even as late as 1865 that the singular, easily saleable book he had promised Hetzel three years earlier would bring him the financial success that had eluded him: "Now, supposing that of these last fifty there were twenty which were unintelligible or repulsive to the newspaper's public, there will still be plenty of material to be able to ask a good price" (letter to Julien Lemer, October 13, 1865).

In the dedicatory preface to Houssaye, Baudelaire shows himself as, among other things, a salesman of his own literary wares. As our first and principal access to the work, the preface provides a vantage point from which to consider the relations of the author/producer not only to his publisher/middleman but also to the reader/consumer. The importance of the latter is suggested in the preface by its designation of the work not as an organic unity but as "neither head nor tail, both head and tail, alternately and reciprocally" (*ni queue ni tête . . . à la fois tête et queue, alternativement et réciproquement*). Considering the emphasis in literary studies on the role of the reader over the last decade, it is surprising that a passage such as the following, and prose poem collections generally, should have attracted so little attention:

> Considérez, je vous prie, quelles admirables commodités cette combinaison nous offre à tous, à vous, à moi et au lecteur. Nous pouvons couper où nous

voulons, moi ma rêverie, vous le manuscrit, le lecteur sa lecture, car je ne suspends pas la volonté rétive de celui-ci au fil interminable d'une intrigue superflue.

[I beg you to consider how admirably convenient this combination is for all of us, for you, for me, and for the reader. We can cut wherever we please, I my dreaming, you your manuscript, the reader his reading; for I do not keep the reader's restive mind hanging in suspense on the threads of an interminable and superfluous plot.]

The fragmented, antiorganic composition of Baudelaire's collection attested to here exemplifies that phenomenon of "ordered disorganization" which is a characteristic feature, as Terdiman remarks, of both the newspaper and the department store. Similarly, individual prose poems—which Baudelaire hoped, as we recall, would be "easily saleable"—bear a strong and, as seems likely, more than incidental resemblance in their form to newspaper "articles" and "faits divers." It is in the newspaper after all that, in Terdiman's words, "page space was measurable in money . . . the column *itself* became readable as a machine to make money." Accordingly, in Baudelaire's preface, the potential reader is clearly envisaged, though certainly not without irony, as a consumer, the texts themselves as products—convenient commodities—to be consumed with as little annoyance as possible.

The author thus emerges not only as a producer of literary wares but also as his own agent, the work of art not as a pure end in itself but as a means for acquiring both an audience and an income. There may never have been a letter or, for that matter, any piece of writing that contained, between the opening "Mon cher ami" and the closing "Votre bien affectionné" more "deep duplicity" [so termed by Walter Benjamin, in his *Charles Baudelaire,* 1973] and calculation than Baudelaire's preface to a new genre. Examples of such duplicity abound: the "whole serpent" Baudelaire dares to dedicate to Houssaye in the hope that some of what he refers to as its "fragments" (*tronçons*) will be sufficiently alive to "please," "amuse," and also no doubt to disturb the reader—both Houssaye and the broader public accessible to him through *La presse*; the statement raising up Aloysius Bertrand's ghost only to banish it into the shadow of his own accomplishment; the concealment of false modesty under the aegis of integrity in Baudelaire's reference to his own work as a mere "accident which anyone else would glory in" (*accident dont tout autre que moi s'enorgueillirait sans doute*). Finally, this duplicity manifests itself in Baudelaire's not terribly subtle attempt to flatter Houssaye by intimating that, no less than Bertrand, Houssaye was—in his efforts to "translate in a song the *Glazier's* strident cry . . . and to express in a lyric prose all the dismal suggestions this cry sends up through the fog of the street to the highest garrets"—Baudelaire's true "mysterious and brilliant model," that same Houssaye who authored the prose poem, "La chanson du vitrier," so acidly parodied by Baudelaire's own **"Le mauvais vitrier."** Following this letter of introduction, it is less a wonder that a number of the later *Petits poèmes en prose* were not published before

Baudelaire's death than that most of them were—and by Houssaye!

Around 1850, Roland Barthes has said, "Literature begins to be confronted with the problem of its own justification: writing starts looking for alibis." In what has become one of its most celebrated passages, Baudelaire's preface (1861-62) refers to "a poetic prose, musical, without rhythm and without rhyme, supple enough and rugged enough [*assez heurtée*] to adapt itself to the lyrical impulses [*mouvements lyriques*] of the soul, the undulations of reverie, the jibes [*soubresauts*] of conscience?" Musicality, the impulses of the soul, dreams, even meditative consciousness—these are the traditional stock-in-trade of Romantic poetry, and especially of the subjective verse lyric. In the *Petits poèmes en prose,* certainly, these have an important role, yet more in a position of negation than affirmation, a negation beneath the weight of the "huge cities" (*villes énormes*) and the "medley of their innumerable interrelations" (*croisement de leurs innombrables rapports*). Speaking of the "lyrical impulses of the soul" is Baudelaire's alibi for presenting the individual not as self-sufficient or transcendent but, rather, as radically situated in the social matrix.

Nowhere is there a clearer presentation of the situatedness of the authorial "I" than in the prose poem, **"A une heure du matin"** (**"One O'Clock in the Morning"**). The demands Baudelaire makes of his prose poetry, that it be supple and tough enough to adapt itself to the undulations of dream and the jolts of consciousness, are those required not by the lyrical soul in splendid isolation but by the individual in society. For the writer, this society includes, most immediately, other writers and potential publishers. Thus, strategically placed after the parodic demolition of Houssaye's "La chanson du vitrier" ("The Song of the Glazier") in Baudelaire's own **"Le mauvais vitrier"** (**"The Bad Glazier"**), **"A une heure du matin"** begins with the double exclamation: "At last! Alone!" (*Enfin! seul!*). That five more exclamations follow before the text begins to recapitulate the day's events in the third paragraph suggests how long it takes the speaker to recover from the encounters about to be listed. How absorbed the speaker is by the social life of his big-city environment is indicated by the text's initial pronoun, which is not the conventional lyric's first-person singular, *je,* but the impersonal third person, *On* (serving in this case in its everyday sense as an alternative for the first person plural). *On* is then followed in the second sentence by the other collective first person plural form, *nous*; only after "the tyranny of the human face has disappeared" does the first *je* of the poem appear, followed by the more intimate first-person privacy of *moi-même* (myself). The first paragraph thus presents a shift from the impersonal and the collective to the private and personal, a shift expressed, significantly, in terms of private ownership, the desire to "possess silence, if not rest" (*nous posséderons le silence, sinon le repos*; my emphasis).

Having arrived home at his solitary room, immediately the speaker double-locks the door: "It seems to me that this turn of the key increases my solitude and strengthens

Painting of Baudelaire in his early twenties, shortly before he wrote La Fanfarlo.

the barricades that currently separate me from the world" (*Il me semble que ce tour de clef augmentera ma solitude et fortifiera les barricades qui me séparent actuellement du monde*). Ironically resonant with the revolution of 1848 in "barricades," this willed separation is undermined by the memories of the day which succeed each other relentlessly in the third paragraph. Following the exclamations, "Horrible life! Horrible city!" the text returns to the impersonal, this time in the form of a sequence of past infinitives: "avoir vu . . . avoir disputé . . . avoir salué . . . avoir distribué . . . être monté . . . avoir fait ma cour . . . m'être vanté . . . avoir nié . . . avoir refusé . . . et donné" (to have seen . . . to have disagreed . . . to have greeted . . . to have distributed . . . to have gone up to . . . to have made my rounds . . . to have boasted . . . to have denied . . . to have refused . . . and given). The effect of this sequence is of a confessional, a kind of litany or mea culpa in which the speaker recounts his *business,* his daily bread. The figures he encounters belong for the most part to his professional milieu, "several men of letters . . . the editor of a review . . . a theatrical director," but include also "twenty or more persons, of whom fifteen were unknown to me . . . a dancer [*une sauteuse*] who asked me to design her a costume for *Venustre* . . . a friend . . . and . . . a perfect rouge." In fact, this second list of acquaintances, encounters, friends, and enemies *also* belongs to the speaker/writer's professional circle, for as the paragraph and its conclusion suggest, the circle continues round indefinitely: "Ugh! is there no end to it?" (*ouf! est-ce bien fini?*).

For the writer, as for every member of a competitive society concerned with getting ahead (or even staying in the same place), no stone can be left unturned. That the speaker turns in the last paragraph—unhappy, in his words, with everyone, including himself—to the consolations of religion ("*Seigneur mon Dieu!*") would but be in keeping with the ideology of his class were it not for his implicit demystification of that same religious idelogy: " . . . *je voudrais bien me racheter . . .*" (I long to redeem myself). The verb *racheter,* with its specifically Christian connotation, "to redeem," should be understood here also in its economic sense, "to buy back," which echoes the verb "to possess" (*nous posséderons*) in the first paragraph. The speaker would like to buy *himself* back, to be in possession of himself, not to be subjected to the laws of the marketplace. Yet no matter how much he pleads to the "souls" of "those [he] has loved and celebrated in song" (*ceux que j'ai aimé . . . ceux que j'ai chantés*) he will not be able to shut himself off from that market and continue to live. Even his double-lock will not keep the "contaminating fumes" (*vapeurs corruptrices*) of the social world from seeping into his most private room or from fixing even his most lyrical self in its matrix.

Knowing this, the speaker prays to God for a strange kind of grace. *Dieu* emerges here as a substitute for the poetic muse, the inspiration that is to allow the speaker to "produce" something ("some beautiful verses") which will set him above his kind, not for the liberation of forgiveness, of self and others, but to prove to himself that he is not "the lowest of men" (*le dernier des hommes*), "inferior to those [he] scorns" (*inférieur à ceux que je méprise*). Although the desire these lines express not to be *inferior* does not necessarily imply a need to feel *superior* to others, the speaker's admitted scorn for those with whom he compares himself strongly suggests such an interpretation. If we are inclined to interpret the speaker's prayer as a desire to be no more than equal to others, then his invocation to God may strike us as sincere and even self-effacing. The fact, however, that the speaker desires not only to redeem himself but also to "boost [his] own pride at the expense of others" (*m'enorgueillir un peu*), may well lead us to interpret his appeal to God, though not his desire to produce beautiful poetry, as at least partially ironic. Christian grace is not given because one has or has not earned it. It is, rather, a gift that may be accorded to even the most unworthy. Thus, an ironic reading seems called for especially by the speaker's desire to *prove* his own worth, and above all to himself (*"qui me prouvent à moi-même"*), rather than to a Christian God who would require no such proof, whether through the creation of beautiful poetry or through any other means. In any case, poetry is here inseparable from what Hegel calls "the world of daily life and of prose." With its sober, forceful indication of the extent to which poets are themselves, like anyone else, trapped in this world of prose and hence no longer able to maintain "that appearance of autonomous and complete vitality and freedom which is the very foundation of beauty," **"A une heure du matin"** offers itself as a paradigmatic text for the *Petits poèmes en prose* as a whole. Although the individual in such a world may desire to see himself as, in Hegel's words, "a sealed unity," he finds himself comprehensible, like the speaker in **"A une heure du matin,"** only through his relationships to other people, on whom he is wholly dependent.

Academic critics have traditionally slighted Baudelaire's prose poetry in favor of the verse poetry of the *Fleurs du mal.* Even so profound and radical a critic as Benjamin managed to all but ignore the *Petits poèmes en prose* in his important studies of Baudelaire's work. It is almost as if Baudelaire criticism has been suffering from a kind of aestheticist repression of that very "world of prose" which Baudelaire thematized in his later work, not just as a pendant or ornament to the *Fleurs du mal,* but to "brush against the grain" of the earlier poems. [In *Défigurations du langage poétique*] Barbara Johnson has noted that, although critics have largely neglected Baudelaire's prose poetry, poets have consistently considered it among his most interesting work. Only relatively recently has the surprising lack of attention given to the *Petits poèmes en prose* in Baudelaire criticism begun to see some redress. In the 1970s in particular, there seems finally to have emerged a broader consensus that the more revolutionary Baudelaire is not necessarily to be found in his verse poetry. Now more than ever before it is possible to speak credibly of what Johnson has called the "second Baudelairean revolution" as equally enduring.

Exemplifying on a small scale the dialogical, heteroglossic, mixed mode of discourse Mikhail Bakhtin associates with the novel and prose forms generally, the prose poem in Baudelaire's hands demonstrates the kind of "self critique of the literary language of the era" Bakhtin has said is carried out not at the level of abstraction but through images of language which are "inseparable from images of various world views and from the living beings who are their agents—people who think, talk, and act in a setting that is social and historically concrete." Far more extensively and concretely than the dialogical struggles enacted in Novalis's and especially in Schlegel's texts, those in Baudelaire's prose poems incorporate discourses other than the predominantly literary and philosophical. This broadening of the dialogical from a virtually exclusive focus on struggles *within* high culture to include a concern with struggles *between* high and low culture is crucial to the social reinscription of the lyric that the prose poem advances as it emerges with Baudelaire. In the remainder of this [essay], I will bring together three prose poems that have not previously been examined in detail in close relation to one another despite several worthwhile studies of them in isolation. The three poems I will consider are those that deal most explicitly with the poor: **"Le joujou du pauvre"** (**"The Poor Child's Toy"**), **"Les yeux des pauvres"** (**"The Eyes of the Poor"**), and **"Assommons les pauvres!"** (**"Let's Beat Down the Poor!"**). Though Baudelaire's treatment of the poor in the *Petits poèmes en prose* is not at all limited to these three texts, they offer an especially useful interpretive constellation. Much of their pathos, like that of Baudelaire's prose poetry and the prose poem generally, stems from their symbolic enactment of the impossibility of resolving existing antagonisms in the absence of the kind of *collective* praxis necessary for such a resolution to come about. Seen in

relation to one another, the three prose poems on the poor suggest an "internal" dynamic, three moments of a single dialectical relation. In the aspiration they figure, both individually and collectively, toward a dialectical resolution of oppositional forces; in their staging of the urgency and extreme difficulty of the same, they offer paradigmatic examples of the prose poem's own gesture as genre.

"In every aspect of daily life in which the individual worker imagines himself to be the subject of his own life," Georg Lukács has remarked, "he finds this to be an illusion that is destroyed by the immediacy of his experience." As a prose poem such as **"A une heure du matin"** suggests, the writer is scarcely more the "subject of his own life" (a lyrical perspective) than any other worker or wage laborer. In its presentation of the lyrical subject's unwilling dependence on others, its imaging of the individual's ineradicable situatedness within determinately social contexts, **"A une heure du matin"** exemplifies the turn taken by the *Petits poèmes en prose* toward more concretely and explicitly social motifs than the verse poetry of the day seems to have allowed. In **"A une heure du matin"** and elsewhere, Baudelaire's prose poetry shows him as having developed, by means of his literary praxis, an intense awareness of himself *as object,* of his sensibility and his texts as exchangeable goods within the commodity structure of society. There is, accordingly, an intimate connection between Baudelaire's awareness of his own precarious situation as a literary producer and the presentation of the poor in the *Petits poèmes en prose*. It is questionable whether this awareness enables Baudelaire to get entirely beyond that contemplative subject-object dualism Lukács describes as characteristic of bourgeois thought. Still, as we shall see, the penultimate poem of the *Petits poèmes en prose,* **"Assommons les pauvres!",** shows signs if not of a breakthrough, then at least of a movement in that direction.

Through its frequent focus on the first-person singular of subjective, "lyrical" consciousness, the prose poem offers, on the one hand, an implicit critique of the putative "objectivity" of prose. On the other hand, by virtue of its dislocation and reinsertion of the self into the social context of third-person narrative (with particular emphasis on the anecdote), the prose poem also suggests a critique of the "subjective" lyric. In the case of Baudelaire, it seems most useful to emphasize the genre's critique of lyric poetry, both because the inventor of the modern prose poem has been primarily known as a writer of the verse lyric and because the prose poem's implied critique of prose becomes foregrounded only somewhat later, in the work, for example, of Rimbaud, Lautréamont, and Max Jacob. In the "ordinary" novel, Barthes has said, "the 'I' is the witness; it is the 'he' who is actor." Thus, the "I" in Baudelaire's prose poems, according to Fritz Nies [in his *Poesie in prosaicher Welt,* 1964], speaks mostly from the standpoint of the observer, "occasionally retreating so far into the background that in many texts it doesn't even make an appearance." This denial of the primacy of the "I" is indeed a prominent aspect of the *Petits poèmes en prose* and an important part of its critique of the verse lyric, but it is only one dimension of this critique and by no means final. [In "A Prose Poem in the Nominal Style: 'Un Hémisphère dans une chevelure,'" *L'Esprit créateur* 13, No. 2 (Summer 1973)] John Lyons has written that the collection comprises mostly narratives, "anecdotes . . . hallucinatory adventures, with the structural core . . . generally a story of someone doing something . . . the protagonist *acts*." That these acts are recounted in the first person as well as in the third person suggests an alternation between lyrical and novelistic, poetic and prosaic perspectives, between "the poet observing himself . . . and the poet observing others" [Fernande De George, "The Structure of Baudelaire's *Petits poèmes en prose*," *L'Esprit créateur* 13, No. 2 (1973)].

In an otherwise admiring letter to Sainte-Beuve (dated January 15, 1866), whom Benjamin considered the poet most responsible before Baudelaire for incorporating social motifs into the lyric, Baudelaire indicates his reservations about the aestheticizing tendencies of his friend's work: "In certain places of Joseph Delorme, I find a little too much of *luths*, of *lyres*, of *harps* and *Jehovahs*. It taints the Parisian poems. Besides, you had come to destroy that." Earlier in the letter, Baudelaire speaks of *Le spleen de Paris* as itself "a new Joseph Delorme attaching its rhapsodic thought to each incident of his idleness and drawing from each object a disagreeable moral." The difference between Baudelaire's treatment of the poor and Sainte-Beuve's is suggested in part by the *disagreeable* moral Baudelaire, in contrast to Saint-Beuve, wishes to draw from the prosaic world. Although Benjamin's analysis of social motifs in Baudelaire's poetry focuses on the *Fleurs du mal,* the **Petits poèmes en prose** displays an even greater emphasis on such motifs, as well as, perhaps, the greater insights; while the verse collection tends to turn mud into gold, poeticizing (versifying) social relations even as it ironizes them. In the prose poems of *Le spleen de Paris,* by comparison, as Suzanne Bernard has said [in *Le poème en prose de Baudelaire jusqu'à nos jours*], "mud stays mud."

Thus, **"Le joujou du pauvre,"** first published in 1862, does not greatly change or poeticize the prosaic objects it excerpts from the essay, "Morale du joujou," which first appeared nine years earlier. Except for some slight additions, including the list of three exemplary toys in the second paragraph and the breaking up of the second paragraph of the original into the prose poem's eight paragraphs, the two texts remain substantially the same. The most striking difference besides these, and the one that makes the prose poem, is the establishment of a symmetrical frame in the form of a two-line opening and two-line closing paragraph. The latter two lines are completely new, the former partially drawn from the earlier text. Inside this frame, with its "*Je*" on one end and "*les deux enfants*" (two children) on the other, the narrator situates himself as a pure observer. The almost immediate shift away from the first person in **"Le joujou du pauvre"** contrasts with the extended first-person anecdote that begins "Morale du joujou," where Baudelaire recounts a personal event from his own childhood as background to his fascination with toys as an adult. The isolation from this original context of the paragraphs that make up the

prose poem effectively cancels much of the subjective, "poetic" first-person intimacy of the earlier essay in favor of a more distanced, objective and "prosaic" account. Although the second paragraph suggests contact between the first and third persons, the subject and object of contemplation, it does so only in the uncertain temporal space between future and imperative, and by means of an ambiguous second person: "When you go out in the morning . . . fill your pockets" (*Quand vous sortirez le matin . . . remplissez vos poches*). Of the poor children who are to receive toys and who would run away like cats to savor them, the speaker says: "You will see their eyes open unbelievably wide" (*Vous verrez leurs yeux s'agrandir démesurément*). There is no guarantee, however, that these children will "actually" receive anything (from us? the speaker? Baudelaire?), as the children well know, "having learned to be wary of man" (*ayant appris à se défier de l'homme*). Contact is postponed indefinitely, leaving speaker and reader suspended in the space/time between two verb tenses.

In the third paragraph, the verb tense changes, and the speaker, who remains unidentified except as an "I" who contemplates the (im)possibility of an "innocent diversion," begins to recount the principal anecdote of the poem, a static portrait. On one side of a fence a wealthy child stands passively on the grass beside a splendid toy; across from him, like an outcast from Eden, "on the highway" (*sur la route*), there is another child described as "pitifully black and grimy" (*sale, chétif, fuligineux*). The two children and their objects are presented in a frozen, dualistic world. What is referred to in "Morale du joujou" as "that immense *mundus* of childhood" is in fact two worlds, the insecure world of poverty and the road separated by "symbolic bars" from the cozy, domestic world of the rich. If the toy is, as Baudelaire writes in the earlier essay, "the first initiation of the child to art," then the literary art to which the poor child receives initiation would certainly be unadorned prose, that of the rich child the aristocratic art of classical French poetry with its intricate rhyme schemes and other aesthetic devices and adornments. The phrase Baudelaire uses to describe the rich child's toy— "*verni, doré, vêtu d'une robe pourpre, et couvert de plumets et de verroteries*" (gilded and shining, dressed in purple, and covered with plumes and glittering beads)— suggests the latter in the preciosity of its diction and subject matter, in the conspicuous assonance and alliteration of "*verni . . . vêtu . . . verroteries*" and "*pourpre . . . plumets,*" and in its concealed approximation of a double alexandrine ("*verni . . . pourpre*" / "*et . . . verroteries*").

Corresponding to this symbolic reading on the literary/aesthetic level, the two worlds of the poor and the rich child suggest on the social level the class relations of proletariat and bourgeoisie. In an earlier verse poem from his "Révolte" cycle, "Abel et Caïn," Baudelaire lays out a similar set of relations, where the race of Cain may be identified with the proletariat and the race of Abel with the bourgeoisie. Recalling not only the poor child "on the road" in **"Le joujou du pauvre"** but also the beggar family in **"Les yeux des pauvres,"** in "Abel et Caïn" Baudelaire writes: "*Race de Caïn, sur les routes / Traîne ta famille* *aux abois"* (Race of Cain, on the roads / drag along your family with your backs to the wall). Like Abel in the biblical version of the story, the rich child in **"Le joujou du pauvre"** stands inside the garden from which the poor child is excluded. In contrast to **"Abel et Caïn,"** however, with its open call to rebellion, the tone of **"Le joujou du pauvre"** is more detached; the speaker is one who keeps his distance and self-possession, "the eye of a connoisseur." The dominant verbs in the latter poem have to do with observation, the calm *durée* of the imperfect tense: *"regardait," "nettoyait"* used to refer to the act of divining "an authentic master under . . . the disgusting patina of misery" (*une peinture idéale sous . . . la répugnante patine de la misère*). The closest the children come to action is, momentarily, in the poor child's "showing" (*montrait*), the rich child's "examining" (*examinait avidement*) the live rat that is the shared focus of their gaze, "drawn from life itself" (*tiré de la vie elle-même*).

The only real center of activity in the poem, the rat the poor child agitates violently, is quite literally caged up. Clothed in a proliferation of adjectives, the children face each other across what seems for the moment of the text a secure partition, but the activity of the poor child exciting the rat inside its cage on one side of the "symbolic bars" is suggestive of the energy that might be released by the proletariat in class struggle. Up to the very end, the speaker of Baudelaire's poem keeps his distance, though the "fraternal" smiles, "of an *equal* whiteness" (*d'une* égale *blancheur*), serve as an ironic reminder that the promises of the French revolution for liberty, fraternity, and equality have been realized only by those on the right side of a class barrier that has yet to be broken down by successful revolutionary praxis. As with the man looking at his own reflection in the prose poem, **"Le miroir"** ("according to the immortal principles of '89, all men are equal before the law" [*d'après les immortels principes de '89, tous les hommes sont egaux en droits*]), an empty formal likeness is here reflected alongside unresolved, potentially explosive difference. The mirror, Pierre Macherey has said: "does not reflect things (in which case the relationship between the reflection and the object would be one of mechanical correspondence). The image in the mirror is deceptive: the mirror enables us to grasp only *relationships* of contradiction. By means of contradictory images the mirror represents and evokes the historical contradictions of the period" [*A Theory of Literary Production,* translated by Geoffrey Will]. The prose poem in Baudelaire's hands is not only the site of a potential and actual confrontation between literary modes, between poetry and prose, it is also the location, as **"Le joujou du pauvre"** makes abundantly clear, of a strong emphasis on societal oppositions, potential and actual antagonisms stemming from class relations. In **"Les yeux des pauvres,"** the second of Baudelaire's poems on the poor we will consider, conflict involves not only class relations and literary antagonisms of the form prose/poetry but also another kind of "generic" conflict, the gender-based sexual antagonisms between men and women.

In **"Le joujou du pauvre,"** as we have seen, the speaker keeps his distance, and with it, his anonymity, consider-

ing the poor from the point of view of a "connoisseur." The overall effect of the poem is to situate poverty as an object of contemplation, as spectacle. In **"Les yeux des pauvres,"** subject—poetry, the speaker, the lyrical "I"— and object—prose, the poor, the narrative "he"—continue to be held apart in a relation of mutual exclusion, but at a closer distance than in **"Le joujou du pauvre."** The latter text, as we have seen, takes the form of a monological anecdote, with the speaker present only as an observer and narrator. **"Les yeux des pauvres,"** by contrast, suggests a dialogical relationship that includes the speaker as a more active participant, though even here his position is best described as one of oscillation: "inside" the frame of the lover's relationship, he remains "outside" the frame of the poor. Suggestive of a dialectical reversal of the subject/object relation in **"Le joujou du pauvre,"** however, the eyes of the poor in the prose poem that bears their name take in the speaker at least as much as he takes in the poor.

"Les yeux des pauvres" begins, like other crucial prose poems such as **"A une heure du matin," "Perte d'auréole"** and **"Assommons les pauvres!",** with an exclamation, one of those linguistic shocks suggesting intensified awareness: "Ah! So you want to know why I hate you today?" At this stage, "you" (*vous*) remains powerfully ambiguous. As opposed to the "you" of **"Le joujou du pauvre,"** which functions primarily to parry attention away from a detached "I," "you" in this case serves to immediately implicate the reader in a way reminiscent of the verse poem "Au lecteur" ("To the Reader"). The reader is of course also implicated by the problematic of innocence and guilt which begins **"Le joujou du pauvre,"** but the emphasis in that poem falls first on the speaker rather than, as here, on the reader. Though we may continue to read "you" in reference to ourselves as readers, and we are indeed implicated, the pronoun begins to take on its other and primary connotation with the attribute, "the most perfect example of feminine impermeability." Beyond this, the first sentence of the second paragraph, "We had spent a long day together which to me had seemed short," places the speaker in a past that separates him from the reader. Thus, as the focus shifts from the second person plural *vous* to the first person plural *nous,* the speaker's place in the narrative gives way to a third "other," his female companion.

The couple, the narrator tells us, has promised to share all their thoughts with each other. These thoughts, however, and the generic/sexual problematic the poem thematizes, are not to be separated from a problem of class relations which stands implacably, in the speaker's words, "directly in front of us." Obtruding on the speaker's romantic desire for a utopian oneness with his female companion—"We had duly promised each other . . . that our two souls would henceforth be but one—a dream which . . . has been realized by none"—is the prosaic reality of class, as well as sexual, difference, and the crisis of conscience which results from the disparity between rich and poor. The contrast between the ornate, lavish surroundings of the new café where the speaker and his lover are seated and the poor man "of about forty, with tired face and graying beard" holding two small boys, one "too weak to walk," could not be more pointedly drawn. All three "in rags," the members of the poor family contemplate the conspicuous display of wealth in front of them with serious eyes and an admiration "equal in degree but differing in kind according to their ages" (*une admiration égale, mais nuancée . . . par l'âge*). Ironically "equal" in their admiration of cultural achievements that do not belong to them but only to a privileged few, the poor, we might say, cannot present themselves, they must be represented. And so here the poor are attributed words we take to be their own in a world that excludes them even as it takes them in: "a house where only people who are not like us can go" (*une maison où peuvent seuls entrer les gens qui ne sont pas comme nous*).

Theirs is the world of prose; the speaker's world, that of the poetic "café neuf" of history and mythology: "All the gold of the poor world had come to adorn those walls" (*on dirait que tout l'or du pauvre monde est venu se porter sur ces murs*). This autocritique of French Romantic poetry's aestheticization of poverty, the poeticization of a prosaic world, is further developed in the beginning of the penultimate paragraph:

> Les chansonniers disent que le plaisir rend l'âme bonne et amollit le coeur. La chanson avait raison ce soir-là, relativement à moi. Non seulement j'étais attendri par cette famille d'yeux, mais je me sentais un peu honteux de nos verres [read also "verses"—*vers*] et de nos carafes, plus grandes que notre soif.

> [Song writers say that pleasure ennobles the soul and softens the heart. The song was right that evening as far as I was concerned. Not only was I touched by this family of eyes, but I was even a little ashamed of our glasses/verses and decanters, bigger than our thirst.]

Like **"Le joujou du pauvre,"** **"Les yeux des pauvres"** presents poverty as an object of contemplation, even delectation, though here, significantly, the eyes of the poor *look back*; the distance between the "I" and the other(s) has diminished. Yet though the poor have come closer and their eyes have engaged the speaker, his response is not to confront what stands right before his eyes but to turn away. What he turns toward is a typical substitute for pressing social concerns—romantic love. The eyes of the poor give way to the eyes of the lover, yet the text ends with the static relation of incommunicability. When the speaker's visual intoxication is dispelled, when the lover speaks, the effect is to increase rather than diminish the sense of irreconcilable generic, sexual, and class differences, to accentuate the distance between men and women as well as between social classes: "'Those people are insufferable with their eyes wide open like carriage doors! Can't you tell the proprietor to send them away?'" ('*Ces gens-là me sont insupportables avec leurs yeux ouverts comme des portes cochères! Ne pourriez-vous pas prier le maître du café de les éloigner d'ici?*').

As at the conclusion of **"Le joujou du pauvre,"** in **"Les yeux des pauvres"** a static set of relations remains firmly in place, unchallenged by any notion of an intervening praxis that might resolve existing tensions. Although the subject/object relation of the former remains completely one-sided, however, with the narrator/subject contemplating the frozen, dichotomized world of rich and poor alike, **"Les yeux des pauvres"** displays a contrasting reciprocity in which the speaker, seated complicitously with his lover in a bourgeois café, contemplates the beggarly characters of his anecdote only to have these objects of his contemplation look back at and even "speak" to him (albeit in his own words). These acts of speech distinguish **"Les yeux des pauvres"** from the voiceless landscape of **"Le joujou du pauvre,"** yet both poems exhibit a fundamentally contemplative orientation to the problem of class relations—significantly, in **"Les yeux des pauvres,"** it is the *eyes* that do the talking. In **"Assommons les pauvres!",** by contrast to these two earlier poems, contemplation gives way to action, an exchange of words to an exchange of blows, reciprocal glances between the speaker and the poor to physical interaction and confrontation. Although the probable consequences of such a confrontation are ambiguously drawn in Baudelaire's poem, the change of emphasis in question recalls Marx's fundamental claim that the resolution of theoretical antitheses ("subjectivity and objectivity, spirituality and materiality, activity and suffering") "is *only* possible in a *practical* way, by virtue of the practical energy of man. Their resolution is therefore by no means merely a problem of understanding but a *real* problem of life, which *philosophy* could not solve precisely because it conceived this problem as *merely* a theoretical one."

Le spleen de Paris combines, as we have noted, a markedly social thematic with lyrical brevity and compression. Although often maintaining the lyric "I," individual prose poems as well as the collection as a whole tend to displace the lyrical subject from the center of attention. In the poems we have looked at so far, we have seen this subject (re)situated within decidedly social contexts. In **"Assommons les pauvres!"** the "I" is much more an explicit focus of attention than in either of the other two poems on the poor:

> Pendant quinze jours je m'étais confiné dans ma chambre, et je m'étais entouré des livres à la mode dans ce temps-là (il y a seize ou dix-sept ans); je veux parler des livres où il est traité de l'art de rendre les peuples heureux, sages et riches, en vingt-quatre heures.

> [For fifteen days I had shut myself up in my room and had surrounded myself with the most popular books of the day (that was sixteen or seventeen years ago); I am speaking of those books that treat of the art of making the people happy, wise and rich in twenty-four hours.]

Since **"Assommons les pauvres!"** was written in 1865, the anecdotal narrative of some sixteen or seventeen years earlier which it recounts takes place around 1848, the year of the failed social revolution that here emerges as the immediate horizon within which to situate Baudelaire's radical formal experimentation in the *Petits poèmes en* *prose.* The subject presented to us has a certain distance from his past which allows him to perceive himself as the speaker of the two previous poems we have considered perceived the poor, that is, as an *object* within the historical process. As a consequence of this temporal distancing, the "I" in **"Assommons les pauvres!"** approaches an awareness of himself as both subject and object.

Following the speaker's self-imposed immersion in social theory, the intensive fifteen-day period of reading alluded to above, he does something that is, if not unheard of, at least fairly unusual among the generally contemplative speakers of Baudelaire's prose poems—he *acts*: "And I left my room with a terrible thirst" (*Et je sortis avec une grande soif*). At first, this activity takes the most familiar, relatively passive form of Baudelairian activity, that of the *flâneur*. We are on the verge of following him, however, into a release of energy that is unsurpassed by any other speaker in Baudelaire's work with the possible exception of "Le mauvais vitrier," that poem to which **"Assommons les pauvres!"** bears perhaps the closest resemblance. The former begins, in a manner suggesting spontaneous individual, much more than collective, praxis: "There are certain natures, purely contemplative and totally unfit for action, which nevertheless, moved by some mysterious and unaccountable impulse, act at times with a rapidity of which they would never have dreamed themselves capable." The amount of time the speaker in **"Assommons les pauvres!"** spends confined in his room reading suggests his contemplative affinity with the earlier speaker. Although his immersion in theoretical problems also suggests the search for a well-grounded praxis that might differ qualitatively from the perverse spontaneity of the speaker in "Le mauvais vitrier," the course of action he chooses is scarcely less perverse, the action's outcome no less ironic. Like his predecessor in "Le mauvais vitrier," the speaker here has his demon or, rather, his good angel, yet in contrast to that of the speaker in the earlier poem, the demon/angel of **"Assommons les pauvres!"** is explicitly linked to philosophy—"Since Socrates had his good Demon, why shouldn't I have my good Angel"—as well as to two *aliénistes* of the era, Lélut and Baillarger, who had maintained that Socrates was insane. The principal difference, the speaker says, between his own demon and that of Socrates, is that his is "a demon of *action*" (*un Démon d'action, un Démon de combat*). His counsel: "'A man is the equal of another only if he can prove it, and to be worthy of liberty a man must fight for it'" (*Celui-là est l'égal d'un autre, qui le prouve, et celui-là seul est digne de la liberté, qui sait le conquérir*).

Such a position is quite different from the prevailing attitudes of the speakers in **"Le joujou du pauvre"** and **"Les yeux des pauvres."** What follows in the text is a parodic example or test case of a noncontemplative, violent approach to solving a "theoretical" problem in which the speaker physically attacks a beggar only to get back twofold everything he delivers to him:

> Tout à coup, ô miracle! ô jouissance du philosophe qui vérifie l'excellence de sa théorie!—je vis cette

antique carcasse se retourner, se redresser . . . le malandrin . . . me pocha les deux yeux, me cassa quatre dents. . . . Par mon énergique médication, je lui avais donc rendu l'orgueil et la vie.

[Suddenly,—O miracle! oh joy of the philosopher when he sees the truth of his theory verified!—I saw that antique carcass turn over, jump up . . . the decrepit vagabond . . . proceeded to give me two black eyes, to knock out four of my teeth. . . . —Thus it was that my energetic medication had restored his pride and given him new life.]

After this "discussion," which ends by mutual agreement, the defeated speaker ironically acknowledges the beggar ("Sir, *you are my equal*"), shares his purse with him, and advises him ("if you are really philanthropic") to apply the same theory to his "colleagues" (*confrères*), supposedly in order to benefit them as well. There is more to this anecdote, to be sure, than a perverse version of the adage, "The Lord helps those who help themselves." In contrast to the speaker of **"Le joujou du pauvre,"** who maintains his contemplative distance from what he observes, the speaker in **"Assommons les pauvres!"** turns dramatically from theory to praxis. What kind of praxis is, of course, another question. Equality, the decisive problematic at the end of **"Le joujou du pauvre,"** is imaged as something to be taken by force—or, if need be, by violent action. But to be taken by whom? The speaker's use of the term *colleagues* sends us back to the title's first-person plural, but the question still arises: Who is the implied "we" of this poem?

As so often in Baudelaire, and as we have already seen in the beginnings of **"Le joujou du pauvre"** and **"Les yeux des pauvres,"** the text sets up an inescapable complicity between author and reader, both producers of the contradictions and antagonisms of the social context and text itself. In this case, however, complicity is no longer that of an aesthetic contemplation that makes of the poor one more commodity for pleasurable though guilty consumption. It is, rather, a complicity of praxis, to "beat down" the poor. Although the directive to commit acts of physical violence against the poor is in all likelihood best understood ironically, the particular kind of irony in question is less certain. However we take it, the question of class affiliation arises, and it is difficult to pin down the speaker's own standpoint toward such an imperative: one of "us," or one of "them." The speaker, who is himself not a beggar, gives us no other immediate clues as to his own class alliance, though if we read the poem in the context of the preceding prose poems, Baudelaire's other writings, and his situation as a literary producer in the age of high capitalism, ample evidence is available: "the literary life, the only element where certain classless beings can breathe" (*la vie littéraire, le seul élément où puissent respirer certains êtres déclassés*). The "we" of **"Assommons les pauvres!"** should stand as a warning to all those intent on "rescuing" Baudelaire's motivations and intentions by assuming a Marxist or historical materialist perspective. One of the problems with such a reading is its tendency to minimize or repress the antisocialist aspects of the poem along with that deep duplicity Benjamin rightly maintained as characteristic of Baudelaire. The ambivalence and contradictoriness Oskar Sahlberg says must be emphasized with regard to Benjamin's work obtain even more in that of Baudelaire [Sahlberg, "Die Widersprüche Walter Benjamin," in *Neue Rundschau* 85 (1974)].

Jean-Paul Sartre's claim that the writers of 1848 missed the chance to ally themselves with the proletariat, "the subject par excellence of a literature of *praxis*," applies particularly well to Baudelaire. Insofar as the literary market of the nineteenth century was first of all, as Sahlberg has remarked, "a great opportunity, and a greater battlefield than it had ever been before," Baudelaire's turn to the prose poem as genre suggests among other things a final attempt to gain for himself a greater share of the rapidly growing bourgeois reading public. Perhaps more important, however, the aesthetic experimentation and social reinscription of the lyric evidenced in the *Petits poèmes en prose* also suggest an effort on Baudelaire's part to create a new and expanded audience by *breaking* with the accepted norms and expectations of bourgeois readers as to what a poem should be. As Claude Pichois has remarked [in his edition of Baudelaire's *Oeuvres complètes*]: "In the modern era, isn't respecting rules—even those that presided over the elaboration of the *Fleurs du mal*—a sign of submission [asservissement]? To respect the hierarchy of genres in the nineteenth century is perhaps to accept the hierarchy of social classes." The wealth of devices and artifice characteristic of rhymed, metrical verse, in particular the classical alexandrine, had become by the mid-nineteenth century its peculiar poverty. Responding to this situation, Baudelaire's prose poetry offers itself as a dialogization, prosification, and relative democratization of the verse lyric and a renunciation of the aestheticist tendencies Baudelaire had earlier praised in the work, for example, of Théophile Gautier. Arising as it does in the wake of the failed social revolution of 1848, the critique of such tendencies manifest in the *Petits poèmes en prose* arrives too late, however; their aesthetic revolution goes underground, to be revived by Rimbaud at that "moment of danger" in the early 1870s when the social force of the proletariat begins to show itself again. Full of contradictions, *Le spleen de Paris* gestures to both bourgeoisie and proletariat, and this double gesturing is responsible for much of the work's tension. Such tension manifests itself nowhere more dramatically than in **"Assommons les pauvres!",** where the ambiguous deictic "we" suggests Baudelaire's unwilling economic solidarity with prostitutes, beggars, and unemployed wage laborers, the true "confrères" of the poet within the commodity structure.

It is well known that Baudelaire once planned to end **"Assommons les pauvres!"** with the apostrophe, *"Qu'en dis-tu, Citoyen Proudhon?"* (What do you say to that, Citizen Proudhon?). With or without the deletion, the text suggests a critical appraisal of Proudhon's social theory. Although Baudelaire had warned as early as 1851 against what he called "socialist sophistry," his sympathies at that time, as earlier in 1848, were on the whole closely allied with those of Proudhon, a writer, he said "whom Europe will always envy us." By 1865, however, the year both of Proudhon's death and of the completion of **"Assommons les pauvres!",** Baudelaire's own relation to the philosopher had grown more complex. In a letter to Narcisse Ancelle on February 8, 1865, Baudelaire concedes the weakness of Proudhon's aesthetic ideas, while defending him in economic matters as "singularly respectable." A year later, in his January 2, 1866, letter to Sainte-Beuve, Baudelaire writes that he will never pardon Proudhon for not having been a dandy; he also defends him, however, as, with pen in hand, "un bon bougre." Despite the fact that this letter to Sainte-Beuve was written on the occasion of Sainte-Beuve's own recent appraisal of Proudhon, its special relevance for **"Assommons les pauvres!"** has been left unaccounted for by previous assessments of the poem. With the statement, "I have read him a lot, and known him a little," the letter does indeed document, as Wolfgang Fietkau has pointed out [in *Schwanengesang auf 1848,* 1978], Baudelaire's intimate acquantaince with Proudhon's work. Beyond this, however, it also suggests, both by what it says and by what it does not say, that **"Assommons les pauvres!"** may be read as a symbolic enactment on Baudelaire's part of his own attempts to come to terms with, on the one hand, the contemplative aesthetic of the "midwife of souls" represented for him by Sainte-Beuve, and, on the other hand, the revolutionary social praxis represented for him by Proudhon. Of Sainte-Beuve's own recently completed work on Proudhon, Baudelaire writes: "I'll say nothing to you . . . You have more than ever the air of a midwife of souls. The same was said, I believe, of Socrates, but the gentlemen Baillarger and Lélut declared, on their conscience, that he was insane." Echoing unmistakably the passage in **"Assommons les pauvres!"** quoted earlier which refers to Socrates, these lines suggest that the speaker's "good angel" may be a composite of both figures: Sainte-Beuve, the poet and aesthetician whom Baudelaire elsewhere called "profound in his skepticism," and Proudhon, the most influential French social theorist of his day.

In his well-known letter to P. V. Annenkov of December 28, 1846, responding to what he considered a grave misunderstanding and misrepresentation of the dialectic in Proudhon's recently published, *Système des contradictions économiques ou philosophie de la misère,* Marx refers to Proudhon as "the declared enemy of every political movement." "The solution of present problems," Marx says, "does not lie for him in public action but in the dialectical rotations of his own head." It is little wonder that Proudhon should have represented for Marx an impediment to social praxis. In a letter written to him as early as May 17, 1846, Proudhon rejected violent revolutionary praxis as a means of social reform because "this supposed means would be quite simply an appeal to force, to the arbitrary." Nevertheless, although Proudhon hoped instead for what he called "slow, measured, rational, philosophical progress" (letter to M. F***, March 2, 1840), Baudelaire thought of him as one of the leading forces behind the February 1848 revolution, a role Proudhon himself privately wished to deny. In the first of three articles on his long-time friend, the socialist chansonnier Pierre Dupont, Baudelaire hails Proudhon as the very embodiment of the "genius of action." Accordingly, whereas the "prohibitive Demon" of **"Assommons les pauvres!"** calls to mind the "poor Socrates" whom Baudelaire associates with Sainte-Beuve in his letter of January 2, the "Demon of action" which the prose poem's speaker claims for himself recalls Baudelaire's vision, if not Marx's, of Proudhon as a philosopher of praxis.

Given the movement enacted in **"Assommons les pauvres!"** from a contemplative theoretical approach to social reality toward one based on praxis, the question remains as to what specific kind of praxis, if any, might be most effective. In the *Petits poèmes en prose* generally, as in **"Assommons les pauvres!"** in particular, possible answers to this question are articulated less through affirmative proposals or suggestions than by negation. The "correct" praxis is inscribed in Baudelaire's poem as a conspicuous absence—collective, perhaps, rather than individualistic. Nowhere a given, it is everywhere to be *fought* for. Yet the possibility that such violence will result in benevolent change coexists at the end of **"Assommons les pauvres!"** with the possibility that it will, instead, make matters worse. In 1865, describing his proposed "universal application of the principle of reciprocity" or "mutualism," Proudhon spoke in favor of "the ancient law of the *talion, an eye for an eye, a tooth for a tooth . . .* so to speak reversed and transferred from criminal law and the infamous practices of the vendetta to economic law, to the workers' tasks and the good offices of free fraternity." That same year, alluding to the failed revolution of seventeen years earlier, **"Assommons les pauvres!"** subjects such a principle to a parodic spectacle: where the speaker pokes out only one of the beggar's eyes, the beggar pokes out both of his; where the speaker knocks out two of the beggar's teeth, the beggar knocks out four. Already in 1848, with reference to the June insurrections, Baudelaire had written: "And see how violence, turmoil, impatience and crime retard the questions rather than advance them." Pointing to an indefinite suspension of the synthesis aimed at by revolutionary praxis rather than its permanent realization, the desperate comedy which **"Assommons les pauvres!"** enacts suggests that one of the manifestations of Proudhon's notion of primitive "exchange in kind" may be physical violence that ends, as the most recent revolution itself had in fact ended, neither in a true dialectical synthesis nor even in a provisional resolution of opposing forces which would be as beneficial to all parties as Proudhon hoped. Although the beggar in **"Assommons les pauvres!"** gets a share of the speaker's purse, both he and the speaker come away badly injured, and the future is no more secure for either of them than it was before their bloody encounter. Resolution, no resolution, a "wrong" solution (beating down the poor),—all these are coterminous at the text's conclusion.

The reader of *Le spleen de Paris* is not bound, in Baudelaire's words, "on the thread of an interminable and superfluous plot." As a collection, it allows for multiple entrances and exits, combinations and recombinations of texts such as the dialectical relation I have (re)constructed among **"Le joujou du pauvre," "Les yeux des pauvres,"**

and **"Assommons les pauvres!"** *Le spleen de Paris* represents an important gesture toward what Benjamin has referred to in "The Author as Producer" [in *Reflections,* translated by Edmund Jephcott] as a "melting-down process of literary forms." In Baudelaire's prose poems, this process is not without its conservative side. Pieces of the thread of the "interminable and superfluous plot" the *Petits poèmes en prose* refuses *as collection* to show up unmistakably in the predominantly anecdotal structures of many of its individual texts. It is not until Rimbaud's *Une saison en enfer* that the prose poem challenges narrative, as it were, from within. What is conservative at one historical juncture, however, may be revolutionary at another. For as much as **"Assommons les pauvres!"** represents a critical turning away on Baudelaire's part from the revolutionary Baudelaire/Proudhon of February 1848 and "universal panaceas . . . against poverty and misery," the text also suggests, as does the prose poem itself as form, at least a partial rejection of the "gilded words" and contemplative aspect of French Romanticism. Proudhon, Sainte-Beuve once remarked to Baudelaire, "should have been the man to whom you were least sympathetic. All these philosophers and socialists want literature to be nothing but a tool of instruction, a moralizing instrument for the people. This is a point of view radically opposed to our own." If the ghost of Proudhon emerges, in **"Assommons les pauvres!"** as now the good demon of action, now the author of dubious social theories, this contradiction is suggestive of a growing ambivalence on Baudelaire's part toward Proudhon in particular and socialist theories in general in the aftermath of the failed February revolution. Despite such ambivalences, the poem's very treatment of Proudhon indicates the extent to which, contrary to what Sainte-Beuve might have expected, Proudhon continued to be for Baudelaire, as he had been in 1848, a figure to be reckoned with, as compelling in his way as the merely "prohibitive demon" of a Sainte-Beuve, the "poor Socrates" of Baudelaire's January 2, 1866, letter.

In the *Petits poèmes en prose,* the anecdotal, teleological narrative aspect of individual texts has the progressive function—at once aesthetic and political—of allowing a more radical (re)insertion of the individual subject into concrete social contexts than the verse poetry of Baudelaire's immediate predecessors and contemporaries, including Sainte-Beuve, had seemed to allow. As resolutely cohesive in its individual texts as it is fragmented as a collection, *Le spleen de Paris* marks the persistence of organicist notions of form even as it begins to effect the break with such notions later manifest in the more radically *anti*-organic texts of a Rimbaud or a Mallarmé. Commenting on Baudelaire's prose poetry, Bernard has not hesitated to speak of the "destructive effect that a philosophical, moral, didactic digression can have on the fragile alchemy of poetry." Yet the very interplay of various modes of discourse manifest in Baudelaire's collection is surely one of its greatest strengths. By staging the interpenetration of such "high" and "low" discourses as those we have seen in this [essay]—including the languages of poetry, prose, salesmanship, private ownership, the artist's milieu, religion, social unrest, history, philosophy, myth, philanthropy, social theory, and political confrontation; the languages as well of adults and children, men and women, rich and poor—Baudelaire's prose poetry demonstrates an acute awareness of how greatly the "fragile alchemy" of mid-nineteenth-century French Romantic poetry was, if anything, in some need of destructive effects. Of the author as producer, Benjamin asks: "Does he have suggestions for the reorientation of the novel, the play, the poem?" Baudelaire's **Petits poèmes en prose** provides just such a suggestion.

Michele Hannoosh (essay date 1988)

SOURCE: "The Function of Literature in Baudelaire's *La Fanfarlo,*" in *L'esprit créateur,* Vol. XXVIII, No. 1, Spring, 1988, pp. 42-55.

[*In the following essay, Hannoosh contends that the relationship depicted in* La Fanfarlo *between the characters and literature provides the key to understanding the novella.*]

Baudelaire's **La Fanfarlo** is a story replete with books, writers, readers, and critics, and yet the function of literature in the narrative has prompted no systematic study. Most of the major elements of the plot turn around a literary object: Samuel is introduced immediately as a writer, and his character defined in terms of his method of reading and the contradictory contents of a "typical" nineteenth-century artist's library; his first encounter with Madame de Cosmelly is dominated by a novel of Walter Scott's, and the second by his own volume of poetry, *Les Orfraies*; he contrives to meet La Fanfarlo by means of his journalism; in the end he is reduced to grinding out books for money and founding a socialist newspaper; long discussions of literature occupy the first half, and allusions to literary characters and works occur throughout. We might ask, then, why literature plays so prominent a role in the story, and to what effect?

On the one hand, the theme reflects the status of parody in the work. The overt use of texts within a text is a convention of parody, which as a genre depends on the same metafictional principle: the incorporation of one work within another, which thereby comments on it. *La Fanfarlo* loosely follows the plot of Balzac's *Béatrix,* as Prévost first argued [in *Baudelaire,* 1953], and in a number of individual episodes parodies Balzac, Musset, Gautier, Laclos and others. The scene with Madame de Cosmelly, as all commentators have noted, is a blatant parody of Romanticism. Baudelaire makes this absurdly clear through not only the agglomeration of Romantic clichés, but also the narrator's highly ironic presentation and sarcastic commentary.

But the parody of Romanticism does not cease there. Samuel's Romantic elucubrations in the first episode are clearly a ruse designed to win Madame de Cosmelly. He knows the tricks—and clichés—of the trade and uses them as skillfully as the narrator himself. He becomes an *object* of mockery, however, in the context of the larger story: the

confident *poseur* considers himself a Valmont, a Lovelace, a Chatterton, a Henri de Marsay, but actually plays right into the hands of his intended victim. This the narrator makes plain by naming the literary models against whom Samuel measures parodically, like these, or with whom he compares (Tartuffe), calling him a fool, and ridiculing *Les Orfraies* as an unoriginal collection of puerile clichés. Samuel is a parody of the seducer, and the story a parody of the plot which he imagines for it: he is used by Madame de Cosmelly when he expects to reap the fruits of her gratitude, and made miserable by La Fanfarlo when he expects to bask eternally in the "contentement savoureux" which loving her has inspired. The would-be hero becomes a victim, the lover an object of scorn, the poet a hankerer after official recognition through the intrigues of his mistress with the minister. At this level too the parody is clear, in the consistently ironic turn of events (the plot abounds in the conventional ironic devices of misunderstanding and quidproquo) and the narrator's condescending final remarks about the degradation of the hero.

While the parody and irony are easily perceptible, their interpretation has proved more difficult. Most commentators concur on the parody of Romanticism in the first half, but take the second as a "serious" statement of a new aesthetic or a "positive" view of Romanticism: the conscious cultivation of detachment, difference, duality, illusion, and irony which distinguishes the dandy and the true artist, an aesthetic of artifice approaching Baudelaire's formula for modernity. But this view neglects to take account of the irony present in the second half. Moreover it raises the crucial problem of motivation in the plot: if Samuel's experience with La Fanfarlo represents the "new" aesthetic to replace the "old" Romantic one of the Madame de Cosmelly episode, why does it fail and decline into ludicrous farce at the end? If Samuel becomes an authentic poet and lover in his affair with the dancer, renouncing the myth of presence, cultivating duality, and detaching himself from passion, why does this change? The reason cannot be that his controlled ironic distance becomes mere "natural passion," as some have argued; the change in their relations on the contrary *causes* this to happen. They deteriorate simply when La Fanfarlo learns of his original plan to win her away from Madame de Cosmelly's husband, and takes revenge on him for having, as she thinks, used her. The central questions of the story thus remain: why is Samuel a victim of *both* Madame de Cosmelly and La Fanfarlo? If we accept that his position toward Madame de Cosmelly was false, a hypocritical role, why after his exhilarating, perfect communion with the dancer must he suffer "toutes les horreurs de ce mariage vicieux qu'on nomme le concubinage"? If the "new" aesthetic is the authentic one, why does it end in the same way as the "old" one? In other words, what precisely does the second half of the story have to do with the first? The answer to these troubling questions, which go to the very heart of the work, can be approached by examining the prominent theme of literature.

In fact a study of this motif reveals the fundamental *similarity* between the two parts, despite the apparent differences between them. Samuel's character changes not in substance, only, perhaps, in manner. Indeed the narrator implies at the end that this ongoing metamorphosis continues beyond the time of his narrative: "J'ai appris récemment qu'il fondait un journal socialiste et voulait se mettre à la politique." The episode with La Fanfarlo ends in disaster because it involves the same problems as his equally disastrous contract with Madame de Cosmelly: both reflect his questionable approach to his readings.

This the narrator presents early on as a main trait of character:

> Un des travers les plus naturels de Samuel était de se considérer comme l'égal de ceux qu'il avait su admirer; après une lecture passionnée d'un beau livre, sa conclusion involontaire était: voilà qui est assez beau pour être de moi!—et de là à penser: c'est donc de moi,—il n'y a que l'espace d'un tiret.

Samuel suffers from the classic quixotic, indeed parodic, problem—confusing his experience with his reading. This makes his protean personality more accurately a motley: "Il était à la fois tous les artistes qu'il avait étudiés et tous les livres qu'il avait lus, et cependant, en dépit de cette faculté comédienne, restait profondément original." He believes himself the author and hero of the books he admires, and thus destroys the distinction between subject and object, self and other. The same trait constitutes the "sophism" of hashish in the *Paradis artificiels,* the excessive optimism which transforms desire into reality, confuses dream with reality, substitutes an image—particularly the idealizing image that is art—for reality. Baudelaire specifies the reason for this in *involontaire:* Samuel's prodigious imagination allows him to go beyond the confines of the self and identify with the *non-moi,* but his laziness and lack of will *condemn* him to doing so. His imagination lacks the concentration and centralization necessary for creation, and, unlike the narrator, sufficient *ironie* to control *surnaturalisme,* as Baudelaire prescribes in *Fusées.*

So completely does Samuel identify with his readings that he is himself a kind of living poem ("la poésie brille bien plus dans sa personne que dans ses œuvres"). But this differs from the practice of the dandy, who cultivates the beautiful in his person. The dandy's tyrannical doctrine fortifies the will and disciplines the soul, qualities conspicuously lacking in Samuel: "Le soleil de la paresse [. . .] lui vaporise et lui mange cette moitié de génie dont le ciel l'a doué." Rather, he fits the description of Pinelli in *Quelques caricaturistes étrangers* ("son originalité se manifesta bien plus dans son caractère que dans ses ouvrages") where Baudelaire refers to the trait by the most damning term of his criticism, *poncif.* Samuel represents the *jeunesse littéraire* criticized in the review of Cladel's *Martyrs ridicules* (1861); this generation is characterized by the same *paraesse,* believes in *génie* rather than the disciplined *gymnastique* necessary to express it, and "découpe sa vie sur le patron de certains romans, comme les filles entretenues s'appliquaient, il y a vingt ans, à ressembler aux images de Gavarni." Samuel iden-

tifies with his readings because he lacks the will to do otherwise; and will, in the *Poème du hachisch,* is the only effective arm against self-deception and solipsism. The reader, on the other hand, constantly encounters an alternative to this method in the narrator's, who from the beginning emphasizes his ironic detachment from the hero and his own text.

Samuel's readings have in particular determined the dualism of his character, indeed of an entire generation of artists like him: Samuel Cramer and Manuela de Monteverde (his pseudonym), male and female, northern and southern, cerebral and sensual, "ambitieux" and "fainéant," "entreprenant" and "paresseux," hypocritical and gullible:

> Les voilà aujourd'hui déchiffrant péniblement les pages mystiques de Plotin ou de Porphyre; demain ils admireront comme Crébillon le fils a bien exprimé le côté volage et français de leur caractère. Hier ils s'entretenaient familièrement avec Jérôme Cardan; les voici maintenant jouant avec Sterne, ou se vautrant avec Rabelais dans toutes les goinfreries de l'hyperbole.

The library matches Samuel's paradoxical personality: mysticism vs. racy libertinage, the metaphysical vs. the farcical, grotesque and obscene, like the volume of Swedenborg and the "livre honteux" open on his table. The narrator is scathing about the vanity and egoism, however unwitting, which permit this identification with and appropriation of another: "Ils sont d'ailleurs si heureux dans chacune de leurs métamorphoses, qu'ils n'en veulent pas le moins du monde à tous ces beaux génies de les avoir devancés dans l'estime de la postérité.—Naïve et respectable impudence!" As the irony implies, such spurious generosity results from a self-deception that would be pernicious were it not ludicrous. But it can have unfortunate consequences, as Samuel will learn: his willingness to appropriate his readings for his own life, his failure to preserve a distinction between the two, make him play into the hands of a superior and more circumspect author, Madame de Cosmelly; and foolishly to reveal the original stratagem because it no longer seems to matter to the new story in which he finds himself, that of La Fanfarlo. Samuel considers himself the author of both stories and fails to see that he may actually be a character in a better author's plot.

The first important episode—Samuel's meeting with Madame de Cosmelly—is dominated by books. He initially becomes aware of her from amidst his books and papers. His memory of their youthful love presents itself in the form of a novel ("il s'était raconté à lui-même, détail par détail, tout ce jeune roman"), which he reappropriates for the present, hoping to reopen the book and continue the story. His means of seduction also involves a book, which provides him with not only the standard pretext for entering into conversation (she has left her volume of Walter Scott on a park bench), but also the occasion to pour forth "un torrent de poésie romantique et banale." Samuel does this not by adopting the manner and attitudes of Scott— he has seen that the volume does not hold her interest— but by berating them and thus asserting his own. His *éreintage* denounces Scott's banal Romantic "bric-à-brac" in favor of a more serious Balzacian modernity of heroes in black suits carrying *cartes de visite,* such as Baudelaire himself extolls in his *Salons* of 1845 and 1846. Scott is accused of piling up gothic clichés and creating lifeless automatons lacking in credible passion, *morale,* and *actualité*: "types connus, dont nul plagiaire de dix-huit ans ne voudra plus dans dix ans." He intends his critique to persuade Madame de Cosmelly of the truth of a more contemporary aesthetic, by which he means to win her. But Baudelaire undermines the effort in a few ways. First, the narrator derides Samuel as an insufferable, self-absorbed bore who insists on expounding his ideas to any who will listen, and, as a further insult, compares this passionate Romantic artist to the most standard images of the bourgeois—the travelling salesman, the industrialist, and the framer of stock ventures:

> Samuel [. . .] rentrait dans la classe des gens *absorbants* [. . .]. Il n'y a entre les commis voyageurs, les industriels errants, les allumeurs d'affaires en commandite et les poètes *absorbants* que la différance de la réclame à la prédication; le vice de ces derniers est tout à fait désintéressé.

Second, Samuel's allusion to eighteen-year old plagiarists rings of firsthand experience, given his habit of making himself the hero and author of everything he reads. If he has evolved into a new modernity, the plagiarist method has changed not at all. Samuel's new aesthetic, as we shall see, is as clichéd and *poncif*-ridden as he here considers Scott's. Third, his espousal of a Balzacian aesthetic constitutes a central irony of the story: the man who considers himself a Balzacian hero does not see that he is following the plot of another Balzacian novel, with an outcome different from his own plans for it: *Béatrix*.

The second meeting with Madame de Cosmelly centers on his own book, *Les Orfraies*. These represent the "folies romantiques" alluded to in the first line of the story, which the narrator here treats with the same scorn that Samuel had earlier shown for Scott: "recueil de sonnets, comme nous en avons tous fait et tous lu, dans le temps où nous avions le jugement si court et les cheveux si longs." [In "Baudelaire-Cramer: La sens des *Orfraies*," in *Du romantisme au surnaturalisme*, 1985] F. Leakey convincingly relates them to Baudelaire's own poems of ca. 1843, which he momentarily renounced and later reworked for the *Fleurs du mal*. As others have observed, the title is parodic, although less for recalling "resounding Romantic" ones [Nathaniel Wing, "The Poetics of Irony in Baudelaire's *La Fanfarlo*," *Neophilologus* 59 (1975)] than for denoting a parodic bird, an "anti-oiseau," as Riffaterre points out in Hugo [*La production du texte,* 1979], and for exaggerating the satanic aspect of Romanticism: these are evil, rapacious birds, "vilains oiseaux." But the parody depends especially on a cliché: "Samuel était fort curieux de savoir si ses *Orfraies* avaient charmé l'âme de cette belle mélancolique, et si *les cris de ces vilains oiseaux* lui avaient parlé en sa faveur" (emphasis mine). We are thus reminded of "pousser des cris d'orfraie," shrieking and squawking, the very parody of lyricism. Samuel's

title, deliberately subverting the lyric tradition of first-generation Romanticism, comically suggests the raucous quality of his own verse, and thereby conveys the narrator's parodic attitude toward the Romanticism of Samuel's generation too.

Their discussion of the *Orfraies* defines his new aesthetic for us: artifice, anatomical descriptions, depravity, funereal subjects, *galanteries* addressed to honest ladies, mystical and platonic offerings to "sultanes de bas lieu." In a long discourse full of Romantic clichés, Samuel explains it as a result of disillusionment and spleen. But the importance of the book lies in the fact that it provides him with a model to follow in his later experience with La Fanfarlo. The narrator comments that the famous "n'oubliez pas le rouge!" incident, where Samuel demands that she make love to him in the costume and make-up of her role as Columbine in a pantomime, is perfectly consistent with the *Orfraies*. The long description of her leg and back match the *descriptions anatomiques* of his volume:

> Tranchée perpendiculairement à l'endroit le plus large, cette jambe eût donné une espèce de triangle dont le sommet eût été situé sur le tibia, et dont la ligne arrondie du mollet eût fourni la base convexe [. . .] sa tête, inclinée vers son pied, [. . .] laissait deviner l'ornière des omoplates, revêtues d'une chair brune et abondante.

The "sujets funèbres" return in the portrayal of the world outside their room: "Le temps était noir comme la tombe"; "le ruisseau, lit funèbre où s'en vont les billets doux et les orgies de la ville"; "la mortalité s'abattait joyeusement sur les hôpitaux." The spicy poetry at which he excels corresponds to the spicy cuisine, literal and metaphorical, which he enjoys with her during their first night. La Fanfarlo herself meets Samuel's desire for an aesthetic of *actualité*: "Fanfarlo la catholique, non contente de rivaliser avec Terpsichore, appela à son secours tout l'art des divinités modernes." More importantly, the affair involves the same *douleurs* and ultimately the disillusionment of the *Orfraies*. The final scene, with La Fanfarlo giving birth to twins, fulfills the prediction which Samuel had made to Madame de Cosmelly: "Il n'est pas de rêve, quelque idéal qu'il soit, qu'on ne retrouve avec un poupard glouton suspendu au sein." The irony has a purpose: in transforming his art into reality according to his habit, he fails to heed the very warning that it imparts.

That Samuel's art can work against him in this way is illustrated by the famous *quiproquo des sonnets*. This episode has been interpreted as useless, a ridiculous instance of his effort to use serious literature for practical ends, and an example of his failure to understand women. But Samuel's ludicrous "mistake" of sending to La Fanfarlo the sonnet intended for Madame de Cosmelly, "où il louait en style mystique sa beauté de Béatrix, [. . .] la pureté angélique de ses yeux, la chasteté de ses démarches, etc.," and to Madame de Cosmelly the "ragoût de galanteries pimentées" intended for La Fanfarlo, matches Madame de Cosmelly's description of the *Orfraies* themselves: "Vous adressez des galanteries [. . .] à des dames, que j'estime assez pour croire qu'elles doivent parfois s'en effaroucher. [. . .] vous réservez votre encens le plus mystique à des créatures bizarres [. . .] et vous vous pâmez platoniquement devant les sultanes de bas lieu." Moreover the reaction of the two women—La Fanfarlo "jeta ce plat de concombres dans la boîte aux cigares," Madame de Cosmelly "ne put s'empêcher de rire aux éclats"—prefigures the outcome of the story: La Fanfarlo effectively discards Samuel as she becomes a "lorette ministérielle," and the narrator predicts that he will end up in that ultimate *boîte aux cigares,* the grave; and Madame de Cosmelly has the last laugh. This seemingly trivial "détail comique," this brief "intermède" in the larger drama, does not merely represent Samuel's ineffectualness in a rather typical Romantic episode, but actually links the two parts of the narrative by representing in miniature the unhappy and comical consequences of transferring literature to reality.

Madame de Cosmelly, for all her pretense of simplicity and naivety, proves herself a more sophisticated reader—and author—than Samuel. She understands the psychology of desire: she knows that her husband grew weary of her "parce qu'elle avait trop d'amour; elle mettait tout son cœur en avant." With Samuel she proceeds more carefully, exploiting the power of suggestion and the provocative effect of the hint, playing a role of candor which she spices up with indications of her capacity for passion and corruption. She describes her efforts at coquetry—the "toilettes folles et somptueuses des femmes de théâtre," the sparkling wit of the *femme du monde,* the rouge, two of which accoutrements Samuel later demands of La Fanfarlo. She recounts her hatred, jealousy, and thirst for vengeance, and, with a metaphor calculated to go straight to the heart of Samuel's desire, depicts her passion as that of a mistress "battue et foulée aux pieds." She understands the attraction of vice ("De quel charme si magique le vice auréole-t-il certaines créatures?") Indeed this "charmante victime" possesses the very "charme magique" which she here attributes to women of low virtue; she bewitches Samuel as completely as the dancer does later.

The narrator calls attention to Madame de Cosmelly's cleverness by twice alluding to Tartuffe:

> Pendant qu'elle sanglotait, Samuel faisait la figure de Tartuffe empoigné par Orgon, l'époux inattendu, qui s'élance du fond de sa cachette, comme les vertueux sanglots de cette dame s'élançaient de son cœur, et venaient saisir au collet l'hypocrisie chancelante de notre poète.

>   . . . . .

> Madame de Cosmelly, cette aimable Elmire qui avait le coup d'œil clair et prudent de la vertu, vit promptement le parti qu'elle pouvait tirer de ce scélérat novice, pour son bonheur et celui de son mari.

As Howell remarks [in "Baudelaire: A Portait of the Artist in 1846," *French Studies* 37 (1983)], Samuel displays exemplary *tartufferie* in this scene, attempting to seduce her with his "patois séminariste." But the comically awk-

ward first comparison presents a Tartuffe already caught out and thus points to the other side of his hypocrisy—his utter stupidity before a more clever impostor, with a better talent for acting: or, as the second comparison makes clear, Elmire, who, like Madame de Cosmelly, uses her foolish suitor to bring her husband round to her side.

But why does Samuel fall into her trap? Why is this hypocrite, with his advanced *faculté comédienne,* his literary culture and his extensive experience of reading and writing, incapable of interpreting her story, with its "marivaudages dramatiques," and her designs properly? Samuel here makes the same mistake as with his readings, takes the story as his own, considers himself its author; the plot should follow his plans for it. The narrator places the blame for this error squarely on his credulity, his ability never to be astonished by anything:

> Il semblait dans sa vie vouloir mettre en pratique et démontrer la vérité de cette pensée de Diderot: "L'incrédulité est quelquefois le vice d'un sot, et la crédulité le défaut d'un homme d'esprit. L'homme d'esprit voit loin dans l'immensité des possible. Le sot ne voit guère de possible que ce qui est."

Samuel's credulity is a function of his vast imagination, which allows him to accept the improbable, and his equally vast laziness, which condemns him to doing so indiscriminately. A better reader must be more of a fool, less bold than Samuel but more sceptical, posing the type of question that the narrator attributes to us here:

> Quelques lecteurs scrupuleux et amoureux de la vérité vraisemblable trouveront sans doute beaucoup à redire à cette histoire, où pourtant je n'ai eu d'autre besogne à faire que de changer les noms et d'accentuer les détails: comment, diront-ils, Samuel, un poète de mauvais ton et de mauvaises mœurs, peut-il aborder aussi prestement une femme comme Madame de Cosmelly? [. . .] Madame de Cosmelly, la discrète et vertueuse épouse, lui verser aussi promptement [. . .] le secret de ses chagrins? A quoi je réponds que Madame de Cosmelly était simple comme une belle âme, et que Samuel était hardi comme les papillons, les hannetons et les poètes. [. . .] La pensée de Diderot explique pourquoi l'une fut si abandonnée, l'autre si brusque et si impudent. Elle explique aussi toutes les bévues que Samuel a commises dans sa vie, bévues qu'un sot n'eût pas commises. Cette portion du public qui est essentiellement pusillanime ne comprendra guère le personnage de Samuel, qui était essentiellement crédule et imaginatif [. . .]

But here the narrator contradicts the lesson that the story appears to teach. He mocks the incredulous, pusillanimous reader like ourselves and taunts us for a scepticism that we have learned from his own ironic voice. In urging us to free our own imagination and accept the story uncritically, he actually sets the trap of the second half, where his relative sympathy for the hero risks blinding us to the differences between them. But to follow him in this would repeat Samuel's error. In accepting the aesthetic which the narrator seems to approve, and taking the second half as serious and positive, we abdicate our will, and condemn ourselves to as rude an awakening at the end as Samuel's own.

If Samuel's credulity derives from an imagination which his laziness prevents him from controlling, a further question arises: what is the source of this laziness, which abandons his identity to every book, author, and hero that he encounters? Madame de Cosmelly provides a significant clue: "je me regardais moins souvent que vous dans la glace." Samuel, fascinated by his own image, finds in his readings a reflexion of himself. Literature constitutes a mirror in which he sees himself as he would like to be, and, following the sophistic logic of the *hachischin,* he persuades himself that he is so. His is thus a fantasizing imagination, as R. Storey argues [in *Pierrots on the Stage of Desire,* 1986], which incorporates the object of its desire into itself; maintaining distance is the duty of the will, and this Samuel lacks. Madame de Cosmelly, on the other hand, equates her mirror with her conscience, and while childishly seeking assurance of her beauty from it, yet refrains from glorifying in the image.

Samuel's experience with La Fanfarlo, then, represents merely another "lecture passionnée d'un beau livre," and entails the same problems as his method of reading generally. She is indeed a work of art, "une harmonie matérielle, [. . .] une belle architecture, plus le mouvement," and his love for her is described as "l'admiration et l'appétit du beau": like his readings, she provides a mirror in which he can contemplate himself, another self to appropriate for his own. But this egotistical approach to art, and to love as an art, bars him from the sense of harmony between self and other that art in the Baudelairean scheme inspires, and brings him only the *tristesse* of the *Orfraies*: "il était souvent seul dans son paradis, nul ne pouvant l'habiter avec lui [. . .] aussi, dans le ciel où il régnait, son amour commençait d'être triste et malade de la mélancolie du bleu, comme un royal solitaire." The *infini* that Samuel thinks he sees in her eyes is only the "gouffre lumineux" in which the *hachischin* "admire sa face de Narcisse." Like the drug, his love "ne révèle à l'individu que l'individu lui-même," and his lonely paradise is a "paradis d'occasion"—as R. Chambers remarks [in *L'ange et l'antomate,* 1971], sterile as well as solitary. The "contentement savoureux" that it evokes in him reflects only the diminished power of his will: by contrast, Balzac's Henri de Marsay, having similarly gorged himself on pleasure, feels the imperious need to assert his will, recuperate and concentrate his identity, in the passage from *La Fille aux yeux d'or* to which the narrator in a footnote here directly refers.

Throughout this section one notices the narrator's sympathy for his hero, in contrast to the irony and sarcasm of earlier. He agrees with Samuel openly on the decoration of the bedroom ("Cramer haïssait profondément, et il avait, selon moi, parfaitement raison [. . .]"), and shares his taste for rich wines and highly seasoned foods. His reflexions on the dance ("c'est la poésie avec des bras et des jambes, c'est la matière [. . .] animée, embellie par le mouvement") match Samuel's view of the body ("une

harmonie matérielle [. . .] une belle architecture, plus le mouvement"). He admires La Fanfarlo as deeply as does Samuel. But he also maintains a distance on him, both in the "n'oubliez pas le rouge!" episode and elsewhere, referring to him with condescension as "le romantique Samuel, l'un des derniers romantiques que possède la France," "le pauvre Samuel," and "l'homme le plus faux, le plus égoïste, le plus sensuel, le plus gourmand, le plus spirituel de nos amis." Moreover, the passages on food and décor are sufficiently exaggerated as to be comical: the ludicrously hyperbolic discourse on truffles, the seriousness with which the narrator professes to take the question of sauces, stews, and seasonings ("question grave et qui demanderait un chapitre grave comme un feuilleton de science"), and his eccentric and vehement abhorrence of large rooms. Baudelaire's irony is subtler in this section than earlier, but nevertheless clear. The narrator's sympathy holds the very danger against which he has warned us in Samuel: we risk taking it for a "serious" aesthetic, identifying ourselves with him and endorsing it as he seems to do, until it is undermined by its failure at the end.

But why does it fail? The credulity which makes him the dupe of Madame de Cosmelly makes him the victim of La Fanfarlo too. Believing himself in control of the story, Samuel commits his fatal *bévue* and reveals the original stratagem. Despite discovering that he has been used by Madame de Cosmelly, he does not learn that the will of another can alter the plot and recast the characters: this time it is La Fanfarlo, who takes the revenge on him that he had expected Madame de Cosmelly to take on her husband. He suffers not because he was caught playing a role, but because he had once again forgotten the role, confused it with reality, and simply and candidly told the truth.

By contrast, in the preceding scene, Madame de Cosmelly demonstrates the importance of playing a role and controlling it carefully. In a clever and exaggerated display of virtue, devotion, and self-sacrifice, she lets her husband know that he has been deceived by his mistress, and drives him away in embarrassed annoyance. But the text suggests the wisdom of her action: "S'il alla chez la Fanfarlo, il y trouva sans doute des vestiges de désordre, des bouts de cigares et des feuilletons." Sending him into the arms of the dancer will restore him to her own by presenting the evidence of the affair with Samuel. Having blurred the distinction between art and life, Samuel can exercise no such control, nor achieve such successful results.

His *bévue,* rather, brings only vulgarisation: La Fanfarlo thickens, becomes a "beauté grasse, propre, lustrée et rusée," and gives birth to twins. Samuel's art too degenerates into procreation, the irony lying not only in his previously expressed repugnance for this, but also in the use of a verb normally reserved for beasts: "Samuel a mis bas quatre livres de science." But this is only the logical consequence of his literary method generally: the *commis voyageur* of the narrator's earlier comparison grows well into his role, peddling books of all types and subjects.

The *Auri sacra fames!* which he places as an epigraph to one of them both acknowledges and flouts his "accursed craving for gold." He continues to have the ironic self-consciousness of earlier and to lack the will to act upon it. If he has "tombé bien bas," he remains the poet of the *Orfraies,* the "dieu de l'impuissance" of the beginning, who adapts himself to everything, even harsh financial circumstances, and consequently succeeds at nothing.

However, the final irony, as Wing has noted, aims not at Samuel but at the reader:

> Pauvre chantre des *Orfraies!* [. . .] J'ai appris récemment qu'il fondait un journal socialiste et voulait se mettre à la politique.—Intelligence malhonnête!—comme dit cet honnête M. Nisard.

The narrator turns the tables on us, leading us to concur with the judgment of bad faith, only to identify us thereby with one whose honesty is ironically placed in doubt, as the *malhonnête/honnête* opposition implies. But the irony does not only reintroduce ambiguities about the hero, as Wing allows. Rather, it makes clear that Samuel's experience applies to readers of the story too. The final sentence unveils, with a flourish, the narrator's designs, into which we find we have unwittingly played. The text thus reminds us of Samuel's essential mistake: we must not be readers like him, confusing ourselves with the narrator, considering ourselves the author of the story, lest we find ourselves similarly caught out, our "honest" views shown to be those of a hypocrite. Irony works with ambiguity but need not be ambiguous, and here the point is clear: the truly honest reader remains distinct from all voices, like Diderot's *sot,* and is ultimately the wiser for it.

Baudelaire presented himself as a poet of the city, and in that capacity as an exemplar of what he called Modernity. We think of him as the inventor of a new kind of poem, in which the poet wanders through the streets of a great city and derives from many such experiences a new tone, indeed a new emotion.

—*Denis Donoghue, "The Poet of Modern Life," The New York Review of Books, February 14, 1991.*

Edward K. Kaplan (essay date 1990)

SOURCE: "Interpreting the Prose Poems: An Amalgam beyond Contradictions," in *Baudelaire's Prose Poems: The Esthetic, the Ethical, and the Religious in "The Parisian Prowler,"* The University of Georgia Press, 1990, pp. 1-18.

[*Kaplan is an American poet and critic. In the following excerpt, he finds that* Le spleen de Paris *addresses the conflict between "compassion and a fervent aestheticism." According to Kaplan, compassion entails community, while fervent aestheticism leads to isolation.*]

Baudelaire's 1855 experiments with lyrical prose quickly faded into the background as he developed autonomous subgenres—"fables of modern life," as I call them. The formalistic problem of the "prose poem" is far less valuable in interpreting them than a focus on their narrator, a Second Empire Parisian poet—a *flâneur,* or urban stroller—who struggles with his conflicting drives. It is remarkable that Baudelaire's early critical essays anticipate, by many years, his new prose genre and the revised second edition of *Les Fleurs du Mal* (1861) which they parallel. In fact, his overall development confirms his conversion from "poetic" idealism to a literature of daily experience.

Questions of form are of course essential and we need an appropriate interpretive model: "These texts include in perfect but minimal form the *Märchen* or wonder-tale, the *Sage* or anecdote, the fable, the allegory, the cautionary tale, the tale-telling contest, the short story, the dialogue, the novella, the narrated dream" (Marie Maclean, *Narrative as Performance: The Baudelairean Experiment,* 1988). Editors have accepted—inappropriately, in my view—Baudelaire's dedication "To Arsène Houssaye," which introduces the twenty-six prose poems serialized in 1862 for *La Presse,* as a preface to the completed collection. **"The Thyrsus"** (**"Le Thyrse,"** first published in 1863) is a more sophisticated model, one which surpasses the binary opposition of prose and poetry which has seduced interpreters. These two prominently analyzed texts grope toward a theory of genre but do not encompass the modern fable. **"The Stranger"** and **"The Old Woman's Despair"** (**"L'Etranger,"** **"Le Désespoir de la vieille"**), which open the collection, define *The Parisian Prowler*'s dynamics more precisely.

Baudelaire's early essays demonstrate the generative tension of his entire work: his personal struggle to maintain both compassion and a fervent estheticism. In 1851, his first reflections on imagination, "Du Vin et du hachisch" (On wine and hashish), warn firmly against intemperate reverie by distinguishing the "good" intoxication of wine, which makes one sociable, from the "bad" ecstasies of hashish, which alienate and enfeeble the dreamer. He concludes by quoting a "musical theoretician," Barbereau, a proxy of his implicit ethic: "I do not understand why rational and spiritual man uses artificial means to achieve poetic beatitude, since enthusiasm and free will suffice to raise him to a supernatural existence." Baudelaire's defense of the will remains uncompromised.

The following year, in "L'Ecole païenne" (The pagan school of poetry), Baudelaire locates the problem in literature. He censures the fastidious, polished poetry of "art for art's sake," notably that of Théodore de Banville. The final paragraphs denounce an obsession with esthetic idealism: "The excessive appetite for form induces monstrous and unknown disorders. Absorbed by the ferocious passion for the beautiful, the notions of the just and the true disappear. The feverish passion for art is an ulcer which devours what remains; and, as the clear absence of the just and the true in art amounts to the absence of art, the entire person vanishes; excessive specialization of one faculty produces nothingness."

The most radical solution is to destroy all art. He goes on to cite the famous incident in Augustine's *Confessions* when the neophyte Christian accompanies his friend Alypius to a brutal Roman circus; they refuse to watch, until the crowd's shouts rouse their curiosity. Baudelaire, as moralist, embraces the convert's asceticism: "I understand the fits of rage of iconoclasts and Moslems against images. I accept entirely Saint Augustine's remorse for his excessive pleasure of the eyes. The danger is so great that I forgive the abolition of the object. The madness of art is the equivalent of the abuse of mind." The shattering of a peddler's windowpanes, at the end of **"The Bad Glazier"** (**"Le Mauvais Vitrier"**), confronts us with a comparable idolatry.

Art—the voluntary creation of significant form—should not be confused with self-titillation. Contradicting his reputation as a dandy, Baudelaire admonishes the overly refined "mind" which denies ethics. A perverse "artist" may relish the idea of beauty and yet ignore its intrinsic rectitude:

> [The madness of art] engenders stupidity, hardness of heart and a boundless pride and self-centeredness. I remember having heard about a joker artist who had received a counterfeit coin: I will keep it for a poor man. The wretch took an infernal pleasure in robbing the poor and at the same time enjoying the benefits of a charitable reputation. I heard another one: Why don't the poor put on gloves to beg? They would make a fortune. And another: He is badly draped; his tatters do not become him.
>
> We should not consider those things as childishness. What the mouth gets used to saying, the heart gets used to believing.

In fact, anecdotes cited in this essay became, fourteen years later, full-fledged fables that demonstrate how an exaggerated *estheticism* can abolish elemental decency. The narrator of **"A Joker"** (**"Un Plaisant,"** first published in *La Presse,* 1862) clamors against a gloved dandy who violates the dignity of a beast; the stroller of **"Widows"** (**"Les Veuves,"** first published in the *Revue Fantaisiste,* 1861) analyzes "in the mourning clothes of the poor, an absence of harmony that makes them more heartbreaking"; and the narrator of **"The Counterfeit Coin"** (**"La Fausse Monnaie,"** first published in *L'Artiste,* 1864), speculates about his friend's false gift.

The critic's moral indignation, in 1852, contrasts sharply with the perceived obscenity of his poetic masterpiece, censored a scant fortnight after publication. Perhaps the author subverted his didacticism even more vehemently after *Les Fleurs du Mal* had been so utterly misunder-

stood, for the magistrates did not fathom the author's ethical irony: "One must depict vice as seductive, for it is seductive" ("Les Drames et les romans honnêtes"). By 1861, when he consolidated his practice of the modern fable, Baudelaire abandoned good conscience as his narrator responds to beggars and other outcasts with cruelty, outrage, or cynicism. His anger (an ironic disguise and often hard to interpret) appears to outweigh his compassion.

There is no deeper tension in Baudelaire's mature work than the conflict of ethics and esthetics, and he grapples with a temperament driven by a powerful animus: "To glorify the worship of images (my great, my only, my primitive passion)" (*Mon cœur mis à nu*). The poet feared that his enthrallment with formal grace would numb his humane concern. Despite his neurotic, self-destructive relationships, he cherished the possibility of ordinary love, while at the same time remaining driven by absolute values. A too "perfect idealization" (the phrase appears in **"A Heroic Death"** [**"Une Mort héroique"**]) might deaden the artist's sympathy with others.

Baudelaire's "second revolution" integrates ethics and art. The thirty-two new poems—and especially the "Tableaux parisiens" (Parisian pictures)—added to the 1861 edition of *Les Fleurs du Mal* undermine the first edition's idealist thrust and depict a conversion to the world as it exists. Briefly stated, the first edition storms the gates of a transcendent kingdom, while the second sanctifies the finite. The three sonnets that conclude the 1857 edition—"La Mort des amants," "La Mort des pauvres," and "La Mort des artistes" (The death of lovers, The death of paupers, The death of artists)—recapitulate the journey toward immortality. The expanded 1861 closure introduces a crucial irony; "La Fin de la journée," "Le Rêve d'un curieux," and "Le Voyage" (The day's end, A curious man's dream, The voyage) reject dreams of afterdeath survival.

The initial and longest section, "Spleen et Idéal" (Spleen and Ideal), defines this conversion. The "Beauty Cycle" (poems numbered 17-21) can be read as a single experience which revises the philosophy of the whole. The 1857 sequence consisted of three allegorical sonnets, "La Beauté," "L'Idéal," and "La Géante" (Beauty, The Ideal, The Giantess). The 1861 sequence is transformed by two major poems, "Le Masque" and "Hymne à la Beauté" (The mask, Hymn to Beauty), which denounce the idolatry enounced by the previous three. The artist becomes a self-aware critic who replaces the transcendent with temporality.

"La Beauté" barricades the frontier and promotes the idealist standard. The Idol herself exclaims: "Je suis belle, ô mortels! comme un rêve de pierre" (I am beautiful, O mortals! like a dream of stone). Beauty is a concept of which the artist can produce only a facsimile, "a *dream* of stone," while reenacting a tragic drama:

> Les poètes, devant mes grandes attitudes,
>
>   . . . . .
>
> Consumeront leurs jours en d'austères études

(Poets, confronting my grandiose poses, . . . will consume their days in austere studies).

Artists can justify their sacrifice, since imagination can transform our perception of daily existence. Refracting the Ideal, Beauty's eyes are "De purs miroirs qui font toutes choses plus belles" (Pure mirrors which make all things more beautiful). As **"The Bad Glazier"** insists with devastating irony, art should "make life [look] beautiful," *faire voir la vie en beau,* as it were, through rose-colored glass.

Then a momentous change occurs. "Le Masque," added in 1861, explodes the romantic heroism of "La Beauté," as the poet recovers reality. The poem interprets an exuberant and seductive sculpture by Ernest Christophe (to whom it is dedicated), which itself allegorizes the relationship between artifice and life. The female statue's body represents "the esthetic":

Vois quel charme excitant la gentillesse donne!
Approchons, et tournons autour de sa beauté

(See what stimulating magic her loveliness bestows!
Let's go closer, and walk around her beauty.)

As he deliberately anatomizes his own adoration, the "critic" discovers "the mask" and translates the allegory. The drama pivots on lines 17-19, which compose one brief, but all the more striking stanza:

O blasphème de l'art! ô surprise fatale!
La femme au corps divin, promettant le bonheur,
Par le haut se termine en monstre bicéphale!

(O blasphemy of art! O fateful surprise! The woman
of body divine, promising happiness, at the top becomes
a two-headed monster!)

The woman's superhuman body renders even more grotesque the contradictory heads that become exposed. These two faces represent truth and falsehood. They have denied nature and its temporality, not simply embellished it. The shocked esthete recognizes the inevitable triumph of the finite.

The final section (lines 20-36) elaborates his conversion in three stages. The poet will denounce—and seemingly reject—the "lying mask" that conceals the suffering mortal. First, the woman's *real* self stands unveiled:

La véritable tête et la sincère face
Renversée à l'abri de la face qui ment.

(the true head and the sincere face tipped back and
sheltered by the lying face)

He then identifies with her as a person, again repeating the word "beauty":

Pauvre grande beauté! Le magnifique fleuve
De tes pleurs aboutit dans mon coeur soucieux;

Ton mensonge m'enivre, et mon âme s'abreuve
Aux flots que la Douleur fait jaillir de tes yeux!

(Great pitiful beauty! The magnificent river of your
tears flows out into my anxious heart; your lie intoxicates
me, and my soul slakes its thirst in the waves
that Pain makes gush from your eyes!)

At the obvious thematic level—and it is of fundamental importance—the poet is roused by the woman's authentic grief. But a subtler problem arises when we try to interpret "Ton mensonge m'enivre." He is *enivré*—intoxicated or inspired—but by what? By her real inner struggle, by her pathetic attempt to mask her mortality? or by the *mensonge* itself, the "lie" of her exterior loveliness? Her "beauty" manifests her need to deny, or transcend, physical frailty. Does his imagination respond to her contradiction, her impotent denial which intensifies her suffering—in brief, from *compassion*? Or does his inspiration flow from a purely imaginative, and illusory, act of empathy—from *poetry*? This ambiguous *ivresse* will energize *The Parisian Prowler* from beginning to end.

"Le Masque" might have ended here, but a third movement, comprising two stanzas of dialogue, completes his consent to the real. Unmasking the person does not suffice; we must understand her, as he asks: "—Mais pourquoi pleure-t-elle?" (But why does she weep?). The answer asserts a simple truth, the banality of which signals the poet's sincerity:

—Elle pleure, insensé, parce qu'elle a vécu!
Et parce qu'elle vit!

(She weeps, mad one, because she has lived! and
because she lives!)

Without any irony of qualification, the poet-critic celebrates the pathos of temporality. Disillusioned, and through a dialectical awareness of artistic illusion itself, the esthete embraces his human solidarity. The woman behind the mask is his "hypocrite lecteur," and of course "son semblable, son frère." This mature, reflective woman remains free of the ambivalence typical of his representations of idealized or frivolous females.

The famous "Hymne à la Beauté" which follows—also added in 1861—answers the "Beauty" sonnet more directly. It dwells upon art's ethical consequences as it reiterates the question:

Viens-tu du ciel profond ou sors-tu de l'abîme,
O Beauté

(Do you come from the deep sky or do you emerge
from the abyss, O Beauty?)

The final two stanzas recapitulate the struggle. The penultimate one abandons the question of human justice and, provisionally, reaffirms the transcendent:

Que tu viennes du ciel ou de l'enfer, qu'importe,
O Beauté! monstre énorme, effrayant, ingénu!
Si ton oeil, ton souris, ton pied, m'ouvrent la porte
D'un Infini que j'aime et n'ai jamais connu?

(What does it matter whether you come from the
heavens or from hell, O Beauty! monster enormous,
frightening, innocent! if your eyes, your smile, your
feet, open for me the door of an Infinite I love and
have never known?)

This closure would typify the idealist 1857 edition, were
it not for the final stanza which weds the esthetic quest to
a moral imperative. Baudelaire's mature poetics subordinates the artist's anguished, unfulfilled desire to his solidarity with ordinary people:

De Satan ou de Dieu, qu'importe! Ange ou Sirène,
Qu'importe, si tu rends,—fée aux yeux de velours,
Rhythme, parfum, lueur, ô mon unique reine!—
L'univers moins hideux et les instants moins
    lourds?

(From Satan or from God, what does it matter! Angel
or Siren, what does it matter, if you—velvet-eyed fairy,
rhythm, perfume, light, O my only queen!—make the
universe less hideous and time less oppressive?)

This presymbolist poetry, enriched with synesthesia—a
confluence of music, odor, sight, and touch—preserves
the Ideal within the world and renders mortality bearable.
A nuanced ethics must surpass the simplistic dualism of
good and evil, for these opposites are normally mixed,
sometimes confused. The "modern" artist still strives to
redeem humanity, but his goal is modest, almost practical. Realistically speaking, Beauty can only alleviate anxiety or ennui—not cure it—as it sanctifies the possible.

Baudelaire's poems are far more subtle than his aphorisms, which retain the all-too-familiar dualistic formulas:
"There are, in every person, all the time, two simultaneous postulations, one toward God, the other toward
Satan." His concepts strained toward the notion of *simultaneity* without reaching it. His terminology, despite its
affinity with Joseph de Maistre's theology of violence,
remains more emotive than logical. Wrestling with his
experience in a necessarily imprecise vocabulary, in life
as in writing, Baudelaire attempted, again and again, to
mend these rifts, to become one: "Even as a child, I felt
in my heart two contradictory feelings, the horror of life
and the ecstasy of life." His Platonic, Catholic, and romantic polarities were unequal to the task.

Baudelaire's 1862 dedication "To Arsène Houssaye," artistic editor of *La Presse,* which is normally reprinted as
a guide to the subsequent collection, appears to refute my
interpretive principle of unity. But the author did not
include that deceptive proclamation in his handwritten
table of contents, and a close analysis reveals the dedication itself to be a disguised parody of the genre: its message can be easily understood as a canny, ironic challenge addressed to a colleague whom he did not respect

but needed to please. Subversive self-contradictions
emerge from the very beginning:

My dear friend, I send you this little work of which it
cannot be said, without injustice, that it has neither
head nor tail, since, on the contrary, everything in it is
both tail and head, alternatively and reciprocally. Consider, I beg you, what admirable convenience that
combination offers us all, you, me, and the reader. We
can cut wherever we want, I my reverie, you the
manuscript, the reader his reading; for I do not bind
the latter's recalcitrant will to the endless thread of a
superfluous plot.

Baudelaire highlights the incompleteness of this inaugu-
ral series. How, at that point, could he predict their definitive conception? This "petit ouvrage . . . n'a ni queue ni
tête, puisque tout, au contraire, y est à la fois tête et
queue." The chiasmus *queue/tête / tête/queue* connotes
totality while the image itself opposes fragmentation to
unity and suggests that each piece can be appreciated
separately. Since each one is both tail and head, we must
accept the collection as coherent. There is no "intrigue
superflue," but there may be separate plots, or a unifying
one. Whatever the case, readers should interpret them
flexibly.

The imagery of segmentation derives from a traditional
organic metaphor: the serpent. The author's jovial permission to "cut" cannot be completely in earnest: "Remove one vertebra, and the two pieces of that tortuous
fantasy will reunite without difficulty. Chop it up into
many fragments, and you will find that each one can exist
separately. In the hope that some of those segments will
be lively enough to please and to divert you, I dare dedicate to you the entire serpent." What author would encourage his editor to mutilate, or even surgically to excise
portions of his manuscript? This was in fact the author's
frustrating battle with Houssaye. Baudelaire waggishly
elaborates conflicting metaphors, for his guiding idea is
not one of disorder and irreconcilable separation but that
of relative autonomy. Sparring with an authority he knew
to be literal-minded, Baudelaire rejects a *"superfluous* plot"
while maintaining the possibility of a sustained development (the hierarchical entity of head and tail).

An astute reader (unlike Houssaye) could restore these
parts, if severed, to their rightful place within a larger,
though serpentine, construction. In the last analysis, however, this discussion is trite. Just as single poems in a
collection—such as Scève's *Délie,* Ronsard's *Les Amours,*
Hugo's *Les Contemplations,* and *Les Fleurs du Mal*—can
be read individually or as stages of a spiritual itinerary, so
The Parisian Prowler can mark a journey of initiation or
comprise discrete experiences which readers might synthesize or not according to their concerns.

The remaining four paragraphs stress, with a playful irony, the author's originality. Baudelaire's rhetorical modesty, unanswered questions, self-deprecatory comparisons,
and italics all express his pride. First he "confesses" that
his project was inspired by a model: "the famous *Gas-*

pard de la nuit of Aloysius Bertrand (a book known to you, to me and to some of our friends, does it not have every right to be called *famous*?)." He overpraises Bertrand's commercially unsuccessful book, while the italicized *"fameux"* (which also implies "infamous") implicitly carves out the differences. Bertrand claimed to be inspired by engravings by Callot and Rembrandt, whereas Baudelaire evokes "modern life, or rather *one* modern and abstract life" in Second Empire Paris. The systematically self-aware critic exercises a far bolder ambition.

Formalistic notions of genre have only recently confirmed Baudelaire's true innovation. His oft-cited definition of "poetic prose" plays only a minor role in the dedication and simply adapts conventional views of romantic lyricism: "Which of us has not, in his ambitious days, dreamed of the miracle of a poetic prose, musical without rhythm and without rhyme, supple enough and choppy enough to fit the soul's lyrical movements, the undulations of reverie, the jolts of consciousness?" It is not this "miracle of a poetic prose" that constitutes an "absolute beginning." Could not Rousseau, Chateaubriand, and Michelet, for example, better serve as models? More significantly, Baudelaire transported the lyrical narrative from nature to the city: "This obsessive ideal [of the prose poem] came to life above all in frequenting enormous cities, in the intersection of their countless relationships." The urban poet is both exemplar and theoretician of the modern self.

The two final paragraphs (surreptitiously) take aim at the main target, Houssaye himself. Baudelaire contrasts his malicious fable **"The Bad Glazier"** with his editor's crudely didactic anecdote, **"The Glazier's Song"** (**"La Chanson du vitrier"**), which illustrates a "democratic" reconciliation of a poor man and a poet. Baudelaire pretends to admire Houssaye's effort to compose verbal music, a "poetic" idealization, from the humble artisan's "strident cry," its "prosaic" reality. He does not state that Houssaye's text only reproduces sentimental commonplaces and democratic propaganda. Nor would his postutopian prowler ever replace poetry with *une chanson,* popular ditties. Read in Erasmian tradition as "paradoxical praise," Baudelaire's compliments translate into a mockery of mediocre writing unredeemed by its lofty intentions.

Baudelaire repudiates both didacticism and imitation, obliquely asserting his pride at *not* "executing *exactly* [his italics] what he planned to do." He had deliberately "remained quite far from his mysterious and brilliant model," Bertrand's *Gaspard de la nuit.* The final line of "Le Voyage" (The voyage), the final poem of the 1861 *Fleurs du Mal,* dramatizes his commitment to innovation above all: "Au fond de l'inconnu pour trouver du *nouveau!*" (Into the depths of the Unknown to find the *new*!). Quite earlier, in "Exposition universelle" (1855), Baudelaire had associated himself with Delacroix's "quality *sui generis,* indefinable and defining this century's melancholy and fervent aspect, something completely new, which makes him a unique artist, wihout progenitor, without precedent, probably without a successor." Without knowing it, Baudelaire had announced his modern fables.

"The Thyrsus" states a theory of the Baudelairean "prose poem" more appropriately than his "dedication" to Houssaye. Commentators have differed on their interpretation of this "theoretical fable," which reflects on its own status as literature. The text begins as a meditation on a caduseus (a wand or baton) entwined with flowers, which then generates an extended metaphor of multiple polarities: "What is a thyrsus? According to its social and poetic meaning, it is a sacerdotal emblem to be held by priests and priestesses celebrating the divinity whose interpreters and servants they are. But physically it is only a staff, a mere staff, a vine pole for hops, a vine support, dry, hard, and straight" [Robert Kopp, in his editor of *Petits poèmes en prose*]. These ideas are not extraordinary, for any work can both mimetically represent experience and translate the story into a message, "le sens moral et poétique." But Baudelaire stresses the *combination* of "prosaic" and "poetic" elements, the interweaving of shapes, colors, and scents, which exercises a mysterious seduction—like "a mystical fandango executed around the hieratic staff."

Baudelaire further tangles the web of dualistic categories as he formulates a confluence of opposites. Interpreters should preserve the genre's integrity by applying the chemist's notion of "amalgam." Baudelaire's dedication of this piece to Franz Liszt, whom he truly admired, announces his most advanced conception:

> The thyrsus is the representation of your astonishing duality, powerful and venerable master, dear Bacchant of mysterious and impassioned Beauty. . . .

> The staff, it is your will, straight, firm, and unshakable; the flowers, the rambling of your fancy around your will; the feminine element executing around the male its prodigious pirouettes. Straight line and arabesque line, intention and expression, tautness of the will, sinuosity of the word, unity of goal, variety of means, all-powerful and indivisible amalgam of genius, what analyst would have the hateful courage to divide and to separate you?

The rhetorical question leaves in suspense the possibility—or advisability—of destroying his prose poems' organic unity. A critic must possess a "détestable courage" in order to disintegrate their "amalgame tout-puissant de génie" and abstract its bisexual vitality. Form is not separable from content nor can concepts replace their concrete (or allegorical) representations. Interpreters must respect the opposing elements without immobilizing their productive tensions.

Binary oppositions can distract us from the strict, condensed structure of the whole which prepares a "total effect." Baudelaire's "amalgam theory" justifies our label "fables of modern life," a plausible model of which appears in his 1857 "New Notes on Edgar Poe". The jolts and shocks which had so impressed Walter Benjamin fit into a rigorous plan: "If the first sentence is not written in order to prepare that final impression, the work fails from the very beginning" [*Oeuvres complètes*]. The narrator gains in his ability to wear many masks: "the author of a short story has a multitude of tones at his disposal, nuances of language, a reasonable tone, sarcasm, humor, repudiated by poetry, and which are like dissonances, attacks against the idea of pure beauty" [*Oeuvres complètes*]. Both Baudelaire and Poe capture the complex dynamics of consciousness.

The Parisian Prowler in fact opens, not with lyrical excursions, but with two brief, prosaic fables—**"The Stranger"** and **"The Old Woman's Despair"** ("L'Etranger," "Le Désespoir de la vieille")—which form a "diptych." It is highly significant that the definitive collection of fifty retains, with their original numbering, the four series of prose poems printed in 1862 for *La Presse*. Their central characters—two outsiders, a man and a woman—establish the conflict between fantasy and reality which will consistently direct the narrator's adventures. Both seek to alleviate their anguish, the one through daydreaming, the other through affectionate gestures. The "enigmatic man" of the first and the "good decrepit woman" of the second speak through the *flâneur* who begins *his* journey through them.

The stranger who lends the first fable its name is a sort of nineteenth-century Meursault, Camus's model of alienation. The narrator asks him basic questions, as might a psychotherapist who probes a patient's life history. The odyssey opens by defining a normal person's sources of being:

> "Tell me, whom do you love the most, you enigmatic man? your father, your mother, your sister, or your brother?"

> "I have neither father, nor mother, nor sister, nor brother."

> "Your friends?"

> "There you use a word whose meaning until now has remained to me unknown."

> "Your fatherland?"

> "I am unaware in what latitude it lies."

> "Beauty?"

> "I would willingly love her, goddess and immortal."

> "Gold?"

> "I hate it as you hate God."

> "So! Then what do you love, you extraordinary stranger?"

> "I love clouds . . . drifting clouds . . . there . . . over there . . . marvelous clouds!"

The interviewer wants to discuss love, but the stranger refuses to concede any common ground to him. He ad-

dresses him with the familiar *tu* while the other, denying any middle-class values, will not reciprocate. The stranger is indeed estranged from God, family, and country—the conventional treasures of bourgeois society. They do not really speak, just swap words.

The stranger mirrors the narrator who, in future guises, longs to participate in a community as a citizen or as an artist. He is the prototypical victim of ennui, a pathological deadening of emotion and will, the "delicate monster" leading us to despair, which threatens the narrator from beginning to end. The stranger appears as an orphan who has renounced his yearning for companionship and repressed all memories, traces of the past with which he might construct a solid identity, while his apathy anesthetizes the pain of unsatisfied yearnings. This unknowable person dreams, not to foster desire, but crudely to evade reality. As he "spaces out," constantly mobile reveries waft him away from others—and from himself.

But the stranger's bleak refusals cannot bury his attachment to love. Other things being equal, he *would* pursue Beauty: "Je l'aimerais volontiers, déesse et immortelle." His use of the conditional tense does not deny a commitment to esthetic perfection. Then why does he separate this spiritual search from community values? Understandably, he repudiates the tainted (and elusive!) security of money as he equates cupidity with official religion, echoing the prophetic warning against identifying God and Mammon. His uncompromising standard of truth and beauty renders all prevailing institutions untenable.

How do we understand the stranger's final response, launching his mind into the emptiness of suspension points . . . ? The narrator had first perceived him as "enigmatic"; he now becomes "extraordinary"—the epithet shifting from bafflement to (an ironic?) admiration. At the end, the stranger's self becomes, in Baudelaire's terms, "vaporized"; as Kierkegaard explains: "So when feeling becomes fantastic, the self is simply volatilized more and more, at last becoming a sort of abstract sentimentality which is so inhuman that it does not apply to any person" (*The Sickness Unto Death*). Reverie relishes its narcissistic plunge into the mind's inner spaces. Nevertheless, the *esthetic stranger* (for that is what he represents) has only temporarily eluded the Other, who summons love's absence. He still dwells with ennui.

The female outsider of **"The Old Woman's Despair,"** quite the contrary, attempts to make tender contact; she is the collection's *ethical stranger*. She too is thwarted—not by her own, voluntary aloofness but by her body. Contradicting the fierce misogyny of later fables, the narrator displays his sympathy for this female victim of time, another little old lady of "Tableaux parisiens." Sweet and lonely, she seeks reciprocal affection and symmetrically contradicts the male outsider's disclaimer, in the first fable, of companionship.

The shriveled little old woman felt quite delighted when she saw the pretty baby whom everyone was entertaining, and whom everyone was trying to please; a pretty creature, as fragile as she, the little old woman, and, like her as well, toothless and without hair.

And she went up to him, trying to make little smiles and pleasant faces at him.

But the terrified child struggled under the kind decrepit woman's caresses, and filled the house with his yelpings.

Then the kind old woman withdrew into her eternal solitude, and she wept alone in a corner, saying to herself, "Ah, for us, unfortunate old females that we are, the age of pleasing has passed, even innocent creatures; and we disgust little children we try to love!"

The kinship of these vulnerable persons, aged and infant, at the beginning and the decline of life, is ironic, and the narrator repeatedly associates her tenderness with her age. She is "la petite vieille ratatinée," "la petite vieille," "la bonne femme décrépite," and "la bonne vieille." Baby and hag are both toothless and bald, but what is attractive in one renders the other repulsive. Beauty is relative, and the "innocent" baby has not yet learned that he has no reason to fear the old woman's smiles.

The narrator states his compassion for her "solitude éternelle"; the adjective labels her estrangement as absolute, essential to her being. And so she views herself as a puppet of biological destiny, one of a multitude of pariahs: "malheureuses vieilles femelles." Aged women, discarded by the young who perceive only exterior and transient loveliness, enter a subhuman category. Woman's superficial "gift of pleasing" is all too fragile.

This tension between ethical pathos versus a compelling passion for ideal Beauty energizes the entire collection: conflicts between fantasy and reality, mental versus social space, innocence versus evil. The rigorously dialectical organization of **"The Old Woman's Despair"** anticipates many other pieces, and its "pivotal sentence" [Robert Kopp, in his edition of *Petits poèmes en prose*]—"But the terrified child . . ."—is the first of several brutal proxies for "the world," which will burst into a dream. Usually the narrator hides his compassion under rude poses. The male "stranger" might represent a positive model of the dandy—were it not for the journalist-narrator's deliberate probing of his intimate aspirations. This diptych, which draws the lines of battle, defines the two strands of "esthetic" and "ethical" fables interwoven throughout *The Parisian Prowler*.

FURTHER READING

Criticism

Aynesworth, Donald. "Humanity and Monstrosity in *Le spleen de Paris*: A Reading of 'Mademoiselle Bistouri.'" *Romanic Review* LXXIII, No. 2 (March 1982): 209-21.

    Contends that the fragmentation, linguistic ambiguity, and eclecticism of *Petits poèmes en prose,* as evidenced in "Mademoiselle Bistouri," reflect the nature of life in the city.

Boyd, Greg. Introduction to *La Fanfarlo,* edited by Kendall E. Lappin, pp. 7-22. Berkeley, Calif.: Creative Arts Book Company, 1986.

    Examines the autobiographical elements, literary influences, and aesthetic principles reflected in *La Fanfarlo.*

Carter, A. E. "Other Prose Works" and "*Le spleen de Paris*." In his *Charles Baudelaire,* pp. 44-6, pp. 109-14. Boston: Twayne Publishers, 1977.

    Brief examinations of *La Fanfarlo* and *Petits poèmes en prose.*

Chesters, Graham. "The Transformation of a Prose-Poem: Baudelaire's 'Crépuscule du soir.'" In *Baudelaire, Mallarmé, Valéry: New Essays in Honour of Lloyd Austin,* edited by Malcolm Bowie, Alison Fairlie, and Alison Finch, pp. 24-37. Cambridge: Cambridge University Press, 1982.

    Demonstrates that Baudelaire's revision of an earlier version of "Le crépuscule du soir" indicates that he consciously employed a highly experimental artistic approach when composing it.

Cohn, Robert Greer. "Baudelaire's Beleaguered Prose Poems." In *Textual Analysis: Some Readers Reading,* edited by Mary Ann Caws, pp. 112-20. New York: The Modern Language Association of America, 1986.

    Epistemological critique of recent critical commentary on *Petits poèmes en prose.* Cohn maintains that informed, well-rounded, and impartial study of *Petits poèmes en prose* proves that many deconstructionist analyses of the prose poems are invalid.

De George, Fernande M. "The Structure of Baudelaire's *Petits poèmes en prose.*" *L'esprit créateur* XIII, No. 2 (Summer 1973): 144-53.

    Contests the view of *Petits poèmes en prose* as a haphazardly assembled group of prose pieces, asserting (with the aid of a schematic graph) that the collection evinces progression and symmetry.

Friedman, Geraldine. "Baudelaire's Theory of Practice: Ideology and Difference in 'Les yeux des pauvres.'" *PMLA* 104, No. 3 (May 1989): 317-28.

    Explores the ideological implications of the disparity between the language used and the events related in "Les yeux des pauvres."

George, Albert J. "Baudelaire." In his *Short Fiction in France, 1800-1850,* pp. 205-08. Syracuse, N.Y.: Syracuse University Press, 1964.

    Argues that *La Fanfarlo* represents the last short fiction written before the emergence of the modern short story in France.

Hackett, C. A. "Baudelaire and Samuel Cramer." *Australian Journal of French Studies* VI, Nos. 2-3 (1969): 317-25.

Studies Samuel Cramer—the protagonist of *La Fanfarlo*—and Baudelaire's relationship to his fictional character.

Hamburger, Michael. Introduction to *Twenty Prose Poems of Baudelaire,* translated by Michael Hamburger, pp. vii-xii. London: Editions Poetry London, 1946.

Asserts that the prose poem genre suited Baudelaire as a moralist and as a sensualist/artist.

Heck, Francis S. "Baudelaire's *La Fanfarlo*: An Example of Romantic Irony." *The French Review* XLIX, No. 3 (February 1976): 328-36.

States that the irony pervading *La Fanfarlo* imbues the story with "a certain originality denied it by its Balzacian plot."

Hiddleston, J. A. "'Chacun son *Spleen*': Some Observations on Baudelaire's Prose Poems." *The Modern Language Review* 86, No. 1 (January 1991): 66-9.

Discusses the ordering and publication of the prose poems.

Howells, Bernard. "Baudelaire: Portrait of the Artist in 1846." *French Studies* 37, No. 4 (October 1983): 426-39.

Examines Baudelaire's aesthetic theory as manifested in *La Fanfarlo* and contemporaneous writings by him.

Johnson, Barbara. "Poetry and Its Double: Two 'Invitations au voyage.'" In her *The Critical Difference: Essays in the Contemporary Rhetoric of Reading,* pp. 23-51. Baltimore: The Johns Hopkins University Press, 1980.

Compares Baudelaire's two versions of "Invitation au voyage"—the verse poem and the prose poem—in order to assess the merit of each as a poetic text.

Kaplan, Edward K. "Baudelaire's Portrait of the Poet as Widow." *Symposium* XXXIV, No. 3 (Fall 1980): 233-48.

Contends that the prose poems "Les foules," "Les veuves," and "Le vieux saltimbanque" and the verse poem "Le cygne" reveal Baudelaire's mature conception of the artist: an individual for whom loss, suffering, and sorrow are the source of creativity.

————. "Baudelaire's Neglected Masterpiece." In *The Parisian Prowler (Le spleen de Paris / Petits poèmes en prose),* translated by Edward K. Kaplan, pp. vii-xi. Athens: The University of Georgia Press, 1989.

Brief introduction to Baudelaire's prose poems.

Klein, Richard. "'Bénédiction'/'Perte d'auréole': Parables of Interpretation." *Modern Language Notes* 85 (1970): 515-28.

Maintains that Baudelaire's contrasting uses of symbolism in the verse poem "Bénédiction" and the prose poem "Perte d'auréole" hold the meanings of the two texts.

Mehlman, Jeffrey. "Baudelaire with Freud: Theory and Pain." *Diacritics* IV, No. 1 (Spring 1974): 7-13.

Postmodernist study applying the psychoanalytic theories of Sigmund Freud to Baudelaire's *Petits poèmes en prose.*

Raitt, A. W. "On *Le spleen de Paris.*" *Nineteenth-Century French Studies* 18, Nos. 1-2 (Fall-Winter 1989-90): 150-64.

Speculates on the evolution of *Petits poèmes en prose,* extrapolating from Baudelaire's lists of projected prose poems as well as the list of the prose poems that comprised *Petits poèmes en prose* in his 1869 *Collected Works.*

Scarfe, Francis. Introduction to *Baudelaire: 'The Poems in Prose,'* with '*La Fanfarlo,*' Volume II, edited and translated by Francis Scarfe, pp. 11-21. London: Anvil Press Poetry, 1989.

Discusses historical and biographical circumstances surrounding the composition and publication of *Petits poèmes en prose* and *La Fanfarlo.*

Schofer, Peter. "You Cannot Kill a Cloud: Code and Context in 'L'etranger.'" In *Modernity & Revolution in Late 19th Century France,* edited by Barbara T. Cooper and Mary Donaldson-Evans, pp. 99-107. Newark: University of Delaware Press, 1992.

Provides a comparative study of the prose poems "L'etranger" and "La soupe et les nuages" using theories of the critic Mikhail Bakhtin. Schofer asserts that interpretation of Baudelaire's prose poems varies depending on the context established by the sequence in which they are read.

Scott, David H. T. "*Le spleen de Paris.*" In *Baudelaire: 'La Fanfarlo' and 'Le spleen de Paris'* by Barbara Wright and David H. T. Scott, pp. 37-92. London: Grant & Cutler, 1984.

Overview of Baudelaire's prose poems.

Shattuck, Roger. "Vibratory Organism: Baudelaire's First Prose Poem." In his *The Innocent Eye: On Modern Literature & the Arts,* pp. 135-48. New York: Farrar, Straus, Giroux, 1984.

Asserts that Baudelaire's earliest prose poem is part of his *Salon de 1856.* According to Shattuck the text—which comprises two paragraphs at the beginning of the third chapter, "On Color"—is "quintessential Baudelaire": "The vocabulary and subtly circular style of the passage carry us to the edge of vertigo."

Swain, Virginia E. "The Legitimation Crisis: Event and Meaning in Baudelaire's 'Le vieux saltimbanque' and 'Une mort héroïque.'" *Romantic Review* LXXIII, No. 4 (November 1982): 452-62.

Examines "Le vieux saltimbanque" and "Une mort héroïque" as commentaries on the interpretation of literature and human experience.

Wing, Nathaniel. "The Poetics of Irony in Baudelaire's *La Fanfarlo,*" *Neophilologus* LIX, No. 2 (April 1975): 165-89.

Finds that irony, in various forms, plays a crucial role in "the examination of the artist and the nature of artistic creation" in *La Fanfarlo.*

————. "On Certain Relations: Figures of Sexuality in Baudelaire." In his *The Limits of Narrative: Essays on Baudelaire, Flaubert, Rimbaud, and Mallarmé,* pp. 19-40. Cambridge: Cambridge University Press, 1986.

Deconstructionist study of Baudelaire's prose poems.

Wohlfarth, Irving. "'Perte d'auréole': The Emergence of the Dandy." *MLN* 85, No. 4 (May 1970): 529-71.
  Interprets "Perte d'auréole" as a metaphor equating the Romantic poet with the dandy, "a figurative, self-styled aristocrat who, for lack of public recognition, has, paradoxically, to confer acknowledgement on himself."

Additional coverage of Baudelaire's life and career is contained in the following sources published by Gale Research: *DISCovering Authors*; *Nineteenth-Century Literature Criticism,* **Vols. 6, 29;** *Poetry Criticism,* **Vol. 1; and** *World Literature Criticism.*

Mikhail Bulgakov
1891-1940

(Born Mikhail Afanasevich Bulgakov. Wrote under the pseudonyms Emma B., F. S-ov, Em. Be., Ivan Bezdomny, M. Ol-Rait, and Neznakomets) Russian novelist, novella and short story writer, dramatist, biographer, and essayist.

INTRODUCTION

Considered one of the foremost satirists of post-revolutionary Russia, Bulgakov is best known for his novel *Master i Margarita* (*The Master and Margarita*), which is recognized as one of the greatest Russian novels of the century. His short stories and fictional sketches, like his other works, often present the adjustment of the Russian intellectual class to life under communist rule. Heavily influenced by Nikolai Gogol, Bulgakov combined fantasy, realism, and satire to ridicule modern progressive society in general and the Soviet system in particular.

Biographical Information

Bulgakov was born in 1891 into a Russian family of the intellectual class in the Ukrainian city of Kiev. Music, literature, and theater were important in the family life of the young Bulgakov, as was religion. His father, a professor at the Kiev theological academy, instilled in his son a belief in God and an interest in spiritual matters that he would retain throughout his life. Bulgakov attended Kiev's most prestigious secondary school, where he earned a reputation for playing practical jokes and inventing stories. He continued his education as a medical student at the University of Kiev and graduated with distinction in 1916. Assigned to noncombat duty in the Russian army during World War I, Bulgakov worked for several months in frontline military hospitals until he transferred to a remote village, where he served as the only doctor for an entire district; his experiences in this position served as the basis for the stories of *Zapiski iunogo vracha* (*Notes of a Young Doctor*).

Bulgakov was discharged in 1918 and abandoned medicine two years later to devote his time to writing pieces for newspapers and magazines. In 1921 he moved to Moscow, where he struggled to support himself and his first wife by editing and writing for various newspapers, but gradually became established as an author. From 1925 to 1928 Bulgakov worked in close association with the Moscow Art Theater as a writer, producer, and occasionally as an actor. His plays were all well received by audiences but denounced by Communist Party critics, and in 1929 his works were banned for their ideological nonconformity. At Bulgakov's request, Soviet leader Joseph Stalin intervened to enable some of his works to be pub-

lished and performed. Bulgakov resigned form the Art Theater in 1936, at which time he became a librettist for the Bolshoi Theater. Though publishing little, he wrote steadily until his death from nephrosclerosis in 1940.

Major Works of Short Fiction

Bulgakov's first published collection of short stories, *D'iavoliada* (*Diaboliad, and Other Stories*), was strongly influenced by Gogol: realism dissolves into fantasy and absurdity, and light comic satire erupts into sudden brutality. Included is his best-known story, "Rokovye iaitsa" ("The Fatal Eggs"), in which a well-meaning scientist discovers a red ray that stimulates growth. The ray is appropriated by a bureaucrat to increase the country's chicken population, but through a mix-up produces instead a crop of giant reptiles that ravage the countryside. "The Fatal Eggs" introduces one of Bulgakov's favorite themes: the consequences of power in the hands of the ignorant. Although written during the same period as *Diaboliad*, Bulgakov's *Notes of a Young Doctor* differs radically in its strict realism and exclusion of the fantastic and grotesque. This collection of autobiographical fiction records his trials as an inexperienced doctor working under primitive conditions, and the difficulties he faced as an educated man among the ignorant, superstitious peasants. Another literary achievement, *Sobach'e serdtse (The Heart of a Dog)*, portrays a scientist's transformation of a dog into a man. The creature develops reprehensible human qualities, and the scientist changes him back into the good-natured dog he once was.

Critical Reception

Most of Bulgakov's short fiction was written early in his career, in the middle of the 1920s. Due to official censorship of his manuscript during his lifetime, Bulgakov's greatest works remained unpublished until after his death. *The Heart of a Dog*, which is ranked among Soviet Russia's best satirical fiction, has never been published in the Soviet Union because of its counterrevolutionary cast. This story has obvious thematic parallels to "The Fatal Eggs" and the two works have elicited similar critical readings. Some critics consider *The Heart of a Dog* a blatant political satire, equating the operation with the Revolution, while others stress a moral and philosophical interpretation of the conflict between the intellectual scientist and the uneducated masses, and of the disastrous results of interfering with a natural process. Commentators have read "The Fatal Eggs" as a satirical treatment of the Russian Revolution, or, less specifically, as a commentary on progress and a rejection of revolution in favor of evolution. Reviewers generally praise the stories of *Notes of a Young Doctor*, especially those evincing attention to dramatic tension, but speculate as to whether the collection might more correctly be considered autobiography than fiction.

PRINCIPAL WORKS

*Short Fiction

D'iavoliada [*Diaboliad, and Other Stories*] 1925
†*Zapiski iunogo vracha* [*Notes of a Young Doctor*; also translated as *A Country Doctor's Notebooks*] 1963
‡*Sobach'e serdtse* [*The Heart of a Dog*] 1969
Sobranie sochinenii (short stories, novels, and dramas) 1982–
Notes on the Cuff, and Other Stories 1991

Other Major Works

Dni Turbinykh [*Days of the Turbins*] (drama) 1926
Zoikina kvartira [*Zoya's Apartment*] (drama) 1926
Belaia gvardiia: Dni Turbinykh [*The White Guard*] (novel) 1927
Bagrovyi ostrov [*The Crimson Island*] (drama) 1928
Kabala sviatosh [*A Cabal of Hypocrites*] (drama) 1936
Posledniye dni (drama) 1943
Beg [*Flight*] (drama) 1957
Zhizn' gospodina de Mol'era [*The Life of Monsieur de Molière*] (biography) 1962

Ivan Vasil'evich (drama) 1964
Tetral'nyi roman [*Black Snow: A Theatrical Novel*] 1965
Blazhenstvo [*Bliss*] (drama) 1966
Master i Margarita [*The Master and Margarita*] (novel) 1966-67
The Early Plays of Mikhail Bulgakov (dramas) 1972

*Many of Bulgakov's short stories and sketches appeared in Russian periodicals and other foreign journals but have not been published in collections.

†Comprised of stories published in Russian periodicals between 1925 and 1927.

‡Written in 1925; translated and published in English in 1968—prior to publication in Russian.

CRITICISM

Helen Muchnic (essay date 1968)

SOURCE: "Laughter in the Dark," in *The New York Review of Books,* Vol. XI, No. 1, July 11, 1968, pp. 26-8.

[*Muchnic is a Russian-born American critic and author. In the following review, she offers a positive assessment of* The Heart of a Dog, *considering it not only a parable about the Russian revolution but also a denunciation of the concepts underlying the revolution.*]

The Heart of a Dog is a variation on [one] of Bulgakov's recurrent themes. In one of his best known, and most uncanny, tales, **"The Fatal Eggs,"** a scientist's discovery of and experiment with a life-giving ray results in the hatching of monstrous reptiles that multiply in uncontrollable profusion and lay waste the land. In ***The Heart of a Dog,*** a renowned surgeon, Professor Preobrazhensky (the name suggests "transfiguration"), who specializes in rejuvenating men and women, tries something new. He operates on a stray dog, replacing its testicles by human testes and its pituitary gland by a human one; and the result, a scientific triumph, is a moral and social disaster: out of a pathetic, lovable mutt there emerges an insolent monstrosity that walks like a man and behaves like a cur. Its language is obscene and its manners intolerable. It demands its rights as a citizen, changes its pet dog's name, Sharik, to the human Sharikov, and gets itself a job with the Moscow City Sanitation Department, which entrusts it with the congenial task of eliminating vagrant cats. It steals, attempts rape, slanders and denounces the Professor himself, and tries to shoot his assistant. At the end, the Professor, recognizing his experiment as a lamentable blunder, turns this "man with the heart of a dog" back to its original state.

[In his preface to ***The Heart of a Dog,*** Michael Glenny] suggests that the story is a parable of the Bolshevik revolution, that "the 'dog' of the story is the Russian people, brutalized and exploited for centuries," the surgeon "the embodiment of the Communist Party—perhaps Lenin himself—and the drastic transplant operation . . . the revolution itself." To my mind, this is only partially true. The parallels cannot be so explicitly drawn. After all, the dog grew up in the Soviet State and was maltreated by Soviet citizens; and if the surgeon returns his homunculus to his original form, does this mean that Lenin wilfully returns the Russian people to their brutalized and exploited pre-revolutionary condition? But the story is indeed a cautionary fable on the menace of crude, illiterate, and unprincipled creatures suddenly exposed to learning and given status and a modicum of power. Sharikov is a kind of Caliban or a grotesque incarnation of Dostoevsky's Smerdyakov. "What have you been reading?" Professor Preobrazhensky asks him, expecting to hear something like *Robinson Crusoe,* and getting instead:

> "That guy . . . What's his name . . . Engel's correspondence with . . . hell, what d'you call him . . . oh—Kautsky."

And what is his opinion of the book?

> "I don't agree."

> "With whom—Engels or Kautsky?"

> "With neither of 'em."

> "That is most remarkable . . . Well what would you suggest instead?"

> "Suggest? I dunno . . . They just write and write all that crap . . . all about some congress and some Germans. . . . Makes my head reel. Take everything away from the bosses, then divide it up . . . "

To Sharikov, it is all perfectly simple: one takes from the haves, like the Professor, and gives to the have-nots, like Sharikov. Preobrazhensky loses his patience. "You belong to the lowest possible stage of development," he thunders, "You are still in the formative stage. You are intellectually weak. All your actions are purely bestial. Yet you allow yourself in the presence of two university-educated men to offer advice, with quite intolerable familiarity, on a cosmic scale and of quite cosmic stupidity, on the redistribution of wealth. . . . "

In such passages as these the social and political implications of Bulgakov's parable are obvious. Yet it seems to me that his meaning lies beyond them. Just as *Black Snow,* through satire on the Moscow Art Theatre, is actually concerned with the broader theme of the artist's plight, so *The Heart of a Dog,* through allusive comments on the revolution, is really denouncing the basic concepts that underly the revolution. The meaning is implicit in what Preobrazhensky says to his assistant: "This, Doctor, is what happens when a researcher, instead of keeping in step with nature, tries to force the pace and lift the veil." The human glands Preobrazhensky had used happened to be a drunkard's and thief's. Perhaps Sharikov would have turned out better had they come from a worthier man. But, Preobrazhensky asks, what if they had been Spino-

za's? Why perform such an operation at all? "What in heaven's name for? That's the point. Will you kindly tell me why one has to manufacture artificial Spinozas when some peasant woman may produce a real one any day of the week?" This is what Bulgakov is writing about: the ominous error, of which the revolution may be an example, in meddling with fundamental processes of nature.

It is not, that is, the social and political so much as the intellectual revolution Bulgakov is satirizing, that drastic change in men's attitudes to life and nature which the Bolsheviks tried to instill, their arrogant assumption that fate lies in men's hands, that they can both know and foresee everything and create whatever they please. It was against this kind of arrogance that Pasternak had also written. "Reshaping life!" he had said through his Doctor Zhivago, "People who can say that have never understood a thing about life. . . . They look on it as a lump of raw material that needs to be processed by them, to be ennobled by their touch. But life is never a material, a substance to be moulded. . . . " Like Pasternak, Bulgakov also quarreled with the self-exalting assumptions of Soviet ideology, but whereas Pasternak's work was a lyrical assertion of what he called "the sublimity of life and the unfathomable values of human existence," Bulgakov's was fantastic grotesquery satirizing human presumption. This is the core of *The Master and Margarita* (it was published in English last fall), a humorous, intricate, philosophic work that seems to be a version of Goethe's *Faust,* but is really a parody of it, transforming the Goethian conception of a world in which illimitable human striving, whatever crimes it may entail, is the essence of virtue, into a daemon-ridden one where helpless men are ruled by incomprehensible fate, where the highest good is an artist's mysterious knowledge of truth and reality, and the finest virtue is self-abnegating devotion.

Bulgakov was unique, with a voice all his own, one of that brilliant group of young Russian writers of the early 1920s who were, most of them, exiled, suppressed, or killed in the Thirties. A humorist and satirist—not so genteel as Olesha, not so light-hearted as Ilf and Petrov, not so Chekovian as Zoshchenko, not so trenchant as Zamyatin—humorous rather than witty, horrifying rather than bitter, he was, in his daemonic fantasy and his uproarious laughter, akin to Gogol, but more intellectual. Interested in rational rather than social man, in man as believer rather than doer, he always began with the actualities of Soviet Russia, but saw them in the context of a larger philosophic scheme, of which *The Master and Margarita* is his finest and grandest statement.

Peter Sourian (essay date 1968)

SOURCE: "Bureaucratic Brute," in *The New York Times Book Review,* July 28, 1968, pp. 5, 16.

[*Sourian is an American critic and novelist. Below, he discusses the political implications of* The Heart of a Dog *and lauds the story's humor, claiming: "implicit always is a passionate and severe humanity."*]

In 1923, Lenin, the tired and ailing wizard of the Revolution, foresaw monstrous possibilities in what he had wrought. In one of his last letters he said, "I am horrified by the bureaucratic procedure of Stalin and Ordjonikidze." In his final letter, written to Stalin himself, he declared, "I must appeal to the Party as a whole and demand your expulsion. You are not fit to be a Communist," and characterized him as an Abdul Hamid with a drunken lust for power.

But it was too late; Lenin's death spared Stalin, and in 1925, in the same month that Mikhail Bulgakov began to write *The Heart of a Dog,* surely realizing how dim were its chances of seeing print, Trotsky was informed by the Central Committee that he must resign his post and that he would be expelled from the party unless he stopped criticizing its policies, whereupon the former War Commissar was ignominiously put in charge of a concessions committee for electrical supplies, leaving the field of power open to the dogs. . . .

After decades of suppression, while the works of mediocre compromisers and kowtowers flourished, Bulgakov's books were finally published in the Soviet Union, albeit in censored form; *The Heart of a Dog,* however, written much earlier, has yet to appear there. . . .

[This] novel would certainly still rankle, having forewarned with comic bitterness and aristocratic contempt of the worst result of the Revolution—a lumpen-authoritarianism leading finally to murder as a solution to "policy" differences.

The foul climate has been well-evoked in that branch of Russian literature published, if at all, outside of Russia: Pasternak, *One Day in the Life of Ivan Denisovich,* Eugenia Ginzburg's noble and horrific account of her own unwarranted sufferings, *Journey Into the Whirlwind,* and so on.

But Bulgakov's novel was not written after the fact. It is prophecy in the true sense—surprising yet ultimately unmysterious. The careful observer of the present, in touch with the past as well, thus plots an arc into the future. Such a small matter as, say, the mildly ominous boorishness of a tenants' committee in the present of 1925 becomes a coordinate on the curve.

[In the introduction to his translation of *The Heart of a Dog,* Michael Glenny states] that Bulgakov, a journalist by trade, published several long stories in the twenties in a satirical vein popular at the time, and of a "'fantastic realism,' in which frightening and often outrageously grotesque ideas are embodied in a narrative of straight deadpan naturalism," reminiscent of Gogol, whose *Dead Souls* was successfully dramatized by Bulgakov.

The Heart of a Dog answers to this general description. Bulgakov's strange wizard is a world-famous Moscow specialist in the transplantation of human glands, Dr. Philip Philipovich, who turns a decent enough mongrel into something worse than either man or dog. The operation, described in the book, is bloody, and Sharik the dog becomes Poligraph Poligraphovich, subsequently a Commissar "for the elimination of vagrant quadrupeds." It rapidly becomes clear that the elimination may not stop with quadrupeds.

No one is more upset by the existence of this bureaucratic brute than the doctor, who is forced to watch Poligraphovich eat at his table, sleep in his apartment, abuse his cook, break his equipment, play Don Juan, and try, in the most cowardly fashion, to ruin him.

Lenin apparently liked to quote Napoleon as saying, "You commit yourself, and then—you see." Fortunately Dr. Philipovich manages at the end to reverse the process he has set in motion, after having publicly reproached himself for his mistake; and when he is charged with the murder of Poligraphovich, he points to Sharik the dog, dozing cozily at his feet.

Such is Bulgakov's unobstrusive skill that it all seems quite believable. The reader sees just how Sharik evolves into Poligraphovich into Commissar. The psychology is sound, the illusion is remarkably well sustained, the humor is never forced, and implicit always is a passionate and severe humanity.

Ellendea Proffer and Carl R. Proffer (essay date 1971)

SOURCE: An introduction to *Diaboliad, and Other Stories* by Mikhail Bulgakov, edited by Ellendea Proffer and Carl R. Proffer, translated by Carl R. Proffer, Indiana University Press, 1972, pp. vii–xx.

[*Ellendea and Carl Proffer are translators, critics, and editors of Russian literature, with a special interest in the writings of Mikhail Bulgakov. In the following excerpt from an essay written in 1971, they provide an overview of the short fiction collected in* Diaboliad, and Other Stories.]

The Irish *filid,* or poet, frequently used his magic talent for satirical purposes, and ancient Irish laws suggest that the authorities came to regard these poetic satirists as a serious social problem. Thus Aithrine the Importunate was eventually walled into his fortress with his sons and daughters and burned. He was not the first nor the last satirist to suffer at the hands of societies and governments fearing the metaphorical swords of the written word. If rats can be rhymed to death, and humans can be skewered on their own folly, so artists like Bulgakov who perform these ritual murders with great skill have never been loved by proponents of systems or men holding power.

A parabolic path led Bulgakov to writing. It began in Kiev, where he was born, the son of a professor of theology in 1891, and swerved to a literary career in Moscow, where, blinded by neurosclerosis and filled with pain-killing narcotics, he died in 1940. Despite boyhood dreams of the theater, he went to medical school at Kiev University and spent his first adult years in ignorant rural areas amputating limbs and healing infections (venereology was his specialty), rather than composing dialogue. When World War I and Revolution raged around Kiev, Bulgakov lived through the city's fourteen changes of power in the refuge of his family's apartment—later transformed into the home of the Turbins in his brilliant first novel *White Guard* (1925) and in his famous play *Days of the Turbins* (1926). He abruptly abandoned medicine in 1919, and after a hungry stay in the Caucasus, where he wrote stories for newspapers and plays for local theaters, Bulgakov moved to Moscow in the bitterly cold winter of 1921. . . .

[*Diaboliad, and Other Stories* represents] the first stage in Bulgakov's career as a prose writer. Besides the dozens of stories Bulgakov wrote in the years 1921-25, he also completed what is probably the best Civil War novel (*White Guard*). The feuilletons were written strictly for money, the novel was a labor of love. The *Diaboliad* collection and the first parts of *White Guard* were both published in 1925, and, with the exception of two slim booklets of reprinted feuilletons (1926), this marked Bulgakov's last appearance in print until after the death of Stalin. Bulgakov's satire was neither gentle nor primitive, and thus could have no success with Party-oriented keepers of the faith. *Diaboliad* provoked a furor of criticism; the journal in which *White Guard* was serialized (*Russia*) was shut down by the Cheka; and Bulgakov's plays *Days of the Turbins* and *Zoya's Apartment* (1926) were subjected to a bewildering sequence of bannings, rewritings by the theaters, and "unbannings." To this day *Diaboliad* is not in the open card catalogue of the Lenin Library in Moscow, and the copies of the almanac *Nedra* have had the stories **"The Fatal Eggs"** and **"Diaboliad"** torn out and Bulgakov's name expunged from their tables of contents—this no doubt a relic of the Stalin era. . . .

"Diaboliad" belongs to the tradition of Russian stories about "little men" and civil servants started by Gogol in "The Nose" and "The Overcoat" and continued less successfully by Dostoevsky in *The Double*. Character types are similar, including civil servant heroes suffering from sexual isolation and menacing superiors. The systemizing world of bureaucracy reduces people to categories, prizing sameness over individuality—and thus it produces frightening doubles. The boundaries which separate people begin to disintegrate, as does the sanity of the hero; when this happens the distinction between the "real" world and a fantastic world is not far behind. Madness and fantasy are age-old satirical devices. Gogol's Poprishchin ("Notes of a Madman") imagines noses living on the moon; Bulgakov's Korotkov sees Underwarr turning first into a phosphorescent black cat (forerunner of Behemoth in *The Master and Margarita*) and then into a white cock smelling of sulphur. Dostoevsky's Golyadkin Sr. loses his identity to an arrogant serial self and Korotkov loses his identity to a similar upstart—through documents, for as Soviet satirists have noted, without identification papers a man is not a man. In Gogol, without a nose a man is not a man.

Stylistic grotesqueries accompany thematic ones. Comic similes and realized metaphors appear on every page

(Underwarr has a voice "like a copper pan"; after the first reference in the simile it is always "clanged the pan" or "rang the pan"). Ordinary verbs of saying are rare; the dialogue is marked by all kinds of "squeaks," "sings," and "mutters" rather than "he saids." Inanimate objects such as type-writers or teapots sing and talk to characters. People are turned into synecdoches (usually colors or clothing), and many minor characters remain nameless except for some dominant feature ("the blond one," "the *kuntush*").

Neither in the use of fantasy nor in stylistic grotesqueries is Bulgakov unique for the mid-twenties. The short story was the dominant genre, and there was a great deal of experimentation in the realm of verbal stylization and fantasy—much of it more radical, and ephemeral, than Bulgakov's style. This was particularly true of the group known as the Serapion Brothers—named after a character in E. T. A. Hoffmann. Their leader, Lev Luntz, wrote a story entitled "Outgoing No. 37" in which a little clerk so fears for a lost document that he turns into that document (as Gogol's hero in *Vladimir Third-Class* turns into that medal). The Kafkaesque atmosphere and fantasy of that story is much like that in **"Diaboliad."** Among the better-known writers one had such experiments as the primitivism of Zamyatin, the ornamentalism of Vsevolod Ivanov, and the brilliant narrative inventions of Zoshchenko. In all of these stories, as in Bulgakov's, characterization suffered at the expense of style—true, sometimes as an intentional reduction of the characters to the status of robots. One of the ways Bulgakov does this—and it is obviously borrowed from Gogol's "The Nose" and Dostoevsky's *The Double*—is the exaggeratedly detailed registering of Korotkov's physical gestures and changes of location.

Korotkov's mortal plunge provides a natural ending, but it is not "the bone of the bone and the blood of the blood of the beginning," as Robert Louis Stevenson has said endings of short stories must be. It is typical of Bulgakov (for example, **"The Fatal Eggs," "A Chinese Tale," "No. 13"**) that what seemed harmless fun and fairly mild topical satire should unexpectedly end in death—which is no laughing matter. Of course, the mixture of satire and death is not unusual; (indeed it has ancient roots), and this is found in works by the best Russian satirists of the twenties—in Zamyatin's *We,* for example, or Zoshchenko's *Tales of Nazar Ilich Sinebryukhov*. But as is frequently the case (recall Gogol's "The Overcoat" again) the reader is faced with the problem of sympathy. If Korotkov has been made flat and ridiculous in the beginning, can we feel his death as a real tragedy? The problem of irony which undercuts irony is one which Bulgakov faces in other stories too, including **"The Fatal Eggs."**

"The Fatal Eggs" is the most famous and ambitious story of [*Diabolad, and Other Stories*]. The Serapion Brothers had helped renew interest in stories with interesting plots (generally classical Russian literature has little plot interest), and works describing adventures enjoyed great popularity. Nor were science-fiction elements entirely new to Russian literature in the twenties. Zamyatin's anti-utopian *We* is the best-known example; Alexei Tolstoy's pro-Soviet tales "Aelita" and "Garin's Death-Ray" soon followed, and Bulgakov returned to this kind of literature in the short novel *Heart of a Dog* (1925) as well as in his later plays. In **"The Fatal Eggs,"** using the plot of H. G. Wells' *The Food of the Gods,* Bulgakov created a horrifying picture of the catastrophe that results when the state interferes in scientific endeavors. The story is brilliant in its details, but as allegory it is somewhat unclear. Although it is the leather-jacketed Feyt and the journalist Bronsky who are responsible for getting the government interested in using the ray for chicken breeding, it is some unknown person who switches the reptile and chicken eggs. This means that the *direct* cause of the reptile invasion is an accidental switching of boxes—which seems rather pointless. Bulgakov's critique of the Revolutionary handling of scientific inventions and the attempt to circumvent natural evolution is presented far more lucidly and logically in *Heart of a Dog*—written only a few months after **"The Fatal Eggs."**

Feyt himself is at first portrayed as an extremely unpleasant man with a Mauser at his hip—but then we suddenly discover that he had been a flute player before the Revolution and that he has a nice wife and is really just a kind, simple man. We are told all of this in chapter eight, which is devoted to an idyllic (and humorous) description of the night on the Sovkhoz: Feyt is fluting, his nice wife is listening—and the next day she is crushed by a giant reptile in a scene described in horrifying naturalistic, clinical detail. This is a shock from which the reader never really recovers; although the deaths that follow are many and frightening, they are expected—except perhaps for Persikov's death at the hands of the Moscow mob.

The reptiles and ostriches, like Napoleon, are finally destroyed not by the Russians, but by an incredible frost. The frost comes at the end of August in true *deus ex machina* fashion. While interesting on first reading, the plot itself is not all-important, which one can conclude from the fact that Bulgakov's basic plot differs from Wells' only in that Persikov is killed—Wells' persecuted scientist escapes the mob and lives out his days in safe obscurity.

Bulgakov's originality consists in the way he adapts the story to the Russian environment—the Deaconess Drozdova's story, for example, is all his own invention. Also in evidence is Bulgakov's great talent for arousing readers' interest by creating an air of mystery and suspense. However, all of these abilities are as nothing when compared with Bulgakov's ability to make the fantastic seem real— as in the description of the giant reptiles ravaging the land. Scientific precision and a proclivity for naturalistic detail might explain the extraordinarily powerful effect of these descriptions of horrible events—but only partially. Perhaps it is explained by the visual nature of Bulgakov's imagination, the fact that whatever he described he had "seen," if only in a nightmare. Elena Sergeevna Bulgakova has related how when dictating Bulgakov would stand staring out a window, interrupting himself only to correct a detail which he could see but was describing imprecise-

ly. In *Theatrical Novel* there is an obviously autobiographical description of a dramatist "merely" transcribing the pictures which of themselves appear before his eyes.

The visual side of Bulgakov's imagination is perhaps most effective in the six scenes of **"A Chinese Tale."** This story is somehow enchanting in its description of a Chinese coolie in the Red Army. Bulgakov's repeated evocation of the coolie's childhood under the hot sun is an effective and touching contrast to the cold of Moscow and the Kremlin wall. The repetition of certain key details, details which are packed with memory and meaning for the character—the kaoliang, the keen-edged shadow, the buckets of ice-cold water—is typical of the mature Bulgakov's prose. The cocaine dream with its careful incorporation of details from the coolie's immediate past and mystical foreshadowing of the future (the Chinaman being rewarded for a decapitation) is another successful feature of the story. (The irreverent references to Lenin make the story unpublishable now.) Bulgakov later used the cocaine, the Finnish knife, and Hellish vision of a Chinese dwelling in Moscow in his play *Zoya's Apartment.*

> **Bulgakov's world is moved by the desire for justice here and now, and his most powerful satire comes from the frustration of that desire**.
>
> —*Ellendea and Carl R. Proffer*

As noted by critics at the time *Diaboliad* was published, **"A Chinese Tale"** appears to be a polemic with Vsevolod Ivanov's celebrated story "Armored-Train 14-69"—which was made into a play and put on at the Moscow Art Theater shortly after Bulgakov's own *Days of the Turbins,* with much less trouble politically. Ivanov also has a Chinese hero, but a *real* hero who joins the Bolsheviks and intelligently and consciously serves the cause. In the end he deliberately sacrifices his life for his comrades, throwing himself under the wheels of a train which has to be stopped. Contrast Bulgakov's coolie, who owes his original acceptance by the Red Army merely to his utterance of three words, the Russian national oath ("Fuck your mother"), and who serves and kills strictly for bread, with not a whisper of ideology.

"The Adventures of Chichikov" is one of Bulgakov's "Gogolisms." The title is the title which Gogol's censors insisted he use above *Dead Souls.* Basically the story uses characters and lines from *Dead Souls* (both Part I and Part II), but other works by Gogol, including *The Inspector General* and "The Nose," are also incorporated parodistically. Much of the narration is composed of bits and pieces of sentences from Gogol—such as the last sentence of the story, which from "again life went parading before me" is from the end of a Homeric simile in *Dead*

Souls. Bulgakov's ironic "dream" ending mimics both Gogol's original version of "The Nose" and the denial of reality in the preface to "The Tale of How Ivan Ivanovich Quarrelled with Ivan Nikiforovich"—the narrator claims it is all fantasy, but the reader knows that it is all too real. For this reason, Bulgakov was attacked by politically minded critics who, like the critics mentioned in *Dead Souls* ("they will come scurrying from their crannies"), saw the story as unpatriotic slander. There are several examples of Gogol's works being updated during the twenties, including Barkanov's long story "How Ivan Ivanovich Made Up with Ivan Nikiforovich" and Meyerhold's surrealistic production of *The Inspector General.* Later Bulgakov was to be the author of the stage version of *Dead Souls* which has been a standard at the Moscow Art Theater for nearly forty years, and he wrote film scripts for both *Dead Souls* and *The Inspector General.* Even before **"The Adventures of Chichikov,"** which is really an overgrown feuilleton, Bulgakov used Gogolian epigraphs, characters, themes, and parodies in several of his feuilletons for *The Whistle* (see especially the hilarious **"Inspector General with a Kicking Out"**).

"No. 13. The Elpit-Rabkommun Building" (from *Rabochaja kommuna*—Workers' Commune) is also a feuilletonistic piece. Its themes (the housing shortage, problems of communal living, "ignorant" or "uneducated" people—*temnye ljudi*) recur in Bulgakov's early humorous works and then in his plays (*Zoya's Apartment, Bliss*), as well as in *The Master and Margarita.* Indeed, the number of the fatal apartment—50—is used again in *The Master and Margarita* (Berlioz's and Woland's apartment), and No. 13 was the Bulgakovs' address in Kiev. In this story the narrator's sympathies seem to lie primarily with the old order, and the ignorant people, the unwashed multitudes represented by Annushka, are to blame for tragedies of this sort. The repeated images and metaphors (the naked stone girl, the fire as beast), the secret servicemen, hints of demonism (the devil is disguised as a snowstorm), allusion to Meyerbeer's *The Huguenots,* and the sudden intrusion of electrifying death are all typical of Bulgakov's fiction.

Three of the feuilletons published in a tiny book called *A Treatise on Housing* (the title story, **"Four Portraits,"** and **"Moonshine Lake"**) are characteristic of the best of Bulgakov's early newspaper humor—which is not to say much. They are not really fiction, and are of interest now mainly for the topical humor—after all, Bulgakov was rather bold to poke fun at pictures of Lenin and Marx. They are also useful for a study of Bulgakov's narrators. Typically these early works had quotations from Worker Correspondent Reporters as epigraphs. Bulgakov would then bring the epigraph to life—a frequent device was a mix-up caused, say, by the combination of a snack bar and a library, or what would occur when the political indoctrination class, choir practice, and the movie "The Daughter of Montezuma" would all take place simultaneously. His success with feuilletons is due in large part to Bulgakov's natural abilities as a storyteller—since feuilletons are unified by the narrator rather than by plot. The narrator-storyteller was one that was natural to Bulgakov,

and he employed him in most of his prose. This narrator is especially visible when a work is long and tends toward the comic. For example, the narrator is fairly unobtrusive in **"Diaboliad,"** but he makes his presence felt in **"The Fatal Eggs."**

The need for refuge in the midst of real and metaphorical storms is a theme which runs through most of Bulgakov's fiction. **"Psalm,"** however, is very unusual for him. He had written feuilletons in which dialogue dominates, and some of the impressionistic devices are used in other stories (especially **"The Raid"**), but **"Psalm"** is wistful, personal, and delicate in a way unusual for the early Bulgakov. Here we have no satire, no science fiction, none of the grotesqueries which dominate virtually all of his other early stories—only a quietly lyrical set of scenes between a lonely man and a lonely woman. It is a touching story, affecting partly because Bulgakov has his characters transform homely details, such as the buttons, into apt symbols of complicated and pathetic situations in a way which we recognize as very human.

Abram in **"The Raid"** also has a very human triumph, a minor victory of quiet inner dignity over the indignity of physical ridiculousness, the arrogance of Yak, and the torment of Revolution. In manner **"The Raid"** is close to the battle scenes in *White Guard,* and to a certain extent, some scenes in **"A Chinese Tale."** This happens when the narrator's mind merges with that of the main character and we see things, estranged, through the eyes of a wounded man—Abram recalls the warmth and unfinished watercolor as the Chinaman had the kaoliang. Stories about the Civil War were probably numerically dominant in the early twenties, and the naturalistic description of physical cruelty can also be found in the tales of Vsevolod Ivanov, Mikhail Slonimsky, and Nikolai Nikitin. The metaphorical, impressionistic description of the storm and attack also owes something to the ornamentalism typical of the twenties, although the light effects are typically Bulgakovian.

"The Crimson Island" was published in the Berlin newspaper *On the Eve* in 1924. "Islands" and "journeys" are ancient devices for presenting utopias or anti-utopias, and obviously Jules Verne, from whom Bulgakov borrows characters and situations, is the most important forerunner in this genre. Both the island and the journey were used frequently by Soviet writers—from Mayakovsky's *Mystery-Bouffe* (1918) to Ehrenburg's *Trust D. E.* (1923) and Valentin Kataev's *Ehrendorf Island* (1924). Bulgakov's story appears to be a parody of the kind of propagandistic stories written after the Revolution, allegories in which history is simplified and characters are either heroes or villains. It is full of hyperbole, gross caricature, incongruous juxtapositions, and funny non sequiturs. It is an amusing piece, but hardly significant; one would not give it much attention if Bulgakov had never written a play called *The Crimson Island.* The play was written in 1927 and premiered at the Kamerny Theater in December 1928. While the play was very popular with the public, the critics violently denounced it as "talentless, toothless, humble" and a "pasquinade on the Revolution." The play is quite different from the story—in fact the basic story is made into a play within the play, and the main theme becomes censorship. So *The Crimson Island* served as the final piece of evidence in the trial by press of Bulgakov, and soon he was run out of Russian literature.

A complete picture of Bulgakov's early prose would also have to include such diverse genres as **"Notes on the Cuff,"** the stories which make up *The Notes of a Young Doctor,* and *Heart of a Dog*. The first of these is a curious work—a fragmentary autobiographical account given the appearance of a fictional feuilleton describing Bulgakov's literary life in the Caucasus (with many famous writers such as Mandelstam and Pilnyak appearing briefly) and then in Moscow's labyrinthine corridors. The six stories which form *The Notes of a Young Doctor,* told in the first person, are again closer to *White Guard,* with little grotesque satire, more in the realistic vein. There are strong echoes of Tolstoy's story "The Snowstorm," Pushkin's story with the same title, and such Chekhov stories as "The Enemies." Here one again finds a hero, common to many of Bulgakov's works at different periods, who suffers agonizing self-doubt, but survives inhuman trials because of his aristocratic sense of human dignity and humane compassion. The young doctor is an aristocrat in ability, as are the scientific heroes of **"The Fatal Eggs,"** *Adam and Eve,* and *Heart of a Dog* All three of these works describe the confident misuse of knowledge which, while promising human good, leads only to injustice and inhumanity.

Bulgakov once referred to himself as a "mystical writer"—but he is only mystical in that he believes there is more to the world than common sense can know. There is no absorption in the other-worldly in his works—even in *The Master and Margarita* he describes Yeshua and his character, not God and His divinity. Bulgakov's world is moved by the desire for justice here and now, and his most powerful satire comes from the frustration of that desire.

In order to support myself I served as a reporter and feuilletonist for the newspapers, and I came to hate these jobs, which have no merit. At the same time I learned to hate editors, I hate them now, and I will hate them the rest of my life.

—Mikhail Bulgakov, as translated by Ellendea Proffer in **Bulgakov, *1984*.**

V. S. Pritchett (essay date 1975)

SOURCE: "Surgical Spirit," in *New Statesman,* Vol. 89, No. 2309, June 20, 1975, p. 807.

[*Pritchett, a modern British writer, is respected for his mastery of the short story and for what critics describe as his judicious, reliable, and insightful literary criticism. Below, he provides a positive assessment of the collection* Notes of a Young Doctor.]

Early experience as practising doctors has more than once given a headstart to a number of novelists and it is easy to see why. They are not bemused by literary tradition; their discipline makes them objective. Their material is waiting for them every day in the surgery; they see society without its clothes, naked and defenceless, frightened or malingering, shameless or struck by fate. What happens when they become story tellers? Most of them become anecdotal in a conventional way; few attain the stature of a Chekhov. The practice of medicine was with him a key to larger matters than physical illness; and he is distinguished from the other great Russians, both in his views on art and society, and by his freedom from the didactic tradition of Russian literature. He did not, like other doctor-writers split in two when he came to write.

Mikhail Bulgakov (1891-1940), on the other hand, does appear to have split. He became known in the NEP [New Economic Policy] period for his fantasies, his mastery of the grotesque and satire in the free ferment that went on for a short time after the Civil War. On this savage subject he was one of several outstanding raw and vivid realists who could rise to the epic note. But between 1925 and 1927 he wrote sketches about his earlier life as a young doctor in the Smolensk region to which he had been sent in 1916. They appeared in magazines and have only lately been collected. They reveal a grave, nervous young man who is discovering for himself the vast gulf of 500 years that separated the Russian peasant from the intelligentsia. The oil lamps of his little provincial hospital seemed to him a lonely beacon which symbolised the battle between light and darkness. Not that the hospitals were poorly equipped: the place he was put in charge of when he qualified—though he had no intern experience whatever—was decent enough; but in those days it lay in a wilderness, and awful roads made it almost inaccessible.

The strain on an inexperienced young man working almost alone, for months on end, was hard to bear. Some doctors collapsed under it, as one reads in the most remarkable of his sketches. It purports to be the diary of a doctor who has become a morphia addict and who with bitter accuracy reports the clinical progress of his own case. A literary writer might easily have fallen into self-dramatisation, but Bulgakov has quietly made the victim his own observer and has thereby given the double focus of psychological truth. I have never read as convincing a study of addiction and Bulgakov's art has given it human reality. It is interesting that the extravagant, later Bulgakov could be so exact and laconic.

That Bulgakov—and his patients—survived those grim times of 1916 in this remote place is a tribute to the courage of a young man rising by force of will over his own fears. He arrived knowing only the text books. He feared his youth made him ridiculous. Almost the moment he arrived he was obliged to amputate the leg of an injured girl; he must have been well-taught for, book in hand, he kept the girl alive. But what he is able to convey is his sense of his own will directing him, as if it were another person, when what he felt was nausea and horror. And nature outside—blizzards, gales, the isolation of the weeks of thaw, and once even a night ride from a dying man with wolves in pursuit and the frozen panic of the horses—added the sense of an elemental struggle. So these straightforward yet extraordinary sketches gain their effect from being also the account of a young man's growth. One begins to see that he became a novelist not because he had material but because he was storing up passion and temperament. It tells us something about him, that his later satires, grotesqueries and fantasies were a protest against melancholy and the standardisation of the Soviet citizen. What happened to him when the brief years of literary freedom came to an end, I don't know: they were years when satire and imagination, the Gogol qualities, burst out. That time before the Union of Soviet Writers got its teeth in has rarely been matched since.

Sigrid McLaughlin (essay date 1978)

SOURCE: "Structure and Meaning in Bulgakov's 'The Fatal Eggs,'" in *Russian Literature Triquarterly,* No. 15, 1978, pp. 263-79.

[*In the following essay, McLaughlin explores the "narrative mechanism" that Bulgakov uses to relate the events of "The Fatal Eggs," thereby demonstrating that the story is not only a social satire but also a commentary on moral and philosophical issues.*]

The critics—irrespective of their political stand—characterize **"The Fatal Eggs"** inevitably and not incorrectly as a social satire. But to view the story exclusively as a social satire is to ignore a number of textual features which strongly suggest that Bulgakov's concerns were moral-philosophical at least as much as social-satirical. The social-satirical interpretation of the story singles out those incidents that show how a society totally inefficient in all its public functions exploits, mistreats, and kills its greatest genius. Yet it ignores the obtrusive fact that the scientist-hero Persikov is a sinner in his own right, obsessed with science, virtually devoid of human qualities and concerns, voluntarily isolated from the political, social, and human world. Persikov sinfully tampers with life by experimenting with an evil life force, the red ray, and by surrendering it to further abuse. Like Goethe's *Zauber-lehrling,* he unleashes hellish forces over which he loses control. Purged of emotions, weak-willed, ethically frail, he becomes a satanist and his science, black magic.

Bulgakov aims at two targets in his story. He exposes to ridicule and censure a society guided by strictly utilitarian principles, and also an individual dehumanized by an obsession. This interpenetration of contemporary satire and serious ethics against a narrative background of fantastic events in **"The Fatal Eggs"** also characterizes Bulgakov's *The Master and Margarita.* **"The Fatal Eggs"** is a more important early work than commonly assumed, and *The Master and Margarita* is not the isolated masterpiece it seemed to be.

The inattention to the serious ethical problems raised in the figure of Persikov is at least partly attributable to Bulgakov's narrative mechanism. Bulgakov chose a reporting consciousness that lacks a firm ethical point of view and consistent judgmental faculties. As a result, a pattern of broken norms in grammar, logic, narrative organization, attitude, and commentary marks the structure of the story. It is a pattern of thwarted conventional expectations. It absorbs the reader's attention and disorients and puzzles him. It is also the prime vehicle of social satire. It makes both victim (Persikov) and villains ludicrous and pitiable. The social functionaries appear at once devilishly evil and intellectually so limited, so subhuman, so naively, unscrupulously and openly opportunistic that they are criminal as well as comic. Similarly, Persikov appears so naively, innocently and childishly out of touch with his surrounding world, he behaves in such a ludicrous and subhuman manner, that he seems to be too comic to be entirely blameworthy for his deeds.

But Bulgakov orients his reader behind the back of his recording consciousness with symbolic patterns and authorially valid remarks. They are the key to the neglected moral-philosophical aspects of the story. Studying the narrative mechanism of the story, i.e., sorting out what is authorially valid and what is unreliable information, allows the story's ethical implications to emerge.

One major source of comic distortion and disorientation is the insensitivity of Bulgakov's recording consciousness to lexical and grammatical conventions. Words from lexical strata conventionally considered incompatible may stand adjacent to each other. Grammatical structures which tradition has associated with certain "styles" and "tones" combine incongruously. Grammatical forms clash with lexical meanings.

Throughout **"The Fatal Eggs"** verbal material from the dominant lexical stratum consisting of words marked in the *Dictionary of the Russian Language* as "colloquial" (*razgovornoe*) and "substandard colloquial" (*prosto-rechie*) is interspersed with words marked obsolete, bookish, or foreign. The resulting combinations are stylistically and semantically incongruous. The pervasive use of colloquial formulations (such as *tak ili inache, dal'she poshlo khuzhe, delo bylo vot v chem*), oral fill words (such as *itak, chut'chut', kaby, vidimo, a vprochem, pravda, prosto uzh, chto li* etc.) as well as diminutives and phonetic transcription of noises, sets an informal oral tone and suggests unpretentiousness, naturalness and truthfulness. On the other hand, the use of bookish or obsolete words (such as *koi, poistine, zasim*), pretentious words of foreign origin (such as *eruditsiia, spich, fenomenal'nyi, perturbatsiia, siurpriz*), and the misuse of difficult technical terms and parts of speech convey affectation and ostentatious grandiloquence. The semantic quality created by the lexical stratum of a given word clashes immediately with the semantic aura of the following word, which comes from a different lexical stratum. Such a collision of semantic realms produces a tension, disorientation and semantic "bulging."

Let us take this sentence as an example: *A tak kak on govoril vsegda uverenno, ibo eruditsiia v ego oblasti u nego byla sovershenno fenomenal'naia, to kriuchok ochen' chasto poiavlialsia pered glazami sobesednikov professora Persikova.* ["And since he always spoke with assurance, for the erudition he had in his field was absolutely phenomenal, the little hook of his bent finger appeared often before the eyes of Professor Persikov's partners in conversation."] Here the informal conjunctions *a* and *tak kak,* the particle *to,* and the diminutive *kriuchok* combine incongruously with the bookish conjunction *ibo* and the pretentious *eruditsiia* and *fenomenal'nyi*. The lexical collocation of the informal and the bookish becomes transferred to the subject described. Persikov becomes familiar as well as strange and distant, ridiculous as well as respectable.

Inappropriate and misleading chapter titles, which first raise and then frustrate expectations, also reflect the (of course carefully manipulated) insensitivity of the recording consciousness to lexical and novelistic conventions. The title of the first chapter, *Curriculum vitae,* e.g., is conventionally out of place in literature. It suggests the dry matter-of-factness and external objectivity of a bureaucracy. The text that follows includes neither factual biographical information, as the title would suggest, nor a novelistic biography with experiences and facts related to character and character development. The numerous dates and figures are a pseudo-tribute to the title; they are irrelevant. The hodge-podge of the conventionally relevant (his wife left him, he had no children, he obtained the chair of zoology, he published this article and that book of such and such length) and the irrelevant (certain frogs and toads died in a particular year, the government requisitioned three of his five rooms in 1919, the clock at the corner of Herzen and Gorokhovaya St. stopped at a quarter past eleven, etc.) creates an incongruity that is comic and, at the same time, disorienting. Upon closer inspection we realize that the details have been selected from Persikov's point of view. Bulgakov allowed the recording consciousness to coincide with Persikov's consciousness. This strategy exposes Persikov as selfish and naive, and at the same time ridicules and belittles revolution and civil war.

Similarly, the title of the last chapter—"A Frosty God on a Machine" (*"Moroznyi bog na mashine"*)—is more than a folk-etymological mutilation of the Latin *deus-ex-machina* (*bog iz mashiny*) in which the Latin *ex* is translated with the Russian *na* (on); it also provokes a host of conventional expectations that are partially met, but in unconventionally comic terms. Just as Bulgakov ridicules the title concept by taking it too literally, i.e., by animating it (what is meant is "Frost as Deus ex Machina"), his narrative mocks its own contrived pseudo-solution, the

sudden frost. The mutilation of the technical term in the title parallels the ironic violation of justice which the frost constitutes. It comes to save villains, not to reinstitute a whole world (as a *deus ex machina* would).

Bulgakov establishes an atmosphere of comic distortion when he makes his recording consciousness break morphological and semantic rules in such combinations as "anti-chicken vaccination" (*"anti-kurinye privivki"*) when "vaccination against the chicken pest" is meant, and "anti-religious sufferings" (*"anti-religioznye ogorcheniia"*) when sufferings from anti-religious activities is intended; and in such phrases as "chicken events," "chicken commissions" "chicken field," "chicken catastrophe" when "events resulting from the chicken pest" etc. is meant.

Similar effects result when the conventions of metaphor are transgressed, namely, if the secondary subject introduces semantic dimensions that are unrelated and basically incompatible with those of the principal subject. The suggested figurative relation of the two subjects then becomes forced and incongruous. Each subject, in fact, retains its literal meaning, and the secondary subject does not unveil hidden semantic dimensions of the principal or develop meaning along the line of semantic similarity. Instead, its semantic realm is logically incongruous with that of the principal subject. Both subjects interact in their confrontation: the secondary subject ridicules the primary subject, making it absurd or illuminating it ironically. Such a collision of metaphoric subjects may also have the effect of putting in question or destroying the laws of logical probability.

Such metaphors occur when the narrative consciousness reverses the conventions of animation, i.e., reduces the human figure and personifies objects and abstract concepts. It reports that "curious heads of people stood above the rural fence and in its cracks" (*"liubopytnye golovy liudei torchali nad derevenskim zaborom i v shcheliakh ego"*) and that Pankrat speaks with the "sleepless cylinder hat on guard" (*"Pankrat govoril bessonnomu dezhurnomu kotelku"*). As a result of such a perspective, human beings disintegrate and become automata.

Violating the laws of reality and logical probability, the narrative consciousness animates the inanimate. We no longer tread on familiar ground when the pest is allowed to walk on our side: "Having reached A in the north, the pest stopped all by itself, because it had nowhere else to go . . . it stopped . . . disappeared and quieted down . . . lingered on . . . did not go any further" (*"Doidia na severe do A, mor ostanovilsia sam soboi po toi prichine, chto itti emu dal'she bylo nekuda . . . ostanovilsia . . . propal i zatikh . . . zaderzhalsia . . . dal'she ne poshel"*). Equal estrangement results from the humanization of animals. A frog is crucified. Sleeping roaches keep their silence and demonstrate their opposition to war communism by disappearing. Mrs. Drozdova's chickens die as human beings. The dying rooster becomes a restless drunkard who "like an animal [!] stared at them." The hen suffers "like a man" and receives parting words on its way to heaven.

By allowing his recording consciousness to create such apparently harmless metaphors as the humanization of the chickens, Bulgakov makes important implicit statements. On the one hand, the humanization of the chicken world imparts tragic proportions to an event that is merely unfortunate. On the other hand, the dominantly colloquial lexicon of the passage undermines the tragic grandeur metaphorically imposed on the events. The context of this episode makes evident that Bulgakov contrived this clash to comment on two circumstances of life during the Twenties: the unsuccessful anti-religious campaigns and the New Economic Policy. At the beginning of the episode Deacon Drozdov is reported to have succumbed to sufferings caused by anti-religious campaigns of the Soviet government. But ironically, his neighbors remain so superstitiously religious that it is entirely natural for the prior of the local church to perform a service on behalf of the chickens afflicted with the "evil eye." As it turns out, praying does just as much, or rather, as little, as government commissions to curb the pest. The NEP, by allowing private enterprise to flourish, gave Drozdov's widow a chance to survive. Despite high taxes and constant changes in regulations, she managed to run a profitable chicken farm. Her chickens were more important to her than people, and with good reason: their death meant her destitution. It is comic and tragic that chickens dominate human life and that the anti-religious campaigns culminate in the deacon's unnecessary death and the survival of primitive religiosity. His chosen narrative consciousness allows Bulgakov to criticize and ridicule the presented facts implicitly.

Bulgakov achieves the same effect when his recording consciousness disregards the expected relationship between grammar and meaning. Conventional expectations are reversed when a weighty syntactical build-up (a host of subordinate clauses) collapses in a short main clause, which moreover has little logical connection with the preceding verbiage. The grammatical logic of the following sentence (based on the construction "it is unknown whether . . . but well known that . . . ") is irreproachable:

Neizvestno, tochno li khoroshi bylo lefortovskie veterinarnye privivki, umely li zagraditel'nye samarskie otriady, udachny li krutye mery, priniatye po otnosheniiu k skupshchikam iaits v Kaluge i Voronezhe, uspeshno li rabotala chrezvychainaia Moskovskaia kommissiia, no khorosho izvestno, chto cherez dve nedeli posle poslednego svidaniia Persikova s Al'fredom v smysle kur v Soiuze bylo sovershenno chisto.

It is unknown whether the Lefortovo veterinary vaccinations were actually valid, whether the Samara roadblock units were skillful, whether the decisive measures undertaken in respect to the egg merchants of Kaluga and Voronezh were successful, whether the Extraordinary Commission in Moscow worked successfully, but it is well known that two weeks after Alfred's last visit with Persikov, it was entirely clean in the Union of Republics as far as chickens were concerned.

The semantic content of the sentence, however, is utterly illogical. What is claimed to be unknown in the first section of the sentence is implicitly reported as familiar in the second section. In other words, since the chickens died, official measures were obviously unsuccessful, though their effect is reported as unknown. Furthermore, the enumeration of the subordinate clauses lacks conventional logical ordering. Different levels of abstraction are mixed. Specific minutiae are followed by general categories: the specific campaign measures normally would be subsumed under the activities of the Moscow commission. Listing items of different levels of abstraction in one coordinating chain transmits the contradictory message that all are of equal or logically graded significance. Here Bulgakov attacks under cover the Soviet preoccupation with "decisive measures" and useless commissions and the government's inability to acknowledge defeat.

Not only grammatical and lexical usage, but also narrative structure and commentary reflect the disorienting qualities of Bulgakov's recording consciousness. Narrative structure fails to comply with the laws of logic and causality; discrimination and judgment proceed in disregard of conventional standards.

Bulgakov wreaks havoc upon conventional expectations of narrative sequence when he begins his story with the report that Persikov entered his study and looked around, and then proceeds to refer to a mysterious "terrifying catastrophe" which began that evening and whose "first cause" was Persikov. The reader expects to hear what Persikov saw when he entered his study or why he looked around. Instead, he is immediately jolted to a different level of abstraction. After the allusion to the catastrophe, a description of the protagonist follows, a description, however, that lacks any information relevant to the catastrophe. It notes the shape of Persikov's head, the tone of his voice, habits of gesture, etc. Of the catastrophe we hear only chapters later.

The chapters consist of dissociated fragments in random order. The narration shifts whimsically from episode to episode, with titles and chapter numbers inserted for no compelling reasons. Chapter VII, for example, first reports the spread of the chicken pest, the reaction of the domestic and foreign press, and Persikov's work in the "chicken domain." Next, in swift succession, it recounts Persikov's rejection of an automobile, a speech by him, his collision with a mysterious stranger, the arrival of Rokk, the strange mood sweeping the country, the death of Persikov's former wife, and a conversation between Pankrat and the Institute's guards. Sometimes chapter titles have little connection with the contents. The chapter "The Deacon's Wife Drozdova" contains only a passing reference to her. "A Chicken Story" devotes about three out of ten pages to "chicken matters."

The unreliability of the recording consciousness becomes particularly disturbing when it passes on fantastic and possible occurrences as facts of equal validity. This combination of two disparate realms throughout **"The Fatal Eggs"** finds symbolic representation in the story's central

A scene from the original 1928 production of The Crimson Island, *Bulgakov's stage adaptation of his 1924 short story of the same title.*

image, the red ray. The ray speeds breeding and increases size; this is scientifically plausible. But its capacity to instill evil is possible only by magic. Similarly implausible events, such as a frost in the middle of August, an invasion of ostriches and reptiles (which, to begin with, could not live in the Russian climate), their victory over the Russian army, the "inexplicably melancholy mood" that befell men and animals on the day before the snakes hatched, are reported as commonplace or strange, monstrous, mysterious, nightmarish or extraordinary; but their truth is taken for granted.

The evaluative commentary of the recording consciousness is equally disorienting. An obvious or trivial fact generates extensive commentary, as e.g., the containment of the chicken pest within the borders of the Soviet Union. In addition, in the commentary, the narrative consciousness avows ignorance of well known facts or pretends knowledge of the unknowable: in the north and east the pest "had no place to go" since "there was water" and "since chickens aren't found in water"; in the south the pest stopped simply, no conjecture given; and in the east it halted "in the most amazing manner at the Polish and Rumanian border." The commentary continues, "Was it the climate [that] was different there or [was it] that the

defensive quarantine measures undertaken by the neighboring governments played a role?" The reader would, of course, know that the climate does not stop at borders and that most likely the quarantine measures halted the pest.

In another such case the recording consciousness ceremoniously admits ignorance of a fact which is of no interest to the reader, and perfectly clear as well. "Dunia, the maid [is said to have] found herself in a copse behind the Sovkhoz and, by coincidence, the red-mustached chauffeur of the battered Sovkhoz truck was there too. What they did, remains unknown." Not only is it no coincidence that the chauffeur was there, but the reader guesses very well what Dunia and the chauffeur were up to. After the reader decides the matter is closed, the narration continues: "They took shelter in the fluid shadow of an elm directly on the chauffeur's outspread leather coat." With this telling piece of information the matter is really closed.

This grotesque inconscience in attitude, commentary, knowledge, and values is part and parcel of the changing identity of the recording consciousness, as a result of which its distance from characters and events also varies. Occasionally it seems to possess a specific identity. Its language is orally and colloquially flavored, and on two occasions it employs the phrase, "let's say" ("skazhem"), which labels it as an observer with limited knowledge. On the other hand, its vocabulary and syntax are often bookish, and much of its information is that of an omniscient teller. In short, the contradictory nature of the commentary prevents us from locating it in a single sane mind. The narrative consciousness shares both the attitudes of the characters and the vision of the author. It sometimes assumes a position above the characters, but, at other times, it descends to their level and plays the part of an objective but limited observer. The result is a constantly and whimsically shifting intellectual distance, which, in turn, contributes to a sense of mistrust in the validity of the narrated information and of the evaluatory commentary.

In the following example the narrative consciousness is cast as an omniscient nonparticipant. It is privileged to know things concealed from the ordinary reporter. Quasi-indirect discourse reports Ivanov's thoughts:

> *Ivanov byl porazhen, sovershenno razdavlen: kak zhe takaia prostaia veshch', kak eta tonen'kaia strela, ne byla zamechena ran'she, chort voz'mi! Da kem ugodno, i khotia by im, Ivanovym, i deistvitel'no, eto chudovishchno! Vy tol'ko posmotrite.*

> Ivanov was surprised, in fact, completely shattered: how could such a simple thing as this thinnish arrow not have been noticed earlier, the devil take it! By anyone, for that matter, why not even by himself, Ivanov. And indeed it was monstrous! You just look.

Similarly, the narrative consciousness summarizes a conversation which could not possibly have been overheard: "and then a conversation took place, the meaning of which could be summed up as follows." Such privilege produces a tone of superiority which is exacerbated by such detached, evaluative commentary as: "Unfortunately, for the republic, no ungifted mediocrity sat at the microscope. No, it was Professor Persikov."

On the other hand, in just as many cases the narrative consciousness loses this privilege of omniscient knowledge and moves to a level identical with or even lower than that of the characters. It speculates about Persikov's thoughts as often as it reports them with confidence: "he probably wanted Pankrat to. . . . " Or it registers incomprehension of Persikov's behavior: "for some reason he accused the People's Commissar of Education of the deaths." It may also assume the role of an objective, disinterested observer, who is ignorant of scientific matters: "One could obviously see something very interesting in the frog's mesentery . . . the two scientists exchanged lively words incomprehensible to simple mortals."

The moral distance of the narrative consciousness, i.e., its attitudes to characters and events, is just as unstable as its intellectual distance. And the reasons for the vacillation in attitude remain obscure. Both Persikov and Rokk, for example, are alternately admired and despised. Persikov is a "first-rate scientist" with an "Eye of genius" who as the "only one in the world possessed something special

apart from knowledge." Rokk also is a "positively great man." Such assertions of greatness remain unproven and are contradicted by equally unproven statements to the contrary. Persikov is "the first cause of the catastrophe," a "swine," and "washes his hands" like Pontius Pilate. Rokk's face makes "an extremely unpleasant impression," and the snake is said to have "released him for repentance." Finally, such similar evaluative phrases as "and to the misfortune of the republic no ungifted mediocrity sat at the microscope" and "Alas! Alas! To the misfortune of the republic the sizzling brain of Alexander Semyonovich Rokk did not break down" equate protagonist and antagonist.

Such contradictory evaluations are further complicated by the fact that the narrative consciousness is sometimes comically detached from Persikov, at other times sympathetically close to him. This makes Persikov both a subhuman marionette and a pathetically human being.

The comic aspects of Persikov's personality involve his physiology and conduct, the absence of motivation for his behavior, and the goals behind his frantic activity. Like Gogol's Akaky Akakievich Bashmachkin (Mr. Shoe), Vladimir Ipatievich Persikov (Mr. Peach) is a ludicrously incomplete man. He is said to have a "croaking" voice, and the mechanical habit of screwing up his eyes and hooking his right index finger. His body and mind are not coordinated. He puts his shoes on the wrong feet, takes them off in the street, smokes an unlit cigarette and passes for a drunkard. When during the miseries of the Civil War he mourns the death of his Surinam toad and ignores the starvation of his own devoted guard, when he thinks of nothing but writing articles on frogs and teaching, examining, and failing students for not knowing that amphibia lack pelvic buds, when we learn that he preferred his frogs to his wife, we can still laugh at this being devoid of consciousness and conscience. He is a caricature of the devoted scientist.

But expressions of sympathy and reports about his emotions constantly undermine this comically detached view of Persikov. "Alas, the garbled name did not save the Professor from the events," the narrative reads. Later, he is a "hunted-down wolf" and said to have been "crucified" by a "furious mob" of "wild animals." Furthermore, Persikov himself is said to experience a fleeting feeling of compassion for the "mechanical man"; and realizing his moral responsibility for his discovery, he momentarily resists inquiry about it and the expropriation of his experimental equipment. When he finds out that his untested discovery has caused a catastrophe, he suffers a stroke and becomes deranged. Turned into a victim of his own obsession and external circumstances, he excites our sympathy. It is as if the narrative consciousness was equipped with a telescope which—when used correctly—would bring Persikov sympathetically close and—when turned around—jolt him to the comic horizon.

Occasionally, a sympathetic close-up is overlaid with a comic distance shot. An event is described that excites the reader's sympathy for Persikov. Persikov's response, however, is so inappropriate that the sympathy is lost amid condescending laughter. Persikov, for example, first loses his experimental chambers and then receives the news of his former wife's death. Persikov starts to cry, but for the wrong reason, the loss of the object, rather than of the human being: "his lips trembled like those of a child from whom one took suddenly, without any reason, his favorite toy." Ironically, a most human attribute, tears, is associated with something most inhuman, in fact, evil. Persikov's humanity is simultaneously asserted and denied.

The most blatant example of the incongruence of situation and conduct—of which the recording consciousness seems entirely unaware—is Persikov's death. When a mad crowd storms the Scientific Institute, he fails to flee to safety and shouts: "This is outright insanity! You are completely wild animals." Ironically, he is mad; his conduct has no logical relation to his insight. As with Gogol's Akaky Akakievich, the details surrounding Persikov's death cast a comic illumination over this tragic event, mixing two perspectives, two kinds of distance.

Since the recording consciousness of the story has proven to be unreliable, Bulgakov has to offer other sources of orientation. These are a symbolic leitmotif and symbolic phrases, and a systematic exposure of inadequate perceptions. He also relies on the reader's information about the historical period during which the catastrophe strikes. Oriented in this way, the reader is able to examine the narrative critically and to see how Bulgakov's narrative mechanism functions to ridicule contemporary social mores.

The most important sign of an authorial point of view and the most significant clue for the interpretation of the story is the symbolic leitmotif "red." The ray which the professor discovers is red, and it is revealed as demonic from the very outset. Though it is called the professor's child, it is a brain child, conceived by a "monstrous, fantastic accident" ("chudovishchnaia sluchainost´") which "leads to the devils knows what." Not sunlight but artificial light produces this false "spirit of life." All creatures that grow under the red ray have a special viciousness. A textual allusion to hell confirms the authorial intent: the chamber in which the scarlet ray appears is compared to hell.

Persikov becomes an instrument of metaphysical evil when he continues to experiment with the red ray, although he has seen and been appalled by its effects upon amoebas. He is tempted to dabble with life as it is given, and he succumbs to the temptation. He sins, driven, like Faust, by an obsessive curiosity; but his obsession, unlike Faust's, is an obsession in the void, and obsession without motivation. The authorial voice is audible when superstitious peasants call Rokk "anti-Christ" and want to kill him who dares to breed chickens unnaturally "by ray." When a superstitious mob kills Persikov, who committed the same sin with amoebas and frogs, the parallel to Rokk becomes clear.

From the outset much factual information about Persikov allows the reader to form a picture of him on the authorial

level. His mourning over the death of his experimental animals in contrast to the unlamented disappearance of his frog-hating wife and the causal reasoning about the starvation of the Institute's faithful watchman ("The cause of his death . . . was the same as that of the poor animals.") suggest that Persikov is a victimizer without human ethical consciousness, devoid of a sense of the value of life and of human limitations and responsibilities, a man with a non-normative, purely rational relationship to natural phenomena. When Persikov comments "very good" to a gory scene of vivisection (. . . "on the glass table a frog—half-choked and struck dumb with fear and pain—was *crucified* on a corkplate, its transparent viscera pulled out of its bloody abdomen into the microscope") the reader agrees with the comment of the dying frog: "you are rotten bastards . . . " Moreover, when Persikov "washes his hands," we encounter another authorial hint at Persikov's moral guilt.

The color red is not only symbolic of metaphysical evil, but of contemporary social-political devilry. The reader cannot avoid seeing **"The Fatal Eggs"** as an allegory of the Civil War, nor can he avoid the implication that revolution and communism share the qualities of the red ray, bring strife and evil, and interfere with the normal social and moral processes. Such interpretation imposes itself when one reads: "In the area, where the red, pointed sword of the ray lay, strange phenomena were taking place. The red strip teemed with life . . . Some force infused them with the spirit of life. They crawled in flocks and fought each other for a place in the ray. Within it a frenzied . . . process of multiplication went on . . . The red strip and the entire disk quickly became overcrowded, and the inevitable struggle began. The newborn ones attacked each other furiously, swallowing each other and tearing each other to shreds . . . The strongest were victorious. And these best ones were terrifying." The victorious invasion of the reptiles produced by the red ray becomes the ruthless "red" conquest during the Civil War.

The symbolic function of "red" becomes more explicit when Moscovites are said to read such journals as *Red Fire, Red Pepper, Red Journal, Red Projector, Red Evening Moscow, The Red Raven,* and *The Red Fighter.* Mr. Rokk collides with Persikov's discovery in his room at the "Red Paris Hotel," and he founds the experimental Sovkhoz "Red Ray." Furthermore, the characters who represent this contemporary "red" society resemble the amoebas in the viciousness of their fight for a place "in the red strip," that is, for material survival and well-being. The journalists, for example, fight with ruthless frenzy for an interview with Persikov; Bronsky, the victorious one, is the worst and most terrifying—like the victorious amoeba under the ray. These representatives of society are, in fact, marked as creatures of the devil. One of the members of the secret police is an "angel"—that is, a fallen angel—in patent leather boots, eyes hidden behind foggy glasses. The word "angel" ironically suggests the Biblical "guardian angel" ("angel khra-nitel´")—the secret police agents have officially come to guard Persikov's life—as well as "okhrana," the feared Third Section (secret police) of Nikolai I. These men betray, use, and destroy Persikov in the name of protecting him and his discovery.

Bronsky, employee of the journal *Red Raven* and member of the secret police possesses several features of the conventional devil. He is a foreigner and wears patent leather boots that resemble hooves. Furthermore he raves ("besnovalsia") and writes devilish stuff ("chertovshchina"). Rokk, similarly is not only greeted by Persikov as "devil"—he materializes when named and appears incognito, like Faust's poodle—but wears a yellow revolver, the color of evil. The "religious" peasants recognize him immediately as "anti-christ." As devil, he also plays the part of fate ("rok" = fate). His physical collision with Persikov suggests the collision of a society which lives according to what is symbolized by red (material survival of the fittest without any moral values), with an unscrupulous individual who experiments with an evil biological force.

Predictably, a disaster ensues. But are society and individual equally responsible for it? How authorially valid is such a statement as "its [the catastrophe's] primary cause was Persikov"? There is sufficient authorial evidence that Persikov is meant to be judged much less severely than the "red" society. Not only is he never equated (by simile or metaphor) with the evil red force he invokes, but he himself is not guided by the "ethical" maxim of the "red" society: the most powerful should survive. In fact, Persikov is unselfish as far as his personal material well-being is concerned. His guilt lies in an obsession with something inhuman and abstract, but nonetheless something outside himself. His fellow-citizens are entirely motivated by petty self-interest. Persikov is shown to have a moral sense, albeit a weak one: he does resist large-scale experimentation with his discovery. And some degree of innocence is suggested when people are said to relate to him as to a child and to find him naive. He is set apart from his society, though in an ambiguous way. He is admired as a great man, but feared as someone not entirely human; people relate to him with "reverence and terror."

More important still, Persikov is allowed to die and thus redeem his moral errors. He becomes the victim of a society which "shoots" him with a black camera; he is metaphorically killed by an inhuman publicity campaign in which political objectives override his individual rights. Voices report, falsely, but in anticipation of the real event, that Persikov was found with his throat slit open. Finally, his society "crucifies" him. Persikov emerges as a person evil in a Faustian sense, who has been victimized by forces even more evil than himself. Persikov gains moral stature by being placed in such an evil social context. Had he been placed in a society guided by traditional Christian ethics, his demonic pursuits would have found external limitations, and he would have been more of a Marlowian Faust. In **"The Fatal Eggs"** he is sinner and saint, victim and victimizer.

Ironically, society, the main culprit, has no chance for (nor is it, implicitly, worthy of) redemption and regeneration. The ignoble invasion of the reptiles chastises it, but only to deprecate it even more. An unnatural natural event is needed to save it, grotesquely and undeservedly, from utter peril, stamping it as incapable of tragedy, heroism or self-impelled regeneration. Had it perished in its fight against self-provoked evil, it could have been tragic; had it won, it could have been heroic. Finally, this solution implies that the "red" evil remains unexorcised from Soviet society.

Under the comic surface of the story, then, lurks a deep authorial concern with individual and social ethics. The introduction of a demonic biological force, supernatural evil, lifts the story out of its purely temporal context and universalizes the particular institutional and human shortcomings the story describes. As a result, the story asks questions about universal ethical principles, the individual's responsibility to himself and to society, and society's responsibility to the individual. The real-life situations and attitudes Bulgakov satirizes become symbolic embodiments of moral and philosophical problems thanks to the complex interplay between a symbolic pattern and his particular recording consciousness.

Helena Goscilo (essay date 1978)

SOURCE: "Points of View in Bulgakov's *Heart of a Dog*," in *Russian Literature Triquarterly,* No. 15, 1978, pp. 281-91.

[*Goscilo is a Scottish-born American critic, editor, and translator who specializes in Russian literature. In the following essay, she discusses the shifts of narrative voice in* The Heart of a Dog.]

Four narrative voices may be distinguished in **Heart of a Dog**: those of Sharik, Bormenthal, Professor Preobrazhensky, and an "impartial" commentator. Whereas the first three offer limited points of view, the fourth (with a few minor exceptions) is omniscient. Structure and point of view furnish mutual reinforcement, for Bulgakov allows the alternations in viewpoint to coincide roughly with the four divisions of the story: Chapters I through IV (pre-operation and operation) are filtered chiefly through Sharik's eyes; Chapter V (immediate post-operative results) comprises Bormenthal's laboratory journal; Chapters VI to IX (long-range effects of transformation) are mostly omniscient narration with occasional flashes from Preobrazhensky's perspective; and the Epilogue (reverse operation) reverts to an omniscient mode, briefly reinstating Sharik as the center of consciousness at the story's close. The impersonal narrator intrudes in all sections, his "objective" commentary disrupting or fusing with the subjective presentation of the three narrator-participants. His vantage point dominates the third section (Chapters VI to IX), for the fleeting insights into Preobrazhensky's inner world are rare. Most of the Epilogue, likewise, unfolds objectively, with only the last two paragraphs proceeding from Sharik. Upon careful examination, these apparently arbitrary shifts prove to be systematic and susceptible to a logical explanation; they are part of a tightly controlled technique.

Sharik, who is unquestionably the least conventional narrator insofar as he is a dog, ceases to narrate once he sheds his canine identity through the operation that transforms him into the objectionable pseudo-human Sharikov. Instead of steering the reader's perceptions, he becomes the chief object of the reader's and the other personae's focus, and justifiably so; he is, after all, the necessary subject of a scientific experiment. Until the metamorphosis, however, Sharik's point of view prevails. Clearly, then, his animal nature is requisite for certain qualities of narration that Bulgakov wishes to accentuate at the beginning and conclusion of the novel.

"Ooooww—oooww—ooow—! Look at me, I'm perishing"—with this desolate howl *cum* piteous exhortation, Sharik launches into eight paragraphs of uninterrupted interior monologue—an extended introduction that serves to kindle the reader's amused interest and capture his affection. To predispose the reader favorably to the mongrel—to move him by the dog's unenviable plight and to insure that he will place in Sharik the trust that one customarily invests in the narrating persona—Bulgakov enlists the aid of two major interrelated devices: he discloses Sharik's inner world directly, reproducing the dog's thought processes, and he transfuses the narrative with infectious humor. Sharik's philosophical musings, peppered with an astringent yet disingenuous commentary on the street-scene he surveys, reveal a broad range of winning qualities: epigrammatic cynical wisdom combined with simplistic naivete, stoic resilience, sensitivity of perceptions, acute moral awareness, and an attractive compassion for the world's unfortunates.

Sharik's endearing traits, moreover, are enhanced by the comic spirit in which the character of the dog is largely conceived. Through a series of corollary incongruities, Bulgakov refines upon the striking fundamental incongruity of a dog who is cogently articulate and, moreover, given to philosophical rumination. By cutting across boundaries that are conventionally assumed to separate the human domain from the purely animal, Bulgakov shrewdly taps a rich vein of humorous possibilities. For instance, Sharik arrives at various information that has conscious significance only for a human, but does so through deductive methods of an unabashedly canine nature. He deduces that it is 4 p.m. (preoccupation with clock time is surely the lamentable prerogative of humans?) from the smell of onions that emanates from the Immaculate (Prechistenka) fire station. Many of his conclusions and observations, in fact, are inspired by odors and the dilemma of acquiring food wherever possible (be it from garbage cans, benevolent cooks, etc.). Yet his observations are riddled with remarks that one is apt to identify only with a human mentality; they evidence a concern with prices, a knowledge of gourmets, and the like. Human values are clearly grafted onto a canine sensibility, and the resulting synthesis is often hilarious and moving.

Humor likewise is generated by the absurdity of Sharik's familiarity with and references to class distinctions and political slogans. An edge is lent to his indignation at the cook who scalded his side, for example, by the fact that the cook's action violated the much-vaunted Soviet doctrine of class solidarity: "The viper—and a proletarian too!" According to Sharik's accurate understanding of socialist stereotypes, at least in their ideal form, the cook's class origins should unite him by a common bond with his own kind (e.g., Sharik). Further, Sharik denounces garbage men (a profession by definition inimical to the canine world?) as "the lowest rubbish of all proletarians." Yet he reveres the memory of Vlas, a cook from Immaculate, for an openhandedness which, Sharik implies, is an outgrowth of Vlas's connections with the upper classes: "He is a grand character, God rest his soul, a gentleman's cook employed by Count Tolstoy's family and not the Food Ration Board." In short, Sharik is a street dog reared on Soviet cliches, but frankly appreciative of the finer things in life and the grandeur that attached to a class now officially defunct. His powers of discrimination enable Sharik to recognize Preobrazhensky immediately as a privileged and superior individual of exacting tastes. Overcome by admiration for the Professor's panache and lordly self-assurance, Sharik is quick to discern later that the insufferably self-righteous Shvonder and his cohorts are "outclassed" by the sybaritic scientist in all senses of the word. Insofar as he opts for an insulated affluence over the evangelical renunciation and continence of the proletariat, Sharik may be classified as a bourgeois.

For the opening segment of the first section, Bulgakov wisely confines the reader to Sharik's vision. By the time that the "little typist's" words of commiseration break into Sharik's sustained interior monologue, his hold on our trust and affection is solid. "The dog Sharik," as the objective narrator later confides, "possessed some secret which enabled him to conquer people's hearts"—including the reader's. At this stage Bulgakov reinforces our liking for the irresistible animal by introducing the omniscient narrative voice, whose very first words stress the pitiful aspect of Sharik's condition—his physical pain, his despair and loneliness, and the poignant "little dog tears" trickling from his eyes. Henceforth, Sharik's perspective and the omniscient mode alternate, the two voices frequently merging so as to become almost indistinguishable. Occasionally, too, narrated interior monologue gives way imperceptibly to interior monologue in its pure form. For example, the paragraph which ushers Preobrazhensky physically into the novel opens with what seems to be an impartial human intonation, yet halfway through it dissolves into Sharik's inimitable manner of speech. And the final sentence of the paragraph subsides into a growl. Such a blend inclines to bolster the reader's faith in Sharik, for it implies that Sharik's knowledgeability is in some way comparable to, if not on a par with, the "impartial" narrator's.

Having secured the reader's friendliness and compassion for Sharik, Bulgakov turns his attention to the task of heightening Preobrazhensky's image by focussing on it from the spunky little dog's stance. Bulgakov permits the scientist to reveal his humane charm personally—through his trenchant pronouncements, his amiable kindliness to Sharik; his consideration for his colleague Bormenthal and his servants Zina and Darya; his clear-headedness and freedom from unreasonable prejudices; his unshakable integrity; and his consummate aplomb in besting such nonentities as Shvonder. Capable of appreciating the spiritual (in art, and most notably opera) and the physical (in all aspects of creature comforts and especially in food—note the considerable space devoted to Preobrazhensky's meals and his enraptured disquisitions on the pleasures of fine cuisine), he emerges as a well-rounded and balanced human being—warm, generous, imaginative, yet disciplined and commonsensical. His own actions and words, as well as the universal homage accorded him, attest to his worth. What inflates Preobrazhensky's image to the proportions of heroic myth, however, is the halo cast over him by Sharik's perceptions. Bulgakov elevates the Professor in the reader's estimation by allowing Sharik to apply consistently to his master a vocabulary associated with magic, riches, and divinity.

Philip Philipovich Preobrazhensky's beard and mustaches are reminiscent of "knights of old"; he is a "dignified benefactor," an "immaculate personage," "a miraculous fur-coated vision," and "the sage of Immaculate" (repeated); he "thunders like an ancient prophet," and he is regularly identified with shining and glittering objects: "the gold rims of his glasses flash"; "a gold chain across his stomach shines with a dull glow"; his study "blazes with light"; his hair shines "like a silver halo"; "his glittering eyes" scrutinize his patients, while his eyeglasses "glitter" and his fox-fur coat "glitters with millions of snow-flakes." Not only do the devoted Bormenthal and a grateful patient observe reverentially that he is "a wizard, a magician," but Sharik, doing "obeisance" to Preobrazhensky after his colorful victory over Shvonder and his cronies, is convinced that his master is "the wizard, the magician, the sorcerer out of those dogs' fairy tales." Preobrazhensky is, indeed, one who performs the magical transformations that his name implies.

The language through which Sharik's enchanted worship of Preobrazhensky is communicated acquires a dubious tinge, however, with the operation. Immediately before he is anesthetised, Sharik glimpses with foreboding the "unusually brilliant lighting" of the operating room presided over by "the high priest," "the patriarch," "the divine figure." Once the mongrel loses consciousness, and as an automatic consequence, his command over point of view, Preobrazhensky "the priest" who "raises his hands as though blessing the unfortunate Sharik's difficult exploit," still shines and glistens with gold as he embarks upon his "conjuring tricks." But his image is contaminated by comparisons with figures of destruction, and the terms in which the operation itself is described reek of violence. Bormenthal is likened to a beast of prey and a tiger, Preobrazhensky to an inspired robber and a satiated vampire, and both to murderers. Furthermore, Bormenthal "shouts," "swoops," "squeezes," "grips," "leaps," "pounces," "pierces," and "plunges," while the Professor "barks," "growls," "roars," and "hisses" as he clenches his teeth, bares them to the gums, becomes "positively awe-inspiring," and flashes "a savage look" at his assistant. It is as though the two were reverting to atavistic

instincts as blood "spurts," the scalpel seems to "leap," and the patient's skull "shakes" and "squeaks." As a result of the emotionally-charged lexicon, the operation suggests the illicit enterprise of predatory beasts.

At this stage, then, Sharik is removed as the intermediary, the link between the professor and the reader. The scientist, who heretofore has impressed us most favorably when viewed through Sharik's partial eyes, becomes a slightly equivocal figure. His treacherous plan, steeped in duplicity, prevents the reader from giving his unqualified approval.

To summarize: in the first part of the novel, Sharik's angle of vision produces humor and wins the reader's fondness for the spirited mongrel. It also aggrandizes Preobrazhensky, the "transformer" of life, and engenders mystery, for Sharik remains ignorant of the significance of Preobrazhensky's conduct, as does the reader even after he learns about the operation to which the unconscious dog, naturally, cannot be privy.

The "great man's" assertion that Sharik is likable is placed in a key position—at the end of the first section—both to mitigate the reader's censorious attitude to Preobrazhensky, and to accentuate the ineffable charm of the mongrel who can no longer be his own spokesman. That charm contrasts dramatically with the provoking obnoxiousness of Sharikov in later parts of the narrative.

Bormenthal's laboratory diary constitutes the comparatively short second section. Its scientific format serves to lend plausibility to the fantastic events it records. Furthermore, the dry nature of what is at base a scientific ledger brings into sharper relief the subjective and emotional elements which penetrate with increasing momentum into Bormenthal's jottings and which humanize the portraits of both doctors. Stimulated by Bormenthal's awed adulation of his idol, the reader's esteem for Preobrazhensky revives. Whatever qualms the violence of the operation may have bred in the reader's mind dwindle in the face of the Professor's scientific brilliance and daring. Moreover, now that Sharik is an object of observation, the reader is distanced from him. Bulgakov's subtle control of narration encourages the reader to accept his own alienation from the being with whom he earlier sympathized so wholeheartedly. In fact, the reader is grateful for the dissociation, for the new developments that Bormenthal registers in Sharikov's (ex-Sharik's) personality coalesce to form a picture of an unscrupulous and somewhat repugnant vulgarian. Crudity, greed, and sloppiness are Sharikov's principal traits; his vocabulary consists primarily of curses and street invective. As Bormenthal dolefully notes, "His swearing is methodical, uninterrupted, and apparently absolutely meaningless." Both doctors, like the reader, find him repellent—a reaction that emerges clearly from Bormenthal's purportedly objective notations.

With the metamorphosis completed and the reader's sympathy transferred from Sharik to Preobrazhensky and his colleague, Bulgakov in the third and major portion of the novel switches to a narration that, with certain modifications, may be called omniscient. At no stage is the reader brought into proximity with Sharikov. The man-dog is seen exclusively from the outside, and whereas Sharik's character was revealed through the inner workings of his desires and thoughts, Sharikov's is shown solely through action. Where Sharik was the appealing and relatively passive victim, Sharikov is the selfish, cowardly, and destructive victimizer who initiates the disastrous incidents that bring his creators to the brink of despair. His infuriating behavior makes it impossible for the reader to cherish anything but amused contempt or vague revulsion for the creature. Perhaps the major reason for our dismayed withdrawal of sympathy is the paradoxical discovery that with his newly acquired human form, Sharikov becomes an utter animal. Those human qualities that made Sharik so winsome are replaced in Sharikov by baser impulses. Boasting distressingly meager intellectual resources, the intractable brute drinks to excess, eats unrestrainedly and grossly, steals, chases cats, and enjoys catching his own fleas with his teeth. Contentious and querulous, he is epicene, coarse, and motivated by pragmatic self-interest to an unprecedented degree. Preobrazhensky succinctly diagnoses the dismal state of affairs when he declares that "Sharikov now only shows traces of canine behavior and . . . [one] must remember that chasing cats is the best of the things he does! The whole horror of it is that he now has not a canine, but a human heart. And the rottenest heart of any existing in nature!"

What contributes substantially to the reader's alienation from Sharikov is the latter's alliance with Shvonder. While Sharik was clearsighted enough to despise the scoundrel's stubborn mediocrity, Sharikov, by contrast, seems drawn to it. In other words, Sharik, his animal nature notwithstanding, was immeasurably more acute, tasteful, and honorable than the pseudo-human Sharikov.

Preobrazhensky, who was formerly well-nigh deified, becomes totally humanized in the third section as his customary composure starts to erode. In addition to the laudable characteristics that he exhibited earlier, he now reveals vulnerability, moral courage, a capacity for self-criticism, and an uncommon readiness to shoulder responsibility. If only through his ability to retain honor and dignity in the midst of havoc and his steadfast fairness and magnanimity to Fyodor, Zina, Darya, and Sharikov's duped little typist, to whom he gives money, he earns the reader's unreserved respect. That the "objective" narrator wishes to redirect our sympathies to Preobrazhensky may be gathered from the fact that it is now he who not unlike Sharik, calls the professor "a gray-haired Faust" and "an ancient king of France." Less a seer than an individual valiantly battling overwhelming odds, the Professor is portrayed as a man beleaguered by doubts, hounded by the inane conjectures and speculations of the press, plagued by the calumnious denunciations of Shvonder, and exasperated beyond endurance by the increasingly abusive humanoid he himself has manufactured. The uneasiness and sufferings that the Professor undergoes are accented in a number of ways: through the narrator's references to both his mental fatigue and his physical deterioration; through Bormenthal's solicitous endeavors to spare Preo-

brazhensky's taut nerves from further irritation by Sharikov's outlandish antics; and through Philip Philipovich's own reflections, which the narrator occasionally presents as narrated interior speech. Secondary characters—Zina, Darya, Fyodor—all commiserate with the scientist's plight, thereby indicating that Sharikov is insupportable by everyone's standards.

Approximately equal attention is allotted in the section to Sharikov's wanton displays of unmitigated idiocy and to the barely mastered sense of outrage they arouse in the professor. The penultimate division of the last chapter in the third section concludes on a note, however, that spotlights the visible signs of Preobrazhensky's psychic strain and distress: "Philip Philipovich merely gestured in despair. And the patient noticed that the professor had becomed stooped and recently seemed to have grown grayer." That is our last close-up of the scientist in the section, and it is one which stirs our compassion.

The narrative of the very short passage that follows unfolds from the standpoint of the "impersonal" commentator who, at appropriate junctures, falls prey to the confused ignorance of Gogol's deceptively ingenuous narrator. He purposely withholds information from the reader even as he actively whets his curiosity. If, indeed, "we are all like Scheherazade's husband, in that we want to know what happens next" [E. M. Forster, *Aspects of the Novel,* 1927], the mystification created by Bulgakov's idiosyncratic teller artfully plays upon our impatience. In order to augment suspense and to keep the reader puzzled as to the true nature of what is called the Professor's "crime," he enigmatically refers to the act as "it," suspends key explanatory sentences in midpoint and leaves them dangling, and repeats the neighbors' subsequent statement about what they witnessed that evening without corroborating or denying its veracity. Such tactics successfully heighten the emotional intensity of an event that essentially stays unidentified until the Epilogue. By contrast to the preceding parts of the novel, which were presented scenically, this passage is handled in the panoramic manner. As a result, summary replaces dramatization, the immediacy of the former scenes vanishes, and the pace is accelerated. Here Bulgakov prepares the reader for the compressed Epilogue that unveils the mystery and rapidly ties up the threads of the novel.

With the Epilogue comes a release in tension, the reemergence of the old Preobrazhensky—"masterful," "energetic," "dignified," "regal"—and a continuation of "impersonal" narration. As soon as Sharikov is summoned upon the scene it becomes clear that he is beginning to revert to Sharik; the Professor's mysterious "crime" is in reality a blessing, for it redresses his central error and reverses the transformation effected by the first operation. Vestiges of the insensate and sulky boor are still perceptible in Sharikov, but his canine aspect is visibly dominant in the final confrontation with Shvonder and the police. Because Bulgakov takes pains to emphasize that Sharikov is undergoing a speedy change to his original shape, the reader correctly anticipates another encounter with Sharik the dog *qua* narrator.

At the close of the novel Sharik has completely regained his canine form and consequently his control over the narrative viewpoint and the reader's responses. The "impartial" voice interjects itself regularly into Sharik's thoughts, but it is unmistakably Sharik who, basking in the domestic equilibrium of his restored paradise, once more admires Preobrazhensky as "the higher being, the powerful benefactor of dogs," and "the gray-haired magician." What is evoked in the concluding passage is the secluded coziness of Chapter III. As in the earlier scenes, the resolute Professor, singing his favorite motif from *Aida*, is absorbed in his scientific research; Sharik gratefully acknowledges his debt to his stylish master and, blessing fate for his rediscovered haven, artlessly speculates upon his background. Not only has Preobrazhensky vindicated Sharik's belief in his magical prowess and beneficence, but he has passed honorably the stringent moral test of acknowledging his colossal blunder. In so doing he has exonerated himself before that reader who insists upon a continuity between ends and means and who deplores man's gratuitous tampering with the processes of nature. Moral strength brings it own rewards; harmony and tranquility reign in the apartment where "the blinds shut out the thick Immaculate night with its lone star."

To a reader attuned to the implications behind the novel's shifts in narration, a return to Sharik's viewpoint is synonymous with a retreat to trust and affection. The reader's faith in a benign presence that oversees the activities of men is affirmed, for the resolution of *Heart of a Dog*, with its triumphant reinstatement of Sharik's naively wise perspective, testifies to Woland's comforting truism [in *Master i Margarita*] that "all will be as it should; that is what the world rests on."

Bulgakov's stories [in *Notes of a Young Doctor*] will often provoke the reader to laughter and still more often bring a smile to his lips, not because they are humorous but because they give intense artistic pleasure, so lively, so talented and realistic is his writing.

—*Vladimir Lakshin, in a review of* Notes of a Young Doctor, *in* Soviet Literature, *February, 1964.*

A. Colin Wright (essay date 1978)

SOURCE: "Development of a Writer, 1891-1921" and "Moscow and Journalism, 1921-24," in *Mikhail Bulgakov: Life and Interpretations,* University of Toronto Press, 1978, pp. 3-31, 32-44.

[*Wright is an English educator, author, and critic. In the following excerpt, he discusses* Notes of a Young Doctor *and the short fiction of Bulgakov that appeared in various Russian journals in the early 1920s.*]

The publication of Bulgakov's medical stories dates from a later period, but he probably made notes for some of them while he was still in Nikolskoe [in the Sychyovka district of Smolensk province in 1916-17], and certainly he made drafts before he left Kiev . . . in 1919. There are nine of them altogether, all except one published in a medical journal, *Meditsinskii rabotnik,* between 1925 and 1927. In order of publication these are: **'First Breech,' 'Snowstorm,' 'Egyptian Darkness,' 'Starry Rash,' 'Towel with a Rooster,' 'The Missing Eye,' 'I Killed,'** and **'Morphine.'** It seems that Bulgakov intended to publish at least some of these as one book, in imitation perhaps of Vikenty Veresaev's very successful *Notes of a Doctor* of 1901. But it was not until 1963 that five of the above were published together, in a small paper edition put out by the 'Ogonek' library, under the title *Notes of a Young Doctor*. Included too was one story, **'Silver Throat,'** not previously published in *Meditsinskii rabotnik,* somewhat revised by the editors to make its details consistent with other stories. The same five stories were reprinted in the authoritative *Selected Prose* edition of 1966, and now Bulgakov's **'Steel Throat'** was substituted, unamended, for the 'Ogonek' editors' **'Silver Throat,'** and placed second instead of third.

It is convenient to treat the six stories of *Notes of a Young Doctor* as one work, leaving aside for the present **'Starry Rash,' 'I Killed,'** and **'Morphine,'** which were not included. Apart from the inconsistencies of **'Steel Throat'** (chronological detail, the narrator's age, the number of his patients) and a few other minor discrepancies, the stories are relatively consistent with each other, linked by setting and characters, principally the narrator, and follow in a definite time sequence. They involve a doctor's first year of practice: his fears because of his inexperience, the operations he performs successfully (an amputation, a tracheotomy, a breech delivery), his own secluded life, the growth of his practice.

Made up of individual incidents over the course of a year, these stories have a charm and simplicity which is extraordinarily appealing, and indeed this collection belongs to the best of Bulgakov. It has received praise, justifiably, from critics and doctors alike. In some ways the stories are almost written to a formula, involving three stages: the narrator's thoughts and fears, or memories of other cases; some sudden happening involving the need for decision and action; and the successful conclusion, bringing about a greater understanding on the part of the narrator. In the six collected stories there is little variation from this set pattern. Underlying them too is an outlook on life which reflects Bulgakov's own, for many of the themes which occur in his later works can be found here in some form or other.

The centre of interest in these stories is the personality of the narrator: a narrator who is all too human, even if he is a qualified doctor. The reader can identify with him precisely because his attitudes are those of all of us in

Bulgakov with his third wife, Elena Sergeevna Shilovskaya, in the early 1930s.

unfamiliar situations. Afraid of his youth and the impression he makes, he deliberately tries to make himself look older, without success. He stands in awe of things he does not understand, instruments in the hospital he is unfamiliar with, the well-stocked pharmacy. While even the assistants and midwives seem to be more experienced than he is, above all he is tormented by the memory of his predecessor, who of course knew everything and compared to whom he is a 'False Dmitry,' an impostor. Objectively, his fears are exaggerated, for we as readers well know that he will come through; but it is for this reason that we can smile upon the narrator's sense of inadequacy, at his feeling cold with fear when faced with a difficult case, at his constant sweat when operating. Bulgakov frequently makes use of an interior monologue or a dialogue with some inner voice to express the narrator's thoughts, which are amusing in that they dwell always on the possibilities of disaster:

' . . . and what will you do about a hernia?' fear stubbornly insisted in the form of a voice.

'I'll sit him in the bath,' I defended myself in a rage. 'In the bath. And I'll try to reduce it.'

'A strangulated one, my dear fellow! What earthly use are baths then! A strangulated one,' fear sang in a demonic voice. 'You'll have to cut him open . . . '

Yet contrasting with this fear there is an equally exaggerated pride, in which the narrator delights: he performs operations without spilling a drop of blood; when his assistants compliment him, as is frequently the case, he pretends to be more experienced or assured than in fact. But he is honest enough to admit to this boasting and to be ashamed of such pretensions. Underneath everything, he knows that potentially he is a good doctor, but still only at the beginning, that he must constantly be learning. It is this that is emphasized in the last story, **'The Missing Eye,'** where after thinking over all that he has been through and learnt he becomes boastful—'I positively cannot imagine their bringing me a case which could stump me . . . '—then makes a mistake which could have cost a boy his eye, and is duly humbled.

These feelings that Bulgakov is describing are common to anyone placed in a position of responsibility: the clinical details are not important so much as the choices the narrator is called upon to make and his own attitude towards them. There is here a certain fundamental honesty.

Bulgakov shows an extraordinary ability to make fun of himself through his narrator: to look humorously at his actions and analyse his inner feelings, his fears, his depressions, his pride in the job he is doing.

In Bulgakov's later work one of the principal themes is that of the writer and his struggle in life. Here his doctor is just as much of an artist, struggling against inner and outer forces, and taking pride in his hard-won professionalism. On a more general level, this applies to any conscientious person. The first struggle is with oneself, one's own treacherous thoughts and the temptation to take the easy way out—'"Die. Die quickly," I thought, "please die. Otherwise what shall I do with you?"' But man finds surprising reserve powers for, despite the cowardice of his thoughts, his inner self takes over and accomplishes things he would not have thought possible. This is no mere accident but, in medicine at least, the result of training and the acquisition of certain attitudes—and the same surely is true of other professions. It leads one to act seemingly against one's own interests, even against common sense—as when, in **'Steel Throat,'** the narrator persuades a mother and grandmother to allow an operation he does not know if he can do. Here, the contrast between the narrator's desires and the words he speaks provides an obvious source of comedy: 'Within myself I thought "What am I doing? I'll just butcher the girl." But I spoke differently: "Hurry up, hurry up, agree! Agree! Look, her nails are already turning blue."' Even in a different situation, when the narrator is almost attacked by wolves when returning from a patient, this inner man takes over, avoiding agonizing decisions in the face of the need for action. It is the same with Bulgakov's later heroes. As men of integrity, all do what they know they must despite the real dangers they face.

In *Notes of a Young Doctor* man's interior struggles are often expressed in physical form, on the down-to-earth level of comfort as opposed to necessity: the narrator is constantly being interrupted—from sleep, from having a bath, from shaving. This is the whole point of the story **'Snowstorm,'** where he is called out from a day of rest to a girl who then dies before the doctor can do anything. What is important is the bath he can at last enjoy, contrasted with the discomforts of the drive and then the cold misery of the return when he and the coachman get lost in the snow. The story is reminiscent of Tolstoy's 'Master and Man' but with the difference that in Tolstoy the main character is a merchant travelling to make a profit, whereas here we have a doctor who is travelling only because of his sense of duty. And he, in contrast to the merchant, lives, swearing that he will never go out again like this— but knowing quite well that he will not refuse when the time comes. This is the first time that Bulgakov uses the image of the snowstorm—emphasized by an epigraph from Pushkin—but we . . . find it again in other of his works. It has been suggested [by A. M. Al'tshuler, in "Bulgakov-Prozaik," *Literaturnaia gazeta,* February 7, 1968] that the storm is the aesthetic equivalent of the Revolution, that the way through it is shown by the lamp of the

hospital symbolizing science and light. But it is hardly necessary to find such a specific reference. Man is simply alone in an apparently hostile world: he cannot tame it or change it, but he can find his own area where there is light and civilization, try to cling on to this and extend it.

A related theme, . . . is the struggle against ignorance, the 'Egyptian darkness' which impedes the growth of civilization and, like the storm, is a force of its own. It finds its expression most often in the ignorance of the peasants, those 'benighted people' who lack understanding and actively prevent enlightenment: the grandmother in **'Steel Throat,'** superstitiously afraid of the surgeon's knife and sure all the child needs is some medicine when she is already on the point of suffocation; a father-in-law who makes a pregnant woman walk five kilometres to the hospital to give birth because he does not want to give her horses for nothing. The story **'Egyptian Darkness'** opens appropriately with a description of physical darkness—in the village where the nearest kerosene lamps are nine kilometres away. There follows a whole series of stories of peasants' stupidity: the woman who gets enough medicine to share it with all the village, or the man who applies mustard plasters on top of his sheepskin coat. And the narrator, determined to struggle with this darkness, gets caught himself with a patient of seeming intelligence who takes all his pills at the same time because he thinks that this will be more effective.

Such themes we can find in many of Bulgakov's feuilletons, and in some of his later works as well. Darkness is not only a matter of ignorance: it is often one of self-interest, narrow-mindedness, dogmatism, or, on a more philosphical level, of evil. And to achieve light in one's own life is a struggle, too, involving both learning and experience: '"One can obtain great experience in the country," I thought as I went to sleep, "but one must just read, read, as much as possible . . . read."'

Of course, there is a more fundamental struggle too, between life and death: the basic *raison d'être* of the doctor. As a medical student Bulgakov had on his wall a sign which read *quod medicamenta non sanat, mors sanat* (Hippocrates): what medicine does not cure, death cures. This might almost have been an epigraph to these stories, when it would sound not as a piece of cynicism but as a grim warning. As a doctor, Bulgakov is aware that death is his one real enemy. 'Death' plays an important role in his other works, too; later he will explore its meaning, the whole problem of immortality and of the life which has gone before, particularly in *The Master and Margarita.* Here it is expressed in simple physical terms. It is always ugly, as opposed to those it threatens who, significantly, are young and beautiful. Theirs is the beauty of life itself, and sometimes, inevitably, it is extinguished.

Such are the human problems which are presented even in these early stories. Yet for all their seriousness, they are humorous, even light-hearted, for the reader knows that in the end all will turn out well, even after the death in **'Snowstorm.'** There is here an optimism that difficulties will be overcome. 'Bulgakov writes lightly and gayly. Only his is the gaiety not of heedlessness but of conquered timidity and inexperience—which makes it the most lasting and intelligent gaiety there can be' [Vladimir Lakshin, in a review of *Notes of a Young Doctor*, in *Soviet Literature*, February 1964]. Bulgakov's light-heartedness stems partly from his condescending treatment of his own narrator and partly from his use of dialogue. He never allows a description to continue too long without inserting dialogue in some form: either another person's words, or the narrator's own thoughts, or the narrator's 'second voice.' In this is reflected at different times the comical speech of the peasant, the seriousness of the medical staff, and of course all the different tones of the narrator himself: fear, pride, boastfulness, urgency. Because we see through the narrator in all his assumed roles, the total effect is a humorous one.

If we turn to the three medical stories not included in *Notes of a Young Doctor*, we find that thematically there is a certain similarity, but the light-hearted tone is absent. **'Starry Rash,'** about the horrors of syphilis, is another story emphasizing the 'darkness,' the ignorance of the peasants. But it is too didactic, and the concern too specific: we are no longer interested in the narrator but in a medical and social problem. So too with **'Morphine,'** a wearisome account of a doctor's addiction (when it was republished in *Russkaia mysl'* in March and April 1970, a whole page of the original was omitted accidentally without its being noticeable). **'I Killed'** is more interesting, showing a doctor taking life in order to escape from the brutal soldiers of the Ukrainian nationalist Petlyura in 1919; but again, it is lacking in humour and hardly belongs in the cycle of the other stories.

Quite apart from the opposition of Bulgakov's widow to publishing **'Morphine,'** it would seem unlikely that he himself intended these three stories to be collected with the others. (He made no attempts even to bring names in **'Morphine'** in line with the rest.) The main reason for setting them aside was undoubtedly an artistic one. The inclusion of any one of them would destroy the collection's present artistic unity, for they take us outside the world of a young doctor in his first year of practice; nor do they have the same uniformity of style.

Notes of a Young Doctor, as it is, makes a consistent, satisfactory whole. Its tone is humorous throughout—and Bulgakov is often at his best when serious issues are combined with comedy. He is, of course, writing in a minor form. A work such as Veresaev's *Notes of a Doctor,* which treats broadly the same subject, is far more weighty and gives a deeper insight into the kind of moral dilemmas a doctor may face. Bulgakov has none of Veresaev's long theoretical discussions. But artistically his work is more satisfying, its strength lying in its careful selection of incidents, which give an *impression* of a young man's problems in his chosen profession. The reader relates to the narrator as a person rather than as a doctor, for in this collection (if not in **'Starry Rash'** and **'Morphine'**) literature comes before medicine. Bulgakov in his stories aimed basically at simplicity as the hallmark of

good writing. In *Notes of a Young Doctor* he achieves this admirably, while raising issues to which he was to devote a lifetime of thought.

. . . . .

Of all the feuilletons Bulgakov wrote at the beginning of the twenties, those published in *Gudok* are the least ambitious from a literary viewpoint. Therein lies their charm. Totally unpretentious, written hastily for monetary reward, they are amusing, simple, and direct: revealing Bulgakov's mastery in just telling a funny story. There are over a hundred readily identifiable stories of this type in *Gudok* for the years between 1923 and 1926, and it is probable that there are other similar ones either overlooked or hiding under unidentified pseudonyms, both in *Gudok* and elsewhere. We may add to these Bulgakov's published volume of *Stories* of 1926, containing a number of reprints from *Gudok,* a number from *Nakanune,* and five more not published earlier but also of the *Gudok* type. (This volume was published by *Smekhach,* a humorous magazine which the 'Gudok' press printed. Another collection of stories, advertised for publication by *Nedra,* never appeared, having apparently been banned.)

The feuilletons are essentially based on true events, on information sent in by the 'working correspondents.' Taken as a whole, they provide a surprisingly vivid picture of life among the ordinary workers in the years following the Revolution and civil war. They are characterized by brevity, by their concentration on one single humorous incident or situation, and by their satirical purpose. They are almost entirely situational comedy, with considerable reliance on dialogue. The style is conversational: Bulgakov, for example, will often add 'serve him right!' to a story where a wrong-doer is caught and punished. Some have a strong plot (as the story about a locksmith who simulates various illnesses to make money on medical payments, until he is caught: **'A Nasty Type'**); some are purely descriptive with scarcely a plot at all. Frequently the emphasis is on abuses brought about by people's ignorance and stupidity, and there is a constant, sometimes expressed, hope that things will improve after those responsible have been made to look foolish.

The feuilletons are described most easily in terms of a few of their recurrent themes. Bureaucracy of one kind or another is perhaps the most prominent target of Bulgakov: workers not getting what they are entitled to (**'The R.K.K.,' 'The Libertine'**); the need to get official stamps and signatures on documents (**'The Trouble with Stamps'**); officiousness or overzealousness making life difficult (**'Skull-Hunters'**); or officialdom being a hiding-place for fraud and deceit (**'False-Dimitry Lunacharsky,' 'A Bewitched Place,' 'How the Local Committee Bought a Present with an Old Woman's Money'**). On the one hand, workers—such as telephone operators—use their job to their own advantage (**'On the Telephone,' 'The Undismayed Operators,'**); on the other, getting paid is a constant problem (**'The Effective Remedy,' 'The Desired Payment,' 'Three Kopecks'**). Party meetings are another theme: speakers do not turn up (**'The Station-Master's**

Cradle') or come with an agenda three years out of date, which is still discussed ('**The Wrong Trousers**'); a drunk gives a lecture on syphilis for women's day ('**Festival with Syphilis**'); another is thrown out of a theatrical performance ('*Inspector General* **with an Ejection**'). Drunkenness itself is a frequent theme ('**A Story of Beer,**' '**On the Usefulness of Alcoholism,**' '**A Drunken Steam-Engine**'). There are stories about the problems of getting rations ('**How Buton Got Married**') or about inefficiencies in the commercial trusts ('**A New Method of Book Distribution**'). As we might expect, there are a number of medical stories too ('**Man with a Thermometer,**' '**The Flying Dutchman**'). And there are more grotesque ones with corpses continuing, by habit, to do what they did when alive ('**Adventures of a Dead Man,**' '**When the Dead Rise from Their Graves,**' '**The Dead Walk**'). Or there are the simple oddities: the shunning of a man with the same name as the White general Wrangel ('**Trick of Nature**') or a dream about the former tsar travelling by tram ('**The Conductor and a Member of the Imperial Family**'). Typical of Bulgakov at his most amusing is '**Political Director of Divine Worship,**' in which a school and a church are in adjoining buildings and everything can be heard from the other—with the result that there is a hilarious dialogue of political and religious slogans, while the deacon gets drunk and is almost converted to communism. Ludicrous and yet all too probable in this new society, exaggerated perhaps and always containing a strong element of social satire—with the author's sympathy on the side of the individual—stories like this had an immediate appeal to *Gudok*'s readers.

One of the earliest feuilletons published there is rather different from the others: '**The Raid,**' concerning a sentry, Abram, who is captured and beaten up by the enemy, only just escaping with his life. Years later, someone in a workers' club is telling of his war adventures and the others turn to Abram, now deaf, never expecting that he will have anything to tell: when he does, they can hardly believe it is true. It is simple and unpretentious, as are the other feuilletons, and very moving. Without humour or satire, describing instead the simple feelings of an ordinary man and his one moment of involuntary heroism, it is a step away from journalism into the realm of literature. . . .

. . . . .

The *Nakanune* feuilletons are altogether more ambitious, longer, and more varied in scope. . . . [We] may divide them into those that are largely literary description and those that tell a definite story. In all of them, Bulgakov is very much the writer of the town, and indeed he has been described as the 'singer' of Moscow in the same way that Pushkin, Gogol, Dostoevsky, and Blok were the singers of St Petersburg.

His descriptions relate entirely to the Moscow he was living in, and specifically to the time of the New Economic Policy, which allowed, temporarily, for the re-

establishment of private enterprise and ownership. Bulgakov describes the 'nepmen'—those who took advantage of the policy—and the new 'red specialists,' also the black market ('**Under a Glass Sky**'). He talks too of the ordinary people in the shops, and the outward show and glitter of the goods there as opposed to the real hunger that still existed ('**Red-stoned Moscow**'). The most successful of such descriptions is '**Forty Times Forty,**' which contrasts the 'heroic' Moscow of 1921 with the new Moscow of the NEP. Starting as a gradual humming of which everyone soon becomes aware, the NEP develops into all the noise of a busy, thriving city, with its bright lights, businesses, fashionable restaurants. Although Bulgakov clearly takes pride in the growth of 'mother Moscow' he has no particular love for the nepmen, whom he fears 'at the thought that they were filling all Moscow, that they had gold ten-rouble coins in their pockets, that they would throw me out of my room, that they were strong, had large teeth, were wicked, with hearts of stone.' Yet he is impressed by the vigour of the new society around him, by such achievements as the impressive Agricultural Exhibition ('**The Golden Town**'), by the new orderliness, which he praises in '**Chanson d'été**' and '**The Capital in My Notebook.**' The second of these particular feuilletons serves as a vehicle for Bulgakov to describe all kinds of things going on in Moscow: reconstruction, nepmen flourishing, the opera, a well-behaved schoolchild, a man so wealthy he is a trillionaire. (These last two scenes appeared in English translation the same year, in *The Living Age*.) He expresses his opinion of the theatre, and in particular his dislike of Meyerhold's 'biomechanics.' He is concerned, too, with what will become of the intelligentsia, but shows optimism, despite everything, that it will survive.

Bulgakov is remarkably fair towards the society he is describing: he does not condemn or praise as a whole, although he does not hesitate to describe his individual likes and dislikes. His own experiences clearly play a large part in what he writes (see, in particular, '**A Day of Our Life,**' with its conversations and with its frustrations), but despite this he never forces his views on the reader or implies that things were better in former times. Indeed, he seems to have accepted the new order, and writes with a simple love of his country, with all its faults. Each piece reads like a 'letter from Moscow'—which, of course, to his readers in Berlin it undoubtedly was. The appeal is mainly to those who know and love Moscow: the interest was in 'what it's like now,' and Bulgakov provides details both of the familiar and the new. Thus in '**Red-stoned Moscow**' he tells what the NEP is like, but finishes with an image of eternal Moscow, with the chimes from the Kremlin bell and the 'Kitay-gorod' lying close by. It is similar in '**Travel Notes,**' which describes a train journey: there is a new Bryansk station, but the same old queues; boys are still selling preserves at stations en route, but illegally, since passengers are now supposed to use the special shops. Even the descriptions of demonstrations against Lord Curzon ('**Lord Curzon's Benefit Day**'—also translated in *The Living Age*) are interesting largely in that they take place against the familiar background of Moscow, for which Bulgakov shows a love that the reader can be expected to share. So, too, in **'Kiev—a Town,'** in all Bulgakov's survey of the recent history, in all his discussions on Kievans as compared with Muscovites, on churches, on the NEP, there lies a basic appeal to the reader's familiarity with Moscow itself, to his love for it—which Bulgakov still shares deeply: 'In a word, a beautiful town, a happy town. The mother of Russian towns.'

Bulgakov shows a remarkable sense of his audience. Today we can still feel something of this appeal—the Russian certainly can—but now for most of us these feuilletons must seem more like period pieces, essays representing journalism of high quality rather than strictly literary writing.

The same may be said of some of those that tell a story. Two such feuilletons, **'Golden Documents'** and **'Sparkling Life'** (both subtitled 'From My Collection'), consist of a number of tales of the same type that are in *Gudok*: four of these even appear alongside them in the 1926 *Stories*. 'Sparkling Life' has some particularly weak items, hardly more than funny jokes. A few other feuilletons too are typical newspaper stories: a friend who has a final fling before being arrested (**'Cup of Life'**), a horse-dealer who makes money by murder (**'The Komarov Case'**), a bank director ruined by his speculator brother (**'The Belobrysov Story'**).

A number, however, demand greater attention. One, **'The Crimson Island,'** a low burlesque on the Revolution, was the basis for a play. . . . More important is **'The Adventures of Chichikov,'** which would be included in the *Diavoliada* collection—and was also at one time forbidden for public reading. It is linked with the other feuilletons in *Nakanune* in that primarily it is a satire on life in Moscow and on the NEP. It differs from them in that it is a comic imitation of Gogol, using not only his situations and characters—mainly but not exclusively from *Dead Souls*—but many of his actual sentences as well. In a 'dream,' Chichikov, the hero of *Dead Souls* (which had 'The Adventures of Chichikov' as an alternative title) reappears in Moscow in Soviet times, and finds there all his old acquaintances. Very little has changed, except for the names. Chichikov first wangles extra rations for himself, following Sobakevich's example, then, inspired by Nozdryov, goes into the export business and builds up a completely non-existent enterprise (in Gogol's original he has, of course, built up an estate of non-existent serfs).

The elements of satire need little elaboration: the little change since Gogol's day, the same people still occupying important positions, the petty crooks such as Chichikov and Nozdryov managing to survive in Soviet times very nicely. There are some clever instances of parody too, with sufficient of Gogol's thought kept intact and combined with the modern situation to create incongruities almost of the type that we find in his own prose. Thus Gogol's famous description of the troika and the Russians' love of speed is applied to the motor car and a rather different picture from the uninterrupted drive through the Russian countryside results:

What Russian does not love a swift ride?

Selifan loved it, too, and therefore at the entrance to Lubyanka he was forced to choose between a trolley car and a plate-glass store window. In a brief instant of time Selifan chose the latter, swerved away from the trolley, and like a whirlwind, screaming 'Help!' drove through the store window.

'The Adventures of Chichikov' is an amusing and witty story, but not perhaps a work of major importance. Its merit lies in its basic idea—the application of Gogol to modern times. The imitation is well sustained, the parallels are ingenious, but beyond this there is not a great deal of depth.

One of the earliest feuilletons deserves to be better known: **'Red Crown (*Historia morbi*)'** of 1922. (The Soviet scholar M. Chudakova suggests that this may be identified with the 'Illness' Bulgakov mentions in his letters—and that it

---

An excerpt from Lyubov Belozerskaya-Bulgakova's biography of her life with Bulgakov:

An entire Pleiade of writers came out of *The Whistle* (how lucky for that magazine!): Mikhail Bulgakov, Yury Olesha—then still only a columnist known as "Zubilo" who wrote in verse on topics of the day, and Valentin Kataev and later his brother Evgeny Petrov, all of them worked there. Olesha remembers those days touchingly in his memoirs.

Later at some festivity at the paper, Olesha read the epigram he'd dedicated to Bulgakov:

> Treating everyone the same
> Clinking his rusty pen
> Was Bulgakov the rewrite man,
> But today he's the evil of the day.

Mikhail Afanasievich [Bulgakov] wrote quickly, almost in bursts. This is what he himself has to say about the matter: "It took me between eighteen and twenty minutes, including time out for smoking and whistling, to write a column of 75 lines. To have it typed, including giggling with the typist, took eight minutes. In a word, a half an hour and it was all finished."

I recently re-read more than a hundred of Bulgakov's feuilletons printed in *The Whistle*. He signed them differently, but in spite of the various pseudonyms it is still possible to recognize his "handwriting." No matter how light Bulgakov himself made of his work as a rewriter, it played a certain role in his creative work by serving as a springboard for his moving to serious literary work. His grasp of plot, his easy dialog, his inventiveness and humor—it is all here.

Lyubov Belozerskaya-Bulgakova, in her My Life with Mikhail Bulgakov, *translated by Margareta Thompson, 1983.*

may also be a stage in the composition of *The White Guard*.) It is about a narrator haunted by the image of his dead brother Kolya, and by that of a man hanged by the White general whom Kolya served. It is a powerful story of the horror and senselessness of the civil war, and the bestiality of the hangings that took place. The responsibility for this, however, lies not with the general alone but also with the narrator, and a bond is formed between the two in their common guilt: 'Who knows, perhaps that dirty begrimed man from the lamppost in Berdyansk comes to you. If so, we suffer justly. I sent Kolya to help you hang others, and you did the hanging.' The burden of accepting such guilt is intolerable: the narrator goes mad. The story is a brilliant precursor to Bulgakov's play *Flight,* where the theme of responsibility and illness brought on by repeated hangings is central.

Four of the *Nakanune* stories were republished in 1926 in a paper book entitled *A Treatise on Housing*—the name of the first of them. This story was originally the first part of a feuilleton entitled **'Moscow of the Twenties'** (the second—about the ruses people employ to obtain or keep an apartment—was not republished). From a literary point of view **'A Treatise on Housing'** is the least satisfactory of the four. The housing shortage in Moscow and the pressures caused by overcrowding are illustrated by a story of three people living in a telephone receiver [sic] and their inevitably muddled conversations, and by the arguments that go on in the author's own apartment block. Although Bulgakov's usual witty style can be appealing ('This winter Natalya Egorovna threw a mop rag on the floor and couldn't unstick it because it was nine degrees above the table and on the floor there were no degrees at all—and it even lacked one') there is a certain facetiousness, particularly in the hyperbole of the telephone receiver, that is annoying; it is neither fantasy nor realism.

The same theme is treated more effectively in **'Four Portraits.'** In the Moscow of that time a person was allowed only a certain amount of 'living space': anyone with more had to accept other lodgers, often total strangers, who could nevertheless not be ejected. The process was known as *uplotnenie*—which is most easily translated as 'doubling up.' The story concerns a man's efforts to prevent this, and our sympathies are entirely with him rather than with the commissions who come to inspect his apartment. He is, in fact, an early example of the 'sympathetic crook' who is to feature in many of Bulgakov's later writings. The third story, **'A Lake of Home-brew,'** describing a drunken brawl which goes on for nearly twenty-four hours in the narrator's own apartment block, is interesting largely for what it tells us about Bulgakov's own life.

Most outstanding, however, is **'A Psalm,'** one of the best stories of this period: about a neighbour's four-year-old boy, his father, who has gone away, and his mother who returns to kiss with the narrator after the boy has gone to bed. It is a most moving story of loneliness yet affection as a result of grief—emphasized by the boy with his ordinary child's concerns and lack of understanding. It is remarkable, too, for its use of leitmotifs: cones of light

from the kerosene lamp; door hinges, which sing pleasantly and unpleasantly; buttons, which are a constant problem for the narrator; and above all the refrain of the poem 'I'll buy shoes to match my coat, and at night I'll sing a psalm, I'll get a dog, and somehow we'll get by.' More than this there is little to hope for.

Two stories in *Rupor* in 1922, **'The Extraordinary Adventures of a Doctor'** and **'Spiritual Séance,'** need not particularly detain us. But two others published in the newspaper *Krasnyi zhurnal dlia vsekh* are far more important: **'No 13—the Elpit House—Workers' Commune'** of 1922 (well known since it was republished in the *Diavoliada* collection) and **'Fire of the Khans'** of 1924. Both have clearly been strongly influenced by Konstantin Fedin's 'The Orchard,' which has an almost identical theme—destruction of the old by fire—and had been published in *Nakanune* (in the same issue as **'Notes on the Cuffs'**) some six months earlier than **'No 13.'** In **'No 13'** the once-elegant five-storey Elpit House becomes, after the Revolution, a workers' commune, but its manager, Khristi, is retained. He tries to keep up the building for its former owner but, when there is an oil shortage, a woman lights a stove she has illegally installed in her apartment, causing a fire. Khristi watches, weeping, as the building burns.

It is arguably Bulgakov's earliest masterpiece—the imitation of Fedin notwithstanding. The main theme is more than nostalgia, it is the difference of two worlds, one of which is characterized by the ignorance and stupidity of the new class. 'We are ignorant people. Benighted people. We fools must be taught,' thinks Annushka, the woman who caused the fire. What was splendid about the past has been destroyed, needlessly, and we cannot help but weep with Khristi at this destruction. We may also see the Elpit House as symbolical of the old régime, with all its luxury and decadence, until taken over by communism, personified in the new name of the building and its inhabitants. Despite hopes for survival, the old is totally destroyed—and indeed, when this story was later published in the *Diavoliada* collection, Soviet critics were not slow to point out Bulgakov's apparent feeling that the change had been for the worse. But Bulgakov's sympathies were not necessarily entirely with the old order. In this story he merely points to certain glories of the past and the neglect that follows from making over their use to those who are unappreciative, or have no sense of history.

A similar theme is the basis of **'Fire of the Khans.'** A group of tourists is shown round the former mansion of the princes Tugay-Beg Ordynsky by the old servant Iona, who clashes ideologically with a most objectionable man dressed only in shorts and a cap. The reader's sympathy is all with Iona, particularly when he gets the better of his opponent. When the others have left, one man returns: the present, disinherited, prince, whom Iona had not recognized. Angry at the treatment of his family and at the new régime, Tugay-Beg sets fire to the house and makes his escape. The theme of the glories of the past and the vulgarity of the new—epitomized in the odious half-naked party member—is still very much present. Iona fulfils a similar role to that of Khristi, by looking after the house for the hoped-for return of the legitimate owner—or indeed to that of the gardener in Fedin's story, who himself burns down the dacha attached to the orchard in disgust. But of the three former owners of house, estate, and orchard, Tugay-Beg, consumed with hatred for the new régime, is the least sympathetic. He is shown as unable to reconcile himself with the new, questioning his own existence in this world, and becoming bitter, malicious as a result.

Bulgakov's own attitude remains ambiguous, although it would appear to be more pessimistic than Fedin's since, although he is not uncritical of the past, he shows greater love for it. In both his stories he struggles to maintain a certain objectivity, describing sadly what he recognizes to be inevitable and showing the futility of struggling against it.

Bulgakov's works before 1924—and some for the following two years—are largely journalistic. In them we can find many stylistic features which would become part of his mature writing: his use of dialogue, his love for a simple direct story, his witty narrator who enjoys making his own comments. It is successful journalism, but would hardly be of great literary interest were it not for Bulgakov's subsequent achievement. In a few stories, however, he shows deeper insights and more universal concerns than is possible in mere reportage. The human emotion portrayed in **'No 13,' 'Fire of the Khans,' 'Red Crown,'** and **'A Psalm'** gives them a more than local interest and makes of them literary works in their own right.

Ellendea Proffer   (essay date 1984)

SOURCE: "The Diaboliad Collection," in *Bulgakov: Life and Work,* Ardis Publishers, 1984, pp. 105-22.

[*In the following excerpt, Proffer provides an overview of the five stories that comprise the 1925 Russian collection* D'iavoliada *(Diaboliad, and Other Stories).*]

The editor Angarsky accepted the long story **"Diaboliad"** for his *Nedra* anthology in the hopes that it would find favor with readers tired of literary experiments which neglected plot. One reader who did regard it as the most important work in *Nedra* No. 4 (1924) was Evgeny Zamyatin, the famous author of the anti-utopian novel *We.* Zamyatin was an influential critic who was still on the board of the Leningrad Writers' Union despite his controversial novel, which could not be published in Russia. He might be considered politically suspect by some, but his literary opinions carried weight.

Since what Zamyatin had to say in his review of the *Nedra* anthology reveals many of the literary and social concerns of the mid-1920s, and provides a context for Bulgakov's place in the literary scene, it deserves attention. Zamyatin dealt severely with most of the works in the collection. He especially disliked Veresaev's *Dead End*

and Serafimovich's *The Iron Flood.* Veresaev, who was on the *Nedra* board, was an old-fashioned writer in all respects, and it is understandable that Zamyatin would have little interest in his work. But Serafimovich's novel, which was to be proclaimed an official classic of Soviet literature, was original in several respects, and had as its hero the masses themselves. Zamyatin expressed annoyance at its operatic tone and uninteresting style, but did find some of the scenes memorable. Another work, Sergeev-Tsensky's "The Professor's Story," gets slightly higher marks as an example of neoclassicism, which Zamyatin declares superior to Serafimovich's "pseudoclassicism." The poetry, in the critic's view, is just as uninspired as most of the prose:

> In its choice of poems, *Nedra* still clings to its realistic virginity—and clings to it so rigidly that the verses of Kirillov, Polonskaya and Oreshin have the sameness of ten-kopek coins: of the six poems published, four even have the same meter—iambic tetrameter. [M. Ginsburg, *A Soviet Heretic: Essays by Yevgeny Zamiatin,* 1970]

The one work which pleased the critic was **"Diaboliad"**:

> The only modern piece in *Nedra* is Bulgakov's **"Diaboliad."** The author unquestionably possesses the right instinct in the choice of his compositional base— fantasy rooted in actual life, rapid, cinematic succession of scenes—one of the few formal frameworks which can encompass our yesterday—1919-1920. The term "cinematic" is all the more applicable to this work since the entire novella is two-dimensional, done on a single plane; everything is on the surface, and there is no depth of scene whatever. With Bulgakov, *Nedra* loses its classical (and pseudoclassical) innocence for what I believe is the first time, and as happens so frequently, the provincial old maid is seduced by the very first brash young man from the capital. The absolute value of this piece, somehow too thoughtless, is not so great, but it would appear that we can expect good things from its author.

"Diaboliad" is a headlong rush into the life of the city, and it is appropriate that the hero commit suicide by leaping from one of the tallest buildings in Moscow. The building in the novella has ten floors, just as the Nirenzee building did, and a vast number of offices and corridors like the House of Labor, where *Gudok* was published. There is a touch of German expressionism in the descriptions and the action, and everything takes place at film speed.

The plot of the novella, like the plots of *Heart of a Dog* and **"The Fatal Eggs,"** turns on a simple but crucial mistake. The meek, quite boring hero, Korotkov, who is employed at a match factory, mishears the name of his boss and reads his signature as *"kal'sony"* (underwear) instead of "Kal'soner" (translated as Underwarr in the English version). Because the hero reads the signature as part of an order, and transmits the order, he is fired. In the course of the tale Korotkov is obsessed with the desire to explain this mistake to his boss. This aim is hopelessly and comically complicated by the fact that there are two sets of doubles involved, his boss's look-alike and his own. In this work the very traditional Russian theme of the double is taken to grotesque extremes as poor Korotkov, accused of being a Don Juan (as his double is), begins to go insane after chasing the two Kalsoners through the endless bureaucratic corridors. He soon concludes that it is all the trick of the devil . . .

Korotkov has also been robbed of his documents, and is thus unable to prove his identity. Since the person who could replace them, his housing manager, is away, there are serious consequences: without his documents Korotkov does not exist. From non-existence to suicide is a short step, as a chase involving the various doubles leads him to the roof and his final jump.

It is hard to take this tale seriously as an indictment of bureaucracy, although the bureaucratic machinery is as wretched as anything found in Saltykov or Sukhovo-Kobylin. Korotkov himself seems to be the source of most of his problems. His own stupidity and hysteria blind him to obvious explanations—one of the two Kalsoners has a beard, one does not, and someone else might have concluded that two different men were involved. Korotkov is something of a parody of the traditional Russian "little man," but it would be straining ingenuity to see the story as a condemnation of an entire society. People with political minds, both pro- and anti-Soviet, will see political aspects of this story, but I think, like Zamyatin, that the plot is merely a pretext for the introduction of a series of dazzling scenes, all based on famous Moscow locations of the early twenties. Bulgakov's customary suggestions of demons and magic are present, at least in the fantasy imagery, and the smell of sulphur—natural to a match factory—suggests a hellish fire. At one point, as Korotkov watches one of the doubles fall, the man seems to metamorphose into a black cat with phosphorescent eyes, which then rolls itself into a ball and jumps through a broken window. Another figure tied to the satanic line is a little old man who frequently turns up, a malevolent force, clearly, whose eyes flash ominously. All of this is the first occurrence of material which will turn up again in *Theatrical Novel* and *The Master and Margarita*.

The comic scenes are less refined than later variants. The typewriter terror scene, for example, is an early version of the office scene in *The Master and Margarita* in which the entire staff is forced to sing in unison by Woland's band. Here Korotkov hallucinates a scene of thirty typists doing a cancan around their desks to the bells of the typewriters, which are playing a foxtrot.

At the end Korotkov decides to jump rather than surrender to his pursuers, but he believes he is going up rather than down, until "the incarnadine sun cracked resoundingly in his head, and he saw nothing more." This description is very close to the one used as Berlioz dies in Bulgakov's last novel.

The influence of Gogol (especially "The Nose" and "The Overcoat") is evident here, and while there are obvious thematic echoes of Dostoevsky's *The Double,* Bulgakov modernizes many devices. The style, with its sudden hallucinatory transformations and incongruities, realized metaphors and detailed registration of character movements, gestures and colors, owes something to the Gogolian-Dostoevskian Natural School of the 1840s; but a number of these devices were characteristic of the 1920s as well. What marks **"Diaboliad"** as modern is its speed and compression. As Zamyatin suggests, things on the surface attract our attention, and there is little real psychology. Instead of interior monologue we have dialogue, for which Bulgakov had a real talent. It is joined by extremely diverse verbs of saying: characters are said to sing, squeak, ring—all somewhat dehumanizing—but rarely simply speak.

The story's exuberance stems from the author's enjoyment of the epoch itself. There is a fascination with elevators, skyscrapers, and public transport; the sound a machine-gun makes is compared to a "deafening" Singer sewing-machine and so on. Like a Charlie Chaplin movie, this work makes use of all the modern machines and settings to contrast with an old-fashioned hero. However, unlike Chaplin, Bulgakov does not mix his ingredients well. The hero's silliness is not balanced by sympathetic traits. Korotkov is very funny when, in his literal way, he hits Dyrkin with a candelabra, but when four pages later Korotkov is dead, the reader may be forgiven for not caring very much. Unlike the hero of *Theatrical Novel,* to whom he bears a real resemblance, Korotkov has no talent to recommend him. He is neurotic at the beginning of the story and insane at the end, little more than a man with an obsession. In this he is like Gogol's Akaky Akakievich, but it is not really possible to care about him. Korotkov lives in a world of mechanical-seeming people, but he himself is an automaton by the end, with few human qualities left.

In this first real try at the fantastic Bulgakov did succeed in combining the grotesquely fantastic with sharply observed details of Moscow life, and required only a better plot to support his style—such as the one he adapted from H. G. Wells for **"The Fatal Eggs."**

The starting point for the plot of Bulgakov's most famous novella [**"The Fatal Eggs"**] is H. G. Wells's *The Food of the Gods,* but as Christine Rydel has pointed out [in "Bulgakov and H. G. Wells," *Russian Literature Triquartely* 15 (1978)], Bulgakov utilized only the first third of the English novel for plot ideas, and the intentions of the two works are quite dissimilar. Wells was a genuine science-fiction writer, and in his novel happily predicted a future in which children are given special food (which, however, causes disasters in the present) and become like gods. Bulgakov was not interested in describing a future order. In all of his fantasy works he does so only once, in the play *Adam and Eve.* **"The Fatal Eggs"** is, like other Bulgakov works, a satire which uses elements of science fiction for the purpose of examining present, not future, problems.

The novella was finished in October 1924, read to friends and colleagues soon after, and first published in the sixth

Nedra anthology, which came out around February 1925. Subsequently it was serialized in *Red Panorama* (*Krasnaia panorama*) in a shortened version, under the title *The Red Ray* (*Krasnyi luch*).

In **"The Fatal Eggs"** events unfold in the most unpredictable fashion. It is a satirical, parodic tale of a scientific experiment gone wrong in the future Soviet Republic of 1928. Among the many satirical targets are journalists, and the story should and can be considered in the context of the mass journalism of the 1920s, as Chudakova points out [in "Archiv M. A. Bulgakova," *Zapiski Otdela Rukorisei,* Vypusk 37 (1976)]. The journalists of the time (and not just in Russia) seemed to share a naive belief that great scientific advances would take place at any moment, and, indeed, that such advances had already taken place. The description of the yellow journalists—as embodied in the character of Bronsky, who actually sets the plot in motion—is pointed and well-informed. Bulgakov's extensive knowledge of the Moscow newspaper world was obviously useful, and there are many inside jokes, distortions of well-known names and parodies of the jargon of the new era.

The basic elements of the work are familiar: an obsessed scientist, his faithful lab assistant, a stunning new discovery, and a terrifying development as the discovery is either misused or misunderstood. But the fact that the setting of Bulgakov's story is 1928, only three years after publication, indicates that science-fiction is not the proper category for this work. Nothing has really changed in those three years and no contemporary reader thought the story was about anything but Moscow in the mid-twenties.

At the beginning of the story the narrator lays the blame for an unspecified catastrophe on the scientist Persikov. Professor Persikov, he says, must be considered "the prime cause of this catastrophe." But Persikov, like so many other erudite characters in Bulgakov's literary world, seems to inspire ambivalent feelings in the author. Bulgakov was fascinated by scholarly expertise and accomplishment—both his father and his brother were experts in their fields—and he himself had envisioned a glamorous future involving microscopes when he first chose a medical career. But at the same time, Bulgakov was painfully aware of what pure scientific curiosity could lead to, such as the gases used during World War I. In Bulgakov's view, it was dangerous to ignore the social and political implications of a discovery—something the Soviet Union, anxious to be in the forefront of science, had a tendency to ignore, at least in the press. Bulgakov respected the highest traditions of science, but was skeptical about scientific rationalism, and the supposed golden age the new science would usher in. Science had all but replaced religion in Soviet popular culture, and the belief in progress through technology was widespread. **"The Fatal Eggs,"** for all its debt to Wells, is really a variation of the Faust theme: man should not try to assume the powers of a god.

Persikov may seem to come from Wells, but he was actually based on a real person, Lyubov's relative, Evgeny

Tarnovsky, a man who was remarkably erudite. Persikov is a Faustian figure, endowed with a quick temper and an all-consuming interest in zoology. His problems begin with his discovery of what a certain red ray does to amoebas which are accidentally caught in it. The ray increases both the size—and the viciousness—of the organisms subjected to it. Rumors of this discovery immediately spread through Moscow.

Unknown to the professor, who doesn't read newspapers because he thinks they only contain gibberish, there is a chicken plague raging through the nation, and various parties are trying to come up with a solution to the shortage of eggs. The journalist Bronsky publicizes the ray; the head of a collective farm, Rokk (translated as Feyt in English, since his name echoes *rok,* the Russian for "fate") reads of the discovery and is certain that it will solve the chicken problem. He comes to Moscow to convince the professor to help.

Feyt is a negative character who shares many of the physical characteristics of Kalsoner from **"Diaboliad."** When he first enters the professor's study the entire scene appears hellish to him, and the professor seems to have the air of Satan.

It is important to remember that the professor is firmly opposed to using the ray to produce enormous chickens by exposing imported eggs to it. The professor declares that the ray has not been sufficiently tested, but a phone call from a mysterious and stern personage of high authority convinces him he has no choice, so he lets the state farm have his specially constructed chambers.

Up to this point the novella is essentially comic: the chicken plague produces all sorts of comic headlines and humorously named commissions. But once Feyt goes off with the chambers, the suspense intensifies—the reader has been warned from the start that some unspecified catastrophe has taken place. At the lyrically described collective farm there are signs from nature that something is wrong: the dogs bark, the birds are silent, the peasants are uneasy. The eggs which were due to hatch under the ray are found empty. Feyt, a leather-jacketed relic of the Civil War, is at this moment incongruously playing the flute, a reminder of his previous profession as a musician. The next day, when Feyt and his wife go for a swim she is suddenly, and horribly, devoured by a giant reptile, and the comedy takes a truly grotesque turn:

> Blood splashed from her mouth, a broken arm slipped out, and little fountains of blood spurted from under the fingernails. Then, almost dislocating its jaws, the snake opened its mouth, quickly slipped its head over Manya's, and began to pull itself over her like a glove over a finger.

The explanation for this is that by an incredible coincidence (like the mistaken identity in **"Diaboliad"**), the Professor's long-awaited shipment of reptile eggs has been switched for Feyt's chicken eggs: the result is that the countryside is infested with giant anacondas and other such creatures instead of the giant egg-laying hens. Who exactly switched the two shipments is unknown, which means that the *direct* cause of the reptile invasion is accidental, and does not involve either Persikov or Feyt. However, there is no doubt that Bulgakov's real theme is the interference of the state in scientific matters—a point not made by Wells.

The deaths that follow the first one are many and horrible, but it is Manya's that shocks the reader. In the midst of this clinically described violence, the comedy persists: in an attempt to distract the monster, Feyt plays the waltz from the opera *Eugene Onegin* on his flute, having dimly remembered that one can charm snakes. However, "the eyes in the foliage instantly began to smolder with implacable hate for the opera."

Bulgakov's ability to give concrete form to the imaginary is, as usual, combined with accurate observations of the real world. For example, the picture of Moscow awaiting its doom, with the atmosphere of panic and mob violence, though set in the future, is based on what Bulgakov saw during the Civil War. Certain figures from the present are carried into this future, such as the cavalry commander who had become legendary ten years before, i.e., Budenny.

The civil hysteria has dire consequences: Persikov is killed by a man who splits his skull open. The professor is described as spreading his arms "as one crucified" just before he is killed. Persikov's institute is destroyed by fire—the end of many things in Bulgakov's fiction.

The giant reptiles are finally exterminated, but not by the soldiers who have mobilized for this task. On the night before the dawn of August 19 (Bulgakov favored the time just before dawn for important events) the monstrous creatures are killed by an incredible summer frost. Like Napoleon, they are defeated by the weather. This chapter is entitled "A Frosty God *Ex Machina,*" and the frost is indeed a sudden, almost off-hand development in terms of the story's plot.

The red ray, the discovery which set everything in motion, is lost forever, since, as the narrator concludes, something besides knowledge was needed, and that something was possessed by only one man in the world—Persikov.

There are only two important characters in **"Fatal Eggs,"** and it seems to me that the story can best be understood through them. Professor Persikov and Feyt are the only two characters who are provided with extensive biographies.

Persikov is the classic scientist, a type which attracted Bulgakov; such characters are usually shown as absorbed in their work, and essentially uninterested in the world around them. I have no doubt that Belozerskaya's relative was the model for certain character traits, but it seems to me that there is another obvious prototype for this character in the person of Pavlov, a world-renowned scientist who disapproved of the Revolution, but kept on working in Russia, ignoring his changed context, and achieving some degree of success.

Persikov is flawed, but he is not really a negative character, although some critics have made that assumption. It is Persikov's genius, his drive to follow something to its logical end, which leads to the developing of the red ray, but it is the phone call from the Kremlin which determines the outcome. One can make the case that Persikov could have somehow destroyed the ray so that no one else could misuse it, or could have fought harder to restrict use of it until he knew more. This is all implied by Persikov's words when he understands that the ray will be used on the eggs, with him or without him: "I wash my hands of this!" Like Pilate, Persikov is overwhelmed by events, and like Pilate, he senses that something wrong is taking place.

Persikov, like the doctor hero of **Heart of a Dog,** is Faustian in certain ways. He is doing a dangerous thing, interfering with natural processes; the point of both stories is the same—that evolution is safer than revolution. But as long as Persikov's experiment remains in his laboratory there is no danger to anyone but himself. This seems to me a key point. Bulgakov is not saying that scientific endeavor should be restricted—as a doctor he saw the benefits which came from the scientific mind at liberty—he is saying instead that such things are best left to scientists. Persikov is not quite as lost in the ivory tower as he seems to be: he exhausts himself helping with the chicken plague, throws a spy out of his office, and in general appears to be an intellectual of the old school, a type for which Bulgakov had great admiration. Persikov's dry, logical approach to life does not prevent him from weeping when he learns of the death of his wife, who had deserted him fifteen years earlier. In general, his brusque, cantankerous exterior is deceiving. The wife, however, is a clue, since in Bulgakov's works absence of a woman indicates a man who is not completely alive. Persikov's sin is one which is always punished in Bulgakov's world: he has become so absorbed in his work that he has lost his interest in the world around him—and the people around him. One of Bulgakov's main points when describing scientists is that they bear responsibility for what they discover—they cannot simply present a weapon, say, to their society and then return to their laboratories with no thought of how their discovery will be used. Persikov is wrong, but he is not an evil force, no matter how devilish he seems to Feyt—who *is* a force for evil.

Feyt is antipathetic in basic ways, and the narrator's treatment of him is ironic. We are told that he has accomplished such feats as the irrigation of Turkestan, and that he began as a musician before the Revolution. These two things do not seem to go together, and the Professor voices the conviction that the man is an ignoramus—which, of course, is quite true. Feyt's biography is thought-provoking: from musician, to editor of a Turkestan newspaper, to member of the local Agricultural Commission, and finally, irrigator of Turkestan, after which he comes back to Moscow. Like Persikov's, his appearance is strangely old-fashioned, but in a different way, since he is still wearing the uniform of the Civil War, a leather jacket and puttees. Feyt's ignorance is of a different order from that of the "dark people" but the results are the same. He notices that the eggs that arrive at the farm seem dirty, but it never occurs to him that they are not chicken eggs. He is a man of action, after all, not an intellectual—but in the end he does not even possess common sense, only a sort of brutal determination.

In the descriptions of the two major characters we may see the basis for an allegorical interpretation of the role of the intelligentsia (Persikov) in breeding the Revolution, as compared to the opportunists (Feyt) who came to power, utterly unprepared for the positions they would occupy. However, the allegory hunters fall into hopeless contradictions when they deal with the specific details of the story. It is tempting to see the red ray itself as a metaphor for Bolshevism, but who is Lenin? Critics have suggested both Feyt and Persikov for this identification, which indicates the problem of decoding the allegory here. The fact that the eggs are switched by accident implies blind forces at work, which in turn connects with Bulgakov's Tolstoyan attitude to history itself. In any case, Feyt's name gives us a clue to his role. Like many other negative characters, such as Stroganov in Bulgakov's play about Pushkin, *Last Days,* Feyt is blind to possible consequences.

This novella should be evaluated not only in the context of the *Diaboliad* collection, but as a companion piece to the other two novellas Bulgakov wrote in the twenties, **"Diaboliad"** itself and *Heart of a Dog*. These works share themes and stylistic devices, as Bulgakov turned from the historical and autobiographical material of the Civil War to modern city life, with its exuberance and contradictions. In this new world Bulgakov finds many traces of the old, despite the new jargon (which he parodies) and the advances of science which are supposed to change the world. The theme of the misuse of science is even stronger in *Heart of a Dog,* which is, unlike **"The Fatal Eggs,"** an unambiguous allegory about the dangers of remaking the world overnight through revolution.

It is appropriate that **"The Fatal Eggs"** was included in the collection *Diaboliad*: as in the story **"Diaboliad,"** there are signs of the devil at work everywhere. Bulgakov was especially amused by rumors of the anti-Christ, and here the peasants spread the rumor that Feyt is none other than he. The secret police are given shoes with toes that resemble hooves, and variations on the phrase "the devil knows" are scattered throughout the tale.

The narrative is a deliberate melange of styles and parodies. At times the events are seen from the point of view of a credulous, dense journalist; at other points the voice is that of an omniscient, ironical narrator. Bulgakov's aim is clearly to get his readers off balance, and in this he succeeds, following perfectly rendered scientific description with very funny semi-literate journalese typical of the yellow press, in which big words are consistently misused. Bulgakov's ear for the speech of this era serves him well. The description of the chicken plague is an *Iliad* of the animal world, containing many comic catalogues. Puns and word distortions, combined with the ignorance of the characters, are further sources of comedy for the reader—and confusion for the characters. The title itself contains a double pun: *rok* (fate) sounds like *Rokk* (Feyt's name in Russian), so that one could hear the title as *Rokk's Eggs* as well as **"The Fatal Eggs."** In Russian the word eggs (*iaitsa*) is the vulgar Russian term corresponding to the English "balls" when describing the male anatomy, so that the title of the story can also be read as *The Fatal Balls* or *Rokk's Balls,* either quite shocking to the Russian ear. Bulgakov continually plays on these double entendres throughout the story. **"The Fatal Eggs"** has a structure based on comic illogic and surprise, with frustration of expectation the norm: chapter titles promise what they do not deliver, and interesting plot lines are deliberately interrupted at crucial points, all leading, of course, to greater suspense.

Whatever its muddiness as allegory, **"The Fatal Eggs"** is a successful work of the imagination. Bulgakov's ability to make the fantastic seem real, the graphic descriptions of the giant reptiles ravaging the land, the rush of the narration—these things are so powerful that the reader tends not to stop and analyze anything. Indeed, according to Mayakovsky, who returned from a trip to America in 1925, one American newspaper had reported the plot of **"The Fatal Eggs"** as if it were true.

Seen against the other notable works of the time, **"The Fatal Eggs"** is especially original and daring. This work immediately convinced both readers and critics that Bulgakov was a writer to watch, and, for many people, **"The Fatal Eggs"** seemed to be the best of Bulgakov's satiric prose. This, however, was only because his real masterpiece of this particular genre of satiric science fiction, *Heart of a Dog,* was never published in the Soviet Union.

"The Fatal Eggs" provoked strong responses from the critics. Some thought it counter-revolutionary, while others were puzzled by the apparent contradictions. One generally hostile critic, D. Gorbov [in "Itogi literaturnogo goda," *Novyi mir,* 1925], was willing, but unable, to attribute an anti-Soviet meaning to the work:

> Despite all readiness to read into it some definite meaning, even more some repudiation of our society (as one of the critics advises us to do), we confess that we couldn't do it: too many threads are left hanging.

Another critic wondered how a work obviously meant for the "White Guardist press" had ended up on the pages of the Soviet periodical *Nedra* [M. Lirov, "Nedra, Kniga 6-ia," *Pechat'i revoliutsiia,* July-September, 1925]. Fyodor Gladkov, the author of *Cement,* accused Bulgakov of feeling culturally superior while "vomiting on our way of life." (This last was in a letter to Gorky, who was an admirer of Bulgakov's story [*Literaturnoe nasledstvo 70. Gor'kii i sovetskie pisateli. Neizdannaia perepiska,* 1971]).

Gorky was not the only one to praise the story. *A New World (Novyi mir)* critic wrote:

Bulgakov's tale is not just light reading. The characters, types and scenes are all topical and pointed. A brief sentence is enough to illuminate an ugly corner of our present life with a bright ray of laughter.

The editor of the respected journal *Red Virgin Soil (Krasnaia nov')*, Voronsky, provided an interesting analysis of this novella some years later, in 1927, when Bulgakov was under attack for a long list of literary sins, including the writing of **"The Fatal Eggs."** Voronsky calls the work unusually talented and caustic, and notes that its basic thesis is that bad can come of a good idea when it ends up in the head of a well-meaning, but ignorant person. This is, he agrees, the right of a writer: why not discuss this problem? But the critic claims that the flaw in Bulgakov's work is that he does not know exactly why he is writing this "lampoon" or what precisely he wants done about the problem.

> At best, this work arouses doubt . . . in the end one doesn't know where he is leading us: perhaps not at all in the direction which our new reader, who values October [i.e., the Revolution] wants to go. ["Pisatel, kniga, chitatel," *Krasnaia nov'*, 1927]

In my view, all of these critics, save Gladkov, are correct. Bulgakov, perhaps afraid of the censorship, perhaps undecided in his own mind, does not follow through. His joke does not have a logical punch line; it is nevertheless very funny.

The critics may have had doubts, but the readers did not. S. N. Sergeev-Tsensky, one of the regular contributors to the almanac, said that Bulgakov's work was the only thing in *Nedra* that wasn't boring [M. Chudakora, "Arkhiv M. A. Bulgakov"].

Bulgakov's most important admirer was Gorky. In his letters from this period Gorky recommended that his correspondents get a copy of *Nedra* and read Bulgakov's tale: "It will make you laugh. It's a witty thing!" Gorky's only complaint was that Bulgakov had not exploited all of the work's possibilities—he had not, for example, included a picture of the giant reptiles advancing on Moscow, which, he said, would have made a "terrifically interesting scene."

In 1926, in a review of Bulgakov's hit play *Days of the Turbins,* an American correspondent mentioned Bulgakov's "first book of short stories which caused a sensation here eighteen months ago because it included a daring skit on some of the weak points in Bolshevist methods. It was called **'The Fatal Eggs'"** [Walter Duranty, "Red Intelligentsia Is Stirred by Play," *New York Times,* November 7, 1926]. This, we may assume, represented general opinion available to a foreign correspondent, and demonstrates why **"The Fatal Eggs"** would eventually be seen as a serious literary transgression. . . .

[The] manuscript Bulgakov submitted to the Nedra publishing house shows that he originally planned that the *Diaboliad* collection would contain the story **"The Fire of the Khans"** as well as the other stories which were finally printed in it. In terms of subject matter this would have made sense; it seems likely that the censorship would not pass the story of an emigre who secretly returns to Russia in order to set fire to his former estate. The stories which were printed, however, are scarcely less provocative, given the requirements of the censorship even in these years, and it is understandable that the collection is still banned in the Soviet Union.

"No. 13. The Elpit-Rabkommun Building," orginally published in 1922, recounts the rise and fall of the Elpit Building, the history of which is based on the Pigit Building where Bulgakov was living. According to Levshin, the details of the building's history are fairly accurate. Bulgakov describes the worst moment in this history— when it was transformed into a workers' commune. The only person standing between this magnificent building and utter ruin is the efficient superintendent, Christy, who had worked at the building since before the Revolution. But Christy cannot save the building from the ignorance of its new inhabitants. When there is no fuel for a week these people start using the little stoves in their rooms, which have no flues, for heat. The result is that the building goes up in flames. At the end of the story, the old woman who has caused the fire, Annushka—no doubt a version of that same Annushka-the-plague from *The Master and Margarita*—has a lucid thought for the first time in her life: "We are ignorant people. Ignorant people. We must be taught, fools that we are . . . "

This is a cautionary tale, firmly rooted in the reality of the life of the people in Bulgakov's building, and the implications of the story are hardly orthodox, even for the early 1920s. In this work we may see Christy as an analogue to the caretaker in **"The Fire of the Khans,"** a man who takes care of a place or property out of love and long association. His efficiency shows him to be the opposite of the Bulgakovian building manager, who is both ineffective and officious. That Christy is essentially an unreconstructed pre-Revolutionary type would not have been overlooked by contemporary readers.

"The Adventures of Chichikov," first published in *Nakanune* in 1922, is an act of homage to Bulgakov's beloved Gogol. Bulgakov later wrote play adaptations and scenarios for *Dead Souls* and *The Inspector General,* but this is his first known "Gogolism." The title of the story is the one which Gogol's censors insisted he use above the title of *Dead Souls;* while Bulgakov uses characters and lines from that novel, he also cannibalizes other works by Gogol, including *The Inspector General* and "The Nose." Much of the material of this story is actually composed of bits and pieces of Gogol's prose, for example, the last line: " . . . and again life went parading before me in its quotidian way." This tale of how Gogol's resurrected scoundrels successfully swindle everyone in NEP-era Moscow makes the point that the Russian corruption which existed before the Revolution is flourishing after as well. Just as all of the illegal deals are coming to a climax, the narrator himself enters the story to rout the rascals, as only a reader of Gogol could. The ending, which shows all the preceding events to have been a dream, mimics both Gogol's original version of "The Nose" and the denial of reality found in the preface to "The Tale of How Ivan Ivanovich Quarreled with Ivan Nikiforovich." This story has a certain charm, and is funny, but it is a distinctly minor work, like most of the other short pieces in the *Diaboliad* collection.

A story which falls outside all of the usual Bulgakovian categories is **"A Chinese Tale,"** first published in 1923. The visual side of Bulgakov's imagination is much in evidence here, as we see what the primitive mind of a Chinese coolie makes of the Red Army and the Civil War. In the end he understands nothing, and is comforted only by the sensual memories of his childhood under the hot sun, in contrast to the cold of Moscow. The repetition of certain key details which are packed with meaning for the character—the kaoliang, the shadow, the buckets of cold water—is characteristic of Bulgakov's serious prose. The coolie's cocaine dream, with its careful incorporation of details from his past and a foreshadowing of his future, is also well done. At the time the *Diaboliad* collection was published, critics took the story to be a polemic with Vsevolod Ivanov's famous "Armored Train 14-69," a story which was made into a play and put on at the Art Theater shortly after Bulgakov's *Days of the Turbins.* Ivanov's story, published in 1922, also has a Chinese hero, who is genuinely heroic, joining the Bolsheviks to serve the cause. In the end he deliberately sacrifices his life for his comrades, throwing himself under the wheels of a train which must be stopped. In contrast, Bulgakov's coolie owes his original acceptance by the Red Army to his utterance of three words in Russian (the only Russian he has picked up)—the oath "Fuck your mother." This coolie serves and kills strictly for bread, and ideology is something quite incomprehensible to him. The story follows the format of titled mini-chapters, but it remains a sort of special exception in Bulgakov's works, a work whose point is elusive, as if it were an exercise in exoticism, under the influence of some well-known works by Bunin and others. But the character, the opium den, and the Finnish knife will return again, in the play *Zoya's Apartment.*

In November of 1924 Bulgakov signed a contract with the Nedra publishing house for a collection of stories. In May 1925, Mospoligraf printed Bulgakov's collection of stories under the general title *Diaboliad (D'iavoliada).* This collection, the only real book to be published during Bulgakov's lifetime, was responsible for much of his reputation among readers and other writers. It contained **"Diaboliad," "The Fatal Eggs," "No. 13. The Elpit-Rabkommun Building," "A Chinese Tale,"** and **"The Adventures of Chichikov."**

The edition was not large, apparently five thousand, and book collectors assert that part of the edition was destroyed, making the book a bibliographic rarity. Despite the small edition, the book helped Bulgakov's reputation, revealing as it did a writer of real talent who used specifically modern Soviet material in an original manner. The book received substantial critical attention, much of it negative, but even if some critics became suspicious of

Bulgakov on the basis of this collection, the editors and publishers greeted **"The Fatal Eggs"** with enthusiasm, since it was a work which would attract and satisfy readers.

The cumulative impression of the stories included in the *Diaboliad* collection is one of dark satire. Bulgakov deliberately selected works which fit the conception of "deviltry," and there is an edge to the humor: major characters die with frequency, and a demonic force appears to operate in all five works. In **"Diaboliad"** a clerk commits suicide after being driven insane by a quirk of fate; in **"The Fatal Eggs"** the major character is murdered by a man, and numerous others by reptiles; in **"No. 13. The Elpit-Rabkommun Building,"** an old woman burns down a building, causing the death of a fireman; in **"A Chinese Tale,"** the Chinese sharp-shooter is bayonetted; in **"The Adventures of Chichikov,"** Gogol's characters find that little has changed in the new Russia.

The diabolic references in these works are ironically misleading. Virtually every time someone says "the devil take it," "the devil only knows," there is an assumption that the devil himself or some other distant force is the explanation of whatever has gone wrong. Closer examination reveals, however, that more often than not, people themselves are to blame for what appears devilish—burning down the house (when specifically warned not to have fires), rushing ahead with a new discovery (when warned it has not been sufficiently tested), and so on. What village story-tellers would ascribe to the work of the devil, Bulgakov sees as human error, human responsibility. His attribution of events to "deviltry" is ironic, like so much else in these works. There *are* terrible forces at work in the world of these stories, but they are human ignorance and cupidity, and not deviltry.

> **Bulgakov was a master at parodying the styles of different social levels, and in *Diaboliad* we find journalese, bureaucratese, folk locutions, epic narrators, political and military jargon and big city street vulgarisms**.
>
> —*Ellendea Proffer*

Bulgakov was a master at parodying the styles of different social levels, and here we find journalese, bureaucratese, folk locutions, epic narrators, political and military jargon and big city street vulgarisms, to name only a few of the linguistic targets. The style is sophisticated, but perhaps too unrestrained, and the marks of the early twenties are visible throughout—synecdoche, exaggerated attention to physiological changes, comic similes and realized metaphors. Bulgakov did this with a surer touch and fresher eye than most of the writers of the period, but his stories are weak structurally, as if they were novels imprisoned in a short form. Equally unsatisfying is the lack of characterization, which is certainly deliberate, since Bulgakov had demonstrated in **"Notes on the Cuff"** that he was perfectly able to characterize briefly but well. This problem may come from Bulgakov's changing ideas about satire. In any case, this collection shows how early the classic Bulgakovian narrator was present, i.e., from the start. Here is the actor-narrator of *The Master and Margarita,* who switches from the style of a well-bred educated man to an incredibly dense yokel. Throughout the collection there are multiple points of view, another characteristic of Bulgakov's longer prose.

There is nothing new for Russian literature in the themes of these stories: the madness of urban and bureaucratic life are prominent in the works of Gogol and Saltykov, two of Bulgakov's favorite writers. But the nineteenth-century writers are very different in style. Bulgakov is laconic where they are lavish. Bulgakov brought something new to this material, a genuinely modern outlook and style, which was also different from the work of his contemporaries. As Altshuler mentions [in *M. A. Gor'kii i russkaii literatura,* 1970], Bulgakov's fantasy differed from that found in the Hoffmannesque works of the Serapion Brothers group. For them, the fantastic world of the soul or spirit was separate, and opposed to, the impoverished world of the senses and the everyday. For Bulgakov, fantasy was a part of the everyday, tightly interwoven with the sensual world, growing right out of it. This required a thorough understanding of the real world, and Bulgakov, like his literary models, was careful to accurately describe the ordinary environments of his heroes as well as the fantastic deformations of that world. Nor can anyone miss the joy he takes in the sights, sounds, and smell of that "ordinary" world which for him is so magical in itself.

Diaboliad as a whole is an interesting collection, especially when judged against the other works of this period, but few critics would have predicted the author's ultimate development as a writer from reading only this. *White Guard* was a far better indicator of the range and depth of Bulgakov's abilities as a writer, but fate decreed that it be published in full only abroad, leaving *Diaboliad* as the only prose by which most readers could judge him.

Teo Forcht Dagi (essay date 1988)

SOURCE: "Medical Ethics and the Problem of Role Ambiguity in Mikhail Bulgakov's 'The Murderer' and Pear S. Buck's 'The Enemy,'" in *Literature and Medicine,* Vol. 7, 1988, pp. 107-22.

[In the following excerpt, Dagi discusses the moral ambiguity embodied in the physician, Dr. Yashvin, in "The Murderer."]

Several years after the October revolution, Dr. Yashvin, an urbane man and excellent surgeon, appears unusually preoccupied during a soirée. The conversation turns to the way in which the public fails to appreciate the moral probity of physicians. If a patient dies, for example, the physician is called a murderer. This appellation, the host argues, is absurd: "'A surgeon with a pistol in his hand— that . . . might be murder. But I've never met any such surgeon in my life. . . . '" To the astonishment of those present, Dr. Yashvin announces that he has killed a man— a patient—deliberately. The night of the soirée is the seventh anniversary of the murder.

Yashvin begins his account of the murder by describing the closing days of the civil war in Kiev, when the White Russian forces were in retreat. The arrival of the Bolsheviks was eagerly anticipated by the populace, not only for ideological reasons, but also because of the atrocities committed under the leadership of the infamous Petlyura, general of the White Army. There had been endless pogroms. Naked bodies were everywhere: the dead were robbed of their clothing and possessions. So commonplace had such atrocities become that Yashvin, like many others, was inured to their horror. His interest in the political aspects of the conflict had long since dwindled into apathy. But after the White forces vandalized his library, he too "'started looking forward to the Bolsheviks' arrival.'"

One evening, upon returning from the hospital where he was an intern, Yashvin was summoned to join Petlyura's forces. He decided, instead, to flee. Packing some meager possessions, he purposefully put an automatic pistol and spare magazine in his pocket. Trying to leave the building surreptitiously, he was intercepted by two troopers and brought before Colonel Leshchenko, one of Petlyura's cavalry commanders and a sadist, who declared that Yashvin would be disciplined for attempting to escape. As Yashvin observed the brutal punishment that was meted out by the Colonel to deserters, he realized that this would most probably be his lot as well.

In the course of battle, the cavalry troop deserted Kiev and moved to Slobodka, guarding Yashvin closely to preclude his escape. New headquarters were established. People were brought in and tortured. Yashvin could not close his ears to the anguished sounds of human agony. When he protested, he was told that the Colonel has discovered "'an organization in Slobodka. Communists and Yids.'" Interrogations were in progress: the tortures continued while Yashvin tended to wounded soldiers.

Suddenly Yashvin was summoned to treat the Colonel, who had just been stabbed by one of the men under interrogation. As Yashvin examined the wound, a woman burst in, distraught, demanding to know why her husband had been shot. In reply, the Colonel said simply, "'"Because he had to be shot, that's why."'" The woman turned contemptuously to Yashvin and exclaimed:

> "'And you're a doctor!' . . .
>
> "'Oh, my God,' . . . 'what a wretch you are . . . you trained at university and yet you can bring yourself to treat this murdering swine . . . tying nice little bandages for *them!* He thrashes a man in the face without cease, till he drives him mad . . . And you're bandaging him!'"

Yashvin did not answer her, but he remembers: "'Everything blurred before my eyes and I felt sick; I knew the most terrible episode in my wretched career as a doctor had begun.'" The woman spat in the Colonel's face. Furiously, he ordered his men to thrash her twenty-five times with a ramrod. Only then did Yashvin protest: "'They're going to beat a *woman?*'" The colonel retorted, "'Now I see what sort of a doctor I've been given!'" Quietly, Yashvin continues his account:

> "I must have fired one of the bullets into his mouth because I remember him swaying on the stool and blood running out of his mouth; . . . Finally he slumped to the floor. As I pulled the trigger, I remember being afraid of losing count and firing the seventh bullet, the last one. 'That'll be for my own death,' I said to myself. The smell of gun powder from the automatic was delicious."

Yashvin escaped by jumping out of a window and hiding during a night filled with artillery barrage. The next morning, Petlyura's men fled. The Bolsheviks were in control, and Yashvin returned to Kiev.

The end of Yashvin's story is met with silence. After a pause, the host cautiously inquires whether Yashvin is certain that Colonel Leshchenko died. Is it possible he was only wounded? "'Oh, don't worry,'" responds Yashvin. "'I killed him all right. Trust my experience as a surgeon.'"

. . . . .

"The Murderer" is a parable in which truth is less important than plausibility. Yashvin serves two purposes for Bulgakov: figuratively, he stands for the virtuous physician; allegorically, he represents the intelligentsia. . . . From the very first, Yashvin is established as a morally significant figure. In the context of post-revolutionary Russia, he is remarkably balanced: cultured, intellectual, educated, and reasonable. His support for the Bolsheviks is highly qualified, perhaps even reluctant. He is neither a radical nor a pacifist and certainly not a fanatic ideologue. No, Yashvin is set slightly apart from his audience: he is, in some vaguely defined way, an admirable individual.

The murder is a secret that the audience neither expects nor quite believes. It belies the character of the man. Yashvin may have killed, but it is inconceivable that he should have murdered. Yet Yashvin is not introduced in a heroic mode. His attempts to escape Petlyura arise from self interest, not principle. In many respects he begins solipsistically. He neither aspires to virtue nor thinks of it: on the contrary, virtue is thrust upon him by circumstance. Early on, like a reporter, Yashvin observes the tragedies that surround him without becoming involved. He attempts to parlay his professional role as a physician into political neutrality. The impossibility of this position becomes evident to the audience before it is acknowledged by Yashvin. It requires external moral indignation to prod Yashvin into action. The woman whose husband has been killed addresses him in stages: first as a physician; next as a person; then as a member of the intelligentsia, a civilized human being; and finally as a morally responsible agent. At each level, a different moral issue is raised as a consequence of distinct roles and role responsibilities. As a doctor, how could Yashvin stand by, witness, and tacitly condone the atrocities he describes? As a person, what must his own moral standard be? As an educated soul and a member of the intelligentsia, would he not know better, would he be ignorant of the differences between right and wrong? And ultimately, on the level of an explicit ethical challenge to Yashvin's conflicting responsibilities in each of these roles, how can Yashvin save the life of an immoral being? Yashvin knowingly has the opportunity to choose between the moral responsibilities of these several roles, and now must do so.

These questions move Yashvin, but do not overcome his moral paralysis. Now, however, he has been sensitized acutely. A relatively more trivial issue releases and captures the full force of his hitherto unexpressed—perhaps even unacknowledged—moral dismay. As the Colonel orders his men to take the woman away to beat her, Yashvin cries out in protest—ostensibly because it is a woman who is about to be beaten. This breach of chivalry becomes the proverbial straw, or, to use a different metaphor, the lens that focuses Yashvin's indignation. Yashvin realizes that the most terrible episode in his career has begun. With this recognition, he transfers himself and the reader from the mode of moral disengagement to that of ethical discourse. This is the critical moment, the instant of moral revelation, when right and wrong are starkly and inescapably contrasted.

Forced to confront the meaning of what he has witnessed, Yashvin can no longer escape. His weak protest as the woman assails him—"Are you talking to me?," as if there were any other possibility—is a gesture of moral defensiveness, akin to Cain's response after the death of Abel. *Alea jacta est:* "this has been the first step." He has acknowledged, however weakly, the moral revelation. Now the question is whether he will find the wherewithal to act.

Ironically, the Colonel's response, parallelling the woman's taunt, is what challenges Yashvin to his core: "Now I see what sort of a doctor I've been given!" Yashvin is left with no choice. He kills the Colonel. He proves what kind of doctor the Colonel has been given. But has he acted as a physician or in some other role? Has he taken unjust advantage of his access to the Colonel? As a physician, is he not prohibited from killing, particularly from killing his own patient? Would a caring physician not feel at least some remorse?

Susanne Fusso (essay date 1989)

SOURCE: "Failures of Transformation in *Sobač'e serdce*," in *Slavic and East-European Journal,* Vol. 33, No. 3, Fall, 1989, pp. 386-99.

Bulgakov's study.

[*In the following essay, Fusso analyzes the scope of political allegory in* The Heart of a Dog *(Sobač'e serdce), concluding that the allegorical level extends beyond "the level of social and political themes, which lie relatively close to the surface . . . , [to] the level of language, where Bulgakov's critique of radical transformation finds perhaps its deepest expression."*]

Bulgakov's *Sobač'e serdce* is the tale of a transformation: a meddling professor turns a perfectly nice dog into an obnoxious man. As recently as 1984, in Ellendea Proffer's biography of Bulgakov [entitled *Bulgakov: Life and Work,* 1984], the story has been read as an allegory of the revolutionary transformation of Russian society, a cautionary tale about the dangers of tampering with nature. Other readers have been understandably dissatisfied with the schematicism of an interpretation that draws an equation between plot events and political events and seems to deny the richness and complexity so characteristic of Bulgakov. Yet, it is impossible to deny the allegorical aura of this fable-like work. If *Sobač'e serdce* is in fact an allegory, it is by no means a simple or naive one. Bulgakov's allegory is both broader and deeper than the political reading in the tradition of *Animal Farm* implies. It has as its frame of reference not only the Marxist revolution but the cult of the new in all its forms: technological, commercial, linguistic, and aesthetic. The allegory is expressed not just in plot and theme, but in every level of the text. In other words, it is a matter not just of *fabula* but of *sjužet* in Tynjanov's sense, permeating style, lexicon, and narrative construction. The allegorical reading can be refined and deepened through a closer look at the process of transformation in *Sobač'e serdce* not just on the level of social and political themes, which lie relatively close to the surface and have been rather thoroughly elucidated, but on the level of language, where Bulgakov's critique of radical transformation finds perhaps its deepest expression. For of all Bulgakov's works *Sobač'e serdce* is the most skeptical about the possibility of instant, irreversible metamorphosis through the magical power of language.

In his study of the fantastic, [*The Fantastic: A Structural Approach to a Literary Genre,* translated by Richard Howard, 1973], Tzvetan Todorov characterizes metamorphosis as a type of transcendence:

> We say readily enough that someone monkeys around, or that he fights like a lion, like an eagle, *etc.* The supernatural begins the moment we shift from words to the things these words are supposed to designate. The metamorphoses . . . constitute a transgression of the separation of matter and mind as it is generally conceived. . . . the transition from mind to matter has become possible.

This formulation reminds us of the beauty, swiftness, and irreversibility of transformation in that encyclopedia of change, Ovid's *Metamorphoses*. In Ovid's work human desire or guilt combines with divine power to effect miraculous and satisfyingly complete transformation. In *Sobač'e serdce,* transformations are human, devoid of theophany, and thus flawed, incomplete, and reversible—mind fails to control or transcend matter. On the highest level of generality, the stubbornly materialistic universe of this work is related to Bulgakov's attitude toward the recent social transformation of Russia, particularly in response to the myth of that transformation propounded by Vladimir Majakovskij.

Sobač'e serdce, written in early 1925 and not published in the Soviet Union until 1987, is set in the Moscow of the immediate past, December, 1924, to January, 1925, at the height of the NÈP period. A mutt named Šarik, who helps narrate the first three chapters, is lured home by the arch-bourgeois reactionary, Professor Filipp Filippovič Preobraženskij. Preobraženskij's scientific interest is in eugenics, the improvement of the human race, but he makes his living and protects his seven-room apartment from consolidation by performing rejuvenation operations on NÈP-men and government officials. After a period of recuperation and fattening up, during which Šarik observes the goings-on in the *poxabnaja kvartirka,* he himself becomes the subject of an experiment. Preobraženskij practices his surgical techniques by transplanting the pituitary gland and testes of a recently deceased criminal, Klim Čugunkin, into the dog. Contrary to the expected outcome—Šarik's death—the dog survives, gradually takes on human shape and the ability to speak, and christens himself Poligraf Poligrafovič Šarikov. Šarikov resists the educational efforts of both Preobraženskij's assistant Bormental, who attempts to drum the rules of bourgeois etiquette into the wretch's head, and the house manager Švonder, who gives him the *Correspondence of Engels and Kautsky* to read and gets him a job purging the city of stray cats. Šarikov's disruptive escapades take on a serious character when he writes a denunciation of Preobraženskij, and the exasperated professor and his assistant perform another operation, reversing the effects of the original one. The story ends with Šarik, scarred but ignorant of his interlude as a man, watching Preobraženskij continue his researches.

Šarik is born *u Preobraženskoj zastavy,* Klim dies there. The entire story proceeds under the sign of *preobraženie,* transfiguration. On the level of style, the work is saturated with similes, metaphors, and metonymies, which have the momentary effect of transforming one thing into another. In narrative fiction, figurative expressions carry more weight than they do in everyday language because of the significance each detail acquires in the process of interpretation. Thus the figures of speech in *Sobač'e serdce,* as several critics have noted, transform the emotional tone of certain key scenes. The kitchen where Preobraženskij's cook, Dar'ja Petrovna, presides is a hell where she toils in *večnaja ognennaja muka,* and where she flays the bodies of defenseless grouse *kak jarostnyj palač.* The fire of her kitchen is transferred to her amorous exploits when she entertains her fireman lover. *Kak demon pristal,* she murmurs to him. *Do čego vy ognennaja!* he answers. The same change in coloration is given to the scene of the operation on Šarik, as an ominous tone begins to pervade the comic work. For example, Preobraženskij is referred to as *žrec,* pagan priest. This epithet, when combined with Preobraženskij's love for *Aida,* reminds us that the major function of the priest in that opera is to offer up the soprano and the tenor as human sacrifices. He is also compared here to a *vdoxnovennyj razbojnik* and a *sytyj vampir*.

Despite the effect of temporary transformation, these similes stay on this side of Todorov's limit between mind and matter. Dar'ja Petrovna remains a very earthly and innocuous servant despite her figurative ties with hell; Preobraženskij, variously referred to as *božestvo, francuzskij rycar'*, and Faust, remains a recognizably human and unheroic figure. The failure of figurative language to realize itself in *Sobač'e serdce* becomes more obvious when compared with the status of figurative language in *Master i Margarita*. Here there is a constant play with realization of commonplace metaphor. The inhabitants of Apartment No. 50 are said to have "mysteriously disappeared," when in fact they have been arrested, but when the Devil comes to town, people begin to vanish instantaneously and by supernatural means. In an homage to Gogol, a bureaucrat's request, *čerti b menja vzjali,* is immediately granted, and his empty suit is left to toil away behind his desk. And when an audience expresses its dissatisfaction by calling for the M. C.'s head to be torn off, their metaphor is instantly realized by the demonic cat Begemot. No such magical realizations of the figurative occur in *Sobač'e serdce.*

Characters are transformed not only through figurative language but by the physiological changes accompanying emotional stress. Preobraženskij is particularly prone to turn an apoplectic red or a ghostly white under the travails caused by Šarikov and Švonder. The expression *on menjalsja v lice* marks the crisis of several scenes. Such changes in appearance are concentrated in the scenes of the two operations on Šarik. In the first, Preobraženskij's face *stalo strašnym;* Bormental's becomes *mjasistyj i raznocvetnyj.* Even the professor's fingers are transformed: *svoimi korotkimi pal'cami. stavšimi točno čudom tonkimi i gibkimi.* In the later scene of the subduing and retransformation of the odious Šarikov, Bormental is seen by the servants *s ne svoim licom,* and a bit later with *zelenoe lico.* Preobraženskij, too *v tot večer sam na sebja ne byl poxož.* Preobraženskij also undergoes a more protracted change in appearance. Under the strain of dealing with Šarikov, he begins to look older and more haggard. When a former patient comes to warn him of Šarikov's denunciation, he notices *čto professor sgorbilsja i daže kak budto posedel za poslednee vremja.* But this change is seen to have been reversed along with the change of Šarikov back into Šarik: *vse mogli ubedit'sja srazu, čto Filipp Filippovič očen' popravilsja v poslednjuju nedelju.*

All these changes are temporary and psychologically motivated. Bulgakov dealt with changes in appearance very differently in his 1924 story **"D'javoliada."** Here the demonic Kal'soner drives his subordinate Korotkov mad by his rapid, supernatural transformations. He goes from being clean-shaven to having a long Assyrian beard and back again, his voice varies from the clang of a copper pan to a sweet falsetto, and he ultimately becomes a black cat and then a white cock that is swallowed up by the earth only to reappear in Kal'soner's original form

(breathing fire this time) to preside over Korotkov's self-destruction. No explanation is offered; the story is so free with the mind-matter limit as to lose all narrative coherence. By contrast, the changes in appearance in *Sobač'e serdce* are well within the bounds of conventional realistic description. It is only in the context of the story's other types of transformation that they become at all remarkable.

An important verbal transformation is laid bare in Šarik's opening "narration." The convention of the satirical canine observer is a very old one, going back at least to Lucian. But Bulgakov introduces a curious twist. This dog's seemingly first-person narrative is contaminated by the voice of an omniscient third-person narrator. In Mirra Ginsburg's English translation Šarik's narration is printed in italics to set it off from the omniscient narrator's voice, but in the Russian the only signal is provided by the narrator's past-tense verb forms, which interrupt Šarik's present tense. Even Šarik's first-person narration, however, is invaded by bits of information that could be known only to the omniscient narrator, thus disturbing the illusion that the dog is speaking. Šarik lets fall certain facts that he could not possibly know at this point, such as Preobraženskij's name and patronymic and the fact that he is *veličina mirovogo značenija, blagodarja mužskim polovym železam.* When Šarik becomes a man, his first utterances are disconnected obscenities and fragments of conversations. Bormental concludes: *Rugan' èta metodičeskaja, bespreryvnaja i, po-vidimomu, soveršenno bessmyslennaja . . . kak budto èto suščestvo gde-to ran'še slyšala brannye slova, avtomatičeski podsoznatel'no zaneslo ix v svoj mozg i teper' izrygaet ix pačkami.* But this contradicts our initial impression of Šarik's command of language—in his opening narration he is coherent, shrewd, and the master of a literary style. The inevitable conclusion is that the opening narration is actually in one voice, but a voice that shifts between an objective presentation and an *imitation* of a dog's-eye view—a kind of ventriloquism. Bulgakov lays bare the convention of representing a character's inner life. The narrator indeed transforms himself into a dog, but it is an imperfect transformation. Gaps and incongruities are left in order to signal that this transformation too remains on the level of figurative language. This is not a dog's narration but a dog-like narration.

When we move to the level of plot, we find that transformation remains the dominant motif. Again, however, transcendence of the mind-matter limit fails to be achieved; verbal transformation remains verbal, and physical change is brought about by physical means. Rejuvenation is evoked in figurative language twice. Šarik, following the sausage held out to him by Preobraženskij, sees a poster with the words: *Vozmožno li omoloežnie?* He answers: *Natural'no, vozmožno. Zapax omolodil menja . . .* Similarly, Dar'ja Petrovna asks her ardent lover: *Čto ty, čisto tebja tože omolodili?* One of Preobraženskij's patients calls him *mag i čarodej,* but his rejuvenation operations are not a magical feat but a technical one, and it is clear that the technique is still imperfect and in need of improvement. The same patient has green hair, as a result of using a dye made by the government cosmetics industry in an attempt to make his appearance match his rejuvenated sexual appetite. When he suggests that a method of rejuvenating hair might be Preobraženskij's next project, the latter replies: *Ne srazu, ne srazu, moj dorogoj.* This imperfect rejuvenation process can be compared with the magical action of Azazello's cream in *Master i Margarita.* The cream instantaneously takes ten years off Margarita's age—both her vitality and her youthful looks are restored in seconds.

The transformation of Šarik into Šarikov is also connected with figurative language. It evokes the whole complex of Russian expressions built on the word *sobaka: sobač'ja sčast'e* (Bulgakov's original title for the work), *sobač'ja žizn', sobake sobač'ja smert',* and a remarkable saying attested by Dal: *Ne bej sobaki, i ona byla čelovekom* (Dal's note: *obraščena v psa za prožorlivost'*). The pejorative connotations of these expressions, though, are more apposite to Klim the man than to Šarik the dog. The obnoxiousness of Šarikov is due not to his canine aspects but to the human legacy of Klim. If he has a *sobač'e serdce,* it is not in the literal sense of a heart actually belonging to a dog. Šarikov has Klim's human heart, which can be called *sobač'e serdce* only in the pejorative figurative sense.

Despite the metaphorical aura and proverbial documentation of the dog-into-man transformation, the transformation of Šarik, like the rejuvenation operations, is a matter of technical skill, not an instantaneous magical feat brought about by language. Bulgakov devotes an entire harrowing chapter to a description of the operation, informed by his own practical experience as a doctor. He emphasizes the intense physicality of surgery, the pressure to accomplish difficult maneuvers quickly, racing against the perishability of the body. He spares no detail of spurting blood or oozing tissue. The action of opening Šarik's cranium is described as a feat of craftsmanship: [*Preobraženskij*] *načal pilit', kak vypilivajut damskij rukodel'nyj jaščik.* Even the seemingly magical change in Šarik's shape after the operation, described in Dr. Bormental's notebook, is eventually shown to be in accordance with physical laws, as defined within the story. Preobraženskij's discovery that the pituitary gland determines the shape (*oblik*) of the organism is the rational explanation for what otherwise would seem to be a supernatural occurrence. The transformation of Šarik lacks magical ease and speed, but it also lacks magical completeness. Šarikov is not a new being, an educable *tabula rasa,* as Bormental thinks. Preobraženskij recognizes that he cannot be educated beyond the limits of Klim Čugunkin. He refines Bormental's definition of their discovery: *Odnim slovom, gipofiz—zakrytaja kamera, opredeljajuščaja čelovečeskoe dannoe lico. Dannoe! . . . a ne obščečelovečeskoe.* Thus this new creature has a past—the past of Klim Čugunkin, petty crook and alcoholic.

Early in the story, when Preobraženskij triumphs over the house committee that seeks to consolidate his apartment, Šarik thinks: *Čto on, slovo, čto li, takoe znaet?* In fact it is not the power of language but the power of Preobražen-

skij's influence over his highly-placed patient that has done the trick. In general, language does not have the magical efficacy in *Sobač'e serdce* that it does in other Bulgakov works, notably *Master i Margarita.* Here we find, as in *Master i Margarita,* the maxim that a person cannot exist without a document. In *Master i Margarita,* the existence of Aloizij Mogaryč is obliterated and denied when his name disappears from the landlord's rentbook (*Nikakogo Mogaryča ne bylo*), and the Master is restored from nonentity (*Ja teper' nikto*) to full-fledged existence when he retrieves his papers. But in the epilogue of *Sobač'e serdce,* the document attesting to the existence of Poligraf Poligrafovič Šarikov is powerless in the face of the physical evidence of the re-caninized Šarik. Another manifestation of the power of language, frequently used by Gogol, is the way in which rumors take on a life of their own and begin to influence events in the physical world. In the Bulgakov work that immediately preceded *Sobač'e serdce,* "Rokovye jajca," rumors about a scientist's experiment ultimately destroy him, when an angry mob bursts into his laboratory and beats him to death. In *Sobač'e serdce,* similar rumors fly, distorting the nature of Preobraženskij's experiment and linking it with the apocalypse, but they have only the minor result of an increase in annoying telephone calls. In one case, language in the form of rumors exerts an influence over life and death; in the other, despite the threat of apocalypse, language fails to be translated into physical action. "Rokovye jajca" bears an interesting relation to *Sobač'e serdce.* It treats similar plot material but in a very different way. Instead of being set in the immediate past it is set in the near future; as a result the events are given a more fantastic treatment. Of course *Sobač'e serdce* belongs to the genre of science fiction, since the physical laws it posits are not those that we know to be valid, and even Preobraženskij's imperfect operation surpasses the technological capabilities of medical science in the 1920s. But although "Rokovye jajca" is also about a scientific experiment gone wrong, its tone and atmosphere are entirely different from those of *Sobač'e serdce.* In "Rokovye jajca," the Moscow landscape is illuminated by moving, speaking advertisements and news stories flashing from the roofs of skyscrapers; the results of Persikov's experiments culminate in scenes of cartoon violence and gore; the giant, malevolent reptiles to which his ray has given birth decimate the Možajsk cavalry and nearly encircle Moscow. In *Sobač'e serdce,* the streets of the city and the psychology of the characters are realistically observed, and the treatment of Preobraženskij's experiment avoids hyperbole—Preobraženskij's troubles with Šarikov occur on a restricted, one might say intimately domestic, scale. Thus although both stories may technically be labeled science fiction, "Rokovye jajca" is much farther removed from traditional psychological realism than is *Sobač'e serdce.*

Sobač'e serdce lacks the quality determined by Todorov as the hallmark of the fantastic: the hesitation between a rational and a supernatural explanation for unusual events. The narration explicitly postulates a rational, scientific explanation for the change in Šarik; within the narrative, physical laws are obeyed. There are no magic or divine transformations here as in *Master i Margarita,* where demonic mountebanks turn rubles into dollars, a beret into a meowing cat, and a human head into a jewelled goblet. *Sobač'e serdce* stays stubbornly within a materialistic universe, where verbal transformations remain figures of speech and physical transformations are difficult, slow, and incomplete.

Why does Bulgakov here discredit the magical power of language, while in other works he allows Todorov's mindmatter limit to be freely transgressed? A clue is provided by the presence in the text of Vladimir Majakovskij. Majakovskij appears precisely in his capacity as *čarodej* for the new Soviet state, utterer of magical incantations designed to influence external reality, high priest of magically realized metaphor. The first reference to Majakovskij appears in Šarik's opening narration. The dog quotes Majakovskij's most famous advertising slogan: *Nigde krome kak v Mossel'prome.* Majakovskij took advertising very seriously; of this slogan he wrote: *Nesmotrja na poètičeskoe uljuljukan'e, sčitaju 'Nigde krome kak v Mossel'prome' poèziej samoj vysokoj kvalifikacii [Polnoe sobranie sočinenijv trinadcati tomax,* 1955-61]. He saw advertising as the industrial and commercial branch of agitation. In a 1923 article, *Agitacija i reklama,* he emphasizes the magical efficacy of good advertising: *Nado zvat', nado reklamirovat', čtob kaleki nemedlenno isceljalis' i bežali pokupat', torgovat', smotret'!* Advertising is the creation of a name that wields persuasive power: *Reklama—èto imja vešči. Kak xorošij xudožnik sozdaet sebe imja, tak sozdaet sebe imja i vešč'. Uvidev na obložki žurnala 'znamenitoe' imja, ostanavlivajutsja kupit'.*

In *Sobač'e serdce,* the "magical" power of advertising is seen from another point of view, as a pathetic deception. Majakovskij's attempts to create powerful names for Soviet products are consistently undermined in the text. His Mossel'prom slogan is wickedly altered by Šarik. When the dog sees the well-dressed Preobraženskij buying a sausage in a state store, he cries: *Začem ona vam? Dlja čego vam gnilaja lošad'? Nigde, krome takoj otravy ne polučite, kak v Mossel'prome.* Throughout the story, Soviet products are shown to be contaminations, substitutions, or pure fictions, as in the case of the galoshes that Majakovskij peddled for Rezinotrest. When Preobraženskij asks Šarikov what will become of all the cats he's strangled in the Purge Bureau, he replies: *Na pol'ty pojdut . . . iz nix belok budut delat' na rabočij kredit.* The cats will, of course, remain cats, despite being called squirrels. The "name of the thing" as advertised fails to change the substandard nature of the thing itself.

Another reference to Majakovskij occurs during a dinner at which Preobraženskij expounds to Bormental his reactionary views on the recent revolution. When Bormental timidly suggests that the sudden disappearance of galoshes and steam heat is due to *razruxa,* Preobraženskij explodes. He calls the word *miraž, dym, fikcija. Čto takoe èto vaša razruxa? Staruxa s kljukoj? Ved'ma, kotoraja vybila vse stekla, potušila vse lampy?* According to Preobraženskij, *razruxa* is an imaginary scapegoat on which people blame their intellectual and physical inabil-

ity to cope with external difficulties. In his view, *razruxa* is in people's heads. *Značit, kogda èti baritony kričat 'bej razruxu!'—ja smejus' . . . Èto označaet, čto každyj iz nix dolžen lupit' sebja po zatylku!*

It is not hard to guess that these "baritones" represent a paranoiacally multiplied Vladimir Majakovskij. It was indeed he who created the fairy-tale figure of *razruxa—trekljataja staruxa* for his *Okna ROSTA* agitational posters in 1920. *Razruxa,* who also appears in act 5 of the 1920 version of *Misterija-buff,* is the embodiment of the forces of chaos and destruction. Hand in hand with her brother *Golod,* she goes about the country smashing machinery and gobbling up workers. Majakovskij depicts her as a bright-green goblin with a bent girder in her mouth.

Both Majakovskij's advertising and his ROSTA windows were ubiquitous in Moscow of the 1920s, and they presented Bulgakov with a vivid image of Majakovskij's approach to the achievement of utopia. Majakovskij creates a world of magic words, of glittering, if as yet nonexistent, consumer goods, of fairy-tale monsters, of heroic Red Army soldiers who can defeat any counterrevolutionary ogre as long as they are armed with the right rhyming couplets. In a 1923 feuilleton, Bulgakov depicts Majakovskij on a balcony, hurling words *tjaželye, kak bulyžniki* onto the crowd below (*Sob. soč.*). If in *Sobač'e serdce* words are denied their usual magical weight and efficacy, it is perhaps because Bulgakov is attempting to counter Majakovskij's magical approach to the large-scale social transformation that forms the background to *Sobač'e serdce*—the 1917 revolutions.

Bulgakov's works of the decade following the Revolution fix on the physical obstacles blocking the path to utopia. He has left us a graphic picture of the lack of food, clothing, and especially living space endured by all Russians in those years. In his 1923 feuilleton **"Sorok sorokov,"** he looks back on the immediate post-Revolutionary period with clear eyes, denying the attempts of poets to change history through wishful assertion. . . .

Like the smaller-scale transformations in *Sobač'e serdce,* the transformation of Russian society is a human production, and limited by human power and skill to cope with physical obstacles. Despite his belief in language, when dealing with the problems of post-Revolutionary Russia Bulgakov is concerned to deny the kind of magical incantation indulged in by Majakovskij and his epigones.

In speaking of the possible achievement of utopia, Bulgakov uses not Majakovskij's term "kommuna" but the term "zolotoj vek" (which he will consider to have arrived when sunflower seeds disappear from the streets of Moscow). The classical allusion reminds us that Bulgakov's attitude toward the past also contrasts with that of Majakovskij. For Majakovskij, the Revolution was a realization of the Futurist metaphor of complete newness, of being able to purge language and literature of its past and to start afresh. Bulgakov, who began his public career in Vladikavkaz defending Puškin in a debate against a Majakovskij clone, approached survivals of the past in a very different spirit. For him the famous Futurist call to "throw Puškin, Dostoevskij, Tolstoj, *etc., etc.,* overboard from the Steamship of Modernity" is not only obnoxious but impracticable. The eighteenth-century odic tradition lives on in Majakovskij just as the unpleasant predilections of Klim Šugunkin live on in Šarikov. Even the most radical invention of the Futurists, *zaum'*, cannot free itself entirely of the past; its most brilliant practitioner, Xlebnikov, relies for the power and resonance of his poetry on the meanings and associations accumulated by Russian phonemes and morphemes over the centuries.

As we have seen, Preobraženskij's transformation of Šarik fails to eradicate the past; the new creature is merely the sum of Klim's character plus a few doggy habits. Although this creates an uncomfortable situation for the professor, there is something comforting in the thought that nothing is really lost, that human transformations fail in completeness and irreversibility. In **"Sorok sorokov,"** Bulgakov's narrator looks out on a panorama of Moscow and sees not only the new but the old—he takes pleasure in recording the former names of buildings and institutions. The skyline is dominated by the "forty forties," the domes of Moscow's ancient churches that have witnessed so many humanly induced transformations. His is not the sour nostalgia of a Preobraženskij but the calm conscientiousness of an historian, noting the outlines of the past that remain ineradicably in the present and the future.

. . . . .

A final, tangential note. One of the most important functions of language is its labeling function. The consequences of accepting a label or having it forced upon one may be of life-and-death magnitude; the wrong label can mean prison, the right one can mean escape from starvation. Among the genres to which *Sobač'e serdce* belongs (the literature of talking dogs, of Faust, of Frankenstein) is the literature of hunger, the literature that investigates what happens when bodily needs and desires corrupt the spirit. (In a sense, *Master i Margarita* belongs to the same genre.) The imperative of the belly was of necessity a vital topic in Soviet literature of the post-1917 era. Even Majakovskij's apocalyptic *Misterija-buff* is really the story of a group of people in search of a decent meal. In *Sobač'e serdce,* Šarik is the character most aware of this imperative, having known starvation, and it is his search for security and satiety that leads to his temporary downfall. He initially resists the name Šarik given him by passersby, on the grounds of inappropriateness: *Šarik—èto značit kruglyj, upitannyj, glupyj, ovsjanku žret, syn znatnyx roditelej, a on loxmatyj, dolgovjazyj i rvanyj, šljajka podžaraja, bezdomnyj pes*. Gradually, however, lulled by the bourgeois comfort of Preobraženskij's home, Šarik changes his identity from vagabond to oatmeal-eating *barskij pes*. He even begins to imagine an aristocratic lineage for himself: *Očen' vozmožno, čto babuška moja sogrešila s vodolazom.*

When Šarik is anesthetized, the last words that float through his head are: *Za čto?* He has perhaps offered the

answer himself in his pre-operative meditations. He admits to himself that he has irrevocably adopted the label *barskij pes* and traded freedom for comfort. *Da i čto takoe volja? Tak, dym, miraž, fikcija, . . . Bred ètix zlosčastnyx demokratov. . . .* Unlike Majakovskij's *razruxa, volja* is not a fairytale witch but a word with a meaningful history. It is for Šarik's failure of courage, his willingness to deny the meaning of freedom, that he is delivered into the hands of his torturers. Šarik is restored to life at the end of *Sobač'e serdce,* but he has no memory of the transformation to which he has been subjected. There is no guarantee that the same thing will not happen again to the unsuspecting dog. The final scene emphasizes the reversibility of change. Whole phrases are repeated from the pre-operation narrative; the original equilibrium of Preobraženskij's apartment has been restored. But the seeds of change also remain, in the form of Preobraženskij's continuing scientific quest. Šarik has been granted at least temporary peace, but light, the awareness of danger that might arm him against it, has been denied.

Although the ending of *Sobač'e serdce* might seem to be a Bulgakovian idyll (drawn shades, humming radiators, intellectual at work), the final line from *Aida* cannot help but evoke the frightening image of the cowled surgeon-executioner; the ominous, threatening side of Preobraženskij's personality is clearly present up to the end. Despite attempts to identify Bulgakov with Preobraženskij, Bulgakov's feuilletons of the 1920s do not deal kindly with people who hang onto seven-room apartments in the midst of a housing shortage. Bulgakov may have had a bourgeois background, but in 1920 he starved along with the proletariat. In **"Sorok sorokov"** his autobiographical narrator describes his Šarik-like position between two worlds. . . . Survival is won by refusing to capitulate to either camp, by persistence and courage in holding onto freedom—freedom from labels.

Bulgakov's position in relation to literary conservatism on the one hand and the *avant-garde* on the other is similar to that of his autobiographical narrator *vis-à-vis* the bourgeoisie and the proletariat. Zholkovsky has subtly analyzed the way in which Bulgakov complicates the familiar carnival opposition between the forces of order (government) and of disorder (revolt) in *Sobač'e serdce*: the professor is both a challenger of the ruling ideology (the Soviet state) and a conservative opponent of disorder, while Šarikov, the carnival clown, is presented not as a liberator but as the villain of the piece. *"Èta paradoksal'naja konfiguracija—produkt togo perexodnogo istoričeskogo momenta, kogda pod Porajdkom, podryvu kotorogo posvjaščen Karnaval, možet ponimat'sja kak staryj, tak i novyj režim"* [A. K. Žolkovskij, "Dialog Bulgakova: Oleši (o kolbase, parade čuvstv i Golgofe)," in *Sintaksis* 20 (1988)]. At the moment when the last have become first, when political (and literary) radicalism have become orthodoxy, the individual who wishes to side with either Order or Disorder may not know where to look. Bulgakov's literary strategies take full account of this bewildering *perexodnyj istoričeskij moment*. He refuses the label either of literary conservative or of avant-gardist; like the narrator of **"Sorok sorokov,"** he *perenjal . . .*

priemy v oboix lagerjax, combining respect for tradition with brilliantly conceived experimentation. *Sobač'e serdce* may be a product of Bulgakov's reaction against the *avant-garde,* but *Master i Margarita,* with its strikingly original blend of psychological realism, horror-movie fantasy, and religious myth, actually makes us believe, contrary to the convictions of its author, that there can be something new under the sun.

Edythe C. Haber (essay date 1992)

SOURCE: "The Social and Political Context of Bulgakov's 'The Fatal Eggs'," in *Slavic Review,* Vol. 51, No. 3, Fall, 1992, pp. 497-510.

[*In the essay below, Haber discusses the satirical parallels between the events following the Bolshevik Revolution and the characters and circumstances in the story "The Fatal Eggs."*]

"The Fatal Eggs," written in 1924 and published in early 1925, was the first of Bulgakov's works to attract widespread attention—and a storm of controversy. Recipient of a few positive reviews as well as uniformly enthusiastic praise—privately expressed—from writers and editors, the novella was also the object of virulent attack from a number of (mostly proletarian) critics. Among the attackers were those who saw the work as a thinly veiled allegory and Professor Persikov's discovery of the "revolutionary" red ray as an allusion to the socialist experiments of the bolsheviks.

While a link between the scientific and socio-political levels of the novella indubitably exists, a strict allegorical reading (in which more recent critics have also been known to engage) is too simplistic to accommodate Bulgakov's rich, complex portrayal of Soviet society. The work's resistance to schematic interpretation, moreover, is compounded by two factors. The first is the myriad of referents associated with its main characters and its central images which operate simultaneously on several planes— the scientific, religio-metaphysical and political—and each level contains multiple meanings, not always easily reconcilable. The second factor, which especially complicates interpretation of the socio-political level, is the blurring of time: while occurring in the near future (1928), the novella contains an intricate web of allusions to events of the immediate past. This essay will focus on the social and political dimensions of **"The Fatal Eggs"** and, by examining in detail the topical realia underlying Bulgakov's fantastic world, reach a more precise understanding than heretofore of these relatively neglected aspects. We should thereby arrive at a greater appreciation of the scope and richness of the work as a whole.

When one turns to the descriptions of Moscow in **"The Fatal Eggs,"** one is struck immediately by the absence of the schematism generally associated with futuristic, allegorical works. Bulgakov's city is, in fact, so far from a straightforward communist utopia (or anti-utopia) that little specifically socialist remains. The noise, lights, rush-

ing cars and teeming crowds render Moscow almost indistinguishable from other modern metropolises like New York or London:

> It [the city] shone, lights danced, died down and flashed up. On Theater Square the white headlights of buses and the green lights of trolleys revolved; above the former Miur and Meriliz, over the added tenth story, an electrical, multi-colored woman was jumping, emitting multi-colored words letter by letter: "workers' credit." In the public garden opposite the Bolshoi Theater, where a multi-colored fountain gushed at night, a crowd pushed and hummed.

In this dynamic urban world, many distinguishing signs of bolshevism are fast fading: "comrade" has virtually disappeared from the vocabulary and civil war garb is entirely replaced by suit jackets even among the proletariat. This is not a depiction of a rationalized, socialist city of the future; rather, it is the Moscow of 1928 from the vantage point of the mixed system of NEP [New Economic Policy] that prevailed in 1924.

> **When one turns to the descriptions of Moscow in "The Fatal Eggs," one is struck immediately by the absence of the schematism generally associated with futuristic, allegorical works.**
>
> —*Edythe C. Haber*

In this regard, **"The Fatal Eggs"** has particularly close ties to Bulgakov's feuilletons published in 1922-1924 in the Berlin "Change of Landmarks" newspaper, *Nakanune.* But the construction and return of plenty of NEP portrayed so vividly in the latter is projected into the near future in the former. The housing crisis, the bane of Bulgakov's early Soviet existence, is at an end and nascent technology and construction have advanced. And if in one *Nakanune* feuilleton a tail coat amazingly materializes among the uniforms and leather jackets of the civil war period, by the time **"The Fatal Eggs"** takes place the entire audience at Persikov's lecture is dressed in evening clothes. In the *Nakanune* pieces, Bulgakov's depiction of the glittering hybrid world of NEP, although far from uncritical, is filled with the optimism and vitality of a recovery period; the Moscow of **"The Fatal Eggs"** in many ways reflects that optimism. Indeed, some reviewers singled out for praise the glowing depiction of Moscow of the future: " . . . the author of a utopian r-r-revolutionary novel could hardly arouse in his readers the same sense of a powerful, joyous country, a true New World" [L-v, *Novyi mir,* 6 (1925)]. Even a more negative reviewer [A. Men'shoi, "Moskva v 1928-m godu," in *Zhizn' iskusstva* 18 (1955)] praised the "beauty" of the contrasts of old and new, the "running, rush, quickness, dynamism of our marvelous days."

The contemporary reader of **"The Fatal Eggs"** associated this glittering, speeding city not only—not even primarily—with the new bolshevik order, but with America. Thus our negative critic [Men'shoi] sums up his impression: "Moscow has started living American-style [*zazhila po-amerikanski*]. Moscow has become entirely Americanized [*obamerikanilas'*]." And there are in the text numerous explicit links between this "New World" and America. Persikov's housing problem, for example, has been solved by the efforts of a "united American-Russian company" which in 1926 "built . . . 15 fifteen-story houses in the center of Moscow and 300 workers' cottages, each containing eight apartments, on the outskirts, thus ending once and for all the terrible and ridiculous housing crisis that so tormented Muscovites in the years 1919-1925." And Persikov himself is lured by Americanisms: he agrees to answer the questions of an impudent journalist because " . . . all the same, there is something American in this scoundrel." Bulgakov depicts this Americanized society with considerable élan, but also with implicit reservations. His city is a place, after all, where artificial light replaces the natural, where the increased speed and growth brought about by technology have also increased the level of ruthlessness.

This process, symptomatic of all modern, technological societies, is analogous to the developments among the amoebae which run amok under Professor Persikov's ray. And there are additional parallels between society and Persikov's laboratory, especially apparent in Professor Persikov's relations with journalists where colored rays and magnification also play a role. One evening, for example, when the professor is out on the street, he is accosted by a journalist and blinded by a "violet ray" apparently from a camera. The next day he sees himself, much magnified, "on the roof, on a white screen, shielding himself with his fists from the violet ray." Such importunate journalists (who also figure in the work that inspired **"The Fatal Eggs,"** H. G. Wells's *Food of the Gods*) are, like the speed, crowds and artificial lights of Moscow, a feature of the modern world as a whole, not just of socialist society: yet another indication that Bulgakov's Moscow cannot be reduced to a schematic vision of the bolshevik future.

At the same time, however, one must avoid the extreme of regarding the city as merely a generalized metropolis. The society of the novella reflects the hybrid system of NEP in which specific features both of the west and of bolshevism play roles. The most salient feature of the latter—and one that emphasizes the parallels between Persikov's laboratory and contemporary society—is central control. If the social Darwinism underlying laissez-faire capitalism in the west is analogous to unfettered natural evolution, the laboratory, with its controlling and manipulating intelligence, is the model for socialism. From the beginning of **"The Fatal Eggs,"** socialist central control, imposed primarily by the GPU [the Russian secret police], co-exists with the elemental urban life typical of all modern cities. When, for example, the journalist Bronskii, "staff member of the Moscow magazines *Red Flame, Red Pepper, Red Journal, Red Projector* and the Moscow newspaper *Red Evening Moscow*," calls upon Persikov, the scientist at first summarily orders him thrown out. But when he learns that Bronskii also works for *Red Raven*, a publication of the GPU, he relents and agrees to see him.

Although the GPU is here and elsewhere a coercive force, relations between the professor and the secret police are not entirely adversarial. Persikov, indeed, summons the GPU when a suspicious character offers him 5,000 rubles to pass his discovery to a foreign government. At that point, parallels between Persikov and the GPU emerge that reinforce the analogies between his control in the laboratory and their control of society as a whole.

Throughout the novella Persikov is portrayed as a "divinity" who tampers with nature in the "hell" of his laboratory; the three GPU agents who come to him are also a blend of the heavenly and the diabolical. The first is "reminiscent of an angel in patent-leather boots. The second, shortish, . . . [is] terribly gloomy . . . " The third, like the professor, is endowed with extraordinary vision and has "amazingly piercing [*koliuchie*] eyes" which, although covered by smoky glasses, "see the study, illuminated and permeated with streams of tobacco smoke, through and through." They, like Persikov, are amazingly knowledgeable and are able to identify a suspicious visitor from a mere glimpse of a galosh he left behind. Grateful to Persikov for his cooperation, the GPU agents offer to control the pesky journalists, to prevent them from disturbing him. Accustomed to total control in his laboratory, Persikov requests that the reporters be shot, just as he killed his irradiated tadpoles when they got out of hand. The response of one of the agents reveals the congruous methods of the secret police and the scientist: " . . . of course that would be good . . . however, such a project is already being worked out [*nazrevaet*] at the Council of Labor and Defense . . . "

Persikov's tragedy in **"The Fatal Eggs"** is that in the course of the novella he himself becomes victim to his belief in scientific control. The GPU not only attempts (and fails) to control forces inimical to him, but they and the government as a whole also repeatedly manipulate the man of genius himself. And so, while Persikov is in one sense a "divinity," a model to his science-worshipping society, at the same time he is but a means to its end: just as a frog is "crucified" by Persikov in a scientific experiment, so in the end is he himself "crucified" in the state's larger social experiment.

The ever-present power of the state, overshadowed at the beginning of the novella by the glitter and dynamism of modern, urban society, emerges only during a national crisis: the chicken plague which first breaks out in a provincial town and soon spreads throughout the country. Not only does the disease show the limitation of scientific control over the forces of nature, as others have noted, it also takes on other levels of meaning, from frivolous to grave. Clearly of the first category are the scabrous associations evoked by the resulting shortage of eggs (eggs in colloquial Russian = balls, testicles); for example, performers at a night club sing: "Oh, mama, what will I do without eggs?" And a feuilleton that lambasts a Mr. Hughes (an allusion to Charles Evans Hughes, American Secretary of State) concludes: "Don't hanker after our eggs, Mr. Hughes—you have your own!"

The ostensibly light-hearted reference to Hughes points to another, non-sexual order of impotence in the Soviet Union and is part of a complex web of political allusion in the novella. The political, indeed international, political significance of the chicken plague is manifest, first of all, by the fact that it ceases immediately at the borders of the Soviet Union. As the narrator comments: "Whether the climate there was different or the defensive-cordoning measures taken by neighboring governments played a role, the fact is that the plague went no farther"; the military terminology (*zagraditel'nye kordonnye mery*) here alludes to the *cordon sanitaire* placed around the Soviet Union by western powers to prevent the spread of the "contagion" of revolution. One also recalls that in the satirical allegory **"The Crimson Island,"** written shortly before **"The Fatal Eggs,"** the revolution itself is termed a "plague" against which a quarantine is enforced by nervous imperialist powers. In **"The Crimson Island,"** the plague is declared over six years after the revolution, at which point the French and British decide to invade the island. And in **"The Fatal Eggs"** (written in the seventh year after the revolution), the plague arouses fear of intervention. A voice from a loudspeaker calls out: "New attempts at intervention! . . . in connection with the chicken plague!"; and a newsboy cries: "Poland is preparing for a nightmarish war!"

Bulgakov envisioned a recurrence of intervention and Polish invasion based on the Soviet political situation shortly before **"The Crimson Island"** and **"The Fatal Eggs"** were written. The fear of intervention arose with French occupation of the Ruhr in early 1923 and the concomitant threat of invasion by France's eastern ally, Poland. This fear was exacerbated when the fiercely anti-bolshevik Lord Curzon came to power in England and in May 1923 presented the Soviets with a very stiff ultimatum. In the very first published entry in his diary, Bulgakov writes of the events leading up to the ultimatum: "There is the smell of a rupture or even of war in the air. . . . It's awful that Poland and Rumania have also begun stirring. . . . In general we are on the eve of [momentous] events." In one of his *Nakanune* feuilletons, **"Benefit Performance for Lord Curzon,"** Bulgakov describes a mass demonstration against the Curzon ultimatum. Chicherin, the principal orator at the demonstration, imputed Lenin's illness as basis for the current crisis since it had convinced the bolsheviks' enemies that "Soviet power is deprived of its firmness and can be overthrown by pressure from without." He concluded: "We firmly await our enemy before our threshold . . . " [quoted in Edward Hallett Carr, *A History of Soviet Russia: The Interregnum, 1923-1924,* 1954]. Thus the chicken plague symbolizes both the revolutionary contagion with which the Soviet Union was threatening other nations and the weakness of the country itself in 1923-1924 when the death of its powerful leader "emasculated" the country and invited foreign invasion.

If the plague imagery in **"The Fatal Eggs"** parallels that in **"The Crimson Island,"** the depiction in the novella of international relations is far more complex. The Soviet Union has not been "quarantined" after all: with its American housing, German scientific equipment and French electric revolvers, among many other things, it appears to enjoy full economic relations with capitalist countries. And while the chicken plague does bring the risk of foreign intervention, it also results in a massive import of eggs. This rather contradictory state of affairs actually reflects the international situation by late 1923 and early 1924 when the Soviet Union, in desperate need of foreign aid for its economic recovery, attempted to normalize relations with western powers by establishing active trade and, in some cases, diplomatic relations. The danger of foreign conflict remained, however, due to Soviet unwillingness to abandon revolutionary activities abroad and to pay its foreign debt. This unstable international situation—broad foreign contact co-existing uneasily with foreign threat—is projected into the future in Bulgakov's fiction.

In addition to this complex of political referents, the chicken plague alludes as well to the chronic agricultural problems with which the country was suffering, in particular to the serious drought that threatened the harvest of 1924. The measures taken in **"The Fatal Eggs"** to combat the chicken plague echo the Soviet government's reactions to the agricultural and international crises of 1923-1924. In July 1924 an "emergency commission for combating the consequences of the deficient harvest" [Carr, *A History of Soviet Russia: Socialism in One Country,* 1958] was set up, a manifestation of the increasing demand placed upon scientists to redirect their attention toward social problems. As Trotsky wrote in *Pravda* in late 1923: " . . . all of us very much need a new orientation on the part of scientists: the adjustment of their attention, their interests, and their efforts to the tasks and demands of the new social structure" ["Science in the Task of Socialist Construction," translated by Frank Manning and George Saunders, in *Problems of Everyday Life and Other Writings on Culture and Science,* 1973. Originally published in *Pravda,* November 24, 1923]. Another, more significant result of this demand was the formation, also in 1924, of a chemists' organization, *Dobrokhim,* whose main task was to find practical uses for chemistry, especially in defense. In **"The Fatal Eggs,"** there are organizations analogous to the "commission for the deficient harvest" and to *Dobrokhim*: the "emergency commission for combating the chicken plague" and *Dobrokur.* Persikov becomes a member of both organizations and follows the path that Trotsky envisioned for scientists in which obligation to the state takes precedence over pure research.

Persikov's intellectual autonomy—like that of actual scientists of the time—is ever more eroded by his civic duties. The real test of his autonomy, however, occurs upon the arrival of Alexander Semenovich Rokk, director of the Red Ray *sovkhoz.* Rokk wants to put the red ray to immediate practical use: to accelerate chicken breeding and thus end the crisis. The professor's confrontation with Rokk is a test that Persikov ultimately fails when, Pilate-like, he declares "I wash my hands" and yields the equipment to the *sovkhoz* chairman. In the hands of Rokk, the ray, without losing its broader implications in modern technological society as a whole, becomes specifically associated with the socialist experiment; it is he who attempts to apply the laboratory model to the real world.

Yet to regard Rokk as simply an undifferentiated communist is a mistaken response to this complex tale; one must define more exactly the position that he occupies in the ideological spectrum in the Moscow of 1928. When he enters Persikov's study, the professor is struck by his revolutionary garb, his leather jacket and "immense mauser pistol," an attire that, the narrator explains, makes him look "strangely old-fashioned" in the Moscow of 1928. He adds: "In 1919 this man would have fit in perfectly, he would have been tolerated in 1924, at its beginning, but in 1928 he was strange." Of special importance is "in 1924, at its beginning," for in January of that year two events occurred which may have led Bulgakov to predict a shift in the Communist Party of the future. The first was the death of Lenin; more significant for **"The Fatal Eggs,"** however, was an early indication that Trotsky would fall from power: a newspaper bulletin, announcing his illness and "leave with full freedom from all duties for a period of no less than two months." In his diary, Bulgakov quotes the bulletin, then commenting: "And so on 8 January 1924 they chucked Trotsky out. God only knows what will happen to Russia." The writer no doubt reacted so strongly to news of Trotsky's "leave" because the bitter struggle taking place within the Communist Party pitted supporters of the ruling triumvirate—Zinoviev, Kamenev and Stalin—against Trotsky and other so-called "deviationists." These latter considered the NEP a retreat from revolutionary socialist principles to be replaced as soon as possible by greater central control of the economy, while the ruling coalition advocated the more popular line of continuing the policy. Thus Bulgakov, having observed the weakening of the more doctrinaire branch of the Party, described the Moscow of **"The Fatal Eggs"** as having a flourishing NEP with zealous revolutionaries such as Rokk virtually extinct—although, as the novella demonstrates, they may reappear at a time of crisis.

Further evidence of Rokk's link with Trotsky's followers can be found by comparing him to the diabolical Shpolianskii in *The White Guard*. Like Shpolianskii. Rokk was an artist before the revolution. However, as former flutist at "the cozy Cinema Enchanted Dreams [*Volshebnye grezy*] in the city of Ekaterinoslav," Rokk parodies the formidable Petersburg poet and critic. The revolution marked a sharp break in Rokk's life, as it did in Shpolianskii's: he replaced his flute with a mauser and began to wander from one end of the country to the other. Himself radically transformed, he set about transforming the nation, both by "enlightening" its populace, as editor of a newspaper in Turkestan, and by altering it physically, as a member of a commission concerned with irrigation there. The image of Rokk at the end of **"The Fatal Eggs"** is also congruous to that of Trotsky himself toward the end of *The White Guard*. In **"The Fatal Eggs,"** the diabolical snakes that hatch from "Rokk's eggs" (an alternative trans-

lation of the novella's title) threaten to invade Moscow just as the poet Rusakov in the novel envisions Satan-Trotsky's legions coming from the "kingdom of the anti-Christ, Moscow" and invading Kiev.

Rokk's convictions and proclivities, moreover, coincide—in travestied form, of course—with Trotsky's. Rokk's unquestioning faith in Persikov's ray (" . . . your ray is so renowned you could even raise elephants, not just chicks") lampoons Trotsky's belief in the power of science and technology to conquer nature. The latter in 1924 imagined that: "Through the machine, man in Socialist society will command nature in its entirety. . . . He will change the course of rivers, and he will lay down rules for the oceans" [*Literature and Revolution,* translated by Rose Strunsky, 1960]. He also envisaged physiological transformations (not in chickens, to be sure, but in people): "Even purely physiologic life will become subject to collective experiments. The human species, the coagulated *homo sapiens,* will once more enter into a state of radical transformation, and, in his own hands, will become an object of the most complicated methods of artificial selection and psycho-physical training. This is entirely in accord with evolution . . . "

Rokk parodies not only Trotsky's pronouncements on science but also his devotion to high art and his belief that in a socialist society masterpieces of the past could enrich and elevate the ignorant proletariat: "What the worker will take from Shakespeare, Goethe, Pushkin, or Dostoievsky, will be a more complex idea of human personality, of its passions and feelings, a deeper and profounder understanding of its psychic forces and of the role of the subconscious, etc. In the final analysis, the worker will become richer." However, when Rokk tests the civilizing effects of culture and tries to charm by playing *Evgenii Onegin* on his flute to a product of "revolutionary" change (one of the giants that has hatched from the "fatal eggs"), the creature proves impervious to high art. It jumps past the *sovkhoz* director and strangles his wife—the first of an untold number of ghastly fatalities that result from his ill-conceived experiment.

Rokk also shares Trotsky's association with the newest, most technological of art forms, the cinema. Such enthusiasm for the medium was, of course, widespread among political and artistic radicals of the time: Lenin himself dubbed film "the most important of all the arts." In "Vodka, the Church, and the Cinema" [in *Problems of Everyday Life,* originally published in *Pravda,* July 12, 1923] Trotsky looked to motion pictures to replace both tavern and church in Russian life, and hoped to "make up for the separation of the church from the socialist state by the fusion of the socialist state and the cinema . . . Having no need of a clergy in brocade, etc., the cinema unfolds on the white screen spectacular images of greater grip than are provided by the richest church. . . . " Early in **"The Fatal Eggs,"** as we have seen, magnified representations created by artificial rays are projected onto Moscow buildings and play a prominent part in the new society. Rokk's revolutionary transformation, to be sure, entails severing his former tie to the cinema and abandoning his cozy bourgeois niche in the "dusty starry satin" of the Enchanted Dreams Movie Theater for the "open sea of war and revolution." The narrator ironically adds: "It turned out that this man was positively great, and of course it was not for him to sit in the lobby of Dreams." Rokk, however, merely transfers the cinematic dream world from the stuffy little theater out into the great world of revolution: he now has the "cinematic" task of creating giant beings by means of an artificial ray. This task, moreover, involves usurpation of the divine-religious function, as do motion pictures in Trotsky's view.

The combination of cinematic motif and religious imagery continues: Rokk's "cinematic" effort to play God having failed, he undergoes a reverse transformation to "Biblical prophet" and entreats two skeptical GPU agents: "Listen to me. Listen. Why don't you believe?" When the agents investigate, they find a "strange cinematic light" illuminating a huge number of giant snakes and on the floor three experimental boxes which resemble "immense cameras." The "enchanted dreams" of Rokk's cinematic past become a nightmare when transferred to the world of reality; the blasphemous attempt at creation results in terrible destruction.

Rokk is not a stereotypical communist; rather, he is associated specifically with Trotsky and others who advocated a return to the accelerated revolutionary processes of war communism. This is not to imply, of course, an identification of Rokk with Trotsky: there is little superficial likeness between the brilliant and urbane co-maker of the Russian revolution and the provincial, semi-educated *sovkhoz* director. Through Rokk, Bulgakov demonstrates instead the untold havoc that could be wrought by Trotsky's grandiose beliefs in the transforming powers of science and art.

The snake incursion itself also has a complex of political referents, domestic and international. The fact that the disaster originates in the countryside—especially at a new Soviet institution, a *sovkhoz*—suggests an analogy between the horrifying outcome of Rokk's experiments and a peasant uprising resulting from over-precipitous attempts to socialize the rural population. Dissatisfaction is expressed by the peasantry in the novella: in response to the thousand human deaths resulting from the plague, a "prophet" appears in Volokolamsk "who proclaim[s] that the chicken plague was caused by none other than the commissars . . ." The peasants then beat "several policemen who were taking chickens away from peasant women" and break windows in the local post office and telegraph station. Another example of peasant dissatisfaction, more closely tied to the basic plot, occurs shortly before the eggs hatch when the housemaid warns Rokk of mortal danger from the peasants: "They say that your eggs are diabolical. . . . They wanted to kill you." The next day, after the appearance of a "well-known troublemaker and sage," the eggs hatch and giant anacondas and ostriches overrun the land.

Bulgakov's concern about disorder in the countryside is confirmed by a diary entry of late 1923 in which he reported that "hooliganism is developing among the young people in the villages" and observed that "We are a savage, dark, unfortunate people." Rural rioting occurred in 1924 and there were murders of *sel'kory* (village correspondents) whose ardent bolshevism, reminiscent of Rokk's, aroused antagonism among the peasants. That Bulgakov linked these disorders to future catastrophe is attested in a diary entry of late 1924, where he comments on a *sel'kor* murder, "Either I have no intuition [*chut'e*] . . . or this is the introduction to a totally unbelievable opera."

The international aspects of the snake incursion are also numerous: within **"The Fatal Eggs"** itself there are references to the threat of intervention; the eggs are of foreign origin and the beasts that hatch from them are exotic; the snakes follow the "Napoleonic" route through burning Smolensk to the threshold of Moscow; Budennyi's cavalry is mobilized as it was during the Polish campaign of the civil war. In Bulgakov's diary entries for 1923 and early 1924, moreover, he expressed numerous times the premonition of impending war or other disaster and occasionally echoed almost verbatim his reaction to the Curzon ultimatum, "we are on the eve of events." These premonitions were linked with particular frequency to the failed German revolution of fall 1923 in whose planning the Russian communists were centrally involved. That Bulgakov was aware of the Soviets' revolutionary activities in Germany is also apparent in his diary: "The Communist Party is bending over backwards [*iz kozhi von lezet*] to incite a revolution in Germany and create havoc." And he speculated on a possible struggle between fascism and communism (which would seem prophetic were it not such a frequent topic in *Pravda* and *Izvestiia* at the time): " . . . who knows, perhaps the world really is splitting into two parts—communism and fascism . . . It is possible that the world really is on the eve of a general skirmish between communism and fascism." It is tempting to draw a connection between the snake invasion and the fascist danger: the giant snakes and ostriches, after all, result from Rokk's attempt to speed up natural processes, and the growth of fascism, in Bulgakov's view, was furthered by the communists' misguided attempts to accelerate revolutionary processes abroad. As he noted in his diary in October 1923: "In Germany, instead of the expected communist revolution, evident and widespread fascism has resulted." But the disaster in **"The Fatal Eggs"** should not be associated only with fascism. That it refers to a broader foreign threat is indicated by a later entry in Bulgakov's diary which comments on the breakdown of an Anglo-Soviet conference: "It would be interesting to know how long the 'Union of Socialist Republics' will last in such a position."

The snake invasion and its ensuing destruction may thus be linked to the more extreme bolshevik policies of 1923-1924, both domestic and foreign. Here, as with the red ray and the chicken plague, Bulgakov has created a capacious symbol which accommodates disparate socio-political referents. It is precisely these broad symbols that make **"The Fatal Eggs"** such an extraordinarily dense work, one which conjures up from beneath its bright and witty surface the entire tangled complex of political events

Bulgakov's last place of residence: the writer's cooperative housing on Nashchokin Lane in Moscow.

engaged his art in current issues, only at an ironic, hypothetical remove; entered a dialogue, both complex and playful, with the prevailing verities; and probed some of the basic assumptions of the new society.

This dialogic stance was a precarious one, at the very limit of the permissible even in the relatively tolerant atmosphere of the mid-1920s. With **Heart of a Dog,** written just a few months after **"The Fatal Eggs,"** Bulgakov fell over the edge; no less than the bolshevik leader Lev Kamenev judged the work "a sharp lampoon on contemporary life, [which] under no circumstance can be published." **Heart of a Dog** was the first of Bulgakov's works to be banned entirely, a harbinger of the writer's total exclusion from print.

Despite the official disfavor his satirical fantasies aroused, however, Bulgakov continued along the path broken by them, a path that led finally to *The Master and Margarita*. In that novel the fantastic is once again grounded in everyday Soviet reality and the many-layered and at times opaque allusiveness of **"The Fatal Eggs"** achieves its fullest artistic realization.

Ronald D. LeBlanc (essay date 1993)

SOURCE: "Feeding a Poor Dog a Bone: The Quest for Nourishment in Bulgakov's *Sobach'e serdtse*," in *The Russian Review,* Vol. 52, No. 1, January, 1993, pp. 58-78.

[*Below, LeBlanc analyzes* The Heart of a Dog *(*Sobach'e serdtse*) as a tale about the need for physical and spiritual sustenance, asserting that Bulgakov's focus on language and imagery pertaining to eating signifies the "deleterious effects that the Bolshevik Revolution and the concomitant victory of the proletariat were having upon the level of culture in Soviet Russia."*]

Mikhail Bulgakov's **Sobach'e serdtse** (1925), most critics would agree, is essentially the tale of a transformation gone awry: it tells the story of how a scientist—through a misguided organ transplant operation—turns "a perfectly delightful dog" into a disgustingly vulgar quasi-human being. As Helena Goscilo explains [in "Point of View in Bulgakov's **Heart of a Dog,**" in *Russian Literature Triquarterly* 15 (1978)], "those human qualities that made Sharik so winsome are replaced in Sharikov by baser impulses." Few readers, I think, would seriously dispute the view that what stands at the center of Bulgakov's satiric novella is this ill-fated transformation of Sharik (the pleasant dog) into Sharikov (the unpleasant man), a change that is generally interpreted as serving to parody the grand social experiment of creating a new species of human being: *homo sovieticus*. It seems to me, however, that readers of **Sobach'e serdtse** tend to overlook a metamorphosis of almost equal significance that occurs earlier in the narrative when Sharik is first taken in off the street by Philipp Philippovich and brought home to live with him. Upon trading his wretched freedom for the material comforts provided in the wealthy doctor's home, this clever canine vagabond rapidly changes his class identity and

and issues of its tumultuous time. The political dimension, moreover, by no means negates other levels of symbolism—whether scientific or metaphysical—that have been discussed by other critics.

"The Fatal Eggs" also provides a vivid illustration of the relations of Bulgakov's art to politics during the NEP. He, together with Zamyatin and a number of others, occupied a middle ground far from those ideologically committed writers (whether of the proletarian or futurist stripe) who placed their art at the service of the state. Nor did he side with those, most notably the Serapion Brothers, who emphasized the autonomy of art in contemporary reality and insisted that a literary work should "live its own life. . . . Not be a copy of nature, but live on an equal footing with nature" [Lev Lunts, "Pochemu my Serapionovy Brat'ia," in *Rodina i drugie proizvedeniia,* 1981]. Especially in his three novellas, **"The Diaboliad"** (1923), **"The Fatal Eggs"** (1924) and *Heart of a Dog* (1925), Bulgakov employed the fantasy typical of the Serapions but transplanted it from some imagined "other" world to everyday Soviet life. By introducing incredible factors into the contemporary socio-political equation (the discovery of the ray of life, the transformation of dog to man), he transforms himself from a homeless mutt to, in his words, a "gentleman's dog" (*barskii pes*). Sharik's initial transformation from a miserable specimen of the lower strata of society to a more genteel member of the privileged class, however, not only advances the novella's central theme of transformation. It also helps to illuminate the widespread search for nourishment that takes place in *Sobach'e serdtse* and thus to reflect the story's abiding concern with alimentation, ingestion, and gustation. This occurs because Bulgakov charts the change of identity in Sharik, much as he does the result of the central transplant operation itself, largely through the language of gastronomy. The author, as I aim to demonstrate in this essay, uses food imagery and eating metaphors as a way to express some of the grave misgivings he harbored about the deleterious effects that the Bolshevik Revolution and the concomitant victory of the proletariat were having upon the level of culture in Soviet Russia. As a result, *Sobach'e serdtse* engages the reader in a discourse that is at once gastronomical and culinary as well as political and psychological.

Within the context of Bulgakov's overall literary oeuvre, such gastronomic or culinary discourse is not unique to *Sobach'e serdtse,* of course. Following in the rich satiric tradition established by such great writers as Molière, Gogol, and Chekhov, Bulgakov tends throughout his works to exploit the comic possibilities of food motifs, very often humorously contrasting physical with spiritual ingestion: that is, he frequently treats eating both as mimesis and as metaphor. Perhaps the most memorable instance of his use of gastronomic satire occurs in *Master i Margarita,* where he portrays the members of the Soviet literary establishment as venal philistines who are more concerned with feeding their bellies than with nourishing either their intellects or their souls. It is entirely appropriate, therefore, that the headquarters of MASSOLIT be housed in a building which bears the significant name (significant in a culinary and etymological as well as a literary and cultural sense) of *Dom Griboedova*: the House of Griboedov (the "mushroom eaters"). Indeed, this ostensible literary "hothouse," under whose roof young artistic talent is supposed to ripen (a place, as Koroviev points out, that is designed to nurture and develop "the future author of a *Don Quixote,* a *Faust* or—who knows?—*Dead Souls!*") [*The Master and Margarita*], is famous primarily for the magnificent restaurant that it houses in two large rooms on the ground floor. "Some of us old inhabitants of Moscow still remember the famous Griboedov," Bulgakov's narrator exclaims at the beginning of a veritable ode that he delivers on the gastronomic wonders of the restaurant.

> But boiled fillets of perch was nothing, my dear Ambrose! What about the sturgeon, sturgeon in a silver-plated pan, sturgeon filleted and served between lobsters' tails and fresh caviar? And *oeufs en cocotte* with mushroom purée in little bowls? And didn't you like the thrushes' breasts? With truffles? The quails à la Genovese? . . . Do you remember, Ambrose? But of course you do—I can see from your lips you remember.

> Not just your salmon or your perch either—what about the snipe, the woodcock in season, the quail, the grouse? And the sparkling wines! But I digress, reader.

Bulgakov proceeds in the novel to make Griboedov House into an infernal netherworld, where poets are depicted as wanton gluttons, much after the manner of those damned souls Dante depicts in his *Divine Comedy,* sinners who, as one critic notes, care "more for stuffing their mouths with food than for opening them with words." [Maggie Kilgour, *From Communion to Cannibalism: An Anatomy of Metaphors of Incorporation,* 1990]. The Soviet literati who inhabit Griboedov House appear to be little more than greedy and vulgar materialists who, to borrow an apt distinction that Lev Tolstoy once made [in *Anna Karenina,* 1877], live more for their stomachs (*dlia briukha*) than for their souls (*dlia dushi*).

In *Sobach'e serdtse,* however, Bulgakov invokes food motifs less to highlight the inherent materialism, baseness, and venality of human beings than to condemn a social system that creates a condition of widespread hunger and misery among its populace. Such a strategy becomes readily apparent from the opening section of the book, which makes a strong impression upon the reader not merely because the narrative point of view is that of a dog but also because that canine perspective is so thoroughly dominated by longings for food, shelter, and warmth. In addition to being made to view the world from the "defamiliarizing" vantage point of a four-legged creature, readers of Bulgakov's novella are also forced to focus upon the lower material aspects of both human and animal existence. As we pursue the thoughts of this homeless and hungry dog, we see that Sharik has been reduced to the indignity of rummaging through garbage cans, searching desperately for sustenance to fight off the looming threat of starvation. Like many a human member of the lower social classes, people who have become severely disenfranchised and alienated under the economic systems of War Communism and now NEP capitalism, Sharik exists on the very margins of his society, forced to live in a harsh and cruel world not of his choosing, where sheer physical survival predominates over all other instinctual urges, psychological desires, and spiritual aspirations. The desperate battle for self-preservation that Sharik wages in the opening section of *Sobach'e serdtse* thus reminds us of the fate of the literary hero in picaresque fiction, who likewise travels through a nightmare world of pain, hunger, and deprivation.

The point of depicting such existential misery is usually ideological, of course, since picaresque novelists generally pursue the satirical aim of exposing and attacking the social inequities that exist within their native societies. As had been the case with Lazarillo de Tormes, Guzmán de Alfarache, and other Spanish picaros, Sharik's struggle for survival is presented to us largely through food imagery and eating metaphors. The contrast between wealth and poverty in the story he tells, for instance, is set up as more than merely a sociological opposition between the gentry class on one hand and the peasantry or proletariat on the other. It also manifests itself in gastronomical terms as a dichotomy between those fortunate people who can afford to dine on fancy dishes at elegant restaurants and those unfortunate others (including dogs like Sharik) who are happy just to feed on the free sausage ends left over by people at Sokolniki Park and to lick to their heart's content the greasy paper in which that sausage is wrapped. At the human (rather than canine) level, the low end of this spectrum of gastronomic polarization between wealth and poverty is occupied by Vasnetsova, the female typist who works in the same building where Sharik is rummaging in the gateway. Like the narrating dog, she too lives at a basic subsistence level that some gastrocritics would call *degré zéro alimentaire*. Because she is a working-class girl who can hardly afford to dine at the expensive Bar Restaurant on Neglinny Avenue, Vasnetsova is forced to eat the stinking soup and putrid meat served in the "Normal Diet" cafeteria (even though such slops hurt her stomach by giving her cramps). Indeed, by story's end this selfsame typist will even be prepared to put up with the indecent sexual advances of the lecherous Sharikov, willing to work for the obnoxious director of the purge section of the Moscow Communal Property Administration, if only to avoid having to eat any longer the unpalatable food served in the Soviet cafeteria. "I'll poison myself!" she exclaims in despair. "Every day in the cafeteria it's corned beef."

This function of food imagery as a measure of socioeconomic status, and thus its use as a narrative device for categorizing the characters in the story along the lines of social class, becomes even more apparent once Professor Preobrazhenskii enters the narrative. When the professor first makes his appearance across the street from the gateway where Sharik is holed up, the canine narrator immediately recognizes that this very distinguished looking personage could hardly be a comrade, but must instead be a member of the privileged class. Sharik then proceeds to describe Philipp Philippovich's gentility in terms that are predominantly gastronomical. Like the French, who according to Sharik know how to "eat well" (*lopaiut bogato*), the professor is not one "to start gobbling [*lopat'*] moldy corned beef." Instead, he too is presumed to "eat plenty" (*est obil'no*). Indeed, Sharik is greatly surprised that a wealthy and cultured gentleman like Professor Preobrazhenskii should be buying sausage in such a shabby little food store when he could easily afford to shop at the more elegant establishments on Okhotnyi Row. "Sir, if you could see what this sausage is made of, you'd never come near that store," Sharik addresses himself mentally to the professor. "Better give it to me."

Because Sharik's whole life seems to constitute little else than the search for a decent meal, it comes as no surprise that the human beings with whom he has the most contact are cooks, a category of people that he again valorizes along the lines of social class. The proletarian cook, who burned Sharik's side by throwing boiling water at the dog when he spotted him scrounging through garbage cans, is, in his opinion, a worthless scoundrel and a scum. In contrast to the heartless cruelty demonstrated by this mean-spirited representative of the working class, Sharik remembers fondly the generosity of a gentry cook named Vlas, who not only treated stray dogs more humanely, but also practiced his culinary craft with much more competence than did his proletarian brethren. "All the old dogs still talk of how Vlas would throw them a bone, and with a solid chunk of meat on it," Sharik reminisces nostalgically:

> May he be blessed for it in the Heavenly Kingdom— a real personality he was, the gentry cook for the family of Count Tolstoy, not one of those nobodies from the Soviet of Normal Diet. The things they do in that Normal Diet, it's more than a dog's brain can comprehend. Those scoundrels make soup of stinking corned beef, and the poor wretches don't know what they're eating.

The "poor wretches" to whom Sharik alludes include, of course, those lower-class folk (such as Vasnetsova) who, given their miserable material conditions, have little choice but to eat such gruesome fare; only dire biological necessity can possibly explain why they are willing to "come running, gobbling it down, lapping it up."

By having Sharik delineate the quality of their respective styles of cooking as one of the principal differences between proletarian cooks who work at the Normal Diet and gentry cooks who work for the family of Count Tolstoy, Bulgakov introduces one of the central motifs in his story: namely, the theme of nourishment. The reader is invited to make the inference that the bulk of the country's population is, like Sharik and Vasnetsova, still desperate for an adequate supply of edible food to eat. Sharik himself broaches this issue of proper alimentation when, after describing how Vasnetsova is resigned to her fate of eating the stinking soup and putrid meat served daily at the Normal Diet cafeteria, he asks rhetorically, "Is that the kind of nourishment she needs?" The more pressing question in this text, however, is: Who can provide the kind of nourishment that is needed by Vasnetsova and, by extension, every working-class citizen in Soviet Russia? For Sharik, the answer is the gentry class, embodied in Vlas, the benevolent and talented *barskii povar,* as well as in the person of Philipp Philippovich, the cultured and imperious gentleman-aristocrat whose characterization by the canine narrator, as we have seen, is dominated by gastronomic imagery (he "eats well," he won't "start gobbling moldy corned beef," he is unafraid "because he is never hungry"). These two personages, Vlas the cook and Preobrazhenskii the host, both of whom are closely associated with the privileged gentry class from tsarist days, seem to hold out the only real hope of adequately nourishing the badly underfed dog. Indeed, when Sharik first sees the professor, the latter is even carrying a source of nourishment in his hand: namely, that piece of "special Cracow sausage" (made up of chopped horsemeat mixed with garlic and pepper) whose smell alone is enough to "rejuvenate" (*omolodil*) the starving canine.

As the professor lures Sharik home with the piece of sausage, the reader of *Sobach'e serdtse* thus sees how Bulgakov, who foreshadows in this scene the "rejuvenation" operation that the dog will soon undergo, is able to link the theme of transformation with the theme of alimentation. As we quickly discover, Philipp Philippovich is willing to feed Sharik some of the tasty "rejuvenating" sausage, but the price exacted in exchange for this sustenance is the renunciation of the dog's freedom, a miserable burden that the hungry, homeless mutt seems only too eager to rid himself of. Resorting to a series of toadying gestures that perhaps emblematize as much Sharik's readiness to act obsequiously toward an authority figure as his eagerness to show his love and devotion to this kindly new benefactor, the servile dog licks Philipp Philippovich's hand, kisses his galoshes, and crawls along the sidewalk on his belly. "I kiss your trousers, my benefactor!" he muses shamelessly. When Preobrazhenskii, after stroking Sharik's midsection, instructs the dog to follow him, the latter confesses that he is prepared to follow his new master "to the end of the world." "You may kick me with your fine suede shoes," Sharik admits, as he kisses the professor's overshoes. "I won't say a word."

To the long list of genres to which *Sobach'e serdtse* may be said to belong (the literature of talking dogs, of Faust, of Frankenstein), Susanne Fusso suggests [in "Failures in Transformation in *Sobac'e serdce*," in *Slavic and East European Journal* 33 (1989)] that we add the "literature of hunger": the literature that, in her words, "investigates what happens when bodily needs and desires corrupt the spirit." Placing Bulgakov's novella within the context of those works of postrevolutionary Soviet literature that addressed the "imperative of the belly" in war-torn Russia, Fusso argues that it is Sharik's "search for security and satiety that leads to his temporary downfall," a demise she traces back directly to the dog's "failure of courage, his willingness to deny the meaning of freedom." There is no disputing the claim that Sharik has indeed traded his freedom for the comfort, security, and stability provided by the professor's apartment, a gastronomic heaven where he believes he has at last found *sobach'e shchast'e* (the novella's original title). Even before Philipp Philippovich rescues Sharik from the streets, we hear the starving mutt confess, "We have the souls of slaves and a wretched fate!" After a few days at the professor's home, Sharik openly admits, in a highly revealing moment of epiphany, that he has now become "a gentleman's dog, an intellectual creature," and he dismissively rejects freedom (in words that echo the professor's own) as nothing more than "a puff of smoke, a mirage, a fiction. . . . A delirium of those wretched democrats." Sharik's renunciation of his liberty is further signalled by his acquiescence in donning a collar and chain, two restraining devices that he is at first ashamed to wear since they make him feel like a convicted criminal. Once Sharik realizes, however, that the collar and chain serve at the same time as social emblems, which indicate his membership in an upper-class household and thus will earn him the respect and admiration of militiamen (as well as the envy of his fellow dogs), he begins to take great pride in his shackles: "A collar is just like a briefcase, the dog quipped mentally and, wagging his behind, proceeded with a lordly air [*kak barin*] up to the second floor."

Given the long-standing Russian cultural tradition of valuing the concerns of the spirit over those of the flesh, there are certainly strong grounds for viewing Sharik's process of gentrification mainly in a political light and thus for condemning the dog's readiness to "sell out" so cheaply—to forfeit so easily his personal freedom and submit to what one critic calls "the seductive but cheap allure of comfort" [Diana L. Burgin, "Bulgakov's Early Tragedy of the Scientist-Creator: An Interpretation of *The Heart of a Dog*," *Slavic and East European Journal* 22 (1978)]. Moreover, the kitchen of the professor's apartment, with its flaming oven, is associated with imagery that makes it as much a hellish domain as a gastronomical paradise. Being nutritionally satisfied and materially comfortable, however, hardly seems to constitute a diabolical moral vice or personal shortcoming on the part of other characters in Bulgakov's novella, as the case of the "sybaritic" [Goscilo] scientist-creator and the well-fed members of his household clearly demonstrates. "Sharik's predilection for the comfort and luxury that are synonymous with a vanishing way of life and with the upper social strata," as Goscilo notes, "makes him, indeed, Preobrazhenskian." Seen primarily in psychological and gastronomical terms, Sharik's search for security and comfort can be understood in a much less negative way, especially when we keep in mind that this poor dog is at first merely seeking some basic nourishment so as to avoid starvation. From the moment Sharik leaves the cold, cruel world of Moscow's back streets and goes to live in the professor's spacious, well-heated, and amply provisioned household, he begins to undergo a personality change that the author, as I suggested at the outset of this article, charts largely through the language of gastronomy. In psychological terms, Sharik gradually moves out of a mode that Roland Barthes, in his Introduction to Brillat-Savarin's *Physiologie du goût* [1975], has characterized as the "realm of necessity" (*l'ordre de besoin*), the domain of survival, which is dominated by hunger, deprivation, and an obsession with food. In Sharik's case, this realm of necessity not only shapes the dog's measurement of time, which is gauged according to the smell of onions emanating from the local firehouse; it also generates its own special gastronomic language, composed of visual as well as olfactory signs used by canines to communicate such notions as "meat," "sausage," "cheese," and other food items.

Once he is removed from his dire existential situation of hunger and homelessness, however, where food and shelter are desperately coveted as basic items of survival and self-preservation, Sharik is soon free to progress to more civilized needs, more elevated desires, and more sophisticated tastes. The warmth, comfort, and security provided by Preobrazhenskii's home allow Sharik to enter into a new psychological realm, one that Barthes calls *l'ordre de desir*: the domain of pleasure, where food now becomes a sign of abundance, plenitude, and extravagance. The seriously underfed Sharik, once a shaggy, lanky, and skinny mutt, quickly "fattens up" while living at the professor's home, where in preparation for the upcoming transplant operation he is allowed by the master of the house to eat all that he wants, despite the strident protests of the servant Zina and her complaint that the dog, who allegedly "eats enough for six," is eating them "out of house and home." "In the course of a week," we are told, "the dog gobbled down as much food as he had eaten during the last month and a half of hunger in the streets." Sharik becomes so sated, in fact, that he is moved to admit at one point that he "can't stand looking at any more food." This once scrawny mutt begins at last truly to deserve the name "Sharik," which, as he himself noted earlier, is supposed to indicate "somebody round, plump, the son of aristocratic parents who gobbles oatmeal." Not only is the quantity of food that Sharik is now able to eat much improved over what he had to survive on while living in the streets, so too is the culinary quality of his present diet far beyond comparison with what he used to have to eat. Freed from the necessity of scrounging through garbage cans in back alleys, eating human leftovers, or licking greasy sausage wrappers at Sokolniki Park, Sharik is now allowed to eat roast beef, mutton bones, and other canine delicacies in the comfort of the professor's elegant dining room.

We might say, borrowing Barthes's terms again, that *l'appetit naturel* within Sharik, whereby he eats to live, has rapidly given way during his stay at the professor's apartment to *l'appetit de luxe,* according to which the fattened dog now lives to eat, dreaming sybaritically of the next sumptuous repast that Dar'ia Petrovna will feed him. Food for the sated Sharik is no longer primarily a means for satisfying basic hunger and thus avoiding starvation; rather it has now become a source of pure pleasure in and of itself, as well as a stimulant for further desire. In a sense, this dog has realized in practice the sentiment expressed earlier by Vasnetsova's embittered lover. "It's my turn to have some fun in life," he had been heard to exclaim, "I've starved long enough in my youth." Whereas the professor's human clients have undergone a rejuvenation operation that enables them better to enjoy sexual pleasures, the dog Sharik has undergone a change that allows him to revel hedonistically in the delights of gastronomical indulgence. This pre-transplant transformation that Sharik's personality undergoes as he moves out of the realm of necessity and into the realm of desire— from *l'appetit naturel* to *l'appetit de luxe,* from hunger to pleasure—parallels the theoretical model of human development formulated by Abraham Maslow, one of the pioneers of the American school of humanistic psychology. According to Maslow's theory of self-actualization [expressed in his *Toward a Psychology of Being,* second edition, 1968], human motives can be arranged in hierarchical form, whereby man's basic physiological needs (to satisfy hunger, thirst, and sex) stand on the bottom rung, followed by the need for safety (security, order, stability), belonging (love and affection), esteem (feelings of self-respect and success), and finally self-actualization. Since the physiological needs at the bottom of Maslow's hierarchical pyramid are the most urgent, they must first be satisfied before man can be freed to seek the higher spiritual goals of the self. More important for the purposes of my analysis, however, is the assumption, implicit in Maslow's theory, that the society in which one lives must be able to provide nourishment, safety, and stability before the individual can even begin to strive for the loftier goals to which human nature innately aspires. Otherwise,

man is destined to struggle incessantly to satisfy his most basic and primitive biological needs.

Maslow's developmental model seems quite applicable in the case of Sharik, who suddenly discovers within himself the existence of higher needs (such as safety, belonging, and esteem) only after he is provided with the basic necessities of life. Once he is fed and his basic physical hunger has been satisfied, Sharik can begin to seek nourishment that is spiritual in nature rather than merely corporeal, psychological rather than simply physiological. He can now appreciate the need for food for the soul as well as the body, sustenance for the mind as well as the stomach. In Western culture, it is true, there is a strong tradition of considering physical and spiritual appetites not as complementary urges, but rather as polarized and opposing ones: the complete satisfaction of bodily appetites, it is often feared, will stupefy the hunger of the spirit and the imagination. The fictional world that Bulgakov creates in *Sobach'e serdtse,* however, seems to resemble the Rabelaisian universe, where "physical hunger must be satisfied first before the process of feeding the spirit with art can even begin" [Kilgour]. Since Sharik's needs for safety, security, and belonging are amply taken care of at the professor's home, the dog is free to entertain thoughts that reflect his desire for higher needs, such as self-esteem and self-actualization. Indeed, he even posits for himself an inherent nobility of spirit when he muses about the possibility that, unbeknownst to anyone, he might well be a "canine prince incognito." It should be noted that a precedent for Sharik's metamorphosis was provided by the professor's able assistant, Doctor Bormental'. He was once a "half-starved" creature himself before Philipp Philippovich nurtured, sheltered, and thus transformed him from a poor medical school student to a valuable and productive member of the scientific community.

> *The Heart of a Dog* begins to suggest that the traditionally disenfranchised classes in Russia—the peasantry, the proletariat, the petty bourgeoisie, the lumpenproletariat—can hardly hope to find the physical or spiritual sustenance that they seek under the culturally bankrupt ideology of Bolshevism.
>
> —*Ronald D. LeBlanc*

By metaphorizing the act of eating in *Sobach'e serdtse* in the way that I have been charting here, Bulgakov makes this bodily function serve in his text as a trope for intellectual, moral, and cultural ingestion. Read as an allegorical tale, Sharik's story begins to suggest that the traditionally disenfranchised classes in Russia—the peasantry, the proletariat, the petty bourgeoisie, the lumpenproletariat—can hardly hope to find the physical or spiritual sustenance that they seek under the culturally bankrupt ideology of Bolshevism, which has instead ushered in the triumph of the venal, the vulgar, and the philistine. When *Sobach'e serdtse* is read as a political allegory, the alimentary imperative elaborated in the opening section of the novella tells us metaphorically that the Soviet regime which came to power with the revolution has been unable to provide sufficient nourishment, either physical or spiritual, for the starving masses in Russia. Bulgakov's political message here reads that Lenin and his Bolshevik cohorts have reneged on the promise they made that first brought them to power in 1917: that is, to bring food to the populace. What the people of Russia need is a moral, spiritual, and cultural leadership that, in addition to providing them literally with their daily bread, is capable of feeding them spiritual food as well, thus nurturing and preserving within them lasting cultural values.

This need for a sustenance that is by nature spiritual, intellectual, and cultural becomes especially acute during the second half of Bulgakov's novella, where narrative attention shifts from Sharik the dog to Sharikov the man. The cultural leadership that Russia so desperately needs is here represented primarily in the person of Philipp Philippovich. Yet this eminent scholar and renowned surgeon, a man whom Andrei Sinyavskii has characterized as a "typical representative of the old Russian intelligentsia" [*Soviet Civilization: A Cultural History,* translated by Joanne Turnbull, 1990], proves to be a somewhat problematic figure to have serve as the ethical center of the story. On one hand, Preobrazhenskii emerges as "the very incarnation of good taste, refinement and intellect" [Burgin], and would thus seem to represent all that Bulgakov values positively about prerevolutionary Russian culture. On the other hand, this "mad scientist" can be seen in a highly negative light as a rather fiendish figure who flourishes materially during the heyday of NEP by performing expensive rejuvenation operations that do little more than cater to the baser instincts of the venal people who can afford them. In gastronomic terms, meanwhile, the vampirish imagery and demonic motifs that occasionally cluster around Philipp Philippovich could be understood to suggest that he not only generously "feeds" Sharik and later Sharikov, but also "feeds upon" them like a bloodthirsty predator.

Nonetheless, Preobrazhenskii emerges as the one character in *Sobach'e serdtse* who reveals most directly to us Bulgakov's intention that the act of eating be understood in this text as a paradigm for the art of living. "Food," the professor observes to Doctor Bormental' at one point, "is a curious thing. You have to know how to eat, and imagine, most people haven't the slightest notion of how to do it. It is not only a matter of knowing what to eat, but also when and how." By focusing on the manner as well as the content of the dining experience, the professor is implying here that under the Soviet regime people have, in a broad sense, somehow lost the ability to make sound judgments or discriminating choices and thus to appreciate the finer things in life; one might say that, in gastronomical as well as cultural terms, they simply have no sense of taste. As Stephen Mennell reminds us, "taste, in food as in other domains of culture, implies discrimination, stan-

dards of good and bad, the acceptance of some things and the rejection of others" [*All Manners of Food: Eating and Taste in England and France from the Middle Ages to the Present,* 1985]. It is against the ostensible absence of such powers of discrimination and appreciation that Philipp Philippovich takes strong issue in his continuing dispute with Comrade Shvonder and the other members of the cultural department of his apartment building's house committee, a dispute, significantly enough, that centers initially upon the issue of the professor's dining room. "Nobody in Moscow has a dining room . . . not even Isadora Duncan," Shvonder and his fellow committee members object when Preobrazhenskii insists upon maintaining what they consider to be an excessive number of rooms in his apartment. When Philipp Philippovich inquires where then is he expected to take his meals, Shvonder suggests that he eat them in the bedroom. "I shall dine in the dining room," the professor thunders back, "allow me to take my meals where all normal people take theirs, that is, in the dining room." The intensity and centrality of this dining room dispute seem to support Mariia Shneerson's contention [in her "Chto mozhet vyiti iz etogo Sharikova?" *Grani* 42 (1988)] that *Sobach'e serdtse* is less about the history of a failed scientific experiment than about a man's battle to defend the integrity of his home—a battle for what she calls "the inviolability of his abode."

In Bulgakov's novella, the *stolovaia* (understood in both its meanings: as a private "dining room" as well as a public "dining hall") is made to function as an indicator of one's good taste, proper manners, and overall cultural development. In sharp contrast to those stinking public cafeterias in which poor Soviet working-class citizens (such as Vasnetsova) are forced to dine on slops, the private dining room in Preobrazhenskii's apartment constitutes a highly cultured setting, characterized by elegant dining, refined tastes, and intelligent conversation. In the tradition established by Plato's *Symposium,* the professor's dining room serves as the scene for philosophical discourse (the province of the mind) as well as banquet feasting (the province of the body). Indeed, Philipp Philippovich, reinforced by the hearty dinner that he has just consumed, proceeds after the meal to thunder forth with pronouncements like an ancient prophet. Having maintained that knowing how to eat—and thus, by extension, how to live—involves knowing "what to talk about while you are at it," he now speaks out sharply against the highly deleterious effect that the discourse of Marxist-Leninist ideology exerts upon the process of alimentation. "If you care about your digestion," he warns Doctor Bormental', "my good advice is: do not talk about Bolshevism . . . at the dinner table. And—heaven preserve us!—don't read any Soviet newspapers before dinner." The professor goes on to explain how the patients at his hospital, whom he had deliberately compelled to read *Pravda* each day, all lost weight as a result. Those patients found, in addition, that their appetites had been ruined, their reflexes dulled, and their state of mind depressed. If eating is understood in *Sobach'e serdtse* as a trope for living, then the novella's political subtext encourages us to comprehend the professor to be saying that the ruling ideology in Soviet Russia gives one a bad case of existential indigestion and spiritual flatulence. The imposition of Marxist doctrine by the Bolsheviks threatens nothing less than the total impoverishment and decline of the country due to cultural malnutrition.

If the first half of Bulgakov's novella is concerned with the starving Sharik and the theme of alimentation mainly in its literal sense of physical hunger, nourishment, and digestion, then in the second half, where Sharikov's story comes to the fore, attention is shifted to the metaphoric aspects of this theme: to poor nourishment in its spiritual, intellectual, and cultural sense. In addition, the discourse of gustation—good taste and judicious discrimination—is now brought into the foreground as Preobrazhenskii and Bormental' increasingly voice their serious misgivings about the savage beast (culturally considered) that their organ transplant operation has succeeded in creating. The irony here, of course, is that this creature turns out to be bestial more because of the vulgar nature of the human being whose organs have been transplanted (Klim Chugunkin) than because of the canine nature of the dog Sharik.

Fear of Russia's imminent cultural collapse as a direct result of the victory of such vulgarity is expressed as early as chapter 3, where this topic dominates the postprandial conversation that takes place between Preobrazhenskii and Bormental' during the initial dining room scene. The professor here launches into a long harangue about the so-called economic "ruin" (*razrukha*) that is said to be threatening their country. Susanne Fusso has shown how Bulgakov, through this motif of *razrukha,* is making allusion to Vladimir Maiakovskii, attempting to counter the Futurist poet's fairy-tale figure (an old witch by the same name in his play, *Misteriia-buff*) who, as the embodiment of the forces of chaos and destruction, "goes about the country smashing machinery and gobbling up workers." Whatever its particular intertextual connections may turn out to be, Preobrazhenskii's diatribe on *razrukha* is clearly directed in a general sense against those who are responsible for the cultural decline that Russia has begun to experience since the Soviets took power. The current problem in the country, according to Philipp Philippovich, is not an imminent economic collapse, attributable to certain elements in the population who are dedicated to wrecking the industrial machinery (and thus the productive capacity) of the young state. The culprit instead is the moral, intellectual, and cultural deterioration that the people of Russia have had to experience ever since the disappearance of the gentry class. All that remains in the wake of the passing of Russia's sociopolitical and cultural aristocracy is a spiritual coarseness that serves as the main target for the author's satiric attack in the novella. Thefts in their apartment building, for example, the professor is quick to remind his loyal assistant, began only after the revolutions of 1917. Philipp Philippovich goes on to excoriate the victorious proletariat not only for stealing his galoshes but also for tracking in dirt on the marble staircase from their muddy boots. What these new people lack, he explains through a highly colorful (if scatological) example, is not so much an adequate supply of material goods as a sense of basic decorum: "If, coming into the bathroom, I will—forgive the expression—begin to urinate past the toilet bowl, and if Zina and Dar'ia Petrovna do the same, I'll have ruin (*razrukha*) in my bathroom. Hence, the ruin is not in the bathrooms, but in people's heads." The point of Professor Preobrazhenskii's bathroom trope is to emphasize that high gentry culture must be preserved, otherwise low plebeian culture will fill the vacuum and come to dominate society. An upper class made up of educated, refined, and well-mannered people must provide the necessary moral leadership in the country and serve as role models for the lower classes. An elite vanguard of civilized people, according to the professor, is needed to show others how to use toilets properly or else the people will degenerate to such barbaric behavior as urinating on the bathroom floor.

One of the more overt manifestations in *Sobach'e serdtse* of this class war—this competition for dominance between high and low culture in Soviet Russia of the 1920s— occurs in the domain of music. The after-dinner conversation in chapter 3 between Preobrazhenskii and Bormental', for instance, is interrupted by the sounds of choral singing that waft into the professor's dining room from the general meeting of the house committee taking place upstairs. The communal, *narodnyi* character of choral singing as a quintessentially proletarian activity is in keeping, of course, with Marx's view that man's alienation within capitalist society stems largely from the division of labor, a system whereby each person abrogates to someone else (invariably a specialist) tasks and activities whose fulfillment might otherwise make us better rounded, more complete and whole human beings rather than badly fragmented ones. The politically incorrect and rabidly undemocratic Professor Preobrazhenskii, who makes it clear that (contra Marx) he is "an advocate of the division of labor," seems to support instead an elitist meritocracy of talent and abilities, whereby only those who are blessed with a beautiful voice and formal training as a singer would undertake to sing songs. A strong supporter of high culture and a steadfast proponent of its preservation, Philipp Philippovich clearly prefers professional operatic singing to amateur choral singing: throughout the text he can be heard repeatedly to hum his favorite line from the libretto for Verdi's *Aida* ("Toward the sacred banks of the Nile"). This contrast between high elitist culture and low popular culture in the realm of music becomes especially palpable after the transplant operation is performed and Sharikov appears. Indeed, one of the most salient indicators of the cultural barbarism of the quasi-human monster that Preobrazhenskii has created, besides his inclination to frequent the circus rather than the theater, is his propensity (shared later by Prisypkin in Maiakovskii's *Klop*) to play the infectious melodies from popular tavern tunes on his balalaika. The infectiousness of such melodies is made evident, of course, by the fact that even the professor himself begins to hum one of these tavern tunes rather than his beloved arias: "The moo-o-n is shining . . . The moo-o-n is shining . . . The moo-o-n is shining . . . Phew, can't get rid of that damned tune!"

Not unlike music, food and eating also come to serve in *Sobach'e serdtse* as a barometer for measuring one's level of cultural development and sophistication. This function of food motifs can be seen in the two very different scenes of dining depicted in the text: the first in chapter 3, before Sharik has undergone the transplant operation, and the second in chapter 7, after Sharikov has been created. Taken together, these two dining scenes succeed in creating a cultural matrix by which the reader can contrast the appallingly savage behavior of the uncouth proletarian Sharikov with the more civilized behavior exhibited at table by the urbane, genteel duo of Preobrazhenskii and Bormental'. The opening of the scene in chapter 3 immediately endows the professor's dining room with an aura of *haute cuisine,* elegant decor, and refined manners:

> Thin slices of salmon and pickled eel were piled on plates adorned with paradisiac flowers and wide black borders. A piece of fine, moist Swiss cheese lay on a heavy board, and near it stood a silver bucket with caviar, set in a bowl of snow. Among the plates stood several slender liqueur glasses and three crystal carafes with liqueurs of different colors. All these objects were arranged on a small marble table, cosily set against a huge sideboard of carved oak filled with glass and silver, which threw off sheaves of light. In the center of the room a table, heavy as a sepulchre, was covered with a white cloth, and on it were two settings, with napkins rolled like papal tiaras, and three dark bottles.

Moreover, the after-dinner conversation between these two civilized, well-educated gentlemen that takes place in this chapter, as we remember, centers upon a general discussion—counterrevolutionary in nature, according to Bormental'—about how proletarian types are lowering the cultural level of people in Soviet Russia (the professor's bathroom trope).

The scene of dining in chapter 7, on the other hand, provides us with a very concrete example of the appalling philistinism that, according to Philipp Philippovich, has triumphed in this society with the advent of socialism. Much like Victorian novelists, for whom "dining rituals take on the serious purpose of defining moral good and upholding class structure" [Helena Michie, *The Flesh Made Word: Female Figures and Women's Bodies,* 1987], Bulgakov uses the evening meal as an opportunity to make gastronomic *savoir faire* into an index of social status: knowing how to eat directly reflects one's knowledge of how to live. The focus in this second scene of dining, as a result, is centered upon the almost total lack of table manners and dining etiquette exhibited by Sharikov. Even before the meal begins, we know Sharikov as an incorrigible slob who has been repeatedly castigated for a lack of manners. He has already been warned, for instance, to put an end to several of his more ungainly habits in the apartment: such as eating sunflower seeds, playing his balalaika, sleeping on the bench in the kitchen, throwing cigarette butts on the floor, swearing, spitting, and catching fleas with his teeth. "You are a savage [*dikar'*]!" Bormental' screams at him in exasperation at one point. Preobrazhenskii, for his part, inquires sardonically, "Where do you think you are? In a tavern?" This uncouth behavior on the part of the savage Sharikov is only further underscored once the scene of dining actually commences. Bormental' initially will not even let Sharikov begin eating until he first tucks in his napkin; indeed, the doctor threatens to have Zina take away Sharikov's food if he doesn't oblige. Then Bormental' must remind Sharikov to use a fork, to offer vodka to others before taking some himself, and to avoid hiccuping at table since it spoils other people's appetites.

These valiant attempts to inculcate some decent table manners and basic rules of dining etiquette seem totally wasted on Sharikov, a gluttonous gourmand who is intent solely on quickly filling his stomach, downing his meal (especially his vodka and brown bread) as rapidly as possible. "Everything with you is like being on parade," he interjects. "A napkin there . . . a necktie here . . . pardon me . . . please . . . merci . . . You are torturing yourselves, just like in tsarist times." Unlike the earlier scene of dining in chapter 3, Preobrazhenskii's after-dinner comments at this meal touch upon the low cultural level not of the people in Soviet Russia generally, but specifically of this one particular representative of popular, proletarian culture. "You are on the lowest rung of development," the professor shouts at Sharikov:

> You are a creature just in the process of formation, with a feeble intellect. All your actions are those of a beast. Yet you permit yourself to speak with utterly insufferable impudence in the presence of two people with a university education—to offer advice on a cosmic scale and of equally cosmic stupidity on how to divide everything . . . And right after gobbling up a boxful of toothpowder too.

Philipp Philippovich ends his harangue against such blatant *nekul'turnost'* (on the part of a creature he has already characterized as a "Neanderthal") with the plea that Sharikov "try to learn, try to become a more or less acceptable member of socialist society." The meal concludes with the professor entreating his ill-mannered guest, "Just behave decently."

Much like the mealtime admonitions rendered earlier by Doctor Bormental', all of Preobrazhenskii's advice comes to naught, as do his efforts in general to educate and "nurture" the vulgar Sharikov, who is referred to in the text as the professor's "charge" (*vospitannik*) and his "ward" (*pitomets*), words that in Russian underscore—at an etymological, lexical level—the notion that Philipp Philippovich has been endeavoring to "feed" (*pitat'*) moral, spiritual, and cultural "food" (*pishcha*) to his creation. In fighting against the deplorable cultural barbarism that is represented by Sharikov (as a loyal defender of the proletarian class) and in attempting to remedy the spiritual malnutrition from which average citizens living under Soviet rule must necessarily suffer, Preobrazhenskii—as we have seen—finds himself pitted directly against Comrade Shvonder and the other members of the house committee. The class war that they wage against each other manifests itself in their efforts to win the cultural as well as ideological loyalties of Sharikov: Philipp Philippovich seeks to inculcate some aristocratic manners, tastes, and values in his creation, while Shvonder's efforts are directed toward raising the political consciousness (and political correctness) of this fledgling proletarian. Where Preobrazhenskii would like to have his "ward" appreciate the Bolshoi Theater's version of the aria "Celeste Aida," Shvonder and his cohorts encourage this new comrade to participate in their weekly sessions of choral singing. Sharikov's education, as Zholkovskii puts it, consists of a general "playing" with culture.

This clash of competing cultural values touches upon reading as well as singing. Thus Shvonder encourages Sharikov to raise his political consciousness by reading Engels' *Correspondence with Kautsky,* which is, according to Preobrazhenskii, an insidious tome that ought to be destroyed by being thrown into the fireplace. The only literary work that Philipp Philippovich mentions (and that Sharikov might thus consider as an alternative to Engels's *Correspondence*) is Daniel Defoe's *Robinson Crusoe.* "And what do you read?" the professor asks Sharikov after the latter mentions that he is a voracious reader. "A picture suddenly flashes through his mind: an uninhabited island, a palm tree, a man in an animal skin and cap. 'I'll have to get him *Robinson*'." This particular choice of text seems significant to me on a number of counts. First of all, *Robinson Crusoe,* understood as the narrative account of how a European man teaches himself to survive in an alien environment outside of civilized society, represents the apotheosis of a "novel of education" (*roman vospitaniia*) and would thus constitute an appropriate aid to Preobrazhenskii in his project to educate or "nurture" (*vospitat'*) his child of creation and to enable the latter to emerge from his primitive state. Moreover, Robinson Crusoe—as a representation of man as an essentially economic animal (*homo economicus*)—epitomizes the type of the rugged individualist; as such, he counterposes directly the collectivist ideology of the Bolsheviks that Shvonder is attempting to inculcate in Sharikov. In addition, Defoe's novel may be said to constitute a classic example of what critics engaged in cultural studies would today characterize as "colonial discourse": that is, Crusoe's narrative account of his adventures is told from the culturally, ethnically, and sexually biased perspective of an empowered White Anglo-Saxon Protestant male from imperialist Europe. As a result, *Robinson Crusoe* constructs the image of the "other" as a savage cannibal in order to have him serve as the direct antithesis of its hero, who is a civilized European man of culture. Defoe's novel creates a dualism of this sort, Maggie Kilgour points out, in an effort to justify subsuming the inferior element in this pairing and thus vindicate cultural cannibalism.

Preobrazhenskii's scheme to nurture and educate Sharikov, it seems to me, shares some striking affinities with this imperialist brand of colonial discourse. For one thing, Sharikov and the proletarian class that he represents are similarly depicted as existing at a primitive level of cultural development, especially when viewed from the perspective of such well-educated members of the cultural elite as Preobrazhenskii and Bormental', who highly val-

ue the achievements of European civilization. Like "Ellochka the Cannibal," the fashion plate in Ilf and Petrov's *Dvenadtsat' stul'ev* who grotesquely cannibalizes not only the Russian language and her husband's meager income but also modern material culture in general, those characters in Bulgakov's novella who belong to the proletariat are invariably portrayed as what the author would deem intellectual and cultural "pygmies." By representing Sharikov, Shvonder, and others of their proletarian ilk as wild, primitive beasts (*dikari*) who are culturally impoverished, Bulgakov advances a discourse that encourages the readers of *Sobach'e serdtse* to share in what Kilgour refers to as "the imperialist desire for total mastery of what is foreign and strange by means of complete appropriation and incorporation." It is curious that the imperialist strategy of cultural cannibalism in *Sobach'e serdtse*—the construction of a hegemonic relationship between high gentry culture and low proletarian culture in Soviet Russia during the 1920s that allows the stronger of the two to devour the weaker one—should include the reading of *Robinson Crusoe,* since Defoe's hero represents a fictional character who is himself obsessively concerned with the threat of actual cannibalism.

This battle over the book in *Sobach'e serdtse*—the competition being waged between Engels's *Correspondence* and Defoe's *Robinson Crusoe* as the appropriate intellectual food to feed the spiritually starving Sharikov—reveals the manner in which Bulgakov (whether wittingly or not) exploits the act of eating not only as a trope for life but also as a metaphor for literature: for the processes of reading and writing as well as living. In its treatment of eating as an act of mental consumption and internalization, Bulgakov's text may be seen to follow a well-established tradition of viewing literature, and especially the knowledge it imparts, as food for the reader's mind. Writers of Western literature, as we know, have frequently compared reading to eating, and writing to cooking. In the "Author's Prologue" to *Gargantua et Pantagruel* [translated by J. M. Cohen, 1987], for example, François Rabelais invites the reader to the verbal feast that he has prepared in the text of his work. Indeed, he compares the reading of his book to the activity of a dog (according to Plato, the most intellectual creature in the world) who breaks open a bone and licks out the delicious marrow hidden within. Similarly, in the introduction to his *History of Tom Jones,* subtitled "Bill of Fare to the Feast," Henry Fielding warns his readers—just as an innkeeper through a menu might warn his customers—what type of literary meal they can expect to be served up in his comic novel and how the author (not unlike a cook) has gone about preparing that fare. "We shall represent Human Nature at first to the keen appetite of the reader," Fielding announces, "in that plain and simple manner in which it is found in the country, and shall hereafter hash and ragoo it with all the high French and Italian seasoning of affectation and vice which courts and cities afford."

Within Russian literature, one of the writers whose verbal art has quite often been described through gastronomical metaphors is, appropriately enough, Nikolai Gogol, perhaps the most famous of all Russian literary gourmands and one of Bulgakov's most revered literary models. Simon Karlinsky, for one, has called Gogol a "word glutton" because of the author's highly exuberant prose style, while Edmund Wilson has compared reading one of Gogol's "far-stretching" paragraphs to eating "a big bowl of Ukrainian soup, full of cabbage and beets and potatoes, chunks of sturgeon and shreds of beef or duck, with a foundation of sour cream." Iurii Ivask likewise makes use of culinary imagery when he describes the Russian author's unique writing style, observing that "Gogol's literary victuals are rich and greasy and full of vitamins, just like the meals prepared according to the instructions of a Pul'kheriia Ivanovna, a Korobochka, or a Petukh." Even one of Gogol's contemporaries, the literary critic Stepan Shevyrev, had recourse to gastronomic analogies when describing the idiosyncratic prose style of this famous Russian writer, comparing *Mertvye dushi* to a pie that had been overstuffed by "an ingenious gastronome who has bought the ingredients without calculating how much he will need, and who does not spare the filling."

All these analogies between gastronomy and literature ought to remind us that both these fields of human endeavor participate actively in a nation's cultural discourse. Eating and speaking are, after all, closely related oral acts, both of which involve the mouth, and there thus exists a natural kinship between the person who prepares a meal and the person who creates a work of literature. As Ronald Tobin has noted [in *Tarte à la crème*], the poet and the cook ought to be seen as quite kindred souls in the sense that they both perform "an archetypal, sacred and creative act that produces original, complex products which change the consumer emotionally, intellectually, and physically." The poet and the cook, in other words, both seek—by engaging in the mediatory activities of their verbal and culinary art—to fulfill what Claude Levi-Strauss has described as the humanist's goal of transforming raw nature (*le cru*) into sophisticated culture (*le cuit*). "Cuisine," as Tobin succinctly puts it, "is the ultimate art of metamorphosis."

In Bulgakov's case, of course, this very sort of metamorphosis through the civilizing process comes to serve as one of the central themes of his story: Preobrazhenskii attempts to transform both Sharik and Sharikov (Klim Chugunkin) from primitive beasts into relatively sophisticated creatures. In a metaliterary sense, meanwhile, the author of *Sobach'e serdtse* may himself be considered a chef who seeks to transform his readers by providing them—in accord with Horace's dictum that literature combine pleasure and benefit—with both food for the stomach (through the novella's rich comic and satiric entertainment) and food for the soul (through its more serious political allegory and psychological analysis). It is all the more unfortunate, therefore, that Soviet Russia's cultural watchdogs, the censors, found Bulgakov's inventive contribution to canine literature not to their taste and thus prevented contemporary Russian readers during the late 1920s from breaking open this juicy literary bone and sucking out its delicious marrow. Instead it has been left to subsequent generations of readers, both inside and outside the author's homeland, to discover and to savor

the tasty, but nourishing artistic treat that Bulgakov has served up for us in *Sobach'e serdtse*.

FURTHER READING

Bibliographies

Proffer, Ellendea. *An International Bibliography of Works by and about Mikhail Bulgakov.* Ann Arbor, Mich.: Ardis, 1976, 133 p.

> Primary and secondary bibliography listing publications in several languages including Russian, English, Dutch, French, German, and Italian.

Terry, Garth M. *Mikhail Bulgakov in English: A Bibliography 1891-1991.* Nottingham, England: Astra Press, 1991, 30 p.

> Index of works by and about Bulgakov in English.

Biographies

Belozerskaya-Bolgakova, Lyubov. *My Life with Mikhail Bulgakov.* Ann Arbor, Mich.: Ardis, 1983, 136 p.

> Personal account by Bulgakov's second wife.

Proffer, Ellendea. *Bulgakov: Life and Work.* Ann Arbor, Mich.: Ardis, 1984, 670 p.

> Comprehensive biographical and critical study of Bulgakov's career.

Criticism

Berman, Michael. "Plays and Stories by a Soviet Chekhov." *The New York Times Book Review* (23 July 1972): 7, 13.

> Positive review of *The Early Plays of Mikhail Bulgakov* and *Diaboliad, and Other Stories.*

Doyle, Peter. "Bulgakov's Satirical View of Revolution in 'Rokovye iaitsa' and *Sobach'e serdtse.*" *Canadian Slavonic Papers* XX, No. 4 (December 1978): 467-82.

> Compares the story "The Fatal Eggs" and the novella *The Heart of a Dog,* "examining the different ways in which each work treats the same theme—the rejection of revolution as a means for achieving human progress."

Friedberg, Maurice. "The Earliest Transplant." *Saturday Review* LI, No. 20 (20 July 1968): 24-5.

> Favorable evaluation of *The Heart of a Dog* in which Friedberg describes contemporary scholarship devoted to Bulgakov's writings as "a successful literary excavation that yields gems whose existence had never been suspected."

Hetényi, Zsuzsa. "Fatal Hearts of the 1920s (On Mikhail Bulgakov's Story *The Heart of a Dog*)," translated by Jonathan Crossan. *Scottish Slavonic Review*, No. 14 (Spring 1990): 181-90.

> Examines the historical context that shaped the philosophical perspective presented in the novella.

Hoover, Marjorie L. A review of *Diaboliad, and Other Stories*. *Studies in Short Fiction* XI, No. 2 (Spring 1974): 218-21.

Summarizes several stories in the *Diaboliad* collection, which receives a mixed assessment from Hoover.

Lakshin, Vladimir. A review of *Notes of a Young Doctor*. *Soviet Literature* (February 1964): 189-90.

Praises the humor and realism of *Notes of a Young Doctor*.

Morgan, Edwin. "The Healer's Art." *The Times Literary Supplement*, No. 3821 (30 May 1975): 584.

Mixed review of *Notes of a Young Doctor*.

Natov, Nadine. *Mikhail Bulgakov*. Boston: Twayne Publishers, 1985, 144 p.

Survey of Bulgakov's life and works.

Proffer, Ellendea. Introduction to *Notes on the Cuff, and Other Stories,* translated by Alison Rice, pp. vii-xix. Ann Arbor, Mich.: Ardis, 1991.

Describes *Notes on the Cuff, and Other Stories* as "a very nervous collection of stories from the start of Bulgakov's career—a nervous man, writing in a nervous time. The cataclysm underlying all of the tension one can sense here is the harrowing experience of the Revolution and Civil War, as well as a brief exposure to World War I."

Sahni, Kalpana. *A Mind in Ferment: Mikhail Bulgakov's Prose*. New Delhi, India: Arnold-Heinemann, 1984, 260 p.

Assesses the prose of Bulgakov "in the context of . . . socio-historical and cultural developments in Post-Revolutionary Russia," noting that he neither belonged to a literary group with ideological aims nor actively participated in politics. Bulgakov "refused the simplistic solutions to art that were demanded of the [Russian] artist and for this he was ostracised."

Soviet Literature 7 (1988).

Issue devoted to Bulgakov; includes autobiographical and biographical material, critical essays, and translations of several short works.

Theroux, Paul. A review of *Diaboliad, and Other Stories*. *The Washington Post Book World* VI, No. 19 (7 May 1972): Part I, p. 4.

Judges *Diaboliad, and Other Stories* "a lively collection" but categorizes Bulgakov's stories as "funny social criticism" rather than "great satire."

"Almost Human." *The Times Literary Supplement*, No. 3471 (5 September 1968): 937.

Positive review of *The Heart of a Dog*.

"Disruptive Moments." *The Times Literary Supplement*, No. 3679 (1 September 1972): 1013.

Brief appraisal of *Diaboliad, and Other Stories*.

Additional coverage of Bulgakov's life and career is contained in the following sources published by Gale Research: *Contemporary Authors,* Vol. 105; and *Twentieth-Century Literary Criticism,* Vols. 2, 16.

Daphne du Maurier
1907-1989

English novelist, short story writer, playwright, biographer, and autobiographer.

INTRODUCTION

The author of popular Gothic romance novels, including *Rebecca* and *Jamaica Inn*, du Maurier also wrote short stories variously described as mystery, suspense, and horror. Among the best known are "The Birds" and "Don't Look Now," which, like several other du Maurier works, have been popularized through film adaptations. Regarded as a talented storyteller, du Maurier used inventive details to animate formulaic plots, and she demonstrated a particular flair for evoking a suspenseful atmosphere in her short stories. Sarah Booth Conroy has commented that du Maurier's stories "have the quality of *deja vu,* legends half remembered, old wives' tales and episodes from epics, with the inevitable but always shocking 'Boo' at the end."

Biographical Information

Du Maurier was born in London to a prominent family. Her mother was an actress and her father was a popular matinee idol and theater manager. Du Maurier was educated privately, and as a young woman rejected a career in acting in order to become a writer. Her first published works were short stories and articles printed mostly in women's magazines. In 1931 she gained notoriety with the publication of her first novel, *The Loving Spirit,* which she wrote during a ten-week stay at her parents' country home on the coast of Cornwall. *The Loving Spirit* became a best seller and gained a degree of critical acclaim. Her first collection of short stories, *The Apple Tree: A Short Novel and Some Stories* (1952), first revealed the writer's macabre side. Du Maurier lived most of her life in Cornwall with her husband and children; she produced more than twenty novels and several collections of short stories there and often used the Cornish coast as her setting. She died in 1989 at the age of eighty-one.

Major Works of Short Fiction

Du Maurier's short stories portray mysterious and fantastic events that intrude upon the lives of ordinary people, often having a catastrophic effect. In "The Birds," human assumptions about the natural order of the world are challenged when birds suddenly turn predatory toward humans. The main character of the piece cannot avoid being destroyed by this inexplicable phenomenon, and the story ends with him, barricaded in his home, listening to the birds peck and scratch their way through the windows and doors. "Don't Look Now" is the story of a husband and wife vacationing in Venice to recover from the recent death of their young daughter. The couple are drawn into

further tragedy by a mysterious chain of events over which they seem to have no control. Du Maurier was interested in human psychology and the circumstances that push people toward mental breakdown. These concerns figure prominently in *The Breaking Point* (1959), which she described as a collection of stories in which "the link between emotion and reason is stretched to the limit of endurance, and sometimes snaps." One story in this collection, "The Alibi," portrays a middle-aged man who feels oppressed by his ordinary life and finds a sense of power and control in fantasizing about murder. His fantasy is realized, for better or for worse, when he is accused of a murder that he committed only in his mind.

Critical Reception

Du Maurier's short stories have received mixed critical responses. While some critics have faulted them for what they perceive as contrived, unbelievable plots and shallow characters, others have argued that du Maurier's narratives are highly imaginative and that her skill as a writer lies in her ability to make compelling use of suspense, atmosphere, and surprising plot twists. John Barkham has commented: "In every case Miss du Maurier painstakingly creates her atmosphere before she begins spinning her web. No fleeting moods or impressions here: the style is deliberate, the pace leisurely, and the stories hold up as stories."

PRINCIPAL WORKS

Short Fiction

The Apple Tree: A Short Novel and Some Stories 1952; also published as *Kiss Me Again Stranger: A Collection of Eight Stories, Long and Short*, 1953; and as *The Birds, and Other Stories*, 1977
The Breaking Point 1959; also published as *The Blue Lenses, and Other Stories*, 1970
Early Stories 1959
The Treasury of du Maurier Short Stories 1960
Don't Look Now 1971; also published as *Not After Midnight*, 1971
Echoes From the Macabre: Selected Stories 1976
The Rebecca Notebook, and Other Memories (notebook, short stories, and essays) 1980
The Rendezvous, and Other Stories 1980
Classics of the Macabre 1987

Other Major Works

The Loving Spirit (novel) 1931
I'll Never Be Young Again (novel) 1932
The Progress of Julius (novel) 1933
Gerald: A Portrait (biography) 1934
Jamaica Inn (novel) 1936
The du Mauriers (biography) 1937
Rebecca (novel) 1938
Frenchman's Creek (novel) 1942
Hungry Hill (novel) 1943
The King's General (novel) 1946
The Parasites (novel) 1949
My Cousin Rachel (novel) 1951
Mary Anne (novel) 1954
The Scapegoat (novel) 1957
The Glass-Blowers (novel) 1963
The Flight of the Falcon (novel) 1965
The House on the Strand (novel) 1969
Rule Britannia (novel) 1972
Myself When Young: The Shaping of a Writer (autobiography) 1977; also published as *Growing Pains: The Shaping of a Writer*, 1977

CRITICISM

John Barkham (essay date 1953)

SOURCE: "The Macabre and the Unexpected," in *The New York Times Book Review*, March 8, 1953, p. 5.

[*In the following review of* Kiss Me Again, Stranger, *Barkham lauds du Maurier's craftsmanship as a mystery writer.*]

In her short stories, as in her novels, Daphne du Maurier is a firm believer in keeping her readers on tenterhooks. She cannot dazzle them with her prose or excite them with her imagination, but at least she baffles them with her mysteries. And baffle them she does, over and over again in this book. Guessing the identity of du Maurier murderers is still likely to remain a favorite indoor sport this spring.

> **In these days of shiny-knobbed science fiction, the old-fashioned story of the supernatural, which used to chill the kids and keep old men from the chimney corner, is becoming something of a rarity. More's the pity. Miss du Maurier can still write them in the grand tradition.**
>
> **—*John Barkham***

These eight tales are the mixture as before. All lean to the macabre, the strange, the unexplained. None of them is bad, and several are very good indeed. No wraiths or clanking ghosts, you understand, but subtle emanations, like a dying tree that bursts ominously into bloom, or a wife who falls under the spell of the mountains. In every case Miss du Maurier painstakingly creates her atmosphere before she begins spinning her web. No fleeting moods or impressions here: the style is deliberate, the pace leisurely, and the stories hold up as stories.

One is a masterpiece of horror. Twenty years ago an Australian named Carl Stephenson wrote a superb short story, "Leningen and the Ants," in which he described a South American planter's epic struggle against a column of jungle ants. It was an adventure you could not forget. Miss du Maurier has matched it with a story in the same genre. **"The Birds"** is set on a peaceful English farm. Its theme? The birds of the world have suddenly and inexplicably turned predatory, and all over the earth have begun to peck, scratch and tear human beings to death. We watch the attack on the farm. Like Leningen, farmer Nat Hocken fights a hair-raising battle against the winged warriors that darken the sky.

Two of the tales are straight studies in crime. There is the elegant marquise who dallies with a young photographer and pushes him over a cliff, only to find herself trapped through a revealing portrait, a piece of very neat plotting. Better still is **"The Motive,"** a skillful unraveling of a seemingly purposeless suicide. Here Miss du Maurier does what J. B. Priestley did so well in his "Dangerous Corner." She opens with a motiveless death, then gradually leads the reader deeper and deeper into the mystery, until at last all the jigsaw pieces fall into place. This kind of progressive revelation requires real craftsmanship.

Have you noticed how often the agent of mystery or evil in a du Maurier story is a woman? Du Maurier women have been bewitching and bewildering their simple-minded menfolk for years, and in these stories they are still at it. The girl who lures a youth into a cemetery, the marquise who kills her lover, the nagging wife who haunts by way of a tree—these are *femmes fatales* who toy with their men and then get them, one way or another. They also leave this reviewer with some interesting theories as to the author's artistic motivations.

In these days of shiny-knobbed science fiction, the old-fashioned story of the supernatural, which used to chill the kids and keep old men from the chimney corner, is becoming somthing of a rarity. More's the pity. Miss du Maurier can still write them in the grand tradition. Try these tales and see how they dwarf those rockets and bug-eyed monsters.

Sylvia Berkman (essay date 1953)

SOURCE: "A Skilled Hand Weaves a Net of Horror," in *New York Herald Tribune Book Review,* March 15, 1953, p. 4.

[*In the following review, Berkman praises* Kiss Me Again, Stranger *for its insightful representation of painful and frightening human experiences.*]

Daphne du Maurier is a specialist in horror. Her creative intelligence is resourceful, her command of eerie atmosphere persuasive and precise, her sense of shock-timing exceptionally skilled. In [*Kiss Me Again, Stranger*] she explores horror in a variety of forms; in the macabre, in the psychologically deranged, in the supernatural, in the fantastic, most painfully of all, in the sheer cruelty of human beings in interrelationship. Yet on the whole the volume offers absorbing rather than oppressive reading because chiefly one's intellect is engaged; the emotional content remains subordinate. Broadly speaking, for the most part these are stories of detection as well, with the contributing elements of excitation, suspense, and climax manipulated with a seasoned hand.

Miss du Maurier is most successful, I believe (as most of us are) when her intentions are unmixed. **"Kiss Me Again, Stranger,"** the title story, adaptly marshals the ingredients best suited to her abilities. Here in a trim, fluently moving narrative she developed an incident in war-torn London, with no purpose beyond the immediate recounting of a sad and grisly tale. A young mechanic, a simple, sensitive, likable good chap, attracted by a pretty usherette at a cinema palace, joins her on her bus ride home, to be led, bewildered, into a cemetery, where her conduct baffles him, to say the least. The girl, so gentle, wistful, languorous, and sleepy, turns out to be psychopathically obsessed, with a vindicative animus against members of the R. A. F. The summary is unjust, for Miss du Maurier

forcibly anchors her story in a strange lonely graveyard atmosphere, with night rain falling cold and dreary on the flat tombs, which both reflects and reinforces the mortal impairment of the young girl's nature and the destruction of the young man's hopes, in a charnel world dislocated by the larger horror of war.

In **"Kiss Me Again, Stranger,"** all separate aspects of the narrative fuse. **"The Birds,"** however, essentially a far more powerful story is marred by unresolved duality of intent. Slowly, with intensifying accurate detail. Miss du Maurier builds up her account of the massed attack of the starving winter birds on humankind, the familiar little land birds, the battalions of gulls bearing in rank upon rank from the sea, the murderous predatory birds of prey descending with ferocious beaks and talons to rip, rend, batter and kill. The struggle involved is the ancient struggle of man against the forces of nature, Robinson Crusoe's struggle to overcome an elemental adversary through cunning, logic, and wit. The turning of this material also into a political fable, with the overt references to control from Russia and aid from America, to my mind dissipates the full impact of a stark and terrifying tale.

> **Daphne du Maurier is a specialist in horror. Her creative intelligence is resourceful, her command of eerie atmosphere persuasive and precise, her sense of shock-timing exceptionally skilled.**
>
> **— Sylvia Berkman**

Monte Verità also clothes parable in an outer aspect of realism, this time for the statement of philosophical axiom: that the residence of truth is harsh, lonely and austere, by an ascent granted only to few, but its attainment the attainment of richest beatitude, even though in the general community below the few spirits who achieve the lofty summit are persecuted through hatred and fear. Again Miss du Maurier is most successful in the establishment of other-worldly atmosphere, the creation of impressive scene, particularly of the clear symbolic peaks of Monte Verità rising pure and unadorned against the sky. Perhaps this kind of story requires a special attitude on the part of the author—E. M. Forster's confident asssumption that the dryad *is* in the tree, if only one looks hard enough; too heavy a grounding in realistic detail can arouse realistic questioning. Here the factual narration of events, in which Anna, forsaking worldly attachments enters the citadel on the heights of Monte Verità, and the subsequent development of the two men who love her, again imposes disunity. Yet *Monte Verità* contains an abundance of integrated incident to sustain the interest; one surely wants to know thc end.

Equally, each of the stories exerts that claim: one surely wants to know the end. **"The Split Second,"** with its investigation of the inter-temporal in the instant of death, represents the author at her most skillful, weaving a logical, firm, constantly tautening web of mystification and suspense. **"The Little Photographer,"** recounting the divertissement of a bored, vain, beautiful marquise with a crippled shopkeeper, in part recalls Thomas Mann's "Little Herr Friedemann"; but Miss du Maurier has given the denouement a characteristic turn (M. Paul is not idly cast as a photographer; he had a way of snapping pictures of his lady after their dalliance in the bracken), and the story ends with a sinister good chill.

Miss du Maurier is not primarily concerned with character. Her figures are presented with swift unhesitating strokes; through them a fairly complicated history unfolds. Yet every account of human action contains its residue of human experience; and Miss du Maurier's main themes, if seriously regarded, are neither haphazard nor trivial: again and again she returns to the consideration of our human predicament, to frustration, destruction, loss, betrayal, and needless suffering, Joyce's themes of the *Dubliners,* conveyed through the obverse method of a decided emphasis on plot. In general in this volume complexities of plot disinfect horror to a pungent and provocative spice.

Malcolm Bradbury (essay date 1959)

SOURCE: "To a Moment of Truth," in *The New York Times Book Review,* October 25, 1959, p. 4.

[*An English novelist and critic, Bradbury is best known as the author of such satiric novels as* Eating People Is Wrong *(1959) and* Stepping Westward *(1965). In the following review of* The Breaking Point, *he expresses several reservations about the individual pieces but calls du Maurier's short stories her best work.*]

[*The Breaking Point*] is a curious and uneven affair. The stories are, claims the author in an introductory note, concerned with the moment of truth that comes in the life of each individual, the moment at which "it is as though the link between emotion and reason is stretched to the limit of endurance, and sometimes snaps." And her theme in the first three stories (**"The Alibi," "The Blue Lenses"** and **"Ganymede"**) is the sudden perception of the reality and the horror that lie beneath the placid and rather dreary face of everyday life.

This is a perennial theme among English novelists, perhaps because English life is so much given over to the mannered and the conventional, and manners provide a cushion against the stricter problems of life. **"Ganymede,"** the best story in the volume, is an exercise in the mode of Thomas Mann's "Death in Venice," about the mythically corrupt Italy which the North European races find a subject both for fascination and fear. The narrator of the story exercises, and suffers for, his corruption in the fetid atmosphere of Venice, but unlike Mann's hero he returns to England to live on, with his corruption. In **"The Alibi"** the hero escapes from the boredom of a conventional life

into fantasies of murder, spending his afternoons painting pictures in a hidden basement, finally paying for his escape by being accused of a murder that he committed only in fantasy. These stories actually seem to me to be better than anything in Miss du Maurier's novels; it is as if the short-story form controls and orders her skill and vision.

Unfortunately this is not always true. Elsewhere, she is successful almost in spite of herself: her virtuosity takes her far beyond the banality of her material. An example in this vein is **"The Archduchess,"** a fable about a mythical European state that has existed in perpetual bliss until it is destroyed by two naughty liberals fermenting revolution. Another is **"The Menace,"** a story about an English film star in a thoroughly unrealized Hollywood— where studio executives worry because they have spent a thousand dollars entertaining a star and where actors eat porridge and go to bed at nine.

If **"The Menace"** is alarming because of the heaviness of the humor ("they jumped in the car and drove the five hundred yards to Barry's place"), **"The Archduchess"** is alarming because of its moral perspective. It is a criticism of skepticism and moral questioning; the Rondese have been a happy race because "all they asked for was life, and life was given them, and happiness, which springs from within," and this state is ruined by doubt. Rondo has a mysterious water of perpetual youth, which gives to those who drink it "that sense of perpetual well-being on waking which a child has before puberty; or perhaps it would be better to say a renewal of wonder."

It is to this glorious state that several of her stories, such as **"The Pool,"** hark back. Even **"The Alibi"** can equally be the story of a man who is destroyed by the flatness of his environment, or the tale of a man who destroys himself by refusing to accept the dreary, the commonplace and the conventional.

In such a story, Miss du Maurier's native powers as a storyteller take over to make the tale a fine and satisfying one; but at times she forsakes her artist's role for polemic, and it is no accident that the stories in which she does this are technically the least successful. We see exposed the narrowness of her range, and what seemed in the better stories to be lapses of tone stand exposed as places where she has gone beyond her powers. In the lesser stories the breaking point of her title seems to be the state of self-destruction that deservedly comes to those who meddle with newfangled Western doubt. When this pervasive conservatism becomes joined with lapses in skill, we find Miss du Maurier's own breaking point.

Margaret Hurley (essay date 1959)

SOURCE: "Behind the Curtain," in *The Saturday Review,* New York, Vol. XLII, No. 45, November 7, 1959, p. 23.

[*In the following review of* The Breaking Point, *Hurley commends du Maurier's talent as a suspense and horror writer, noting particularly her ability to create realistic settings and believable characters.*]

Daphne du Maurier's collection of short stories *The Breaking Point* leaves no doubt as to the author's talent as a crackerjack raconteuse. Each selection is a masterpiece—sometimes of suspense, chicanery, insidious evil, in other instances of sensitivity and perception, as in the case of **"The Pool,"** a heartrending story about the brink of adolescence. She takes the reader by the icy hand and leads him behind the curtain to view the characters on their ways to their own breaking points.

If you read a book of short stories as I do, starting at page one and proceeding in an orderly manner, you will be exposed to the experiences of compulsive murder and the horrors of base propaganda. Then the thought comes to mind: Miss du Maurier can conjure up a scene, an atmosphere; the suspense is shattering; she can make characters live and breathe; but where, oh where is her sense of humor? Any relief in sight? Or is this *my* breaking point?

Have another go at it. Turn the page to **"The Menace."** It is a cool breeze for a fevered brow—a hilarious story of the career of a Hollywood matinee idol whose greatest emotional excitement is evoked by the sight of a nice bowl of porridge. Tall, broad-shouldered, hipless, provocatively homely, completely deadpan, dumb beyond belief, this heart-throb leaves the fans writhing in their seats. His vast popularity might have gone on for years except for the "feelies"—a new movie technique by which the theatres are wired and audiences actually "feel" the personalities projected on the screen. Unfortunately, our hero's sawdust composition fails to register with the wiring apparatus. The ensuing efforts of his wife (yes, he has one—a mom type), his manager, his coach, his agent, and other partners interested in his career, to rouse **"The Menace"** to an emotional pitch sufficient to vibrate the sex-appeal detector are funny and rowdy in the extreme. His particular "breaking point" is a happy one.

The book closes with the **"The Limpet,"** which is particularly satisfying because the main character is one familiar to everybody. You've known her and I've known her—a mean, selfish, devious, stupid creature who screens her puny schemes behind a façade of nauseating nice-Nellyisms.

Throughout these stories, Daphne du Maurier demonstrates her talent in ferrting out and describing the subtleties and foibles of human nature.

Richard Sullivan (essay date 1959)

SOURCE: "Du Maurier Collection: Polished but Shallow," in *Chicago Tribune*, Part 7, November 15, 1959, p. 7.

[*Sullivan is an American novelist and critic. In the following negative review of* The Breaking Point, *he perceives du Maurier's approach to human interactions as shallow and calculated.*]

The prose written by Daphne du Maurier is both grammatical and efficient. It is a prose well practiced in story telling, and over the years it has given pleasure to a multitude of readers. But perhaps—at least as exhibited in *The Breaking Point*—it is a deceptive prose, which conceals in a pleasant, experienced way the essential shallowness of its approach to human entanglements.

The stories which make up this collection may all be accurately summed up by the book's collective title. Each piece deals with a person brought, one way or another, to something like a breaking point; and then this person breaks, one way or the other.

There is a story about a man of business who turns artist and is ironically destroyed, after having plotted other destructions. There is one about a movie star, inept, inadequate, inarticulate, but the idol of millions. The irony of the one story is as obviously underlined as the intended satire of the other.

Several of the pieces are out and out fantasies; and the volume as a whole leans toward the fantastic. One excellent story, **"The Blue Lenses,"** combines fantasy with insight to make a memorable little commentary upon human nature. But in general this is a book marked not by wisdom or insight but by crafty invention.

Invention itself is a great gift for a story teller. But unless it is backed up by a deep concern about people invention can degenerate to mere trickiness. And these stories are generally too tricky to be satisfying as accounts in words of people in action.

They seem, indeed, these polished stories, to rise not out of life or the contemplation of life but out of a careful calculation as to what cooked-up material may next be presented, efficiently and grammatically, to a multitude of readers. Even expert craftsmanship, when it stoops to calculation of this sort, can hardly be praised.

Margaret Millar (essay date 1971)

SOURCE: A review of *Don't Look Now,* in *The New York Times Book Review,* October 17, 1971, pp. 56-7.

[*A Canadian novelist and nonfiction writer, Millar is a critically acclaimed author of several mystery and suspense novels. In the following mixed review of* Don't Look Now, *she suggests that while du Maurier's stories are intriguing and entertaining, some have manipulative plots and unbelievable, superficial characters.*]

[*Don't Look Now*] is a collection of five uneasy pieces. In each one the reader is given an intriguing situation, a series of neatly planted clues and a generous number of plot twists, the kind of thing that Bennett Cerf has lovingly referred to as shenanigans. His taste for shenanigans must be shared by a great many readers: Miss du Maurier has been a household word for more than 30 years, and the most famous Rebecca in the world today is not from

Sunnybrook Farm or the Book of Genesis but from a lonely old English mansion called Manderley.

In the title story, **"Don't Look Now,"** Laura and John return to Venice, the scene of their honeymoon 10 years previously. In a restaurant they meet elderly twin sisters from Scotland, one of whom is blind. She is also psychic, and she tells Laura that she has just seen her little daughter who had recently died at the age of 5. Laura is a ready believer. To her husband's alarm she contrives a further meeting with the twins. The psychic warns her of danger if she and John remain in Venice. When a telegram arrives from England with news of the illness of her other child, Laura makes arrangements to fly home immediately. John, who stays behind to take care of their car and baggage, escorts her as far as the landing launch.

That afternoon as he is thinking of Laura winging her way back to England he sees her on a tourist-filled ferry steaming down the Grand Canal. The twin sisters are close beside her and Laura is looking distressed. John assumes her flight was canceled, and she is returning to the hotel. But she fails to show up, and he doesn't know the name of the sisters or where they are staying. Here the plot begins to thicken when it should quicken.

Is Laura really dead? No. Are the sisters dead? No. Is the story dead? A bit. Miss du Maurier is not at her best writing in the third person. Her most effective prose is done in the first person, which keeps her from sprawling and gives her better emotional control of her characters. Laura and John are superficial and dull. Seen from another angle they might have come across as mysterious and cool.

While **"Don't Look Now"** is a tale of the supernatural, **"The Breakthrough"** combines the supernatural with superscience. At a secret Government installation on the northwest coast of England, experiments are being conducted on blast. The purpose is to transmit waves that will strike specific targets rather than destroy indiscriminately like sonic booms. The not-so-mad scientist, Maclean, is trying to apply the same principle to promote high-frequency response between individuals, in this case a young man dying of leukemia and an idiot child whose psychic energy is extra strong because her brain did not develop. Miss du Maurier put more genuine feeling into these two characters than in others in the book. As for the story, I guarantee you'll remember it every time you visit a secret experimental station on the northwest coast of England.

In **"Not After Midnight"** a British schoolteacher, Timothy Grey, is spending his holidays on the island of Crete. He rents a seaside chalet whose previous occupant, a young man writing a book on archeological finds and their connection with Greek mythology, had drowned during a midnight swim. Grey, interested only in his painting, tries to avoid the other hotel guests but finds himself unable to avoid a middle-aged American couple named Stoll. Stoll is a heavy drinker and a bully whose mousey wife tolerates his outbursts mainly because she is deaf.

Every day the Stolls rent a boat and go fishing, but they return to their chalet empty-handed, or at least without any fish. Then they suddenly leave the hotel after delivering a gift to Grey, an ancient jug decorated with the head of Silenos and three of his fellow satyrs.

Puzzled by the gift and the Stolls's mysterious actions, Grey rents the boat they'd been using and investigates. The investigation reveals a shocker of an ending which has little to do with either science or the supernatural.

In **"A Border-Line Case,"** a young actress is bewildered by her father's dying words, which seem to indicate that she is at fault. Attempting to discover the source of her guilt, she sorts through the clues her father left behind: photographs, an address book and a scrap of paper with a list of dates on it and the name of the man who'd been best man at her parents' wedding: Nicolas Barry, Lough Torrah, Eire. So it's off to Ireland for our heroine.

The Irish complications that follow seem to have been inserted merely to throw readers off and keep them from guessing the ending, a legitimate ploy but one that should be kept under stricter control.

"The Way of the Cross" concerns six adults and a boy on a one-day guided tour of Jerusalem. Shenanigans in the Holy City are the same as those in Peoria, Ill., but the Biblical names give them a little more class. Miss Dean, the spinster, almost drowns in the Pool of Bethesda; Lady Althea loses the caps on her front teeth outside the Church of All Nations; the young bride is seduced in the Garden of Gethsemane; her seducer, Foster, a plastics manufacturer, is mistaken for a thief on the Via Dolorosa; Mrs. Foster tells some straight truths in the Garden of Joseph of Arimathea, and the Rev. Mr. Babcock suffers an attack of *turista* in the Church of the Holy Sepulchre. Jerusalem, Jerusalem!

Only the 9-year-old boy and the 5,000-year-old city seem very real. The other characters used to flesh out the story are mainly flab. Some sort of message comes across about Christianity and humility but the vibes are weak.

Richard Kelly (essay date 1987)

SOURCE: "The World of the Macabre: The Short Stories," in *Daphne Du Maurier,* Twayne Publishers, 1987, pp. 123-40.

[*Kelly is an American critic and educator. In the following excerpt from his book-length biographical and critical study of du Maurier, he concludes that her characters often remain undefined and secondary to her formulaic plots, and that her best short stories are those that break out of this pattern, such as "Ganymede," "Don't Look Now," and "The Birds."*]

Before she embarked on her career as a novelist du Maurier had published a few of her short stories in the *Bystander,* a magazine edited by her maternal uncle, William Comyns Beaumont. She continued writing short stories during the next five decades, many of which appeared in such women's magazines as the *Ladies Home Journal* and *Good Housekeeping*. Most of these tales were later collected and published in *The Apple Tree,* 1952 (entitled *Kiss Me Again, Stranger* in the American edition), *The Breaking Point,* 1959, *Not After Midnight,* 1971 (entitled *Don't Look Now* in the American edition), and *The Rendezvous and Other Stories,* 1980. *Echoes from the Macabre,* published in 1976, is a composite of selected stories from the earlier collections. Finally, some of the stories that appeared in these earlier books are reprinted, along with a few previously uncollected essays and early tales, in *The Rebecca Notebook and Other Memories,* 1980.

Although some of du Maurier's novels, such as *The House on the Strand* and *The Flight of the Falcon,* acknowledge the workings of the unconscious mind, most of her short stories focus upon this sixth sense and explore the region of the mind that borders upon reason and madness, the natural and the supernatural. In her preface to *The Breaking Point,* du Maurier writes, "There comes a moment in the life of every individual when reality must be faced. When this happens, it is as though a link between emotion and reason is stretched to the limit of endurance, and sometimes snaps." Two of her tales that study this breaking point, **"The Birds,"** and **"Don't Look Now,"** have been indelibly etched upon millions of minds through the enormously popular films by Alfred Hitchcock and Nicholas Roeg.

"The Birds" is an excellent short story that has been turned into a very bad motion picture. "On December the third the wind changed overnight and it was winter," the story opens. This sudden shift in the weather sets the tone for the catastrophic change in the natural order of things to follow. The tale focuses upon an English farmer, Nat Hocken, his wife and children. As the cold begins to bite into both the land and Nat's body, he notices that there are more birds than usual, both over the sea and land. That night he hears pecking at the windows of his home. The birds are trying to get in, and when he goes to investigate the noise one of them pecks at his eyes. Some fifty birds then fly through the open window in his children's room, and he manages to kill most of them amidst the hysterical cries of the children.

The next day the family discusses the bizarre occurrence. Nat explains that the east wind must have affected the behavior of the birds and caused them to seek shelter in his house. When his daughter, Jill, says that they tried to peck at her brother's eyes, Nat again offers a rational explanation. "Fright made them do that. They didn't know where they were, in the dark bedroom."

Later that day, Nat sees what he thinks are white caps out at sea, but they turn out to be hundreds of thousands of gulls: "They rose and fell in the trough of the seas, heads to the wind, like a mighty fleet at anchor, waiting on the tide." When he returns home his wife informs him that there was an announcement on the radio stating that "it's everywhere. In London, all over the country. Something

has happened to the birds." A later bulletin says that "The flocks of birds have caused dislocation in all areas."

"Dislocation" is a key word in this story, for it identifies the fundamental disruption in the natural order of things. Man, who is ordained to have dominion over the birds and the beasts, suddenly has his authority threatened. There is not only a dislocation in the great chain of being but within people's minds. Reason and serenity are displaced by fear and panic in this unexpected reversion to a Darwinian world of the survival of the fittest.

Realizing that neither the government nor the military could do anything to help at this point, Nat assumes the thinking of a survivalist: "Each householder must look after his own." Life within his small farmhouse takes on the character of Londoners during the air raids: the family huddles together, food is carefully accounted for, windows and other openings are sealed up, as they prepare for the invasion. The next day the birds continue to gather ominously in the sky and in the fields. On his way home Nat is viciously attacked by a gull, and during his panic a dozen other gulls join in. "If he could only keep them from his eyes. They had not learnt yet how to cling to a shoulder, how to rip clothing, how to dive in mass upon the head, upon the body. But with each dive, with each attack, they became bolder."

Safe at home again, Nat has his wounds treated by his wife, and his children become terrified at the sight of the blood. The battle is now in earnest. The parents do their best to keep the children distracted, but their gut fear shows in their faces and in their actions. That night thousands of birds assault the house, breaking the windows, screaming down the chimney. Using all of his energy and resourcefulness, Nat manages to get his family through the harrowing hours. Daylight brings a degree of safety, for the birds seem to settle quietly in the fields.

Nat goes to the home of his neighbor, the Triggs, to see if he can get some food for his family and discovers the mutilated bodies of the couple. Mr. Trigg is lying next to his telephone, and his wife, an umbrella and a few dead birds at her side, is lying on her bedroom floor. Nat gathers up some food and returns home. This time he barricades his house with barbed wire around the boarded windows and chimney. He works feverishly as his wife and children sleep and then joins them in the hope that his small world is secure.

The story ends with Nat lighting up his last cigarette and listening to the attack of the birds:

> The smaller birds were at the window now. He recognized the light taptapping of their beaks, and the soft brush of their wings. The hawks ignored the windows. They concentrated their attack upon the door. Nat listened to the tearing sound of splintering wood, and wondered how many millions of years were stored in those little brains, behind the stabbing beaks, the piercing eyes, now giving them this instinct to destroy mankind with all the deft precision of machines.

*Du Maurier in 1947, on the staircase of Menabilly,
her home on the Cornish coast.*

By limiting the focus of her story upon Nat Hocken and his family du Maurier manages to convey the effect of a believable claustrophobic nightmare. The birds may be attacking people throughout the world, but du Maurier wisely keeps the story within the confines of one person's family (though, of course, Nat hears reports of the birds turning predatory in London). The Hocken family becomes a microcosm of an apparent world-wide disaster, and the conclusion of the story clearly suggests that the birds will destroy all the people on earth.

During recent years there have been stories and films featuring everything from rabbits to ants as man's final enemy. Du Maurier's story, however, was something of a shocker at the time, and her choice of birds as the destroyers was particularly effective. Birds have long been associated with peacefulness, beauty, freedom, spirituality, music, and poetry. Unlike ants, frogs, rats, bees, and the other assortments of creatures that go on the rampage in contemporary science fiction tales, birds are attractive and elusive creatures. By making them relentless, almost calculating predators, du Maurier revolutionizes the traditional symbolism of birds, and her story conjures up the nightmarish imagery of the paintings by Hieronymus Bosch, in which grotesque birds with stabbing beaks threaten the rational order of things. Du Maurier plays upon the archetypal fear of having one's eyes pierced by having Nat several times throughout the story exclaim in the midst of an attack that he must protect his eyes.

One other nice touch in the story is that du Maurier does not offer some pseudo-scientific explanation for the birds' behavior. Given an ordered and reasonable world, her characters attempt to explain the phenomena in terms they can understand—a shift in the weather or migration patterns. They gradually discover, however, that their life-long assumptions about reason and order do not apply, that their world has suddenly become absurd, a bad dream in which rules of logic and common sense no longer work. The end result is that human beings are forced to act like animals themselves, with survival as their solitary goal.

Alfred Hitchcock became interested in du Maurier's story after he read the headlines of a Santa Cruz newspaper: "A Sea Bird Invasion Hits Coastal Homes." Realizing that there was no plot or character development in the short story, Hitchcock knew he would have to get someone, preferably a novelist, who could expand the story and make it suitable for a film. He turned to the novelist Evan Hunter.

Hunter's final story line is as follows: A rich San Francisco socialite named Melanie Daniels (played by Tippi Hedren) meets a brash young lawyer named Mitch Brenner (played by Rod Taylor) in a pet shop. Despite Mitch's arrogant manner, Melanie is attracted to him, and she travels by boat to his home in Bodega Bay to deliver a pair of love birds his young sister wanted. Returning to town, Melanie is attacked by a swooping gull that wounds her head. Later she accepts an invitation to Mitch's home for dinner, despite his mother's disapproval of her. The birds in the area, meantime, show signs of erratic behavior. Melanie goes to help out at the sister's birthday party the next day, and during the party a flock of gulls attacks the children. The school teacher, Annie Hayworth (played by Suzanne Pleshette), was formerly in love with Mitch and provides the love triangle.

The violence increases as a flock of sparrows pours into the house through the chimney. A neighboring farmer and his wife are pecked to death; another attack leads to an explosion of a gasoline tank; and Annie is killed while trying to protect her students. Finally, Melanie, Mitch, his mother and sister, barricade the house against a brutal onslaught of birds. During a lull the next day, Mitch gets his car, and he drives the terrified group away slowly down a road surrounded by birds.

Hitchcock did not want any stars in his film. He told Hunter, "I'm the star, the birds are the stars—and you're the star." Apart from the famous stage actress Jessica Tandy, who played the mother, there were no well-known actors in the film. Hitchcock chose Suzanne Pleshette, a newcomer, over Anne Bancroft for the role of the school-teacher. He gave Tippi Hedren and Rod Taylor their first leading roles. A great expense of time and money went into the birds themselves: mechanical birds, animated birds, and real birds. Two men, wearing protective gloves, threw live birds at Tippi Hedren during the climactic scene. Hours were spent in shooting this scene in a caged room as Hedren attempted to act under the constant bombardment of feathers and beaks. Once a frightened bird left a deep gash on her lower eye lid, and the terror in the cage became more than mere acting.

If a lesser figure than Hitchcock had produced this film it is doubtful that it would have received such enormous notoriety. It is without a doubt the worst film version of a du Maurier story. Evan Hunter's script is largely devoted to the dull and unbelievable love story between Mitch and Melanie. The audience must sit through over an hour of poor acting and vapid dialogue before the birds get their chance to star. The nightmare effect of du Maurier's story is diminished beyond recall, with the exception of one excellent scene in which Melanie sits outside the school house waiting for Mitch's sister. As she sits there smoking a cigarette, a jungle-gym set in the background ominously fills up with large blackbirds.

Brendal Gill, in the *New Yorker,* observes that the film "doesn't arouse suspense, which is, of course, what justifies and transforms the sadism that lies at the heart of every thriller. Here the sadism is all too nakedly, repellently present. . . . If this picture is a hit, the Audubon Society has an ugly public-relations problem on its hands." Most of the major newspapers and magazines attacked this film with the vehemence of the predatory birds themselves. Before long, the critics were busily attacking each other. Gary Arnold in *Moviegoer* ridicules the opinions of Peter Bogdanovich and Andrew Sarris, who contend that *The Birds* is Hitchcock's greatest artistic achievement. Arnold observes that Evan Hunter's script lies at the heart of the film's failure: "Since the people in the film are so shallow, so lacking in the qualities and complexities of human beings, the birds themselves lose a good deal of force both as terrorizers and possible symbols. Assaulting vacant, passive, cardboard figures proves very little, I think, about what men are like or what they may have in store for themselves."

In a prefatory note to *The Breaking Point,* du Maurier writes that "In this collection of stories, men, women, children, and a nation are brought to the breaking point. Whether the link [between emotion and reason] snaps, the reader must judge for himself." The two most memorable tales in this volume are **"The Alibi"** and **"Ganymede."**

"The Alibi" is the story of a homicidal personality. Middle-aged, married, and bored with the routine of his life, James Fenton feels that he has become a puppet, constrained by social customs and manners. Then, one day, he suddenly becomes aware of a sense of power within himself: "His was the master-hand that set the puppets jiggling." He looks at the quiet, apathetic houses along the street and begins to express his new-found power in psychopathic terms: "They don't know, those people inside, how one gesture of mine, now, at this minute, might alter their world. A knock on the door, and someone answers—a woman yawning, an old man in carpet slippers, a child sent by its parents in irritation; and according to what I will, what I decide, their whole future will be decided. Faces smashed in. Sudden murder. Theft. Fire. It was as simple as that."

Pretending he is an artist, Fenton rents a basement room in a rundown section of the city, "the air of poverty and decay" presenting "a contrast to the houses in his own small Regency square." As in Victorian pornography, the victim of the upper-class manipulator is the lower-class woman. The only tenants in this slum dwelling are an Austrian woman named Anna Kaufman and her young boy Johnnie. Fenton plans to murder them both, believing that this act will demonstrate both his power and freedom as a human being.

Spending several hours in these lodgings each day (he tells his wife that he is working late at the office), Fenton becomes intensely interested in his paintings, first done as part of his charade but later taken seriously. Meanwhile, Anna has become very dependent upon him for companionship and money, and, when he says that he is going to take another apartment where he hopes to finish up his series of paintings, she becomes morose. He gathers up his materials and is about to leave when she asks him if he would throw away a package that she gives him. A policeman sees him drop the package into a trashcan and shows up at his home later to arrest him for disposing of a dead fetus.

Fenton confesses to the police and to his wife that indeed he was keeping this apartment where he painted nearly every day but that his relationship with Anna was an innocent one, all of which is true. When the police take him to the lodgings he discovers that Anna has turned on the gas and killed herself and Johnnie. Both the police and his wife believe that he murdered them, and Fenton, in an act of ironic despair, cries out, "All right, I'll confess everything. I was her lover, of course, and the child was mine. I turned on the gas this evening before I left the house. I killed them all." The story ends with Fenton's false confession, a confession to a crime he had committed only in his imagination. His fantasy of power and freedom thus brings about his destruction.

Fenton's dissatisfaction with the routines and customs of middle-class life proves to be his undoing. Although the focus of this story is upon the melodrama of potential murder, its structure argues for the acceptance of conventional values. If one ventures out to become a sort of Nietzschean superman, imposing his own will upon events and becoming a law unto himself, then he is destroyed. In this case, the hero plants the seeds of self-destruction by merely fantasizing his plan for gratuitous murder. Of course, if one is a writer, like du Maurier, she may commit fictional murders with impunity and still retain her firm belief in the conventional manners and customs that hold her world so firmly together.

Influenced by Thomas Mann's "Death in Venice," du Maurier constructs a very compelling story in **"Ganymede."** The narrator is a classics scholar from England on holiday in Venice. Fired from his teaching position for "unsavoury practices," this sad and rather lonely man falls in love with a handsome young Italian waiter whom he christens "Ganymede." The middle-aged scholar imagines himself as Zeus being served by this young cupbearer, and the fantasy provides him intense happiness during his stay in the hotel. Before long, however, he becomes involved with the boy's family and promises to get the young man a good-paying job in England. It becomes clear that there is a great gap between the scholar's and the boy's interests. The narrator considered giving him his prized collection of Shakespeare's plays but decides not to when he discovers that the boy really would like to have an Elvis Presley record. Their relationship develops, and the scholar's fantasy continues to grow when suddenly tragedy brings his homosexual dream to an end. While the boy is water-skiing, the narrator mishandles the tow line, and the boy is dragged under the propeller of the boat and killed. The narrator pays for all of the funeral expenses, and his life, as he says, "has become rather different." With no living relative except his sister, whom he sees occasionally, he is once again facing the void. He concludes his tale by announcing that he has a little present for the fifteen-year-old boy training to be a waiter. He bought him a Perry Como record.

Du Maurier seems to be at her best in her more commonplace tales, such as this one and *The Parasites,* where she is not seeking melodramatic or supernatural effects. Like the Reverend Davey, the narrator is one of her "freaks," a social outcast who attempts to manipulate other people to satisfy his loneliness and unhappiness. Like Davey, who pays homage to the Druidical gods, Fenton identifies himself with the Greek god, Zeus. He is a sympathetic character until the end of the story where we learn that he is about to engage another young boy for his pleasure. Du Maurier's choice of first-person point of view is especially effective here, since it disallows any judgmental statements by an omniscient narrator. As far as the scholar is concerned, he is living a normal life, unwittingly revealing his selfishness, his pitiful loneliness, and his corruption. Above all else, he is guilty of hubris, an arrogant pride bred from sexual passion. When he first sees his "Ganymede" he remarks: "I myself was above him, did not exist in his time; and this self who was non-existent knew with every nerve fibre, every brain cell, every blood corpuscle that he was indeed Zeus, the giver of life and death, the immortal one, the lover; and that the boy who came towards him was his own beloved, his cup-bearer, his slave, his Ganymede." Having inadvertently brought about the death of his first cupbearer, this would-be-Zeus descends from his classical heaven to the lowly world again, with a Perry Como record under his arm, to seduce his next young boy. Du Maurier's grotesque sense of humor here is brilliant.

It often happens that a novel or short story is overshadowed by the film upon which it is based. *Gone with the Wind, The Wizard of Oz,* and *Rebecca* are cases in point. **"Don't Look Now,"** the first story in *Not After Midnight,* may not be as well known as *Rebecca* but Nicholas Roeg's translation of the tale into film is one of the happiest marriages between fiction and film in recent years.

Du Maurier opens her story with a compellingly suspenseful sentence: "'Don't look now,' John said to his wife, 'but there are a couple of old girls two tables away who

are trying to hypnotise me.'" John and Laura, an English couple, are on vacation in Venice in an attempt to distract themselves from the memory of the recent death of their young daughter, Christine, who died of meningitis. The two women sitting in the restaurant behind them are identical twins, only one of them is blind. They are wearing mannish clothes, and John jokingly speculates that they are lesbians or male twins in drag or hermaphrodites. Laura goes to the restroom, and when she returns she tells John that the blind twin told her that she saw their daughter Christine sitting between them and that she was laughing. Laura learned that one sister is a retired doctor from Edinburgh and that the other one has studied the occult all her life and was very psychic. "It's only since going blind," she tells John, "that she has really seen things, like a medium."

John is an unbeliever, but upon seeing the blind sister's sightless eyes fixed upon him, "He felt himself held, unable to move, and an impending sense of doom, of tragedy, came upon him. His whole being sagged, as it were, in apathy, and he thought, 'This is the end, there is no escape, no future.'" These thoughts prove to be prophetic. A believer in such psychic forces as precognition and spirit communication, du Maurier allows the Tiresias-like sister to set the stage for the psychic drama to follow.

While John and Laura later roam through the back alleys of Venice in search of a restaurant they hear a scream. John catches a fleeting glimpse of a small figure that suddenly creeps from a cellar entrance below one of the houses opposite him and jumps into a boat below. "It was a child," he tells Laura, "a little girl—she couldn't have been more than five or six—wearing a short coat over her minute skirt, a pixie hood covering her head."

When they get to the restaurant they run into the twin sisters again. This time the blind woman tells Laura that Christine is trying to tell their parents that they are in danger in Venice, that they should leave as soon as possible. Laura reports the warning to John and adds, "the extraordinary thing is that the blind sister says you're psychic and don't know it. You are somehow *en rapport* with the unknown, and I'm not." John, as it turns out, is indeed psychic, and his refusal to believe in the supernatural eventually leads to his death.

A telephone call from London informs John and Laura that their son, Johnnie, is ill. Laura leaves Venice on a boat to catch a plane back home, and John is supposed to drive home the next day. John boards a ferry to fetch his car, and when another ferry passes him he thinks he sees Laura on it: "Laura, in her scarlet coat, the twin sisters by her side, the active sister with her hand on Laura's arm, talking earnestly, and Laura herself, her hair blowing in the wind, gesticulating, on her face a look of distress." John returns to his hotel to wait for her, but when she fails to show up he tries to track down the sisters. When he checks at the restaurant, the proprietor informs him of a murderer at large: "A grizzly business. One woman found with her throat slit last week—a tourist too—and some old chap discovered with the same sort of knife wound this morning. They seem to think it must be a maniac, because there doesn't seem to be any motive."

John reports his missing wife to the police, but soon afterwards he receives a call from London informing him that his son's appendicitis operation was successful and that his wife would like to speak to him. John has no explanation for his vision earlier in the day: "The point was he *had* seen all three of them on the vaporetto. It was not another woman in a red coat. The women *had* been there, with Laura. So what was the explanation? That he was going off his head? Or something more sinister?" He tries desperately to convince himself that the whole business was a mistake, an hallucination. What he is unable to recognize at this point is that his vision is perfectly clear, only what he saw was a scene in the immediate future, namely that of Laura and the two sisters riding the ferry to his funeral.

John talks to the blind sister, and she explains that he had looked into the future but he naturally refuses to credit that explanation. He then proceeds to walk along the back alleys and suddenly sees the little girl with the pixie hood again "running as if her life depended upon it. . . . She was sobbing as she ran, not the ordinary cry of a frightened child, but the panic-stricken intake of breath of a helpless being in despair." He hears someone pursuing her and, thinking that they are both in danger of the homicidal maniac, he follows the child up the stairs within a courtyard and into a room leading off a small landing. He slams the door shut and bolts it, unwittingly sealing his fate: "The child struggled to her feet and stood before him, the pixie-hood falling from her head on to the floor. He stared at her, incredulity turning to horror, to fear. It was not a child at all but a little thick-set woman dwarf, about three feet high, with a great square adult head too big for her body, grey locks hanging shoulder-length, and she wasn't sobbing anymore, she was grinning at him, nodding her head up and down."

He hears the police banging on the door. Suddenly the details of the past few days come together to form a horrifyingly clear picture: the figure he mistook for a child is the psychopathic killer, the blind sister was correct in the warning she conveyed to him through his dead daughter—his life was in danger, and the vision he had of the twin sisters with Laura was in fact an image of the future, as they will now proceed in such fashion to his funeral.

The dwarf withdraws a knife from her sleeve and hurls it at him with hideous strength piercing his throat. The creature begins gibbering in the corner, the police continue hammering on the door, and the sounds gradually grow fainter for him as he thinks, "Oh, God, what a bloody silly way to die."

The gothic setting of a decaying Venice, the mad dwarf, the recurring glimpses into the future, the suspense, and the violence all go to make up an exciting story. Characteristically, du Maurier does not develop her characters to the point where we can have any strong feelings of sympathy for them. Instead, we watch with curiosity what *hap-*

pens to them. Life in a du Maurier tale is not so much depth of feeling as it is a sequence of events that eventually spell out the characters' fates. On a psychological level there is a suggestion here that John feels guilty for the death of his daughter, a feeling that makes him sensitive to the distress of the creature in the pixie hood, but du Maurier seems more concerned with his precognition than with his memories and how they affect his future.

The film *Don't Look Now* appeared in 1973, directed by Nicholas Roeg and starring Donald Sutherland as John, Julie Christie as Laura, Hilary Mason as the blind sister, and Clelia Matania as the other sister. In the picture John is an architect. After Christine accidentally drowns, the bereaved parents leave England and go to Venice, where John works at repairing the statuary and mosaics of a church.

Roeg uses the imagery of the film to draw events together. Christine, for example, is wearing a red slicker when she drowns. The malicious dwarf is also wearing a red slicker, making John's concern for her safety more compelling. When the film opens John is examining a slide of a church interior, and the top of the dwarf's red hood shows over one of the benches towards the rear of the church. A bleeding-red stain appears across the slide shortly before John has a premonition that something is wrong. He runs outside and sees the body of his daughter floating in the pond.

Another image is established at the opening of the film. Christine is riding her bicycle, and the camera focuses upon the front wheel going over a pane of glass, shattering it. When John is stabbed at the end of the film, all of the imagery comes together in his mind. He sees Laura and the sisters on the funeral boat, the bleeding stains across the slide, and in his death agony he kicks out a pane of glass with his foot. The sights and sounds associated with Christine's death close in upon him as his blood pumps from the large wound in his neck staining the floor.

Roeg also develops a nice contrast between pagan and Christian imagery in the film, something only vaguely hinted at in du Maurier's story. In Catholic Venice John earns his livelihood restoring the Christian images. Though we do not get the impression that either he or Laura are devout Christians, there is a scene in which Laura lights a votive candle for Christine. Set against the traditional Catholic images are those of a pagan world: the blind seer (Tiresias), the séance, and the malignant dwarf of folklore.

All of these images are timeless, floating between and connecting future, present, and past. The long scene of John and Laura's love-making is also consistent with the premonitory theme of the film. Throughout their passionate interlude there are frequent images of their getting dressed—flash-forwards. Pauline Kael observes that this scene "relates to the way eroticism is displaced throughout; dressing is splintered and sensualized, like fear and death—death most of all, with splashes of red." The film

Du Maurier in 1929.

itself, she contends, is a mosaic of premonitions, and the dislocations are eroticized: "rotting Venice, the labyrinthine city of pleasure, with its crumbling, leering gargoyles, is obscurely, frighteningly sensual" ["Labyrinths," *New Yorker* 49, December 24, 1973].

Du Maurier's cool indifference to her characters, her clinical observation of their movements through the fate she has predestined for them, allows Roeg to flesh out this tale with a rich elegance and sensuality to create what Kael calls a "Bor-gesian setting—the ruins tokens of a mysteriously indifferent universe. . . . the romanticism isn't of the traditional Gothic variety but a coolly enigmatic sexiness." Things are not what they seem in this dislocated world. A child in a red raincoat becomes a murderer. John's pursuit of the image of his daughter leads to his death, which is ironical in that her spirit warned him to leave Venice. The weird sisters—reminiscent of the ancient fates—are sometimes seen snickering together. Are they charlatans or seers? The erotic is not found in bed but in dressing and in the sinister streets of a deserted Venice and in the upper room in which John is alone with the grotesque dwarf. In short, Roeg turns du Maurier's gothic thriller into an erotic nightmare. As Kael says, "the picture is the fanciest, most carefully assembled Gothic enigma yet put on the screen."

"A Border-Line Case" is a curious story of romantic incest. The narrator is a young actress named Shelagh

Money. She attempts to amuse her ailing father by showing him some photographs from the family album. She will soon play the role of Cesario in *Twelfth Night* and pushes her hair behind her head to ape the character. Upon seeing this, her father suddenly stares at her with a look of horror and disbelief on his face and then dies. The tale then takes on the character of a detective story as Shelagh attempts to discover why her assumed appearance triggered her father's death.

After considerable digging for information, Shelagh tracks down her father's old friend, Nick Barry. Despite the fact that he is an older man, she falls in love with him and discovers that he is an Irish sympathizer who has organized a terrorist group in an attempt to unify Ireland. She soon enjoys a sexual interlude with him in the back of a grocery truck as he and his men head towards a terrorist attack on the border of Northern Ireland.

More probing leads to an amazing discovery. Nick was once ungraciously received by her mother and to seek revenge he "had a rough-and-tumble with her on the sofa." Knowing all of this, Shelagh comments: "He's deceived my father, deceived my mother (serves her right), deceived the England he fought for for so many years, tarnished the uniform he wore, degraded his rank, spends his time now, and has done so for the past twenty years, trying to split this country wider apart than ever." His reckless, adventuresome spirit, however, overwhelms her, and she confesses she loves him and is willing to throw over her theatrical career in order to "come and throw bombs with you."

She returns to London and to the stage and soon receives a letter from Nick informing her that he is going to America to work on a book. He encloses a photograph of himself with a note written across the back: "Nick Barry as Cesario in *Twelfth Night*." She realizes then that Nick is her father and that her presumed father, upon seeing her in a similar pose, had awakened "from a dream that had lasted twenty years. Dying, he discovered truth." The story ends with Shelagh planning to leave the theater in order to dedicate herself to a life as a terrorist, "for only by hating can you purge away love, only by sword, by fire."

The chief interest in this preposterous story is the oedipal feelings of the narrator. Incest comes into play here as Shelagh enjoys a sexual encounter with her father during a dangerous trip to the Irish border. The likelihood of being caught or killed adds to the thrill of the relationship. Shelagh does not at the time realize that the older man is her father. Her pleasure lies in being sexually dominated by a person long associated with her parent. When she discovers that Nick is indeed her father, she expresses no feelings of guilt or anguish but rather a strong determination to follow in his radical, violent ways. The adolescent and shrill tone of the story makes it unbelievable. It is compelling only as a youthful female fantasy of a sexually frustrated young woman.

"The Way of the Cross" is an entertaining account of an ill-sorted group of English pilgrims in Jerusalem. After the vicar of Little Bletford succumbs to an attack of influenza, the Reverend Edward Babcock is assigned the task of guiding the interesting group of tourists around the holy city. Lady Althea Mason, the most prominent of the party, is a vain, stuffy, wealthy woman whose mind is preoccupied with her looks and with social status. Her husband is a retired army colonel who sees everything from the military perspective of the 1940s. Jim Forster is the managing director of an up-and-coming plastics firm. A lecher, he later seduces Jill Smith, a young woman on her honeymoon. His wife, Kate Forster, expresses concern mainly for such topics as world poverty and starvation. Bob Smith and his bride, Jill, are attempting to come to terms with their new relationship. Miss Dean is a seventy-year-old spinster, perhaps the only member of the group actually interested in the historical tour. She is strongly attached to the vicar of Little Bletford, and Reverend Babcock's sudden replacement of her pastor spoils her idyll. Robin is the nine-year-old grandson of the Masons. Reminiscent of Browning's Pippa (in *Pippa Passes*), he is free, outspoken, intelligent, precocious, and unaffected by the mad constraints of those around him.

Colonel Mason comes to realize during the tour that the military has consumed his entire life. He tells Babcock that he would have been given command of his regiment but that he had to leave the army due to Althea's illness. Robin reports this conversation to Althea, who is overcome by doubt, guilt, and bewilderment. She had always thought that her husband was content in his garden and in arranging his military papers and books in the library.

Althea's complacency is further shocked when she loses the caps from her front teeth after biting into a piece of hard bread. She looks into a mirror: "The woman who stared back at her had two small filed pegs stuck in her upper gums where the teeth should have been. They looked like broken matchsticks, discoloured, black. All trace of beauty had gone. She might have been some peasant who, old before her time, stood begging at a street corner."

Jill Smith, who had allowed Jim Foster to make love to her the previous day, begins to feel guilty for deceiving her husband during their honeymoon, especially since they are in the Holy Land. Jim, meanwhile, gets caught up in a mob when he is chased by the police for refusing to pay for a cheap medallion from a street merchant. Miss Dean wanders off to the Pool of Bethesda to gather some of its miraculous waters into a vial. She plans to bring the water back to the vicar in hopes of winning his continued approval. She slips on a damp stone, however, falls into the pool and almost drowns in the holy water. Even the Reverend Babcock manages to humiliate himself when, at the Chapel of Golgotha, he has an attack of diarrhea from some bad chicken he ate and passes out and fouls himself lying on the church floor. Like Jonathan Swift, du Maurier takes especial delight in focusing upon the repulsiveness of the human body (the description of Lady Althea's mouth) and upon fecal humor.

In the last scene we see most of the principals sitting together, physically or emotionally changed from what they were twenty-four hours earlier. Miss Dean sits silently with a blanket over her knees. Lady Althea is also silent, a chiffon scarf masking the lower part of her face. She, too, has a blanket over her knees, and the Colonel holds her hand beneath it. The Smiths more openly hold hands. The Forsters sit on either side of Miss Dean, and Reverend Babcock, in a change of clothes, sits next to Robin. The story ends with Robin saying that he wishes he could have stayed two more days. Babcock asks why and Robin replies, "Well, you never know. Of course it's not very probable in this day and age, but we might have seen the Resurrection."

The central theme of this story is that one must know the truth before he or she can be free. A Jewish workman tells Robin that tomorrow is the Feast of the Unleavened Bread, "the Festival of our Freedom," and that "everyone, everywhere, wanted freedom from something." Babcock learns humility; the Forsters are separated; the Masons are closer together; and Miss Dean is chastened.

Unlike most of du Maurier's short stories, which are terribly earnest and usually dependent upon the supernatural for their effect, this one is remarkably simple. The light, mocking tone of the narrator, the quickly but deftly drawn characters, and the clever setting that contrasts their personal concerns with great moments in Christianity give this tale a charm and cogency lacking in her other stories.

Although *The Rendezvous and Other Stories* was published in 1980, all of the stories were written between 1930 and 1950. Why du Maurier chose to resurrect them is not clear, for they clearly do not further her reputation as a writer. Only her most die-hard fans, with minds clouded by her past success, could celebrate the publication of this collection. Paul Ableman, a reviewer for the *Spectator,* cleverly reviews this book by con-structing an inner debate between his sentimental and rational mind. The rational mind, which prevails in the end, offers some of the following damning observations: the characters in the stories are wooden and unconvincing; the plots creak and depend upon outrageous coincidence; the prose is sloppy and chaotic "and the whole volume hardly contains a shapely sentence"; the dialogue consists of "rent-a-line prefabricated units"; there is an absence of "exact observation, authority over language, convincing motivation, significant plot or, to be brief, any evidence whatsoever of true literary ability."

"The Rendezvous" is one of the better stories in this volume. Robert Scrivener, a well-known English novelist, lives a lonely life until he begins corresponding with a young woman from Geneva named Annette Limoges. She flatters him in her letters, and soon the author becomes infatuated with his unseen correspondent. Scheduled to give a lecture in Geneva, he arranges to meet Annette there. He is dazzled by her beauty and longs to make love to her. It turns out, however, that she has fallen in love with a local bathing attendant named Alberto, a handsome fellow half Scrivener's age. Desperate to declare his love for her but too proud to be rejected in favor of the youth, Scrivener goes along with their joyful company, even to the point of tolerating their making love in his room when he is away from the hotel. He comes to the realization that his fame may win a beautiful young woman's attention but that it cannot compete with the sexual attraction of a younger man.

There are some interesting aspects of this story that suggest that du Maurier is constructing a rationalization and a defense for the sort of popular fiction she writes. One of Scrivener's friends, a popular novelist whose works sell in "ridiculous numbers," implies that Scrivener is "a fake, without the wide experience of life that his novels appeared to possess" because he has never been married or had a lover. Scrivener is an elitist, careful to praise books that are unlikely to sell but that show some constructive approach to world problems. He "did not permit himself to be spoilt by his success, and he was careful to tell his friends that he would never be tempted by offers from Hollywood to prostitute his work upon the screen. As a matter of fact, no such offers came, but this was beside the point." Obviously believing that she herself has had a wide experience of life, du Maurier uses Scrivener as an example of the limited literary purist, a strawman to be devastated by his private needs, which, ironically, are depicted in a Hollywood motion picture.

After his lecture in Geneva Scrivener receives a note from Annette telling him that she and Alberto will be using his apartment that evening. In despair, Scrivener goes to a theater where he sees a movie about a middle-aged man whose life turns sour and who murders his wife and falls in love with his step-daughter. Identifying with the hero, Scrivener weeps uncontrollably and sees the works he has written as lost to him "across the wasted years of his own dull, empty life." When the film credits are run he suddenly realizes that the picture was based upon his writer friend's best-selling novel that he had always despised.

The autobiographical fable embedded within this tale, then, argues that du Maurier's wide experience, her best-selling novels, and her concessions to Hollywood are all meritorious. The elitist writers may have the adulation of the snobbish literary establishment but real life moves on a lower, more powerful plane, and the elitist will one day come to realize that.

In most of her short fiction du Maurier is primarily interested in conclusions and in the events that lead to those conclusions. Character, atmosphere, language, social commentary—all are of secondary interest to her as she plunges her undefined characters into a sequence of events that inextricably lead them to a predestined, usually surprising, fate. Her stories present life in neat, tidy little packages. Her characters are manipulated by their contrived future, their every gesture and word leading to a preconceived conclusion. Du Maurier's best stories avoid this easy pattern in favor of a more complex, ambiguous view of life. **"The Birds," "Don't Look Now," "The Way of the Cross,"** and **"Ganymede"** are four of her most convincing and entertaining stories. Like *Rebecca* and *The*

Parasites, two of her best novels, they convey a cogent sense of the terror and comedy of ordinary human life.

Margaret Forster (essay date 1993)

SOURCE: "The Breaking Point 1946-1960" and "Death of the Writer 1960-1989," in *Daphne du Maurier: The Secret Life of the Renowned Storyteller,* Doubleday, 1993, pp. 205-312, 313-416.

[*Forster is an English novelist, biographer, and critic. In the following excerpt from her authorized biography of du Maurier, she examines the stories collected in* The Apple Tree.]

[In the winter of 1949, Daphne] wrote a new collection of short stories [*The Apple Tree*] which were a completely new departure. These were strange, morbid stories, in which deep undercurrents of resentment and even hatred revealed far more about Daphne's inner fantasy life than any novel had ever done. ('All those stories have inner significance for problems of that time,' she later wrote.) They included a novella, *Monte Verita,* which completely bewildered Victor Gollancz [du Maurier's publisher], who commented: 'I don't understand the slight implication that there is something wrong with sex.' This novella is about a woman, Anna, who is mesmerized by a mysterious sect who live in a secret world in the mountains in Central Europe. She joins them and disappears. The whole point of the story is that in her 'Monte Verita' Anna has found a spiritual happiness she could never find with her husband or any man. Sexual love between a man and a woman no longer means anything to her, and all the young women who became part of her sect are now saved from 'the turmoil of a brief romance turning to humdrum married life'. What disturbed Victor most was that in the first version Anna, once she is safe in her Monte Verita, turns into a *man*. At Victor's insistence, Daphne changed this and Anna remains a woman but, as he had picked up, the general drift of this highly metaphorical story *is* that there is something wrong with sex between men and women— it spoils relationships, it drains energy, it gets in the way of self-fulfilment. Written by a woman who was in the middle of her first love-affair with another woman for twenty years, it seems strikingly significant.

The title story, **'The Apple Tree'**, seems even more so. It tells of a man who, after his wife has died, notices an apple tree, which has never borne blossom or fruit, suddenly flourishing. He becomes convinced that the tree represents his wife, whom he never really loved because 'she always seemed to put a blight on everything' and because they had lived 'in different worlds . . . their minds not meeting'. All his efforts go into trying to destroy the tree, but in the end, when finally he has hacked it into logs and given it away, he trips over its root and is trapped in the snow. It is very hard to decide quite how Daphne intended this story to be read: is the hatred of the man for his dead wife justified, or does he get his deserts? Or is the whole story meant to damn marriages in which true minds do not meet—as in her own. . . . Whatever the origin of **'The Apple Tree'**, it was all of a piece with the volume's general theme of sex as trouble, in one way or another, of the sexual urge causing violence and even murder.

Two of the other four stories very forcibly emphasized this and have a distinctly nasty tone to them. **'The Little Photographer'** tells of a rich woman on holiday who has everything she wants except a lover (her husband is not with her). She finds herself wanting to have a love-affair, as long as it can be 'a thing of silence' with a stranger, so that it is just sex and nothing more. She sets her sights on a crippled photographer whom she meets while working on a cliff. She asks him, 'Why don't you kiss me?' and he does, which gives her a delicious furtive sense of excitement—'What she did was without emotion of any sort, her mind and affections quite untouched.' But eventually sex with the photographer becomes a boring ritual. One day she doesn't turn up. He is distraught and says she is his life, he cannot do without her. He tells her she is wicked when she offers him money to go away, and she pushes him over the cliff. Her husband arrives to take her home and she thinks she has got away with both the love-affair (in which there was no love) and the murder, but on the last page it is made clear that she will not do so and will be condemned to a future life of guilt and blackmail.

All the details of the plot in this unpleasant story are incredible, but the atmosphere is convincing. The coldness of the woman, her contempt for the poor photographer, her ruthlessness—all these repel but fascinate. The woman's ideal, 'passion between strangers', sex as something to discard, is ugly but argued with such conviction that the attempt at the end to make her pay some sort of price seems weak. Another story, **'Kiss Me Again, Stranger'**, has an even more brutal view of sex. A young mechanic picks up a cinema usherette. They go into a cemetery and she tells him to kiss her but that she likes him silent. He feels himself falling in love with her and starts fantasizing about their future together. He leaves her reluctantly and goes home. Next day he reads about the murder of an RAF man and realizes that the murderess was his girl. The plot is totally unbelievable, but once again the atmosphere is not.

After such macabre happenings, the other two stories in this collection come as a relief, although here again, in one of them at least, there are autobiographical connections freely acknowledged by the author. **'The Old Man'** is a simply told story which turns out to be a spoof. The old man is described as big and strong. He lives by a lake with his wife but has driven his children away, so he can be alone with her, 'which is what he has always wanted'. In the last three lines it is revealed that the old man is, in fact, a swan. Often, after she had written this story, Daphne would refer to Tommy [her husband] as 'just like **"The Old Man"**'—wanting her to himself, jealous, she believed, of the attention she gave her children, especially Kits [their son]. 'But that is not the whole significance of the story,' she commented. 'The real significance is that Moper [Tommy] must not kill his only begotten son but kill the petty

jealous *self* which is his hidden nature, and so rise again.' This, she thought, 'is the truth behind Christianity and all the religions'. But the story she liked best, and which 'just came bubbling out', fitted into no pattern. **'The Birds'** is a wholly atmospheric story, beautifully paced and unmarred by the intricacies of plot which sometimes spoiled Daphne's original ideas. The tension of birds attacking humans in hordes is sustained throughout. The birds themselves, shuttling on window-sills, pecking at glass panes, swooping in from the sea in millions, are horrifyingly real. ' **"The Birds"**, wrote Victor Gollancz, elated, 'is a masterpiece.'

The whole collection thrilled him, but he was firm in telling Daphne that he did not at all like two other stories she added—**'No Motive'** and **'Split Second'**. She was, he told her, 'one of the few authors . . . with whom I can be frank'. **'No Motive'** jarred on him and **'Split Second'** was poor. Daphne, as ever, accepted his judgement and dropped these two stories. She told him he really was 'the *only* publisher in the world' even though she was 'a tinge sorry' about **'Split Second'**. He was 'dynamic, exuberant, tender, intolerant and the only publisher for me'. Victor responded that she was 'beautiful, adorable, gracious, charming and good'. This was indeed the high-water mark of their relationship as author and publisher. But Victor warned her that even though he loved the stories she must brace herself for shocked reviews—the violence in them would be noted and probably found abhorrent coming from the pen of the 'romantic' writer she was supposed to be. He was, on the whole, right. Nancy Spain in the *Daily Express* in particular was revolted by the stories and attacked the author. Victor replied to her in a storming letter . . . , only to be soundly told off by Nancy Spain in turn. Her review, which he had called 'low-down', was, she wrote, perfectly accurate—the stories were 'all concerned with malformation, hatred, blackmail, cruelty and murder' and he shouldn't object to her saying so. Anyone writing such stories was surely sick.

Daphne's own response was to ask who Nancy Spain was and then to dismiss all the reviewers as 'nearly always indifferent writers who can't make a living from their own books and are forced to make a living through shoddy journalism . . . kicking at writers more successful than themselves is probably the only thrill they ever get'. Victor was, in fact, doing her no favours by encouraging her to take this attitude, so that soon she was no longer able to detect genuine and potentially helpful criticism. But it was a pity this collection did not merit more attention, and that it was **'The Birds'** which monopolized any attention it did get, because it was a huge improvement on Daphne's previous short stories of her early years.

Not only were these new stories better written, they also showed a shift in the balance of power between the sexes which she had been working out for some twenty years now in her novels. The women were no longer pathetic and exploited, the men no longer always powerful and dominant. Now, women were often in control and making men suffer. Women had become quite vicious creatures, perfectly capable of tricking, and even killing, men as they had been tricked and killed in the early stories. Daphne's friends and family were rather taken aback at this strain of brutality she displayed, but she was unrepentant and talked cheerfully of 'my macabre tastes' without seeming to fear any significance being read into them. But this collection was highly important: it represented a change not only in Daphne's style but in her subject-matter—her 'macabre tastes' at last were acknowledged and given an outlet, reflecting the confusion of her inner self.

FURTHER READING

Biography

Cook, Judith. *Daphne: A Portrait of Daphne du Maurier.* London: Bantam Press, 1991, 321 p.

Study of du Maurier's life and work. Cook describes du Maurier as "a strange, self-contained and introverted woman, a woman who had suffered an emotional onslaught in her early years, the blighting effect of which never left her."

Forster, Margaret. *Daphne du Maurier: The Secret Life of the Renowned Storyteller.* New York: Doubleday, 1993, 457 p.

Detailed account of du Maurier's life and career, including critical analysis and biographical interpretation of her works. Forster provides many previously unknown details about du Maurier's life, which she gathered from the letters and personal recollections of du Maurier's family, particularly her children, and her close friends.

Leng, Flavia. *Daphne du Maurier: A Daughter's Memoir.* Edinburgh: Mainstream Publishing, 1994, 206 p.

Childhood reminiscence focusing on family relationships and life at Menabilly.

Malet, Oriel, ed. *Daphne du Maurier: Letters from Menabilly, Portrait of a Friendship.* London: Weidenfeld and Nicolson, 1993, 303 p.

Collection of letters from du Maurier to her close friend and fellow author Oriel Malet. The letters, dating from the early 1950s to January 1981, discuss family and friends, the craft of writing, and books.

Criticism

Bleiler, E. F. "More Words and Pictures." *The Washington Post Book World* (December 27, 1987): 8.

Appreciates du Maurier's stories in *Classics of the Macabre* but finds the collection overall "an overproduced coffee-table book."

D'Ammassa, Don. Review of *Classics of the Macabre.* *Science Fiction Chronicle* 9, No. 5 (February 1988): 42.

Praises du Maurier's sense of timing and suspense and, noting the illustrations by Michael Foreman, calls it "a beautiful collection."

Ross, Mary. "Stories of Lives in Crisis." *New York Herald Tribune Book Review* (October 25, 1959): 13.

Favorable review of *The Breaking Point* in which Ross compliments du Maurier's storytelling ability.

Shallcross, Martyn. "Sinister Stories." In his *The Private World of Daphne du Maurier*, pp. 135-55. London: Robson Books, 1991.

Discusses the film adaptations of two of du Maurier's most famous short stories, "The Birds" and "Don't Look Now."

Siaulys, Anthony. Review of *Don't Look Now. Best Sellers* 31, No. 15 (November 1971): 353-54.

Positive assessment of *Don't Look Now*, noting that du Maurier has "the mark of a great suspense writer."

Smith, Harrison. "The Anatomy of Terror." *The Saturday Review*, New York (March 14, 1953): 29, 52.

Review of *Kiss Me Again, Stranger*, in which Smith finds that du Maurier "has the gift of making believable the unbelievable."

Additional coverage of du Maurier's life and career is contained in the following sources published by Gale Research: *Contemporary Authors*, Vols. 5-8 (rev. ed.), 128; *Contemporary Authors New Revision Series*, Vol. 6; *Contemporary Literary Criticism*, Vols. 6, 11, 59; *Major 20th-Century Writers*; and *Something about the Author*, Vols. 27, 60.

Hamlin Garland
1860-1940

(Born Hannibal Hamlin Garland) American short story writer, novelist, autobiographer, essayist, and critic.

INTRODUCTION

The short fiction of Hamlin Garland combines the principles of literary realism with the author's concern for oppressed Midwestern farmers in the decades following the American Civil War. The result is a closely-knit group of stories that illustrate the hardships of rural labor, debunking the myth of idyllic farm life that had prevailed in the United States since the country's inception. The stories, especially in his initial collection, *Main-Travelled Roads,* also proved influential in their use of descriptive detail, their inclusion of Garland's populist political views, and their omission of the sentimental characters and plot devices that were common in the literature of the late 1800s. For all of these reasons, Garland is viewed as a seminal author whose impact is evident on a number of writers, including his immediate literary descendants such as Frank Norris and Stephen Crane, as well as twentieth-century authors like Sherwood Anderson, Sinclair Lewis, and John Steinbeck. A later collection of his short stories, *The Book of the American Indian,* has also been praised for its progressive attitude toward the problems faced by Native Americans at the turn of the century. A prolific author, Garland also produced several well-respected autobiographical volumes and a series of Western adventure novels that made him a popular success but have been harshly criticized by scholars.

Biographical Information

Born on a farm near New Salem, Wisconsin, in 1860, Garland spent his childhood in various parts of the "Middle Border"—the recently-settled regions of the Midwestern United States that stretched from the Mississippi Valley to the western edge of the Great Plains. In Wisconsin, Iowa, and the Dakota Territory (now South Dakota), his father and mother established a number of farms, and Garland became familiar with agricultural work at an early age. After attending school at a seminary in Osage, Iowa, he travelled through the eastern United States for a time before becoming a homestead farmer in the Dakota Territory in 1883. The next year he gave up his farm and returned to the East, hoping to further his education in Boston. Having little money and few contacts in the city, his studies consisted of long days of reading in the public library; he soon became immersed in the ideas of prominent philosophers and economists of the 1800s, especially those of Herbert Spencer and Henry George. The lat-

ter's proposal of a "Single Tax" on land values was aimed at alleviating the economic burden suffered by small farmers, and Garland soon became an avid proponent of George's ideas. Garland also became acquainted with novelist William Dean Howells at this time, and Howells's ideas on realistic and "local color" literature, as well as his influence in the world of letters, helped to guide Garland's writing career. In 1887 Garland returned briefly to South Dakota to visit his family, and his close observation of the hardships of farm life inspired the first of the short stories that would become part of *Main-Travelled Roads.* Following the book's publication, he campaigned for Henry George's People's Party and wrote a number of novels that were fictional arguments for George's populist movement, but his involvement with the Single Tax and other reform causes began to wane in the mid-1890s. Garland moved to Chicago in 1894, where he became involved in the city's cultural circles and began a family with his wife Zulime Taft Garland. He lived there until 1916, though he frequently travelled around the country, especially to the Far West, conducting research for his books. Garland later resided in New York City and then in California, where he died in 1940.

Major Works of Short Fiction

Garland's first book, *Main-Travelled Roads,* presents the literary techniques, characters, and ideas that have established his reputation as a writer. As a pioneer of realistic and local color literature, his work in the volume graphically describes the lives and surroundings of his characters. Many of the stories, including "The Return of the Private" and "Up the Coulé," concern Middle Border natives who return to their homeland and find their friends and families struggling with lives of grim labor. Women, in particular, are depicted as victims of the region's harsh conditions; in "A Branch Road," Will Hannan returns to the midwest to find his former sweetheart Agnes living in ill health on a squalid farm, married to a callous husband who cares little for her suffering. Garland's female characters sometimes flee from their dreary lives, as Agnes does in "A Branch Road," while others, including the protagonist of "Mrs. Ripley's Trip," are resigned to their rural toil. In placing blame for the suffering of farm families, Garland targeted the economic and political conditions of the time and used his stories as a means of lobbying for change. The primary evil in the author's eyes was a tax system that encouraged speculation and victimized the small land owner. "Under the Lion's Paw," from *Main-Travelled Roads,* is one of many Garland stories that take up this issue, arguing for the adoption of the Henry George's Single Tax system.

Garland's most prolific period as a short story writer lasted from the late 1880s to the mid-1890s. In this period he produced the stories that appeared in the various editions of *Main-Travelled Roads,* as well as those collected in *Prairie Folks, Wayside Courtships,* and *Other Main-Travelled Roads.* These books have much in common, featuring rural or small town locales, and are often considered companion volumes. In the latter three, Garland at times invokes a lighter, more humorous tone than in *Main-Travelled Roads,* while other stories continue to emphasize realistic principles and provide somber portrayals of life in the Midwest. At roughly the same time that he was composing his Midwestern stories, he was also writing novels. After producing several works of long fiction that were intended to promote various reform issues, he began to publish romantic adventure novels in the late 1890s. These books are typically set in the Rocky Mountains and feature romances between rugged Western men, such as forest rangers and calvary captains, and beautiful women who have recently arrived from the East. Such plots were a radical departure for Garland, a writer who, just a few years prior, had practiced and vocally supported realistic fiction.

The author's later short fiction is collected in two volumes. The stories in *They of the High Trails* feature western mountain settings, and, as their titles indicate, they attempt to delineate various characters common in the region such as "The Cow-boss" and "The Trail Tramp." *The Book of the American Indian,* in contrast, returns to issues of social reform, confronting the status and legacy of Native Americans in the western United States. The book depicts the cruel treatment Indians received from settlers and the difficulties tribal people face in adapting to the modern world. Despite these obstacles, stories such as "Wahiah—A Spartan Mother" and the novella "The Silent Eaters" suggest that the Native Americans must change their way of life in order to exist in the white man's world.

Critical Reception

Main-Travelled Roads is considered an important publication in nineteenth-century American literature. Critics cite its value both as an innovative collection of realistic short fiction and as a social artifact that provides insight into rural American life and the reform movements of the time. Reviewers have, on occasion, criticized the didactic qualities of the book and its overwhelming emphasis on the grim aspects of farm life. Other scholars, however, have found that it is Garland's strident social and political concerns that make *Main-Travelled Roads* his most powerful work, and these qualities are also noted in many of the related stories published in other Middle Border volumes. Much criticism on Garland is devoted to the abrupt change in writing style that is reflected in his romantic works of popular fiction; the most-prevalent theories attribute the change to the author's dwindling commitment to social causes and his desire for popular and financial success. The stories in *They of the High Trails* are generally viewed as similar to Garland's adventure novels and therefore dismissed or ignored by critics. *The Book of the American Indian,* however, has received largely positive notices, especially from contemporary critics. Many have praised the author's exhaustive research and his effective use of the fictional format to address the relationship between native tribes and Euro American settlers. Though the overall quality of Garland's writing is viewed as strangely uneven, scholars largely agree that his finest fictional work is found in his short stories. As Thomas A. Bledsoe writes, "Hamlin Garland produced a handful of minor masterpieces, of which *Main-Travelled Roads* is the finest. For them he deserves to be remembered . . . as an artist who, for a brief time at least, knew his craft and practiced it honestly."

PRINCIPAL WORKS

Short Fiction

*Main-Travelled Roads 1891
Prairie Folks 1893
Wayside Courtships 1897
Other Main-Travelled Roads 1910
They of the High Trails 1916
The Book of the American Indian 1923

*Various enlarged editions of *Main-Travelled Roads* were published in 1899, 1922, and 1930.

Novels

Jason Edwards, An Average Man 1892
A Little Norsk 1892
A Member of the Third House 1892
A Spoil of Office: A Story of the Modern West 1892
Rose of Dutcher's Coolly 1895
The Spirit of Sweetwater 1898
Boy Life on the Prairie 1899
The Eagle's Heart 1900
Her Mountain Lover 1901
The Captain of the Gray-Horse Troop 1902
Hesper 1903
The Light of the Star 1904
The Tyranny of the Dark 1905
Money Magic 1907
The Shadow World 1908
*Cavanagh, Forest Ranger: A Romance of the Mountain
    West* 1910
Victor Ollnee's Discipline 1911
The Forester's Daughter 1914

Autobiographies

A Son of the Middle Border 1917
A Daughter of the Middle Border 1921
Trail-Makers of the Middle Border 1926
Back-Trailers from the Middle Border 1928
Roadside Meetings 1930
Companions on the Trail 1931
My Friendly Contemporaries 1932
Afternoon Neighbors 1934
Hamlin Garland's Diaries 1968

Other Major Works

Under the Wheels: A Modern Play in Six Scenes (play)
    1890
*Prairie Songs: Being Chants Rhymed and Unrhymed of
    the Level Lands of the Great West* (poetry) 1893
*Crumbling Idols: Twelve Essays on Art, Dealing Chiefly
    with Literature, Painting and the Drama* (essays) 1894
Ulysses S. Grant: His Life and Character (biography)
    1898
The Trail of the Goldseekers (nonfiction) 1899
Forty Years of Psychic Research (nonfiction) 1936
The Mystery of the Buried Cross (nonfiction) 1939
*Hamlin Garland's Observations on the American Indian,
    1895-1905* (nonfiction) 1976

CRITICISM

William Dean Howells (essay date 1891)

SOURCE: "Editor's Study," in *Critical Essays on Hamlin
Garland,* edited by James Nagel, G. K. Hall & Co., 1982,
pp. 35-6.

[*A prominent figure in nineteenth-century American literature, Howells was one of the leading advocates and
practitioners of literary realism in the United States. He
offered early encouragement for Garland's writing, and
in the following excerpt, he declares* Main-Travelled Roads
*to be an accurate depiction of the Midwestern farmer's
plight as well as "a work of art."*]

. . . At present we have only too much to talk about in a
book so robust and terribly serious as Mr. Hamlin Garland's volume called **Main-Travelled Roads**. That is what
they call the highways in the part of the West that Mr.
Garland comes from and writes about; and these stories
are full of the bitter and burning dust, the foul and tram-
pled slush of the common avenues of life: the life of the
men who hopelessly and cheerlessly make the wealth that
enriches the alien and the idler, and impoverishes the
producer. If any one is still at a loss to account for that
uprising of the farmers in the West, which is the translation of the Peasants' War into modern and republican
terms, let him read **Main-Travelled Roads** and he will
begin to understand, unless, indeed, Mr. Garland is painting the exceptional rather than the average. The stories
are full of those gaunt, grim, sordid, pathetic, ferocious
figures, whom our satirists find so easy to caricature as
Hayseeds, and whose blind groping for fairer conditions
is so grotesque to the newspapers and so menacing to the
politicians. They feel that something is wrong, and they
know that the wrong is not theirs. The type caught in Mr.
Garland's book is not pretty; it is ugly and often ridiculous; but it is heart-breaking in its rude despair. The story
of a farm mortgage as it is told in the powerful sketch
"Under the Lion's Paw" is a lesson in political economy, as well as a tragedy of the darkest cast. **"The Return
of the Private"** is a satire of the keenest edge, as well as
a tender and mournful idyl of the unknown soldier who
comes back after the war with no blare of welcoming
trumpets or flash of streaming flags, but foot-sore, heart-
sore, with no stake in the country he has helped to make
safe and rich but the poor man's chance to snatch an
uncertain subsistence from the furrows he left for the
battle-field. **"Up the Coulé,"** however, is the story which
most pitilessly of all accuses our vaunted conditions,
wherein every man has the chance to rise above his brother and make himself richer than his fellows. It shows us
once for all what the risen man may be, and portrays in
his good-natured selfishness and indifference that favorite ideal of our system. The successful brother comes back
to the old farmstead, prosperous, handsome, well dressed,
and full of patronizing sentiment for his boyhood days
there, and he cannot understand why his brother, whom
hard work and corroding mortgages have eaten all the joy
out of, gives him a grudging and surly welcome. It is a
tremendous situation, and it is the allegory of the whole
world's civilization: the upper dog and the under dog are
everywhere, and the under dog nowhere likes it.

But the allegorical effects are not the primary intent of
Mr. Garland's work: it is a work of art, first of all, and we
think of fine art; though the material will strike many
gentilities as coarse and common. In one of the stories,
"Among the Corn Rows," there is a good deal of burly,

broad-shouldered humor of a fresh and native kind; in **"Mrs. Ripley's Trip"** is a delicate touch, like that of Miss Wilkins; but Mr. Garland's touches are his own, here and elsewhere. He has a certain harshness and bluntness, an indifference to the more delicate charms of style; and he has still to learn that though the thistle is full of an unrecognized poetry, the rose has a poetry too, that even overpraise cannot spoil. But he has a fine courage to leave a fact with the reader, ungarnished and unvarnished, which is almost the rarest trait in an Anglo-Saxon writer, so infantile and feeble is the custom of our art; and this attains tragical sublimity in the opening sketch, **"A Branch Road,"** where the lover who has quarrelled with his betrothed comes back to find her mismated and miserable, such a farm wife as Mr. Garland has alone dared to draw, and tempts the broken-hearted drudge away from her loveless home. It is all morally wrong, but the author leaves you to say that yourself. He knows that his business was with those two people, their passions and their probabilities. He shows them such as the newspapers know them.

The Atlantic Monthly (essay date 1892)

SOURCE: A review of *Main-Travelled Roads,* in *The Atlantic Monthly,* Vol. LXIX, No. CCCCXII, February, 1892, p. 266.

[*In the following excerpt, the anonymous critic comments on Garland's "earnest" depiction of rural toil in* Main-Travelled Roads *and cautions that the unremitting despair of the stories borders on dullness.*]

Whoever fares with Mr. Garland along his ***Main-Travelled Roads*** is still no farther from the South than the Mississippi Valley, but the environment is unmistakably the West. The color, the light, the life, the movement, the readiness to turn from melancholy feeling to humorous perception,—all these are gone, together with the ameliorating negro; and in their places, produced by a massive, crude force which will have to be reckoned with in our literature, is one overwhelming impression of grinding, unremunerated toil. Mr. Garland's West is not the beckoning Occident—familiar to our imaginations, if not to our hopes—of enterprise and "push" and fortune that may be had for fighting, if not for asking. His West is on the other side of the shield. The right to vote and an American education cannot, he would have us believe, raise men and women who are really no more than beasts of burden much above the level of an oppressed peasantry, except that knowledge and rights confer on them the dignity of a sharper unhappiness. The remembrance of Mr. Garland's people, after the book is laid aside, is, strangely enough, that of a class, and not of individuals,—of a vast company, with worn, stolid faces, toiling in the fields all day without remission. Even the Angelus is denied them; and if they heard it, our fellow-countrymen would know too much to bow their heads before a superstition. They go home from work to grim cleanliness or grim squalor, as the case may be, and the dreariness of the farmer is exceeded, as ever, by the dreariness of the farmer's wife. One reads and is convinced, and then cries out that it is impossible; that this writer, so terribly in earnest, must be mistaken; that in his enthusiasm for Mr. Howells he has married Russian despair and French realism. Certain echoes, however, from the Mississippi Valley and from other tracts in the West hint that Mr. Garland may be telling the mere truth. If he is, the sum of human grief and suffering is still greater than we had supposed. Meanwhile, writing is writing, and Mr. Garland must accept and take to heart the warning that monotony is the danger of the earnest man.

Brander Matthews (essay date 1892)

SOURCE: "American Fiction Again," in *Cosmopolitan,* Vol. XII, No. 5, March, 1892, pp. 636-40.

[*Matthews was an influential American critic and educator of the late-nineteenth and early-twentieth centuries. In the following excerpt, he praises the insight and originality of* Main-Travelled Roads, *while noting several flaws in the collection.*]

Mr. Garland paints his pictures boldly; or rather should I call his work etching, vigorously done, with many a firm stroke, well bitten in the bath. These are rugged figures that he draws and the shadows they cast are grim and hard. The trouble with most of us men of letters is that we go on writing stories about ladies and gentlemen instead of telling the lives of men and women. It is the merit of Mr. Garland that he is able to interest us in the plain people, as Lincoln called them. It is the merit of Mr. Garland that he has something to say. He has not learned yet how to say it in the easiest way and with the least friction; sometimes his style creaks and there is a sense of strain; sometimes he draws our attention to the picturesqueness of his materials, to their epic quality, not having yet found out how to let his story speak for itself. When work is as strong as this, its author's silence is more eloquent than can be any finger post of self-congratulation.

But these blemishes are trifles. There is no doubt that Mr. Garland has the root of the matter in him. He has insight into humanity; he has power to make us see and feel and think; he has sympathy. He can show us the dignity of labor and the uselessness of it. This note of pessimism, heard now and again in these virile tales, is the only thing about them which is not American. If America does not spell Hope, then our experiment here is a failure and we may as well confess it and quit. The life Mr. Garland sets before us, not without gentle pathos, is dull and barren, but it is not a loveless life; it is not a life that ought to be hopeless, though the author seems to hint that it is. Nature is beautiful enough and bountiful enough to make existence worth the struggle, though the struggle be wearisome and ceaseless. The main-travelled roads of the western country are not more lonely or more desolate than the streets of a great city here in the East. Perhaps, in trying to grasp all the facts, Mr. Garland has let this truth slip through his fingers.

I do not know which of these six stories to praise the most highly. Perhaps **"The Return of the Private"** has the deepest and simplest pathos, but there is one line that jars on the sense of fairness; . . . it intimates that when there came a call to arms, the rich man shirked his duty to the Union; this is a fling wholly unworthy of the writer of a tale as sober as this and as honest. In the second of the six, the one called **"Up the Coulé"**, the reader wonders whether in ten years the returned prodigal could have forgotten the life of his boyhood so completely as to wear a fancy tennis costume with no thought of its incongruity. In the next story, **"Among the Corn Rows,"** there is nothing misplaced and we accept this Theocritan idyl without question. The proposal is most delicately presented, and the truthfulness of the situation is beyond peradventure. The resulting runaway match is wholly without any flavor of cheap romanticism.

These *Main-Travelled Roads* have not before been trodden by the feet of a story teller, and Mr. Hamlin Garland is a pioneer, fortunately for him. "In a highly polished country, where so much genius is monthly employed in catering for public amusement," wrote Sir Walter Scott in the preface to *Ivanhoe,* the first novel in which he crossed the border and chose an English subject instead of a Scotch, "a fresh topic, such as [the author of *Waverley*] had the happiness to light upon is the untasted spring in the desert—

Men bless their stars aud call it luxury."

Carl Van Doren (essay date 1922)

SOURCE: "Hamlin Garland," in *Critical Essays on Hamlin Garland,* edited by James Nagel, G. K. Hall & Co., 1982, pp. 147-51.

[*Van Doren was an American educator, editor, and author. In the following essay, he recognizes Garland as the literary predecessor to later writers, such as Sinclair Lewis, whose fiction painted a bleak picture of rural America. Van Doren also argues that most of Garland's novels do not equal the achievement of his short stories and autobiographical volumes because his long fiction often ignores the author's authentic experiences.*]

The pedigree of the most energetic and important fiction now being written in the United States goes unmistakably back to that creative uprising of discontent in the eighties of the last century which brought into articulate consciousness the larger share of the aspects of unrest which have since continued to challenge the nation's magnificent, arrogant grand march.

The decade had Henry Adams for its bitter philosopher, despairing over current political corruption and turning away to probe the roots of American policy under Jeffer-

son and his immediate successors; had the youthful Theodore Roosevelt for its standard-bearer of a civic conscience which was, plans went, to bring virtue into caucuses; had Henry George for its spokesman of economic change, moving across the continent from California to New York with an argument and a program for new battles against privilege; had Edward Bellamy for its Utopian romancer, setting forth a delectable picture of what human society might become were the old iniquities reasonably wiped away and cooperative order brought out of competitive chaos; had William Dean Howells for its annalist of manners, turning toward the end of the decade from his benevolent acceptance of the world as it was to stout-hearted, though soft-voiced, accusations brought in the name of Tolstoy and the Apostles against human inequality however constituted; had—to end the list of instances without going outside the literary class—Hamlin Garland for its principal spokesman of the distress and dissatisfaction then stirring along the changed frontier which so long as free land lasted had been the natural outlet for the expansive, restless race.

Heretofore the prairies and the plains had depended almost wholly upon romance—and that often of the cheapest sort—for their literary reputation; but Garland, who had tested at first hand the innumerable hardships of such a life, became articulate through his dissent from average notions about the pioneer. His earliest motives of dissent seem to have been personal and artistic. During that youth which saw him borne steadily westward, from his Wisconsin birthplace to windy Iowa and then to bleak Dakota, his own instincts clashed with those of his migratory father as the instincts of many a sensitive, unremembered youth must have clashed with the dumb, fierce urges of the leaders of migration everywhere. The younger Garland hungered on the frontier for beauty and learning and leisure; the impulse which eventually detached him from Dakota and sent him on a trepid, reverent pilgrimage to Boston was the very impulse which, on another scale, had lately detached Henry James from his native country and had sent him to the ancient home of his forefathers in the British Isles.

Mr. Garland could neither feel so free nor fly so far from home as James. He had, in the midst of his raptures and his successes in New England, still to remember the plight of the family he had left behind him on the lonely prairie; he cherished a patriotism for his province which went a long way toward restoring him to it in time. Sentimental and romantic considerations, however, did not influence him altogether in his first important work. He had been kindled by Howells in Boston to a passion for realism which carried him beyond the suave accuracy of his master to the somber veracity of *Main-Travelled Roads, Prairie Folks,* and *Rose of Dutcher's Coolly.* This veracity was more than somber; it was deliberate and polemic. Mr. Garland, ardently a radical of the school of Henry George, had enlisted in the crusade against poverty, and he desired to tell the unheeded truth about the frontier farmers and their wives in language which might do something to lift the desperate burdens of their conditions. Consequently his passions and his doctrines joined hands to fix the direction of his art; he both hated the frontier and hinted at definite remedies which he thought would make it more endurable.

It throws a strong light upon the progress of American society and literature during the past generation to point out that the service recently performed by [Sinclair Lewis's novel] *Main Street* was, in its fashion, performed thirty years ago by **Main-Travelled Roads**. Each book challenges the myth of the rural beauties and the rural virtues; but whereas Sinclair Lewis, in an intellectual and satiric age, charges that the villagers are dull, Mr. Garland, in a moral and pathetic age, charged that the farmers were oppressed. His men wrestle fearfully with sod and mud and drought and blizzard, goaded by mortgages which may at almost any moment snatch away all that labor and parsimony have stored up. His women, endowed with no matter what initial hopes or charms, are sacrificed to overwork and deprivations and drag out maturity and old age on the weariest treadmill. The pressure of life is simply too heavy to be borne except by the ruthless or the crafty. Mr. Garland, though nourished on the popular legend of the frontier, had come to feel that the "song of emigration had been, in effect, the hymn of fugitives." Illusion no less than reality had tempted Americans toward their far frontiers, and the enormous mass, once under way, had rolled stubbornly westward, crushing all its members who might desire to hesitate or to reflect.

The romancers had studied the progress of the frontier in the lives of its victors; Mr. Garland studied it in the lives of its victims: the private soldier returning drably and mutely from the war to resume his drab, mute career behind the plow; the tenant caught in a trap by his landlord and the law and obliged to pay for the added value which his own toil has given to his farm; the brother neglected until his courage has died and proffered assistance comes too late to rouse him; and particularly the daughter whom a harsh father or the wife whom a brutal husband breaks or drives away—the most sensitive and therefore the most pitiful victims of them all. Mr. Garland told his early stories in the strong, level, ominous language of a man who had observed much but chose to write little. Not his words but the overtones vibrating through them cry out that the earth and the fruits of the earth belong to all men and yet a few of them have turned tiger or dog or jackal and snatched what is precious for themselves while their fellows starve and freeze. Insoluble as are the dilemmas he propounded and tense and unrelieved as his accusations were, he stood in his methods nearer, say, to the humane Millet than to the angry Zola. There is a clear, high splendor about his landscapes; youth and love on his desolate plains, as well as anywhere, can find glory in the most difficult existence; he might strip particular lives relentlessly bare but he no less relentlessly clung to the conviction that human life has an inalienable dignity which is deeper than any glamor goes and can survive the loss of all its trappings.

Why did Mr. Garland not equal the intellectual and artistic success of **Main-Travelled Roads, Prairie Folks,** and *Rose of Dutcher's Coolly* for a quarter of a century? At the outset he had passion, knowledge, industry, doctrine, approbation, and he labored hard at enlarging the sagas of which these books were the center. Yet *Jason Edwards, A Spoil of Office, A Member of the Third House* are dim names and the Far Western tales which succeeded them grow too rapidly less impressive as they grow older. The rise of historical romance among the American followers of Stevenson at the end of the century and the subsequent rise of flippancy under the leadership of O. Henry have both been blamed for the partial eclipse into which Mr. Garland's reputation passed. As a matter of fact, the causes were more fundamental than the mere fickleness of literary reputation or than the demands of editors and public that he repeat himself forever. In that first brilliant cycle of stories this downright pioneer worked with the material which of all materials he knew best and over which his imagination played most eagerly. From them, however, he turned to pleas for the single tax and to exposures of legislative corruption and imbecility about which he neither knew nor cared so much as he knew and cared about the actual lives of working farmers. His imagination, whatever his zeal might do in these different surroundings, would not come to the old point of incandescence.

Instead, however, of diagnosing his case correctly Mr. Garland followed the false light of local color to the Rocky Mountains and began the series of romance narratives which further interrupted his true growth and, gradually, his true fame. He who had grimly refused to lend his voice to the chorus chanting the popular legend of the frontier in which he had grown up and who had studied the deceptive picture not as a visitor but as a native, now became himself a visiting enthusiast for the "high trails" and let himself be roused by a fervor sufficiently like that from which he had earlier dissented. In his different way he was as hungry for new lands as his father had been before him. Looking upon local color as the end—when it is more accurately the beginning—of fiction, he felt that he had exhausted his old community and must move on to fresher pastures.

Here the prime fallacy of his school misled him: he believed that if he had represented the types and scenes of his particular region once he had done all he could, when of course had he let imagination serve him he might have found in that microcosm as many passions and tragedies and joys as he or any novelist could have needed for a lifetime. Here, too, the prime penalty of his school overtook him: he came to lay so much emphasis upon outward manners that he let his plots and characters fall into routine and formula. The novels of his middle period—such as *Her Mountain Lover, The Captain of the Gray-Horse Troop, Hester, The Light of the Star, Cavanagh, Forest Ranger*—too frequently recur to the romantic theme of a love uniting some powerful, uneducated frontiersman and some girl from a politer neighborhood. Pioneer and lady are always almost the same pair in varying costumes; the stories harp upon the praise of plains and mountains and the scorn of cities and civilization. These romances, much value as they have as documents and will long continue to have, must be said to exhibit the frontier as self-conscious, obstreperous, given to insisting upon its difference from the rest of the world. In ordinary human intercourse such insistence eventually becomes tiresome; in literature no less than in life there is a time to remember local traits and a time to forget them in concerns more universal.

What concerns of Mr. Garland's were universal became evident when he published *A Son of the Middle Border*. His enthusiasms might be romantic but his imagination was not; it was indissolubly married to his memory of actual events. The formulas of his mountain romances, having been the inventions of a mind not essentially inventive, had been at best no more than sectional; the realities of his autobiography, taking him back again to **Main-Travelled Roads** and its cycle, were personal, lyrical, and consequently universal. All along, it now appeared, he had been at his best when he was most nearly autobiographical: those vivid early stories had come from the lives of his own family or of their neighbors; *Rose of Dutcher's Coolly* had set forth what was practically his own experience in its account of a heroine—not hero—who leaves her native farm to go first to country college and then to Chicago to pursue a wider life, torn constantly between a passion for freedom and a loyalty to the father she must tragically desert.

In a sense *A Son of the Middle Border* supersedes the fictive versions of the same material; they are the original documents and the *Son* the final redaction and commentary. Veracious still, the son of that border appears no longer vexed as formerly. Memory, parent of art, has at once sweetened and enlarged the scene. What has been lost of pungent vividness has its compensation in a broader, a more philosophic interpretation of the old frontier, which in this record grows to epic meanings and dimensions. Its savage hardships, though never minimized, take their due place in its powerful history; the defeat which the victims underwent cannot rob the victors of their many claims to glory. If there was little contentment in this border there was still much rapture. Such things Mr. Garland reveals without saying them too plainly: the epic qualities of his book—as in Mark Twain's *Life on the Mississippi*—lie in its implications; the tale itself is a candid narrative of his own adventures through childhood, youth, and his first literary period.

This autobiographic method, applied with success in *A Daughter of the Middle Border* to his later life in Chicago and all the regions which he visited, brings into play his higher gifts and excludes his lower. Under slight obligation to imagine, he runs slight risk of succumbing to those conventionalisms which often stiffen his work when he trusts to his imagination. Avowedly dealing with his own opinions and experiences, he is not tempted to project them, as in the novels he does somewhat too frequently, into the careers of his heroes. Dealing chiefly with action not with thought, he does not tend so much as elsewhere to solve speculative problems with sentiment instead of with reflection. In the *Son* and the *Daughter* he has the fullest chance to be autobiographic without disguise.

Here lies his best province and here appears his best art. It is an art, as he employs it, no less subtle than humane. Warm, firm flesh covers the bones of his chronology. He imparts reality to this or that occasion, like a novelist, by reciting conversation which must come from something besides bare memory. He rounds out the characters of the persons he remembers with a fulness and grace which, lifelike as his persons are, betray the habit of creating characters. He enriches his analysis of the Middle Border with sensitive descriptions of the "large, unconscious scenery" in which it transacted its affairs. If it is difficult to overprize the documentary value of his saga of the Garlands and the McClintocks and of their son who turned back on the trail, so is it difficult to overpraise the sincerity and tenderness and beauty with which the chronicle was set down.

Peter Phillip (essay date 1923)

SOURCE: "Plain Tales from the Plains: Hamlin Garland on the Red Man," in *The New York Times Book Review*, October 14, 1923, p. 5.

[*In the following review of* The Book of the American Indian, *Phillip praises Garland's stories about Native Americans as a valuable addition to the literature of the United States.*]

[**The Book of the American Indian**] is a joint tribute to the Saga of the American Indian by two artists who knew him intimately and loved him. A great deal of mawkish sentiment has obscured our fictional studies: the romantic evil of Fenimore Cooper continues to haunt us in fiction and the drama. A utilitarian school has viciously rationalized for popular consumption the vanishing folk tales and customs of the Red Man. Mr. Garland stands between them in his endeavor to share with us his accurate knowledge of a noble subject, giving it a dignity along with its romance that makes it significant in our national story. Had these tales been written of a similar period in the expansion of France one can imagine what the French Academy would have done for them.

Like an American Kipling he has made this period of contacts between our urgent and ruthless civilization and that of a primitive society relevant to our American life. It is more than a matter of entertainment; it is a service to American literature. These plain tales from our American plains have a more valid claim upon our attention than many of the sources of cultural inspiration from Europe which have already become shadowy in our national life, and should become part of the prescribed reading for our youth. Our very phrases, our ways of living and playing are heavily indebted to the storehouse of the Red Man.

Mr. Garland has not hesitated to recall melancholy episodes along with the brave and gay. With his intimate knowledge of the setting he has given us the Red Man's point of view with consummate artistry. Mr. Garland turns our eyes eastward to meet the threatening, engulfing forces, material, economic and physical of the white intruder. These devastating forces produce various reactions from the free, primitive society they threaten with their iron horse, their superior weapons, their economic and social systems. Mr. Garland has not failed to recapitulate the impatience and ignorance of which we were guilty in these first painful contacts, to remind us that for all his primitive condition the Indian lived and fought under as fine a code as his opponent. He knows that Mr. Kipling would have us forget that he ever presumed to advise us on our "new-caught, sullen peoples, half-devil and half-child."

In stories like **"Wahiah"** and **"The Iron Khiva"** we cannot fail to understand the sacrifice of tradition that involved so simple a matter as bringing Indian youth to our schools. Discipline is the basis of both the red and white systems. But Wahiah, a Spartan mother, is human. She is torn by the idea of submitting her proud boy to the stranger's discipline, fearful that the fine, free spirit of his ancestors will be broken in the stranger's hands. The nice play of instinct and intelligence under the mother's love is delicately suggested by Mr. Garland. Likewise in **"The Iron Khiva,"** as the tribe identifies the corrugated iron schoolhouse, we get our most intransigeant type, the Quaker schoolmaster, pitting his indomitable will against the combined tribe. The codes of red and white in this case are nearly alike; both are relentless and are strangely based upon such human elements as love and duty. In addition Mr. Garland does not neglect redskin psychology, the fact that the Iron Khiva is dangerously akin to the system of pauperization and bondage that are part of their new life on the cramped reservation.

It is in stories like these of conflict between the two races that Mr. Garland is a supreme artist. Such were the themes that engaged Kipling in India. We are given many a little classic like **"Storm Child"** which is comparable with "The Luck of Roaring Camp," or a love idyl with its inarticulate suffering like "Nistina." Mr. Garland's **"Story of Howling Wolf,"** **"Lone Wolf's Old Guard"** and **"Drifting Crane"** are typical of an ugly period, and remained to be written with this simplicity and poignancy if only to remind us that the Indian still requires our infinite tact and understanding. They furnish us with national texts, for lynching and mob law are still national vices, and the Indian Bureau is still capable of showing some of its old brand of cynicism in a Bursum bill. Stories like these will play an important part in strengthening our national conscience against recurrent dangers.

"The Story of Howling Wolf" should become a schoolroom classic. The proud, sensitive chief watches his tribe embracing the White Man's ways. But he has already suffered insult and brutality, and it is hard to forget. The agent of the reservation finally wins him by compelling his respect. Howling Wolf is conscious of his ancient grudge, and is anxious to carry on his person a testimony of his change of heart; the agent draws up for him this statement: "I am Howling Wolf. Long I hated the White Man. Now my heart is good." He puts aside his tribal

pride, and though a chief, gets a wagon and team like his former subjects and goes to work.

But Howling Wolf's first trip to the raw settlement involves him in disaster. He stares, like a child, at the store windows, admiring the strange wares and eager to adopt the new life. While engaged in this form of education a drunken cowboy insults him. The Indian, ignorant of the storm of abuse, extends his hand in friendship, as taught him by his beloved agent. The cowboy spits in his hand and the trouble begins. Then follows his identification by the mob, when he simply offers his letter patent. There is a wild shot by the cowboy which wounds another white man, and Howling Wolf is jailed. The agent has no power outside the reservation. The chief languishes in jail until one day the Sheriff, anxious to see a ball game, takes his prisoner along. But Howling Wolf thinks he is going to furnish a Roman holiday, and in terror attempts to escape. The rest is a familiar version of a man hunt. Howling Wolf is almost lynched, but for the priest who rescues him. Thereafter he will never forget what he suffered, despite the friendship of his agent and the priest. And such memories are plentiful "east of Suez where the best is like the worst."

The longest story, almost a novelette in this generous collection, is **"The Silent Eaters."** We are here given an epitome of all those ruthless forces that threatened and finally extinguished an ancient civilization. The greed for gold and land so poignantly told in **"Lone Wolf's Old Guard,"** the distrust of a distant Government whose benignance was too often travestied by unscrupulous land agents and settlers, by cruel and ignorant agents of reservations, and against these the Red Man's respect for the soldiers, whom he alone trusted because they had fought him fairly. But in addition to these Mr. Garland has accomplished the difficult task of giving us the Indian's version of the Custer fight. Mr. Garland has painstakingly kept to fact in his fiction. It is of such material that history is often written and here it appears in its most attractive form.

This harvest of Mr. Garland's craftsmanship crowns a life spent in service to literature, and like a true son of the West he has gone back to a native theme. Those who saw a primitive civilization disintegrating are growing few; those who are still able to record what they saw are far between. Though we are condemned to botanize over the remains of what we wantonly destroyed, in pages like these the spirit of Indian life will survive to dignify the human claim we reluctantly concede to the original American. If they do no more than prick our conscience as to a national responsibility toward an ancient race which, as the Indian Bureau reminds us, is slowly increasing, then they will bring their greatest honor to a distinguished American writer.

Dorothy Anne Dondore (essay date 1926)

SOURCE: "The Realism of the Mississippi Valley," in *The Prairie and the Making of Middle America: Four*

Centuries of Description, The Torch Press, 1926, pp. 328-44.

[*In the excerpt below, Dondore discusses the grim portrayals of rural life in Garland's short stories, recognizing them as truthful depictions drawn from the author's own experiences.*]

[Hamlin Garland] wrote some of the most widely discussed of western short stories; he created the most complete and artistic portrayal of the epic lure that in three centuries drew the line of migration from the Atlantic to the Pacific; he flung down the gauntlet to Eastern critics in his [1894] volume of essays *Crumbling Idols;* in his work appears not only the fullest presentation but the most satisfying explanation of the ironic paradox that has caused the Middle West, a region celebrated since its discovery in the most hyperbolic terms—"a region of enchantment," "a terrestrial Paradise," "the Garden of the World"—to be the source of our harshest literary realism.

His artistic theories he promulgated early, the keynote to them being struck in the dedication to his volume of essays already mentioned:

> To the men and women of America who have the courage to be artists.

There he promulgates the code of the realist, proclaiming the local novel as the most promising and sincere of the literary attempts of the day; there he suggests the possibilities of new fields in fiction; there he cries for an interpretation of our common life in painting and sculpture; there with true midland fervor he heralds Chicago as the coming cultural centre, prophesying the original nature of the literature resulting from the great interior spaces of the South and West; there he makes impassioned appeal to the "Sayer and Doers of this broad, free inland America of ours." . . .

His longer tales such as *A Little Norsk* or *Rose of Dutchers's Coolly* have flaws in structure and a sentimentality that weaken them decidedly; too many of his later books seem purely commercialized; but the stories . . . collected for us in *Main-Travelled Roads* (1891), *Other Main-Travelled Roads* (1910), and *Prairie Folks* (1893), form next to the *Son of the Middle Border* his most significant work.

Almost all of them are unrelievedly gloomy. Shanty-like cabins, the inmates of which are crowded together much as in a New York tenement, with unplastered lofts, furnace-like bedrooms, small steaming kitchens—these are the settings. Buzzing flies swarm around almost always; crying children scuffle underfoot; outside reeks the barnyard, torrid in the sunlight, gluey with muck in a storm. In such habitations the toiling men and women sink at times almost to the level of the beasts. Warped with poverty and toil, they take on the labor mask of a Daddy Deering, the hideous outward semblance of a Lucretia Burns. But their physical ugliness is as nothing in the face of their spiritual degradation. A life of savage toil produces equally savage passions; absolute sway over one's beasts tends to produce a desire for equally absolute sway over one's fellows as is demonstrated in such tales as **"William Bacon's Man"** or **"A Preacher's Love Story"**; the lack of adequate recreation causes a petty question of property to bring about **"A Division in the Coolly"**; absence of the outward luxuries of life is intensified by the complete omission of its spiritual graces. The careless brutality of her husband, the nagging of her "in-laws" make Agnes Kinney's daily life a literal hell; years of unrecognized labor bring to Lucretia Burns dreadful rebellion at last. As Douglas Radbourn [one of Garland's characters in *Other Main-Travelled Roads*] sums up the situation,

> Men who toil terribly in filthy garments day after day and year after year cannot easily keep gentle; the frost and grime, the heat and cold, will soon or late enter into their souls. The case is not all in favor of the suffering wives and against the brutal husbands. If the farmer's wife is dulled and crazed by her routine, the farmer himself is degraded and brutalized.

There are other brighter aspects of the picture, but they do not mitigate, rather they accentuate, its essential sombreness. Mr. Garland admits in his preface to *Other Main-Travelled Roads* that "youth and love are able to transform a bleak prairie town into a poem, and to make of a barbed-wire lane a highway of romance"; yet, watching the merrymaking at the Grove Schoolhouse, the gaiety of the racing drivers, the shy "coupling-off" in the intermissions of farm labor, we are confronted always by the question of how long the youthful love will last, how long before the rosy laughing girls will be transformed into gray and shapeless slatterns, the dashing youths, into surly brutes. The landscape, marred only by the habitations of man, loses no whit of the beauty it bore to the dreaming eyes of the prairie boy; but [as Garland wrote in *A Son of the Middle Border*] "how much of consolation does the worn and weary renter find in the beauty of cloud and tree or in the splendor of the sunset?—Grace of flower does not feed or clothe the body, and when the toiler is both badly clothed and badly fed, birdsong and leaf-shine cannot bring content."

The most terrible thing about all the stories is the hopelessness of their outlook; most of the characters seem come to an absolute impasse. The hero of **"A Stop-Over at Tyre"** is literally forced by circumstances into a marriage that strikes the death-blow to all his ambitions. In **"Up the Coolly"** the inequalities of opportunity and environment make the brother who went to New York rich and successful, the younger who stayed behind and took up the father's burdens poor and oppressed with a bitter sense of failure. The tales are filled with scenes that are symbolic—poor Martha in **"Before the Low Green Door"** who doesn't care to live but who never thought she'd die so early and unsatisfied; Simeon Burns trying to puzzle out the situation over which Democrats and Republicans, Grangers and Greenbackers disputed while hard-working, discouraged farmers in bewildered and wordless resentment toiled on; the despair of poor Haskins [in **"Under the Lions Paw"**] after his years of killing and fruitless labor,

He was under the lion's paw. . . . He was hid in a mist, and there was no path out.

The toilers are indeed of the Main Travelled Road—the road arid and brown with the choking dust of the summer; desolate with the dingy mud and stinging snow of the winter; the road long and wearisome, almost always ungracious to the laboring feet that traverse it.

The denunciation of the stories was immediate and bitter. "Editorials and criticisms poured into the office," says Mr. Garland, "all written to prove that my pictures of the middle border were utterly false." And, as a matter of fact, the charges of distortion and untruth persist yet today. Yet scene after scene, character after character in the much-maligned tales can be paralleled in the pages of the autobiographical volume [*A Son of the Middle Border*]. And after all the criticism availed little save to solidify the author's purpose; he had, he asserts, the confidence of truth behind him; and if ever he were tempted to waver he had but to think of his father and mother in the Dakotas. For on another visit he had found another dry year upon the land and the settlers deeply disheartened.

> The holiday spirit of eight years before had entirely vanished. In its place was a sullen rebellion against government and against God. . . . Two of my father's neighbors had gone insane over the failure of their crops. Several had slipped away "between two days" to escape their debts, and even little Jessie, who met us at the train, brave as a meadow lark, admitted that something gray had settled down over the plain. [From *A Son of the Middle Border*.]

On that same withered treeless plain, with no shade save that cast by the little cabin, the weary mother gave out at last; on that plain the resolute father unable to face crop failures year after year, although he still wanted to try irrigation in Montana, was persuaded to turn his back on the West, almost convinced of the elusiveness of the pot of gold at the foot of the rainbow.

> After nearly a third of a century of migration, the Garlands were about to double on their trail, and their decision was deeply significant. It meant that a certain phase of American pioneering had ended, that "the woods and prairie lands" having all been taken up, nothing re-mained but the semi-arid valleys of the Rocky Mountains. "Irrigation" was a new word and a vague word in the ears of my father's generation, and had little of the charm which lay in the "flowery savannahs" of the Mississippi valley. In the years between 1865 and 1892 the nation had swiftly passed through the buoyant era of free land settlement, and now the day of reckoning had come. [From *A Son of the Middle Border*.]

Granville Hicks (essay date 1935)

SOURCE: "Struggle and Fight," in *The Great Tradition: An Interpretation of American Literature Since the Civil War*, revised edition, Macmillan Publishing Company, 1935, pp. 142-48.

[*Hicks was an American literary critic whose famous study* The Great Tradition: An Interpretation of American Literature Since the Civil War *(1933) established him as the foremost advocate of Marxist critical thought in Depression-era America. In the following excerpt from that book, he offers a brief assessment of Garland's career and maintains that the power of the author's best work, his short stories, stems from his identification with Midwestern farmers and the agrarian reform movement of the 1880s and 1890s.*]

[From the 1860s to the 1880s, Middle Western farmers] had not shared in the prosperity of the post-war years, and yet the West felt the depression of 1873 quite as sharply as the East. In the Patrons of Husbandry and the Greenback Party they recorded their discontent, but the good crops of the early eighties led them to abandon their struggle. In 1889, however, the wheat crop was only one-third of what it had been in 1885, and money was scarce and interest rates high. Countless farmers, attracted to the West by land agents' promises of prosperity, labored from sunrise to sunset, only to deliver the fruits of their toil into the hands of bankers and railroad magnates. Though agricultural production grew, the lot of the farmer did not improve, and the proportion of tenant farmers increased. It was no wonder that organizers of the People's Party, campaigning up and down the agricultural states, met with a response that suggested the enthusiasm of the crusades. It was not a narrow nor a fantastic program they advocated: they wanted financial reform, an income tax, postal savings banks, public ownership of the means of transportation and communication, and the restriction of the possession of land to actual producers. The farmers became conscious not only of their own ills but also of the oppression of other classes, and they proposed measures that they believed would protect the downtrodden everywhere.

It would have been strange if that wave of revolt, so charged with emotion, had not had its literary effect. Its spokesman was Hamlin Garland, who, in the late eighties, returned to Minnesota after two or three years of self-education in Boston. He looked about him, and for the first time he really saw the middle border. He saw his family and their neighbors, defeated, downhearted, degraded. "I perceived beautiful youths becoming bowed and bent," he afterwards wrote. "Some of my playmates opened their acrid hearts to me. . . . Every house I visited had its individual message of sordid struggle and half-hidden despair. . . . All the gilding of farm life melted away. The hard and bitter realities came back upon me in a flood." And he not only saw; he felt, surging within himself, the bitter resentment that was rousing the West to action. Joseph Kirkland, who had written two painstakingly accurate novels of rural life, *Zury* and *The McVeys*, told Garland that he was the first dirt farmer in literature and should make the most of that fact. Kirkland was wiser than he knew: Garland's power sprang from his identification with the farmer's cause. Ed Howe, who had published *The Story of a Country Town* in 1883, knew and portrayed the harshness of life on the middle border, but he was a bitter, disappointed newspaper man, whose bitterness set him apart from instead of allying him with his neighbors. Garland came from a farming family, had worked on a farm, had farmers for friends and neighbors, and he made their cause his cause and their enemies his enemies.

In his play, *Under the Wheel,* Garland's sympathies were all with the Edwardses, who, escaped from the slums of Boston, have been led to the West by the extravagant promises of unprincipled speculators, to be beaten down by the harshness of nature and the greed of men. Crude as the play is, the scene laid in the boomer's office is effective propaganda, and the climax of the fourth scene, when hail comes instead of the longed-for rain, is moving drama. And though the tragedy of the Edwards family is complete, the play holds out promise to the farmer. "Courage," one character says, "you will yet live to see the outposts of the enemy carried, and Linnie will live to see a larger and grander abolition cause, carried to a bloodless Appomattox, the abolition of industrial slavery. . . . Over us the shadow still hangs, but far in the west, a faint, ever-widening crescent of light tells of clear skies beyond."

It was in this spirit that Garland wrote the stories in *Main-Traveled Roads* and *Prairie Folks,* though he made no such attempt at direct propaganda as he had made in his play. The former is dedicated "to my father and mother whose half-century pilgrimage on the main-traveled road of life has brought them only toil and deprivation." As we read of the unhappiness of the woman in **"The Branch-Road,"** the contrast between Howard and Grant in **"Up the Coolly,"** the reception of Ed Smith in **"The Return of the Private,"** Haskins' defeat in **"Under the Lion's Paw,"** we know what toil and deprivation are. Garland does not neglect the humor and kindness of the people of the middle border, but he places these pleasanter characteristics against a background of dull, monotonous, ceaseless struggle. The stories are not merely honest—and honesty was rare at the time they were written; they are stirring stories, by virtue of the power of the protest that is implicit in them. And there is some of the same power in passages of *A Spoil of Office* and *Rose of Dutcher's Coolly.*

Reading *Crumbling Idols,* a collection of literary essays, one sees that Garland never fully realized why he had written so surely and soundly in his short stories. His conscious aim was simply to do for the middle border what other local color writers were doing for their sections; that his alliance with the most vital force in his region had made his work superior to that of the ordinary sectionalist he never understood. He protested against slavish subservience to tradition, but he was as much in bondage to Victorian prudishness as any of his contemporaries. He praised the heroism of labor and called for the abolition of special privilege, but he also glorified the sturdy individualism of the pioneer and preached the doctrine of success. His veritism was no stronger than

Howells' realism, and his acceptance of the most sentimental of the regionalists indicates the superficiality of his theories.

Perhaps it was because Garland so imperfectly understood what he had done that he abandoned so readily the high ground on which he at first established himself. After the first five or six years of literary activity his career is almost pure tragedy. Reading his many autobiographical volumes, we find that even as a boy he felt the urge of the pioneer to better his circumstances: he wanted to succeed, to raise himself and his immediate family out of the slough of poverty. In accordance with this ambition he went east to prepare himself for literature. When he returned, equipped with standards by which to measure the misery of middle border life, and armed with the revealing theories of Henry George, his sympathies reached out beyond the Garlands and the McClintocks to embrace the whole class to which they belonged. This zeal made not merely a reformer but a writer of him. He no longer fumblingly sought for subjects and methods; his life had a center, a purpose, that concentrated all his experience and imaginative power. The result was the finest stories yet written of American farm life—direct, comprehensive, moving, and savagely honest.

[The stories in *Main-Travelled Roads* and *Prairie Folks*] are not merely honest—and honesty was rare at the time they were written; they are stirring stories, by virtue of the power of the protest that is implicit in them.

—Granville Hicks

The fiction thus inspired laid the foundation of a literary career, and gradually Garland realized his ambition for his family. Though far from wealthy, he found himself on the road to comfort and respectability. Accepted in literary and academic circles, he became fastidious and a little contemptuous of dirt and disorder. "The reform impulse was steadily waning," he wrote, describing the middle nineties. *"Looking Backward,* like *Progress and Poverty,* was a receding, fading banner." He forsook Populism and Bryanism for more respectable causes, and good naturedly confessed that his days of controversial writing were over, that he was "in league with the capitalistic forces of society." Young writers such as Norris and Dreiser he only half-heartedly accepted; on the other hand, his own acceptance by the academicians was a constant joy.

He yielded to the temptations of the new popular magazines with their higher prices. S. S. McClure candidly advised him, "Drop your literary pose," and he did his best to obey. When he established himself in Chicago and his family on the old Wisconsin homestead, his ties with the struggling farmers were broken. "The pen," he said with pardonable pride, "had proved itself to be mightier than the plow. Going east had proved more profitable than going west." But this deracination involved the finding of new themes, and these he sought in the farther, wilder West. "I perceived," he wrote, "that almost any character I could imagine could be verified in this amazing mixture." He embarked upon a career as romantic novelist, and, as he has boasted, anticipated Zane Grey. Between 1900 and 1917 he wrote a series of highly colored tales of western adventure, with one or two experiments in the novel of psychic experience and an occasional venture in the profitable field of juvenile fiction. But during these years he was unhappy and restless. His novels achieved no spectacular success, the money that his new responsibilities and tastes demanded was not forthcoming, and his creative powers grew constantly feebler. Finally he began to write his autobiography, emphasizing the heroism of the pioneer rather than the cruel realities of agrarian oppression, and throwing over everything the charm of reminiscence. When at last *A Son of the Middle Border* was published, and was greeted by Howells' flattering review, the road to success was open. Garland had found a way to utilize the only vital experiences of his life while maintaining his new standards of respectability. Other autobiographical volumes followed, each one a step to greater comfort and a more impeccable standing. The rebel had vanished. "The poor are almost obsolete," he wrote in one of his autobiographies. In another he referred to "the all-conquering genius of Mussolini." And in the campaign of 1932, speaking as "a theoretical radical," he endorsed the candidacy of Herbert Hoover.

It is interesting to speculate as to what might have happened to Hamlin Garland if he had kept his loyalty to the humble, hapless farmers of his early stories, and had extended his loyalty to embrace urban as well as rural laborers. He might have avoided the whole period of unhappy experimentation in romanticism, and he might have ended, not as a complacent and garrulous chronicler of past glories, but as the great novelist he once gave promise of becoming. But the seeds of failure were there from the first. Perhaps the sources of his ultimate defeat were not far removed from the sources of his first victories. The embattled farmers were themselves individualists, each forgetting the cause of his class once his own success was achieved.

Walter Fuller Taylor (essay date 1942)

SOURCE: "Hamlin Garland," in *The Economic Novel in America,* 1942. Reprint by Octagon Books, 1964, pp. 148-83. Originally published by the University of North Carolina Press.

[*Taylor was an American critic and educator whose books include* A Literary History of the United States *(1948). In the following excerpt, Taylor traces the economic and social influences that shaped Garland's fiction. The critic* *also offers an explanation for why Garland stopped including reform topics in his writing, arguing that by the mid-1890s, "the cultural foundation on which [Garland] had hitherto stood was dissolving."*]

More systematic than the scattered deliverances of Mark Twain, and of more artistic importance than the now forgotten novels of several score journalists and reformers, is the work of Hamlin Garland. With Garland, both as man and as artist, economics and economic reform were, over a period of some ten years, a major interest. Prior to, and during, this decade, many influences converged upon Garland's maturing personality; in the course of it, he produced a unique body of work in which these forces were shaped by the creative imagination into forms more or less artistic; toward its close, he was already being diverted from this characteristic expression, and his work was beginning to reveal that indirection, that temporary frustration, even, which has so curiously baffled our American commentators.

Of the backgrounds out of which Garland's work emerged, that of his youth on the middle border in Iowa is so fundamental that it calls less for elaboration than for the merest resumé. Certain scattered, idyllic memories he retained, to be sure, of a childhood passed among the coulées of Wisconsin; but it was the life on the Iowa prairie, where he lived from his tenth through his twentieth year, that furnished the real matrix of his imagination. From this source, chiefly, came the myriad concrete images that give his descriptive writing its individual color and tone and texture—sights of low, treeless horizons and the waving of ripe wheat; sounds of turningplows thrusting through grassroots embedded in black loam; the lurch of plowhandles, the rasp of cornhusks, the bite and weight of the prairie blizzard. Here in Iowa, too, under the Spartan regime on his father's farm, he first learned that the satisfaction of work might be outweighed by its tortures: by the man's ache of fatigue, by his irritation over the threshing of fly-lanced horses or the stench of cattle stalls; still more [as he described in *A Son of the Middle Border*], by the woman's perpetual treadmill of "cooking, sewing, washing, churning, and nursing the sick."

The middle border society, into which he had been so early adopted as to be virtually a native, Garland took, throughout his life, curiously for granted; he never became more than vaguely aware of such a different region as the South, or of such a different class as the urban proletariat. The Garlands and most of their neighbors were native American stock—sturdy, hard-working, moderately well-to-do, religious folk. A kind of agrarian middle class, they formed an outpost of the midwestern rural democracy of Lincoln, with a vein of backwoodsy angularity and rudeness in their collective character, and more than a vein of the restlessness of the pioneer. Living among these people, the youth Garland assumed, with no serious question, the premises common in our agrarian democracy before the Civil War. Politically, he assumed a democratic tradition, heightened by memories of a heroic struggle fought ostensibly for the cause of human freedom. Socially, he took for granted the equality with which his folk mingled in sports, in the church, in neighborhood fairs, and in sociables of the Grange. Economically, he assumed the Western principle of the pre-emption and exploitation of the public lands. Indeed, at the very time when he came on the book which awakened his first serious thought on social problems, the *Progress and Poverty* of Henry George, he was himself engaged in homesteading in Dakota.

Yet even while he was absorbing the viewpoints of his Iowa society, Garland was, though with no clearly defined intention, preparing his escape from it into a life less physically exacting, more intellectually satisfying; and here, too, the Border society provided him with his main bearings. Through the "Seminary" at Osage, it provided him at least an introduction to culture—a sense of the value of literature and of the power of the written or spoken word. The heated discussions of the townspeople over the writings of Bob Ingersoll, especially "The Mistakes of Moses," helped crystallize his religious independence and agnosticism. The reading of Eggleston's *The Hoosier Schoolmaster* in *Hearth and Home* gave him his first taste of the romanticizing of the common regional life of the West. A sermon delivered by a young Methodist minister stimulated his awareness of the value of art and beauty—a theme which recurs like a refrain in his maturer work. To his homestead in Dakota he carried copies of Taine, of Chambers' *Encyclopedia of English Literature,* and of Greene's *Short History of the English People.* Altogether, if his coming to Boston in 1883 was that of a passionate pilgrim in search of a richer culture, it was also that of a pilgrim who knew with unusual clearness what things he was seeking.

For eight or ten years, after his removal to Boston, Garland developed with a rapidity, with an overwhelming energy, which suggests a major creative genius. Beginning in the obscurity of a cheap lodging house, reading fourteen hours a day from the shelves of the Boston public library, he presently found work as teacher in a school of oratory; formed a dozen profitable associations in literary and artistic Boston; wrote book reviews, thirty-odd short stories, two plays, three novels, and much of the material for a book of critical essays; associated himself with the reform journal, the *Arena,* and with its aid toured the West to observe the Populist movement at first hand; and, all this while, acquired and developed his views on philosophy, on literature, and on economics. In the growth of this threefold view of life—philosophical, aesthetic, and social—lies the key to this first period in Garland's career.

That Garland, when he came to Boston, was already inclined to a natural rather than a supernatural view of life, is indicated by his previous interest in Ingersoll and Taine. Now, in Boston, it was to the nineteenth-century scientists and their interpreters that he naturally turned—to Fiske, to Darwin, and, most of all, to Herbert Spencer. From these masters, however, Garland did not derive, for himself, a scientific method of thought. Instead, he accepted, almost without question, the main conclusions of Spencer. He came to look upon Spencer as the greatest living thinker, and he accepted the authority of the Synthetic Philosophy as that of a new and more plausible Bible which, to him, endued the universe with a rationally acceptable harmony and order.

Under such influences, the remnants of Garland's belief in Christian theology, including his belief in an after-life, sloughed quietly away; but the loss of the elder faith brought to him no such suffering as it had brought, say, to Carlyle. For within Spencer's Synthetic Philosophy had lingered much of the optimism of the Enlightenment, and in the thought of Garland, as in that of other Spencerians, the idea of the evolving of all things from the simple to the complex was fused with an assumption of indefinite progress. The belief that the evolutionary process extends to human society gave sanction to Garland's radicalism and instructed him to welcome reform. The belief that the evolutionary process extends also to the arts—he once planned to write literary histories of the evolution of English and American ideals—gave sanction to his bold disregard of many established classics and to his attempt to strike out a literary way of his own—Veritism. The loss of any faith in a future life only called for a more vigorous attempt to make the present life tolerable; the individualism of Spencer, which might have stood in the way of Garland's interest in any socialistic program of economic reform, only confirmed him in his discipleship to Henry George; and, in short, the Synthetic Philosophy furnished, with Garland, a most favorable nourishment for the growth of literary and economic radicalism.

In the forming of his scheme of aesthetics, Garland drew upon sources more complex and varied than those which had contributed to his general philosophy. Of the European critics and artists, Taine attracted him by his naturalistic interpretation of literary history, Eugene Véron by his opposition to the French Academy, and Max Nordau by his savage treatment of the "Conventional Lies" of our civilization. Garland admired, too, the great dramatists and novelists of Norway and Russia, whom he regarded as being "almost at the very summit" of modern authorship [*Roadside Meetings*]. Of the American authors, Whitman, whose *Leaves of Grass* he read in 1883, "changed the world" for him, taught him the "mystery of the near at hand," and let loose upon him "the spiritual significance of America" [*A Son of the Middle Border*]. Besides the poetry of Whitman, Garland read also the *Specimen Days* and especially the vigorous *Democratic Vistas,* with its caustic romantic critique of the commercialism of the Gilded Age. Whitman himself he visited in Camden, approaching the elder poet with the respect due to "one of the very greatest literary personalities of the century" [*Roadside Meetings*]. Of other American authors, it was chiefly Howells who taught him to look upon fiction as a fine art. Above all, however, he studied the works of the local colorists—Eggleston, Kirkland, in fact, almost every significant author of American regional fiction; and it is from this literary type that his own earliest work most immediately derives.

No less curiously instructive than these influences which Garland accepted are those which he rejected; for, if there were certain masters whom he admired, there were others against whom he was more or less consciously in revolt. The New England school he referred to as "eminent but bookish"; men like Bulwer, Scott, and Hugo he disliked because of their "aristocracy" [*Crumbling Idols*]. Many of the classics of the past, he felt, had by the inescapable processes of social evolution lost their validity for the present: "Shakespeare, Wordsworth, Dante, Milton, are fading away into mere names—books we should read but seldom do" [*Crumbling Idols*]. In this complex of rejection and assimilation, it is difficult, of course, to find any very systematic set of principles; but of one main drift we may be reasonably sure: Garland accepted and assimilated chiefly those influences he thought pertinent to the shaping of a literature which should deal powerfully, truthfully, and, if possible, beautifully, with the secular life of his contemporary America; and those influences which he felt inimical to a realistic literary treatment of our democracy, he rejected.

From such materials, and from their interaction with his own personality, Garland developed his own, individual scheme of aesthetics—a fusion of insurgency, realism, and ethical earnestness. As an insurgent—that is, as a rebellious individualist—he holds first of all that the true artist must be a creator, not an imitator. Excessive bookishness hinders rather than helps the artist. He may be warped or destroyed by libraries; he is made by vital contact with life. In the task of creation, he must free himself from the dominance of literary centers; he must thrust aside all models, even living writers, and "consciously stand alone" before life and before nature. Rebellion is therefore prerequisite to creation; "the iconoclast is a necessity" [*Crumbling Idols*].

Moreover, only by such independence of mind can an author arrive at that entire truthfulness for which Garland preferred a stronger name than realism—Veritism. The essence of Veritism is complete sincerity in the treatment of such phases of contemporary life as are known to the author. To the apprentice writer, Garland's counsel is,

> Write of the things of which you know most, and for which you care most. By so doing you will be true to yourself, true to your locality, and true to your time. [*Crumbling Idols*]

By this basic principle of truthfulness, Garland's emphasis on the value of local color in literature is, to his own mind at least, justified. The presence of local color in a work of fiction means that the writer "spontaneously reflects the life that goes on around him"; it gives a novel "such quality of texture and background that it could not have been written in any other place or by anyone else than a native." Because of the organic union of truthfulness and local color, the latter is "demonstrably the life of fiction," and is a factor in the greatness of many of the classics both of modern and of ancient times [*Crumbling Idols*].

Veritism—fidelity to the truth—was, moreover, an ethical principle with Garland as well as an aesthetic; for the truthful portraiture of the unjust and evil necessarily suggests, by contrast, the ideally just and good. By delineating the ugliness and strife of the present, the artist aims to hasten the age of beauty and peace. The Veritist

> sees life in terms of what it might be, as well as in terms of what it is; but he writes of what is, and, at his best, suggests what is to be. [*Crumbling Idols*]

Hence the artist may adopt the aim of spreading everywhere the reign of justice and yet keep his artistic interests paramount—provided only that he convey his social message not by preaching, but by exemplifying, "not by direct expression, but by placing before the reader the facts of life as they stand related to the artist" [*Crumbling Idols*]. Veritist and indirect propagandist are one. Seen in this light, the social bearing of fiction need in no way interfere with its aesthetic values, which are to afford the writer "keen creative delight" and to enrich the experience of the reader by touching, lifting, and exalting him.

On the whole, Garland's aesthetics are as individualistic as his general philosophy of life; and the individualism of both is of a piece with that of his sociology. While still a homesteader, himself sharing in the disposal of the public domain, Garland, as we have seen, read *Progress and Poverty* and accepted George's thesis that the root of social evils is monopoly of land. Some years later, this abstract conviction was transformed into personal loyalty; George spoke in Boston, and his impressive power, his sincere altruism, and his personal charm combined to make of Garland a disciple. Garland joined the Anti-Poverty society which George's visit had called into being, and attended and addressed its meetings. Later, while living temporarily in New York, he fell into the habit of visiting "the Prophet and his delightful family," and became an observer, if not an intimate, of the circle of reformers that foregathered about George [*A Son of the Middle Border*].

Sensitive as he was to every appeal to humanitarian feeling, Garland could hardly, if he would, have escaped the general humanitarian temper of the times, of which the work of George was only one of many manifestations. The influences he met with in the circle of George were reinforced by numerous others. His connection with B. O. Flower and the *Arena* brought him into fellowship first with another Eastern group of social critics, and later with the Western leaders of Populism. The time was one in which he could awaken an enthusiastic interest in the Single Tax in his friends the Hernes, or argue against socialism in the company of Howells. It was, in short, an era of "parlor-socialists, single-taxers, militant populists, Ibsen dramas, and Tolstoyan encyclicals against greed, lust, and caste" [*Roadside Meetings*]. Upon Garland, the effect of this welter of reform movements was chiefly to deepen his concern for social justice. Only one phase of the reform program provided him with intellectual meat. From his all but religious discipleship to Henry George, he was not diverted.

The sociology of Garland is, then, a simpler version of the sociology of George. Equally with George, Garland is aware, sensitively aware, of the curse of poverty and the burden of human suffering; and he is capable of an equally burning hatred of social injustice. Along with George—and, indeed, with the thinkers of the eighteenth-century Enlightenment—he assumes that the primary causes of human suffering do not lie in the beneficent scheme of Nature, but in the imperfect and unjust laws of man. His particular concern is, of course, with that scheme of law which allows the speculator to monopolize the natural resources of the earth. He assumes, with George, that the destruction of monopoly and of speculative values in land is the crucial task of the economic reformer, the one stroke needful to insure the restoration of the buoyant prosperity that had accompanied the era of the open frontier.

> The effect of the tax on land values is precisely like that of opening new land to settlement. It brings it out of the speculator's hands into the settler's hands. It passes out of the hands of the monopolist into the hands of the contractor and builder. ["The Single Tax in Actual Operation," in *Arena,* Vol. X, No. 57 (June 1894)]

More explicitly than George, Garland rejects all tendencies toward collectivism. The sufferings of the victims of society are not due, as the Socialists claim, to free competition, but to the lack of free competition—in short, to monopoly. Not the paternal care of the government, but opportunity merely, is the need of the average American citizen. Given a chance, the average man is industrious enough and frugal enough to be trusted with the management of his own affairs; and the interference of government with his business ought therefore, Jeffersonian fashion, to be diminished rather than increased.

Moreover, the restoration of opportunity, and the consequent abolition of poverty, are not economic aims merely; they are aesthetic as well. With William Morris, Garland believed that widespread social injustice dwarfs the growth of art. If he lacked Morris's profound understanding of the creative values of craftsmanship, he at least realized that if the arts are ever to have meaning for the populace in general, poverty must first be alleviated. The exhausted sweatshop girl or farm hand has no chance to care for beauty. Hence, "if you would raise the standard of art in America you must first raise the standard of living. . . ." "With leisure to enjoy and means to purchase to his refining taste, the common man would be no longer a common man, and art, genuine art, with free and happy intellects before it, would no longer be the poor, begging thing that it seems now" ["The Land Question and Its Relation to Art and Literature," in *Arena,* Vol. IX (January 1894)]. . . .

Since Garland himself has so emphasized his concern over social injustice, one is surprised to find, on examining his stories, that less than a third deal, even indirectly, with economic reform. One story, **"Black Ephram,"** is vaguely humanitarian, but devoid of any bearing on the specific economic causes of suffering in Garland's own time. Two others, **"A Day of Grace"** and **"The Test of Elder Pill,"** express Garland's opposition to the hell-fire evangelism

and emotional excesses of much rural religion. Nine stories, such as **"The Sociable at Dudley's,"** are regional narratives, concerned with local color and with the peculiar folkways of a remote rural community. The subjects of ten others, including **"The Return of a Private,"** are general and miscellaneous; and among these at least one, **"God's Ravens,"** deals with provincial life much in the idyllic manner from which Garland supposed he had broken away. By the most liberal interpretation, the need for economic reform and the influence of economic conditions are major themes in only nine stories: **"A Branch Road," "Up the Coulée," "Among the Corn Rows," "Under the Lion's Paw," "A Day's Pleasure," "Sim Burns's Wife," "A Stop-Over at Tyre," "An Alien in the Pines,"** and **"Before the Low Green Door."**

The economic creed expressed in these nine stories is as simply conceived as it is powerfully driven home. That because of economic injustice rural life is now barren and intolerably painful; that such suffering must be relieved, and such barrenness enriched; and that these gains may be had by the one thoroughgoing act of destroying all monopolistic holdings in land—this is Garland's platform. All in all, it is the sufferings and the spiritual deformity of the victims of society that he renders most powerfully. Among these victims, there is the farmer Sim Burns:

> The man thrust his dirty, naked feet into his huge boots, and, without washing his face or combing his hair, went out to the barn to do his chores.

> He was a type of the average prairie farmer. . . .

> No grace had come or ever could come into his life. Back of him were generations of men like himself, whose main business had been to work hard, live miserably, and beget children to take their places when they died.

And beside the portrait of the man there is that of his wife, Lucretia, who, after a day of vexations and sufferings and quarrels, wears a pitifully tired, almost tragic, face—

> long, thin, sallow, hollow-eyed. The mouth had long since lost the power to shape itself into a kiss, and had a droop at the corners, which seemed to announce a breaking down at any moment into a despairing wail. The colorless neck and sharp shoulders sagged painfully.

There is power in portrayals such as these, the unforgettable power of a profound indignation which has found truthful and adequate voice. And these two are reinforced by other descriptions of equal force—that of Grant MacLane in **"Up the Coulée";** those of such farm women as Mrs. Sam Markham in **"A Day's Pleasure"** and the dying Matilda in **"Before the Low Green Door"**—descriptions that say all that need be said about the futility of the lives, women's lives especially, that never escape from the imprisonment of poverty.

Besides descriptive portrayal, Garland's one other important method of economic teaching is the illustration of some economic principle or problem in a series of imagined events. In **"A Stop-Over at Tyre,"** he suggests the economic effect of premature marriage in preventing a man from his intended career; in **"A Branch Road"** he suggests the problem, whether a woman should remain faithful to a marriage in which she is being wrecked by unhappiness and overwork. In **"Under the Lion's Paw,"** the most admirably executed of all the stories, he illustrates the effect of land monopoly on the farmer Haskins, who, when he buys the place he has worked as a tenant, is compelled to pay for his own improvements and to accept terms that make of him an economic slave. The economics of **"Under the Lion's Paw"** is, of course, straight out of *Progress and Poverty;* Garland himself has spoken of the work [in *Roadside Meetings*] as a single-tax story; and, indeed, its relation to George's main thesis is precisely that of example to theorem in mathematics. Not the least triumph of Garland's work is that he successfully translates the abstractions of George into such concrete, human, dramatic, and moving terms.

Description and exemplification, then, are the common fictional methods of Garland. Mindful of Howells's counsel to exemplify and not to preach, he was almost overcareful in avoiding the explicit statement of any economic views, particularly his own. Rarely, he has his characters discuss some industrial problem of the times; even more rarely, he employs a chorus character to inculcate his own views. Chief of these characters is the radical, Radbourn, who, in **"Sim Burns's Wife,"** protests against the "horrible waste of life involved in it all," who wishes to "preach discontent, a noble discontent," and whose program of practical reform involves

> the abolition of all indirect taxes, the State control of all privileges the private ownership of which interfered with the equal rights of all. He would utterly destroy speculative holdings of the earth. He would have land everywhere brought to its best use, by appropriating ground rents to the use of the state.

And yet, even in the stories that are definitely economic in purpose, the didactic element is not obtruded. The economic teaching is suspended, as it were, in a current of more purely fictional elements, especially of the kind common among local color stories. In characterization, for example, there is an abundance of *genre* paintings, like those of Mrs. Ripley and Uncle Ethan Ripley, or the Yohe boys in **"The Sociable at Dudley's."** In the talk of Garland's people, a Western rural idiom, which gives an impression of entire naturalness, abounds. The natural scene, the prairie background, while not insisted on as is the Tennessee mountain scenery in Miss Murfree's stories, is skillfully, often beautifully, employed.

Indeed, to one who came to Garland's stories without any preconceptions, their principal merit might seem to reside in the sheer craftsmanship of the writer. Stimulated by the artistic example of his friend Howells, situated independently, at liberty to take his time and brood over his materials until he brought them to full creation, Garland, writing and rewriting, wrought out his stories with the conscious artistry of the master craftsman. The result is a carefully wrought expansion of scene, a deliberate build-up and calculation of effect, and a plausibility dependent on the aesthetically consistent use of precisely the right detail, that are beyond praise. Often the movement of the story culminates in some dramatic or even melodramatic climax—the quietly intense talk of Grant and Howard MacLane in **"Up the Coulée,"** or Haskins' narrowly averted murder of the speculator Butler in **"Under the Lion's Paw."** Richly suggestive, intensely human touches abound; the language, intentionally rugged, intensifies at times into restrained rhythmic beauty. Underneath the surface, unobtruded but continually felt, the force of the author's profound indignation urges the stories along. Above all, Garland knows when to close, and how to strengthen his conclusions by abandoning direct statement for impressive restraint and suggestion. When, in **"Up the Coulée,"** the prosperous Howard MacLane learns the entire tragedy of his brother's defeat by the poverty he could have relieved, we are told only,

> The two men stood there, face to face, hands clasped, the one fair-skinned, full-lipped, handsome in his neat suit; the other tragic, sombre in his softened mood, his large, long, rugged Scotch face bronzed with sun and scarred with wrinkles that had histories, like sabrecuts on a veteran, the record of his battles.

The reception of *Main-Travelled Roads* was a puzzling affair, at least to Garland. The book sold steadily, to be sure, but mostly in the East; its sale in the West remained small for many years. Certain critics, unprepared for Garland's relentless truth-telling, evinced an antagonism which the author found astonishing. But he had the cordial appreciation of Flower, Mary Wilkins, Howells, and others; and although conservatives like Edward Fuller might look at him askance, he had at least become a force.

. . . . .

With the completion of [his third novel of economic fiction] *A Spoil of Office*, we are brought to the verge of that break in Garland's career—that disintegration, so far as his social aims are concerned—which has so piqued the curiosity of our historians and critics. . . .

Interpretations of Garland's change of policy are as numerous as the historians and critics who have attacked the problem. . . . The basic, the original factor, however, appears to have been, as [Vernon Louis Parrington, in *The Beginnings of Critical Realism in America,*] suggests, the decline of the middle-class protest against industrialism—or, more exactly, the diversion of that protest from its agrarian and romantic expression into other forms.

Although there is some reason for believing that the middle-class drive for social justice was already losing force as early as 1892, the definite outward symptom of that decline, and one of the decisive turning-points in American history, was the defeat of William Jennings Bryan and of the Populist-Democratic fusion in 1896. Thenceforward, Populism was no longer a national power, and the force of events directed the liberal elements in the Democratic party toward other issues. The inflation for which the free-silver men had for years ineffectually struggled, followed naturally upon the discovery of new gold fields and an enormous increase in the world-supply of gold; the trough of a world-wide economic depression was passed; once more America, the middle border included, knew prosperity; and the quest for social justice lost the tragically dynamic motive power of unusual and widespread suffering. The Spanish-American and Philippine wars tended, likewise, to divert popular attention from domestic reforms; so that, when Bryan undertook his second campaign for the presidency, he found it expedient to crystallize the democratic and humanitarian sentiment of the country about the issue of imperialism instead of economic reform. The middle-class opposition to the plutocracy was carried on for a while only by isolated groups of single-taxers, nationalists, and others, and by the occasional novel of some critic or humanitarian. When, presently, that protest again received a national hearing—in the work of the muck-rakers and in the progressive movement led by Theodore Roosevelt—it was under the leadership of other men, and under the influence of another time-spirit, than that which had given it focus in the Gilded Age. . . .

In brief, the middle nineties, whether considered from the viewpoint of factual history, or that of the leadership of public opinion, or that of *belles-lettres,* were a time when certain powerful forces, which had come to focus within the two preceding decades, were rapidly disintegrating. The culture of antebellum, agrarian America, its protagonists now grown old, its way of life fast becoming only a memory, its forces spent in the effort to transform or control the Machine Age, had lived its active life and was ready for whatever doubtful immortality might belong to an influence and a heritage.

In the middle nineties, therefore, Garland held the unenviable position of a spokesman for a disintegrating movement, of a survivor of a fast disappearing culture. The social, the cultural foundation on which he had hitherto stood was dissolving, and it behooved him either to find another stance, or to retire from literature as a vocation. Moreover, if he were to marry, to create a home, to realize himself completely in a normal human life, he must find a stance that promised economic security. His fundamental problem (although he himself never stated it in just these terms) was simply a problem of literary survival in a rapidly changing *milieu.* Stated in another way, his was the problem of discovering, as journalist and free lance writer, materials and methods interesting enough to the public to command an adequate income, an income by which he might realize his aims, not as a member of society but as an individual, not as a social prophet, but simply as a man. These materials he was already finding in the local color, the romance, of the Rocky Mountain West.

Grant C. Knight (essay date 1951)

SOURCE: "The Search for Reality," in *The Critical Period in American Literature,* The University of North Carolina Press, 1951, pp. 43-67.

[*In this excerpt, Knight details the events that inspired Garland's fiction and analyzes the stories in* Main-Travelled Roads, Prairie Folks, *and* Wayside Courtships.]

[William Dean] Howells had no more admiring and articulate defender than Hamlin Garland, who had somehow picked up the title of Professor. Lecturing on Howells at Avon-by-the-Sea, Garland quoted his friend's definition of realism as "the truthful treatment of material" and rightly appraised it as a revolutionary step in the history of the American novel; he went on to assert that [Howells's novel] "*A Modern Instance* is the greatest, most rigidly artistic novel ever written by an American, and ranks with the great novels of the world." The two men had in 1891 a kind of master-and-disciple relationship, with the older one encouraging the other to go on with his composition of stories which were so realistic that only a radical magazine like *The Arena* would print them; in fact, **"Up the Coolly"** and **"A Branch Road"** were too strong even for that doughty periodical. Six of these stories Garland issued in a volume with the title of *Main-Travelled Roads,* the outstanding contribution to American realism in 1891 and one of the classic collections of American short stories. *Main-Travelled Roads* did not break utterly with the Genteel Tradition—Garland was never to do that—but it did inch closer to such a rupture than any other important American writing had come by that date.

In his "Editor's Study" [in *Harper's New Monthly Magazine,* LXXXIII, 639] Howells gladly welcomed this "robust and terribly serious" book, commending the stories for their art, their strength, their courage, and rejoicing that they would "strike many gentilities as coarse and common." With an oblique allusion to his own rationale of criticism he wrote:

> If any one is still at a loss to account for that uprising of the farmers in the West which is the translation of the Peasants' War into modern and republican terms, let him read *Main-Travelled Roads,* and he will begin to understand, unless, indeed, Mr. Garland is painting the exceptional rather than the average. The stories are full of those gaunt, grim, sordid, pathetic, ferocious figures, whom our satirists find so easy to caricature as Hayseeds, and whose blind groping for fairer conditions is so grotesque to the newspapers and so menacing to the politicians. They feel that something is wrong, and they know that the wrong is not theirs. The type caught in Mr. Garland's book is not pretty; it is ugly and often ridiculous, but it is heart-breaking in its rude despair.

The passage displays more than Howells's gratification at finding he had a stalwart ally; it reveals, too, that he sympathized with the revolting farmer of the 1890's. The main facts of that revolt must be outlined here briefly not only because they made Garland a writer but also because they helped mightily to form the disposition, the receptive mood, for realism which was expanding over the nation. Thousands of Americans, losing during that rebellion some of their more romantic illusions about their country and inspired by a deeply-rooted puritanic culture which, as with Howells and Garland and Stephen Crane, craved the truth no matter how much it hurt, were reluctantly revising their opinions about their opportunities and at the same time becoming more ready to accept a literature which would mirror the life they knew.

By the late eighties and early nineties the farmer of the West and South, whether or not he realized that the Civil War had brought victory to industry and finance, began to see himself as an economic casualty. The bankers, the manufacturers, even the mill workers were organized and receiving favors from the government while he was left to fend for himself, and the fending was becoming less and less tolerable. He bought in a dear market and sold in a cheap one; Kansas farmers received eight or ten cents a bushel for wheat which the New York broker priced at one dollar a bushel. He had little to say about the price of the commodities he dealt in, and nothing at all about the prices of the things he bought. He reasoned that he was at the mercy of stock market manipulators, of the railroads which by virtue of their monopolies could fix discriminatory freight rates, and of the Wall Street bankers who ultimately held the farm mortgages, and he came to hate them all bitterly. Because his property was land, he could not conceal its existence or its value and so could not escape, as he thought business men often did, the burden of taxation. The tariff, he thought, was devised so as to keep him in economic peonage. He was the victim of the drought and other acts of God. Like the other westerner, the silver man, his fortune was being taken from him by the ruthless gold man of the East. Congress, the courts, the governors, and legislatures were all the creatures of an oligarchy that lived upon his sweat and blood and hunger; he produced, the others fattened and lived luxuriously upon the harvest of his toil.

The farmers had tried to organize, too, in the hope of obtaining redress for their grievances, but the Grange, the Agricultural Wheel, the Corn-growers' Association, and the Farmers' Alliance had little success. Then in May of 1891 delegates representing the embattled farmers and reformers of various sects met in a convention at Cincinnati to call for the formation of a third party to be named the People's Party of the United States of America. Meeting in St. Louis the following year, delegates of the Populists drew up a platform that has not been equalled in our history for forthright wrathful language as it described the class struggle here and abroad. Among other charges it thundered:

> We meet in the midst of a nation brought to the verge of ruin. Corruption dominates the ballot box, the legislatures, the Congress, and touches even the ermine of the bench. . . . The newspapers are subsidized or muzzled; public opinion silenced; business prostrated, our homes covered with mortgages, labor impoverished,

and the land concentrated in the hands of the capitalists. The urban population are denied the right of organization for self-protection; imported pauperized labor beats down their wages; a hireling standing army, unrecognized by our laws, is established to shoot them down. . . . The fruits of the toil of millions are boldly stolen to build up colossal fortunes, unprecedented in the history of the world, while the possessors despise the republic and endanger liberty. . . . The national power to create money is appropriated to enrich bondholders; silver . . . has been demonetized to add to the purchasing power of gold by decreasing values of all forms of property as well as human labor; and the supply of currency is purposely abridged to fatten usurers, bankrupt enterprise, and enslave industry. A vast conspiracy against mankind has been organized on two conztinents and is taking possession of the world. If not met and overthrown at once it forebodes terrible convulsions, the destruction of civilization, or the establishment of an absolute despotism.

In the 1892 election the Populist candidate for president carried the states of Colorado, Kansas, Nevada, and Utah, and received over a million votes, thereby so frightening the eastern conservative press that it advertised the three Populist United States senators and eleven representatives and their friends as agents of subversion. The Populist party continued strong in the elections of 1894 but was practically absorbed by the Democratic party in 1896. By 1900 it was admittedly dead.

All this ferment of words, passions, and occasional lawlessness called loudly for interpretation by a writer of fiction who believed in Howells's definition of realism. Hamlin Garland had met many of the leaders of the revolt, studied them shrewdly, penetrated through their rhetorical fulminations to the wrongs that incited them, and written sketches of them for *The Arena*. His interest was not that of the mere observer or doctrinaire; it was that of a man who had from childhood been familiar with the toil, the deprivations, the poverty, and the frustrations of a farmer's life. Interest is, in truth, much too mild a word to describe his feeling, which was one of hot anger— anger not just because of the economic oppression under which the farmer fretted but even more largely because of the attendant indignities to the human spirit. He saw that unrequited toil could break the heart as well as the body; he knew from his experiences in Wisconsin and Iowa and Dakota how meager were the pleasures of the lonely farmer and his wife, how few those refinements and beauties which can make humble life tolerable. And he knew that this farming couple and its children, the grim odorous battle with nature, the heroism in the face of failure and death, the piety and the cherished culture, the pathetic ambitions for the young, had never been given a completely honest treatment in American literature. It was his aim and his achievement to give that treatment, first in essays, then in stories.

The idea of writing fiction about his native region would possibly never have occurred to Garland had he remained there all his life. To the middle westerner Boston was the hub of literary America and literature was a thing removed

Garland at the Ordway, South Dakota, homestead where he began work on Main-Travelled Roads.

from ordinary life. No one had written adequately about the Middle West except Edward Eggleston, whose *The Hoosier Schoolmaster* Garland read in serial form in 1871 and later recognized as a milestone in his literary progress. But it was only after several years of residence in Boston that he began to acquire the perspective and the creed necessary for the successful handling of the Border in writing. First he penned a series of articles about prairie life in the different seasons. Then, with revived interest in his material and a dream of fame to be found in the field of realistic writing, he left for his former home in the summer of 1887. In May of that year he had read Kirkland's *Zury, the Meanest Man in Spring County* (1887), and on his way to Iowa he stopped in Chicago to see the author of that epic of stinginess. Kirkland, acquainted with some of Garland's sketches, advised him to write fiction.

As Garland drew nearer home he was more and more struck with the gracelessness of the dwellings, the lack of color and charm everywhere, the futility of life, especially of woman's life, on a farm. And when he reached Osage and was greeted by his old friends, worn out with their labors and discouraged by their prospects, he remembered the gospel of [Henry George's] *Progress and Poverty,* which he had read in 1883. Thus with Eggleston, Kirkland, and Henry George as stimuli, and with his "perception of the sordid monotony of farm life" to give him a new emotional relationship to the land, he began to write his first short story while with his parents. However, most of the *Main-Travelled Roads* stories were written in the two years following his return to Boston, where he was further inspired by hearing George lecture and by the friendship of Howells. In 1889, called home by the serious illness of his mother, he was confirmed in his

impression of the drabness and sorrow of existence on the plains and resumed his writing in what he described as a mood of bitter resentment. When he dedicated the first edition of **Main-Travelled Roads** to his father and mother he acknowledged that their "half-century pilgrimage on the main-travelled road of life" had "brought them only toil and privation."

Of the six stories in this volume two retain some of the heat in which they were written and first read. Because it is not so much propaganda as it is the record of a clash in temperaments, a clash which grew out of the nature of life itself, **"Up the Coolly"** has the more lasting effect upon a sensitive reader. Though derived directly from Garland's experience, it is finely and patiently imagined. Garland's return to his old home was not marked by the harsh collision of personalities which forms the plot of **"Up the Coolly,"** but it could have been, and the story otherwise follows loosely the details of that visit. Howard McLane, through whose eyes the unhappy situation unfolds, is a successful dramatist and actor, an item which is not autobiographical, though the fact that Garland's brother Franklin was moderately successful on the stage at the time may have suggested McLane's profession. But McLane's response to the landscape, his feelings upon seeing his mother, his attempt to help in the hay field, the changes in land ownership, the increase in foreign settlers, McLane's determination to find a comfortable home for his mother, his wish to spend Thanksgiving with her—all these things correspond with facts later set forth in *A Son of the Middle Border* (1917). One small detail of the story which is interestingly autobiographical is McLane's selection of silk dress material as a gift for his mother and of General Grant's *Personal Memoirs* for his brother.

These were the gifts which Garland purchased for mother and father respectively with the first money he earned by writing.

In the light of what Garland was trying to do, and in view of the theory of fiction which he was to put into print in 1894, it is just to value his fiction in proportion to its artistic and realistic use of the prairie as he knew it. He did use it freely, sympathetically, observantly; a close reading of his stories and his Middle Border series demonstrates how consistently and faithfully he introduced into the stories himself, his family, his neighbors, and the incidents of farm life in his section. But the values of **"Up the Coolly"** transcend those of mere realism. Howard McLane, beaten, smouldering, scarred and weary, is not only a man envious of his brother's fortune and stung by that brother's cavalier neglect. He is also a symbol of a great and inexplicable failure of justice, a denial of the old maxims about thrift and industry and integrity, a mockery of the proclamations of the patriotic orator, a kind of modern Job, tormented not by divine but by economic determinism. A character like that allows but one solution to the complication he created, and Garland, rejecting all temptations to compromise with romanticism, proved himself a genuine realist by bringing **"Up the Coolly"** to an unorthodox but satisfying end.

"The Return of a Private" has probably been reprinted more often than any other of the *Main-Travelled Roads* stories. Although it has nothing to do with battle, it is the first memorable American story to have as its prime intent the throwing of suspicion upon the glory of a soldier's service to his country. Bierce had made war a thing of chance and carnage but he had also ascribed to many of his military men a debonair courage that veiled some of the horror of their profession. Garland's private has no shred of glory left him as he returns to his farm after being discharged—no committee meets him, no flags wave, no official makes a speech, no drums and bugles welcome the weary, sick, impoverished ex-soldier whose health has been undermined and whose farm has deteriorated during the three years he was in blue. He came back, it is true, to a loving wife and to three children, but he also came back to a mortgage, to weedy acres, to a future darkened by the fact that his machinery had been stolen by a tenant. Had Stephen Crane told the story of Private Smith he might have jeered at the penalized idealist. Garland, writing with no illusions but with a kind of sad wonderment, had his hero assume his new duties and burdens with a stout heart. "His war with the South was over, and his fight, his daily running fight with nature and against the injustice of his fellow-man, was begun again," was his concluding comment.

This story, describing the return of Garland's father after the Civil War, is completely autobiographical. Almost all of the narrative particulars, from the reading of tea leaves by the Widow Gray (Widow Green in real life) to the youngest son's fear of his stranger father, appear in the first chapter of *A Son of the Middle Border*. **"A Branch Road"** also contains autobiographical elements, although the plot was invented. Two of Garland's favorite themes

are here interwined with deceptive skill: men and women separate themselves from each other by a perverse, jealous reserve, and the life of the prairie woman was frequently close to the unendurable. In this story Will Hannan saves Agnes Dingman, whom he had loved seven years before, from the nagging and bullying of her husband by eloping with her and her baby. Such an application of the principles of realism must have been somewhat embarrassing to Howells when he came to review *Main-Travelled Roads*; guardedly he conceded that the story was morally all wrong but that the author had left the reader to say that himself. "He knows that his business was with those two people, their passions and their probabilities," he wrote. Surely he must have realized that by this evasion he had inferentially contradicted the doctrine of the need to unite art and morality which he had preached zealously in *Criticism and Fiction*.

"Among the Corn-Rows," with a considerably lighter tone, belongs to local color rather than to propaganda. It has, to be sure, its serious angles in the difficulties of a young man who tries as Garland did in 1883 to live unmarried on his land claim; in the consciousness of the Norwegians that they are regarded as queer by their neighbors; and in Julia Petersen's exhausting and well-nigh hopeless drudgery. But its key is that of aspiration and young love, and all ends well in an elopement to which Garland gave a romantic lift. **"Mrs. Ripley's Trip,"** the first of the stories Garland wrote for this collection and one grafted upon an anecdote told him by his mother, is another addition to local color literature, reminiscent, in its effective use of dialect and its understanding of concealed affection, of the narratives by Mary E. Wilkins, particularly "The Revolt of Mother." Yet even this half-playful story has its heavy undertone in the evidence of ever-present toil and near-poverty. For twenty-three years Jane Ripley had "stuck right to the stove an' churn without a day or night off"; after her visit East, relates Garland, she "took up her burden again, never more thinking to lay it down." That last sentence, like several of Garland's closing sentences, admirably suits the Biblical cadence to the sober emotion.

Better known than any of the preceding stories with the exception of **"The Return of a Private"** is **"Under the Lion's Paw,"** written in 1890 when Garland was a disciple of Henry George and a member of the Anti-Poverty Society. Sometimes dubbed Garland's Single Tax story, this one thrusts its truth into the conscience of the modern reader as patly as it did in the 1890's, for it explains concretely how increasing real estate values may enrich a landlord who has not done a stroke of contributing or productive labor. Though Garland wrote with creditable restraint, the fury of Timothy Haskins, the tenant farmer, is quickly and fully communicated from story to reader, who is almost ready to excuse the murderous assault which the overworked man came near to perpetrating but which Garland wisely prevented.

These six stories have many of the qualities of enduring literature. They crystalize the revolt of an important section of the American people. Their images convey the impressions of an aroused observer who intended to tell the truth about that part of humanity which he knew. And those impressions are set down with acuteness and dexterity, for without employing any of the tricks of the popular sentimentalist of his day Garland evokes compassion for his unhappy characters and compels us to await eagerly the outcome of their humble fortunes. His men and women are copied without much alteration from persons with whom he had lived and worked; they are not the rustic clowns of traditional drama and story but figures of true comic and tragic proportions; persons who laugh and shout and dance, who try to preserve their inherited cultures on a barren frontier, whose bodies and minds are cramped by undeserved want and the lack of opportunity for self-improvement, who speak with the tongues of real farmers and who love and hate and quarrel and worship like ordinary Americans of their part of the country. Garland did not, to be sure, tell the whole truth; he did not reproduce the full vigor of barnyard speech nor did he pry into the shadowed corners of small towns or of farmhouses. Yet he did not shrink from informing us that if too many of his settlers of the Middle Border lived meanly, some of them were also mean. Almost all of them are in one way or another the victims of an economic derangement, but Garland avoided the superficiality of the maladroit propagandist by refusing to make everyone heroic or even wholesome. There they are, with the movements and minds of real persons: hardworking or shiftless, sober or drunken, kind or brutal, planning a better future or plodding through their days with scarcely more than animal persistence. They are completely alive, completely convincing. They exist.

This authenticity was one reason for the lively censure with which *Main-Travelled Roads* was greeted in 1891. Garland, hurt, it would seem, for many years by the reception given this book, tells us in the thirty-first chapter of *A Son of the Middle Border* that the people he was trying to help execrated him as a bird fouling its own nest, that "statistics were employed to show that pianos and Brussels carpets adorned almost every Iowa farmhouse," that editorials and reviews insisted that tilling the soil was a noble occupation quite unlike the picture he had drawn. He was accused over the country of fomenting class hatred, of associating with cranks like Henry George and Walt Whitman, of falsifying the good life in America. When the dissent was not abusive it was skeptical; *The Atlantic Monthly* [LXIX] voiced the feeling of the cloistered conscience by remarking that if these stories were true then "the sum of human grief and suffering is still greater than we had supposed" and by hoping that "in his enthusiasm for Mr. Howells" Garland had "married Russian despair and French realism"—an indirect criticism that was notably confused.

In these stories the incidents, and the order in which they are related, are equally persuasive. They have the unhurried rhythm which assures the reader that they have not been pressed or teased into shape but have grown naturally. The hand of the writer is almost invisible as his farm people sow and reap, cook and eat, court and marry, grow old and die. Brief as is their individual appearance upon the page, they contribute to an epic effect, to a sense of the vast heaving organism which uses soil and sun and rain to produce life but which is constantly at war with itself to bring on death. The plots are, in the best meaning of the word, serious, and because they are effortlessly constructed and utterly true they will keep *Main-Travelled Roads* alive as long as books are read. Garland never did better writing.

Other editions of this work, with added stories, came out in 1893 and 1899, and Garland continued his purpose partially in two other collections of short stories, *Prairie Folks* (1893) and *Wayside Courtships* (1895)—partially, because there is less bitterness and crusading in these tales and more of a rendering into fiction of the Middle Border scene apart from its economic sickness.

"**Daddy Deering,**" with excellent accounts of threshing and hog-killing and dancing, does again emphasize the ceaseless unavailing labor of the farmer, but "**The Sociable at Dudley's**" and "**Saturday Night on the Farm**" turn to the lighter moments of rural life; the former is one of the most thoroughly autobiographical of Garland's stories. The tragic note resounds again in "**Sim Burns's Wife,**" "**A Day's Pleasure,**" "**Before the Green Door,**" and "**A Division in the Coolly,**" in all of which the author, drawing upon his memories of his mother, sister, and women friends, grieves over the rigorous conditions under which prairie women lived out their days. "**Sim Burns's Wife**" is also another Single Tax tract, with Garland's sentiments expressed movingly by the young lawyer, David Radbourn. "**An Alien in the Pines**" contains realistic descriptions of the Wisconsin lumber camps, probably based upon Garland's visit to that region and on conversations with his father, who had worked there.

In three stories Garland dealt with the type of religion found on the Border, particularly with the revival, which in "**Elder Pill: the Country Preacher**" and "**A Day of Grace**" is described as an occasion for hell-fire preaching and hysterical response but which in "**A Preacher's Love Story**" unites a neighborhood in friendship instead of gloom. One of the best additions is "**The Creamery Man,**" which to an unwary reader is a comedy of courtship involving a young delivery man, a proud farmer's daughter, and a clumsy, unattractive German girl; actually it expresses, with a kind of homely poetry appropriate to the milieu, a knowledge that tears lie at the bottom of even commonplace human relationships.

In contrast with the farm stories, Garland's stories of small town life are less melancholy and at the same time less interesting and less important. Bluff Siding and Tyre are names which he used for his Middle Border towns, and while they seem to represent the typical rather than specific places they are doubtless related to Onalaska and Osage, the towns of that kind which Garland knew. "**God's Ravens**" is a miniature revolt against the village almost a generation before [Sinclair Lewis's] *Main Street* appeared. Its hero, Robert Bloom, leaves Chicago for his health and goes back to his native town in Wisconsin, only to recoil from what he finds there:

"Oh, I can't stand these people! They don't know anything. They talk every rag of gossip into shreds. 'Taters, fish, hops; hops, fish, and 'taters. They've saved and pinched and toiled till their souls are pinched and ground away. You're right. They are caricatures. They don't read or think about anything in which I'm interested. This life is nerve-destroying. Talk about the health of the village life! it destroys body and soul.

But he changes his mind after his neighbors nurse him through a grave illness.

Sentimental, likewise, is **"A 'Good Fellow's' Wife,"** with a dénouement that is possible but lucky. Two of Garland's social ideas get into this story: Belle Sanford doubts the rightness of taking money for which one has not worked, and she finds that she cannot fulfill herself by being dependent upon her husband, a theme which Garland was to expand in *Rose of Dutcher's Coolly* (1895). **"Some Village Cronies"** is an affectionate recital of what happens in a small store when men foregather on a cold night, and here Garland drew again upon a familiar setting since he had seen in an uncle's store the horseplay of a village social center. The boarding-house in which the action of **"A Stop-Over at Tyre"** is laid resembles the one in Osage in which Garland stayed while attending the Cedar Valley Seminary; the persons of the story are also taken from real life, but the similarity ends there since actually the girl and the salesman eloped, whereas in the narrative they marry, forsake high ambitions, and settle down to a hollow life in a dull little town.

Besides using the thirty-three *Main-Travelled Roads* stories as vehicles for his insurgency, Garland produced in 1892 three propaganda novels. Two of them, *Jason Edwards* and *A Spoil of Office,* proclaim the injustice of land monopoly; the last, *A Member of the Third House,* shows the attempt of a carrier corporation to corrupt a state legislature. All three, however well-intentioned, are so amateurish in execution that they do not seem to be the work of the same man who wrote **"Up the Coolly"**; the first and third suffer especially in having been hurriedly converted from plays into fiction, with a result that their characters are wooden and their action predictable. In *A Member of the Third House,* by way of illustration, the scene between Brennan and his paramour creaks shamefully, and when in the same novel Garland wrote:

> *"Now* I say, irrevocably, the investigation must go on, and I will testify."
>
> Helene looked from one to the other in dismay and bewilderment. Brennan appeared on the other side of the shrubs, listening to the conversation.

we know we are reading stage directions rather than the deliberately developed narrative of a good novelist. Garland's generosity and enthusiasm simply got the better of his art.

But that enthusiasm, canalized more calmly in the earlier accounts, made him a leader in the revolution against nineteenth-century romanticism. By his brave and veracious use of western materials he had, he thought, set an example for, or at least been the forerunner of William Allen White, Albert Bigelow Paine, Stewart Edward White, Jack London, Emerson Hough, George Ade, Meredith Nicholson, Booth Tarkington, and Rex Beach, and though his opinion may be too inclusive it is easy to believe that he was also an encouragement to Willa Cather, O. E. Rölvaag, Ellen Glasgow, and Ruth Suckow. Moreover, when in 1893 he attended the Literary Congress at the World's Fair he became the most vocal spokesman for the new realism, debating (too warmly, he sometimes felt) with Eugene Field, Alice French, and Mary Hartwell Catherwood, the last of whom after writing realistically of the Northwest between 1878 and 1882 had become a mild apostate. Stories of country life, declared Garland, would be false if they mentioned sunshine and roses and strawberries without speaking of dust and mud and snow. He did not object to beauty in description—Howells had taught him the need of that kind of relief from drabness, and he wrote as he felt of the purple hills, the swell and fall of farm land, the sunsets, the tints of fruits and grains. What he was opposing was the insincere, aristocratic conception of literature which would shut its eyes to the general unhappiness of the common man living in quiet desperation.

Sinclair Lewis on the influence of Garland's early fiction:

I read [*Main-Travelled Roads* and *Rose of Dutcher's Coolly*] as a boy in a prairie village in Minnesota—just such an environment as was described in Mr. Garland's tales. They were vastly exciting to me. I had realized in reading Balzac and Dickens that it was possible to describe French and English common people as one actually saw them. But it had never occurred to me that one might without indecency write of the people of Sauk Centre, Minnesota, as one felt about them. Our fictional tradition, you see, was that all of us in Midwestern villages were altogether noble and happy; that not one of us would exchange the neighborly bliss of living on Main Street for the heathen gaudiness of New York or Paris or Stockholm. But in Mr. Garland's *Main-Travelled Roads* I discovered that there was one man who believed that Midwestern peasants were sometimes bewildered and hungry and vile— and heroic. And, given this vision, I was released; I could write of life as living life.

Sinclair Lewis, "The American Fear of Literature," in The Man From Main Street: Selected Essays and Other Writings, 1904-1950, *edited by Harry E. Maule and Melvin H. Cane, Random House, 1953.*

Bernard I. Duffey (essay date 1953)

SOURCE: "Hamlin Garland's 'Decline' from Realism," in *American Literature,* Vol. XXV, No. 1, March, 1953, pp. 69-74.

[*Duffey is an American educator and critic whose books include* Modern American Literature *(1951). Below, he asserts that for Garland "reform and realism were never in themselves primary literary or intellectual pursuits," and that he largely made use of these ideas in his writing so that he could further his literary success. For a response to Duffey's argument, see the 1954 essay by James D. Koerner.*]

The place of Hamlin Garland in the history of American writing is by this time a familiar and even a conventionalized one. He is pictured as the turn-of-century young Westerner full of an anger against the injustices of Middle-Border life bred out of a combination of a hard upbringing and an early exposure to [Henry] George's single-tax doctrine, who wrote the reformist stories contained in ***Main-Travelled Roads***. Thereafter, for reasons never made entirely clear, he sold his Western, reformist, and realistic birthright to produce the long series of inanities which comprises his later work, redeeming himself for a brief moment only in *A Son of the Middle Border*. Such an account of Gerland's career does have the prima-facie evidence of his published books to recommend it, though at least one significant event therein, the appearance of the sentimentalized *A Little Norsk* in 1892, will not entirely square. But once this first layer of evidence is pierced, a somewhat different pattern of motives is made apparent. The specific period in question would be that falling between 1884 and 1893, the years, respectively, of Garland's arrival in Boston after breaking with his farmboy's life, and of his subsequent move to Chicago to establish himself as a leading light of the upward-aspiring Western metropolis. It was during these nine years that all of Garland's realistic fiction and drama was published, and, though his collection of critical essays, *Crumbling Idols,* appeared in 1894, the essays themselves were largely written between 1891 and 1893. The details of Garland's convictions and practice during his Boston years remain unexplored, however, and it is from such detail that the account of Garland's "decline" may have to be altered.

Garland told the story of his Boston years twice over, with a number of conflicting particulars, in *A Son of the Middle Border* (1917) and in *Roadside Meetings* (1930). The tale is that of a Dakota boy come East, devoted to high though somewhat vague ends—partly elocutionary, partly literary, but mostly undefined. His chief motive was that of escape from the bleak life of Dakota to the attractive New England country and the cultural life of Boston which his grandmother had eulogized frequently and which he had glimpsed briefly on an earlier visit. His great desire was that of escape, though the positive goal was little understood. Garland's departure from the Middle West was far from being that of a determined writer, prophet, or reformer. His life there had been monotonous; it held no promise and seemed to him thoroughly unsat-

isfactory. The impetus to his leaving came when a Methodist minister named Bashford, traveling west from his Portland, Maine, church, learned of Garland's vaguely intellectual and oratorical interests and suggested that Boston was the logical place for him to go. He gave Garland letters of introduction (which later proved valueless), and, with only their prospects, Garland sold his claim and departed for the East. He had less than $150 in his pocket.

His first few months in Boston were spent between a hall bedroom in Boylston Street and the reading room of the public library, where he read widely though without plan or particular end. After some months he met a Doctor Brown, head of the Boston School of Oratory, whom he impressed and from whom he obtained work as a teacher. This connection, through most of his Boston years, remained his chief support. From 1884 until the summer of 1887 his time was largely spent in making acquaintances, turning from one interest to another as opportunities arose. He gave a series of lectures on the art of Edwin Booth by means of which he met Charles Hurd, literary editor of the *Transcript,* for whom he did some reviewing. Through his *Transcript* connection he met Howells, who was kind to him and urged him to write on the West. He wrote a series of Western sketches in a nostalgic mood, one of which was published in the *New American Magazine* as early as 1886, and some short stories patterned after Hawthorne.

In the summer of 1887 he returned to the West for his first visit. In Chicago he stayed briefly with Joseph Kirkland, who, like Howells, urged him to write Western fiction, and while with his parents heard from his mother the story of **"Mrs. Ripley's Trip"** which he wrote up into the earliest of the ***Main-Travelled Roads*** tales. These experiences fired his embryonic hopes of becoming a storyteller of the West. Upon his return to Boston he immediately set to work writing and produced [as he wrote in *Roadside Meetings*] "several short stories and a novelette." It was through this fall and winter of 1887 and 1888 that Garland's emergence as a writer began. His earlier work had been without positive character, done as it was upon sudden inspiration or opportunity. It had not been particularly realistic and indeed, in his earliest reviews for the *Transcript,* he had attacked realism. His campaign now, however, had a definite outline. "My plan of battle was to 'aim high and keep shooting,' " he declared, "and to Gilder of the *Century* and Henry M. Alden of *Harper's* (high judges and advocates of local color in fiction) I sent the first of my almost illegible manuscripts" [*Roadside Meetings*]. The choice of words is important. As Garland made clear in his memoirs, neither Gilder nor Alden had much use for realism, and much less for the "preaching" of Garland's own realism, but Gilder, especially, was at this time favoring "local color" work. It seems likely that Garland made his approach to Gilder as a local colorist and not as a reformer or grim realist though the exact stories he submitted at this time cannot be ascertained. His earliest letter to Gilder contained a caution on this point ". . . I aim to be true to the life I am depicting and to deal not with abnormal phases so much as with representative phases." [In a footnote, Duffey explains that all correspondence referred to between Garland and Gilder is contained in the Richard Watson Gilder Collection of The New York Public Library.] **"Mrs. Ripley's Trip"** was declined by Alden of *Harper's,* though it was accepted by John Foord of *Harper's Weekly.* Gilder, declared Garland, accepted one of these early stories, and if this be **"A Spring Romance,"** published by the *Century* in June of 1891, the first of Garland's stories printed by Gilder, it seems certain that Garland's commitment to a sentimentalized and quaint local color as his best literary hope was made at the outset of his career.

Before the spring of 1890, or during the two years following his return from his first Western visit, Gilder was Garland's chief literary target. Though the latter published some in *Harper's Weekly,* it was the "aristocratic" *Century* which was his great hope. His aim was that of literary success, not reform, and it was to be achieved by playing the main chance. He submitted **"The Test of Elder Pill"** [reprinted as **"Elder Pill, Preacher,"** in *Other Main-Travelled Roads*] to Gilder and upon his advice revised the offensive speech of one of its characters. He wrote and rewrote explicitly for Gilder the saccharine **"Ol' Pap's Flaxen,"** beginning as early as October, 1889, and altered a "maternity scene" in it which caused offense to the editor. He contemplated a series of Western poems with illustrations by Frederick Remington for Gilder's use and assured the editor of the propriety of certain aspects of **"Flaxen's"** plot. He accepted Gilder's rejection of **"A Prairie Heroine,"** written just after his return to Boston from a second visit West in 1889, as being "a little too obviously preaching . . . a falling off from the artistic standpoint" and assured him on this occasion as on others that he would "submit to any reasonable change" in his work to make it acceptable for Gilder's use. In connection with **"A Stop Over at Tyre,"** he read Gilder a lengthy sermon on the dignity and strength of colloquial language, but consented to "soften down the lingual sins of Albert." The instances could be multiplied, but the evidence as to Garland's intentions during this first stage of his career seems sufficiently clear.

His realistic and reformist writing came only upon the opening to him of another chance for literary success and one demanding that type of work. In 1889 B. O. Flower inaugurated the "radical" *Arena* magazine, hospitable to articles on free silver, the Farmer's Alliance, the Populist movement, and other subjects of a Western and reformist sort. It was to Flower that Garland submitted **"A Prairie Heroine"** after the story had been declined by Gilder because of its "preaching" tendencies, though Garland later declared that he "had no thought of sending it to either Gilder or Alden." And this pattern of submitting work to Flower only after it had been declined by Gilder was to be repeated often. **"Elder Pill"** appeared in the *Arena* despite Garland's revision of it for Gilder's taste. *A Member of the Third House,* in its dramatic form, was offered first to Gilder, as was **"Up the Cooly,"** the first story in *Main-Travelled Roads*. On one occasion Garland tried to

squeeze Gilder by informing him that a story had gone to the *Arena* which would have gone to the *Century*, "only you have two or three of my stories now." *Jason Edwards,* whether in its narrative or dramatic form is unclear, was sent to Gilder with a hope so fervent that Garland could describe himself as "praying like a dervish" that Gilder might give Garland "a chance to make his story suitable for your use." The drama, however, appeared in the *Arena* in July of 1890. Most telling, perhaps, was Garland's assurance to Gilder of his right intentions, written probably in early 1890 during the first period of his radical contributions to the *Arena* and perhaps therefore in reassurance: "the single-tax with me means International copyright, the Sermon on the Mount, and vacations for everybody."

So long as the *Arena* remained useful to him Garland continued to supply it with the kind of reform writing which Flower valued. His contributions included numerous stories, essays, and poems, and one full-length play. In 1891 and again in 1892 Garland toured the country at Flower's expense gathering material for his *Arena* contributions and laying the groundwork for his later career. But as his success with the old-line magazines waxed, his attachment to the *Arena,* reform, and realism waned, and after 1895 he had little to do with the *Arena* though he was careful to keep up his connections with *Harper's* and the *Century* despite his move to Chicago.

A survey of Garland's magazine publication through 1895 makes apparent the extent to which his writing was shaped by the vagaries of editorial taste. The great bulk of his work, two novels, five short stories, and eleven articles appeared in the *Arena,* and, with the exception of **"Under the Lion's Paw,"** which was taken by Foord of *Harper's Weekly,* the *Arena* contributions include all of Garland's writing that may be classified as reformist or realistic beyond the limits of local color. Gilder took **"A Spring Romance"** and **"Ol' Pap's Flaxen"** for the *Century*. Alden published **"Evangel in Cyrene"** and **"God's Ravens."** Three stories in addition to **"Under the Lion's Paw"** were taken by *Harper's Weekly*. A scattering of articles appeared in the *Forum,* the *Atlantic,* and the *New England Magazine*. These sedulously avoided the reforming note, though the *Forum* articles were concerned with the West as a subject for fiction.

It might be too much to say that Garland's realistic work came into being entirely because of the editorial hospitality of Benjamin Flower, though such a claim would not be far wide of the mark. But one may, with justice, argue that for Hamlin Garland reform and realism were never in themselves primary literary or intellectual pursuits. They were accessory for a time to his campaign for intellectual and literary success. To the extent that they served his end, he used them; but he seemed from the beginning never to hesitate over any necessary compromises. His trade was learned at the fountainhead of the Eastern genteel tradition, and it was from that tradition, with occasional lapses in favor of Flower, Howells, Kirkland, or other sufficiently useful persons, that he drew his identity and his rewards.

Thomas A. Bledsoe (essay date 1953)

SOURCE: An introduction to *Main-Travelled Roads* by Hamlin Garland, edited by Thomas A. Bledsoe, Rinehart & Co., 1954, pp. ix-xl.

[*Bledsoe is an American author, editor, and educator. In this excerpt, he comments on Garland's genesis as a fiction writer and his ultimate deterioration, but the critic upholds the artistic achievement of* Main-Travelled Roads, *maintaining that Garland "produced a handful of minor masterpieces" in his career.*]

1

It would be easy to see in Hamlin Garland one of the minor tragedies of American literature. In the contrast between the bitter realism of *Main-Travelled Roads* and the complacent romanticizing of *They of the High Trails,* its later counterpart, there is a sense of a good man gone wrong that has the overtones of an American tragedy. Garland's rebellion was so intense and his conformity so ingenuous that one cannot help speculating on what might have happened had he not lost, as Howells wrote to Henry Fuller in 1904, the "simplicity of his ideal, such as it was when he had *Main-Travelled Roads* under his feet, and throbbed with his fine angry sympathy for 'the familiar and the low.'"

But it is idle to wonder. Garland reflects the large American tragedy of success and the deeper psychological tragedy of emotional conviction without intellectual stays; his literary defections are the inevitable result of his background and his character. He was, as H. L. Mencken once termed him, a stranger on Parnassus. A more fruitful attitude than regret for his decline is gratitude for the handful of minor masterpieces that were the by-product of his essentially nonliterary and highly moral indignation.

Hamlin Garland was born in West Salem, Wisconsin, in 1860. His father, Richard Garland, was a Maine man with an itch for the frontier that carried him to Wisconsin, to Iowa, and to Dakota, from which last outpost Hamlin, in 1884, deserted the prairie, mortgaging for two hundred dollars a homestead whose freezing nights "permanently chilled [his] enthusiasm for pioneering the plain." With this meager capital, young Garland set out for Boston, in the hope of training at Harvard for his chosen career of teaching. The Harvard lectures, however, were not open to a friendless young westerner with no further academic background than the amenities of the Osage, Iowa, Seminary, and he turned perforce to the Boston Public Library. This seemed to him a tragic deprivation: some of the most moving chapters of *A Son of the Middle Border,* his autobiographical account of the early years, record the loneliness and real heroism of his struggle. Friendless and half starving, he spent his days in the library and his nights "making detailed studies of the habits of the cockroaches" in his eight by ten room. Actually the desperate urgency of this winter was the best thing that could have

happened to him; these bleak days were the catalyst for the brief years when he was vital and alive.

He grew steadily paler, thinner, and shabbier; but he grew also in wisdom, learning things neither Harvard nor the prairies would have taught him. From the limiting shore of an education circumscribed by the Osage Seminary and by desultory reading in Shakespeare, Milton, Taine, and Henry George, he plunged into the flood waters of contemporary intellectual controversy:

> I read both day and night, grappling with Darwin, Spencer, Fiske, Helmholtz, and Haeckel—all the masters of evolution whose books I had not hitherto been able to open. . . . Among other proscribed books I read Whitman's *Leaves of Grass,* and without doubt that volume changed the world for me as it did for many others. . . . The spiritual significance of America was let loose on me. . . . Under the influence of Spencer I traced a parallel development of the Arts and found a measure of scientific peace. Under the inspiration of Whitman I pondered the significance of democracy and caught some part of its spiritual import. With Henry George as guide I discovered the main cause of poverty and suffering in the world.

It was a new world Hamlin Garland had discovered. It had no relation as yet to the prairie world he had left behind him; paradoxically, it was very much a part of the urban life of which he felt so little a part. It was the world of *avant-garde* radicalism, and Garland, grinding away in the gloomy reading room of the public library, became a working member of a group of whose existence he was as yet hardly aware—the radical intellectuals, the earnest young men and women with advanced views on art and society. That he himself was no intellectual, then or ever that all he read was only half-assimilated, was of no consequence. He had a fearsome positiveness, an absolute certainty of belief in all his views, no matter how recently won, no matter how soon to be lost. In the space of a winter he became an evolutionist, a Whitmanesque democrat, a single taxer, a disciple of the new realism. Alone and friendless as he still was, depending for recreation on free lectures at the Young Men's Union and rare trips to the theater where, from the peanut gallery, he watched his idol Edwin Booth, he had nonetheless arrived. It needed only circumstance—and this was soon to come—to catapult him into the center of Boston radicalism.

What he was, after the intensity of these labors, Garland himself never really understood; but it is important that we see him, emerging stooped and hungry from the threshold of the Public Library, with success in Boston at hand. Once, speculating about the warmth with which Boston intellectuals received him, Garland surmised that "perhaps they were surprised at finding so much intelligence in a man from the Plains." A good deal of his charm was precisely his anomalous acquaintance with the current intellectual patter: this gawky westerner, with his awkward manners and rusty suit, was to be the season's literary curiosity. But the urgent honesty that kept him at his chores in the library combined with his natural friendliness to delight as well as startle his sophisticated new acquaintances; both his sincerity and his ingenuousness impressed them. He lectured with almost equal success on Edwin Booth, about whom he knew a good deal, and Victor Hugo, the Modern German Novel, and The Modern American Novel, about all of which, in varying degrees, he knew considerably less. His audiences considered him a rough diamond and were entranced by his vigor.

The sum of these paradoxes, is, in embryo, the author of **Main-Travelled Roads**. He had not thus far even thought of being a creative writer; his literary intentions were to write essays and perhaps a history of American literature. Nor, more importantly, despite his reading of Henry George, had the fundamental catalytic urge of moral indignation at the plight of the border people as yet overwhelmed him. But this is our man—ingenuous, half-educated, fearsomely earnest, spiritually, despite his apprenticeship to Herbert Spencer, one of Kingsley's muscular Christians. As a commentator in the *Literary World* [No. 27 (February 22, 1896)] subsequently described him:

> We may mention, as a matter of curiosity, considering what some periods of Mr. Garland's life have been, that he uses neither tobacco or liquor in any form, and has never had any taste for the sort of life that too commonly, though not always, goes with cigars and beer.

In short, a moralist. In the overwhelming moral intensity of this lonely frequenter of the Boston Public Library we shall find a key to the whole man and a necessary ingredient of his best writing. It was exactly this earnestness that gave him his start in intellectual Boston.

2

One night, during one of the lectures at the Young Men's Union, he was so impressed by the speaker, Dr. Moses True Brown, that he ventured to congratulate him after the program. The form of his approval—acquaintance with several quotations from Darwin's *Expression of the Emotions*—so impressed Brown that he gave Garland a place first as a free student and subsequently as Instructor in Literature in his Boston School of Oratory. Success followed quickly. Mrs. Payne, a literary resident of Hyde Park, sponsored a series of lectures that netted him ninety dollars and, more important, the backing of Charles Hurd, the influential literary editor of the *Transcript*. He wrote a sketch, "The Western Corn Husking," which "included the mud and cold of the landscape as well as its bloom and charm," and sold it to the *New American Magazine*. His first published story, **"Ten Years Dead,"** which combined the influence of Hawthorne with a foreshadowing of his own midwestern realism, appeared in *Every Other Saturday* in 1885. When he revisited Dakota in 1887 he could pass as a successful Professor of Literature and a man who had dabbled in writing.

It is easy to let Garland speak for himself. For one who has described himself [in a letter to the author—Bledsoe] as a "modest old fellow," he has had a remarkable pen-

chant for self-revelation: two series of autobiographies occupied him during the last twenty-five years of his life. Certainly it would be hard to find a more moving description of his 1887 trip, and of a subsequent one in 1889 when his mother suffered a stroke, than his own in *A Son of the Middle Border*:

> All that day I had studied the land. . . . The lack of color, of charm in the lives of the people anguished me. I wondered why I had never before noticed the futility of woman's life on the farm. I asked myself, "Why have these stern facts never been put into our literature as they have been used in Russia and England? Why has this land no story tellers like those who have made Massachusetts and New England illustrious? . . .

> I perceived the town from the triple viewpoint of a former resident, a man from the city, and a reformer, and every minutest detail of dress, tone, and gesture revealed new meaning for me. Fancher and Gammon were feebler certainly, and a little more querulous with age, and their faded beards and rough hands gave pathetic evidence of the hard wear of wind and toil. At the moment nothing glozed over the essential tragic futility of their existence. . . .

> Obscurely forming in my mind were two great literary concepts—that truth was a higher quality than beauty, and that to spread the reign of justice should everywhere be the design of the artist. The merely beautiful in art seemed petty, and success at the cost of the happiness of others a monstrous egotism. In the spirit of these ideals I returned to my small attic room in Jamaica Plain and set to work to put my new conceptions into some sort of literary form. . . .

> I began to write, composing in the glow of a flaming conviction. With a delightful (and deceptive) sense of power, I graved with a heavy hand, as if upon brazen tablets, picture after picture of the plain. . . . "Give us charming love stories," pleaded the editors. "No, we've had enough of lies," I replied. "Other writers are telling the truth about the city . . . and it appears to me that the time has come to tell the truth about the barn yard's daily grind. . . . For me the mud and the sweat and the dust exist. They still form a large part of life on the farm, and I intend that they shall go into my stories in their proper proportions. . . ."

> I resumed my writing in a mood of bitter resentment, with full intention of telling the truth about western farm life, irrespective of the land-boomer or the politicians.

This is the Garland of **Main-Travelled Roads**. The moral indignation these visits aroused galvanized him into writing, in quick succession, the stories of this volume; significantly, the first of them, **"Mrs. Ripley's Trip,"** was begun at the homestead in Dakota and based on a story told him by his mother. Shortly after his return to Boston, his resentment was further channelized. At a meeting of the Anti-Poverty League he volunteered as a speaker; a review of his harangue by his friend Chamberlain, the Listener of the *Transcript,* placed him "with one leap . . . [in] the limelight of conservative Boston's disapproval." He was now both a reformer and a writer; by 1888, when **"Mrs. Ripley's Trip"** appeared in *Harper's Weekly,* he had become an active propagandist for the single tax.

As a writer and an active campaigner, Garland became the literary spokesman for the discontented farmers of the Middle Border, whose bitterness was epitomized in the Populist revolt of the nineties. He met the prophet of San Francisco, Henry George, creator of the single tax, and became his personal as well as literary disciple; he was a protégé of B. O. Flower, the radical editor of the *Arena,* who suggested and published *Main-Travelled Roads.* In 1891, on a commission from the *Arena,* he toured the rebellious West and completed his Populist novel, *A Spoil of Office;* in the fall of this year he became a campaign speaker for the Peoples' Party of Iowa. For one who in 1885 had been friendless and half starving, the range of his acquaintants half a dozen years later among the social and intellectual radicals of the day is astonishing. In his travels for the *Arena* he met most of the Populist leaders, including such spectacular characters as Mary Ellen ("raise more hell and less corn") Lease, on whom the character of Ida Wilbur in *A Spoil of Office* is partly based; there is hardly a writer of social fiction in the period whom he did not know. William Dean Howells, the most eminent of them all, became his close friend and adviser; in his efforts to convert Howells to the single tax he was the link between Howells and Henry George. Our lonely frequenter of the Boston Public Library had become a public figure, a notorious realist and radical.

It is important, however, to remember the private motivations of this public man. Of no other prominent radical of the time can it be said that his rebellion was finally of so personal a character. Garland had a large gift for translating his private emotions into public abstractions; he could not help interpreting his bitterness over his mother's illness and poverty as a concern for universal Truth and Justice. It was not that he was dishonest; he simply never understood that he was rationalizing. Inevitably, five years later, when his mother was comfortably resettled in Wisconsin, when he had become established, moderately well-off, and accustomed to comfort and respectability, he must feel that not himself but the times had changed, and that in the western romances he had begun to write he was continuing the realism and regionalism of his earlier work.

The fact is that Garland's convictions, for all their facade of public proclamation, were always personal and emotional; our comparison of his theory and practice will suggest how little he understood the things he felt. Behind the successful reformer and realist stands the young man we saw on the steps of the Library, the ingenuous, half-educated moralist. Fundamentally he has changed remarkably little. His new sophistication is more apparent than real; his dedication to writing and the earnestness with which he advanced his theories of veritism (his term for realism) and local color are only a transmutation of his earlier vague determination to be a Professor and an essayist; and his characteristic moral fervor has now found a definite channel—indignation at the plight of the farmer, at the hardships he found his family and friends enduring.

It was the focusing of his resentment that was crucial for the author of *Main-Travelled Roads.* This fact Garland himself bitterly denied. He was at great pains to insist that his "reform notions were subordinate to . . . [his] desire to take honors as a novelist." It is significant that this misconception was not entirely window dressing for his later conservatism; in the years of his vitality his relations with two prominent editors indicate that to a considerable degree he believed it even then.

The editor who really liked Garland's most original work was B. O. Flower, who supported and publicized him indefatigably. But it was Richard Watson Gilder, the eminent and polite editor of the *Century,* whose praise, then and later, Garland really valued, despite the fact that the border stories Gilder printed were second-rate, while Flower bought his best work. When, for example, Garland submitted **"A Prairie Heroine"** to the *Arena,* Flower accepted it with this stipulation:

> I note that you have cut out certain paragraphs of description with the fear, no doubt, that the editor would object to them. I hope you will restore the manuscript to its original form and return it. When I ask a man to write for me, I want him to utter his mind with perfect freedom.

In contrast, **"A Girl of Modern Tyre,"** [**"A Stop-Over at Tyre"**] a trite romance whose virtue in book form is a bleak ending in which an ill-considered marriage ruins a man's career, was printed by Gilder with the addition of the following paragraph:

> Albert and Maud still live in the homestead in Tyre. In the five years that have elapsed since that party with Hartly he has been a hard worker as principal of the village school. His friends say he ought to be in a larger field of labor, and he has sweet dreams of doing something in the great splendid world, which he realizes at times is sweeping by him; but three little mouths have come into the world demanding bread, and three pairs of childish eyes hold him prisoner, though a willing one.

In these pathetic clichés, even in the days of his bitterest realism, his future is foreshadowed. For Garland they were the only possible result of Gilder's warning "not to leave beauty out of the picture"; when Howells, more perceptive but still misunderstanding the nature of Garland's talent, cautioned him not to forget "the rose," he was pointing the same way. Without moral indignation, banality was the only place Hamlin Garland could go.

3

The fact is that Garland took in not only himself but his most perceptive contemporaries; of all his intimates, only Henry Fuller, I think, really understood him. Garland's violent theories of regionalism and veritism, which so delighted Howells and horrified more conventional critics, had little to do with the real power of his best writing. His critical preachments created a sensation that, as far as his own work was concerned, was a fraud.

But the tumult was tremendous. Even after Garland's own retreat into romance, one critic replied to his "Sanity in Fiction" [in *North American Review* No. 176 (March 1903)], an article largely devoted to Howells, under the title "Insanity in Criticism" [James E. Rooth, Jr., in *Critic* No. 43 (August 1903)]. In the *Atlantic Monthly* [December 1895] a critic discussing *Crumbling Idols,* which was published in Chicago in 1894 by the enterprising new firm of Stone and Kimball, suggested that it "should have had for a cover design a dynamite bomb," instead of the peaceful wheat sheaf with which the art-minded publishers had decorated it. Edward Everett Hale, Jr., reviewing the same book [in *Dial* No. 17 (July 1, 1894)], remarked that Garland "is not persuasive; he is bellicose, obstreperous, blatant. Nobody could possibly agree with him, whatever he said." That this book, a turgid combination of Whitman, realism, and regionalism, should arouse such a furor (Walter Page, editor of the *Forum,* estimated that over a thousand editorials were written on its main thesis) is a tribute both to Garland's vigor and to the dissociation he was able to create between his theory and his practice.

Only when moved by violent moral indignation could Hamlin Garland discard the romantic clichés his fundamentally conventional cast of mind made natural for him. When he was indignant he suddenly became a man with an honest literary talent: he forgot formulas and plunged directly into what he had to say.

—*Thomas A. Bledsoe*

When Howells, in 1910, after Garland's escape into themes which were, by his own description, "happily quite outside the controversial belt," begged him to "be true to the dream of thy youth—the dream of an absolute and unsparing veritism," he was expressing in fundamentally irrelevant terms his regret at the decay of Garland's writing. Even the dreariest of Garland's later romances have a regional and veritist purpose: **"Marshall's Capture,"** perhaps the low point of the very low level of his later fiction, was based on a "true story," just as was **"Mrs. Ripley's Trip."**

The truth is that the indignant conservatives who attacked *Main-Travelled Roads* as a polemic were right. It is the

quality of indignation that gives these stories their power. This is not to say that the stories are tracts, but that this quality is essential to Garland's curious creative process. Only when moved by violent moral indignation could Hamlin Garland discard the romantic clichés his fundamentally conventional cast of mind made natural for him. When he was indignant he suddenly became a man with an honest literary talent: he forgot formulas and plunged directly into what he had to say. It follows that his talent was for short stories and not for novels, since novels demand intellectual development as well as emotional intensity, and, for the same reason, for stories of situation rather than plot.

These assumptions exactly describe the stories of *Main-Travelled Roads*. They are stories of situation, inspired by moral indignation, concerned with typical situations familiar to the author. These are the invariable elements of Garland's best work; lacking them, it becomes banal. Local color, even an intense familiarity with his subject matter, is not enough; this is evidenced by the mediocre Border stories of the other collections, or by a story like **"Old Sid's Christmas"** (which appeared in *Harper's Weekly* in 1889, three months after the publication of **"Under the Lion's Paw"** in the same magazine), which is sentimental and nostalgic and was too bad even for Garland to reprint. These stories, none of which displays any resentment, are not only dull but artistically crude.

Conversely, in a later period, when the general level of his work had become complacent, noncontroversial, and utterly dreary, he became momentarily aroused over the plight of the American Indians and wrote about them a series of stories very nearly equal to his best work. He knew no more about the Indians than the cowboys and mountain people about whom he was then romanticizing so fatuously (he knew them all from personal experience, and fairly well), but the injustice of their treatment at the hands of the white man galvanized him momentarily into the peculiar tensions of his art. A story like "Outlaw" [later published as **"The Story of Howling Wolf"**] would seem perfectly characteristic to a reader who knew Garland only from the six original stories of *Main-Travelled Roads*; **"Marshall's Capture,"** which appeared in the same magazine eighteen months after "Outlaw," would seem the work of another man.

Likewise, a concern for the average man (only the typical provides a basis for a generalized moral) characterizes only his best work. The most obvious paradox in his later romances is his effort to imbue these unique adventures with a general and "sociologic" (one of his favorite words) significance. Nor is moral indignation alone sufficient: the querulous and ignorant Jeremiads of the later autobiographies are the dull complaints of a provincial moralist in a world he never made and wants no part of.

4

The first edition of *Main-Travelled Roads* . . . was published by the Arena Publishing Company in 1891 and contained six stories. Four of these had appeared in *Harper's Weekly* and the *Arena;* two others, **"Up the Coulé"** and **"A Branch Road,"** appeared here for the first time. The foreword and dedication characterize the spirit of the book; it was indeed, as Garland later described it, a volume with a "message of acrid accusation." Time has not diminished the power of this indictment; these stories remain a minor classic of American Fiction. Their portrayal of man's struggles against the forces of nature and an unjust society is as moving today as when **Main-Travelled Roads** aroused a furious clamor against its brutalization of what editors liked to regard as the noblest of vocations, tilling the soil of the American prairie.

Perhaps the word which best describes the spirit which informs these stories is *guilt.* For Garland it was guilt of a very personal kind, guilt over the plight of his family, and especially of his mother. Like many another nineteenth-century moralist who survived to view with horror the twentieth century's concern with sex and frustration, he was beset by complexes which are the commonplaces of the psychiatrist's couch. Chief among these was the violence of his affection for his mother and the depth of the sense of guilt which leaving or neglecting her caused him. In **Main-Travelled Roads** this appears most directly in the most powerful and in a sense most autobiographical of the stories, **"Up the Coulé."** Compare Howard's feeling on first seeing the little town again with Garland's on seeing Fancher and Gammon; consider Howard's—and Garland's—emotions on seeing his mother: "This was his mother—the woman who bore him, the being who had taken her life in her hand for him; and he, in his excited and pleasurable life, had neglected her!"

It appears again, transmuted, in Will Hannan's reparation to Agnes, in **"A Branch Road,"** where Garland's guilt over the plight of a prairie mother leads him, for one of the very few times in all his fiction, to endorse breaking the moral code, as Will carries Agnes into a materially improved but illicit future. It is evident in **"The Return of a Private"**—the private is Garland's father—where the mother occupies an equal share of a stage that might this once have been the father's, in Mrs. Ripley's and Mrs. Haskin's hardships, in the drudgeries which Julia Peterson not only has grown up with but is moving toward in her escape with Rob.

To be aware of this is to be reminded of the private and personal character of Garland's stories of the average man; it also helps us to identify the importance of accurate reporting in them. Garland is by no means simply a reporter, but in all his best work there is an unmistakable sense of authenticity.

The reader of these border stories who is familiar with the details of Garland's life is constantly discovering incidents and people taken directly from the author's experience, but no such biographical acquaintance is needed to validate the reality of these pictures. The home from which Will rescues Agnes in **"A Branch Road,"** the slop and mud of the farmyard or the details of the party in **"Up the Coulé,"** the driving weariness of the plowing in **"Among the Corn-Rows"**: in such characteristic episodes we do not need to be convinced that Garland has told us what midwestern farm life in the eighties was really like. We know that this is how it was, and share the author's bitterness at the emptiness and drudgery of these lives.

We share, too, his sense of the beauty of the Dakota prairies, of the definite hills and abrupt coulés of Wisconsin, of the good fellowship and human decency of Stephen Council and Old Widder Gray. We share, that is, his sense of the basic paradox which animates each of these stories and around which centers the indignation which enabled him to project them: the conflict between Good—man's better nature, the simple beauties of the land—and Evil, the injustice of society, the grasping selfishness that speculation fosters, the bitterness of the struggle with nature which injustice necessitates. In all these stories the large drama between Good and Evil—both with capital letters—is played out.

This struggle is not, to be sure, without its ambivalences. In part Garland belongs to an old and honored tradition; in the long controversy over nature and society he is philosophically in the primitivists' camp. It was this traditional distrust of urban society that Henry Fuller noted in "The Downfall of Abner Joyce," a satire on Garland to which we will return: "Abner, on his return to the town, found its unpleasant precincts more crowded than ever with matters of doubtful propriety." This attitude appears frequently in Garland's own work; in the city portion of *Jason Edwards,* for example, where all the premises have an effluvium of evil; in a verse like this one from *Boy Life on the Prairie:*

> With heart grown weary of the heat
> And hungry for the breath
> Of field and farm, with eager feet
> I trod the pavement dry as death
> Through city streets where crime is born
> And sudden—lo, a ridge of corn!

Garland knew the rigors of farm life too well, however, to buy this romantic notion whole hog, and he is at constant pains to show that nature is a hard taskmaster. All the stories in [**Main-Travelled Roads**] develop this hardship at one point or another, and such treatments, along with his announced intention to give the mud and sweat and dust of farm life their due place in literature, added to the clamor **Main-Travelled Roads** produced and to his subsequent reputation as a realistic critic of the rigors of prairie existence. That he was the latter should not, however, blind us to the fact that nature for Garland was beneficent as well as demanding. At times in his stories her arbitrary cataclysms are the final cause of human disaster: in **"Under the Lion's Paw"** it is four years of grasshoppers that drive Haskins penniless out of Kansas; in *Jason Edwards* it is a hailstorm that leads to Jason's ruin and death. But such catastrophes are characteristically the final blows that bring down an already ruined structure. Both Haskins and Edwards are had by the land speculators—Haskins, driven on to Kansas in the first place by the high price of unoccupied land, comes back to be trapped by Butler; Edwards, having left the city for the free West, is already ruined by the speculators when a heart attack gives him release.

In all of these stories, that is, those who willingly traffic in inhumanity are the villains, and in all of them the conflict between Justice and Injustice is displayed, either on stage or in the wings. Sometimes, as in **"A Branch-Road,"** it is at first peripheral, the outcome of an ordinary lover's quarrel; sometimes, as in **"Under the Lion's Paw,"** the conflict is a dramatized sermon on Henry George's single tax and the evils of unearned increment; sometimes, as in **"Up the Coulé,"** the depth of Garland's own guilt and the final hopelessness of the average western farmer unite in a bitter indictment. But always Garland reflects a romantic moralism which was much a part of his times and much at odds with the scientific realism he thought he believed in. It is also much at odds with the spirit which, in Crane, in Norris, in Dreiser, was to animate his younger contemporaries.

Because of this it is important to realize that Garland was no naturalist, nor even one of the writers of the nineties who most nearly practiced the formula of naturalism. A capsule definition of naturalism is difficult—if for no other reason than because naturalism existed as much by the violation of its precepts as the practice of them—but a basic tenet was certainly a belief in determinism, a conviction of the importance of forces rather than individuals, a certainty that individual moral responsibility was not important because in the end individuals were not important.

Hamlin Garland's people provide an interesting variant on this theme. He was well schooled in the importance of the social machine and the hopelessness of individuals caught in its meshes. But he never wrote without a sense of individual responsibility. Butler is no less responsible and no less personally evil because he profits by an iniquitous social scheme; Grant McLane's tragedy is his own moral responsibility as much as Howard's: it is not merely that he has been trapped by circumstance but that, as Laura cries out, he has accepted it. It is against the backdrop of the American Dream of the right and responsibility of every man to be free, to succeed, that Garland's tragedies display themselves. A belief in this dream, and an indignation against whatever frustrates it, informs his writing as it does not that of his naturalistic contemporaries. For all the hopelessness of some of these stories, Hamlin Garland's world, unlike Stephen Crane's, for example, remains an optimistic one. For Crane the universe was indifferent, which for practical purposes meant hostile; for Garland, in spite of the muck and sweat of the farmyard, the universe was friendly if only man would make it so. Thus Crane's Maggie goes down alone to inevitable death; Garland's Agnes Dingman is led by Will into new life.

And so Garland wrote these indignant—and nostalgic—stories of the middle border; and five years later, when his mother had been safely returned to Wisconsin and he no longer had intense personal reminders that society was still making it hard for the good and poor man, he moved further west and began to write heroic romances about the cowboy and the highlander, epic figures in the westward expansion of the American Dream.

Of all the stories in *Main-Travelled Roads,* **"Among the Corn-Rows"** perhaps most delicately illustrates the tensions of Garland's moral universe. It is significant that this story has frequently been reprinted without the first section, the account of Rob's life on the Dakota prairie that gives it its framework. Without this preface the story seems a prairie idyll, but Garland, for all his sense of the beauty and heroism of the country, could not write it simply as that. What excited his creativeness was the conflict between beauty and the social system which would inevitably warp the innocent hopes of Julia's escape into the frustrations of Mrs. Ripley's trip. This insight is adumbrated through Rob's life in Dakota, where the beauty of the landscape and the friendliness of the homesteaders cannot conceal the loneliness and drudgery for which a prairie wife is destined, and through the tyranny of Julia's father, a tyranny which reflects a society in which inhumanity is justified as a means of survival. The beauty and hope are there—but in the America of the eighties, Hamlin Garland tells us, they are being frustrated by a society which denies the fulfillment which is Rob's and Julia's by right.

5

The question with which Garland's critics have chiefly concerned themselves is the explanation of his change from the realism of *Main-Travelled Roads* and *Jason Edwards* to the conventional romanticizing of such later novels as *Hesper* and *The Captain of the Gray-Horse Troop.* Carl Van Doren, making the first serious attack on this problem in the *Nation* in 1921 [No. 113 (Nov. 23)], viewed this long flirtation with romance as the result of Garland's being misled by the false light of local color, and saw in *A Son of the Middle Border* and *A Daughter of the Middle Border* a return to the frontier in which "memory, parent of art, has at once sweetened and enlarged the scene." Although the querulous trend of Garland's subsequent autobiographies has since made it impossible to view this period, as Van Doren then could, as his greatest, the notion that *A Son of the Middle Border* is his best work has remained a popular one.

A contrast between *A Son of the Middle Border* and *Main-Travelled Roads* is fruitful. In my own view the autobiography is inferior to the stories, being both more uneven and less original, but such an evaluative comparison of works in disparate forms is of less value than the insights these separate outgrowths of the same period in the author's life can give into the qualities of his work.

A Son of the Middle Border is in a sense the reverse of the coin. Its power derives from its reconsideration of the material which gave rise to the stories and from its partial recapture of the mood in which they were created. It has the wider range of tone to be expected from a book which is the retrospect of later years: it is sometimes nostalgic ("Oh those blessed days, those entrancing nights! How fine they were then, and how mellow they are now!"); sometimes indignant ("Fling away my convictions! It were as easy to do that as to cast out my bones."); sometimes apologetic ("Alas! Each day made me more and more the dissenter." "I do not defend this mood, I merely report it.") It is weakest in the opening nostalgic account of his early childhood and the closing sentimental story of the trip that meant family reunion. In the long intervening section, which carries him from the hardships of a farm boyhood to the climax of his rebellion, it recaptures vicariously a good deal of the power of the days of his vitality; it is one of the genuinely significant American autobiographies, and an essential book for anyone who wishes to understand the time. But it never approaches the intensity of *Main-Travelled Roads*.

This fact has been denied. H. L. Mencken, [in *Prejudices: First Series,* 1919], for example, who properly pegged Garland as a Puritan and a moralist (seduced into literature under false pretenses, was Mencken's explanation), considered *A Son of the Middle Border* his best book because it was a significant, naive record of fact, though lacking in beauty. *Main-Travelled Roads* he dismissed as a tract; we call these stories art, he maintained, only because American criticism always mistakes a poignant document for art. In this opinion Mencken has had considerable, if less violent, company. The notion that Garland is only a reporter, that these stories are valuable chiefly as documents, has had wide currency.

The trouble with this explanation is, as they used to say on the middle border, that it won't wash. When Henry James received Garland pleasantly on a visit to England and spoke well of his work, James was recognizing the qualities Mencken denied: not merely beauty—and there is a good deal of beauty—but art. It is impossible to examine any of these stories carefully without coming away impressed with the very considerable literary skill that is operating in them.

Part of this, it is true, is the result of Garland's native gift for reportage. He seems, for one thing, to have had almost total recall of the most minute particulars of prairie life. In his description of the threshing and the dinner in **"A Branch Road,"** of the party in **"Up the Coulé,"** the sense of authentic detail is unmistakable. He also had a well nigh perfect ear for the patterns of border speech, a talent that is evidenced on every page. But these abilities, or something like them, are a part of the equipment of any writer of consequence; what matters is that Garland had the skill to select from and order these materials in an artistically effective way.

I have already noted that Garland was a master of situation rather than of plot. He had also, however, a genuine talent for ordering his situations to produce a cumulative result, and for developing each of them in a thoroughly convincing way. **"The Return of a Private"** is one of the simplest illustrations of this. It is divided into three major scenes: the veterans' return to La Crosse, the wife's loneliness and the dinner at Widder Gray's, and the reunion. These episodes are as sharply separated as the scenes of a play, and each of them is developed in the most careful detail. In the first the hardship and aloneness, the companionship and mutual consideration of men returning from war is sharply etched; the second is a marvelously convincing picture of a Sunday dinner in the West; the third moves surely from the uncertainty of first meeting to the fulfillment of being at last at home. But none of these scenes is static: they build cumulatively on each other and are cumulatively developed within themselves. We pick up the father as a returning fragment of a dispersed army and leave him bidding a temporary goodbye to his neighbors in his own country; we see the wife in her loneliness and desertion and follow her into a companionship which is a foretaste of her life after her husband's return: the reunion begins in the most painful strangeness and ends in ecstatic security.

This is a great deal more than reporting; it is narrative art of a rather high order, built on a careful and complex (even in one of the most simply developed of the stories) arrangement which moves steadily toward the resolution. And this order always directly serves the theme; Garland makes full use of his intimate knowledge of midwestern life, but he never lets it get the better of him. Unlike the reporter, he uses detail not merely to make what *happened* vivid, but to flesh out a theme—the germ which moral indignation planted—by incidents which may or may not have happened but undeniably could have. Unlike the tract writer, he is not concerned simply with the moral; he develops his idea with the most credible realistic detail, detail so rich it has a life and significance of its own. And so, in **"The Return of a Private,"** he uses an incident from his own family history to protest the lot of the average western farmer, in a story which remains an artistically effective fiction.

The same sort of balance between inner theme and external reality is to be found in his characters. Were he either a reporter or a preacher, we could expect his people to be types. Since he is something of both, as well as something more—an artist—they are at once individual and typical. The Ripleys represent countless elderly farm couples, but at the same time they are individuals in their own right: the skill with which Garland portrays their hostility and love, their indifference and sympathy, the whole ambivalence of their long intimacy, can only be described as art. Similarly, Grant McLane is both a symbol and a memorable character; Haskins is a classic victim of the evils the single tax would remedy, and at the same time a man whom the chance sight of his daughter stays in the act of murder.

How Garland came by this skill—these, his best stories, are almost the first thing he ever wrote—remains a mystery. His exercise of it requires the presence of a deeply felt theme, always a theme of protest; somehow this intensity prompts him to enter chronology at the psychologically correct moment, to move surely through a skil-

To Whom it May Concern:

This book was mainly written in Boston during the winter of 1887–8. It is a faithful statement of my conception of the working farmer's life at that time. It sprang from my own experiences as the son of a prairie farmer. I was not a boarder—I was a "full hand" from my thirteenth to my twenty-first year.—Times have changed the conditions here so often, but the working farmer is still a lonely figure on the border.

Hamlin Garland

Chicago.
Dec. 1915.

This account of the creation of Main-Travelled Roads *was written by Garland in 1917, twenty-six years after the book's initial publication.*

fully developed sequence of themes, and to end when resolution has been achieved. He utilizes surprisingly subtle effects. Consider the frame of **"Under the Lion's Paw,"** whose theme is the evils of unearned increment, a sermon on the single tax. The story opens with "the last of autumn and the first day of winter coming together," in a magnificent picture of late fall plowing. Haskins appears in the dark and snow and mud; he enters the warmth and light of the farm kitchen—a step into the security Council's kindness and generosity are to bring him. It ends on a well-stocked farm in the brightness of an autumn afternoon, with only the fall plowing remaining before the Haskins are to take the trip home (a ritual act for the frontiersman) they have earned. We leave Haskins, triumphant over nature which had seemed so hostile just three years before, but defeated by the evil Butler represents, "seated dumbly on the sunny pile of sheaves, his head sunk into his hands." In this identity of seasons, in the contrast of barrenness and plenty, of darkness and light, an artistry is at work which subtly reinforces the theme—that not nature but man's iniquity is the primal evil.

One other aspect of Garland's art deserves mention—his attempt to make *Main-Travelled Roads* a coherent and unified book, not simply a collection of related stories. To this end he utilized the dedication, the opening epigraph, and a series of epigraphs at the head of each story. He arranged the stories purposefully. **"A Branch Road,"** which opens the book, is a story of young love; **"Mrs. Ripley's Trip,"** which closes it, concerns the ashes of an old one. **"Up the Coulé"**, the second story, deals with a young man who, unlike Will Hannan, returned home too late. **"Among the Corn-Rows"** offers relief from the grimness of the preceding story, and **"The Return of a Private"** renews the mood of somberness. **"Under the Lion's Paw"** is a commentary on the "daily running fight against the injustice of his fellow-men" with which **"The Return of a Private"** ends. In the whole book, in short, Garland made a conscious effort to follow the method he systematically used in the stories—to develop theme through a planned sequence of scenes. And, to a considerable extent, he succeeded. Read straight through like a novel, the book is more powerful than any of the individual stories.

Hamlin Garland's was not a major talent. His career as a writer of consequence was one of the briefest in American letters; it was also one of the most paradoxical. At the time he was doing his best and most honest work he was conducting a questionable flirtation with Richard Watson Gilder and furnishing him with second-rate and acceptable stories. With B. O. Flower, editor of the *Arena,* he was at once doing his finest work, stories of violent protest of the here and now, and dabbling in psychography. But these things are not the final issue. Whatever the reason, and in whatever way, Hamlin Garland produced a handful of minor masterpieces, of which *Main-Travelled Roads* is the finest. For them he deserves to be remembered, and I think will be, as an artist who, for a brief time at least, knew his craft and practiced it honestly.

James D. Koerner (essay date 1954)

SOURCE: "Comment on 'Hamlin Garland's "Decline" from Realism'," in *American Literature,* Vol. XXVI, No. 3, November, 1954, pp. 427-32.

[*Koerner is an American critic and educator. Here, he presents a rebuttal to Bernard Duffey's 1953 argument regarding Garland's sincerity as realist and a writer of protest fiction. Koerner maintains that Garland's social consciousness was evident prior to the beginning of his publishing career and that the author's "honestness of purpose" was affirmed by many of his contemporaries.*]

Bernard I. Duffey's paper, "Hamlin Garland's 'Decline' from Realism," in the March, 1953, issue of *American Literature* seems to me unreasonable in its basic inference and in its lack of solid support. Briefly stated, Duffey's position is that Garland was from the beginning the complete literary opportunist who pretended admiration for such men as Howells and Benjamin Orange Flower only so far as they were useful in getting him on as a writer, blithely rejecting them when it was expedient to do so. On the strength of a few phrases from *Roadside Meetings* and some extracts from the letters of Garland to Gilder of the *Century,* Duffey would reverse the traditional picture of the young Garland as a green and stumbling, and desperately sincere, writer of protest and reform.

But the bulk of evidence that can be marshaled from such sources as Garland's books of fiction and autobiography, his letters and notebooks, and from testimonials of his contemporaries, points not to the literary opportunist, but to a writer who, whatever his artistic shortcomings, was completely sincere in his exposure of life in the Middle Border.

Let it be admitted at once that Garland's efforts at reform suffered a precipitate decline in favor of more remunerative stuff after 1894, when he had become a fairly established writer. Garland attempted to explain this in several places, the main reason being that by 1894 he felt that he had said all that he had to say about the oppressed farmers of the Middle Border and that [as he wrote in *A Daughter of the Middle Border,* 1921] "to attempt to recover the spirit of my youth would not only have been a failure, but a bore." And undoubtedly it would have been.

Duffey cites for major support the Garland-Gilder correspondence. This correspondence merely proves, no more and no less, that Garland was willing to alter his stories in some respects to meet editorial requirements—a fact that Garland himself never denied. But if this makes him a fundamentally insincere writer, he at least lies with the most immortal of bedfellows.

The point is that, in the absence of a reliable biography, and of less speculative evidence that Duffey has mustered, there is no real reason to disbelieve Garland's own account of the Boston years and the genesis of *Main-*

Travelled Roads. The outlines of the story are well known, but there are some points that Duffey seems to have overlooked.

To begin with, Garland's social conscience had been awakened long before he met B. O. Flower *or* Gilder. By the time he came East, he was already a confirmed Single Taxer, sharing from intimate experience the Populist grievance; and his early years in Boston where he went about proselytizing whenever he could, served to enflame, not to dampen, this reforming zeal. Duffey asserts that Garland's "reformist writing came only upon the opening to him of another chance for literary success," that is, his first meeting with B. O. Flower, founder and editor of the *Arena*. But as a matter of fact, all of the stories that comprise the volume for which Garland is most famous as a writer of protest, **Main-Travelled Roads**, were written before he had even met Flower. And so were many of the other stories that Garland furiously turned out after his second visit home to Dakota in 1888. Among these was the story that Duffey alludes to in support of his idea that Garland turned reformer only after meeting Flower, **"A Prairie Heroine,"** one of the most bitter of all Garland's Middle Border tales. It was ultimately published by Flower as **"Lucretia Burns"** but was written before the two men were acquainted.

Flower undoubtedly gave Garland an easier publishing outlet than he was accustomed to, and financed the writing of much of Garland's weaker stuff, but Duffey has reversed the significance of the original connection between the two men. Flower, being "constitutionally predisposed," as David H. Dickason has observed [in *American Literature,* XIV (May 1942)], "toward any literary work inspiring amelioration of society's evils and injustices," was immediately attracted to Garland upon seeing **"A Prairie Heroine,"** and wrote to him explaining the sociological purpose of the *Arena*. Flower records the delight he felt when, upon meeting Garland for the first time in 1890, he discovered that Garland was already a devoted reformer and Single Taxer; and adds that he listened to Garland's story of how *Progress and Poverty* had "opened a new world to him, a world of hope and inspiration, when all life seemed hopeless and chaotic" [in *Progressive Men, Women, and Movements of the Last Twenty-Five Years,* 1914]. Whatever might have been the subsequent influence of Flower, Garland certainly did not opportunistically turn reformer after meeting him; he had been actively on the reform trail under his own power since 1887.

Even more important for Garland than the connection with Flower was his friendship with Howells, his first important literary acquaintance in Boston. Duffey refers to Howells, along with Flower and Kirkland, as being for Garland another of the "sufficiently useful persons" to warrant cultivating. This is an extremely misleading assertion. There is not an iota of evidence to suggest that Garland sought out Howells because he could be "sufficiently useful" to a struggling young writer. They met through the efforts of Charles Hurd of the Boston *Transcript,* for whom Garland, having acquired before he came

East an immense regard for Howells's writing, favorably reviewed *The Minister's Charge*. Although their first interview was rather in the nature of peasant visiting king, a thirty years' friendship was begun that was always warm and frequently intimate, and that went far beyond the bounds of Howells's usefulness. Looking back on Howells's death in 1920, Garland refers to it, at a time when there was simply no need for a hypocritical statement, as putting an end "to the longest and most important friendship of my life" [*My Friendly Contemporaries,* 1932].

Far from following Howell's lead in social criticism, or seeking his approval, Garland found himself on occasion recommending to Howells a little more preaching in his books. In one of his first letters to Garland, Howells wrote, in answer to Garland's query as to why the case for justice was not made more explicit in *Annie Kilburn,* that the book was "from first to last a cry for *justice,* not alms. . . . Read Mr. Peck's sermon. It could hardly have been expected that he should preach the single tax, but short of that, what more would you have?" [from a letter dated Nov. 6, 1888, *Life in Letters of William Dean Howells,* ed. Mildred Howells, 1928]. And, again, in January of the same year, we find Howells writing to Garland, in apologetic vein, explaining his inability to share in the reform sentiment as fully as Garland. Howells remembers Garland at this time—that is, the years 1887-1890, before Garland's connection with Flower and the *Arena*—as being "a realist to the point of idealism," and goes on to describe a Garland sharply at variance with Duffey's conception: ". . . he was such an ardent believer in Henry George's plan for abolishing poverty that with his heart and hopes fixed on a glorious morrow for all men he took no thought of his own narrow day. He seems at that time to have gone about preaching Georgism equally with Veritism in the same generous self-forgetfulness" [from "Mr. Garland's Books," *North American Review,* CXCVI, 523-24 (Oct. 1912)]. It seems clear, then, that this friendship was not due to any opportunistic vein in Garland's makeup, but to the real affection and respect that each man carried for the other.

Nor did the critics and reviewers of his early work, many of whom knew Garland personally, find anything in his character or writings to suggest insincerity. Indeed, sincerity is the virtue for which he was most frequently cited—sometimes the only one. Joseph E. Chamberlain, for example, remarks that Garland "has no earthly motive than the exact portrayal of truth. . . . Nothing could induce him to seek success by factitious work or meretricious means. . . . He would sacrifice the personal opportunity to the idea if it were the very last opportunity he had" ["Hamlin Garland's Work," *Writer,* V, October, 1891]. The reviewer [in "New Figures in Literature and Art," *Atlantic Monthly,* LXXVI, December, 1895] finds much to quarrel with in **Main-Travelled Roads,** but adds: "These faults would have worked sad havoc" had they appeared in the work of "a less obviously sincere writer." By no means were all the reviewers and critics of the time enthusiastic about Garland, but any disapproval they had of him was invariably on artistic grounds. However else Garland may have impressed his contemporaries, his integrity and honestness of purpose, which Duffey has called sharply into doubt, were never questioned.

Is there, then, a reasonable explanation for Garland's sudden desertion of the reform spirit? Undoubtedly he saw in the early months of 1893 the possibility of greater success in the kind of popular literature that editors like Gilder were seeking. Moreover, he had at no time proposed to dedicate his life to reform; and by 1893 he felt, especially in view of the poor reception of his three novels of protest written under the aegis of Flower and the *Arena,* that he had little more to add to his work already done in this area. And with his growing attachment to local color, he abandoned the enthusiasms of his youth.

Approving Garland's motives, and merely understanding them, involves a distinction that ought to be respected. The fact that Garland, after becoming an established writer, moved away from reform writing in favor of something that paid better does not prove, *ipso facto,* that he was simply an opportunist; and assuming even that he was opportunistic under the pressures of family, depleted material, and editorial requirements like those of Gilder, does it mean that he wrote nothing of integrity and was not serious in his earlier, and better, books? It means merely that he was opportunistic in a certain way for a certain time. But the weight of evidence, literary and biographical, supports the idea of Garland as one of our pioneer writers of protest and exposure, distinguished in his early work by one quality above all others: sincerity.

Walt Whitman was remarkably prophetic, though wrong in his conclusion, when, after meeting Garland at Camden in January of 1889, he said to Traubel [quoted in *Walt Whitman in Camden,* 1914]:

> Garland looks like a man who is bound to last—to go on from very good to very much better; but you can never tell: there are so many dangers—so many ways for the innocent to be betrayed: in the clutter, clatter, crack of metropolitan ambitions, jealousies, bribes, so many ways for a man, unless he is a giant, unless he is possessed of brutal strength and independence—so many ways for him to go to the devil. I look for Garland to save himself from this fate.

Garland of course did not save himself, as he himself recognized, and never fulfilled the promise of the early work; but that work still remains an important and completely honest contribution to the American literature of protest.

Donald Pizer (essay date 1960)

SOURCE: "The Local Colorist as Social Reformer (1888-1890)," in *Hamlin Garland's Early Work and Career,* University of California Press, 1960, pp. 59-78.

[*Pizer is an American critic and educator and a prominent authority on Garland's life and works, having served* *as editor for the author's* Diaries *(1968) and the novel* Rose of Dutcher's Coolly *(1970). In the following excerpt, the critic analyzes* Main-Travelled Roads *and* Prairie Folks, *asserting that the high quality of the two collections results from Garland's emphasis on issues of social life and social injustice.*]

Most of the stories Garland wrote during 1888-1890 were collected in *Main-Travelled Roads* and *Prairie Folks.* Since he later made additions to both of these volumes, it should be clear that in referring to them I mean the 1891 edition of *Main-Travelled Roads,* which contained six stories, and the 1893 *Prairie Folks,* containing nine stories. Though *Prairie Folks* followed *Main-Travelled Roads* by two years, its stories were written contemporaneously with those of *Main-Travelled Roads.* Indeed, Garland thought of the second collection as a "companion volume" to the first [as stated in a letter to Herbert S. Stone, Dec. 19, 1893], and was planning its publication within a year of the appearance of *Main-Travelled Roads.* The latter has become, for several reasons, Garland's best-known work of fiction, whereas *Prairie Folks* has gone out of print and is rarely discussed. But the two are clearly related and should be examined together.

Main-Travelled Roads and *Prairie Folks* are remarkably coherent books, considering that they are composed of short stories written for individual publication over a period of several years. For one thing, they have a consistent and reappearing geography and cast. The middle border, to Garland, was not a place out west, but a geographical reality, populated by people he knew who belonged in a specific locality with specific characteristics.

There are three "matters" in Garland's middle-border fiction. Rock River and Cedarville are neighboring towns in northeastern Iowa, and in the stories set there farmers Councill, Jennings, and Ridings appear again and again. Elder Wheat exhorts in several. Milton Jennings, Radbourn, Bradley Talcott, and Lily Graham are initially students at the Rock River Seminary and later professional people of the town. Lime Gilman marries his Marietta and settles down; Mr. and Mrs. Ripley grow older; and Judge Brown, teacher Knapp, and editor Foster go about their duties. Not so well represented in these early collections, but flourishing nevertheless, are Bluff Siding and Tyre in the coulee region of western Wisconsin, where family groups predominate. The McLanes and the McTurgs, the Grays and the McIlvaines appear in story after story. Lastly, there are the rival towns of Boomtown and Belleplain in the "Jim" River Valley of Dakota. Here Judge Sid Balser is a perennial speculator in land, and farmers Wilson and Rodemaker, businessmen Whiting and Graham, and editor Seagraves aid in the settlement of the area. Besides being knit together by the continual reappearance of character and place, the stories are also unified by Garland's conception of them as composing a full and complex picture of Western life. In *Main-Travelled Roads* this idea is communicated (in the epigraph and in the lines before each story) by the metaphor of a Western road—its varying condition, countryside, and travelers symbolizing the diversity of Western life. Middle-border life was frequently tragic, Garland stated, but it was also, especially for the young, often joyous and exhilarating. Though the Western road is usually "hot and dusty" or "desolate and drear," it "does sometimes cross a rich meadow where the songs of the larks and bobolinks and blackbirds are tangled" [from the epigraph to *Main-Travelled Roads*]. In *Prairie Folks* the device of a few lines of verse before each story is used to introduce the prairie type or social scene to be portrayed. In both collections Garland was conscious of his role as a Western local colorist whose function was to depict the richness of Western life, to capture its "sentiments." He had been "true to particulars and to the provincial," to that of which he knew and cared the most, he wrote to friends in explaining his intentions in *Main-Travelled Roads,* and had proved his "theory" that "the mystery and significance of high heaven falls like the sun-light on the far Iowan prairie as well as upon the Rhine, the Rhone, and the Righi" [quoted from letters to Brander Matthews (Mar. 15, 1892) and Louise Chandler Moulton (June 11, 1891)].

Main-Travelled Roads is dominated by two long, previously unpublished stories which are similar in several ways. Both **"A Branch-Road"** and **"Up the Coulé"** exemplify social themes controlling much of Garland's thought and writing of this period. Both stories strikingly and poignantly reveal his sense of guilt toward those of his family he had left behind in the West. In both, the plot centers on the return of a recreant to his home and on his ineffectual attempt to right his wrong. And in both, the personal injury committed is made doubly tragic by the prevalent social injustice which heightens and accentuates it.

In **"A Branch-Road,"** Will Hannan leaves home in a fit of jealousy, despite his love for Agnes Dingman, his youthful sweetheart. He returns some years later to find that Agnes, having been forced into marriage by economic necessity, is dominated by her coarse, bullying husband. Moreover, the hard lot of a farm wife has destroyed her beauty and crushed her spirit. Will rescues her from both farm and husband, but it is clear that he saves only the shell of the girl he knew and loved.

As Howells remarked in his review of *Main-Travelled Roads* [*Harpers Monthly,* LXXXIII. (Sept. 1891)], the conclusion of the story, in which Will and Agnes run off together, was by conventional standards "morally wrong." But to Garland, who had been influenced by the Spencerian doctrine of woman's right to individuality, by the contemporary struggle (stoutly supported by the *Arena*) for woman's rights, and by Ibsen, the conclusion had a morality of its own. Like Spencer, Garland believed that the political and social subjection of woman was a survival of an older stage of social evolution and was increasingly unjustified in an era of growing devotion to individual freedom and personality. Garland wrote in [in the *Standard,* Oct. 8, 1890]:

> I believe in individual liberty. I believe the progress of the ages has been toward a fuller expansion of average individual souls, toward altruism and high average personality. In my far-off ideal world the liberty of

man and woman is bounded only by the equal rights of others. Woman stands there as independent of man as man is independent of woman. Both individuals with no must or shall, save the great law of nature which will at last, under a free sky and upon a free earth, produce indeed the survival of the best.

When Will offers Agnes a true "partnership" in marriage, promising her understanding and the opportunity and the leisure to pursue her own interests, Agnes can accept his offer without sacrificing her moral integrity. There is no immorality, but rather a more advanced morality, one more in step with the evolutionary emergence of individual rights and personality.

If Agnes is ground down by farm life and by the social convention that permits a husband to tyrannize his wife, Grant McLane, in **"Up the Coulé,"** is defeated by the lack of opportunity which is the fate of the farmer under monopolistic land practices. Howard McLane, his comparatively prosperous brother, had neglected his obligation to those he had left behind on the coulee farm, and farm life has embittered and coarsened them. Now, despite the aid that Howard offers, life is over for Grant, as it is for Agnes.

Garland made clear that Grant McLane's defeat is not merely the result of his brother's neglect. Grant himself points out the overpowering evils of contemporary farm conditions:

> "The worst of it is . . . a man can't get out of it [hard work and poverty] during his lifetime, and *I* don't know that he'll have any chance in the next—the speculator'll be there ahead of us."

The rest laughed, but Grant went on grimly:

> "Ten years ago Wess, here, could have got land in Dakota pretty easy, but now it's about all a feller's life's worth to try it. I tell you things seem shuttin' down on us fellers."

"Plenty o' land to rent," suggested some one.

> "Yes, in terms that skin a man alive. More than that, farmin' ain't so free a life as it used to be. This cattle-raisin' and butter-makin' makes a nigger of a man. Binds him right down to the grindstone and he gets nothin' out of it—that's what rubs it in. He simply wallers around in the manure for somebody else. I'd like to know what a man's life is worth who lives as we do? How much higher is it than the lives the niggers used to live?"

In both stories someone who has escaped from the farm returns and tries to aid the one whom he has left to face farm life unassisted. In each instance, however, farm life has taken its toll and crushed the one remaining behind. Only pity and material comfort can be offered—gone is the chance for a full life, for self-development and self-realization. This loss is the true tragedy of Agnes and

Grant. Life will be made easier for both, but for neither will it be possible to undo the terrible deprivation of individual opportunity wreaked by farm conditions.

"A Branch-Road" and **"Up the Coulé"** are two of Garland's most powerful stories. They derive much of their strength from their integration of his sense of guilt—had he not left his parents and sister on the prairie?—with his indignation toward prevalent social conditions. He was seldom again to achieve such a high level of personal involvement and emotional intensity, even though these were the qualities necessary to raise his fiction above the commonplace.

Garland's purpose, in many of his stories, had been to "debunk" idyllic pictures of farm life, and he gave this theme explicit expression several times. Radbourn, in **"Sim Burns's Wife,"** tells the town-bred Lily Graham: "'Writers and orators have lied so long about "the idyllic" in farm life, and said so much about the "independent American farmer," that he himself has remained blind to the fact that he's one of the hardest-working and poorest-paid men in America.'" In **"Old Daddy Deering,"** Garland himself, in describing a threshing, made a clear-cut distinction between the "picturesque" and "familiar" views:

> A spectator riding along the road would have remarked upon the lovely setting for this picturesque scene—the low swells of prairie, shrouded with faint, misty light from the unclouded sky, the flaming colors of the trees, the faint sound of cow-bells, and the cheery sound of the machine. But to be a tourist and to be a toiler in a scene like this are quite different things.

Generally, however, Garland's exposition of the anti-idyllic was implicit in his depiction of farm life. **"Among the Corn-Rows,"** for example, is an obvious antidote to conventional portraits of bucolic courtship. Julie Peterson, sweating and straining behind a plow in the July heat, and Rob Rodemaker, giving himself ten days to find a wife—someone to cook for him and to dispel the loneliness of his Dakota shanty—are as far from conventional rustic lovers as is possible.

The same debunking tendency pervades one of Garland's best-known stories, **"The Return of a Private."** Again the personal note—"Private Smith" is Garland's father—vitalizes the story. But also, as in **"Up the Coulé,"** in which the countryside looks rich and sleek to Howard McLane until he views his brother's farmyard, Garland brings the reader up close and reveals the truth beneath the gloss of the soldier's life. Private Smith returns from war against the South without fanfare, worn and ill, but only to take up again his "daily running fight with nature and against the injustice of his fellowmen."

In several of the stories Garland stated single-tax ideas directly. Grant McLane complains of speculation and of the unreasonable demands made upon the farmer because of high rent and low prices. Rob Rodemaker has gone to Dakota to escape the high price of land in the East, and Hank Wilson wonders why the Indian must constantly be driven west when "'There's land enough for us all, or ought to be.'" **"Under the Lion's Paw"** is a classic exemplification of single-tax doctrine. The Haskins family, forced to settle in western Kansas by the high price of land farther east, are eaten out by grasshoppers. Aided by a kindly farmer, they rent a farm in Iowa from Jim Butler, a landlord who "believed in land speculation as the surest way of getting rich." After three years of "ferocious labor," Haskins is ready to buy. Butler, however, realizing the increased value of the farm, doubles the original price. The story closes with Haskins crushed and helpless under the lion's paw of land-lordism. In *Prairie Folks,* **"Sim Burns's Wife"** is Garland's only overt single-tax story. Here Radbourn explains that the hardship and the bleakness of the Burnses' life are a result of the land system and that those striving for a better life for all must preach the "noble discontent" of land reform.

These instances of explicit single-tax propaganda are exceptional, for Garland usually followed Howells and "exemplified" rather than "preached." Most of the stories that are the product of his reaction to Western conditions picture these conditions in single-tax terms rather than advocate the single tax. So he constantly emphasized such interlocking themes as the contrast between a narrow-minded, poverty-stricken farmer and a rich and beautiful countryside; the intellectual and cultural barrenness of Western life; and the prevalence of solitude in the West, for Garland believed that all these were caused by current land policy.

The stories of *Prairie Folks* are particularly indicative of the range of Garland's depiction of Western life. **"Sim Burns's Wife," "The Test of Elder Pill,"** and **"Drifting Crane"** are in varying degrees polemical. The first is one of Garland's strongest indictments of farm conditions. The second dramatizes a Spencerian distrust of the "barbarism" of evangelism and calls for an "earnest morality" to replace "antiquated terrorism." **"Drifting Crane,"** the only story in the collection not set in Iowa, is a plea for understanding of the Indian displacement problem. The rest of the stories are in Garland's other vein of Western fiction, retelling yarns familiar enough to be folk tales and chronicling the older life now gone by. The best of these stories are less "stories" than artistic renderings of the anecdotal store of American country people. There is scarcely any plot and little depth of character. Rather, the material is that which is common to experience everywhere: of the clever salesman and the gullible old man and his slightly shrewish wife; of youthful love and rivalry at a church sociable; of the hired hand winning the farmer's daughter; of the return to one's birthplace, after a long absence, when one is old. This is the common stuff of humanity, not the extravagance and picturesqueness often equated with local color.

When Garland ventured outside this "plotless" subject matter, which he did increasingly as his middle-border material ran thin, he was unsuccessfully forced to contrive plot and character. In his Rocky Mountain novels and stories, for example, he was apt to exploit local-color details within a conventional pattern of plot and character, and his fiction declined in quality. This tendency is already evident in **"Saturday Night on the Farm,"** the last published of the stories in *Prairie Folks*. Lime Gilman, a strong, blond, chivalrous, abstemious giant, is forced to fight Steve Nagle, a drunkard and braggart, to protect a boy. Lime wins, and virtue and right are triumphant. For it was only when man was pitted against social evil that Garland could conceive of tragedy, of the fall of a worthy man. His strong and conventional moral view of life refused to accept this defeat, and he indignantly pictured it as tragedy. But it is this same cast of mind which could not frame a tragic relationship between individuals, which lapsed into stereotypes of character and plot when evil and good moved out of the readily grasped social world into the subtler one of human relations.

In *Main-Travelled Roads* and *Prairie Folks,* however, Garland's incapacity to go beyond the conventional in human relations seldom appears. His themes and subject matter were primarily social—the depiction of Western social life and the dramatization of oppression of the individual by social injustice. The stories of the two collections, by embodying both his response to and his conception of the West, represent the best work he was ever to do in fiction.

Garland's feeling for reform was complicated by a second ambition, dearer to the heart of the young Westerner than the first. He wanted to be a literary success. He wanted to be accepted. And under the guise of preferring art to reform, Garland gradually began to compromise—and to succeed.

—Claude Simpson, in "Hamlin Garland's Decline," in **Southwest Review, Winter, 1941.**

James K. Folsom (essay date 1966)

SOURCE: "The Vanishing American," in *The American Western Novel,* College University Press, 1966, pp. 141-76.

[*In the following excerpt, Folsom examines Garland's treatment of Native American assimilation into Euro American society. The critic finds that most of the stories in* The Book of the American Indian *promote the idea that "the Indian must change," but that "The Story of Howling Wolf" illustrates the difficulty of this process.*]

In many ways Hamlin Garland's Indian studies are a transition between traditional and modern literary treatments of the Indian. Both **"The Silent Eaters"**—a fictionalized biography of Sitting Bull—and the short stories which together make up *The Book of the American Indian* (1923) are written out of a feeling of indignation over unjust treatment of the Indian; and both as well have a very definite social reference which, in the weakest of the stories, deteriorates into a thinly disguised program of social action. Yet this program is significantly different from earlier fictional discussions of the Indian problem; for, as Garland sees, the problem itself has changed. No longer is it conceived in terms of how best to defeat the Indians; rather it has become the question of how best to rehabilitate a defeated enemy. **"The Silent Eaters"** and the stories in *The Book of the American Indian* are rather specifically concerned with providing answers to this problem, and the method of explication Garland uses is closely related to the idea of Indian conversion [to the white man's way of life]. Garland, however, sees that the question of whether the old ways are "good" or "bad" must be approached differently in order for it to have any relevance to the actual world. As a result, the standard plot of escape fiction, the story of the reactionary old chief who is replaced by the modern progressive young Indian is put in a different perspective. Where the escapist plot concerns itself primarily with the events leading to the subjugation of the Indian, after which he is converted, Garland focuses primarily upon the Indian's condition after his subjugation, and hence emphasizes the absolute necessity for his conversion; and where the escapist plot concerns itself primarily with the description of unmotivated event, Garland's primary concern is with the nature of the process of conversion.

This is most clearly seen in **"The Silent Eaters,"** which in format most closely resembles the escapist plot. In this biographical account of the Sioux chief Sitting Bull, Garland presents an expanded metaphor for the decline of the Sioux nation, from its early proud self-sufficiency to its final utter dependence upon the whites. Garland tells his story with considerable skill, especially when he succeeds in generalizing the character of Sitting Bull from that of a conventional "bad" Indian into a sympathetic type of the Sioux nation in general. And just here is the focus of Garland's story; for **"The Silent Eaters"** universalizes the particular figure of Sitting Bull into a general statement of the nature of that historic process which has inevitably ended with the triumph of the whites and the subjugation of the Indians.

Such a focus enables Garland to establish a double point of view toward his material. While he can admire Sitting Bull's courage, resourcefulness, and so on, at the same time he may consistently condemn these qualities as out of place in the white world inevitably to come. Hence Sitting Bull can be personally admired, but at the same time the position for which he stands need not be affirmed. Garland establishes this double viewpoint by means of his narrator, a young Sioux Indian named Iapi. When Sitting Bull finally surrenders, Iapi is befriended by a Lieutenant Davies of the U.S.Army, who gives him the opportunity for education in the white man's ways, even sending him East to study. Lieutenant Davies has a great respect both for the Indians as a race and for education as a means to ameliorate their unhappy reservation conditions. "The plains Indian was a perfect adaptation of organism to environment," he once tells Iapi, who also tells us that "he looked upon each people as the product of its conditions." The moral is not far to seek, nor does it escape Iapi. Now that the environment is changed, the organism must change with it, and Iapi's role must be that of the educator of his people.

The creation of the character of Iapi is Garland's only major fictional tampering with the historic facts of the life of Sitting Bull. Such a character as Iapi, however, is admirably suited for telling Sitting Bull's story. He is first of all an Indian, and his white ways are only superimposed upon the virtues of what Lieutenant Davies calls "a wonderful race." Hence he can be sympathetic to Indian ways without appearing condescending, and at the same time need not pretend to be anything other than outraged over the excesses and outrages which various whites perpetrate upon his people. His white schooling, on the other hand, has given him another perspective on Indian history which enables him to interpret Sitting Bull not in a personal light but in a historic one. From this historic perspective Sitting Bull, however admirably he may appear as a character, is nevertheless the voice of the past. "He epitomized the epic, tragic story of my kind," Iapi sums up. "His life spanned the gulf between the days of our freedom and the death of every custom native to us. He saw the invader come and he watched the buffalo disappear. Within the half century of his conscious life he witnessed greater changes and comprehended more of my tribe's tragic history than any other red man." But this elegy for Sitting Bull and the heroic past is alloyed with optimism; for the future belongs to Iapi.

The present pessimism and future optimism which Garland notes as the process of Indian history in **"The Silent Eaters"** are by no means confined to this least fictional of his treatments of the Indian. The historic process of evolution described specifically (and by Lieutenant Davies, at least, in pseudo-scientific Social Darwinian terms) here is also clearly illustrated by the various stories in *The Book of the American Indian*.

The general philosophical burden of these various tales is that, like it or not, the Indian must change. This is emphasized by a recurrent image which is made explicit in a number of the stories, that the Indian's trail has ended, and that the white man's road is the only one left for the Indians to follow. Even when not explicit, this image is always close to the surface. For instance, **"Wahiah—A Spartan Mother"** tells of the necessity for Indian children to adopt the white man's ways. In this story Wahiah realizes that she must send her son Atokan to the Indian school, no matter how much the reactionary Indians may disapprove of it. When Atokan refuses to go, the schoolteacher gives him a whipping, and Wahiah, in a clearly symbolic gesture, breaks the boy's bow and arrows, his "symbols of freedom," and after saying only "Obey" leaves Atokan at the school.

The theme is most clearly stated in one of the best stories in the book, **"Rising Wolf—Ghost Dancer."** Rising Wolf, who tells the story of his life himself, recounts how as a young brave he had become a medicine man. He had an honorable position in the tribe before the white men came and, Garland makes clear, he was no cynical prestidigitator but one who sincerely believed in the value of his medicine. After the Indian defeat, Rising Wolf and the rest of his tribe had been sent to a reservation where all had heard of the Ghost Dance. To a medicine man and hence presumably something of an authority on the subject, the idea of the Ghost Dance seemed to make some sense, and he became a convert. The Ghost Dance, Rising Wolf and the other Indians believed, was to operate by magic. The Indians were to dance for four days, and on the fourth day the white men would disappear and the buffalo return, and all Indians, alive or dead, would be reunited on the rejuvenated earth.

The ending of the story describes, in a very sensitively handled tragicomic manner, the Dance itself. The whites, fearing that the gathering dancers represent a threat to civil order, send soldiers to watch lest the dance prove hostile in intent. Of course the Indians, confident of their "medicine," are peaceable in the extreme. For four days they dance, and when they have finished Rising Wolf retires to rest satisfied with a job well done and sure that when he wakes the following morning the whites will have vanished and the buffalo returned.

When he awakes the millennium has unaccountably been delayed; the whites are still there. Convinced by the visible proof that the Ghost Dance in particular and Indian medicine in general have both been in error, he renounces them and resolves to take up white ways. The conclusion of the story is worth examination in detail.

> "When I rose, it was morning. I flung off my blanket, and looked down on the valley where the tepees of the white soldiers stood. I heard their drums and their music. I had made up my mind. The white man's trail was wide and dusty by reason of many feet passing thereon, but it was long. The trail of my people was ended.

> "I said, 'I will follow the white man's trail. I will make him my friend, but I will not bend my neck to his burdens. I will be cunning as the coyote. I will ask him to help me to understand his ways, and then I will prepare the way for my children. Maybe they will outrun the white man in his own shoes. Anyhow, there are but two ways. One leads to hunger and death, the other leads where the poor white man lives. Beyond is the happy hunting ground, where the white man cannot go'"

The general similarity between the conclusion of **"Rising Wolf"** and the more detailed interpretation of history in **"The Silent Eaters"** is obvious. What is perhaps not so obvious are the implications inherent in Garland's choice of Rising Wolf for his hero. In the character of Rising Wolf, Garland has combined the two points of view represented in **"The Silent Eaters"** by Sitting Bull and Iapi. By making Rising Wolf first a medicine man and then a believer in the Ghost Dance, Garland has made him symbolically stand for the most reactionary and unprogressive elements in the old order; his conversion to white ways, however anthropologically dubious and psychologically untenable it may seem, represents Garland's deeply held belief that the Indian can be made to accept these ways. Even the most reactionary Indian, when once he understands the hard facts of history, can adjust to the new life forced on him by its inevitable processes.

Garland's insistence upon the inevitability of change relieves him from the fictional necessity to choose sides and accept either white or red ways without qualification; he need not categorically defend or excuse either whites or Indians. Hence villains as well as heroes can be either white or red, and in fact there are many white villains in *The Book of the American Indian*. As a general rule, these white villains are missionaries, for whom Garland has little respect. The general tone of *The Book of the American Indian* is, if not exactly anti-religious, certainly anti-clerical and anti-missionary. One of the most poignant stories, **"The Iron Kiva,"** clearly shows Garland's typical attitude; it tells of two Indian children who kill themselves rather than let the white missionary take them away to school in the East. Significantly, the children like the idea of the white man's school, but distrust and fear the missionaries.

Garland's white heroes are usually Indian agents and schoolteachers, whose tolerance and kindliness stand in none too subtle contrast to missionary bigotry. The agents and schoolteachers are sympathetic to those Indian ways which are not immediately harmful and do not stand in the way of the Indians' education. They view the process of education as basically one of training the Indians in the use of unfamiliar skills which he will need to survive in the white man's world. The missionaries, in contrast, view the educational process as one of total ruthless eradication of Indian customs. Without sympathy for or understanding of the Indians, the missionaries are helpless either to convert them or to ameliorate their lot. To rehabilitate the Indian, Garland says, it is not necessary to turn him into a white man; Indian customs need not be entirely blotted out, as the missionaries would have it. The Indian desperately needs training in the general skills of civilized life, for in order to survive he must become literate and learn how to use the white man's agricultural tools. But further than this, education should not go; it is possible to assent to the truth of mathematics without swearing undying allegiance to the Apostles' Creed.

Ultimately Garland's point is that the Indian can and should be allowed to have the best of both white and red worlds. Like Iapi and Rising Wolf, the modern Indian can keep the cultural traditions of his fathers and combine them successfully with the demands of life in a world dominated by white values. Perhaps, as Rising Wolf suggests, if he is cunning enough he can outstrip the white man on his own grounds.

This is true of all the stories in *The Book of the American Indian* with the exception of the best one, **"The Story of Howling Wolf."** In this somber tale the often complacent "long view" of history which justifies particular present hardship is subjected to serious qualification. When the story opens Howling Wolf hates white men because his brother had been killed for sport by cowboys seven years before. He has never forgiven the whites and has taken a vow to kill the men responsible for his brother's death, but the Indian agent manages to talk him out of his lust for vengeance. Howling Wolf is strongly influenced by the example of the Indian agent, with whom he makes friends, and, renouncing his savage ways, determines to turn himself into the kind of Indian white men will respect. He even gets the agent to write him a paper which, he ingenuously thinks, "will tell [all men] that my heart is made good." This paper, which he carries with him as a sort of passport, says "I am Howling Wolf. Long I hated the white man. Now my heart is good and I want to make friends with all white men. I want to work with a plow and live in a house like the white man. These are my words. [Signed] Howling Wolf."

Armed with his passport, Howling Wolf does what a sober, industrious Indian should and gets a job hauling hides. But when he transports a wagonload of hides to town the whites laugh at him and spurn his offers of friendship. A cowboy picks a fight with him and fires a wild shot which hits another white man in the knee. The outraged citizenry assume that Howling Wolf has fired the shot, and are all for lynching him until he gives them the paper which, when they read it, cools their anger, and they compromise their earlier position by throwing Howling Wolf into jail on more or less general principles. The agent's efforts to have Howling Wolf released are futile. One day Howling Wolf, who has borne up patiently throughout the whole affair, is taken from jail by the sheriff, who wants to attend a baseball game and is afraid to leave the Indian unattended. Howling Wolf thinks he is being taken to his execution, so he tries to escape; but he is apprehended by a group of cowboys who lasso him and drag him behind their horses for amusement. A Catholic priest manages to make the cowboys stop, albeit only after Howling Wolf has apparently been dragged to death. Though he finally recovers, he is "so battered, so misshapen that his own wife did not know him." Howling Wolf's attempt to civilize himself has ended disastrously; he will speak only to the priest and the agent, and when he dies no white man knows where his grave is hidden.

In many ways **"The Story of Howling Wolf"** is an exact inversion of the other stories in *The Book of the American Indian*. Howling Wolf's story, like Iapi's and Rising Wolf's, is a description of education; but what he learns stands in direct opposition to the lesson the other progressive Indians have been taught. Howling Wolf's education is much like Sitting Bull's; that the whites are cruel, selfish, and not to be trusted.

The most sobering aspect of **"The Story of Howling Wolf"** and what sets it apart from the other stories is Garland's conception of the limited possibilities for goodness in the nature of man. In the brutal and savage "civilized" world to which Howling Wolf is introduced, there is little room for the optimism which Garland elsewhere shows. Evil in this story is not a product of the conflict between different social values, a conflict which, the other stories lead us to believe, can be smoothed away when one set of social values disappears; rather evil is understood as an expression of the bestiality in man, and social values are not its causes but the ways in which it is made manifest in the world. To such a view history cannot possibly appear optimistic; for all hopes of meliorating human life depend upon the assumption that man's character can be changed for the better. In **"The Story of Howling Wolf"** such is simply not the case. The parable of history in this story resembles that in the Leatherstocking Tales. Change is certain, but it does not represent progress; history records the frustration of hope.

Lewis O. Saum   (essay date 1972-73)

SOURCE: "Hamlin Garland and Reform," in *The South Dakota Review*, Vol. 10, No. 4, Winter, 1972-73, pp. 36-62.

[*In the following excerpt, Saum reviews the various reform movements that Garland promoted in his short stories and asserts that, despite his consideration of society's ills in his early works, Garland was initially optimistic regarding human potential. The critic also proposes that Garland's eventual rejection of fictional protest resulted from a waning of his optimism and the growing opposition to literary realism at the turn of the century.*]

Hamlin Garland's writing of the 1890's foreshadowed various of the twentieth century reform activities and persuasions. Far too commonly he has been seen as having a monistic focus on Midwestern farm life. This essay will attempt to indicate first that he gave literary treatment to a multiplicity of reform urges, among which agrarianism may not have been even the most prominent. Secondly, the essay will attempt to make more meaningful Garland's removal from the realm of protest realism by viewing it in the context of the intellectual currents of the turn of the century.

Literary critics and historians have claimed both too much and too little for the son of the middle border. On the one hand, they admiringly present him as a wrathful man heaping artistic scorn and indictment upon the prevalent cruelty of the American system. On the other hand, they impatiently dismiss him as one who fled the uninspiring Midwest kitchen because he could not stand the heat, subsequently betaking himself to the Rocky Mountain realm of comfortable romance. Of course, part of that disparity in assessment stems from the fact that Garland's writing changed around the turn of the century, not only in locale but in subject matter and import. But there is more involved than changes in a man's writing over the course of time. The tensions between romance and realism, pessimism and optimism, the ugly and the benign

appear not only when we compare *Main-Travelled Roads* with, say, *Her Mountain Lover*. The ambiguity readily appears when those supposedly grim works of the 1890's are viewed by themselves.

Focusing on one side of the Garlandian coin has caused some to exaggerate the element of protest in his early works. Of course, in the autobiographical *A Son of the Middle Border* Garland himself raised questions about the dearth of "stern facts" in the nation's literature. Certainly there is accuracy in the view that *Main-Travelled Roads* represented, at least in part, "a protest against the romantic portrayal of the Middle West" [Lars Ahnebrink, *The Beginnings of Naturalism in American Fiction,* 1961]. But it is far too much to say that the stories of *Main-Travelled Roads* have unity of theme in "the ugliness, the monotony, the bestiality, the hopelessness of life on the farm" [Lucy Lockwood Hazard, *The Frontier American Literature,* 1961]. On the "long and wearyful" road Garland presented futility, even desperation. But the same track, he noted, crossed "a rich meadow where the songs of the larks and the bobolinks are tangled." Thus, at the sunny conclusion of **"Among the Corn Rows,"** "the katydids sang to the liquid contralto of the river in its shallows." As Garland mused years later [in *Roadside Meetings*]: "the book was less austere than it appeared to the critic."

Other Main-Travelled Roads follows the same ambivalent vein. Two of the stories in that collection convey the severest sentiments that Garland ever committed to paper. But much of the remainder seems meant to substantiate the hopeful contention at the end of the preface: "youth and love are able to transform a bleak prairie town into a poem, and to make of a barbed-wire land a highway to romance." . . .

In his introduction to the Rinehart edition of *Main-Travelled Roads* [1954] Thomas A. Bledsoe emphasized the disparity between Garland's theoretical pronouncements in *Crumbling Idols* and the literary creations which he achieved. Bledsoe detected a dissociation of theory from practice so marked as to border upon "fraud"—a militant radicalism as goal, happy conventionalities as realization. Here, it seems to me, Bledsoe has fallen into an error which he generally avoids in that excellent essay. He focuses his attention on one part of the theory just as others have focused their attention on some one part of Garland's realized output. As in nearly any Garland work, happy, positive and optimistic sentiments pervade the credo called *Crumbling Idols*. For example, Garland anticipated that the literature soon to emanate from the Pacific Coast region will deal "with the wholesome love of honest men for honest women, with the heroism of labor, (and) the comradeship of men." It will pronounce the truth, he tells us. But the truth has little in it that is dangerous or cataclysmic. In an almost fatuous tone, he informs us that in the soon to be written far western literature

> The lovers who wander down the aisles of orange or lemon or pepper trees will not marvel at blooms and shrubs. Their presence and perfume will be familiar

and lovely, not strange. The stark lines of the fir and the broad-sword thrust of the banana-leaf will not attract their surprised look. All will be as friendly and grateful as the maple or the Lombardy poplar to the Iowa school-boy.

This is not the realism of wretchedness and protest, it is the realism of happy and unawed familiarity. "I am overwhelmed," he wrote, "by the majesty, the immensity, the infinite charm of the life that goes on around me" [*Crumbling Idols: Twelve Essays on Art Dealing Chiefly with Literature, Painting and the Drama,* 1894].

Hamlin Garland possessed a lively vision of a better order. He consciously eschewed the past because he considered it ugly. He criticized the present but viewed it as a beckoning doorway to a bright and wholesome future. Few essays can match *Crumbling Idols* in its hopefully, even ebulliently, prophetic tone. In it Garland used evolution as his philosophical point of departure. To Henry Adams [in *The Education of Henry Adams,* 1907] evolution offered the source of wryly sophisticated jest—a principle the unfolding of which put Ulysses S. Grant in the White House instead of a George Washington. To us, the late nineteenth century penchant for evolutionism appears often as a misanthropic law of the jungle invoked by the strong to oppress the weak, as the brutal theme of survival of the fittest and the atavistic "red in tooth and claw." To Garland, it meant something far different— human progress. "Metamorphosis," he tell us [in *Crumbling Idols*], "is the law of all living things," and traditional thought and training had failed to recognize its working. Thus, the conventional and traditional outlook

> is essentially hopeless. It blinds the eyes of youth to the power and beauty of the life and literature around him. It worships the past, despises the present, and fears the future. Such teaching is profoundly pessimistic . . .

For Garland, pessimism bordered on anathema.

He assured his readers that he would attack the blemishes of his day—but never out of morbid fascination nor for sheer titillation. Rather, he would do so out of a thoroughly positive and constructive impulse. The central import of *Crumbling Idols* appears in a chapter titled, appropriately enough, "Literary Prophecy":

> The realist or veritist is really an optimist, a dreamer. He sees life in terms of what it might be, as well as in terms of what it is . . . (He) sees a more beautiful and peaceful future social life . . . Therefore he is encouraged to deal truthfully and at close grapple with the facts of his immediate present . . . He aims to hasten the age of beauty and peace by delineating the ugliness and warfare of the present . . . He sighs for a lovelier life. He is tired of warfare and diseased sexualism and Poverty the mother of Envy . . . Because he is sustained by love and faith in the future, he can be mercilessly true. He strikes at thistles, because he knows the unrotted seed of loveliness and peace needs but sun and the air of freedom to rise to flower and fragrance.

In light of this pronouncement of purpose, I cannot accept Bledsoe's charge that Garland divorced literary theory from literary practice. And, if in some broad sense Garland erred, he did so for the least damning, the most excusable, of reasons—a too great faith in human potential. Those often contrivedly happy circumstances and denouements mentioned earlier represent more than the marks of an uncritical naif. Garland's discontent was authentic. (He called it a mood of "sad severity.") In his efforts to give "the unrotted seed of loveliness and peace" some "sun and the air of freedom," he struck at a good many "thistles."

People motivated by a reform ethos rarely maintain singleness of purpose. When they destroy one barrier to human felicity, they quickly find other related ones upon which to expend effort. Though Hamlin Garland is understandably connected with agrarian protest, he too had a breadth of vision which encompassed various evils of the late nineteenth century. Most likely, he looked upon the problems of the time not as distinct and separate phenomena but as interrelated reflections of some fundamental failure of approach. Still, if only for purposes of analysis, we can isolate and itemize the concerns which he felt for his society.

In the late nineteenth century one of the prime dimensions of reform appeared in the religious realm. The social gospel movement urged churchly functions more immediately meaningful than the purveying of spiritual balm, the holding out of hope for individual salvation and the promising of untold rewards in the hereafter as recompense for sufferings borne here. Religion, this movement insisted, must succour the needy in a direct and physical fashion. It must make the *world* a better place in which to live. Few could have agreed more fully than Hamlin Garland. With a frequency unreflected in **Main-Travelled Roads,** he accusingly presented humans whose lives had been thwarted and broken by acceptance of anachronistic and inhuman creeds.

At times, the son of the middle border indulged in gratuitous rancor, as when he introduced a divinity student for no apparent reason than to write him off as "an affected, brainless creature" [*A Member of the Third House*]. In more reasoned terms, he found two major faults with the religious institutions of his time. First, he felt an especial abhorrence for certain evangelistic forms. In the autobiographical *Boy Life on the Prairie* he recalled that for several years his neighborhood "had been darkened and made austere by the work of an 'evangelist' who came preaching the wickedness of natural man and the imminence of death." He never forgave that evangelist. **"A Day of Grace"** delivers his severest indictment of the primitive, orgiastic and psychopathic excesses of the revival. In the story a group of Garland's beloved youths attend a revival out of curiosity but one, a girl appropriately named Grace, nearly falls under the exhorter's morbidly hypnotic spell. But then the stolid Ben, speaking for the author, rescues the girl by challenging the revivalist in the most direct fashion: "'God damn ye. Get out o' way. I'll kill ye if you lay a hand on her'." As they ride home under the stars "heaven" seemed very near and "hell" was back at the revival:

> A moment later, as the demoniacal chorus of yells, songs, incantations, shrieks, groans, and prayers swelled high, a farmer's wife on the left uttered a hoarse cry and stiffened and fell backward upon the ground. She rolled her head from side to side. Her eyes turned in; her lips wore a maniac's laugh, and her troubled brow made her look like the death mask of a tortured murderer, the hell horror frozen on it.

With equal determination and greater frequency he arraigned the less frenzied religious forms which counseled resignation in the face of worldly unjustices on the premise that all would be righted by the blessings of the hereafter. Typically, Garland used women protagonists to communicate his disgust with narcotizing preaching. Lucretia Burns of *Prairie Folks,* one of his truly tragic figures, lives a life of overpowering destitution and hardship. A thoughtless husband and the farm have combined to break her utterly. "'I've worked like no nigger ever worked . . . I've had enough t' drive an Indian crazy . . . I'd take poison if it wa'n't f'r the young ones.'" When the salving hope of "another world" is called to her attention, she recoils angrily: "Don't talk that. I don't want that kind o' comfort. I want a decent chance here. I want 'o rest an' be happy now." Garland injects himself into the tale in the guise of a young intellectual pondering the plight of those like Lucretia Burns. The humanistic reform impulse informs his pronouncement that "'the very religion they hear is soporific. They are taught to be content here that they may be happy hereafter. Suppose there isn't any hereafter?'". . . .

Late in life Garland recalled [in *Roadside Meetings*] with a tinge of guilt the unintended offense which he had given in the home of acquaintances in France. At dinner, he had allowed a glass of precious vintage wine to stand by his plate untouched so long that his hostess inferred his displeasure. He knew that he had been written off as a savage and he tried to explain by references to his early life among "simple and abstemious folk." On that occasion, his "untutored palate" caused him remorse. In his writings however he viewed abstention both as honorable and as necessary to the harmonious working of human affairs. In the 1890's this youthful and self-proclaimed *enfant terrible* may have been discomfitted by what amounted to restrictive posture in regard to alcohol. Still, like many reformers, he hopefully anticipated the general curtailment of its use.

Garland rarely delivered himself of sustained frontal assaults upon the traffic which exercised so many reform-minded people. Rather, he portrayed alcohol as an integral facet of the settings in which human beings went astray. In *Other Main-Travelled Roads* the "alien in the pines" attempts to re-order a life disrupted if not ruined by drink. In the same book, the story, **"A Fair Exile,"** conveys a diatribe against the divorce racket in Dakota and delivers a characteristically tangential blow at demon rum. The "fair exile"—a prospective divorcee—represents besmirched

womanhood. But, as she points out, little could be expected of one who has a brute for a husband and "a big Chicago brewer for a father." Against such a background, her flight to a divorce colony full of men with "hot leering eyes" and "liquor-laden breath" appeared more understandable, if no less tawdry. Because he saw his own background as marked by wholesome simplicity, Garland practiced literary dissociation where liquor was concerned. He made it a trapping of an alien and distasteful milieu. Ordinarily the city was that enemy country and, when Garland depicted the urban scene, he readily detected the noxious and demoralizing fumes of strong drink. . . .

Of course, Garland's reputation rests upon his airing of the grievances and problems of rural America. After a period of self-directed training in the libraries of Boston the young man returned to the West and surveyed the scenes of misery and poverty which generated his mood of severity of the early 1890's. His best and bitterest efforts went into painting the "savage and unrelenting" [as he termed it in *Roadside Meetings*] pictures inspired by that visit—**"Up the Coulé," "Under the Lion's Paw," "Lucretia Burns,"** and **"Before the Low Green Door."** Indeed, his disgust and outrage, conjoined with the impact of a philosophical vogue, moved Garland toward a position of naturalistic fatalism. Thus, one frequently finds the metaphorical emblems of pessimistic determinism in his writings of the period. In **"Up the Coulé"** farmer Grant McLane compares himself to "a fly in a pan of molasses." In the autobiographical *Roadside Meetings* Garland reiterated what for him was a compelling simile by referring to the nation's agrarians as held helpless like "flies in a pool of tar." Jason Edwards' daughter Alice sees life as a "relentless, horrible struggle," and Bailey of **The Mocassin Ranch** considers men's actions as the groupings of "animaliculae"—"battling, breeding, dying."

But, as Lars Ahnebrink has shown, the true spirit of the son of the middle border had informing principles far removed from grim determinism. Even in his darkest moments, Garland maintained his sanguine persuasion and eschewed the despair which he occasionally expressed. He insisted that the wretched farm conditions could be improved; indeed, they could be perfected.

Garland suggested two general means of correcting the deplorable situation to which he had given dramatic documentation. First, farmers must organize. Through coherent political activism they could balance the unfair fight which they waged against the town and the economic middlemen. . . .

More spectacularly, Garland called for the implementation of the Henry George single tax system. In *Progress and Poverty* George had pondered the grimly paradoxical fact that poverty spread in our society quite as inexorably as did progress. He reasoned that the key to the riddle inhered in our land system. Those who owned no land faced the Sisyphean task of paying ever higher rents for the property they used—property the value of which *they* rather than the *owners* worked to appreciate. While time and renters enhanced the value of property, owners gleaned the "unearned increment." By George's view, justice demanded that owners should receive only that income from their holdings which resulted from their own efforts to improve it. Appreciation in value which came as a natural result of the country's growth belonged not to the individual, because he had done nothing to earn it. It belonged to society, and society should confiscate it in the form of a tax—a single tax sufficient for all governmental needs. In *Progress and Poverty* Garland saw the basic cause of and cure for the depressed conditions of the farm population. . . .

As Henry Smith has noted [in *Virgin Land: The American West as Symbol and Myth,* 1957], the son of the middle border achieved his best synthesis of reform persuasion and literary depiction in the story **"Under the Lion's Paw."** Here, Garland stated forcefully and artistically the cruel logic of the conditions which beset and debilitated the American farmer. He neglected only one ingredient— the solution. Victimized by natural calamity in Kansas, Tim Haskins removes to Iowa where human greed treats him no better. Like nearly all of Garland's characters, Haskins has the ability to achieve; by Herculean effort he makes that run-down farm fairly bloom. Jim Butler, the ugly embodiment of an unjust land system, undoes his accomplishments. Butler, the author informs us, "believed in land speculation as the surest way of getting rich." While he does nothing, the growth of the country aggrandizes the worth of his holdings. Haskins, having achieved a relative prosperity offers to buy the farm which he has rented and worked for the past three years. But its owner, recognizing the enhanced value of the place, quotes a price double that of the original arrangement. The painful dialogue accentuates the identities of victim and oppressor as Haskins angrily points to the fruits of his own efforts:

"But *you* had nothin' t'do about that. It's my work and my money."

"You bet it was; but it's my land."

"But *you've* done nothing . . . You hain't added a cent. I put it all there myself . . . I worked an' sweat to improve it . . . I'm kickin' about payin' you twice f'r my own things,—my own fences, my own kitchen, my own garden."

"*Your* improvements! The law will sing another tune . . . It's the law. The reg'lar thing. Everybody does it."

Because the law sang another tune, the farmer was helpless.

Things could have been different, however, and ultimately, by Garland's telling, they will be. Turning to the past, he has the village radical of *Jason Edwards* recount errors already committed:

"If we hadn't give away s'much land to the railroad an' let landsharks gobble it up, an' if we'd taxed 'em as we ought to, we wouldn't be crowded way out here

where it can't rain without blowing hard enough to tear the ears off a cast-iron bulldog—"

Turning forward, Garland's young intellectual, after having viewed the torments of Sim Burns and his wife Lucretia, projects into the future and outlines "his plan of action":

The abolition of all indirect taxes; the State control of all privileges the private ownership of which interfered with the equal right of all. He would utterly destroy speculative holdings of the earth. He would have land everywhere brought to its best use, by appropriating all ground rents to the use of the State . . .

This, we assume, would assure the felicity of Sim Burns and his wife.

Garland impressed most people with his depictions of farm conditions and his appeals for betterment. However, he wove into his protest literature another, final theme which exceeds the farm in prevalence and, it seems to me, in importance. He called it "The Real Woman-question" [in *A Spoil of Office*]. Quite likely, Garland felt a sizeable burden of disquietude, if not outright guilt, for having forsaken his parents in the bleak country setting. He dedicated **Main-Travelled Roads** to his father and mother "whose half-century pilgrimage on the main-travelled road of life has brought them only toil and deprivation . . ." But his emotional intensity followed a narrower channel; his mother and her numberless counterparts most centrally exercised his concern. In his recollections he went quickly from the general to the compelling particular— from the farm blight to the blight of womanhood. Like Ole Rölvaag, he operated from the assumption—sometimes tacit, sometimes explicit—that the women bore the ghastliest burdens of the pioneering process.

Indeed, almost any evil to which Garland pointed hurriedly eventuated in a cross borne by the females of the species. All other injustices had their upshot and logical finality in suffering womanhood. Who suffered under the influence of an out-dated and inhuman religion? Everyone, of course, but women were more susceptible to the hurt. Thus, it is the girl Grace who nearly succumbs to the morbid sway of the exhorter in **"A Day of Grace."** Religion's soporific resignation re-enforces the hopelessness of Sim Burns' wife Lucretia. And in his most acrimonious story, **"Before the Low Green Door,"** the dying farm wife has long felt the verdict of utter futility pronounced by the spiritual values of her time. When the world drank, wives and daughters suffered for it. . . .

The "fair exile" [in the story **"A Fair Exile"**], driven to a Dakota divorce colony by a husband who consumes liquor and a father who produces it, now must run the gauntlet of drummers and ne'er-do-wells—"wild beasts roused by the presence of prey," eyes gleaming with "relentless lust." . . .

Though villainy as well as heroism abounds in Garland's works of the 1890's, to only one woman did he ascribe a malicious spirit. In **"A Division in the Coolly"** a quite undeveloped character craftily exacerbates the rift between two sisters who have quarreled over an inheritance. This general absence of feminine knavery conveys implicitly what Garland often expounded explicitly. Whatever ugly fates befell people, especially women, the blame belonged to men. In **"Sim Burn's Wife"** Garland has Lily the schoolteacher concede that "the case is not all in favor of the suffering wives, and against the brutal husbands." But the admission appears awkward, weighted and contrived. Lily muses in a more Garlandian vein when she recognizes women as "the crowning wonder and beauty of God's world." As they ride the train to Heron Lake and a divorce court, the young lawyer—here speaking for the author—ominously tells the "fair exile": "You're on the road to hell!" But this represents a judgment upon male society, not upon the young girl who though "naturally pure," was now reduced to being a "lamb among lustful wolves." Speaking for his sex, the lawyer informs her that "'we are responsible . . . for every tragic, incomplete woman's life.'" . . .

Garland's abandonment of reformist realism has generally been explained in one of two ways. The more charitable contention first made by his friend Henry Blake Fuller in "The Downfall of Abner Joyce" [in *Under the Skylights,* 1901] holds that Garland, an amiable fellow by nature, made a comfortable acquiescence in the style of life to which success exposed him. "Yes," Fuller wrote, "Abner had made his compromise with the world." According to others, Garland's realistic posture had the marks of calculation and opportunism. He had, with an eye to "the main chance," used protest realism as a means to the end of success and prominence.

The two, of course, are closely related. But an aspect of the latter has gone largely unnoticed. That is the possibility that Garland's desertion of realism and naturalism might well have been quite as opportunistic (or as intellectually justifiable, or as *au courant*) as his previous championing of those things. At various levels, realism and naturalism were arousing impatience, boredom and antipathy. At the popular level, newspapers of the period frequently used Howells, the exemplar of realism, as the object of caustic jibes. His opposition to the hanging of the Chicago anarchists in the wake of the Haymarket affair moved the Minneapolis *Tribune* [October 31, 1887] to mordant aspersion. "Those of the anarchists," according to an editorial, "who have read the novels written by Mr. Howells are said to be willing to let the law take its course." In the same context the Washington *Post* noted simply: "Poor Howells. Realism has driven him mad" [November 6, 1887]. In 1882 the St. Louis *Spectator* [November 4, 1882] noted that many were reading *A Modern Instance,* and all were disappointed. In describing the characters of the novel, the *Spectator* employed a term that would become a byword—"Commonplace." In that connection the Boston *Globe* uneasily reported a London journal's contention that the burgeoning dime novel was "'a beautiful, unconscious protest against Mr. Howells and realism'" [June 19, 1883].

This discontent did not confine itself to popular journals. William Marion Reedy of *The Mirror* judged the Chicago *Chap-Book* a fine publication, but "too everlastingly devoted to Mr. Hamlin Garland to be a continual delight to sane people" [quoted in *The Man in the "Mirror"* by Max Putzel, 1963]. In whimsical fashion Eugene Field—poet, art critic and humorist—told in 1893 of "The Battle of the Realists and Romancists." As point of departure he used the "famous intellectual wrestling-match" between Garland and Mrs. Mary Hartwell Catherwood at a writers' congress.

> Garland is one of the apostles of realism. Mrs. Catherwood has chosen the better part. . . . Mr. Garland's heroes sweat and do not wear socks. . . . Mrs. Catherwood's heroes—and they are the heroes we like—are aggressive, courtly, picturesque fellows. . . . Mr. Garland's *in hoc signo* is a dung-fork or a butter-paddle; Mrs. Catherwood's is a lance or an embroidery needle. Give us the lance and its companion every time.

Continuing the playfulness, Field explained that "in an evil hour" Garland had fallen under the "baleful influences of William D. Howells, and—there you are." The author of "Sharps and Flats" felt that Garland was not so far gone as to be beyond redemption, "if he will only keep away from Howells. In all solemnity we declare it to be our opinion that Howells is the only bad habit Garland has" [*The Writings in Prose and Verse of Eugene Field,* 1901].

At a vast remove in temperament from Field, Ambrose Bierce wrote more biting disparagement of the school that Garland and Howells represented. He dismissed the former as one who wrote "with the corn-fed enthusiasm of the prairies," as an illustration of the "Western mind which has discovered that marks can be made on paper with a pen." "Cato Howells"—law-giver of the realistic school—demanded fuller treatment. Howells and those of "the Reporter School," Bierce wrote in 1897, "hold that what is not interesting in life becomes interesting in letters—the acts, thoughts, feelings of commonplace people, the lives and loves of noodles, nobodies, ignoramuses and millionaires; of the village vulgarian, the rural maiden whose spiritual grace is not incompatible with the habit of falling over her own feet . . ." The "prodigal excess" of detail was precisely that which "bores us our whole lives through." The writer who could not see that life is "picturesque, enchanting, astonishing, terrible, is denied the gift and faculty divine, and being no poet can write no prose" [*Collected Works of Ambrose Bierce,* 1911].

On the last day of 1899 the Portland *Oregonian* carried a lengthy review of George E. Woodberry's *The Heart of Man.* Few books, the reviewer contended, "evidenced more fully the revolt against realism (re-baptized naturalism) now sweeping over the world." In 1908 Chesterton [in *Orthodoxy,* 1945] reviled the realist school on grounds similar to that of Bierce. "A baby," he remarked, "is about the only person, I should think, to whom a modern realistic novel could be read without boring him." A few years later James Branch Cabell compounded the indictment. Realistic literature was not only boring but psychologically insupportable [*Beyond Life,* 1919]. As Garland observed in his diary in 1900 on the occasion of his fortieth birthday, "life will not bear close investigation. It yields depressing results at best. At its worst it is not a road to be retravelled" [*The Diaries of Hamlin Garland,* 1968].

The desertion of realism and naturalism placed Garland in consonance with some of the best thought of the time, as well as some of the most popular. In the essay, "The Present Dilemma in Philosophy," William James in 1906 wrote of the "progress of science" which had implied "the enlargement of the material universe and the diminution of man's importance." This growth of "naturalistic or positivistic feeling" meant that "the romantic spontaneity and courage are gone, the vision is materialistic and depressing" [*Pragmatism,* 1922]. Treating European thought, H. Stuart Hughes tells of the "intellectual revolution" of the 1890's—"The Revolt against Positivism" [*Consciousness and Society,* 1958]. Recalling his own experiences in *The Romantic 90's* [1926] Richard LeGallienne wrote that the "motive philosophy" of that decade was "the will to romance," "the modern determination to escape from the deadening thraldom of materialism." James at one level, Garland at another represent that "modern determination" in America. "Do these little fellows, the so-called realists," Bierce asked in 1897, "ever think of the goodly company which they deny themselves by confining themselves to their clumsy feet and pursuing their stupid noses through the barren hitherland, while just beyond the Delectable Mountains lies in light the Valley of Dreams . . . ?" [quoted in *A Daughter of the Middle Border*]. Shortly, Garland crossed the Delectable Mountains to the Valley of Dreams. And, as he noted later, ". . . I found myself almost popular" [*Collected Works*].

In a variety of ways Garland has lent a heated voice to the emotional and intellectual questioning which presaged the twentieth century "age of reform." In portraying lives thwarted by outworn institutions he occasionally lapsed into a tone so deeply censorious as to border on despair. The dying farm woman in **"Before the Low Green Door"** finds no comfort whatever in thoughts of the hereafter because she senses that "God himself"—if there be—could never compensate for what she had suffered. Far more commonly, Garland equivocated. He skirted hopelessness by accepting the central contention of the Henry George ethos—suffering came from faults in human laws and institutions, not from the dictates of nature nor the designs of God. He pronounced his disgust at hardship and injustice about him, but always with the felicitous assumption that man could will and work a better future. As an artist he might have to depict a scene of present anguish in order to corrode a "steel chain of ideas" [as Eric Goldman stated in *Rendezvous with Destiny,* 1952] binding society to the past. But that necessity did not undermine his conviction that the future is filled with "magnificent promise" [*Crumbling Idols*]. . . .

Thus, the man's apostasy might be viewed in yet another way. Given the fact that his protest realism was so fully

predicated on optimism, one might well infer that a weakening of that optimism begot the change. In recent years historians have tended to view the turn-of-the-century period as one that witnessed the "end of innocence" and the "loss of confidence." Surely, Garland fits that pattern. Personally, there was the disturbing awareness of physical aging, and a muted bitterness over literary potential unrealized. Cultural and societal changes had an equally disquieting effect. Cities overrun by alien hordes, demagogy in politics, the literary obsession with "sensual love" and "atavistic morals" led to the conclusion that "our world is disintegrating" [as Garland termed it in his diaries]. Here, the aged Garland was in tune with the philosophic despair of Joseph Wood Krutch's *The Modern Temper* and Walter Lippmann's *A Preface to Morals*. His flight to insipid and banal romance and to the realm of the mystic and the occult seems at least understandable. Talcott, Tuttle, Rose Dutcher and other Garlandians of the 1890's often seem unsatisfyingly buoyant. But they were reform figures. As G. K. Chesterton put it [in *Charles Dickens: A Critical Study,* 1906], "The optimist is a better reformer than the pessimist; and the man who believes life to be excellent is the man who alters it most." *Crumbling Idols* expresses it well: "Because he is sustained by love and faith in the future, he can be mercilessly true." When Garland ceased to be "mercilessly true," he was no longer sustained by "love and faith in the future."

Henry Nash Smith on the importance of Garland's short fiction:

Garland's early stories are not a literary achievement of the first or even of the second rank, but they mark the end of a long evolution in attitudes. It had at last become possible to deal with the Western farmer in literature as a human being instead of seeing him through a veil of literary convention, class prejudice, or social theory.

Henry Nash Smith, in his Virgin Land: The American West as Symbol and Myth, *Vintage Books, 1950.*

Jack L. Davis (essay date 1978)

SOURCE: "Hamlin Garland's Indians and the Quality of Civilized Life," in *The Critical Reception of Hamlin Garland: 1891-1978,* Charles L. P. Silet, Robert E. Welch, and Richard Boudreau, eds., The Whitston Publishing Company, 1985, pp. 426-39.

[*In the following essay, Davis argues that the stories in* The Book of the American Indian *and the novel* The Captain of the Gray-Horse Troop *reflect Garland's chang-*

ing attitude toward Native American assimilation. In these works, the critic maintains, Garland attempted to "work out a concept which acknowledged the value of traditional Indian society and yet which showed the Indian could benefit by civilization."]

Hamlin Garland's reputation today is fairly secure as a chronicler of Euro-American civilization establishing itself in the northern Midwest. In the early and latter phases of his fiction, as Donald Pizer [in *American Literary Realism*, 1 (Fall 1967)], Jay Martin [in *Harvests of Change*, 1967], and Robert Gish [in *Hamlin Garland: The Far West*, 1976] have noted, Garland attacked the myth of the easy, good life in the old Northwest and introduced Eastern readers to the arduous physical and social realities on the raw middle border. *Main-Travelled Roads* (1891) and *Rose of Dutcher's Coolly* (1895) are the best known examples of that early realistic fiction. Yet in his middle phase of over two decades, beginning in 1895, Garland turned his attention farther west, apparently discarding everything he had previously said about the need for literature to deal with the unpleasant as well as the pleasant aspects of life. As a consequence, most of his work during this middle period is viewed as a temporary abdication of Garland's undisputed gift for delineating the hard realities of western life.

However, Robert Gish has recently suggested that this very phase, when Garland betook himself farther west to meet ranchers, miners, Indian agents, and sundry tribes of native Americans, is the most interesting to contemporary students of western literature. It is true that most of the dozen novels and many stories of this Far West period simply invoke the romanticized vision of the West Garland strove so hard to puncture earlier. Yet the Indian material, the stories written mainly between 1895 and 1905 but later collected in *The Book of the American Indian* (1923) and also the novel *The Captain of the Gray-Horse Troop* (1902) are truly landmark treatments of Indians. They suggest that Garland was not simply escaping back into the mythology of ideal life in the West, but actually was extending the trenchant criticism begun in his early work.

During his travels in the Far West, Garland found the Indian increasingly crucial to his design for critiquing the failure of American westerners to create a worthy civilization. But it took him a long time to discover precisely what Indian culture disclosed about the deficiencies of white civilization. Early in his Indian studies Garland himself thought he was dealing solely with the Indian problem—that is, how to help the Indian walk the white man's road and how to reform abuses of the reservation system. Only slowly did he realize that the Indian problem was primarily a white one.

Garland's fascination with the Indian began in a serious way with a trip to the Southwestern pueblos of Acoma, Isleta, Laguna, and Zuni in 1895. He then traveled back up to Montana and the Dakotas, then in 1900 down to Oklahoma, where he visited John Seeger to hear tales about the Indian way of life. Later that year on the Stand-

ing Rock reservation he was fortunate enough to speak, through interpreters, with warriors of the late Sitting Bull. The novella **"The Silent Eaters"** comes out of this last experience. In all, Garland visited over a dozen reservations; gained the confidence of several Indian agents; and learned something about the conditions and feelings of American natives around the turn of the century. That education naturally focused his attention upon the pressing problems of assimilation and reservation abuses. Thus, it is no surprise that both *The Captain of the Gray-Horse Troop* and *The Book of the American Indian* are usually discussed in terms of those two issues. Indisputably, Garland was a reformer at heart; nor was he content to make his point in fiction. He also published [in *North American Review*, 174 (April 1902)] a closely argued policy statement which proposed explicit alternatives to governmental policies administered on reservations. And by the standards of American thinking in 1902, his proposals were penetrating and persuasive.

But as important as Garland's sleuthing of reservation ills was, it is not the sole issue in his Indian material. Rather he was on the track of a more substantive, if more subtle, question. Would civilization actually bring the defeated aborigines the good life? This problem, of course, has been with Western civilization ever since its technologically and numerically superior peoples have overrun others and imposed their standards upon them. Inevitably, the same disquieting question was working at the back of Garland's mind, and it gave a distinctively troubled cast to his Indian fiction. Its presence, indeed, creates the running dialogue that makes this work absorbing to today's reader.

Early, Garland's bottom-line belief was that the process of civilization was irreversible. He believed the imperative of social evolution dictated that the red man must henceforth walk the white man's road. But as a result of his observations on Indian reservations, Garland came to see that Indian ways had their own values; so he compromised by advocating that the Indian maintain his own identity while walking the road toward civilization. This more enlightened view, however, raised a number of paradoxes and forced Garland into a closer examination of Indian resistance. He became determined to discover "the soul of the Indian," as one of his fictive spokesmen put it. And at that point he opened himself to the seductive possibility that native life possessed a quality missing from, but perhaps necessary to, American civilization. Thus, Garland worked himself into that classic dilemma of double cultural vision which has been with our tradition ever since Sir Thomas More used Vespucci's account of the Inca empire to create a vision of an ideal society in *Utopia* (1517). And no less prestigious American predecessors than Cooper, Hawthorne, Thoreau, and Melville had at times suggested that native culture might be a viable referent against which basic failures of American culture could be judged.

The best place to begin tracing Garland's search for the essential, and differentiating, essence of Indianness is an almost offhand remark he wrote in a travel essay, "Hit-ting the Trail" (*McClure's Magazine,* 12 [February, 1899], pp. 298-304). In a brilliant synecdoche he compares the Indian trail with the white man's road. The red man's path is "always indirect, accommodating, patient of obstruction—an adjustment, not a ravage. It alarms nothing. It woos every wild thing. It never disfigures. It sacrifices itself. It loses itself in nature." Further, "the Trail is poetry; a wagon road is prose; the railroad, arithmetic." These images may be taken simply as romantic hyperbole directed invidiously against that supremely practical American temperament [Alexis] De Tocqueville desparingly noted [in *Democracy in America,* 1942 edition]. They are that, but more. The synecdoche is so marvelously accurate about the quality of Indian thinking that even Levi-Strauss would be hard pressed to improve on it, although he devoted an entire volume to analyzing "the savage mind." As Garland traveled deeper into Indian country he learned more of its almost intangible quality. He recorded of his experiences there that "it has given me blessed release from care and worry and the troubled thinking of our modern day. It has been a return to the primitive and peaceful. Whenever the pressures of our complex city life thin my blood and benumb my brain, I seek relief on the trail; and when I hear the coyote waking to the yellow dawn my cares fall from me—I am happy" (*McClure's Magazine,* p. 304). It is this elusive peace of mind, happiness, which becomes the motif of his Indian fiction. And while he was no pioneer in discovering the paradox that civilization prized material advancement often at the expense of peace of mind, he recognized here a central objection of Indians to walking the white man's road.

Though Garland never quite resolved this paradox, a good share of his Indian fiction works in that direction. The key term, which eluded him, is what a more recent writer has called "quality." Robert Persig in *Zen and the Art of Motorcycle Maintenance* [1974], has argued that quality is what our form of civilization conspicuously lacks. It emerges only when one is perfectly attuned to his environment and situation. As he says: "Peace of mind isn't at all superficial. . . . It's the whole thing. . . . The reason for this is that peace of mind is a prerequisite for a perception of that Quality which is beyond romantic Quality and classical Quality and which unites the two." In Persig's view cultures tend to approach the world either in the romantic (intuitive) way or classical (analytical) way. He argues that Western tradition has been so obsessively rationalistic that it has failed to achieve a holistic sense of being, a caring identification with the environment. Ultimately, this was the recognition towards which Garland was working. If technical advances could only be forced upon the Indian by inculcating him with the calculative mentality of white culture, he might be more victim than beneficiary. Thus, Garland tried to work out a concept which acknowledged the value of traditional Indian society and yet which showed how the Indian could benefit by civilization. As we follow his thinking through several key stories in *The Book of the American Indian* and selected episodes of *The Captain of the Gray-Horse Troop,* the overall direction of Garland's thought will become clear.

"Drifting Crane" was the first Indian story, appearing first in *Harper's* in 1890 before its collection in ***The Book of the American Indian*** (New York: Harper, 1923). Its dramatic effect is achieved by juxtaposing two representatives of the competing cultures in what amounts to a stereotypical white man versus red man confrontation. A white rancher moves out on newly taken Indian land and is visited by the local chief, Drifting Crane, who views him as an invader. Garland describes the meeting thus: "It was a thrilling, a significant scene. It was in absolute truth the meeting of the modern vidette of civilization with one of the rearguard of retreating barbarism. Each man was a type; each was wrong, and each was right. The Indian was as true and noble from the barbaric point of view as the white man. He was a warrior and a hunter; made so by circumstances over which he had no control." Here Garland has acknowledged the presence of two standards, barbaric and civilized; but clearly the latter is of a higher order. As Persig points out, the basic structure for all Western knowledge is a hierarchy. In this case, Garland simply follows Lewis Henry Morgan's hierarchy of social evolution: savage, barbaric, and civilized. The significant law here is that lower cultures have fewer human rights.

It takes Garland a while to locate the nature of cultural superiority. It is not found in the character of the rancher, although he is a courageous, not a vicious, person. Rather Garland says: "The settler represented the unflagging energy and fearless heart of the American pioneer. Narrow-minded, partly brutalized by hard labor and a lonely life, yet an admirable figure for all that. As he looked into the Indian's face he seemed to grow in height. He felt behind him all the weight of millions of westward-moving settlers; he stood the representative of an unborn state." The fallacy of manifest destiny was not yet apparent to Garland, although the modern reader will see in this passage the rationale of one Western nation which used this philosophy to justify conquest, reservation-like concentration camps, and genocidal pogroms against an allegedly inferior race.

The settler then takes down his rifle from the wall. It is:

> The magazine rifle, most modern of guns; he patted the stock, pulled the crank, throwing a shell into view.

> "You know the thing, chief?" The Indian nodded slightly.

> "Well, I'll go when—this—is—empty."

The images are perhaps the most revealing thing in the dialogue. White superiority is based upon force backed by technological skill, especially in weaponry. Yet the rancher's machismo is disturbed by a curious note of ambivalence. Not oblivious of the great chief's dignity, he muses "there's land enough for us all, or ought to be. I don't understand—Well, I'll leave it to Uncle Sam." This would be the last time Garland let the ranchers off so easily. In later fiction they become a favorite bete noir, as they deliberately provoke reservation Indians into hostilities as an excuse for retaliatory preemption of more native land.

"The Story of Howling Wolf," first published in 1903, stands midway in philosophy between **"Drifting Crane"** and the concluding story, **"The Silent Eaters."** Here the traditionalist chief is transmuted into one ready to walk the white road, accepting the reservation agent, a just cavalry officer, as his role model. Carrying a note from the agent attesting to his peaceable character, Howling Wolf seeks to widen his experiences with white people by visiting a nearby town. Unfortunately, the townspeople have just been whipped by local yellow journalism into hysteria by false accounts of uprisings on the reservation. Howling Wolf is treacherously attacked and thrown in jail. And then tricked into thinking his freedom is being granted, he is ironically delivered into the hands of a mob during a Fourth of July celebration at which he is ridden down, beaten, dragged behind horses, mutilated, and left for dead. Miraculously, his iron constitution sustains him, but he is left a blind and bitter wreck of a once magnificent warrior. The savage irony of Howling Wolf's story suggests that Garland is beginning to think assimilation poses less of an Indian problem than a white one. The author's distrust of cowboys and ranchers, especially of the Far Western types observed in his travels, surfaces unmistakably. He is out to expose sensationally what he terms "the cruel, leering, racial hate of the border man, to whom the red man is big game." Not only is the story an outraged protest against white brutality, it discloses that the Indian has become primarily a symbolic problem. Since he had, by this time, been defeated militarily and reduced to beggary on barren reservations, he posed no material threat. Garland intuits that something crucial lies beneath the continuing need to vindictively and falsely hound the very people one professes to be leading into a higher level of existence. He has no answer yet to this mystery.

The concluding tale in *The Book of the American Indian* is the novella **"The Silent Eaters,"** which takes its name from Sitting Bull's trusted executive council, men of probity who eat in silence, disdaining any frivolity, while they meditate upon the difficulties of their chief's losing struggle to retain cultural hegemony for his defeated people. The narrator, Iapi, is son to one Silent Eater. He has been encouraged by Sitting Bull and Lieutenant Davies, a typical Garland military hero and intellectual, to learn about white ways. Davies, a man trained in classical logic, admonishes Iapi that "knowledge is power. . . . Study, acquire words, the white man's wisdom, then you will be able to defend the rights of your people." Sadly, by following this advice, Iapi becomes trapped between the opposing forces represented by Sitting Bull, the conservator of traditional values, and the Indian-hating agent, who is characterized by the author as "hard, unimaginative, and jealous of his authority. He was also a bigot and it is hard for anyone not a poet or a philosopher to be just to a people holding a different view of the world. Race hatred and religious prejudices stand like walls between the red man and the white." Here Garland not only amplifies the note of cultural relativity sounded earlier, he suggests that civilization breeds racial and religious intolerance pre-

Garland at work, circa 1885.

cisely because it has convinced all but poets and philosophers that its vision of civilized man is the only one. And to turn to Persig again, we see uncovered the commonest fallacy of classical thinking, the idea that of all alternative hypotheses about reality, there is only a single correct one. Ergo, civilized man has the only true way of life and the only true religion. All other humans of all other persuasions are wrong, and their insistence upon false culture and religion simply verifies their unworthiness. They are a threat. When one understands this thinking, the antagonism toward all things Indian becomes a little clearer.

In **"The Silent Eaters,"** then, an absolutist culture confronts and methodically sets out to destroy a pluralistic one. The reason is simply its inability to see the quality of pluralistic vision or the higher vision which Persig claims contains both with equanimity. And that is precisely the resolution Garland seeks—how the Indian can retain his vision and still assimilate white ways. But only in the character of the great Sitting Bull do we find the possibility of such transcendence, and he is adamantly opposed to assimilation, at least under the present circumstances. His character is most insightfully drawn. The Bull has been a shrewd and moral politician since his early manhood, an inveterate peacemaker who is brilliant in detecting and defusing threats against the wellbeing of the people, and a genius at ratiocination who empirically evaluates the evidence about the Ghost Dance and finds its validity wanting. Yet this paragon of wisdom, justice, and forebearance is destroyed by the viciousness of a conquering people determined to turn the vanquished into carbon copies of themselves. Sitting Bull, however, is allowed the last word on this issue, commenting tartly that if the Great Spirit had wanted Indians to be white people, he would have made them white. So much for the claim that there exists an hierarchal order of races.

Besides the character of Sitting Bull, we do not learn much about Indian personality and culture. One exception comes in the opening lines when Garland, this time poet rather than philosopher, invokes the tranquility of Plains life before the white man came. In the spring when grass sprang back to life, creeks flowed again, and the sun waxed warmer, there was a time of matchless beauty, harmony, and plenty. This seamless unity of beauty was matched by the serenity and peace of mind in Plains Indian villages. But later in the story, Garland hints that white people find these same golden plains hostile and lonely. There are indeed alternative realities. The white man carried on to the plains his antagonism to nature and subverted the natural order of things. This is the kind of progress Garland begins to find disturbing.

As a philosophic statement, **"The Silent Eaters"** exposes the mendacity of white protestations to improve the quality of barbaric life. The Sioux are systematically relocated to the poorest land, dispossessed of their horses and hunting gear, and dispersed from their communal village pattern once tribal leadership in governance and sacred ceremonies has been destroyed. Then they are asked to farm this worthless land, emulating the life patterns of the alienated and materialistic settlers who pushed them out. The final straw for many Indians was the implacable desire of agents, missionaries, and teachers to destroy in their children any respect for their elders or traditional values and beliefs. It is very difficult in this portrait, which was solidly grounded upon Garland's personal investigation of reservations, to find a key to assimilation without the loss of Indian integrity. Yet Garland was still convinced that if abuses were corrected, the best of the two worlds could be brought together. His before-mentioned article, "The Red Man's Present Needs," articulately sets before the American public the need and possibilities of each reform.

In the same year as this article, 1902, Garland also attempted to put his theories about bridging the two cultures into fictive action. His chief spokesman is Captain Curtis, the title hero in *The Captain of the Gray-Horse Troop*. The author's paternalism toward Indians is disappointingly obvious when Curtis's superior officer offers him an assignment as reservation agent: "You'll have a clear field for experiment at Smith. You can try all your pet theories on the Tetong." It would seem these Indians are reduced to little more than subjects of amateur experimentation in psycho-cultural engineering. This is not a promising start.

After Curtis takes over as agent, he and his ethnologist friend Lawson, as well as the young artist and aristocrat Elsie, debate the proper diagnosis and treatment of the Tetong problem. On one side are the enlightened men, on the other Elsie, who as daughter of the arch-conservative Senator Brisbane defends the genocidal assimilation approach of the U. S. War Department then administering the reservation system. Ultimately, Curtis wins the lovely Elsie to his side, though with a surprising concession, for she is artist enough to see that Curtis's rationalistic theories negelct the aesthetics of human life.

As Garland, through Curtis, struggles toward a principle to reconcile white and red realities, he first examines the doctrine of progress as Western peoples conceive it. Curtis muses that it may not be necessary for his Tetong charges to immediately, or ever, progress to the intensive agricultural and industrial techniques of Euro-Americans. Early in the novel he reflects that "the older I grow the less certain I am that any race of people has a monopoly of the virtues. I do not care to see the 'little people' of the world civilized in the way in which the word is commonly used. . . . If I could, I would civilize only to the extent of making life easier and happier—the religious beliefs, the songs, the native dress—all these things I would retain. What is life for, if not this?" While this judicious view moves Garland closer to the solution he seeks, an Indian might reply that Garland's assumptions are based upon a highly inaccurate history. It was the white man's arrival, introduction of European diseases, and wholesale seizure of land that destroyed for Indians their easy and happy life. But Garland was working toward an important principle. If the Indians themselves could determine which elements of foreign culture they wanted to adopt, a healthy balance between red and white might be struck. After all, the Sioux had radically transformed their society by integrating the European horse. Incidentally, one should note that Captain Curtis actually subverts his espousal of retaining native customs. Only at special ceremonies are the Tetong encouraged to wear native garb and remember their traditions.

In fact, Garland had not done his homework well at all. He pictures the frustrating difficulties of getting the Tetongs to become farmers. While it is probably true they relied extensively during the past hundred years upon a hunting economy, they were by no means ignorant of agriculture. But the exasperated agent Curtis maligns the intellectual capacity and motivation of red people. Though the Tetong have faithfully planted unfamiliar crops according to Curtis's instructions, they just cannot get the hang of farming: "These child-like souls said: 'Behold we have done our part, now let Mother Earth and Father Sun bring forth the harvest. We cannot ripen the grain; we can only wait. Besides we are weary'." In short, they are too lazy to weed and cultivate their crops by the workaholic standards of white people. Nor do they grasp the nature of a plant's life cycle: "The seed and the apple are too far apart" in time for them to see the connection. As we know now, and Garland should have been able to discover from narratives of exploration, Indian botanists were among the foremost in the world. They had domesticated numerous plants like maize before the dawn of European civilization. In fact, over four-sevenths of the United States' present agricultural produce is from Indian-developed crops.

By pandering to the worst suspicions of his audience about Indian intellective capacity, Garland measurably weakens the case for equitable treatment. If Indians are genetically and culturally thousands of years behind white people, how can the differences be bridged by simply eliminaing abuses on reservations? And how can the Indian expect to be assimilated on equal terms? Garland's answer is to go slow. As Captain Curtis explains: "They have developed like ourselves through countless generations of life under relatively stable conditions. These moderial conditions are giving way, are vanishing, but the mental traits they formed will persist. Think of this when you are impatient with them." This passage represents a vacillation back to Garland's earlier belief that white civilization is destined to make over the rest of the world in its image. He failed to indicate here, as he well knew, that the scientific approach of Western culture has severe limitations in providing the good life. As Persig has noted, Western-style rationality has worked very well since the Renaissance. And "so long as the need for food, clothing, and shelter is dominant [the scientific approach] will continue to work." But he warns that when such needs no longer overwhelm people, they will discover that "the whole structure of reason, handed down to us from ancient times, is no longer adequate. It begins to be seen for what it really is—emotionally hollow, esthetically meaningless and spiritually empty."

Garland is manifestly dissatisfied with Curtis's advice, since it ignores Western civilization's deficiencies, the prime target of his earlier fiction. But he is in a quandry about how the Tetong should be led along the white man's road. The best he can do is have Captain Curtis vow to stay on the reservation "till I can demonstrate my theory that, properly led, the people can be made happy." And a few pages later we learn what that entails: "To be clean, to be peaceful, to be happy—these are precepts I would teach them." Unfortunately for Garland, he has the whole thing backwards. The Tetongs were undoubtedly cleaner, more peaceful, and happier folks before civilization arrived. However, it is true that once they have been deprived of their considerable land base, they needed to learn something about the scientific approach in order to survive.

Garland does intuit the unnerving possibility of Indians becoming totally rational like whites. They will undoubtedly then lose their aesthetic and spiritual sensibilities as Persig suggests Western civilization did after the Renaissance. Garland's recognition of this vital truth appears when Captain Curtis chides Elsie for painting an old Tetong as a mindless Indian beggar. Curtis insists that "Crawling Elk is the annalist and story teller of his tribe. He carries the 'winter count' and the sacred page, and can tell you of every movement of the Tetongs for more than a century and a half. His mind is full of poetry, and his conceptions of earth and sky are beautiful. He knows little that white men know, and cares for very little what the white man fights for, but his mind teems with the lore of the mysterious universe into which he has been thrust, and which he has studied for seventy-two years. In the eyes of God, I am persuaded there is no great difference between old Crawling Elk and Herbert Spencer. The circle of Spencer's knowledge is wider, but is as far from

including the infinite as the redman's story of creation." And a moment later, Curits concludes: "All these things, and many more, you must learn before you can represent the soul of the redman. You can't afford to be unjust." Nor does Garland wish to be unfair. This long paragraph was as close as he would come to granting the Indian a complete, independent, and poetic construction of reality second only to that produced by the best mind of the Western world. That was more than almost any other white writer or anthropologist of the time would allow. Its weakness, as Persig would tell us, is that one cannot create a hierarchy of poetic and rational constructions of reality. They are inherently equal and complementary. Somehow they need to be combined: the red man's direct apprehension of nature's unity and the white man's breaking down nature into controllable entities.

In an effort to amalgamate both the poetic and rational modes, Garland reaches for a principle capable of that synthesis. Sensing that the essential quality of Indian life lies in the realm of aesthetics, but beyond language, Garland has Captain Curtis finally acknowledge the deficiency of a purely intellectual solution to the Indian (or for that matter, white) problem. Curtis confesses to his artistic fiancee, "you've given me a dim notion of a new philosophy. I haven't organized it yet, but it's something like this: Beauty is a sense of fitness, harmony. This sense of beauty—call it taste—demands positively a readjustment of the external facts of life, so that all angles, all suffering and violance, shall cease. If all men were lovers of the beautiful, the gentle, then the world would be suave and genial, and life harmoniously colored, like your own studio, and we would campaign only against ugliness. *To civilize would mean a totally different thing.* I'm not quite clear on my theory yet, but perhaps you can help me out" [my italics]. Philosophically speaking, this is the high point of *The Captain of the Gray-Horse Troop*. But Elsie proves quite unable to help Curtis develop his insight, which is frittered away in the remaining pages of the novel.

In a remarkably parallel passage from *Zen and the Art of Motorcycle Maintenance,* Persig supplies the explanation Garland sought. Persig too finds ugliness pervasive, the real enemy of the good life. But he argues that ugliness does not reside in modern technology nor its materials: "Real ugliness lies in relationships between people who produce the technology and the things they produce, which results in a similar relationship between the people who use the technology and the things they use." By this he means that in the West products of technology are not created out of a sense of identity between the craftsman and the material: "It is this identity [which non-Western people have] that modern, dualistically conceived technology lacks." In short, ugliness of spirit is what plagues Western civilization. By a curious paradox, once nature has been reduced to the manipulatable, material level, it becomes ordinary. And while it can be made to yield the physical aspects of the good life, its sacredness is lost. As Curtis noticed, the Tetong winced at the idea of tearing the breast of mother earth with a plow. It violated their carefully developed sense of identity with nature.

Persig believes the impasse between these disparate approaches can be hurdled. He argues that "the way to solve the conflict between human values and technological needs is not to run away from technology. That's impossible. The way to resolve the barriers of dualistic thought that prevent a real understanding of what technology is—not exploitation of nature, but a fusion of nature and the human spirit into a new kind of creation that transcends both." He adds that every dimension of human existence involves problems which admit of either a beautiful or ugly solution. To achieve beauty, Persig explains just what civilizing means, the principle for which Curtis groped. The requirements are "both an ability to see what 'looks good' [the Indian's well-developed aesthetic sensibility] and an ability to understand the underlying methods to arrive at that 'good' [the white man's scientific method]."

Therefore, we can conclude that Garland came very close to an understanding of the real issues involved in assimilation of Indian people. He would have come full circle to recognize that the Indian world needed less from the white world than vice versa, although both would have profited from each other. But the old Indian life, whose beauty Garland so keenly appreciated, was already whole and complete, being based upon a spiritual sense of identity with the material/spiritual world. Ugliness of spirit was discouraged there, nature was revered rather than exploited, and one's fellow man was respected despite his race or creed. The aboriginal Sioux and Tetong may have been inferior in material possessions, but not in things of the spirit.

Pushed to its logical conclusion, *The Captain of the Gray-Horse Troop* is a continuation of Garland's earlier criticism of our failure to establish a worthy civilization in America. Had we learned from the first Americans how to limit technology so it did not diminish man's identity with the wondrous world around him, there would not be the ugliness of spirit that so enraged Garland—the avariciousness of land-hungry ranchers, the leering racial brutality of drunken cowboys, the crookedness of traders, and the sanctimoniousness of missionaries and other emissaries of white culture who despised the very people they attempted to help. To Garland's credit, he opened a fruitful trail for later critics of our national culture. And his intuition that the Indian was crucial to understanding our failed culture proved perfectly accurate.

Leland Krauth (essay date 1982)

SOURCE: "Hamlin Garland: Realist of Old Age," in *Mid-America,* Vol. IX, 1982, pp. 23-37.

[*In the following excerpt, Krauth examines Garland's depiction of the elderly in* Main-Travelled Roads *and* Prairie Folks, *maintaining that the author gave "serious, extended, and successful treatment to a subject that is more often skirted in American literature—old age."*]

When he is remembered at all, Hamlin Garland is recalled in literary history as a writer who took the right trail in the beginning, as the realist of *Main-Travelled Roads,* only to wander astray into the thin atmosphere of rocky mountain romance in the end. Garland has been praised for opening the Midwest to fiction more authentically than his regional predecessors, writers like Edward Eggleston, E. W. Howe, and Joseph Kirkland; for fulfilling Howells' dictum that the commonplace is the proper subject for the realist; and for instilling into the main-stream of American writing a capacious yet gritty humanitarian sympathy. But he has, I believe, also done one other notable thing: he has given serious, extended, and successful treatment to a subject that is more often than not skirted in American literature—old age.

Garland's consideration of old people is especially notable because it runs counter to the prevailing myths embodied in the classic literature of our culture. Whitman [in *Leaves of Grass*] gave voice to the image that has stirred the American literary imagination most deeply:

> As Adam early in the morning,
> Walking forth from the bower refresh'd with sleep
> Behold me where I pass . . .

Our literature has been predisposed to see America in Edenic terms, as the New World garden, and to see the archetypal Americans as the New Adam and the New Eve, wandering hand-in-hand their solitary way, perpetually beginning anew. With their emphasis upon youthful innocence and change, our Edenic myths exclude *a priori* the elderly whose characters tend to be fixed and whose knowledge has come from a gradual accumulation of experience. In this context, Garland's depiction of the aged is both a needed counterbalance and a daring experiment. . . .

Garland himself outlived his generation of realists, "The Class of the '70s" as Warner Berthoff has called them [in The *Ferment of Realism,* 1965], that included Stephen Crane and Frank Norris. But long before he was old himself, Garland was haunted by visions of the elderly, by images of people who had, as he put it in one of the prosey, sentimental verses he sometimes mistook for poetry, grown old together:

> F'r forty years next Easter day,
>   Him and me in wind and weather
> Have been a-gittin' bent 'n' gray,
>   Moggin' along together.
>   [From *Prairie Songs.*]

The "bent 'n' gray" loom large in Garland's fiction from the first, partly because they were pivotal in his life. As Garland repeatedly made clear, the immediate impetus behind *Main-Travelled Roads* was his return from the East, first in 1887 and then again in 1888, to the prairie home of his aged parents in Ordway, South Dakota, where he discovered both regional poverty and familial distress. With a lacerating mixture of pity and guilt, he witnessed [as he recounted in the preface to *Main-Travelled Roads,*

1922] "the ugliness, the endless drudgery, and the lone-liness of the farmer's lot," and he found his parents, es-pecially his mother, hopelessly "imprisoned" in that drea-ry life. Most critics have emphasized the general aware-ness of hard times instilled in Garland by his returns, but it seems clear that what stirred his creativity, as it cut closest to the bone of his compassion, was the plight of his aging parents. Garland got the idea for the first of the **Main-Travelled Roads** stories, **"Mrs. Ripley's Trip,"** from his mother, and he wrote most of it in between grinding work with his fifty-nine year old father as a stacker in the wheat harvest. In a real sense, Garland's aged and strug-gling parents—to whom he dedicated his book—provided the models as well as the inspiration for **Main-Travelled Roads**.

Old people are central to the book. They appear in one role or another in all six of the original stories, and they are prominent in four of them. Garland creates his old people in the spirit of the realist—or more exactly, in the spirit of what he would come to call "veritism," which was for him a combination of truth to things as they are and to individual perception. In *Crumbling Idols* he sum-marized the essence of his version of realism in this in-juction: "Write of those things of which you know most, and for which you care most. By so doing you will be true to yourself, true to your locality, and true to your time." Garland's old people are perfect examples of this theory. While they are patterned after his family mem-bers, about whom Garland cared deeply, they represent quite convincingly the Middle Border region in its time of agrarian struggle. They appear as the debilitated survi-vors of the hardships of Midwestern life.

On the face of it, the most commonplace feature of Gar-land's elderly characters is their attachment to the land. Of course the heroes of our literature are often found absorbed in the natural world, whether that world is a receding frontier, a whale-haunted ocean, a Mississippi flowing insistently South, or a rocky mountain peak ris-ing starkly from the plains. Garland's aged characters, however, inhabit a more down-to-earth landscape; they are simply living on farms. Garland frames the opening and closing of the book with realistic scenes of old peo-ple at work on the land. In the first story, **"A Branch-Road,"** old man Kinney, who is, Garland says, a "Hard-featured, wiry old man," "entering his second childhood," is pictured beginning "to limp painfully" as he goes through the daily chore of "driving the cows" out to pas-ture, and in the last story of the original six, **"Mrs. Rip-ley's Trip,"** old Ethan Ripley is seen "husking all alone in the field, his spare form rigged out in two or three ragged coats, his hands inserted in a pair of gloves minus nearly all the fingers, his thumbs done up in 'Stalls', and his feet thrust into huge coarse boots." Both men are bent and stiff, weary from work, poverty, and age. Like Kin-ney and Ripley, all the elderly of **Main-Travelled Roads** are locked into a farm life that yields only a marginal existence at best. They are enslaved on the land, and while its natural beauty provides intermittent satisfaction, there is no retirement from their grinding work short of death.

Garland's old people of the Middle Border do not live in consonance with the deeper rhythms of the natural world. Max Westbrook has pointed out that the seminal Western hero has an intimate relationship with nature in its most profound dimension; he is, Westbrook says, one who has experienced at some moment the sacred "original cre-ation" and thereafter knows the essential "unity" of all things [in an essay in *The Westering Experience in Amer-ican Literature,* edited by Merrill Lewis and L. L. Lee, 1977]. For all of their direct contact with the land, Gar-land's old people have no such knowledge. They do not take from the land ultimate truth, but only labor to eke out a living. They are not extraordinary Western heroes but ordinary Midwestern people, a part of the land in its nonmythic actuality.

The young people of **Main-Travelled Roads** often try to sever themselves from the land. Will Hannan, Agnes Kin-ney, Howard McLane, Rob Rodemaker, and Julia Peter-son all leave their Middle Border farms for such places East and West as New York, South Dakota, and Arizona. In their desire to escape, to flee from home, as well as in their mobility, they are typical of the figures who popu-late most American fiction, characters who are, more often than not, on the run, lighting out for the territories—or if they start there, for the cities—to get away from or to catch up with the rest. Further, in their urgent exodus Garland's younger people trace a pattern that will become distinctive in Midwestern literature—a path of departure followed by such later figures as Anderson's George Willard, Lewis's Carol Kennicott, and Fitzgerald's Nick Carraway, to mention only a few. Garland's old people, on the other hand, are sedentary. And this makes them unique. They are confined to their regional homes by economic necessity, by the exhaustion of old age, and, most importantly, by choice. Of all the elderly people in **Main-Travelled Roads** only one, Mrs. Ripley, leaves the region, and she does so simply to visit her family in the state of New York. Significantly, having begun **Main-Travelled Roads** with the flight of young Will Hannan, Garland ends the volume with the return of old Mrs. Ripley, who comes back to her husband, her grandson, and her work—to stay.

At the emotional and normative center of **Main-Travelled Roads** is the home. With the single exception of old wid-ow Gray in **"The Return of a Private,"** all of Garland's old people are married couples—home-folk "Moggin' along together," as he put it in his poem. In all six of the stories Garland depicts families which include more than one generation. While he is attentive to the hardships of farming and the snares of capitalism, issues which make **Main-Travelled Roads** protest fiction, Garland envisions the ultimate threat arising from these conditions as the loss of the family home. Fully two-thirds of the stories turn upon either the fact or the possibility of dispossession. Such loss looms as the ultimate horror, for home is the core of life in Garland's Middle Border. Lapsing at one point into Victorian sentimentality, Garland observes,

> There is no despair as deep as the despair of a homeless man or woman. To roam the roads of the country or

the streets of the city, to feel there is no rood of ground on which the feet can rest, to halt weary and hungry outside lighted windows and hear laughter and song within—these are the hungers and rebellions that drive men to crime and women to shame.

The homes Garland cherishes are uniformly dilapidated, realistic emblems of Midwestern poverty and deprivation. Yet they are enlivened by the spirit of their aged inhabitants, especially the old women.

For all of his interest in realism, Garland was, as Jay Martin has observed, "a maker and follower of myth and romance" [*Harvests of Change,* 1967]. His imagination, even at its most factual, strained to lift its creations into larger configurations of meaning. In ***Main-Travelled Roads*** this inclination results in a glorification of the Aged Mother. While the Mother figure obviously derives from Garland's own mother, to find in the type, as some critics have, only an embarrassingly unconscious Oedipal love is to miss Garland's indication of universality. Old Window Gray, old Mother Council, old Mrs. Ripley are virtually mythologized as avatars of love; they are Garland's equivalents of the archetypal Great Earth Mother who is the source and sustainer of life. Garland describes Old Widow Gray, the quintessence of the type, in quasisacramental language as the "visible incarnation of hospitality," and he compares the aged Mother Council to the sun and endows her with the power to instill vitality into those lifeless in body and spirit. Garland is too realistic to bestow full mythic stature upon the Mothers of the Middle Border, but he sees them all as elemental forces, universal nourishers, timeless figures of unconditional, enduring charity.

These almost mythic women live in a world that is not only real but even shabby. The widow Gray's parlor, a best-room carpeted with "a faded and patched rag" rug, is decorated, Garland says, by a "horrible white-and-green-striped wall-paper" and "a few ghastly effigies of dead members of the family hung in variously-sized oval walnut frames." Whatever the failures of taste here (the room is Garland's counterpart to the Grangerford parlor in *Huckleberry Finn*), the family portraits attest to a sense of the past. Unlike the typical heroes of our literature who are so bereft of history as to exist primarily in space, not time, Garland's old people are linked to the past. They have family as well as personal histories. Both resentments, like the Hannans' dislike of the Kinneys in **"A Branch-Road,"** and loyalties, like the McTurgs' ties to the MacLanes in **"Up the Coulé,"** linger through generations. The young are identified as the son or daughter of their parents, and the old are defined by the time they—or their parents—first settled in the region. Garland's old people naturally conceive of themselves in time as well as place, as Jane Ripley does when she explains her desire for a trip, "I ain't been away't stay overnight for thirteen years in this house, 'n' it was just so in Davis Country for ten more." Having lived out their histories, the aged retell them to newcomers with dignified restraint—in "Western fashion," Garland says, slowly, equitably, trading one long lifestory for another.

Embodying the past, Garland's old people represent not only continuity but also an ethic of communal cooperation, the code of "help" that obtained of necessity when the land was first settled. The sense of mutuality that informed such pioneer tasks as house-roofing, barn-raising, and harvesting lives on in the elderly people of ***Main-Travelled Roads***. It leads the old Councils first to take-in the Haskins family and then to back their effort to farm with advice, seed, stock, and labor. And it prompts old widow Gray to help feed Private Smith's family while he is at war. In the later additions to ***Main-Travelled Roads*** this ethic of cooperation degenerates into what one critic [Anthony Channell Hilfer in *The Revolt From the Village 1915-1930,* 1969] has called Garland's "ersatz glorification of small-town togetherness," but in the original stories the code convincingly animates the old people. For while Garland is, as Donald Pizer has pointed out [in *Realism and Naturalism in Nineteenth-Century American Fiction,* 1960], a romantic individualist, he deviates from romantics like Emerson and Thoreau in his outright celebration of communal living, both in the extended families headed by the elderly and in the larger rural society knit together by a common past.

Perhaps most importantly Garland's old people—like Faulkner's after him—endure. Despite their deprivations and sufferings, despite their drudgery and poverty, they survive, and their survival is in itself a kind of triumph. For Garland their spirit is unconquerable. Interwining the ideas of a harsh land, of home and family, of mutual concern, and of a binding past, Garland conveys the spirit of his old people in the image of old Mrs. Ripley returning from her once-in-a-lifetime trip:

> And off up the road the indomitable little figure trudged, head held down to the cutting blast. Little snow-fly, a speck on a measureless expanse, crawling along with painful breathing, and slipping, sliding steps—"Gittin' home to Ripley an' the boy."

In ***Main-Travelled Roads*** Garland envisions the Midwest as a coherent culture: built upon a series of family farms, centered in the values of the home, animated by an ethic of communal cooperation, and bound together by the past living on into the present in the old people. Garland creates a dramatic and symbolic representation of the cohesion of the Middle Border ethos in **"Up the Coulé,"** when William McTurg plays, for the young and the old, for the permanent community members and the temporarily estranged native sons, the old fiddle tunes of frontier settlement. As McTurg plays the old songs of Westward dreaming, the people of the Middle Border sense their common past and so draw together in their present. Personal resentments, intellectual differences, economic disparities, and separate generations are all bridged as the region's music sounds the past. The moment of transfiguring music is, however, heavy with melancholy, for McTurg's music reminds the community of unrealized hopes as well as heroic achievements.

Ignored in criticism, the aged William McTurg is one of the most significant figures in ***Main-Travelled Roads***.

Garland depicts him as an embodiment of the past: he is a patriarchal figure—a grizzled old man with white "hair and beard" and "great lion-like head," a "soft-voiced giant" who, despite his years, holds himself as "erect as an Indian." McTurg's enormous strength, instinctive kindness, and aesthetic appreciation of the land's austere beauty represent the noble qualities of the early pioneers. Most importantly, old McTurg is the native artist who expresses in his music the heritage of the region. Unlike the elderly mothers who suffer the ills of advancing age but who in their maternal aspect seem to rise beyond time, out of history to the realm of myth, Garland's regional artist is time-bound, linked to a specific moment of heroic settlement. His traditional materials express again and again the emotions, aspirations, and endeavors of a bygone era. In *Main-Travelled Roads* both the character of this artist and his art are honored.

But in *Prairie Folks,* one of the sequels to *Main-Travelled Roads,* the native artist becomes a displaced person, as change overtakes Garland's Middle Border. In **"Daddy Deering,"** for instance, Garland conveys with considerable power both the coming of old age and the passing of an heroic era. Deering, described as a "gaunt old man of sixty years" or "older," as a "giant" with a body as "bony and tough as hickery," is a variant of the aged William McTurg, and like McTurg, Deering is both prodigious worker of the land and its native artist. As a former logger, farmer, horse trader, cattle herder, hog butcher, and grain harvester, he is the epitome of the passing Middle Border life, and "above all else," Garland tells us, he loves to "play the fiddle for dances." With more grim honesty than pathos, Garland shows Deering's gradual but steady loss of physical prowess, a decline that finally leaves him crippled in his hands and lame in his legs. His diminished state terrifies him; it makes him, Garland observes, begin "to think and to tremble," for it brings "age and decay close to him." Deering's demise strips him of his heroic stature as an invincible pioneer. At the same time, the changing culture of the region denies him his place as its artist, and for Deering—and no doubt for Garland—this is more tragic than physical decay.

In his early old age Deering is able to fiddle for the local dances, sitting in a chair on the kitchen table "as if it were a throne," bearing himself with a "rude sort of grace and a certain dignity," playing the songs filled with "old-time memories." Although the young people delight more in his "antics" than his "tunes," they are nevertheless "immensely pleased" with him. But as an even newer generation comes of age, as the old neighbors die, as the young migrate West or to the cities, as, Garland says, "the wholesome simplicity of pioneer days is lost," Daddy Deering becomes not only unwanted as a musician but even unwelcome as a "visitor." He says flatly of himself, "I'm left out," and ironically his plain, laconic statement marks him indelibly as a Middle Border man, even as it expresses his exclusion from the region's present life. The utterance is Garland's epitaph for all his time-bound heroes, who become obsolete when the prairie lands are broken, when their own Herculean bodies decay, and when their traditional music falls upon indifferent young ears.

FURTHER READING

Bibliography

Bryer, Jackson R., and Harding, Eugene. *Hamlin Garland and the Critics: An Annotated Bibliography.* Troy, N.Y.: The Whitston Publishing Co., 1973, 282 p.

A list of writings on Garland that distinguishes between reviews of his works, periodical articles about the author, and criticism published in books.

Silet, Charles L. P. *Henry Blake Fuller and Hamlin Garland: A Reference Guide.* Boston: G. K. Hall, 1977, 148 p.

Bibliography of works related to Garland.

Biography

Holloway, Jean. *Hamlin Garland: A Biography.* Austin: University of Texas Press, 1956.

Study of Garland's life and times.

Criticism

French, Warren. "What Shall We Do about Hamlin Garland?" *American Literary Realism 1870-1910* 3, No. 4 (Fall 1970): 283-89.

Opposes the positive commentary on Garland's works and asserts that the author's importance stems from his role as "an American type—the man who made it too quickly and then hung around too long."

Harrison, Stanley R. "Hamlin Garland and the Double Vision of Naturalism." *Studies in Short Fiction* VI, No. 5 (Fall 1969): 548-56.

Maintains that Garland uses natural forces to create both conflict and respite for his characters.

Kaye, Frances W. "Hamlin Garland's Feminism." In *Women and Western American Literature,* edited by Helen Winter Stauffer and Susan J. Rosowski, pp. 135-61. Troy, N.Y.: The Whitston Publishing Co., 1982.

Argues that Garland "was the only male author of literary significance who specifically endorsed in his writing woman's rights, woman suffrage, and woman's equality in marriage."

Keiser, Albert. "Travelling the White Man's Road." In his *The Indian in American Literature,* pp. 279-92. New York: Oxford University Press, 1933.

Analyzes Garland's depiction of Native Americans and pronounces it "one of the most systematic as well as sympathetic treatments of the American native and his problem."

Nagel, James, ed. *Critical Essays on Hamlin Garland.* Boston: G. K. Hall, 1982, 372 p.

Presents a selection of essays and reviews on Garland's writings.

Pizer, Donald. "Herbert Spencer and the Genesis of Hamlin Garland's Critical System." *TSE: Tulane Studies in English* 7 (1957): 153-68.

    Traces evolutionary philosopher Herbert Spencer's influence on Garland's life and works.

Reamer, Owen J. "Garland and the Indians." *New Mexico Quarterly* XXXIV, No. 3, (Autumn 1964): 257-80.

    Details Garland's visits to various reservations in the 1890s and analyzes the stories in *The Book of the American Indian.*

Thacker, Robert. "'Twisting toward insanity': Landscape and Female Intrapment in Plains Fiction." *North Dakota Quarterly* 52, No. 3 (Summer 1984): 181-94.

    Discusses Garland's novella *The Moccasin Ranch* as it portrays a woman's reaction to the stark atmosphere of the Great Plains.

Silet, Charles L. P., Welch, Robert E., and Boudreau, Richard, eds. *The Critical Reception of Hamlin Garland.* Troy, N.Y.: The Whitston Publishing Co., 1985, 462 p.

    Reprints selected criticism on Garland's writings.

Additional coverage of Garland's life and career is contained in the following sources published by Gale Research: *Contemporary Authors,* **Vol. 104;** *Dictionary of Literary Biography,* **Vols. 12, 71, 78; and** *Twentieth Century Literary Criticism,* **Vol. 3.**

Henry Lawson
1867-1922

(Full name Henry Archibald Hertzberg Lawson; also wrote under the pseudonym John Lawrence) Australian short story writer, poet, and autobiographer.

INTRODUCTION

Lawson is highly regarded for his realistic short stories about the Australian "bush," or inland wilderness. Many critics note that his deceptively simple writing style foreshadowed that of many later writers, and his vivid realism and exploration of the concept of mateship, or male comraderie in the bush, influenced an entire generation of Australian writers. Although Lawson produced only two important short fiction collections, he nonetheless is considered a landmark figure in Australian literature.

Biographical Information

Lawson was born near Grenfell in New South Wales. He left school at fourteen to work with his father as a painter and builder, and when his parents separated in 1883 he moved with his mother to Sydney. Lawson published his first book, *Short Stories in Prose and Verse*, in 1894. A slim volume of poetry and short fiction privately printed on his mother's press, it attracted little attention, although it contained stories which would be recognized as among Lawson's best when reprinted two years later in *While the Billy Boils*, a collection that made him nationally famous. In 1897 he moved to New Zealand for a year, where Lawson was temporarily able to overcome incipient alcoholism and concentrate on writing. In 1900 Lawson traveled to England, where he published his most successful short story collection, *Joe Wilson and His Mates*. He returned to Australia in 1902. Progressing alcoholism, an unhappy marriage, and declining literary output and quality marked the last twenty years of his life.

Major Works of Short Fiction

Critics agree that Lawson's best work is contained in the short story volumes *While the Billy Boils* and *Joe Wilson and His Mates*. Concerned with the hardships of living in the bush, several of these early stories describe the inherent obstacles to human habitation of the region and portray the roughness and cruelty exhibited by people living in such difficult conditions. Lawson's harsh, vivid descriptions countered a tradition in Australian literature that romanticized the outback and idealized its inhabitants. In many of the stories, however, Lawson also depicted kind-

ness in his characters and celebrated the idealistic concept of mateship. In "The Union Buries Its Dead," from *While the Billy Boils*, a group of men loyally attend the funeral of an unfamiliar fellow union member simply because he has no family or friends in the area, but they nevertheless callously make a farce of the ceremony and fail even to recall the man's name after they learn it. The central stories of *Joe Wilson of His Mates*—"Joe Wilson's Courtship," "Brighten's Sister-in-Law," "'Water Them Geraniums,'" and "A Double Buggy at Lahey's Creek"—are linked pieces that follow the courtship, marriage, subsequent hardships, loss of affection, and tentative reconciliation of a young man and woman in the outback.

Critical Reception

Critics highly commend Lawson's achievements in *While the Billy Boils* and *Joe Wilson and His Mates,* in particular the realistic themes and unadorned narrative style of these collections. Lawson wrote authentic stories that overturned false and romantic conceptions of Australian life; as a result, he was acclaimed as a spokesman for the Australian people.

PRINCIPAL WORKS

Short Fiction

Short Stories in Prose and Verse (short stories and poetry)
   1894
While the Billy Boils 1896
*On the Track 1900
*Over the Sliprails 1900
The Country I Come From 1901
Joe Wilson and His Mates 1901
Children of the Bush (short stories and poetry) 1902
The Rising of the Court (short stories and poetry) 1910
Triangles of Life, and Other Stories 1913
The Prose Works of Henry Lawson 1937
The Stories of Henry Lawson. 3 vols. 1964
Henry Lawson: Short Stories and Sketches (short stories
   and sketches) 1972

Other Major Works

In the Days when the World Was Wide, and Other Verses
   (poetry) 1896
Verses Popular and Humorous (poetry) 1900
The Skyline Riders (poetry) 1910
A Coronation Ode and Retrospect (poetry) 1911
For Australia, and Other Poems (poetry) 1913
My Army! O, My Army!, and Other Songs (poetry) 1915
Poetical Works of Henry Lawson. 3 vols. (poetry) 1925
Collected Verse. 3 vols. (poetry) 1967-69
Henry Lawson: Letters 1890-1922 (letters) 1970
Henry Lawson: Autobiographical and Other Writings
   (autobiography and nonfiction) 1972

*Subsequently published jointly as On the Track and Over the
Sliprails.

CRITICISM

Henry Lawson (essay date 1894)

SOURCE: An excerpt in *An Annotated Bibliography of
Henry Lawson,* edited by George Mackaness, Angus and
Robertson, 1951, pp. 1-3.

[*In the following passage, which was originally published
as the preface to* Short Stories in Prose and Verse *(1894),
Lawson introduces the stories in his first collection, emphasizing the Australian nature of the work.*]

This is an attempt to publish, in Australia, a collection
of sketches and stories at a time when everything Australian, in the shape of a book, must bear the imprint of
a London publishing firm before our critics will conde-
scend to notice it, and before the 'reading public' will
think it worth its while to buy nearly so many copies as
will pay for the mere cost of printing a presentable volume.

The Australian writer, until he gets a 'London hearing' is
only accepted as an imitator of some recognised English
or American author; and, as soon as he shows signs of
coming to the front, he is labelled 'The Australian Southey',
'The Australian Burns' or 'The Australian Bret Harte',
and, lately, 'The Australian Kipling'. Thus, no matter how
original he may be, he is branded, at the very start, as a
plagiarist, and by his own country, which thinks, no doubt,
that it is paying him a compliment and encouraging him,
while it is really doing him a cruel and an almost irreparable injury.

But, mark! As soon as the Southern writer goes 'home'
and gets some recognition in England, he is 'So-and-So,
the well-known Australian author whose work has attracted so much attention in London lately'; and we first hear
of him by cable, even though he might have been writing
at his best for ten years in Australian.

The same paltry spirit tried to dispose of the greatest of
modern short story writers—as 'The Californian Dickens', but America wasn't built that way—neither was Bret
Harte.

To illustrate the above growl: a Sydney daily paper, reviewing the *Bulletin*'s 'Golden Shanty' when the first edition came out, said of my story, **'His Father's Mate'**,
that it stood out distinctly as an excellent specimen of that
kind of writing which Bret Harte set the world imitating
in vain, and being 'full of local colour, it was no unworthy copy of the great master'. That critic evidently hasn't
studied the 'great master' any more than he did my yarn,
or Australian goldfield life.

Then he spoke of another story as also having the 'Californian flavor'. For the other writers I can say that I feel
sure they could point out their scenery, and name, or, in
some cases, introduce 'the reader' to their characters in
the flesh. The first seventeen years of my life was spent
on the goldfields, and, therefore, I don't need to go back,
in imagination, to a time before I was born, and to a
country I had never seen, for literary material.

This pamphlet—I can scarcely call it a volume—contains
some of my early efforts, and they are sufficiently crude
and faulty. They have been collected and printed hurriedly, with an eye to Xmas, and without experienced editorial assistance, which last, I begin to think, was sadly
necessary.

However, we all hope to do better in future, and I shall
have more confidence in my first volume of verse which
will probably be published some time next year. The stories and sketches were originally written for the *Bulletin,
Worker, Truth, Antipodean Magazine,* and the *Brisbane
Boomerang,* which last was one of the many Australian
publications which were starved to death because they
tried to be original, to be honest, to pay for and encourage Australian literature, and, above all, to be Australian,
while the 'high average intelligence of the Australians'
preferred to patronize thievish imported rags of the 'Faked-
Bits' order.

David G. Ferguson (essay date 1896)

SOURCE: "Mr. Lawson's New Book," in *Henry Lawson Criticism: 1894-1971,* edited by Colin Roderick, Angus and Robertson, 1972, pp. 44-8.

[*In the following essay, originally published in 1896, Ferguson offers a positive assessment of* While the Billy Boils.]

The sketches collected by Mr Henry Lawson, under the title *While the Billy Boils,* give him an assured place amongst the few Australian prose writers; a place much safer, I venture to think, than that yet gained for him by his verse. The quality seems to me to be better sustained, and the touch finer and more certain. But, in prose, as in verse, all Mr Lawson's work so far is marked by one striking characteristic—it would be premature yet to call it positively a defect—a very pronounced and narrow restriction in the choice of material. Whether this is due to his own limitations, or is the result of enforced and deliberate choice remains to be proved by his future work.

However, taking the present book as we find it, dealing as it does with little more than a single phase of Australian life, it is impossible to deny it very high praise indeed. I know of no writer who has dealt with this phase of our life on anything like the same scale, with anything like the same truth and vigour. The shearer's shed, the shepherd's humpy, the cockatoo selector, the station cook, the fossicker, the swagman, the bush shanty, the bush spieler—he has transferred them whole into his pages, and there they stand, with the full glare of the Australian sun on them, harsh and unlovely of aspect for the most part, yet never quite without a chastening touch of humour or pathos, and always and unmistakably alive.

The collection comprises something over fifty tales and sketches, and while it is safe criticism to say that some of them might with advantage have been omitted (especially if the critic wisely forbears to particularise), it may also safely be said that, in the whole number, a really uninteresting one would be hard to find. We are introduced to quite a gallery of entertaining rascals, whose sayings and doings are chronicled with unctuous relish. They euchre the bush publican, outwit the station cook, clandestinely remove swags and ironing tables to evade distraint, get stringy-bark palings and shingles out of mountain-ash, and behave in all sorts of picturesquely reprehensible ways. In **"His Father's Mate"**, **"When the Sun Went Down"**, and many other stories, we get simple, unrestrained pathos.

A glance at some of Mr Lawson's bits of description will show with what eyes he has looked on life in the bush. Here, for example, is a passage telling how a city tradesman, who went away hopefully to "settle on the land", found out what grubbing meant—

> He found a soft place between two roots on one side of the first tree, made a narrow, irregular hole, and burrowed down till he reached a level where the tap-root was somewhat less than four feet in diameter, and

not quite as hard as flint; then he found he hadn't room to swing the axe, so he hewed out another ton or two of earth—and rested. Next day he sank a shaft on the other side of the gum; and after tea, over a pipe, it struck him that it would be a good idea to burn the tree out, and so use up the logs and lighter rubbish lying round. So he widened the excavation, rolled in some logs and set fire to them—with no better results than to scorch the roots. Tom persevered. He put the trace harness on his horse, drew in all the logs within half a mile, and piled them on the windward side of the gum; and during the night the fire found a soft place, and the tree burnt off about six feet above the surface, falling on a squatter's boundary fence, and leaving the ugliest kind of stump to occupy the selector's attention—which it did for a week. He waited till the hole cooled, and then he went to work with pick, shovel, and axe; and even now he gets interested in drawings of machinery, such as are published in the agricultural weeklies, for getting out stumps without graft.

In the same sketch . . . is a line that strikes the note of the author's treatment of the feminine element, wherever it appears in his stories.

> Then he arranged with his sweetheart to be true to him and wait whilst he went West and made a home. She drops out of the story at this point.

All Mr Lawson's women, broadly speaking—true, there are not many—fall into one of two categories: the woman that marries and wears her heart out, and the one that waits and breaks it. Here is the drover's wife, the "gaunt, sunbrowned bushwoman", who is pictured to the life in Mr Mahony's accompanying illustration—

> She is used to being left alone. She once lived like this for eighteen months. As a girl she built the usual castles in the air; but all her girlish hopes and aspirations have long been dead. She finds all the excitement and recreation she needs in the *Young Ladies' Journal,* and, Heaven help her! takes a pleasure in the fashion plates. . . .

> She has few pleasures to think of as she sits here alone by the fire, on guard against a snake. All days are much the same to her; but on Sunday afternoon she dresses herself, tidies the children, smartens-up baby, and goes for a lonely walk along the bush track, pushing an old perambulator in front of her. She does this every Sunday. She takes as much care to make herself and the children look smart as she would if she were going to do the block in the city. . . .

The following is a characteristic bit of scenery:—

> Bush all round—bush with no horizon, for the country is flat. No ranges in the distance. The bush consists of stunted, rotten, native apple trees. No undergrowth. Nothing to relieve the eye save the darker green of a few sheoaks which are sighing above the narrow, almost waterless creek. Nineteen miles to the nearest sign of civilisation—a shanty on the main road.

In another place Mr Lawson thus describes the surroundings of a border town:—

> The country looks as though a great ash-heap had been spread out there, and mulga scrub and firewood planted—and neglected.

He almost seems to have gone out of his way to justify the description of his native country by a renegade Australian of his (afterwards happily converted) as "the worst country that ever the Lord had the sense to forget". Once, indeed, and only once I think between cover and cover, do we find a bit of landscape with colour in it. It is a vision that comes to a bushman in Sydney, where he was getting something done to his eyes. He was going blind.

> He saw the dark blue ridges in the sunlight, the grassy sidings and flats, the creek with clumps of sheoak here and there, the course of the willow-fringed river below, the distant peaks and ranges fading away into a lighter azure, the granite ridge in the middle distance, and the rocky rises, the stringy-bark and the apple tree flats, the scrubs, and the sunlit plains—and all.

One would like to quote in full—but it is too long—the passage that tells how the daily milking is done in districts outside the jurisdiction of the Board of Health; but the following description of a selector's boy feeding a "poddy"—a calf weaned too early—is a fair sample of its truthfulness and of some of its other qualities:—

> He carries the skim-milk to the yard in a bucket made out of an oil-drum—sometimes a kerosene tin—seizes a calf by the nape of the neck with his left hand, inserts the dirty forefinger of his right into its mouth, and shoves its head down into the milk. The calf sucks, thinking it has a teat, and pretty soon it butts violently—as calves do to remind their mothers to let down the milk—and the boy's wrist gets barked against the jagged edge of the bucket. He welts that calf in the jaw, kicks it in the stomach, tries to smother it with its nose in the milk, and finally dismisses it with the assistance of the calf-rope and a shovel, and gets another.

Here is a fine little picture:—

> It was a stout, dumpy swag, with a red blanket outside, patched with blue, and the edge of a blue blanket showing in the inner rings at the end. The swag might have been newer; it might have been cleaner; it might have been hooped with decent straps, instead of bits of clothes line and green hide—but otherwise there was nothing the matter with it, as swags go.

Add "the twisted towel which served for a shoulder strap", and none but a person hard to please would say there *was* anything the matter with it, as swags go.

Only one more quotation:—

> We met one [old mate of our father's] to-day, and had a yarn with him, and afterwards we got thinking, and

somehow began to wonder whether those ancient friends of ours were, or were not, better and kinder to their mates than we of the rising generation are to our fathers; *and the doubt is painfully on the wrong side.*

The italics are mine (time-honoured phrase!). Not that there is anything intrinsically remarkable in the passage, but how on earth did it stray into Mr Lawson's book? *Que diable va-t-il faire dans cette galère?* It is not in Mr Lawson's own style; it is a distinct and glaring lapse into another and an alien method. The method of Mr Lawson's school, to which he closely adheres, with such rare exceptions that they may be left out of account, is purely objective. The author places the subject in an appropriate light, and then stands aside and lets you look at it. He has nothing to say about it, no comment to make; the thing must tell its own tale. Of course the comment is there all the same, only you must look for it not in what the author says, but in what he leaves out. That shows his point of view. This brings us round again to the question of our author's limitations. What Mr Lawson leaves out may be comprehensively exemplified in a sentence: There is not a horse in the book, from title page to imprint—not one horse!

The decline of Henry Lawson:

The remaining twenty years of Lawson's life were a dismal anticlimax to the promise of his youth, and throw little light on the body of work for which he is now remembered. If he had died, say in 1898, there is little of his important work that we would have lost, and we would have had the satisfaction of lamenting a great writer cut down in his prime. "At thirty," A. G. Stephens remarked, "he had worked out his alluvial field of youth: his mind lost vigor," and Lawson himself admits that "I had lost the thunder, both far and near, the almighty sympathy, the splendid crudity and the sledgehammer force of simplicity of that lonely boy's song". Indeed, while the fragment of autobiography the *Bulletin* published in January 1899 ("Pursuing Literature in Australia") is interesting in many ways, it is most interesting in that it reads like the long-range recollections of some elderly laureate of literature, full of honours, and confident—not to say complacent—in the knowledge of the long and busy career behind him. But it was written by a young man of thirty-one, assumed by many to be only approaching the full deployment of his powers. Lawson had genius, but not the driving ambition or staying power that takes genius to its goal. To put it another way, he had the insights of genius but not its perspectives.

Stephen Murray-Smith, in Henry Lawson,
Lansdowne Press, 1962.

John Farrell (essay date 1896)

SOURCE: A review of *While the Billy Boils*, in *Henry Lawson Criticism: 1894-1971*, edited by Colin Roderick, Angus and Robertson, 1972, pp. 55-8.

[*In the following essay, originally published in 1896,*

Farrell lauds Lawson's treatment of Australian themes and settings.]

As in his verse, Mr Lawson here [in *While the Billy Boils*] treats of certain aspects of everyday life peculiar to Australia, and certain phases of human nature common to mankind. But prose has advantages over the other form of composition which are obvious. "Rhymes are so few in this world of ours", and the necessity for having a given number of them, in accordance with a set scheme, sometimes compels even the most capable writers of verse to use words which are not the best available to express what is intended. In these pages the writer seems more at his ease than when dealing with the same general range of subjects in his poems. So much at ease does he seem, indeed, that they form the most excellent, and, in a literary sense, the most faultless, set of delineations of bush and back-blocks life which has yet been produced in Australia. In his versified writings, Mr Lawson did not let his imagination run far away from the realities in the case, as there may be a temptation to do. In these sketches imagination never obtrudes as a disturbing element. The thing seen or heard is, in such parts of it as are striking and characteristic, reproduced with an exactitude not marred by over-coloring or over-striving for effect. No book could be more unmistakably the product of experience and observation. It may be thought that some of the incidents recorded are not of such size or consequence as to deserve a place beside others more dramatic or impressive. But hardly anything can be found here which is not actual and, in some degree, representative. What could be more true and natural than the depiction, in **"An Old Mate of your Father's",** of how the two old-time diggers, sitting pensively among the deserted shafts, would "absently pick up pieces of quartz and slate, rub them on their sleeves, look at them in an abstracted manner, and drop them again." They "would talk of some old lead they had worked on: 'Hogan's party was here on one side of us; Macintosh was here on the other; Mac. was getting good gold, and so was Hogan; now, why the blanky blank weren't we on gold?' And the mate would always agree that there was 'gold in them ridges and gullies yet, if a man had only the money to get at it.' And then perhaps the guv'nor would show him a spot where he intended to put down a shaft some day—the old man was always thinking of putting down a shaft."

We have among the fifty-odd sketches and short tales here given some vivid pictures of life in the bush and in the city, on the wallaby, in the shearing-shed, on the selection, in the steerage of intercolonial vessels, in the men's hut, and the cheap Sydney boarding-house, and in the meaner Sydney streets, where pushism prospers. The writer has had to take a good deal of work for his stomach's sake—any work that could be had; sufficient to carry him on to the next place, wherever it might be. He has had hard experiences, but being endowed with a very active power of observation and excellent literary capacity, he has made better use of his experiences than most are able to do. The sketches have in them a quality of concise and exact statement, of sufficient description, and of suggestiveness, which continually reminds one of how far Rud-

yard Kipling can make language go in serving his ends. Mitchell, the ordinary human swagman, with his far-back devices for getting along at the cost of the squatter, his self-confidence, and his Alnaschar-like plans for the future, is almost as perfect a portrait as Mulvaney. Steelman and his humble disciple Smith are true types of greatness and humility, coupled with a desire to learn, as existing among the race of bush spielers and gentlemen of adventure. If anybody wants a true delineation of the soft-hearted, shy, wordless, big, unintellectual youth of the pastoral bush, let him read **"Malachi"**. And whoso cannot perceive the beauty, the naturalness, the completeness, and power in the touching story **"Going Blind"** must be of some such material as the lawyer who pronounced the "Ancient Mariner" to be "great rubbish", and thereby became known to posterity.

It is rather singular that the distinctive agricultural life of Australia has yet found so little representation in song or story. That of the pastoral pursuit has claimed the almost exclusive attention of descriptive and imaginative writers who go beyond city limits for their subjects. Yet there is a rich field among the free selectors which some able writer will yet exploit. Mr Lawson enters it once or twice in this book. In **"A Day on a Selection",** some of the peculiarities of that state of life which it does not please Providence to allow back-blocks husbandmen to escape from, are presented. It is Sunday morning, and the selector stands against the fence with another selector. "His arms rest on the top rail of the fence, his chin rests on his hands, his pipe rests between his fingers, and his eyes rest on a white cow that is chewing her cud at the opposite end of the fence. The neighbor's arms rest on the top rail also, his chin rests on his hands, his pipe rests between his fingers, and his eyes rest on the cow. They are talking about that cow. They have been talking about her for three hours." Here is an idyllic glimpse of the milking-yard of a bush dairy farm, with the son of the house in the character of milk-maid: —"Sometimes the boy sticks his head into the cow's side, hangs on by a teat, and dozes, while the bucket, mechanically gripped between his knees, sinks lower and lower, until it rests on the ground. Likely as not he'll doze until his mother's shrill voice startles him with an inquiry as to whether he intends to get that milking done to-day; other times he is aroused by the plunging of the cow, or knocked over by a calf which has broken through a defective panel in the pen. In the latter case the youth gets tackle on to the calf, detaches its head from the teat with the heel of his boot, and makes it fast somewhere. Sometimes the cow breaks or loosens the leg-rope and gets her leg into the bucket, and then the youth clings desperately to the pail, and hopes she'll get her hoof out without spilling the milk. Sometimes she does; more often she doesn't—it depends on the strength of the boy and the pail, and on the strategy of the former. Anyway, the boy will lamb the cow down with a jagged yard shovel, let her out, and bail up another."

In Mr Lawson's prose sketches the quality of humor is more apparent than in his poems. This is chiefly because personal characteristics are more largely dealt with. Sometimes the humor is imitative, as when a dog's "chawingup apparatus" is referred to; and then it is worse than unrelieved gloom. Americanism does not fit in with things Australian. But these aberrations are infrequent and trivial. In **"His Country, After All"**, **"The Shearing of the Cook's Dog"**, and **"Settling on the Land"**—notwithstanding the exaggerations of the latter—Mr Lawson shows how well he can handle humor which does not depend on the use of outré and incongruous phraseology. Some of his terms would bear modification, in the interests of refinement, but if that were done, the "true talk" of the dramatis personae would not be represented. Of the stories, if they may rightly be so-called, there are half-a-dozen fit to rank with the best short tales ever written. Of these, **"The Drover's Wife"** is perhaps the best; but it would be hard to find in **"Arvie Aspinall's Alarm Clock"**, **"The Bush Undertaker"**, **"His Father's Mate"**, **"A Visit of Condolence"**, and **"An Unfinished Love Story"**, faults which are worth considering, in view of their high merit. Author and publishers can be equally congratulated on a book which is in every respect equal to anything yet produced in Australia, and which, as a contribution to our characteristic literature, has claims of its own which cannot fail to be widely recognised.

C. Hartley Grattan (essay date 1958)

SOURCE: "Some Blokes Down Under," in *The New York Times Book Review,* February 9, 1958, p. 4.

[*Grattan was an American educator and critic with a special interest in Australian literature. In the following review, he provides an overview of the major themes of Lawson's short fiction.*]

Up to this moment, only those American readers who have chanced upon the writings of Henry Lawson in English or Australian editions have had the very great pleasure of savoring the work of this master of the short fictional narrative. Now Lyle Blair has arranged the first publication of a selection of stories and verses [*The Selected Works of Henry Lawson*], and it is to be fervently hoped that what he has assembled will find its way into the hands of every last American who enjoys making literary discoveries.

I am not at all certain that it was wise to mix Lawson's poetry with his prose to allow the use of the word "Works," though of course he wrote verse. Whatever may be thought of the poems, anybody who can read such stories as **"The Drover's Wife," "A Double Buggy at Lahey's Creek," "The Union Buries its Dead,"** and **"The Loaded Dog,"** all included here, and not raise a cheer is surely suffering from hardening of the mind and emotions.

Henry Lawson (1867-1922) was the son of a wandering Norwegian sailor (Larsen) and an Australian mother. The father is a shadowy figure, dogged by failure to adapt to bush life, but the mother, after the collapse of the marriage, became a vigorous journalistic exponent of women's rights in Sydney. Henry was but indifferently educated in bush schools—"no good at arithmetic and never

learned to spell"—and he made his literary debut while still working as a carriage and house painter. His literary derivation was from Dickens and Bret Harte, and he profited enormously from the exacting discipline of the editors of *The Bulletin* (a raffish political and literary journal).

Politically aligned with labor's reformism and nationalism, he was brother-in-law of famous Left-Wing Labor Premier of New South Wales, John Thomas ("Jack") Lang. Emotionally identified with the common working "bloke," Lawson permeated his stories with the emotions of the people with whom he identified himself. His love-hate for the harsh Australian environment, his insistence upon the sacredness of mateship coupled with a sardonic view of the human being as he comported himself, his mixed-up pro-Australia anti-imperial patriotism and his tasteless lapses into an often didactic sentimentalism, all characteristic of his "blokes," are reflected in the selections Mr. Blair here offers.

Lawson was a prolific writer. About 150 stories by him were put between hard covers during his lifetime and frequently reprinted in Australia, and a forthcoming all-inclusive edition will add fifty to sixty more. Then there is his poetry, which, all told, makes a fat book, and his non-fictional topical journalism. Yet with all this he never made a satisfactory living for long at a time, and he inevitably became as much of a casual laborer (literary style) as any of his characters. His life was hard, and became harder as the well of his material ran lower and lower; eventually he fell victim to drink, as he tried to make beer make him feel the way he should have felt without beer.

A sorry tale, but rather a Lawsonesque tale, all in all. Nevertheless, in his lifetime he won high praise not only from Australian but from English and French critics, and since his death his work has been translated into a variety of languages, including Russian. Now at long last he arrives in America, and it is a happy circumstance that he is presented visually in David Low's utterly charming caricature-portrait made when Low was on *The Bulletin* in Sydney and Lawson was a contributor. This shows us the gallant old literary warrior. It would have added to one's pleasure if Mr. Blair had also slipped in a reproduction of Lionel Lindsay's splendid etched head of Lawson, which shows him as literary artist. A copy of this drawing (one of fifty printed) has hung in my home for twenty years. It shows a fascinatingly powerful face that inevitably commands, even from casual observers, the urgent, fervent inquiry, "Who is that?"

Chris Wallace-Crabbe (essay date 1964)

SOURCE: "Lawson's *Joe Wilson*: A Skeleton Novel," in *Australian Literary Studies*, Vol. 1, No. 3, June, 1964, pp. 147-54.

[*In the essay below, Wallace-Crabbe examines the themes of "Joe Wilson's Courtship," "Brighten's Sister-in-law,"*

"'Water Them Geraniums,'" and "A Double Buggy at Lahey's Creek," asserting that the four stories are "the nearest Lawson ever came to transcending the bounds of his unassertive short story form and writing something in which he could look at human relations more substantially, more expansively."]

Henry Lawson remains unquestionably our greatest short story writer. Indeed he is one of our greatest prose writers, a man whose achievement stands there in the *Prose Works,* square and solid and unmistakable. At the same time, we cannot pretend not to notice his limitations, which are considerable: to put it simply, Lawson worked within a very limited range in terms of form, of emotional variety, of the kinds of experience he could grasp and set down clearly. Within these narrow bounds his remarkable art came to fruition and, in time, fell away.

A cluster of themes run together through Lawson's stories. These are extremely persistent and they have obvious origins in his private life, wherein the pain of family tensions can only have been reinforced by the affliction of early deafness. Again and again we are brought up against loneliness, failure, the false haven of alcoholism and a compulsive insistence upon the gossamer precariousness of human happiness. Far from being able to participate imaginatively in the optimism of his age, Lawson portrayed life as a vale of tears, or if not of tears at least of patient stoicism and bitter humour. His characters have very little satisfying contact with one another: there is the hard-won mateship of the bush tracks, certainly, but this does not seem so much a lasting thing as a kind of tolerant alliance against the forces of the world.

Lawson's materials are so heavily charged with emotion that he slides all too frequently into the troughs of self-pity: stories like **'His Father's Mate'**, **'Black Joe'** and **'Two Boys at Grinder Brothers'** show how easily a tender heart could succumb to the blandishments of tear-jerking. But in his best work he faces up to the harshness of his world, faces up to his emotions—pity, fear, despair, loneliness, self-indulgence—and portrays them with great accuracy and conciseness. The crisp clarity of the prose exemplifies his control: his achievement in creating a 'style' is at the same time an achievement in gaining self-knowledge.

Although they transparently draw on the experience of a sensitive adolescent, Lawson's finest stories are a rigorously adult achievement. Among these mature and deeply moving works I would class **'The Drover's Wife'**, **'The Union Buries Its Dead'** and **'Going Blind'**. Along with, yet unmistakably above, these stand the four linked stories which comprise the *Joe Wilson* sequence [**'Joe Wilson's Courtship'**, **'Brighten's Sister-in-Law'**, **'"Water Them Geraniums"'** and **'A Double Buggy at Lahey's Creek'**]: four stories which were, significantly, among the last effective stories he produced, since the quality of his writing from 1901 onward fell away rapidly. *Joe Wilson* was written when the collapse of Lawson's life was directly confronting him; it is a triumph snatched out of the teeth of despair.

> **We cannot pretend not to notice Lawson's limitations, which are considerable: to put it simply, Lawson worked within a very limited range in terms of form, of emotional variety, of the kinds of experience he could grasp and set down clearly.**
>
> **—Chris Wallace Crabbe**

The four interlocked stories of *Joe Wilson* are the nearest Lawson ever came to transcending the bounds of his unassertive short story form and writing something in which he could look at human relations more substantially, more expansively. The sequence is, in miniature (or in the form of a skeleton), his 'big novel'. His attempts to weave the four pieces of narrative into a larger pattern for which he presumably did not have the stamina, reveal themselves in very interesting ways.

'Joe Wilson's Courtship' begins the sequence. Here is the first stage of Lawson's portrait of Joe, the debilitatingly sensitive protagonist of the stories: a young man who plainly has much in common with the author himself. But there are two Joes. Joe Wilson is both narrator and main actor in the sequence, the story beginning with the older Joe looking back on the young man that once he was:

> There are many times in this world when a healthy boy is happy. When he is put into knickerbockers, for instance, and 'comes a man to-day', as my little Jim used to say. When they're cooking something at home that he likes. When the 'sandy blight' or measles breaks out amongst the children. . . .
>
> I wasn't a healthy-minded, average boy; I reckon I was born for a poet by mistake, and grew up to be a bushman, and didn't know what was the matter with me—or the world—but that's got nothing to do with it.
>
> There are times when a man is happy. When he finds out that the girl loves him. When he's just married. When he's a lawful father for the first time, and everything's going on all right: some men make fools of themselves then—I know I did. I'm happy to-night because I'm out of debt and can see clear ahead, and because I haven't been easy for a long time.

This opening is strikingly casual, yarn-like; the older Joe is a garrulous, relaxed figure, inclined to wax philosophical but perhaps a little world-weary. His tone suggests the considerable distance in time between the present and the occurrences he is recalling—and, as we see soon enough, an equally large gap between the man he was and the man he is now.

Such a leisurely beginning is unusual for Lawson ([in *The Australian Tradition: Studies in a Colonial Culture,* 1958] A. A. Phillips has noted his tendency to plunge into the heart of things from the very first sentence) but it is by no means as aimless as it may look at first glance. The flashes to and fro in time—back to schooldays and forward again to the years of all too wordly wisdom—begin to indicate the wider perspectives of *Joe Wilson.* This apparently casual chatter is loaded with implications for events ahead: I need only single out Joe's insistence that he wasn't 'a healthy-minded, average boy', and the familiarity with debts and depression in his present life. On top of this, a distinctly ominous tone is struck by the piece of advice which follows in the next paragraph: 'Make the most of your courting days, you young chaps, and keep them clean, for they're about the only days when there's a chance of poetry and beauty coming into this life.'

This first story follows a simple enough series of events, tracing the courtship through a number of scenes and situations, which delineate Joe's relationship with his workmate Jack Barnes, his growing awareness of the girl who is nicknamed 'Possum', his bungling, his shyness, his need to be jockeyed along by Jack. All this is achieved concisely, perceptively, humorously. Of particular interest is the sketch of Jack and Joe early on:

> Jack was sentimental too, but in a different way. I was sentimental about other people—more fool I!—whereas Jack was sentimental about himself. Before he was married, and when he was recovering from a spree, he'd write rhymes about 'Only a boy, drunk by the roadside', and that sort of thing; and he'd call 'em poetry, and talk about signing them and sending them to the *Town and Country Journal.* But he generally tore them up when he got better. The bush is breeding a race of poets, and I don't know what the country will come to in the end.

There is a strong element of Lawson in both these characters. Both, for instance, have a dangerous weakness for alcohol; both are sensitive and sentimental, though Jack has plainly toughened up a good deal more than Joe has. Interestingly enough, it is Jack who gets cast in the role of would-be poet, which gives the narrator the opportunity for a mildly cynical wisecrack. But Jack is also the more practical of the two. He is obliged to keep planning the courtship for his nervous workmate: in fact he has to keep bullying Joe into making a move of some kind.

A lot of the material which has gone into this story is demonstrably autobiographical. In Bertha Lawson's reticent little book, *My Henry Lawson,* we find an account of relations between Henry and his wife that has affinities with the *Joe Wilson* stories. For example, Bertha came from Gippsland, as Mary probably does, and had a more genteel upbringing than her husband-to-be. More significant is the resemblance between the introverted, isolated Joe, with his extraordinary difficulties of communication, and Lawson's own destructively manic-depressive temperament; prolonged failures of communication are a prominent feature of both marriages.

However, the full impact of these tensions is not felt until later in the sequence. At this stage Joe's awkwardness is wholly engaging and gently entertaining, as in the humorous passage where the clothesline breaks and he bumbles along to assist Mary. Joe's courtship goes ahead in an easy-paced, unemphatic unfolding of narrative, with a minimum of interpolation from the backward-looking narrator. The highlight of the action is Joe's fight with Romany, a silly, unheroic affair; Romany, an ugly customer on the surface, is an unhappy outcast, disliked by his fellow workers. This misfit is the man whom shy, sensitive Joe has to knock about:

> I felt the reaction pretty bad. I didn't feel proud of the affair at all. I thought it was a low brutal business all round.

Romany's downfall leads obliquely to Joe's triumph, which is ironic since Joe's rival for Mary is somebody quite different, a confident jackeroo. Long afterwards, in '**A Double Buggy at Lahey's Creek**', it is partly his catching another glimpse of Romany that spurs Joe on to buying the double buggy and nursing his marriage out of one of its black periods. On such slender threads of narrative are the four stories strung together.

After an absent-minded proposal, the first story ends on the note of old Black's reminiscence when Joe goes to ask for Mary's hand. This is not only a nicely turned conclusion; it also parallels another kind of nostalgic reminiscence: that of the older Joe at the very beginning. And we realize that not much has been made of the presence of the narrator. That ominously resigned note has not been fully justified as yet: the hints of '**Joe Wilson's Courtship**' look forward to, and open out into, events to come.

'**Brighten's Sister-in-Law**' passes over Joe's marriage, over the birth of a son, over a period when the Wilsons have been living in the scruffy town of Gulgong, such past events being sketched in by means of apparently random memories and flashbacks. We have come to a time when Joe decides to take up a small selection and the story turns on a terrible fit that seizes his delicate son, Jim, on the track to Lahey's Creek. The whole tone of this second story is darker. The voice of the narrator has lost some of its easy-going quality and his emphasis falls more obviously on loneliness, separation, fear. We can see why young men were advised to 'make the most of their courting days': the world of maturity is so harsh and uncompromising that all one can do is to grasp at early, transient pleasures. For a sense is growing in the narrative of disasters constantly looming up in life. Young Jim's fits, Joe's recollections of helpless drinking sprees, the glimpses of marital conflict, all these become part of the natural pattern of existence.

One thing that emerges is the way Joe's isolation is growing worse. Here, surely, we have the fullest picture Lawson was ever to paint of his own increasing loss of contact, loss of confidence. Here we have the self-questioning of the deaf, unhappy writer, his life already disintegrating, his talent soon to do the same, gathering up fragments to shore against his ruins. At this late point in his career, in the figure of Joe Wilson—Joe the narrator and Joe the actor together—Lawson was able to create a piece of self-analysis more ambitious than anything else in his writing.

Even young Jim notices his father's progressive alienation and in sidelong glances from the narrative we are shown relations with Mary beginning to deteriorate. A passage early in the story reveals how things are going:

> This sort of talk from Mary always bored me and made me impatient with her, because I knew it all too well. I never worried for myself, only for Mary and the children. And often, as the days went by, I said to myself, 'I'll take more notice of Jim and give Mary more of my time, just as soon as I can see things clear ahead a bit.' And the hard days went on, and the weeks, and the months, and the years—Ah, well!

> Mary used to say, when things would get worse, 'why don't you talk to me, Joe? Why don't you tell me your thoughts, instead of shutting yourself up in yourself and brooding—eating your heart out? It's hard for me: I get to think you're tired of me, and selfish. I might be cross and speak sharp to you when you are in trouble. How am I to know, if you don't tell me?'

> But I didn't think she'd understand.

This, I believe, is what the whole sequence is about. There are four distinct stories about widely different incidents, ranging from the gentle, charming comedy of the courtship to the grim emptiness of worn-out Mrs Spicer's death at the end of '"Water Them Geraniums"', but the common factor to them all is Joe: Joe as narrator trying to pull the threads of his past life into some shape, Joe as awkward young pioneer trying to build his life, Joe as uncommunicative husband, Joe as sensitive, introverted man, constantly hurt by what he sees and feels around him.

The figure of Brighten's sister-in-law plays a key role in the story that bears her name. She is the kind of failure that Joe seems fated to become. Her strength and her weakness run close together. Her insight, her humane imagination, the loving care which she bestows on Jim in nursing him out of his fit: these are aspects of the idealism which has, it appears, driven her out of the busy world and banished her to a wretched wayside shanty. Her background is vague, the story being that 'she'd been a hospital matron in the city . . . and there were yarns about her. Some said she got the sack for exposing the doctors—or carrying on with them—I didn't remember which'. But, given the insight with which this woman comprehends the tensions existing between Joe and Mary, we are left in no doubt that her failure is inextricably connected with her warm humanity.

Two women in these stories throw light back onto Joe's situation. These are Brighten's sister-in-law and poor old Mrs Spicer. Both women are failures or near-failures who keep on struggling against the slings and arrows of an intolerable universe; both have affinities with similar courageous women elsewhere in Lawson's fiction, with the Drover's Wife, for example. Perhaps they represent something of the battling feminism of Lawson's mother?

For Joe Wilson these two women are, first of all, images of what could happen to Mary. The sight of a battered bushwoman fills young Joe with fears for his young wife, at present so fresh and confident; throughout the third part of the sequence the Spicer's selection lies alongside the Wilsons' newly taken up land like a horrible cautionary tale.

Then again, both women are embodiments for young Joe of the threat of personal defeat that haunts him in a world of perpetual insecurity. His own potential alcoholism could all too easily drag him down, just as that unnamed indiscretion drove a woman from a Sydney hospital to a shanty on a disused bush road. And, as I have suggested, the proximity of Spicer's selection shadows forth the way in which vicissitudes of wind and weather could reduce him to a scratching poverty. Furthermore, in old Joe, the narrator, we hear the voice of a world-weariness which is in some ways comparable with the weariness of the two women; his spirit of garrulous futility, his memories of ways that were once open to him and now are closed for ever, the oblique, self-reproachful indications of his later life, all these things reinforce the note of weather-beaten acceptance, which is the most that Lawson's older characters have managed to wring out of life.

Thirdly, both Brighten's sister-in-law and Mrs Spicer are more perceptive than young Joe; both are capable of seeing into his marriage. The ex-matron, after the crisis with young Jim's fit has passed, has a long talk with Mary, who is then, Joe notices, 'extra gentle for the next few days'. And even dotty old Mrs Spicer, having observed Mary's attempts at civilizing a primitive shack in hard, lonely country manages to blurt out: 'What-did-you-bring-her-here-for?' In other words, their apparently disconnected stories keep bearing back on the central preoccupations of *Joe Wilson*—a man's fragile personality and his attempts to sustain human communication, to prevent himself from becoming completely alienated from family and society.

'A Double Buggy at Lahey's Creek' is, like the first story, a straightforward account of relations between Joe and Mary, and it recounts the coming of a period of material success. The conclusion might suggest an optimistic ending to the sequence, until we look back and recall how much of the narrative has depicted obstinacy, argument, conflict, until we recall the intermittent world-weariness of the narrator and weigh the final impact of such an aside as this:

> What women some men are! But the time came, and not many years after, when I stood by the bed where Mary lay, white and still; and, amongst other things, I kept saying, 'I'll give in, Mary—I'll give in,' and then I'd laugh. They thought I was raving mad, and took me from the room. But that time was to come.

In short, we are given no encouragement to see the glow of domestic peace which concludes **'A Double Buggy'** as anything but a transient condition. We come away from *Joe Wilson* still affected by the feeling that drought and illness, loneliness and disagreement provide the norm in Lawson's vision of life.

All this is frail and modest enough, it must be admitted; the limitations of Lawson's talent are seen in his reliance on brief hints and flashbacks instead of the full dramatic presentation that a full-scale novel could provide. But it is impossible not to admire his concentration on what he knows and what he has felt. *Joe Wilson* is a clean, economical work, its human insights relentlessly frank. It stands high among the achievements of Australian fiction. Perhaps even its tentative, skeletal structure emerges in the long run as a paradoxical virtue, serving to reinforce the quality of painful and reticent plainness which characterizes the whole sequence.

Cecil Mann (essay date 1964)

SOURCE: An introduction to *The Stories of Henry Lawson, first series,* edited by Cecil Mann, Angus and Robertson, 1964, pp. vii-xiv.

[*In the following excerpt, Mann outlines Lawson's career and assesses his significance as a short story writer.*]

Henry Lawson, never one without literary honour, has now already attained, or been invested with, a nationally unique status. He has become personally a romantic legend. At his best a great writer in his medium, he appears in this present concept as one who is himself seen first, standing in the forefront of his literary fame. As thus popularly known, legendary and alive in the legend, he occupies here much the same position that Robert Burns holds among Scots, and has not had to wait even half the time specified by his overseas counterpart: "Don't be afraid. I'll be more respected a hundred years after I am dead than I am at present." With both of them it is essentially a literary phenomenon. Whether or not, in the sum of permanence or the test of human values, there have been greater Scots, or greater Australians, there has been no writer of either country with quite the same common touch, the same simple human appeal that each of these has in his own different style; and there has been none, either, who so wholly took over, as each of these did, the natural voice of his country and made it naturally his own. In Burns the voice may often speak Lowland dialect, now in need of translating even for Scots, and many of the gold-mining, shearing and other terms and contemporary references in Lawson may be similarly dated and, for exactness, in some need of interpretation even for Australians; but in both of them the idiom is so nationally right and the simplicity so true that Scots or Australians understand their man well enough for a' that.

The close resemblance to Burns, in this way at least, seems at present clearly obvious; though, if it is not too greatly risking the wrath of Caledonia, it might be suggested that such national uniqueness indicates that a country has no really wide and varied literary greatness; and that, while Burns's position may be permanent, Lawson's in the long run may change, and he may become the most outstanding writer and literary figure of a period, rather than of a people. Australia's own story is, after all, barely through its first chapter.

For the present, though, Lawson's national position stands very much the same as that of Burns, and looks just as secure. It would seem, too, that Lawson had himself grown consciously aware of this peculiar shared identity of theirs—and had forethought of some latterday developments as well—when he dipped his pen in a simmering of the self-pity from which they both rather hopelessly suffered and splashed it over idolators at "Robbie's Statue". Earlier, in the preface to his first published book, he had sharply resented, as critical parochialism, his being labelled, in a literary sense, "the Australian Robert Burns"; but his own outlook, narrowed by an obsession of personal frustration and honed by "republican" enthusiasm, was itself sharply parochial then, and the critic, whoever he was, had at least an unconscious foretaste of truth, touching on their broader, and now most plainly marked, com-

Caricature of Lawson.

mon legendary identity. The differences between them—in character, appearance, work, surroundings, education (particularly), outlook on life at large and especially on the feminine half of it, and in other ways also—are as wide as the dividing seas; but as well as their distinct major resemblance sundry minor likenesses not peculiar to themselves will come to mind. The human note which each of them struck is without doubt most warming and endearing—but then, so is that of others of their literary stature elsewhere, a close example, perhaps, Charles Lamb, the number of whose cherishing admirers has also been legion, without any hope of raising Elia to anything like the nationally representative position of either Burns or Lawson. Both of them, Lawson and Burns—though not altogether alone in this, either—are freely repetitive in a good deal of their work: Burns, in his themes (or theme) and images alike, to the extent that his whole poetic statement can once and for all be very quickly taken in; Lawson in that respect also, as well as in repeated plots and movable scenes, and in varied use of the same character-names and place-names, sparing him the trouble of fresh invention in his prose. (Still, if Mitchell, Stiffner and one or two others seem to be each several different persons, in physical appearance as well as in character, this at least has the brand of Australian casualness on it, and no one ever more deliberately and successfully created the illusion of writing under that brand than Lawson.) Again, both Burns and Lawson eked out the richness of their genius with old material refurbished to the point of re-creating it and making it original anew: Burns, the songs warmed by more than the fire at firesides under thatched roofs; Lawson, the yarns drawled at camp-fires or spun wherever else men mellowed their hearts in companionship and mateship together. Both of them, too, were satirists on personally felt or imagined contemporary failures to fill vague ideals; and in both of them the satire not surprisingly fades; the song, or story, stays. But, however far any such associated comparisons might be carried, it is still in the one major resemblance that they come naturally to mind together: each of them distinctively his own countrymen's affectionately regarded representative national writer—a generally allotted status and stature all the more remarkable in that, as Burns has been not unkindly called "the singer and satirist of a parish", so Lawson may, without disparagement, be as truly called the poet, storyteller, satirist of a strip of colony, if not chiefly of a decade . . . that great decade of the 1890s, in which Australia, with Lawson in some measure portraying its national being, first took on shape and form.

Certainly no one would question the importance of that decade in Henry Lawson's life's work. It holds virtually the whole of his masterpiece writing; indeed anyone might "know Lawson"—in a literary sense—without prospecting beyond its fringes. Taken all in all, the reader can thus know his Lawson on, say, less than a score each of the poems and of the stories and sketches—"Ballad of the Drover", "The Sliprails and the Spur", "When Your Pants Begin to Go", "Sweeney", "Faces in the Street", "The Star of Australasia", perhaps one or two more of the "prophetic" pieces with the beat of the brass band shak-

ing their ragged lines, a few examples of Lawson's having sometimes written a better verse version than his prose version of an identical bush narrative, and a limited personal selection from the rest; and in the prose, **"The Drover's Wife"**, **"Send Round the Hat"**, **"Bill the Ventriloquial Rooster"**, **"The Loaded Dog"**, **"A Wild Irishman"**, **"The Union Buries Its Dead"**, **"A Double Buggy at Lahey's Creek"**, **"The Geological Spieler"**, **"The Bush Undertaker"**, the curiously neglected sketch-masterpiece of sustained humour accurately and perhaps affectionately titled **"The Darling River"**, a filling of the more familiar others, and some of the early but little known minor sketch gems to be found in the Third Series of [*The Stories of Henry Lawson,* edited by Cecil Mann]. But—as can surely be fairly suggested—to gain anything like real personal familiarity with one well worth knowing (on his own account, no less than on account of the unique place he occupies in Australian lore) it is necessary to read him closely, verse and prose, a great deal more extensively.

The reason scarcely needs elaborating: with a completeness hard to match in fiction and semi-fictional writing anywhere, or in any writing whatever outside that of the few honestly direct personal essayists and autobiographers, he threaded both the fine and the coarse, the strong and the frayed strands of his life experience, and of himself, through the bulk of his work, fictional and non-fictional, prose and verse. . . .

[In *The Stories of Henry Lawson*] an attempt is made to project a passably accurate character-mosaic of Henry Lawson pieced together mainly from his writing, not overlooking that, in any such design, a strong measure of commonsense caution is called for. Many people have been misled by taking him always with solemn literalness. He was, first and last, a fictionizer, a master storyteller—one, moreover, whose inspiration was often necessity—and where fact was troublesome in any of his work the semblance was near enough. Also, he was in himself paradox in person. Instances are endless; to give a few examples:

There would seem to be ample proof in his repetitiveness of one kind and another that he was naturally blessed with the gift of laziness; yet the amount of his work would seem to deny it. Again, as many have spoken of his "hatred" as of his "love" for the bush; actually, it would seem that his heart was in the bush always, but that he was never truly contented when he was there; indeed, he feared the bush life. Unlike Dr Johnson—the small-townite turned Londoner entire—he remained a recognizable bushman to the end, and yet was never wholly at home without the feel of the pavements under his feet. He was for ever restless, and never adventurous—a berth in the *Royal Tar,* taking the original New Australians in search of a socialist Utopia in South America, was not for him; nor were the Western Australian goldfields on either of his two visits to the West, however alluring the golden glitter, and however disappointing were Albany and (later) Perth as Meccas for unemployed eastern States' tradesmen. To mention one other paradox, he was the voice of the common man; yet there was more than fictional convenience in his admiration for an aristocratic past.

That by no means completes the tale of paradox, but it is enough to underline the final paradox it clearly spells out: that, while there is always more than risk in taking anything from his pen—fictional or non-fictional—with confident literalness, any biographer of him is unlikely to find a field richer in personal payable gold than his total work. In this same respect, he was, too, habitually careless: his quotations—even of his own verse—are frequently wrong or are memory paraphrases: in this, as in such simple tools of trade as spelling and punctuation, he was, after hard trying, ultimately content to leave it "to the comps". In the MS. of "A Fragment of Autobiography"— to quote one significant instance—there are three attempts at spelling "Norwegian", all different. The fact that in these particular entries he was referring to his father—"he . . . was a Norweegean sailor"—makes these spellings specially notable. Poverty of schooling falls far short of explaining them, and they certainly do not signify that he disliked his father, which would possibly be a Freudian interpretation. The brief autograph record of his early days—the most successful of his several attempts at autobiography—leaves no doubt that he was very fond of his father, Peter Larsen, even beyond the recorded admiration he had for his maternal grandfather, Henry Albury, or perhaps for anybody else. The clear significance, then, in his variety of spelling would seem to be that it indicates more than mere habitual carelessness. There is ample evidence that, although he was acutely self-conscious about his educational shortcomings, and for a time tried to bridge the needlessly self-torturing lack, he found even the simplest learning difficult—not that this was any disadvantage in his work; rather the contrary. His genius was in narrative writing: the one great literary quality in all his work is simplicity—storytelling as simple and realistic as language and close (if not very extensive) observation can manage: his scant schooling and little learning were not only sufficient for that purpose but were the very essence of his style and method.

This is not to suggest that he was what is vaguely termed a "natural" writer. For all his casual carelessness in various unimportant respects, he could, when he wished, be a competent and careful craftsman—never more careful than when careless casualness seems most apparent. Indeed that effect of apparent careless casualness is just what he chiefly deliberately aimed at; as much an element of his storytelling as his first-person method, which, in story after story, leaves the impression of listening to one relating a simple factual account, instead of an impression of reading artfully contrived fiction. This effect of the spoken rather than of the written word, of the voice rather than the pen, is not restricted to his use of the first-person method: it seems just as clearly present in the best of his other work; instance **"The Bush Undertaker"** as a masterpiece example. The effect is of listening to simple yarning; of hearing something being told to pass away the time at the campfire; and, in one guise and another, the yarn-spinner, more often than not, is Henry Lawson. This, too, seems something significantly different from the force

of a writer's character investing his work with life, which is there in every good writer. It is an intimate quality, an intimate contact; but spoken, not written. Perhaps it finally explains Lawson's nationally unique status. The voice rather than the pen, and by the voice we know him—it could well be, also, the most important technical element in his workmanship and his literary achievement. Through it we have the woof and warp, the design, colour and pattern, the entire texture of these collected stories and sketches. By it they are as close bound together as Lawson himself is inseparably bound in with them. As well as their individual identity, as prose masterpieces or mere straws of journalism, they clearly have this unified completeness also. They are held together thus, by voice, as a composite work, a single book, rather than only a collection of assorted writings scattered over a lifetime. In sum they are the book of that life—a book which provides the key to our legendary Lawson.

Apparent careless casualness is just what Lawson chiefly deliberately aimed at; as much an element of his storytelling as his first-person method, which, in story after story, leaves the impression of listening to one relating a simple factual account, instead of an impression of reading artfully contrived fiction.

—Cecil Mann

Here, then, in one spoken word and another, is a subject for a series which Hogarth, mixing his pigments with some binding of sentiment, might have portrayed. It is a story never far from the normal common level of humanity, but, in the mirage of legend at least, not altogether without some touches of the picturesque. A story stemming off from factual Kentish yeomen: big, bearded men, silhouetted in the mirage of legend against retreating vistas of green country England. Included there, a dubious supposed tinge of gipsy origins; fancied and fostered by none more favourably than by Henry Lawson himself; conjuring up in the mirage hooded carts and lithe Romany poachers, crones crouched over smoky night-fires, back along the misted byways to wherever legends begin. That is the maternal side; the background of the literary mother— strong, formidable, feared—who had her own share of fame as the early feminist leader Louisa Lawson. On the other side, again, of the beginnings, the Norwegian sailor-navigator ancestry; venturing out to any foreign landfall; coming to visible life here in this new-old south in an imagined leap ashore by one of them from his ship, with the glitter of gold beckoning him on. So to the unbroken bush ("the stony, barren ridges", Lawson said, over and over); the mining claims around Grenfell and there-abouts; sinking their golden holes or duffers almost as chance fell out. Of birth there on 17th June 1867, in a gold-seeker's tent; a poor and humble place. "There was one born in a manger", he reminds us, not without personal inference; implying, with a foot on the rail, his own Messianic complex and purpose: this a paradox for moralizers whose morality begins and ends with a dry throat. He reminds us, further, that the one there also humbly born was a storyteller, too: that one of His stories was of a man, a good Samaritan, who befriended a stranger: "the stranger's friend": the creed of friendship, of mateship: creed and literary theme enough for a lifetime. A warming creed of generous helpfulness, of man's humanity to man; freely granted by many of his fellow-men to Henry Lawson. It is there, for him, in the ordinary ways of friendship, mateship, good-fellowship, springing from one and another of those significantly many friends, mates and companions, almost from when, in early youth, he left bush work for a painter's trade in the city. Also, it is there in extraordinary ways. It secures the Government appointment for him as "teacher" at the "little Maori school" on his second work-seeking venture to New Zealand, where and when, with his young wife doing most of the teaching, he did some of the best of his writing. It is there again, with a State Governor leading in the Good Samaritan role, sending them off from Sydney, at the end of the 1890s and at the peak of Lawson's achievement and fame, ambitiously to England, with the grand hopes unrealized, and thence the sorry retreat, ending in broken marriage, and the long, depressive decline. Again it is there, years later, in wartime 1916, in the well-intentioned, and fantastic, conspiracy of his city mates and friends and admirers to "save him from himself" by getting him away, once more under Government sponsorship, to the then "dry" Murrumbidgee Irrigation Area, expecting him to rusticate, and grow fruit, drink water, and publicize the new settlement.

In those, and in other respects also, Henry Lawson's is a lifetime without the remotest parallel anywhere in our literary records. Writing the cold truth . . . asking more of a man than he has in him to give . . . it is often a darkened lifetime, sinking deep, under a weight of self-pity and remorse, even to the sordid; saved and lifted again at the end by spontaneous national acknowledgement; tribute; acclaim; sorrow; regret; and something of the sound of a sigh of relief. One never altogether without honour now gone from the living, on 2nd September 1922; the forming nation of his reforming thoughts pausing for a moment to think of him; a solemn State funeral: and Bohemia, too, in its fashion, burying its dead.

A. A. Phillips (essay date 1965)

SOURCE: "Henry Lawson Revisited," in *Meanjin,* Vol. XXIV, No. 100, 1965, pp. 5-17.

[In the following essay, Phillips offers a stylistic and thematic analysis of Lawson's short fiction.]

Revisiting Henry Lawson, reading straight through all his most significant work, has proved for me a surprising experience. Before I enlarge on the surprise, I had better declare myself on the begged question in my first sentence. What constitutes the significant part of Lawson's work?

First, I have ignored his verse. That is only partly because it is not consistently good enough to be patiently readable in quantity. Mainly I have set it aside because I am uncertain how truly it contains the mind of its writer. Too often, one feels, the ballads are not by Henry Lawson. They are the work of a persona, bearing his name and cashing his cheques, who assumed the rôle of the Australian folk-voice. Lawson himself, I suspect, never recognised the histrionic element which the hypnosis of rhythm created within him.

I have also taken little account of the stories which Lawson wrote during the long and painful period of his decline. That period begins—with a distressing obviousness—in **'The Romance of the Swag'** volume. Again it was not merely the inferiority of the writing which induced my disregard. Literary work may be bad and yet tell us much about the mind of its writer. No student of Wordsworth, for example, dare disregard his dullnesses. These later stories of Lawson have not the same value, because in them he has lost the fine edge of his perception and of his truth to himself. What was a sensitive recognition of human values has become dogma, a preacher's assertion of the importance of kindliness. Moreover, that ventriloquial folk-voice which had usually dictated the ballads now speaks also through the prose.

Lawson's prose-work falls into clearly marked periods. There is a short preparatory phase in which the dominant influence is that of Dickens. Then, in *While the Billy Boils,* Lawson comes, with astonishing swiftness, to mastery of his highly original art. Most of the stories in these two volumes are handled with the confidence of a matured technician who has filled a wilderness of wastepaper baskets with preliminary failures—as Lawson had not.

There follows in *On the Track and Over the Slip-Rails* a period of recession. The conceptions are more conventional, the touch is less consistently sure; and the sentimental element in Lawson appears to be growing dominant. Then he triumphantly returns to form with his master-piece, the *Joe Wilson* volume.

Lawson here appears to be on the edge of an exciting development, which never takes place. It is one of the most painful disappointments in literary history. One can accept the deaths of an Emily Brontë or a Keats, despite one's sense of the loss which they probably cost us—for death at least has dignity; but this living collapse of a talent which seemed about to add depth to its already achieved sureness and originality—this is almost unendurable.

And here I had better digress; for I have used the word 'sentimental' and we need to come to terms with it. It is an awkward word—all the more because it happens to be two words. There is sentiment, which is comparatively respectable, and there is sentimentality which is a term of abuse—almost a four-letter word, in fact, if one doesn't check the arithmetic. For each of these, 'sentimental' is the adjectival representative.

That is not the only complexity. What is the difference between 'sentiment' and 'sentimentality'? Is it merely a matter of degree and of subjective response? Do we use them as we use the words 'sweet' and 'sugary', saying 'sentiment' when there is about as much of it as one can take, and 'sentimentality' when there is so much that it makes one sick? Perhaps we often do; yet we feel that there is a qualitative rather than a quantitative difference between them.

I distrust definitions. If words were really definable, literature—poetry at least—would be impossible. Its tool of words would not slice finely enough. But if we are to use in company these terms, we had better avoid confusion by resorting to the approximation of definition.

Sentiment, then, it seems to me, is the expression of a scale of values which prefers the tendernesses of human response to the virilities, the softnesses to the strengths. The man of sentiment will find a readier sympathy for St. Francis than for Marcus Aurelius, for Botticelli than for Michelangelo, for Schubert than for Sibelius. He will incidentally prefer the emotional to the intellectual approach.

Lawson, at his best, has a surprisingly rigorous sense of truth—we do not expect it because there is so much of the naïve in his composition, and because his writing-method is so deceptively casual in its effect.

—*A. A. Phillips*

Sentimentality is the indulgence in the pleasure of that emotionalism for its own sake and at the expense of truth. Example reveals more than definition, and the revealing example here is Mozart's music—full of sentiment and unerringly avoiding sentimentality.

You will observe that, in terms of my definitions, sentimentality is not merely an over-extension of sentiment, the Aristotelian extreme of the virtuous mean (if sentiment is a virtue). It is different in kind. We use for the one quality a word derived from the other because sentimentality is the besetting temptation to which the man of sentiment is exposed.

Lawson was certainly a man of sentiment. He had a tenacious regard for the tendernesses of human response, and he seems scarcely interested in most of the virilities. He is also often a sentimentalist. His verse is full of sentimentality, and there is much in his later prose. It does occur, too, in the stories of the good period—but remarkably little for a writer so exposed to sentimentalist temptation by the strength of his sentiment. Lawson, at his best, has a surprisingly rigorous sense of truth—we do not expect it because there is so much of the naïve in his

composition, and because his writing-method is so deceptively casual in its effect.

It is an illuminating exercise to read the *Joe Wilson* stories with this problem in mind. Here is a work which unreservedly expresses the view of life of a man of sentiment. Yet after the first page or two, there is scarcely a moment of sentimentality, scarcely a touch which is not controlled by a rigorous sense of truth. It is a masterly feat of tight-rope walking.

There are readers who will deny this, who will regard the whole conception of *Joe Wilson* as sentimentalist. They would be wrong, basically ignorant of the nature of life. They are, in fact, sentimentalists-in-reverse, who have lost their sense of truth through a debilitating fear of sentiment.

But it is time that I returned to the surprise which I mentioned in my opening paragraph. Let me approach it through a cursory consideration of one aspect of Lawson criticism.

The earlier commentators frequently defended Lawson against the charge that he was too gloomy, too melancholy, too pessimistic—the term varies. The curious thing is that, while one often meets the defence, one never comes across the accusation—or, at least, I have not in the course of a somewhat superficial search.

[In *Australian Literature,* Volume 1] Morris Miller thus refutes the anonymous view: 'Prevalence of the pathetic note must not deceive us into assuming that his main note is marked by pessimism. . . . Lawson never forgot the element of risk in living, and its occasional accompaniment of sorrow and distress. But he also knows its positive side . . . his stories manifest an evenly-balanced mental perspective of life'.

It is not an impressive defence; the writer of vision does not hedge his bets about life in the manner which Miller's treatment suggests Lawson did.

H. M. Green, who writes very well about Lawson, defends him against the same charge, basing his plea on the ground that after all Lawson often wrote humorously. This, of course, just won't wash. As Lawson himself said— Green quotes the remark—'There seems a quiet sort of sadness always running through outback humour, alleged or otherwise'. This is true of more than the outback variety of humour. It is quite false to equate the humorous with the optimistic. A comic writer may be as desperate as Swift, as melancholy as Thurber. A quiet sort of gloom does run through most of Lawson's humour.

Vance Palmer in *National Portraits* has given us the best short summation of Lawson, and one which is in many ways in advance of the views of Palmer's contemporaries; but he stresses little the melancholic flavour of Lawson's best writing.

Later critics have been on the whole more aware of Lawson's dark tone. Cecil Hadgraft in his *History of Austra-*

lian Literature clearly recognises it; but he usually applies to it the word 'pathos'. It is true that Lawson does often pull out the pathetic stop; but it is not, it seems to me, his pathos which is the true source of his darkness of tone.

Perhaps that element has been best described by H. P. Heseltine in his article on 'The Literary Heritage' (*Meanjin*, No. 1, 1962). Unhappily, he has there entangled his perceptions with a thesis—a process which is always rather hard on perceptions, and the more so here because, in my view, the thesis won't work out.

This recognition, then, forms a small part of the expressed views about Lawson. Yet, revisiting him as I have done, with his more triumphant qualities already established in my mind, one's strongest first impression is of the depth and the persistence of Lawson's melancholy, the darkness of his view of the human condition.

That is revealed in many facets of his work. There is the dismal tone, insistently recurrent, of his landscape settings. One could assemble a sizeable anthology of passages such as this:

> The country looks just as bad for a hundred miles round Hungerford, and beyond that it gets worse—a barren, blasted wilderness that doesn't even howl. If it howled it would be a relief.

> A hot, breathless, blinding sunrise—the sun having appeared suddenly above the ragged edge of the barren scrub like a great disc of molten steel. No hint of a morning breeze before it, no sign of earth or sky to show that it is morning—save the position of the sun.

> It was blazing hot outside and smothering hot inside the weatherboard and tin shanty at Dead Dingo, a place on the cleared road, where there was a pub and a police station, and which was sometimes called 'Roasted' and other times 'Potted Dingo'—nicknames suggested by the everlasting drought and the vicinity of the one-pub township of Tinned Dog.

Against these one can set a celebration of the splendours of the Australian scene, written in London under the influence of nostalgia, and cast in a rhetorical style uncharacteristic of Lawson—and not half so effective as his usual dry precision: there is a short lyrical passage setting the background for Joe Wilson's proposal: and that is about all. If one assembled the meteorological statistics, one would probably find that the total rainfall in the *Collected Works of Henry Lawson* was about three inches.

Once, indeed, the drought does break back o' Bourke. It must have been an occasion to set the cockies carolling hymns of praise. Does Lawson? No! **'In a Wet Season'** is a superbly accurate delineation of a misery of dampness, as dismal as the more customary pictures of drought.

It may be argued—it often has been—that the Australian scenes which Lawson best knew, about Gulgong and

Bourke, *are* dismal, that Lawson was merely setting down what was there to be seen. True, no doubt; but when a man really knows a countryside, when it has seeped into his blood, he usually finds in it elements of beauty, and if he is a writer he wants to communicate his sense of its beauty. Lawson's love for Australia certainly came from deeper levels than the ventriloquial folk-voice, but it hardly colours at all his picture of the Australian scene. Reading Lawson's work consecutively, one becomes more and more convinced that he was not merely objectively delineating the New South Wales plains; he was projecting on to them the landscape of his own soul.

There is a similar quality in Lawson's recordings of Australian society. He celebrates Australia as the land of splendid opportunity only when he is speaking through the ventriloquial folk-voice. The tone is very different when he speaks from himself. His chosen human material is the men of the roads, rejects from an unjust society, the slum's victims, the selectors struggling thin-lipped against a hostile nature which plays with loaded dice, their wives facing slow spiritual destruction through hardship and loneliness.

Again it can be argued that Lawson wrote his best work during a period of drought and economic depression, and again one becomes progressively convinced that it is an insufficient explanation, that there are subjective compulsions controlling his emphases.

There is a virtual admission of this in the view of himself which Lawson often presents. I have written elsewhere [*The Australian Tradition*] that 'Lawson, as unassumingly humble a writer as ever lived, knew very well that he belonged to the tragic élite of the sensitive'. I might have added that he consistently regarded this distinction as his curse. There is almost a refrain through his work of such remarks as this:

> I wasn't a healthy-minded average boy; I reckon I was born for a poet by mistake, and grew up to be a bushman, and didn't know what was the matter with me—or the world. . . . [**'Joe Wilson's Courtship'**]

> I only drank because I felt less sensitive, and the world seemed a lot saner and better and kindlier when I had a few drinks. . . . It is better to be thought 'wild' than to be considered eccentric or ratty. [**'Joe Wilson's Courtship'**]

> I often think how at sunset, the past must come home to a new-chum black sheep, sent out to Australia and drifted into the bush. I used to think that they couldn't have much brains, or the loneliness would drive them mad. [**'Past Carin''**]

> They all seemed to forget him as they came into the Heads; they had their own troubles to attend to. But I didn't forget him. I wish sometimes that I didn't take so much notice of things. [**'They Wait on the Wharf in Black'**]

There is another kind of remark that forms something like an undercurrent refrain through Lawson's work:

The procession numbered fifteen, fourteen souls following the broken shell of a soul. Perhaps not one of the fourteen possessed a soul any more than the corpse did—but that doesn't matter. ['**The Union Buries Its Dead**']

If we saw our married lives as others see them, half of us would get divorced. ['**Barney Take Me Home Again**']

A man doesn't shoot himself when he's going to be made a lawful father for the first time, unless he can see a long way into the future. ['**A Hero in Dingo-Scrubs**']

Taken in isolation, these comments suggest a man of cynical temperament. Such an interpretation of Lawson is, of course, wildly absurd. They express rather a profound melancholy, shaped into the irony which Lawson used to stiffen himself to endurance.

There is an even more significant recurrence in Lawson's work, this time of a theme—the theme of the man loaded with a guilty past. He bears it usually with nobility, and with a growth in tenderness, and he is always sympathetically presented. There is Bogg of Geebung, the derelict remittance-man with a broken love-affair long ago, who ends in the river. There is the Oracle who has caused the death of the woman he loved: there is the Hero of Redclay who has gone to jail on a false accusation because he has seduced a decent girl, and can only defend himself by revealing his presence in her bedroom: there is Doc Wilde, bearing some guilt from his American past, and assuaging his despair with whisky, cynicism and acts of kindness. Even Peter McLaughlan's saintliness and understanding, it is ultimately revealed, are created by memory of an early guilt. And so one could go on.

It is by far the most frequently repeated theme in Lawson's work. And it is plainly the symbol of something profoundly important to him in his sense of the human condition.

Finally, let me draw your attention to two of Lawson's stories. One is '**The Union Buries its Dead**'. To-day we see it as one of his greatest. Perhaps the most remarkable thing about it is that it ever got itself written in the Australia of the 1890s. For, in its implicit view of the function of literature, in its manner and method, it is a mid-twentieth century story. It is barely credible that it could be written so long before the general establishment of its kind of literary approach, by an unschooled writer with no theories about his art. It only becomes credible if we assume that the story was forced upon Lawson by a profound need to shape what it declares.

It has sometimes been suggested that this story celebrates the spirit of mateship. That is only a minor thread in its weave. Its real purpose is almost the reverse—to declare the loneliness of the human condition and the deadliness of human indifference.

The story which immediately follows '**The Union**' is a very short episode, of little apparent importance. It is called '**On the Edge of the Plain**'. In it Mitchell describes his return home after he has been reported dead, the excitement of his reception, and how his family made him promise never to leave home again. Then comes the ironic twist typical of the Mitchell stories. His mate comments that he has broken his promise:

> Mitchell stood up, stretched himself, and looked dolefully from his heavy swag to the wide, hot, shadeless cotton-bush plain ahead.

> 'Oh, yes', he yawned, 'I stopped at home for a week, and then they began to growl because I couldn't get any work to do'.

There follows the characteristic prolonging echo of a Lawson story's ending:

> The mate guffawed and Mitchell grinned. They shouldered the swags, with the pup on top of Mitchell's, took up their billies and water-bags, turned their unshaven faces to the wide, hazy distance, and left the timber behind them.

Let me emphasize that the story is called '**On the Edge of the Plain**'. It is an improbable title. The plain is merely the setting in which Mitchell relates the episode—it has nothing to do with the tale's nominal subject-matter. Can we believe that Lawson would have chosen the title if the story's tail-piece had not had a compelling significance for him—and, indeed, it does give that sketch a depth which only Lawson could have achieved with such material?

Two men, bearing the burden of the ironic and painful past, assuaging each other's loneliness, as they face the drought-stricken deadliness of a plain—here is a revealing symbol of Lawson's view of the human condition.

I could cite further evidence, but perhaps I have given enough to convince you of the justice of the accusation brought by those anonymous detractors whom the early critics attempted to answer. They were unjust, of course, in one way—for the crime which they arraigned is no crime. A writer is entitled to as dark a melancholy as his experience or his digestion may impose upon him, provided that he conveys it with truth and imaginative vitality—as Lawson certainly does.

No doubt the detractors were moved partly by the discomfortableness of Lawson's attitude, which was disconcerting to simple minds, partly by their feeling that Lawson's pessimism betrayed the self-confident Australianism of which he was an admired representative. But they had a more legitimate justification. There is something not quite right about Lawson's melancholy. Lawson's life is the terrible story of a man who accepted defeat almost before he had begun. The taint of that defeatism is in the melancholy of his writing. It is too surrendering, it won't hit back at the fate with the loaded dice. That obsession with the figure of the man with the guilty past—I don't think it arises from a subconscious sense of guilt in Lawson, although that is a possible explanation. I believe that Lawson used that figure because the guilty man is impelled to a sympathy with the defeated.

Despite the blood on the wattle, Lawson lacked the temperament of the rebel. He suggests too much the attitude of Hamlet as (wrongly) interpreted by Coleridge. Furphy was right in what he meant when he said that Lawson was too feminine—though one must dissent from the sex-intolerance, and ignorance, implied by the term Furphy used. Moreover, as I have said, Lawson was indifferent to the virilities of human response—too indifferent to achieve a balanced view of life. Lawson often suggests to us the attitude of Maxim Gorki; but he was incapable of that acceptance of the brutalities of instinctual response which gives perspective to the Russian's tenderness. To put it bluntly, Lawson hadn't quite got the guts which a writer needs.

Lawson was aware of this. The character of Joe Wilson was, or became, largely a self-portrait. That is the point of Lawson's remark in the post-script: 'I know Joe Wilson very well'. He also writes, 'I had an idea of making Joe Wilson a strong character. Whether he is or not, the reader must judge. It seems to me that the man's sentimental selfishness, good-nature, "softness", or weakness—call it what you like—developed as I wrote on.'

I have suggested that the early critics of Lawson denied the intensity of his melancholy, that the later critics, although more aware of it, seldom emphasize its significance. For myself, in my memoried impression of Lawson before my revisitation, awareness of that quality was not deeply etched. Were we all wrong? Well, critics often are wrong, but not quite so wrong as this, surely. And if memoried impressions of a writer do not carry one deeper into his work than any formal analysis, literature would not be the profound and subtle art which it is. Moreover if Lawson were only this sombre figure, he might have compelled admiration, but he could not have won the kind of affection which he did, from the sort of people who felt it.

There is, in truth, a more positive side to his work which alters the whole tone of the impression which he leaves. Before I discuss that positive aspect, let me first establish an element which affects the lighting of the Lawsonian picture.

Despite his sense of the pain and loneliness of living, Lawson never presents to us the tragic view of existence. That is only partly because he lacked the passion and the feeling for the virilities which the tragic needs. Lawson was never articulate about ideas, and one is therefore forced to speak for him with an impertinent over-confidence. As I see it then, Lawson did not merely fail to reach the tragic view. He positively rejected it. Had he been capable of abstract expression, I think he would have said that it was a sentimentalism, sacrificing truth to a large emotionalism.

> Lawson often suggests to us the attitude of Maxim Gorki; but he was incapable of that acceptance of the brutalities of instinctual response which gives perspective to the Russian's tenderness. To put it bluntly, Lawson hadn't quite got the guts which a writer needs.
>
> —*A. A. Phillips*

It is a view for which there is something to be said. In that story I quoted a few pages back, Mitchell knew the bitterness of the exile, but not the relief of a tragic confrontation of it. He put the pup on the swag, and walked on. And what he walked on was a plain—that is an essential part of the symbol. For Lawson the un-tragic tragedy of life is that it has not the satisfaction of peaks, however grim.

Lawson, and most of those of his Australian contemporaries who wrote fiction, worked within the convention of naturalism. That was not simply because it was the mode to which they were accustomed, a handily-established technique which stood ready for use; for Lawson, at least, refashioned the technique of the story in his own way—he plainly had no need for the crutch of a ready-made writing method. He used the mode of naturalism because he needed it to reflect his attitude towards life. His conceptions demanded that he keep within the scale of life-as-it-is-lived.

The abstractions of the critical vocabulary are too flavourless to convey this point expressively. Will you permit me, then, to approach it obliquely?

In introducing *Lear* to students I have sometimes said: 'This is not essentially a play about a great king in a barbaric age. Go into a hundred suburban homes at random, and in one of them, you will find the play of *Lear* enacting itself. There is Joe O'Leary, a bossy old chap who has created a good business as a master-builder. He's old and tired and a bit soft now; so he retires and makes the business over to his two daughters to avoid death-duties. He is going to live with each of his daughters in turn. But he's a difficult old chap, and they're tougher types than he realizes. He spoils the grand-children, interfering with maternal discipline. He wants his meals when he wants them, and that upsets domestic routine. He invites old cronies in for beer-parties, and other people's beer-parties in your own house are hard to take. So the daughters get together to present an ultimatum: either he does what he's told, or he can go to the Old Men's Home.'

So far, so good, and you can carry the parallel rather further—but not much. There are things in *Lear* which cannot be thus translated. Joe O'Leary does not grandly curse his daughters; he declines into lachrymose querulousness. He does not achieve an insanity which illuminates the world by lightning-flashes; he goes, rather try-ingly, soft in the head.

What Shakespeare has done, for valid artistic purposes, is to enlarge the scale from living-as-it-is. That change has enabled him to illuminate certain truths better than the naturalistic scale could. But it has entailed also certain losses. As I have tried to suggest, in changing the scale, Shakespeare has changed the quality, too, of the experi-ence. The element of truth which Shakespeare thus lost—and which was not needed for his kind of vision—was important to the Lawsonian conception. It was necessary for him to keep the scale of living-as-it-is; and he evolved his delicate and original technique in the light of this need.

Let me illustrate through a passage in which Lawson is preparing for the culminating symbol of *Joe Wilson*—the purchase of the double buggy:

> I thought of getting the turn-out while she was laid up, keeping it dark from her until she was on her feet, and then showing her the buggy standing in the shed. But she had a bad time, and I had to have the doctor regularly, and get a proper nurse, and a lot of things extra: so the buggy idea was knocked on the head. I was set on it too; I'd thought of how, when Mary was getting up and getting strong, I'd say one morning, 'Go round and have a look in the shed, Mary; I've got a few fowls for you', or something like that—and follow her round to watch her eyes when she saw the buggy. I never told Mary about that—it wouldn't have done any good.

Trivial, you may think, merely sentimentalist. No; Law-son is here virtually saying, 'Depth of emotion is not truthfully recorded through such expressions as the rhet-oric of Antony and Cleopatra. Those who know the actu-ality of living know that it is on this scale that we feel most deeply'.

Tucking into the back of our minds this recognition by Lawson of the scale of living-as-it-is, let us return to the consideration of the positive element in his work. It ap-pears most obviously in his emphasis on endurance. Law-son, Heaven knows, was himself no Stoic; but he thor-oughly understood and admired the bushman's stoicism. As he displays it to us in his writing, it is not a force which goes on the offensive. It does not meet and subdue the Fate with the loaded dice. But it is not negative, it is not satisfied with mere survival; it has its positive aim, and its moderate triumph.

To understand that aim, we must return to Lawson, the man of sentiment, the convinced believer in the value of the tendernesses. Here lies the aim and the triumph of his Stoics. Against all the odds, they maintain the value of the tendernesses. Under the pain, the loneliness and the burden of guilt, they summon their strength, and preserve unhardened hearts.

Lawson was, of course, well aware that the Common Man often failed to maintain the tendernesses, and the sensitiv-ity from which they spring. He did not blink at that fact. Again and again, he records in some sharp ironic phrase his bitterness at that failure—you will find it, for exam-ple, in **'The Union Buries its Dead'**. But Lawson never made this failure the central theme of a story, because the positive achievement was more important.

One could cite many stories which declare this theme. One of the clearest is **'Going Blind'**. Sentimental as it seems, it is precisely true, and it admirably declares the triumph of the bushman's stoicism in maintaining the supremacy of tenderness. Or one might instance Andy of **'Telling Mrs. Baker'**, who could 'keep a promise and nothing else', and who endured the—for him—repulsive task of telling a pack of lies, because that is what loyalty and human decency demand. A strangely trivial example, you may think, of triumphant Stoicism. Or is it rather an admirable example of Lawson's firmness in preserving the scale of living-as-it-is? Here let me remind you of a detail of the symbolism of **'On the Edge of the Plain'**. On Mitchell's swag, there rides a puppy.

Perhaps the best example of the expression of the two aspects of Lawson's view of life is his master-work, the Joe Wilson stories. It is a work, not a series of stories which happen to be linked, for each incident has its pur-poseful place in illuminating the theme of the whole. It was written when the Lawsons were running their Maori school, a time when Lawson was as close to happiness as he was capable of coming. He was off the drink. Even more important, he had leisure and some measure of se-curity. He did not need to snatch at an incident, in order to turn it into a story because he needed the cheque. At last he could write entirely as he wanted to write. Not that he had ever been the kind of pot-boiler who tells comfort-ing lies to please the customers; but he had lacked that freedom from pressure which lets the conception flower into the right declaring form.

In these stories, as I have said, he was writing of himself. He is also, more fully than ever before, writing from him-self. You can sense him saying, 'Now I am going to get said what I feel about living'.

I wish I had left myself space to discuss fully these un-der-regarded stories. Let me at least, in passing, point to the skill with which, in the opening story, Lawson keeps us aware of the pain and insecurity of living without destroying the required atmosphere of confident young love: to the economy with which Brighten's sister-in-law is created as a symbol of the maintenance of tenderness through endurance against the hostility of fate: to the way in which Mrs. Spicer is made to hang over Mary Wilson, threatening her with her own probable future, and to the deepening effect which this threat gives to the following story: to the classic rightness of the husband-and-wife quarrel.

But the most impressive achievement is the culminating symbol of the purchase of the double buggy—and that in two ways. First there is the sureness of touch with which Lawson prevents this idyllic last incident from degenerat-

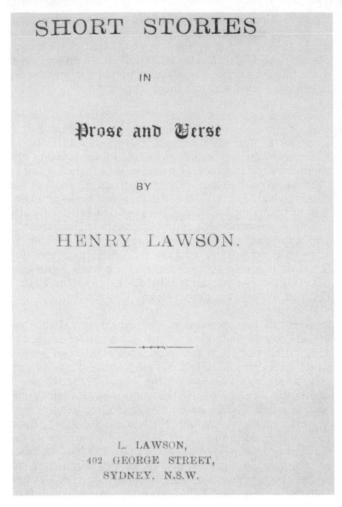

Facsimile of the title-page of Lawson's first book.

ing into the lie of a happy ending. We are deeply moved by it, we are charmed by it; but we are never in danger of mistaking it for finality.

Even more impressive is the rightness of the symbol for conveying what Lawson wants to say about the nature of living. It would hopelessly diminish its effectiveness to attempt a translation of that symbolism. 'Life is a painful business: marriage, even with love, is a difficult relationship: loneliness is inescapable; but there is an insecure triumph when a Joe Wilson buys his wife a double buggy'. How hopelessly inadequate that is; and how right Lawson makes it. I could wish that Patrick White would study these stories and perhaps learn from them to recognise the comparative crudity of his own theory of literary symbolism—and I do not say that in scorn of a writer whom I largely admire. Indeed, one should add, in common fairness, that White can do much that is quite outside Lawson's limited range.

Perhaps it is as well that I have no space to analyse these stories in detail. I doubt if it would get us anywhere. What I would rather wish to do is to send you back to their re-reading with a sharper responsiveness, prepared

to find in them what is surely there—a subtle communication of a view of the nature of living, far deeper than their framework of narrative suggests, and unspoiled by their occasional naïvetés.

These stories particularly well illustrate the central truth about Lawson. The needed modification of his desperate view of the human condition is provided by his sentiment, his sense of the insecurely triumphant survival of tenderness through endurance. The sentiment is the more convincing because of the rigour with which Lawson keeps within the scale of living-as-it-is. It is the more impressive and moving because it was formed within the matrix of a defeated man's dark melancholy.

Colin Roderick (essay date 1966)

SOURCE: "Henry Lawson as Short Story Writer," in *Henry Lawson: Poet and Short Story Writer,* Angus and Robertson, 1966, pp. 43-66.

[*In the following excerpt, Roderick places Lawson's fiction in the context of the modern short story and the Australian short story.*]

[What] is the nature of the short story? What characterizes it as an art form?

We could arrive at its nature by taking a historical view of it. We could see how the modern short story began independently with Hans Andersen in Denmark, Gogol in Russia, and Edgar Allan Poe in America. Thence we might trace it through to the present time. From any volume of Charles Dickens's weekly magazine, *Household Words,* we could see how Dickens first essayed the form in the 1850's. We could see how he approached it after many years of writing novels—none better—and how he failed because he applied to it the art of the novel. These historical elements we shall touch briefly—all too briefly—as we pass through the first part of our examination of Lawson's work. For the moment we shall take the end result of this historical development, as shown in two or three modern short stories, and ascertain from them the chief characteristics of this form of art. Let us examine first one of the stories in that very useful collection of Australian work by Mr Hadgraft and Mr Wilson [*A Century of Australian Short Stories,* 1963], "The Woman From the Bend", by Don Edwards, a Sydney writer who died as recently as 1963. Notice how the story begins. (The beginning of a short story is often an important clue to its quality.) Here it is:

> Ever since his wife died and he had moved in from Wilson's farm, "Lofty" Gibson had lived in the old hut on the bank of the creek.

Let us examine that sentence. What do we get from it? In the first place we get an immediate mental picture of Gibson's physical attributes. He was "Lofty" Gibson: a lanky type of man. He lived in an old hut: he was careless, unambitious; he'd finished with striving for something better. His wife was dead: combined with the title, this knowledge, conveyed in the first five words, immediately puts our minds into a state of expectation: there's going to be a woman in the case. Here's a fellow who has given life away; but something's going to happen. In fewer than thirty words we are plunged into the heart of the story.

Now, leaving Australia for America, here is the opening of a Hemingway story, "Fifty Grand":

> "How are you going yourself, Jack?" I asked him.
>
> "You seen this Walcott?" he says.
>
> "Just in the gym."
>
> "Well," Jack says, "I'm going to need a lot of luck with that boy."

Those two exchanges make the pace for the whole story. You expect to read a story about the world of the prize-fighter. Obviously Jack is either scared stiff, or, as we suspect from our knowledge of the peculiarities of the boxing game, he is up to no good and means to take a dive, as the saying goes. With those few words Hemingway sets the tone of his story and creates an atmosphere in which the reader expects to experience suspense.

The writing in both stories is pithy and to the point. Both stories are upon you at once and bear you along swiftly.

This is an essential of the modern short story. After all, it is a short story: there's no room in it for the discursiveness of the novel. There's no room to describe the environment in detail, no time to go in for full-length portraits of the characters involved. It was right and proper for Dickens to give us massive word pictures of Mr Pickwick; very proper when he published his novel in parts and had to remind readers from month to month what his characters looked like. This was an acceptable convention for the novel. But a writer of the short story today has a great advantage over Dickens. The writers of a century have taught him how unnecessary it is for us to have a tip-to-toe description of his characters. The conventions established in that time enable us to form a firm enough image of them without the details.

Now let us see how Lawson measures up to this test of terseness, the capacity to plunge the reader into the heart of the story, the ability to paint his characters in a few strokes. Take first **"An Old Mate of Your Father's"**:

> You remember when we hurried home from the old bush school how we were sometimes startled by a bearded apparition, who smiled kindly down on us, and whom our mother introduced, as we raked off our hats, as "An old mate of your father's on the diggings, Johnny".

Or take this opening, from **"They Wait on the Wharf in Black"**:

> We were coming back from West Australia, steerage—Mitchell, the Oracle, and I. I had gone over saloon, with a few pounds in my pocket. Mitchell said this was a great mistake—I should have gone over steerage with nothing but the clothes I stood up in, and come back saloon with a pile.

Those are not unusual examples of Lawson's manner: if you look at a dozen more of his stories, you will find more than half of them just as terse.

Now the astonishing thing about this is that Lawson wrote them all at least seventy years ago, before anyone had even begun to think about analysing the technique of the modern short story, before critics had even begun to talk about it as a distinctive art form. Even at that early stage he had grasped the essential air of implication, rather than statement, that the good short story possesses.

No one can say how he did it. Perhaps the fact that he was disciplined by the limitations of space in the Sydney *Bulletin* and the *Worker* had something to do with it. But essentially it was his natural medium. The fact is that Lawson's grasp of this modern form was far in advance of the understanding of his contemporaries. Price Warung, who wrote some good stories himself, reviewed **While the Billy Boils** in the Bathurst *Free Press* when the book appeared in 1896. Like most of the other critics of the day, he paid tribute to Lawson's ability to see beneath the surface of life, but like them, he found in many of the stories "a lack of balance, an absence of constructive power". Such gems as **"Enter Mitchell"** and **"Hungerford"** he wrote down as "bald sketches, scribbled on the rude and shaky editorial table—perhaps an inverted gin-case—of a back-block newspaper for five shillings".

Today Lawson's power to capture a mood or a wisp of sentiment is understood and appreciated; in Price Warung's day it was something new.

The idea of writing a story without some attempt at developing character was something most of Lawson's contemporaries could not grasp. Dialogue, too, was expected, mainly because it helped the writer to develop his characters. Nowadays we agree that characterization, that is, the development of character, and dialogue, that is, the expression of character in action, are not essentials of the short story: they belong to the art of the novel. In the short story it is enough merely to suggest character. As for dialogue, if you look at another story of our own time, "The Persimmon Tree", by Marjorie Barnard—also in Mr Hadgraft and Mr Wilson's book—you will see that dialogue is not essential to the short story. Lawson realized this seventy years ago, when he wrote things like **"Settling on the Land"**. He was to prove its truth again and again, in such stories as **"'Dossing Out' and 'Camping'"**, **"Mr Smellingscheck"**, **"A Rough Shed"**, **"The Man Who Died"**, and so on.

The best modern short stories teach us that what is essential is pattern. The story must be so constructed that its conclusion issues naturally from its beginning. Its form is far from being stylized: its pattern may appear to be as casual and artless as life itself. Yet it must create a belief that it is going somewhere: it may not drift aimlessly along. It must capture the mind by its implication of purpose. It may, and very often will, appear to lack constructive power, as Price Warung said. It may seem to leave the pattern incomplete. But so does life. Life almost always leaves you to guess at what's to come. Any short story that leaves you completely informed is artistically deficient. It ought so to work on your mind that you continue to pursue its implications beyond the writer's words. This requires a sinewy style, a style sparing of words, a style that says little but implies much.

Mr Hadgraft, in referring to the story by John Lang, "The Ghost Upon the Rail", puts his finger on one of its deficiencies in these words: "As a short story it is too lengthy for its content, and the temptation to cut it by at least a quarter was very tantalizing." In the modern sense it isn't a short story at all. But it serves a useful purpose in enabling us to appreciate what Lawson did for the Australian short story in its infancy.

"The Ghost Upon the Rail" was written under the influence of Charles Dickens. Furthermore, it was written for Charles Dickens. It first appeared in *Household Words*. Like most of the other stories that Lang wrote for Dickens, it plays the same game of under-rating the reader as Dickens does through novel after novel. Now in the novel this is fine enough, but in the short story it reminds one of the frills and furbelows in which Victorian parents dressed their children.

The short story cannot bear the weight of its literary parent's clothing. It cannot carry the verbiage loaded on it by Dickens and by the Merediths and Hardys who followed in the Dickens tradition. Do not think that this is to condemn either Dickens or them. On the contrary, they were inheritors of a great tradition—a tradition of leisure and elegance and culture that expressed itself becomingly in the novel. They had no inclination towards the impressionist technique that marks the short story. So we read John Lang's tale, not as a short story, but as a novel in miniature. Its opening paragraph is an example of what the short story writer avoids—the laboured enumeration of detail, the cultivated nature of the writing, divorced from the common idiom. It is wooden, slow-moving. But turn to Henry Lawson's story, **"The Drover's Wife"**. Notice first how the setting jumps at you from the first sentence:

> The two-roomed house is built of round timber, slabs, and stringy-bark, and floored with split slabs.

Lawson was the first Australian to use the speech rhythms and the idiom of everyday life in a wide range of expression in the short story. Compare the sentence I have just quoted with the language in the story by "Tasma" in Mr Hadgraft and Mr Wilson's book. She takes three pages to describe a gum-tree. On the second page she says:

> Every succeeding season had stamped it [i. e., the gum-tree] with hieroglyphics of its own to the interpretation

of which only nature could furnish the key. Becoming warty as it reached maturity, and discharging its acrid juices less frequently than in its more expansive and full-blooded days, it had acquired a seasoned appearance as compared with the gum-trees around it, that gave it all the dignity of a Chiron in the world of the Eucalypti. A close examination of its seared bark would have brought to light a succession of short horizontal indentations, succeeding each other at somewhat irregular intervals from about four feet above the ground to within a few feet of its throwing out a branch—a proof that, if time be measured by impressions, the gum-tree was older than the most aged oak in Britain—for what English tree can remember a time when naked savages scaled it, and scooped out hollows for the reception of their monkey-toes?

When you read this, you cannot help saying, "So what? Get on with the story." No doubt "Tasma's" readers of 1870 enjoyed playing this game of literary hide-and-seek, working out the cultural puzzles she invented for them. It was good fun; but it was not the short story. It was Dickens all over again, suffocating the story with literary frills and furbelows. If you want the real thing, a terse evocation of a gum-tree and what the sight of one conveys to the beholder, read Lawson's short story, **"His Country—After All"**: Lawson's gum-tree is "gnarled and twisted and ragged"—"'a thunderin' old blue-gum!' said the traveller." "Tasma" stuns you with words and buries you under centuries of culture:

> Besides the indentations afore-mentioned—not to be twisted by the most acute decipherer of cuneiform inscriptions into signifying anything more than *points d'appui* for aboriginal fingers and toes—there were some characters inscribed on the opposite side of the tree, which favoured the supposition that they were channels for the outlet of some idea.

The short story cannot tolerate this burden of irrelevant culture. It must paint a succession of swift pictures in words instinct with the culture embedded in the life of the people; "Tasma" paints her pictures with a lexicon.

While Dickens and his disciples continued in the traditional English approach to the new literary form, revolutionary changes were taking place in peoples' reading habits. Dickens himself took part in this revolution with *Household Words,* but he did not become part of it. Periodicals began to multiply in the 1830's. The demand for fiction in America at this time was answered by the periodical. At the same time the man appeared who reconciled the story with the periodical. In doing that, he laid out the fundamental design of the modern short story. This was Edgar Allan Poe. He had a personality nervous, tense, restless. These characteristics made his short stories sharp, gave them an air of suspense, as, for example, in "The Pit and the Pendulum". Poe was never serene, never comfortable; but he was a great artist. His influence on the short story, in form, atmosphere, mood, technique, was universal. It extended, as far as mood and atmosphere go, to the youthful Henry Lawson: it inspired one of his earliest stories, **"The Third Murder"**; he laughed at it in **"The Ghostly Door"**.

Of the influence of Gogol on the Australian short story we cannot be so sure. The Russian short story began with him. His influence on the short story in other countries was less immediate than Poe's; but that he did influence it is beyond question. His influence was one of approach rather than of mood. I do not know that Lawson ever read Gogol, although of course it is possible. Nevertheless, it would be hard to guess which of the two men was speaking in these words: "I believe the lives of ordinary human folk, rich or poor, good or bad, exciting or dull, are the only material a writer need ever seek." It was Gogol who said that, and Lawson who of all Australian short story writers has given it widest application.

In reading Lawson's stories, we realize that we are in the company of a man with a wonderfully swift eye. Up to his time, as I have suggested, there was no one to teach Lawson to analyse the art of the short story, although it is possible that through his father he may have caught one point in his technique subconsciously from Hans Andersen, namely, the way in which he ends many of his stories.

The three stories by Lawson that are in Mr Hadgraft and Mr Wilson's anthology are good illustrations of the mode that the short story was just coming to at about the time Lawson wrote. He had much the same nervous temperament as Poe, but he did not have Poe's morbidity. This nervous tension you see in **"The Drover's Wife"**; and this element, in varying degrees of intensity, you find in all great short stories.

Lawson's conscious masters at the outset of his career were in mood and tone Edgar Allan Poe, and in flavour Bret Harte. The influence of Poe he soon outgrew, since criminal morbidity was not to his liking. The influence of Bret Harte lasted longer; but Lawson's touch was so much finer, his tact for poetic truth so much firmer, his insight into the heart of humanity so much deeper, that whereas Bret Harte is anchored to his period, Henry Lawson has emerged as timeless.

Nevertheless, Bret Harte did have something that was of value to Lawson. It was contact with the "lives of ordinary human folk"—to use Gogol's phrase. There is ample internal evidence to show that it was Bret Harte who taught Lawson to go to the humour of everyday life for the patterns of his stories. I do not use the word "humour" in the sense of jocularity only, but also to signify the disposition and temper of human behaviour in a particular society, the mood of a social group, the complex of its attitudes, the spice of its temperament—all the social materials that combine to produce its distinctive patterns of behaviour. Lawson was indebted to Bret Harte for direction to the behaviour patterns—the humour—of the workaday world. But I would stress that Lawson did not copy Bret Harte. Where inferior artists might have merely imitated him, and in fact did, Lawson's analytical mind grasped the fundamental principle: he did not paint Californian Aus-

tralians, but drew from the life. The derivation of his humour was not literary, but social: it was the humour of Australian society.

The social outlook of English writers at the time was foreign to Lawson's method. As I have said, the tradition in England had become one of a learned, and leisured, culture. When you search the literature of the short story in nineteenth-century England, you find nothing that reflects the national humour. Certainly the English novelists did not forsake the common earth. You have only to read Elizabeth Gaskell, Dickens, Trollope, and Hardy to recognize that; and there were many others. But the short story did not take root in it. Even if *Punch* had gone in for the short story, I doubt that the picture would have altered. As the title of an anthology, *Short Stories from Punch* somehow sounds impossible; it was impossible, because the humour of *Punch* was strictly Harrovian. Of the life of the "lower classes" it took the conventional Harrovian view. It was left to the colonial and American writers to shape the popular humour into short stories, as Lawson did in the Joe Wilson stories, in **"That Pretty Girl in the Army"**, **"The Romance of the Swag"**, and many others. For illustrations of the tribute he extracted from the folk tale, I mention only **"The Loaded Dog"**, **"The Mystery of Dave Regan"**, and **"The Ironbark Chip"**.

These three illustrate Lawson's mastery of that important feature of the short story that we have already mentioned—speed. As you read **"The Loaded Dog"**, you do not realize that the action of the central incident takes only a few minutes: it happens in the time it takes to read the story. And how does Lawson move the story along so fast? Simply by the economical use of everyday words in their natural order: you might almost say, the natural words in their natural order—the popular idiom. Andy sees the dog alongside him with a live dynamite cartridge in its mouth, the fuse hissing and spitting. How does Lawson get Andy under way? Here it is:

> Andy's legs started with a jolt: his legs started before his brain did, and he made after Dave and Jim. And the dog followed Andy.

At this point we ought perhaps to pause and sum up the features so far mentioned that determine whether any piece purporting to be a short story has a real claim to be one. These are terseness, immediate impact, swift movement, and a recognizable pattern free of cultural impediment. The writing must be incisive. The writer must be in touch with the humour of his social group. He must be in tune with the rhythm of its life. To be talented, he must have clarity of vision, a swift eye penetrating enough to see the significance of detail to the work of art as a whole; he must have a power of original observation and analysis. If his work is to endure, he must avoid contrivance, that is, he must be natural in idiom and faithful to the inner life of his characters.

Can we go further than this and say what characteristics distinguish a short story as Australian? I think we can. The key is in our social history.

Just as Gogol set the tone and colour of the Russian short story through contact with the life of the Russian folk, or as Bret Harte first exhibited the colour of the American short story by reference to American frontier life, so, in Australia, the artist arrived whose moment of insight corresponded with the social moment. The striking thing is not that Henry Lawson was able to give direction and colour to the Australian short story, but that society should have presented him with material that impelled him irresistibly to put it on paper.

In saying this, I do not suggest that Lawson's contemporaries were devoid of one or more of the three main elements that conspire to give the Australian short story its distinguishing colour. What I do say is that those elements first reached their full bloom in Lawson's work, and in it harmonized with the poetry of human life. We could take a story like **"Send Round the Hat"** or **"The Union Buries Its Dead"** and dissect it to isolate these three essential elements of the Australian short story. That would be one way to arrive at them. But if we were to do that, we should be less than just to at least two of his contemporaries, Price Warung and Steele Rudd. And we should be working backwards from Lawson instead of using the evidence of other witnesses. If we take the two writers I mentioned, we shall avoid seeing Lawson as an isolated phenomenon. We shall instead see him fall into his historical place as the first thorough-going delineator of the nature of Australia and its people.

Let us go first to Price Warung. Price Warung, we know, drew the material for most of his short stories from the Imperial convict system of 1788 to 1850. He looked into convict records with a sympathetic eye. What he saw aroused in him the same kind of feeling as the victims of the system themselves had experienced. So Price Warung's writing is a reflection of theirs. They did indeed write, some of them well—biographies, memoirs, plays, novels, verse. The sentiments that we discern in their work give a clue to the first of the primary elements of the Australian short story. These convict writers were men without social rights and responsibilities. Their writings and songs expressed the degraded man's longing for dignity and the broken man's for happiness. The rebellious man expressed himself ironically: he concealed his resentment beneath mocking deference. If we put those things down, and add satire, we get one mood, the mood that reflects the exercise of the comic spirit in adverse circumstances. And what does that all add up to? In short, the sardonic mood.

The Imperial convict system gave birth to the sardonic mood of the Australian. It was the dominating attitude of the convict writers. Price Warung caught it from them and transferred it to his own writing. It was a mood that did not die with the convict system. It was kept alive by the severity of the gold-licensing laws. Immediately after that, land settlement brought men like Lawson's own father face to face with a more remorseless master than either convict overseer or goldfield officer: this was the land itself. These ex-diggers had no knowledge of the husbandry necessary to make the soil productive; the agriculturist will tell you that we still have not mastered the

land. Drought, flood, fire, the very deficiencies of the soil itself—these were the agents that kept the sardonic mood alive in our people until the master of the Australian short story gave it its finest literary expression. I shall do no more at this point than refer you to the story called **"Hungerford"** to show that Lawson was an inheritor of the sardonic tradition. We shall refer to other stories later.

The next important social element to influence the short story in this country was expressed most broadly, and most plainly, by the Queensland writer, Steele Rudd. Much has been written about the nature of this man's writing, all of it stressing his homeliness, his earthiness. But it is more significant than that: it does more than describe the cocky's life. It expresses the bond between place and spirit that exists in all significant literature, whatever its local origin—whether the writer is Mark Twain, Charles Dickens, Tchekov, or Steele Rudd. Steele Rudd concentrated on bringing the Australian story into contact with the Australian earth. And unless a story is associated with the Australian ethos, unless it mirrors a pattern of Australian life, it is hard to see how it can be called Australian. From it there must emanate something of the creative power of the environment that has nurtured the artist who produces it.

Does Lawson possess this power? There is no need to mention individual stories to prove that he does possess it: it is in almost all of them. But to see it emerging conspicuously in his early work, read **"Bill, The Ventriloquial Rooster"**, **"The Bush Undertaker"**, **"They Called Him 'Ally' for Short"**, or **"Rats"**. It is this characteristic that led H. M. Green to say of Lawson [in *An Outline of Australian Literature*, 1930]: "To read him in a foreign country is to breathe the air of home."

The third element that distinguishes the Australian short story is embedded in the social psychology of our people. But I am hard put to it to find another writer of Lawson's time who expressed it half so plainly as he did. We find it well portrayed in the story, **"Send Round the Hat"**.

Lawson wrote this story in 1901, in the gloom of a London fog. In it his mind flew back to Bourke—"Bourke in the early nineties". He thought of his mates of 1892, of the wide assortment of characters depicted in the story. In recollection stimulated by distant absence, he glimpsed a prevalent characteristic of Australian social behaviour, the characteristic that forms this third element. He summed it up in the title of the story. He found its focus in his main character, Bob Brothers, nicknamed "the Giraffe". What was there in the Giraffe that led Lawson to use him as a symbol for this characteristic?

> The Giraffe . . . was well known in Bourke and to many shearers who came through the great dry scrubs from hundreds of miles round. He was stakeholder, drunkard's banker, peacemaker where possible, referee or second to oblige the chaps when a fight was on, big brother or uncle to most of the children in town, final court of appeal when the youngsters had a dispute over a foot-race at the school picnic, referee at their fights, and *he was the stranger's friend. . . . He was always helping someone or something.* Now it was a

bit of a "darnce" that he was gettin' up for the "girls"; again it was Mrs Smith, the woman whose husban' was drowned in the flood in the Bogan River lars' Crismas, or that there poor woman down by the Billabong—her husban' cleared out and left her with a lot o' kids. Or Bill Something, the bullocky, who was run over by his own waggon, while he was drunk, and got his leg broke.

Well, there it is. We need go no further. The Giraffe was a symbol for a moral attitude of our people that you notice more in the country than in the city because it's more easily seen in the country—a sense of social interdependence irrespective of class or creed: the sort of thing you often read about in the papers. We have all heard of such cases: for example, when a widow's house is burnt down and the men of the place build another one; or when a family is flooded out and relief comes at once from the community; or when a child is lost in the bush and the countryside turns out to look for it. This feeling of social brotherhood was born of the isolation of communities in the Australian bush; it has not disappeared with the years. (Not long ago the townsfolk of Moree raised £2000 to send one of their number to Los Angeles for a tumour operation that meant the welfare of his wife and family.)

In Lawson's work there is unity of mood, there is purpose and pattern, there is fidelity to life and the rhythm of life. In him there is penetrating and sympathetic observation. He is economical in both word and action.

—Colin Roderick

Henry Lawson was the first Australian writer to notice how powerful an element this feeling of social obligation is in the composition of individual Australians. It exists elsewhere, of course, but with us it is noticeable.

I call this element in our behaviour social humanism, understanding by the word "humanism", as used in this context, neither the cultural attitude of Renaissance Europe nor the modern materialist philosophy so called. I use the term "social humanism" to suggest an ethical attitude that aims at promoting individual happiness consistent with the general welfare of the community. This, I suggest, is a dominating force in our social conduct: it colours our politics and our legislation; it distinguishes our national character; it has led to the establishment of unique industrial tribunals; it is ingrained in us. Many Australian writers have given expression to it; but Lawson was the first.

Likewise he was the first to blend all three of these prominent Australian elements in the Australian short story.

In his work there is unity of mood, there is purpose and pattern, there is fidelity to life and the rhythm of life. In him there is penetrating and sympathetic observation. He is economical in both word and action. In him is the sardonic mood, the humour of the Australian people; he has a strong sense of social interdependence, what I call "social humanism". These are the stuff of his stories; but there is more yet in them: the resonant quality that raises his art to the level of timelessness, the thing that makes him great. This, in a word, is poetry.

How are we to discern this poetic quality in Lawson's stories?

Consider the truthfulness of his idiom—what I called the natural words in their natural order. We could never find in Lawson such a sentence as this from Price Warung:

> Not suspecting the relationship of the young transport to Bess, he did not doubt the truth of her avowal, although he was shocked at it.

Lawson's language is yours and mine:

> He was the last of his tribe and a King: but he had built that woodheap hollow.

Those words live, not so much because they are the sort of simple words we use in daily talk, but for three other reasons: they are graphic; they are charged with emotion; and they reflect something of the eternal sadness that Lawson found in life.

Even when Lawson does diverge from the terseness of his narrative to introduce a cultural reference, it is one that goes to the marrow of the story, not a mere decoration that diverts you from it. As an example of this, take Alligator's tussle with the snake in **"The Drover's Wife"**. The dog has the snake by the tail. I quote now:

> Alligator gives another pull, and he has the snake out—a black brute, five feet long. The head rises to dart about, but the dog has the enemy close to the neck. He is a big, heavy dog, but quick as a terrier. He shakes the snake as though he felt the original curse in common with mankind.

What is "the original curse", and how does this cultural reference reinforce the message of the story? Simply this. In the book of Genesis we read:

> *And the Lord God said unto the Serpent, Because thou hast done this, thou art cursed above all cattle, and above every beast of the field; upon thy belly shalt thou go, and dust shalt thou eat all the days of thy life; and I will put enmity between thee and the woman, and between thy seed and her seed; it shall bruise thy head, and thou shalt bruise his heel.*

> Thud! Thud!—the snake's back is broken. . . . Thud! Thud!—its head is crushed.

And the drover's wife

lifts the mangled reptile on the point of her stick, carries it to the fire, and throws it in: then piles on the wood and watches the snake burn. . . . The dirty-legged boy stands for a moment in his shirt, watching the fire. Presently he looks up at her, sees the tears in her eyes, and, throwing his arms round her neck, exclaims:

"Mother, I won't never go drovin'; blast me if I do!"

And she hugs him to her worn-out breast and kisses him; and they sit thus together while the sickly daylight breaks over the bush.

Unto the woman he said, I will greatly multiply thy sorrow and thy conception.

This kind of prose has the force of elemental poetry. Its simplicity is its truth; its truth is its enduring strength. "I can never read the story of the Drover's Wife," an experienced editress said to me once, "and I have read it a hundred times, without the tears coming to my eyes."

Lawson's reference to "the original curse", you see, rather than slowing up the thought, adds depth and power to it. I do not know any short story in three literatures that more powerfully illustrates the ancient theme: *"Unto the woman he said, 'I will multiply thy sorrow and thy conception'."* What admirable insight Lawson shows here! The woman, the child, the snake! Symbols of the creative and destructive forces of life that are as old as man himself. You will understand from these comments that I meant when I said of Lawson elsewhere, "A great deal of his poetic feeling, and the best of his art, went into his short stories."

For a blend of the three elements that characterize the Australian story at its best, consider **"The Union Buries Its Dead"**. This is not a panegyric on the creed of mateship, as has often been said, but a sardonic analysis of it. "The 'defunct',"—notice how Lawson puts bite even into this; not "the 'deceased'" or "the 'dead'", but "the defunct", with its sardonic overtones of absolute finality—

The "defunct" was a young Union labourer, about twenty-five, who had been drowned the previous day while trying to swim some horses across a billabong of the Darling.

He was almost a stranger in town, and the fact of his having been a Union man accounted for the funeral. The police found some Union papers in his swag, and called at the General Labourers' Union Office for information about him. That's how we knew. The secretary had very little information to give. The departed was a "Roman", and the majority of the town were otherwise—but Unionism is stronger than creed. Liquor, however, is stronger than Unionism; and when the hearse presently arrived, more than two-thirds of the funeral were unable to follow.

How different the tone of this story is from that of **"The Drover's Wife"**: there you felt the stirring of an infinite pity for sorrow-laden humanity; here resentment against

death and the manner of its coming. Yet they are philosophically consistent: man is born to sorrow as the sparks fly upwards.

More than seventy years have passed since Lawson wrote those two stories, but time has not minimized their power. When he reprinted **"The Union Buries Its Dead"** in *Short Stories in Prose and Verse* he gave it the sub-title, "A Sketch From Life and Death". Perhaps it is because the story brings us up suddenly against the fact of death, death robbed of sentimentality, intractable death, bleak, rigid, cold, unsparing, that it has this timeless power to attract even as it repels, a power gained from the marriage of fear and fascination that makes the fact of death an eternal mystery.

Lawson has the power to bring the rhythm of human behaviour into the rhythm of his writing because he has caught the harmony of life, the harmony of man with his universe.

—Colin Roderick

In such a story as this, as in **"The Drover's Wife"**, **"'Water Them Geraniums'"**, **"The Babies in the Bush"**, **"Across the Straits"**, **"Payable Gold"**, **"A Hero in Dingo Scrubs"**, and many more, Lawson mirrors the restlessness of humanity. In his best work he gives rein to the poetic imagination. So there comes into his stories that measure of poetry without which the short story to us today is dry, sapless. This quality we see in such a story as Judith Wright's "The Weeping Fig". The great short stories of the world have always had it. There is poetry in "The Outcasts of Poker Flat", as there is in "Stragglers"; in Maupassant's "Father" as in Lawson's **"Pretty Girl in the Army"**. What marks the literary quality of such stories is the degree to which they are instinct with the poetry of life. And if you ask, "What is the poetry of life?" what shall I answer? It is something that cannot be physically described, unlike this building: yet there is poetry in the form of this building, in the impression it conveys to the mind, in its harmonious proportions, in the harmony of its design with the idea of its function, the harmony of its design with the landscape. What is the poetry of life but the writer's understanding of harmony, harmony between himself and his fellow creatures, between himself and his environment? To understand man's place in nature is to begin to appreciate life and the harmony of life. The modern short story seeks to explain that harmony by illuminating man's place in the world. The sensitive mind of such an artist as Lawson discerns what he takes to be a truthful reflection of man's place in the universe. Then he sets it down so that we too discern it for truth. Robert Browning put it well:

We're made so that we love
First when we see them painted, things we have
   passed

Perhaps a hundred times nor cared to see;
And so they are better, painted—better to us,
Which is the same thing. Art was given for that.
God uses us to help each other so,
Leading our minds out.

The best of Lawson's stories do lead our minds out to
grasp the moment of truth that is at the heart of his poetry. Seen through his eyes, the moment of truth takes
shape and bodies forth the essential poetry within it. And
if you ask me, as well you may, "How shall I know that
I recognize in Lawson the moment of truth?" I answer,
"Be sure, above all, that you understand the import of his
symbol." Ask yourself, "Have I understood the phase of
life he is presenting? How far into the life of man does
the story take me?" This is the first rule: go deep—deep
into the European tradition—to get understanding. Having got that, ask yourself, "Does the story ring true? Are
the people who work out this phase of life credible?" Do
not say, "Have I met people like them?" but rather, "Could
I have met people like them?" If the answer seems to you
to be, "Yes, such people could exist, and the phase of life
they embody is within the bounds of possibility," examine then the intensity of feeling with which Lawson presents this phase of life and the degree of sympathy that he
exhibits for his characters. Does he seem to live with
them? Does he awaken feeling for them? Do you find his
story emotionally satisfying? Does its theme come through
to you naturally? If it does, you will see, as like as not,
that it uses the natural words in their natural order. You
will respond to the rhythm of its characters' behaviour,
not only for what they do, but also for what they say and
how they say it; for speech is only a form of behaviour.

Lawson has the power to bring the rhythm of human behaviour into the rhythm of his writing because he has
caught the harmony of life, the harmony of man with his
universe. It is important to keep in mind that this harmony is a spiritual force, reconciling the restless human race
to its habitation and to whatever destiny awaits it, linking
the life of the individual with universal life, as Dryden
put it long ago:

From harmony, from heavenly harmony
    This universal frame began:
From harmony to harmony
    Through all the compass of the notes it ran,
    The diapason closing full in man.

So for us, who are of the family of man, it must ever be.
As for Lawson, man was his theme, the world of men his
counterpoint. His pre-eminence among us rests on his
deeper insight into the spiritual force that works in man;
for this was the power that enabled him to blend its varied notes into pleasing harmony.

Brian Matthews (essay date 1968)

SOURCE: "*The Drover's Wife* Writ Large: One Measure
of Lawson's Achievement," in *Meanjin,* Vol. XXVII, No.
112, March, 1968, pp. 54-66.

[*In the following essay, Matthews determines the significance of "The Drover's Wife" and "'Water Them Geraniums,'" maintaining that the stories are a "crucial stage
in Lawson's artistic development."*]

'**The Drover's Wife**' is almost certainly one of Henry
Lawson's best known stories. Relentlessly anthologized,
it deserves its eminence, even if the attention of most
readers and many editors has been too much focused upon
the pioneering aspects of the story or its skilfully controlled suspense. It is no doubt true that '**The Drover's
Wife**' pictures 'the self-sacrificing lonely life of the bushwoman, who in those days helped to lay the foundation of
our prosperity' [according to Colin Roderick, in the introduction to *Henry Lawson, Fifteen Stories*], but I feel that
the story's real significance and merit are better appreciated if it is seen as a crucial stage in Lawson's artistic
development. With stories like '**The Union Buries Its
Dead**' and '**The Bush Undertaker**' it impresses as one
of the successive refinements of Lawson's elusively apocalyptic vision of the bush. But '**The Drover's Wife**' is
perhaps especially intriguing because, with '**Water Them
Geraniums**'—a second, more ambitious attempt at a similar theme—it provides some measure of Lawson's achievement up to and including *Joe Wilson,* his greatest work.

'**The Drover's Wife**' opens with a series of flat, documentary observations. The tone is dispassionate, if a little pessimistic and there is a general impression of unyielding
realism.

> The two-roomed house is built of round timber, slabs,
> and stringy-bark, and floored with split slabs . . . Bush
> all round—bush with no horizon, for the country is
> flat . . . no undergrowth . . . Nothing to relieve the eye
> save the darker green of a few she-oaks which are
> sighing above the narrow, almost waterless creek.
> Nineteen miles to the nearest sign of civilization . . .

Yet despite this apparently neutral monotone and the
clipped, naturalistic piecing together of staccato descriptions, there is nevertheless a subtly implied sense of involvement, of belonging: one feels the bush as the common enemy. The toneless documentation is not as taut
and mechanical as might at first appear: there is a perceptible stress on the prospect of the encircling bush and on
the remoteness of even the most pathetic form of human
life—'a shanty on the main road'. This emphasis unobtrusively invites us not only to *envisage* the drab scene, but
even more to realize and savour the potential horror of
the situation.

This quiet flexibility of style continually undercuts the
stern, seemingly dispassionate observations: without losing the documentary flavour Lawson can, for example,
accommodate a sort of tight-lipped humour. 'He is a
moment late . . . the boy's club comes down and skins the
aforesaid nose.' Again, as the story progresses, the narrator becomes at times identified with the emotions and
reactions of the woman:

> She finds all the excitement and recreation she needs
> in the *Young Ladies' Journal,* and Heaven help her!

takes pleasure in the fashion plates.

or

> She does this every Sunday. . . . There is nothing to see,
> however, and not a soul to meet. . . . This is because of
> the everlasting, maddening, sameness of the stunted
> trees—that monotony which makes a man long to break
> away and travel as far as trains can go. . . .

The resumption, at various points throughout the woman's reminiscences, of the purely documentary narrative tone helps to give the present situation a hard immediacy in contrast to the controlled gentleness, even softness of tone, that characterizes much of her memories. This documentary quality also helps, by virtue of its toughness and self-imposed limitations, to avoid undue sentimentality in a story that at least runs the risk of that sort of failure. Lawson does permit himself a gesture in the last sentence:

> And she hugs him to her worn-out breast and kisses
> him; and they sit thus together, while the sickly daylight
> breaks over the bush.

But in the context of the story this admittedly well-worn tableau seems to me to succeed remarkably. It reinforces that sense of implacable continuity, of a life being lived, that is so strong throughout the story, and uses the natural scene to suggest emotional and spiritual exhaustion.

Lawson's view of life here is characteristically sombre. The odds are heavily stacked against the drover's wife: the elements, loneliness, hardships, fear, littleness in face of the vast, indifferent, natural world—all these attack and defeat her. Her survival through the present situation is quite immaterial. We can gauge her desperation by simply reflecting how utterly small is her present victory—the killing of one snake—in comparison with the fear and strain she has gone through to achieve it. Lawson's flashback method has not merely served to reveal her whole life in the space of one brief incident, it has endowed that incident with an intensity of emotion, fear and spiritual exhaustion which accumulates as it were from her vivid memories of past hardships. Nor is this crisis the last, but merely one in a succession: her reminiscences are equally a drab blueprint for her future. The only bright spot is that Tommy, in a flash of sympathetic insight, promises he 'won't never go drovin''—a significantly negative assurance. Her husband's return is never a real factor in the story: 'if he has a good cheque when he comes back he will give most of it to her', but 'she has not heard from her husband for six months, and is anxious about him'. His nebulous existence is underlined by the fact that she actually has to 'invent' him on certain occasions:

> She generally tells the suspicious-looking stranger that
> her husband and two sons are at work below the dam,
> or over at the yard. . . .

For all its terse delineations and the oppressive, threatening atmosphere so felicitously evoked by the blend of past and present, it is the deep human sympathy of the story which adds a new dimension to Lawson's talent for portraying the bush and its captives. The woman emerges as a loving, fearful, determined human being: though, as a character, she remains a shadowy figure, the revealed pattern of her life endows her, if not with a personal individuality, at least with a profound and poignant humanity. The plight of the drover's wife is hopeless, but susceptible of deep compassion and understanding. The story implies that human attributes may well be the ennobling and enduring consolation in a ruthless and spiritually debilitating environment. In 'The Drover's Wife' the 'Lawson country' is taking shape: life there is insidiously cruel and potentially tragic, but—in this story at least—human worth perhaps prevents it from being a bad joke.

'The Drover's Wife', for all its virtues, is nevertheless a study of a human situation rather than an impression from within it. The documentary style and the stance of the narrator—as a severely sympathetic onlooker—enhance this effect. In 'The Drover's Wife' the very organization, with its flashbacks commenting on and intensifying a central situation in the present, has the neatness and unity of careful, controlled observation. This is in no way a contradiction of the various merits previously claimed for the story: the picture of her plight is vivid and compassionate, the pathos enhanced, not dissipated, by the documentation. But while we are strongly aware of the stresses and fears she constantly endures and the abrasive effect on her character and personality, the actual processes by which she seeks to adjust mentally and emotionally to her situation, and the effects on her of this adjustment, remain obscure. This is partly because the observant, fairly detached onlooker can obviously explore such depths to a limited extent only, and partly because Lawson, it seems, had simply not developed his craft to that point (though the whole concept of 'The Drover's Wife' shows it is coming within his scope). Her courage and steadfastness against mainly physical hardships are no doubt part of the reason why the story is so often accepted as a fine tribute to the pioneers.

It is interesting then to find Lawson returning to the same theme later on and treating it in an entirely different way. 'Water Them Geraniums' is not simply a study or a document. It is sprawling, untidy, full of the inconsequential asides and indirections of life; it conforms only to the broadest logic—that of time and change drawing events and characters irresistibly onwards, and its climax, as it happens, is life's own inevitable climax. Mrs Spicer, and indeed Joe and Mary, are all fighting physical hardships, but Lawson is now less interested in the actual battle; he is exploring the effect on the personalities of the people themselves, and on their efforts to communicate with one another. One could not speak of the nature of the communication in 'The Drover's Wife' because there was none. In this story Lawson was on the verge of discoveries about the effect of the bush on people's minds and hearts, but he was unable to carry this interest very far. The bush was fires, drownings, drought, loneliness— an opponent to be physically confronted. It is in the Joe Wilson stories that the emphasis shifts in various intriguing ways. One of the most impressive achievements of **'Water Them Geraniums'** is the sense of alienation that runs so strongly through the story: the environment again becomes a divisive force, but in a way that transcends the mere physical separations of earlier stories.

Joe and Mary set off for Lahey's Creek against a backdrop of the same unpromising, monochromatic bush that provided such a tight, vivid opening description for **'The Drover's Wife'**:

> Mary drove with me the rest of the way to the creek, along the lonely branch track, across native apple-tree flats. It was a dreary, hopeless track. There was no horizon, nothing but the rough ashen trunks of the gnarled and stunted trees in all directions, little or no undergrowth, and the ground . . . as bare as the road, for it was a dry season . . . I wondered what I should do with the cattle if there wasn't more grass on the creek.
>
> Mary and I didn't talk much along this track. . . . And I suppose we both began to feel pretty dismal as the shadows lengthened. I'd noticed lately that Mary and I had got out of the habit of talking to each other. . . . But then I thought, 'It won't last long—I'll make life brighter for her by and by.'

It is not only the personal, looser, less cryptic and less consciously tight-lipped style that is different here: the bush is being seen not just as a symbol of the physical hardships and troubles, but as an active force working invisibly towards the alienation of one human being from another. Communication between Joe and Mary has broken down so that even the smallest efforts towards genuine relationship either seem impossibly complicated, or are better put off to another time 'when things brighten up a bit'. The thrall of the bush, it seems, is the constant hope of better times—'something better and brighter' when 'everything will be alright' and Joe will be able to 'win her back again'. But human contact apparently cannot stand such a search in such unrelenting surroundings. Here then, Lawson moves into a new dimension of existence within the familiar context, one which so transcends the earlier 'physical' view of the bush, that that view itself becomes a symbol of the higher significance, and no longer an end in itself; as, for example, when Lawson interrupts Joe's moody reflection on the puzzling intricacies of his marriage:

> In this sort of country a stranger might travel for miles without seeming to have moved, for all the difference there is in the scenery. The new tracks were 'blazed'— that is, slices of bark cut off from both sides of trees, within sight of each other, in a line, to mark the track until the horses and wheel marks made it plain . . . a bushman a little used to the country soon picks out the differences amongst the trees, half unconsciously as it were, and so finds his way about.

The physical surroundings mirror Joe's state of mind: a faceless country where it is difficult to tell if your directions are right, or if you have moved at all. Joe badly needs the track ahead to be blazed (the word stands out artlessly in inverted commas!) to find something familiar he can cling to, or some sign he can follow that shows others have gone the same way.

Whether intuitive or deliberated, this seems to me one of those master strokes which so frequently lie beneath the deceptive surfaces of Lawson's best work; so completely integrated into the mood and spirit of the writing that the effect is wrought almost on the subconscious. (Here it will be noted that the description under discussion not only *deals* with directions and the lack of them, but is in itself involved and repetitious: the technical explanation of 'blazing', the repeating of the word 'track' produce an over-all impression of intricacy rather than clarity.) Even more important, though, it shows Lawson working at a new level, the familiar environment being explored not only as a physical obstacle to man, but as a pervasive, often divisive influence on human relationships and man's efforts to comprehend his fellows and himself in a pitiless land.

Again, their shack in the bush is at first glance a replica of that in **'The Drover's Wife'**, and of many another in Lawson's stories. But where the emphasis previously had been on the material deficiencies and primitiveness of the place (the rough slabs, the 'ground' floor, the chinks and draughts), the house at Lahey's Creek is framed in a context of alienation: Mary's first glimpse of it follows suddenly upon Joe's depressed musings on the strange, half-understood failure of their relationship.

> It's an awful thing to me, now I look back to it, to think how far apart we had grown, what strangers we were to each other. It seems, now, as though we had been sweethearts long years before, and had parted, and had never really met since.
>
> The sun was going down when Mary called out:
>
> 'There's our place, Joe!'

Instead of breaking his gloomy train of thought with the possibility of something a little more hopeful, the house for that brief instant becomes in Joe's sombre eyes a symbol of the very failure he has been brooding on:

> She hadn't seen it before, and somehow it came new and with a shock to me, who had been out here several times.

One infers that it is a shock because the miserable shack stands as a part of the whole environment whose unreasonable demands and strange influence have, in some way that Joe cannot quite grasp, brought them to their own personal crisis. The lengthy naturalistic description of the property that follows shows the house to be indeed miserable and depressing: but Lawson no longer relies on such details to evoke atmosphere; the real impact of the house had already been established before even a slab of it was described; its oppressive connotations are enhanced

Portrait of Lawson.

by the final, inconsequential remark that 'the man who took up this selection left it because his wife died there.'

In this uneasy atmosphere, enclosed yet divided by the bush, Joe and Mary grope their way through the imponderable silences and the strained snatches of conversation that increase their remoteness from each other, until the crisis is temporarily relieved, though not resolved, by a quarrel. 'We quarrelled badly then—that first hour in our new home. . . .' The causes of this quarrel, of course, run deeper than the mere sight of the house or the dismal prospect of Lahey's Creek, but it is on the other hand the stolid, unpromising surroundings that provoke the train of thought: their situation appears so grim that conflicts and doubts arise as to whether Joe has amounted to anything. The homecoming thus finally disintegrates and the failure, which Joe in retrospect attributes to the callous influence of the surroundings, hangs like a cloud over them, even after the worst wounds are seemingly patched up. 'Somehow I didn't feel satisfied with the way things had gone.'

One of the reasons that leads Joe to blame the place for their troubles is his shocked glimpse of the Spicer family. In fact, the 'Lonely Track' that Joe and Mary have just traversed through the bush, and the 'Lonely Track' on which they find themselves, spiritually directionless and apart, both lead ineluctably to Mrs Spicer, the gloomy colossus of the story and one of Lawson's finest achievements.

Mrs Spicer is the drover's wife writ large; where the latter was steadfast and had about her (though not to the story's detriment) a suggestion of 'the woman-of-the-west', Mrs Spicer is flawed and a little confused.

> I supposed the reason why she hadn't gone mad through hardship and loneliness was that she hadn't either the brains or the memory to go farther than she could see through the trunks of the 'apple-trees'.

She stands as a horrible example of what Mary might become; this is implicit in the counterbalance of the two parts of the story—**'The Lonely Track'** and **'Past Carin''**—and explicit at particular points, for example:

> I didn't feel like going to the woman's house that night; I felt . . . that this was what Mary would come to if I left her here.

and

> 'What-did-you-bring-her-here-for? She's only a girl.'

Against the competence of the drover's wife in so many situations, Mrs Spicer's life seems a flurry of pathetic, often unsuccessful efforts to make headway against a sea of shortcomings and threats. It is true that she deals with similar, sometimes identical situations (e.g. the fire) but where the drover's wife's courageous efforts evoke admiration and some compassion, Mrs. Spicer is—for all her undeniable courage and tenacity—often pathetic and pitiable.

The reason why this second version of **'The Drover's Wife'** is so different (despite the fact that it contains much reworked material) is that Lawson is exploring another and more ambitious dimension, and again one is struck by the sense of alienation. Mrs Spicer is a personality in process of disintegration. She faces the hardships of each day, not with the intense determination that almost seemed like composure in the drover's wife, but with a doggedness that has lost sight of the purpose and is animated only by habit. She has gone beyond the stages of physical separation and alienation from her husband, though once they were painful enough:

> 'I remember when we lived on the Cudgegong River . . . the first time Spicer had to go away from home I nearly fretted my eyes out. . . . He's been away drovin' in Queenslan' as long as eighteen months at a time since then. . . . But . . . I don't mind—I somehow seem to have got past carin'. Besides—besides, Spicer was a very different man then to what he is now. He's got so moody and gloomy at home, he hardly ever speaks.'

Her plight is far worse than this: she is a personality at war, alienated from her innermost self and switching unsurely from one 'self' to the other, no longer certain which is meaningful.

> Her voice sounded, more than anything else, like a voice coming out of a phonograph . . . and not like a voice coming out of her. But sometimes, when she got outside her everyday life on this selection she spoke in a sort of—in a sort of lost groping-in-the-dark kind of voice.

Doggedness, and a rather heavy cheerfulness are common characteristics of the 'selection' side of Mrs Spicer; on 'smothering' hot mornings, or 'bitter, black rainy mornings' she is already toiling at sunrise, and accepts help with a matter-of-factness that belies her inadequacy to cope:

> 'Thenk yer, Mr Wilson. Do yer think we're ever goin' to have any rain?'

or

> 'Thenk yer, Mr Wilson. This drop of rain's a blessin'! Come in and have a dry at the fire and I'll make yer a cup of tea.'

Her descriptions of the 'ploorer' and the mad squatter are similarly down-to-earth just this side of being humorous, and always with the not quite convincing implication that these events were simply routine and unremarkable.

But it is her 'groping' voice that reveals Mrs Spicer to herself, shows the extent to which she has been brutalized and hurt, turned away from a gentleness and gentility to which she has the last shreds of a genuine response. Such outbursts are so alien to what she has become and to her surroundings, that they are invariably followed by an embarrassed and pathetic disclaimer, a shocked, too-hurried return to the safety of the other self, that only needs to talk about rain and drought and 'ploorer' and milkers to sound safely normal.

> 'Oh, I don't know what I'm talkin' about! You mustn't take any notice of me, Mrs Wilson—I don't often go on like this. I do believe I'm gittin' a bit ratty at times. It must be the heat and the dullness.'

This sort of uneasy explanation, with its rather ghastly flippancy, occurs again and again to cover up the softer, almost ethereal musings that take control of her conversation at various times. Her whole nature seems to be in fragments, with the pieces re-arranging themselves into this pattern or that, according to what the situation, seen through her pained, half-nostalgic, half-comprehending eyes, evokes. There is, in fact, more than a little truth in Mrs Spicer's disturbed protestations. She seems on the verge of madness—the ultimate alienation, from oneself and from the world. It would be a gentle vague madness, but madness nevertheless. And Lawson is, of course, well aware of this final complexity to which his quiet, deceptive probings in this new dimension have led him. For madness, or the fear of it, pervades the story utterly.

Because they so constantly and consciously walk this knife-edge of madness, Joe and Mary and Mrs Spicer have about them implicitly a pathetically intense desire to remain linked with some broader, ill-defined stream of life, from which they doggedly refuse to see themselves as disqualified simply because of their surroundings; disqualification will come only if they *succumb* to their surroundings. It is this consciousness of and determination to belong to a vital, humane existence that so sharpens the compassion in this story in comparison with **'The Drover's Wife'**. In the latter, the woman herself, and the shadowy figures who moved on the periphery of her small world, were bush people, their life was bush life and their trials were those that the implacable bush presented. This vision produced a dramatic and moving story—a compassionate picture of a determined woman fighting to preserve her own spirit, her family and some sort of reasonable existence against the depradations of hardship and dangers of various kinds. All this is equally true of **'Water Them Geraniums'**—but the story goes much further than this. The alienation already discussed applies not only to the individual characters and their relationships with each other, it applies to them as a group: they confront not only hardships and dangers, not only failure of personal communications; they are fighting to remain in the human race, to be members of a stream of existence which, for all its faults, ennobles them, while failure to remain members brutalizes and decivilizes them. No such implication was apparent in the powerful but simpler **'Drover's Wife'**, and it is this I think which at once makes **'Water Them Geraniums'** a more deeply compassionate story, and suggests that Lawson's art has assumed a breadth and a power in relation to which the bush milieu of his stories no longer stands as a limiting factor.

The references to madness collectively make up one important way by which this 'broader stream of life' is suggested, and membership of it made to seem valuable. For about all these references there is a sort of duality: the emphasis is not so much on the madness itself as on its effect—the terrible separation or dissociation from life that it brings with it. In comparison with this fate, it seems, almost anything is acceptable. Better to be something of a fool than be sufficiently sensitive and imaginative for the insidious surroundings to produce this gradual alienation from life itself:

> I often think how, at sunset, the past must come home to a new-chum black sheep, sent out to Australia and drifted into the bush. I used to think that they couldn't have much brains, or the loneliness would drive them mad.

Even the more or less inevitable 'strangeness' that is the lot of any habitual bush dweller, expresses itself in a partial spiritual separation from the rest of the world:

> You'll sometimes sit of an evening and watch the lonely track, by the hour, for a horseman or a cart or someone that's never likely to come that way—someone, or a stranger, that you can't and don't really expect to see. I think that most men who have been alone in the bush for any length of time—and married couples too—are more or less mad . . . it is generally the husband who is painfully shy and awkward when strangers come.

There is an intimacy, a longing and a deliberative weight even about the rhythm of this musing revelation that deeply impress the seriousness of the problem. One feels above all a desire to belong, a dread of letting things slip too far. With a scarcely noticeable but characteristic complexity, Lawson is suggesting that this very desire is so strong that it becomes a form of madness itself (quite distinct from the 'strangeness' of solitude) if thwarted too long.

> . . . watch the lonely track, by the hour, for a horseman or a cart, or someone that's never likely to come that way—someone, or a stranger, that you can't and don't really expect to see.

This dread of dissociation from existence is further implied in the very seriousness of the references to madness. There is a horrible fascination about it—this insidious yielding to the inscrutable invitations of the bush and contracting out of the human race—but it is never funny. The bushman in the horrors is a bizarre figure—perhaps the nearest approach in the story to a humorous madman—but he *does* go and hang himself, and his grotesque corpse *does* exercise a hideous attraction to which not only the children yield. And it is impossible in retrospect to remember Mrs Spicer's off-hand reference—'He had two saddle-straps in his hand'—without the slow realization that the whole incident, however curious, may have had a chill and insane determination running through it.

The possibility that Mrs Spicer's life and death may prefigure the fate of others, reinforces the compassion one must feel for people struggling so desperately to remain involved in humanity. Her death is not simply the result of hardships and heartbreaks (as, for example, we might imagine the death of the drover's wife *would* be); it is the climax, and paradoxically the greatest triumph in a long struggle to remain a 'member': in death she affirms a humanity and a sense of purpose which her confused and disintegrating personality was losing in life. Mrs Spicer stands as a ghastly glimpse into the future for Mary, but not only for Mary. In her pathetic clinging to niceties, innocent pretensions and etiquettes that she can neither sustain nor properly remember, Mrs Spicer stakes her dwindling claim to belonging; at the same time she not only emphasizes, unwittingly, the grotesque irrelevance of such observances in that environment, but sounds a grim warning that the bush may be the death of womanhood, and not merely of some of the refinements affected by woman. Her unsuccessful attempts to maintain appearances (which persist right up to her last breath) are an important part of the ever more confused flurry of her life:

> 'Mother told Annie not to say we was hungry if yer asked; but if yer give us anythink to eat, we was to take it an' say thenk yer, Mrs Wilson.'

> 'I wish you wouldn't come down any more till I'm on my feet, Mrs Wilson. The children can do for me.'

> ' . . . the place is in such a muck and it hurts me.'

> . . . we'd see her bustle round, and two or three fowls fly out the front door, and she'd lay hold of a broom . . . and flick out the floor, with a flick or two round in front of the door perhaps.

All of these, and the many other examples, have that strangely ambivalent character that Lawson so artlessly achieves. The actions themselves are essentially feminine, as is the mind that sees the necessity for them; yet the situation is so pathetic, the efforts, however well-intended, so pitiable, that her womanhood seems somehow undermined, its character changed by the stress of unreasonable demands. This feeling is enhanced by fleeting impressions that circumstances have made her rather masculine in some ways:

> . . . She was gaunt and flat-chested and her face was 'burnt to a brick' . . . She had brown eyes, nearly red, and a little wild-looking at times, and a sharp face— ground sharp by hardship—the cheeks drawn in.

> I've . . . seen her trudging about the yard . . . ankle-deep in black, liquid filth—with an old pair of blucher boots on, and an old coat of her husband's . . .

In the context of her spiritual disintegration her little attempts at frippery and appearance emerge, not so much as pride (though this is partly the case) but rather as her personal effort to cling to the stream of life. There is much more than hurt pride in the anguished recognition:

> 'Oh, I don't think I'll come up next week, Mrs Wilson.'

> ' . . . the visits doesn't do me any good. I get the dismals afterwards.'

Rather the recognition seems to come from an impression, however vague, that her dissociation from herself and from life is worsening, in comparison with someone whose trial has only just begun. Mrs Spicer's 'dismals' are more than injured pride at a patched tablecloth or a deficient cutlery set.

She is a warning, not just to Mary but to all women, that their very personalities may be distorted, their characteristic femininity denatured, as deprivation, inadequacy, makeshift and longing take their physical, mental and spiritual toll; and that they may pass into a limbo where existence is not that of woman or man, but one of confused, dissociated sensations—pain, nostalgia, bitterness, despair.

In **'Water Them Geraniums'** there is, then, a depth and quality of compassion not found in **'The Drover's Wife'**. Its poignancy and impact derive from Lawson's delicate understanding of man's desperate need to know himself involved in humanity (perhaps this is the real Lawson mateship?) and his fear and horror when, for whatever reason, he begins to lose himself and his human landmarks in the labyrinths of alienation and endless physical stress; and Lawson sees this fate as perhaps being highly likely in the Australian bush environment. Perhaps, even more important, Lawson's style has developed to such a point in this story that he can realize these elusive ideas with such subtlety that the writing actually *embodies* the intricacies, doubts and confusions, rather than being a description of them.

The legend of Henry Lawson:

With Lawson dead, the adulation started. A public subscription was started, an artist commissioned, and a hideously unlifelike statue was erected in Hyde Park, Sydney, to the memory of Australia's National Poet. In the years that followed, eulogies were written about the man, mainly saccharine in content and uncritical in intent. Luckily, time has taken care of much of this. The legend of Lawson is now almost dead. Indeed, the *Oxford Book of Australian Verse* contains but one poem by Lawson. At last, uncluttered by sentiment, Lawson is being appraised as the artist he was.

There can be no doubt that Lawson was the finest short story writer that Australia has produced, a writer of international stature. No other Australian has yet, either in the novel or the short-story form, approached him as an interpreter of both the humor and the harshness of the young country. He wrote as an Australian, using the Australian idiom without the constraint that makes so many Australian writers appear weak imitations of overseas stylists.

Lyle Blair, in the introduction to The Selected Works of Henry Lawson, *Michigan State University, 1957.*

John Maddocks (essay date 1977)

SOURCE: "Narrative Technique in Lawson's Joe Wilson Stories," in *Southerly*, Vol. 37, No. 1, March, 1977, pp. 97-107.

While the Joe Wilson stories are generally considered to represent Henry Lawson's prose style at its best, little attention has been paid to the narrative technique on which that style depends.

Joe, as narrator, attains the successful balance of objectivity and imaginative evocation sought in Lawson's previous stories. The older Joe Wilson maintains an almost objective detachment in the narration of his own earlier life. This tone of detachment is struck in the generalizing reflections of the opening of **"Joe Wilson's Courtship"**: "There are many times in this world when a healthy boy is happy". The balance between this objective tone and that of personal reminiscence is soon introduced: "I wasn't a healthy-minded, average boy . . .". The balance created by the narrative voice allows for shifts in perspective throughout the story. Whenever there is a danger that the self-revelatory aspect of the narration may approach indulgence, as when Joe tells us that

> I reckon I was born for a poet by mistake, and grew up to be a Bushman, and didn't know what was the matter with me—or the world—but that's got nothing to do with it.

there is a shift to a detached generalization like "There are times when a man is happy . . .". The obvious depth of the revelation about not being average, and being born for a poet, has, of course, everything "to do with it", and the attempt to gloss over this aspect of personality in fact creates a strong impression about Joe's nature. We are drawn away from the impression for the moment by a return to the objective "There are times".

What may appear to be a discursive introduction is actually a skilful evocation of the tone and content of the story, and an establishing of the quality of Joe's narrative voice.

Joe Wilson is a man of considerable experience, an older, but not necessarily wiser, married man. Joe attempts to express his experience and the depth of his personal feelings in a detached manner, and to cover his more emotional reflections with generalizations. Having claimed that

> the happiest time in a man's life is when he's courting a girl and finds out for sure that she loves him and hasn't a thought for anyone else.

—having exposed a gentleness—he turns to a tone of almost patronizing distance: "Make the most of your courting days, you young chaps . . .". The effect of this alternation of tone is to create an impression of Joe as a sensitive man who has been hurt by experience. But those who miss the purpose of this technique, and who mistake the instruction to "young chaps" for moralizing from the point of view of the cheap advantage of age will not be able to explain the equanimity of "In short he is—well, a married man. And when he knows all this, how much better or happier is he for it?"

This discontinuous and apparently rambling narrative has in fact effectively and economically introduced the theme of the major Joe Wilson stories—an attempt to portray uncompromisingly the range of Joe's personal experiences within marriage, to speak of the woe, and the happiness. In the space of a few paragraphs we have been given an impression of Joe as father and husband, have glimpsed his youth, and been given hints of his possible adultery and marriage failure. All these aspects of Joe's experience are portrayed in the ensuing stories. And, most importantly, the balance of the narrative voice is established, a balance by which Joe, a sensitive and reticent character, is able gradually to reveal his deepest personal emotions.

One of the finest achievements of the Joe Wilson stories is the full realization of a personality and his experiences by means of an impressionist technique. This impressionism is created by the position of memory in the narrative, a memory which selects in its reflective processes the primary material to be included in the story. The narrator, as vehicle for memory, also interprets and includes glimpses of the present in relation to the past, which results in not merely a flashback effect, but a shifting perspective closer to superimposition in film. In describing the "first glimpse I got of Mary". Joe uses such a superimposition:

> There was a wide, old-fashioned brick-floored verandah in front, with an open end: there was ivy climbing up the verandah post on one side and a baby-rose on the other, and a grape-vine near the chimney. We rode up to the end of the verandah, and Jack called to see if there was anyone at home, and Mary came trotting out; so it was in the frame of vines that I first saw her.

> More than once since then I've had a fancy to wonder whether the rose-bush killed the grape-vine or the ivy smothered 'em both in the end. I used to have a vague idea of riding that way some day to see. You do get strange fancies at odd times.

There is in this passage the initial framing of Mary in the vines, the recall of a first impression, followed immediately by the movement to a later time, with its impression of decay and death in "whether the rose-bush killed the grape-vine". The purpose of the later impression is, of course, to contrast some of the bitterness and harshness of the love relationship with its first glowing freshness. And the contrast is masterfully achieved. The superimposition of the later impression on the earlier, which appears to be merely the inclusion of a rather casual reflection, creates a depth of insight for the reader which would be difficult to achieve any other way. The technique allows us a passing, but penetrating, glimpse of Joe's strange fancies, and of the course of the relationship of Joe and Mary that produces their presence in Joe's mind.

Joe Wilson as narrator is an essentially psychological construct. The narrative is centred in the processes of Joe's consciousness, in his reactions to people and events recorded internally. This is demonstrated by the way that external events are described succinctly whilst passing on to the central concern—Joe's recalled impression: "Jack asked her if the boss was in. He did all the talking". These preliminary facts being dispensed with, we move to the recollection of Mary:

> I saw a little girl rather plump, with a complexion like a New England or Blue Mountain girl. . . . She had the biggest and brightest eyes I'd seen round there, dark, hazel eyes, as I found out afterwards, and bright as a 'possum's. No wonder they called her 'Possum.

This highly selective description gives the reader a mere impression of Mary; of the aspects of her which Joe notices. That is, we see only, and consciously, Joe's Mary—a record available only through the process of his visual perception, and not a literal accumulation of detail. The external world in these stories is presented only by the impressions arising from Joe's response to it, refined through the processes of memory. Joe himself is included in the picture of past events by means of such recalled responses: "I felt a sort of comfortable satisfaction in the fact that I was on horseback: most Bushmen look better on horseback". The effect of this remembered feeling is to create an image of the younger Joe as a Bushman, as a type. But the image itself is a product of the function of memory.

Although the story appears to unfold sequentially—with a linear progression from Joe's introduction to Mary to his proposal—there are constant changes in the time perspective which qualify and overlay the sequential narrative. The opening of the story, with its mature reflections on marriage, tends to contain (but not reduce) the impact of the emotions of the younger man. Joe's impetuosity, his romanticism, his bashfulness are fully presented, but are continually placed in a balanced perspective by the discontinuous interpretative entries of the older Joe. An example is the reflective comment on the fight with Romany:

> Looking back, I think there was a bit of romance about it: Mary singing under the vines to amuse a jackaroo dude, and a coward going down to the river in the moonlight to fight for her.

The effect of the shifting narrative perspective is to ensure that any romance is eclipsed, and to create a tone of world weariness, of the dissolution of youthful hopes. This effect is most successfully achieved in the ending of **"Joe Wilson's Courtship"**. The romantic climax of the clumsy proposal with its innocence and naïvety is completely placed by the final scene depicting Joe's approach to Old Black for Mary's hand. Black's bitterness towards his wife is made evident, and the story ends with a masterfully evoked sense of impermanence, of the inevitable dissolution of romantic aspiration. We are left with the final image of an old man conveying that feeling of inev-

itability to a younger man. And it is conveyed by impression only, by hint, and with unusual power:

> "What did you say, Boss?" I said.
>
> "Nothing Joe," he said. "I was going to say a lot, but it wouldn't be any use. My father used to say a lot to me before I was married."

The failure of Black's marriage, and more than mere failure, a sense of disillusion for which no one can be prepared or forewarned, is carried by these sentences. And that important Lawsonian device, the reflective pause, is used to convey the unspeakable:

> I waited a good while for him to speak.
>
> "Well, Boss," I said, "What about Mary?"
>
> "Oh! I suppose that's all right Joe," he said. "I—I beg your pardon. I got thinking of the days when I was courting Mrs Black."

The nostalgia of Black for his courting days has, of course, already been undercut by his present position and bitterness towards his wife. This ends the story neatly on the theme of the transitory joy of courtship. But there is a further significance in Black's "that's all right, Joe". It is an echo of the statement that would have been the climax of the story had it been merely romantic: "'Mary,' I said, 'would you marry a chap like me?' And that was all right". The very different tone of "all right" in Black's later statement gives the phrase a strongly ironic quality.

It is clear from a close reading of **"Joe Wilson's Courtship"** that Lawson was trying to achieve an intensification of experience of a different nature from that of the full dramatic presentation of a novel. His use of discontinuous narrative enables him to escape the confines of a strictly sequential time scheme and plot development, and to include only those events and characters important to his impressionistic style.

In the Joe Wilson sequence of **"Joe Wilson's Courtship"**, **"Brighten's Sister-in-Law"**, **"'Water Them Geraniums'"**, **"A Double Buggy at Lahey's Creek"** and **"Drifting Apart"**, intensification of experience is centred upon an event or character, and is depicted in terms of Joe's responses. The fight with Romany, little Jim's convulsions, the strangeness of Mrs Spicer, stimulate Joe's gaining of insight into existence. These incidents and characters also force Joe to reflect on his own psychological processes. On his way to fight Romany, for example, Joe, in hastily deciding that this incident is to be the turning point of his life, reflects that "A man can think a lot in a flash sometimes". A major aspect of the story becomes a study of Joe's psychological reactions to the stress of the fight. We gain impression after impression of these reactions, which take precedence in Joe's memory:

> I was thinking fast, and learning more in three seconds than Jack's sparring could have taught me in three

weeks. I fancy that a fighting man, if he isn't altogether an animal, suffers more mentally than he does physically. . . . I thought hard into the future, even as I fought the fight only seemed something that was passing.

In **"Brighten's Sister-in-Law"** we again find this type of "flash" insight of Joe's, which occurs while little Jim is being attended to by the nurse: "I thought of Mary and the funeral—and wished that that was past. All this in a flash, as it were". Joe's recorded psychological reactions are not merely mundane or conventional, but have a revelatory, confessional tone:

> I felt that it would be a great relief, and only wished the funeral was months past. I felt—well, altogether selfish. I only thought for myself.

Joe is aware that this is not the way he is supposed to be thinking, and that a more normal feeling would be to be thinking only of his sick child. But this is not merely an attempt to be confessionally honest or coldly realistic. It is a continuation of a theme of these stories concerning unusual or extreme states of mind emanating from intense experiences. In **"Brighten's Sister-in-Law"**, the aspect of strangeness is accentuated from the beginning. Jim is described as being an "old-fashioned child", and Joe implies some connection between this aspect of personality and Jim's convulsions. Jim's disjointed conversation and behaviour become a progression of signs of impending illness:

> When I went to lift him in he was lying back, looking up at the stars in a half-dreamy, half-fascinated way that I didn't like. Whenever Jim was extra old-fashioned, or affectionate, there was a danger.

Joe, alone in the Bush at night with a sick child, has become involved, as in his fight with Romany, in a decisive struggle which will severely test his mind and emotions. The internal narrative allows the reader to experience this struggle in terms of responses and feelings:

> I was mad with anxiety and fright: I remember I kept saying, "I'll be kinder to Mary after this! I'll take more notice of Jim."

The sense of strangeness and tension would probably become melodramatic if it was not for the narrative viewpoint. The inclusion of the apparition pointing to Brighten's farm would be almost ridiculous if not for Joe's consciousness being the vehicle for its interpretation:

> —Now, it might have been that I was all unstrung, or it might have been a patch of sky outlined in the gently moving branches, or the blue smoke rising up. But I saw the figure of a woman, all white, come down, down, nearly to the limbs of the trees, point on up the main road and then float up and up and vanish, still pointing. I thought Mary was dead! Then it flashed on me—

What would otherwise be a rather clumsy piece of plot machinery, or too strenuous a concession to the supernat-

ural and strange elements of the story, becomes a means of possible psychological insight because of Joe's own account of his state of mind immediately before the hallucination:

> Then I lost nerve and started blundering backward and forward between the waggon and the fire, and repeating what I'd heard Mary say the last time we fought for Jim: "God! don't take my child! God! don't take my boy!"

In this context the hallucination becomes the manifestation of a severely distracted state of mind. It is as if Joe's memory, which already holds the information about Brighten's Sister-in-Law, fails to operate rationally under stress, and his mind instead throws out an image revealing the information.

The success of **"Brighten's Sister-in-Law"** is dependent on the fidelity of the narrator in recording his responses and impressions. Joe is regarding his consciousness with detachment, as if its functions are not really under control, but merely *happen*:

> I felt cold all over then and sick in the stomach—but *clear-headed* in a way: strange, wasn't it? I don't know why I didn't get down and rush into the kitchen to get a bath ready.

This confessional honesty, only possible in an internal narrative, is undoubtedly a great achievement of the Joe Wilson stories. It is a very convincing form of psychological realism.

It is, then, the consciousness of Joe Wilson, as presented in his narrative, that is the subject of these stories. Neither Brighten's Sister-in-Law, or even Mrs Spicer, are the true subjects of the stories in which they feature so prominently. These characters become ultimately important because of what they represent for Joe at the time of their appearance, and for the significance of the impressions of them created in Joe's consciousness.

Mrs Spicer is undoubtedly important as a representative type; the downtrodden Bushwoman. But if she is representative, like, say, the Drover's Wife, she is not representative in the same way. Mrs Spicer is most important as representing something for Joe. She is a symbol of the wretchedness awaiting him, and particularly, awaiting Mary. The full sketch of Mrs Spicer in Part Two of **"'Water Them Geraniums'"** would be of greatly reduced significance, and in no real way different from, say, the portrait of the Bush Undertaker (another mad or "ratty" inhabitant of Lawson's Bush) if we did not have the preceding knowledge of Joe's depressed state in Part One before she makes her real appearance.

Mrs Spicer is introduced after Joe and Mary have their first argument at Lahey's Creek. The argument is chiefly interesting because of the insight we gain into Joe's character and personality, an insight gained by the technique of allowing the reader to experience the gap between what

Joe is saying to Mary and what he is thinking in response to her words:

> "And what sort of a place was Gulgong, Joe?" asked Mary quietly. (I thought even then in a flash what sort of a place Gulgong was. A wretched remnant of a town on an old abandoned goldfield. . . .)

The distance between Joe's words in argument with Mary, and his actual recognition of his own weaknesses and wrong views, creates an impression of discontent which far exceeds the particular subject of the argument. The sense of discontent is heightened dramatically by the intervention of the older Joe with a bitter reflection:

> But the time came, and not many years after, when I stood by the bed where Mary lay, white and still, and, amongst other things, I kept saying, "I'll give in, Mary—I'll give in," and then I'd laugh. They thought that I was raving mad, and took me from the room.

This dismal image of the end of Joe and Mary's relationship, a vision of Joe's ultimate discontent, failure, and even madness, sets the tone of the narrative for the introduction of Mrs Spicer as a symbol of desperation, the introduction of the bushwoman who precedes Mary to the state of being "past carin'".

Joe's feeling of marital failure is matched by his recognition of the personal weaknesses which he feels underlie his general failure: "I was not fit to 'go on the land' . . . I had only drifted here through carelessness, brooding, and discontent". And into the midst of these reflections on failure, this mental landscape of desolation, is introduced the figure of Mrs Spicer, the "gaunt haggard Bush-woman".

Mrs Spicer represents even more than "what Mary would come to if I left her here". She is the embodiment of the madness of the Bush, the representation of a mind driven beyond "carin'", beyond normal feelings and responses. And rather than being a merely individual study of this condition, she is presented as being an extension of a state of mind common to all who spend a long time alone in the Bush:

> I think that most men who have been alone in the Bush for any length of time—and married couples too—are more or less mad.

The commonness of madness in the Bush makes Mrs Spicer less an eccentric to be identified as outside normal experience, and more a natural development of the conditions common to all Bush inhabitants. It is significant that Joe himself has had some experience of Bush madness, and can thus act as a credible interpreter of Mrs Spicer's condition. Mary, however, is outside this experience, and this intensifies the relationship of shared understanding between Joe and Mrs Spicer: "Mary thought her a little mad at times. But I seemed to understand". Joe's understanding of Mrs Spicer is crucial to the creation of her as a character of stature.

Mrs Spicer, as reflected in and presented by Joe's narrative consciousness, represents not so much a fully drawn character as a state of being. She is the true objective correlative of the desolation of the Bush, and of Joe's discontent with Bush life. Her disjointed conversations, with their bitter reflections on a harsh existence, and their anecdotes of men hanging themselves in despair, create the impression of a personality that has lost its full range of normal response, that has gradually narrowed in the face of a limited and harsh environment. Mrs Spicer is in the state of being (progressively) "past carin'". But this state does not have any equanimity or philosophical resignation of a positive kind. It is rather an almost total disintegration of human sensibility. For example, when Mary asks Mrs Spicer about her loneliness during the long absences of her husband, she replies "'I don't mind—I somehow seem to have got past carin'". Mrs Spicer's self-awareness has been reduced to the knowledge that she is "past carin'", and "ratty", or mad.

Mrs Spicer represents, then, the disintegration of civilized habits in the harsh Bush environment. That Mrs Spicer had once had such habits is indicated when Mary notices that she "had been used to table napkins at one time in her life". This observation both places Mary at a considerable distance from the experience of Mrs Spicer's present condition, adding to the former's aura of innocence, and skilfully creates an impression of the early Mrs Spicer and the extent of her downfall. And it is Joe who possesses and conveys the full knowledge of what Mrs Spicer's state of being really is. Mary is largely outside this knowledge, gaining only a partial insight into its full significance, and this increases her potential as a victim of the Bush.

> **In the Joe Wilson sequence, Lawson has most successfully presented his preoccupation with the intricacies and manifestations of the deep suffering of existence, and the attempts of the human spirit to come to terms with that suffering.**
>
> **—*John Maddocks***

Mrs Spicer herself indicates to Joe both her awareness of his recognition of the cause of her state of mind, and their complicity in the implications that the recognition may have for Mary:

> She said nothing for a long time, and seemed to be thinking in a puzzled way. Then she said suddenly:
>
> "What-did-you-bring-her-here-for? She's only a girl."
>
> "I beg pardon, Mrs Spicer?"

Joe's politely evasive "I beg pardon" attempts to conceal what is in fact a feeling shared by both Joe and Mrs

Spicer. For the reader already has the record of Joe's reaction on first encountering Mrs Spicer:

> I felt—and the thought came like a whip-stroke on my heart—that this was what Mary would come to if I left her here.

It is this relationship of Joe, as narrator, with Mrs Spicer and their shared knowledge of the possible effect of the Bush on human sensibility, which makes **"'Water Them Geraniums'"** the finest story of the Joe Wilson series. Lawson has achieved a narrative balance which allows a powerful creation of impression with a minimum of conventional plot. **"Joe Wilson's Courtship"** and **"Brighten's Sister-in-Law"** have a far greater element of plot development than **"'Water Them Geraniums'"**. The creation of Mrs Spicer does not rely on the pretext of an event like courtship or the sickness of a child, or on any sequential development of such events. **"'Water Them Geraniums'"** records the interaction of characters in a shared experience—living in the Bush. And in this interaction we see most clearly the personality and consciousness of the narrator. Unlike, say, the fight with Romany, or the midnight dash to Brighten's house, the events of **"'Water Them Geraniums'"** are comparatively unexceptional.

What is conveyed most strongly by the story is a sense of depression, of a type of grinding anguish. And Lawson, in so doing, has created his "strange dream" of the Bush:

> It is when the sun goes down on the dark bed of the lonely Bush, and the sunset flashes like a sea of fire and then fades, and then glows out again, like a bank of coals, and then burns away to ashes—it is then that old things come home to one. And strange, new-old things too, that haunt and depress you terribly, and that you can't understand.

Joe and Mrs Spicer share this mystical knowledge of the Bush, a knowledge which may lead to anguish and madness, and which is incomprehensible to the uninitiated. It is the exploration of this anguish through the narrative consciousness of Joe, located most powerfully in his reaction to and relationship with Mrs Spicer, that gives the story such a depth of insight into human nature.

Lawson has here most successfully presented his preoccupation with the intricacies and manifestations of the deep suffering of existence, and the attempts of the human spirit to come to terms with that suffering. The quality of narrative in the Joe Wilson sequence is undoubtedly the high point of Lawson's literary production.

D. R. Jarvis (essay date 1980)

SOURCE: "Narrative Technique in Lawson," in *Australian Literary Studies,* Vol. 9, No. 3, May, 1980, pp. 367-73.

In fashioning his short story form Lawson made, as A. A. Phillips has noted in 'The Craftsmanship of Lawson' [in

Watercolor of Lawson.

The Australian Tradition, 1958], considerable technical departures from the primarily narrative aims of the form at the time. Lawson kept the story or narrative element to a minimum but was nevertheless able to create, with great economy, sufficient framework to support his sketches without their becoming shapeless. The chief device of these frameworks is Lawson's narrator, and the diminution of the story element naturally casts the discourse element, the rhetoric of the narrator, into prominence. It will be argued in this essay that contrasts between the story and the narrator's discourse point to a problematic realism and a documentary intention on the narrator's part. Furthermore, the rhetoric of the narrator, particularly that of the 'I' who masquerades as Lawson himself as distinct from other personae like Mitchell or Joe Wilson, invites comparison with the artistic aims of the author, the real Henry Lawson. The role of the narrator in a story like **'The Spooks of Long Gully'**, when viewed from this perspective, indicates that Lawson's aims may have been more complex than much modern criticism has allowed.

Colin Roderick is a modern critic who, in his essay 'Lawson's Mode and Style' [in *Henry Lawson Criticism,* ed. Colin Roderick, 1972], considers the technique of the fictitious Henry Lawson who sometimes acts as narrator in

Lawson's stories. Roderick points out that this narrator impersonated Lawson so successfully that many of his attributes and experiences were ascribed to the real Lawson. Roderick's sample disentanglement of the fictional and factual in the narrator is intended to show how Lawson created a vivid, real, but imagined world. By contrast, the old Lawson criticism mistook the stories for factual reporting. The modern tendency, having the benefit of the facts established by the biographers, is to say the old criticism neglected the artistry of Lawson's 'fictive world'. But the old Lawson criticism was responding to the salient feature of Lawson's narrative technique, and the modern tendency leads attention away from it, away from the aesthetic standpoints implicit in the technique. By masquerading as the real Henry Lawson the narrator gains for the story the illusion of non-fiction. The technique also implies certain authorial convictions about literary artifice and its effect on the value or authenticity of the work. This is precisely the effect in the piece Roderick discusses in some detail, **'The Romance of the Swag'**. Only a prodigious knowledge of Lawson's biography enables one to isolate the fictional elements. The more important effect is the sketch's implicit disclaimer of literary artifice. By masquerading as the personal memoir of the real Henry Lawson the piece purports not to be a story but a note on outback slang and customs which the author records in the spirit of a historian or folklorist.

This narrator is usually present even when the story is told by a character like Mitchell. A. A. Phillips wrote that Lawson's narrator was the 'prime character—especially if he is Mitchell—adding a perspective to the story'. But strictly, Mitchell is not the narrator in most of his stories—as Phillips seems aware when he refers to the technique as 'reported narrative'. Even when the story is almost entirely the direct speech of Mitchell it is mostly introduced by another narrator. **'Two Dogs and a Fence'** begins with '"Nothing makes a dog madder", said Mitchell.' **'One-Eyed Dogs'** opens with '"Knocking around the country," said Mitchell, in a sentimental mood'—here the narrator's part is significant though small for he is able to disclaim sentimentality while nevertheless reporting Mitchell's speech faithfully. **'The Bull-Run Style'** begins 'One day I asked my mate Mitchell what the "bull-run" style of architecture was'. Here the 'I' is explicit, and he is both past auditor and present reporter of the story.

Such gestures on the narrator's part emphasise and objectify the two complementary aspects of any speech. All speech is both statement and enunciative act. Some linguists make a distinction between two modes of language—between sentences which contain references to the situation of enunciation and the subjectivity of the speaker and those that do not. For example, 'he entered the room' is impersonal. The simple past tense narrates the act stripped of its existential complexity. It is reduced to its essential elements. The perfect tense of 'he has entered the room' is, by contrast, an act of discourse. The perfect tense explicitly distinguishes the enunciation of the sentence in time from the event itself. It much more strongly implies the presence of a 'speaker'. The latter is discourse as opposed to narrative. The gestures of Lawson's narrator point to a similar internal distinction between the story and its manner of presentation, between the referents (the descriptions of characters and incidents) and the discourse (the rhetoric of a narrator). In the opening of **'One-Eyed Dogs'** the narrator indicates that the reader should be wary of Mitchell's rhetoric, and the reader may infer the narrator's aesthetic standpoint that sentimentality is an inappropriate mood for story-telling. When, in **'The Union Buries Its Dead'**, the narrator tells us he has 'left out the wattle' and 'neglected to mention the heart-broken old mate', he is making a similar denunciation of sentimental rhetoric found in an inferior type of story and at the same time asserting the reality of his story. He is saying that the reader ought not to expect romantic conventions and sentimental idealisations from him. It is significant that his gesture occurs just after his own elaborate speculation that the sods falling on the coffin might well have evoked powerful sentimental responses in the most sensitive of those present. 'But do not be fooled', his subsequent gesture seems to be saying, 'my language is merely intended to make you refer to a reality.'

Perhaps the best example of this kind of manoeuvre occurs in **'Getting Back on Dave Regan'** where Jimmy Nowlett begins his yarn with:

> You might work this yarn up. I've often thought of doin' it meself, but I ain't got the words. I knowed a lot of funny an' rum yarns about the Bush, an' I often wished I had the gift o' writin'. I could tell a lot better yarns than the rot they put in books sometimes, but I never had no eddication. But you might be able to work this yarn up—as yer call it.

This brilliant opening is replete with implications. Firstly, the person being addressed is not the reader or auditor but the implicit narrator, Henry Lawson the story-writer. As in **'One-Eyed Dogs'** the narrator's referent is an account of facts and events, not the facts and events themselves as in **'The Union'** where the narrator was actually present. Secondly, the narrator appears to have been somewhat embarrassed by Jimmy's suggestion that he work the yarn up—a phrase which Jimmy ascribes to him. He has ignored Jimmy's suggestion—based on an unsophisticated admiration for literary artifice—and faithfully transcribed the yarn. So scrupulous is he that he even includes Jimmy's introductory remarks which contain damaging imputations about his integrity as a realist and an authentic recorder of the bush. Thus, thirdly, although the entire story is the faithfully recorded direct speech of Jimmy Nowlett, it is subtly framed by the narrator's 'negative' rhetoric. That is, the absence of authorial interference constitutes an implicit claim on the narrator's part for the scrupulous authenticity of the facts of his material.

The distinction between narrative and discourse also involves a temporal contrast between the past (the referential time-scale) and the present (the time-scale of the narrator's enunciation). The temporal situation of the narrator can usually be identified as being at considerable distance from that of the events described. The reader's impression, which is complementary to the narrator's standpoint of realism, is that the narrator is an experienced man looking back dispassionately on the past. The narrator's mode is more that of the historian than that of *littérateur*. In the first examples this is only marginally suggested in the simple past tenses of ' . . . said Mitchell' or 'One day I asked Mitchell . . .' but in **'The Union Buries Its Dead'** the perfect tense of the narrator's remarks about the wattle and the old mate explicitly refers to the time-scale of the telling of the story. When the narrator says 'I have left out the wattle—because it wasn't there', his past tense ('wasn't') refers to the referential time-scale while his perfect tense refers to his telling of the story. He means *'In the above* I have left out the wattle'; he is referring to the story *up to that point.* This temporal distinction is also apparent in Joe Wilson. In **'Water Them Geraniums'** Joe narrates that 'Mary kept her head pretty well through the first months of loneliness' but then comments: *'Weeks* rather, I should say . . .'. In a gesture similar to those of the realist narrator Joe checks an impulse to exaggerate the facts of his material—and this restraint occurs in the 'present'—as he is speaking. In short, as much as the narrator tries to employ the realistic and impersonal mode of the *récit* or narrative which uses a temporal system based on the aorist and designed to exclude the present of the speaker, he is continually lapsing into the mode of discourse which reveals his subjectivity and his different situation in time. The reader is continually reminded of the 'meta-drama' in the narrative frame: the struggle of the narrator to check those impulses which threaten to jeopardise his integrity as a realist and therefore the authenticity of the story.

The conspicuousness of the occasions when the narrator can be identified as being youthful testifies to the typicality of his usual role of experienced memoirist-historian. One such occasion occurs in **'They Wait On The Wharf in Black'** in which both the narrator (the 'I') and Mitchell are auditors of Tom the digger's story. The narrator evinces a youthful sensitivity with 'I wish sometimes I didn't take so much notice of things' while his view of Mitchell is that the latter is an older hardened bushman 'who hadn't seemed to be noticing anything in particular'. His view that Mitchell was not noticing anything is an erroneous one as it turns out, but the present tense of his 'I wish . . .' indicates he is still, as he recounts the story, in that youthful state, whereas his other comments might have been taken as coming from the usual narrator distanced in time. In this story the narrator is more like the narrator in **'The Hero of Redclay'**—a youthful 'apprentice' to Mitchell.

It is worth noting that in stories with a framed 'inner' narrative such as **'Getting Back On Dave Regan'** and **'They Wait On The Wharf In Black'** there are three time-scales. There is the 'present' in which the narrator speaks; there is the referential time-scale, the time in the past when the narrator was told the yarn (these first two are only implicit in **'Getting Back On Dave Regan'**, in Jimmy's introductory remarks); and, further back in the past, the time in which the framed story occurred. This multiplicity of time-scales is also a feature of **'The Spooks Of Long Gully'**. Before moving on to **'The Spooks'** it is also worth noting, in recapitulation, that the narrator's

disclaimers of literary artifice and conventions of sentimentality such as the heart-broken old mate are directed at a particular kind of literary art. The narrator has a quarrel with its poetics. A more detailed discussion of this poetics and of Lawson's reasons for making his narrator criticise it is beyond the scope of these notes. Nevertheless, it seems clear that Lawson's narrator has allegiance to an 'opposing' poetics of realism or naturalism.

In **'The Spooks Of Long Gully'** this narrator is faced with perhaps his most formidable problems. The situation is not as simple as in **'The Union Buries Its Dead'** where he could unequivocally declare that the wattle and the old mate were not there. Strictly, none of the ghost yarns has any 'real' referent. The narrator is faced with the task of distinguishing the 'real' ghosts (the local folklore) from the 'fictional' ghosts (the yarns told from impure and ulterior motives). All the paraphernalia and attitudes of the realist are objectified in the narrator. He collects 'all the available information'; he scrupulously rejects 'unreliable' information; he even revisits the area of Long Gully to engage in 'field work'. In short, he seems to approach his task in the scientific spirit of the Zolaesque realist or the anthropologist. At the same time, however, those subjective impulses in the narrator which could cast doubt on his credibility are also present. In the introductory section the narrator explains the childish aspirations and superstitions which form the context of his first two memoirs of boyhood ghosts. The ambitions to become 'mounted troopers, bushrangers, and jockeys' and the naive beliefs in 'ghosts and fairies' are meant to contrast with the narrator's present scientific realism. But there is also his curious admission that as a boy he told 'stories' to avoid punishment 'even as we now do to avoid starving'. His play on the ambiguity of 'stories' compromises his present writing. It is implied that his motives might not be purely scientific. And ironically, it is the impurity of a personal motive, that of self-aggrandisement, which casts doubt on the authenticity of Jim Bullock's and Fred Dunn's ghosts in the two boyhood memoirs which follow.

The next section is the 'field work' section in which the narrator revisits the area to conduct interviews with locals reputed to have seen ghosts. The narrator's 'I . . . collected all the available information concerning the spooks', 'I interviewed Jim Block' or 'It was also reported that . . .' do little in their semblance of factual reporting to allay the reader's increasing doubts about the narrator's credibility. Some of the narrator's interviewees are even more scrupulous than he, and decline to elaborate on what they are uncertain of having seen or suggest to him that he might ask someone else. In view of his later rejection of the evidence of 'old Boozer Reid' on account of its lurid, artificial and exorbitant character, it is curious that the narrator seems not to notice the most obvious explanation for the spooks seen by Corny George who 'died in the delirium tremens a few weeks later'. He also seems contemptuous of the 'Local heathens' who insinuate that the Irishwoman's vision of the angel Gabriel is the result of 'Gin'. Similarly, the fact that some of the local children had been in the habit of teasing War Kee when he was alive is, for the narrator, the explanation for their subsequent dismay at his ghostly re-appearance. It does not seem to occur to him that their guilt might account for the appearance of the Chinaman's ghost itself.

The short final section purports to be a kind of 'author's note'. He begins by pompously attesting the validity of the information he has provided: 'I collected a great deal of evidence besides the above; but it is mostly unreliable, and so I refrain from publishing it.' He then goes on to explain his criteria of selection. His aim has been to record the local folklore, the 'respectable spooks of Long Gully'; he does not, of course, attempt to insist that even these spooks worthy of inclusion in his record were real. His scientific realism does not permit him to share in the superstitiousness of the outback community as he had done in his boyhood. On the contrary, he has rejected a considerable amount of evidence such as that of Boozer Reid not because its spooks were not real, but on the grounds of stylistic features in the yarns which suggest that they have been 'worked up'—to use Jimmy Nowlett's phrase. Boozer Reid's yarn was too 'disjointed and lurid, and so evidently overdrawn and exaggerated'. In the narrator's poetics an overly 'literary' style indicates a lack of sincerity in the informant. Those informants who have mastered a plain, realistic style have been included in the record. The story of the ghost seen by Ted Phipps, recounted by his brother Joe, is an example. But of course, the narrator has been obviously blind to 'extra-textual' indicators which also could call an informant's sincerity into question. Corny George, for example, is another boozer. And young Joe Phipps is clearly out to impress the visitor from the city: 'A young drover named Joe Phipps didn't see any ghost himself, but his brother Ted did.' The last phrase betrays a slight anxiety on Joe's part that he might be excluded from the visiting researcher's report unless he can come up with a ghost story. Ted, moreover, is away 'on the Lachlan', so his story cannot be tested.

Truth, realism and historical accuracy are essential to the moral-ideological aspect of Lawson's artistic purposes, his aim to bring the social conditions of the working classes to notice and thus to possible remedy.

—D. R. Jarvis

The theoretical issues hinted at in Jimmy Nowlett's introductory remarks in **'Getting Back On Dave Regan'**, the questions of literary artifice and selectivity versus artistic truth and realism, are given in **'The Spooks'** an extended and complex treatment by means of the satirical dismantling of the narrator's realist pose and his confusing application of its criteria. That the narrator masquerades in these, and in many other stories, as Lawson himself raises the question of the significance of realism and historical documentation in the real Lawson's artistic purposes. As

Peter Quartermaine convincingly argues in his recent article 'The "Literary Photographs" of Henry Lawson' [in *Australian Literary Studies*, 1978], the evidence of Lawson's creative and other writings indicates that he would probably have welcomed those early critics who praised his work for its 'photographic' realism. That is, when those critics meant by such analogies that 'His writings are photographs hardly idealised at all', and not that his writings were photographs in the sense in which photography is often compared to painting, in the sense of mere mechanical reproduction. The narrator's sardonic reminder in **'The Union Buries Its Dead'** that we can expect no sentimental idealisations from him, only a fidelity to the facts of his material, is typical of his realist standpoint. Among Lawson's other writings 'The Australian Cinematograph' and 'If I Could Paint' also indicate that Lawson himself was to a large extent convinced of the artistic value of realistic representation.

To emphasise such elements is to go against the current of much modern Lawson criticism. In the modern view such an emphasis would be to neglect Lawson's imaginative qualities and to display 'ignorance of his artistic purpose'. Yet if a documentary element is a significant part of those purposes then photographic representation and realism would be useful qualities. It has already been remarked that the role of Lawson's narrator often seems close to that of the historian, folklorist or even the social anthropologist. Such a role is consistent with the temporal situation of the narrator and is clearly dominant in **'The Romance of the Swag'** and in **'The Spooks'** where it is dramatised in the narrator's nostalgia for his boyhood in the bush 'when we were mostly true to each other' and his return to document the local ghost lore. A documentary intention is also evident in much of Lawson's other writings. For example, in 'The Golden Nineties' which first appeared in the *Australian Star* in 1899, Lawson wrote that 'The nineties—our nineties—are dying and, when they are dead, a hundred years of history will be deader for ever than the years of the histories of most other countries. History might repeat itself but never the first century of a new country. He clearly feels that, unless recorded, this history could soon be lost forever. The contemporary critics also valued the documentary element in Lawson's writings. The writer [in *Henry Lawson Criticism*] who admired his 'photographs' went on to say that they depicted 'a phase of Australian life . . . that is destined to pass away. In this respect they will be of immense value to the future historian of Australia.'

Truth, realism and historical accuracy are also essential to the moral-ideological aspect of Lawson's artistic purposes, his aim to bring the social conditions of the working classes to notice and thus to possible remedy. As Colin Roderick observes in his 'Introduction' to *Henry Lawson Criticism*, even those contemporary critics who had different political views recognised the function of Lawson's 'realism' in this respect: 'In many cases it is not literary criticism at all, but approval or disapproval of the social or political portrait which the writers believed was Lawson's attempt at a photographic representation of some aspect of actual Australian life.' Of course, the argument of such criticism is often that 'realism', by definition, ought not to exhibit so obvious a political or ideological partisanship. To be set against this, however, is the fact that from its beginning nineteenth-century realism was associated with egalitarian and socialistic ideology. In their 1864 Preface to *Germinie Lacerteux* the De Goncourts, hardly otherwise noted for their egalitarian sympathies, are compelled to speak of the 'right' of the 'low classes' to be represented in the novel. In that other famous expression of the realist's position, 'The Experimental Novel', Zola says [in *The Experimental Novel and Other Essays*, 1893], that the novelist's task is to document the social conditions and processes so that 'legislators and . . . men of affairs' can regulate 'these phenomena in such a way as to develop the good and reject the bad, from the point of view of their utility to man'. In a real sense, the conflict between the subjectivity of the author, his artistic selectivity and moral-ideological sympathies on the one hand, and the dictates of 'science' and 'realism' on the other has always been a problem for literary realism. The awareness of this conflict and the rigour of 'impersonality' needed to overcome it is raised to its highest degree in Flaubert.

A call such as Peter Quartermaine's for the reinstatement of 'photographic' realism and documentation to their rightful place in Lawson's artistic purposes is a timely correction of a tendency to neglect their significance in modern Lawson studies, but at the same time it threatens to obscure the contradictions in realism itself. The foregoing discussion of Lawson's narrator has, if anything, pointed to the presence in him of contradictory impulses rather than an uncomplicated allegiance to 'the facts' or 'truth'. His mode is always that of discourse rather than that of the narrative in which 'no one speaks'.

One other complicating factor in Lawson's narrative technique which might be noted in conclusion is the prevalence of the 'reported narrative'. In many cases the narrator is dealing not with the historical facts but with accounts or interpretations of the facts. In a sense, literature, unlike photography or painting, can have no real connection at all with the objective world. When a writer declares he is a realist we know he is choosing an inference from the physical, social or cultural world and making *it* the real; it almost goes without saying that in literature, which is never more than language, an entirely sociocultural system, realism or the real has absolutely no part. It is with accounts or interpretations of the world that the narrator is dealing in **'The Spooks'** and, significantly, he sees realism not in terms of fidelity to the objective world—the subject of 'spooks' itself precludes this—but in terms of the manner or style of the interpretation which reflects the sincerity or truthfulness of the interpreter.

Harry Heseltine (essay date 1982)

SOURCE: "Between Living and Dying: The Ground of Lawson's Art," in *The Uncertain Self: Essays in Australian Literature and Criticism,* Oxford University Press, Melbourne, 1986, pp. 42-55.

[*In the following essay, which was originally published in* Overland *in 1982, Heseltine evaluates Lawson's cultural significance, asserting that his realistic treatment of Australian themes and settings validates his reputation as a major literary artist.*]

The strident controversy that attended the publication of *In Search of Henry Lawson* in 1978 in some measure obscured what must surely be the most obvious implication of Manning Clark's title: that his subject still awaits a full and true discovery. The conflicting views of Clark and Colin Roderick [whose views are enumerated in his introduction to *Henry Lawson: Short Stories and Sketches 1888-1922*], indeed, merely schematized a prevailing pattern in Lawson commentary. Virtually every new account of our most enigmatic author has achieved its own conviction only at the expense of blotting out some of the central features of its predecessors. It is not my aim here to support either Clark or Roderick in their opposing claims concerning Lawson as a profoundly representative figure of our culture. What I do assert is that neither (at least in *In Search of Henry Lawson* and Dr Roderick's response to that work) provides adequate reasons why, through and in his writings, Lawson can be claimed to be profoundly representative of anything. It is not enough repeatedly to claim that Lawson 'knew what life was all about'; nor, on the other hand, to insist simply that 'his work mirrors the yearning of man to refine the human condition'. If the public property we call Henry Lawson is to be worth anyone's ownership, there must be demonstrated in his writing particular proofs of an actively searching, successfully expressed creative imagination.

In other words, as often as competing arguments about Lawson's cultural significance are raised, it becomes the responsibility of literary criticism to submit his work, once again, to its own procedures—the only procedures by which, in the long run, we can test whether he merits the high national importance imputed to him by Manning Clark, or Colin Roderick, or anyone else. To address myself to that task is precisely my aim in this essay. Not that I shall offer anything so pretentious as 'My Henry Lawson' or 'Henry Lawson: A Revaluation'. My modest purpose is to examine a comparatively small and well-defined part of Lawson's prose writing with the intention of demonstrating in it one instance of that creative dynamism which, multiplied a hundredfold, is the mark of the major literary artist.

My starting point then, is the year 1892, a 'year [as Manning Clark would phrase it] of miracles' in Lawson's life. Clark sees 1893-94, too, as 'halcyon years'. And there would be few to dissent from his belief that it was during the three- to four-year period from 1892 to 1895 that Lawson reached the high-water mark of his career. Some of the major stories of that time will constitute my subject; the ground of Lawson's art, my theme. In adopting that phrase I do not wish primarily to indicate the importance of place in Lawson's prose narratives. Enough has been made, for instance, of the bush as a source of passion, meaning, value in his tales. The meaning of 'ground' that I have chiefly in mind is its musical one: 'the plainsong or melody on which a descant is raised'. Now all great writers have such 'melodies' playing to their inner ear; their books become the descants raised upon them. If we can detect even one such motif stated and restated in Lawson's stories, we will have at least one possible starting point for arguing his mastery as a writer, and consequently his importance as a figure in our culture.

One particular interplay between ground and descant, one source of creative dynamism, has struck me more forcibly than before in the re-reading of Lawson's work demanded of me by the Clark-Roderick conflict of opinions. I can identify it most clearly in that story which, as Clark would have it, initiates the golden period of Lawson's artistic life. **'A Day on a Selection'** was published in 1892. Only four pages long, this bitter, plotless snapshot of up-country living has generated some remarkably diverse responses. Here, for instance, is Manning Clark's comment:

> In this work a wondrous thing began to happen. On the surface it was a description by a man who had begun to feel bitter about life . . . On the surface the life of the selector seemed hopeless . . . At the end of the story an attempt is made to portray the majesty and absurdity of life in the bush . . . He had managed to confer a might, a power and a glory on what had previously been dismissed by the cringers to overseas culture as the affairs of the sliprail, the cow-yard and the chook-house.

This, by way of contrast, is Denton Prout's assessment of the same story, in *Henry Lawson: the Grey Dreamer*:

> The whole sketch . . . is filled with scorn for the fantasy-ridden idealists who live in a world of slip-shod incompetence and haven't the willpower, "guts", or initiative to improve their lot by physical action . . . It is a picture of the "bad" side of the "intellectual ferment" of the nineties.

Such divergencies of opinion I find neither surprising nor distressing. For there is that in Lawson's own words which permits, enforces even, a range of response limited only by the number of his readers. To me, the unavoidable feature of **'A Day on a Selection'** is its style of scrupulous meanness, a style which, in reducing human life to mere event and observable action, evacuates from the whole performance the possibility of guiding its readers to any single moral or emotional judgement. In **'A Day on a Selection'** Lawson, no less than Joyce in *Dubliners,* remains within or behind or beyond his handiwork, allowing the primal facts to speak as they will. It is perhaps the first thoroughly (and compellingly) depersonalized work of fiction in Australian literary history. The means of achieving this remarkable *tour de force* (and it is nothing less) are obvious enough—the consistent use of the passive voice ('A boy is seen to run' . . . 'The thick milk is poured into a slop bucket'), the recurrent elision of narrative connections, the dependence on a tone of voice wholly apart from the action or any moral significance

that might conceivably attach to it. The full result of Lawson's method is a representation of the enigma of sheer existence, of that order of human experience captured by T. S. Eliot in 'The Hollow Men':

> Shape without form, shade without colour,
> Paralysed force, gesture without motion.

My allusion to Eliot is neither arbitrary nor, as I believe, unwarranted. For in **'A Day on a Selection'** Lawson committed himself, at the beginning of his major phase, to the depiction of that state of spiritual nullity, that kind of life-in-death, in which the author of 'The Waste Land' was so expert. Even before 1892, indeed, there had been preliminary soundings of what during the middle years of the decade was to become the very ground of his most important fiction. As early as 1890, in the Albany *Observer,* he had surveyed the inhabitants of the continent's western third and dismissed them in a single phrase: *'the people of West Australia have no existence'.* As social observation, the remark must be allowed a measure of exaggeration; as the expression of one man's state of mind and heart, it registers the personal vision for which Lawson, in succeeding years, had to invent plots and characters, that it might enjoy a local habitation and a name.

The exact phrase, 'they have no existence', does not occur (to the best of my knowledge) in any of the major stories of 1892-95. They exhibit, however, their own recurring verbal motif, summing up the hollowness that Lawson felt in himself and sensed in so much that he looked out on: 'it doesn't matter'. The phrase occurs, almost parenthetically, in **'A Day on a Selection'**:

> Sometimes the boy's hand gets tired and he lets some of the milk run over, and gets into trouble; but it doesn't matter much, for the straining-cloth has several sizeable holes in the middle.

It forms the theme of the old shepherd's obituary spoken over his friend's remains in **'The Bush Undertaker'**: 'Brummy . . . it's all over now; nothin' matters now— nothin' didn't ever matter, nor—nor don't'. Its most striking appearance is in the climax of **'The Union Buries Its Dead'**:

> [The grave digger] tried to steer the first few shovelfuls gently down against the end of the grave with the back of the shovel turned outwards, but the hard, dry Darling River clods rebounded and knocked all the same. It didn't matter much—nothing does.

The whole of **'The Union Buries Its Dead'**, as we now see, is probably less in praise of union solidarity than in recognition of that state of spiritual paralysis which its author could project so tellingly upon his characters because (we must believe) he knew it so well himself. Every significant element in the story testifies to this view— action, setting, comedy, social observation, most of all, perhaps, its rejection of the sentimental comfort of literary convention ('I have left out the wattle—because it wasn't there'—). Even the detail which so taxed Colin

Roderick—the shadow cast by a fence at noon—can be explained (if not finally defended) in terms of this reading of the tale. Richer and more fully dramatized than 'A Day on a Selection', 'The Union Buries Its Dead' yet takes up exactly the same theme: 'shade without colour, / Paralysed force, gesture without motion'.

'The Union Buries Its Dead' appeared in the *Bulletin* on 16 April 1893—during the year, that is to say, which followed the publication of 'A Day on a Selection'. These two stories portray with a thoroughness never surpassed in Lawson's canon his sense that it is man's lot to be held somewhere between living and dying. To the very extent, however, that they succeeded in sounding the groundtone of his fiction, they represented a barrier to its further development. It is not to my purpose to enquire into the psychological genesis of the tune which played so insistently to Lawson's inner ear, merely to examine its energizing effects on his creative patterns. Even within the limits of such an enquiry, however, it is possible to suggest that few human beings could bear to remain stalled in that perception of nullity which characterizes 'The Union Buries Its Dead'—particularly one as alert as Lawson was to human potentiality. In such a situation Lawson almost inevitably sought for a release from the imaginative impasse he had revealed to himself in his art. The mode and substance of that release are to be detected in a new descant he began to raise upon the ground of his narratives, a descant first unmistakably heard in 'The Bush Undertaker', published in the *Antipodean* of Christmas 1892.

Colin Roderick finds the primary significance of 'The Bush Undertaker' in its traffic with the Australian bush:

> [Lawson] wanted to retain the notion of Nature's indifference to human activity, to leave the impression of the bush brooding over the grim episode . . .

This view or something like it represents the common wisdom about the story, and has accordingly directed a good deal of attention towards the well-known final paragraph—especially the critical acumen (or otherwise) exhibited by Lawson and his editors in the various alterations and omissions of the early printings:

> And the sun sank again on the grand Australian bush— the nurse and tutor of eccentric minds, the home of the weird, and much that is different from things in other lands.

Whatever uncertainty Lawson may have felt about the ending of 'The Bush Undertaker' is of less consequence, it seems to me, for his representation of the Australian bush than for his status as a creative artist in the culture in which perforce he operated. I shall return to this issue later; for the time being, however, I wish to comment on a strand of meaning in the story much less obvious than the impact of the bush—what might be called its inside narrative. I do so not for the sake of contesting prevailing interpretations but in order to lay bare what I have described as the descant that Lawson came to weave about the theme of spiritual nullity.

The main action of 'The Bush Undertaker' takes place on Christmas Day. The heavy-handedness of the irony should not, however, blind us to its importance. For the tale is last, if not first, a tale of death and rebirth. The opening sequence, wherein a solitary shepherd goes in search of some old bones in what is probably an Aboriginal grave, does more than establish the pathological eccentricity of an individual condemned to a solitary life in a remote corner of the bush. It establishes the motif of the (here quite literal) resurrection of the dead: the nature of the bones may remain problematical, but they are most certainly exhumed. The narrative then develops along a line of ironic counterpoint: after the shepherd has uncovered the long-dead occupant of the grave, he discovers an unburied body, that of his old friend Brummy, awaiting ritual committal to the earth. It may be imputing too great a subtlety to Lawson to discover a pun in his description of the skeleton as 'thunderin' jumpt-up bones', yet observation of the possible play on words confirms the prevailing meaning and emphasis of the entire tale.

The fugal opposition between the shepherd's Christmas dinner of 'boggabri and salt meat', on the one hand, and the meal the goanna makes of Brummy's remains, on the other, cannot be gainsaid. Nor is it possible to overlook the resolution of opposing themes—of death and rebirth— in the closing scene. As the shepherd commits the remains of his old mate to the ground, his hope is that Brummy will find 'a great an' gerlorious rassaraction'. For all the grotesque comedy of its realized action, 'The Bush Undertaker' finds its deepest motivation in the juxtaposition of an absolutely hopeless, sterile existence with the possibility of redemptive change.

I make this claim for 'The Bush Undertaker' with all the greater confidence because exactly the same dynamic structure can be shown to inform many of Lawson's other stories of the same period. It is foreshadowed, for instance, even in the city tales which precede the great bush studies of 1892-95. The irony, thus, of dating Arvie Aspinall's death (in 'Arvie Aspinall's Alarm Clock') during the Easter holidays may be as heavily pathetic as the Christmas setting of 'The Bush Undertaker' is deliberately grotesque; it points quite as clearly to Lawson's dream of renewal. Nor should it go unnoticed that in 'Jones's Alley' Mrs Aspinall lived in dread of her husband's 'daily resurrection', and that rescue from imminent eviction at the end of the story takes on the appearance of a funeral:

> When the funeral reached the street, the lonely "trap" was, somehow, two blocks away in the opposite direction, moving very slow, and very upright, and very straight, like an automaton.

After these tentative experiments Lawson was ready to confront, in story after story, death-in-life with the hope of release by dying into a new identity. A recurring feature of this interplay between the ground of his art and the new motif he wove around it is set out with singular clarity at the beginning of 'The Mystery of Dave Regan':

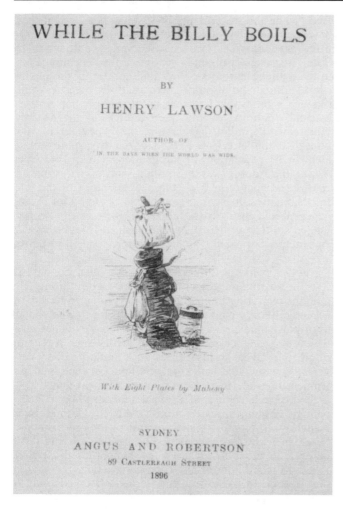

WHILE THE BILLY BOILS

BY

HENRY LAWSON

AUTHOR OF
'IN THE DAYS WHEN THE WORLD WAS WIDE'

With Eight Plates by Mahony

SYDNEY
ANGUS AND ROBERTSON
89 CASTLEREAGH STREET
1896

Facsimile of the title-page of perhaps Lawson's most famous short story collection.

"And then there was Dave Regan," said the traveller.

"Dave used to die oftener than any other bushman I knew. He was always being reported dead and turnin' up again."

Time and again the pattern is repeated. The bush worker disappears up-country, seemingly dead, only to return, unannounced, to his former surroundings. Time and again the faint hope that he may be renewed, especially through the influence of romantic love, is disappointed. The expression of the pattern may be comic (as in **'The Mystery of Dave Regan'**), pathetic, grotesque, but its activating elements remain the same. Mitchell, for instance, is made to undergo a representative experience in one of the briefest pieces Lawson ever wrote, **'A Love Story'**. 'He went up-country and was reported dead', says Mitchell to his mate, patently projecting his own case onto an imaginary third person. But there is no comic sequel to this disappearance:

"He was reported to have been drowned while trying to swim his horses across a billabong. His girl broke her heart—and mended it again; then he turned up

alive, and drier than ever, and married her, and broke her heart for certain. And—she died."

The only release he can know is the bitter, familiar comment 'Ah, well—never mind . . . The billy's boiling, Joe'. Mitchell is required to suffer a remarkably similar experience in **'On the Edge of a Plain'**, while the situation to which Lawson condemns him in **'Some Day'** is even harsher. He speaks his tale of lost love from the outback itself, the outback from which he knows he will never return. Descended into purgatory, he knows that there can be no resurrection.

If the farthest reaches of the bush could hold an itinerant pastoral worker like Mitchell captive for months or years, Lawson knew of other ways in which the Australian earth could literally swallow those who inhabit its surface. The conditions of shallow-shaft gold mining, with which he was so early familiar, provided him (as it did later Henry Handel Richardson) with potent images. The motif of the miner dying underground was quite as vivid to him as that of the pastoral worker wandering the land in hope of resurrection. Indeed, exactly that motif is at the heart of the very first of Lawson's prose narratives, **'His Father's Mate'**. In that piece the father's desire to work underground is the direct cause of his son Isley's death, through a fall to the base of the mine shaft. As an afterpiece to the main action, the long-lost elder son returns home to find his father dead of a broken heart.

The ironic symmetry of **'His Father's Mate'** clearly prefigures the design of **'The Bush Undertaker'**, while its substance is repeated in a number of important stories, notably **'When the Sun Went Down'**. This tale tells of a quarrel between two brothers, both helping to sink the same shaft. The quarrel is resolved (before the sun goes down) when the elder brother Tom saves Jack from a cave-in, only to die of heart failure at the very moment the rescue is effected. As one brother is resurrected into life, the other goes down into the darkness of death. **'The Golden Graveyard'**, by way of contrast, uses the mining material to create a comic variation of Lawson's central theme. In their search for a rich reef of gold, Dave Regan and his mates drive straight underneath a cemetery, literally uncovering the coffins of the dead as they strike towards their hoped-for wealth. In a farcical climax, one of the diggers momentarily thinks he has met the devil when he comes face to face with a Negro driving in to the gold from another direction. It is life, however, which finally triumphs—life in the form of drunken Mrs Middleton, as she saves her husband's grave from threatened despolation by the diggers.

Comic, pathetic, or tragic, the hope (never more than half-believed in) that there may be some release from the state of death-in-life by a redemptive rebirth is the animating force behind nearly every significant story that Lawson wrote in the middle years of the 1890s. In many, as in **'Brummy Usen'**, it determines both the substance and the mode of the telling. Brummy, thus, experiences the rare difficulty of being declared unofficially dead by his bush companions and subsequently being unable to convince them of his continued existence. He becomes that loneliest type in all Lawson's range of characters—the solitary traveller, the 'hatter'. The terrible detachment of his life from the rest of humanity is revealed in the conclusion of the story, when the narrator unwittingly reveals that, in recounting Brummy's history, he has been recounting his own.

Perhaps, however, the most extreme instance in Lawson's fiction of the 'hatter' as a man condemned to live, in Eliot's phrase, 'in death's other kingdom', is the story entitled **'Rats'**, first published in the *Bulletin* of 3 June 1893. Its experiential extremity is further complicated by an ambiguity of meaning quite as marked as that which attaches to **'A Day on a Selection'**. The ambiguity in the case of **'Rats'**, however, derives less from any scrupulous meanness of style than from rival interpretations produced by its alternative endings. The editorial crux is the propriety or otherwise of printing a single sentence as a coda to the main narrative:

> And late that evening a little withered old man with no corks round his hat and with a humorous twinkle instead of a wild glare in his eyes called at a wayside shanty, had several drinks, and entertained the chaps with a yarn about the way in which he had "had" three "blanky fellers" for some tucker and "half a caser" by pretending to be "barmy".

That sentence did not appear in the original *Bulletin* printing; it was added for **Short Stories in Prose and Verse** (1894), and completely altered the meaning and tone of the tale. The later version uses the final sentence to produce a sort of 'trick' ending to which the entire episode must be regarded as leading. Without the coda, however, **'Rats'** becomes accessible to a much more ambiguous and, I believe, satisfying interpretation. The opening scene, thus, in which Sunlight, Macquarie, and Milky first see the hatter apparently struggling with a human opponent in the middle of a dusty track, becomes crucial in establishing the ground-tone of Lawson's meaning. The three shearers are sufficiently interested by the prospect of witnessing a fight to abandon their 'smoke-oh' and move, without undue haste, towards the encounter. Their interest becomes urgent, however, when they decide that one of the participants is a woman:

> "It's a funny-lookin' feller, the other feller," panted Milky. "He don't seem to have no head. Look! he's down—they're both down! They must ha' clinched on the ground. No! they're up an' at it again . . . Why, good Lord! I think the other's a woman!"

It is only when a sexual element is introduced into the scene that 'they dropped swags, water-bags and all, and raced forward'. While it is certainly possible to account for this haste as a gesture of outback chivalry, it is quite as fair to regard it as the behaviour of sexually frustrated men excited by the prospect of near contact with a woman. Neither interpretation is invalidated by the fact that when the shearers come near the hatter they discover that he is in fact wrestling with his swag.

Even when the truth of the matter has been established, however, the behaviour of the three shearers continues to offer psychological interest. Seemingly untouched by Rats's neurotically disabled condition, they encourage him in his pathetic parody of the ritual contest of the boxing ring. Sunlight and his mates take a sadistic pleasure in the old man's antics that Lawson is at no pains whatsoever to conceal. If, however, the overt actions of the shearers vibrate with implicit aggression, the behaviour of Rats himself in the latter part of the story is even more ambivalent in its psychological implications. 'Well, old Rats, what's the trouble?' asks Sunlight, and his question encapsulates what is perhaps the deepest motif of the tale. Rats's manifest behaviour cannot be accounted for by any generalized appeal to the alienating effects of the prolonged solitude in the Australian bush. It is reported with an exactness of detail which demands a detailed response.

Once the symbolic boxing match has been concluded, Rats, borrowing a piece of meat for bait, goes through the motions of fishing in the dust. There is no need to rely on accepted literary convention to account for this behaviour as displaced male sexuality. There is ample evidence elsewhere in Lawson's own fiction to justify such a reading of **'Rats'**. Rivers in his stories are regularly (if not universally) associated with romantic love between men and women; one tale in particular, moreover, provides striking evidence in support of a sexual understanding of Rats's pathetic angling in a sterile bush track. In **'The Hero of Redclay'**, Mitchell tells the narrator of the sad history of 'Lachlan', who has condemned himself to a living death outback in order to preserve the honour of the girl he loved. Mitchell himself had been peripherally involved in that history, to the extent that he had observed some of the meetings between 'Lachlan' and his girl while he himself was fishing. Mitchell's report of one such incident leaves no doubt that his fishing excursion was a quite direct attempt to 'catch' a woman of his own:

> "About a week before that I was down in the bed of the Redclay Creek fishing for 'tailers'. I'd been getting on all right with the housemaid at the Royal . . . She mentioned one day, yarning, that she liked a stroll by the creek sometimes in the cool of the evening. I thought she'd be off that day, so I said I'd go for fish after I'd knocked off. I thought I might get a bite. Anyway, I didn't catch Lizzie—tell you about that some other time."

Rats's fumbling with meat and string, that is to say, may be seen as the symbolic gesture of a man spiritually paralysed through prolonged deprivation of the company of women. So understood, the whole story must properly end at the comment which insists on the ambivalent existence of a man completely without hope of restoration:

> When they turned their heads again, Rats was still fishing: but when they looked back for the last time before entering the timber, he was having another row with his swag; and Sunlight reckoned that the trouble arose out of some lies which the swag had been telling about the bigger fish it caught.

So radical a reading of **'Rats'** must provoke questions about Lawson's intentions in writing the story, about the validity of a commentary so completely based on a doubtful text. My own position on the matter is simple enough. Whatever Lawson's conscious 'intentions', his imagination was demonstrably capable of entertaining at least two possible interpretations of the same events. My inclination in such a situation is to prefer the richer reading. In any case, if there is any discrepancy between the pattern that Lawson finally decided on and that urged on him by the deeper promptings of his imagination, the question of primary interest concerns the nature of that discrepancy and the reasons for its appearance. An inspection of the whole range of Lawson's stories written in the middle 1890s, furthermore, reveals that indecision about the final status of a text is by no means unique to **'Rats'**. On the contrary, variant printings of the stories seem to be the rule rather than the exception. To be sure, many of the textual emendations can be accounted for, as Colin Roderick has pointed out, by the interference of editors less perceptive than Lawson himself. Even those which can be shown to have authorial sanction are often the result of Lawson's desire to heighten, say, the dramatic impact of a particular tale, or the naturalness of its idiom. Nevertheless, the very fact that Lawson had to suffer (and accept) frequent editorial interference indicates something of the uncertain status of the Australian writer of his generation. His own need, furthermore, to tinker with his texts (sometimes with profound consequences) suggests that such uncertainty was not entirely a matter of external pressure; it existed within the man himself, as a radical element of his creative apparatus. Manning Clark is, thus, right to draw attention to the codas so often appended to Lawson's stories. In perceiving them, however, as a 'signature tune, a Lawson comment . . . on life in general', he was missing much of their significance in the larger patterns of Lawson's art. For nowhere more than in these end pieces and in Lawson's seemingly unavoidable need to tinker with them is there more acute evidence of his uncertainty about his own self, the very basis of his being. The textual history of these final paragraphs suggests as potently as any other data marshalled by Clark the actuality of that divided and ambivalent self which the whole sweep of *In Search of Henry Lawson* aims to demonstrate.

Curiously, however, what might be construed as fundamental weaknesses in his life and personality proved to be the strength and buttress of his art. The great stories of his flowering time are precisely those in which he refuses to let ambivalence, uncertainty, distress be resolved by the comforts of doctrine, any absolutes of belief or action. His primal sense, that is to say, of human existence held between living and dying stubbornly opposes the seductive symbols of death and rebirth to which it is so regularly submitted. However great the temptation to convert the motif of resurrection into a faith, an explanatory myth, he steadfastly refused to succumb, at least in the middle 1890s, to any certitude which would falsify his sense of the enigmatic, the ambivalent, in man's life. The Christmas and Easter symbols of **'The Bush Undertaker'** and **'Arvie Aspinall's Alarm Clock'** are, in spite of their diagnostic value, patently machinery (or at most uneasy

devices for injecting sympathetic irony into the writing). Unlike T. S. Eliot, Lawson would never have occasion to write an 'Ash Wednesday'; the integrity of his great tales of the middle 1890s resides in his determination to hold the balance between the spiritual wasteland he perceived in his own and other lives and the tantalizing but illusory promise of rebirth he could not help but entertain.

I should make it plain that I claim no status for the patterns I am imputing to Lawson's fiction other than what in theatrical terms would be called the sub-text to a script. In other words, I do not wish to challenge the validity of orthodox readings of such tales as **'Rats'**, **'The Bush Undertaker'**, **'A Day on a Selection'**, and **'The Union Buries its Dead'**, which locate their meanings in the interchange between men and the Australian bush. All that I wish to suggest is that the manifest meanings of these stories can be made to bear the burden of cultural representativeness and value so often demanded of them in part because the 'melodies' I have attempted to describe can be heard, by the well-tuned ear, playing at their very core. It is also, and finally, true that, just as from the late 1890s on Lawson's life began its long disintegration, so too did his art begin to lose the authority it derived from the tense balance it had once held between the ground-tone of existential disease and the several variations on the theme of resurrection. From the end of the decade on, indeed, Lawson's career had at least this in common with Christopher Brennan's: both men acted on the metaphoric prophecies of self-destruction that they had dared to create in the flowering time of their imagination. Just as the latter part of Brennan's career is, in a sense, contained and predicted in 'The Forest of Night', so too is Lawson's life, from, say, his journey to England on, characterized by episodes in which he sought to destroy the old Adam of his former self and rise into a new and changed identity. One thinks, for instance, of the burning of his manuscripts upon his arrival in England—a symbolic *auto-da-fé*; of the abortive leap from the cliff at Fairy Bower; of the multifarious *personae* tried and discarded in the letters of his later years.

Such episodes in his life find their parallel in the conduct of his later fiction. The nexus between his awareness of spiritual paralysis and his dreams of release is all too often shattered, leaving him stranded between polarized extremes. By way of example I might cite **'That Pretty Girl in the Army'**, composed in 1901 and first published in the following year in *Children in the Bush*. In that tale Lawson reverts to material he had gathered on his trip to Bourke in 1892. Where, in the stories written immediately after that outback expedition, the motif of romantic love had been expressed with a tactful restraint, in **'That Pretty Girl in the Army'** his treatment of women undergoes a complete polarization. On the one hand there is the sentimentalization of the 'pretty girl' of the title; on the other, an attitude towards female sexuality which produces perhaps the only coarse jest that Lawson allowed into his fiction:

The Army prayed, and then a thin "ratty" little woman bobbed up in the ring; she'd gone mad on religion as women do on woman's rights and hundreds of other things. She was so skinny in the face, her jaws so prominent, and her mouth so wide, that when she opened it to speak it was like a ventriloquist's dummy and you could almost see the cracks open down under her ears.

"They say I'm cracked!" she screamed in a shrill, cracked voice. "But I'm not cracked—I'm only cracked on the Lord Jesus Christ! That's all I'm cracked on—." And just then the Amen man of the Army—the Army groaner we called him, who was always putting both feet in it—just then he blundered forward, rolled up his eyes, threw his hands up and down as if he were bouncing two balls, and said, with deep feeling: "Thank the Lord she's got a crack in the right place!"

No story, however, more fully measures the extent to which the deepest controls of Lawson's imagination collapsed along with the externals of his life than **'The Man Who Was Drowned'**, not printed in Lawson's lifetime and probably composed about 1908. Its opening paragraph gives the clearest indication of the value it had for Lawson:

This is the story of a man who went away and died— or was supposed to be dead. Supposed to be drowned. He was a writer. I might have made him a "great" artist, actor, singer, musician, or poet, or anything else out of the common and great—or in the common, rather, and "great", as "great" things go now; but he was a writer. He was a writer who had been widely known and had written for many years. And he found that the more he wrote, and the more widely known he became, the less money he got for it. Perhaps it was because of the drink—and perhaps private worries had been the cause of the drink. No time nor space to enter into the mystery of drink here.

To dispel any doubt that Lawson is, in fact, writing of himself, he identifies his protagonist in the second paragraph by one of his considerable range of pseudonyms: 'Maybe his name was John Lawrence'. **'The Man Who Was Drowned'**, in other words, must be read as a prolonged and uncontrolled fantasy in which Lawson, bitter and aggrieved at himself and the world, gives way uncritically to the dream of dying into a new life.

There were of course temporary reversals of the trend— the Joe Wilson stories spring instantly to mind. By and large, however, after 1895 Lawson found it increasingly difficult to bring his fantasies under the command of his creative imagination. That fragile balance between the personal ground-tone of his fiction and the vision of Australian life that he constructed upon it more and more slipped away from his control. Only rarely could he repeat the triumphs of the major phase; hardly ever could he find some new vision of his own uncertain self to give his life and art new impetus. Near the beginnings of his sad decline, however, one story stands out, and for a single scene. In **'The Blinding of One-Eyed Bogan'** Lawson strikes off an unforgettable image. His protagonist is briefly revealed, blinded in the act of saving a policeman

sent to effect his arrest, naked and alone by the side of the life-giving waters of the River Darling:

. . . I've often thought since what a different man Bogan seemed without his clothes and with the broken bridge of his nose and his eyes covered by the handkerchiefs. He was clean shaven, and his mouth and chin are his best features, and he's clean limbed and well hung. I often thought afterwards that there was something of a blind god about him as he stood there naked by the fire on the day he saved Campbell's life . . .

A fleeting glimpse of man as Adonis-Lear, and no more. Unable to find release from his wasteland, increasingly paralysed by its sterility, Lawson was condemned in his later years to the composition of fragments to shore against the ruins of his life.

Ken Stewart (essay date 1983)

SOURCE: "'The Loaded Dog': A Celebration," in *Australian Literary Studies,* Vol. 11, No. 2, October, 1983, pp. 152-61.

[*In the following essay, Stewart examines two chief characteristics of Lawson's fiction, "human gregariousness" and "the hardness of things."*]

The Loaded Dog inhabits the background of millions of Australian minds, where he jostles amiably and vitally amongst the stiffer corpses and tutored shades of Bell Birds, My Country and Gallant Cook sailing from Albion. There is nothing dutiful, however, about the way the dog lingers in our minds. He is approved. He remains voluntarily, neither as an official and required patriotic cliché of the olden times, like the land of sweeping plains, nor as a drilled and tinkling set piece, like 'Bell Birds', learnt by rote without a meaning. In a central and formative position in Australian popular literary culture, the Loaded Dog grins and slobbers and wags his tail with the inerasable certainty of a figure in a nursery rhyme.

In spite of its popularity, the story has received little attention from commentators. Lawson's critics, I suspect, have assumed that a straightforward legendary yarn written within a recognizable tradition does not require discussion. There is also the possibility that a popular, 'happy' story that lacks characteristic Lawsonian sombreness has been held necessarily to lack seriousness. To put the work aside and unexamined on these grounds is hazardous. The comic simplicity and folk acceptance of popular writing is often inseparable from its accessible human seriousness: the appeal of the story itself courts explanation. I believe that a discussion of its meaning, artistry and cultural significance can help us to appreciate the significance of Lawson's comic celebration of a dream, and that the context of Lawson's fiction itself best establishes the concepts that give meaning to the comic world of **'The Loaded Dog'**. The two central and inseparable preoccupations in his stories that are most helpful, and which I shall need to define in my own way, are 'human gregariousness' and 'the hardness of things', my labels for what are frequently accepted as quintessentially Lawsonian themes.

Lawson's emphasis on gregariousness is obvious and elusive: obvious, because we attest to it in every story about loneliness, isolation, mateship, neighbourliness, the masculine bush ethos, love, husband and wife, madness, the bush itself as humans experience it; potentially elusive, because we may so easily fail to perceive that he alone among authors of recognised stature writes of little else: this instinct and need within the human species, its potential and limitations, the forms it may take and the effects of its repression, are virtually his exclusive subject, determining action and plot, or passivity and plotlessness, and the complexity of his narrative tone, as well as defining the area in which his insight into human behaviour and human nature operates. It is possible for characters to live by themselves in Furphy's fiction, for example, without becoming mad, or eccentric, or intolerably deprived; and if, like Tom Collins, the loner may be judged as rather fussy, pedantic and self-deluding—then, such is life. Such *isn't* life for Lawson: the gregarious impulse, in his view of the nature of things, is dominant and paramount; the loner is to be perceived as a curious individual, like Mr Smellingscheck, whose mystique and mystery derive from the fact that he is *not* gregarious. The isolate in Lawson is eccentric; or mad; or sulky, sullen and selfish; or intolerably deprived. The salvation of the Bush Undertaker, and of the swagman 'Rats', is that they create their own gregarious reality from illusion. The Drover's Wife is an archetypal image of maternal isolation and loneliness— intolerably deprived. The urgency and extensiveness of Lawson's preoccupation with the gregarious impulse is artistically valid (his art validates it) but it is almost exclusive: nobody climbs Mount Everest, or experiences an epiphany or invents the wheel, or is 'justified' through romantic love or religious experience, or occupies himself in any way satisfactorily, unless it be gregariously; and the author's values and priorities adjust themselves to this perspective on human lives.

Lawson's subject, then, is the instinct of human beings for human company and contact: to huddle, to be, and to interact, preferably warmly, with others of the species. His first person narrators are 'insiders'. They write critically, ambivalently and loyally from inside the group, accommodating themselves to the bullies and big kids, like Barcoo Rot and One Eyed Bogan; the innocuously stupid, like Tom Hall; and the hard cases, like Mitchell. The relationship of the narrator to the group establishes the paradox of conformity as a theme or problematic element within many of the stories, (for example, **'Lord Douglas'**, **'The Union Buries Its Dead'**, and **'Telling Mrs Baker'**), but gregarious solidarity must win, or at least continue. In **'The Union Buries Its Dead'** it is not the loner's death that is disturbing; it is Lawson's evocation of the fear that a man, or all men, could be cut off from the human race, unredeemed by the gregarious impulse, locked without recognition within the individual self. His Union is a huddle of schoolboys; the verandah

of the Bourke Imperial is like the quadrangle of a segregated boys' secondary school. Although the characters in these settings are not 'types', they are realised psychologically only to the extent that social rituals and the breaking of them permit and define. They are real people whom the reader gets to know socially, but not intimately; and their mores and routines, the unwritten rules for gregarious behaviour, are, as Hal Porter would write, 'equally of air and of iron'. From time to time a fight breaks out in the quadrangle; and occasionally, as in **'That Pretty Girl in the Army'**, a strange foreign creature called a girl wanders into alien precincts, and you have to patronise her delicately and watch your language. The exclusiveness of Lawson's preoccupation with the lights and shades of human gregariousness provides a context for discussing the Loaded Dog—he is the gregarious impulse incarnate, canonised and canine-ised.

Lawson's second pervasive assumption is 'the hardness of things'. The most universal practice amongst sane people in his fiction is overt worry, in the manner of Joe Wilson, or the suppression of outward concern, as with Mitchell. His celebrated 'realism' is flecked with constant emotional regret: external reality is not his subject—the narrator's emotional response, his voice, is the subject. The difference between Lawson's **'Ah, well'** and Furphy's 'Such is Life', or rather his many 'Such is Life's, is that Lawson's expresses a direct emotional avowal, whereas Furphy's characters offer a more cerebral diversity of clinching observations in the face of the variety and enigma of life itself. 'Ah, well' expresses *felt* resignation: it is a kind of sad moan. The contrast with 'Such is Life' is illustrated inadvertently by Manning Clark in Volume IV of *A History of Australia*:

> Ned Kelly walked to his death in the Old Melbourne Gaol in the morning of 11 November 1880. His mother had urged him to die like a Kelly. Some said he looked frightened and morose and only managed to utter a lame 'Ah well, I suppose it has come to this'. Others said he summed it all up in that sardonic Australian remark 'Such is Life'.

Lawson's positives, then, charity, neighbourliness, even madness, toughness and shrewdness, are really the valued arms of strugglers against the hardness of things. Lawson never states despair: he intones something grim. Even 'It didn't matter much—nothing does' is a fluctuation of the voice, rather than a considered conclusion; and it is a voice which is not so much meditating, as actually expressing the moment's reaction to a continuing burden. There is an undefined or lost ideal behind Lawson's writing: it is life *without* the hardness of things; it is the relief of that pressure which creates his narrator's burdened tone.

That Lawson, unlike Furphy and Baynton, implicitly uses such an ideal as a gauge of the quality of reality is illustrated by his attacks on the romanticism and optimism of other Australian writers. These attacks in fact indicate his self-delusion, because they illustrate *his* romantic longing:

They put in shining rivers and grassy plains, and western hills, and dawn and morn, and forest boles of gigantic size—everything, in fact, which is not and never was in bush scenery or language; and the more the drought bakes them the more inspired they become. Perhaps they unconsciously see the bush as it should be, and their literature is the result of craving for the ideal.

The angry bitterness is revealing. It is as though Lawson would really like to 'put in shining rivers and grassy plains' but the truth prevents him, and makes him angry with those who do. In the phrase 'they unconsciously see the bush as it should be', he gives himself away, by implying that the bush 'should be' an Arcadian dream world. Clearly, and ironically, Lawson's literature is equally 'the result of a craving for the ideal' of the optimists he attacks, albeit in conjunction with his constant emotional rediscovery that the world is not ideal. 'Oh, may the grass grow green and tall'. In Tom Collins' ridicule of *Geoffry Hamlyn* and other romantic novels, by way of contrast, we find no 'craving for the ideal' and total scorn of Kingsley's literary concoction, which Tom would never *want* as a substitute for bush life. The irony in Furphy's superior implication that life may be more romance-like than Tom perceives does not alter the fact that neither Collins nor Furphy endorses a romantic literary projection, or even dreams of 'the' ideal.

Lawson's fascination with ideal and real, and with illusion and reality, triggers the creative impulse behind several of his best known stories. It leads him to examine perspectives on a seeming innocence or state of grace, a condition in which the Hardness of Things dissolves or loses its oppressiveness, and in which altruism and generosity are unsullied by hard experience, and may work as an agent of good. These stories, however, work to conclude that the Hardness of Things itself explains or modifies any initial, magical *appearance* of innocence or grace, and reduces it to the status of very unmagical experience. 'That's the way of it', comments Donald McDonald at the end of **'That Pretty Girl in the Army'**, 'with a woman it's love or religion; with a man it's love or the devil'. That Pretty Girl, whose initial mystique is of altruism, beauty and spiritual quality, so far from transcending the Hardness of Things through some unusual bestowed grace or inherent innocence or goodness, is eventually to be perceived as simply the product and the victim of this ordinary hardness in life: apparent innocence becomes an explicable delusion. Mrs Baker, too, must remain deluded: the hardness of things is *too* hard for her to be told. The Giraffe, to whom we have begun to respond for his innocence and natural generosity, is as close as Lawson gets to sainthood. But in Lawson's world, where there are many martyrs and no saints, the Giraffe has to start saving his money, and is despatched on the train to marriage, which in Lawson is virtually a synonym for Paradise Lost. 'I wish I could immortalize him!', writes the narrator, longing for the ideal, but thereby confirming that he cannot. The Giraffe has never really changed hardbitten humanity; it has changed him.

The innocent and gregarious potential of the carefully named Bob Brothers, incidentally, is given a non-human referent. 'The Giraffe' is not merely a nickname to designate our awkward lanky appearance. The name becomes associated with naive, gangling, yet noble, taller than life generosity: he is, in this setting, an exotic legendary beast, to immortalise—if that were possible. In **'The Loaded Dog'** the device is used in reverse: the dog is gauche, stupid, blundering, generous, gregarious and innocent; and the dog is a mate, with a human name, 'Tommy'. And he is 'immortalised'.

'The Loaded Dog' inverts or softens Lawson's characteristic hard reality: the weight of the Hardness of Things is taken from the narrator's shoulders. As such, it is Lawson's most thorough-going bestowal of grace upon a superficially recognisable reality—the comic celebration of a dream. The Dog is idealised Mateship. Innocent, gregarious, happy, loyal and unworried, he is accordingly the unwitting instrument of the forces of good in a triumph over those adversaries of mateship, selfishness, greed and solitary bastardry. And because he is ideal, he is allowed only to be a dog. He is briefly let off the chain in a holiday world where the grim work-a-day forces of the Hardness of Things are replaced on their regular melancholy rounds by a literary Providence, who rewards gregariousness and goodness of heart and punishes bastards. No worries. Those slender-witted, virgin-souled schoolboys Andy, Dave and Jim experience literary alarm, but never a real care; and the Ideal, the Dog, is incapable of anxiety. The story is therefore more than simply farce or slapstick. It is what happens to Lawson's imagination when he discards his characteristic assumptions. It is not reality, but its yardstick is reality. As a bush yarn that works within the traditional frame of reference of comic romance it is an archetypal, speculative and, certainly, serious story; and its seriousness is fully definable only within the wider context of Lawson's complete prose fiction.

From the Drover's Dog to Kerr's cur and the apparently innocent dingo of Ayer's Rock, dogs are legendary mates or bastards in Australian bush culture. Lawson's bush is a prodigious literary kennel. Although his dogs are not invariably man's best friend, and his kangaroo dogs are emphatically repugnant and untrustworthy, most dogs in Lawson are the gregarious adjunct and loyal companion, the mate, of their owners. The indefatigable 'Alligator' is courageous and loyal; the practical 'Five Bob', though perhaps not the full quid, is a devoted gravedigger's labourer; and that unfortunate poodle who is the victim of an ungracious tonsorial operation in **'The Shearing of the Cook's Dog'** is so much his owner's mirror image that the cook is 'narked for three days' not by the indignity of the act, but because 'they'll think me a flash man in Bourke' with the dog 'trimmed up like that'. Both versions of the morose **'That there dog of mine'** exploit the received wisdom that the dog is man's close and faithful friend: in the original version, in which the dog eats his dead master, this sentiment is the source of the nihilistic grotesquerie; in the revised version, it is a means of endorsing and illustrating mateship. The moral of **'Two Dogs and a Fence'** is that men, like dogs, will quarrel stupidly over a barrier, 'yet if those same two dogs were to meet casually outside they might get chummy at once, and be the best of friends, and swear everlasting mateship, and take each other home'. Lawson's dogs, then, are only human, but more so; and sometimes ideally so. The Loaded Dog is gregarious innocence, the epitome of idealised Mateship; and his skulking adversary is brooding, selfish, stand-offish bastardry.

The story begins quietly and deliberately, with two pages of down to earth detail concerning the technology of cartridge making and fishing. Lawson's method is not only to establish an authentic if somewhat idyllic calm before the explosion, but also to allow the tale gradually to forge and validate its own folk significance: it works slowly at first towards the genre of the apocryphal story and heightened folk yarn, from an initial immersion in genial pedestrian actuality:

> They used the old-fashioned blasting-powder and time fuse. They'd make a sausage or cartridge of blasting powder in a skin of strong calico or canvas, the mouth sewn and bound round the end of the fuse; they'd dip the cartridge in mellow tallow to make it water-tight, get the drill-hole as dry as possible, drop in the cartridge with some dry dust, and wad and ram with stiff clay and broken brick . . .

The narrator here is confirming his bush credentials. The reader is to assent to this practical mystique, to nod approvingly at the bushmen's and the narrator's know-how, and to perceive the wisdom and rituals of the ethos, 'as bushmen do'.

It is not until after the introduction of the dog that the story transcends the pleasantly mundane. Then the vitality of the imagery, the apocryphal exaggerations of the yarn, the slapstick conventions, and the ritualised posturing towards the reader, establish a 'do you remember the time' quality which is confirmed by the concluding lines:

> And most of this is why, for years afterwards, lanky, easy going bushmen, riding lazily past Dave's camp, would cry, in a lazy drawl and with just a hint of the nasal twang:

> 'Ello, Da-a-ve! How's the fishin' gettin' on, Da-a-ve?'

That is Lawson's cheerful but certain reminder to the reader that the teller of a tale is licensed to blur reality with the shine of myth: the reader should not necessarily believe that the land of once-upon-a-time is a real place.

Lawson's use of the apocryphal yarn, and of anecdote as a literary device, is diverse and uneven. At his worst his stories are straitjacketed by the boring conventions of tall tale garrulity which have lingered into Frank Hardy's Billy Borker yarns and into the futile maundering that still passes for humour on some radio programmes. The original version of **'Rats'**, in which in a final sentence we learn that the little old man is yarning in the pub about

'the way which he had "had" three "blanky fellers" for some tucker and "half a caser" by pretending to be "Barmey"' is inferior to the final version because, as Brian Kiernan has pointed out [in *Henry Lawson*,] 'the disturbing implications of the sketch are lost in the factitiously well made story version'—or, to extend the point, the reader feels that *he* has been 'had' by the author, since the subtleties of the reader's uncertainty and disturbance are reduced to the engineered certainty and bar-room bravado of a conventional yarn.

In other stories, and in various ways, Lawson deflates the apocryphal and romantic elements of the recollected yarn: **'Send Round the Hat'** and **'The Chinaman's Ghost'** are examples. In **'The Bush Undertaker'** he demythologises a conventional apocryphal yarn, not by suggesting that it is spurious, but actually by confirming that the ordinary ingredients of a seemingly far-fetched tale constitute a grotesquely credible heightened reality: its 'truth' may not be exactly literal, but neither is it apocryphal. Lawson uses certain elements of the yarn to affirm that the story is *not* a yarn.

In **'The Loaded Dog'** we work towards the avowedly apocryphal, but from the beginning we respond to glimmerings of idyll:

> Dave Regan, Jim Bentley and Andy Page were sinking a shaft at Stoney Creek in search of a rich gold quartz reef which was supposed to exist in the vicinity. There is always a rich reef supposed to exist in the vicinity: the only questions are whether it is ten feet or hundreds beneath the surface, and in which direction.

Although the narrator is rather cynical about this golden dream, a holiday quest for El Dorado, his tone is indulgent. We are not in work-a-day reality, for the mates have gone fishing as well as gold-seeking; and fishing is a traditional literary escape, from Izaac Walton to Huck Finn. Moreover, Lawson's not-so-good earth has suddenly become extravagantly bountiful:

> There was plenty of fish in the creek, fresh-water bream, cod, cat-fish and tailers. The party were fond of fish, and Andy and Dave of fishing.

The creek is neither in flood nor in a dry, hard bed; and the weather seems uncharacteristically clement.

The cartridge is a 'formidable bomb'. The emphasis on its destructive potential is unstinting,—indeed, Dave has engineered an elaborate device 'to increase the force of the explosion'. To argue, therefore, that Lawson even here tinges his bush humour with the constant threat of crude violence and destruction is understandable; but I do not believe that we are invited to respond to the threat of the cartridge except insofar as it is primarily a familiar comic clowning device, the equivalent of the double bunger of the later Tom and Jerry animated cartoon. Although there is some sadism within the convention itself, appropriate to the 'sadistic' bush tradition that countless stories and cartoons in the *Bulletin* of the period unpleasantly exploit, it is remarkable that this element has been greatly softened in comparison with other examples in the *Bulletin,* and has been transformed in context from 'realistic' sadistic humour into a distanced, almost comic cartoon stylisation. As we are to discover, the Providence of Lawson's comedy, unlike the Fates of his reality, will use the destructive power of the cartridge to achieve a poetic justice and a happy retributive ending. The dog itself makes a belated *grande entrance*:

> They had a big black young retriever dog—or rather an overgrown pup, a big, foolish, four-footed mate, who was always slobbering round them and lashing their legs with his heavy tail that swung round like a stockwhip. Most of his head was usually a red, idiotic, slobbering grin of appreciation of his own silliness. He seemed to take life, the world, his two-legged mates, and his own instinct as a huge joke.

The impression is immediate, exaggerated, almost Dickensian, and unforgettable: the sudden juxtaposition of this colourful caricature against the genial pedestrian rituals of pragmatic bush technology confirms the dog's status as the larger than life subject of the yarn. He is not only a mate; he is a gangling, gauche, madly friendly, stupidly generous mate—a caricature of his own masters, and a satirical but delighted idealisation of bush gregariousness. This description together with the action that follows emphasises the vitality of the forces the dog embodies, the reversal of the usual Lawsonian passivity.

The dog is proper instinct, graced by a freedom from all worry and malice; and in his innocence he is necessarily stupid, the archetypal saint and fool, an ideal who cannot be killed off by the immense and random destructiveness of the cartridge. A bush dog, he grins 'sardonically'; 'they loved him for his goodheartedness'; life for him is 'a huge joke': the seeds of the moral allegory are sown, and germinate within the farcical action—all his goodhearted, game-playing, fun loving, faithful, gregarious responses actually cause the slapstick.

As in an animated cartoon, which the technique anticipates, a series of poses and attitudes make up a set of ritualised 'frames': Dave and Andy running in divergent directions; Jim shinnying up a sapling; the 'big pup' laying the cartridge 'as carefully as a kitten' at the foot of the tree; the sputtering fuse; Jim hiding in a hole; the dog grinning 'sardonically down at him, as if he thought it would be a good lark to drop the cartridge down on Jim'. Farcical action is pictorialized. The technique may derive from pantomime stage tradition and circus clowning; and from the black and white pen drawing which helped to popularise the *Bulletin*. It is hard to think of examples before Lawson which better exploit it through the medium of the written word.

Providence in the shape of a benevolent Lawson has the retriever arrive at the natural home of mates and bushmen, the pub, where he goes 'in under the kitchen, amongst the piles': a plausible, Hades-like moral setting in which

to find the sworn enemy of mateship and gregariousness, the troll of the Bush, ensconced in selfish solitary brooding. This particular *bête noire* is a *chien jaun,* a nameless, 'vicious, yellow mongrel cattle dog' . . . 'sulking and nursing his nastiness under there'. He sounds like the kind of *person* Lawson finds distasteful, a canine Barcoo Rot, 'A sneaking, fighting thieving canine, whom neighbours had tried for years' to put down.

At this stage a mock-epic assemblage of the clan or pack, a sort of grand dog Union, gathers at the pub, and to the fray:

> Nearly a dozen other dogs came from round all the corners and under the buildings—spidery, thievish, cold-blooded kangaroo dogs, mongrel sheep and cattle dogs, vicious black and yellow dogs—that skip after you in the dark, nip your heels, and vanish without explaining—and yapping, yelping small fry. They kept at a respectable distance round the nasty yellow dog, for it was dangerous to go near him when he thought he had found something which might be good for a dog or cat.

Lawson's dogs here are scruffy, unheroic witnesses, as are his unionists in other contexts; the 'one-eyed cattle dog' of this company is perhaps a counterpart of 'One-Eyed Bogan'. The parallel, however, is no more than a suggestion: the essential, and literally redeeming, characteristic of the dogs is that they stick together, gregariously. They are an audience within an audience to be viewed by the drinkers at the pub; both audiences will be viewed by the reader. The dogs, as the story's inner circle, will be required to engage in the ritual witnessing of the central providential purgation of evil and restitution of right. We are told that they are to remember this cautionary epic ritual all their lives.

> He sniffed at the cartridge twice, and was just taking a third cautious sniff when—It was very good blasting powder—a new brand that Dave had recently got up from Sydney; and the cartridge had been excellently well made. Andy was very patient and painstaking in all he did, and nearly as handy as the average sailor, with needles, twine, canvas, and rope.

The 'big bang' is narrated with a comedian's timing, but the amusing ironical understatement of 'it was very good blasting powder . . .', protracted within a return to the prosaics of Dave's and Andy's practical credentials, anticipates carefully the sensationally juxtaposed apocryphal exaggeration which insists on the incredible 'folk' status of the yarn:

> Bushmen say that the kitchen jumped off its piles and on again. When the smoke and dust cleared away. . . .

What is happening is that Lawson is insinuating into the narrative the rules and terms by which the Loaded Dog is to remain in our minds: he is to be remembered as legend, as the hero of a happy bush instance in which the hardness of things is overcome and destroyed, in which gre-

Lawson standing in front of his North Sydney house c. 1920.

gariousness actually triumphs and endures in the imagination. The dogs disperse to go home, to seek their ancestral birthplaces, to remember the lesson and nurse their cautionary wounds; but laughter is restored to all ordinary decent humanity, in hyperbolic quantities of segregated squawks, hysterics and shrieks.

Life resumes with this grand cautionary memory, and with universal good cheer, gregariously established; and the dog will finally be put back on the chain. But the triumph of Mateship incarnate, of the Loaded Dog as total gregariousness with Providence on its side, of myth as a lingering armament against the workaday reality which must be returned to, is celebrated by the ritual of his final victorious appearance before the reading audience:

> And the dog that had done it all, 'Tommy', the great, idiotic mongrel retriever, came slobbering round Dave and lashing his legs with his tail, and trotted home after him, smiling his broadest, longest and reddest smile of amiability.

That **'The Loaded Dog'** has become Australia's greatest bush nursery yarn is not only the serious compliment it deserves; it is also the enduring evidence that Lawson's literary instructions and gestures within the story, which require that it assume that kind of status as a popular yarn, have been heeded with an authenticating delight and affection.

Brian Matthews   (essay date 1983)

SOURCE: "Eve Exonerated: Henry Lawson's Unfinished Love Stories," in *Who Is She?*, edited by Shirley Walker, St. Martin's Press, 1983, pp. 37-55.

[*In the following essay, Matthews examines the role of women in Lawson's short stories.*]

In his harsh review of *While The Billy Boils* [found in *Henry Lawson Criticism*, 1972] A. G. Stephens makes so many damaging criticisms that it is easy to overlook one of the strangest and most quixotic of them, especially as it occurs in the last two sentences and is more or less a "throw-away". "Not the best", he suggests, "but the most promising [stories] are those which tell **'An Unfinished Love Story'**." "Here, for the first time, Lawson ceases to describe characteristics and starts to create characters." This is a rather gnomic pronouncement in several ways. What are the other stories which, it is implied, also tell an unfinished love story? Even interpreted as literally as possible, the remark could only refer to a very few stories: **"He'd Come Back"** perhaps; **"Bogg of Geebung"**, **"The Drover's Wife"**, **"Drifted Back"**, **"Some Day"** . . . ? These would at least be candidates but they are not at all obvious or even satisfactory choices. Outside of them, it's difficult to see what else might qualify. Moreover, even when Stephens's implied definition is stretched to breaking point, only two of these could remotely be regarded as creating characters rather than describing characteristics. The other three, **"He'd Come Back"**, **"Drifted Back"**

and **"Bogg of Geebung"** are, on the face of it, some of the slightest pieces in the whole collection. They are precisely the sort of thing to which Stephens takes energetic exception elsewhere in the same review: " . . . here a mouthful of salt, there one of pepper", "scrappy and disconnected", "detached sketches", "slight skeins", "half-a-hundred taps to strike half-a-dozen blows", etc.

What did Stephens see in **"An Unfinished Love Story"**? Probably not much. It is the last point he makes in his review and it has all the hallmarks of reviewer's twitch—that surrender to home-grown aphorism, slick generalization, neat phrase-turning or cavalier throwaway which casts little or no light on the work but makes the reviewer look rather good so long as no one reads too closely. Stephens's special trick here is to adapt the story's title neatly to his own apparent purpose, but in doing so he commits himself to a generalization about *While The Billy Boils* which will not stand a moment's scrutiny. And yet . . . *Something* caught Stephens's attention even if almost subliminally, and it was something more intriguing, more substantial than can be conveyed by the glib distinction between describing characteristics and creating characters. If Lawson is creating characters in **"An Unfinished Love Story"**, Brook is not one of them. He is a thoroughly recognizable figure—the world-hardened city man returning with only contempt or at best weary curiosity to his bush origins, who takes advantage (just exactly what advantage is not clear) of an inexperienced farm girl. There is something desolating and deathly about Brook. In a collection where names and characters recur constantly, Brook, whose "father was dead [and whose] other relations had moved away" is never heard of or mentioned in any other story. His return to the city where, "'after hours', he staggered in through a side entrance to the lighted parlour of a private bar" is like a grateful descent into a subworld. But Lizzie is much more interesting and perhaps it is only the relative mediocrity of the story, *pace* Stephens, that makes it seem extravagant to see her not as a new departure in Lawsonian characterization (which, as far as I can see, she is not) but as an example of a pattern the recognition of which is crucial to our understanding of Lawson's portrayal of women.

There is a certain passiveness about Lizzie, but it is more like what *The Dawn* referred to as feminine "passive force" than anything describable as submissiveness. Lizzie's demeanour is constantly characterized as "grave", "solemn", "reflective", "thoughtful", "pondering"; she deliberates and her essential innocence is communicated by this deliberation which is always suggesting that she has no ready-made reactions drawn from pleasant or bitter experience in life or love. Her answers are carefully and reasonably thought out; they are not recollections or interpretations of experience. Lawson skilfully enhances this impression of an innocent, unspoiled mind addressing complex and personal matters with untutored genuineness, by reporting much of what she decides and replies in short, scrupulously unambiguous sentences. This method has the added effect of making her appear silent, withdrawing, but also self-contained. We don't often, as it were, hear her voice:

She thought a while, and then she asked him if he was glad to go.

She thought a good long while, and then she said she was.

She reflected so as to be sure; then she said she hadn't.

She pondered over this for some minutes as a result of which she said she thought that she did.

Lizzie accepts Brook's attentions "with the greatest of gravity". After the first kiss, during which her lack of emotion gives way to "agitation", she "obeys" Brook's further urgings "just as a frightened child might". Her breathless confusion, her sudden torrent of words ("We must go now" / "We really must go now" / "I don't know—I can't promise" / "I don't like to promise" etc.) stand in pointed contrast to her earlier reticence and deliberation. Yet with all this, and despite her acceptance of Brook's urgent authority and ready rationalizations, Lizzie's "passive force" seems always more impressive, more substantial than Brook's persuasions: it is not that she won't be hurt by him but that she remains—no matter what the outcome of their insignificant encounter—on another plane from him, *profoundly* different. As for the outcome, it is always obvious Brook will abandon her: every move he has made has been both calculated and shallow and in response to her sense of "wonder" he feels only curiosity. When the truth can no longer be avoided, she shows "some emotion for the first time, or, perhaps the second—maybe the third time—in that week of her life". "They say Lizzie broke her heart that year", the story concludes, "but, then, the world does not believe in such things nowadays".

It seems, though, that Lawson does. If anything distinguishes the story it is the kind of love which it is within Lizzie's power to bestow: "the wonder in her expression—as if something had come into her life which she could not realize" has a transforming effect upon her presence in the story. Her innocence, which Lawson has been at pains to establish and which is not simple sexual inexperience or ignorance but a kind of pristineness (she has never loved anyone but she knows what love is), is enhanced by this incipient transformation. There is something utopian in this view of woman and the sense of utopianism disappointed informs the saddened conclusion as well as the ruthless realism of the portrait of Brook and his motives. Brook—and the disbelieving "world"—are Experience to her Innocence. Lawson seems to have a personal investment in the idealism of his portrait of Lizzie while, at the same time, sadly admitting and demonstrating that this is not the kind of world in which such idealism can long live untainted. He returns to the point in a sequel story, **"Thin Lips and False Teeth"**, in which Brook dreams of Lizzie during a feverish, hungover sleep:

> He began to dream pretty coherently. He thought he was back on the old selection where he had spent a holiday some two or three years previously. He was

sitting, in the twilight, on a log among some saplings, with the selector's niece—a country girl of nineteen—by his side . . . Next he was on his knees in the dirt before the log, with his arms folded on top of it, and his forehead resting on his wrists. He seemed crushed down by some horrible load of trouble. A light girlish hand was laid gently on his bowed head . . . She understood, then! She understood! The simple, innocent bush girl! Oh God!

It is Lizzie's brand of innocence here which makes her the healer of his ills. She has nothing of his experience of the world, she is a "country girl", only "nineteen", "girlish", "simple", "innocent", a "bush girl"—one could scarcely miss the emphasis—but she "understands". From some resource that is not reason, experience, the lessons of the years, she derives her healing knowledge. The source seems to be what Lawson sees as a uniquely feminine innocence.

Awake, Brook resolves to seek out this "something pure", the "rest and peace" represented by the vision of Lizzie; he will "breathe awhile in an atmosphere of innocence". But it is too late. Lizzie has already been tainted by the world—by his previous rejection—has already written him a pathetic, pleading and vulnerable letter, has already—as a result of having given in vain "the first love of her life"—married the oafish James Bullock. "How cruelly dull and dreary her life must be in such a place", Brook reflects, before retreating once more to the city.

Lizzie's story adds, in retrospect, further substance and some explanation to **"The Drover's Wife"**. The two stories are placed almost together in the second half of *While The Billy Boils,* separated—perhaps as a kind of momentary relief—only by **"Steelman's Pupil"**; so if the book is read in sequence it is almost inevitable that some connections between them will become evident. The drover's wife is well advanced along a road on which Lizzie has taken only the first fatal steps. She is long past bestowing her life's first love. "As a girl she built the usual castles in the air; but all her girlish hopes and aspirations have long been dead." She has known great hardship and "has few pleasures to think of"; she has learned so well to endure the loneliness she once hated that she would now "feel strange away from it". Her husband, who may "forget sometimes that he is married" is "careless, but a good enough husband". "She is glad when [he] returns, but she does not gush or make a fuss about it . . . She seems contented with her lot." Nevertheless, her plight is truly desperate and her tears at the end of the story are silent recognition of the knowledge that she is doomed forever to this life of successive crises, of loneliness, of gradual decline as her strength and her will to endure are eroded. Tommy's assurance that he "won't never go drovin'" only twists the knife. She knows, as does the reader, that he will go his own way, inevitably. "How cruelly dull and dreary her life [is] in such a place."

There are some important similarities between these two portrayals. While the nature of the bush and bush life is a powerful force in the imminent disintegration of both women, so also is the nature of man. Both are in one way or another abandoned by a man (the drover's wife has been alone for six months at the time the incident takes place); both have a husband who is at best "good enough"; both have suffered the destruction of innocent visions—the drover's wife's "girlish hopes and aspirations" are dead; Lizzie's sense of "wonder . . . as if something had come into her life which she could not realize" has been brutally dissipated, leaving her broken-hearted. Explicitly in **"An Unfinished Love Story"** and less obviously in **"The Drover's Wife"**, there is a suggestion that a crucial factor in the actual or imminent decline of the woman has been her involvement with an unworthy man. Even in **"The Drover's Wife"** such an inference is available and receives more than bare emphasis when Tommy makes his vow: the actual emptiness of his impulsive assurance, the certainty that he *will* go away, seems to point to something in the nature of things between men and women. Tommy's outburst is implicitly a criticism of his father as a man unworthy of the wife who endures so much because of his absence. But Tommy will do the same thing. In **"An Unfinished Love Story"**, of course, the unworthiness of Brook is unmistakable.

There aren't many other women in *While the Billy Boils* but Lizzie's small tragedy does seem to have a brief prefiguration in **"Some Day"**. Here, the redoubtable Mitchell tells of the "one little girl" he "was properly struck on":

> I think she was the best little girl that ever lived, and about the prettiest. She was just eighteen, and didn't come up to my shoulder; the biggest blue eyes you ever saw, and she had hair that reached down to her knees, and so thick you couldn't span it with two hands—brown and glossy—and her skin was like lilies and roses. Of course, I never thought she'd look at a rough, ugly, ignorant brute like me, and I used to keep out of her way and act a little stiff towards her; . . . I thought . . . she pitied me because I was such a rough, awkward chap. I was gone on that girl and no joking; and I felt quite proud to think she was a countrywoman of mine.

The pattern is the same: the man either is or, as in this case, fancies he is unworthy of the woman. She for her part is perfection. Lizzie was not physically striking but had an innocence, a pristine quality as I have called it, which Brook—belatedly—recognized as setting her absolutely apart. Edie Brown is physically beautiful with ideal attributes: lustrous hair, blue eyes, perfect skin fit for comparison with the lilies and roses of tradition; and so on. Her innocence, her unspoilt quality, is suggested by the twice-used term "*little* girl". The real or imagined unworthiness of the man in both **"An Unfinished Love Story"** and **"Some Day"** destroys the possibilities which the woman's transcendent qualities put within his reach. In each case, the woman is forced to make a declaration which is painful to her pride and natural modesty: she abandons momentarily and with difficulty what Lawson portrays as a natural demureness that comes not from subservience but from self-awareness, in an attempt to begin the process of realizing the potential she feels rightly or wrongly exists in the relationship. In each case the man rejects this plea and leaves her. Lizzie's life is ruined by it; we don't hear about Edie though the experience will clearly do her no good judging from the intensity of her reactions. And in each case it is, in the final judgment, "the world"—the nature of things between men and women—that is the problem: "the world does not believe in such things nowadays"; "Damn the world, say I", concludes Mitchell.

On the evidence of these three stories, together with the fleeting glimpses one gets in sketches and vignettes like **"Drifted Back"**, **"Bogg of Geebung"** and others, it begins to look as if, in Lawson's eyes, men are simply not worthy of women. He tends to place women on a pedestal or alternatively, portray them as if they have been treated shamefully if not so placed. Thus idealised, they are basically beyond the reach of men, either because the men are frankly no good or because in the presence of ideal womanhood, they think they are no good. When women leave their pedestals to enter the world of men, it is like leaving Eden: their innocence becomes permanently scarred by rejection or other kinds of ill-treatment; the vision of love either disintegrates completely or degenerates to mere propinquity; loving sacrifice collapses into a dogged endurance that might well appear more and more meaningless as time passes. There is, it seems, rarely a middle way. That, at any rate, is how it looks in *While The Billy Boils,* a work which, considering its deservedly classic status, has remarkably little to say about the relationships between men and women, or, more particularly, about women. Nevertheless, what it does say tends to linger in the mind: **"Some Day"** is the bitterest of the earliest group of Mitchell sketches; **"The Drover's Wife"** is a fascinating, endlessly challenging portrait; and as for Lizzie, it is not surprising she caught A. G. Stephens's jaundiced eye even if he didn't pause to work out what it was he had glimpsed. In these three pieces, and very tenuously elsewhere, Lawson begins to worry around the edges of a conflict—that between woman as ideal (because that is the way he inclines to see her) and a world, a reality, in which, as he clearly realizes, that ideal cannot continue to exist without some concessions, some deterioration from its pristine original. Men inhabit the evil world. Women—the women he values—are beyond it and are tarnished almost invariably by entering it. In *While The Billy Boils* this conflict is barely sketched; if he'd said no more on the matter it would have been impossible to proceed even this far. But in fact, he has a great deal more to say: in later books it becomes a major preoccupation and the pattern arguably visible in *While The Billy Boils* becomes familiar and entrenched.

On The Track and *Over the Sliprails* have much to say about women and the woman problem (or "the sex problem") mostly through the medium of Mitchell. There are discussions on the matter (**"Mitchell on Matrimony"**, or **"Mitchell on Women"**, **"Mitchell on the 'Sex' and Other 'Problems'"**—the very titles have a didactic ring) and cases and examples are canvassed (**"The Story of the Oracle"**, **"A Case for the Oracle"**). There are more ambitious, plotted stories (**"The Selector's Daughter"** and **"The Hero of Redclay"**) but these owe a great deal to standard melodramatic plots and much less to Lawson's own inspiration which, for various reasons, is faltering in both these books. (Even so, Ruth Wilson in **"The Hero of Redclay"** is "pretty, and ladylike, and [keeps] to herself" and "most of the single men . . . and some of the married ones . . . were gone on her" but could not bring themselves to approach her; she gives herself to Jack Drew who is unworthy of her but whom she hopes will reform and who finally leaves her rather than have her name besmirched. She never recovers from the shock and dies of brain fever: a familiar pattern grafted onto a borrowed situation.)

In the Mitchell sketches—which incidentally lose much of their punch and profundity as they become more diffuse and didactic—Mitchell grapples with the problem of understanding women and makes a poor fist of it. In **" . . . On Matrimony"** he decides that trying to understand women "would be only wasted brain power that might just as well be spent on the blackfellow's lingo; because by the time you've learnt it they'll be extinct, and woman'll be extinct before you've learnt her". The rest of his reflection, fragmented and even a little muddled, consists of musings on how a woman's inevitably domestic career might be made more comfortable by a thoughtful husband! In having Mitchell put these views, no matter how sympathetically, Lawson was at odds even then with much feminine (and not only feminist) opinion and entirely in conflict with his mother who, only a year before the composition date of this sketch, had thundered in *The Dawn* editorial:

> A woman's life should not be bounded by domesticity, not as a means of showing her dislike for that sphere, but for the highest good of those within it. The true mother gathers the riches of intellect, education, and ethics that she may administer them to those at home. [June, 1896]

But it is evident that Lawson could not have accommodated such views even had he been ideologically inclined to because he was haunted by the sense that once the woman became part of the man's world the result was a Fall. His vision of her was such that no man was worthy of her. Mitchell's meanderings in **" . . . On Matrimony"** are shot through with this assumption: "I don't think we ever understood women properly . . . I don't think we ever will"; " . . . a man changes after he's married . . . it comes like a cold shock to her and all her air-castles vanish"; " . . . a woman's love is her whole existence, while a man's love is only part of his". Equally, his listener, Joe, who is heading home to his wife, can tell a story only of subtle decline: "I might have made a better husband than I did" he admits "seriously and rather bitterly"; "I might have made her a good deal more happy and contented without hurting myself much". His stern avowal that he is "going to try and make up for it" when he gets back "this time" makes little headway against this prevailing impression of decay, an impression intensified by the final revelation that Mitchell, for all his apparent awareness of women's needs, lost his wife to "another kind of fellow".

In **"Mitchell on the 'Sex' And Other 'Problems'"** the muddle is much greater. This is partly because the "sex problem" is confusedly mixed up with several other unrelated matters, but also because, it seems, Mitchell is frustrated by the imponderability of the whole thing: " . . . the rotten 'sex-problem' sort of thing is the cause of it all", he says vaguely, attributing to the "sex problem" most of the world's political and social ills. Once again, there are strong indications of a "Fall" mentality, a strengthening conviction that when unworthy man does more than worship a good woman from afar, only decline and destructive complexities can result. Polygamy, monogamy, promiscuity—none has really provided an answer to the corrosion that eats into relationships between men and women:

> In the Bible times they had half a dozen wives each, but we don't know for certain how *they* got on. The Mormons tried it again, and seemed to get on all right till we interfered. We don't seem to be able to get on with one wife now . . . The "sex problem" troubled the Turks so much that they tried three. Lots of us try to settle it by knocking round promiscuously, and that leads to actions for maintenance and breach of promise cases and all sorts of trouble. Our blacks settle the "sex problem" with a club, and so far I haven't heard any complaints from them.

The last alternative is, both in its extremity and its underlying desire to have the whole problem somehow go away, as good an indication as any of a strain of desperation never far from the surface of this diatribe.

The lack of control in this sketch, its muddle and indecisiveness, may be attributed, of course, to a number of causes, but one of them is certainly the "problem" of the title. Lawson's own frustrations and confusions are evident: they are caused by his inability or, at best, profound reluctance to see any middle ground between Ideal Woman and the inevitably fallen and deteriorating state which follows upon that woman entering the world of reality, the evil world, the world of men. This is why the conclusion of the sketch, which might conceivably have been mildly humorous, is so significant: it makes explicit at last the anguished desire for simplicity, for a utopia of the sexes, which was recognizable to varying degrees in **"The Drover's Wife"**, **"An Unfinished Love Story"**, **"Some Day"** and **" . . . On Matrimony"**:

> Trying to find out things is the cause of all the work and trouble in this world. It was Eve's fault in the first place—or Adam's rather, because it might be argued that he should have been master. Some men are too lazy to be masters in their own homes, and run the show properly; some are too careless, and some too drunk most of their time, and some too weak. If Adam and Eve hadn't tried to find out things there'd have been no toil and trouble in the world today; there'd have been no bloated capitalists, and no horny-handed working men, and no politics, no free trade and protection—and no clothes. We'd have all been running round in a big Garden of Eden with nothing on, and nothing to do except loaf, and make love, and lark, and laugh, and play practical jokes on each other . . .
>
> That would have been glorious. Wouldn't it, Joe? There'd have been no "sex problem" then.

Here is simplicity—don't try to find out things—and utopia—"nothing to do except loaf and make love . . ."—and no sex problem at all. The fact that it is men's ills that are catalogued now comes as no surprise. The blame for the loss of Eden, traditionally seen as beginning with Eve, is transferred to Adam with a deliberation which draws to it maximum attention. It is man who is unworthy, it is man's transgressions and omissions from which evils flow. The fallen world is characteristically man's world. Eve has been exonerated.

In other stories of *On The Track* and *Over the Sliprails* a similar tendency is discernible though there are variations on the basic pattern. In **"No Place For A Woman"** the entry of the woman into the man's world is an actual, physical event: Mary, "a jolly girl when [he] married her", insists on joining Howlett in the remote bush. He, in common with so many of Lawson's men, resists her descent into his world—it's "no place for a woman". But she does come and decline and disaster follow. In **"The House That Was Never Built"** young Brassington marries "the brightest, best, good-heartedest, an' most lady-like little girl in the district". He arranges for a magnificent two-storey house to be built and ready for them on their return from the honeymoon. Only the best will do for her: "Do you think I'd ask that girl to live in a hut? . . . She ought to live in a palace!" But they are scarcely married when tragedy strikes. The young wife succumbs to the madness that is in the family. Brassington himself becomes a bush nomad intermittently obsessed with finishing the house as if somehow this completion would restore all the other losses. Then there is the hero of Redclay who cannot speak in his own defence as this would involve revealing he'd "taken advantage of a poor, unprotected girl because she loved him"; and The Oracle who "thinks that . . . most men would deceive women if they could" and who must agonizingly tear himself away from the "sort of girl that can love a man for six weeks and lose him forever, and yet go on loving him to the end of her life—and die with his name on her lips" in order to honour a commitment to another, lesser, woman. And there is Bob Baker (**"Telling Mrs Baker"**) whose wife was "a good little woman . . . a damned sight too good for the Boss". As much as any of Lawson's women, Mrs Baker is scarred by contact with an unworthy man. Only careful and concentrated lying by the two bushmen allows her to remember him as her "poor, dear, kind, dead husband", —an intensely ironic description, carefully arranged by Lawson, in which only the last adjective is true. The fact that he is dead is his only saving grace and, together with a complicated and desperate structure of lies and distortions, provides the only condition in which she can credibly remember him with affection. In another variation on the basic Lawsonian pattern, the woman is being shielded from the reality. Nothing has changed: the man is totally worthless, unworthy of her and represents only disaster and decline for her. But the bushmen reconstruct the real world so that, aided by some rationalizing on her part, she can regard him forever more as worthy, and their relationship as a successful one which only death interrupted. But it is all lies: ". . . he was a selfish man as far as his wife and children were concerned . . . they had

to suffer for it in the end" and, when he was in his death throes, he "cursed everything; he cursed his wife and children, and yelled that they were dragging him down to hell. He died raving mad. It was the worst case of death in the horrors of drink that I ever saw or heard of in the Bush".

Of course, much else can be said about these stories. The bush, the *place* hastens and exacerbates the rifts between men and women as Lawson sees it. It might not be so bad elsewhere, away from loneliness, hardship, uncertainty. It is, literally, no place for a woman. But it is obviously not *only* that which works the evil: the fault is in the nature of the universe and, above all, in the nature of man; not woman.

Lawson's finest work, *Joe Wilson,* is among other things a detailed working out of this pattern which comes to dominate his fiction whereever it deals seriously with love between man and woman. This quartet of stories begins with a clear statement of the "fall" theme: love begins to decline almost as soon as it is born:

> I think the happiest time in a man's life is when he's courting a girl and finds out for sure that she loves him and hasn't a thought for anyone else. Make the most of your courting days, you young chaps, and keep them clean, for they're about the only days when there's a chance of poetry and beauty coming into this life. Make the best of them and you'll never regret it the longest day you live. They're the days that the wife will look back to, anyway, in the brightest of times as well as in the blackest, and there shouldn't be anything in those days that might hurt her when she looks back. Make the most of your courting days, you young chaps, for they will never come again.

Innocence is replaced by Experience: "A married man knows all about it . . . if he's inclined that way, [he] has three times the chance with a woman than a single man has . . . he knows just how far he can go . . . he takes [women] and things for granted . . . And, when he knows all this, how much better or happier is he for it?" **"Joe Wilson's Courtship"**, edenic as it is at one level—with "the Possum's" beauty and innocence and Joe's stumbling transformation as he falls in love—is shot through with sombre reminders of inevitable decay, of "fall". The older Joe, who is narrating the story, pauses often to lament the failures and regrets that have burdened their lives since those days of courtship; and old Black, whose permission Joe must ask in order to marry Mary, sadly prefigures the decline that will inevitably be the lot of Joe and Mary, for all their present commitment to each other.

> "Well, what is it, Joe?"
>
> "I—well, the fact is, I want little Mary."
>
> He puffed at his pipe for a long time, then I thought he spoke.
>
> "What did you say, Boss?" I said.
>
> "Nothing, Joe," he said. "I was going to say a lot, but

it wouldn't be any use. My father used to say a lot to me before I was married."

I waited a good while for him to speak.

"Well, Boss," I said, "What about Mary?"

"Oh! I suppose that's all right, Joe," he said. "I—I beg your pardon. I got thinking of the days when I was courting Mrs Black."

Like other Lawson women before they descend into the world of men, there is something (and it does not have to be obvious physical beauty) which distinguishes Mary from all around her, which makes her seem unspoilt:

I saw a *little girl*, rather plump, with a complexion like a New England or Blue Mountain girl, or a girl from Tasmania or from Gippsland in Victoria. Red and white girls were very scarce in the Solong district. She had the biggest and brightest eyes I'd seen round there, dark hazel eyes, as I found out afterwards, and bright as a "possum's". No wonder they called her Possum. I forgot at once that Mrs Jack Barnes was the prettiest girl in the district. [my emphasis]

Like other Lawson men at this point of decision, Joe feels unworthy and therefore reluctant:

. . . somehow, whenever a girl took any notice of me I took it for granted that she was only playing with me, and felt nasty about it.

. . .

"My wife knows little 'Possum'," said Jack. "I'll get her to ask her out to our place and let you know."

I reckoned that he wouldn't get me there then, and made a note to be on the watch for tricks.

. . .

"What did you tell her?"

"Oh, nothing in particular. She'd heard all about you before."

"She hadn't heard much good, I suppose," I said.

"Well, that's true as far as I could make out."

. . .

. . . I reckoned that I was a fool for thinking for a moment that she might give me a second thought, except by way of kindness.

But unlike so many of his predecessors in Lawson's fiction, Joe does win Mary. The stories that follow the courtship anatomize their life together and represent certainly Lawson's most extended attempt—but in some ways his *only* real attempt—to portray in detail and to understand

the middle way that lies between, on the one hand, an ideal of woman, woman "on a pedestal", for whom no man is worthy and, on the other, the inevitably disastrous result of that woman's descending into a world of unworthy men. It is not only a near-novel; it aspires to be, at last, a finished love story. Joe and Mary function in "the world"—that world that Mitchell damns and that doesn't believe in such things as heart-broken women. But the pattern of their relationship, though much elaborated in comparison with earlier stories and sketches, remains quite recognizable. Their marriage, despite moments of tenderness and intimacy, is a process of decay and decline. This is partly and powerfully due to the nature of the bush in which they live which implacably wears away at their resilience, their mutual tolerance and love and their sense of meaning; but it is also the fault of that larger "world" in which men, including Joe, are simply unworthy of and unable properly to love and cherish women like Mary. His weakness for drink, his indecision, his stubborn pride, his spurning of Mary's "passive force", his rejection of that strange "understanding" which Brook, in his dream, saw in Lizzie—all these are contributors to their failure. (It is significant that, when "not many years after" he stands "by the bed where Mary lay, white and still", he repeats over and over to her, "I'll give in, Mary—I'll give in".) Their moments of closest understanding and their important reconciliations are not so much the results of a process of relationship in which bonds strengthen and can withstand pressures, as ecstatic but necessarily momentary returns to their own Eden—that time of courtship when life was uncomplicated and there was a chance for poetry and beauty:

. . . I think we got to understand each other better that night. And at last Mary said, "Do you know, Joe, why, I feel tonight just—just like I did the day we were married."

And somehow I had that strange, shy sort of feeling too.

. . . When the train swung round the horn of the crescent of hills in which Haviland lay there wasn't any need for acting. There was the old homestead, little changed, and as fair as it seemed in those faraway days . . . when that lanky scamp, Joe Wilson, came hanging round after "Little Possum", who was far too good for the likes of him . . .

There was no need for humbugging now. The trouble was to swallow the lumps in my throat. Mary . . . was staring out with wide-opened eyes, and there were tears in them . . . Then suddenly she turned from the window and looked at me, her eyes wide and brimming . . .

I jumped up and sat down by her side, and put my arm round her; she put her arms round my neck and her head down on my chest, and cried . . .

It seems to me true to say of Lawson's fictional women that they "become not so much a complementary sex as a separate species" and if, as I think is also true, "Lawson's treatment of women lacks sexual intensity" (in comparison, say, with Barbara Baynton who is superior to Lawson in this respect alone) this may well be importantly due to the fact that his particular presentation of them rarely allows of their being for long, or even at all, in clearly sexual contexts. [Both of these quotations are from Vincent Buckley's introduction to Brian Matthews' *The Receding Wave,* 1972.] They are either idealized—creatures in comparison with whom men feel, fancy themselves to be or indeed are, unworthy—or they enter into the world of men, the real and un-ideal world, only at the price of decay and decline precisely because they have thrown in their lot with the unworthy.

Why Lawson should have developed this view of women in his fiction is a question which can no doubt be answered in a number of ways. It does, however, seem to me consistent with his weakness for the romantic and the melodramatic. The impulse to put women on a pedestal is both romantic—because it seeks to turn the flesh and blood human being into some sort of vision—and melodramatic—because it removes her from the real and complicated world into the realm of starkly opposed good and bad. Such idealization is above all a simplifying move: if woman will only stay on her pedestal she can be properly adored without the necessity of coping with the complexities of relationship, the difficulties of understanding her, and oneself in relation to her. "Trying to find out things is the cause of all the work and trouble . . ." Lawson was constantly wanting woman on a pedestal while just as constantly conceding that she could not and would not stay there, reality dictated this. Thus, so many of his women are portrayed initially in idealized terms and yet come to grief and decay and loss and rejection subsequently. He sees that they must "enter" the real world but that entry, as far as he is concerned, can lead only to their being tainted. His own behaviour towards both Mary Cameron and Bertha Bredt was intensely idolizing and idealizing, scarcely allowing the relationships their calmer, more mundane moments. Like Brook in his dream of Lizzie, Lawson seems to have seen Bertha as healer, restorer of peace and innocence:

> Rest, for your eyes are weary, girl—you have
>   driven the worst away—
> The ghost of the man that I might have been is
>   gone from my heart to-day;
> We'll live for life and the best it brings till our
>   twilight shadows fall;
> My heart grows brave, and the world, my girl, is a
>   good world after all.

It is just possible also that Lawson took some of his idealizing tendency where women were concerned from his mother. Louisa certainly had a splendid vision of the role women might play, once liberated to do so, in the revolutionizing of political and social life. But her ideals were above all credible, eminently realizable; indeed, *The Dawn*—as we might expect—had no time whatsoever for the kind of idealization which immobilized women on a pedestal:

The man who talks of women as darling angels, offers this exaggerated verbiage, which no one believes, in lieu of fair recognition, just as he who talks of chivalry offers a temporary homage to hide a permanent robbery of individual liberty, doffing his hat to the sex in general but keeping his wife well under his thumb. Women are not angels but human creatures, and they need human recognition. They cannot do without this Earth and the men who are upon it, therefore they need the same kind of justice as men do.

If Lawson's impulse to idealize women owes anything at all to his mother's vision of the political and social revolution which she saw women as capable of spearheading, it totally lacks Louisa's dynamism and earthiness. Where Lawson's fiction deals in any way substantially and seriously with women—and over the whole of his work from the almost womanless *While The Billy Boils* through to the preoccupation with the "sex problem", women play relatively little part—the pattern is almost invariable: he would prefer them to "do without this Earth" and especially to do without "the men who are upon it".

Expecting impossibilities of women, Lawson was doomed to disappointment. Descending into the world of men his women, even the best and most admirable of them, become like men. It is a hallmark of Lawson's enduring, slowly disintegrating women that they lose their femininity, they become rather masculine. The drover's wife wears her husband's trousers to fight the fire and is attacked, in mistake, by the dog; her "surroundings are not favourable to the development of the 'womanly' or sentimental side of nature". Mrs Spicer wears "an old coat of her husband's" and is "gaunt and flat-chested . . . her face . . . 'burnt to a brick'". It is not the bush alone that causes these ravages: Mrs Aspinall who lives in Jones's Alley, is

a haggard woman. Her second husband was supposed to be dead, and she lived in dread of his daily resurrection. Her eldest son was at large, but, not being yet sufficiently hardened in misery, she dreaded his getting into trouble . . . She could buy off the son for a shilling or two and a clean shirt and collar, but she couldn't purchase the absence of the father at any price—*he* claimed what he called his "conzugal rights" as well as his board, lodging, washing and beer. She slaved for her children and nag-nag-nagged them ever-lastingly . . . She had the spirit of a bullock. Her whole nature was soured.

It is not only the bush, not only the remorseless city and slums that produce these effects. It is, just as importantly, life with men. Even the frankly "bad" women in Lawson's fictional world are, most often, originally the victims of men: the Giraffe's comment on the prostitutes in Bourke is typical: "I s'pose they're bad, but I don't s'pose they're worse than men has made them."

Henry Lawson's love stories are almost always unfinished: communication between man and woman always breaks down, or often enough, scarcely begins. The Giraffe may *possibly* be heading for marital bliss; *perhaps* Jack Moonlight will have a successful reunion with Hannah. But the picture overall is grim: men and women stand little chance of successful, sustained loving communion because Lawson seems unable to shake himself free of the conviction that such involvement represents for the woman a descent, an entry into a kind of world which can only undermine and possibly destroy her. No continuity, no "finish" is possible in his depictions of women encountering men, because the inevitable "fall" that is the fate of women entering the world of men breaks off relationship, sours and destroys it.

That the image of woman which develops in Lawson's fiction—woman as an idealized figure which contact with man corrupts—owed something to a growing tendency towards self-hatred in Lawson himself, seems quite likely. His haunted fear of failure and accelerating sense that a life over which he had never exercised effective control was running more and more out of hand, enters increasingly into his fiction in the form of male characters who "damn the world", turn to drink, make a virtue of failure and who deceive, disappoint or irremediably wound their loyal women. By 1909, Lawson's conviction of personal unworthiness, his hatred of self, had developed to the point where he adopted a pseudonym (John Lawrence) and began writing and, on occasions apparently, conversing in his own version of Scots dialect. This whole process in Lawson's life and his fiction comes to a pathetic culmination in **"The Man Who Drowned"**, in which Lawrence/Lawson returns from the depths of failure and degradation, literally a "new man", clear of eye, steady of hand, once more the brilliant writer. It is a desperate fantasy that Lawson so obviously wished would come true, in which the old, failed and hated self is cast off in favour of one more acceptable. The story not only emphasizes the extent of the revulsion Lawson was feeling against himself, but also testifies to the persistence of his views about the unworthiness of men generally in their relationships with women and the impossibility of such relationships with women ever prospering or flowering:

> John Lawrence was separated from his wife, but that should go without saying: a mere unimportant detail—a matter of very minor importance. Except amongst the working people, married folk live less and less together every year: and they'll end up by not living together at all—only marrying and getting separated and divorced for the excitement or the notoriety of the thing. And perhaps getting re-married, re-separated, and re-divorced, until the novelty wears, and they have leisure to think of the happy homes they might have had. It was John Lawrence's fault, of course (though he was a teetotaller at the time). It always is.

Despite the amazing (and, from the point of view of Lawson's fantasies of regeneration, embarrassing) nature of John Lawrence's transformation, his blame with respect to the failure of his marriage is never questioned. "It was John Lawrence's fault . . . It always is", is meant of course to strike a note of heavy, tolerant irony: but its essential truth within the story's context is not mitigated. Lawrence (and Lawson) accepts his blame: the estranged wife is referred to always with respect, even a kind of residual affection. In contrast to the sailors who are uneasy about the loyalty of their wives and sweethearts, John Lawrence is "content",

knowing his "practical little wife" notwithstanding the gulf now between them would not precipitately deem him dead; and he reserves implicit praise for "the wife of the Governor General who was the only one to visit Mrs Lawrence" as against those who "thought little or nothing of her being . . . too much taken up with their own littlenesses and dignities . . ." In the moment of his triumph, John Lawrence asks that the fund money be turned over to his wife and children in clear expiation for those times, recorded earlier in the story, when he was gaoled for failure to pay maintenance. In this story, even as Lawson fantasizes about the shedding of a hated and unworthy self, he portrays a man who was unworthy of the woman he married and who, despite regeneration, remains so. **"The Man Who Drowned"** is one extreme of the self-hatred that grew in Lawson over a long period and which may do something towards explaining the invariable unworthiness of his male characters in so many situations but especially in their relationships with women.

> **That the image of woman which develops in Lawson's fiction—woman as an idealized figure which contact with man corrupts—owed something to a growing tendency towards self-hatred in Lawson himself, seems quite likely.**
>
> —*Brian Matthews*

In his later years, Lawson said and wrote some venomous things about women: **"The She Devil"**—an unpleasant diatribe about "a national danger, a national crime . . . a national shame"—and his preface to Vance Marshall's *The World of The Living Dead,* in which he urges amendment of the laws "to provide against" the woman "with the glib, lying tongue", hysterical women and "The Great Australian Nag" are only two of the more obvious examples. To a large extent, however, these outbursts proceeded from specific, personal grievances associated with his separations from Bertha, the final judicial separation (June 1903) and his several imprisonments thereafter for failure to pay alimony and maintenance. Even at his most vindictive his basic attitude towards women in general remains adulatory. He resolves the potential contradiction (idolizing women, putting them on a pedestal, yet attacking them as "she devils") by simply discriminating between womanhood *per se* and certain evil aberrations:

> . . . I must have it understood that this article is no slur on the women of Australia as a body. I don't suppose there is any man in the country who admires and respects pure womanhood more than I do.

Even in sketches as late as the documentary/fictional meanderings based on his time in the Yanco Irrigation Area, he continues to portray women as special, as creatures to be looked up to, creatures with capacities, awarenesses and merits which men can and should admire but which, in the nature of things, they can never emulate: "they are very brave, and very strong in faith, and very kind and very gentle in illness or trouble". Falling "in love" with Jim Grahame's two and a half year old daughter, Bonnie, Lawson characteristically reminds us that he is unworthy of her: she was "a child who believed I was everything I should have been". Her innocent and lovingly meant gift of three white feathers has, of course, a sinister and insulting connotation in 1916: the two images—the unspoilt and loving girl, the unregenerate, unworthy man wryly accepting an ambiguous and yet sadly appropriate gift— summarize, somehow, all Lawson's portrayals of woman, and of man in self-exile from her in the sure knowledge of his own unworthiness.

. . .

> The wife is well. She's a gem. Matrimony is good and right, but . . . Oh, Jack! "it plays hell with your notions of duty"—to your chums.
>
> And what were our notions of duty, in the abstract? Never mind, Jack. I think the creed of the Chaps, Coves, and Fellows is the grandest of all.

So wrote Lawson to Brereton from New Zealand (April 1897). The letter was probably dashed off (it was certainly overdue) and shouldn't be burdened with a second glance. Yet, like A. G. Stephens's throwaway aside with which this essay opened, this concluding paragraph of the letter is curiously revealing, irresistably arresting. All Lawson's women are gems. And the creed of the chaps, coves and fellows is so earth-bound, so shot through with failures, regrets, shames and self-blame, that aspiration towards the pure world of gems is scarcely possible, and if persisted with, results only in the dulling of the gem.

Lawson's alcoholic lifestyle:

If he drank spirits he became belligerent, and quite savage about men like A. G. Stephens; if he drank beer he became morose and sentimental. The next day, just to reassure himself and prove to his wife and the world what manner of man he was, he would be up with the dawn to write feverishly in his room. On days when the hangover was of such massive proportions that creative work became an impossibility, and the only respite from pain and remorse seemed to be an act which would postpone the onset of the hangover, he still, as in previous years, returned to the *Bulletin* office on the morning after to make a pathetic plea to J. F. Archibald for a sixpence or a shilling. Archibald, a man of great compassion, would say: 'Tchk-tchk. This is terrible! For God's sake try and pull yourself together. (Giving him enough money to keep a hangover at bay.) Get a good drink and go home and try to eat something. Get your wife to get you some broth or something. Stay in over Sunday and bring it to me on—No. Send your wife in, and keep away from the office next week.' And Archibald would wander over to the shop where he bought his bait for the weekend fishing he loved, his thumb dredging his waistcoat pocket to find enough money to pay for prawns, or squid or yellow-tail, while Lawson scampered to the watering house for the one thing he believed in his madness would make him feel better.

Manning Clark, in In Search of Henry Lawson, *MacMillan, 1978.*

John Barnes (essay date 1986)

SOURCE: An introduction to *The Penguin Henry Lawson: Short Stories,* edited by John Barnes, Penguin Books, 1986, pp. 1-16.

[*In the excerpt below, Barnes traces the evolution of Lawson criticism and provides a laudatory assessment of his achievement as a short story writer.*]

Story-telling is an ancient art, but the idea of the short story as a distinct literary form is comparatively recent. Today the term 'short story' covers a range of possibilities, and we are less likely than the readers of a century ago to regard the short story as the poor relation of the novel. There perhaps still lingers a suspicion that the fiction writer without a novel to his credit has, so to speak, failed to measure up to the real test of creativity, no matter how fine that writer's short fiction may impress us as being. And in our assessment of the achievements of a short-story writer, we incline perhaps to regard most highly those stories which best bear comparison with novels. It is certainly true that critical discussion of Henry Lawson's prose writing has been coloured by the assumption—sometimes unconscious—that in being 'only a short-story writer' he was less than if he had been a novelist. . . .

In Lawson's lifetime a combination of factors tended to cloud perception of what was distinctive about his writing. There was the general expectation that as he matured he would write a novel (or a sequence of connected stories), a 'big' work, no matter how commonplace, being regarded as of a higher order of creation than a piece of short fiction. The prevailing taste was for short stories with a strong narrative interest—'story' in the simplest sense—and Lawson was most highly praised by local critics for those works in which he came nearest to the conventional. But probably the most influential factor was Lawson's standing as a national figure. 'Henry Lawson is the voice of the bush, and the bush is the heart of Australia', proclaimed A. G. Stephens of the *Bulletin,* when reviewing his first book, ***Short Stories in Prose and Verse,*** in 1895, and that view of his uniquely representative status is still potent, at least for older readers. For some of us, our responses to Lawson's writing still tend to get mixed up with feelings about 'the real, the true Australia'. Manning Clark's recent *In Search of Henry Lawson* (which he describes as 'a hymn of praise to a man who was great of heart') states the basic proposition on which the 'Lawson legend' rests: 'Australia is Lawson writ large'. Clark's book shows just how strong the romantic conception of the 'national voice' remains, at least where Lawson is concerned.

The historical function of Lawson's writing is undeniable. At a time of burgeoning nationalism, he was stimulated by a notion of 'Australianness', and was himself a source of stimulus to others. In his stories where he writes as one of the bush people he describes, Lawson impressed his contemporaries as a reporter and observer, opening their eyes to the reality around them. Reviewing *While the Billy Boils in* 1896, Price Warung clearly had reservations about the literary quality of the stories, but no doubt about their documentary value. 'We do not yet, we Australians, know our country', he wrote, going on to praise Lawson's knowledge and concluding, 'Whatever else may be said of it, certain it is that this book must make Australians know their Australia better'. Another reviewer—like Price Warung, inclined to devalue Lawson's stories as being no more than 'photographs'—thought that they would help 'to correct false and create fresh impressions of Australian life among all who are amiably or earnestly interested in learning what our National Characteristics are and towards what they may be tending'. Yet another found 'the genuine Australia' in *While the Billy Boils* and (in the rhetoric to which Lawson's admirers were prone) wrote: 'Of this Australia Henry Lawson is the poet, the prophet, the singer, and the portal-keeper of its temple'. By the end of his life, the belief that Lawson was 'the poet prophet of Australia' (in the words of his aristocratic benefactor, Earl Beauchamp) had taken firm root, and more and more in the years that followed it affected how he was read.

The historical function of Lawson's writing is undeniable. At a time of burgeoning nationalism, he was stimulated by a notion of 'Australianness', and was himself a source of stimulus to others.

—John Barnes

The 'Lawson legend' was not groundless—legends seldom are—but it was a partial and distorting view of a writer of individual gifts, and it fostered an uncritical attitude which discouraged intelligent scrutiny of what he had written. Lawson's writing did strike his contemporaries with the effect of a revelation. What he offered, though, was not an inclusive transcript of bush life but an intense and narrow personal vision. His famed knowledge of the bush was comparatively limited, his direct experience of the Outback being confined to that one soul-searing trip to Bourke and Hungerford which lasted in all less than a year. The precision of detail and the feeling of intimacy with which life in the countryside was portrayed in his writing led some of the early readers to think of him as primarily concerned with describing various phases of Australian life. Very soon, though, there were objections that his work did not portray the whole truth about the bush or about Australia in general. The argument was really beside the point. As Frank Sargeson—himself a fine short-story writer who learnt from Lawson—once pointed out, Lawson was not a realist, in the usual sense of the word: 'He looked at the desolation of the Australian inland, and he saw his own interior desolation'. Lawson, he went on to say, 'uses naturalistic phenomena to express his inward-looking vision'.

This 'inward-looking vision' was very different from the 'gospel of mateship' with which Lawson has been identified, on the basis of a selective reading of his work. True, mateship was a phenomenon of the bush life, and Lawson writes about it often. True also, the impulse to idealise the facts of mateship, and to sentimentalise relationships between men, is there from the beginning (his very first story—of a father and son—is entitled **'His Father's Mate'**). But the insistence on the value of mateship as the most important human relationship is an aspect of Lawson's decline. *Children of the Bush,* which appeared in 1902, marks the turning point in Lawson's artistic life. It contains a number of stories in which mateship is celebrated, stories like **'Send Round the Hat'**, which are heart-warming and quite lacking in the hard-edged authenticity of the best stories in *While the Billy Boils*. The bush life which Lawson now lovingly evokes is a touched-up 'photograph', in which sentiment predominates over emotion. Lawson himself, one might say, could not face reality as he had once done, and retreated into sentimental re-writing of his own achievement. Indeed, one could say that his early collapse contributed to falsification of what he had done in the short creative period of his life.

To those who saluted Lawson as 'the voice of Australia', literary considerations were of secondary importance, and the struggling artist was hardly discernible in the almost mystically conceived National Writer. A most common formulation in the obituary articles was that Lawson was the 'Poet of Australia', a kind of antipodean Burns, whose writings were a treasure house of Australianness. When half a century later Colin Roderick collected Lawson's verse in three substantial volumes, it was apparent how little of it could be considered poetry. The essential criticism had been made as long ago as 1902 by Edward Garnett, the most perceptive critic Lawson encountered, when he wrote: 'Like a voice speaking to you through a bad telephone, the poems convey the speaker's meaning, but all the shades of original tone are muffled, lost or hidden'. There would be general agreement now that Lawson's verse is marginal to his achievement, thus reversing the preference of his own day.

However, although we may now claim that we are no longer blinkered in our view of Lawson—at least, not to the extent that previous generations were—we can hardly claim to have seen him steadily, and certainly not whole. Anyone looking over the quite extensive body of critical comment on Lawson must be struck by the almost patronising way in which his work—especially his prose work—was discussed, even by his admirers, before A. A. Phillips's essay in 1948 argued the case for Lawson as a craftsman. Although Phillips's own acceptance of the essential outline of the Lawson legend did close off lines of speculation that he might profitably have followed, his perception that Lawson was a conscious innovator—aiming at a minimum of 'plot'—directed attention to the previously neglected formal aspects of the stories. Brian Matthews effected a further reorientation of Lawson studies when in the first full-length critical study of the stories, *The Receding Wave* (1972), he argued that Lawson's decline was not mainly the result of personal circumstances but had its origin in the very nature of his talent. Odd though it may seem, considering how much has been written about Lawson, it is only since Matthews's book that the stories have begun to receive sustained critical attention. Scholarly study has now revealed aspects of the man and his writing that hitherto were hidden or ignored. There is as yet no adequate biography, but biographical accounts have now got beyond anecdote and admiration, and an illuminating Freudian study by French academic Xavier Pons has identified psychological issues with which Lawson's eventual biographer will have to deal.

'I don't know about the merit or value of my work', wrote Lawson in '"Pursuing Literature" in Australia', a bitter *apologia* in the *Bulletin* in 1899, 'all I know is that I started a shy, ignorant lad from the bush, under every disadvantage arising from poverty and lack of education, and with the extra disadvantage of partial deafness thrown in.' He did not exaggerate the disadvantages, but they can be seen in another light as not being disadvantages at all, as far as the writer was concerned. Many have sought to imitate Lawson's simplicity of style, but no other Australian writer has managed so well to create that effect of natural, unaffected Australian speech, which is Lawson's hallmark. A few years of elementary education in 'the old bark school', taught by a teacher whose weak points were 'spelling, English grammar and singing', may not seem much of a preparation for a writing career; and Lawson was always rather defensive on the point, easily hurt by the criticisms of his 'cultured critics'. But though his spelling was always shaky and he suffered from feelings of inferiority, Lawson's very lack of education meant that his style was largely formed on the speech of the people amongst whom he lived. He had learnt to read from *Robinson Crusoe,* and Defoe's plain style undoubtedly had some influence on the formation of his own. Lawson read little throughout his life and took little from what he did read. The absence of pretension, and of self-conscious literariness, enabled Lawson to write in a genuinely simple style. He had confidence in the vernacular as literary language (most other Australian writers have thought it suitable only for humorous effects) because he knew no other. His prose at its best shows him acutely aware of tone and inflection as registers of feeling in the voice. His deafness may have shut out a great deal in his adult life, while preserving uncorrupted the memory of voices heard in childhood.

Asked by an aspiring writer what was the best early training for a writer, Hemingway replied, 'an unhappy childhood'. Lawson might well have given the same answer. More important than the vivid memories of places and people was the intense loneliness he felt. He was the eldest child of a foreign father and an Australian-born mother. His father was Nils Larsen, a Norwegian sailor who had left his ship to join the gold rushes in 1855. His mother, Louisa, who changed the family name when registering her son's birth in 1867, was the dominant parent in the marriage: a remarkable woman of great determination, she had literary talent and encouraged her son to write. Lawson's parents were the models for the couple in **'A Child in the Dark, and a Foreign Father'**, though it

would be a mistake to take the story as straight autobiography. In his 'Fragment of Autobiography', a meandering and patchy account of his early years, Lawson touched on the misery of his childhood, but shied away from looking closely at the family situation:

> Home life, I might as well say here, was miserably unhappy, but it was fate—there was no one to blame. It was the result of one of those utterly impossible matches so common in Australia. I remember a child who, after a violent and painful scene, used to slip out in the dark and crouch down behind the pig-stye and sob as if his heart would break.

A weak, dreamy boy, whose aunts always said that he should have been a girl, and whom town boys called 'Barmy Harry', Lawson knew periods when he seemed to live on his own: 'when Mother and brothers, but not so often Father, seemed to go completely out of my life'. Later in the autobiography he remarks: 'As I grew the feeling of loneliness and the desire to be alone increased'. The partial deafness which afflicted him from the age of nine added to his isolation. 'I wasn't a healthy-minded, average boy', says Joe Wilson (in **'Joe Wilson's Courtship'**), and there is no doubt that he speaks for Lawson.

The Lawson family was broken up in 1883 when the parents separated. Henry and the other children went with their mother to Sydney, where she became a prominent advocate of women's rights, founding *Dawn,* the first Australian feminist journal in 1888, and publishing her son's first book, **Short Stories in Prose and Verse,** in 1894. Lawson's early years had been spent in the countryside around Mudgee in New South Wales, where his father had variously been a prospector, selector, and carpenter, but from 1883 onward Sydney became his home base. Lawson's life was never settled for very long, but it was always to Sydney that he returned after his various trips—to back o' Bourke, to Western Australia (twice), to New Zealand (twice), and to England. These journeys brought him fresh 'copy' (Lawson favoured the journalist's term though he did not have the journalist's approach to writing) in the shape of new impressions, but they did not fundamentally alter his vision of things. The impulse to write grew out of the keenness of his youthful feeling. Looking back late in his life, Lawson knew that he had lost the power he had possessed when he began to write as 'the lonely boy who felt things deeply and wrote with his heart's blood'.

The *Bulletin,* begun in Sydney in 1880, invited contributions of verse and prose from its readers, and it was here that Lawson was first published, in 1887. The editor and part-founder, J. F. Archibald, was an important figure in Lawson's life—the first, and perhaps the most decisive of the father-figures on whom Lawson depended. A gifted journalist, his attitude towards writing was summed up in the phrase he regularly used: 'Boil it down'. For his part, Lawson had no guiding notions of 'style', and although the influence of Dickens, Bret Harte, and later Mark Twain, is there in some of his stories, he was not apprenticed to any literary master. Archibald encouraged his own natural instinct as a writer, with advice which Lawson remembered as follows:

> Every man has at least *one* story; some more. Never write until you have something to write about; *then* write. Write and re-write. Cut out every word from your copy that you can possibly do without. Never strain after effect; and, above all, always avoid anticlimax.

Lawson's comment was 'I think I did all that naturally from the first', and there is no reason to doubt him. In the same passage, Lawson offers a rare insight into his thinking on form:

> Archibald in those days, preferred the short story to the short sketch. I thought the short story was a lazy man's game, second to 'free' verse, compared with the sketch. The sketch, to be really good, must be good in every line. But the sketch-story is best of all. ('Three or Four Archibalds and the Writer')

In modern usage the term 'short story' embraces what Lawson and his contemporaries called 'the sketch'. During the twentieth century writers have greatly extended the range of the short story to the point where the 'story' has become inessential. Lawson's preference for the 'sketch-story' aligns him with those modern writers since Chekhov who have aimed at suggestiveness rather than explicitness. Introducing a collection of short stories, *Capajon*, in 1933, Edward Garnett praised Hemingway's 'amazing power of suggesting more in three pregnant words than other authors do in ten', but shrewdly observed in passing that 'Lawson gets even more feeling observation and atmosphere into a page than does Hemingway'.

Apart from Garnett, however, the critics of Lawson's time failed almost completely to appreciate the artistic worth of his sketches. Worse than that, Stephens in his *Bulletin* review of *While the Billy Boils* was dismissive of the 'fragmentary impressions' which he thought could have been written as 'a single plotted, climaxed story which would make a permanent mark'. It was a line of criticism which disturbed Lawson and continued to worry him over the years. Stephens was right in judging the collection to be very uneven—the same point could be made about all the collections of Lawson's stories—but his review, in effect, advised Lawson to write against the grain of his talent. Though Lawson responded by telling his publisher, George Robertson, 'My line is writing short stories and sketches in prose and verse. I'm not a novelist', and asking, 'If you were a builder, would you set the painters to do the carpentering?', the criticism shook his self-confidence and discouraged him from experimenting further with sketches or sketch-stories. Over the next six years Lawson several times persuaded himself that he was capable of writing a novel, and his failures added to the depression and despair that finally broke him. . . .

In Lawson's writing life two journeys mark important stages: the first was to Bourke and Hungerford in 1892,

returning to Sydney in the following year, and the second was to England in 1900, returning in 1902.

Of the stories written before Lawson went out to Bourke, . . . [two] are among his most admired works. **'The Drover's Wife'**, written when he was only twenty-five, was the first in which he found an individual voice. It is more of a sketch than a story (in Lawson's terms), the anecdote of the snake being used to provide a framework within which he evokes the woman's life. What could have been exploited for its external interest, and presented as sensational or farcical (as it would have been by other *Bulletin* writers of the day), becomes typical of the daily threat to existence. Much discussion of the story has concentrated on the ending, which many readers have thought sentimental. Phillips implicitly defends Lawson against the charge in the course of demonstrating his art, asking what naive writer would have resisted the temptation to put an epithet before 'bush' in the final sentence. The point is well made. The writing is firm, restrained, economical; and the two adjectives which are used in that final sentence—the woman's breast is 'worn-out' and the daylight is 'sickly'—show a considerable literary tact. Far from laying it on thick, Lawson attempts to establish the emotional significance of the moment with minimal effects. This concluding tableau of mother and son is not designed to wring further pathos out of the situation, but to give it a symbolic dimension. The boy's attempt to comfort his mother—'Mother, I won't never go drovin'; blast me if I do!'—brings into focus feelings that inhere in the predicament of the drover's wife. The boy is dependent for his survival on the mother he tries to comfort; he cannot replace the absent father and husband; his 'manly' promise to his mother, with its implication that his father was weak in submitting to necessity and leaving the family, reveals his child's vulnerability and helplessness. If **'The Drover's Wife'** is susceptible to a sentimental interpretation, it is partly because the central image of mother and son—I should emphasise that I see the final scene as aiming at something more complex and more subtle than is achieved in the supposed climax of the killing of the snake—is perilously close to cliché in its conception, and throughout the sketch Lawson's notion of the woman is too close to the stereotype of the bush heroine.

Yet **'The Drover's Wife'** is an impressive work to come from a young inexperienced writer. Along with **'The Bush Undertaker'**, it can be accommodated by the conventional view of Lawson as the sympathetic chronicler of bush life, but such an approach does not do justice to either story. In both Lawson is attempting—not wholly successfully—to create images which will define and express feelings he would have been incapable of analysing or explaining. The old hatter muttering 'I am the rassaraction' over the grave is cut off from all consolation, all hope that existence has some meaning. Uncharacteristically, in the final paragraph, Lawson distances himself from the grotesque figure he has portrayed, in sharp contrast to his identification with the 'hollow men' of **'The Union Buries Its Dead'**, which was written a year or so later, when he was working in the Bourke district.

A poster of the film based on Lawson's collection of short stories While the Billy Boils.

The trip to Bourke and Hungerford—arranged by Archibald who was concerned by Lawson's heavy drinking—brought a new energy and toughness to his writing, as **'The Union Buries Its Dead'** bears witness. He went up-country with no illusions about what he would find. A month or so earlier he had been told by 'Banjo' Paterson in the pages of the *Bulletin:*

> You had better stick to Sydney and make merry
>   with the 'push',
> For the bush will never suit you, and you'll never
>   suit the bush.

The two writers had engaged in a verse controversy, in which Lawson attacked the account Southern poets gave of the inland, and Paterson had written 'In Defence of the Bush'. Arriving in Bourke in a dry season, Lawson wrote to his aunt: 'The bush between here and Bathurst is horrible. I was right and Banjo wrong'. In the same letter he told her 'I got a lot of good points for copy on the way up', and 'Took notes all the way up'. Out of the journey came **'In a Dry Season'**, which, like **'The Union Buries Its Dead'** and probably **'Hungerford'**, was written close to the event. These three sketches . . . are 'good in every line', and repay the close attention which they may not seem to invite. Written as newspaper sketches (the form of which, I suppose, had descended from the periodical essays of the previous century), they assume a local audience, alert to local references (to Tyson in **'The Union Buries Its Dead'**, and to Clancy in **'Hungerford'**, for instance). These sketches display a remarkable sureness and economy of treatment, and give the impression of a man writing out of an intensity of feeling untroubled by doubts about form.

It is relevant to note here that a number of commentators have been inclined to suggest that Lawson spoiled a good story when he included the passage beginning 'I have left out the wattle . . .' in **'The Union Buries Its Dead'**. Such criticism assumes that Lawson's purpose was to tell a story, and that he intruded himself to draw attention to his avoidance of the stock conventions. But this 'Sketch from Life', as it was subtitled when first published, was not thought of by Lawson as a work of fiction: it was a personal impression, and the passage simply emphasised the writer's fidelity to fact in writing up his 'copy'. (That the stock emotive devices he disdains here appealed to him is plain enough from weaker stories in which he falls back upon such consoling falsities.) Placed as it is, following the painfully detailed description of the actual burial, in which the narrator, insisting that 'It doesn't matter much—nothing does', has shown how much he feels it does matter, the comment restores the unemotional reporting tone, which the narrator adopts as the representative of the union. The verbal ironies which accumulate through the sketch (more accurately sketch-story) make it a powerful revelation of what Lawson perceived as 'the Out Back Hell' (as he calls it elsewhere).

'Hungerford' is another expression of Lawson's bleak vision. On the surface a mere 'newspaper sketch', it illustrates superbly his ability to charge detail with emotional significance while leaving the meaning of the whole to emerge through implication. In this instance, the experience of going to Hungerford becomes an experience of human absurdity and futility. As a town, a centre of 'civilisation', Hungerford is a ludicrous and horrifying negation of all meaning in human endeavour. The road stops short of the town; there is a rabbit-proof fence with rabbits on both sides of it; the river on the banks of which the town is sited flows only when it floods; and, most absurd of all, the colonial border divides the town in two. And the surrounding landscape is an image of desolation which appalls the onlooker. The humour of the sketch is in the tradition of bush leg-pulling, but the effect is intentionally the reverse of comic.

Much of what Lawson wrote in the next few years was under the stimulus of the Bourke experience, though nothing else approached the direct personal intensity of these early sketches. The work, collected in *While the Billy Boils,* while uneven, contains some fine examples of sketch-stories with Mitchell as the narrator within the story framework. The economy and poise of such sketch-stories as **'On the Edge of a Plain'**, **'Some Day'**, and **'Our Pipes'** is very impressive. One thinks of Chekhov's remark in a letter to Gorki: 'When a man spends the least possible number of movements over some definite action, that is grace'. These stories, seemingly insubstantial, suggest much more than they state—and so much more than *can* be stated. They are all implication. To do anything like justice to the delicate precision of their art one would have to explore them in more detail than is possible here. The appropriate comparison is with a poem rather than with a conventional story. Lawson works on a small scale, and the very brevity of the work is essential to its effect. To add and elaborate would be to destroy the effect. [Some of his stories] show, as Edward Garnett said, that Lawson 'has the faculty of bringing life to a focus, of making it typical.'

An important element in Lawson's success with these slight stories is his use of Mitchell, the shrewd, kindly, and philosophical swagman. A version of Lawson, a persona rather than a fully developed character, he replaces the author as narrator or teller of yarns in a number of stories, allowing the author to create perspective. Mitchell is on the track, a man on his own except when he finds a mate to travel with; one could suggest that as a literary creation he is related to the Romantic outcast figure of the Wanderer. Mitchell's stories give glimpses of his past, but the manner of telling and the related small actions that are described work together to have the teller reveal more than he realises. Mitchell is not so much a character to be explored in connected stories as an instrument by which Lawson can create states of feeling and so define his sense of being human. **'On the Edge of a Plain'** is, in this respect, a perfect story. To a modern reader of Chekhov, the art of this little story is quickly recognised, but the originality of what Lawson was doing on his own went unremarked when *While the Billy Boils* was published in 1896.

Most critics would now agree that Lawson is at his strongest in *While the Billy Boils* and *Joe Wilson and His*

Mates. . . . Joe Wilson and His Mates was the product of his first year in England. Lawson's decision to leave Australia grew out of his conviction that if he were to succeed as a writer he had to get away. Although *While the Billy Boils* and *In the Days When the World was Wide* had won acclaim in Australia, his life had become increasingly desperate: he had married in 1896 but by 1900 there were strains in the marriage; his alcoholism had become so bad that he had voluntarily entered an inebriates' home; his writing did not earn him a sufficient income; he was depressed and distracted by the constant need to earn money, and he was tormented by the sense that he could not do himself justice working under the conditions that prevailed in Australia. The encouragement of English editors and publishers led him to decide to try to survive as a full-time writer in London. The ordeal that he underwent during the two-year stay in England (his wife became mentally unstable and had to be hospitalised for long periods, and he was responsible for the care as well as the support of two infants) has only recently been told. By the time he returned to Australia in mid-1902 his marriage was virtually over, he was exhausted, and there had been a marked decline in his writing. Before the end of that year he had attempted suicide. He never recovered from the crisis of that time, and although he continued to write over the next twenty years—he was writing the night he died in September 1922—after 1902 there are only occasional flickers of the imaginative power he had previously shown. As a writer his life was tragically short: the work on which his current reputation rests was all done between 1892 and 1902.

[In *The Penguin Henry Lawson: Short Stories,* I printed] the Joe Wilson stories in the order in which they were written, not as they were arranged in *Joe Wilson and His Mates*. I have done this to encourage readers to consider each story individually. To read the group of four stories as if they constitute 'a single plotted, climaxed story' (the model Stephens had recommended) is to put the emphasis in the wrong place and, incidentally, to pass over quite significant inconsistencies between the stories as a result of changes in conception from one to the other. '**Brighten's Sister-in-law**', the first story Lawson wrote after his arrival in England, was the longest he had ever written up to that time. Lawson was aiming at writing a short story rather than his preferred story-sketch, and seeking to respond to the voices that urged on him the superiority of the extended narrative. It is a leisurely story, in which he exploits the freedom allowed by the autobiographical mode of narration, but the core of its meaning is located in the narrator's perception of the woman as a suffering soul. The source of her tragedy is not stated directly, nor does Joe Wilson reflect on what he sees, the woman's behaviour towards the father and son being in itself a form of revelation to the reader. In the final form of the story the link between the lonely woman without husband or child and the Wilsons is delicately suggested: her fate could be theirs.

'**Brighten's Sister-in-law**' had been an important advance for Lawson, in that he had preserved the essence of the 'sketch-story', with its focus on the moment of aware-ness, within an extended narrative, such as he had never managed before. His next Joe Wilson story ["**A Double Buggy at Lahey's Creek**"] attempted less and was a more even performance. By now Lawson was thinking of a Joe Wilson series, but in the next story ["'**Water Them Geraniums**'"] he had obvious difficulty in controlling the direction of the narrative, and what was intended as the story of how the Wilson settled on the land became the story of Mrs Spicer (the drover's wife writ large, as Brian Matthews says). This story has some very fine passages, including the initial episode in which Joe Wilson hears Mrs Spicer summon Annie to 'water them geraniums'. The description of the pathetic flower patch outside the Spicer hut is an outstanding example of how deftly and subtly Lawson could suggest the symbolic dimension of an experience.

There were more attempts at Joe Wilson stories, but the only other one Lawson chose to include in *Joe Wilson and His Mates* was '**Joe Wilson's Courtship**', which is set earlier in time than the envisaged sequence and narrated in a gently reminiscent manner. Like the earlier monologue, '**An Old Mate of Your Father's**', this story has all the charm of tender recollection without losing a sense of the real. The ending—with Joe Wilson asking Black for permission to marry Mary—is another of those short episodes in which Lawson was so effective: it is virtually a 'story-sketch' in itself.

> **Henry Lawson's fate seems especially bitter in that he was misread and frustrated as an artist in the country which praised him highly while he lived and honoured him with a state funeral when he died.**
>
> —*John Barnes*

'**Telling Mrs Baker**' and '**The Loaded Dog**' were both written in England in the same period as the Joe Wilson stories. In the first Lawson displays a confident control of narrative, and it is only after one has started to reflect upon the view of character that it offers that one realises the unexamined emotionalism on which the whole situation is based. The idealising of the bushmen ('They are grand men—they are noble') contrasts with the realistic observation of earlier stories, and signals Lawson's turning away from the painfully real into a consoling dream-world of the bush, in which the gospel of mateship is lived out. . . .

['**The Loaded Dog**' and a few other stories] illustrate Lawson's success as a humorous writer. The term 'humorous writer' is, in itself, a limiting one, and I would agree with the view that, though he wrote many enjoyable comic sketches and stories, Lawson's individual distinction is not to be found there. **'The Geological Spieler'**, the best of several stories in which Steelman and Smith appear, shows Lawson's characteristic use of ironic reversal, but the story does remain within the conventions of frontier humour which Mark Twain popularised. **'The Iron-bark Chip'**, which similarly relies upon a sudden twist, has more of the feel of local experience about it. The hilarious farce of **'The Loaded Dog'** centres on the action of the dog, but Lawson raises the story above the level of stock farce by making what happens the result of Dave Regan's bright idea; with a few strokes at the end, Lawson puts the episode into perspective as a Dave Regan yarn, part of the communal memory of the bush. . . . [The] Mitchell yarn, **'Bill, the Ventriloquial Rooster'**, is [highly] successful in giving the flavour of bush humour.

There is no hint of humour in [**'A Child in the Dark, and a Foreign Father'**, a story of significance] because it is of very great biographical interest, and also because it so clearly marks the end of Lawson's creative period. In his autobiography Lawson quotes a friend's advice to him on a projected book about bush people: 'Treated ruthlessly, Rousseaulike, without regard to your own or others' feelings, what a notable book yours would be!' **'A Child in the Dark, and a Foreign Father'** may well have been begun under the influence of such advice. According to Lawson, he had intended to write a novel, and had begun work in England. The story was finished after his return to Australia in 1902 and before his suicide attempt that same year. In this version of what were obviously distressing childhood memories, there is an impersonality of tone that is quite uncharacteristic, and an absence of those evocative impressionistic descriptions which carry so much emotional force in his best work. Like **'The Drover's Wife'** this story deals with the relationship of parent and child, but it is the work of a man who has lost the power to see into the heart of things. . . .

Lawson's achievement as a short-story writer . . . is not to be measured by the bulk of his collected works. His writing will be read by Australians for all sorts of reasons that have nothing to do with his literary qualities, but his claim to recognition as a writer in the larger English-speaking world rests, I believe, on the stories [in which] . . . he stands apart from his *Bulletin* contemporaries—and successors—who understood the short story as a form of yarn-spinning, and no more than that. Reading these stories one starts to develop Lawson's own haunting sense of 'what-might-have-been'. The delicacy of his art met with little appreciation in a culture which valued the 'slap-dash' as being 'dinkum', and he never realised his full potential. Henry Lawson's fate seems especially bitter in that he was misread and frustrated as an artist in the country which praised him highly while he lived and honoured him with a state funeral when he died.

FURTHER READING

Bibliography

Mackaness, George, ed. *An Annotated Bibliography of Henry Lawson.* Sydney: Angus and Robertson, 1951, 99 p.
    Primary and secondary bibliography of Lawson's work.

Biography

Clark, Manning. *In Search of Henry Lawson.* South Melbourne: MacMillan Co. of Australia, 1978, 143 p.
    Romanticized biography of Lawson.

Prout, Denton. *Henry Lawson: The Grey Dreamer.* London: Angus and Robertson, 1963, 306 p.
    In his acccount of Lawson's life, Prout extensively quotes Lawson's work correspondence and reminis-cences of family and acquaintances.

Criticism

Barnes, John. "Lawson and the Short Story in Australia." *Westerly*, No. 2 (July 1968): 83-7.
    Discusses the influence of Lawson on the short story in Australia.

Lawson, Alan. "The Framing of 'The Loaded Dog'." *Quadrant* XXIX, No. 5 (May 1985): 63-5.
    Suggests a possible source for Lawson's short story.

Matthews, Brian. "'The Nurse and Tutor of Eccentric Minds': Some Developments in Lawson's Treatment of Madness." *Australian Literary Studies* 4, No. 2 (1970): 251-57.
    Traces Lawson's treatment of madness through examination of a few of his short stories.

———. *The Receding Wave: Henry Lawson's Prose.* Melbourne: Melbourne University Press, 1972, 196 p.
    A close examination of Lawson's major works. Matthews offers an explanation for Lawson's decline and demonstrates that the sentimental excesses that mar Lawson's work are carefully suppressed in his best stories.

Murray-Smith, Stephen. *Henry Lawson.* Melbourne: Lansdowne Press, 1962, 48 p.
    Critical and biographical study.

Phillips, A. A. *Henry Lawson.* New York: Twayne, 1970, 159 p.
    Book-length biography with critical information on Lawson's short stories.

Roderick, Colin, ed. *Henry Lawson Criticism: 1894-1971.* Sydney: Angus and Robertson, 1972, 514 p.
    Thorough compilation of criticism on Lawson, with a lengthy and informative biographical and critical intro-

duction. This is an excellent source of commentary by
many early critics, particularly A. G. Stephens.

———. *The Real Henry Lawson*. Adelaide, Australia: Rigby,
1982, 208 p.
    Critical biography of Lawson.

Turner, Graeme. "Mateship, Individualism and the Production
of Character in Australian Fiction." *Australian Literary
Studies* 11, No. 4 (October 1984): 447-57.
    Analyzes the Australian theme of mateship as evidenced
in Lawson's short story "Telling Mrs. Baker."

Additional coverage of Lawson's life and career is contained in the following sources published by Gale Research: *Contemporary Authors*, Vol. 120; and *Twentieth-Century Literary Criticism*, Vol. 27.

Gordon Lish
1934-

(Full name Gordon Jay Lish) American short story writer, novelist, and editor.

INTRODUCTION

Lish is considered one of the most influential editors in publishing, and critics credit him with promoting new aesthetic movements in contemporary fiction. In his own short stories, he employs a variety of innovative narrative styles, often abandoning traditional narrative forms in favor of a variety of metafictional techniques. Lish's work is not commercially popular, and commentators have a mixed assessment of his fiction; according to Brian Evenson, Lish's impact lies in that he "is not afraid to violate taboo, to render discourse extravagant, to speak of that which others dare not, in his relentless exploration of the abscession of the human heart."

Biographical Information

Lish was born in Hewlett, New York. In his adolescence, he was treated in a mental health facility for hypermania. During his rehabilitation, Lish met the poet Hayden Carruth, who was to be a major influence on his writing. He graduated with a bachelor's degree in English with honors from the University of Arizona in 1959 and attended a year of graduate study at San Francisco State College in 1960. Lish worked as an English instructor at a California high school from 1961 until 1963, while also working as a radio broadcaster. In 1963, he became director of linguistic studies at Behavioral Research Laboratories in Menlo Park, California, where, in 1964, he wrote the textbook *English Grammar*. Lish garnered popular and critical attention in 1969 when he accepted the position of fiction editor at *Esquire* magazine. Using the influential publication as a vehicle to introduce new fiction by emerging authors, he promoted the work of such writers as Cynthia Ozick, Reynolds Price, T. Coraghessan Boyle, and Barry Hannah. Lish left *Esquire* in 1977 to become a senior editor with the publishing firm of Alfred A. Knopf, where he continued to champion new fiction, introducing such writers as Raymond Carver, David Leavitt, Amy Hempel, and William Ferguson. In 1987 Lish founded the literary journal, *The Quarterly*, which also showcases the works of contemporary authors. In addition to his career in literary publishing, Lish has conducted writing seminars in New York City and served as a lecturer at Yale and Columbia University.

Major Works of Short Fiction

Most of the stories in Lish's first collection, *What I Know So Far*, are narrative monologues delivered in repetitive and often disjointed language. The narrators in these stories fre-

quently reminisce about their childhood experiences, and critics have noted Lish's obsessive first-person narration and lack of plot, characterization, and linear progression. The most widely discussed piece in the volume, "For Jeromé—with Love and Kisses," is a parody of J. D. Salinger's story, "For Esmé—with Love and Squalor." The story centers on a father's efforts to resuscitate his relationship with his estranged son, who has become a famous author. The reclusive son is a fictional parody of J. D. Salinger himself. Some critics have called the piece exploitative, but others have praised it as an innovative satire. The stories in Lish's second short story collection, *Mourner at the Door*, are brief pieces in which he uses repetitive language to convey the excited psychological states of his characters. In "The Death of Me," for example, the narrator begins a meditation on his childhood: "I wanted to be amazing. I wanted to be so amazing. I had already been amazing up to a certain point. But I was tired of being at that point. I wanted to go past that point." Classified as a comic novella, Lish's next work of short fiction, *Zimzum*, consists of six sections that are thematically linked. As was the case with his earlier short fiction, critics have extended a mixed assessment of Lish's fusion of fiction, biography, and autobiographical elements.

Critical Reception

Lish's works have elicited a wide range of critical responses. Some critics have concluded that his first-person narrations are engaging and compelling and effectively convey intimate psychological portraits of his characters. Other commentators have suggested, however, that Lish's repetitive language often operates as a self-conscious gimmick that alienates readers from his characters. Although some critics fault Lish for the lack of plot and the absence of linear progression in his short fiction, he is widely commended for his ability to use innovative narrative techniques to create a broad range of voices and characterizations.

PRINCIPAL WORKS

Short Fiction

What I Know So Far 1984
Mourner at the Door 1988
Zimzum 1993

Other Major Works

English Grammar (textbook) 1964
Dear Mr. Capote (novel) 1983
Peru (novel) 1986
Extravaganza: A Joke Book (novel) 1989
My Romance (novel) 1991

CRITICISM

Alan Friedman (essay date 1984)

SOURCE: "Writers as Tricksters," in *The New York Times Book Review,* April 22, 1984, p. 13.

[*In the following positive review of* What I Know So Far, *Friedman focuses on the plot and style of "For Jeromé—with Love and Kisses."*]

When you read a writer as terribly clever as Gordon Lish, an inescapable question comes up—is he only clever? I doubt it. I think he's earnest and reckless besides. Mr. Lish, who made his mark first as the fiction editor of *Esquire* and then as a publisher's editor, has lately chosen to join the madding crowd of authors he has edited. I say this because, to judge from the two books he has written recently, he seems obsessed with writers—with their magical power as tricksters and big shots, with their vanities and inanities, with their techniques of deception, including self-deception.

Dear Mr. Capote was an eccentric first novel that earned justified high marks when it appeared last year. Sensational, it is difficult to read because it is written in the form of a long disjointed letter from a homicidal maniac to the famous author. . . . Among Mr. Lish's terrifying perceptions was one that particularly appealed to me—the discovery by the letter writer, your ordinary subliterate madman, that fancy words can serve as agents of death. Fancy words, uncomprehended, could confuse unwary victims (readers too? one wonders), conveniently turning them toward the killer's knife. The killer's line of attack, begun with a word, was through the eye and into the brain.

Now we have *What I Know So Far,* a collection of Mr. Lish's short stories. Short they certainly are—two to four pages long, for the most part—and edgy and subtle. To call them stories, however, is mere force of habit. Some of them do tell a tale of sorts, but even these read like riddles and satires or like sketches and blackouts. Some of them resemble narrative essays, bearing titles like **"Fear: Four Examples"** and **"How to Write a Novel"** (which is really about several kinds of suffering other than writing a novel). But virtually every story, whatever else it may be, is a monologue delivered by a first-person narrator who characterizes himself as he speaks his piece. His voice is everything; other characters have walk-on roles, but they hardly count. Never mind. It turns out that the author of these 18 stories is a cunning ventriloquist who can throw his voice with lethal accuracy. His narrators do not merely characterize themselves, they skewer themselves.

The first story, for example, is narrated by a man who is very likely sane in a clinical sense. Yet he is so detached, deaf to tones and uninterested in other people that he can commit an act of violent insanity without so much as noticing it. His wife, he tells us, cries at night. He wonders why, but only vaguely. In his repellent voice, he manages to narrate the story of another man's downfall without once realizing that what he has in fact recorded is his own catastrophe.

The longest story is the one most likely to command the attention of readers. A longwinded Jewish joke, it's also a literary "in" joke, perhaps even a cruel one. No one is likely to forget how often Philip Roth has been accused of fostering anti-Semitism (among other things) for allowing his mordant wit to bite the hand of the mother who fed him. Mr. Lish now bravely sinks his teeth into the Jewish father. He does so through a comical letter from father to son. But its jokiness is deceptive. Under the story's winking and whining, beneath its smiles of compassion, lies a satire that snarls.

It's called **"For Jeromé—With Love and Kisses,"** a kitschy echo of the title of J. D. Salinger's heart-rending story "For Esmé—With Love and Squalor.". . .

The premise of this sunny piece of savagery is that the retired or widowed parents of the most famous Jewish writers in America now live in Florida, all of them together at the Seavue Spa Oceanfront Garden Arms and Apartments. They play cards, they one-up each other, they compare their children's triumphs in the literature business. Murray Mailer and Burt Bellow live there, as do Gus Krantz, Dora Robbins, Mort Segal, Charlie Heller, a certain Mrs. Roth, the victorious Allen family (temporarily located in the penthouse) and "the Malamuds on 6, a one-bedroom facing front." The honor rolls on. And among all these literary Moms and Pops, only J. D.'s father—and a mysterious Mrs. Pinkowitz—have trouble getting in touch with their famous kids.

Can't J. D.'s father simply pick up the phone? No, because these days his "hermit" sonny boy has a *new* unlisted phone number. . . . By turns furious, cajoling, abject, hectoring, breast-beating, unctuous, crude and crafty, [J. D.'s father is] especially ticked off because his "boychikel" has abbreviated those two gorgeous names, Jerome David. With a quip, he swears he'll stop lecturing. "If I ever utter one more word in this department, may I inherit the Waldorf-Astoria and drop dead in every room." But he's unable to stop.

And I can't, without ruining the suspense on which Mr. Lish's fable turns, reveal its ending—its punch line. It's a haymaker, all right. Thrown at the jaw of Mrs. Pinkowitz's son, Tommy, who turns out to be quite as real a writer as J. D., this literary sideswipe strikes me as exploitative. Yet I suppose that Jews and gentiles alike will read **"For Jerome—With Love and Kisses"** as a work of broad humor and high hilarity.

Dennis Drabelle (essay date 1984)

SOURCE: "Playing the Game of 'What If . . .'," in *Book World—The Washington Post*, May 20, 1984, pp. 3, 13.

[*Below, Drabelle provides a mixed assessment of the short stories in* What I Know So Far.]

In his introduction to a recent anthology, *Great Esquire Fiction*, L. Rust Hills, the magazine's fiction editor, credits his predecessor Gordon Lish with founding the New Fiction. Since Hills doesn't define this category beyond singling out two exemplars reprinted in the anthology—William Kotzwinkle's hilarious "Horse Badorties Goes Out" and T. Coraghessan Boyle's wicked "Heart of a Champion"—let me try my hand. In a time of egregious turmoil (1969-77), these and dozens more stories published under Lish's imprimatur offered rude, gabdrunk, disorienting, fearful alternatives to mainstream magazine fiction.

Many of the New fictions rely heavily on outlandish suppositions, some of these not far removed from the "What If" segments of the original *Saturday Night Live*. In **"Heart of a Champion,"** for instance, the premise is that Lassie has a sex life. The trick (by which I mean art) is to extend such potent *données* full length without sacrificing spontaneity to design.

"For Jerome—with Love and Kisses," the longest story in Lish's collection [*What I Know So Far*], belongs to the "What If" school, and it's a lulu. As the title indi-

cates—by punning on J. D. Salinger's "For Esmé—with Love and Squalor"—the story is a send-up of America's second most elusive literary hermit. (You might try to identify numero uno as we move along.) The premise is that Mr. Ess, J. D.'s widowed father, a resident of Miami's Seavue Spa Oceanfront Garden Arms and Apartments, has some bones to pick with his famous son and sits down to write a kvetching letter.

For one thing, Jerome has just changed from one unlisted phone number to another without notifying guess whom. Has the son's obsession with privacy gone so far as to freeze out his sole surviving parent? If it's reached that stage, Mr. Ess might as well do himself in. "One mini-wink," he writes, "and your father will be only too happy and glad to make you a present of his own dead body."

[What crowns **"For Jeromé—with Love and Kisses"**] with glory is Mr. Ess' acrid, self-lacerating, guilt-dispensing tone. He's the most spellbinding Jewish complainant since Stanley Elkin's "Bailbondsman" raised his voice in outrage, and the story is a classic screed. . . .

Among the 17 other stories, I marked half-a-dozen for rereading some rainy day—not a bad percentage as story collections go. One of these, **"For Rupert—with No Promises,"** augments Lish's debt to Salinger by purporting to extend the Glass family saga. **"Guilt"** is an affecting story of an emotion that needs no foundation in fact. **"Frank Sinatra or Carleton Carpenter"** memorably depicts the bogies that plague earnest parents. **"Fear: Four Examples"** is notable if only for a wonderful phrase: the narrator suffers from a "rogue cramp."

Other stories in the collection are irritatingly obscure. Owing to the excessive archness of their narrative voices, they manage to fall on their faces and make the reader feel clumsy. No matter. **"For Jerome—with Love and Kisses"** alone is reason enough for you to buy Lish's book—and for J. D. to mend his ways.

Anne Tyler (essay date 1984)

SOURCE: "Uncommon Characters," in *The New Republic*, Vol. 190, No. 21, May 28, 1984, pp. 33-4.

[*Tyler is an American novelist and short story writer who is known for her fictional portraits of family life in works such as* Searching for Caleb *(1976) and* Dinner at the Homesick Restaurant *(1982). Often considered a Southern regionalist, Tyler has been most influenced by Eudora Welty, an author to whom she is frequently compared. In the following review, she provides a negative assessment of the short fiction in* What I Know So Far.]

Mention Gordon Lish and most readers will think of short stories, logically enough. Gordon Lish was fiction editor at *Esquire* for a number of years, and has edited three short story anthologies. This is what makes it so odd that of the two books he has written—a novel [*Dear Mr. Ca-*

pote] and a collection of stories [*What I Know So Far*]—it's the novel that's the stunner. . . .

The characters in the short story collection, *What I Know So Far,* remain peculiarly distant. The single exception is the narrator of **"Guilt,"** which is a strong and affecting study of a boy grown just past the curls-and-dimples stage whose mother finds a neighbor child more beautiful. (Yes, just like the mother in *Dear Mr. Capote.*) But the other stories—seventeen of them—seem less stories than "turns," in the theatrical sense. The author steps forward, presents a little piece, and retreats. Next, please.

"For Rupert—with No Promises" is his J. D. Salinger turn. ("Wall-to-wall cigars and three packs of Raleighs a day for almost twenty-five years, and I get cancer of the goddamn *spleen,*" a character says. And "He could be the President of the United goddamn *States,* or change the theory of zero, and *this* won't stop him. My being dead, I mean—my dying.")

And speaking of J. D. Salinger, we also have **"For Jerome—with Love and Kisses,"** which is a letter to "Jay-deezie darling, dear cutie fellow, sweetheart, cutie guy" from the man who keeps calling himself "I your father." Mr. Salinger Senior lives at the Seavue Spa Oceanfront Garden Arms and Apartments in Florida with his neighbors Mrs. Roth, Mr. and Mrs. Bellow, Mr. and Mrs. Malamud, the Elkins, the Potoks . . . oh, and poor, poor Gert Pinkowitz, whose son Thomas had to go and "get cute" and change his name to Pynchon. This is entertaining for a while, but when you come right down to it it's just a very long dialect joke—albeit one with a powerful punch line.

Then there are the more serious pieces. **"Fear: Four Examples"** describes in three pages the various kinds of anguish, both grand and trivial, that the father of a daughter can experience. **"How to Write a Poem,"** while it dumps us with a thud at the end, has at its core an ingenious, mad, deceptively reasonable idea. The narrator is a poem-stealer; he's good at detecting the moment in a poem when the poet has suddenly "seen it coming at him—an ordinary universe, the itemless clutter of an unraveling world."

> Maybe I don't like poets—or people. But I just love to catch a poet at it, and then to test myself against the thinglessness that made him cut and run. What I do is I pick it up where the poet's nerve dumped him, where he just couldn't stand to see there's still nothing in a place where something never was.

> It's no big deal. You just face down what he, in his chickenheart, couldn't. Then you type your version up and sign your name. Next thing you do is get it printed as your own, sit back and listen to them call you brave.

On occasion, a story's briefness is its only drawback: **"How to Write a Novel"** has much of the eerie, sad quality of *Dear Mr. Capote,* except that it's over and done with so quickly we can't fully experience it. **"Two Families"** reads like a writer's preliminary notes for a plot—and only the very sketchiest of notes, scrawled on the back of a matchbook. In fact, several of these stories are so skeletal, so

elliptical, so connect-the-dots that readers feel overworked. Wait a minute, we want to say, who's getting paid for telling this?

"This is my first major rule," says the hero of *Dear Mr. Capote.* "Think a thing all the way through. I say you have not thought it through enough when you come out on the same side you started on." For Gordon Lish, ironically, the novel seems to be the form in which he does his best thinking-through. *What I Know So Far* is a hit-and-run book. *Dear Mr. Capote* hits and stays.

Robert Jones (essay date 1987)

SOURCE: "Writing the Troubling Truth," in *Commonweal,* Vol. CXIV, No. 15, September 11, 1987, pp. 501-04.

[*In the essay below, Jones discusses the defining characteristics of Lish's fiction.*]

The public fascination with the mess F. Scott Fitzgerald made of his life encouraged the confusion in popular culture that sees serious writers as something like movie stars who can type. What is significant about Fitzgerald's peculiar fame is that even when he was alive, he was more famous than his novels. His and Zelda's escapades were known to people who did not ordinarily read, and his years in Hollywood and the excesses that felled him made him seem no different from any other actor on a downhill binge. And despite his torture in his last years at being unable to write and shame at having been reduced to a studio hack, he came to personify a kind of glamour that the public associated with writers. In the fifty years since Fitzgerald's death, our literary icons are even more victimized by the prevailing cult of personality, so that now more than ever, a writer's work is incidental to the life. The likes of Philip Roth and Eudora Welty compete for space opposite starlets and sports stars in the pages of weekly magazines.

There is little to be learned by the example of even the most famous of contemporary lives, yet there is now almost no secondary literary figure who is not the subject of a biography. And of some writers, like Virginia Woolf, there is no aspect of her life, including her account ledgers, that is not exposed. But to what purpose? We don't need scores of books on Virginia Woolf. But even less do we need full-scale biographies of decent but unexceptional writers like James Gould Cozzens and Louise Bogan. Long after their books lie unread by anyone but graduate students, their personal misery is resurrected as somehow meaning more than the common sorrow of yet another life unhappily lived.

There is a desperateness to this scavenging of graveyards, as if every life of even fleeting notoriety must be examined for clues to life's purpose. What is handed down as part of the cultural memory is inconsequential data. One can only be thankful for the obscure origins of Homer and Plato.

Of all the writers at work in America, there is one who is presently receiving an astonishing amount of press attention, not so much for the books he writes—which are among the best of contemporary fiction—but for his rather expansive personality. Within the past year or so, Gordon Lish has been called "Captain Fiction," in the pages of *Vanity Fair;* a "cultural commissar" with "more power than *The New Yorker,*" in *The Mississippi Review;* the subject of endless speculation about his supposedly Machiavellian teaching methods in the pages of *Spy* magazine; and most curiously, in an article in *The New Republic* this fall, as something akin to a literary monster—because of his triple hat of author, editor, and teacher—who is almost singlehandedly destroying modern writing.

It is instructive to watch someone being adopted by the media and turned into a "personality" before our eyes. The very democracy of fame in which everyone becomes equally well-known and, within that context, equally pointless, declaws even the mightiest. Popularizing is a kind of strait jacket that presents writers publicly in ways that are easily digestible, so that any threat in what they say, or what they represent, is defused. If what is known about them is how many dogs or nervous breakdowns they have had, or in Lish's case, rumors of the spell he induces in his students, then the work drifts away from center stage. The act of writing serves merely as a vehicle for becoming famous, not for what the writing might tell us about the way we live.

Gordon Lish has plenty to tell us about the way we live now, but it is easier to hear about his seduction of young minds, so that he is portrayed as the Reverend Moon to the literary set. But what should trouble readers is what Lish says about how we are imprisoned by memory and are undermined by fear. For this is the message found in his books and where he achieves the only power that should concern us: as a teller of truth.

Accustomed as we are to the elegiac pull of the great modernist writers, we have come to see memory as a kind of imaginative resting place. But what if there is no peace to be found and the return to the past reveals simply the horrors that were always there and continue to thrive in the unconscious? As a writer, Gordon Lish is obsessed with our attempts to become unentangled by the past. His novel *Peru,* published last year, tells us that personal history can never really be remade, but is replayed incessantly in images unloosed by the imagination. Memory becomes a kind of cul de sac in which we are constantly flung back into the past, just as we think we have hidden ourselves in the present.

To enter the world of Lish's fiction, we must think for a moment of the most unspeakable thing we have done—or thought of doing—and then imagine it unfolding before us as a real event. And how we could be swept away as it took possession of our consciousness and grew, so that all life would be overwhelmed by that one moment. Or imagine murdering someone and keeping it secret from even those closest to you. The pressure of that secret would build over time until it began to choke you. Lish

is fascinated with the revelation of our most terrible thoughts because in speaking them, we disclose what is truest about ourselves. This is not to say that we are all monsters, but that in our secrets, we are most stripped of evasion and the social conventions that make us able to slip more easily into lies.

The tension in every mind between an essentially truth-telling consciousness and the utterance of the unspeakable is fundamental to Lish's vision. He often chooses violence as his theme—for example, the serial killer in *Dear Mr. Capote,* or the child murderer in *Peru*—and because of this, he is frequently, and facilely, dismissed as a sensationalist. But violence is a necessary subject for him. Its extreme images allow Lish to describe the pressure of guilt upon thought and how the memory of the unspeakable and the compulsion to confess form the ground to experience.

What should trouble readers is what Lish says about how we are imprisoned by memory and are undermined by fear. For this is the message found in his books and where he achieves the only power that should concern us: as a teller of truth.

—Robert Jones

In *Peru* the narrator tells of how he went outside to play and it began to rain and so he sat inside the garage and:

> kept feeling funny and out of the ordinary, as if I were in some kind of trouble and that certain things I didn't exactly know about yet were probably dangerously unfinished, lying lopsided somewhere and being dangerous, and it made me feel a terrible wildness, this strange feeling, it made me feel as if I had to feel the wildness if I was ever going to get rid of the strange feeling, which I think, to my way of thinking as a child, was the worse one, the feeling before the feeling of wildness, the feeling of incompletion and of chaos, a feeling of things getting started and of never getting them over with.

This terrible wildness, this feeling of being swept away by the power of our own imagination reveals the hugeness of the world and what tiny things we are in proportion to it. Lish shares with Freud the idea that human beings step into a malevolent world and thereby receive their education to reality. But for Lish, we are never assimilated to this catastrophic entry into experience.

There is something almost pre-modern in Lish's understanding of how we awaken to the world and find ourselves assaulted by a never-ending stream of images. He does not give us the familiar, repressed human mind, but one that sees everything as if for the first time: not just things and events, but ordinary human emotion. There is a rawness to his characters' response to the world and a sense of being so freshly stunned that they seem to have dropped into the present age from some other period.

As the narrator in *Peru* reflects from middle-age upon the time he killed his playmate, Steven Adinoff, in the sandbox, he speaks about how it felt then and says, "I'll tell you something else—which is that the way you felt when you were six is the way you still feel. Getting older doesn't get you any further away from the feeling, it just gets you further away from telling the truth about it to anybody." We carry in our hearts the dislocation of the child being struck with the dizziness that is the first awareness of our separateness. But it would be a mistake to sentimentalize Lish's idea of the child shadowing our passage into adulthood. His six-year-old in *Peru* is a murderer, after all. Lish is fascinated by children because each one of them is like the original human placing an expectant foot on earth. And all there is to know is waiting for them to come upon like a loose board in the floor.

One of our greatest myths is that in knowledge is freedom, and that by understanding the world, we find our place within it. Lish is obsessed with what we can learn, but he inverts the romantic notion of knowledge as liberation by telling us that we never get far from where we began. As the epigraph to his collection of short stories, **What I Know So Far,** he chose this quotation from Adorno: "Of the world as we know it, it is impossible to be enough afraid." Fear is the natural partner to the awakening of consciousness, and the more we know about experience, the more we learn to be afraid.

The perversity of the human mind is that this fear accelerates the compulsion to know. But we are unequipped to choose the thing—if anything exists—that might save us or at least halt for a moment the unrelenting barrage of images that pass before us. To recognize Lish's difference in this regard from other writers, think of one of the great passages in stream-of-consciousness writing, Bernard's final summation in *The Waves*:

> But it is a mistake, this extreme precision, this orderly and military progress, a convenience, a lie. There is always deep below it. . . . There is nothing one can fish up with a spoon, nothing one can call an event. Yet it is alive too and deep, this stream . . . Whatever sentence I extract whole and entire from the cauldron is only a string of six little fish that let themselves be caught while a million others leap and sizzle. . . . How impossible to order them rightly, to detach one separately, or to give the effect of the whole.

Even when describing the loss of the self, Bernard marvels at the richness of the parts that make up the whole of life and celebrates how consciousness—vast, potent, and imprecise—brings into harmony only one small aspect of the mutable variety experience offers us.

Lish, too, describes what consciousness is like. There is a randomness to the way thought follows thought in his characters' minds, and a weird, almost primal rhythm to his prose, that makes some passages in his books seem closer to mirroring the way we think than any of his modernist predecessors. But he is as far as one can go from reveling in the haphazard continuity found in Woolf's "rushing stream of broken dreams."

Consciousness for Lish functions as a kind of weapon, sometimes self-inflicted, sometimes pointed out towards the world. To read him is to remember the peculiar power of the mind, of how we can make something exist simply by thinking it. We tend to see the mind as something independent of the world outside. But in Lish's view, everything we can believe or conjure or fantasize begins to live in our line of horizon. When reading his books, one cannot imagine a street in a suburb he might describe, or a department store in Manhattan, or even a television set in a bedroom, without his character being part of the act of seeing it. This is not simply the case of the exterior world emerging through the thoughts of his characters; there is no world seen without the self. Lish goes the Cartesian "I think, therefore I am" one better by replacing it with: "I think, therefore *it is.*"

We make things exist. There is a giddy ecstasy to the realization of our power to be so wildly self-creating, but also an exhaustion and despair. . . .

Lish's characters are obsessed with understanding what has happened to them, but the very limitlessness of experience propels them into the nightmare of knowledge:

> There was just the day which was so hot and sitting on the curb and thinking to myself . . . "It's hot," "It's lot," "It's not," "It's top," "It's mop," "It's mop," "It's nop," "Tip top," "Sip," "Hip hop," and so on and so forth—and on and on and on . . . It's the closest you ever get to feeling that you yourself are God or that if there wasn't any God, then that this would be the same thing which he was, that it was God who could rhyme all of the words, or at least which did once.

> But there is a God, so you give up.

From the epigraph to *Peru* which is the child's poem, "One two buckle my shoe," to the six-year-old's mad rhyme of "hot," Lish shows us the fevered underside of Croce's idea of language as perpetual creation. A word for anything imaginable exists, and then a word that means the same thing, and a word that sounds like it, and on and on until language itself dissolves in unmeaning.

And yet, there is nothing without words. Lish tells us that the very structure of seeing is a linguistic one. If experience is viewed as one hallucination unfolding into the next, and each one imploding in its turn upon the mind, then language is the only means we have to objectify this experience. Language brings us (literally) out of our minds; by naming, we give things a form by which they appear as something other than the self. And it is only in this attempt to create a distance from ourselves, however tenuous or even illusory, that we can make the amorphous movement of experience seem concrete.

Lish takes nothing for granted, even the fact that we speak and see. His books possess unnerving power because in them we rediscover the strangeness of our minds and the queer sounds we utter to explain ourselves. Listen, sometime, to a person chatter in a foreign tongue that you don't understand and consider how odd the trail of nonsensical syllables appears to the uneducated ear. This is the state Lish brings us to in our own language, the place where words begin in all their complexity and mystery. . . .

In the modern literature that has endured, memory is a way of recharting lost territory. Think of Joyce's Dublin or Nabokov's Russia. They lay claim to the harmony found in experience after the fact. Memory attains a kind of mythic power to liberate and remake the world through language, so that we might come to peace with the past. Lish suggests that language and memory lack the convenience of forgetting. Once something is named, it is irrevocable. His characters remain trapped in the past because memory's return only replays all that has happened to them. They want what each of us wants: a second chance. But for Lish, there are no fresh starts.

"Peru" means many things in his novel, but I believe in part it is an anagram of the word "pure." His characters speak themselves to a frenzy to try to empty themselves of the memory of what they've done, as if discourse could wash away a stain. The language of reminiscence seeks the emptiness we all desire in our hearts but fail to find, the kind of purity with which we begin life and lose ever after. Memory is meant to return us there, but instead it is the judge we each possess that reminds us what is truest about ourselves and just how far we have strayed.

Gordon Lish's critics are quick to jump on him (and his so-called disciples) because they are presumed to offer us only a tiny segment of life, and a nasty one at that. In the *New Republic,* Sven Birkerts, one of a new breed of neoconservative literary critics, misreads Lish and some of his authors, like Amy Hempel, and suggests that

> . . . their work represents an abrogation of literary responsibility. If fiction is to survive as more than a coterie sport, it must venture something greater than a passive reflection of fragmentation and unease. Indeed it must manifest intelligence, moral seriousness, and relentlessness. And I would add, comprehensiveness and scope.

Arnold Bennett would be proud. "Literary responsibility" is the kind of pious term that has a nice ring and is essentially meaningless. To create an image of how life appears to one is the only "responsibility" we can reasonably expect of any artist.

In his attack on Hegel's idealism, Adorno wrote: "the whole is the untrue." To seek the whole story, the narrative that will explain the scope and range of life, is an understandable dream. But this desire often forsakes the world as it is for a fantasy of how it ought to be. Writers like Gordon Lish understand how humbled we are by the vastness of experience. And yet, the writer's subterfuge is to seize the smallest part and reveal the truth entirely through the language of fragments.

It's easy to get the impression that Lish wants to offend his readers, wants to slap them in the face until they just can't stand him.

—Marcia Froelke Coburn, in the **Chicago Tribune,** *May 15, 1988.*

Sven Birkerts (essay date 1987)

SOURCE: "The School of Gordon Lish," in *An Artificial Wilderness: Essays on 20th-Century Literature,* William Morrow and Company, Inc., 1987, pp. 251-63.

[*Birkerts is an American critic. In the following excerpt, he traces Lish's influence as an editor and fiction writer.*]

> When I had my interview with Arnold Gingrich at *Esquire* and he asked me what kind of fiction I was going to be publishing, I said, "The new fiction." He said, "What's that?" I said, "I'll get out there and find it, Mr. Gingrich."
>
> —Lish

Longtime readers of American fiction will probably have noticed certain changes in the product during the last few decades. A good deal of the gravity, scope, and narrative energy seems to have gone out of our prose. Formerly there were lives, fates. Now, increasingly, we greet disembodied characters who move about in a generic sort of present. Events on the page are dictated less by complex causes than by authorial fiat. While adherents of the poststructuralist disciplines may find this exalting and confirming, the "dear Reader" tacitly addressed by a more traditional fiction registers a growing despair.

The first signs of disturbance came during the late sixties, when writers like Donald Barthelme, Kurt Vonnegut, Robert Coover, John Barth, and E. L. Doctorow began to assault the narrative norms. Different as their subversions were—they included surreal disjunctions, the mixing of high and low genres, and the use of self-reflexive "metafictional" techniques—the end was the same: the sustaining pretenses of fiction were powerfully undermined. The influence of this attack was felt in every quarter; even professedly rearguard stylists found it ever more difficult to generate the necessary authority.

The spirit of playful subterfuge and interrogation vanished, however, along with the counterculture. In its place

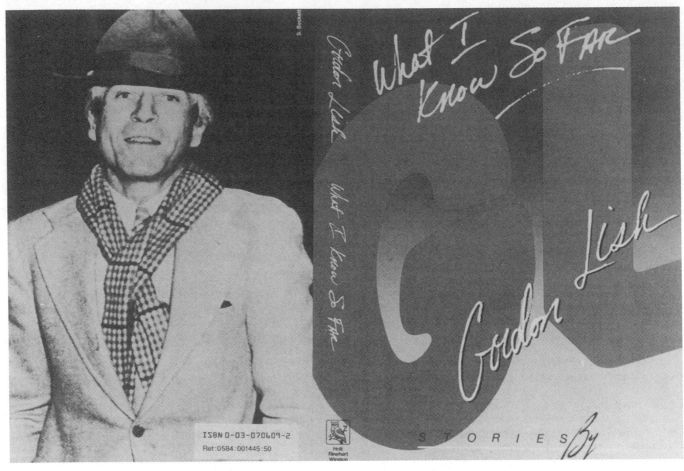

Dust jacket for Lish's first collection of short fiction (1984).

there appeared a deep unease. Fiction writers neither resumed the old ways nor went on with the dare of the new. In a climate of social instability, both the novel and the story drew in their wings. Raymond Carver, Ann Beattie, Frederick Barthelme, and others tried to forge a prose out of whatever had not been decimated by their predecessors. Rooting their work in an indefinite present, they refused to essay the creation of coherent fictional worlds. Their example caught on. Styles everywhere became numbly diaristic. Structures were collage derived. The episode, the paragraph, the sentence, the phrase were the new units of composition. The literary glamour of the seventies attached to the fragmented writings of Renata Adler and Joan Didion, and an army of epigones rose up to follow.

If fiction was once an empire on which the sun never set, it is no longer. Nowadays we rarely meet with a work that tries to bring a larger social context to life, or that explores with any conviction what it means to live in an era of broken connections. In this media culture, fiction seems no longer charged with the mirroring of reality. And yet words keep coming. A whole new generation of prose stylists advances behind the Barthelmes, Carvers, Adlers, and Beatties, a generation that studies the moves and devices of these "masters" as avidly as midcentury writers studied Hemingway, Faulkner, and Joyce.

In casting about for some way to give the new tendencies a habitation and a name, we might do worse than fix upon a particular office at the firm of Alfred A. Knopf, in which sits an energetic and outspoken editor named Gordon Lish. Lish is right now very much at the epicenter of American literary publishing. For one thing, he edits a fair number of "hot" young novelists and story writers. But there are his other activities as well. Lish has for years conducted highly selective fiction workshops in New York and elsewhere—not infrequently assisting his stars into print and into publishing careers. He has also launched a magazine, *The Quarterly,* which is subsidized and distributed through the Random House network. (The first issue appeared in the spring of 1987.) On top of all this, Lish is himself a determined practitioner of post-Carver fiction, with a story collection and two novels to his credit.

Lish's diversified enterprise, and his literary and practical influence, have drawn extremes of response. Nothing could have been more worshipful, for instance, than Amy Hempel's 1985 article in *Vanity Fair* ("Captain Fiction," it was called), which opened with this bold-faced blurb: "Gordon Lish is the Lee Strasberg of American fiction." Writing as a student and a published discovery of Lish's, Hempel fizzed exuberantly about his qualities as a teacher, dwelling upon his idiosyncrasy, his assertive candor, his engagement ("For thirteen weeks it is a class in which first Lish and then his students get the spirit and testify"), and not least, his willingness to perform extramural services for the deserving.

A more astringent view of this activity of discovery and promotion is to be found in Joe David Bellamy's essay "A Downpour of Literary Republicanism" in a recent issue of the *Mississippi Review* (1986). Bellamy suggests that Lish is in some ways as important as *The New Yorker.* Calling him a "cultural commissar" and identifying his aesthetic with Republican conservatism (for its interest in outer, documentary narrative, as opposed to inner, subjective experimentation), Bellamy concludes by goggling at the power that Lish commands: "possibly enough to make it rain if he wants it to rain."

Hempel has evidently passed too many mesmerized hours staring at her book contract, Bellamy too many brooding over his Saul Steinberg poster of New York; but surely some truth can be shaken out of both. Lish does command power. He has gone on from his early days of publishing and proselytizing for writers like Carver in *Esquire,* where he was fiction editor for eight years, to put together a distinctive, if not universally appealing, roster of talents for Knopf. His list includes Anderson Ferrell, Barry Hannah, Hempel, Bette Howland, Janet Kauffman, Raymond Kennedy, Nancy Lemann, Michael Martone, Bette Pesetsky, Mary Robison, Leon Rooke. And he has abetted a career or two; a few years back, for instance, Lish secured a contract for his student Anderson Ferrell on the strength of a few paragraphs of prose.

Still, it's obviously foolish to think of the man as omnipotent. While he will extol the trust placed in him by Knopf's president, Robert Gottlieb—"No question," says Lish, "I am able to indulge my fantasies at the expense of a powerful organization"—he does have a tether. He has tried for years to put across one of his favorite stylists, Stanley G. Crawford, author of the novella *Log of the S.S. The Mrs. Unguentine,* without success. Nor could Lish be called capricious. Ferrell's short novel *Where She Was* (1985) is a sharply realized work of prose; it amply deserves to have been published. The issue, perhaps, is not so much that Lish can indulge his fantasies, but that so few other editors manage to do the same.

What finally makes Lish exceptional among editors is his devotion to the young. A photocopied announcement for *The Quarterly* advised that the magazine "is open to all comers, but will doubtless prove to be particularly hospitable to the work of the young and unsung." Lish is frank about his predilections and his agenda. "If I were given the option of publishing the fourth great work by author A," he states, "and the OK first book by author B, I would be inclined to go with the OK first book."

But he also admits to an ambition greater than just discovering the publishable young. Lish wants to find and train the next titleholder, the future Great American Novelist. He uses the analogy of a boxing coach: "I can tell

you how to take the guy, though I can't do it myself." And the guy, the writer that Lish admires above all others and hence is determined to unseat, is . . . Harold Brodkey.

Harold Brodkey? Yes, emphatically. Lish admits no reservations to his adoration. Brodkey-love swamps every other subject of conversation, though Lish will, to be fair, also sing arias of praise for Cynthia Ozick and Don DeLillo. He is convinced, in part on the strength of published work, but especially by what he has read of the legendary (some would say too legendary) work in progress *A Party of Animals,* that Brodkey is the prose master of our century. He acknowledges, of course, the credibility problem that comes with declaring the preeminence of a novelist whose major work is still under wraps, but as he puts it, "The evidence is before me . . . and there it is."

Lish cites as the cardinal virtues of Brodkey's prose its intelligence, its moral seriousness, its relentlessness. He particularly admires what he sees as the author's willingness always to remake himself. "I don't think there's anyone who is coming onto the page so ferociously," he says. "I read Brodkey and I can't catch my breath." Brodkey presents, for Lish, in every way the opposite of the writing represented by Saul Bellow, whose fiction he derides as pretentious and predictable. Asked if anyone can challenge this Goliath, he smiles. "Somewhere out there is a young writer who has what it takes."

It's hard to get things square. Here we have Lish's testimony on behalf of Brodkey, a writer well along in his career, who is working with a perfectionist's resolve on a grand novel, refusing to publish before he's ready. There we have the example of Lish himself, editor and evangelist of the unsung, doing everything he can to get their young work in front of an audience, hoping that one of them will be the next Brodkey. But there is still a greater contradiction. Where Brodkey's prose aims at grandeur, at a dynamic totality that can embrace ideas, psychological motivations, moral and spiritual questioning, Lish's progeny come across almost without exception as purveyors of the slight and the fragmented. They are sculptors of sentences rather than worlds. Their hunt for essences bypasses existence. Ferocity is nowhere in evidence.

Of course Lish's authors are not all of a single stripe. Though they tend to youthfulness, and their productions to slimness—each one can be read in an evening—there seems to be little similarity between a book like Leon Rooke's *Shakespeare's Dog* (1983), which looks at the bard through the eyes of his randy and highly verbal dog, Mr. Hooker, and the pruned contemporaneity of a story collection by Mary Robison or Amy Hempel. And between these two poles we get the denser domestic portraits of Janet Kauffman and the airy biographical fantasies of Michael Martone. But underneath the variegated surface, behind the sentence-by-sentence expertise, are indications of what is either a new aesthetic or else a crisis in the art. Whichever it is, it has very little to do with Brodkey, Ozick, or DeLillo.

Joe David Bellamy's charge of "literary Republicanism" is misleading when applied to this group of writers. Doubtless Bellamy had Carver's fiction in mind when he coined the epithet. And while Carver's fidelity to grim middle- and lower-class exteriors, and to a tactic of unstated motivation, has been influential, things have changed since his heyday in the early seventies. Lish's writers take a much freer hand with subject matter, voice, and narrative exposition. And what has passed into their fiction, whether from Carver, Beattie, or the spirit of the time, is a total refusal of larger social connection. Indeed, in this respect, Lish's authors are only a case in point. Most of contemporary fiction is similarly skewed. Characters are shown as moving in contained worlds, alone, or with family, friends, and lovers. Everything beyond the local is alien chaos. The social fabric, once the complex and comprehensive subject of fiction, can no longer be found. Nor is there any attempt, as in the novels of Don DeLillo, to make a subject out of this very absence of social bonds. Among these writers a centripetal isolation prevails; the world never extends illusionistically beyond the cast assembled on the stage. This might explain why so many of these books are slight. The writers have shorn themselves, or they have been shorn of, a central resource.

Lish's own work is relevant here, for he preaches what he practices. The stories in his 1977 collection, **What I Know So Far,** progress by way of an anxious staccato, building their episodic structures along the fault lines of discontinuous speech patterns. The sentences capture the reader with their erratic and colloquial beat: "Alan Silver moved in. He moved in when there were seven houses and four still going up. He was twelve. Maybe I was nine by then. So that's the boys from two houses. The other five had boys in them too." They deny him, however, any kind of stable fictional order. Lish's novel *Dear Mr. Capote* (1983) worked similarly, though the subject matter was horrific: the colloquial jumps came out of the mouth of a demented serial killer. But *Peru* (1986), his most recent novel, achieves an eerie profundity absent from the other work. For Lish has finally matched his talky, nipped-off style to its ideal subject—the gradual recovery of a repressed childhood memory. The flat word-sounds and incessant repetitions eventually reveal the violent psyche of a lonely child. Needless to say, nothing exists beyond the recursive monody of the narrator's voice and the handful of images that it summons up. Lish, then, is the paradigmatic Lish author.

Greg Johnson (essay date 1988)

SOURCE: "Isn't It Gothic?" in *The Georgia Review,* Vol. XLII, No. 4, Winter, 1988, pp. 840-49.

[*Johnson is an American novelist, short story writer, poet and critic. Below, he provides a stylistic analysis of* Mourner at the Door.]

The attempt to define and evaluate literary Gothicism has created an ongoing controversy among critics and scholars, primarily because the term "Gothic" has achieved the kind of connotative vagueness—rather like that other free-floating term, "Romantic"—that inspires its use in a startling variety of contexts. In his recent study of Gothic fiction, *In the Circles of Fear and Desire* (University of Chicago Press, 1985), William Patrick Day insists that too often critics "expand the term to a point where it is no longer useful" and that "ambiguity, a conflict between fear and terror, does not make a novel Gothic." Yet even Day acknowledges that the Gothic is the most enduring fictional genre and that it bears a meaningful relationship to modern literature because "both traditions are colored by a sense of crisis, breakdown, and collapse." Similarly, he suggests that Freudian psychology has validated the thematic concerns of Gothic fiction and that the basic function of this antirealistic genre—"to escape from conventional life and articulate and define the turbulence of psychic existence"—has remained unchanged.

In American fiction, after notable achievements in the genre by Charles Brockden Brown and Edgar Allan Poe, followed by a brief resuscitation in Henry James's *The Turn of the Screw,* the familiar Gothic staples—a moldering mansion, a defenseless heroine, and a pervasive atmosphere of violence and terror—virtually disappeared. Yet the subgenre we term "Southern Gothic," typified by such works as Faulkner's *Absalom, Absalom!* and Carson McCullers' *Reflections in a Golden Eye,* is generally accepted as having meaningfully adapted certain Gothic conventions—especially an atmosphere of brooding fatalism and a focus upon extreme psychological states—to the spiritual condition of a defeated South, even as it eliminated the supernatural elements that characterized the generative eighteenth-century British Gothics of Horace Walpole and Ann Radcliffe.

Most contemporary fiction described as "gothic"—the uncapitalized spelling growing more common as the term's connotations become more far-ranging—often bears little or no relationship either to the supernatural or to the American South. Instead, recent novels and stories most often reflect the original Gothic conventions in flamboyantly hyperbolic, self-reflexive or parodic forms. Gothic conventions, in fact, have become less conspicuous than what might be termed a Gothic sensibility: a tendency to focus upon the violent extremes of human behavior; to suggest the distortions of perception and feeling created by personal isolation; to explore the depths of memory, fear, and longing; or simply to indulge in verbal pyrotechnics and a playfully macabre tone—indulgences at once Poe-like and postmodernist—when writing about pain, madness, or death. For some contemporary writers the Gothic realm also provides an escape from the constraints of conventional plot structure, character development, motivation, and even credibility itself, demanding that the reader not merely suspend disbelief but toss it to the winds.

Although Gothic fiction has often suffered at the hands of critics who consider it less than "serious," it is no less worthy of thoughtful attention than any other form of imaginative work. Indeed, since it is more daring, more challenging to both the writer's and reader's imaginations, and at times seemingly more attuned to the turbulent unconscious processes informing all genuine art, such fiction might be considered especially noteworthy. (The origins of the Gothic as a commercially successful genre, combined with its tendency to express the most lurid of our repressed fantasies and fears, has surely contributed to disapproval from more conservative critical quarters.) Clearly, whatever permutations the genre has undergone, the Gothic still offers contemporary writers an opportunity for fictional experimentation of various kinds: as a means of parodying realist conventions, as a rich alternative to the meiotic thinness of minimalist fiction, or as a way of exploring the blatantly subversive nature of the writer's own imagination. . . .

But unlike Philip Roth (whose narrators are no less self-absorbed than Lish's, and whose work is also concerned with memory, confession, and the nature of fiction), Lish seems unable or unwilling to forge any substantial artistic statement out of his obsessive themes.

—Greg Johnson

It's not surprising that contemporary Gothicism often focuses upon textuality itself, the crumbling mansions of earlier Gothic authors recast as a house of fiction currently haunted by the friable, "ghostly" power of language and by the writer's own relentless self-consciousness. In his 1985 novel, *Peru,* Gordon Lish effectively united psychological obsession and flamboyant fictional artifice in his brooding narrative of a man (named Gordon) haunted by the memory of a violent act he committed (or might have committed) as a child. The novel's implicit commentary on the unreliable nature of memory and of narrative itself, when combined with an aura of profound psychological unease that was present throughout, achieved moments of extraordinary power. Unfortunately, this power is almost wholly missing from the glibly self-conscious pieces—one hesitates to call them stories—in Lish's new collection, *Mourner at the Door.* Although some of these brief offerings bring over from *Peru* the deliberately monotonous repetition, the brooding, and the overheated psychological states that might be termed Gothic in nature, here Lish replaces the powerful subtext that distinguished his novel with gimmicky, superficial remarks on the inadequacy of fictional conventions and of language as a representational medium. The book is a rehash, in short, of insights already achieved—and with far more originality and skill—by much experimental writing of the sixties and early seventies, especially that of John Barth, Donald Barthelme, and Robert Coover.

In particular, Lish carries his fondness for iteration to obnoxious extremes. From **"The Death of Me"**: "I wanted to be amazing. I wanted to be so amazing. I had al-

ready been amazing up to a certain point. But I was tired of being at that point. I wanted to go past that point. I wanted to be more amazing than I had been. . . ." Or from **"Knowledge"**: "You're not really telling me that that is what all of this fuss is about. Is that what all of this fuss is about? I cannot believe that this is what all of this fuss is about. Is that what you have been making such a fuss about?" This sort of thing gets very old very quickly, and it suggests not a love of experimentation but a poverty of imagination; the repetition often seems the only means Lish has of filling his pages.

Of course, many of the techniques of experimental fiction have now become conventions in their own right, the most outworn of which—a fiction writer speaking directly to his readers about the process of writing fiction—is also Lish's favorite. A piece titled **"Shit"** begins: "I like talking about people sitting on toilets. It shows up in the bulk of my speech. Wherever at all in keeping with things, I try to work it in. You just have to look back at stories I have had printed to see that I am telling the truth." Similarly, **"Leopard in a Temple"** begins: "Look, let's make it short and sweet. Who anymore doesn't go crazy from overtures, from fanfares, from set-ups, from preambles, from preliminaries? So, okay, here is the thing—this is my Kafka story."

Occasionally these pieces offer an engaging, raucous humor and a powerfully felt impression of Jewish family life that recall the work of Joseph Heller or Philip Roth. But unlike Roth (whose narrators are no less self-absorbed than Lish's, and whose work is also concerned with memory, confession, and the nature of fiction), Lish seems unable or unwilling to forge any substantial artistic statement out of his obsessive themes. Thus we get the strenuous insistence and defensiveness of this volume's jacket copy—which, as *Harper's Magazine* reported, was written by Lish himself: "whatever judgment the reader takes away with him from his experience with *Mourner at the Door,* no reader will go away from these pages unshaken by the force of their sentences, nor will any reader not know why it is that Gordon Lish has so powerfully and indelibly entered the literary history of this century." Let us charitably presume (as *Harper's* did not, using "But Enough About You" as a headline for its report) that Lish is here attempting to parody the inflated rhetoric of jacket blurbs rather than to inflate his own reputation, yet "force" and "power" are exactly what this volume lacks. In their place the reader is offered cuteness and self-indulgence in nearly all of these pieces. Like the jacket copy, they suggest a good deal of posturing and a squandered talent.

Gordon Lish with Amy Penn   (interview date 1988)

SOURCE: Interview by Amy Penn, originally published in *INTERVIEW Magazine,* Brant Publications, January, 1988, pp. 94-5, 101.

[In the following interview, Lish discusses aspects of his career as an editor, teacher, and writer.]

[Penn]: *Where have you taught writing?*

[Lish]: I've taught at Yale, Columbia and NYU. Now I only teach privately. I run workshops in the spring and fall, two at a time—one meets on Tuesday nights, the other on Thursday nights—from six to twelve o'clock.

Who are some of the writers who have studied with you?

Amy Hempel and Anderson Ferrel are two who are well known. I can tell you two names you will certainly know as the years wear on: Mark Richard and Yannick Murphy. I predict the highest returns for two others: Jennifer Allen and Ted Pejovich. While making predictions, I'll say that William Tester will be knocking you flat presently. One of my former students is Christopher Coe, and he has published his first book, a splendid novella called *I Look Divine.*

Do you consider yourself first and foremost a writer or a teacher?

I feel most centered in myself and most useful to the world as a teacher. I feel most possessed of a kind of unpredictable exuberance when I am teaching, so that surely, to offer a quick judgment, I'd want to claim that my personality is actually that of a teacher. Writing does not leave me with the kind of enduring satisfaction that teaching does. When I am obliged to review sentences that I have put into the world, I find it difficult to continue having an affection for them. Not so for what I produce as a teacher. As a writer, the best I've done strikes me as not nearly good enough.

Are there certain qualities you have found to be consistent in the writers you have taught?

Yes. I believe that each of these writers has widened my own purchase on the world, on my heart, on my own perception of myself moving through the world. I can't imagine my taking on a writer who in some way did not engage a visceral response matched by an intellectual response. I have to feel myself overwhelmed and opened up to visions that would not have already occurred to me. I don't look to these prospects to confirm what I already know, but rather to surprise, to unsettle, to refresh, to jog me to the side a goodish distance. So that when there comes a writer like Yannick Murphy or Mark Richards, two persons whose work could not be more unlike the kind of work I myself would produce, I'm stunned and loudly exhilarated by the prospect for extension of not myself, but of what I know and feel. These writers are not continuous with what my own impulses are. They occur to me as prophets to my being in the world. They enlarge my own experience rather than confirm my own experience, by persuading me that these things are in the world. These things are in the world somewhere, and I, without their guidance, would not have seen these things.

Let's discuss Lish's Laws.

Lish's Laws seem to be almost obnoxious now, but I know I've stated them. They're evolving with the time. If one has

to be a writer, to be a teacher, one has to maintain a certain rate of growth. If not, you're not doing your work anymore. I would revise the term *laws* to read something like principles, claims or adulations.

To be a writer, one has to tell the truth, and one has to tell the hardest truth that is available in one. One has to tell one's own truth. One has to risk everything to capture that truth; one has to reach down inside of oneself to the zone of most crucial danger, to the zone where, in fact, one may even be unsettling one's notion of oneself and therefore destabilizing one's personality. Through means of acoustical pressure, through means of thematic pressure, one must extrude that acuity and get it onto the page so that it can be seen. I think that this task is accomplished chiefly as a function of courage, of the will, and then of an absolutely unrelenting industry.

If we are bent on rendering our acuity precisely as we understand it to be in our deepest, deepest selves, then I think, all things being equal, we have a very rich prospect of making an important noise in national literature. I'm only talking about the procedure—how one begins to elucidate a story, to find a story in oneself, a story of such rank as to merit the attention of persons who are all day long confronted with the shrieks of humanity. As we come to the end of the century, how does one properly engage intelligent attention in a world that is screaming for excellent reason into the ears of everyone out there all day long? How does one make, within that frame, a noise of the kind that warrants the attention of one's proper audience? One has to find in oneself the place of greatest jeopardy, and then with a kind of surfeit of recklessness and courage, go beyond even that to uncover yet another kind of disqualifying and contradicting truth. The writer must each time redouble his efforts to probe more deeply, and more deeply and more deeply, knowing that as he does so he gains the fuel, the energy for an important fiction discourse. It is the only way for a writer to confront the horrific discouragement of being in a world with people who are smarter than he is, who know more, who feel more, who have more, who have had more experience and who will again and again surpass him in capturing the attention. It seems to me that one must come to terms with the interior object and find one's stories within it.

> **To be a writer, one has to tell the truth, and one has to tell the hardest truth that is available in one. One has to tell one's own truth.**
>
> **—Gordon Lish**

Let's touch on the method to your madness. You'll throw anything from a student's divorce to his bank account in his face. Do you have any idea of how some of your students leave your classroom and what you may have evoked in them?

Yes. I don't think anyone leaves untouched or unaffected. I think some go away ultimately disapproving, ultimately undone; many go away with at least a way of thinking about writing, an attitude about being an artist. I think that an increasingly remarkable share of these students are able to go away with a strong sense of what is requisite for the page. People have transformed themselves within a matter of two or three meetings. At the same time, I've observed persons who have been with me for four, five, six workshops—that is to say many, many hours of the most vehement instruction—who are probably worse off than when they came to me, because what they had, what they believed in, has been taken from them, and nothing has been put in its place. Which is not to say that I have not put anything in its place, but rather I claim that such persons have been unable to install anything in its place. I think that inability is frequently a function of age. The older we get, the more difficult it is to take on new ways of behaving, and that's largely what my kind of teaching is about. It's about another way to behave. If by a certain age you've gotten through life managing your environment with a certain relation to language, it is extraordinarily difficult to set that aside, and that's really what's required. So sometimes it seems to me the younger candidates make the better students.

You've said that if you're going to write, you're going to write. You're going to write at three in the morning, you're going to write if you're half asleep. . . .

Absolutely. Even without the search for an alibi for failing to write—funeral services for a family member, illness—the body, your own body, wants you to fail, and it will always offer up alibis for you to fail. I think one makes this a daily oblation; it's an undertaking that must be habitual in the face of every kind of worldly interference from spouses or children or colleagues. None of us lives in the world alone. So in order to establish the kind of discipline that is requisite to doing important writing, one has to be prepared to anger a lot of people a lot of the time, because one is obliged again and again to say, "No, I must be in my space now and do what I do in that space."

I cannot believe that anything important is earned without not only great strife for oneself, but also great rupture around one. It's a question of making these choices. What are you willing to pay? I believe you've got to pay through the nose in order to achieve the kind of speech that will matter in history. Because the faculty for writing is like a muscle; if it is not exercised regularly and to its stress point, it will never be a healthy muscle. You have to do this kind of thing without cease, whatever the claims on your attentions. You have to exploit yourself as insistently and as dangerously as you can, and you have to be comparably prepared to exploit everything around you. No one is claiming that the modality of the artistic life is an admirable one or even one which is suffused with

civic goodness. On the contrary, it may be that the process of creating art of a kind that will have a life in history will necessarily interfere very astringently with the processes of living life. I think that's a rather fair exchange, not an unholy one at all. It is a liaison that establishes a sort of demon in the self. One has to want this greatly.

I believe that we all want to stick out in the world, that the least of us has a profound impulse to distinguish himself from everyone else on earth, and I believe the doing of art—creativity—is the way we chiefly go about this kind of thing. The bulk of us are deprived of such opportunities. If we are determined to stick out to such extremes as to be given account of in history, then the price for doing so is going to be exorbitant.

What are your expectations for yourself as a writer?

I have a collection of short stories called **Mourner at the Door** coming out in March. But what I want to write is *Extravaganza,* a novel I've been working on for six years. I want it to be a novel that brings to the page the configuration of the most secret pressure in me. In the last twelve versions that I've written of this book, I've discovered that I have yet to uncover that pressure. I'm well aware of what it is, but I'm yet to have the grip on it to be able to put it down. I keep teasing around the edges of it, then tart it up to make it handsomer, more genial, more congenial. In the version I'm beginning now, the only real challenge is to be the equal to what I know the task must be. It is not really a challenge that is literary, because I have the means to do the work. I know how to make the sentences. I have to find the courage to utter those sentences. As of a week or so ago, I did not have the courage, but this morning I believe I do.

Where does that courage come from?

It comes in part from recklessness, part from fearlessness, part from desire and part, I think, from the will to dissolve the self. If you want badly enough what all of us want—to dissolve oneself, to fall out of time, to fall out of history, to swoon—then you may be willing to let go of ego just long enough to have something which appears to be courage. I think that if you are enough overcome by that feeling, you may, for a bit of time, be willing to let go of your vanity, your shame, your ego, so that you can dissolve with an audience watching. That's what I want.

Let's talk about the new magazine that you're editing.

I have persuaded the key officers at Random House to back me in a literary magazine, an adventure that is called *The Quarterly.* As an activity, it brings to a kind of closure a tremendous impulse in me, which is to find ways to shout about that for which I have great affection. The magazine represents an extraordinarily open forum for the unsigned and undiscovered who are writing in English. I hope to claim that I've been discovering a great, great number of them each time we come out. What I'm doing is singing as loud as I can my praises for them. I can't begin to tell you how greatly I am restored by this activity.

Do you think that anything exists for writers in New York that is "homey"?

That is homey in the sense of community? I'm not really able to answer this question with accuracy because of my age. I can think of a number of networks where young writers come together, sometimes socially, sometimes professionally, that must give them some sense of being in communion with one another. Given my age and my isolation, I have such a feeling of fellowship with a group of writers, and we often are in touch with each other. These would be Don DeLillo, Cynthia Ozick, Harold Brodkey chiefly. It would be extended to Harold Bloom and Denis Donoghue. These are people with whom I'll have some regular intercourse—by telephone, over lunch—but nothing that would constitute the regular contact that I think younger artists do have and do require and should profit from. I'm not willing to believe that writers of my age are necessarily improved by such contact on an intense basis. My hunch is that it is a diversion from activities they should most probably be at. One must rid oneself of alibis if one wants to do this kind of work. I don't know if I can talk to someone coherently in the course of writing a novel, and I find myself distracted all the time. A novel might take a year or take me eight months or something of that sort. I'm incessantly distracted. The only time I find myself really focused in contradistinction of that distraction is when I'm teaching. It's very difficult for me to draw myself from it otherwise, so that my spouse and my children, I'm sure, pay a certain price. My friends definitely do, because I'm not in touch and not available for friendship in the way that one would like to be. If I think about the writers I admire most, they tend to be isolated. They tend not to need or wish for the company of others very much. One's family seems to be about the size of it.

Is writing lonely?

Writing isn't lonely in the most important sense, because when you do it, you are in touch with your best friend, so the loneliness can be abridged in those terms. Also, a writer can suppose to himself that by doing his work, he is fashioning a bridge to other lone souls in space and in time—that he is in conversation with the most secret place in himself and others. I am most willing to sense a kind of consort when I am truly engaged in a conversation with my deepest self. I then feel as if I'm Gordon Lish. Gordon and not even Lish. As if I'm Gordy. As if I'm suddenly emptied of all the impedimenta that interfered with my having access to Gordy: my age, the world I live in, the lies I tell all day long, all the fraudulences in the world that make life do-able, of which we all are immeasurably guilty. I'm not entirely convinced that the routine complaint of loneliness really suffices to answer the entire question. Of course, you do it by yourself. You can't even count on anyone else in your immediate camp to put up with the sort of behavior you create around you when you are doing this sort of thing. You really ought not to ask anyone into it; you oughtn't read to your spouse or your children or your par-

ents and so on. I think that you go into the bathroom and you do your business.

MacDonald Harris (essay date 1988)

SOURCE: "Going Crazy with Pencil and Paper," in *Los Angeles Times Book Review,* March 13, 1988, pp. 3, 7.

[*Harris, pseudonym of Donald Heiney, is an American novelist and critic. In the following essay, he offers a favorable review of the stories in* Mourner at the Door.]

By all evidence, Gordon Lish is a remarkable person. He is better known as an editor than as a fiction writer. For a number of years, he was the fiction editor of *Esquire;* more recently he has been an editor at Alfred A. Knopf and the founder and editor of *The Quarterly,* a magazine which has sought to bring the work of younger, often experimental American writers to the attention of a wider public. He has taught in various universities, and was at one time the director of linguistic studies at a research laboratory. As if this weren't enough, he is the author of two novels and a previous volume of stories, **What I Know So Far.**

The first sentence of the first story in [**Mourner at the Door**] is, "I wanted to be amazing." It is about a boy's summer experience in camp, but Lish writes it with a heartfelt emphasis; there can be no doubt that it is a wish he shares with his character. In fact, his talent is a special one. His fiction has a sheen transparency to it, the polished surface of a simple and perfectly designed machine, yet one with something slightly fey or odd to it. Some of these pieces are not stories at all; they are just collections of clever language. But they are very clever. He is good at monologues, and in **Mourner at the Door,** it becomes clear that his real specialty is something he himself invented, the obsessive monologue of clichés addressed to a silent listener. **"The Merry Chase"** consists of seven pages of stereotyped formulas for putting people down. It ends, "You think I am talking just to hear myself talk?" **"Spell Bereavement"** is a variation on the technique; the narrator's sister and mother alternate on the telephone, upbraiding him for not feeling anything for his father's death and browbeating him about coming home for the funeral. He doesn't speak a word. At the end, it turns out that the reason for his silence is that he is "going crazy with a pencil and paper," getting down all these wonderful insults to put them in a story.

These pieces are not for the lazy or slow reader; they are in a kind of telegraphese, an intricate and repetitive post-modern style located somewhere near the intersection of Gertrude Stein and Donald Barthelme. One consists almost entirely of women's names, culminating with that of his own wife, and another of place-names from an atlas, including several sites of Nazi death camps. They are not exactly suitable for your old Aunt Harriet; one of them is entirely about vomiting, and another about excretion, although Lish doesn't call it that. There is a

not be negative. Be not negativized. Befriend

negativity not. Shun negativity. Eschew negativity.

Send down negativity. Turn a cold shoulder to

negativity. Never know the name of negativity. Make

yourself the assassin of negativity. Let negativity

not enter in. Keep negativity out. Go away from

negativity. Take flight from negativity. Rid thy

house of negativity. Be free of negativity. Tear up

the taproot of negativity. Throw off the garment of

negativity. Eat not of the nutriment of negativity.

Worry negativity. Usher negativity away. Shut your

door to negativity. Spurn negativity. Scorn it.

Smite it. Never call out to the servants of

negativity. Hate negativity. No, no, not to summon

negativity's jinn. Unlearn negativity. Do unto

negativity as you would the unclean. Let not your mind

2

Page from the typescript for Lish's "Philosphical Statements," written in 1991.

smart-aleck, know-it-all quality about all of them that you can find amusing or annoying, according to your taste. **"Behold the Incredible Revenge of the Shifted P.O.V."** is a long ramble about a grandmother clock, and it shifts point of view at the end, thus the title. If you haven't been hanging around writing schools, you don't know that P.O.V. is shorthand for point of view. You may not even know what point of view means; so much the worse for you. Lish gives you no help at all, and he seems to delight in your discomfort. In short, he puts you down.

While you are still staggering, or annoyed, you come to **"Fish Story,"** a fish story in which the narrator tells you how, as a boy, he caught 12 fish with a fence picket, a length of Venetian blind cord, and no hook. Then he smirks, "He'll bite on any fool thing, your silly blowfish will. But so for that matter, will your friendly reader—hook, line and sinker. I mean, since it is all the same in the end, and if it is all the same to you, give me human nature every time— and the equally hideous fishing of men." Is he comparing himself to Jesus? No, probably he means just that he is a clever writer.

The pieces in *Mourner at the Door* are not for the lazy or slow reader; they are in a kind of telegraphese, an intricate and repetitive post-modern style located somewhere near the intersection of Gertrude Stein and Donald Barthelme.

—*MacDonald Harris*

It's impossible to give the full effect of these pieces by quoting short fragments of them, because they depend for their effect on the very weight and monotony of iteration. This is a style that Lish experimented with in his 1984 collection, *What I Know So Far,* and in this book, he brings it to a high and refined pitch. *Mourner at the Door* has a beautiful unity of style, 27 stories in the same mode, with slight variations as though they were a musical composition; it is more like the "Goldberg Variations" than it is like the latest rock album. The jacket copy suggests that after reading it, the reader will "know why it is that Gordon Lish has so powerfully and indelibly entered the literary history of this century." That's a little strong, but it can be said that he certainly does not write like an editor. He writes like a writer who has trouble with editors, who want to change his writing all around and make it more normal and grammatical and less personal than it is. Luckily, Lish has enough clout in the publishing world so they can't do that to him.

Josh Rubins (essay date 1988)

SOURCE: "Bygone Haircuts and Other Stories," in *The New York Times Book Review,* April 3, 1988, p. 11.

[*In the following negative review of* Mourner at the Door, *Rubins maintains that Lish's short fiction is "so mannered, so derivatively styled, as to cancel out all intimacy and empathy."*]

From Huck Finn to Holden Caulfield, "Call me Ishmael" to "So it goes," the calling up of home-grown voices, narrators who address us in the unbuttoned vernacular with conversational immediacy, has been one of the impudent glories of American fiction. Backwoodsy or ethnic, laconic or rambling, the most commanding of these straight talkers take a shortcut into the reader's imagination. We seem to be getting the story firsthand, unvarnished and unpackaged, instead of through a literary sieve—especially when the narrator is also at the center of the action.

Gordon Lish's first novel, *Dear Mr. Capote,* which was cast in the form of a serial killer's letter to the author of *In Cold Blood,* was very much a bravura performance in this informal-monologue tradition. Mr. Lish's nameless New York psychopath unburdened himself in a disarmingly colloquial voice, mixing Runyonesque locutions with garbled clichés (à la Archie Bunker) and casual obscenities. The contrast between the narrator's chatty spiel and his horrific confessions gave rise to mordantly amusing effects. The book's essential flatness could be taken as a skillful reflection of the madman's deformed sensibility. (*Peru,* a second, less forceful mock-memoir, also tackled the theme of violence alienated from feeling.) Yet, for all the craft and energy on display in this impersonation, one could never forget—not even for one of suspended disbelief's fractional moments—that the voice of *Dear Mr. Capote* was being artificially, laboriously produced by a sophisticated ventriloquist.

In Mr. Lish's short stories, unfortunately, not only are you aware of a ventriloquist at work: you keep seeing his lips move. Both *What I Know So Far* and this second, even slighter collection [*Mourner at the Door*] offer fragments of nakedly autobiographical free association. Some of the new material—the ambivalent mourning of a father's death, the panicky love for a child growing up too fast—comes with built-in emotional clout. But the first-person voices in these 27 pieces, though fitted out with the soul-baring vocabulary of the analyst's couch, are so mannered, so derivatively styled, as to cancel out all intimacy and empathy.

The "I" in *Mourner at the Door* almost always affects some form of inarticulate confusion—a familiar enough pose in post–*Catcher in the Rye* American letters, but one rarely so unconvincingly assumed. Each "I mean" and "I guess," every "sort of" and "I don't know," seems painfully calculated. One solemn anecdote, **"Resurrection,"** leans mercilessly on the narrator's verbal shrugs involving "thing": "the country thing," "the house-guest thing," "the big thing," "the whole thing" and—raising the specter of unintentional parody—"this burnished thing the April light can sometimes get to be at maybe five o'clock. . . ."

Nor do the story-by-story variations on this faux-naïf drawl add much authenticity. When the delivery is recognizably Jewish (as it often is), the broad, studied inflections register more as feeble echoes—of Stanley Elkin, Saul Bellow, Philip Roth—than as cadences particular to "the story of Gordon Lishnofski." When the monologues turn themselves into run-on sentences, alphabetical lists or numbered paragraphs (there's a virtual compendium of once-trendy literary gimmicks here), they seem to do so out of fecklessness rather than psychological or intellectual necessity. And when the narrator adopts a benumbed, incantatory tone suggestive of partial lobotomy or terminal irony—as in **"The Death of Me,"** a meditation on childhood's delusions of grandeur—the arch aping of Gertrude Stein distracts from any frail kernel of content:

"I wanted to be amazing," this story's narrator begins. "I wanted to be so amazing. I had already been amazing up to a certain point. But I was tired of being at that point. I wanted to go past that point. I wanted to be more amazing than I had been up to that point. I wanted to do something which went beyond that point and which went beyond every other point and which people would look at and say that this was something which went beyond all other points and which no other boy would ever be able to go beyond, that I was the only boy who could, that I was the only one."

It's the scarcity of substance, in fact, that forces the synthetic voicings in **Mourner at the Door** into such constant, unflattering focus. Tiny silvers of reminiscence—about sexual conquests, bygone haircuts, an aunt's compulsive joke-telling—fail to take on larger resonance, despite cheaply manipulative punch lines that invoke concentration camps and cancer. In four redundant sketches, the narrator is tormented by the interchangeable kvetchings, cartoonishly exaggerated yet short on satiric brio, of his tetchy wife and generic Jewish mother. Clinical tidbits—a married couple's obsession with vomiting, a friendless spinster's devotion to a dubious pet—settle for freak-show bathos. Most undernourished of all, however, are Mr. Lish's post-modernist attempts to make a concert program out of authorial throat-clearing—with self-pitying ruminations on the ordeal of Being a Writer.

In only one story is the modesty of Mr. Lish's material matched by a relaxed, relatively unpretentious voice, one that flickers, at least, with genuineness. The narrator of **"Fish Story"** presents his growing-up-Jewish memories—mostly about a make-shift fishing expedition in quest of a "real American" boyhood—as a low-key stand-up comic's frankly light-weight shtick. ("I am not saying that what happened converted an indoors type to an outdoors one. I still get closest to God somewhere where you can control the light.") Yet, in its last paragraph, even this wry recollection succumbs to preciousness: the memoirist, musing portentou.ly on "the equally hideous fishing of men," reminds us that, just like a blowfish, "your friendly reader" will "bite on any fool thing."

Mr. Lish, an influential fiction editor for some 20 years (primarily at *Esquire* magazine and Alfred A. Knopf),

surely knows better. But "any fool thing"—the flotsam and jetsam of a would-be writer's notebook—all too precisely describes the contents of this self-conscious, dispiriting collection.

Erin McGraw (essay date 1988)

SOURCE: "Universes," in *The North American Review*, Vol. 273, No. 3, September, 1988, pp. 64-8.

[*Below, McGraw provides an unfavorable review of the stories in* Mourner at the Door.]

It is not immobility that afflicts Gordon Lish's characters in the stories that make up *Mourner at the Door.* These are characters capable of taking some kind of action in the world, who attempt, sometimes, to reach out to one another. There is, however, an enormous amount of *talking* that has to be got through before any action can be essayed, talk that backtracks, second-guesses, and assures the reader several times that this action, once arrived at, will be worth the wait. One story begins this way:

Don't tell me. Do me a favor and let me guess. Be honest with me, tell the truth, don't make me laugh. Tell me, don't make me have to tell you, do I have to tell you that when you're hot you're hot, that when you're dead you're dead? Because you know what I know? I know you like I know myself, I know you like the back of my hand, I know you like a book, I know you inside out. You know what? I know you like you'll never know.

Another like this:

My wife says, "Look at you. Just look at you. How can you look like that? Why don't you take a good look at yourself? Look at me, don't you have any idea of what you look like? What do you think people are going to think when they look at you? Tell me, how can you go around looking like that? Do you know what you look like? You couldn't conceivably know what you look like. Who would believe that anyone could look like that? I can't believe what you look like . . ."

Another like this:

I wanted to be amazing. I wanted to be so amazing. I had already been amazing up to a certain point. But I was tired of being at that point. I wanted to go past that point. I wanted to be more amazing than I had been up to that point. I wanted to do something which went beyond that point and which went beyond every other point and which people would look at and say that this was something which went beyond all other points and which no other boy would ever be able to go beyond, that I was the only boy who could, that I was the only one.

The collection contains 27 stories, many of them quite short, but all sharing this quality of hysteria, until the reader wants to snarl back at the book, "Quit *shouting* at me!" The prose is arch and self-conscious throughout, and narrative snappiness, the sense of the heard voice, becomes a tic. The narrative voice is what Lish is best known for, but it is turned into a burlesque of itself in this collection as characters natter on and on. Many of the stories are, at one level or another, about the writing of stories, but as we are forced to hear them in the voice of these consistently neurotic, compulsive narrators, we lose interest in what story *could* be told, and are left with the irritation of hearing the same scale, the same riff, practiced again and again and again.

> The characters in *Mourner at the Door* are like children tugging at our sleeve, whining louder and louder, afraid their concerns are being overlooked, and we end by feeling *nagged* by these stories, left no decent room to consider or respond or breathe.
>
> —*Erin McGraw*

The stories are also remarkably uncharitable. They are, first of all, uncharitable toward their characters. The people of *Mourner at the Door* speak in the circular, agitated manner of those under great stress, like people just released from est or therapy, people who feel they have the right to claim the floor. Their monologues are small journeys of self-discovery, and self-hate pours forth, as characters discover in themselves the capacity for cruelty, or cowardice, or cynicism. In fiction, in life, the frenzy of talk is sometimes earned, is sometimes the hallmark of emotional release. But presented as it is here, endlessly, that frenzy is cheapened; we have the impression that these people were yammering before we came into the room and will be yammering after we leave.

But the stories are also uncharitable toward the reader, who isn't permitted for even a moment the illusion that she will be left alone to put things together. Everything is carefully delineated and laid out, and the characters are tremendously anxious to explain themselves to us. This is not to say, of course, that the characters' explanations of their own behavior is always to be accepted—in general, I am inclined to judge these people less harshly than they judge themselves. But they're like children tugging at our sleeve, whining louder and louder, afraid their concerns are being overlooked, and we end by feeling *nagged* by these stories, left no decent room to consider or respond or breathe.

There are some fine moments in *Mourner at the Door.* "The Friend" is quite moving (it is also richer in traditional narrative than most of the stories in the collection—largely in the third person, it covers a separate landscape, a realm we are allowed to imagine). And "History, or the Four Pictures of Vludka" is shocking in the best revealing, necessary sense—even those things we hold most solemn and sacred are rooted, after all, in the world; even martyrs were human. Even as we cannot approach the hor-

ror of the death camps, we are drawn to them: We *made* them. This is a moment of pain because the reader is as one with the narrator, not knowing what to do with the wretched knowledge we carry, are heirs to. But too often this excellence breaks down into shock-for-shock's sake, with Lish scrambling for effects in the spirit of a seventh-grader telling fart jokes. (The justly notorious "Shit" begins, "I like talking about people sitting on toilets.")

The collection ends with "Fish Story," a story more modulated in tone than most, that concerns a man remembering the day in his New York City-bred childhood that he decided, in the finest Wheaties and Jack Armstrong tradition, to catch a fish. To his amazement, when he dips his line of knotted Venetian blind cord into the inlet, he pulls up a full string of blowfish.

> He'll bite on any fool thing, your silly blowfish will. But so, for that matter, will your friendly reader—hook, line, and sinker. I mean, since it is all the same in the end, and if it is all the same to you, give me human nature every time—and the equally hideous fishing of men.

It is only too apt—that readers will suck onto anything, however unnourishing, however inappropriate. It is the view that pervades the book, that readers will gobble down whatever mingy little insights are let down by the one who sets out to haul us poor and dumb creatures in.

Irving Malin   (essay date 1988)

SOURCE: A review of *Mourner at the Door,* in *The Review of Contemporary Fiction,* Vol. VIII, No. 3, Fall, 1988, pp. 157-58.

[*Malin is an American critic. In the following laudatory review, he praises Lish's use of language in his short fiction.*]

I must quote the following long epigraph because it is the key to Lish's amazing collection:

> It is reported that Wittgenstein's last words were these: "Tell them that I had a wonderful life." Perhaps he did and perhaps he did not—have a wonderful life. But how could Wittgenstein have known one way or the other? As to a further matter, suppose that these were not the words—suppose the words were German words. What I want to know is this—is it the same thing to have a wonderful life in another language? Or put it this way—if another language was the the language that Wittgenstein had it in, then how could it have been a wonderful life?

If we look at the twisted, tortured paths of these sentences we see that Lish is trying to understand the relationship of "life" to "language," of the "world" to the "word." Do "words" have any significance in our lives? How do we gain knowledge? Can we ever bridge the gap between experience and description—an experience

---

Lish on the major enemies of great fiction:

Fear: "That's why so many writers drink or take drugs. It's fear, it's fear, it's fear, it's fear, it's embarrassment, it's anxiety, it's fear, it's fear."

Self-consciousness: "One has to find a way to uncover the heart."

Money: "If I can't outpull everyone else as a function of my alacrity as an editor, I quit. I don't want to make this magazine [*Esquire*] the best it can be simply as a function of Knopf having very deep pockets."

Hollywood: "But of course anybody who volunteers himself for that sort of whoredom gets exactly what he's set up for. We all open our legs for something."

Gordon Lish with Lisa Grunwald, in Esquire, *March, 1989.*

---

itself!—of experience? The epigraph contains sardonic, "metaphysical" circles.

I have spent so much time on the epigraph that I cannot do justice to the brilliant stories. The stories are, first of all, deliberately short. They inform us that basic questions of "life" are abrupt, shocking, and minimal. The stories are "amazing"—to use one of Lish's favorite words—because they recognize that we (or the characters or, rather, the words) cannot offer full explanation.

"The Death of Me" repeats compulsively that "I wanted to be amazing. I wanted to be so amazing. I had already been amazing up to a certain point. But I was tired of being at that point. I wanted to go past that point." Consider the repetitions, the ritualistic compulsions. What is the "point"? Isn't the "point" Wittgenstein's? How do we move past the past? How do we go beyond? And how do we ever know, if we do? The story doesn't inform us, doesn't give answers. It ends in a kind of silence as the adults merely pat the child-narrator on the head.

I quote lines from other stories. Here are some from **"Last Descent to Earth"**: "One had words galore. One had words to burn. One had to beat them off with a stick. I myself had words to kill, and did away with as many as one could." The narrator wants to destroy "words"—to *kill* them, to *burn* them—because he recognizes that we live in a fallen world in which we cannot understand our "descent."

In another story, we have the ending: "Adjectives—oh *Christ!*" There is the linkage between "description" and religion. Can we ever get answers? Can we get to the point of life and death?

I merely list titles: **"Don't Die," "Spell Bereavement"** (a pun?), **"Agony," "Knowledge," "The Death of Me."** I see that Lish cannot control his anguish of non-knowledge, his inability to capture meanings. Now I understand that his previous works—full of murder, torture,

sadism—fit into the pattern I have been tracing. They also deal with frustrated narrators who try desperately to find final solutions.

Why does Lish give us **Mourner at the Door** as the title of this book? We recognize that *we* are before the doors of Heaven; we can't get *in* because we don't know the right words, the passwords. We mourn our inabilities, our "death-in-life" (whatever these words *mean*). We remain silent, hoping, perhaps, that silence is the answer.

Lish's collection is an important literary event, a book which uses words to battle words. It is a murder-suicide because it gets to the "point" in an amazing manner. It wins as it loses.

David Seabrook (essay date 1990)

SOURCE: "'What We Write About When We Write About Gordon Lish'," in *The New American Writing: Essays on American Literature Since 1970,* edited by Graham Clarke, Vision Press, 1990, pp. 123-38.

[*In the following excerpt, Seabrook examines Lish's work in the context of minimalist fiction and discusses the unconventional narrative techniques utilized in* What I Know So Far.]

In its Fall and Winter issues of 1988 the *Michigan Quarterly Review* published 'A Symposium on Contemporary American Fiction': solicited contributions from more than seventy authors on their preferences in current American writing. Many opted for brief, breathy endorsements, sometimes of each other; a few writers, inured to interrogation, declined to name names. Strewn through these responses is the general rant on the subject of minimalist writing, and when the name of Gordon Lish is finally invoked it is to make the rant more specific and also to specify why he has not been mentioned before: [According to Daniel Stern,] 'The so-called "minimalist" writers—some people have called them the children of Gordon Lish—are thin, self-regarding, narcissistic. . . .' Lish is the grey eminence behind this literary anorexia, the chief offender in what, elsewhere in the symposium, Raymond Carver refers to as the 'stale debate' of 'Minimalism v. Maximalism'.

The term's obfuscatory appeal is strengthened, in Carver's case, by the notion that his stories are both cosmetically confounding and obscurely traditional, *à la* Hemingway, for the studied eschewal of all but the middle of a narrative is nothing less than an urbane acknowledgement of its incompleteness. Many of the symposium's contributors, in common with British and American reviewers, adopt a correspondingly traditional view of his work, assessing the deployment of computerized rigour in the service of some higher, humanistic purpose. Carver and Lish both have claims to be regarded as minimalists, yet Lish seems to have been penalized for his appropriation of the end rather than the middle. Despite the acquisition of favourable reviews at home, his is a notable absence from the *Michigan Quarterly Review's* symposium of 'distinguished American fiction writers'; in Britain, where his short story collection remains unavailable, his name is practically unknown.

Lish's early work, the short stories that form the collection *What I Know So Far* (1984), seems to blot its own letter of introduction through its forfeiture of recognizable literary aims—character, momentum, resolution—for the cultivation of a breezy anonymity. Lish's pennywise ratepayers fret over sons, wives, vagrants, and insist on their citizenhood. Yet living liaises with language to alter the status of a soliloquy and the presuppositions of its speaker: 'The wife insisted she would tell her version first. I was instantly interested because of the word' ('**Everything I Know**'). Conventional narration is jettisoned in favour of what can be termed literal figurations, in which narrative revelation is redefined as verbal process, whose speakers, as the sum of their sentences, bear semantic, rather than psychological scars. The content of the stories, which concern themselves with codes, shapes, surfaces, and, of course, stories and poems, animates them as suburban farce whilst enshrining anxiety as form. The fear is of what will take space, not place: 'But you're looking at this and thinking these are really truths. You're thinking why make sentences if all they do is fool' ('**Imp Among Aunts**').

The resultant pressure postulates a fever chart that may be read sociologically or psycho-semantically, as the speaker of '**The Psoriasis Diet**' (*psoriasis:* 'skin disease marked by red patches covered with scales', O.E.D.) is discovering:

> *Psoriasis*
> I've seen worse words. Besides, it got me on education, being as how I took up an interest in language right after. I started with all the pee-ess words and just kept on after that. There was no stopping me, I can tell you.
>
> There was no stopping it, either.

This is figuration as disfigurement in which each sentence spoken is another skin sloughed, and in tandem with this exfoliation Lish's own lexicon is laid waste, acceding to the slow death of dyslexias. As the narrator declares as the voice closes:

> Not anachronism.
> *Anachorism.*
> Look it up.

Experimentation ebbs into euthanasia, to which the reading (as writing) process is seen to be analogous. Elsewhere the stories trumpet their demise rather more discordantly:

> It is why I am not very interested in people—nor in myself. We all of us know exactly what to say, and say it—the man who sat with me making a drama out of his half-finished glass; I, speaking to him then and speaking to you now; you, reading and making your mind up about this page.
>
> There is no escape from this. Nor is it any longer necessary to act as if there might be.
>
> (‘**What Is Left to Link Us**’)

This is the point at which the tortuous tramlines of Borgesian legerdemain and *nouvelle roman* tendentiousness converge. A route to nowhere, in fact. The psoriasis victim sheds tears as well as skin.

The ascendancy of a counter-impulse discontinues this cycle of the self-defining dilemma. Lish flees claustrality and consecrates a structuralist shibboleth in a deferral to his reader as writer, surfacing in Ian Hamilton's bedevilled biography of J. D. Salinger [*In Search of J. D. Salinger*] as a parenthetical footnote to a legend when the book's rubble of conjecture finally yields an *aperçu* of genuine interest:

> There have been Salinger spoofs: in 1977 *Esquire* published a story called '**For Rupert—With No Promises**' and there were rumours that Salinger had written it (the piece was actually composed by the magazine's fiction editor, Gordon Lish). . . .

'Spoof' sits oddly in the story's proximity; the wheedling and wonder of Salinger's style is cleaved to down to the high-school italics, yet the virulence of its refutation makes it more taunt that treat. In an address to his brother's son the narrator Buddy warns him of imminent danger at the hands of his father, the terminally ill Smithy. Adamant that his ex-wife has poisoned the teenager against him, he fears for the life of 5-year-old Rupert, his second and best-loved boy: 'Some way none of us can predict, my firstborn will stalk my second, find a way to hurt *him* because my death *robs* him of his chance to hurt *me*.' Murder is the proposed solution 'and if you are your father's son, Chap, you will see he has a point'.

'**For Rupert**' begins its assault on the Salinger code with Buddy's commendations of 'a Viennese logician', presumably Wittgenstein, as a prelude to his brother's 'reasoned argument', whose obeisance to the dictates of logic 'could give the Viennese logician cards and spades'. The wayward mysticism of Salinger's Glass family is then called briskly to heel by the Old Testament authority of Lish's scenario, which offers 'No Promises', of reprieve or anything else. It is perhaps the voice of a readership (the readership that thought it was reading Salinger) appalled at its own assertiveness in the face of such desertion.

'**For Jerome—with Love and Kisses**' counters the logical proposition with the emotional outburst. Chicago meat importer Sol Salinger does not expect another novel, a telephone call will suffice. 'Please God, Heaven should make a miracle and your father should live that long, you won't have to worry, his number is in the book.' Hyperbolic, semetic musicality stresses family ties and the story does service as a trenchant rebuttal of Kafka's 'Letter to his Father', orphaning a parent into a jeremiad of his own in which anonymity shades sleekly into stature. Lish broadens the plain man's philosophy of his speakers to encompass the philistinism of the cultural entrepreneur; Sol takes the eponymous liberty with his son's name, for as the European 'Jerome' he is better placed for the Nobel Prize: 'A medal! Thousands and thousands of dollars and a medal!'

Lish's exploitation of the public face of American letters forms the cornerstone of his achievement here. . . .

> In *Mourner at the Door,* one story is about vomit, another about constipation, another about masturbation. Now if they were enlightening or entertaining stories about vomit, constipation or masturbation, that would be one thing. These, however, are just as inane and repetitive as the rest of the book.
>
> —*Ralph Novak, in* People Weekly, *May 9, 1988.*

Michael Harris (essay date 1993)

SOURCE: "Lish's Narrator is a Many-Layered Thing," in *Los Angeles Times,* September 20, 1993, p. E3.

[*In the following mixed review of* Zimzum, *Harris describes Lish's writing as solipsistic and lacking substance.*]

By now, we know we have to take Gordon Lish as he is. We know he isn't going to wriggle out of the pupa of his established personality and suddenly flap his wings as a writer of taste, moderation, balance and moral acuity—an E. M. Forster, say.

No, the Lish we've encountered before, as a bad-boy editor at *Esquire* and Knopf, as a controversial teacher of writing and as the author of provocative fictions (*Dear Mr. Capote, Peru, My Romance*), is the same Lish we get here.

Zimzum—no telling what the title means—is a typical Lish novel, short and crowded. The crowding isn't due to the number of characters and incidents. There is only one real character, the narrator, who is more or less Lish himself. It's due to the number of inflections, or layers, that Lish is able to pile onto the narrator's voice.

At the most basic level—call him Lish One—the narrator is an ordinary guy beset by life's problems. His wife is "burning up" with an undiagnosed ailment; he must live in freezing cold and in the roar of multiple air conditioners. His lover is emotionally just as chilly. A "Mr. Fix-It Man" refuses to return a sex toy the narrator took in for repairs. His parents are threatened with eviction from a nursing home for "acting up." Fairness, decency, the simplest human contact seem unobtainable.

Before long, though, we feel uneasy about Lish One. His troubles are ludicrous as well as poignant. He lacks—another Forster word—perspective. He bends our ear with

the obsessive sense of grievance, the numbing monotony of the drunk on the next bar stool. We begin to see him in a different way: as Lish Two. We blame *him* rather than the state of the world—and blame the neurotic author for losing control of the story.

The author is ready for us. You want control? he asks. I'll give you more control than you ever thought possible. And, indeed, we come to see that what we took for mere rant and diatribe is actually rhetoric polished to a very high gloss, crafted for us by—let's call him Lish Three.

Take this sentence from the opening chapter, a reminiscence of childhood: "I saw the men who were the drivers who had on sunglasses on who were sitting up on the seat." When we read that sentence on the page, we want to grab an editor's blue pencil and cross out the second *on.* But when we read it aloud, in the context of similar sentences, we find that the joke is on us: This really *is* how people talk.

Or take the second chapter, in which the narrator longs for sex and replays his whole erotic past—the names of the women, the things they did, the cities they did them in. Far from arousing desire, as pornography is supposed to do, it beats the language of desire to death. It's a leaden parody of porn that first depresses us and then—especially when read aloud—makes us giggle. You see? Lish Three asks. Isn't humor a sign of perspective? There isn't criticism you can make of me that I haven't anticipated. Believe me, I'm *covered.*

What happens when we finally grow tired of all this game-playing, skillful as it is, and demand more substance from the story? Enter Lish Four, who is like Lish One, only more sophisticated, encompassing as he does all the Lishes in between. Lish Four asserts that he *is* in pain—that the game-playing wouldn't have been necessary if he hadn't had to overcome what he has assumed all along would be our contempt for him. His appeals to the reader become more personal and pointed:

> Is this what you think, that I am just sitting here making a spectacle of myself from telling you this? Nobody has [anyone else's] welfare at heart. . . . I do not know why I am bothering trying to communicate to you.

And in the sex chapter, after the depression and the mockery, Lish Four leads us into another, more elusive emotion. The crazy catalogue of past couplings reminds us that, indeed, nothing is more evanescent and irrecoverable than sexual experience, no matter how vivid it seemed at the time. We feel a different kind of sadness, and then, unexpectedly, a bit of desire after all.

Is Lish covered? Not completely. He still lacks some of the novelist's most basic equipment: an interest in the world outside himself. He's a solipsist, and knows it, and knows *we* know it. All his elaborate fictional strategies are a compensation for that lack, like a blind man's sharpened hearing. It's entertaining to see him walk down the sidewalk as sure-footedly as he does, tapping with the cane of that remarkable voice; but we can't ever expect him to run.

Brian Evenson (essay date 1993)

SOURCE: A review of *Zimzum,* in *The Review of Contemporary Fiction,* Vol. XIII, No. 3, Fall, 1993, pp. 214-15.

[*Below, Evenson offers a stylistic analysis of* Zimzum.]

Lish is not afraid to violate taboo, to render discourse extravagant, to speak of that which others dare not, in his relentless exploration of the abscession of the human heart. A consummate stylist, Lish offers up sentences near perfect in their rhythmical and tonal qualities. *Zimzum* advances through sentential variation and permutation, employing the formal repetition common to musical arrangement, to liberate the powers of the utterance. The result is a brilliant, dark, comic novella, a book unique in American literature.

Zimzum consists of six discrete sections, from two to fifty-five pages. The first four sections practice a non-paragraphing whose seamlessness rivals Márquez's *Autumn of the Patriarch* and Bernhard's *Correction.* The sections are linked by a common theme: people are little more than objects, even for their dearest friends and family. We use others—and in turn are used by others—for selfish purposes.

The opening section, **"Paragraph,"** confronts a boy named Lish with the enigmatic appearance of a boy in an iron lung at his beach. **"Sentences"** charts an anguished older man's attempts to soften the hell of attending his dying wife by recalling past sexual escapades. But remembrance intensifies, rather than dissipates, his grief. The strongest section, **"July the Fifteenth, 1988,"** is a crazed, selfish narrator's recounting of the collapse of his life through the events of a single day—his wife's discovery of an unspecified illness, his parents' misbehavior at a rest home, and his being made to shop for a dildo with his lover. The narrator insists, in increasingly harried fashion, on others' insensitivity—failing to acknowledge his own ill-usage of others. The narrators of **"Sentences"** and **"July the Fifteenth"** verge on madness. Lish, like Jonathan Swift, refuses to present an overarching judgment of his narrators, allowing them instead to condemn themselves. He trusts the reader's ability to perceive and judge his narrator's madness—and in so doing to judge oneself. In **"July the Fifteenth,"** the narrator's insistence on having been ill-treated is enough to reveal his moral blindness to a careful reader, but not to himself. **"Sentences"** critiques erotica in the way Lish's *Dear Mr. Capote* critiques criminal biography. Working by exhaustion, Lish allows the narrator to heap up libidinal evidence against himself until titillation gives way to desperation, rupturing the thin membrane containing the narrator's anguish. What begins as seeming erotics ends with humanity stripped of flesh, nerves exposed.

"July the Fifteenth" is followed by perhaps Lish's only female narrator. The language in this section is cultured, beautifully controlled, and utterly convincing. The female narrator reexposes the theme, offsetting its harsher expressions elsewhere.

With the first narrator named Lish, and with other narrators recalling the press's parody of Lish, *Zimzum* initially seems to encourage biographical reading. Like Denis Diderot and Michel Leiris, Lish is unafraid of fleshing his fiction through biography. However, his fictionalizing transforms biography into something entirely other. *Zimzum* refuses to provide simple answers to the question of biography's relation to fiction, the novella's last two sections poking fun at those who do. Michel Leiris's words are relevant: "I reveal all, but only to hide better." There will doubtless be those who insist on reading *Zimzum* in light of Lish's public persona (another fiction) rather than in the fiction's own terms. To do so is to neglect the book's real power.

The sections, initially seeming disparate, prove on further reading to be complexly interlinked. *Zimzum* gains in complexity from reading to reading. *Zimzum* reasserts Lish's strengths as an original writer of fiction, proving Lish the rule by which those writing progressive, formally perfected fiction shall be measured.

Additional coverage of Lish's life and career is contained in the following sources published by Gale Research: *Contemporary Authors,* Vols. 113, 117; *Contemporary Literary Criticism,* Vol. 45; and *Dictionary of Literary Biography,* Vol. 130.

Robert Musil
1880-1942

Austrian novella writer, novelist, essayist, dramatist, and poet.

INTRODUCTION

Musil is regarded by some as among the greatest writers of the twentieth century. His innovative novels and novellas use an expressionistic style to explore the nature of human consciousness and to convey the disparity between rational and nonrational aspects of existence. Rather than offering traditional, realistic narratives, these works often employ subjective points of view to represent the inner thoughts and impressions of characters. In Musil's fiction, as Kathleen O'Connor has pointed out, "thoughts are the events."

Biographical Information

Musil was born in Klagenfurt, Austria, and raised in an unorthodox household. For forty years his emotionally unstable mother openly maintained an extramarital liaison with an engineer who eventually moved in with the family. Commentators have observed that as a result of this unusual arrangement many of Musil's writings reflect familial and sexual tensions. Musil's father, also an engineer, enrolled his son at the age of twelve at the military academy at Eisenstadt. Two years later Musil was sent to the senior military academy at Mährisch-Weisskirchen. He made use of his experiences there in his first novel, *Die Verwirrungen des Zöglings Törless* (1906; *The Confusions of Young Törless*). Musil went on to earn a degree in engineering and later attended the University of Berlin to study philosophy, mathematics, and psychology. Philosopher Friedrich Nietzsche's critiques of traditional conceptions of the self and consciousness had a profound impact on Musil's subsequent writings. His 1911 novella collection *Vereinigungen* (*Unions*) shows the influence of Nietzsche and other philosophers and represents a radical experiment in the subjective presentation of character and action. Before devoting himself solely to writing, Musil worked as an engineer, a librarian, and an editor; served as an officer in World War I; and held various government positions. From 1922 to 1938 Musil subsisted on what little money he could make as a writer and on financial support from patrons in Vienna and Berlin. He published a second collection of novellas, *Drei Frauen* (*Three Women*), in 1924 and was awarded the Literature Prize of the City of Vienna the same year. Beginning in 1923 Musil worked on the massive novel *Der Mann ohne Eigenschaften* (*The Man without Qualities*), two volumes of which were published in his lifetime but which ultimately remained unfinished. After the Austrian unification with Germany in 1938, Musil and his wife emigrated to Switzerland, where he died four years later.

Major Works of Short Fiction

Between writing *Young Törless,* the novel that marked the beginning of his career, and *The Man without Qualities*, the master work that remained unfinished at its end, Musil composed dramas, poems, novellas, and numerous essays. His principal short fiction consists of the five novellas comprising *Unions* and *Three Women*. In *Die Vollendung der Liebe* (*The Perfecting of a Love*) and *Die Versuchung der stillen Veronika* (*The Temptation of Quiet Veronica*) in the first collection, Musil focused on the thoughts and feelings of his female protagonists as they interact with men. Nearly plotless, these works represent the author's experimentation with the depiction of subjective psychological states. Despite the titles of *Three Women* and of the individual pieces comprising the collection, the main characters of *Grigia, Tonka,* and *Die Portugiesin* (*The Lady from Portugal*) are men who all have careers that define their identities: engineer, scientist, and soldier (jobs Musil himself performed in his own life). All three men become involved with mysterious women in relationships that cause identity crises requiring them to attempt some sort of resolution between the rational aspects of life, to which they themselves are predisposed, and the nonrational aspects represented by their lovers.

Critical Reception

Although Musil is often ranked with James Joyce, Thomas Mann, and Marcel Proust as one of the most important writers in modern literature, his work has received much less critical attention than that of his peers. Moreover, many critics have viewed his novellas as important mainly for what they reveal about *The Man without Qualities*; as Charles N. Genno has argued, "all of his earlier works may be considered as preparation for his last great novel." Other critics, however, have judged Musil's short fiction as valuable in its own right. Frederick G. Peters, for example, has described *The Lady from Portugal* as "artistically the most perfect of all of Musil's fiction." Whether seen as preliminary experiments leading to his major novels or as independent achievements in the depiction of human psychology, Musil's novellas are commonly heralded for their significant contributions to the development of modernist fiction.

PRINCIPAL WORKS

Short Fiction

Vereinigungen [*Unions*] 1911
†*Drei Frauen* [*Three Women*] 1924
Die Amsel [*The Blackbird*] 1928

Other Major Works

Die Verwirrungen des Zöglings Törless [*The Confusions of Young Törless*] (novel) 1906
Die Schwärmer [*The Enthusiasts*] (drama) 1921
"Isis und Osiris" (poetry) 1923
Vinzenz und die Freundin bedeutender Männer [*Vinzenz and the Lady Friend of Important Men*] (drama) 1923
Der Mann ohne Eigenschaften [*The Man without Qualities*] 3 vols. (unfinished novel) 1930-43
Nachlass zu Lebzeiten (essays) 1936

*Contains the novellas *Die Vollendung der Leibe* (*The Perfecting of a Love*; also translated as *The Completion of Love*) and *Die Versuchung der stillen Veronika* (*The Temptation of Quiet Veronica*).

†Contains the novellas *Grigia, Die Portugiesin* (*The Lady from Portugal*), and *Tonka*.

CRITICISM

Burton Pike (essay date 1961)

SOURCE: "*Unions* (1911)," in *Robert Musil: An Introduction to His Work*, Cornell, 1961, pp. 57-70.

[*An American critic and educator specializing in German literature, Pike is the editor of* Robert Musil: Selected

Writings *(1986) and* Precision and Soul: Essays and Addresses of Robert Musil *(1990). In the following excerpt, he discusses Musil's "expressionistic" narrative technique in* Unions, *finding it more successful in* The Completion of Love *than in* The Temptation of Silent Veronica. *Elsewhere in Musil criticism the title* The Completion of Love *has been translated as* The Perfecting of a Love.]

[The two stories in *Unions*]—called "novellas" (*Novellen*) on the cover of the first edition and "two tales" (*zwei Erzählungen*) on the title page—present two attitudes toward love between the sexes, the yea-saying and the nay-saying. These works might best be characterized as attitude studies rather than character studies. The heroine of the first story is a sensualist with nymphomaniac tendencies who glories in her feelings, while the heroine of the second is a psychotic ignorant woman who expresses her strong sensual love in unnatural ways and finds a negative pleasure, as well as frustration, in withholding it from natural completion. Both heroines are examples of that *Ausnahmemoral,* or morality of exception (fundamentally a behavioristic concept), which so fascinated Musil in his observation of life.

The first story, **The Completion of Love,** has an atmosphere of warmth and tenderness not found elsewhere in Musil. The atmosphere of the second story, **The Temptation of the Silent Veronika,** is one of frustration. The two tales thus complement each other, the more so in that they have a common base of erotic, sexual love. But eroticism and sex are not presented for their own sake in *Unions*—it is hard to imagine these stories hiding behind a suggestive cover on a drugstore bookrack—but for what they represent; Musil's treatment of sex is closer to that of a manual of abnormal psychology than to the school of Henry Miller. The adultery that is the incident of the first story actually bestows a final perfection upon the marriage it "disturbs"; the refusal to love in the second story leads to near suicide and waste of individual potentialities. The basic assumption of both stories is that fulfillment of the potentiality of the individual is desirable, however unconventional such fulfillment might prove to be. The heroines of these stories are for all practical purposes the only characters in them; and one never loses the feeling in reading *Unions* that in spite of Musil's impressionistic technique these women tend more toward being clinical case studies than individuals with problems. This feeling seems to derive in part from the author's detachment from his heroines; in both stories observation is a much more important element than identification.

This detachment vitiates the two stories in that it makes the characters, for all the psychological subtlety with which they are presented, singularly colorless. To appreciate this one need only compare Musil's Claudine and Veronika with the heroine of a similar and nearly contemporary story by Gertrude Stein, "Melanctha" in *Three Lives* (1908). Musil's detachment from his heroines also seems to be responsible for the reader's impression that as a whole these works are considerably less impressive than the individual scenes and observations of which they are composed. Still, while *Unions* might be obscure to the reader from a rational point of view, he finds himself responding emotionally with some degree of empathy. This is especially true of **The Temptation of the Silent Veronika.** The impressionistic technique which is responsible for this effect deserves closer attention, especially since after pushing it to the breaking point in **Veronika** Musil abandoned it almost entirely in his later writing.

Musil's impressionistic technique becomes somewhat clearer if we think of impressionistic technique in painting and of what "impressionism" in general is. In this connection some of the observations made by Richard Hamann in his book *Der Impressionismus in Leben und Kunst (Impressionism in Life and Art)* are illuminating. Speaking of impressionist painting Hamann notes that it is concerned with individual figures rather than groups (one notes the extreme concentration in Musil's stories on the heroines). He further observes that impressionist painting avoids large connecting color surfaces, concentrating rather on building up each surface from innumerable little spots and points of different tones. This latter process is also the one that Musil has used in **Unions,** and when thought of in these terms the stories become more comprehensible. In a philosophical discussion of impressionism which draws heavily, significantly enough, on Mach and the philosopher Heinrich Rickert, Hamann says that in impressionism psychological states (*Seelenzustände*) have become the real object of fiction (*Dichtung*). And when Hamann summarizes the basic characteristics of impressionism he almost seems to be talking about **Unions**. These major characteristics are: thinking and speaking in images, exaggeration, the animation of thought, and, instead of a systematic unity, a "monism of gradual transitions" which recalls Musil's theory of literature as "the path of the smallest steps." A critical examination of these two stories will help to give a clearer idea of an important phase of Musil's art.

The Completion of Love

According to Musil's stepdaughter this was Musil's favorite work, and the only one of his works which he reread. The action of the story can be quickly sketched. The heroine, Claudine, leaves her husband to visit a small town where her daughter by one of a number of earlier illicit love affairs is at school. On the train she meets a bearded stranger; several days later she allows him to seduce her. But if ever in literature action was incidental, or rather accidental, it is in **The Completion of Love**.

The story opens in the middle of a dialogue between husband and wife. The first sentence, a question, sets up the story: "You really can't come along?" Claudine asks her husband. The husband's replies show a certain irritation. A note of intimacy and looming separation, as in the later story **Grigia,** is immediately struck in this conversation. For some time the speakers are referred to only as "the man" and "the woman." The first few pages establish their complete mental union; they follow each other's unspoken thoughts and feelings perfectly. But the husband's irritation and their agreement that "every brain is something lonely" indicate a subterranean tension.

The man remains undeveloped in the story; from the second page Musil's images focus exclusively on the woman. As the story proceeds, one feels that Claudine's latent hostility toward her husband is a defensive means of preserving her own identity—an element we shall see later in Maria in *The Visionaries* and in Agathe in *The Man without Qualities*.

In a Rilkean passage the couple thinks of a "third," of many thirds who form a counter to their Adam-and-Eve relationship. Their conversation is highly stylized and borders on the metaphysical; the images are almost exclusively of erotic sensuality, for instance: "Then one of them said, and it was as if one lightly stroked a violin. . . . "

Musil uses imagery involving ordinary objects in Claudine's environment, such as a clock, or snow, to communicate to the reader not her feelings and thoughts themselves but her impressions of them. The reader is thus presented with a nebulous impressionism that is apparently meant to correspond to the half-conscious half-unconscious continuum which occupies the mind during its waking hours; or, to put it more precisely, Musil here seems to be operating on a level *between* the conscious and the unconscious. Rather than using free association, or showing the content of thought in the mind of his protagonist, Musil is here presenting instead the subjective impressions which they create in that mind as they well up into the area of semiconsciousness.

Musil's thought-impressionism—I do not think that "stream of consciousness" is the right term for this process—is much less direct than similar techniques used by Joyce and Woolf, and considerably less directed; Claudine is not going to any lighthouse, much less returning to the earth-mother after an Odyssean quest. Where Joyce and Woolf use the stream-of-consciousness technique as a means to an end, Musil's technique is both means and end. This would explain the importance of the story line in Joyce and Woolf and its unimportance in **The Completion of Love**. In this respect Musil is somewhat closer to his compatriot Schnitzler, except that the latter uses the technique in a much more formal and straightforward manner, usually presenting as taking place in the minds of his characters a relatively logical association of conscious ideas. But Musil is here closest of all to Gertrude Stein and to her idea of presenting essence rather than substance. One might say that Musil encounters the same basic difficulty as Joyce, Woolf, and Stein in that he is trying to verbalize what are essentially nonverbal processes—which may be regarded as an attempt to overcome one of the basic limitations of literature as an art. The interesting term "stream of *consciousness*" is itself an indication of this difficulty, since what is really meant by it is a stream of semi- or subconsciousness. The following passage from **The Completion of Love** is an example of what Musil is trying to do here:

> Und während sie ihr Herz schlagen fühlte, als trüge sie ein Tier in der Brust,—verstört, irgendwoher in sie verflogen,—hob sich seltsam ihr Leib in seinem stillen Schwanken und schloss sich wie eine grosse, fremde,

nickende Blume darum, durch die plötzlich der in unsichtbare Weiten gespannte Rausch einer geheimnisvollen Vereinigung schaudert, und sie hörte leise das ferne Herz des Geliebten wandern, unstet, ruhelos, heimatlos in die Stille klingend wie ein Ton einer über Grenzen verwehten, fremdher wie Sternlicht flackernden Musik, von der unheimlichen Einsamkeit dieses sie suchenden Gleichklangs wie von einer ungeheuren Verschlingung ergriffen, weit über alles Wohnland der Seelen hinaus.

("And while she felt her heart beating, as if she bore a beast in her breast—disturbed, fled somewhere within her—her body rose strangely in its silent oscillation and closed itself around it like a large, strange, nodding flower, through which, suddenly, the ecstasy of a secret union, stretched into invisible distances, shudders; and she heard softly the distant heart of her beloved wander, sounding fluttering, restless, homeless in the silence like a note of music blown over borders, flickering strange like starlight, a note seized as by a monstrous maze by the uncanny loneliness of the consonance which was seeking her, sounding far beyond all that land where souls are at home.")

This kind of erotic imagistic impressionism builds up for pages on end, giving the reader an excellent impression of the waves of feeling that sweep over Claudine; as psychological characterization it is extremely effective. Musil's ability to give a convincing impression of the thought processes of nonintellectual or even ignorant women, such as Claudine and Veronika, is one of his most striking gifts. There are in every one of his works women of one or the other stamp, from the prostitute Božena in *The Confusions of Young Törless* to Bonadea and even Diotima in *The Man without Qualities.*

In its erotic imagistic impressionism *Unions* might also be compared with one of the most ambitious attempts to convey passion through music, Wagner's *Tristan and Isolde.*

Musil might have used as a motto for both these stories Novalis' phrase "the mysterious pathway leads within," for nowhere else in his works is the physical world so shadowy. There is no physical description at all of Claudine or her husband and only the most fleeting description of the other characters. Externals, such as the description of the room in which the conversation between Claudine and her husband takes place, are systematically subordinated to internal states of feeling and through imagery made to reflect these internal states. Indeed the external world is so dependent on the internal in this story—as opposed to *The Confusions of Young Törless,* where the external world exists as a separate, objective reality— that at one point the school town and its houses change as Claudine's feelings change. The real processes of both stories in *Unions* go on in the minds of the heroines, as Musil indicates when he speaks, in reference to Claudine, of "the great context of feeling of her existence, braided through the years." It is, in other words, the web of feeling rather than action which constitutes for Musil in these stories the important plane of human activity. The enormous slowing-down of both time and action in order to

concentrate on the subtle shadings of feeling—one again thinks of *Tristan and Isolde*—is what Musil referred to in connection with *Unions* as "the maximally laden path, the path of the smallest steps."

Claudine takes the train alone to go see her daughter. Separated from her husband for the first time, she feels herself psychologically and erotically vulnerable, and finds herself sinking into her emotional past, which had been effectively forgotten in her complete devotion to her husband. Claudine does not regret this past, which time has dimmed: "Nothing remained of it but the memory of a strange cloud of feelings, which had confused and aroused her for a while like a cloak suddenly thrown over her head, and which had then swiftly slid to the floor." Although in her earlier life she had yielded repeatedly to her nymphomaniac tendencies—her daughter had been the result of a momentary fascination with an American dentist—Claudine, who prefigures in this respect the nymphomaniac Bonadea in *The Man without Qualities,* had never lost the belief "that everything she did did not basically touch her, and essentially had nothing to do with her." Like Törless, she is conscious of a deep inner life paralleling, but not connected with, her outer daily life.

The body of the story establishes not Claudine's individuality but her isolation, the isolation which seems to be in Musil's works the prime mark of the *condition humaine.* Claudine lives in a silent world of feelings which is mirrored in the muffling snow, a very prominent element in the story. Speech rarely intrudes into this world, and when it does it usually breaks her mood. Her isolation appears the more marked when compared with the harmony of her relationship with her husband at the beginning of the story, where speech is seen merely as an extension of inner silence.

It is, then, against a background of separation, isolation and eroticism that the incident of *The Completion of Love,* the seduction of Claudine, occurs, and it occurs as a complete and almost comical accident. The bearded stranger, a *Ministerialrat* (a government official), first comes to her attention on the train; the rest of the story, approximately the second half, is concerned with the slow crystallization of her feeling around this "third" who comes between her and her husband. It is a crystallization in the specifically Stendhalian sense of the term, and one feels that the author of *On Love* would have been enchanted by *The Completion of Love.* It must, however, be emphasized that the *Ministerialrat* is as accidental an object for Claudine's feeling as Basini was for Törless', and this accidentality here provides Musil with an occasion for some of his sharpest irony. The man preens himself on his ability as an irresistible lady-killer, unaware of the ridiculous picture he presents to Claudine and to the reader, who sees him through Claudine's eyes.

The *Ministerialrat* is the ironical element in *The Completion of Love*; Claudine's relationship with her husband is treated with tender seriousness. It is perhaps not accidental that the vehicle of the irony in this story is one of Musil's most successful characterizations; the man is perfectly sketched in his few banal remarks and equally banal actions. In his opening gambit to Claudine on the train he compares the landscape ("an idyll, an enchanted island") to a beautiful woman. Claudine's reaction to this remark sets the tone for her subsequent attitude toward him: "'How silly,' thought Claudine, but she did not find the right answer immediately." In this first interchange the attitudes of both are established, and the rest of the story is elaboration.

The *Ministerialrat* obviously prides himself that it is his elegant technique which, after several days of hesitation on her part, conquers Claudine. She, however, is no Emma Bovary, and yields to him for reasons which have nothing to do with him at all but well up from her past emotions. The most urgent of these reasons seem to be her basic sense of insecurity and an outburst of suppressed resentment and hostility against her husband; when the man asks her if she loves her husband, Claudine replies "trembling and decidedly": "No, no, I don't love him at all." In this total failure of mental contact between the lady and her seducer Musil is again demonstrating how his characters operate on different levels without breaking through to each other. The dominant impression even of Claudine's intimate relationship with her husband is that neither of them understood the other as well as they thought. This failure of contact becomes at times grotesquely comic: "Then the Ministerialrat kissed her: 'So you love me?' And Claudine still found the strength to object: 'No, I love being with you, the fact, the accident, that I'm with you. One could be sitting with the Eskimos. In sealskin pants. And have hanging breasts. And find that pretty.'"

On a more serious level, Claudine's submission seems to be a way of proving her own identity vis-à-vis her husband, whom she loves. Sexual union with this stranger, contrasting with the intercourse she has had with her husband early in the story, is for her a token of reunion with her husband, an overcoming, in some obscure sense, of her hostility. And as a result of this experience, which takes place in "a small town cut off from reality," Claudine understands her love for her husband. The final sentence of **The Completion of Love** is: "And very far away, as children say of God that He is great, she had an idea of her love."

The Temptation of the Silent Veronika

An earlier version of this story, **The Enchanted House** (*Das verzauberte Haus*), is a traditional, almost banal tale of seduction. The transformation into the shimmering abstract impressionism of **The Temptation of the Silent Veronika** is startling. Even upon repeated readings one cannot say precisely what *happens* in the finished version. And yet as an impression of a situation seen chiefly through the eyes of an ignorant, mentally disturbed woman, much as the first part of Faulkner's *The Sound and the Fury* is seen from the point of view of the idiot deafmute Benjy, this story is effective, although in the last analysis its effectiveness seems limited.

Veronika, who foreshadows Clarisse in *The Man without Qualities,* has committed sodomy with a dog, and has—perhaps—had intercourse with Johannes, who is, as far as one can gather, a relative of some sort (he belongs to the same family and lives in the same house). She also has apparently unfulfilled sexual urges toward Demeter, a third member of the family and household. A man with the name of the Greek goddess of the fruits of the earth Demeter is, as one might expect, rude, vital, and earthy. (In the earlier version Demeter, a soldier, is the leading male character and far more prosaic.) Veronika refuses three times to marry Johannes, a weak, sensitive character who is frustrated by her withdrawal from him. She sends him off to commit suicide, but once he is gone from the strange house Johannes sensibly refuses to oblige. Veronika is left in the house with Demeter to become a frustrated sexless creature like her aged spinster aunt.

Veronika's ruling passion appears to be a fear of sterility. This is expressed in her frank conversations with Johannes about his lack of virility and Demeter's apparent abundance of it. Veronika compares their house to "a world in which we are alone, a sad world in which everything becomes crooked and strange as if under water"—which is very much the way this world looks to the reader. Veronika's isolation, of the most extreme sort, is behind the solid wall of her psychosis; like Claudine, but in a negative rather than a positive way, she lives largely in a world of remembered feelings rather than present actions. In a specific description of a kind quite rare in Musil's works Veronika is described from Johannes' point of view; the essence of this description is an impression of wild, almost animal sensuality.

One curious feature of this story is the conversation. It is not at all realistic, but rather as if one person's feelings were speaking directly with those of another in exaggerated verbalized pictures without passing through the "censor" of the superego. Characteristic is the remark that Veronika makes to Johannes: "You are sometimes as impersonal and withdrawn as a candle in the dark, which is nothing itself and only makes the darkness larger and more visible." This kind of conversation is not to be found in *The Confusions of Young Törless* nor, except at the beginning, in **The Completion of Love**. In both these latter works characters' states of feeling are presented imagistically, but conversation between characters is of the everyday variety. The conversation in **The Temptation of the Silent Veronika** is also at the opposite extreme from that in *The Man without Qualities,* in which both id and ego are burned away and conversation involves only the superego. This difference reflects Musil's different orientation in the two works; in the early story he is interested in presenting an example of irrational behavior, while in the later novel the background of such behavior is a much more important element.

The Temptation of the Silent Veronika has certain affinities of mood and language with Rilke's *The Notebooks of Malte Laurids Brigge,* which appeared in 1910, a year before **Unions**. Rilke succeeds better than Musil in presenting a decaying neurotic household, perhaps because of the pervasive sense of morbid autobiographical introspection in *Malte* which is totally absent from Musil's work. Musil, in trying to use lyric language clinically, and maintaining through his technique a detached objectivity, succeeds here only in being opaque. In this respect *The Temptation of the Silent Veronika* differs also from the morbid rural visions of the Austrian poet Georg Trakl (1887-1914): although the garment Musil wears in his story was put on for the occasion, as its sophisticated imagery and somewhat clinical handling show, the same is not true of Rilke and Trakl, whose methods were an organic part of their subjects and of themselves.

In *The Temptation of the Silent Veronika* Musil carries the impressionistic technique of *The Completion of Love* one step farther along his "maximally laden path," and one step too far. All one can see in this story are individual spots of color; the spots do not combine, as they do in the first story, into the impression of a form. It is significant that in his subsequent works Musil abandoned this kind of impressionism; in the later stories *Grigia* and *The Portuguese Lady,* for instance, the characters are much more clearly defined while the *setting* is used as the base of impressionistic evocation.

But whatever its merits compared with other works, *The Temptation of the Silent Veronika* remains an interesting experiment on Musil's part to see how far he could carry his attempt to express feelings through words. And taken as a whole, *Unions* is one of the most interesting experiments in modern fiction.

Frank Kermode (essay date 1966)

SOURCE: A preface to *Five Women* by Robert Musil, translated by Eithne Wilkins and Ernest Kaiser, Delacorte Press, 1966, pp. 7-13.

[*Kermode is an English critic who combines modern critical methods with traditional scholarship. In his discussions of modern literature Kermode has embraced many of the concepts of structuralism and phenomenology. He characterizes all human knowledge as affected by the perceptual and emotional limitations of human consciousness. Because perceptions of life and the world change, so do human knowledge and the meaning attached to things and events. Thus, Kermode maintains, a work of art has no single fixed meaning, but a multiplicity of possible interpretations. In the following excerpt, he discusses the ambiguities of plot, character, and description in Musil's novellas, claiming that they "reflect the ambiguities of human reality."*]

Three Women (*Grigia, The Lady from Portugal, Tonka*) was published in the middle of a great literary period and stands comparison with its contemporaries. *Unions,* thirteen years earlier, has rather more the character of the *fin de siècle* (as indeed may be said of *Death in Venice*), but Musil valued it highly, perhaps because it contains, in a different blend and without irony, the same constituents—

a nervous obliquity, a mystique of the erotic, a deep interest in the borders of the human mind, those uneasy frontiers with the human body and with inhuman reality—that go to the making of *The Man Without Qualities*.

Musil's is notoriously a world in political collapse, the end of a great empire; but more central to his poetic writing (at times he makes one think of a prose Rilke) is the sense of a world in metaphysical collapse, a universe of hideously heaped contingency, in which there are nonetheless transcendent human powers. These he represents always by the same complex and various image of eroticism, which reaches its fullest expression in the big novel. *The Man Without Qualities* has among its themes nymphomania, incest and sex murder, not at all for their prurient interest but as indices of the reaches of consciousness. Moosbrugger, the murderer, thinks, when he is not killing, that he is by his personal effort holding together the world; the story of the love between Ulrich, the book's hero, and his sister was, according to Musil, to take us to the "farthest limits of the possible and unnatural, even of the repulsive"; and yet if one theme can be called central in *The Man Without Qualities* it is this one, and nobody could think Musil anything but overwhelmingly serious in his treatment of it. Erotic ecstasy is beyond good and evil ("all moral propositions refer to a sort of dream condition that's long ago taken wing") and exemplifies the power of our consciousness to cross the borderline formerly protected by what are now the obsolete fortresses of traditional ethics and metaphysics.

Throughout his career Musil explored this borderline. He kept a notebook on medieval mysticism and labeled it "Borderline Experiences." It interested him that the mystic, speaking of his incommunicable experience of God, will usually do so by analogies with erotic pleasure. Ulrich, a considerable authority on love-making, decides that the transformation of a sane man into a frothing lunatic by the pleasures of the bed is only "a special case of something far more general"—namely, our ability to undergo a quasi-erotic metamorphosis of consciousness which gives us what is in effect a second state of consciousness interpolated into the ordinary one. Like E. M. Forster, whose greatest novel, *A Passage to India,* came out in the same year as *Three Women,* Musil believed that the heightening of consciousness which makes possible the order and the perceptions of good fiction has something in common with erotic feeling; and meaningless contingency is the enemy of novels as well as love. For Musil the two metamorphoses of consciousness—art and love—ran together, and the sheer polymorphousness of the erotic was the subject as well as the analogue of his fiction.

To some extent this was already the case in *Young Törless,* and it is altogether so in [Musil's novellas]. All have erotic themes, and most are concerned with female eroticism and with love as a means to some kind of knowledge. Here, as in the later novel, love is extremely various and free of the considerations of parochial ethics. In *Quiet Veronica* it is bestial, in *The Perfecting of a Love* it is profligate. *Grigia* and *Tonka* are variants of the medieval *pastourelle*—the seduction, in *Grigia,* of a peasant girl by a man of higher social class, and in *Tonka* of a shopgirl by a student; but in either case the sexual situation is a figure for what is beyond sex. To study the behavior of people in love is, for Musil, to study the human situation at its quick. Even when there is only delighted animality, or when, as in *Tonka,* there is an avowed absence of love and of intellectual communion, in a milieu of poverty and disease, sex remains the central ground for Musil's study of the potentialities of human consciousness.

The earliest of these stories is *The Temptation of Quiet Veronica,* which appeared in an earlier and very different version as *The Enchanted House* in 1908. One's first thought is to relate this story, in its later form, to the literature of the Decadence; but its opaque surface, and the erotic feeling which occasionally pierces it, reflect Musil's preoccupation with the penetrating of reality by consciousness under the stimulus of sex. In short, it is not a failed attempt at the literature of neurasthenia, but a perhaps overworked statement of what we have seen to be Musil's principal theme. What we remember is not the pathology but Veronica's sense of her own body as she undresses, and Johannes, on the point of suicide, sensing himself as somehow rooted in the randomness of life. *The Perfecting of a Love* has a stronger and more visible story, and again there is a touch of romantic agonizing— "voluptuous enervated horror . . . nameless sin." But there is also much to distinguish it from run-of-the-mill decadence: the sharp picture of the amber twist issuing from a teapot on the first page; the detached view of Claudine dressing ("all her movements took on something of oafishly sensual affectation"); the sexuality of the stranger, which causes "a scarcely perceptible displacement of the surrounding world." Finally sex, represented as a defense against the "horribly gaping contingency of all one does," achieves a low and commonplace realization in the hotel cut off by snow; and from a body disagreeably swelling with lust emerges an image of love and union. *The Perfecting of a Love* cost Musil more nervous effort than any other work, and it is curiously central to his achievement. It is entirely lacking in the worldly irony and the "essayism" with which, in the great novel, he tried to relate its themes to the whole surface of modern life; but it is for all that a work which, in its uncommunicative, oblique fashion, expresses an understanding of human capacity, an intelligent and modern creativeness, comparable with those displayed in the contemporary writings of Lawrence and Thomas Mann.

By the time *Three Women* was published, thirteen years later, Musil had given up this somewhat hermetic manner, though he had not, as yet, developed the ironical discursiveness of *The Man Without Qualities*. Standing between his early and late manners, this book nevertheless has the same preoccupation with the erotic metamorphosis of consciousness and might also have been called *Unions*. The difference from the earlier work could be expressed as a new willingness to find a place in his stories for straight narrative (the "low, atavistic" element in fiction which Forster comically deplored and which

troubles most experimental novelists). Not that this simpler form of satisfaction has the effect of making the stories simple, considered as a whole. They are still parables, and still, in the manner of parables, refuse to submit themselves to any single interpretation. In *Grigia,* Homo is distinguished from the peasant community by his association with urban technology as well as urban civility; there is a futile rape of the land as well as easy seduction of women. Homo rediscovers the pleasant animality of sex, and with it a love for his absent wife and perhaps even for death. The climax of the tale has an insoluble ambiguity; but it is worth noting that ambiguity is a property not only of the narrative but also of the texture of the book. There are many passages of strange resonant poetry, for instance the description of behavior of hay when used as a love-bed. *Grigia* has the obliquity of high intelligence and idiosyncratic creativity. So too has *The Lady from Portugal,* though its parable announces itself more clearly because its elements—love and union, spirituality and sickness—are placed at a great historical distance. And if *Tonka* is the best of all the stories, it is so not in virtue of its more down-to-earth theme, but because one senses in it a stricter relation between the narrative and the texture.

The story of *Tonka* seems almost commonplace beside the others, but that is only because of its superficial resemblance to the stories of Zola or the De Goncourts or George Moore. It treats of the quasi-mystical aspects of sex in the least promising of relationships. The liaison is of apparently low power; there is nothing involved that can be called love, indeed there is hardly any discernible communication between the pair. On the other hand there is a curious lack of amorous or spiritual self-aggrandizement, there is goodness and nature. Above all there is guilt, but even guilt somehow escapes the conventional categories and remains as it were unattached to real personalities. When Shakespeare's Cressida was unfaithful, Troilus could not believe his senses: "This is and is not Cressida." In the same situation Tonka steadfastly *is* Tonka, the "nobly natural" shopgirl who has nevertheless quite certainly been unfaithful. These ambiguities reflect the ambiguities of human reality; Musil once wrote that he saw no reason in the world why something cannot be simultaneously true and false, and the way to express this unphilosophical view of the world is by making fictions. As Tonka's lover notices when he debates with himself the question of marrying or leaving her, the world is as a man makes it with his fictions; abolish them and it falls apart into a disgusting jumble.

All these stories have obvious autobiographical elements, roots in Musil's personal life; but much more important is their truth to his extraordinarily intelligent and creative mind. They are elaborate attempts to use fiction for its true purposes, the discovery and registration of the human world. As with all works of genius, they suggest a map of reality with an orientation at first strange and unfamiliar. And though it is true that the experience of *The Man Without Qualities* is one involving a more permanent change of consciousness in the reader, these works also require his serious attention.

Christine Oertel Sjögren (essay date 1972)

SOURCE: "An Inquiry into the Psychological Condition of the Narrator in Musil's *Tonka*," in *Monatshefte*, Vol. 64, No. 2, Summer, 1972, pp. 153-61.

[*In the following essay, Sjögren contends that the nameless narrator of Musil's* Tonka *exhibits the symptoms of schizophrenia.*]

Strictly speaking, there is no narrator formally interposed between author and reader in Musil's *Erzählung Tonka,* since the story is told in the third person; however, it must be noted that the point of view given is exclusively that of the protagonist, an unnamed "he." Memories of the protagonist are recalled haphazardly as in life, with little attention to accurate chronology, and are recounted without any correction by the author. Relinquishing his prerogative of "unhampered omniscience," the author almost never intrudes into the report, but pretends to submerge himself into the mind of the protagonist, imposing upon himself the limitations of that consciousness. Werner Hoffmeister, who considers this work "das interessanteste und unkonventionellste Prosastück in Robert Musils Frühwerk," points out that it evidences an "einmalige Verquickung von Erzähler und Hauptperson bei Benutzung der unpersönlichen dritten Person," a technique which offers both "objektive Außensicht und subjektive Innensicht" [*Studien zur erlebten Rede bei Thomas Mann und Robert Musil,* 1965]. Clearly, the protagonist must be considered a kind of narrator, despite the objective stance he pretends to assume by using the third person in order perhaps to persuade us of the unbiased nature of his report.

As Gerhard Friedrich observes [in "Robert Musils *Tonka,*" *Die Sammlung* 15, 1960], the subjectivity of the protagonist's memory requires the reader to make an effort himself to ascertain what really happened. Where the protagonist's memory is sketchy, the author does not fill in any missing parts; where the protagonist's chronology is vague, the author does not make it more definite, but lets him grope through his remembrances haphazardly, lifting up one fragment, then another, as he finds them.

The memories have an expressionistic quality, as is apparent already in the first sentences: "An einem Zaun. Ein Vogel sang. Die Sonne war dann schon irgendwo hinter den Büschen. Der Vogel schwieg. Es war Abend." These are broken pieces of experiences, hurled up from subconscious depths, where past events lie unordered by sequential logic. In the resulting random presentation of events, chronology and causality are dissolved, and everything is simultaneously present in what Benno von Wiese [in "Die Amsel," *Die deutsche Novelle von Goethe bis Kafka. Interpretationen* II, 1962] calls "ein Kraftfeld des Potentiellen, dessen jeweilige Aktualisierung dem Menschen dann in der Zeit aufgetragen ist."

The protagonist's personal participation in the events presented solely from his point of view makes it likely that the report is not disinterested but rather biased in favor of his own image. Any emotion aroused in him by the events will also color the narration. In fact, the total personality of the protagonist must be taken into account in evaluating the report. "N," as we shall call the narrator-protagonist, is like a lens through which the reader perceives deflected images that give a distorted view of what really happened.

In one sense, N's report is the record of his quest for the truth about Tonka, who is long since dead. As N gropes through the fog of the past, some images are blurred and others are oddly askew. His uncertainty regarding the events of the past becomes apparent already in the first pages. Attempting to recall his first meeting with Tonka, he gets lost in a maze of possibilities before he finally penetrates all the "Märchen" and arrives at something like "Wahrheit" and "etwas Wirkliches." Then he presents her in a series of vignettes, which do not give a clear picture either, because her image often becomes entangled with the misty shadows and lights in the morass of his memory.

The events of the story are as follows: While in his year of military service young N notices Tonka, an attractive working girl, as they pass each other on a street. Upon learning that the young girl lives with her aunt and is employed in a fabric shop, he arranges, through a little ruse, that she be given a position in his home, as companion and nurse to his aged grandmother. These circumstances give N the opportunity to become well acquainted with her. The young people enjoy each other's company, and after some time they become lovers. When the grandmother dies and it appears that Tonka is to be dismissed from the household without adequate compensation for her services, N asks her to stay with him and he will take care of her. Although N's mother strongly disapproves of the affair, nevertheless he and Tonka remain together. After passing his doctoral examinations in science, N leaves his parental home and moves to another city with Tonka. There he continues his chemical research, while Tonka takes a job that will support them both and attends night school to enhance her earning capacity.

Some years later Tonka one day finds herself to be pregnant. However, N calculates that according to the calendar, he was absent at the time of conception. Tonka denies infidelity, and the pregnancy remains unexplained and apparently unexplainable. Convinced that he is not the father, N becomes doubly sure upon learning that Tonka is seriously ill with a disease that could have been transmitted only by the father. He now faces the decision whether to accept the extremely high scientific probability that Tonka betrayed him or to believe in the innocence and integrity of Tonka, as it radiates from her face and her whole being.

N cannot commit himself to Tonka in faith, nor can he reach certainty about her infidelity. Meanwhile Tonka is dismissed from her position, money becomes short, and Tonka's health fails. With Tonka's fading, N achieves a breakthrough in his scientific research by perfecting an invention which he believes will bring benefit to mankind. After her death he carries on an illustrious career in his field. He adjudges Tonka to have been valuable in making him a better person, and he feels her little warm shadow on his brilliant life like a blessing.

Through the eyes of the narrator, the story of Tonka, while sad and mysterious, is still the story of his own success. A promising scientist at a time of life when he is most exposed, allows himself to be swept into a romantic relationship which causes him much pain but eventually leads to his self-fulfillment as a contributor to the well-being of mankind. His sufferings have enriched him with human sensitivity rare among his professional peers. From his viewpoint, Tonka's life is a sacrifice to the noble cause of his genius, and her pregnancy a supernatural event that gives him insight into the realm of the spiritual. Relegating Tonka to the realm of myth and religion ("das war die Welt des Gesalbten, der Jungfrau und Pontius Pilatus"), he transforms her into an event of the spirit. He relishes the thought of her as a poem, a call from the beyond. His last words about Tonka elevate her to the realm of poetry: "Da fiel ihm nebenbei ein wie ein Gedicht, zu dem man den Kopf wiegt, das war gar nicht Tonka, mit der er gelebt hatte, sondern es hatte ihn etwas gerufen."

N's evaluation of Tonka and of her influence upon his life has heretofore been taken at face value. A representative commentary is that of Wilhelm Braun [in "An Interpretation of Musil's Novelle *Tonka*," *Monatshefte* 53, No. 2, February 1961]: "Some intimation of the divine had come into the life of the hero that was to change him forever. We can now see the whole novelle as an educational experience of the hero. He has finished his invention, he is ready for life, but he has also been changed into a better man. Even though his awareness of all this might last a second, it is the kind that is inescapable."

Such a summary dismissal of Tonka as a little emissary from the beyond, sent to teach N something, to bring him success and a happy life, does not really give the *Erzählung* a happy ending, even if we were likewise to dismiss Tonka's life as unimportant in itself and concentrate purely upon N as the hero. Gerhard Friedrich is one of the few critics who does not entirely focus upon N's fate, but accords Tonka the tragic human fate which he feels Musil intended for her: "Aus den Tagebüchern ist zu ersehen, daß Musil von allem Anfang an das Schicksal Tonkas tragisch verstanden wissen wollte. Er kommt in seinen Aufzeichnungen mehrfach auf das Wort 'Tragödie' zurück und, verbunden damit, sieht er in Tonka ein 'Opfer der Notwendigkeit.'"

The very form of the story forbids our accepting N's complacent remarks upon his good fortune, for it is only after Tonka's death that he tells his story and relives its beauty and horror, its idyll and its nightmares. Clearly the problem of Tonka is one that he cannot solve or dismiss. The paragraph preceding the last of the story conveys the ambiguity of N's situation, and the questionable state he is in. While he congratulates himself on his good fortune and basks in his comfort, a sudden eruption of horror rends the mask of his equanimity:

Er stand im Licht und sie lag unter der Erde, aber alles in allem fühlte er das Behagen des Lichts. Bloß wie er da um sich sah, blickte er plötzlich einem der vielen Kinder ringsum in das zufällig weinende Gesicht; es war prall von der Sonne beschienen und krümmte sich wie ein gräßlicher Wurm nach allen Seiten: da schrie die Erinnerung in ihm auf: Tonka! Tonka! Er fühlte sie von der Erde bis zum Kopf und ihr ganzes Leben. Alles, was er niemals gewußt hatte, stand in diesem Augenblick vor ihm, die Binde der Blindheit schien von seinen Augen gesunken zu sein.

An extraordinary reaction to the sight of a weeping child! Its face is convulsed like an ugly worm, and suddenly the memory of Tonka arises in him, not as a "Gedicht, zu dem man den Kopf wiegt," not as a comforting little shadow, but as a scream that tears the bandage of blindness from his eyes. The scream of memory that wells up, is it a scream of Tonka's or is it a scream of his own distress? The unexpected revelation is transitory, but it illustrates how vulnerable are his defenses—an ordinary common phenomenon could without forewarning shatter his protective shield of contentment and thrust at him a terrifying vision.

The sight of the weeping child recalls Tonka to him, because once while in her company he saw a child's face in this guise. The ugliness so mercilessly exposed by the strong sunlight seems to N as basic as death to the meaning of life, and he was annoyed with Tonka for not penetrating behind the appearances of things to find their real significance.

If we subject N's account of his relationship with Tonka to a close analytical scrutiny, perhaps we too can find the true significance of the incident with the child and penetrate behind the appearance of the narrator to his true state.

When Tonka first meets N he is suspicious of all appearances, and from the beginning of their acquaintance he undertakes to fathom her being, not, however, in regard to what is real about her, but in regard to what might be false. He notes that the house she lives in as a child has elegant draperies, but they merely hide from sight a shameful business within, namely prostitution. The procuress there puts on a false front of respectability by sending her daughter to the best schools. Cousin Julie, who sometimes chats with Tonka, is not the pleasant girl she seems, but an easy make and a disgrace to the family. Nothing in Tonka's environment seems quite authentic: the aunt is not really an aunt but a cousin, the aunt's son is not a legitimate child, the grandmother is not really the grandmother but a sister of the grandmother, the only true relative is dead. Even Tonka's name, with its Slavic ending, is not quite right, since she was baptized in German as Antonie. The language on the street is not pure, but a curious mixture of German and Czech. N ponders the influence all this falseness may have had upon Tonka. When she yields to his importunate sexual demands, he sees no real evidence of her virginity and he questions whether her tears and her reluctance are genuine or merely a trap to possess him the more fully.

It is strikingly evident from the narrative that sex is a major concern in N's quest of reality. No matter what the point of departure, N's thoughts tend toward the problem of falseness in the area of sex. Preoccupied with thoughts of prostitution, adultery, and promiscuity, N shows an obsession with the shamefulness of illicit sexual activity. Cousin Julie is "eine Schande," prostitution is "schändlich," and he hopes that Tonka still has a sensitivity to "Schande."

In his relationship with Tonka, N's obsession with sex takes the form of jealousy. The first hint of his jealousy appears when he tells of Tonka at her work. After noting that she is employed in a textile shop, he suddenly mentions the two foppish young sons of the proprietor. A weighty "Aber" introduces them in a statement that is logically a non sequitur but psychologically a revealing trend of his thoughts. Even after Tonka has left her position, he is still irritated when the shop is mentioned ("Es ärgerte ihn, wenn sie durch irgend etwas noch mit dem Geschäft zusammenhing").

He begins to accompany her whenever she goes out "weil er sich nicht traute, sie allein zu lassen." Any man they encounter on the street is suspected of being her seducer. The jealousy mingled with his uncertainty tortures him, and his relationship with Tonka becomes a bramble of thorns ("ein Dornengerank"), ("das . . . Dornengerank in seinem Kopf") which remains permanently in his mind. He cannot determine whether Tonka is trustworthy or not because all her actions can be interpreted in two ways ("Wie waren alle zweideutig"), and even her silence could betoken either innocence or stubbornness. Finally her silence could mean what is uppermost in his mind: "Schande für ihn."

While trying to extract from Tonka a confession of guilt he is at the same time harassing physicians to pronounce her innocent. He embarks on a lengthy series of medical consultations in a kind of mania ("eine Art medizinischer Prozeßsucht") to ascertain whether Tonka's child could have been conceived without a man as agent, and learns that in all the history of medicine there is no record of such an instance. The only incriminating evidence he ever finds against Tonka is a little mark on the calendar, which is not enough proof to save him from the uncertainty which is so "annihilating," but cannot be dismissed.

Thus he lingers in a state of indecision which threatens to destroy him ("das Vernichtende war doch gerade, daß man keins von beiden tat"). As his thoughts waver between faith and doubt, his emotions also vacillate with pathological rapidity. Anguish batters him "wie ein Sturm," howls about him ("heulte um alle Ecken seiner Festigkeit") until he wants to scream "Hilf mir, hilf du mir! Hier knie ich vor dir!" or consolation comes suddenly with the thought that he will be near Tonka forever, like God.

Tonka's mysterious pregnancy is not the reason for N's obsession with sexual "Schande" nor the cause of his jealousy and tortured uncertainty, for traces of these aberrations can be observed much earlier. The source of his disorder can be found in his childhood, when he experiences a prolonged disturbance that climaxes in a particular traumatic incident which he remembers with sharp poignancy.

In N's childhood there is, besides Mother and Father, an Uncle Hyazinth, who is not a "real" nucle, but a friend of the parents, "einer jener Onkel, welche die Kinder vorfinden, wenn sie die Augen aufschlagen." The boy N gradually realizes that, in fact, Hyazinth is his mother's lover. Distressed by the deception his mother practices and confused by the show of restraint and sublimation with which the lovers delude themselves, N endures a troubled and angry childhood. Late one night while traveling by train with his mother and Hyazinth, N has the impression that his mother is resting with tender familiarity against Hyazinth, who is holding her hand. As N leans forward in rage, trying to see more clearly, the two adults are sitting properly apart. The whole process repeats itself as the boy experiences the agony caused by his mother's exhibition of sexual betrayal, and by his own uncertainty: "So groß war die durch das ungenaue Sehen hervorgerufene Qual oder so ungenau durch die Qual in der Dunkelheit das Sehen." His witness to his mother's adulterous actions at a time when normal incestuous Oedipal desires may not yet be completely resolved, inflicts a psychological wound of incalculable depth. With Tonka's pregnancy the factors both of adultery and of uncertainty seem to be present again. In a repetition compulsion he relives the agonizing event of his childhood, but this time more specifically as the victim.

When N's childhood experience is interpreted as a trauma affecting his whole later orientation, his behavior becomes comprehensible. The report takes on aspects of a case study of personality disintegration, as N exhibits increasingly the symptoms of psychosis. N, the scientist who supposedly embodies the technological spirit of the age, adopts childish, irrational superstitions. Like his mother, he begins to regard Tonka as the cause of all their misfortune, "geradezu als ein böses Zeichen, das Unglück vorbedeutete." He discards a fine old ring he likes and wears instead a flashy new one that brings him luck. He grows a beard because he is luckier when he doesn't shave. He plays the horses and regards his losses as a sinister omen.

The beard which makes him look unlike himself ("entstellte ihn") is also a mark of self-estrangement. He begins to look upon both himself and Tonka as alien beings: "er war fremd. Und wer war Tonka? . . . ein fremdes Geschöpf." A paranoia becomes evident in his sensation of hostility around him ("von Feindseligkeiten umgeben"), as he feels pursued by people on the street as by a pack of hounds. His bad luck in gambling persuades him that even supernatural powers wish him ill.

His disorientation in the world of material things becomes acute as everything seems to fall apart into senseless, isolated fragments ("So zerfällt sie in sinnlose Einzelheiten . . . traurig getrennt"), and the furnishings of his room lose their equilibrium ("hatten etwas Schiefes, Vornübergeneigtes, fast Fallendes"). Hypersensitive to others' consciousness, he is nauseated by the intermingling and collisions of many spheres of human awareness: "ein ekelhaftes Durcheinander."

More and more he loses his footing in the everyday world, as hallucinations fill his waking hours. With detachment he observes spooklike figures, formerly objects of his jealousy, doing, singly or in combinations, "das Fürchterlichste." He sees Tonka clear-blue as moonlight against kaleidoscopic colors, no longer denying her guilt. He dreams his own dreams, and he dreams such dreams as Tonka might have of him.

However, fantasy and dream do not possess him in entirety. His being is sharply split in two: one part is lost in illusions; the other operates in the rational world with great success. As his emotional self progressively degenerates, his intellectual self reaches a high level of precise and objective vision. As Wilhelm Braun has noted, N's behavior now becomes almost schizophrenic. In the area of his scientific research he deals pragmatically with the laws of probability, and he reinforces his investigations with courage, confidence, intuition, and a healthy determination to succeed. Here he sets reasonable limits to his questioning instead of indulging in infinite speculation, as with Tonka: "hätte er jeden Zweifel so prüfen wollen, wie er mit Tonka tat, so wäre er niemals zum Ende gekommen: Denken heißt, nicht zuviel denken, und ohne etwas Verzicht auf das Grenzenlose der Erfindungsgabe läßt sich keine Erfindung machen."

The deep division within him is never bridged, but is still evident at the end of his narrative. While he marks the contrast between his own situation and that of Tonka: "Er stand im Licht und sie lag unter der Erde" the worm, the image of death in life, pierces his delusion of well-being and he senses Tonka "von der Erde bis zum Kopf." The realization of the dead Tonka within him is more than sad recollection or empathy: it is the harrowing revelation of deadness within himself. While one part of his split personality basks in the sunlight of success, the other is in darkness. Translated into non-poetic terms, this flash of truth is the sudden and brief awareness of his schizophrenia.

Although N's classical symptoms of schizophrenia are demonstrable, it would not do justice to the rich complexity of the story to regard N only in the clinical light of Freudian psychology. On one level of meaning N is indeed psychotic; the Freudian interpretation is valid as far as it goes. A psychological approach to the narrator is a useful preliminary study, for it establishes that his orientation toward reality is basically unsound. Reaching a judgment about N's reliability is decidedly a first step toward interpreting the story according to the author's conception.

Frederick G. Peters (essay date 1978)

SOURCE: "Three Mysterious Women: *Grigia, The Lady from Portugal, Tonka,*" in *Robert Musil, Master of the*

Hovering Life: A Study of the Major Fiction, Columbia University Press, 1978, pp. 105-87.

[*In the following excerpt, Peters interprets* The Lady from Portugal *from a psychoanalytic perspective.*]

The second story [*The Lady from Portugal*] in the trilogy *Three Women* is set (as was the first story, *Grigia*) in a geographical area that is intentionally vague, in a region situated between North and South and in a world at once specifically medieval and yet enveloped in the timelessness of the fairy tale. Generations earlier, the Ketten family had come from the North and stopped, as did Homo, on the threshold of the South near the Brenner pass in Italy. It is in such an ambiguous geographical setting that Musil treats once again the conflict between reason and mysticism. And it is because of the way in which the present Herr von Ketten eventually resolves this duality (which, as in *Grigia,* Musil treats as an internal psychological conflict between the male and female principles) that he manages to escape the destiny of all the previous heads of his family. Generation after generation, all of them had died before reaching their sixtieth birthday. Each one of them had been cut down by death as soon as he had completed a great task. Ketten also accomplishes a great task, by which and through which his life becomes defined. Like his ancestors, he, too, suffers a "death," but is then, as if by a miracle, reborn and restored to life with his family and the others for whom he is responsible.

The Wolf and His Moonlady

Because of the importance to this story of the conflict within Ketten of the male and female principles as Musil understood them, Musil goes to great pains to describe husband and wife in terms that are not only at once both concrete and symbolic, but also at first antagonistic. Throughout the story, Musil compares Ketten's life and nature to that of a wolf, a ferocious beast of prey who pursues his goal inexorably and without deviation. If Ketten can get what he wants by honest means, he does so; but, if not, he uses methods both violent and cunning. He is alert, cruel, and aggressive. Ketten is also compared with the landscape surrounding his family seat. The castle stands on a sheer and lonely cliff. Five hundred feet below a torrent of water rages so loudly that no sound can penetrate from the outer world into the castle; nor can any sound from the castle reach the outer world. The patterns in which the woods rise and fall on the mountainsides bestow an air of savagery and violence upon the landscape. The atmosphere surrounding the stunted trees and ragged cliffs is chilly and the countryside is described as being inhabited by stags, wild boars, wolves, dragons, and perhaps even the unicorn. Eagles soar in the clouds above, and demons and spirits seem to lurk in the upper air. After his courtship in Portugal, a land of beauty described in terms of the gentle blue waves of the sea, Ketten brings his wife home to his castle. Although she had assumed that the landscape would be in some way similar to the nature of her husband, what she sees as she rides up to the castle for the first time is something "unimag-

Musil at his desk in Geneva, 1941.

inably hideous." Her first impulse is to flee. But she forces herself to remain by assuming that the castle and the landscape have a beauty of their own, "like a man's ways, to which one had to become accustomed."

Ketten, for his part, perceives his lady from Portugal as being more than merely a very beautiful woman from the South. She is an unceasing mystery to him, an enchantment that can never be dispelled: "Embracing the woman, might he not suddenly be brought up short by the force of some magical resistance?" On one occasion, when she is standing on the steps waiting to mount her horse, she seems to Ketten as if she were about to step into the saddle and ride off into an Other World. Amid the continuing violence of Ketten's life, she blooms silently as a rose; she is also compared to a pearl necklace that could easily be crushed but which nevertheless continues to exist in the everyday world, absolutely invulnerable. Eventually a legend arises among the people that Ketten has sold his soul to the Devil, who now lives in his castle disguised as a beautiful woman. It is significant that husband and wife rarely seem to talk to each other. And yet, everything that is meaningful in Ketten's life is in some way connected with his lady's existence, an uncanny existence that cannot be expressed discursively in language or comprehended by reason. Ketten's intense love

for his "moonlady" reflects a deep and secret yearning of his soul. Compared with this feeling, he takes no joy in increasing his worldly possessions and in expanding his household.

Ketten's wife, the lady from Portugal, is a close literary relation of Homo's mistress, Grigia. From a Jungian perspective, both women represent the anima figure, Grigia a lower stage of its development and the Portugese lady a higher one. The first stage . . . is often represented by an Eve, a woman who expresses only the instinctual and biological needs of man. The second stage is represented by a figure like Faust's Helen, who embodies not only the sexual but also the aesthetic elements of man's nature. The Portugese lady may be regarded as embodying this higher aspect. The way in which the anima figure first manifests itself in *Grigia* is different from the way it is introduced in *The Lady from Portugal,* and this difference determines the utter dissimilarity of atmospheres pervading the two works. Homo rides into Grigia's world, into the world of the anima, and his attitude toward her causes the story to be enveloped by a sentimental and romantically pastoral mood. But in *The Lady from Portugal,* it is the woman who rides into the man's world; the story therefore takes place in a violent, masculine, and almost primeval setting.

The Temptation of the Warrior

When Ketten brings his bride home after a year-long courtship in Portugal, he is eighteen years old. He spends the next twelve years almost without interruption in a war with the Bishop of Trent, a war that the Ketten family has been waging on and off for generations. Musil indicates the presence of ambivalence in Ketten's sense of identity by the fact that he bears two names, the German "von Ketten" (North) and the Italian "delle Catene" (South). The narrator comments, further, that Ketten himself did not know whether he revealed his true self during the one-year period of his graceful courtship in the South, throughout which he had behaved in accordance with the rules of feminine society, or only in all the other years of incessant and brutal warfare. Because his existence as a human being is defined by his role in the external world as leader of the army against the Bishop's forces, he must resist the temptations of his wife's world. Ketten must play the role of man, as understood in his society. For in the world of medieval northern Italy, life is war and the man who kills survives. It is Ketten's dilemma that he must fight and murder while at the same time feeling drawn toward another alien and ambiguous world whose human expression appears in his gentle and silent wife. Her very being seems always to be "luring him on into some Other Realm." This is the world of religious feeling; it is the realm of God, as both Johannes and Homo designated it. But it is also a realm that negates all those virtues and vices required by a war lord in order to achieve victory over his enemies.

Musil describes Ketten's attitude toward these two worlds of being in terms of the sun and the moon: "To command is a thing of clarity; such a life is day-bright, solid to the touch, and the thrust of a spear under an iron collar that has slipped is as simple as pointing one's finger at something and being able to say: This is *this*. But the other thing is as alien as the moon." Out of this other soft and ambiguous world no commands are given and none are received, for it is sufficient unto itself. Sometimes in the evenings when Ketten is sitting at the campfire, half-dreaming and in a state of total physical exhaustion, this Other World seems to creep out of the shadows toward him and threatens to undo his manly strength and determination. The same question that Homo had asked himself expresses in a most lucid and dramatic fashion the dilemma of Ketten's life: "Kill, and yet feel the presence of God? . . . Feel the presence of God and yet kill?"

Ketten resists the temptation and manages to remain keen, alert, and cruel, happy in the knowledge that he is still able to "cause others to die without that other thing," i.e., the mystical realm, intruding to paralyze all activity. While there never seemed to be a point in Homo's life where he considered the possibility of resisting the temptation of the mystical realm, the thought never occurs to Ketten that he could ever surrender to the Bishop and yield to this alien world. Ketten is filled with "the happiness of not yielding, and this was the very soul of his soul." Homo's family will survive without him. Ketten, however, must defend his wife, sons, and subjects by waging

aggressive war. There is no alternative for him: Ketten must repress the same impulse in which Homo, having once discovered it, indulged himself to the point where life became irrelevant to him.

It is clear—to continue the comparison between *Grigia* and *The Lady from Portugal*—that the relationship of the protagonist to mysticism is different in both stories. The duality in *Grigia* was that between two forms of mysticism: Homo's love-at-a-distance for his wife (contemplative mysticism) and his attraction to the exotic Grigia (dionysian mysticism). The glory of Homo's one moment of eternal "reunion" with his wife caused the sexual attraction for Grigia to fade by comparison into insignificance, although their relationship continued to drift on. The final struggle was one between Homo's passive drifting off into death and his instinctual desire to live. Because of the intensity and purity of the mystical "reunion" with his wife, Homo relinquished his life almost with an air of indifference. In *The Lady from Portugal,* however, the initial conflict is between Ketten's everyday duties to the world as a man and his attraction to the mystical realm in general, for both dionysian and contemplative mysticism are present in one woman. From a Jungian point of view, Ketten has married his anima: Madonna-like wife and exotic temptress are one. It is obvious, then, that neither *Grigia* nor *The Lady from Portugal* can be regarded as merely describing a superficial conflict between man and woman. Neither Grigia nor the lady are simple, external, active female temptresses, to whom the male protagonist must succumb or from whom he must flee. It is true that Homo succumbs. And in *The Lady from Portugal,* Ketten is always in flight. In the twelve years of war, Ketten in fact never spends more then twelve hours at home: "Doubtless he feared to stay at home longer, just as a tired man dare not sit down." But the conflict is essentially endopsychic. Both Homo and Ketten are dealing with an impulse from within themselves that manifests itself externally in the form of a particular woman. The unconscious nature of this psychological dynamic explains why Homo felt such an irrational attraction for Grigia as well as why Ketten chose to marry such an exotic woman from the South. Both women are able to accommodate the projection of the protagonist's repressed feminine soul, a repression that had been required on behalf of the pursuit of extremely masculine professions: that of scientist and soldier.

Victory and Decline

The Bishop falls ill and dies, and the cathedral chapter, being without its leader, decides to sue for peace. A war that has lasted for four generations comes to an end. After having spent almost every waking moment of his life and every ounce of his strength in the violent pursuit of a specific goal, Ketten suddenly finds himself with nothing to do but to manage his estates, a task that his wife had discharged adequately enough during the twelve years of his absence. (A striking parallel exists here between Ketten's life and that of the author. It will be recalled that Musil suddenly lost his job in 1922 due to cutbacks in government expenditures, thus ending a twelve-year period of steady employment that had begun with his marriage. This was a traumatic experience for Musil who, at 42, was twelve years older than the 30-year-old Ketten, but it finally permitted him to devote himself entirely to his creative work as a writer. Ketten, too, now faces a traumatic turning point in his life.) A man who has been defined and supported mainly by his profession as a soldier is now expected to return to a life of tranquility and passivity. The prospect for his declining years is a life of boredom and meaninglessness, circumscribed by the duties of the farmer—"no goal," as the narrator comments, "for a great lord." Then, while traveling home, Ketten is stung by a fly, whereupon he falls into deep and protracted illness. Ketten, who had won his war with the Bishop and who had survived hundreds of dangerous engagements on the battle field as well as numerous wounds from the enemy, is defeated by a fly. Or, more precisely, the success of the fly's attack is merely an external sign of the fact that Ketten's life, now without its high goal, has fallen into a state of total vulnerability. He no longer possesses a reason to fight and to survive.

Ketten's fever continues to linger on. While his wife chalks secret signs on his door and bedposts, learned doctors are called from distant places. But nothing helps. Ketten becomes ever more isolated in his suffering. This man, who had once stood squarely in the middle of wordly events, now feels that the world is steadily receding from him. For days and even weeks, he is only vaguely aware of what is happening around him. Previously, he had never remained very long in the presence of his wife, because "if he had ever remained longer, he would have had to be truly as he was"—an oblique statement which implicitly, though only tentatively, suggests that his deepest impulse is to surrender as did Homo. Cared for by his wife, he will now be forced into confronting whatever his true nature might really be, for the persona of the soldier, the professional disguise, will gradually be burned away by the fever.

Jung once stated [in *The Practice of Psychotherapy*] that a significant number of his patients were not suffering from any clinically definable neurosis, but rather from the aimlessness and senselessness of their daily existence. It is at such periods in the individual's life that he tends to fall either mentally or physically ill. However, such illness can be regarded as the first stage of a process in which the individual moves toward greater psychological health: illness may indeed be the transitional stage through which the individual passes as he outgrows the first half of his psychic development and enters the second half. Ketten's illness functions in precisely this fashion. While the individual's prime task in the first half of his life is concerned with his adaptation to the demands of the external environment, his task in the second half is, as Jacobi writes, directed toward "the so-called 'initiation into the inner reality,' a deeper self-knowledge and knowledge of humanity, a 'turning back' (*reflectio*) to the traits of one's nature that have hitherto remained unconscious or become" [Jolande Jacobi, *The Psychology of C. G. Jung,* 1968]. The following observation made by another Jungian analyst, M.-L. von Franz, is relevant to the diag-

nosis not only of Ketten's illness but also of the "higher" function of this illness in contributing towards his psychic development: "The actual process of individuation—the conscious coming-to-terms with one's own inner center (psychic nucleus) or Self—generally begins with a wounding of the personality and the suffering that accompanies it" [M.-L. von Franz, "The Process of Individuation," in *Man and His Symbols,* ed. Carl G. Jung, 1971].

M.-L. von Franz also draws attention to one theme which persistently occurs in the fairy tales of different cultures and is also directly related to the subject of Musil's story, namely, the suffering of the individual psyche at the beginning of the individuation process: "Beneath the surface a person is suffering from a deadly boredom that makes everything seem meaningless and empty. Many myths and fairy tales symbolically describe this initial stage in the process of individuation by telling of a king who has fallen ill or grown old." Jung in his psychotherapy often made much reference to the quests of heroes in fairy tales in order to illuminate the state of a patient's psyche. In *The Lady from Portugal,* Musil may well have presented an aesthetic version of his own inner psychic condition which, because of its high degree of objectification, appears to the reader as a self-contained, sophisticated exercise in the fairy tale genre. The symbolic manner in which Musil was able to capture the inner life of the individual by the aesthetic means of a fairy-tale-like story is illuminated by Jung's explanation of the origin and function of all fairy tales. In Jung's thought, fairy tales represent an aesthetic formulation of various developmental stages of the psyche of a race or culture as a whole, and the literature of Jungian psychology refers to a number of fairy tales which are analagous to the one that Musil wrote.

During the course of his illness, Ketten eventually feels that he has died and is surprised that dying was so peaceful. At the same time, he also feels that he is standing somewhere at the periphery of life, as though he might be able to come back to life again. What it is that will make it possible for him to return to life is not yet clear. However, Ketten believes that only part of his being has gone on ahead into death, and that his bones have been left behind on the bed. Ketten sees his wife bending over him and he looks directly into her face. At this point halfway between life and death, Ketten experiences the equivalent of Veronica's and Homo's mystical moment of "reunion." In a vision, he sees himself and his wife arise together out of his dead body and walk quietly into the distance. The Ketten resting in bed as well as the Ketten walking with his wife in the distance seem to be cradled in some gigantic and benevolent hand: "Doubtless that was God," he thinks. Veronica's and Homo's respective mystical moments differ in a significant manner from that of Ketten: their experience is one of "melting," of "flowing" into the beloved, of a union so total that the personalities dissolve. In Ketten's ephiphany, on the other hand, he and his wife appear and remain as two separate and independent individuals, existing side by side in total equality. This epiphany proves to be prophetic of the couple's happy fate after Ketten has overcome his crisis.

Time continues to pass without any significant change occurring in Ketten's condition until the day on which a fearful thought suddenly grips his mind. He realizes that if he is going to return to life, he must gather together all of his will-power now. If he is not to die completely, he must exert his will upon the course of events in daily reality; he must will an action (as Veronica felt she had to recall a repressed memory in order to prevent herself from degenerating into insanity). As is consonant with Ketten's behavior before his illness, he kills. The first stage of his recovery is indicated by his ordering the killing of a wolf. Why it is that he chooses specifically a wolf as his victim requires further elaboration. During Ketten's absence in the field, his wife had adopted a wolf. She was particularly attracted to the wolf because it reminded her of her husband. (This relationship between a woman and an animal is reminiscent of that between Veronica and her dog, although the sexual aspect of the attraction is not overtly mentioned by Musil in the case of the Portugese lady except indirectly and ironically when she once wonders whether her two sons are really hers, for they remind her of two young wolves rather than of two children.) It may be recalled that throughout the story the narrator has often compared Ketten's behavior with that of a wolf. It is clear that Ketten, his wife, and Musil's reader cannot help but be quite conscious of the parallel between the man and the wolf. Without informing his wife, Ketten, who is still too weak to carry out the action himself, orders a serving man to kill the beast. What Ketten has done is to destroy the usurper; for in his feverish mind, the wolf seemed more like the vigorous Ketten he once had been than this man now victimized and broken by suffering and illness. By means of this violent action, Ketten has begun the process of recovering his old identity. When the Portuguese lady learns what her husband has done, her blood seems at first to freeze in her veins. But she accepts and in fact welcomes his act of violence, for in this decision she, too, recognizes the return of the vigorous man she had married twelve years before. She goes to his bedside, "and for the first time he looked her straight in the eyes again." His shame has passed and he is now able to gaze at his wife, feeling himself to be truly her husband.

The Little Cat from the World Beyond

An interpretation of the complex function of the little cat in this story presents many difficulties. The following analysis will be informed by two perspectives: first, the transformation of the cat into human being and, second, the cat's life and death as a secular analogue to the religious drama of the sacrifice of the scapegoat.

Although he has willed an action by having the wolf killed, Ketten is unable by his own powers to reach the second stage of recovery, and it seems to him that only some miracle from outside can now alter his situation for the better. The bearer of the miracle arrives one day quite unexpectedly and unannounced at the gate of the castle. A more inauspicious beginning for a miracle can hardly be imagined. It is a small cat who arrives, but it is a rather strange cat. This cat insists upon entering the castle through the front gate as human beings do and not by climbing over the wall cat-fashion. The cat also strikes everyone as possessing a slightly sadder and more meditative air than is appropriate for a mere kitten. It also seems to lack something, and "this absence of whatever would have made it into an ordinary kitten—was like a second presence, a hovering double, perhaps, or a faint halo surrounding it." It is the absence of something in cat-nature that makes the kitten more than an animal and relates it to human beings. In the context of Musil's psychology, to be a human being means (among other things) to lack to a greater or lesser extent something in or of animal nature; man is the only animal who has lost his instincts. What takes the place of this absence in man and in this particular cat? The unnatural psychological vacuum, caused by the absence of instinctual nature, becomes "filled" with illness and suffering.

Musil's story of the humanization and eventual spiritualization of the cat by means of illness represents an artistic climax in the history of an idea that has received analogous formulations in German romanticism, Christianity, philosophy, and psychoanalysis. . . .

In a spirit nearer to the romantics and Nietzsche than to Freud, Musil treated the process of psychological heightening through suffering, but chose to do so in the context of medieval Europe. Because he set the story in a religious world, the metaphors provided by Christian theology became available to him. And as the work of C. G. Jung has revealed, religious metaphors give dramatic and objective expression to profound psychological truths and processes that are the same in every age.

The cat in ***The Lady from Portugal*** becomes sick and, like Ketten, grows ever weaker. After three days, its vomiting and filth have become so unbearable that Ketten, with feelings of great guilt, has the cat forcibly removed to a peasant's house outside the castle walls. But the cat returns and continues its physical decline. The cat's intense and sustained suffering seems to be transforming it into a human being. Heine's statement is particularly relevant here: "I believe that by suffering even animals could be made human." Ketten has the distinct feeling that his "illness and its deathly gentleness had been transformed into that little animal's body and so were no longer merely within him." He believes that his own destiny is "being vicariously accomplished in this little cat already half released from earthly bonds." As Ketten killed the wolf, his wife now orders that the cat be taken away and destroyed. With the death of the cat and its illness, Ketten's illness passes and he returns to life.

It is the Portuguese lady who, not surprisingly, has the first intuition into the meaning of the "miracle," into the significance of the cat's appearance, illness, and death. She says to Ketten: "If God could become man, then He can also become a kitten." She intuitively recognizes the intrinsically religious nature of the cat's last passion and her insight receives further confirmation from the narrator, who stresses the religious connotations of the cat's sickness: he terms the cat's suffering "its martyrdom" and describes its struggles as a trial of strength between the cat's "imperceptible halo and the dreadful filth." In reality—if one may distinguish between the characters' reactions and the objective world from which their reactions arose—this final episode merely tells of a somewhat odd-looking kitten, who happens to catch a disease and finally dies in an extremely wretched manner. The religious significance is projected upon the cat by Ketten and his wife.

Jung's psychology offers some illuminating insights into why, how, and for what purpose such projections occur. The presupposition for Jung's theories about the religious impulse is his belief . . . that its expression is as important for the psychic health of the individual as are the equally natural expressions of sexual and aggressive urges. By means of ritual and drama, religions have given external form in action and verbal formulae to certain profound psychological needs. Fordham explains dogma as being "the product of conscious thought working on and refining the raw material of the unconscious" [Frieda Fordham, *An Introduction to Jung's Psychology,* 1961]. Thus, dogma and ritual may be regarded as crystallized forms of original mystical experiences that take place prior to and are more profound than their eventual expression in orthodox religious terms. Jung identified the fundamental forms that the external religious drama takes in the West: organized religion expresses "the living process of the unconscious in the form of the drama of repentance, sacrifice, and redemption" [*Psychology and Religion: West and East*]. In *The Lady from Portugal,* Musil has presented a story whose central mystery is closely related to a religious drama: the sacrifice of the scapegoat which brings salvation to the sick in mind and body.

While Ketten is a foe of the Church, the Bishop—so Ketten's chaplain tells him—is able to pray to God, and this must prove of ultimate disadvantage to Ketten's interests. It is a decided irony, therefore, that when the Bishop becomes ill he dies, while Ketten is saved by the kind of sacrifice and redemption that is at the heart of Christian theology. Ketten's situation, in this regard, is analogous to the relationship between the individual and the Church in the modern world as analyzed by Jung. Although modern man may possess a religious impulse that is in no way inferior to the drive experienced by his medieval brothers, he is no longer able to return to the Church and to find in the Christian drama of Christ's suffering and self-sacrifice for man a satisfactory expression of the "living processes of the unconscious." In place of the search for God, the modern individual is in search of that mysterious entity "the whole man," which represents the culmination of the individuation process. Jung expressed this historical change as follows: "There is no deity in the [modern] mandala, nor is there any submission or reconciliation to a deity. The place of the deity seems to be taken by the wholeness of man." The problem that the contemporary Church faces arises from the fact that modern man is no longer able to feel the presence of God within its walls. Musil once noted in his

diaries that the Church was the "ruin of the Other Condition (*des andern Zustandes*)." Today's unfortunate situation has occurred for two reasons, Jung asserted: first, the Church's creed and ritual have become so elaborate and obscure that they have degenerated into mere formalities and, second, the Church (as in Musil's *The Lady from Portugal*) reveals a face to the believer that little distinguishes it from any secular power bent upon increasing its political power and extending its ownership of land. Ultimately, it is the Bishop who appears as the warrior and Ketten who undergoes a profound religious transformation. In this sense, Ketten is really a representative of modern man who continues to undergo profound psychological transformations but who no longer interprets them in the context of metaphors provided by Christian theology. Jung believed that his own "process of individuation" provided man with a new series of metaphors for the expression of spiritual experience in the modern world.

A few observations may now be offered by way of summarizing the function of the animal and animal metaphors in Musil's fiction up to this point. First, characters are often "debased" and identified with animals: Basini behaves like a pig, Claudine's stranger is compared to a goat, Demeter is associated with a dog, and Grigia is identified with a cow. The function of such metaphors is clear: certain human beings are thereby reduced to the animal level or, more specifically, they are transformed into sexual objects. Such characters function in the narrative as projections of the protagonist in a state of dionysian mysticism, the major examples of which are found in *The Temptation of Quiet Veronica* and *Grigia*. The thought once occurred to Veronica that an animal would be like the Other Dimension. Not only does she compare the sensual Demeter with a dog but the priestlike Johannes as well. And just as Johannes seems to have lost the instincts of the lower animals so too has the cat in *The Lady from Portugal*. Both Johannes and the cat are associated with animals, but in their aura of impersonality (which is present in all animals) and in the absence of animal instincts, they become in the minds of Veronica and the Kettens, respectively, the bearers of a projected religious impulse. It is the martyred cat alone of all the other animals (dogs, pigs, cows) mentioned above who brings salvation: the cat is the bearer of the miracle whereby Ketten, who feels that he has already died, achieves a resurrection of the body. In *Grigia* Homo's religious impulse remained merely at the level of a profound feeling. In *The Lady from Portugal,* Ketten's religious feelings are given symbolic expression in the drama of the sufferings and death of the little cat.

It should be noted also that although such religious terms as "spiritual," "resurrection," and "salvation" have been used in this analysis of the function of the cat in *The Lady from Portugal*—for the story is set during an age of faith—Musil's narrative never transcends the secular plane of existence. As is also the case in Jung's writings, religious experience provides metaphors for psychological occurrences. But whereas Jung analyzes these psychological processes from within, Musil merely indicates from outside what may be occurring within the psyche of the protagonist. The act of psychologizing is left to the reader.

The Climb into Manhood

At some indefinite point during Ketten's illness a young Portuguese knight, a childhood friend of Ketten's wife, had arrived at the castle for an extended visit. In front of this radiantly healthy young man, Ketten "lay in the grass like a dog, filled with shame." As the days passed, suspicions arose in Ketten's mind that his wife and her friend were deceiving him. But he was unable, because of his debilitated state, either to investigate his suspicions or to take any immediate and decisive action, as he would have done in times long gone by when he had been the great and forceful warrior. Suffering had now become his new occupation. After his illness passes, however, Ketten firmly decides that if his wife does not send the knight away, he will kill him in spite of all the rules of hospitality. Nevertheless, although Ketten finally makes a decision, he finds himself unable to act upon it and to carry out the kind of task that he had previously found to be so easy to accomplish. For now, after his illness, fighting and killing strike him as being a "senseless, alien mode of action." This revaluation and striking reversal of his former style of life provide the most graphic indication of the change that illness and suffering have wrought upon his psyche. On the other hand, it is not in Ketten's nature to continue to suffer his suspicions quietly. Moreover, although he is over his physical illness because of the miracle of the cat, he has not yet recovered his self. The miracle of the cat was a passive occurrence: Ketten had merely watched and believed that the cat had taken on his illness. Therefore, although Ketten was cured of his physical illness, he is not yet a whole man. He knows intuitively that "he would never be wholly well again if he did not wrench himself free of all this." The Portuguese knight provides the pretext for a second act of will that completes Ketten's final stage of recovery just as the murder of the wolf signified the first step in his return to health.

Ketten recalls that he had once consulted a soothsaying woman who had made him the following prophecy: "You will be cured only when you accomplish a task." Suddenly a thought comes to him. As a boy, he had always wanted to climb the cliff on top of which the castle was built. The accomplishment of this feat will be the task, the "trial by ordeal," through which Ketten will regain himself. It is a suicidal task, he knows, for no human being can scale such a sheer and high cliff. Nevertheless, he begins to climb at nightfall and as he climbs he feels that it is not he but the little cat from "the world beyond" who is returning to the castle in this fashion. As the cat had entered the castle as a human being, a human being is now entering the castle like a cat. Sweat pours from his body and waves of heat flash through his limbs. By means of this supreme physical exertion combined with the risk of sudden death, he has duplicated to a great extent the situation on the field of battle. Ketten recaptures and re-enters his body and his earlier spirit by accomplishing the task: "it was strange to feel how in this struggle with death strength and health came flowing back into his

limbs." He reaches the castle and "with his strength his ferocity had also returned." With dagger at his side, he climbs through the window and into the bedroom of the young knight. But the bed is empty. He immediately goes to his wife's bedroom and is overjoyed to find that the knight is not there either. A servant tells Ketten that the knight had ridden away at the rising of the moon. Considering the Portuguese lady's identification with the moon, we may safely interpret this remark as meaning that Ketten's wife herself had sent him away. In this regard, the Portuguese lady would be following the pattern set by the two earlier Musil women, who also eventually either reject or leave men associated solely with vitality and sexuality: Claudine leaves the stranger and returns to her husband and Veronica rejects Demeter utterly. The Portuguese lady is startled by Ketten's entry and sits up in bed "as though in her dreams she had been waiting for this." She knows that her husband has finally returned to her after twelve years of battle and many months of illness.

In *Grigia* and *The Lady from Portugal,* Musil has presented women who exert a profound effect upon the life of the male protagonist. Whether as a particular, although somewhat strange woman (if Musil's narrative is read on a literal level) or whether as the feminine element within the male psyche (if the narrative is "internalized" for the purposes of psychological interpretation), she functions to lure the protagonist toward the "other side." The temptation of the protagonist in *Grigia* leads to his death, although the preconditions for his disintegration were already present within himself before he met his peasant mistress. (Grigia was herself no more directly responsible for Homo's death than Tadzio was for the collapse and death of Gustav von Aschenbach in "Death in Venice.") The Portuguese lady also tempts the protagonist to experience another dimension—either of life in general or one existing within his own psyche: it is a world of gentleness, patience, suffering, passivity, and intuition.

The fact that Homo dies and Ketten is reborn reflects the differing relationship of the protagonist to the mystical realm in the two stories. It would have been conveniently symmetrical to be able to argue that while Grigia represents a mysticism that destroys, the lady from Portugal is a force that saves. But such an interpretation places too great a significance upon the women as characters; the essential difference in these two stories is one that exists between the two male protagonists. It should also be pointed out that the Portuguese lady does not save Ketten: at most she is able to chalk magic signs on his door. She can but nurse him; only something that seems to transcend the human altogether, only "a miracle" followed by the exertion of Ketten's own mental and physical powers is able to save him. But as a representative of that other aspect of life, which Ketten as a warrior had had to repress, the lady from Portugal introduces her husband to and nurses him through that realm in which miracles occur, a realm where scientific thought and rational proof bow before intuition and faith. Unlike Homo, Ketten passes through this Other World, makes contact with its deepest level near the point of death, and emerges beyond it. Thus Ketten's relationship to his wife and to the Other Realm as represented by the cat finally serves only to enlarge his personality, to widen and deepen his understanding of life.

Musil has on occasion been misinterpreted as suggesting that psychological perfection is to be found in the hermaphroditic ideal. But as Veronica's perfect mystical moment could not be sustained in time and was eventually destroyed, so the hermaphroditic balance, if it occurs, also passes. For Musil always returns to reality, to "possible possibilities." Ketten may well experience the mystical world of his wife, a feminine dimension within himself, in such an intense fashion that the ferocious wolf within him almost dies. But he eventually returns into his old self. In this regard, Musil and Jung are in agreement. Fordham wrote: "A man, for instance, by accepting and learning to know his anima, may become more receptive, or he may develop his intuition or his feeling, but he cannot possess himself of those qualities." Feminine qualities may be present in him in the form of compassion, mercy, sensitivity, and so forth, but they will remain in a sense only worthy accretions, additions to his fundamental self that are necessary to produce a more balanced life. Ketten remains essentially what he was before, tempered by the opposite way of life without undergoing a total conversion to it. Ketten began as the ferocious wolf, became a climbing cat who had come back from the dead, and ends not as half-wolf, half-cat, but as a wolf again. But although he aggressively defends what is his, he is no longer "cruel as a knife." He is glad, therefore, that the Portuguese knight has escaped and that he will not need to kill him. In Ketten we now recognize neither a very worldly wolf nor an otherworldly cat, but a balanced human being—a rather rare phenomenon in Musil's fiction.

Ronald M. Paulson (essay date 1981)

SOURCE: "Myth and Fairy Tale in Robert Musil's *Grigia*," in *Turn of the Century: German Literature and Art, 1880-1915,* edited by Gerald Chapple and Hans H. Schulte, Bouvier Verlag, 1981, pp. 135-48.

[*In the following essay, Paulson discusses the mythological elements of Musil's* Grigia.]

Robert Musil's *Grigia* is a story with a very simple plot and very little development of characters, yet it continues to be read and discussed nearly sixty years after its first publication. Two reasons for the continuing interest in *Grigia* suggest themselves. The first is that Musil uses vivid, though enigmatic, imagery and striking metaphors, both of which engage the attention of the reader. Secondly, throughout the story Musil gives indications of a hidden meaning underlying the story. The story opens with the paragraph: "Es gibt im Leben eine Zeit, wo es sich auffallend verlangsamt, als zögerte es weiterzugehen oder wollte seine Richtung ändern. Es mag sein, daß einem in dieser Zeit leichter ein Unglück zustößt." The subject of the story, it is clear from the first paragraph, is life itself. It is life which slows down; it is the person *to* whom things happen. Most stories are an attempt to make some

statement about human life, but few of them begin with a statement about life in the abstract. The use of allegorical sounding names and emblematic imagery also points to a hidden meaning. In addition there are references to "secret aesthetic laws" which govern the phenomena described in the story and phrases spoken in an unusual dialect, the meaning of which are deliberately left vague and which seem ominous. The obscurity of the story prevents it from being an allegory despite the allegorical elements, and the expectations of clarity raised in the reader by such elements greatly emphasize the obscurity.

A related aspect of *Grigia* which engages the reader's attention is the fairy-tale atmosphere created in the story. Again, such elements are used to indicate a hidden meaning in the story. The wandering inhabitants of the valley tell tales of gems growing out of the ground like flowers: " . . . und diese unheimlich schönen Märchengebilde verstärkten noch mehr den Eindruck, daß sich unter dem Aussehen dieser Gegend, das so fremd vertraut flackerte wie die Sterne in mancher Nacht, etwas sehnsüchtig Erwartetes verberge." The forest of the region is called a "Märchenwald," and a number of descriptions of the forest and landscape are reminiscent of fairy-tale descriptions. In general the elements of the modern fairy tale enumerated by Hartmut Geerken in his collection of Expressionist fairy tales are to be found in *Grigia*: "An Zaubersprüchen, Verwandlungen, magischen Situationen, der vermenschlichten Tier- und Pflanzenwelt, der mühelosen Aufhebung der Raum- und Zeitkategorie erkennt man das Märchen bis in unsere Tage" ["Zur Märchendichtung im 20. Jahrhundert," in *Die Goldene Bombe: Expressionistische Märchendichtungen und Grotesken,* ed. Hartmut Geerken, 1970]. The unintelligible words of the peasants resemble magical formulas, and of one of these unusual remarks Homo gives an obvious explanation of the origin and meaning; but the narrator adds: "Aber es konnte auch etwas Seltsameres sein." Homo undergoes a temporary transformation in the forest idyll scene, and his entry of the mine shaft at the end of the story certainly *seems* to be a prelude to a transformation. Jewels grow from the ground; crystals live under the moss; when cows move their mouths, they seem to pray, and in general a kind of primitive animism and anthropomorphism underlies the story. Time is suspended in the final scene: "Sie regten sich stundenlang nicht. Tage mochten vergangen sein und Nächte. . . . " At least from the time of the romantics to the present the fairy tale has been regarded by students of literature and psychology as pointing to a higher reality (or perhaps a deeper level of the psyche), and as a result the fairy-tale elements also point to a hidden meaning in the story.

For Musil the term "Märchen" is somewhat broader than usual and includes myth (in the present paper no distinction is made between myth and religion). It is said of Tonka, for example: "Tonka war in die Nähe tiefer Märchen gerückt. Das war die Welt des Gesalbten, der Jungfrau und Pontius Pilatus." The world of "Märchen," as is stated in the same passage, is one in which the concept of truth does not exist, and by the end of the story it is clear that it is the realm of the ineffable, the mystical, beyond logical categories. Tonka remains "ein halbgeborener Mythos," but the thought of her after her death leads the protagonist to a kind of enlightenment: "Alles, was er niemals gewußt hatte, stand in diesem Augenblick vor ihm, die Binde der Blindheit schien von seinen Augen gesunken zu sein. . . . " There is certainly some irony involved in Musil's use of the word "Märchen" to designate something as serious as religion, and Musil himself uses the term in *Tonka* to mean "illusion": "Aber war es überhaupt so gewesen? Nein, das hatte er sich erst später zurechtgelegt. Das war schon das Märchen. . . . " However, one is dealing here with a kind of experience which occurs in a realm where the ordinary categories of truth and falsity do not apply, a realm of "analogical" rather than discursive thought, a realm of *mythos* rather than *logos*. Musil's own term for this realm was the "*Nicht-tratiöide*."

Nietzsche, of whom Musil wrote that his own work was an echo, regarded myth as an attempt to break the bonds imposed on our perception by rationality. . . . If there is any one quality which characterizes Musil's writing it is a boldness, some might even say a recklessness, in associating concepts with one another and inventing metaphors, and there is an undeniable dream-like quality in the story brought about by the chaos of vivid imagery, coupled with realistic detail, for example real place names such as Selvot (Selva) and Gronleit (Gronlait). Homo's own perception of his life in the mountains has a dreamy quality. He perceives it as " . . . gar nicht mehr Wirklichkeit, sondern ein in der Luft schwebendes Spiel." Musil also saw a similarity between myths and dreams and spoke of myths as "Menschheitsträume."

Of course the most conventional use of myths in modern literature takes the form of allusions to various mythological figures or incidents. In Nietzsche's early writings Apollo and Dionysus are used to symbolize antithetical elements in civilization, while in his later writings the opposition is between Dionysus and Christ, the Crucified One, who for present purposes is to be regarded as a mythological figure. While Dionysus faces death and self-sacrifice with purpose and determination, the Crucified One accepts death meekly and with resignation. Homo passes through both stages: in the forest idyll scene Homo overcomes his fear of death: "Von diesem Tag an war er von einer Bindung befreit . . . der Bindung an das Lebendigseinwollen, dem Grauen vor dem Tode." The knowledge of impending death does not cause Homo to indulge in an orgy of sensual gratification, contrary to his own expectations, but produces a calm satisfaction in him which makes him the sultan of his existence. The notion of prevailing over one's life by accepting destiny ("Er erkannte die persönliche Vorsehung, welche sein Leben in diese Einsamkeit gelenkt hatte . . . ") stands in stark contrast to the passive acceptance of death at the end of the story: " . . . er war in diesem Augenblick vielleicht schon zu schwach, um ins Leben zurückzukehren, wollte nicht oder war ohnmächtig geworden." In the story, Homo begins as an apollonian individual leading a rationally ordered existence, he experiences a dionysian self-overcoming and affirmation of life and then a Pauline negation of life.

Mankind undergoes a temporary dionysian experience, but fails to produce "der neue Mensch."

In a more general way an atmosphere appropriate for relating myths is created by such things as the time frame of the story. The story begins in May when Homo is separated from his wife, a symbolic birth, and ends at harvest time with his death. One might say the story fills a mythological year. The repeated emphasis on the primitivity of the mountain people also helps to establish this milieu. The houses of the village look from one angle like "ein vorweltliches Pfahldorf," and it is said of the women:

> . . . die Tücher, die sie am Kopf und gekreuzt über der Brust trugen, waren billiger Kattundruck moderner Fabrikmuster, aber durch irgend etwas in den Farben oder deren Verteilung wiesen sie weit in die Jahrhunderte der Altvordern zurück. Das war viel älter als Bauerntrachten sonst, weil es nur ein Blick war, verspätet, durch all die Zeiten gewandert, trüb und schwach angelangt aber man fühlte ihn dennoch deutlich auf sich ruhn, wenn man sie ansah.

The most prosaic products of modern mass production are unable to hide the primitive, dionysian element present in the women. The atmosphere of the story in general calls to mind the very dawn of civilization.

In his 1927 review of Alfred Döblin's *Manas,* Musil expressed the opinion that, while we know the ancient myths better today than they were known by the ancients themselves, they remain fragments for us, and the suspension of disbelief necessary for the creation of new myths is lacking. The need for magic and religious ecstasy is now filled by lyrical poetry and "die Wolkenburg der Musik." While Musil did not believe it was possible to create a new mythology—a project which has preoccupied German authors at least since the time of Friedrich Schlegel—he did employ mythological allusions and did create a myth-like atmosphere in *Grigia*, as has been remarked by Jost Hermand among others [Jost Hermand, "Musils *Grigia*," *Monatshefte* 54, 1962]. Kaiser and Wilkins took note of allusions to the Isis-Osiris myth some years ago [Ernst Kaiser and Eithne Wilkins, *Robert Musil: Eine Einführung in das Werk,* 1962]. Specifically, the association of Grigia with a cow is reminiscent of the close association of Isis with a cow, at least in the Isis cults which followed the time of the ancient Egyptians, and the comparison of Grigia with a scarab beetle brings to mind the sacred beetle of the ancient Egyptians. Annie Reniers-Servranckx has pointed out [in *Robert Musil: Konstanz und Entwicklung von Themen, Motiven und Strukturen in den Dichtungen,* 1972] that both Isis and the scarab beetle are associated with the idea of resurrection.

Little has been done since Kaiser and Wilkins to discover specific mythological allusions in the story. Reniers-Servranckx has noted allusions to Demeter in *Grigia,* and Jost Hermand points out in a general way the importance of mythology in the story but, aside from a reference to the myth of Antaeus and Gaea, he adds nothing to the recognition of specific myths. A number of writers have recognized that the rock rolled in front of the opening of the mine shaft and the fact that Grigia's middle name is Maria are allusions to Christian mythology. The allusions to Christian tradition, like the allusions to Egyptian mythology, are related to the idea of resurrection, and in general, as Jung pointed out [in *Symbole der Wandlung: Analyse zu einer Schizophrenie,* 1952], the cave (here a mine shaft) is a symbol of death and rebirth and of the maternal womb. Resurrection is also the most reasonable interpretation of the "return" to which Grigia's husband refers near the end of the story in the cryptic statement: " . . . das Zruckkemma is halt schwer." Another veiled allusion to resurrection is the description of cows lying on a hillside: " . . . [die Rinder] blickten den Vorübergehenden nicht an, noch ihm nach, sondern hielten das Antlitz unbewegt dem erwarteten Licht entgegen, und ihre gleichförmig langsam mahlenden Mäuler schienen zu beten." Of course the use of the sunrise as a symbol of resurrection considerably antedates Christianity.

The "Wiedervereinigung" referred to in Homo's forest idyll should not be seen merely as a reunion with his wife (after all, it is at this point that Homo virtually breaks all contact with his wife and child, refusing to answer her letters, etc.), but as a symbolic re-entry of the womb for the purpose of being reborn. It is paradoxical, of course, that the self must be given up in order to be born, but in a 1914 essay Musil describes a mystical experience brought about by love (like Homo's forest idyll): "Das Wollen löst sich, wir sind nicht wir selbst und doch zum erstenmal wir selbst." The symbolic rebirth of Christ from the tomb and the rebirth of Osiris from Isis are of course the resurrection theme in a slightly different guise, and it is this theme which unites the mystery religions.

The influence of the Greco-oriental mystery religions (including the Isis-Osiris rites) on the beliefs and practices of Christianity were a matter of intense speculation in the late nineteenth and early twentieth century, and it is not surprising to find other references to the mystery cults in *Grigia*. One reference to the Isis-Osiris rites which anticipates the notion of partaking of the body of God is the description of slaughtered pig hanging from the branch of a lone birch tree over a fire, since Frazer reports [in *The Golden Bough*] that pigs were slaughtered and eaten as sacrifices to Osiris, and were in fact regarded as ritual representations of the god himself. Jung also discusses the practice of hanging sacrifices from trees as a symbolic preparation for rebirth, and the discusses the practice of devouring the dead god. These themes are discussed by Jung as important elements in both Christian and Osirian ritual. Another, more whimsical reference to the Isis-Osiris myth is found in the name Mozart Amadeo Hoffingott, since Mozart's *Die Zauberflöte* is concerned with a priest of Isis and contains the well-known hymn, "O Isis und Osiris."

Allusions to the Egyptian mysteries are more important in the story than has hitherto been realized, but there are also allusions to the Eleusinian mysteries, in particular to the mysteries of Demeter and Dionysus. Dionysus is regarded by both ancient and modern authors as the Greek counterpart of Osiris, since Dionysus (called Dithyram-

bos 'the Twice-Born') was torn to pieces and devoured by Titans, according to cult lore, just as Osiris was torn to pieces by Set. Dionysus was then reborn after his heart was placed in the thigh of Zeus, or in another version, was devoured by Zeus. The same theme is found in Musil's poem "Isis und Osiris," in which Isis devours Osiris' penis to give birth to him, and each devours the other's heart in order to partake of the nature of the other. The theme of devouring the body of the dead god is further alluded to in the enumeration of the supplies carried into the mountains by the peasant women: " . . . sie trugen köstliche, seltene Last, Brot, Fleisch und Wein. . . . " The word "Fleisch" is superfluous if this is to be regarded as an allusion to the Christian sacrament, and may be regarded as an intrusion of mortality. In fact the discussion in which the enumeration occurs leads directly to a presentiment of death: " . . . wenn man an einer Wiese vorbeikam, vermochte auch ein alter Bauer dort zu stehn und winkte mit der Sense wie der leibhafte Tod." Later in the story the meat is revealed to be tainted and the cause of *Fleischvergiftung*. If *Fleish* is understood here to mean the animal or sensual side of human nature, the passages are consistent with the eroticism which pervades the story. It is also consistent with the comparisons of sexual activity with eating and drinking: "Er dachte an die Küsse zurück und fühlte sie schnalzen . . . Er stellte sich das Kommende vor und mußte wieder an die Bauernart zu essen denken; sie kauen langsam, schmatzend, jeden Bissen würdigend. . . . " A comparison of kissing to drinking is made after Homo's first overt sexual advances to Grigia: "Nun küßte er sie auch zum Siegel, und ihre Lippen schnalzten danach, so wie sich Lippen befriedigt von einem Trinkgefäß lösen, dessen Rand sie gierig umfat hielten." Homo's experience of love as a sacrament has a double meaning. The feeling of love is a sacred thing, but erotic activity is also a kind of ritual leading to the "other condition."

A more specific allusion to Dionysus is found in the figure of the young man who is tied to a tree for stealing wine. Since he believes he is going to be hanged, he calls to mind the "hanged god" of Frazer, who is identified with Dionysus (or, in more Germanic contexts with Odin). The specific references to wine are less important for introducing the dionysian theme than are the references to other kinds of intoxication. The wall-paper in Homo's room, for example, causes a kind of ecstasy:

> [Es gab eine] Tapete mit einem unsagbar wirren, geschmacklosen, aber durchaus unvollendbaren und fremden Muster. Und einen Schaukelstuhl aus Rohr; wenn man sich in diesem wiegt und die Tapete anschaut, wird der ganze Mensch zu einem auf- und niederwallenden Gewirr von Ranken . . .

This is an allusion to Dionysus, both as a symbol of mystical intoxication and as the god of the vine, both the grape vine and the ivy. The connection of savagery and intoxication is also dionysian: "Man brauchte sich nur zu erinnern, daß man hier unter Wilden lebte, so entstand schon ein Rausch in der Hitze des engen, von gärendem Heu hochgefüllten Raumes."

A reference to the Nietzschean identification of music with the dionysian spirit is found in the passage describing the playing of a recording of *Tosca* to a group of drunken men. In the scene music, sexuality, madness, and intoxication are perceived as one:

> Ihre Röcke blähten sich vor Bewegung, dieses Auf und Nieder, dieses eine Weile lang angepreßte Stillliegen an einem Ton, und wieder sich Heben und Sinken, und bei alldem dieses Verströmen, und immer doch noch von einer neuen Zuckung Gefaßtwerden, und wieder Ausströmen: war Wollust. Homo fühlte, es war nackt jene auf alle Dinge in den Städten verteilte Wollust, die sich von Totschlag, Eifersucht, Geschäften, Automobilrennen nicht mehr unter-scheiden kann—es war gar nicht mehr Wollust, es war Abenteuersucht—nein, es war nicht Abenteuersucht, sondern ein aus dem Himmel niederfahrendes Messer, ein Würgengel, Engelswahnsinn, der Krieg?

War arises from the dionysian, i.e., libidinal, impulses of European (repressed) sexuality, and these impulses are seen as underlying the activities of modern urban life. The decadent condition of the peasantry is expressed by a partial primitivism. In a truly primitive condition the society would have both apollonian and dionysian elements, i.e., both the animal drives and a system of taboos and religious prescriptions regulating them, but the decadent condition of the peasants in *Grigia* leaves them no control over their drives. The breakdown in the social order which has reduced the peasants to a state of animality is a result of isolation, but clearly a similar breakdown occurs in societies in a much more violent way as a result of war. Dionysian elements stand at the beginning and end of the process.

In addition to the dionysian and Egyptian mythological allusions, there are allusions to the mysteries of Demeter, the Earth Mother. Annie Reniers-Servranckx points out: "[Grigia] wird mit der Erde und der Umwelt (dem Inneren des Berges) identifiziert, mit dem Heu, der Ernte, dem Sommer. Homo könnte sie auch Demeter nennen . . . " She points out too that a character in Musil's earlier fiction is also named Demeter. The specific similarities between Grigia and Musil's Demeter (ironically a male character) are their close connection with animal sensuality—Demeter is symbolized by a rooster—and the fact that both are juxtaposed with a more 'spiritual' lover: Grigia with Homo's wife, Demeter with the priestly Johannes. The horses and pig already mentioned are strongly associated with Demeter; in fact there is some speculation that originally Demeter *was* a pig in the myths, and one important myth relates that Demeter sealed herself in a cave, and at this time her head was that of a horse. When Homo and Grigia are sealed in the tunnel: "Sie zeterte sogleich wie ein Schwein und rannte sinnlos gegen den Fels wie ein scheues Pferd."

Numerous allusions to Grigia as an Earth Mother figure also strengthen the identification with Demeter, and incidentally with Isis. Homo finds Grigia squatting in a potato field: "Er wußte, sie hat nichts als zwei Röcke an, die trockene Erde, die durch ihre schlanken, rauhen Finger

rann, berührte ihren Leib." Here the woman conceived of as Earth Mother and the earth conceived of as a womb are in close proximity. Similarly, during a description of sexual intercourse between Homo and Grigia, it is stated: "Noch einmal rann Grigia wie weich trockene Erde durch ihn. . . . " The promiscuity attributed to the women of the region accords with the hetaerism associated with rites to insure fertility of the earth (the earth being understood as being open to fertilization from any quarter). The facts that Homo and Grigia enter the mine shaft in the Fall and that the last scene they view is a harvest are also significant since harvest time is the time for rites associated with Demeter and Dionysus. The peasant woman in *Grigia* who instigates the crisis which ultimately leads to Homo's death is described as being in a debilitated condition: " . . . es war fast als hätten sich stets das gesunde Leben ihrer Kinder und das gestörte ihres Gesichts gegenseitig als Eindrücke zu Null aufgehoben." Her feebleness reflects the debilitated condition of the earth (the mother) contrasted with the wealth of the harvest (the children). In some unexplained way Homo believes the woman is responsible for Grigia's refusal to lie with him in the hay: " . . . nur von daher [from the condition of the peasant woman and her children] könne das Beunruhigende gekommen sein. . . . " This state of affairs leads Homo to take Grigia into the mine shaft and thus brings about his death. The impoverished condition of the earth calls for sacrifice, and Homo is chosen to be that sacrifice in a way reminiscent of Frazer's hypothesis of the origin of kingship (also discussed by Freud [in *Totem and Taboo*]). Frazer believed that kings originally were strangers chosen to reign for a short time and then to be sacrificed as representatives of a deity. Homo and his colleagues certainly act like kings or gods in relation to the local peasants: "Sie schütteten Geld unter die Leute und walteten wie die Götter."

Homo becomes a sacrifice symbolising the destruction of the male principle in procreation, and such a sacrifice in turn symbolizes the rebirth of the creative principle. This symbolism is found in the rites of all the mystery cults discussed above; it is expressed most clearly in *Grigia* by the mine shaft (read: cave) symbol, because, as Jung states, the cave is a symbol of the maternal womb to which re-entry is achieved by death. There is direct evidence that Musil was interested in the idea of re-entry of the womb, and of course the allusions to re-entry of the womb in Hoffmann's "Bergwerke" (which become explicit in Hofmannsthal's reworking of the material) are of importance in this regard. Furthermore, because of Grigia's being identified with the Earth Mother, she may be regarded as a mother figure in the story, and this helps to explain the feeling one has that the scene of discovery at the end of the story repeats a primal fantasy of the discovery by the father of incestuous wishes in the male child. Homo's wife is also a mother figure, however, first because of the fact that she is the mother of Homo's son, but also because of the symbolic birth which Homo experiences when separated from her. Jung discusses such a symbolic birth (the origin of individuality) as a necessary part of the mother-child relationship. The contrast between Homo's idealized love for his wife and his animal lust for Grigia also parallels the opposition of mother (virgin) versus sexual partner (prostitute), an idea which is reflected in the ending of *Die Verwirrungen des Zöglings Törless,* where the apartment of the prostitute Bozena (behind tangles of vegetation) is juxtaposed with the scent of Törless' mother.

In conclusion, Grigia, as a representative of Demeter, and as the object of Homo's sensual desire, symbolizes nature and *eros.* Homo's wife represents a more spiritual kind of love, Christian love or *agape,* and indeed the spirit in general. The two women, who scarcely exist as characters in their own right, serve as the goals of Homo's own yearning for nature on the one hand and the spirit on the other. Homo resembles the peasants whom he treats as animals in that he becomes partially primitive; his civilized principles are loosened but not given up entirely, and he partly overcomes his estrangement from nature by his relationship with Grigia, although nature is still described as "giftig" and threatening. Homo loses his fear of death by means of a mystical experience which he can have only when he is cut off from civilization, but he does not thereby become a primitive in Rousseau's sense of a person who is in harmony with nature. A number of paradoxes arise from this situation: The development of man's spirituality presupposes a disturbance of man's unity with nature, otherwise man would view his own death and decay with the same equanimity with which he observes the death and rebirth of nature in the seasonal cycle. Man's fear of death compels him to develop a spiritual nature which enables him to see beyond the finitude of nature into eternity. Civilized man is not only separated from nature, but learns to fear it as the source of death, and to turn to the spirit as the source of eternal life, but life without nature would not be worth living, since few people would choose to exist as disembodied spirits. Homo represents a civilized man who is freed from the distraction of civilization and is brought face to face with his own fear of death. He overcomes his fear of death, but at the expense of widening the gulf between himself and nature. He is fatally attracted to nature, however, and his will—itself an expression of nature or life—has been weakened by his attraction to the spirit, and so he must die. The only alternative would be to create a synthesis between nature and spirit which would indeed render man immortal, but this is clearly impossible.

Michael W. Jennings (essay date 1984)

SOURCE: "Mystical Selfhood, Self-Delusion, Self-Dissolution: Ethical and Narrative Experimentation in Robert Musil's *Grigia,*" in *Modern Austrian Literature,* Vol. 17, No. 1, 1984, pp. 59-77.

[*In the following excerpt, Jennings argues that Homo's search for a unified identity in* Grigia *is undermined by his self-delusion.*]

Grigia opens with a brief recounting of the geologist Homo's station in life. The sententious introductory paragraph sets up his life as a normal and perhaps even par-

adigmatic one: "Es gibt im Leben eine Zeit, wo es sich auffallend verlangsamt, als zögerte es weiterzugehen oder wollte seine Richtung ändern." Homo's concerns and problems indeed seem chosen for their typicality: his spouse, child and profession have all presented him with difficulties. The recurrence of and importance attributed to the idea of "Trennbarkeit" signals, however, the emergence of a particular problem which marks Homo as a man apart. The notion of separability first emerges in association with Homo's work. Asked to accompany his wife and child to a spa, he refuses, since "es kam ihm vor, als würde er dadurch zu lange *von sich getrennt,* von seinen Büchern, Plänen, und seinem Leben" (emphasis added).

Homo's work had not always seemed so important to him; the earliest stage in his life mentioned in the text is one at which he and his wife had been inseparable. This love, however, "war durch das Kind *trennbar* geworden" (emphasis added). Homo seems to fear nothing so much as separation from himself, from his identity, yet paradoxically it had been first his wife and later his work that furnished him with a sense of self. An image emerges of a man searching outside himself for a stable center for his identity. The transient nature of Homo's self-understanding is underlined when, two days after the departure of wife and child, he abandons the books and plans which had only shortly before seemed so central to his existence and joins a mining expedition. Homo sets out on a journey, a motif which, especially in conjunction with the idea of caves and mining, is characteristic of the Romantics. Like the works from which the motif is clearly borrowed (e.g. *Heinrich von Ofterdingen, Der Runenberg*), *Grigia* emerges as the portrayal of Homo's journey inward toward a new identity.

As even this briefest recounting of the earliest events in the novella indicates, *Grigia* deals with the resolution of the tension between the two areas, the reconciliation of the interiority and identity of the individual with a reality which seems to dictate universal and immutable ethical laws: "love your wife, nurture your child." The recurrence of this problem complex in Musil's works—one need only think of Törleß, von Ketten, or even Ulrich—has led to a uniform thematic reading of *all* his works. Hence the interpretations of *Grigia* by Kaiser and Wilkins, Reniers-Servranckx, Tober, and Eibl, in which Homo's central mystical experience is viewed as the resolution of the tension which separates world and individual. *Grigia* does not, however, in any sense represent a reconciliation of the two poles. The narrative structure of the novella suggests another alternative.

The paragraph dealt with above, the second in the novella, already reveals the extent to which Musil breaks with traditional narrative technique; his departure is radical enough to have elicited characterizations of *Grigia* as a "Prosaskizze" or even an "Erzählexperiment." As Brigitte Röttger first pointed out [in *Erzählexperiment: Studien Zur Robert Musils "Drei Frauen" and "Vereinigunen,"* 1973], the narrative perspective of the novella shifts from that of an authorial narrator, evident in the sententious opening paragraph and at intervals throughout the text, to that of a figural narrator. A significant portion of *Grigia* is narrated, in other words, from a standpoint all but identical to that of Homo's consciousness. The coexistence of these two narrative modes in one text is of course not in itself problematic. *Grigia* and its narrative technique demand attention, however, due to the presence of a conflict within the novella which is discernible only at the level of narration. The conflict of narrative voices which I will describe below stands, in fact, as a metaphor for a larger dissonance which defines Homo's ongoing relationship to the world in which he lives.

This conflict between authorial and figural voices is evident in the frequent juxtaposition in one sentence of the two distinct narrative perspectives. The following sentence, which comments upon Homo's refusal to accompany his family, is typical: "Er empfand seinen Widerstand als eine große Sehnsucht, es war aber vielleicht eher eine Selbstauflösung." The differing conclusions to be drawn regarding Homo's life, the first his own, the second that of the authorial narrator, point to a need on the part of the "frame" narrator to adjust and even correct Homo's perspective. Such adjustment and correction takes several forms in *Grigia*. In addition to the direct contradiction discussed here the authorial voice employs devices such as the sententious commentary of the introduction, or, strikingly, the ironization of Homo's pronouncements. The authorial irony is evident, for example, in the revised estimate of the number of nightingales which are flushed from their cover upon Homo's entrance into the valley: "wenn nicht hundert, so doch sicher zwei Dutzend." Why, then, does Homo's perspective require such correction?

A possible, if partial, answer becomes evident early in the text. Even when the perspective remains constant, adhering solely to that of figural narration, contradictions arise which cannot be accounted for by the intrusion of another perspective. Not long after Homo's appeal to his career, to his books and plans, as justification for his failure to accompany his family to a spa, another, unrelated ground for his decision is cited: "Er empfand bloß einen heftigen Widerwillen gegen Bade- und Gebirgsorte." Despite this stated distaste for mountains, Homo immediately accepts the invitation to join the expedition headed into the Italian mountains. These contradictions can be explained by recourse not to the narrative perspective, but only to Homo's consciousness from which the narration emanates. Thus, the notion of separability points to more than the search for an identity; Homo's consciousness is characterized by a certain lack of unity. His first experiences on his journey illustrate the exact nature of the problem. Upon entering his room in the town of P., Homo's attention is drawn to three objects. "Es gab da drei Dinge, die ihm auffielen. Betten von einer unsagbar kühlen Weichheit in schöner Mahagonischale. Eine Tapete mit einem unsagbar wirren, geschmacklosen, aber durchaus unvollendbaren fremden Muster. Und ein Schaukelstuhl aus Rohr."

This passage of figural narration bears unmistable marks of a deep-seated disorientation, and it is again the mode of narration which reveals the nature of the problem. First, the *aber* inserted between logically sequential adjectives

not only disrupts the flow of the narrative, but also points to an inability to recognize the quality of congruence. Secondly, the repetition of the adverb *unsagbar* points to a failure to lend to perception an articulable form. Finally and most importantly the adjectives employed to describe the wallpaper (*wirr, fremd, unvollendbar*) share one characteristic: they reveal less the nature of the wallpaper than that of Homo. The pattern is confusing and strange to Homo, who is incapable of completing its impression in his mind. So strong, in fact, is this reflexive quality of the description, that a literal inversion of the elements involved occurs: " . . . wenn man sich in diesem wiegt und die Tapete anschaut, wird der ganze Mensch zu einem auf- und niederwallenden Gewirr von Ranken." The observing consciousness, in attempting to order its perceptions, finds itself instead shaped by the very objects under observation. Whereas Blake could state that he became what he beheld and thereby assert the synthetic power of the poet's vision, Homo's very identity proves so unstable as to render him susceptible to frequent and damaging incursions by an apparently hostile world. Underlying Homo's inability to define himself is a deficiency in his ability to order reality.

The experience in the *Gasthof* is not an isolated one; evidence of Homo's inability to synthesize spatially and temporally the elements of the perceived world is everywhere in *Grigia*. His first impressions of the Fersena valley are typical. Villas there seem to be grouped according to "ein ihnen unbekanntes, eigentümliches Formgesetz," while the valley itself resists assimilation into a coherent image, remaining instead "eine leere, gugelhupfförmige Welt." This frustrated longing to comprehend the structure of his world remains with Homo after his mystical experience. Even groups of horses seem to conspire against him: "[die Pferde] standen dann in Gruppen auf der Wiese oder legten sich nieder, aber sie gruppierten sich immer irgendwie scheinbar regellos in die Tiefe, so daß es nach einem geheim verabredeten ästhetischen Gesetz genau so aussah wie die Erinnerung an die kleinen grünen, blauen und rosa Häuser unter dem Selvot." This reference to the villas, which, as we have seen, also lacked a "Formgesetz," serves to emphasize the ongoing nature of Homo's problem: his mysticism has not alleviated the tension between self and world. Furthermore, not only spatial relationships frustrate Homo. The narration betrays a frequent lack of sense for sequence: the figural narration refers repeatedly to objects and events as if the reader were already familiar with them, when in fact their explanation follows later. We hear thus . . . of a black pig: "An diese Birke war mit einem in der Luft hängenden Bein noch das schwarze Schwein gebunden"; the definite article implies a familiarity which we in fact gain only later, as the slaughtering of the pig is described. The frequent confusion in temporal relationships is a further sign of Homo's failure to order his world.

We have seen that Homo had sought a firm basis for his sense of self first in his wife, then in his work, and finally in the expedition. Yet not only his identity, but also his ability to make sense of his physical environment is significantly impaired. To Homo the world poses an endless impenetrable problem. It seems to him that it holds back from him the key to its form, order, and even its meaning. Musil had stated that the discovery of the "Struktur der Welt" was the task of fiction. This structure remains veiled for Homo, and his search for it is frustrated by his inability to order the data of sense perception. Homo is plagued, in other words, by a malfunction in the Kantian synthetic. His journey to find the self is occasioned not by a rejection of an inflexible exterior reality, but instead by a radical failure to assume an identity commensurable with that reality.

Mozart Amadeo Hoffingott's mining expedition not only provides a vehicle by means of which Homo searches for help, but the methods of the expedition also provide him with a way of living in the world. A contrast is quickly established between the expedition, which has at its disposal "gewaltige amerikanische Mittel," and the "merkwürdige Leute" of the valley, whose "Voreltern waren zur Zeit der tridentinischen Bischofsmacht als Bergknappen aus Deutschland gekommen, und sie saßen heute noch eingesprengt wie ein verwitterter deutscher Stein zwischen den Italienern." The expedition, a concrete manifestation of, and at the same time a metaphor for modern post-industrial capitalism, intrudes upon an archaic society so unchanging as to have become all but an organic component of its natural environment. The encounter between the historical and economic world orders predictably occasions a violent confrontation when the expedition attempts to bend the valley and its inhabitants to its own purposes. The reader is granted only a brief glimpse of the actual methods of the expedition, but this one glimpse is graphic in its details:

> . . . dort rief eine scharfe Herrenstimme aus den schwatzend wartenden Weibern eins nach dem andern vor, und es wurde der große leere Rückenkorb so lang befrachtet, *bis die Knie sich bogen und die Halsadern anschwollen.* War solch ein hübsches junges Weib beladen, *so hing ihm der Blick bei den Augen heraus* und *die Lippen blieben offen stehen;* es trat in die Reihe, und auf das Zeichen begannen *diese stillgewordenen Tiere* hintereinander langsam *in langen Schlangenwegen* ein Bein vor das andre bergan zu setzen (emphasis added).

Two motifs which will become dominant in Homo's relationship with the woman Grigia are here prefigured. First, the inhabitants, particularly the women, of the valley are exploited. Secondly and more importantly for Homo's subsequent actions, they are reduced to a level of bestiality. In the course of the novella the valley natives gradually are deprived of all human characteristics and come to be identified with animals. Grigia is at once the name of Magdalena Maria Lenzi and of her cow.

A curtain of obfuscation and euphemism descends upon the activities of the expedition following this vision of inhuman exploitation. Homo attempts to justify the reduction of the women to bestiality, by pointing out, for example, that they could occasionally reclaim some part of their burden for their own use, and "darum trugen sie es gerne, und dankten noch den Männern, welche den

Segen in die Berge gebracht hatten." Capitalism, in other words, far from representing the mere opportunistic exploitation or even pragmatic development of economic potential, in fact carries a quasi-divine dispensation. Not only do the members of the expedition bring a "blessing," but, as Homo puts it, they "walteten wie die Götter." The image presented to the victim (and to the reader by means of figural narration) is that of modern economic principles in the process of bringing about a creative and beneficial transformation of preindustrial society. The creative, semi-divine self-understanding of the expedition (encapsulated in the name Mozart Amadeo Hoffingott, in which the transfiguring power of the absolute is augmented by reference to Mozart's creative potential *and* fulfillment) becomes explicit in the following description of the changes worked upon the valley: "Aus den Männern *bildeten* sie Arbeitspartien . . . aus den Weibern *formierten* sie Trägerkolonnen. . . . Das steinerne Schulhaus ward in eine Faktorei *verwandelt*" (emphasis added). To the men who make up this force which intrudes upon the archaic population, the swollen veins, protruding lips, and buckling legs of the women are inconsequential beside the creative splendor. Notably the significance of this vision of society lies not in the result of the expedition's actions, that is, not in any quantifiable or experientially ascertainable benefit to society, but rather in the quality of the action itself; realization of creative potential is its own reward.

Homo plays out his fate upon a stage provided by these larger intentions of the expedition, and his actions become a microcosm of the larger effort of recreating the valley. Both aspects of the capitalism Musil depicts, its apparently beneficial facade and its actually pernicious and degrading effect, are translated in the person of Homo onto a personal level. In this sense Homo is Everyman— the Everyman of modern society who participates, however unwittingly, in a delusion. Homo's answer to his inability to correctly perceive and synthesize reality is thus precisely that of the expedition as a whole. Rather than come to terms with the new world, Homo will recreate it in an image better suited to his own limitations— in fact, Homo must become godlike. Unable to divine the inherent form and significance of his world, Homo instead imposes through a creative stratagem a shape and meaning of his own.

His means of doing so is figurative language. Just as the expedition employs euphemism to its own ends, so too does Homo find a trope eminently suited to his task: the simile. No fewer than ten similes occur in the two paragraphs given over to Homo's first description of valley and village. The description differentiates itself from earlier descriptions in the novella (of the *Gasthof,* e.g.) in its reliance upon the simile; through it Homo tries to reshape the valley in his consciousness. By making "Schluchten" of "Straßen," "Friedhofskränze" of "Laub," and "Bäche" of "Gassen" Homo rejects the inherent form and significance of these objects and imposes a personal meaning upon them. Jörg Kühne has discussed Musil's use of the simile in general and asserts that the simile serves to bring home the insubstantiality of the world as viewed from consciousness and to lend to the world a reality based in language: "Einer seltsam unfesten, rätselnden Beziehung des Ichs zur Wirk-lichkeit entspringt hier das Gleichnis" [*Das Gleichnis: Studien zur inneren Form von Robert Musils Roman "Der Mann ohne Eigenschaften,"* 1968]. The simile is in **Grigia** at once a sign of Homo's search for a new place in the world and the emblem of the overcoming of his synthetic deficiencies. His entry into the valley is indeed an entry into a "Märchenwelt," but the magical attributes do not exist independently in the world of the valley: they emanate from Homo's new interpretation. Only in this sense can we understand Homo's remark that the valley is something "sehnsüchtig Erwartetes" which was at the same time "fremd vertraut." Through his poeticization of the valley the alien has become at once familiar and possessed of a particular, if hermetic, meaning. In Homo, then, we see the activities of the expedition, in which mastery over men and things seems to be obtained by means of their creative transformation played out on a linguistic level. Just as the expedition alters not only the economic relationships which had pertained to the valley, but also actually mutilates the identity of the inhabitants, so too does Homo, beginning here with his physical environment but soon proceeding to human beings, seek to impose an arbitrary shape upon his world.

The power wielded by the expedition and, in a different way, by Homo bears within it a dangerous element. Even though through the narrative voice Homo seems to create for himself a secure environment within which he can establish an identity, a discrepancy yawns between his newly created world and the reality which remains unchanged for all but him. His life in the valley is a "schönes Leben" primarily because the world and life itself have ceased to make claims upon him:

> . . . man wurde hier nicht, wie sonst überall in der Welt, geprüft, was für ein Mensch man sei,—ob verläßlich, mächtig und zu fürchten oder zierlich und schön—sondern was immer für ein Mensch man war und wie immer man über die Dinge des Lebens dachte, man fand Liebe, weil man den Segen gebracht hatte.

The implications of the passage are clear: even a man unable to function adequately within the bounds of the outside world can nonetheless thrive in the hermetic world created in the valley. And the conditions Homo describes do seem to represent a desirable balance between the needs of the inhabitants and the desires of the expedition. The friendliness and even sexual willingness of the native women is presented, for example, as nothing less than a character trait; the story of the counterfeit husband with its implication of the absolute interchangeability of sexual partners emphasizes nothing if not this. Homo of course exploits the situation, inviting the women into the hay and confining his speech with them to the level of innuendo: "Du bist noch eine Jungfrau?" Reality is, however, at odds with Homo's vision of the world: the women's accessibility results not from any inherent sexual drive but from the prospect of monetary gain. Riches are the blessing brought to the valley.

Sketch of Musil by his wife, Martha.

Whether or not Homo is aware of this contradiction is irrelevant here. For whatever reason, he is concerned to shield his behavior by attributing his successes to reasons that exist only in his imagination. Figural narration allows Homo to do so while maintaining the appearance of objectively reporting the circumstances of life in the valley. His strategy here is remarkably similar to that lent by Kafka to many of his protagonists. The reader is drawn into the world as it is interpreted by the narrating consciousness without being at first aware of the radical subjectivity which informs that perspective. Only later does it become clear that things are not what they are made to seem.

As long as Homo's vision had been focused on his physical environment, his transformation of the world had remained benign; the ruse of figural narration seems pointless. As, however, that vision is increasingly extended so as to encompass even greater areas of the world, Homo's self-delusion becomes pernicious. When ambient reality is relegated to a secondary level, when the locus of significance is shifted from a variety of centers to one, in this case Homo's consciousness, a form of solipsism emerges. Without ties to the world which continues to exist around him Homo's identity is cast adrift, and he opens himself to domination by that world.

Musil's essays make it clear that the claims of the "nicht-ratioïdes Gebiet," that is, that altered, mystical state of transcendence which emphasizes the inner man, must be balanced and held in check with a solid grounding in the physical, rationally deducible world. In one sense the tension between the two realms is that which exists between radically individual facts and occurrences on the one hand and general laws and properties on the other. Musil can thus write in "Skizze der Erkenntnis des Dichters": "Der bedeutende Mensch ist der, welcher über die größte Tatsachenkenntnis *und* die größte ratio zu ihrer Verbindung verfügt." Insofar as *Grigia* represents an ethical experiment in the sense discussed above, it shows the result of a failure to reconcile these two spheres; Homo's actions constitute nothing less than the wholesale rejection of one in favor of the other, in favor of absolute interiority.

This is nowhere clearer than in the mystical experience at the heart of the novella. Homo receives a letter from his child and concludes that since his family knows where he is staying, he now had nothing further to explain to them. Thus freed from all prior constraints, he has the following vision.

> Er sank zwischen den Bäumen mit den giftgrünen Bärten aufs Knie, breitete die Arme aus, was er so noch nie in seinem Leben getan hatte, and ihm war zu Mut, als hätte man ihm in diesem Augenblick sich selbst aus den Armen genommen. Er fühlte die Hand seiner Geliebten in seiner, ihre Stimme im Ohr, alle Stellen seines Körpers waren wie eben erst berührt, er empfand sich selbst wie eine von einem anderen Körper gebildete Form.

Those reading of *Grigia* for which the novella is a preliminary treatment of material ultimately destined for *Der Mann ohne Eigenschaften* view this passage, which culminates in Homo's purported "Wiedervereinigung da" with a "Geliebte," as an early version of the "anderer Zustand" experience and as an example of the idea of "Fernliebe." I agree with the idea of connecting this passage with the later novel but take issue with the manner in which the passage is evaluated. Homo's rejection of and liberation from the world too often takes on the contours of a positive and even courageous act.

Homo's encounter with a "tiefe Religion" is triggered not by any perceived need to gain transcendence but by contact with a nature that has been transformed in his mind. Just before the experience cited above the figural narrator offers the following vision of nature:

> Ein Märchenwald von alten Lärchenstämmen, zartgrün behaarten, stand auf smaragdener Schräge. Unter dem Moos mochten violette und weiße Kristalle leben. Der Bach fiel einmal mitten im Wald über einen Stein so, daß er aussah wie ein großer silberner Steckkamm.

This is an eroticized nature, a nature whose indifference has been mistaken for enticement. In the "Wiedervereinigung da" experience Homo equates nature itself with the inhabitants of the valley, who are associated with nature; the experience furnishes Homo with a transition from an imagined domination of nature to an actual mastery over "natural" persons, and especially Grigia herself. Homo has given himself over to his fictional world, and life in the outside world has become irrelevant. One is reminded of Tieck's crazed Christian at the end of *Der Runenberg,* unable to distinguish base rock and precious stone, as

Homo "fühlte wie . . . eine für ihn bestimmte Zauberwelt den Boden mit Gold und Edelsteinen unter seinen Füßen." Homo's "Wiedervereinigung da" has reinforced, but in no way changed, those impulses within him that had become obvious much earlier in the novella. Like the experience in the *Gasthof* this is an inversion experience. Whereas, however, the first experience had demonstrated the mutability of Homo's consciousness, the second serves as an instigation for Homo to articulate his newfound mastery over the world. He is now "Sultan seiner Existenz," free to continue a life based upon the sort of solipsism which pervades the following passage: "Es gab eine zart scharlachfarbene Blume, es gab diese in keines anderen Mannes Welt, nur in seiner, so hatte es Gott geordnet."

This mystical experience is in a way a transcendence of the world, but a transcendence whose dangers far outweigh its ecstasies. These dangers become explicit in Homo's relationship to Grigia. In the affair with Grigia two trends momentarily united in the experience in the meadow again diverge. First, Homo's increasing subjugation of all that is natural finds its final object in the person of Grigia, and leads ironically to his final loss of both the real and the imagined worlds. In the moment of "Wiedervereinigung" the *unio* with nature had surprised Homo: "seltsamerweise war mit seiner Aufregung ein Bild der rings um den Wald blühenden Wiesen verbunden." Homo is unable to grasp the necessary reciprocity latent in that statement. Grigia is, to be sure, for Homo a natural phenomenon, "ein schlankes giftiges Pilzchen" who grows from her shoes "wie aus wilden Wurzeln"; he loses sight, however, of the importance of a nature that exists apart from him as he sinks ever deeper into his transfiguration of the world. Whereas Homo might have established through Grigia a new point of contact to reality, she instead becomes a cipher, the one-dimensional object of Homo's libidinous drives.

Secondly, Homo increasingly interprets his mastery over the subjugated world as a sign of approaching divinity. The messianic overtones which proliferate toward the end of the novella serve as a mask behind which Homo's salacious intentions are sanitized and even justified. When he kisses Grigia, for example, the figural narrator comments that Homo does not know "ob er dieses Weib liebte, oder ob ihm ein Wunder bewiesen werde, und Grigia nur der Teil einer Sendung war, die ihn mit seiner Geliebten in Ewigkeit weiter verknüpfte." This delusion is in fact so powerful that it ultimately eclipses the drive which it conceals. Homo dies a lonely death in the shaft, making no effort to escape. His messianic pretensions are laid to rest in an ironic fashion as Grigia's husband rolls the stone across the entrance to his tomb. For Homo there will be neither resurrection, "Himmelfahrtstage," nor "Wiedervereinigung." Instead of a new and stable identity he has achieved the dissolution of his personality predicted for him in the opening lines of the novella by the authorial narrator.

Homo's journey inward culminates not in a new certainty but rather in a void. The dissolution of Homo's physical and spiritual life is the direct result of his delusion; his road inward had led him through an untrammeled mysticism. Without the "Grundsätze" of the rational world, which must serve as the checks and balances of the inner life, his journey is a destructive one.

Todd Kontje (essay date 1987)

SOURCE: "Motivating Silence: The Recreation of the 'Eternal Feminine' in Robert Musil's *Tonka*," in *Monatshefte*, Vol. 79, No. 2, Summer, 1987, pp. 161-71.

[*In the following excerpt, Kontje analyzes the elements of power and domination in the relationship between the unnamed narrator and the eponymous character in Musil's* Tonka.]

Robert Musil's *Tonka* is a blatantly mysterious story. Like Joseph in the Gospel according to Matthew, or like the Marquise von O . . . in Kleist's novella, the unnamed male protagonist of Musil's work is confronted with an enigmatic pregnancy. Midway through the tale we learn that Tonka has become pregnant at a time when her lover was out of town. Tonka nevertheless insists until her death that she has not been unfaithful. In all probability she is lying, either consciously or unconsciously, but it is at least conceivable that a modern miracle has occurred. Whatever the correct explanation of Tonka's pregnancy may be, both she and the baby die before the answer is revealed.

Thus *Tonka* is structured in such a way as to frustrate the conventional expectations of its readers. In a typical narrative such a problem would be introduced for the purpose of keeping the reader's attention until the solution was revealed towards the end of the work. In *Tonka,* however, our perspective is limited to that of the unnamed character who retrospectively narrates an episode of his youth which remains rationally inexplicable. The persistence of this mystery within the text, in turn, requires a different strategy on the part of the reader. Because we will never know the source of her pregnancy we are compelled to direct our attention to the thematic significance of this unanswered question. . . .

[Robert Peters, in *Robert Musil: Master of the Hovering Life,* 1978] stands out among critics by reminding us of the ethical problems in the work which are usually bypassed in the attempt to ascertain its religious, psychological, or philosophical significance. The following essay will be devoted to the elaboration and modification of issues raised by Peters' analysis of the work. First, Peters sees the protagonist's guilt primarily in terms of a personal flaw, whereas I will emphasize his status as a typical representative of the particular ideology which governs the sexual relations between upper-class men and lower-class women in many works of European literature of the eighteenth, nineteenth, and early twentieth centuries. The young man's "love" for Tonka expresses itself primarily in terms of his need to dominate her in a number of ways. Second, I will consider the function of the epistemological problems which are raised by the unsolved mystery of Tonka's pregnancy. If knowledge and power are shown to be intimately connected in the first half of Musil's text, then the persistent enigma of Tonka's pregnancy precipitates the systematic frustration of the protagonist's attempts at domination. Finally, I will examine the protagonist's role as the narrator of the text. Consistent with his treatment of Tonka during her life, the act of narration marks one more attempt on his part to assert control over her after her death, by either inculpating her on the basis of circumstantial evidence, or exonerating her as a twentieth-century Madonna, but in any case rendering her comprehensible. Yet because Tonka has died with her secret, these attempts remain at the level of hypothetical conjectures, which reveal less about Tonka than the mind of the narrator and the ideology he perpetuates.

In many ways *Tonka* is anything but a traditional work of literature. It not only introduces a mystery which is never solved, but also fails to provide a name for one of its two central characters, the young man who later recounts the work through the unusual technique of *erlebte Rede*. The story itself, however, follows a pattern familiar at least since the Sturm und Drang period of German literature. Goethe's *Faust* is only the most famous example of a work which contains a configuration repeated in Heinrich Leopold Wagner's *Die Kindermörderin,* J. M. R. Lenz's *Die Soldaten,* and Schiller's *Kabale und Liebe.* A cultivated man of high social status has a brief affair with what is perceived as a simple, natural girl of the lower classes. Marriage is inconceivable, an unwanted pregnancy often results, and the conclusion is generally tragic, at least for the woman. The same basic pattern is repeated and varied in European literature throughout the nineteenth century in works such as Gustave Flaubert's *Madame Bovary,* Gottfried Keller's "Regine," Thomas Hardy's *Tess of the D'Urbervilles,* and Arthur Schnitzler's *Liebelei.*

Musil clearly draws on this tradition in the basic outline of the plot of *Tonka*. A gifted young scientist of a respectable family meets a young working girl during his year of military service. To the deep distress of his mother, the relationship threatens to become more serious than is socially acceptable when the young man takes Tonka to live with him while he pursues his studies at the university. However, she soon becomes pregnant under suspicious circumstances and dies with her stillborn child, leaving him to continue a successful career without remorse.

Their relationship is marked by social and economic inequality from the beginning. While the young man pursues a career destined to bring him both financial rewards and high social status, Tonka is systematically exploited in each of the three jobs she fills in the course of the novella. Her first job in a cloth factory results in constant irritation to her hands. She receives a mere pittance from the young man's family when his grandmother dies earlier than expected. Finally, her last employer fires her when he learns that she is pregnant.

The young man's attitude towards Tonka seems ambivalent at first. On the one hand, he does seem genuinely attracted to her and makes several attempts to help her. It is he who arranges to have Tonka care for his grandmother, and when his grandmother dies, he offers to care for her. Later, when Tonka is underpaid by her last employer, he makes up the difference with his own money. On the other hand, it becomes increasingly evident that these actions are motivated more by a need to dominate Tonka than genuine sympathy. This is particularly evident in the young man's attitude to Tonka's last employer. To her this man seems "eine übermenschliche Macht" because of her complete financial dependence on him. After she has been driven out of her job we learn that he too "bewunderte heimlich diesen schäbigen, kleinen, namenlosen Kaufmann," not from the perspective of the cowed employee, but rather because he is a decisive man who does not hesitate to sacrifice an individual to the needs of his business.

The young man's social and economic dominance of Tonka extends further to the intellectual realm. While he pursues his education and inventions, she has little time and seemingly less ability to acquire academic knowledge. What fragments of knowledge have clung to Tonka from her older, now deceased brother and her brief visit to night school are greeted with at best bemused condescension, never genuine interest on the part of the young man. More often than not, his impatience with her reticence in conversation turns towards the assertion of force.

Thus the social, financial, and intellectual inequality between Tonka and the young man results in a relationship in which he is unquestionably in control. His treatment of Tonka fluctuates between patronizing attention and the direct assertion of his authority. These tendencies intensify when the young man decides it is time to begin having sexual relations with Tonka. His friend Baron Mordansky has already set the mood for the type of affair which follows when he comments on the harvest for his uncle's sugar factory, "wo Hunderte solcher Bauernmädchen auf den Fabriksfeldern arbeiten und sich den Gutsinspektoren und deren Gehilfen in allem so willig unterwerfen sollen wie Negersklaven." The first open expression of the young man's interest in Tonka occurs after she has received the small amount of money for the care of his grandmother. He goes upstairs and watches her pack without being noticed, until she turns and starts, at which point he "freute sich über ihre Verlegenheit." He sets the date for their first sexual intercourse "wie ein Gerichtsvollzieher!" She prepares for the event in silence, "als würde sie von der Macht des 'Herrn' unterjocht." Finally, just before the consummation of the act, his sense of anxiety and helplessness is coupled with "Entsetzen über ihre Undankbarkeit."

A crucial change is introduced immediately after this remarkably unromantic "wedding night." Several years are passed over in silence to bring us to the problem of Tonka's pregnancy, which dominates the second half of the work. If in the first part of the story the nature of the sexual act epitomizes the general pattern of the young man's complete power over Tonka, then the mysterious pregnancy in the second half of the work functions to frustrate each of the ways in which he formerly controlled her. The young man is threatened sexually by Tonka's pregnancy, because it suggests the possibility of a rival lover. Yet the alternative explanation, namely that some sort of modern miracle has taken place, is equally threatening to his scientific intellect, as it would indicate a serious shortcoming in his understanding of the world. This sexual and intellectual dilemma precipitated by Tonka's pregnancy leads to economic and social denigration as well. When Tonka loses her last job he is thrust into the soup kitchens of the impoverished lower class. The intellectual frustration surrounding Tonka's pregnancy results further in a turn towards superstition. He begins to bet on horses and makes a futile try at the lottery. His irrational decision to wear a cheap ring in place of an old family heirloom not only supplies further evidence of his growing superstition, but can be seen as a symbolic representation of his lost social status. The story thus falls neatly into two halves, the first demonstrating the young man's social, intellectual, financial, and sexual dominance of Tonka, the second inverting this pattern through the unresolved mystery of Tonka's pregnancy.

Given this interpretation of *Tonka,* one would logically expect to find the protagonist utterly crushed, perhaps, even suicidal by the end of the work. The actual ending, however, is quite the opposite. Much like Goethe's Faust, who awakens refreshed and without a trace of guilt at the beginning of the second part of the drama, Musil's protagonist experiences the death of Tonka as a release from a troubled phase of his life. "Er stand im Licht und sie lag unter der Erde, aber alles in allem fühlte er das Behagen des Lichts." The sight of a crying child reminds him of the charmingly innocent way in which "Tonka 'hatte' nur 'Kinder gern'." She has brought a touch of warmth into his world, "das ihn etwas besser machte als andere, weil auf seinem glänzenden Leben ein kleiner warmer Schatten lag." To be sure, Tonka herself is no longer able to share this warmth—"Das half Tonka nichts mehr. Aber ihm half es." And that, presumably, is all that really matters.

It is quite possible to take this happy ending at face value. One critic summarized the events of the work as follows: "We can now see the whole novelle as an educational experience of the hero. He has finished his invention, he is ready for life, but he has also been changed into a better man" [Wilhelm Braun, "An Interpretation of Musil's Novelle 'Tonka'," *Monatshefte* 53, 1961]. But who says that he has become a better man? Not an omniscient third-person narrator, but the protagonist himself. From the opening pages of the work it is clear that the story is told from the perspective of the now older scientist, who is looking back over an incident of his youth. He chooses to set the work in the third person because it gives his account of the events a guise of objectivity. The narrative as a whole is less a disinterested presentation of the facts than a highly self-interested attempt on the part of the protagonist to justify himself at the expense of Tonka, to gain a triumph over her after her death which was denied him during her life.

The caution one must exercise when reading this novella is summed up nicely in a seemingly peripheral comment in the midst of the young man's agonized attempts to determine the source of Tonka's pregnancy. He lists a series of situations in which one assumes that a given interpretation is correct, while admitting that it is at least theoretically possible that this particular incident may be an exception. The first example is the following: "Kommst du zu einem Kaufmann und eröffnest nicht eine Aussicht, die bald seine Begehrlichkeit reizt, sondern hältst ihm eine lange Rede über die Zeiten und das, was ein reicher Mann eigentlich tun müßte, so weiß er, du bist gekommen, um ihm sein Geld zu stehlen." This passage provides us with a small example of the sort of ambiguity which pervades Musil's *Tonka*. Because people do not always say what they mean, each utterance has to be interpreted by its addressee. Tonka says she is innocent, but the facts speak against her. Is she lying or telling the truth? Is it ever possible to be absolutely certain that we have correctly understood our interlocutor? Yet this passage does not merely raise an abstract philosophical problem. If the salesman's deceptive speech is not interpreted correctly, the result may well be financial ruin for his victim, just as Tonka's repeated assertions of her innocence despite her pregnancy push the young man into the crisis sketched above.

When at some later date the scientist begins to recount this event, he still is not sure of what actually happened. How did the affair with Tonka begin? One memory is presented, but then quickly corrected, only to be reasserted a few lines later. It is this hesitant, even self-contradictory beginning of the story which led Rudolf Schier to see affinities between this work and the *nouveau roman*: "Das bedeutet aber, daß die in der traditionellen Epik bestehende Verbindung zwischen Erzählung und Wirklichkeit, Sprache und Welt, weitgehend verloren gegangen ist" ["Robert Musils 'Tonka' als Vorläufer des *nouveau roman*," *Etudes Germaniques* 32, 1977]. However, one need only look at the content of the various fragments which begin the novella to realize that this is hardly an adumbration of the postmodern condition, but rather a clear attempt on the part of the narrator to cast doubt on Tonka's moral character, and therefore to justify his suspicion that she has been in fact unfaithful to him. Tonka grew up in the house of her "aunt" who allowed cousin Julie, a prostitute, to come to visit. Tonka was permitted to associate with the female prisoners, "auch meist Prostituierte," at an early age. Next door to the house was a bordello, and Tonka played with the daughter of the proprietress. None of the family relationships are quite what they seem, with the exception of the "aunt's" illegitimate son. This opening segment ends with the comment that Tonka, although still a virgin at this time, was one of those women about whom one cannot be quite sure on the wedding night, due to "physiologische Zweideutigkeiten, wo selbst die Natur nicht ganz klar Aufschluß gibt, und im gleichen Augenblick, wo das wieder vor der Erinnerung stand, wußte er: auch der Himmel war gegen Tonka."

This comment marks the beginning of a process which runs parallel to the narrator's attempt to establish a log-ical, if inconclusive, explanation for Tonka's behavior. She is not merely unfaithful—she is cursed by heaven! That is, if a rational explanation for her pregnancy cannot be established, it can still be accounted for in terms of the traditional symbolism of Western culture. God has singled Tonka out, either to curse her, or in an alternative interpretation offered later in the work, to sanctify her: "Tonka war in die Nähe tiefer Märchen gerückt. Das war die Welt des Gesalbten, der Jungfrau und Pontius Pilatus, und die Ärzte sagten, daß Tonka geschont und gepflegt werden müßte, sollte sie ihren Zustand überdauern." In a third attempt at a symbolic interpretation she becomes neither virgin nor whore, but simply Nature, a mysterious, unfathomable being whose essence is mystery: "Sie war Natur, die sich zum Geist ordnet; nicht Geist werden will, aber ihn liebt und uner-gründlich sich ihm anschloß wie eins der vielen dem Menschen zugelaufenen Wesen."

As noted above, readers have been quick to adopt the vocabulary of the narrator uncritically in their efforts to understand who Tonka is or what she represents. But we must bear in mind that Tonka herself remains silent in this work. All we have are the narrator's perspectives on this enigmatic figure, with no guarantee that they have any validity. While the narrator can never shed any light on the object of his investigation, his various attempts do reveal a good deal about himself and the purposes of his interpretations of Tonka. Whether Tonka really "is" a miraculous virgin, a despicable whore, or nature incarnate is beside the point; what matters is that these are the categories which present themselves to the narrator as the only logical explanations for her pregnancy.

The very passages which seem to grant symbolic richness to the figure of Tonka are therefore actually motivated by a complete ignorance of her true nature. In this sense we can see a direct parallel between the narrator's account of Tonka and the dubious productions of his "uncle" Hyacinth. Hyacinth is introduced as an "Oberfinanzrat und nebenher noch ein vielgelesener deutscher Dichter, dessen Erzählungen große Auflagen erreichten." Despite their great popularity, his stories are poor. For all of Hyacinth's attempts at intellectual profundity, "seine Gedanken waren daher so beschaffen, daß sie desto größer erschienen, je leerer sie waren, indem sie sich über die Jahrtausende und größten Fragen ausdehnten." There is thus an inverse proportion between the pretentiousness of the novels and their actual worth, which finds an ironic parallel in the scope of their public success. The public, in other words, finds itself in the position of the person confronted by the shady businessman in the anecdote recalled above, but in their case they fail to see through the literary charlatan.

The public success of this verbal huckster is further crowned by a private triumph over the young man's mother. As a child the future scientist admired the seemingly selfless love of Hyacinth for his mother, but when he grew older he realized that Hyacinth was actually attracted to her because he could exploit her ideals as a source for his novels, "wahrscheinlich weil sie als Offizierstochter von Ehr- und Charaktervorstellungen gehalten und, diese lebhaft ausstrahlend, jene Festigkeit der Grundsätze besaß, die er für die Ideale seiner Bücher brauchte, während ihm dunkel ahnte, daß die Flüssigkeit seiner Rede und Erzählergabe gerade davon kam, daß sie seinem Geist fehlte." The suspicion that Hyacinth's attraction to the protagonist's mother is linked to her ability to inspire bombastic, but highly profitable prose is confirmed when Hyacinth is asked to write a letter to the protagonist's father in the place of his ailing mother: "Was soll ich denn schreiben?—er, welcher der Mutter bogenlange Episteln bei jeder Trennung schrieb!"

The example of Hyacinth's duplicity causes the young man to reject any sort of poetic mysticism in his life. "Der vielseitig Begabte studierte Chemie und stellte sich taub gegen alle Fragen, die nicht klar zu lösen sind, ja er war ein fast haßerfüllter Gegner solcher Erörterungen und ein fanatischer Jünger des kühlen, trocken phantastischen, Bogen spannenden neuen Ingenieurgeistes." Yet despite this professed rejection of anything but the most sober and precise sort of scientific language, we frequently find the protagonist using language in a way in which the words seem to become detached from any direct communicative purpose. At one point he finds himself defending Tonka's seeming lack of emotion to his mother by pointing out that some people don't cry easily, "nicht weil es ihn wichtig zu sagen dünkte, sondern weil ihn seine Redegeschicklichkeit reizte." Later he spends considerable effort writing quite poetic letters to first his mother and then to Tonka, which however he never mails. Whereas the normal letter is written to establish communication between two individuals, here writing becomes a private exercise whose content has less significance than the act of writing itself: "Da erst fiel ihm ein, daß er die Briefe nie abgeschickt hatte; sie waren ja nicht mit Sicherheit seine Meinung, sondern eben ein Zustand, der sich nicht anders helfen kann als mit Schreiben."

This condition evidently persists in the scientist after Tonka's death, causing him to recall the event again in the narrative we read. Like his mother for Hyacinth, she becomes the impetus for his seemingly profound allusions to questions of philosophy, religion, and language, while relegating the fate of Tonka to a matter of indifference, just as in *Die Verwirrungen des Zöglings Törleß* we are encouraged to consider the problem of Basini's sufferings as one of those "trivial concerns for trivial minds" [Peters]. What separates Musil's *Tonka* from the work of Hyacinth, however, is the subtle way in which it reveals the duplicitous character of the narrator. The heavy artillery of literary symbolism is brought to bear on an enigmatic target, but the shots explode into darkness, revealing only the location of the ramparts from which they were launched. That the young man is able to walk away from the experience with more of a smug grin than a mortal wound is indicative more of his willful self-deception than any real victory. This becomes particularly evident in his last encounters with the mortally ill Tonka, in which the question of his belief in her comes closest to its resolution: "Er sprach nie das Wort aus: ich glaube dir. Obgleich er längst an sie glaubte. Denn er glaubte ihr bloß so, daß er nicht länger alle Folgen daraus auch vor seinem Verstand einstehen wollte. Es hielt ihn heil und an der

Erde fest, daß er das nicht tat." His sanity is only retained by deliberately ignoring the full consequences of his half-hearted belief. One is again reminded of Törleß, who serenely leaves the boarding school and the battered Basini behind, while aware that "das Eigentliche, das Problem, saß fest." Peace of mind is bought by ignoring the questions which bothered them, rather than finding a solution.

This element of bad faith in the seeming maturity of the young man at the end of *Tonka* suggests a motivation for one of the most radical aspects of the work, the fact that its protagonist remains unnamed. As Tonka's pregnancy progresses and her changing physical appearance becomes a constant reminder of the threat she poses to the young man's ability to maintain control over either her or himself, he decides to grow a beard. Like his turn to superstition in this period of crisis, the beard becomes a symbol of his increasing alienation from his former self, which involves an increased aggression towards Tonka: "Und da man nichts weiß, wünschte er Tonka vielleicht zuweilen tot, damit dieses unerträgliche Leben ein Ende finde, und mochte den Bart bloß deshalb, weil er alles verstellte und verbarg." However, as soon as Tonka has left the house to go to the hospital, he has his beard shaved off: "Nun war er wieder mehr er selbst." Yet as we have seen, Tonka's departure only removes the constant reminder of the problem posed by her pregnancy but not the problem itself. Thus the alleged recovery of the young man's true identity masks this fact in a way which directly parallels his avoidance of the consequences of his "belief" in Tonka during the last days of her life. His namelessness, in turn, can be understood as a reflection of the dissonance which lies just beneath the surface of the uplifting tonality of the final paragraphs of the work. The happy ending is paid for with the deliberate willingness to put some problems into the dark in order to claim that one is standing in a comforting light.

To what extent is Musil to be identified with this narrator? Even the staunchest formalist would have to admit that there is some strong evidence for equating the author with his fiction in the case of this particular text. In the early drafts of the story, found in Musil's diary of 1905, the protagonist is named Robert. His lover's name is not Tonka, but Herma, the name of Musil's early lover Herma Dietz, whom he compares to his mother, Hermine Musil. The figure of Hyacinth directly parallels the actual situation in Musil's household as a child, where his mother openly maintained an intimate relationship with Heinrich Reiter while remaining married to Alfred Musil.

However intriguing the evidence of Musil's diaries may be, it would be a mistake to reduce *Tonka,* completed nearly twenty years later, to a piece of camouflaged autobiography. The strength of the work lies in its manipulation of a familiar literary archetype, not its private significance for its author. Musil takes the familiar story of a woman who suffers at a man's expense and complicates it by introducing the unresolved problem of Tonka's pregnancy, resulting in the symbolic frustration of the young man's attempt to assert his power over Tonka.

The situation is further complicated by the young man's role as narrator of the text. Narration becomes an exercise in compensating for repressed frustration by turning mystery into myth. Thus the enigma of Tonka's pregnancy which results in the inversion of the familiar pattern of the man's cultural, intellectual, and class dominance of the woman in the plot of the text becomes the primary motivation for the narrator's attempt to interpret Tonka's silence in terms of the old clichés of woman as nature, virgin, or whore. In this way Musil's *Tonka* becomes a powerful comment on the resiliency of the ideology which is both defeated and resurrected in the course of the work.

Lowell A. Bangerter (essay date 1989)

SOURCE: "Looking Inside: *Unions*," in *Robert Musil,* Continuum, 1989, pp. 43-57.

[*An American critic and educator, Bangerter is the author of* German Writing since 1945 *(1988) as well as studies of Johann Schiller and Hugo von Hofmannsthal. In the following exerpt, he argues that the "unions" referred to in the title of* Unions *are ones that take place within the protagonists rather than between individuals.*]

An important distinguishing feature of Musil's literary art is the deliberate de-emphasis of structured plot and sequential narrative in favor of illustrating and illuminating his ideas about mortal existence. Characters and their relationships become the vehicles that the author uses to explore theme variations and possibilities for response to the phenomena, problems, and questions of human life. In the slender volume *Unions,* which contains the two novellas *The Perfecting of a Love* and *The Temptation of Quiet Veronica,* Musil experimented with a creative technique that pushed to a new extreme the development of this tendency in his writings. Focusing almost completely on the thoughts and feelings of the respective female protagonists, he subordinated any sense of story line and perspective to a precise rendering of their inner worlds in a dense, carefully constructed web of metaphors. The resulting literature is extremely complex and difficult to understand. Musil himself suggested that in order to appreciate the stories, the reader should contemplate and ponder them like pieces of visual art. His diary reveals that he regarded *Unions* as something entirely different from traditional narrative prose, something that could best be understood by removing it from any association with the concept: "book." He felt that the stories would better communicate their meaning if they were separated into pages that could be placed on display under glass and exchanged at appropriate intervals.

The style of *Unions* is abstract and lyrical. There is a pronounced absence of real specifics concerning time and place. The physical world is often subdued and shadowy or excluded entirely. Instead of a connected flow of events, the narrative substance consists mainly of floods of thought, surges of emotion, and intense projections of feelings and sensations. Musil consciously associated the two novellas with the poetry of ideas, and the heavy fabric of metaphors and images forces the reader to approach these writings from precisely that kind of perspective. In a letter to Franz Blei, Musil pointed out that his usage of stylistic devices in *Unions,* especially symbolic and parabolic forms of expression, deviated from the norm. He insisted that such components of his writing were not secondary, decorative trappings, but rather primary aspects of the narrative and critical elements of its structure.

The overall effect of this approach is very poetic, and the lyrical aspect contributes directly to the penetration of the protagonists' inner worlds, or, as Musil termed it, "the boring into the psychological dimension" that is the author's major purpose. Eithne Wilkins and Ernst Kaiser [in "Musil und die Quadraturzel aus minus eins," in *Robert Musil: Leben, Werk, Wirkung,* ed. Karl Dinklage, 1960] have accurately summed up the role of lyricism in *Unions* as follows: "Through the lyrical element there arises in these novellas a greater density of symbols than is present in the more discursive works, but these too are full of suggestions of new, still half-hidden horizons of consciousness, of indications of a boundary and what lies mysteriously behind it, of that which is extreme and the borderline case."

In addition to the stylistic density of the novellas, the obscurity of Musil's primary focus contributes to the difficulty that is typically encountered in the attempt to interpret *Unions*. Experience with traditional narrative prose, in which relationships between characters carry much of the story weight, tempts the reader to relate the volume's title to the establishment and failure of connections between portrayed individuals and to seek in that equation the central meanings of the respective stories. Musil's own comments indicate that such an interpretation must lead to misunderstanding of his intent. The "unions" that are important take place *within* the protagonists, and the author is more concerned with the devaluation of all causality, and with the problems of self-betrayal and the relationship of the individual to his ideals than with the ties between his heroines and the men in their lives.

The first of the narratives in *Unions, The Perfecting of a Love,* lays bare the inner life of Claudine, a woman whose physical trip to visit her daughter at a boarding school in an isolated town provides the external guideposts for a parallel voyage into the depths of her own soul. The outward happenings of the story are minimal. After leaving her husband alone, Claudine takes the train to the city where her daughter is studying and there eventually allows herself to be seduced by a man who remains a stranger. Paradoxically, she seems to experience her unfaithfulness as a process of perfecting her love for her husband, and what transpires within her during the period of her separation from him forms the real substance of the novella.

As was the case with the main character of *Young Törless,* the point of departure for Claudine's journey into herself is a potent tension that arises from an increasing sense of spiritual isolation. The opening scene of *The*

Perfecting of a Love, which is peculiar for its intensity of concrete detail, invokes a feeling of loneliness on several levels at once. Claudine and her husband sit drinking tea as though suspended in what Frederick Peters has described [in *Robert Musil, Master of the Hovering Life,* 1978] as "an impressionistic painting, a still life of fruits and flowers or lifeless puppets rather than of two human beings." There is an immediate sense of something at once beautiful and fragile that cannot survive outside of the hermetically closed sphere in which it now exists.

Conversation between husband and wife, and the author's representation of their thoughts, intensify the mood of separation from the world that is evoked by the rich but sterile minutiae of their environment. The focus of their discussion is a sexual deviant about whom they have been reading. Like some peculiar apparition, the man identified only as G. haunts their thoughts and stimulates consciousness of their personal isolation. Their contemplation of the criminal, his deeds, and motivations leads unerringly to the concluding question: "Yes indeed, isn't every mind solitary?" The response to the query is only silence, a signal to the reader that the focus has shifted away from G. and back to the people who are thinking about him, and the result is an overwhelmingly cold, harsh impression of intense isolation. It is then from this perspective of loneliness that the nature of Claudine's actual relationship with her husband is revealed.

The two characters are described as feeling that the secret of their union rests upon the solitude that they experience. Their vision of the surrounding world is almost opaque, a fact that makes them seem to cling to one another. With a sense of coldness around them, they derive warmth from the peculiar joining of one to the other that forces them internally into a larger whole. Although aloneness has brought the two of them together, their relationship is flawed because they remain unable to perfect their union on any external plane. Proceeding from that state of affairs, Claudine's journey quickly transforms itself into the search for an alternative solution to the problem, within herself.

The physical events that occur after Claudine leaves home represent an intensification of her isolation in both time and space. The time element is especially important. In the description of her departure there is an immediate shift in narrative focus from Claudine's present to her past, and the greatest emphasis is given to things that contributed to an earlier sense of separation from everything around her. As she waits at the railway station, she remembers when she experienced passionate acts that virtually humiliated her because of their violence, even though she remained continually aware that nothing she did really had any important impact upon her or meaning for her life. Her memory is then juxtaposed with the present in which she feels uneasy about the people around her and is moved to seek refuge within herself. Once she is on the train, its soft rocking movements and the view of nature passing outside the window enable her to complete her escape into solitude. Subsequently, when ele-

ments of the external world threaten to intrude and the people around her begin to touch her thoughts, she is able to retreat without difficulty into an inner place where she is left only with a feeling of her own insignificance that causes her to drift within herself toward an indefinite goal. By the time she reaches the city where her daughter is, her mood is such that she views the town itself as cut off from reality, and she is prepared for the encounter that will enable her to reach her goal. Her readiness is signaled by an inexpressible yearning for some man who is as misunderstood and lonely as she is. Such an individual, she believes, would be characterized by a tenderness that would have the power to subdue the external, material world, while maintaining the perfect security of the inner, spiritual realm through a balanced consciousness of the self. Clearly, what she yearns for is union with her own deepest being.

Claudine's encounter with the isolated boarding-school town is like Törless's stay at the academy in that her interpretations of events are colored and confused by an awareness of the world's apparent doubleness. At one point the narrator says that each thing she sees appears to illuminate surrounding things in a reciprocal manner that makes them appear to echo one another in a broader pattern of vision. Frederick Peters relates this phenomenon more closely to the kind of search for identity that Musil described in his first novel by arguing that the city "functions as a geographical metaphor for the Other Realm that lies beyond the frontier of everyday life."

Claudine's experience differs from that of Törless, however, because her perception of duplication is primarily temporal rather than spatial. Even the "echo" metaphor cited above places the emphasis on repetition in *time*. For Claudine, the "Other Realm" is the past. All of her experiences seem to be repetitions of earlier ones, and even her words have the ring of things that she has spoken previously. Accordingly, her entry into the internal world where the union with self can be perfected is tied to her return to the former spiritual state in which she can perform again acts of physical passion that have no real effect on her.

Critics who interpret what happens to Claudine as a true perfecting of her love for her husband overlook the fact that on a real plane, union with him, even a spiritual one, and the return to the past are mutually exclusive. It is the physical and mental separation from her husband that permits her to slide back into her former life, while dwelling in that past brings a sadness that she cannot associate with a normal longing for love. On the contrary, the feeling within her seems to move her away from the intense relationship with her husband in the real world, and toward some other, as yet indistinguishable goal. The impression that she has is one of being on a road to a particularly sublime loneliness in which she is exposed to the harsh elements of an empty wasteland.

Alone in her room after her arrival, Claudine is engulfed by dreams from her early life. There she recognizes that she is not attracted to the stranger that she has been watching, but only by the intense anticipation of the ecstasy that she will experience in the confrontation with her own deepest being. In that moment of longing for self she has a premonition of the "mysterious union" that is coming, and it is again connected with an image that emphasizes distance from rather than proximity to her loved one. The narrator presents it as an act of hearing the distant, restless, homeless wandering of her husband's heart. The sounds that her spirit detects form a strange kind of flickering music that touches her with a profound sense of loneliness, and the loneliness in turn becomes a catalyst that enables her to transcend the former limits of her soul.

Like Törless, Claudine discovers the duality of her own nature by peering into the "Other Realm." The aspect belonging to the world from which she has come is the ideal Claudine that cannot live without the mate she has left behind. During her return to the past, however, she is dominated by another, baser, more sensual self that the author presents in animalistic metaphors. During the night, for example, she wakes up and goes to the window to look out at the falling snow. She is described specifically as being keenly aware that her feet touch the ground like those of some animal.

The confrontation with her animal self becomes more intense with each incident that takes place. At the boarding school, when she talks with the teachers about her daughter (who is a product of a disinterested physical-animal act in her promiscuous past), she experiences a strange but meaningful vision in which a peculiar something seems to rise from the shadows, confronting her with the impression of a huge, shaggy, evil-smelling beast. Her initial inclination to lash out at it and drive it away is destroyed by a sudden realization: The changing expressions on the apparition's face are extremely familiar; in some unknown fashion they mirror her own.

This encounter with the animal side of her being is the turning point in the narrative. Its effect on her is extremely powerful. Immediately afterward she attempts to envision her husband, with the result that she can no longer see him as clearly or as near to her as before. It is at that point that she considers a variety of possibilities for action and concludes that the spiritual merging with her husband can only be consummated *within herself* when all external events become meaningless. In that context, the physical attraction that she has for the nameless official who has been trying to win her favor provides the opportunity for her to achieve the perfect union that she desires.

The civil servant becomes an outward symbol for her animal self, and her intended sexual submission to him without emotional involvement, the ultimate proof of her accomplishment, is equated in her mind with sodomy. Her subsequent mental behavior then emphasizes the increasing dominance of the animal element within her. On the night when her potential seducer remains outside her door without knocking, she later looks out into the empty hallway and responds silently to what has happened. In presenting what takes place within her, the narrator describes her sudden impulse to throw herself to the ground and kiss the footprints on the rug, comparing this feeling of arousal to the animal actions of a bitch in heat.

When the stranger finally follows her to her room, the author again transforms her metaphorically into an animal. Upon hearing his footsteps on the stairs behind her, she mentally distances herself from what is happening, while her physical reaction is to tremble "like an animal hunted down, deep in the forest." On that level she surrenders to him. For Claudine, the stranger too is an animal, but without identity. As Frederick Peters has pointed out, "a particular man with a particular history . . . could not have conquered her."

The major metaphors that form the skeleton of *The Perfecting of a Love* suggest a variety of possibilities for union on different levels, ranging from disinterested or totally submissive mechanical coupling to intensely spiritual unification. While the animal metaphors are the most graphic of these, the most important ones pertain to Claudine's perception of her relationship to her distant husband. Her peculiar notion that the sexual affair with a stranger will mysteriously enable her to perfect the marital bond is a troublesome problem that can be resolved only through recognition that the love tie itself is but a metaphor for something else. That fact becomes clear in the progression of thoughts that builds to a critical climax during the night that Claudine spends away from the civil servant.

What happens to Claudine in her room is prefigured in a train of thought that she entertains while sitting with the stranger before going upstairs. The temptation to submit herself to him causes her to project a mental image of a union in which her spirit disowns and abandons her body, leaving it open to the physical, sensual, even murderous assaults of the stranger, while at the same time experiencing the constancy of her physical being as an enduring presence around the soul that she can only define as a sickness. Like Törless, she is looking for a means to make contact with her deepest essence.

The experience that occurs when she is alone is generated not by her love for her husband but by her overt denial of it. During her conversation with the stranger, he had asked her whether she loved her husband, and she had given a negative response. As she ponders the significance of this lie, it becomes for her a gateway to the "Other Realm," a place where she is no longer subject to the binding force of her ideals.

While sitting in her room, anticipating the adventure in which she will commit adultery and yet remain somehow aloof from the act, she feels a dangerous excitement that she associates with the very concept of betraying her husband. This feeling enables her to transcend the limits of physical reality. Spiritually, she moves into a state in which her soul is beyond the reach of other people. The narrator describes this ethereal domain as "the void that sometimes gapes for an instant behind all ideals." Once the door to this place of total isolation has been opened, her mind can lead her to the fulfillment that she seeks.

The moment of perfection comes neither in sexual union with the stranger nor in the envisioned spiritual joining with her husband, but in the achievement of oneness within herself. Musil describes it as an instant of closing up the soul against all foreign elements. Perfection is realized in a dreamlike state where the contradictions of life are dissolved in the trembling light of an intense and undefiled love. Viewed from this perspective, the subsequent sexual affair with the civil servant becomes an anti-climax that verifies only her attainment of a state of internal harmony that renders physical entanglements completely meaningless.

Like Claudine, the central figure of *The Temptation of Quiet Veronica* searches for a means to become one with her innermost self. For Veronica, the process of realizing internal unity involves the rejection of normal sexual activity in the belief that she can reach a more significant relationship with her friend Johannes on a higher, more spiritual plane. The focal event of her quest is a peculiar, semimystical experience that leads only briefly to perfect oneness because it cannot be sustained in the real world.

The Temptation of Quiet Veronica has been called Musil's most abstract narrative, primarily because of its lack of any substantial realistic story line. While the literary presentation develops the relationships between three main characters who live together in an old house, aside from opaque conversations and descriptions of a few minor happenings, the only external action is Johannes's departure by train for the coast, followed a day later by the arrival of a letter from him containing the news that he has not committed suicide as Veronica expected him to do. Everything else that is offered for the reader's examination occurs within the characters, primarily Veronica, with no more than general, indefinite reference to factors of time and space.

In many respects, *The Temptation of Quiet Veronica* offers an intensification of the central themes in *The Perfecting of a Love*. Once more the point of departure for the female protagonist's excursion into the uttermost recesses of her soul is a profound state of spiritual aloneness. Musil's employment of the house's indistinct, almost timeless, realm as a metaphor for separation from reality is particularly powerful. It is, in the words of Frederick Peters, "as if three people were each living in complete isolation in a shadowy dreamlike world at the still bottom of a deep pool of water. They seem to wander about the house in varying states of agonized emotional tension, now and then engaging in elliptical conversations as they glide past each other."

The most visible symptom of the insulating void that exists between the major figures is their inability to communicate effectively to each other their thoughts and feelings. Musil conveys the spoken word's failure to bring about interpersonal union by presenting as conversation what seem to be random pieces of monologues that never go

anywhere. By this means he forces the reader into the stream-of-consciousness pattern that leads in a sequence of complex metaphors into the inner world of his central character.

Critical factors in Veronica's failure to participate in normal human interaction are the pronounced tensions that exist between her and the two male figures Johannes and Demeter. Strong parallels are visible between the respective relationships and the corresponding elements that permit different aspects of Claudine's nature to respond to her husband and to the unnamed civil servant in *The Perfecting of a Love*. In each of the Veronica situations, however, the strain placed on ties between individuals and the metaphors that represent those connections are more extreme than those of the first novella.

For Claudine, the physical separation of the train trip combined with her mental retreat into the past place enough distance between her and her husband to enable her to "perfect" her love by transcending its bonds and achieving unity within herself. In the case of Veronica, a far more drastic parting is necessary for her to find what she is seeking. Johannes suggests to her that they leave the house and go away together in order to find a common focus around which they can join their lives. Veronica rejects his proposal, and when he renews it she responds in words that define both her perception of him and the only circumstances under which she can envision union between them on any level. She says: "Surely no human being can be so impersonal, only an animal . . . yes, perhaps if you were going to die." The real reason why Veronica cannot accept Johannes on his terms is that she sees him as an animal. Only through the complete destruction of that image, that is, only through his death, can he become something with which she can possibly unite on a mystical plane.

In *The Perfecting of a Love* Musil employs the animal metaphors most pointedly to depict and highlight Claudine's perception of the stranger and her approach to the sexual encounter with him. Vivid symbols of the same kind are used to characterize the relationship between Veronica and Demeter.

Like the civil servant, Demeter represents mechanical, completely physical intercourse that has no meaning. After Demeter has made a sexual proposition to her, Veronica tells Johannes about it. Her description reveals the lack of significance that such an act would have for either her or Demeter. She presents what happened as a natural, mechanical event, a deed that was meaningless, according to Demeter, because nobody would know about it, and it would therefore have no relationship to things in the external world of reality. To emphasize the incident's triviality, she concludes by insisting that Demeter meant nothing at all to her.

Although Veronica does not feel anything *for* Demeter, he does have a powerful impact upon her that is conditioned by her tendency to relate him to specific animal images. At one point, for example, as she watches the chickens in the yard beneath the window, she senses that she has been thinking about something that she cannot identify. Demeter comes and stands next to her and his presence acts as a catalyst that brings her elusive thought into focus. She has been thinking about the rooster below. While relating the incident to Johannes, she tells him how the thought suddenly came to her that Demeter must be like the rooster.

In his diary Musil wrote that he originally intended to present Veronica as a figure caught between two antagonistic tendencies, the sensuality that dominated her thoughts, and an internal longing for balance. Demeter and Johannes are the respective external stimuli that alternately focus her awareness on the two forces that struggle within her and through their conflict make it impossible for her to reach a permanent internal harmony. Each represents a temptation that must be faced if Veronica is to come to grips with her own destiny.

Frederick Peters has argued that Veronica's awareness of Demeter's animal essence, in the scene where she relates him to the rooster, is a primary "precipitating agent" for the return of a repressed sexual memory that explains why she rejects his physical advances. While it is certainly true that what she finally brings herself to recall holds the key to the tension that she feels with respect to sexual activity, there is no clear causal relationship in the text between the rooster scene and the regeneration of the memory that occurs several pages later. The attempt to link the two events so closely places a false emphasis on the relationship between Veronica and Demeter. What is important about the sudden awakening within her of the experience from her childhood is that it explains why she can unite with *neither* Johannes *nor* Demeter in the real world.

As Veronica attempts to deal with her internal conflict, she goes through a process that corresponds to Claudine's retreat into the past. Over a period of weeks she is deluged with mental pictures from her early life. The direct stimulus for the final critical memory is an exchange of calls by two birds, and it seems to Veronica in retrospect that similar birdcalls have heralded the other flashes of remembrance. At the sound of the birds' song, Veronica suddenly sees a time when she had loved the fur of a large Saint Bernard dog. On a particular day, as she lies beside the dog, her mind roams through peculiar fantasies with sexual overtones. She closes her eyes for a while, and when she opens them again, the dog is looking at her. At this point she becomes aware of the dog's sexual arousal, as she catches sight of its penis protruding from the fur. When she tries to get up, the dog licks her face, and she is unable to move. It is as though she is an animal herself, and emotionally she struggles between her fears concerning what is happening and some peculiar feeling of ecstasy that she does not understand.

The meaning of this vision of the past for Veronica's attitudes toward Johannes and Demeter is vividly clear. For years she has carried within her the suppressed knowledge of an experience that has in effect reduced her to an

animal at the sexual mercy of a large dog. Her mental association of Johannes and Demeter with various animal images, including dogs, creates an unconscious equation of their relationships with what has transpired when she was a teenager. For that reason she is totally incapable of submitting to the real-world desires of either male figure. With respect to Johannes in particular, that fact is hammered home in a mental association in which she relates him directly to the dog of her memory. As she feels the intensity of his gaze resting upon her, within her mind he assumes the characteristics of a large exhausted animal that is lying on her, and that she cannot push away. This association calls forth again the vision of that afternoon in her past. In the act of mentally reliving the traumatic event from her youth, she overcomes it and opens the way for her brief encounter with inner oneness.

After Johannes departs by train for the coast, where, Veronica believes, he will commit suicide, she returns to her room and retreats into an internal world where she contemplates the possibility of achieving union with him on a mystical plane. There the souls would become joined in a fashion that is impossible in the realm of physical reality. In the process of her examination of that prospect, her sense of ecstasy intensifies. She seems to wallow in the vision of Johannes's impending death and in her own yearning to unite with his soul. As the intensity of feeling increases, however, she experiences the revelation of what really lies at the heart of her innermost longing: "She had begun dimly to realise that it was not Johannes but herself that she experienced with such palpable sensuality."

What follows is the enjoyment of what Frederick Peters has called "the moment of ultimate narcissism." Suddenly Johannes loses importance as a being in his own right. He becomes a vehicle for Veronica's observation of herself. A mystical union of souls occurs in which she penetrates beyond the physical trappings of her body into the innermost reaches of herself. She seems to see herself through Johannes's eyes, and to experience not only his spiritual touch but also his sense of contact with her.

The semi-mystical experience that permits Veronica to become one with her own soul brings about the same kind of resolution of the basic problems of insecurity and spiritual loneliness that Claudine achieves. The union with self that results from the attempt to "perfect a love" demands in the real world a rejection of that love. Complete oneness with the soul and an emotional tie to another individual are mutually exclusive because, as Veronica learns, it is the soul of living people that makes them unable to love, regardless of how much they may yearn to do so.

When Veronica learns that Johannes is still alive, the news destroys any hope that she might have of maintaining the state of inner unity that she has achieved the night before. Her mental vision of his death was a necessary bridge to the "Other Realm" in which the union could occur. Without it, her endeavors to regain what she has experienced cause her to drift into the void between the reality from which she has excluded herself and the transcendent world that she can no longer reach. From physical isolation in the old house, she has moved into the devastating loneliness of mental illness, a realm where there is "perhaps only a sadness . . . like walls painted by fever and delusions, and between those walls the words spoken by the sane and healthy have no resonance, but fall to the ground, meaningless. . . . "

Barbara Mabee (essay date 1992)

SOURCE: "Images of Woman in Musil's *Tonka*: Mystical Encounters and Borderlines between Self and Other," in *The Michigan Academician,* Vol. XXIV, No. 2, Winter, 1992, pp. 369-81.

[*In the following excerpt focusing on* Tonka, *Mabee discusses the women in Musil's novellas, arguing that their association with nature and imagination makes them "catalysts for illumination" and "mirrors to the male protagonists' fragmented selves in the post-enlightenment world with its emphasis on scientific formulation."*]

Recalling to consciousness a rationally inexplicable episode of his youth, the nameless young scientist in Robert Musil's *Tonka,* the third novella in his trilogy *Drei Frauen (Three Women,* 1924), encounters woman as the Other. As narrator-protagonist, distancing himself in a third-person narratorial style, he ponders the effects of his friendship with the mysterious, simple servant girl Tonka. The stream-of-consciousness narrative unfolds in retrospect as the narrator's confrontation with himself and his memories of events surrounding his affair with her. In fragmented and tension-filled memory processes, the young man attempts to unravel the "tangle of thorns" that overtook his scientific mind upon encountering Tonka's non-rational world, her oneness with nature, and her peculiar "language of the totality of things"—a language of silence, songs, and aphasia. Tonka functions, as critics have frequently pointed-ed out, as an unparticipating foil or catalyst in the narrator's search for truth and meaning in his life. Her existence in images that she evokes in the scientist poses questions of borderlines between self and Other and of woman's absence as Other in a science-oriented world.

In my analysis of *Tonka,* I intend to examine underlying reasons for Tonka's simultaneous portrayal of a tainted and idealized woman with subversive powers, leading Musil's narrator to the "other condition"—to the mystical world and creative/imaginative realm of the poet or *Dichter.* Furthermore, I will focus on the polarities that Musil sets up between male and female, and on the masculine-feminine split in the post-enlightenment individual. For these foci, it is essential to establish initially the context for "Tonka" within the trilogy.

In each of the three stories in the cycle, *Grigia, Die Portugiesin (The Lady from Portugal)* and *Tonka,* the narrator describes the effect of "the feminine" on the male, as the protagonist is confronted with a previously unknown side of himself—in Jungian terms, his "anima"—

and comes to a better understanding of selfhood. This process of self-discovery and self-creation is mediated in all three cases by a woman who represents a different cultural milieu and a foreign, irrational, incomprehensible dimension of the male's existence. The title figures open a doorway to a mystical realm, a new level of consciousness for the respective men. Musil calls this realm the "other condition" ("anderer Zustand"), a concept that presents an intangible, mysterious, and inspirational world, as we find it in the writings by Christian, Jewish, and oriental mystics. Musil's concept, however, is less indebted to the mystics as to the Austrian physicist-philosopher Ernst Mach (Musil's 1908 dissertation is on Mach, 1836-1916) and to Nietzsche. Musil describes this realm as a shadow-like double of our world, as the moment when a normal sense of the world is burst. This condition is experienced in love, in contemplation, or in mystic vision. In this "other condition" there is neither purpose nor cause, good or evil, but a mysterious rising and falling tide ("unio mystica") in which our nature flows together with that of other human beings or objects.

In *Grigia,* the protagonist Homo embarks upon what becomes a journey into the primeval state of consciousness and the primeval past. He goes to a remote Italian village, where every woman greets any man seductively as her missing husband. Homo's alluring peasant mistress Grigia is depicted as a woman governed by instinct and irrationalism. She takes him away from civilization into a mining shaft, symbolically the womb or cave, where he is ready to meet death after a last moment of erotic ecstasy that brings him into an unusually close union with his wife rather than his lover. In *Die Portugiesin,* cast in a medieval setting on the border between Austria and Italy, real and unreal events merge and interweave with one another. The knight, Herr von Ketten, brings a Portuguese woman with mysterious female spirituality to his castle. After eleven years of marriage, interspersed with frequent absences due to his continual, somewhat mysterious fights with the Bishop of Trent, von Ketten finally achieves self-definition and harmony between his conflicting selves of love for warfare and caring gentleness as he faces a severe illness. His Portuguese wife functions as an active and life-embracing facilitator in his rebirth and metamorphosis into a real human being, capable of connecting masculine and feminine principles within himself. Also in *Tonka,* the reader encounters Musil's preoccupation with those situations in which the normal and habitual patterns of an individual's life have been suddenly disrupted. Here it is the compulsory one-year military service near the Czech border that parallels the lengthy trip away from home and family in *Grigia* and the encounter with a foreigner in *Die Portugiesin.* The vulnerable protagonist in each of the situations is thrown into a world of new relationships and experiences. The young scholar in *Tonka* meets the young woman as he is emotionally vulnerable during his year of military service and makes attempts to sever his close ties to his parental home.

In all three stories Musil's male characters meet a part of themselves in their female lovers and are forced to examine borders between self and Other. Readers find traditional images of woman as nature, virgin, and whore, as portrayed for example by Sandra Gilbert and Susan Gubar in their seminal study of women writers in *The Madwoman in the Attic* or in the 1989 study by Alison Jaggar and Susan Bordo, *Gender/Body/Knowledge*. In Musil's cycle *Drei Frauen,* these images undergo close scrutiny and a reexamination by the narrators. Musil takes the reader on a journey to explore the female figures in relation to "the other condition," the mystical realm that already medieval mystics, in whom Musil was much interested, frequently likened to certain kinds of erotic experiences.

Antithetical impressions of Tonka become intertwined in the fourteen vignettes, ranging from virgin in the "world of the Anointed, of the Virgin, and of Pontius Pilate" to Tonka as whore and unfaithful lover in the sixth episode. The mysterious pregnancy in this episode, occurring miraculously during a time of his travel and absence and followed by Tonka's insidious disease, an infection of the blood, becomes the focal point of the narrator's reflections on Tonka's natural goodness and kindness amidst poverty in a small Austrian town by the Czech border. Her tainted pregnancy and her kind of goodness "that a dog might have had" are equally mysterious to him:

> It was astonishing with what sureness she rejected everything crude, coarse, uncivilized in whatever guise it came her way. . . . And yet she lacked any urge to rise beyond her own orbit into a higher sphere. She remained pure and unspoilt like Nature herself. . . . She was Nature adjusting itself to Mind, not wanting to become Mind, but loving it and inscrutably attaching itself to it.

Her refusal to let go of her connectedness with nature intrigues him again and again. She is protected by the moon, a symbol which in folklore is associated with the Moon-mother and other female principles. In the imagination of the young, ambitious chemist, Tonka is present as a "sign," "hallucination," "fairy tale," and as a "half-born myth"—"a snowflake falling all alone in the midst of a summer's day." This central image of the snowflake takes on parabolic character in its miraculous singularity, impossible purity and innocence that can-not survive the stark scrutiny of the dissecting intellect in the empirical world of science in the post-enlightenment world. The image comes from the region of irrationality and dreams and points to the borderlines where subconscious thoughts become conscious ones. The snowflake captures Tonka's close connection with nature, and implicitly alludes to her mysterious pregnancy. Her unproven infidelity and resulting pregnancy completely unsettle the scientist, who is accustomed to clear-cut answers and a "fanatical disciple of the cool soberly fantastical, world-encompassing spirit of modern technology."

The male encounter with female sensuality has been likened to Faust's awe of the "eternal feminine" in his lover Gretchen. Renate Gerulaitis, Lowell Bangerter, and Todd Kontje have placed Tonka in the literary tradition of Goethe's Gretchen (in *Faust*) as the prototype for the German and European lower-class woman, presented in clichés of the innocent, passive, self-sacrificing child of nature, whose sacrificial death raises the stature of their socially and educationally superior "fickle lovers" [Gerulaitis, *Michigan Academician* 15, No. 3, Spring 1983; Bangerter, *Robert Musil*, 1989; Kontje, *Monatshefte* 79, No. 2, 1987]. I agree with the notion that Tonka joins Faust's Gretchen in the apotheosis of the "eternal feminine," in her exemplary role of self-sacrifice and suffering so that her male lover may grow emotionally, spiritually and professionally. However, I intend to show how Musil tarnishes the very image of female goodness and uses the mysterious pregnancy as a literary device to explore border regions, in which irrational, mystical and mythical conceptions collide with rational ones and approach the creative realm of the poet or *Dichter*.

Female silence, sensibility, and humility are continually juxtaposed with "the authority of the 'master'" and subtly undermine it, thereby creating a subversive undercurrent in the text. Seen in this light, I maintain that Musil draws on but goes beyond the eighteenth-century German literary tradition of the virtuous female from the middle or lower classes who is seduced by a man of high social status and whose life ends tragically, often in suicide or infanticide, when she is accused of not adhering to female virtue and bourgeois morality. The male protagonist in *Tonka* in the next-to-last episode sees himself confronted with the limitation of his scientific mind and with his domination over Tonka and femaleness in general: "there is a realm where she is grand, noble, and good, where she is not a little shopgirl, but his equal, deserving a great destiny." . . .

Significantly, from the beginning the narrator in the novella encapsulates Tonka's and his world with borders. Even the first sentence expresses in the image of the hedge a transition that the narrator uncovers in short, incomplete sentences from his innermost depth:

> At a hedge. A bird was singing. And then the sun was somewhere down behind the bushes. The bird stopped singing. It was evening, and the peasant girls were coming across the fields, singing. What little things! Is it petty if such little things cling to a person? Like burrs? That was Tonka. Infinity sometimes flows in droplets.

This description is not reality but the consciousness of the narrator, who sees Tonka as nature (sun, bird), silent and clinging femaleness in need of male protection. The farmgirls' singing in the fields suggests a parallel to Tonka, who, like Gretchen in *Faust,* expresses herself not in words but in songs that have the same simplicity as those sung by farmgirls in the fields. The young scientist strains to remember the first time he saw the poor salesgirl from a Czech bordertown where "inhabitants of those back streets talked a queer mixture of the two languages." In this flash of memory, Tonka first emerges in the vicinity of a border, "standing by a hedge that time, in front of the dark open doorway of a cottage." The dark open doorway may be understood as a foreshadowing of Tonka's role in the narrator's life—that of introducing him to the darker zones in life to which the scientific mind cannot apply proofs and logic. The singing and subsequent silence of the bird in the introductory scene ("A bird was singing. . . . The bird stopped singing") throws a first light on Tonka's silent nature and her closeness to flora and fauna. We do not hear the words of the Slavic songs she translates as we do with Gretchen's songs; instead we witness the narrator joining hands and singing child-like with Tonka because it "seemed to him that she was very lonely." Tonka's self-expression in song is untouched by any civilization process and accounts, in the narrator's view, for her being thought stupid and insensitive, because by the standards of a developed culture, language is the highest level of communication in the human realm. In memories of shared walks, Tonka's teaching him about the beauty of nature stands out. However, he can only momentarily join in her joy over a "long-stemmed flower" until immediate doubts and disgust over her naivety set in and he is made aware of his own broken relationship with nature: "If she had been trained to think like her companion, at that moment Tonka would have realized that Nature consists of nothing but ugly things one hardly notices and which live as sadly far apart from each other as the stars in the night-sky."

Antithetical references to Tonka's noticing "tiny blades" of moss and to the scientist's brutal statement "that Nature consists of nothing but ugly little things" highlight the paradox in the consciousness of the narrator, whose trained mind wants to dissect the harmony within nature while envying its unity. The same inner split is evident when the narrator fondly remembers their joint singing episodes during peaceful evenings, but dismisses them with the outburst, "and even if the whole thing was foolishness, the dusk itself was at one with their feelings." The scientist longs to experience the close union he once had with Tonka and with nature. In his memory processes, her presence unites his own intellect and feelings. However, as soon as he puts into words what she meant to him, he is confused. Any time he points to a positive quality in Tonka, he reverses it after a few moments and sees only a simple-minded country girl.

Only in the world of dreams does the scientist's imagination sustain Tonka's virtues for any length of time. He describes Tonka's nature and her genuine connectedness with nature in "brightcolored dreamrooms," in which she stands with an infinite smile. His love for her in the realm of dreams, however, continually clashes with a love that would not manifest itself in his "waking life," causing him to feel like a "victim of doppelgänger-trickery." He simply "could not bring himself to set the light behind Tonka." In the area of science, which one approaches with rational thought processes, the scientist is not bothered by improbabilities; there he works with self-confidence and assurance. However, in the social realm, he lacks all security. He does not dare to trust his feelings and react to Tonka's mysterious pregnancy with faith rather than severe doubt. Tonka lives in zones he usually prefers to close off: "The shadowy being, the unreal element in him, struggled for words, and the realization that everything

ought to be measured by quite different standards almost broke surface. But, like all understanding, even this was ambiguous and without certainty." His thoughts carry him into an unreal zone of shadows and his imagination sets images and memories in motion: A ray of light is cast on a "small suburban room" in which his mother appears as a negative vision with falsified letters on Tonka's unfaithfulness. . . .

The scientist in *Tonka* continually attempts to approach the "other condition," as he is trying to get in touch again with his imagination and his feelings through Tonka. It is striking how many images and references to the double or *Doppelgänger* are already contained in the novella from 1922. . . . The narrator/protagonist refers to his duality and multiplicity in perspective as the "world of windows," *"Doppelgänger-spiel."* In his mystical encounter with Tonka as his lover, he looks desperately for points of contact and possibilities of union with her. He longs "to discover the inner man," his own humanness. In his words, Tonka had become a "mission" to him. She encourages the narrator to bare his inner self, which stands vulnerable and unprotected in his memories and moments of self-mirroring.

Tonka, Grigia, and the Portuguese woman function undoubtedly as catalysts for illumination and as mirrors to the male protagonists' fragmented selves in the post-enlightenment world with its emphasis on scientific formulation. In Musil's unfinished novel *Der Mann ohne Eigenschaften* (*The Man without Qualities*), published in parts between 1930 and 1952, he develops the "other condition" more fully through the figure of the complementary double in the juxtaposition of the brother/sister relationship of Ulrich and Agathe, two complementary halves of the fragmented individual longing for the platonic whole. In *Tonka,* the reader initially encounters the scientist/narrator in a self-assured way in an empirically proven reality:

> He was in favor of doing away with the emotions. He was the antagonist of poetry, kindness, virtue, simplicity. Song birds need a branch to perch on, and the branch a tree, and the tree the dumb brown earth to grow in; but he flew, he was between the ages, he was somewhere in mid-air. . . . For the time being the thing was to be as tough and austere as on an expedition.

Only gradually is he able to get in touch with parts of his repressed half.

Ironically, the narrator uses poetic and metaphorical language as he paints an image of his encounter with Tonka, whom he portrays as the embodiment of everything that he is not and that he opposes. Tonka, the singing bird, needs a branch, while he is free to be suspended in the air. Yet this stage is soon made less secure, as we find out in the second part of the novella about Tonka's mysterious pregnancy. Tonka does not defend herself against his reproaches but remains devoted "like a dog." The narrator's self-mirroring is closely connected with his memories and images of Tonka. Even though she has limited ability to express her thoughts, she can express empathy and fully understand her lover's innermost thoughts. She shows a deep understanding for the tension-filled relationship of the scientist with his mother and his parental home in general. In many exhausting dreams the smile of his mother appears, full of pity and ridicule for him. Most likely the double standard and unfaithfulness of Musil's own mother in their home contribute to the narrator's constant vacillating between Tonka as angel and *femme fatale,* between dreaming of the "palace of goodness where they would live united and never part again," and cursing her as whore and fallen virgin. Toward the end of the novella, the scientist wavers between closeness and distance from Tonka, between exuberant presentation of Tonka in ecstatic images of nature and self-approaches that cause in him a pathological condition such that he has anxiety attacks and can't even close his own shirt buttons. Becoming superstitious, he hides behind a ring that is to bring him luck and a beard that is to provide him with a mask. He even plays with Tonka in the horse lottery. Logic no longer functions as an anchoring place in his private life, even though ironically he completes his studies at the time of Tonka's death.

Tonka's presence in song, dream, and fairy tale signifies the narrator's longing for a world beyond empirical studies and scientific inventions, for a paradisical state beyond good and evil: "Tonka was now living in the deep world of fairy-tale. It was the world of the Anointed, of the Virgin, and of Pontius Pilate." In these lines we have reminiscences of the apotheosis of the eternal feminine in *Faust,* whose male protagonist never questions the goodness and purity of Gretchen. The scientist of the twentieth century, however, even while surrounded by Tonka's presence in his flashbacks, cannot lose himself fully to the "other condition"; he remains linked to the earth and to his own career and success in the scientific world: "The world lay around him. He realized indeed, that he had been changed in some way and that in time he would be yet again man, but this was, after all, his own doing and not really any merit of Tonka's. . . . He stood in the light and she lay under the ground, but all in all what he felt was the cheer and comfort of the light." Yet the scientist could not bring himself to utter the thought 'I believe in you!' with conviction. He remained torn and doubtful until the end: "And even supposing everything were like that, who could be sure of it? He was still saying that when Tonka died." His clinging to the earth underscores that he had only caught a glimpse of the "other condition" but could not reach it completely. He was neither capable of giving himself over to unconditional love nor to an intense emotional life. Only in brief moments of his memory journey had he been able to melt together like a snowflake with Tonka's natural, wholesome, giving character and her silent intuition. However, he had come to understand the essence of Tonka's sensitivity and its impact on him: "From that time on much came to his mind that made him a little better than other people, because there was a small warm shadow that had fallen across his brilliant life."

Final references by the narrator to a "gleam when the travelling coat opened" and to "many children round about" indicate a forward motion to a utopia that would not deny a "brilliant life" and self-assertion to Tonka. Fleeting moments of epiphany have revealed to him the absence of the other from his love and from his world of reason and logic. His willingness to trust Tonka, and to relate to her in dialogic love as "Thou" instead of a reified, distant "It" came too late for her. In the end, the image of Tonka as an unseasonal, fragile snowflake that was forced to disappear and die silently next to the scientist's brilliant invention fades into the image of the "cheer and comfort of the light" that engulfs the narrator and his text.

The encounter with Tonka's aphasic liveliness in this memory narrative becomes a mystical encounter for the narrator and the reader in a technological, post-enlightenment age. Elisabeth Albertsen's study [*Ratio und 'Mystik' im Werk Robert Musils,* 1968] poignantly captures Tonka as a mystical paradox in an irreligious, science-oriented world that only knows mysticism without God. The doubting mind of the scientist distrusts anything that lacks scientific proof, yet he seeks a path to an inner, second reality that links the feminine with his intellectual vision. Because of his ambivalence, he must immediately destroy his images of ideal femaleness. The literary tradition of the Gretchen-figure with her attributes of the "eternal feminine" and her sacrificial role becomes subverted in the novella. In the face of rapid advances in science and technology, Musil reveals how difficult it is for the scientifically-minded male to understand and appreciate a woman's duality of being close to nature and her body and to the realm of the imagination and spirituality. In spite of Tonka's death in childbirth, the focus in the novella is not on female sacrificial death, particularly when seen in the context of the role of women in the trilogy. By limiting Tonka's life to "a sacrifice to the noble cause of his [the scientist's] genius," one overlooks the realm of the creative poet in the story. Significantly, in *Grigia,* the male protagonist with his symbolic name Homo ("Everyman") is left by his earth-bound female lover to die in the mining shaft. Also in the second novella, it is the male protagonist who briefly contemplates suicide or murder of his Portuguese wife's former lover. Perhaps Tonka and the other female characters in Musil's cycle *Three Women* point to a deconstruction of the masculine and feminine and to a diffusion of female "otherness." Musil's use of the *Doppelgänger* in *Tonka* suggests a search for a double, or the "second self," which does not instill fear but potentially dissolves the borderline between masculinity and femininity.

FURTHER READING

Biography

Erickson, Susan J. "Writer's Block: Robert Musil and the Mother." *Substance* 41 (1983): 79-90.

    A "psycho-biographical essay" focusing on the author's relationship with his mother. Erickson also discusses the autobiographical aspects of Musil's fiction.

Silone, Ignazio. "Encounters with Musil," trans. Reinhard Mayer and Raija Koli. *Salmagundi,* No. 61 (Fall 1983): 90-8.

> Silone, who was an acquaintance of Musil while he lived in Switzerland, describes his memories of the writer and disputes some accounts of Musil's last few years.

Criticism

Boa, Elizabeth J. "Austrian Ironies in Musil's 'Drei Frauen'." *The Modern Language Review* 63 (1968): 119-31.

> Examines Musil's ironic treatment of the searches for identity in the novellas comprising *Three Women.*

Erickson, Susan. "The Psychopoetics of Narrative in Robert Musil's 'Die Portugiesin'." *Monatshefte* 78, No. 2 (Summer 1986): 167-81.

> Discusses the depiction of consciousness and selfhood in *The Lady from Portugal.*

Genno, Charles N. "Observations of Love and Death in Musil." *Neophilologus* LXVII, No. 1 (January 1983): 118-25.

> Examines the interrelated themes of love and death as they appear throughout Musil's major works.

Gerulaitis, Renate. "Gretchen's Fickle Lovers." *Michigan Academician* XV, No. 3 (Spring 1983): 401-12.

> Compares the character Tonka from the novella of the same name to similar female characters in works by Johann Wolfgang von Goethe.

Kirchberger, Lida. "Musil's Trilogy: An Approach to 'Drei Frauen'." *Monatshefte* LV, No. 4 (April-May 1965): 167-82.

> Using ideas drawn from the work of Sigmund Freud, Kirchberger examines the relations between the sexes as a theme running through *Three Women.*

Langman, F. H., and Langman, E. A. "A Tale of Robert Musil's." *The Critical Review* 11 (1968): 91-100.

> Provides a "straightforward explication" of *The Temptation of Quiet Veronica* in an attempt to counter what these writers believe have been critical misreadings of the novella.

Luft, David S. *Robert Musil and the Crisis of European Culture 1880-1942.* Berkeley: University of California Press, 1980, 323 p.

> Analysis of Musil's works in their historical and ideological contexts. Luft also provides a bibliography which lists both the German and English editions of Musil's works, as well as books, dissertations, and articles about them.

Lungstrum, Janet. "Conceiving the Text: Nietzschean Inspiration in Musil's *Tonka.*" *The German Quarterly* 64, No. 4 (Fall 1991): 488-500.

> Examines *Tonka* in relation to the philosophical writings of Friedrich Nietzsche.

O'Connor, Kathleen. *Robert Musil and the Tradition of the German Novelle.* Riverside, Calif.: Ariadne Press, 1992, 181 p.

> Detailed study of Musil's narrative technique in his short fiction.

Paulson, Ronald M. "A Re-interpretation of Some of the Symbols in Robert Musil's *Die Portugiesin.*" *Modern Austrian Literature* 13, No. 2 (1980): 111-21.

> Discusses the religious symbolism in *The Lady from Portugal.*

Sokel, Walter H. "Kleist's Marquise of O., Kierkegaard's Abraham, and Musil's Tonka: Three Stages of the Absurd as the Touchstone of Faith." *Wisconsin Studies in Contemporary Literature* VIII, No. 4 (Fall 1967): 505-16.

> Discusses the conflict between faith and reason in the modern world as expressed in works by Heinrich Kleist, Søren Kierkegaard, and Musil.

Wilson, Catherine. "Morality and the Self in Robert Musil's *The Perfecting of a Love.*" *Philosophy and Literature* 8, No. 2 (October 1984): 222-35.

> Discusses questions regarding the "philosophical conceptions of action, judgment, and experience" raised by *The Perfecting of a Love.*

Additional coverage of Musil's life and career is contained in the following sources published by Gale Research: *Contemporary Authors,* Vol. 109; *Dictionary of Literary Biography,* Vols. 81, 124; and *Twentieth-Century Literary Criticism,* Vol. 12.

Gérard de Nerval
1808-1855

(Born Gérard Labrunie) French poet, short story writer, playwright, translator, novelist, essayist, and critic.

INTRODUCTION

Widely regarded as a precursor of the Symbolists and the Surrealists, Nerval was one of the first writers to explore the realm of the subconscious, suggesting that "the dream is a second life." Remembered for his vivid delineation of the illusory mental states such as dreams and hallucinations, and for the far-reaching influence of his artistic vision, Nerval presented images in his works that originated from such diverse sources as cabalism, mythology, religion, fantasy, and the occult. His themes were directed by several persistent personal obsessions, and his greatest creative energy resulted from the insanity that plagued him much of his life.

Biographical Information

Nerval was a small child when his mother died while assisting her husband, a surgeon in the Napoleonic army, on his tours of Germany. He was raised by a great-uncle in the Valois, the charming rural region of France that was to remain in his memory—and appear in *Sylvie* and other works—as an idyllic landscape of childhood perfection. During his schooling in Paris, he displayed precocious literary talent, publishing at age twenty a translation of Johann Wolfgang von Goethe's *Faust,* which the great poet himself acclaimed. His belletristic reputation thus established, Nerval became a member of the *Jeune-France,* a group of Romantic artists and writers who challenged the established classical school not only with radical artistic theories but with flamboyant dress and eccentric behavior. Nerval delighted his comrades one afternoon by parading through the Palais-Royal gardens with a lobster on a leash of blue ribbon. "He does not bark," Nerval declared, "and he knows the secrets of the deep." But Nerval's carefree Bohemian life became troubled as increasingly severe money problems and mental difficulties befell him. The fact that he had never known his mother haunted Nerval, making him susceptible, even as a boy, to profound infatuations with women, who are depicted in various guises throughout his writing as unattainable embodiments of ideal femininity. The most enduring of these unrequited passions was for an actress, Jenny Colon, whose aloofness and early death hastened the deterioration of Nerval's mental health. Soon after Jenny died, Nerval, always an avid traveler, embarked on a journey to the Orient. This trip excited his imagination with mystical and exotic motifs and provided material for *Voyage en Orient (Journey to the Orient).* Ironically, the madness which plagued Nerval heightened his artistic sensibility, and it was in his final, most painful years that he produced his greatest works: the fine, pure narratives and

enigmatic, expressive sonnets. Seemingly a victim of his own tormented vision, forty-six-year-old Nerval was found hanging from a railing in a dank Paris alley with the last pages of *Aurélia* in his pocket.

Major Works of Short Fiction

Nerval's short fiction was largely affected by the author's recurrent battles with insanity. "His works, far from suffering from his madness, seem to be enhanced by it, or even contingent upon it," commented H. Kay Moon. The author's prose pieces contain fantastic elements, the theme of the double, or doppelgänger, autobiographical elements, hallucinations, dreams, and humor. Nerval's mastery as an artist began with *Journey to the Orient,* a book of travel essays interjected with fictional elements. In 1854, a compilation of short stories and poetry titled *Les Filles de feu (Daughters of Fire)* was published, containing Nerval's lauded tale, *Sylvie.* In this story that merges dream with reality, the narrator, Gérard, struggles with his love for a mythic female personae, Aurélie-Adrienne, and a real woman Sylvie. In Gérard's mind, Aurélie and Adrienne are fantastic images of ideal women who eventually merge into one figure. His illusory search for the perfect love ruins his chances for a relationship with the real Sylvie. Kari Lokke summarized the message in *Sylvie*: "Paradoxically . . . the wistful, delicate beauty of *Sylvie*, Nerval's stylistic and tonal masterpiece, is created by Nerval's combination of this mythic and esthetic vision of the Valois and its women with the melancholy realization that such a sublimated mode of interaction leads away from the present and the love of a real human being to an ideal past or a utopian future." The author's last achievement, *Aurélia*, presents the world of dreams as another life. This story, inspired by unattainable love, features a narrator who, after falling into a hallucinatory state, begins to see his doppelgänger. The tale depicts the two different states of being in which the narrator and his double exist.

Critical Reception

Sylvie and *Aurélia*, written during periods of madness, are Nerval's most critically acclaimed prose pieces. His earlier short fiction did not receive much attention; according to Moon, they "merely represent Nerval's ability to follow the literary current of his time." Overall, critics have lauded the author's work for its visionary quality, which influenced many later writers. Charles Baudelaire and the Symbolists were inspired by his use of cryptic symbols and his fascination with hallucinatory states. The Surrealists celebrated Nerval as a spiritual ancestor, a courageous pioneer in the exploration of the subconscious. Also, Nerval's re-creation of scenes from memory and reverie evokes stream-of-consciousness and prefigures the work of Marcel Proust, who, in his *Marcel Proust on Art and Literature 1896-1919,* called Nerval "assuredly one of the three or four greatest writers of the nineteenth century."

PRINCIPAL WORKS

Short Fiction

Voyage en Orient [*Journey to the Orient*] 1851
Les Illuminés 1852
Les Filles du feu [*Daughters of Fire*] (novellas and poetry) 1854
Le Rêve et la Vie [*Dreams and Life*] (short stories and poetry) 1855; includes *Aurélia*
Sylvie: Recollections of Valois 1887
Œuvres Complètes. 10 vols. 1926-32
Aurélia [*Aurelia*] 1932
Selected Writings (short stories and poetry) 1957
Œuvres complémentaires 1959-
Œuvres 2 vols. 1960-61

Other Major Works

Faust [translator] (poetry) 1828
Léo Burckart (drama) 1839
Lorely: souvenirs d'Allemagne (travel essays) 1852
Les Chiméres [*The Chimeras*] (poetry) 1854; published in *Les Filles du feu*

CRITICISM

Arthur Symons (essay date 1898)

SOURCE: "The Problem of Gérard de Nerval," in *The Fortnightly Review,* Vol. LXII, No. CCCLXXIII, January, 1898, pp. 81-91.

[*Symons was a critic, poet, dramatist, short story writer, and editor who first gained notoriety in the 1890s as an English decadent. Eventually, he established himself as one of the most important critics of the modern era. In his book* The Symbolist Movement in Literature *(1899), Symons provided his English contemporaries with an appropriate vocabulary with which to define the aesthetic of symbolism; furthermore, he laid the foundation for much of modern poetic theory by discerning the importance of the symbol as a vehicle by which a "hitherto unknown reality was suddenly revealed." In the following excerpt, Symons discusses the effect of madness on Nerval's works, concluding that Nerval is "only inspired, only really wise, passionate, collected, only really master of himself, when he is insane."*]

It is not necessary to exaggerate the importance of the half-dozen volumes which make up the works of Gérard de Nerval. He was not a great writer: he had moments of greatness; and it is the particular quality of these moments which is of interest for us. There is the entertaining, but not more than entertaining *Voyage en Orient*; there is the estimable translation of *Faust,* and the admirable versions from Heine; there are the volumes of short stories and sketches, of which even *Les Illuminés,* in spite of the promise of its title, is little more than an agreeable compilation. But there remain three compositions: the sonnets, *Le Rêve et la Vie,* and *Sylvie*; of which *Sylvie* is the most objectively achieved, a wandering idyl, containing some folk-songs of Valois, two of which have been translated by Rossetti; *Le Rêve et la Vie* being the most intensely personal, a narrative of madness, unique as madness itself; and the sonnets, a kind of miracle, which may be held to have created something at least of the method of the later Symbolists. These three compositions, in which alone Gérard is his finest self, all belong to the periods when he was, in the eyes of the world, actually mad. The sonnets belong to two of these periods, *Le Rêve et la Vie* to the last, *Sylvie* was written in the short interval between the two attacks in the early part of 1853. We have thus the case of a writer, graceful and elegant when he is sane, but only inspired, only really wise, passionate, collected, only really master of himself, when he is insane. It may be worth looking at a few of the points which so suggestive a problem presents to us.

Gérard de Nerval lived the transfigured inner life of the dreamer. "I was very tired of life!" he says. And like so many dreamers, who have all the luminous darkness of the universe in their brains, he found his most precious and uninterrupted solitude in the crowded and more sordid streets of great cities. He who had loved the Queen of Sheba, and seen the seven Elohims dividing the world, could find nothing more tolerable in mortal conditions, when he was truly aware of them, than the company of the meanest of mankind, in whom poverty and vice, and the hard pressure of civilization, still leave some of the original vivacity of the human comedy. The real world seeming to be always so far from him, and a sort of terror of the gulfs holding him, in spite of himself, to its flying skirts, he found something at all events realisable, concrete, in these drinkers of Les Halles, these vagabonds of the Place du Carrousel, among whom he so often sought refuge. It was literally, in part, a refuge. During the day he could sleep, but night wakened him, and that restlessness which the night draws out in those who are really under lunar influences, set his feet wandering, if only in order that his mind might wander the less. The sun, as he mentions, never appears in dreams; but, with the approach of night, even the most solid and short-sighted of us becomes a little visionary.

Crains, dans le mur aveugle, un regard qui t'épie!

he writes in one of his great sonnets; and that fear of the invisible watchfulness of nature was never absent from him. It is one of the terrors of human existence that we may be led at once to seek and to shun solitude; unable to bear the mortal pressure of its embrace, unable to endure the nostalgia of its absence. "I think man's only happy when he forgets himself," says some one in the *Duchess of Malfy;* and, with Gérard, there was Adrienne to forget, and Jenny Colon the actress, and the Queen of Sheba. But to have drunk of the cup of dreams is to have drunk of the cup of eternal memory. The past, and, as it seemed to him, the future were continually with him; only the present fled continually from under his feet. It was only by the effort of this contact with people who lived, so sincerely, in the day, the minute, that he could find even a temporary foothold. It was something to hold back all the stars, and the darkness beyond them, and the interminable approach and disappearance of all the ages, if only for the space between tavern and tavern, where he could open his eyes on so frank an abandonment to the common drunkenness of most people in this world, here for once really living the symbolic intoxication of their ignorance.

Like so many dreamers of illimitable dreams, it was the fate of Gérard to incarnate his ideal in the person of an actress. The fatal transfiguration of the footlights, in which reality and the artificial change places with so fantastic a regularity, has drawn many moths into its flame, and will draw more, as long as men persist in demanding illusion of what is real, and reality in what is illusion. The Jenny Colons of the world are very simple, very real, if one will but refrain from assuming them to be a mystery. But it is the penalty of all imaginative lovers to create for themselves the veil which hides from them the features of the beloved. It is their privilege, for it is incomparably more entrancing to fancy oneself in love with Isis than to know that one is in love with Manon Lescaut. The picture of Gérard, after many hesitations, revealing to the astonished Jenny that she is the incarnation of another, the shadow of a dream, that she has been Adrienne and is

about to be the Queen of Sheba; her very human little cry of pure incomprehension, "Mais vous ne m'aimez pas!" and her prompt refuge in the arms of the "jeune premier ridé;" if it were not of the acutest pathos, would certainly be of the most quintessential comedy. For Gérard, so sharp an awakening was but like the passage from one state to another, across that little bridge of one step which lies between heaven and hell, to which he was so used in his dreams. It gave permanency to the trivial, crystallising it, in another than Stendhal's sense; and when death came, changing mere human memory into the terms of eternity, the darkness of the spiritual world was lit with a new star, which was henceforth the wandering, desolate guide of so many visions. The tragic figure of Aurélia, which comes and goes through all the labyrinths of dream, is now seen always "as if lit up by a lightning-flash, pale and dying, hurried away by dark horsemen."

The dream or doctrine of the reincarnation of souls, which has given so much consolation to so many questioners of eternity, was for Gérard (need we doubt?) a dream rather than a doctrine, but one of those dreams which are nearer to a man than his breath. "This vague and hopeless love," he writes in *Sylvie,* "inspired by an actress, which night by night took hold of me at the hour of the performance, leaving me only at the hour of sleep, had its germ in the recollection of Adrienne, flower of the night, unfolding under the pale rays of the moon, rosy and blonde phantom, gliding over the green grass, half bathed in white mist. . . . To love a nun under the form of an actress! . . . and if it were the very same! It is enough to drive one mad!" Yes, "il y a de quoi devenir fou," as Gérard had found; but there was also, in this intimate sense of the unity, perpetuity, and harmoniously recurring rhythm of nature, not a little of the inner substance of wisdom. It was a dream, perhaps refracted from some broken, illuminating angle, by which madness catches unseen light, that revealed to him the meaning of his own superstition, fatality, malady:—"During my sleep, I had a marvellous vision. It seemed to me that the goddess appeared before me, saying to me: 'I am the same as Mary, the same as thy mother, the same also whom, under all forms, thou hast always loved. At each of thine ordeals I have dropt yet one more of the masks with which I veil my countenance, and soon thou shalt see me as I am!'" And in perhaps his finest sonnet, the mysterious "Artémis," we have, under other symbols, and with the deliberate inconsequence of these sonnets, the comfort and despair of the same faith. . . .

Who has not often meditated, above all what artist, on the slightness, after all, of the link which holds our faculties together in that sober health of the brain which we call reason? Are there not moments when that link seems to be worn down to so fine a tenuity that the wing of a passing dream might suffice to snap it? The consciousness seems, as it were, to expand and contract at once, into something too wide for the universe, and too narrow for the thought of self to find room within it. Is it that the sense of identity is about to evaporate, annihilating all, or is it that a more profound identity, the identity of the whole sentient universe, has been at last realised? Leaving the concrete world on these brief voyages, the fear is, that we may not have strength to return, or that we may lose the way back. Every artist lives a double life, in which he is for the most part conscious of the illusions of the imagination. He is conscious also of the illusions of the nerves, which he shares with every man of imaginative mind. Nights of insomnia, days of anxious waiting, the sudden shock of an event, any one of these common disturbances may be enough to jangle the tuneless bells of one's nerves. The artist can distinguish these causes of certain of his moods from those other causes which come to him because he is an artist, and are properly concerned with that invention which is his own function. Yet is there not some danger that he may come to confuse one with the other, that he may "lose the thread" which conducts him through the intricacies of the inner world?

The supreme artist, certainly, is the furthest of all men from this danger; for he is the supreme intelligence. Like Dante, he can pass through hell unsigned. With him, imagination is vision; when he looks into the darkness, he sees. The vague dreamer, the insecure artist and the uncertain mystic at once, sees only shadows, not recognising their outlines. He is mastered by the images which have come at his call; he has not the power which chains them for his slaves. "The kingdom of Heaven suffers violence," and the dreamer who has gone tremblingly into the darkness is in peril at the hands of those very real phantoms who are the reflection of his fear.

The madness of Gérard de Nerval, whatever physiological reasons may be rightly given for its outbreak, subsidence, and return, I take to have been essentially due to the weakness and not the excess of his visionary quality, to the insufficiency of his imaginative energy, and to his lack of spiritual discipline. He was an unsystematic mystic; his "Tower of Babel in two hundred volumes," that medley of books of religion, science, astrology, history, travel, which he thought would have rejoiced the heart of Pico della Mirandola, of Meursius, or of Nicholas of Cusa, was truly, as he says, "enough to drive a wise man mad." "Why not also," he adds, "enough to make a madman wise?" But precisely because it was this "amas bizarre," this jumble of the perilous secrets in which wisdom is so often folly, and folly so often wisdom. He speaks vaguely of the Kabbala; the Kabbala would have been safety to him, as the Catholic Church would have been, or any other reasoned scheme of things. Wavering among intuitions, ignorances, half-truths, shadows of falsehood, now audacious, now hesitating, he was blown hither and thither by conflicting winds, a prey to the indefinite.

Le Rêve et la Vie, the last fragments of which were found in his pockets after his suicide, scrawled on scraps of paper, interrupted with Kabbalistic signs and "a demonstration of the Immaculate Conception by geometry," is a narrative of a madman's visions by the madman himself, yet showing, as Gautier says, "la raison froide assise au chevet de la fiévre chaude, l'hallucination s'analysant elle-même par un suprême effort philosophique." What is curious, yet after all natural, is that part of the narrative seems to be contemporaneous with what it describes, and

part subsequent to it; so that it is not as when De Quincey says to us, such or such was the opium-dream that I had on such a night; but as if the opium-dreamer had begun to write down his dream while he was yet within its coils. "The descent into hell," he calls it twice; yet does he not also write: "At times I imagined that my force and my activity were doubled; it seemed to me that I knew everything, understood everything; and imagination brought me infinite pleasures. Now that I have recovered what men call reason, must I not regret having lost them?" But he had not lost them; he was still in that state of double consciousness which he describes in one of his visions, when, seeing people dressed in white, "I was astonished," he says, "to see them all dressed in white; yet it seemed to me that this was an optical illusion." His cosmical visions are at times so magnificent that he seems to be creating myths; and it is with a worthy ingenuity that he plays the part he imagines to be assigned to him in his astral influences.

> First of all I imagined that the persons collected in the garden (of the madhouse) all had some influence on the stars, and that the one who always walked round and round in a circle regulated the course of the sun. An old man, who was brought there at certain hours of the day, and who made knots as he consulted his watch, seemed to me to be charged with the notation of the course of the hours. I attributed to myself an influence over the course of the moon, and I believed that this star had been struck by the thunderbolt of the Most High, which had traced on its face the imprint of the mask which I had observed.

> I attributed a mystical signification to the conver-sations of the warders and to those of my companions. It seemed to me that they were the representatives of all the races of the earth, and that we had undertaken between us to re-arrange the course of the stars, and to give a wider development to the system. An error, in my opinion, had crept into the general combination of numbers, and thence came all the ills of humanity. I believed also that the celestial spirits had taken human forms, and assisted at this general congress, seeming though they did to be concerned with but ordinary occupations. My own part seemed to me to be the re-establishment of universal harmony by Kabbalistic art, and I had to seek a solution by evoking the occult forces of various religions.

So far we have, no doubt, the confusions of madness, in which what may indeed be the symbol is taken for the thing itself. But now observe what follows:—

> I seemed to myself a hero living under the very eyes of the gods; everything in nature assumed new aspects, and secret voices came to me from the plants, the trees, animals, the meanest insects, to warn and to encourage me. The words of my companions had mysterious messages, the sense of which I alone understood; things without form and without life lent themselves to the designs of my mind; out of com-binations of stones, the figures of angles, crevices, or openings, the cut of leaves, out of colours, odours, and sounds, I saw unknown harmonies come forth. "How is it," I said to myself, "that I can possibly have lived so long outside

nature, without identifying myself with her? All things live, all things are in motion, all things correspond; the magnetic rays emanating from myself or others traverse without obstacle the infinite chain of created things: a transparent network covers the world, whose loose threads communicate more and more closely with the planets and the stars. Now a captive upon the earth, I hold converse with the starry choir, which is feelingly a part of my joys and sorrows."

To have thus realised that central secret of the mystics, from Pythagoras onwards, the secret which the Smaragdine Tablet of Hermes betrays in its "As things are below, so are they above"; which Boehme has classed in his teaching of "signatures", and Swedenborg has systematised in his doctrine of "correspondences"; does it matter very much that he arrived at it by way of the obscure and fatal initiation of madness? Truth, and especially that soul of truth which is poetry, may be reached by many roads; and a road is not necessarily misleading because it is dangerous or forbidden. Here is one who has gazed at light till it has blinded him; and for us all that is important is that he has seen something, not that his eyesight has been too weak to endure the pressure of light overflowing the world from beyond the world.

Alison Fairlie (essay date 1961)

SOURCE: "An Approach to Nerval," in *Studies in Modern French Literature*, 1961, pp. 87-103.

[*In the excerpt below, Fairlie examines themes, form, and tone in* Sylvie.]

Sylvie used to be read as a delightful country idyll. Reaction set in and it became 'le poème de la fin du monde', a 'bilan de la faillite'—'Sylvie s'achève en débâcle'. Here I disagree, and think that the undertones of the last chapter have been overlooked, and with them some of the use of themes and form throughout the story.

The outline is simple: the narrator had pursued in the actress Aurélie the reflection of the 'idéal sublime' once seen in the child Adrienne; not only had this reflection of the ideal proved illusory but in its pursuit he had let slip Sylvie, 'la douce réalité'. Summarized in this form, it sounds like an obvious temptation to various kinds of insufferable romanticization: it might either glorify the ideal as a metaphysical super-reality, or twist round to give an equally spurious glorification to the lost Sylvie, or finally exalt loss, anguish and hankering after the impossible as superior values in themselves. And the story is often presented as if Nerval were doing one or other or all of these. Quite the contrary. The obsession by Adrienne and Aurélie is worked out not in supernatural but in human terms, and every detail of background is made to suggest that it is as fallacious as it is gripping and lovely. The narrator is neither psychopath nor prophet; he analyses lucidly the conditions which cause sensitive minds in his generation to set woman on a pedestal and fear to approach her, since feelings have been distorted in the moulds both of inherited idealism and of inherited cyni-

cism. Then, though Adrienne deliberately suggests the archetypal figures of Queen and Saint, Aurélie the Enchantress and the Siren, and Sylvie the strange Fairy, yet the sense of dream and illusion that surrounds them is woven from the live details of an everyday world with its children's games and folk-songs, its plays in the convent or on the Paris stage. The hero is haunted by the idea that Aurélie strangely recalls Adrienne, but the echoes between them are called up in terms of the real world, by suggestive sense-impressions of the two kinds most evocative in Nerval: play of light and modulations of voice. Aurélie sings on the stage as Adrienne had in the garden or the convent play; the stage lighting casts a circle round her head as the moon in the garden or the halo in the mystery-play had done for Adrienne. And constantly the illusory nature of his worship is suggested. From the first sentence he mocks gently at his passion as he sits every night in the theatre 'en grande tenue de soupirant', among a thinly-scattered audience in frumpish clothes, watching his idol in a second-rate play. Adrienne is made mysterious by the half-light of sunset or moonrise, and wreathed in swirls of evening mist; in the convent play her halo is of gilded cardboard. Lucidly and consciously the dream is presented as lovely but a mere imagining: the narrator punctures it with 'Reprenons pied sur le réel', Aurélie with her pointed 'Vous cherchez un drame, voilà tout', and Sylvie, questioned as to any strange connection between Adrienne and Aurélie, with a burst of gay laughter at the very idea.

The pursuit of the ideal proved illusory, and because of it he has lost Sylvie. Here was the opportunity for the large-scale disillusion in romantic terms: Nerval has delicately avoided it. There is no psychological analysis, simply the tiny details of everyday life which the reader must juxtapose with the past: the Sylvie who had never heard of Rousseau now reads *La Nouvelle Héloïse* and sees the countryside in terms of Walter Scott; instead of sitting with her green cushion and lace-bobbins she works in a glove-factory; in her bedroom the old-fashioned 'trumeau' has given place to something more modern; instead of folk-songs she sings fashionable operas in sophisticated style. She had seemed the opposite of Aurélie, but she has followed the same pattern: Aurélie will marry the devoted and useful 'jeune premier ridé' and Sylvie too realizes that 'il faut songer au solide' so is engaged to the village baker. Yet he does not erect her into a lost ideal in her turn: when he reflects on what he might have had it is in the form: 'Là était le bonheur *peut-être, cependant . . .* '

Nerval has refused to inflate either dream or reality, or to confuse the two. His particular sense of irony is vital; an irony quite without bitterness. When the narrator comes back to beg Sylvie to save him from his obsessions, at the key point we have what might have been seen as the Interruption of Fate. But here it is no large-scale incident or dramatic lamentation: simply Sylvie's brother and the baker in a benevolent state of post-ball fuddledness blundering their wavering course through the undergrowth at daybreak, and without recriminations all go home together. When he returns to the scenes of his childhood, there is the dangerous opportunity for the obligatory romantic set-piece. But the two things which survive from the past are not the lofty emotions: they are the intellectual and the touchingly comic. Through the eighteenth-century characters who decked the countryside with their maxims now so out of date comes the realization that *'la soif de connaître* restera éternelle'. And childhood memories are evoked not through lofty symbols but from the odd bits and pieces dug up by the amateur archaeologist and most of all from a stuffed dog and an ancient parrot who 'me regarda de cet oeil rond, bordé d'une peau chargée de rides, qui fait penser au regard expérimenté des vieillards'. The theme of loss and persistence finds an individual dimension in that live comic glance of ancient and friendly irony.

Then there comes, in the last chapter, the very opposite of a 'bilan de la faillite'. As always, Nerval's method is not to analyse feeling or to sum up explicitly (though one sentence, with a graceful apology, brings home the value of experience, even with its bitterness). What he does is to take a series of tiny details, each of which is deliberately directed to calling up something almost unnoticed from earlier in the story, and through both details and tone to convey the rebirth of all that seemed lost, in a cycle of repetitive and satisfying pattern. It is some years later, and now, time after time, the narrator sets out from Paris for the old country inn, arriving in the evening. In his inn room he finds the 'trumeau au-dessus de la glace'. There is no statement but we must recognize it as that same old-fashioned object which had decked Sylvie's room in childhood and been banished as she grew sophisticated. The odd collection of 'bric-à-brac' recalls that in his own room at the beginning of the story, later given up. He wakes in the morning and sees round the inn window the same flowers that grew round Sylvie's in childhood; looks out over the same countryside with its memories of eighteenth-century thinkers and lovers. Every word contributes not to a sense of failure but to the joy and renewal of a fresh country morning: 'Après avoir rempli mes poumons de l'air si pur, je descends gaiement . . . ' His foster-brother greets him with the familiar nicknames of childhood. Sylvie's children play round the ruins of the castle, the 'tours de brique' recalling the background where he first saw Adrienne; they practise for the archery festival which had been part of his own memories at the beginning and was linked with druidical traditions from a further past. The cycle of repetitive pattern has caught up in the present all that seemed to have disappeared. He and Sylvie read together old tales now out of date. Again the tone mixes loveliness with gentle mockery: he and Sylvie are part of a permanent human experience but one that will not take itself melodramatically: 'Je l'appelle quelquefois Lolotte et elle me trouve un peu de ressemblance avec Werther, moins les pistolets, qui ne sont plus de mode.' Nostalgia and mockery have achieved a gentle reconciliation with the world as it is, and out of the elusive, the fallacious, the fragmentary or the lost, has come, as in the *Chimères*, the persistent ritual of human traditions.

Again form as well as theme deliberately evokes a play of opposites, a setting of the elusive and the chaotic against the patterned and the permanent. Memories apparently evoked at random are in fact grouped round a meticulous time-sequence and complex echoes of detail. There is a deliberate sense of inconsequentiality: events which would normally be prepared, stressed and led up to seem to flicker past almost unimportantly; then there come the sudden transformation scenes where we stand outside time and the characters become exemplars: a hushed circle listens to Adrienne singing and 'nous pensions être au Paradis'; or the boy and girl stand dressed up in the old wedding-clothes: 'Nous étions l'époux et l'épous pour tout un beau matin d'été.'

The whole story has of course created the palimpsest of the past beneath the present. To pick out the extraordinary tissue of allusions to different ages is to make it sound an artificial and strange amalgam: Herculaneum, the Queen of Trebizond, Apuleius, Dante, the neo-platonists and the druids, Virgil and Rousseau, the Tiburtine Sybil and the Song of Solomon, the Carolingian, Valois and Medici monarchs—but all are intimately and relevantly evoked by a fresh and real countryside and a personal experience. If the air of the story is given to the elusive and the fugitive, the accompaniment constantly and irresistibly suggests a timeless world where the present catches up the echoes of the past.

Sylvie obviously takes on a new richness when the reader knows Nerval's other works and Nerval's reading. The theme of the 'double' (here the foster-brother) has all kinds of undertones. Nerval has worked fascinating coincidences between themes suggested by works and authors as startlingly different as the *Pastor Fido* and Rétif de la Bretonne, the *Roman Comique,* the *Songe de Poliphile* and *Wilhelm Meister.* To recognize them is to be brought back once again to the coincidence of experience across the ages, the weaving of parallel patterns out of disparate elements.

There is one particular tone that I should suggest is distinctively nervalian in the world of *Sylvie.* What he has specially picked out from the past are those traditions that stand outside the accepted line of greatness. Sainte-Beuve and Baudelaire had talked of how all the 'great' subjects had already been monopolized, and how beauty must now be drawn from the prosaic, the horrible or the bizarre. Nerval quietly turns to more neglected material. The themes he takes up have stood outside the margin of the great tradition for two opposite reasons: some because they were too mannered and artificial, others for their naivety, simplicity and halting clumsiness. From the outmoded and the neglected Nerval brings a gentle mockery at whatever is odd or stiff or strange, and a sense of the permanent human value so particular in its loveliness and its oddity. So he consciously chooses the note of the Gessner pastoral, the ancient idyll, or the country-side of the pre-romantics with its elaborately natural parks and its deliberately constructed ruins, its sentimental moral maxims carved on temples and trees, its delightful conventionalizing of the ceremonies of antiquity in the stylized engravings of the *Voyage du Jeune Anacharsis,* and all its delicate formality: 'les traces fugitives d'une époque où le naturel était affecté.' And on the other hand the folk-songs attract him because they are limping and irregular, sung by young voices haltingly imitating the quavers of old age. Elsewhere he loves them because they are 'ces mélodies d'un style *suranné*', and even 'des airs anciens *d'un mauvais goût sublime*'.

Loveliness is evoked through the *suranné* and what is outside accepted taste, and is the more penetrating for that. Aurélie shines out from a second-rate play, in a dowdy theatre; Adrienne enchants as a mechanically propelled angel with a cardboard halo; Sylvie dressed up as a bride is all the more charming for the outmoded sleeves, the material yellowed with age, the faded ribbons and tinsel, the 'deux éventails de nacre un peu cassés', and the whole gentle air of the ridiculous of a Greuze village wedding. In the background of this scene stand the portraits of the old aunt and her husband, perhaps the most nervalian touch of all. No great paintings: the local artist has done his doubtful best in the charming and half-ridiculous conventions of his day, with their mixed stiffness and grace; but through this laborious and well-meant art, and the necessary pose with the obligatory bird on curved finger, there shines the personality of the gay mischievous girl, now a bent old woman, beside the self-consciously pink-and-white martial air of her husband the gamekeeper, and the two come alive again in the boy and girl who borrow their clothes, while the naive, halting country songs the old aunt remembers from her pompous village wedding seem to go back to the tradition of the Song of Solomon. From both the limpingly natural and the elaborately formalized Nerval weaves his sense of tenderness, irony and final persistence.

Nerval wrote of Goethe, 'Le génie n'aperçoit pas un chaos sans qu'il lui prenne envie d'en faire un monde.' The world he himself creates exercises a hallucinatory fascination as the reader moves further into the intertwining suggestions of age-long traditions, whether familiar or strange. The present article has deliberately concentrated on one or two simple points. The reader who has once been captured by Nerval will sooner or later find himself both deeply grateful for the recent research which has made possible the understanding of so many details, and impelled, deliberately or instinctively, to look further at the allusions that have not yet been elucidated.

The Nervalian moment has the strange characteristic of being at one and the same time unique, eternal, replacing all the others, and yet depending for what is its intensity and even its existence, on an identical past that it must conjure around itself to give itself signification and life.

—*Georges Poulet, in "Nerval," in* The Metamorphoses of the Circle, *1966.*

H. Kay Moon (essay date 1965)

SOURCE: "Gérard de Nerval: A Reappraisal," in *Brigham Young University Studies,* Vol. VII, No. 1, Autumn, 1965, pp. 40-52.

[*Here, American educator and critic Moon surveys Nerval's life, short fiction, and influence on later literature. Moon states that Nerval is "best when he is autobiographical."*]

Unfortunately, scholars have generally neglected or ignored Gérard de Nerval as a possible precursor to modern tendencies in literature. It will be my purpose in the pages that follow to (1) explore the elements of his biography that seem to contribute to an understanding of his development as a writer, (2) venture a few observations regarding his short prose fiction, and (3) suggest briefly the possible extent of his relevancy in the flood of literary trends since his time.

Seven months after his birth in May, 1808, Gérard de Nerval was left with a wet nurse in the village of Loisy, near Mortefontaine. Upon the death of his mother two years later, he was sent to live with a great-uncle in Mortefontaine. By the time his father returned some seven years later to take him to Paris and begin his studies, the Valois countryside had etched its indelible impression upon Gérard's sensitive nature. When school days were over, he invariably returned to Mortefontaine to his childhood friends, as he later returned to try to capture his childhood memories. A great many of the details of his life in Mortefontaine are found in his *Sylvie* and *Promenades et souvenirs*. There is no question that the region of Valois had a great effect upon his life and his subsequent works. Especially significant was Sylvie, who came from the neighboring hamlet of Loisy, and who provided him with a kind of pagan balance to the other elusive, mystic love whom he also came to "know" in the region of Valois, i.e. his Adrienne. He walked and played with Sylvie, and with her learned to know and love the countryside and its people. She was the principal object of his nostalgic reminiscence in the story that bears her name.

Adrienne, whom Gérard, accompanied by Sylvie, met at a village festival, was to become for him a Pandora and a Beatrice—at once his tormentor and savior. The few extant facts regarding this event would indicate that the person Gérard met and kissed in a dance in the above-mentioned festival was the worldly Sophie Dawes, who by marriage to Baron Adrien de Feuchères, could claim the far more glamorous title of Mme de Feuchéres. It is apparent that Gérard was either not aware of her true identity, or the ideal woman that he saw in this Adrienne could not be erased by ugly realities. His quixotic pursuit of this ideal love was to be the foremost quest of his life.

Another Valois influence on Gérard was his great-uncle's musty attic library, which was replete with books of theosophic and cabalistic deliberations. There were nondescript treatises on Buddhism, alchemy, magic and germane theosophies, neo-Platonic, Orphic and Pythagorean myths. Gérard would amuse himself for hours in the fantasy of this discarded library. His great-uncle's own pantheistic bent was also destined to affect him, though he was constantly in touch with Catholic dogma in Valois, largely through the efforts of one of his aunts. He was ultimately to represent in his own beliefs an admixture of pagan and Christian elements which led him on one occasion to claim adherence to seventeen different religions.

Gérard was also a more than passive reader of Jean Jacques Rousseau, who had spent his last years near Montefontaine. The fact that his most characteristic writing is, like Rousseau's, confessional suggests that he was spiritually drawn to the eighteenth century *philosophe*. But the importance of his Parisian life and education cannot be minimized. He owes his initial literary success to the knowledge of German which his father had been careful to impart to him in the earliest years of his instruction, for his translation of Goethe's *Faust* in 1827 was his first literary effort of rewarding merit. It betrays not only an adequate knowledge of German, but more important, an affinity for the Faust theme.

One of the most singular events in his life and works is his platonic love affair with Jenny Colon, an actress in whom Gérard saw the reembodiment of his ideal love, Adrienne. Ironically, Jenny was almost as worldly as Sophie Dawes, his Adrienne. Gérard's love for her was destined, from the moment it was conceived, to dominate the remainder of his life. He first saw Jenny Colon early in the year 1834, but it was several months later that he actually met her. It is doubtful that he ever possessed her, though he lavished gifts and money on her and founded *Le Monde dramatique,* an elegantly edited theatrical magazine, for the dual purpose of swelling her reputation and pleasing his father, who never approved of his son's literary penchant. But Gérard proved, like Balzac, to be a genius of financial disaster. Although some of the foremost names of the day contributed to its publications, *Le Monde dramatique* was destined shortly to pass into other hands, and finally into oblivion, for it soon became a mere altar upon which Gérard made anonymous adorations and sacrifices to Jenny until it had devoured the whole of the modest legacy he had received in 1835. It was at about that time, too, that he chose his pseudonym, Nerval, from a field (Clos be Nerval) near Mortefontaine, which belonged to his great-uncle's family. Jenny not only received limitless adoration and favors from him, but it was for her that he wrote the bulk of his unsuccessful plays. Ironically, his best play, *Leo Burckart,* was written after Jenny Colon had left him.

Gérard traveled frequently. He went often to Italy, and in fact traveled all over the European continent, and visited extensively Egypt and the Near East. He wrote many accounts of his travels, but most notable is his *Voyage en Orient,* which exposes his preoccupations with cabalistic and esoteric religions. The embroidery of his account lends it charm and interest. His letters to his unimaginative father describe the trail of reality in his itinerary. The trail of charming fancy is followed in *Voyage en Orient.*

The last decade, approximately, of Gérard's life was punctuated by periods of actual insanity and confinement. He had lived for many years in a twilight state in which the line of demarcation between dream and reality was to him very dim. It disappeared entirely at intervals, the first of which occurred on February 28, 1841, when he was confined to Dr. Emile Blanche's asylum. It is even believed that he suffered two such confinements that year. A series of reverses and further mental strain precipitated a relapse in the form of a sort of cataleptic fall and consequent chest injury in 1851. For this seizure he was sent for a brief period to Dr. Dubois' private asylum. He was once more interned there in the spring of 1853, but again only briefly. Between this confinement and the subsequent relapse of the following year, he wrote *Sylvie*. In 1854 he was committed again to the care of Dr. Emile Blanche, in whom he expressed complete trust. He was released for the last time in October of that year. Between periods of confinement his life was characterized by hallucinations and vagabond wanderings into the Parisian underworld, with which, by now, he was well acquainted. His subjective description of these wanderings, and some of the accompanying hallucinations, appear in *Les Nuits d'octobre*. In spite of his demented condition, this period was one of his more fruitful, and is unequivocally the most important. The uncompleted manuscript of his *Aurélia* left the asylum with him in his penultimate release. The final pages were found in his pocket following his death on January 26, 1855. He died, it is commonly conceded, by hanging himself with an apron string which he maintained at various times was the corset string of Madame de Maintenon or Marguerite de Valois, or, more often, the Queen of Sheba's garter.

II

Nerval's early prose works are by no means as significant as the final burst of literary activity in the last few years of his life. They mostly reflect the influence of his great-uncle's molding attic library. They represent a type of horror story then in vogue. His output was not very great. He is best when he is autobiographical. Even the stories in which he supposedly avoids his own preoccupations are fraught with overtones of the Adrienne love theme. For example, his *Jemmy,* which is a translation of an obscure story by the German author Charles Sealsfield, portrays the same scene found in *Sylvie* between Gérard and Adrienne. At a harvest festival, Jemmy and Toffel, surrounded by a group of young people, are obliged by custom to exchange kisses. The tone is idyllic—pastoral in essence. Its setting is in America, its theme is largely one of primitivism à la Chateaubriand. This and other stories merely represent Nerval's ability to follow the literary current of his time.

It is, of course, of greater pertinence to consider the more typical style of Nerval's *Sylvie* and *Aurélia*. The former is a conscious attempt to reconstruct his childhood through a work of art. It represents his primitivism, his reaction against the prevalent materialism, his own "recherche du temps perdu." It is autobiographical, written with a type of pre-Proustian flash-back technique. It is the key to his obsession for the ideal woman, whom he saw personified first in Adrienne, then in Jenny Colon, who was to him a kind of Pythagorean reincarnation of Adrienne. *Sylvie* reveals Gérard's concept of ideal womanhood, his Venus in three phrases. Jean Gaulmier explains it thus:

> Sylvie . . . nous donne aussi une image des Trois Vénus: dès le premier chapitre, l'actrice Jenny-Aurélia prend figure de déesse infernale aux feux de la rampe qui l'éclairait d'en bas et Gérard éprouve devant elle une terreur sacrée: Je craignais de troubler le miroir magique qui me renvoyait son image. Au chapitre II, Adrienne, reine du pays d'enfance, est la Vénus céleste, véritable vision paradisiaque. Enfin, la complexe Sylvie, après l'apparition d'Adrienne en sainte, Sylvie qui a perdu sa pureté primitive, qui fabrique des gants à la mécanique au lieu de son ancienne dentelle, qui chante l'opéra et a oublié les vieilles romances, Sylvie devient, elle aussi, une sorte de Vénus infernale.

> [Sylvie . . . also gives us an image of the three Venuses. From the first chapter, the actress Jenny-Aurélia assumes the form of an infernal goddess under the glare of the footlights which illuminated her from below and Gérard feels a sacred terror before her. "I feared to disturb the magic mirror that sent me her image." In the second chapter, Adrienne, queen of the land of childhood, is the celestial Venus, a true paradisiacal vision. Finally, the complex Sylvie, after the appearance of Adrienne as a saint, Sylvie, who has lost her primitive purity, who makes gloves with a machine instead of the lace-work of former years, who sings opera and has forgotten the old ballads, Sylvie too becomes a kind of infernal Venus.]

Gérard's fascination with time and memory is arresting.

Aurélia, his most important work, is, again, autobiographical, or more specifically confessional. It is Gérard's symbolic descent into hell, his personal *Divine Comedy.* He describes quite faithfully, if we can count on his own word, his hallucinations, his visions—his insanity. This work is the summation of his cabalistic, Pythagorean, pantheistic, and Christian tendencies. It is his portrayal of his mental strife. Unattainable love was the cause of his madness, and represents for him his salvation. His manias become apparent, allegedly at least, to the initiated in psychology. He was plagued with feelings of guilt for the outrages he had committed against his love for Aurélia (ideal woman), because he had indulged in "facile love affairs" [L. H. Sebilotte, *Le Secret de Gérard de Nerval,* 1948]. He had profaned her memory. He also felt pangs of guilt for his compromise of doctrine, though he never felt that he could embrace Christianity alone. His descent into hell teaches him the way to atone for these sins. He fancies that in these visions he is able to learn secrets withheld from him in his normal consciousness. He sometimes regrets his conscious state and awaits anxiously the time for his visionary sleep, but for the most part his visions are frightful trials to which he is subjected. It is, in Dantesque fashion, his Aurélia that represents to him his salvation when she appears and assures him:

> L'épreuve à laquelle tu étais soumis est venue à son terme; ces escaliers sans nombre que tu te fatiguais à descendre ou à gravir étaient les liens mêmes des anciennes illusions qu'embarrassaient ta pensée, et maintenant rappelle-toi le jour où tu as imploré la Vierge sainte et où, la croyant morte, le délire s'est emparé de ton esprit. Il fallait que ton voeu lui fût porté par une âme simple et dégagée des liens de la terre. Celle-là s'est rencontrée près de toi, et c'est pourquoi it m'est permis à moi-même de venir et de t'encourager.

> [The ordeal you have undergone is coming to an end; these countless stairways which wore you out so going up and down are the bonds of old illusions that impeded your thoughts; now remember the day when you implored the Holy Virgin and, thinking her dead, were possessed of a frenzy of the mind. Your vow must be carried to her by a simple soul, one free from the ties of the earth. She is near you and that is why I myself have been permitted to come and encourage you (Translation by Geoffrey Wagner).]

His *Aurélia* is not his only account of a descent into hell. There is another of a sort in *Les Nuits d'octobre,* in which he tells of his nocturnal wanderings and the progressively horrifying descent into the Parisian underworld. In fact, his guide at one point tells him, as Virgil to Dante, "Or sie forte ed ardito; omai si scende per si fatte scale" ["Be strong and bold; only through such steps does one descend here"].

As though anticipating that his reader might doubt the verisimilitude of his account, Gérard states in *Aurélia,*

> Si je ne pensais que la mission d'un écrivain est d'analyser sincèrement ce qu'il éprouve dans les grâces circonstances de la vie, et si je ne me proposais un but que je crois utile, je m'arrêterais ici, et je n'essayerais pas de décrire ce que j'éprouvai ensuite dans une série de visions insensées peut-être, ou vulgairement maladives. . . .

> [If I did not think that a writer's duty is to analyze with sincerity what he feels in grave moments of life, and if I had not in view to be useful, I would stop here, and make no attempt to describe my later experiences in a series of visions which were either insane or, vulgarly, diseased (Translation by Geoffrey Wagner.)]

This passage is illustrative of his very personal style. The tonal unity in this work, as in *Sylvie,* is impeccable. It is a tone of madness, analyzed with seemingly cold objectivity, which arouses a curious observation regarding Nerval's latest literary output, i.e., that his works, far from suffering from his madness, seem to be enhanced by it, or even contingent upon it.

"Le bon Gérard" was not capable of the consistently mordant satire of Merimée, but satire does appear in his works. Nothing in all his writings is more delightfully whimsical than his account of his relationship with his Mohammedan slave Zeynab (Z'n'b). What could have greater exotic appeal than this Malaysian with almond-shaped eyes, pearl-like teeth, long, burnished hair, tawny skin, and a regal air of distinction, and what could be more in keeping with a romantic bent? But on the other hand, what could be more useless? Their relationship was hardly exotic. She was quite ignorant, she could not cook or sew, and she could not learn French in order to interpret for him; but his moral reservations would not admit of placing her back on the slave market. She was little more than extra weight in his travel plans. But, he observed, "Her smile was delightful!" The satirical elements are typically good-natured, by no means bitter nor abusive, but even this would tend to contribute to the decline of Romanticism, because he is, after all, laughing at its exaggerated exoticism.

III

Defining the extent of an author's influence is at best an elusive task. Gérard de Nerval's role and importance are still being assessed. Guy Michaud, the latest authority on French Symbolism, points out that Nerval went well beyond his fellow *Romantiques* in establishing norms for passing from Romanticism to modern tendencies. Arthur Symons [in *The Symbolist Movement in Literature,* 1911] traces the origin of symbolist literature to Nerval, largely on the basis of the ideas and style apparent in *Aurélia*. Gérard's opening statement, "Le rêve est une seconde vie," simple as it is, supplies an initial basis for Symons' claim on him as the father of the symbolists' and surrealists' muse. Symons further maintains that Gerard's genius, " . . . to which madness had come as the liberating, the precipitating spirit, disengaging its finer essence, consisted in a power of materializing vision, whatever is most volatile and unseizable in vision, and without losing the sense of mystery, or that quality which gives its charm to the intangible." Certainly, Gérard represents a change in libido, a shift from the visible to the invisible, or more specifically, from the material to the spiritual, which is in essence the basis of Symbolism. [In *Gérard de Nerval, Poet, Traveler, Dreamer,* 1951] S. A. Rhodes, whether accurate or not in his evaluation, is certain that Baudelaire felt his influence, and through him " . . . the long lineage of symbolist, post symbolist, and surrealist poets, all of whom experienced what Jean Cocteau has described as the 'incalculable . . . repercussion . . . of a Nerval. . . '."

The duality theme in *Aurélia* is identical to the symbolic duality of Hakim-Biamr-Allah and Yousouf, who appear in a tale in *Voyage en Orient*. In this tale, Yousouf, who is Hakim's double, strikes the first blow that fells Hakim, just as Gérard's double, who in one of his visions is his mortal enemy, prepares to strike him. This "double" of Gérard's is undoubtedly the phase of his personality responsible for his own death, which is symbolically prefigured in the tale of Hakim and Yousouf. Gérard and his spiritual twin die together, just as Hakim and Yousouf, one inflicting the death blow upon the other. This is the epitome of Nerval's power to "materialize vision."

Marcel Schwob, whom no less an authority than Pierre Champion places squarely in the mainstream of Symbol-ism, offers affinities for Nerval which tend to substantiate Symons' postulation regarding Nerval's contribution to the development of Symbolism. Schwob no doubt heard his father speak of Nerval, for the elder Schwob had been associated with him and Charles Baudelaire in the printing of a literary review, the *Corsaire Satan.* While still a teen-ager, Schwob wrote an erotic version of *Faust,* and about two years later another work, "Les vierges du feu," which bears notable resemblance to *Les Filles du feu* by Nerval. Also, Schwob gave the title *Les Faux-Saulniers* to one of his *contes,* after Nerval's *Faux-Saulniers, Histoire de l'abbé de Bucquoy,* his sentimental journey through the countryside of his childhood. While still in his youth, Schwob composed a "Ballade pour Gérard de Nerval pendu à la fenêtre d'un bouge." Recently, in 1959, John A. Green has brought to light an article written my Schwob with the title "La chanson populaire," the essential theme of which he shows to derive from Nerval's statement in "Chansons et légendes populaires de Valois" that the old "Chansons populaires" represent "la memoire et la vie des bonnes gens du temps passé;" therefore, continues Nerval, "il serait à desirer que de bons poètes modernes missent à profit l'inspi-ration naïve de nos peres, et nous rendissent . . . une foule de petits chefs-d'oeuvre qui se perdent." [" . . . the memory and life of good folk of yesteryear; . . . it would be desirable if good modern poets were to profit by the simple inspiration of our fore-fathers and return to us a wealth of little masterpieces which are disappearing."] Moreover, it is apparent that this admiration for Nerval follows Schwob even in his mature years. According to his dossier at the Archives Nationales, on December 12, 1894 (nine years before his death), he requested fifteenth-century documents formerly communicated to Nerval, probably for no greater purpose than to review material in which Nerval had shown a lively interest. He had learned from Nerval's comments regarding the documents that they contained an autobiography of Angélique de Longueval, about whom Nerval wrote in *Les Filles du feu.* Schwob seemed bent on utilizing the same material to compose a play, perhaps in an attempt to surpass his master, but death overtook him before the project could be completed.

A close relative of Symbolism is its descendant Surrealism. [As defined in *Dictionary of World Literature*] "Surrealism aims to transcend the accepted limitation of reality, to bring into literature material hitherto unused, the dream and the automatic association, and to synthesize the experiences of the conscious and unconscious minds." Its basic idea is derived " . . . from a combination of dadaism with Freud: the automatic, illogical, uncontrolled fantasies and associations of the mind represent a higher reality than the realistic . . . world" [cited in *Reader's Companion to World Literature,* 1956]. This, certainly, defines the basic approach in *Aurélia.* It is thus that André Breton, author of the surrealist manifesto, is able to declare, "It seems indeed that Nerval possessed exactly the spirit we claim kinship with." On the other hand, though Gérard sometimes preferred his dream world to the world of reality, he rarely failed to recognize the difference between them. C. G. Jung states the case [in *Psychological Types,* 1933] for many of the surrealists: "Intellect remains imprisoned within itself so long as it does not voluntarily sacrifice its supremacy, and admit the value of other claims. It shrinks from taking a step beyond itself, and will not allow that it does not possess universal validity, for everything outside its own view is nothing but phantasy." Gérard was always willing to "admit the value of other claims." For the surrealists, the insane world is a mere prolongation of experience in the sane. The subtitle of *Aurélia* is *Le Rêve et la vie,* not *ou* la vie, and Gérard opens the narrative with "Le rêve est une seconde vie," *another* life, not a prolongation of the conscious world. Hence the difference between him and his spiritual twin, his double. Though the general spirit and tone of his writing is very closely akin to Surrealism, there is that basic difference.

Another unexplored possibility as regards Nerval's range of influence is Latin America. Following the belated Romantic movement in that area, which was obviously on the decline in 1870, the writers of that generation demanded, for the most part, a more subdued treatment of verse than had been practiced by the followers of Byron and Hugo. The Modernist movement in Latin America captures and characterizes much of the spirit of Nerval's writing, particularly the nostalgic reverie and the accompanying disdain of materialism evident in *Sylvie*. The following might have been part of their manifesto:

> Nous vivions alors dans une époque étrange . . . L'homme matériel aspirait au bouquet de roses qui devait le régénérer par les mains de la belle Isis; la déesse éternellement jeune et pure nous apparaîssait dans les nuits, et nous faisait honte de nos heures de jours perdus. L'ambition n'était cependant pas de notre âge, et l'avide curée qui se faisait alors des positions et des honneurs nous éloignait des spheres d'activité possibles. Il ne nous restait pour asile que cette tour d'ivoire des poètes, où nous montions toujours plus haut pour isoler de la foule. A ces points élevés où nous guidaient nos maîtres, nous respirons enfin l'air pur des solitudes, nous buvions l'oubli dans la coupe d'or des légendes, nous étions ivres de poésie et d'amour. Amour, hélas! des formes vagues, des teintes roses et bleues, de fantômes métaphysiques!

> [We were then living in a strange period. . . . Material man longed for the bouquet of roses which would regenerate him from the hands of the divine Isis; the goddess in her eternal youth and purity appeared to us by night and made us ashamed of our wasted days. We had not reached the age of ambition, and the greedy scramble for honors and positions caused us to stay away from all possible spheres of activity. The only refuge left to us was the poet's ivory tower, which we climbed, ever higher, to isolate ourselves from the mob. Led by our masters to those high places we breathed at last the pure air of solitude, we drank oblivion in the legendary golden cup, and we got drunk on poetry and love. Love, however, of vague forms, of blue and rosy hues, of metaphysical phantoms! (Translation by Geoffrey Wagner).]

This finds an echo in Darìo's own statement [quoted in *An Anthology of Spanish American Literature*, 1946], "Yo detesto la vida y el tiempo en que me tocó nacer" ["I detest the life and the time in which it was my lot to be born"]. Compare the above quotation from *Sylvie* with the following definition of Modernism [from G. Dundas-Craig, *The Modernist Trend in Spanish American Poetry* 1934]: "Modernism may be described as the literary expression of that mood of unrest and of dissatisfaction with the prevailing worship of material success that marked the last few years of the nineteenth century. The young idealist of those days felt himself thrown by fate into an environment to which he did not belong. He had a soul above the sordid aims of his fellowmen, and his art and his ideals were things beyond their comprehension."

The term "ivory tower," for which Gérard more than perhaps anyone else was responsible, was adopted by the Modernists. Their inspiration was admittedly French, their champion Rubén Darìo an avid reader of all the nineteenth-century masters. Their disdain of the materialistic led them, like Nerval, to explore new doctrines, desire new experiences, discover new truths. Julián del Casal was attracted by Japanese verse patterns and philosophy, Amado Nervo was a student of Buddhism, and James Freyre ardently studied Scandinavian mythology and philosophy, and particularly the works of Emmanuel Swendenborg, likewise a favorite of Nerval's.

It is difficult to assess the extent of Gérard's influence, through his preoccupation with time and memory, on Marcel Proust. It is known that Proust read him extensively and regarded him highly, but did Nerval make any contribution to his literary output? Perhaps Proust would have written just as much, just as well, and perhaps he would have said it just the same way if Nerval had never existed. But the style of *Sylvie,* the nostalgic search for his lost childhood, and his idea of involuntary memory in *Aurélia* suggests that Proust built his novels on the foundation laid by Nerval. Jacques de Lacretelle recalls one of his last visits to Proust, when the latter spoke of Nerval and quoted some of his poetry. As Lacretelle departed, he tells us, " . . . il me parut que Nerval et lui s'étaient unis pour me donner la clef de son oeuvre" [" . . . it seemed to me that Nerval and he had united to give me the key to his work"]. Proust himself, in an unpublished notebook in the possession of Madame Mante-Proust, acknowledges, however indirectly, " . . . a more than normally ardent friendship . . . a shared taste." The following passage from *Sylvie* suggests, at the least, a "shared taste":

> Je regagnai mon lit et je ne pus y trouver le repos. Plongé dans une demisomnolence, toute ma jeunesse repassait en mes souvenirs. Cet état, où l'esprit résiste encore aux bizarres combinaisons du songe, permet souvent de voir se presser en quelques minutes les tableaux les plus saillants d'une longue période de la vie.

> [I went to bed but could not rest. Lost in a kind of half-sleep, all my youth passed through my memory again. This state, when the spirit still resists the strange combinations of dreams, often allows us to compress into a few moments the most salient pictures of a long period of life (Translation by Geoffrey Wagner).]

What, finally, is Nerval's bearing, if any, upon the twentieth century? This is, of course, impossible to determine definitively. He is not widely read; it is not the direct influence of his works that constitutes his present significance. The "mal du siècle" of which he was a victim is still extant. The disdain of materialism which characterized his generation still exists. This feeling, persisting in the guise of existentialist nausea, is not his doing, nor is he the first to introduce the relativity of truth. But in this area, his ideas are still relevant, even though they are only the echo of ideas already expressed in previous ages. "What may I believe?" was Gérard's constant query. He felt a kinship with a certain Mohammedan cult which, aside from its Pythagorean foundation that always attracted Gérard, held truth and error to be equally deceptive. "God knows, we do not!" was their cry. This spirit permeates Gérard's works and echoes in the minds of those, like André Gide, who find it impossible to stipulate definitively the difference between truth and error, and those who in far greater extremity, like van Gogh or Hölderlin, belong with Gérard de Nerval to the group of "great abnormals."

Bettina L. Knapp (essay date 1980)

SOURCE: "Isis: The Cult of the Madonna," in *Gérard de Nerval: The Mystic's Dilemma*, The University of Alabama Press, 1980, pp. 226-36.

[*In the following excerpt, American educator and author Knapp explores the religious aspects of* Isis *and the role of the female in the work.*]

Nerval's narrative *Isis* (1845) is an expression of his syncretistic approach to religion and, in particular, an example of the immense role played by the feminine principle in his cosmology.

Isis takes place in Herculaneum and Pompeii, cities destroyed by the eruption of Mt. Vesuvius A.D. 79. It is night. The moon shines brilliantly and the illusion of the past grandeur of these cities is complete. Nerval tells us that an ambassador in Naples had given a costume ball a few years earlier and in so doing had revived all the ancient Roman customs for the festivities: the dance, the chariot races, the temples with their vestal virgins, the stores and merchants with their wares. This "palingensian attempt," wrote Nerval, was interesting, but the most fascinating ceremony of them all took place at sundown in the "admirable" temple to Isis.

The physical features of this house of worship are then described: the two altars in the temple, the statues of Isis, and the two vases containing holy water on either side of the entrance, which he compares with the fonts in Catholic churches. Nerval then outlines the rituals involved in the secret cult of Isis while underscoring the similarities existing between the Egyptian and Christian rites. The high priest, together with his deacons, recite special prayers and litanies, burn incense on the altar while flutes play softly in the background; sistrums are sounded by the

devout and the life story of Isis is enacted before the congregation in pantomime or in symbolic dances. The most awe-inspiring part of the entire ceremony, according to Nerval, took place when the high priest, with his deacons standing on either side of him, covered his hands with the fine linen of his robe and elevated the holy water, which contained the living presence of Osiris, before the worshippers. The devout then raised their hands heavenward and expressed "the miracle of divine mercy" and cried out: "We have found it and we—all of us—are joyous!"

Nerval then focuses his attention upon Lucius Apuleius and his initiation into the Isis mysteries, as recorded in *The Golden Ass*. Nerval underscores the affinities existing between the ancient Egyptian Isis cult of the Madonna and the worship of the Virgin Mary in the Christian religion.

For Nerval, Isis was a positive manifestation of the Great Mother archetype. He viewed her as he did the Virgin Mary, as a figure with outstretched arms, always ready to comfort and hold him in her embrace. Nerval pointed out many similarities between Isis and the Virgin Mary. Not only are there "a thousand analogous details in the ceremonies" involved in their worship, but in the many concrete depictions of them. Both Isis and the Virgin Mary held their child-god in their arms; both held a cross, gave milk, were born under the same sign of the zodiac, were featured with a moon placed either below their thrones or in the background, wore a glowing nimbus around their head. Isis was a *mediatrix* between man and the divine; Mary, between the sinner and God. And, Nerval adds, "the adoration by man of a Celestial Mother whose child is the hope of the world is not only understandable, it is a necessity."

The worship of the eternal feminine (the Great Mother, Mother Nature or the Madonna) dates back not only to Egyptian mystery cults but to the very dawn of history. In China and Japan, for example, the mother goddess Kuan-yin was most frequently depicted with her child in her arms or lap and she was considered a savior and a symbol of mercy and gentleness. In India, Sakti or Kali Durga, the Great Mother was equally beneficial in her relationships with men. In the ancient world, along the Tigris, Euphrates, and Nile rivers and in Asia Minor, she was worshipped under many names: Ishtar, Isis, Atargatis, Rhea, Cybele, Artemis, among others. During the last years of paganism there was an attempt to unify worship throughout the ancient world. Isis became this composite figure known as "The Divine Mother, The Blessed Queen of Heaven." The cult of the Virgin Mary was a continuation of this tradition.

Nerval lists the various names under which Isis was worshipped in antiquity: Venus, Ceres, Persephone.

CELESTIAL VENUS: (Aphrodite): In this manifestation she acted through her son Eros (Cupid), enabling all of mankind to unite, to come together. Eros, the god of relatedness, enacted his mother's wishes.

TERRESTRIAL CERES: (Demeter): The corn goddess, the origin and source of all that grows on earth. When her daughter Persephone was taken from her, she became barren. She was productive only during the six months of the year when her daughter was returned to her: summer-winter.

INFERNAL PERSEPHONE: (Hecate): Ruler of the dead, of the ghosts. She watched over the living as well.

Together, these three goddesses, as embodied in Isis, represent a totality. The three have their psychological equivalents. Venus, for example, represents man's need to unite, to relate to others, to strive for spiritual values. Ceres stands for his earthly aspects, his desire to reproduce, his conscious and daily activities. Persephone symbolizes man's unconscious, that tremulous realm where fears, rancor, as well as secret positive forces rumble.

During the early centuries of Christianity, when the ancient world was declining and new ways were taking hold, a struggle between matriarchal and patriarchal traditions was widespread. Isis worship was a powerful force at this time. As the bearer of a divine child under mysterious circumstances, as a wife who bore her husband's death with strength and who brought about his renewal in her son—all possibilities and mysteries lived within her. Because she remained one of the most important factors in Egyptian religion, she posed a severe threat to early Christians and repeated attempts were made by them (following Hebrew tradition), to wipe out the Madonna cult. St. Paul, the harbinger of patriarchal Christianity, did his best to unseat matriarchal worship as witnessed by his attitude toward Diana. We read in Acts:

Demetrius, a silversmith, which made silver shrines for Diana, brought no small gain unto craftsman . . . (19:24) . . . but almost throughout all Asia, this Paul hath persuaded and turned away much people, saying that they be no gods, which are made with hands (19:26).

So that not only this our craft is in danger to be set at nought; but also that the temple of the great goddess Diana should be despised, and her magnificence should be destroyed, whom all Asia and the world worshippeth (19:27).

And when they heard these sayings, they were full of wrath and cried out, saying, Great is Diana of the Ephesians (19:28).

As a result of the suppression of matriarchal deities, certain strange Christian sects developed during the early Christian centuries. The Collyridians, in the fifth century, worshipped the Virgin Mary in the same manner as the ancient Egyptians and Greeks had adored Isis and Diana. The orthodox Epiphanius halted such rites and declared: "Let Mary be held in honour, and let the Father and the Son and the Holy Ghost be adored, but let no one adore Mary" [according to C. G. Jung, in *Psychology and Religion,* 1963].

At Ephesus, the center of the Artemis-Diana Madonna cult, a council of Christian bishops gave Mary the title of "Theotokos," "Mother of God," an appellation that took on the power of dogma. It was "she who gave birth to God," who became the "vessel that was found worthy to contain Him whom heaven and earth cannot contain because of the vastness of His glory." The Virgin Mary became the transmitter of the divine "mystery."

In early Christianity the cult of the Virgin, therefore, had not yet been strongly integrated into church doctrine. The miracles of the Virgin in the Middle Ages and in later history (Lourdes and Fatima, for example) were individual expressions of an immense need among the people. In the western church, the ancient cult of the Virgin was "replaced by the institution of the Church" [States Marie-Louise von Franz in *The Golden Ass of Apuleis,* 1970]. Priests remained celibate, monks were tonsured, just as Isis worshippers had also always remained chaste. All these deprivations were signs of an inner sacrifice. The union between the physical priest and the spiritual female principle in Roman Catholicism is represented by the celebration of the first Mass read by the priest. This is his most solemn moment. The priest is the bridegroom who is marrying the church (Mary) and is giving up the human woman for complete union with her spiritual manifestation. He is in effect becoming the "bride of God" and the "bride of Christ" and in this sense, he "is feminine." The extreme need Christians felt for the female principle became manifest in the twentieth century with the proclamation of the Assumption of the Virgin Mary as dogma. Her Assumption was a "prototype of man's bodily resurrection. As Bride of God and Queen of Heaven . . . " [Jung].

For Nerval, Isis and the Virgin Mary filled an aching void in his heart and soul.

While describing Lucius' deep immersion in the Isis mysteries, Nerval was in effect projecting his own inner contents onto Isis. She became for him a composite figure: the Egyptian goddess Isis and the hyperdulian Virgin Mary.

> **Like Lucius, Nerval could not adapt to his times. He suffered intensely because of an inability to relate to or understand women. He had never been given the kind of maternal love so necessary to a child during his early years.**
>
> *—Bettina L. Knapp*

Lucius was born in North Africa (A.D. 155), studied in Carthage and Athens, and spent several years traveling and learning the mysteries implicit in a variety of occult arts. In his novel *The Golden Ass* he relates the tale of his transformation from man to donkey. Because he had attempted to learn certain secrets in the art of magic from a slave girl, with whom he was having a love affair, he had violated certain religious laws. He was punished for his transgressions by Isis, who felt he was unprepared to comprehend fully the occult arts whose secrets he had not merited but had tried to win through deceit. The rest of the volume deals with Lucius' adventures as an ass, the suffering and humiliations he endured, his final initiation into the Isis mysteries, his transformation back to man, and his departure for Rome, where he became an eminent lawyer—always working, thereafter, in complete harmony with his deity, Isis.

Why should Lucius have been drawn to Isis worship and not to Mithraism or Christianity? In a growing patriarchal society, Lucius, who suffered from a mother complex, could not relate to the prevailing form of worship. He needed a *mediatrix* who would help him express his feelings and give him the experience necessary to handle people and situations. Only through the positive aspects of the Great Mother, the bearer of the feeling principle, could he come to know and experience a sense of belonging. Once such feelings of warmth could be enjoyed, he would be able to go one step further and know redemption which, in psychological terms, means fulfillment.

Nerval suffered from similar problems. Like Lucius, he could not adapt to his times. He suffered intensely because of an inability to relate to or understand women. He had never been given the kind of maternal love so necessary to a child during his early years. Whenever he did fall in love, therefore, he divinized, adulated and worshipped the object of his projections. Because of this naïve view of women, he neglected to take into consideration their negative side and, as such, not only became vulnerable but was the recipient of their destructive aspects. The more powerful his hurt after loving such women as Jenny Colon and Marie Pleyel, the more isolated he felt and the greater was his despair. The agony of life became almost unbearable. As a way of release, he began fantasizing about women. Rather than worshipping living beings, as he had done in the past, he resorted to spiritualized women, divinities: Isis, the Virgin Mary, or some celestial force—a star. In so doing, he felt safe. He could not be rejected. He would never experience alienation. But he was withdrawing from life, slowly withering away.

The fact that Isis first appeared to Lucius in a dream is significant in our study of Nerval. Real life at this juncture in Nerval's earthly sojourn was experienced only on an unconscious level. Everyday existence was peripheral. His dream world had become the most intense and exciting part of his experience. Nerval does not merely translate Lucius' description of Isis in his narrative; he paraphrases it, incorporating his own subjective feelings in the picture.

> Her long thick hair fell in tapering ringlets on her divine neck, and was crowned with an intricate chaplet in which was woven every kind of flower. Just above

her brow shown a "silvery moon"; vipers rising on either side of the blond partings of her hair. Her robe, with its myriad reflections, changing with the folds, from the purest white to saffron-colored yellow, from which its flame red seems to be borrowed; her mantle, deep black, is bordered with a luminous fringe; her right hand holds the bronze sistrum, which sings out clearly; in her left hand, is the golden vase in the form of a gondola.

Isis is associated with the "silvery moon." Let us recall that moon worship was the product of a matriarchal society that antedated patriarchal sun worship in Egypt. Since the moon reflects color, it symbolizes the unconscious, as opposed to the sun, which is linked to thinking or consciousness. Because the moon at its fullest has the greatest power over all things (vegetative, animal, mineral) it is believed to govern life and death. Likewise, the moon, as incorporated in the Isis deity in the above description, may be said to have ruled over the psyches of both Apuleius and Nerval.

When Nerval writes, "Just above her brow shown a silvery moon," this image recalls Plato's third eye: it paves the way for inner vision. The "silvery" part of the moon image takes on the value of a mirror; it shines, reflects, and projects whatever comes into its range. When looking at the "silvery moon" one sees oneself as an object outside of oneself or in projection. Accustomed to a subjective evaluation of oneself, one is frequently unable to recognize or accept such an image. Confrontation with this other self is meaningful. It forces another attitude into focus, engendering new insights, as does the dream, that unconscious depiction of conscious events. Through the "silvery moon" Lucius (and hopefully Nerval) first understands his need for Isis. Only she can replenish what had been drained, fecundate what had been stunted: his capacity to express his feelings openly, to relate to others.

The crown of multiformed and multityped flowers on her "divine neck" not only stands for the goddess's beauty, freshness, and fertility, but injects the notion of spring, seasonal change and, therefore, of death and rebirth—the transitory nature of creation. It is interesting to note that Egyptians frequently brought all types of flowers to their feasts to underscore the reality of death and to encourage people to enjoy life. Flowers had always been associated with Greek and Roman goddesses, and the celestial flower with the Virgin Mary. Because of their shape, flowers have come to symbolize the world and its center. As such, they are considered archetypes of the soul. Such an act expressed an unconscious desire to penetrate the very heart of creation, the dawn of their own beings. Psychologically, it expressed a desire and need to return to their past, to experience a rebirth on a higher level—the goal of all initiations and mystery cults.

The vipers "rising on either side of the blond partings of her hair" also indicate an intense need for transformation. Vipers, snakes, and serpents stand for a most primitive strata within the unconscious and are associated with energy. They are catalyzing forces. Didn't the snake inspire

Eve to pick the forbidden fruit from the Tree of Knowledge, thereby disobeying God and disrupting the smooth-running patriarchal order? In *The Book of the Dead* (XVII) the reptile was the first living creature to believe in the sun god Ra and to greet him as he emerged from the waters. Because the snake sheds its skin, it represents the eternal force of renewal, regeneration, and resurrection. Since the snake is strong, and fights fearlessly, it is given the tasks, in myths and legends, of guarding springs, caves, and hidden treasures. The psychological implications of snake symbolism are vast. If not properly understood or handled, the snake (as energy) may become destructive, shedding evil and poison, as in the Perseus-Medusa tale. But if the "snake" energy is properly channeled and accepted as part of life's active process existence can be enriched. Within Isis, then, there live both positive and negative forces, but neither Lucius nor Nerval had yet learned to cope with this dynamic entity. Lucius had violated her secret. His rash act indicates his inexperience with the negative side of the female principle and an inability to cope with it. He suffered Isis' wrath. Nerval, who had always overlooked the negative side of the feminine principle, was forever confronted with its destructive force.

The four colors mentioned in the description of Isis (black, white, yellow, red) may be interpreted alchemically as an expression of a need for initiation. Initiation requires confrontation with pain, fear, and anguish, self-discipline and control. Completing such a trial successfully may lead to a fuller and more wholesome existence.

The black in Isis' "black mantle" represents the first phase in the alchemical transformative process. During this period all matter coalesces, churns. Black, for the alchemist, does not necessarily represent evil, but rather the "world beyond" or the "inner world." In Genesis we read:

> . . . and the earth was without form, and void: and darkness was upon the face of the deep (1:2).

Chaos and turbulence exist in the void—but also the creative element. In darkness, germination takes place. Richard Wagner and Victor Hugo considered black, when surrounded by light, a maternal and fecundating principle. Psychologically, only through a descent into the unconscious can illumination be experienced and former attitudes transformed. Orpheus' journey into Hades (grottoes, caves) is a quest to reach the darkest point within, the center, after which inner development or germination may occur. Christ also descended into Hell for three days, after which his soul was redeemed and resurrected. A descent into self or a withdrawal from the world is an outer expression of an inner process. Isis' black mantle indicates that within her lives a world *in potentia,* burgeoning forces of all sorts—spiritual and physical.

White and yellow ("white to saffron-colored yellow") are associated in alchemical terminology with purity, gold, and the sun. They represent the coming to consciousness of an idea or attitude, the emerging of the rational thinking functions, the ordering of heretofore turbulent forces. In Sparta, China, and certain African countries, white is

associated with death. Such death can be the end of a previously held philosophical or psychological attitude. In Lucius' case, through his initiation into the Isis mysteries his transformation back to man occurred—from black to gold. Not so for Nerval, who could only experience his initiation into the Isis (Mary) cult vicariously (cerebrally) and, therefore, not authentically.

"Flame red" (or blood) is the alchemical color that imitates the creation of life or the philosopher's stone. Red stands for the very essence of life, the vital force without which nothing could exist. In Egyptian tombs (and in prehistory), corpses, as well as the inside of many coffins, were painted red, indicating that life was eternal and existed after death, though in a different form. In that Isis wore red, she represented both the living and the dead: celestial, earthly, and underworld attitudes.

Lucius was now ready to experience her as a totality, as a living incarnation of the philosopher's stone, a means through which purification and the individuating process could be achieved. But Nerval could only long for such an experience. As a nineteenth-century Christian he could not revert back to Isis worship, nor, as a student of religion in general, could he find fulfillment in the "perfect" image of the Virgin Mary. Because she represented only one aspect of human nature, she could not help him cope with the evils and difficulties of life. To worship her meant further withdrawal from life.

Isis carried "the bronze sistrum" in her right hand. The sistrum was an instrument sounded during the religious ceremony to ward off any evil ghosts or destructive forces. The bell sounded during Catholic mass, which calls attention to the solemn moment at hand and drives away all that is unholy in the Isis ceremony. The fact that Isis holds the sistrum in her right hand—always associated with consciousness—indicates that she stands for a rational way of life and is in the process of relegating all chaotic and tenebrous thoughts and emotions to another sphere. Lucius and Nerval, in their attempts to experience Isis as a totality, are given the means to bring order out of turbulence, accord out of discord.

"In her left hand is the golden vase in the form of a gondola." The left hand ("sinistra") is the dreamer, or so the saying goes. It represents the forces of the unconscious, the underworld—man's shadowy, mysterious, secretive, and arcane regions, the source of his creativity. The fact that the vase is made of gold, the most precious and the purest of metals, implies the immense value placed upon it and its contents. It is shaped like a gondola to indicate Isis' power over sea-faring vessels. Isis was the goddess of navigators, a function inherited by the Virgin Mary. But the water contained within the vessels is of great import.

The elevation of the holy water to honor Isis was the most solemn moment in the service. The water from the Nile was placed in the golden vessel, symbolizing the body and essence of Osiris, the world fertilizer. Osiris, who represented the father spirit of the living and the dead, came to life during the morning and evening services, each time the high priest showed the people the *hydria,* the golden vessel that was then adored. The water, as the carrier of the divine essence, power, or mana, was capable of bringing about rebirth, healing, miracles, and cures of all sorts, like the waters of Lourdes for the Catholic. The part played by the holy water for the Egyptian is comparable to the transsubstantiation in the Catholic service. The fact that the holy water is contained in a vessel (a female symbol because of its containing quality) implies the blending of the masculine (water) and the feminine forces (vase) or the uterus in which the foetus is born and grows. The female "receptacle" is then a *mediatrix* between the uncreated and the created. In the Isis mysteries, water symbolizes an eternally mobile world and as a result Osiris is in the process of being reborn in his son Horus and bequeathing his powers to him. Isis, in that she holds the vessel in her hand, becomes the vehicle through which the mystery occurs, the rebirth of the living God. Only through the woman, as represented by Isis, may Lucius and Nerval experience rebirth—that is, the renaissance of the Eros or feeling principle within them.

Lucius prayed most fervently to Isis to transform him back to a man and in so doing experienced the greatest of all turmoils. [Franz explains that when] an animal acts like an animal "he is in harmony with himself," but when a man acts like one, it is an indication of inner chaos.

> You see me here, Lucius, in answer to your prayer. I am Nature, the universal Mother, mistress of all the elements, primordial child of time, sovereign of all things spiritual, queen of the dead, queen also of the immortals, the single manifestation of all gods and goddesses that are. My god governs the shining heights of Heaven, the whole-some sea-breezes, the lamentable silence of the world below. Though I am worshipped in many aspects, known by countless names, and propitiated with all manner of different rites, yet the whole round earth venerates me . . . call me by my true name, namely, queen Isis.

Why did Isis transform Lucius into an ass? Why not into some other animal? The ass was considered by Isis to be the most "hateful" of all animals. The ass was the animal of Osiris' murderer, Set. But the ass also had positive features: he was the sacred animal to such youthful savior gods as Dionysus, Attis, and Tammuz; and the ass carried Christ around Jerusalem and was present at his birth in Bethlehem. Saturn is associated with the ass and, therefore, is endowed with such characteristics as helplessness, creativity, suffering, depression.

As an ass, Lucius was in a state of despair. A composite of destructive and evil forces (Set), of gentleness (Christ carrier), of helplessness (Saturn), he suffered from the conflicts raging between his various traits (his animal form and his human soul). The intensity of his pain brought him to his senses. Turmoil and suffering are part and parcel of all initiations; they brought illumination or light, making him worthy of bearing his name, Lucius—*lucere,* "light."

Light came to Lucius only when he looked at his situation objectively, when he became aware—through Isis—of his inadequate life attitude. The ancient religions (alchemy, masonry, and other occult sects have continued this tradition) believed that the "eternal personality is established in this life and not projected into a postmortal sphere." One must therefore try to experience inner evolution within his mortal state so as to build both body and soul to as high a level as possible. Christianity, on the contrary, stresses an afterlife in which there is hope of redemption—hope of immortality after the last judgment. It was to Lucius's advantage to experience the anguish of initiation on earth. As a Christian, the choice was open to Nerval. He was not driven by that inner compulsion for perfection, and he knew that no matter what the fault or sin, he could or would eventually be pardoned in the hereafter.

Thus, Nerval was not concerned with Lucius's peregrinations as an ass. He could not identify with these aspects of Lucius's mystery. He projected only on Lucius's adoration of Isis and her divine intervention on his behalf. Though he did not quote Lucius's prayer to Isis, "O Blessed Queen of Heaven," which was later used by the Catholic Church in worship of the Virgin Mary, did look upon her as an eternal and universal principle, as a living corpus, an all-embracing and comforting power.

Lucius' actual initiation was kept a secret. Isis had wisely counseled him to do so.

> Only remember, and keep these words of mine locked tight in your heart, that from now onwards until the very last day of your life you are devoted to my service. It is only right that you should devote your whole life to the goddess who makes you a man again. Under my protection you will be happy and famous, and when at the destined time of your life, you descend to the land of the ghosts, there too in the subterranean hemisphere you shall have frequent occasion to adore me. . . . Further, if you are found to deserve my divine protection by careful obedience to ordinance of my religion by perfect chastity, you will become aware that I, and I alone, have power to prolong your life beyond the limits of appointed destiny.

Initiation can never be revealed since it is a subjective experience. An inner transformation must be lived out on an individual basis, as are birth and death. If the secrets of initiation are related to another, the entire experience loses point and power. The ancients were well aware of the importance of such secrecy. Herodotus never reveals the essence of the mysteries he witnessed in honor of Osiris in front of the Temple of Athens, at Saïs in the Delta.

> It is on this lake that the Egyptians act by night in what they call their Mysteries, the Passion of that being whose name I will not speak. All the details of these performances are known to me, but—I will say no more.
>
> [Georges Nagel, "The Mysteries of Osiris in Ancient Egypt," *Eranos Yearbooks* II, 1955]

Nor did Christ reveal any facts concerning his initiation, his descent into Hell.

When Nerval visited the Temple of Isis at Pompeii, he underwent a numinous experience that permitted him to understand—though only cerebrally—the complexities of his own problems, problems that face many sensitive people today who find it difficult to exteriorize their feelings. Nerval was incapable of relating to those about him. He needed a *mediatrix,* an intercessor, some force to temper life's cruel ways. Isis, the Queen of Heaven, the Mother of God, the World Principle, the Redeemer, as Nerval called her, understood and loved mankind. She would react and become a helping force to those who took both her positive and negative sides into consideration. If one aspect of her personality was accorded more respect than the other, imbalance resulted within the votary's psyche, making him vulnerable to her power.

Just as Isis had helped Lucius in his battle with life, so Nerval looked toward her and the Virgin Mary, to succor him.

> O nature! O eternal mother! Have mortals come to the point of rejecting all hope and all prestige. O Goddess of Saïs! Has the most brazen of your followers, while raising your sacred veil, come face to face with death?

We know nothing of Nerval's descent into self, into darkness. To penetrate one's inner realm is to undergo the greatest mystery of all!

Peter S. Thompson (essay date 1983)

SOURCE: "*Sylvie*: The Method of Myth," in *Nineteenth-Century French Studies,* Vol. XII, Nos. 1 & 2, Fall-Winter, 1983, pp. 96-104.

[*Below, Thompson addresses the function of myth in* Sylvie, *focusing on Nerval's use of colors and treatment of memory to suggest a fantastic world. The critic finds in the story an overflowing of the "unreal from amid the real."*]

Gérard de Nerval's *Sylvie* provides not only evidence of the author's predilection for an "other," "spiritual," or mythical world—a possible escape from time—but also an example in itself of transcending myth. Since it is meant to both celebrate and exemplify a timeless spirituality, *Sylvie* suggests this aspect of its own critique: how well, or with what emphasis, do we recall the story after the passage of time? Some recall best the character Sylvie, the countryside of Le Valois, the fêtes, the ruined architecture. Others may retain a strong physical impression of nature, in its misty, diaphanous portrayal. In general, memory favors the Valois vignettes, which are the fantastic or mythical portion of the story—the same visions which come to the sleepless narrator in his Paris rooms. So much has been written about fantasy and myth in *Sylvie* that we take these words as a simple summary of creative intent. The narrative decision, as well as the mythic flavor of the story, is subtle and shifting. Nerval has not

constructed a simple literary flight of fantasy, which might seem somewhat gratuitous even in relation to his own experiences in love. When one takes account of the evocations of Paris, the hours spent at the theater, the narrator's trip to Germany, Sylvie's sophistication and marriage, Aurélie's disenchantment with the narrator, and the action which moves the narrator back and forth between Paris and Le Valois, the impression of fantasy contracts, and with it some of the visual impressions which Nerval confers only upon Le Valois. It then becomes clear that Nerval's story is not merely a myth-like creation, but a story about such creative attempts. It is not too demanding of the mythical portion of *Sylvie* to stress its genuine power—its hold on the reader's memory; it instruments Nerval's belief in dream or myth as access to the timeless, the spiritual. It is equally important to emphasize the role of the non-mythical parts of *Sylvie*—the narrative poise that places us in a colorless Paris and invokes fantasy as a theme or symbol, as in the extravagant worship of the actress Aurélie.

The force of *Sylvie* arises in an effect of *épanchement* of the unreal from amid the real. Nerval's narrative emphasizes that fantasy is ineluctably based in reality; a close textual analysis like that of Léon Cellier reveals that this emphasis is reflected in the structure of the story. The story's mythical ambience is naturally clarified by this understanding. It is most important to pay attention to levels of explicitness both in Nerval's emphasis on the thread of reality in the narrative and in his cultivation of the spiritual and the relatively fantastic. The atmosphere, as we will see, is tightly contrived: "From both the limpingly natural and the elaborately formalized, Nerval weaves his sense of tenderness, irony, and final persistence" [Alison Fairlie, "An Approach to Nerval," in *Studies in Modern French Literature,* 1961]. With respect to "the elaborately formalized," we should be aware of the conventional mechanism of his atmosphere of myth, that is, his use of symbol and metaphor. More significantly, though less remarked by Nervalian scholarship, there is a peculiar use of abstraction which assists this mechanism. This assistance may have been unconscious with Nerval; it enters the reader's consciousness only gradually, or at some distance from the story. It is this underlying technique of abstraction that accomplishes the exemplary purpose of myth—especially with regard to Nerval's avowed desire to defeat time—which is to preserve itself well in memory.

The explicitness of mythical elements, and of both the narrator's satisfaction and his disappointment with his fantasies, tends to lessen the need to include Nerval's other works in this discussion. It is not important either to thoroughly relate the Aurélie sequences in *Sylvie* to Jenny Colon, and the antecedence of the Nerval-Colon letters to the writing of *Sylvie,* as a demonstration not only of Aurélie's real counterpart but of Nerval's real experience with love and illusion. Again, we can allow the story its own esthetic isolation from the author, and its effective, if somewhat hermetic, self-explanation.

The story begins in Paris, with the exposition of Aurélie's power over the narrator. She is not presented visually, except in a vague description of the luster created about her by the manipulation of stage lights. This detail may be the first glimpse of the narrator's complicated attitude; his poetic sensitivity seems aroused by these stage lights, but their mention also reveals a more cynical awareness of his love's object. Pierre Moreau, ascribing three categories of love to Sylvie, Adrienne, and Aurélie, emphasizes the "poetic" and the "bohemian" of the relationship with the last. This one is the most passionate and "affranchi" of the three visions of woman; it is an early introduction to the idea of loss of self ("Je me sentais vivre en elle" [*Sylvie, Suivi de Léo Bruckart et d'Aurélia,* ed. Henri Clouard, 1946]) in romantic fantasy. It is significant, then, that this opening passage is followed by an analytical glance at the narrator's epoch. It was a time of "enthousiasmes vagues," "espoirs incertains," in which, it is emphasized, poetic vision was isolated—drunk with love and art in an ivory tower. The poetic vision of love was vague, a "phantom of metaphysics"; above all, "il fallait qu'elle [the woman beloved] apparût reine ou déesse, et surtout n'en pas approcher." This epoch is affirmed as a basis of reality in the story by the narrator's relation of his time to others, to that of the *Fronde,* of the *Régence,* of the *Directoire.* So the question of love, the vision of woman, has been proposed, as well as the implicit idea of fantasy, but effusiveness in the narrative has quickly been subjected to history. The description of the era in the fourth and fifth paragraphs of *Sylvie* broaches the study of fantasy by proposing its essential dependence on reality; the fantasy to follow appears less gratuitous, or less literary, because it is the effect of established causes. This is the basis of an insistent demonstration that the relationship of fantasy to reality is problematical.

We can understand the obsession of Nerval's narrator only by outlining a thread of reality throughout the story—reality as an interruption of fantasy, as the kind of backdrop suggested above, and as an emphasis on present time as opposed to the past. After the narrator's effusion over Aurélie, after the memory of his uncle saying that nature forgot to give actresses "a heart," after the evocation of the epoch's love for a distant "queen" or "goddess," comes a scene presenting the narrator in a club or *salon.* It is the same evening as in the opening lines of the story, and he has just come from the theater. Interrogated, in this mundane setting, the narrator says of Aurélie, "C'est une image que je poursuis, rien de plus." There, in the reading room, the narrator picks up a newspaper in which a financial item reveals that he has become rich; Aurélie is accessible. Now the narrator rejects her accessibility—refusing to kill love with gold, and pretending that she would not be bought anyway. Yet his attention is coincidentally turned from Aurélie to Sylvie; it is in this newspaper that, moments later, he sees a notice of the archers' fête at Loisy. Instantly, in a passage which impressed Marcel Proust, there arises what the narrator calls a "série d'impressions" of the fête he remembers. The first chapter ends leaving the narrator standing with the newspaper and a flood of memories.

In the second chapter similar devices underline an intrusion of reality into the mythical air of the fête—one fête

in particular at which Adrienne, as well as Sylvie, was present. The chapter might have begun with "Je me souvenais de . . ." in order to continue the flow of impressions which ended the previous chapter. Nerval, however, cuts off this *épanchement* of the past by taking care to establish the narrator at home in his bed. It is only the first five lines which attach the "thread of reality" this way, but Nerval obviously wants to establish for the *rêverie* a starting point in reality. The narrator is sleepless; Nerval even explains that near-sleep provides the mechanism for reviewing long periods of life in only a few minutes. The following chapter returns the narrator's awareness to Paris. It opens with a quick deflation of the previous dreaming. The narrator explains what he has just realized, that his love for Aurélie originated with Adrienne. "Il y a de quoi devenir fou!" he exclaims; "Reprenons pied sur le réel." His thinking shifts to Sylvie, who will come to symbolize (for him) the real, the natural. He briefly presents his relationship with her, and he decides to attend the present fête at Loisy. His description of the journey supports a real setting in time and place; towns are named along the way—like Gonesse, which recalls the *Ligue* and the *Fronde.*

The next three chapters are an uninterrupted segment of Le Valois descriptions. There persists a schematic encapsulation of this type of account by implications of the real, the present. The moment of memory is firmly situated in the real, and the words "recomposons le souvenir" underline the narrator's control and coordination of the memory impressions. More particularly, he demonstrates a mechanism for a new, spontaneous tone in his release of *rêverie;* he passes through Châalis—"encore un souvenir!" The power, here, of the name of a town is clearly reminiscent of moments in Proust's work; the simple efficacity of this mechanism suggests itself to the narrator as apt for the treatment of memory or *Rêverie.* Then the particularly dream-like chapter, "Châalis," ends with a remarkable emphasis on the present situation of the narrator, placing him at the moment of composition: "En me retraçant ces détails, j'en suis à me demander s'ils sont réels, ou bien si je les ai rêvés."

Now, these shifts in time, and several phrases which evoke the process of composition, may raise some dissatisfaction with the manipulation of fantasy by the author. This is only because the reader does not at first assume the rigor with which Nerval has delineated the relationship of fantasy to reality. Although this is a subtle problem and can only be resolved with a complete reading, the third chapter introduces a clarifying element. The narrator speaks of wanting, at that moment, to write the story of loving Sylvie and Adrienne simultaneously. He is a gifted writer; it is revealed that Aurélie stars in a play that he has written for her, and he later writes for her troupe. In the last chapter, "Dernier Feuillet," he says "Telles sont les chimères qui charment et égarent au matin de la vie. J'ai essayé de les fixer sans beaucoup d'ordre, mais bien des coeurs me comprendront. Les illusions tombent, l'une après l'autre, comme les écorces d'un fruit, et le fruit, c'est l'expérience. Sa saveur est amère; elle a pourtant quelque chose d'âcre qui fortifie—qu'on me pardonne ce style vieilli." So the fact that the story is written is part of the story; this added element of authenticity becomes an instrument of Nerval's portrayal of an individual's fantasy. The awareness of art, or of the time of composition, refers us to the real setting—the sober Parisian life of a hard working writer, from which fantasy provides escape. As suggested earlier, the authentic escape value of the narrator's fantasy is enhanced by less explicit elements of his narration: the almost painterly vividness of the Le Valois descriptions, which emerge as antithesis and negation of the Parisian reality.

There is no descriptive intensity outside of Le Valois; Aurélie herself is only a thematic emblem of fantasy, hardly described until she goes to Le Valois and is disguised as Adrienne, when a different register of description is engaged: "Aurélie, en amazone avec ses cheveux blonds flottants, traversait la forêt comme une reine d'autrefois, et les paysans s'arrêtaient éblouis.—Mme. de F . . . était la seule qu'ils eussent vue si imposante et si gracieuse dans ses saluts." At this point Nerval, having established a thematic basis of reality, and thus assured the authentic evolution of fantasy, is free to indulge his penchant for the Valois ambience of love, innocent play, timelessness. The description of the Temple de La Philosophie, the fêtes, Adrienne's drama at Châalis, develops the essence of this fantasy; its significance as an effusion away from the real is underscored by a vividness in both its overall exoticism and the colors of its physical impression on the narrator. We also sense here an effacement of the structure of reality, which is partly explained by a lack of decisiveness on the narrator's part. He preserves an ambivalence toward the present, the Parisian, the terms of real life and love. The attempt to turn this simple ambivalence into a satisfying integration of reality and fantasy is the most important Nervalian theme. And the importance of the ending of *Sylvie,* in "Dernier Feuillet," is that it concludes the narration without integrating the real and the unreal—without solving, and anesthetizing, the narrator's ambivalence toward reality.

The present narrator's great contribution is his peculiar application of art and artifice to this same indecisiveness. In a broad sense, the artifice rests on a technique of abstraction. Pierre Moreau has demonstrated a technique of evocative simplicity in the rustic descriptions of Le Valois. Given the effusive, vague nature of much of the Valois memories, Moreau's attention to simplicity, to a "goût de réalité," in the visual sense, points to an abstraction of selected concrete details to enforce some vivid structure in the precious fabrication of memories and illusions. *Sylvie* derives narrative structure from the abstraction of idea which has Le Valois geographically remote from the narrator. Indeed, the name of the region—"Châalis" is also an example—is an abstraction, a Proustian concentration of images and emotions which is neatly transportable through time, and from which an *épanchement* of memory or narrative can be released with any desired degree of accuracy. Symbolism, such as the concentration of theme in the dog preserved by taxidermy, is also part of this technical simplicity. Nerval was, of course, aware of the force of the abstract symbol; he was familiar with

Martines de Pasqually and the related thesis of *syncrétisme,* in which symbols are derived from the spiritual world and produce isolated reconciliations of the real and the spiritual. Jean Richer, in another context, cites this passage, familiar to Nerval, from Martines' *Traité de La Réintégration*: "Par la contemplation de ses propres idées et l'abstraction de tout ce qui tient au monde extérieur et au corps, l'homme pouvait s'élever à la notion parfaite de l'essence universelle et à la domination des esprits." We notice, as a possible application of this theory, that Nerval is adroit in using fog or mist both as a symbol of hazy inaccessibility and as a simplification of detail: certain scenes are drawn from the mist as from a haze of memory, thus appearing both vivid and remote. This is an abstraction.

There is a better example of what we should interpret broadly as abstraction. The sensation of simple physical contrasts and of a painterly deposition of color, sometimes combined with a specific symbolism, seems to extend the technique of abstraction to include color. Color, in *Sylvie,* tends to affect readers more impressionistically than naturally. Proust found an atmosphere of blue or purple prevalent in the Valois mist. Jean-Pierre Richard remarks on the use of red to fundamentally complement the pervading green of the Valois scenes. He emphasizes the contrastive colorfulness of the château, particularly the contrast of the lambent bricks and the gray or black of the slate roof. Here is the description: "Je me représentais un château du temps de Henri IV avec ses toits pointus couverts d'ardoises et sa face rougeâtre aux encoignures dentelées d'ormes et de tilleuls, dont le soleil couchant perçait le feuillage de ses traits enflammés." Moreau calls attention to other painterly traits in descriptive parts of *Sylvie.* One is the tableau quality (in the sense of a theatrical tableau) with which Nerval establishes some scenes. Another is the conscious deployment of color, the alertness to visual art shown, for example, in the words "des rougers du soir *sur* le vert sombre de la forêt," and "la bruyère rose relève le vert des fougères."

The contrast of red and green, with the values attributed by Richard or the quasi-symbolism that Baudelaire found in this opposition, occurs three times in *Sylvie.* Perhaps there is symbolism in the "bleu et rose" of the star *Aldébaran,* related to love of Sylvie. This pink and blue opposition occurs four times in all: once again as the colors of Sylvie's room; in the pink figures of saints and angels on the blue ceiling of a chapel at Châalis; as the colors of the "formes vagues" of typical love for men of the narrator's epoch. Another simple opposition, perhaps symbolic, presents itself in the black eyes and blond hair of Sylvie. Poulet has called attention to this; apparently Gautier and others recognized a romantic standard in this description. The château mentioned earlier and physical descriptions of people appear practically as lists of colors. The colors are stark and relatively unobstructed by other detail. They are pure in hue. We should note that virtually all the use of color in *Sylvie* fits this pattern, tending toward contrasts of two, as here: "Les grands chênes d'un vert uniforme n'étaient variés que par les troncs blancs des bouleaux . . . " Here again is the typical formula: "les nénuphars jaunes et blancs"; "la façade jaune et les contrevents verts"; "Le portrait d'un jeune homme du bon vieux temps souriait avec ses yeux noirs et sa bouche rose."

Did Nerval see these visual effects simply as aids to our imagination, or was their simplicity part of the effort at "abstraction de tout ce qui tient au monde extérieur"? Or did he intuit that the very effects which serve the theme of memory, and convey the selective sensation of memory, would by these efforts gain a peculiar hold on our memory? The physical descriptions do achieve this hold, thus contributing to Jeanne-Marie Durry's "universalisation du souvenir" [*Nerval et le mythe*, 1956], adding collective weight or appeal to a personal myth, and joining not only an esthetic but an experiential dimension to Nerval's story. Since the conscious use of this technique is problematical, especially in view of the possible Martinesian influence, a further analysis of the artistic potential of some types of abstraction may be helpful. Perhaps the presentation of hashish in *Voyage en Orient* is a clue to Nerval's general appreciation of abstraction. Nerval was certainly familiar with the effects of the drug, one of which is the breaking down of contexts, the revelation of objects in some extreme essence, some simplest abstraction. An object's purely sensual impression is often intensified in this way. A correlative process is the breakdown of contextual organization of impressions already stored in the subconscious, so that the memory of an object can leap forth from seemingly unfathomable depths because one has summoned it by seeing another object which is worlds apart contextually speaking—different in function, for example—though it has a startling similarity of shape, odor or color. In fact, [Durry writes that] Nerval mentions a "memory enhancing" effect of the drug: "Le hachich n'avait fait que développer un souvenir enfoui au plus profond de mon âme, car ce visage divin m'était connu. Par exemple, où l'avais-je vu déjà? Dans quel monde nous étions-nous recontrés? Quelle existence antérieure nous avait mis en rapport? C'est ce que je ne saurais dire." Such a remark emphasizes the depths of the subconscious, which, in the context of fantasy, is Nerval's raw material; he points out that thoughts and memories can travel such distances as to become almost unrecognizable, and be received as signals from another world or former life. This may be part of the confusion of the "souvenir du réel" and the "souvenir de l'iréel" that Durry speaks of. In any case the process is the same; be it through altering of consciousness or through Nerval's creation of a vivid suggestion and its reception in the reader's mind, some process of abstraction facilitates an object's movement between the natural world and the transcendental realm of communicable thought and idea. Thus the use of color in *Sylvie* is more than a merely vivid technique of description, and more than an efficacious symbolism. With its taste of abstraction, this simplicity or selectivity of color seems particularly apt for the kind of fantasy which, like myth or fable, endures in memory and transcends time.

The colors convey their own spirituality and their own metaphoricalness, almost in the sense of the typical compulsive metaphor of *Sylvie*. This effect may in the end seem rather patent; naturally it still does not jeopardize the authenticity of the writing narrator whose artifice and imagination, and whose particular urge to defeat time, are explicit. In fact these colors articulate most convincingly the collusion between an explicit fantasy and such comparatively covert elements as Nerval's sense of abstraction. Even the casual reader recognizes the obviously metaphorical nymph and symbolic clock. One gradually recognizes that they not only explain the narrator's vision, his metaphorical and mythicizing impulse, but serve as a compelling example of it. It is only as we come to value this exemplary myth that we finally appreciate the least explicit but most effective instruments of our sympathy with the sleepless narrator: colors in the mist, luminous memories of Le Valois.

On similarities between *Sylvie* and Nerval's life:

Sylvie indeed resembles one of those shrines of seaside Venus, slight counterparts of Cnidian Aphrodite's citadel, which grateful travellers (the Anthology records) established here and there along the shores of the Graeco-Roman world, its materials pathetically commemorating the artist's voyage, polished and whitened spars of the wreck he had escaped, brittle flukes of weed he had gathered, struggling inshore over the treacherous rocks, with the goddess herself, who appears to ride the calm, enshrined among shells and flowers and stars of mica. For Gérard's story too is a tribute of gratitude and the record of a happy escape. But the dangers he had escaped from were still close at hand, just as the shrine still echoed to the sound of the sea. Even the smoothness of his style suggests the tumult just beneath the surface. Gérard, we know, wrote against, as it were in spite of, the appalling press and tangle of his ideas.

Peter Quennell, in "Gérard de Nerval," in Baudelaire and the Symbolists, *revised edition, Weiden Feld and Nicolson, 1954.*

Anne-Marie Smith (essay date 1984)

SOURCE: "*Pandora*'s Quality of Figure," in *Paragraph*, Vol. 4, October, 1984, pp. 62-82.

[*In the following essay, Smith describes the quality of figuration in* Pandora *that prevents the novella from succumbing to abstraction, disorder, and senselessness. She also delineates the differences between* Pandora *and "Les Amours de Vienne," the earlier sketch by Nerval on which the novella is based.*]

From its inception Nerval's *Pandora* was fraught with anxiety and confusion. Both the text and its criticisms profess bewilderment. Tracing the tensions which form the history of *Pandora* gives us a sense of Nerval's marginal position, of the rewriting of unfinished fragments amid the response of confusion and lack of understanding from the readers of his letters and text. Alienated by his publisher-readers, he tried desperately to control the destiny of *Pandora*. In December 1853, he wrote to George Bell, a regular correspondent: 'Informez-vous je vous prie des épreuves d'une nouvelle intitulée 'Pandora' dont je voudrais corriger la fin. ('Please make enquiries about the proofs of a novella entitled "Pandora" of which I'd like to correct the ending'.) Then eleventh months later in a letter to the writer, Louis Ulbach, he reacted angrily to what he perceived to be editorial misprision, 'Je pars pour Saint Germain. J'ai les poches pleines de copie que je remporte de peur de les perdre. Vous êtes cause, du moins l'administration compliquée de la revue est cause que j'ai donné au Mous-quetaire des fragments bizarres que Dumas a imprimés sans faire observer que cela n'a ni queue, ni tête' ('I'm leaving for Saint Germain. My pockets are full of copy which I'm taking away with me for fear of losing it. It is your fault, or at least the fault of the journal's complicated administration, that I gave to the "Mous-quetaire" some bizarre fragments which Dumas printed without pointing out that these have neither head nor tail'). In 1861 Ulbach, preceded a publication of Nerval's letter with the following remarks, 'Je me souviens du 'manuscrit bizarre qui me fut remis par Gérard de Nerval pour la Revue de Paris, des bouts de papier de toutes dimensions de toute provenance entremêlés de figures cabalistiques' ('I remember the bizarre manuscript which Gérard de Nerval gave me for the Revue de Paris, bits of paper of all shapes and sizes, from all possible sources, intermingled with cabbalistic figures').

The text was submitted to a movement between curtailment due to its apparent incommunicability and consequent regeneration due to the writer's persistence, which is a movement the fiction espouses in all its forms. It is as if the narrator of the fiction were anticipating the frustrated communication the writer of the text experienced and moreover as if this fury of confusion and frustration were anticipating the history of *Pandora*'s critical reception; as if then 'the scene of the critical debate (were) a repetition of the scene dramatized in the text . . . unwittingly participat(ing) in it' [Shoshana Felman, 'Turning the Screw of Interpretation', *Literature and Psychoanalysis,* 1982], and the text itself were 'thematizing its own invention and prefiguring its own reception' [Paul de Man, in his introduction to *Towards an Aesthetic of Reception,* 1982].

For more than a century Pandora was thought unreadable. The text continued to generate denials of comprehension, or was recognized only for its: 'pathologie nervalienne', for what it reflected of 'l'égarement due poéte alors inquiété par la folie' [Michel Jeanneret, '*Pandora* de Nerval, Essai d'intérprétation', *Critique*, 1973], (the aberration of the poet now troubled by madness) or for its 'forme impartaite, déroutante' [Jean Senelier, *Un Amour Inconnu de Gérard de Nerval*, 1966], for having 'l'air d'être un écrit occasional fait de quelques tombeés' (the appearance of being an incidental piece, of windfalls put together) and 'quelque chose de déconcertant, d'irritant, de bizarre' ('something disconcerting, annoying, bizarre' [Raymond Jean, 'Une Lecture de *la Pandora*', *La Poétique du Désir*, 1974]). Such readings can comment only on the bewilderment *Pandora* arouses for they make of discontinuity and disconnection merely bewilderment and not text.

Pandora was published in various forms and continued to generate confusion, until in 1968 the Nerval critic le père Guillaume, re-arranged various fragments of the text and was acclaimed for having recovered a century's lost meaning, [Jeanneret stated] 'le père Guillaume remonte aux sources et pour la première fois publie une *Pandora* douée de cohérence et de profondeur. . . . In 1975 Jean Senelier attacked Guillaume's enterprise and produced his own fiercely defended edition of the Pandora manuscripts, nevertheless acknowledging the text's resistance to his project: 'Il s'y manifeste une discordance interne'. Yet may readability be conferred by such editorial gestures of reform? Is not the source of an immense readability to be found rather in the *refractory* nature of the text, its tangential resistance to interpretation, its literal unreadability. The tangentiality which traverses both the fiction and the history of *Pandora* is its claim to literarity. In the words of Jacques Derrida [in 'Living On: Border Lines', *Deconstruction and Criticism,* 1979], ' . . . unreadability does not arest reading, does not leave it paralysed in the face of an opaque surface: rather it starts reading and writing (. . .) moving again'.

So might not *Pandora*'s 'weak' points, the ghosts of unintelligibility and indeterminacy which have haunted and inhibited the text for more than a century prove to be the very source of its generative power? This generative power of the text inhibits that refracted, tangential space which is the domain of the figural language. A reading which catches its momentum attends seriously to the symptoms of the figural: to 'an excess', to the 'more than we can recuperate as semantically relevant' (Norman Bryson [in 'Discourse, Figure', *Word and Image,* 1981]), that is to the *incongruous,* the *anachronistic,* to leaks in the text which are strange and yet familiar, both excessive and inalienable: to the 'strangely familiar' Freudian Uncanny: 'un-heimlich'. These tangential leaks in a text's framework make up its *figurality*—an elusive but fundamental quality. Derrida [in 'Fors', in Nicolas Abraham and Maria Torok's *Cryptonomie, Le Verbier de L'homme aux Loups,* 1976] defines this difficult paradox of the figural: 'cela meme que pour en être la condition (du discours) lui échapperait par essence' ('That which being the very condition of discourse, would by its very essence escape discourse').

Thirteen years before he wrote *Pandora*, Nerval published *Le Voyage en Orient*, where in the introduction, 'Vers l'orient', he included a section 'Les Amours de Vienne' of which *Pandora* is perceptibly a rewritten version. 'Les Amours de Vienne' is a radical part of the Pandora text, as are the letters and constantly corrected manuscripts which surround its publication. It is in 'Les Amours de Vienne' that we first encounter the narrator's preoccupation with a woman he meets at the theatre door in Vienna. This woman becomes veiled in enigma and ambiguity as she is confused with the various fleeting female figures in the text until we no longer know whether she is the 'charmante jeune fille blonde', 'ouvrière', the latter's 'maîtresse', 'Caterina Colossa' or 'femme du monde'. But then this fluidity suddenly shifts to an illusion of shape, to her identification with 'La Vénitienne de Gozzi':

Mon ami, imagine que c'est une beauté de celles que nous avons tant de fois rêvées,—la femme idéale des tableaux de l'école italienne, la Vénitienne de Gozzi, *bionda egrassota,* la voilà trouvée! Je regrette de n'être pas assez fort en peinture pour t'en indiquer tous les traits Figure-toi une tête ravissante, blonde, blanche, une peau incroyable, à croire qu'on l'ait conservée sous des verres; les traits les plus nobles, le nez aquilin, le front haut, la bouche en cerise; puis un col de pigeon gros et gras, arrêté par un collier de peries; puis des épaules blanches et fermes, où il y a de la force d'Hercule et de la faiblesse et du charme de l'enfant d deux ans. J'al expliqué à cette beauté qu'elle me plaisait surtout—parce qu'elle était pour ainsi dire *Austro-Vénitienne,* et qu'elle réalisait en elle seule le Saint-Empire romain, ce qui a paru peu la toucher.

(Imagine, my friend, (that she's) a beauty like those we've so often dreamt,—the ideal woman of paintings of the italian school, Gozzi's Venetian, 'blonda e grassota', here she is. I regret not being sufficiently well-versed in painting to show you her every feature. Imagine a rav-ishing head, blonde, white, incredible skin, as if preserved under glass; the most noble features, aquiline nose, cherry mouth, a pigeon's neck plump and soft, fastened with a pearl necklace, then shoulders white and firm, where there is a strength of Hercules and the fragility and charm of the child. I explained to this beauty that she pleased me especially—because she was so to speak Austro-Venetian, and that she embodied in herself alone the Holy Roman Empire, which seemed immaterial to her.)

Yet such apparently concrete references with the status of cliche, 'la femme idéale', 'de l'école italienne', and 'la Vénitienne de Gozzi' betray all the signs of an apology for fantasy: 'imagine que', and 'tant de fois révées'. Inscribed within this illusory identification there is a gesture of apology; 'je regrette de n'être pas'assez fort en peinture pour t'en indiquer tous le traits', the regret for a lack. He regrets not being sufficiently well-versed in painting to show her every feature. And yet the text moves forward as if in attempted description of her: 'une tête ravissante . . . puis des épaules blanches et fermes', yet there is no fixity for the image must evaporate or shift, inscribed as it is within the speculative 'figure-toi', 'à croire que', and 'pour ainsi dire'. The regret for a lack becomes an elaboration on the lack, a comment on the capacity of language *per medium* to betray at once solidity and fluidity, to leak its figurality. So a profession of incompetence, *Recusatio* is here a rhetorical figure which inverts the literal apology to *apologia,* a written defence. The regret for a lack veils ingenuity. Woman remains undefined in the realms of art and language and we are left only with an indication of her infinite dimension: 'qu'elle réalisait en elle seule le Saint-Empire romain' with the inference, nevertheless, that this is at once the key to her attractiveness: 'qu'elle me plaisait surtout', and yet quite immaterial to her: 'ce qui a peu la toucher'.

The opening to **Pandora** exposes the same shifting amalgam of knowing and not knowing or imagining. The text's opening gesture of inclusion and familiarity: 'Vous l'avez tous connue, o mes amis!' ('You have all know her, o my

friends!') is almost immediately checked and closed, as it were, by a quasi-assertive, quasi-unsure allusion to her as an indecipherable enigma: 'c'etait bien à elle peut-être,—à elle, en vérité,—que pouvait s'appliquer l'indéchif-frable énigme . . . ', ('it was to her indeed perhaps,—to her, in truth,—that might refer the indecipherable enigma . . . '.) This invitation to conjecture is echoed in the final statement of the paragraph which feigns to define her: 'Enfin *la Pandora* c'est tout dire, car je ne veux pas dire tout'. Pandora speaks for itself; I don't want to give everything away. So might Nerval speak of a text whose title, meaning 'gift of all', 'all gifted', is itself a single indication of multiplicity. In the shifts from certainty to possibility then, Pandora, text and figure in the text, wavers between definitely being an indecipherable enigma and perhaps not; between that which we all know: 'Vous l'avez tous connue', and that which is completely closed to us: 'une indéchiffrable enigme'. Textually she is a free signifier like Poe's 'purloined letter', Lacan's 'pur signifiant' whose narrative is an allegory of the signifier.

The reader must contend with the paradox of overindulgent detail running concurrently with explicit witholding of information throughout the text. Reading is tantalized by a wealth of reference to the foreign, the Vinnese, the intertextual, and yet the reader is denied indulgence in a 'good story' since all this, interwoven with the narrator's own affabulations, seems to yield no cohesion. The narrative nevertheless survives on the drift of metonymic linking. As the text's obscure female figures, 'Les Amours de Vienne', espouse a movement which in poetic terms can only be described as metonymic displacement, Vienna, the textual context, remains the only apparent continuum amidst the cinema of women, a vast forum for elusive objects of desire: '*L'odor di femina* est partout dans l'air'. [In a footnote, the critic states that '"Odor di femina", italicized in the text is a quote from Da Ponte's libretto to Mozart's "Don Giovanni"'.] We witness in 'Les Amours de Vienne' a series of encounters with the narrator taking the hand of female *variantes* who come and go between theatre and café. Interest is sustained by frequent reference to time and place giving the illusion of a point to the 'drama' for both narrator and reader. Yet these are illusory *points de repère* for never is interaction defined on an actual level, only through discourse; that is, only through the narrator's reported attempts at communication; which report little but a sense of inevitable incommunicability. So discourse paves the way to sexual encounter while always keeping it at bay. The text in its movement and timing might evoke comparison with scenes of café-théâtre, or that other Viennese drama, Schnitzler's *La Ronde,* but it resists this resemblance because at the very crux of the Pandora narrative lies language's persistant witholding of action.

The narrator, a foreigner to Vienna, originally sought a woman who might teach him the language: *le patois* qui se parle à Vienne' ('the patois spoken in Vienna'), and insists, 'Il est donc important que je cherche quelque jolie personne de la ville qui veuille bien me mettre au courant du langage usuel' ('It is therefore important for me to look for some pretty native who won't mind informing me of the idiom'.) So the movement of the text is motivated by this wish, by a desire confusing two objects: woman, and language which will be his verbal currency. Yet throughout written and verbal encounter, comprehension is continually suspended, deferred to further rendezvous. Each woman leaves him confounded, speaks a language which only bewilders, to leave a misinterpretable and therefore infinitely interpretable confusion of tongues. Vienna assumes the dimensions of Babel, the scene of linguistic confusion, of a vast forum containing the dissimilarities of many a race and language. Linguistic confusion is manifest on a concrete level in the text's italicized reference in foreign language and on an abstract level in the text's dialogue: 'Comme elle me l'a dit fort agréablement elle ne sait bien aucune langue, mais un peu trois langues' ('As she very pleasantly told me she knew no language well, but three languages a little'), and 'Pandant la route elle me disait des phrases en toutes sortes de langues, ce qui fait que je comprenais à la rigueur' ('On the way she spoke to me in sentences from all kinds of languages which meant I hardly understood'). Each person speaks for himself: 'Je lui dit en bon allemand qu'elle comprend blen et parle mal' ('I told her in good German which she understands well and speaks badly'), which means that any mutual comprehension must fall into abeyance or be deferred. This is a phenomenon not only operative in verbal communication, for 'Il n'est pas moins difficile de déchiffrer son écriture que sa parole'. ('It is no less difficult to decipher her writing than her speech'), but the threat of bewilderment incumbent upon all language. As we read here the narrator's fear of unintelligibility before another's system of writing, 'J'ai peur que ses caractères ne solt d'aucune langue' ('I fear her characters belong to no language'), so might we read of Nerval's bewilderment before another's system of writing, 'Je ne comprends rien à votre imprimerie. Il n'y a pas de caractères pour imprimer ma suite' ('I don't understand anything of your printing press. There are no characters to print my follow-up'); the persistent threat of incommunicability. His denying any understanding of her words leaves the narrator both bound and free to conjecture her meaning: 'Je m'imagine sur la foi d'un verbe d'une consonnance douteuse, qu'elle veut dire que . . . ' ('I [delude myself with the] fancy, on the faith of a verb of questionable consonance, that she means that . . . ') and to structure possible meaning only by pronunciation: 'Sa prononciation me change un peu le sens des mots' ('Her pronunciation changes a little the meaning of words for me'). Language here performs but does not state. Each to his/her own words and his/her conjecture seems to be the order of things—which inevitably fosters a climate of misunderstanding; 'nous recommençons à ne plus nous entendre sur un mot'. ('We begin again to no longer understand a word of each other'.) It is with the excuse of being infinitely confounded that the narrator leaves his reader the addressee of a meta-language on dialogue never disclosed and escapes having to reveal content.

After a long section of reported dialogue, which the narrator qualifies as 'le fil des événements' ('the thread of events / the course of things'), we are left with little indication of any real event. The figural, 'that which being

the very condition of discourse might by its very essence escape discoures', the gap in understanding which is the condition of discourse, both inhabits and inhibits communication. In the same way, a passage which begins 'Il fallait bien cependant un peu de mise en scène à mes aventures romanesques, car tu n'es pas au bout'. ('I ought to have set the scene of my romantic ventures for you a little because you've not yet come to the end') and seems to promise literal description, leaves a residual doubt about the very possibility of literal description. The description of Vienna is strangely provisional, 'Suppose que . . . ' ('Suppose that . . . '), 'Tu aurais ainsi und ideé . . . ' ('You would then have an idea . . . '). It is both imaginative and provocative, 'Ne vas-tu pas penser tout de suite . . . ' ('Are you not going immediately to think . . . '), evokes the city's hostility to the aimless dreamer, the wanderer, and defeats first impressions. The description of the scene of the fiction sets most evocatively the scene of the text, that is to say it escapes its literal function of setting the scene. Vienna *is* the writing, with that split investment in the rich and the poor, the material and the fluid. Rich overwhelming concrete reference is inscribed within the insubstantial abstraction which is nevertheless its lifeline. The writing is split between a quasi-fetishist investment in time, place, culture and myth—in the salient features of a European capital on one hand, and a tributary movement of desire in all its indeterminacy on the other. The narrator's movement within and struggle with, the foreign city which harbours the confusion of many a currency and language is closely aligned to the writer's disappearance within, and struggle with, the language which is his medium and its capacity to contain and still those fleeting Viennese women, his subject. The writing becomes the subject.

In this light, description of a Viennese tavern whose centre has been vacated for dance leaves space for a movement of dance which functions structurally throughout this text which is, in a sense, choreocentric. It is the pause and abandon of dance which choreographs Nerval's writing; a seductive, elusive to-ing and fro-ing of language which elaborately defers dialogue, sexual encounter and conclusion. In description of 'la décoration' of this 'pièce principale' whose centre is dance floor, we have once again both a scene of the fiction and a scene of the writing: it is elaborately rococo, cradled within a complex network, generative like the vinebranch with shootleaves 'pampres', and containing the intricacy and pattern of lattice-work 'treillages'. Description of this room's inhabitants conjures up a mixed society in primitive disguise, reflection of the bizarre heterogeneity of the Viennese population whose presence is uncannily repeated in this text which proposes Vienna as the mythic forum for the encounter of many a language and race. Yet this is somehow a myth the text disbelieves, for heterogeneity and difference inhabit most intensely the figures of the narrator and 'ses Amours', while repeated reference to their mixed entourage, 'les Moldaves, Hongrois, Bohémiens et autres . . . ', 'Les Slaves, les Magyares, les Tyroliens, Illyriens et autres . . . ', begins to function as cliché. The heterogeneity and difference which inhabit those female figures: 'Les Amours de Vienne' is assumed into an illusion of homogeneity by the title/name of the later text *Pandora*. Yet such is the etymology of that eponym that it defeats naming, for 'gift of all', 'all gifted', 'all the gifts' only splinters further tenable definition. The female figures which traverse the text bear the title's confusion, inviting definition in so many words, yet with an indefatigable imprecision which thwarts all fixity.

It has become apparent that within the descriptive dynamics of this story, there is a kind of 'figural embedding' at work, which, to cite Ross Chambers [in a paper given at the University of London in 1981, entitled 'Story and Situation'], would consist of 'the incorporation into the narrative of a figure, in the sense of a personnage but also in the sense of an image which is representative, in some sense, of "art", of the production and reception of narrative'. In *Pandora* we find figures whose movement corresponds to the production of the text and whose configuration we can call a 'poetry of poetry', to use a term cited by Paul de Man; 'Poesie der Poesie' in relation to the literary theory of Hans Robert Jauss, 'the figure of a poetic voice . . . whose song (corresponds to) a production of the text'. Such is the figure of woman in the Nervalian text then, the woman of 'Les Amours de Vienne' later named Pandora, who embraces the whole extraordinary conjurings of Nerval's imagination; at once nameless, or when named, amalgamating multiple and 'contradictory' features, so described as to be beyond recognition; seemingly artificial, she is given to self-abandon, infinitely seducible, yet she is never seduced. The narrative espouses her pursuit, nevertheless, and the paths of seduction, though circuitous, are incredibly compliant: 'Vous en remarquez une (femme), vous la suivez, alors elle fait des coudes et des zigzags de rues en rues. Puis choisissez un endroit un peu désert pour l'aborder et jamais elle ne refusera de répondre' ('You notice one, [a woman], you follow her, so she twists and turns from street to street. Then choose a quiet place to approach her and she will never refuse to respond'); 'toute femme que vous abordez se laisse prendre le bras, reconduire' ('every woman you approach lets herself be taken by the arm, and led away'); and 'Personne ne me dispute la conquête de la veille' ('Nobody disputes my conquest of the previous day'). This figure of woman is inextricably linked with other textual figures, to 'la valse', the movement of her abandonment; 'elles s'abandonnent à la valse avec une ardeur singulière' ('they abandon themselves to the waltz with peculiar ardour'), and to the clouds of dust the waltz creates amid the spirals of tobacco smoke. The narrator remarks that the vertiginous spirals of the waltz in smoky Viennese cafés and taverns are assumed as part of the general spectacle and are not just distraction: 'l'on dîne et l'on soupe toujours au milieu des danses et de la musique, et le galop serpente autour des tables sans inquiéter les dîneurs' ('We have dinner and supper always amid dances and music, the dance winds between the tables without worrying those eating'). The narrator soon inclines towards apology as if for the gratuitousness of the preceding detail: 'Peut-être ai-je tort de t'écrire tout ce qui précède. Je dois te faire l'effet d'un malheureux, d'un cuistre, d'un voyageur léger qui ne représente son pays que dans les tavernes et qu'on goût immodéré de bière

impériale et d'impressions fantasques entraîne à de trop faciles amours' ('Perhaps I'm wrong to write all this so far. I must be giving the impression of an unhappy man, an ill-bred pedant, a frivolous traveller who only represents his country in taverns and who through an immoderate taste for imperial beer and whim-sical impressions is led to easily into love'); but this (too) is a rhetorical apology. It has become increasingly perceptible on close analysis that, in this text, what might appear to be gratuitous description in fact carries the momentum of figural language, that the ornament is part of the argument, of the whole textual structure, in much the same way that in musical figuration a cadenza may be both elaboration and argument and yet like a dance, have no need of resolution. If in figural inscription the ornament is part of the argument then its figures, the figural subjects in the text, define the strategy of that text's discourse. The text is auto-theoretical.

Repeated reference to 'café' and 'taverne', then, may seem textual trivia, yet they assume auto-theoretical status when accorded figural significance. Indeed Gérard de Nerval indicates just this when he says of *Les Nuits d'Octobre*: 'Vous avez raison de croire que le spectacle continuel de scènes de cabaret et de bals de barrière n'a rien de sain pour l'esprit. Aussi ne faut-il pas s'y complaire' ('You are right to think that the perpetual spectacle of cabaret scenes and local dances is no good for one's sanity but they mustn't be taken for granted'). 'Café' and 'taverne' are, in fact, 'where it's all at' in Vienna, the text's plenum and fundamental locus, and always the scene of the narrator's writing: 'Je t'écris d'un café où j'attends que l'heure sonne' ('I'm writing to you from a café where I'm waiting for the hour to strike'), and 'Je t'écris d'un café où j'attends l'heure du spectacle' ('I'm writing to you from a café where I'm waiting until the performance begins'), 'Je t'écris non pas de ce cabaret enfumé . . . je vais te parler d'un autre cabaret non moins enfumé . . . ' ('I'm not writing to you from that smoky cabaret . . . I'm going to tell you about another, no less smoky, cabaret'). Of the 'cabaret enfumé' we read: 'à l'autre bout étaient l'homme qui a perdu son reflet et l'homme qui a perdu son ombre discutant fort gravement' ('at the other end were the man who has lost his reflection and the man who has lost his shadow in very serious discussion'), and we are reminded of these Hoffmanesque figures whe, crossing Vienna with his usual 'rapidité,' and 'fureur d'investigation', the narrator finds himself 'nez à nez . . . avec le monsieur qui me servait d'ombre' ('face to face . . . with the man who served as my shadow'). This 'monsieur' is a textual reminder of 'le jeune homme qui n'avait pas de femme, (qui) s'assit auprès de moi' ('the young man without a woman who sat beside me'), which in turn refers back to the previous observation: 'Personne ne me dispute la conquête de la veille, quoique l'un des individus soit sans femme' ('Nobody disputes my conquest of the previous day despite the fact that one individual is without a woman'). We become aware that there is within the text a shadowy figurc without a woman, a figure who has a certain affinity with the narrator if only because he sits beside him and serves as his shadow. 'L'homme qui a perdu son reflet' and 'l'homme qui a perdu son ombre',

Memorial stone of Nerval in the town of Senlis in northern France.

might in different light, be the same figure, yet there is a confrontation between the narrator and his shadow in which it appears that each is in constant pursuit of the other. The shadowy figure is in a situation uncannily akin to the narrator's own. The narrator is able to relieve his companion's anxiety about Viennese police censure vis à vis foreigners and particularly the French. This reassurance depends on his consultation with a certain 'directeur', 'ancien poète lyrique, . . . passé à la police, en prenant de L'âge, à peu près comme on se *range* après les folies de la jeunesse . . . ' ('former lyric poet, . . . turned policeman when he got old, almost like becoming stable after the follies of youth' . . .). All we learn about the encounter is 'Nous avons causé littérature' ('We talked literature'), and it is after this that the narrator admits, 'Et moi-même, je me regarde comme un poète étranger, égaré dans cette société mi-parti d'aristocratie brillante et de populaire en apparence insoucieux' ('And I myself, I regard myself as a foreign poet, lost in this society which is partly brilliantly aristocratic and partly apparently carefree vulgar'). We reach such a confusion of identities, of figures relayed and fragmented by time and maturity: 'les folies de la jeunesse', and by distance and language: the difference and vulnerability of an 'étranger égaré', such a confusion of identities as might only occur between the writer and a reader who has been constantly teased into suspense by the text's continual promise and concomitant deferral of revelation: 'Cest que le dénouement que tu auras prévu en lisant les premièrs pages a été suspendu tout ce temps' ('The denouement you will have expected while reading the first pages has been suspended all this

time'), 'mais décidément l'encre est trop mauvaise, et j'ajourne la suite de mais observations' ('but decidely the ink is too bad, and I'll defer my next observations'), 'J'hésite à te continver ma confession o mon ami! comme tu peux voir que j'al longtemps hésité à t'envoyer cette lettre' ('I continue my confession with some reluctance my friend! as you can see that I've long been reluctant to send you this letter'). Then 'Les Amours de Vienne' concludes with an ultimate *mise en suspens* as it were: 'La dame me retient en me demandant si (J'allais écrire une phrase qui serait une indication). Enfin sache seulement qu'elle me demande un petit service que je peux lui rendre' ('the lady detained me, asking me if [I was going to write a sentence which would be an indication]. Just remember that she asked me to do her a small favour'). He is to do a favour for this woman who has dismissed everyone else present, with the pretext that she has a letter for him, only to confide when alone with him that she has no letter to give him. We can only conclude that his favour involves writing the letter that she has feigned to mean to write, like Pandora herself (in the text of that name, ***Pandora***) of whom we are told on first encounter: 'Une lettre qu'elle faisait semblant d'écrire n'avancait guère . . . ' ('A letter she pretended to be writing hardly progressed . . . '). As if, with retrospective knowledge that a letter will be written, the narrator describes how Pandora pretends to be writing at the moment. An allusion to pretence, and to her lack of success or want of conclusion, is the excuse for leaving content unrevealed, to be invented; it is an invitation to the reader to conjecture, like the excuse of infinite confusion or misunderstanding which leaves the content of dialogue unrevealed in 'Les Amours de Vienne', and like the indecipherable enigma posited as Pandora's definition in the opening to *Pandora*. It is as if unrevealed content has become a paradigm of reading, an abstract like the mythic Pandora's box which harbours the conjecture of all who care to guess. This box becomes an instrument of the text which constantly teases conjecture while persistently denying textual representation: 'La Pandora c'est tout dire car je ne veux pas dire tout'. Pandora is a narrative which says things in other words; it corresponds to Paul de Man's 'allegory of figure' [from 'Excuses', *Allegories of Reading,* 1979].

In one *Pandora* manuscript, Nerval introduces his text: 'Je suis obligé d'expliquer que *Pandora* fait suite aux aventures que j'ai publiées autre fois dans le Revue de Paris, et réimprimés dans l'introduction do mon Voyage en Orient, sous ce titre: *"les Amours de Vienne"*' (I am obliged to explain that Pandora is a sequel to ventures which I published in the past in la Revue de Paris, and reprinted in the introduction to my Voyage en Orient, under the title: 'les Amours de Vienne'), and in so doing acknowledges a link over a gap in time between the two text. *Pandora* written thirteen years after 'Les Amours de Vienne', remembers this text and repeats its gestures. It is memory which lends the intensity of time and reflection to what I have called *Pandora*'s opening gesture of familiarity: 'Vous l'avez tous connu, ô mes amis!'. This is an ironic intensity for is it not Pandora's nature to be encountered, 'connue', and yet remain unknown 'inconnue'?

Pandora possesses the intensity of repeated gesture and is different from 'Les Amours de Vienne' in its betrayal of a more urgent sense of drama, perceptible within textual manifestations of the narrator's anger. These betray an edge of anxiety dramatized within the problematics of the story. There is as well more evidence of conflict in the *Pandora* text where the strange inhabitants of 'Les Amours de Vienna', 'le lombard', 'le Magyar' and 'le Bohème' have become rival suitors for the intractable Pandora. Pursuit of her is now interwoven with references to his difference from these 'others' feared preferred. The narrator's first scene with Pandora is heralded by a metonymic reference to her presence, a disguising of her: 'il faisait très froid à Vienne la veille de Saint Sylvestre et je me plaisais beaucoup dans le boudoir de la Pandora' ('It was very cold in Vienna on New Year's Eve and I was very pleasantly occupied in Pandora's boudoir'). She has previously been disguised in a rhetorical apostrophe to Vienna and we are scarcely given time to remember this before the metonymy shifts as the coldness here evoked with reference to Vienna re-occurs to veil recurring references to Pandora's presence in the text: 'Je traversai les glacis couverts de neige et je rentrai à Léopoldstadt' ('I crossed the snow-covered slopes and returned to Léopoldstadt'). Here 'la Pandora' is heralded in the guise of 'La Kathi' who coldly thwarts his desire in a demand for payment of money he does not possess, a textual reminder of his preoccupation with her possible preference for rich barons as lovers. She leaves him suffering from not being preferred and re-experiencing his lack of means to win her. Not surprisingly the situation engenders some kind of reparation, be it only symbolic 'Je me fis cire, car la neige avait fort détérioré ma chaussure' ('I had my footwear waxed, for the snow had done much damage'). But the cold strikes again, symbolically castrating, after the charade fiasco: 'le sourire glacé des spectatrices . . . me remplit d'épouvante' ('the frozen smile of the female spectators . . . filled me with terror'), as if Pandora in all her disguises is watching him in total derision. When moments of difference occur in the text the narrator's compensatory virtues would seem to have their source in his lyrical outpourings and demonstrations of sensibility: 'Je n'ai pu moi-même planter le clou symbolique dans le tronc chargé de fer . . . ', 'mais j'ai versé mes plus douces larmes et les plus purs effusions de mon coeur', 'j'ai attendri de mes chants d'amour', and 'promené mes rêveries' ('I myself have not been able to set the symbolic nail in the iron-laden trunk . . . , but I've shed my sweetest tears, poured out from my heart the purest effusions, I've moved to pity with my songs of love, and followed the paths of reverie'); the emotive exposition of a Romantic vulnerability, which has led him to fall prey to many a Pandora. Yet this is a rhetorical lyricism, for within it we might discern the intention and irony that he, the narrator, is separated from these 'others' by a language which is both the relief of compensation and the pain of difference.

In *Pandora,* there is a remarkable development upon the movement of 'Les Amours de Vienne', a development crucial to this reading: as the female figures of the text, who all represent Pandora as she does them, displace each other in their dance through the text, changing partners; so the letter, first signifying in his first scene with her, changes hands as, unwritten or unread, it is submitted to the same movement of traceless circularity. Content is always withheld, yet the scene of the writing is described: 'Une lettre qu'elle faisait semblant d'écrire n'avançait guère et les délicieuses pattes de mouche de son écriture s'entremêlaient follement avec je ne sais queis arpèges qu'elle tirait par instant des cordes de sa harpe' ('A letter written in an elusive hand confused with occasional mysterious pluckings at the strings of a harp'), itself disguised as a gilded siren, undetermined like the text, holds mystery and irrational charm. Yet is it not the same letter which re-occurs throughout *Pandora* as a sign of the writing, as unsubstantial evidence of figural language, just as in 'Les Amours de Vienne' a series of insubstantial verbal encounters established a similar movement of deferred or suspended conclusion? Is it not now perceptible that in scenes with the structure of dialogue or of letter-sending, Nerval is presenting the most remarkable figural espousal of the writing of his text, is defining the strategy of his own discourse?

The narrator re-encounters the letter of the first scene with Pandora, when in search of a postal order from his uncle. The mandate reappears transformed for the narrator to sign in the charade scene. In the second instance it remains unopened but illuminated by the rays of the sun. The form of the writing is perceptible yet content still withheld: 'Un rayon de soleil tombait d'aplomb sur cette lettre insidieuse. Les lignes s'y suivaient impitoyablement sans le moindre croisement de mandat sur la poste d'effets de commerce. Elle ne contenait de toute évidence que des maximes de morale et des conseils d'économie' ('A beam of sunlight fell directly onto that insidious letter. The lines of writing followed each other relentlessly without the slightest crossing made by a billed postal order. It obviously contained only moralising maxims and advised economy'). Hoping for money, he finds only language. We remember a contest of means between the narrator and those who might be preferred to him, invariably a contest between language and worldly riches, for the narrator has no money as such, rather he possesses a verbal currency by which the very contest is mediated. Might not this reference be read as a figural counter-image of this text, which located in the oppositional world of desire and *écriture,* splits itself from the world of order and writes against the prescriptive language of 'maximes de morale et conseils d'économie'?

The contents of the letter are indirectly disclosed, they are recalled to the narrator when he arrives home, 'J'y trouvai une lettre qui me rappelait que je devais participer à une brillante représentation où assisterait une partie de la cour et de la diplomatie. Il s'agissait de jouer des charades. Je pris mon rôle avec humeur car je ne l'avais guère étudié'. ('I found a letter there which reminded me that I had to participate in a brilliant performance which would be attended by members of the court and diplomats. We were to play charades. I took my role temperamently as I had hardly studied it'). The symbolic letter chain continues as we recall that members of 'la cour' and 'la diplomatie' figure frequently in the text and most notably in the charade game and in the dream where they are peceptibly in conflict with the narrator's desire and provoke a considerable outburst of temperament. With its shifts, displacements and toings and froings of time and object of desire, the spiral dancing movement of the text is in itself an enactment of language, like both the charade game and the dream; the writer's role, then, like the narrator's, is conflictual and temperamental. We remember that, when rejected by 'La Kathi' in preference for her baron—a richer rival, the narrator indulges in an illusion of freedom and extravagance while the writing nevertheless betrays anxiety about a responsibility he is at pains to forget, the responsibility of his role: 'me voilà libre. Je descends le faubourg en étudiant mon rôle que je tenais à la marin' ('Free I went through the outskirts of the town studying the role I held in my hand'). The role in his hand is a preoccupation which teases his extravagant desire, for amidst the indulgence he encounters his own guilt; the woman he meets is weary and reproachful and amidst verbal extravagances such as 'je m'inondai', 'j'arrosai' and 'regorgaient' grimace the sweet nothings of Nuremberg: 'fanfreluches', 'bamboches', 'et poupées'. The role is a reminder of commitment to time and space, to the 'rendez-vous positif', (the illusory *point de repère* articulated in repeated reference to time and place throughout 'Les Amours de Vienne') and anxiety about the rendez-vous is soon manifest as the feared preferred appear in disguise. Again the narrator must set himself apart from

these others. This he claims to do in the cherishing of memory, space for protection or so it seems, from Pandora creator of artifice. In the 'souvenir chéri' he fosters an illusion of keeping time to himself, only to be informed on arrival at the rendez-vous that impromptu charade games have been invented to *kill time*—a figural insight into this text, which enacts its own theory of writing; in which disguise, displacement and repetition create an illusion of coincidence and confusion, a synchronicity which suspends the logic of time; the arrival at the 'rendez-vous positif'.

Figurally the whole charade game might be a fictional parody of the text itself in which a frivolous burlesque detracts from a nevertheless perceptible significance. Under one disguise or another the rival suitors assume that which, theoretically, can only be the role of the writer himself: it is to them that poetry, soliloquy and tragic declamation appear to belong. Deprived of his own language, then, and seduced by the charm of Pandora, the narrator is in danger of having to play their game, but he intervenes as 'le destin' of this *'Roman Comique'*, this charade, to put an end to the potential loss and robbery of his language. He does this by forgetting his words and the language which is his role: 'Je fis manquer la représentation'. He forgets his words exactly as the writing forgets its words. In dialogue without words and letters without words, representation is 'missed', 'made to fail': 'manqué'. The narrator's forgetting of words (assigned by them) allows him to spoil their game and re-appropriate language for himself. It is he therefore, who takes over letter-writing: 'Et j'écrivis à la déesse une lettre d'un style abracadabrant. Je lui rappelais les souffrances de Prométhée quand il mit au jour une créature aussi dépravée qu'elle. Je critiquai sa boîte à malice et son ajustement de bayadère. J'osai même m'attaquer à ses pieds serpentins que je voyais passer insidieusement sous sa robe' ('I wrote the goddess a letter in an amazing style. I reminded her of Prometheus' suffering when he gave birth to a creature as depraved as she. I criticised her box of tricks and her oriental dancing costume. I even dared affront her serpentine feet which I glimpsed moving insideously beneath her dress'). A temporary narrational break with Pandora veils a swing to critical distance. This 'créature dépravée' has given rise to much suffering. Her 'boîte à malice' is the source of all her artifice. Her oriental dancing and veiled sinuosity, like her writing 'pattes de mouches (qui) s'entremêlaient follement', and her 'lettre insidieuse', have rendered her elusive and indeterminable. This letter which the narrator writes as a reminder, 'quatre pages d'un style abracadabrant' resembles and recalls the Pandora text itself ('des bouts de papier de toutes dimensions entremêles de figures cabalistiques').

The charade game is followed by a dream which repeats it and also conjures the displaced re-appearance of figures previously evoked, of elements transposed from other parts of the text. Pandora appears dancing as she danced in the charade and as the entranced narrator tries to touch her, she shifts to represent another female figure, 'l'altière Catherine, impératrice de toutes les Russies' (a combined textual memory of 'La Kathi' remembered for her exigency, and the 'auguste archiduchesse' evoked earlier in rhetorical nostalgia). In his dream the narrator himself appears as a prince figure who almost falls for the empress's beguiling game. The dream, however stages a temporary finale: 'elle avait disparu pour l'éternité', until, remembering the 'grenats' which decorated Pandora's oriental costume in the charade, the narrator swallows 'quelques pépins de grenade'. Then, as if in memory of the deprivation of his role, the threat of castration experienced during the charade game, he finds himself decapitated and his head left on an oriental doorstep, 'à la porte du serail'. The charade itself is recalled in the dream by the anouncement of 'Une opéra en trois actes', a metaphoric reference to the three act charade game, and the forgetting of the narrator's words is an event transposed onto three sister figures, 'soeurs du ciel', encountered in the dream, 'qui avaient oublié la langue des hommes' ('who had forgotten the language of men').

Both the charade and the dream seem metaphorically condensed in the next scene, during which the narrator stands his ground when in conflict with the now familiar 'aliens' of the text and makes a symbolic refusal to recognise the language of the other: 'Ils se mirent à causer dans une langue que j'ignorais, mais je ne lâchai pas un pouce de terrain' ('They began to talk in a language unknown to me, but I didn't give an inch [of ground]'). He is nevertheless forced to retreat from those who do not speak the same language and returns home to find a letter, the text's first and last, both rehearsal and repeat performance, '*répétition*': Je reçus un billet de répétition qui me rejoignait d'apprendre le rôle de Valbelle pour jouer une pièce intitulée 'Deux mots dans la forêt'. He refuses to act in this play of language, 'je repartis', assumes a critical distance from the drama: 'et je repartis pour Salzbourg où j'allai réfléchir amèrement dans l'ancienne maison de Mozart, habitée aujourd'hui par un chocolatier' ('And I left for Salzburg where I went to reflect bitterly in Mozart's former home now occupied by a chocolate maker'). From Vienna to Salzburg where an enterprise of petty indulgence has appropriated the former home of a musical genius, an apparent inversion of cultural values but one with rhetorical significance. As if Art must in the end encounter economics. We witness a similar instance of bathos, a fall from the high hopes of fantasy to the material world of worldly riches when, encountered at Pandora's haunting reappearance (a year to the day of their first meeting), her box spills only gilded artifice.

Yet the box of unrevealed content, a paradigm of reading, remains abstractly inscribed within *Pandora* until the final words of the text suddenly stop naming writing as it were, to reinscribe Pandora within the Prometheus myth (in which she was sent by Jupiter to punish Prometheus for hubris), and thereby to reveal unnamable agony: 'O Jupiter! quand finira mon supplice?' ('O Jupiter! when will my torment end?') The struggle is prefigured in the despair of the text's epigraphic quotation from Goethe's *Faust*, and is echoed within the text by Pandora's tormenting question uttered at the moment of her inevitable reappearance, 'Où as-tu caché le feu du ciel que tu dérobas

à Jupiter?' ('Where have you hidden the fire of the gods, stolen from Jupiter?') This only intensifies an already painful awareness of the excessive nature of his desire (dilemma both Faustian and Promethean) and here of the dilemma of a languagebound creature too aware of language's lack. It is here in the end a cruel reference to his Promethean situation which opens an old wound: 'car je sens encore à mon front le bec éternel du vautour dont Alcide m'a délivré' ('I still feel at my forehead the perpetual pecking of the vulture from which I was delivered by Alcides'), and recalls the suffering evoked in the specular letter to Pandora: 'Je lui rappelais les souffrances de Prométhée quand il mit au jour une créature aussi dépravée qu'elle'. The *Pandora* text is worried, *tracassé,* by these references to wounding and suffering. The dancing spiral movement is interrupted as the cries from Faust and Prometheus tear the fabric of the text, for these are universal figures whose mythic torment here remembered, breaks out from the Viennese referentiality of the test they frame. Betrayed, is the ironic despair of one who calls in the knowledge that there will be no response from the figure invoked. This agonising invocation of a mythic god is a futile question masking a groan which wrenches the text apart, leaving a weeping wound. The narrator's sudden identifications with Prometheus betray the denial of communication with a pain which is his. The wound erupts into reading to spread pain throughout the text. It functions as a rhetorical trope, performs a crisis of meaning. The absent subject assumes presence as pain and Pandora assumes absence as the lack his despair speaks. Then the language of the text's opening gesture: ' . . . *la Pandora* c'est tout dire, car je ne veux pas dire tout' reverberates with the ironic tension of an ineffable. It is a well of cruel irony which holds the writer victim, and therefore blind to the irony yet experiencing the cruelty; a cruel irony which speaks in spite of him to betray one still subject to torture when delivered of the experience of it: 'Car je sens encore à mon front le bec éternel du vautour dont Alcide m'a délivré'. The words of a figure whose ineffable pain is a self-inflicted wound leave us with the haunting memories or phantom pains of the psyche.

Pandora invokes a reading which attends to its figural quality, both to a rhetorical irony which makes representation fail and instead names writing, and to the unnamable residue this leaves, the presence and cruel irony of a wound which painfully leaks the subject. To recognize *Pandora*'s quality of figure is to accede to a peculiar textuality which will both resist and overrun the assigning of limits.

Ross Chambers (essay date 1984)

SOURCE: "Seduction Renounced: 'Sylvie' as Narrative Act," in *Story and Situation: Narrative Seduction and the Power of Fiction,* University of Minnesota Press, 1984, pp. 97-122.

[*Here, Chambers analyzes several narrative approaches in* Sylvie *and comments on themes in the novella.*]

The Narration of Madness

Why [. . .] does the narrator produce the narrative act that is *Sylvie*? "Si j'écrivais un roman," he says (and [. . .] it is precisely *not* a romance he is writing), "jamais je ne pourrais faire accepter l'histoire d'un coeur épris de deux amours simultanés." This means that, in the antiromance he does give us, the purpose is not to resolve differences and contradictions by means of seductive discourse but to make sense of something that is, on the face of it, implausible, or more accurately, to have this implausibility "accepted"—by means of a narrative act that might be called, not seductive, but therapeutic. In this way, although from a slightly unexpected angle, *Sylvie* demonstrates a certain similarity with *Aurélia*: in both texts, the problem is the narration of a form of madness, an experience of doubleness which common judgment might regard as unlikely. To have others accept this story, for the narrator, is a way of having them accept *himself,* by making believable for them what he himself considers strange or aberrant: here, the fact of being capable of "deux amours simultanés." As a first step toward having others accept him, he must presumably, therefore, begin by achieving an understanding of himself—and the narrative does offer certain characteristics of a self-analysis (whose primary *destinataire* is identical with its *destinateur*). But it is also clear that, for the narrator, self-understanding and self-acceptance are insufficient and that acceptance of self needs to be validated by the acceptance of others. An implication of this is that the narration of *Sylvie* will be carried out by an "I" who is attempting to understand what is incomprehensible in his own existence but in a framework of concern for the values and perspectives of a readership that is assumed to be, by definition, unsympathetic to the madness represented by a heart capable of double love, and hence to the narrator's basic program. So, the problem of acceptance resolves partly into that of rendering the actual sensation of double love (i.e., making it acceptable as a possibility in lived experience) and partly into that of obtaining some positive evaluation of this madness (i.e., making it acceptable in ethical or social terms).

This, in turn, implies a rhetorical tactic—or more accurately a double rhetoric—designed, on the one hand, to obtain the reader's involvement in the adventure and, on the other, to elicit his or her understanding judgment. Let us begin with the latter. The double-loving heart is in love, first, with a twofold image (Adrienne-Aurélie) representing the mirage of cyclical extratemporality and second, with a real figure (Sylvie) who embodies the linear temporality of history and change. A "therapeutic" account of their double love must then incorporate, and make acceptable, both the desire that has Adrienne-Aurélie as its object and the desire that concerns Sylvie (and we will see that this is indeed what happens). But part of the rhetorical tactic consists of an initial displacement of the idea of madness, which comes to refer only to the love of Adrienne-Aurélie (i.e., "simultaneous" love): "Aimer une religieuse sous la forme d'une actrice! . . . et si c'était la même!—Il y a de quoi devenir fou! . . . Reprenons pied sur le réel." In this context, the lover of Sylvie, whose

desire has a real object, tends to appear as the ancestor of the narrator himself, since the latter inherits the experience of the former and incorporates into his narration the disenchanted view of "illusions" and "chimères" that, precisely, we see Sylvie's lover acquiring. For this narrator, the way to make the hero's capacity for "deux amours simultanés" acceptable is to classify as madness the attractive notion of simultaneity (along with the conception of time it applies) while projecting as sensible only respect for the linear time he associates with "la douce réalité." That this involves a certain betrayal is indisputable—he is betraying both the hero's heart, with its double love, and his own narrative program, since in order to bring about acceptance of his double-loving heart he is obliged to deny half of his desire.

However, these are the terms in which, referring apparently to his love for Aurélie, he is led to conclude: "Telles sont les chimères qui charment et égarent au matin de la vie." The act of deixis—relegating the *narré,* slightly disdainfully, to a distanced status that clearly separates it from the moment of *narration,* and hence from the narrating "I," is eloquent in its implications. "J'ai essayé de les fixer . . . ," the text continues: here the narrating "I" appears ("je"), but taking responsibility only for the *récit,* having no other task than to stabilize through writing the chimeras of the past. (In which, it is true, he displays a certain fidelity to that past, since to "fix" a chimera is to reinforce its principal charm, its resistance to linear time). What follows, however, continues to insist on the distance between the time for illusions and the time for narration: "J'ai essayé de les fixer *sans beaucoup d'ordre,* mais bien des cœurs me comprendront." To "fix" a chimera "sans beaucoup d'ordre" is to compromise what is essentially *order* by transposing it into the world in which entropy is the master—the world of time; it is an essentially unfaithful way of being faithful to it, since it subordinates fixity to the lack of order characteristic of the universe of temporal flow and change. "Mais"—this "but" is a crucial one—such is the very condition of gaining the acceptance of others: "bien des cœurs me comprendront," for it is not in spite of the disorder of presentation that the chimeras are now comprehensible but because of the narrative disorder, which functions as a sign of the narrator's allegiance to the world of time. In this way—the chimeras becoming acceptable *as illusions,* precisely—"bien des cœurs *me* comprendront."

This means that the narrator "I," having distanced himself from youthful illusions, is appealing for understanding, not of them, but for himself. And appropriately, he follows up immediately with a passage in praise of experience (the recognition of linear time) that, separating him from his illusions, has made him what he is. "Les illusions tombent l'une après l'autre, comme les écorces d'un fruit, et le fruit c'est l'expérience." It is as if the writing "I" of the narrator—"qu'on me pardonne ce style vieilli," he says a few lines later, displaying his awareness of being a writer (and a writer addressing an audience assumed to be out of tune with the charms of nostalgia)—is defining himself in opposition to the desiring "I" he once was, since his erstwhile double desire has now split into "chimères" on the one hand and on the other "expérience," that is, renunciation. It is ironic, then, that the understanding he needs as the subject of a strange desire can only be obtained by presenting himself as a (now reformed) writing "I."

Throughout the story, the narrator presents to the implied reader (the "hearts" who are entrusted with "understanding" him) this reassuring persona. The "I" who speaks in the text speaks *in place of,* not on behalf of, the "I" he once was; and to do so he uses language that distinguishes him carefully from his former dream-ridden self. This is a language of philosophical wisdom and cultured serenity, the language of one who has learned to "take things as they may be." What he calls "le monde des rêveries" is duly gratified with his comprehension, and he shows himself a most judicious analyst of psychological phenomena and states of semiconsciousness, about which he produces considered observations: "Cet état, où l'esprit résiste encore aux bizarres combinaisons du songe, permet souvent de voir se presser en quelques minutes les tableaux les plus saillants d'une longue période de vie." For the main value to which he now subscribes is the thirst for knowledge, the "soif de connaître" he attributes to humankind as its only eternal characteristic, a desire of the mind replacing the desire of the heart as "mobile de toute force et de toute activité." And the tradition in which he now seems to situate himself in order to judge and understand matters of the heart is the tradition of the philosophers, from Lucretius and Virgil, as he says, to Montaigne, Descartes, and Rousseau.

But this same distance that intervenes, by the nature of his philosophical investigation, between himself and the manifestations of his erotic desire (such as memory and dreams), can be seen also when the narrator concerns himself, as a folklorist and historian (that is, a Parisian) with the area of experience of which Sylvie is an embodiment, the folk culture of the Valois. The peasants, who are "peu étymologistes de leur nature," as he says, are ignorant of what he, the narrator, knows, that is, the historical dimension of the customs, monuments, and manner of speech of the region. Once, as a child, he had shared their unawareness: " . . . nous formions le cortège . . . —sans savoir que nous ne faisions que répéter d'âge en âge une fête druidique, survivant aux monarchies et aux religions nouvelles." But soon—having been sent away to school, having lived in Paris, having traveled abroad— the young man who was initially indistinguishable from the peasant population began to return among them with forms of knowledge (historical, archaeological, geographical, literary) that set him apart. The story of his alienation from Sylvie does not involve only the changes on her side, setting the hardworking and practical girl apart from an idle and chimerical poet; it results also from the hero's increasingly "Parisian" culture that gives him a stranger's viewpoint on Valois life, whether he is evaluating the continuity of its traditions in his role as historian or whether, in his poetic moments, he is nostalgically lamenting the changes that take place there.

The alienation that comes to separate the hero "I" from Sylvie clearly foreshadows the narrator "I"'s alienation from "himself." In this respect, the narrative voice can be seen in the final analysis as being almost equally removed from the part of the hero's heart that loved Sylvie as it is from the part of his heart that is now judged to have been a victim of illusion in the form of "simultaneous" loves. The *only* continuity connecting the speaker with the personage on whose behalf he speaks is "experience"—but "experience" is the experience of loss, it is a principle of discontinuity in that it is disillusioning, separating one not only from what one calls "chimères" but from the *whole* of one's past—from the love of Sylvie as well as from the love of Adrienne-Aurélie. The upshot is that, in the way the connotational field of "madness" ("folie") was initially restricted, for tactical reasons, so as to cover not both of the hero's loves in their incompatibility but only the love of Adrienne-Aurélie as love of the simultaneous, now the term "chimères," in the summing-up phrase that introduces the *Dernier Feuillet,* comes in a compensatory way to acquire a broadened range of significance, referring both to the disillusioning courtship of Sylvie and to the hopeless love for Aurélie(-Adrienne), and consequently distancing the whole of the hero "I"'s adventure.

But what this means is that, in rejecting both sides of his double love as "chimères," the narrator is also recognizing their solidarity. And this is the solidarity that can now be found—but with a positive valorization—if one looks again at the formulation of the narrator "I"'s program in the phrase "J'ai essayé de les fixer sans beaucoup d'ordre." A new reading is possible, which corresponds to the other half of the rhetorical tactic (the part that consists of obtaining the reader's adherence to, or involvement with, the lived experience of double love). In this reading, instead of seeing in the oxymoronic "fixer"/"sans beaucoup d'ordre" the sign of a deliberate distancing, it is perceived as a paradoxical collocation indexing a narrative project no less strange than the hero's own double love, since it attempts to be no less respectful of the continuity characteristic of "chimères" than of the discontinuity recognized by disenchantment and experience. There is no incompatibility here—as we will see in due course—with the narrator "I" who espouses the stance of philosophical wisdom; but this statement of his narrative program can be seen as an *échangeur,* a switching device, which allows the definition of a distanced mode of narration to reverse itself into an invitation, or appeal, for a sympathetic, and indeed empathetic (nondistanced), mode of reading. The narrator who is so anxious to distinguish himself from the hero he once was is also no less anxious for his narrative to be read as the faithful reflection of the double postulation that once occupied the hero's heart—the postulation he now wishes to have "accepted" by those "hearts" that are capable of "understanding." His success, which depends partly on *distancing the narrative act* from the narrative content, depends equally on a second and absolutely complementary tactic, which aims to achieve the *reader's adherence* to the self-same narrative content.

Hence, the presence in the story of a series of *models for reading* that function as indices of the narrative code, models of order and disorder none of which is individually capable of being applied to the narrative in its full extent but that cumulatively form a complex that covers the whole. These models, logically speaking, are opposed to each other; yet they are simultaneously valid; in this way, they call for a reading of what is perhaps an impossible totality, but a totality that would, if one could achieve it, transcend the opposed categories, the logical oppositions in the text. Thanks to this, the reader's "heart" would be the place where understanding might take place of the double loves that the mind can accept only as "chimères," as "folie." The reader would now apprehend the text *simultaneously* in the mode of order and permanence and in the mode of disorder and change; such a reader's heart would become, in relation to the text, "épris d'un double amour."

Festivity, Theatre, Ruins

The first reading model is that of festivity (*la fête*) as a celebration of cultural continuity and repetition, as in the "fête de l'arc," which, we have already seen, recurs "d'âge en âge . . . survivant aux monarchies et aux religions nouvelles," surviving—that is—the course of history itself. The emblem of the *fête* is the procession ("cortège"), itself an image of repetition within continuity, whether it be the "cortège de l'arc" or the girls' round dance on the lawn or the "gracieuse *théorie* renouvelée des jours antiques," which turns a later "fête de l'arc" into what is at once a reproduction of Watteau's *Voyage à Cythère* and an "image des galantes solennités d'autre-fois." Once more, I do not intend to underscore here, after so much criticism, from the Proust of *Contre Sainte-Beuve* to Sarah Kofman, the ways in which the text of *Sylvie* lends itself to a reading that focuses on its repetitive structures, its thematics of similarity, its temporal minglings and confusions of period with period. This has been the classic reading of the *nouvelle*.

I will note instead that festivities, in the tale, are subject to a kind of degenerative trend, as a result of which their significance as a mere "image," a "*mirage* de la gloire et de la beauté" (my emphasis), gradually comes to predominate. Even of the round dance on the lawn it is said, symptomatically, that "nous *pensions* être en paradis" (my emphasis); but it is the scene of the pseudowedding at the home of the aunt—with its disguised participants, their consciousness of their own disguise as Greuzean "accordés de village," the many allusions to the passing of time and the brevity of happiness—that most clearly illustrates the fragility of the *fête,* its theatrical quality. One might think also of the village dance that is going on in chapters III through VII while the hero, his mind alive with memory, makes his nocturnal dash through the Valois countryside toward Loisy: it symbolizes memory as the *fête* of the mind, on the one hand, but, on the other, it prepares for the morning-after-the-night-before mood of the following day, with its overcast ("maussade") weather, its sleepy villagers, and the hero's own sense of fatigue, growing disenchantment, and final abandonment of the Valois and everything for which it has, up to that point, stood. In this respect, the supper party with Père Dodu, a modest festivity whose subdued mood is specifically attributed to the fact that it follows the livelier *fête* of the night before, is

symptomatic: it typifies a mood that prevails in a narrative that itself "comes after" and is a festivity "de lendemain de fête." The festive character of *Sylvie* derives from the *memories* of previous festivities rather than from any direct or immediate rendering of what are contrastingly described as "les fêtes *naïves* de notre jeunesse" (my emphasis).

So, there is a mental component in the festivity model, and a consequent vulnerability with respect to everyday reality, that invite comparison with the theatre, the place of illusions. The opening words of *Sylvie* ("Je sortais d'un théâtre où tous les soirs je paraissais aux avant-scènes en grande tenue de soupirant") teach us that the whole text can be read as the story of an *emergence from the theatre* into cold daylight. In point of fact, things are more complex, since part of the narrative is devoted also to the story of the hero's *entry* into the world of the theatre, that is, to an account of how he came to the point of appearing every evening "en grande tenue de soupirant," as the lover of Aurélie, and this narrative is conducted in tandem with that of the events (the exciting night of memories, the disenchanting day in the Valois, the courtship of Aurélie) that cured him of his addiction to a *romanesque* and theatrical conception of love and thus brought him out of this world of inauthenticity. "Ce n'était donc pas l'amour," he says at the culminating point of this process "Mais où donc est-il?" If the *fête* figures what is genuinely comforting in the phenomenon of memory, then the theatre figures the false hold memory can exert, the fascination it has for a mind caught up in love of an "image" and unable or unwilling to disturb the "magic mirror" of simultaneity that has him in its thrall. In the theatre, there is no real continuity of past and present, only a resemblance that masks their actual discontinuity; and although the actress may *remind* one of the nun, the two are not identical. To believe in their identity, therefore, is to be subject to an illusion, a "chimère," and indeed only the distance the hero is so careful to maintain between himself and the actress makes it possible for him to protect the "image" for which he longs.

From the very start, then, there is a hint of the vulnerability of the theatrical experience when it enters into contact with the real, and this is confirmed by the gradual degeneration of the theatrical theme as the story develops. Thus, in the episode of the "wedding" at the home of the old aunt, the reference is to the fairy plays of the Théâtre des Funambules, with their magical, but palpably false, dénouements. With respect to Châalis, where he recalls the performance of a "mystère des anciens temps" in which Adrienne appeared, "transfigurée par son costume," the narrator finds he can no longer be certain whether the details, as he says, are "real" or whether he has "dreamed" them; and this *mental* theatre will soon become the initiatory *hell* in which, courting Aurélie, as a latter-day figuration of the redemptive goddess Isis, the hero passes "par tous les cercles de ces lieux d'épreuves qu'on appelle théâtres." In this way, the theatre as a place of initiation becomes retrospectively identified with the Parisian club ("cercle") in which the young men of the time, the hero among them, indulged in "rêves renouvelés d'Alexandrie" and "l'homme matériel aspirait au bouquet de roses qui devait le regénérer par les mains de la belle Isis"—a club that, as the narrator knows, was an ivory tower. "Vue de près, la femme réelle révoltait notre ingénuité; il fallait qu'elle apparût reine ou déesse, et surtout n'en pas approcher." The theatrical theme has brought us back full circle, then, to the narrator in his "grande tenue de soupirant"—but it is this whole dreamworld "renouvelé d'Alexandrie" that is destined to collapse when once it comes, at last, into contact with reality. The travels with Aurélie's company, the hero's declaration of love to her, "au château, près d'Orry, sur la même place verte où pour la première fois j'avais vu Adrienne," and her refusal of his hand are a structural repetition and thematic confirmation of the disenchantment brought about already by the return to the Valois in the night of memories, followed by the disillusioning wanderings of the day and the collapse of the hero's aspirations at Père Dodu's supper party, with the announcement of Sylvie's forthcoming marriage.

As a self-acknowledged inheritor of the Enlightenment, and a reader of the Abbé Terrasson in particular, Nerval quite naturally associated the idea of the theatre as a place of initiatory ordeal with that of *artifice*. Everywhere in the text, the magical illusion is deflated by reference to the material means that produce it—the footlights that shine on Aurélie from below, the twisting sun of the Funambules stage, the gilt cardboard producing a "cercle de lumière" about the head of Adrienne—so that what is mediated for the hero is not a passage from the profane to the sacred but from illusion to reality, a process of disenchantment that is also a discovery of the real. Here there is doubtless a lesson for the reader who is first invited to share the hero's fascination with an art of illusion and then to join him in discovering the theatrical machinery, the "clockwork" that underlies it, and, hence, in renouncing it. One should not be content to read *Sylvie* in submission to the "charm" of a narrative constructed according to the theatrical principle of resemblance; one must also conceive one's reading as an initiation into the artifices of the tale, the seductive secrets of its "miroir magique," and hence as an *emergence* out of this fascinating but deceptive world into the real. For, in "Sylvie," alongside the *fête* (whose patron is Adrienne) and the theatre (presided over by Aurélie), there is also a whole art of lucidity, of the "après-fête," of the daylight world of time. This art has, of course, as its representative the figure of Sylvie.

Sylvie is the one who remains, who survives in the world of time. Present like Adrienne in the hero's childhood and like Aurélie in his young manhood, she is the only one of the three to remain present in his life at the end, in other words, the only one who participates in his life as *narrator*. But in this way and for this reason, she is associated with the whole idea of *aftermath*: after the nocturnal *fêtes* (dominated by Adrienne), Sylvie is there the next day, ready to walk with the hero (although she sometimes disappears on account of fatigue, leaving him significantly alone); after the breakup with the theatrical Aurélie who then fades from the hero's life, Sylvie is still there,

with her husband and children, unavailable as an object of love but always willing to welcome him as a friend and a visitor. She is the patron of an art of the *residual*—which both signifies the power of entropy and yet resists its force—and she invites us to read *Sylvie* in terms of "making do" with what is "left over" (another name for which is *bricolage*).

Hence, the persistent motif of "bric-à-brac" in the tale. It is a manifestation of the dispersion, destruction, and disorder produced by the passing of time; but it is evidence also of a human need to preserve these residual objects so as to use them as a point of departure for memory, and even to collect them—"sans beaucoup d'ordre"—into a more or less harmonious blend that might serve as a monument in the present to the past. "Au milieu de toutes les splendeurs du bric-à-brac qu'il était d'usage de réunir à cette époque," what stands out in the hero's fashionably decorated apartment is a Renaissance clock that, demonstrating his airy ignorance of temporality, he never winds. But his later visit to his dead uncle's house—with its antique furniture, its engravings, the stuffed dog "que j'avais connu vivant" and the parrot "qui vit toujours"—can only inspire a more complex attitude to time, and one more respectful of its power. Yet, at the end, when the narrator returns to his room in a Valois inn, "dernier retour vers le bric-à-brac, auquel j'ai depuis longtemps renoncé" (a very Nervalian phrase in its quiet enunciation of paradox), he rediscovers the objects (an eiderdown, an old tapestry, the "trumeau") that in his last visit as hero to Sylvie's room he had missed; and as well he notes yet again the permanent characteristic of the village cottages, the trail of creeper and roses around the window frame. Here we see, then, the persistence of this particular reading model, since the narrator remains faithful to his *taste* for "bric-à-brac" (and to the possibilities of temporal survival it represents) even while announcing that he has "long since" renounced the passing *fashion* of his youth, with its too ambitious aspirations (cf. "toutes les *splendeurs* du bric-à-brac," "pour *restaurer* dans sa couleur locale un appartement d'autrefois"). Like Sylvie herself, then, but unlike the *fête* and the theatre, "bric-à-brac" provides a reading model for which the narrator himself continues to stand guarantee.

Alongside "bric-à-brac," ruins offer a more noble version of what an art of leftovers might be; and this, too, is a model to which the narrator remains faithful to the end, since on the last page we find him walking with Sylvie's family near the "débris des vieilles tours de brique" of the château of Dammartin. But the special relevance of ruins to the narrator's art is demonstrated by the gardens of Ermenonville, with their reminders of the eighteenth-century vogue for *constructing* ruins. One such reminder is the temple to Urania, a "ruine moderne" in which the festivities of the "fête de l'arc" take place; but more important is the temple to Philosophy, "que son fondateur n'a pas eu le bonheur de terminer. . . . Cet édifice inachevé n'est déjà plus qu'une ruine." Here ruins appear simultaneously as what survives the destructiveness of time and as a symbol of what an art that is respectful of the conditions of reality can nevertheless construct.

And it is in this respect that they symbolize also the type of "philosophy" that the narrator achieves at the end of his adventure, a philosophy whose components are renunciation but also a certain ineradicable aspiration. What must be renounced is, of course, the need for a "dénoûment," and the unfinished state of the temple to Philosophy stands for the very conditions of temporal life to which the narrator must submit: his narrative is indeed characterized by a certain failure to end, by a sense of the ongoing quality of life. But the very existence of the temple, evidence as it is in its half-finished state of the power of time, is also a manifestation of a powerful human principle that the text sees as escaping from time, because it is eternal, a principle that—far from seeking illusory satisfaction in endings, derives from the eternal *absence* of satisfaction and indeed *relies* on this lack in its confident proclamation of the permanence of a certain form of desire, the desire to comprehend.

> *Rerum cognoscere causas:*—Oui, ce temple tombe comme tant d'autres, les hommes, oublieux ou fatigués, se détourneront de ses abords, la nature indifférente reprendra le terrain que l'art lui disputait; mais la soif de connaître restera éternelle, mobile de toute force et de toute activité!

In this need to understand we recognize, of course, the narrator "I" who so carefully distinguishes himself from the hero "I" as a victim of erotic desire, the folly of double love; or, to put it more accurately, this is the point at which we see the narrator "I" constitute himself by the reversal of values in which the desire to know and to understand comes to replace erotic desire. At this point, too, we realize that the reading models of the text can be classified in terms of their relevance, on the one hand, to a reading of the text as *énoncé* (its structures, intimately tied up as they are with the adventure of the hero as lover) and, on the other, to the apprehension of the text as *énonciation* (its function as narrative act, which is no less intimately tied to the narrator's project as philosopher). To read *Sylvie* as *énoncé* is to read it as a *fête* through attention to the paradigmatic equivalences, the repetitions and resemblances that constitute the text. To read it as *énonciation* is to read in terms of "bric-à-brac" and ruins, to be sensitive to the way in which someone is reconstructing his past out of the vestiges of the present—reconstructing it the better to comprehend it, and to make it comprehensible. These are not two opposed modes of reading; they are not mutually exclusive, but complementary.

And what mediates them is the theatrical reading, which is also a reading of structures, but of the syntagmatic structures of the *énoncé,* those that convey the story of an evolution, a change. This reading makes of the reader himself or herself an initiate, following in the path traced by the hero in his *emergence from the theatre,* his transformation into the narrator. The reader passes from a certain dazzled reception of the text as *fête,* a magical illusion, to awareness of the presence of a narrator (philosopher, *bricoleur*), and hence of the narrative act, with

its necessary clockwork of narrative artifice. This *informed* reader will now focus on the narrative act as an art of making do with leftovers, of constructing from them a temple, not to love, but to wisdom—an ongoing and never completed activity. And like the narrator, this reader will take as motto the Lucretian *rerum cognoscere causas,* a phrase that for the narrator "I" signifies his need to understand the whys and wherefores of his youthful errors and of his emergence out of them into the philosophical wisdom he now professes. For the reader, it signifies the need to understand the narration, in "Sylvie," through identification with the narrator—an identification that takes the form of *experiencing the narration as the narrator has experienced his life,* that is, as an initiation into wisdom.

"Bien des cœurs me comprendront"—it is now easier to see why the narrator is so confident in this affirmation. He is relying on the reading of the text itself to convert them, that is, by imposing on them the itinerary he himself has followed, through festivity, entry into the theatre and emergence from it, into exploration of the real and the discovery of "philosophy." The two halves of his rhetorical tactic—the distancing of the narrator from the narrated, the involvement of the reader in the narrated—come together here, since the outcome of the reader's involvement with the hero's adventure is identification with the distanced attitude that has become that of the narrator. What they define, however, is a curiously solipsistic narrative, in which the subject of enunciation can envision being understood only by an addressee who has been shaped by the narrative in his own image. And the renunciation of seduction, which in the narrative content makes the narrator out of the hero, appears finally as a seductive device in its own right, since it functions to lead the reader imperceptibly along (*sub-ducere* is the source of "to seduce" and "to subdue"), through the power of the narrative *act,* into union with the narrator "I."

Residues

When one looks in *Sylvie* for explicit thematization of the act of reading, one quickly sees that it is connected with the theme of the residual, whose significance is not exhausted by the "philosophical" interpretation we have just explored. For the narrator, "recompos(er) les souvenirs" also means reconstituting a lost capital, and the "economic" significance both of the hero's adventure and of the narrator's activity needs some examination. At the point when his adventure begins, the hero—addicted to the theatre and a denizen of the "tour d'ivoire des poètes, où nous montions toujours plus haut pour nous isoler de la foule"—is also financially *ruined.* An opportunity then presents itself to make good the vestiges ("débris") of his fortune:

> Dans les débris de mon opulence se trouvait une somme assez forte en titres étrangers. Le bruit avait couru que, négligés longtemps, ils allaient être reconnus; ce qui venait d'avoir lieu à la suite d'un changement de

ministère. Les fonds se trouvaient déjà cotés très haut; je redevenais riche.

How then to exploit this sudden wealth? Should he buy Aurélie with gold? The young hero cannot stomach such materialism: it would mean "toucher du doigt mon idéal"— and, as he says, "ce n'est pas à mon âge que l'on tue l'amour avec de l'or". His plunge into the world of dreams and illusions is, then, a turning away from the option of reaping gain from his wealth: "Mon regard parcourait vaguement le journal que je tenais encore, et j'y lus ces deux lignes: *Fête du Bouquet provincial.* . . . " The journey back to the Valois begins here.

We now know that it is an error. With his platonic ideals, his "amour, hélas! des formes vagues, des teintes roses et bleues, des fantômes métaphysiques," the young poet is involving himself in an adventure whose only outcome can be disenchantment. He emerges, as we have seen, as the narrator of "Sylvie," a philosopher now reconciled with the world of work to the extent that he himself practices an art of narration inspired by a workmanlike trade, that of the clockmaker, even though, more modestly, his own practice of it appears as a *bricolage* with *bric-à-brac*. In this sense, he has returned to the initial question of the appropriate manner of exploiting his leftover wealth: the Aurélie option has been disposed of (through his refusal to buy her and his failure to realize his double love in the Valois), and he proposes now to construct from his *residuals* (which Sylvie continues to represent) something positive, corresponding to the human "soif de connaître." It seems, then, that the correct response to the sudden possibility of fortune the hero was vouchsafed lay not in the latter's impulsive adventure but in the narrator's assumption of the work of narration, of which *Sylvie* is the outcome and embodiment.

So, it is not irrelevant that, at the moment the chance of fortune is offered him, the hero figures as a reader. "En sortant, je passai par la salle de lecture, et machinalement je regardai un journal. C'était, je crois, *pour y voir le cours de la Bourse*" (my emphasis). But instead of this reading, in the economic-productive mode, his eye falls accidentally on "ces deux lignes: *Fête du Bouquet provincial*," and he is off on his madcap adventure in the Valois. It is as if he has missed his chance: instead of reading the market rates, he slips into a world of dreams and "chimères." He will not read again until at the end of the text we find the narrator "I" giving an account of his quiet pursuits when now he visits the Valois to see Sylvie. He walks with Sylvie near the "débris des vieilles tours de briques du château," and: "Tandis que ces petits s'exercent, au tir des compagnons de l'arc, à ficher dans la paille les flèches paternelles, nous lisons quelques poésies ou quelques pages de ces livres si courts qu'on ne fait plus guère." The reference to the still vital tradition of the archers' festival (the *fête du Bouquet*), together with the allusion to the theme of residue, underscores the positional equivalence (at the beginning of the adventure, at the end of the narrative) of these two reading episodes, the reading of the newspaper and the reading of one of "ces livres si courts qu'on ne fait plus guère." But the differences are

important. The lonely newspaper reader was too much of a "poet" to grasp his chance; but here he is now reading in company, and in the company of the beloved woman whom, previously, the "poet" had let slip through his fingers. The narrator's mode of reading seems a compensation for the false mode of reading into which the hero allowed himself to slip.

The intertext of this final passage quite clearly includes the Paolo and Francesca episode in Dante, another and very famous reading situation. But the Dantean model is what is being denied here, since reading together is not a prelude to passion in this case, but the sign that an affair is over, a reward for renunciation. Sylvie and the narrator are reading together because they are *no longer* lovers, because they have changed: having renounced the "chi-mères" of love, the narrator now discovers a form of compensatory happiness in a relationship *mediated by a literary text*. It is the happiness of communication, taking the place of the impossible happiness of the "fantômes métaphysiques"—for it is difficult not to see this picture of the narrator and Sylvie reading together as the representation of two "hearts" that *understand* each other through the mediation of a shared text, that is, as a figure of the realization of the narrator's narrative program.

What, then, is the book they are reading? The words "quelques pages de ces livres si courts qu'on ne fait plus guère" read like a reference to *Sylvie* itself, with its unfinished, fragmentary quality ("quelques pages . . . ") and its old-fashioned mode (cf. "qu'on me pardonne ce style vieilli" and "ces livres qu'on ne fait plus guère"), not to mention its brevity. The more explicit reference is, of course, to *Werther*, which is alluded to in the opening sentence of the same paragraph: "Je l'appelle quelquefois Lolotte, et elle me trouve un peu de ressemblance avec Werther, moins les pistolets, qui ne sont plus de mode." But this sentence itself serves to define *Sylvie* as an aftermath, belonging to a literary genre once popular but now outdated, one of "ces livres . . . *qu'on ne fait plus guère,*" a leftover. It is a late-coming, and passion-free, version of *Werther*. So, the scene in which the narrator "I" and Sylvie bend their heads together over the fragment of a residual and short text can only be an embedding of the relationship that the text of *Sylvie* as narrative act seeks to create between its narrator and its understanding narratee, between "I" and the many "hearts" that may be assumed to comprehend. . . . And the slightly ironic distinction the characters themselves make between their own relationship and that of Goethe's characters—a distinction that distributes the two situations on either side of the dividing line between "romance" and nonromance—not only confirms *Sylvie*'s belonging to the afterstage of a literary tradition that has undergone significant evolution but it also underlines the appeal being made to an understanding readership—one, that is, that, like the narrator, has *transcended* the stage of "romance."

For, in the course of the story, Sylvie's own taste as reader has been formed precisely by the influence of the future narrator. Her original inclination was for the sentimental romances of Auguste Lafontaine, and it was the future narrator who first mentioned to her the *Nouvelle Héloïse.* Her reading of this seductive romance consequently represents in her own evolution something like the theatrical ordeal the hero undergoes (and the reader of "Sylvie" with him) in his own brush with *le romanesque*: "Vous m'avez parlé autrefois de la *Nouvelle Héloïse,* je l'ai lue, et j'ai frémi d'abord en tombant sur cette phrase: 'Toute jeune fille qui lira ce livre est perdue.' Cependant j'ai passé outre, me fiant sur ma raison." We have already noted how narrowly Sylvie escaped the illusions of identification: the ordeal that she has survived in this way, thanks to her natural good sense ("raison"), is precisely the ordeal that qualifies her as the appropriate reader for a text like *Sylvie,* which needs a reader who is both attuned to the seduction of illusion (able to "understand" it) and aware of the superior claims of philosophical sense, or wisdom. Her experience, her initiation into reading at the future narrator's hands, is consequently an exact model for the initiatory experience that the implied reader of *Sylvie* is led to undergo in his or her own passage through the ordeal of the *fête* and the theatre—the experience that constitutes such a reader as fit to "understand" the narrator "I." . . .

[In] discovering the virtues of narrative work, the narrator "I" becomes worthy of hardworking Sylvie at precisely the moment when he learns that she is no longer available. She cannot provide a model for the work of narration because she is about to become, as a *pâtissière,* the opposite of what she has been heretofore: a town dweller, a shopkeeper, and, in short, a *bourgeoise.* And so it is Père Dodu, the clockmaker-*bricoleur,* who provides the narrative model. But what can now be perceived is that Sylvie eluded the hero at that point only as a possible wife (on the plane of the "chimères" of love) and that in becoming a *bourgeoise* she constitutes herself on a new plane as the ideal partner for the narrator "I"—the appropriate reader for his "philosophical" enterprise of narration. As a reader, one may assume that she is realistic and serious-minded, but also a tad sentimental, her taste having been formed by her reading of novelists such as Scott, Rousseau, and Goethe, but being informed also by her own "solid" values—the very values that the narrator presupposes in the "hearts" he expects to understand him. In short, it was not on the plane of emotional relationships but on the plane of literary communication that Sylvie and the narrator were destined to form a couple.

The hovering presence of the husband in the reading scene at the end—he fixes lunch while they read—and that of the children, sending their pre-Freudian arrows with a thud into the targets, certainly suggest that the reading couple is a compensation, and a sublimation, for another coupling. But it is true that the narrator "I" has regained, in his own terms, what the hero "I" lost in the world of erotic illusion. And what he has regained is something solid, for, economically speaking, it is clear that, where the hero failed, the narrator has succeeded in making good the vestiges of his lost fortune. What, indeed, is an artist's capital unless it be the "débris," the residue of life that is

called experience? Is experience not the "fruit"—the profit—one derives from one's existential losses? "Les illusions tombent l'une après l'autre, comme les écorces d'un fruit, et le fruit, c'est l'expérience." The contrast is clear with "l'amère tristesse que laisse un songe évanoui," the only type of profit that can be hoped for by a poet such as the hero, with his love of "teintes roses et bleues" and his proclivity for the ivory tower. In the final analysis, *Sylvie* appears as a text that thinks of itself in terms of a commercial conception of literature, renouncing values like the *romanesque,* enthusiasm, the dream, and madness as *unprofitable* and turning toward a public whose values, embodied in the character of Sylvie, are those of a petty shopkeeper.

What does this mean? Has Nerval capitulated, abandoned the values of poetry, of lyricism, of "folie"? It is essential to distinguish the narrator "I" of Sylvie from the historical Nerval who more or less contemporaneously was introducing into a parallel text, *Aurélia,* a narrator who is diametrically opposed, as a spokesperson for madness, to the narrator of *Sylvie.* But it is difficult not to postulate that *Sylvie* does represent an attempt on Nerval's part, per medium of his narrator, to overcome a sense of personal alienation and to regain a place in the bourgeois society that had marginalized him, both as "poet" and as "madman." In light of Nerval's biography—Gérard Labrunie was the son of a doctor and the heir to a fortune he rapidly squandered—this appeal to middle-class values makes sense. Baudelaire, too, was obsessed throughout his life by the memory of a squandered fortune, his consequent infantilization (his remaining wealth was placed in trust), and the urgency of compensating for this disastrous loss through artistic work. Nerval, even more than Baudelaire, is one to whom *all* the senses of the word *alienation* apply: small wonder if the practice of art came to seem to him a means of struggling for "acceptance."

At the same time, there is something *rusé* in the narrative program of *Sylvie.* The reader who experiences the reading of the text as an *emergence from the theatre* must first of all enter into it, enter—in other words—into the experience of the hero's "madness." Even if such a reader does come eventually to share the narrator "I"'s carefully distanced situation, he or she can no longer maintain watertight divisions between such categories as folly and wisdom, reason and dream. In *Sylvie*—much as in *Aurélia,* there is "épanchement du songe dans la vie réelle"— such divisions are thoroughly permeable; and, for a "philosophical" reader, there is some risk in "accepting"—in Rimbaud's phrase—"l'histoire d'une de mes folies." Between *Aurélia* and *Sylvie,* there is certainly a very different distribution of functions between hero and narrator (madness and writing), but the two texts do combine as parts of a common project. Indeed, to the (very considerable) extent that *Aurélia* itself displays a measurable gap between the adventure and its narration, one can see in it the same cleavage as in *Sylvie* between faithfulness to experience and desire for rehabilitation. The social diagnosis in each case must, then, be the same.

On the significance of memory in *Sylvie*:

Memory in *Sylvie* is an alternating structure, at times spectator and subject, at others actor and object, unable to see itself from a distance. The narrator cannot see the past as an object separate from the present. In remembering his past experiences in the theater and differentiating them from his experiences in the present, the narrator describes the different levels which exist within his language in the present. Past and present are metaphors for a discrepancy between the narrator's self-image and the structure of his own language. His memory of repeated returns to the theater contains within it the two elements which will be distinguished from one another throughout the story—a spectator for whom illusions are objects, like the "médaillons charmants" that the uncle uses to decorate his snuff-boxes, and a subject who participates fully in the experience of illusion, viewing fiction from the inside rather than from the outside.

> *Phyllis Jane Winston, in* "Aurélia: *The Madman as Master of Invention," in* Nerval's Magic Alphabet, *Peter Lang, 1989.*

Kari Lokke (essay date 1987)

SOURCE: "Woman: The Other as Sister," in *Gérard de Nerval: The Poet as Social Visionary*, French Forum, Publishers, Inc., 1987, pp. 65-103.

[*In the excerpt below, Lokke discusses Nerval's depiction of women in his short fiction.*]

One glance at the titles of Nerval's major works shows women to be the heart, the center, of his fictional and poetic universe: *Les Filles du feu* (*Angélique, Sylvie, Jemmy, Octavie, Isis, Corilla, Emilie*), *Pandora, Aurélia, Les Chimères* ("Myrtho," "Delfica," "Artémis"). . . .

This poet, who never knew his mother, who never married, who seemed most at ease with women when separated from them by the costumes, theatrical makeup and footlights of the stage, compensated for their absence in his life by granting them overwhelming power and presence in his art. The contemporary critic, inevitably looking at Nerval through the lens of current psychological and feminist theory, cannot help responding to such an obviously compensatory effort with a certain skepticism. Such an artist, one assumes, must be telling us much more about himself, his own fears, needs and projections, than about the reality of 19th-century womanhood.

Nevertheless, the almost preternatural sensitivity to the plight of victims of economics, political and religious persecution reflected in so many of Nerval's works suggests that he might be equally sensitive to the oppression of women as a social injustice in need of commentary and correction. And in fact, as an artist, Nerval, like Blake, seems to have been endowed with a visionary imagination so subjective that, following the laws of Hegel's dialectic, it becomes objective and impersonal as well as concrete and historical. A careful look at Nerval's fiction-al portrayal of the social roles imposed upon women by patriarchal society reveals a remarkably modern critique of marriage and the bourgeois family as vehicles for entrapping, timing and breaking the female spirit. Once again, just as Nerval understood and elucidated the role played by ideological and political repression in the creation of mental illness, so his works consistently portray women, both in their strengths and in their vulnerabilities, as pitted against the constraints of patriarchal society.

Yet Nerval is certainly not first and foremost a conscious social theorist or critic, and perhaps the most striking feature of his poetic presentation of woman is his mythification of the feminine. Woman is daughter, wife, mother, mistress and worker for Nerval, but she is also saint, victim, goddess, siren, courtesan, amazon and witch. How does one reconcile these seemingly opposing impulses—a clear and explicit sympathy with women as victims of societal oppression and an even more powerful urge to view women through the strictures of age-old archetypes, perhaps even misogynistic stereotypes?

This tension between a progressive historical view of woman's evolving social roles and an apparently conservative mythological presentation of her seemingly ahistorical essence characterizes Nerval's portrayal of woman from beginning to end of his œuvre. In fact the relationship between social and mythological woman in Nerval's work is one of interpenetration and creative complementarity. It is in the socially determined and accepted roles of mother, wife and daughter that Nerval shows women to be oppressed and unnecessarily limited. And, paradoxically, it is his seemingly restrictive stereotypes of witch, siren, queen and saint that in fact release and celebrate the power of women.

This conception of the role of myth in cultural imagination follows the lead of Nina Auerbach's eloquent study of 19th-century British images of womanhood, *Woman and the Demon: The Life of a Victorian Myth*. Auerbach asserts that the process of understanding and demystifying male myths of womanhood should include the task of searching those same archetypes for the subversive and emancipatory power they enclose. She suggests that feminist criticism should move beyond its earlier simplistic condemnation of myths of womanhood to a rediscovery of myth as a source of contemporary strength: "Woman's freedom is no longer simple initiation into historical integrity, but the rebirth of mythic potential. The mythologies of the past as well have become stronger endowments than oppressions." Interpretative revaluation of myth can act as a corrective to what Auerbach terms the "sleek complacency" of modernist formalism, as well as to the lack of imaginative spirit and promise in behaviorist and empiricist research:

> The allegiance of feminism in the early 1970's was to the social sciences, whose demographic charts and statistics affirmed the reality of our half-life in society—and nothing else. But lives are inspired by beliefs before they are immortalized in statistics. It may be time for feminists to circle back to those

"images" of angels and demons, nuns and whores, whom it seemed so easy and so liberating to kill, in order to retrieve a less tangible, but also less restricting, facet of woman's history than the social sciences can encompass.

Nerval's obsessive fascination with the enigma of the feminine creates in his poetry a kind of ideal repository of 19th-century myths of woman. The archetypes of mother, saint, amazon, courtesan, siren—protean, self-transformatory images that recur incessantly, blend into and flow out of one another—form the heart of all of Nerval's major works. It is almost as if the absence of close relationships with women in his personal life allowed Nerval the distance needed to present a kind of panoramic view of 19th-century woman's social and mythic essence. The complementary relationship between Nerval's mythic and social representations of women can perhaps best be demonstrated by showing that for Nerval mythic woman often has precisely those powers denied or repressed by her social roles of daughter, wife and worker. Finally, what is of ultimate interest, as Mary Harper suggests in ["Recovering the Other: Women and the Orient in the Writings of Early Nineteenth-Century France," in *Critical Matrix* 1, No. 3, 1985] is not "any simple opposition between myth and 'reality,'" but rather "the blurring of the boundaries between them—not as a seamless narrative but rather as a tangled web of attitudes which need to be explored." My discussion will seek to render evident the connections between Nerval's criticism of patriarchy and his mythification of women. . . .

Nerval's most important collection of fiction is entitled *Les Filles du feu,* daughters of fire. Before Nerval's women are mothers or lovers, they are daughters, not of earthly men and women, but of the creative, active and rebellious Promethean element of fire. Yet they are daughters of earthly parents as well, parents who represent the demands of social order and hierarchy against the demands of the free spirit. Thus it is the figure of Iphigenia under the knives of her father Agamemnon and the priest Calchas, Iphigenia sacrificed to "la vieille autorité du prêtre et du souverain," to the demands of war and nationalism, who stands as central symbol of woman in Nerval's introduction to this series of novellas. In his dedication to Alexandre Dumas, Nerval creates a narrative persona, one of his many fictional doubles, who is an actor imagining himself in the role of Achilles. Achilles, as lover of Iphigenia, is trying to save her from martyrdom. Yet the modern ironic self-consciousness of Nerval's actor prevents him from taking his own role seriously, though he presents Iphigenia's plight with empathy and intensity of feeling:

> l'entrais comme la foudre au milieu de cette action forcée et cruelle; je rendais l'espérance aux mères et le courage aux pauvres filles, sacrifiées toujours à un devoir, à un Dieu, à la vengeance d'un peuple, à l'honneur ou au profit d'une famille! . . . car on comprenait bien partout que c'était là l'histoire éternelle des mariages humains. Toujours le père livrera sa fille par ambition, et toujours la mère la vendra avec avidité;

> mais l'amant ne sera pas toujours cet honnête Achille, si beau, si bien armé, si galant et si terrible, quoiqu'un peu rhéteur pour un homme d'épée!

Yet despite—or in fact precisely because of—the beauty and superiority of these lovers, both the Greek witnesses and the French audiences, Nerval suggests, are desirous of the sacrifice of Iphigenia as scapegoat: "Chacun s'est dit déjà qu'il fallait qu'elle mourût pour tous, plutôt que de vivre pour un seul; chacun a trouvé Achille trop beau, trop grand, trop superbe!" Daughters, then, like the archetypal son in Nerval's "Christ aux Oliviers" and like the victims of religious and political persecution described in Chapter I, are scapegoats of a cruel and authoritarian social order.

The first of *Les Filles du feu* is *Angélique,* written in 1850 and originally published together with the story of l'abbé de Bucquoy in *Le National.* In his research for "les Bucquoy sous toutes les formes" Nerval discovers the diary of Angélique de Longueval, his elusive abbé's great aunt who, in disobedience to her father, eloped with a servant to embark on a life of exile, hardship and brutalization at the hands of her husband. Because Nerval's aims are primarily esthetic and spiritual rather than political, his depiction of women as an oppressed social group often seems more a product of unconscious sympathy and sensitivity than one of a conscious commitment to the emancipation of women. With *Angélique* it is almost as if Nerval had unconsciously asked himself a question analogous to Virginia Woolf's "What if Shakespeare had been a woman?" For in the life of Angélique de Longueval Nerval shows how the courage, determination and will to freedom characteristic of "Les Bucquoys" manifested themselves in a woman unable to move about in society on her own, bound to the "protection" of a husband or a father. Angélique, Nerval writes, represents "l'opposition même en cotte hardie." As Ross Chambers suggests, she shares with her descendant l'abbé de Bucquoy "l'hérédité valoise, grande source de rebelles et de ligueurs de tous camps."

Angélique tells her story in her own voice as Nerval quotes long passages from her diary. Nerval mirrors her naïve, straightforward and unflinching style in his own restrained, almost matter-of-fact narration of her profoundly tragic life story. Thus he resurrects the historical voice of a woman whose name had been effaced from the genealogical records of her family. As he states ironically, "Angélique n'était pas en odeur de sainteté dans sa famille, et cela paraît en ce fait qu'elle n'a pas même été nommée dans la généalogie de sa famille." Although all her brothers are listed, "on ne parle pas de la fille."

Angélique, Nerval suggests, is an exceptional human being, "d'un caractère triste et rêveur," an early victim of Romantic melancholy. Before she had reached twenty years of age, two men had been murdered as punishment for their passion for her, uniting in truly Nervalian fashion love, death and sorrow in a seemingly indissoluble whole. It is almost easier to see Angélique as a fictional creation, an angel-anima, rather than as a historical personage. She is in fact clearly Nerval's sister soul—note the relationship of equality—a personage, like so many of Nerval's fictional characters, with whom Nerval cannot help identifying. The line between fact and fiction, between historical and imaginative reality, is never clear for Nerval. In one of his letters to Jenny Colon Nerval admits that he conceives of his life "comme un roman," and he makes the following confession in the dedication of *Les Filles du feu* to Alexandre Dumas:

> Il est, vous le savez, certains conteurs qui ne peuvent inventer sans s'identifier aux personnages de leur imagination [. . . .] l'on arrive pour ainsi dire à s'incarner dans le héros de son imagination, si bien que sa vie devienne la vôtre et qu'on brûle des flammes factices de ses ambitions et de ses amours!

As much as Nerval emphasizes that Angélique's passionate and dreamy character creates her fate, he also makes it clear that the restrictions placed on her as a woman and daughter force a person of such passionate determination to rebel. Once again, with Nerval sympathetic identification produces acute insight into the realities of political and social oppression. For Nerval Angélique is like the heroine of the folk song he records in the seventh letter of the text, a brave heroine who refuses to reject her poor lover and is, therefore, sentenced by her father to confinement in a tower that will become a tomb:

> —Ma fille, il faut changer d'amour . . .
> Ou vous resterez dans la tour.
>
> —J'aime mieux rester dans la tour,
>
> Mon père, que de changer d'amour!

After the death of her first lover at the hands of her father, Angélique had begged him to introduce her into the world in the hopes that she would find someone to free her from the memory of "ce mort éternel," as Nerval calls him. It appears that the count ignored her wishes, as her later attempts to forget her love for La Corbinière, her father's servant, are frustrated by the lack of any occupation or company worthy of her. She cannot be satisfied with the concerns traditionally assumed to be the province of women. Thus when La Corbinière is forced to spend a year in Paris, she succumbs to depression and melancholy, distracted only by their exchange of letters. She writes, "Je n'avais pas d'autre divertissement, [. . .] car les belles pierres, ni les belles tapisseries et beaux habits, sans la conversation des honnêtes gens, ne me pouvaient plaire. . . . "

Angélique finally resolves to leave the prison of her father's castle with his servant, her lover. Love seeks to invalidate class distinctions here, just as it does in the *Histoire du Calife Hakem* and just as it seeks to transcend international warfare and hatred in *Emilie*. Love, no matter how strong, is not all-powerful, for Angélique, a victim of a societal and familial repetition compulsion, chooses a husband who is every bit as insensitive and tyrannical as her father. Her search for freedom only subjugates her more deeply to an oppressive and tragic fate.

Her account of their life together reveals her husband's nightmarish brutality and stupidity. After escaping with the family silver, she quickly changes into men's clothing so as to avoid detection and capture. One evening when they are resting at an inn, La Corbinière is questioned about the "demoiselle vêtue en homme" who is accompanying him. Nerval isolates his proprietary response and records it with condemnatory silence: "Ouida, Monsieur . . . Pourquoi avez-vous quelque chose à dire là-dessus? Ne suis-je pas maître de faire habiller ma femme comme il me plaît?." Similarly, there seems to be a kind of silent horror behind Nerval's matter-of-fact quoting of the passage in Angélique's diary where she records her lover's "cavalier" response to having accidentally shot her: "Il dit seulement à ceux qui le blâmaient de son imprudence: 'C'est un malheur qui m'est arrivé . . . je puis dire à moi-même, puisque c'est ma femme'."

The fleeing couple, exhausted, sick and nearly starving, finally reach Italy, where they are married. As a woman exiled from family and home, Angélique is subjected to the advances and propositions of a number of men, but she remains true to her husband, even following him when he is forced by their poverty to join the Austrian army. La Corbinière falls critically ill with a fever, and Angélique nearly dies of the combined effects of a miscarriage and exposure. Doubtless Nerval associates Angélique with his own mother, who followed her husband, an army surgeon, into battle six months after Nerval was born, and died two years later in Silesia, never having seen her infant again. It is, however, Angélique, rather than her husband, who appears to have the greater physical endurance, for she nurses him back to health, obtains a pardon for him when he is detained for desertion and eventually leads him back to Verona. In Verona they set up a home, but are soon forced by his debauchery and profligacy to open up a tavern.

All of Angélique's love and devotion are rewarded by murderous brutality on her husband's part. After witnessing her exchange greetings with a passing army officer, La Corbinière tries to strangle her, nearly kicks her to death and feels justified in threatening to eviscerate her if she ever speaks to the man again. Beginning with this event, her story is no longer recounted in her own voice. Angélique has been silenced, perhaps by shame and misery. Her diary stops here, and the sparse facts of her last years are known through the manuscript of her cousin, a Celestine monk to whom she appealed for help in her last years. When Angélique finally receives a pardon from her mother and wishes to return to France, her husband refuses, fearing that he will be executed there. Finally, after the death of both her parents they return to France, where La Corbinière dies and Angélique lives out the rest of her life in ignominy and the most abject poverty.

Angélique is Nerval's portrait of a lady, his tribute to a woman who, once she had committed herself to a husband, never complained and never wavered: "en constatant quelques malheureuses dispositions de celui qu'elle ne nomme jamais, elle n'en dit pas de mal un instant. Elle se borne à constater les faits,—et l'aime toujours, en épouse platonicienne et soumise à son sort par le raisonnement." As mythic vision, the appropriately named Angélique is a strange melding of scandalous fallen woman and self-sacrificing saint, revealing to the careful reader the proximity of these two dialectically opposed images. These stereotypes in fact both contain and reveal her strength of will and endurance of spirit. She refuses to succumb to the tyranny and brutality of either her father or her husband, remaining true to her conception of love and outliving both men, refusing the traditional escape of death, suicide or seclusion in a convent usually reserved for the fictional fallen woman/saint.

Yet there is something Brechtian as well, perhaps unconsciously so, in Nerval's portrait of this "good woman." Like Brecht's Shen Te, she does not want to "count the cost" of going with the man she loves. During all her hardships her constant refrain is a simple "Voyez [. . .] ce que c'est de l'amour." This heart-rending exclamation cannot but frustrate and even anger a modern reader who wishes in vain for Angélique that she wake up to a consciousness of her right to personal freedom and dignity and that she leave her brutish husband. This discrepancy between character and reader consciousness, as in Brecht's plays, is a highly effective tool of social criticism. *Angélique* stands as an implicit critique of a social and familial structure that made it almost impossible for her to give serious consideration to leaving her husband even after his debauchery and cruelty had reduced her to utter misery.

. . . . .

The exquisite novella *Sylvie* is in fact structured around the opposition between real and mythic woman, between Sylvie, "la douce réalité," and Adrienne-Aurélia, "l'idéal sublime," becoming in the end a highly self-conscious critique of the tendency to view other human beings as a mirror of one's own psychic, esthetic or mythic projections.

Sylvie is immediately self-conscious, beginning as it does in the realm of theater, with Gérard acknowledging that he is playing a role: "je paraissais aux avant-scènes en grande tenue de soupirant." He worships not a real woman, but "une apparition," who, he imagines, egotistically enough, lives only for him: "Je me sentais vivre en elle, et elle vivait pour moi seul. [. . .] Elle avait pour moi toutes les perfections, elle répondait à tous mes enthousiasmes [. . .] ." There is little self-delusion in Gérard's attitude, however. In a highly ironic expression of self-mockery he speaks of the "paradoxes platoniques" of his generation: "Amour, hélas! des formes vagues, des teintes roses et bleues, des fantômes métaphysiques! Vue de près, la femme révoltait notre ingénuité; il fallait qu'elle apparût reine ou déesse, et surtout n'en pas approcher." He feels no jealousy for his beloved's suitors ("C'est une image que je poursuis, rien de plus,") because he does not wish to know the real woman, fearful that she is not equal to her magical image, that she is not a reflection of his

own soul: "Je craignais de troubler le miroir magique qui me renvoyait son image."

Dreams of this ideal woman, who he suspects may in reality be a heartless materialist, kept by the gold of his era, mysteriously call forth an image of feminine purity from an earlier time, Adrienne, the beautiful, blond, aristocratic child whom Gérard kissed and crowned with a laurel wreath in a magical childhood memory of a nostalgic folk dance on the lawn of a beautiful château. This young, ethereal beauty, as a source of "pensées douleureuses que la philosophie de collège était impuissante à calmer," inspired in Gérard "un amour impossible et vague." Adrienne was soon "consecrated" (one is tempted to read "sacrificed") by her family to a religious life, so that she was never more than a glimmering "mirage de gloire et de la beauté" for him.

In the world of myth, opposition exists only to be negated; the actress-demi-mondaine and the saintly nun become one in Gérard's reverie:

> Cet amour vague et sans espoir, conçu pour une femme de théâtre, qui tous les soirs me prenait à l'heure du spectacle, pour ne me quitter qu'à l'heure du sommeil, avait son germe dans le souvenir d'Adrienne, fleur de la nuit éclose à la pâle clarté de la lune, fantôme rose et blond glissant sur l'herbe verte à demi baignée de blanches vapeurs.

Yet it is precisely the fluid, nebulous metamorphic quality of these dream images that provokes a response of terror and desperation in the conscious, rational mind: "Aimer une religieuse sous la forme d'une actrice! . . . et si c'était la même!—Il y a de quoi devenir fou! C'est un entraînement fatal où l'inconnu vous attire comme le feu follet fuyant sur les joncs d'une eau morte . . . ".

For help, for a touchstone to reality, it is to another woman that Gérard turns, to the peasant girl Sylvie, his childhood friend whose heart was once broken by his attentions to the aristocratic Adrienne:

> Et Sylvie que j'aimais tant, pourquoi l'ai-je oubliée depuis trois ans? . . . C'était une bien jolie fille, et la plus belle de Loisy! . . . Elle existe, elle, bonne et pure de coeur sans doute. [. . .] Elle m'attend encore . . . Qui l'aurait épousée? elle est si pauvre!

If Aurélie and Adrienne are not valued in and for themselves, but as fulfillment of a mystic fantasy, then Sylvie is also not perceived as a human being with her own needs and wants, but as a poor peasant who has suspended her life for three years waiting for the preoccupied Parisian to return to her.

And Gérard resolves to return to her and to marry her, hoping to build a life together on what remains of the inheritance he has almost totally squandered. The reverie of his return to her on the "triste route [. . .] de Flandre" is flooded with memories of the joys he has shared with Sylvie in the past: an annual festival imagined by Gérard as a recreation of Watteau's *Voyage à Cythère* with Sylvie in the role of smiling Aphrodite, the "Vénus populaire" of the *Voyage en Orient*; the picturesque room of Sylvie, the fine lacemaker; their walks together along the flower-filled fields. Most significant is their enactment, in the wedding costumes of Sylvie's aunt, of a playful yet deeply nostalgic wedding celebration that has overtones of a mystical marriage. Together they sing "le naïf épithalame qui accompagnait les mariés rentrant après la danse." "Nous répétions ces strophes si simplement rythmées, [. . .] amour-euses et fleuries comme le cantique de l'Ecclésiaste; nous étions l'époux et l'épouse pour tout un beau matin d'été."

This marriage never leaves the realm of fantasy, however, and when the voyager finally reaches the real Sylvie of the present, it is too late. In the reverie of his journey Gérard has once again become haunted, obsessed, with the spirit of Adrienne, this time as actress-nun participant in an apocalyptic mystery play. Sylvie, then, above all else becomes a means of escaping this obsessive memory risen from the Nervalian netherworld between the empirical and the imaginary:

> Tout à coup je pensai à l'image vaine qui m'avait égaré si longtemps.
>
> "Sylvie, dis-je, arrêtons-nous ici, le voulez-vous?
>
> Je me jetai à ses pieds; je confessai en pleurant à chaudes larmes mes irrésolutions, mes caprices; j'évoquai le spectre funeste qui traversait ma vie.
>
> —Sauvez-moi! ajoutai-je, je reviens à vous pour toujours."

Sylvie, however, is a real woman with a life of her own. When Gérard finally returns to her, she is an incarnation of the changes that urbanization and industrialization have brought to his idealized world of the Valois. Her simple dress has been replaced by city fashion, her folk songs by phrased operatic arias, and her quaint bedroom is decorated in a more practical modern style. Most poignantly, her beautiful and delicate lace is gone, sacrificed to the law of supply and demand. She is now a glovemaker, and her room is invaded by an iron instrument, a machine that holds the gloves while they are being sewn.

Furthermore, her poet-lover sacrificed his chance with her when he chose to leave for Italy instead of carrying their fictional and theatrical marriage into reality. As Sylvie says, "les choses ne vont pas comme nous voulons dans la vie. [. . .] Ah, que n'êtes-vous revenu alors! Mais vous étiez, disait-on, en Italie." At one time, she admits, she had imagined herself and her costumed lover as Rousseau's Julie and Saint-Preux, but now she has pledged herself to another, to "le grand frisé," Gérard's "frère de lait," or foster brother, another Nervalian double figure. True to the archetypal pattern of the double, "le grand frisé" will marry Sylvie, leaving the poet-narrator a "Werther, moins les pistolets," as he ironically imagines himself, to long for his Lotte and to muse wistfully when he visits her and her children: "là était le bonheur peut-être; cependant. . . ."

As Rousseau's Julie and Goethe's Lotte, Sylvie takes on a life in the realm of fiction as the novella closes. She also seems to move from reality into the realm of myth. Already in her aunt's quaint bridal costume, she becomes in Gérard's imagination "la fée des légendes éternellement jeune" of the Théâtre des Funambules. By the end of the novel she is elevated to the level of goddess; with her "sourire athénien" she is the warm, smiling "Vénus populaire": "Sylvie m'échappait par ma faute; mais la revoir un jour avait suffi pour relever mon âme: je la plaçais désormais comme une statue souriante dans le temple de la Sagesse. Son regard m'avait arrêté au bord de l'abîme."

Just as Sylvie is transfigured and idealized, so Aurélie moves from the realm of theater, illusion and myth into reality. And just as Sylvie now has the power to inspire him, so Aurélie teaches him a lesson in the reality—not the illusion—of love. When Gérard finally meets Aurélie, confesses his fascination and admits to the authorship of extravagant anonymous love letters, her response is sympathetic, yet matter-of-fact: "Vous êtes bien fou; mais revenez me voir . . . Je n'ai jamais pu trouver quelqu'un qui sût m'aimer. [. . .] Si c'est bien pour moi que vous m'aimez [. . .]."

Gérard, however, learns the painful lesson that it is not for herself that he loves Aurélie. When he brings her to the world of Adrienne, having persuaded her theater company to perform there, he imagines he will finally unite Aurélie and Adrienne, the actress and the nun, and his dream will be complete. "J'avais projeté de conduire Aurélie au château, près d'Orry, sur la même place verte où pour la première fois j'avais vu Adrienne." Aurélie comes to him on horseback "en amazone, avec ses cheveux blonds flottants," "comme une reine d'autrefois." In this moment of mythical climax Gérard sees Aurélie not only as actress-nun, not only as courtesan-saint, but also as powerful amazon-queen, thus prefiguring the apocalyptic conclusion of *Aurélia,* where, as Berthe Reymond notes in ["Le Myth Feminin dans l'oeuvre de Nerval," in *Etude de Letters,* 6, No. 4, 1963], "les trois images de l'actrice, la sainte et l'amazone [. . .] se fondent [. . .] dans celle de la Médiatrice chevauchant vers la Jérusalem céleste."

Once again, however, the real woman steps out from under the burden of Gérard's projection:

> Nulle émotion ne parut en elle. Alors je lui racontai tout; je lui dis la source de cet amour entrevu dans les nuits, rêvé plus tard, réalisé en elle. Elle m'écou-tait sérieusement et me dit: "Vous ne m'aimez pas! Vous attendez que je vous dise: 'La comédienne est la même que la religieuse'; vous cherchez un drame, voilà tout, et le dénoûment vous échappe. Allez, je ne vous crois plus."

Aurélie's sophistication and clear-mindedness communicate what Sylvie had only gently suggested, that Gérard does not love her, but only wishes to use her as material for the unfinished drama that constitutes her life: "Cette parole fut un éclair. Ces enthousiasmes bizarres que j'avais ressentis si longtemps, ces rêves, ces pleurs, ces désepoirs et ces tendresses . . . ce n'était donc pas l'amour? Mais où donc est-il?"

From the very first line of the text, the self-conscious poet-narrator is keenly aware of his own tendency to view women as actresses in a comedy, goddesses in a myth he has created. But by the end of the novella, Sylvie and Aurélie have shown him how potentially harmful, exploitative and lacking in love this tendency to estheticize and mythologize the real, flesh-and-blood woman can be. Gérard begins to take responsibility for his esthetic vision and mythological projection and not to confuse it with true love of, and concern for, another human being. Thus the lucidity of his self-consciousness has been heightened and clarified by a moral dimension. Paradoxically, then, the wistful, delicate beauty of *Sylvie,* Nerval's stylistic and tonal masterpiece, is created by Nerval's combination of this mythic and esthetic vision of the Valois and its women with the melancholy realization that such a sublimated mode of interaction leads away from the present and the love of a real human being to an ideal past or a utopian future.

In Nerval's earlier and simpler work *Corilla* (1839) the same dilemma stands out in much bolder relief. *Corilla,* a kind of drama in miniature, gives expression, as does *Sylvie,* to the opposition between reality and illusion through the metaphors of doubling, the mask and the theater. The plot is age-old: the prima donna Corilla, pursued by two men, disguises herself in an effort to discover which one truly loves her. She arranges simultaneous meetings with Fabio, the idealist, at the Villa Reale and with Marcelli, the realist, at the baths of Neptune—an occult, astrological symbol of illusion, dream and the ideal—as if to suggest that she knows and can communicate to each man what he lacks.

In the end, however, she concludes that neither Fabio the poet and platonic lover nor Marcelli the Don Juan and sensualist loves her. Once again it is woman who holds the wisdom and power of human relationships:

> Pardonnez-moi d'avoir été comédienne en amour comme au théâtre, et de vous avoir mis à l'épreuve tous deux. Maintenant, je vous l'avouerai, je ne sais trop si aucun de vous m'aime [. . .]. Le seigneur Fabio n'adore en moi que l'actrice peut-être, et son amour a besoin de la distance et de la rampe allumée; et vous, seigneur Marcelli, vous me paraissez vous aimer avant tout le monde, et vous émouvoir difficilement dans l'occasion. Vous êtes trop mondain, et lui trop poète.

Corilla holds herself aloof from both men, who are really only loving themselves through her.

The moral and psychological dilemma presented by *Corilla* and *Sylvie* is transformed, transfigured in *Aurélia* by the death of Jenny-Aurélia. Gerard is no longer torn between the real woman and the mythological projection. The drama of *Aurélia* takes place, as he writes, "toute entière dans les mystères de mon esprit." Thus the poet-narrator accepts responsibility for his purely mythological vision and no longer forces it upon a real woman. True to the dialectic of Nerval's work as a whole, however, the subjectivity of *Aurélia* transforms itself into its opposite and creates a historical vision of the oppression of woman and the potentiality of her utopian future.

Expiation of a crime against woman is the motivating force behind the entire narrative of *Aurélia,* as the first chapter indicates: "Une dame que j'avais aimée longtemps et que j'appellerai du nom d'Aurélia, était perdue pour moi" (I, 359). Gérard considers himself "Condamné par celle que j'aimais, coupable d'une faute dont je n'espérais plus le pardon." The novella concludes with the miraculous pardon won through the experience of a series of trials and effected by the combined figures of the Christ-like Saturnin and the goddess Aurélia, united in the image of the sacred Rose-Pearl. As François Constans emphasizes, [in his "Sur la pelouse de Mortefontaine," in *Gérard de Nerval de vant le destin*], the poet's spiritual journey concludes with the defication of Aurélia and the journey towards "la Jérusalem céleste":

> Avant de décrire la vision qui l'assure de son salut, il est allé jusqu'à mettre la médiatrice sur le même rang que le Juge de l'Univers! "Oh! que ma grande amie est belle! Elle est si grande qu'elle pardonne au monde, et si bonne qu'elle m'a pardonné!" L'espérance chrétienne est ici transcendée par un délirant syncrétisme d'espoirs. Plus précisément, le Christ et Isis, conciliés en Aurélia, concourent à la "réintégration" de Gérard selon la formule théosophique.

Central to this process of redemption is Gérard's recognition not only of his individual guilt in relation to Aurélia, but also his acknowledgment of the collective guilt of man in his crimes against woman. The "plot" of *Aurélia* is the story of the narrator's growing awareness of the magnitude and significance of these crimes. From the first chapters woman is identified with and celebrated as nature in Nerval's own delicate expression of the Romantic rebellion against Western man's worship of the rational and the technological. Woman is goddess of nature for Nerval, a nature threatened with destruction:

> La dame que je suivais, développant sa taille élancée dans un mouvement qui faisait miroiter les plis de sa robe en taffetas changeant, entoura gracieusement de son bras nu une longue tige de rose trémière, puis elle se mit à grandir sous un clair rayon de lumière, de telle sorte que peu à peu le jardin prenait sa forme, et les parterres et les arbres devenaient les rosaces et les festons de ses vêtements; tandis que sa figure et ses bras imprimaient leurs contours aux nuages pourprés du ciel. Je la perdais de vue à mesure qu'elle se transfigurait, car elle semblait s'évanouir dans sa propre grandeur. "Oh! ne fuis pas! m'écriai-je . . . car la nature meurt avec toi!"

Woman is the garden of Eden, the ouroboros, feminine symbol of divinity, the snake without sin, curled in a circle of infinity, completion and openness. This "déesse rayonnante" guides the evolution of humanity until a group of sorcerers impose upon others "les leçons funestes de leurs sciences" along with tradition, hierarchy and priestly ritual:

> Cette grandeur imposante et monotone, réglée par l'étiquette et les cérémonies hiératiques, pesait à tous sans que personne osât s'y soustraire. Les vieillards languissaient sous le poids de leurs couronnes et de leurs ornements impériaux, entre des médecins et des prêtres, dont le savoir leur garantissait l'immortalité. Quant au peuple, à tout jamais engrené dans les divisions des castes, il ne pouvait compter ni sur la vie, ni sur la liberté.

Death and destruction of woman, *l'Etoile,* and nature are the result. Gérard sees a woman crying out and fighting for her life: "Fut-elle sauvée? Je l'ignore. Les dieux, ses frères, l'avaient condamnée; mais au-dessus de sa tête brillait l'Etoile du soir, qui versait sur son front des rayons enflammés."

Sophia, the ouroboros, image of wisdom, wholeness and unity, is severed by the sword of dualism, rationality and conflict, which has produced religions that are agents of carnage like that between Christians and Moors:

> Partout mourait, pleurait ou languissait l'image souffrante de laMère éternelle.... on voyait se renouveler toujours une scène sanglante d'orgie et de carnage.... La dernière se passait à Grenade, où le talisman sacré s'écroulait sous les coups ennemis des chrétiens et des Maures. [. . .] Ce sont les tronçons divisés du serpent qui entoure la terre . . . Séparés par le fer, ils se rejoignent dans un hideux baiser cimenté par le sang des hommes.

In this mythological history Nerval prefigures more explicit 20th-century discussions of the intimate relationship between the glorification of rationality, the technological subjugation of nature and the oppression of women found in works as varied as André Breton's *Arcane 17,* Horkheimer and Adorno's *Dialectic of Enlightenment* and Susan Griffin's *Woman and Nature.*

In the final chapters of *Aurélia* visions of the violation of women stand in opposition to revelatory experiences of correspondence, harmony and unity: "Comment [. . .] ai-je pu exister si longtemps hors de la nature sans m'identifier à elle? Tout vit, tout agit, tout se correspond; les rayons magnétiques émanés de moi-même ou des autres traversent sans obstacle la chaîne infine des choses créées; c'est un réseau transparent qui couvre le monde." An understanding of the intricate balance of nature and of the interpenetration of all life and matter provokes the horrific and prophetic insight that technological mastery of nature's secrets without equivalent moral awareness could lead to apocalyptic annihilation of the earth:

> Si l'électricité [. . .] qui est le magnétisme des corps physiques, peut subir une direction qui lui impose des lois, à plus forte raison des esprits hostiles et tyran-

niques peuvent asservir les intelligences et se servir de leurs forces divisées dans un but de domination. C'est ainsi que les dieux antiques ont été vaincus et asservis par des dieux nouveaux; c'est ainsi [. . .] que les nécromants dominaient des peuples entiers, dont les générations se succédaient captives sous leur sceptre éternel. [. . .] rien n'est indifférent, rien n'est impuissant dans l'univers; un atome peut tout dissoudre, un atome peut tout sauver!

In the face of this horror it is to the principles of love and relatedness embodied for Gérard in the goddess Isis-Mary-Aphrodite that he appeals for the spiritual values necessary to combat such terror and destruction. Realistically, however, he fears that the oppression of woman has rendered her nearly powerless: "'Que peut-elle, vaincue, opprimée peut-être, pour ses pauvres enfants?' Pâle et déchiré, le croissant de la lune s'amincissait tous les soirs et allait bientôt disparaître; peut-être ne devions-nous plus le revoir au ciel!" The image of a woman's dismembered, bleeding body graphically depicts the carnage and fragmentation that for Nerval is human history:

> Je crus alors me trouver au milieu d'un vaste charnier où l'histoire universelle était écrite en traits de sang. Le corps d'une femme gigantesque était peint en face de moi, seulement ses diverses parties étaient tranchées comme par le sabre; d'autres femmes de races diverses et dont les corps dominaient de plus en plus présentaient sur les autres murs un fouillis sanglant de membres et de têtes, depuis les impératrices et les reines jusqu'aux plus humbles paysannes. C'était l'histoire de tous les crimes [. . . .] "Voilà, me disais-je, ce qu'a produit la puissance déférée aux hommes."

The efforts to heal the French soldier that immediately follow this vision clearly take on symbolic significance as an attempt to heal the wounds of humanity's age-old plague of war and bloodshed. From this moment on, the tone of the text changes as the combined mediatory and redemptive powers of Saturnin and Aurélia redeem the world in Gérard's imagination and usher in the reign of peace and harmony created by women rulers and by the female divinities of Isis-Mary-Sophia.

The Nervalian narrators and protagonists gather their honey and abscond, giving obscure and unconvincing reasons for their failure to make peace with woman—ill health, bad timing, restlessness, misunderstanding, the presence of rivals, themselves also ineffectual.

—Kari Lokke

In the mythical world of *Aurélia* the reconciliation between man and woman, the mystical, alchemical marriage that is lacking in Nerval's other works, takes place. . . .

[In] *Sylvie* and *Corilla* women function as spiritual and emotional healers and as teachers who are out of the reach of the male protagonists. As Aurélie so wisely observes in *Sylvie,* there seems to be conclusion to the comedy of love Nerval writers for his heroes and leading ladies. Women seem to challenge traditional plot lines and narrative devices, as Mary Harper asserts: "The strange equivocation of these encounters with women [. . .], the narrative inconclusiveness with which they seem to be associated, call attention to the disruptive presence of women in the plot as figures who persistently defy the narrator's attempts to 'fix' his direction, and organize his narrative." The Nervalian narrators and protagonists gather their honey and abscond, giving obscure and unconvincing reasons for their failure to make peace with woman—ill health, bad timing, restlessness, misunderstanding, the presence of rivals, themselves also ineffectual.

This pattern of behavior also forms the narrative structure and the thematic content of two of Nerval's most troubling texts: *Octavie* and *Pandora.* In *Octavie* Gérard hovers, hummingbird-like, over three flowers—the ideal Parisian love, avatar of Jenny Colon, named Aurélie-Aurélia in his other texts; her dark mirror, the mysterious woman of the night met on the streets of Naples; and the bright, playful undine Octaive, his swimming partner in the Mediterranean. These three images of Venus—the ideal Vénus-Uranie, the demonic underworld temptress and the smiling Aphrodite—metamorphose into one another in Gérard's consciousness and make it impossible for him to separate the real women, the individual human beings, one from another.

It is precisely the metamorphic, even volcanic (following the metaphors of the Vesuvian landscape) quality of these mythic images that gives them their power to overwhelm Nerval's voyager-narrator. The heart of the text—Gérard's escape from his unrequited Parisian love to the Neapolitan landscape, both bright and joyous as well as dark and mysterious—reveals that the attempt to run away from woman only brings her presence more fully and powerfully to mind. For Nerval fear of woman is fear of life; this fear calls forth her image in the form of seductive, easeful death.

Gérard recognizes in a mysterious, gypsy-like foreigner Aurélia's dark mirror image: "Il me prit fantaisie de m'étourdir pour tout un soir, et de m'imaginer que cette femme, dont je comprenais à peine le langage, était vous-même, descendue à moi par enchantement." Paradoxically, this image of death in the form of a gypsy-sorceress has infinitely more vigor and life than the cold, abstract and distant creation and recipient of Gérard's desperate love letters. The dark Middle Easterner speaks a beautiful and mysterious language and lives in a room described with the fascination of occult significance: a picture of Saint Rosalie, Nerval's saintly patroness crowned with roses, a treatise on divination, a table of the four elements and corresponding mythical beings, spectacular jewelry and a black madonna ornamented with gold: "cette femme, aux manières étranges, royalement parée, fière et capricieuse, m'apparaissait comme une de ces magiciennes

de Thessalie à qui l'on donnait son âme pour un rêve." She is surrounded by a warm and kindly mother and a beloved son. A dark madonna, both embodying and breaking out of her stereotype, she stands among her religious relics, proudly comforting and consoling her crying infant.

Gérard, "L'Inconsolé," will, however, not be comforted. His sadness is as simple as it is profound:

> O dieux! je ne sais quelle profonde tristesse habitait mon âme, mais ce n'était autre chose que la pensée cruelle que je n'étais pas aimé. J'avais vu comme le fantôme du bonheur, j'avais usé de tous les dons de Dieu, j'étais sous le plus beau ciel du monde, en présence de la nature la plus parfaite, du spectacle le plus immense qu'il soit donné aux hommes de voir, mais à quatre cents lieues de la seule femme qui existât pour moi, et qui ignorait jusqu'à mon existence. N'être pas aimé et n'avoir pas l'espoir de l'être jamais!

And now he adds to his sorrow the guilt of having desecrated the image of his ideal love in the night spent with this "fantôme," his "facile conquête."

The eternally restless Nervalian narrator makes it clear that he cannot make peace either with woman or with nature and that the two processes are somehow intertwined. Each of the three women is in fact mythically mirrored in the magical Italian landscape conjured up by *Octavie.* Octavie herself, child-nymph-undine, first seen swimming in the Mediterranean and presenting Gérard with the gift of a fish caught in her own hands, is the bright blue Italian sea and sky. Vesuvius, erupting the night Gérard spends with his gypsy-sorceress, unites heaven and hell in a cataclysmic movement, powerful as the divine and demonic madonnas of his dreams. Contemplation of this magnificent landscape brings nothing but the desire for death.

Only the thought of the young, innocent and bright Octavie saves him from suicide. Like Sylvie, who saves him, "au bord de l'abîme," from the haunting apparition of Adrienne-Aurélia, so Octavie rescues him from the severity of his ideal Venus as well as the temptations of her dark double. And once again, as with Sylvie, a marriage takes place with Octavie only on a figurative, ritualistic level as they reenact the rites of Isis and Osiris at the temple of Pompeii. Finally, again as in *Sylvie,* the world of myth becomes an oppressive burden preventing closer contact with the real woman Octavie:

> En revenant, frappé de la grandeur des idées que nous venions de soulever, je n'osai lui parler d'amour . . . Elle me vit si froid qu'elle m'en fit reproche. Alors je lui avouai que je ne me sentais plus digne d'elle. Je lui contai le mystère de cette apparition qui avait réveillé un ancien amour dans mon coeur, et toute la tristesse qui avait succédé à cette nuit fatale où le fantôme du bonheur n'avait été que le reproche d'un parjure.

Here the text breaks, informing the reader in the next line that Gérard has vanished, that this mythic Pompeian reality lies in the far distant past: "Hélas, que tout cela est loin de nous!" The conclusion is doubly melancholic, doubly nostalgic, as Gérard relates the story of a second trip to Naples when he returned from his voyage to the Middle East, to find Octavie married to a famous painter. With this marriage, she added to the care of her crippled father the burden of a husband, for the young man was struck with a complete paralysis as soon as he married Octavie. Imprisoned by his "atroce jalousie," Octavie cannot even walk freely through the beauties of the Neapolitan landscape. This spectacle of sorrow is intolerable to Gérard, and he leaves, wondering, as in *Sylvie,* if he has not abandoned with Octavie all hope of happiness: "Le bateau qui me remenait à Marseille emporta comme un rêve le souvenir de cette apparition chérie, et je me dis que peut-être j'avais laissé là le bonheur. Octavie en a gardé près d'elle le secret."

Yet in place of the domestic idyll of *Sylvie, Octavie* gives us the picture of feminine youth, beauty and delicacy of feeling imprisoned by a monstrous husband, image of "ce géant noir qui veille éternellement dans la caverne des génies, et que sa femme est forcée de battre pour l'empêcher de se livrer au sommeil!" *Octavie* thus ends with a radical opposition of man and woman. Octavie, symbol of joy and life, is opposed to her father and husband, the embodiments of sickness, paralysis and stricture, who are extreme images of the narrator's own fears of impotence and ineffectuality. Like Fouqué's Undine and true to her archetype, the mermaid Octavie is under the surveillance of a powerful male spirit who regulates the entrance of such a refreshing being into "humanity."

Why, then, this radical disharmony between man and woman to which *Octavie* testifies from beginning to end? Nerval gives his reader a clue in the question posed at the end of the text: "Faut-il voir dans un tel tableau les marques cruelles de la vengeance des dieux!" The happiness of a union with a woman such as Octavie provokes a vengeful response on the part of the gods, who cannot bear to witness such happiness on earth. As is so often the case in Nerval's oeuvre, the gods are presented here as petty and vindictive, certainly of no greater moral stature than their human antagonists and perhaps even incapable themselves, like Jehovah's earthly representative Solomon, of the happiness they deny others.

Pandora, one of Nerval's most enigmatic and disturbing texts, also presents the battle of the sexes in terms of divine vengeance, elaborating the problem in more detail and perhaps even suggesting some answers to the question posed at the end of *Octavie*. There is no more misogynistic myth than the tale of Pandora, the tale of a curse in the form of a woman placed upon humankind and upon Prometheus in retaliation for his theft of fire from the gods. And of course it is Pandora's curiosity that opens the forbidden box and gives pain, suffering and evil to the world.

Certainly *Pandora* seems Nerval's most misogynistic tale. His "artificieuse Pandora" is a temptress and a tease, a true incarnation of "la belle dame sans merci." Always

evasive, her taunts are nevertheless blatantly sexual as she mocks Gérard's timidity and impotence by naming him her little "prêtre" and by calling out a sexual challenge in her last words to him: "Où as-tu caché le feu du ciel que tu dérobas à Jupiter?" (*Pandora*). *Pandora* is without doubt a tale of sexual fear, frustration and humiliation, as the Freudian analysis of L.-H. Sebillote [*Le Secret de Gérard de Nerval,* 1948] emphasizes. The atmosphere of the tale is so sexually charged that it is almost impossible to take at face value such exclamations as "Je n'ai pu moi-même planter le clou symbolique dans le tronc chargé de fer (Stock-im-Eisen)" or " . . . ma bourse était vide! Quelle honte!"

After a salon performance where Gérard forgets his part, and Pandora, "froide Etoile," seems to take joy in this humiliation, Gérard writes to his "déesse" in a "style abracadabrant":

> Je lui rappelais les souffrances de Prométhée, quand il mit au jour une créature aussi dépravée qu'elle. Je critiquai sa boîte à malice et son ajustement de bayadère. J'osai même m'attaquer à ses pieds serpentins, que je voyais passer insidieusement sous sa robe.

He compensates for his feeling of humiliation by raping her in a dream where she appears as the archetypal seductress and as an embodiment of female power:

> Je la voyais dansant toujours avec deux cornes d'argent ciselé, agitant sa tête empanachée, et faisant onduler son col de dentelles gauffrés sur les plis de sa robe de brocart.

> Qu'elle était belle en ses ajustemens de soie et de pourpre levantine, faisant luire insolemment ses blanches épaules, huilées de la sueur du monde. Je la domptai en m'attachant désespérément à ses cornes, et je crus reconnaître en elle l'altière Catherine, impératrice de toutes les Russies.

François Constans, in his "Nerval et l'amour platonique: 'la Pandora,'" argues convincingly that Pandora appears here as an avatar of the Syrian goddess Astarté-Dercéto, figure of "l'érotisme déchaîné," a horned goddess who is also serpentine and amphibious, "mi-femme, mi-poisson." She, then, is the dark side of the undine-mermaid Octavie. The rape of Pandora-Dercéto becomes a recreation of the original sin, as Gérard, like his many mythical predecessors, blames woman for the consequences of his own desire:

> Malheureuse! lui dis-je, nous sommes perdus par ta faute, et le monde va finir! Ne sens-tu pas qu'on ne peut plus respirer ici? L'air est infecté de tes poisons, et la dernière bougie qui nous éclaire encore tremble et pâlit déjà au souffle impur de nos haleines . . . De l'air! de l'air! Nous périssons.

Yet *Pandora* is much more than a tired rerendering of the myth of male anxiety before female sexuality and power.

Placed in the context of Nerval's work as a whole, it can even be seen as a radical rereading of the tale of Pandora. If one remembers Nerval's glorification of such Promethean figures as Adoniram, Hakem and Antéros, Pandora's last words—"Où as-tu caché le feu du ciel que tu dérobas à Jupiter?"—become less a sexual provocation than a provocation to the poet-narrator to acknowledge his theft of creative and sexual fire from the gods, to take responsibility for it and to use it. And Gérard's response can be read as his desire to deny his own Promethean nature and to capitulate to the tyrant god Jupiter: "Je ne voulus pas répondre: le nom de Prométhée me déplaît toujours singulièrement, car je sens encore à mon flanc le bec éternel du vautour dont Alcide m'a délivré. O Jupiter! quand finira mon supplice?" Seen from this perspective, Pandora is not so much an evil temptress as she is a "fille du feu" calling to the frightened poet-narrator to accept his inheritance and his destiny as "enfant-génie du feu."

Such an interpretation is corroborated by the mysterious opening paragraph of the text:

> Vous l'avez tous connue, ô mes amis! la belle Pandora du théâtre de Vienne. Elle vous a laissé sans doute, ainsi qu'à moi-même, de cruels et doux souve-nirs! C'était bien à elle peut-être,—à elle, en vérité,—que pouvait s'appliquer l'indéchiffrable énigme gravée sur la pierre de Bologne: AELIA LAELIA.—Nec vir, nec mulier, nec androgyna, etc. "Ni homme, ni femme, ni androgyne, ni fille, ni jeune, ni vieille, ni chaste, ni folle, ni pudique, mais tout cela ensemble . . . " Enfin la Pandora, c'est tout dire,—car je ne veux pas dire tout.

Thanks to Jean Richer, we know that AELIA LAELIA is the name given the philosopher's stone by the 17th-century alchemist Nicolas Bernaud. Here [in "Nerval et l'amour platonique,"] is Constans's succinct summary of Richer's findings:

> Grâce à la sagacité de Jean Richer on sait que ce double nom désignait la pierre philosophale que les alchimistes tenaient de composer au feu de leurs athanors, le premier élément qui signifierait "Fille du Soleil" (Hélios) représentant l'or alchimique, le second désignant "la force et l'essence de la lune" (ou argent vulgaire). Et, toujours selon Richer, Nerval pourrait avoir appris d'un autre écrivain occultiste au pseudonyme pro-méthéen, Epimetheus Franciscus, que l'androgyne alchimique luni-solaire portait le nom de Pandora. Rappelant un mythe du feu et, par un raffinement d'interprétation étymologique, faisant songer à l'étalon traditionnel de la richesse, l'or, figure de tout don (pan dôron), le nom de la mythique créature était bien fait pour aimenter l'attention des artisans du Grand Œuvre, systématiquement curieux de symboles à la fois séculaires, hermétiques et savants.

Suddenly the text is turned on its head. As an embodiment of the philosopher's stone, Pandora represents all that is most valuable; she is the ever-evasive goal of the spiritual seeker's quest, the union or marriage of oppo-

sites. Somehow for Nerval this goal is incarnated in woman, not only in her saintly side or in her role as medium, but also in her most frightening and seductive self, in "la complexité déroutante de l'âme féminine," composed, as Constans suggests, of coexistent contraries. Considering the myth of her origin, it is hardly surprising that Pandora should be so valued; all the gods vied in giving her their most extravagant gifts at her creation. Yet Prometheus rejected her, sensing the deceit implicit in Zeus's gift of the beautiful box. Nerval, on the other hand, may be implying that it would have been well worth it to take the risk and to marry Pandora, just as he repeatedly revealed the wisdom of his sympathy for the devil and his understanding that human progress is based upon a pact with forces that law and order label demonic.

Jean Guillaume suggests that the phrase "ni androgyne" quoted by Nerval in **Pandora** vitiates an alchemical interpretation based upon the search for androgyny and the union of opposites. Nevertheless, as he also recognizes, this negation, "ni androgyne," is reversed by the concluding phrase, "mais tout cela ensemble." The esoteric and alchemical context and connotations of the AELIA LAELIA formula cannot, in my opinion, be discounted, as Guillaume seeks to do. Rather, they should be combined with his assertion that Nerval, in **Pandora,** envisages "le problème psychologique ou moral posé par l'étonnante complexité d'un personnage immédiat (bien que non réductible pour autant à un seul être"). Once again we seem to have arrived at the notion of a self that is a dynamic and active union of opposites, of coexistent contraries.

Nerval's Pandora is in fact a quintessential embodiment of the enigmatic, indifferent, self-sufficient woman, the type and essence of the "eternal feminine," who is at the center of Sarah Kofman's incisive essay "The Narcissistic Woman: Freud and Girard" [in *Diacritics,* 1980]. Kofman suggests that narcissistic women may in truth represent a threat to the male ego by virtue of their healthy self-love, their affirmative self-sufficiency. The intellectualizations of Freud and Girard, as they are exposed by Kofman, seem strikingly dishonest in the light of the fearful fascination of Nerval's narrative persona and his intuition that Pandora's completeness is something he envies, something he himself seeks. Perhaps Nerval's monism and his conception of a collective self free him from Freud's need to condemn narcissism ethically, for if humans are all part of a collective self, then all love is, in a positive and healthy sense, love of self.

The alchemical enigma AELIA LAELIA connects **Pandora** with two little-known Nervalian fragments, **L'Ane d'or** and **Le Comte de Saint-Germain.** Both narratives begin with a segment entitled "Une Ame sans corps" that is the story of the strange fate of the cynic philosopher Pérégrinus-Proteus, "l'inventeur du suicide le plus extraordinaire qu'on ait vu sur ce globe." He demonstrated the key to eternal life to his disciples by incinerating himself in a public square and distilling himself into an eternally wandering soul without a body, an impalpable and floating spirit.

Posing as "l'Incréé, le Radical et l'Absolu," as the father of eclecticism, pleading "la cause du néant," he insulted the gods of all religions and was, therefore, excluded from all their heavens. Thus he is forced to move from foreign body to foreign body, entering them as their spirits leave them:

> Je me suis vu enfant, homme, femme tour à tour, mourant comme les autres, par hasard ou par destinée; mon âme a parcouru toute l'échelle humaine, j'ai été roi, empereur, cacique, artiste, bourgeois, soldat, Grec, Indien, Américain, Français même.

Since he has been everything, he identifies with nothing, no body, no sex, no class; in fact, he literally is Nothing in his own rendering of the AELIA LAELIA formula: "Je suis donc celui qui n'est ni mort, ni vivant; ni ombre, ni corps; ni élu, ni damné; ni historique ni fabuleux."

This same Pérégrinus-Proteus is incarnated in the fantastic historical figure of the comte de Saint-Germain in the Nervalian story of the same title. Here the alchemical formula appears as an almost identical, though extended, version of the introduction to **Pandora**:

> Aux Dieux Mânes: Aelia Laelia Crispis qui n'est ni homme ni femme ni hermaphrodite: ni fille, ni jeune, ni vieille, ni chaste, ni prostituée, ni pudique, mais tout cela ensemble, qui n'est ni morte de faim, et qui n'a été tuée, ni par le fer, ni par le poison mais par ces trois choses: n'est ni au ciel, ni dans l'eau, ni dans la terre; mais est partout.

Pérégrinus in this tale is more tragic, less light-hearted, as he confesses that he burned himself on Mount Olympus in revolt against Jupiter and that he therefore now suffers the vengeance of Jehovah: "il . . . s'écria en baissant la tête et pleurant: 'Jéhovah! Jéhovah! mon père . . . ne t'es-tu pas assez vengé.'"

This Pérégrinus-Proteus, this "âme sans corps," is Nerval's metaphor for the human self, reminding one of the notion of Brahman as "neti, neti, neither this nor that." Coming back from the dead, he is told, "Revenez à vous-même . . . ," and his response is an untroubled "D'abord, qu'est-ce que c'est que moi-même?" What, then, is the relationship between this iconoclastic philosopher and Pandora, seductress and femme fatale? Perhaps it is that in women this mythical, protean, self-transformatory quality of the self is much easier to see, that woman is by definition less easy to categorize than man, who molds himself to the status quo and the social order. For Nerval historical woman is on the outside of the power structure, always slipping out and away from man's attempt to pin her down and categorize her. She embodies what Nina Auerbach calls the disruptive power of the myth of self-transformation and self-transfiguration, a myth that is profoundly threatening to hierarchy and authority, to the realm of God the Father.

Woman holds the key to realization of the self, a key she will present to man only when she is permitted free expression of her own nature, both mythic and real. Without Pandora Nerval's Prometheus is chained in perpetual suffering and servitude to Jupiter-Jehovah. It is hardly surprising that Nerval describes, however mockingly, a visit by Pérégrinus to a political rally celebrating the "evadism" of his time:

> —L'évadaïsme, c'est la nouvelle synthèse du grand Evadam.—Cette formule renferme les noms de l'homme-femme, Eve et Adam . . . L'androgyne, le père et la mère. Les deux êtres séparés n'en font plus qu'un; l'homme est réuni à la femme, et la femme à l'homme; l'antagonisme des deux sexes n'existe plus, l'homme est libre, la femme est libre, tout le monde est libre.

Evadism was the religion of Ganneau, the Mapah, whose name is composed of the first syllables of *mater* and *pater,* a religion founded in principles of androgyny. As Busst emphasizes in his essay on the androgyne, evadism celebrated the hermaphrodite as a symbol of the emancipation of women and the ideals of the French Revolution. Busst quotes Ganneau's disciple, L.-Ch. Caillaux, as he praises his leader: "C'est un homme qui proteste intégralement contre la forme religieuse, politique, sociale, comme n'étant que l'expression monstrueuse de l'absorption de la femme par l'homme, du pauvre par le riche, du faible par le fort." In fact, social mystics as varied as Ballanche, Leroux and Enfantin all propounded variations on the theme, central to Nerval's work, that true human progress depended upon the breakdown of barriers between men and women, rich and poor, West and East, not through appropriation of one by the other, but through equalization of power inequities.

Nerval, too iconoclastic to adhere to any party line and too sophisticated to believe in any simplistic formula for human liberation, nevertheless shares the belief that future human progress would be based upon the emancipation of women. This belief unites him in spirit with the utopian socialists of his time and distinguishes him from the liberal feminists of his day, who were convinced that emancipation of men would inevitably free women as well. My analysis of Nerval's poetic and political vision of women joins that of Stéphane Michaud's *Muse et Madone* in its emphasis upon the bonds that unite 19th-century utopian feminism with the work of poets like Jean-Paul, Novalis, Nerval and Baudelaire. As Michaud writes in the introduction to this informative and provocative study, "Je me suis en effet efforcé de montrer que la flamme mystique qui brille dans les ténèbres baudelairiennes et la mélancolie nervalienne n'était pas radicalement distincte à son origine de celle qui luit dans le combat des femmes prolétaires de 1848." Perhaps a new picture of Nerval is coming into view, one in which his works are seen to constitute a self-conscious meditation on the complexity of woman's social and mythic essence and evolution, a celebration of the gifts a free Pandora could bring to humanity.

> Nerval derived a passionate joy from his conviction that he was a part of the great chain of souls and of the universal harmony. His fear that it might in some way be attacked by evil did not weaken his determination to be accepted and to prove himself worthy to participate in this communion.
>
> —*Norma Rinsler, in "Gérard de Nerval's Celestical City and the Chain of Souls," in* Studies in Romanticism, *1963.*

Susan Noakes (essay date 1988)

SOURCE: "Nerval: Reading between the Lines," in *Timely Reading: Between Exegesis and Interpretation,* Cornell, 1988, pp. 135-56.

[*In the following excerpt, Noakes observes the significance of time in* Aurélia *and comments on the relationship between the narrator and his double in the novella.*]

The Failed Dialectic of Exegesis and Interpretation

Aurélia begins with a catalogue of the narrator's mental library and his statement that his readings have driven him mad: "[Cette folie] est la faute de mes lectures" (My readings bear the blame for [this madness]). It is important to distinguish this statement from Francesca's, for Nerval's narrator sees his madness as the fault not of his books but of his readings of those books, of the mistaken way he has interpreted them. Again, near the end of the story a voice from the beyond reproaches the narrator for his failure as a reader: "Tout cela était fait pour t'enseigner le secret de la vie, et tu n'as pas compris. Les religions et les fables, les saints et les poètes s'accordaient à expliquer l'énigme fatale, et tu as mal interprété. . . . Maintenant il est trop tard!" (All that was done to teach you the secret of life, and you have not understood. Religions and myths, the saints and the poets agree in explaining the enigma of fate, and you have misinterpreted. . . . Now it is too late). The narrator's last important human contact in the story is with one final interpreter of the "fatal enigma," "un interprète sublime . . . prédestiné à entendre ces secrets de l'âme que la parole n'oserait transmettre ou ne réussirait pas à rendre. C'était l'oreille de Dieu" (a sublime interpreter . . . predestined to understand these secrets of the soul which language would not dare to convey or would not succeed in rendering. It was the ear of God). But the ear not being an organ of speech, the sublime interpreter does not pass on the messages received, so that at the end of the story the narrator is, by his own qualitative standards, still illiterate.

If this reference to God as the ultimate interpreter calls to mind the theological framework in which Dante presents

reading, the association is certainly no accident: of the four authors listed at the beginning of *Aurélia,* Dante is the one whom Nerval mentions most frequently throughout his writings. Perhaps his key allusion to Dante appeared three years before the publication of *Aurélia,* in *Les Nuits d'octobre* (*October nights*). The narrator, about to be introduced to the Parisian market by a friend, recalls Rousseau's invective against the "moeurs des villes" (city ways; Nerval, *Oeuvres*) and remarks, in a tongue-in-check reference to the opening of the *Inferno:* "Si je n'étais sûr d'accomplir une des missions douleureuses de l'écrivain, je m'arrêterais ici" (If I were not sure of carrying out one of the writer's painful tasks, I would stop here). Since the tense of the main clause is the present (not the past) conditional, it is clearly the narrator as writer, as well as the nocturnal *flâneur,* the urban vagabond, who "would stop"; the doubling parallels that of Dante the poet and Dante the character. The Dantesque allusion then becomes explicit as the friend quotes *Inferno* XVII (the Geryon episode):

> . . . mais mon ami me dit comme Virgile à Dante: "Or sie forte e ardito;—omai si scende per sì fatte scale . . . "
>
> A quoi je répondis sur un air de Mozart: "Andiam'! andiam'! andiamo bene."
>
> —Tu te trompes! reprit-il, ce n'est pas là l'enfer; c'est tout au plus le purgatoire. Allons plus loin.
>
> (But my friend said to me, as Vergil did to Dante: "Now be strong and daring;—henceforth one goes down on stairs made like this . . . " To which I answered, with a snatch from Mozart: "Let's go! Let's go! Indeed, let's go." "You're mistaken!" he said, "that's not Hell; at most, it's Purgatory. Let's go farther on.")

The narrator's response in misremembered words from an erotic seduction scene in Mozart's *Don Giovanni* are as lightheartedly inappropriate as his friend's Dantesque quotation. Indeed, misreading ("Tu te trompes!") is the point of this comic passage, in which Nerval pokes fun at the impulse to emulate Dante which frequently emerges in his work, inevitably to be frustrated.

Dante's theologically grounded view of "reading" represented for Nerval a totally unattainable ideal. Dante's pilgrim can "hear" Beatrice as an indicator pointing to Mary, who in turn indicates the Divine Word (*Paradiso* XXIII. 70-75; cf. *Paradiso* IV; 1-12), without either finding himself lost in a series of signifiers without end (ceaseless interpretation) or conflating the signifiers and the historical moments of their appearance so as to lose the essential human sense of their difference (deadening exegesis). Dante's model, in other words, can remain fully open to continuous *change* in meaning without resulting in an ultimate *lack* of meaning; indeed, constant change in meaning and ultimate meaningfulness are, in this fully dialectical model, inextricably interdependent.

But the narrator of *Aurélia* cannot find ultimate meaning in what he reads. Like the pilgrim in Paradise, he sees people as signs that point to something else, but for him this something else is always another word, or a person seen as a word—something to be further interpreted, not final. The narrator's failure in reading is like that of the young Dante: "I have deified my love and I have worshipped [her]." One woman dissolves into another, and still another:

> La déesse m'apparaissait, me disant: "Je suis la même que Marie, la même que ta mère, la même aussi que sous toutes les formes tu as toujours aimée. A chacune de tes épreuves, j'ai quitté l'un des masques dont je voile mes traits, et bientôt tu me verras telle que je suis."

> (The goddess appeared to me, saying to me: "I am the same as Mary, the same as your mother, the same one also under all the forms whom you have always loved. At each of your trials, I have dropped one of the masks with which I always veil my face, and soon you will see me as I am.")

When Beatrice pointed to Mary, it was as the incarnatrix of the eternal Word; Nerval's goddess is a metaphor for metaphor, for things that stand for other things that lead back in an endless series.

Near the end of the fifth chapter in the first part, one of the narrator's friends asks tearfully: "N'est-ce pas que c'est vrai qu'il y a un Dieu?" (Isn't it true that there is a God?). In effect, he wants to be reassured that all the words the narrator has said, all the symbols he has seen as pointing each to the next, must point to something final. "'Oui!' lui dis-je avec enthousiasme" ('Yes!' I said to him with enthusiasm). The narrator goes on: "Quel bonheur je trouvai d'abord dans cette conviction!" (What happiness I found at first in this conviction!). Later, however, his certainty vanishes.

Temporal Irony

Because the Dantesque model of reading does not work for him, Nerval must devise a narrative structure wholly different from Dante's. The *Commedia,* on the other hand, is the product of the tension between two narrative perspectives, that of narrator and that of pilgrim. These two figures stand at different points along a "then/now" axis. In *Aurélia,* on the other hand, Nerval uses two voices not separated by a fixed moment of conversion to "new life," distinguishing "then" from "now." These voices are so equal in narrative power that the reader would be unable to decide which voice is the "original" and which the "double" did not the voice that speaks the first words of the story also end it. And yet, because the two voices have functioned in such perfect polyphony throughout the tale, it is the voice of the double, which does not speak at the end, that gives *Aurélia* its unwritten afterword. The story's ending appears unsatisfactory if judged by the criteria of traditional narrative structure, for although at an explicit level it asserts itself as a conclusion, at another

level the story's problem continues after the story's end. It is the voice of the double that gives the ending this continuing quality and makes it, rather than a narrative failure, a narrative tour de force.

The conceptual basis for the temporal double in *Aurélia* is the physical double often encountered in romantic narrative. It first appears shortly after the narrator falls into a hallucinatory fit in the night streets of Paris. Taken to a police station, he senses the presence of his double behind him as he lies stretched on a cot and later believes he sees his friends taking the double out of the station, mistaking it for the narrator. When his friends finally retrieve him, denying that they came to the station earlier in the evening, the narrator continues to be troubled by the knowledge of the existence of his double. He later realizes that his beloved Aurélia, already lost once, to Death, will be taken in by the same fraud that deceived his friends. Then, dreaming that he is in a room where a group has gathered to await the arrival of a bridegroom, he remarks, "J'imaginai que celui qu'on attendait était mon *double,* qui devait épouser Aurélia, et je fis un scandale qui sembla consterner l'assemblée" (I imagined the person they were awaiting was my *double,* who was to marry Aurélia, and I made a scene that seemed to upset everyone). Threatened with physical violence, the narrator prepares to fight back, and his upraised arm is stopped only by a woman's mournful cry. He awakens, knowing that the cry was real, not a dream, and that the voice was the dead Aurélia's.

Two details in the depiction of the traditional physical double suggest the willed blindness toward the threat of death which forms the conceptual basis for Nerval's temporal double: first, the narrator decides not to look at the double; second, he recalls that seeing one's double indicates death's approach. Since the narrator's death would bring the narration to an end, his refusal to advance from intuiting the double's presence to seeing it makes possible the continuation of the story. He merely glimpses someone of his size retreating from the room. His later violence directs itself toward those who are awaiting the double's appearance, not toward the double itself, and no second appearance of the physical double is represented in *Aurélia.*

Rather than growing out of a struggle between the narrator and his physical double, the story develops from the tension between the narrator and his temporal double. The narrator, in other words, maintains his existence as narrator by ignoring the commentaries of the temporal double, which tend to undermine his own story. Like the physical one, the temporal double must be glimpsed only in passing. The relation between the two voices is not at all that between two characters (narrator-then/narrator-now) but rather that between two texts. Each text reads the other and comments upon it; each finds in the other a gloss that modifies its own value and meaning. But the relation between text and commentary is not regular and continuous, with the two laid out in a predictable pattern as they are in the *Vita nuova* or the *Epistre Othéa.* Instead, single discourse often splits in two at the most unexpected junctures, just when the narrator's voice has imposed itself as univocal.

An especially disorienting eruption of the voice of the temporal double occurs as early as the story's second paragraph. Up to that point, the temporal structure is simple. The narrator states that he has, in a time prior to the time in which he is writing, gone through "une longue maladie" (a long illness), which he associates with "rêve" (dream), the "monde invisible" (the invisible world), "limbes" (limbo), and "le monde des Esprits" (the Spirit world). By the time he begins his story, he has come back from the other world to the world of "ce que les hommes appellent la raison" (what men call reason). It is a straightforward then/now structure: "then," the narrator was sick, asleep, and imagining; "now," he is healthy, awake, and reasoning.

But this clear structure is rendered ambiguous by the verbs of the last sentence of the second paragraph. In the penultimate sentence the narrator refers to the ecstasies that his imagination brought him during his period of sickness, now past. His voice, firmly grounded in the time frame in which he is writing, describes his past self as past. "Parfois, je croyais ma force et mon activité doublées; il me semblait tout savoir, tout comprendre; l'imagination m'apportait des délices infinies" (Sometimes, I thought my strength and activity were doubled; it seemed to me that I knew everything, understood everything; imagination brought me infinite ecstasies). But the verbs of the last sentence of the paragraph move the narrator backward for an instant into the realm of those lost ecstasies. Instead of being the person he was in the preceding sentence, someone who was once blessed with "imagination" and "ecstasies" but is so blessed no longer, he becomes someone who still possesses these gifts but, balanced on a threshold, anticipates the approaching moment when he will have to give them up: "En recouvrant ce que les hommes appellent la raison, faudra-t-il regretter de les avoir perdues?" (Recovering what men call reason, will it be necessary to regret having lost them?)

The first element to be noted in this important sentence is the tense of the verb *falloir*. The clarity of the then/now structure would have been better maintained if *falloir* had been placed in the present tense: *faut-il*. It would then be clear that the narrator continued to speak from the healthy, awake, reasoning viewpoint of "now," asking whether "now" he should regret having lost the "délices" "then": "faut-il regretter de les avoir perdues?" The structure would have been clarified even further if the participial phrase that opens the sentence had been based on a past rather than a present participle. But Nerval's use of the future tense, "faudra-t-il," makes the question quite a different one, blurring what had been a clear demarcation between past and present. The lack of temporal specificity of the phrase "en recouvrant" permits modulation away from the tense norms already established, though not in itself implying any deviation. The narrator, with "faudra-t-il," asks whether he will have to regret the loss of the "délices" in the future when he experiences it; the loss has yet to occur. The voice that says "faudra" cannot have

returned from the "monde invisible"; that voice speaks from a moment prior to the time in which the two preceding sentences are written.

What is important about the form "faudra" is not merely that it is in the future tense but rather that its tense deviates slightly from the pattern established by the immediate context. It does not initiate a flashback or a reverie of any substantial duration; its power lasts no longer than the ellipsis which follows the question mark: "faudra-t-il regretter de les avoir perdues? . . . " Not a change in the color or line of the whole canvas of *Aurélia,* it is only one very light brushstroke, but a brushstroke that nonetheless changes the appearance of everything around it. The two paragraphs that precede this sentence establish a norm for the use of tenses and the description of temporality from which *faudra* deviates just enough to call the norm into question. They have together formed a prologue to the account that begins with the third paragraph: "Cette *Vita nuova* a eu pour moi deux phases. Voici les notes qui se rapportent à la première" (This *New Life* has had two phases for me. Here are the notes relating to the first).

As the prologue closes, what it explicitly announces about the account to come is thus cast into a new light, if only for an instant. The assertion of the first two paragraphs that the narrator has returned from the state labeled "maladie" is, with the syntactic structure, called into question. The reader must look back and reevaluate what has gone before. This instant of questioning passes but leaves the question behind, even as the narrative returns to the clear temporal order set up by the main body of the prologue. In a move crucial to the rhetorical structure of the work, Nerval has rendered visible the discrepancy between the two narrative voices that will tell the story. If his next sentence, the first of the text proper, hides the discrepancy once again, that does not mean that the reader is to forget what has been glimpsed: the crucial sentence embodies the moment of transition between two states of being and two moments of knowing, which—according to the first paragraph—it is the purpose of *Aurélia* to describe. "Les premiers instants du sommeil sont l'image de la mort; un engourdissement nébuleux saisit notre pensée, et nous ne pouvons déterminer l'instant précis où le moi, sous une autre forme, continue l'oeuvre de l'existence" (The first instants of sleep are the image of death; a vague numbness takes hold of our thought, and we cannot fix the precise instant in which the I, in another form, continues the work of existence). The final sentence of the prologue, then, not only treats but also exemplifies the breaking through of past into present. It is particularly important to *Aurélia* because it shows for the first time how the story's themes will be worked out in its structures.

Reading between (the Lines of) Past and Present

The opening paragraphs of *Aurélia* thus announce, in detail as well as in general terms, both the structure and the themes of the work as a whole. In his prologue Nerval writes *about* and also *in* two periods of time. The two might be called "remembered time," time past, the time of sickness; and "text time," the present time of narration, the time of recovered health. The prologue might then be described as written *in* the time of recovered health *about* the time of sickness—except for "faudra," a word spoken in the time of sickness about the time of recovered health, to which it looks forward with some ambivalence. Thus, to label the period of sickness as "remembered time" or "past time," implying that it is definitely over when *Aurélia* begins, is to falsify the story's temporal structure and to simplify Nerval's conception of memory. Similarly, to label the period of recovered health as "text time" or "present time," implying that the entire text is written in that time frame, is to fail to perceive *Aurélia*'s complexity. Even the opening paragraphs, which establish the traditional setting of the traveler returned and about to tell the story of his journey, are not written entirely from the point of view of the "returned" time frame.

The only satisfactory labels for the time frames the story is written about and in are those suggested by the subtitle, "le rêve et la vie" (dream and life), or "dream time" and "life time." Dream time is to be associated with the double, life time with the one who is doubled. In the first sentence of *Aurélia,* the realm of dream is given a secondary status with respect to the realm of life: "Le Rêve est une seconde vie." The implication is that a dream is a duplicating of life, a mode of being and knowing modeled on life. But considering *Aurélia* as a whole, it is by no means clear that the "second life" is inferior merely because it is second.

The entire story presents itself as an inquiry into one question: is the dream state, as compared with the waking state, a time of diminished or of heightened awareness? But by asking which voice has access to the truth, that of the Double or that of the one who is doubled, Nerval poses two more general problems deriving from the relation between time and knowing. The first has to do with time conceived as normative, predictably continuous, the stable background against which events are measured and through which events are described. The second has to do with time conceived as moving.

The first problem is posed directly by the tenses, which ordinarily function according to conventions. The conventions pertaining to the relation of one tense to another effectively restrict what is seen or, more particularly, what is spoken or written about what is seen. They keep the individual speaker in conformity with those notions accepted a priori by a linguistic community as to what is "then" and what is "now," for example; they thus privilege some moments as present and relegate others to nonpresent status. In order to question these notions, *Aurélia* must break the syntactic conventions on which they depend.

The second, more complex problem is how to conceive time as moving, a vehicle of transition. Nerval's extended speculation about the way change occurs from one form of understanding to another depends upon explorations of this problem. His concern with this process is suggested

by the line from the story's first paragraph already cited: "We cannot fix the precise instant in which the I, in another form, continues the work of existence." The moment of transition is indeed itself the unknown which is to be explored ("nous ne pouvons déterminer") and not merely a passage toward the unknown. To understand the moment of transition is to understand a process that changes the known into the unknown, perhaps the most powerful kind of alchemy.

Death must form a part of this inquiry, even if only at one remove, as figured in sleep; for it is death that places a limit on both human time and human knowledge, and the limit position is always the one that promises the explorer the greatest rewards. The twilight consciousness, whether a transition to the darkness of death or to the darkness of sleep, is a state in which the self knows it is passing from one mode of being to another but is unable to determine at exactly what moment that passing occurs. It knows it is experiencing something that it does not understand, that seems just beyond its grasp. The twilight state is, then, the point of intersection between the known and the unknown; in it the self does not know whether to say: "I am awake; I will sleep" or "I was awake; I do sleep." When it does not know what time it is, it recognizes the extent of its own ignorance.

It was in this focus on the difficult moment of transition between two modes of being and two time frames that Marcel Proust found the strength of Nerval's narrative technique. Commenting on Nerval's *Sylvie,* Proust noted [in "Gérard Nerval," printed in the Pléiade volume *Contre Sainte-Beuve: Précédé de pastiches et mélanges*] that "One is obliged at every moment to turn the preceding pages to see where one is, whether it is present or recollection of the past." He describes his own desire to fix the "pictures" seen in the moments of transition between one state of consciousness and another: "Sometimes, at the moment of falling asleep, one perceives them, one wishes to fix and define their charm, and then one awakens and sees them no more, one lets oneself go and before one has been able to fix them one is asleep, as if the understanding were not permitted to see them." Proust found that Nerval had not only succeeded in seizing such moments as isolated instances but had also been able to see in these moments general patterns: "these mysterious laws of thought which I have often wished to express and which I find expressed in *Sylvie*." What is great and "inexpressible" in *Sylvie* "is not in the words [but] all mixed in between the words."

This is even more the case in *Aurélia,* where the movement from one time frame to another and back again is more rapid still than in *Sylvie*. It is to be glimpsed in the relations between words, specifically between verbs, rather than in individual words themselves. The way the verbs refer to each other and thus give rise to the effect Proust notes may be seen in a paragraph in which the narrator asks himself whether the figure glimpsed in the police station was "the *Double* of the legends." What is at issue throughout this paragraph is, once again, the relation between time and knowing, between the way the narrator knows the earthly world, "vie," and the way he knows the supernatural world, "rêve." Nerval's use of tenses in this paragraph to mark off different periods of time and the attitudes toward "vie" and "rêve" in each period is careful and regular, once again establishing a definite norm with respect to which deviation can be noted. The first sentence begins: "Je ne sais comment expliquer . . . " (I don't know how to explain . . .). The time frame is the present: the moment of writing is life time rather than dream time. "Mais quel était donc cet esprit . . . " (But who, then, was this spirit . . .): this standard use of the imperfect tense makes clear that the spirit's existence has some undefined duration, but its context by no means suggests that this duration extends into the moment of *Aurélia*'s writing. "N'avais-je pas été frappé de l'histoire de ce chevalier qui combattit toute une nuit dans une forêt contre un inconnu qui était lui-même?" (Had I not been struck by the story of that knight who fought all night in a forest against an unknown who was himself?) The past imperfect tense beginning this sentence emphasizes that the narrator, in the present, knows not only that the Double's appearance in the police station took place in the past but also that something occurred ("N'avais-je pas été frappé . . . ") in an even more distant past. That is, the paragraph shows a clear sense of the distinctions among discrete periods of time.

But the paragraph ends in temporal as well as epistemological ambiguity: "Quoi qu'il en soit, je crois que l'imagination humaine n'a rien inventé qui ne soit vrai, dans ce monde ou dans les autres, et je ne pouvais douter de ce que j'avais *vu* si distinctement" (Whatever the case may be, I believe the human imagination has invented nothing that is not true, in this world or in the other, and I could not doubt what I had so distinctly *seen;* original emphasis). This sentence moves from a present-tense affirmation of belief in the truth of the imagined to an imperfect-tense assertion of inability to doubt that truth.

Although, with respect to verbal convention, there is nothing even slightly aberrant in Nerval's use of tenses here, the relation between the two principal verbs creates precisely the effect of uncertainty that Proust describes. Each of the two coordinate independent clauses carries the same message—belief in imagination in the first clause, and non-doubt of vision in the second—yet each of them is constructed around a different tense. The impact of the imperfect tense in this context is clearer when one considers how the two clauses would function together if the present tense, the near past tense, or the past definite tense were substituted for the imperfect (necessitating tense changes elsewhere in the sentence as well):

> je crois que l'imagination humaine n'a rien inventé qui ne soit vrai . . . et je ne *puis* douter de ce que j'ai vu . . .

> je crois que l'imagination humaine n'ait rien inventé qui ne soit vrai . . . et je n'*ai pu* douter de ce que j'ai vu . . .

> je crus que l'imagination humaine n'avait rien inventé

que ne fut vrai . . . et je ne *pus* douter de ce que j'avais vu. . . .

What is significant is the effect of the juxtaposition of the imperfect with other tenses, for it indicates that whether the narrator's belief in his vision of the Double continues into the moment of narrating the story is an unsettled question. It would have been answered affirmatively by the first two of the foregoing models, negatively by the third. It is instead left open, because to provide an answer to this question would be to eliminate the problem that is the story's motive force. A grammarian has described the imperfect tense (from *imperfectus,* not completely finished or carried out) in the following terms: "There are [implicit in the imperfect tense] limits . . . but one does not see them (*or does not want to see them*)."

That the inability to doubt the imagination is expressed in the imperfect tense indicates that the narrator does not see the beginning or the end of his inability to doubt. Indeed, it is crucial to *Aurélia* that the narrator see neither a moment when he begins to believe nor a moment when he ceases to believe his imagination. There must be no discoverable dividing line between belief and unbelief, for the narrator must know that his visions are simultaneously false and true. *Aurélia* is subtitled "le rêve *et* la vie," not "le rêve *ou* la vie." Dream and life are concurrent.

The ambiguous relation between two selves, two time frames, and two ways of knowing is, in *Aurélia,* most typically expressed in this way, through the juxtaposition of a verb in the imperfect tense with a verb in some other tense. To paraphrase Proust, it is in the space "mixed between" imperfect tense verbs and verbs in other tenses that the narrator's double makes its presence, or its presentness, felt. The narrator generally relegates to a clearly demarcated past time, cut off from the present, those attitudes characteristic of dream. He speaks in tenses indicating that the past is over and that he is, at the moment of writing the description, cured of the delusions he describes. Often, however, there is a sudden movement from those tenses that represent cut-off past time to an imperfect tense implying that the dream attitudes have not been banished and that dream continues in wakefulness. A traditional description of the French imperfect tense is "a present in the past." Nerval's use of the imperfect, however, often inverts this formula by bringing the past into the present.

Sometimes in *Aurélia,* other tenses in various combinations also serve to create rapid shifts in temporal perspective. As Proust says of the earlier *Sylvie,* one must constantly look back to see whether one is reading about a state of vision or a return from vision. Each verb, in fact, must be questioned in a deliberate attempt to slow the fluctuations in temporal perspective: that is, to understand them rather than simply to feel their effect. The initial theme of *Aurélia* is made manifest in its structure; the reader must try to measure just how distant dream time is from life time at particular moments in the narrative, thus imitating the narrator's inquiry.

Authorial Mastery, Readerly Madness

But the oscillation between temporal perspectives which struck Proust as innovative is, however remarkable, new in only a quite specific sense. Rapid changes in the narrator's viewpoint occur in any number of well-known texts and are designated by the traditional rhetorical term "irony." What is unusual about Nerval's changes in perspective is that they are temporal; they are, nonetheless, not different in structure from other types of irony, all of which are based on doubling. In *Aurélia* it is the time frame fixed at the very start of the story which is made to appear double in structure. The temporal irony consists in oscillation between this time frame and another, between one that is continuous and one discontinuous with the moment of the opening of the narrative. The moment of beginning to write signifies a time frame in which the narrator records: "Je vais essayer . . . de transcrire les impressions" (I am going to try . . . to transcribe the impressions). Transcription is his characteristic activity in this—rather than in the imagining—time frame, and it is the concept of transcription that is undercut by the temporal irony.

The time frame of transcription is to be associated at first with "vie" more than with "rêve." In the time of "vie," the narrator claims, an effort is made to transcribe—that is, to double or repeat graphically—the experiences of the time of "rêve." In fact, though, the time in which the imaginative experiences to be transcribed occur and the time in which the actual transcription takes place are one and the same; that is, the writing time is not and cannot be double in structure. As it is made to appear doubled, however, there occurs a redistribution of connotation between the paired terms of the subtitle, coloring all the concepts associated with each. The relative positions of "rêve" and "vie" are nearly inverted as the notion that the fiction is a transcription of past feelings remembered rather than a present creation of them in writing becomes more convincing. "Vie," clearly associated with transcribing time at the outset, becomes more and more associated with the fictive remembered time as the second life takes on increasingly privileged status, becoming a more deeply real form of life than the "first."

The fictive doubling of the writing time, with the consequent redistribution of value from "rêve" to "vie," is brought about by the same device that is used to achieve doubling within the story: repetition. Characters, events, images, and ideas that are presented as occurring in one time and therefore as temporally discrete are shown to be similar to those occurring in another time and are no longer temporally discrete but part of a repetitive temporal structure. In the second part of *Aurélia* there is an especially striking example of such a metamorphosis of something that is single, first, into something that is related by similarity to something else and, then, into something that is part of a repetitive series extending across time.

> Pendant mon sommeil, j'eus une vision merveilleuse. Il me semblait que la déesse m'apparaissait, me disant: 'Je suis la même que Marie, la même que ta mère, la même aussi que sous toutes les formes tu as toujours aimée. A chacune de tes épreuves, j'ai quitté l'un des masques dont je voile mes traits, et bientôt tu me verras telle que je suis.'
>
> (During my sleep, I had a marvelous vision. It seemed to me that the goddess appeared to me, saying: "I am the same as Mary, the same as your mother, as well as the same woman whom you have always loved in all the different forms. At each of your trials, I have dropped one of the masks with which I always veil my face, and soon you will see me as I am.")

Such extensions of what are essentially metaphors into the temporal realm unify—or, rather, constitute—the narrative. Because two images are similar, the two time periods in which they occur seem to reflect each other. One moment, so mirrored in another, will therefore appear to have been extended, and the resemblance between what occurs within the two moments will be taken as duration, just as reflections in a sequence of mirrors will be taken as depth.

In the same way, one moment of writing is made to seem doubled through the creation of apparent repetition. The writing, it is claimed, is not discrete, something unto itself, but rather a copy of something else, for example, an insight or inner experience. The relationship of similarity between insight or experience, on the one hand, and a copy, on the other, creates the double structure of the writing. Once this double structure is established, it is metamorphosed from a doubling derived from similarity to a doubling extended over time. Metaphor becomes history. The insight or inner experience is said to be a memory, an inner copy of an event that occurred in the past. In the writing, then, by means of the same two-step process used in the story, what is written in the present is cast onto the screen of the past. The present thus appears to acquire duration, a quality that it cannot, in fact, possess.

One of the important consequences of such literary metamorphosis is a fundamental change in the status of the writer, a change that may be the writer's primary motivation in bringing about the metamorphosis. A synchrony that recalls human limitation becomes instead a synchrony that implies omniscience. The synchronic reality, an image written in a single passing moment, is fictionalized into a diachronic narrative structured through repetition, and this repetition in turn suggests a synchrony visible from a point of view larger than that of mortal beings.

Nerval described the desire to perceive such a superhuman synchrony in the preface to his translation of *Faust*; the preface, published in 1840, anticipates the concerns of *Aurélia,* interpreting Goethe's work in terms of the relation between time and knowledge:

> Cet infini toujours béant, qui confond la plus fort raison humaine, n'effraye point le poète de *Faust;* il s'attache à en donner une définition et une formule. . . . Bien plus, non content d'analyser le vide et l'inexplicable de l'infini présent, il s'attaque de même à celui du passé. Pour lui, comme pour Dieu sans doute, rien ne finit, ou du moins rien ne se transforme que la matière. . . . Il serait consolant de penser, en effet, que rien ne meurt de ce qui a frappé l'intel-ligence, et que l'éternité conserve dans son sein une sorte d'histoire universelle,

visible par les yeux de l'âme, synchronisme divin, qui nous ferait participer un jour à la science de Celui qui voit d'un seul coup d'oeil tout l'avenir et tout le passé.

(This always gaping infinite, which confounds the strongest human intelligence, does not at all frighten the poet of *Faust*; he is intent on giving a definition of and a formula for it. . . . What's more, not satisfied with analyzing the abyss and the unexplain-able of the present infinite, he takes on as well that of the past. For him, as for God no doubt, nothing ends, or at least nothing is transformed but matter. . . . It would be comforting to think, in fact, that nothing of what has struck the understanding dies, and that eternity preserves in its breast a kind of divine synchronism, which would one day make us participate in the knowledge of the One who sees in a single glance all the future and all the past.) . . .

[Baudelaire once asserted] the immortality of everything that has ever been thought. Did such immortality exist, both exegesis and interpretation would be fully possible. But, even though this "synchronisme divin" is not available to mortals, at least something quite like it can be constructed, through writing. The one who constructs it— that is, the one who convincingly presents him- or herself as seeing from a point of view beyond that actually available to a finite being—is elevated to a superior position. The writer's position is especially privileged when a conviction is awakened, in the writer as well as others, that she or he actually has seen a "synchronisme divin" and not merely constructed it. The reader will follow the same impulse toward immortality when pursuing exegetical reading with too much passion.

Nerval, perhaps unfortunately for his personal equanimity, recognized the falsity of any sense of authorial mastery over time and the reading process. Traces of irony in his description of Goethe's undertaking indicate mockery of the writer who pretends to an understanding which is, for temporal reasons, unavailable to him: "Bien plus, non content d'*analyser le vide* et l'inexplicable de l'*infini présent*. . . . Pour lui, comme pour Dieu *sans doute* . . . " Nerval's awareness of the futility of undertaking a project that demands a knowledge exceeding human temporal limits had made him describe ironically his **Les Filles du feu** (**The Daughters of Fire**) in which he had believed he was capturing the series of all his past lives (Nerval, **Oeuvres**), as a "livre infaisable" (unwriteable book). The slightly later **Aurélia** is in this sense even more "unwriteable."

If only fleetingly, **Aurélia** makes visible what exists in invisible form in other works. Temporal doubling has the same form as the writer's relationship to his or her language, insofar as writing is a creation of duration for a lived moment that vanishes: the moment of writing. The temporally doubled structure is, however, a simplification. Writing meant to be read, so far as its writer knows (and hopes), potentially exists in an infinity of future moments, which the writer envisions by reference to a series of past moments that he or she purports to be "transcribing." The moments associated with writing are thus multiple rather than merely double.

When schematically reduced to two, however, these moments may be described as the relative present and the relative past. . . . In relation to the author, the present is the time *of* writing, and the past is a remembered experience *about which* he or she writes in an effort to make the moment of that remembered experience recur in some future moment when the text is read. In relation to the reader, the present is the time of reading (which was the writer's future), and the past is the time of writing (which was the writer's present) as well as, in some cases, the time about which the writer seems to write. The writer has no real access to the future (the reader's present), just as the reader has no access to the writer's present (the reader's past). Yet each struggles to have what cannot be had, to see what cannot be seen.

To simplify the model further, one might say that the past always belongs to the author as the present belongs to the reader, and that each wants to possess not only his or her own time frame but also the other's. Each has one but is driven to seek another. At times, a dialectical exchange between moments may seem to occur in passing, as it does in the fictive structure Nerval constructed by means of temporal irony. More often, however, the attempt at exchange will be felt to end in failure—as it does for the narrator, whose madness is, he says, caused by his readings.

It is never quite possible to read both in the past and in the present. One inevitably reads in only one moment while nonetheless desiring to read in two: that is, to make one's mind live in a moment other than one's own, to know something as it was known (or, from the writer's viewpoint, will be known) at another time. The "other" moment in which one wishes to have one's mind exist, however, is always the province of someone else: for the reader, the author; for the author, the reader. For this reason, author and reader are often seen as inevitably locked in struggle; and the author (like Boccaccio) imagines the reader's victory as bringing dismemberment, while the reader imagines the author's victory as bringing madness. In fact, however, they struggle not against each other but against the common enemy: time.

On Nerval's dream explorations in *Aurélia*:

"The dream is a second life," wrote Nerval at the outset of *Aurélia*, and it is the domain of the dream that he sets out to investigate. Yet *Aurélia* is not simply strict reportage of the images that he confronted in his subliminal realm; it is also a work of art and, as such, is a composite of distilled, refined material, devoid of all extraneous, peripheral material. Nerval offers the reader symbols of extreme density and complexity, images left from the inroads made on his psyche by the works of men like Boehme, Cazotte, Bosch, and Saint-Martin. Nerval's unconscious meanderings manifest themselves in archetypal material that, after having been churned and turned about within his own prima materia, emerges in *Aurélia* as an entity unto itself.

Bettina L. Knapp, in "Aurélia," in Gérard de Nerval: The Mystic's Dilemma, *The University of Alabama Press, 1980.*

George MacLennan (essay date 1992)

SOURCE: "Gérard de Nerval: 'Madness Tells Her Story'," in *Lucid Interval: Subjective Writing and Madness in History*, Fairleigh Dickinson University Press, 1992, pp. 177-95.

[*Below, MacLennan studies Nerval's subjective portrayal of madness in* Aurélia *and relates the tale to other nineteenth-century French literature. He examines the story's conclusion and reviews Nerval's use of visionary sequences and dream narratives.*]

Gérard's sojourn in the asylum in the final episodes of *Aurélia* parallels George Trosse's experience in Glastonbury and Cowper's in St Albans. Each protagonist undergoes a spiritual resurrection in a place of healing. In *Aurélia*, however, the asylum, for all its historical specificity, remains a fictional construction. The tension between autobiographical history and autobiographical fiction reflects the tension which characterises the work as a whole: as an autobiographical discourse, it is bound up with the relevant historical and biographical contexts, but as a writing of subjectivity it is independent of them. The two levels of discourse subvert each other. Meanwhile, the relationship between the life and the work itself remains problematic: the narrative of Gérard's recovery is coherent, but in biographical terms that very coherence is fictional.

The ambivalence of Nerval's actual relationship with Dr Blanche and his establishment is not apparent in *Aurélia*, yet traces can be detected in a description of Gérard's private room at the asylum: 'On the whole I found nearly everything that I had possessed there.' The asylum, seemingly, provides Gérard with a space in which to realise a sense of identity. For Nerval, however, home was not a private interior: it was located by memories of his maternal uncle's house in Loisy, and comprised an entire locality. As *Sylvie* shows, this is not a space which Gérard can reinhabit, for it no longer exists in reality: the sites of childhood still exist, but their meaning derives from the lost plenitude of the childhood world.

A domestic retreat might conceivably have compensated Nerval for that alienating objectivisation of social reality which he saw occurring in contemporary life. In *Sylvie* both Gérard's 'old-fashioned apartment,' full of 'bric-a-brac splendours,' and his celebrated proposal that 'the only refuge left to us was the poet's ivory tower' imply a domestic aesthetic of the type which assumed increasing importance as the century progressed—the private 'palace of art' into which sensitive souls such as Huysmans's des Esseintes could withdraw from the insufferable vulgarities of the era. For Nerval, however, the private interior was usually a point of departure, and he was rarely *chez lui*.

Dr Blanche attempted to persuade Nerval not merely to take up residence in his clinic, but to treat it as a home. In a period when a settled domicile acquires a psychological character, Blanche was evidently concerned about his patient's chronic *vagabondage*. In October 1853, he took delivery of Nerval's possessions and installed them in a private room at Passy, seeking, in effect, to anchor him to a stable environment. As reported in *Aurélia*, however, the personal possessions that surround Gérard obstinately refuse to coalesce into the domestic circumference of a centred self:

> I found there the debris of my various fortunes, the confused remains of several sets of furniture scattered or resold over the past twenty years. It is a junk heap as bad as Doctor Faust's. A tripod table with eagles' heads, a console supported on a winged sphinx, a Seventeenth-Century commode, and Eighteenth-Century bookcase, a bed of the same period, with an oval-ceilinged baldequin covered with scarlet damask (. . .), a rustic dresser laden with faïence and Sèvres porcelain, most of it somewhat damaged; a hookah brought back from Constantinople, a large alabaster cup, a crystal vase; some wood panelling from the destruction of an old house I had once lived in on the site of the Louvre.

The list of antiques, exotic curios and bric-à-brac, all of it lacking in use value, continues for half a page further. The disparate and heterogeneous nature of this collection, so far from placing Gérard, bears witness to his endemic displacement: 'For some days I amused myself by rearranging all these things, creating in this narrow attic a bizarre ensemble composed of palace and hovel, that aptly summarises my wandering existence.'

The age of the commodity had dawned with the Paris of the Second Empire and Gérard's room in the asylum is a fantastic version of the commodified private interior of the mid-nineteenth century. Like that interior, it perpetuates the connection which is traced between person, property and desire in the bourgeois era, but in the inverted forms of heterogeneity, eccentricity and lack of permanence. Under these conditions bourgeois reality becomes extravagant, fantastic and unstable. Later in the century, Maupassant's naturalist fiction took an increasingly fantastic turn as his mental condition deteriorated (he was to be another patient of Dr Blanche's at Passy). One of his later stories, 'Qui sait?' (1890) would have delighted Marx: it concerns a roomful of furniture which comes to life one night and makes its way out of the house. Some time later, the narrator inspects an antique shop full of bric-à-brac, where he discovers his furniture. By the end of the story he has taken refuge in a private mental clinic. Nerval's possessions, although not so fantastically animated, were scarcely more restful in their effect: 'Dr Blanche thought he had done well in re-establishing him in his past; that would help him, he hoped, to cope better with his solitude. On the contrary, the reappearance of his fondest memories provoked an acute crisis of exaltation; he wept day and night (. . .). After several days, the doctor decided to suspend the experiment and moved him to another room' [Pierre Petitfils, *Nerval*, 1986].

In a psychoanalytic study of *Sylvie* [*Nerval: le charme de la répétition: lecture de 'Sylvie,'* 1979], Sarah Kofman has itemised 'narcissistic' female motifs in Nerval's *oeuvre*:

rhythmically repetitive rounds, accompanied by songs with set refrains, garlands, bowers [*berceaux de fleurs*]— these have a maternal, protective value; they are linked to the cycle of natural fecundity, to the cycle of the seasons, to that of woman; they are linked to the moon, to the cult of Artemis-Isis, to that of the Great Mother and her avatars. They refer to the need to be regenerated and reborn through maternal exhalation, to the desire to be enclosed in an enveloping uterine form.

In Nerval, such female-maternal circles are rarely if ever 'enveloping' in the claustrophobic sense of the reference to the uterus. None of the womb motifs noted by Kofman involve an interior space; all, on the contrary, are situated in the open, and associated with nature. From an historical point of view, this alfresco emphasis is untypical. In his paper, 'The Uncanny' ['Das Unheimliche,' 1955], Freud assimilates the female womb to a home: 'It often happens that neurotic men declare there is something uncanny about the female genital organs. This *unheimlich* place, however, is the former *Heim* [home] of all human beings, to the place where each one of us has lived once upon a time and in the beginning.' According to Freud, this (repressed) association is primeval, but the literature he cites tells a rather different story. His final example, immediately prior to this identification of womb and home, is a story encountered in the *Strand* magazine which exemplifies the Victorian-Edwardian genre of the haunted house story, 'about a young married couple who move into a furnished house (. . .).' In Nerval, the non-interiority of the womb corresponds to the non-materiality (and non-sexuality) of the ideal female, which in turn derives from the absence of the mother. Conversely, if the domestic interior rarely constitutes for him a womb-like space of retreat from the reality of the world at large this is because he does not associate it with the image of the mother presiding over hearth and home. His lack of interest in the forms of bourgeois reality extends to the private sphere.

As well as seeking to surround Nerval with a homelike space, Blanche further sought to integrate him into a surrogate family. [According to Petitfils] 'Dr Blanche held it to be important that his establishment was above all a family dwelling: the boarders' meals were shared and presided over by the doctor's family (his mother and sister) and his assistants.' Blanche married in the summer of 1854 while Nerval was absent from the clinic on the ill-fated journey to Germany. When he returned to Blanche's care in August, the doctor sought to assert a paternal authority over his patient. Nerval resisted this: in a letter written on October 17, and left behind at Passy for Blanche to discover, he insisted on his seniority in years: 'You are young! in fact I forget what age separates us, because I still act as a young man, which stops me from perceiving that I am several years older than you.' As the letter continues, Nerval transfers his own sense of rivalry to his doctor:

> I saw you at your father's so young that I took advantage of my presumed state of madness to inspire the friendship of a young lady (. . .). Do you want me to think and let it be thought that, from that period, a

dark jealousy has made you unjust towards me . . . Perhaps even this cruel sentiment will be newly manifested here. I fear to go too far, and in order to reassure you, I need to appeal to my entire life. Never having aspired to the wives or mistresses of my friends, I wish to always rank you among these (. . .).

> (*Pléiade*)

The letter continues with a bizarre paragraph which seems to provide evidence of derangement. It is not, however, incoherent: full of masonic references, it resumes the themes of seniority and rivalry in a pseudo-occult language:

> I don't know whether you are *three years* old or *five,* but I am more than *seven* and I have *metals* hidden in Paris. If you have for yourself the Gr . . . B . . . I will tell you that I call myself the *terrible brother* I will even be the *terrible sister* if need be. Belonging in secret to the *Order of the Nopses,* which is German, my rank permits me to play my cards openly . . . Tell it to your superiors, for I don't suppose that great secrets have been confided to a simple [brother] who should find me *very Respectable* (X). But I am sure that you are more than that. If you have the right to pronounce the word [. . .] [hieroglyph inserted] (that is to say *Mac-Benac* and I write it in the Oriental way), if you say *Jachin,* I say *Boaz,* if you say *Boaz* I say *Jehova,* or even *Machenac* . . . But I know very well that we are only joking (*Pléiade*).

Ross Chambers [in *Nerval et la poétique du voyage,* 1969] argues that Blanche's marriage aligned him, for Nerval, with the double who, in *Aurélia,* is scheduled to marry the beloved. Bearing this perception in mind, the above paragraph can be linked to the climactic encounter with the double in the final dream of Part One of *Aurélia* (which Nerval had only recently completed): Gérard raises his arm 'to make a sign which appeared to me to have magical power.' This aggressive contest is converted into a reciprocal gesture of healing in the asylum at the end of *Aurélia*: 'the spirit figure [Saturninus] placed his hand upon my forehead, as I had done, the night before, when I had endeavoured to magnetize my companion.' But in the real as against the symbolic asylum, matters turned out differently. Nerval's stay at Passy in 1854 reverses the narrative sequence: the letter of October 17 shows his relations with Blanche in the light of the occult and latently sexual contest which ends Part One of *Aurélia.*

At a climactic point in the narrative of recovery, Nerval exploded any normative implications by inserting the radically heterogeneous lyricism of the 'Mémorables'. This rhapsodic prose sequence seeks to enact the immediacy of transcendental revelation: 'A star shone suddenly and revealed the secret of the world of worlds to me. Hosannah! Peace on earth and glory in heaven!.' The 'Mémorables' constitutes a maternally inspired writing of nonidentity: birth and creation are joyful and effortless because they do not involve the painful labour of producing a substantial entity: 'In the Himalayas a little flower is born. (. . .) A silver pearl shone in the sands; a golden pearl sparkled in the sky . . . The world was created.' The inspired writer is fecund rather than potent: 'the world was created. Chaste loves, divine sighs!'; 'the air quivers, and light harmoniously bursts the budding flowers [*fleurs naissantes*]. A sigh, a shiver of love comes from the swollen womb of the earth.' Breathing and sighing are intimately allied with fecundity. Inspired language, transcending the concerns of the ego, is selfless. The various equivocations, doubts and questionings of the confessional discourse of identity evanesce: the visionary prose consists of a flowing succession of declarative and lyrical statements, untroubled by either introspective self-examination or temporal succession (they fluctuate between present and past tenses). The writer is released from the labour-pains of reproducing an identifiable self through his autobiographical discourse. Inspired language is diffuse and gentle, 'a soft foreign tongue,' different in kind from the self-analytical discourse of identity.

As the studies [in 'Illuminism, utopia, mythology,' *The French romantics,* 1984] of Frank Paul Bowman have shown, the imagery of the 'Mémorables' is embedded in the syncretistic, illuminist and utopian thought of the period. The message of the Romantic visionaries, and of the 'Mémorable', concerns 'the utopian and apocalyptic dream of justice and unity, the spiritualisation of matter and humanity, the disappearance of the ancient anathema' [Bowman, 'Une lecture politique de la folie réligieuse ou "théomanie",' *Romantisme,* 1979]. The resurrection of the son coincides with the Second Coming ('glad tidings') and announces an end of history: 'peace on earth and glory in heaven.' Celebrating a paradisal transformation of reality, the texture of the prose further enacts the positive overcoming of identity in language. A relay of song threads together time and space in an animate texture which is both turned inwards and returned outwards: 'the choir of stars unfolds itself in infinity; it turns away and returns upon itself, contracts and expands.' Revealed secrets, emergence from sheltered grottoes, music and song—these images subsist in a language which itself opens outwards in a responsive rhythm—the rhythm of an inspired language which aspires to the status of revelation.

However, the visionary momentum of the 'Mémorables' is not sustained: The visionary sequence is abruptly succeeded by dream narratives: 'I found myself *in spirit* at Saardam, which I visited last year': Nerval had in fact visited Saardam in 1852. We find ourselves once more in the presence of an autobiographical narrator, relating his dreams to his lived experience. Bowman [in '"Mémorables" d'*Aurélia,* signification et situation générique,' *French Forum,* 1986] has argued that these dream narratives are continuous with the visionary sequence, and carry over its utopian theme. Nevertheless it remains true that the immediacy and transparency of the visionary prose sequence is problematised by the return of a voice which no longer acts as a transparent medium of revelation and is identifiably that of an autobiographical and psychological subject. Loss of transparency is confirmed by the discourse which follows: 'I resolved to fix my dream state and learn its secret.' This is a subject who is by no means certain of the meaning of his dreams and who now confronts sleep and dream as a threat to the integrity of the ego: 'Is it not possible to control this attractive and fear-

ful chimera, to rule the spirits of the night which play with our reason?.' In seeking to unriddle the enigma of his dreams, Gérard engages in a discourse of psychological introspection. Seeking to come to terms with his own psychological identity, he is aware of being divided between two modes of being ('Sleep takes up a third of our lives'). From the side of the ego he must attempt to reestablish the link between the disjoined spheres: 'Who knows if there is not some link between those two existences and if it is not possible for the soul to re-tie it [*de le nouer*] now. From that moment on I devoted myself to trying to find the meaning of my dreams.'

In *The interpretation of dreams* [1976], Freud admitted the existence of dream-thoughts which defeat analysis: 'there is at least one spot in every dream at which it is unplumbable—a navel, as it were, that is its point of contact with the unknown.' Subsequently, the psychoanalyst Guy Rosolato has proposed that this node or knot serves as the metaphor of a relationship with a maternal dimension which escapes knowing—*a relation d'inconnu.* Gérard's reference to the problematic link [*lien*] between the two existences of life and dream (a link which must be retied) can be interpreted in these terms [from Guy Rosolato's *La relation d'inconnu,* 1978]: 'The sleep into which the sleeper plunges can be assimilated to the maternal container for a primordial identification. The navel indicates (. . .) that which is *not recognised* concerning the originally lived relationship between the child and its mother, but which is daily reproduced in sleep where the desire of the dream is condensed.'

For Rosolato, the hollow of the navel is superimposed on the female fissure [*fente*] which constitutes the dark abyss of the 'unknown' on which object-relations are founded. In this way (and bearing in mind Gérard's own quest for meaning) he provides us with a means of interpreting the second of the dream-narratives which succeed the visionary sequence:

> in front of me there opened an abyss into which there rushed in tumult the frozen waves of the Baltic. It seemed that the whole ofthe Neva with its blue waters were to be swallowed up in this fissure in the globe. The ships of Cronstadt and Saint Petersburg bobbed at anchor, ready to break away and vanish in the abyss, when a divine radiance from above lighted the scene of this desolation. In the bright beam of light piercing the mist, I saw the rock on which stands the statue of Peter the Great. Above this solid pedestal clouds rose in groups, piling up to the zenith.

It is the rocklike image of the father-emperor who restores stability to a world threatened by a watery abyss. A similar contrast recurs in Gérard's subsequent consideration of the problem of dream-imagery: 'the strangeness of certain pictures, which are like the grimacing reflections of real objects on a surface of troubled water.' The masculine-paternal identity is re-established over against an unstable female dimension which is both fascinating and disturbing ('cette chimère attrayante et redoutable'), and which eludes male knowledge. In this view, it is the unknown fissure of female sexuality which haunts the psychological subject as that which is not known, but against which he will react as the assumptions of sanity require he must: '"Why should I not," I asked myself, "at last force those mystic gates, armed with all my will-power, and dominate my sensations instead of being subject to them?"' The image, not fortuitously, is one of rape and domination.

Michel Foucault [in *The History of Sexuality, Vol. 1: An Introduction,* 1980] has proposed that 'the society that emerged in the nineteenth century—bourgeois, capitalist or industrial society—call it what you will—did not confront sex with a refusal of recognition. On the contrary, it put into operation an entire machinery for producing true discourses concerning it.' Dr Labrunie was, at an early date, an exponent of this development: 'On brumaire 9, XIV (1806), he submitted his thesis on "The Dangers of the Deprivation and Abuse of Venereal Pleasure in Women" (. . .). The chosen subject—a study of hysterical manifestations in women due to either a lack or an abuse of sexual relations—announces the direction in which he will later specialise—female illnesses and gynaecology' [Petitfils]. There is some evidence that Dr Labrunie's son found the prospect of physical sexuality a disturbing one: Sebillote [in *Le secret de Gérard de Nerval,* 1948] has underlined the significance of the statement in *Sylvie,* 'Seen at close quarters the real woman revolted our ingenuous souls.' Nerval's openly acknowledged tendency to idealise and spiritualise women can be understood as a reaction against his father's medical interests. However in proposing to force apart the gates of dream he is once more his father's son: it is the psychological subject who finds the female space of the unknown threatening rather than liberating, and who now undertakes a quest for knowledge as means of control in an act of historical reason. If Nerval is nowhere more radical than in the 'Mémorables', he is nowhere more normative than in the passages which follow the 'Mémorables' and which reflect on the problematic relationship between dream and reality. The therapeutic discourse of identity which results anticipates the project of Freud's *Interpretation of dreams* in proposing to investigate the meaning of dreams in the context of a self-analytical autobiography.

Rosolato proposes that the umbilical knot of the navel is the corporeal metaphor of a relationship with a female sexual orifice, and with the womb as interior container. This female 'unknown' poses a double threat to masculine definitions of reality: it is that fissure which, as absence of the phallus, undermines the solidity of the object-world; equally, it presents the seductive phantasy of a 'regressive' return to the uterus. In this way the doctor, typically, would project the onus of madness onto the female: 'Thus we see converging in an interiorisation which, singularly, makes the psychical apparatus a *container,* possessing therefore a feminine value, everything which escapes the signifying organisation and its totalisation—sexuality represented in femininity itself, madness and the real' [Rosolato]. The key term here is 'interiorisation.' In *Aurélia,* dream has represented a spiritual realm which may be 'psychical,' but which is not psychologi-

cal. On the penultimate page of the text, however, this spiritual dimension is seemingly lost. As it becomes the object of introspection and self-analysis, dream acquires the meaning of an interiorised madness. On the final page of the text, Gérard returns his attention to the figure who, in the asylum, sums up the simultaneous representations of madness and interiorisation—the young madman. Turned in on himself and sustained by a life-support system, Gérard confronts in him an embodiment of self-withdrawal into the interiorised enclosure of the uterus.

Entry into sleep involves a descent into a 'vague underground cavern.' Going to sleep is an 'image of death,' but the cavern also suggests a uterus. The space of the tomb and that of the womb converge in this dangerous transitional moment.

In chapter VIII of Part One of *Aurélia,* Gérard, in the course of a sequence of dream-visions, witnesses the unfolding of an occult world history. Necromancers parthenogenetically reproduce themselves in uterine sepulchres:

> These necromancers, exiled to the ends of the earth, had agreed to transmit their power to one another. Surrounded by women and slaves, each of their sovereigns was assured of being born again in the form of one of his children. Their life lasted a thousand years. When they were about to die, powerful cabalists shut them up in well-guarded tombs where they were fed elixirs and life-giving substances. They preserved the semblance of life for a long time. Then, as the chrysalis spins its cocoon, they fell asleep for forty days to be born again as a little child which was later called to the kingdom.

These male wombs are malignant parodies of the female womb: they do not produce new life but endlessly reproduce the Oedipal self. In the asylum, Gérard, remembering the necromancers, exclaims, 'Ah misery! (. . .) we live again in our sons as we have lived in our fathers.' The necromancers are bad versions of the father-doctor. In the narrative of recovery, the good father embodies an historically determined reality-principle, but this good father is inescapably accompanied by a negative double. The bad father asserts his presence in a fantasmatic perversion of history: the threat of a pathological loss of reality resides in his continuing influence.

In *Aurélia,* an open, undefined maternal 'womb' is readily translated into the material closure of the paternal tomb. In Part One, Gérard dreams of a woman whose form coalesces with the landscape of a garden, but this in turn is nightmarishly transformed into a graveyard:

> gradually the whole garden blended with her own form (. . .). I lost her as she became transfigured, for she seemed to vanish in her own immensity. 'Don't leave me!' I cried. 'For nature dies with you.' (. . .) I threw myself on a fragment of ruined wall, at the foot of which lay the bust of a woman. I lifted it up and felt convinced it was of *her* . . . I recognized the beloved features and as I stared around me I saw that

the garden had become a graveyard, and I heard voices crying: 'The universe is in darkness.'

Subsequently, (in an episode which corresponds to the relapse of 1851) Gérard, visiting a friend, admires the view from a terrace. While descending a stairway he falls, hurting his chest. He believes himself mortally wounded and rushes into the centre of a garden: 'I felt happy to be dying this way, at this hour, surrounded by the trees, trellises, autumn flowers. It was, however, no more than a swoon.' Later, as fever takes hold, he 'remembers' that the view he had admired overlooked the cemetery where Aurélia is buried. Again, a garden or landscape is transformed into a cemetery; again a site saturated with maternal implications is juxtaposed with the graveyard of the dead beloved. Gérard rushes into the garden as into the maternal circle which will transform death into rebirth, but this transition is denied: the open, pastoral space congeals into the enclosure of the tomb, and Gérard is plunged once more into delirious dreams. In the climax of this sequence, the dead beloved, trapped in a material, reified form (represented in the dream as a sculpted bust) is claimed by the hostile double who rules in the underworld: 'I imagined that the man they were waiting for was my *double,* and that he was going to marry Aurélia.'

In the asylum, the situation of the young madman resumes the episode of the necromancers. '[the necromancers] were fed elixirs and life-giving substances'; '[the young man] was made to swallow liquid and nutritious substances by means of a long rubber tube inserted into his stomach.' Nerval had originally written 'By means of a long tube of rubber inserted into a nostril he was made to swallow a fairly large quantity of semolina and chocolate.' The revision, while highlighting the womb-image, brings the madman's situation into closer rapport with that of the necromancers. Given this rapport, his delusive perception is symbolically accurate: 'I was buried in a certain graveyard.' His trance equates dream and madness just as his state of suspended animation equates womb and tomb: in confronting this figure, Gérard confronts the embodiment of a nexus of concerns which bear directly on his own experiences of sleep, dream and madness. The madman's delusion that he inhabits a tomb expresses, for ·Gérard, the deadly interiorisation of madness itself as a psychopathological condition. In *Aurélia,* the 'uterine' womb, so far from being a maternal space, is both deathly and paternal. The meanings of the asylum are balanced between this negative condition of stasis and a positive release from enclosure, with the young madman positioned at the point of balance.

In seeking to heal him, Gérard magnetises him, then sings to him. In this way he re-establishes a connection with the maternal-transcendental realm celebrated in the 'Mémorables'. As in the 'Mémorables', song evokes an answering response: 'I had the happiness of seeing that he heard them, and he repeated certain parts of the songs.' Reawakened from the deathly sleep of the paternal tomb, the young man is linked with the resurrected son of the 'Mémorables'.

This renewed maternal influence enables a positive revaluation of the paternal roles—soldier, doctor and gynaecologist—which are redistributed between Gérard and the madman. Gérard is thus able to care for the afflicted young man, where Nerval's father had failed to care for him in his crises. We should, then, conclude that a psychological recovery would reintegrate the spiritual values of the maternal sphere with the stabilising norms of the paternal sphere. Such a recovery would reconcile the spirit world with contemporary historical reality, notably the Crimean war, which is implicated in the imagery of the dream-narratives. Recovered from the fatal divide which polarises the mother and the father, reality itself would then fulfil its utopian potential. The possibility of such an outcome is intimated in the happy conclusion to the 'historical' dream-narrative: the solid statue of Peter the Great, having stabilised the threatening abyss and re-established the historical world, is surrounded by ethereal female forms who bring a message of harmony which is at once visionary and historical:

> In the bright beam of light piercing the mist, I saw the rock on which stands the statue of Peter the Great. Above this solid pedestal clouds rose in groups, piling up to the zenith. They were laden with radiant, heavenly forms, among which could be distinguished the two Catherines and the empress Saint Helen accompanied by the loveliest Princesses of Muscovy and Poland. Their gentle expressions, directed towards France, lessened the distance by means of long crystal telescopes. By that I saw that our country had become the arbiter of the old quarrel of the East, and they were awaiting its solution. My dream ended in the sweet hope that peace would at last be granted us.

Nevertheless this cannot but seem a secondary, compromised version of the visionary radicality of the "Mémorables." As the maternal and paternal figures return to their ordained roles, and as the ecstatic dream-language returns to a discourse of identity, the celebration of holy madness is suspended. It recedes on an horizon of utopian possibility, becoming a dream from which the sleeper must awaken. With that awakening, the utopian priority cedes to a medical one, the healing of a damaged reality to the healing of a damaged self, represented in the figure of the young madman.

FURTHER READING

Bibliography

Villas, James. *Gérard de Nerval: A Critical Bibliography, 1900 to 1967.* Columbia: University of Missouri Press, 1968, 118 p.

> Annotated bibliography of criticism on Nerval published from 1900 to 1967.

Biography

Rhodes, S. A. *Gérard de Nerval, 1808-1855: Poet, Traveler, Dreamer.* New York: Philosophical Library, 1951, 416 p.

The only full-length English biography of Nerval. The author presents critical commentary incidental to biographical information.

Symons, Arthur. "Gérard de Nerval." In his *The Symbolist Movement in Literature*, pp. 10-36. New York: E. P. Dutton, 1908.

Surveys Nerval's life and writings and describes the author's role in the Symbolist movement.

Whitridge, Arnold. "Gérard de Nerval." In his *Critical Ventures in Modern French Literature,* pp. 45-64. New York: Charles Scribner's Sons, 1924.

Largely biographical essay offering brief critical commentary.

Wood, Michael. "Gérard de Nerval: (1808-1855)." In *European Writers: The Romantic Century,* edited by Jacques Barzun, pp. 943-69. New York: Charles Scribner's Sons, 1985.

Capsule of Nerval's life and career.

Criticism

Bowman, Frank Paul. "The 'Mémorables' of Nerval's *Aurélia.*" In his *French Romanticism: Intertextual and Interdisciplinary Readings,* pp. 167-81. Baltimore: The Johns Hopkins Uni-versity Press, 1990.

States the significance of "Mémorables," the last section of *Aurélia.*

Brombert, Victor. "Nerval's Privileged Enclosures." In his *The Romantic Prison: The French Tradition,* pp. 120-32. Princeton, N. J.: Princeton University Press, 1978.

Explores the "motif of the facetious prison, blending parody and melancholy, [that] recurs in Nerval's work."

Carpenter, Scott D. "Figures of Interpretation in Nerval's *Aurélia.*" *Nineteenth-Century French Studies* XVII, No. 1 (Fall 1988): 152-60.

Explains various ways of interpreting madness as manifested in *Aurélia.*

Carroll, Robert C. "Romanesque Seduction in Nerval's *Sylvie.*" *Nineteenth-Century French Studies* V, Nos. 3-4 (Spring-Summer 1977): 222-35.

Studies Sylvie's literature-induced transformation from an attractive naif to a lonely, disenchanted girl.

Chambers, Ross. "Water in 'Sylvie'." *Modern Language Review* LVIII, No. 4 (1963): 500-06.

Describes how the presence of water images in *Sylvie* works on many levels: to illuminate character, evoke metaphor, and unify themes.

―――. "Speed and Delay in Nerval." *Australian Journal of French Studies* 1, No. 1 (1964): 40-57.

Perceives a connection in Nerval's works between travel and escape from the "time-bound life of reality."

―――. "Narrative as Oppositional Practice: Nerval's *Aurélia.*" *Stanford French Review* VIII (Spring 1984): 55-73.

Interprets *Aurélia* as an oppositional prac-tice, meaning that "the narrator is always, to some extent, at the mercy of the narratee because the 'authority' to narrate derives from an act of authorization on the part of the other, and this authorization will be accorded or withheld according to the 'interest,' 'power,' 'profit,' etc., the narrative is judged to have by that other, the narratee."

Dubruck, Alfred. *Gérard de Nerval and the German Heritage.* London: Mouton & Co., 1965, 136 p.

Observes the German influence on Nerval's works.

Dunn, Susan. "Nerval: Transgression and the *Amendement Riancey.*" *Nineteenth-Century French Studies* XII, Nos. 1 and 2 (Fall-Winter 1983): 86-95.

Comments on how Nerval's writings were affected by his fear of transgression with his literature, which was exacerbated by the formation of the 1851 censorship law *amendement Riancey.*

―――. "Nerval and Money: The Currency of Dreams." *Nineteenth-Century French Studies* XIX, No. 1 (Fall 1990): 54-64.

Discusses the role of money in Nerval's life and many of his works.

Felman, Shoshana. "Gérard de Nerval: Writing, Living, or Madness as Autobiography." In her *Writing and Madness,* translated by Martha Noel Evans, Shoshana Felman, and Brian Massumi, pp. 59-77. Ithaca, N.Y.: Cornell University Press, 1985.

Presents Nerval's view on madness and expounds on the antithetical relationship between rationality and insanity in *Aurélia.*

George, Albert J. "Gérard de Nerval." In his *Short Fiction in France, 1800-1850,* pp. 208-16. Syracuse, N.Y.: Syracuse University Press, 1964.

Analyzes Nerval's contribution to the development of various styles of French short fiction.

Gilbert, Claire. *Nerval's Double: A Structural Study.* University, Miss.: Romance Monographs, Inc., 1979, 199 p.

Contemplates the theme of the double, or doppelgänger, in Nerval's works.

Haskell, Eric T. "Picturing Nerval's *Aurélia*: Illustration as Interpretation." *Word and Image* 3, No. 4 (October-December 1987): 248-58.

Studies the illustrations of *Aurélia,* finding them a means to interpreting the text. Commenting on the scarcity of illustrations, Haskell states that "perhaps it is this very idea of fixing, framing or immobilizing the dream [depicted in the novella] that seems to have distanced illustrators from *Aurélia.*"

Hiddleston, J. A. "'Sous les arbres sacrés': Trees and Divinities in Nerval." In *Myth and Legend in French Literature: Essays in Honour of A. J. Steele,* edited by Keith Aspley, David Bellos, and Peter Sharratt, pp. 173-83. London: The Modern Humanities Research Association, 1982.

Explores the sigificance of images of trees in Nerval's writings.

Huige, Frida F. L. "Nerval's 'Aurélia': Schizophrenia and Art." *American Imago* 22, No. 4 (Winter 1965): 255-74.

Suggests that Nerval's mental illness was probably a form of schizophrenia and that "to understand his work, one must delve into the troubled mind of the author." Huige ponders the effect of schizophrenia on *Aurélia.*

————. *Gérard de Nerval: The Mystic's Dilemma.* University: The University of Alabama Press, 1980, 372 p.

Critical study of Nerval's works.

Newmark, Kevin. "The Forgotten Figures of Symbolism: Nerval's *Sylvie.*" *Yale French Studies,* No. 74 (1988): 207-29.

Explores symbolism, especially historical and linguistic models, in *Sylvie.*

Noakes, Susan. "Self-Reading and Temporal Irony in *Aurélia.*" *Studies in Romanticism* 16, No. 1 (Winter 1977): 101-19.

Examines the narrative structure of *Aurélia,* which represents an attempt to "narrate in two time periods simultaneously."

Olson Padgett, Jacqueline. "Spirits and Their Bodies: Images of Woman in Nerval's *Sylvie.*" *Kentucky Romance Quarterly* XXVII, No. 3 (1980): 327-33.

Aims to define the spiritual and physical roles of women in *Sylvie.*

Porter, Laurence M. "Mourning and Melancholia in Nerval's *Aurélia.*" *Studies in Romanticism* 15, No. 2 (Spring 1976): 289-306.

Analyzes the psychological makeup of the narrator of *Aurélia,* concluding that "his preoccupation with the dead—Aurélia, ancestors, lost civilizations and gods— betray his secret hope to end a world where he has been defeated."

Poulet, Georges. "Nerval." In his *The Metamorphoses of the Circle,* pp. 166-81. Baltimore: The Johns Hopkins University Press, 1966.

Surveys the circular aspects of Nerval's writings. Poulet declares that with a circle "we are able to figure for ourselves the place, either mental or real, in which we find ourselves, and to locate within it, what surrounds us, or that with which we surround ourselves. Its simplicity, its perfection, its ceaseless universal application, makes it the foremost of those recurring and chosen forms which we discover at the base of all beliefs."

Quennell, Peter. "Books in General." *The New Statesman and Nation* XLI, No. 1055 (26 May 1951): 596, 598.

Reviews S. A. Rhodes's biography on Nerval and provides a capsule of Nerval's life and literary achievements.

Radcliff-Umstead, Douglas. "Cainism and Gérard de Nerval." *Philological Quarterly* XLV, No. 2 (April 1966): 395-408.

Discusses Nerval's conversion from Cainism—the exalting of the biblical Cain as a hero instead of as a villain— to Christianity in his life and writings. Radcliff-Umstead remarks on the transformation: "From his shaking his fist at God in *Voyage en Orient,* through the Promethean tortures of *La Pandora,* after his failure to make a Cain out of Christ in *Les Chimeres,* to the Laura love which pointed to his Catholic conversion in *Aurélia,* a certain inching forward and painful progressing with some backward slips become manifest."

Raitt, A. W. "Time and Instability in Nerval's *Sylvie.*" *Modern Language Review* 83, No. 4 (October 1988): 843-51.

Comments on "warping" and "dissonances" created by verb tenses and anachronism in *Sylvie.* According to Raitt, the reader is intentionally disorientated and "made to share the narrator's anguish at his inability to find a stable point amid the endlessly moving planes of time."

Rinsler, Norma. "Gérard de Nerval and the Divinities of Fire." *French Studies* XVII, No. 2 (April 1963): 136-47.

Delves into Nerval's relationship with his father and its effect upon his life and literature.

————. "Gérard de Nerval, Fire and Ice." *Modern Language Review* LVIII (1963): 495-99.

Examines the contrasting presence of fire and ice images in Nerval's writings. Rinsler contends that in Nerval's works fire is a symbol of life and cold is a "dangerous element."

————. "Gérard de Nerval's Celestial City and the Chain of Souls." *Studies in Romanticism* II (1963): 87-106.

Studies Nerval's use of "images of the celestial city and of the universal chain of souls, which prove to be primarily images of the human family and its bonds of affection" throughout his literary pieces.

————. "Gérard de Nerval: The Goddess and the Siren." *Philological Quarterly* XLIII, No. 1 (January 1964): 99-111.

Examines some images representing a "feminine principle" in Nerval's writings.

Sullivan, Dennis G. "The Function of the Theater in the Work of Nerval." *Modern Language Notes* 80 (1965): 610-17.

States that the theater appealed to Nerval as "an instrument which defines the correspondence" between the temporal world and the eternal realm. Sullivan finds the theater as an important concept for understanding *Sylvie* and *Aurélia.*

"World of a Visionary." *The Times Literary Supplement* No. 2933 (16 May 1958): 261-62.

Gives an overview of Nerval's literary career and describes Geoffrey Wagner's translation *Selected Writings of Gérard de Nerval* as "monotonous and indigestible."

Ulmer York, Holly. "Nerval's *Aurélia: À la Recherche du Signe Effacé.*" *French Forum* 11, No. 1 (January 1986): 19-27.

Ponders the language of the dream world in *Aurélia,* describing it as "the innate language of every individual."

Villas, James. "Present State of Nerval Studies: 1957 to 1967." *French Review* XLI, No. 2 (November 1967): 221-31.
    Provides commentary on important critical studies on Nerval published in the period.

Warren, Rosanna. "The 'Last Madness' of Gérard de Nerval." *The Georgia Review* XXXVII, No. 1 (Spring 1983): 131-38.
    Attempts to provide a better understanding of Nerval's works. Warren contends that "all too often [Nerval's] devotees only manage to present him as a crazed packrat of esoteric lore."

Winston, Phyllis Jane. *Nerval's Magic Alphabet.* New York: Peter Lang, 1989, 135 p.
    Considers the role of language in depicting madness in Nerval's works.

Additional coverage of Nerval's life and career is contained in the following source published by Gale Research: *Nineteenth-Century Literature Criticism,* **Vol. 1.**

Ruth Suckow
1892-1960

American short story writer, novelist, memoirist, and essayist.

INTRODUCTION

Suckow is best known for her fiction focusing on rural and small-town life in the American midwest in the early twentieth century. Critics note that her fiction often explores the tension between small-town tradition and need for individual expression and self-development. While Suckow was compared to other women writers such as Sarah Orne Jewett, Harriet Beecher Stowe, and Willa Cather, and was regarded by commentators as a regionalist or local colorist, later evaluations of her work have noted that her stories incorporate themes that transcend the narrow scope of her work.

Biographical Information

Suckow was born in Hawarden, Iowa, daughter of a Congregationalist minister and his wife. Although her family moved often, the majority of Suckow's formative years were spent in rural Iowa, and her experiences were reflected later in her short fiction and novels. Following her graduation from high school, she matriculated at Grinnell College. In 1913, Suckow attended the Curry School of Expression in Boston, and subsequently enrolled at the University of Denver, from which she received an MA in English. Suckow worked as a beekeeper, and when her father relocated to Earlville, Iowa, she established her own apiary there. Meanwhile she pursued a writing career, and in 1918, she published her first poems. She began to submit short fiction to the periodical *Midland*, which subsequently published a number of Suckow's early stories. *Iowa Interiors*, her first collection, was published in 1926 and brought her to the attention of H. L. Mencken, who himself accepted many of Suckow's work for his magazines. Subsequently, her short fiction appeared frequently in periodicals such as *Smart Set, American Mercury, Century Magazine*, and *Midland*. Failing health eventually required Suckow to spend more and more time in the warmer climates of Arizona and California. She died in Claremont, California in 1960.

Major Works of Short Fiction

While Suckow originally gained fame for her work as a novelist, some critics assert that short fiction is her most effective genre. Her first collection, *Iowa Interiors*, demonstrates the defining characteristics of her stories, in particular the provincial setting, usually in Iowa; a dearth of action and a wealth of realistic detail; and themes that include generational conflict, alienation from small-town tradition and values, and the inability to express feelings within a family or community setting. In "Uprooted," her

first published short story, the children of an older couple living in Iowa meet to discuss the fate of their parents as they age. The most prosperous son, Sam, manipulates his most passive and least affluent sibling into taking responsibility for them. Suckow characteristically invests the story with symbolic detail of the meeting which functions to build a sense of familiarity and intensify the tension between the homey, old-fashioned world of the older couple and the brash, fast-moving world of their son.

Critical Reception

Despite Suckow's critical and commercial popularity in the 1920s and 1930s, some contemporary commentators have indicted her short fiction as narrow and monotonous. In her time, her work was labelled "feminist," as it often focuses on female characters as they struggle to find self-fulfillment under patriarchal, provincial circumstances. Yet most critics recognize Suckow's role as observer and recorder of small-town life, and they praise her deft characterizations and use of realistic detail in her stories. It is noted that while Suckow presents the drawbacks to provincial life, she also depicts much of its beauty and tranquility as well. As Leedice McAnelly Kissane asserts: "Her awareness of life with its complexities and its sadness, no less than her artist's touch in creating the illusion of reality, distinguishes the whole of her work."

PRINCIPAL WORKS

Short Fiction

The Best of the Lot 1922; published in journal *Smart Set*
Other People's Ambitions 1923; published in *Smart Set*
A Part of the Institution 1923; published in *Smart Set*
Iowa Interiors 1927
Children and Older People 1931
Carry-Over (short stories and novels) 1936
Some Others and Myself 1952
A Ruth Suckow Omnibus (short stories and novels) 1988

Other Major Works

Country People (novel) 1924
The Odyssey of a Nice Girl (novel) 1925
The Bonney Family (novel) 1928
Cora (novel) 1929
The Kramer Girls (novel) 1930
The Folks (novel) 1934
New Hope (novel) 1942
A Memoir (essay) 1952
The John Wood Case (novel) 1959

CRITICISM

Herbert Asbury (essay date 1926)

SOURCE: "The American Interior," in *New York Herald Tribune Books,* October 3, 1926, pp. 6-7.

[*An American journalist and author, Asbury published works about the operations of the underworld in Chicago, New York City, New Orleans, and San Francisco. In the following essay, he examines the characters and the major themes of* Iowa Interiors.]

[The stories in *Iowa Interiors*] are the first of Miss Suckow's shorter works to appear in book form, and reading them is, to me, like meeting a host of old and not very desirable acquaintances, for I was born and reared among just the sort of people with whom she has concerned herself. I know of no other writer who can portray so clearly the hideous drabness of existence on the farms and in the hamlets of the American interior, or who can so faithfully set down the petty selfishness or the vicious current of hatred which dominate human intercourse in the corn country. Her characters are terribly authentic, and in recounting their trivial doings she paints a brilliantly cruel picture of the utter futility of life which is bounded on one side by a row of corn and on all others by intolerance and stupidity. The people of whom she

writes are born, they spend their lives in dreary, soul-shattering toil and in a fuming, fretful worry, and then they die, without having caught more than a fleeting glimpse of a beauty of living which they can neither capture nor understand. And not understanding, they inveigh against it, and damn with gossip those who strive to find it.

It is generally the custom of those who would write about humanity beyond the Alleghenies to proclaim that the small town or country woman is obsessed by sex, and that her whole life is a constant torment because of Freudian inhibitions. But Miss Suckow, knowing whereof she writes, puts sex in its proper place, which is one of relatively small importance. There is sex in her stories, to be sure, just as there is sex in the corn country, but in these tales it is secondary to and almost submerged by a fearful dreariness which not even passion can overcome. The truth is that the farm woman of the Middle West has no time to worry over sex; even in its romantic aspects it is a negligible quantity in the life of a woman who must clamber out of bed at daybreak to cook breakfast for a horde of hungry farm hands, and who must then labor almost without ceasing for the next fourteen or sixteen hours. She scarcely knows that there is such a thing as sex; it becomes an important and compelling influence only at camp meetings, at basket dinners, and at other religious orgies where all sorts of emotions are aroused by the evangelistic lash. And even then she seldom realizes what is the matter with her; she generally thinks that she has "got religion." However, there is always plenty of opportunity to learn.

For these people Miss Suckow has an immense sympathy, and a great pity also, but neither blinds her to their mental and spiritual squalor. The material from which she constructs her stories is petty, because the people of whom she writes are petty, but she manipulates it with extraordinary skill. She is not dependent upon the sharp clash of dramatic incident or the obscure twistings of an involved plot; she obtains her effects by a methodical piling up of significant trivialities, and by erecting layer after layer of jealousies, backbitings and hatreds with which the small town mind is for the most part occupied. She has an amazing gift for characterization, and produces a picture so uncanny in its clearness and truth that one is almost ashamed to read, and is conscious of an uncomfortable feeling that one has learned too much about the littleness of the human soul.

Several of Miss Suckow's best known stories are in this volume, among them **"The Golden Wedding," "Wanderers," "A Start in Life," "Mame"** and **"The Daughter."** They are all fine, but to my mind the best is **"Wanderers,"** the story of a small town preacher, an absurd and utterly futile figure. He attempts the impossible task of translating the teachings of his Master into terms of human conduct, and of course steps on the toes of the best people and the big business men of his town, the paying members of his church. He is finally bounded from his charge; he has been "talked about" because he displayed a little kindness towards a woman who has the reputation of being "a little too gay"; that is, she laughed and found joy in living, she danced occasionally with men other than her husband, and she wore good clothing and perhaps powdered her nose. It is a variation of the old story of Mary Magdalene, with the usual difference that a Biblical harlot is a mint, while a small town harlot is never anything but a harlot. Nor is it necessary for her to be an actual practitioner of the ancient art; she need only be "a little too gay."

In **"A Start in Life"** Miss Suckow tells the story of Daisy Switzer, a Skinny, homely child who must "work out" to help her mother. She starts eagerly, filled with pride that she is to earn money and begin the great adventure of life, and imagining that Elmer and Edna Kruse will still be **"Elmer and Edna"** after she has become their servant. Her mind cannot grasp the difference and her realization of her changed condition is just sufficient to fill her with torturing, bewildered resentment. Miss Suckow leaves Daisy alone in the kitchen, a pathetically tragic figure submerged by a dreadful ache which she cannot understand, and weeping silently without tears, for she had "the cold knowledge that no one would notice or comfort her."

H. L. Mencken (essay date 1926)

SOURCE: A review of *Iowa Interiors,* in *American Mercury,* Vol. IX, No. 35, November, 1926, pp. 382-83.

[*Mencken was one of the most influential figures in American literature from the First World War until the early years of the Great Depression. His strongly individualistic, irreverent outlook on life and his vigorous, invective-charged writing style helped establish the iconoclastic spiritc of the Jazz Age and significantly shaped the direction of American literature. Mencken was an early and emphatic supporter of Suckow's writing, and in the following laudatory review, he praises her ability to create credible characters.*]

In Miss Suckow's stories situation is usually of small significance: the salient thing is the anatomizing of character. Who among us can manage that business with greater penetration and understanding, with a finer feeling for the tragedy of everyday, with a more moving evocation of simple poetry? Who, indeed, at home or abroad, has ever published a better first book of short stories than [*Iowa Interiors*]? Of its sixteen stories, not one is bad—and among the best there are at least five masterpieces. I mean by a masterpiece a story that could not imaginably be improved—one in which the people are overwhelmingly real, and not a word can be spared. All of these people are simple Iowa peasants. In other hands they would slide inevitably into stock types, ludicrous and artificial. But Miss Suckow differentiates them sharply, and into every one she breathes something of the eternal tragedy of man. Her talent is not unlike that of Sherwood Anderson, but her mind is more orderly than his: she gropes and guesses less, and is hence more convincing. There are moments when he far surpasses her, but her average, it seems to me, is at least as high

as his. She is unquestionably the most remarkable woman now writing short stories in the Republic; all the rest, put beside her, seem hollow and transparent.

The Outlook (essay date 1926)

SOURCE: A review of *Iowa Interiors,* in *The Outlook,* Vol. 144, No. 11, November 10, 1926, pp. 342-43.

[*In the following review, the critic provides a positive assessment of* Iowa Interiors.]

"Local color fiction" is snubbed and scorned by the present-day critics who accept the work of Ruth Suckow as of distinguished merit. Local color fiction belongs, Carl Van Doren has told us, to "a now moribund cult" which was freighted with sentimentality and tinctured with respectability. Miss Suckow, on the contrary, is approved as a realist and an ironist who conveys without illusion the barrenness, the grossness, and the commonplaceness of rural life. She is, and she does; but on her Iowa farmlands she is blood-kin to Rose Terry Cooke gathering huckleberries on her New England hills, to Mary Wilkins Freeman, and to Mary Murfree among her Tennessee mountains. Their sentimentality, their respectability, are simply part of the legend with which to-day's *intelligentsia* are investing all American life and letters prior to 1905. The bleak realism of Rose Terry Cooke's story "Freedom Wheeler's Controversy with Providence," the delicate, detached irony of Mrs. Freeman's "New England Nun," are the same colors that we find on the palette from which Miss Suckow paints her *Iowa Interiors*.

Miss Suckow has published two novels, but her art is essentially that of the local colorist, and its best expression is episodic, through the short story. In her novels—*Country People* and *The Odyssey of a Nice Girl*—the lack of strong or sustained plot structure, the enveloping detail of environment, give a sense of monotony that even the flesh-and-blood reality of her people does not overcome. But in her shorter work there is no such flattening. Here we have single episodes, *genre* studies focused on a central figure or a small group of figures, all complete, proportioned, sharing in or moved by some common experience.

Seldom has a book received a more fitting title than has been bestowed upon this first collection of Miss Suckow's short stories. As always, her native State furnishes her, not with backgrounds alone, but with "interiors," using the word in a human and spiritual sense. For here we come to understand and feel the influences that have controlled the lives and molded the natures of the men and women in the run-down farmhouses set beside sun-steeped pastures or in the little hamlets with their willow trees and dusty streets. It is a round of unending farm toil, of village community life with its immense interrelationships, its bickerings and obstinacies. There are the old German settlements, still richly foreign in speech and living; the communities made up almost entirely of farmers of English birth and descent; the thriving towns, with their success and progress; the ubiquitous automobile; but even with wealth there is little change in the rooted life of the soil. One gains a sense of the perpetual flow of the generations—nothing new, after all, but endless, slightly varied repetitions; and one realizes that human relationships—not books, or plays, or "public events"—furnish the one undying spark that kindles human interest. There is no lightness in these episodes. Mostly they are somber: the dependence and the demands of old age, of poverty and failure after a lifetime of toil, are themes that recur constantly. The opening story, **"A Start in Life,"** is quite unforgettable in its reflection of the awakening to reality of the little girl who leaves home for the first time to "work out;" curiously, for all its complete difference, it recalls Katharine Mansfield. All the stories are detached, cool, impersonal; but underneath their quiet surface, their detailed rendering of a pattern of life, there are pity and understanding.

Florence Haxton Britten (essay date 1931)

SOURCE: "Sparrows of Iowa," in *New York Herald Tribune Books,* August 16, 1931, p. 6.

[*In the following review, Britten commends the variety of characters and themes that Suckow depicts in her fiction.*]

Within her field—the lives of the meagre-minded in the small towns of "Ioway"—Miss Ruth Suckow's work carries the final authority of utter perfection. She is like a brilliant laboratory worker who sets off a certain field of research for her own and works unceasingly—with a devotion that amounts almost to tenderness, and a commitment to accuracy which leaves no place conceivable for humor—to discover and record the precise (and consequently beautiful) truth.

The people she has chosen to examine, with her immense seriousness, are the little people, the sparrows of life. The Watkinses, the Bensons, the Kempers are not citizens of the great world: they are of the very fibre of the towns in which they live. They are persistent grubbers: and they have no hifalutin notions of the dignity of labor; only a matter-of-fact acceptance of its necessity. Both the children and the older people of Miss Suckow's fictive world are pitiful—not because they are consciously unhappy or deprived, but because they live in a world in which necessity and their own limitations have so closely battened down the edges of their horizons that no view remains at all, and there is no space for dreams. Their only joys are small joys, of peace, and order in the small things immediately about them.

Every one of the fourteen short stories in *Children and Older People* is a full-bodied entity, and the range both of theme and of personalities is rather astonishingly wide. **"Eminence,"** a cool, regretful little story of the outstanding child in a small town is a far trek, emotionally and in materials, from **"Midwestern Primitive,"** the story of a primly ambitious tearoom-keeper who suffers acutely from the supposed handicap of her old mother's wholesome Europeanisms. The most vigorous story—and personality—of the collection is **"A Great Mollie,"** the tale of a hearty rather masculine countrywoman who loved to tink-

er with her Ford and drive long joggling miles over the countryside selling underwear and corselets. She thought once of raising skunks for profit, and once of opening a beauty parlor in Chicago. She always got on better with the men.

> Suckow is like a brilliant laboratory worker who sets off a certain field of research for her own and works unceasingly—with a devotion that amounts almost to tenderness, and a commitment to accuracy which leaves no place conceivable for humor—to discover and record the precise (and consequently beautiful) truth.
>
> —*Florence Haxton Britten*

Miss Suckow has an extraordinary faculty for getting inside these people of hers and making them live. The plot in each of these small tales is complete, with the emotional culmination and decline clearly enunciated. There is a trick here of indicating the inevitable outcome and stopping well short of it—thus skillfully heightening the reader's sense of the implacability of a life in which living is a burden that must be shouldered afresh each day and mere being is carrying on. And for a painstaking capacity to say the subtly unsayable, Miss Suckow ranks with Katherine Mansfield herself.

There is no magic here, or swift legerdemain; Miss Suckow's structure is built slowly and solidly; it will last. If there are no crazy chinks in it through which one can see the stars, at any rate its broad windows permit one to look, with utmost sympathy, down the street of little people.

Fred T. Marsh (essay date 1931)

SOURCE: "Ruth Suckow, Historian of the Prairie Town," in *The New York Times Book Review*, August 23, 1931, p. 4.

[*In the following excerpt, Marsh praises the perceptiveness and depth of the stories in* Children and Older People.]

[In *Children and Older People*] Ruth Suckow continues to write of the same people, the same environment, and with the same acute perceptiveness as always. Like all her stories these are studies of her own people executed with the economy of the born artist. She remains the historian in fiction of the American folk of the Western prairie towns and farms; and she remains, fundamentally, as completely the determinist as Dreiser. Like an Iowa landscape all her tales are leveled out and the lives of the people of whom she writes are devoid of great crises. These lives, like the prairies, are undulating. She sees them, stretching out over the years, colored by sown patches of joy and sorrow, bitterness and primitive beauty, desolation of spirit and small satisfactions. And in each of her short stories she picks up the thread of a life at some moment when the swell and ebb of an emotion are most decidedly marked.

But there is passion inherent in all her work. And those who, because they do not care for the literature of the commonplace or for homely realism, accuse her of being, in her work, deficient in emotional power, are themselves blind to what is apparent to others who have an inherent sympathetic understanding of one aspect of both literature and life. It is probably true that Ruth Suckow will never have anything like universal appeal. If some of us have greater admiration for her books than we know how to justify in criticism, others read them only to ask with lifted eyebrow that most disconcerting of all questions, "What of it?" One can reply only by putting more questions. Is not all life a subject for art? Has not Ruth Suckow given us profound insight into the lives of a contemporary folk? It only happens that these people are of mixed strain, descendants of pioneers, without as yet a culture, but advanced products of the new American civilization.

The stories in this volume mark no gain over Miss Suckow's earlier work—although, perhaps, in certain instances, there is evidence of a growing gentleness in approach to character—nor do they show any signs of a falling off. Her career, like her Iowa landscapes, like her people, like each of her volumes, remains on a level plane. But even the prairies dip and swell, and the first story in the book, **"Eminence,"** stands on a little crest of its own.

It is Christmas eve. Mr. and Mrs. Watkins are on their way to the church for the festivities. Mr. Watkins carries little Florentine in his arms—Florentine of the pale little face and starry eyes, the pride of her parents if not of the whole Sunday school.

The exercises begin. Little Florentine waits her turn in agony. Her head is hot, her little hands are cold, her dry lips mumble over and over again the first line of the song she must sing. Other children might fail, but too much depends on Florentine for her even to falter. Her mama and papa, her teacher, all the other children and their parents are expecting her success.

Her name is called. Florentine goes to the platform, shaking, determined to go through her part and then die. But as soon as she starts the words come easy, her knees stop trembling, she is intoxicated with a sense of victory while her little bell-like voice rings out clear and pure.

After the program comes the Christmas tree and little Florentine gets the largest package containing the biggest doll ever seen. All the children flock around to look at it and touch it; and the parents shower Mr. and Mrs. Watkins with congratulations on Florentine's brilliant performance. All three Watkinses are proud and happy and exalted folk. But then—imperceptibly—the atmosphere changes. The

---

An excerpt from "Susan and the Doctor" :

Susan started going with the boys early. Too early. Her mother had died, and there was no one to look after her. Her father had affairs of his own on his hands.

Susan's escapades, from the time she was thirteen, had been a source of talk in the town where she lived. But they seemed all to have happened in a past that was now incredible. People had almost forgotten that she had once gone with Buddie Merton and Carl Flannigan and Chuck Myers and Pat Dougherty—her affair had been going on for so many years with the Doctor.

And it had obscured not only her relations to other men, but almost everything else about Susan. People did not think about the long and steady efficiency of her position in the Farmers Bank, where she had risen from clerk to assistant cashier, and where she was actually a stand-by. When they went into the bank, and up to Susan's little barred window, they did not see her—slim, shining-haired, immaculate—as the cashier who dealt out nickels and dimes and bills with swift, experienced, white fingers. They did not recall how her present security was due to herself alone. She had never depended upon her father for a living. She had never depended upon anyone. She had borrowed money and taken a business course and then asked old Henry Houghton for a place in the bank; and it was upon that first meager and grudging admission that she had lived and put money aside and paid for the always fashionable perfection of her tailored clothes and the smartness of her hats. They looked through the little window at her white hands and smooth hair, and thought:

"I wonder how her affair is coming on with the Doctor!" Oh, yes! Susan was handy, and she was bright. She made some of those pretty clothes herself—knitted scarves when scarves were in fashion, and embroidered collar and cuff sets when they were the thing. She kept her two rooms and kitchenette at Mrs. Calverton's in exquisite order. Women did admit that. And there were men in town who said that no one in that bank knew as much about its business as Susan. But all that seemed irrelevant to the consistent interest of her love affair.

Ruth Suckow, in Twentieth Century Short Stories, *selected by Sylvia Chatfield Bates, Houghton Mifflin, 1933.*

Watkinses see that other children are coming in for praise too. Some of the cruder little boys and girls, unmindful of Florentine's triumph, begin chasing each other around the aisles, shouting and laughing. Older people gather together in little groups and discuss entirely extraneous matters. A few, even, whisper that the Watkinses are altogether too given to showing off their kid, that next year some other child should have a chance, that that doll was much too expensive and ostentatious a present for a Sunday School tree. And the minister's wife goes bustling around saying over and over again, "They were *all* good."

Her hour of glory over, Florentine grows tired and forlorn waiting at the door saying good-byes while her father and mother seek to squeeze out the last word of compliment that is to be had. Then papa takes her up proudly in his comfortable arms and the three plow, their way home through the snow. On the way mama, still beaming with pride, reminds Florentine that the beautiful new doll is only for special occasions and that on no account must she let any of the other children play with it. "Remember how Kitty ruined your little piano. This doll is much too expensive for that."

Half the stories are concerned with children. **"Big Kids and Little Kids"** is one of the most poignant of them all in its understanding of the joys and agonies of childhood over what blundering grown folks, however fond and well meaning, see as mere trivialities.

The stories of adults are of a more somber caste. **"Mrs. Kemper"** is a short portrait of an unloved woman. **"The Spinster and the Cat"** contains some extraordinary descriptive passages and a touch of grim realistic humor. **"Susan and the Doctor"** is a fine revealing short story on an old theme, briefly and poignantly executed.

If Ruth Suckow has limited the range of her subjects to a single environment, the realities in her books are true to all American life; more, they are universal; for by remaining true to her own understanding she has remained true to universals. She stands out among the group of American writers of recognized reputation as one who has never strayed from her own field nor been tempted by the possibilities inherent in achieving a tour-de-force. And in staying at home she has seen the world.

Anzja Yezierska (essay date 1952)

SOURCE: "Seven Tales and a Fact," in *The New York Times Book Review,* January 6, 1952, p. 4.

[*Yezierska was a Russian-born novelist and short story writer whose works chronicle the early twentieth-century Jewish immigrant experience in the United States. Her protagonists search for the "American Dream" while contending with a new and sometimes hostile environment. In the following review, Yezierska commends the themes and realistic characters of* Some Others and Myself.]

[The seven stories of *Some Others and Myself*] have the quiet realism that distinguishes all Ruth Suckow's work. As always, she is more interested in capturing the essence of character than in plotting a story. She has the gift of summing up a life in a few phrases, as in **"Aunt Amy,"** the story of a middle-aged woman to whom nothing had ever happened: "She was a princess in a tower of innocence whose door had never been opened." In the old, the shelved, the mediocre, in seemingly drab, colorless lives, Ruth Suckow finds color and drama. The theme of compensation runs through many of the stories. In **"Eltha,"** a stolid farm-woman submerged in the round of cooking awakens to true motherhood at sight of her child, stricken with polio, "lying helpless on the bed, like Snow White in her crystal coffin." The author turns

failure inside out, reveals spiritual grandeur even in defeat, in **"Merrittsville,"** the story of a town hit by the Depression.

You put the book down with the feeling that you've looked deep into the hearts of real people. With one or two exceptions they have not found the right answer to their lives. But they rise out of the page to haunt you and make you aware that we are greater than we know.

Mencken, who published Ruth Suckow's first stories in *The Smart Set,* spoke of her as "The voice of the voiceless. Through her, the dumb speak." In 1924, her first novel, *Country People,* was serialized in *Century Magazine,* chronicling three generations of German Americans through the hardships of pioneer life in Iowa. Though Miss Suckow has written chiefly of German immigrants of the Middle West, her work is not merely "regional." Her seven novels and numerous short stories have a universal quality that ranked her among the three or four most distinguished women writers of the Nineteen Twenties. Ten years of silence have vitalized her craftsmanship with religion—the belief that "truth is a living, growing, increasing revelation." *Some Others and Myself* leaves the impression of large reserves still unexplored, of greater books to come.

John T. Flanagan (essay date 1953)

SOURCE: A review of *Some Others and Myself,* in *American Literature,* Vol. XXIV, No. 4, January, 1953, pp. 568-69.

[*Flanagan is an American educator and critic. In the following excerpt, he offers a negative review of the short stories in* Some Others and Myself.]

It is almost thirty years ago now that Ruth Suckow first attracted attention by the blunt, terse short stories of Iowa farm life that she contributed to the *Midland,* the *American Mercury,* and other magazines. Eventually collected in *Iowa Interiors* and subsequent volumes, these tales revealed their author as an observant realist who lacked both the satirical attitude and the acidity of the more sensational rebels against village life but who nevertheless wrote with quiet authority about simple people and simple lives. Miss Suckow's work was neither flamboyant nor melodramatic. She dealt with Iowa farm folk in commonplace situations, with hired girls, with peripatetic ministerial families, with renters, with old couples selling out and moving to town, with large families celebrating festivals or natal days. Pathos was more common than tragedy in her stories, and humor was rarer than sympathy. Her stock themes tended to be loneliness, the imminence of death, the approach of senility, the dullness of routine, and the desolate, circumscribed lives of spinsters and widows. In various novels and collections of tales Miss Suckow approached such subjects from different angles. They were as much her province as rural Iowa was her background.

In the last dozen years Miss Suckow has published little fiction, but the seven stories included in *Some Others and*

Myself suggest her continued interest in familiar material. Lonely and deserted women dominate these rather dreary tales. The wasted lives sketched here are still pathetic rather than tragic, but the narrator's art has become diffuse and repetitive. Overloaded with the kind of details that Willa Cather objected to in her crusade for selective realism, the stories drag. The women, to be sure, are recognizable individuals, but they are neither interesting nor vivid. Best perhaps of the seven printed here is the joint portrait, **"Mrs. Vogel and Ollie."**

On the other hand, the long "memoir" which covers over one hundred pages of this somewhat lopsided book turns out to be one of Miss Suckow's best pieces of writing. It is basically autobiographical and it reveals a good deal about the author's youth, her family, her various residences, ministerial life in a succession of small towns, and even clerical politics (the seamy side of parochial existence), but its chief interest is its portrait of her father, the Reverend W. J. Suckow—for fifty years a Congregational minister in Iowa. Her father is Miss Suckow's real hero, a liberal clergyman, independent in mind and actions, unaggressive and unambitious, quietly faithful to his principles, and courageous enough to bring up his family without fear of orthodoxy in the temperate zone. A reader familiar with Miss Suckow's earlier stories will recognize themes and situations here and will look interestedly at the whole fabric from which she cut her pieces. But her father is more vivid than many of her imagined characters, and it is obviously his influence that led his daughter to the Quaker doctrines of religion and ethics which she holds today. "A Memoir" is as successful a piece of writing as any of Miss Suckow's fictions and it shares the qualities of her best stories— simplicity, dignity, quiet observation, fidelity to fact, sympathy, and understanding.

John T. Frederick (essay date 1954)

SOURCE: "The Nineteen Twenties," in *The Palimpsest*, Vol. XXXV, No. 2, February, 1954, pp. 61-74.

[*An American educator, critic, and author, Frederick wrote two novels about Midwestern farm life. In the following excerpt, he compliments Suckow's creation of authentic milieus in her writing but stresses that people are her real interest—"people in their relation to other people and to their communities."*]

The Second World War and the mid-century have given us a new perspective in relation to the literary output of the 1920's. Perhaps we have not yet attained the historical distance requisite for decisive critical evaluation, but we can be much more sure of our judgments than we could be twenty years ago. In rereading the work of Ruth Suckow, therefore, I was happy to realize freshly and more fully than ever before—how good her books are. . . . In my work as a book reviewer, and a teacher of contemporary literature (and, presumably, for my sins), it has been my lot to read hundreds upon hundreds of new books of fiction through these years. At the same time I've been studying older American fiction—Hawthorne, Melville, Howells, James—year after year. It is against this background and with this perspective that I have reviewed Ruth Suckow's work, and that I believe it to be a part of American literature in the precise sense, marked by values that are durable and truly distinguished. She is the one all-Iowan writer for whom I can make this claim with confidence.

It is obvious that Ruth Suckow's early experience as the daughter of a Congregational minister gave her rich material. The life in half-a-dozen Iowa towns is beautifully recorded by Miss Suckow in her most recent delightful book, *Some Others and Myself* (1952). But it is the spirit in which Miss Suckow used this material that made possible her achievement—a spirit neither partisan nor hostile—and her dedicated power as a writer that produced it. The town is *there* in her work, just as it was, for better or worse, set down neither with love nor with hate— save love for the living fact of whatever hue, hatred of the writer's besetting weaknesses of distortion and artifice. Her "New Hope," in her novel of that name, and her "Morning Sun," of *The Bonney Family,* are only the brightest of a whole gallery of towns in Miss Suckow's novels and stories, all firmly individualized, authentic, seen with penetration and in significant aspects. Can anyone ever get more of the atmosphere of an Iowa town of fifty years ago through a single detail than she does in the picture of little Wilfred Bonney bringing home the family cow? "Women getting supper smiled to see him trotting down the wide road through the soft warm dust patterned with shadows of leaves and branches, talking companionably to the cow."

A sense of place *as place* is strong and omnipresent in Ruth Suckow's work. Essence of Iowa is on an opening page of *The Bonney Family*:

> There was something lush and rank about the midwestern summer—the moisture in the heat, the loftiness of elm branches with their dense foliage, the hot nasturtiums along the walk to the barn.

She has a special genius for houses: that of *The Kramer Girls,* that of the Grunewald sisters in **"One of Three Others,"** that of the old couple in **"Uprooted"** are fused with the inmost experience of the story in each case and contribute substantially to it. Though small towns afford the backgrounds of most of Miss Suckow's books, she can etch sharply the raw, new residential district of "The Rapids" in *The Kramer Girls,* and touch deftly the college town of "Vincent Park" (where, to the horror of a professor's wife from New England, "some of the professors had actually never been abroad, and two or three of them had never even been *east*") in *The Bonney Family.*

But people are Miss Suckow's real concern, of course— people in their relation to other people and to their communities. The town is very strongly felt as social background in **"Susan and the Doctor"** of *Children and Older*

People. Often a child's mind is the center of illumination for the community, as in **"The Man of the Family"** of the same volume, with the boy beginning to earn money by working at the drugstore. It is the extensive use of the child's point of view in *New Hope* which lends the town of that name its special interest, and the novel part of its high distinction. The world of high school youngsters is sensitively revealed in the adolescent Ruth of *The Kramer Girls*. It is the strong sense of a totality of such relationships that makes Miss Suckow's towns so real and so important. Social distinctions exist in these towns; there are the relatively rich and the relatively poor, the privileged and the unprivileged. The boundaries change. Of the deaf spinsters in **"One of Three Others"**—"All three belonged to leading families; or what had been leading families"—and are so no longer. In nothing is Miss Suckow's mastery of her material more sure than in her ability to present people at extremes of the social scale with equal force and equal sympathy. In **"Mrs. Vogel and Ollie"** of *Some Others and Myself* we have a grand assortment of outcasts and misfits—the foul-mouthed Dee Slack, the mildly insane Queen Victoria Allerdyce, One-legged Joe, Mrs. Fickel—the hangers-on who relish Mrs. Vogel's sympathy and Ollie's coffeecake. They are portrayed very clearly, with abundance of sharp detail, but with no malice, no tinge of exploitation. In the same volume, in **"An Elegy for Alma's Aunt Amy,"** we have the other extreme:

> They were Middle-Western ladies. They were workers. Idleness—such an idea of ladyhood—filled them with disdain. They had known some early hardships. Although Mrs. Root was well-to-do—and Mr. Root had been "an awful good husband"—her fingers were a little knotted, and her figure was spread, and she had an ample, motherly bosom. Mrs. Root was getting elderly, but there was not much that went on in the town without her. She baked her marvelous angel cakes for the church suppers, and helped make the coffee for the high school banquet; and people came to her for roses for the graduation exercises and for snowballs on Decoration Day. No kind of domestic crisis daunted her. . . . She would have been ashamed not to be found capable in any purely human emergency.

The close relation of town and farm is almost universally present in Miss Suckow's work: as social contrast or conflict, as economic interdependence, or as mere physical nearness. Sarah, of *The Bonney Family*, "was possessed with a desire to get out to the open road beyond the streetcar tracks, where she could feel the wind cold against her face and see the dark, moist country look of the shocked corn." In the two thousand words of the story, **"Retired"** *(Iowa Interiors),* she has achieved the finest portrayal of the retired farmer in all American literature. She has seen more clearly than any other writer the recurring dramatic situation, within Iowa families, of contrasts and conflicts between those who stay on the farm and those who leave it, and has treated it more thoroughly, with many variations of character and incident: most fully in *The Folks,* but also with especial poignancy in *New Hope* and in such stories as **"A Rural Community"** and **"Four Generations."**

As social history Miss Suckow's work is more inclusive than it would seem at first; and it is always and wholly authentic.

—John T. Frederick

The modification, external and internal, of Iowa towns and cities by commercial and industrial changes is rarely a major theme in Miss Suckow's work, but it is not neglected. Sarah Bonney, returning to Morning Sun after World War I, finds many changes:

> . . . stretches of new paving, stucco houses of a very modern quaintness, a chain store with a brilliant red front in place of Anderson's old grocery on Main Street. . . . Fourteenth Street dresses, cheaply up to date and slightly askew at the seams, in the windows long sacred to bolts of "reliable" linen. Cars were parked thick round the court house, and people no longer took leisurely summer outings on the river. There was only one old row-boat for hire.

As social history, then, Miss Suckow's work is more inclusive than it would seem at first; and it is always and wholly authentic. But "sharply set in time and place" as her people unfailingly are, they are also unfailingly "treated as eternal souls." To grasp this truth with some fullness is to begin to measure the achievement of Ruth Suckow as a writer.

Leedice McAnelly Kissane (essay date 1969)

SOURCE: "Beauty" and "Quests," in *Ruth Suckow,* Twayne Publishers, Inc., 1969, pp. 26-41, 42-65.

[Kissane was an American educator and critic. In the following excerpt, she provides a thematic analysis of Suckow's early short stories and short novels.]

All [Suckow's] early stories are low-keyed, with a note of sadness. They deal with somber themes—death and illness, poverty, deprivation, old age, and loneliness. Of the sixteen that were later gathered and published in *Iowa Interiors,* all but three or four are about old people. Because of these subjects, critics often commented that Miss Suckow chose her subjects from the unlovely aspects of life. Yet, paradoxically, the purpose which motivated her was to grasp a moment of beauty and preserve it. The beauty she perceived and that she again and again celebrated is appreciated the more keenly as the circumstances are seen in their unadorned reality.

To Ruth Suckow, with her uncompromising honesty, to "prettify" was to desecrate. If life is truly beautiful and worthy to be loved, she seems to say, its quality should be tested by the everyday situations and not by the unusual ones. . . .

In choosing her subject matter, Ruth Suckow deliberately took a new path—that of depicting everyday people in the hampering circumstances of day-to-day existence. . . .

The early stories have a lyric quality. Some are very short: **"Retired"** is six pages; **"The Resurrection,"** five. They present a situation, make it recognizable by actual details from its setting, breathe life into it, and let it stand, a messenger of beautiful truth, like a poem. The elements of nature are used to convey and intensify meaning. In **"A Home-coming"** and in **"A Rural Community"** this imagery is more elaborate than in the briefer stories. Nature is often used to set a mood—the bleakness of a cold rainy day pervades **"A Start in Life"**; the urgency of incipient spring makes itself felt in **"Retired."**

Though the stories move through time toward a crucial moment, they tend to be more pictorial than dramatic. Sometimes the moment is frozen into immobility by some device such as the taking of the photograph in **"Four Generations"** or the look on the mother's dead face in **"The Resurrection."** Some are epiphanic like those of Anton Chekhov whom Miss Suckow much admired. Often a cumulative effect is built up from a series of random happenings as in **"Renters"** or **"Mame,"** or from a patterned sequence as in **"Golden Wedding."** Though the stories are simple, they show a surprising variety in method. The narrator is frequently objective, but occasionally she moves inside her central character's mind, and when she does, she renders thought into appropriate speech patterns with great naturalness. There is never any evidence of experimenting. In each case, the method exactly fits the story, as if the inspiration had brought with it its own manner of telling.

The situation in **"The Resurrection"** is sketched with a few simple strokes—the grandmother is lying dead in the parlor, and the family is summoned by the undertaker to view her body, now prepared for burial. Her beauty and remoteness startle them all. The littlest grandchild thinks of the transformation wrought by frost upon the familiar world of outdoors. Her daughters, used to their unobtrusive, hard-working mother, are moved by the unexpected grandeur of her presence. But the climax is her old husband's half-dazed recognition that, through the mysterious power of death, this strange loveliness has emerged—the spirit of her virgin girlhood, which only he among all who now behold her has seen before. Dimly he perceives that he has witnessed a resurrection; then he sinks back to everydayness as he comments to his granddaughter, "Your grandma looks—real nice, don't she, Nellie?"

"The Resurrection" has an almost stylized precision about it. Yet its very starkness suggests depths of emotion beneath. Many years later, in **"A Memoir,"** the author spoke of looking upon her own mother's face in death: "My mother's face, young and beautiful as I could never re-member having seen it, marks of her long illness erased and the best look of her lovely young girlhood come back."

"Four Generations," mentioned above, is essentially pictorial—the taking of a family picture in which, as the title indicates, four generations are represented: the old German grandfather; his son Charlie, a prosperous Iowa banker; Katherine, Charlie's daughter, home on a visit from the East; and her little Phyllis, the great-grandchild and center of the group. The group is thrown into brilliant relief by the brightness of the hot July sun on the deep green of the grass and the snowball bushes which form the background. Interest focuses on the four figures brought to life by skillful touches—Grandpa's frail hands clasping his knotted stick, Charlie's luminous bald skull, the tense cords in Katherine's neck, and little Phyllis's delicate arms, damp with the heat. Off at the side other family members draw back against the house, careful "not to get in the picture."

Actually the picture *is* the story. It is external, but revealing. The sequences of interior monologue only bear out what the picture itself suggests: Charlie's baffled resentment at the distance between himself and his only daughter and grandchild; Grandpa's disappointment that he has nothing to say to Charlie, now a "town man," not a farmer; and Katherine's shrinking from the "feminine grossness" of the women's conversation, as she contrasts her relatives with her husband's family and their New England ways that she feels actually closer to now than to these Iowa ones. The final scene rounds out the piece—pictorial once more, but this time with sound—as Phyllis, up from her nap, approaches her great-grandfather as he sits quietly smoking in the doorway of his small house. Like an inquisitive bird, she hovers, draws back, approaches tentatively. To lure and keep her, the old man speaks gently, quizzically: "Is dis a little yellow bird? Can it sing a little song? No? Den Grandpa will have to sing one to you." And he quaveringly sings the old German folk song "Du, Du, liegst mir im Herzen."

Critics often commented that Miss Suckow chose her subjects from the unlovely aspects of life. Yet, paradoxically, the purpose which motivated her was to grasp a moment of beauty and preserve it.

—Leedice McAnelly Kissane

The symmetry of this work, together with its vivid picturization, gives it an exquisite unity. It is far from slight, however; it suggests a number of themes central to Miss Suckow's thinking and reinforced in her later works. The four generations, so close together in the opening picture (the photographer keeps urging them to move closer), are actually divided and torn apart by differences. The conflict between town and country is here, that between Eastern and Midwestern culture, the German versus the New England tradition, and the never-ending strife between the generations. The final scene resolves the paradox as great-grandfather and little grandchild draw together. The rifts and resentments that trouble those in middle life mean little to the very old and the very young; they hold in common their love for the fundamentals of simplicity and beauty.

"A Home-coming" conveys its meaning through the flower imagery that suffuses its descriptions. A flower fancier, Ruth Suckow nowhere shows her indigenous quality more truly than in her accurate knowledge of what blooms and when in Iowa gardens. Even the place names in **"A Home-coming"** are suggestive of flowers. The town is Spring Valley; the street is Summer Street; and the girl, no longer young, who returns to her home there is named Haviland, suggesting the fragility of pretty china, often flowered. Not much happens in this rather leisured story—it is situation merely—but the flower symbolism gives it poignancy.

Laura Haviland has spent her best years traveling about with and waiting on her restless, demanding mother. Now, the mother dead, she has come back to find everything changed. The town has adopted new ways, her home shows the effect of long neglect, and her childhood friends are now brittle matrons. The pathos is in the drained vitality of Laura, who cannot find the zest either to make a new life or to adjust to the changes of the old one. She is like a wilted flower, her hands supple but lifeless.

In the back yard of her old home, once full of flowers, there are only fallen petals of the syringa, their scent bringing a thought of Mark, the lover she relinquished long ago. The grass under the catalpa tree is sprinkled with white ruffly blossoms edged in sepia, tacitly suggesting the wedding gown unworn and her own wasted flowering. A lone wild violet left blooming she greets with a soft cry, "Darling—beautiful." But there are no "spring beauties" in their old place by the little cobwebbed cellar window.

Wistfulness, gentleness, and flowerlike fragility give this story its special tone, but without its confrontation of evil it would remain merely sweetly sad. The evil is selfish maternal domination, which the author represents in a metaphor of force and violence that yet remains perfectly in keeping with her chosen imagery of plants and flowers:

> She thought of herself at twenty, when her mother and she had left the first time for Florida. How she had felt aching, bleeding, *as if she had been torn up by the roots.* How she had said to Mark: "We will certainly be home in the spring." So they had—and then had had to go again. Her mother's need of her *creeping about her like tendrils, fastening on her and holding her tight.* She had said to Mark: "I feel . . . it isn't fair to you" and his always unbelievable acquiescence. That same year he had married a girl from Fort Weston. . . . (Italics mine.)

Now Laura has come to realize that what she has been born for is not hers. Nothing is hers except the old house, the trees, the fallen petals on the lawn.

"A Rural Community" also shows a character, this one a young man, who returns to his native environment. In contrast to most of Ruth Suckow's Iowans, Ralph Cheney is, like the author, a writer, a traveled person, hence one capable of making comments in his own voice; and the tone is reflective and poetic, rich in symbolism. Ralph's return takes place in the autumn, and many of his impressions resemble the author's journal entries for that season: "One slender young cottonwood, yellow as a goldfinch and as lyric in its quality, stood in a meadow, alone." The glowing and transient colors, seen against the unchanging landscape, point up the tension between change and permanence—the dominant impression of his visit. The remembered line of hills on the horizon reminds him of the eternal verities, suggesting the stability that he misses in his transient life. Another kind of permanence, that of human personality, is expressed by his old foster mother, who exclaims on recognizing him: "It's the look in your eyes—I'd have known ye anywhere."

Ralph's foster parents mourn that he has no wife and that his newspaper work takes him to all corners of the world. Gazing at the display of family photographs in the parlor—weddings, first babies, then family groups with children growing up to engage in the same unending cycle—the wanderer recognizes the difference in the point of view of these rural relatives: "Human relationships were what they understood, the things to which they clung." But Ralph's fate is not so tragic as Laura's fruitless life—it is only rootless—and he suffers merely a mild nostalgia at the sight of familiar scenes.

When he takes the night train for the East, he feels that his visit has done him good: " . . . All night long, as he lay half sleeping, swinging lightly with the motion of the train, he was conscious of that silent spreading country outside, over which changes passed like the shadows of the clouds across the pastures; and it gave him a deep quietude." The play of the ephemeral shadows over the everlasting rocks of the pastures is a revelation that speaks to Ralph's soul and serves as the key symbol of the story. Natural beauty serves in a transcendental way to represent that "something overpowering in nature" that the author writes of in her journal.

In another of the stories, **"Retired,"** nature speaks to the inner consciousness of man. Seth Patterson, an old retired farmer, on an early spring day ambles down town on an errand for his wife, drops in at several places along Main Street, exchanges small talk with cronies who hang out at the produce store, and in the late afternoon trudges back home. On the first warm day in March everything suggests planting time to Seth. "Won't be long now till the ground's ready," he mutters. Though Seth is at loose ends and discontented with his aimless life, feeling, as he says, "crabbed and helpless, sitting around just gassing with the ground getting soft and the sky blue" his story does more than point out the need for educating for retirement and old age. His response to the vital urgency of the day with its scent of melting snow, fresh mud, and bright clean air indicates a mystical partnership of man with nature.

Seth Patterson represents a special kind of attainment. His reaction to the March weather is proof of what his kind of life has made him—he is inarticulate, wordless as the forces of nature themselves, but he is acutely aware of them and perfectly attuned to their call. In his own way, the old farmer is completely at home in his world. To attribute futility to such a life, as some readers have done, is to misunderstand the meaning Miss Suckow has so carefully planted.

In **"A Start in Life"** natural conditions provide a metaphor for the cold, unsympathetic world. The weather is rainy and bleak as twelve-year-old Daisy Switzer goes to work as a hired girl for a promised dollar and a half a week. Ironically named (she is a homely little thing), she suggests a straggling flower beaten down by the rain. There is a chill about everything in this story—the bare, clean, new little house; the cool, offhand treatment of the young Kruses in their determination not to make Daisy one of the family. "You must help me," Edna reminds her. "You know we got you to help me." The coldness affects Daisy, for children, even the not-very-sensitive-ones, like Daisy, suffer when there is nobody to care about them. As the rainy twilight sets in, Daisy sadly sees the truth of what her mother has told her: "This isn't like visiting."

"Renters" projects a similarly pessimistic outlook for the Mutchler family. Echoes of Hamlin Garland sound in the hopeless frustration of the hard-working husband who is turned off the farm he has made prosperous by owners who now see the place as a desirable haven for one of their relatives. "They expect a man to take care of it like it was his own," Fred says bitterly, "and then any time they can send him off." He goes on: "What's a fellow gonna do? He works and does the best he can with the land he's on, and then they want it for someone else. And if he don't work, he has to leave. He has to leave anyway. There ain't nothing in it for the renter. There's nothing unless a fellow owns the land he's on."

His wife Beth has thoughts even more corrosively cynical: "Fred made her angry. Under the savage bitterness of some of his words there was always that something appealing, something childish and ready to trust people, in his eyes. Oh, he was a good worker and he was honest, but it needed *something more than that to get ahead. Something hard was what it needed.* Old lady Hunt had it, and Mrs. Foster showed it in that bright, glittering, mean smile she could turn upon you. *Why wasn't Fred like that?*"

Though Miss Suckow pays some attention to the injustice of "the system" as it affects individuals like Fred Mutchler and Daisy, she is for the most part concerned with "universals"; and the short story **"Mame"** illustrates this concern. There are touches of fatalism here. Mame and her husband Alick have always been unfortunate, and the rest of the family says it does no good to help them.

"Why did there seem to have to be one like that in every large family? All the hard knocks and none of the good things. Why did life seem to have it in for folks like Mame?"

But sociological explanations of their problems are of less concern in this story than the nature of Mame herself— she is self-sacrificing (almost too good-hearted, the brothers agree). She has looked after the younger children and has stood by her Alick whom she insisted on marrying after the accident that left him crippled. Mame and Alick moved into the old home to care for her parents through their old age and final illnesses. Mame has always put her own welfare after that of those she loves. Now that her plight is becoming desperate because Alick is too lame and feeble to work and because the small country town offers few opportunities for her and her daughter to earn money, she has appealed to Louie, the brother she feels closest to, to drive over from his home in the county seat to discuss what can be done.

Nothing is done, as it turns out, beyond Louie's giving Mame a check for twenty dollars to meet overdue payments on her sewing machine. This is one of Miss Suckow's masterly delineations of a situation which is left unresolved—but its very insolubility reveals the strength of the forces set against each other. Louie, a prospering businessman, suffers from his own ambivalent feelings— grateful affection for his sister who he knows is "the best and truest among his brothers and sisters," and selfish inclination to follow the lead of his wife and his other relatives in avoiding involvement with Mame and Alick's problems.

The physical objects in the old, run-down house where Mame and Alick live contribute to his mixed feelings. He is impatient with the doors that won't catch, with the rocking chair that threatens to capsize: "Didn't these people ever fix anything when it was coming to pieces?" At the same time, everything reminds him of the old days, his sister's unfailing goodness, and the fact that "he never felt at home anywhere else in just the same way as here on this old familiar lounge with Mame." Mame's solicitude for him—"You look kind o' thin, Louie"—shows her readiness to turn from her own troubles to thoughts of others. Ineffectual though she is, Mame's character is the bright touch of beauty in this all-too-human struggle between head and heart that Louie epitomizes.

"Golden Wedding" is another example of Miss Suckow's treatment of universal themes cloaked in the specific details of a recognizable situation. This account of the fiftieth wedding anniversary of an old Iowa couple takes them through the winter day just as it happens: the trip in the bobsled to their daughter's farm home, the big dinner attended by all the relatives, the sleigh ride in the afternoon, the taking of photographs, supper, and finally the return to their home and the resumption of their everyday existence.

The old wife's consciousness illumines the narration. Throughout the perfectly rendered incidents and embedded in her reactions are indications of a long-standing conflict of personalities:

> Why did Pa have to be so mean—and just today? He wouldn't admit that the celebration would be held in spite of the snowstorm; he never wanted to admit that anything was going to turn out right. But she still held to this blind faith of hers, and he to his objections. She pulling ahead, he pulling back.

> And that old tie he wanted to put on, just because, as he said, "Nobody would want to come out in all this snow just to eat dinner with us." He wanted to tarnish the glory of the occasion—pull it down to his level. The old tie was a blow at her importance as his wife—at their marriage—at her pride as a bride of fifty years.

However, as the events of the day rise to their climax, old Mrs. Willey feels her faith justified. The presence of the minister elevates the family dinner to an occasion. The table is decked with the best silverware and table linen that the family can boast; the food is sumptuously beyond the ordinary. She and Pa preside at the head of the table, she cuts the cake, and Pa even makes a speech. In the gaiety of their after-dinner ride through the snow in a sled decorated with the slogan "Just Married," he goes so far as to raise aloft their clasped hands to signal passersby.

As the celebration dwindles to its end, though, the commonness of everyday asserts itself, and Pa resumes his usual stance. He only grunts when she attempts to relive the events of the day in bedtime conversation. As she lingers over the putting away of her best clothes and trinkets, he orders her crossly to come to bed. "Pa would never talk to her," she mourns. "He'd talk more to anybody than to her."

"Golden Wedding" takes its form from the traditional Prothalamion, a celebration of the ritual of marriage from the donning of ceremonial attire in the early morning, through each observance of the day to the disrobing and union of the wedding night. But the ceremony is manqué—defective. Not all its poignancy resides in the travesty of re-enacting in age and disillusionment what was once made beautiful by youth and hope. Here, as Miss Suckow would say, particularity has its importance, too.

Old Angie Willey is more than merely the bride figure. She has a life of her own, shaped by her kind of environment, and conditioned by fifty years of intimacy with a tenaciously opposed personality. Hers is the immemorial quest of the self to know and fulfill itself; and in this quest, marriage in general and her marriage partner in particular have worked against her. "She pulling ahead, he pulling back" is the way she puts it.

Her old husband, though harsh and insensitive, is not entirely the villain of the piece; their life of narrow conformity is much to blame. Angie's spiritual gropings can find no expression beyond the clichés of the local paper, and her innate love of beauty has rigidified into a pinched regard for seemliness. Undeniably, she is warped and frus-

trated, though no more so than many another old person on whom life has inflicted its hard teachings. As an individual with thoughts of her own to cherish, she ends her day in finding contentment within herself.

"Uprooted," Miss Suckow's first published story, still stands as one of her very best and as an exemplar of her philosophy about the writing of fiction. This philosophy she was later to discuss in magazine pieces—"I Could Write if Only" and "The Short Story"—and in talks at writers' conferences. The details in **"Uprooted"** serve not only to set the tone or to provide background for the narrative, but also to perform a part in the resolution of the story. The Shafer "relationship," three married children and their spouses, gather at their parents' home to decide who is to "take" the old people, now no longer able to live alone. The action takes place in the parlor, described with the most specific realism—musty air, old photographs, flowered carpet, doilies tied to the chairs with ribbons, illustrated Bible, and all—and in the bedroom where the old mother weeps at the prospect of being separated from her "things," and where Sam, eldest and best-off of the family, persuades her to move in with her daughter by promising that she "can take everything in the house if she wants to"—he'll build on a room to Hat's house if necessary.

The amount of enmity, jealousy, and self-protectiveness underlying the discussion in the parlor almost justifies an early critic's judgment that Ruth Suckow's works principally succeed in showing "the petty selfishness, the vicious current of hatred which dominate human intercourse in the corn country" [Herbert Asbury, in *New York Tribune Books,* October 3, 1926]. Sam controls the situation because of his financial standing and also because he is his mother's first-born and her favorite. But he is not allowed to settle everything without some struggle—with his acerbic sister-in-law Jen, his obstinate if inarticulate sister Hat, and even his mother herself, whose withered person, pathetic in the tearfulness of old age, rouses some remnants of filial tenderness. There is ironic humor in his middle-aged businessman's eagerness to get through with all this and go home to the comfortable leather chair "whose hollows are his own," while at the same time he tells himself impatiently, "How strange it is that people seem to take root in a place!"

The outcome of the story is pessimistic, even cynical, in that the burden of caring for the old people is foisted on the one least able to bear it because she is also least adept at protecting herself. Heartache is foreseen for the old parents; that they are already aware that they can no longer control their future is indicated by the mother's bitter words: "They've fixed it among 'em." The author's purpose, however, is not limited to ironic commentary. The compromise on which the settlement hangs involves the mother's "things," so dear to her that she will not consent to abandon them. At the beginning, they are meticulously described, one by one, in a way remindful of Huck Finn's description of the Grangerford parlor a half-century earlier. Looked at in this light, the doilies and knick-knacks are pure Americana—genuine bits of local color. They also set the stage for the action, a fitting background for the family conclave taking place in their midst. Graceless, materialistic, yet eminently respectable, the character of the Shafer family is reflected in the primly placed, decorous furnishings.

They serve to illustrate a deeper meaning. The author remarks: "Those things were all about him now," as Sam paces about the parlor after settling things with his mother. "He could not look at the pampas grass sticking up absurd and stiff from the blue painted vase. The elaborate lace curtains tied back with cords of red plush, the sea shell beside the door, the ingrain carpet, musty smelling, and patterned all over with great sprawling cornucopias of roses—his muttered "Oh, pshaw" betrays his softened feelings as he half turns to the bedroom to repudiate his decision. Then he shrugs and puts the impulse from him.

At this point the furnishings act as mute reminders of family ties. The room where they stand is a shrine, seldom used, but representative of family solidarity and status. As Sam dimly senses, the old home-maker who has long cherished these articles feels more than affection for them—her very life is bound up with them. Instinctively, like an uprooted plant that can survive in its new place only if packed and cushioned by its own soil, she insists on surrounding herself with the same familiar objects she has always lived with. Finally, in their power to participate in and affect human destiny, these things are raised to a certain momentousness. They have almost the stature of a protagonist in the working out of the story. The author's genuine feeling for concreteness has made possible a happy harmony between the physical setting and the characters, or, as she would put it, between localism and universality.

Later when this story was gathered with the others into *Iowa Interiors,* critics were quick to liken them to the works of the Dutch genre painters. The precision of detail and the luminous clarity of the Dutch interiors, it was often pointed out, were the very qualities the Iowa writer achieved in her word paintings. Of all the stories in the volume, **"Uprooted"** owns the most apt affinity with the title. In her concern with domestic scenes, the author presents a number of interiors done with meticulous care; but on none has she concentrated the passion of attention she gives the Shafer parlor.

The name of the collection has a symbolic bearing, of course. It is plain that Miss Suckow meant her interiors to be the same ones that Howthorne had in mind when he coined his famous phrase in connection with his masterpiece: "the interiors of the human heart."

. . . . .

Interspersed with the jewel-like short stories that Miss Suckow produced with such plenitude in the early 1920's were three examples of a form she always favored—the short novel or novelette. Sinclair Lewis, who considered her *Country People* as also belonging to this genre, named its author among the masters of this "swift-winged form,"

as he called it. Toward the end of her life, Miss Suckow mentioned in a letter to a friend that she was "absorbed in writing some long short stories" which she hoped might eventually make a small volume. She commented that she found the form "beguiling," though "that length of story is difficult to place—it seems to fit nowhere."

These early novelettes, which came out in *Smart Set* between November, 1992, and October, 1923, resulted from the same creative urge as the short stories; and they have the same poetic genesis. Though their greater length poses difficulties, Ruth Suckow's art is equal to sustaining their unity of impression and their singleness of emotional impact. In each case she takes a single character as a focus of interest, and one dominating trait is traced throughout almost the entire life span with the effects and outcomes it brings. With admirable control, she never deviates from this central concern, though scenes and incidents are fitted out with a wealth of imagined detail.

[Suckow's] editors showed some reluctance to accept these longer pieces. [Her editor, George Jean] Nathan reminded her of the magazine's general limit of fifteen thousand words but conceded that "*A Part of the Institution* is good enough to make any magazine editor break his rules." The decision to feature them as "novels complete in one issue" was a fortunate one since they are actually fairly short, between twenty-two thousand and twenty-five thousand words.

Favorite themes of Ruth Suckow are treated in these three stories. *The Best of the Lot* deals with sacrifice, the familiar situation of the unmarried daughter spending her life and energies in family duties and the care of elderly parents. *Other People's Ambitions* presents another Suckow concern, that of tyranny, one human being victimizing another for selfish aggrandizement. *A Part of the Institution* is a semi-satirical treatment of the small denominational college of the Middle West; its theme is the pitfall of false or weak idealism. Because these novelettes have never been reprinted and so have not received the critical attention they probably deserve, they need to be examined in some detail.

The Best of the Lot, which first appeared in the November, 1922, issue of *Smart Set,* is a simple account of the life of Jennie Robinson, a little country girl who devotes herself to her shiftless family, slaving to raise them to respectability, insisting on standards of behavior and education for her brood of brothers and sisters, all of whom are ordinary. Though Jennie achieves a measure of success with them for a time, it is at the cost of sacrificing her own chance to marry. Later, she gives up her humble teaching career to care for her aging and invalid parents. The brothers and sisters, selfish and indifferent, leave home early, abandoning Jennie to a state of neglected poverty. At length, after her mother's death, she is left completely alone in her elderly house. Now a quaint little spinster, her energies and ambitions drained, her only outside occupation is keeping up the family graves in the cemetery.

Though Jennie reminds us of Mary in **"The Daughter"** and Laura Haviland in **"A Home-coming,"** she is as she should be in this lengthy work, more fully realized. We see her grow and change throughout the years. Engaging glimpses are given of her—small, neat, and industrious as she flies about the hotel dining room where she works, little beads of sweat glistening on her forehead and upper lip. She conscientiously admonishes her little sisters: "No, no, Jennie says no. Nellie knows better."

Of the three novelettes, this one is the most indigenous. Descriptive passages are true to rural Iowa. There are touches of beauty in the commonplace scenes. The Robinson children play out in the grove, described as follows:

> They would spend whole hours there, in the green leafy dimness, where they could just hear the sounds from the road. They picked wild flowers, wild gooseberries, raspberries and chokecherries, May apples and butternuts. The grass was long and fine, marked with the faint shiny tracks of wagon wheels. They lay on their backs and watched the leaves move against the blue sky.

More than the other two, this novelette is a forerunner of the novels to come. The opening farm scenes are similar to some of those in *Country People;* for example, there are the little frowzy-headed country children whose mother has too much to do. The earlier Jennie with her furious energy and ambition, her ability to organize her family, resembles Cora in the novel of that name. Jennie's brother Charlie is an embryonic Carl (later described in *The Folks*), whose conformity is at war with his better nature.

As in the short stories, Miss Suckow relies on generalized comment to round out her characters and set the tone. "People said: 'I guess Jennie Robinson hardly knows what to do. I wonder what she lives on'." Jennie's relatives and the family doctor expand the comment. Doc Zimmerli says: "I'd take Jennie any time. The best of the lot, too good for the rest of them." Though scrupulously detached as always, the author reveals compassion for Jennie. Her sacrifice is made to appear admirable, but there is regret for the seemingly useless waste of excellent human material in unrewarded and unappreciated self-abnegation. Like a number of the short stories, this novel closes with a puzzled and unreconciled protest against the way things are. As Doc puts it: "It was queer how the ones that deserved the most got the least half the time in this world."

Dreiser's influence and that of other contemporaries in the school of Naturalistic determinism are felt in this work. Early in the story occurs this statement about Jennie's parents: "The two breeded like animals, without volition or knowledge of any kind, not wanting more, but accepting the warning of another with a worried sense of fatality." This bluntness is not typical of Miss Suckow. It departs from her usual reticence, doing violence to her policy of "staying out of the story, of letting the characters live."

Ruth Suckow's apparent desire to register protest against things as they are also strains the credibility of this novel.

Though misfortunes and the selfish neglect of the rest of the family make a victim of Jennie, one feels that she lets down too easily: that the indomitable Jennie of childhood years would not turn into the passive, inhibited old maid she becomes. Though facing destitution, she lacks initiative to do anything for herself—she even shrinks from peddling a line of toilet goods among her friends and neighbors. Jennie did well in college, yet later her intellectual life seems insufficient to sustain her or to suggest means of escape.

The same objections could be raised as to Mary's limpness in **"The Daughter"** and to Laura Haviland who, though still in her thirties, lacks energy to resume living her own life after her mother's death. The fact that Ruth Suckow herself suffered from physical inadequacy in her middle years comes to mind. But, to look a bit deeper, Jennie and the others she resembles seem doomed by their own self-sacrificing natures. They can give unstintingly of themselves for others but not for themselves. That their weakness may be the result of a subverted maternal impulse is not understood by the possessors nor by those around them.

Their society approves the sacrifice of these maiden daughters and encourages the mothers to expect it. As Miss Suckow wrote, with some asperity: "Most of these widows had once been farmer's wives with enormous families; and each one had providentially one daughter left to her for her sole benefit. It was so nice for the mothers, everyone said sympathetically. 'Such a comfort to her that she has Mary.' These women had led the average lives, with the average mixture of pleasure and joy in their sorrows; but still it was felt that, as women and mothers, a 'comfort' was due each of them." The daughters, on their part, respond both to the prevailing mores and to their own inner promptings to tenderness in caring for their helpless parents. "She felt as deep a loyalty, a responsibility, to her mother as she would have felt to her child," is said of one of these sacrificing women in an early short story by Miss Suckow.

Although Mencken and Nathan both warmly admired *The Best of the Lot,* Nathan expressed reservations about the next novelette, *Other People's Ambitions*. He wrote: "Your story, *Other People's Ambitions,* pleases us, and we are accepting it. While it does not seem to us to be quite so good a piece of work as *The Best of the Lot,* it still contains an ample measure of excellent writing." The editor does not explain his statement, but one can guess that he missed in this novel the Iowa background Miss Suckow was in the habit of re-creating with such effortless authenticity. Most of the action in the new novel takes place in Denver, which the author also knew well; and it must be said that her close knowledge of sanitariums and the peripatetic health seekers that frequent them is capably utilized. But the familiar setting in Iowa is lacking.

The main character in this work is a young man, Harold Swisher, the son of a wealthy and domineering Iowa manufacturer. Harold, a graduate of a liberal college, is opposed to the career in the family industry envisioned for him by his father, tries it for a year, and suffers a physical breakdown. After a stay in a Denver sanitarium, he regains a measure of health and determines to remain in the congenial Colorado climate and live the kind of life he desires. His father, after helping him obtain a not-too-strenuous job that would maintain him, declares he will do no more for him and leaves him free to follow his inclinations. Harold's future looks fairly hopeful in an unspectacular way when May appears on the scene.

May's situation is that of one of Ruth Suckow's not-so-young maidens devoted to the care of her widowed mother, but with a difference. This maiden is designing and determined, and she sees in Harold a means of achieving married status and a home that she can dominate. She snares him without great difficulty when her mother's death heightens his sympathy toward her, and the two begin their version of love in a cottage.

After a short idyllic interval, during which May revels in organizing and decorating the house and Harold dreams of a life of continued beauty and leisure, their cross-purposes become plain, and May shows herself a more formidable tyrant than Harold's father. A selfish materialist rendered acutely unhappy by others' good fortune and possessions, she nags her husband continually. She longs for the luxuries of apartment dwelling, better cars and clothes, a standard of living that to her spells success. She keeps at Harold to exert himself to make more money, to secure a higher-salaried position, to induce his family to shower them with luxuries. He is able to resist her for a time—the birth of a child satisfies her restlessness temporarily—but she is the stronger of the two; and, though he is aware that his health will suffer, he yields to her urgings. They leave behind their peaceful, half-rural existence; he attempts a more strenuous, less congenial type of work, worries about it, and sickens. His early ailment reasserts itself, this time with more virulence, and in a few months he is dead.

Superficially, this plot resembles that of a dozen slick magazine stories. The domestic wrangling between husband and wife, May's specific wants, the detailed descriptions of their way of life, their house, car, and, later, their baby—all are familiar. In her skill in presenting domestic details like these, Miss Suckow resembled popular women's magazine writers of her time. She had a sure understanding of feminine nature together with an overweening love for the concrete appurtenances of daily living—"the things of use and wont," to quote one of her most laudatory critics.

Miss Suckow's works differ from typical magazine fiction, however, primarily in her basic attitude toward her material—an attitude quietly but unmistakably manifested. In this novel she is deadly serious. Harold and May are locked in a death struggle, not a frothy married lovers' dispute. The fate of the individual forced to yield to other people's ambitions is extinction. Irony, rare in the regulation "slick" story, is also implicit in the assump-

tions of the other characters about Harold. His sisters complain that he will not do as other people do. He is queer from the start. In college his cronies are a Professor Quarton and a mousy girl named Quigley, (the initial "Q" is indicative of their queerness). The life Harold desires for himself is a modest existence with leisure to cultivate and appreciate beauty. To his relatives and May, this is no life at all; and they assert that he lacks ambition. But the title betrays the distinction between the ambition of these others and Harold's vision of life which is beyond their abilities to conceive.

The word "ambition" in the title is perfectly chosen. To Miss Suckow's Midwesterners, it possessed connotations closely tied in with the prevailing system of values. "Ambition" was a highly favorable term implying a whole list of virtues; outstanding among them was the proclivity of exerting oneself to the utmost of his powers—"to work till he dropped." In that society and in that era, leisure was discredited; it was equated with idleness and closely associated with dissipation and evil. Buried somewhere in the meaning of ambition was also the ruthlessness necessary to achieving material success, a hardness akin to cruelty that would not brook interference. Ruth Suckow's people did not advocate cruelty, but they accepted it as an ingredient of ambition. The end justified the means, and the aim of life was "getting ahead."

Harold, who has felt the brush of dark wings in his collapse and during his sojourn in the sanitarium, knows the futility of the dream of "getting ahead." His own dream is different. Others discredit it and he is not allowed to realize it, but it is a not less worthy dream because of that. On the contrary, its difficulty of attainment even implies something of its loftiness. In the best sense, Harold is the truly ambitious one after all.

Other People's Ambitions resembles regulation magazine fiction in its organization and plotting, and it is tighter and smoother than many of the author's other works. The struggle rises to its climax in a series of engagements between the protagonists, subsiding between times to stretches of everyday existence under a sort of armed truce. The narrative is crisp and clear, like the Colorado atmosphere; and it lacks the nostalgic overtones of Ruth Suckow's Iowa pieces. It furnishes an indication of the kind of writer she might have become had she more often ventured into worlds she knew less well: shallower, perhaps; more obviously fictional; but possibly even more acceptable to the popular taste. But she is less herself, and surely less poetic. Nathan may have had something of this in mind in his unexplained reservations about ***Other People's Ambitions***.

Needless to say, the ending of this novelette is completely at odds with the happy ending expected of magazine fiction. Indeed, the off-beat quality of its conclusion is at odds with most fiction, breaking sharply with the rule against dragging in new characters and situations at the close. But Ruth Suckow always insisted that her kind of stories obeyed no rules except their own. In this one, she seemed to feel the need of a commentator on Harold's tragedy and sketched her in, complete with her situation, so that the final paragraph is an entire little short story in itself.

> . . . . The wife of the president of the seed house [where Harold worked], a discerning woman, made thoughtful by ill health which had forced her out of social life, had only touched his life at the outskirts. But she thought of it, wondered about it. It was one more note in her bewilderment concerning the world—why it should have been. The whole story, as she had had it from her husband and had made it out for herself, was one of those things whose existence she simply could not understand. One of the things that made her suddenly look at her husband, with his pink, kindly face and neat little optimistic definitions of life, with sudden, wondering, alien eyes.

The dominant note of *The Best of the Lot* is pathos; that of *Other People's Ambitions* is tragedy. But that of *A Part of the Institution* is satire. Hester Harris is another of Miss Suckow's self-abnegating old maids; but we have to smile at her mistaken devotion, for the object of her love is not another human being but an institution of learning—little, self-centered, self-satisfied Adams College. Hester can not escape her fanatical loyalty to Adams. She was born and bred in Adamsville, in its shadow; her mother is a distant connection of its founding family, and Hester's childhood home is a rooming house for women students. College activities absorb her interests from the beginning; the co-eds are the heroines of her dreams. She prays to grow up a popular, "all-around" Adams girl. In time her hopes are realized. Blessed with a singularly sweet smile and a nature marked by willingness to serve, she is recognized as a true "Adams type"—one thoroughly imbued with Adams ideals.

In Miss Suckow's analysis of Iowa earlier referred to, she writes of the "milk-and-watery idealism" in the colleges of the state, particularly the denominational colleges. At Adams, idealism is implicit in the student-body prayer meetings, in the powerful influence of the Y.M. and Y.W.C.A.'s, and in the missionary spirit which yearly impels a number of students to volunteer to carry the Adams spirit to benighted countries. But the flaw exists in the emphasis on conformity—the pressure on individuals to adjust to the group pattern. The conformity most favored consists in joining all campus organizations of prestige and, through energetic and faithful membership plus political finagling, working into control of these. It is expected that active, "all-around" students will wear themselves out in extra-curricular activity (some literally kill themselves), but the sacrifice is highly regarded as being made "for dear old Adams."

Hester performs as a true Adams co-ed. Her successful four years in college are marred by only a slight defection when during her junior year she falls in love with Joe Forrest, a quiet, rebellious boy who dares to question the worth of the Adams ideals. Hester ardently tries to make a convert of Joe; but when she fails and he is suspended, she flees back with something like relief to the shelter of the group and resumes her active campus life with zeal. Her friends have followed her affair with Joe disapproving-

ly; they feel he is "not the person for her." But when he is gone, there is nobody. Though Hester is a prominent senior, she has lost her chances with the popular Adams men.

After her graduation, Hester's desire to serve, to devote her life to promoting Adams ideals, traps her into accepting a poorly paid "scrub faculty" position at the college. For a time she throws herself into the ungrateful job with eagerness; then she is needed to help with a special endowment campaign; eventually she becomes one of the president's assistants, a "part of the institution," whose old-fashioned mien earns her the ridicule of younger office girls and the contemptuous nickname of "Hetty G." Reduced to existing in housekeeping rooms with her failing mother, she lives in anticipation of the reunions with her classmates at commencement times. The final glimpse of her is after one of these, bidding her old friends goodbye on the station platform of Adamsville. Mature, worldly, and successful, they respond to her eager affection with a pitying fondness she only partly understands. Obviously, Hester is the perpetual college student, one not very different from the character in Irwin Shaw's "Eighty Yard Run," reliving the glory of his achievement in college football. Hester, too, has failed to grow up. She is the victim of her college successes, when she represents the perfect embodiment of the group's ideals.

Miss Suckow's presentation of Hester is knowledgeable but gentle. Hester is silly in her unthinking devotion to Adams and in her pleasure in her popularity as a campus figure; but she is nevertheless warm-hearted, hard-working, and loyal—richly endowed with the feminine traits of a successful wife and mother. She should be part of a family, not of an institution—the very word reflects the coldness, the barrenness of poor Hester's fate. The institution has exploited her, utilizing her sincerity and unquestioning devotion in poorly paid, drudging work. But even Adams College is gently dealt with. A nostalgic glow surrounds the buildings, the trysting places, the college pranks, the good times, and most of all the young people themselves. Bunty and Ellen, Jinny, Joe, Big Bill, and Jay are amazingly vital individuals, full of high spirits and shining with youthful promise. Like the later *New Hope,* the Adams community has Utopian qualities of freshness and faith; but the ideals on which it rests are weakly defined and readily adaptable by hypocritical selfseekers.

In *A Part of the Institution* is found some of the best writing in the novelettes. There is no sentimentality, but warmth and understanding pervade it. The satire is light, inducing many a smile. There is naturalness in the speech patterns, for example in the child Hester's fervent prayer, "Make me like my darlingest, belovedest Helen and be taken into EBB—if it pleases Thee that I should—but, oh, *please* dear Heavenly Father because I can't bear to live if I'm not," and her mother's admonition: "Darling, mamma likes to see you good, but you make such long prayers when it's so cold. Your little feet are like ice. Can't you do part of your praying in bed?"

The description of the hot Iowa summer when Mrs. Harris and Hester shut themselves in their darkened house and wait for fall to bring back coolness and life to the town is at the same time utterly realistic and also symbolic of an existence narrowed and circumscribed, dependent upon one agency—the institution: "That summer seemed endlessly long and dull. Hot—every day worse than the one before. The nights were terrible. Hester and her mother did not pretend to do regular cooking. After a little lunch, they each took a bath, put on their nightgowns, and tried to read and sleep in the darkened back parlor until the worst heat of the day was over. . . . The town was nothing without the college people. How could she ever stand it until fall?"

There are other examples throughout this work of style and content wholly in harmony. The large trees that droop over Hester as she walks away from the station at the end convey the author's sure feeling for Iowa atmosphere as well as regret for the futility of Hester's wasted life: "Humphrey had left her. Her steps seemed loud on the wide cement walk. The tall elms stood up thick-leaved, motionless, as they would all through the long hot summer, throwing gray dappled shadows on the asphalt. There was that after-commencement feeling—a growing languor, a sadness and a uselessness in the fragrance that floated out over the thick, moist, solid, mid-June heat."

Margaret Stewart Omrcanin (essay date 1972)

SOURCE: "Short Story Writer," in *Ruth Suckow: A Critical Study of Her Fiction,* Dorrance & Company, 1972, pp. 154-80.

[*In the following excerpt, Omrcanin outlines Suckow's philosophy of short fiction writing, asserting that her stories "remain the best expression of her narrative purpose and method."*]

Ruth Suckow expressed herself more often and more explicitly on the subject of the short story than on any other aspect of her writing. In two magazine articles, the preface to **Carry-Over,** and in an unpublished essay written from lecture notes presented to college and university groups, she has made a number of observations about her own concept of short story writing.

In 1927 in an article in *Saturday Review of Literature,* she protested efforts to define and formalize the method of writing short stories. As the one vigorous native expression of American life in fiction, the short story, she believed, must be unrestricted in form if it is to retain vitality and originality. She observed regretfully that Poe's definition, the evidence of his struggle for originality and perfection in the chaos of early American literature, boomeranged.

> It was the chaos, the unevenness, the diversity of American life that made short stories such a natural artistic expression in the first place. . . . It [the short story] was the first eager, hasty way of snatching little treasures of art from the great abundance of unused, uncomprehended material. Short stories were a way of making America intelligible to itself.
>
> ["The Short Story," *Saturday Review of Literature,* Nov. 19, 1927.]

The imposition of standards presupposes that beauty is a rule and not an effect. In denying the efficacy of definition she insists, "If that effect is poignant, deep, and lasting, then the right means have been used." Short stories may be whatever the author has power to make them— "A running commentary upon life; fireflies in the dark; questions and answers; fragments, or small and finished bits of beauty."

In a later article, in *The Outlook,* she directed her comments to aspiring writers in "search for the master-key" for successful writing, and again denied the efficacy of a single approach:

> there is one important door which, through eager fumbling, may be opened. It is the door to consciousness. When that mysterious region is entered, we can do without our keys.
>
> ["I Could Write if Only—," *The Outlook,* Mar. 21, 1928.]

She discusses the writer's response to the realm of consciousness in the essay, "Development of a Story." Citing as a valid explanation of the desire to record an impression in enduring form, she quotes a statement made by an eleventh century Japanese novelist, Lady Murasaki:

> We write because something, in our own life or in the lives of others, has so impressed us, for good or evil, that it must never be lost. There must never come a time, we feel, when people do not know about it.

She selects for discussion in the essay a single hypothetical incident that might occur within a child's experience, and then suggests possible methods by which a writer, as experiencer and spectator, translates the experience into some creative experience. Among others she indicates two possible methods that describe the creative processes through which many of her own stories seem to have evolved. A writer may, she says, translate his knowledge of the world at large back into a small world and tell his story from the viewpoint of a child. He may show the quality and the implication of human experience through his evocation of a childhood drama, not necessarily the same, in which he himself has participated or which he has witnessed. "Yet it may be the same scene, or his memory of it, added to or substracted from to get what is essential." He may, on the other hand, carry on into adult terms of emotion and experience what so impressed him in an experience of childhood. In either case the artist transforms the real and the actual that have impressed his consciousness, and fashions in an original design an experience that has the quality of the real, but is not the real.

> It may be written quickly, while the impression is fresh. It may stay in the writer's mind for years, almost for a life-time. Observations, reflections, experiences, insights, cluster around it—broadening, deepening, enlarging. Our author "finds the right form." This comes to him in a flash, or the form is slowly perfected. Instance is balanced against instance, with light thrown from one to the other, in order to illuminate the situation

and to test out what holds true in general. Finally the writer is able to tell a story, perhaps very far from that which holds "the germ," regardless of the method used which is no longer autobiography slightly veiled (the silver cord unbroken) but has undergone a sea change of imagination.

Her short stories were her first published fiction, and they remain the best expression of her narrative purpose and method. In them she portrays the underlying sadness of existence in those whom Florence Haxton Britton called the "sparrows of life" [in *New York Herald Tribune Books,* August 16, 1931]. Her characteristic concern for the minute detail of environment, which sometimes obstructs narrative and gives a sense of monotony in longer work, is her most effective technique in presenting a single situation with fullness and meaning. Her artistry lies chiefly in her capacity to select and marshal details that evoke the implication of a situation and to penetrate with sensitivity the incommunicable responses conspiciously suppressed or submerged in her inarticulate characters. In her deft treatment of a single episode she communicates the essense of a character, the texture of an experience or mood, the meaning in a situation, or the subtleties of human relations.

No pattern can be defined with exactness to describe the method in every story. The revelation of an emotional experience may require the narrative to illuminate a moment or a day in a character's life, or even an entire life span. She is adept in limiting her selection of material to what is necessary and in choosing the most effective method for her particular purpose in each story. Her talent in the short story from her first publications has been recognized for its vigor and originality.

> She, like Sherwood Anderson, became a pioneering figure in the history of the American story, and if now her gifts seem less extraordinary than they did when H. L. Mencken first praised her work, it is because others have tried to follow the path she made. No short story writer in this country has done more to release the story from dulling "requirements of the trade." No writer has been more scrupulous in maintaining a high level of accomplishment.
>
> [Harold Blodgett, *The Story Survey,* 1939]

The stories collected in *Iowa Interiors* and *Children and Older People* are similar in subjects and themes—the rural scene with its impoverished and circumscribed lives. Underlying almost every theme are irony, pathos, and bitterness. In each episode her narrative method is adapted to the revelation of some inner response, a character trait, or a pattern of life. The situation is usually commonplace, uncomplicated and not dependent on dramatic incident or sharp conflict. Yet in each small tale plot is "complete with emotional culmination and decline clearly enunciated." She has greater concern for capturing the essence of character than for plotting a story. In H. L. Mencken's words, "the salient thing is the anatomizing of character" which he believed her to achieve with "penetration and understanding" [*American Mercury* IX, November, 1976].

The stories in these volumes have such familiar homespun situations as the gathering of families in reunions and councils; an anniversary celebration; a Christmas entertainment; a family vacation; Iowans touring in California; the reopening of a homeplace long closed, and the return to one's birthplace. Among the people are sensitive children, the failures, the disappointed and the unrequited, and the aged pathetic in their isolation. Small tragedies grow out of such relationships as those between a young girl and her first employers, a sacrificing daughter and a selfish mother, a reliable but unfortunate member of a family and the more prosperous brothers and sisters, old folks and the younger generation, renter and landowner, a minister and church members, a sensitive and sentimental woman and a grumbling pessimistic husband.

In her deft treatment of a single episode Suckow communicates the essense of a character, the texture of an experience or mood, the meaning in a situation, or the subtleties of human relations.

—*Margaret Stewart Omrcanin*

Characteristic of subject interest and skills are the stories that focus on a group of figures sharing in an act or moved by some common experience. The situation provides the means for exploring the interrelationships with which she is so frequently preoccupied. The revelation of emotions aroused by a situation that touches the lives of a family group becomes more important than what happens in the story. The situation is sometimes viewed through the perspective of one character. These stories are penetrating family portraits that reveal the characters' thoughts and emotions as well as their external appearances. Stories that illuminate motives and emotions of a group of characters responding to a single situation include: **"Uprooted," "Four Generations," "Mame," "A Rural Community,"** and **"The Resurrection."**

"Uprooted," her first story, portrays family members assembled to make a difficult decision. In an atmosphere of suspicion and hostilities, brothers and sisters are gathered in the dank chill and close musty air of the Shafer's parlor. The children and the old people are excluded.

Dominant in the family council was Sam, the successful brother from Omaha, who took the lead and assumed a brisk cheerfulness. He sat large, amenable, prosperous. His wife, Lou, spoke with a "majestic sweetness that created an instant atmosphere of suspicion," and sat with smiling unconcern "with her large hard bosom plastered with silver and beading, and her maddening air of being only remotely, and by virtue of her own graciousness, connected with the affairs of the Shafer family."

Art, the brother who was a preacher, spoke in his ministerial tone, "for which he hated himself," and searched for excuses on a moral basis. His wife, Jen, sat "ready to fly off the handle if anyone winked."

Mattie, a "bulkily built woman who seemed to overflow the small cane-seated rocking-chair," wore a look of protesting stupidity. Her husband, little Henry, summoned from his feed store, "swung his foot and examined the cracks in his fingertips. No one needed to consider him."

From the beginning there is conflict in the selfish scheming and distrust among them. Their hypocrisy is obvious in every statement. More poignant is the mute resentment of the old mother unwilling to admit dependency and the slow comprehension of the old man who had the "unfathomable look of old peasantry." He had "grown sweeter, vaguer, and more useless with the years."

The physical and emotional setting is presented in the opening scene.

> The sense of conspiracy that attends family conclaves lay heavy upon them. The air was thick with undercurrents of feeling, schemes, secret alliances and antipathies. They had all eaten too much and they sat with the discomfort of middle age in the stiff old-fashioned chairs. The three men were making a pretence that the whole affair amounted to nothing. They refused to meet the meaning glances, full of dire warning and portent, which their wives cast at them from time to time. Whenever, in a pause of the furious squeaking of Jen's rocking-chair, the clatter of dishes and shrill children's voices sounded loud from the kitchen, they were suddenly stricken, condemned with an obscure sense of guilt.

When the conversation shifts from neutral topics the pretense of a pleasant gathering is shattered. The cleared throats, the solemn quiet, and the shifting of positions mark the tenseness. In their evasive statements, lacking any subtlety, all express concern but decline to assume responsibility. Silently they seem to settle on the one least articulate and also least able financially to shoulder the burden. There is no love, sympathy or gentle sentiment among these people who neither feel nor comprehend the old people's attachment to home. Together they resolve nothing. But alone with the old woman her favorite son Sam, the most affluent, wins her trust.

The old lady distrusts all the others, but puts a pathetically mistaken confidence in Sam which he betrays by directing the action against her will. He resolves the problem hastily by proposing the home of his defenseless sister. He knows Hat is incapable of opposing him.

Through their expressed statements and the analysis of unspoken reservations, Miss Suckow reveals the pretenses and jealousies of these characters. She communicates with feeling the mute and resentful submissiveness of the aged and the inarticulate. Characteristic of her subdued irony is the solicitous comment of Jen: "It's good they [the old folks] have their children to look after them."

Often attitudes of characters are indicated by a consciousness of physical details as in Sam Shafer's observation of his sister-in-law. "He smiled sardonically as he saw Jen's tense listening back." Henry, the poorest, who had the least to say, sat swinging his foot and sucking in his breath. When a suggestion was made that affected his home, "he sniffed slightly but made no answer." All of the characters have something of obstinacy and selfishness and the only judgment implicit in the story is in Sam's reflection, "But it was too bad that the way of life was as it was."

Another story which explores thoughts and feelings of family members studied in juxtaposition is **"Four Generations."** In this instance conflict does not evolve from the incident itself but from the long-cherished and innate feelings that are merely brought to a sharp focus by the situation. An old homeplace is the scene of a family reunion at which four generations are represented. The story has more the static quality of a picture; in it the characters are ranged as in the photograph for which they pose.

While a heavy stolid country group waits against the wall of the farmhouse, four members of the family stand before the snowbushes to be photographed. Each one is described largely in physical details observable by those waiting.

Grandpa sits in his chair, small, bent like a little old troll, his blue far-apart peasant eyes with their still gaze, his thin silvery beard, hands gnarled from years of work, wearing the checked shirt of an old farmer. Next to him is his son Charlie, a small town banker, dressed in the easy garments of good quality and yet a trifle careless. Charlie's daughter Katherine is slender, haggard, worn, with dark intelligent weak eyes behind her thick-rimmed glasses. The child Phyllis, dressed in a yellow frock vivid as a canary bird, has "liquid brown eyes" and shining gold-brown hair, her bare arms round and soft and tiny, white and moist in the heat.

Both the party, waiting the right light for the photographer, and the onlookers are conscious of every detail of the setting in the brightest, hottest time of day—the flowers and green foliage, the orchard and the "green spreading cornfields where little silvery clouds of gnats went shimmering over the moist richness of the leaves." At the moment for the picture their breathless silence is emphasized by the contrast of the long whirr and rush of a car on the brown country road beyond the grove.

The rest of the day lags for the visiting relatives from town eager to get away. The inaction provides a quiet appropriate for exploration of the moods and feelings of the individuals who were photographed. Every analysis points to the persistent theme of the unfathomable disparities between generations—each is an enigma to the previous.

The great grandfather, like Grandpa Stille and Chris Schwietert in the novels, is uncertain and bewildered. Alienated from his children, he lives in the memory of the past. The old man had little to talk about with his son, a town man, banker, who smoked cigars and rode in a new car. The two sit silently in sight of the automobile, a coach with blue draperies on the windows. It is always a reminder of Charlie's wealth, his separation from the country family, and his readiness to leave the farm. Charlie is unsuccessful in drawing his father into a conversation about business or the crops. The only thing comprehensible in the old man's reverie is the muttering, "Dot was all so long ago."

In the long silence Charlie too reminisces with resentment at his own daughter's aloofness. Unlike her country cousins she had studied music and art, gone to college, married, and lived in the East. In her fastidiousness with Phyllis and her rigid attention to schedule she did not allow her father much freedom to enjoy his grandchild.

Katherine among the "womenfolks" is offended by the feminine grossness and vulgarities in the country women's talk which she has associated from her childhood with the family's visits to the country. She feels no ties to this ancestral home so unlike the quiet old frame house in New England that belonged to her husband's family. The fragile daintiness of the child Phyllis seems most incongruous with this rustic setting.

In the account of her few minutes alone with her grandfather the story takes on a touch of that tenderness which in Suckow's stories often relieves the drab and prosaic element that is so pervasive. As her grandfather rocked in the doorway of his room Phyllis stood outside and watched.

> The late afternoon sunlight shimmered in the fine texture of his thin silvery beard. It brought out little frostings and marks and netted lines on his old face in which the eyes were so blue. One hand lay upon his knee. She stared wonderingly at the knots that the knuckles made, the brownish spots, the thick veins, the queer look of the skin between the bones. She looked at his black pipe, his funny little cap, his slippers with the tufted flowers. . . .

> He stretched out his hand slowly and cautiously, as if it were a butterfly poised just outside his door. A sudden longing to get this small pretty thing nearer, an ingenuous delight, possessed him now that he was alone with her.

Old songs had been murmuring in his mind and in a faint quavering voice he sang one to the child. For a moment she was quite near, they understood each other. Then suddenly, instinctively aware of the strangeness of the place, she flitted away to her mother.

The story successfully evokes a scene and notes effectively such ironic contrasts and incongruities in the situation as the pose for the photograph that suggests an intimacy, closeness and pride in continuity that denies the actual lack of understanding, and the reunion in the ancestral home that is bitterly alien to the younger generation. It also contains the delicate touch suggested in the momentary grasp of some fleeting awareness of gentleness in usually stolid lives.

It may be said that in its lack of narrative action and static quality **"Four Generations"** is hardly a story. But it produces effectively a poignant impression. It also has interest in its inclusion of so many subjects, themes, and motifs of later stories and novels: the immigrant ancestry, the remote German grandfather; the conflict between generations; the movement from country to town; the preference for the East among the young; and the contrasts between rural and town members of the family. In this story, written in 1924, the character types selected to represent each generation are ones that receive repeated and extended treatment in longer fiction.

"Mame" also is a story that involves the relationships of a family group. The willingness to shift responsibility and to rationalize guilt feelings characterizes this family exactly as it does the Shafers in **"Uprooted."** Mame's letter stating her need to raise money for taxes is the occasion for her brother Louie's visit to the farm. Little happens to change the status quo. Mame and the other family members emerge through the conversation and the thoughts of the brother Louie. Her generosity, sacrifice, affection, and hard work all become known through Louie's rationalization of his need to avoid too great a sympathy.

On his way to the country he stopped first at his brother George's house. In the prosperous and hearty household his foreboding about Mame was minimized. The brothers agreed "there would always be something" with Mame and her husband, that "they were bound to be unfortunate." Exasperation was the accepted family attitude to Mame.

When he comes upon Mame's blind and crippled husband, Alick, whose "eyes were filmed and uncertain, his face sunken in mournful, hopeless lines," Louie's "eyes slid away from the painful sight. He would not admit it to his sympathies—must not, could not." His prudence would not let him pity. In Alick, Miss Suckow portrays the bitter and pathetic suspicion of the dependent and infirm. Mame's appearance tells the story of her life of toil. "She was a loosely built woman with straggling hair that had once been red, a corded neck and a kindly, sunken, helpless face." In her presence Louie is conscious of guilt for her eleven years of sacrifice for the old folks before they died. He had a remorseful affection for her, but it was tempered with his fear of his wife, the need for caution, and an irritation at her helplessness. Everything on the place was in poor repair like the "old rocker" that was still loose on its standard and came forward with a jerk that rasped Louie's nerves.

He is able to maintain a sympathetic attitude without obligation beyond a twenty-dollar payment on a sewing machine. This gift made him feel less guilty for what he did not plan to do. He also protects others in the family by discouraging Mame's plan to move in with them. In his resistance to any consciousness of affection or attachment to his home place, he is much like Sam in **"Uprooted,"** who is eager to get away from the sight of the wretchedness. The relationship between Mame and Louie is like that of the mother and Sam in the first story. In

Suckow at work.

her simplicity and trust Mame feels that Louie is more kindly than the others and puts more confidence in him than he deserves. Mame's troubles become more remote as he drives toward home; by the end of the trip he can almost dismiss any sense of guilt or responsibility. This story presents the poverty of the rural life, the pathos and ill temper of the afflicted, the impatience of the prosperous with the unfortunate, and the uncomplaining acceptance of hardship. Here as well as in **"Uprooted"** Suckow perceives the drab, the mean, and the selfish among the rural folks.

Another story in which the situation is a visit to the old homeplace is **"A Rural Community."** The main character, Ralph Chapin, has grown away from the rural life in his years of writing and travel. In the story he is more an observer and interpreter than a participant in any action. More sophisticated than the villagers, he possesses a self-awareness that they do not have. No longer a part of their life, he shares in it through his reminiscence and associations with the past. The country scene, the folk gatherings, the people, their conversation and rural ways are all seen through this perspective. He analyzes with some nostalgia his own responses to childhood scenes revisited and looks objectively at those who have stayed close to their own soil. In so doing he sees both the stability and the circumscribed pattern of their lives. This is one of the few stories in which a character becomes the interpreter of the rural life.

The story in which a family group is portrayed is sometimes merely a revelation of a momentary emotional response of one of the characters. In **"The Resurrection"** Suckow writes of an old woman's appearance in death—inexplicable and inscrutable. The familiarity of the beauty and strangeness which awes her children and grandchildren is perceptible only to her husband, an old man. He knows the look and half unconsciously struggles to know its meaning: it is the spirit of her girlhood—the spirit that had underlain the acquiescence, the seeming patience of everyday; her thoughtfulness that the children might not be frightened; her sense of propriety to look her best on important occasions; her religious spirit. A little hurt that the toil and familiar way of their life together had not erased her girlhood beauty, yet proud and tearful, he is unable to speak any of these thoughts. None of the emotion that stirred him is detected in his restrained comment, "Your Grandma looks—real nice—don't she, Nellie?"

The revelation of a character is achieved in some stories through the narration of a single incident that illuminates an entire life by arousing reflections and observations, his own or others. A retrospective view gives meaning to the incident in relation to a pattern that extends over a period of time. The essential qualities of the character are brought into focus by some situation in which the story "picks up the thread of a life at some moment when the swell and ebb of an emotion are most decidedly marked." The stories convey a sense of the totality of a life determined by some combination of circumstances or psychological factors. Largely concerned with her spinsters and her aged people, these portraits resemble the effect produced with brevity in the epitaphs of "Spoon River."

In **"A Home-coming"** the description of the town of Spring Valley, the almost forgotten Summer Street with its drabness and old houses, and the musty, gloomy interior of the Haviland house all prepare for the introduction of Laura Haviland. Her return to Spring Valley and her reopening of her house create interest in the townspeople. A visit from a friend of her youth is the main incident for stimulating Laura's sad feelings and her reflections on her past life.

Every detail emphasizes the consciousness of a spent life—of its loneliness, emptiness, and uselessness. The darkness of the room and the gloom of the unused house claim her attention more than that of the caller. Absorbed in bitter thoughts of her lost youth and empty future, she listens to her visitor's conversation with only polite attention. The demand for her help which had destroyed her opportunity for making a life no longer exists. Her hopes for marriage and her interest in music, like all other desires, had been relinquished to her mother's demands.

The poignancy of the story is achieved through the creation of atmosphere and the evocation of feeling. The return to the gloom of the unused house emphasizes for Laura more sharply the emptiness of her life without purpose, ambition, or meaning—all destroyed by family claims. Life here is a kind of entombment in the musty atmosphere of the neglected house and furnishings of outmoded splendor. In the realization of her loneliness Laura likens her life to Summer Street, which youthful drivers pass by, laughing and gay, because it "doesn't go anywhere."

"The Daughter" is a story with a similar theme. It has more of bitterness than the sad melancholy of **"A Home-coming."** The pervasive atmosphere of this story is the morbid gloom of sickness and death created by the descriptions of the place and people, all unlovely. It tells the meagre life story of Mary Lane who had cared patiently for an invalid mother. To her even the recurring spring brought sadness with a sense of time passing, and unfilfillment. Since her high school years Mary had been engaged to Henry Acres, a clerk in a hardware store who had never lost the country look. The delayed marriage took place after her mother's death. Mary was frail and broken and never escaped the sense of her mother's presence. After one year she died in childbirth.

In a second marriage her husband recovered from his loneliness and overcame the shy and clumsy ways for which Mary had pitied him. The child grew up with queer ways—she was sensitive, unresponsive, and reticent, a mystery to her stepmother but not to the ladies of the town who said, "It was easy enough to see whose daughter she was." The story, like *Country People*, reveals the lives with a conciseness and economy of analysis that communicate their meagreness.

"Susan and the Doctor" develops a similar subject and theme in which Susan's love affair with the doctor obscures all the rest of her life. The town maintained a consistent concern with the prolonged courtship. At first, Susan was a figure of interest and mystery, but later, one of pity.

While the doctor's obligation to an aging mother and aunt prevented their marriage, the lonely quiet surgeon found sustainment and release from his gloom in the reassuring devotion of Susan. Her own tastes, interests, and personality were submerged in her love for him which had to remain unsatisfied. But her dissatisfaction and apathy turned to fear when the doctor made no proposal after his mother's death. Forgetful of the love affair bound up with the old days of gloom, he turned to a girl younger and gayer than Susan had become. Emotionally depleted, Susan became resentful of the patronage of old beaux and the pitying tone of older women. Regardless of her own determination that her life was not finished, the women would never look at Susan as long as she lived in the town without thinking of the doctor.

"Mrs. Kemper" is a story of a woman's need for the security of affection. The women in the town observed her nervous manner and sunken figure and wondered why she need look like such a "bedraggled piece," a woman who had a nice home and a good husband, someone to look after her, and not a real trouble in the world. A timidity of manner and a halting approach spoiled all her attempts at sociability and dignity. Like Lillian White in *The Folks*, Mrs. Kemper required the assurance of her husband's love. She could never be sure he had forgotten the dead girl he had first loved. Because he had never said he loved her, a furtive uncertainty prevented her pleasure in her husband's success, their well-furnished country home, her social position, and even in her own sons. She dared not claim any of them.

> All her own treasures were sunk within herself, within this drooping pallor, and could never be loosened . . . she could not possess even herself without the key that had never been laid in her hand.

Her own brightness, laughter, and tenderness were all thwarted by her timid uncertainty. A lifetime of repression and humiliating suffering is compressed into the sketch of her life.

Miss Suckow's stories of the aged depict the meagreness and futility of their entire existence. The characters and the situations are much alike. The details of a single day's routine in the life of Seth Patterson in the story **"Retired"** epitomize the vacuousness in the lives of her inactive old people. The feeling of uselessness experienced by all of these characters is expressed in Seth's thought, "When a man's work was over, what was there to live for, anyway?" The loneliness and yearning for home that the old feel in unfamiliar settings is the theme of **"A Pilgrim and a Stranger,"** In **"Just Him and Her"** reliance on each other gives the only meaning to the lives of an isolated couple. They feel their age that was setting them apart from everything else, was pulling them together. So necessary are they to each other that their lives seem to stop almost simultaneously. The death of one follows that of the other after only a day's interval. In these three stories the sense of leftover, lingering life prevails, revealed in the characters' restricted activities, the limitations of their conversations, and even in the furnishings of their homes. In the nostalgia for the farm these old men show some of the most sensitive responses to the beauties of the rural scene that are to be found in the stories.

While characters always control the plot, some stories are more compact and are more sharply focused on a single incident to illuminate the character. One pattern in the stories is the narration of a single episode presented chronologically in the natural order of events, with dramatization of a conflict culminating in an emotional experience. The significance is in the single incident which has its beginning and end within the story and its action usually confined to a single day or some short period of time. These stories convey a greater sense of movement than those previously discussed.

"A Start in Life" is the story of Daisy Switzer's first day of hiring out. In the one day's happenings she realizes the difference between her status as the oldest child in her own home and that of a hired girl in the home of a young farm couple. Unaware of the anxious fatalism beneath her mother's warning, "this ain't like visiting," and unconscious of her homeliness, the skinny, unappealing child "stood at the little mirror preening herself," eager to wear her best ribbon. The child's pride at "starting to earn" and her anticipation of the venture are contrasted with the mother's sadness in her knowledge that Daisy "had so many things to learn." Every action and every word exchanged emphasize the contrast in moods. The day itself has a "cold rainy loneliness" and "chilly wind." The drive with Daisy seated in the back seat of Elmer's car which skidded over muddy roads soon puts her own weathered house out of sight.

Her arrival is temporarily ignored as the couple go in the house ahead of her and exchange conversation about their plans for the day. Her telescope with her clothes is almost forgotten and left in the car. A little saddened by the parting with home, Daisy still has the child's eagerness "to prick up her sharp little ears" at the mention of a ride later in the day and to watch hungrily where Edna put the sack of lemon drops. In her confidence that she is one of the household she leaves her unpacking for later in order to be "where the rest of them are." Throughout the afternoon Edna's efforts to clarify Daisy's status are persistent with the reminder "You know we got you to help." From Edna's impatience with her clumsiness and forgetfulness, the indifference to the child's efforts at conversation and to her complaints of a toothache, Daisy begins to feel a queer ache. "She sensed something different in the atmosphere than she had ever known before." The greatest rebuff is from the children. Her efforts to play with them send them crying to their mother. The lowered voices behind shut doors are only partially understood. But the consciousness of her new status, which she had been

unable to comprehend in her mother's sadness and Edna's efforts to exclude her, becomes painfully real when the family drive away in the car and leave her at home.

> There wasn't anything, really, to be done at home. That was the worst of it. They just didn't want to take her. They all belonged together. . . . She was an outsider.

The baby's rompers scattered on the rug and the Big Ben clock in the kitchen ticking loudly were reminders of her desolate loneliness.

> Her ugly little mouth contorted into a grimace of weeping. But silent weeping, without any tears; because she already had the cold knowledge that no one would notice or comfort it.

Every detail of the girl's appearance, her home, the drive, the chill and rain of the day, the trivial incidents, and the conversation in the household emphasize the pathos of the situation. Her final clear perception of her own desolateness is anticipated by every word and action of the story which gradually affect her own consciousness.

"The Man of the Family" is the story of a young boy's emotions. Very little action takes place in the story, but Gerald Rayburn, like Daisy Switzer, assumes mature responsibility. On the day of the school picnic he goes to work in Floyd Oberholzer's drug store to help support his mother widowed by his father's accidental death. On this holiday for other school children he sets about with dogged earnestness to learn the new job. With silent concentration he keeps busy at the little jobs made for him by the druggist and his wife.

His attitude toward his new role is expressed in numerous little actions which he identifies with his growing maturity. When his sister comes to the drug store, he rebukes her for wasting her time and money. At home he takes on his father's pattern; he washes his hands in the kitchen, drinks coffee for supper, accepts the extra servings because he had worked hard, and after supper sits on the porch.

He is at the same time stirred by boyish feelings—his disappointment at missing the picnic, the aching pain when he thinks about his father, and his burning embarrassment at a conversation overheard in the drugstore about his mother and a widower. But "above that ache of unmanly tears he felt a hard exultance in his new role." The culmination of this new feeling is expressed in the protective attitude to his mother and his rough dismissal of Art Fox, the widower, who comes to the house with a box of strawberries for the family. Resentfully he declines the gift and tells Art his mother is not at home.

> He was the man of the house now. Art Fox could stay at home where he belonged. This was *their* home. She was *his* mother. . . . They wouldn't laugh any more in the drugstore. They wouldn't talk about her.

His mother's resentment at his hostility is softened when she sees how proud he is of his strength. "He was only a little boy, after all—her little boy, sitting small and pitiful and unapproachable in the twilight."

The emotional impact is in its portrayal of Gerald's pride in responsibility along with his boyish sufferings. In this as in other stories of hardship and toil details are recorded with objectivity and restraint.

"Eminence" depicts the temporary joy of a child who has performed brilliantly turning almost imperceptibly into a bewildered loneliness. The parents of Florentine Watkins were vain in their desire for her superiority in everything—appearance, performance, and possessions. From the opening of the story with Mr. Watkins proudly carrying Florentine in his arms until the end where he carried her home through the snow, the parents were self-consciously proud of her superiority and tensely alert to hear every word of praise.

As the parents made their way through the church they were "thrillingly aware of the whispers all around them." Sunday School teachers, parents, and older girls gathered around the child in eager delight to admire the prettiest child in the Sunday School with her pale-gold curls, who was wearing white slippers and a white silk dress and a crown of silver paper tipped at the center with a star. Florentine, aware that she was the star of the evening, stood on the register, a little princess, small, calm, and sure of herself.

> Beneath her little smile, the glory of the occasion, of the moment, of the worship, was shining and singing through her.

During the program Mr. and Mrs. Watkins smiled slightly and clapped perfunctorily. They could not give ready applause until after Florentine's performance. Waiting for her turn, Florentine sat whispering her piece over and over to herself, almost in terror as she realized she "was Florentine Watkins. The whole church expected her to do well. . . . She could not breathe or live until this was over. She moistened her lips and moved one cold little hand. She was the most miserable one on the program."

While Florentine spoke, her mother's eyes were fixed in an agony of watchfulness on that small face, and afterwards "her heart steadied into a happy, elated beat as she drank in the applause." She could be happy that her child was the best on the program. Florentine accepted the homage with sweet childish royalty, but in her mind under all the glory was a tremulous, shining wonder that craved to be reassured.

The entertainment was followed by a party and a distribution of gifts. Florentine received an enormous doll, expensive and beautifully dressed. "She was mute with a surfeit of bliss." Other children crowded around her—their reactions of excitement, wonder, disappointment, and envy were noted by Mrs. Watkins. Soon satiated with the vision of the fairy princess and the big doll, the children drifted off to enjoy their own modest presents and to play games in which Florentine was not included. Other children received attention and praise. Florentine, who had

been noticed by everyone, was no longer one of them. As she looked after the other girls with a strange loneliness, she felt timid and no longer cared what people said. At the end of the program, the proud father carried her home and the anxious mother, mindful "that tomorrow will be here," was eager to put her to bed.

The nervousness of the attentive parents, the child's strain to excel, the childish perfection of her performance, and the admiration of the church members came to a climax of glory for Florentine. After the gift of the doll, however, the atmosphere changed. Other parents revealed envy, jealousy, and disapproval. "The Watkinses, on the very peak of glory in showing it off, did not know," and they remained insensitive to the child's loneliness and to the emptiness of her life, as unreal as that of the expensive doll she "must never let any of the girls handle."

The situation and occasion that provide setting for the little drama involve more personalities in the interplay of feelings—the parents and child, other parents and other children. The narrator moves from one to the other in recording actions, conversations, responses. A complete little drama is fully enacted between the arrival and departure of Mr. and Mrs. Watkins.

In **"Good Pals"** a couple's desire to fulfill a youthful romantic dream to watch a sunrise from a mountain peak is frustrated by the demanding needs of their frightened child who is left behind at a halfway cabin. The story presents more conflict of characters in relation to a particular incident and a desired achievement than is customary in Miss Suckow's stories. Here she shows her ability to present with feeling and delicacy the beauties of a scene other than the Iowa countryside and to give reality to characters who have a capacity for a physical delight in the beauty of the natural world. In describing the mountain climb she communicates with vitality their sensory response to the primal freshness and savage hugeness of the scene as the party comes upon the splendor of great pines, the plunging waterfall, the abundant wild flowers, the chipmunks and birds, and the chill fresh snow. The weariness of the toiling climb is also real.

The story centers on Hazel Benson's mingled feelings—her own youthful eagerness and romantic sentiment, her maternal protectiveness of the children, her sympathy and her resentment toward her husband's impatience at being disappointed. The conflict in loyalties to husband and children is resolved in a compromise that makes each more comprehensible to the other and strengthens the bonds of understanding and affection.

The Bensons have only done things they could all do together, but on this vacation Roy and Hazel plan to fulfill the dream they have had since their college days, to climb Black's Peak. The children's first protest at being left is pacified when they agree to stop at the halfway point for the rest of the night. Roy and Hazel have just started their dangerous climb in the moonlight when a frantic cry takes them back to the cabin where one of the children is sobbing in terror, the caretaker certain he is in great agony. Hazel immediately recognizes the cry as one of fear and not pain. She recalls a former occasion when he wakened in a strange place. Sympathetic to the child's fear she is defensive against Roy's impatience and at the same time resentful that he agrees to make the climb alone. Her grievance, however, lessens when he returns in a short time, unwilling to go without her. They compromise on a less difficult climb they can all make and half remorseful Roy and Hazel comfort each other in their disappointment.

In the experience of Miss Suckow's characters moments of exaltation that lift commonplace lives from their every day existence are rare and transient. The closeness of the familiar and the ordinary presses upon them while the dingy happenings of every day tarnish their splendor. **"Golden Wedding"** is a story of the celebration of a couple's anniversary. It is another of the stories that portrays character through the narrative of a single incident.

The dramatic conflict is one of character revealed in the responses to the events of the day—a day of unusual importance in the ordinary uneventful lives of Mr. and Mrs. Willey. Mrs. Willey's hopefulness, sentiment, and sensitivity struggle against her husband's pessimistic grumblings, his insistence on the prosaic, and his uncommunicative disposition. In the developments of the day she experiences that exaltation her spirit longs for, but by evening the radiance of the day begins to elude her.

It is through little details that conflict is expressed. Angie Willey, in anticipation of the festive spirit of the day, puts on her grey silk dress, lace collar and brooch to look her best before the people who, she is confident, will join them at her granddaughter's house. Asa, reluctant to acknowledge any excitement of the occasion, grumbles about putting on his best tie, utters forebodings about the weather, and doubts that anyone else will get out in the snow. This characteristic insistence on their insignificance and meagreness seems to Angie to deny their one achievement of continuity.

Beginning with the bobsled ride to the granddaughter's house the excitement mounts. The strangeness of the falling snow in the new, pure whiteness makes all feel the exhilaration of a festival. The cheerful welcome, the air of preparation in the subdued bustle, the perfect order of the mission table, the chairs set so neatly suggest something beyond the ordinary. Mrs. Willey's expectations are gratified when friends arrive shouting and waving from a bobsled. The dinner is the big event—the abundance of a harvest dinner served on a table set with the best china, silver, and tumblers in a room festively decorated with yellow crepe paper, wedding bell and cake. The occasion is enlivened by the arrival of a telegram from an absent son, the minister's speech, the presentation of an engraved silver loving cup, and even a speech from Mr. Willey.

After the dinner comes a ride in a sleigh furbished and decked with sleigh bells. The merriment in the greetings of friends adds to the hilarity. The stop at the photographer's climaxes the day's happy intoxication. Even the old man is lifted above the gloom and forebodings as he

raises his wife's hands clasped in his and shouts back at the people.

The happiness of the day gradually slips away. When the sleigh returns the best of the sunshine is over. At the granddaughter's house, friends are gone, and the women are weary. But they revive their cheer for the night meal of remnants after the outsiders have left.

Back at her own home standing bleak and silent with no shine from the windows and no smoke from the chimney, Mrs. Willey enters "with the feeling of a traveller from splendid scenes who still carries a trace of their radiance with him to shed upon the familiar home." In the house together there is nothing for the couple to do; alone they have so little to say. Their room is too familiar, their knowledge of each other too intimate for their speech to go outside its daily boundaries. Mrs. Willey wants to linger and talk about the details of the day; he is impatient to go to sleep. A thin bitterness "seeped through her proud exaltation, tincturing it with the familiar quality of every day." She knows she has to keep to herself her incommunicable thoughts both of beauty and bitterness.

In the story is the characteristic treatment of country scenes, houses and furnishings, family gatherings, and characters whose incommunicable thoughts are smothered in commonplace utterances. The excitement that mounts to an exhilarating peak is but a brief interlude that cannot restrain for long the intrusion of the drabness in their daily existence. The order of the story that begins and ends in the plain home of the old couple emphasizes its theme. The narrative movement toward a culminating but transient happiness dramatizes briefly the life of Angie Willey with its fleeting moments of brightness.

In two stories [Suckow] uses a moderately satirical approach to her treatment of characters and situations. In **"Midwestern Primitive"** the situation is slight—a tourist party from the East stops for dinner at a country inn near a small Iowa town. Two characters are portrayed with an almost satiric, but not unsympathetic touch.

In the story, Mrs. Hohenschus, a stubborn German peasant, refuses to dress or act according to the manner her daughter thinks proper. The daughter Bert manages The Hillside Inn. Bert has made every effort to make her dining room conform in decoration and service to the city tearooms photographed in her cooking magazines and has copied the napkins, decorations, and menus that appear in household publications. She is both bewildered and hurt when this special party from the city take delight in Mrs. Hohenschus's dandelion wine, her old-fashioned garden, her geraniums planted in old brown tile, and her plush album. They encourage her to make her naive revelations of family history in a "voice rich with chuckles and drolleries of German inflection," while they show their disappointment in the obvious standardization of decorations and menu where they expected to find rusticity.

The situation is one that might have been presented with Sinclair Lewis's biting sarcasm to ridicule the visitors as well as Bert for their standards of conformity. In the whole recital only Mrs. Hohenschus is free from pretense. Yet in the presentation there is a sympathetic understanding of Bert's defeat and disappointment.

The story **"Auntie Bissel,"** appearing in the volume *Some Others and Myself,* was written and first published in 1935. Like the others in the book, it is the sketch of an unusual character who lived intimately and vividly in the memory of the narrator. Otherwise it is unlike any of the other stories in that collection or in the earlier volumes. It is beyond the shadow of gloom and suffering, of sickness, age, and death.

In Reverton, Iowa, in the early 1900s Auntie Bissel had lived in a regulation house which could have been preserved as a museum enshrining all the bad taste of the period. After her husband's death, she moved to California where some years later an Iowa friend visited her. There in the golden sunshine of southern California, the matron from Iowa blossomed in the atmosphere of youthful happiness. With a comic touch almost unique in her stories, she describes Auntie Bissel's fulfillment in the humanly conjured fairy land.

Her visitor found her living in a semi-Spanish house with a gleaming up-to-date porcelain kitchen, her appearance and dress evidence of her new good fortune. The great coil of hair formerly worn in a topknot was bobbed and frizzled. With an effervescent delight she took her visitor to see all the marvelous sights in her newly found Paradise, climaxed by a trip to an elaborate memorial park with a mausoleum, the "most effulgent blossom of this civilization." It best symbolizes the ideals to which Auntie Bissel responded.

In that resting place the ancient gloomy symbols have been replaced by a statue of a child, the symbol of "eternal youth and invulnerable happiness." It represents a curious mixture of an exalted worship of the ancient and a modern up-to-date aspect. The ashes of the great reposed in urns more grandiose than those of ancient Greeks.

> those of other humbler ones . . . were stowed away in what resembled nothing so much as glorified white marble post-office boxes—and to make the resemblance complete, and to give the whole idea of burial the personal touch, these boxes were labeled with "exact reproductions" in everlasting bronze of the actual autographs of the owners.

This extravaganza of a grandiose American dream is the only instance where Miss Suckow looks critically at the superficialities in American culture. But in the presentation of this farcical and melodramatic tribute to birth and death there is no barb in her portrayal of Auntie Bissel's delightful naïveté.

The stories collected in *Some Others and Myself* (1952) are a departure from her familiar objective portrayals of commonplace lives. They are less compact, intensely personal sketches of the unusual and the non-typical, differing from earlier stories in narrative method, tone, and attitude. In five of the seven stories the narrator is a first person observer with an intimate knowledge of the characters whose lives are sketched with a gentleness and tenderness. The narrator's tone sometimes approaches that of the personal essay more than of the short story and allows the author greater freedom of interpretation. Mood, however, more than structure distinguishes these stories from earlier ones.

> **In retrospective mood and with deft strokes Suckow creates her vignettes, lavishing on each the art, care, and attention that produce the reality of a bygone time.**
>
> *—Margaret Stewart Omrcanin*

She continued in them to be the marvelous observer, but in these stories her impressions are more than clear reflections. In three of the stories, **"Mrs. Vogel and Ollie," "An Elegy for Alma's Aunt Amy,"** and **"One of Three Others,"** the narrator reminisces from the point of view of one who returns to scenes where years before she had been charmed by the rare qualities of the women she depicts. In retrospective mood and with deft strokes she creates her vignettes, lavishing on each the art, care, and attention that produce the reality of a bygone time. In all the stories of the volume there is a sense of picturesque but decaying charm in which ghosts of a life gone by linger with an enchanting tenderness. There are touches of the macabre, the mysterious, the fanciful, and the childlike wonder. Interpreter as well as narrator, she searches for meaning in the lives of the "odd discards, half hidden . . . and yet spectacular." These fond tributes to characters she had known and loved are inspired by the same appealing quality she eulogizes in her sketch of Amy Root.

> Her life was an air that sounded muted and interwoven with others, with no one ever to play and to make audible its separate music.

Some shadow of sorrow or mystery pervades the atmosphere of most of the stories and the lives of the characters. In **"One of Three Others,"** Jennie Gruenwald's deafness and later her mental aberration enshroud her life in half darkness. In her late years only a few intimate friends can recall the charm of the woman who became an aged and withered child clutching a rag doll. There is charm in the slight madness and childlike wonder of Mrs. Vogel whose yard is like an "outdoor attic, full of horticultural relics," and her orchard "a witch's orchard" with its fallen misshapen fruit nested in the matted grass. In **"Merrittsville,"** a faded gentility and an air of mystery impress a visitor with the feeling that "the clocks were stopped and the whole household lived on in an unmeaning timelessness after time was over." The spiritual grandeur of her husband's nobility lives in the memory of his widow. The sad and waning beauty of Amy Root reveals some sense of disappointment held and cherished. The faded flower of her girlhood lingers about the room with the little reed rocker, her satin sachet on the dresser, and the old-fashioned perfume bottles tied at the neck with blue ribbons. In her shadowy role in her sister's home she keeps her life closed in the box of faded photographs and keepsakes shown only to intimate friends in a kind of plea for recognition of the unanswered claims of her pretty girlhood. In the story **"Eltha,"** an ethereal quality and a sad enchantment of a stricken child give her the appearance of "Snow White lying in trance in her crystal coffin." Another story [**"Memorial Eve"**] reveals memories of family sorrows and pent-up sufferings struggling for release as a woman visits family graves on Memorial Eve in an atmosphere of impending war.

In her last collection of stories and in her last novel, both of which came after the ten-year interval from 1942-52 without publication, Suckow's art shows a less stark realism and a less rigid objectivity. The retrospective view of the stories is not unlike that of the "Memoir" with which they were published. They could and probably do contain much actuality—memories stored up from childhood impressions of the old ladies to whom she was always attracted. A fondness for the nostalgic and an interest in the eccentric, flavor these reminiscences, most of them about women in the twilight of life. But in their somber and sad lives there is less sense of futility and bitterness, and more courage and dignity expressed simply and movingly.

A woman in **"One of Three Others"** accepts with resignation the burden of a helpless sister and lavishes upon her all her care and goodness of heart. The strength of the ordinary daughter, Ollie Vogel, remains firm and reliable in contrast to the whimsical fancies and aberrations of her childlike mother. Mrs. Merritt and her daughter are sustained in their poverty by the memory of her husband's integrity. Mabel Mosher in **"Memorial Eve"** releases her pent-up suffering by easing the bitter aloofness between two families. **"Eltha"** is the story of the confining and wearing care of an afflicted child which becomes a service of love transcending duty and ennobling a mother.

In one of the stories Miss Suckow's own regard for the significant in life and in fiction is ascribed to a character to whom the story of Judge Merritt is disclosed. The judge's experience had been a disaster resulting from the bank failures of the depression. When his wife recounted the details to George and Mary Sedgewick, who were paying guests in the Merritt home, George Sedgewick fitted the bit of local history into the "framework of social-economic reference." But Mary expressed a consistent attitude of Miss Suckow's when she contended

> that what happened in a particular way, under its own particular terms and circumstances, mattered too. A particular instance mattered.

Setting forth the particular circumstances in the destinies of non-spectacular lives remains the purpose of all

Suckow's fiction. The variation of her method in her later stories points to the extension of her earlier purpose but not to a contradiction. In 1951 she reiterated a previously stated concept but with some expansion of her original idea. Her last publications indicate that the statement described her intention for later writing.

> On my own part, I would liken a story (as I would like to tell a story) to a reflection in very clear water, which seems to give back the scene itself, but with a depth and a slight mystery, sense of atmosphere and meaning, there being a current in the stream as well. I also feel more and more that slight touch of elegance . . . may be given by the author and in this way add a certain personality.

Abigail Ann Hamblen (essay date 1978)

SOURCE: *Ruth Suckow*, Boise State University, 1978, 48 p.

[*In the following excerpt, Hamblen explores the role of suffering in Suckow's short fiction, especially feelings of loneliness, rejection, and helplessness in her characters.*]

Among [the] fundamental problems of human existence, Ruth Suckow's fiction examines the important problem of individual isolation. Every serious writer has been forced to recognize this problem and to make it part of his picture of human life. Ruth Suckow's work is full of lonely people. . . .

Loneliness is, of course, only one problem that besets mankind. It is probably no more distressing, in the long run, than old age. Some of Ruth Suckow's earliest stories have to do with elderly people. In one short story after another, she takes up the theme of old age with its attendant illnesses, discouragement, and bitterness. Most of her novels have old people as subsidiary characters. Suckow has drawn them with sure strokes and has shown us, with compassion, that "the sunset years" are not always a "golden age." In one place, for instance, she speaks of five retired farmers sitting about in the "produce house." They are "rough and weather-stained like old furniture that had been left out in the weather."

In the short story **"Retired,"** big Seth Patterson, who has come to town to live, feels his health deteriorating: there is a heavy sensation in his chest. But what if it does seem to be getting worse? It does not matter. If a man cannot work any more, what is the use of living? Old Enos Bush of **"A Pilgrim and a Stranger"** has a similar feeling about his illness. Taken with his wife to stay in his son's home, far from their own town, he will not admit that the change of climate is beneficial. He resents the solicitude of the family and the presence of other old derelicts whom he sees on park benches, "so rootless, so homeless and strange." He wants to be home, and if he cannot be there, he does not mind dying.

All older people seem to find themselves lonely, with a loneliness that can never be assuaged. They suffer the solitude of those who have been cut off from other generations. Enos Bush and his wife feel that they no longer have any connection with their pleasant son, even though they are living with him: "They had never since they had first come in the spring, dreamed of intruding even their interest upon him."

The old German grandfather in **"Four Generations"** feels a gulf between himself and his son. The description of him sitting in his hickory chair is like a picture done in soft tints:

> Small, bent like a little old troll, foreign with his black cambric skullcap, his blue, far-apart peasant eyes with their still gaze, his thin, silvery beard. His hands, gnarled from years of farm work in a new country, clasped the homemade knotted stick that he held between his knees. His feet, in old felt slippers with little tufted wool flowers, were set flat on the ground.

What possible rapport can he have with the plumpish, small-town, prosperous banker who is no longer his young helper in the fields and who has a fine car and smokes expensive cigars? He goes into his reverie and mutters at times, "Ach, ja, ja, ja . . . dot was all so long ago." . . .

Equally pathetic is the plight of the old couple in **"The Uprooted."** The parlor, where their children meet to decide what to do about them, is dank with a "close, musty air." Meanness is almost palpable in the little group of men and women who, without the parents themselves being present, are going to make decisions about them. The old mother, weeping in her dingy bedroom, is not an appealing sight. "Her thin gray hair, streaked with brown . . . was wildly disheveled. The tiny braid . . . was slowly uncoiling like a bit of twisted wire . . . her wrinkled brown cheek drawn up with crying."

But emptiness, loneliness, poverty, and illness may be bearable if one has no bitterness and no straining sense of frustration. Many people come to their last years with a feeling that life has cheated them. Innocent and trusting, the Nobles of **"Wanderers"** find that their best is not good enough for the tiny church they try to serve. Only disappointment and a knowledge of betrayal lie ahead for them . . .

Not long after she wrote **"The Uprooted,"** Suckow wrote a strange little story which she called **"The Resurrection."** It has its place with her other stories of old people because it concerns the elderly, but it also goes beyond old age in order to deal with death. Here, with characteristic insight, she shows that death does not have to be merely the end of life. It can be a triumph that sweeps away the sordidness of decay and decline, a triumph that negates the disappointments of the last years. . . .

Old age may be bitter and full of pain, dull with frustration, or perhaps terrifyingly empty. But with its remote beauty, death is also capable of granting individuality and meaning. Looking at his wife in her coffin, the old husband of the story is touched by awe and wonder, for she lies before him self-contained and untouched, a personality complete and radiant, whom he has never really known. Death has smoothed away the marks of life and has revealed a wonderful, immortal thing. Realizing the power of death, the very aged can take heart. Dying can sometimes be the ultimate satisfaction.

If it had no other excellence, Ruth Suckow's fiction would still be notable for its portrayal of women and for its delineation of problems peculiar to them. As Leedice Kissane says [in *Ruth Suckow,* 1969], she "is always convincing when exploring the depths of the feminine consciousness."

From teen-agers to ancient grandmothers, her women move through the stories and novels, their perplexities and desires vivid and unforgettable. In Suckow's fiction the viewpoint is almost always feminine, a narrative strategy which is calculated to appeal to feminine readers and to raise questions in the minds of the masculine.

The problems of these women are many and various, but in almost every case they fit into one of three categories. The first of these is the necessity for sacrifice. Too often women must give their all to husband, lover, children, or parents. A second concerns a woman's relationship with a husband or lover, particularly the difficulty a woman has in trying to communicate with the man she loves. The third, and by far the most important problem to anyone searching for social significance, is the conflict which can be caused by a woman's desire to give up everything for romantic or sexual love.

Writing about the novel *Cora,* one reviewer remarked that Ruth Suckow is "The champion of women who have not yet found their place in a society that offers the conflicting inducements of independence and domesticity" (*The Bookman,* July, 1930). Although true, the statement does not go quite far enough. "Domesticity" is a weak word to apply to the rapture of surrender for which most Suckow women long.

Disturbingly, from a survey of the whole body of Ruth Suckow's fiction, a single impression stands out: she invariably sees women as victims. They are not necessarily victims of society or of men. Often, indeed, they are conquered by their own biology. To put the matter crudely—simply because they are female they crave a mate, not only to satisfy a physical hunger, but also for emotional security. By virtue of being *women,* they must suffer. Leedice Kissane phrases this problem in another way: "sacrifice is coincident with feminine destiny—a conviction that runs through all Miss Suckow's fiction." . . .

In Ruth Suckow's fiction, as a whole, there are a variety of feminine characters. Some of her women are strong and ambitious, but they lack the saving ingredient of ruthlessness that would let them succeed as [the protagonist of *Cora*] does. Consider **"A Great Mollie,"** first published under the title, **"As Strong as a Man."** With what gusto Mollie wrestles with her old Ford when she drives about the country selling underwear! She is big, hearty, and avid for life. Her selling seems purely incidental in the course of her busy days. Has a woman's hen run away? Mollie will catch it for her. Does another customer find herself behind with her ironing? Mollie will finish it for her. She will even stay to dinner and joke with the husband. Then she will help him "figure out" just what is wrong with his cider press.

Her vitality is enormous, overwhelming. Great possibilities have always existed for her somewhere in the future. Her life has been a series of projects, vigorously pursued but unsuccessful. The skunk-farm idea failed, and so did the raising of violets and the breeding of goldfish. But surely somewhere there is something to take up her tremendous energy, something in which she can triumph. In the city, perhaps, if she can get away, she can go into business. Visions mist her eyes. These visions are all the life—all the "success"—she will ever have, tied as she is to a brother whose only pleasure is to potter about building bird houses, and tied to a sister whose one passion is housework. For, strong as she seems, Mollie is not able to extricate herself from family ties, family bickering, and the small, nagging demands of every day.

Something of Mollie's vitality characterizes Jessie Grunewald, who appears in **"One of Three Others."** Jessie suffers wild flares of useless rage against the things which each day asks of her. She could have done so many things! She is large enough to encompass the world, but instead, frustrated by poverty and by some strange quirk in her own temperament, she lives out her days in the old home at the edge of town, storming at her tiny, self-contained sister.

A great many Suckow women are susceptible to passionate love or give themselves in passionate devotion to duty. Susan in **"Susan and the Doctor"** is strong, even hard. Yet her affair with the doctor, which she carries on for some years, takes control of her whole personality. She becomes more understanding of others, the whole of her familiar world takes on a new aspect, and she knows more joy than she had ever thought possible. Margaret Ferguson of *The Folks* involves herself in an intense, passionate love that takes over her whole life. In much the same way, Cora succumbs to a vacation romance, for a short time letting herself live blindly, dazed with happiness.

As for passionate devotion, nothing could be more moving than Ollie Vogel's story in **"Mrs. Vogel and Ollie."** Papa, dying, has asked that she keep Mama happy, and Ollie strives to do so, knowing that Mama, dear and sweet and delightful as she is, cannot bear unhappiness. Mama loves to have neighbors come in for coffee of an afternoon, and she loves to feed tramps. She also loves to play about in the frowsy garden and to go fishing. She is able to enjoy all these things because Ollie endlessly cooks, bakes, washes dishes, weeds vegetable plots, and keeps house. When her mother is gone, Ollie is left alone, deserted by those who were wont to "drop in" day after day. "Oh, they could all come back," she bursts out bitterly, "and I'd bake cake and cookies, if they'd just recognize they wouldn't have had all those good times if there hadn't

been somebody to stand at the stove! Well, I know I'm ordinary. Maybe cooking was my part."

The Suckow world has its weak women, too, and they are drawn with the same kind of compassionate but relentless detail which Suckow has afforded the others. Spoiled by her parents, Marjorie Schloessel of *The Odyssey of a Nice Girl,* is often bewildered and uncertain about just what she wants from life. *The Kramer Girls* tells the story of Rose, who is often too easily led by others.

Ruth Suckow's women are of great interest in the light of the underlying theme—the victimization of women, for the only women she shows to be happy and fulfilled are those who live on the surface of life. The others are always conscious of a hidden yearning, of a vital lack.

—*Abigail Ann Hamblen*

In contrast, Suckow creates portraits of women who are happy because they are content to live on the bright surface of life. In **"Auntie Bissel"** the central character is an extrovert, gaily, exuberantly fatuous, a delightful creature. Her house, with its fringed "throws" and cushions and tiny, rumpling rugs, with its fat pug dog and its wonderful cooking, has a "rich aura of the commonplace brought to a climax." One unforgettable decoration is Gracie's picture, which immortalizes the little daughter who, as Auntie Bissel says with ready tears in her round eyes, has "fallen asleep." No one is surprised to learn that when she has been left a widow, Auntie Bissel goes to California to revel in sunshine and youth. There she adores the "stars" and child actors, grows misty-eyed on excursions to Forest Lawn, and tints her hair golden and her lips poppy-red.

Moreover, who can be more fun than the old German hausfrauen, Mrs. Hohenschuh in **"Mid-Western Primitive,"** as well as Mrs. Vogel? One can almost feel their presence. One can almost see their beaming smiles and their heavy, shapeless figures. One can almost hear their hearty "Ach, I don't know." They are so successfully whole—all of a piece—in their looks, in their voices, and in their attitudes, that only quotations can impart their flavor. Consider Mrs. Vogel. "She was past seventy when I knew her. Her figure was motherly, her walk a grandmotherly waddle, the thick little curls at the nape of her fat neck were silvered. But her eyes were young. Looking into them suddenly—when she came to the door exuding welcome—there was always that shock of delight: the marvel of discovering, within the shining brown of the old woman's gaze, the world of childhood all intact and joyously alive."

Ruth Suckow's women are of great interest in the light of the underlying theme—the victimization of women, for the only women she shows to be happy and fulfilled are those who live on the surface of life. The others are always conscious of a hidden yearning, of a vital lack.

Rarely does she show us a marriage or even an extramarital relationship that is perfectly satisfying. Mrs. Schwietert, for instance, loves her husband, but must acknowledge that he does not provide adequately for their children. Her face shows "a compression of the lips, and tears in her quiet gray eyes." Mrs. Ferguson of *The Folks* is a fortunate wife. She harbors a feeling of discontent, a confused impression that she has had to sacrifice too much of herself for her family. Hazel of **"Good Pals"** feels herself cut off from her husband by the maternity she had welcomed. The old free, loving companionship is gone, no matter how tenderly she tries to renew it, and the claims of the children are too insistent. In **"Susan and the Doctor"** a girl's life is enriched and made meaningful by a passionate love affair; yet even here there is hidden resentment. Susan feels at times that she must give up too much for her lover.

Even the mores which help to stabilize society work against women. For generations these mores have implied the dependence of women upon men—"second class citizenship" as the Women's Liberation movement says. Ruth Suckow subtly suggests this dependence with her description of Mrs. Emerson's problem in *The Bonney Family*. The Emersons' daughter has made an unfortunate marriage. Mr. Emerson has set the son-in-law up in business for the last time and has told Geraldine that this time if the young man does not succeed, she may come home, but only without him. "And he ought to know Geraldine won't do that," Mrs. Emerson says tearfully to her friend. The home is comfortable, and Mrs. Emerson is a petted wife. But her husband, after all, is the only one who can say whether the daughter may come home to live and to bring a husband. "If Mrs. Emerson won, she would have to win by weeping and pleading—because Mr. Emerson was indulgent; not because it was she who was right."

An apt summary of the feminine plight in Cora's dark brooding appears just after her daughter is born. Those around her think that the baby will be a "comfort." "As if it could be any comfort to have brought another girl baby into the world to find everything leagued against her—find that, no matter what she did or what she wanted, she was between the devil and the deep sea!"

Reading [Suckow's] fiction, one is conscious of a pervasive *Welt Schmerz,* for she emphasizes the universal problems of loneliness, of old age, and of feminine frustration. Even in their happiest moments, her men and women are conscious of an underlying vein of sadness. Few writers have been able to convey pure agony as tellingly as she does: for instance, Lillian's terrible mute suffering in *The Folks* as she sees Carl slipping away from her; and in the same novel, Margaret's wrenching despair when her lover leaves her. Some of the short stories, notably **"Experience,"** take up the theme of ag-

ony. Here a young woman must face the death of the man she loves. In doing so, she discovers that not to feel the almost unbearable pain of her loss would mean that she must feel an emptiness even more dreadful.

Essentially, then, Ruth Suckow sees life as an ordeal. No one may escape suffering. There is no relationship, however beautiful and satisfying, that does not have its inner core of discontent, of bitterness, and of disappointment. In her quiet "Memoir" Suckow says that she herself had experienced the sadness of loss, the pain of temporary alienation from a father to whom she was devoted, and that she had undergone the bewildering search for a philosophy that she could live by when she found that the old beliefs were untenable. But in her early middle age she found that one may triumph over pain and grief and doubt. She found her personal answer in the core of the Judeo-Christian religion—the Gospel of Love. For her, "Love" was not a cant word. It seems to have meant, quite simply, an emotion of utter selflessness that can change a person's life from one of despair to one of shining triumph. In many cases, as she points out, loving is very difficult. But eventually it will transform any situation.

Some of her later fiction illustrates this concept explicitly. The short story which she is said to have liked the most, **"Eltha,"** is a good example. Written in the first person, the story tells of a farm wife whose little daughter is stricken with a paralyzing disease that must have been poliomyelitis. For more than ten years the child lies helpless on the sheet-draped couch, unable to speak, probably not even sentient. Her mother, the Aunt Clara of the narrator, looks after her tenderly. Aunt Clara has much to do, since she has three other children and is noted for her wonderful cooking, but in order to care for the child she must frequently interrupt every activity: "Only for a few minutes could Eltha be left alone." Because one or the other must always be there, mother and father can never leave the house together. Few relatives are free to help, and if they are, they are unable to understand the wants of the little girl. Moreover, they are not able to interpret "those discordant, strangled sounds, which to Aunt Clara tell so much."

Years of devotion go by, and then at the age of thirteen the little patient catches the flu and dies. The pitying relatives all breathe the words "mercy," "release," and "relief." Life on the farm goes on; the other children grow up; Aunt Clara and her husband, both neat and frugal, attain a measure of comfort.

But when after a lapse of time, the narrator pays a visit, she is struck by her aunt's character:

> A blending of qualities: of passionate feeling with clinging love, feminine shrinking and timidity with womanly strength; daily kindness, deep if limited intuitive understanding; still deeper tenderness—informed, almost too much informed, by suffering. . . .

> Yet the thing that stayed with me was a single gesture—her turning from the stove, with face flushed, and eyes

open so that for a moment I looked clear into their depths, and saying to me:

"I miss Eltha."

With that the young niece realizes that Aunt Clara's maternal duty toward a stricken child had indeed been transformed and glorified by love. "Her service was love, and could not be fathomed."

As a short story, **"Eltha"** is not as good as some other stories by Suckow. A conscientious critic could point out faults of structure and some prolixity. But as a statement of affirmation it is flawless. . . .

Through all her fiction Ruth Suckow sought something. She sought the means of meeting the immense problems of loneliness, old age, and the frustration of cherished dreams. She sought an alternative to the restless search for a happy end to all endeavors. In her seeking she was forced to reject the one organization that was supposed to be able to help, for the church failed her.

But eventually life itself gave her what she sought. Life led her back to the ideals of her early beliefs to show her that the answer is rooted in love, in the love that can come from sorrow and pain. This love is unquenchable and immortal. It is the love which the church had been established to promote. Illness, despair, and death will come, but love can arise from them. Through love one can triumph over these dreadful adversaries.

From the gentle resignation of her first published work, a quatrain, she arrived at the triumph of her last novel. . . .

She had found a way not only to accept grief, loneliness, and pain, but also to transform them. She had found that life will never conquer the spirit that has discovered the unyielding strength of love.

Ruth Suckow is a regional writer. In many short stories, in several novels, especially in *The Folks,* she anatomizes Midwestern life and gives us incomparable pictures of Midwestern people and their environment. But she has also done much more. She has shown us universals. She has given her readers an understanding of fundamental human problems in quiet inland places. She has shown not only the amazing force of love on a midland farm, but also the tragedy that can strike average people in an Iowa town. Her works stand as proof that one need not go to far and exotic lands or to famous cities in order to live profoundly.

Fritz Oehlschlaeger (essay date 1980)

SOURCE: "The Art of Ruth Suckow's 'A Start in Life'," in *Western American Literature,* Vol. XV, No. 3, November, 1980, pp. 177-86.

[*In the following essay, Oehlschlaeger examines the first story in* Iowa Interiors, *"A Start in Life," which, he says, demonstrates "the meanness, repression, and degrada-*

tion that occur when economic relations between people supplant human ones."]

When Ruth Suckow's first volume of short stories, *Iowa Interiors,* appeared in 1926, no less a critic than H. L. Mencken hailed the book with unqualified enthusiasm:

> Who . . . has ever published a better first book of short stories than this one? Of the sixteen stories, not one is bad—and among the best there are at least five master-pieces. I mean by masterpiece a story that could not imaginably be improved—one in which the people are overwhelmingly real and not a word can be spared. All of these people are simple Iowa peasants. In other hands they would slide inevitably into stock types, ludicrous and artificial. But Miss Suckow differentiates them sharply, and into every one she breathes some-thing of the eternal tragedy of man. Her talent is not unlike Sherwood Anderson's, but her mind is more orderly than his. She gropes and guesses less and is hence more convincing.
>
> [*American Mercury* IX, November 1926]

Despite Mencken's praise, however, Miss Suckow's rep-utation has been modest at best. She is generally men-tioned, with varying degrees of favor, in the standard works on American regionalism and local color fiction. . . . All of these works are unquestionably sympathetic, but none has done enough to illuminate the particular quality of Suckow's short fiction that Mencken praised—her fine artistic command of language and detail. Indeed, in Suck-ow's best stories, "not a word can be spared."

In his review of *Iowa Interiors,* Mencken did not identify specifically the five stories he deemed masterpieces. But I feel sure that one of these must have been the volume's opening story, **"A Start in Life."** In no story is Miss Suckow's sure command of the significant surface—her ability to make every detail count—more apparent. What I propose, then, is to look carefully at the art of this deceptively simple tale of a hired girl's first day of work. My purpose is dual: to reveal the thematic and artistic preoccupations of a remarkable short story, and, by ex-posing the story's artistry, to assert the value of Ruth Suckow's fiction.

As its title suggests, **"A Start in Life"** is a story of initiation, in this case the initiation of a young girl into a life of grinding economic necessity and subservience. The story's outward action can be very simply told. Suckow focuses on Daisy Switzer's first day of work as a hired girl in a rural community of Iowa. The opening scenes of the story take place at the Switzer's house, as Daisy's harried mother, herself a hired domestic, works frantically to get her daughter ready to go to her new position. Daisy is then picked up by her employer, an up-and-coming young farmer named Elmer Kruse, and driven to the Kruse farm, where she spends the day learn-ing her duties. When she arrives at the farm, Daisy overhears Mrs. Kruse's mentioning to her husband that she would like to go for a drive to her mother's late in the afternoon: a drive that Daisy looks forward to through-out the day. The story's crisis occurs, then, when the Kruses decide not to ask Daisy to go driving with them. Being excluded brings Daisy her first awareness of her status. Mrs. Switzer had told Daisy that going to work for the Kruses would not be like "visiting." By the end of the story, Daisy has begun to understand her mother's meaning.

Although the two most thorough studies of Suckow's fic-tion [Leedice McAnelly Kissane, *Ruth Suckow,* 1969, and Margaret Stewart Omrcanin, *Ruth Suckow: A Critical Study of Her Fiction,* 1972] tend to underplay her interest in sociological and economic issues, it seems to me that **"A Start in Life"** is best read as social criticism. What Daisy Switzer begins to understand at the end of the story is what it means to be regarded simply as a commodity. What Ruth Suckow dramatizes is the dehumanization that occurs when the labor of one person is owned by another. Moreover, Miss Suckow directly attributes Daisy's deg-radation to her lack of economic power; we are carefully told that Daisy has inherited neither property nor status from her dead father. Thus the story is an implicit criti-cism of the American dream: in a community where land above all is power, the landless remain poor and subser-vient from generation to generation.

What Daisy does inherit from her father is brilliantly sug-gested by the opening scene, which takes place in the bedroom of the Switzer home. Throughout that scene, Suckow focuses on a central symbol, a "battered tele-scope" which is the only luggage available to carry Dai-sy's belongings to the Kruse farm. As she attempts to pack Daisy's clothes into the old telescope bag, Mrs. Switzer looks at it with a "helpless, anxious fatalism that it would have to do somehow." This line later reverber-ates with striking irony when we are told that the tele-scope "was an old thing, hadn't been used since her husband, Mert, had 'left off canvassing' before he died. And he had worn it all to pieces." Thus Daisy's legacy—and burden—is the very symbol of her father's landless-ness, the telescope that he had carried as a traveling sales-man—one who in a rural community is without land, power, and the accompanying status. Mrs. Switzer's know-ing "fatalism" surfaces again when she says to Daisy of the telescope, "'Well, you'll have to take it the way it is'." This statement applies with fine irony to all of Dai-sy's legacy. In the telescope that Daisy carries out the door, Suckow has found an appropriate symbol of the girl's inheritance from a father who was "battered" and "worn all to pieces" by work in a world where he had no place.

The powerlessness that results from the Switzers' eco-nomic condition is also carefully suggested by Suckow's opening description. The Switzers' lack of control over their own lives extends even to the most trivial of life's details:

> Daisy's things were scattered over the dark brown quilt and the rumpled sheet that were dingy and clammy in this damp weather. So was the whole bedroom, with

its sloping ceiling and old-fashioned square-paned windows, the commode that they used for a dresser, littered with pin tray, curlers, broken comb, ribbons, smoky lamp, all mixed up together; the door of the closet open, showing the confusion of clothes and shabby shoes.

Yet Daisy seems quite undisturbed by her chaotic sur-roundings and blissfully unaware of the reality of her economic condition. Bound by the egoism of the child, she looks forward eagerly to beginning work and feels "important in her small world." Her mother of course understands the reality of working for other people and tries delicately to prepare Daisy for the blows her ego is about to receive. The result is some finely understated moments that gain additional irony as the story unfolds. When Daisy realizes, for instance, that she will not be able to take all of her clothes, she suggests that she will pick them up some week when she rides into town with the Kruses. To this her mother cautions, in a line that directly anticipates the story's climax, "'Yes, but maybe they won't always be bringing you in'." Or, as Daisy stands in front of the mirror adjusting her ribbons, Mrs. Switzer says, "'You needn't be so anxious to fix yourself up. This ain't like going visiting'." Such is the under-statement of a parent who wants to prepare the child's ego for the shocks and changes of experience without destroying it altogether.

The first step in Daisy's coming to self-awareness occurs at the end of the story's first section as the car in which she is riding pulls away from the Switzer house. Sudden-ly she has "a startled view of home": its shabbiness, the litter in the yard and the unkempt grass, the solemn faces of her brother and sister, the drawn face of her mother. As she sees the "playthings they had used yesterday," Daisy is seized by a sharp sense of separation and begins to wave frantically, both to her mother and to the life of protection she is leaving behind. For a moment Daisy's mother seems to share this brief epiphany; she waves back to Daisy and then stands for "a little while" in the yard, as if in recognition of the moment's significance. The reader is poised for a revelation from Mrs. Switzer, but Suckow denies us this revelation and closes the section instead with two lines of cutting ironic force: "Then came the harsh rasp of the old black iron pump that stood out under the box-elder tree. She was pumping water to leave for the children before she went off to work." The utterly impersonal working of the pump here is a revelation in itself; Suckow seems almost to suggest that work has lit-erally obliterated Mrs. Switzer's personality. And in the final sentence Suckow manages an irony that any femi-nist will appreciate when she implicitly attacks the dis-tinction between Mrs. Switzer's pumping water for the children and the domestic "work" for pay that she goes off to do.

As she leaves her mother's home, Daisy begins to seek emotional identification with the Kruses, who subtly but determinedly insist that she learn her place as the hired girl. Indeed much of the emotional force of the story's later sections derives from Suckow's juxtaposing Daisy's need for inclusion in the Kruse family with the Kruses' insistence on her exclusion. Daisy's identification with the Kruses begins on the ride to the farm. She feels "the grandeur of having a ride" and is "proud . . . of going out with Elmer and Edna." She wants to know the names and ages of the Kruse children, though she does not ask these, and she hopes that the Kruses will take her to the movies on Saturday nights. She even begins to feel a pride in the Kruses' power and status in the community: "Elmer and Edna were just young folks; but Mrs. Metzinger said that they had more to start with than most young farmers did, and that they were hustlers. Daisy felt that the pride of this belonged to her too, now."

But there are subtle suggestions, even in section two of the story, that Daisy's attempts to identify with the Kruses will prove to be futile. When Daisy gets into the car, for instance, Mr. Kruse puts her in the back seat next to a bag of groceries, an obvious act of distancing that even Daisy seems instinctively to recognize: "She wished she were in the front seat with Elmer. She didn't see why he hadn't put her there." Moreover, the distancing largely accomplishes its purpose, as very little conversation passes between Kruse and Daisy on the way to the farm. He offers nothing about his family or about the people whose farms they pass on the way. When Daisy finally breaks the silence, "calling out" from her distance, "'Say, how much farther is your place?'," Kruse blurts out, "'What's that?'," obviously taken aback by her familiarity. Later, when Daisy arrives at the farm, she is left to stand forlornly on the porch while the Kruses enter the house, their attention taken up with their own children. Elmer Kruse also neglects to bring in Daisy's telescope until reminded by his wife to get "'Her valise—or whatever it is—out in the car.'" Finally, when Daisy tries to share something of her own life with Mrs. Kruse, she is quickly reminded of her status. Remarking on the Kruse children, Daisy says to Edna, "'I didn't know both of your children was boys. I thought one of 'em was a girl. That's what there is at home now—one boy and one girl'." Clearly Daisy is trying here to elicit some emotional response, some evidence of interest, from Edna. But Edna barely acknowledges Daisy's remark about her family; instead she seeks immediately to establish the proper distance between herself and this too familiar little girl: "'You know we got you to help me,' she reminded."

The tension between Daisy and Edna Kruse becomes the major focus of the story's third section. With a few deft strokes, Suckow characterizes Edna as a cool, efficient, and capable woman. As she did earlier in drawing Mrs. Switzer, Suckow uses details of setting to suggest the personality and condition of Edna Kruse. A vision of order and cleanliness, the Kruse house stands in stark contrast to the Switzer household. When Daisy arrives at the Kruses' she is led up "bright new stairs" into a hall where "two strips of very clean rag rug were laid over the shining yellow of the floor." The floor of Daisy's room also has the look of bright varnish, a look that dominates the Kruse household. But for all its cleanliness and enforced order—or perhaps because of them—the Kruse house seems cold to Daisy: she is "chilly" as she stands in "the bright little kitchen . . . with the white oilcloth on the table, the baby's varnished high chair and his little fat, mottled hands." The chill flows from Edna Kruse herself, a severe young woman whose concern for propriety makes her suppress every generous impulse toward Daisy.

Edna's behavior toward Daisy also reflects her habit of control. At this point we should remember what Daisy's friend Mrs. Metzinger said of the Kruses: they "had more to start with than most young farmers did, and . . . they were hustlers." What the Kruses have is land, and with it, power, the ability to control their own lives. That ability is suggested by Suckow's descriptions of their almost obsessively ordered house, just as the chaos of Mrs. Switzer's house functions to suggest her basic lack of power. The ability and desire to exercise power dictate Edna's treatment of Daisy as well. In the process Daisy is dehumanized, reduced from person to commodity. Edna does this without malice, and that is what makes it even more terrifying. She simply insists that her relationship to Daisy be a purely economic one, the relationship between employer and labor. But what Suckow reveals, in a subtly understated way, is the brutal insensitivity that such a fundamentally dehumanized relationship necessitates.

Edna's degradation of Daisy manifests itself in her language. Despite her apparently kind intentions, Edna speaks to Daisy only in commands or sarcasm. Edna's concern for propriety appears in several statements to Daisy of the following kind: "'You must help, you know. That's what you are supposed to do.'" When she is not directly insisting that Daisy learn the duties of her place, Edna employs sarcastic rebukes. When Daisy's efficiency fails to meet Edna's expectations, for instance, she is met with, "'You might bring me a dish, Daisy'" or "'Now you might take Billy into the kitchen out of my way, Daisy, and amuse him'." Each of these statements may seem inoffensive in itself, but Suckow builds them up carefully and unobtrusively until they unmistakably suggest Edna's subtle degradation of Daisy.

Even more effective is Suckow's emphasis on the difference between Edna's treatment of her own children and her treatment of Daisy. When Daisy first arrives at the farmhouse, she is left to stand on the porch while the Kruses carry their own two children inside. Later, when she first picks up the baby Billy and he breaks into tears, Daisy is rebuked while Edna comforts her son and even Elmer fusses over him. Edna's way of comforting her son is very revealing: "'Don't cry, Billy. The girl didn't mean anything.'" Here Daisy is only the girl, stripped of identity and self-worth. Edna is telling her son implicitly that this is no one he will ever have to worry about, only "the girl," the hired girl (there may even be a frightening play of words on Daisy's not "meaning anything"). In a later scene, Daisy seeks comfort from Edna by complaining of a toothache. Again Suckow stresses the difference in Edna's responses to Daisy and to her own children. Edna answers only "'That's too bad'" to Daisy's complaint while at the same time giving "a secret little smile at the baby asleep on a blanket and a pillow in one corner of the shiny leather davenport."

Still another scene pits Daisy directly against one of the Kruse children in a conflict that is filled with symbolic suggestion about Daisy's condition and ultimate hopes. Edna asks Daisy to entertain Billy by playing with his building blocks. Daisy is delighted by this request, undoubtedly because she sees it as a gesture on Edna's part toward including her in the family. Indeed Daisy feels "a thrill of comfort" as she leads Billy to the kitchen, where she previously had felt only chilled. As she had earlier in the car, Daisy feels a sense of pride in what belongs to the Kruses, these marvellous blocks out of which "she could make something really wonderful." Daisy's pathetic longing for inclusion in some human community manifests itself in what she begins to make of the blocks: "She put the blocks together with great interest. She knew what she was going to make—it was going to be a new house; no, a new church." But the new church is never completed; Billy knocks it down, sweeping the blocks across the floor of the kitchen. Daisy's immediate response is to pull him away to a far corner of the room, where he sobs until Edna arrives to comfort him and again rebuke Daisy: "'Never mind, lover . . . Of course he can play with his blocks. They're Billy's blocks, Daisy . . . He doesn't like to sit and see you put up buildings'." Edna's logic is brutally clear: what Daisy wants, what she aspires to, simply does not matter. Only Billy matters, because he owns the blocks. Power and worth lie in possession, in property; those like Daisy who are without it can only hope to serve those who have it.

What happens to Daisy is terrifying precisely because it is so commonplace: Suckow's achievement lies in exposing to us the meanness, repression, and degradation that occur when economic relations between people supplant human ones.

—*Fritz Oehlschlaeger*

The story's climatic moment occurs just after Daisy's confrontation with Edna over the blocks. It is a climax that confirms Daisy's status as commodity. Earlier in the day Edna had indicated to her husband that she would like to go for a late afternoon drive to her mother's. Daisy overheard this, assumed she would be included in the ride, and looked forward to it throughout the day. But Edna has resolved otherwise. When it is time for them to leave, Edna confers with her husband, a conversation that Daisy partially overhears:

> 'Kind of hate to go off . . . I know, but if we once start . . . not a thing all day . . . what we got her for . . . ' [ellipses Suckow's].

The scene provides an apt metaphor for Daisy's relationship to all the forces, economic and social, that control her life. Her fate is determined in another room, by voices that she can hardly hear and whose meaning she does not comprehend. Daisy is merely a commodity, to be used and manipulated by those with greater power than she has. She is not fully human to the Kruses, a fact that Suckow suggests unequivocally in this climatic scene. After the Kruses have obviously decided not to take Daisy with them, Elmer Kruse hurries outside to busy himself with warming up the car. He apparently feels guilty at excluding Daisy, but he feels neither sufficiently obligated to Daisy nor sufficiently courageous to offer her an explanation. He simply avoids her. Edna Kruse similarly treats Daisy as a non-person. She says only, "'We're going for a little ride, Daisy'" and then rattles off a series of chores to keep Daisy busy while they are away. And at this point Suckow includes one telling detail that says everything about the relationship between the Kruses and Daisy; while Edna is assigning these duties, "she did not look at Daisy."

All of this is not lost on Daisy. She comes to a clear recognition of her status as an "outsider" in the Kruse house, and she begins to sense the full meaning of "starting in to earn." She has learned, in short, a crucial lesson in survival. But such survival comes only with great cost, as Suckow implies in the story's richly suggestive final paragraph:

> Her ugly little mouth contorted into a grimace of weeping. But silent weeping, without any tears; because she already had the cold knowledge that no one would notice or comfort it.

Daisy has already begun to learn that survival as a hired girl, as labor, requires emotional repression—requires her to be less fully and responsively human than she might otherwise be. In short, Daisy must accept the definition of herself forced upon her by the Kruses: she must become a commodity in order to avoid further hurt and pain to herself. Such is a "cold knowledge" indeed.

Alfred Kazin once argued that there was "more significant terror of a kind" in the fiction of Sinclair Lewis "than in a writer like Faulkner or the hard-boiled novelists, for it is the terror immanent in the commonplace." I think much the same might be said of Ruth Suckow's **"A Start in Life,"** as well as of several other stories in *Iowa Interiors*. Certainly the story creates a kind of terror, the terror of Daisy's isolation and progressive dehumanization by the Kruses. And it is a terror skillfully created by Suckow out of the most ordinary of situations, the most commonplace of life's details. Indeed what happens to Daisy is terrifying precisely because it is so commonplace: Suckow's achievement lies in exposing to us the meanness, repression, and degradation that occur when economic relations between people supplant human ones. That achievement is a considerable one, more than enough to earn Miss Suckow Mencken's praise and our continued attention and respect.

Fritz Oehlschlaeger (essay date 1986)

SOURCE: "A Book of Resolutions: Ruth Suckow's *Some Others and Myself*," in *Western American Literature,* Vol. XXI, No. 2, August, 1986, pp. 111-21.

[*In the following essay, Oehlschlaeger speculates that the stories in* Some Others and Myself *received less critical attention than Suckow's previous efforts because of their informal, reflective style, but maintains that this style is suited to the overall purpose of the author, which is to allow the significance of the stories to be perceived collectively rather than individually.*]

Despite the praise of so distinguished a critic as H. L. Mencken, who compared her favorably to Sherwood Anderson, Ruth Suckow has not received a great deal of critical attention. When her fiction has been discussed, most of the interpretation and praise have been given to her novels of generational change and family conflict, *Country People* (1924) and *The Folks* (1934), and to her first book of short stories, *Iowa Interiors* (1926). One volume that has received almost no attention is her last book of short stories, *Some Others and Myself* (1952). The neglect of these stories is no doubt due to what [Leedice McAnelly Kissane, in *Ruth Suckow,* 1969] has called "their relaxed and some-what discursive" manner. Clearly the stories in *Some Others and Myself* do lack the tight plotting and disciplined concentration of effect that one expects from the short story. In their sprawling, meditative style, they seem at times more properly reminiscences or personal essays. But I would argue that this style is precisely suited to the purposes of these stories and that the significant aesthetic effects of *Some Others and Myself* must be sought in the volume as a whole rather than in its individual parts. Looked at in this way, *Some Others and Myself* reveals both its great beauty, which is a beauty of resolution rather than of conflict, and Suckow's best quality as a writer, a certain Jamesian fineness of mind that refuses ever to simplify the human.

Some Others and Myself consists of seven stories, only two of which had been previously published. The volume closes with Suckow's autobiographical work, "A Memoir", which was also given separate publication in 1952. Of the stories, five take place in the small Iowa towns that generally provide the setting for Suckow's fiction, while a sixth, **"Merrittsville,"** is set in a small Kentucky town. The remaining story, **"Auntie Bissel,"** traces a transplanted Iowan to her home in California. Five of the stories are narrated in the first person, with the "I" involved at times as a participant, largely in remembered action, but more frequently as an observer and listener. The other two stories are narrated in the third person through central female figures whose experience conforms in some degree to Suckow's and whose points of view dominate their respective stories. The pattern of both individual stories and of the volume as a whole is one of return and resolution. In the first story, **"One of Three Others,"** the narrator returns to visit a pair of aged sisters, antithetical in many ways, who have lived together, somewhat stormily, throughout their lives. In the second story, **"Mrs.**

Vogel and Ollie," the narrator remembers a pair of women, here a mother and daughter, whose lives were also linked through many years. The third story, **"Merrittsville,"** moves the action away from Iowa to a Kentucky town where Mary Redmond and her painter husband hear the story of the town's chief citizen's financial collapse and heroic efforts to repay his creditors. The next story, **"Auntie Bissel,"** moves the scene to California, which Suckow satirizes pointedly.

"An Elegy for Alma's Aunt Amy" marks a return to Iowa and a return by the narrator to visit a mother and daughter whom she had known years earlier. In **"Memorial Eve,"** Mabel Mosher returns to honor the family graves in the home town from which she has long been absent. In the final story, **"Eltha,"** the narrator remembers the family of an aunt and uncle whose life was dominated largely by the care of a child afflicted with polio and left virtually insentient. The story beautifully balances the first in the book, **"One of Three Others,"** with its depiction of the Grunewald sisters, one of whom is nearly deaf and almost as demanding on her sister as Eltha, the stricken child, is on her mother. Interestingly, in a letter to her publisher, Suckow identified these two stories, **"One of Three Others"** and **"Eltha,"** as being those closest to actual reminiscence. Even as she designed the volume, then, Suckow repeated the patterns so dominant throughout the stories: she began with what was nearest to her, moved away from it, and then returned.

As my descriptions of the stories make obvious, *Some Others and Myself* is a book of women. Suckow begins the book's first story, **"One of Three Others,"** with an explanation that her purpose is to record and recognize the lives of women that would otherwise remain unnoticed. "We have doubtless all heard talk of good old days," she begins, "when society was rightly balanced, because women were women." Such superficial cultural assessment depends on an assumption that Suckow wittily assails:

> The assumption holds of a standard Woman, correctly situated inside the household, important but submissive, keeping her cellar stocked with home canning—an American pioneer version, more robust if less lovely, of the lace-capped Victorian lady seated in her low chair, occupied with needlework, lifting her dovelike gaze at the entrance of the lord and master. I heard such an allusion only a few hours ago in an oration on the radio.

Suckow's subjects are not representatives of this "standard Woman" but others who are "left out of the oration." These are women "deeply marked by that conception of 'inside the home' with all its assumptions," but they are marked in ways that no sociological analysis of the condition of women can fathom. These women are literally "half hidden" from view, and it is to bring their lives to light that Suckow writes.

If *Some Others and Myself* is a book of women, then, it also is a book of persons, for Suckow repeatedly emphasizes the concrete person's transcendence of all categories. In this purpose lies the reason for her stories' relative loose-ness and meditative quality. Suckow is not so much inter-ested here in the hard edge of character, which the tightly unified short story can brilliantly reveal, as she is in depth of character, which develops and discloses itself only through long experience. The depth of her characters' lives emerges not from a single dramatic action or gesture but from long-sustained, repetitive actions. Because the drama of her "half hidden" women plays itself out only over a long course of time, Suckow turns to a relatively free form that combines a focus on the present with recollection and meditative interpretation of character. This is not to say that she abandons the devices of the short story altogether. Several of the stories lead to moments of climactic percep-tion or epiphany, and her command of the significant sur-face of detail to reveal character is everywhere apparent.

Two purposes of *Some Others and Myself,* then, are to make visible the lives of otherwise invisible women and to insist on the irreducibility of concrete persons. A third purpose is suggested by the book's title, which points not only to the fact that it contains stories and a memoir but also and more significantly to the self's necessary rela-tionship to others. Whatever the self is, Ruth Suckow insists, it becomes so only among other selves. The nar-rator of several of the stories realizes this as she returns to the others who have been such a part of her own past. Again and again she discovers the close, sometimes suf-focating, interdependence of others and at the same time the role of those others in making her what she is.

All of Suckow's themes are evident in **"One of Three Others,"** which focuses on the Grunewald sisters, Jessie and Jennie, and their life together in the family house after the deaths of their father and brother, both success-ful businessmen widely loved for their liberality. The sisters are a study in contrast. Jessie is large, robust and rather sloppy, full of big-hearted generosity and kind-ness; Jennie is small and pretty, quiet, immaculate, and self-contained. Jennie, whom the narrator knows only as a woman of seventy and older, has been nearly deaf since girlhood, but she does not seem "a damaged creature." Instead her deafness has only intensified her own quali-ties, especially her devotion to home and the memory of her parents and brother, a devotion she elevates to a kind of piety. Jessie, on the other hand, is full of plans: to "take up nursing," to "study undertaking," "to be a flo-rist, to run a restaurant, [to] give massage." Jessie's plans founder on the rocks of family tradition, causing her more than occasional resentment of Jennie and her familial piety. But Suckow resists any easy categorization of Jessie as a victim. The "old ways and ideas and ties" come to seem "concentrated" to Jessie in the "dark, faint-voiced, ever-present figure" of her deaf and iron-willed sister, "but what really held Jessie were the ties themselves" and her own way of honoring them.

Two incidents will illustrate the conflict between the sis-ters and the story's wonderful blend of comedy and seri-ousness. While setting the table one evening, the sisters quarrel over which set of silverware to use. After the always more liberal Jessie has set out the "good silver,"

Jennie "took it off and put on the old tarnished German silver," so suggestive to her of their parents and the past. Jessie then "shouted, tossed the German silver back in the drawer," and "banged the good silver on the table," all loudly enough, of course, so that for once her near-deaf sister could not ignore her. Jennie, however, refused to eat with the good silver and went back for her own, at which point Jessie yielded, as she characteristically did in their conflicts, though not without tears. Significantly, neither woman seems to have considered the possibility of their each using a different setting.

A second revealing incident occurs in the cemetery, where Jessie and the narrator have gone walking. Jessie, inter-ested in people and the larger community, knows "the history of almost every grave." She and the narrator are "off in a corner" discussing the graves of another family when the "little dark figure" of Jenny, with hat and bas-ket, enters at the gate and pointedly ignores their greet-ing. Later at the house, there is a "storm" between the sisters, for Jennie has considered it "impious to feel an interest in any but the graves of the family and perhaps a few close friends." She goes to the cemetery only "for business."

In the closing pages of the story, the narrator returns to visit the sisters after Jennie has become quite old, immo-bile, and somewhat senile. What she finds is that the two have "reached a kind of resolution." At the last Jennie has had to turn to Jessie, knowing "like the neighbors, that one could ask Jessie anything." On the other hand, "now that Jennie was helpless, Jessie had an object" on which to "lavish all her care and goodness of heart." Such close-ness meant that now their "revulsions" were "often at their strongest," but still "at last their interdependence was acknowledged and felt." During the last visit between them, Jennie quite surprisingly recognizes the narrator, saying, "'She looks good.'" It is a minor moment in the story but nevertheless something of an epiphany for the narrator, for it reveals what the always guarded Jennie had never quite acknowledged: that she considered the narrator a friend. At the close of the story, the focus is firmly on Jennie. "I suppose anyone could name her state senility," comments Suckow, always skeptical of catego-ries, "but what does that term describe?" "Why use fixed terms about life?". Jennie was "still Jennie" to the end, though more intensely. Her so-called aberrant behaviors were only more intense versions of things she had always done. She started little brush fires at the corners of the yard because she was always proud of wasting nothing, and she sat clutching a rag doll in the same way she had caught up small visiting children or her beloved cat years earlier. Even in this final ugliness, Jennie Grunewald seems "'a little wonder'" to Suckow, and one "certainly off the pattern of the standard Woman."

The next several stories in Suckow's volume amplify the themes introduced in **"One of Three Others."** **"Mrs. Vogel and Ollie"** presents a mother and daughter who are as close as the Grunewald sisters. A woman of child-like innocence, Mrs. Vogel becomes the center of an unusual human communion consisting of a local poet, a

Marxist handyman, a former town beauty now "in a state of advanced ruin," the "last survivor of a pioneer group of Middle-European tree grubbers," and a rather coarse "widow woman" who loves lewd stories. For years this group gathers in Mrs. Vogel's kitchen, where there is always a great Germanic plenty of coffee, cookies, and cakes, mostly supplied by Ollie, whose retiring quality causes her to be overshadowed by her mother. In the latter part of the story, however, the narrator discovers a depth of strength in Ollie that she had not previously seen. Mrs. Vogel is now dead, and Ollie tells the narrator a tragic story of her brother's supposedly accidental death. Hansie's death was actually a suicide, but Ollie protected her mother from this fact for years. Thus Ollie, at great cost to herself, has paradoxically been the source of her mother's innocence.

Suckow's artistic credo emerges clearly in **"Merrittsville."** When Gene and Mary Redmond stop at a tourist home, they hear from Mrs. Judge Merritt the story of her late husband's catastrophic financial losses during a recession and his heroic attempts to pay back his creditors by sacrificing all. Gene, a painter, finds the story quite typical, able to be "fixed into the framework of social-economic reference," but to Mary it seems "old and fresh at the same time." She sees nobility in the Judge's refusal to take advantage of the bankruptcy laws and a refreshing deviation from type in the story's "not going on to any of the more familiar denouements, of the penitentiary, suicide, or getting off personally scot-free." As the story closes, Mary is reflecting some years later on her husband's paintings from the period and on a photograph of the Judge given her by Mrs. Merritt. The paintings she finds "highly representative of Gene's work at the time—thoroughly typical"; in short, they are failed art, the art of one who, believing only in the typical, failed to see the living particularities of experience. The Judge's picture, by contrast, seems "to have grown stronger and clearer instead of dimmer with time."

The movement away from Iowa continues in **"Auntie Bissel,"** whose title character is a widow resettled in a "semi-Spanish" house in southern California, which Suckow depicts as a dream factory reminiscent of Nathanael West's Hollywood. The satire concentrates on a particularly vulgar mausoleum where the ashes of the "stars" repose in "urns more grandiose than those of the ancient Greeks." Despite the falseness of her environment, however, Auntie Bissel remains essentially innocent and worthy of respect. To her "pure naivete," California is simply a source of wonder. Once again the person is, for Suckow, greater than any external analysis can apprehend.

In contrast to the garrulous Auntie Bissel is the quiet, decorous Amy Ramsey, who has once lived in California but returned to Iowa. The dignity of **"An Elegy for Alma's Aunt Amy"** derives from precise emotional and ethical notation. One of seven children, Miss Ramsey stayed with her father after her mother's death, thus ensuring her spinsterhood. But toward her family she holds no resentment. She has been somewhat disappointed in life, and indeed she "cherishes" that disappointment be-

cause it is part of her history. But it does not affect her essential charm and freshness, or the "slight, fine humility" that is the dominant feature of her character.

The need to abandon resentment is the theme of **"Memorial Eve,"** in which Mrs. Mabel Mosher returns to her home town to honor the dead on Decoration Day. Mrs. Mosher has long been away from this town and cemetery because of a bitter conflict between her family and another family, the Dollingers, occasioned by the First World War. The Dollingers used their influence to keep their son out of the War, which in indirect but nevertheless significant ways has claimed both Mabel's husband and brother. But when Mrs. Mosher sees Roswell Dollinger and his wife tending their own family's lot, she recognizes a chance "to get rid of her own accumulation of poisonous resentments." In a potentially melodramatic moment deftly lightened by Suckow, Mabel speaks to the Dollingers, who appear somewhat absurd. Mrs. Dollinger stands with her mouth open, while he "struggled to his feet, raised his hand confusedly as if to lift his hat, seemed to have forgotten he wasn't wearing one." The comic relief is welcome, but it in no way undercuts the fundamental seriousness of Mabel's reconciliation to her former community.

"Eltha," the final story in *Some Others and Myself,* is one that Suckow rightly considered to be among her best. The story beautifully balances the collection's opening story; reaffirms the need, stressed throughout the book, for an organic link between past and present; and recapitulates the volume's major themes: the heroism of half-hidden women, the person's transcendence of categories, and the self's creation through its life with others. In the narrator, too, we see the by now familiar patterns of withdrawal, return, and maturation, here in response to suffering and its place in human life.

"Eltha" focuses on the effects of a nearly, perhaps completely, insentient child on the lives of others, her mother especially, but also her father, twin sister, brothers, and cousin, the narrator. The narrator begins by remembering her yearly visits as a child to Aunt Clara and Uncle Ernie's, moves next to a later Thanksgiving visit when she has become a young woman and Eltha has been dead for some years, and concludes by reflecting on the family after her aunt, too, has died and her uncle has remarried.

The relationship between the dependent Eltha and the devoted Clara recalls that between the Grunewald sisters in the year before Jennie's death and gives final climactic emphasis to Suckow's theme of human interdependence. Clara emerges as a heroine throughout, not through grand gestures but through the patient daily care of the child. Indeed Clara seems to make less of the care than those who see the relationship of mother and daughter only from the outside. They speak frequently in commiseration of "Poor Clara!" but for her the care is something very much "taken for granted" and unworthy of others' pity. Here again Suckow emphasizes the person's resistance to categorization; in almost existentialist fashion, she insists that what can be seen by observers from outside is simply not commensurate with the reality one lives from within.

There is discussion among the aunts and other cousins as to whether Eltha "'realized,'" and one aunt, "sounding medically learned," declares authoritatively that "the brain was numbed, in a certain center. 'She *doesn't* know. And it's merciful.'" But Clara insists that Eltha does "know" and that the child communicates to her through what seem to others only her "little unco-ordinated movements, and sounds." Similarly, when Eltha dies, a general judgment of "mercy" and "relief" goes up, and the narrator does find life at her aunt and uncle's "easier, warmer, less austere." But the one "thing that stayed" with the narrator from her Thanksgiving visit some years after Eltha's death was "a single gesture" of Clara's, an impulsive "turning from the stove, with face flushed, and eyes open so that for a moment I looked clear into their depths, and saying to me: 'I miss Eltha'." Others might see Eltha's death as a mercy or release, but for Clara it was a deep loss. Suckow underscores her point about the differences between "outside" and "inside" perceptions in the narrator's reflection on her aunt's revelatory statement: "The figure of the afflicted child became wholly human. I sensed communication in the strangled sounds, the unfocused violet gaze that used to make me afraid." To any external view, Eltha's life might seem as wasted or blighted as it is possible for a life to be, but when the narrator is privileged to see Eltha even for a moment from within her mother's view, she sees her as "wholly human." Obviously Eltha can do nothing we would define as useful; she can perform no ordinary human functions that are observable or measurable from outside. She frightens the narrator with her unfocused gaze, as others like her frighten all of us, because she seems at once both human and disturbingly non-human. Suckow's presentation of Eltha thus climaxes the personalist theme she has developed throughout *Some Others and Myself*. Against all functionalist definitions of the person, Suckow shows that what makes Eltha "wholly human" is her ability to communicate some inwardness, however muffled and indistinct, to a receptive Thou, in this case her mother.

The epiphany between Clara and the narrator also climaxes the latter's education in suffering, a subordinate motif developed with great honesty by Suckow throughout the story. As a child the narrator sympathized with the suffering of animals on the farm, even that of the flies Aunt Clara caught on big sheets of fly paper. These the narrator tried to save, "with exquisite care pulling out the little threadlike legs of those strugglers who might still be rescued." But for her cousin Eltha the narrator's "pity was more or less abstract"; indeed Eltha's "signs of illness" were "a kind of outrage" to the "feeling of health" the narrator sensed both inside and all around her. The difficulties of her aunt and uncle were similarly incomprehensible; since they were "grown people," their "sufferings were in a different world." When the narrator later returns after Eltha's death, she at least does feel "relief," for she is "glad" she "would not have to see Eltha." At that time the narrator would have feared seeing Eltha even more than she had as a child, because she "would have comprehended more" and could no longer escape by going "to the aid of the flies." On that visit, however, the narrator arrives at a deeper understanding of suffering. Her aunt

comments that she had "never liked that old fly paper either," but that "there were many things you had to do, it seemed, especially on a farm." It is this orientation to duty that the narrator comes to admire finally and which helps her to overcome her fear of suffering. From Clara she learns that one does what one must, no matter how much suffering one encounters, or experiences oneself, or incidentally creates.

"Eltha" closes with a brief reassertion of the interdependence of human lives and an affirmation of continuity with the past. First the narrator speculates on the effect that Eltha and her mother's relationship has had on the other members of the family. After Eltha's death, her always sensitive brother Don fell ill, perhaps in search of the tenderness his mother had previously given Eltha. The narrator poses the possibility of such an explanation for Don's illness, but she states, too, that she "dare not try" to suggest it definitively. In short, she recognizes the limits of any external view of character and the final mystery of human personality. But after his mother's death in middle age, Don "brooded upon her," spending his time tending the flowers at her grave. When Don died, Uncle Ernie also turned to the "lost companionship" of his wife. He "took to going out to the cemetery" and neglected his duties at home, thus causing a greater burden to fall on Eltha's twin sister, Deltha, and delaying her marriage. No one is at fault in this sequence of human events; indeed everyone in *Some Others and Myself* is beheld in the clear light of a charity that is beyond all judgment. But the desire for a full view of the human situation requires the narrator to explain the sense of "shadow" surrounding Aunt Clara that has always stayed in her mind. Clara possessed such a depth of tenderness that others turned instinctively in their suffering to her, even to her remembered presence after death, and thus perhaps weakened themselves. The story concludes, however, on a fully affirmative note. Uncle Ernie is remarried, this time to a widow, Carrie, Clara's sister. His act, moreover, represents a full acceptance of his past, for Carrie has been the only person whom Clara trusted sufficiently to be left with the care of Eltha from time to time. All are happy about this marriage, for they see in it what Suckow has been finding and affirming throughout her volume: the process of "keeping continuity with the past and going on into the fresh future."

Some Others and Myself closes with Suckow's "A Memoir," much of it devoted to remembrances of her father, a Congregationalist minister, and to her own relationship to the church, one that changed over the years. Without analyzing the work in great detail, I would like to suggest here how it recapitulates some of the stories' themes. Suckow begins by attacking the conventional assumptions surrounding ministers' daughters, two of which she finds particularly prevalent. One, influenced by "the pattern of the vicar's daughter in English Victorian novels," assumes that the daughters "of parsons must have followed an orthodox pattern of behavior and belief dutifully and uninquiringly, out of filial obedience." A second insists that "frustration" and "rebellion" are the dominant attitudes of the minister's child, whose home life was always rigidly authoritarian and narrowly pietistic. Neither stereotype bears very much relation to experience.

Suckow's father was no more an authoritarian figure than she was a frustrated daughter. Instead she emphasizes his liberality. For her he embodied the spirit of charity that she brings to her characterization. Only once did he become intolerant, during the First World War, when "he became one of those preachers who ardently presented arms." This temporary loss of balance in her father contributed to Suckow's decision to leave the church, a decision that occupies a central place in her memoir. Nevertheless the final movement of "A Memoir" is, like that of the stories of *Some Others and Myself,* one of reconciliation and return. At the end of her memoir, Suckow describes her decision to join again an organized religious body, the Society of Friends. She chooses the Quakers specifically because with them she has found, especially in "renewed circumstances of world warfare," "the one best hope of creative religious action in places of tension and conflict—the best hope of making concrete reality of Paul's injunction to overcome evil with good." But the more general decision to return to organized faith derives from the same mature vision of human interdependence that illuminates her stories. At the end of "A Memoir," Suckow testifies, in a spirit beyond all sectarianism, to her own lived sense of the great Pauline idea of the Body of Christ. In the church, "one finds oneself among the people, a member with and of them, thoroughly—and sometimes I feel outstandingly!—limited and fallible also." From first to last *Some Others and Myself* gives testimony to the way we "find" ourselves, in both senses of the word, among the people, those "actual companions" whom Emerson once beautifully called "the mystic officials to whom the universe has delegated its whole pleasure for us."

Additional coverage of Suckow's life and career is contained in the following sources published by Gale Research: *Contemporary Authors,* Vol. 113; and *Dictionary of Literary Biography,* Vols. 9, 102.

Appendix:

Select Bibliography of General Sources on Short Fiction

BOOKS OF CRITICISM

Allen, Walter. *The Short Story in English*. New York: Oxford University Press, 1981, 413 p.

Aycock, Wendell M., ed. *The Teller and the Tale: Aspects of the Short Story* (Proceedings of the Comparative Literature Symposium, Texas Tech University, Volume XIII). Lubbock: Texas Tech Press, 1982, 156 p.

Averill, Deborah. *The Irish Short Story from George Moore to Frank O'Connor*. Washington, D.C.: University Press of America, 1982, 329 p.

Bates, H. E. *The Modern Short Story: A Critical Survey*. Boston: Writer, 1941, 231 p.

Bayley, John. *The Short Story: Henry James to Elizabeth Bowen*. Great Britain: The Harvester Press Limited, 1988, 197 p.

Bennett, E. K. *A History of the German Novelle: From Goethe to Thomas Mann*. Cambridge: At the University Press, 1934, 296 p.

Bone, Robert. *Down Home: A History of Afro-American Short Fiction from Its Beginning to the End of the Harlem Renaissance*. Rev. ed. New York: Columbia University Press, 1988, 350 p.

Bruck, Peter. *The Black American Short Story in the Twentieth Century: A Collection of Critical Essays*. Amsterdam: B. R. Grüner Publishing Co., 1977, 209 p.

Burnett, Whit, and Burnett, Hallie. *The Modern Short Story in the Making*. New York: Hawthorn Books, 1964, 405 p.

Canby, Henry Seidel. *The Short Story in English*. New York: Henry Holt and Co., 1909, 386 p.

Current-García, Eugene. *The American Short Story before 1850: A Critical History*. Twayne's Critical History of the Short Story, edited by William Peden. Boston: Twayne Publishers, 1985, 168 p.

Flora, Joseph M., ed. *The English Short Story, 1880-1945: A Critical History*. Twayne's Critical History of the Short Story, edited by William Peden. Boston: Twayne Publishers, 1985, 215 p.

Foster, David William. *Studies in the Contemporary Spanish-American Short Story*. Columbia, Mo.: University of Missouri Press, 1979, 126 p.

George, Albert J. *Short Fiction in France, 1800-1850*. Syracuse, N.Y.: Syracuse University Press, 1964, 245 p.

Gerlach, John. *Toward an End: Closure and Structure in the American Short Story*. University, Ala.: The University of Alabama Press, 1985, 193 p.

Hankin, Cherry, ed. *Critical Essays on the New Zealand Short Story*. Auckland: Heinemann Publishers,

1982, 186 p.

Hanson, Clare, ed. *Re-Reading the Short Story*. London: MacMillan Press, 1989, 137 p.

Harris, Wendell V. *British Short Fiction in the Nineteenth Century*. Detroit: Wayne State University Press, 1979, 209 p.

Huntington, John. *Rationalizing Genius: Ideological Strategies in the Classic American Science Fiction Short Story*. New Brunswick: Rutgers University Press, 1989, 216 p.

Kilroy, James F., ed. *The Irish Short Story: A Critical History*. Twayne's Critical History of the Short Story, edited by William Peden. Boston: Twayne Publishers, 1984, 251 p.

Lee, A. Robert. *The Nineteenth-Century American Short Story*. Totowa, N. J.: Vision / Barnes & Noble, 1986, 196 p.

Leibowitz, Judith. *Narrative Purpose in the Novella*. The Hague: Mouton, 1974, 137 p.

Lohafer, Susan. *Coming to Terms with the Short Story*. Baton Rouge: Louisiana State University Press, 1983, 171 p.

Lohafer, Susan, and Clarey, Jo Ellyn. *Short Story Theory at a Crossroads*. Baton Rouge: Louisiana State University Press, 1989, 352 p.

Mann, Susan Garland. *The Short Story Cycle: A Genre Companion and Reference Guide*. New York: Greenwood Press, 1989, 228 p.

Matthews, Brander. *The Philosophy of the Short Story*. New York, N.Y.: Longmans, Green and Co., 1901, 83 p.

May, Charles E., ed. *Short Story Theories*. Athens, Oh.: Ohio University Press, 1976, 251 p.

McClave, Heather, ed. *Women Writers of the Short Story: A Collection of Critical Essays*. Englewood Cliffs, N. J.: Prentice-Hall, 1980, 171 p.

Moser, Charles, ed. *The Russian Short Story: A Critical History*. Twayne's Critical History of the Short Story, edited by William Peden. Boston: Twayne Publishers, 1986, 232 p.

New, W. H. *Dreams of Speech and Violence: The Art of the Short Story in Canada and New Zealand*. Toronto: The University of Toronto Press, 1987, 302 p.

Newman, Frances. *The Short Story's Mutations: From Petronius to Paul Morand*. New York: B. W. Huebsch, 1925, 332 p.

O'Connor, Frank. *The Lonely Voice: A Study of the Short Story*. Cleveland: World Publishing Co., 1963, 220 p.

O'Faolain, Sean. *The Short Story*. New York: Devin-Adair Co., 1951, 370 p.

Orel, Harold. *The Victorian Short Story: Development and Triumph of a Literary Genre*. Cambridge: Cambridge University Press, 1986, 213 p.

O'Toole, L. Michael. *Structure, Style and Interpretation in the Russian Short Story*. New Haven: Yale University Press, 1982, 272 p.

Pattee, Fred Lewis. *The Development of the American Short Story: An Historical Survey*. New York: Harper and Brothers Publishers, 1923, 388 p.

Peden, Margaret Sayers, ed. *The Latin American Short Story: A Critical History*. Twayne's Critical History of the Short Story, edited by William Peden. Boston: Twayne Publishers, 1983, 160 p.

Peden, William. *The American Short Story: Continuity and Change, 1940-1975*. Rev. ed. Boston: Houghton Mifflin Co., 1975, 215 p.

Reid, Ian. *The Short Story*. The Critical Idiom, edited by John D. Jump. London: Methuen and Co., 1977, 76 p.

Rhode, Robert D. *Setting in the American Short Story of Local Color, 1865-1900*. The Hague: Mouton, 1975, 189 p.

Rohrberger, Mary. *Hawthorne and the Modern Short Story: A Study in Genre*. The Hague: Mouton and Co., 1966, 148 p.

Shaw, Valerie. *The Short Story: A Critical Introduction*. London: Longman, 1983, 294 p.

Stephens, Michael. *The Dramaturgy of Style: Voice in Short Fiction*. Carbondale, Ill.: Southern Illinois University Press, 1986, 281 p.

Stevick, Philip, ed. *The American Short Story, 1900-1945: A Critical History*. Twayne's Critical History of the Short Story, edited by William Peden. Boston: Twayne Publishers, 1984, 209 p.

Summers, Hollis, ed. *Discussion of the Short Story*. Boston: D. C. Heath and Co., 1963, 118 p.

Vannatta, Dennis, ed. *The English Short Story, 1945-1980: A Critical History*. Twayne's Critical History of the Short Story, edited by William Peden. Boston: Twayne Publishers, 1985, 206 p.

Voss, Arthur. *The American Short Story: A Critical Survey*. Norman, Okla.: University of Oklahoma Press, 1973, 399 p.

Walker, Warren S. *Twentieth-Century Short Story Explication: New Series, Vol. 1: 1989-1990*. Hamden, Conn.: Shoe String, 1993, 366 p.

Ward, Alfred C. *Aspects of the Modern Short Story: English and American*. London: University of London Press, 1924, 307 p.

Weaver, Gordon, ed. *The American Short Story, 1945-1980: A Critical History*. Twayne's Critical History of the Short Story, edited by William Peden. Boston: Twayne Publishers, 1983, 150 p.

West, Ray B., Jr. *The Short Story in America, 1900-1950*. Chicago: Henry Regnery Co., 1952, 147 p.

Williams, Blanche Colton. *Our Short Story Writers*. New York: Moffat, Yard and Co., 1920, 357 p.

Wright, Austin McGiffert. *The American Short Story in the Twenties*. Chicago: University of Chicago Press, 1961, 425 p.

CRITICAL ANTHOLOGIES

Atkinson, W. Patterson, ed. *The Short-Story*. Boston: Allyn and Bacon, 1923, 317 p.

Baldwin, Charles Sears, ed. *American Short Stories*. New York, N.Y.: Longmans, Green and Co., 1904, 333 p.

Charters, Ann, ed. *The Story and Its Writer: An Introduction to Short Fiction*. New York: St. Martin's Press, 1983, 1239 p.

Current-García, Eugene, and Patrick, Walton R., eds. *American Short Stories: 1820 to the Present*. Key Editions, edited by John C. Gerber. Chicago: Scott, Foresman and Co., 1952, 633 p.

Fagin, N. Bryllion, ed. *America through the Short Story*. Boston: Little, Brown, and Co., 1936, 508 p.

Frakes, James R., and Traschen, Isadore, eds. *Short Fiction: A Critical Collection*. Prentice-Hall English Literature Series, edited by Maynard Mack. Englewood Cliffs, N.J.: Prentice-Hall, 1959, 459 p.

Gifford, Douglas, ed. *Scottish Short Stories, 1800-1900*. The Scottish Library, edited by Alexander Scott. London: Calder and Boyars, 1971, 350 p.

Gordon, Caroline, and Tate, Allen, eds. *The House of Fiction: An Anthology of the Short Story with Commentary*. Rev. ed. New York: Charles Scribner's Sons, 1960, 469 p.

Greet, T. Y., et. al. *The Worlds of Fiction: Stories in Context*. Boston, Mass.: Houghton Mifflin Co., 1964, 429 p.

Gullason, Thomas A., and Caspar, Leonard, eds. *The World of Short Fiction: An International Collection*. New York: Harper and Row, 1962, 548 p.

Havighurst, Walter, ed. *Masters of the Modern Short Story*. New York: Harcourt, Brace and Co., 1945, 538 p.

Litz, A. Walton, ed. *Major American Short Stories*. New York: Oxford University Press, 1975, 823 p.

Matthews, Brander, ed. *The Short-Story: Specimens Illustrating Its Development*. New York: American Book Co., 1907, 399 p.

Menton, Seymour, ed. *The Spanish American Short Story: A Critical Anthology*. Berkeley and Los Angeles: University of California Press, 1980, 496 p.

Mzamane, Mbulelo Vizikhungo, ed. *Hungry Flames, and Other Black South African Short Stories*. Longman African Classics. Essex: Longman, 1986, 162 p.

Schorer, Mark, ed. *The Short Story: A Critical Anthology*. Rev. ed. Prentice-Hall English Literature Series, edited by Maynard Mack. Englewood Cliffs, N. J.: Prentice-Hall, 1967, 459 p.

Simpson, Claude M., ed. *The Local Colorists: American Short Stories, 1857-1900*. New York: Harper and Brothers Publishers, 1960, 340 p.

Stanton, Robert, ed. *The Short Story and the Reader*. New York: Henry Holt and Co., 1960, 557 p.

West, Ray B., Jr., ed. *American Short Stories*. New York: Thomas Y. Crowell Co., 1959, 267 p.

Short Story Criticism Indexes

Literary Criticism Series
Cumulative Author Index

SSC Cumulative Nationality Index
SSC Cumulative Title Index

How to Use This Index

The main references

Calvino, Italo
  1923-1985.....CLC 5, 8, 11, 22, 33, 39,
                                73; SSC 3

list all author entries in the following Gale Literary Criticism series:

BLC = *Black Literature Criticism*
CLC = *Contemporary Literary Criticism*
CLR = *Children's Literature Review*
CMLC = *Classical and Medieval Literature Criticism*
DA = *DISCovering Authors*
DC = *Drama Criticism*
HLC = *Hispanic Literature Criticism*
LC = *Literature Criticism from 1400 to 1800*
NCLC = *Nineteenth-Century Literature Criticism*
PC = *Poetry Criticism*
SSC = *Short Story Criticism*
TCLC = *Twentieth-Century Literary Criticism*
WLC = *World Literature Criticism, 1500 to the Present*

The cross-references

See also CANR 23; CA 85-88;
  obituary CA 116

list all author entries in the following Gale biographical and literary sources:

AAYA = *Authors & Artists for Young Adults*
AITN = *Authors in the News*
BEST = *Bestsellers*
BW = *Black Writers*
CA = *Contemporary Authors*
CAAS = *Contemporary Authors Autobiography Series*
CABS = *Contemporary Authors Bibliographical Series*
CANR = *Contemporary Authors New Revision Series*
CAP = *Contemporary Authors Permanent Series*
CDALB = *Concise Dictionary of American Literary Biography*
CDBLB = *Concise Dictionary of British Literary Biography*
DLB = *Dictionary of Literary Biography*
DLBD = *Dictionary of Literary Biography Documentary Series*
DLBY = *Dictionary of Literary Biography Yearbook*
HW = *Hispanic Writers*
JRDA = *Junior DISCovering Authors*
MAICYA = *Major Authors and Illustrators for Children and Young Adults*
MTCW = *Major 20th-Century Writers*
NNAL = *Native North American Literature*
SAAS = *Something about the Author Autobiography Series*
SATA = *Something about the Author*
YABC = *Yesterday's Authors of Books for Children*

Abasiyanik, Sait Faik 1906-1954
  See Sait Faik
  See also CA 123

Abbey, Edward 1927-1989...... CLC 36, 59
  See also CA 45-48; 128; CANR 2, 41

Abbott, Lee K(ittredge) 1947-...... CLC 48
  See also CA 124; DLB 130

Abe, Kobo 1924-1993..... CLC 8, 22, 53, 81
  See also CA 65-68; 140; CANR 24; MTCW

Abelard, Peter c. 1079-c. 1142 ... CMLC 11
  See also DLB 115

Abell, Kjeld 1901-1961........... CLC 15
  See also CA 111

Abish, Walter 1931-.............. CLC 22
  See also CA 101; CANR 37; DLB 130

Abrahams, Peter (Henry) 1919- ..... CLC 4
  See also BW 1; CA 57-60; CANR 26;
  DLB 117; MTCW

Abrams, M(eyer) H(oward) 1912-... CLC 24
  See also CA 57-60; CANR 13, 33; DLB 67

Abse, Dannie 1923-............ CLC 7, 29
  See also CA 53-56; CAAS 1; CANR 4, 46,
  46; DLB 27

Achebe, (Albert) Chinua(lumogu)
  1930- ..... CLC 1, 3, 5, 7, 11, 26, 51, 75;
                              BLC; DA; WLC
  See also BW 2; CA 1-4R; CANR 6, 26, 47;
  CLR 20; DLB 117; MAICYA; MTCW;
  SATA 40; SATA-Brief 38

Acker, Kathy 1948- .... CLC 45
  See also CA 117; 122

Ackroyd, Peter 1949-.......... CLC 34, 52
  See also CA 123; 127

Acorn, Milton 1923-.............. CLC 15
  See also CA 103; DLB 53

Adamov, Arthur 1908-1970 ..... CLC 4, 25
  See also CA 17-18; 25-28R; CAP 2; MTCW

Adams, Alice (Boyd) 1926- ... CLC 6, 13, 46
  See also CA 81-84; CANR 26; DLBY 86;
  MTCW

Adams, Andy 1859-1935......... TCLC 56
  See also YABC 1

Adams, Douglas (Noel) 1952- ... CLC 27, 60
  See also AAYA 4; BEST 89:3; CA 106;
  CANR 34; DLBY 83; JRDA

Adams, Francis 1862-1893....... NCLC 33

Adams, Henry (Brooks)
  1838-1918 .... TCLC 4, 52; DA
  See also CA 104; 133; DLB 12, 47

Adams, Richard (George)
  1920- .... CLC 4, 5, 18
  See also AITN 1, 2; CA 49-52; CANR 3,
  35; CLR 20; JRDA; MAICYA; MTCW;
  SATA 7, 69

Adamson, Joy(-Friederike Victoria)
  1910-1980 .... CLC 17
  See also CA 69-72; 93-96; CANR 22;
  MTCW; SATA 11; SATA-Obit 22

Adcock, Fleur 1934-.............. CLC 41
  See also CA 25-28R; CANR 11, 34;
  DLB 40

Addams, Charles (Samuel)
  1912-1988 .... CLC 30
  See also CA 61-64; 126; CANR 12

Addison, Joseph 1672-1719 .... LC 18
  See also CDBLB 1660-1789; DLB 101

Adler, C(arole) S(chwerdtfeger)
  1932- .... CLC 35
  See also AAYA 4; CA 89-92; CANR 19,
  40; JRDA; MAICYA; SAAS 15;
  SATA 26, 63

Adler, Renata 1938-.......... CLC 8, 31
  See also CA 49-52; CANR 5, 22; MTCW

Ady, Endre 1877-1919 .... TCLC 11
  See also CA 107

Aeschylus
  525B.C.-456B.C. .... CMLC 11; DA

Afton, Effie
  See Harper, Frances Ellen Watkins

Agapida, Fray Antonio
  See Irving, Washington

Agee, James (Rufus)
  1909-1955 .... TCLC 1, 19
  See also AITN 1; CA 108;
  CDALB 1941-1968; DLB 2, 26

Aghill, Gordon
  See Silverberg, Robert

Agnon, S(hmuel) Y(osef Halevi)
  1888-1970 .... CLC 4, 8, 14
  See also CA 17-18; 25-28R; CAP 2; MTCW

Agrippa von Nettesheim, Henry Cornelius
  1486-1535 .... LC 27

Aherne, Owen
  See Cassill, R(onald) V(erlin)

Ai 1947-................... CLC 4, 14, 69
  See also CA 85-88; CAAS 13; DLB 120

Aickman, Robert (Fordyce)
  1914-1981 .... CLC 57
  See also CA 5-8R; CANR 3

Aiken, Conrad (Potter)
  1889-1973 ... CLC 1, 3, 5, 10, 52; SSC 9
  See also CA 5-8R; 45-48; CANR 4;
  CDALB 1929-1941; DLB 9, 45, 102;
  MTCW; SATA 3, 30

Aiken, Joan (Delano) 1924-........ CLC 35
  See also AAYA 1; CA 9-12R; CANR 4, 23,
  34; CLR 1, 19; JRDA; MAICYA;
  MTCW; SAAS 1; SATA 2, 30, 73

Ainsworth, William Harrison
  1805-1882 .... NCLC 13
  See also DLB 21; SATA 24

Aitmatov, Chingiz (Torekulovich)
  1928-...................... CLC 71
  See also CA 103; CANR 38; MTCW;
  SATA 56

Akers, Floyd
  See Baum, L(yman) Frank

Akhmadulina, Bella Akhatovna
  1937-...................... CLC 53
  See also CA 65-68

Akhmatova, Anna
  1888-1966 .... CLC 11, 25, 64; PC 2
  See also CA 19-20; 25-28R; CANR 35;
  CAP 1; MTCW

Aksakov, Sergei Timofeyvich
  1791-1859 .... NCLC 2

Aksenov, Vassily................. CLC 22
  See also Aksyonov, Vassily (Pavlovich)

Aksyonov, Vassily (Pavlovich)
  1932-...................... CLC 37
  See also Aksenov, Vassily
  See also CA 53-56; CANR 12

Akutagawa Ryunosuke
  1892-1927 .... TCLC 16
  See also CA 117

Alain 1868-1951 .... TCLC 41

Alain-Fournier.................... TCLC 6
  See also Fournier, Henri Alban
  See also DLB 65

Alarcon, Pedro Antonio de
  1833-1891 .... NCLC 1

Alas (y Urena), Leopoldo (Enrique Garcia)
  1852-1901 .... TCLC 29
  See also CA 113; 131; HW

Albee, Edward (Franklin III)
  1928- ...... CLC 1, 2, 3, 5, 9, 11, 13, 25,
                            53, 86; DA; WLC
  See also AITN 1; CA 5-8R; CABS 3;
  CANR 8; CDALB 1941-1968; DLB 7;
  MTCW

Alberti, Rafael 1902-.............. CLC 7
  See also CA 85-88; DLB 108

Alcala-Galiano, Juan Valera y
  See Valera y Alcala-Galiano, Juan

Alcott, Amos Bronson 1799-1888 .. NCLC 1
  See also DLB 1

Alcott, Louisa May
  1832-1888 .... NCLC 6; DA; WLC
  See also CDALB 1865-1917; CLR 1;
  DLB 1, 42, 79; JRDA; MAICYA;
  YABC 1

Aldanov, M. A.
  See Aldanov, Mark (Alexandrovich)

Aldanov, Mark (Alexandrovich)
  1886(?)-1957 .... TCLC 23
  See also CA 118

Aldington, Richard 1892-1962...... CLC 49
  See also CA 85-88; CANR 45; DLB 20, 36,
  100

Aldiss, Brian W(ilson)
1925- .... CLC 5, 14, 40
See also CA 5-8R; CAAS 2; CANR 5, 28;
DLB 14; MTCW; SATA 34

Alegria, Claribel 1924-............ CLC 75
See also CA 131; CAAS 15; DLB 145; HW

Alegria, Fernando 1918-.......... CLC 57
See also CA 9-12R; CANR 5, 32; HW

Aleichem, Sholom .... TCLC 1, 35
See also Rabinovitch, Sholem

Aleixandre, Vicente 1898-1984 ... CLC 9, 36
See also CA 85-88; 114; CANR 26;
DLB 108; HW; MTCW

Alepoudelis, Odysseus
See Elytis, Odysseus

Aleshkovsky, Joseph 1929-
See Aleshkovsky, Yuz
See also CA 121; 128

Aleshkovsky, Yuz .... CLC 44
See also Aleshkovsky, Joseph

Alexander, Lloyd (Chudley) 1924- .. CLC 35
See also AAYA 1; CA 1-4R; CANR 1, 24,
38; CLR 1, 5; DLB 52; JRDA; MAICYA;
MTCW; SAAS 19; SATA 3, 49, 81

Alfau, Felipe 1902-.............. CLC 66
See also CA 137

Alger, Horatio, Jr. 1832-1899..... NCLC 8
See also DLB 42; SATA 16

Algren, Nelson 1909-1981 .... CLC 4, 10, 33
See also CA 13-16R; 103; CANR 20;
CDALB 1941-1968; DLB 9; DLBY 81,
82; MTCW

Ali, Ahmed 1910-................ CLC 69
See also CA 25-28R; CANR 15, 34

Alighieri, Dante 1265-1321 .... CMLC 3

Allan, John B.
See Westlake, Donald E(dwin)

Allen, Edward 1948-.............. CLC 59

Allen, Paula Gunn 1939-.......... CLC 84
See also CA 112; 143; NNAL

Allen, Roland
See Ayckbourn, Alan

Allen, Sarah A.
See Hopkins, Pauline Elizabeth

Allen, Woody 1935- .... CLC 16, 52
See also AAYA 10; CA 33-36R; CANR 27,
38; DLB 44; MTCW

Allende, Isabel 1942- .... CLC 39, 57; HLC
See also CA 125; 130; DLB 145; HW;
MTCW

Alleyn, Ellen
See Rossetti, Christina (Georgina)

Allingham, Margery (Louise)
1904-1966 .... CLC 19
See also CA 5-8R; 25-28R; CANR 4;
DLB 77; MTCW

Allingham, William 1824-1889 ... NCLC 25
See also DLB 35

Allison, Dorothy E. 1949-........ CLC 78
See also CA 140

Allston, Washington 1779-1843.... NCLC 2
See also DLB 1

Almedingen, E. M. .... CLC 12
See also Almedingen, Martha Edith von
See also SATA 3

Almedingen, Martha Edith von 1898-1971
See Almedingen, E. M.
See also CA 1-4R; CANR 1

Almqvist, Carl Jonas Love
1793-1866 .... NCLC 42

Alonso, Damaso 1898-1990 .... CLC 14
See also CA 110; 131; 130; DLB 108; HW

Alov
See Gogol, Nikolai (Vasilyevich)

Alta 1942-...................... CLC 19
See also CA 57-60

Alter, Robert B(ernard) 1935-...... CLC 34
See also CA 49-52; CANR 1, 47

Alther, Lisa 1944-.............. CLC 7, 41
See also CA 65-68; CANR 12, 30; MTCW

Altman, Robert 1925-............ CLC 16
See also CA 73-76; CANR 43

Alvarez, A(lfred) 1929-.......... CLC 5, 13
See also CA 1-4R; CANR 3, 33; DLB 14,
40

Alvarez, Alejandro Rodriguez 1903-1965
See Casona, Alejandro
See also CA 131; 93-96; HW

Amado, Jorge 1912-..... CLC 13, 40; HLC
See also CA 77-80; CANR 35; DLB 113;
MTCW

Ambler, Eric 1909-............ CLC 4, 6, 9
See also CA 9-12R; CANR 7, 38; DLB 77;
MTCW

Amichai, Yehuda 1924- ...... CLC 9, 22, 57
See also CA 85-88; CANR 46, 46; MTCW

Amiel, Henri Frederic 1821-1881 .. NCLC 4

Amis, Kingsley (William)
1922- .. CLC 1, 2, 3, 5, 8, 13, 40, 44; DA
See also AITN 2; CA 9-12R; CANR 8, 28;
CDBLB 1945-1960; DLB 15, 27, 100, 139;
MTCW

Amis, Martin (Louis)
1949- .... CLC 4, 9, 38, 62
See also BEST 90:3; CA 65-68; CANR 8,
27; DLB 14

Ammons, A(rchie) R(andolph)
1926- .... CLC 2, 3, 5, 8, 9, 25, 57
See also AITN 1; CA 9-12R; CANR 6, 36;
DLB 5; MTCW

Amo, Tauraatua i
See Adams, Henry (Brooks)

Anand, Mulk Raj 1905-........... CLC 23
See also CA 65-68; CANR 32; MTCW

Anatol
See Schnitzler, Arthur

Anaya, Rudolfo A(lfonso)
1937- .... CLC 23; HLC
See also CA 45-48; CAAS 4; CANR 1, 32;
DLB 82; HW 1; MTCW

Andersen, Hans Christian
1805-1875 .. NCLC 7; DA; SSC 6; WLC
See also CLR 6; MAICYA; YABC 1

Anderson, C. Farley
See Mencken, H(enry) L(ouis); Nathan,
George Jean

Anderson, Jessica (Margaret) Queale
.... CLC 37
See also CA 9-12R; CANR 4

Anderson, Jon (Victor) 1940- .... CLC 9
See also CA 25-28R; CANR 20

Anderson, Lindsay (Gordon)
1923-1994 .... CLC 20
See also CA 125; 128; 146

Anderson, Maxwell 1888-1959 ..... TCLC 2
See also CA 105; DLB 7

Anderson, Poul (William) 1926- .... CLC 15
See also AAYA 5; CA 1-4R; CAAS 2;
CANR 2, 15, 34; DLB 8; MTCW;
SATA-Brief 39

Anderson, Robert (Woodruff)
1917- .... CLC 23
See also AITN 1; CA 21-24R; CANR 32;
DLB 7

Anderson, Sherwood
1876-1941 .... TCLC 1, 10, 24; DA;
SSC 1; WLC
See also CA 104; 121; CDALB 1917-1929;
DLB 4, 9, 86; DLBD 1; MTCW

Andouard
See Giraudoux, (Hippolyte) Jean

Andrade, Carlos Drummond de ...... CLC 18
See also Drummond de Andrade, Carlos

Andrade, Mario de 1893-1945..... TCLC 43

Andreas-Salome, Lou 1861-1937... TCLC 56
See also DLB 66

Andrewes, Lancelot 1555-1626 .... LC 5

Andrews, Cicily Fairfield
See West, Rebecca

Andrews, Elton V.
See Pohl, Frederik

Andreyev, Leonid (Nikolaevich)
1871-1919 .... TCLC 3
See also CA 104

Andric, Ivo 1892-1975 .... CLC 8
See also CA 81-84; 57-60; CANR 43;
DLB 147; MTCW

Angelique, Pierre
See Bataille, Georges

Angell, Roger 1920-.............. CLC 26
See also CA 57-60; CANR 13, 44

Angelou, Maya
1928- .... CLC 12, 35, 64, 77; BLC; DA
See also AAYA 7; BW 2; CA 65-68;
CANR 19, 42; DLB 38; MTCW;
SATA 49

Annensky, Innokenty Fyodorovich
1856-1909 .... TCLC 14
See also CA 110

Anon, Charles Robert
See Pessoa, Fernando (Antonio Nogueira)

Anouilh, Jean (Marie Lucien Pierre)
1910-1987 ...... CLC 1, 3, 8, 13, 40, 50
See also CA 17-20R; 123; CANR 32;
MTCW

Anthony, Florence
See Ai

Anthony, John
See Ciardi, John (Anthony)

Anthony, Peter
See Shaffer, Anthony (Joshua); Shaffer, Peter (Levin)

Anthony, Piers 1934- .... **CLC 35**
See also AAYA 11; CA 21-24R; CANR 28; DLB 8; MTCW

Antoine, Marc
See Proust, (Valentin-Louis-George-Eugene-) Marcel

Antoninus, Brother
See Everson, William (Oliver)

Antonioni, Michelangelo 1912- ..... **CLC 20**
See also CA 73-76; CANR 45

Antschel, Paul 1920-1970
See Celan, Paul
See also CA 85-88; CANR 33; MTCW

Anwar, Chairil 1922-1949 .... **TCLC 22**
See also CA 121

Apollinaire, Guillaume .. **TCLC 3, 8, 51; PC 7**
See also Kostrowitzki, Wilhelm Apollinaris de

Appelfeld, Aharon 1932- .... **CLC 23, 47**
See also CA 112; 133

Apple, Max (Isaac) 1941-........ **CLC 9, 33**
See also CA 81-84; CANR 19; DLB 130

Appleman, Philip (Dean) 1926- ..... **CLC 51**
See also CA 13-16R; CAAS 18; CANR 6, 29

Appleton, Lawrence
See Lovecraft, H(oward) P(hillips)

Apteryx
See Eliot, T(homas) S(tearns)

Apuleius, (Lucius Madaurensis)
125(?)-175(?) .... **CMLC 1**

Aquin, Hubert 1929-1977......... **CLC 15**
See also CA 105; DLB 53

Aragon, Louis 1897-1982........ **CLC 3, 22**
See also CA 69-72; 108; CANR 28; DLB 72; MTCW

Arany, Janos 1817-1882........ **NCLC 34**

Arbuthnot, John 1667-1735.......... **LC 1**
See also DLB 101

Archer, Herbert Winslow
See Mencken, H(enry) L(ouis)

Archer, Jeffrey (Howard) 1940- .... **CLC 28**
See also BEST 89:3; CA 77-80; CANR 22

Archer, Jules 1915- .... **CLC 12**
See also CA 9-12R; CANR 6; SAAS 5; SATA 4

Archer, Lee
See Ellison, Harlan (Jay)

Arden, John 1930- .... **CLC 6, 13, 15**
See also CA 13-16R; CAAS 4; CANR 31; DLB 13; MTCW

Arenas, Reinaldo
1943-1990 .... **CLC 41; HLC**
See also CA 124; 128; 133; DLB 145; HW

Arendt, Hannah 1906-1975 .... **CLC 66**
See also CA 17-20R; 61-64; CANR 26; MTCW

Aretino, Pietro 1492-1556 .... **LC 12**

Arghezi, Tudor................... **CLC 80**
See also Theodorescu, Ion N.

Arguedas, Jose Maria
1911-1969 .... **CLC 10, 18**
See also CA 89-92; DLB 113; HW

Argueta, Manlio 1936-............ **CLC 31**
See also CA 131; DLB 145; HW

Ariosto, Ludovico 1474-1533........ **LC 6**

Aristides
See Epstein, Joseph

Aristophanes
450B.C.-385B.C.... **CMLC 4; DA; DC 2**

Arlt, Roberto (Godofredo Christophersen)
1900-1942 .... **TCLC 29; HLC**
See also CA 123; 131; HW

Armah, Ayi Kwei 1939-.... **CLC 5, 33; BLC**
See also BW 1; CA 61-64; CANR 21; DLB 117; MTCW

Armatrading, Joan 1950-.......... **CLC 17**
See also CA 114

Arnette, Robert
See Silverberg, Robert

Arnim, Achim von (Ludwig Joachim von Arnim) 1781-1831 .... **NCLC 5**
See also DLB 90

Arnim, Bettina von 1785-1859.... **NCLC 38**
See also DLB 90

Arnold, Matthew
1822-1888 ..... **NCLC 6, 29; DA; PC 5; WLC**
See also CDBLB 1832-1890; DLB 32, 57

Arnold, Thomas 1795-1842 ...... **NCLC 18**
See also DLB 55

Arnow, Harriette (Louisa) Simpson
1908-1986 .... **CLC 2, 7, 18**
See also CA 9-12R; 118; CANR 14; DLB 6; MTCW; SATA 42; SATA-Obit 47

Arp, Hans
See Arp, Jean

Arp, Jean 1887-1966............... **CLC 5**
See also CA 81-84; 25-28R; CANR 42

Arrabal
See Arrabal, Fernando

Arrabal, Fernando 1932-... **CLC 2, 9, 18, 58**
See also CA 9-12R; CANR 15

Arrick, Fran...................... **CLC 30**

Artaud, Antonin 1896-1948 ..... **TCLC 3, 36**
See also CA 104

Arthur, Ruth M(abel) 1905-1979.... **CLC 12**
See also CA 9-12R; 85-88; CANR 4; SATA 7, 26

Artsybashev, Mikhail (Petrovich)
1878-1927 .... **TCLC 31**

Arundel, Honor (Morfydd)
1919-1973 .... **CLC 17**
See also CA 21-22; 41-44R; CAP 2; CLR 35; SATA 4; SATA-Obit 24

Asch, Sholem 1880-1957 .... **TCLC 3**
See also CA 105

Ash, Shalom
See Asch, Sholem

Ashbery, John (Lawrence)
1927- ...... **CLC 2, 3, 4, 6, 9, 13, 15, 25, 41, 77**
See also CA 5-8R; CANR 9, 37; DLB 5; DLBY 81; MTCW

Ashdown, Clifford
See Freeman, R(ichard) Austin

Ashe, Gordon
See Creasey, John

Ashton-Warner, Sylvia (Constance)
1908-1984 .... **CLC 19**
See also CA 69-72; 112; CANR 29; MTCW

Asimov, Isaac
1920-1992 ...... **CLC 1, 3, 9, 19, 26, 76**
See also AAYA 13; BEST 90:2; CA 1-4R; 137; CANR 2, 19, 36; CLR 12; DLB 8; DLBY 92; JRDA; MAICYA; MTCW; SATA 1, 26, 74

Astley, Thea (Beatrice May)
1925- .... **CLC 41**
See also CA 65-68; CANR 11, 43

Aston, James
See White, T(erence) H(anbury)

Asturias, Miguel Angel
1899-1974 .... **CLC 3, 8, 13; HLC**
See also CA 25-28; 49-52; CANR 32; CAP 2; DLB 113; HW; MTCW

Atares, Carlos Saura
See Saura (Atares), Carlos

Atheling, William
See Pound, Ezra (Weston Loomis)

Atheling, William, Jr.
See Blish, James (Benjamin)

Atherton, Gertrude (Franklin Horn)
1857-1948 .... **TCLC 2**
See also CA 104; DLB 9, 78

Atherton, Lucius
See Masters, Edgar Lee

Atkins, Jack
See Harris, Mark

Atticus
See Fleming, Ian (Lancaster)

Atwood, Margaret (Eleanor)
1939- ..... **CLC 2, 3, 4, 8, 13, 15, 25, 44, 84; DA; PC 8; SSC 2; WLC**
See also AAYA 12; BEST 89:2; CA 49-52; CANR 3, 24, 33; DLB 53; MTCW; SATA 50

Aubigny, Pierre d'
See Mencken, H(enry) L(ouis)

Aubin, Penelope 1685-1731(?)........ **LC 9**
See also DLB 39

Auchincloss, Louis (Stanton)
1917- .... **CLC 4, 6, 9, 18, 45**
See also CA 1-4R; CANR 6, 29; DLB 2; DLBY 80; MTCW

Auden, W(ystan) H(ugh)
1907-1973 ...... **CLC 1, 2, 3, 4, 6, 9, 11, 14, 43; DA; PC 1; WLC**
See also CA 9-12R; 45-48; CANR 5; CDBLB 1914-1945; DLB 10, 20; MTCW

Audiberti, Jacques 1900-1965 ...... **CLC 38**
See also CA 25-28R

Audubon, John James
1785-1851 .... **NCLC 47**

Auel, Jean M(arie) 1936-.......... **CLC 31**
See also AAYA 7; BEST 90:4; CA 103; CANR 21

Auerbach, Erich 1892-1957....... **TCLC 43**
See also CA 118

Augier, Emile 1820-1889 . . . . **NCLC 31**

August, John
See De Voto, Bernard (Augustine)

Augustine, St. 354-430 . . . . **CMLC 6**

Aurelius
See Bourne, Randolph S(illiman)

Austen, Jane
1775-1817 . . . . **NCLC 1, 13, 19, 33; DA;**
WLC
See also CDBLB 1789-1832; DLB 116

Auster, Paul 1947- . . . . **CLC 47**
See also CA 69-72; CANR 23

Austin, Frank
See Faust, Frederick (Schiller)

Austin, Mary (Hunter)
1868-1934 . . . . **TCLC 25**
See also CA 109; DLB 9, 78

Autran Dourado, Waldomiro
See Dourado, (Waldomiro Freitas) Autran

Averroes 1126-1198 . . . . **CMLC 7**
See also DLB 115

Avison, Margaret 1918- . . . . **CLC 2, 4**
See also CA 17-20R; DLB 53; MTCW

Axton, David
See Koontz, Dean R(ay)

Ayckbourn, Alan
1939- . . . . **CLC 5, 8, 18, 33, 74**
See also CA 21-24R; CANR 31; DLB 13;
MTCW

Aydy, Catherine
See Tennant, Emma (Christina)

Ayme, Marcel (Andre) 1902-1967 . . . **CLC 11**
See also CA 89-92; CLR 25; DLB 72

Ayrton, Michael 1921-1975 . . . . **CLC 7**
See also CA 5-8R; 61-64; CANR 9, 21

Azorin . . . . **CLC 11**
See also Martinez Ruiz, Jose

Azuela, Mariano
1873-1952 . . . . **TCLC 3; HLC**
See also CA 104; 131; HW; MTCW

Baastad, Babbis Friis
See Friis-Baastad, Babbis Ellinor

Bab
See Gilbert, W(illiam) S(chwenck)

Babbis, Eleanor
See Friis-Baastad, Babbis Ellinor

Babel, Isaak (Emmanuilovich)
1894-1941(?) . . . . . . **TCLC 2, 13; SSC 16**
See also CA 104

Babits, Mihaly 1883-1941 . . . . **TCLC 14**
See also CA 114

Babur 1483-1530 . . . . **LC 18**

Bacchelli, Riccardo 1891-1985 . . . . . **CLC 19**
See also CA 29-32R; 117

Bach, Richard (David) 1936- . . . . **CLC 14**
See also AITN 1; BEST 89:2; CA 9-12R;
CANR 18; MTCW; SATA 13

Bachman, Richard
See King, Stephen (Edwin)

Bachmann, Ingeborg 1926-1973 . . . . . **CLC 69**
See also CA 93-96; 45-48; DLB 85

Bacon, Francis 1561-1626 . . . . **LC 18**
See also CDBLB Before 1660

Bacon, Roger 1214(?)-1292 . . . . . . **CMLC 14**
See also DLB 115

Bacovia, George . . . . **TCLC 24**
See also Vasiliu, Gheorghe

Badanes, Jerome 1937- . . . . **CLC 59**

Bagehot, Walter 1826-1877 . . . . . . **NCLC 10**
See also DLB 55

Bagnold, Enid 1889-1981 . . . . **CLC 25**
See also CA 5-8R; 103; CANR 5, 40;
DLB 13; MAICYA; SATA 1, 25

Bagrjana, Elisaveta
See Belcheva, Elisaveta

Bagryana, Elisaveta
See Belcheva, Elisaveta
See also DLB 147

Bailey, Paul 1937- . . . . **CLC 45**
See also CA 21-24R; CANR 16; DLB 14

Baillie, Joanna 1762-1851 . . . . **NCLC 2**
See also DLB 93

Bainbridge, Beryl (Margaret)
1933- . . . . **CLC 4, 5, 8, 10, 14, 18, 22, 62**
See also CA 21-24R; CANR 24; DLB 14;
MTCW

Baker, Elliott 1922- . . . . **CLC 8**
See also CA 45-48; CANR 2

Baker, Nicholson 1957- . . . . **CLC 61**
See also CA 135

Baker, Ray Stannard 1870-1946 . . . **TCLC 47**
See also CA 118

Baker, Russell (Wayne) 1925- . . . . . . **CLC 31**
See also BEST 89:4; CA 57-60; CANR 11,
41; MTCW

Bakhtin, M.
See Bakhtin, Mikhail Mikhailovich

Bakhtin, M. M.
See Bakhtin, Mikhail Mikhailovich

Bakhtin, Mikhail
See Bakhtin, Mikhail Mikhailovich

Bakhtin, Mikhail Mikhailovich
1895-1975 . . . . **CLC 83**
See also CA 128; 113

Bakshi, Ralph 1938(?)- . . . . **CLC 26**
See also CA 112; 138

Bakunin, Mikhail (Alexandrovich)
1814-1876 . . . . **NCLC 25**

Baldwin, James (Arthur)
1924-1987 . . . . . . **CLC 1, 2, 3, 4, 5, 8, 13,**
15, 17, 42, 50, 67; BLC; DA; DC 1;
SSC 10; WLC
See also AAYA 4; BW 1; CA 1-4R; 124;
CABS 1; CANR 3, 24;
CDALB 1941-1968; DLB 2, 7, 33;
DLBY 87; MTCW; SATA 9;
SATA-Obit 54

Ballard, J(ames) G(raham)
1930- . . . . **CLC 3, 6, 14, 36; SSC 1**
See also AAYA 3; CA 5-8R; CANR 15, 39;
DLB 14; MTCW

Balmont, Konstantin (Dmitriyevich)
1867-1943 . . . . **TCLC 11**
See also CA 109

Balzac, Honore de
1799-1850 . . . . **NCLC 5, 35; DA; SSC 5;**
WLC
See also DLB 119

Bambara, Toni Cade
1939- . . . . **CLC 19; BLC; DA**
See also AAYA 5; BW 2; CA 29-32R;
CANR 24; DLB 38; MTCW

Bamdad, A.
See Shamlu, Ahmad

Banat, D. R.
See Bradbury, Ray (Douglas)

Bancroft, Laura
See Baum, L(yman) Frank

Banim, John 1798-1842 . . . . **NCLC 13**
See also DLB 116

Banim, Michael 1796-1874 . . . . . . **NCLC 13**

Banks, Iain
See Banks, Iain M(enzies)

Banks, Iain M(enzies) 1954- . . . . **CLC 34**
See also CA 123; 128

Banks, Lynne Reid . . . . **CLC 23**
See also Reid Banks, Lynne
See also AAYA 6

Banks, Russell 1940- . . . . **CLC 37, 72**
See also CA 65-68; CAAS 15; CANR 19;
DLB 130

Banville, John 1945- . . . . **CLC 46**
See also CA 117; 128; DLB 14

Banville, Theodore (Faullain) de
1832-1891 . . . . **NCLC 9**

Baraka, Amiri
1934- . . . . **CLC 1, 2, 3, 5, 10, 14, 33;**
BLC; DA; PC 4
See also Jones, LeRoi
See also BW 2; CA 21-24R; CABS 3;
CANR 27, 38; CDALB 1941-1968;
DLB 5, 7, 16, 38; DLBD 8; MTCW

Barbellion, W. N. P. . . . . **TCLC 24**
See also Cummings, Bruce F(rederick)

Barbera, Jack (Vincent) 1945- . . . . . . **CLC 44**
See also CA 110; CANR 45

Barbey d'Aurevilly, Jules Amedee
1808-1889 . . . . **NCLC 1; SSC 17**
See also DLB 119

Barbusse, Henri 1873-1935 . . . . **TCLC 5**
See also CA 105; DLB 65

Barclay, Bill
See Moorcock, Michael (John)

Barclay, William Ewert
See Moorcock, Michael (John)

Barea, Arturo 1897-1957 . . . . **TCLC 14**
See also CA 111

Barfoot, Joan 1946- . . . . **CLC 18**
See also CA 105

Baring, Maurice 1874-1945 . . . . **TCLC 8**
See also CA 105; DLB 34

Barker, Clive 1952- . . . . **CLC 52**
See also AAYA 10; BEST 90:3; CA 121;
129; MTCW

Barker, George Granville
1913-1991 . . . . **CLC 8, 48**
See also CA 9-12R; 135; CANR 7, 38;
DLB 20; MTCW

Barker, Harley Granville
See Granville-Barker, Harley
See also DLB 10

Barker, Howard 1946-............ **CLC 37**
See also CA 102; DLB 13

Barker, Pat 1943-.............. **CLC 32**
See also CA 117; 122

Barlow, Joel 1754-1812 .... **NCLC 23**
See also DLB 37

Barnard, Mary (Ethel) 1909-....... **CLC 48**
See also CA 21-22; CAP 2

Barnes, Djuna
1892-1982 ... **CLC 3, 4, 8, 11, 29; SSC 3**
See also CA 9-12R; 107; CANR 16; DLB 4,
9, 45; MTCW

Barnes, Julian 1946-.............. **CLC 42**
See also CA 102; CANR 19; DLBY 93

Barnes, Peter 1931- .... **CLC 5, 56**
See also CA 65-68; CAAS 12; CANR 33,
34; DLB 13; MTCW

Baroja (y Nessi), Pio
1872-1956 .... **TCLC 8; HLC**
See also CA 104

Baron, David
See Pinter, Harold

Baron Corvo
See Rolfe, Frederick (William Serafino
Austin Lewis Mary)

Barondess, Sue K(aufman)
1926-1977 .... **CLC 8**
See also Kaufman, Sue
See also CA 1-4R; 69-72; CANR 1

Baron de Teive
See Pessoa, Fernando (Antonio Nogueira)

Barres, Maurice 1862-1923 .... **TCLC 47**
See also DLB 123

Barreto, Afonso Henrique de Lima
See Lima Barreto, Afonso Henrique de

Barrett, (Roger) Syd 1946- .... **CLC 35**

Barrett, William (Christopher)
1913-1992 .... **CLC 27**
See also CA 13-16R; 139; CANR 11

Barrie, J(ames) M(atthew)
1860-1937 .... **TCLC 2**
See also CA 104; 136; CDBLB 1890-1914;
CLR 16; DLB 10, 141; MAICYA;
YABC 1

Barrington, Michael
See Moorcock, Michael (John)

Barrol, Grady
See Bograd, Larry

Barry, Mike
See Malzberg, Barry N(athaniel)

Barry, Philip 1896-1949......... **TCLC 11**
See also CA 109; DLB 7

Bart, Andre Schwarz
See Schwarz-Bart, Andre

Barth, John (Simmons)
1930- ...... **CLC 1, 2, 3, 5, 7, 9, 10, 14,
27, 51; SSC 10**
See also AITN 1, 2; CA 1-4R; CABS 1;
CANR 5, 23; DLB 2; MTCW

Barthelme, Donald
1931-1989 ...... **CLC 1, 2, 3, 5, 6, 8, 13,
23, 46, 59; SSC 2**
See also CA 21-24R; 129; CANR 20;
DLB 2; DLBY 80, 89; MTCW; SATA 7;
SATA-Obit 62

Barthelme, Frederick 1943-........ **CLC 36**
See also CA 114; 122; DLBY 85

Barthes, Roland (Gerard)
1915-1980 .... **CLC 24, 83**
See also CA 130; 97-100; MTCW

Barzun, Jacques (Martin) 1907-.... **CLC 51**
See also CA 61-64; CANR 22

Bashevis, Isaac
See Singer, Isaac Bashevis

Bashkirtseff, Marie 1859-1884 ... **NCLC 27**

Basho
See Matsuo Basho

Bass, Kingsley B., Jr.
See Bullins, Ed

Bass, Rick 1958-................. **CLC 79**
See also CA 126

Bassani, Giorgio 1916-............. **CLC 9**
See also CA 65-68; CANR 33; DLB 128;
MTCW

Bastos, Augusto (Antonio) Roa
See Roa Bastos, Augusto (Antonio)

Bataille, Georges 1897-1962 .... **CLC 29**
See also CA 101; 89-92

Bates, H(erbert) E(rnest)
1905-1974 .... **CLC 46; SSC 10**
See also CA 93-96; 45-48; CANR 34;
MTCW

Bauchart
See Camus, Albert

Baudelaire, Charles
1821-1867 ..... **NCLC 6, 29; DA; PC 1;
SSC 18; WLC**

Baudrillard, Jean 1929-............ **CLC 60**

Baum, L(yman) Frank 1856-1919 ... **TCLC 7**
See also CA 108; 133; CLR 15; DLB 22;
JRDA; MAICYA; MTCW; SATA 18

Baum, Louis F.
See Baum, L(yman) Frank

Baumbach, Jonathan 1933- ...... **CLC 6, 23**
See also CA 13-16R; CAAS 5; CANR 12;
DLBY 80; MTCW

Bausch, Richard (Carl) 1945- ...... **CLC 51**
See also CA 101; CAAS 14; CANR 43;
DLB 130

Baxter, Charles 1947-.......... **CLC 45, 78**
See also CA 57-60; CANR 40; DLB 130

Baxter, George Owen
See Faust, Frederick (Schiller)

Baxter, James K(eir) 1926-1972 .... **CLC 14**
See also CA 77-80

Baxter, John
See Hunt, E(verette) Howard, (Jr.)

Bayer, Sylvia
See Glassco, John

Baynton, Barbara 1857-1929...... **TCLC 57**

Beagle, Peter S(oyer) 1939-......... **CLC 7**
See also CA 9-12R; CANR 4; DLBY 80;
SATA 60

Bean, Normal
See Burroughs, Edgar Rice

Beard, Charles A(ustin)
1874-1948 .... **TCLC 15**
See also CA 115; DLB 17; SATA 18

Beardsley, Aubrey 1872-1898 ..... **NCLC 6**

Beattie, Ann
1947- .... **CLC 8, 13, 18, 40, 63; SSC 11**
See also BEST 90:2; CA 81-84; DLBY 82;
MTCW

Beattie, James 1735-1803 .... **NCLC 25**
See also DLB 109

Beauchamp, Kathleen Mansfield 1888-1923
See Mansfield, Katherine
See also CA 104; 134; DA

Beaumarchais, Pierre-Augustin Caron de
1732-1799 .... **DC 4**

**Beauvoir, Simone (Lucie Ernestine Marie
Bertrand) de**
1908-1986 .... **CLC 1, 2, 4, 8, 14, 31, 44,
50, 71; DA; WLC**
See also CA 9-12R; 118; CANR 28;
DLB 72; DLBY 86; MTCW

Becker, Jurek 1937-............ **CLC 7, 19**
See also CA 85-88; DLB 75

Becker, Walter 1950-............. **CLC 26**

Beckett, Samuel (Barclay)
1906-1989 ...... **CLC 1, 2, 3, 4, 6, 9, 10,
11, 14, 18, 29, 57, 59, 83; DA; SSC 16;
WLC**
See also CA 5-8R; 130; CANR 33;
CDBLB 1945-1960; DLB 13, 15;
DLBY 90; MTCW

Beckford, William 1760-1844 .... **NCLC 16**
See also DLB 39

Beckman, Gunnel 1910-........... **CLC 26**
See also CA 33-36R; CANR 15; CLR 25;
MAICYA; SAAS 9; SATA 6

Becque, Henri 1837-1899........ **NCLC 3**

Beddoes, Thomas Lovell
1803-1849 .... **NCLC 3**
See also DLB 96

Bedford, Donald F.
See Fearing, Kenneth (Flexner)

Beecher, Catharine Esther
1800-1878 .... **NCLC 30**
See also DLB 1

Beecher, John 1904-1980........... **CLC 6**
See also AITN 1; CA 5-8R; 105; CANR 8

Beer, Johann 1655-1700............. **LC 5**

Beer, Patricia 1924-.............. **CLC 58**
See also CA 61-64; CANR 13, 46, 46;
DLB 40

Beerbohm, Henry Maximilian
1872-1956 .... **TCLC 1, 24**
See also CA 104; DLB 34, 100

Beerbohm, Max
See Beerbohm, Henry Maximilian

Begiebing, Robert J(ohn) 1946-..... **CLC 70**
See also CA 122; CANR 40

Behan, Brendan
1923-1964 .... **CLC 1, 8, 11, 15, 79**
See also CA 73-76; CANR 33;
CDBLB 1945-1960; DLB 13; MTCW

Behn, Aphra
1640(?)-1689 .... **LC 1; DA; DC 4; WLC**
See also DLB 39, 80, 131

Behrman, S(amuel) N(athaniel)
1893-1973 .... **CLC 40**
See also CA 13-16; 45-48; CAP 1; DLB 7,
44

Belasco, David 1853-1931 .... **TCLC 3**
See also CA 104; DLB 7

Belcheva, Elisaveta 1893- .... **CLC 10**
See also Bagryana, Elisaveta

Beldone, Phil "Cheech"
See Ellison, Harlan (Jay)

Beleno
See Azuela, Mariano

Belinski, Vissarion Grigoryevich
1811-1848 .... **NCLC 5**

Belitt, Ben 1911-................. **CLC 22**
See also CA 13-16R; CAAS 4; CANR 7;
DLB 5

Bell, James Madison
1826-1902 .... **TCLC 43; BLC**
See also BW 1; CA 122; 124; DLB 50

Bell, Madison (Smartt) 1957- ...... **CLC 41**
See also CA 111; CANR 28

Bell, Marvin (Hartley) 1937-..... **CLC 8, 31**
See also CA 21-24R; CAAS 14; DLB 5;
MTCW

Bell, W. L. D.
See Mencken, H(enry) L(ouis)

Bellamy, Atwood C.
See Mencken, H(enry) L(ouis)

Bellamy, Edward 1850-1898 ...... **NCLC 4**
See also DLB 12

Bellin, Edward J.
See Kuttner, Henry

Belloc, (Joseph) Hilaire (Pierre)
1870-1953 .... **TCLC 7, 18**
See also CA 106; DLB 19, 100, 141;
YABC 1

Belloc, Joseph Peter Rene Hilaire
See Belloc, (Joseph) Hilaire (Pierre)

Belloc, Joseph Pierre Hilaire
See Belloc, (Joseph) Hilaire (Pierre)

Belloc, M. A.
See Lowndes, Marie Adelaide (Belloc)

Bellow, Saul
1915- ...... **CLC 1, 2, 3, 6, 8, 10, 13, 15,**
25, 33, 34, 63, 79; DA; SSC 14; WLC
See also AITN 2; BEST 89:3; CA 5-8R;
CABS 1; CANR 29; CDALB 1941-1968;
DLB 2, 28; DLBD 3; DLBY 82; MTCW

Bely, Andrey .... **TCLC 7; PC 11**
See also Bugayev, Boris Nikolayevich

Benary, Margot
See Benary-Isbert, Margot

Benary-Isbert, Margot 1889-1979 ... **CLC 12**
See also CA 5-8R; 89-92; CANR 4;
CLR 12; MAICYA; SATA 2;
SATA-Obit 21

Benavente (y Martinez), Jacinto
1866-1954 .... **TCLC 3**
See also CA 106; 131; HW; MTCW

Benchley, Peter (Bradford)
1940- .... **CLC 4, 8**
See also AAYA 14; AITN 2; CA 17-20R;
CANR 12, 35; MTCW; SATA 3

Benchley, Robert (Charles)
1889-1945 .... **TCLC 1, 55**
See also CA 105; DLB 11

Benedikt, Michael 1935- .... **CLC 4, 14**
See also CA 13-16R; CANR 7; DLB 5

Benet, Juan 1927-................ **CLC 28**
See also CA 143

Benet, Stephen Vincent
1898-1943 .... **TCLC 7; SSC 10**
See also CA 104; DLB 4, 48, 102; YABC 1

Benet, William Rose 1886-1950 ... **TCLC 28**
See also CA 118; DLB 45

Benford, Gregory (Albert) 1941-.... **CLC 52**
See also CA 69-72; CANR 12, 24;
DLBY 82

Bengtsson, Frans (Gunnar)
1894-1954 .... **TCLC 48**

Benjamin, David
See Slavitt, David R(ytman)

Benjamin, Lois
See Gould, Lois

Benjamin, Walter 1892-1940 ..... **TCLC 39**

Benn, Gottfried 1886-1956......... **TCLC 3**
See also CA 106; DLB 56

Bennett, Alan 1934- .... **CLC 45, 77**
See also CA 103; CANR 35; MTCW

Bennett, (Enoch) Arnold
1867-1931 .... **TCLC 5, 20**
See also CA 106; CDBLB 1890-1914;
DLB 10, 34, 98

Bennett, Elizabeth
See Mitchell, Margaret (Munnerlyn)

Bennett, George Harold 1930-
See Bennett, Hal
See also BW 1; CA 97-100

Bennett, Hal .... **CLC 5**
See also Bennett, George Harold
See also DLB 33

Bennett, Jay 1912-................ **CLC 35**
See also AAYA 10; CA 69-72; CANR 11,
42; JRDA; SAAS 4; SATA 41;
SATA-Brief 27

Bennett, Louise (Simone)
1919- .... **CLC 28; BLC**
See also BW 2; DLB 117

Benson, E(dward) F(rederic)
1867-1940 .... **TCLC 27**
See also CA 114; DLB 135

Benson, Jackson J. 1930-.......... **CLC 34**
See also CA 25-28R; DLB 111

Benson, Sally 1900-1972 .... **CLC 17**
See also CA 19-20; 37-40R; CAP 1;
SATA 1, 35; SATA-Obit 27

Benson, Stella 1892-1933......... **TCLC 17**
See also CA 117; DLB 36

Bentham, Jeremy 1748-1832 ..... **NCLC 38**
See also DLB 107

Bentley, E(dmund) C(lerihew)
1875-1956 .... **TCLC 12**
See also CA 108; DLB 70

Bentley, Eric (Russell) 1916-....... **CLC 24**
See also CA 5-8R; CANR 6

Beranger, Pierre Jean de
1780-1857 .... **NCLC 34**

Berendt, John (Lawrence) 1939-.... **CLC 86**
See also CA 146

Berger, Colonel
See Malraux, (Georges-)Andre

Berger, John (Peter) 1926- ...... **CLC 2, 19**
See also CA 81-84; DLB 14

Berger, Melvin H. 1927- .... **CLC 12**
See also CA 5-8R; CANR 4; CLR 32;
SAAS 2; SATA 5

Berger, Thomas (Louis)
1924- .... **CLC 3, 5, 8, 11, 18, 38**
See also CA 1-4R; CANR 5, 28; DLB 2;
DLBY 80; MTCW

Bergman, (Ernst) Ingmar
1918- .... **CLC 16, 72**
See also CA 81-84; CANR 33

Bergson, Henri 1859-1941 .... **TCLC 32**

Bergstein, Eleanor 1938- .... **CLC 4**
See also CA 53-56; CANR 5

Berkoff, Steven 1937-............. **CLC 56**
See also CA 104

Bermant, Chaim (Icyk) 1929- ...... **CLC 40**
See also CA 57-60; CANR 6, 31

Bern, Victoria
See Fisher, M(ary) F(rances) K(ennedy)

Bernanos, (Paul Louis) Georges
1888-1948 .... **TCLC 3**
See also CA 104; 130; DLB 72

Bernard, April 1956- .... **CLC 59**
See also CA 131

Berne, Victoria
See Fisher, M(ary) F(rances) K(ennedy)

Bernhard, Thomas
1931-1989 .... **CLC 3, 32, 61**
See also CA 85-88; 127; CANR 32;
DLB 85, 124; MTCW

Berriault, Gina 1926- .... **CLC 54**
See also CA 116; 129; DLB 130

Berrigan, Daniel 1921-............. **CLC 4**
See also CA 33-36R; CAAS 1; CANR 11,
43; DLB 5

Berrigan, Edmund Joseph Michael, Jr.
1934-1983
See Berrigan, Ted
See also CA 61-64; 110; CANR 14

Berrigan, Ted.................... **CLC 37**
See also Berrigan, Edmund Joseph Michael,
Jr.
See also DLB 5

Berry, Charles Edward Anderson 1931-
See Berry, Chuck
See also CA 115

Berry, Chuck...................... **CLC 17**
See also Berry, Charles Edward Anderson

Berry, Jonas
See Ashbery, John (Lawrence)

Berry, Wendell (Erdman)
1934- .... **CLC 4, 6, 8, 27, 46**
See also AITN 1; CA 73-76; DLB 5, 6

Berryman, John
1914-1972 ...... **CLC 1, 2, 3, 4, 6, 8, 10,**
13, 25, 62
See also CA 13-16; 33-36R; CABS 2;
CANR 35; CAP 1; CDALB 1941-1968;
DLB 48; MTCW

Bertolucci, Bernardo 1940- .... **CLC 16**
See also CA 106

Bertrand, Aloysius 1807-1841 .... **NCLC 31**

Bertran de Born c. 1140-1215 ..... **CMLC 5**

Besant, Annie (Wood) 1847-1933 ... **TCLC 9**
See also CA 105

Bessie, Alvah 1904-1985. .... **CLC 23**
See also CA 5-8R; 116; CANR 2; DLB 26

Bethlen, T. D.
See Silverberg, Robert

Beti, Mongo................. **CLC 27; BLC**
See also Biyidi, Alexandre

Betjeman, John
1906-1984 .... **CLC 2, 6, 10, 34, 43**
See also CA 9-12R; 112; CANR 33;
CDBLB 1945-1960; DLB 20; DLBY 84;
MTCW

Bettelheim, Bruno 1903-1990 ...... **CLC 79**
See also CA 81-84; 131; CANR 23; MTCW

Betti, Ugo 1892-1953 .... **TCLC 5**
See also CA 104

Betts, Doris (Waugh) 1932-.... **CLC 3, 6, 28**
See also CA 13-16R; CANR 9; DLBY 82

Bevan, Alistair
See Roberts, Keith (John Kingston)

Bialik, Chaim Nachman
1873-1934 .... **TCLC 25**

Bickerstaff, Isaac
See Swift, Jonathan

Bidart, Frank 1939- .... **CLC 33**
See also CA 140

Bienek, Horst 1930-............ **CLC 7, 11**
See also CA 73-76; DLB 75

Bierce, Ambrose (Gwinett)
1842-1914(?) .... **TCLC 1, 7, 44; DA;
SSC 9; WLC**
See also CA 104; 139; CDALB 1865-1917;
DLB 11, 12, 23, 71, 74

Billings, Josh
See Shaw, Henry Wheeler

Billington, (Lady) Rachel (Mary)
1942-........................ **CLC 43**
See also AITN 2; CA 33-36R; CANR 44

Binyon, T(imothy) J(ohn) 1936- .... **CLC 34**
See also CA 111; CANR 28

Bioy Casares, Adolfo
1914- ...... **CLC 4, 8, 13; HLC; SSC 17**
See also CA 29-32R; CANR 19, 43;
DLB 113; HW; MTCW

Bird, Cordwainer
See Ellison, Harlan (Jay)

Bird, Robert Montgomery
1806-1854 .... **NCLC 1**

Birney, (Alfred) Earle
1904- .... **CLC 1, 4, 6, 11**
See also CA 1-4R; CANR 5, 20; DLB 88;
MTCW

Bishop, Elizabeth
1911-1979 ...... **CLC 1, 4, 9, 13, 15, 32;
DA; PC 3**
See also CA 5-8R; 89-92; CABS 2;
CANR 26; CDALB 1968-1988; DLB 5;
MTCW; SATA-Obit 24

Bishop, John 1935-............... **CLC 10**
See also CA 105

Bissett, Bill 1939-............... **CLC 18**
See also CA 69-72; CAAS 19; CANR 15;
DLB 53; MTCW

Bitov, Andrei (Georgievich) 1937-... **CLC 57**
See also CA 142

Biyidi, Alexandre 1932-
See Beti, Mongo
See also BW 1; CA 114; 124; MTCW

Bjarme, Brynjolf
See Ibsen, Henrik (Johan)

Bjornson, Bjornstjerne (Martinius)
1832-1910 .... **TCLC 7, 37**
See also CA 104

Black, Robert
See Holdstock, Robert P.

Blackburn, Paul 1926-1971 ...... **CLC 9, 43**
See also CA 81-84; 33-36R; CANR 34;
DLB 16; DLBY 81

Black Elk 1863-1950 .... **TCLC 33**
See also CA 144; NNAL

Black Hobart
See Sanders, (James) Ed(ward)

Blacklin, Malcolm
See Chambers, Aidan

Blackmore, R(ichard) D(oddridge)
1825-1900 .... **TCLC 27**
See also CA 120; DLB 18

Blackmur, R(ichard) P(almer)
1904-1965 .... **CLC 2, 24**
See also CA 11-12; 25-28R; CAP 1; DLB 63

Black Tarantula, The
See Acker, Kathy

Blackwood, Algernon (Henry)
1869-1951 .... **TCLC 5**
See also CA 105

Blackwood, Caroline 1931- .... **CLC 6, 9**
See also CA 85-88; CANR 32; DLB 14;
MTCW

Blade, Alexander
See Hamilton, Edmond; Silverberg, Robert

Blaga, Lucian 1895-1961.......... **CLC 75**

Blair, Eric (Arthur) 1903-1950
See Orwell, George
See also CA 104; 132; DA; MTCW;
SATA 29

Blais, Marie-Claire
1939- .... **CLC 2, 4, 6, 13, 22**
See also CA 21-24R; CAAS 4; CANR 38;
DLB 53; MTCW

Blaise, Clark 1940-............... **CLC 29**
See also AITN 2; CA 53-56; CAAS 3;
CANR 5; DLB 53

Blake, Nicholas
See Day Lewis, C(ecil)
See also DLB 77

Blake, William
1757-1827 ..... **NCLC 13, 37; DA; WLC**
See also CDBLB 1789-1832; DLB 93;
MAICYA; SATA 30

Blasco Ibanez, Vicente
1867-1928 .... **TCLC 12**
See also CA 110; 131; HW; MTCW

Blatty, William Peter 1928-......... **CLC 2**
See also CA 5-8R; CANR 9

Bleeck, Oliver
See Thomas, Ross (Elmore)

Blessing, Lee 1949-............... **CLC 54**

Blish, James (Benjamin)
1921-1975 .... **CLC 14**
See also CA 1-4R; 57-60; CANR 3; DLB 8;
MTCW; SATA 66

Bliss, Reginald
See Wells, H(erbert) G(eorge)

Blixen, Karen (Christentze Dinesen)
1885-1962
See Dinesen, Isak
See also CA 25-28; CANR 22; CAP 2;
MTCW; SATA 44

Bloch, Robert (Albert) 1917-1994 ... **CLC 33**
See also CA 5-8R; 146; CAAS 20; CANR 5;
DLB 44; SATA 12

Blok, Alexander (Alexandrovich)
1880-1921 .... **TCLC 5**
See also CA 104

Blom, Jan
See Breytenbach, Breyten

Bloom, Harold 1930- .... **CLC 24**
See also CA 13-16R; CANR 39; DLB 67

Bloomfield, Aurelius
See Bourne, Randolph S(illiman)

Blount, Roy (Alton), Jr. 1941- ..... **CLC 38**
See also CA 53-56; CANR 10, 28; MTCW

Bloy, Leon 1846-1917............ **TCLC 22**
See also CA 121; DLB 123

Blume, Judy (Sussman) 1938-... **CLC 12, 30**
See also AAYA 3; CA 29-32R; CANR 13,
37; CLR 2, 15; DLB 52; JRDA;
MAICYA; MTCW; SATA 2, 31, 79

Blunden, Edmund (Charles)
1896-1974 .... **CLC 2, 56**
See also CA 17-18; 45-48; CAP 2; DLB 20,
100; MTCW

Bly, Robert (Elwood)
1926- .... **CLC 1, 2, 5, 10, 15, 38**
See also CA 5-8R; CANR 41; DLB 5;
MTCW

Boas, Franz 1858-1942.......... **TCLC 56**
See also CA 115

Bobette
See Simenon, Georges (Jacques Christian)

Boccaccio, Giovanni
1313-1375 .... **CMLC 13; SSC 10**

Bochco, Steven 1943-............. **CLC 35**
See also AAYA 11; CA 124; 138

Bodenheim, Maxwell 1892-1954 ... **TCLC 44**
See also CA 110; DLB 9, 45

Bodker, Cecil 1927- .... **CLC 21**
See also CA 73-76; CANR 13, 44; CLR 23;
MAICYA; SATA 14

Boell, Heinrich (Theodor)
1917-1985 .... **CLC 2, 3, 6, 9, 11, 15, 27,
32, 72; DA; WLC**
See also CA 21-24R; 116; CANR 24;
DLB 69; DLBY 85; MTCW

Boerne, Alfred
See Doeblin, Alfred

Bogan, Louise 1897-1970 . . . . . **CLC 4, 39, 46**
See also CA 73-76; 25-28R; CANR 33;
DLB 45; MTCW

Bogarde, Dirk . . . . **CLC 19**
See also Van Den Bogarde, Derek Jules
Gaspard Ulric Niven
See also DLB 14

Bogosian, Eric 1953- . . . . **CLC 45**
See also CA 138

Bograd, Larry 1953- . . . . **CLC 35**
See also CA 93-96; SATA 33

Boiardo, Matteo Maria 1441-1494 . . . . **LC 6**

Boileau-Despreaux, Nicolas
1636-1711 . . . . **LC 3**

Boland, Eavan (Aisling) 1944- . . . **CLC 40, 67**
See also CA 143; DLB 40

Bolt, Lee
See Faust, Frederick (Schiller)

Bolt, Robert (Oxton) 1924- . . . . **CLC 14**
See also CA 17-20R; CANR 35; DLB 13;
MTCW

Bombet, Louis-Alexandre-Cesar
See Stendhal

Bomkauf
See Kaufman, Bob (Garnell)

Bonaventura . . . . **NCLC 35**
See also DLB 90

Bond, Edward 1934- . . . . **CLC 4, 6, 13, 23**
See also CA 25-28R; CANR 38; DLB 13;
MTCW

Bonham, Frank 1914-1989 . . . . **CLC 12**
See also AAYA 1; CA 9-12R; CANR 4, 36;
JRDA; MAICYA; SAAS 3; SATA 1, 49;
SATA-Obit 62

Bonnefoy, Yves 1923- . . . . **CLC 9, 15, 58**
See also CA 85-88; CANR 33; MTCW

Bontemps, Arna(ud Wendell)
1902-1973 . . . . **CLC 1, 18; BLC**
See also BW 1; CA 1-4R; 41-44R; CANR 4,
35; CLR 6; DLB 48, 51; JRDA;
MAICYA; MTCW; SATA 2, 44;
SATA-Obit 24

Booth, Martin 1944- . . . . **CLC 13**
See also CA 93-96; CAAS 2

Booth, Philip 1925- . . . . **CLC 23**
See also CA 5-8R; CANR 5; DLBY 82

Booth, Wayne C(layson) 1921- . . . . . **CLC 24**
See also CA 1-4R; CAAS 5; CANR 3, 43;
DLB 67

Borchert, Wolfgang 1921-1947 . . . . . **TCLC 5**
See also CA 104; DLB 69, 124

Borel, Petrus 1809-1859 . . . . **NCLC 41**

Borges, Jorge Luis
1899-1986 . . . **CLC 1, 2, 3, 4, 6, 8, 9, 10,
13, 19, 44, 48, 83; DA; HLC; SSC 4;
WLC**
See also CA 21-24R; CANR 19, 33;
DLB 113; DLBY 86; HW; MTCW

Borowski, Tadeusz 1922-1951 . . . . . . **TCLC 9**
See also CA 106

Borrow, George (Henry)
1803-1881 . . . . **NCLC 9**
See also DLB 21, 55

Bosman, Herman Charles
1905-1951 . . . . **TCLC 49**

Bosschere, Jean de 1878(?)-1953 . . . **TCLC 19**
See also CA 115

Boswell, James
1740-1795 . . . . **LC 4; DA; WLC**
See also CDBLB 1660-1789; DLB 104, 142

Bottoms, David 1949- . . . . **CLC 53**
See also CA 105; CANR 22; DLB 120;
DLBY 83

Boucicault, Dion 1820-1890 . . . . . . **NCLC 41**

Boucolon, Maryse 1937-
See Conde, Maryse
See also CA 110; CANR 30

Bourget, Paul (Charles Joseph)
1852-1935 . . . . **TCLC 12**
See also CA 107; DLB 123

Bourjaily, Vance (Nye) 1922- . . . . **CLC 8, 62**
See also CA 1-4R; CAAS 1; CANR 2;
DLB 2, 143

Bourne, Randolph S(illiman)
1886-1918 . . . . **TCLC 16**
See also CA 117; DLB 63

Bova, Ben(jamin William) 1932- . . . . **CLC 45**
See also CA 5-8R; CAAS 18; CANR 11;
CLR 3; DLBY 81; MAICYA; MTCW;
SATA 6, 68

Bowen, Elizabeth (Dorothea Cole)
1899-1973 . . . . . . **CLC 1, 3, 6, 11, 15, 22;
SSC 3**
See also CA 17-18; 41-44R; CANR 35;
CAP 2; CDBLB 1945-1960; DLB 15;
MTCW

Bowering, George 1935- . . . . **CLC 15, 47**
See also CA 21-24R; CAAS 16; CANR 10;
DLB 53

Bowering, Marilyn R(uthe) 1949- . . . **CLC 32**
See also CA 101

Bowers, Edgar 1924- . . . . **CLC 9**
See also CA 5-8R; CANR 24; DLB 5

Bowie, David . . . . **CLC 17**
See also Jones, David Robert

Bowles, Jane (Sydney)
1917-1973 . . . . **CLC 3, 68**
See also CA 19-20; 41-44R; CAP 2

Bowles, Paul (Frederick)
1910- . . . . **CLC 1, 2, 19, 53; SSC 3**
See also CA 1-4R; CAAS 1; CANR 1, 19;
DLB 5, 6; MTCW

Box, Edgar
See Vidal, Gore

Boyd, Nancy
See Millay, Edna St. Vincent

Boyd, William 1952- . . . . **CLC 28, 53, 70**
See also CA 114; 120

Boyle, Kay
1902-1992 . . . . . **CLC 1, 5, 19, 58; SSC 5**
See also CA 13-16R; 140; CAAS 1;
CANR 29; DLB 4, 9, 48, 86; DLBY 93;
MTCW

Boyle, Mark
See Kienzle, William X(avier)

Boyle, Patrick 1905-1982 . . . . **CLC 19**
See also CA 127

Boyle, T. C.
See Boyle, T(homas) Coraghessan

Boyle, T(homas) Coraghessan
1948- . . . . **CLC 36, 55; SSC 16**
See also BEST 90:4; CA 120; CANR 44;
DLBY 86

Boz
See Dickens, Charles (John Huffam)

Brackenridge, Hugh Henry
1748-1816 . . . . **NCLC 7**
See also DLB 11, 37

Bradbury, Edward P.
See Moorcock, Michael (John)

Bradbury, Malcolm (Stanley)
1932- . . . . **CLC 32, 61**
See also CA 1-4R; CANR 1, 33; DLB 14;
MTCW

Bradbury, Ray (Douglas)
1920- . . . **CLC 1, 3, 10, 15, 42; DA; WLC**
See also AITN 1, 2; CA 1-4R; CANR 2, 30;
CDALB 1968-1988; DLB 2, 8; MTCW;
SATA 11, 64

Bradford, Gamaliel 1863-1932 . . . . . **TCLC 36**
See also DLB 17

Bradley, David (Henry, Jr.)
1950- . . . . **CLC 23; BLC**
See also BW 1; CA 104; CANR 26; DLB 33

Bradley, John Ed(mund, Jr.)
1958- . . . . **CLC 55**
See also CA 139

Bradley, Marion Zimmer 1930- . . . . . **CLC 30**
See also AAYA 9; CA 57-60; CAAS 10;
CANR 7, 31; DLB 8; MTCW

Bradstreet, Anne
1612(?)-1672 . . . . **LC 4; DA; PC 10**
See also CDALB 1640-1865; DLB 24

Brady, Joan 1939- . . . . **CLC 86**
See also CA 141

Bragg, Melvyn 1939- . . . . **CLC 10**
See also BEST 89:3; CA 57-60; CANR 10;
DLB 14

Braine, John (Gerard)
1922-1986 . . . . **CLC 1, 3, 41**
See also CA 1-4R; 120; CANR 1, 33;
CDBLB 1945-1960; DLB 15; DLBY 86;
MTCW

Brammer, William 1930(?)-1978 . . . . **CLC 31**
See also CA 77-80

Brancati, Vitaliano 1907-1954 . . . . . **TCLC 12**
See also CA 109

Brancato, Robin F(idler) 1936- . . . . . **CLC 35**
See also AAYA 9; CA 69-72; CANR 11,
45; CLR 32; JRDA; SAAS 9; SATA 23

Brand, Max
See Faust, Frederick (Schiller)

Brand, Millen 1906-1980 . . . . **CLC 7**
See also CA 21-24R; 97-100

Branden, Barbara . . . . **CLC 44**

Brandes, Georg (Morris Cohen)
1842-1927 . . . . **TCLC 10**
See also CA 105

Brandys, Kazimierz 1916- . . . . **CLC 62**

Branley, Franklyn M(ansfield)
1915- .... **CLC 21**
See also CA 33-36R; CANR 14, 39;
CLR 13; MAICYA; SAAS 16; SATA 4,
68

Brathwaite, Edward Kamau 1930-... **CLC 11**
See also BW 2; CA 25-28R; CANR 11, 26,
47; DLB 125

Brautigan, Richard (Gary)
1935-1984 .... **CLC 1, 3, 5, 9, 12, 34, 42**
See also CA 53-56; 113; CANR 34; DLB 2,
5; DLBY 80, 84; MTCW; SATA 56

Braverman, Kate 1950- .... **CLC 67**
See also CA 89-92

Brecht, Bertolt
1898-1956 ...... **TCLC 1, 6, 13, 35; DA;**
DC 3; WLC
See also CA 104; 133; DLB 56, 124; MTCW

Brecht, Eugen Berthold Friedrich
See Brecht, Bertolt

Bremer, Fredrika 1801-1865 ..... **NCLC 11**

Brennan, Christopher John
1870-1932 .... **TCLC 17**
See also CA 117

Brennan, Maeve 1917- .... **CLC 5**
See also CA 81-84

Brentano, Clemens (Maria)
1778-1842 .... **NCLC 1**
See also DLB 90

Brent of Bin Bin
See Franklin, (Stella Maraia Sarah) Miles

Brenton, Howard 1942- .... **CLC 31**
See also CA 69-72; CANR 33; DLB 13;
MTCW

Breslin, James 1930-
See Breslin, Jimmy
See also CA 73-76; CANR 31; MTCW

Breslin, Jimmy .... **CLC 4, 43**
See also Breslin, James
See also AITN 1

Bresson, Robert 1907- .... **CLC 16**
See also CA 110

Breton, Andre 1896-1966... **CLC 2, 9, 15, 54**
See also CA 19-20; 25-28R; CANR 40;
CAP 2; DLB 65; MTCW

Breytenbach, Breyten 1939(?)- .. **CLC 23, 37**
See also CA 113; 129

Bridgers, Sue Ellen 1942- .... **CLC 26**
See also AAYA 8; CA 65-68; CANR 11,
36; CLR 18; DLB 52; JRDA; MAICYA;
SAAS 1; SATA 22

Bridges, Robert (Seymour)
1844-1930 .... **TCLC 1**
See also CA 104; CDBLB 1890-1914;
DLB 19, 98

Bridie, James................... **TCLC 3**
See also Mavor, Osborne Henry
See also DLB 10

Brin, David 1950- .... **CLC 34**
See also CA 102; CANR 24; SATA 65

Brink, Andre (Philippus)
1935- .... **CLC 18, 36**
See also CA 104; CANR 39; MTCW

Brinsmead, H(esba) F(ay) 1922- .... **CLC 21**
See also CA 21-24R; CANR 10; MAICYA;
SAAS 5; SATA 18, 78

Brittain, Vera (Mary)
1893(?)-1970 .... **CLC 23**
See also CA 13-16; 25-28R; CAP 1; MTCW

Broch, Hermann 1886-1951....... **TCLC 20**
See also CA 117; DLB 85, 124

Brock, Rose
See Hansen, Joseph

Brodkey, Harold 1930-........... **CLC 56**
See also CA 111; DLB 130

Brodsky, Iosif Alexandrovich 1940-
See Brodsky, Joseph
See also AITN 1; CA 41-44R; CANR 37;
MTCW

Brodsky, Joseph .. **CLC 4, 6, 13, 36, 50; PC 9**
See also Brodsky, Iosif Alexandrovich

Brodsky, Michael Mark 1948- ..... **CLC 19**
See also CA 102; CANR 18, 41

Bromell, Henry 1947-.............. **CLC 5**
See also CA 53-56; CANR 9

Bromfield, Louis (Brucker)
1896-1956 .... **TCLC 11**
See also CA 107; DLB 4, 9, 86

Broner, E(sther) M(asserman)
1930- .... **CLC 19**
See also CA 17-20R; CANR 8, 25; DLB 28

Bronk, William 1918-.............. **CLC 10**
See also CA 89-92; CANR 23

Bronstein, Lev Davidovich
See Trotsky, Leon

Bronte, Anne 1820-1849......... **NCLC 4**
See also DLB 21

Bronte, Charlotte
1816-1855 ... **NCLC 3, 8, 33; DA; WLC**
See also CDBLB 1832-1890; DLB 21

Bronte, (Jane) Emily
1818-1848 .... **NCLC 16, 35; DA; PC 8;**
WLC
See also CDBLB 1832-1890; DLB 21, 32

Brooke, Frances 1724-1789 .... **LC 6**
See also DLB 39, 99

Brooke, Henry 1703(?)-1783 .... **LC 1**
See also DLB 39

Brooke, Rupert (Chawner)
1887-1915 .... **TCLC 2, 7; DA; WLC**
See also CA 104; 132; CDBLB 1914-1945;
DLB 19; MTCW

Brooke-Haven, P.
See Wodehouse, P(elham) G(renville)

Brooke-Rose, Christine 1926- ...... **CLC 40**
See also CA 13-16R; DLB 14

Brookner, Anita 1928- ...... **CLC 32, 34, 51**
See also CA 114; 120; CANR 37; DLBY 87;
MTCW

Brooks, Cleanth 1906-1994 ..... **CLC 24, 86**
See also CA 17-20R; 145; CANR 33, 35;
DLB 63; MTCW

Brooks, George
See Baum, L(yman) Frank

Brooks, Gwendolyn
1917- ...... **CLC 1, 2, 4, 5, 15, 49; BLC;**
DA; PC 7; WLC
See also AITN 1; BW 2; CA 1-4R;
CANR 1, 27; CDALB 1941-1968;
CLR 27; DLB 5, 76; MTCW; SATA 6

Brooks, Mel...................... **CLC 12**
See also Kaminsky, Melvin
See also AAYA 13; DLB 26

Brooks, Peter 1938-............... **CLC 34**
See also CA 45-48; CANR 1

Brooks, Van Wyck 1886-1963...... **CLC 29**
See also CA 1-4R; CANR 6; DLB 45, 63,
103

Brophy, Brigid (Antonia)
1929- .... **CLC 6, 11, 29**
See also CA 5-8R; CAAS 4; CANR 25;
DLB 14; MTCW

Brosman, Catharine Savage 1934-.... **CLC 9**
See also CA 61-64; CANR 21, 46, 46

Brother Antoninus
See Everson, William (Oliver)

Broughton, T(homas) Alan 1936- ... **CLC 19**
See also CA 45-48; CANR 2, 23

Broumas, Olga 1949-.......... **CLC 10, 73**
See also CA 85-88; CANR 20

Brown, Charles Brockden
1771-1810 .... **NCLC 22**
See also CDALB 1640-1865; DLB 37, 59,
73

Brown, Christy 1932-1981........ **CLC 63**
See also CA 105; 104; DLB 14

Brown, Claude 1937-........... **CLC 30; BLC**
See also AAYA 7; BW 1; CA 73-76

Brown, Dee (Alexander) 1908- .. **CLC 18, 47**
See also CA 13-16R; CAAS 6; CANR 11,
45; DLBY 80; MTCW; SATA 5

Brown, George
See Wertmueller, Lina

Brown, George Douglas
1869-1902 .... **TCLC 28**

Brown, George Mackay 1921-.... **CLC 5, 48**
See also CA 21-24R; CAAS 6; CANR 12,
37; DLB 14, 27, 139; MTCW; SATA 35

Brown, (William) Larry 1951-...... **CLC 73**
See also CA 130; 134

Brown, Moses
See Barrett, William (Christopher)

Brown, Rita Mae 1944- ..... **CLC 18, 43, 79**
See also CA 45-48; CANR 2, 11, 35;
MTCW

Brown, Roderick (Langmere) Haig-
See Haig-Brown, Roderick (Langmere)

Brown, Rosellen 1939-............ **CLC 32**
See also CA 77-80; CAAS 10; CANR 14, 44

Brown, Sterling Allen
1901-1989 .... **CLC 1, 23, 59; BLC**
See also BW 1; CA 85-88; 127; CANR 26;
DLB 48, 51, 63; MTCW

Brown, Will
See Ainsworth, William Harrison

Brown, William Wells
1813-1884 .... **NCLC 2; BLC; DC 1**
See also DLB 3, 50

Browne, (Clyde) Jackson   1948(?)-... CLC 21
See also CA 120

Browning, Elizabeth Barrett
1806-1861 ..... NCLC 1, 16; DA; PC 6;
WLC
See also CDBLB 1832-1890; DLB 32

Browning, Robert
1812-1889 .... NCLC 19; DA; PC 2
See also CDBLB 1832-1890; DLB 32;
YABC 1

Browning, Tod   1882-1962 .... CLC 16
See also CA 141; 117

Bruccoli, Matthew J(oseph)   1931- .. CLC 34
See also CA 9-12R; CANR 7; DLB 103

Bruce, Lenny .... CLC 21
See also Schneider, Leonard Alfred

Bruin, John
See Brutus, Dennis

Brulard, Henri
See Stendhal

Brulls, Christian
See Simenon, Georges (Jacques Christian)

Brunner, John (Kilian Houston)
1934- .... CLC 8, 10
See also CA 1-4R; CAAS 8; CANR 2, 37;
MTCW

Bruno, Giordano   1548-1600........ LC 27

Brutus, Dennis   1924- .... CLC 43; BLC
See also BW 2; CA 49-52; CAAS 14;
CANR 2, 27, 42; DLB 117

Bryan, C(ourtlandt) D(ixon) B(arnes)
1936- .... CLC 29
See also CA 73-76; CANR 13

Bryan, Michael
See Moore, Brian

Bryant, William Cullen
1794-1878 .... NCLC 6, 46; DA
See also CDALB 1640-1865; DLB 3, 43, 59

Bryusov, Valery Yakovlevich
1873-1924 .... TCLC 10
See also CA 107

Buchan, John   1875-1940 .... TCLC 41
See also CA 108; 145; DLB 34, 70; YABC 2

Buchanan, George   1506-1582 .... LC 4

Buchheim, Lothar-Guenther   1918- ... CLC 6
See also CA 85-88

Buchner, (Karl) Georg
1813-1837 .... NCLC 26

Buchwald, Art(hur)   1925-......... CLC 33
See also AITN 1; CA 5-8R; CANR 21;
MTCW; SATA 10

Buck, Pearl S(ydenstricker)
1892-1973 .... CLC 7, 11, 18; DA
See also AITN 1; CA 1-4R; 41-44R;
CANR 1, 34; DLB 9, 102; MTCW;
SATA 1, 25

Buckler, Ernest   1908-1984......... CLC 13
See also CA 11-12; 114; CAP 1; DLB 68;
SATA 47

Buckley, Vincent (Thomas)
1925-1988 .... CLC 57
See also CA 101

Buckley, William F(rank), Jr.
1925- .... CLC 7, 18, 37
See also AITN 1; CA 1-4R; CANR 1, 24;
DLB 137; DLBY 80; MTCW

Buechner, (Carl) Frederick
1926-.................. CLC 2, 4, 6, 9
See also CA 13-16R; CANR 11, 39;
DLBY 80; MTCW

Buell, John (Edward)   1927-........ CLC 10
See also CA 1-4R; DLB 53

Buero Vallejo, Antonio   1916- ... CLC 15, 46
See also CA 106; CANR 24; HW; MTCW

Bufalino, Gesualdo   1920(?)-........ CLC 74

Bugayev, Boris Nikolayevich   1880-1934
See Bely, Andrey
See also CA 104

Bukowski, Charles
1920-1994 .... CLC 2, 5, 9, 41, 82
See also CA 17-20R; 144; CANR 40;
DLB 5, 130; MTCW

Bulgakov, Mikhail (Afanas'evich)
1891-1940 .... TCLC 2, 16; SSC 18
See also CA 105

Bulgya, Alexander Alexandrovich
1901-1956 .... TCLC 53
See also Fadeyev, Alexander
See also CA 117

Bullins, Ed   1935- .... CLC 1, 5, 7; BLC
See also BW 2; CA 49-52; CAAS 16;
CANR 24, 46, 46; DLB 7, 38; MTCW

Bulwer-Lytton, Edward (George Earle Lytton)
1803-1873 .... NCLC 1, 45
See also DLB 21

Bunin, Ivan Alexeyevich
1870-1953 .... TCLC 6; SSC 5
See also CA 104

Bunting, Basil   1900-1985.... CLC 10, 39, 47
See also CA 53-56; 115; CANR 7; DLB 20

Bunuel, Luis   1900-1983 .. CLC 16, 80; HLC
See also CA 101; 110; CANR 32; HW

Bunyan, John   1628-1688 .. LC 4; DA; WLC
See also CDBLB 1660-1789; DLB 39

Burford, Eleanor
See Hibbert, Eleanor Alice Burford

Burgess, Anthony
CLC 1, 2, 4, 5, 8, 10, 13, 15, 22, 40, 62,
81
See also Wilson, John (Anthony) Burgess
See also AITN 1; CDBLB 1960 to Present;
DLB 14

Burke, Edmund
1729(?)-1797 .... LC 7; DA; WLC
See also DLB 104

Burke, Kenneth (Duva)
1897-1993 .... CLC 2, 24
See also CA 5-8R; 143; CANR 39; DLB 45,
63; MTCW

Burke, Leda
See Garnett, David

Burke, Ralph
See Silverberg, Robert

Burney, Fanny   1752-1840 .... NCLC 12
See also DLB 39

Burns, Robert
1759-1796 ..... LC 3; DA; PC 6; WLC
See also CDBLB 1789-1832; DLB 109

Burns, Tex
See L'Amour, Louis (Dearborn)

Burnshaw, Stanley   1906-..... CLC 3, 13, 44
See also CA 9-12R; DLB 48

Burr, Anne   1937- .... CLC 6
See also CA 25-28R

Burroughs, Edgar Rice
1875-1950 ....TCLC 2, 32
See also AAYA 11; CA 104; 132; DLB 8;
MTCW; SATA 41

Burroughs, William S(eward)
1914- .... CLC 1, 2, 5, 15, 22, 42, 75;
DA; WLC
See also AITN 2; CA 9-12R; CANR 20;
DLB 2, 8, 16; DLBY 81; MTCW

Burton, Richard F.   1821-1890.... NCLC 42
See also DLB 55

Busch, Frederick   1941- ... CLC 7, 10, 18, 47
See also CA 33-36R; CAAS 1; CANR 45;
DLB 6

Bush, Ronald   1946- .... CLC 34
See also CA 136

Bustos, F(rancisco)
See Borges, Jorge Luis

Bustos Domecq, H(onorio)
See Bioy Casares, Adolfo; Borges, Jorge
Luis

Butler, Octavia E(stelle)   1947- ..... CLC 38
See also BW 2; CA 73-76; CANR 12, 24,
38; DLB 33; MTCW

Butler, Robert Olen (Jr.)   1945-..... CLC 81
See also CA 112

Butler, Samuel   1612-1680 .... LC 16
See also DLB 101, 126

Butler, Samuel
1835-1902 ...... TCLC 1, 33; DA; WLC
See also CA 143; CDBLB 1890-1914;
DLB 18, 57

Butler, Walter C.
See Faust, Frederick (Schiller)

Butor, Michel (Marie Francois)
1926-.............. CLC 1, 3, 8, 11, 15
See also CA 9-12R; CANR 33; DLB 83;
MTCW

Buzo, Alexander (John)   1944-...... CLC 61
See also CA 97-100; CANR 17, 39

Buzzati, Dino   1906-1972 .... CLC 36
See also CA 33-36R

Byars, Betsy (Cromer)   1928-....... CLC 35
See also CA 33-36R; CANR 18, 36; CLR 1,
16; DLB 52; JRDA; MAICYA; MTCW;
SAAS 1; SATA 4, 46, 80

Byatt, A(ntonia) S(usan Drabble)
1936- .... CLC 19, 65
See also CA 13-16R; CANR 13, 33;
DLB 14; MTCW

Byrne, David   1952-.............. CLC 26
See also CA 127

Byrne, John Keyes   1926-
See Leonard, Hugh
See also CA 102

Byron, George Gordon (Noel)
1788-1824 . . . . . NCLC **2, 12; DA; WLC**
See also CDBLB 1789-1832; DLB 96, 110

C. 3. 3.
See Wilde, Oscar (Fingal O'Flahertie Wills)

Caballero, Fernan 1796-1877 . . . . . **NCLC 10**

Cabell, James Branch 1879-1958 . . . **TCLC 6**
See also CA 105; DLB 9, 78

Cable, George Washington
1844-1925 . . . . **TCLC 4; SSC 4**
See also CA 104; DLB 12, 74

Cabral de Melo Neto, Joao 1920- . . . **CLC 76**

Cabrera Infante, G(uillermo)
1929- . . . . **CLC 5, 25, 45; HLC**
See also CA 85-88; CANR 29; DLB 113;
HW; MTCW

Cade, Toni
See Bambara, Toni Cade

Cadmus and Harmonia
See Buchan, John

Caedmon fl. 658-680 . . . . **CMLC 7**
See also DLB 146

Caeiro, Alberto
See Pessoa, Fernando (Antonio Nogueira)

Cage, John (Milton, Jr.) 1912- . . . . . **CLC 41**
See also CA 13-16R; CANR 9

Cain, G.
See Cabrera Infante, G(uillermo)

Cain, Guillermo
See Cabrera Infante, G(uillermo)

Cain, James M(allahan)
1892-1977 . . . . **CLC 3, 11, 28**
See also AITN 1; CA 17-20R; 73-76;
CANR 8, 34; MTCW

Caine, Mark
See Raphael, Frederic (Michael)

Calasso, Roberto 1941- . . . . **CLC 81**
See also CA 143

Calderon de la Barca, Pedro
1600-1681 . . . . **LC 23; DC 3**

Caldwell, Erskine (Preston)
1903-1987 . . . . **CLC 1, 8, 14, 50, 60**
See also AITN 1; CA 1-4R; 121; CAAS 1;
CANR 2, 33; DLB 9, 86; MTCW

Caldwell, (Janet Miriam) Taylor (Holland)
1900-1985 . . . . **CLC 2, 28, 39**
See also CA 5-8R; 116; CANR 5

Calhoun, John Caldwell
1782-1850 . . . . **NCLC 15**
See also DLB 3

Calisher, Hortense
1911- . . . . **CLC 2, 4, 8, 38; SSC 15**
See also CA 1-4R; CANR 1, 22; DLB 2;
MTCW

Callaghan, Morley Edward
1903-1990 . . . . **CLC 3, 14, 41, 65**
See also CA 9-12R; 132; CANR 33;
DLB 68; MTCW

Calvino, Italo
1923-1985 . . . . . **CLC 5, 8, 11, 22, 33, 39,
73; SSC 3**
See also CA 85-88; 116; CANR 23; MTCW

Cameron, Carey 1952- . . . . **CLC 59**
See also CA 135

Cameron, Peter 1959- . . . . **CLC 44**
See also CA 125

Campana, Dino 1885-1932 . . . . **TCLC 20**
See also CA 117; DLB 114

Campbell, John W(ood, Jr.)
1910-1971 . . . . **CLC 32**
See also CA 21-22; 29-32R; CANR 34;
CAP 2; DLB 8; MTCW

Campbell, Joseph 1904-1987 . . . . **CLC 69**
See also AAYA 3; BEST 89:2; CA 1-4R;
124; CANR 3, 28; MTCW

Campbell, Maria 1940- . . . . **CLC 85**
See also CA 102; NNAL

Campbell, (John) Ramsey 1946- . . . . **CLC 42**
See also CA 57-60; CANR 7

Campbell, (Ignatius) Roy (Dunnachie)
1901-1957 . . . . **TCLC 5**
See also CA 104; DLB 20

Campbell, Thomas 1777-1844 . . . . **NCLC 19**
See also DLB 93; 144

Campbell, Wilfred . . . . **TCLC 9**
See also Campbell, William

Campbell, William 1858(?)-1918
See Campbell, Wilfred
See also CA 106; DLB 92

Campos, Alvaro de
See Pessoa, Fernando (Antonio Nogueira)

Camus, Albert
1913-1960 . . . . **CLC 1, 2, 4, 9, 11, 14, 32,
63, 69; DA; DC 2; SSC 9; WLC**
See also CA 89-92; DLB 72; MTCW

Canby, Vincent 1924- . . . . **CLC 13**
See also CA 81-84

Cancale
See Desnos, Robert

Canetti, Elias
1905-1994 . . . . **CLC 3, 14, 25, 75, 86**
See also CA 21-24R; 146; CANR 23;
DLB 85, 124; MTCW

Canin, Ethan 1960- . . . . **CLC 55**
See also CA 131; 135

Cannon, Curt
See Hunter, Evan

Cape, Judith
See Page, P(atricia) K(athleen)

Capek, Karel
1890-1938 . . . . . **TCLC 6, 37; DA; DC 1;
WLC**
See also CA 104; 140

Capote, Truman
1924-1984 . . . . . . **CLC 1, 3, 8, 13, 19, 34,
38, 58; DA; SSC 2; WLC**
See also CA 5-8R; 113; CANR 18;
CDALB 1941-1968; DLB 2; DLBY 80,
84; MTCW

Capra, Frank 1897-1991 . . . . **CLC 16**
See also CA 61-64; 135

Caputo, Philip 1941- . . . . **CLC 32**
See also CA 73-76; CANR 40

Card, Orson Scott 1951- . . . . **CLC 44, 47, 50**
See also AAYA 11; CA 102; CANR 27, 47;
MTCW

Cardenal (Martinez), Ernesto
1925- . . . . **CLC 31; HLC**
See also CA 49-52; CANR 2, 32; HW;
MTCW

Carducci, Giosue 1835-1907 . . . . . . **TCLC 32**

Carew, Thomas 1595(?)-1640 . . . . **LC 13**
See also DLB 126

Carey, Ernestine Gilbreth 1908- . . . . **CLC 17**
See also CA 5-8R; SATA 2

Carey, Peter 1943- . . . . **CLC 40, 55**
See also CA 123; 127; MTCW

Carleton, William 1794-1869 . . . . . . **NCLC 3**

Carlisle, Henry (Coffin) 1926- . . . . . . **CLC 33**
See also CA 13-16R; CANR 15

Carlsen, Chris
See Holdstock, Robert P.

Carlson, Ron(ald F.) 1947- . . . . **CLC 54**
See also CA 105; CANR 27

Carlyle, Thomas 1795-1881 . . **NCLC 22; DA**
See also CDBLB 1789-1832; DLB 55; 144

Carman, (William) Bliss
1861-1929 . . . . **TCLC 7**
See also CA 104; DLB 92

Carnegie, Dale 1888-1955 . . . . **TCLC 53**

Carossa, Hans 1878-1956 . . . . **TCLC 48**
See also DLB 66

Carpenter, Don(ald Richard)
1931- . . . . **CLC 41**
See also CA 45-48; CANR 1

Carpentier (y Valmont), Alejo
1904-1980 . . . . **CLC 8, 11, 38; HLC**
See also CA 65-68; 97-100; CANR 11;
DLB 113; HW

Carr, Caleb 1955(?)- . . . . **CLC 86**

Carr, Emily 1871-1945 . . . . **TCLC 32**
See also DLB 68

Carr, John Dickson 1906-1977 . . . . . . **CLC 3**
See also CA 49-52; 69-72; CANR 3, 33;
MTCW

Carr, Philippa
See Hibbert, Eleanor Alice Burford

Carr, Virginia Spencer 1929- . . . . **CLC 34**
See also CA 61-64; DLB 111

Carrier, Roch 1937- . . . . **CLC 13, 78**
See also CA 130; DLB 53

Carroll, James P. 1943(?)- . . . . **CLC 38**
See also CA 81-84

Carroll, Jim 1951- . . . . **CLC 35**
See also CA 45-48; CANR 42

Carroll, Lewis . . . . **NCLC 2; WLC**
See also Dodgson, Charles Lutwidge
See also CDBLB 1832-1890; CLR 2, 18;
DLB 18; JRDA

Carroll, Paul Vincent 1900-1968 . . . . **CLC 10**
See also CA 9-12R; 25-28R; DLB 10

Carruth, Hayden
1921- . . . . . . **CLC 4, 7, 10, 18, 84; PC 10**
See also CA 9-12R; CANR 4, 38; DLB 5;
MTCW; SATA 47

Carson, Rachel Louise 1907-1964 . . . **CLC 71**
See also CA 77-80; CANR 35; MTCW;
SATA 23

Carter, Angela (Olive)
1940-1992 ...... **CLC 5, 41, 76; SSC 13**
See also CA 53-56; 136; CANR 12, 36;
DLB 14; MTCW; SATA 66;
SATA-Obit 70

Carter, Nick
See Smith, Martin Cruz

Carver, Raymond
1938-1988 ... **CLC 22, 36, 53, 55; SSC 8**
See also CA 33-36R; 126; CANR 17, 34;
DLB 130; DLBY 84, 88; MTCW

Cary, (Arthur) Joyce (Lunel)
1888-1957 .... **TCLC 1, 29**
See also CA 104; CDBLB 1914-1945;
DLB 15, 100

Casanova de Seingalt, Giovanni Jacopo
1725-1798 .... **LC 13**

Casares, Adolfo Bioy
See Bioy Casares, Adolfo

Casely-Hayford, J(oseph) E(phraim)
1866-1930 .... **TCLC 24; BLC**
See also BW 2; CA 123

Casey, John (Dudley) 1939- .... **CLC 59**
See also BEST 90:2; CA 69-72; CANR 23

Casey, Michael 1947- .... **CLC 2**
See also CA 65-68; DLB 5

Casey, Patrick
See Thurman, Wallace (Henry)

Casey, Warren (Peter) 1935-1988 ... **CLC 12**
See also CA 101; 127

Casona, Alejandro .... **CLC 49**
See also Alvarez, Alejandro Rodriguez

Cassavetes, John 1929-1989 .... **CLC 20**
See also CA 85-88; 127

Cassill, R(onald) V(erlin) 1919- ... **CLC 4, 23**
See also CA 9-12R; CAAS 1; CANR 7, 45;
DLB 6

Cassity, (Allen) Turner 1929- .... **CLC 6, 42**
See also CA 17-20R; CAAS 8; CANR 11;
DLB 105

Castaneda, Carlos 1931(?)- .... **CLC 12**
See also CA 25-28R; CANR 32; HW;
MTCW

Castedo, Elena 1937- .... **CLC 65**
See also CA 132

Castedo-Ellerman, Elena
See Castedo, Elena

Castellanos, Rosario
1925-1974 .... **CLC 66; HLC**
See also CA 131; 53-56; DLB 113; HW

Castelvetro, Lodovico 1505-1571 ..... **LC 12**

Castiglione, Baldassare 1478-1529 ... **LC 12**

Castle, Robert
See Hamilton, Edmond

Castro, Guillen de 1569-1631 .... **LC 19**

Castro, Rosalia de 1837-1885 ..... **NCLC 3**

Cather, Willa
See Cather, Willa Sibert

Cather, Willa Sibert
1873-1947 .... **TCLC 1, 11, 31; DA;
SSC 2; WLC**
See also CA 104; 128; CDALB 1865-1917;
DLB 9, 54, 78; DLBD 1; MTCW;
SATA 30

Catton, (Charles) Bruce
1899-1978 .... **CLC 35**
See also AITN 1; CA 5-8R; 81-84;
CANR 7; DLB 17; SATA 2;
SATA-Obit 24

Cauldwell, Frank
See King, Francis (Henry)

Caunitz, William J. 1933- .... **CLC 34**
See also BEST 89:3; CA 125; 130

Causley, Charles (Stanley) 1917- ..... **CLC 7**
See also CA 9-12R; CANR 5, 35; CLR 30;
DLB 27; MTCW; SATA 3, 66

Caute, David 1936- .... **CLC 29**
See also CA 1-4R; CAAS 4; CANR 1, 33;
DLB 14

Cavafy, C(onstantine) P(eter) ...... **TCLC 2, 7**
See also Kavafis, Konstantinos Petrou

Cavallo, Evelyn
See Spark, Muriel (Sarah)

Cavanna, Betty .... **CLC 12**
See also Harrison, Elizabeth Cavanna
See also JRDA; MAICYA; SAAS 4;
SATA 1, 30

Caxton, William 1421(?)-1491(?) ..... **LC 17**

Cayrol, Jean 1911- .... **CLC 11**
See also CA 89-92; DLB 83

Cela, Camilo Jose
1916- .... **CLC 4, 13, 59; HLC**
See also BEST 90:2; CA 21-24R; CAAS 10;
CANR 21, 32; DLBY 89; HW; MTCW

Celan, Paul ...... **CLC 10, 19, 53, 82; PC 10**
See also Antschel, Paul
See also DLB 69

Celine, Louis-Ferdinand
.... **CLC 1, 3, 4, 7, 9, 15, 47**
See also Destouches, Louis-Ferdinand
See also DLB 72

Cellini, Benvenuto 1500-1571 .... **LC 7**

Cendrars, Blaise
See Sauser-Hall, Frederic

Cernuda (y Bidon), Luis
1902-1963 .... **CLC 54**
See also CA 131; 89-92; DLB 134; HW

Cervantes (Saavedra), Miguel de
1547-1616 ...... **LC 6, 23; DA; SSC 12;
WLC**

Cesaire, Aime (Fernand)
1913- .... **CLC 19, 32; BLC**
See also BW 2; CA 65-68; CANR 24, 43;
MTCW

Chabon, Michael 1965(?)- .... **CLC 55**
See also CA 139

Chabrol, Claude 1930- .... **CLC 16**
See also CA 110

Challans, Mary 1905-1983
See Renault, Mary
See also CA 81-84; 111; SATA 23;
SATA-Obit 36

Challis, George
See Faust, Frederick (Schiller)

Chambers, Aidan 1934- .... **CLC 35**
See also CA 25-28R; CANR 12, 31; JRDA;
MAICYA; SAAS 12; SATA 1, 69

Chambers, James 1948-
See Cliff, Jimmy
See also CA 124

Chambers, Jessie
See Lawrence, D(avid) H(erbert Richards)

Chambers, Robert W. 1865-1933 ... **TCLC 41**

Chandler, Raymond (Thornton)
1888-1959 .... **TCLC 1, 7**
See also CA 104; 129; CDALB 1929-1941;
DLBD 6; MTCW

Chang, Jung 1952- .... **CLC 71**
See also CA 142

Channing, William Ellery
1780-1842 .... **NCLC 17**
See also DLB 1, 59

Chaplin, Charles Spencer
1889-1977 .... **CLC 16**
See also Chaplin, Charlie
See also CA 81-84; 73-76

Chaplin, Charlie
See Chaplin, Charles Spencer
See also DLB 44

Chapman, George 1559(?)-1634 ...... **LC 22**
See also DLB 62, 121

Chapman, Graham 1941-1989 ..... **CLC 21**
See also Monty Python
See also CA 116; 129; CANR 35

Chapman, John Jay 1862-1933 ..... **TCLC 7**
See also CA 104

Chapman, Walker
See Silverberg, Robert

Chappell, Fred (Davis) 1936- .... **CLC 40, 78**
See also CA 5-8R; CAAS 4; CANR 8, 33;
DLB 6, 105

Char, Rene(-Emile)
1907-1988 .... **CLC 9, 11, 14, 55**
See also CA 13-16R; 124; CANR 32;
MTCW

Charby, Jay
See Ellison, Harlan (Jay)

Chardin, Pierre Teilhard de
See Teilhard de Chardin, (Marie Joseph)
Pierre

Charles I 1600-1649 .... **LC 13**

Charyn, Jerome 1937- .... **CLC 5, 8, 18**
See also CA 5-8R; CAAS 1; CANR 7;
DLBY 83; MTCW

Chase, Mary (Coyle) 1907-1981 ...... **DC 1**
See also CA 77-80; 105; SATA 17;
SATA-Obit 29

Chase, Mary Ellen 1887-1973 .... **CLC 2**
See also CA 13-16; 41-44R; CAP 1;
SATA 10

Chase, Nicholas
See Hyde, Anthony

Chateaubriand, Francois Rene de
1768-1848 .... **NCLC 3**
See also DLB 119

Chatterje, Sarat Chandra 1876-1936(?)
See Chatterji, Saratchandra
See also CA 109

Chatterji, Bankim Chandra
1838-1894 .... **NCLC 19**

Chatterji, Saratchandra . . . . TCLC 13
See also Chatterje, Sarat Chandra

Chatterton, Thomas 1752-1770 . . . . LC 3
See also DLB 109

Chatwin, (Charles) Bruce
1940-1989 . . . . CLC 28, 57, 59
See also AAYA 4; BEST 90:1; CA 85-88;
127

Chaucer, Daniel
See Ford, Ford Madox

Chaucer, Geoffrey
1340(?)-1400 . . . . LC 17; DA
See also CDBLB Before 1660; DLB 146

Chaviaras, Strates 1935-
See Haviaras, Stratis
See also CA 105

Chayefsky, Paddy . . . . CLC 23
See also Chayefsky, Sidney
See also DLB 7, 44; DLBY 81

Chayefsky, Sidney 1923-1981
See Chayefsky, Paddy
See also CA 9-12R; 104; CANR 18

Chedid, Andree 1920- . . . . CLC 47
See also CA 145

Cheever, John
1912-1982 . . . . . . CLC 3, 7, 8, 11, 15, 25,
64; DA; SSC 1; WLC
See also CA 5-8R; 106; CABS 1; CANR 5,
27; CDALB 1941-1968; DLB 2, 102;
DLBY 80, 82; MTCW

Cheever, Susan 1943- . . . . CLC 18, 48
See also CA 103; CANR 27; DLBY 82

Chekhonte, Antosha
See Chekhov, Anton (Pavlovich)

Chekhov, Anton (Pavlovich)
1860-1904 . . . . . TCLC 3, 10, 31, 55; DA;
SSC 2; WLC
See also CA 104; 124

Chernyshevsky, Nikolay Gavrilovich
1828-1889 . . . . NCLC 1

Cherry, Carolyn Janice 1942-
See Cherryh, C. J.
See also CA 65-68; CANR 10

Cherryh, C. J. . . . . CLC 35
See also Cherry, Carolyn Janice
See also DLBY 80

Chesnutt, Charles W(addell)
1858-1932 . . . . TCLC 5, 39; BLC; SSC 7
See also BW 1; CA 106; 125; DLB 12, 50,
78; MTCW

Chester, Alfred 1929(?)-1971 . . . . CLC 49
See also CA 33-36R; DLB 130

Chesterton, G(ilbert) K(eith)
1874-1936 . . . . TCLC 1, 6; SSC 1
See also CA 104; 132; CDBLB 1914-1945;
DLB 10, 19, 34, 70, 98; MTCW;
SATA 27

Chiang Pin-chin 1904-1986
See Ding Ling
See also CA 118

Ch'ien Chung-shu 1910- . . . . CLC 22
See also CA 130; MTCW

Child, L. Maria
See Child, Lydia Maria

Child, Lydia Maria 1802-1880 . . . . NCLC 6
See also DLB 1, 74; SATA 67

Child, Mrs.
See Child, Lydia Maria

Child, Philip 1898-1978 . . . . CLC 19, 68
See also CA 13-14; CAP 1; SATA 47

Childress, Alice
1920-1994 . . CLC 12, 15, 86; BLC; DC 4
See also AAYA 8; BW 2; CA 45-48; 146;
CANR 3, 27; CLR 14; DLB 7, 38; JRDA;
MAICYA; MTCW; SATA 7, 48, 81

Chislett, (Margaret) Anne 1943- . . . . CLC 34

Chitty, Thomas Willes 1926- . . . . CLC 11
See also Hinde, Thomas
See also CA 5-8R

Chomette, Rene Lucien 1898-1981
See Clair, Rene
See also CA 103

Chopin, Kate . . . . . . TCLC 5, 14; DA; SSC 8
See also Chopin, Katherine
See also CDALB 1865-1917; DLB 12, 78

Chopin, Katherine 1851-1904
See Chopin, Kate
See also CA 104; 122

Chretien de Troyes
c. 12th cent. - . . . . CMLC 10

Christie
See Ichikawa, Kon

Christie, Agatha (Mary Clarissa)
1890-1976 . . . . . . CLC 1, 6, 8, 12, 39, 48
See also AAYA 9; AITN 1, 2; CA 17-20R;
61-64; CANR 10, 37; CDBLB 1914-1945;
DLB 13, 77; MTCW; SATA 36

Christie, (Ann) Philippa
See Pearce, Philippa
See also CA 5-8R; CANR 4

Christine de Pizan 1365(?)-1431(?) . . . . LC 9

Chubb, Elmer
See Masters, Edgar Lee

Chulkov, Mikhail Dmitrievich
1743-1792 . . . . LC 2

Churchill, Caryl 1938- . . . CLC 31, 55; DC 5
See also CA 102; CANR 22, 46; DLB 13;
MTCW

Churchill, Charles 1731-1764 . . . . LC 3
See also DLB 109

Chute, Carolyn 1947- . . . . CLC 39
See also CA 123

Ciardi, John (Anthony)
1916-1986 . . . . CLC 10, 40, 44
See also CA 5-8R; 118; CAAS 2; CANR 5,
33; CLR 19; DLB 5; DLBY 86;
MAICYA; MTCW; SATA 1, 65;
SATA-Obit 46

Cicero, Marcus Tullius
106B.C.-43B.C. . . . . CMLC 3

Cimino, Michael 1943- . . . . CLC 16
See also CA 105

Cioran, E(mil) M. 1911- . . . . CLC 64
See also CA 25-28R

Cisneros, Sandra 1954- . . . . . . CLC 69; HLC
See also AAYA 9; CA 131; DLB 122; HW

Clair, Rene . . . . CLC 20
See also Chomette, Rene Lucien

Clampitt, Amy 1920-1994 . . . . CLC 32
See also CA 110; 146; CANR 29; DLB 105

Clancy, Thomas L., Jr. 1947-
See Clancy, Tom
See also CA 125; 131; MTCW

Clancy, Tom . . . . CLC 45
See also Clancy, Thomas L., Jr.
See also AAYA 9; BEST 89:1, 90:1

Clare, John 1793-1864 . . . . NCLC 9
See also DLB 55, 96

Clarin
See Alas (y Urena), Leopoldo (Enrique
Garcia)

Clark, Al C.
See Goines, Donald

Clark, (Robert) Brian 1932- . . . . CLC 29
See also CA 41-44R

Clark, Curt
See Westlake, Donald E(dwin)

Clark, Eleanor 1913- . . . . CLC 5, 19
See also CA 9-12R; CANR 41; DLB 6

Clark, J. P.
See Clark, John Pepper
See also DLB 117

Clark, John Pepper
1935- . . . . CLC 38; BLC; DC 5
See also Clark, J. P.
See also BW 1; CA 65-68; CANR 16

Clark, M. R.
See Clark, Mavis Thorpe

Clark, Mavis Thorpe 1909- . . . . CLC 12
See also CA 57-60; CANR 8, 37; CLR 30;
MAICYA; SAAS 5; SATA 8, 74

Clark, Walter Van Tilburg
1909-1971 . . . . CLC 28
See also CA 9-12R; 33-36R; DLB 9;
SATA 8

Clarke, Arthur C(harles)
1917- . . . . . . CLC 1, 4, 13, 18, 35; SSC 3
See also AAYA 4; CA 1-4R; CANR 2, 28;
JRDA; MAICYA; MTCW; SATA 13, 70

Clarke, Austin 1896-1974 . . . . CLC 6, 9
See also CA 29-32; 49-52; CAP 2; DLB 10,
20

Clarke, Austin C(hesterfield)
1934- . . . . CLC 8, 53; BLC
See also BW 1; CA 25-28R; CAAS 16;
CANR 14, 32; DLB 53, 125

Clarke, Gillian 1937- . . . . CLC 61
See also CA 106; DLB 40

Clarke, Marcus (Andrew Hislop)
1846-1881 . . . . NCLC 19

Clarke, Shirley 1925- . . . . CLC 16

Clash, The
See Headon, (Nicky) Topper; Jones, Mick;
Simonon, Paul; Strummer, Joe

Claudel, Paul (Louis Charles Marie)
1868-1955 . . . . TCLC 2, 10
See also CA 104

Clavell, James (duMaresq)
1925-1994 . . . . CLC 6, 25
See also CA 25-28R; 146; CANR 26;
MTCW

Cleaver, (Leroy) Eldridge
1935- .... CLC 30; BLC
See also BW 1; CA 21-24R; CANR 16

Cleese, John (Marwood) 1939- ..... CLC 21
See also Monty Python
See also CA 112; 116; CANR 35; MTCW

Cleishbotham, Jebediah
See Scott, Walter

Cleland, John 1710-1789 .... LC 2
See also DLB 39

Clemens, Samuel Langhorne 1835-1910
See Twain, Mark
See also CA 104; 135; CDALB 1865-1917;
DA; DLB 11, 12, 23, 64, 74; JRDA;
MAICYA; YABC 2

Cleophil
See Congreve, William

Clerihew, E.
See Bentley, E(dmund) C(lerihew)

Clerk, N. W.
See Lewis, C(live) S(taples)

Cliff, Jimmy .... CLC 21
See also Chambers, James

Clifton, (Thelma) Lucille
1936- .... CLC 19, 66; BLC
See also BW 2; CA 49-52; CANR 2, 24, 42;
CLR 5; DLB 5, 41; MAICYA; MTCW;
SATA 20, 69

Clinton, Dirk
See Silverberg, Robert

Clough, Arthur Hugh 1819-1861.. NCLC 27
See also DLB 32

Clutha, Janet Paterson Frame 1924-
See Frame, Janet
See also CA 1-4R; CANR 2, 36; MTCW

Clyne, Terence
See Blatty, William Peter

Cobalt, Martin
See Mayne, William (James Carter)

Coburn, D(onald) L(ee) 1938- ...... CLC 10
See also CA 89-92

Cocteau, Jean (Maurice Eugene Clement)
1889-1963 .... CLC 1, 8, 15, 16, 43; DA;
WLC
See also CA 25-28; CANR 40; CAP 2;
DLB 65; MTCW

Codrescu, Andrei 1946- .... CLC 46
See also CA 33-36R; CAAS 19; CANR 13,
34

Coe, Max
See Bourne, Randolph S(illiman)

Coe, Tucker
See Westlake, Donald E(dwin)

Coetzee, J(ohn) M(ichael)
1940- .... CLC 23, 33, 66
See also CA 77-80; CANR 41; MTCW

Coffey, Brian
See Koontz, Dean R(ay)

Cohen, Arthur A(llen)
1928-1986 .... CLC 7, 31
See also CA 1-4R; 120; CANR 1, 17, 42;
DLB 28

Cohen, Leonard (Norman)
1934- .... CLC 3, 38
See also CA 21-24R; CANR 14; DLB 53;
MTCW

Cohen, Matt 1942- .... CLC 19
See also CA 61-64; CAAS 18; CANR 40;
DLB 53

Cohen-Solal, Annie 19(?)- .... CLC 50

Colegate, Isabel 1931- .... CLC 36
See also CA 17-20R; CANR 8, 22; DLB 14;
MTCW

Coleman, Emmett
See Reed, Ishmael

Coleridge, Samuel Taylor
1772-1834 .. NCLC 9; DA; PC 11; WLC
See also CDBLB 1789-1832; DLB 93, 107

Coleridge, Sara 1802-1852 .... NCLC 31

Coles, Don 1928- .... CLC 46
See also CA 115; CANR 38

Colette, (Sidonie-Gabrielle)
1873-1954 ...... TCLC 1, 5, 16; SSC 10
See also CA 104; 131; DLB 65; MTCW

Collett, (Jacobine) Camilla (Wergeland)
1813-1895 .... NCLC 22

Collier, Christopher 1930- .... CLC 30
See also AAYA 13; CA 33-36R; CANR 13,
33; JRDA; MAICYA; SATA 16, 70

Collier, James L(incoln) 1928- ..... CLC 30
See also AAYA 13; CA 9-12R; CANR 4,
33; CLR 3; JRDA; MAICYA; SATA 8,
70

Collier, Jeremy 1650-1726 .... LC 6

Collins, Hunt
See Hunter, Evan

Collins, Linda 1931- .... CLC 44
See also CA 125

Collins, (William) Wilkie
1824-1889 .... NCLC 1, 18
See also CDBLB 1832-1890; DLB 18, 70

Collins, William 1721-1759 .... LC 4
See also DLB 109

Colman, George
See Glassco, John

Colt, Winchester Remington
See Hubbard, L(afayette) Ron(ald)

Colter, Cyrus 1910- .... CLC 58
See also BW 1; CA 65-68; CANR 10;
DLB 33

Colton, James
See Hansen, Joseph

Colum, Padraic 1881-1972........ CLC 28
See also CA 73-76; 33-36R; CANR 35;
CLR 36; MAICYA; MTCW; SATA 15

Colvin, James
See Moorcock, Michael (John)

Colwin, Laurie (E.)
1944-1992 .... CLC 5, 13, 23, 84
See also CA 89-92; 139; CANR 20, 46, 46;
DLBY 80; MTCW

Comfort, Alex(ander) 1920-........ CLC 7
See also CA 1-4R; CANR 1, 45

Comfort, Montgomery
See Campbell, (John) Ramsey

Compton-Burnett, I(vy)
1884(?)-1969 ...... CLC 1, 3, 10, 15, 34
See also CA 1-4R; 25-28R; CANR 4;
DLB 36; MTCW

Comstock, Anthony 1844-1915 .... TCLC 13
See also CA 110

Conan Doyle, Arthur
See Doyle, Arthur Conan

Conde, Maryse 1937- .... CLC 52
See also Boucolon, Maryse
See also BW 2

Condillac, Etienne Bonnot de
1714-1780 .... LC 26

Condon, Richard (Thomas)
1915- .... CLC 4, 6, 8, 10, 45
See also BEST 90:3; CA 1-4R; CAAS 1;
CANR 2, 23; MTCW

Congreve, William
1670-1729 ... LC 5, 21; DA; DC 2; WLC
See also CDBLB 1660-1789; DLB 39, 84

Connell, Evan S(helby), Jr.
1924- .... CLC 4, 6, 45
See also AAYA 7; CA 1-4R; CAAS 2;
CANR 2, 39; DLB 2; DLBY 81; MTCW

Connelly, Marc(us Cook)
1890-1980 .... CLC 7
See also CA 85-88; 102; CANR 30; DLB 7;
DLBY 80; SATA-Obit 25

Connor, Ralph .... TCLC 31
See also Gordon, Charles William
See also DLB 92

Conrad, Joseph
1857-1924 .... TCLC 1, 6, 13, 25, 43, 57;
DA; SSC 9; WLC
See also CA 104; 131; CDBLB 1890-1914;
DLB 10, 34, 98; MTCW; SATA 27

Conrad, Robert Arnold
See Hart, Moss

Conroy, Pat 1945-............. CLC 30, 74
See also AAYA 8; AITN 1; CA 85-88;
CANR 24; DLB 6; MTCW

Constant (de Rebecque), (Henri) Benjamin
1767-1830 .... NCLC 6
See also DLB 119

Conybeare, Charles Augustus
See Eliot, T(homas) S(tearns)

Cook, Michael 1933- .... CLC 58
See also CA 93-96; DLB 53

Cook, Robin 1940- .... CLC 14
See also BEST 90:2; CA 108; 111;
CANR 41

Cook, Roy
See Silverberg, Robert

Cooke, Elizabeth 1948- .... CLC 55
See also CA 129

Cooke, John Esten 1830-1886 ..... NCLC 5
See also DLB 3

Cooke, John Estes
See Baum, L(yman) Frank

Cooke, M. E.
See Creasey, John

Cooke, Margaret
See Creasey, John

Cooney, Ray .... CLC 62

Cooper, Douglas 1960-. . . . . CLC **86**

Cooper, Henry St. John
See Creasey, John

Cooper, J. California. . . . . CLC **56**
See also AAYA 12; BW 1; CA 125

Cooper, James Fenimore
1789-1851 . . . . NCLC **1, 27**
See also CDALB 1640-1865; DLB 3;
SATA 19

Coover, Robert (Lowell)
1932- . . . . . CLC **3, 7, 15, 32, 46**; SSC **15**
See also CA 45-48; CANR 3, 37; DLB 2;
DLBY 81; MTCW

Copeland, Stewart (Armstrong)
1952- . . . . CLC **26**

Coppard, A(lfred) E(dgar)
1878-1957 . . . . TCLC **5**
See also CA 114; YABC 1

Coppee, Francois 1842-1908 . . . . . . TCLC **25**

Coppola, Francis Ford 1939-. . . . . . . CLC **16**
See also CA 77-80; CANR 40; DLB 44

Corbiere, Tristan 1845-1875 . . . . . NCLC **43**

Corcoran, Barbara 1911-. . . . . CLC **17**
See also AAYA 14; CA 21-24R; CAAS 2;
CANR 11, 28; DLB 52; JRDA; SATA 3,
77

Cordelier, Maurice
See Giraudoux, (Hippolyte) Jean

Corelli, Marie 1855-1924. . . . . TCLC **51**
See also Mackay, Mary
See also DLB 34

Corman, Cid. CLC **9**
See also Corman, Sidney
See also CAAS 2; DLB 5

Corman, Sidney 1924-
See Corman, Cid
See also CA 85-88; CANR 44

Cormier, Robert (Edmund)
1925- . . . . CLC **12, 30**; DA
See also AAYA 3; CA 1-4R; CANR 5, 23;
CDALB 1968-1988; CLR 12; DLB 52;
JRDA; MAICYA; MTCW; SATA 10, 45

Corn, Alfred (DeWitt III) 1943-. . . . CLC **33**
See also CA 104; CANR 44; DLB 120;
DLBY 80

Cornwell, David (John Moore)
1931- . . . . CLC **9, 15**
See also le Carre, John
See also CA 5-8R; CANR 13, 33; MTCW

Corso, (Nunzio) Gregory 1930-. . . CLC **1, 11**
See also CA 5-8R; CANR 41; DLB 5, 16;
MTCW

Cortazar, Julio
1914-1984 . . . . . . CLC **2, 3, 5, 10, 13, 15,
33, 34**; HLC; SSC **7**
See also CA 21-24R; CANR 12, 32;
DLB 113; HW; MTCW

Corwin, Cecil
See Kornbluth, C(yril) M.

Cosic, Dobrica 1921-. . . . . CLC **14**
See also CA 122; 138

Costain, Thomas B(ertram)
1885-1965 . . . . CLC **30**
See also CA 5-8R; 25-28R; DLB 9

Costantini, Humberto
1924(?)-1987 . . . . CLC **49**
See also CA 131; 122; HW

Costello, Elvis 1955-. . . . . CLC **21**

Cotter, Joseph Seamon Sr.
1861-1949 . . . . TCLC **28**; BLC
See also BW 1; CA 124; DLB 50

Couch, Arthur Thomas Quiller
See Quiller-Couch, Arthur Thomas

Coulton, James
See Hansen, Joseph

Couperus, Louis (Marie Anne)
1863-1923 . . . . TCLC **15**
See also CA 115

Coupland, Douglas 1961-. . . . . CLC **85**
See also CA 142

Court, Wesli
See Turco, Lewis (Putnam)

Courtenay, Bryce 1933-. . . . . CLC **59**
See also CA 138

Courtney, Robert
See Ellison, Harlan (Jay)

Cousteau, Jacques-Yves 1910-. . . . . . CLC **30**
See also CA 65-68; CANR 15; MTCW;
SATA 38

Coward, Noel (Peirce)
1899-1973 . . . . CLC **1, 9, 29, 51**
See also AITN 1; CA 17-18; 41-44R;
CANR 35; CAP 2; CDBLB 1914-1945;
DLB 10; MTCW

Cowley, Malcolm 1898-1989 . . . . CLC **39**
See also CA 5-8R; 128; CANR 3; DLB 4,
48; DLBY 81, 89; MTCW

Cowper, William 1731-1800. . . . . . . NCLC **8**
See also DLB 104, 109

Cox, William Trevor 1928- . . . CLC **9, 14, 71**
See also Trevor, William
See also CA 9-12R; CANR 4, 37; DLB 14;
MTCW

Coyne, P. J.
See Masters, Hilary

Cozzens, James Gould
1903-1978 . . . . CLC **1, 4, 11**
See also CA 9-12R; 81-84; CANR 19;
CDALB 1941-1968; DLB 9; DLBD 2;
DLBY 84; MTCW

Crabbe, George 1754-1832. . . . . . . NCLC **26**
See also DLB 93

Craig, A. A.
See Anderson, Poul (William)

Craik, Dinah Maria (Mulock)
1826-1887 . . . . NCLC **38**
See also DLB 35; MAICYA; SATA 34

Cram, Ralph Adams 1863-1942. . . . TCLC **45**

Crane, (Harold) Hart
1899-1932 . . . . TCLC **2, 5**; DA; PC **3**;
WLC
See also CA 104; 127; CDALB 1917-1929;
DLB 4, 48; MTCW

Crane, R(onald) S(almon)
1886-1967 . . . . CLC **27**
See also CA 85-88; DLB 63

Crane, Stephen (Townley)
1871-1900 . . . . TCLC **11, 17, 32**; DA;
SSC **7**; WLC
See also CA 109; 140; CDALB 1865-1917;
DLB 12, 54, 78; YABC 2

Crase, Douglas 1944-. . . . . CLC **58**
See also CA 106

Crashaw, Richard 1612(?)-1649. . . . . LC **24**
See also DLB 126

Craven, Margaret 1901-1980. . . . . . . CLC **17**
See also CA 103

Crawford, F(rancis) Marion
1854-1909 . . . . TCLC **10**
See also CA 107; DLB 71

Crawford, Isabella Valancy
1850-1887 . . . . NCLC **12**
See also DLB 92

Crayon, Geoffrey
See Irving, Washington

Creasey, John 1908-1973. . . . . CLC **11**
See also CA 5-8R; 41-44R; CANR 8;
DLB 77; MTCW

Crebillon, Claude Prosper Jolyot de (fils)
1707-1777 . . . . LC **1**

Credo
See Creasey, John

Creeley, Robert (White)
1926- . . . . . CLC **1, 2, 4, 8, 11, 15, 36, 78**
See also CA 1-4R; CAAS 10; CANR 23, 43;
DLB 5, 16; MTCW

Crews, Harry (Eugene)
1935-. . . . . CLC **6, 23, 49**
See also AITN 1; CA 25-28R; CANR 20;
DLB 6, 143; MTCW

Crichton, (John) Michael
1942-. . . . . CLC **2, 6, 54**
See also AAYA 10; AITN 2; CA 25-28R;
CANR 13, 40; DLBY 81; JRDA;
MTCW; SATA 9

Crispin, Edmund . . . . CLC **22**
See also Montgomery, (Robert) Bruce
See also DLB 87

Cristofer, Michael 1945(?)-. . . . . CLC **28**
See also CA 110; DLB 7

Croce, Benedetto 1866-1952 . . . . . . TCLC **37**
See also CA 120

Crockett, David 1786-1836 . . . . NCLC **8**
See also DLB 3, 11

Crockett, Davy
See Crockett, David

Crofts, Freeman Wills
1879-1957 . . . . TCLC **55**
See also CA 115; DLB 77

Croker, John Wilson 1780-1857 . . NCLC **10**
See also DLB 110

Crommelynck, Fernand 1885-1970 . . CLC **75**
See also CA 89-92

Cronin, A(rchibald) J(oseph)
1896-1981 . . . . CLC **32**
See also CA 1-4R; 102; CANR 5; SATA 47;
SATA-Obit 25

Cross, Amanda
See Heilbrun, Carolyn G(old)

Crothers, Rachel 1878(?)-1958. . . . . TCLC **19**
See also CA 113; DLB 7

Croves, Hal
See Traven, B.

Crowfield, Christopher
See Stowe, Harriet (Elizabeth) Beecher

Crowley, Aleister.................**TCLC 7**
See also Crowley, Edward Alexander

Crowley, Edward Alexander 1875-1947
See Crowley, Aleister
See also CA 104

Crowley, John 1942-.............**CLC 57**
See also CA 61-64; CANR 43; DLBY 82;
SATA 65

Crud
See Crumb, R(obert)

Crumarums
See Crumb, R(obert)

Crumb, R(obert) 1943-...........**CLC 17**
See also CA 106

Crumbum
See Crumb, R(obert)

Crumski
See Crumb, R(obert)

Crum the Bum
See Crumb, R(obert)

Crunk
See Crumb, R(obert)

Crustt
See Crumb, R(obert)

Cryer, Gretchen (Kiger) 1935-......**CLC 21**
See also CA 114; 123

Csath, Geza 1887-1919..........**TCLC 13**
See also CA 111

Cudlip, David 1933-..............**CLC 34**

Cullen, Countee
1903-1946......**TCLC 4, 37; BLC; DA**
See also BW 1; CA 108; 124;
CDALB 1917-1929; DLB 4, 48, 51;
MTCW; SATA 18

Cum, R.
See Crumb, R(obert)

Cummings, Bruce F(rederick) 1889-1919
See Barbellion, W. N. P.
See also CA 123

Cummings, E(dward) E(stlin)
1894-1962......**CLC 1, 3, 8, 12, 15, 68;
DA; PC 5; WLC 2**
See also CA 73-76; CANR 31;
CDALB 1929-1941; DLB 4, 48; MTCW

Cunha, Euclides (Rodrigues Pimenta) da
1866-1909.................**TCLC 24**
See also CA 123

Cunningham, E. V.
See Fast, Howard (Melvin)

Cunningham, J(ames) V(incent)
1911-1985.................**CLC 3, 31**
See also CA 1-4R; 115; CANR 1; DLB 5

Cunningham, Julia (Woolfolk)
1916-......................**CLC 12**
See also CA 9-12R; CANR 4, 19, 36;
JRDA; MAICYA; SAAS 2; SATA 1, 26

Cunningham, Michael 1952-.......**CLC 34**
See also CA 136

Cunninghame Graham, R(obert) B(ontine)
1852-1936.................**TCLC 19**
See also Graham, R(obert) B(ontine)
Cunninghame
See also CA 119; DLB 98

Currie, Ellen 19(?)-..............**CLC 44**

Curtin, Philip
See Lowndes, Marie Adelaide (Belloc)

Curtis, Price
See Ellison, Harlan (Jay)

Cutrate, Joe
See Spiegelman, Art

Czaczkes, Shmuel Yosef
See Agnon, S(hmuel) Y(osef Halevi)

Dabrowska, Maria (Szumska)
1889-1965.................**CLC 15**
See also CA 106

Dabydeen, David 1955-..........**CLC 34**
See also BW 1; CA 125

Dacey, Philip 1939-..............**CLC 51**
See also CA 37-40R; CAAS 17; CANR 14,
32; DLB 105

Dagerman, Stig (Halvard)
1923-1954.................**TCLC 17**
See also CA 117

Dahl, Roald 1916-1990.....**CLC 1, 6, 18, 79**
See also CA 1-4R; 133; CANR 6, 32, 37;
CLR 1, 7; DLB 139; JRDA; MAICYA;
MTCW; SATA 1, 26, 73; SATA-Obit 65

Dahlberg, Edward 1900-1977...**CLC 1, 7, 14**
See also CA 9-12R; 69-72; CANR 31;
DLB 48; MTCW

Dale, Colin.....................**TCLC 18**
See also Lawrence, T(homas) E(dward)

Dale, George E.
See Asimov, Isaac

Daly, Elizabeth 1878-1967........**CLC 52**
See also CA 23-24; 25-28R; CAP 2

Daly, Maureen 1921-.............**CLC 17**
See also AAYA 5; CANR 37; JRDA;
MAICYA; SAAS 1; SATA 2

Damas, Leon-Gontran 1912-1978...**CLC 84**
See also BW 1; CA 125; 73-76

Daniel, Samuel 1562(?)-1619........**LC 24**
See also DLB 62

Daniels, Brett
See Adler, Renata

Dannay, Frederic 1905-1982.......**CLC 11**
See also Queen, Ellery
See also CA 1-4R; 107; CANR 1, 39;
DLB 137; MTCW

D'Annunzio, Gabriele
1863-1938.................**TCLC 6, 40**
See also CA 104

d'Antibes, Germain
See Simenon, Georges (Jacques Christian)

Danvers, Dennis 1947-...........**CLC 70**

Danziger, Paula 1944-...........**CLC 21**
See also AAYA 4; CA 112; 115; CANR 37;
CLR 20; JRDA; MAICYA; SATA 30,
36, 63

Dario, Ruben 1867-1916....**TCLC 4; HLC**
See also CA 131; HW; MTCW

Darley, George 1795-1846........**NCLC 2**
See also DLB 96

Daryush, Elizabeth 1887-1977....**CLC 6, 19**
See also CA 49-52; CANR 3; DLB 20

Daudet, (Louis Marie) Alphonse
1840-1897.................**NCLC 1**
See also DLB 123

Daumal, Rene 1908-1944........**TCLC 14**
See also CA 114

Davenport, Guy (Mattison, Jr.)
1927-..........**CLC 6, 14, 38; SSC 16**
See also CA 33-36R; CANR 23; DLB 130

Davidson, Avram 1923-
See Queen, Ellery
See also CA 101; CANR 26; DLB 8

Davidson, Donald (Grady)
1893-1968.............**CLC 2, 13, 19**
See also CA 5-8R; 25-28R; CANR 4;
DLB 45

Davidson, Hugh
See Hamilton, Edmond

Davidson, John 1857-1909.......**TCLC 24**
See also CA 118; DLB 19

Davidson, Sara 1943-.............**CLC 9**
See also CA 81-84; CANR 44

Davie, Donald (Alfred)
1922-.................**CLC 5, 8, 10, 31**
See also CA 1-4R; CAAS 3; CANR 1, 44;
DLB 27; MTCW

Davies, Ray(mond Douglas) 1944-..**CLC 21**
See also CA 116

Davies, Rhys 1903-1978...........**CLC 23**
See also CA 9-12R; 81-84; CANR 4;
DLB 139

Davies, (William) Robertson
1913-.....**CLC 2, 7, 13, 25, 42, 75; DA;
WLC**
See also BEST 89:2; CA 33-36R; CANR 17,
42; DLB 68; MTCW

Davies, W(illiam) H(enry)
1871-1940.................**TCLC 5**
See also CA 104; DLB 19

Davies, Walter C.
See Kornbluth, C(yril) M.

Davis, Angela (Yvonne) 1944-......**CLC 77**
See also BW 2; CA 57-60; CANR 10

Davis, B. Lynch
See Bioy Casares, Adolfo; Borges, Jorge
Luis

Davis, Gordon
See Hunt, E(verette) Howard, (Jr.)

Davis, Harold Lenoir 1896-1960....**CLC 49**
See also CA 89-92; DLB 9

Davis, Rebecca (Blaine) Harding
1831-1910.................**TCLC 6**
See also CA 104; DLB 74

Davis, Richard Harding
1864-1916.................**TCLC 24**
See also CA 114; DLB 12, 23, 78, 79

Davison, Frank Dalby 1893-1970...**CLC 15**
See also CA 116

Davison, Lawrence H.
See Lawrence, D(avid) H(erbert Richards)

Davison, Peter (Hubert) 1928- ..... **CLC 28**
See also CA 9-12R; CAAS 4; CANR 3, 43;
DLB 5

Davys, Mary 1674-1732............ **LC 1**
See also DLB 39

Dawson, Fielding 1930- .... **CLC 6**
See also CA 85-88; DLB 130

Dawson, Peter
See Faust, Frederick (Schiller)

Day, Clarence (Shepard, Jr.)
1874-1935 .... **TCLC 25**
See also CA 108; DLB 11

Day, Thomas 1748-1789............ **LC 1**
See also DLB 39; YABC 1

Day Lewis, C(ecil)
1904-1972 .... **CLC 1, 6, 10; PC 11**
See also Blake, Nicholas
See also CA 13-16; 33-36R; CANR 34;
CAP 1; DLB 15, 20; MTCW

Dazai, Osamu .... **TCLC 11**
See also Tsushima, Shuji

de Andrade, Carlos Drummond
See Drummond de Andrade, Carlos

Deane, Norman
See Creasey, John

**de Beauvoir, Simone (Lucie Ernestine Marie
Bertrand)**
See Beauvoir, Simone (Lucie Ernestine
Marie Bertrand) de

de Brissac, Malcolm
See Dickinson, Peter (Malcolm)

de Chardin, Pierre Teilhard
See Teilhard de Chardin, (Marie Joseph)
Pierre

Dee, John 1527-1608 .... **LC 20**

Deer, Sandra 1940-............... **CLC 45**

De Ferrari, Gabriella .... **CLC 65**

Defoe, Daniel
1660(?)-1731 .... **LC 1; DA; WLC**
See also CDBLB 1660-1789; DLB 39, 95,
101; JRDA; MAICYA; SATA 22

de Gourmont, Remy
See Gourmont, Remy de

de Hartog, Jan 1914-............. **CLC 19**
See also CA 1-4R; CANR 1

de Hostos, E. M.
See Hostos (y Bonilla), Eugenio Maria de

de Hostos, Eugenio M.
See Hostos (y Bonilla), Eugenio Maria de

Deighton, Len .... **CLC 4, 7, 22, 46**
See also Deighton, Leonard Cyril
See also AAYA 6; BEST 89:2;
CDBLB 1960 to Present; DLB 87

Deighton, Leonard Cyril 1929-
See Deighton, Len
See also CA 9-12R; CANR 19, 33; MTCW

Dekker, Thomas 1572(?)-1632....... **LC 22**
See also CDBLB Before 1660; DLB 62

de la Mare, Walter (John)
1873-1956 .. **TCLC 4, 53; SSC 14; WLC**
See also CDBLB 1914-1945; CLR 23;
DLB 19; SATA 16

Delaney, Franey
See O'Hara, John (Henry)

Delaney, Shelagh 1939-........... **CLC 29**
See also CA 17-20R; CANR 30;
CDBLB 1960 to Present; DLB 13;
MTCW

Delany, Mary (Granville Pendarves)
1700-1788 .... **LC 12**

Delany, Samuel R(ay, Jr.)
1942- .... **CLC 8, 14, 38; BLC**
See also BW 2; CA 81-84; CANR 27, 43;
DLB 8, 33; MTCW

De La Ramee, (Marie) Louise 1839-1908
See Ouida
See also SATA 20

de la Roche, Mazo 1879-1961...... **CLC 14**
See also CA 85-88; CANR 30; DLB 68;
SATA 64

Delbanco, Nicholas (Franklin)
1942- .... **CLC 6, 13**
See also CA 17-20R; CAAS 2; CANR 29;
DLB 6

del Castillo, Michel 1933- .... **CLC 38**
See also CA 109

Deledda, Grazia (Cosima)
1875(?)-1936 .... **TCLC 23**
See also CA 123

Delibes, Miguel .... **CLC 8, 18**
See also Delibes Setien, Miguel

Delibes Setien, Miguel 1920-
See Delibes, Miguel
See also CA 45-48; CANR 1, 32; HW;
MTCW

DeLillo, Don
1936- ..... **CLC 8, 10, 13, 27, 39, 54, 76**
See also BEST 89:1; CA 81-84; CANR 21;
DLB 6; MTCW

de Lisser, H. G.
See De Lisser, Herbert George
See also DLB 117

De Lisser, Herbert George
1878-1944 .... **TCLC 12**
See also de Lisser, H. G.
See also BW 2; CA 109

Deloria, Vine (Victor), Jr. 1933-.... **CLC 21**
See also CA 53-56; CANR 5, 20; MTCW;
NNAL; SATA 21

Del Vecchio, John M(ichael)
1947- .... **CLC 29**
See also CA 110; DLBD 9

de Man, Paul (Adolph Michel)
1919-1983 .... **CLC 55**
See also CA 128; 111; DLB 67; MTCW

De Marinis, Rick 1934-........... **CLC 54**
See also CA 57-60; CANR 9, 25

Demby, William 1922-....... **CLC 53; BLC**
See also BW 1; CA 81-84; DLB 33

Demijohn, Thom
See Disch, Thomas M(ichael)

de Montherlant, Henry (Milon)
See Montherlant, Henry (Milon) de

Demosthenes 384B.C.-322B.C. .... **CMLC 13**

de Natale, Francine
See Malzberg, Barry N(athaniel)

Denby, Edwin (Orr) 1903-1983..... **CLC 48**
See also CA 138; 110

Denis, Julio
See Cortazar, Julio

Denmark, Harrison
See Zelazny, Roger (Joseph)

Dennis, John 1658-1734........... **LC 11**
See also DLB 101

Dennis, Nigel (Forbes) 1912-1989.... **CLC 8**
See also CA 25-28R; 129; DLB 13, 15;
MTCW

De Palma, Brian (Russell) 1940-.... **CLC 20**
See also CA 109

De Quincey, Thomas 1785-1859 ... **NCLC 4**
See also CDBLB 1789-1832; DLB 110; 144

Deren, Eleanora 1908(?)-1961
See Deren, Maya
See also CA 111

Deren, Maya .... **CLC 16**
See also Deren, Eleanora

Derleth, August (William)
1909-1971 .... **CLC 31**
See also CA 1-4R; 29-32R; CANR 4;
DLB 9; SATA 5

Der Nister 1884-1950........... **TCLC 56**

de Routisie, Albert
See Aragon, Louis

Derrida, Jacques 1930-............ **CLC 24**
See also CA 124; 127

Derry Down Derry
See Lear, Edward

Dersonnes, Jacques
See Simenon, Georges (Jacques Christian)

Desai, Anita 1937-............ **CLC 19, 37**
See also CA 81-84; CANR 33; MTCW;
SATA 63

de Saint-Luc, Jean
See Glassco, John

de Saint Roman, Arnaud
See Aragon, Louis

Descartes, Rene 1596-1650 .... **LC 20**

De Sica, Vittorio 1901(?)-1974 ..... **CLC 20**
See also CA 117

Desnos, Robert 1900-1945........ **TCLC 22**
See also CA 121

Destouches, Louis-Ferdinand
1894-1961 .... **CLC 9, 15**
See also Celine, Louis-Ferdinand
See also CA 85-88; CANR 28; MTCW

Deutsch, Babette 1895-1982 .... **CLC 18**
See also CA 1-4R; 108; CANR 4; DLB 45;
SATA 1; SATA-Obit 33

Devenant, William 1606-1649 ...... **LC 13**

Devkota, Laxmiprasad
1909-1959 .... **TCLC 23**
See also CA 123

De Voto, Bernard (Augustine)
1897-1955 .... **TCLC 29**
See also CA 113; DLB 9

De Vries, Peter
1910-1993 .... **CLC 1, 2, 3, 7, 10, 28, 46**
See also CA 17-20R; 142; CANR 41;
DLB 6; DLBY 82; MTCW

Dexter, Martin
See Faust, Frederick (Schiller)

Dexter, Pete 1943- . . . . CLC **34, 55**
See also BEST 89:2; CA 127; 131; MTCW

Diamano, Silmang
See Senghor, Leopold Sedar

Diamond, Neil 1941- . . . . CLC **30**
See also CA 108

di Bassetto, Corno
See Shaw, George Bernard

Dick, Philip K(indred)
1928-1982 . . . . CLC **10, 30, 72**
See also CA 49-52; 106; CANR 2, 16;
DLB 8; MTCW

Dickens, Charles (John Huffam)
1812-1870 . . . . . . NCLC **3, 8, 18, 26, 37;**
DA; SSC **17;** WLC
See also CDBLB 1832-1890; DLB 21, 55,
70; JRDA; MAICYA; SATA 15

Dickey, James (Lafayette)
1923- . . . . CLC **1, 2, 4, 7, 10, 15, 47**
See also AITN 1, 2; CA 9-12R; CABS 2;
CANR 10; CDALB 1968-1988; DLB 5;
DLBD 7; DLBY 82, 93; MTCW

Dickey, William 1928-1994 . . . . . . CLC **3, 28**
See also CA 9-12R; 145; CANR 24; DLB 5

Dickinson, Charles 1951- . . . . CLC **49**
See also CA 128

Dickinson, Emily (Elizabeth)
1830-1886 . . NCLC **21;** DA; PC **1;** WLC
See also CDALB 1865-1917; DLB 1;
SATA 29

Dickinson, Peter (Malcolm)
1927- . . . . CLC **12, 35**
See also AAYA 9; CA 41-44R; CANR 31;
CLR 29; DLB 87; JRDA; MAICYA;
SATA 5, 62

Dickson, Carr
See Carr, John Dickson

Dickson, Carter
See Carr, John Dickson

Diderot, Denis 1713-1784 . . . . LC **26**

Didion, Joan 1934- . . . . . CLC **1, 3, 8, 14, 32**
See also AITN 1; CA 5-8R; CANR 14;
CDALB 1968-1988; DLB 2; DLBY 81,
86; MTCW

Dietrich, Robert
See Hunt, E(verette) Howard, (Jr.)

Dillard, Annie 1945- . . . . CLC **9, 60**
See also AAYA 6; CA 49-52; CANR 3, 43;
DLBY 80; MTCW; SATA 10

Dillard, R(ichard) H(enry) W(ilde)
1937- . . . . CLC **5**
See also CA 21-24R; CAAS 7; CANR 10;
DLB 5

Dillon, Eilis 1920- . . . . CLC **17**
See also CA 9-12R; CAAS 3; CANR 4, 38;
CLR 26; MAICYA; SATA 2, 74

Dimont, Penelope
See Mortimer, Penelope (Ruth)

Dinesen, Isak . . . . CLC **10, 29;** SSC **7**
See also Blixen, Karen (Christentze
Dinesen)

Ding Ling . . . . CLC **68**
See also Chiang Pin-chin

Disch, Thomas M(ichael) 1940- . . . CLC **7, 36**
See also CA 21-24R; CAAS 4; CANR 17,
36; CLR 18; DLB 8; MAICYA; MTCW;
SAAS 15; SATA 54

Disch, Tom
See Disch, Thomas M(ichael)

d'Isly, Georges
See Simenon, Georges (Jacques Christian)

Disraeli, Benjamin 1804-1881 . . NCLC **2, 39**
See also DLB 21, 55

Ditcum, Steve
See Crumb, R(obert)

Dixon, Paige
See Corcoran, Barbara

Dixon, Stephen 1936- . . . . . CLC **52;** SSC **16**
See also CA 89-92; CANR 17, 40; DLB 130

Dobell, Sydney Thompson
1824-1874 . . . . NCLC **43**
See also DLB 32

Doblin, Alfred . . . . TCLC **13**
See also Doeblin, Alfred

Dobrolyubov, Nikolai Alexandrovich
1836-1861 . . . . NCLC **5**

Dobyns, Stephen 1941- . . . . CLC **37**
See also CA 45-48; CANR 2, 18

Doctorow, E(dgar) L(aurence)
1931- . . . . . CLC **6, 11, 15, 18, 37, 44, 65**
See also AITN 2; BEST 89:3; CA 45-48;
CANR 2, 33; CDALB 1968-1988; DLB 2,
28; DLBY 80; MTCW

Dodgson, Charles Lutwidge 1832-1898
See Carroll, Lewis
See also CLR 2; DA; MAICYA; YABC 2

Dodson, Owen (Vincent)
1914-1983 . . . . CLC **79;** BLC
See also BW 1; CA 65-68; 110; CANR 24;
DLB 76

Doeblin, Alfred 1878-1957 . . . . TCLC **13**
See also Doblin, Alfred
See also CA 110; 141; DLB 66

Doerr, Harriet 1910- . . . . CLC **34**
See also CA 117; 122; CANR 47

Domecq, H(onorio) Bustos
See Bioy Casares, Adolfo; Borges, Jorge
Luis

Domini, Rey
See Lorde, Audre (Geraldine)

Dominique
See Proust, (Valentin-Louis-George-Eugene-)
Marcel

Don, A
See Stephen, Leslie

Donaldson, Stephen R. 1947- . . . . . . CLC **46**
See also CA 89-92; CANR 13

Donleavy, J(ames) P(atrick)
1926- . . . . CLC **1, 4, 6, 10, 45**
See also AITN 2; CA 9-12R; CANR 24;
DLB 6; MTCW

Donne, John
1572-1631 . . . . LC **10, 24;** DA; PC **1**
See also CDBLB Before 1660; DLB 121

Donnell, David 1939(?)- . . . . CLC **34**

Donoghue, P. S.
See Hunt, E(verette) Howard, (Jr.)

Donoso (Yanez), Jose
1924- . . . . CLC **4, 8, 11, 32;** HLC
See also CA 81-84; CANR 32; DLB 113;
HW; MTCW

Donovan, John 1928-1992 . . . . CLC **35**
See also CA 97-100; 137; CLR 3;
MAICYA; SATA 29

Don Roberto
See Cunninghame Graham, R(obert)
B(ontine)

Doolittle, Hilda
1886-1961 . . . . . CLC **3, 8, 14, 31, 34, 73;**
DA; PC **5;** WLC
See also H. D.
See also CA 97-100; CANR 35; DLB 4, 45;
MTCW

Dorfman, Ariel 1942- . . . . CLC **48, 77;** HLC
See also CA 124; 130; HW

Dorn, Edward (Merton) 1929- . . . CLC **10, 18**
See also CA 93-96; CANR 42; DLB 5

Dorsan, Luc
See Simenon, Georges (Jacques Christian)

Dorsange, Jean
See Simenon, Georges (Jacques Christian)

Dos Passos, John (Roderigo)
1896-1970 . . . . . . CLC **1, 4, 8, 11, 15, 25,**
34, 82; DA; WLC
See also CA 1-4R; 29-32R; CANR 3;
CDALB 1929-1941; DLB 4, 9; DLBD 1;
MTCW

Dossage, Jean
See Simenon, Georges (Jacques Christian)

Dostoevsky, Fedor Mikhailovich
1821-1881 . . . . . . NCLC **2, 7, 21, 33, 43;**
DA; SSC **2;** WLC

Doughty, Charles M(ontagu)
1843-1926 . . . . TCLC **27**
See also CA 115; DLB 19, 57

Douglas, Ellen . . . . CLC **73**
See also Haxton, Josephine Ayres;
Williamson, Ellen Douglas

Douglas, Gavin 1475(?)-1522 . . . . LC **20**

Douglas, Keith 1920-1944 . . . . TCLC **40**
See also DLB 27

Douglas, Leonard
See Bradbury, Ray (Douglas)

Douglas, Michael
See Crichton, (John) Michael

Douglass, Frederick
1817(?)-1895 . . . . NCLC **7;** BLC; DA;
WLC
See also CDALB 1640-1865; DLB 1, 43, 50,
79; SATA 29

Dourado, (Waldomiro Freitas) Autran
1926- . . . . CLC **23, 60**
See also CA 25-28R; CANR 34

Dourado, Waldomiro Autran
See Dourado, (Waldomiro Freitas) Autran

Dove, Rita (Frances)
1952- . . . . CLC **50, 81;** PC **6**
See also BW 2; CA 109; CAAS 19;
CANR 27, 42; DLB 120

Dowell, Coleman 1925-1985 . . . . CLC **60**
See also CA 25-28R; 117; CANR 10;
DLB 130

Dowson, Ernest Christopher
1867-1900 .... **TCLC 4**
See also CA 105; DLB 19, 135

Doyle, A. Conan
See Doyle, Arthur Conan

Doyle, Arthur Conan
1859-1930 ...... **TCLC 7; DA; SSC 12;
WLC**
See also AAYA 14; CA 104; 122;
CDBLB 1890-1914; DLB 18, 70; MTCW;
SATA 24

Doyle, Conan
See Doyle, Arthur Conan

Doyle, John
See Graves, Robert (von Ranke)

Doyle, Roddy 1958(?)- .... **CLC 81**
See also AAYA 14; CA 143

Doyle, Sir A. Conan
See Doyle, Arthur Conan

Doyle, Sir Arthur Conan
See Doyle, Arthur Conan

Dr. A
See Asimov, Isaac; Silverstein, Alvin

Drabble, Margaret
1939- .... **CLC 2, 3, 5, 8, 10, 22, 53**
See also CA 13-16R; CANR 18, 35;
CDBLB 1960 to Present; DLB 14;
MTCW; SATA 48

Drapier, M. B.
See Swift, Jonathan

Drayham, James
See Mencken, H(enry) L(ouis)

Drayton, Michael 1563-1631 .... **LC 8**

Dreadstone, Carl
See Campbell, (John) Ramsey

Dreiser, Theodore (Herman Albert)
1871-1945 ...... **TCLC 10, 18, 35; DA;
WLC**
See also CA 106; 132; CDALB 1865-1917;
DLB 9, 12, 102, 137; DLBD 1; MTCW

Drexler, Rosalyn 1926- .... **CLC 2, 6**
See also CA 81-84

Dreyer, Carl Theodor 1889-1968.... **CLC 16**
See also CA 116

Drieu la Rochelle, Pierre(-Eugene)
1893-1945 .... **TCLC 21**
See also CA 117; DLB 72

Drinkwater, John 1882-1937 ...... **TCLC 57**
See also CA 109; DLB 10, 19

Drop Shot
See Cable, George Washington

Droste-Hulshoff, Annette Freiin von
1797-1848 .... **NCLC 3**
See also DLB 133

Drummond, Walter
See Silverberg, Robert

Drummond, William Henry
1854-1907 .... **TCLC 25**
See also DLB 92

Drummond de Andrade, Carlos
1902-1987 .... **CLC 18**
See also Andrade, Carlos Drummond de
See also CA 132; 123

Drury, Allen (Stuart) 1918- .... **CLC 37**
See also CA 57-60; CANR 18

Dryden, John
1631-1700 ... **LC 3, 21; DA; DC 3; WLC**
See also CDBLB 1660-1789; DLB 80, 101,
131

Duberman, Martin 1930- .... **CLC 8**
See also CA 1-4R; CANR 2

Dubie, Norman (Evans) 1945- ...... **CLC 36**
See also CA 69-72; CANR 12; DLB 120

Du Bois, W(illiam) E(dward) B(urghardt)
1868-1963 ...... **CLC 1, 2, 13, 64; BLC;
DA; WLC**
See also BW 1; CA 85-88; CANR 34;
CDALB 1865-1917; DLB 47, 50, 91;
MTCW; SATA 42

Dubus, Andre 1936- ... **CLC 13, 36; SSC 15**
See also CA 21-24R; CANR 17; DLB 130

Duca Minimo
See D'Annunzio, Gabriele

Ducharme, Rejean 1941- .... **CLC 74**
See also DLB 60

Duclos, Charles Pinot 1704-1772 ..... **LC 1**

Dudek, Louis 1918- .... **CLC 11, 19**
See also CA 45-48; CAAS 14; CANR 1;
DLB 88

Duerrenmatt, Friedrich
1921-1990 ...... **CLC 1, 4, 8, 11, 15, 43**
See also CA 17-20R; CANR 33; DLB 69,
124; MTCW

Duffy, Bruce (?)- .... **CLC 50**

Duffy, Maureen 1933- .... **CLC 37**
See also CA 25-28R; CANR 33; DLB 14;
MTCW

Dugan, Alan 1923- .... **CLC 2, 6**
See also CA 81-84; DLB 5

du Gard, Roger Martin
See Martin du Gard, Roger

Duhamel, Georges 1884-1966 ...... **CLC 8**
See also CA 81-84; 25-28R; CANR 35;
DLB 65; MTCW

Dujardin, Edouard (Emile Louis)
1861-1949 .... **TCLC 13**
See also CA 109; DLB 123

Dumas, Alexandre (Davy de la Pailleterie)
1802-1870 .... **NCLC 11; DA; WLC**
See also DLB 119; SATA 18

Dumas, Alexandre
1824-1895 .... **NCLC 9; DC 1**

Dumas, Claudine
See Malzberg, Barry N(athaniel)

Dumas, Henry L. 1934-1968 ..... **CLC 6, 62**
See also BW 1; CA 85-88; DLB 41

du Maurier, Daphne
1907-1989 ...... **CLC 6, 11, 59; SSC 18**
See also CA 5-8R; 128; CANR 6; MTCW;
SATA 27; SATA-Obit 60

Dunbar, Paul Laurence
1872-1906 ...... **TCLC 2, 12; BLC; DA;
PC 5; SSC 8; WLC**
See also BW 1; CA 104; 124;
CDALB 1865-1917; DLB 50, 54, 78;
SATA 34

Dunbar, William 1460(?)-1530(?) .... **LC 20**
See also DLB 132, 146

Duncan, Lois 1934- .... **CLC 26**
See also AAYA 4; CA 1-4R; CANR 2, 23,
36; CLR 29; JRDA; MAICYA; SAAS 2;
SATA 1, 36, 75

Duncan, Robert (Edward)
1919-1988 .... **CLC 1, 2, 4, 7, 15, 41, 55;
PC 2**
See also CA 9-12R; 124; CANR 28; DLB 5,
16; MTCW

Dunlap, William 1766-1839 .... **NCLC 2**
See also DLB 30, 37, 59

Dunn, Douglas (Eaglesham)
1942- .... **CLC 6, 40**
See also CA 45-48; CANR 2, 33; DLB 40;
MTCW

Dunn, Katherine (Karen) 1945- ..... **CLC 71**
See also CA 33-36R

Dunn, Stephen 1939- .... **CLC 36**
See also CA 33-36R; CANR 12; DLB 105

Dunne, Finley Peter 1867-1936.... **TCLC 28**
See also CA 108; DLB 11, 23

Dunne, John Gregory 1932-........ **CLC 28**
See also CA 25-28R; CANR 14; DLBY 80

**Dunsany, Edward John Moreton Drax
Plunkett** 1878-1957
See Dunsany, Lord
See also CA 104; DLB 10

Dunsany, Lord................... **TCLC 2**
See also Dunsany, Edward John Moreton
Drax Plunkett
See also DLB 77

du Perry, Jean
See Simenon, Georges (Jacques Christian)

Durang, Christopher (Ferdinand)
1949- .... **CLC 27, 38**
See also CA 105

Duras, Marguerite
1914- ...... **CLC 3, 6, 11, 20, 34, 40, 68**
See also CA 25-28R; DLB 83; MTCW

Durban, (Rosa) Pam 1947-........ **CLC 39**
See also CA 123

Durcan, Paul 1944-............ **CLC 43, 70**
See also CA 134

Durkheim, Emile 1858-1917 ...... **TCLC 55**

Durrell, Lawrence (George)
1912-1990 .... **CLC 1, 4, 6, 8, 13, 27, 41**
See also CA 9-12R; 132; CANR 40;
CDBLB 1945-1960; DLB 15, 27;
DLBY 90; MTCW

Durrenmatt, Friedrich
See Duerrenmatt, Friedrich

Dutt, Toru 1856-1877.......... **NCLC 29**

Dwight, Timothy 1752-1817...... **NCLC 13**
See also DLB 37

Dworkin, Andrea 1946- .... **CLC 43**
See also CA 77-80; CANR 16, 39; MTCW

Dwyer, Deanna
See Koontz, Dean R(ay)

Dwyer, K. R.
See Koontz, Dean R(ay)

Dylan, Bob 1941- ...... **CLC 3, 4, 6, 12, 77**
See also CA 41-44R; DLB 16

Eagleton, Terence (Francis) 1943-
See Eagleton, Terry
See also CA 57-60; CANR 7, 23; MTCW

Eagleton, Terry .... **CLC 63**
See also Eagleton, Terence (Francis)

Early, Jack
See Scoppettone, Sandra

East, Michael
See West, Morris L(anglo)

Eastaway, Edward
See Thomas, (Philip) Edward

Eastlake, William (Derry) 1917- ..... **CLC 8**
See also CA 5-8R; CAAS 1; CANR 5;
DLB 6

Eastman, Charles A(lexander)
1858-1939 .... **TCLC 55**
See also NNAL; YABC 1

Eberhart, Richard (Ghormley)
1904- .... **CLC 3, 11, 19, 56**
See also CA 1-4R; CANR 2;
CDALB 1941-1968; DLB 48; MTCW

Eberstadt, Fernanda 1960- .... **CLC 39**
See also CA 136

Echegaray (y Eizaguirre), Jose (Maria Waldo)
1832-1916 .... **TCLC 4**
See also CA 104; CANR 32; HW; MTCW

Echeverria, (Jose) Esteban (Antonino)
1805-1851 .... **NCLC 18**

Echo
See Proust, (Valentin-Louis-George-Eugene-)
Marcel

Eckert, Allan W. 1931- .... **CLC 17**
See also CA 13-16R; CANR 14, 45;
SATA 27, 29

Eckhart, Meister 1260(?)-1328(?) .. **CMLC 9**
See also DLB 115

Eckmar, F. R.
See de Hartog, Jan

Eco, Umberto 1932- .... **CLC 28, 60**
See also BEST 90:1; CA 77-80; CANR 12,
33; MTCW

Eddison, E(ric) R(ucker)
1882-1945 .... **TCLC 15**
See also CA 109

Edel, (Joseph) Leon 1907- ...... **CLC 29, 34**
See also CA 1-4R; CANR 1, 22; DLB 103

Eden, Emily 1797-1869 .... **NCLC 10**

Edgar, David 1948- .... **CLC 42**
See also CA 57-60; CANR 12; DLB 13;
MTCW

Edgerton, Clyde (Carlyle) 1944- .... **CLC 39**
See also CA 118; 134

Edgeworth, Maria 1767-1849 ...... **NCLC 1**
See also DLB 116; SATA 21

Edmonds, Paul
See Kuttner, Henry

Edmonds, Walter D(umaux) 1903- .. **CLC 35**
See also CA 5-8R; CANR 2; DLB 9;
MAICYA; SAAS 4; SATA 1, 27

Edmondson, Wallace
See Ellison, Harlan (Jay)

Edson, Russell .... **CLC 13**
See also CA 33-36R

Edwards, Bronwen Elizabeth
See Rose, Wendy

Edwards, G(erald) B(asil)
1899-1976 .... **CLC 25**
See also CA 110

Edwards, Gus 1939- .... **CLC 43**
See also CA 108

Edwards, Jonathan 1703-1758 .... **LC 7; DA**
See also DLB 24

Efron, Marina Ivanovna Tsvetaeva
See Tsvetaeva (Efron), Marina (Ivanovna)

Ehle, John (Marsden, Jr.) 1925- .... **CLC 27**
See also CA 9-12R

Ehrenbourg, Ilya (Grigoryevich)
See Ehrenburg, Ilya (Grigoryevich)

Ehrenburg, Ilya (Grigoryevich)
1891-1967 .... **CLC 18, 34, 62**
See also CA 102; 25-28R

Ehrenburg, Ilyo (Grigoryevich)
See Ehrenburg, Ilya (Grigoryevich)

Eich, Guenter 1907-1972 .... **CLC 15**
See also CA 111; 93-96; DLB 69, 124

Eichendorff, Joseph Freiherr von
1788-1857 .... **NCLC 8**
See also DLB 90

Eigner, Larry .... **CLC 9**
See also Eigner, Laurence (Joel)
See also DLB 5

Eigner, Laurence (Joel) 1927-
See Eigner, Larry
See also CA 9-12R; CANR 6

Eiseley, Loren Corey 1907-1977 ..... **CLC 7**
See also AAYA 5; CA 1-4R; 73-76;
CANR 6

Eisenstadt, Jill 1963- .... **CLC 50**
See also CA 140

Eisenstein, Sergei (Mikhailovich)
1898-1948 .... **TCLC 57**
See also CA 114

Eisner, Simon
See Kornbluth, C(yril) M.

Ekeloef, (Bengt) Gunnar
1907-1968 .... **CLC 27**
See also CA 123; 25-28R

Ekelof, (Bengt) Gunnar
See Ekeloef, (Bengt) Gunnar

Ekwensi, C. O. D.
See Ekwensi, Cyprian (Odiatu Duaka)

Ekwensi, Cyprian (Odiatu Duaka)
1921- .... **CLC 4; BLC**
See also BW 2; CA 29-32R; CANR 18, 42;
DLB 117; MTCW; SATA 66

Elaine .... **TCLC 18**
See also Leverson, Ada

El Crummo
See Crumb, R(obert)

Elia
See Lamb, Charles

Eliade, Mircea 1907-1986 .... **CLC 19**
See also CA 65-68; 119; CANR 30; MTCW

Eliot, A. D.
See Jewett, (Theodora) Sarah Orne

Eliot, Alice
See Jewett, (Theodora) Sarah Orne

Eliot, Dan
See Silverberg, Robert

Eliot, George
1819-1880 .... **NCLC 4, 13, 23, 41; DA;
WLC**
See also CDBLB 1832-1890; DLB 21, 35, 55

Eliot, John 1604-1690 .... **LC 5**
See also DLB 24

Eliot, T(homas) S(tearns)
1888-1965 ..... **CLC 1, 2, 3, 6, 9, 10, 13,
15, 24, 34, 41, 55, 57; DA; PC 5; WLC 2**
See also CA 5-8R; 25-28R; CANR 41;
CDALB 1929-1941; DLB 7, 10, 45, 63;
DLBY 88; MTCW

Elizabeth 1866-1941 .... **TCLC 41**

Elkin, Stanley L(awrence)
1930- ... **CLC 4, 6, 9, 14, 27, 51; SSC 12**
See also CA 9-12R; CANR 8, 46, 46;
DLB 2, 28; DLBY 80; MTCW

Elledge, Scott .... **CLC 34**

Elliott, Don
See Silverberg, Robert

Elliott, George P(aul) 1918-1980 ..... **CLC 2**
See also CA 1-4R; 97-100; CANR 2

Elliott, Janice 1931- .... **CLC 47**
See also CA 13-16R; CANR 8, 29; DLB 14

Elliott, Sumner Locke 1917-1991 ... **CLC 38**
See also CA 5-8R; 134; CANR 2, 21

Elliott, William
See Bradbury, Ray (Douglas)

Ellis, A. E. .... **CLC 7**

Ellis, Alice Thomas .... **CLC 40**
See also Haycraft, Anna

Ellis, Bret Easton 1964- .... **CLC 39, 71**
See also AAYA 2; CA 118; 123

Ellis, (Henry) Havelock
1859-1939 .... **TCLC 14**
See also CA 109

Ellis, Landon
See Ellison, Harlan (Jay)

Ellis, Trey 1962- .... **CLC 55**

Ellison, Harlan (Jay)
1934- .... **CLC 1, 13, 42; SSC 14**
See also CA 5-8R; CANR 5, 46, 46; DLB 8;
MTCW

Ellison, Ralph (Waldo)
1914-1994 .... **CLC 1, 3, 11, 54, 86;
BLC; DA; WLC**
See also BW 1; CA 9-12R; 145; CANR 24;
CDALB 1941-1968; DLB 2, 76; MTCW

Ellmann, Lucy (Elizabeth) 1956- .... **CLC 61**
See also CA 128

Ellmann, Richard (David)
1918-1987 .... **CLC 50**
See also BEST 89:2; CA 1-4R; 122;
CANR 2, 28; DLB 103; DLBY 87;
MTCW

Elman, Richard 1934- .... **CLC 19**
See also CA 17-20R; CAAS 3; CANR 47

Elron
See Hubbard, L(afayette) Ron(ald)

Eluard, Paul .... **TCLC 7, 41**
See also Grindel, Eugene

Elyot, Sir Thomas 1490(?)-1546 ..... **LC 11**

Elytis, Odysseus 1911- .... **CLC 15, 49**
See also CA 102; MTCW

Emecheta, (Florence Onye) Buchi
1944- .... **CLC 14, 48; BLC**
See also BW 2; CA 81-84; CANR 27;
DLB 117; MTCW; SATA 66

Emerson, Ralph Waldo
1803-1882 ...... **NCLC 1, 38; DA; WLC**
See also CDALB 1640-1865; DLB 1, 59, 73

Eminescu, Mihail 1850-1889 ..... **NCLC 33**

Empson, William
1906-1984 .... **CLC 3, 8, 19, 33, 34**
See also CA 17-20R; 112; CANR 31;
DLB 20; MTCW

Enchi Fumiko (Ueda) 1905-1986.... **CLC 31**
See also CA 129; 121

Ende, Michael (Andreas Helmuth)
1929- .... **CLC 31**
See also CA 118; 124; CANR 36; CLR 14;
DLB 75; MAICYA; SATA 42, 61

Endo, Shusaku 1923- ..... **CLC 7, 14, 19, 54**
See also CA 29-32R; CANR 21; MTCW

Engel, Marian 1933-1985......... **CLC 36**
See also CA 25-28R; CANR 12; DLB 53

Engelhardt, Frederick
See Hubbard, L(afayette) Ron(ald)

Enright, D(ennis) J(oseph)
1920- .... **CLC 4, 8, 31**
See also CA 1-4R; CANR 1, 42; DLB 27;
SATA 25

Enzensberger, Hans Magnus
1929- .... **CLC 43**
See also CA 116; 119

Ephron, Nora 1941- .... **CLC 17, 31**
See also AITN 2; CA 65-68; CANR 12, 39

Epsilon
See Betjeman, John

Epstein, Daniel Mark 1948- .... **CLC 7**
See also CA 49-52; CANR 2

Epstein, Jacob 1956- .... **CLC 19**
See also CA 114

Epstein, Joseph 1937-............. **CLC 39**
See also CA 112; 119

Epstein, Leslie 1938- .... **CLC 27**
See also CA 73-76; CAAS 12; CANR 23

Equiano, Olaudah
1745(?)-1797 .... **LC 16; BLC**
See also DLB 37, 50

Erasmus, Desiderius 1469(?)-1536.... **LC 16**

Erdman, Paul E(mil) 1932- .... **CLC 25**
See also AITN 1; CA 61-64; CANR 13, 43

Erdrich, Louise 1954-.......... **CLC 39, 54**
See also AAYA 10; BEST 89:1; CA 114;
CANR 41; MTCW; NNAL

Erenburg, Ilya (Grigoryevich)
See Ehrenburg, Ilya (Grigoryevich)

Erickson, Stephen Michael 1950-
See Erickson, Steve
See also CA 129

Erickson, Steve .... **CLC 64**
See also Erickson, Stephen Michael

Ericson, Walter
See Fast, Howard (Melvin)

Eriksson, Buntel
See Bergman, (Ernst) Ingmar

Eschenbach, Wolfram von
See Wolfram von Eschenbach

Eseki, Bruno
See Mphahlele, Ezekiel

Esenin, Sergei (Alexandrovich)
1895-1925 .... **TCLC 4**
See also CA 104

Eshleman, Clayton 1935-.......... **CLC 7**
See also CA 33-36R; CAAS 6; DLB 5

Espriella, Don Manuel Alvarez
See Southey, Robert

Espriu, Salvador 1913-1985........ **CLC 9**
See also CA 115; DLB 134

Espronceda, Jose de 1808-1842... **NCLC 39**

Esse, James
See Stephens, James

Esterbrook, Tom
See Hubbard, L(afayette) Ron(ald)

Estleman, Loren D. 1952- .... **CLC 48**
See also CA 85-88; CANR 27; MTCW

Eugenides, Jeffrey 1960(?)- .... **CLC 81**
See also CA 144

Euripides c. 485B.C.-406B.C. .... **DC 4**
See also DA

Evan, Evin
See Faust, Frederick (Schiller)

Evans, Evan
See Faust, Frederick (Schiller)

Evans, Marian
See Eliot, George

Evans, Mary Ann
See Eliot, George

Evarts, Esther
See Benson, Sally

Everett, Percival L. 1956-......... **CLC 57**
See also BW 2; CA 129

Everson, R(onald) G(ilmour)
1903- .... **CLC 27**
See also CA 17-20R; DLB 88

Everson, William (Oliver)
1912-1994 .... **CLC 1, 5, 14**
See also CA 9-12R; 145; CANR 20; DLB 5,
16; MTCW

Evtushenko, Evgenii Aleksandrovich
See Yevtushenko, Yevgeny (Alexandrovich)

Ewart, Gavin (Buchanan)
1916- .... **CLC 13, 46**
See also CA 89-92; CANR 17, 46, 46;
DLB 40; MTCW

Ewers, Hanns Heinz 1871-1943 ... **TCLC 12**
See also CA 109

Ewing, Frederick R.
See Sturgeon, Theodore (Hamilton)

Exley, Frederick (Earl)
1929-1992 .... **CLC 6, 11**
See also AITN 2; CA 81-84; 138; DLB 143;
DLBY 81

Eynhardt, Guillermo
See Quiroga, Horacio (Sylvestre)

Ezekiel, Nissim 1924-............ **CLC 61**
See also CA 61-64

Ezekiel, Tish O'Dowd 1943- .... **CLC 34**
See also CA 129

Fadeyev, A.
See Bulgya, Alexander Alexandrovich

Fadeyev, Alexander.............. **TCLC 53**
See also Bulgya, Alexander Alexandrovich

Fagen, Donald 1948-.............. **CLC 26**

Fainzilberg, Ilya Arnoldovich 1897-1937
See Ilf, Ilya
See also CA 120

Fair, Ronald L. 1932-............. **CLC 18**
See also BW 1; CA 69-72; CANR 25;
DLB 33

Fairbairns, Zoe (Ann) 1948- .... **CLC 32**
See also CA 103; CANR 21

Falco, Gian
See Papini, Giovanni

Falconer, James
See Kirkup, James

Falconer, Kenneth
See Kornbluth, C(yril) M.

Falkland, Samuel
See Heijermans, Herman

Fallaci, Oriana 1930-............. **CLC 11**
See also CA 77-80; CANR 15; MTCW

Faludy, George 1913-............. **CLC 42**
See also CA 21-24R

Faludy, Gyoergy
See Faludy, George

Fanon, Frantz 1925-1961..... **CLC 74; BLC**
See also BW 1; CA 116; 89-92

Fanshawe, Ann 1625-1680 .... **LC 11**

Fante, John (Thomas) 1911-1983 ... **CLC 60**
See also CA 69-72; 109; CANR 23;
DLB 130; DLBY 83

Farah, Nuruddin 1945-....... **CLC 53; BLC**
See also BW 2; CA 106; DLB 125

Fargue, Leon-Paul 1876(?)-1947 ... **TCLC 11**
See also CA 109

Farigoule, Louis
See Romains, Jules

Farina, Richard 1936(?)-1966 .... **CLC 9**
See also CA 81-84; 25-28R

Farley, Walter (Lorimer)
1915-1989 .... **CLC 17**
See also CA 17-20R; CANR 8, 29; DLB 22;
JRDA; MAICYA; SATA 2, 43

Farmer, Philip Jose 1918-....... **CLC 1, 19**
See also CA 1-4R; CANR 4, 35; DLB 8;
MTCW

Farquhar, George 1677-1707........ **LC 21**
See also DLB 84

Farrell, J(ames) G(ordon)
1935-1979 .... **CLC 6**
See also CA 73-76; 89-92; CANR 36;
DLB 14; MTCW

Farrell, James T(homas)
1904-1979 .... **CLC 1, 4, 8, 11, 66**
See also CA 5-8R; 89-92; CANR 9; DLB 4,
9, 86; DLBD 2; MTCW

Farren, Richard J.
See Betjeman, John

Farren, Richard M.
See Betjeman, John

Fassbinder, Rainer Werner
1946-1982 . . . . CLC 20
See also CA 93-96; 106; CANR 31

Fast, Howard (Melvin) 1914- . . . . . . CLC 23
See also CA 1-4R; CAAS 18; CANR 1, 33;
DLB 9; SATA 7

Faulcon, Robert
See Holdstock, Robert P.

Faulkner, William (Cuthbert)
1897-1962 . . . . . CLC 1, 3, 6, 8, 9, 11, 14,
18, 28, 52, 68; DA; SSC 1; WLC
See also AAYA 7; CA 81-84; CANR 33;
CDALB 1929-1941; DLB 9, 11, 44, 102;
DLBD 2; DLBY 86; MTCW

Fauset, Jessie Redmon
1884(?)-1961 . . . . CLC 19, 54; BLC
See also BW 1; CA 109; DLB 51

Faust, Frederick (Schiller)
1892-1944(?) . . . . TCLC 49
See also CA 108

Faust, Irvin 1924- . . . . CLC 8
See also CA 33-36R; CANR 28; DLB 2, 28;
DLBY 80

Fawkes, Guy
See Benchley, Robert (Charles)

Fearing, Kenneth (Flexner)
1902-1961 . . . . CLC 51
See also CA 93-96; DLB 9

Fecamps, Elise
See Creasey, John

Federman, Raymond 1928- . . . . . . CLC 6, 47
See also CA 17-20R; CAAS 8; CANR 10,
43; DLBY 80

Federspiel, J(uerg) F. 1931- . . . . CLC 42

Feiffer, Jules (Ralph) 1929- . . . . CLC 2, 8, 64
See also AAYA 3; CA 17-20R; CANR 30;
DLB 7, 44; MTCW; SATA 8, 61

Feige, Hermann Albert Otto Maximilian
See Traven, B.

Feinberg, David B. 1956- . . . . CLC 59
See also CA 135

Feinstein, Elaine 1930- . . . . CLC 36
See also CA 69-72; CAAS 1; CANR 31;
DLB 14, 40; MTCW

Feldman, Irving (Mordecai) 1928- . . . . CLC 7
See also CA 1-4R; CANR 1

Fellini, Federico 1920-1993 . . . . . CLC 16, 85
See also CA 65-68; 143; CANR 33

Felsen, Henry Gregor 1916- . . . . CLC 17
See also CA 1-4R; CANR 1; SAAS 2;
SATA 1

Fenton, James Martin 1949- . . . . CLC 32
See also CA 102; DLB 40

Ferber, Edna 1887-1968 . . . . CLC 18
See also AITN 1; CA 5-8R; 25-28R; DLB 9,
28, 86; MTCW; SATA 7

Ferguson, Helen
See Kavan, Anna

Ferguson, Samuel 1810-1886 . . . . . NCLC 33
See also DLB 32

Ferling, Lawrence
See Ferlinghetti, Lawrence (Monsanto)

Ferlinghetti, Lawrence (Monsanto)
1919(?)- . . . . CLC 2, 6, 10, 27; PC 1
See also CA 5-8R; CANR 3, 41;
CDALB 1941-1968; DLB 5, 16; MTCW

Fernandez, Vicente Garcia Huidobro
See Huidobro Fernandez, Vicente Garcia

Ferrer, Gabriel (Francisco Victor) Miro
See Miro (Ferrer), Gabriel (Francisco
Victor)

Ferrier, Susan (Edmonstone)
1782-1854 . . . . NCLC 8
See also DLB 116

Ferrigno, Robert 1948(?)- . . . . CLC 65
See also CA 140

Feuchtwanger, Lion 1884-1958 . . . . . TCLC 3
See also CA 104; DLB 66

Feuillet, Octave 1821-1890 . . . . . . NCLC 45

Feydeau, Georges (Leon Jules Marie)
1862-1921 . . . . TCLC 22
See also CA 113

Ficino, Marsilio 1433-1499 . . . . LC 12

Fiedeler, Hans
See Doeblin, Alfred

Fiedler, Leslie A(aron)
1917- . . . . CLC 4, 13, 24
See also CA 9-12R; CANR 7; DLB 28, 67;
MTCW

Field, Andrew 1938- . . . . CLC 44
See also CA 97-100; CANR 25

Field, Eugene 1850-1895 . . . . NCLC 3
See also DLB 23, 42, 140; MAICYA;
SATA 16

Field, Gans T.
See Wellman, Manly Wade

Field, Michael . . . . TCLC 43

Field, Peter
See Hobson, Laura Z(ametkin)

Fielding, Henry
1707-1754 . . . . LC 1; DA; WLC
See also CDBLB 1660-1789; DLB 39, 84,
101

Fielding, Sarah 1710-1768 . . . . LC 1
See also DLB 39

Fierstein, Harvey (Forbes) 1954- . . . CLC 33
See also CA 123; 129

Figes, Eva 1932- . . . . CLC 31
See also CA 53-56; CANR 4, 44; DLB 14

Finch, Robert (Duer Claydon)
1900- . . . . CLC 18
See also CA 57-60; CANR 9, 24; DLB 88

Findley, Timothy 1930- . . . . CLC 27
See also CA 25-28R; CANR 12, 42;
DLB 53

Fink, William
See Mencken, H(enry) L(ouis)

Firbank, Louis 1942-
See Reed, Lou
See also CA 117

Firbank, (Arthur Annesley) Ronald
1886-1926 . . . . TCLC 1
See also CA 104; DLB 36

Fisher, M(ary) F(rances) K(ennedy)
1908-1992 . . . . CLC 76
See also CA 77-80; 138; CANR 44

Fisher, Roy 1930- . . . . CLC 25
See also CA 81-84; CAAS 10; CANR 16;
DLB 40

Fisher, Rudolph
1897-1934 . . . . TCLC 11; BLC
See also BW 1; CA 107; 124; DLB 51, 102

Fisher, Vardis (Alvero) 1895-1968 . . . . CLC 7
See also CA 5-8R; 25-28R; DLB 9

Fiske, Tarleton
See Bloch, Robert (Albert)

Fitch, Clarke
See Sinclair, Upton (Beall)

Fitch, John IV
See Cormier, Robert (Edmund)

Fitzgerald, Captain Hugh
See Baum, L(yman) Frank

FitzGerald, Edward 1809-1883 . . . . NCLC 9
See also DLB 32

Fitzgerald, F(rancis) Scott (Key)
1896-1940 . . . . TCLC 1, 6, 14, 28, 55;
DA; SSC 6; WLC
See also AITN 1; CA 110; 123;
CDALB 1917-1929; DLB 4, 9, 86;
DLBD 1; DLBY 81; MTCW

Fitzgerald, Penelope 1916- . . . CLC 19, 51, 61
See also CA 85-88; CAAS 10; DLB 14

Fitzgerald, Robert (Stuart)
1910-1985 . . . . CLC 39
See also CA 1-4R; 114; CANR 1; DLBY 80

FitzGerald, Robert D(avid)
1902-1987 . . . . CLC 19
See also CA 17-20R

Fitzgerald, Zelda (Sayre)
1900-1948 . . . . TCLC 52
See also CA 117; 126; DLBY 84

Flanagan, Thomas (James Bonner)
1923- . . . . CLC 25, 52
See also CA 108; DLBY 80; MTCW

Flaubert, Gustave
1821-1880 . . . . NCLC 2, 10, 19; DA;
SSC 11; WLC
See also DLB 119

Flecker, (Herman) James Elroy
1884-1915 . . . . TCLC 43
See also CA 109; DLB 10, 19

Fleming, Ian (Lancaster)
1908-1964 . . . . CLC 3, 30
See also CA 5-8R; CDBLB 1945-1960;
DLB 87; MTCW; SATA 9

Fleming, Thomas (James) 1927- . . . . CLC 37
See also CA 5-8R; CANR 10; SATA 8

Fletcher, John Gould 1886-1950 . . . TCLC 35
See also CA 107; DLB 4, 45

Fleur, Paul
See Pohl, Frederik

Flooglebuckle, Al
See Spiegelman, Art

Flying Officer X
See Bates, H(erbert) E(rnest)

Fo, Dario 1926- . . . . CLC 32
See also CA 116; 128; MTCW

Fogarty, Jonathan Titulescu Esq.
See Farrell, James T(homas)

Folke, Will
See Bloch, Robert (Albert)

Follett, Ken(neth Martin) 1949- .... **CLC 18**
See also AAYA 6; BEST 89:4; CA 81-84;
CANR 13, 33; DLB 87; DLBY 81;
MTCW

Fontane, Theodor 1819-1898 ..... **NCLC 26**
See also DLB 129

Foote, Horton 1916- .... **CLC 51**
See also CA 73-76; CANR 34; DLB 26

Foote, Shelby 1916- .... **CLC 75**
See also CA 5-8R; CANR 3, 45; DLB 2, 17

Forbes, Esther 1891-1967......... **CLC 12**
See also CA 13-14; 25-28R; CAP 1;
CLR 27; DLB 22; JRDA; MAICYA;
SATA 2

Forche, Carolyn (Louise)
1950- .... **CLC 25, 83, 86; PC 10**
See also CA 109; 117; DLB 5

Ford, Elbur
See Hibbert, Eleanor Alice Burford

Ford, Ford Madox
1873-1939 .... **TCLC 1, 15, 39, 57**
See also CA 104; 132; CDBLB 1914-1945;
DLB 34, 98; MTCW

Ford, John 1895-1973............. **CLC 16**
See also CA 45-48

Ford, Richard 1944-.............. **CLC 46**
See also CA 69-72; CANR 11, 47

Ford, Webster
See Masters, Edgar Lee

Foreman, Richard 1937-.......... **CLC 50**
See also CA 65-68; CANR 32

Forester, C(ecil) S(cott)
1899-1966 .... **CLC 35**
See also CA 73-76; 25-28R; SATA 13

Forez
See Mauriac, Francois (Charles)

Forman, James Douglas 1932-...... **CLC 21**
See also CA 9-12R; CANR 4, 19, 42;
JRDA; MAICYA; SATA 8, 70

Fornes, Maria Irene 1930-...... **CLC 39, 61**
See also CA 25-28R; CANR 28; DLB 7;
HW; MTCW

Forrest, Leon 1937- .... **CLC 4**
See also BW 2; CA 89-92; CAAS 7;
CANR 25; DLB 33

Forster, E(dward) M(organ)
1879-1970 ..... **CLC 1, 2, 3, 4, 9, 10, 13,
15, 22, 45, 77; DA; WLC**
See also AAYA 2; CA 13-14; 25-28R;
CANR 45; CAP 1; CDBLB 1914-1945;
DLB 34, 98; DLBD 10; MTCW;
SATA 57

Forster, John 1812-1876 .... **NCLC 11**
See also DLB 144

Forsyth, Frederick 1938-...... **CLC 2, 5, 36**
See also BEST 89:4; CA 85-88; CANR 38;
DLB 87; MTCW

Forten, Charlotte L. .... **TCLC 16; BLC**
See also Grimke, Charlotte L(ottie) Forten
See also DLB 50

Foscolo, Ugo 1778-1827......... **NCLC 8**

Fosse, Bob .... **CLC 20**
See also Fosse, Robert Louis

Fosse, Robert Louis 1927-1987
See Fosse, Bob
See also CA 110; 123

Foster, Stephen Collins
1826-1864 .... **NCLC 26**

Foucault, Michel
1926-1984 .... **CLC 31, 34, 69**
See also CA 105; 113; CANR 34; MTCW

Fouque, Friedrich (Heinrich Karl) de la Motte
1777-1843 .... **NCLC 2**
See also DLB 90

Fournier, Henri Alban 1886-1914
See Alain-Fournier
See also CA 104

Fournier, Pierre 1916- .... **CLC 11**
See also Gascar, Pierre
See also CA 89-92; CANR 16, 40

Fowles, John
1926- .... **CLC 1, 2, 3, 4, 6, 9, 10, 15, 33**
See also CA 5-8R; CANR 25; CDBLB 1960
to Present; DLB 14, 139; MTCW;
SATA 22

Fox, Paula 1923-.................. **CLC 2, 8**
See also AAYA 3; CA 73-76; CANR 20,
36; CLR 1; DLB 52; JRDA; MAICYA;
MTCW; SATA 17, 60

Fox, William Price (Jr.) 1926- ..... **CLC 22**
See also CA 17-20R; CAAS 19; CANR 11;
DLB 2; DLBY 81

Foxe, John 1516(?)-1587 .... **LC 14**

Frame, Janet .... **CLC 2, 3, 6, 22, 66**
See also Clutha, Janet Paterson Frame

France, Anatole.................... **TCLC 9**
See also Thibault, Jacques Anatole Francois
See also DLB 123

Francis, Claude 19(?)- .... **CLC 50**

Francis, Dick 1920-...... **CLC 2, 22, 42**
See also AAYA 5; BEST 89:3; CA 5-8R;
CANR 9, 42; CDBLB 1960 to Present;
DLB 87; MTCW

Francis, Robert (Churchill)
1901-1987 .... **CLC 15**
See also CA 1-4R; 123; CANR 1

Frank, Anne(lies Marie)
1929-1945 .... **TCLC 17; DA; WLC**
See also AAYA 12; CA 113; 133; MTCW;
SATA 42

Frank, Elizabeth 1945-............ **CLC 39**
See also CA 121; 126

Franklin, Benjamin
See Hasek, Jaroslav (Matej Frantisek)

Franklin, Benjamin 1706-1790... **LC 25; DA**
See also CDALB 1640-1865; DLB 24, 43,
73

Franklin, (Stella Maraia Sarah) Miles
1879-1954 .... **TCLC 7**
See also CA 104

Fraser, (Lady) Antonia (Pakenham)
1932- .... **CLC 32**
See also CA 85-88; CANR 44; MTCW;
SATA 32

Fraser, George MacDonald 1925-.... **CLC 7**
See also CA 45-48; CANR 2

Fraser, Sylvia 1935-.............. **CLC 64**
See also CA 45-48; CANR 1, 16

Frayn, Michael 1933-...... **CLC 3, 7, 31, 47**
See also CA 5-8R; CANR 30; DLB 13, 14;
MTCW

Fraze, Candida (Merrill) 1945-..... **CLC 50**
See also CA 126

Frazer, J(ames) G(eorge)
1854-1941 .... **TCLC 32**
See also CA 118

Frazer, Robert Caine
See Creasey, John

Frazer, Sir James George
See Frazer, J(ames) G(eorge)

Frazier, Ian 1951-................ **CLC 46**
See also CA 130

Frederic, Harold 1856-1898...... **NCLC 10**
See also DLB 12, 23

Frederick, John
See Faust, Frederick (Schiller)

Frederick the Great 1712-1786 ...... **LC 14**

Fredro, Aleksander 1793-1876..... **NCLC 8**

Freeling, Nicolas 1927- .... **CLC 38**
See also CA 49-52; CAAS 12; CANR 1, 17;
DLB 87

Freeman, Douglas Southall
1886-1953 .... **TCLC 11**
See also CA 109; DLB 17

Freeman, Judith 1946-............ **CLC 55**

Freeman, Mary Eleanor Wilkins
1852-1930 .... **TCLC 9; SSC 1**
See also CA 106; DLB 12, 78

Freeman, R(ichard) Austin
1862-1943 .... **TCLC 21**
See also CA 113; DLB 70

French, Albert 1944(?)- .... **CLC 86**

French, Marilyn 1929-...... **CLC 10, 18, 60**
See also CA 69-72; CANR 3, 31; MTCW

French, Paul
See Asimov, Isaac

Freneau, Philip Morin 1752-1832.. **NCLC 1**
See also DLB 37, 43

Freud, Sigmund 1856-1939 .... **TCLC 52**
See also CA 115; 133; MTCW

Friedan, Betty (Naomi) 1921-...... **CLC 74**
See also CA 65-68; CANR 18, 45; MTCW

Friedman, B(ernard) H(arper)
1926- .... **CLC 7**
See also CA 1-4R; CANR 3

Friedman, Bruce Jay 1930-.... **CLC 3, 5, 56**
See also CA 9-12R; CANR 25; DLB 2, 28

Friel, Brian 1929-........... **CLC 5, 42, 59**
See also CA 21-24R; CANR 33; DLB 13;
MTCW

Friis-Baastad, Babbis Ellinor
1921-1970 .... **CLC 12**
See also CA 17-20R; 134; SATA 7

Frisch, Max (Rudolf)
1911-1991 ..... **CLC 3, 9, 14, 18, 32, 44**
See also CA 85-88; 134; CANR 32;
DLB 69, 124; MTCW

Fromentin, Eugene (Samuel Auguste)
1820-1876 .... **NCLC 10**
See also DLB 123

Frost, Frederick
See Faust, Frederick (Schiller)

Frost, Robert (Lee)
1874-1963 .... CLC 1, 3, 4, 9, 10, 13, 15,
26, 34, 44; DA; PC 1; WLC
See also CA 89-92; CANR 33;
CDALB 1917-1929; DLB 54; DLBD 7;
MTCW; SATA 14

Froude, James Anthony
1818-1894 .... NCLC 43
See also DLB 18, 57, 144

Froy, Herald
See Waterhouse, Keith (Spencer)

Fry, Christopher   1907-....... CLC 2, 10, 14
See also CA 17-20R; CANR 9, 30; DLB 13;
MTCW; SATA 66

Frye, (Herman) Northrop
1912-1991 .... CLC 24, 70
See also CA 5-8R; 133; CANR 8, 37;
DLB 67, 68; MTCW

Fuchs, Daniel   1909-1993 .... CLC 8, 22
See also CA 81-84; 142; CAAS 5;
CANR 40; DLB 9, 26, 28; DLBY 93

Fuchs, Daniel   1934-.............. CLC 34
See also CA 37-40R; CANR 14

Fuentes, Carlos
1928-...... CLC 3, 8, 10, 13, 22, 41, 60;
DA; HLC; WLC
See also AAYA 4; AITN 2; CA 69-72;
CANR 10, 32; DLB 113; HW; MTCW

Fuentes, Gregorio Lopez y
See Lopez y Fuentes, Gregorio

Fugard, (Harold) Athol
1932-.... CLC 5, 9, 14, 25, 40, 80; DC 3
See also CA 85-88; CANR 32; MTCW

Fugard, Sheila   1932-............. CLC 48
See also CA 125

Fuller, Charles (H., Jr.)
1939-............ CLC 25; BLC; DC 1
See also BW 2; CA 108; 112; DLB 38;
MTCW

Fuller, John (Leopold)   1937-....... CLC 62
See also CA 21-24R; CANR 9, 44; DLB 40

Fuller, Margaret .... NCLC 5
See also Ossoli, Sarah Margaret (Fuller
marchesa d')

Fuller, Roy (Broadbent)
1912-1991 .... CLC 4, 28
See also CA 5-8R; 135; CAAS 10; DLB 15,
20

Fulton, Alice   1952-.............. CLC 52
See also CA 116

Furphy, Joseph   1843-1912........ TCLC 25

Fussell, Paul   1924-.............. CLC 74
See also BEST 90:1; CA 17-20R; CANR 8,
21, 35; MTCW

Futabatei, Shimei   1864-1909 ...... TCLC 44

Futrelle, Jacques   1875-1912 ...... TCLC 19
See also CA 113

Gaboriau, Emile   1835-1873 ...... NCLC 14

Gadda, Carlo Emilio   1893-1973 .... CLC 11
See also CA 89-92

Gaddis, William
1922-..... CLC 1, 3, 6, 8, 10, 19, 43, 86
See also CA 17-20R; CANR 21; DLB 2;
MTCW

Gaines, Ernest J(ames)
1933-......... CLC 3, 11, 18, 86; BLC
See also AITN 1; BW 2; CA 9-12R;
CANR 6, 24, 42; CDALB 1968-1988;
DLB 2, 33; DLBY 80; MTCW

Gaitskill, Mary   1954-............. CLC 69
See also CA 128

Galdos, Benito Perez
See Perez Galdos, Benito

Gale, Zona   1874-1938 .... TCLC 7
See also CA 105; DLB 9, 78

Galeano, Eduardo (Hughes)   1940-... CLC 72
See also CA 29-32R; CANR 13, 32; HW

Galiano, Juan Valera y Alcala
See Valera y Alcala-Galiano, Juan

Gallagher, Tess   1943-.... CLC 18, 63; PC 9
See also CA 106; DLB 120

Gallant, Mavis
1922-........... CLC 7, 18, 38; SSC 5
See also CA 69-72; CANR 29; DLB 53;
MTCW

Gallant, Roy A(rthur)   1924-....... CLC 17
See also CA 5-8R; CANR 4, 29; CLR 30;
MAICYA; SATA 4, 68

Gallico, Paul (William)   1897-1976 ... CLC 2
See also AITN 1; CA 5-8R; 69-72;
CANR 23; DLB 9; MAICYA; SATA 13

Gallup, Ralph
See Whitemore, Hugh (John)

Galsworthy, John
1867-1933 .... TCLC 1, 45; DA; WLC 2
See also CA 104; 141; CDBLB 1890-1914;
DLB 10, 34, 98

Galt, John   1779-1839............ NCLC 1
See also DLB 99, 116

Galvin, James   1951-.............. CLC 38
See also CA 108; CANR 26

Gamboa, Federico   1864-1939...... TCLC 36

Gann, Ernest Kellogg   1910-1991.... CLC 23
See also AITN 1; CA 1-4R; 136; CANR 1

Garcia, Cristina   1958-............ CLC 76
See also CA 141

Garcia Lorca, Federico
1898-1936 .... TCLC 1, 7, 49; DA;
DC 2; HLC; PC 3; WLC
See also CA 104; 131; DLB 108; HW;
MTCW

Garcia Marquez, Gabriel (Jose)
1928-.... CLC 2, 3, 8, 10, 15, 27, 47, 55,
68; DA; HLC; SSC 8; WLC
See also AAYA 3; BEST 89:1, 90:4;
CA 33-36R; CANR 10, 28; DLB 113;
HW; MTCW

Gard, Janice
See Latham, Jean Lee

Gard, Roger Martin du
See Martin du Gard, Roger

Gardam, Jane   1928-.............. CLC 43
See also CA 49-52; CANR 2, 18, 33;
CLR 12; DLB 14; MAICYA; MTCW;
SAAS 9; SATA 28, 39, 76

Gardner, Herb .... CLC 44

Gardner, John (Champlin), Jr.
1933-1982 ..... CLC 2, 3, 5, 7, 8, 10, 18,
28, 34; SSC 7
See also AITN 1; CA 65-68; 107;
CANR 33; DLB 2; DLBY 82; MTCW;
SATA 40; SATA-Obit 31

Gardner, John (Edmund)   1926-..... CLC 30
See also CA 103; CANR 15; MTCW

Gardner, Noel
See Kuttner, Henry

Gardons, S. S.
See Snodgrass, W(illiam) D(e Witt)

Garfield, Leon   1921-.............. CLC 12
See also AAYA 8; CA 17-20R; CANR 38,
41; CLR 21; JRDA; MAICYA; SATA 1,
32, 76

Garland, (Hannibal) Hamlin
1860-1940 .... TCLC 3; SSC 18
See also CA 104; DLB 12, 71, 78

Garneau, (Hector de) Saint-Denys
1912-1943 .... TCLC 13
See also CA 111; DLB 88

Garner, Alan   1934-............... CLC 17
See also CA 73-76; CANR 15; CLR 20;
MAICYA; MTCW; SATA 18, 69

Garner, Hugh   1913-1979 .... CLC 13
See also CA 69-72; CANR 31; DLB 68

Garnett, David   1892-1981 .... CLC 3
See also CA 5-8R; 103; CANR 17; DLB 34

Garos, Stephanie
See Katz, Steve

Garrett, George (Palmer)
1929- .... CLC 3, 11, 51
See also CA 1-4R; CAAS 5; CANR 1, 42;
DLB 2, 5, 130; DLBY 83

Garrick, David   1717-1779 .... LC 15
See also DLB 84

Garrigue, Jean   1914-1972 .... CLC 2, 8
See also CA 5-8R; 37-40R; CANR 20

Garrison, Frederick
See Sinclair, Upton (Beall)

Garth, Will
See Hamilton, Edmond; Kuttner, Henry

Garvey, Marcus (Moziah, Jr.)
1887-1940 .... TCLC 41; BLC
See also BW 1; CA 120; 124

Gary, Romain .... CLC 25
See also Kacew, Romain
See also DLB 83

Gascar, Pierre .... CLC 11
See also Fournier, Pierre

Gascoyne, David (Emery)   1916- .... CLC 45
See also CA 65-68; CANR 10, 28; DLB 20;
MTCW

Gaskell, Elizabeth Cleghorn
1810-1865 .... NCLC 5
See also CDBLB 1832-1890; DLB 21, 144

Gass, William H(oward)
1924- ... CLC 1, 2, 8, 11, 15, 39; SSC 12
See also CA 17-20R; CANR 30; DLB 2;
MTCW

Gasset, Jose Ortega y
See Ortega y Gasset, Jose

Gates, Henry Louis, Jr. 1950-...... **CLC 65**
See also BW 2; CA 109; CANR 25; DLB 67

Gautier, Theophile 1811-1872 ..... **NCLC 1**
See also DLB 119

Gawsworth, John
See Bates, H(erbert) E(rnest)

Gaye, Marvin (Penze) 1939-1984 ... **CLC 26**
See also CA 112

Gebler, Carlo (Ernest) 1954-....... **CLC 39**
See also CA 119; 133

Gee, Maggie (Mary) 1948-........ **CLC 57**
See also CA 130

Gee, Maurice (Gough) 1931-....... **CLC 29**
See also CA 97-100; SATA 46

Gelbart, Larry (Simon) 1923- ... **CLC 21, 61**
See also CA 73-76; CANR 45

Gelber, Jack 1932-........ **CLC 1, 6, 14, 79**
See also CA 1-4R; CANR 2; DLB 7

Gellhorn, Martha (Ellis) 1908-.. **CLC 14, 60**
See also CA 77-80; CANR 44; DLBY 82

Genet, Jean
1910-1986 ... **CLC 1, 2, 5, 10, 14, 44, 46**
See also CA 13-16R; CANR 18; DLB 72;
DLBY 86; MTCW

Gent, Peter 1942-................ **CLC 29**
See also AITN 1; CA 89-92; DLBY 82

Gentlewoman in New England, A
See Bradstreet, Anne

Gentlewoman in Those Parts, A
See Bradstreet, Anne

George, Jean Craighead 1919-...... **CLC 35**
See also AAYA 8; CA 5-8R; CANR 25;
CLR 1; DLB 52; JRDA; MAICYA;
SATA 2, 68

George, Stefan (Anton)
1868-1933 .... **TCLC 2, 14**
See also CA 104

Georges, Georges Martin
See Simenon, Georges (Jacques Christian)

Gerhardi, William Alexander
See Gerhardie, William Alexander

Gerhardie, William Alexander
1895-1977 .... **CLC 5**
See also CA 25-28R; 73-76; CANR 18;
DLB 36

Gerstler, Amy 1956-.............. **CLC 70**

Gertler, T. .... **CLC 34**
See also CA 116; 121

Ghalib 1797-1869 .... **NCLC 39**

Ghelderode, Michel de
1898-1962 .... **CLC 6, 11**
See also CA 85-88; CANR 40

Ghiselin, Brewster 1903- .... **CLC 23**
See also CA 13-16R; CAAS 10; CANR 13

Ghose, Zulfikar 1935-............. **CLC 42**
See also CA 65-68

Ghosh, Amitav 1956- .... **CLC 44**

Giacosa, Giuseppe 1847-1906 ...... **TCLC 7**
See also CA 104

Gibb, Lee
See Waterhouse, Keith (Spencer)

Gibbon, Lewis Grassic .... **TCLC 4**
See also Mitchell, James Leslie

Gibbons, Kaye 1960- .... **CLC 50**

Gibran, Kahlil
1883-1931 .... **TCLC 1, 9; PC 9**
See also CA 104

Gibson, William 1914-........ **CLC 23; DA**
See also CA 9-12R; CANR 9, 42; DLB 7;
SATA 66

Gibson, William (Ford) 1948-... **CLC 39, 63**
See also AAYA 12; CA 126; 133

Gide, Andre (Paul Guillaume)
1869-1951 .... **TCLC 5, 12, 36; DA;
SSC 13; WLC**
See also CA 104; 124; DLB 65; MTCW

Gifford, Barry (Colby) 1946-....... **CLC 34**
See also CA 65-68; CANR 9, 30, 40

Gilbert, W(illiam) S(chwenck)
1836-1911 .... **TCLC 3**
See also CA 104; SATA 36

Gilbreth, Frank B., Jr. 1911-....... **CLC 17**
See also CA 9-12R; SATA 2

Gilchrist, Ellen 1935-.. **CLC 34, 48; SSC 14**
See also CA 113; 116; CANR 41; DLB 130;
MTCW

Giles, Molly 1942- .... **CLC 39**
See also CA 126

Gill, Patrick
See Creasey, John

Gilliam, Terry (Vance) 1940-....... **CLC 21**
See also Monty Python
See also CA 108; 113; CANR 35

Gillian, Jerry
See Gilliam, Terry (Vance)

Gilliatt, Penelope (Ann Douglass)
1932-1993 .... **CLC 2, 10, 13, 53**
See also AITN 2; CA 13-16R; 141; DLB 14

Gilman, Charlotte (Anna) Perkins (Stetson)
1860-1935 .... **TCLC 9, 37; SSC 13**
See also CA 106

Gilmour, David 1949-............. **CLC 35**
See also CA 138

Gilpin, William 1724-1804....... **NCLC 30**

Gilray, J. D.
See Mencken, H(enry) L(ouis)

Gilroy, Frank D(aniel) 1925-........ **CLC 2**
See also CA 81-84; CANR 32; DLB 7

Ginsberg, Allen
1926- ...... **CLC 1, 2, 3, 4, 6, 13, 36, 69;
DA; PC 4; WLC 3**
See also AITN 1; CA 1-4R; CANR 2, 41;
CDALB 1941-1968; DLB 5, 16; MTCW

Ginzburg, Natalia
1916-1991 .... **CLC 5, 11, 54, 70**
See also CA 85-88; 135; CANR 33; MTCW

Giono, Jean 1895-1970......... **CLC 4, 11**
See also CA 45-48; 29-32R; CANR 2, 35;
DLB 72; MTCW

Giovanni, Nikki
1943- ...... **CLC 2, 4, 19, 64; BLC; DA**
See also AITN 1; BW 2; CA 29-32R;
CAAS 6; CANR 18, 41; CLR 6; DLB 5,
41; MAICYA; MTCW; SATA 24

Giovene, Andrea 1904-............. **CLC 7**
See also CA 85-88

Gippius, Zinaida (Nikolayevna) 1869-1945
See Hippius, Zinaida
See also CA 106

Giraudoux, (Hippolyte) Jean
1882-1944 .... **TCLC 2, 7**
See also CA 104; DLB 65

Gironella, Jose Maria 1917-....... **CLC 11**
See also CA 101

Gissing, George (Robert)
1857-1903 .... **TCLC 3, 24, 47**
See also CA 105; DLB 18, 135

Giurlani, Aldo
See Palazzeschi, Aldo

Gladkov, Fyodor (Vasilyevich)
1883-1958 .... **TCLC 27**

Glanville, Brian (Lester) 1931-...... **CLC 6**
See also CA 5-8R; CAAS 9; CANR 3;
DLB 15, 139; SATA 42

Glasgow, Ellen (Anderson Gholson)
1873(?)-1945 .... **TCLC 2, 7**
See also CA 104; DLB 9, 12

Glaspell, Susan (Keating)
1882(?)-1948 .... **TCLC 55**
See also CA 110; DLB 7, 9, 78; YABC 2

Glassco, John 1909-1981 .... **CLC 9**
See also CA 13-16R; 102; CANR 15;
DLB 68

Glasscock, Amnesia
See Steinbeck, John (Ernst)

Glasser, Ronald J. 1940(?)-........ **CLC 37**

Glassman, Joyce
See Johnson, Joyce

Glendinning, Victoria 1937-........ **CLC 50**
See also CA 120; 127

Glissant, Edouard 1928-....... **CLC 10, 68**

Gloag, Julian 1930- .... **CLC 40**
See also AITN 1; CA 65-68; CANR 10

Glowacki, Aleksander
See Prus, Boleslaw

Glueck, Louise (Elisabeth)
1943- .... **CLC 7, 22, 44, 81**
See also CA 33-36R; CANR 40; DLB 5

Gobineau, Joseph Arthur (Comte) de
1816-1882 .... **NCLC 17**
See also DLB 123

Godard, Jean-Luc 1930-........... **CLC 20**
See also CA 93-96

Godden, (Margaret) Rumer 1907-... **CLC 53**
See also AAYA 6; CA 5-8R; CANR 4, 27,
36; CLR 20; MAICYA; SAAS 12;
SATA 3, 36

Godoy Alcayaga, Lucila 1889-1957
See Mistral, Gabriela
See also BW 2; CA 104; 131; HW; MTCW

Godwin, Gail (Kathleen)
1937- .... **CLC 5, 8, 22, 31, 69**
See also CA 29-32R; CANR 15, 43; DLB 6;
MTCW

Godwin, William 1756-1836...... **NCLC 14**
See also CDBLB 1789-1832; DLB 39, 104,
142

Goethe, Johann Wolfgang von
1749-1832 . . . . NCLC 4, 22, 34; DA;
PC 5; WLC 3
See also DLB 94

Gogarty, Oliver St. John
1878-1957 . . . . TCLC 15
See also CA 109; DLB 15, 19

Gogol, Nikolai (Vasilyevich)
1809-1852 . . . . NCLC 5, 15, 31; DA;
DC 1; SSC 4; WLC

Goines, Donald
1937(?)-1974 . . . . CLC 80; BLC
See also AITN 1; BW 1; CA 124; 114;
DLB 33

Gold, Herbert 1924- . . . . CLC 4, 7, 14, 42
See also CA 9-12R; CANR 17, 45; DLB 2;
DLBY 81

Goldbarth, Albert 1948- . . . . CLC 5, 38
See also CA 53-56; CANR 6, 40; DLB 120

Goldberg, Anatol 1910-1982 . . . . CLC 34
See also CA 131; 117

Goldemberg, Isaac 1945- . . . . CLC 52
See also CA 69-72; CAAS 12; CANR 11,
32; HW

Golding, William (Gerald)
1911-1993 . . . . CLC 1, 2, 3, 8, 10, 17, 27,
58, 81; DA; WLC
See also AAYA 5; CA 5-8R; 141;
CANR 13, 33; CDBLB 1945-1960;
DLB 15, 100; MTCW

Goldman, Emma 1869-1940 . . . . . . TCLC 13
See also CA 110

Goldman, Francisco 1955- . . . . CLC 76

Goldman, William (W.) 1931- . . . . CLC 1, 48
See also CA 9-12R; CANR 29; DLB 44

Goldmann, Lucien 1913-1970 . . . . . . CLC 24
See also CA 25-28; CAP 2

Goldoni, Carlo 1707-1793 . . . . LC 4

Goldsberry, Steven 1949- . . . . CLC 34
See also CA 131

Goldsmith, Oliver
1728-1774 . . . . LC 2; DA; WLC
See also CDBLB 1660-1789; DLB 39, 89,
104, 109, 142; SATA 26

Goldsmith, Peter
See Priestley, J(ohn) B(oynton)

Gombrowicz, Witold
1904-1969 . . . . CLC 4, 7, 11, 49
See also CA 19-20; 25-28R; CAP 2

Gomez de la Serna, Ramon
1888-1963 . . . . CLC 9
See also CA 116; HW

Goncharov, Ivan Alexandrovich
1812-1891 . . . . NCLC 1

Goncourt, Edmond (Louis Antoine Huot) de
1822-1896 . . . . NCLC 7
See also DLB 123

Goncourt, Jules (Alfred Huot) de
1830-1870 . . . . NCLC 7
See also DLB 123

Gontier, Fernande 19(?)- . . . . CLC 50

Goodman, Paul 1911-1972 . . . . CLC 1, 2, 4, 7
See also CA 19-20; 37-40R; CANR 34;
CAP 2; DLB 130; MTCW

Gordimer, Nadine
1923- . . . . CLC 3, 5, 7, 10, 18, 33, 51, 70;
DA; SSC 17
See also CA 5-8R; CANR 3, 28; MTCW

Gordon, Adam Lindsay
1833-1870 . . . . NCLC 21

Gordon, Caroline
1895-1981 . . . CLC 6, 13, 29, 83; SSC 15
See also CA 11-12; 103; CANR 36; CAP 1;
DLB 4, 9, 102; DLBY 81; MTCW

Gordon, Charles William 1860-1937
See Connor, Ralph
See also CA 109

Gordon, Mary (Catherine)
1949- . . . . CLC 13, 22
See also CA 102; CANR 44; DLB 6;
DLBY 81; MTCW

Gordon, Sol 1923- . . . . CLC 26
See also CA 53-56; CANR 4; SATA 11

Gordone, Charles 1925- . . . . CLC 1, 4
See also BW 1; CA 93-96; DLB 7; MTCW

Gorenko, Anna Andreevna
See Akhmatova, Anna

Gorky, Maxim . . . . TCLC 8; WLC
See also Peshkov, Alexei Maximovich

Goryan, Sirak
See Saroyan, William

Gosse, Edmund (William)
1849-1928 . . . . TCLC 28
See also CA 117; DLB 57, 144

Gotlieb, Phyllis Fay (Bloom)
1926- . . . . CLC 18
See also CA 13-16R; CANR 7; DLB 88

Gottesman, S. D.
See Kornbluth, C(yril) M.; Pohl, Frederik

Gottfried von Strassburg
fl. c. 1210- . . . . CMLC 10
See also DLB 138

Gould, Lois . . . . CLC 4, 10
See also CA 77-80; CANR 29; MTCW

Gourmont, Remy de 1858-1915 . . . . TCLC 17
See also CA 109

Govier, Katherine 1948- . . . . CLC 51
See also CA 101; CANR 18, 40

Goyen, (Charles) William
1915-1983 . . . . CLC 5, 8, 14, 40
See also AITN 2; CA 5-8R; 110; CANR 6;
DLB 2; DLBY 83

Goytisolo, Juan
1931- . . . . CLC 5, 10, 23; HLC
See also CA 85-88; CANR 32; HW; MTCW

Gozzano, Guido 1883-1916 . . . . PC 10
See also DLB 114

Gozzi, (Conte) Carlo 1720-1806 . . NCLC 23

Grabbe, Christian Dietrich
1801-1836 . . . . NCLC 2
See also DLB 133

Grace, Patricia 1937- . . . . CLC 56

Gracian y Morales, Baltasar
1601-1658 . . . . LC 15

Gracq, Julien . . . . CLC 11, 48
See also Poirier, Louis
See also DLB 83

Grade, Chaim 1910-1982 . . . . CLC 10
See also CA 93-96; 107

Graduate of Oxford, A
See Ruskin, John

Graham, John
See Phillips, David Graham

Graham, Jorie 1951- . . . . CLC 48
See also CA 111; DLB 120

Graham, R(obert) B(ontine) Cunninghame
See Cunninghame Graham, R(obert)
B(ontine)
See also DLB 98, 135

Graham, Robert
See Haldeman, Joe (William)

Graham, Tom
See Lewis, (Harry) Sinclair

Graham, W(illiam) S(ydney)
1918-1986 . . . . CLC 29
See also CA 73-76; 118; DLB 20

Graham, Winston (Mawdsley)
1910- . . . . CLC 23
See also CA 49-52; CANR 2, 22, 45;
DLB 77

Grant, Skeeter
See Spiegelman, Art

Granville-Barker, Harley
1877-1946 . . . . TCLC 2
See also Barker, Harley Granville
See also CA 104

Grass, Guenter (Wilhelm)
1927- . . . . . CLC 1, 2, 4, 6, 11, 15, 22, 32,
49; DA; WLC
See also CA 13-16R; CANR 20; DLB 75,
124; MTCW

Gratton, Thomas
See Hulme, T(homas) E(rnest)

Grau, Shirley Ann
1929- . . . . CLC 4, 9; SSC 15
See also CA 89-92; CANR 22; DLB 2;
MTCW

Gravel, Fern
See Hall, James Norman

Graver, Elizabeth 1964- . . . . CLC 70
See also CA 135

Graves, Richard Perceval 1945- . . . . CLC 44
See also CA 65-68; CANR 9, 26

Graves, Robert (von Ranke)
1895-1985 . . . . . . CLC 1, 2, 6, 11, 39, 44,
45; PC 6
See also CA 5-8R; 117; CANR 5, 36;
CDBLB 1914-1945; DLB 20, 100;
DLBY 85; MTCW; SATA 45

Gray, Alasdair (James) 1934- . . . . . . CLC 41
See also CA 126; CANR 47; MTCW

Gray, Amlin 1946- . . . . CLC 29
See also CA 138

Gray, Francine du Plessix 1930- . . . CLC 22
See also BEST 90:3; CA 61-64; CAAS 2;
CANR 11, 33; MTCW

Gray, John (Henry) 1866-1934 . . . . TCLC 19
See also CA 119

Gray, Simon (James Holliday)
1936- . . . . CLC 9, 14, 36
See also AITN 1; CA 21-24R; CAAS 3;
CANR 32; DLB 13; MTCW

Gray, Spalding 1941- . . . . **CLC 49**
See also CA 128

Gray, Thomas
1716-1771 . . . . . . **LC 4; DA; PC 2; WLC**
See also CDBLB 1660-1789; DLB 109

Grayson, David
See Baker, Ray Stannard

Grayson, Richard (A.) 1951- . . . . **CLC 38**
See also CA 85-88; CANR 14, 31

Greeley, Andrew M(oran) 1928- . . . . **CLC 28**
See also CA 5-8R; CAAS 7; CANR 7, 43;
MTCW

Green, Brian
See Card, Orson Scott

Green, Hannah
See Greenberg, Joanne (Goldenberg)

Green, Hannah . . . . **CLC 3**
See also CA 73-76

Green, Henry . . . . **CLC 2, 13**
See also Yorke, Henry Vincent
See also DLB 15

Green, Julian (Hartridge) 1900-
See Green, Julien
See also CA 21-24R; CANR 33; DLB 4, 72;
MTCW

Green, Julien . . . . **CLC 3, 11, 77**
See also Green, Julian (Hartridge)

Green, Paul (Eliot) 1894-1981 . . . . . . **CLC 25**
See also AITN 1; CA 5-8R; 103; CANR 3;
DLB 7, 9; DLBY 81

Greenberg, Ivan 1908-1973
See Rahv, Philip
See also CA 85-88

Greenberg, Joanne (Goldenberg)
1932- . . . . **CLC 7, 30**
See also AAYA 12; CA 5-8R; CANR 14,
32; SATA 25

Greenberg, Richard 1959(?)- . . . . **CLC 57**
See also CA 138

Greene, Bette 1934- . . . . **CLC 30**
See also AAYA 7; CA 53-56; CANR 4;
CLR 2; JRDA; MAICYA; SAAS 16;
SATA 8

Greene, Gael . . . . **CLC 8**
See also CA 13-16R; CANR 10

Greene, Graham
1904-1991 . . . . **CLC 1, 3, 6, 9, 14, 18, 27,
37, 70, 72; DA; WLC**
See also AITN 2; CA 13-16R; 133;
CANR 35; CDBLB 1945-1960; DLB 13,
15, 77, 100; DLBY 91; MTCW; SATA 20

Greer, Richard
See Silverberg, Robert

Greer, Richard
See Silverberg, Robert

Gregor, Arthur 1923- . . . . **CLC 9**
See also CA 25-28R; CAAS 10; CANR 11;
SATA 36

Gregor, Lee
See Pohl, Frederik

Gregory, Isabella Augusta (Persse)
1852-1932 . . . . **TCLC 1**
See also CA 104; DLB 10

Gregory, J. Dennis
See Williams, John A(lfred)

Grendon, Stephen
See Derleth, August (William)

Grenville, Kate 1950- . . . . **CLC 61**
See also CA 118

Grenville, Pelham
See Wodehouse, P(elham) G(renville)

Greve, Felix Paul (Berthold Friedrich)
1879-1948
See Grove, Frederick Philip
See also CA 104; 141

Grey, Zane 1872-1939 . . . . **TCLC 6**
See also CA 104; 132; DLB 9; MTCW

Grieg, (Johan) Nordahl (Brun)
1902-1943 . . . . **TCLC 10**
See also CA 107

Grieve, C(hristopher) M(urray)
1892-1978 . . . . **CLC 11, 19**
See also MacDiarmid, Hugh
See also CA 5-8R; 85-88; CANR 33;
MTCW

Griffin, Gerald 1803-1840 . . . . **NCLC 7**

Griffin, John Howard 1920-1980 . . . . **CLC 68**
See also AITN 1; CA 1-4R; 101; CANR 2

Griffin, Peter 1942- . . . . **CLC 39**
See also CA 136

Griffiths, Trevor 1935- . . . . **CLC 13, 52**
See also CA 97-100; CANR 45; DLB 13

Grigson, Geoffrey (Edward Harvey)
1905-1985 . . . . **CLC 7, 39**
See also CA 25-28R; 118; CANR 20, 33;
DLB 27; MTCW

Grillparzer, Franz 1791-1872 . . . . . . **NCLC 1**
See also DLB 133

Grimble, Reverend Charles James
See Eliot, T(homas) S(tearns)

Grimke, Charlotte L(ottie) Forten
1837(?)-1914
See Forten, Charlotte L.
See also BW 1; CA 117; 124

Grimm, Jacob Ludwig Karl
1785-1863 . . . . **NCLC 3**
See also DLB 90; MAICYA; SATA 22

Grimm, Wilhelm Karl 1786-1859 . . **NCLC 3**
See also DLB 90; MAICYA; SATA 22

Grimmelshausen, Johann Jakob Christoffel
von 1621-1676 . . . . **LC 6**

Grindel, Eugene 1895-1952
See Eluard, Paul
See also CA 104

Grisham, John 1955- . . . . **CLC 84**
See also AAYA 14; CA 138; CANR 47

Grossman, David 1954- . . . . **CLC 67**
See also CA 138

Grossman, Vasily (Semenovich)
1905-1964 . . . . **CLC 41**
See also CA 124; 130; MTCW

Grove, Frederick Philip . . . . **TCLC 4**
See also Greve, Felix Paul (Berthold
Friedrich)
See also DLB 92

Grubb
See Crumb, R(obert)

Grumbach, Doris (Isaac)
1918- . . . . **CLC 13, 22, 64**
See also CA 5-8R; CAAS 2; CANR 9, 42

Grundtvig, Nicolai Frederik Severin
1783-1872 . . . . **NCLC 1**

Grunge
See Crumb, R(obert)

Grunwald, Lisa 1959- . . . . **CLC 44**
See also CA 120

Guare, John 1938- . . . . **CLC 8, 14, 29, 67**
See also CA 73-76; CANR 21; DLB 7;
MTCW

Gudjonsson, Halldor Kiljan 1902-
See Laxness, Halldor
See also CA 103

Guenter, Erich
See Eich, Guenter

Guest, Barbara 1920- . . . . **CLC 34**
See also CA 25-28R; CANR 11, 44; DLB 5

Guest, Judith (Ann) 1936- . . . . **CLC 8, 30**
See also AAYA 7; CA 77-80; CANR 15;
MTCW

Guild, Nicholas M. 1944- . . . . **CLC 33**
See also CA 93-96

Guillemin, Jacques
See Sartre, Jean-Paul

Guillen, Jorge 1893-1984 . . . . **CLC 11**
See also CA 89-92; 112; DLB 108; HW

Guillen (y Batista), Nicolas (Cristobal)
1902-1989 . . . . . **CLC 48, 79; BLC; HLC**
See also BW 2; CA 116; 125; 129; HW

Guillevic, (Eugene) 1907- . . . . **CLC 33**
See also CA 93-96

Guillois
See Desnos, Robert

Guiney, Louise Imogen
1861-1920 . . . . **TCLC 41**
See also DLB 54

Guiraldes, Ricardo (Guillermo)
1886-1927 . . . . **TCLC 39**
See also CA 131; HW; MTCW

Gunn, Bill . . . . **CLC 5**
See also Gunn, William Harrison
See also DLB 38

Gunn, Thom(son William)
1929- . . . . **CLC 3, 6, 18, 32, 81**
See also CA 17-20R; CANR 9, 33;
CDBLB 1960 to Present; DLB 27;
MTCW

Gunn, William Harrison 1934(?)-1989
See Gunn, Bill
See also AITN 1; BW 1; CA 13-16R; 128;
CANR 12, 25

Gunnars, Kristjana 1948- . . . . **CLC 69**
See also CA 113; DLB 60

Gurganus, Allan 1947- . . . . **CLC 70**
See also BEST 90:1; CA 135

Gurney, A(lbert) R(amsdell), Jr.
1930- . . . . **CLC 32, 50, 54**
See also CA 77-80; CANR 32

Gurney, Ivor (Bertie) 1890-1937 . . . **TCLC 33**

Gurney, Peter
See Gurney, A(lbert) R(amsdell), Jr.

Guro, Elena 1877-1913 . . . . **TCLC 56**

Gustafson, Ralph (Barker) 1909-.... **CLC 36**
See also CA 21-24R; CANR 8, 45; DLB 88

Gut, Gom
See Simenon, Georges (Jacques Christian)

Guthrie, A(lfred) B(ertram), Jr.
1901-1991 .... **CLC 23**
See also CA 57-60; 134; CANR 24; DLB 6;
SATA 62; SATA-Obit 67

Guthrie, Isobel
See Grieve, C(hristopher) M(urray)

Guthrie, Woodrow Wilson 1912-1967
See Guthrie, Woody
See also CA 113; 93-96

Guthrie, Woody .... **CLC 35**
See also Guthrie, Woodrow Wilson

Guy, Rosa (Cuthbert) 1928-........ **CLC 26**
See also AAYA 4; BW 2; CA 17-20R;
CANR 14, 34; CLR 13; DLB 33; JRDA;
MAICYA; SATA 14, 62

Gwendolyn
See Bennett, (Enoch) Arnold

H. D. .... **CLC 3, 8, 14, 31, 34, 73; PC 5**
See also Doolittle, Hilda

H. de V.
See Buchan, John

Haavikko, Paavo Juhani
1931- .... **CLC 18, 34**
See also CA 106

Habbema, Koos
See Heijermans, Herman

Hacker, Marilyn 1942- .... **CLC 5, 9, 23, 72**
See also CA 77-80; DLB 120

Haggard, H(enry) Rider
1856-1925 .... **TCLC 11**
See also CA 108; DLB 70; SATA 16

Haig, Fenil
See Ford, Ford Madox

Haig-Brown, Roderick (Langmere)
1908-1976 .... **CLC 21**
See also CA 5-8R; 69-72; CANR 4, 38;
CLR 31; DLB 88; MAICYA; SATA 12

Hailey, Arthur 1920- .... **CLC 5**
See also AITN 2; BEST 90:3; CA 1-4R;
CANR 2, 36; DLB 88; DLBY 82; MTCW

Hailey, Elizabeth Forsythe 1938-... **CLC 40**
See also CA 93-96; CAAS 1; CANR 15

Haines, John (Meade) 1924-....... **CLC 58**
See also CA 17-20R; CANR 13, 34; DLB 5

Haldeman, Joe (William) 1943-..... **CLC 61**
See also CA 53-56; CANR 6; DLB 8

Haley, Alex(ander Murray Palmer)
1921-1992 .... **CLC 8, 12, 76; BLC; DA**
See also BW 2; CA 77-80; 136; DLB 38;
MTCW

Haliburton, Thomas Chandler
1796-1865 .... **NCLC 15**
See also DLB 11, 99

Hall, Donald (Andrew, Jr.)
1928- .... **CLC 1, 13, 37, 59**
See also CA 5-8R; CAAS 7; CANR 2, 44;
DLB 5; SATA 23

Hall, Frederic Sauser
See Sauser-Hall, Frederic

Hall, James
See Kuttner, Henry

Hall, James Norman 1887-1951 ... **TCLC 23**
See also CA 123; SATA 21

Hall, (Marguerite) Radclyffe
1886(?)-1943 .... **TCLC 12**
See also CA 110

Hall, Rodney 1935- .... **CLC 51**
See also CA 109

Halleck, Fitz-Greene 1790-1867 .. **NCLC 47**
See also DLB 3

Halliday, Michael
See Creasey, John

Halpern, Daniel 1945- .... **CLC 14**
See also CA 33-36R

Hamburger, Michael (Peter Leopold)
1924- .... **CLC 5, 14**
See also CA 5-8R; CAAS 4; CANR 2, 47;
DLB 27

Hamill, Pete 1935-............... **CLC 10**
See also CA 25-28R; CANR 18

Hamilton, Clive
See Lewis, C(live) S(taples)

Hamilton, Edmond 1904-1977....... **CLC 1**
See also CA 1-4R; CANR 3; DLB 8

Hamilton, Eugene (Jacob) Lee
See Lee-Hamilton, Eugene (Jacob)

Hamilton, Franklin
See Silverberg, Robert

Hamilton, Gail
See Corcoran, Barbara

Hamilton, Mollie
See Kaye, M(ary) M(argaret)

Hamilton, (Anthony Walter) Patrick
1904-1962 .... **CLC 51**
See also CA 113; DLB 10

Hamilton, Virginia 1936-.......... **CLC 26**
See also AAYA 2; BW 2; CA 25-28R;
CANR 20, 37; CLR 1, 11; DLB 33, 52;
JRDA; MAICYA; MTCW; SATA 4, 56,
79

Hammett, (Samuel) Dashiell
1894-1961 .... **CLC 3, 5, 10, 19, 47;
SSC 17**
See also AITN 1; CA 81-84; CANR 42;
CDALB 1929-1941; DLBD 6; MTCW

Hammon, Jupiter
1711(?)-1800(?) .... **NCLC 5; BLC**
See also DLB 31, 50

Hammond, Keith
See Kuttner, Henry

Hamner, Earl (Henry), Jr. 1923- ... **CLC 12**
See also AITN 2; CA 73-76; DLB 6

Hampton, Christopher (James)
1946-....................... **CLC 4**
See also CA 25-28R; DLB 13; MTCW

Hamsun, Knut .... **TCLC 2, 14, 49**
See also Pedersen, Knut

Handke, Peter 1942- .. **CLC 5, 8, 10, 15, 38**
See also CA 77-80; CANR 33; DLB 85,
124; MTCW

Hanley, James 1901-1985 ... **CLC 3, 5, 8, 13**
See also CA 73-76; 117; CANR 36; MTCW

Hannah, Barry 1942-.......... **CLC 23, 38**
See also CA 108; 110; CANR 43; DLB 6;
MTCW

Hannon, Ezra
See Hunter, Evan

Hansberry, Lorraine (Vivian)
1930-1965 ...... **CLC 17, 62; BLC; DA;
DC 2**
See also BW 1; CA 109; 25-28R; CABS 3;
CDALB 1941-1968; DLB 7, 38; MTCW

Hansen, Joseph 1923-............. **CLC 38**
See also CA 29-32R; CAAS 17; CANR 16,
44

Hansen, Martin A. 1909-1955..... **TCLC 32**

Hanson, Kenneth O(stlin) 1922-.... **CLC 13**
See also CA 53-56; CANR 7

Hardwick, Elizabeth 1916- .... **CLC 13**
See also CA 5-8R; CANR 3, 32; DLB 6;
MTCW

Hardy, Thomas
1840-1928 ...... **TCLC 4, 10, 18, 32, 48,
53; DA; PC 8; SSC 2; WLC**
See also CA 104; 123; CDBLB 1890-1914;
DLB 18, 19, 135; MTCW

Hare, David 1947- .... **CLC 29, 58**
See also CA 97-100; CANR 39; DLB 13;
MTCW

Harford, Henry
See Hudson, W(illiam) H(enry)

Hargrave, Leonie
See Disch, Thomas M(ichael)

Harjo, Joy 1951- .... **CLC 83**
See also CA 114; CANR 35; DLB 120;
NNAL

Harlan, Louis R(udolph) 1922-..... **CLC 34**
See also CA 21-24R; CANR 25

Harling, Robert 1951(?)- .... **CLC 53**

Harmon, William (Ruth) 1938-..... **CLC 38**
See also CA 33-36R; CANR 14, 32, 35;
SATA 65

Harper, F. E. W.
See Harper, Frances Ellen Watkins

Harper, Frances E. W.
See Harper, Frances Ellen Watkins

Harper, Frances E. Watkins
See Harper, Frances Ellen Watkins

Harper, Frances Ellen
See Harper, Frances Ellen Watkins

Harper, Frances Ellen Watkins
1825-1911 .... **TCLC 14; BLC**
See also BW 1; CA 111; 125; DLB 50

Harper, Michael S(teven) 1938- .. **CLC 7, 22**
See also BW 1; CA 33-36R; CANR 24;
DLB 41

Harper, Mrs. F. E. W.
See Harper, Frances Ellen Watkins

Harris, Christie (Lucy) Irwin
1907-....................... **CLC 12**
See also CA 5-8R; CANR 6; DLB 88;
JRDA; MAICYA; SAAS 10; SATA 6, 74

Harris, Frank 1856(?)-1931....... **TCLC 24**
See also CA 109

Harris, George Washington
1814-1869 . . . . **NCLC 23**
See also DLB 3, 11

Harris, Joel Chandler 1848-1908 . . . **TCLC 2**
See also CA 104; 137; DLB 11, 23, 42, 78,
91; MAICYA; YABC 1

Harris, John (Wyndham Parkes Lucas)
Beynon 1903-1969
See Wyndham, John
See also CA 102; 89-92

Harris, MacDonald . . . . **CLC 9**
See also Heiney, Donald (William)

Harris, Mark 1922- . . . . **CLC 19**
See also CA 5-8R; CAAS 3; CANR 2;
DLB 2; DLBY 80

Harris, (Theodore) Wilson 1921- . . . . **CLC 25**
See also BW 2; CA 65-68; CAAS 16;
CANR 11, 27; DLB 117; MTCW

Harrison, Elizabeth Cavanna 1909-
See Cavanna, Betty
See also CA 9-12R; CANR 6, 27

Harrison, Harry (Max) 1925- . . . . . . **CLC 42**
See also CA 1-4R; CANR 5, 21; DLB 8;
SATA 4

Harrison, James (Thomas)
1937- . . . . **CLC 6, 14, 33, 66**
See also CA 13-16R; CANR 8; DLBY 82

Harrison, Jim
See Harrison, James (Thomas)

Harrison, Kathryn 1961- . . . . **CLC 70**
See also CA 144

Harrison, Tony 1937- . . . . **CLC 43**
See also CA 65-68; CANR 44; DLB 40;
MTCW

Harriss, Will(ard Irvin) 1922- . . . . . . **CLC 34**
See also CA 111

Harson, Sley
See Ellison, Harlan (Jay)

Hart, Ellis
See Ellison, Harlan (Jay)

Hart, Josephine 1942(?)- . . . . **CLC 70**
See also CA 138

Hart, Moss 1904-1961 . . . . **CLC 66**
See also CA 109; 89-92; DLB 7

Harte, (Francis) Bret(t)
1836(?)-1902 . . . . **TCLC 1, 25; DA;
SSC 8; WLC**
See also CA 104; 140; CDALB 1865-1917;
DLB 12, 64, 74, 79; SATA 26

Hartley, L(eslie) P(oles)
1895-1972 . . . . **CLC 2, 22**
See also CA 45-48; 37-40R; CANR 33;
DLB 15, 139; MTCW

Hartman, Geoffrey H. 1929- . . . . **CLC 27**
See also CA 117; 125; DLB 67

Haruf, Kent 19(?)- . . . . **CLC 34**

Harwood, Ronald 1934- . . . . **CLC 32**
See also CA 1-4R; CANR 4; DLB 13

Hasek, Jaroslav (Matej Frantisek)
1883-1923 . . . . **TCLC 4**
See also CA 104; 129; MTCW

Hass, Robert 1941- . . . . **CLC 18, 39**
See also CA 111; CANR 30; DLB 105

Hastings, Hudson
See Kuttner, Henry

Hastings, Selina . . . . **CLC 44**

Hatteras, Amelia
See Mencken, H(enry) L(ouis)

Hatteras, Owen . . . . **TCLC 18**
See also Mencken, H(enry) L(ouis); Nathan,
George Jean

Hauptmann, Gerhart (Johann Robert)
1862-1946 . . . . **TCLC 4**
See also CA 104; DLB 66, 118

Havel, Vaclav 1936- . . . . **CLC 25, 58, 65**
See also CA 104; CANR 36; MTCW

Haviaras, Stratis . . . . **CLC 33**
See also Chaviaras, Strates

Hawes, Stephen 1475(?)-1523(?) . . . . . **LC 17**

Hawkes, John (Clendennin Burne, Jr.)
1925- . . . . . . **CLC 1, 2, 3, 4, 7, 9, 14, 15,
27, 49**
See also CA 1-4R; CANR 2, 47; DLB 2, 7;
DLBY 80; MTCW

Hawking, S. W.
See Hawking, Stephen W(illiam)

Hawking, Stephen W(illiam)
1942- . . . . **CLC 63**
See also AAYA 13; BEST 89:1; CA 126;
129

Hawthorne, Julian 1846-1934 . . . . . **TCLC 25**

Hawthorne, Nathaniel
1804-1864 . . . . . . **NCLC 39; DA; SSC 3;
WLC**
See also CDALB 1640-1865; DLB 1, 74;
YABC 2

Haxton, Josephine Ayres 1921-
See Douglas, Ellen
See also CA 115; CANR 41

Hayaseca y Eizaguirre, Jorge
See Echegaray (y Eizaguirre), Jose (Maria
Waldo)

Hayashi Fumiko 1904-1951 . . . . . . **TCLC 27**

Haycraft, Anna
See Ellis, Alice Thomas
See also CA 122

Hayden, Robert E(arl)
1913-1980 . . . . . . **CLC 5, 9, 14, 37; BLC;
DA; PC 6**
See also BW 1; CA 69-72; 97-100; CABS 2;
CANR 24; CDALB 1941-1968; DLB 5,
76; MTCW; SATA 19; SATA-Obit 26

Hayford, J(oseph) E(phraim) Casely
See Casely-Hayford, J(oseph) E(phraim)

Hayman, Ronald 1932- . . . . **CLC 44**
See also CA 25-28R; CANR 18

Haywood, Eliza (Fowler)
1693(?)-1756 . . . . **LC 1**

Hazlitt, William 1778-1830 . . . . . . **NCLC 29**
See also DLB 110

Hazzard, Shirley 1931- . . . . **CLC 18**
See also CA 9-12R; CANR 4; DLBY 82;
MTCW

Head, Bessie 1937-1986 . . . **CLC 25, 67; BLC**
See also BW 2; CA 29-32R; 119; CANR 25;
DLB 117; MTCW

Headon, (Nicky) Topper 1956(?)- . . . **CLC 30**

Heaney, Seamus (Justin)
1939- . . . . **CLC 5, 7, 14, 25, 37, 74**
See also CA 85-88; CANR 25;
CDBLB 1960 to Present; DLB 40;
MTCW

Hearn, (Patricio) Lafcadio (Tessima Carlos)
1850-1904 . . . . **TCLC 9**
See also CA 105; DLB 12, 78

Hearne, Vicki 1946- . . . . **CLC 56**
See also CA 139

Hearon, Shelby 1931- . . . . **CLC 63**
See also AITN 2; CA 25-28R; CANR 18

Heat-Moon, William Least . . . . **CLC 29**
See also Trogdon, William (Lewis)
See also AAYA 9

Hebbel, Friedrich 1813-1863 . . . . . . **NCLC 43**
See also DLB 129

Hebert, Anne 1916- . . . . **CLC 4, 13, 29**
See also CA 85-88; DLB 68; MTCW

Hecht, Anthony (Evan)
1923- . . . . **CLC 8, 13, 19**
See also CA 9-12R; CANR 6; DLB 5

Hecht, Ben 1894-1964 . . . . **CLC 8**
See also CA 85-88; DLB 7, 9, 25, 26, 28, 86

Hedayat, Sadeq 1903-1951 . . . . **TCLC 21**
See also CA 120

Hegel, Georg Wilhelm Friedrich
1770-1831 . . . . **NCLC 46**
See also DLB 90

Heidegger, Martin 1889-1976 . . . . . . **CLC 24**
See also CA 81-84; 65-68; CANR 34;
MTCW

Heidenstam, (Carl Gustaf) Verner von
1859-1940 . . . . **TCLC 5**
See also CA 104

Heifner, Jack 1946- . . . . **CLC 11**
See also CA 105; CANR 47

Heijermans, Herman 1864-1924 . . . **TCLC 24**
See also CA 123

Heilbrun, Carolyn G(old) 1926- . . . . . **CLC 25**
See also CA 45-48; CANR 1, 28

Heine, Heinrich 1797-1856 . . . . **NCLC 4**
See also DLB 90

Heinemann, Larry (Curtiss) 1944- . . **CLC 50**
See also CA 110; CANR 31; DLBD 9

Heiney, Donald (William) 1921-1993
See Harris, MacDonald
See also CA 1-4R; 142; CANR 3

Heinlein, Robert A(nson)
1907-1988 . . . . . . **CLC 1, 3, 8, 14, 26, 55**
See also CA 1-4R; 125; CANR 1, 20;
DLB 8; JRDA; MAICYA; MTCW;
SATA 9, 69; SATA-Obit 56

Helforth, John
See Doolittle, Hilda

Hellenhofferu, Vojtech Kapristian z
See Hasek, Jaroslav (Matej Frantisek)

Heller, Joseph
1923- . . . . **CLC 1, 3, 5, 8, 11, 36, 63; DA;
WLC**
See also AITN 1; CA 5-8R; CABS 1;
CANR 8, 42; DLB 2, 28; DLBY 80;
MTCW

Hellman, Lillian (Florence)
1906-1984 ...... **CLC 2, 4, 8, 14, 18, 34, 44, 52; DC 1**
See also AITN 1, 2; CA 13-16R; 112; CANR 33; DLB 7; DLBY 84; MTCW

Helprin, Mark 1947- ..... **CLC 7, 10, 22, 32**
See also CA 81-84; CANR 47; DLBY 85; MTCW

Helvetius, Claude-Adrien
1715-1771 .... **LC 26**

Helyar, Jane Penelope Josephine 1933-
See Poole, Josephine
See also CA 21-24R; CANR 10, 26

Hemans, Felicia 1793-1835 ...... **NCLC 29**
See also DLB 96

Hemingway, Ernest (Miller)
1899-1961 .... **CLC 1, 3, 6, 8, 10, 13, 19, 30, 34, 39, 41, 44, 50, 61, 80; DA; SSC 1; WLC**
See also CA 77-80; CANR 34; CDALB 1917-1929; DLB 4, 9, 102; DLBD 1; DLBY 81, 87; MTCW

Hempel, Amy 1951- .... **CLC 39**
See also CA 118; 137

Henderson, F. C.
See Mencken, H(enry) L(ouis)

Henderson, Sylvia
See Ashton-Warner, Sylvia (Constance)

Henley, Beth .... **CLC 23**
See also Henley, Elizabeth Becker
See also CABS 3; DLBY 86

Henley, Elizabeth Becker 1952-
See Henley, Beth
See also CA 107; CANR 32; MTCW

Henley, William Ernest
1849-1903 .... **TCLC 8**
See also CA 105; DLB 19

Hennissart, Martha
See Lathen, Emma
See also CA 85-88

Henry, O. .... **TCLC 1, 19; SSC 5; WLC**
See also Porter, William Sydney

Henry, Patrick 1736- .... **LC 25**
See also CA 145

Henryson, Robert 1430(?)-1506(?). ... **LC 20**
See also DLB 146

Henry VIII 1491-1547 .... **LC 10**

Henschke, Alfred
See Klabund

Hentoff, Nat(han Irving) 1925- ..... **CLC 26**
See also AAYA 4; CA 1-4R; CAAS 6; CANR 5, 25; CLR 1; JRDA; MAICYA; SATA 27, 42, 69

Heppenstall, (John) Rayner
1911-1981 .... **CLC 10**
See also CA 1-4R; 103; CANR 29

Herbert, Frank (Patrick)
1920-1986 ...... **CLC 12, 23, 35, 44, 85**
See also CA 53-56; 118; CANR 5, 43; DLB 8; MTCW; SATA 9, 37; SATA-Obit 47

Herbert, George 1593-1633 .... **LC 24; PC 4**
See also CDBLB Before 1660; DLB 126

Herbert, Zbigniew 1924- .... **CLC 9, 43**
See also CA 89-92; CANR 36; MTCW

Herbst, Josephine (Frey)
1897-1969 .... **CLC 34**
See also CA 5-8R; 25-28R; DLB 9

Hergesheimer, Joseph
1880-1954 .... **TCLC 11**
See also CA 109; DLB 102, 9

Herlihy, James Leo 1927-1993 ...... **CLC 6**
See also CA 1-4R; 143; CANR 2

Hermogenes fl. c. 175- .... **CMLC 6**

Hernandez, Jose 1834-1886 ...... **NCLC 17**

Herrick, Robert
1591-1674 .... **LC 13; DA; PC 9**
See also DLB 126

Herring, Guilles
See Somerville, Edith

Herriot, James 1916- .... **CLC 12**
See also Wight, James Alfred
See also AAYA 1; CANR 40

Herrmann, Dorothy 1941- .... **CLC 44**
See also CA 107

Herrmann, Taffy
See Herrmann, Dorothy

Hersey, John (Richard)
1914-1993 .... **CLC 1, 2, 7, 9, 40, 81**
See also CA 17-20R; 140; CANR 33; DLB 6; MTCW; SATA 25; SATA-Obit 76

Herzen, Aleksandr Ivanovich
1812-1870 .... **NCLC 10**

Herzl, Theodor 1860-1904 .... **TCLC 36**

Herzog, Werner 1942- .... **CLC 16**
See also CA 89-92

Hesiod c. 8th cent. B.C.- .... **CMLC 5**

Hesse, Hermann
1877-1962 .... **CLC 1, 2, 3, 6, 11, 17, 25, 69; DA; SSC 9; WLC**
See also CA 17-18; CAP 2; DLB 66; MTCW; SATA 50

Hewes, Cady
See De Voto, Bernard (Augustine)

Heyen, William 1940- .... **CLC 13, 18**
See also CA 33-36R; CAAS 9; DLB 5

Heyerdahl, Thor 1914- .... **CLC 26**
See also CA 5-8R; CANR 5, 22; MTCW; SATA 2, 52

Heym, Georg (Theodor Franz Arthur)
1887-1912 .... **TCLC 9**
See also CA 106

Heym, Stefan 1913- .... **CLC 41**
See also CA 9-12R; CANR 4; DLB 69

Heyse, Paul (Johann Ludwig von)
1830-1914 .... **TCLC 8**
See also CA 104; DLB 129

Hibbert, Eleanor Alice Burford
1906-1993 .... **CLC 7**
See also BEST 90:4; CA 17-20R; 140; CANR 9, 28; SATA 2; SATA-Obit 74

Higgins, George V(incent)
1939- .... **CLC 4, 7, 10, 18**
See also CA 77-80; CAAS 5; CANR 17; DLB 2; DLBY 81; MTCW

Higginson, Thomas Wentworth
1823-1911 .... **TCLC 36**
See also DLB 1, 64

Highet, Helen
See MacInnes, Helen (Clark)

Highsmith, (Mary) Patricia
1921- .... **CLC 2, 4, 14, 42**
See also CA 1-4R; CANR 1, 20; MTCW

Highwater, Jamake (Mamake)
1942(?)- .... **CLC 12**
See also AAYA 7; CA 65-68; CAAS 7; CANR 10, 34; CLR 17; DLB 52; DLBY 85; JRDA; MAICYA; SATA 30, 32, 69

Hijuelos, Oscar 1951- ...... **CLC 65; HLC**
See also BEST 90:1; CA 123; DLB 145; HW

Hikmet, Nazim 1902(?)-1963....... **CLC 40**
See also CA 141; 93-96

Hildesheimer, Wolfgang
1916-1991 .... **CLC 49**
See also CA 101; 135; DLB 69, 124

Hill, Geoffrey (William)
1932- .... **CLC 5, 8, 18, 45**
See also CA 81-84; CANR 21; CDBLB 1960 to Present; DLB 40; MTCW

Hill, George Roy 1921- .... **CLC 26**
See also CA 110; 122

Hill, John
See Koontz, Dean R(ay)

Hill, Susan (Elizabeth) 1942- .... **CLC 4**
See also CA 33-36R; CANR 29; DLB 14, 139; MTCW

Hillerman, Tony 1925- .... **CLC 62**
See also AAYA 6; BEST 89:1; CA 29-32R; CANR 21, 42; SATA 6

Hillesum, Etty 1914-1943 .... **TCLC 49**
See also CA 137

Hilliard, Noel (Harvey) 1929-...... **CLC 15**
See also CA 9-12R; CANR 7

Hillis, Rick 1956-................ **CLC 66**
See also CA 134

Hilton, James 1900-1954......... **TCLC 21**
See also CA 108; DLB 34, 77; SATA 34

Himes, Chester (Bomar)
1909-1984 .... **CLC 2, 4, 7, 18, 58; BLC**
See also BW 2; CA 25-28R; 114; CANR 22; DLB 2, 76, 143; MTCW

Hinde, Thomas .... **CLC 6, 11**
See also Chitty, Thomas Willes

Hindin, Nathan
See Bloch, Robert (Albert)

Hine, (William) Daryl 1936-....... **CLC 15**
See also CA 1-4R; CAAS 15; CANR 1, 20; DLB 60

Hinkson, Katharine Tynan
See Tynan, Katharine

Hinton, S(usan) E(loise)
1950- .... **CLC 30; DA**
See also AAYA 2; CA 81-84; CANR 32; CLR 3, 23; JRDA; MAICYA; MTCW; SATA 19, 58

Hippius, Zinaida .... **TCLC 9**
See also Gippius, Zinaida (Nikolayevna)

Hiraoka, Kimitake 1925-1970
See Mishima, Yukio
See also CA 97-100; 29-32R; MTCW

Hirsch, E(ric) D(onald), Jr.   1928-... CLC 79
See also CA 25-28R; CANR 27; DLB 67;
MTCW

Hirsch, Edward   1950- .... CLC 31, 50
See also CA 104; CANR 20, 42; DLB 120

Hitchcock, Alfred (Joseph)
1899-1980 .... CLC 16
See also CA 97-100; SATA 27;
SATA-Obit 24

Hitler, Adolf   1889-1945......... TCLC 53
See also CA 117

Hoagland, Edward   1932- .... CLC 28
See also CA 1-4R; CANR 2, 31; DLB 6;
SATA 51

Hoban, Russell (Conwell)   1925- .. CLC 7, 25
See also CA 5-8R; CANR 23, 37; CLR 3;
DLB 52; MAICYA; MTCW; SATA 1,
40, 78

Hobbs, Perry
See Blackmur, R(ichard) P(almer)

Hobson, Laura Z(ametkin)
1900-1986 .... CLC 7, 25
See also CA 17-20R; 118; DLB 28;
SATA 52

Hochhuth, Rolf   1931-....... CLC 4, 11, 18
See also CA 5-8R; CANR 33; DLB 124;
MTCW

Hochman, Sandra   1936-......... CLC 3, 8
See also CA 5-8R; DLB 5

Hochwaelder, Fritz   1911-1986...... CLC 36
See also CA 29-32R; 120; CANR 42;
MTCW

Hochwalder, Fritz
See Hochwaelder, Fritz

Hocking, Mary (Eunice)   1921- ..... CLC 13
See also CA 101; CANR 18, 40

Hodgins, Jack   1938-.............. CLC 23
See also CA 93-96; DLB 60

Hodgson, William Hope
1877(?)-1918 .... TCLC 13
See also CA 111; DLB 70

Hoffman, Alice   1952-............. CLC 51
See also CA 77-80; CANR 34; MTCW

Hoffman, Daniel (Gerard)
1923- .... CLC 6, 13, 23
See also CA 1-4R; CANR 4; DLB 5

Hoffman, Stanley   1944-............ CLC 5
See also CA 77-80

Hoffman, William M(oses)   1939- ... CLC 40
See also CA 57-60; CANR 11

Hoffmann, E(rnst) T(heodor) A(madeus)
1776-1822 .... NCLC 2; SSC 13
See also DLB 90; SATA 27

Hofmann, Gert   1931-............. CLC 54
See also CA 128

Hofmannsthal, Hugo von
1874-1929 .... TCLC 11; DC 4
See also CA 106; DLB 81, 118

Hogan, Linda   1947-.............. CLC 73
See also CA 120; CANR 45; NNAL

Hogarth, Charles
See Creasey, John

Hogg, James   1770-1835.......... NCLC 4
See also DLB 93, 116

Holbach, Paul Henri Thiry Baron
1723-1789 .... LC 14

Holberg, Ludvig   1684-1754......... LC 6

Holden, Ursula   1921-............. CLC 18
See also CA 101; CAAS 8; CANR 22

Holderlin, (Johann Christian) Friedrich
1770-1843 .... NCLC 16; PC 4

Holdstock, Robert
See Holdstock, Robert P.

Holdstock, Robert P.   1948-........ CLC 39
See also CA 131

Holland, Isabelle   1920- .... CLC 21
See also AAYA 11; CA 21-24R; CANR 10,
25, 47; JRDA; MAICYA; SATA 8, 70

Holland, Marcus
See Caldwell, (Janet Miriam) Taylor
(Holland)

Hollander, John   1929-...... CLC 2, 5, 8, 14
See also CA 1-4R; CANR 1; DLB 5;
SATA 13

Hollander, Paul
See Silverberg, Robert

Holleran, Andrew   1943(?)-......... CLC 38
See also CA 144

Hollinghurst, Alan   1954-.......... CLC 55
See also CA 114

Hollis, Jim
See Summers, Hollis (Spurgeon, Jr.)

Holmes, John
See Souster, (Holmes) Raymond

Holmes, John Clellon   1926-1988.... CLC 56
See also CA 9-12R; 125; CANR 4; DLB 16

Holmes, Oliver Wendell
1809-1894 .... NCLC 14
See also CDALB 1640-1865; DLB 1;
SATA 34

Holmes, Raymond
See Souster, (Holmes) Raymond

Holt, Victoria
See Hibbert, Eleanor Alice Burford

Holub, Miroslav   1923-............. CLC 4
See also CA 21-24R; CANR 10

Homer   c. 8th cent. B.C.- ..... CMLC 1; DA

Honig, Edwin   1919- .... CLC 33
See also CA 5-8R; CAAS 8; CANR 4, 45;
DLB 5

Hood, Hugh (John Blagdon)
1928-.................... CLC 15, 28
See also CA 49-52; CAAS 17; CANR 1, 33;
DLB 53

Hood, Thomas   1799-1845........ NCLC 16
See also DLB 96

Hooker, (Peter) Jeremy   1941-...... CLC 43
See also CA 77-80; CANR 22; DLB 40

Hope, A(lec) D(erwent)   1907- .... CLC 3, 51
See also CA 21-24R; CANR 33; MTCW

Hope, Brian
See Creasey, John

Hope, Christopher (David Tully)
1944- .... CLC 52
See also CA 106; CANR 47; SATA 62

Hopkins, Gerard Manley
1844-1889 .... NCLC 17; DA; WLC
See also CDBLB 1890-1914; DLB 35, 57

Hopkins, John (Richard)   1931-...... CLC 4
See also CA 85-88

Hopkins, Pauline Elizabeth
1859-1930 ....TCLC 28; BLC
See also BW 2; CA 141; DLB 50

Hopkinson, Francis   1737-1791 ...... LC 25
See also DLB 31

Hopley-Woolrich, Cornell George   1903-1968
See Woolrich, Cornell
See also CA 13-14; CAP 1

Horatio
See Proust, (Valentin-Louis-George-Eugene-)
Marcel

Horgan, Paul   1903- .... CLC 9, 53
See also CA 13-16R; CANR 9, 35;
DLB 102; DLBY 85; MTCW; SATA 13

Horn, Peter
See Kuttner, Henry

Hornem, Horace Esq.
See Byron, George Gordon (Noel)

Horovitz, Israel (Arthur)   1939-..... CLC 56
See also CA 33-36R; CANR 46; DLB 7

Horvath, Odon von
See Horvath, Oedoen von
See also DLB 85, 124

Horvath, Oedoen von   1901-1938... TCLC 45
See also Horvath, Odon von
See also CA 118

Horwitz, Julius   1920-1986......... CLC 14
See also CA 9-12R; 119; CANR 12

Hospital, Janette Turner   1942-..... CLC 42
See also CA 108

Hostos, E. M. de
See Hostos (y Bonilla), Eugenio Maria de

Hostos, Eugenio M. de
See Hostos (y Bonilla), Eugenio Maria de

Hostos, Eugenio Maria
See Hostos (y Bonilla), Eugenio Maria de

Hostos (y Bonilla), Eugenio Maria de
1839-1903 .... TCLC 24
See also CA 123; 131; HW

Houdini
See Lovecraft, H(oward) P(hillips)

Hougan, Carolyn   1943- .... CLC 34
See also CA 139

Household, Geoffrey (Edward West)
1900-1988 .... CLC 11
See also CA 77-80; 126; DLB 87; SATA 14;
SATA-Obit 59

Housman, A(lfred) E(dward)
1859-1936 ...... TCLC 1, 10; DA; PC 2
See also CA 104; 125; DLB 19; MTCW

Housman, Laurence   1865-1959..... TCLC 7
See also CA 106; DLB 10; SATA 25

Howard, Elizabeth Jane   1923- ... CLC 7, 29
See also CA 5-8R; CANR 8

Howard, Maureen   1930- ..... CLC 5, 14, 46
See also CA 53-56; CANR 31; DLBY 83;
MTCW

Howard, Richard 1929- ...... **CLC 7, 10, 47**
See also AITN 1; CA 85-88; CANR 25;
DLB 5

Howard, Robert Ervin 1906-1936... **TCLC 8**
See also CA 105

Howard, Warren F.
See Pohl, Frederik

Howe, Fanny 1940- .... **CLC 47**
See also CA 117; SATA 52

Howe, Irving 1920-1993........... **CLC 85**
See also CA 9-12R; 141; CANR 21;
DLB 67; MTCW

Howe, Julia Ward 1819-1910 ..... **TCLC 21**
See also CA 117; DLB 1

Howe, Susan 1937-............... **CLC 72**
See also DLB 120

Howe, Tina 1937-................ **CLC 48**
See also CA 109

Howell, James 1594(?)-1666 .... **LC 13**

Howells, W. D.
See Howells, William Dean

Howells, William D.
See Howells, William Dean

Howells, William Dean
1837-1920 .... **TCLC 7, 17, 41**
See also CA 104; 134; CDALB 1865-1917;
DLB 12, 64, 74, 79

Howes, Barbara 1914- .... **CLC 15**
See also CA 9-12R; CAAS 3; SATA 5

Hrabal, Bohumil 1914-........ **CLC 13, 67**
See also CA 106; CAAS 12

Hsun, Lu .... **TCLC 3**
See also Shu-Jen, Chou

Hubbard, L(afayette) Ron(ald)
1911-1986 .... **CLC 43**
See also CA 77-80; 118; CANR 22

Huch, Ricarda (Octavia)
1864-1947 .... **TCLC 13**
See also CA 111; DLB 66

Huddle, David 1942- .... **CLC 49**
See also CA 57-60; CAAS 20; DLB 130

Hudson, Jeffrey
See Crichton, (John) Michael

Hudson, W(illiam) H(enry)
1841-1922 .... **TCLC 29**
See also CA 115; DLB 98; SATA 35

Hueffer, Ford Madox
See Ford, Ford Madox

Hughart, Barry 1934-............. **CLC 39**
See also CA 137

Hughes, Colin
See Creasey, John

Hughes, David (John) 1930- .... **CLC 48**
See also CA 116; 129; DLB 14

Hughes, (James) Langston
1902-1967 ..... **CLC 1, 5, 10, 15, 35, 44;**
BLC; DA; DC 3; PC 1; SSC 6; WLC
See also AAYA 12; BW 1; CA 1-4R;
25-28R; CANR 1, 34; CDALB 1929-1941;
CLR 17; DLB 4, 7, 48, 51, 86; JRDA;
MAICYA; MTCW; SATA 4, 33

Hughes, Richard (Arthur Warren)
1900-1976 .... **CLC 1, 11**
See also CA 5-8R; 65-68; CANR 4;
DLB 15; MTCW; SATA 8;
SATA-Obit 25

Hughes, Ted
1930- .... **CLC 2, 4, 9, 14, 37; PC 7**
See also CA 1-4R; CANR 1, 33; CLR 3;
DLB 40; MAICYA; MTCW; SATA 27,
49

Hugo, Richard F(ranklin)
1923-1982 .... **CLC 6, 18, 32**
See also CA 49-52; 108; CANR 3; DLB 5

Hugo, Victor (Marie)
1802-1885 .. **NCLC 3, 10, 21; DA; WLC**
See also DLB 119; SATA 47

Huidobro, Vicente
See Huidobro Fernandez, Vicente Garcia

Huidobro Fernandez, Vicente Garcia
1893-1948 .... **TCLC 31**
See also CA 131; HW

Hulme, Keri 1947- .... **CLC 39**
See also CA 125

Hulme, T(homas) E(rnest)
1883-1917 .... **TCLC 21**
See also CA 117; DLB 19

Hume, David 1711-1776............. **LC 7**
See also DLB 104

Humphrey, William 1924-........ **CLC 45**
See also CA 77-80; DLB 6

Humphreys, Emyr Owen 1919-..... **CLC 47**
See also CA 5-8R; CANR 3, 24; DLB 15

Humphreys, Josephine 1945-.... **CLC 34, 57**
See also CA 121; 127

Hungerford, Pixie
See Brinsmead, H(esba) F(ay)

Hunt, E(verette) Howard, (Jr.)
1918- .... **CLC 3**
See also AITN 1; CA 45-48; CANR 2, 47

Hunt, Kyle
See Creasey, John

Hunt, (James Henry) Leigh
1784-1859 .... **NCLC 1**

Hunt, Marsha 1946-.............. **CLC 70**
See also BW 2; CA 143

Hunt, Violet 1866-1942 .... **TCLC 53**

Hunter, E. Waldo
See Sturgeon, Theodore (Hamilton)

Hunter, Evan 1926- .... **CLC 11, 31**
See also CA 5-8R; CANR 5, 38; DLBY 82;
MTCW; SATA 25

Hunter, Kristin (Eggleston) 1931-... **CLC 35**
See also AITN 1; BW 1; CA 13-16R;
CANR 13; CLR 3; DLB 33; MAICYA;
SAAS 10; SATA 12

Hunter, Mollie 1922-............. **CLC 21**
See also McIlwraith, Maureen Mollie
Hunter
See also AAYA 13; CANR 37; CLR 25;
JRDA; MAICYA; SAAS 7; SATA 54

Hunter, Robert (?)-1734............ **LC 7**

Hurston, Zora Neale
1903-1960 .... **CLC 7, 30, 61; BLC; DA;**
SSC 4
See also BW 1; CA 85-88; DLB 51, 86;
MTCW

Huston, John (Marcellus)
1906-1987 .... **CLC 20**
See also CA 73-76; 123; CANR 34; DLB 26

Hustvedt, Siri 1955-.............. **CLC 76**
See also CA 137

Hutten, Ulrich von 1488-1523....... **LC 16**

Huxley, Aldous (Leonard)
1894-1963 ..... **CLC 1, 3, 4, 5, 8, 11, 18,**
35, 79; DA; WLC
See also AAYA 11; CA 85-88; CANR 44;
CDBLB 1914-1945; DLB 36, 100;
MTCW; SATA 63

Huysmans, Charles Marie Georges
1848-1907
See Huysmans, Joris-Karl
See also CA 104

Huysmans, Joris-Karl.............. TCLC 7
See also Huysmans, Charles Marie Georges
See also DLB 123

Hwang, David Henry
1957- .... **CLC 55; DC 4**
See also CA 127; 132

Hyde, Anthony 1946-............. **CLC 42**
See also CA 136

Hyde, Margaret O(ldroyd) 1917- ... **CLC 21**
See also CA 1-4R; CANR 1, 36; CLR 23;
JRDA; MAICYA; SAAS 8; SATA 1, 42,
76

Hynes, James 1956(?)-............ **CLC 65**

Ian, Janis 1951- .... **CLC 21**
See also CA 105

Ibanez, Vicente Blasco
See Blasco Ibanez, Vicente

Ibarguengoitia, Jorge 1928-1983.... **CLC 37**
See also CA 124; 113; HW

Ibsen, Henrik (Johan)
1828-1906 .... **TCLC 2, 8, 16, 37, 52;**
DA; DC 2; WLC
See also CA 104; 141

Ibuse Masuji 1898-1993........... **CLC 22**
See also CA 127; 141

Ichikawa, Kon 1915-.............. **CLC 20**
See also CA 121

Idle, Eric 1943-................. **CLC 21**
See also Monty Python
See also CA 116; CANR 35

Ignatow, David 1914-...... **CLC 4, 7, 14, 40**
See also CA 9-12R; CAAS 3; CANR 31;
DLB 5

Ihimaera, Witi 1944- .... **CLC 46**
See also CA 77-80

Ilf, Ilya.......................TCLC 21
See also Fainzilberg, Ilya Arnoldovich

Immermann, Karl (Lebrecht)
1796-1840 .... **NCLC 4**
See also DLB 133

Inclan, Ramon (Maria) del Valle
See Valle-Inclan, Ramon (Maria) del

Infante, G(uillermo) Cabrera
See Cabrera Infante, G(uillermo)

Ingalls, Rachel (Holmes) 1940- . . . . . **CLC 42**
See also CA 123; 127

Ingamells, Rex 1913-1955 . . . . **TCLC 35**

Inge, William Motter
1913-1973 . . . . **CLC 1, 8, 19**
See also CA 9-12R; CDALB 1941-1968;
DLB 7; MTCW

Ingelow, Jean 1820-1897 . . . . **NCLC 39**
See also DLB 35; SATA 33

Ingram, Willis J.
See Harris, Mark

Innaurato, Albert (F.) 1948(?)- . . **CLC 21, 60**
See also CA 115; 122

Innes, Michael
See Stewart, J(ohn) I(nnes) M(ackintosh)

Ionesco, Eugene
1909-1994 . . . . **CLC 1, 4, 6, 9, 11, 15, 41,
86; DA; WLC**
See also CA 9-12R; 144; MTCW; SATA 7;
SATA-Obit 79

Iqbal, Muhammad 1873-1938 . . . . . **TCLC 28**

Ireland, Patrick
See O'Doherty, Brian

Iron, Ralph
See Schreiner, Olive (Emilie Albertina)

Irving, John (Winslow)
1942- . . . . **CLC 13, 23, 38**
See also AAYA 8; BEST 89:3; CA 25-28R;
CANR 28; DLB 6; DLBY 82; MTCW

Irving, Washington
1783-1859 . . . . **NCLC 2, 19; DA; SSC 2;
WLC**
See also CDALB 1640-1865; DLB 3, 11, 30,
59, 73, 74; YABC 2

Irwin, P. K.
See Page, P(atricia) K(athleen)

Isaacs, Susan 1943- . . . . **CLC 32**
See also BEST 89:1; CA 89-92; CANR 20,
41; MTCW

Isherwood, Christopher (William Bradshaw)
1904-1986 . . . . **CLC 1, 9, 11, 14, 44**
See also CA 13-16R; 117; CANR 35;
DLB 15; DLBY 86; MTCW

Ishiguro, Kazuo 1954- . . . . . . **CLC 27, 56, 59**
See also BEST 90:2; CA 120; MTCW

Ishikawa Takuboku
1886(?)-1912 . . . . **TCLC 15; PC 10**
See also CA 113

Iskander, Fazil 1929- . . . . **CLC 47**
See also CA 102

Ivan IV 1530-1584 . . . . **LC 17**

Ivanov, Vyacheslav Ivanovich
1866-1949 . . . . **TCLC 33**
See also CA 122

Ivask, Ivar Vidrik 1927-1992 . . . . . . **CLC 14**
See also CA 37-40R; 139; CANR 24

Jackson, Daniel
See Wingrove, David (John)

Jackson, Jesse 1908-1983 . . . . **CLC 12**
See also BW 1; CA 25-28R; 109; CANR 27;
CLR 28; MAICYA; SATA 2, 29;
SATA-Obit 48

Jackson, Laura (Riding) 1901-1991
See Riding, Laura
See also CA 65-68; 135; CANR 28; DLB 48

Jackson, Sam
See Trumbo, Dalton

Jackson, Sara
See Wingrove, David (John)

Jackson, Shirley
1919-1965 . . . . . **CLC 11, 60; DA; SSC 9;
WLC**
See also AAYA 9; CA 1-4R; 25-28R;
CANR 4; CDALB 1941-1968; DLB 6;
SATA 2

Jacob, (Cyprien-)Max 1876-1944 . . . **TCLC 6**
See also CA 104

Jacobs, Jim 1942- . . . . **CLC 12**
See also CA 97-100

Jacobs, W(illiam) W(ymark)
1863-1943 . . . . **TCLC 22**
See also CA 121; DLB 135

Jacobsen, Jens Peter 1847-1885 . . **NCLC 34**

Jacobsen, Josephine 1908- . . . . **CLC 48**
See also CA 33-36R; CAAS 18; CANR 23

Jacobson, Dan 1929- . . . . **CLC 4, 14**
See also CA 1-4R; CANR 2, 25; DLB 14;
MTCW

Jacqueline
See Carpentier (y Valmont), Alejo

Jagger, Mick 1944- . . . . **CLC 17**

Jakes, John (William) 1932- . . . . **CLC 29**
See also BEST 89:4; CA 57-60; CANR 10,
43; DLBY 83; MTCW; SATA 62

James, Andrew
See Kirkup, James

James, C(yril) L(ionel) R(obert)
1901-1989 . . . . **CLC 33**
See also BW 2; CA 117; 125; 128; DLB 125;
MTCW

James, Daniel (Lewis) 1911-1988
See Santiago, Danny
See also CA 125

James, Dynely
See Mayne, William (James Carter)

James, Henry
1843-1916 . . . . . . **TCLC 2, 11, 24, 40, 47;
DA; SSC 8; WLC**
See also CA 104; 132; CDALB 1865-1917;
DLB 12, 71, 74; MTCW

James, M. R.
See James, Montague (Rhodes)

James, Montague (Rhodes)
1862-1936 . . . . **TCLC 6; SSC 16**
See also CA 104

James, P. D. . . . . **CLC 18, 46**
See also White, Phyllis Dorothy James
See also BEST 90:2; CDBLB 1960 to
Present; DLB 87

James, Philip
See Moorcock, Michael (John)

James, William 1842-1910 . . . . . **TCLC 15, 32**
See also CA 109

James I 1394-1437 . . . . **LC 20**

Jameson, Anna 1794-1860 . . . . **NCLC 43**
See also DLB 99

Jami, Nur al-Din 'Abd al-Rahman
1414-1492 . . . . **LC 9**

Jandl, Ernst 1925- . . . . **CLC 34**

Janowitz, Tama 1957- . . . . **CLC 43**
See also CA 106

Jarrell, Randall
1914-1965 . . . . **CLC 1, 2, 6, 9, 13, 49**
See also CA 5-8R; 25-28R; CABS 2;
CANR 6, 34; CDALB 1941-1968; CLR 6;
DLB 48, 52; MAICYA; MTCW; SATA 7

Jarry, Alfred 1873-1907 . . . . **TCLC 2, 14**
See also CA 104

Jarvis, E. K.
See Bloch, Robert (Albert); Ellison, Harlan
(Jay); Silverberg, Robert

Jeake, Samuel, Jr.
See Aiken, Conrad (Potter)

Jean Paul 1763-1825 . . . . **NCLC 7**

Jefferies, (John) Richard
1848-1887 . . . . **NCLC 47**
See also DLB 98, 141; SATA 16

Jeffers, (John) Robinson
1887-1962 . . . . **CLC 2, 3, 11, 15, 54; DA;
WLC**
See also CA 85-88; CANR 35;
CDALB 1917-1929; DLB 45; MTCW

Jefferson, Janet
See Mencken, H(enry) L(ouis)

Jefferson, Thomas 1743-1826 . . . . **NCLC 11**
See also CDALB 1640-1865; DLB 31

Jeffrey, Francis 1773-1850 . . . . **NCLC 33**
See also DLB 107

Jelakowitch, Ivan
See Heijermans, Herman

Jellicoe, (Patricia) Ann 1927- . . . . . . **CLC 27**
See also CA 85-88; DLB 13

Jen, Gish . . . . **CLC 70**
See also Jen, Lillian

Jen, Lillian 1956(?)-
See Jen, Gish
See also CA 135

Jenkins, (John) Robin 1912- . . . . **CLC 52**
See also CA 1-4R; CANR 1; DLB 14

Jennings, Elizabeth (Joan)
1926- . . . . **CLC 5, 14**
See also CA 61-64; CAAS 5; CANR 8, 39;
DLB 27; MTCW; SATA 66

Jennings, Waylon 1937- . . . . **CLC 21**

Jensen, Johannes V. 1873-1950 . . . . **TCLC 41**

Jensen, Laura (Linnea) 1948- . . . . . . **CLC 37**
See also CA 103

Jerome, Jerome K(lapka)
1859-1927 . . . . **TCLC 23**
See also CA 119; DLB 10, 34, 135

Jerrold, Douglas William
1803-1857 . . . . **NCLC 2**

Jewett, (Theodora) Sarah Orne
1849-1909 . . . . **TCLC 1, 22; SSC 6**
See also CA 108; 127; DLB 12, 74;
SATA 15

Jewsbury, Geraldine (Endsor)
1812-1880 . . . . **NCLC 22**
See also DLB 21

Jhabvala, Ruth Prawer
1927- . . . . **CLC 4, 8, 29**
See also CA 1-4R; CANR 2, 29; DLB 139;
MTCW

Jiles, Paulette 1943- . . . . **CLC 13, 58**
See also CA 101

Jimenez (Mantecon), Juan Ramon
1881-1958 . . . . **TCLC 4; HLC; PC 7**
See also CA 104; 131; DLB 134; HW;
MTCW

Jimenez, Ramon
See Jimenez (Mantecon), Juan Ramon

Jimenez Mantecon, Juan
See Jimenez (Mantecon), Juan Ramon

Joel, Billy . . . . **CLC 26**
See also Joel, William Martin

Joel, William Martin 1949-
See Joel, Billy
See also CA 108

John of the Cross, St. 1542-1591 . . . . **LC 18**

Johnson, B(ryan) S(tanley William)
1933-1973 . . . . **CLC 6, 9**
See also CA 9-12R; 53-56; CANR 9;
DLB 14, 40

Johnson, Benj. F. of Boo
See Riley, James Whitcomb

Johnson, Benjamin F. of Boo
See Riley, James Whitcomb

Johnson, Charles (Richard)
1948- . . . . **CLC 7, 51, 65; BLC**
See also BW 2; CA 116; CAAS 18;
CANR 42; DLB 33

Johnson, Denis 1949- . . . . **CLC 52**
See also CA 117; 121; DLB 120

Johnson, Diane 1934- . . . . **CLC 5, 13, 48**
See also CA 41-44R; CANR 17, 40;
DLBY 80; MTCW

Johnson, Eyvind (Olof Verner)
1900-1976 . . . . **CLC 14**
See also CA 73-76; 69-72; CANR 34

Johnson, J. R.
See James, C(yril) L(ionel) R(obert)

Johnson, James Weldon
1871-1938 . . . . **TCLC 3, 19; BLC**
See also BW 1; CA 104; 125;
CDALB 1917-1929; CLR 32; DLB 51;
MTCW; SATA 31

Johnson, Joyce 1935- . . . . **CLC 58**
See also CA 125; 129

Johnson, Lionel (Pigot)
1867-1902 . . . . **TCLC 19**
See also CA 117; DLB 19

Johnson, Mel
See Malzberg, Barry N(athaniel)

Johnson, Pamela Hansford
1912-1981 . . . . **CLC 1, 7, 27**
See also CA 1-4R; 104; CANR 2, 28;
DLB 15; MTCW

Johnson, Samuel
1709-1784 . . . . **LC 15; DA; WLC**
See also CDBLB 1660-1789; DLB 39, 95,
104, 142

Johnson, Uwe
1934-1984 . . . . **CLC 5, 10, 15, 40**
See also CA 1-4R; 112; CANR 1, 39;
DLB 75; MTCW

Johnston, George (Benson) 1913- . . . **CLC 51**
See also CA 1-4R; CANR 5, 20; DLB 88

Johnston, Jennifer 1930- . . . . **CLC 7**
See also CA 85-88; DLB 14

Jolley, (Monica) Elizabeth 1923- . . . **CLC 46**
See also CA 127; CAAS 13

Jones, Arthur Llewellyn 1863-1947
See Machen, Arthur
See also CA 104

Jones, D(ouglas) G(ordon) 1929- . . . . **CLC 10**
See also CA 29-32R; CANR 13; DLB 53

Jones, David (Michael)
1895-1974 . . . . **CLC 2, 4, 7, 13, 42**
See also CA 9-12R; 53-56; CANR 28;
CDBLB 1945-1960; DLB 20, 100; MTCW

Jones, David Robert 1947-
See Bowie, David
See also CA 103

Jones, Diana Wynne 1934- . . . . **CLC 26**
See also AAYA 12; CA 49-52; CANR 4,
26; CLR 23; JRDA; MAICYA; SAAS 7;
SATA 9, 70

Jones, Edward P. 1950- . . . . **CLC 76**
See also BW 2; CA 142

Jones, Gayl 1949- . . . . **CLC 6, 9; BLC**
See also BW 2; CA 77-80; CANR 27;
DLB 33; MTCW

Jones, James 1921-1977 . . . . **CLC 1, 3, 10, 39**
See also AITN 1, 2; CA 1-4R; 69-72;
CANR 6; DLB 2, 143; MTCW

Jones, John J.
See Lovecraft, H(oward) P(hillips)

Jones, LeRoi . . . . **CLC 1, 2, 3, 5, 10, 14**
See also Baraka, Amiri

Jones, Louis B. . . . . **CLC 65**
See also CA 141

Jones, Madison (Percy, Jr.) 1925- . . . **CLC 4**
See also CA 13-16R; CAAS 11; CANR 7

Jones, Mervyn 1922- . . . . **CLC 10, 52**
See also CA 45-48; CAAS 5; CANR 1;
MTCW

Jones, Mick 1956(?)- . . . . **CLC 30**

Jones, Nettie (Pearl) 1941- . . . . **CLC 34**
See also BW 2; CA 137; CAAS 20

Jones, Preston 1936-1979 . . . . **CLC 10**
See also CA 73-76; 89-92; DLB 7

Jones, Robert F(rancis) 1934- . . . . **CLC 7**
See also CA 49-52; CANR 2

Jones, Rod 1953- . . . . **CLC 50**
See also CA 128

Jones, Terence Graham Parry
1942- . . . . **CLC 21**
See also Jones, Terry; Monty Python
See also CA 112; 116; CANR 35; SATA 51

Jones, Terry
See Jones, Terence Graham Parry
See also SATA 67

Jones, Thom 1945(?)- . . . . **CLC 81**

Jong, Erica 1942- . . . . . . **CLC 4, 6, 8, 18, 83**
See also AITN 1; BEST 90:2; CA 73-76;
CANR 26; DLB 2, 5, 28; MTCW

Jonson, Ben(jamin)
1572(?)-1637 . . . . **LC 6; DA; DC 4; WLC**
See also CDBLB Before 1660; DLB 62, 121

Jordan, June 1936- . . . . **CLC 5, 11, 23**
See also AAYA 2; BW 2; CA 33-36R;
CANR 25; CLR 10; DLB 38; MAICYA;
MTCW; SATA 4

Jordan, Pat(rick M.) 1941- . . . . **CLC 37**
See also CA 33-36R

Jorgensen, Ivar
See Ellison, Harlan (Jay)

Jorgenson, Ivar
See Silverberg, Robert

Josephus, Flavius c. 37-100 . . . . . . **CMLC 13**

Josipovici, Gabriel 1940- . . . . **CLC 6, 43**
See also CA 37-40R; CAAS 8; CANR 47;
DLB 14

Joubert, Joseph 1754-1824 . . . . **NCLC 9**

Jouve, Pierre Jean 1887-1976 . . . . . . **CLC 47**
See also CA 65-68

Joyce, James (Augustine Aloysius)
1882-1941 . . . . . . **TCLC 3, 8, 16, 35; DA;
SSC 3; WLC**
See also CA 104; 126; CDBLB 1914-1945;
DLB 10, 19, 36; MTCW

Jozsef, Attila 1905-1937 . . . . **TCLC 22**
See also CA 116

Juana Ines de la Cruz 1651(?)-1695 . . . **LC 5**

Judd, Cyril
See Kornbluth, C(yril) M.; Pohl, Frederik

Julian of Norwich 1342(?)-1416(?) . . . . **LC 6**
See also DLB 146

Just, Ward (Swift) 1935- . . . . **CLC 4, 27**
See also CA 25-28R; CANR 32

Justice, Donald (Rodney) 1925- . . **CLC 6, 19**
See also CA 5-8R; CANR 26; DLBY 83

Juvenal c. 55-c. 127 . . . . **CMLC 8**

Juvenis
See Bourne, Randolph S(illiman)

Kacew, Romain 1914-1980
See Gary, Romain
See also CA 108; 102

Kadare, Ismail 1936- . . . . **CLC 52**

Kadohata, Cynthia . . . . **CLC 59**
See also CA 140

Kafka, Franz
1883-1924 . . . . **TCLC 2, 6, 13, 29, 47, 53;
DA; SSC 5; WLC**
See also CA 105; 126; DLB 81; MTCW

Kahanovitsch, Pinkhes
See Der Nister

Kahn, Roger 1927- . . . . **CLC 30**
See also CA 25-28R; CANR 44; SATA 37

Kain, Saul
See Sassoon, Siegfried (Lorraine)

Kaiser, Georg 1878-1945 . . . . **TCLC 9**
See also CA 106; DLB 124

Kaletski, Alexander 1946- . . . . **CLC 39**
See also CA 118; 143

Kalidasa fl. c. 400- . . . . **CMLC 9**

Kallman, Chester (Simon)
    1921-1975 .... **CLC 2**
    See also CA 45-48; 53-56; CANR 3

Kaminsky, Melvin 1926-
    See Brooks, Mel
    See also CA 65-68; CANR 16

Kaminsky, Stuart M(elvin) 1934- ... **CLC 59**
    See also CA 73-76; CANR 29

Kane, Paul
    See Simon, Paul

Kane, Wilson
    See Bloch, Robert (Albert)

Kanin, Garson 1912-.............. **CLC 22**
    See also AITN 1; CA 5-8R; CANR 7;
    DLB 7

Kaniuk, Yoram 1930-............ **CLC 19**
    See also CA 134

Kant, Immanuel 1724-1804 ...... **NCLC 27**
    See also DLB 94

Kantor, MacKinlay 1904-1977 ...... **CLC 7**
    See also CA 61-64; 73-76; DLB 9, 102

Kaplan, David Michael 1946- ...... **CLC 50**

Kaplan, James 1951- .... **CLC 59**
    See also CA 135

Karageorge, Michael
    See Anderson, Poul (William)

Karamzin, Nikolai Mikhailovich
    1766-1826 .... **NCLC 3**

Karapanou, Margarita 1946-....... **CLC 13**
    See also CA 101

Karinthy, Frigyes 1887-1938 ...... **TCLC 47**

Karl, Frederick R(obert) 1927-..... **CLC 34**
    See also CA 5-8R; CANR 3, 44

Kastel, Warren
    See Silverberg, Robert

Kataev, Evgeny Petrovich 1903-1942
    See Petrov, Evgeny
    See also CA 120

Kataphusin
    See Ruskin, John

Katz, Steve 1935-............... **CLC 47**
    See also CA 25-28R; CAAS 14; CANR 12;
    DLBY 83

Kauffman, Janet 1945-............ **CLC 42**
    See also CA 117; CANR 43; DLBY 86

Kaufman, Bob (Garnell)
    1925-1986 .... **CLC 49**
    See also BW 1; CA 41-44R; 118; CANR 22;
    DLB 16, 41

Kaufman, George S. 1889-1961..... **CLC 38**
    See also CA 108; 93-96; DLB 7

Kaufman, Sue .... **CLC 3, 8**
    See also Barondess, Sue K(aufman)

Kavafis, Konstantinos Petrou 1863-1933
    See Cavafy, C(onstantine) P(eter)
    See also CA 104

Kavan, Anna 1901-1968...... **CLC 5, 13, 82**
    See also CA 5-8R; CANR 6; MTCW

Kavanagh, Dan
    See Barnes, Julian

Kavanagh, Patrick (Joseph)
    1904-1967 .... **CLC 22**
    See also CA 123; 25-28R; DLB 15, 20;
    MTCW

Kawabata, Yasunari
    1899-1972 ..... **CLC 2, 5, 9, 18; SSC 17**
    See also CA 93-96; 33-36R

Kaye, M(ary) M(argaret) 1909-..... **CLC 28**
    See also CA 89-92; CANR 24; MTCW;
    SATA 62

Kaye, Mollie
    See Kaye, M(ary) M(argaret)

Kaye-Smith, Sheila 1887-1956..... **TCLC 20**
    See also CA 118; DLB 36

Kaymor, Patrice Maguilene
    See Senghor, Leopold Sedar

Kazan, Elia 1909-........... **CLC 6, 16, 63**
    See also CA 21-24R; CANR 32

Kazantzakis, Nikos
    1883(?)-1957 .... **TCLC 2, 5, 33**
    See also CA 105; 132; MTCW

Kazin, Alfred 1915- .... **CLC 34, 38**
    See also CA 1-4R; CAAS 7; CANR 1, 45;
    DLB 67

Keane, Mary Nesta (Skrine) 1904-
    See Keane, Molly
    See also CA 108; 114

Keane, Molly .... **CLC 31**
    See also Keane, Mary Nesta (Skrine)

Keates, Jonathan 19(?)-........... **CLC 34**

Keaton, Buster 1895-1966 .... **CLC 20**

Keats, John
    1795-1821 ... **NCLC 8; DA; PC 1; WLC**
    See also CDBLB 1789-1832; DLB 96, 110

Keene, Donald 1922- .... **CLC 34**
    See also CA 1-4R; CANR 5

Keillor, Garrison .... **CLC 40**
    See also Keillor, Gary (Edward)
    See also AAYA 2; BEST 89:3; DLBY 87;
    SATA 58

Keillor, Gary (Edward) 1942-
    See Keillor, Garrison
    See also CA 111; 117; CANR 36; MTCW

Keith, Michael
    See Hubbard, L(afayette) Ron(ald)

Keller, Gottfried 1819-1890....... **NCLC 2**
    See also DLB 129

Kellerman, Jonathan 1949- .... **CLC 44**
    See also BEST 90:1; CA 106; CANR 29

Kelley, William Melvin 1937-...... **CLC 22**
    See also BW 1; CA 77-80; CANR 27;
    DLB 33

Kellogg, Marjorie 1922-............ **CLC 2**
    See also CA 81-84

Kellow, Kathleen
    See Hibbert, Eleanor Alice Burford

Kelly, M(ilton) T(erry) 1947-....... **CLC 55**
    See also CA 97-100; CANR 19, 43

Kelman, James 1946-.......... **CLC 58, 86**

Kemal, Yashar 1923- .... **CLC 14, 29**
    See also CA 89-92; CANR 44

Kemble, Fanny 1809-1893 .... **NCLC 18**
    See also DLB 32

Kemelman, Harry 1908-........... **CLC 2**
    See also AITN 1; CA 9-12R; CANR 6;
    DLB 28

Kempe, Margery 1373(?)-1440(?) ..... **LC 6**
    See also DLB 146

Kempis, Thomas a 1380-1471 .... **LC 11**

Kendall, Henry 1839-1882....... **NCLC 12**

Keneally, Thomas (Michael)
    1935- ...... **CLC 5, 8, 10, 14, 19, 27, 43**
    See also CA 85-88; CANR 10; MTCW

Kennedy, Adrienne (Lita)
    1931- .... **CLC 66; BLC; DC 5**
    See also BW 2; CA 103; CAAS 20; CABS 3;
    CANR 26; DLB 38

Kennedy, John Pendleton
    1795-1870 .... **NCLC 2**
    See also DLB 3

Kennedy, Joseph Charles 1929-
    See Kennedy, X. J.
    See also CA 1-4R; CANR 4, 30, 40;
    SATA 14

Kennedy, William 1928-... **CLC 6, 28, 34, 53**
    See also AAYA 1; CA 85-88; CANR 14,
    31; DLB 143; DLBY 85; MTCW;
    SATA 57

Kennedy, X. J.................... **CLC 8, 42**
    See also Kennedy, Joseph Charles
    See also CAAS 9; CLR 27; DLB 5

Kent, Kelvin
    See Kuttner, Henry

Kenton, Maxwell
    See Southern, Terry

Kenyon, Robert O.
    See Kuttner, Henry

Kerouac, Jack ..... **CLC 1, 2, 3, 5, 14, 29, 61**
    See also Kerouac, Jean-Louis Lebris de
    See also CDALB 1941-1968; DLB 2, 16;
    DLBD 3

Kerouac, Jean-Louis Lebris de 1922-1969
    See Kerouac, Jack
    See also AITN 1; CA 5-8R; 25-28R;
    CANR 26; DA; MTCW; WLC

Kerr, Jean 1923-................. **CLC 22**
    See also CA 5-8R; CANR 7

Kerr, M. E. .... **CLC 12, 35**
    See also Meaker, Marijane (Agnes)
    See also AAYA 2; CLR 29; SAAS 1

Kerr, Robert .... **CLC 55**

Kerrigan, (Thomas) Anthony
    1918- .... **CLC 4, 6**
    See also CA 49-52; CAAS 11; CANR 4

Kerry, Lois
    See Duncan, Lois

Kesey, Ken (Elton)
    1935- ...... **CLC 1, 3, 6, 11, 46, 64; DA;**
                                              WLC
    See also CA 1-4R; CANR 22, 38;
    CDALB 1968-1988; DLB 2, 16; MTCW;
    SATA 66

Kesselring, Joseph (Otto)
    1902-1967 .... **CLC 45**

Kessler, Jascha (Frederick) 1929-.... **CLC 4**
    See also CA 17-20R; CANR 8

Kettelkamp, Larry (Dale) 1933- .... **CLC 12**
See also CA 29-32R; CANR 16; SAAS 3;
SATA 2

Keyber, Conny
See Fielding, Henry

Keyes, Daniel 1927- .... **CLC 80; DA**
See also CA 17-20R; CANR 10, 26;
SATA 37

Khanshendel, Chiron
See Rose, Wendy

Khayyam, Omar
1048-1131 .... **CMLC 11; PC 8**

Kherdian, David 1931- .... **CLC 6, 9**
See also CA 21-24R; CAAS 2; CANR 39;
CLR 24; JRDA; MAICYA; SATA 16, 74

Khlebnikov, Velimir .... **TCLC 20**
See also Khlebnikov, Viktor Vladimirovich

Khlebnikov, Viktor Vladimirovich 1885-1922
See Khlebnikov, Velimir
See also CA 117

Khodasevich, Vladislav (Felitsianovich)
1886-1939 .... **TCLC 15**
See also CA 115

Kielland, Alexander Lange
1849-1906 .... **TCLC 5**
See also CA 104

Kiely, Benedict 1919- .... **CLC 23, 43**
See also CA 1-4R; CANR 2; DLB 15

Kienzle, William X(avier) 1928- .... **CLC 25**
See also CA 93-96; CAAS 1; CANR 9, 31;
MTCW

Kierkegaard, Soren 1813-1855.... **NCLC 34**

Killens, John Oliver 1916-1987..... **CLC 10**
See also BW 2; CA 77-80; 123; CAAS 2;
CANR 26; DLB 33

Killigrew, Anne 1660-1685........... **LC 4**
See also DLB 131

Kim
See Simenon, Georges (Jacques Christian)

Kincaid, Jamaica 1949- ... **CLC 43, 68; BLC**
See also AAYA 13; BW 2; CA 125;
CANR 47

King, Francis (Henry) 1923- ..... **CLC 8, 53**
See also CA 1-4R; CANR 1, 33; DLB 15,
139; MTCW

King, Martin Luther, Jr.
1929-1968 .... **CLC 83; BLC; DA**
See also BW 2; CA 25-28; CANR 27, 44;
CAP 2; MTCW; SATA 14

King, Stephen (Edwin)
1947- ...... **CLC 12, 26, 37, 61; SSC 17**
See also AAYA 1; BEST 90:1; CA 61-64;
CANR 1, 30; DLB 143; DLBY 80;
JRDA; MTCW; SATA 9, 55

King, Steve
See King, Stephen (Edwin)

Kingman, Lee.................... CLC 17
See also Natti, (Mary) Lee
See also SAAS 3; SATA 1, 67

Kingsley, Charles 1819-1875 ..... **NCLC 35**
See also DLB 21, 32; YABC 2

Kingsley, Sidney 1906-............ **CLC 44**
See also CA 85-88; DLB 7

Kingsolver, Barbara 1955-...... **CLC 55, 81**
See also CA 129; 134

Kingston, Maxine (Ting Ting) Hong
1940- .... **CLC 12, 19, 58**
See also AAYA 8; CA 69-72; CANR 13,
38; DLBY 80; MTCW; SATA 53

Kinnell, Galway
1927- .... **CLC 1, 2, 3, 5, 13, 29**
See also CA 9-12R; CANR 10, 34; DLB 5;
DLBY 87; MTCW

Kinsella, Thomas 1928- .... **CLC 4, 19**
See also CA 17-20R; CANR 15; DLB 27;
MTCW

Kinsella, W(illiam) P(atrick)
1935- .... **CLC 27, 43**
See also AAYA 7; CA 97-100; CAAS 7;
CANR 21, 35; MTCW

Kipling, (Joseph) Rudyard
1865-1936 ...... **TCLC 8, 17; DA; PC 3;
SSC 5; WLC**
See also CA 105; 120; CANR 33;
CDBLB 1890-1914; DLB 19, 34, 141;
MAICYA; MTCW; YABC 2

Kirkup, James 1918- .... **CLC 1**
See also CA 1-4R; CAAS 4; CANR 2;
DLB 27; SATA 12

Kirkwood, James 1930(?)-1989 ...... **CLC 9**
See also AITN 2; CA 1-4R; 128; CANR 6,
40

Kis, Danilo 1935-1989 .... **CLC 57**
See also CA 109; 118; 129; MTCW

Kivi, Aleksis 1834-1872........ **NCLC 30**

Kizer, Carolyn (Ashley)
1925- .... **CLC 15, 39, 80**
See also CA 65-68; CAAS 5; CANR 24;
DLB 5

Klabund 1890-1928.............. **TCLC 44**
See also DLB 66

Klappert, Peter 1942-............ **CLC 57**
See also CA 33-36R; DLB 5

Klein, A(braham) M(oses)
1909-1972 .... **CLC 19**
See also CA 101; 37-40R; DLB 68

Klein, Norma 1938-1989 .... **CLC 30**
See also AAYA 2; CA 41-44R; 128;
CANR 15, 37; CLR 2, 19; JRDA;
MAICYA; SAAS 1; SATA 7, 57

Klein, T(heodore) E(ibon) D(onald)
1947- .... **CLC 34**
See also CA 119; CANR 44

Kleist, Heinrich von
1777-1811 .... **NCLC 2, 37**
See also DLB 90

Klima, Ivan 1931-................ **CLC 56**
See also CA 25-28R; CANR 17

Klimentov, Andrei Platonovich 1899-1951
See Platonov, Andrei
See also CA 108

Klinger, Friedrich Maximilian von
1752-1831 .... **NCLC 1**
See also DLB 94

Klopstock, Friedrich Gottlieb
1724-1803 .... : **NCLC 11**
See also DLB 97

Knebel, Fletcher 1911-1993........ **CLC 14**
See also AITN 1; CA 1-4R; 140; CAAS 3;
CANR 1, 36; SATA 36; SATA-Obit 75

Knickerbocker, Diedrich
See Irving, Washington

Knight, Etheridge
1931-1991 .... **CLC 40; BLC**
See also BW 1; CA 21-24R; 133; CANR 23;
DLB 41

Knight, Sarah Kemble 1666-1727 ..... **LC 7**
See also DLB 24

Knister, Raymond 1899-1932...... **TCLC 56**
See also DLB 68

Knowles, John
1926- .... **CLC 1, 4, 10, 26; DA**
See also AAYA 10; CA 17-20R; CANR 40;
CDALB 1968-1988; DLB 6; MTCW;
SATA 8

Knox, Calvin M.
See Silverberg, Robert

Knye, Cassandra
See Disch, Thomas M(ichael)

Koch, C(hristopher) J(ohn) 1932- ... **CLC 42**
See also CA 127

Koch, Christopher
See Koch, C(hristopher) J(ohn)

Koch, Kenneth 1925- .... **CLC 5, 8, 44**
See also CA 1-4R; CANR 6, 36; DLB 5;
SATA 65

Kochanowski, Jan 1530-1584....... **LC 10**

Kock, Charles Paul de
1794-1871 .... **NCLC 16**

Koda Shigeyuki 1867-1947
See Rohan, Koda
See also CA 121

Koestler, Arthur
1905-1983 .... **CLC 1, 3, 6, 8, 15, 33**
See also CA 1-4R; 109; CANR 1, 33;
CDBLB 1945-1960; DLBY 83; MTCW

Kogawa, Joy Nozomi 1935-........ **CLC 78**
See also CA 101; CANR 19

Kohout, Pavel 1928-.............. **CLC 13**
See also CA 45-48; CANR 3

Koizumi, Yakumo
See Hearn, (Patricio) Lafcadio (Tessima
Carlos)

Kolmar, Gertrud 1894-1943....... **TCLC 40**

Komunyakaa, Yusef 1947-......... **CLC 86**
See also DLB 120

Konrad, George
See Konrad, Gyoergy

Konrad, Gyoergy 1933- ...... **CLC 4, 10, 73**
See also CA 85-88

Konwicki, Tadeusz 1926-..... **CLC 8, 28, 54**
See also CA 101; CAAS 9; CANR 39;
MTCW

Koontz, Dean R(ay) 1945-......... **CLC 78**
See also AAYA 9; BEST 89:3, 90:2;
CA 108; CANR 19, 36; MTCW

Kopit, Arthur (Lee) 1937- .... **CLC 1, 18, 33**
See also AITN 1; CA 81-84; CABS 3;
DLB 7; MTCW

Kops, Bernard 1926-.............. **CLC 4**
See also CA 5-8R; DLB 13

Kornbluth, C(yril) M. 1923-1958.... **TCLC 8**
See also CA 105; DLB 8

Korolenko, V. G.
See Korolenko, Vladimir Galaktionovich

Korolenko, Vladimir
See Korolenko, Vladimir Galaktionovich

Korolenko, Vladimir G.
See Korolenko, Vladimir Galaktionovich

Korolenko, Vladimir Galaktionovich
1853-1921 .... **TCLC 22**
See also CA 121

Kosinski, Jerzy (Nikodem)
1933-1991 .... **CLC 1, 2, 3, 6, 10, 15, 53,**
70
See also CA 17-20R; 134; CANR 9, 46, 46;
DLB 2; DLBY 82; MTCW

Kostelanetz, Richard (Cory) 1940- .. **CLC 28**
See also CA 13-16R; CAAS 8; CANR 38

Kostrowitzki, Wilhelm Apollinaris de
1880-1918
See Apollinaire, Guillaume
See also CA 104

Kotlowitz, Robert 1924-............ **CLC 4**
See also CA 33-36R; CANR 36

Kotzebue, August (Friedrich Ferdinand) von
1761-1819 .... **NCLC 25**
See also DLB 94

Kotzwinkle, William 1938- ... **CLC 5, 14, 35**
See also CA 45-48; CANR 3, 44; CLR 6;
MAICYA; SATA 24, 70

Kozol, Jonathan 1936-............ **CLC 17**
See also CA 61-64; CANR 16, 45

Kozoll, Michael 1940(?)- .... **CLC 35**

Kramer, Kathryn 19(?)- .... **CLC 34**

Kramer, Larry 1935- .... **CLC 42**
See also CA 124; 126

Krasicki, Ignacy 1735-1801 .... **NCLC 8**

Krasinski, Zygmunt 1812-1859 .... **NCLC 4**

Kraus, Karl 1874-1936............ **TCLC 5**
See also CA 104; DLB 118

Kreve (Mickevicius), Vincas
1882-1954 .... **TCLC 27**

Kristeva, Julia 1941- .... **CLC 77**

Kristofferson, Kris 1936- .... **CLC 26**
See also CA 104

Krizanc, John 1956-............... **CLC 57**

Krleza, Miroslav 1893-1981........ **CLC 8**
See also CA 97-100; 105; DLB 147

Kroetsch, Robert 1927- ...... **CLC 5, 23, 57**
See also CA 17-20R; CANR 8, 38; DLB 53;
MTCW

Kroetz, Franz
See Kroetz, Franz Xaver

Kroetz, Franz Xaver 1946- .... **CLC 41**
See also CA 130

Kroker, Arthur 1945-............. **CLC 77**

Kropotkin, Peter (Aleksieevich)
1842-1921 .... **TCLC 36**
See also CA 119

Krotkov, Yuri 1917-.............. **CLC 19**
See also CA 102

Krumb
See Crumb, R(obert)

Krumgold, Joseph (Quincy)
1908-1980 .... **CLC 12**
See also CA 9-12R; 101; CANR 7;
MAICYA; SATA 1, 48; SATA-Obit 23

Krumwitz
See Crumb, R(obert)

Krutch, Joseph Wood 1893-1970.... **CLC 24**
See also CA 1-4R; 25-28R; CANR 4;
DLB 63

Krutzch, Gus
See Eliot, T(homas) S(tearns)

Krylov, Ivan Andreevich
1768(?)-1844 .... **NCLC 1**

Kubin, Alfred 1877-1959 .... **TCLC 23**
See also CA 112; DLB 81

Kubrick, Stanley 1928-............ **CLC 16**
See also CA 81-84; CANR 33; DLB 26

Kumin, Maxine (Winokur)
1925- .... **CLC 5, 13, 28**
See also AITN 2; CA 1-4R; CAAS 8;
CANR 1, 21; DLB 5; MTCW; SATA 12

Kundera, Milan
1929- .... **CLC 4, 9, 19, 32, 68**
See also AAYA 2; CA 85-88; CANR 19;
MTCW

Kunene, Mazisi (Raymond) 1930-... **CLC 85**
See also BW 1; CA 125; DLB 117

Kunitz, Stanley (Jasspon)
1905- .... **CLC 6, 11, 14**
See also CA 41-44R; CANR 26; DLB 48;
MTCW

Kunze, Reiner 1933-............. **CLC 10**
See also CA 93-96; DLB 75

Kuprin, Aleksandr Ivanovich
1870-1938 .... **TCLC 5**
See also CA 104

Kureishi, Hanif 1954(?)-........... **CLC 64**
See also CA 139

Kurosawa, Akira 1910-............ **CLC 16**
See also AAYA 11; CA 101; CANR 46, 46

Kushner, Tony 1957(?)- .... **CLC 81**
See also CA 144

Kuttner, Henry 1915-1958........ **TCLC 10**
See also CA 107; DLB 8

Kuzma, Greg 1944-............... **CLC 7**
See also CA 33-36R

Kuzmin, Mikhail 1872(?)-1936 .... **TCLC 40**

Kyd, Thomas 1558-1594....... **LC 22; DC 3**
See also DLB 62

Kyprianos, Iossif
See Samarakis, Antonis

La Bruyere, Jean de 1645-1696...... **LC 17**

Lacan, Jacques (Marie Emile)
1901-1981 .... **CLC 75**
See also CA 121; 104

Laclos, Pierre Ambroise Francois Choderlos
de 1741-1803 .... **NCLC 4**

Lacolere, Francois
See Aragon, Louis

La Colere, Francois
See Aragon, Louis

La Deshabilleuse
See Simenon, Georges (Jacques Christian)

Lady Gregory
See Gregory, Isabella Augusta (Persse)

Lady of Quality, A
See Bagnold, Enid

La Fayette, Marie (Madelaine Pioche de la
Vergne Comtes 1634-1693...... **LC 2**

Lafayette, Rene
See Hubbard, L(afayette) Ron(ald)

Laforgue, Jules 1860-1887........ **NCLC 5**

Lagerkvist, Paer (Fabian)
1891-1974 .... **CLC 7, 10, 13, 54**
See also Lagerkvist, Par
See also CA 85-88; 49-52; MTCW

Lagerkvist, Par
See Lagerkvist, Paer (Fabian)
See also SSC 12

Lagerloef, Selma (Ottiliana Lovisa)
1858-1940 .... **TCLC 4, 36**
See also Lagerlof, Selma (Ottiliana Lovisa)
See also CA 108; SATA 15

Lagerlof, Selma (Ottiliana Lovisa)
See Lagerloef, Selma (Ottiliana Lovisa)
See also CLR 7; SATA 15

La Guma, (Justin) Alex(ander)
1925-1985 .... **CLC 19**
See also BW 1; CA 49-52; 118; CANR 25;
DLB 117; MTCW

Laidlaw, A. K.
See Grieve, C(hristopher) M(urray)

Lainez, Manuel Mujica
See Mujica Lainez, Manuel
See also HW

Lamartine, Alphonse (Marie Louis Prat) de
1790-1869 .... **NCLC 11**

Lamb, Charles
1775-1834 .... **NCLC 10; DA; WLC**
See also CDBLB 1789-1832; DLB 93, 107;
SATA 17

Lamb, Lady Caroline 1785-1828.. **NCLC 38**
See also DLB 116

Lamming, George (William)
1927- .... **CLC 2, 4, 66; BLC**
See also BW 2; CA 85-88; CANR 26;
DLB 125; MTCW

L'Amour, Louis (Dearborn)
1908-1988 .... **CLC 25, 55**
See also AITN 2; BEST 89:2; CA 1-4R;
125; CANR 3, 25, 40; DLBY 80; MTCW

Lampedusa, Giuseppe (Tomasi) di ... **TCLC 13**
See also Tomasi di Lampedusa, Giuseppe

Lampman, Archibald 1861-1899 .. **NCLC 25**
See also DLB 92

Lancaster, Bruce 1896-1963........ **CLC 36**
See also CA 9-10; CAP 1; SATA 9

Landau, Mark Alexandrovich
See Aldanov, Mark (Alexandrovich)

Landau-Aldanov, Mark Alexandrovich
See Aldanov, Mark (Alexandrovich)

Landis, John 1950-............... **CLC 26**
See also CA 112; 122

Landolfi, Tommaso 1908-1979... **CLC 11, 49**
See also CA 127; 117

Landon, Letitia Elizabeth
    1802-1838 .... NCLC 15
    See also DLB 96

Landor, Walter Savage
    1775-1864 .... NCLC 14
    See also DLB 93, 107

Landwirth, Heinz 1927-
    See Lind, Jakov
    See also CA 9-12R; CANR 7

Lane, Patrick 1939- .... CLC 25
    See also CA 97-100; DLB 53

Lang, Andrew 1844-1912 .... TCLC 16
    See also CA 114; 137; DLB 98, 141;
    MAICYA; SATA 16

Lang, Fritz 1890-1976 .... CLC 20
    See also CA 77-80; 69-72; CANR 30

Lange, John
    See Crichton, (John) Michael

Langer, Elinor 1939- .... CLC 34
    See also CA 121

Langland, William
    1330(?)-1400(?) .... LC 19; DA
    See also DLB 146

Langstaff, Launcelot
    See Irving, Washington

Lanier, Sidney 1842-1881 .... NCLC 6
    See also DLB 64; MAICYA; SATA 18

Lanyer, Aemilia 1569-1645 .... LC 10

Lao Tzu .... CMLC 7

Lapine, James (Elliot) 1949- .... CLC 39
    See also CA 123; 130

Larbaud, Valery (Nicolas)
    1881-1957 .... TCLC 9
    See also CA 106

Lardner, Ring
    See Lardner, Ring(gold) W(ilmer)

Lardner, Ring W., Jr.
    See Lardner, Ring(gold) W(ilmer)

Lardner, Ring(gold) W(ilmer)
    1885-1933 .... TCLC 2, 14
    See also CA 104; 131; CDALB 1917-1929;
    DLB 11, 25, 86; MTCW

Laredo, Betty
    See Codrescu, Andrei

Larkin, Maia
    See Wojciechowska, Maia (Teresa)

Larkin, Philip (Arthur)
    1922-1985 .... CLC 3, 5, 8, 9, 13, 18, 33,
                               39, 64
    See also CA 5-8R; 117; CANR 24;
    CDBLB 1960 to Present; DLB 27;
    MTCW

Larra (y Sanchez de Castro), Mariano Jose de
    1809-1837 .... NCLC 17

Larsen, Eric 1941- .... CLC 55
    See also CA 132

Larsen, Nella 1891-1964 ..... CLC 37; BLC
    See also BW 1; CA 125; DLB 51

Larson, Charles R(aymond) 1938-... CLC 31
    See also CA 53-56; CANR 4

Lasker-Schueler, Else 1869-1945 .. TCLC 57
    See also DLB 66, 124

Latham, Jean Lee 1902-.......... CLC 12
    See also AITN 1; CA 5-8R; CANR 7;
    MAICYA; SATA 2, 68

Latham, Mavis
    See Clark, Mavis Thorpe

Lathen, Emma .... CLC 2
    See also Hennissart, Martha; Latsis, Mary
    J(ane)

Lathrop, Francis
    See Leiber, Fritz (Reuter, Jr.)

Latsis, Mary J(ane)
    See Lathen, Emma
    See also CA 85-88

Lattimore, Richmond (Alexander)
    1906-1984 .... CLC 3
    See also CA 1-4R; 112; CANR 1

Laughlin, James 1914-............ CLC 49
    See also CA 21-24R; CANR 9, 45; DLB 48

Laurence, (Jean) Margaret (Wemyss)
    1926-1987 .. CLC 3, 6, 13, 50, 62; SSC 7
    See also CA 5-8R; 121; CANR 33; DLB 53;
    MTCW; SATA-Obit 50

Laurent, Antoine 1952- .... CLC 50

Lauscher, Hermann
    See Hesse, Hermann

Lautreamont, Comte de
    1846-1870 .... NCLC 12; SSC 14

Laverty, Donald
    See Blish, James (Benjamin)

Lavin, Mary 1912-...... CLC 4, 18; SSC 4
    See also CA 9-12R; CANR 33; DLB 15;
    MTCW

Lavond, Paul Dennis
    See Kornbluth, C(yril) M.; Pohl, Frederik

Lawler, Raymond Evenor 1922- .... CLC 58
    See also CA 103

Lawrence, D(avid) H(erbert Richards)
    1885-1930 .... TCLC 2, 9, 16, 33, 48;
                              DA; SSC 4; WLC
    See also CA 104; 121; CDBLB 1914-1945;
    DLB 10, 19, 36, 98; MTCW

Lawrence, T(homas) E(dward)
    1888-1935 .... TCLC 18
    See also Dale, Colin
    See also CA 115

Lawrence of Arabia
    See Lawrence, T(homas) E(dward)

Lawson, Henry (Archibald Hertzberg)
    1867-1922 .... TCLC 27; SSC 18
    See also CA 120

Lawton, Dennis
    See Faust, Frederick (Schiller)

Laxness, Halldor .... CLC 25
    See also Gudjonsson, Halldor Kiljan

Layamon fl. c. 1200-............ CMLC 10
    See also DLB 146

Laye, Camara 1928-1980 ... CLC 4, 38; BLC
    See also BW 1; CA 85-88; 97-100;
    CANR 25; MTCW

Layton, Irving (Peter) 1912-..... CLC 2, 15
    See also CA 1-4R; CANR 2, 33, 43;
    DLB 88; MTCW

Lazarus, Emma 1849-1887........ NCLC 8

Lazarus, Felix
    See Cable, George Washington

Lazarus, Henry
    See Slavitt, David R(ytman)

Lea, Joan
    See Neufeld, John (Arthur)

Leacock, Stephen (Butler)
    1869-1944 .... TCLC 2
    See also CA 104; 141; DLB 92

Lear, Edward 1812-1888 .... NCLC 3
    See also CLR 1; DLB 32; MAICYA;
    SATA 18

Lear, Norman (Milton) 1922- ...... CLC 12
    See also CA 73-76

Leavis, F(rank) R(aymond)
    1895-1978 .... CLC 24
    See also CA 21-24R; 77-80; CANR 44;
    MTCW

Leavitt, David 1961-.............. CLC 34
    See also CA 116; 122; DLB 130

Leblanc, Maurice (Marie Emile)
    1864-1941 .... TCLC 49
    See also CA 110

Lebowitz, Fran(ces Ann)
    1951(?)- .... CLC 11, 36
    See also CA 81-84; CANR 14; MTCW

Lebrecht, Peter
    See Tieck, (Johann) Ludwig

le Carre, John .... CLC 3, 5, 9, 15, 28
    See also Cornwell, David (John Moore)
    See also BEST 89:4; CDBLB 1960 to
    Present; DLB 87

Le Clezio, J(ean) M(arie) G(ustave)
    1940- .... CLC 31
    See also CA 116; 128; DLB 83

Leconte de Lisle, Charles-Marie-Rene
    1818-1894 .... NCLC 29

Le Coq, Monsieur
    See Simenon, Georges (Jacques Christian)

Leduc, Violette 1907-1972......... CLC 22
    See also CA 13-14; 33-36R; CAP 1

Ledwidge, Francis 1887(?)-1917 ... TCLC 23
    See also CA 123; DLB 20

Lee, Andrea 1953- .... CLC 36; BLC
    See also BW 1; CA 125

Lee, Andrew
    See Auchincloss, Louis (Stanton)

Lee, Don L. .... CLC 2
    See also Madhubuti, Haki R.

Lee, George W(ashington)
    1894-1976 .... CLC 52; BLC
    See also BW 1; CA 125; DLB 51

Lee, (Nelle) Harper
    1926- .... CLC 12, 60; DA; WLC
    See also AAYA 13; CA 13-16R;
    CDALB 1941-1968; DLB 6; MTCW;
    SATA 11

Lee, Helen Elaine 1959(?)- .... CLC 86

Lee, Julian
    See Latham, Jean Lee

Lee, Larry
    See Lee, Lawrence

Lee, Lawrence 1941-1990......... CLC 34
    See also CA 131; CANR 43

Lee, Manfred B(ennington)
1905-1971 .... **CLC 11**
See also Queen, Ellery
See also CA 1-4R; 29-32R; CANR 2;
DLB 137

Lee, Stan 1922-................ **CLC 17**
See also AAYA 5; CA 108; 111

Lee, Tanith 1947-................ **CLC 46**
See also CA 37-40R; SATA 8

Lee, Vernon .... **TCLC 5**
See also Paget, Violet
See also DLB 57

Lee, William
See Burroughs, William S(eward)

Lee, Willy
See Burroughs, William S(eward)

Lee-Hamilton, Eugene (Jacob)
1845-1907 .... **TCLC 22**
See also CA 117

Leet, Judith 1935- .... **CLC 11**

Le Fanu, Joseph Sheridan
1814-1873 .... **NCLC 9; SSC 14**
See also DLB 21, 70

Leffland, Ella 1931- .... **CLC 19**
See also CA 29-32R; CANR 35; DLBY 84;
SATA 65

Leger, Alexis
See Leger, (Marie-Rene Auguste) Alexis
Saint-Leger

Leger, (Marie-Rene Auguste) Alexis
Saint-Leger 1887-1975........ **CLC 11**
See also Perse, St.-John
See also CA 13-16R; 61-64; CANR 43;
MTCW

Leger, Saintleger
See Leger, (Marie-Rene Auguste) Alexis
Saint-Leger

Le Guin, Ursula K(roeber)
1929- .... **CLC 8, 13, 22, 45, 71; SSC 12**
See also AAYA 9; AITN 1; CA 21-24R;
CANR 9, 32; CDALB 1968-1988; CLR 3,
28; DLB 8, 52; JRDA; MAICYA;
MTCW; SATA 4, 52

Lehmann, Rosamond (Nina)
1901-1990 .... **CLC 5**
See also CA 77-80; 131; CANR 8; DLB 15

Leiber, Fritz (Reuter, Jr.)
1910-1992 .... **CLC 25**
See also CA 45-48; 139; CANR 2, 40;
DLB 8; MTCW; SATA 45;
SATA-Obit 73

Leimbach, Martha 1963-
See Leimbach, Marti
See also CA 130

Leimbach, Marti .... **CLC 65**
See also Leimbach, Martha

Leino, Eino .... **TCLC 24**
See also Loennbohm, Armas Eino Leopold

Leiris, Michel (Julien) 1901-1990... **CLC 61**
See also CA 119; 128; 132

Leithauser, Brad 1953-............ **CLC 27**
See also CA 107; CANR 27; DLB 120

Lelchuk, Alan 1938-............... **CLC 5**
See also CA 45-48; CAAS 20; CANR 1

Lem, Stanislaw 1921-........ **CLC 8, 15, 40**
See also CA 105; CAAS 1; CANR 32;
MTCW

Lemann, Nancy 1956-............. **CLC 39**
See also CA 118; 136

Lemonnier, (Antoine Louis) Camille
1844-1913 .... **TCLC 22**
See also CA 121

Lenau, Nikolaus 1802-1850 ...... **NCLC 16**

L'Engle, Madeleine (Camp Franklin)
1918- .... **CLC 12**
See also AAYA 1; AITN 2; CA 1-4R;
CANR 3, 21, 39; CLR 1, 14; DLB 52;
JRDA; MAICYA; MTCW; SAAS 15;
SATA 1, 27, 75

Lengyel, Jozsef 1896-1975.......... **CLC 7**
See also CA 85-88; 57-60

Lennon, John (Ono)
1940-1980 .... **CLC 12, 35**
See also CA 102

Lennox, Charlotte Ramsay
1729(?)-1804 .... **NCLC 23**
See also DLB 39

Lentricchia, Frank (Jr.) 1940-...... **CLC 34**
See also CA 25-28R; CANR 19

Lenz, Siegfried 1926-............. **CLC 27**
See also CA 89-92; DLB 75

Leonard, Elmore (John, Jr.)
1925- .... **CLC 28, 34, 71**
See also AITN 1; BEST 89:1, 90:4;
CA 81-84; CANR 12, 28; MTCW

Leonard, Hugh.................... **CLC 19**
See also Byrne, John Keyes
See also DLB 13

Leopardi, (Conte) Giacomo
1798-1837 .... **NCLC 22**

Le Reveler
See Artaud, Antonin

Lerman, Eleanor 1952-............ **CLC 9**
See also CA 85-88

Lerman, Rhoda 1936-............. **CLC 56**
See also CA 49-52

Lermontov, Mikhail Yuryevich
1814-1841 .... **NCLC 47**

Leroux, Gaston 1868-1927........ **TCLC 25**
See also CA 108; 136; SATA 65

Lesage, Alain-Rene 1668-1747........ **LC 2**

Leskov, Nikolai (Semyonovich)
1831-1895 .... **NCLC 25**

Lessing, Doris (May)
1919- ..... **CLC 1, 2, 3, 6, 10, 15, 22, 40;**
DA; SSC 6
See also CA 9-12R; CAAS 14; CANR 33;
CDBLB 1960 to Present; DLB 15, 139;
DLBY 85; MTCW

Lessing, Gotthold Ephraim
1729-1781 .... **LC 8**
See also DLB 97

Lester, Richard 1932-............ **CLC 20**

Lever, Charles (James)
1806-1872 .... **NCLC 23**
See also DLB 21

Leverson, Ada 1865(?)-1936(?) .... **TCLC 18**
See also Elaine
See also CA 117

Levertov, Denise
1923- ...... **CLC 1, 2, 3, 5, 8, 15, 28, 66;**
PC 11
See also CA 1-4R; CAAS 19; CANR 3, 29;
DLB 5; MTCW

Levi, Jonathan.................... **CLC 76**

Levi, Peter (Chad Tigar) 1931-..... **CLC 41**
See also CA 5-8R; CANR 34; DLB 40

Levi, Primo
1919-1987 .... **CLC 37, 50; SSC 12**
See also CA 13-16R; 122; CANR 12, 33;
MTCW

Levin, Ira 1929-................. **CLC 3, 6**
See also CA 21-24R; CANR 17, 44;
MTCW; SATA 66

Levin, Meyer 1905-1981 .... **CLC 7**
See also AITN 1; CA 9-12R; 104;
CANR 15; DLB 9, 28; DLBY 81;
SATA 21; SATA-Obit 27

Levine, Norman 1924-............ **CLC 54**
See also CA 73-76; CANR 14; DLB 88

Levine, Philip 1928-.. **CLC 2, 4, 5, 9, 14, 33**
See also CA 9-12R; CANR 9, 37; DLB 5

Levinson, Deirdre 1931-........... **CLC 49**
See also CA 73-76

Levi-Strauss, Claude 1908- .... **CLC 38**
See also CA 1-4R; CANR 6, 32; MTCW

Levitin, Sonia (Wolff) 1934- .... **CLC 17**
See also AAYA 13; CA 29-32R; CANR 14,
32; JRDA; MAICYA; SAAS 2; SATA 4,
68

Levon, O. U.
See Kesey, Ken (Elton)

Lewes, George Henry
1817-1878 .... **NCLC 25**
See also DLB 55, 144

Lewis, Alun 1915-1944............ **TCLC 3**
See also CA 104; DLB 20

Lewis, C. Day
See Day Lewis, C(ecil)

Lewis, C(live) S(taples)
1898-1963 ..... **CLC 1, 3, 6, 14, 27; DA;**
WLC
See also AAYA 3; CA 81-84; CANR 33;
CDBLB 1945-1960; CLR 3, 27; DLB 15,
100; JRDA; MAICYA; MTCW;
SATA 13

Lewis, Janet 1899-.............. **CLC 41**
See also Winters, Janet Lewis
See also CA 9-12R; CANR 29; CAP 1;
DLBY 87

Lewis, Matthew Gregory
1775-1818 .... **NCLC 11**
See also DLB 39

Lewis, (Harry) Sinclair
1885-1951 ..... **TCLC 4, 13, 23, 39; DA;**
WLC
See also CA 104; 133; CDALB 1917-1929;
DLB 9, 102; DLBD 1; MTCW

Lewis, (Percy) Wyndham
1884(?)-1957 .... **TCLC 2, 9**
See also CA 104; DLB 15

Lewisohn, Ludwig 1883-1955...... **TCLC 19**
See also CA 107; DLB 4, 9, 28, 102

Lezama Lima, Jose 1910-1976 ... **CLC 4, 10**
See also CA 77-80; DLB 113; HW

L'Heureux, John (Clarke) 1934-.... **CLC 52**
See also CA 13-16R; CANR 23, 45

Liddell, C. H.
See Kuttner, Henry

Lie, Jonas (Lauritz Idemil)
1833-1908(?)................ **TCLC 5**
See also CA 115

Lieber, Joel 1937-1971............. **CLC 6**
See also CA 73-76; 29-32R

Lieber, Stanley Martin
See Lee, Stan

Lieberman, Laurence (James)
1935-..................... **CLC 4, 36**
See also CA 17-20R; CANR 8, 36

Lieksman, Anders
See Haavikko, Paavo Juhani

Li Fei-kan 1904-
See Pa Chin
See also CA 105

Lifton, Robert Jay 1926-......... **CLC 67**
See also CA 17-20R; CANR 27; SATA 66

Lightfoot, Gordon 1938-.......... **CLC 26**
See also CA 109

Lightman, Alan P. 1948-......... **CLC 81**
See also CA 141

Ligotti, Thomas 1953- .... **CLC 44; SSC 16**
See also CA 123

Liliencron, (Friedrich Adolf Axel) Detlev von
1844-1909................ **TCLC 18**
See also CA 117

Lilly, William 1602-1681.......... **LC 27**

Lima, Jose Lezama
See Lezama Lima, Jose

Lima Barreto, Afonso Henrique de
1881-1922................ **TCLC 23**
See also CA 117

Limonov, Eduard.................. **CLC 67**

Lin, Frank
See Atherton, Gertrude (Franklin Horn)

Lincoln, Abraham 1809-1865..... **NCLC 18**

Lind, Jakov .... **CLC 1, 2, 4, 27, 82**
See also Landwirth, Heinz
See also CAAS 4

Lindbergh, Anne (Spencer) Morrow
1906-...................... **CLC 82**
See also CA 17-20R; CANR 16; MTCW;
SATA 33

Lindsay, David 1878-1945....... **TCLC 15**
See also CA 113

Lindsay, (Nicholas) Vachel
1879-1931 .... **TCLC 17; DA; WLC**
See also CA 114; 135; CDALB 1865-1917;
DLB 54; SATA 40

Linke-Poot
See Doeblin, Alfred

Linney, Romulus 1930- .... **CLC 51**
See also CA 1-4R; CANR 40, 44

Linton, Eliza Lynn 1822-1898.... **NCLC 41**
See also DLB 18

Li Po 701-763................. **CMLC 2**

Lipsius, Justus 1547-1606......... **LC 16**

Lipsyte, Robert (Michael)
1938-.................... **CLC 21; DA**
See also AAYA 7; CA 17-20R; CANR 8;
CLR 23; JRDA; MAICYA; SATA 5, 68

Lish, Gordon (Jay) 1934-.. **CLC 45; SSC 18**
See also CA 113; 117; DLB 130

Lispector, Clarice 1925-1977....... **CLC 43**
See also CA 139; 116; DLB 113

Littell, Robert 1935(?)- .... **CLC 42**
See also CA 109; 112

Little, Malcolm 1925-1965
See Malcolm X
See also BW 1; CA 125; 111; DA; MTCW

Littlewit, Humphrey Gent.
See Lovecraft, H(oward) P(hillips)

Litwos
See Sienkiewicz, Henryk (Adam Alexander
Pius)

Liu E 1857-1909................ **TCLC 15**
See also CA 115

Lively, Penelope (Margaret)
1933-.................... **CLC 32, 50**
See also CA 41-44R; CANR 29; CLR 7;
DLB 14; JRDA; MAICYA; MTCW;
SATA 7, 60

Livesay, Dorothy (Kathleen)
1909-.................. **CLC 4, 15, 79**
See also AITN 2; CA 25-28R; CAAS 8;
CANR 36; DLB 68; MTCW

Livy c. 59B.C.-c. 17............ **CMLC 11**

Lizardi, Jose Joaquin Fernandez de
1776-1827................ **NCLC 30**

Llewellyn, Richard
See Llewellyn Lloyd, Richard Dafydd
Vivian
See also DLB 15

Llewellyn Lloyd, Richard Dafydd Vivian
1906-1983 .... **CLC 7, 80**
See also Llewellyn, Richard
See also CA 53-56; 111; CANR 7;
SATA 11; SATA-Obit 37

Llosa, (Jorge) Mario (Pedro) Vargas
See Vargas Llosa, (Jorge) Mario (Pedro)

Lloyd Webber, Andrew 1948-
See Webber, Andrew Lloyd
See also AAYA 1; CA 116; SATA 56

Llull, Ramon c. 1235-c. 1316..... **CMLC 12**

Locke, Alain (Le Roy)
1886-1954 .... **TCLC 43**
See also BW 1; CA 106; 124; DLB 51

Locke, John 1632-1704 .... **LC 7**
See also DLB 101

Locke-Elliott, Sumner
See Elliott, Sumner Locke

Lockhart, John Gibson
1794-1854 .... **NCLC 6**
See also DLB 110, 116, 144

Lodge, David (John) 1935-........ **CLC 36**
See also BEST 90:1; CA 17-20R; CANR 19;
DLB 14; MTCW

Loennbohm, Armas Eino Leopold 1878-1926
See Leino, Eino
See also CA 123

Loewinsohn, Ron(ald William)
1937-..................... **CLC 52**
See also CA 25-28R

Logan, Jake
See Smith, Martin Cruz

Logan, John (Burton) 1923-1987..... **CLC 5**
See also CA 77-80; 124; CANR 45; DLB 5

Lo Kuan-chung 1330(?)-1400(?)...... **LC 12**

Lombard, Nap
See Johnson, Pamela Hansford

London, Jack.. **TCLC 9, 15, 39; SSC 4; WLC**
See also London, John Griffith
See also AAYA 13; AITN 2;
CDALB 1865-1917; DLB 8, 12, 78;
SATA 18

London, John Griffith 1876-1916
See London, Jack
See also CA 110; 119; DA; JRDA;
MAICYA; MTCW

Long, Emmett
See Leonard, Elmore (John, Jr.)

Longbaugh, Harry
See Goldman, William (W.)

Longfellow, Henry Wadsworth
1807-1882 .... **NCLC 2, 45; DA**
See also CDALB 1640-1865; DLB 1, 59;
SATA 19

Longley, Michael 1939-........... **CLC 29**
See also CA 102; DLB 40

Longus fl. c. 2nd cent. -.......... **CMLC 7**

Longway, A. Hugh
See Lang, Andrew

Lopate, Phillip 1943-............. **CLC 29**
See also CA 97-100; DLBY 80

Lopez Portillo (y Pacheco), Jose
1920-...................... **CLC 46**
See also CA 129; HW

Lopez y Fuentes, Gregorio
1897(?)-1966................ **CLC 32**
See also CA 131; HW

Lorca, Federico Garcia
See Garcia Lorca, Federico

Lord, Bette Bao 1938-............ **CLC 23**
See also BEST 90:3; CA 107; CANR 41;
SATA 58

Lord Auch
See Bataille, Georges

Lord Byron
See Byron, George Gordon (Noel)

Lorde, Audre (Geraldine)
1934-1992 .... **CLC 18, 71; BLC**
See also BW 1; CA 25-28R; 142; CANR 16,
26, 46, 46; DLB 41; MTCW

Lord Jeffrey
See Jeffrey, Francis

Lorenzo, Heberto Padilla
See Padilla (Lorenzo), Heberto

Loris
See Hofmannsthal, Hugo von

Loti, Pierre .... TCLC 11
See also Viaud, (Louis Marie) Julien
See also DLB 123

Louie, David Wong   1954- .... CLC 70
See also CA 139

Louis, Father M.
See Merton, Thomas

Lovecraft, H(oward) P(hillips)
1890-1937 .... TCLC 4, 22; SSC 3
See also AAYA 14; CA 104; 133; MTCW

Lovelace, Earl   1935-.............. CLC 51
See also BW 2; CA 77-80; CANR 41;
DLB 125; MTCW

Lovelace, Richard   1618-1657........ LC 24
See also DLB 131

Lowell, Amy   1874-1925 .... TCLC 1, 8
See also CA 104; DLB 54, 140

Lowell, James Russell   1819-1891 .. NCLC 2
See also CDALB 1640-1865; DLB 1, 11, 64,
79

Lowell, Robert (Traill Spence, Jr.)
1917-1977 ... CLC 1, 2, 3, 4, 5, 8, 9, 11,
15, 37; DA; PC 3; WLC
See also CA 9-12R; 73-76; CABS 2;
CANR 26; DLB 5; MTCW

Lowndes, Marie Adelaide (Belloc)
1868-1947 .... TCLC 12
See also CA 107; DLB 70

Lowry, (Clarence) Malcolm
1909-1957 .... TCLC 6, 40
See also CA 105; 131; CDBLB 1945-1960;
DLB 15; MTCW

Lowry, Mina Gertrude   1882-1966
See Loy, Mina
See also CA 113

Loxsmith, John
See Brunner, John (Kilian Houston)

Loy, Mina .... CLC 28
See also Lowry, Mina Gertrude
See also DLB 4, 54

Loyson-Bridet
See Schwob, (Mayer Andre) Marcel

Lucas, Craig   1951-.............. CLC 64
See also CA 137

Lucas, George   1944-............. CLC 16
See also AAYA 1; CA 77-80; CANR 30;
SATA 56

Lucas, Hans
See Godard, Jean-Luc

Lucas, Victoria
See Plath, Sylvia

Ludlam, Charles   1943-1987 ..... CLC 46, 50
See also CA 85-88; 122

Ludlum, Robert   1927- .... CLC 22, 43
See also AAYA 10; BEST 89:1, 90:3;
CA 33-36R; CANR 25, 41; DLBY 82;
MTCW

Ludwig, Ken...................... CLC 60

Ludwig, Otto   1813-1865.......... NCLC 4
See also DLB 129

Lugones, Leopoldo   1874-1938 ..... TCLC 15
See also CA 116; 131; HW

Lu Hsun   1881-1936 .... TCLC 3

Lukacs, George .... CLC 24
See also Lukacs, Gyorgy (Szegeny von)

Lukacs, Gyorgy (Szegeny von)   1885-1971
See Lukacs, George
See also CA 101; 29-32R

Luke, Peter (Ambrose Cyprian)
1919- .... CLC 38
See also CA 81-84; DLB 13

Lunar, Dennis
See Mungo, Raymond

Lurie, Alison   1926-........ CLC 4, 5, 18, 39
See also CA 1-4R; CANR 2, 17; DLB 2;
MTCW; SATA 46

Lustig, Arnost   1926-.............. CLC 56
See also AAYA 3; CA 69-72; CANR 47;
SATA 56

Luther, Martin   1483-1546 .... LC 9

Luzi, Mario   1914-................ CLC 13
See also CA 61-64; CANR 9; DLB 128

Lynch, B. Suarez
See Bioy Casares, Adolfo; Borges, Jorge
Luis

Lynch, David (K.)   1946-.......... CLC 66
See also CA 124; 129

Lynch, James
See Andreyev, Leonid (Nikolaevich)

Lynch Davis, B.
See Bioy Casares, Adolfo; Borges, Jorge
Luis

Lyndsay, Sir David   1490-1555 ...... LC 20

Lynn, Kenneth S(chuyler)   1923-.... CLC 50
See also CA 1-4R; CANR 3, 27

Lynx
See West, Rebecca

Lyons, Marcus
See Blish, James (Benjamin)

Lyre, Pinchbeck
See Sassoon, Siegfried (Lorraine)

Lytle, Andrew (Nelson)   1902-...... CLC 22
See also CA 9-12R; DLB 6

Lyttelton, George   1709-1773........ LC 10

Maas, Peter   1929- .... CLC 29
See also CA 93-96

Macaulay, Rose   1881-1958 ..... TCLC 7, 44
See also CA 104; DLB 36

Macaulay, Thomas Babington
1800-1859 .... NCLC 42
See also CDBLB 1832-1890; DLB 32, 55

MacBeth, George (Mann)
1932-1992 .... CLC 2, 5, 9
See also CA 25-28R; 136; DLB 40; MTCW;
SATA 4; SATA-Obit 70

MacCaig, Norman (Alexander)
1910- .... CLC 36
See also CA 9-12R; CANR 3, 34; DLB 27

MacCarthy, (Sir Charles Otto) Desmond
1877-1952 .... TCLC 36

MacDiarmid, Hugh
.... CLC 2, 4, 11, 19, 63; PC 9
See also Grieve, C(hristopher) M(urray)
See also CDBLB 1945-1960; DLB 20

MacDonald, Anson
See Heinlein, Robert A(nson)

Macdonald, Cynthia   1928-...... CLC 13, 19
See also CA 49-52; CANR 4, 44; DLB 105

MacDonald, George   1824-1905 ..... TCLC 9
See also CA 106; 137; DLB 18; MAICYA;
SATA 33

Macdonald, John
See Millar, Kenneth

MacDonald, John D(ann)
1916-1986 .... CLC 3, 27, 44
See also CA 1-4R; 121; CANR 1, 19;
DLB 8; DLBY 86; MTCW

Macdonald, John Ross
See Millar, Kenneth

Macdonald, Ross..... CLC 1, 2, 3, 14, 34, 41
See also Millar, Kenneth
See also DLBD 6

MacDougal, John
See Blish, James (Benjamin)

MacEwen, Gwendolyn (Margaret)
1941-1987 .... CLC 13, 55
See also CA 9-12R; 124; CANR 7, 22;
DLB 53; SATA 50; SATA-Obit 55

Macha, Karel Hynek   1810-1846 .. NCLC 46

Machado (y Ruiz), Antonio
1875-1939 .... TCLC 3
See also CA 104; DLB 108

Machado de Assis, Joaquim Maria
1839-1908 .... TCLC 10; BLC
See also CA 107

Machen, Arthur.................... TCLC 4
See also Jones, Arthur Llewellyn
See also DLB 36

Machiavelli, Niccolo   1469-1527 .. LC 8; DA

MacInnes, Colin   1914-1976...... CLC 4, 23
See also CA 69-72; 65-68; CANR 21;
DLB 14; MTCW

MacInnes, Helen (Clark)
1907-1985 .... CLC 27, 39
See also CA 1-4R; 117; CANR 1, 28;
DLB 87; MTCW; SATA 22;
SATA-Obit 44

Mackay, Mary   1855-1924
See Corelli, Marie
See also CA 118

Mackenzie, Compton (Edward Montague)
1883-1972 .... CLC 18
See also CA 21-22; 37-40R; CAP 2;
DLB 34, 100

Mackenzie, Henry   1745-1831 .... NCLC 41
See also DLB 39

Mackintosh, Elizabeth   1896(?)-1952
See Tey, Josephine
See also CA 110

MacLaren, James
See Grieve, C(hristopher) M(urray)

Mac Laverty, Bernard   1942-....... CLC 31
See also CA 116; 118; CANR 43

MacLean, Alistair (Stuart)
1922-1987........CLC 3, 13, 50, 63
See also CA 57-60; 121; CANR 28; MTCW;
SATA 23; SATA-Obit 50

Maclean, Norman (Fitzroy)
1902-1990 .... CLC 78; SSC 13
See also CA 102; 132

MacLeish, Archibald
1892-1982 . . . . CLC **3, 8, 14, 68**
See also CA 9-12R; 106; CANR 33; DLB 4,
7, 45; DLBY 82; MTCW

MacLennan, (John) Hugh
1907-1990 . . . . CLC **2, 14**
See also CA 5-8R; 142; CANR 33; DLB 68;
MTCW

MacLeod, Alistair 1936- . . . . CLC **56**
See also CA 123; DLB 60

MacNeice, (Frederick) Louis
1907-1963 . . . . CLC **1, 4, 10, 53**
See also CA 85-88; DLB 10, 20; MTCW

MacNeill, Dand
See Fraser, George MacDonald

Macpherson, (Jean) Jay 1931- . . . . . . CLC **14**
See also CA 5-8R; DLB 53

MacShane, Frank 1927- . . . . CLC **39**
See also CA 9-12R; CANR 3, 33; DLB 111

Macumber, Mari
See Sandoz, Mari(e Susette)

Madach, Imre 1823-1864 . . . . NCLC **19**

Madden, (Jerry) David 1933- . . . . CLC **5, 15**
See also CA 1-4R; CAAS 3; CANR 4, 45;
DLB 6; MTCW

Maddern, Al(an)
See Ellison, Harlan (Jay)

Madhubuti, Haki R.
1942- . . . . CLC **6, 73; BLC; PC 5**
See also Lee, Don L.
See also BW 2; CA 73-76; CANR 24;
DLB 5, 41; DLBD 8

Maepenn, Hugh
See Kuttner, Henry

Maepenn, K. H.
See Kuttner, Henry

Maeterlinck, Maurice 1862-1949 . . . TCLC **3**
See also CA 104; 136; SATA 66

Maginn, William 1794-1842 . . . . . . NCLC **8**
See also DLB 110

Mahapatra, Jayanta 1928- . . . . CLC **33**
See also CA 73-76; CAAS 9; CANR 15, 33

Mahfouz, Naguib (Abdel Aziz Al-Sabilgi)
1911(?)-
See Mahfuz, Najib
See also BEST 89:2; CA 128; MTCW

Mahfuz, Najib . . . . CLC **52, 55**
See also Mahfouz, Naguib (Abdel Aziz
Al-Sabilgi)
See also DLBY 88

Mahon, Derek 1941- . . . . CLC **27**
See also CA 113; 128; DLB 40

Mailer, Norman
1923- . . . . . . CLC **1, 2, 3, 4, 5, 8, 11, 14,
28, 39, 74; DA**
See also AITN 2; CA 9-12R;
CANR 28; CDALB 1968-1988; DLB 2,
16, 28; DLBD 3; DLBY 80, 83; MTCW

Maillet, Antonine 1929- . . . . CLC **54**
See also CA 115; 120; CANR 46, 46;
DLB 60

Mais, Roger 1905-1955 . . . . TCLC **8**
See also BW 1; CA 105; 124; DLB 125;
MTCW

Maistre, Joseph de 1753-1821 . . . . NCLC **37**

Maitland, Sara (Louise) 1950- . . . . . . CLC **49**
See also CA 69-72; CANR 13

Major, Clarence
1936- . . . . CLC **3, 19, 48; BLC**
See also BW 2; CA 21-24R; CAAS 6;
CANR 13, 25; DLB 33

Major, Kevin (Gerald) 1949- . . . . CLC **26**
See also CA 97-100; CANR 21, 38;
CLR 11; DLB 60; JRDA; MAICYA;
SATA 32

Maki, James
See Ozu, Yasujiro

Malabaila, Damiano
See Levi, Primo

Malamud, Bernard
1914-1986 . . . . . . CLC **1, 2, 3, 5, 8, 9, 11,
18, 27, 44, 78, 85; DA; SSC 15; WLC**
See also CA 5-8R; 118; CABS 1; CANR 28;
CDALB 1941-1968; DLB 2, 28;
DLBY 80, 86; MTCW

Malaparte, Curzio 1898-1957 . . . . . TCLC **52**

Malcolm, Dan
See Silverberg, Robert

Malcolm X . . . . CLC **82; BLC**
See also Little, Malcolm

Malherbe, Francois de 1555-1628 . . . . . LC **5**

Mallarme, Stephane
1842-1898 . . . . NCLC **4, 41; PC 4**

Mallet-Joris, Francoise 1930- . . . . . . CLC **11**
See also CA 65-68; CANR 17; DLB 83

Malley, Ern
See McAuley, James Phillip

Mallowan, Agatha Christie
See Christie, Agatha (Mary Clarissa)

Maloff, Saul 1922- . . . . CLC **5**
See also CA 33-36R

Malone, Louis
See MacNeice, (Frederick) Louis

Malone, Michael (Christopher)
1942- . . . . CLC **43**
See also CA 77-80; CANR 14, 32

Malory, (Sir) Thomas
1410(?)-1471(?) . . . . LC **11; DA**
See also CDBLB Before 1660; DLB 146;
SATA 33, 59

Malouf, (George Joseph) David
1934- . . . . CLC **28, 86**
See also CA 124

Malraux, (Georges-)Andre
1901-1976 . . . . . . CLC **1, 4, 9, 13, 15, 57**
See also CA 21-22; 69-72; CANR 34;
CAP 2; DLB 72; MTCW

Malzberg, Barry N(athaniel) 1939- . . . CLC **7**
See also CA 61-64; CAAS 4; CANR 16;
DLB 8

Mamet, David (Alan)
1947- . . . . CLC **9, 15, 34, 46; DC 4**
See also AAYA 3; CA 81-84; CABS 3;
CANR 15, 41; DLB 7; MTCW

Mamoulian, Rouben (Zachary)
1897-1987 . . . . CLC **16**
See also CA 25-28R; 124

Mandelstam, Osip (Emilievich)
1891(?)-1938(?) . . . . TCLC **2, 6**
See also CA 104

Mander, (Mary) Jane 1877-1949 . . . TCLC **31**

Mandiargues, Andre Pieyre de . . . . . . CLC **41**
See also Pieyre de Mandiargues, Andre
See also DLB 83

Mandrake, Ethel Belle
See Thurman, Wallace (Henry)

Mangan, James Clarence
1803-1849 . . . . NCLC **27**

Maniere, J.-E.
See Giraudoux, (Hippolyte) Jean

Manley, (Mary) Delariviere
1672(?)-1724 . . . . LC **1**
See also DLB 39, 80

Mann, Abel
See Creasey, John

Mann, (Luiz) Heinrich 1871-1950 . . . TCLC **9**
See also CA 106; DLB 66

Mann, (Paul) Thomas
1875-1955 . . . . TCLC **2, 8, 14, 21, 35, 44;
DA; SSC 5; WLC**
See also CA 104; 128; DLB 66; MTCW

Manning, David
See Faust, Frederick (Schiller)

Manning, Frederic 1887(?)-1935 . . . TCLC **25**
See also CA 124

Manning, Olivia 1915-1980 . . . . . . CLC **5, 19**
See also CA 5-8R; 101; CANR 29; MTCW

Mano, D. Keith 1942- . . . . CLC **2, 10**
See also CA 25-28R; CAAS 6; CANR 26;
DLB 6

Mansfield, Katherine
. . . . TCLC **2, 8, 39; SSC 9; WLC**
See also Beauchamp, Kathleen Mansfield

Manso, Peter 1940- . . . . CLC **39**
See also CA 29-32R; CANR 44

Mantecon, Juan Jimenez
See Jimenez (Mantecon), Juan Ramon

Manton, Peter
See Creasey, John

Man Without a Spleen, A
See Chekhov, Anton (Pavlovich)

Manzoni, Alessandro 1785-1873 . . NCLC **29**

Mapu, Abraham (ben Jekutiel)
1808-1867 . . . . NCLC **18**

Mara, Sally
See Queneau, Raymond

Marat, Jean Paul 1743-1793 . . . . LC **10**

Marcel, Gabriel Honore
1889-1973 . . . . CLC **15**
See also CA 102; 45-48; MTCW

Marchbanks, Samuel
See Davies, (William) Robertson

Marchi, Giacomo
See Bassani, Giorgio

Margulies, Donald . . . . CLC **76**

Marie de France c. 12th cent. - . . . . CMLC **8**

Marie de l'Incarnation 1599-1672 . . . . LC **10**

Mariner, Scott
See Pohl, Frederik

Marinetti, Filippo Tommaso
1876-1944 . . . . TCLC **10**
See also CA 107; DLB 114

Marivaux, Pierre Carlet de Chamblain de
1688-1763 .... LC 4

Markandaya, Kamala .... CLC 8, 38
See also Taylor, Kamala (Purnaiya)

Markfield, Wallace 1926- .... CLC 8
See also CA 69-72; CAAS 3; DLB 2, 28

Markham, Edwin 1852-1940 ...... TCLC 47
See also DLB 54

Markham, Robert
See Amis, Kingsley (William)

Marks, J
See Highwater, Jamake (Mamake)

Marks-Highwater, J
See Highwater, Jamake (Mamake)

Markson, David M(errill) 1927- .... CLC 67
See also CA 49-52; CANR 1

Marley, Bob .... CLC 17
See also Marley, Robert Nesta

Marley, Robert Nesta 1945-1981
See Marley, Bob
See also CA 107; 103

Marlowe, Christopher
1564-1593 ..... LC 22; DA; DC 1; WLC
See also CDBLB Before 1660; DLB 62

Marmontel, Jean-Francois
1723-1799 .... LC 2

Marquand, John P(hillips)
1893-1960 .... CLC 2, 10
See also CA 85-88; DLB 9, 102

Marquez, Gabriel (Jose) Garcia
See Garcia Marquez, Gabriel (Jose)

Marquis, Don(ald Robert Perry)
1878-1937 .... TCLC 7
See also CA 104; DLB 11, 25

Marric, J. J.
See Creasey, John

Marrow, Bernard
See Moore, Brian

Marryat, Frederick 1792-1848 .... NCLC 3
See also DLB 21

Marsden, James
See Creasey, John

Marsh, (Edith) Ngaio
1899-1982 .... CLC 7, 53
See also CA 9-12R; CANR 6; DLB 77;
MTCW

Marshall, Garry 1934- .... CLC 17
See also AAYA 3; CA 111; SATA 60

Marshall, Paule
1929- .... CLC 27, 72; BLC; SSC 3
See also BW 2; CA 77-80; CANR 25;
DLB 33; MTCW

Marsten, Richard
See Hunter, Evan

Martha, Henry
See Harris, Mark

Martial c. 40-c. 104 .... PC 10

Martin, Ken
See Hubbard, L(afayette) Ron(ald)

Martin, Richard
See Creasey, John

Martin, Steve 1945- .... CLC 30
See also CA 97-100; CANR 30; MTCW

Martin, Violet Florence
1862-1915 .... TCLC 51

Martin, Webber
See Silverberg, Robert

Martindale, Patrick Victor
See White, Patrick (Victor Martindale)

Martin du Gard, Roger
1881-1958 .... TCLC 24
See also CA 118; DLB 65

Martineau, Harriet 1802-1876.... NCLC 26
See also DLB 21, 55; YABC 2

Martines, Julia
See O'Faolain, Julia

Martinez, Jacinto Benavente y
See Benavente (y Martinez), Jacinto

Martinez Ruiz, Jose 1873-1967
See Azorin; Ruiz, Jose Martinez
See also CA 93-96; HW

Martinez Sierra, Gregorio
1881-1947 .... TCLC 6
See also CA 115

Martinez Sierra, Maria (de la O'LeJarraga)
1874-1974 .... TCLC 6
See also CA 115

Martinsen, Martin
See Follett, Ken(neth Martin)

Martinson, Harry (Edmund)
1904-1978 .... CLC 14
See also CA 77-80; CANR 34

Marut, Ret
See Traven, B.

Marut, Robert
See Traven, B.

Marvell, Andrew
1621-1678 ..... LC 4; DA; PC 10; WLC
See also CDBLB 1660-1789; DLB 131

Marx, Karl (Heinrich)
1818-1883 .... NCLC 17
See also DLB 129

Masaoka Shiki .... TCLC 18
See also Masaoka Tsunenori

Masaoka Tsunenori 1867-1902
See Masaoka Shiki
See also CA 117

Masefield, John (Edward)
1878-1967 .... CLC 11, 47
See also CA 19-20; 25-28R; CANR 33;
CAP 2; CDBLB 1890-1914; DLB 10, 19;
MTCW; SATA 19

Maso, Carole 19(?)- .... CLC 44

Mason, Bobbie Ann
1940- .... CLC 28, 43, 82; SSC 4
See also AAYA 5; CA 53-56; CANR 11,
31; DLBY 87; MTCW

Mason, Ernst
See Pohl, Frederik

Mason, Lee W.
See Malzberg, Barry N(athaniel)

Mason, Nick 1945- .... CLC 35

Mason, Tally
See Derleth, August (William)

Mass, William
See Gibson, William

Masters, Edgar Lee
1868-1950 ...... TCLC 2, 25; DA; PC 1
See also CA 104; 133; CDALB 1865-1917;
DLB 54; MTCW

Masters, Hilary 1928- .... CLC 48
See also CA 25-28R; CANR 13, 47

Mastrosimone, William 19(?)- ...... CLC 36

Mathe, Albert
See Camus, Albert

Matheson, Richard Burton 1926- ... CLC 37
See also CA 97-100; DLB 8, 44

Mathews, Harry 1930- .... CLC 6, 52
See also CA 21-24R; CAAS 6; CANR 18,
40

Mathews, John Joseph 1894-1979... CLC 84
See also CA 19-20; 142; CANR 45; CAP 2;
NNAL

Mathias, Roland (Glyn) 1915- ...... CLC 45
See also CA 97-100; CANR 19, 41; DLB 27

Matsuo Basho 1644-1694 .... PC 3

Mattheson, Rodney
See Creasey, John

Matthews, Greg 1949- .... CLC 45
See also CA 135

Matthews, William 1942- .... CLC 40
See also CA 29-32R; CAAS 18; CANR 12;
DLB 5

Matthias, John (Edward) 1941- ...... CLC 9
See also CA 33-36R

Matthiessen, Peter
1927- .... CLC 5, 7, 11, 32, 64
See also AAYA 6; BEST 90:4; CA 9-12R;
CANR 21; DLB 6; MTCW; SATA 27

Maturin, Charles Robert
1780(?)-1824 .... NCLC 6

Matute (Ausejo), Ana Maria
1925- .... CLC 11
See also CA 89-92; MTCW

Maugham, W. S.
See Maugham, W(illiam) Somerset

Maugham, W(illiam) Somerset
1874-1965 ...... CLC 1, 11, 15, 67; DA;
SSC 8; WLC
See also CA 5-8R; 25-28R; CANR 40;
CDBLB 1914-1945; DLB 10, 36, 77, 100;
MTCW; SATA 54

Maugham, William Somerset
See Maugham, W(illiam) Somerset

Maupassant, (Henri Rene Albert) Guy de
1850-1893 .... NCLC 1, 42; DA; SSC 1;
WLC
See also DLB 123

Maurhut, Richard
See Traven, B.

Mauriac, Claude 1914- .... CLC 9
See also CA 89-92; DLB 83

Mauriac, Francois (Charles)
1885-1970 .... CLC 4, 9, 56
See also CA 25-28; CAP 2; DLB 65;
MTCW

Mavor, Osborne Henry 1888-1951
See Bridie, James
See also CA 104

Maxwell, William (Keepers, Jr.)
1908- .... **CLC 19**
See also CA 93-96; DLBY 80

May, Elaine 1932- .... **CLC 16**
See also CA 124; 142; DLB 44

Mayakovski, Vladimir (Vladimirovich)
1893-1930 .... **TCLC 4, 18**
See also CA 104

Mayhew, Henry 1812-1887 ...... **NCLC 31**
See also DLB 18, 55

Maynard, Joyce 1953- .... **CLC 23**
See also CA 111; 129

Mayne, William (James Carter)
1928- .... **CLC 12**
See also CA 9-12R; CANR 37; CLR 25;
JRDA; MAICYA; SAAS 11; SATA 6, 68

Mayo, Jim
See L'Amour, Louis (Dearborn)

Maysles, Albert 1926- .... **CLC 16**
See also CA 29-32R

Maysles, David 1932- .... **CLC 16**

Mazer, Norma Fox 1931- .... **CLC 26**
See also AAYA 5; CA 69-72; CANR 12,
32; CLR 23; JRDA; MAICYA; SAAS 1;
SATA 24, 67

Mazzini, Guiseppe 1805-1872 .... **NCLC 34**

McAuley, James Phillip
1917-1976 .... **CLC 45**
See also CA 97-100

McBain, Ed
See Hunter, Evan

McBrien, William Augustine
1930- .... **CLC 44**
See also CA 107

McCaffrey, Anne (Inez) 1926- ...... **CLC 17**
See also AAYA 6; AITN 2; BEST 89:2;
CA 25-28R; CANR 15, 35; DLB 8;
JRDA; MAICYA; MTCW; SAAS 11;
SATA 8, 70

McCall, Nathan 1955(?)- .... **CLC 86**
See also CA 146

McCann, Arthur
See Campbell, John W(ood, Jr.)

McCann, Edson
See Pohl, Frederik

McCarthy, Charles, Jr. 1933-
See McCarthy, Cormac
See also CANR 42

McCarthy, Cormac 1933- ..... **CLC 4, 57, 59**
See also McCarthy, Charles, Jr.
See also DLB 6, 143

McCarthy, Mary (Therese)
1912-1989 ... **CLC 1, 3, 5, 14, 24, 39, 59**
See also CA 5-8R; 129; CANR 16; DLB 2;
DLBY 81; MTCW

McCartney, (James) Paul
1942- .... **CLC 12, 35**

McCauley, Stephen (D.) 1955- ..... **CLC 50**
See also CA 141

McClure, Michael (Thomas)
1932- .... **CLC 6, 10**
See also CA 21-24R; CANR 17, 46, 46;
DLB 16

McCorkle, Jill (Collins) 1958- ...... **CLC 51**
See also CA 121; DLBY 87

McCourt, James 1941- .... **CLC 5**
See also CA 57-60

McCoy, Horace (Stanley)
1897-1955 .... **TCLC 28**
See also CA 108; DLB 9

McCrae, John 1872-1918 .... **TCLC 12**
See also CA 109; DLB 92

McCreigh, James
See Pohl, Frederik

McCullers, (Lula) Carson (Smith)
1917-1967 .... **CLC 1, 4, 10, 12, 48; DA;
SSC 9; WLC**
See also CA 5-8R; 25-28R; CABS 1, 3;
CANR 18; CDALB 1941-1968; DLB 2, 7;
MTCW; SATA 27

McCulloch, John Tyler
See Burroughs, Edgar Rice

McCullough, Colleen 1938(?)- ...... **CLC 27**
See also CA 81-84; CANR 17, 46, 46;
MTCW

McElroy, Joseph 1930- .... **CLC 5, 47**
See also CA 17-20R

McEwan, Ian (Russell) 1948- ... **CLC 13, 66**
See also BEST 90:4; CA 61-64; CANR 14,
41; DLB 14; MTCW

McFadden, David 1940- .... **CLC 48**
See also CA 104; DLB 60

McFarland, Dennis 1950- .... **CLC 65**

McGahern, John
1934- .... **CLC 5, 9, 48; SSC 17**
See also CA 17-20R; CANR 29; DLB 14;
MTCW

McGinley, Patrick (Anthony)
1937- .... **CLC 41**
See also CA 120; 127

McGinley, Phyllis 1905-1978 ...... **CLC 14**
See also CA 9-12R; 77-80; CANR 19;
DLB 11, 48; SATA 2, 44; SATA-Obit 24

McGinniss, Joe 1942- .... **CLC 32**
See also AITN 2; BEST 89:2; CA 25-28R;
CANR 26

McGivern, Maureen Daly
See Daly, Maureen

McGrath, Patrick 1950- .... **CLC 55**
See also CA 136

McGrath, Thomas (Matthew)
1916-1990 .... **CLC 28, 59**
See also CA 9-12R; 132; CANR 6, 33;
MTCW; SATA 41; SATA-Obit 66

McGuane, Thomas (Francis III)
1939- .... **CLC 3, 7, 18, 45**
See also AITN 2; CA 49-52; CANR 5, 24;
DLB 2; DLBY 80; MTCW

McGuckian, Medbh 1950- .... **CLC 48**
See also CA 143; DLB 40

McHale, Tom 1942(?)-1982 ...... **CLC 3, 5**
See also AITN 1; CA 77-80; 106

McIlvanney, William 1936- .... **CLC 42**
See also CA 25-28R; DLB 14

McIlwraith, Maureen Mollie Hunter
See Hunter, Mollie
See also SATA 2

McInerney, Jay 1955- .... **CLC 34**
See also CA 116; 123

McIntyre, Vonda N(eel) 1948- ..... **CLC 18**
See also CA 81-84; CANR 17, 34; MTCW

McKay, Claude ..... **TCLC 7, 41; BLC; PC 2**
See also McKay, Festus Claudius
See also DLB 4, 45, 51, 117

McKay, Festus Claudius 1889-1948
See McKay, Claude
See also BW 1; CA 104; 124; DA; MTCW;
WLC

McKuen, Rod 1933- .... **CLC 1, 3**
See also AITN 1; CA 41-44R; CANR 40

McLoughlin, R. B.
See Mencken, H(enry) L(ouis)

McLuhan, (Herbert) Marshall
1911-1980 .... **CLC 37, 83**
See also CA 9-12R; 102; CANR 12, 34;
DLB 88; MTCW

McMillan, Terry (L.) 1951- ..... **CLC 50, 61**
See also BW 2; CA 140

McMurtry, Larry (Jeff)
1936- .... **CLC 2, 3, 7, 11, 27, 44**
See also AITN 2; BEST 89:2; CA 5-8R;
CANR 19, 43; CDALB 1968-1988;
DLB 2, 143; DLBY 80, 87; MTCW

McNally, T. M. 1961- .... **CLC 82**

McNally, Terrence 1939- ...... **CLC 4, 7, 41**
See also CA 45-48; CANR 2; DLB 7

McNamer, Deirdre 1950- .... **CLC 70**

McNeile, Herman Cyril 1888-1937
See Sapper
See also DLB 77

McPhee, John (Angus) 1931- ...... **CLC 36**
See also BEST 90:1; CA 65-68; CANR 20,
46, 46; MTCW

McPherson, James Alan
1943- .... **CLC 19, 77**
See also BW 1; CA 25-28R; CAAS 17;
CANR 24; DLB 38; MTCW

McPherson, William (Alexander)
1933- .... **CLC 34**
See also CA 69-72; CANR 28

Mead, Margaret 1901-1978 .... **CLC 37**
See also AITN 1; CA 1-4R; 81-84;
CANR 4; MTCW; SATA-Obit 20

Meaker, Marijane (Agnes) 1927-
See Kerr, M. E.
See also CA 107; CANR 37; JRDA;
MAICYA; MTCW; SATA 20, 61

Medoff, Mark (Howard) 1940- ... **CLC 6, 23**
See also AITN 1; CA 53-56; CANR 5;
DLB 7

Medvedev, P. N.
See Bakhtin, Mikhail Mikhailovich

Meged, Aharon
See Megged, Aharon

Meged, Aron
See Megged, Aharon

Megged, Aharon 1920- .... **CLC 9**
See also CA 49-52; CAAS 13; CANR 1

Mehta, Ved (Parkash) 1934- .... **CLC 37**
See also CA 1-4R; CANR 2, 23; MTCW

Melanter
See Blackmore, R(ichard) D(oddridge)

Melikow, Loris
See Hofmannsthal, Hugo von

Melmoth, Sebastian
See Wilde, Oscar (Fingal O'Flahertie Wills)

Meltzer, Milton 1915-............ **CLC 26**
See also AAYA 8; CA 13-16R; CANR 38;
CLR 13; DLB 61; JRDA; MAICYA;
SAAS 1; SATA 1, 50, 80

Melville, Herman
1819-1891 .... **NCLC 3, 12, 29, 45; DA;**
SSC 1, 17; WLC
See also CDALB 1640-1865; DLB 3, 74;
SATA 59

Menander
c. 342B.C.-c. 292B.C.... **CMLC 9; DC 3**

Mencken, H(enry) L(ouis)
1880-1956 .... **TCLC 13**
See also CA 105; 125; CDALB 1917-1929;
DLB 11, 29, 63, 137; MTCW

Mercer, David 1928-1980.......... **CLC 5**
See also CA 9-12R; 102; CANR 23;
DLB 13; MTCW

Merchant, Paul
See Ellison, Harlan (Jay)

Meredith, George 1828-1909 ... **TCLC 17, 43**
See also CA 117; CDBLB 1832-1890;
DLB 18, 35, 57

Meredith, William (Morris)
1919-............... **CLC 4, 13, 22, 55**
See also CA 9-12R; CAAS 14; CANR 6, 40;
DLB 5

Merezhkovsky, Dmitry Sergeyevich
1865-1941 .... **TCLC 29**

Merimee, Prosper
1803-1870 .... **NCLC 6; SSC 7**
See also DLB 119

Merkin, Daphne 1954-............ **CLC 44**
See also CA 123

Merlin, Arthur
See Blish, James (Benjamin)

Merrill, James (Ingram)
1926-........ **CLC 2, 3, 6, 8, 13, 18, 34**
See also CA 13-16R; CANR 10; DLB 5;
DLBY 85; MTCW

Merriman, Alex
See Silverberg, Robert

Merritt, E. B.
See Waddington, Miriam

Merton, Thomas
1915-1968 .. **CLC 1, 3, 11, 34, 83; PC 10**
See also CA 5-8R; 25-28R; CANR 22;
DLB 48; DLBY 81; MTCW

Merwin, W(illiam) S(tanley)
1927- ... **CLC 1, 2, 3, 5, 8, 13, 18, 45, 86**
See also CA 13-16R; CANR 15; DLB 5;
MTCW

Metcalf, John 1938-............. **CLC 37**
See also CA 113; DLB 60

Metcalf, Suzanne
See Baum, L(yman) Frank

Mew, Charlotte (Mary)
1870-1928 .... **TCLC 8**
See also CA 105; DLB 19, 135

Mewshaw, Michael 1943-.......... **CLC 9**
See also CA 53-56; CANR 7, 47; DLBY 80

Meyer, June
See Jordan, June

Meyer, Lynn
See Slavitt, David R(ytman)

Meyer-Meyrink, Gustav 1868-1932
See Meyrink, Gustav
See also CA 117

Meyers, Jeffrey 1939- .... **CLC 39**
See also CA 73-76; DLB 111

Meynell, Alice (Christina Gertrude Thompson)
1847-1922 .... **TCLC 6**
See also CA 104; DLB 19, 98

Meyrink, Gustav .... **TCLC 21**
See Meyer-Meyrink, Gustav
See also DLB 81

Michaels, Leonard
1933- .... **CLC 6, 25; SSC 16**
See also CA 61-64; CANR 21; DLB 130;
MTCW

Michaux, Henri 1899-1984 ..... **CLC 8, 19**
See also CA 85-88; 114

Michelangelo 1475-1564........... **LC 12**

Michelet, Jules 1798-1874 ...... **NCLC 31**

Michener, James A(lbert)
1907(?)-.......... **CLC 1, 5, 11, 29, 60**
See also AITN 1; BEST 90:1; CA 5-8R;
CANR 21, 45; DLB 6; MTCW

Mickiewicz, Adam 1798-1855 ..... **NCLC 3**

Middleton, Christopher 1926-...... **CLC 13**
See also CA 13-16R; CANR 29; DLB 40

Middleton, Richard (Barham)
1882-1911 .... **TCLC 56**

Middleton, Stanley 1919-...... **CLC 7, 38**
See also CA 25-28R; CANR 21, 46, 46;
DLB 14

Middleton, Thomas 1580-1627........ **DC 5**
See also DLB 58

Migueis, Jose Rodrigues 1901-..... **CLC 10**

Mikszath, Kalman 1847-1910 ..... **TCLC 31**

Miles, Josephine
1911-1985 .... **CLC 1, 2, 14, 34, 39**
See also CA 1-4R; 116; CANR 2; DLB 48

Militant
See Sandburg, Carl (August)

Mill, John Stuart 1806-1873 ..... **NCLC 11**
See also CDBLB 1832-1890; DLB 55

Millar, Kenneth 1915-1983 .... **CLC 14**
See also Macdonald, Ross
See also CA 9-12R; 110; CANR 16; DLB 2;
DLBD 6; DLBY 83; MTCW

Millay, E. Vincent
See Millay, Edna St. Vincent

Millay, Edna St. Vincent
1892-1950 ...... **TCLC 4, 49; DA; PC 6**
See also CA 104; 130; CDALB 1917-1929;
DLB 45; MTCW

Miller, Arthur
1915- .... **CLC 1, 2, 6, 10, 15, 26, 47, 78;**
DA; DC 1; WLC
See also AITN 1; CA 1-4R; CABS 3;
CANR 2, 30; CDALB 1941-1968; DLB 7;
MTCW

Miller, Henry (Valentine)
1891-1980 .... **CLC 1, 2, 4, 9, 14, 43, 84;**
DA; WLC
See also CA 9-12R; 97-100; CANR 33;
CDALB 1929-1941; DLB 4, 9; DLBY 80;
MTCW

Miller, Jason 1939(?)- .... **CLC 2**
See also AITN 1; CA 73-76; DLB 7

Miller, Sue 1943-................. **CLC 44**
See also BEST 90:3; CA 139; DLB 143

Miller, Walter M(ichael, Jr.)
1923- .... **CLC 4, 30**
See also CA 85-88; DLB 8

Millett, Kate 1934-............... **CLC 67**
See also AITN 1; CA 73-76; CANR 32;
MTCW

Millhauser, Steven 1943-....... **CLC 21, 54**
See also CA 110; 111; DLB 2

Millin, Sarah Gertrude 1889-1968 .. **CLC 49**
See also CA 102; 93-96

Milne, A(lan) A(lexander)
1882-1956 .... **TCLC 6**
See also CA 104; 133; CLR 1, 26; DLB 10,
77, 100; MAICYA; MTCW; YABC 1

Milner, Ron(ald) 1938-....... **CLC 56; BLC**
See also AITN 1; BW 1; CA 73-76;
CANR 24; DLB 38; MTCW

Milosz, Czeslaw
1911- ... **CLC 5, 11, 22, 31, 56, 82; PC 8**
See also CA 81-84; CANR 23; MTCW

Milton, John 1608-1674... **LC 9; DA; WLC**
See also CDBLB 1660-1789; DLB 131

Min, Anchee 1957-............... **CLC 86**

Minehaha, Cornelius
See Wedekind, (Benjamin) Frank(lin)

Miner, Valerie 1947- .... **CLC 40**
See also CA 97-100

Minimo, Duca
See D'Annunzio, Gabriele

Minot, Susan 1956- .... **CLC 44**
See also CA 134

Minus, Ed 1938-................. **CLC 39**

Miranda, Javier
See Bioy Casares, Adolfo

Mirbeau, Octave 1848-1917....... **TCLC 55**
See also DLB 123

Miro (Ferrer), Gabriel (Francisco Victor)
1879-1930 .... **TCLC 5**
See also CA 104

Mishima, Yukio
...... **CLC 2, 4, 6, 9, 27; DC 1; SSC 4**
See also Hiraoka, Kimitake

Mistral, Frederic 1830-1914 ...... **TCLC 51**
See also CA 122

Mistral, Gabriela........... **TCLC 2; HLC**
See also Godoy Alcayaga, Lucila

Mistry, Rohinton 1952-.......... **CLC 71**
See also CA 141

Mitchell, Clyde
See Ellison, Harlan (Jay); Silverberg, Robert

Mitchell, James Leslie 1901-1935
See Gibbon, Lewis Grassic
See also CA 104; DLB 15

Mitchell, Joni 1943-. . . . . CLC 12
See also CA 112

Mitchell, Margaret (Munnerlyn)
1900-1949 . . . . TCLC 11
See also CA 109; 125; DLB 9; MTCW

Mitchell, Peggy
See Mitchell, Margaret (Munnerlyn)

Mitchell, S(ilas) Weir 1829-1914 . . TCLC 36

Mitchell, W(illiam) O(rmond)
1914- . . . . CLC 25
See also CA 77-80; CANR 15, 43; DLB 88

Mitford, Mary Russell 1787-1855. . NCLC 4
See also DLB 110, 116

Mitford, Nancy 1904-1973. . . . . CLC 44
See also CA 9-12R

Miyamoto, Yuriko 1899-1951 . . . . . TCLC 37

Mo, Timothy (Peter) 1950(?)- . . . . . . CLC 46
See also CA 117; MTCW

Modarressi, Taghi (M.) 1931- . . . . . . CLC 44
See also CA 121; 134

Modiano, Patrick (Jean) 1945- . . . . . CLC 18
See also CA 85-88; CANR 17, 40; DLB 83

Moerck, Paal
See Roelvaag, O(le) E(dvart)

Mofolo, Thomas (Mokopu)
1875(?)-1948 . . . . TCLC 22; BLC
See also CA 121

Mohr, Nicholasa 1935- . . . . . . CLC 12; HLC
See also AAYA 8; CA 49-52; CANR 1, 32;
CLR 22; DLB 145; HW; JRDA; SAAS 8;
SATA 8

Mojtabai, A(nn) G(race)
1938- . . . . CLC 5, 9, 15, 29
See also CA 85-88

Moliere 1622-1673 . . . . LC 10; DA; WLC

Molin, Charles
See Mayne, William (James Carter)

Molnar, Ferenc 1878-1952. . . . . . . TCLC 20
See also CA 109

Momaday, N(avarre) Scott
1934- . . . . CLC 2, 19, 85; DA
See also AAYA 11; CA 25-28R; CANR 14,
34; DLB 143; MTCW; NNAL; SATA 30,
48

Monette, Paul 1945-. . . . . CLC 82
See also CA 139

Monroe, Harriet 1860-1936. . . . . . . TCLC 12
See also CA 109; DLB 54, 91

Monroe, Lyle
See Heinlein, Robert A(nson)

Montagu, Elizabeth 1917- . . . . NCLC 7
See also CA 9-12R

Montagu, Mary (Pierrepont) Wortley
1689-1762 . . . . LC 9
See also DLB 95, 101

Montagu, W. H.
See Coleridge, Samuel Taylor

Montague, John (Patrick)
1929- . . . . CLC 13, 46
See also CA 9-12R; CANR 9; DLB 40;
MTCW

Montaigne, Michel (Eyquem) de
1533-1592 . . . . LC 8; DA; WLC

Montale, Eugenio 1896-1981 . . . CLC 7, 9, 18
See also CA 17-20R; 104; CANR 30;
DLB 114; MTCW

Montesquieu, Charles-Louis de Secondat
1689-1755 . . . . LC 7

Montgomery, (Robert) Bruce 1921-1978
See Crispin, Edmund
See also CA 104

Montgomery, L(ucy) M(aud)
1874-1942 . . . . TCLC 51
See also AAYA 12; CA 108; 137; CLR 8;
DLB 92; JRDA; MAICYA; YABC 1

Montgomery, Marion H., Jr. 1925- . . CLC 7
See also AITN 1; CA 1-4R; CANR 3;
DLB 6

Montgomery, Max
See Davenport, Guy (Mattison, Jr.)

Montherlant, Henry (Milon) de
1896-1972 . . . . CLC 8, 19
See also CA 85-88; 37-40R; DLB 72;
MTCW

Monty Python
See Chapman, Graham; Cleese, John
(Marwood); Gilliam, Terry (Vance); Idle,
Eric; Jones, Terence Graham Parry; Palin,
Michael (Edward)
See also AAYA 7

Moodie, Susanna (Strickland)
1803-1885 . . . . NCLC 14
See also DLB 99

Mooney, Edward 1951-
See Mooney, Ted
See also CA 130

Mooney, Ted . . . . CLC 25
See also Mooney, Edward

Moorcock, Michael (John)
1939- . . . . CLC 5, 27, 58
See also CA 45-48; CAAS 5; CANR 2, 17,
38; DLB 14; MTCW

Moore, Brian
1921- . . . . CLC 1, 3, 5, 7, 8, 19, 32
See also CA 1-4R; CANR 1, 25, 42; MTCW

Moore, Edward
See Muir, Edwin

Moore, George Augustus
1852-1933 . . . . TCLC 7
See also CA 104; DLB 10, 18, 57, 135

Moore, Lorrie . . . . CLC 39, 45, 68
See also Moore, Marie Lorena

Moore, Marianne (Craig)
1887-1972 . . . . CLC 1, 2, 4, 8, 10, 13, 19,
47; DA; PC 4
See also CA 1-4R; 33-36R; CANR 3;
CDALB 1929-1941; DLB 45; DLBD 7;
MTCW; SATA 20

Moore, Marie Lorena 1957-
See Moore, Lorrie
See also CA 116; CANR 39

Moore, Thomas 1779-1852. . . . . NCLC 6
See also DLB 96, 144

Morand, Paul 1888-1976 . . . . CLC 41
See also CA 69-72; DLB 65

Morante, Elsa 1918-1985. . . . . CLC 8, 47
See also CA 85-88; 117; CANR 35; MTCW

Moravia, Alberto. . . . . . . CLC 2, 7, 11, 27, 46
See also Pincherle, Alberto

More, Hannah 1745-1833 . . . . NCLC 27
See also DLB 107, 109, 116

More, Henry 1614-1687. . . . . LC 9
See also DLB 126

More, Sir Thomas 1478-1535 . . . . LC 10

Moreas, Jean. . . . . TCLC 18
See also Papadiamantopoulos, Johannes

Morgan, Berry 1919- . . . . CLC 6
See also CA 49-52; DLB 6

Morgan, Claire
See Highsmith, (Mary) Patricia

Morgan, Edwin (George) 1920-. . . . . CLC 31
See also CA 5-8R; CANR 3, 43; DLB 27

Morgan, (George) Frederick
1922- . . . . CLC 23
See also CA 17-20R; CANR 21

Morgan, Harriet
See Mencken, H(enry) L(ouis)

Morgan, Jane
See Cooper, James Fenimore

Morgan, Janet 1945- . . . . CLC 39
See also CA 65-68

Morgan, Lady 1776(?)-1859. . . . . . NCLC 29
See also DLB 116

Morgan, Robin 1941-. . . . . CLC 2
See also CA 69-72; CANR 29; MTCW;
SATA 80

Morgan, Scott
See Kuttner, Henry

Morgan, Seth 1949(?)-1990 . . . . CLC 65
See also CA 132

Morgenstern, Christian
1871-1914 . . . . TCLC 8
See also CA 105

Morgenstern, S.
See Goldman, William (W.)

Moricz, Zsigmond 1879-1942 . . . . . TCLC 33

Morike, Eduard (Friedrich)
1804-1875 . . . . NCLC 10
See also DLB 133

Mori Ogai . . . . TCLC 14
See also Mori Rintaro

Mori Rintaro 1862-1922
See Mori Ogai
See also CA 110

Moritz, Karl Philipp 1756-1793 . . . . . . LC 2
See also DLB 94

Morland, Peter Henry
See Faust, Frederick (Schiller)

Morren, Theophil
See Hofmannsthal, Hugo von

Morris, Bill 1952-. . . . . CLC 76

Morris, Julian
See West, Morris L(anglo)

Morris, Steveland Judkins 1950(?)-
See Wonder, Stevie
See also CA 111

Morris, William 1834-1896 . . . . NCLC 4
See also CDBLB 1832-1890; DLB 18, 35, 57

Morris, Wright 1910-... **CLC 1, 3, 7, 18, 37**
See also CA 9-12R; CANR 21; DLB 2;
DLBY 81; MTCW

Morrison, Chloe Anthony Wofford
See Morrison, Toni

Morrison, James Douglas 1943-1971
See Morrison, Jim
See also CA 73-76; CANR 40

Morrison, Jim................... **CLC 17**
See also Morrison, James Douglas

Morrison, Toni
1931-.. **CLC 4, 10, 22, 55, 81; BLC; DA**
See also AAYA 1; BW 2; CA 29-32R;
CANR 27, 42; CDALB 1968-1988;
DLB 6, 33, 143; DLBY 81; MTCW;
SATA 57

Morrison, Van 1945-............. **CLC 21**
See also CA 116

Mortimer, John (Clifford)
1923-.................... **CLC 28, 43**
See also CA 13-16R; CANR 21;
CDBLB 1960 to Present; DLB 13;
MTCW

Mortimer, Penelope (Ruth) 1918-.... **CLC 5**
See also CA 57-60; CANR 45

Morton, Anthony
See Creasey, John

Mosher, Howard Frank 1943-...... **CLC 62**
See also CA 139

Mosley, Nicholas 1923-........ **CLC 43, 70**
See also CA 69-72; CANR 41; DLB 14

Moss, Howard
1922-1987 .... **CLC 7, 14, 45, 50**
See also CA 1-4R; 123; CANR 1, 44;
DLB 5

Mossgiel, Rab
See Burns, Robert

Motion, Andrew 1952-............. **CLC 47**
See also DLB 40

Motley, Willard (Francis)
1909-1965 .... **CLC 18**
See also BW 1; CA 117; 106; DLB 76, 143

Motoori, Norinaga 1730-1801 .... **NCLC 45**

Mott, Michael (Charles Alston)
1930-.................... **CLC 15, 34**
See also CA 5-8R; CAAS 7; CANR 7, 29

Mowat, Farley (McGill) 1921- ..... **CLC 26**
See also AAYA 1; CA 1-4R; CANR 4, 24,
42; CLR 20; DLB 68; JRDA; MAICYA;
MTCW; SATA 3, 55

Moyers, Bill 1934-................ **CLC 74**
See also AITN 2; CA 61-64; CANR 31

Mphahlele, Es'kia
See Mphahlele, Ezekiel
See also DLB 125

Mphahlele, Ezekiel 1919-..... **CLC 25; BLC**
See also Mphahlele, Es'kia
See also BW 2; CA 81-84; CANR 26

Mqhayi, S(amuel) E(dward) K(rune Loliwe)
1875-1945 .... **TCLC 25; BLC**

Mr. Martin
See Burroughs, William S(eward)

Mrozek, Slawomir 1930-........ **CLC 3, 13**
See also CA 13-16R; CAAS 10; CANR 29;
MTCW

Mrs. Belloc-Lowndes
See Lowndes, Marie Adelaide (Belloc)

Mtwa, Percy (?)-................. **CLC 47**

Mueller, Lisel 1924-........... **CLC 13, 51**
See also CA 93-96; DLB 105

Muir, Edwin 1887-1959 .... **TCLC 2**
See also CA 104; DLB 20, 100

Muir, John 1838-1914 .... **TCLC 28**

Mujica Lainez, Manuel
1910-1984 .... **CLC 31**
See also Lainez, Manuel Mujica
See also CA 81-84; 112; CANR 32; HW

Mukherjee, Bharati 1940-......... **CLC 53**
See also BEST 89:2; CA 107; CANR 45;
DLB 60; MTCW

Muldoon, Paul 1951-.......... **CLC 32, 72**
See also CA 113; 129; DLB 40

Mulisch, Harry 1927-............. **CLC 42**
See also CA 9-12R; CANR 6, 26

Mull, Martin 1943-.............. **CLC 17**
See also CA 105

Mulock, Dinah Maria
See Craik, Dinah Maria (Mulock)

Munford, Robert 1737(?)-1783 .... **LC 5**
See also DLB 31

Mungo, Raymond 1946-........... **CLC 72**
See also CA 49-52; CANR 2

Munro, Alice
1931-........ **CLC 6, 10, 19, 50; SSC 3**
See also AITN 2; CA 33-36R; CANR 33;
DLB 53; MTCW; SATA 29

Munro, H(ector) H(ugh) 1870-1916
See Saki
See also CA 104; 130; CDBLB 1890-1914;
DA; DLB 34; MTCW; WLC

Murasaki, Lady................. **CMLC 1**

Murdoch, (Jean) Iris
1919- ...... **CLC 1, 2, 3, 4, 6, 8, 11, 15,**
22, 31, 51
See also CA 13-16R; CANR 8, 43;
CDBLB 1960 to Present; DLB 14;
MTCW

Murnau, Friedrich Wilhelm
See Plumpe, Friedrich Wilhelm

Murphy, Richard 1927-........... **CLC 41**
See also CA 29-32R; DLB 40

Murphy, Sylvia 1937-............. **CLC 34**
See also CA 121

Murphy, Thomas (Bernard) 1935-... **CLC 51**
See also CA 101

Murray, Albert L. 1916-........... **CLC 73**
See also BW 2; CA 49-52; CANR 26;
DLB 38

Murray, Les(lie) A(llan) 1938- ..... **CLC 40**
See also CA 21-24R; CANR 11, 27

Murry, J. Middleton
See Murry, John Middleton

Murry, John Middleton
1889-1957 .... **TCLC 16**
See also CA 118

Musgrave, Susan 1951- .... **CLC 13, 54**
See also CA 69-72; CANR 45

Musil, Robert (Edler von)
1880-1942 .... **TCLC 12; SSC 18**
See also CA 109; DLB 81, 124

Musset, (Louis Charles) Alfred de
1810-1857 .... **NCLC 7**

My Brother's Brother
See Chekhov, Anton (Pavlovich)

Myers, Walter Dean 1937- ... **CLC 35; BLC**
See also AAYA 4; BW 2; CA 33-36R;
CANR 20, 42; CLR 4, 16, 35; DLB 33;
JRDA; MAICYA; SAAS 2; SATA 27, 41,
71

Myers, Walter M.
See Myers, Walter Dean

Myles, Symon
See Follett, Ken(neth Martin)

Nabokov, Vladimir (Vladimirovich)
1899-1977 ..... **CLC 1, 2, 3, 6, 8, 11, 15,**
23, 44, 46, 64; DA; SSC 11; WLC
See also CA 5-8R; 69-72; CANR 20;
CDALB 1941-1968; DLB 2; DLBD 3;
DLBY 80, 91; MTCW

Nagai Kafu...................... **TCLC 51**
See also Nagai Sokichi

Nagai Sokichi 1879-1959
See Nagai Kafu
See also CA 117

Nagy, Laszlo 1925-1978............ **CLC 7**
See also CA 129; 112

Naipaul, Shiva(dhar Srinivasa)
1945-1985 .... **CLC 32, 39**
See also CA 110; 112; 116; CANR 33;
DLBY 85; MTCW

Naipaul, V(idiadhar) S(urajprasad)
1932-.......... **CLC 4, 7, 9, 13, 18, 37**
See also CA 1-4R; CANR 1, 33;
CDBLB 1960 to Present; DLB 125;
DLBY 85; MTCW

Nakos, Lilika 1899(?)-............ **CLC 29**

Narayan, R(asipuram) K(rishnaswami)
1906-................... **CLC 7, 28, 47**
See also CA 81-84; CANR 33; MTCW;
SATA 62

Nash, (Fredric) Ogden 1902-1971 .. **CLC 23**
See also CA 13-14; 29-32R; CANR 34;
CAP 1; DLB 11; MAICYA; MTCW;
SATA 2, 46

Nathan, Daniel
See Dannay, Frederic

Nathan, George Jean 1882-1958 ... **TCLC 18**
See also Hatteras, Owen
See also CA 114; DLB 137

Natsume, Kinnosuke 1867-1916
See Natsume, Soseki
See also CA 104

Natsume, Soseki .... **TCLC 2, 10**
See also Natsume, Kinnosuke

Natti, (Mary) Lee 1919-
See Kingman, Lee
See also CA 5-8R; CANR 2

Naylor, Gloria 1950-........ **CLC 28, 52; BLC; DA**
See also AAYA 6; BW 2; CA 107;
CANR 27; MTCW

Neihardt, John Gneisenau
1881-1973 .... CLC 32
See also CA 13-14; CAP 1; DLB 9, 54

Nekrasov, Nikolai Alekseevich
1821-1878 .... NCLC 11

Nelligan, Emile 1879-1941 .... TCLC 14
See also CA 114; DLB 92

Nelson, Willie 1933- .... CLC 17
See also CA 107

Nemerov, Howard (Stanley)
1920-1991 .... CLC 2, 6, 9, 36
See also CA 1-4R; 134; CABS 2; CANR 1,
27; DLB 6; DLBY 83; MTCW

Neruda, Pablo
1904-1973 ..... CLC 1, 2, 5, 7, 9, 28, 62;
DA; HLC; PC 4; WLC
See also CA 19-20; 45-48; CAP 2; HW;
MTCW

Nerval, Gerard de
1808-1855 .... NCLC 1; SSC 18

Nervo, (Jose) Amado (Ruiz de)
1870-1919 .... TCLC 11
See also CA 109; 131; HW

Nessi, Pio Baroja y
See Baroja (y Nessi), Pio

Nestroy, Johann 1801-1862 ...... NCLC 42
See also DLB 133

Neufeld, John (Arthur) 1938- ...... CLC 17
See also AAYA 11; CA 25-28R; CANR 11,
37; MAICYA; SAAS 3; SATA 6, 81

Neville, Emily Cheney 1919- .... CLC 12
See also CA 5-8R; CANR 3, 37; JRDA;
MAICYA; SAAS 2; SATA 1

Newbound, Bernard Slade 1930-
See Slade, Bernard
See also CA 81-84

Newby, P(ercy) H(oward)
1918- .... CLC 2, 13
See also CA 5-8R; CANR 32; DLB 15;
MTCW

Newlove, Donald 1928- .... CLC 6
See also CA 29-32R; CANR 25

Newlove, John (Herbert) 1938- ..... CLC 14
See also CA 21-24R; CANR 9, 25

Newman, Charles 1938- .... CLC 2, 8
See also CA 21-24R

Newman, Edwin (Harold) 1919- .... CLC 14
See also AITN 1; CA 69-72; CANR 5

Newman, John Henry
1801-1890 .... NCLC 38
See also DLB 18, 32, 55

Newton, Suzanne 1936- .... CLC 35
See also CA 41-44R; CANR 14; JRDA;
SATA 5, 77

Nexo, Martin Andersen
1869-1954 .... TCLC 43

Nezval, Vitezslav 1900-1958 ...... TCLC 44
See also CA 123

Ng, Fae Myenne 1957(?)- .... CLC 81

Ngema, Mbongeni 1955- .... CLC 57
See also BW 2; CA 143

Ngugi, James T(hiong'o) .... CLC 3, 7, 13
See also Ngugi wa Thiong'o

Ngugi wa Thiong'o 1938- ..... CLC 36; BLC
See also Ngugi, James T(hiong'o)
See also BW 2; CA 81-84; CANR 27;
DLB 125; MTCW

Nichol, B(arrie) P(hillip)
1944-1988 .... CLC 18
See also CA 53-56; DLB 53; SATA 66

Nichols, John (Treadwell) 1940- .... CLC 38
See also CA 9-12R; CAAS 2; CANR 6;
DLBY 82

Nichols, Leigh
See Koontz, Dean R(ay)

Nichols, Peter (Richard)
1927- .... CLC 5, 36, 65
See also CA 104; CANR 33; DLB 13;
MTCW

Nicolas, F. R. E.
See Freeling, Nicolas

Niedecker, Lorine 1903-1970 .... CLC 10, 42
See also CA 25-28; CAP 2; DLB 48

Nietzsche, Friedrich (Wilhelm)
1844-1900 .... TCLC 10, 18, 55
See also CA 107; 121; DLB 129

Nievo, Ippolito 1831-1861 .... NCLC 22

Nightingale, Anne Redmon 1943-
See Redmon, Anne
See also CA 103

Nik. T. O.
See Annensky, Innokenty Fyodorovich

Nin, Anais
1903-1977 ...... CLC 1, 4, 8, 11, 14, 60;
SSC 10
See also AITN 2; CA 13-16R; 69-72;
CANR 22; DLB 2, 4; MTCW

Nissenson, Hugh 1933- .... CLC 4, 9
See also CA 17-20R; CANR 27; DLB 28

Niven, Larry .... CLC 8
See also Niven, Laurence Van Cott
See also DLB 8

Niven, Laurence Van Cott 1938-
See Niven, Larry
See also CA 21-24R; CAAS 12; CANR 14,
44; MTCW

Nixon, Agnes Eckhardt 1927- ...... CLC 21
See also CA 110

Nizan, Paul 1905-1940 .... TCLC 40
See also DLB 72

Nkosi, Lewis 1936- .... CLC 45; BLC
See also BW 1; CA 65-68; CANR 27

Nodier, (Jean) Charles (Emmanuel)
1780-1844 .... NCLC 19
See also DLB 119

Nolan, Christopher 1965- .... CLC 58
See also CA 111

Norden, Charles
See Durrell, Lawrence (George)

Nordhoff, Charles (Bernard)
1887-1947 .... TCLC 23
See also CA 108; DLB 9; SATA 23

Norfolk, Lawrence 1963- .... CLC 76
See also CA 144

Norman, Marsha 1947- .... CLC 28
See also CA 105; CABS 3; CANR 41;
DLBY 84

Norris, Benjamin Franklin, Jr.
1870-1902 .... TCLC 24
See also Norris, Frank
See also CA 110

Norris, Frank
See Norris, Benjamin Franklin, Jr.
See also CDALB 1865-1917; DLB 12, 71

Norris, Leslie 1921- .... CLC 14
See also CA 11-12; CANR 14; CAP 1;
DLB 27

North, Andrew
See Norton, Andre

North, Anthony
See Koontz, Dean R(ay)

North, Captain George
See Stevenson, Robert Louis (Balfour)

North, Milou
See Erdrich, Louise

Northrup, B. A.
See Hubbard, L(afayette) Ron(ald)

North Staffs
See Hulme, T(homas) E(rnest)

Norton, Alice Mary
See Norton, Andre
See also MAICYA; SATA 1, 43

Norton, Andre 1912- .... CLC 12
See also Norton, Alice Mary
See also AAYA 14; CA 1-4R; CANR 2, 31;
DLB 8, 52; JRDA; MTCW

Norton, Caroline 1808-1877 ...... NCLC 47
See also DLB 21

Norway, Nevil Shute 1899-1960
See Shute, Nevil
See also CA 102; 93-96

Norwid, Cyprian Kamil
1821-1883 .... NCLC 17

Nosille, Nabrah
See Ellison, Harlan (Jay)

Nossack, Hans Erich 1901-1978 ..... CLC 6
See also CA 93-96; 85-88; DLB 69

Nostradamus 1503-1566 .... LC 27

Nosu, Chuji
See Ozu, Yasujiro

Notenburg, Eleanora (Genrikhovna) von
See Guro, Elena

Nova, Craig 1945- .... CLC 7, 31
See also CA 45-48; CANR 2

Novak, Joseph
See Kosinski, Jerzy (Nikodem)

Novalis 1772-1801 .... NCLC 13
See also DLB 90

Nowlan, Alden (Albert) 1933-1983 .. CLC 15
See also CA 9-12R; CANR 5; DLB 53

Noyes, Alfred 1880-1958 .... TCLC 7
See also CA 104; DLB 20

Nunn, Kem 19(?)- .... CLC 34

Nye, Robert 1939- .... CLC 13, 42
See also CA 33-36R; CANR 29; DLB 14;
MTCW; SATA 6

Nyro, Laura 1947- .... CLC 17

Author Index

Oates, Joyce Carol
1938- ...... **CLC 1, 2, 3, 6, 9, 11, 15, 19, 33, 52; DA; SSC 6; WLC**
See also AITN 1; BEST 89:2; CA 5-8R; CANR 25, 45; CDALB 1968-1988; DLB 2, 5, 130; DLBY 81; MTCW

O'Brien, Darcy 1939- .... **CLC 11**
See also CA 21-24R; CANR 8

O'Brien, E. G.
See Clarke, Arthur C(harles)

O'Brien, Edna
1936- ... **CLC 3, 5, 8, 13, 36, 65; SSC 10**
See also CA 1-4R; CANR 6, 41; CDBLB 1960 to Present; DLB 14; MTCW

O'Brien, Fitz-James 1828-1862... **NCLC 21**
See also DLB 74

O'Brien, Flann .... **CLC 1, 4, 5, 7, 10, 47**
See also O Nuallain, Brian

O'Brien, Richard 1942- .... **CLC 17**
See also CA 124

O'Brien, Tim 1946- .... **CLC 7, 19, 40**
See also CA 85-88; CANR 40; DLBD 9; DLBY 80

Obstfelder, Sigbjoern 1866-1900... **TCLC 23**
See also CA 123

O'Casey, Sean
1880-1964 .... **CLC 1, 5, 9, 11, 15**
See also CA 89-92; CDBLB 1914-1945; DLB 10; MTCW

O'Cathasaigh, Sean
See O'Casey, Sean

Ochs, Phil 1940-1976............. **CLC 17**
See also CA 65-68

O'Connor, Edwin (Greene)
1918-1968 .... **CLC 14**
See also CA 93-96; 25-28R

O'Connor, (Mary) Flannery
1925-1964 .... **CLC 1, 2, 3, 6, 10, 13, 15, 21, 66; DA; SSC 1; WLC**
See also AAYA 7; CA 1-4R; CANR 3, 41; CDALB 1941-1968; DLB 2; DLBD 12; DLBY 80; MTCW

O'Connor, Frank .... **CLC 23; SSC 5**
See also O'Donovan, Michael John

O'Dell, Scott 1898-1989........... **CLC 30**
See also AAYA 3; CA 61-64; 129; CANR 12, 30; CLR 1, 16; DLB 52; JRDA; MAICYA; SATA 12, 60

Odets, Clifford 1906-1963 .... **CLC 2, 28**
See also CA 85-88; DLB 7, 26; MTCW

O'Doherty, Brian 1934-........... **CLC 76**
See also CA 105

O'Donnell, K. M.
See Malzberg, Barry N(athaniel)

O'Donnell, Lawrence
See Kuttner, Henry

O'Donovan, Michael John
1903-1966 .... **CLC 14**
See also O'Connor, Frank
See also CA 93-96

Oe, Kenzaburo 1935- .... **CLC 10, 36, 86**
See also CA 97-100; CANR 36; MTCW

O'Faolain, Julia 1932- .... **CLC 6, 19, 47**
See also CA 81-84; CAAS 2; CANR 12; DLB 14; MTCW

O'Faolain, Sean
1900-1991 .... **CLC 1, 7, 14, 32, 70; SSC 13**
See also CA 61-64; 134; CANR 12; DLB 15; MTCW

O'Flaherty, Liam
1896-1984 .... **CLC 5, 34; SSC 6**
See also CA 101; 113; CANR 35; DLB 36; DLBY 84; MTCW

Ogilvy, Gavin
See Barrie, J(ames) M(atthew)

O'Grady, Standish James
1846-1928 .... **TCLC 5**
See also CA 104

O'Grady, Timothy 1951- .... **CLC 59**
See also CA 138

O'Hara, Frank
1926-1966 .... **CLC 2, 5, 13, 78**
See also CA 9-12R; 25-28R; CANR 33; DLB 5, 16; MTCW

O'Hara, John (Henry)
1905-1970 .... **CLC 1, 2, 3, 6, 11, 42; SSC 15**
See also CA 5-8R; 25-28R; CANR 31; CDALB 1929-1941; DLB 9, 86; DLBD 2; MTCW

O Hehir, Diana 1922- .... **CLC 41**
See also CA 93-96

Okigbo, Christopher (Ifenayichukwu)
1932-1967 ..... **CLC 25, 84; BLC; PC 7**
See also BW 1; CA 77-80; DLB 125; MTCW

Olds, Sharon 1942-........ **CLC 32, 39, 85**
See also CA 101; CANR 18, 41; DLB 120

Oldstyle, Jonathan
See Irving, Washington

Olesha, Yuri (Karlovich)
1899-1960 .... **CLC 8**
See also CA 85-88

Oliphant, Laurence
1829(?)-1888 .... **NCLC 47**
See also DLB 18

Oliphant, Margaret (Oliphant Wilson)
1828-1897 .... **NCLC 11**
See also DLB 18

Oliver, Mary 1935-............. **CLC 19, 34**
See also CA 21-24R; CANR 9, 43; DLB 5

Olivier, Laurence (Kerr)
1907-1989 .... **CLC 20**
See also CA 111; 129

Olsen, Tillie
1913- .... **CLC 4, 13; DA; SSC 11**
See also CA 1-4R; CANR 1, 43; DLB 28; DLBY 80; MTCW

Olson, Charles (John)
1910-1970 ..... **CLC 1, 2, 5, 6, 9, 11, 29**
See also CA 13-16; 25-28R; CABS 2; CANR 35; CAP 1; DLB 5, 16; MTCW

Olson, Toby 1937- .... **CLC 28**
See also CA 65-68; CANR 9, 31

Olyesha, Yuri
See Olesha, Yuri (Karlovich)

Ondaatje, (Philip) Michael
1943- .... **CLC 14, 29, 51, 76**
See also CA 77-80; CANR 42; DLB 60

Oneal, Elizabeth 1934-
See Oneal, Zibby
See also CA 106; CANR 28; MAICYA; SATA 30

Oneal, Zibby .... **CLC 30**
See also Oneal, Elizabeth
See also AAYA 5; CLR 13; JRDA

O'Neill, Eugene (Gladstone)
1888-1953 ...... **TCLC 1, 6, 27, 49; DA; WLC**
See also AITN 1; CA 110; 132; CDALB 1929-1941; DLB 7; MTCW

Onetti, Juan Carlos 1909-1994 ... **CLC 7, 10**
See also CA 85-88; 145; CANR 32; DLB 113; HW; MTCW

O Nuallain, Brian 1911-1966
See O'Brien, Flann
See also CA 21-22; 25-28R; CAP 2

Oppen, George 1908-1984 .... **CLC 7, 13, 34**
See also CA 13-16R; 113; CANR 8; DLB 5

Oppenheim, E(dward) Phillips
1866-1946 .... **TCLC 45**
See also CA 111; DLB 70

Orlovitz, Gil 1918-1973 .... **CLC 22**
See also CA 77-80; 45-48; DLB 2, 5

Orris
See Ingelow, Jean

Ortega y Gasset, Jose
1883-1955 .... **TCLC 9; HLC**
See also CA 106; 130; HW; MTCW

Ortiz, Simon J(oseph) 1941-....... **CLC 45**
See also CA 134; DLB 120; NNAL

Orton, Joe .... **CLC 4, 13, 43; DC 3**
See also Orton, John Kingsley
See also CDBLB 1960 to Present; DLB 13

Orton, John Kingsley 1933-1967
See Orton, Joe
See also CA 85-88; CANR 35; MTCW

Orwell, George
.... **TCLC 2, 6, 15, 31, 51; WLC**
See also Blair, Eric (Arthur)
See also CDBLB 1945-1960; DLB 15, 98

Osborne, David
See Silverberg, Robert

Osborne, George
See Silverberg, Robert

Osborne, John (James)
1929- .... **CLC 1, 2, 5, 11, 45; DA; WLC**
See also CA 13-16R; CANR 21; CDBLB 1945-1960; DLB 13; MTCW

Osborne, Lawrence 1958- .... **CLC 50**

Oshima, Nagisa 1932- .... **CLC 20**
See also CA 116; 121

Oskison, John Milton
1874-1947 .... **TCLC 35**
See also CA 144; NNAL

Ossoli, Sarah Margaret (Fuller marchesa d')
1810-1850
See Fuller, Margaret
See also SATA 25

Ostrovsky, Alexander
1823-1886 .... **NCLC 30**

Otero, Blas de 1916-1979......... **CLC 11**
See also CA 89-92; DLB 134

Otto, Whitney 1955-.............. **CLC 70**
See also CA 140

Ouida........................ **TCLC 43**
See also De La Ramee, (Marie) Louise
See also DLB 18

Ousmane, Sembene 1923- .... **CLC 66; BLC**
See also BW 1; CA 117; 125; MTCW

Ovid 43B.C.-18(?).......... **CMLC 7; PC 2**

Owen, Hugh
See Faust, Frederick (Schiller)

Owen, Wilfred (Edward Salter)
1893-1918 ...... **TCLC 5, 27; DA; WLC**
See also CA 104; 141; CDBLB 1914-1945;
DLB 20

Owens, Rochelle 1936-.............. **CLC 8**
See also CA 17-20R; CAAS 2; CANR 39

Oz, Amos 1939- ... **CLC 5, 8, 11, 27, 33, 54**
See also CA 53-56; CANR 27, 47; MTCW

Ozick, Cynthia
1928- .... **CLC 3, 7, 28, 62; SSC 15**
See also BEST 90:1; CA 17-20R; CANR 23;
DLB 28; DLBY 82; MTCW

Ozu, Yasujiro 1903-1963 .... **CLC 16**
See also CA 112

Pacheco, C.
See Pessoa, Fernando (Antonio Nogueira)

Pa Chin .... **CLC 18**
See also Li Fei-kan

Pack, Robert 1929-................ **CLC 13**
See also CA 1-4R; CANR 3, 44; DLB 5

Padgett, Lewis
See Kuttner, Henry

Padilla (Lorenzo), Heberto 1932-... **CLC 38**
See also AITN 1; CA 123; 131; HW

Page, Jimmy 1944-................ **CLC 12**

Page, Louise 1955-................ **CLC 40**
See also CA 140

Page, P(atricia) K(athleen)
1916- .... **CLC 7, 18**
See also CA 53-56; CANR 4, 22; DLB 68;
MTCW

Paget, Violet 1856-1935
See Lee, Vernon
See also CA 104

Paget-Lowe, Henry
See Lovecraft, H(oward) P(hillips)

Paglia, Camille (Anna) 1947-....... **CLC 68**
See also CA 140

Paige, Richard
See Koontz, Dean R(ay)

Pakenham, Antonia
See Fraser, (Lady) Antonia (Pakenham)

Palamas, Kostes 1859-1943 .... **TCLC 5**
See also CA 105

Palazzeschi, Aldo 1885-1974 .... **CLC 11**
See also CA 89-92; 53-56; DLB 114

Paley, Grace 1922-.... **CLC 4, 6, 37; SSC 8**
See also CA 25-28R; CANR 13, 46, 46;
DLB 28; MTCW

Palin, Michael (Edward) 1943-..... **CLC 21**
See also Monty Python
See also CA 107; CANR 35; SATA 67

Palliser, Charles 1947-............ **CLC 65**
See also CA 136

Palma, Ricardo 1833-1919 .... **TCLC 29**

Pancake, Breece Dexter 1952-1979
See Pancake, Breece D'J
See also CA 123; 109

Pancake, Breece D'J............... **CLC 29**
See also Pancake, Breece Dexter
See also DLB 130

Panko, Rudy
See Gogol, Nikolai (Vasilyevich)

Papadiamantis, Alexandros
1851-1911 .... **TCLC 29**

Papadiamantopoulos, Johannes 1856-1910
See Moreas, Jean
See also CA 117

Papini, Giovanni 1881-1956 ...... **TCLC 22**
See also CA 121

Paracelsus 1493-1541 .... **LC 14**

Parasol, Peter
See Stevens, Wallace

Parfenie, Maria
See Codrescu, Andrei

Parini, Jay (Lee) 1948- .... **CLC 54**
See also CA 97-100; CAAS 16; CANR 32

Park, Jordan
See Kornbluth, C(yril) M.; Pohl, Frederik

Parker, Bert
See Ellison, Harlan (Jay)

Parker, Dorothy (Rothschild)
1893-1967 .... **CLC 15, 68; SSC 2**
See also CA 19-20; 25-28R; CAP 2;
DLB 11, 45, 86; MTCW

Parker, Robert B(rown) 1932-...... **CLC 27**
See also BEST 89:4; CA 49-52; CANR 1,
26; MTCW

Parkin, Frank 1940-.............. **CLC 43**

Parkman, Francis, Jr.
1823-1893 .... **NCLC 12**
See also DLB 1, 30

Parks, Gordon (Alexander Buchanan)
1912- .... **CLC 1, 16; BLC**
See also AITN 2; BW 2; CA 41-44R;
CANR 26; DLB 33; SATA 8

Parnell, Thomas 1679-1718 .... **LC 3**
See also DLB 94

Parra, Nicanor 1914- .... **CLC 2; HLC**
See also CA 85-88; CANR 32; HW; MTCW

Parrish, Mary Frances
See Fisher, M(ary) F(rances) K(ennedy)

Parson
See Coleridge, Samuel Taylor

Parson Lot
See Kingsley, Charles

Partridge, Anthony
See Oppenheim, E(dward) Phillips

Pascoli, Giovanni 1855-1912 ...... **TCLC 45**

Pasolini, Pier Paolo
1922-1975 .... **CLC 20, 37**
See also CA 93-96; 61-64; DLB 128;
MTCW

Pasquini
See Silone, Ignazio

Pastan, Linda (Olenik) 1932- ...... **CLC 27**
See also CA 61-64; CANR 18, 40; DLB 5

Pasternak, Boris (Leonidovich)
1890-1960 ...... **CLC 7, 10, 18, 63; DA;
PC 6; WLC**
See also CA 127; 116; MTCW

Patchen, Kenneth 1911-1972... **CLC 1, 2, 18**
See also CA 1-4R; 33-36R; CANR 3, 35;
DLB 16, 48; MTCW

Pater, Walter (Horatio)
1839-1894 .... **NCLC 7**
See also CDBLB 1832-1890; DLB 57

Paterson, A(ndrew) B(arton)
1864-1941 .... **TCLC 32**

Paterson, Katherine (Womeldorf)
1932-..................... **CLC 12, 30**
See also AAYA 1; CA 21-24R; CANR 28;
CLR 7; DLB 52; JRDA; MAICYA;
MTCW; SATA 13, 53

Patmore, Coventry Kersey Dighton
1823-1896 .... **NCLC 9**
See also DLB 35, 98

Paton, Alan (Stewart)
1903-1988 ...... **CLC 4, 10, 25, 55; DA;
WLC**
See also CA 13-16; 125; CANR 22; CAP 1;
MTCW; SATA 11; SATA-Obit 56

Paton Walsh, Gillian 1937-
See Walsh, Jill Paton
See also CANR 38; JRDA; MAICYA;
SAAS 3; SATA 4, 72

Paulding, James Kirke 1778-1860.. **NCLC 2**
See also DLB 3, 59, 74

Paulin, Thomas Neilson 1949-
See Paulin, Tom
See also CA 123; 128

Paulin, Tom..................... **CLC 37**
See also Paulin, Thomas Neilson
See also DLB 40

Paustovsky, Konstantin (Georgievich)
1892-1968 .... **CLC 40**
See also CA 93-96; 25-28R

Pavese, Cesare 1908-1950 .... **TCLC 3**
See also CA 104; DLB 128

Pavic, Milorad 1929- .... **CLC 60**
See also CA 136

Payne, Alan
See Jakes, John (William)

Paz, Gil
See Lugones, Leopoldo

Paz, Octavio
1914- .... **CLC 3, 4, 6, 10, 19, 51, 65;
DA; HLC; PC 1; WLC**
See also CA 73-76; CANR 32; DLBY 90;
HW; MTCW

Peacock, Molly 1947-............. **CLC 60**
See also CA 103; DLB 120**

Peacock, Thomas Love
    1785-1866 .... NCLC 22
    See also DLB 96, 116

Peake, Mervyn   1911-1968 ...... CLC 7, 54
    See also CA 5-8R; 25-28R; CANR 3;
    DLB 15; MTCW; SATA 23

Pearce, Philippa .... CLC 21
    See also Christie, (Ann) Philippa
    See also CLR 9; MAICYA; SATA 1, 67

Pearl, Eric
    See Elman, Richard

Pearson, T(homas) R(eid)   1956- .... CLC 39
    See also CA 120; 130

Peck, Dale   1968(?)- .... CLC 81

Peck, John   1941- .... CLC 3
    See also CA 49-52; CANR 3

Peck, Richard (Wayne)   1934- ...... CLC 21
    See also AAYA 1; CA 85-88; CANR 19,
    38; CLR 15; JRDA; MAICYA; SAAS 2;
    SATA 18, 55

Peck, Robert Newton   1928- .... CLC 17; DA
    See also AAYA 3; CA 81-84; CANR 31;
    JRDA; MAICYA; SAAS 1; SATA 21, 62

Peckinpah, (David) Sam(uel)
    1925-1984 .... CLC 20
    See also CA 109; 114

Pedersen, Knut   1859-1952
    See Hamsun, Knut
    See also CA 104; 119; MTCW

Peeslake, Gaffer
    See Durrell, Lawrence (George)

Peguy, Charles Pierre
    1873-1914 .... TCLC 10
    See also CA 107

Pena, Ramon del Valle y
    See Valle-Inclan, Ramon (Maria) del

Pendennis, Arthur Esquir
    See Thackeray, William Makepeace

Penn, William   1644-1718 .... LC 25
    See also DLB 24

Pepys, Samuel
    1633-1703 .... LC 11; DA; WLC
    See also CDBLB 1660-1789; DLB 101

Percy, Walker
    1916-1990 .... CLC 2, 3, 6, 8, 14, 18, 47,
                                            65
    See also CA 1-4R; 131; CANR 1, 23;
    DLB 2; DLBY 80, 90; MTCW

Perec, Georges   1936-1982 .... CLC 56
    See also CA 141; DLB 83

Pereda (y Sanchez de Porrua), Jose Maria de
    1833-1906 .... TCLC 16
    See also CA 117

Pereda y Porrua, Jose Maria de
    See Pereda (y Sanchez de Porrua), Jose
    Maria de

Peregoy, George Weems
    See Mencken, H(enry) L(ouis)

Perelman, S(idney) J(oseph)
    1904-1979 ... CLC 3, 5, 9, 15, 23, 44, 49
    See also AITN 1, 2; CA 73-76; 89-92;
    CANR 18; DLB 11, 44; MTCW

Peret, Benjamin   1899-1959 .... TCLC 20
    See also CA 117

Peretz, Isaac Loeb   1851(?)-1915 ... TCLC 16
    See also CA 109

Peretz, Yitzkhok Leibush
    See Peretz, Isaac Loeb

Perez Galdos, Benito   1843-1920 ... TCLC 27
    See also CA 125; HW

Perrault, Charles   1628-1703 .... LC 2
    See also MAICYA; SATA 25

Perry, Brighton
    See Sherwood, Robert E(mmet)

Perse, St.-John .... CLC 4, 11, 46
    See also Leger, (Marie-Rene Auguste) Alexis
    Saint-Leger

Peseenz, Tulio F.
    See Lopez y Fuentes, Gregorio

Pesetsky, Bette   1932- .... CLC 28
    See also CA 133; DLB 130

Peshkov, Alexei Maximovich   1868-1936
    See Gorky, Maxim
    See also CA 105; 141; DA

Pessoa, Fernando (Antonio Nogueira)
    1888-1935 .... TCLC 27; HLC
    See also CA 125

Peterkin, Julia Mood   1880-1961 .... CLC 31
    See also CA 102; DLB 9

Peters, Joan K.   1945- .... CLC 39

Peters, Robert L(ouis)   1924- .... CLC 7
    See also CA 13-16R; CAAS 8; DLB 105

Petofi, Sandor   1823-1849 .... NCLC 21

Petrakis, Harry Mark   1923- .... CLC 3
    See also CA 9-12R; CANR 4, 30

Petrarch   1304-1374 .... PC 8

Petrov, Evgeny .... TCLC 21
    See also Kataev, Evgeny Petrovich

Petry, Ann (Lane)   1908- ...... CLC 1, 7, 18
    See also BW 1; CA 5-8R; CAAS 6;
    CANR 4, 46, 46; CLR 12; DLB 76;
    JRDA; MAICYA; MTCW; SATA 5

Petursson, Halligrimur   1614-1674 .... LC 8

Philipson, Morris H.   1926- .... CLC 53
    See also CA 1-4R; CANR 4

Phillips, David Graham
    1867-1911 .... TCLC 44
    See also CA 108; DLB 9, 12

Phillips, Jack
    See Sandburg, Carl (August)

Phillips, Jayne Anne
    1952- .... CLC 15, 33; SSC 16
    See also CA 101; CANR 24; DLBY 80;
    MTCW

Phillips, Richard
    See Dick, Philip K(indred)

Phillips, Robert (Schaeffer)   1938- ... CLC 28
    See also CA 17-20R; CAAS 13; CANR 8;
    DLB 105

Phillips, Ward
    See Lovecraft, H(oward) P(hillips)

Piccolo, Lucio   1901-1969 .... CLC 13
    See also CA 97-100; DLB 114

Pickthall, Marjorie L(owry) C(hristie)
    1883-1922 .... TCLC 21
    See also CA 107; DLB 92

Pico della Mirandola, Giovanni
    1463-1494 .... LC 15

Piercy, Marge
    1936- .... CLC 3, 6, 14, 18, 27, 62
    See also CA 21-24R; CAAS 1; CANR 13,
    43; DLB 120; MTCW

Piers, Robert
    See Anthony, Piers

Pieyre de Mandiargues, Andre   1909-1991
    See Mandiargues, Andre Pieyre de
    See also CA 103; 136; CANR 22

Pilnyak, Boris .... TCLC 23
    See also Vogau, Boris Andreyevich

Pincherle, Alberto   1907-1990 ... CLC 11, 18
    See also Moravia, Alberto
    See also CA 25-28R; 132; CANR 33;
    MTCW

Pinckney, Darryl   1953- .... CLC 76
    See also BW 2; CA 143

Pindar   518B.C.-446B.C. .... CMLC 12

Pineda, Cecile   1942- .... CLC 39
    See also CA 118

Pinero, Arthur Wing   1855-1934 ... TCLC 32
    See also CA 110; DLB 10

Pinero, Miguel (Antonio Gomez)
    1946-1988 .... CLC 4, 55
    See also CA 61-64; 125; CANR 29; HW

Pinget, Robert   1919- .... CLC 7, 13, 37
    See also CA 85-88; DLB 83

Pink Floyd
    See Barrett, (Roger) Syd; Gilmour, David;
    Mason, Nick; Waters, Roger; Wright,
    Rick

Pinkney, Edward   1802-1828 ..... NCLC 31

Pinkwater, Daniel Manus   1941- .... CLC 35
    See also Pinkwater, Manus
    See also AAYA 1; CA 29-32R; CANR 12,
    38; CLR 4; JRDA; MAICYA; SAAS 3;
    SATA 46, 76

Pinkwater, Manus
    See Pinkwater, Daniel Manus
    See also SATA 8

Pinsky, Robert   1940- .... CLC 9, 19, 38
    See also CA 29-32R; CAAS 4; DLBY 82

Pinta, Harold
    See Pinter, Harold

Pinter, Harold
    1930- ..... CLC 1, 3, 6, 9, 11, 15, 27, 58,
                                    73; DA; WLC
    See also CA 5-8R; CANR 33; CDBLB 1960
    to Present; DLB 13; MTCW

Pirandello, Luigi
    1867-1936 ..... TCLC 4, 29; DA; DC 5;
                                            WLC
    See also CA 104

Pirsig, Robert M(aynard)
    1928- .... CLC 4, 6, 73
    See also CA 53-56; CANR 42; MTCW;
    SATA 39

Pisarev, Dmitry Ivanovich
    1840-1868 .... NCLC 25

Pix, Mary (Griffith)   1666-1709 .... LC 8
    See also DLB 80

Pixerecourt, Guilbert de
    1773-1844 .... NCLC 39

Plaidy, Jean
See Hibbert, Eleanor Alice Burford

Planche, James Robinson
1796-1880 . . . . NCLC 42

Plant, Robert 1948- . . . . CLC 12

Plante, David (Robert)
1940- . . . . CLC 7, 23, 38
See also CA 37-40R; CANR 12, 36;
DLBY 83; MTCW

Plath, Sylvia
1932-1963 . . . . . CLC 1, 2, 3, 5, 9, 11, 14,
17, 50, 51, 62; DA; PC 1; WLC
See also AAYA 13; CA 19-20; CANR 34;
CAP 2; CDALB 1941-1968; DLB 5, 6;
MTCW

Plato 428(?)B.C.-348(?)B.C. . . . . CMLC 8; DA

Platonov, Andrei . . . . TCLC 14
See also Klimentov, Andrei Platonovich

Platt, Kin 1911- . . . . CLC 26
See also AAYA 11; CA 17-20R; CANR 11;
JRDA; SAAS 17; SATA 21

Plick et Plock
See Simenon, Georges (Jacques Christian)

Plimpton, George (Ames) 1927- . . . . . CLC 36
See also AITN 1; CA 21-24R; CANR 32;
MTCW; SATA 10

Plomer, William Charles Franklin
1903-1973 . . . . CLC 4, 8
See also CA 21-22; CANR 34; CAP 2;
DLB 20; MTCW; SATA 24

Plowman, Piers
See Kavanagh, Patrick (Joseph)

Plum, J.
See Wodehouse, P(elham) G(renville)

Plumly, Stanley (Ross) 1939- . . . . . . CLC 33
See also CA 108; 110; DLB 5

Plumpe, Friedrich Wilhelm
1888-1931 . . . . TCLC 53
See also CA 112

Poe, Edgar Allan
1809-1849 . . . . . NCLC 1, 16; DA; PC 1;
SSC 1; WLC
See also AAYA 14; CDALB 1640-1865;
DLB 3, 59, 73, 74; SATA 23

Poet of Titchfield Street, The
See Pound, Ezra (Weston Loomis)

Pohl, Frederik 1919- . . . . CLC 18
See also CA 61-64; CAAS 1; CANR 11, 37;
DLB 8; MTCW; SATA 24

Poirier, Louis 1910-
See Gracq, Julien
See also CA 122; 126

Poitier, Sidney 1927- . . . . CLC 26
See also BW 1; CA 117

Polanski, Roman 1933- . . . . CLC 16
See also CA 77-80

Poliakoff, Stephen 1952- . . . . CLC 38
See also CA 106; DLB 13

Police, The
See Copeland, Stewart (Armstrong);
Summers, Andrew James; Sumner,
Gordon Matthew

Pollitt, Katha 1949- . . . . CLC 28
See also CA 120; 122; MTCW

Pollock, (Mary) Sharon 1936- . . . . . . CLC 50
See also CA 141; DLB 60

Pomerance, Bernard 1940- . . . . CLC 13
See also CA 101

Ponge, Francis (Jean Gaston Alfred)
1899-1988 . . . . CLC 6, 18
See also CA 85-88; 126; CANR 40

Pontoppidan, Henrik 1857-1943 . . . TCLC 29

Poole, Josephine . . . . CLC 17
See also Helyar, Jane Penelope Josephine
See also SAAS 2; SATA 5

Popa, Vasko 1922- . . . . CLC 19
See also CA 112

Pope, Alexander
1688-1744 . . . . LC 3; DA; WLC
See also CDBLB 1660-1789; DLB 95, 101

Porter, Connie (Rose) 1959(?)- . . . . . CLC 70
See also BW 2; CA 142; SATA 81

Porter, Gene(va Grace) Stratton
1863(?)-1924 . . . . TCLC 21
See also CA 112

Porter, Katherine Anne
1890-1980 . . . . . . CLC 1, 3, 7, 10, 13, 15,
27; DA; SSC 4
See also AITN 2; CA 1-4R; 101; CANR 1;
DLB 4, 9, 102; DLBD 12; DLBY 80;
MTCW; SATA 39; SATA-Obit 23

Porter, Peter (Neville Frederick)
1929- . . . . CLC 5, 13, 33
See also CA 85-88; DLB 40

Porter, William Sydney 1862-1910
See Henry, O.
See also CA 104; 131; CDALB 1865-1917;
DA; DLB 12, 78, 79; MTCW; YABC 2

Portillo (y Pacheco), Jose Lopez
See Lopez Portillo (y Pacheco), Jose

Post, Melville Davisson
1869-1930 . . . . TCLC 39
See also CA 110

Potok, Chaim 1929- . . . . CLC 2, 7, 14, 26
See also AITN 1, 2; CA 17-20R; CANR 19,
35; DLB 28; MTCW; SATA 33

Potter, Beatrice
See Webb, (Martha) Beatrice (Potter)
See also MAICYA

Potter, Dennis (Christopher George)
1935-1994 . . . . CLC 58, 86
See also CA 107; 145; CANR 33; MTCW

Pound, Ezra (Weston Loomis)
1885-1972 . . . . . . CLC 1, 2, 3, 4, 5, 7, 10,
13, 18, 34, 48, 50; DA; PC 4; WLC
See also CA 5-8R; 37-40R; CANR 40;
CDALB 1917-1929; DLB 4, 45, 63;
MTCW

Povod, Reinaldo 1959-1994 . . . . CLC 44
See also CA 136; 146

Powell, Anthony (Dymoke)
1905- . . . . CLC 1, 3, 7, 9, 10, 31
See also CA 1-4R; CANR 1, 32;
CDBLB 1945-1960; DLB 15; MTCW

Powell, Dawn 1897-1965 . . . . CLC 66
See also CA 5-8R

Powell, Padgett 1952- . . . . CLC 34
See also CA 126

Powers, J(ames) F(arl)
1917- . . . . CLC 1, 4, 8, 57; SSC 4
See also CA 1-4R; CANR 2; DLB 130;
MTCW

Powers, John J(ames) 1945-
See Powers, John R.
See also CA 69-72

Powers, John R. . . . . CLC 66
See also Powers, John J(ames)

Pownall, David 1938- . . . . CLC 10
See also CA 89-92; CAAS 18; DLB 14

Powys, John Cowper
1872-1963 . . . . CLC 7, 9, 15, 46
See also CA 85-88; DLB 15; MTCW

Powys, T(heodore) F(rancis)
1875-1953 . . . . TCLC 9
See also CA 106; DLB 36

Prager, Emily 1952- . . . . CLC 56

Pratt, E(dwin) J(ohn)
1883(?)-1964 . . . . CLC 19
See also CA 141; 93-96; DLB 92

Premchand . . . . TCLC 21
See also Srivastava, Dhanpat Rai

Preussler, Otfried 1923- . . . . CLC 17
See also CA 77-80; SATA 24

Prevert, Jacques (Henri Marie)
1900-1977 . . . . CLC 15
See also CA 77-80; 69-72; CANR 29;
MTCW; SATA-Obit 30

Prevost, Abbe (Antoine Francois)
1697-1763 . . . . LC 1

Price, (Edward) Reynolds
1933- . . . . CLC 3, 6, 13, 43, 50, 63
See also CA 1-4R; CANR 1, 37; DLB 2

Price, Richard 1949- . . . . CLC 6, 12
See also CA 49-52; CANR 3; DLBY 81

Prichard, Katharine Susannah
1883-1969 . . . . CLC 46
See also CA 11-12; CANR 33; CAP 1;
MTCW; SATA 66

Priestley, J(ohn) B(oynton)
1894-1984 . . . . CLC 2, 5, 9, 34
See also CA 9-12R; 113; CANR 33;
CDBLB 1914-1945; DLB 10, 34, 77, 100,
139; DLBY 84; MTCW

Prince 1958(?)- . . . . CLC 35

Prince, F(rank) T(empleton) 1912- . . CLC 22
See also CA 101; CANR 43; DLB 20

Prince Kropotkin
See Kropotkin, Peter (Aleksieevich)

Prior, Matthew 1664-1721 . . . . LC 4
See also DLB 95

Pritchard, William H(arrison)
1932- . . . . CLC 34
See also CA 65-68; CANR 23; DLB 111

Pritchett, V(ictor) S(awdon)
1900- . . . . CLC 5, 13, 15, 41; SSC 14
See also CA 61-64; CANR 31; DLB 15,
139; MTCW

Private 19022
See Manning, Frederic

Probst, Mark 1925- . . . . CLC 59
See also CA 130

Prokosch, Frederic 1908-1989.... **CLC 4, 48**
See also CA 73-76; 128; DLB 48

Prophet, The
See Dreiser, Theodore (Herman Albert)

Prose, Francine 1947-............. **CLC 45**
See also CA 109; 112; CANR 46, 46

Proudhon
See Cunha, Euclides (Rodrigues Pimenta) da

Proulx, E. Annie 1935- .... **CLC 81**

Proust, (Valentin-Louis-George-Eugene-)
    Marcel
    1871-1922 ... **TCLC 7, 13, 33; DA; WLC**
See also CA 104; 120; DLB 65; MTCW

Prowler, Harley
See Masters, Edgar Lee

Prus, Boleslaw 1845-1912 .... **TCLC 48**

Pryor, Richard (Franklin Lenox Thomas)
    1940-...................... **CLC 26**
See also CA 122

Przybyszewski, Stanislaw
    1868-1927 .... **TCLC 36**
See also DLB 66

Pteleon
See Grieve, C(hristopher) M(urray)

Puckett, Lute
See Masters, Edgar Lee

Puig, Manuel
    1932-1990 ... **CLC 3, 5, 10, 28, 65; HLC**
See also CA 45-48; CANR 2, 32; DLB 113;
    HW; MTCW

Purdy, Al(fred Wellington)
    1918-................ **CLC 3, 6, 14, 50**
See also CA 81-84; CAAS 17; CANR 42;
    DLB 88

Purdy, James (Amos)
    1923-............ **CLC 2, 4, 10, 28, 52**
See also CA 33-36R; CAAS 1; CANR 19;
    DLB 2; MTCW

Pure, Simon
See Swinnerton, Frank Arthur

Pushkin, Alexander (Sergeyevich)
    1799-1837 .... **NCLC 3, 27; DA; PC 10;**
                                             WLC
See also SATA 61

P'u Sung-ling 1640-1715 .... **LC 3**

Putnam, Arthur Lee
See Alger, Horatio, Jr.

Puzo, Mario 1920-......... **CLC 1, 2, 6, 36**
See also CA 65-68; CANR 4, 42; DLB 6;
    MTCW

Pym, Barbara (Mary Crampton)
    1913-1980 .... **CLC 13, 19, 37**
See also CA 13-14; 97-100; CANR 13, 34;
    CAP 1; DLB 14; DLBY 87; MTCW

Pynchon, Thomas (Ruggles, Jr.)
    1937- ..... **CLC 2, 3, 6, 9, 11, 18, 33, 62,**
                     72; DA; SSC 14; WLC
    See also BEST 90:2; CA 17-20R; CANR 22,
    46, 46; DLB 2; MTCW

Qian Zhongshu
See Ch'ien Chung-shu

Qroll
See Dagerman, Stig (Halvard)

Quarrington, Paul (Lewis) 1953-.... **CLC 65**
See also CA 129

Quasimodo, Salvatore 1901-1968 ... **CLC 10**
See also CA 13-16; 25-28R; CAP 1;
    DLB 114; MTCW

Queen, Ellery.................... **CLC 3, 11**
See also Dannay, Frederic; Davidson,
    Avram; Lee, Manfred B(ennington);
    Sturgeon, Theodore (Hamilton); Vance,
    John Holbrook

Queen, Ellery, Jr.
See Dannay, Frederic; Lee, Manfred
    B(ennington)

Queneau, Raymond
    1903-1976 .... **CLC 2, 5, 10, 42**
See also CA 77-80; 69-72; CANR 32;
    DLB 72; MTCW

Quevedo, Francisco de 1580-1645.... **LC 23**

Quiller-Couch, Arthur Thomas
    1863-1944 .... **TCLC 53**
See also CA 118; DLB 135

Quin, Ann (Marie) 1936-1973 .... **CLC 6**
See also CA 9-12R; 45-48; DLB 14

Quinn, Martin
See Smith, Martin Cruz

Quinn, Simon
See Smith, Martin Cruz

Quiroga, Horacio (Sylvestre)
    1878-1937 .... **TCLC 20; HLC**
See also CA 117; 131; HW; MTCW

Quoirez, Francoise 1935-........... **CLC 9**
See also Sagan, Francoise
See also CA 49-52; CANR 6, 39; MTCW

Raabe, Wilhelm 1831-1910 .... **TCLC 45**
See also DLB 129

Rabe, David (William) 1940-... **CLC 4, 8, 33**
See also CA 85-88; CABS 3; DLB 7

Rabelais, Francois
    1483-1553 .... **LC 5; DA; WLC**

Rabinovitch, Sholem 1859-1916
See Aleichem, Sholom
See also CA 104

Radcliffe, Ann (Ward) 1764-1823 .. **NCLC 6**
See also DLB 39

Radiguet, Raymond 1903-1923 .... **TCLC 29**
See also DLB 65

Radnoti, Miklos 1909-1944 .... **TCLC 16**
See also CA 118

Rado, James 1939-............... **CLC 17**
See also CA 105

Radvanyi, Netty 1900-1983
See Seghers, Anna
See also CA 85-88; 110

Rae, Ben
See Griffiths, Trevor

Raeburn, John (Hay) 1941-........ **CLC 34**
See also CA 57-60

Ragni, Gerome 1942-1991 .... **CLC 17**
See also CA 105; 134

Rahv, Philip 1908-1973 .... **CLC 24**
See also Greenberg, Ivan
See also DLB 137

Raine, Craig 1944-............... **CLC 32**
See also CA 108; CANR 29; DLB 40

Raine, Kathleen (Jessie) 1908- ... **CLC 7, 45**
See also CA 85-88; CANR 46, 46; DLB 20;
    MTCW

Rainis, Janis 1865-1929 .... **TCLC 29**

Rakosi, Carl..................... **CLC 47**
See also Rawley, Callman
See also CAAS 5

Raleigh, Richard
See Lovecraft, H(oward) P(hillips)

Rallentando, H. P.
See Sayers, Dorothy L(eigh)

Ramal, Walter
See de la Mare, Walter (John)

Ramon, Juan
See Jimenez (Mantecon), Juan Ramon

Ramos, Graciliano 1892-1953 ..... **TCLC 32**

Rampersad, Arnold 1941-.......... **CLC 44**
See also BW 2; CA 127; 133; DLB 111

Rampling, Anne
See Rice, Anne

Ramuz, Charles-Ferdinand
    1878-1947 .... **TCLC 33**

Rand, Ayn
    1905-1982 ...... **CLC 3, 30, 44, 79; DA;**
                                             WLC
See also AAYA 10; CA 13-16R; 105;
    CANR 27; MTCW

Randall, Dudley (Felker)
    1914- .... **CLC 1; BLC**
See also BW 1; CA 25-28R; CANR 23;
    DLB 41

Randall, Robert
See Silverberg, Robert

Ranger, Ken
See Creasey, John

Ransom, John Crowe
    1888-1974 .... **CLC 2, 4, 5, 11, 24**
See also CA 5-8R; 49-52; CANR 6, 34;
    DLB 45, 63; MTCW

Rao, Raja 1909- .... **CLC 25, 56**
See also CA 73-76; MTCW

Raphael, Frederic (Michael)
    1931- .... **CLC 2, 14**
See also CA 1-4R; CANR 1; DLB 14

Ratcliffe, James P.
See Mencken, H(enry) L(ouis)

Rathbone, Julian 1935-........... **CLC 41**
See also CA 101; CANR 34

Rattigan, Terence (Mervyn)
    1911-1977 .... **CLC 7**
See also CA 85-88; 73-76;
    CDBLB 1945-1960; DLB 13; MTCW

Ratushinskaya, Irina 1954- .... **CLC 54**
See also CA 129

Raven, Simon (Arthur Noel)
    1927-...................... **CLC 14**
See also CA 81-84

Rawley, Callman 1903-
See Rakosi, Carl
See also CA 21-24R; CANR 12, 32

Rawlings, Marjorie Kinnan
    1896-1953 .... **TCLC 4**
See also CA 104; 137; DLB 9, 22, 102;
    JRDA; MAICYA; YABC 1

Ray, Satyajit 1921-1992....... **CLC 16, 76**
See also CA 114; 137

Read, Herbert Edward 1893-1968.... **CLC 4**
See also CA 85-88; 25-28R; DLB 20

Read, Piers Paul 1941- ...... **CLC 4, 10, 25**
See also CA 21-24R; CANR 38; DLB 14;
SATA 21

Reade, Charles 1814-1884 .... **NCLC 2**
See also DLB 21

Reade, Hamish
See Gray, Simon (James Holliday)

Reading, Peter 1946- .... **CLC 47**
See also CA 103; CANR 46, 46; DLB 40

Reaney, James 1926- .... **CLC 13**
See also CA 41-44R; CAAS 15; CANR 42;
DLB 68; SATA 43

Rebreanu, Liviu 1885-1944 .... **TCLC 28**

Rechy, John (Francisco)
1934- .... **CLC 1, 7, 14, 18; HLC**
See also CA 5-8R; CAAS 4; CANR 6, 32;
DLB 122; DLBY 82; HW

Redcam, Tom 1870-1933 .... **TCLC 25**

Reddin, Keith.................... **CLC 67**

Redgrove, Peter (William)
1932- .... **CLC 6, 41**
See also CA 1-4R; CANR 3, 39; DLB 40

Redmon, Anne.................... **CLC 22**
See also Nightingale, Anne Redmon
See also DLBY 86

Reed, Eliot
See Ambler, Eric

Reed, Ishmael
1938- ... **CLC 2, 3, 5, 6, 13, 32, 60; BLC**
See also BW 2; CA 21-24R; CANR 25;
DLB 2, 5, 33; DLBD 8; MTCW

Reed, John (Silas) 1887-1920 ...... **TCLC 9**
See also CA 106

Reed, Lou........................ **CLC 21**
See also Firbank, Louis

Reeve, Clara 1729-1807 .... **NCLC 19**
See also DLB 39

Reich, Wilhelm 1897-1957........ **TCLC 57**

Reid, Christopher (John) 1949-..... **CLC 33**
See also CA 140; DLB 40

Reid, Desmond
See Moorcock, Michael (John)

Reid Banks, Lynne 1929-
See Banks, Lynne Reid
See also CA 1-4R; CANR 6, 22, 38;
CLR 24; JRDA; MAICYA; SATA 22, 75

Reilly, William K.
See Creasey, John

Reiner, Max
See Caldwell, (Janet Miriam) Taylor
(Holland)

Reis, Ricardo
See Pessoa, Fernando (Antonio Nogueira)

Remarque, Erich Maria
1898-1970 .... **CLC 21; DA**
See also CA 77-80; 29-32R; DLB 56;
MTCW

Remizov, A.
See Remizov, Aleksei (Mikhailovich)

Remizov, A. M.
See Remizov, Aleksei (Mikhailovich)

Remizov, Aleksei (Mikhailovich)
1877-1957....................**TCLC 27**
See also CA 125; 133

Renan, Joseph Ernest
1823-1892 .... **NCLC 26**

Renard, Jules 1864-1910 .... **TCLC 17**
See also CA 117

Renault, Mary............... **CLC 3, 11, 17**
See also Challans, Mary
See also DLBY 83

Rendell, Ruth (Barbara) 1930- .. **CLC 28, 48**
See also Vine, Barbara
See also CA 109; CANR 32; DLB 87;
MTCW

Renoir, Jean 1894-1979 .... **CLC 20**
See also CA 129; 85-88

Resnais, Alain 1922-.............. **CLC 16**

Reverdy, Pierre 1889-1960 .... **CLC 53**
See also CA 97-100; 89-92

Rexroth, Kenneth
1905-1982 ...... **CLC 1, 2, 6, 11, 22, 49**
See also CA 5-8R; 107; CANR 14, 34;
CDALB 1941-1968; DLB 16, 48;
DLBY 82; MTCW

Reyes, Alfonso 1889-1959 .... **TCLC 33**
See also CA 131; HW

Reyes y Basoalto, Ricardo Eliecer Neftali
See Neruda, Pablo

Reymont, Wladyslaw (Stanislaw)
1868(?)-1925 .... **TCLC 5**
See also CA 104

Reynolds, Jonathan 1942- .... **CLC 6, 38**
See also CA 65-68; CANR 28

Reynolds, Joshua 1723-1792....... **LC 15**
See also DLB 104

Reynolds, Michael Shane 1937- .... **CLC 44**
See also CA 65-68; CANR 9

Reznikoff, Charles 1894-1976 .... **CLC 9**
See also CA 33-36; 61-64; CAP 2; DLB 28,
45

Rezzori (d'Arezzo), Gregor von
1914- .... **CLC 25**
See also CA 122; 136

Rhine, Richard
See Silverstein, Alvin

Rhodes, Eugene Manlove
1869-1934 .... **TCLC 53**

R'hoone
See Balzac, Honore de

Rhys, Jean
1890(?)-1979 .... **CLC 2, 4, 6, 14, 19, 51**
See also CA 25-28R; 85-88; CANR 35;
CDBLB 1945-1960; DLB 36, 117; MTCW

Ribeiro, Darcy 1922- .... **CLC 34**
See also CA 33-36R

Ribeiro, Joao Ubaldo (Osorio Pimentel)
1941- .... **CLC 10, 67**
See also CA 81-84

Ribman, Ronald (Burt) 1932- .... **CLC 7**
See also CA 21-24R; CANR 46, 46

Ricci, Nino 1959-................. **CLC 70**
See also CA 137

Rice, Anne 1941- .... **CLC 41**
See also AAYA 9; BEST 89:2; CA 65-68;
CANR 12, 36

Rice, Elmer (Leopold)
1892-1967 .... **CLC 7, 49**
See also CA 21-22; 25-28R; CAP 2; DLB 4,
7; MTCW

Rice, Tim(othy Miles Bindon)
1944- .... **CLC 21**
See also CA 103; CANR 46

Rich, Adrienne (Cecile)
1929- .... **CLC 3, 6, 7, 11, 18, 36, 73, 76;
PC 5**
See also CA 9-12R; CANR 20; DLB 5, 67;
MTCW

Rich, Barbara
See Graves, Robert (von Ranke)

Rich, Robert
See Trumbo, Dalton

Richards, David Adams 1950-...... **CLC 59**
See also CA 93-96; DLB 53

Richards, I(vor) A(rmstrong)
1893-1979 .... **CLC 14, 24**
See also CA 41-44R; 89-92; CANR 34;
DLB 27

Richardson, Anne
See Roiphe, Anne (Richardson)

Richardson, Dorothy Miller
1873-1957 .... **TCLC 3**
See also CA 104; DLB 36

Richardson, Ethel Florence (Lindesay)
1870-1946
See Richardson, Henry Handel
See also CA 105

Richardson, Henry Handel.......... **TCLC 4**
See also Richardson, Ethel Florence
(Lindesay)

Richardson, Samuel
1689-1761 .... **LC 1; DA; WLC**
See also CDBLB 1660-1789; DLB 39

Richler, Mordecai
1931- .... **CLC 3, 5, 9, 13, 18, 46, 70**
See also AITN 1; CA 65-68; CANR 31;
CLR 17; DLB 53; MAICYA; MTCW;
SATA 27, 44

Richter, Conrad (Michael)
1890-1968 .... **CLC 30**
See also CA 5-8R; 25-28R; CANR 23;
DLB 9; MTCW; SATA 3

Riddell, J. H. 1832-1906 .... **TCLC 40**

Riding, Laura.................... **CLC 3, 7**
See also Jackson, Laura (Riding)

Riefenstahl, Berta Helene Amalia 1902-
See Riefenstahl, Leni
See also CA 108

Riefenstahl, Leni.................. **CLC 16**
See also Riefenstahl, Berta Helene Amalia

Riffe, Ernest
See Bergman, (Ernst) Ingmar

Riggs, (Rolla) Lynn 1899-1954 .... **TCLC 56**
See also CA 144; NNAL

Riley, James Whitcomb
1849-1916 .... **TCLC 51**
See also CA 118; 137; MAICYA; SATA 17

Riley, Tex
See Creasey, John

Rilke, Rainer Maria
1875-1926 . . . . **TCLC 1, 6, 19; PC 2**
See also CA 104; 132; DLB 81; MTCW

Rimbaud, (Jean Nicolas) Arthur
1854-1891 . . . . . **NCLC 4, 35; DA; PC 3;**
WLC

Rinehart, Mary Roberts
1876-1958 . . . . **TCLC 52**
See also CA 108

Ringmaster, The
See Mencken, H(enry) L(ouis)

Ringwood, Gwen(dolyn Margaret) Pharis
1910-1984 . . . . **CLC 48**
See also CA 112; DLB 88

Rio, Michel 19(?)- . . . . **CLC 43**

Ritsos, Giannes
See Ritsos, Yannis

Ritsos, Yannis 1909-1990 . . . . **CLC 6, 13, 31**
See also CA 77-80; 133; CANR 39; MTCW

Ritter, Erika 1948(?)- . . . . **CLC 52**

Rivera, Jose Eustasio 1889-1928 . . . **TCLC 35**
See also HW

Rivers, Conrad Kent 1933-1968 . . . . . . **CLC 1**
See also BW 1; CA 85-88; DLB 41

Rivers, Elfrida
See Bradley, Marion Zimmer

Riverside, John
See Heinlein, Robert A(nson)

Rizal, Jose 1861-1896 . . . . **NCLC 27**

Roa Bastos, Augusto (Antonio)
1917- . . . . **CLC 45; HLC**
See also CA 131; DLB 113; HW

Robbe-Grillet, Alain
1922- . . . . . . **CLC 1, 2, 4, 6, 8, 10, 14, 43**
See also CA 9-12R; CANR 33; DLB 83;
MTCW

Robbins, Harold 1916- . . . . **CLC 5**
See also CA 73-76; CANR 26; MTCW

Robbins, Thomas Eugene 1936-
See Robbins, Tom
See also CA 81-84; CANR 29; MTCW

Robbins, Tom . . . . **CLC 9, 32, 64**
See also Robbins, Thomas Eugene
See also BEST 90:3; DLBY 80

Robbins, Trina 1938- . . . . **CLC 21**
See also CA 128

Roberts, Charles G(eorge) D(ouglas)
1860-1943 . . . . **TCLC 8**
See also CA 105; CLR 33; DLB 92;
SATA 29

Roberts, Kate 1891-1985 . . . . **CLC 15**
See also CA 107; 116

Roberts, Keith (John Kingston)
1935- . . . . **CLC 14**
See also CA 25-28R; CANR 46, 46

Roberts, Kenneth (Lewis)
1885-1957 . . . . **TCLC 23**
See also CA 109; DLB 9

Roberts, Michele (B.) 1949- . . . . **CLC 48**
See also CA 115

Robertson, Ellis
See Ellison, Harlan (Jay); Silverberg, Robert

Robertson, Thomas William
1829-1871 . . . . **NCLC 35**

Robinson, Edwin Arlington
1869-1935 . . . . **TCLC 5; DA; PC 1**
See also CA 104; 133; CDALB 1865-1917;
DLB 54; MTCW

Robinson, Henry Crabb
1775-1867 . . . . **NCLC 15**
See also DLB 107

Robinson, Jill 1936- . . . . **CLC 10**
See also CA 102

Robinson, Kim Stanley 1952- . . . . . . **CLC 34**
See also CA 126

Robinson, Lloyd
See Silverberg, Robert

Robinson, Marilynne 1944- . . . . **CLC 25**
See also CA 116

Robinson, Smokey . . . . **CLC 21**
See also Robinson, William, Jr.

Robinson, William, Jr. 1940-
See Robinson, Smokey
See also CA 116

Robison, Mary 1949- . . . . **CLC 42**
See also CA 113; 116; DLB 130

Rod, Edouard 1857-1910 . . . . **TCLC 52**

Roddenberry, Eugene Wesley 1921-1991
See Roddenberry, Gene
See also CA 110; 135; CANR 37; SATA 45;
SATA-Obit 69

Roddenberry, Gene . . . . **CLC 17**
See also Roddenberry, Eugene Wesley
See also AAYA 5; SATA-Obit 69

Rodgers, Mary 1931- . . . . **CLC 12**
See also CA 49-52; CANR 8; CLR 20;
JRDA; MAICYA; SATA 8

Rodgers, W(illiam) R(obert)
1909-1969 . . . . **CLC 7**
See also CA 85-88; DLB 20

Rodman, Eric
See Silverberg, Robert

Rodman, Howard 1920(?)-1985 . . . . . **CLC 65**
See also CA 118

Rodman, Maia
See Wojciechowska, Maia (Teresa)

Rodriguez, Claudio 1934- . . . . **CLC 10**
See also DLB 134

Roelvaag, O(le) E(dvart)
1876-1931 . . . . **TCLC 17**
See also CA 117; DLB 9

Roethke, Theodore (Huebner)
1908-1963 . . . . . . **CLC 1, 3, 8, 11, 19, 46**
See also CA 81-84; CABS 2;
CDALB 1941-1968; DLB 5; MTCW

Rogers, Thomas Hunton 1927- . . . . . **CLC 57**
See also CA 89-92

Rogers, Will(iam Penn Adair)
1879-1935 . . . . **TCLC 8**
See also CA 105; 144; DLB 11; NNAL

Rogin, Gilbert 1929- . . . . **CLC 18**
See also CA 65-68; CANR 15

Rohan, Koda . . . . **TCLC 22**
See also Koda Shigeyuki

Rohmer, Eric . . . . **CLC 16**
See also Scherer, Jean-Marie Maurice

Rohmer, Sax . . . . **TCLC 28**
See also Ward, Arthur Henry Sarsfield
See also DLB 70

Roiphe, Anne (Richardson)
1935- . . . . **CLC 3, 9**
See also CA 89-92; CANR 45; DLBY 80

Rojas, Fernando de 1465-1541 . . . . . . **LC 23**

Rolfe, Frederick (William Serafino Austin
Lewis Mary) 1860-1913 . . . . . . **TCLC 12**
See also CA 107; DLB 34

Rolland, Romain 1866-1944 . . . . . . **TCLC 23**
See also CA 118; DLB 65

Rolvaag, O(le) E(dvart)
See Roelvaag, O(le) E(dvart)

Romain Arnaud, Saint
See Aragon, Louis

Romains, Jules 1885-1972 . . . . **CLC 7**
See also CA 85-88; CANR 34; DLB 65;
MTCW

Romero, Jose Ruben 1890-1952 . . . **TCLC 14**
See also CA 114; 131; HW

Ronsard, Pierre de
1524-1585 . . . . **LC 6; PC 11**

Rooke, Leon 1934- . . . . **CLC 25, 34**
See also CA 25-28R; CANR 23

Roper, William 1498-1578 . . . . **LC 10**

Roquelaure, A. N.
See Rice, Anne

Rosa, Joao Guimaraes 1908-1967 . . . **CLC 23**
See also CA 89-92; DLB 113

Rose, Wendy 1948- . . . . **CLC 85**
See also CA 53-56; CANR 5; NNAL;
SATA 12

Rosen, Richard (Dean) 1949- . . . . **CLC 39**
See also CA 77-80

Rosenberg, Isaac 1890-1918 . . . . **TCLC 12**
See also CA 107; DLB 20

Rosenblatt, Joe . . . . **CLC 15**
See also Rosenblatt, Joseph

Rosenblatt, Joseph 1933-
See Rosenblatt, Joe
See also CA 89-92

Rosenfeld, Samuel 1896-1963
See Tzara, Tristan
See also CA 89-92

Rosenthal, M(acha) L(ouis) 1917- . . . **CLC 28**
See also CA 1-4R; CAAS 6; CANR 4;
DLB 5; SATA 59

Ross, Barnaby
See Dannay, Frederic

Ross, Bernard L.
See Follett, Ken(neth Martin)

Ross, J. H.
See Lawrence, T(homas) E(dward)

Ross, Martin
See Martin, Violet Florence
See also DLB 135

Ross, (James) Sinclair 1908- . . . . **CLC 13**
See also CA 73-76; DLB 88

Rossetti, Christina (Georgina)
1830-1894 . . . **NCLC 2; DA; PC 7; WLC**
See also DLB 35; MAICYA; SATA 20

Rossetti, Dante Gabriel
    1828-1882 .... **NCLC 4; DA; WLC**
    See also CDBLB 1832-1890; DLB 35

Rossner, Judith (Perelman)
    1935- .... **CLC 6, 9, 29**
    See also AITN 2; BEST 90:3; CA 17-20R;
    CANR 18; DLB 6; MTCW

Rostand, Edmond (Eugene Alexis)
    1868-1918 .... **TCLC 6, 37; DA**
    See also CA 104; 126; MTCW

Roth, Henry   1906- .... **CLC 2, 6, 11**
    See also CA 11-12; CANR 38; CAP 1;
    DLB 28; MTCW

Roth, Joseph   1894-1939 .... **TCLC 33**
    See also DLB 85

Roth, Philip (Milton)
    1933- ...... **CLC 1, 2, 3, 4, 6, 9, 15, 22,**
    31, 47, 66, 86; DA; WLC
    See also BEST 90:3; CA 1-4R; CANR 1, 22,
    36; CDALB 1968-1988; DLB 2, 28;
    DLBY 82; MTCW

Rothenberg, Jerome   1931- .... **CLC 6, 57**
    See also CA 45-48; CANR 1; DLB 5

Roumain, Jacques (Jean Baptiste)
    1907-1944 .... **TCLC 19; BLC**
    See also BW 1; CA 117; 125

Rourke, Constance (Mayfield)
    1885-1941 .... **TCLC 12**
    See also CA 107; YABC 1

Rousseau, Jean-Baptiste   1671-1741 ... **LC 9**

Rousseau, Jean-Jacques
    1712-1778 .... **LC 14; DA; WLC**

Roussel, Raymond   1877-1933 ..... **TCLC 20**
    See also CA 117

Rovit, Earl (Herbert)   1927- .... **CLC 7**
    See also CA 5-8R; CANR 12

Rowe, Nicholas   1674-1718 .... **LC 8**
    See also DLB 84

Rowley, Ames Dorrance
    See Lovecraft, H(oward) P(hillips)

Rowson, Susanna Haswell
    1762(?)-1824 .... **NCLC 5**
    See also DLB 37

Roy, Gabrielle   1909-1983 .... **CLC 10, 14**
    See also CA 53-56; 110; CANR 5; DLB 68;
    MTCW

Rozewicz, Tadeusz   1921- .... **CLC 9, 23**
    See also CA 108; CANR 36; MTCW

Ruark, Gibbons   1941- .... **CLC 3**
    See also CA 33-36R; CANR 14, 31;
    DLB 120

Rubens, Bernice (Ruth)   1923- ... **CLC 19, 31**
    See also CA 25-28R; CANR 33; DLB 14;
    MTCW

Rudkin, (James) David   1936- ...... **CLC 14**
    See also CA 89-92; DLB 13

Rudnik, Raphael   1933- .... **CLC 7**
    See also CA 29-32R

Ruffian, M.
    See Hasek, Jaroslav (Matej Frantisek)

Ruiz, Jose Martinez .... **CLC 11**
    See also Martinez Ruiz, Jose

Rukeyser, Muriel
    1913-1980 .... **CLC 6, 10, 15, 27**
    See also CA 5-8R; 93-96; CANR 26;
    DLB 48; MTCW; SATA-Obit 22

Rule, Jane (Vance)   1931- .... **CLC 27**
    See also CA 25-28R; CAAS 18; CANR 12;
    DLB 60

Rulfo, Juan   1918-1986 .... **CLC 8, 80; HLC**
    See also CA 85-88; 118; CANR 26;
    DLB 113; HW; MTCW

Runeberg, Johan   1804-1877 ...... **NCLC 41**

Runyon, (Alfred) Damon
    1884(?)-1946 .... **TCLC 10**
    See also CA 107; DLB 11, 86

Rush, Norman   1933- .... **CLC 44**
    See also CA 121; 126

Rushdie, (Ahmed) Salman
    1947- .... **CLC 23, 31, 55**
    See also BEST 89:3; CA 108; 111;
    CANR 33; MTCW

Rushforth, Peter (Scott)   1945- ..... **CLC 19**
    See also CA 101

Ruskin, John   1819-1900 .... **TCLC 20**
    See also CA 114; 129; CDBLB 1832-1890;
    DLB 55; SATA 24

Russ, Joanna   1937- .... **CLC 15**
    See also CA 25-28R; CANR 11, 31; DLB 8;
    MTCW

Russell, (Henry) Ken(neth Alfred)
    1927- .... **CLC 16**
    See also CA 105

Russell, Willy   1947- .... **CLC 60**

Rutherford, Mark .... **TCLC 25**
    See also White, William Hale
    See also DLB 18

Ryan, Cornelius (John)   1920-1974 ... **CLC 7**
    See also CA 69-72; 53-56; CANR 38

Ryan, Michael   1946- .... **CLC 65**
    See also CA 49-52; DLBY 82

Rybakov, Anatoli (Naumovich)
    1911- .... **CLC 23, 53**
    See also CA 126; 135; SATA 79

Ryder, Jonathan
    See Ludlum, Robert

Ryga, George   1932-1987 .... **CLC 14**
    See also CA 101; 124; CANR 43; DLB 60

S. S.
    See Sassoon, Siegfried (Lorraine)

Saba, Umberto   1883-1957 .... **TCLC 33**
    See also CA 144; DLB 114

Sabatini, Rafael   1875-1950 .... **TCLC 47**

Sabato, Ernesto (R.)
    1911- .... **CLC 10, 23; HLC**
    See also CA 97-100; CANR 32; DLB 145;
    HW; MTCW

Sacastru, Martin
    See Bioy Casares, Adolfo

Sacher-Masoch, Leopold von
    1836(?)-1895 .... **NCLC 31**

Sachs, Marilyn (Stickle)   1927- ..... **CLC 35**
    See also AAYA 2; CA 17-20R; CANR 13,
    47; CLR 2; JRDA; MAICYA; SAAS 2;
    SATA 3, 68

Sachs, Nelly   1891-1970 .... **CLC 14**
    See also CA 17-18; 25-28R; CAP 2

Sackler, Howard (Oliver)
    1929-1982 .... **CLC 14**
    See also CA 61-64; 108; CANR 30; DLB 7

Sacks, Oliver (Wolf)   1933- .... **CLC 67**
    See also CA 53-56; CANR 28; MTCW

Sade, Donatien Alphonse Francois Comte
    1740-1814 .... **NCLC 47**

Sadoff, Ira   1945- .... **CLC 9**
    See also CA 53-56; CANR 5, 21; DLB 120

Saetone
    See Camus, Albert

Safire, William   1929- .... **CLC 10**
    See also CA 17-20R; CANR 31

Sagan, Carl (Edward)   1934- .... **CLC 30**
    See also AAYA 2; CA 25-28R; CANR 11,
    36; MTCW; SATA 58

Sagan, Francoise .... **CLC 3, 6, 9, 17, 36**
    See also Quoirez, Francoise
    See also DLB 83

Sahgal, Nayantara (Pandit)   1927- ... **CLC 41**
    See also CA 9-12R; CANR 11

Saint, H(arry) F.   1941- .... **CLC 50**
    See also CA 127

St. Aubin de Teran, Lisa   1953-
    See Teran, Lisa St. Aubin de
    See also CA 118; 126

Sainte-Beuve, Charles Augustin
    1804-1869 .... **NCLC 5**

Saint-Exupery, Antoine (Jean Baptiste Marie
    Roger) de
    1900-1944 .... **TCLC 2, 56; WLC**
    See also CA 108; 132; CLR 10; DLB 72;
    MAICYA; MTCW; SATA 20

St. John, David
    See Hunt, E(verette) Howard, (Jr.)

Saint-John Perse
    See Leger, (Marie-Rene Auguste) Alexis
    Saint-Leger

Saintsbury, George (Edward Bateman)
    1845-1933 .... **TCLC 31**
    See also DLB 57

Sait Faik .... **TCLC 23**
    See also Abasiyanik, Sait Faik

Saki .... **TCLC 3; SSC 12**
    See also Munro, H(ector) H(ugh)

Sala, George Augustus .... **NCLC 46**

Salama, Hannu   1936- .... **CLC 18**

Salamanca, J(ack) R(ichard)
    1922- .... **CLC 4, 15**
    See also CA 25-28R

Sale, J. Kirkpatrick
    See Sale, Kirkpatrick

Sale, Kirkpatrick   1937- .... **CLC 68**
    See also CA 13-16R; CANR 10

Salinas (y Serrano), Pedro
    1891(?)-1951 .... **TCLC 17**
    See also CA 117; DLB 134

Salinger, J(erome) D(avid)
1919- ...... **CLC 1, 3, 8, 12, 55, 56; DA;
SSC 2; WLC**
See also AAYA 2; CA 5-8R; CANR 39;
CDALB 1941-1968; CLR 18; DLB 2, 102;
MAICYA; MTCW; SATA 67

Salisbury, John
See Caute, David

Salter, James 1925- .... **CLC 7, 52, 59**
See also CA 73-76; DLB 130

Saltus, Edgar (Everton)
1855-1921 .... **TCLC 8**
See also CA 105

Saltykov, Mikhail Evgrafovich
1826-1889 .... **NCLC 16**

Samarakis, Antonis 1919- .... **CLC 5**
See also CA 25-28R; CAAS 16; CANR 36

Sanchez, Florencio 1875-1910..... **TCLC 37**
See also HW

Sanchez, Luis Rafael 1936- .... **CLC 23**
See also CA 128; DLB 145; HW

Sanchez, Sonia 1934- ... **CLC 5; BLC; PC 9**
See also BW 2; CA 33-36R; CANR 24;
CLR 18; DLB 41; DLBD 8; MAICYA;
MTCW; SATA 22

Sand, George
1804-1876 ...... **NCLC 2, 42; DA; WLC**
See also DLB 119

Sandburg, Carl (August)
1878-1967 .... **CLC 1, 4, 10, 15, 35; DA;
PC 2; WLC**
See also CA 5-8R; 25-28R; CANR 35;
CDALB 1865-1917; DLB 17, 54;
MAICYA; MTCW; SATA 8

Sandburg, Charles
See Sandburg, Carl (August)

Sandburg, Charles A.
See Sandburg, Carl (August)

Sanders, (James) Ed(ward) 1939- ... **CLC 53**
See also CA 13-16R; CANR 13, 44;
DLB 16

Sanders, Lawrence 1920- .... **CLC 41**
See also BEST 89:4; CA 81-84; CANR 33;
MTCW

Sanders, Noah
See Blount, Roy (Alton), Jr.

Sanders, Winston P.
See Anderson, Poul (William)

Sandoz, Mari(e Susette)
1896-1966 .... **CLC 28**
See also CA 1-4R; 25-28R; CANR 17;
DLB 9; MTCW; SATA 5

Saner, Reg(inald Anthony) 1931- .... **CLC 9**
See also CA 65-68

Sannazaro, Jacopo 1456(?)-1530...... **LC 8**

Sansom, William 1912-1976....... **CLC 2, 6**
See also CA 5-8R; 65-68; CANR 42;
DLB 139; MTCW

Santayana, George 1863-1952..... **TCLC 40**
See also CA 115; DLB 54, 71

Santiago, Danny .... **CLC 33**
See also James, Daniel (Lewis); James,
Daniel (Lewis)
See also DLB 122

Santmyer, Helen Hoover
1895-1986 .... **CLC 33**
See also CA 1-4R; 118; CANR 15, 33;
DLBY 84; MTCW

Santos, Bienvenido N(uqui) 1911-... **CLC 22**
See also CA 101; CANR 19, 46, 46

Sapper .... **TCLC 44**
See also McNeile, Herman Cyril

Sappho fl. 6th cent. B.C.-.... **CMLC 3; PC 5**

Sarduy, Severo 1937-1993 .... **CLC 6**
See also CA 89-92; 142; DLB 113; HW

Sargeson, Frank 1903-1982 .... **CLC 31**
See also CA 25-28R; 106; CANR 38

Sarmiento, Felix Ruben Garcia
See Dario, Ruben

Saroyan, William
1908-1981 ..... **CLC 1, 8, 10, 29, 34, 56;
DA; WLC**
See also CA 5-8R; 103; CANR 30; DLB 7,
9, 86; DLBY 81; MTCW; SATA 23;
SATA-Obit 24

Sarraute, Nathalie
1900- .... **CLC 1, 2, 4, 8, 10, 31, 80**
See also CA 9-12R; CANR 23; DLB 83;
MTCW

Sarton, (Eleanor) May
1912- .... **CLC 4, 14, 49**
See also CA 1-4R; CANR 1, 34; DLB 48;
DLBY 81; MTCW; SATA 36

Sartre, Jean-Paul
1905-1980 .... **CLC 1, 4, 7, 9, 13, 18, 24,
44, 50, 52; DA; DC 3; WLC**
See also CA 9-12R; 97-100; CANR 21;
DLB 72; MTCW

Sassoon, Siegfried (Lorraine)
1886-1967 .... **CLC 36**
See also CA 104; 25-28R; CANR 36;
DLB 20; MTCW

Satterfield, Charles
See Pohl, Frederik

Saul, John (W. III) 1942- .... **CLC 46**
See also AAYA 10; BEST 90:4; CA 81-84;
CANR 16, 40

Saunders, Caleb
See Heinlein, Robert A(nson)

Saura (Atares), Carlos 1932-....... **CLC 20**
See also CA 114; 131; HW

Sauser-Hall, Frederic 1887-1961.... **CLC 18**
See also CA 102; 93-96; CANR 36; MTCW

Saussure, Ferdinand de
1857-1913 .... **TCLC 49**

Savage, Catharine
See Brosman, Catharine Savage

Savage, Thomas 1915- .... **CLC 40**
See also CA 126; 132; CAAS 15

Savan, Glenn 19(?)- .... **CLC 50**

Sayers, Dorothy L(eigh)
1893-1957 .... **TCLC 2, 15**
See also CA 104; 119; CDBLB 1914-1945;
DLB 10, 36, 77, 100; MTCW

Sayers, Valerie 1952-............. **CLC 50**
See also CA 134

Sayles, John (Thomas)
1950- .... **CLC 7, 10, 14**
See also CA 57-60; CANR 41; DLB 44

Scammell, Michael .... **CLC 34**

Scannell, Vernon 1922- .... **CLC 49**
See also CA 5-8R; CANR 8, 24; DLB 27;
SATA 59

Scarlett, Susan
See Streatfeild, (Mary) Noel

Schaeffer, Susan Fromberg
1941- .... **CLC 6, 11, 22**
See also CA 49-52; CANR 18; DLB 28;
MTCW; SATA 22

Schary, Jill
See Robinson, Jill

Schell, Jonathan 1943-............ **CLC 35**
See also CA 73-76; CANR 12

Schelling, Friedrich Wilhelm Joseph von
1775-1854 .... **NCLC 30**
See also DLB 90

Schendel, Arthur van 1874-1946... **TCLC 56**

Scherer, Jean-Marie Maurice 1920-
See Rohmer, Eric
See also CA 110

Schevill, James (Erwin) 1920-....... **CLC 7**
See also CA 5-8R; CAAS 12

Schiller, Friedrich 1759-1805 .... **NCLC 39**
See also DLB 94

Schisgal, Murray (Joseph) 1926-..... **CLC 6**
See also CA 21-24R

Schlee, Ann 1934-................ **CLC 35**
See also CA 101; CANR 29; SATA 36, 44

Schlegel, August Wilhelm von
1767-1845 .... **NCLC 15**
See also DLB 94

Schlegel, Friedrich 1772-1829 .... **NCLC 45**
See also DLB 90

Schlegel, Johann Elias (von)
1719(?)-1749 .... **LC 5**

Schlesinger, Arthur M(eier), Jr.
1917- .... **CLC 84**
See also AITN 1; CA 1-4R; CANR 1, 28;
DLB 17; MTCW; SATA 61

Schmidt, Arno (Otto) 1914-1979.... **CLC 56**
See also CA 128; 109; DLB 69

Schmitz, Aron Hector 1861-1928
See Svevo, Italo
See also CA 104; 122; MTCW

Schnackenberg, Gjertrud 1953-..... **CLC 40**
See also CA 116; DLB 120

Schneider, Leonard Alfred 1925-1966
See Bruce, Lenny
See also CA 89-92

Schnitzler, Arthur
1862-1931 .... **TCLC 4; SSC 15**
See also CA 104; DLB 81, 118

Schor, Sandra (M.) 1932(?)-1990 ... **CLC 65**
See also CA 132

Schorer, Mark 1908-1977 .... **CLC 9**
See also CA 5-8R; 73-76; CANR 7;
DLB 103

Schrader, Paul (Joseph) 1946-...... **CLC 26**
See also CA 37-40R; CANR 41; DLB 44

Schreiner, Olive (Emilie Albertina)
1855-1920 .... **TCLC 9**
See also CA 105; DLB 18

Schulberg, Budd (Wilson)
1914- . . . . CLC 7, 48
See also CA 25-28R; CANR 19; DLB 6, 26, 28; DLBY 81

Schulz, Bruno
1892-1942 . . . . TCLC 5, 51; SSC 13
See also CA 115; 123

Schulz, Charles M(onroe) 1922- . . . . CLC 12
See also CA 9-12R; CANR 6; SATA 10

Schumacher, E(rnst) F(riedrich)
1911-1977 . . . . CLC 80
See also CA 81-84; 73-76; CANR 34

Schuyler, James Marcus
1923-1991 . . . . CLC 5, 23
See also CA 101; 134; DLB 5

Schwartz, Delmore (David)
1913-1966 . . . . . . CLC 2, 4, 10, 45; PC 8
See also CA 17-18; 25-28R; CANR 35;
CAP 2; DLB 28, 48; MTCW

Schwartz, Ernst
See Ozu, Yasujiro

Schwartz, John Burnham 1965- . . . . CLC 59
See also CA 132

Schwartz, Lynne Sharon 1939- . . . . . CLC 31
See also CA 103; CANR 44

Schwartz, Muriel A.
See Eliot, T(homas) S(tearns)

Schwarz-Bart, Andre 1928- . . . . CLC 2, 4
See also CA 89-92

Schwarz-Bart, Simone 1938- . . . . CLC 7
See also BW 2; CA 97-100

Schwob, (Mayer Andre) Marcel
1867-1905 . . . . TCLC 20
See also CA 117; DLB 123

Sciascia, Leonardo
1921-1989 . . . . CLC 8, 9, 41
See also CA 85-88; 130; CANR 35; MTCW

Scoppettone, Sandra 1936- . . . . CLC 26
See also AAYA 11; CA 5-8R; CANR 41;
SATA 9

Scorsese, Martin 1942- . . . . CLC 20
See also CA 110; 114; CANR 46, 46

Scotland, Jay
See Jakes, John (William)

Scott, Duncan Campbell
1862-1947 . . . . TCLC 6
See also CA 104; DLB 92

Scott, Evelyn 1893-1963 . . . . CLC 43
See also CA 104; 112; DLB 9, 48

Scott, F(rancis) R(eginald)
1899-1985 . . . . CLC 22
See also CA 101; 114; DLB 88

Scott, Frank
See Scott, F(rancis) R(eginald)

Scott, Joanna 1960- . . . . CLC 50
See also CA 126

Scott, Paul (Mark) 1920-1978 . . . . CLC 9, 60
See also CA 81-84; 77-80; CANR 33;
DLB 14; MTCW

Scott, Walter
1771-1832 . . . . NCLC 15; DA; WLC
See also CDBLB 1789-1832; DLB 93, 107,
116, 144; YABC 2

Scribe, (Augustin) Eugene
1791-1861 . . . . NCLC 16; DC 5

Scrum, R.
See Crumb, R(obert)

Scudery, Madeleine de 1607-1701 . . . . . LC 2

Scum
See Crumb, R(obert)

Scumbag, Little Bobby
See Crumb, R(obert)

Seabrook, John
See Hubbard, L(afayette) Ron(ald)

Sealy, I. Allan 1951- . . . . CLC 55

Search, Alexander
See Pessoa, Fernando (Antonio Nogueira)

Sebastian, Lee
See Silverberg, Robert

Sebastian Owl
See Thompson, Hunter S(tockton)

Sebestyen, Ouida 1924- . . . . CLC 30
See also AAYA 8; CA 107; CANR 40;
CLR 17; JRDA; MAICYA; SAAS 10;
SATA 39

Secundus, H. Scriblerus
See Fielding, Henry

Sedges, John
See Buck, Pearl S(ydenstricker)

Sedgwick, Catharine Maria
1789-1867 . . . . NCLC 19
See also DLB 1, 74

Seelye, John 1931- . . . . CLC 7

Seferiades, Giorgos Stylianou 1900-1971
See Seferis, George
See also CA 5-8R; 33-36R; CANR 5, 36;
MTCW

Seferis, George . . . . CLC 5, 11
See also Seferiades, Giorgos Stylianou

Segal, Erich (Wolf) 1937- . . . . CLC 3, 10
See also BEST 89:1; CA 25-28R; CANR 20,
36; DLBY 86; MTCW

Seger, Bob 1945- . . . . CLC 35

Seghers, Anna . . . . CLC 7
See also Radvanyi, Netty
See also DLB 69

Seidel, Frederick (Lewis) 1936- . . . . . CLC 18
See also CA 13-16R; CANR 8; DLBY 84

Seifert, Jaroslav 1901-1986 . . . . . CLC 34, 44
See also CA 127; MTCW

Sei Shonagon c. 966-1017(?) . . . . . . CMLC 6

Selby, Hubert, Jr. 1928- . . . . . CLC 1, 2, 4, 8
See also CA 13-16R; CANR 33; DLB 2

Selzer, Richard 1928- . . . . CLC 74
See also CA 65-68; CANR 14

Sembene, Ousmane
See Ousmane, Sembene

Senancour, Etienne Pivert de
1770-1846 . . . . NCLC 16
See also DLB 119

Sender, Ramon (Jose)
1902-1982 . . . . CLC 8; HLC
See also CA 5-8R; 105; CANR 8; HW;
MTCW

Seneca, Lucius Annaeus
4B.C.-65 . . . . CMLC 6; DC 5

Senghor, Leopold Sedar
1906- . . . . CLC 54; BLC
See also BW 2; CA 116; 125; CANR 47;
MTCW

Serling, (Edward) Rod(man)
1924-1975 . . . . CLC 30
See also AAYA 14; AITN 1; CA 65-68;
57-60; DLB 26

Serna, Ramon Gomez de la
See Gomez de la Serna, Ramon

Serpieres
See Guillevic, (Eugene)

Service, Robert
See Service, Robert W(illiam)
See also DLB 92

Service, Robert W(illiam)
1874(?)-1958 . . . . . . TCLC 15; DA; WLC
See also Service, Robert
See also CA 115; 140; SATA 20

Seth, Vikram 1952- . . . . CLC 43
See also CA 121; 127; DLB 120

Seton, Cynthia Propper
1926-1982 . . . . CLC 27
See also CA 5-8R; 108; CANR 7

Seton, Ernest (Evan) Thompson
1860-1946 . . . . TCLC 31
See also CA 109; DLB 92; JRDA; SATA 18

Seton-Thompson, Ernest
See Seton, Ernest (Evan) Thompson

Settle, Mary Lee 1918- . . . . CLC 19, 61
See also CA 89-92; CAAS 1; CANR 44;
DLB 6

Seuphor, Michel
See Arp, Jean

**Sevigne, Marie (de Rabutin-Chantal) Marquise
de** 1626-1696 . . . . LC 11

Sexton, Anne (Harvey)
1928-1974 . . . . CLC 2, 4, 6, 8, 10, 15, 53;
DA; PC 2; WLC
See also CA 1-4R; 53-56; CABS 2;
CANR 3, 36; CDALB 1941-1968; DLB 5;
MTCW; SATA 10

Shaara, Michael (Joseph Jr.)
1929-1988 . . . . CLC 15
See also AITN 1; CA 102; DLBY 83

Shackleton, C. C.
See Aldiss, Brian W(ilson)

Shacochis, Bob . . . . CLC 39
See also Shacochis, Robert G.

Shacochis, Robert G. 1951-
See Shacochis, Bob
See also CA 119; 124

Shaffer, Anthony (Joshua) 1926- . . . . CLC 19
See also CA 110; 116; DLB 13

Shaffer, Peter (Levin)
1926- . . . . CLC 5, 14, 18, 37, 60
See also CA 25-28R; CANR 25, 47;
CDBLB 1960 to Present; DLB 13;
MTCW

Shakey, Bernard
See Young, Neil

Shalamov, Varlam (Tikhonovich)
1907(?)-1982 . . . . CLC 18
See also CA 129; 105

Shamlu, Ahmad 1925- . . . . CLC 10

Shammas, Anton 1951-............. **CLC 55**

Shange, Ntozake
        1948- .... **CLC 8, 25, 38, 74; BLC; DC 3**
        See also AAYA 9; BW 2; CA 85-88;
        CABS 3; CANR 27; DLB 38; MTCW

Shanley, John Patrick 1950-....... **CLC 75**
        See also CA 128; 133

Shapcott, Thomas William 1935- ... **CLC 38**
        See also CA 69-72

Shapiro, Jane.................... **CLC 76**

Shapiro, Karl (Jay) 1913- .. **CLC 4, 8, 15, 53**
        See also CA 1-4R; CAAS 6; CANR 1, 36;
        DLB 48; MTCW

Sharp, William 1855-1905 .... **TCLC 39**

Sharpe, Thomas Ridley 1928-
        See Sharpe, Tom
        See also CA 114; 122

Sharpe, Tom.................... **CLC 36**
        See also Sharpe, Thomas Ridley
        See also DLB 14

Shaw, Bernard.................. **TCLC 45**
        See also Shaw, George Bernard
        See also BW 1

Shaw, G. Bernard
        See Shaw, George Bernard

Shaw, George Bernard
        1856-1950 .... **TCLC 3, 9, 21; DA; WLC**
        See also Shaw, Bernard
        See also CA 104; 128; CDBLB 1914-1945;
        DLB 10, 57; MTCW

Shaw, Henry Wheeler
        1818-1885 .... **NCLC 15**
        See also DLB 11

Shaw, Irwin 1913-1984....... **CLC 7, 23, 34**
        See also AITN 1; CA 13-16R; 112;
        CANR 21; CDALB 1941-1968; DLB 6,
        102; DLBY 84; MTCW

Shaw, Robert 1927-1978 .... **CLC 5**
        See also AITN 1; CA 1-4R; 81-84;
        CANR 4; DLB 13, 14

Shaw, T. E.
        See Lawrence, T(homas) E(dward)

Shawn, Wallace 1943- .... **CLC 41**
        See also CA 112

Shea, Lisa 1953-................. **CLC 86**

Sheed, Wilfrid (John Joseph)
        1930- .... **CLC 2, 4, 10, 53**
        See also CA 65-68; CANR 30; DLB 6;
        MTCW

Sheldon, Alice Hastings Bradley
        1915(?)-1987
        See Tiptree, James, Jr.
        See also CA 108; 122; CANR 34; MTCW

Sheldon, John
        See Bloch, Robert (Albert)

Shelley, Mary Wollstonecraft (Godwin)
        1797-1851 .... **NCLC 14; DA; WLC**
        See also CDBLB 1789-1832; DLB 110, 116;
        SATA 29

Shelley, Percy Bysshe
        1792-1822 .... **NCLC 18; DA; WLC**
        See also CDBLB 1789-1832; DLB 96, 110

Shepard, Jim 1956-................ **CLC 36**
        See also CA 137

Shepard, Lucius 1947- .... **CLC 34**
        See also CA 128; 141

Shepard, Sam
        1943- .... **CLC 4, 6, 17, 34, 41, 44; DC 5**
        See also AAYA 1; CA 69-72; CABS 3;
        CANR 22; DLB 7; MTCW

Shepherd, Michael
        See Ludlum, Robert

Sherburne, Zoa (Morin) 1912-...... **CLC 30**
        See also AAYA 13; CA 1-4R; CANR 3, 37;
        MAICYA; SAAS 18; SATA 3

Sheridan, Frances 1724-1766........ **LC 7**
        See also DLB 39, 84

Sheridan, Richard Brinsley
        1751-1816 ... **NCLC 5; DA; DC 1; WLC**
        See also CDBLB 1660-1789; DLB 89

Sherman, Jonathan Marc.......... **CLC 55**

Sherman, Martin 1941(?)-......... **CLC 19**
        See also CA 116; 123

Sherwin, Judith Johnson 1936-... **CLC 7, 15**
        See also CA 25-28R; CANR 34

Sherwood, Frances 1940-.......... **CLC 81**

Sherwood, Robert E(mmet)
        1896-1955 .... **TCLC 3**
        See also CA 104; DLB 7, 26

Shestov, Lev 1866-1938 .... **TCLC 56**

Shiel, M(atthew) P(hipps)
        1865-1947.................. **TCLC 8**
        See also CA 106

Shiga, Naoya 1883-1971.......... **CLC 33**
        See also CA 101; 33-36R

Shilts, Randy 1951-1994 .... **CLC 85**
        See also CA 115; 127; 144; CANR 45

Shimazaki Haruki 1872-1943
        See Shimazaki Toson
        See also CA 105; 134

Shimazaki Toson................ **TCLC 5**
        See also Shimazaki Haruki

Sholokhov, Mikhail (Aleksandrovich)
        1905-1984 .... **CLC 7, 15**
        See also CA 101; 112; MTCW;
        SATA-Obit 36

Shone, Patric
        See Hanley, James

Shreve, Susan Richards 1939-...... **CLC 23**
        See also CA 49-52; CAAS 5; CANR 5, 38;
        MAICYA; SATA 41, 46

Shue, Larry 1946-1985........... **CLC 52**
        See also CA 145; 117

Shu-Jen, Chou 1881-1936
        See Hsun, Lu
        See also CA 104

Shulman, Alix Kates 1932- ...... **CLC 2, 10**
        See also CA 29-32R; CANR 43; SATA 7

Shuster, Joe 1914- .... **CLC 21**

Shute, Nevil.................... **CLC 30**
        See also Norway, Nevil Shute

Shuttle, Penelope (Diane) 1947- ..... **CLC 7**
        See also CA 93-96; CANR 39; DLB 14, 40

Sidney, Mary 1561-1621 .... **LC 19**

Sidney, Sir Philip 1554-1586.... **LC 19; DA**
        See also CDBLB Before 1660

Siegel, Jerome 1914- .... **CLC 21**
        See also CA 116

Siegel, Jerry
        See Siegel, Jerome

Sienkiewicz, Henryk (Adam Alexander Pius)
        1846-1916 .... **TCLC 3**
        See also CA 104; 134

Sierra, Gregorio Martinez
        See Martinez Sierra, Gregorio

Sierra, Maria (de la O'LeJarraga) Martinez
        See Martinez Sierra, Maria (de la
        O'LeJarraga)

Sigal, Clancy 1926-................ **CLC 7**
        See also CA 1-4R

Sigourney, Lydia Howard (Huntley)
        1791-1865 .... **NCLC 21**
        See also DLB 1, 42, 73

Siguenza y Gongora, Carlos de
        1645-1700 .... **LC 8**

Sigurjonsson, Johann 1880-1919... **TCLC 27**

Sikelianos, Angelos 1884-1951 .... **TCLC 39**

Silkin, Jon 1930- .... **CLC 2, 6, 43**
        See also CA 5-8R; CAAS 5; DLB 27

Silko, Leslie (Marmon)
        1948-................. **CLC 23, 74; DA**
        See also AAYA 14; CA 115; 122;
        CANR 45; DLB 143; NNAL

Sillanpaa, Frans Eemil 1888-1964... **CLC 19**
        See also CA 129; 93-96; MTCW

Sillitoe, Alan
        1928-.......... **CLC 1, 3, 6, 10, 19, 57**
        See also AITN 1; CA 9-12R; CAAS 2;
        CANR 8, 26; CDBLB 1960 to Present;
        DLB 14, 139; MTCW; SATA 61

Silone, Ignazio 1900-1978 .... **CLC 4**
        See also CA 25-28; 81-84; CANR 34;
        CAP 2; MTCW

Silver, Joan Micklin 1935- .... **CLC 20**
        See also CA 114; 121

Silver, Nicholas
        See Faust, Frederick (Schiller)

Silverberg, Robert 1935- .... **CLC 7**
        See also CA 1-4R; CAAS 3; CANR 1, 20,
        36; DLB 8; MAICYA; MTCW; SATA 13

Silverstein, Alvin 1933- .... **CLC 17**
        See also CA 49-52; CANR 2; CLR 25;
        JRDA; MAICYA; SATA 8, 69

Silverstein, Virginia B(arbara Opshelor)
        1937-..................... **CLC 17**
        See also CA 49-52; CANR 2; CLR 25;
        JRDA; MAICYA; SATA 8, 69

Sim, Georges
        See Simenon, Georges (Jacques Christian)

Simak, Clifford D(onald)
        1904-1988 .... **CLC 1, 55**
        See also CA 1-4R; 125; CANR 1, 35;
        DLB 8; MTCW; SATA-Obit 56

Simenon, Georges (Jacques Christian)
        1903-1989 .... **CLC 1, 2, 3, 8, 18, 47**
        See also CA 85-88; 129; CANR 35;
        DLB 72; DLBY 89; MTCW

Simic, Charles 1938-... **CLC 6, 9, 22, 49, 68**
        See also CA 29-32R; CAAS 4; CANR 12,
        33; DLB 105

Simmons, Charles (Paul) 1924-..... CLC 57
See also CA 89-92

Simmons, Dan 1948-.............. CLC 44
See also CA 138

Simmons, James (Stewart Alexander)
1933-....................... CLC 43
See also CA 105; DLB 40

Simms, William Gilmore
1806-1870 .... NCLC 3
See also DLB 3, 30, 59, 73

Simon, Carly 1945-.............. CLC 26
See also CA 105

Simon, Claude 1913-....... CLC 4, 9, 15, 39
See also CA 89-92; CANR 33; DLB 83;
MTCW

Simon, (Marvin) Neil
1927-.......... CLC 6, 11, 31, 39, 70
See also AITN 1; CA 21-24R; CANR 26;
DLB 7; MTCW

Simon, Paul 1942(?)-.............. CLC 17
See also CA 116

Simonon, Paul 1956(?)-........... CLC 30

Simpson, Harriette
See Arnow, Harriette (Louisa) Simpson

Simpson, Louis (Aston Marantz)
1923-................. CLC 4, 7, 9, 32
See also CA 1-4R; CAAS 4; CANR 1;
DLB 5; MTCW

Simpson, Mona (Elizabeth) 1957-... CLC 44
See also CA 122; 135

Simpson, N(orman) F(rederick)
1919-....................... CLC 29
See also CA 13-16R; DLB 13

Sinclair, Andrew (Annandale)
1935-..................... CLC 2, 14
See also CA 9-12R; CAAS 5; CANR 14, 38;
DLB 14; MTCW

Sinclair, Emil
See Hesse, Hermann

Sinclair, Iain 1943-.............. CLC 76
See also CA 132

Sinclair, Iain MacGregor
See Sinclair, Iain

Sinclair, Mary Amelia St. Clair 1865(?)-1946
See Sinclair, May
See also CA 104

Sinclair, May................. TCLC 3, 11
See also Sinclair, Mary Amelia St. Clair
See also DLB 36, 135

Sinclair, Upton (Beall)
1878-1968 ...... CLC 1, 11, 15, 63; DA;
WLC
See also CA 5-8R; 25-28R; CANR 7;
CDALB 1929-1941; DLB 9; MTCW;
SATA 9

Singer, Isaac
See Singer, Isaac Bashevis

Singer, Isaac Bashevis
1904-1991 .... CLC 1, 3, 6, 9, 11, 15, 23,
38, 69; DA; SSC 3; WLC
See also AITN 1, 2; CA 1-4R; 134;
CANR 1, 39; CDALB 1941-1968; CLR 1;
DLB 6, 28, 52; DLBY 91; JRDA;
MAICYA; MTCW; SATA 3, 27;
SATA-Obit 68

Singer, Israel Joshua 1893-1944... TCLC 33

Singh, Khushwant 1915-........... CLC 11
See also CA 9-12R; CAAS 9; CANR 6

Sinjohn, John
See Galsworthy, John

Sinyavsky, Andrei (Donatevich)
1925-....................... CLC 8
See also CA 85-88

Sirin, V.
See Nabokov, Vladimir (Vladimirovich)

Sissman, L(ouis) E(dward)
1928-1976 .... CLC 9, 18
See also CA 21-24R; 65-68; CANR 13;
DLB 5

Sisson, C(harles) H(ubert) 1914-..... CLC 8
See also CA 1-4R; CAAS 3; CANR 3;
DLB 27

Sitwell, Dame Edith
1887-1964 .... CLC 2, 9, 67; PC 3
See also CA 9-12R; CANR 35;
CDBLB 1945-1960; DLB 20; MTCW

Sjoewall, Maj 1935-................ CLC 7
See also CA 65-68

Sjowall, Maj
See Sjoewall, Maj

Skelton, Robin 1925-.............. CLC 13
See also AITN 2; CA 5-8R; CAAS 5;
CANR 28; DLB 27, 53

Skolimowski, Jerzy 1938-......... CLC 20
See also CA 128

Skram, Amalie (Bertha)
1847-1905 .... TCLC 25

Skvorecky, Josef (Vaclav)
1924-................. CLC 15, 39, 69
See also CA 61-64; CAAS 1; CANR 10, 34;
MTCW

Slade, Bernard.................. CLC 11, 46
See also Newbound, Bernard Slade
See also CAAS 9; DLB 53

Slaughter, Carolyn 1946-.......... CLC 56
See also CA 85-88

Slaughter, Frank G(ill) 1908- ...... CLC 29
See also AITN 2; CA 5-8R; CANR 5

Slavitt, David R(ytman) 1935-.... CLC 5, 14
See also CA 21-24R; CAAS 3; CANR 41;
DLB 5, 6

Slesinger, Tess 1905-1945 .... TCLC 10
See also CA 107; DLB 102

Slessor, Kenneth 1901-1971....... CLC 14
See also CA 102; 89-92

Slowacki, Juliusz 1809-1849 ..... NCLC 15

Smart, Christopher 1722-1771........ LC 3
See also DLB 109

Smart, Elizabeth 1913-1986........ CLC 54
See also CA 81-84; 118; DLB 88

Smiley, Jane (Graves) 1949- .... CLC 53, 76
See also CA 104; CANR 30

Smith, A(rthur) J(ames) M(arshall)
1902-1980 .... CLC 15
See also CA 1-4R; 102; CANR 4; DLB 88

Smith, Anna Deavere 1950-........ CLC 86
See also CA 133

Smith, Betty (Wehner) 1896-1972... CLC 19
See also CA 5-8R; 33-36R; DLBY 82;
SATA 6

Smith, Charlotte (Turner)
1749-1806 .... NCLC 23
See also DLB 39, 109

Smith, Clark Ashton 1893-1961 .... CLC 43
See also CA 143

Smith, Dave.................. CLC 22, 42
See also Smith, David (Jeddie)
See also CAAS 7; DLB 5

Smith, David (Jeddie) 1942-
See Smith, Dave
See also CA 49-52; CANR 1

Smith, Florence Margaret 1902-1971
See Smith, Stevie
See also CA 17-18; 29-32R; CANR 35;
CAP 2; MTCW

Smith, Iain Crichton 1928- .... CLC 64
See also CA 21-24R; DLB 40, 139

Smith, John 1580(?)-1631 .... LC 9

Smith, Johnston
See Crane, Stephen (Townley)

Smith, Lee 1944-.............. CLC 25, 73
See also CA 114; 119; CANR 46; DLB 143;
DLBY 83

Smith, Martin
See Smith, Martin Cruz

Smith, Martin Cruz 1942-......... CLC 25
See also BEST 89:4; CA 85-88; CANR 6,
23, 43; NNAL

Smith, Mary-Ann Tirone 1944-..... CLC 39
See also CA 118; 136

Smith, Patti 1946- .... CLC 12
See also CA 93-96

Smith, Pauline (Urmson)
1882-1959 .... TCLC 25

Smith, Rosamond
See Oates, Joyce Carol

Smith, Sheila Kaye
See Kaye-Smith, Sheila

Smith, Stevie.............. CLC 3, 8, 25, 44
See also Smith, Florence Margaret
See also DLB 20

Smith, Wilbur (Addison) 1933-..... CLC 33
See also CA 13-16R; CANR 7, 46, 46;
MTCW

Smith, William Jay 1918-.......... CLC 6
See also CA 5-8R; CANR 44; DLB 5;
MAICYA; SATA 2, 68

Smith, Woodrow Wilson
See Kuttner, Henry

Smolenskin, Peretz 1842-1885.... NCLC 30

Smollett, Tobias (George) 1721-1771 .. LC 2
See also CDBLB 1660-1789; DLB 39, 104

Snodgrass, W(illiam) D(e Witt)
1926-........... CLC 2, 6, 10, 18, 68
See also CA 1-4R; CANR 6, 36; DLB 5;
MTCW

Snow, C(harles) P(ercy)
1905-1980 .... CLC 1, 4, 6, 9, 13, 19
See also CA 5-8R; 101; CANR 28;
CDBLB 1945-1960; DLB 15, 77; MTCW

Snow, Frances Compton
See Adams, Henry (Brooks)

Snyder, Gary (Sherman)
1930- . . . . CLC 1, 2, 5, 9, 32
See also CA 17-20R; CANR 30; DLB 5, 16

Snyder, Zilpha Keatley 1927- . . . . . . CLC 17
See also CA 9-12R; CANR 38; CLR 31;
JRDA; MAICYA; SAAS 2; SATA 1, 28,
75

Soares, Bernardo
See Pessoa, Fernando (Antonio Nogueira)

Sobh, A.
See Shamlu, Ahmad

Sobol, Joshua . . . . CLC 60

Soderberg, Hjalmar 1869-1941 . . . . TCLC 39

Sodergran, Edith (Irene)
See Soedergran, Edith (Irene)

Soedergran, Edith (Irene)
1892-1923 . . . . TCLC 31

Softly, Edgar
See Lovecraft, H(oward) P(hillips)

Softly, Edward
See Lovecraft, H(oward) P(hillips)

Sokolov, Raymond 1941- . . . . CLC 7
See also CA 85-88

Solo, Jay
See Ellison, Harlan (Jay)

Sologub, Fyodor . . . . TCLC 9
See also Teternikov, Fyodor Kuzmich

Solomons, Ikey Esquir
See Thackeray, William Makepeace

Solomos, Dionysios 1798-1857 . . . NCLC 15

Solwoska, Mara
See French, Marilyn

Solzhenitsyn, Aleksandr I(sayevich)
1918- . . . . . . CLC 1, 2, 4, 7, 9, 10, 18, 26,
34, 78; DA; WLC
See also AITN 1; CA 69-72; CANR 40;
MTCW

Somers, Jane
See Lessing, Doris (May)

Somerville, Edith 1858-1949 . . . . . . TCLC 51
See also DLB 135

Somerville & Ross
See Martin, Violet Florence; Somerville,
Edith

Sommer, Scott 1951- . . . . CLC 25
See also CA 106

Sondheim, Stephen (Joshua)
1930- . . . . CLC 30, 39
See also AAYA 11; CA 103; CANR 47

Sontag, Susan 1933- . . . CLC 1, 2, 10, 13, 31
See also CA 17-20R; CANR 25; DLB 2, 67;
MTCW

Sophocles
496(?)B.C.-406(?)B.C. . . . . . CMLC 2; DA;
DC 1

Sorel, Julia
See Drexler, Rosalyn

Sorrentino, Gilbert
1929- . . . . CLC 3, 7, 14, 22, 40
See also CA 77-80; CANR 14, 33; DLB 5;
DLBY 80

Soto, Gary 1952- . . . . CLC 32, 80; HLC
See also AAYA 10; CA 119; 125; DLB 82;
HW; JRDA; SATA 80

Soupault, Philippe 1897-1990 . . . . . . CLC 68
See also CA 116; 131

Souster, (Holmes) Raymond
1921- . . . . CLC 5, 14
See also CA 13-16R; CAAS 14; CANR 13,
29; DLB 88; SATA 63

Southern, Terry 1926- . . . . CLC 7
See also CA 1-4R; CANR 1; DLB 2

Southey, Robert 1774-1843 . . . . NCLC 8
See also DLB 93, 107, 142; SATA 54

Southworth, Emma Dorothy Eliza Nevitte
1819-1899 . . . . NCLC 26

Souza, Ernest
See Scott, Evelyn

Soyinka, Wole
1934- . . . . CLC 3, 5, 14, 36, 44; BLC;
DA; DC 2; WLC
See also BW 2; CA 13-16R; CANR 27, 39;
DLB 125; MTCW

Spackman, W(illiam) M(ode)
1905-1990 . . . . CLC 46
See also CA 81-84; 132

Spacks, Barry 1931- . . . . CLC 14
See also CA 29-32R; CANR 33; DLB 105

Spanidou, Irini 1946- . . . . CLC 44

Spark, Muriel (Sarah)
1918- . . . . CLC 2, 3, 5, 8, 13, 18, 40;
SSC 10
See also CA 5-8R; CANR 12, 36;
CDBLB 1945-1960; DLB 15, 139; MTCW

Spaulding, Douglas
See Bradbury, Ray (Douglas)

Spaulding, Leonard
See Bradbury, Ray (Douglas)

Spence, J. A. D.
See Eliot, T(homas) S(tearns)

Spencer, Elizabeth 1921- . . . . CLC 22
See also CA 13-16R; CANR 32; DLB 6;
MTCW; SATA 14

Spencer, Leonard G.
See Silverberg, Robert

Spencer, Scott 1945- . . . . CLC 30
See also CA 113; DLBY 86

Spender, Stephen (Harold)
1909- . . . . CLC 1, 2, 5, 10, 41
See also CA 9-12R; CANR 31;
CDBLB 1945-1960; DLB 20; MTCW

Spengler, Oswald (Arnold Gottfried)
1880-1936 . . . . TCLC 25
See also CA 118

Spenser, Edmund
1552(?)-1599 . . . . LC 5; DA; PC 8; WLC
See also CDBLB Before 1660

Spicer, Jack 1925-1965 . . . . . . CLC 8, 18, 72
See also CA 85-88; DLB 5, 16

Spiegelman, Art 1948- . . . . CLC 76
See also AAYA 10; CA 125; CANR 41

Spielberg, Peter 1929- . . . . CLC 6
See also CA 5-8R; CANR 4; DLBY 81

Spielberg, Steven 1947- . . . . CLC 20
See also AAYA 8; CA 77-80; CANR 32;
SATA 32

Spillane, Frank Morrison 1918-
See Spillane, Mickey
See also CA 25-28R; CANR 28; MTCW;
SATA 66

Spillane, Mickey . . . . CLC 3, 13
See also Spillane, Frank Morrison

Spinoza, Benedictus de 1632-1677 . . . . LC 9

Spinrad, Norman (Richard) 1940- . . . CLC 46
See also CA 37-40R; CAAS 19; CANR 20;
DLB 8

Spitteler, Carl (Friedrich Georg)
1845-1924 . . . . TCLC 12
See also CA 109; DLB 129

Spivack, Kathleen (Romola Drucker)
1938- . . . . CLC 6
See also CA 49-52

Spoto, Donald 1941- . . . . CLC 39
See also CA 65-68; CANR 11

Springsteen, Bruce (F.) 1949- . . . . . . CLC 17
See also CA 111

Spurling, Hilary 1940- . . . . CLC 34
See also CA 104; CANR 25

Spyker, John Howland
See Elman, Richard

Squires, (James) Radcliffe
1917-1993 . . . . CLC 51
See also CA 1-4R; 140; CANR 6, 21

Srivastava, Dhanpat Rai 1880(?)-1936
See Premchand
See also CA 118

Stacy, Donald
See Pohl, Frederik

Stael, Germaine de
See Stael-Holstein, Anne Louise Germaine
Necker Baronn
See also DLB 119

Stael-Holstein, Anne Louise Germaine Necker
Baronn 1766-1817 . . . . NCLC 3
See also Stael, Germaine de

Stafford, Jean 1915-1979 . . . CLC 4, 7, 19, 68
See also CA 1-4R; 85-88; CANR 3; DLB 2;
MTCW; SATA-Obit 22

Stafford, William (Edgar)
1914-1993 . . . . CLC 4, 7, 29
See also CA 5-8R; 142; CAAS 3; CANR 5,
22; DLB 5

Staines, Trevor
See Brunner, John (Kilian Houston)

Stairs, Gordon
See Austin, Mary (Hunter)

Stannard, Martin 1947- . . . . CLC 44
See also CA 142

Stanton, Maura 1946- . . . . CLC 9
See also CA 89-92; CANR 15; DLB 120

Stanton, Schuyler
See Baum, L(yman) Frank

Stapledon, (William) Olaf
1886-1950 . . . . TCLC 22
See also CA 111; DLB 15

Starbuck, George (Edwin) 1931- . . . . CLC 53
See also CA 21-24R; CANR 23

Stark, Richard
  See Westlake, Donald E(dwin)

Staunton, Schuyler
  See Baum, L(yman) Frank

Stead, Christina (Ellen)
  1902-1983 . . . . **CLC 2, 5, 8, 32, 80**
  See also CA 13-16R; 109; CANR 33, 40;
  MTCW

Stead, William Thomas
  1849-1912 . . . . **TCLC 48**

Steele, Richard 1672-1729 . . . . **LC 18**
  See also CDBLB 1660-1789; DLB 84, 101

Steele, Timothy (Reid) 1948- . . . . **CLC 45**
  See also CA 93-96; CANR 16; DLB 120

Steffens, (Joseph) Lincoln
  1866-1936 . . . . **TCLC 20**
  See also CA 117

Stegner, Wallace (Earle)
  1909-1993 . . . . **CLC 9, 49, 81**
  See also AITN 1; BEST 90:3; CA 1-4R;
  141; CAAS 9; CANR 1, 21, 46, 46;
  DLB 9; DLBY 93; MTCW

Stein, Gertrude
  1874-1946 . . . . . . **TCLC 1, 6, 28, 48; DA;**
  WLC
  See also CA 104; 132; CDALB 1917-1929;
  DLB 4, 54, 86; MTCW

Steinbeck, John (Ernst)
  1902-1968 . . . . . . **CLC 1, 5, 9, 13, 21, 34,**
  45, 75; DA; SSC 11; WLC
  See also AAYA 12; CA 1-4R; 25-28R;
  CANR 1, 35; CDALB 1929-1941; DLB 7,
  9; DLBD 2; MTCW; SATA 9

Steinem, Gloria 1934- . . . . **CLC 63**
  See also CA 53-56; CANR 28; MTCW

Steiner, George 1929- . . . . **CLC 24**
  See also CA 73-76; CANR 31; DLB 67;
  MTCW; SATA 62

Steiner, K. Leslie
  See Delany, Samuel R(ay, Jr.)

Steiner, Rudolf 1861-1925 . . . . **TCLC 13**
  See also CA 107

Stendhal
  1783-1842 . . . . . **NCLC 23, 46; DA; WLC**
  See also DLB 119

Stephen, Leslie 1832-1904 . . . . **TCLC 23**
  See also CA 123; DLB 57, 144

Stephen, Sir Leslie
  See Stephen, Leslie

Stephen, Virginia
  See Woolf, (Adeline) Virginia

Stephens, James 1882(?)-1950 . . . . . . **TCLC 4**
  See also CA 104; DLB 19

Stephens, Reed
  See Donaldson, Stephen R.

Steptoe, Lydia
  See Barnes, Djuna

Sterchi, Beat 1949- . . . . **CLC 65**

Sterling, Brett
  See Bradbury, Ray (Douglas); Hamilton,
  Edmond

Sterling, Bruce 1954- . . . . **CLC 72**
  See also CA 119; CANR 44

Sterling, George 1869-1926 . . . . . . **TCLC 20**
  See also CA 117; DLB 54

Stern, Gerald 1925- . . . . **CLC 40**
  See also CA 81-84; CANR 28; DLB 105

Stern, Richard (Gustave) 1928- . . . **CLC 4, 39**
  See also CA 1-4R; CANR 1, 25; DLBY 87

Sternberg, Josef von 1894-1969 . . . . . **CLC 20**
  See also CA 81-84

Sterne, Laurence
  1713-1768 . . . . **LC 2; DA; WLC**
  See also CDBLB 1660-1789; DLB 39

Sternheim, (William Adolf) Carl
  1878-1942 . . . . **TCLC 8**
  See also CA 105; DLB 56, 118

Stevens, Mark 1951- . . . . **CLC 34**
  See also CA 122

Stevens, Wallace
  1879-1955 . . . . **TCLC 3, 12, 45; DA;**
  PC 6; WLC
  See also CA 104; 124; CDALB 1929-1941;
  DLB 54; MTCW

Stevenson, Anne (Katharine)
  1933- . . . . **CLC 7, 33**
  See also CA 17-20R; CAAS 9; CANR 9, 33;
  DLB 40; MTCW

Stevenson, Robert Louis (Balfour)
  1850-1894 . . . . **NCLC 5, 14; DA;**
  SSC 11; WLC
  See also CDBLB 1890-1914; CLR 10, 11;
  DLB 18, 57, 141; JRDA; MAICYA;
  YABC 2

Stewart, J(ohn) I(nnes) M(ackintosh)
  1906- . . . . **CLC 7, 14, 32**
  See also CA 85-88; CAAS 3; CANR 47;
  MTCW

Stewart, Mary (Florence Elinor)
  1916- . . . . **CLC 7, 35**
  See also CA 1-4R; CANR 1; SATA 12

Stewart, Mary Rainbow
  See Stewart, Mary (Florence Elinor)

Stifle, June
  See Campbell, Maria

Stifter, Adalbert 1805-1868 . . . . . . **NCLC 41**
  See also DLB 133

Still, James 1906- . . . . **CLC 49**
  See also CA 65-68; CAAS 17; CANR 10,
  26; DLB 9; SATA 29

Sting
  See Sumner, Gordon Matthew

Stirling, Arthur
  See Sinclair, Upton (Beall)

Stitt, Milan 1941- . . . . **CLC 29**
  See also CA 69-72

Stockton, Francis Richard 1834-1902
  See Stockton, Frank R.
  See also CA 108; 137; MAICYA; SATA 44

Stockton, Frank R. . . . . **TCLC 47**
  See also Stockton, Francis Richard
  See also DLB 42, 74; SATA 32

Stoddard, Charles
  See Kuttner, Henry

Stoker, Abraham 1847-1912
  See Stoker, Bram
  See also CA 105; DA; SATA 29

Stoker, Bram . . . . **TCLC 8; WLC**
  See also Stoker, Abraham
  See also CDBLB 1890-1914; DLB 36, 70

Stolz, Mary (Slattery) 1920- . . . . **CLC 12**
  See also AAYA 8; AITN 1; CA 5-8R;
  CANR 13, 41; JRDA; MAICYA;
  SAAS 3; SATA 10, 71

Stone, Irving 1903-1989 . . . . **CLC 7**
  See also AITN 1; CA 1-4R; 129; CAAS 3;
  CANR 1, 23; MTCW; SATA 3;
  SATA-Obit 64

Stone, Oliver 1946- . . . . **CLC 73**
  See also CA 110

Stone, Robert (Anthony)
  1937- . . . . **CLC 5, 23, 42**
  See also CA 85-88; CANR 23; MTCW

Stone, Zachary
  See Follett, Ken(neth Martin)

Stoppard, Tom
  1937- . . . . . . **CLC 1, 3, 4, 5, 8, 15, 29, 34,**
  63; DA; WLC
  See also CA 81-84; CANR 39;
  CDBLB 1960 to Present; DLB 13;
  DLBY 85; MTCW

Storey, David (Malcolm)
  1933- . . . . **CLC 2, 4, 5, 8**
  See also CA 81-84; CANR 36; DLB 13, 14;
  MTCW

Storm, Hyemeyohsts 1935- . . . . **CLC 3**
  See also CA 81-84; CANR 45; NNAL

Storm, (Hans) Theodor (Woldsen)
  1817-1888 . . . . **NCLC 1**

Storni, Alfonsina
  1892-1938 . . . . **TCLC 5; HLC**
  See also CA 104; 131; HW

Stout, Rex (Todhunter) 1886-1975 . . . **CLC 3**
  See also AITN 2; CA 61-64

Stow, (Julian) Randolph 1935- . . **CLC 23, 48**
  See also CA 13-16R; CANR 33; MTCW

Stowe, Harriet (Elizabeth) Beecher
  1811-1896 . . . . **NCLC 3; DA; WLC**
  See also CDALB 1865-1917; DLB 1, 12, 42,
  74; JRDA; MAICYA; YABC 1

Strachey, (Giles) Lytton
  1880-1932 . . . . **TCLC 12**
  See also CA 110; DLBD 10

Strand, Mark 1934- . . . . . . **CLC 6, 18, 41, 71**
  See also CA 21-24R; CANR 40; DLB 5;
  SATA 41

Straub, Peter (Francis) 1943- . . . . . . **CLC 28**
  See also BEST 89:1; CA 85-88; CANR 28;
  DLBY 84; MTCW

Strauss, Botho 1944- . . . . **CLC 22**
  See also DLB 124

Streatfeild, (Mary) Noel
  1895(?)-1986 . . . . **CLC 21**
  See also CA 81-84; 120; CANR 31;
  CLR 17; MAICYA; SATA 20;
  SATA-Obit 48

Stribling, T(homas) S(igismund)
  1881-1965 . . . . **CLC 23**
  See also CA 107; DLB 9

Strindberg, (Johan) August
  1849-1912 . . . . . . **TCLC 1, 8, 21, 47; DA;**
  WLC
  See also CA 104; 135

Stringer, Arthur 1874-1950 .... TCLC 37
See also DLB 92

Stringer, David
See Roberts, Keith (John Kingston)

Strugatskii, Arkadii (Natanovich)
1925-1991 .... CLC 27
See also CA 106; 135

Strugatskii, Boris (Natanovich)
1933- .... CLC 27
See also CA 106

Strummer, Joe 1953(?)- .... CLC 30

Stuart, Don A.
See Campbell, John W(ood, Jr.)

Stuart, Ian
See MacLean, Alistair (Stuart)

Stuart, Jesse (Hilton)
1906-1984 .... CLC 1, 8, 11, 14, 34
See also CA 5-8R; 112; CANR 31; DLB 9,
48, 102; DLBY 84; SATA 2;
SATA-Obit 36

Sturgeon, Theodore (Hamilton)
1918-1985 .... CLC 22, 39
See also Queen, Ellery
See also CA 81-84; 116; CANR 32; DLB 8;
DLBY 85; MTCW

Sturges, Preston 1898-1959 .... TCLC 48
See also CA 114; DLB 26

Styron, William
1925- .... CLC 1, 3, 5, 11, 15, 60
See also BEST 90:4; CA 5-8R; CANR 6, 33;
CDALB 1968-1988; DLB 2, 143;
DLBY 80; MTCW

Suarez Lynch, B.
See Bioy Casares, Adolfo; Borges, Jorge
Luis

Su Chien 1884-1918
See Su Man-shu
See also CA 123

Suckow, Ruth 1892-1960
See also CA 113; DLB 9, 102; SSC 18

Sudermann, Hermann 1857-1928 .. TCLC 15
See also CA 107; DLB 118

Sue, Eugene 1804-1857 .... NCLC 1
See also DLB 119

Sueskind, Patrick 1949- .... CLC 44
See also Suskind, Patrick

Sukenick, Ronald 1932- ..... CLC 3, 4, 6, 48
See also CA 25-28R; CAAS 8; CANR 32;
DLBY 81

Suknaski, Andrew 1942- .... CLC 19
See also CA 101; DLB 53

Sullivan, Vernon
See Vian, Boris

Sully Prudhomme 1839-1907 ...... TCLC 31

Su Man-shu .... TCLC 24
See also Su Chien

Summerforest, Ivy B.
See Kirkup, James

Summers, Andrew James 1942- ..... CLC 26

Summers, Andy
See Summers, Andrew James

Summers, Hollis (Spurgeon, Jr.)
1916- .... CLC 10
See also CA 5-8R; CANR 3; DLB 6

Summers, (Alphonsus Joseph-Mary Augustus)
Montague 1880-1948 .... TCLC 16
See also CA 118

Sumner, Gordon Matthew 1951-.... CLC 26

Surtees, Robert Smith
1803-1864 .... NCLC 14
See also DLB 21

Susann, Jacqueline 1921-1974...... CLC 3
See also AITN 1; CA 65-68; 53-56; MTCW

Suskind, Patrick
See Sueskind, Patrick
See also CA 145

Sutcliff, Rosemary 1920-1992 ...... CLC 26
See also AAYA 10; CA 5-8R; 139;
CANR 37; CLR 1; JRDA; MAICYA;
SATA 6, 44, 78; SATA-Obit 73

Sutro, Alfred 1863-1933........... TCLC 6
See also CA 105; DLB 10

Sutton, Henry
See Slavitt, David R(ytman)

Svevo, Italo .... TCLC 2, 35
See also Schmitz, Aron Hector

Swados, Elizabeth 1951- .... CLC 12
See also CA 97-100

Swados, Harvey 1920-1972 .... CLC 5
See also CA 5-8R; 37-40R; CANR 6;
DLB 2

Swan, Gladys 1934- .... CLC 69
See also CA 101; CANR 17, 39

Swarthout, Glendon (Fred)
1918-1992 .... CLC 35
See also CA 1-4R; 139; CANR 1, 47;
SATA 26

Sweet, Sarah C.
See Jewett, (Theodora) Sarah Orne

Swenson, May
1919-1989 .... CLC 4, 14, 61; DA
See also CA 5-8R; 130; CANR 36; DLB 5;
MTCW; SATA 15

Swift, Augustus
See Lovecraft, H(oward) P(hillips)

Swift, Graham (Colin) 1949- .... CLC 41
See also CA 117; 122; CANR 46, 46

Swift, Jonathan
1667-1745 ...... LC 1; DA; PC 9; WLC
See also CDBLB 1660-1789; DLB 39, 95,
101; SATA 19

Swinburne, Algernon Charles
1837-1909 ...... TCLC 8, 36; DA; WLC
See also CA 105; 140; CDBLB 1832-1890;
DLB 35, 57

Swinfen, Ann.................... CLC 34

Swinnerton, Frank Arthur
1884-1982 .... CLC 31
See also CA 108; DLB 34

Swithen, John
See King, Stephen (Edwin)

Sylvia
See Ashton-Warner, Sylvia (Constance)

Symmes, Robert Edward
See Duncan, Robert (Edward)

Symonds, John Addington
1840-1893 .... NCLC 34
See also DLB 57, 144

Symons, Arthur 1865-1945 .... TCLC 11
See also CA 107; DLB 19, 57

Symons, Julian (Gustave)
1912- .... CLC 2, 14, 32
See also CA 49-52; CAAS 3; CANR 3, 33;
DLB 87; DLBY 92; MTCW

Synge, (Edmund) J(ohn) M(illington)
1871-1909 .... TCLC 6, 37; DC 2
See also CA 104; 141; CDBLB 1890-1914;
DLB 10, 19

Syruc, J.
See Milosz, Czeslaw

Szirtes, George 1948-............. CLC 46
See also CA 109; CANR 27

Tabori, George 1914-............. CLC 19
See also CA 49-52; CANR 4

Tagore, Rabindranath
1861-1941 .... TCLC 3, 53; PC 8
See also CA 104; 120; MTCW

Taine, Hippolyte Adolphe
1828-1893 .... NCLC 15

Talese, Gay 1932-................ CLC 37
See also AITN 1; CA 1-4R; CANR 9;
MTCW

Tallent, Elizabeth (Ann) 1954- ..... CLC 45
See also CA 117; DLB 130

Tally, Ted 1952-................. CLC 42
See also CA 120; 124

Tamayo y Baus, Manuel
1829-1898 .... NCLC 1

Tammsaare, A(nton) H(ansen)
1878-1940 .... TCLC 27

Tan, Amy 1952- .... CLC 59
See also AAYA 9; BEST 89:3; CA 136;
SATA 75

Tandem, Felix
See Spitteler, Carl (Friedrich Georg)

Tanizaki, Jun'ichiro
1886-1965 .... CLC 8, 14, 28
See also CA 93-96; 25-28R

Tanner, William
See Amis, Kingsley (William)

Tao Lao
See Storni, Alfonsina

Tarassoff, Lev
See Troyat, Henri

Tarbell, Ida M(inerva)
1857-1944 .... TCLC 40
See also CA 122; DLB 47

Tarkington, (Newton) Booth
1869-1946 .... TCLC 9
See also CA 110; 143; DLB 9, 102;
SATA 17

Tarkovsky, Andrei (Arsenyevich)
1932-1986 .... CLC 75
See also CA 127

Tartt, Donna 1964(?)-............. CLC 76
See also CA 142

Tasso, Torquato 1544-1595 .... LC 5

Tate, (John Orley) Allen
1899-1979 .... CLC 2, 4, 6, 9, 11, 14, 24
See also CA 5-8R; 85-88; CANR 32;
DLB 4, 45, 63; MTCW

Tate, Ellalice
See Hibbert, Eleanor Alice Burford

Tate, James (Vincent) 1943- ... CLC 2, 6, 25
See also CA 21-24R; CANR 29; DLB 5

Tavel, Ronald 1940- .... CLC 6
See also CA 21-24R; CANR 33

Taylor, C(ecil) P(hilip) 1929-1981... CLC 27
See also CA 25-28R; 105; CANR 47

Taylor, Edward 1642(?)-1729.... LC 11; DA
See also DLB 24

Taylor, Eleanor Ross 1920-........ CLC 5
See also CA 81-84

Taylor, Elizabeth 1912-1975 ... CLC 2, 4, 29
See also CA 13-16R; CANR 9; DLB 139;
MTCW; SATA 13

Taylor, Henry (Splawn) 1942-...... CLC 44
See also CA 33-36R; CAAS 7; CANR 31;
DLB 5

Taylor, Kamala (Purnaiya) 1924-
See Markandaya, Kamala
See also CA 77-80

Taylor, Mildred D. .... CLC 21
See also AAYA 10; BW 1; CA 85-88;
CANR 25; CLR 9; DLB 52; JRDA;
MAICYA; SAAS 5; SATA 15, 70

Taylor, Peter (Hillsman)
1917- ...... CLC 1, 4, 18, 37, 44, 50, 71;
SSC 10
See also CA 13-16R; CANR 9; DLBY 81;
MTCW

Taylor, Robert Lewis 1912-........ CLC 14
See also CA 1-4R; CANR 3; SATA 10

Tchekhov, Anton
See Chekhov, Anton (Pavlovich)

Teasdale, Sara 1884-1933.......... TCLC 4
See also CA 104; DLB 45; SATA 32

Tegner, Esaias 1782-1846........ NCLC 2

Teilhard de Chardin, (Marie Joseph) Pierre
1881-1955 .... TCLC 9
See also CA 105

Temple, Ann
See Mortimer, Penelope (Ruth)

Tennant, Emma (Christina)
1937- .... CLC 13, 52
See also CA 65-68; CAAS 9; CANR 10, 38;
DLB 14

Tenneshaw, S. M.
See Silverberg, Robert

Tennyson, Alfred
1809-1892 .. NCLC 30; DA; PC 6; WLC
See also CDBLB 1832-1890; DLB 32

Teran, Lisa St. Aubin de .... CLC 36
See also St. Aubin de Teran, Lisa

Terence 195(?)B.C.-159B.C....... CMLC 14

Teresa de Jesus, St. 1515-1582 ...... LC 18

Terkel, Louis 1912-
See Terkel, Studs
See also CA 57-60; CANR 18, 45; MTCW

Terkel, Studs .... CLC 38
See also Terkel, Louis
See also AITN 1

Terry, C. V.
See Slaughter, Frank G(ill)

Terry, Megan 1932-.............. CLC 19
See also CA 77-80; CABS 3; CANR 43;
DLB 7

Tertz, Abram
See Sinyavsky, Andrei (Donatevich)

Tesich, Steve 1943(?)-.......... CLC 40, 69
See also CA 105; DLBY 83

Teternikov, Fyodor Kuzmich 1863-1927
See Sologub, Fyodor
See also CA 104

Tevis, Walter 1928-1984 .... CLC 42
See also CA 113

Tey, Josephine.................. TCLC 14
See also Mackintosh, Elizabeth
See also DLB 77

Thackeray, William Makepeace
1811-1863 .... NCLC 5, 14, 22, 43; DA;
WLC
See also CDBLB 1832-1890; DLB 21, 55;
SATA 23

Thakura, Ravindranatha
See Tagore, Rabindranath

Tharoor, Shashi 1956-............ CLC 70
See also CA 141

Thelwell, Michael Miles 1939-..... CLC 22
See also BW 2; CA 101

Theobald, Lewis, Jr.
See Lovecraft, H(oward) P(hillips)

Theodorescu, Ion N. 1880-1967
See Arghezi, Tudor
See also CA 116

Theriault, Yves 1915-1983......... CLC 79
See also CA 102; DLB 88

Theroux, Alexander (Louis)
1939- .... CLC 2, 25
See also CA 85-88; CANR 20

Theroux, Paul (Edward)
1941- .... CLC 5, 8, 11, 15, 28, 46
See also BEST 89:4; CA 33-36R; CANR 20,
45; DLB 2; MTCW; SATA 44

Thesen, Sharon 1946-............ CLC 56

Thevenin, Denis
See Duhamel, Georges

Thibault, Jacques Anatole Francois
1844-1924
See France, Anatole
See also CA 106; 127; MTCW

Thiele, Colin (Milton) 1920-....... CLC 17
See also CA 29-32R; CANR 12, 28;
CLR 27; MAICYA; SAAS 2; SATA 14,
72

Thomas, Audrey (Callahan)
1935-................. CLC 7, 13, 37
See also AITN 2; CA 21-24R; CAAS 19;
CANR 36; DLB 60; MTCW

Thomas, D(onald) M(ichael)
1935-............... CLC 13, 22, 31
See also CA 61-64; CAAS 11; CANR 17,
45; CDBLB 1960 to Present; DLB 40;
MTCW

Thomas, Dylan (Marlais)
1914-1953 ... TCLC 1, 8, 45; DA; PC 2;
SSC 3; WLC
See also CA 104; 120; CDBLB 1945-1960;
DLB 13, 20, 139; MTCW; SATA 60

Thomas, (Philip) Edward
1878-1917 .... TCLC 10
See also CA 106; DLB 19

Thomas, Joyce Carol 1938-........ CLC 35
See also AAYA 12; BW 2; CA 113; 116;
CLR 19; DLB 33; JRDA; MAICYA;
MTCW; SAAS 7; SATA 40, 78

Thomas, Lewis 1913-1993 .... CLC 35
See also CA 85-88; 143; CANR 38; MTCW

Thomas, Paul
See Mann, (Paul) Thomas

Thomas, Piri 1928-............... CLC 17
See also CA 73-76; HW

Thomas, R(onald) S(tuart)
1913- .... CLC 6, 13, 48
See also CA 89-92; CAAS 4; CANR 30;
CDBLB 1960 to Present; DLB 27;
MTCW

Thomas, Ross (Elmore) 1926-...... CLC 39
See also CA 33-36R; CANR 22

Thompson, Francis Clegg
See Mencken, H(enry) L(ouis)

Thompson, Francis Joseph
1859-1907 .... TCLC 4
See also CA 104; CDBLB 1890-1914;
DLB 19

Thompson, Hunter S(tockton)
1939- .... CLC 9, 17, 40
See also BEST 89:1; CA 17-20R; CANR 23,
46, 46; MTCW

Thompson, James Myers
See Thompson, Jim (Myers)

Thompson, Jim (Myers)
1906-1977(?) .... CLC 69
See also CA 140

Thompson, Judith .... CLC 39

Thomson, James 1700-1748........ LC 16

Thomson, James 1834-1882...... NCLC 18

Thoreau, Henry David
1817-1862 ...... NCLC 7, 21; DA; WLC
See also CDALB 1640-1865; DLB 1

Thornton, Hall
See Silverberg, Robert

Thurber, James (Grover)
1894-1961 ... CLC 5, 11, 25; DA; SSC 1
See also CA 73-76; CANR 17, 39;
CDALB 1929-1941; DLB 4, 11, 22, 102;
MAICYA; MTCW; SATA 13

Thurman, Wallace (Henry)
1902-1934 .... TCLC 6; BLC
See also BW 1; CA 104; 124; DLB 51

Ticheburn, Cheviot
See Ainsworth, William Harrison

Tieck, (Johann) Ludwig
1773-1853 .... NCLC 5, 46
See also DLB 90

Tiger, Derry
See Ellison, Harlan (Jay)

Tilghman, Christopher 1948(?)-..... CLC 65

Tillinghast, Richard (Williford)
1940- .... CLC 29
See also CA 29-32R; CANR 26

Timrod, Henry 1828-1867 .... NCLC 25
See also DLB 3

Tindall, Gillian 1938-.............. CLC 7
  See also CA 21-24R; CANR 11

Tiptree, James, Jr. .... CLC 48, 50
  See also Sheldon, Alice Hastings Bradley
  See also DLB 8

Titmarsh, Michael Angelo
  See Thackeray, William Makepeace

Tocqueville, Alexis (Charles Henri Maurice
    Clerel Comte) 1805-1859..... NCLC 7

Tolkien, J(ohn) R(onald) R(euel)
    1892-1973 .... CLC 1, 2, 3, 8, 12, 38;
                                       DA; WLC
  See also AAYA 10; AITN 1; CA 17-18;
    45-48; CANR 36; CAP 2;
    CDBLB 1914-1945; DLB 15; JRDA;
    MAICYA; MTCW; SATA 2, 32;
    SATA-Obit 24

Toller, Ernst 1893-1939......... TCLC 10
  See also CA 107; DLB 124

Tolson, M. B.
  See Tolson, Melvin B(eaunorus)

Tolson, Melvin B(eaunorus)
    1898(?)-1966 .... CLC 36; BLC
  See also BW 1; CA 124; 89-92; DLB 48, 76

Tolstoi, Aleksei Nikolaevich
  See Tolstoy, Alexey Nikolaevich

Tolstoy, Alexey Nikolaevich
    1882-1945 .... TCLC 18
  See also CA 107

Tolstoy, Count Leo
  See Tolstoy, Leo (Nikolaevich)

Tolstoy, Leo (Nikolaevich)
    1828-1910 ...... TCLC 4, 11, 17, 28, 44;
                           DA; SSC 9; WLC
  See also CA 104; 123; SATA 26

Tomasi di Lampedusa, Giuseppe 1896-1957
  See Lampedusa, Giuseppe (Tomasi) di
  See also CA 111

Tomlin, Lily...................... CLC 17
  See also Tomlin, Mary Jean

Tomlin, Mary Jean 1939(?)-
  See Tomlin, Lily
  See also CA 117

Tomlinson, (Alfred) Charles
    1927- .... CLC 2, 4, 6, 13, 45
  See also CA 5-8R; CANR 33; DLB 40

Tonson, Jacob
  See Bennett, (Enoch) Arnold

Toole, John Kennedy
    1937-1969 .... CLC 19, 64
  See also CA 104; DLBY 81

Toomer, Jean
    1894-1967 ...... CLC 1, 4, 13, 22; BLC;
                           PC 7; SSC 1
  See also BW 1; CA 85-88;
    CDALB 1917-1929; DLB 45, 51; MTCW

Torley, Luke
  See Blish, James (Benjamin)

Tornimparte, Alessandra
  See Ginzburg, Natalia

Torre, Raoul della
  See Mencken, H(enry) L(ouis)

Torrey, E(dwin) Fuller 1937-....... CLC 34
  See also CA 119

Torsvan, Ben Traven
  See Traven, B.

Torsvan, Benno Traven
  See Traven, B.

Torsvan, Berick Traven
  See Traven, B.

Torsvan, Berwick Traven
  See Traven, B.

Torsvan, Bruno Traven
  See Traven, B.

Torsvan, Traven
  See Traven, B.

Tournier, Michel (Edouard)
    1924-.................. CLC 6, 23, 36
  See also CA 49-52; CANR 3, 36; DLB 83;
    MTCW; SATA 23

Tournimparte, Alessandra
  See Ginzburg, Natalia

Towers, Ivar
  See Kornbluth, C(yril) M.

Townsend, Sue 1946-............. CLC 61
  See also CA 119; 127; MTCW; SATA 48,
    55

Townshend, Peter (Dennis Blandford)
    1945-.................... CLC 17, 42
  See also CA 107

Tozzi, Federigo 1883-1920....... TCLC 31

Traill, Catharine Parr
    1802-1899 .... NCLC 31
  See also DLB 99

Trakl, Georg 1887-1914........... TCLC 5
  See also CA 104

Transtroemer, Tomas (Goesta)
    1931-...................... CLC 52, 65
  See also CA 117; 129; CAAS 17

Transtromer, Tomas Gosta
  See Transtroemer, Tomas (Goesta)

Traven, B. (?)-1969............. CLC 8, 11
  See also CA 19-20; 25-28R; CAP 2; DLB 9,
    56; MTCW

Treitel, Jonathan 1959-.......... CLC 70

Tremain, Rose 1943-.............. CLC 42
  See also CA 97-100; CANR 44; DLB 14

Tremblay, Michel 1942-........... CLC 29
  See also CA 116; 128; DLB 60; MTCW

Trevanian........................ CLC 29
  See also Whitaker, Rod(ney)

Trevor, Glen
  See Hilton, James

Trevor, William
    1928- .... CLC 7, 9, 14, 25, 71
  See also Cox, William Trevor
  See also DLB 14, 139

Trifonov, Yuri (Valentinovich)
    1925-1981 .... CLC 45
  See also CA 126; 103; MTCW

Trilling, Lionel 1905-1975.... CLC 9, 11, 24
  See also CA 9-12R; 61-64; CANR 10;
    DLB 28, 63; MTCW

Trimball, W. H.
  See Mencken, H(enry) L(ouis)

Tristan
  See Gomez de la Serna, Ramon

Tristram
  See Housman, A(lfred) E(dward)

Trogdon, William (Lewis) 1939-
  See Heat-Moon, William Least
  See also CA 115; 119; CANR 47

Trollope, Anthony
    1815-1882 ...... NCLC 6, 33; DA; WLC
  See also CDBLB 1832-1890; DLB 21, 57;
    SATA 22

Trollope, Frances 1779-1863..... NCLC 30
  See also DLB 21

Trotsky, Leon 1879-1940......... TCLC 22
  See also CA 118

Trotter (Cockburn), Catharine
    1679-1749 .... LC 8
  See also DLB 84

Trout, Kilgore
  See Farmer, Philip Jose

Trow, George W. S. 1943-........ CLC 52
  See also CA 126

Troyat, Henri 1911-.............. CLC 23
  See also CA 45-48; CANR 2, 33; MTCW

Trudeau, G(arretson) B(eekman) 1948-
  See Trudeau, Garry B.
  See also CA 81-84; CANR 31; SATA 35

Trudeau, Garry B.................. CLC 12
  See also Trudeau, G(arretson) B(eekman)
  See also AAYA 10; AITN 2

Truffaut, Francois 1932-1984....... CLC 20
  See also CA 81-84; 113; CANR 34

Trumbo, Dalton 1905-1976 .... CLC 19
  See also CA 21-24R; 69-72; CANR 10;
    DLB 26

Trumbull, John 1750-1831....... NCLC 30
  See also DLB 31

Trundlett, Helen B.
  See Eliot, T(homas) S(tearns)

Tryon, Thomas 1926-1991....... CLC 3, 11
  See also AITN 1; CA 29-32R; 135;
    CANR 32; MTCW

Tryon, Tom
  See Tryon, Thomas

Ts'ao Hsueh-ch'in 1715(?)-1763....... LC 1

Tsushima, Shuji 1909-1948
  See Dazai, Osamu
  See also CA 107

Tsvetaeva (Efron), Marina (Ivanovna)
    1892-1941 .... TCLC 7, 35
  See also CA 104; 128; MTCW

Tuck, Lily 1938-................. CLC 70
  See also CA 139

Tu Fu 712-770.................... PC 9

Tunis, John R(oberts) 1889-1975 ... CLC 12
  See also CA 61-64; DLB 22; JRDA;
    MAICYA; SATA 30, 37

Tuohy, Frank .... CLC 37
  See also Tuohy, John Francis
  See also DLB 14, 139

Tuohy, John Francis 1925-
  See Tuohy, Frank
  See also CA 5-8R; CANR 3, 47

Turco, Lewis (Putnam) 1934- ... CLC 11, 63
  See also CA 13-16R; CANR 24; DLBY 84

Turgenev, Ivan
    1818-1883 ...... NCLC 21; DA; SSC 7;
                                    WLC

Turgot, Anne-Robert-Jacques
    1727-1781 .... LC 26

Turner, Frederick 1943- .... CLC 48
    See also CA 73-76; CAAS 10; CANR 12,
    30; DLB 40

Tutu, Desmond M(pilo)
    1931- .... CLC 80; BLC
    See also BW 1; CA 125

Tutuola, Amos 1920- ... CLC 5, 14, 29; BLC
    See also BW 2; CA 9-12R; CANR 27;
    DLB 125; MTCW

Twain, Mark
    ... TCLC 6, 12, 19, 36, 48; SSC 6; WLC
    See also Clemens, Samuel Langhorne
    See also DLB 11, 12, 23, 64, 74

Tyler, Anne
    1941- .... CLC 7, 11, 18, 28, 44, 59
    See also BEST 89:1; CA 9-12R; CANR 11,
    33; DLB 6, 143; DLBY 82; MTCW;
    SATA 7

Tyler, Royall 1757-1826 .... NCLC 3
    See also DLB 37

Tynan, Katharine 1861-1931 .... TCLC 3
    See also CA 104

Tyutchev, Fyodor 1803-1873 ..... NCLC 34

Tzara, Tristan .... CLC 47
    See also Rosenfeld, Samuel

Uhry, Alfred 1936- .... CLC 55
    See also CA 127; 133

Ulf, Haerved
    See Strindberg, (Johan) August

Ulf, Harved
    See Strindberg, (Johan) August

Ulibarri, Sabine R(eyes) 1919- ..... CLC 83
    See also CA 131; DLB 82; HW

Unamuno (y Jugo), Miguel de
    1864-1936 .... TCLC 2, 9; HLC; SSC 11
    See also CA 104; 131; DLB 108; HW;
    MTCW

Undercliffe, Errol
    See Campbell, (John) Ramsey

Underwood, Miles
    See Glassco, John

Undset, Sigrid
    1882-1949 .... TCLC 3; DA; WLC
    See also CA 104; 129; MTCW

Ungaretti, Giuseppe
    1888-1970 .... CLC 7, 11, 15
    See also CA 19-20; 25-28R; CAP 2;
    DLB 114

Unger, Douglas 1952- .... CLC 34
    See also CA 130

Unsworth, Barry (Forster) 1930- .... CLC 76
    See also CA 25-28R; CANR 30

Updike, John (Hoyer)
    1932- ...... CLC 1, 2, 3, 5, 7, 9, 13, 15,
        23, 34, 43, 70; DA; SSC 13; WLC
    See also CA 1-4R; CABS 1; CANR 4, 33;
    CDALB 1968-1988; DLB 2, 5, 143;
    DLBD 3; DLBY 80, 82; MTCW

Upshaw, Margaret Mitchell
    See Mitchell, Margaret (Munnerlyn)

Upton, Mark
    See Sanders, Lawrence

Urdang, Constance (Henriette)
    1922- .... CLC 47
    See also CA 21-24R; CANR 9, 24

Uriel, Henry
    See Faust, Frederick (Schiller)

Uris, Leon (Marcus) 1924- ...... CLC 7, 32
    See also AITN 1, 2; BEST 89:2; CA 1-4R;
    CANR 1, 40; MTCW; SATA 49

Urmuz
    See Codrescu, Andrei

Ustinov, Peter (Alexander) 1921- .... CLC 1
    See also AITN 1; CA 13-16R; CANR 25;
    DLB 13

Vaculik, Ludvik 1926- .... CLC 7
    See also CA 53-56

Valdez, Luis (Miguel)
    1940- .... CLC 84; HLC
    See also CA 101; CANR 32; DLB 122; HW

Valenzuela, Luisa 1938- ... CLC 31; SSC 14
    See also CA 101; CANR 32; DLB 113; HW

Valera y Alcala-Galiano, Juan
    1824-1905 .... TCLC 10
    See also CA 106

Valery, (Ambroise) Paul (Toussaint Jules)
    1871-1945 .... TCLC 4, 15; PC 9
    See also CA 104; 122; MTCW

Valle-Inclan, Ramon (Maria) del
    1866-1936 .... TCLC 5; HLC
    See also CA 106; DLB 134

Vallejo, Antonio Buero
    See Buero Vallejo, Antonio

Vallejo, Cesar (Abraham)
    1892-1938 .... TCLC 3, 56; HLC
    See also CA 105; HW

Valle Y Pena, Ramon del
    See Valle-Inclan, Ramon (Maria) del

Van Ash, Cay 1918- .... CLC 34

Vanbrugh, Sir John 1664-1726 ...... LC 21
    See also DLB 80

Van Campen, Karl
    See Campbell, John W(ood, Jr.)

Vance, Gerald
    See Silverberg, Robert

Vance, Jack .... CLC 35
    See also Vance, John Holbrook
    See also DLB 8

Vance, John Holbrook 1916-
    See Queen, Ellery; Vance, Jack
    See also CA 29-32R; CANR 17; MTCW

**Van Den Bogarde, Derek Jules Gaspard Ulric
    Niven** 1921-
    See Bogarde, Dirk
    See also CA 77-80

Vandenburgh, Jane .... CLC 59

Vanderhaeghe, Guy 1951- .... CLC 41
    See also CA 113

van der Post, Laurens (Jan) 1906- ... CLC 5
    See also CA 5-8R; CANR 35

van de Wetering, Janwillem 1931- .. CLC 47
    See also CA 49-52; CANR 4

Van Dine, S. S. .... TCLC 23
    See also Wright, Willard Huntington

Van Doren, Carl (Clinton)
    1885-1950 .... TCLC 18
    See also CA 111

Van Doren, Mark 1894-1972..... CLC 6, 10
    See also CA 1-4R; 37-40R; CANR 3;
    DLB 45; MTCW

Van Druten, John (William)
    1901-1957 .... TCLC 2
    See also CA 104; DLB 10

Van Duyn, Mona (Jane)
    1921- .... CLC 3, 7, 63
    See also CA 9-12R; CANR 7, 38; DLB 5

Van Dyne, Edith
    See Baum, L(yman) Frank

van Itallie, Jean-Claude 1936-....... CLC 3
    See also CA 45-48; CAAS 2; CANR 1;
    DLB 7

van Ostaijen, Paul 1896-1928 ..... TCLC 33

Van Peebles, Melvin 1932- ...... CLC 2, 20
    See also BW 2; CA 85-88; CANR 27

Vansittart, Peter 1920-............ CLC 42
    See also CA 1-4R; CANR 3

Van Vechten, Carl 1880-1964 ...... CLC 33
    See also CA 89-92; DLB 4, 9, 51

Van Vogt, A(lfred) E(lton) 1912-..... CLC 1
    See also CA 21-24R; CANR 28; DLB 8;
    SATA 14

Varda, Agnes 1928- .... CLC 16
    See also CA 116; 122

Vargas Llosa, (Jorge) Mario (Pedro)
    1936- .... CLC 3, 6, 9, 10, 15, 31, 42, 85;
                                        DA; HLC
    See also CA 73-76; CANR 18, 32, 42;
    DLB 145; HW; MTCW

Vasiliu, Gheorghe 1881-1957
    See Bacovia, George
    See also CA 123

Vassa, Gustavus
    See Equiano, Olaudah

Vassilikos, Vassilis 1933-.......... CLC 4, 8
    See also CA 81-84

Vaughan, Henry 1621-1695......... LC 27
    See also DLB 131

Vaughn, Stephanie................. CLC 62

Vazov, Ivan (Minchov)
    1850-1921 .... TCLC 25
    See also CA 121; DLB 147

Veblen, Thorstein (Bunde)
    1857-1929 .... TCLC 31
    See also CA 115

Vega, Lope de 1562-1635........... LC 23

Venison, Alfred
    See Pound, Ezra (Weston Loomis)

Verdi, Marie de
    See Mencken, H(enry) L(ouis)

Verdu, Matilde
    See Cela, Camilo Jose

Verga, Giovanni (Carmelo)
    1840-1922 .... TCLC 3
    See also CA 104; 123

Vergil 70B.C.-19B.C. .... CMLC 9; DA

Verhaeren, Emile (Adolphe Gustave)
    1855-1916 .... TCLC 12
    See also CA 109

Verlaine, Paul (Marie)
1844-1896 . . . . NCLC 2; PC 2

Verne, Jules (Gabriel)
1828-1905 . . . . TCLC 6, 52
See also CA 110; 131; DLB 123; JRDA;
MAICYA; SATA 21

Very, Jones 1813-1880 . . . . NCLC 9
See also DLB 1

Vesaas, Tarjei 1897-1970 . . . . CLC 48
See also CA 29-32R

Vialis, Gaston
See Simenon, Georges (Jacques Christian)

Vian, Boris 1920-1959 . . . . TCLC 9
See also CA 106; DLB 72

Viaud, (Louis Marie) Julien 1850-1923
See Loti, Pierre
See also CA 107

Vicar, Henry
See Felsen, Henry Gregor

Vicker, Angus
See Felsen, Henry Gregor

Vidal, Gore
1925- . . . . . CLC 2, 4, 6, 8, 10, 22, 33, 72
See also AITN 1; BEST 90:2; CA 5-8R;
CANR 13, 45; DLB 6; MTCW

Viereck, Peter (Robert Edwin)
1916- . . . . CLC 4
See also CA 1-4R; CANR 1, 47; DLB 5

Vigny, Alfred (Victor) de
1797-1863 . . . . NCLC 7
See also DLB 119

Vilakazi, Benedict Wallet
1906-1947 . . . . TCLC 37

Villiers de l'Isle Adam, Jean Marie Mathias
Philippe Auguste Comte
1838-1889 . . . . NCLC 3; SSC 14
See also DLB 123

Vinci, Leonardo da 1452-1519 . . . . LC 12

Vine, Barbara . . . . CLC 50
See also Rendell, Ruth (Barbara)
See also BEST 90:4

Vinge, Joan D(ennison) 1948- . . . . . . CLC 30
See also CA 93-96; SATA 36

Violis, G.
See Simenon, Georges (Jacques Christian)

Visconti, Luchino 1906-1976 . . . . CLC 16
See also CA 81-84; 65-68; CANR 39

Vittorini, Elio 1908-1966 . . . . . . CLC 6, 9, 14
See also CA 133; 25-28R

Vizinczey, Stephen 1933- . . . . CLC 40
See also CA 128

Vliet, R(ussell) G(ordon)
1929-1984 . . . . CLC 22
See also CA 37-40R; 112; CANR 18

Vogau, Boris Andreyevich 1894-1937(?)
See Pilnyak, Boris
See also CA 123

Vogel, Paula A(nne) 1951- . . . . CLC 76
See also CA 108

Voight, Ellen Bryant 1943- . . . . CLC 54
See also CA 69-72; CANR 11, 29; DLB 120

Voigt, Cynthia 1942- . . . . CLC 30
See also AAYA 3; CA 106; CANR 18, 37,
40; CLR 13; JRDA; MAICYA;
SATA 33, 48, 79

Voinovich, Vladimir (Nikolaevich)
1932- . . . . CLC 10, 49
See also CA 81-84; CAAS 12; CANR 33;
MTCW

Voloshinov, V. N.
See Bakhtin, Mikhail Mikhailovich

Voltaire
1694-1778 . . . LC 14; DA; SSC 12; WLC

von Daeniken, Erich 1935- . . . . CLC 30
See also AITN 1; CA 37-40R; CANR 17,
44

von Daniken, Erich
See von Daeniken, Erich

von Heidenstam, (Carl Gustaf) Verner
See Heidenstam, (Carl Gustaf) Verner von

von Heyse, Paul (Johann Ludwig)
See Heyse, Paul (Johann Ludwig von)

von Hofmannsthal, Hugo
See Hofmannsthal, Hugo von

von Horvath, Odon
See Horvath, Oedoen von

von Horvath, Oedoen
See Horvath, Oedoen von

von Liliencron, (Friedrich Adolf Axel) Detlev
See Liliencron, (Friedrich Adolf Axel)
Detlev von

Vonnegut, Kurt, Jr.
1922- . . . . . . CLC 1, 2, 3, 4, 5, 8, 12, 22,
40, 60; DA; SSC 8; WLC
See also AAYA 6; AITN 1; BEST 90:4;
CA 1-4R; CANR 1, 25;
CDALB 1968-1988; DLB 2, 8; DLBD 3;
DLBY 80; MTCW

Von Rachen, Kurt
See Hubbard, L(afayette) Ron(ald)

von Rezzori (d'Arezzo), Gregor
See Rezzori (d'Arezzo), Gregor von

von Sternberg, Josef
See Sternberg, Josef von

Vorster, Gordon 1924- . . . . CLC 34
See also CA 133

Vosce, Trudie
See Ozick, Cynthia

Voznesensky, Andrei (Andreievich)
1933- . . . . CLC 1, 15, 57
See also CA 89-92; CANR 37; MTCW

Waddington, Miriam 1917- . . . . CLC 28
See also CA 21-24R; CANR 12, 30;
DLB 68

Wagman, Fredrica 1937- . . . . CLC 7
See also CA 97-100

Wagner, Richard 1813-1883 . . . . NCLC 9
See also DLB 129

Wagner-Martin, Linda 1936- . . . . CLC 50

Wagoner, David (Russell)
1926- . . . . CLC 3, 5, 15
See also CA 1-4R; CAAS 3; CANR 2;
DLB 5; SATA 14

Wah, Fred(erick James) 1939- . . . . . . CLC 44
See also CA 107; 141; DLB 60

Wahloo, Per 1926-1975 . . . . CLC 7
See also CA 61-64

Wahloo, Peter
See Wahloo, Per

Wain, John (Barrington)
1925-1994 . . . . CLC 2, 11, 15, 46
See also CA 5-8R; 145; CAAS 4; CANR 23;
CDBLB 1960 to Present; DLB 15, 27,
139; MTCW

Wajda, Andrzej 1926- . . . . CLC 16
See also CA 102

Wakefield, Dan 1932- . . . . CLC 7
See also CA 21-24R; CAAS 7

Wakoski, Diane
1937- . . . . CLC 2, 4, 7, 9, 11, 40
See also CA 13-16R; CAAS 1; CANR 9;
DLB 5

Wakoski-Sherbell, Diane
See Wakoski, Diane

Walcott, Derek (Alton)
1930- . . . . CLC 2, 4, 9, 14, 25, 42, 67, 76;
BLC
See also BW 2; CA 89-92; CANR 26, 47;
DLB 117; DLBY 81; MTCW

Waldman, Anne 1945- . . . . CLC 7
See also CA 37-40R; CAAS 17; CANR 34;
DLB 16

Waldo, E. Hunter
See Sturgeon, Theodore (Hamilton)

Waldo, Edward Hamilton
See Sturgeon, Theodore (Hamilton)

Walker, Alice (Malsenior)
1944- . . . . CLC 5, 6, 9, 19, 27, 46, 58;
BLC; DA; SSC 5
See also AAYA 3; BEST 89:4; BW 2;
CA 37-40R; CANR 9, 27;
CDALB 1968-1988; DLB 6, 33, 143;
MTCW; SATA 31

Walker, David Harry 1911-1992 . . . . CLC 14
See also CA 1-4R; 137; CANR 1; SATA 8;
SATA-Obit 71

Walker, Edward Joseph 1934-
See Walker, Ted
See also CA 21-24R; CANR 12, 28

Walker, George F. 1947- . . . . CLC 44, 61
See also CA 103; CANR 21, 43; DLB 60

Walker, Joseph A. 1935- . . . . CLC 19
See also BW 1; CA 89-92; CANR 26;
DLB 38

Walker, Margaret (Abigail)
1915- . . . . CLC 1, 6; BLC
See also BW 2; CA 73-76; CANR 26;
DLB 76; MTCW

Walker, Ted . . . . CLC 13
See also Walker, Edward Joseph
See also DLB 40

Wallace, David Foster 1962- . . . . CLC 50
See also CA 132

Wallace, Dexter
See Masters, Edgar Lee

Wallace, (Richard Horatio) Edgar
1875-1932 . . . . TCLC 57
See also CA 115; DLB 70

Wallace, Irving 1916-1990 . . . . **CLC 7, 13**
See also AITN 1; CA 1-4R; 132; CAAS 1;
CANR 1, 27; MTCW

Wallant, Edward Lewis
1926-1962 . . . . **CLC 5, 10**
See also CA 1-4R; CANR 22; DLB 2, 28,
143; MTCW

Walpole, Horace 1717-1797 . . . . **LC 2**
See also DLB 39, 104

Walpole, Hugh (Seymour)
1884-1941 . . . . **TCLC 5**
See also CA 104; DLB 34

Walser, Martin 1927- . . . . **CLC 27**
See also CA 57-60; CANR 8, 46, 46;
DLB 75, 124

Walser, Robert 1878-1956 . . . . **TCLC 18**
See also CA 118; DLB 66

Walsh, Jill Paton . . . . **CLC 35**
See also Paton Walsh, Gillian
See also AAYA 11; CLR 2; SAAS 3

Walter, Villiam Christian
See Andersen, Hans Christian

Wambaugh, Joseph (Aloysius, Jr.)
1937- . . . . **CLC 3, 18**
See also AITN 1; BEST 89:3; CA 33-36R;
CANR 42; DLB 6; DLBY 83; MTCW

Ward, Arthur Henry Sarsfield 1883-1959
See Rohmer, Sax
See also CA 108

Ward, Douglas Turner 1930- . . . . **CLC 19**
See also BW 1; CA 81-84; CANR 27;
DLB 7, 38

Ward, Mary Augusta
See Ward, Mrs. Humphry

Ward, Mrs. Humphry
1851-1920 . . . . **TCLC 55**
See also DLB 18

Ward, Peter
See Faust, Frederick (Schiller)

Warhol, Andy 1928(?)-1987 . . . . **CLC 20**
See also AAYA 12; BEST 89:4; CA 89-92;
121; CANR 34

Warner, Francis (Robert le Plastrier)
1937- . . . . **CLC 14**
See also CA 53-56; CANR 11

Warner, Marina 1946- . . . . **CLC 59**
See also CA 65-68; CANR 21

Warner, Rex (Ernest) 1905-1986 . . . . **CLC 45**
See also CA 89-92; 119; DLB 15

Warner, Susan (Bogert)
1819-1885 . . . . **NCLC 31**
See also DLB 3, 42

Warner, Sylvia (Constance) Ashton
See Ashton-Warner, Sylvia (Constance)

Warner, Sylvia Townsend
1893-1978 . . . . **CLC 7, 19**
See also CA 61-64; 77-80; CANR 16;
DLB 34, 139; MTCW

Warren, Mercy Otis 1728-1814 . . . **NCLC 13**
See also DLB 31

Warren, Robert Penn
1905-1989 . . . . **CLC 1, 4, 6, 8, 10, 13, 18,**
39, 53, 59; DA; SSC 4; WLC
See also AITN 1; CA 13-16R; 129;
CANR 10, 47; CDALB 1968-1988;
DLB 2, 48; DLBY 80, 89; MTCW;
SATA 46; SATA-Obit 63

Warshofsky, Isaac
See Singer, Isaac Bashevis

Warton, Thomas 1728-1790 . . . . **LC 15**
See also DLB 104, 109

Waruk, Kona
See Harris, (Theodore) Wilson

Warung, Price 1855-1911 . . . . **TCLC 45**

Warwick, Jarvis
See Garner, Hugh

Washington, Alex
See Harris, Mark

Washington, Booker T(aliaferro)
1856-1915 . . . . **TCLC 10; BLC**
See also BW 1; CA 114; 125; SATA 28

Washington, George 1732-1799 . . . . . . **LC 25**
See also DLB 31

Wassermann, (Karl) Jakob
1873-1934 . . . . **TCLC 6**
See also CA 104; DLB 66

Wasserstein, Wendy
1950- . . . . **CLC 32, 59; DC 4**
See also CA 121; 129; CABS 3

Waterhouse, Keith (Spencer)
1929- . . . . **CLC 47**
See also CA 5-8R; CANR 38; DLB 13, 15;
MTCW

Waters, Roger 1944- . . . . **CLC 35**

Watkins, Frances Ellen
See Harper, Frances Ellen Watkins

Watkins, Gerrold
See Malzberg, Barry N(athaniel)

Watkins, Paul 1964- . . . . **CLC 55**
See also CA 132

Watkins, Vernon Phillips
1906-1967 . . . . **CLC 43**
See also CA 9-10; 25-28R; CAP 1; DLB 20

Watson, Irving S.
See Mencken, H(enry) L(ouis)

Watson, John H.
See Farmer, Philip Jose

Watson, Richard F.
See Silverberg, Robert

Waugh, Auberon (Alexander) 1939- . . **CLC 7**
See also CA 45-48; CANR 6, 22; DLB 14

Waugh, Evelyn (Arthur St. John)
1903-1966 . . . . . . **CLC 1, 3, 8, 13, 19, 27,**
44; DA; WLC
See also CA 85-88; 25-28R; CANR 22;
CDBLB 1914-1945; DLB 15; MTCW

Waugh, Harriet 1944- . . . . **CLC 6**
See also CA 85-88; CANR 22

Ways, C. R.
See Blount, Roy (Alton), Jr.

Waystaff, Simon
See Swift, Jonathan

Webb, (Martha) Beatrice (Potter)
1858-1943 . . . . **TCLC 22**
See also Potter, Beatrice
See also CA 117

Webb, Charles (Richard) 1939- . . . . . . **CLC 7**
See also CA 25-28R

Webb, James H(enry), Jr. 1946- . . . . **CLC 22**
See also CA 81-84

Webb, Mary (Gladys Meredith)
1881-1927 . . . . **TCLC 24**
See also CA 123; DLB 34

Webb, Mrs. Sidney
See Webb, (Martha) Beatrice (Potter)

Webb, Phyllis 1927- . . . . **CLC 18**
See also CA 104; CANR 23; DLB 53

Webb, Sidney (James)
1859-1947 . . . . **TCLC 22**
See also CA 117

Webber, Andrew Lloyd . . . . **CLC 21**
See also Lloyd Webber, Andrew

Weber, Lenora Mattingly
1895-1971 . . . . **CLC 12**
See also CA 19-20; 29-32R; CAP 1;
SATA 2; SATA-Obit 26

Webster, John 1579(?)-1634(?) . . . . **DC 2**
See also CDBLB Before 1660; DA; DLB 58;
WLC

Webster, Noah 1758-1843 . . . . **NCLC 30**

Wedekind, (Benjamin) Frank(lin)
1864-1918 . . . . **TCLC 7**
See also CA 104; DLB 118

Weidman, Jerome 1913- . . . . **CLC 7**
See also AITN 2; CA 1-4R; CANR 1;
DLB 28

Weil, Simone (Adolphine)
1909-1943 . . . . **TCLC 23**
See also CA 117

Weinstein, Nathan
See West, Nathanael

Weinstein, Nathan von Wallenstein
See West, Nathanael

Weir, Peter (Lindsay) 1944- . . . . **CLC 20**
See also CA 113; 123

Weiss, Peter (Ulrich)
1916-1982 . . . . **CLC 3, 15, 51**
See also CA 45-48; 106; CANR 3; DLB 69,
124

Weiss, Theodore (Russell)
1916- . . . . **CLC 3, 8, 14**
See also CA 9-12R; CAAS 2; CANR 46, 46;
DLB 5

Welch, (Maurice) Denton
1915-1948 . . . . **TCLC 22**
See also CA 121

Welch, James 1940- . . . . **CLC 6, 14, 52**
See also CA 85-88; CANR 42; NNAL

Weldon, Fay
1933- . . . . **CLC 6, 9, 11, 19, 36, 59**
See also CA 21-24R; CANR 16, 46, 46;
CDBLB 1960 to Present; DLB 14;
MTCW

Wellek, Rene 1903- . . . . **CLC 28**
See also CA 5-8R; CAAS 7; CANR 8;
DLB 63

Weller, Michael   1942- . . . . **CLC 10, 53**
  See also CA 85-88

Weller, Paul   1958- . . . . **CLC 26**

Wellershoff, Dieter   1925- . . . . **CLC 46**
  See also CA 89-92; CANR 16, 37

Welles, (George) Orson
  1915-1985 . . . . **CLC 20, 80**
  See also CA 93-96; 117

Wellman, Mac   1945- . . . . **CLC 65**

Wellman, Manly Wade   1903-1986 . . **CLC 49**
  See also CA 1-4R; 118; CANR 6, 16, 44;
  SATA 6; SATA-Obit 47

Wells, Carolyn   1869(?)-1942 . . . . . . **TCLC 35**
  See also CA 113; DLB 11

Wells, H(erbert) G(eorge)
  1866-1946 . . . . **TCLC 6, 12, 19; DA;**
                                          SSC 6; WLC
  See also CA 110; 121; CDBLB 1914-1945;
  DLB 34, 70; MTCW; SATA 20

Wells, Rosemary   1943-. . . . . **CLC 12**
  See also AAYA 13; CA 85-88; CLR 16;
  MAICYA; SAAS 1; SATA 18, 69

Welty, Eudora
  1909- . . . . . . **CLC 1, 2, 5, 14, 22, 33; DA;**
                                          SSC 1; WLC
  See also CA 9-12R; CABS 1; CANR 32;
  CDALB 1941-1968; DLB 2, 102, 143;
  DLBD 12; DLBY 87; MTCW

Wen I-to   1899-1946 . . . . **TCLC 28**

Wentworth, Robert
  See Hamilton, Edmond

Werfel, Franz (V.)   1890-1945 . . . . . . **TCLC 8**
  See also CA 104; DLB 81, 124

Wergeland, Henrik Arnold
  1808-1845 . . . . **NCLC 5**

Wersba, Barbara   1932-. . . . . **CLC 30**
  See also AAYA 2; CA 29-32R; CANR 16,
  38; CLR 3; DLB 52; JRDA; MAICYA;
  SAAS 2; SATA 1, 58

Wertmueller, Lina   1928- . . . . **CLC 16**
  See also CA 97-100; CANR 39

Wescott, Glenway   1901-1987. . . . . . . **CLC 13**
  See also CA 13-16R; 121; CANR 23;
  DLB 4, 9, 102

Wesker, Arnold   1932- . . . . **CLC 3, 5, 42**
  See also CA 1-4R; CAAS 7; CANR 1, 33;
  CDBLB 1960 to Present; DLB 13;
  MTCW

Wesley, Richard (Errol)   1945-. . . . . . . **CLC 7**
  See also BW 1; CA 57-60; CANR 27;
  DLB 38

Wessel, Johan Herman   1742-1785 . . . . **LC 7**

West, Anthony (Panther)
  1914-1987 . . . . **CLC 50**
  See also CA 45-48; 124; CANR 3, 19;
  DLB 15

West, C. P.
  See Wodehouse, P(elham) G(renville)

West, (Mary) Jessamyn
  1902-1984 . . . . **CLC 7, 17**
  See also CA 9-12R; 112; CANR 27; DLB 6;
  DLBY 84; MTCW; SATA-Obit 37

West, Morris L(anglo)   1916-. . . . . **CLC 6, 33**
  See also CA 5-8R; CANR 24; MTCW

West, Nathanael
  1903-1940 . . . . . **TCLC 1, 14, 44; SSC 16**
  See also CA 104; 125; CDALB 1929-1941;
  DLB 4, 9, 28; MTCW

West, Owen
  See Koontz, Dean R(ay)

West, Paul   1930- . . . . **CLC 7, 14**
  See also CA 13-16R; CAAS 7; CANR 22;
  DLB 14

West, Rebecca   1892-1983 . . **CLC 7, 9, 31, 50**
  See also CA 5-8R; 109; CANR 19; DLB 36;
  DLBY 83; MTCW

Westall, Robert (Atkinson)
  1929-1993 . . . . **CLC 17**
  See also AAYA 12; CA 69-72; 141;
  CANR 18; CLR 13; JRDA; MAICYA;
  SAAS 2; SATA 23, 69; SATA-Obit 75

Westlake, Donald E(dwin)
  1933- . . . . **CLC 7, 33**
  See also CA 17-20R; CAAS 13; CANR 16,
  44

Westmacott, Mary
  See Christie, Agatha (Mary Clarissa)

Weston, Allen
  See Norton, Andre

Wetcheek, J. L.
  See Feuchtwanger, Lion

Wetering, Janwillem van de
  See van de Wetering, Janwillem

Wetherell, Elizabeth
  See Warner, Susan (Bogert)

Whalen, Philip   1923- . . . . **CLC 6, 29**
  See also CA 9-12R; CANR 5, 39; DLB 16

Wharton, Edith (Newbold Jones)
  1862-1937 . . . . . . **TCLC 3, 9, 27, 53; DA;**
                                          SSC 6; WLC
  See also CA 104; 132; CDALB 1865-1917;
  DLB 4, 9, 12, 78; MTCW

Wharton, James
  See Mencken, H(enry) L(ouis)

Wharton, William (a pseudonym)
  . . . . **CLC 18, 37**
  See also CA 93-96; DLBY 80

Wheatley (Peters), Phillis
  1754(?)-1784 . . . . **LC 3; BLC; DA; PC 3;**
                                          WLC
  See also CDALB 1640-1865; DLB 31, 50

Wheelock, John Hall   1886-1978 . . . . **CLC 14**
  See also CA 13-16R; 77-80; CANR 14;
  DLB 45

White, E(lwyn) B(rooks)
  1899-1985 . . . . **CLC 10, 34, 39**
  See also AITN 2; CA 13-16R; 116;
  CANR 16, 37; CLR 1, 21; DLB 11, 22;
  MAICYA; MTCW; SATA 2, 29;
  SATA-Obit 44

White, Edmund (Valentine III)
  1940- . . . . **CLC 27**
  See also AAYA 7; CA 45-48; CANR 3, 19,
  36; MTCW

White, Patrick (Victor Martindale)
  1912-1990 . . **CLC 3, 4, 5, 7, 9, 18, 65, 69**
  See also CA 81-84; 132; CANR 43; MTCW

White, Phyllis Dorothy James   1920-
  See James, P. D.
  See also CA 21-24R; CANR 17, 43; MTCW

White, T(erence) H(anbury)
  1906-1964 . . . . **CLC 30**
  See also CA 73-76; CANR 37; JRDA;
  MAICYA; SATA 12

White, Terence de Vere
  1912-1994 . . . . **CLC 49**
  See also CA 49-52; 145; CANR 3

White, Walter F(rancis)
  1893-1955 . . . . **TCLC 15**
  See also White, Walter
  See also BW 1; CA 115; 124; DLB 51

White, William Hale   1831-1913
  See Rutherford, Mark
  See also CA 121

Whitehead, E(dward) A(nthony)
  1933- . . . . **CLC 5**
  See also CA 65-68

Whitemore, Hugh (John)   1936-. . . . . **CLC 37**
  See also CA 132

Whitman, Sarah Helen (Power)
  1803-1878 . . . . **NCLC 19**
  See also DLB 1

Whitman, Walt(er)
  1819-1892 . . . . . **NCLC 4, 31; DA; PC 3;**
                                          WLC
  See also CDALB 1640-1865; DLB 3, 64;
  SATA 20

Whitney, Phyllis A(yame)   1903-. . . . **CLC 42**
  See also AITN 2; BEST 90:3; CA 1-4R;
  CANR 3, 25, 38; JRDA; MAICYA;
  SATA 1, 30

Whittemore, (Edward) Reed (Jr.)
  1919- . . . . **CLC 4**
  See also CA 9-12R; CAAS 8; CANR 4;
  DLB 5

Whittier, John Greenleaf
  1807-1892 . . . . **NCLC 8**
  See also CDALB 1640-1865; DLB 1

Whittlebot, Hernia
  See Coward, Noel (Peirce)

Wicker, Thomas Grey   1926-
  See Wicker, Tom
  See also CA 65-68; CANR 21, 46, 46

Wicker, Tom   . . . . **CLC 7**
  See also Wicker, Thomas Grey

Wideman, John Edgar
  1941- . . . . **CLC 5, 34, 36, 67; BLC**
  See also BW 2; CA 85-88; CANR 14, 42;
  DLB 33, 143

Wiebe, Rudy (Henry)   1934-. . . **CLC 6, 11, 14**
  See also CA 37-40R; CANR 42; DLB 60

Wieland, Christoph Martin
  1733-1813 . . . . **NCLC 17**
  See also DLB 97

Wiene, Robert   1881-1938. . . . . **TCLC 56**

Wieners, John   1934-. . . . . **CLC 7**
  See also CA 13-16R; DLB 16

Wiesel, Elie(zer)
  1928- . . . . **CLC 3, 5, 11, 37; DA**
  See also AAYA 7; AITN 1; CA 5-8R;
  CAAS 4; CANR 8, 40; DLB 83;
  DLBY 87; MTCW; SATA 56

Wiggins, Marianne   1947-. . . . . **CLC 57**
  See also BEST 89:3; CA 130

Wight, James Alfred 1916-
See Herriot, James
See also CA 77-80; SATA 44, 55

Wilbur, Richard (Purdy)
1921- .... **CLC 3, 6, 9, 14, 53; DA**
See also CA 1-4R; CABS 2; CANR 2, 29;
DLB 5; MTCW; SATA 9

Wild, Peter 1940- .... **CLC 14**
See also CA 37-40R; DLB 5

Wilde, Oscar (Fingal O'Flahertie Wills)
1854(?)-1900 .... **TCLC 1, 8, 23, 41; DA;**
            SSC 11; WLC
See also CA 104; 119; CDBLB 1890-1914;
DLB 10, 19, 34, 57, 141; SATA 24

Wilder, Billy .... **CLC 20**
See also Wilder, Samuel
See also DLB 26

Wilder, Samuel 1906-
See Wilder, Billy
See also CA 89-92

Wilder, Thornton (Niven)
1897-1975 ...... **CLC 1, 5, 6, 10, 15, 35,**
            82; DA; DC 1; WLC
See also AITN 2; CA 13-16R; 61-64;
CANR 40; DLB 4, 7, 9; MTCW

Wilding, Michael 1942- .... **CLC 73**
See also CA 104; CANR 24

Wiley, Richard 1944- .... **CLC 44**
See also CA 121; 129

Wilhelm, Kate .... **CLC 7**
See also Wilhelm, Katie Gertrude
See also CAAS 5; DLB 8

Wilhelm, Katie Gertrude 1928-
See Wilhelm, Kate
See also CA 37-40R; CANR 17, 36; MTCW

Wilkins, Mary
See Freeman, Mary Eleanor Wilkins

Willard, Nancy 1936- .... **CLC 7, 37**
See also CA 89-92; CANR 10, 39; CLR 5;
DLB 5, 52; MAICYA; MTCW;
SATA 30, 37, 71

Williams, C(harles) K(enneth)
1936- .... **CLC 33, 56**
See also CA 37-40R; DLB 5

Williams, Charles
See Collier, James L(incoln)

Williams, Charles (Walter Stansby)
1886-1945 .... **TCLC 1, 11**
See also CA 104; DLB 100

Williams, (George) Emlyn
1905-1987 .... **CLC 15**
See also CA 104; 123; CANR 36; DLB 10,
77; MTCW

Williams, Hugo 1942- .... **CLC 42**
See also CA 17-20R; CANR 45; DLB 40

Williams, J. Walker
See Wodehouse, P(elham) G(renville)

Williams, John A(lfred)
1925- .... **CLC 5, 13; BLC**
See also BW 2; CA 53-56; CAAS 3;
CANR 6, 26; DLB 2, 33

Williams, Jonathan (Chamberlain)
1929- .... **CLC 13**
See also CA 9-12R; CAAS 12; CANR 8;
DLB 5

Williams, Joy 1944- .... **CLC 31**
See also CA 41-44R; CANR 22

Williams, Norman 1952- .... **CLC 39**
See also CA 118

Williams, Tennessee
1911-1983 ..... **CLC 1, 2, 5, 7, 8, 11, 15,**
    19, 30, 39, 45, 71; DA; DC 4; WLC
See also AITN 1, 2; CA 5-8R; 108;
CABS 3; CANR 31; CDALB 1941-1968;
DLB 7; DLBD 4; DLBY 83; MTCW

Williams, Thomas (Alonzo)
1926-1990 .... **CLC 14**
See also CA 1-4R; 132; CANR 2

Williams, William C.
See Williams, William Carlos

Williams, William Carlos
1883-1963 .... **CLC 1, 2, 5, 9, 13, 22, 42,**
          67; DA; PC 7
See also CA 89-92; CANR 34;
CDALB 1917-1929; DLB 4, 16, 54, 86;
MTCW

Williamson, David (Keith) 1942- .... **CLC 56**
See also CA 103; CANR 41

Williamson, Ellen Douglas 1905-1984
See Douglas, Ellen
See also CA 17-20R; 114; CANR 39

Williamson, Jack .... **CLC 29**
See also Williamson, John Stewart
See also CAAS 8; DLB 8

Williamson, John Stewart 1908-
See Williamson, Jack
See also CA 17-20R; CANR 23

Willie, Frederick
See Lovecraft, H(oward) P(hillips)

Willingham, Calder (Baynard, Jr.)
1922- .... **CLC 5, 51**
See also CA 5-8R; CANR 3; DLB 2, 44;
MTCW

Willis, Charles
See Clarke, Arthur C(harles)

Willy
See Colette, (Sidonie-Gabrielle)

Willy, Colette
See Colette, (Sidonie-Gabrielle)

Wilson, A(ndrew) N(orman) 1950- .. **CLC 33**
See also CA 112; 122; DLB 14

Wilson, Angus (Frank Johnstone)
1913-1991 .... **CLC 2, 3, 5, 25, 34**
See also CA 5-8R; 134; CANR 21; DLB 15,
139; MTCW

Wilson, August
1945- .. **CLC 39, 50, 63; BLC; DA; DC 2**
See also BW 2; CA 115; 122; CANR 42;
MTCW

Wilson, Brian 1942- .... **CLC 12**

Wilson, Colin 1931- .... **CLC 3, 14**
See also CA 1-4R; CAAS 5; CANR 1, 22,
33; DLB 14; MTCW

Wilson, Dirk
See Pohl, Frederik

Wilson, Edmund
1895-1972 .... **CLC 1, 2, 3, 8, 24**
See also CA 1-4R; 37-40R; CANR 1, 46, 46;
DLB 63; MTCW

Wilson, Ethel Davis (Bryant)
1888(?)-1980 .... **CLC 13**
See also CA 102; DLB 68; MTCW

Wilson, John 1785-1854 .... **NCLC 5**

Wilson, John (Anthony) Burgess 1917-1993
See Burgess, Anthony
See also CA 1-4R; 143; CANR 2, 46, 46;
MTCW

Wilson, Lanford 1937- .... **CLC 7, 14, 36**
See also CA 17-20R; CABS 3; CANR 45;
DLB 7

Wilson, Robert M. 1944- .... **CLC 7, 9**
See also CA 49-52; CANR 2, 41; MTCW

Wilson, Robert McLiam 1964- ..... **CLC 59**
See also CA 132

Wilson, Sloan 1920- .... **CLC 32**
See also CA 1-4R; CANR 1, 44

Wilson, Snoo 1948- .... **CLC 33**
See also CA 69-72

Wilson, William S(mith) 1932- ..... **CLC 49**
See also CA 81-84

Winchilsea, Anne (Kingsmill) Finch Counte
1661-1720 .... **LC 3**

Windham, Basil
See Wodehouse, P(elham) G(renville)

Wingrove, David (John) 1954- ...... **CLC 68**
See also CA 133

Winters, Janet Lewis .... **CLC 41**
See also Lewis, Janet
See also DLBY 87

Winters, (Arthur) Yvor
1900-1968 .... **CLC 4, 8, 32**
See also CA 11-12; 25-28R; CAP 1;
DLB 48; MTCW

Winterson, Jeanette 1959- .... **CLC 64**
See also CA 136

Wiseman, Frederick 1930- .... **CLC 20**

Wister, Owen 1860-1938 .... **TCLC 21**
See also CA 108; DLB 9, 78; SATA 62

Witkacy
See Witkiewicz, Stanislaw Ignacy

Witkiewicz, Stanislaw Ignacy
1885-1939 .... **TCLC 8**
See also CA 105

Wittig, Monique 1935(?)- .... **CLC 22**
See also CA 116; 135; DLB 83

Wittlin, Jozef 1896-1976 .... **CLC 25**
See also CA 49-52; 65-68; CANR 3

Wodehouse, P(elham) G(renville)
1881-1975 ... **CLC 1, 2, 5, 10, 22; SSC 2**
See also AITN 2; CA 45-48; 57-60;
CANR 3, 33; CDBLB 1914-1945;
DLB 34; MTCW; SATA 22

Woiwode, L.
See Woiwode, Larry (Alfred)

Woiwode, Larry (Alfred) 1941-... **CLC 6, 10**
See also CA 73-76; CANR 16; DLB 6

Wojciechowska, Maia (Teresa)
1927- .... **CLC 26**
See also AAYA 8; CA 9-12R; CANR 4, 41;
CLR 1; JRDA; MAICYA; SAAS 1;
SATA 1, 28

Wolf, Christa 1929- . . . . **CLC 14, 29, 58**
See also CA 85-88; CANR 45; DLB 75;
MTCW

Wolfe, Gene (Rodman) 1931- . . . . **CLC 25**
See also CA 57-60; CAAS 9; CANR 6, 32;
DLB 8

Wolfe, George C. 1954- . . . . **CLC 49**

Wolfe, Thomas (Clayton)
1900-1938 . . . **TCLC 4, 13, 29; DA; WLC**
See also CA 104; 132; CDALB 1929-1941;
DLB 9, 102; DLBD 2; DLBY 85; MTCW

Wolfe, Thomas Kennerly, Jr. 1931-
See Wolfe, Tom
See also CA 13-16R; CANR 9, 33; MTCW

Wolfe, Tom . . . . **CLC 1, 2, 9, 15, 35, 51**
See also Wolfe, Thomas Kennerly, Jr.
See also AAYA 8; AITN 2; BEST 89:1

Wolff, Geoffrey (Ansell) 1937- . . . . . **CLC 41**
See also CA 29-32R; CANR 29, 43

Wolff, Sonia
See Levitin, Sonia (Wolff)

Wolff, Tobias (Jonathan Ansell)
1945- . . . . **CLC 39, 64**
See also BEST 90:2; CA 114; 117; DLB 130

Wolfram von Eschenbach
c. 1170-c. 1220 . . . . **CMLC 5**
See also DLB 138

Wolitzer, Hilma 1930- . . . . **CLC 17**
See also CA 65-68; CANR 18, 40; SATA 31

Wollstonecraft, Mary 1759-1797 . . . . . **LC 5**
See also CDBLB 1789-1832; DLB 39, 104

Wonder, Stevie . . . . **CLC 12**
See also Morris, Steveland Judkins

Wong, Jade Snow 1922- . . . . **CLC 17**
See also CA 109

Woodcott, Keith
See Brunner, John (Kilian Houston)

Woodruff, Robert W.
See Mencken, H(enry) L(ouis)

Woolf, (Adeline) Virginia
1882-1941 . . . . **TCLC 1, 5, 20, 43, 56;**
DA; SSC 7; WLC
See also CA 104; 130; CDBLB 1914-1945;
DLB 36, 100; DLBD 10; MTCW

Woollcott, Alexander (Humphreys)
1887-1943 . . . . **TCLC 5**
See also CA 105; DLB 29

Woolrich, Cornell 1903-1968 . . . . **CLC 77**
See also Hopley-Woolrich, Cornell George

Wordsworth, Dorothy
1771-1855 . . . . **NCLC 25**
See also DLB 107

Wordsworth, William
1770-1850 . . . . **NCLC 12, 38; DA; PC 4;**
WLC
See also CDBLB 1789-1832; DLB 93, 107

Wouk, Herman 1915- . . . . **CLC 1, 9, 38**
See also CA 5-8R; CANR 6, 33; DLBY 82;
MTCW

Wright, Charles (Penzel, Jr.)
1935- . . . . **CLC 6, 13, 28**
See also CA 29-32R; CAAS 7; CANR 23,
36; DLBY 82; MTCW

Wright, Charles Stevenson
1932- . . . . **CLC 49; BLC 3**
See also BW 1; CA 9-12R; CANR 26;
DLB 33

Wright, Jack R.
See Harris, Mark

Wright, James (Arlington)
1927-1980 . . . . **CLC 3, 5, 10, 28**
See also AITN 2; CA 49-52; 97-100;
CANR 4, 34; DLB 5; MTCW

Wright, Judith (Arandell)
1915- . . . . **CLC 11, 53**
See also CA 13-16R; CANR 31; MTCW;
SATA 14

Wright, L(aurali) R. 1939- . . . . **CLC 44**
See also CA 138

Wright, Richard (Nathaniel)
1908-1960 . . . . **CLC 1, 3, 4, 9, 14, 21, 48,**
74; BLC; DA; SSC 2; WLC
See also AAYA 5; BW 1; CA 108;
CDALB 1929-1941; DLB 76, 102;
DLBD 2; MTCW

Wright, Richard B(ruce) 1937- . . . . . . **CLC 6**
See also CA 85-88; DLB 53

Wright, Rick 1945- . . . . **CLC 35**

Wright, Rowland
See Wells, Carolyn

Wright, Stephen Caldwell 1946- . . . . **CLC 33**
See also BW 2

Wright, Willard Huntington 1888-1939
See Van Dine, S. S.
See also CA 115

Wright, William 1930- . . . . **CLC 44**
See also CA 53-56; CANR 7, 23

Wu Ch'eng-en 1500(?)-1582(?) . . . . **LC 7**

Wu Ching-tzu 1701-1754 . . . . **LC 2**

Wurlitzer, Rudolph 1938(?)- . . . **CLC 2, 4, 15**
See also CA 85-88

Wycherley, William 1641-1715 . . . . **LC 8, 21**
See also CDBLB 1660-1789; DLB 80

Wylie, Elinor (Morton Hoyt)
1885-1928 . . . . **TCLC 8**
See also CA 105; DLB 9, 45

Wylie, Philip (Gordon) 1902-1971 . . . **CLC 43**
See also CA 21-22; 33-36R; CAP 2; DLB 9

Wyndham, John . . . . **CLC 19**
See also Harris, John (Wyndham Parkes
Lucas) Beynon

Wyss, Johann David Von
1743-1818 . . . . **NCLC 10**
See also JRDA; MAICYA; SATA 27, 29

Yakumo Koizumi
See Hearn, (Patricio) Lafcadio (Tessima
Carlos)

Yanez, Jose Donoso
See Donoso (Yanez), Jose

Yanovsky, Basile S.
See Yanovsky, V(assily) S(emenovich)

Yanovsky, V(assily) S(emenovich)
1906-1989 . . . . **CLC 2, 18**
See also CA 97-100; 129

Yates, Richard 1926-1992 . . . . . **CLC 7, 8, 23**
See also CA 5-8R; 139; CANR 10, 43;
DLB 2; DLBY 81, 92

Yeats, W. B.
See Yeats, William Butler

Yeats, William Butler
1865-1939 . . . . . **TCLC 1, 11, 18, 31; DA;**
WLC
See also CA 104; 127; CANR 45;
CDBLB 1890-1914; DLB 10, 19, 98;
MTCW

Yehoshua, A(braham) B.
1936- . . . . **CLC 13, 31**
See also CA 33-36R; CANR 43

Yep, Laurence Michael 1948- . . . . . . **CLC 35**
See also AAYA 5; CA 49-52; CANR 1, 46,
46; CLR 3, 17; DLB 52; JRDA;
MAICYA; SATA 7, 69

Yerby, Frank G(arvin)
1916-1991 . . . . **CLC 1, 7, 22; BLC**
See also BW 1; CA 9-12R; 136; CANR 16;
DLB 76; MTCW

Yesenin, Sergei Alexandrovich
See Esenin, Sergei (Alexandrovich)

Yevtushenko, Yevgeny (Alexandrovich)
1933- . . . . **CLC 1, 3, 13, 26, 51**
See also CA 81-84; CANR 33; MTCW

Yezierska, Anzia 1885(?)-1970 . . . . . **CLC 46**
See also CA 126; 89-92; DLB 28; MTCW

Yglesias, Helen 1915- . . . . **CLC 7, 22**
See also CA 37-40R; CAAS 20; CANR 15;
MTCW

Yokomitsu Riichi 1898-1947 . . . . . . **TCLC 47**

Yonge, Charlotte (Mary)
1823-1901 . . . . **TCLC 48**
See also CA 109; DLB 18; SATA 17

York, Jeremy
See Creasey, John

York, Simon
See Heinlein, Robert A(nson)

Yorke, Henry Vincent 1905-1974 . . . **CLC 13**
See also Green, Henry
See also CA 85-88; 49-52

Yosano Akiko 1878-1942 . . . . **PC 11**

Yoshimoto, Banana . . . . **CLC 84**
See also Yoshimoto, Mahoko

Yoshimoto, Mahoko 1964-
See Yoshimoto, Banana
See also CA 144

Young, Al(bert James)
1939- . . . . **CLC 19; BLC**
See also BW 2; CA 29-32R; CANR 26;
DLB 33

Young, Andrew (John) 1885-1971 . . . . **CLC 5**
See also CA 5-8R; CANR 7, 29

Young, Collier
See Bloch, Robert (Albert)

Young, Edward 1683-1765 . . . . **LC 3**
See also DLB 95

Young, Marguerite 1909- . . . . **CLC 82**
See also CA 13-16; CAP 1

Young, Neil 1945- . . . . **CLC 17**
See also CA 110

Yourcenar, Marguerite
1903-1987 . . . . **CLC 19, 38, 50**
See also CA 69-72; CANR 23; DLB 72;
DLBY 88; MTCW

Yurick, Sol 1925- .... **CLC 6**
    See also CA 13-16R; CANR 25

Zabolotskii, Nikolai Alekseevich
        1903-1958 .... **TCLC 52**
    See also CA 116

Zamiatin, Yevgenii
    See Zamyatin, Evgeny Ivanovich

Zamyatin, Evgeny Ivanovich
        1884-1937 .... **TCLC 8, 37**
    See also CA 105

Zangwill, Israel 1864-1926. .... **TCLC 16**
    See also CA 109; DLB 10, 135

Zappa, Francis Vincent, Jr. 1940-1993
    See Zappa, Frank
    See also CA 108; 143

Zappa, Frank .... **CLC 17**
    See also Zappa, Francis Vincent, Jr.

Zaturenska, Marya 1902-1982. .... **CLC 6, 11**
    See also CA 13-16R; 105; CANR 22

Zelazny, Roger (Joseph) 1937- ..... **CLC 21**
    See also AAYA 7; CA 21-24R; CANR 26;
        DLB 8; MTCW; SATA 39, 57

Zhdanov, Andrei A(lexandrovich)
        1896-1948 .... **TCLC 18**
    See also CA 117

Zhukovsky, Vasily 1783-1852 .... **NCLC 35**

Ziegenhagen, Eric .... **CLC 55**

Zimmer, Jill Schary
    See Robinson, Jill

Zimmerman, Robert
    See Dylan, Bob

Zindel, Paul 1936- ... **CLC 6, 26; DA; DC 5**
    See also AAYA 2; CA 73-76; CANR 31;
        CLR 3; DLB 7, 52; JRDA; MAICYA;
        MTCW; SATA 16, 58

Zinov'Ev, A. A.
    See Zinoviev, Alexander (Aleksandrovich)

Zinoviev, Alexander (Aleksandrovich)
        1922- .... **CLC 19**
    See also CA 116; 133; CAAS 10

Zoilus
    See Lovecraft, H(oward) P(hillips)

Zola, Emile (Edouard Charles Antoine)
        1840-1902 ...... **TCLC 1, 6, 21, 41; DA;**
                                          WLC
    See also CA 104; 138; DLB 123

Zoline, Pamela 1941- .... **CLC 62**

Zorrilla y Moral, Jose 1817-1893. . **NCLC 6**

Zoshchenko, Mikhail (Mikhailovich)
        1895-1958 .... **TCLC 15; SSC 15**
    See also CA 115

Zuckmayer, Carl 1896-1977. .... **CLC 18**
    See also CA 69-72; DLB 56, 124

Zuk, Georges
    See Skelton, Robin

Zukofsky, Louis
        1904-1978 .... **CLC 1, 2, 4, 7, 11, 18;**
                                          PC 11
    See also CA 9-12R; 77-80; CANR 39;
        DLB 5; MTCW

Zweig, Paul 1935-1984. .... **CLC 34, 42**
    See also CA 85-88; 113

Zweig, Stefan 1881-1942 .... **TCLC 17**
    See also CA 112; DLB 81, 118

SSC Cumulative Nationality Index

AMERICAN

Aiken, Conrad (Potter) 9
Anderson, Sherwood 1
Baldwin, James (Arthur) 10
Barnes, Djuna 3
Barth, John (Simmons) 10
Barthelme, Donald 2
Beattie, Ann 11
Bellow, Saul 14
Benet, Stephen Vincent 10
Bierce, Ambrose (Gwinett) 9
Bowles, Paul (Frederick) 3
Boyle, Kay 5
Boyle, T(homas) Coraghessan 16
Cable, George Washington 4
Calisher, Hortense 15
Capote, Truman 2
Carver, Raymond 8
Cather, Willa Sibert 2
Cheever, John 1
Chesnutt, Charles W(addell) 7
Chopin, Kate 8
Coover, Robert (Lowell) 15
Crane, Stephen (Townley) 7
Davenport, Guy (Mattison 16
Dixon, Stephen 16
Dubus, Andre 15
Dunbar, Paul Laurence 8
Elkin, Stanley L(awrence) 12
Ellison, Harlan (Jay) 14
Faulkner, William (Cuthbert) 1
Fitzgerald, F(rancis) Scott (Key) 6
Freeman, Mary Eleanor Wilkins 1
Gardner, John (Champlin) 7
Garland, (Hannibal) Hamlin 18
Gass, William H(oward) 12
Gilchrist, Ellen 14
Gilman, Charlotte (Anna) Perkins (Stetson)
    13

Gordon, Caroline 15
Grau, Shirley Ann 15
Hammett, (Samuel) Dashiell 17
Harte, (Francis) Bret(t) 8
Hawthorne, Nathaniel 3
Hemingway, Ernest (Miller) 1
Henry, O. 5
Hughes, (James) Langston 6
Hurston, Zora Neale 4
Irving, Washington 2
Jackson, Shirley 9
James, Henry 8
Jewett, (Theodora) Sarah Orne 6
King, Stephen (Edwin) 17
Le Guin, Ursula K(roeber) 12
Ligotti, Thomas 16
Lish, Gordon (Jay) 18
London, Jack 4
Lovecraft, H(oward) P(hillips) 3
Maclean, Norman (Fitzroy) 13
Malamud, Bernard 15
Marshall, Paule 3
Mason, Bobbie Ann 4
McCullers, (Lula) Carson (Smith) 9
Melville, Herman 1, 17
Michaels, Leonard 16
Nabokov, Vladimir (Vladimirovich) 11
Nin, Anais 10
Oates, Joyce Carol 6
O'Connor, (Mary) Flannery 1
O'Hara, John (Henry) 15
Olsen, Tillie 11
Ozick, Cynthia 15
Paley, Grace 8
Parker, Dorothy (Rothschild) 2
Phillips, Jayne Anne 16
Poe, Edgar Allan 1
Porter, Katherine Anne 4
Powers, J(ames) F(arl) 4

Pynchon, Thomas (Ruggles 14
Salinger, J(erome) D(avid) 2
Singer, Isaac Bashevis 3
Steinbeck, John (Ernst) 11
Suckow, Ruth 18
Taylor, Peter (Hillsman) 10
Thurber, James (Grover) 1
Toomer, Jean 1
Twain, Mark 6
Updike, John (Hoyer) 13
Vonnegut, Kurt 8
Walker, Alice (Malsenior) 5
Warren, Robert Penn 4
Welty, Eudora 1
West, Nathanael 16
Wharton, Edith (Newbold Jones) 6
Wright, Richard (Nathaniel) 2

ARGENTINIAN

Bioy Casares, Adolfo 17
Borges, Jorge Luis 4
Cortazar, Julio 7
Valenzuela, Luisa 14

AUSTRALIAN

Lawson, Henry (Archibald Hertzberg) 18

AUSTRIAN

Kafka, Franz 5
Musil, Robert (Edler von) 18
Schnitzler, Arthur 15

CANADIAN

Atwood, Margaret (Eleanor) 2
Gallant, Mavis 5
Laurence, (Jean) Margaret (Wemyss) 7
Munro, Alice 3

COLOMBIAN
Garcia Marquez, Gabriel (Jose) 8

DANISH
Andersen, Hans Christian 6
Dinesen, Isak 7

ENGLISH
Ballard, J(ames) G(raham) 1
Bates, H(erbert) E(rnest) 10
Carter, Angela (Olive) 13
Chesterton, G(ilbert) K(eith) 1
Clarke, Arthur C(harles) 3
Conrad, Joseph 9
de la Mare, Walter (John) 14
Dickens, Charles (John Huffam) 17
Doyle, Arthur Conan 12
du Maurier, Daphne 18
Hardy, Thomas 2
James, Montague (Rhodes) 16
Kipling, (Joseph) Rudyard 5
Lawrence, D(avid) H(erbert Richards) 4
Lessing, Doris (May) 6
Maugham, W(illiam) Somerset 8
Pritchett, V(ictor) S(awdon) 14
Saki 12
Wells, H(erbert) G(eorge) 6
Wodehouse, P(elham) G(renville) 2
Woolf, (Adeline) Virginia 7

FRENCH
Balzac, Honore de 5
Barbey d'Aurevilly, Jules Amedee 17
Baudelaire, Charles 18
Camus, Albert 9
Colette, (Sidonie-Gabrielle) 10
Flaubert, Gustave 11
Gide, Andre (Paul Guillaume) 13
Lautreamont, Comte de 14
Maupassant, (Henri Rene Albert) Guy de
   1
Merimee, Prosper 7
Nerval, Gerard de 18
Villiers de l'Isle Adam, Jean Marie Mathias
   Philippe Auguste 14
Voltaire 12

GERMAN
Hoffmann, E(rnst) T(heodor) A(madeus)
   13
Mann, (Paul) Thomas 5

IRISH
Beckett, Samuel (Barclay) 16
Bowen, Elizabeth (Dorothea Cole) 3
Joyce, James (Augustine Aloysius) 3
Lavin, Mary 4
Le Fanu, Joseph Sheridan 14
McGahern, John 17
O'Brien, Edna 10
O'Connor, Frank 5
O'Faolain, Sean 13
O'Flaherty, Liam 6
Wilde, Oscar (Fingal O'Flahertie Wills) 11

ITALIAN
Boccaccio, Giovanni 10
Calvino, Italo 3
Levi, Primo 12

JAPANESE
Kawabata, Yasunari 17

Mishima, Yukio 4

NEW ZEALANDER
Mansfield, Katherine 9

POLISH
Schulz, Bruno 13

RUSSIAN
Babel, Isaak (Emmanuilovich) 16
Bulgakov, Mikhail (Afanas'evich) 18
Bunin, Ivan Alexeyevich 5
Chekhov, Anton (Pavlovich) 2
Dostoevsky, Fedor Mikhailovich 2
Gogol, Nikolai (Vasilyevich) 4
Tolstoy, Leo (Nikolaevich) 9
Turgenev, Ivan 7
Zoshchenko, Mikhail (Mikhailovich) 15

SCOTTISH
Spark, Muriel (Sarah) 10
Stevenson, Robert Louis (Balfour) 11

SOUTH AFRICAN
Gordimer, Nadine 17

SPANISH
Cervantes (Saavedra), Miguel de 12
Unamuno (y Jugo), Miguel de 11

SWEDISH
Lagerkvist, Par 12

SWISS
Hesse, Hermann 9

WELSH
Thomas, Dylan (Marlais) 3

SSC Cumulative Title Index

"The Abandoned House" (Michaels) **16**:316

"L'abandonné" (Maupassant) **1**:259

"The Abbé Aubain" (Merimee) **7**:290, 292, 295, 300

"The Abbey Grange" (Doyle) **12**:60, 62

ABC Book (Tolstoy) **9**:386-87

"The Abduction from the Seraglio" (Barthelme) **2**:46, 51-2

"El abejorro" (Unamuno) **11**:312

Abel Sánchez (Unamuno)
See *Abel Sánchez: Una historia de pasión*

Abel Sánchez: Una historia de pasión (*Abel Sánchez*) (Unamuno) **11**:314, 317, 325, 337-39, 345, 347, 349, 351

Die Abenteuer in der Sylvesternacht (Hoffmann) **13**:188-89, 210

"The Abortion" (Walker) **5**:412, 414

"About How Ivan Ivanovič Quarreled with Ivan Nikiforovič" (Gogol)
See "The Tale of How Ivan Ivanovich Quarrelled with Ivan Nikiforovich"

"About Love" (Chekhov) **2**:139, 141, 143, 157

"Abroad" (Gordimer) **17**:157, 160

"The Absence of Mr. Glass" (Chesterton) **1**:131

"Absent-Mindedness in a Parish Choir" (Hardy) **2**:206, 215, 217

"Absolution" (Fitzgerald) **6**:46, 77, 81, 83-4, 86, 100, 102-03

"Acceptance of Their Ways" (Gallant) **5**:139-40

"The Accompanist" (Pritchett) **14**:263, 273

"An Account of Some Strange Disturbances in an Old House on Aungier Street" (Le Fanu)
See "Some Strange Disturbances in an Old House on Augier Street"

"Ace in the Hole" (Updike) **13**:351-52

"El acercamiento a Almotásim" ("The Approach to Almotasim"; "The Approach to al Mu'tasim") (Borges) **4**:4, 16

"The Achievement of the Cat" (Saki) **12**:314, 327

"Achilles' Heel" (O'Connor) **5**:370, 372

Acia (Turgenev)
See *Asya*

"Across the Bay" (Bates) **10**:118, 134

"Across the Straits" (Lawson) **18**:220

Actions and Reactions (Kipling) **5**:272, 283-85

"The Actor and the Alibi" (Chesterton) **1**:138

"Acts of God" (Boyle) **16**:157

"Adam, One Afternoon" (Calvino) **3**:112

Adam, One Afternoon, and Other Stories (Calvino)
See *L'entrada en guerra*

"Adam's Death" (Boyle) **5**:57

"Ad Astra" (Faulkner) **1**:147

"Adieu" (Balzac) **5**:17-18, 22, 24, 31, 33

"The Adjuster" (Fitzgerald) **6**:46

"The Admiralty Spire" (Nabokov) **11**:124-25

"The Admirer" (Singer) **3**:378, 384

"Admiring the Scenery" (O'Faolain) **13**:284-86, 288, 297, 300, 302-05, 307, 309

"Adoration" (Gilchrist) **14**:157

"Ad porcos" (Bioy Casares) **17**:56

"Adrift Just Off the Islets of Langerhans: Latitude 38 54'N, Longitude 00'13"W" (Ellison) **14**:109-11, 115, 118-21

"The Adulterous Woman" (Camus)
See "La femme adultère"

"Adultery" (Dubus) **15**:74, 76, 87, 89-90, 92-4, 98, 100

Adultery, and Other Choices (Dubus) **15**:72-3, 75-6, 80-1, 92

"Advancing Luna—and Ida B. Wells" (Walker) **5**:412-13

"Adventure" (Anderson) **1**:18, 58

"The Adventure" (Lagerkvist)
See "Äventyret"

"An Adventure from a Work in Progress" (Thomas) **3**:402, 407

"The Adventure of a Clerk" (Calvino) **3**:116

"Adventure of a Photographer" (Calvino) **3**:111

"The Adventure of a Poet" (Calvino) **3**:111, 116

"The Adventure of a Reader" (Calvino) **3**:112

"Adventure of a Traveller" (Calvino) **3**:111

"The Adventure of Charles Augustus Milverton" (Doyle) **12**:61

"The Adventure of Gloria Scott" (Doyle) **12**:57

"The Adventure of Lieutenant Jergounoff" (Turgenev)
See "Istoriya leytenanta Ergunova"

"The Adventure of Peter Black" (Doyle) **12**:50

"The Adventure of Shoscombe Old Place" (Doyle) **12**:51-2, 63

"The Adventure of Six Napoleone" (Doyle) **12**:55

"The Adventure of the Black Fisherman" (Irving) **2**:241, 247

"The Adventure of the Blanched Soldier" (Doyle) **12**:51-2

"The Adventure of the Blue Carbuncle" (Doyle) **12**:55, 66, 68, 73-4

"The Adventure of the Cardboard Box" (Doyle) **12**:62-4

"The Adventure of the Copper Beeches" (Doyle) **12**:51, 55, 58-9, 68, 71-3

"The Adventure of the Creeping Man" (Doyle) **12**:52, 63-4

"The Adventure of the Dancing Men" (Doyle) **12**:49, 51

"The Adventure of the Empty House" (Doyle) **12**:61

"The Adventure of the Engineer's Thumb" (Doyle) **12**:51, 58, 66, 68, 72-4

"The Adventure of the Englishman" (Irving) **2**:262

"The Adventure of the German Student" (Irving) **2**:241, 256-57, 261

"The Adventure of the Golden Pince-Nez" (Doyle) **12**:62

"The Adventure of the Greek Interpreter" (Doyle) **12**:51, 55

"The Adventure of the Illustrious Client" (Doyle) **12**:54, 64

"The Adventure of the Mason" (Irving) **2**:266

"The Adventure of the Missing Three-Quarter" (Doyle) **12**:50-2

"Adventure of the Mysterious Picture" (Irving) **2**:261, 265

"The Adventure of the Mysterious Stranger" (Irving) **2**:261

"The Adventure of the Naval Treaty" (Doyle) **12**:50-1, 58-60

"The Adventure of the Noble Bachelor" (Doyle) **12**:53, 66, 71, 75

"The Adventure of the Norwood Builder" (Doyle) **12**:51-2

"The Adventure of the Red-Headed League" (Doyle) **12**:50, 54-5, 66, 70-1, 73

"The Adventure of the Reigate Puzzle" (Doyle) **12**:58-9

"The Adventure of the Retired Colourman" (Doyle) **12**:50

"The Adventure of the Second Stain" (Doyle) **12**:51, 53, 62

"The Adventure of the Silver Blaze" (Doyle) **12**:51

"The Adventure of the Speckled Band" (Doyle) **12**:58-9, 66, 68, 71, 73-4

"The Adventure of the Stockbroker's Clerk" (Doyle) **12**:50-1, 55

"The Adventure of the Sussex Vampire" (Doyle) **12**:52, 63

"The Adventure of the Three Gables" (Doyle) **12**:52, 64

"The Adventure of the Veiled Lodger" (Doyle) **12**:52, 63

"The Adventure of the Yellow Face" (Doyle) **12**:50-2, 58

"The Adventure of Wisteria Lodge" (Doyle) **12**:62-3

Adventures du Baron de Gangan (Voltaire) **12**:340

Adventures in the Skin Trade, and Other Stories (Thomas) **3**:396, 403-04

"Adventures of a Dead Man" (Bulgakov) **18**:90

"The Adventures of Chichikov" (Bulgakov) **18**:73-4, 91, 98-9

"The Adventures of Françoise and Suzanne" (Cable) **4**:49

Adventures of Gerard (Doyle) **12**:81-2

The Adventures of Sherlock Holmes (Doyle) **12**:68, 72-4

"The Adventures of the Bruce-Partington Plans" (Doyle) **12**:51-2, 55-6

"Advice to Young Men" (Chesnutt) **7**:14

"Aepyornis Island" (Wells) **6**:388, 399

"The Aeroplanes at Brescia" (Davenport) **16**:161, 165, 167, 170, 176, 197

"Los afanes" (Bioy Casares) **17**:87, 95

"Afar a Bird" (Beckett) **16**:123, 125-26

"The Affair at 7, Rue de M----" (Steinbeck) See "L'affaire du l'avenue de M----"

"The Affair at Coulter's Notch" (Bierce) **9**:49

"The Affair at Grover Station" (Cather) **2**:102

"L'affaire du l'avenue de M----" ("The Affair at 7, Rue de M----") (Steinbeck) **11**:255-56, 258

"An Affair of Honor" (Nabokov) **11**:117

"An Affair of Outposts" (Bierce) **9**:60, 96

"L'affichage céleste" ("Celestial Publicity") (Villiers de l'Isle Adam) **14**:377, 381-83, 390, 396

"The Aficionados" (Carver) **8**:50

"Afloat" (Beattie) **11**:10-11, 13, 29

Afloat (Maupassant) See *Sur l'eau*

"Afonka Bida" (Babel) **16**:52, 58

"Africa Emergent" (Gordimer) **17**:57, 160, 174

"The African Magician" (Gordimer) **17**:156, 162, 173-74

"African Morning" (Hughes) **6**:116-17, 122

African Stories (Lessing) **6**:189-91, 196, 212, 214-15, 217-18

"After Dark in the Playing Fields" (James) **16**:251

"After Dinner" (Cortazar) **7**:70

"After Fourteen Years" (O'Connor) **5**:381, 387, 392

"After Holbein" (Wharton) **6**:422-23

After-Hours (Cortazar) See *Deshoras*

After Lazarus: A Filmscript (Coover) **15**:58-9, 61

"After Lunch" (Cortazar) **7**:70

"An Afternoon Miracle" (Henry) **5**:162, 181

"Afternoon of an Author" (Fitzgerald) **6**:60

"Afternoon of a Playwright" (Thurber) **1**:424

"Afternoon Waltz" (O'Hara) **15**:277, 284

"An Afternoon with the Old Man" (Dubus) **15**:74

After Such Pleasures (Parker) **2**:273-74

"After the Ball" ("The Morning after the Ball") (Tolstoy) **9**:367, 379, 388, 394-95

"After the Battle" (Babel) **16**:12, 26-28, 30, 52, 54, 57-8

"After the Denim" (Carver) **8**:14

"After the Fair" (Thomas) **3**:399

"After the Game" (Dubus) **15**:86, 100

"After the Race" (Joyce) **3**:205, 208-09, 226, 231, 234, 247-48

"After the Storm" (Hemingway) **1**:216, 234

"After the Winter" (Chopin) **8**:93

"Afterward" (Wharton) **6**:433

"Agafia" (Chekhov) **2**:155

"Agatha" (O'Hara) **15**:282-83

Age (Calisher) **15**:12-14

"The Age of Genius" ("The Genial Epoch") (Schulz) **13**:336, 344

"Agony" (Lish) **18**:283

Ahasverus död (*The Death of Ahasuerus*) (Lagerkvist) **12**:184, 186-90, 192, 198

"Ahí, pero dónde, cómo" (Cortazar) **7**:61-2

Ahí y ahora (*There and Now*) (Cortazar) **7**:91

Ah King (Maugham) **8**:374, 378

"El ahogado más hermoso del mundo" ("The Handsomest Drowned Man in the World: A Tale for Children") (Garcia Marquez) **8**:160, 167-70, 183, 186

"Ah, Well" (Lawson) **18**:243

"Ah, Woe Is Me" (Gordimer) **17**:152, 160, 167

"Airwaves" (Mason) **4**:1

Akëdysséril (Villiers de l'Isle Adam) **14**:378-79, 383-84, 386, 388-90

"An Akoulina of the Irish Midlands" (Lavin) **4**:182-83

"Albert" (Tolstoy) **9**:376, 389-90, 393

"Albert Savarus" (Balzac) **5**:27

"Alec" (O'Connor) **5**:371, 390

"El aleph" ("The Aleph") (Borges) **4**:25, 28, 31-2, 34

"The Aleph" (Borges) See "El aleph"

El aleph (*The Aleph, and Other Stories, 1933-1969*) (Borges) **4**:15, 18-20, 34, 36, 39-41

The Aleph, and Other Stories, 1933-1969 (Borges) See *El aleph*

"Alexander" (Bates) **10**:111-12, 124, 132

"Alguien desordena estas rosas" ("Someone Has Disturbed the Roses") (Garcia Marquez) **8**:154, 158

"Alguien que anda por ahí" ("Someone Walking Around") (Cortazar) **7**:83-7, 90-1

The Alhambra (Irving) **2**:242-46, 251, 254, 265, 268

"The Alibi" (du Maurier) **18**:127, 132

"Alice Long's Dachsunds" (Spark) **10**:360, 362, 367, 371

"Alicia's Diary" (Hardy) **2**:211, 214

"The Alien Corn" (Maugham) **8**:356-57, 366, 369, 378-79

"An Alien Flower" (Gallant) **5**:124, 132-33

"An Alien in the Pines" (Garland) **18**:154, 160

"The Aliens" (McCullers) **9**:342-43, 347, 354, 356

"The Alien Skull" (O'Flaherty) **6**:262, 280

"Alix de Morainville" (Cable) **4**:60

"Alix's Refusal" (Colette) **10**:292

"Alkmene" (Dinesen) **7**:165

"Allal" (Bowles) **3**:69

"All, All Wasted" (Aiken) **9**:12, 14

"Allan and Adelaide: An Arabesque" (Ligotti) **16**:286

"All at One Point" (Calvino) **3**:103, 108

"Allegiance" (Taylor) **10**:375-79

"Aller et retour" (Barnes) **3**:7-8, 10, 14-17, 24

"All Fires the Fire" (Cortazar) See "Todos los fuegos el fuego"

All Fires the Fire, and Other Stories (Cortazar) See *Todos los fuegos el fuego*

All Gone (Dixon) **16**:218

"All Hallows" (de la Mare) **14**:70, 71, 83, 92

"The Alligators" (Updike) **13**:356

"All Lovers Love the Spring" (Gordon) **15**:104-05

"All Saints" (Bowen) **3**:40, 42

"The All-Seeing" (Nin) **10**:303-04

"All Shook Up" (Boyle) **16**:144-45

"All Sorts of Impossible Things" (McGahern) **17**:299, 304, 309

"All Souls'" (Wharton) **6**:423, 426-27

"All Strange Away" (Beckett) **16**:117

"All That Glitters" (Clarke) **3**:134

"All the Birds Come Home to Roost" (Ellison) **14**:124

"All the Dead Pilots" (Faulkner) **1**:147

"All the Girls He Wanted" (O'Hara) **15**:248, 255, 264, 266

"ALL the Good People I've Left Behind" (Oates) **6**:250, 252-53

All the Good People I've Left Behind (Oates) **6**:247-48, 250, 252-54

"All the King's Horses" (Vonnegut) **8**:434

"All the Other Stories" (Calvino) **3**:101

All the Sad Young Men (Fitzgerald) **6**:46, 94

"All the Sounds of Fear" (Ellison) **14**:105

"All the Time in the World" (Clarke) **3**:135

"Al-Mamon" (Gogol) **4**:83

"Alma Redeemed" (Malamud) **15**:235

"The Almond Tree" (de la Mare) **14**:80

"The Aloe" (Mansfield) **9**:279, 282, 284, 301-03, 309

"Aloha Oe" (London) **4**:269

"Alone" (O'Hara) **15**:248, 265, 267, 274-76

"Alone" (Singer) **3**:360-61, 364

Alone Against Tomorrow: Stories of Alienation in Speculative Fiction (Ellison) **14**:143-47

"Along the Edges" (McGahern) **17**:319

"An Alpimalyan Dialogue" (Turgenev) **7**:335

"An Alpine Idyll" (Hemingway) **1**:210, 217

"The Altar of the Dead" (James) **8**:269, 302, 304, 307-09

Altogether: The Collected Stories of W. Somerset Maugham (Maugham)
    See *East and West: The Collected Short Stories of W. Somerset Maugham*

Altogether: The Collected Stories of W. Somerset Maugham (Maugham) **8**:356, 358, 360, 370, 380, 382

"Always Something to Do in Salinas" (Steinbeck) **11**:253

"Alyosha the Pot" (Tolstoy) **9**:379, 389

"El amante liberal" ("The Generous Lover"; "The Liberal Lover") (Cervantes) **12**:3, 5, 7-8, 14-16, 18, 34, 44

"Les amants de Tolède" (Villiers de l'Isle Adam) **14**:390, 394, 397

"Amargura para tres sonámbulos" ("Bitterness for Three Sleepwalkers"; "Bitter Sorrow for Three Sleepwalkers") (Garcia Marquez) **8**:154-55, 157-58, 182

Amateurs (Barthelme) **2**:47

"The Ambitious Guest" (Hawthorne) **3**:182, 186-87

"The Ambitious Sophomore" (Vonnegut) **8**:431

"Ambrose His Mark" (Barth) **10**:41, 45-6, 53-4, 56, 60-1, 63, 89, 95, 97-8, 100

"Ambuscade" (Faulkner) **1**:170, 177

"American Honeymoon" (Benet) **10**:149

"The American's Tale" (Doyle) **12**:81, 84-5

"The American Wife" (O'Connor) **5**:373

"Les âmes du purgatoire" ("The Souls in Purgatory") (Merimee) **7**:283-84, 289-90, 292

"Les amies de pension" (Villiers de l'Isle Adam) **14**:378, 396

"Los amigos" ("The Friends") (Cortazar) **7**:70, 88-9

"Am I Not Your Rosalind?" (Thurber) **1**:420, 425

"Amnesty" (Gordimer) **17**:182, 184, 187-88, 191

"Among the Corn Rows" (Garland) **18**:142, 144, 154, 159, 168-69, 172, 176, 180

Among the Lost People (Aiken) **9**:6, 28

"Among the Massagetae" (Hesse) **9**:244

"Among the Paths to Eden" (Capote) **2**:74-5

"Among Those Present" (Benet) **10**:154

Gli amori difficili (Difficult Loves) (Calvino) **3**:111-13, 116-18

"El amor que asalta" (Unamuno) **11**:312-13

"Amour" (Maupassant) **1**:278, 280

"L'amour du naturel" (Villiers de l'Isle Adam) **14**:396

"L'amour suprême" (Villiers de l'Isle Adam) **14**:379, 384-85, 387, 390, 396

L'amour suprême (Villiers de l'Isle Adam) **14**:378, 396-97

"An Amusing Adventure" (Zoshchenko) **15**:399

"Amy Foster" (Conrad) **9**:143

"Anabella's Hat" (Michaels) **16**:309

Analytical Studies (Balzac)
    See *Etudes analytiques*

"An Anarchist" (Conrad) **9**:157, 179, 181-83, 185

"Ancestors" (Woolf) **7**:381, 389

"& Answers" (Oates) **6**:232

And Other Stories (O'Hara) **15**:286

"A & P" (Updike) **13**:372, 398-99

"Andrea" (O'Hara) **15**:285

"Andreas Thameyer's Last Letter" (Schnitzler)
    See "Andreas Thameyers letzter brief"

"Andreas Thameyers letzter brief" ("Andreas Thameyer's Last Letter") (Schnitzler) **15**:377

"Andrei Kolosov" (Turgenev) **7**:313, 320, 323-24, 335, 339-40, 359

André Walter (Gide) **13**:59

"Andrey Satchel and the Parson and Clerk" (Hardy) **2**:215

"Androcles and the Army" (O'Connor) **5**:369, 374

"Andromache" (Dubus) **15**:73-4, 81

"And Then" (Barthelme) **2**:47

"The Andventure of the Devil's Foot" (Doyle) **12**:63

"L'ane" (Maupassant) **1**:259

Anecdotes of Destiny (Dinesen) **7**:175

L'Ane d'or (Nerval) **18**:371

"The Angel" (Andersen) **6**:15

"The Angel at the Grave" (Wharton) **6**:414

"Angelic Butterfly" (Levi) **12**:278

Angélique (Nerval) **18**:362-65

"Angel Levine" (Malamud) **15**:168, 170-71, 173, 203-04, 207-09, 214, 220

"The Angel of the Bridge" (Cheever) **1**:96, 100, 110

"The Angel of the Odd" (Poe) **1**:407-08

"The Angel Was a Yankee" (Benet) **10**:154, 160

Angry Candy (Ellison) **14**:141-42

"Angst" (Oates) **6**:241

"Anna" (Dubus) **15**:96

"Anna on the Neck" (Chekhov) **2**:131, 157

"Anna, Part I" (Gilchrist) **14**:157-60

"Anner Lizer's Stumblin' Block" (Dunbar) **8**:120-21, 129, 136

"Annette Delarbre" (Irving) **2**:241, 251, 259

"Gli anni-lucci" (Calvino) **3**:92

"Anniversary" (Aiken) **9**:13, 31

"An Anniversary" (de la Mare) **14**:79, 84, 89

"Ann Lee's" (Bowen) **3**:54

Ann Lee's (Bowen) **3**:37, 39-40, 55

"Ann Lisbeth" (Andersen) **6**:14-15

"L'annonciateur" ("Azraël") (Villiers de l'Isle Adam) **14**:381-87, 389-90, 395-96

"Anonymiad" (Barth) **10**:40, 43-4, 46-8, 52, 54-6, 64, 74, 78-80, 83, 86-8, 90-1, 98-9 100-02

"An Anonymous Story" ("A Story without a Title") (Chekhov) **2**:130-31, 157-58

"Another Man's Wife" (Anderson) **1**:39

"Another Pair of Hands" (Spark) **10**:370

"Another Part of the Sky" (Gordimer) **17**:151

"Another Story" (Cheever) **1**:112

"Another Time" (O'Brien) **10**:346-47

"Another Wife" (Anderson) **1**:31, 50-1

"The Answer Depends" (O'Hara) **15**:262

"Answer to Prayer" (Wells) **6**:392

"The Antchar" (Turgenev) **7**:318-19

The Antheap (Lessing) **6**:189-91, 193-94, 196

"Antigona" ("Antigone") (Bunin) **5**:113

"Antigone" (Bunin)
    See "Antigona"

"The Antique Ring" (Hawthorne) **3**:189, 191

"The Antiquities of Elis" (Davenport) **16**:170, 176, 178, 195-96

"Antonie" ("Le médaillon") (Villiers de l'Isle Adam) **14**:382

"Antónov Apples" (Bunin) **5**:81, 100

"Antonovskie jabloki" (Bunin) **5**:98-9

"The Ant's Wedding" (Levi) **12**:275, 277

"Anxiety" (Paley) **8**:411-12

"Any Reasonable Offer" (Vonnegut) **8**:433

"Anywhere Out of the World" (Baudelaire)
    See "N'importe où hors du monde"

"Apacalipsis de Solentiname" ("Apocalypse at Solentiname") (Cortazar) **7**:83, 86, 88, 90-1

"The Ape" (Pritchett) **14**:271

"The Ape Lady in Retirement" (Boyle) **16**:148, 154

"Apocalypse at Solentiname" (Cortazar)
    See "Apacalipsis de Solentiname"

"The Apostate" (London) **4**:263, 291-92

"An Apostle of the Tulles" (Harte) **8**:247-49

"The Apparatus for the Chemical Analysis of the Last Breath" (Villiers de l'Isle Adam)
    See "L'appareil pur l'analyse chimique du dernier soupir"

"L'appareil pur l'analyse chimique du dernier soupir" ("The Apparatus for the Chemical Analysis of the Last Breath") (Villiers de l'Isle Adam) **14**:379, 396

"Apparition" (Maupassant) **1**:265, 281

"Appearance and Reality" (Maugham) **8**:380

"Appearances" (O'Hara) **15**:290

"The Apple" (Wells) **6**:359, 383

"Apples and Pears" (Davenport) **16**:185-89

Apples and Pears, and Other Stories (Davenport) **16**:183-89, 199-200

"The Apple Tree" (Bowen) **3**:33, 41

"The Apple Tree" (du Maurier) **18**:137-38

"The Apple Tree" (Mansfield) **9**:282, 284

The Apple Tree: A Short Novel and Some Stories (Kiss Me Again, Stranger: A Collection of Eight Stories, Long and Short) (du Maurier) **18**:126, 130, 137

"The Apple-Tree Table" (Melville) **1**:294-95, 298

"The Approach to Almotasim" (Borges)
    See "El acercamiento a Almotásim"

"The Approach to al Mu'tasim" (Borges)
    See "El acercamiento a Almotásim"

"April Fish" (Gallant) **5**:151

"April in Paris" (Le Guin) **12**:232

"Apropos of the Wet Snow" ("Concerning Wet Snow") (Dostoevsky) **2**:169, 187

Apt Pupil (King) **17**:262-66, 271, 273

"The Aquatic Uncle" (Calvino)
See "Lo zio acquativo"

Arabesques (Gogol) **4**:104

"Araby" (Joyce) **3**:202-03, 205, 208, 217-18, 225, 231, 234, 237, 242, 245-46, 249

"Arcadian London" (Dickens) **17**:123

"Archangel" (Updike) **13**:390, 397

"The Archduchess" (du Maurier) **18**:127

"Ardagh" (Le Fanu)
See "The Fortunes of Sir Robert Ardagh"

"Ardessa" (Cather) **2**:99, 110-11

"Are These Actual Miles?" (Carver) **8**:47

"Are You a Doctor?" (Carver) **8**:9-10, 18, 32, 34, 47

"Argamak" (Babel) **16**:27-8, 52, 56

"The Argentine Ant" (Calvino)
See *La formica Argentina*

"Argon" (Levi) **12**:255-57, 259, 264

"The Argonauts of North Liberty" (Harte) **8**:214, 216-17, 223

"The Argonauts of the Air" (Wells) **6**:359, 367, 374, 380, 383, 388, 403

"The Argument" (Dixon) **16**:211

"Ariadna" (Chekhov)
See "Ariadne"

"Ariadne" ("Ariadna") (Chekhov) **2**:131-32, 157

"The Aristocrat" (Pritchett) **14**:270, 293, 296

"Armande" (Colette) **10**:274-75, 293

"Las armas secretas" ("Secret Weapons") (Cortazar) **7**:50, 53-8, 70-1

"Army of Occupation" (Boyle) **5**:64, 74-5

Around the Day in Eighty Worlds (Cortazar)
See *La vuelta al día en ochenta mundos*

"Arrangement in Black and White" (Parker) **2**:274-75, 278, 280, 283, 286

"Arrangements" (Dixon) **16**:216

"The Arrest of Lieutenant Golightly" (Kipling) **5**:288, 290

"The Arrow of Heaven" (Chesterton) **1**:128

"Arsène Guillot" (Merimee) **7**:279, 290-92, 300

"Art and Mr. Mahoney" (McCullers) **9**:332, 343, 345-46, 354, 359

"Artemis, the Honest Well-Digger" (Cheever) **1**:107-08

"Arthur Jermyn" (Lovecraft) **3**:258, 264

"The Artificial Nigger" (O'Connor) **1**:343, 345, 347, 353

"Artificial Roses" (Garcia Marquez) **8**:185

"The Artist at Work" (Camus)
See "Jonas ou l'artiste au travail"

"The Artistic Career of Corky" (Wodehouse) **2**:342

"The Artist of the Beautiful" (Hawthorne) **3**:169-71, 174, 183-84

"An Artist's Story" ("The House with a Mezzanine"; "The House with an Attic"; "The House with the Maisonette") (Chekhov) **2**:131, 139, 157

"The Art of Book-Making" (Irving) **2**:254

"The Art of Living" (Gardner) **7**:224-28, 235, 240

The Art of Living, and Other Stories (Gardner) **7**:223-28, 235

"The Artus Exchange" (Hoffmann)
See "Der Artushof"

"Der Artushof" ("The Artus Exchange") (Hoffmann) **13**:183, 223

"Arvie Aspinall's Alarm Clock" (Lawson) **18**:201, 238, 241

"Ash-Cake Hannah and Her Ben" (Dunbar) **8**:122

Ashenden; or, The British Agent (Maugham) **8**:365, 367, 376-78, 380, 383

"The Ash-Tree" (James) **16**:225, 229-30, 232, 234-36, 240-41, 251, 253, 256

"Asigh" (Lavin) **4**:167-68, 181-83

"The Aspern Papers" (Bellow) **14**:25

The Aspern Papers (James) **8**:275, 300, 321-22, 324, 332, 335

"Asphodel" (Welty) **1**:467-69, 472

An Aspidistra in Babylon: Four Novellas (*The Grapes of Paradise: Four Short Novels*) (Bates) **10**:122

"The Assassination of John Fitzgerald Kennedy Considered as a Downhill Motor Race" (Ballard) **1**:70-1, 75

"Assault" (Oates) **6**:243

"The Assembly" (Borges)
See *El congreso*

"The Assembly" (Gallant) **5**:147

Assembly (O'Hara) **15**:251, 252, 261, 279, 280-81, 287

"The Assessor of Success" (Henry) **5**:187

Assez (*Enough*) (Beckett) **16**:71, 76-8, 83, 87, 95-9, 122, 135

"The Assignation" (Poe) **1**:394

"The Assistant" (O'Hara) **15**:279, 285

"The Assistant Producer" (Nabokov) **11**:113, 128

"Assommons les pauvres" ("Let's Beat Down the Poor") (Baudelaire) **18**:34, 47, 49-53

"As Strong as a Man" (Suckow)
See "A Great Mollie"

"Assumption" (Beckett) **16**:72

"Astley's" (Dickens) **17**:134

"The Astronomer" (Updike) **13**:389

Asya (*Acia*) (Turgenev) **7**:320, 323-24, 326-27, 334, 337, 339, 347-52, 360

"At a Dinner of Atheists" (Barbey d'Aurevilly)
See "A un dîner d' athées"

"At Age Forty-Seven" (Zoshchenko) **15**:407

"At Chênière Caminada" (Chopin) **8**:95, 99, 110

"At Christmas-Time" (Chekhov) **2**:130-31

"At Daybreak" (Calvino) **3**:109

"At First Sight" (de la Mare) **14**:71, 74, 89

"At Geisenheimer's" (Wodehouse) **2**:355

"Athénaïse" (Chopin) **8**:66, 72-3, 78, 86, 96, 99, 113-14

"At Home" (Chekhov) **2**:139, 142, 155, 157-58

"At One O'Clock in the Morning" (Baudelaire)
See "A une heure du matin"

"At Paso Rojo" (Bowles) **3**:59, 61-2, 66, 79

"The Atrocity Exhibition" (Ballard) **1**:75

The Atrocity Exhibition (*Love and Napalm: Export U.S.A.*) (Ballard) **1**:70-1, 76-8, 80-3

"Atrophy" (Wharton) **6**:424

"At Sallygap" (Lavin) **4**:169, 171-72, 175, 178-79, 182

"At Shaft 11" (Dunbar) **8**:120-21, 127, 129, 131, 136, 139-40, 143

"Attack" (O'Connor) **5**:371, 391

"An Attack of Nerves" ("A Nervous Breakdown") (Chekhov) **2**:153, 155-56

"An Attack on Lenin" (Zoshchenko) **15**:407

"Attalie Brouillard" (Cable) **4**:59

"At the Barber's" (Zoshchenko) **15**:407-08

"At the Bay" (Mansfield) **9**:278, 280, 282-83, 286, 288-92, 300, 302, 305-07, 309

"At the 'Cadian Ball" (Chopin) **8**:72, 91, 95, 99, 106-07

"At the Drug Store" (Taylor) **10**:398-400, 418

"At the End of the Mechanical Age" (Barthelme) **2**:47

"At the End of the Passage" ("The End of the Passage") (Kipling) **5**:264, 271-72, 274, 278, 280-81, 290-91

"At the Krungthep Plaza" (Bowles) **3**:80

"At the Landing" (Welty) **1**:468

"At the Mouse Circus" (Ellison) **14**:115

"At the Prophet's" (Mann) **5**:323

"At the Rainbow's End" (London) **4**:286

"At the Rendezvous of Victory" (Gordimer) **17**:171

"At the Seminary" (Oates) **6**:255-56

"At the Tolstoy Museum" (Barthelme) **2**:31, 35, 40, 48, 56

"Attractive Modern Homes" (Bowen) **3**:54

"L'auberge" (Maupassant) **1**:265

L'auberge rouge ("The Red Inn") (Balzac) **5**:18, 31, 33

"An Auction" (Crane) **7**:108, 110

"August" (Schulz) **13**:330-31, 339

"Augustus" (Hesse) **9**:234

"Au large" (Cable) **4**:58-9

"A un dîner d' athées" ("At a Dinner of Atheists") (Barbey d'Aurevilly) **17**:6-8, 11-12, 17, 19-20, 33-4, 37, 43-4

"A une heure du matin" ("At One O'Clock in the Morning") (Baudelaire) **18**:19, 41-2, 45-7, 49

"Aunt Gertrude" (Pritchett) **14**:263, 271

"Auntie Bissel" (Suckow) **18**:413, 422, 424

"Aunt Lucy's Search" (Chesnutt) **7**:13

"Aunt Lympy's Interference" (Chopin) **8**:84

"Aunt Mandy's Investment" (Dunbar) **8**:121, 127, 137, 143, 147

"Aunt Mimy's Son" (Chesnutt) **7**:28

"Aunt Tempy's Revenge" (Dunbar) **8**:122

"Aunt Tempy's Triumph" (Dunbar) **8**:122

"Auprès d'un mort" (Maupassant) **1**:281

Aurélia (Nerval) **18**:334-37, 355, 361-62, 366-68, 373-81, 383-84

"The Aurelian" (Nabokov) **11**:130

Aus dem Leben eines bekannten Mannes (Hoffmann) **13**:187, 189

"Au Seabhac" (O'Flaherty) **6**:286-89

"The Author of Beltraffio" (James) **8**:300, 304-05, 345, 350

"The Author of the Acacia Seeds and Other Extracts from the 'Journal of the Association of Therolinguistics'" (Le Guin) **12**:230, 235

"The Author's Chamber" (Irving) **2**:265

"An Author's Confession" (Gogol) **4**:83

"Author's Outline of 'The Mute'" (McCullers) **9**:343

"Autobiography" (Atwood) **2**:15

"An Autobiography" (Gallant) **5**:133

"Autobiography: A Self-Recorded Fiction" (Barth) **10**:41-2, 46, 53-4, 60, 64, 72, 76-9, 80, 84, 91 97-8

"Die Automate" (Hoffmann) **13**:209, 213-14, 219

"Au tombeau de Charles Fourier" (Davenport) **16**:168-69, 175, 177, 191, 193

"La autopista del sur" ("The Southern Thruway") (Cortazar) **7**:54-5, 61

"Autre étude de femme" (Balzac) **5**:32-3, 35-6, 39

"Autres temps" (Wharton) **6**:424-26, 436

"Autumn I" (Mansfield) **9**:284

"Autumn II" (Mansfield) **9**:284

"Autumn II" (Mansfield)
See "The Wind Blows"

"Gli avangnardisti a Mentone" (Calvino) **3**:97

"Avec la bebe-sitter" (Updike) **13**:385

"L'aventure de Walter Schnafs" (Maupassant) **1**:263

"Äventyret" ("The Adventure") (Lagerkvist) **12**:181, 191

"Averroes's Search" (Borges)
See "La busca de Averroes"

"L'aveu" (Maupassant) **1**:263, 274

"Avey" (Toomer) **1**:441, 443-45, 451, 453, 458-59

"An Awakening" (Anderson) **1**:34, 44-5

"Awakening" (Babel) **16**:36, 41-2, 59

"The Awakening" (Clarke) **3**:143, 148

"The Awakening of Rollo Podmarsh" (Wodehouse) **2**:344

"The Awful Gladness of the Mate" (Wodehouse) **2**:356

"Axolotl" (Cortazar) **7**:58, 63-4, 66-7, 70-5, 81

"Azathoth" (Lovecraft) **3**:273

"Azélie" (Chopin) **8**:110

"Azraël" (Villiers de l'Isle Adam)
See "L'annonciateur"

"Baa, Baa, Black Sheep" (Kipling) **5**:277-78, 283, 293

"Las babas del diablo" ("Blow-Up"; "The Devil's Spittle") (Cortazar) **7**:54, 65-6, 68-9, 86

"Babes in the Woods" (Henry) **5**:193

"The Babes in the Woods" (O'Connor) **5**:380

"Babette's Feast" (Dinesen) **7**:166, 195

"The Babies in the Bush" (Lawson) **18**:220

"The Babylon Lottery" (Borges)
See "La lotería en Babilonia"

"Babylon Revisited" (Fitzgerald) **6**:47, 51, 53, 60, 63-4, 72, 74, 76, 81, 85-6, 99-100, 104

"The Baby Party" (Fitzgerald) **6**:46, 94-5

"The Babysitter" (Coover) **15**:30, 38, 40, 48, 50-1

"A Baby Tramp" (Bierce) **9**:87

"The Bachelor's Supper" (Aiken) **9**:6, 13

"Bachmann" (Nabokov) **11**:124

"The Back Drawing-Room" (Bowen) **3**:40, 54

"The Background" (Saki) **12**:311

"The Back of Beyond" (Maugham) **8**:375

"The Backwater" (Turgenev) **7**:320, 335

"Bad Company" (de la Mare) **14**:80, 88, 90

"A Bad Day" (Nabokov) **11**:132-33

"Bad Dreams" (Taylor) **10**:379-80, 384, 389, 393

"The Bad Glazier" (Baudelaire)
See "Le mauvais vitrier"

"The Bag" (Saki) **12**:315

"Bagombo Snuff Box" (Vonnegut) **8**:433, 437

"The Bagpipes of Spring" (Benet) **10**:150

"The Bailbondsman" (Elkin) **12**:93, 95, 106-07, 110, 112, 114, 116

"The Baker's Dozen" (Saki) **12**:328

"The Balcony" (Irving) **2**:266

"Le bal de sceaux" (Balzac) **5**:4, 29

"A Ballad" (Bunin)
See "Ballada"

"A Ballad" (McGahern) **17**:315, 317

"Ballada" ("A Ballad") (Bunin) **5**:115

"The Ballad of the Sad Café" (McCullers) **9**:322-26, 329, 331-32, 334-35, 338, 341-42, 344-46, 350, 353, 355, 358

The Ballad of the Sad Cafe: The Novels and Stories of Carson McCullers (McCullers) **9**:332

"The Ballet of Central Park" (Boyle) **5**:66

"The Balloon" (Barthelme) **2**:31, 33, 36, 42

"The Balloon Hoax" (Poe) **1**:406

"Balthazar's Marvelous Afternoon" (Garcia Marquez)
See "La prodigiosa tarde de Baltazar"

"The Baluchiterium" (Updike) **13**:348, 360

"Bang-Bang You're Dead" (Spark) **10**:353, 356-60, 364-65, 367, 370

"Bank Holiday" (McGahern) **17**:306, 311, 317-18, 321

"Banquet in Honor" (Hughes) **6**:122

"The Banquet of Crow" (Parker) **2**:280, 285

"Un baptême" (Maupassant) **1**:256, 259, 284

"Baptizing" (Munro) **3**:331, 339-40

Barabbas (Lagerkvist) **12**:178-8, 183, 185, 187, 189, 193-4, 197-203

"Bara no Yūrei" ("The Ghost of the Rose") (Kawabata) **17**:242

"Barbados" (Marshall) **3**:299-300, 302-04, 306-08, 316-17

"Barbara of the House of Grebe" (Hardy) **2**:204, 209, 214-15, 221

"The Barbecue" (Dixon) **16**:206, 211

"The Barber" (Bates) **10**:112

"A Barefaced Lie" (West) **16**:402-03

"The Barefoot Saint" (Benet) **10**:145, 153

"Barker's Luck" (Harte) **8**:222, 244

"Barn Burning" (Faulkner) **1**:163, 165

"Barney Take Me Home Again" (Lawson) **18**:211

Il barone rampante (*The Baron in the Trees*) (Calvino) **3**:89-91, 93-5, 99, 117-18

The Baron in the Trees (Calvino)
See *Il barone rampante*

"The Barrel" (Maupassant) **1**:269

"The Barricade" (Hemingway) **1**:208

"The Barrow" (Le Guin) **12**:210, 213, 216, 218, 247-48

"Bartleby, the Scrivener: A Story of Wall-Street" (Melville) **1**:293, 295, 297-98, 303-04, 311, 317, 322-23, 325, 328, 331; **17**:326-92

"The Basement" (Lagerkvist) **12**:179, 182, 196-7

"Basil and Cleopatra" (Fitzgerald) **6**:50

"Basilisk" (Ellison) **14**:102-05

"Bás na Bó" (O'Flaherty) **6**:287-88

"The Basque and Bijou" (Nin) **10**:326

"Batard" ("Diable—A Dog") (London) **4**:288-89

"The Bath" (Carver) **8**:15, 19-24, 26-7, 30, 39, 56-60

"Bathhouse and People" (Zoshchenko) **15**:

"Battleground" (King) **17**:261

"The Battler" (Hemingway) **1**:242, 244-45, 247

"Der bau" ("The Burrow") (Kafka) **5**:206, 209, 241

"Baum Gabriel, 1935 - ( )" (Gallant) **5**:137-38

"Bavarian Gentians" (Lawrence) **4**:233

"Baxter's Procrustes" (Chesnutt) **7**:15

"A Ballad" (Bunin)
See "Ballada"

Bayou Folk (Chopin) **8**:65-8, 72, 77, 84, 88-9, 93, 97, 103-08, 110-11, 114

"The Beach Murders" (Ballard) **1**:72-4

"The Beach of Falesá" (Stevenson) **11**:269, 279, 283-84, 286-87, 296, 299

"The Beach Party" (Grau) **15**:148, 160

"The Bear" (Faulkner) **1**:148, 152-58, 167, 172-74, 182

"The Beard" (Singer) **3**:375

"A Bear Hunt" (Faulkner) **1**:177

"The Bear-Hunt" (Tolstoy) **9**:387

The Beast in Me, and Other Animals: A New Collection of Pieces and Drawings about Human Beings and Less Alarming Creatures (Thurber) **1**:425

"The Beast in the Jungle" (James) **8**:302, 307-09, 320, 326, 338-40, 342, 347

Beasts and Super-Beasts (Saki) **12**:288, 291, 294-96, 307-09, 313-14, 323, 329, 332

"The Beast That Etcetera" (Ellison)
See "The Beast That Shouted Love at the Heart of the World"

"The Beast That Shouted Love at the Heart of the World" ("The Beast That Etcetera") (Ellison) **14**:106-07, 115, 117

Beatrice (Schnitzler)
See *Frau Beate und ihr Sohn*

"The Beauties" (Chekhov) **2**:156

"A Beautiful Child" (Capote) **2**:81

"The Beautiful Stranger" (Jackson) **9**:272

"The Beautiful Suit" (Wells) **6**:361-62, 376, 391

"Beauty" (O'Flaherty) **6**:262, 285

"Beauty Spots" (Kipling) **5**:280

"La beca" (Unamuno) **11**:312

"Because of the Dollars" (Conrad) **9**:152

Bech: A Book (Updike) **13**:356, 366-68, 379-82

"Bech Enters Heaven" (Updike) **13**:380, 383

"Bech in Rumania" (Updike) **13**:380

"Bech Panics" (Updike) **13**:380-81

"Bech Swings?" (Updike) **13**:380

"Bech Takes Pot Luck" (Updike) **13**:380

"The Becker Wives" (Lavin) **4**:166-67, 184-90, 192

"Becky" (Toomer) **1**:445, 456-58

"The Bedfordshire Clanger" (Bates) **10**:117

"The Bees" (Zoshchenko) **15**:407-08

"Before Breakfast" (Cather) **2**:93-4

"Before Eden" (Clarke) **3**:127

"Before the Law" (Kafka)
See "Vor dem gesetz"

"Before the Low Green Door" (Garland) **18**:148, 154, 160, 182-83, 185

"Before the Party" (Maugham) **8**:359, 362, 366-67, 372

"Before the War" (Atwood) **2**:16

"The Beggar and the Diamond" (King) **17**:295

The Beggar Maid: Stories of Flo and Rose (Munro)
See *Who Do You Think You Are?*

"The Beggars" (O'Flaherty) **6**:276-78

"The Beginning" (Grau) **15**:162

A Beginning, and Other Stories (de la Mare) **14**:79, 85, 89, 92

"The Beginning of an Idea" (McGahern) **17**:307, 323

"The Beginning of Something" (Dixon) **16**:207, 214

"Beginnings" (Coover) **15**:45-6

Title Index

"Behind the Scenes at a Whist Game" (Barbey d'Aurevilly)
See "Le dessous de cartes d'une partie de whist"
"Behind the Singer Tower" (Cather) 2:99, 103-04, 111
"Behind the Times" (Doyle) 12:89
"Behold the Incredible Revenge of the Shifted P.O.V." (Lish) 18:280
"Behold the Key" (Malamud) 15:169, 181, 222
Beim Bau der Chinesischen Mauer (*The Great Wall of China, and Other Pieces; The Great Wall of China: Stories and Reflections*) (Kafka) 5:206
"Being Moral" (Michaels) 16:311
"Belaja lošad'" (Bunin) 5:98
"The Belated Travellers" (Irving) 2:262
"Un bel gioco dura poco" (Calvino) 3:97
"Belize" (Gilchrist) 14:157-58
"The Bell" (Andersen) 6:6-8, 15, 30, 33
"The Bell" (de la Mare)
See "Out of the Deep"
"The Bella Lingua" (Cheever) 1:93, 106, 112
The Bellarosa Connection (Bellow) 14:50, 56, 58-61
"Bella vista" (Colette) 10:274
"La belle Dorothée" ("Dorothée") (Baudelaire) 18:3-7
"Bellerophoniad" (Barth) 10:44, 49-52, 54, 56, 61, 64-9, 91-3, 101-02
"Belles Demoiselles Plantation" (Cable) 4:48, 53, 62-4, 66-7, 73-4
"La Belle Zoraïde" (Chopin) 8:71, 87, 90-1, 106
"The Bell-Ringer of Angels" (Harte) 8:214, 248-49
"The Bell-Tower" (Melville) 1:298, 303
"The Belobrysov Story" (Bulgakov) 18:91
"Below the Mill Dam" (Kipling) 5:268, 283
"The Bench" (Dixon) 16:207-08, 212-13
"The Bench of Desolation" (James) 8:277, 304
"Beneath the Cards of a Game of Whist" (Barbey d'Aurevilly)
See "Le dessous de cartes d'une partie de whist"
"Beneath the Willow-Tree" (Andersen) 6:30
"Benediction" (Fitzgerald) 6:45, 57-8
"The Benefit of the Doubt" (London) 4:291
"Benefit Performance for Lord Cuzon" (Bulgakov)
See "Lord Curzon's Benefit Day"
"Benighted" (de la Mare) 14:90
"Benito Cereno" (Melville) 1:293, 295-300, 303-04, 310-12, 320-23, 328, 330; 17:328, 338, 361
"The Bênitou's Slave" (Chopin) 8:89
"Benjamin Button" (Fitzgerald)
See "The Curious Case of Benjamin Button"
Benya Krik the Gangster, and Other Stories (Babel) 16:14
"An Beo" (O'Flaherty) 6:286-88
"Ber-Bulu" (Hammett) 17:222
"Berenice" (Poe) 1:396, 398
"Berestechko" (Babel) 16:9, 27-8, 31, 52, 55-7
"Die Bergwerke zu Falun" (Hoffmann) 13:205, 209-11, 218, 220, 252, 255, 257
"Bernadette" (Gallant) 5:122, 125, 139
"Bernice Bobs Her Hair" (Fitzgerald) 6:58, 96
"Berry" (Hughes) 6:121, 142

"Bertie Changes His Mind" (Wodehouse) 2:356
"Bertram and Bini" (Kipling) 5:274
"The Beryl Coronet" (Doyle) 12:52, 58, 66, 71-3
"Bess" (Phillips) 16:336, 338-39
"The Best China Saucer" (Jewett) 6:166
Best Ghost Stories of J. S. Le Fanu (Le Fanu) 14:237
"Bestiario" (Cortazar) 7:57-8, 77-8
Bestiario (*Bestiary*) (Cortazar) 7:50-1, 53-4, 69-70
Bestiary (Cortazar)
See *Bestiario*
The Best of Arthur C. Clarke: 1937-1971 (Clarke) 3:149
The Best of H. E. Bates (Bates)
See *Seven by Five: Stories 1926-61*
The Best of Saki (Saki) 12:320
The Best of Simple (Hughes) 6:137
The Best of the Lot (Suckow) 18:400-01, 403
"Best-Seller" (Henry) 5:159
The Best Short Stories of J. G. Ballard (Ballard) 1:74
"The Best Years" (Cather) 2:93-4, 105
"The Bet" (Chekhov) 2:130
"La bête à Maître Belhomme" (Maupassant) 1:259, 273, 281
"The Betrayer of Israel" (Singer) 3:383
Die Betrogene ("The Black Swan"; "The Deceived") (Mann) 5:313-16, 324-26, 340-42
"Betrothed" (Chekhov) 2:131, 139, 143, 149, 151
"Betty" (Atwood) 2:14, 22
"Between Men" (Lessing) 6:197, 200, 207
"Between the Devil and the Deep Sea" (Kipling) 5:268
"Between Zero and One" (Gallant) 5:134, 144
"Bewitched" (Wharton) 6:422, 427
"A Bewitched Place" (Bulgakov) 18:89
"The Bewitched Spot" (Gogol)
See "Zakoldovannoe mesto"
"Beyond" (Faulkner) 1:162
"Beyond the Bayou" (Chopin) 8:89, 104
"Beyond the End" (Barnes)
See "Spillway"
"Beyond the Pale" (Kipling) 5:261-62, 273
"Beyond the Wall of Sleep" (Lovecraft) 3:258, 268
"Bezhin Meadow" (Turgenev)
See "Byezhin Prairie"
"La biblioteca de Babel" ("The Library of Babel") (Borges) 4:6-7, 18, 29
"Bicycles, Muscles, Cigarettes" (Carver) 8:10, 20, 42
"Les bienfaits de la lune" (Baudelaire) 18:4
"The Bienfilâtre Sisters" (Villiers de l'Isle Adam)
See "Les demoiselles de Bienfilâtre"
"Big Bertha Stories" (Mason) 4:2
"Big Black Good Man" (Wright) 2:364
"Big Blonde" (Parker) 2:273-74, 276, 278-81, 284
"Big Boy Leaves Home" (Wright) 2:360-61, 363, 365, 367-69, 371-76, 379-81, 386-90
"The Big Broadcast of 1938" (Barthelme) 2:26
"Big Claus and Little Claus" (Andersen)
See "Little Claus and Big Claus"
"Big Fiddle" (Boyle) 5:66-8

"Big Game" (Boyle) 16:156-57
"Big Game Hunt" (Clarke) 3:133-34
"The Big Garage" (Boyle) 16:140-42
"Big Kids and Little Kids" (Suckow) 18:393
"The Big Knockover" (Hammett) 17:200-1, 215, 219, 224, 230
The Big Knockover: Selected Stories and Short Novels (Hammett) 17:201-4, 212
"Big Mama's Funeral" (Garcia Marquez)
See "Los funerales de la Mamá Grande"
Big Mama's Funeral (Garcia Marquez)
See *Los funerales de la Mamá Grande*
"Big Meeting" (Hughes) 6:119, 122, 132-33
"The Big Outside World" (Beattie) 11:25
"Big Two-Hearted River" (Hemingway) 1:208, 214, 220, 231, 234, 240, 243-48
"Big Wheels: A Tale of the Laundry Game" ("Milkman 2") (King) 17:275
"Les bijoux" (Maupassant) 1:273, 286, 288
"The Bill" (Malamud) 15:169, 175, 202, 222-23
"Bill" (Powers) 4:375, 381-82
"Billenium" (Ballard) 1:68-9, 75
"Bill the Ventriloquial Rooster" (Lawson) 18:206, 218, 263
Billy Budd, Sailor: An Inside Narrative (Melville) 1:294-303, 305-16, 318, 321, 329
Bing (*Ping*) (Beckett) 16:76-85, 122
"Biografía de Tadeo Isidoro Cruz" ("Biography of Tadeo Isidoro Cruz"; "The Life of Tadeo Isidoro Cruz") (Borges) 4:9
"Biography of Tadeo Isidoro Cruz" (Borges)
See "Biografía de Tadeo Isidoro Cruz"
"Bird" (Hesse) 9:244
A Bird in the House (Laurence) 7:246-49, 251, 253-60, 262-64, 266-72
"A Bird of Bagdad" (Henry) 5:196
"The Bird of Travel" (de la Mare) 14:66, 67, 80, 85, 90
"The Birds" (du Maurier) 18:125-26, 130, 137-38
"Birds" (Schulz)
See "Ptaki"
"The Birds and the Foxes" (Thurber) 1:426, 431
"Birds on the Western Front" (Saki) 12:314
"Birth" (Nin) 10:299-305
"Birth" (O'Flaherty) 6:262
"A Birthday" (Mansfield) 9:281, 284, 302-03
"The Birthday of the Infanta" (Wilde) 11:364-65, 372, 374, 376, 382-83, 394-97, 399, 407-09
"The Birthmark" (Hawthorne) 3:159, 168-70, 178, 183-84, 189, 191-94
"The Bisara of Pooree" (Kipling) 5:262, 265
"The Bishop" (Chekhov) 2:131, 148-49, 157-58
"The Bishop of Borglum" (Andersen) 6:18
"The Bishop's Beggar" (Benet) 10:156
"The Bishop's Robe" (Singer) 3:374
"A Bit of Shore Life" (Jewett) 6:166
"A Bit of Young Life" (Gordimer) 17:153, 168
"Bitterness for Three Sleepwalkers" (Garcia Marquez)
See "Amargura para tres sonámbulos"
"Bitter Sorrow for Three Sleepwalkers" (Garcia Marquez)
See "Amargura para tres sonámbulos"
"Blacamán el bueno vendedor de milagros" (Garcia Marquez)

See "Blacamán the Good, Vendor of
    Miracles"
"Blacamán the Good, Vendor of Miracles"
    ("Blacamán el bueno vendedor de milagros")
    (Garcia Marquez) **8**:167-69, 186
"Blackberry Winter" (Warren) **4**:387-94, 396-
    99, 401-04
"The Blackbird" (O'Flaherty) **6**:268, 280
"Blackbird Pie" (Carver) **8**:51
"The Black Bird's Mate" (O'Flaherty) **6**:280
"Black Boy" (Boyle) **5**:56
"The Black Cat" (Poe) **1**:389-90, 406, 408
"Black Death" (Hurston) **4**:142
"Black Ephram" (Garland) **18**:154
"The Black Friar" (Chekhov)
    See "The Black Monk"
"Black Is My Favorite Color" (Malamud)
    15:173-74, 207-09
"A Black Jack Bargainer" (Henry) **5**:162, 170
"Black Joe" (Lawson) **18**:202
"The Black Madonna" (Lessing) **6**:189, 193,
    196-97, 212, 214
"The Black Madonna" (Spark) **10**:350-52,
    355, 359, 361, 366, 368
"The Black Magic of Barney Haller"
    (Thurber) **1**:415
"The Black Mare" (O'Flaherty) **6**:264, 281
"The Black Mate" (Conrad) **9**:179
"The Black Monk" ("The Black Friar")
    (Chekhov) **2**:126, 131-32, 143, 147-48
"The Black Prince" (Grau) **15**:147, 150, 156,
    151, 164
The Black Prince, and Other Stories (Grau)
    15:148-52, 154, 156, 160, 164
"The Black Rabbit" (O'Flaherty) **6**:274, 281
"The Black Swan" (Mann)
    See *Die Betrogene*
"Black Tickets" (Phillips) **16**:325, 327-28
Black Tickets (Phillips) **16**:325, 327-31, 333-
    34, 336-37, 339
"The Black Veil" (Dickens) **17**:117, 121, 125-
    26
"Black Venus" (Carter) **13**:17-20, 32-35
Black Venus (*Saints and Strangers*) (Carter)
    13:13-15, 17-18
"The Black Wedding" (Singer) **3**:359, 375-76
Blandings Castle (Wodehouse) **2**:346-47, 353
"The Blank Page" (Dinesen) **7**:200
"The Blast of the Book" (Chesterton) **1**:131
Le blé en herbe (Colette) **10**:262
"Blessed Assurance" (Hughes) **6**:123-24
"A Blessed Deceit" (Dunbar) **8**:122
"The Blessed Man of Boston, My
    Grandmother's Thimble, and Fanning
    Island" (Updike) **13**:400
"The Blessing" (Powers) **4**:368-70, 373
"Blessings" (Dubus) **15**:85
"Bless Me, Father" (Dubus) **15**:83
"Der blinde Geronimo und sein Bruder"
    ("Blind Geronimo and His Brother")
    (Schnitzler) **15**:343, 345, 377
"Blinder" (Gordimer) **17**:171, 194
"Blindfold" (Oates) **6**:231
"Blind Frank" (Steinbeck) **11**:203
"Blind Geronimo and His Brother"
    (Schnitzler)
    See "Der blinde Geronimo und sein Bruder"
"Blind Girls" (Phillips) **16**:328
"The Blinding of One-Eyed Bogan" (Lawson)
    18:242
"Blind Lightning" (Ellison) **14**:113-15, 117

"Blind Love" (Pritchett) **14**:259, 261, 266,
    268, 280-81, 285-86, 289
Blind Love, and Other Stories (Pritchett)
    14:255, 267
"The Blind Man" (Chopin) **8**:100
"The Blind Man" (Lawrence) **4**:231, 233-36,
    242-46
"Bliss" (Mansfield) **9**:276, 279-80, 295, 297,
    299, 301, 305-07, 309-11, 314
Bliss, and Other Stories (Mansfield) **9**:279,
    281
"The Blizzard" (Singer) **3**:374
"The Blond Beast" (Wharton) **6**:435
"Blood" (Singer) **3**:356, 358, 364, 375
"Blood-Burning Moon" (Toomer) **1**:443, 445,
    450, 452-53, 458
"Bloodfall" (Boyle) **16**:141-42, 144, 151
"The Blood-Feud of Toad-Water" (Saki)
    12:328
"Blood Lust" (O'Flaherty) **6**:261, 269, 277,
    283
"The Blood of the Martyrs" (Benet) **10**:142,
    152, 154, 156
"Blood of the Walsungs" (Mann)
    See *Wälsungenblut*
"Blood, Sea" (Calvino)
    See "Il sangue, il mare"
"Bloodshed" (Ozick) **15**:302, 304, 306, 317
Bloodshed and Three Novellas (Ozick) **15**:302,
    304-06, 308-10, 315, 317-18, 323, 326, 333
"Blood-Swollen Landscape" (Oates) **6**:250
"The Bloody Chamber" (Carter) **13**:5-9, 11-
    12, 17, 23, 26-28, 30
The Bloody Chamber, and Other Stories
    (Carter) **13**:5-8, 17, 23, 27-8, 30
"The Bloomsbury Christening" (Dickens)
    17:110-11, 116, 120, 136
"The Blow" (O'Flaherty) **6**:260, 282, 287
"Blow-Up" (Cortazar)
    See "Las babas del diablo"
"Blue and Green" (Woolf) **7**:374-75, 398
"Bluebeard's Egg" (Atwood) **2**:17, 21
Bluebeard's Egg (Atwood) **2**:17-18, 20-2
"The Blue Cross" (Chesterton) **1**:119, 123,
    133, 135, 138
"The Blue-Eyed Buddhist" (Gilchrist) **14**:158
"Bluegill" (Phillips) **16**:335-38
"The Blue Hotel" (Crane) **7**:104-06, 108-16,
    127, 129, 142-43, 145, 151-52, 154-55
"Blue Island" (Powers) **4**:368, 372
"Bluejay Yarn" (Twain) **6**:310
"The Blue Lenses" (du Maurier) **18**:127-28
"The Blue Moccasins" (Lawrence) **4**:220
"Blue Moon" (Phillips) **16**:335-36, 338
"The Blue Room" (Merimee)
    See "La chambre bleue"
"The Blues I'm Playing" (Hughes) **6**:121-22,
    129, 134-36
"Blumfeld, an Elderly Bachelor" (Kafka)
    5:243-44
"The Boarding House" (Dickens) **17**:110,
    113, 117, 120
"The Boarding House" (Joyce) **3**:201, 205-07,
    234, 237, 247-48
"The Boar-Pig" (Saki) **12**:295, 307, 320, 325
Bödeln (Lagerkvist) **12**:177, 180, 182, 185,
    193, 197
"Bodies in the Moonlight" (Hughes) **6**:117-
    18, 127
The Body (King) **17**:263-64, 267, 272, 276-78,
    280, 284-85

"The Body-Snatcher" (Stevenson) **11**:269-70,
    282, 296, 306
"Bogg of Geebung" (Lawson) **18**:248, 250
"The Bog King's Daughter" (Andersen)
    See "The Marsh King's Daughter"
"The Bohemian Girl" (Cather) **2**:96-7, 101,
    103-05, 108
"Boitelle" (Maupassant) **1**:263
"The Bold Dragoon" (Irving) **2**:256
"Bombard" (Maupassant) **1**:263
"The Bomb Shop" (O'Faolain) **13**:314
"Bona and Paul" (Toomer) **1**:444, 446, 450,
    452-54, 458-62
"Bonaventure" (Gallant) **5**:144
*Bonaventure: A Prose Pastoral of Acadian
    Louisiana* (Cable) **4**:48, 50-1, 53, 58-60, 62,
    73, 75
"The Bond" (Singer) **3**:385, 387
"Bone Bubbles" (Barthelme) **2**:31
"The Bone Setter" (Le Fanu)
    See "The Ghost and the Bone Setter"
"Bones of Contention" (O'Connor) **5**:371,
    377
Bones of Contention, and Other Stories
    (O'Connor) **5**:364, 371, 377, 380, 382
"The Bonfire" (O'Hara) **15**:283
"Le bonheur dans le crime" ("Happiness in
    Crime") (Barbey d'Aurevilly) **17**:6-8, 11,
    13-16, 19-20, 26, 44
"Les bons chiens" (Baudelaire) **18**:39
"Bon Voyage" (Benet) **10**:149
"The Book" (Schulz)
    See "Księga"
A Book (Barnes) **3**:3-4, 14, 22, 26
"The Book-Bag" (Maugham) **8**:357, 360-61,
    375, 378
"The Bookkeeper's Wife" (Cather) **2**:99, 110
"Book of Harlem" (Hurston) **4**:155
The Book of the American Indian (Garland)
    18:146, 177-79, 186-88
"The Book of the Dead" (Kawabata)
    See "Shisha no Sho"
"The Book of the Grotesque" (Anderson)
    1:57
Book That Doesn't Bite (Valenzuela)
    See *Libro que no muerde*
"The Border Line" (Lawrence) **4**:219, 238
"A Border-Line Case" (du Maurier) **18**:129,
    135
"A Born Farmer" (Jewett) **6**:156, 158
"A Born Genius" (O'Faolain) **13**:283-84, 309,
    312, 314
"The Boscombe Valley Mystery" (Doyle)
    12:66, 68-71, 73-4
"The Bottle" (Zoshchenko) **15**:404
"The Bottle Imp" (Stevenson) **11**:268-69, 283,
    296, 298
"A Bottle of Perrier" (Wharton) **6**:423-24
"The Bottomless Well" (Chesterton) **1**:122
"Boule de suif" (Maupassant) **1**:255-57, 259,
    263, 266, 269, 271-76, 281-83, 286-88, 290
"Boulôt and Boulotte" (Chopin) **8**:88, 102-03
"The Bouquet" (Chesnutt) **7**:3, 16, 22-3, 29-
    30, 33, 36
"La bourse" (Balzac) **5**:29
"Bow Down, Isaac" (Aiken) **9**:7, 13, 42
"The Bowl" (de la Mare) **14**:87
"The Bowmen of Shu" (Davenport) **16**:184-
    85, 187-88
"Boxes" (Carver) **8**:43
"A Box of Ginger" (Calisher) **15**:5, 15, 17

"Box Seat" (Toomer)   **1**:440, 443, 445-48, 450-53, 458

"A Box to Hide In" (Thurber)   **1**:414, 417

A Boy and His Dog (Ellison)   **14**:99-100, 115, 117, 124, 128-29, 138, 140-41

"The Boy and the Bayonet" (Dunbar)   **8**:122, 147

"A Boy Asks a Question of a Lady" (Barnes)   **3**:10-11

Boyhood (Tolstoy)
See *Otrochestvo*

"Boy in Rome" (Cheever)   **1**:100

"The Boy Knows the Truth" (Singer)   **3**:380

"Boys and Girls" (Munro)   **3**:321, 343-44

"The Boy Who Hated Girls" (Vonnegut)   **8**:431

Bracebridge Hall (Irving)   **2**:240, 244-46, 251, 254-55, 258-59, 265

"Brain Damage" (Barthelme)   **2**:32-3, 39-40, 42, 47, 55

"Brainsy" (O'Faolain)   **13**:291, 312

"A Branch Road" (Garland)   **18**:143, 150, 154-56, 159, 168-70, 172, 175-76, 192-93

"The Brand-New Approach" (Bioy Casares)   **17**:75

"The Brandon House and the Lighthouse" (Jewett)   **6**:154, 167

"Die Brautwahl" ("The Coice of a Bride") (Hoffmann)   **13**:186

"Brazil" (Marshall)   **3**:299, 300, 302-04, 306, 317

"Bread" (Atwood)   **2**:19-20

"Bread Alone" (O'Hara)   **15**:248-49

"Bread Alone" (O'Hara)   **15**:248-49

"The Bread of Charity" (Turgenev)   **7**:318

"Breakfast" (Bowen)   **3**:54

"Breakfast" (Cortazar)
See "Desayuno"

"Breakfast" (Steinbeck)   **11**:225-26, 233-34, 238-39, 241

Breakfast at Tiffany's (Capote)   **2**:67-76, 78-9, 81

The Breaking Point (du Maurier)   **18**:127-28, 130, 132

"Breaking Strain" (Clarke)   **3**:144, 150

"Breaking the News" (Nabokov)   **11**:117

"The Breaking Up of the Winships" (Thurber)   **1**:419, 435

The Break of Day (Colette)
See *La naissance du jour*

"The Breakthrough" (du Maurier)   **18**:129

"Breath from the Sky" (McCullers)   **9**:342, 345, 354-55

The Breathing Method (King)   **17**:265-67, 272-73, 280

"The Breech" (Hammett)   **17**:217

"Brethren" ("Brothers") (Bunin)   **5**:80-2, 87-8, 93-7, 106, 115

"The Bridal Night" (O'Connor)   **5**:363-64, 371, 377, 380, 383, 390, 395, 398

"The Bridal Party" (Fitzgerald)   **6**:48, 61

"Bridal Sheets" (Lavin)   **4**:165, 167, 180-81

"The Bride Comes to Yellow Sky" (Crane)   **7**:104-05, 108-09, 116-17, 126-27, 149, 151

"The Bridegroom" (Gordimer)   **17**:154

"The Bridegroom's Body" (Boyle)   **5**:58-63, 66, 68

"The Bride of Christ" (Gordimer)   **17**:157

The Bride of Innisfallen (Welty)   **1**:476, 479, 484, 495

"The Bridge" (Dixon)   **16**:216

"The Bridge-Builders" (Kipling)   **5**:267, 283, 294

"The Brief Cure of Aunt Fanny" (Dunbar)   **8**:122, 149

"The Brief Début of Tildy" (Henry)   **5**:171

"The Brigade Commander" (Babel)   **16**:26, 29, 50

"The Brigadier" (Turgenev)
See "Brigadir"

The Brigadier and the Golf Widow (Cheever)   **1**:94-5, 100

"Brigadir" ("The Brigadier") (Turgenev)   **7**:316, 320-21, 324, 337, 358

"The Brigands" (Villiers de l'Isle Adam)
See "Les brigands"

"Les brigands" ("The Brigands") (Villiers de l'Isle Adam)   **14**:381, 395-96

"Bright and Morning Star" (Wright)   **2**:363, 368, 373, 375, 377, 379-83, 387-88, 391-92

"The Bright Day" (Grau)   **15**:159

"Brighten's Sister-in-Law" (Lawson)   **18**:202-03, 229-30, 232, 241, 262

"Brigid" (Lavin)   **4**:167

"The Brilliant Leaves" (Gordon)   **15**:104, 108-09, 116, 139, 142

"Brillo" (Ellison)   **14**:123

"Bring, Bring" (Aiken)   **9**:12-13, 40

Bring! Bring! (Aiken)   **9**:3, 5, 6, 28

"British Guiana" (Marshall)   **3**:299-300, 302, 305, 317

"The Broken Giraffe" (O'Hara)   **15**:286

"The Broken Heart" (Irving)   **2**:243, 245

"Broken Sword" (Chesterton)
See "The Sign of the Broken Sword"

"Broken Wings" (James)   **8**:304, 306

"A Broken World" (O'Faolain)   **13**:283-84, 287, 293, 298, 300, 302, 306, 309, 316-17

"Brokers' and Marine-Store Shops" (Dickens)   **17**:133

"Bronze Leaves and Red" (Davenport)   **16**:198

"The Brooch" (Faulkner)   **1**:165

"Brooklyn" (Marshall)   **3**:300, 302, 304-05, 307-08, 314-17

"Brooksmith" (James)   **8**:304, 306

"Broomsticks" (de la Mare)   **14**:68, 69, 87

Broomsticks, and Other Tales (de la Mare)   **14**:82, 86

"The Brother" (Coover)   **15**:33, 35, 48, 59

"Brother" (O'Brien)   **10**:345

"Brother Boniface" (Lavin)   **4**:183

"Brother Death" (Anderson)   **1**:32, 37, 39, 50-1, 56-7

"Brother Earl" (Anderson)   **1**:52

"The Brotherhood Movement" (Bioy Casares)   **17**:75

"Brothers" (Anderson)   **1**:52

"Brothers" (Bunin)
See "Brethren"

"Brothers and Sisters" (Le Guin)   **12**:210-11, 213-16, 249-50

"The Brown Hand" (Doyle)   **12**:62, 64

"Brown of Calaveras" (Harte)   **8**:214, 236, 244, 246-48

"Brugglesmith" (Kipling)   **5**:266

"Brummy Usen" (Lawson)   **18**:239

"The Brushwood Boy" (Kipling)   **5**:266-67, 273-74, 283

"The Brute" (Conrad)   **9**:152, 176, 183

"La bûche" (Maupassant)   **1**:274

"The Bucket of Blood" (O'Hara)   **15**:281

"Buckeye Hollow Inheritance" (Harte)   **8**:218

"Buckthorne and His Friends" (Irving)   **2**:241, 251, 261-62

"The Buckwheat" (Andersen)   **6**:7, 12, 18, 34

"Buddy" (Dixon)   **16**:217

"Build-Up" (Ballard)   **1**:68, 76-7

"An Buille" (O'Flaherty)   **6**:286-89

"The Bulgarian Poetess" (Updike)   **13**:367, 374-75, 378, 380-81

"The Bull-Run Style" (Lawson)   **18**:233

"The Bull That Thought" (Kipling)   **5**:279, 286

"The Bully" (Dubus)   **15**:74

"A Bundle of Letters" (James)   **8**:299

"Bunner Sisters" (Wharton)   **6**:418, 422, 433

"The Burglar's Christmas" (Cather)   **2**:100

"The Burning" (Welty)   **1**:476, 479, 484

"The Burning Baby" (Thomas)   **3**:399, 407

"The Burning Eyes" (Gordon)   **15**:128-29, 142

"The Burning House" (Beattie)   **11**:10, 13, 22, 29

The Burning House (Beattie)   **11**:7, 9, 10-12, 19, 22-4, 26-7, 29, 32

"The Burrow" (Kafka)
See "Der bau"

"Burutu Moon" (Hughes)   **6**:118

"The Bus" (Singer)   **3**:381-82

"La busca de Averroes" ("Averroes's Search") (Borges)   **4**:26, 37, 41

"The Bush Undertaker" (Lawson)   **18**:201, 206-07, 218, 221, 237-39, 241, 245, 259

"The Business Man" (Poe)   **1**:407

"Busride" (Cortazar)
See "Omnibus"

"The Bus to St. James's" (Cheever)   **1**:100, 106

"A Busy Day in a Lawyer's Office" (Chesnutt)   **7**:14

"A Busy Man" (Nabokov)   **11**:133

"Butterball's Night" (Cortazar)
See "La noche de Mantequilla"

"The Butterfly" (Chekhov)   **2**:126

"The Butterfly" (O'Hara)   **15**:282

"The Butterfly and the Traffic Light" (Ozick)   **15**:298, 313

"Byezhin Prairie" ("Bezhin Meadow") (Turgenev)   **7**:316, 345

"By Moonlight" (Mansfield)   **9**:286

"By My Troth, Nerissa" (Aiken)   **9**:13

"By the People" (Faulkner)   **1**:178

"By the Road" (Bunin)   **5**:106

"By the Water" (Bowles)   **3**:71-2

"By the Waters of Babylon" ("The Place of the Gods") (Benet)   **10**:154, 157

Byways (Hesse)   **9**:230

"The Byzantine Omelet" (Saki)   **12**:295

"The Cabalist of East Broadway" (Singer)   **3**:374, 383-84

"The Caballero's Way" (Henry)   **5**:167

Cabbages and Kings (Henry)   **5**:155, 160, 162-63, 167-69, 172

"The Cabin" (Carver)   **8**:50

"The Cabinet of Edgar Allan Poe" (Carter)   **13**:16-18, 20

"La cachet d'onyx" (Barbey d'Aurevilly)   **17**:9-13, 17-18

"Cadence" (Dubus)   **15**:73-4, 100

"Café des exilés" (Cable)   **4**:58, 62, 68

"The Cage Birds" (Pritchett)   **14**:284, 298

"Cahoots" (Dunbar)   **8**:122, 132, 145

"Cain Rose Up" (King)   **17**:274

Cakes and Ale and Twelve Stories (Maugham)   **8**:384

"El calamar opta por su tinta" (Bioy Casares) **17**:95

"Caline" (Chopin) **8**:94

"The Caliph and the Cad" (Henry) **5**:158

"The Caliph, Cupid, and the Clock" (Henry) **5**:158

"Call at Corazón" (Bowles) **3**:59, 61-2, 66, 69, 77, 79

"Calling Cards" (Bunin)
　See "Vizitnye kartochki"

"Calling Jesus" (Toomer) **1**:445, 447, 450

"Call Me, Call Me" (O'Hara) **15**:252

"The Call of Blood" (Cervantes)
　See "La fuerza de la sangre"

"The Call of Cthulhu" (Lovecraft) **3**:258, 261, 263-64, 269-70, 274, 278, 280, 283, 290

"The Call of the Tame" (Henry) **5**:191, 194

"A Call on Mrs. Forrester" (Thurber) **1**:431

"The Calm" (Carver) **8**:14, 42

"Le Calmant" ("The Calmative") (Beckett) **16**:73-5, 87, 89-91

"The Calmative" (Beckett)
　See "Le Calmant"

"The Camberwell Beauty" (Pritchett) **14**:262-63, 266, 272

The Camberwell Beauty, and Other Stories (Pritchett) **14**:267, 301, 305

Cambio de armas (*Other Weapons*) (Valenzuela) **14**:352, 355, 359, 366-67, 372

"The Camel's Back" (Fitzgerald) **6**:45, 59, 96-7

"The Canals of Mars" (Boyle) **5**:55

"The Canary" (Mansfield) **9**:282, 306, 310, 313

"A Canary for One" (Hemingway) **1**:209, 217, 232, 237

Canary in a Cat House (Vonnegut) **8**:428

Candide; or, Optimism (Voltaire)
　See *Candide; ou, L'optimisme*

·*Candide; ou, L'optimisme* (*Candide; or, Optimism*) (Voltaire) **12**:338-44, 347-55, 357-62, 364-65, 368-69, 372-74, 376-78, 383-90, 393-6, 400

"Candleshine" (Benet) **10**:149

Cane (Toomer) **1**:439-55, 458-60, 462

"The Cane in the Corridor" (Thurber) **1**:420, 422

"Can I Stay Here?" (O'Hara) **15**:262, 283

"Canon Alberic's Scrap-Book" (James) **16**:232, 234-36, 238, 242, 248, 250-52, 255-57

Can Such Things Be? (Bierce) **9**:59

"The Canterbury Pilgrims" (Hawthorne) **3**:185-86

"The Canterville Ghost: A Hylo-Idealistic Romance" (Wilde) **11**:372, 376, 399-401, 407

"Can You Carry Me?" (O'Hara) **15**:270

The Cape Cod Lighter (O'Hara) **15**:281-82

"Cape Race" (de la Mare) **14**:82, 86, 89

"The Capital in My Notebook" (Bulgakov) **18**:90

"The Capital of the World" (Hemingway) **1**:217, 232, 234, 245

"The Captain" (Dubus) **15**:93

"The Captain" (Michaels) **16**:305, 307-10

"Captain Boldheart" (Dickens) **17**:124

"The Captain of 'The Camel'" (Bierce) **9**:80

"The Captains" (Jewett) **6**:154, 167

"Captain Sands" (Jewett) **6**:167

"The Captain's Doll" (Lawrence) **4**:197, 204, 210-12, 223-26, 234-36, 239-40

"The Captain's Son" (Taylor) **10**:396-97, 399, 402

"The Captive" (Gordon) **15**:105-06, 110, 117, 128, 133

"The Captive" (Kipling) **5**:283

"The Captive" (Singer) **3**:374, 384

"The Captives" (Benet) **10**:154

"The Captured Shadow" (Fitzgerald) **6**:49

"The Captured Woman" (Barthelme) **2**:46

"The Carafe" (Zoshchenko) **15**:407-08

"Carancro" (Cable) **4**:58

"Las caras de la verdad" (Bioy Casares) **17**:59

"Carbon" (Levi) **12**:257, 259, 262, 265, 268, 280

"Carcassonne" (Faulkner) **1**:181

"The Cardinal's First Tale" (Dinesen) **7**:162-63, 172, 186, 194, 198

"The Cardinal's Third Tale" (Dinesen) **7**:168, 200

"Cards" (Beattie) **11**:26, 29

"The Career of Nightmares" (Ligotti) **16**:293

"Careful" (Carver) **8**:26, 31, 35, 51

"Careless Talk" (Bowen) **3**:31

"Careless Talk" (Gallant) **5**:151

"A Careless Widow" (Pritchett) **14**:300

A Careless Widow, and Other Stories (Pritchett) **14**:300

"The Caress" (O'Flaherty) **6**:267

"Caricature" (Singer) **3**:359, 375

"La caricia más profunda" ("The Most Profound Caress") (Cortazar) **7**:58, 61, 94

"Carma" (Toomer) **1**:456-57

Carmen (Merimee) **7**:276, 280-82, 285-86, 290, 294-96, 305-06, 308

"Carmilla" (Le Fanu) **14**:221, 223, 225, 233-38, 243-45, 251

"Carnival" (Dinesen) **7**:190-91

"Carpe Noctem, If You Can" (Thurber) **1**:424

"The Carriage Lamps" (Crane) **7**:104

Carry On, Jeeves (Wodehouse) **2**:337, 346

Carry-Over (Suckow) **18**:404

"Carta a un senorita en París" ("Carta a un srta. en París"; "Letter to a Young Lady in Paris") (Cortazar) **7**:56-7, 61, 70-1

"Carta a un srta. en París" (Cortazar)
　See "Carta a un senorita en París"

"Cartoon" (Coover) **15**:60

"The Cartouche" (de la Mare) **14**:79

"The Car We Had to Push" (Thurber) **1**:431

"The Caryatids" (Dinesen) **7**:167, 191-92, 203-04

"Casa Anna" (Taylor) **10**:379

"La casa de Asterión" ("The House of Asterión") (Borges) **4**:7, 10, 25

"El casamiento engañoso" ("The Deceitful Marriage") (Cervantes) **12**:21, 24, 33-4, 37-8, 40

Casanovas Heimfahrt (*Casanova's Homecoming*) (Schnitzler) **15**:352, 371, 376

Casanova's Homecoming (Schnitzler)
　See *Casanovas Heimfahrt*

"Casa tomada" ("The House Taken Over") (Cortazar) **7**:53, 81

"Un cas de divorce" (Maupassant) **1**:286

"Le cas de Madame Luneau" (Maupassant) **1**:259, 286

The Case-Book of Sherlock Holmes (Doyle) **12**:62

"A Case for the Oracle" (Lawson) **18**:250

"A Case History" (O'Hara) **15**:252, 280

"A Case in a Thousand" (Beckett) **16**:72

"The Case of 'Ca'line': A Kitchen Monologue" (Dunbar) **8**:122, 127, 147

"A Case of Identity" (Doyle) **12**:49, 51, 59, 66-8, 70-1, 73

"The Case of Lady Sannox" (Doyle) **12**:64

"The Case of Lieutenant Yelaghin" (Bunin)
　See "The Elaghin Affair"

"The Cask of Amontillado" (Poe) **1**:378, 394, 407-08

"Cassandra" (Mansfield) **9**:282

"Cassation" ("A Little Girl Tells a Story to a Lady") (Barnes) **3**:6, 10, 16, 24-5

"The Cassowary" (Bowen) **3**:33

"Castaway" (Clarke) **3**:125, 135-36, 149

"Casting the Runes" (James) **16**:227, 230, 233, 236, 245, 248, 252-53, 255

"The Castle of Crossed Destinies" (Calvino) **3**:101-02

The Castle of Crossed Destinies (Calvino)
　See *Illl castello dei destini incrociati*

The Casuarina Tree (Maugham) **8**:366-67, 371, 374

The Cat (Colette)
　See *La chatte*

"Catalina" (Villiers de l'Isle Adam) **14**:397

"A Catastrophe" (Wells) **6**:389

"The Catbird Seat" (Thurber) **1**:422, 425, 431-32, 435

"The Catch" (Gordimer) **17**:151-52, 166

"The Catechist" (Barthelme) **2**:37, 39, 55

"Cathedral" (Carver) **8**:26, 30, 34-5, 40-1, 43-4, 48-9, 51

Cathedral (Carver) **8**:17, 20, 23, 26-8, 30-2, 34, 39-40, 46, 49, 55-61

"The Cat in the Hat for President" (Coover) **15**:45-6

"Cat in the Rain" (Hemingway) **1**:244-45

"The Cat Jumps" (Bowen) **3**:41, 53

The Cat Jumps (Bowen) **3**:33, 41

"Catman" (Ellison) **14**:109-10

"A Cat Named Dempsey" (Benet) **10**:154

"The Cats of Ulthar" (Lovecraft) **3**:262

"The Cat That Walked by Himself" (Kipling) **5**:284

"The Cattle Dealers" (Chekhov) **2**:128

Il cavaliere inesistente (*The Invisible Knight*; *The Nonexistent Knight*) (Calvino) **3**:90-1, 99, 106-07, 117

"Cavanelle" (Chopin) **8**:94, 108, 111

"Cavar un foso" (Bioy Casares) **17**:95

"Caviar" (Boyle) **16**:144

"Cefalea" (Cortazar) **7**:58

"The Celebrated Jumping Frog of Calaveras County" (Twain) **6**:300, 309-12, 316-21

"La céleste aventure" (Villiers de l'Isle Adam) **14**:390

"The Celestial Plot" (Bioy Casares) **17**:85

The Celestial Plot (Bioy Casares)
　See *La trama celeste*

"Celestial Publicity" (Villiers de l'Isle Adam)
　See "L'affichage céleste"

"The Celestial Railroad" (Hawthorne) **3**:178, 181, 183

Les célibataires (Balzac)
　See *Le curé de Tours*

"El celoso extremeño" ("The Jealous Extremaduran"; "The Jealous Hidalgo") (Cervantes) **12**:3-4, 8, 14, 16-17, 21, 23, 33-4, 37, 39

"The Cemetery at Kozin" (Babel) **16**:27-8, 31, 55

"The Cemetery in the Demesne" (Lavin)
4:166, 176

"Centaur in Brass" (Faulkner) 1:177

"Ceremonias de rechazo" ("Rituals of
Rejection") (Valenzuela) 14:355, 358-59

"Cerium" (Levi) 12:256, 258, 265, 280

A Certain Lucas (Cortazar)
See *Un tal Lucas*

"Chacun sa chimère" (Baudelaire) 18:4-5, 17-
18, 35

"Chagrin d'Amour" (Hesse) 9:231, 235

"The Chain Smoker" (Pritchett) 14:286

"The Chair" (Davenport) 16:185, 187

"Châli" (Maupassant) 1:259

"The Challenge" (O'Flaherty) 6:277-78

"Chambers" (Dickens) 17:123

"La chambre 11" (Maupassant) 1:288

"La chambre bleue" ("The Blue Room")
(Merimee) 7:277, 296-97

Chambre d'hotel (*Chance Aquaintances*)
(Colette) 10:269-70

"Le chambre double" ("The Double
Chamber") (Baudelaire) 18:5, 8, 18

"The Champ" (Boyle) 16:140-41, 151-52

Le Champ d'Oliviers (Maupassant) 1:273, 283

"The Champion of the Weather" (Henry)
5:159

Chance Aquaintances (Colette)
See *Chambre d'hotel*

*A Changed Man, The Waiting Supper, and
Other Tales* (Hardy) 2:210-11, 214-15, 220-
21

"A Change of Heart" (Jewett) 6:156, 158

A Change of Light, and Other Stories
(Cortazar) 7:62-3

"Chanson d'été" (Bulgakov) 18:90

"La chanson vitrier" ("The Glazier's Song")
(Baudelaire) 18:63

"Le chant du coq" (Villiers de l'Isle Adam)
14:396

Les chants de Maldoror: Chant premier
(Lautreamont) 14:167-212

"Le chapeau chinois" (Villiers de l'Isle Adam)
See "Le secret de l'ancienne musique"

"The Chaplet" (Saki) 12:288

"A Chapter in the History of a Tyrone
Family" (Le Fanu) 14:220, 237, 239, 247

"Charity" (O'Flaherty) 6:264

"Charles" (Jackson) 9:249

"Charlie" (Chopin) 8:84, 86

Charlie in the House of Rue (Coover) 15:47,
59-60

"Charlie's Greek" (O'Faolain) 13:320

"Charlotte Esmond" (Bates) 10:112

"A Charm" (Kipling) 5:283

"The Charmed Spot" (Gogol)
See "Zakoldovannoe mesto"

"Charnel House of the Moon" (Ligotti)
16:277

"An Charraig Dhubh" (O'Flaherty) 6:287

"Chasy" ("The Watch") (Turgenev) 7:324-
25, 327, 358

"Le chat-qui-pelote" (Balzac)
See "La maison du chat-qui-pelote"

La chatte (*The Cat*) (Colette) 10:225-56, 262,
265, 269-71, 276-77

"Chattery Teeth" (King) 17:295

"The Cheapjack" ("The New Teacher")
(O'Connor) 5:371, 389

"An Chcarc Uisce" (O'Flaherty) 6:287

"The Cheery Soul" (Bowen) 3:32, 54

"The Cheese Stands Alone" (Ellison) 14:127

"Le chef d'oeuvre inconnu" ("The Unknown
Masterpiece") (Balzac) 5:12, 16, 23, 48-9

Chéri (Colette) 10:253-55, 257-58, 262, 267,
270, 277-78, 282, 285-86 288

"Chesniki" (Babel) 16:26, 50, 58

"The Chestnut Tree" (Pritchett) 14:271

"Che ti dice la patria?" (Hemingway) 1:232

"A cheval" (Maupassant) 1:278, 280

"Un cheval de race" (Baudelaire) 18:6, 20

"La chevelure" (Baudelaire) 18:8

"Chichi Haha" ("Father and Mother")
(Kawabata) 17:245-46

"Chickamauga" (Bierce) 9:53-7, 64, 68, 70,
75, 77, 87

"Chicken-Grethe" (Andersen) 6:7

"Chief Justice Harbottle" (Le Fanu)
See "Mr. Justice Hartbottle"

"The Chief Mourner of Marne" (Chesterton)
1:128, 138

"Le chien" (Maupassant) 1:259

"Le chien et le flacon" (Baudelaire) 18:17, 33

"The Child" (Bates) 10:112

"The Child Born Out of the Fog" (Nin)
10:301, 303

"Childhood" (Hesse)
See "Kinderseele"

Childhood (Tolstoy) 9:374-76, 380, 383, 399,
401-03

Childhood (Tolstoy)
See *Detstvo*

"Childhood: At Grandmother's" (Babel)
16:36

"A Child in the Dark, and a Foreign Father"
(Lawson) 18:258, 263

"The Child in the Grave" ("The Dead Child")
(Andersen) 6:15, 26

"The Child of God" (O'Flaherty) 6:262, 269-
70, 281

"The Children" (Oates) 6:225

Children and Older People (Suckow) 18:391,
394, 405

Children of the Bush (Lawson) 18:241, 257

Children of the Frost (London) 4:258, 282,
285-88

"The Children of the Zodiac" (Kipling)
5:283, 286

"Children on Their Birthdays" (Capote) 2:61,
63-6, 70, 72-3, 75-8

"The Children's Campaign" (Lagerkvist)
See "Det lilla fälttåget"

"A Child's Dream of a Star" (Dickens)
17:124, 131

"The Child's Evening Prayer" (Andersen)
6:15

"A Child's Heart" (Hesse) 9:227

"The Child That Went with the Fairies" (Le
Fanu) 14:223

"The Child Who Favored Daughter" (Walker)
5:403, 409-11

"Childybawn" (O'Faolain) 13:288, 297, 301

"The Chimera" (Cheever) 1:97, 105

Chimera (Barth) 10:44, 48-53, 55-7, 60-1,
64-5, 68-9, 70-2, 74, 81, 83-4, 91, 93-5 100-
04

The Chimes (*Christmas Chimes*) (Dickens)
17:99, 101, 103-09, 115, 127, 129-30, 132

"The Chinago" (London) 4:263

"The Chinaman's Ghost" (Lawson) 18:245

"A Chinese Tale" (Bulgakov) 18:72-4, 99

"The Chink in Armor" (O'Hara) 15:254-55

"A Chip of Glass Ruby" (Gordimer) 17:155,
161, 173, 181

"Chistyi ponedel'nik" ("The First Monday in
Lent") (Bunin) 5:114

"The Choice" (Wharton) 6:418

"A Choice of Profession" (Malamud) 15:170,
173, 175, 220-21

"The Chords of Youth" (Bates) 10:139

"The Chorus Girl" (Chekhov) 2:130, 137,
139

"The Christening" (Lawrence) 4:197, 202,
234

"A Christian Education" (Warren) 4:390,
394, 396

"Christmas" (McGahern) 17:298, 302

"Christmas" (Nabokov) 11:132-33

"The Christmas Banquet" (Hawthorne)
3:181, 183

"Christmas by Injunction" (Henry) 5:162

A Christmas Carol (Dickens) 17:99, 101, 103-
04, 108, 113-20, 124, 127, 129-30, 132, 139,
143, 145-48

"A Christmas Carol for Harold Ross" (Boyle)
5:64

Christmas Chimes (Dickens)
See *The Chimes*

"A Christmas Dinner" (Dickens) 17:110, 116

"Christmas Eve" (Gogol)
See "Noč pered roždestvom"

"The Christmas Eves of Aunt Elise: A Tale of
Possession in Old Grosse Pointe" (Ligotti)
16:271, 278, 283

"Christmas Gift" (Warren) 4:388-90, 394

"Christmas is a Sad Season for the Poor"
(Cheever) 1:107

"Christmas Jenny" (Freeman) 1:191

"A Christmas Memory" (Capote) 2:67, 72-3,
75-6

"Christmas Morning" (O'Connor) 5:378

"A Christmas Party and a Wedding"
(Dostoevsky)
See "A Christmas Tree and a Wedding"

"A Christmas Song" (Bates) 10:117

"A Christmas Tree and a Wedding" ("A
Christmas Party and a Wedding")
(Dostoevsky) 2:171, 190, 193-95, 197

"Christmas with Two Children's Stories"
(Hesse) 9:241, 244

"Chromium" (Levi) 12:256, 268

"The Chronic Argonauts" (Wells) 6:388

Chronicle of a Death Foretold (Garcia
Marquez)
See *Crónica de una muerte anunciada*

Chronicles of Bustos Domecq (Bioy Casares)
See *Crónicas de Bustos Domecq*

The Chronicles of Clovis (Saki) 12:287-88,
293, 323, 330-35

Chronicles of Golden Friars (Le Fanu) 14:220,
245

Chronopolis (Ballard) 1:69, 84

Chronopolis, and Other Stories (Ballard) 1:71

"The Chrysanthemums" (Steinbeck) 11:207,
210, 214, 221, 223-37, 240-41, 244

"Chu Chu, The Devotion of Enriquez" (Harte)
8:228

"An Chulaith Nua" (O'Flaherty) 6:287

"Chun Ah Chun" (London) 4:269

"The Church at Novograd" (Babel) 16:25,
28, 52, 56

"The Church That Was at Antioch" (Kipling)
5:272

"The Church with an Overshot Wheel"
(Henry) 5:163, 180-81

"The Chymist" (Ligotti)   **16**:266, 269, 271, 280-81, 283

"Cicadas" (Bunin)   **5**:82

"Cicely's Dream" (Chesnutt)   **7**:22-3, 33-4, 37

"Ciclismo en Gringnan" ("Cycling in Gringnan") (Cortazar)   **7**:95

"The Cigarstore Robbery" (Hemingway)   **1**:208

"The Cinderella Waltz" (Beattie)   **11**:8

Cinnamon Shops (Schulz)   **13**:326-27, 332, 343-44

"A Circle in the Fire" (O'Connor)   **1**:343-44, 347, 356

"Circle of Prayer" (Munro)   **3**:348

"The Circular Ruins" (Borges)
   See "Las ruinas circulares"

"The Circular Valley" (Bowles)   **3**:66, 69-71, 79

"The Circus" (Porter)   **4**:331-34, 340, 353

"The Circus at Denby" (Jewett)   **6**:150, 155, 167

"The Circus Horse" (Colette)   **10**:292

"The Circus in the Attic" (Warren)   **4**:387-89, 391, 395-98, 404

The Circus in the Attic, and Other Stories (Warren)   **4**:387-90, 393, 396-97

"Citizen" (Pritchett)   **14**:297

"The City" (Hesse)   **9**:230, 235

"The City" (Updike)   **13**:403, 409

"City Boy" (Michaels)   **16**:301, 303, 312, 321

"City Life" (Barthelme)   **2**:40

City Life (Barthelme)   **2**:30-5, 37-9

"A City of Churches" (Barthelme)   **2**:37, 39, 41, 54

"The City of Dreadful Night" (Henry)   **5**:188, 197

"City of London Churches" (Dickens)   **17**:123

"A City of the Dead, a City of the Living" (Gordimer)   **17**:171, 174, 191

"Civil War" (O'Flaherty)   **6**:262, 274

Claire Lenoir (Villiers de l'Isle Adam)   **14**:376

The Clairvoyant (Gass)   **12**:148

"Clancy in the Tower of Babel" (Cheever)   **1**:107

"Clara" (O'Brien)   **10**:333

"Clara Milich" (Turgenev)
   See "Klara Milich"

"Clarence" (Harte)   **8**:222, 251-52

Claudine à l'école (*Claudine at School*) (Colette)   **10**:269

Claudine at School (Colette)
   See *Claudine à l'école*

"Clave para un amor" (Bioy Casares)   **17**:58

"Clay" (Joyce)   **3**:205, 209, 211, 221-22, 226, 233-34, 237, 247

"A Clean, Well-Lighted Place" (Hemingway)   **1**:216, 230, 232, 237-38

"A Cleared Path" (Gilman)   **13**:141-42

"The Clear Track" (O'Hara)   **15**:289

"The Clemency of the Court" (Cather)   **2**:96, 100, 103, 105

"Clementina" (Cheever)   **1**:100, 107

"The Clerk's Tale" (Pritchett)   **14**:271

"A Clever-Kids Story" (Beattie)   **11**:6, 15-16

"The Clever Little Trick" (Zoshchenko)   **15**:404

The Clicking of Cuthbert (Wodehouse)   **2**:344, 354

"The Climber" (Mason)   **4**:3

"The Cloak" (Gogol)
   See "The Overcoat"

"The Clock" (Baudelaire)

See "L'horloge"

"Clone" (Cortazar)   **7**:69-71

"Closed Space" (Beckett)   **16**:123, 126

"Clothe the Naked" (Parker)   **2**:275, 280-81, 286

"Cloud, Castle, Lake" (Nabokov)   **11**:108-09, 127

The Cloven Viscount (Calvino)
   See *Il visconte dimezzato*

"Clowns in Clover" (Gordimer)   **17**:153

The Club of Queer Trades (Chesterton)   **1**:120, 122, 139

"Clytie" (Welty)   **1**:466, 468, 471, 481, 495

"C. Musonius Rufus" (Davenport)   **16**:169, 171, 175, 177, 191

"The Coach House" (Chekhov)   **2**:128

"The Cobweb" (Saki)   **12**:296

"Cock-a-Doodle-Doo!" (Melville)   **1**:295, 298, 303, 305, 322; **17**:363

"Cockadoodledoo" (Singer)   **3**:358

"Cock Crow" (Gordon)   **15**:123-24, 126

"Cockroaches" (Schulz)   **13**:333-34

"Cocky Olly" (Pritchett)   **14**:300

"Coco" (Maupassant)   **1**:275

"The Cocoons" (Ligotti)   **16**:282-84

"Un coeur simple" ("A Simple Heart") (Flaubert)   **11**:37, 45-6, 54-6, 58-66, 70-1, 80-1, 84, 87, 91, 94, 96-9, 101, 103

"Un coeur simple" (Maupassant)   **1**:286

"The Coice of a Bride" (Hoffmann)
   See "Die Brautwahl"

"Cold Autumn" (Bunin)   **5**:115-16

"A Cold, Calculating Thing" (O'Hara)   **15**:252

"The Cold House" (O'Hara)   **15**:258, 265

"Colic" (O'Flaherty)   **6**:271

Collages (Nin)   **10**:305-06, 308

Collected Ghost Stories (James)   **16**:227, 230-32, 239, 241, 246, 249, 251, 255

The Collected Short Stories of Conrad Aiken (Aiken)   **9**:9, 12, 28, 41

The Collected Stories (Babel)   **16**:6, 8, 11, 14, 17, 19, 21, 25, 35, 41, 59

Collected Stories (Boyle)   **16**:155

Collected Stories (Garcia Marquez)   **8**:182-84

Collected Stories (Lavin)   **4**:174

Collected Stories (Lessing)   **6**:196, 218-19

Collected Stories (Malamud)
   See *The Stories of Bernard Malamud*

Collected Stories (Mansfield)   **9**:281

The Collected Stories (McGahern)   **17**:318, 322

Collected Stories (O'Connor)   **5**:398

Collected Stories (Pritchett)   **14**:301

Collected Stories I (Spark)   **10**:359-60, 368

Collected Stories: 1939-1976 (Bowles)   **3**:65, 68-9

The Collected Stories of Caroline Gordon (Gordon)   **15**:137-38, 141

The Collected Stories of Colette (Colette)   **10**:280, 291

The Collected Stories of Hortense Calisher (Calisher)   **15**:7-8, 15, 19, 21

The Collected Stories of Isaac Bashevis Singer (Singer)   **3**:383-84

The Collected Stories of Katherine Anne Porter (Porter)   **4**:347, 351, 358, 361

The Collected Stories of Peter Taylor (Taylor)   **10**:389

The Collected Stories Of Seán O'Faoláin (O'Faolain)   **13**:313

Collected Stories of William Faulkner (Faulkner)   **1**:151, 161-62, 177, 181

Collected Works (Bunin)   **5**:99

Collected Works of Henry Lawson (Lawson)   **18**:210

Collected Writings (Bierce)   **9**:75

"The Collection" (Pritchett)   **14**:296, 298

"Collectors" (Carver)   **8**:11, 19

"Le collier" (Maupassant)   **1**:259

"Colloquy" (Jackson)   **9**:252

"The Colloquy of Monos and Una" (Poe)   **1**:401-02

Le Colonel Chabert (Balzac)   **5**:8, 18, 24-7

The Colonel Has No One to Write Him (Garcia Marquez)
   See *El colonel no tiene quien le escribe*

"Colonel Julian" (Bates)   **10**:117

Colonel Julian, and Other Stories (Bates)   **10**:115-17

El colonel no tiene quien le escribe (*The Colonel Has No One to Write Him*; *No One Writes to the Colonel*) (Garcia Marquez)   **8**:162, 185, 192-97

"The Colonel's Awakening" (Dunbar)   **8**:121, 127, 131, 148

"The Colonel's Lady" (Maugham)   **8**:366, 380

"Colonel Starbottle for the Plaintiff" (Harte)   **8**:229

"Colonel Starbottle's Client" (Harte)   **8**:216, 245

"El coloquio de los perros" ("The Dialogue of the Dogs"; *The Dogs' Colloguy*) (Cervantes)   **12**:4, 8, 14-16, 21, 24, 26-8, 33-4, 37-8,

"Colorado" (Beattie)   **11**:4-5, 7, 17

"Colour and Line" ("Line and Colour") (Babel)   **16**:22, 27, 59

"The Colour Out of Space" (Lovecraft)   **3**:261, 263, 267-69, 274, 281, 290-91

Columba (Merimee)   **7**:276-77, 280-83, 290, 294-95, 300-05, 308

"Come Again Tomorrow" (Gordimer)   **17**:165

"Come Along, Marjorie" (Spark)   **10**:355-57, 359, 365, 370

Come Along with Me (Jackson)   **9**:254

Come Back, Dr. Caligari (Barthelme)   **2**:26-9, 31, 37-9, 46, 49, 51

Comédie humaine (*The Human Comedy*) (Balzac)   **5**:6-13, 16-17, 19-20, 26-33, 43, 48

"Les comédiens sans le savoir" (Balzac)   **5**:31

"A Comedy in Rubber" (Henry)   **5**:158

"Come on a Coming" (Dixon)   **16**:208

"Come On Back" (Gardner)   **7**:224-25, 227-28, 235, 240-41

"Come Out the Wilderness" (Baldwin)   **10**:2-3, 5, 7-9

"The Comet" (Schulz)
   See "Kometa"

"The Comforts of Home" (O'Connor)   **1**:343-44, 351, 353, 365

"Coming Apart" (Walker)   **5**:412-14

"Coming, Aphrodite!" (Cather)   **2**:91-2, 95, 104, 111-12

"Coming, Eden Bower!" (Cather)   **2**:111-12, 114

"Coming Home" (Bowen)   **3**:40

"Coming into His Kingdom" (McGahern)   **17**:302, 322

"The Coming Out of Maggie" (Henry)   **5**:171, 197

"A Committee-Man of 'The Terror'" (Hardy)   **2**:220

The Common Chord (O'Connor) 5:364-65, 371, 378, 380, 383-84

"A Common Confusion" (Kafka) 5:207

"A Commonplace Story" (Gordimer) 17:167

"The Common Round" (Mansfield) 9:304

"Common Sense Should Tell You" (O'Hara) 15:250

"Cómo perdí la vista" (Bioy Casares) 17:83

Company (Beckett) 16:100-02, 110-12, 115, 129, 134, 137

"Company for Gertrude" (Wodehouse) 2:346

"A Company of Laughing Faces" (Gordimer) 17:155-56, 161

"The Company of Wolves" (Carter) 13:5, 7, 9, 13-14, 27, 28

"The Compartment" (Carver) 8:26, 32, 35

The Compass Rose (Le Guin) 12:235

"A Compatriot" (Bunin) 5:81

"The Complaint Ledger" (Chekhov) 2:130

Complete Collected Stories (Pritchett) 14:302-03, 305

The Complete Fiction of Bruno Schulz (Schulz) 13:342

"The Complete Life of John Hopkins" (Henry) 5:159, 188

The Complete Works of Nathanael West (West) 16:367

The Completion of Love (Musil)
See "Vollendung der Liebe"

"Comrades" (Gordimer) 17:186, 188

Le Comte de Saint-Germain (Nerval) 18:371

"Comte Hippolit" (Hoffmann)
See "Der Vampyrismus"

"Concerning the Bodyguard" (Barthelme) 2:44

"Concerning Wet Snow" (Dostoevsky)
See "Apropos of the Wet Snow"

"Condemned Door" (Cortazar) 7:69

Condensed Novels, and Other Papers (Harte) 8:225, 230, 249

"The Condominium" (Elkin) 12:93-5, 106-07, 110

"Conducta en los velorios" ("Our Demeanor at Wakes") (Cortazar) 7:92

"The Conductor and a Member of the Imperial Family" (Bulgakov) 18:90

"The Cone" (Wells) 6:361, 383

"Coney Island" (Beattie) 11:25-6, 29

"The Conference" (Singer) 3:385, 388

"A Conference of the Powers" (Kipling) 5:259

"The Confessional" (O'Faolain) 13:293

"The Confession of Brother Grimes" (Warren) 4:390, 394, 396

"Confidencias de un lobo" (Bioy Casares) 17:53, 56

"Le *confitéor* de l'artiste" (Baudelaire) 18:4-5, 8, 18

"A Conflict Ended" (Freeman) 1:196-97, 199

"Confused" (Singer) 3:384

"The Conger Eel" (O'Flaherty) 6:269, 274

El congreso ("The Assembly"; *The Congress*) (Borges) 4:27-8

The Congress (Borges)
See *El congreso*

"The Conjurer's Revenge" (Chesnutt) 7:6-7, 10, 18, 42

The Conjure Woman (Chesnutt) 7:2-5, 7-12, 14, 26, 30, 33, 38-40, 43

"The Conjuring Contest" (Dunbar) 8:122, 149

"Con legítimo orgullo" ("With Justifiable Pride") (Cortazar) 7:94

"The Connoisseur" (de la Mare) 14:70, 82

The Connoisseur, and Other Stories (de la Mare) 14:70

"The Connor Girls" (O'Brien) 10:334, 341

"A Conquest of Humility" (Freeman) 1:198

"The Conscript" (Balzac) 5:12-13

"Consequences" (Cather) 2:110-11, 115

"Conservatory" (Barthelme) 2:51

"The Consolations of Horror" (Ligotti) 16:261, 271, 277-78, 283, 285, 288, 294

"A Consolatory Tale" (Dinesen) 7:164, 186, 193, 200

"The Constant Tin Soldier" (Andersen)
See "The Steadfast Tin Soldier"

"A Constellation of Events" (Updike) 13:402

"Conte de fin d'été" (Villiers de l'Isle Adam) 14:390

Contes cruels (*Sardonic Tales*) (Villiers de l'Isle Adam) 14:377-78, 380-81, 391, 395-96, 403, 411

Contes cruels: Nouveaux contes cruels (Villiers de l'Isle Adam) 14:404, 412

Contes de la bécasse (Maupassant) 1:257

Contes drolatiques (*Droll Stories*) (Balzac) 5:19-21

Contes philosophiques (Balzac)
See *Romans et contes philosophiques*

"The Contessina" (Bowen) 3:40

"The Contest" (Paley) 8:388, 394, 398

"The Contest of the Minstrels" (Hoffmann)
See "Der Kampf der Sänger"

The Continental Op (Hammett) 17:212-13, 217, 227

"Continuity of Parks" (Cortazar) 7:54, 70, 83

"The Contract" (Anderson) 1:52

"Contrition" (Dubus) 15:74, 83

"The Convalescence of Jack Hamlin" (Harte) 8:247, 249

"The Conventional Wisdom" (Elkin) 12:99

"A Conversation" (Aiken) 9:14

"A Conversation" (Turgenev) 7:335

"Conversation at Night" (Bunin)
See "A Night Conversation"

"Conversation in the Atomic Age" (O'Hara) 15:250, 258

"The Conversation of Eiros and Charmion" ("Eiros and Charmion") (Poe) 1:402

"Conversation Piece, 1945" ("Double Talk") (Nabokov) 11:109-10, 112-13, 127

"Conversations at Night" (Le Guin) 12:211, 213, 216

"Conversations in a Dead Language" (Ligotti) 16:271, 275, 292, 294, 297

"Conversations with Goethe" (Barthelme) 2:51

"A Conversation with My Father" (Paley) 8:390, 392, 395, 399-402, 405, 407, 415-16, 418

"Converse at Night" (Dinesen) 7:168, 171, 186

"The Conversion of Aurelian McGoggin" (Kipling) 5:261, 274

"The Conversion of Sum Loo" (Cather) 2:102

"The Conversion of William Kirkwood" (McGahern) 17:305, 323

"The Convert" (Lavin) 4:165-68

"A Convert of the Mission" (Harte) 8:216, 254

"Cookie" (Taylor) 10:382, 390

"Cool Air" (Lovecraft) 3:258, 262, 274

A Cool Million: The Dismantling of Lemuel Pitkin (West) 16:343-48, 354-56, 362, 366, 379-85, 387-94, 399-400, 402-03, 405-08, 411, 415, 418

"The Cop and the Anthem" (Henry) 5:173, 187

"Copenhagen Season" (Dinesen) 7:166, 169-71, 186, 190-91

"Un coq chanta" (Maupassant) 1:272

"Cora Unashamed" (Hughes) 6:109-10, 118-19, 121-23, 129

"La corde" ("The Rope") (Baudelaire) 18:35, 39

"The Coreopsis Kid" (Calisher) 15:5, 15-17

Corilla (Nerval) 18:362, 367, 369

"Corkscrew" (Hammett) 17:216, 222, 230

"The Cornet Yelagin Affair" (Bunin)
See "The Elaghin Affair"

"The Corn Planting" (Anderson) 1:37

"Corporal of Artillery" (Dubus) 15:73

"Correspondence" (McCullers) 9:332-34, 343, 345, 358

A Correspondence (Turgenev) 7:317-18, 320, 324-26, 328, 361

"A Correspondence Course" (Gordimer) 17:171, 173, 193

"The Corsican Inn" (Pritchett) 14:268, 298

"Cortísimo metraje" ("Short Feature") (Cortazar) 7:95

"Cosmic Casanova" (Clarke) 3:133

Le cosmicomiche (*Cosmicomics*) (Calvino) 3:92-6, 98-100, 103-04, 106-07, 110, 112, 116-17

Cosmicomics (Calvino)
See *Le cosmicomiche*

Cosmopolitans (Maugham) 8:366, 380

"The Cost of Living" (Gallant) 5:130, 140-41, 149

"The Cost of Living" (Malamud) 15:173-75

Costumes by Eros (Aiken) 9:4, 28

"The Cottagette" (Gilman) 13:126, 145

"Councillor Krespel" (Hoffmann)
See "Rat Krespel"

"A Council of State" (Dunbar) 8:122, 124-25, 128, 136, 141, 144, 150

"A Council of War" (Gilman) 13:143

"Counsel for Oedipus" (O'Connor) 5:370

"The Counterfeit Coin" (Baudelaire)
See "La fausse monnaie"

"Counterparts" (Joyce) 3:200-01, 205, 209, 226, 231, 234, 246, 249

"Countess" (Le Fanu)
See "A Passage in the Secret History of an Irish Countess"

Counting (Phillips) 16:332

"The Counting-House" (Turgenev) 7:313

"Count Magnus" (James) 16:228-30, 232, 237-38, 243, 245, 250-52, 256

"The Count of Crow's Nest" (Cather) 2:100, 102

"The Count of Monte Cristo" (Calvino) 3:93, 95-6

"Country" (Phillips) 16:327

"The Country Church" (Irving) 2:244

"The Country Doctor" (Kafka)
See "Ein landarzt"

A Country Doctor's Notebook (Bulgakov)
See *Zapiski iunogo vracha*

"The Country Funeral" (McGahern) 17:319-22, 324

"The Country Husband" (Cheever) **1**:90, 100-02

"The Country Inn" (Turgenev)
See "The Inn"

"The Country of the Blind" (Wells) **6**:361-62, 368-73, 376-79, 383-84, 391-92, 399-400, 405

The Country of the Blind, and Other Stories (Wells) **6**:359-61, 366, 380, 391-92

The Country of the Pointed Firs (Jewett) **6**:152, 154-55, 157, 162-66, 168-69, 174-82

"Country Society" (Bates) **10**:118

"A Country Tale" (Dinesen) **7**:168-69

"The Count's Courtship" (de la Mare) **14**:66, 81, 86

"The Coup de Grâce" (Bierce) **9**:55-6, 75-7

"Le coup de pistolet" (Merimee) **7**:277

"A Couple of Fools" (Bates) **10**:131

"A Couple of Hamburgers" (Thurber) **1**:418-19

"The Courting of Dinah Shadd" (Kipling) **5**:260, 263-64, 274

"The Courting of Sister Wisby" (Jewett) **6**:152, 160, 162, 178

"Court in the West Eighties" (McCullers) **9**:342, 345, 356

"A Courtship" (Faulkner) **1**:151, 178

"Courtship" (O'Brien) **10**:334, 341

"The Courtship of Mr. Lyon" ("Mr. Lyon") (Carter) **13**:6, 9, 25, 30-31

"Cousin Larry" (Parker) **2**:280, 283

"Cousin Poor Lesley and the Lousy People" (Elkin) **12**:117

"Cousins" (Bellow) **14**:43, 46, 58

"Cousin Teresa" (Saki) **12**:295, 302, 312

Covering End (James) **8**:296

"The Coward" (Barnes) **3**:18-22

"A Coward" (Wharton) **6**:414

"The Cow's Death" (O'Flaherty) **6**:274

"The Cowslip Field" (Bates) **10**:120, 131-32, 139

"The Coxon Fund" (James) **8**:317, 348

Crab Apple Jelly (O'Connor) **5**:362, 364, 371, 377-78, 380, 383

"The Cracked Looking-Glass" (Porter) **4**:327, 329-30, 339-40, 342, 360

"Cracker Prayer" (Hughes) **6**:138

The Crapshooter (Steinbeck) **11**:248

"Crazy, Crazy, Now Showing Everywhere" (Gilchrist) **14**:154

"The Crazy Hunter" (Boyle) **5**:58-9, 61-3, 65-6, 68-9

The Crazy Hunter: Three Short Novels (Boyle) **5**:66

"Crazy Sunday" (Fitzgerald) **6**:47, 52, 60-1, 77-9

"The Creamery Man" (Garland) **18**:160

"The Creamery Manager" (McGahern) **17**:320, 322

"Created He Them" (London) **4**:253

"The Creative Impulse" (Maugham) **8**:369, 378-79

"The Creative Instinct" (Maugham) **8**:358

"The Creature" (O'Brien) **10**:332-33

"The Creatures" (de la Mare) **14**:65, 80, 83, 85

Creatures of Circumstance (Maugham) **8**:380

"A Credibility Gap" (Gordimer) **17**:157

Credos and Curios (Thurber) **1**:424

"The Creeping Siamese" (Hammett) **17**:224

"Cremona Violin" (Hoffmann) **13**:225

"Le crépuscule du soir" ("Evening Twilight") (Baudelaire) **18**:5, 8, 17, 33

"Cressy" (Harte) **8**:221

"Crevasse" (Faulkner) **1**:147

"Crewe" (de la Mare) **14**:73, 80, 84, 88-9, 90-1

"The Cricket on the Hearth" (Dickens) **17**:103, 116, 127-28

"Criers and Kibitzers, Kibitzers and Criers" (Elkin) **12**:94-5, 116-18

"Le crime au père Boniface" (Maupassant) **1**:274

"The Crime of Gabriel Gale" (Chesterton) **1**:124

"The Crime of Professor Sandwich" (Benet) **10**:149

"Crimes of Conscience" (Gordimer) **17**:171, 174, 193

"The Crime Wave at Blandings" (Wodehouse) **2**:344, 346, 349

"Criminal Courts" (Dickens) **17**:115

"The Crimson Curtain" (Barbey d'Aurevilly)
See "Le rideau cramoisi"

"The Crimson Island" (Bulgakov) **18**:74, 91, 110

"The Cripple" (Andersen) **6**:13

"The Crisis" (Zoshchenko) **15**:400

"Critical Mass" (Clarke) **3**:134

"Critique de la vie quotidienne" (Barthelme) **2**:39-40, 42, 55

"Croatoan" (Ellison) **14**:115-17, 128

Crónica de una muerte anunciada (*Chronicle of a Death Foretold*) (Garcia Marquez) **8**:167, 173-82, 186, 190, 200-04

Crónicas de Bustos Domecq (*Chronicles of Bustos Domecq*) (Bioy Casares) **17**:48, 52, 74-5, 84, 86

Cronopios and Famas (Cortazar)
See *Historia de cronopios y de famas*

The Croquet Player (Wells) **6**:400-02

"Crossbones" (Michaels) **16**:302

"Cross-Country Snow" (Hemingway) **1**:217, 244

"Crossing into Poland" (Babel) **16**:25, 28-9, 31, 33

"Crossing the Border" (Oates) **6**:248-49

Crossing the Border: Fifteen Tales (Oates) **6**:226-29, 231, 247-48, 250, 253-54

"Crossing the Line" (McGahern) **17**:315, 323

"Crossing the Zbruck" (Babel) **16**:51-4, 56, 58

"Crouch End" (King) **17**:295

"Crowds" (Baudelaire)
See "Les foules"

"The Crow in the Woods" (Updike) **13**:400

"A Crown of Feathers" (Singer) **3**:374

A Crown of Feathers, and Other Stories (Singer) **3**:374-76, 380, 382, 384

"The Croxley Master" (Doyle) **12**:89

"Cruce de caminos" (Unamuno) **11**:312-13

Crucial Instances (Wharton) **6**:413

"The Cruel Master" (Oates) **6**:237

The Cruise of "The Breadwinner" (Bates) **10**:129-30

The Crusade of the Excelsior (Harte) **8**:245

"The Crystal Egg" (Wells) **6**:383, 389-91, 393-94, 404-05

"The Crystal Fantasy" (Kawabata)
See "Suishō Gensō"

"Crystals" (Calvino) **3**:108-09

"Cuarta versión" ("Fourth Version") (Valenzuela) **14**:355, 367

"The Cuckoo Clock" (Pritchett) **14**:269, 298

"The Cuckoo-Spit" (Lavin) **4**:172, 176, 183, 185

"Cuello de gatito negro" ("Throat of a Black Cat") (Cortazar) **7**:61, 69

"Cunner-Fishing" (Jewett) **6**:155, 167

"The Cupboard of the Yesterdays" (Saki) **12**:310, 328

"Cupid's Arrows" (Kipling) **5**:261

"A Cup of Cold Water" (Wharton) **6**:424

"Cup of Life" (Bulgakov) **18**:91

"The Cup of Life" (Bunin) **5**:90, 92, 109

The Cup of Life (Bunin) **5**:90

"A Cup of Tea" (Mansfield) **9**:310

"The Curb in the Sky" (Thurber) **1**:418, 425

"The Cure" (Cheever) **1**:89

"The Cure" (Colette) **10**:280

Le curé de Tours (*Les célibataires*; *The Curé of Tours*) (Balzac) **5**:5, 7-8, 18, 25-6

The Curé of Tours (Balzac)
See *Le curé de Tours*

"The Curfew Tolls" (Benet) **10**:154

"El curioso impertinente" ("The Impertinent Curiosity"; "Meddlesome Curiosity") (Cervantes) **12**:3-4, 9-15

"The Curious Case of Benjamin Button" ("Benjamin Button") (Fitzgerald) **6**:59, 79-80, 92

"The Curse" (Clarke) **3**:124, 143-44

"The Curtain Blown by the Breeze" (Spark) **10**:356, 359, 361, 370-71

"A Curtain of Green" (Welty) **1**:465-67, 469, 471, 476, 481-82, 484, 487, 496

"The Custard Heart" (Parker) **2**:275, 280-81, 286

"The Custody of the Pumpkin" (Wodehouse) **2**:346-47

"Custom-Made Bride" (Vonnegut) **8**:432, 436

"The Custom of the Country" (O'Connor) **5**:370-71, 384, 387, 389

"Customs" (Oates) **6**:227, 248-50

"Cut" (Dixon) **16**:204, 210

"Cut Glass Bowl" (Fitzgerald) **6**:57

"Cy" (Dixon) **16**:207, 211

"Cycling in Gringnan" (Cortazar)
See "Ciclismo en Gringnan"

"The Cyclone" (Hesse) **9**:230-32, 235

"Cyprian's Narrative" (Hoffmann)
See "Der Vampyrismus"

"Dada" (Boyle) **16**:141, 143

"Daddy Deering" ("Old Daddy Deering") (Garland) **18**:160, 176, 194

"The Daemon Lover" (Jackson) **9**:267, 272

The Daffodil Sky (Bates) **10**:118-19

"The Dagger with Wings" (Chesterton) **1**:130-31

"Dagon" (Lovecraft) **3**:258, 262, 268, 272-73, 282, 285, 289

"The Daisy" (Andersen) **6**:3, 7

Daisy Miller: A Study (James) **8**:264, 274, 291, 298-99, 309-14, 334, 336-38

"Daisy Overend" (Spark) **10**:359-60

"Dalyrimple Goes Wrong" (Fitzgerald) **6**:45, 57

"The Dance at Chevalier's" (Cather) **2**:101, 105, 107

"Dance of the Happy Shades" (Munro) **3**:321, 328-30, 335, 346

Dance of the Happy Shades (Munro) **3**:320, 322, 328-29, 331, 335, 343-44, 347

"Dancing Girls" (Atwood) **2**:6-8, 10, 12

Dancing Girls, and Other Stories (Atwood) **2**:3-7, 10, 13-16, 20-2

"The Dancing Mistress" (Bowen) 3:30, 43, 54
"The Dandy Frightening the Squatter"
  (Twain) 6:300
"Dandy Jim's Conjure Scare" (Dunbar)
  8:122, 149
"Danger!" (Doyle) 12:80
"The Danger in the House" (Thurber) 1:429
"The Danger of Shadows" (Benet) 10:160
A Dangerous Perfume (Nin) 10:306
"Les dangers de l'inconduite" (Balzac) 5:4
"Daniel Webster and the Ides of March"
  (Benet) 10:153, 158
"Daniel Webster and the Sea Serpent" (Benet)
  10:144, 153, 158
"Danny" (Jewett) 6:150, 167
"Dante and the Lobster" (Beckett) 16:64, 69,
  92-3
"Dante Street" (Babel) 16:59
"Daoine Bochta" (O'Flaherty) 6:287, 289
"Daphne's Lover" (Taylor) 10:400, 416-17
"Darcy in the Land of Youth" (O'Connor)
  5:371
"The Dark" (Updike) 13:348
Dark Alleys (Bunin)
  See *Dark Avenues*
"Dark Avenues" (Bunin) 5:115
Dark Avenues (*Dark Alleys*) (Bunin) 5:82, 90,
  113-16
"A Dark Brown Dog" (Crane) 7:130
"The Dark Chamber" (Ligotti) 16:296
"The Dark City" (Aiken) 9:13-14, 31
"The Dark Glasses" (Spark) 10:356
"The Dark Men" (Dubus) 15:77-9
"Darkness Box" (Le Guin) 12:232
"The Dark Walk" (Taylor) 10:392, 411
"The Darling" (Chekhov) 2:131-32, 135
"Darling" (Dixon) 16:207, 211
"The Darling River" (Lawson) 18:206
"The Darning Needle" (Andersen) 6:20
"A Dashing Fellow" (Nabokov) 11:117
"Datos para entender a los perqueos" ("Some
  Facts for Understanding the Perkians")
  (Cortazar) 7:95
"Datura Fastuosa" (Hoffmann) 13:221-23,
  225-26
"The Daughter" (Suckow) 18:389, 401, 409
"Daughter of Albion" (Chekhov) 2:126
"A Daughter of the Aurora" (London) 4:286
"The Daughter of the Regiment" (Kipling)
  5:260
"Daughters" (Anderson) 1:52
"The Daughters of the Late Colonel"
  (Mansfield) 9:280-81, 300, 303-06, 310
"The Daughters of the Vicar" (Lawrence)
  4:197-98, 202, 204, 212, 233
"Daumier" (Barthelme) 2:39, 42, 49, 55
"De Daumier-Smith's Blue Period" (Salinger)
  2:293, 301, 315
"The Daunt Diana" (Wharton) 6:421, 428
"Dave's Neckliss" (Chesnutt) 7:18
"David Swan" (Hawthorne) 3:160
Da Vinci's Bicycle (Davenport) 16:173-74,
  176-77, 179-80, 182-83, 185, 187, 190, 193-
  98
"Dawn" (Powers) 4:370
"The Dawn in Erewhon" (Davenport)
  16:162-67, 169-70, 176, 183, 185-86, 197
"The Day before the Revolution" (Le Guin)
  12:231, 234, 241
Daybreak (Schnitzler)
  See *Spiel im Morgengrauen*
"A Day in Coney Island" (Singer) 3:374

"A Day in the Jungle" (Jackson) 9:258
Daylight and Nightmare (Chesterton) 1:140
"A Day of Grace" (Garland) 18:154, 160,
  181, 183
"A Day of Our Life" (Bulgakov) 18:90
"Day of the Butterfly" (Munro) 3:329-30,
  337
"The Day of the Dying Rabbit" (Updike)
  13:359-61
The Day of the Locust (West) 16:345-49, 355-
  57, 359-62, 364, 366-67, 369-74, 379, 381,
  383-85, 387-89, 394, 396, 399-402, 406-08,
  411, 414-15, 418
"A Day on a Selection" (Lawson) 18:200,
  237-38, 240-41
"The Day Resurgent" (Henry) 5:188
"Days" (O'Hara) 15:253
Day's End and Other Stories (Bates) 10:111
"A Day's Lodging" (London) 4:253
"Days of Sunshine" (Benet) 10:149
"A Day's Pleasure" (Garland) 18:154, 160
"Dayspring Mishandled" (Kipling) 5:270,
  278, 282-83, 299-303
"A Day's Work" (Capote) 2:81
"A Day's Work" (Porter) 4:339-40, 342, 360
The Day's Work (Kipling) 5:266-68, 273-74,
  283, 294-95
"The Day the Dam Broke" (Thurber) 1:426,
  428, 432
"The Day the Pig Fell into the Well"
  (Cheever) 1:100
"The Deacon" (Updike) 13:361
"The Dead" (Joyce) 3:202-06, 208, 210-11,
  214-15, 217, 223-26, 228, 232-40, 242-45,
  247, 249
"The Dead" (Oates) 6:225, 234, 254
"The Dead Are Silent" (Schnitzler)
  See "Der toten schweigen"
"The Dead Child" (Andersen)
  See "The Child in the Grave"
"The Dead Fiddler" (Singer) 3:369, 384
Dead Leaves (Garcia Marquez)
  See *La hojarasca*
"Dead Mabelle" (Bowen) 3:30, 44, 54
"The Dead Man" (Borges)
  See "El muerto"
"The Dead Queen" (Coover) 15:43-6
"The Dead Season" (Schulz)
  See "Martwy sezon"
"The Dead Sexton" (Le Fanu) 14:238
"The Dead Walk" (Bulgakov) 18:90
"Dead Yellow Women" (Hammett) 17:201,
  222-24, 226, 230
"The Deal" (Michaels) 16:301-03
"Dean of Men" (Taylor) 10:390, 399, 415,
  418
"Dear John" (Updike) 13:367
"Death" (Anderson) 1:30, 42
"Death" (Calvino) 3:110
"Death and the Cherry Tree" (Bates) 10:121
"Death and the Child" (Crane) 7:100-01,
  104-08
"Death and the Compass" (Borges)
  See "La muerte y la brújula"
"Death and the Senator" (Clarke) 3:147
"The Deathbird" (Ellison) 14:115, 118, 138,
  140-41, 143, 145-46
Deathbird Stories: A Pantheon of Modern Gods
  (Ellison) 14:118, 121
"Death Constant beyond Love" (Garcia
  Marquez)
  See "Muerte constante más allá der amor"

"Death in Midsummer" (Mishima) 4:313-14,
  318, 321-22
Death in Midsummer, and Other Stories
  (Mishima) 4:313-18, 321-23
"A Death in the Country" (Benet) 10:142,
  149, 156-57
"A Death in the Desert" (Cather) 2:90-1, 98,
  103, 105, 113
"Death in the Woods" (Anderson) 1:31, 37-8,
  40, 50-2, 56, 58-62
Death in the Woods (Anderson) 1:31, 37,
  50-1, 56
Death in Venice (Mann)
  See *Der Tod in Venedig*
"The Death of a Bachelor" (Schnitzler)
  15:343
The Death of Ahasuerus (Lagerkvist)
  See *Ahasverus död*
Death of a Huntsman (Bates) 10:119-20, 128-
  29
"The Death of a Kinsman" (Taylor) 10:415
"The Death of a Traveling Salesman" (Welty)
  1:466, 472, 481, 493, 497
"Death of Distant Friends" (Updike) 13:404
"The Death of Dolgushov" (Babel) 16:12, 24,
  28-30, 41, 53, 58
"The Death of Edward Lear" (Barthelme)
  2:49, 52
"The Death of Halpin Frayser" (Bierce) 9:70,
  85-6
The Death of Ivan Ilych (Tolstoy)
  See *Smert Ivana Ilyicha*
"The Death of Justina" (Cheever) 1:100
"The Death of Ligoun" (London) 4:287
"The Death of Me" (Lish) 18:275, 281, 283
"The Death of Me" (Malamud) 15:174, 216,
  227
The Death of Methusaleh, and Other Stories
  (Singer) 3:389
"The Death of Methusalah" (Singer) 3:389
"The Death of Mrs. Sheer" (Oates) 6:224
"The Death of Stevie Long" (O'Faolain)
  13:315
"The Death of the Lion" (James) 8:281, 306,
  317
"The Death of the Prophet" (Baldwin) 10:17
"Deaths at Sea" (Dubus) 15:90
Debits and Credits (Kipling) 5:275, 279, 283,
  296
"Debris" (Coover) 15:47
"The Debt" (Wharton) 6:421, 429
"A Debt of Honour" (Pritchett) 14:255, 298
"Debts" (Paley) 8:399, 403, 407
"Un début dans la vie" (Balzac) 5:8-9
Decameron (Boccaccio) 10:163-247
"The Deceitful Marriage" (Cervantes)
  See "El casamiento engañoso"
"The Deceived" (Mann)
  See *Die Betrogene*
"The Decision" (O'Hara) 15:250, 252, 254-
  55, 258
"Décoré" (Maupassant) 1:256, 263
"Découverte" (Maupassant) 1:259
"DeDe's Talking, It's Her Turn" (Gilchrist)
  14:154
"Dedication" (King) 17:295
"Deep End" (Ballard) 1:69
Deephaven (Jewett) 6:150, 154-57, 165-69
"Deephaven Cronies" (Jewett) 6:150, 167
"Deephaven Excursions" (Jewett) 6:150, 168
"Deephaven Society" (Jewett) 6:154, 167
"Deer in the Works" (Vonnegut) 8:438

"Deer Season" (Beattie)　**11**:6

"Defeat" (Boyle)　**5**:66

"The Defeated" (Gordimer)　**17**:151

"The Defeat of the City" (Henry)　**5**:184

"The Defection of Mary Ann Gibbs" (Dunbar)　**8**:122

"A Defender of the Faith" (Dunbar)　**8**:122, 132

"The Defenestration of Ermintrude Inch" (Clarke)　**3**:134

"A Defensive Diamond" (Saki)　**12**:296, 327

"The Deliberation of Mr. Dunkin" (Dunbar)　**8**:119, 121, 131, 136, 143

The Delicate Nature (Bates)　**10**:118

"The Delicate Prey" (Bowles)　**3**:59-63, 66, 72, 77

A Delicate Prey and Other Stories (Bowles)　**3**:58-65, 67, 70-2, 76-7, 79-80

"Delivering" (Dubus)　**15**:75, 81, 89, 96

"The Delta at Sunset" (Ballard)　**1**:69

"Delta Autumn" (Faulkner)　**1**:166

Delta of Venus (Nin)　**10**:305, 307, 324-25, 327

"The Deluge at Norderney" (Dinesen)　**7**:163, 170, 174, 176, 179-80, 182-83, 186, 190, 195-98, 200, 204

"Delusion for a Dragon Slayer" (Ellison)　**14**:108, 118, 120

"Les demoiselles de Bienfilâtre" ("The Bienfilâtre Sisters") (Villiers de l'Isle Adam)　**14**:377-81, 383, 385-86, 393, 396, 411

"A Demon" (O'Brien)　**10**:347

"The Demon Lover" (Bowen)　**3**:31-2, 41, 50-2, 54

The Demon Lover and Other Stories (Bowen)　**3**:30-3, 41, 44, 48, 50-2

"The Demonstrators" (Welty)　**1**:488

"Dentistry and Doubt" (Updike)　**13**:351, 354, 395

"Departure" (Anderson)　**1**:31, 42, 45-6

Le dépeupleur (*The Lost Ones*) (Beckett)　**16**:71-2, 76-7, 88, 94, 98, 102, 105-07, 115, 123

"Derletzebrief eines literaten" ("The Last Letter of a Litterateur") (Schnitzler)　**15**:355, 361-64

"Derring-Do" (Capote)　**2**:81

"Desayuno" ("Breakfast") (Cortazar)　**7**:95

"The Desborough Connections" (Harte)　**8**:220

"A Descent into the Maelström" (Poe)　**1**:385, 400, 402

"Descent of Man" (Boyle)　**16**:142, 148-49, 153

"The Descent of Man" (Wharton)　**6**:428-29

The Descent of Man (Wharton)　**6**:420-21

Descent of Man, and Other Stories (Boyle)　**16**:140-41, 143-44, 149-50, 154

"The Deserter" (Babel)　**16**:35

"A Desertion" (Crane)　**7**:106

"Le désespoir de la vieille" ("The Old Woman's Despair") (Baudelaire)　**18**:17, 32, 59, 64-5

Deshoras (*After-Hours; Off-Hours*) (Cortazar)　**7**:79

"Le désir de peindre" (Baudelaire)　**18**:6-7, 18

"Le désir d'être un homme" ("The Desire to Be a Man") (Villiers de l'Isle Adam)　**14**:381, 384, 387, 389-90, 396

"Desire" (Beattie)　**11**:11, 20

Desire (O'Flaherty)　See *Dúil*

"The Desired Payment" (Bulgakov)　**18**:89

"Désirée's Baby" (Chopin)　**8**:66, 68, 74-6, 81-4, 91-2, 99, 103, 105-06

"Desire in November" (Calvino)　**3**:112

"The Desire to Be a Man" (Villiers de l'Isle Adam)　See "Le désir d'être un homme"

"A Desperate Character" (Turgenev)　See "Otchayanny"

"Le dessous de cartes d'une partie de whist" ("Behind the Scenes at a Whist Game"; "Beneath the Cards of a Game of Whist") (Barbey d'Aurevilly)　**17**:7, 10-12, 15, 17-21, 27-8, 30-4, 38-9, 43-4

"The Destruction of Kreshev" (Singer)　**3**:358-59, 368, 375, 383-84

"Details of a Sunset" ("Katastrofa") (Nabokov)　**11**:131, 133

Detstvo (*Childhood*) (Tolstoy)　**9**:374-76, 380, 383, 399, 401-03

"Deutsches Requiem" (Borges)　**4**:9, 18, 24-6, 30, 37, 40-2

"Deux amis" (Maupassant)　**1**:275

"Deux augures" ("Two Augurs") (Villiers de l'Isle Adam)　**14**:381, 395-96

"Les deux rêves" (Balzac)　**5**:31

"The Devil" (Tolstoy)　**9**:377-78

"The Devil and Daniel Webster" (Benet)　**10**:143-44, 152-54, 156-58

"The Devil and Irv Cherniske" (Boyle)　**16**:151, 153

"The Devil and Tom Walker" (Irving)　**2**:241, 247-48, 250-51, 254, 262

"The Devil in the Belfry" (Poe)　**1**:407

"The Devil's Race-Track": Mark Twain's Great Dark Writings (Twain)　**6**:336

"The Devil's Spittle" (Cortazar)　See "Las babas del diablo"

"The Devoted Friend" (Wilde)　**11**:375-76, 380, 386, 395, 398, 407, 409

"The De Wets Come to Kloof Grange" (Lessing)　**6**:186, 189

"Le diable" (Maupassant)　**1**:270, 284

"Diable—A Dog" (London)　See "Bâtard"

"Diaboliad" ("D'javoliada") (Bulgakov)　**18**:72, 74, 93-5, 97, 99, 104, 113

Diaboliad, and Other Stories (Bulgakov)　See *D'iavoliada*

Les diaboliques (*Weird Women*) (Barbey d'Aurevilly)　**17**:2-4, 7-8, 10-13, 15, 17-21, 24-5, 30, 33-4, 39-41, 43-4

"Diagnosis" (Wharton)　**6**:424

"Dial F for Frankenstein" (Clarke)　**3**:145

"Diálogo del espejo" ("Dialogue in a Mirror") (Garcia Marquez)　**8**:154-56, 182

"Dialogue" (Lessing)　**6**:200-04

"Dialogue in a Mirror" (Garcia Marquez)　See "Diálogo del espejo"

"The Dialogue of the Dogs" (Cervantes)　See "El coloquio de los perros"

Dialogues de bêtes (Colette)　**10**:261, 272

"El diamante de Villasola" (Unamuno)　**11**:312

"The Diamond as Big as the Ritz" (Fitzgerald)　**6**:46-7, 58-60, 88, 92, 100-02

"A Diamond Guitar" (Capote)　**2**:67

"The Diamond Maker" (Wells)　**6**:383, 388, 408

"The Diamond Mine" (Cather)　**2**:91-2

"The Diamond Necklace" (Maupassant)　See "La parure"

"The Diamond of Kali" (Henry)　**5**:184

"Diary, 1900" (Hesse)　**9**:230

"Diary of a Madman" ("A Madman's Diary"; "Notes of a Madman") (Gogol)　**4**:82-3, 88, 91, 98, 100-01, 105-07, 122, 124, 126, 128-29

"The Diary of a Madman" (Tolstoy)　See *Zapiski sumasshedshego*

"The Diary of an African Nun" (Walker)　**5**:402, 404

"Diary of a Sixteen-Year-Old" (Kawabata)　See "Jūrokusai no Nikki"

"The Diary of a Superfluous Man" (Turgenev)　See "Dnevnik lishnego cheloveka"

"The Diary of Mr. Poynter" (James)　**16**:223-24, 229-30, 232-33, 235, 249, 255

"A Diary of Sudden Death; By a Public-Spirited Observer on the Inside" (Bierce)　**9**:83

"The Diary of the Rose" (Le Guin)　**12**:230, 237-38

D'iavoliada (*Diaboliad, and Other Stories*) (Bulgakov)　**18**:72-3, 91-2, 97-100

"Dichter und Komponist" (Hoffmann)　**13**:191

"Dick Boyle's Business Card" (Harte)　**8**:216, 252

"Dickon the Devil" (Le Fanu)　**14**:223

"Diddling Considered as One of the Exact Sciences" (Poe)　**1**:407

"Did I Invite You?" (Pritchett)　See "Did You Invite Me?"

"Did You Invite Me?" ("Did I Invite You?") (Pritchett)　**14**:285, 298

"The Die-Hard" (Benet)　**10**:154

"An die Musik" (Le Guin)　**12**:211-12, 214, 219-20, 222-23, 245, 250

"Dieu d'amour" (Wharton)　**6**:428

Different Seasons (King)　**17**:262-67, 271-73, 275, 282, 284

Difficult Loves (Calvino)　See *Gli amori difficili*

"Difficult People" (Chekhov)　**2**:155

"Di grasso" (Babel)　**16**:10-11, 16, 36, 41, 59

"The Dilettante" (Mann)　**5**:320, 323, 330, 335-37

"The Dilettante" (Wharton)　**6**:424

"A Dill Pickle" (Mansfield)　**9**:309-10

"Ding Dong" (Beckett)　**16**:93

Ding Dong Bell (de la Mare)　**14**:90, 92

"A Dinner at Poplar Walk" (Dickens)　**17**:120

"The Dinosaurs" (Calvino)　**3**:103, 109

"Díoltas" (O'Flaherty)　**6**:287-88

"El dios de los toros" (Bioy Casares)　**17**:68, 70

"Direction of the Road" (Le Guin)　**12**:234

"The Discarded" (Ellison)　**14**:103, 113-15, 117

"The Disciple" (Aiken)　**9**:4, 12-13

"Discord" (O'Faolain)　**13**:284-286, 288, 293, 309, 315

"The Discounters of Money" (Henry)　**5**:159

"Discourse on the *Tachanka*" (Babel)　**16**:27, 55

"A Disgrace to the Family" (Boyle)　**5**:64

"Disillusioned" (de la Mare)　**14**:83, 86

"Disillusionment" (Mann)　**5**:321, 330

"The Disinherited" (Bowen)　**3**:33, 41, 45, 48-9, 51

"The Disintegration Machine" (Doyle)　**12**:79

"The Dismissal" (Bowles)　**3**:75, 80

Disorder and Early Sorrow ("Early Sorrow") (Mann)　**5**:310-12, 323, 350

"The Displaced Person" (O'Connor) **1**:335-36, 338, 343-45, 347, 359

"Distance" ("Everything Stuck to Him") (Carver) **8**:4-5, 29, 42, 59

"Distance" (Oates) **6**:236-37

"Distance" (Paley) **8**:416-17

"The Distance of the Moon" (Calvino)
See "La distanza della luna"

"The Distances" (Cortazar)
See "Lejana"

"A Distant Episode" (Bowles) **3**:59, 61-2, 66-9, 72, 78

"Distant Music" (Beattie) **11**:4, 6-7, 17

"La distanza della luna" ("The Distance of the Moon") (Calvino) **3**:92, 103, 107, 109

Distortions (Beattie) **11**:2-5, 11-12, 15-16, 18-23, 26-8, 30-2,

"The Distracted Preacher" (Hardy) **2**:203, 205, 208, 213-15, 219-21

"The Disturber" (Villiers de l'Isle Adam)
See "L'inquiéteur"

"The Disturber of Traffic" (Kipling) **5**:283

"The Ditch" (O'Flaherty) **6**:265

"The Diver" (Dinesen) **7**:163, 167-68, 171

"The Diver" (Pritchett) **14**:260-61, 288-89, 299

A Diversity of Creatures (Kipling) **5**:275, 282-84

"Dividends" (O'Faolain) **13**:300

"The Division" (Turgenev) **7**:318

"A Division in the Coolly" (Garland) **18**:148, 160, 184

"Divorcing: A Fragment" (Updike) **13**:387

"Dizzy-Headed Dick" (Dunbar) **8**:122

"D'javoliada" (Bulgakov)
See "Diaboliad"

"Djinn, No Chaser" (Ellison) **14**:127

"Djouûmane" (Merimee) **7**:285, 296-98

"Djuna" (Nin) **10**:300-01, 317

"Dnevnik lishnego cheloveka" ("The Diary of a Superfluous Man"; "The Journal of a Superfluous Man") (Turgenev) **7**:314, 318-20, 339

"Las doce figuras del mundo" (Bioy Casares) **17**:70

"The Dock-Witch" (Ozick) **15**:297, 300, 312-13, 326

"Doc Marlowe" (Thurber) **1**:414

"Doc Mellhorn and the Pearly Gates" (Benet) **10**:143, 154, 159-60

"The Doctor" (Dubus) **15**:70, 77-9

"The Doctor" (Gallant) **5**:135, 139

"The Doctor and the Doctor's Wife" (Hemingway) **1**:208, 217, 234, 241, 245

Doctor Brodie's Report (Borges)
See *El informe de Brodie*

"Dr. Bullivant" (Hawthorne) **3**:164

"Doctor Chevalier's Lie" (Chopin) **8**:73

"Dr. Heidegger's Experiment" (Hawthorne) **3**:154, 178, 186-87

Doctor Jekyll and Mr. Hyde (Stevenson) **11**:265, 268-69, 282-83, 286-89, 291, 293, 295
See *The Strange Case of Dr. Jekyll and Mr. Hyde*

Doctor Martino, and Other Stories (Faulkner) **1**:180

"The Doctor of Hoyland" (Doyle) **12**:88

"A Doctor of Medicine" (Kipling) **5**:285

"The Doctors" (Barnes) **3**:9-10

"The Doctor's Case" (King) **17**:295

"The Doctor's Son" (O'Hara) **15**:247, 252, 256-57, 265-66, 286

The Doctor's Son, and Other Stories (O'Hara) **15**:249, 263, 264-67, 273-74

"A Doctor's Visit" (Chekhov) **2**:127, 156-58

"The Doctor's Wife" (Ozick) **15**:297, 300, 313-14

"The Dog" (Turgenev) **7**:316, 321, 323-24, 326, 335-36, 338

"Dog Days" (Dixon) **16**:217

"Doge und Dogressa" (Hoffmann) **13**:183-84

"The Dog Hervey" (Kipling) **5**:275, 284-85

"A Dog Named Trilby" (Hughes) **6**:122

"Dog Scent" (Zoshchenko) **15**:406

The Dogs' Colloguy (Cervantes)
See "El coloquio de los perros"

"Dolan's Cadillac" (King) **17**:294

"The Doll" (Chesnutt) **7**:17

Dollari e vecchie mondane (*Dollars and the Demi-Mondaine*) (Calvino) **3**:91

Dollars and the Demi-Mondaine (Calvino)
See *Dollari e vecchie mondane*

"The Doll's House" (Mansfield) **9**:280, 282, 286, 301-05, 308, 311, 313

"Dolph Heyliger" (Irving) **2**:241, 247-48, 251, 254, 256, 259-60

"The Dolt" (Barthelme) **2**:38, 52

"A Domestic Dilemma" (McCullers) **9**:323, 331-32, 343, 353-54, 356, 359-60

"Domestic Life in America" (Updike) **13**:385-86, 388-89

Domestic Relations: Short Stories (O'Connor) **5**:371, 375

"Don" (Dixon) **16**:207, 212

"Doña Faustina" (Bowles) **3**:64, 66, 80, 83

Donde viven las águilas (*Up Among the Eagles*) (Valenzuela) **14**:366

"Don Joaquin" (Cable) **4**:58

"Don Juan (Retired)" (O'Connor) **5**:369, 371

"Don Juan's Temptation" (O'Connor) **5**:366, 371, 389

"Le donneur d'eau bénite" (Maupassant) **1**:281

"Les dons des fées" (Baudelaire) **18**:17, 19, 43

"El don supremo" (Bioy Casares) **17**:53

"Don't Die" (Lish) **18**:283

"Don't Let Them" (Cortazar)
See "No te dejes"

"Don't Look Now" (du Maurier) **18**:129-30, 133, 137

Don't Look Now (du Maurier)
See *Not after Midnight*

"The Doom of the Darnaways" (Chesterton) **1**:131, 138

"The Door: A Prologue of Sorts" (Coover) **15**:33, 35, 51

"The Doorbell" (Nabokov) **11**:133

"The Door in the Wall" (Wells) **6**:361-62, 368-70, 376, 381, 383-84, 391-92, 404, 406

"The Door of Opportunity" (Maugham) **8**:357, 374

"The Door of the Trap" (Anderson) **1**:27, 39, 52

"Doorways" (McGahern) **17**:299, 308-09, 318-19, 321

"Die Doppeltgänger" (Hoffmann) **13**:206

"El Dorado: A Kansas Recessional" (Cather) **2**:101, 105

"Doroga" ("The Road") (Babel) **16**:36, 59

"Dorothée" (Baudelaire)
See "La belle Dorothée"

"Las dos doncelas" ("The Two Maidens") (Cervantes) **12**:4-5, 14, 17-18, 21, 26, 34, 37, 44

"Dos fantasías memorables" (Borges) **4**:16

Dos madres (*Two Mothers*) (Unamuno) **11**:313, 323-25, 327, 347, 356

"'Dossing Out' and 'Camping'" (Lawson) **18**:215

"Do the Dead Sing?" (King)
See "The Reach"

A Double-Barrelled Detective Story (Twain) **6**:295

"Double Birthday" (Cather) **2**:99, 113-15

"A Double Buggy at Lahey's Creek" (Lawson) **18**:201-06, 229, 262

"The Double Chamber" (Baudelaire)
See "Le chambre double"

"A Double-Dyed Deceiver" (Henry) **5**:182

"Une double famille" (Balzac) **5**:22, 29-31

"The Double Happiness Bun" (Gilchrist) **14**:154

La double méprise ("The Double Mistake") (Merimee) **7**:276, 281, 283, 286, 290-92, 304

"The Double Mistake" (Merimee)
See *La double méprise*

".007" (Kipling) **5**:266, 268, 279

"Double Talk" (Nabokov)
See "Conversation Piece, 1945"

"The Doves' Nest" (Mansfield) **9**:280

The Doves' Nest, and Other Stories (Mansfield) **9**:281

"Down at the Dinghy" (Salinger) **2**:290-91, 295-96, 298-300, 314

"Down by the Riverside" (Wright) **2**:360-61, 363, 365-69, 371, 374-75, 379-81, 387, 390-91

"Downers" (Michaels) **16**:308

"Downhill" (Beattie) **11**:17, 28

"Down Pens" (Saki) **12**:306

"The Downward Path to Wisdom" (Porter) **4**:339-40, 342, 359

"The Dowry of Angyar" (Le Guin) **12**:219, 224

"Do You Like It Here?" (O'Hara) **15**:266

"Do You Want to Make Something Out of It?" (Thurber) **1**:428

"Draft" (Beckett) **16**:108

"The Dragon" (Spark) **10**:367, 370

"The Dragon at Hide and Seek" (Chesterton) **1**:140

"The Dragon's Teeth" (Gordon)
See "One against Thebes"

"Dramas" (O'Brien) **10**:346

"Un drame au bord de la mer" ("A Seashore Drama") (Balzac) **5**:11-13, 16, 26, 31

"Drawing Names" (Mason) **4**:5

"Drawing Room B" (O'Hara) **15**:250

"The Dream" (Turgenev)
See "Son"

"Dreamer in a Dead Language" (Paley) **8**:410

"The Dreamers" (Dinesen) **7**:167, 170, 174, 191, 195, 197-98, 200, 209

"The Dreaming Child" (Dinesen) **7**:165, 171

"The Dreaming in Nortown" (Ligotti) **16**:284

"Dream Journeys" (Hesse) **9**:230-32, 236

Dream Journeys (Hesse) **9**:230

The Dream Life of Balso Snell (West) **16**:345-47, 349-51, 354, 361-67, 369, 377, 379, 383-87, 389-90, 393-94, 396-98, 402-03, 406-11, 415, 417

"Dream of a Mannikin; or, The Third Person" (Ligotti) **16**:261, 263, 265, 271, 273, 275-78, 283, 288

"The Dream of an Hour" (Chopin)
See "The Story of an Hour"

"The Dream of a Queer Fellow" (Dostoevsky)
See "The Dream of a Ridiculous Man"

"The Dream of a Ridiculous Man" ("The Dream of a Queer Fellow") (Dostoevsky) **2**:166, 183, 185

"A Dream of Armageddon" (Wells) **6**:360, 383-84, 391, 404

"A Dream of Oblómov's Grandson" (Bunin) **5**:81, 90

"The Dream of the Gods" (Hesse) **9**:243

"Dreams" (Chekhov) **2**:156

"Dream Sequence" (Hesse) **9**:234-35

"The Dreams in the Witch-House" (Lovecraft) **3**:258, 260, 263, 268, 272, 274-76, 282

"The Dreams of Chang" (Bunin) **5**:80-1, 83-4, 93

"A Dreary Story" ("A Dull Story") (Chekhov) **2**:126, 131, 143, 150, 156

Drei Frauen (*Three Women*) (Musil) **18**:292-93, 297, 322-23, 325

"Drenched in Light" (Hurston) **4**:136-38, 149-50

"A Dresden Lady in Dixie" (Chopin) **8**:94

"The Dress" (Thomas) **3**:399, 408

"Dressed Like Summmer Leaves" (Dubus) **15**:87

"Dr. Faustus" (Benet) **10**:145

"Drifted Back" (Lawson) **18**:248, 250

"Drifting Apart" (Lawson) **18**:229

"Drifting Crane" (Garland) **18**:147, 176, 187-88

"Drink to Me Only with Labyrinthine Eyes" (Ligotti) **16**:265, 269, 271, 274, 276, 278, 294

"Dr. Locrian's Asylum" (Ligotti) **16**:269, 278-80, 283, 296

"Le droit du passé" (Villiers de l'Isle Adam) **14**:396

Droll Stories (Balzac)
See *Contes drolatiques*

"The Drover's Wife" (Lawson) **18**:201-02, 206, 216-17, 219-23, 225-27, 248-51, 259, 263

"The Drowned Giant" (Ballard) **1**:68, 74

"The Drowned Girl" (Gogol)
See "Majskaja noč, ili Vtoplennica"

"Drowne's Wooden Image" (Hawthorne) **3**:185

"Drowning" (Boyle) **16**:142, 151, 156

"The Drummer of All the World" (Laurence) **7**:245, 248-50, 256, 260-61, 272

The Drummer of the Eleventh North Devonshire Fusiliers (Davenport) **16**:199-200

"The Drums of the Fore and Aft" (Kipling) **5**:264-65, 269, 273

"The Drunkard" (O'Connor) **5**:369, 371, 378

"Drunkard's Death" (Dickens) **17**:116, 125

"The Drunkard's Dream" (Le Fanu) **14**:220, 222-23

"A Drunken Steam-Engine" (Bulgakov) **18**:90

"Drunk with Love" (Gilchrist) **14**:157

Drunk with Love (Gilchrist) **14**:156-59

"Dr. Voke and Mr. Veech" (Ligotti) **16**:261, 265, 276, 284

"The Dryad" (Andersen) **6**:7

"Dry September" (Faulkner) **1**:148, 180-81

Dry Valley (Bunin)
See *Sukhodol*

Dubliners (Joyce) **3**:201-03, 205-07, 210, 213-14, 216-18, 224-26, 228-30, 233-35, 237-39, 244-45, 247-49

"The Duchess" (Cheever) **1**:106

"The Duchess and the Bugs" (Thurber) **1**:430

"The Duchess and the Jeweller" (Woolf) **7**:377, 388

"The Duchess at Prayer" (Wharton) **6**:413, 415, 428

La Duchesse de Langeais (Balzac) **5**:43-5, 47

"The Duchess of Hamptonshire" (Hardy) **2**:204

"The Duckling" (Andersen)
See "The Ugly Duckling"

"The Ducks" (Carver) **8**:10

"Dudley for the Dartmouth Cup" (Taylor) **10**:379

"The Duel" (Borges)
See "El duelo"

"The Duel" (Chekhov) **2**:131, 143, 145, 150-51, 155, 157

"The Duel" (Conrad) **9**:163, 183

"The Duel" (Henry) **5**:191

"El duelo" ("The Duel") (Borges) **4**:20, 27

"The Duel of Dr. Hirsch" (Chesterton) **1**:138

"A Duel without Seconds" (Barnes) **3**:13

"Dúil" (O'Flaherty) **6**:286, 288-89

Dúil (*Desire*) (O'Flaherty) **6**:285-89

"Duke of Portland" (Villiers de l'Isle Adam) **14**:381, 384, 388, 390-91, 393-96

"The Duke's Reappearance" (Hardy) **2**:210

Dulcima (Bates) **10**:117-18

"The Dulham Ladies" (Jewett) **6**:160

"Dullborough Town" (Dickens) **17**:123

"A Dull Story" (Chekhov)
See "A Dreary Story"

"Dulse" (Munro) **3**:346

"Dummy" (Carver) **8**:5, 29, 34

"The Dunwich Horror" (Lovecraft) **3**:258-59, 263, 269-70, 274-76, 290-92, 294

"Dunyazadiad" (Barth) **10**:48-9, 51, 54, 56, 61, 66, 68-9, 71, 91, 93-7, 101-05

Duo (*The Married Lover*) (Colette) **10**:262-65, 269

"The Duplicity of Hargraves" (Henry) **5**:159, 171

"During the Jurassic" (Updike) **13**:360, 387

"Dusie" (Barnes) **3**:10, 16

"Dusk" (Saki) **12**:296, 305, 315

"Dusk before Fireworks" (Parker) **2**:273-74, 281, 284-85

"Dutch Courage" (Kipling) **5**:264

"Dwarf House" (Beattie) **11**:15-16

"Dying" (Schnitzler)
See "Sterben"

"The Dynamiter" (Stevenson)
See *The New Arabian Nights*

"Each Other" (Lessing) **6**:197, 200, 214, 218

"Early Afternoon" (O'Hara) **15**:248, 274

"Early Coaches" (Dickens) **17**:133

"Early Sorrow" (Mann)
See *Disorder and Early Sorrow*

Early Stories (Bowen) **3**:40

"The Ears of Johnny Bear" ("Johnny Bear") (Steinbeck) **11**:207-08, 225, 229-30, 233-34, 242-44

"Earth, Moon" (Boyle) **16**:142

"Earth's Holocaust" (Hawthorne) **3**:162, 181-82, 189

East and West: The Collected Short Stories of W. Somerset Maugham (*Altogether: The Collected Stories of W. Somerset Maugham*) (Maugham) **8**:356, 358, 360, 370, 382

"The Easter Egg" (Saki) **12**:298, 306, 329

"The Easter Egg Party" (Bowen) **3**:43, 47

"Easter Eve" (Chekhov) **2**:130

"The Easter of the Soul" (Henry) **5**:188

"The Easter Wedding" (Dunbar) **8**:122, 136

"Eating Out" (Michaels) **16**:308

"Eating the Placenta" (Dixon) **16**:208

"The Eccentric Seclusion of the Old Lady" (Chesterton) **1**:120

"Echo" (Barth) **10**:42, 47, 52-4, 59-61, 75-6, 80-1, 85, 89, 95, 99, 102

"The Echo" (Bowles) **3**:59, 61-2, 66, 72, 77, 79

"Echoes" (Dinesen) **7**:173-74

Echoes from the Macabre (du Maurier) **18**:130

"Echo's Bones" (Beckett) **16**:106-08

Eclogues (Davenport) **16**:183, 187-89

L'école des femmes (*The School for Wives*) (Gide) **13**:72, 95, 100-02, 104, 105

"Eddie" (Schulz) **13**:334

"Eddie Mac" (McGahern) **17**:305

"The Edge of the Evening" (Kipling) **5**:269

"The Edge of the World" (Cheever) **1**:88

"The Editor Regrets..." (Pritchett) **14**:297

"Edmund" (Hesse) **9**:230-31, 236

"An Education" (Ozick) **15**:302, 305, 316-17

"The Educational Experience" (Barthelme) **2**:53

"The Education of Audrey" (Mansfield) **9**:301

"Edward and Pia" (Barthelme) **2**:30

"Edward Randolph's Portrait" (Hawthorne) **3**:179, 182

"The Effective Remedy" (Bulgakov) **18**:89

"Effigy of War" (Boyle) **5**:63-4

Les égarements de Minne (Colette) **10**:257

"The Egg" (Anderson)
See "The Triumph of the Egg"

"The Egg" (Anderson)
See "The Triumph of the Egg"

"The Egg Race" (Updike) **13**:386

"L'église" (Balzac) **5**:14, 23, 31

"Egotism; or, The Bosom Serpent" (Hawthorne) **3**:159, 178, 183, 189

"Egotists" (O'Faolain) **13**:309

"An Egyptian Cigarette" (Chopin) **8**:99

"Egyptian Darkness" (Bulgakov) **18**:86, 88

"Eidolons" (Ellison) **14**:142

"1830" (Davenport) **16**:161, 165-66, 170, 183

Eight Men (Wright) **2**:364, 366, 370, 386, 388

"Eight O'Clock One Morning" (Grau) **15**:149, 160

"Eiros and Charmion" (Poe)
See "The Conversation of Eiros and Charmion"

"The Elaghin Affair" ("The Case of Lieutenant Yelaghin"; "The Cornet Yelagin Affair"; "The Elaghin Case"; "The Yelagin Affair") (Bunin) **5**:82-3, 85, 87, 103, 108-09, 115, 119

The Elaghin Affair, and Other Stories (Bunin) **5**:82

"The Elaghin Case" (Bunin)
See "The Elaghin Affair"

"The Elder Lady" (Borges) **4**:19

"The Elder Mother" (Andersen)
See "The Elder-Tree Mother"

Title Index

"Elder Pill, Preacher" ("The Test of Elder Pill") (Garland) **18**:154, 160, 163, 176

"The Elder-Tree Mother" ("The Elder Mother"; "The Elm-Tree Mother") (Andersen) **6**:3-4, 14, 24

Eldorado (Lessing) **6**:191, 194-95

"Eleanor's House" (Cather) **2**:99, 103

"Elegy for a Freelance" (Carter) **13**:4

"An Elegy for Alma's Aunt Amy" (Suckow) **18**:393, 395, 413, 422, 424

"Elementals" (Benet) **10**:145

"Der Elementargeist" (Hoffmann) **13**:215

"Elements of True Manhood" (Jewett) **6**:167

"Elephant" (Carver) **8**:43

"Elethia" (Walker) **5**:413

"The Elevator" (Coover) **15**:30-1,38-40,48, 50

"Eleven O'Clock" (Pritchett) **14**:270

"The Elfin Mound" (Andersen) **6**:7

"Elias" (Tolstoy) **9**:388

Eligible Men (Elkin)
See *Searches and Seizures*

"Die Elixiere des Teufels" ("Elixirs of the Devil") (Hoffmann) **13**:188

"Elixirs of the Devil" (Hoffmann)
See "Die Elixiere des Teufels"

"Elizabeth" (Jackson) **9**:252, 266, 270-71

"Elizabeth Stock's One Story" (Chopin) **8**:100

"Ella and the Chinese" (O'Hara) **15**:263

"Elmer and Edna" (Suckow) **18**:390

"The Elm-Tree Mother" (Andersen)
See "The Elder-Tree Mother"

"An Eloquence of Grief" (Crane) **7**:130

"Elsie in New York" (Henry) **5**:194

"Eltha" (Suckow) **18**:393, 414, 417-18, 422, 424-25

"L'elu des rêves" (Villiers de l'Isle Adam) **14**:390, 393

"Em" (Dixon) **16**:210

"The Emancipator" (Gilchrist) **14**:157-59

"The Embarkment for Cythera" (Cheever) **1**:93

"An Embarrassing Situation" (Chopin) **8**:72

"Emelyan and the Empty Drum" (Tolstoy)
See "The Empty Drum"

"Emeryt" ("The Old Age Pensioner"; "The Retired Man") (Schulz) **13**:328

Emilie (Nerval) **18**:362, 364

"Eminence" (Suckow) **18**:391-92, 411

"Emmanuele! Emmanuele!" (Gordon) **15**:107-08, 121, 138, 142

"Emma Zunz" (Borges) **4**:16, 18-19, 23, 37, 39, 40

"Emotional Bankruptcy" (Fitzgerald) **6**:50

"The Emperor's New Clothes" (Andersen) **6**:10-11, 13, 16, 18, 26, 30

"The Empire of the Ants" (Wells) **6**:361, 365, 382, 391-92, 403

"The Empty Amulet" (Bowles) **3**:76

"The Empty Drum" ("Emelyan and the Empty Drum") (Tolstoy) **9**:377, 380, 388

"An Empty Purse" (Jewett) **6**:156

"The Enamored Youth" (Hesse) **9**:243

"The Encantadas; or, The Enchanted Isles" (Melville) **1**:293, 297-99, 303-04, 308, 310-11, 321-22, 329

"The Enchanted Bluff" (Cather) **2**:97, 102, 104-05, 108

"An Enchanted Garden" (Calvino)
See "Un giardino incantato"

The Enchanted House (Musil)
See *Die Versuchung der Stillen Veronika*

"The Enchanted Kiss" (Henry) **5**:159, 163

"The Enchanted Sea-Wilderness" (Twain) **6**:337

"The Enchanted Spot" (Gogol)
See "Zakoldovannoe mesto"

"The Enchantress" (Bates) **10**:123

The Enchantress, and Other Stories (Bates) **10**:123

"An Encounter" (Coover) **15**:46

"An Encounter" (Joyce) **3**:201, 205, 208, 217-18, 225-26, 230, 232, 234, 237, 247

"Encounter at Dawn" (Clarke) **3**:127, 135, 143

Encounters (Bowen) **3**:29, 40

"Encounter with Evil" (Cortazar)
See "Encuentro con el mal"

"Encrucijada" (Bioy Casares) **17**:53, 56

"Encuentro con el mal" ("Encounter with Evil") (Cortazar) **7**:94

"The End" (Beckett)
See "La Fin"

"The End" (Borges)
See "El fin"

"Endicott of the Red Cross" (Hawthorne) **3**:175-76

"Ending" (Grau) **15**:163

"The End of a Good Man" (O'Faolain) **13**:288, 293

"The End of Something" (Hemingway) **1**:208, 234, 244-45

"The End of the Duel" (Borges) **4**:20, 33-4

End of the Game (Cortazar)
See *Final del juego*

"The End of the Old Folks' Home" (Babel) **16**:24

"The End of the Passage" (Kipling)
See "At the End of the Passage"

"The End of the Story" (London) **4**:256

"The End of the Tether" (Conrad) **9**:140-41, 143, 145

"The End of the World" (Turgenev) **7**:335

The End of the World, and Other Stories (Gallant) **5**:130

"The End of Wisdom" (Chesterton) **1**:140

"L'endormeuse" (Maupassant) **1**:284

"The Enduring Chill" (O'Connor) **1**:342-43, 356, 365

"An Enduring Friendship" (O'Faolain) **13**:297

"Enemies" (Chekhov) **2**:158

"Enemies" (Gordimer) **17**:153, 187

"The Enemies" (Gordon) **15**:119

"The Enemies" (Thomas) **3**:407-09

"The Enemies to Each Other" (Kipling) **5**:283

"En famille" (Maupassant) **1**:259-60, 263, 272, 274, 278

"L'enfant malade" (Colette) **10**:274-76

"Engineer-Private Paul Klee Misplaces an Aircraft between Milbertschofen and Cambrai, March 1916" (Barthelme) **2**:49, 54

"England, My England" (Lawrence) **4**:212-13, 229, 231-32, 235

England, My England, and Other Stories (Lawrence) **4**:202, 230-31, 233-37

"England versus England" (Lessing) **6**:199, 218

"The English Spanish Girl" (Cervantes)
See "La Española inglesa"

"English Writers on America" (Irving) **2**:244, 254

"L'enlèvement de la rédoute" ("The Taking of the Redoubt") (Merimee) **7**:278, 280-81, 283, 287-89

"The Enlightenments of Pagett, M. P." (Kipling) **5**:261

Enormous Changes at the Last Minute (Paley) **8**:391-92, 397, 407-08, 410-11, 415

"The Enormous Radio" (Cheever) **1**:106, 109

The Enormous Radio, and Other Stories (Cheever) **1**:89, 92, 95, 98-100

"Enough" (Turgenev) **7**:323, 325, 336

Enough (Beckett)
See *Assez*

"Enragée" (Maupassant) **1**:274

"Enter a Dragoon" (Hardy) **2**:215

"Enter Mitchell" (Lawson) **18**:215

"Enter the Fanatic" (Ellison) **14**:103

"The Entomologist" (Cable) **4**:50

L'entrada en guerra (*Adam, One Afternoon, and Other Stories*) (Calvino) **3**:97, 116

L'entrave (*The Shackle*) (Colette) **10**:257, 272

"Entrevue à Solesmes" (Villiers de l'Isle Adam) **14**:386, 396

"Entropy" (Pynchon) **14**:308, 312-13, 316-17, 319-22, 324, 330, 334, 339-44, 347-49

L'envers du music-hall (Colette) **10**:291

"En voyage" (Maupassant) **1**:280

"Envy: or, Yiddish in America" (Ozick) **15**:297-301, 304, 309, 312, 314, 316, 321

"En wagon" (Maupassant) **1**:263

"EPICAC" (Vonnegut) **8**:429

"Epilogue: The Photographer" (Munro) **3**:332, 338, 340, 343

"Les epingles" (Maupassant) **1**:263, 286

"Episode" (Maugham) **8**:380

"Episode in the Life of an Ancestor" (Boyle) **5**:54, 70

"An Episode of Cathedral History" (James) **16**:226, 229-30, 232, 240, 244, 246, 248, 252, 255

"An Episode of War" (Crane) **7**:104, 109-10

"Epitaph" (O'Brien) **10**:345, 347

"Eric Hermannson's Soul" (Cather) **2**:96, 100-01, 105, 107

"The Erl-King" (Carter) **13**:9, 27-28

"Ermolai and the Miller's Wife" (Turgenev)
See "Yermolai and the Miller's Wife"

"Ernst in Civilian Clothes" (Gallant) **5**:133, 138

"Eros Rampant" (Updike) **13**:387

"Errand" (Carver) **8**:43

"Error" (Singer) **3**:377

"An Error in Chemistry" (Faulkner) **1**:179

"Esarhaddon, King of Assyria" (Tolstoy) **9**:380, 388

"The Escape" (Mansfield) **9**:293

The Escaped Cock (Lawrence)
See *The Man Who Died*

"Escapement" (Ballard) **1**:68

"La escritura del Dios" ("The God's Script") (Borges) **4**:7, 23, 28-9

"La escuela de noche" ("The School by Night") (Cortazar) **7**:91

"Eskimo" (Munro) **3**:347

"Esmé" (Saki) **12**:305, 330-33

"La Española inglesa" ("The English Spanish Girl") (Cervantes) **12**:3-5, 7-8, 14-16, 18, 35, 44

El espejo de la muerte (Unamuno) **11**:312

"La espera" ("The Waiting") (Borges) **4**:5, 16, 37-9

"Esse est percipi" (Bioy Casares) **17**:75

The Essential Ellison: A 25-Year Retrospective (Ellison) **14**:136, 143-47

"Estación de la mano" ("Season of the Hand") (Cortazar) **7**:94

"Esther" (Toomer) **1**:445, 450-51, 457, 459

"Esther Kreindel the Second" (Singer) **3**:363

"Eterna" (Lavin) **4**:184, 189

The Eternal Husband (Dostoevsky)
See *Vechny muzh*

The Eternal Smile and Other Stories (Lagerkvist) **12**:180-88, 192, 195, 197-98

"The Eternity of Forms" (London) **4**:255-56, 295

"Ethan Brand" (Hawthorne) **3**:159, 179-80, 182

Ethan Frome (Wharton) **6**:415-17, 419, 422, 438-39

"The Ethics of Pig" (Henry) **5**:166

"L'etonnant couple moutonnet" (Villiers de l'Isle Adam) **14**:384

"L'etranger" ("The Stranger") (Baudelaire) **18**:4-5, 8, 59, 64

"Etude de femme" (Balzac) **5**:31

Etudes analytiques (*Analytical Studies*) (Balzac) **5**:8-9, 31

Études de moeurs au XIXe siècle (Balzac) **5**:3

Etudes philosophiques (*Philosophic Studies*) (Balzac) **5**:8-9, 12, 31, 48

"Eugénie Grandet" (Barthelme) **2**:40

"Euphrasie" (Chopin) **8**:69-70

"Eva está dentro de su gato" ("Eva Inside Her Cat") (Garcia Marquez) **8**:154-55

"Eva Inside Her Cat" (Garcia Marquez)
See "Eva está dentro de su gato"

"Evangel in Cyrene" (Garland) **18**:163

"Eveline" (Joyce) **3**:205, 226, 231, 234, 247-48

"Evening" (Babel) **16**:27-8, 50, 52-3, 54, 56

"Evening at Home" (Boyle) **5**:63-4

"The Evening's at Seven" (Thurber) **1**:417, 425

"An Evening's Entertainment" (James) **16**:231, 234, 237

Evenings on a Farm near Dikanka (Gogol)
See *Vechera ná khutore bliz Dikanki*

"Evening Twilight" (Baudelaire)
See "Le crépuscule du soir"

"An Evening with Dr. Faust" (Hesse) **9**:230, 236

"Events of That Easter" (Cheever) **1**:93

Eventyr, fortalte for bøorn (*Fairy Tales*; *New Stories*; *Stories*; *Stories Told for Children*; *Wonder Stories Told for Children*; *Wonder Tales*; *Wonder Tales for Children*) (Andersen) **6**:8, 12, 15, 22, 30

"Everybody Was Very Nice" (Benet) **10**:142, 144, 153

"An Every-Day Girl" (Jewett) **6**:156-59

"Everyday Use" (Walker) **5**:402-03, 406, 416-17

"Everything I Know" (Lish) **18**:284

"Everything in Its Right Place" (Andersen) **6**:4, 22-3

"Everything Stuck to Him" (Carver)
See "Distance"

"Everything That Rises Must Converge" (O'Connor) **1**:341, 363

Everything That Rises Must Converge (O'Connor) **1**:341-43

"Eve's Diary" (Twain) **6**:295

"The Eviction" (O'Flaherty) **6**:277, 280

Det eviga leendet (Lagerkvist) **12**:180-8, 192, 195, 197-8

"Evil Allures, but Good Endures" (Tolstoy) **9**:388

"The Evil Angel" (Lagerkvist)
See "Den onda ängeln"

"The Evil Guest" (Le Fanu) **14**:221, 247

Evil Sagas (Lagerkvist)
See *Onda sagor*

"The Evils of Spain" (Pritchett) **14**:270, 285

Evil Tales (Lagerkvist)
See *Onda sagor*

"Excellent People" (Chekhov) **2**:155

"The Executor" (Spark) **10**:362, 366, 368, 370

Exemplary Novels (Cervantes) **12**:5-8, 19-29, 33
See *Novelas exemplares*

Exemplary Stories (Cervantes)
See *Novelas exemplares*

Exemplary Tales (Cervantes)
See *Novelas exemplares*

Exile and the Kingdom (Camus)
See *L'éxil et le royaume*

"Exile of Eons" (Clarke) **3**:144

L'éxil et le royaume (*Exile and the Kingdom*) (Camus) **9**:103-05, 108-11, 118, 122, 125-26, 131, 134

"An Exorcism" (Malamud) **15**:180, 183, 193-94

"The Expansion of the Universe" (Gilchrist) **14**:157

"Expedition to Earth" (Clarke) **3**:150

Expedition to Earth (Clarke) **3**:124, 135, 149-50

"The Expelled" (Beckett)
See "L'Expulsé"

"Experience" (Suckow) **18**:417

"Les expériences du Docteur Crookes" (Villiers de l'Isle Adam) **14**:396

"The Experiment" (James) **16**:251

"The Experimental World" (Lagerkvist) **12**:195

"Experiment in Luxury" (Crane) **7**:136, 138

"An Experiment in Misery" (Crane) **7**:102, 108-09, 129, 136, 138, 145

"The Explanation" (Barthelme) **2**:35, 40-1, 55

The Exploits of Brigadier Gerard (Doyle) **12**:81-2

"L'Expulsé" ("The Expelled") (Beckett) **16**:66, 71, 73-4, 87-8, 90-1

Extracts from Captain Stormfield's Visit to Heaven (Twain) **6**:295, 303, 339

"The Extraordinary Adventures of a Doctor" (Bulgakov) **18**:92

"Extraordinary Little Cough" (Thomas) **3**:394, 403, 406, 411-12

"Extreme Magic" (Calisher) **15**:4-5

Extreme Magic (Calisher) **15**:4-5, 23-7

Extreme Magic: A Novella and Other Stories (Calisher) **15**:

"Extricating Young Gussie" (Wodehouse) **2**:342

"The Eye" (Bowles) **3**:75, 80

"The Eye" (Powers) **4**:368

"The Eye Altering" (Le Guin) **12**:231, 238

"The Eye of Allah" (Kipling) **5**:283, 285

"The Eye of Apollo" (Chesterton) **1**:121, 136

The Eye of the Heron (Le Guin) **12**:231, 235

"Eye of the Lynx" (Ligotti) **16**:269-70

"The Eyes" (Wharton) **6**:424, 426, 428, 430, 433

"The Eye's Journey" (Nin) **10**:303, 305

Eyes of a Blue Dog (Garcia Marquez) **8**:182

"The Eyes of the Panther" (Bierce) **9**:87

"The Eyes of the Poor" (Baudelaire)
See "Les yeux des pauvres"

"Eye-Witness" (Oates) **6**:251-52

"A Fable" (Lavin) **4**:183

Fables for Our Time and Famous Poems Illustrated (Thurber) **1**:415, 417, 422, 424, 426-27

"The Face" (de la Mare) **14**:79, 82, 84, 86, 89

"A Face from Atlantis" (Gordimer) **17**:152-53

"The Face in the Target" (Chesterton) **1**:122

"The Face of Helene Bournow" (Ellison) **14**:118

"The Faces of the Medal" (Cortazar) **7**:63

Face to Face (Gordimer) **17**:157, 165

Facino Cane (Balzac) **5**:26, 31, 33

"The Facts in the Case of M. Valdemar" (Poe) **1**:379, 385, 400

"The Facts of Life" (Maugham) **8**:380

"The Fad of the Fisherman" (Chesterton) **1**:122

"The Failure of David Berry" (Jewett) **6**:151

"A Faint Heart" ("A Weak Heart") (Dostoevsky) **2**:170-72, 191-92, 195

"The Fair at Sorotchintsy" (Gogol)
See "Soročinskaja jamarka"

"A Fair Exile" (Garland) **18**:182-83

"The Fairy Goose" (O'Flaherty) **6**:261-62, 269-70, 272, 275, 281, 285

"Fairy-Kist" (Kipling) **5**:284

"Fairy Tale" (Chesterton) **1**:136

Fairy Tales (Andersen)
See *Eventyr, fortalte for bøorn*

"Faith" (Hammett) **17**:217

"The Faith Cure Man" (Dunbar) **8**:122, 128-29

"Faithfulness" (Nin) **10**:306

"Faith, Hope, and Charity" (McGahern) **17**:299, 309, 317

"Faith in a Tree" (Paley) **8**:408

"Faith in the Afternoon" (Paley) **8**:392, 398, 406, 408

"The Faithless Wife" (O'Faolain) **13**:296

"The Faith of Men" (London) **4**:258-59, 282, 285, 287

"Faldum" (Hesse) **9**:235

"Falk" (Conrad) **9**:143, 147, 151-52

"The Fall" (Pritchett) **14**:286, 298

"Fallen" (Mann)
See "Gefallen"

"The Fallguy's Faith" (Coover) **15**:47

"The Falling Dog" (Barthelme) **2**:55

"Falling in Love in Ashton, British Columbia" (Oates) **6**:230

"Falling Rocks, Narrowing Road, Cul-de-sac, Stop" (O'Faolain) **13**:296

"The Falling Sleet" (Dostoevsky) **2**:165

"The Fall of Edward Barnard" (Maugham) **8**:370

"The Fall of Joseph Timmins" (O'Flaherty) **6**:262

"The Fall of the House of Usher" (Poe) **1**:377, 379-80, 383, 385-86, 391, 398-99, 403-07

"The Fall River Axe Murders" (Carter) **13**:14-18, 20

"The False Collar" (Andersen) **6**:7

"False Dawn" (Kipling) **5**:261

False Dawn (The 'Forties) (Wharton) 6:439-40

"False-Dmitry Lunacharsky" (Bulgakov) **18**:89

"Fame" (Walker) **5**:412

"The Familiar" ("The Watcher") (Le Fanu) **14**:221, 223-26, 228, 233-36, 238-41, 247-48, 250

"A Family Affair" (Chopin) **8**:84, 86

"The Family de Cats" (Dinesen) **7**:177

"Family Evening" (O'Hara) **15**:290

"A Family Feud" (Dunbar) **8**:120-21, 131, 140, 148

Family Happiness (Tolstoy)
See *Semeinoe schaste*

"Family in the Wind" (Fitzgerald) **6**:47, 60, 62

"A Family Man" (Pritchett) **14**:299

A Family Party (O'Hara) **15**:292-93

"Family Vitriol" (Zoshchenko) **15**:388

"The Famous Gilson Bequest" (Bierce) **9**:87-8

"The Fanatic" (O'Flaherty) **6**:276, 288

A Fanatic Heart: Selected Stories of Edna O'Brien (O'Brien) **10**:340-41

"Fancy Flights" (Beattie) **11**:21, 28

"Fancy's Show-Box" (Hawthorne) **3**:160, 190-91

"The Fancy Woman" (Taylor) **10**:374-77, 386, 389, 398, 400, 406-07, 415

La Fanfarlo (Baudelaire) **18**:9, 11-14, 19-27, 37, 54

"Fanny and Annie" (Lawrence) **4**:232, 234-35

The Fantasies of Harlan Ellison (Ellison) **14**:143-47

Fantasiestüeke in Callots Manier (Hoffmann) **13**:186, 203, 217

Fantastic Fables (Bierce) **9**:59, 75

Fantomas against the Multinational Vampires (Cortazar)
See *Fantomas contra los vampiros multinacionales*

Fantomas contra los vampiros multinacionales (*Fantomas against the Multinational Vampires*) (Cortazar) **7**:60

Far Away from Anywhere Else (Le Guin)
See *Very Far Away from Anywhere Else*

"Faraway Image" (Cortazar)
See "Lejana"

"A Far-Away Melody" (Freeman) **1**:191

"Farce Normande" (Maupassant) **1**:272

"The Far Distant Journey" (Bates) **10**:121

"Farewell" (Barthelme) **2**:51

"Farewell" (Powers) **4**:381

"Farewell! Farewell! Farewell!" (Aiken) **9**:4, 12, 14

"The Farewell Murder" (Hammett) **17**:220, 230-31

"Farewell to Earth" (Clarke) **3**:128

"The Fascination of the Pool" (Woolf) **7**:408, 410-12

"The Fast" (Singer) **3**:355, 361

"Fast Lanes" (Phillips) **16**:335-37

Fast Lanes (Phillips) **16**:332-39

"Fat" (Carver) **8**:3, 29, 42-3, 54

"The Fatal Eggs" (Bulgakov)
See "Rokovye iaitsa"

"The Fate of the Freiherr von Leisenbohg" (Schnitzler)
See "Das schicksal des Freiherr von Leisenbohg"

"The Fat Girl" (Dubus) **15**:74, 77, 80, 94

"The Father" (Babel) **16**:48-9

"The Father" (Carver) **8**:9, 18, 50-1, 55

"The Father" (O'Hara) **15**:290-91

"Father Alexey's Story" (Turgenev)
See "Rasskaz ottsa Aleksaya"

"Father and I" (Lagerkvist) **12**:179, 192, 196-97

"Father and Mother" (Kawabata)
See "Chichi Haha"

"Father and Son" (Hughes) **6**:109, 119, 121-22, 141-42

"Fathers and Sons" (Hemingway) **1**:212, 216, 230, 240-42

"The Fathers' Daughters" (Spark) **10**:361, 366

Father Sergius (Tolstoy) **9**:377-78, 397

"Father's Last Escape" (Schulz)
See "Ostatnia ucieczka ojca"

"A Father's Story" (Dubus) **15**:76, 87, 93, 98-9

"A Father-to-Be" (Bellow) **14**:3, 22-3, 25, 27, 30-1

"Fatimas and Kisses" (O'Hara) **15**:279, 283

"La fausse monnaie" ("The Counterfeit Coin") (Baudelaire) **18**:35, 39-40, 60

Faust (Turgenev) **7**:320, 323-25, 328, 334-35, 337

"The Favourite" (O'Brien) **10**:330, 332

"Fear: Four Examples" (Lish) **18**:266, 268

"The Fear of Nice" (Nin) **10**:306

"The Fear That Walks by Noonday" (Cather) **2**:100

"The Feast of Crispian" (Ballard) **1**:72

"The Feast of Nemesis" (Saki) **12**:296, 299

"Feathers" (Carver) **8**:24, 31-2, 34-5, 44

"Feathertop" (Hawthorne) **3**:158, 179

"Federigo" (Merimee) **7**:283, 287, 289, 299-300

"Fedora" (Chopin) **8**:87, 100

"Fedor Kuzmich" (Tolstoy) **9**:389

"Feed My Lambs" (O'Faolain) **13**:291, 312

"Fellow-Townsmen" (Hardy) **2**:202-03, 207, 215-16, 228-31

La femme abandonnée (Balzac) **5**:8, 31

"La femme adultère" ("The Adulterous Woman") (Camus) **9**:103, 105, 108-110, 114-16, 119, 126-28,

La femme cachée (Colette) **10**:274-76

"La femme de Paul" (Maupassant) **1**:259, 261

"La femme sauvage et la petite-maîtresse" (Baudelaire) **18**:33

"La femme vertueuse" (Balzac) **5**:4, 29

"Les fenêtres" (Baudelaire) **18**:6, 9

"Die Fermate" (Hoffmann) **13**:183

"Le fermier" (Maupassant) **1**:274, 285

"Fern" (Toomer) **1**:441, 444, 457-58, 460

"Ferragus" (Balzac) **5**:43-6

"The Ferry of Unfulfillment" (Henry) **5**:158, 186

"The Ferry; or, Another Trip to Venice" (Cortazar) **7**:63

le Festin de Pierre (Moliere)
See *le Festin de Pierre*

"The Festival" (Lovecraft) **3**:263, 269, 274, 292, 294-95

"Festival with Syphilis" (Bulgakov) **18**:90

"Fever" (Carver) **8**:26-8, 30, 33-4, 40

"Fever Flower" (Grau) **15**:152, 156, 159

"A Few Crusted Characters" (Hardy) **2**:206, 209, 214-15, 217, 219-20

"A Few Trips and Some Poetry" (O'Hara) **15**:286

Fiabe Italiene (*Italian Folktales*) (Calvino) **3**:105, 119

"An Fiach" (O'Flaherty) **6**:287

Ficciones, 1935-1944 (*Fictions*) (Borges) **4**:15-16, 18-20, 41

"La ficelle" ("A Piece of String") (Maupassant) **1**:259, 262, 284, 286, 288

Fictions (Borges)
See *Ficciones, 1935-1944*

"The Fiddler" (Melville) **1**:304; **17**:361, 363

"The Fiddler of the Reels" (Hardy) **2**:216-22, 224-25

"The Field Devil" (Hesse) **9**:231, 235

"Field of Flowers" (Aiken) **9**:5, 12-13

"A Field of Snow on a Slope of the Rosenberg" (Davenport) **16**:174, 176, 180-82, 195, 198

"The Field of Vision" (Le Guin) **12**:233

"La fiesta del Monstruo" (Bioy Casares) **17**:48, 50-2

"The Fifth Quarter" (King) **17**:295

"Fifty Dollars" (Elkin) **12**:103

"Fifty Grand" (Hemingway) **1**:209, 211, 218, 232, 234-35, 248

"Fifty-Seven Views of Fujiyama" (Davenport) **16**:184-85, 188

Fifty Stories (Boyle) **5**:65

"The Fight" (Anderson) **1**:31, 50

"The Fight" (O'Flaherty) **6**:269

"The Fight" (Thomas) **3**:402, 406, 411-12

"The Fig Tree" (Porter) **4**:340, 352-53

"The Fig Tree" (Pritchett) **14**:263

"The Figure in the Carpet" (James) **8**:265, 280, 299, 301-02, 304, 306-07

"Filboid Studge, The Story of a Mouse that Helped" (Saki) **12**:288, 300

Files on Parade (O'Hara) **15**:264-65

La fille aux yeux d'ors (Balzac) **5**:44, 46-7

"Les filles de Milton" ("Les trois filles de Milton") (Villiers de l'Isle Adam) **14**:387, 390

Les filles du feu (Nerval) **18**:336, 362-64, 379

"Filmer" (Wells) **6**:403, 406

"Un fils" (Maupassant) **1**:275

"Filthy with Things" (Boyle) **16**:156-57

"La Fin" ("The End") (Beckett) **16**:72-5, 87-91

"El fin" ("The End") (Borges) **4**:10

Final del juego (*End of the Game*) (Cortazar) **7**:50-1, 53, 62-3, 69-70, 79

"A Final Note on Chanda Bell" (Thurber) **1**:421

"The Final Problem" (Doyle) **12**:57, 60

"Final Trophy" (Ellison) **14**:127

"A Financial Failure" (Jewett) **6**:158

"The Find" (Gordimer) **17**:184, 187

La fin de Chéri (*The Last of Chéri*) (Colette) **10**:255, 257, 260-61, 264, 267-68, 270-71, 285-87

"Finding a Girl in America" (Dubus) **15**:76, 87, 93, 98-9

Finding a Girl in America (Dubus) **15**:74, 78, 81

"The Finding of Martha" (Dunbar) **8**:122

"The Finding of Zach" (Dunbar) **8**:122, 128, 147

"Fine Accommodations" (Hughes) **6**:131, 133

"A Fine Beginning" (Thomas) **3**:403

The Finer Grain (James) **8**:276, 302

"The Finest Diner in the World" (Villiers de l'Isle Adam)
  See "Le plus beau dîner du monde"
Finest Short Stories of Seán O'Faoláin (The Stories of Seán O'Faoláin) (O'Faolain) **13**:292, 297, 308
"The Finest Story in the World" (Kipling) **5**:273, 280
"Fingal" (Beckett) **16**:93
"Fingers and Toes" (Michaels) **16**:302, 311
"Finis" (London) **4**:256
"The Finish of Patsy Barnes" (Dunbar) **8**:122, 125, 128, 137
"Finn" (Michaels) **16**:302-03
"Fire and Cloud" (Wright) **2**:361, 363, 365, 368, 371, 373, 375, 379-81, 383-84, 387
"The Fire and the Hearth" (Faulkner) **1**:182
"The Fireman's Death" (O'Flaherty) **6**:284
"Fire of the Khans" (Bulgakov) **18**:92, 98
Fires: Essays, Poems, Stories, 1966-1982 (Carver) **8**:18, 30, 32, 40-1, 45, 50, 57-60
"The Fires Within" (Clarke) **3**:125, 129, 135, 143, 149
Fireworks: Nine Profane Pieces (Carter) **13**:2-3, 8-9, 14
"Fire Worship" (Hawthorne) **3**:182
"First Blood" (Fitzgerald) **6**:50
"First Breech" (Bulgakov) **18**:86
"The First-Class Passenger" (Chekhov) **2**:130
"First Confession" (O'Connor) **5**:364, 366, 386, 389
"The First Countess of Wessex" (Hardy) **2**:204, 208-09
"First Encounter" (Clarke) **3**:128
"A First Family of Tasajara" (Harte) **8**:216, 218
The First Forty-Nine Stories (Hemingway) **1**:230, 240
"First Love" (Babel) **16**:9, 17, 36, 41, 59
"First Love" (Nabokov) **11**:108, 128
"First Love" (Welty) **1**:467-69, 482
First Love (Beckett)
  See *Premier amour*
First Love (Turgenev)
  See *Pervaya lyubov'*
"First Manhattans" (Gilchrist) **14**:157, 159
"The First Monday in Lent" (Bunin)
  See "Chistyi ponedel'nik"
"The First of April" (Barnes) **3**:13
"The First Poet" (London) **4**:256
"The First Report of the Shipwrecked Foreigner to the Kadanh of Derb" (Le Guin) **12**:231, 241
"The First Seven Years" (Malamud) **15**:168, 189, 212, 221
"First Sorrow" (Kafka) **5**:239
"The First Sunday in June" (Jewett) **6**:159
"The First Year of My Life" (Spark) **10**:364, 366, 368
"The Fir-Tree" ("The Little Fir Tree") (Andersen) **6**:6, 14, 18, 30, 40
"The Fisherman and His Soul" (Wilde) **11**:365, 369, 371, 376, 383-84, 386-87, 394-99, 407-09
"Fish for Friday" (O'Connor) **5**:369
"Fish Story" (Lish) **18**:280-82
"The Fish Supper" (Aiken) **9**:14
"Fishy" (Pritchett) **14**:269
"Fits" (Munro) **3**:347
"The Five-Forty-Eight" (Cheever) **1**:100
"Five Intimate Interviews" (Levi) **12**:275

"The Five Orange Pips" (Doyle) **12**:66, 68, 70, 72-4
"Five Peas from One Pod" (Andersen) **6**:35
"The Five White Mice" (Crane) **7**:104, 106, 126, 150
Fizzles (Beckett)
  See *Foirades*
"The Flag" (Bates) **10**:116
"The Flame" (Bates) **10**:139
"Flanagan and His Short Filibustering Adventure" (Crane) **7**:100-01, 151
Flappers and Philosophers (Fitzgerald) **6**:45-6, 56-8
"The Flats Road" (Munro) **3**:331-32
"Flavia and Her Artists" (Cather) **2**:98, 103
"Flavours of Exile" (Lessing) **6**:191, 211
"The Flax" (Andersen) **6**:7
La fleur de l'age (Colette) **10**:274, 276
"Les fleurs" (Ligotti) **16**:269, 277, 288
"Fleurs de ténèbres" ("Flowers of Darkness") (Villiers de l'Isle Adam) **14**:395-96
"Flight" (Grau) **15**:163
"Flight" (O'Hara) **15**:279, 285
"Flight" (Steinbeck) **11**:207-09, 225, 229, 231-34, 236-37, 244
"Flight" (Updike) **13**:367, 370, 384, 388, 392-95
"Flight and Pursuit" (Fitzgerald) **6**:56
Flight into Darkness (Schnitzler)
  See *Flucht in die Finsternis*
"The Flight of Pigeons from the Palace" (Barthelme) **2**:37, 40, 55-6
"The Flight of the Israelites" (Ballard) **1**:72
"The Fling" (Carver) **8**:4, 34
"Flip, a California Romance" (Harte) **8**:253, 255
"The Flip of a Coin" (Maugham) **8**:376-77
"The Floating Truth" (Paley) **8**:399
"The Flood" (Anderson) **1**:51
"Una flor amarilla" ("A Yellow Flower") (Cortazar) **7**:52
"Florence Green is 81" (Barthelme) **2**:27
"The Flower Garden" (Jackson) **9**:249, 252
"Flowering Judas" (Porter) **4**:329, 339-40, 342, 344, 346, 349-51, 356
Flowering Judas, and Other Stories (Porter) **4**:326-28, 347, 351, 354, 365
"The Flowering of the Strange Orchid" (Wells) **6**:361, 365, 394-96, 404
"The Flowers" (Walker) **5**:402
"Flowers for Marjorie" (Welty) **1**:466, 487-88
"Flowers of Darkness" (Villiers de l'Isle Adam)
  See "Fleurs de ténèbres"
"Flowers of the Abyss" (Ligotti) **16**:282, 284
Flucht in die Finsternis (*Flight into Darkness*) (Schnitzler) **15**:344, 368, 370, 378, 381, 383-84
"Flute Dream" (Hesse) **9**:234
"The Flute Player" (O'Flaherty) **6**:281
"The Fly" (Mansfield) **9**:282-84, 307, 312-13
"Fly Away Ladybird" (Aiken) **9**:13-14
"The Flying Dutchman" (Bulgakov) **18**:90
"The Flying Man" (Wells) **6**:397-98
"The Flying Stars" (Chesterton) **1**:119, 127, 129
"A Flying Start" (Gallant) **5**:147
"The Flying Trunk" (Andersen) **6**:7, 30
"The Fly in the Ointment" (Pritchett) **14**:271, 298

"Fly Paper" (Hammett) **17**:202, 215-16, 220, 222
"The Fog Man" (Boyle) **16**:157
Foirades (*Fizzles; For to end yet again and Other Fizzles; Pour finir encour et Autres Foirades*) (Beckett) **16**:100, 123-28
Folks from Dixie (Dunbar) **8**:118-21, 123, 127-29, 131, 140-41, 143, 145-46
"Foma, the Wolf" (Turgenev) **7**:316
"The Food of the Gods" (Clarke) **3**:133-34
"Fool about a Horse" (Faulkner) **1**:177
"The Foolish Butterfly" (O'Flaherty) **6**:264, 278-79
"Foothold" (Bowen) **3**:40, 44
The Foot Journey to Amager (Andersen) **6**:4
"Footprints in the Jungle" (Maugham) **8**:359, 361, 374-75
"Footsteps in the Footprints" (Cortazar) **7**:63
"For a Good Purpose" (Levi) **12**:278
"For a Place in the Sun" (Grau) **15**:155
"The Forbidden Buzzards" (Saki) **12**:315, 326
"Force Majeure" (Levi) **12**:274-75, 277
"The Force of Blood" (Cervantes)
  See "La fuerza de la sangre"
"The Force of Circumstance" (Maugham) **8**:372, 375
"For Conscience' Sake" (Hardy) **2**:207, 212, 214-15, 220
"For Dear Life" (Gordimer) **17**:192
"Foreign Affairs" (O'Faolain) **13**:322
Foreign Affairs, and Other Stories (O'Faolain) **13**:296, 308, 313-14
"The Foreigner" (Jewett) **6**:156, 174-76
"The Foreign Policy of Company 99" (Henry) **5**:197
"For Esmé--with Love and Squalor" (Salinger) **2**:289, 293-97, 299-300, 303-05, 314, 316-18
"The Forest" (Le Guin) **12**:213, 216, 247-48
"The Forest of the South" (Gordon) **15**:105, 107, 118
The Forest of the South (Gordon) **15**:104, 108, 116, 137
"The Forged Coupon" (Tolstoy) **9**:379
"Forgetting" (O'Brien) **10**:343
"Forging Ahead" (Fitzgerald) **6**:50
"Forgiveness in Families" (Munro) **3**:331
"The Forgotten Enemy" (Clarke) **3**:124
" A Forgotten Poet" (Nabokov) **11**:109-10, 112
"For Jeromé—With Love and Kisses" (Lish) **18**:266-68, 284
"The Forks" (Powers) **4**:374, 382
"La forma de la espada" ("The Shape of the Sword") (Borges) **4**:10, 25, 42
"La forma dello spazio" ("The Form of Space") (Calvino) **3**:92, 109
"For Marse Chouchoute" (Chopin) **8**:89
La formica Argentina ("The Argentine Ant") (Calvino) **3**:91-2, 98, 117
"The Form of Space" (Calvino)
  See "La forma dello spazio"
"For Rupert—With No Promises" (Lish) **18**:267-68, 284
"The Forsaken" (Turgenev) **7**:318-19
"Forschungen eines hundes" ("Investigations of a Dog") (Kafka) **5**:206, 229, 238, 241
"Forsythe and Forsythe" (Gilman) **13**:141
"For the Duration of the War" (Saki) **12**:285, 326
"For to end yet again" (Beckett) **16**:123, 127, 129

For to end yet again and Other Fizzles
(Beckett)
See *Foirades*
"The Fortunes of Sir Robert Ardagh"
("Ardagh") (Le Fanu) **14**:220-21, 223, 239,
247, 251
"The Fortune Teller" (Spark) **10**:367, 370
Forty Stories (Barthelme) **2**:56
"Forty Times Forty" (Bulgakov) **18**:90
"The Foster Portfolio" (Vonnegut) **8**:432, 435
"Le fou et la Vénus" (Baudelaire) **18**:3, 6, 8,
15, 17
"Les foules" ("Crowds") (Baudelaire) **18**:31,
38
"The Found Boat" (Munro) **3**:346
"The Fountains" (Le Guin) **12**:211, 213, 247-
48
The Four-Dimensional Nightmare (Ballard)
1:68
Four Faultless Felons (Chesterton) **1**:126, 132
"The Four Fists" (Fitzgerald) **6**:58
"Four Generations" (Suckow) **18**:395-96,
405-07, 415
"The Four Meetings" (James) **8**:334
The Four Million (Henry) **5**:155, 171-72, 192
Four Past Midnight (King) **17**:280-84
"Four Portraits" (Bulgakov) **18**:74, 92
"The Four Seasons" (Gallant) **5**:130, 135,
137-38
"Four Stories About Lovers" (Beattie) **11**:17
"14 Stories" (Dixon) **16**:208-09, 214
14 Stories (Dixon) **16**:204-05, 207-10, 214-15
"The Fourth Alarm" (Cheever) **1**:101, 110
"The Fourth Day Out from Santa Cruz"
(Bowles) **3**:61-2, 72
"Fourth Version" (Valenzuela)
See "Cuarta versión"
"The Fox" (Lawrence) **4**:197, 203-04, 210-12,
223-26, 229, 231, 235-36
"The Fqih" (Bowles) **3**:68
"The Fragile Age" (Grau) **15**:156
"A Fragment of Stained Glass" (Lawrence)
4:202
"Frail Vessel" (Lavin) **4**:165, 167, 183-84
"The Frame" (Dixon) **16**:205, 207, 211
"Frame-Tale" (Barth) **10**:40, 42, 48, 79, 81,
84-5, 89, 97
"The *Francis Spaight*" (London) **4**:262, 291
"The Franklin Stove" (Dixon) **16**:210, 214-15
"Frank Sinatra or Carleton Carpenter" (Lish)
18:267
"Franny" (Salinger) **2**:291, 293, 297, 302-03,
305
Franny and Zooey (Salinger) **2**:297, 304, 318
Frau Beate und ihr Sohn (*Beatrice*) (Schnitzler)
15:345-46
"Frau Brechenmacher Attends a Wedding"
(Mansfield) **9**:301
"Die Frau des Richters" ("The Judge's Wife")
(Schnitzler) **15**:371
Fräulein Else (Schnitzler) **15**:344-47, 367-69,
375
"Das Fräulein von Scudéri" (Hoffmann)
13:181, 205-06, 209, 220, 225-26
"Free" (O'Hara) **15**:248, 270
"Freedom's a Hard-Bought Thing" (Benet)
10:143, 154, 156
"The Freeholder Ovsyanikov" ("Ovsianko the
Freeholder") (Turgenev) **7**:313, 344
"Free Will and the Commendatore" (Bioy
Casares) **17**:73

"Das Fremde Kind" ("The Strange Child")
(Hoffmann) **13**:192, 194-95, 199-200
"French Harvest" (Boyle) **5**:64
"The Freshest Boy" (Fitzgerald) **6**:49, 58,
80-1, 84-6
"Freud's Room" (Ozick) **15**:318-19
"Freya of the Seven Isles" (Conrad) **9**:142-43,
149
"Friday's Footprint" (Gordimer) **17**:154
Friday's Footprint (Gordimer) **17**:153-54, 165,
168, 184
"The Friend" (Lish) **18**:282
"A Friend and Protector" (Taylor) **10**:382,
418
"Friendly Brook" (Kipling) **5**:275, 279
"A Friend of Kafka" (Singer) **3**:384
A Friend of Kafka, and Other Stories (Singer)
3:370, 373, 375
"A Friend of the Earth" (Thurber) **1**:422,
427
"Friend of the Family" (Boyle) **5**:55
The Friend of the Family (*The Village of
Stepanchikovo*) (Dostoevsky) **2**:164, 172,
175-76
"A Friend of the World" (Bowles) **3**:64, 83
"Friends" (Beattie) **11**:4-5, 7
"The Friends" (Cortazar)
See "Los amigos"
"Friends" (Paley) **8**:409-10
"A Friend's Death" (Dixon) **16**:217
"Friends from Philadelphia" (Updike)
13:350-51, 354
"Friends of the Family" (O'Connor) **5**:371
"The Friends of the Friends" (James) **8**:270,
316
"Froim grach" (Babel) **16**:27
"The Frolic" (Ligotti) **16**:261, 263, 269, 271,
276, 283, 286, 288
"From a Refugee's Notebook" (Ozick)
15:306-07
"From a Window in Vartou" (Andersen) **6**:4
"From Each according to His Ability" (Henry)
5:159
"From the Cabby's Seat" (Henry) **5**:158
"From the Childhood of Saint Francis of
Assisi" (Hesse) **9**:231, 235
"From the Diary of a New York Lady" ("New
York Lady") (Parker) **2**:278, 286
"From the Fifteenth District" (Gallant)
5:136-37
From the Fifteenth District (Gallant) **5**:135-37
"The Frontier" (Bates) **10**:116
"A Froward Child" (de la Mare) **14**:82, 86,
89
"The Frozen Fields" (Bowles) **3**:65-6, 79, 84
"The Fruitful Sleeping of the Rev. Elisha
Edwards" (Dunbar) **8**:122, 127
"The Frying Pan" (O'Connor) **5**:371, 389
"La fuerza de la sangre" ("The Call of Blood";
"The Force of Blood") (Cervantes) **12**:3, 5,
14-16, 18-22, 33, 36-7, 39-40, 44
"Fugue" (O'Faolain) **13**:302-03, 314
"Full Employment" (Levi) **12**:278-79
"The Fullness of Life" (Wharton) **6**:424
"Los funerales de la Mamá Grande" ("Big
Mama's Funeral") (Garcia Marquez)
8:155, 162, 174, 185, 187, 191, 198
Los funerales de la Mamá Grande (*Big Mama's
Funeral*; *The Funeral of Mama Grand*;
Mama Grande's Funeral) (Garcia Marquez)
8:169-70, 183, 185, 187, 189

The Funeral of Mama Grand (Garcia
Marquez)
See *Los funerales de la Mamá Grande*
"Funes el memorioso" ("Funes the
Memorious") (Borges) **4**:19-20, 30
"Funes the Memorious" (Borges)
See "Funes el memorioso"
"Fur" (Saki) **12**:295
"The Fur Coat" (O'Faolain) **13**:288, 314
"The Furious Seasons" (Carver) **8**:5, 50
Furious Seasons, and Other Stories (Carver)
8:4, 30, 32, 34, 46, 50, 57-8
"The Furnished Room" (Henry) **5**:156, 171,
174, 180-81, 184, 187-89
Further Fables for Our Time (Thurber) **1**:426-
28
"The Future, If Any, of Comedy; or, Where
Do We Not-Go from Here?" (Thurber)
1:424
"Gabriel-Ernest" (Saki) **12**:316, 331
The Gadsbys (Kipling)
See *The Story of the Gadsbys*
"A Gala Dress" (Freeman) **1**:196, 201
"Le galant tireur" (Baudelaire) **18**:6, 18, 36-7
"Gale" (Schulz) **13**:335
"La gallina di reparto" (Calvino) **3**:98
"Galway Bay" (O'Flaherty) **6**:265, 269, 282
"Galya Ganskaya" (Bunin) **5**:114
"Gambara" (Balzac) **5**:16, 26
"Gambler's Luck" (Hoffmann)
See "Spielerglück"
"The Gambler, the Nun, and the Radio"
(Hemingway) **1**:218, 234
"The Game" (Barthelme) **2**:40
"The Game of Backgammon" (Merimee)
See "La partie de trictrac"
"Games without End" (Calvino) **3**:109
"Ganymede" (du Maurier) **18**:127, 132, 137
"The Garden" (Bowles) **3**:64, 68, 80
"The Garden at Mons" (Hemingway) **1**:208,
236
"The Gardener" (Kipling) **5**:276, 279, 282-83,
296-97
"The Gardener" (Lavin) **4**:181
"The Gardener and the Family" (Andersen)
6:15
"The Garden Lodge" (Cather) **2**:90, 98, 103
"The Garden of Eden" (Andersen) **6**:30, 37
The Garden of Forking Paths (Borges)
See *El jardín de senderos que se bifurcan*
"Garden of Paradise" (Andersen) **6**:7
"The Garden of the Forking Paths" (Borges)
See "El jardín de senderos que se bifurcan"
"The Garden of Time" (Ballard) **1**:71, 74, 77
"The Garden Party" (Mansfield) **9**:276, 280,
282, 284, 286, 309-11, 313
The Garden Party, and Other Stories
(Mansfield) **9**:275-76, 281
"A Garden Story" (Jewett) **6**:156, 158-59
"Gargantua" (Calisher) **15**:9, 15, 19, 21
A Garland of Love (Bioy Casares)
See *Guirnalda con amores*
"Gaspar Ruiz" (Conrad) **9**:151, 157, 179, 181
Gäst hos verkligheten (*Guest of Reality*)
(Lagerkvist) **12**:180-82, 185, 197
"Le gâteau" (Baudelaire) **18**:8, 18
"Le gâteau" (Maupassant) **1**:274, 286
"The Gate of the Hundred Sorrows" (Kipling)
5:262, 265
"The Gatewood Caper" (Hammett) **17**:220,
222
"Gaudissart" (Balzac)

See "L'illustre Gaudissart"

"The Gauzy Edge of Paradise" (Gilchrist) **14**:153-54

"A Gay Adventure" (Zoshchenko)
See "A Gay Little Episode"

"A Gay Little Episode" ("A Gay Adventure") (Zoshchenko) **15**:395

"Gazebo" (Carver) **8**:14-15, 19-20

"Gedali" (Babel) **16**:8-10, 25, 27-30, 52-3, 55, 57-8

"Gefallen" ("Fallen") (Mann) **5**:319, 323, 351-53

"Gehenna" (Aiken) **9**:10, 12-13, 30

"Das Gelübde" (Hoffmann) **13**:209-11

"Gemcrack" (Phillips) **16**:328

"The General" (O'Hara) **15**:276-77, 285-86

"The Generations of America" (Ballard) **1**:82

"The Generous Lover" (Cervantes)
See "El amante liberal"

"Generous Pieces" (Gilchrist) **14**:150

Geneviéve (Gide) **13**:72, 100-05

"The Genial Epoch" (Schulz) **13**:328
See "The Age of Genius"

"The Genius" (O'Connor) **5**:376

"Gentian" (Freeman) **1**:197

"The Gentle Art" (Gordimer) **17**:161, 184

"The Gentle Boy" (Hawthorne) **3**:164, 167, 181, 185-87

The Gentle Grafter (Henry) **5**:155, 162, 172, 182

"The Gentleman from Cracow" (Singer) **3**:358, 368, 383-84

"The Gentleman from New Orleans" (Chopin) **8**:99

"The Gentleman from San Francisco" (Bunin) **5**:80-3, 85, 87-90, 92, 94-7, 117

The Gentleman from San Francisco (Bunin) **5**:90

"A Gentleman of Bayou Têche" (Chopin) **8**:88, 103

"A Gentleman's Friend" (Chekhov) **2**:137-39

"A Gentle Soul" (Lavin) **4**:165-66, 168

"The Gentry" (O'Hara) **15**:286

"The Geological Spieler" (Lawson) **18**:206, 263

"The Geometry of Love" (Cheever) **1**:97, 101

"George Silverman's Explanation" (Dickens) **17**:124

"George Thurston" (Bierce) **9**:67-9, 76-7

"Georgia's Ruling" (Henry) **5**:162, 164, 170

"The Geranium" (O'Connor) **1**:364

Gerbersau (Hesse) **9**:231

"A German Idyll" (Bates) **10**:113

"The German Refugee" ("The Jewish Refugee") (Malamud) **15**:171, 173-74, 176, 213, 216, 221, 235-36

"A Germ Destroyer" (Kipling) **5**:290

"Gesammelte Erzählungen und Märchen" (Hoffmann) **13**:217

"Get Thee to a Monastery" (Thurber) **1**:429

"Getting Back on Dave Regan" (Lawson) **18**:233-35

"Getting into the Set" (Updike) **13**:402

"Getting Lucky" (Michaels) **16**:309, 316

"Getting off the Altitude" (Lessing) **6**:190, 214

Getting Through (McGahern) **17**:299, 303-04, 306-09, 322-23

"Getzel the Monkey" (Singer) **3**:359

"The Ghost" (Andersen) **6**:30

"The Ghost and the Bone Setter" ("The Bone Setter") (Le Fanu) **14**:216, 219, 221, 239

"A Ghostly Chess Game" (London) **4**:294

"The Ghostly Door" (Lawson) **18**:217

"The Ghost of the Rose" (Kawabata)
See "Bara no Yūrei"

Ghosts (Wharton) **6**:426-27, 430

Ghost Stories and Mysteries (Le Fanu) **14**:237

Ghost Stories and Tales of Mystery (Le Fanu) **14**:217, 220-21

Ghost Stories of an Antiquary (James) **16**:222, 226-27, 229-31, 237-39, 242, 245, 250-51, 255, 258

"The Giant Mole" (Kafka) **5**:206

"The Giant's House" (Benet) **10**:149

"The Giant Wistaria" (Gilman) **13**:128, 130-31, 138-140

"Un giardino incantato" ("An Enchanted Garden") (Calvino) **3**:90, 97, 112

"The Gift" (Steinbeck) **11**:209-10, 212-13, 232-34, 237

"A Gift from the City" (Updike) **13**:353-54

"Gift from the Stars" (Clarke) **3**:128

"The Gift of the Magi" (Henry) **5**:166, 171-72, 181-82, 184-85, 187-88

"The Gift of the Prodigal" (Taylor) **10**:407-08, 418

"Gifts" (Singer) **3**:389

Gigi (Colette) **10**:269-70, 272-74, 293

"Gigolo and Gigolette" (Maugham) **8**:366, 379

"The Gilded Six-Bits" (Hurston) **4**:135-36, 138, 151-52

"Gimpel Tam" ("Gimpel the Fool") (Singer) **3**:352, 355, 363, 365-68, 375, 382-84, 389

Gimpel Tam und andere Dertseylungen (*Gimpel the Fool, and Other Stories*) (Singer) **3**:370

"Gimpel the Fool" (Singer)
See "Gimpel Tam"

Gimpel the Fool, and Other Stories (Singer)
See *Gimpel Tam und andere Dertseylungen*

"The Gingerbread House" (Coover) **15**:33, 38, 41, 48

"The Gioconda of the Twilight Noon" (Ballard) **1**:69

"Girl" (Henry) **5**:163, 182

"The Girl" (Oates) **6**:232

"The Girl and the Habit" (Henry) **5**:158, 164

"The Girl from California" (O'Hara) **15**:281

"The Girl I Left Behind Me" (Spark) **10**:356

"The Girl in the Pink Hat" (Gilman) **13**:126

"A Girl Named Peter" (Bates) **10**:115-16

"A Girl of Modern Tyre" (Garland)
See "A Stop-Over at Tyre"

"The Girl of My Dreams" (Malamud) **15**:217, 239, 240, 242-43

The Girl on the Baggage Truck (O'Hara) **15**:250-51, 271-72

"Girls and the Land" (Gilman) **13**:144

"The Girl Who Had Been Presented" (O'Hara) **15**:263, 266

"The Girl Who Trod on the Loaf" (Andersen) **6**:13

"The Girl with the Cannon Dresses" (Jewett) **6**:157

"The Girl with the Flaxen Hair" (Grau) **15**:147, 150, 158, 165

"The Girl with the Silver Eyes" (Hammett) **17**:219, 221, 228, 230

"The Girl with the Stoop" (Bowen) **3**:54

"Gitanette" (Colette) **10**:292

"La gitanilla" ("The Gypsy Maid") (Cervantes) **12**:3-4, 6-8, 15-18, 21, 23-5, 33-4, 38-40, 44

"Giulia Lazzari" (Maugham) **8**:377

"The Given Case" (James) **8**:316

"Giving Birth" (Atwood) **2**:3-4, 6-10, 12, 14, 16

"Giving Blood" (Updike) **13**:373, 386

G. K. Chesterton: Selected Short Stories (Chesterton) **1**:135

"Glad Ghosts" (Lawrence) **4**:220, 230

"Gladius Dei" (Mann) **5**:310, 323, 329, 331

"Glamour" (Benet) **10**:142, 144, 154

"The Glamour" (Ligotti) **16**:280

"The Glass Mountain" (Barthelme) **2**:34, 40

"The Glass Scholar" (Cervantes)
See "El licienciado vidriera"

"The Glazier's Song" (Baudelaire)
See "La chanson vitrier"

"A Gleam" (Mann) **5**:322-23

"The Gleaner" (Bates) **10**:113, 128

"Gleanings from Snow Country" (Kawabata) **17**:251, 253, 255, 257

Glenda (Cortazar)
See *Queremos tanto a Glenda*

"The Glendale People" (O'Hara) **15**:282-83

"Gloire et malheur" (Balzac) **5**:4, 29

Gloomy People (Chekhov) **2**:146

"Glory in the Daytime" (Parker) **2**:273-74, 280, 283

"The Glory Machine" (Villiers de l'Isle Adam)
See "La machine à gloire"

"Glossolalia" (Barth) **10**:42-3, 45, 47, 54-5, 80, 90, 94-5, 97-8

"Gluck" (Hoffmann) **13**:225

"The Gnats" (Pritchett) **14**:299

"A Goatherd at Luncheon" (Calvino) **3**:116

"The Go-Away Bird" (Spark) **10**:350-56, 358-59, 361, 366, 368, 370

The Go-Away Bird, and Other Stories (Spark) **10**:350-53

"Go Back to Your Precious Wife and Son" (Vonnegut) **8**:436

"The Goblin at the Grocer's" ("The Pixy and the Grocer") (Andersen) **6**:30, 34, 41

"Gobseck" (Balzac) **5**:18, 22, 24, 28, 31, 33

"The Goddess" (Oates) **6**:231

The Goddess and Other Women (Oates) **6**:231, 243

"Godliness" (Anderson) **1**:18, 42, 57

"Godman's Master" (Laurence) **7**:245-46, 249-50, 252-53, 261, 263

"The Godmother" (Chopin) **8**:100

"The God of His Fathers" (London) **4**:258, 286-87

The God of His Fathers (London) **4**:264, 282, 285-87

"The God of the Gongs" (Chesterton) **1**:127

"Go Down, Moses" (Faulkner) **1**:148, 154, 165-67, 173, 180-83

"God Rest You Merry, Gentlemen" (Hemingway) **1**:216

"God Sees the Truth but Waits" (Tolstoy) **9**:382, 386-87

"God's Little Traveling Salesman" (Lagerkvist) **12**:196

"The Godson" (Tolstoy) **9**:388

"God's Ravens" (Garland) **18**:154, 160, 163

"The God's Script" (Borges)
See "La escritura del Dios"

"God's Wrath" (Malamud) **15**:217

"The Go-Getter" (Wodehouse) **2**:346

"The Going Away of Liza" (Chopin) **8**:71

"Going Blind" (Lawson) **18**:200, 202, 213

"Going into Exile" (O'Flaherty) **6**:261, 269, 276-77, 281-82, 284

"Going Places" (Michaels) **16**:302-03, 311-13

Going Places (Michaels) **16**:301-03, 306-08, 310, 314-16, 322

"Going to Meet the Man" (Baldwin) **10**:3, 5, 7, 10, 17-18, 20

Going to Meet the Man (Baldwin) **10**:2, 4, 6, 8-9, 12, 17

"Going to Naples" (Welty) **1**:476, 484

"Going Under" (Dubus) **15**:82, 87, 89-90

"Gold" (Levi) **12**:256, 258

"The Gold Bug" (Poe) **1**:378, 390

"The Gold Dress" (Benet) **10**:160

"The Golden Age" (Cheever) **1**:106

"The Golden Apples" (Welty) **1**:473-74, 479, 483-85, 492, 494, 497

"The Golden Bessie" (Benet) **10**:144, 146

"Golden Documents" (Bulgakov) **18**:91

"Der goldene Topf" (*The Golden Pot: Fairy Tale of Our Times*) (Hoffmann) **13**:186, 189, 192-95, 197, 199-205, 208, 215, 218-19, 223, 226

"Golden Gate" (Hughes) **6**:138

"The Golden Graveyard" (Lawson) **18**:239

"The Golden Horseshoe" (Hammett) **17**:200, 210, 219, 222-23, 225

"Golden Land" (Faulkner) **1**:167

The Golden Oriole (Bates) **10**:123-24

The Golden Pot: Fairy Tale of Our Times (Hoffmann)
See "Der goldene Topf"

"The Golden Town" (Bulgakov) **18**:90

"Golden Wedding" (Suckow) **18**:389, 396, 398-99, 412

"The Goldfish" (Pritchett) **14**:297

"Gold Is Not Always" (Faulkner) **1**:177

"A Gold Slipper" (Cather) **2**:91

"The Gold That Glittered" (Henry) **5**:188

"The Gold Watch" (McGahern) **17**:304, 309-10, 315, 317, 320-21, 323-24

"Gone Away" (Bowen) **3**:53

"The Gonzaga Manuscripts" (Bellow) **14**:3, 22-3, 25

"Goodbye and Good Luck" (Paley) **8**:388, 391, 394, 396, 398

"Goodbye, My Brother" (Cheever) **1**:89, 99, 103-05, 108

"Goodbye to Goodbye" (Dixon) **16**:207

"Good-by, Jack" (London) **4**:269

"Good Climate, Friendly Inhabitants" (Gordimer) **17**:181

"The Good Corn" (Bates) **10**:118

"Good Country People" (O'Connor) **1**:335, 343-45, 350, 356, 359-60

"A 'Good Fellow's' Wife" (Garland) **18**:161

"Good-for-Nothing" ("She Was Good for Nothing"; "She Was No Good") (Andersen) **6**:4, 14, 26, 30

"The Good Girl" (Bowen) **3**:33

"Good Humor" (Andersen) **6**:7

"A Good Job Gone" (Hughes) **6**:109, 121-22, 128, 140, 142

"A Good Location" (O'Hara) **15**:278-79

"A Goodly Life" (Bunin) **5**:81, 90, 92

A Good Man Is Hard to Find (O'Connor) **1**:339, 344, 347-48, 356, 358, 360-63, 371

"Good Pals" (Suckow) **18**:411, 417

"Good Samaritan" (O'Hara) **15**:286

Good Samaritan, and Other Stories (O'Hara) **15**:273, 286

"The Good Soldier" (London) **4**:291

"A Good Temper" (Andersen) **6**:30, 36

"The Good Trip" (Le Guin) **12**:232

"Goodwood Comes Back" (Warren) **4**:387, 389-90, 394, 396

"The Goophered Grapevine" (Chesnutt) **7**:4-6, 9-10, 41

"Gooseberries" (Chekhov) **2**:136-37, 139, 141-43, 155-57

"Gooseberry Winter" (Mason) **4**:6

"Goose Fair" (Lawrence) **4**:197

"The Gospel according to Mark" (Borges) **4**:20, 28, 30

"Gothic Horror" (Ligotti) **16**:287

"A Gourdful of Glory" (Laurence) **7**:245-46, 248-50

"Gracchus the Huntsman" (Kafka)
See "Der jäger Gracchus"

"Grace" (Joyce) **3**:202, 205-06, 208, 210-11, 214-15, 225-26, 232-235, 237, 247-48

"Grace Called" (Dixon) **16**:217

"Grace Calls" (Dixon) **16**:217

"Graduation" (Dubus) **15**:73-4

"Graffiti" (Cortazar) **7**:83, 85-6, 91

"Grail" (Ellison) **14**:127

"A Grain as Big as a Hen's Egg" (Tolstoy) **9**:388

"Grammar of Love" (Bunin) **5**:89-90, 93, 106

"La grande bretèche" (Balzac) **5**:11-12, 14-15, 18-19, 31, 35-9

"The Grande Malade" ("The Little Girl Continues") (Barnes) **3**:5-6, 9-10, 16, 24-6

"Grandfather and Grandson" (Singer) **3**:374

"The Grand Vizier's Daughter" (O'Connor) **5**:381

"El gran serafin" (Bioy Casares) **17**:53

El gran serafin (Bioy Casares) **17**:53, 56, 59

The Grapes of Paradise (Bates) **10**:121-22

The Grapes of Paradise: Four Short Novels (Bates)
See *An Aspidistra in Babylon: Four Novellas*

The Grass God (Bates) **10**:118

"The Grasshopper" (Chekhov) **2**:155

"The Grave" (Porter) **4**:329-34, 340-42, 344, 352, 354, 365

"The Grave by the Handpost" (Hardy) **2**:210

"The Gravedigger" (Singer) **3**:378

"Graven Image" (O'Hara) **15**:248-49, 270

"The Grave of the Famous Poet" (Atwood) **2**:3-5, 7, 10-11, 16

"Graveyard Day" (Mason) **4**:7

"The Graveyard Shift" (King) **17**:262

"Gravity" (Beattie) **11**:10, 13

"Gray Days" (Colette) **10**:292

"Gray Matter" (King) **17**:261-62

"The Gray Mills of Farley" (Jewett) **6**:156

"The Gray Wolf's Ha'nt" (Chesnutt) **7**:7, 10-11, 40

"Greasy Lake" (Boyle) **16**:144-45, 151-52, 156-57

Greasy Lake, & Other Stories (Boyle) **16**:143-46, 148, 153

Great Battles of the World (Crane) **7**:104

"The Great Brown-Pericord Motor" (Doyle) **12**:65, 79

"The Great Carbuncle" (Hawthorne) **3**:157, 159, 181-82, 184-85, 188

"The Great Dark" (Twain) **6**:331-42, 350-53

"A Great Day for Bonzo" (Bates) **10**:120

Great Days (Barthelme) **2**:44, 46

"The Greater Festival of Masks" (Ligotti) **16**:261, 271, 273, 280, 283

The Greater Inclination (Wharton) **6**:413

"The Greatest Love of Don Juan" (Barbey d'Aurevilly)
See "Le plus bel amour de Don Juan"

"The Greatest Man in the World" (Thurber) **1**:420, 431

"The Greatest People in the World" (Bates) **10**:114

The Greatest People in the World, and Other Stories (Bates) **10**:138

"The Greatest Television Show on Earth" (Ballard) **1**:71

"The Great Good Place" (James) **8**:269, 282, 302, 304, 306-07

"The Great Interrogation" (London) **4**:265, 286

"The Great Keinplatz Experiment" (Doyle) **12**:80

"A Great Mollie" ("As Strong as a Man") (Suckow) **18**:391, 415

"The Great Mountains" (Steinbeck) **11**:209, 212-14, 232, 237

"The Great Mutation" (Levi) **12**:276

"Greatness" (Benet) **10**:154

"The Great Road" (Bunin) **5**:87

"A Great Sorrow" (Andersen) **6**:4, 7

"The Great Stone Face" (Hawthorne) **3**:159, 178, 182, 184

"The Great Swinglefield Derby" (Benet) **10**:155

"Great Uncle Crow" (Bates) **10**:132

"The Great Wall of China" (Kafka) **5**:206

The Great Wall of China, and Other Pieces (Kafka)
See *Beim Bau der Chinesischen Mauer*

The Great Wall of China: Stories and Reflections (Kafka)
See *Beim Bau der Chinesischen Mauer*

"The Great Wave" (Lavin) **4**:167-68, 174, 184

The Great Wave, and Other Stories (Lavin) **4**:166

"The Great Winglebury Duel" (Dickens) **17**:110, 116-17

"The Greek Dancing Girl" (Schnitzler) **15**:343

"The Green Banana" (Powers) **4**:379

"Green Christmas" (Benet) **10**:149

"The Green Door" (Henry) **5**:159, 190

"The Green Grave and the Black Grave" (Lavin) **4**:166-67, 174, 180, 184

"Green Hell" (Boyle) **16**:140-42

"Green Holly" (Bowen) **3**:32, 54

"The Green Isle in the Sea" (Thurber) **1**:417

"Greenleaf" (O'Connor) **1**:343, 358, 360

"The Green Man" (Chesterton) **1**:129

"The Green Room" (de la Mare) **14**:71-2, 83, 86-7, 91

"Green Tea" (Le Fanu) **14**:222-25, 227, 229, 231-35, 237-38, 240, 242, 249-51

"A Green Thought" (Michaels) **16**:303

Green Water, Green Sky (Gallant) **5**:123, 144, 146

"The Green Wax" (Colette) **10**:292, 295

"Greenwich Fair" (Dickens) **17**:125, 134

"Greenwich Time" (Beattie) **11**:12

"Gregory's Island" (Cable)
See "The Solitary"

La grenadière (Balzac) **5**:8, 16

"Gretchen's Forty Winks" (Fitzgerald) **6**:46

"The Grey Champion" (Hawthorne) **3**:164, 167, 171, 175-76, 178, 186-87

"Grey Seagull" (O'Flaherty) **6**:262

"A Grey Sleeve" (Crane) **7**:103, 106

"Gribiche" (Colette) **10**:281

"Grief" (Andersen) **6**:26

"Grigia" (Musil) **18**:289, 292-93, 297-99, 302-13, 322, 325

Grimscribe: His Lives and Works (Ligotti) **16**:279-80, 282-85, 293, 294, 296

"Grippes and Poche" (Gallant) **5**:147

"The Grisly Folk" (Wells) **6**:382

"The Grit of Women" (London) **4**:286, 288

"Grjotgard Ålvesøon and Aud" (Dinesen)
See "Grjotgard Ålvesøon og Aud"

"Grjotgard Ålvesøon og Aud" ("Grjotgard Ålvesøon and Aud") (Dinesen) **7**:177

"The Grocery Store" (Malamud) **15**:234-35

A Group of Noble Dames (Hardy) **2**:203-07, 209, 212-13, 220-21

"The Growing Stone" (Camus)
See "La pierre qui pousse"

"The Growtown 'Bugle'" (Jewett) **6**:156, 159

"The Guardian" (de la Mare) **14**:79, 85, 89, 91

"Guardian Angel" (Clarke) **3**:149

"Guayaquil" (Borges) **4**:20, 27

"The Guest" (Camus)
See "L'hôte"

"The Guest" (Elkin) **12**:94, 117-18

"A Guest at Home" (Jewett) **6**:156, 158-59

Guest of Reality (Lagerkvist)
See *Gäst hos verkligheten*

"Guests" (Dixon) **16**:217

"Guests" (Taylor) **10**:389-90, 394, 404, 415, 417

"Guests from Gibbet Island" (Irving) **2**:241, 247-48

"Guests of the Nation" (O'Connor) **5**:369, 375-76, 379-82, 384, 388-89, 393

Guests of the Nation (O'Connor) **5**:363, 370, 375, 377-80, 382, 384, 387, 390-93

"A Guide to Berlin" (Nabokov) **11**:134

"Guilt" (Lish) **18**:267-68

"The Guilty Party—An East Side Tragedy" (Henry) **5**:188, 198

Guilty Pleasures (Barthelme) **2**:39, 41

Guirnalda con amores (*A Garland of Love*) (Bioy Casares) **17**:53, 87, 95

"The Gulf Between" (Calisher) **15**:5, 7, 15, 18

"The Gully of Bluemansdyke" (Doyle) **12**:84-5

The Gully of Bluemansdyke and Other Stories (Doyle)
See *Mysteries and Adventures*

"Gumption" (Hughes) **6**:131, 133

"The Gun" (O'Hara) **15**:262

"The Gunboat and Madge" (O'Hara) **15**:286

"Gusev" (Chekhov) **2**:128-29, 143, 147

"The Gutting of Couffignal" (Hammett) **17**:206, 222, 224, 229-30

"Guy de Maupassant" ("Maupassant") (Babel) **16**:4, 5, 15, 20, 36, 42, 59

"Gwilan's Harp" (Le Guin) **12**:231

"The Gypsy Feeling" (Nin) **10**:306

"The Gypsy Maid" (Cervantes)
See "La gitanilla"

"Habakuk Jephson's Statement" (Doyle) **12**:85

"An Habitation Enforced" (Kipling) **5**:283

"The Habit of Loving" (Lessing) **6**:218

"Hacienda" (Porter) **4**:327, 329-30, 346, 351

"Hackney Coach Stands" (Dickens) **17**:111

"Hadjii murád" (Tolstoy)
See "Khadzi murat"

Hadji Murád (Tolstoy) **9**:376, 378, 394-97

"The Hag" (Turgenev) **7**:335

"The Haile Selassie Funeral Train" (Davenport) **16**:173-74, 177, 183, 194

"Die Haimatochare" (Hoffmann) **13**:187

"The Hair" (Carver) **8**:50-1

"Hair" (Faulkner) **1**:147, 151

"Hair Jewellery" (Atwood) **2**:3, 5-7, 10-11, 14, 16

"The Hairless Mexican" (Maugham) **8**:369, 376

Hair O' the Chine (Coover) **15**:47-8

"The Hair Shirt" (Powers) **4**:380

"Haïta the Shepherd" (Bierce) **9**:49, 87

"Halberdier of the Little Rheinschloss" (Henry) **5**:181, 196

"Hale Hardy and the Amazing Animal Woman" (Beattie) **11**:11, 16, 28

"Half a Grapefruit" (Munro) **3**:334, 342

"The Half-Husky" (Laurence) **7**:253, 270

"Hal Irwin's Magic Lamp" (Vonnegut) **8**:437

"The Hall of Fantasy" (Hawthorne) **3**:181

"The Hallucination" (Oates) **6**:250

"The Hammer of God" (Chesterton) **1**:124, 130, 136

"Hand" (Atwood) **2**:20

"Handcarved Coffins: A Nonfiction Account of an American Crime" (Capote) **2**:80-2

"Hand in Glove" (Bowen) **3**:54

"The Hand of Emmagene" (Taylor) **10**:397-98, 402, 404

"Hands" (Anderson) **1**:32-3, 42, 44, 57

"Handsome Is as Handsome Does" (Pritchett) **14**:268-69, 291, 298

"The Handsomest Drowned Man in the World: A Tale for Children" (Garcia Marquez)
See "El ahogado más hermoso del mundo"

"Hand upon the Waters" (Faulkner) **1**:179

"Hanka" (Singer) **3**:377

"Hannes" (Hesse) **9**:243

"The Happiest I've Been" (Updike) **13**:354

"Happiness" (Chekhov) **2**:130, 156

"Happiness" (Lavin) **4**:182, 185

"Happiness in Crime" (Barbey d'Aurevilly)
See "Le bonheur dans le crime"

"Happy" (Beattie) **11**:14

"The Happy Autumn Fields" (Bowen) **3**:31-2, 50-1

"The Happy Couple" (Maugham) **8**:380

"A Happy Death" (Lavin) **4**:165, 167

"Happy Endings" (Atwood) **2**:15, 19-20

"The Happy Failure" (Melville) **1**:303

Happy Families Are All Alike (Taylor) **10**:380, 389, 410

"The Happy Family" (Andersen) **6**:18

"The Happy Prince" (Wilde) **11**:365, 372, 376-78, 380, 386, 389-90, 394-96, 402-03, 406-08

The Happy Prince, and Other Tales (Wilde) **11**:365-66, 375, 377, 381, 386, 390, 393, 402

"Happy Valley" (Taylor) **10**:394, 397

"Hapworth 16, 1924" (Salinger) **2**:308, 314

"A Harbinger" (Chopin) **8**:71

"The Harbinger" (Henry) **5**:158

"The Hard Passage" (Hesse) **9**:231-32, 234, 236, 243

"Hard Sell" (Boyle) **16**:150

"The Hard Sellers" (Levi) **12**:279

"The Hardy Tin Soldier" (Andersen)
See "The Steadfast Tin Soldier"

"Hari to Ciarasu to Kiri" ("Needle and Glass and Fog") (Kawabata) **17**:242, 254

"The Harness" (Steinbeck) **11**:207, 225, 228, 230, 232-35, 240-41, 243-44

"Harper and Wilton" (Spark) **10**:356

"Harrison Bergeron" (Vonnegut) **8**:427, 434

"Harv Is Plowing Now" (Updike) **13**:348-49, 375

"The Hat" (Boyle) **16**:149, 154-55

"The Hat Act" (Coover) **15**:31, 33-4, 48, 59

The Hat on the Bed (O'Hara) **15**:259-60, 282-83

"The Haunted Baronet" (Le Fanu) **14**:220, 223-24, 237, 245

"The Haunted Boy" (McCullers) **9**:330, 332, 343, 345, 354, 356, 358

"The Haunted Dolls' House" (James) **16**:230, 237, 244, 256

"A Haunted House" (Woolf) **7**:369, 374-75, 389-90, 392, 399

A Haunted House, and Other Short Stories (Woolf) **7**:372, 374, 386, 388, 400

"The 'Haunted House' in Royal Street" (Cable) **4**:53, 59, 61, 75-6

The Haunted Man and the Ghost's Bargain (Dickens) **17**:127-32

"The Haunted Mind" (Hawthorne) **3**:181

"The Haunter of the Dark" (Lovecraft) **3**:259, 263, 273-75, 279, 284

"The Haunting of the Tiled House" (Le Fanu) **14**:224, 226

"Hautot père et fils" (Maupassant) **1**:270, 280, 285, 288

"De Havilland Hand" (Gilchrist) **14**:163-64

"Having a Wonderful Time" (Ballard) **1**:79

"The Hawk" (O'Flaherty) 269, 274, 279

"The Haymaking" (Lavin) **4**:167

"He" (Lovecraft) **3**:259, 262, 283, 289

"He" (Porter) **4**:327-30, 339-40, 349-50, 354, 360

"Head and Shoulders" (Fitzgerald) **6**:45, 57, 96-7

"The Head-Hunter" (Henry) **5**:166

"The Headless Hawk" (Capote) **2**:61-3, 66, 69, 72, 75-6

"The Head of Babylon" (Barnes) **3**:19-20

"The Head of the Family" (Chekhov) **2**:127

"Heads" (Dixon) **16**:219

"Heads of Houses" (Taylor) **10**:389-90, 404, 415-16

"Heartbreak" (Andersen) **6**:30, 32, 35

"Heartburn" (Calisher) **15**:2, 6

"Hear the Nightingale Sing" (Gordon) **15**:107, 118

"Heart of a Champion" (Boyle) **16**:140-43, 157

"Heart of a Champion" (Lish) **18**:267

The Heart of a Dog (Bulgakov)
See *Sobach'e serdtse*

The Heart of a Goof (Wodehouse) **2**:329, 350

Heart of Darkness (Conrad) **9**:140-41, 143-44, 148-56, 160, 168, 171, 173, 175-76, 178, 188-92, 196-207

The Heart of Happy Hollow (Dunbar) **8**:120-22, 127-29, 131-32, 141, 145

The Heart of the West (Henry) **5**:155, 172, 182

"Hearts and Crosses" (Henry) **5**:155, 181

"Hearts of Oak and Bellies of Brass"
(McGahern) **17**:298, 302, 307-09
"Heat" (Dixon) **16**:211
"The Heat of the Sun" (O'Faolain) **13**:283,
292, 311
The Heat of the Sun: Stories and Tales
(O'Faolain) **13**:290, 307, 313
"The Heavenly Animal" (Phillips) **16**:327-28,
330
"Heaven on a Summer Night" (Beattie) **11**:29
"The Hector Quesadilla Story" (Boyle)
16:145, 151
"He'd Come Back" (Lawson) **18**:248
"The Hedgehog" (Saki) **12**:316
"He Don't Plant Cotton" (Powers) **4**:368
"Heimkehr" ("Homecoming") (Kafka) **5**:254
"Heinrich" (Bunin) **5**:114
"Heinrich von ofter dinger" (Hoffmann)
13:218
"An Heiress of Red Dog" (Harte) **8**:248
"The Heir of the McHulishes" (Harte) **8**:217,
252
"He is barehead" (Beckett) **16**:123-24, 126-27
"Hejda" (Nin) **10**:300, 303
Det heliga landet (Lagerkvist) **12**:198
Hellbox (O'Hara) **15**:250, 255, 257-58, 264-
65, 267
"Hello Fine Day Isn't It?" (Oates) **6**:248-50
"Hello Jack" (Michaels) **16**:309
"Hello, Tib" (Aiken) **9**:13
"Un hemisphère dans une chevelure"
(Baudelaire) **18**:5-7, 17
"The Hen" (Saki) **12**:296
"Henne Fire" (Singer) **3**:370, 383-84
"Henry and the Gold Mine" (Benet) **10**:154
Henry Lawson, Fifteen Stories (Lawson)
18:221
"He of the Assembly" (Bowles) **3**:68, 83-4
"Herakleitos" (Davenport) **16**:162-63, 166,
170
"Herbert West--Reanimator" (Lovecraft)
3:282, 293-94
"Her Boss" (Cather) **2**:111
Here and Beyond (Wharton) **6**:422
"Here Comes the Maples" (Updike) **13**:374,
386-87
"Here Come the Tigers" (Thurber) **1**:429
*Here Lies: The Collected Stories of Dorothy
Parker* (Parker) **2**:274-76
Los heréticos (*The Heretics*) (Valenzuela)
14:366
The Heretics (Valenzuela)
See *Los heréticos*
"Here to Learn" (Bowles) **3**:75, 79-80
"Here We Are" (Parker) **2**:273-74, 281, 283
"Her First Ball" (Mansfield) **9**:282-83, 286,
304, 310-11
"Her Housekeeper" (Gilman) **13**:142, 145
"L'héritage" (Maupassant) **1**:256, 259-60,
263, 270, 276, 283
"The Heritage of Dedlow Marsh" (Harte)
8:254
"Her Ladyship's Private Office" (Turgenev)
7:337
"Her Letters" (Chopin) **8**:92, 98-9, 112-13
Hermann Lauscher (Hesse)
See *Hinterlassene Schriften und Gedichte von
Hermann Lauscher*
"The Hermit and the Wild Woman"
(Wharton) **6**:428
The Hermit and the Wild Woman (Wharton)
6:420, 435

"The Hermits" (Dinesen) **7**:177
"Her Need" (Taylor) **10**:404
Herod and Mariamne (Lagerkvist)
See *Mariamne*
"Hérodias" (Flaubert) **11**:37, 46, 50-3, 55-6,
61-5, 70-1, 81-2, 84-7, 91-3, 96-9, 101, 103
"A Heroic Death" (Baudelaire)
See "Une mort héroïque"
"A Hero in Dingo-Scrubs" (Lawson) **18**:211,
220
"The Heroine" (Dinesen) **7**:165, 168, 195
"L'héroïsme du docteur Hallidonhill" (Villiers
de l'Isle Adam) **14**:397
"The Hero of Redclay" (Lawson) **18**:234,
240, 250-51
"A Hero's Death" (Lagerkvist) **12**:182, 195
"Her Own People" (Warren) **4**:389-90, 395,
399
"Her Quaint Honor" (Gordon) **15**:104, 107,
119, 123
"Her Sense of Timing" (Elkin) **12**:119
"Her Son" (Wharton) **6**:423-24
"Her Sweet Jerome" (Walker) **5**:402, 405-06,
419
"Her Table Spread" (Bowen) **3**:34-6, 38, 41,
51
"Her Virginia Mammy" (Chesnutt) **7**:16, 23,
33-5, 37
"He Thinks He's Wonderful" (Fitzgerald)
6:47, 49
"Hey Sailor, What Ship?" (Olsen) **11**:164
"Hey! Taxi!" (Aiken) **9**:4, 12-13
"Hidden Art" (Maclean) **13**:279
"Hidden Treasure" (Zoshchenko) **15**:395
"Hide and Seek" (Clarke) **3**:124-26, 133, 150
"Hiding Man" (Barthelme) **2**:26, 41-2, 54
"High" (Oates) **6**:252
"The High Constable's Wife" (Balzac) **5**:19
"The Higher Abdication" (Henry) **5**:180-81
"The Higher Pragmatism" (Henry) **5**:187
"High Ground" (McGahern) **17**:306, 311-12,
314-15, 324
High Ground (McGahern) **17**:304-06, 309-12,
322-23
"The High Point" (O'Hara) **15**:252
"High School" (Beattie) **11**:26, 29
"High-Water Mark" (Harte) **8**:210, 232
"El hijo de su amigo" (Bioy Casares) **17**:48-
52
"The Hill of the Elves" (Andersen) **6**:31
"Hills Like White Elephants" (Hemingway)
1:210, 217, 232, 234
"The Hilton's Holiday" (Jewett) **6**:152
"Him" (Atwood) **2**:20
"Him with His Foot in His Mouth" (Bellow)
14:40, 42-6
*Him with His Foot in His Mouth, and Other
Stories* (Bellow) **14**:40, 42, 50, 56, 58
*Hinterlassene Schriften und Gedichte von
Hermann Lauscher* (*Hermann Lauscher; The
Posthumous Writings and Poems of Hermann
Lauscher*) (Hesse) **9**:229-30, 235, 243
"His Chest of Drawers" (Anderson) **1**:52
"His Country, After All" (Lawson) **18**:201,
216
"His Excellency" (Maugham) **8**:365, 377
"His Father" (Steinbeck) **11**:246, 252
"His Father's Mate" (Lawson) **18**:197-98,
201-02, 239, 257
"His Father's Son" (Wharton) **6**:421, 424,
435
"His Finest Hour" (Updike) **13**:355

"His General Line of Business" (Dickens)
17:123
*His Last Bow: Some Reminiscences of Sherlock
Holmes* (Doyle) **12**:50, 64
"His Last Bow: The War Service of Sherlock
Holmes" (Doyle) **12**:62
"His Mother" (Gallant) **5**:135, 137
"Hissen som gick ner i helvete" ("The Lift
That Went Down into Hell") (Lagerkvist)
12:182, 196
L'histoire de Fenni (Voltaire) **12**:341, 343
Histoire des treize (*The Thirteen*) (Balzac) **5**:5,
45-7
L'histoire du Calife Hakem ("Legend of Khalif
Hakem") (Nerval) **18**:364
"L'histoire d'une fille de ferme" (Maupassant)
1:257, 259, 261, 272, 274-75
Histoires insolites (Villiers de l'Isle Adam)
14:378, 384, 396-97
Historia de cronopios y de famas (*Cronopios
and Famas*) (Cortazar) **7**:50, 53, 60, 91-2,
94
"Historia del guerrero y de la cautiva"
("History of the Warrior and the Captive";
"Story of the Warrior and the Captive")
(Borges) **4**:29
"Historia prodigiosa" (Bioy Casares) **17**:59
Historia prodigiosa (Bioy Casares) **17**:58
Historias desaforados (Bioy Casares) **17**:86-7
Historia universal de la infamia (*History of
Infamy; A Universal History of Infamy*)
(Borges) **4**:4, 17
"History Lesson" (Clarke) **3**:124, 133, 143-44
History of Infamy (Borges)
See *Historia universal de la infamia*
"The History of Lieutenant Ergunov"
(Turgenev)
See "Istoriya leytenanta Ergunova"
"The History of the Hardcomes" (Hardy)
2:215
"History of the Warrior and the Captive"
(Borges)
See "Historia del guerrero y de la cautiva"
"History, or the Four Pictures of Vludka"
(Lish) **18**:282
"The Hitch-Hikers" (Welty) **1**:466, 468, 481,
487-88, 494
"The Hobo and the Fairy" (London) **4**:255
"Hoboes That Pass in the Night" (London)
4:291
"Hog Pawn" (Faulkner) **1**:178
La hojarasca (*Dead Leaves; Leaf Storm*)
(Garcia Marquez) **8**:154-55, 158, 160, 162,
171, 184, 193
"Holding Her Down" (London) **4**:291
"The Hole" (Dixon) **16**:206, 208
"The Hole in the Wall" (Chesterton) **1**:122
"Holiday" (Porter) **4**:347, 349-50, 355
"Holiday Romance" (Dickens) **17**:124
"The Hollow Boy" (Calisher) **15**:10, 14
"The Hollow of the Three Hills" (Hawthorne)
3:154, 157, 180-81
"The Holy Door" (O'Connor) **5**:365, 367,
371, 384, 390
"The Holy Land" (Lagerkvist) **12**:198
"The Holy Six" (Thomas) **3**:399, 407-08
"Homage to Isaac Babel" (Lessing) **6**:196-99,
214
"Homage to Switzerland" (Hemingway)
1:211

"Hombre de la esquina rosada" ("Hombres de las orillas"; "Man on the Pink Corner"; "The Pink Corner Man"; "Streetcorner Man") (Borges) 4:10, 14-16

"El hombre en el umbral" ("The Man on the Threshold") (Borges) 4:4, 40-1

"Hombres de las orillas" (Borges) See "Hombre de la esquina rosada"

"Home" (Boyle) 5:57

"Home" (Gordimer) 17:178, 180, 186, 188, 190-91

"Home" (Grau) 15:163

"Home" (Hughes) 6:109, 118-19, 121-22, 133

"Home" (Phillips) 16:325, 327-28, 330

"Home" (Updike) 13:397-98

"Homecoming" (Grau) 15:148, 152

"The Homecoming" (Hesse) 9:231, 235

"Homecoming" (Kafka) See "Heimkehr"

"A Homecoming" (Suckow) 18:396-97, 401, 409

"The Home-Coming of 'Rastus Smith" (Dunbar) 8:122, 135

"Home Delivery" (King) 17:295

A Home for the Highland Cattle (Lessing) 6:189-91, 195-96

"Home to Marie" (Beattie) 11:30-1, 34

Home Truths: Selected Canadian Stories (Gallant) 5:138, 141, 143-44, 147

L'homme aux quarante écus (The Man with Forty Ecus) (Voltaire) 12:342, 346

"Un homme d'affaires" (Balzac) 5:32

"The Honest Quack" (Chesterton) 1:133

"An Honest Soul" (Freeman) 1:198, 201

"An Honest Thief" (Dostoevsky) 2:166, 171, 193

"An Honest Woman" (Gilman) 13:126

"Honey" (Beattie) 11:33-4

"Honeymoon" (O'Brien) 10:331, 333

"The Honeymoon" (Pritchett) 14:298

"The Honey Tree" (Jewett) 6:156, 158

"Honolulu" (Maugham) 8:359, 371-72

Honorine (Balzac) 5:18, 31, 33

"The Honour of Israel Gow" (Chesterton) 1:134, 137

"The Hook" (O'Flaherty) 6:264, 269

"Hopeless" (Atwood) 2:20

"Hopes Rise" (Boyle) 16:156-57

"Hop-Frog" (Poe) 1:408

"Horatio Sparkins" (Dickens) 17:110, 120, 137

"Horatio's Trick" (Beattie) 11:30-1, 34

"Horizon" (O'Hara) 15:267-68

"Le horla" (Maupassant) 1:259, 262, 265, 269, 273, 283-84, 286-88

"L'horloge" ("The Clock") (Baudelaire) 18:6

"Horn Came" (Beckett) 16:123-24, 126

"Horn of Plenty" (Gordimer) 17:152, 166

"The Horror at Red Hook" (Lovecraft) 3:258, 262, 289

"The Horror in the Museum" (Lovecraft) 3:279

"The Horror of the Heights" (Doyle) 12:62, 76-7, 79-80

"The Horse-Dealer's Daughter" (Lawrence) 4:202-03, 231-33, 235-36, 240

The Horse Knows the Way (O'Hara) 15:262, 283

"A Horseman in the Sky" (Bierce) 9:50, 55-6, 60, 68

Horses and Men (Anderson) 1:23, 25, 27, 30, 46, 50

"The Horse's Ha" (Thomas) 3:409

"A Horse's Name" (Chekhov) 2:130

"Horses of the Night" (Laurence) 7:255, 259, 262-63, 270

"Horses--One Dash" ("One Dash—Horses") (Crane) 7:104, 106, 108, 125-26, 149, 153-54

"A Horse's Tale" (Twain) 6:303

"The Horse-Stealers" (Chekhov) 2:130

"Horsie" (Parker) 2:273-75, 280, 283-84

"The Hospital Patient" (Dickens) 17:115

"A Host of Furious Fancies" (Ballard) 1:79

"Hot and Cold Blood" (Fitzgerald) 6:46

"L'hôte" ("The Guest") (Camus) 9:103, 105, 109-11, 113, 118-19, 120-26, 128, 135

"Hotel Behind the Lines" (Boyle) 5:74

"Hotel Kid" (O'Hara) 15:248, 265-66

"Hot-Foot Hannibal" (Chesnutt) 7:7, 10-11, 40

"The Hound" (Faulkner) 1:177

"The Hound" (Lovecraft) 3:258, 262, 274, 276, 282

"The Hounds of Fate" (Saki) 12:288, 298, 306

"The Hour and the Years" (Gordimer) 17:151

An Hour Beyond Midnight (Hesse) See Eine Stunde hinter Mitternacht

"The Hours after Noon" (Bowles) 3:64-6, 80, 82

"The Hour That Stretches" (Ellison) 14:128

"The House" (de la Mare) 14:86, 90, 92

"The House" (Le Guin) 12:213, 248-49

"Houseboat" (Nin) 10:303-05

"The Housebreaker of Shady Hill" (Cheever) 1:111

The Housebreaker of Shady Hill, and Other Stories (Cheever) 1:89-92, 95, 100

"Housecoming" (Grau) 15:

"The Household" (Irving) 2:265

"The House in Turk Street" (Hammett) 17:218, 220-21

"Housekeeper" (Grau) 15:163-64

"The House of Asterión" (Borges) See "La casa de Asterión"

"House of Flowers" (Capote) 2:67, 69, 72, 75

"The House of My Dreams" (O'Brien) 10:331, 333, 345

A House of Pomegranates (Wilde) 11:362, 364-65, 375, 376-77, 381, 384, 394, 398, 407-08

The House of Pride, and Other Tales of Hawaii (London) 4:268-69, 283

"The House of the Dead Hand" (Wharton) 6:428

"House of the Sleeping Beauties" (Kawabata) See "Nemureru Bijo"

House of the Sleeping Beauties, and Other Stories (Kawabata) 17:234-35, 240-41, 246

"The House on Maple Street" (King) 17:295

"The House Surgeon" (Kipling) 5:272, 275, 284-85

"The House Taken Over" (Cortazar) See "Casa tomada"

"The House That Johnny Built" (O'Connor) 5:363, 371

"The House That Was Never Built" (Lawson) 18:252

"The House with a Mezzanine" (Chekhov) See "An Artist's Story"

"The House with an Attic" (Chekhov) See "An Artist's Story"

"The House with the Maisonette" (Chekhov) See "An Artist's Story"

"How about This?" (Carver) 8:32

"How a Good Man Went Wrong" (Chesnutt) 7:14

"Howard and the Spinach" (Steinbeck) 11:203

"How Auntie Fedos'ja Chatted with Lenin" (Zoshchenko) 15:407

"How Brother Parker Fell from Grace" (Dunbar) 8:122

"How Buton Got Married" (Bulgakov) 18:90

"How Can I Tell You?" (O'Hara) 15:260, 291

"How Dasdy Came Through" (Chesnutt) 7:13

"Howe's Masquerade" (Hawthorne) 3:154, 187

"How I Finally Lost My Heart" (Lessing) 6:197, 200-01, 206, 220

"How It Was Done in Odessa" (Babel) See "How Things Were Done in Odessa"

"How I Write My Songs" (Barthelme) 2:52

"How Lenin Bought a Boy a Toy" (Zoshchenko) 15:407

"How Lenin Outsmarted the Police" (Zoshchenko) 15:407

"How Lenin Quit Smoking" (Zoshchenko) 15:407

"How Lenin Studied" (Zoshchenko) 15:407

"How Lenin Was Given a Fish" (Zoshchenko) 15:407

"How Many Midnights" (Bowles) 3:60, 69, 72, 79

"How Mickey Made It" (Phillips) 16:335-37, 339

"How Mr. Hogan Robbed a Bank" (Steinbeck) 11:256-58

"How Much Land Does a Man Need?" (Tolstoy) 9:377, 388

"How Much Shall We Bet?" (Calvino) 3:104

"How Pearl Button was Kidnapped" (Mansfield) 9:302

"How Santa Claus Came to Simpson's Bar" (Harte) 8:223-24, 227, 236, 244

"How Sleep the Brave" (Bates) 10:139

How Sleep the Brave, and Other Stories (Bates) 10:138

"How the Brigadier Bore Himself at Waterloo" (Doyle) 12:82

"How the Brigadier Came to the Castle of Gloom" (Doyle) 12:81

"How the Brigadier Held the King" (Doyle) 12:82

"How the Brigadier Lost His Ear" (Doyle) 12:82

"How the Brigadier Played for a Kingdom" (Doyle) 12:

"How the Brigadier Slew the Brothers of Ajaccio" (Doyle) 12:81

"How the Brigadier Slew the Fox" (Doyle) 12:82

"How the Brigadier Triumphed in England" (Doyle) 12:82

"How the Brigadier Was Tempted by the Devil" (Doyle) 12:82

"How the Brigadier Won His Medal" (Doyle) 12:82

"How the King Held the Brigadier" (Doyle) 12:82

"How the Local Committee Bought a Present with an Old Woman's Money" (Bulgakov) **18**:89
"How Things Were Done in Odessa" ("How It Was Done in Odessa") (Babel) **16**:44-5, 48-9
"How to Grow a Wisteria" (O'Brien) **10**:330
"How to Love America" (Updike) **13**:387
"How to Write a *Blackwood* Article" (Poe) **1**:405
"How to Write a Novel" (Lish) **18**:266, 268
"How to Write a Poem" (Lish) **18**:268
"How to Write a Short Story" (O'Faolain) **13**:296
"The Human Being and the Dinosaur" (Thurber) **1**:426, 430
The Human Comedy (Balzac)
   See *Comédie humaine*
"The Human Element" (Maugham) **8**:357, 366, 378
"The Human Fly" (Boyle) **16**:154
"Human Habitation" (Bowen) **3**:55
"The Human Thing" (O'Faolain) **13**:316
"A Humble Romance" (Freeman) **1**:196
A Humble Romance, and Other Stories (Freeman) **1**:191, 194-95, 197, 201
"A Humorous Southern Story" (Chesnutt) **7**:13
"The Hunchback in the Park" (Thomas) **3**:400
A Hundred Camels in the Courtyard (Bowles) **3**:68
Hunger (Lessing) **6**:190, 192-93, 195-97
"A Hunger-Artist" (Kafka)
   See "Ein Hungerkünstler"
"Hungerford" (Lawson) **18**:215, 261
"Ein Hungerkünstler" ("A Hunger-Artist") (Kafka) **5**:207-09, 220, 225, 237-40
"The Hungry" (Mann) **5**:319, 322-23, 330
The Hungry Ghosts (Oates) **6**:241, 243
"Hunktown" (Mason) **4**:8
"Hunted Down" (Dickens) **17**:124
"Hunter" (Grau) **15**:163
"The Hunter" (Hammett) **17**:217
"The Hunter Gracchus" (Kafka)
   See "Der jäger Gracchus"
"The Hunter's Waking Thoughts" (Gallant) **5**:151
"Hunting" (Zoshchenko) **15**:407-08
"A Hunting Accident" (Gordimer) **17**:165, 193
"The Huntsman" (Chekhov) **2**:155
"Hurricane Hazel" (Atwood) **2**:21-3
"The Husband" (Bowles) **3**:80
"Hyacinth" (Saki) **12**:302
"Die Hyänen" (Hoffmann)
   See "Der Vampyrismus"
"The Hyannis Port Story" (Vonnegut) **8**:436
"Hydrogen" (Levi) **12**:259, 262, 264
"The Hyena" (Hoffmann)
   See "Der Vampyrismus"
"The Hyena" (Bowles) **3**:64-5, 68, 80
"Hygeia at the Solito" (Henry) **5**:182
"Hymeneal" (O'Faolain) **13**:291, 314
"The Hypnotist" (Bierce) **9**:75
"The Hypothesis of Failure" (Henry) **5**:184
"I and My Chimney" (Melville) **1**:298, 304, 322, 326-27; **17**:359, 363
"Ib and Christine" (Andersen) **6**:14
"Ibn Hakkan al-Bokhari, Dead in His Labryinth" (Borges) **4**:30, 35

I Cannot Get You Close Enough (Gilchrist) **14**:163-65
"The Ice House" (Gordon) **15**:104, 118, 139
"The Ice Maiden" (Andersen) **6**:12, 19, 26, 34-5, 37
"The Ice Palace" (Fitzgerald) **6**:57-8, 88, 96-7, 100, 103
"The Ice Wagon Going down the Street" (Gallant) **5**:139, 144
"Icicles" (Gass) **12**:123, 133, 167, 168
"Iconography" (Atwood) **2**:15, 20
"I Could See the Smallest Things" (Carver) **8**:19, 34-5
"Ida" (Bunin) **5**:106-07, 116-20
"The Idea" (Carver) **8**:7
"An Ideal Craftsman" (de la Mare) **14**:88
"An Ideal Family" (Mansfield) **9**:282, 284
"The Idealist" (Nin) **10**:306
I den tiden (*In That Time*) (Lagerkvist) **12**:179
"The Idiots" (Conrad) **9**:179
"Idiots First" (Malamud) **15**:171-75, 195, 197, 204-05, 214, 216, 219-20, 225, 243
Idiots First (Malamud) **15**:170-72, 174, 188, 197, 213-14, 220, 225, 227, 235
"An Idle Fellow" (Chopin) **8**:73, 78, 98
"El ídolo" (Bioy Casares) **17**:87
"El ídolo de las cícladas" ("The Idol of the Cyclades") (Cortazar) **7**:57-8, 69-70, 76, 78
"The Idol of the Cyclades" (Cortazar)
   See "El ídolo de las cícladas"
"Une idylle" (Maupassant) **1**:256, 270
"An Idyll of North Carolina Sand-Hill Life" (Chesnutt) **7**:14
"The Idyl of Red Gulch" (Harte) **8**:210, 217, 236-37, 246
"'If I Forget Thee, O Earth'" (Clarke) **3**:124, 126, 143
"If I Should Open My Mouth" (Bowles) **3**:64, 68-9, 80, 83, 85
"If I Were a Man" (Gilman) **13**:126
"If the River Was Whiskey" (Boyle) **16**:146-48, 150, 152, 154, 156
If the River Was Whiskey (Boyle) **16**:146, 148-49, 153-54
"If They Knew Yvonne" (Dubus) **15**:69, 71, 90, 100
"If You Don't Want to Live I Can't Help You" (Calisher) **15**:5
"I Gave Up before Birth" (Beckett) **16**:123, 125-26
"Ignat" (Bunin) **5**:100
"Ignaz Denner" (Hoffmann) **13**:183, 186, 209
"Ignaz Denner" (Hoffmann) **13**:
"I Have No Mouth and I Must Scream" (Ellison) **14**:97-9, 107, 110, 112-15, 117-18, 124-25, 130-31, 138-39, 141, 143-47
I Have No Mouth and I Must Scream (Ellison) **14**:143-47
"Ike and Nina" (Boyle) **16**:144-45, 151
"I Killed" (Bulgakov) **18**:86, 89
"I Know Who I Love" (Jackson) **9**:258, 270-71
Il[l] castello dei destini incrociati (*The Castle of Crossed Destinies*) (Calvino) **3**:99-102, 106, 114, 116, 118
"Il Conde" (Conrad) **9**:151, 160, 179, 184
"I Live on Your Visits" (Parker) **2**:283
Ill Seen Ill Said (Beckett)
   See *Mal vu mal dit*
"The Illuminated Man" (Ballard) **1**:69
Les illuminés (Nerval) **18**:328

"An Illusion in Red and White" (Crane) **7**:104
"L'illustre Gaudissart" ("Gaudissart"; "The Illustrious Gaudissart") (Balzac) **5**:18, 26
"The Illustrious Gaudissart" (Balzac)
   See "L'illustre Gaudissart"
"The Illustrious Kitchen Maid" (Cervantes)
   See "La ilustre fregona"
"The Illustrious Serving Wench" (Cervantes)
   See "La ilustre fregona"
"I Look Out for Ed Wolfe" (Elkin) **12**:94-5, 99, 102, 117-18
"I Love You Very Dearly" (Aiken) **9**:13-14, 29
"Il sangue, il mare" ("Blood, Sea") (Calvino) **3**:109-10
"La ilustre fregona" ("The Illustrious Kitchen Maid"; "The Illustrious Serving Wench") (Cervantes) **12**:4, 6-8, 15, 17-18, 36-7, 40
"Il viccolo di Madama Lucrezia" (Merimee) **7**:283-84, 290, 295-96, 306-07
"I'm a Fool" (Anderson) **1**:23, 25, 27, 30, 37-8, 40, 48-50
The Image, and Other Stories (Singer) **3**:384-86
"An Image of Success" (Gordimer) **17**:154
"The Image of the Lost Soul" (Saki) **12**:285, 305
"Images" (Munro) **3**:326, 338, 343-44
"The Image Trade" (Pritchett) **14**:300, 305
"Imaginary Countries" (Le Guin) **12**:211-13, 217-19, 248
"An Imaginative Woman" (Hardy) **2**:215, 220, 223, 225
"Imagine a Day at the End of Your Life" (Beattie) **11**:30, 33-4
"Imagined Scenes" (Beattie) **11**:2, 18, 21
Imagine Kissing Pete (O'Hara) **15**:250, 272
"The Immigrant Story" (Paley) **8**:406, 409
"The Immortal" (Borges)
   See "El inmortal"
"The Immortals" (Bioy Casares) **17**:75
"Imp Among Aunts" (Lish) **18**:284
"The Imp and the Crust" (Tolstoy) **9**:377, 388
"Impatience de la foule" ("The Impatient Mob") (Villiers de l'Isle Adam) **14**:381, 388, 394
"The Impatient Mob" (Villiers de l'Isle Adam)
   See "Impatience de la foule"
"An Imperfect Conflagration" (Bierce) **9**:75
"The Impertinent Curiosity" (Cervantes)
   See "El curioso impertinente"
"Impertinent Daughters" (Lessing) **6**:215
"The Impossible Man" (Ballard) **1**:75-7
"The Impossible Marriage" (O'Connor) **5**:372, 374
"The Impresario" (Singer) **3**:389
"The Impressions of a Cousin" (James) **8**:316
"Impulse" (Aiken) **9**:6, 13, 24-5, 27, 32
"In a Café" (Lavin) **4**:183, 185, 189
"In a Dry Season" (Lawson) **18**:210, 261
"In a Far Country" (London) **4**:264, 267-68, 279, 281-82, 284-86, 290
In a German Pension (Mansfield) **9**:284, 288, 301
In a Glass Darkly (Le Fanu) **14**:214, 225, 230, 234-35, 239-41, 243-45, 248-49
"In a Grove" (O'Hara) **15**:251
"In Amalfi" (Beattie) **11**:30-3
"In and Out of Old Nachitoches" (Chopin) **8**:103, 105, 113

"In Another Country" (Hemingway) **1**:209, 230-32, 234

"In a Public Place" (Oates) **6**:237

"In a Strange Town" (Anderson) **1**:50

"In a Thousand Years' Time" (Andersen) **6**:30

"In Autumn" (Bunin) **5**:114

"In a Wet Season" (Lawson) **18**:210

"In Bed One Night" (Coover) **15**:47

In Bed One Night and Other Brief Encounters (Coover) **15**:46

"The Incarnation of Krishna Mulvaney" (Kipling) **5**:259, 262

"Incest" (Updike) **13**:355

"An Inch and a Half of Glory" (Hammett) **17**:217

"An Incident in the Park" (Oates) **6**:248-49

"An Incident on the Volga" (Zoshchenko) **15**:404

"Incipit vita nova" (Hesse) **9**:231

"L'inconnue" ("The Unknown Woman") (Villiers de l'Isle Adam) **14**:379-81, 393

The Incredulity of Father Brown (Chesterton) **1**:128

"The Independence of Silas Bollender" (Dunbar) **8**:127, 134

"An Independent Thinker" (Freeman) **1**:196

"In der Strafkolonie" ("In the Penal Colony") (Kafka) **5**:218, 223-24, 229-30, 235-36, 240, 249-52

"The Indian" (Updike) **13**:348, 387

"Indian Camp" (Hemingway) **1**:214, 219, 234, 240-41, 244-45

"The Indian Sign" (Thurber) **1**:425

"Indian Summer" (Barnes) **3**:12, 22

"The Indian Summer of Dry Valley Johnson" (Henry) **5**:162

"The Indian Uprising" (Barthelme) **2**:35-6, 38, 42, 46, 53

"An Indiscreet Journey" (Mansfield) **9**:303, 317

The Indulgent Husband (Colette) **10**:261-62, 269-70

"I Never Seen Anything Like It" (O'Hara) **15**:265

"The Inevitable White Man" (London) **4**:266

"In Exile" (Chekhov) **2**:157

"The Inexperienced Ghost" (Wells) **6**:400

The Infant Prodigy (Mann) See *Das Wunderkind*

"The Infernal Parliament" (Saki) **12**:322

"In Football Season" (Updike) **13**:367, 375, 404

El informe de Brodie (*Doctor Brodie's Report*) (Borges) **4**:17-20, 26-7

"The Informer" (Conrad) **9**:157, 179, 182-86

L'Ingénu (Voltaire) **12**:338-39, 341-43, 362, 364-68, 394

L'ingénue libertine (Colette) **10**:257, 262

"An Ingènue of the Sierra" (Harte) **8**:244, 252

"The Ingrate" (Dunbar) **8**:122-23, 128-29, 136, 142-43, 149

"In Greenwich There Are Many Gravelled Walks" (Calisher) **15**:2, 10

"The Inherited Clock" (Bowen) **3**:31-2

"Inkalamu's Place" (Gordimer) **17**:157

"In Kew Gardens" (Malamud) **15**:235

"In Lilliput" (O'Faolain) **13**:308, 314

In Love and Trouble: Stories of Black Women (Walker) **5**:401-03, 405, 407, 411-12, 418-19, 422

"In Memory of L. I. Shigaev" (Nabokov) **11**:124, 126, 145

"La inmiscusión terrupta" ("Meddlance Tersplat") (Cortazar) **7**:95

"El inmortal" ("The Immortal") (Borges) **4**:7-8, 10-12, 14, 18-20, 26-7

"In My Life" (Dubus) **15**:70, 77, 79, 81

"The Inn" ("The Country Inn"; "The Wayside Inn") (Turgenev) **7**:315, 320, 323, 325, 337, 359

"Innocence" (Bates) **10**:113

"Innocence" (McGahern) **17**:321

The Innocence of Father Brown (Chesterton) **1**:119-21, 124-25

"The Innocence of Reginold" (Saki) **12**:321, 328

"Inochi no Ki" ("The Tree of Life") (Kawabata) **17**:246

In Old Plantation Days (Dunbar) **8**:120-22, 127-29, 132, 134, 141, 145, 148

In Our Time (Hemingway) **1**:206-08, 212, 214-15, 234-36, 238, 243-45

"In Paris" (Bunin) **5**:114

"L'inquiéteur" ("The Disturber") (Villiers de l'Isle Adam) **14**:382

"The Inquisition" (O'Flaherty) **6**:264, 284

"In Sabine" (Chopin) **8**:90, 99, 103

"In Shadow" (Jewett) **6**:150, 168

"Inside and Outside" (Hesse) **9**:230-32, 236

"An Inside Outside Complex" (O'Faolain) **13**:296, 309, 320

"The Insoluble Problem" (Chesterton) **1**:128

"Inspector General with a Kicking Out" (Bulgakov) **18**:74, 90

"*Inspector General* with an Ejection" (Bulgakov) See "*Inspector General* with an Ejection"

"Installation #6" (Beattie) **11**:30-1,

"Instant of the Hour After" (McCullers) **9**:342, 344-45, 354, 359-60

"Instrucciones para John Howell" (Cortazar) **7**:62

"Instructions for the Third Eye" (Atwood) **2**:16-17

"Instructions on How to Dissect a Ground Owl" (Cortazar) **7**:92

"In St. Valentine's Church" (Babel) **16**:25, 53, 55, 57-8

"Intensive Care Unit" (Ballard) **1**:79

"Intercession" (Updike) **13**:355

"L'interdiction" (Balzac) **5**:8, 16, 26

"An Interest in Life" (Paley) **8**:389-90, 396-99, 415-18

"The Interference of Patsy Ann" (Dunbar) **8**:122, 132

"The Interlopers" (Saki) **12**:285, 317

"Interlopers at the Knap" (Hardy) **2**:203, 205, 207, 216, 229-31

"Interlude in a Book Shop" (Powers) **4**:368-69

"Intermission" (Coover) **15**:60-1

"An International Episode" (James) **8**:299, 302

"The Interrupted Class" (Hesse) **9**:229-30, 232-33, 235-36

"L'intersigne" ("The Sign") (Villiers de l'Isle Adam) **14**:377, 379, 381-82, 394-96, 403-04, 407-11, 413, 415

"The Intervention of Peter" (Dunbar) **8**:121, 127, 140

"An Interview" (Colette) **10**:292

"The Interview" (Singer) **3**:387

"The Interview" (Thurber) **1**:420

"Interview with a Lemming" (Thurber) **1**:417

In That Time (Lagerkvist) See *I den tiden*

"In the Absence of Angels" (Calisher) **15**:5

In the Absence of Angels (Calisher) **15**:2, 4-5

"In the Abyss" (Wells) **6**:366, 389, 403, 408-09

"In the Alley" (Elkin) **12**:94

"In the Autumn of the Year" (Oates) **6**:247

"In the Avu Observatory" (Wells) **6**:361

"In the Basement" (Babel) **16**:13, 15, 22, 36, 41, 59

"In the Bosom of the Country" (O'Faolain) **13**:283, 295, 322

In the Cage (James) **8**:302-05, 329, 331

"In the Carquinez Woods" (Harte) **8**:216, 223, 227, 233, 244, 251

"In the Cart" (Chekhov) **2**:156-58

In the Days When the World Was Wide, and Other Verses (Lawson) **18**:262

"In the Direction of the Beginning" (Thomas) **3**:396, 402, 407, 409

"In the Fifties" (Michaels) **16**:308

"In the Forest" (de la Mare) **14**:81-2, 87-8

"In the Forests of the North" (London) **4**:265, 280

"In the Heart of the Heart of the Country" (Gass) **12**:123-24, 128-29, 133-35, 141, 152, 157-66, 171, 173

In the Heart of the Heart of the Country, and Other Stories (Gass) **12**:123

"In the Hours of Darkness" (O'Brien) **10**:333

"In the House of Suddhu" (Kipling) **5**:265

In the Land of Dreamy Dreams (Gilchrist) **14**:150-55, 158-59, 161-62

"In the Matter of a Private" (Kipling) **5**:260

"In the Middle of the Fields" (Lavin) **4**:183, 185

In the Middle of the Fields, and Other Stories (Lavin) **4**:172

In the Midst of Life (Bierce) See *Tales of Soldiers and Civilians*

"In the Miro District" (Taylor) **10**:395, 397, 400-02, 408-09, 411

In the Miro District, and Other Stories (Taylor) **10**:397-99, 404

"In the Mist" (O'Hara) **15**:262

"In the Morning Sun" (O'Hara) **15**:248, 265-66

"In the Orchard" (Woolf) **7**:411

"In the Penal Colony" (Kafka) See "In der Strafkolonie"

"In the Pride of His Youth" (Kipling) **5**:274

"In the Ravine" ("In the River") (Chekhov) **2**:128, 131-32, 145, 156-57

"In the River" (Chekhov) See "In the Ravine"

"In the Rukh" (Kipling) **5**:287

"In the Same Boat" (Kipling) **5**:284-85

"In the Shadow of Another World" (Ligotti) **16**:277-78, 284

"In the Square" (Bowen) **3**:31

"In the Train" (O'Connor) **5**:364, 371, 376-77, 381-82, 388, 395

"In the Tules" (Harte) **8**:244

"In the Tunnel" (Gallant) **5**:130-31, 144

"In the Vault" (Lovecraft) **3**:262

"In the Warehouse" (Oates) **6**:232

"In the White Night" (Beattie) **11**:25-6, 28

In This World (Hesse) **9**:230

"Intimacy" (Carver) **8**:43

"Intimations" (Michaels) **16**:302-03
"In Time" (Dixon) **16**:217-18
"In Time Which Made a Monkey of Us All"
    (Paley) **8**:403
"Into Egypt" (Benet) **10**:154-56
"Into the Comet" (Clarke) **3**:147
"Intoxication" (Oates) **6**:252
"Intracom" (Le Guin) **12**:235
"In Transit" (Gallant) **5**:150
In Transit: Twenty Stories (Gallant) **5**:150
"The Introducers" (Wharton) **6**:424, 437-38
"The Introduction" (Woolf) **7**:381, 390-91,
    393, 395, 397, 399
"The Intruder" (Borges)
    See "La intrusa"
"The Intruder" (Dixon) **16**:204, 214
"The Intruder" (Dixon) **16**:214
"An Intruder" (Gordimer) **17**:158, 181
"La intrusa" ("The Intruder") (Borges) **4**:14-
    15, 20, 37, 40-1
"L'inutile beauté" (Maupassant) **1**:273, 275,
    286-87
The Invention of Morel (Bioy Casares) **17**:53-
    61, 64-7, 75, 83-5, 90, 94-5
"The Invention of Photography in Toledo"
    (Davenport) **16**:169, 174, 179, 194
"The Invention of the Horse Collar" (Updike)
    13:360
"The Inverted Forest" (Salinger) **2**:309
"Investigations of a Dog" (Kafka)
    See "Forschungen eines hundes"
"The Invincible Slave-Owners" (Dinesen)
    7:177, 196
The Invisible Knight (Calvino)
    See *Il cavaliere inesistente*
"The Invisible Man" (Chesterton) **1**:130, 134,
    136, 142
"L'invitation au voyage" (Baudelaire) **18**:5-6,
    8, 17, 35-6
"Invite" (O'Hara) **15**:253
"Invulnerable" (Ellison) **14**:127
"In Youth Is Pleasure" (Gallant) **5**:128-29,
    134, 143, 148
"Ionitch" (Chekhov)
    See "Ionych"
"Ionych" ("Ionitch") (Chekhov) **2**:128, 131-
    32, 155
Iounn the Weeper (Bunin) **5**:90
Iowa Interiors (Suckow) **18**:389-90, 395, 405,
    418, 421-22
"I Passed By Your Window" (Pritchett)
    14:299
"I Remember Babylon" (Clarke) **3**:131
"I Remember! I Remember!" (O'Faolain)
    13:320-21
I Remember! I Remember! (O'Faolain)
    13:288-89, 293, 311
"Irina" (Gallant) **5**:128-32, 137
"Iris" (Hesse) **9**:234, 243
"Irish Revel" (O'Brien) **10**:341
"Iron" (Levi) **12**:256-57, 259, 262
"The Ironbark Chip" (Lawson) **18**:217, 263
"The Iron Khiva" (Garland) **18**:147, 179
"An Irrevocable Diameter" (Paley) **8**:390
"Isaac" (Michaels) **16**:303
Isabelle (Gide) **13**:42-3, 68-70, 72-3, 77-8,
    94-9
Isis (Nerval) **18**:338, 362
"La isla a mediodía" ("The Island at Noon")
    (Cortazar) **7**:55-6, 61
"The Island at Noon" (Cortazar)
    See "La isla a mediodía"

"The Island Dream" (Hesse) **9**:229-33, 235
"An Island Princess" (Bates) **10**:123
Island Tales (London)
    See *On the Makaloa Mat*
"The Isle of Voices" (Stevenson) **11**:269, 283
"I Spend My Days in Longing" (O'Hara)
    15:283
"I Stand Here Ironing" (Olsen) **11**:163-64,
    166, 171, 177-80, 188, 190, 192-93, 195, 197
"Is There Nowhere Else Where We Can
    Meet?" (Gordimer) **17**:159, 168, 172
"Istoriia moei golubiatni" ("The Story of a
    Mouse"; "The Story of My Dovecot")
    (Babel) **16**:9, 15, 17, 20, 36, 41, 59
"Istoriya leytenanta Ergunova" ("The
    Adventure of Lieutenant Jergounoff"; "The
    History of Lieutenant Ergunov";
    "Lieutenant Yergunov's Story"; "The Story
    of Lieutenant Ergunov") (Turgenev) **7**:316,
    321, 326, 337, 358-59
"The Italian Banditti" (Irving) **2**:251, 261
Italian Folktales (Calvino)
    See *Fiabe Italiene*
"Italian Robber" (Irving) **2**:255
"Italian Sunshine" (Babel) **16**:27-8, 52-3, 55-7
"Itchy" (Hammett) **17**:218
"It Grows on You" (King) **17**:295
"Ithaka" (Davenport) **16**:178-79, 185, 194-95
"It May Never Happen" (Pritchett) **14**:263-
    65, 286, 301, 305
It May Never Happen, and Other Stories
    (Pritchett) **14**:270
"It Must Have Been Spring" (O'Hara) **15**:266
Its Image on the Mirror (Gallant) **5**:122-23,
    135, 140, 148-49
"It's Just Another Day in Big Bear City,
    California" (Beattie) **11**:11, 15, 21
"It's Just the Way It Is" (Bates) **10**:114, 137,
    139
"It's Perfectly True" (Andersen) **6**:30
"It Was the Devil's Work" (O'Flaherty)
    6:259
"It Wouldn't Break Your Arm" (O'Hara)
    15:248, 263, 266
"Ivan FederovičŠpon'ka and His Aunt"
    (Gogol)
    See "Ivan FederovičŠpon'ka i ego tetsuška"
"Ivan FederovičŠpon'ka i ego tetsuška" ("Ivan
    FederovičŠpon'ka and His Aunt") (Gogol)
    4:105, 117, 121
"Ivan the Fool" (Tolstoy) **9**:377, 380-81, 388
"Ivory, Apes, and People" (Thurber) **1**:426
"L'ivrogne" (Maupassant) **1**:274
"Ivy Day in the Committee Room" (Joyce)
    3:201, 205-06, 210-11, 214, 218-21, 225-26,
    228, 231, 234, 237, 240, 242, 248
"Ivy Gripped the Steps" (Bowen) **3**:31-2, 38,
    41, 48, 51
"I Want to Know Why" (Anderson) **1**:20,
    23, 27, 35, 37-8, 40, 48-9, 62
"I Was a Teenage Grave Robber" (King)
    17:268
"I Will Not Let Thee Go, Except Thou Bless
    Me" (Updike) **13**:358
"I Would Have Saved Them If I Could"
    (Michaels) **16**:307-08, 313, 322
I Would Have Saved Them If I Could
    (Michaels) **16**:305-06, 308, 310-11, 314, 316
"The Izu Dancer" (Kawabata)
    See "Izu no Odoriko"
"Izu no Odoriko" ("The Izu Dancer")
    (Kawabata) **17**:240-43, 249-50, 252

"Jachid and Jechidah" (Singer) **3**:357, 363,
    375
"Jack and Gill of the Sierras" (Harte) **8**:214
"The Jackdaw" (Hesse) **9**:243-44
"Jack the Dullard" (Andersen) **6**:11
"Jacob and the Indians" (Benet) **10**:143-44,
    154
Jacob Pasinkov (Turgenev)
    See *Yakov Pasynkov*
"Der jäger Gracchus" ("Gracchus the
    Huntsman"; "The Hunter Gracchus")
    (Kafka) **5**:210
"The Jama" (O'Hara) **15**:278, 285
"James Francis and the Star" (O'Hara)
    15:278, 284-85
"Jamesie" (Powers) **4**:368, 371-72
"Jane" (Maugham) **8**:356, 378-79
"Janice" (Jackson) **9**:266
"Jan the Unrepentant" (London) **4**:286
"Janus" (Beattie) **11**:25-7
"El jardín de senderos que se bifurcan" ("The
    Garden of the Forking Paths") (Borges)
    4:5, 8, 10-11, 13, 16, 18-19, 28
El jardín de senderos que se bifurcan (*The
    Garden of Forking Paths*) (Borges) **4**:4, 18
"The Jaunt" (King) **17**:276
"Jazz, Jive and Jam" (Hughes) **6**:143-44, 146
"The Jealous Extremaduran" (Cervantes)
    See "El celoso extremeño"
"The Jealous Hens" (O'Flaherty) **6**:262, 280
"The Jealous Hidalgo" (Cervantes)
    See "El celoso extremeño"
"Jean-ah Poquelin" (Cable) **4**:67-70, 72-3
"Jeeves and the Dog MacIntosh" (Wodehouse)
    2:355-56
"Jeeves and the Greasy Bird" (Wodehouse)
    2:344
"Jeeves and the Yuletide Spirit" (Wodehouse)
    2:356
"Jeff Brigg's Love Story" (Harte) **8**:216
"Jeffty Is Five" (Ellison) **14**:124-25
"The Jelly-Bean" (Fitzgerald) **6**:58-9
"Jemima, the Mountain Girl" (Fitzgerald)
    6:45, 58
Jemmy (Nerval) **18**:334, 362
"Je ne parle pas français" (Mansfield) **9**:280,
    284, 295-96, 310
"Jenny Garrow's Lovers" (Jewett) **6**:156-58,
    166
"Jericho's Brick Battlements" (Laurence)
    7:252, 259, 267
"Jerry and Molly and Sam" (Carver) **8**:12
"Jesse and Meribeth" (Munro) **3**:347, 349
"The Jest of Jests" (Barnes) **3**:18
"Je Suis le Plus Malade des Surréalistes" (Nin)
    10:303-04, 306
"Je suis perdu" (Taylor) **10**:380-81, 416
"Die Jesuiterkirche in G." (Hoffmann)
    13:183
"Jésus-Christ en Flandre" (Balzac) **5**:14, 16-
    17, 23
"Jesus upon Honshu" (Updike) **13**:360
"The Jet Set" (O'Hara) **15**:283, 287-88
"Le jeu des grâces" (Villiers de l'Isle Adam)
    14:387
"The Jew" (Turgenev) **7**:316, 320, 324, 359
"The Jewbird" (Malamud) **15**:171, 173-75,
    189, 195, 197-99, 200-02, 204, 220, 235, 240
"The Jewels of the Cabots" (Cheever) **1**:101
"The Jewess" (Babel) **16**:35
"The Jew from Babylon" (Singer) **3**:389
"The Jewish Refugee" (Malamud)

See "The German Refugee"
"The Jilting of Granny Weatherall" (Porter)
4:327-28, 340, 348, 356-58
"The Jilting of Jane" (Wells)   6:360, 392
"Jim Blaine and His Grandfather's Old Ram"
(Twain)   6:310
"Jimmy and the Desperate Woman"
(Lawrence)   4:219, 238
"Jimmy Goggles the God" (Wells)   6:360
"Jimmy Rose" (Melville)   1:303-04, 325-26;
17:359, 363
"Jim's Big Brother from California" (Harte)
8:254
"Jimsella" (Dunbar)   8:119, 121, 127, 129,
143, 146
"Jim's Probation" (Dunbar)   8:122, 127
"Jim Sullivan's Adventures in the Great
Show" (Le Fanu)   14:219
"Jo" (O'Connor)   5:382
"The Jockey" (McCullers)   9:322, 332, 347,
358
Joe Wilson and His Mates (Lawson)   18:202-
05, 208-09, 213, 221, 252, 261-62
"Joe Wilson's Courtship" (Lawson)   18:202-
03, 210, 228-29, 232, 252, 258, 262
"John Barleycorn Lives" (Boyle)   16:142-43
"John Barrington Cowles" (Doyle)   12:85-6
"John Bull" (Irving)   2:244, 251, 253
"John Charles Tapner" (Davenport)   16:180,
193
"John Inglefield's Thanksgiving" (Hawthorne)
3:189
"John Napper Sailing through the Universe"
(Gardner)   7:214, 216-17, 222, 233, 235,
238
"John Nicholson's Predicament" (Stevenson)
See "The Misadventures of John Nicholson"
"Johnny Bear" (Steinbeck)
See "The Ears of Johnny Bear"
"Johnny Pye and the Fool-Killer" (Benet)
10:142-44, 148, 154, 156-57, 159-60
"John Redding Goes to Sea" (Hurston)
4:136-38, 149, 153
"Johnsonham, Jr." (Dunbar)   8:135, 148
"Joining Charles" (Bowen)   3:30, 47
Joining Charles (Bowen)   3:30, 33, 40
"Joke" (Dixon)   16:207
"The Joke on Eloise Morey" (Hammett)
17:218, 222
"A Joker" (Baudelaire)
See "Un plaisant"
"The Joker's Greatest Triumph" (Barthelme)
2:28, 34
"The Jokers of New Gibbon" (London)   4:266
"The Jolly Corner" (James)   8:296, 304, 306,
308-09, 326-29
"Jonas ou l'artiste au travail" ("The Artist at
Work") (Camus)   9:103, 105, 108-09, 119,
129-35
"Jones's Alley" (Lawson)   18:238
"Jorinda and Jorindel" (Gallant)   5:138, 141-
44
"Josephine" (O'Flaherty)   6:264
"Josephine the Singer, or the Mouse Folk"
(Kafka)
See "Josephine the Songstress"
"Josephine the Songstress" ("Josephine the
Singer, or the Mouse Folk") (Kafka)   5:231,
240, 242
"Joshua" (Grau)   15:156, 168, 164
"Le joueur généreux" (Baudelaire)   18:19, 41

"Le joujou du pauvre" ("The Poor Child's
Toy") (Baudelaire)   18:33-4, 47-51, 53
"Journal" (Michaels)   16:314, 317
"The Journal of a Superfluous Man"
(Turgenev)
See "Dnevnik lishnego cheloveka"
"The Journal of J. P. Drapeau" (Ligotti)
16:277, 283, 286
Journal of Katherine Mansfield (Mansfield)
9:281, 294
"A Journey" (Gordimer)   17:177, 180, 183,
187-88, 190
"The Journey" (Irving)   2:244, 265
"A Journey" (O'Brien)   10:333
"The Journey" (Porter)   4:352, 358, 363
"A Journey" (Wharton)   6:423
"Journey to Polessie" (Turgenev)   7:335
Journey to the East (Hesse)
See *Die Morgenlandfahrt*
"Joy" (Singer)   3:360, 363-64, 368
"The Joy of Nelly Deane" (Cather)   2:98, 104
"The Joy of the Just" (Gardner)   7:226-28
"J's Marriage" (Coover)   15:33, 35, 48, 59
"Juanita" (Chopin)   8:98, 110-11
"Juan Manso" (Unamuno)   11:312
"Juan Muraña" (Borges)   4:19-20
"Judas" (O'Connor)   5:368-69, 378, 381
"Judgement Day" (O'Connor)   1:343, 365
"The Judge's Wife" (Schnitzler)
See "Die Frau des Richters"
"The Judgment" (Kafka)
See "Das Urteil"
"A Judgment in the Mountains" (Benet)
10:156
"The Judgment of Dungara" (Kipling)   5:262
"A Judgment of Paris" (Dunbar)   8:122, 128,
136
"Jug of Silver" (Capote)   2:63, 65-6, 70
The Jules Verne Steam Balloon (Davenport)
16:198-200
Julia Bride (James)   8:311-13, 343-45, 347-51
Julie de Carneilhan (Colette)   10:269-70
"July the Fifteenth, 1988" (Lish)   18:286
"Jumbo's Wife" (O'Connor)   5:390
"Jump" (Gordimer)   17:178, 181-82, 185, 187,
190-91
Jump, and Other Stories (Gordimer)   17:177-
89, 191
"June Recital" (Welty)   1:474, 480, 483, 485,
495, 497
"The Jungle" (Bowen)   3:30, 33, 49
The Jungle Book (Kipling)   5:277, 287, 292
Jungle Books (Kipling)   5:279, 282, 285, 287-
88, 292-94
"Jupiter Doke, Brigadier-General" (Bierce)
9:96, 98-100
"Jupiter Five" (Clarke)   3:124, 129, 134-35,
149
"Jurge Dulrumple" (O'Hara)   15:282
"Jūrokusai no Nikki" ("Diary of a Sixteen-
Year-Old") (Kawabata)   17:248
"A Jury Case" (Anderson)   1:50
"Just a Little One" (Parker)   2:281
"Just Before the War with the Eskimos"
(Salinger)   2:300
"Just Him and Her" (Suckow)   18:409
"A Justice" (Faulkner)   1:147, 177, 181
"Justice" (O'Hara)   15:287-88
"Just like Little Dogs" (Thomas)   3:403, 406,
411-12
"Just Meat" (London)   4:253-54, 262-63, 291
"Just One More Time" (Cheever)   1:100

Just So Stories (Kipling)   5:273, 279, 287, 293
"Just Tell Me Who It Was" (Cheever)   1:90
"Kabnis" (Toomer)   1:440, 442-44, 446-48,
451-54, 457, 459-60
"Kacheli" ("The Swing") (Bunin)   5:113
"Der Kampf der Sänger" ("The Contest of the
Minstrels") (Hoffmann)   13:182,212
"The Kanaka Surf" (London)   4:257, 266
"Karain" (Conrad)   9:143
"Karintha" (Toomer)   1:441, 452, 455-56, 459
"Kärleken och döden" ("Love and Death")
(Lagerkvist)   12:195
"Karl-Yankel" (Babel)   16:13, 16, 22
"Kartofel'nyy el'f" (Nabokov)
See "The Potato Elf"
"Kashtánka" (Chekhov)   2:130
"Kas'ian of the Beautiful Lands" (Turgenev)
7:343-45
"Katastrofa" (Nabokov)
See "Details of a Sunset"
"Kata Ucle" ("One Arm") (Kawabata)
17:235, 240-41, 246-47
"Kate Lancaster's Plan" (Jewett)   6:167
"Kazimír Stanislávovich" (Bunin)   5:81
"Keela, the Outcast Indian Maiden" (Welty)
1:468, 470, 497
"Keeping Fit" (Gordimer)   17:177, 185, 187-
88, 190
"Keep Your Pity" (Boyle)   5:55
"Keesh, the Son of Keesh" (London)   4:287-
88
Le képi (*The Képi*) (Colette)   10:274, 292-93,
295
The Képi (Colette)
See *Le képi*
"Kerfol" (Wharton)   6:426-28, 431-32
"Kew Gardens" (Woolf)   7:368, 370-71, 374-
76, 378, 382-83, 385, 387-88, 392, 398-99,
404-07
Kew Gardens (Woolf)   7:382
"The Key" (Welty)   1:468
"The Keystone" (Powers)   4:376, 381
"The Key to My Heart" (Pritchett)   14:268
"Kezia and Tui" (Mansfield)   9:282
"Khadzi murat" ("Hadjii murád") (Tolstoy)
9:376, 378, 394-97
"Khor and Kalinych" (Turgenev)   7:313, 342,
362
"Khozyaika" ("The Landlady") (Dostoevsky)
2:163, 170-71, 173-74, 181, 191, 193
Khozyain i rabotnik (*Master and Man*)
(Tolstoy)   9:368, 372, 377, 382-86
"Kidnapped" (Kipling)   5:274
"The Kid Nobody Could Handle" (Vonnegut)
8:432
"The Kid's Whistling" (Updike)   13:355
"Kierkegaard Unfair to Schlegel" (Barthelme)
2:31, 38-9, 54
"Kiev—a Town" (Bulgakov)   18:91
"The Kill" (Boyle)   5:64
"Killed at Resaca" (Bierce)   9:67, 75-7
"The Killers" (Hemingway)   1:211, 218-19,
234-36, 242
"Killing" (Updike)   13:402-03, 409
"The Killing Ground" (Ballard)   1:76
"Killings" (Dubus)   15:75, 88, 94, 96-7, 100-
01
"Kin" (Welty)   1:475-76, 487
"Kinderseele" ("Childhood") (Hesse)   9:218
"The Kindest Thing to Do" (Gordimer)
17:166-67
"The King" (Babel)   16:17-18, 42-4, 48-9, 59

Title Index

"King Bee" (Boyle) **16**:148, 155
"The King Business" (Hammett) **17**:222
"King Gregor and the Fool" (Gardner) **7**:234
"A King Lear of the Steppes" (Turgenev)
See "Stepnoy Korol 'Lir"
"A King Listens" (Calvino) **3**:119
"The King of Folly Island" (Jewett) **6**:154
The King of Folly Island and Other People
(Jewett) **6**:154
"The King of Greece's Tea Party"
(Hemingway) **1**:208
"The King of the Cats" (Benet) **10**:143-44,
158
"The King of the Desert" (O'Hara) **15**:248-
49, 270
"The King of the Foxes" (Doyle) **12**:64
"King Pest" (Poe) **1**:406
"King's Ankus" (Kipling) **5**:293
"The King's Bride" (Hoffmann)
See "Königsbraut"
The King's Indian: Stories and Tales (Gardner)
7:213-21, 226, 228-29, 235
"The King Who Lived on Air" (Bates)
10:112
"King Yu" (Hesse) **9**:244
"Kinjū" ("Of Birds and Beasts") (Kawabata)
17:235, 240-41
"The Kiss" (Babel) **16**:16, 59
"The Kiss" (Carter) **13**:17
"The Kiss" (Chekhov) **2**:126, 156
"The Kiss" (Chopin) **8**:72, 111-12
"Kiss Me Again, Stranger" (du Maurier)
18:126, 138
*Kiss Me Again, Stranger: A Collection of Eight
Stories, Long and Short* (du Maurier)
See *The Apple Tree: A Short Novel and Some
Stories*
"The Kitchen" (O'Faolain) **13**:311, 320
"The Kitchen Child" (Carter) **13**:17-18
"The Kite" (Maugham) **8**:380
"Kitty" (Bowles) **3**:76, 80
"Kitty the Wren" (O'Faolain) **13**:309
"Klara Milich" ("Clara Milich") (Turgenev)
7:321, 324, 326-28, 334, 338, 362
"Klee Dead" (Coover) **15**:33, 37, 41
"Kleine Fabel" ("Little Fable") (Kafka)
5:254
Der kleine Herr Friedemann (*Little Herr
Friedemann*) (Mann) **5**:319, 323, 327, 332,
334, 336
"Die Kleine Komödie" ("The Little Comedy")
(Schnitzler) **15**:377
Klein und Wagner (Hesse) **9**:218, 227, 236-40
Klein Zaches gennant Zinnober (*Little Zack*)
(Hoffmann) **13**:192-93, 195, 197, 199, 200,
218-19
"Klingsor's Last Summer" (Hesse) **9**:218,
220, 227, 240-41
Klingsor's Last Summer (Hesse)
See *Klingsors letzter Sommer*
Klingsors letzter Sommer (*Klingsor's Last
Summer*) (Hesse) **9**:219, 227, 238-39
"The Knife and the Naked Chalk" (Kipling)
5:284, 292
"A Knight-Errant of the Foothills" (Harte)
8:249
"Knight's Gambit" (Faulkner) **1**:178-81
Knight's Gambit (Faulkner) **1**:151, 178-79
"The Knock at the Manor Gate" (Kafka)
5:206
"Knock...Knock...Knock" (Turgenev)
See "Stuk...stuk...stuk"

"Knowledge" (Lish) **18**:275, 283
"Knox" (Ellison) **14**:102, 104-05
"Kochergà" (Zoshchenko) **15**:398
"The Komarov Case" (Bulgakov) **18**:91
"Kometa" ("The Comet") (Schulz) **13**:330,
335
Konarmiia (*Red Cavalry*) (Babel) **16**:2-7,
9-21, 23-7, 29-31, 35-36, 42, 49-54, 56-60
"Königsbraut" ("The King's Bride")
(Hoffmann) **13**:192, 195-96, 198-200, 223,
226
"Konkin" (Babel) **16**:50
"Konkin's Prisoner" (Babel) **16**:26, 28
"Koolau the Leper" (London) **4**:269
"Korea" (McGahern) **17**:298, 322
"Kreisler's Certificate" (Hoffmann) **13**:212
Kreitserova sonata (*The Kreutzer Sonata*)
(Tolstoy) **9**:363, 377-78, 396, 403-06
The Kreutzer Sonata (Tolstoy)
See *Kreitserova sonata*
"Kroy Wen" (Boyle) **5**:55
"Księga" ("The Book") (Schulz) **13**:328, 334-
36, 338
"£1000 for Rosebud" (O'Faolain) **13**:295,
318, 320, 322
"Labour Day Dinner" (Munro) **3**:346
"The Labyrinth" (Nin) **10**:317, 319
"The Ladder" (Pritchett) **14**:296
"Ladies and Gentleman" (Spark) **10**:356
"El lado de la sombra" (Bioy Casares) **17**:95
El lado de la sombra (Bioy Casares) **17**:87, 95
"The Ladybird" (Lawrence) **4**:219, 231, 238-
39
"The Lady Cornelia" (Cervantes)
See "La Señora Cornelia"
"Lady Eleanore's Mantle" (Hawthorne) **3**:184
"The Lady from Guatemala" (Pritchett)
14:268
"The Lady from the Land" (Thurber) **1**:424
"The Lady Icenway" (Hardy) **2**:205
"The Lady in the Looking-Glass: A
Reflection" (Woolf) **7**:375-76, 378-80, 388,
392, 399, 407-12
"Lady Lucifer" (O'Faolain) **13**:300-02, 304-
07
"Lady Mottisfont" (Hardy) **2**:208
"A Lady of Bayou St. John" (Chopin) **8**:72,
84, 87, 91, 106, 110
"The Lady of Moge" (Le Guin) **12**:211, 213
"The Lady of the House of Love" (Carter)
13:9, 28
"The Lady of the Lake" (Malamud) **15**:168,
178, 181, 217, 220
"The Lady of the Sagas" (O'Connor) **5**:371
"The Lady Penelope" (Hardy) **2**:209
"A Lady Slipper" (Dunbar) **8**:122
"The Lady's Maid" (Mansfield) **9**:303, 311
"The Lady's Maid's Bell" (Wharton) **6**:427
"Lady with a Lamp" (Parker) **2**:273-74, 280,
285
"The Lady with the Dog" ("Lady with the
Little Dog") (Chekhov) **2**:127-28, 131-33,
135, 150, 155, 157
"Lady with the Little Dog" (Chekhov)
See "The Lady with the Dog"
"The Lady with the Pet Dog" (Oates) **6**:234
"The Lagoon" (Conrad) **9**:143-44, 152
"De la grafología como ciencia aplicada" ("On
Graphology As an Applied Science")
(Cortazar) **7**:95
"A Lake of Home-brew" (Bulgakov) **18**:92
"The Lament" (O'Flaherty) **6**:276

"The Lamentable Comedy of Willow Wood"
(Kipling) **5**:261
Laments for the Living (Parker) **2**:272, 274
"The Lame Shall Enter First" (O'Connor)
1:343-45, 356, 365
"The Lamias" (Wells) **6**:380
"A Lamp in the Window" (Capote) **2**:80
"The Lamplighter" (Dickens) **17**:124
"The Lamp of Psyche" (Wharton) **6**:424, 427
"Lance" (Nabokov) **11**:108
"The Land and the Water" (Grau) **15**:161
"Ein landarzt" ("The Country Doctor")
(Kafka) **5**:213, 216, 230, 246
"The Landing" (O'Flaherty) **6**:264, 269, 273,
276-77
"Landing in Luck" (Faulkner) **1**:177
"The Land Ironclads" (Wells) **6**:374, 380,
403
"The Landlady" (Dostoevsky)
See "Khozyaika"
"A Landlocked Sailor" (Jewett) **6**:156
"The Landlord" (Pritchett) **14**:255, 296
A Landlord's Morning ("The Morning of a
Landed Proprietor") (Tolstoy) **9**:376, 399
"The Landowner" (Turgenev) **7**:313
"The Landscape Chamber" (Jewett) **6**:154
"Land Where My Fathers Died" (Dubus)
15:81, 86
"The Land Where There Is No Death" (Benet)
10:160
The Langoliers (King) **17**:280, 282-84
The Langston Hughes Reader (Hughes)
6:122-23
Lantern Slides (O'Brien) **10**:345-46
"Le lapin" (Maupassant) **1**:263, 274
"Lappin and Lapinova" (Woolf) **7**:376-77,
388, 393-94, 398
"L'Lapse" (Barthelme) **2**:40
"Laquelle est la vraie?" ("Which Is the True
One?") (Baudelaire) **18**:6
"The Last" (Dixon) **16**:217
"The Last Adventure of the Brigadier" (Doyle)
12:83
"The Last Asset" (Wharton) **6**:424-25
"The Last Cab Driver, and the First Omnibus
Cad" (Dickens) **17**:121, 125
The Last Circle (Benet) **10**:160
"The Last Day in the Field" (Gordon)
15:120, 128, 142
Last Days (Oates) **6**:254
"Last Days in Deephaven" (Jewett) **6**:167
"The Last Demon" (Singer) **3**:383
"Last Descent to Earth" (Lish) **18**:283
"The Last Dream of the Old Oak" ("Old Oak
Tree's Last Dream") (Andersen) **6**:18, 40
"The Last Feast of Harlequin" (Ligotti)
16:274, 277-80, 282-83, 287, 289, 297
"The Last Fiddling of Mordaunts Jim"
(Dunbar) **8**:122, 149
"The Last Flight of Father" (Schulz)
See "Ostatnia ucieczka ojca"
"The Last Galley" (Doyle) **12**:80
"The Last Gas Station" (Grau) **15**:148-49,
152, 154, 160
"The Last Kiss" (Gordimer) **17**:154
"The Last Leaf" (Henry) **5**:185
"The Last Leaf" (Porter) **4**:339, 352-53, 358,
361
"The Last Letter of a Litterateur" (Schnitzler)
See "Derletzebrief eines literaten"
"Last May" (Dixon) **16**:203

"The Last Mohican" (Malamud) **15**:169, 171, 175, 179, 181-82, 187, 192-93, 195-96, 211-12, 219, 222

"The Last Night in the Old Homè" (Bowen) **3**:41

The Last of Chéri (Colette)
See *La fin de Chéri*

"The Last of the Belles" (Fitzgerald) **6**:46-8, 100, 103

"The Last of the Legions" (Benet) **10**:143, 154

"The Last Pearl" (Andersen) **6**:36

"The Last Resort" (Dixon) **16**:215-16

Last Round (Cortazar)
See *Ultimo round*

Last Tales (Dinesen) **7**:162, 166, 171, 175-76, 180-81, 191, 198, 200

"The Last Tea" (Parker) **2**:274, 285

"The Last Throw" (Pritchett) **14**:273

"The Last Trolley Ride" (Calisher) **15**:11

The Last Trolley Ride (Calisher) **15**:5

"The Last Visit" (Aiken) **9**:13, 29-30

"The Last Voyage of the Ghost Ship" (Garcia Marquez)
See "El último viaje del buque fantasma"

Last Words (Crane) **7**:103

The Last Worthless Evening (Dubus) **15**:81, 85-6, 96

"A Late Encounter with the Enemy" (O'Connor) **1**:356

"The Late Henry Conran" (O'Connor) **5**:369, 371, 398

"The Latehomecomer" (Gallant) **5**:130, 133, 136-37

"Late, Late Show" (O'Hara) **15**:278-79

Late Prose (Hesse) **9**:230

Later the Same Day (Paley) **8**:412, 419

"A Late Supper" (Jewett) **6**:166

"The Latin Scholar" (Hesse) **9**:230-32, 235

"The Laughing Man" (Salinger) **2**:293, 296, 299, 313-14, 316

Laughing to Keep from Crying (Hughes) **6**:111-12, 116, 119, 121-22, 127, 131, 133

"Laughter" (O'Connor) **5**:390-91

"Lavin" (McGahern) **17**:302, 322

"Lavinia: An Old Story" (Paley) **8**:412

"The Law Breaker" (O'Hara) **15**:283

"The Lawn Party" (Beattie) **11**:6-7

"The Law of Life" (London) **4**:287-89, 292

"The Law of the Jungle" (Cheever) **1**:99

"Layaways" (Dixon) **16**:206, 208

"Lazy Sons" (Calvino) **3**:112

"Léa" (Barbey d'Aurevilly) **17**:9-11

"Lead" (Levi) **12**:264, 268, 281

"The Leader of the People" (Steinbeck) **11**:207-10, 212-13, 217-18, 220-21, 233, 236, 242

"A Leaf From the Sky" (Andersen) **6**:6

"Leaf Season" (Updike) **13**:401

Leaf Storm (Garcia Marquez)
See *La hojarasca*

"The Leaf Sweeper" (Spark) **10**:356, 366

"The League of Old Men" (London) **4**:265, 287

"The Leaning Tower" (Porter) **4**:331, 339-40

The Leaning Tower, and Other Stories (Porter) **4**:331, 347, 352

"The Leap" (Barthelme) **2**:45, 55

"The Leap" (Oates) **6**:250, 252

"The Leap Frog" (Andersen) **6**:7, 10

"Learning to Be Dead" (Calvino) **3**:113

"Learning to Fall" (Beattie) **11**:10, 13, 22-3, 29

"A Lear of the Steppes" (Turgenev)
See "Stepnoy Korol 'Lir"

"The Leather Funnel" (Doyle) **12**:65-6, 76

"Leaves" (Updike) **13**:375-77, 379

"Leaving School" (Gordimer) **17**:166

"Leaving the Yellow House" (Bellow) **14**:22-3, 25-6, 32-3, 35, 37

"Lechery" (Phillips) **16**:325, 327-28, 337

"Lecturer in Morphology" (James) **16**:251

"The Lees of Happiness" (Fitzgerald) **6**:45, 58-9

"The Legacy" (Woolf) **7**:376-77, 388, 393-95

"The Legend" (Wharton) **6**:429, 437

"La légende de l'éléphant blanc" (Villiers de l'Isle Adam) **14**:397

"La légende de Saint-Julien l'Hospitalier" ("The Legend of Saint Julien Hospitaller"; "The Legend of Saint Julien the Hospitator"; "Saint Julien") (Flaubert) **11**:37-9, 42, 45, 53, 55, 61, 63, 65, 70, 78-9, 81, 84, 89-92

"La légende du Mont-Saint-Michel" (Maupassant) **1**:285, 288

"Legend of Khalif Hakem" (Nerval)
See *L'histoire du Calife Hakem*

"Legend of Prince Ahmed Al Kemel, or The Pilgrim of Love" (Irving) **2**:267

"The Legend of Saamstadt" (Harte) **8**:250

"The Legend of Saint Julien Hospitaller" (Flaubert)
See "La légende de Saint-Julien l'Hospitalier"

"The Legend of Saint Julien the Hospitator" (Flaubert)
See "La légende de Saint-Julien l'Hospitalier"

"The Legend of Sleepy Hollow" (Irving) **2**:239, 241, 243-51, 253, 255, 259-60

"Legend of the Arabian Astrologer" (Irving) **2**:267

"The Legend of the Moor's Legacy" (Irving) **2**:246, 254, 268

"Legend of the Rose of Alhambra" (Irving) **2**:246, 268

"Legend of the Three Beautiful Princesses" (Irving) **2**:267

"Lejana" ("The Distances"; "Faraway Image") (Cortazar) **7**:52, 56-7, 81

"The Lemon" (Thomas) **3**:396, 399, 407-08

"Lemonade" (Lavin) **4**:166

"Lenin and the Firewood" (Zoshchenko) **15**:407

"Lenin and the Sentry" (Zoshchenko) **15**:407, 409

"Lenin and the Stovemaker" (Zoshchenko) **15**:407

"Leonard" (O'Hara) **15**:278

"The Leonardo" (Nabokov) **11**:117

"Un león en el bosque de Palermo" (Bioy Casares) **17**:95

"Leopard George" (Lessing) **6**:186, 190

"Leopard in a Temple" (Lish) **18**:275

"The Leper's Helix" (Coover) **15**:59

Lessness (Beckett)
See *Sans*

"The Lesson" (O'Hara) **15**:290

"The Lesson of the Master" (James) **8**:279, 282, 302

"Let's Beat Down the Poor" (Baudelaire)
See "Assommons les pauvres"

"A Letter" (Babel) **16**:27-8, 50

"The Letter" (Maugham) **8**:359, 361, 367, 373-74, 382

"The Letter" (Oates) **6**:236

"The Letter" (O'Flaherty) **6**:262, 265, 276, 280

"Letter from His Father" (Gordimer) **17**:169, 171

"A Letter from Home" (Lessing) **6**:199

"The Letters" (Wharton) **6**:424-25, 427, 436

Letters from the Underworld (Dostoevsky)
See *Zapiski iz podpol'ya*

"Letters to the Editore" (Barthelme) **2**:40

"A Letter That Never Reached Russia" (Nabokov) **11**:132

"The Letter That Was Never Mailed" (Barnes) **3**:13

"Letter to a Young Lady in Paris" (Cortazar)
See "Carta a un senorita en París"

"The Letter Writer" (Singer) **3**:360, 384

"Let There Be Honour" (Boyle) **5**:56

"Let There Be Light" (Clarke) **3**:130

"Letting Go" (Grau) **15**:161-62

Lettre d'un Ture (Voltaire) **12**:359

Let Your Mind Alone! and Other More or Less Inspirational Pieces (Thurber) **1**:414, 422-23, 426

Leutnant Gustl (*Lieutenant Gustl; None but the Brave*) (Schnitzler) **15**:345, 351-53, 375

"Levitation" (Ozick) **15**:307, 318

Levitation: Five Fictions (Ozick) **15**:306, 312, 318-19

"Liaisons Dangereuses" (Zoshchenko) **15**:399

"The Liar" (Faulkner) **1**:177

"The Liar" (James) **8**:275, 296, 318, 320-21

"Liars" (O'Faolain) **13**:312

"The Liars" (Pritchett) **14**:285-86, 296

"The Liberal Lover" (Cervantes)
See "El amante liberal"

"The Liberation of Jake Hanley" (Oates) **6**:230

"The Libertine" (Bulgakov) **18**:89

"Liberty" (O'Faolain) **13**:296, 322-23

"The Library Horror" (Gardner) **7**:226

"The Library of Babel" (Borges)
See "La biblioteca de Babel"

"The Library of Byzantium" (Ligotti) **16**:278-80

The Library Policeman (King) **17**:282-84

Libro que no muerde (*Book That Doesn't Bite*) (Valenzuela) **14**:366, 368

"Lichen" (Munro) **3**:347-49

"El licenciado vidriera" ("The Glass Scholar"; "Master Glass") (Cervantes) **12**:4, 8, 14-15, 17, 36, 38-40

"A Lickpenny Lover" (Henry) **5**:163, 171, 186

"The Lie" (Carver) **8**:34

"Lieutenant" (O'Hara) **15**:248-49

Lieutenant Gustl (Schnitzler)
See *Leutnant Gustl*

"Lieutenant Yergunov's Story" (Turgenev)
See "Istoriya leytenanta Ergunova"

"Life" (O'Flaherty) **6**:260, 269, 271, 277-78, 280

"The Life and Adventures of Matthew Pavlichenko" (Babel)
See "The Life Story of Pavlichenko"

"The Life and Work of Professor Roy Millen" (Warren) **4**:387, 389-90, 395, 400

"A Life at Angelo's" (Benet) **10**:144

"Life Everlastin'" (Freeman) **1**:192, 195

"The Lifeguard" (Beattie)   **11**:16

"Lifeguard" (Updike)   **13**:348, 350, 398-99

"Life Hutch" (Ellison)   **14**:112-15, 117

"Life Is Better than Death" (Malamud)   **15**:173-75, 223

"Life Isn't a Short Story" (Aiken)   **9**:9, 13-14, 32, 40

"The Life of Imagination" (Gordimer)   **17**:158, 172

"Life of Ma Parker" (Mansfield)   **9**:281, 310, 313-14

"The Life of Nancy" (Jewett)   **6**:152

"The Life of Pavlichenko" (Babel)
   See "The Life Story of Pavlichenko"

"The Life of Tadeo Isidoro Cruz" (Borges)
   See "Biografía de Tadeo Isidoro Cruz"

"Life on the Earth" (Gilchrist)   **14**:162

Life's Handicap (Kipling)   **5**:274, 291

Life's Little Ironies (Hardy)   **2**:205-08, 210, 212, 214-16, 220, 222-23

"Life Story" (Barth)   **10**:43, 47-8, 51-5, 73-4, 77-80, 83, 85-7, 91, 97-8, 100

"The Life Story of Pavlichenko" ("The Life and Adventures of Matthew Pavlichenko"; "The Life of Pavlichenko") (Babel)   **16**:28, 51-2

"Life Vanquished" (Lagerkvist)   **12**:187

"Life with Freddie" (Wodehouse)   **2**:344

"The Life You Save May Be Your Own" (O'Connor)   **1**:343-44, 348-49, 356, 359-60

"The Lift" (Doyle)   **12**:78, 80

"The Lift That Went Down into Hell" (Lagerkvist)
   See "Hissen som gick ner i helvete"

"Ligeia" (Poe)   **1**:377, 379-80, 385, 393-97, 399

"Light" (O'Flaherty)   **6**:265, 280

"A Light Breath" (Bunin)
   See "Light Breathing"

"Light Breathing" ("A Light Breath") (Bunin)   **5**:81, 93, 104

"Light Can Be Both Wave and Particle" (Gilchrist)   **14**:162

Light Can Be Both Wave and Particle (Gilchrist)   **14**:161-62

"The Lighter When Needed" (O'Hara)   **15**:252

"The Lighthouse" (Bates)   **10**:115-17

"Lightning" (Barthelme)   **2**:51

"The Lightning-Rod Man" (Melville)   **1**:298, 303-04; **17**:361

"The Light of the World" (Hemingway)   **1**:242, 245

"The Light-Years" (Calvino)   **3**:104

"Like All Other Men" (McGahern)   **17**:321

"Like a Queen" (Anderson)   **1**:31, 52-3

"Like Glass" (Beattie)   **11**:13

"Like Mother Used to Make" (Jackson)   **9**:272

"Like Old Times" (O'Hara)   **15**:250

"Like That" (McCullers)   **9**:342, 345, 354-55

"Like the Sad Heart of Ruth" (Taylor)   **10**:376, 410

"Liking Men" (Atwood)   **2**:20

"Lilacs" (Chopin)   **8**:72, 87, 108-10, 112

"Lilacs" (Lavin)   **4**:171

"Liliana llorando" ("Liliana Weeping") (Cortazar)   **7**:62-3

"Liliana Weeping" (Cortazar)
   See "Liliana llorando"

"The Lilies" (Chopin)   **8**:93

Lilít e altri racconti ("Lilith, and Other Stories"; *Moments of Reprieve*) (Levi)   **12**:260, 263, 272-73, 276, 280

"Lilith" (Nin)   **10**:317, 319

"Lilith, and Other Stories" (Levi)
   See *Lilít e altri racconti*

"Det lilla fälttåget" ("The Children's Campaign") (Lagerkvist)   **12**:179, 182, 195

"Lily Daw and the Three Ladies" (Welty)   **1**:470, 482, 497

"The Lily's Quest" (Hawthorne)   **3**:181

"Limbo" (Lavin)   **4**:167

Limits and Renewals (Kipling)   **5**:278, 283

"The Limpet" (du Maurier)   **18**:128

"Line and Colour" (Babel)
   See "Colour and Line"

"Lion" (Faulkner)   **1**:182

The Lion of Comarre (Clarke)   **3**:145, 148

"A Lion on the Freeway" (Gordimer)   **17**:164, 191-92

"The Lion's Den" (Pritchett)   **14**:271

"Lions, Harts, Leaping Does" (Powers)   **4**:371, 377-78, 380, 384

"The Lion's Skin" (Maugham)   **8**:379

"Lips to Lips" (Nabokov)   **11**:117

"Lispeth" (Kipling)   **5**:262

"Lispet, Lispett & Vaine" (de la Mare)   **14**:60, 80, 85

"Listening" (Paley)   **8**:420

"Le lit 29" (Maupassant)   **1**:274

"The Literary Life of Laban Goldman" (Malamud)   **15**:235

"Literary Talk" (Michaels)   **16**:316

"The Litigants" (Singer)   **3**:385

"Little Bessie" (Twain)   **6**:339

"Little Bull" (Cortazar)
   See "Torito"

"A Little Child Shall Lead Them" (Harper)   **15**:371

"The Little Chill" (Boyle)   **16**:148, 155

"Little Claus and Big Claus" ("Big Claus and Little Claus"; "Little Klaus and Big Criticism") (Andersen)   **6**:4, 11, 13, 16, 18, 26, 30, 37

"A Little Cloud" (Joyce)   **3**:205, 209-10, 226, 231, 234, 245, 248

"The Little Comedy" (Schnitzler)
   See "Die Kleine Komödie"

The Little Comedy, and Other Stories (Schnitzler)   **15**:371

"The Little Cousins" (Taylor)   **10**:383-84

"Little Curtis" (Parker)   **2**:274, 280-81, 283

"Little Did I Know" (Calisher)   **15**:7

The Little Disturbances of Man (Paley)   **8**:388, 391, 395, 407, 410, 414

"Little Dog" (Hughes)   **6**:109, 121-23, 129-30, 142

"Little Fable" (Kafka)
   See "Kleine Fabel"

"The Little Farm" (Bates)   **10**:116

"The Little Fir Tree" (Andersen)
   See "The Fir-Tree"

"A Little Free Mulatto" (Chopin)   **8**:105

"Little French Mary" (Jewett)   **6**:155

"The Little Girl" (Mansfield)   **9**:281, 284, 315-16

The Little Girl, and Other Stories (*Something Childish, and Other Stories*) (Mansfield)   **9**:281, 301

"The Little Girl Continues" (Barnes)
   See "The Grande Malade"

"The Little Girl's Room" (Bowen)   **3**:33, 43

"Little Girls Wiser than Men" (Tolstoy)   **9**:388

"A Little Girl Tells a Story to a Lady" (Barnes)
   See "Cassation"

"The Little Governess" (Mansfield)   **9**:283

"The Little Gray Goat" (Zoshchenko)   **15**:407-09

"The Little Hero" (Dostoevsky)   **2**:171, 189-90

Little Herr Friedemann (Mann)
   See *Der kleine Herr Friedemann*

"The Little Hours" (Parker)   **2**:274, 281

"The Little House" (Bowles)   **3**:76

"The Little House" (Jackson)   **9**:270-71

"Little Ida's Flowers" (Andersen)   **6**:3-4, 6, 23, 30

"Little Klaus and Big Criticism" (Andersen)
   See "Little Claus and Big Claus"

"Little Lizzy" (Mann)   **5**:322-23, 327, 331, 334-36

"A Little Local Color" (Henry)   **5**:191

"The Little Man in Black" (Irving)   **2**:242

"The Little Match Girl" ("The Little Match Seller") (Andersen)   **6**:18-9, 25-6, 30, 41

"The Little Match Seller" (Andersen)
   See "The Little Match Girl"

"The Little Mermaid" ("The Little Sea-Maid") (Andersen)   **6**:6-7, 11-13, 18, 26-30, 36-7, 40-1

"The Little Mother" (O'Connor)   **5**:371-72

Little Novels (Schnitzler)   **15**:342-43

"A Little of Chickamauga" (Bierce)   **9**:99

"Little Old Spy" (Hughes)   **6**:131

"The Little Photographer" (du Maurier)   **18**:127, 138

Little Poems in Prose (Baudelaire)
   See *Petits poèmes en prose: Le spleen de Paris*

"The Little Prince" (Lavin)   **4**:165-67, 183

"The Little Regiment" (Crane)   **7**:102, 106

The Little Regiment, and Other Episodes of the American Civil War (Crane)   **7**:102

"The Little Sea-Maid" (Andersen)
   See "The Little Mermaid"

"The Little Shoemakers" (Singer)   **3**:356, 375, 378, 383-84

"Little Tembi" (Lessing)   **6**:191, 197

"Little Tuk" (Andersen)   **6**:3-4

"The Little Virgin" (Hughes)   **6**:127

"The Little White Dog" (O'Flaherty)   **6**:280

"Little Willie" (Gordimer)   **17**:154

"A Little Woman" (Kafka)   **5**:239

Little Zack (Hoffmann)
   See *Klein Zaches gennant Zinnober*

Lives of Girls and Women (Munro)   **3**:323, 325-28, 330-33, 335-36, 338-46

"Lives of the Poets" (Atwood)   **2**:3-4, 6, 10-11

"The Living" (Lavin)   **4**:167

"Living" (Paley)   **8**:391, 408-09, 416

"A Living Relic" (Turgenev)   **7**:321-22, 326, 337

"Livingstone's Companions" (Gordimer)   **17**:157, 173

Livingstone's Companions (Gordimer)   **17**:157-58, 168, 181, 186, 189

"Livvie" (Welty)   **1**:467, 469, 471

"Lizards in Jamshyd's Courtyard" (Faulkner)   **1**:177

"Ljubka the Cossack" (Babel)   **16**:48

"The Loaded Dog" (Lawson)   **18**:201, 206, 217, 242, 244-45, 248, 262-63

"The Loan" (Malamud) **15**:169, 212, 216, 220, 234

"A Lodging for the Night: A Story of François Villon" (Stevenson) **11**:269, 279, 284-86

"Lofty" (Beattie) **11**:29

"Lofty" (O'Connor) **5**:382

"Logarithms" (Singer) **3**:388

"Logging and Pimping and 'Your Pal, Jim'" (Maclean) **13**:260, 270-71

"Lokis" (Merimee) **7**:276-77, 283, 285-86, 296-99

"The Lone Charge of Francis B. Perkins" (Crane) **7**:108

"The Loneliest Man in the U.S. Army" (Boyle) **5**:55

"Loneliness" (Anderson) **1**:30, 44

"Loneliness" (Schulz) **13**:330

"The Lonely One" (Grau) **15**:155

"A Lonely Ride" (Harte) **8**:210

"Lonely Rock" (O'Connor) **5**:371-72

"The Lonely Track" (Lawson) **18**:225

"The £1,000,000 Bank-Note" (Twain) **6**:303, 328-30

"Lone Wolf's Old Guard" (Garland) **18**:147

"Long Black Song" (Wright) **2**:360-63, 365, 367, 369, 371, 374, 376, 379-81, 387

"The Long Day" (Gordon) **15**:104, 106, 119, 139-40

"The Long Distance Runner" (Paley) **8**:397-98, 408-09, 415

"The Longest Day of the Year" (Beattie) **11**:30, 34

"The Longest Science Fiction Story Ever Told" (Clarke) **3**:133

"A Long Fourth" (Taylor) **10**:374-77, 379, 387-88, 397-400, 402

A Long Fourth, and Other Stories (Taylor) **10**:375-76, 381, 384-86, 395

"Long, Long Ago" (Bunin) ´**5**:82

"The Long Road to Ummera" (O'Connor) **5**:362-65, 378, 380, 383, 388-89, 397-98

"The Long Run" (Wharton) **6**:418, 424-25, 436

The Long Valley (Steinbeck) **11**:207-08, 210, 221, 225-27, 229-34, 236, 239-40, 244-45, 249

"The Long Walk to Forever" (Vonnegut) **8**:424

"Look at All Those Roses" (Bowen) **3**:55

Look at All Those Roses (Bowen) **3**:33, 39, 41

"Look How the Fish Live" (Powers) **4**:368, 373-74, 376-77

Look How the Fish Live (Powers) **4**:375-76, 380-82

Looking Backwards (Colette) **10**:293

"Looking for Mr. Green" (Bellow) **14**:3, 22-3, 25, 27-8, 30-2

"The Looking Glass" (de la Mare) **14**:66, 84, 87, 90

"The Loons" (Laurence) **7**:255, 259, 270

"Loophole" (Clarke) **3**:125, 148-50

"Loopy Ears" (Bunin)
See "Petlistye ushi"

Lord Arthur Savile's Crime, and Other Stories (Wilde) **11**:407

"Lord Arthur Savile's Crime: A Study of Duty" (Wilde) **11**:362, 366-69, 371, 373, 375-77, 394, 399-402

"Lord Curzon's Benefit Day" ("Benefit Performance for Lord Cuzon") (Bulgakov) **18**:90, 110

"Lord Douglas" (Lawson) **18**:243

"Lord Emsworth Acts for the Best" (Wodehouse) **2**:346, 348

"Lord Emsworth and the Girl Friend" (Wodehouse) **2**:346-49

"Lord Mountdrago" (Maugham) **8**:369, 380

"The Lord of the Dynamos" (Wells) **6**:361, 365-67, 375-76, 381-82, 396-97

"The Lord's Day" (Powers) **4**:380-81

"The Los Amigos Fiasco" (Doyle) **12**:81

"A Losing Game" (Powers) **4**:370

"De los reyes futures" (Bioy Casares) **17**:54

"Loss" (Oates) **6**:236

"Loss of Breath" (Poe) **1**:407

"The Lost" (Boyle) **5**:57, 74-6

"The Lost Art of Twilight" (Ligotti) **16**:269, 271, 273

"Lost Ball" (Bates) **10**:123

"The Lost Blend" (Henry) **5**:163

"Lost Face" (London) **4**:265, 289

Lost Face (London) **4**:265, 283, 288

"Lost Hearts" (James) **16**:230, 232-33, 236-39, 241-42, 245, 250-51, 255-56

"Lost in the Funhouse" (Barth) **10**:35, 37, 39, 41-3, 46-8, 52-4, 57, 61, 63, 65, 67, 80, 84-5, 88-9, 95, 97-100

Lost in the Funhouse: Fiction for Print, Tape, Live Voice (Barth) **10**:38-43, 45, 48-50, 52-60, 63-5, 67, 73-85, 87-91, 94-5, 97-9, 100-03

"The Lost Legion" (Kipling) **5**:272-75, 285

"The Lost Letter" (Gogol)
See "Propavšaja gramotax"

"A Lost Lover" (Jewett) **6**:156, 159, 166

"The Lost Novel" (Anderson) **1**:31

"Lost on Dress Parade" (Henry) **5**:158, 189

The Lost Ones (Beckett)
See *Le dépeupleur*

"The Lost Reflection" (Hoffmann)
See "Das Verlorene Spiegelbild"

"The Lost Track" (de la Mare) **14**:80, 84

"The Lost Turkey" (Jewett) **6**:156

"La lotería en Babilonia" ("The Babylon Lottery"; "The Lottery in Babylon"; "The Lottery of Babylon") (Borges) **4**:5-7, 11-12, 14

"The Lottery" (Jackson) **9**:249-52, 254-55, 258, 261, 264-70

"The Lottery in Babylon" (Borges)
See "La lotería en Babilonia"

"The Lottery of Babylon" (Borges)
See "La lotería en Babilonia"

The Lottery; or, The Adventures of James Harris (Jackson) **9**:249

"The Lotus-Eater" (Maugham) **8**:379

"The Loudest Voice" (Paley) **8**:388

"Louisa" (Freeman) **1**:196

"Louisa, Please Come Home" (Jackson) **9**:267, 272

"Louise" (Saki) **12**:322

"Loulou; or, The Domestic Life of the Language" (Atwood) **2**:18, 21, 23

"Lou, the Prophet" (Cather) **2**:96, 100, 105

"Love" (Bowen) **3**:33, 41

"Love" (Paley) **8**:419

"Love" (Zoshchenko) **15**:399

"Love seventy-seven" (Cortazar) **7**:93

"Love among the Haystacks" (Lawrence) **4**:197

"Love and Death" (Lagerkvist)
See "Kärleken och döden"

"Love and Death" (Oates) **6**:225, 254

"Love and Lethe" (Beckett) **16**:68, 72, 93

Love and Napalm: Export U.S.A. (Ballard)
See *The Atrocity Exhibition*

"Love and Russian Literature" (Maugham) **8**:378

Love and Will (Dixon) **16**:211, 216-19

"Love. Friendship." (Oates) **6**:227-28

"Love Has Its Own Action" (Dixon) **16**:204, 210, 214

"Love in a Wych Elm" (Bates) **10**:133

"Love is for Lovers" (Lavin) **4**:166

"Love Life" (Mason) **4**:9

Love Life (Mason) **4**:28

"The Lovely April" (Grau) **15**:153

"The Lovely Lady" (Lawrence) **4**:220

The Lovely Lady, and Other Stories (Lawrence) **4**:230, 238

"The Lovely Leave" (Parker) **2**:277, 280, 285-86

"The Lovely Myfwanwy" (de la Mare) **14**:69

"The Lovely Troubled Daughters of Our Old Crowd" (Updike) **13**:403

The Love Object (O'Brien) **10**:330, 341

"The Love of Elsie Barton: A Chronicle" (Warren) **4**:389-91, 394

"Love of Life" (London) **4**:253, 265, 272-73, 278, 288-89, 291-92

Love of Life, and Other Stories (London) **4**:252, 264-65, 282, 285, 288-89

"Love on the Bon-Dieu" (Chopin) **8**:89

"Love-o'-Women" (Kipling) **5**:266, 276, 279

"The Love-Philtre of Ikey Schoenstein" (Henry) **5**:182

"The Lover" (Bowen) **3**:40

"The Lover" (Walker) **5**:413-14

"The Lovers" (Andersen) **6**:7

"Lovers" (O'Flaherty) **6**:282

"Lovers of the Lake" (O'Faolain) **13**:288, 295, 297

Love Scene (Coover) **15**:

"The Loves of Lady Purple" (Carter) **13**:3-5

"The Love Song of the Conquering Lovers" (Turgenev)
See "Pesn' torzhestruyushchey lyubvi"

"A Love Story" (Bowen) **3**:41, 54

"A Love Story" (Lawson) **18**:239

"Love Suicides" (Kawabata) **17**:258

"Love's Young Dream" (O'Faolain) **13**:315, 319-20

"Loving Memory" (Lavin) **4**:166, 168

"The Lowboy" (Cheever) **1**:112

"Low-Flying Aircraft" (Ballard) **1**:73-4, 83

Low-Flying Aircraft, and Other Stories (Ballard) **1**:71-3

"Low-Lands" (Pynchon) **14**:308, 310, 312, 321-22, 324, 329, 334-35, 340-42, 344, 347-48

"Luani of the Jungle" (Hughes) **6**:127

"Luc and His Father" (Gallant) **5**:147

"Lucas, His Modesty" (Cortazar)
See "Lucas, sus pudores"

"Lucas, His Partisan Arguments" (Cortazar)
See "Lucas, sus discusiones partidarias"

"Lucas, sus discusiones partidarias" ("Lucas, His Partisan Arguments") (Cortazar) **7**:94

"Lucas, sus pudores" ("Lucas, His Modesty") (Cortazar) **7**:94

"Lucerne" (Tolstoy) **9**:376, 389-91, 393

"The Luceys" (O'Connor) **5**:371, 378, 381-83, 389

"An Luchóg" (O'Flaherty) **6**:287

"The Luck of Roaring Camp" (Harte) **8**:208, 210, 219, 225-26, 228, 231-32, 237-39, 241, 243-44, 245, 249, 251-52, 255, 257

The Luck of Roaring Camp, and Other Sketches (Harte) **8**:219, 229, 236, 238, 255-56

"The Lucksmith" (Benet) **10**:148

"The Lucky Fist" (Benet) **10**:147-48

"The Lucky Pair" (Lavin) **4**:173, 183

"Lucretia Burns" (Garland) **18**:173, 182

"Lucy" (de la Mare) **14**:69, 87

"Lucy Grange" (Lessing) **6**:191

"The Luftbad" (Mansfield) **9**:307

"Lui?" (Maupassant) **1**:265-66, 281

"The Lull" (Saki) **12**:295-96, 299, 306, 324

"Lulu" (Hesse) **9**:243

"The Lumber Room" (Saki) **12**:293, 297, 308-09, 320

"Luna e G N A C" ("The Moon and GNAC") (Calvino) **3**:97

"Lunch" (Bowen) **3**:40

"La lune de pluie" ("The Rainy Moon") (Colette) **10**:281

"The Lurking Fear" (Lovecraft) **3**:258, 260, 281

"The Lynching of Jube Benson" (Dunbar) **8**:121-22, 126, 128-30, 132, 136

"Lynx Hunting" (Crane) **7**:104

"Ma'ame Pélagie" (Chopin) **8**:87, 105

"The Macbeth Murder Mystery" (Thurber) **1**:426

"La machine à gloire" ("The Glory Machine") (Villiers de l'Isle Adam) **14**:377, 379, 383, 396

"The Machine-Gun Corps in Action" (O'Connor) **5**:369, 371, 390-91

"Mac in Love" (Dixon) **16**:203, 209-10, 213

"Mackintosh" (Maugham) **8**:359, 370, 372

"Madame Celestine's Divorce" (Chopin) **8**:72-3, 84, 91

"Madame Délicieuse" (Cable) **4**:48, 56, 67, 69-71

Madame Delphine (Cable) **4**:48, 51-2, 56-7, 67, 75-8

"Madame Zilensky and the King of Finland" (McCullers) **9**:322, 330, 332, 347, 357-58

"Made in Heaven" (Updike) **13**:404

"The Madeline Wherry Case" (O'Hara) **15**:262, 283, 287-88, 290

"Mademoiselle Bistouri" (Baudelaire) **18**:15-16, 19, 36, 38, 42

Mademoiselle Coeur-Brisé (West)
   See *Miss Lonelyhearts*

"Mademoiselle O" (Nabokov) **11**:108, 113, 128

"Mademoisselle Fifi" (Maupassant) **1**:256, 259, 274, 287

"The Mad Lomasneys" (O'Connor) **5**:363, 370-71, 378, 383, 389

"A Madman's Diary" (Gogol)
   See "Diary of a Madman"

"The Madness of Ortheris" (Kipling) **5**:260

"Mad Night of Atonement" (Ligotti) **16**:276-77, 288, 292, 295, 297

"A Madonna of the Trenches" (Kipling) **5**:271

"A Mæcenas of the Pacific Slope" (Harte) **8**:216, 255

"Maelstrom II" (Clarke) **3**:129, 147

"The Maenads" (Cortazar) **7**:69-70

"Ma femme" (Maupassant) **1**:280

"The Magazine" (Singer) **3**:374

"Magic" (Porter) **4**:327-30, 339-40, 360

"The Magic Barrel" (Malamud) **15**:168, 170, 172, 176, 186, 188, 192, 195-96, 211, 213, 217, 221, 227-34, 239, 241-43

"Magic Fishbone" (Dickens) **17**:124

"The Magician" (Singer) **3**:375

The Magic of Shirley Jackson (Jackson) **9**:252

"The Magic Poker" (Coover) **15**:31, 38, 41-2, 48, 50, 53-6

"Magna Mater" (Oates) **6**:232

"Magna . . . Reading" (Dixon) **16**:217

"Magna Takes the Calls" (Dixon) **16**:207

"Magnetism" (Fitzgerald) **6**:61

"Magnolia Flower" (Hurston) **4**:136

"The Mahatma's Little Joke" (London) **4**:294

"Maiden, Maiden" (Boyle) **5**:56, 65

"The Maid of Saint Phillippe" (Chopin) **8**:71

"The Maid's Shoes" (Malamud) **15**:173, 175

"Maidstone Comfort" (Gilman) **13**:144

"La main" (Maupassant) **1**:281

"The Main Death" (Hammett) **17**:213

"La main d'ecorché" (Maupassant) **1**:281

"Main Road" (Pritchett) **14**:269, 286, 298

Main-Travelled Roads (Garland) **18**:142-46, 148, 150, 155-56, 158-75, 177, 180-81, 183, 186, 191-94

La maison de Claudine (*My Mother's House*) (Colette) **10**:278-79

"La maison du bonheur" (Villiers de l'Isle Adam) **14**:384, 387, 390, 396

"La maison du chat-qui-pelote" ("Le chat-qui-pelote") (Balzac) **5**:21-2, 29, 31-3

La maison nucingen (Balzac) **5**:31

"La maison Tellier" (Maupassant) **1**:256-57, 259-60, 263, 266, 271-72, 274, 276, 282-83, 287

"The Maja" (Nin) **10**:326

"Majesty" (Fitzgerald) **6**:47

"The Majesty of the Law" (O'Connor) **5**:364-66, 369, 371, 377, 381, 389, 395, 398

"The Major of Hussars" (Bates) **10**:117

"Majskaja noč, ili Vtoplennica" ("The Drowned Girl"; "A May Night; or, The Drowned Maiden") (Gogol) **4**:118-19

"Making a Change" (Gilman) **13**:126, 141-42

"Making a Night of It" (Dickens) **17**:116, 122

"Making Arrangements" (Bowen) **3**:54

"Making Changes" (Michaels) **16**:301-02, 311-12

"The Making of a New Yorker" (Henry) **5**:194

The Making of Ashenden (Elkin) **12**:93, 95, 106-07, 110, 114-16

"Making Poison" (Atwood) **2**:17

"Making Westing" (London) **4**:263

"Malachi" (Lawson) **18**:200

"The Malice of Inanimate Objects" (James) **16**:251

"The Maltese Cat" (Kipling) **5**:279

Mal vu mal dit (*Ill Seen Ill Said*) (Beckett) **16**:129-30, 132, 134-37

Mama Grande's Funeral (Garcia Marquez)
   See *Los funerales de la Mamá Grande*

"Mame" (Suckow) **18**:389, 396, 398, 405, 407

"Mammon and the Archer" (Henry) **5**:195

"Mammy Peggy's Pride" (Dunbar) **8**:121, 128, 131

"Mamouche" (Chopin) **8**:93

"The Manager" (O'Hara) **15**:283

"A Man Alone at Lunch" (Aiken) **9**:14

"Man and Daughter in the Cold" (Updike) **13**:361

"A Man and His Dog" (Mann) **5**:312

"The Man and the Snake" (Bierce) **9**:53, 88

"A Man and Two Women" (Lessing) **6**:198, 200-01, 203, 208

"A Man by the Name of Ziegler" (Hesse) **9**:230, 235

"The Man Child" (Baldwin) **10**:4, 7-8, 10, 17

"The Man from Archangel" (Doyle) **12**:85-8

"A Man from Fort Necessity" (Benet) **10**:151, 154

"A Man from Glasgow" (Maugham) **8**:380

"The Man from Mars" (Atwood) **2**:3, 5-7, 10-11, 14, 21

"The Mangler" (King) **17**:262

"The Man Higher Up" (Henry) **5**:166, 193

"Manhole 69" (Ballard) **1**:68

"The Maniac" (Oates) **6**:243

"Manikin" (Michaels) **16**:301, 303, 311-12

"The Man in a Case" (Chekhov)
   See "The Man in a Shell"

"The Man in a Shell" ("The Man in a Case") (Chekhov) **2**:139, 141, 143, 155, 157

"The Man in the Brown Coat" (Anderson) **1**:21, 27

"Man in the Drawer" (Malamud) **15**:189, 191, 216

"The Man in the Passage" (Chesterton) **1**:136

"The Man of Adamant" (Hawthorne) **3**:171, 185

"Man of All Work" (Wright) **2**:388

"Man of Letters" (Dixon) **16**:210, 215

"The Man of No Account" (Harte) **8**:236

"The Man of the Crowd" (Poe) **1**:379

"The Man of the Family" (Bowen) **3**:45

"The Man of the Family" (Suckow) **18**:395, 410

"The Man of the Forests" (Hesse) **9**:243

"The Man of the House" (O'Connor) **5**:371

"The Man of the World" (O'Connor) **5**:386

"Man on the Pink Corner" (Borges)
   See "Hombre de la esquina rosada"

"The Man on the Threshold" (Borges)
   See "El hombre en el umbral"

"The Man on the Tractor" (O'Hara) **15**:259, 283

"Man's Fate" (Dubus) **15**:88

"The Man's Story" (Anderson) **1**:39, 52

"The Man That Corrupted Hadleyburg" (Twain) **6**:293-95, 301-03, 305-09, 325, 334-35, 345

"The Man That Stopped" (O'Connor) **5**:371

"The Man That Was Used Up" (Poe) **1**:407-08

"The Mantle of Whistler" (Parker) **2**:273, 283

"A Man to Be Trusted" (O'Hara) **15**:286

The Man Upstairs, and Other Stories (Wodehouse) **2**:347

"Manuscript Found in a Pocket" (Cortazar)
   See "Manuscrito hallado en un bolsillo"

"Manuscrito hallado en un bolsillo" ("Manuscript Found in a Pocket") (Cortazar) **7**:61-2, 69

"The Man Who Became a Woman" (Anderson) **1**:30, 37, 48-50

"The Man Who Could Not Shake Hands" (King) **17**:266

"The Man Who Could Work Miracles: A Pantoum in Prose" (Wells) **6**:367, 375, 383, 389, 404-06

"The Man Who Died" (Lawson) **18**:215

The Man Who Died (*The Escaped Cock*)
(Lawrence) **4**:212, 220-21, 226, 238
"The Man Who Had to Talk to Somebody"
(O'Hara) **15**:265-66
"The Man Who Invented Sin" (O'Faolain)
13:293, 301, 306, 314, 318
"The Man Who Kicked Cancer's Ass"
(Gilchrist) **14**:163
"The Man Who Killed a Shadow" (Wright)
2:366, 385-86
The Man Who Knew Too Much (Chesterton)
1:121-22, 125-26
"The Man Who Lived Underground" (Wright)
2:364, 366, 370, 373-74, 377, 379, 387-88
"The Man Who Loved His Kind" (Woolf)
7:373, 376, 381, 388
"The Man Who Loved Islands" (Lawrence)
4:197, 212-17, 221, 230, 233, 238
"The Man Whom Women Adored" (Oates)
6:255
"The Man Who Ploughed the Sea" (Clarke)
3:134
"The Man Who Saw the Flood" (Wright)
2:366
"The Man Who Turned into a Statue" (Oates)
6:224
"The Man Who Was" (Kipling) **5**:293
"The Man Who Was Almos' a Man" (Wright)
2:366, 376, 388
"The Man Who was Drowned" (Lawson)
18:242, 255
"The Man Who Would Be King" (Kipling)
5:262, 264, 273, 278, 282, 291, 299
"A Man with a Conscience" (Maugham)
8:379
"Man with a Thermometer" (Bulgakov)
18:90
The Man with Forty Ecus (Voltaire)
See *L'homme aux quarante écus*
"The Man without a Temperament"
(Mansfield) **9**:284, 314
"The Man with the Broken Arm" (O'Hara)
15:252
"The Man with the Twisted Lip" (Doyle)
12:51, 59, 68, 70, 74-5
The Man with Two Left Feet (Wodehouse)
2:327
"Many Are Disappointed" (Pritchett) **14**:255,
259, 269, 271, 282, 284, 297
Many Inventions (Kipling) **5**:266, 273, 283,
287
"The Map of Love" (Thomas) **3**:399, 402,
407
The Map of Love (Thomas) **3**:410
"The Mappined Life" (Saki) **12**:290, 297,
305, 310, 313, 321, 323
Les marana (Balzac) **5**:8, 26, 31
"Maravillosas ocupaciones" ("Marvelous
Pursuits") (Cortazar) **7**:92
"The Marble Works" (Hesse) **9**:230-31, 234-
35
"The March" (McCullers) **9**:332, 354, 360
Märchen (Hesse) **9**:244
"Ein Märchen aus der neuen Zeit" (Hoffmann)
13:218-19
"Marching through Boston" (Updike) **13**:386
"The Marchioness of Stonehenge" (Hardy)
2:204, 217
"The March of Progress" (Chesnutt) **7**:27-8,
37
Marcovaldo: or, The Seasons in the City
(Calvino)

See *Marcovaldo ouvero le stagioni in citta*
Marcovaldo ouvero le stagioni in citta
(*Marcovaldo: or, The Seasons in the City*)
(Calvino) **3**:106-07
"El mar del tiempo perdido" ("The Sea of
Lost Time") (Garcia Marquez) **8**:155, 167-
68, 172
"María Concepción" (Porter) **4**:326, 328, 330,
339-40, 346, 349
"Maria-Fly" (de la Mare) **14**:86-7
Mariamne (*Herod and Mariamne*) (Lagerkvist)
12:198-99, 201-03
"Marie, Marie, Hold On Tight" (Barthelme)
2:34, 40
Mario and the Magician (Mann)
See *Mario und der Zauberer*
Mario und der Zauberer (*Mario and the
Magician*) (Mann) **5**:310-12, 337, 340-41,
353-59
"The Marker" (Coover) **15**:37
"Markheim" (Stevenson) **11**:266, 268-69, 276,
278-79, 281-82, 292, 297
"Marklake Witches" (Kipling) **5**:285
"The Mark of the Beast" (Kipling) **5**:271,
273-74, 280, 299
"The Mark on the Wall" (Woolf) **7**:368, 370-
71, 378, 382-83, 385-88, 392, 397-98, 405,
409
The Mark on the Wall (Woolf) **7**:382
*Mark Twain's "Which Was the Dream?" and
Other Symbolic Writings of the Later Years*
(Twain) **6**:331
"Marmalade" (O'Faolain) **13**:322
El marqués de Lumbría (Unamuno) **11**:313,
323-24
"Die Marquise de la Pivadière" (Hoffmann)
13:188
"Marrakesh" (Munro) **3**:346
"Marriage à la mode" (Mansfield) **9**:279, 310
"The Marriage Feast" (Lagerkvist) **12**:179,
196
"The Marriage of Phaedra" (Cather) **2**:98,
103
Marriages and Infidelities (Oates) **6**:224, 234,
254
"The Married Couple" (Kafka) **5**:206-07
The Married Lover (Colette)
See *Duo*
"A Married Man's Story" (Mansfield) **9**:282,
311
"Marroca" (Maupassant) **1**:257
"The Marry Month of May" (Henry) **5**:163
"Marshall's Capture" (Garland) **18**:167
"Marshall's Dog" (Beattie) **11**:18, 20-3
"The Marsh King's Daughter" ("The Bog
King's Daughter") (Andersen) **6**:13-15,
35-7
Marshlands (Gide)
See *Paludes*
"Marsh Rosemary" (Jewett) **6**:150
"Mars Jeems's Nightmare" (Chesnutt) **7**:7-8,
10, 40
"Martin's Close" (James) **16**:232, 237, 252,
256
"Martwy sezon" ("The Dead Season")
(Schulz) **13**:326-27, 334
"Maruja" (Harte) **8**:216, 244, 251
"The Marvelous Girl" (Pritchett) **14**:261
"Marvelous Pursuits" (Cortazar)
See "Maravillosas ocupaciones"
"Mary" (Mansfield) **9**:284
"Mary" (O'Hara) **15**:266

"Mary and Norma" (O'Hara) **15**:252, 281
"Mary Button's Principles" (Gilman) **13**:141
"Maryelle" (Villiers de l'Isle Adam) **14**:378,
381-82, 384, 393, 396
"Mary Postgate" (Kipling) **5**:279, 281-83
"Mary's Piece" (Dixon) **16**:210
"Mary Winosky" (Hughes) **6**:117-19
"The Masculine Principle" (O'Connor) **5**:366,
371-72, 381, 388-89
"Masculine Protest" (O'Connor) **5**:387
"The Mask of the Bear" (Laurence) **7**:254,
259, 263
"Le masque" (Maupassant) **1**:274, 286
"The Masque of the Red Death" (Poe) **1**:379,
389-90, 398, 406
"Masquerade of a Dead Sword" (Ligotti)
16:269, 273, 277-78
"Massimilla doni" (Balzac) **5**:16
"The Mass Island" (O'Connor) **5**:372
"Master" (Carter) **13**:4
Master and Man (Tolstoy)
See *Khozyain i rabotnik*
Master Flea (Hoffmann)
See *Meister Floh: Ein Märchen in seiben
Abenteuern zweier Freunde*
"Master Glass" (Cervantes)
See "El licenciado vidriera"
"Master John Horseleigh, Knight" (Hardy)
2:210
"Master Misery" (Capote) **2**:63-5, 72-3, 75,
78
"The Masters" (Le Guin) **12**:223, 232-33, 241
Matteo Falcone (Merimee) **7**:278, 280-81, 283,
285, 287-89, 300-01
"A Matter of Chance" (Nabokov) **11**:123-24,
126
"A Matter of Doctrine" (Dunbar) **8**:122
"A Matter of Prejudice" (Chopin) **8**:93
"A Matter of Principle" (Chesnutt) **7**:16, 23,
33-6
"Maupassant" (Babel)
See "Guy de Maupassant"
"Le mauvais vitrier" ("The Bad Glazier")
(Baudelaire) **18**:6, 16, 18, 34, 45, 60-1, 63
"May Day" (Fitzgerald) **6**:45, 57-9, 74-6, 96-
101
"A May Night; or, The Drowned Maiden"
(Gogol)
See "Majskaja noč, ili Vtoplennica"
"The Mayor" (O'Hara) **15**:260
"The Maypole of Merry Mount" (Hawthorne)
3:164-67, 180-81, 183-84, 187, 188
"May-Ry" (Calisher) **15**:15-16
"May you learn to open the door to go out to
play" (Cortazar)
See "que sepa abrir la puerta para ir a
jugar"
"Mazes" (Le Guin) **12**:230, 235
"Me and Miss Mandible" (Barthelme) **2**:26-7,
35, 47, 49, 53
"Mearbhall" (O'Flaherty) **6**:287-89
"Me Cago en la Leche (Robert Jordan in
Nicaragua)" (Boyle) **16**:151
"Meccana d'amore" (Levi) **12**:276
"Un mécène" (Villiers de l'Isle Adam)
See "Le tueur de cygnes"
"Le médaillon" (Villiers de l'Isle Adam)
See "Antonie"
"Meddlance Tersplat" (Cortazar)
See "La inmiscusión terrupta"
"Meddlesome Curiosity" (Cervantes)
See "El curioso impertinente"

"Medicine Men of Civilisation" (Dickens) 17:123

"Meditations in Monmouth Street" (Dickens) 17:115, 117, 121

"The Medusa" (Ligotti) 16:274, 294, 297

"The Meeting" (Borges) 4:20

"The Meeting" (Cortazar)
See "Reunión"

"The Meeting" (Dixon) 16:210

"A Meeting" (O'Faolain) 13:293-95, 309, 316

"Meeting Aline" (Dixon) 16:212-13

"Meeting a Moscow Acquaintance in the Detachment" (Tolstoy) 9:389-90

"A Meeting in Rauch" (Bioy Casares) 17:95-6

"A Meeting in Space" (Gordimer) 17:158

"A Meeting South" (Anderson) 1:37, 52-3

"A Meeting with Medusa" (Clarke) 3:128, 130, 132, 135-36, 138-40, 146

Meet Mr. Mulliner (Wodehouse) 2:325, 338

"Meiosis" (Calvino) 3:109

Meister Floh: Ein Märchen in seiben Abenteuern zweier Freunde (Master Flea) (Hoffmann) 13:186, 192, 195, 197-200, 218-19, 225

Meister Martin (Hoffmann) 13:182

"Mejdoub" (Bowles) 3:68

"The Melancholy Hussar of the German Legion" (Hardy) 2:214-15, 220

"Mellonta Tauta" (Poe) 1:401, 406

"Melmoth Converted" (Balzac)
See "Melmoth réconcilié"

"Melmoth réconcilié" ("Melmoth Converted") (Balzac) 5:12, 31

"A Member of the Family" (Spark) 10:364, 367

"The Memento" (Henry) 5:185

Memnon; ou, La sagesse humaine (Voltaire) 12:340-42, 357, 379-81, 383, 392-94, 396-97, 399-401

"A Memoir" (Suckow) 18:396

"Mémoires d'un fou" (Flaubert) 11:71

"Memoirs" (Balzac) 5:11

Memoirs from Underground (Dostoevsky)
See *Zapiski iz podpol'ya*

The Memoirs of a Billiard-Marker (Tolstoy) 9:375

Memoirs of a Madman (Tolstoy)
See *Zapiski sumasshedshego*

The Memoirs of Sherlock Holmes (Doyle) 12:49-51, 59

"Memorial" (Munro) 3:331

"Memorial Eve" (Suckow) 18:414, 422, 424

"Memories of D. H. Lawrence" (Thurber) 1:414

"Memories of Yugashima" (Kawabata)
See "Yugashima no Omoide"

"A Memory" (Lavin) 4:178-79, 182-83

"A Memory" (Welty) 1:466, 469-70, 472

"The Memory of Martha" (Dunbar) 8:122

"Memphis" (Gilchrist) 14:159

"Memphis" (Mason) 4:10

"The Menace" (du Maurier) 18:127-28

"Menelaiad" (Barth) 10:39, 43, 47-51, 54, 58, 60-1, 75-6, 80, 90, 97-8, 100-02

"Men in the Storm" (Crane) 7:108, 110, 136-37, 145

"The Men of Forty Mile" (London) 4:267, 282, 284, 286

"A Mental Suggestion" (Chopin) 8:72, 100

"Menudo" (Carver) 8:43

"Menuet" (Maupassant) 1:278

Men without Women (Hemingway) 1:209-12, 214, 216-17

"Men with Their Big Shoes" (Jackson) 9:270

"A Mercenary" (Ozick) 15:302, 304, 316-17, 333-35

"The Merchant of Heaven" (Laurence) 7:245-46, 249-50, 255, 260

"Mercury" (Levi) 12:264, 268, 281

"A Mercury of the Foothills" (Harte) 8:214, 249

"A Mere Interlude" (Hardy) 2:211, 215

"Mère Pochette" (Jewett) 6:156

"La mère sauvage" (Maupassant) 1:277-78

"Merle" (Marshall) 3:317

Merle: A Novella, and Other Stories (Marshall)
See *Reena, and Other Stories*

"The Merman" (Hesse) 9:242-43

"Merrittsville" (Suckow) 18:393, 413, 422, 424

"The Merry Chase" (Lish) 18:278

"The Merry Men" (Stevenson) 11:268, 281-82, 303, 306

"Mesmeric Revelation" (Poe) 1:401

"Le message" (Balzac) 5:8, 31, 40-1, 43

"Message in a Bottle" (Gordimer) 17:156

"La messe de l'athée" (Balzac) 5:16, 26, 31

"A Mess of Pottage" (Dunbar) 8:122, 124, 128

"Mes vingt-cinq jours" (Maupassant) 1:274

"Metamorphoses" (Cheever) 1:94, 100

"The Metamorphosis" (Oates) 6:225, 234

The Metamorphosis (Kafka)
See *Die verwandlung*

"Metzengerstein" (Poe) 1:379

"The Mexican" (London) 4:291

"The Mexican General" (Bellow) 14:37-8, 40

"Mexico" (Gilchrist) 14:161-63

"The Mex Would Arrive at Gentry's Junction at 12:10" (Coover) 15:43-6

"The Mezzotint" (James) 16:232, 237, 240, 243-44, 251-52, 255, 257

"Michael's Wife" (O'Connor) 5:377

"Michel Siniagin" (Zoshchenko) 15:399

Micromégas (Voltaire) 12:341, 343, 390-94

The Middle-Aged Man on the Flying Trapeze: A Collection of Short Pieces (Thurber) 1:413, 420, 423

"A Middle-Class Education" (Oates) 6:246

"The Middle Drawer" (Calisher) 15:7, 15, 19-21

The Middle Years (James) 8:291, 299-300

"Midnight at Tim's Place" (Thurber) 1:429

"Midnight Magic" (Mason) 4:11

"Midnight Mass" (Bowles) 3:75, 80

Midnight Mass (Bowles) 3:75-6, 79-80

"A Midsummer Knight's Dream" (Henry) 5:184

"Midsummer Night Madness" (O'Faolain) 13:295, 301-02, 304, 309, 314-15

Midsummer Night Madness, and Other Stories (O'Faolain) 13:284, 292, 308, 312-13, 316-17

"Mid-western Primitive" (Suckow) 18:391, 412, 416

"Miggles" (Harte) 8:209-10, 236, 254

"El milagro secreto" ("The Secret Miracle") (Borges) 4:29-30, 37

"A Mild Attack of Locusts" (Lessing) 6:191

"Miles City, Montana" (Munro) 3:347-48

"Milford Junction, 1939: A Brief Encounter" (Coover) 15:61

"Milking Time" (O'Flaherty) 6:262, 277

"Milk Is Very Good for You" (Dixon) 16:204, 210, 214

"The Milkmaid of Samaniago" (Coover) 15:36

"Milkman 2" (King)
See "Big Wheels: A Tale of the Laundry Game"

"The Mill" (Bates) 10:126, 130-31, 133

"Millie" (Mansfield) 9:302

"A Millionaire of Rough and Ready" (Harte) 8:254

"Mine" (Carver) 8:30, 34

"The Minister's Black Veil" (Hawthorne) 3:154, 159-60, 164, 171, 177-78, 184, 186-87

"The Minister's Books" (Benet) 10:154, 160

"Ministers of Grace" (Saki) 12:334

Minne (Colette) 10:257

"The Minority Committee" (Dunbar) 8:127

"The Miracle" (O'Connor) 5:388

"The Miracle at Ballinspittle" (Boyle) 16:148, 151-2, 154-55

"The Miracle of Purun Bhagat" ("Purun Bhagat") (Kipling) 5:295

"The Miracle of Tepayac" (Steinbeck) 11:249-51

"Miracles" (Singer) 3:385-86

"Miranda over the Valley" (Dubus) 15:69-70, 85, 87

Mirgorod (Gogol) 4:86-7, 117

Miriam (Capote) 2:61-2, 64, 66, 69, 73-5, 78-9, 83

"Le miroir" (Baudelaire) 18:16, 49

"The Mirror" (O'Flaherty) 6:260, 265, 276-77, 279

"The Mirror" (Singer) 3:364, 368, 375

The Mirror Maker (Levi)
See *Racconti e Saggi*

"The Misadventures of John Nicholson" ("John Nicholson's Predicament") (Stevenson) 11:269, 282, 303, 305-06

"A Miscellany of Characters That Will Not Appear" (Cheever) 1:93, 100

"The Miser" (O'Connor) 5:371

"Misery" (Chekhov) 2:128, 130, 155

"A Misfortunate Girl" (Turgenev)
See "Neschastnaya"

"The Misogamist" (Dubus) 15:75

"Miss Baker" (Pritchett) 14:269

"Miss Brill" (Mansfield) 9:287, 299, 307, 309, 312-13

"Miss Chauncey" (Jewett) 6:168

"Miss Duveen" (de la Mare) 14:68, 83-4, 87

"Miss Gunton of Poughkeepsie" (James) 8:311

"Miss Harriet" (Maupassant) 1:259, 271, 274, 280, 285-87

"Missing" (de la Mare) 14:70, 80, 83, 87-8, 92

"The Missing Eye" (Bulgakov) 18:86-7

"The Missing Line" (Singer) 3:389

"The Mission of Jane" (Wharton) 6:424-25

"The Mission of Mr. Scatters" (Dunbar) 8:122, 132, 137, 147

"Miss Jemima" (de la Mare) 14:69

"Miss Leonora When Last Seen" (Taylor) 10:390, 401, 406, 407, 409, 415

Miss Lonelyhearts (Mademoiselle Coeur-Brise) (West) 16:345-49, 351-52, 354, 356-57, 359-60, 362, 364, 366-67, 369, 375-81, 383-86, 389-90, 394-402, 404, 407-08, 411, 415, 417

"Miss Manning's Minister" (Jewett) 6:156, 159

"Miss Mary Pask" (Wharton) **6**:431

"Miss Miller" (de la Mare) **14**:87

"Miss Pinkerton's Apocalypse" (Spark) **10**:350, 355, 359, 366

"Miss Plarr" (Ligotti) **16**:280

"Miss Sydney's Flowers" (Jewett) **6**:157, 166, 168

"Miss Tempy's Watcher's" (Jewett) **6**:151, 156

"Mrs. Bullfrog" (Hawthorne) **3**:180

"Mrs. Moysey" (Bowen) **3**:30, 33, 40, 42

"Mrs. Windermere" (Bowen) **3**:40, 54

"Miss W." (O'Hara) **15**:258

"Miss Willie Lou and the Swan" (Benet) **10**:148

"Miss Winchelsea's Heart" (Wells) **6**:391

"Miss Witherwell's Mistake" (Chopin) **8**:84, 86

"Miss Yellow Eyes" (Grau) **15**:158, 164

The Mist (King) **17**:265, 268-71, 273-76, 283

"A Mistake" (Zoshchenko)
See "A Slight Mistake"

"The Mistaken Milliner" (Dickens) **17**:135

"The Mistake of the Machine" (Chesterton) **1**:131

"Mr. Higginbotham's Catastrophe" (Hawthorne) **3**:154

"Mr. Kempe" (de la Mare) **14**:70, 80, 85, 90

"Mr. Lyon" (Carter)
See "The Courtship of Mr. Lyon"

Mr. (Calvino)
See *Palomar*

"Mister Palomar in the City" (Calvino) **3**:113, 115

"Mister Palomar's Vacation" (Calvino) **3**:113

"Mitchell on Matrimony" (Lawson) **18**:250-51

"Mitchell on the 'Sex,' and Other 'Problems'" (Lawson) **18**:250

"Mitchell on Women" (Lawson) **18**:250

"Mitosis" (Calvino) **3**:109-10

Mitsou (Colette) **10**:257, 271-74

The Mixture as Before (Maugham) **8**:379

"M'liss" (Harte) **8**:210, 219, 222, 224-25, 231-32, 234

"Mlle de Scudèry" (Hoffmann) **13**:202

"The Mnemogogues" (Levi) **12**:279

"Mobile" (Ballard) **1**:68

The Mocassin Ranch (Garland) **18**:182

"The Mock Auction" (Lavin) **4**:183

"The Mocking-Bird" (Bierce) **9**:64, 67-8, 96

"The Model" (Nin) **10**:326

A Model for Death (Bioy Casares) **17**:48, 74

"A Model Millionaire: A Note of Admiration" (Wilde) **11**:362, 399, 401, 407

"The Moderate Murderer" (Chesterton) **1**:132

"Modern Love" (Boyle) **16**:148, 154-56

A Modern Lover (Lawrence) **4**:230

"Moebius Strip" (Cortazar) **7**:69

"Mohammed Fripouille" (Maupassant) **1**:275

"The Mohican" (Nin) **10**:303

"Mojave" (Capote) **2**:79-80

"Molly" (Dubus) **15**:86, 90-1

"The Moment" (Aiken) **9**:5, 13-14, 41

"The Moment before the Gun Went Off" (Gordimer) **17**:178, 187, 189-90

"Moments of Being: 'Slater's Pins Have No Points'" ("Slater's Pins Have No Points") (Woolf) **7**:375, 388-89, 391-92, 398, 408-10

Moments of Reprieve (Levi)
See *Lilít e altri racconti*

"Monday or Tuesday" (Woolf) **7**:371, 374-75, 390, 392, 397-98, 402

Monday or Tuesday (Woolf) **7**:367-69, 371, 374, 392, 398-401, 404

Monde Comme il va (Voltaire) **12**:340, 393-94

"The Money Diggers" (Irving) **2**:251, 261-62

"Monk" (Faulkner) **1**:165, 179

"The Monkey" (Dinesen) **7**:163, 167, 170, 173, 200-01, 203

"The Monkey" (King) **17**:274-75, 290-91, 293

"Monkey Nuts" (Lawrence) **4**:231, 234-35

"Monologue of Isabel Watching It Rain in Macondo" (Garcia Marquez) **8**:194

"Mon oncle Jules" (Maupassant) **1**:277

"Mon oncle Sosthène" (Maupassant) **1**:263, 272

"Monsieur les deux chapeaux" (Munro) **3**:348

"Monsieur Parent" (Maupassant) **1**:259-60, 283

The Monster (Crane) **7**:103-05, 107, 114, 116, 131, 134, 138, 146-48

The Monster, and Other Stories (Crane) **7**:104

Monte Verità (du Maurier) **18**:126, 137

A Month by the Lake, and Other Stories (Bates) **10**:122, 139-40

"A Monument of French Folly" (Dickens) **17**:124

"The Moon and GNAC" (Calvino)
See "Luna e G N A C"

"Moon-Face" (London) **4**:252, 258-59

Moon-Face, and Other Stories (London) **4**:252

"The Moon in Letters" (Bierce) **9**:78

"The Moon in the Orange Street Skating Rink" (Munro) **3**:348-49

"Moon Lake" (Welty) **1**:474, 486

"A Moonlight Fable" (Wells) **6**:376

"Moonlight on the Snow" (Crane) **7**:108

"Moonshine Lake" (Bulgakov) **18**:74

The Moons of Jupiter (Munro) **3**:346-47

"Moon-Watcher" (Clarke) **3**:127-28

"The Mordivinian Sarafin" (Bunin)
See "Mordovskiy sarafan"

"Mordovskiy sarafan" ("The Mordivinian Sarafin") (Bunin) **5**:82, 106-08

"More Alarms at Night" (Thurber) **1**:428

More Ghost Stories of an Antiquary (James) **16**:231, 238, 251-52, 255, 258

More Pricks than Kicks (Beckett) **16**:64-8, 70-2, 76, 78, 87, 92-4, 106, 108

"More Stately Mansions" (Updike) **13**:402, 409

"More Stately Mansions" (Vonnegut) **8**:433

More Stories by Frank O'Connor (O'Connor) **5**:371

Die Morgenlandfahrt (*Journey to the East*) (Hesse) **9**:227-29, 240-41, 244-45

"Morning" (Barthelme) **2**:45, 55

"The Morning" (Updike) **13**:375

"The Morning after the Ball" (Tolstoy)
See "After the Ball"

"The Morning of a Landed Proprietor" (Tolstoy)
See *A Landlord's Morning*

"A Morning Walk" (Chopin) **8**:98

"Morphine" (Bulgakov) **18**:86, 89

"Morris in Chains" (Coover) **15**:31, 50-1

"The Mortal Coil" (Lawrence) **4**:235

"Mortality and Mercy in Vienna" (Pynchon) **14**:308, 310, 312, 320, 322-25, 328, 342-43, 347-49

"Mort and Mary" (O'Hara) **15**:248

The Mortgaged Heart (McCullers) **9**:341-44, 355-57, 359

"Une mort héroïque" ("A Heroic Death") (Baudelaire) **18**:15-16, 18, 27, 29-30, 34, 60

"The Mortification of the Flesh" (Dunbar) **8**:127

Mosaïque (Merimee) **7**:287-88, 290, 300

"Mosby's Memoirs" (Bellow) **14**:22, 24-5

Mosby's Memoirs, and Other Stories (Bellow) **14**:22-3, 25, 56

"Moscas y arañas" (Bioy Casares) **17**:87-9

"Moscow of the Twenties" (Bulgakov) **18**:92

"The Moslem Wife" (Gallant) **5**:135-38

Mosses from an Old Manse (Hawthorne) **3**:155, 160, 174, 180, 185

"The Most Extraordinary Thing" (Andersen) **6**:11

"The Most Profound Caress" (Cortazar)
See "La caricia más profunda"

"Motel Architecture" (Ballard) **1**:79

"The Moth" (Wells) **6**:383

"Mother" (Anderson) **1**:33, 44

"Mother" (Barnes) **3**:22, 26

"A Mother" (Joyce) **3**:205, 210-11, 234, 237, 245, 247, 249

"Mother and Child" (Hughes) **6**:119, 142

"Mother and Daughter" (Lawrence) **4**:205, 220

"Mother and Son" (O'Flaherty) **6**:262

"The Mother Hive" (Kipling) **5**:279

"Motherhood" (Anderson) **1**:27

"Mother Matilda's Book" (O'Faolain) **13**:293, 297

"The Mother of a Queen" (Hemingway) **1**:211

"The Motive" (Cortazar) **7**:69-70

"The Motive" ("No Motive") (du Maurier) **18**:125, 138

"Mouche" (Maupassant) **1**:273, 284

"The Mound" (Lovecraft) **3**:270-71, 274, 279

"The Mountain Tavern" (O'Flaherty) **6**:277-78, 281, 284

The Mountain Tavern, and Other Stories (O'Flaherty) **6**:262-65, 278, 283

"Mountjoy" (Irving) **2**:242

Mourner at the Door (Lish) **18**:275, 277-78, 280-83

"The Mourners" (Malamud) **15**:203, 205, 214, 217-18, 222-23, 225, 227

"The Mouse" (Lavin) **4**:167, 182

"The Mouse" (Nin) **10**:299-303, 319

"The Mouse and the Woman" (Thomas) **3**:399-402, 408

"La moustache" (Maupassant) **1**:274

"The Moviemaker" (Dixon) **16**:211

"Movies" (Dixon) **16**:206, 208, 214

Movies (Dixon) **16**:205-08, 211, 214-15

"The Moving Finger" (King) **17**:294

"The Moving Finger" (Wharton) **6**:414

"Moving Spirit" (Clarke) **3**:134

"The Mower" (Bates) **10**:124, 131-32

"Mowgli's Brothers" (Kipling) **5**:293

"Moxon's Master" (Bierce) **9**:72, 88

"Mr and Mrs Dove" (Mansfield) **9**:305

"Mr. and Mrs. Elliot" (Hemingway) **1**:208

"Mr. Arcularis" (Aiken) **9**:5-6, 9, 12-13, 15, 18-19, 33-41

"Mr. Bruce" (Jewett) **6**:157, 166

"Mr. Cass and the Ten Thousand Dollars" (O'Hara) **15**:248

"Mr. Coffee and Mr. Fixit" (Carver) **8**:18-19, 32-3, 59-60

"Mr. Cornelius Johnson, Office Seeker" (Dunbar) **8**:122, 125, 128, 131, 141, 144

"Mr. Durant" (Parker) **2**:274

Mr. Featherstone Takes a Ride (Bates) **10**:124

"Mr. Foolfarm's Journal" (Barthelme) **2**:40

"Mr. Groby's Slippery Gift" (Dunbar) **8**:122

"Mr. Harrington's Washing" (Maugham) **8**:369, 377, 383

"Mr. Humphreys and His Inheritance" (James) **16**:230-32, 234, 245, 252-53, 258

"Mr. Icky" (Fitzgerald) **6**:58

"Mr. Jack Hamlin's Mediation" (Harte) **8**:248-49

"Mr. Jones" (Wharton) **6**:426-27

"Mr. Justice Harbottle" (James) **16**:238

"Mr. Justice Hartbottle" ("Chief Justice Harbottle") (Le Fanu) **14**:223-25, 232-34, 236-38, 240-41, 248

"Mr. Know-All" (Maugham) **8**:366

"Mr. Minns and His Cousin" (Dickens) **17**:121, 125

Mr. Mulliner Speaking (Wodehouse) **2**:338

"Mr. Peebles' Heart" (Gilman) **13**:126

"Mr. Potter Takes a Rest Cure" (Wodehouse) **2**:355-56

"Mr. Powers" (Gordon) **15**:143

"Mr. Preble Gets Rid of His Wife" (Thurber) **1**:418

"Mr. Prokharchin" (Dostoevsky) **2**:170, 191-94

"Mrs. Bathurst" (Kipling) **5**:266, 278-79, 281

"Mrs. Billingsby's Wine" (Taylor) **10**:392, 401-02

"Mrs. Bonny" (Jewett) **6**:150, 168

"Mrs. Brown" (O'Hara) **15**:248

"Mrs. Dalloway in Bond Street" (Woolf) **7**:381-82

Mrs. Dalloway's Party (Woolf) **7**:381-82, 388, 392

"Mrs. Fay Dines on Zebra" (Calisher) **15**:3, 7

"Mrs. Galt and Edwin" (O'Hara) **15**:248, 266

"Mrs. Hofstadter on Josephine Street" (Parker) **2**:283

"Mr. Skelmersdale in Fairyland" (Wells) **6**:391-92

"Mrs. Kemper" (Suckow) **18**:393, 409

"Mrs. Mean" (Gass) **12**:123, 134,138-9

"Mr. Smellingscheck" (Lawson) **18**:215

"Mrs. Merrill's Duties" (Gilman) **13**:141

"Mrs. Mobry's Reason" (Chopin) **8**:71

"Mrs. Parkins's Christmas Eve" (Jewett) **6**:156, 159

"Mrs. Powers' Duty" (Gilman) **13**:141

"Mrs. Reinhardt" (O'Brien) **10**:333

Mrs. Reinhardt, and Other Stories (O'Brien) **10**:333

"Mrs. Rinaldi's Angel" (Ligotti) **16**:280, 292, 294-95, 297

"Mrs. Ripley's Trip" (Garland) **18**:143, 159, 162-63, 165-67, 172, 192

"Mrs. Skagg's Husbands" (Harte) **8**:234, 244

"Mrs. Stratton of Oak Knoll" (O'Hara) **15**:252, 280

"Mrs. Todd's Shortcut" (King) **17**:275

"Mrs. Vincent" (Bates) **10**:117

"Mrs. Vogel and Ollie" (Suckow) **18**:394-95, 413, 416, 422-23

"Mrs. Whitman" (O'Hara) **15**:264

"Mr. Taylor's Funeral" (Chesnutt) **7**:18

"MS. Found in a Bottle" (Poe) **1**:379, 391-92, 398

"Mt. Pisgah's Christmas Possum" (Dunbar) **8**:121, 127, 131, 136

"The Mudfog Association" (Dickens) **17**:121

"Muerte constante más allá der amor" ("Death Constant beyond Love") (Garcia Marquez) **8**:167, 169-72, 186

"La muerte y la brújula" ("Death and the Compass") (Borges) **4**:4, 10, 16, 19-24, 28-30, 35-6

"El muerto" ("The Dead Man") (Borges) **4**:4-5, 8-9, 23, 37-9

"Les muets" ("The Silent Men") (Camus) **9**:103, 105, 108, 110, 116, 119, 121-22, 125

"Mule in the Yard" (Faulkner) **1**:177

Mules and Men (Hurston) **4**:133-36, 139-49, 153, 155-56, 158-59

Mulliner Nights (Wodehouse) **2**:338

"Mumu" (Turgenev) **7**:315, 320, 323, 326, 352-57, 363

"A Municipal Report" (Henry) **5**:156, 165, 171-72, 179, 182, 192

"The Murder" (Chekhov) **2**:150

"The Murder" (Steinbeck) **11**:207, 210, 225, 229-33, 235, 244, 247, 254

"Murder at Cobbler's Hulk" (O'Faolain) **13**:296

"Murder at Full Moon by Peter Pym" (Steinbeck) **11**:254-55

"The Murdered Cousin" (Le Fanu) See "A Passage in the Secret History of an Irish Countess"

"The Murderer" (Bulgakov) **18**:101

"Murderers" (Michaels) **16**:306, 308-11, 316, 321

Murder in the Dark (Atwood) **2**:15, 17-20

"The Murders in the Rue Morgue" (Poe) **1**:378, 387, 389, 395, 406

"Muriel" (Gardner) **7**:234

"The Muse of the Coming Age" (Andersen) **6**:7

"The Muse's Tragedy" (Wharton) **6**:414, 428

"Museums and Women" (Updike) **13**:348, 375

Museums and Women, and Other Stories (Updike) **13**:356-61, 366-68

"Music" (de la Mare) **14**:92

"Music" (Gilchrist) **14**:154

"Music" (Nabokov) **11**:122, 125

"Music for Chameleons" (Capote) **2**:80

Music for Chameleons (Capote) **2**:79-81

"Music from Spain" (Welty) **1**:474, 495

"The Music Lesson" (Cheever) **1**:100

"The Music Lover" (Gardner) **7**:223, 225-26, 238

"The Music of Erich Zann" (Lovecraft) **3**:269

"The Music of the Moon" (Ligotti) **16**:278

"The Music on the Hill" (Saki) **12**:288, 315, 331, 334

"The Music School" (Updike) **13**:348, 375

The Music School (Updike) **13**:352, 354, 356, 366-67, 374-76, 378, 380

"The Music Teacher" (Cheever) **1**:106

"The Mutability of Literature" (Irving) **2**:251, 254

"Mute" (Atwood) **2**:16

"Muttsy" (Hurston) **4**:136, 138, 151

"Muza" (Bunin) **5**:114

"My Aunt" (Irving) **2**:242

"My Da" (O'Connor) **5**:388

"My Daily Horse" (Valenzuela) **14**:366

"My Father" (Michaels) **16**:321

"My Father Joins the Fire Brigade" (Schulz) **13**:335

"My Father Leaves Home" (Gordimer) **17**:177, 182-85

"My First Goose" (Babel) **16**:9, 10, 16, 28, 30, 53-4, 57-8

"My First Protestant" (O'Connor) **5**:386-87

"My First Two Women" ("The Pretender") (Gordimer) **17**:152

"My Heart Is Broken" (Gallant) **5**:141

My Heart Is Broken (Gallant) **5**:122-23, 130, 139-41

"My Kinsman, Major Molineux" (Hawthorne) **3**:164-65, 167, 171, 175-76, 179-80, 182-83, 186-87, 189

"My Lady Brandon and the Widow Jim" (Jewett) **6**:154

"My Life" (Chekhov) **2**:128, 130-32, 135-36, 145, 155, 157

My Life and Hard Times (Thurber) **1**:413-14, 419, 421-24, 426-28, 435

"My Life with R. H. Macy" (Jackson) **9**:252, 267

"My Love, My Umbrella" (McGahern) **17**:302, 308-09, 318, 323

"My Metamorphosis" (Harte) **8**:254

"My Molly" (Lavin) **4**:167

My Mother's House (Colette) See *La maison de Claudine*

"My Mother's Life" (Lessing) **6**:216

"My Mother's Mother" (O'Brien) **10**:334

"My Name is Everyone" ("Who Am I This Time?") (Vonnegut) **8**:433, 437

"My Neighbor" (Kafka) **5**:206

"My Oedipus Complex" (O'Connor) **5**:368-69, 378, 386-87

"My Old Man" (Hemingway) **1**:208, 219, 234, 245

"My Own True Ghost-Story" (Kipling) **5**:272-73

"My Pretty Pony" (King) **17**:294

"My Professions" (Zoshchenko) **15**:400

"Myra Meets His Family" (Fitzgerald) **6**:56, 96

"My Side of the Matter" (Capote) **2**:61-2, 65, 70, 83-5

"My Son Austin" (O'Faolain) **13**:284

Mysteries and Adventures (*The Gully of Bluemansdyke and Other Stories*) (Doyle) **12**:58-9

"Mysterious Kôr" (Bowen) **3**:31-2, 39, 41-2, 44, 53

"The Mysterious Lodger" (Le Fanu) **14**:238

The Mysterious Stranger (Twain) **6**:294-99, 301-02, 305-06, 312-16, 322-25, 331, 334, 345-50, 353

"The Mystery of Dave Regan" (Lawson) **18**:217, 238-39

"A Mystery of Heroism" (Crane) **7**:102, 106, 109

"The Mystery of Marie Rogêt" (Poe) **1**:386, 388, 400, 406

"The Mystery of Sasassa Valley, a South African Story" (Doyle) **12**:84

"The Mystics of Muelenburg" (Ligotti) **16**:263, 267, 276, 278, 283-84, 286-87, 295

"Myten om människorna" ("The Myth of Mankind") (Lagerkvist) **12**:181

"The Myth of Mankind" (Lagerkvist) See "Myten om människorna"

"Myths of the Near Future" (Ballard) **1**:78-9

Myths of the Near Future (Ballard) **1**:78-9, 82

"My Uncle John" (Irving) **2**:242

My Uncle Silas (Bates) **10**:117, 130-31

"My Vocation" (Lavin) **4**:167

"My Warszawa: 1980" (Oates) **6**:255

My World—And Welcome to It (Thurber) **1**:420

Nabokov's Dozen (Nabokov) **11**:108, 110, 126-28, 130

"Nabo: The Black Man Who Made the Angels Wait" (Garcia Marquez) **8**:154-55, 157-58, 183, 185

Nachstücke (Hoffmann) **13**:180, 182, 186-88, 234

Nada menos que todo un hombre (Unamuno) **11**:313-14, 320-22, 324-25, 327, 345, 351-52

"The Nails in Mr. Caterer" (Hammett) **17**:224

La naissance du jour (*The Break of Day*) (Colette) **10**:262, 274, 278-79, 285

"Naked" (Michaels) **16**:311

"Nakedness" (Updike) **13**:387

"Naked Nude" (Malamud) **15**:171, 173-75, 183, 192-94, 222

"Na kraj sveta" (Bunin) **5**:98

"The Name-Day" (Saki) **12**:317

"The Name-Day Party" ("The Party") (Chekhov) **2**:128, 130-31, 133, 149, 155-56

"The Nameless City" (Lovecraft) **3**:262-63, 269, 274, 276

"Names" (Dixon) **16**:204

"The Namesake" (Cather) **2**:97, 103-04, 113

"The Name, the Nose" (Calvino) **3**:119

"Namgay Doola" (Kipling) **5**:262

"Nancy Culpepper" (Mason) **4**:13

"Nanette: An Aside" (Cather) **2**:101

"The Nap" (de la Mare) **14**:70, 79, 83, 86, 88

"A Narrow Heart: The Portrait of a Woman" (Gordon) **15**:122-23, 126

"A Nasty Type" (Bulgakov) **18**:89

"Nathalie" (Bunin) **5**:87, 113, 115

Natica Jackson (O'Hara) **15**:278, 284-85

"The National Pastime" (Cheever) **1**:100

"A Nation of Wheels" (Barthelme) **2**:40

"Native of Winby" (Jewett) **6**:155

"Natural Boundaries" (Oates) **6**:248-50

"A Natural History of the Dead" (Hemingway) **1**:211

Natural Stories (Levi)
See *Storie naturali*

"Nature" (Turgenev) **7**:335

The Nature of Love (Bates) **10**:117-21

"The Naughty Boy" (Andersen) **6**:30, 32

"The Navigator Returns to His Country" (Bioy Casares) **17**:94

"Na xutore" (Bunin) **5**:98

"The Necklace" (Maupassant)
See "La parure"

"The Necklace" (Pritchett) **14**:280, 299, 305

"The Necktie" (Aiken) **9**:5, 9, 13-14

"A Need for Something Sweet" (Gordimer) **17**:193-94

"Needle and Glass and Fog" (Kawabata)
See "Hari to Ciarasu to Kiri"

"The Needlecase" (Bowen) **3**:41

"The Negro in the Drawing Room" (Hughes) **6**:121-22

"The Neighborhood" (O'Hara) **15**:279

"The Neighboring Families" (Andersen) **6**:7

"Neighbors" (Carver) **8**:4-6, 9-10, 34, 42, 47, 54

"Neighbors" (Singer) **3**:384

Neighbors (Hesse) **9**:230

"A Neighbor's Landmark" (James) **16**:236, 252, 254

"Neighbour Rosicky" (Cather) **2**:105, 115-17

"Neighbours" (de la Mare) **14**:87

"Neighbours" (Pritchett) **14**:277

"Neil MacAdam" (Maugham) **8**:376

"Neither the Most Terrifying nor the Least Memorable" (Valenzuela) **14**:367

"Nelse Hatton's Revenge" ("Nelse Hatton's Vengeance") (Dunbar) **8**:119, 121, 127, 140, 143

"Nelse Hatton's Vengeance" (Dunbar)
See "Nelse Hatton's Revenge"

"Nelson Redline" (Hammett) **17**:217

"Nemureru Bijo" ("House of the Sleeping Beauties") (Kawabata) **17**:235-41, 243-45

"Neron tiple o el calvario de un inglé" (Unamuno) **11**:312

"A Nervous Breakdown" (Chekhov)
See "An Attack of Nerves"

Nervous People, and Other Stories (Zoshchenko) **15**:405-07

"Neschastnaya" ("A Misfortune Girl"; "The Unfortunate"; "An Unhappy Girl") (Turgenev) **7**:321, 324, 326, 336-38, 358-59

"Nethescurial" (Ligotti) **16**:284, 293

"Neutron Tide" (Clarke) **3**:133

"Never Bet the Devil Your Head" (Poe) **1**:407

"Nevskij Avenue" (Gogol)
See "Nevsky Prospect"

"Nevsky Prospect" ("Nevskij Avenue") (Gogol) **4**:95, 122, 124-25, 128

"The New Accelerator" (Wells) **6**:367, 391, 393, 404, 406

The New Arabian Nights ("The Dynamiter") (Stevenson) **11**:268-70, 280

"The New Atlantis" (Le Guin) **12**:220

"The New Catacomb" (Doyle) **12**:49

"The New Country House" (Chekhov)
See "The New Villa"

"New Day" (O'Hara) **15**:248

"The New Dress" (Woolf) **7**:373, 376, 381-82, 387, 393, 395

"New Dresses" (Mansfield) **9**:281

"The New Englander" (Anderson) **1**:27, 30, 39, 46-7, 53, 55

"A New England Nun" (Freeman) **1**:192, 197, 199

A New England Nun, and Other Stories (Freeman) **1**:191, 194-95, 197

"A New England Prophet" (Freeman) **1**:197

"New Eve and Old Adam" (Lawrence) **4**:220

"The New House" (Bowen) **3**:40, 54

"The New Man" (Lessing) **6**:191, 198

"A New Method of Book Distribution" (Bulgakov) **18**:90

"The New Moon Party" (Boyle) **16**:143-44, 146

"The New Music" (Barthelme) **2**:55

"A New Refutation of Time" (Borges) **4**:5

"News for the Church" (O'Connor) **5**:371, 383, 385, 389

"News from the Sun" (Ballard) **1**:78-9

New Stories (Andersen)
See *Eventyr, fortalte for bøorn*

"The New Suit" (O'Flaherty) **6**:287

"The New Teacher" (O'Connor)
See "The Cheapjack"

"The New Villa" ("The New Country House") (Chekhov) **2**:131, 156

"A New-Wave Format" (Mason) **4**:14

"The New Year" (Dickens) **17**:116

New Year's Eve (The 'Seventies) (Wharton) **6**:439-40, 442

"New York by Campfire Light" (Henry) **5**:159

"New York Lady" (Parker)
See "From the Diary of a New York Lady"

New York Quartet (Wharton)
See *Old New York*

"New York to Detroit" (Parker) **2**:274, 280, 285

"The Next Tenants" (Clarke) **3**:135

"The Next Time" (James) **8**:281, 317

"Nice Girl" (Anderson) **1**:52

"A Nice Quiet Place" (Fitzgerald) **6**:80

The Nick Adams Stories (Hemingway) **1**:240

"Nickel" (Levi) **12**:268, 280

"The Nigger" (Barnes) **3**:5, 10-11, 14, 22

"Night" (Bunin) **5**:100, 108, 114

"Night" (O'Brien) **10**:345

"A Night among the Horses" (Barnes) **3**:5-7, 10, 14, 16, 22-4

"A Night at Greenway Court" (Cather) **2**:100

"A Night at the Fair" (Fitzgerald) **6**:49

A Night at the Movies, or You Must Remember This (Coover) **15**:57, 61, 63

"The Night before Prohibition" (Aiken) **9**:12, 14

"The Night-Born" (London) **4**:266, 291

"The Night Came Slowly" (Chopin) **8**:98, 110-11

"The Night Club in the Woods" (Calisher) **15**:5, 8

"A Night Conversation" ("Conversation at Night") (Bunin) **5**:81, 90-1

"The Night Driver" (Calvino) **3**:109

"The Night Face Up" (Cortazar)
See "La noche boca arriba"

"The Night Flier" (King) **17**:295

"A Night for Love" (Vonnegut) **8**:433

A Night in Acadie (Chopin) **8**:66-8, 77, 84, 93-4, 97, 110-14

"The Nightingale" (Andersen) **6**:7, 16, 27, 30, 32-4, 37, 40

"The Nightingale and the Rose" (Wilde) **11**:372, 375-76, 378-79, 386-87, 389, 393, 395, 402-04, 406-09

"A Night in New Arabia" (Henry) **5**:184

"A Night in the Woods" (Barnes) **3**:18

Nightlines (McGahern) **17**:298, 301-03, 306-09, 320, 322

"Nightmares" (Cortazar)
See "Pesadillas"

Nightmares and Dreamscapes (King) **17**:293-96

"The Night of Denial" (Bunin) **5**:82

"The Night of the Curlews" (Garcia Marquez)
See "La noche de los alcaravanes"

"Night of the Great Season" (Schulz)
See "Noc wielkiego sezonu"

"A Night on the Divide" (Harte) **8**:216, 253

Night Pieces after the Manner of Callot (Hoffmann)
See *Phantasiestüeke in Callots Manier*

"Nightpiece with Figures" (O'Connor) **5**:382, 385, 391-92

Night Run to the West (Bates) **10**:119

"Night-Sea Journey" (Barth) **10**:41-3, 45-8, 53-4, 56-7, 60-1, 75-6, 80, 90, 97-8, 80, 84, 87, 89, 91, 97-100

Night Shift (King) **17**:261-62, 273-76, 294

"Nights in Europe's Ministeries" (Cortazar)
See "Noches en los ministerios de Europa"
"Night Sketches" (Hawthorne) 3:189, 191
"The Nights of Goliadkin" (Bioy Casares)
See "Las noches de Goliadkin"
"Night Surf" (King) 17:269
"The Night the Bed Fell" (Thurber) 1:428
"The Night the Favorite Came Home"
(Gordimer) 17:161
"The Night the Ghost Got In" (Thurber)
1:428, 432
"The Night-Worker" (Pritchett) 14:297
"N'importe où hors du monde" ("Anywhere
Out of the World") (Baudelaire) 18:5, 40
"Nimram" (Gardner) 7:223-27, 235, 238, 241
"The Nine Billion Names of God" (Clarke)
3:134-35, 137, 145
"Nine Lives" (Le Guin) 12:231-33
Nine Stories (Salinger) 2:289-91, 299, 312-13,
316, 318-19
"Nineteen Fifty-Five" (Walker) 5:412, 414
"1957, a Romance" (Gilchrist) 14:150
"1944" (Gilchrist) 14:150
"1934" (Phillips) 16:326, 328, 337
"1939" (Taylor) 10:381-82, 385, 416
"Ninety Minutes Away" (O'Hara) 15:259
Nine Women (Grau) 15:161-64
"Nitrogen" (Levi) 12:255, 265, 268
"No. 44, The Mysterious Stranger" (Twain)
6:331
"A No-Account Creole" (Chopin) 8:90, 103
"Nobody Knows" (Anderson) 1:34, 45
"Nobody Said Anything" (Carver) 8:54
"La noche boca arriba" ("The Night Face
Up"; "On His Back under the Night")
(Cortazar) 7:52, 54, 57, 64, 69-71, 81
"La noche de los alcaravanes" ("The Night of
the Curlews") (Garcia Marquez) 8:154-55,
159, 183
"La noche de Mantequilla" ("Butterball's
Night") (Cortazar) 7:89, 91
"Las noches de Goliadkin" ("The Nights of
Goliadkin") (Bioy Casares) 17:70, 74
"Noches en los ministerios de Europa"
("Nights in Europe's Ministeries")
(Cortazar) 7:94
"No Country for Old Men" (O'Faolain)
13:314
"Noč pered roždestvom" ("Christmas Eve")
(Gogol) 4:86, 118
Noctuary (Ligotti) 16:291, 292, 294, 296-97
"Nocturnal Games" (Hesse) 9:244
"Noc wielkiego sezonu" ("Night of the Great
Season") (Schulz) 13:327, 334, 344
"No Harm Trying" (Fitzgerald) 6:69-70
"Noisy Flushes the Birds" (Pritchett) 14:305
"No-Man's-Mare" (Barnes) 3:11-12, 22
"No More the Nightingales" (Bates) 10:116-
17
"No Morning After" (Clarke) 3:149
"No Motive" (du Maurier)
See "The Motive"
"Nona" (King) 17:274
None but the Brave (Schnitzler)
See Leutnant Gustl
"None of That" (Lawrence) 4:219, 230
The Nonexistent Knight (Calvino)
See Il cavaliere inesistente
The Nonexistent Knight and the Cloven
Viscount (Calvino)
See Il visconte dimezzato

"No, No, Go Not to Lethe" (Aiken) 9:6, 9,
14, 41
No One Writes to the Colonel (Garcia
Marquez)
See El colonel no tiene quien le escribe
Noon Wine (Porter) 4:327-30, 339-40, 347,
349-52, 355-56, 359-60
"No Place for a Woman" (Lawson) 18:252
"No Place for You, My Love" (Welty) 1:476,
479, 484, 493
"No Place Like" (Gordimer) 17:158
No Relief (Dixon) 16:203, 209-10, 213, 215
"Norman and the Killer" (Oates) 6:224, 226
"Un normand" (Maupassant) 1:288
"Nos Anglais" (Maupassant) 1:263
"A Nose" (de la Mare) 14:69
"The Nose" (Gogol) 4:82-4, 91-5, 97, 124-25,
127-29
I nostri antenati (Our Ancestors) (Calvino)
3:91-2, 106, 117
"Not After Midnight" (du Maurier) 18:129
Not after Midnight (Don't Look Now) (du
Maurier) 18:128, 130, 133
"Not a Leg to Stand On" (Boyle) 16:144-45
"The No-Talent Kid" (Vonnegut) 8:431
"Not a Very Nice Story" (Lessing) 6:188,
197, 220
"Not Charles" (Dixon) 16:206, 208, 214
"No te dejes" ("Don't Let Them") (Cortazar)
7:95
"Notes by Flood and Field" (Harte) 8:210
"Notes for a Case History" (Lessing) 6:198,
200, 208, 218
Notes from the Underground (Dostoevsky)
See Zapiski iz podpol'ya
"Notes of a Madman" (Gogol)
See "Diary of a Madman"
The Notes of a Young Doctor (Bulgakov)
See Zapiski iunogo vracha
"Notes on the Cuffs" (Bulgakov) 18:75, 92,
100
"Notes on the Writing of Horror: A Story"
(Ligotti) 16:269, 271, 277-78, 284, 286-87,
293, 295
"Not for Publication" (Gordimer) 17:155
Not for Publication, and Other Stories
(Gordimer) 17:154, 168, 181, 183
"Not for the Sabbath" (Singer) 3:381
Nothing Ever Breaks Except the Heart (Boyle)
5:63
"The Nothing Machine" (O'Hara) 15:282
"Nothing Missing" (O'Hara) 15:248, 270
Nothing Serious (Wodehouse) 2:345
Nothing So Monstrous (Steinbeck) 11:206
"Not Sixteen" (Anderson) 1:52
"No Use to Talk to Me" (Le Guin) 12:231
Nouveaux contes cruels (Villiers de l'Isle
Adam) 14:378, 396, 398
Nouvelles (Beckett) 16:72-5, 87
Novelas exemplares (Exemplary Novels;
Exemplary Stories; Exemplary Tales)
(Cervantes) 12:2-3, 5, 16, 29-34, 36-40, 44
"A Novel in Nine Letters" (Dostoevsky)
2:170
Novels and Stories (Stevenson) 11:287
"November Night" (Hesse) 9:230-31, 234
"Novembre" (Flaubert) 11:71
"Now I Lay Me" (Hemingway) 1:220, 241,
247
"No Witchcraft for Sale" (Lessing) 6:186,
190-91

"Now Sleeps the Crimson Petal" (Bates)
10:123
"Now We Know" (O'Hara) 15:248, 265, 270
"Now: Zero" (Ballard) 1:68
"The Nuisance" (Lessing) 6:186, 217
Les nuits d'Octobre (October Nights) (Nerval)
18:334-35, 350, 373
"Number 13" (James) 16:230, 232, 248, 250-
52
"No. 13: The Elpit-Rabkommun Building"
(Bulgakov) 18:72, 74, 92, 98-9
"No. 16" (Bowen) 3:41
"A Nursery Tale" (Nabokov) 11:123, 125
"Nurse's Stories" (Dickens) 17:123
"Nutcracker" (Hoffmann) 13:192, 194-95,
197, 199-200, 213
La nuvola di smog (Smog) (Calvino) 3:98,
111-12, 117
"Nyarlathotep" (Lovecraft) 3:269, 273
"The Oar" (O'Flaherty) 6:262, 265, 274, 276-
77
"La obra" (Bioy Casares) 17:95
Obscure Destinies (Cather) 2:92, 115, 117-18
"The Occasional Garden" (Saki) 12:311-12,
325
"L'occhio del padrone" (Calvino) 3:97
"Occult Memories" (Villiers de l'Isle Adam)
See "Souvenirs occulte"
"An Occurrence at Owl Creek Bridge"
(Bierce) 9:49-50, 53-6, 60-1, 75, 77-82,
85-6, 89, 92, 95
"The Ocean" (Cheever) 1:94, 111
"The Ocean" (Mason) 4:15
"O City of Broken Dreams" (Cheever) 1:89,
107
Octaedro (Cortazar) 7:60
"The Octascope" (Beattie) 11:6, 14
Octavie: L'illusion (Nerval) 18:362, 369-70
"October and June" (Henry) 5:182
October Nights (Nerval)
See Les nuits d'Octobre
"Odalie Misses Mass" (Chopin) 8:93
"The O. D. and Hepatitis Railroad or Bust"
(Boyle) 16:151
"Das öde Haus" (Hoffmann) 13:185
"Odessa" (Babel) 16:35, 59
The Odessa Stories (Babel)
See The Odessa Tales
The Odessa Tales (The Odessa Stories; Tales of
Odessa) (Babel) 16:5, 9, 13, 17-18, 20-2, 35,
42, 44, 49
"The Odor of Sanctity" (Benet) 10:146-47
"An Odor of Verbena" (Faulkner) 1:171
"The Odour of Chrysanthemums" (Lawrence)
4:197-98, 202, 220, 230
"An Odyssey of the North" (London) 4:251,
258, 278, 282-84, 289, 291
"The Oedipus Complex" (Pritchett) 14:271,
285
Oeuvres (Nerval) 18:379
Oeuvres complètes (Baudelaire) 18:9, 20, 32,
35, 37-8, 52, 63-4
"Of Birds and Beasts" (Kawabata)
See "Kinjū"
"Of Emelya, the Fool" (Bunin) 5:82
"Offerings" (Mason) 4:16
"Offerings" (O'Flaherty) 6:262, 264, 281
Off-Hours (Cortazar)
See Deshoras
"The Office" (Munro) 3:322, 325, 340, 343
"An Official Position" (Maugham) 8:379

"The Offshore Pirate" (Fitzgerald) **6**:45, 56, 58-9, 96-7

"Of Love: A Testimony" (Cheever) **1**:88, 99

"Of Sanctity and Whiskey" (O'Faolain) **13**:291

"Oft in a Stilly Night" (O'Brien) **10**:345-46

"O'Halloran's Luck" (Benet) **10**:154, 158-59

"An Ohio Pagan" (Anderson) **1**:27, 30, 39

Ohio Pastorals (Dunbar) **8**:127, 134

"Oh, My Name Is William Kidd" (Benet) **10**:154

"O How She Laughed!" (Aiken) **9**:6, 9, 14

Oh What a Paradise It Seems (Cheever) **1**:108, 113-15

"Oh Whistle and I'll Come to You, My Lad" (James) **16**:225, 228, 230, 232-33, 235-37, 240, 251-54, 256-57

"Oifig an Phoist" ("The Post Office") (O'Flaherty) **6**:280, 287, 289

"Olalla" (Stevenson) **11**:269, 282, 296, 298

"O Lasting Peace" (Gallant) **5**:124, 133

"Ol' Bennet and the Indians" (Crane) **7**:103

"Old Abe's Conversion" (Dunbar) **8**:122, 146

"The Old Adam" (Lawrence) **4**:220

"The Old Age Pensioner" (Schulz)
See "Emeryt"

"Old-Age Pensioners" (O'Connor) **5**:369

"The Old Apple Dealer" (Hawthorne) **3**:189

"Old Aunt Peggy" (Chopin) **8**:89

"The Old Bachelor's Nightcap" (Andersen) **6**:12

"The Old Beauty" (Cather) **2**:93-4

The Old Beauty and Others (Cather) **2**:93

"The Old Bird, a Love Story" (Powers) **4**:368, 371, 373

"An Old Boot" (Lavin) **4**:165, 168

"The Old Chevalier" (Dinesen) **7**:163, 165-66, 169, 175

"The Old Chief Mshlanga" (Lessing) **6**:186, 189, 196-97, 213

Old Creole Days (Cable) **4**:47, 49-58, 60-2, 64-8, 75-6, 78

"Old Daddy Deering" (Garland)
See "Daddy Deering"

"Old Earth" (Beckett) **16**:123, 126

"Old Esther Dudley" (Hawthorne) **3**:186

"The Old Faith" (O'Connor) **5**:369, 372, 385, 398

"Oldfashioned" (McGahern) **17**:304-05, 308, 311, 317-18, 320, 323

"Old Fellows" (O'Connor) **5**:366, 389

"The Old Forest" (Taylor) **10**:403, 409-10, 416, 418-20, 424

The Old Forest (Taylor) **10**:410

"The Old Friends" (Gallant) **5**:124, 133

Old Friends and New (Jewett) **6**:165-66, 168

"Old Garbo" (Thomas) **3**:403-06, 410-12

"The Old House" (Andersen) **6**:4, 25

"The Old Hunter" (O'Flaherty) **6**:264, 280

"Old John's Place" (Lessing) **6**:186, 190, 211, 213-14, 217

"Old Love" (Singer) **3**:376, 384

Old Love (Singer) **3**:380-82

The Old Maid (The 'Fifties) (Wharton) **6**:439-41

"The Old Man" (Coover) **15**:46

"The Old Man" (du Maurier) **18**:138

"Old Man" (Faulkner) **1**:159-61, 167-68

"The Old Man" (Singer) **3**:355-56

The Old Man and the Sea (The Sea in Being) (Hemingway) **1**:222-24, 226-28, 238-39, 247-50

"Old Man at the Bridge" (Hemingway) **1**:234

"The Old Manse" (Hawthorne) **3**:159, 174, 184

"The Old Master" (O'Faolain) **13**:284, 287, 300, 309

"An Old Mate of Your Father's" (Lawson) **18**:200, 215, 262

"Old Mortality" (Gilchrist) **14**:151

Old Mortality (Porter) **4**:327, 329-34, 338, 340-42, 346-52, 361-65

"Old Mr. Marblehall" (Welty) **1**:466, 471, 498

"Old Mrs. Crosley" (Gilman) **13**:143

"Old Mrs. Harris" (Cather) **2**:97, 102, 115-17

"Old News" (Hawthorne) **3**:174

Old New York (New York Quartet) (Wharton) **6**:439-40, 442

"Old Oak Tree's Last Dream" (Andersen)
See "The Last Dream of the Old Oak"

"The Old Order" (Porter) **4**:339-40, 348, 350-54, 358, 361-62, 365

"Old Portraits" (Turgenev)
See "Starye portrety"

"Old Red" (Gordon) **15**:106, 119-21, 129-30, 141, 143

Old Red, and Other Stories (Gordon) **15**:116, 131, 137

"Old Sid's Christmas" (Garland) **18**:167

"The Old Stock" (Calisher) **15**:14-15, 18-19

"The Old Street Lamp" (Andersen) **6**:4, 7

"The Old System" (Bellow) **14**:22, 24-5, 27

"Old Tar" (Mansfield) **9**:301

"Old Things" (Mason) **4**:17

"Old Ticonderoga" (Hawthorne) **3**:174

"An Old Time Christmas" (Dunbar) **8**:122, 125, 128, 133, 144

"The Old Woman" (O'Flaherty) **6**:277-78, 280

"An Old Woman and Her Cat" (Lessing) **6**:188

"The Old Woman's Despair" (Baudelaire)
See "Le désespoir de la vieille"

"Old-World Landowners" (Gogol)
See "Starosvetskie Pomeščiki"

"Ole Luköie" ("The Sandman") (Andersen) **6**:12

"Ole Underwood" (Mansfield) **9**:278, 302

Olinger Stories: A Selection (Updike) **13**:350, 354, 366, 368-69, 404

"Olive" (O'Hara) **15**:264

"The Olive Garden" (Gordon) **15**:118, 138, 142-43

"Ol' Pap's Flaxen" (Garland) **18**:163

"Omnibus" ("Busride") (Cortazar) **7**:50, 54, 56

"Omnibuses" (Dickens) **17**:112, 137

"On a Field, Rampant" (Elkin) **12**:94-6, 99, 101, 118

"On a Mountain" (Bierce) **9**:61

"On an Amateur Beat" (Dickens) **17**:124

"On Angels" (Barthelme) **2**:32, 38

"On Approval" (Saki) **12**:314

"On A Wagon" (Singer) **3**:375

"Once Upon a Time" (Gordimer) **17**:177, 183, 185, 187, 190-91

"Den onda ängeln" ("The Evil Angel") (Lagerkvist) **12**:179, 195

Onda sagor (Evil Sagas; Evil Tales) (Lagerkvist) **12**:179

"One against Thebes" ("The Dragon's Teeth") (Gordon) **15**:119, 123, 126, 138-39

"One Arm" (Kawabata)
See "Kata Ucle"

"One Christmas at Shiloh" (Dunbar) **8**:122, 138, 146

"One Christmas Eve" (Hughes) **6**:109

"One Dash—Horses" (Crane)
See "Horses--One Dash"

"One Day After Saturday" (Garcia Marquez) **8**:185

"One Day of Happiness" (Singer) **3**:385-86

"One-Eyed Dogs" (Lawson) **18**:233

"One Friday Morning" (Hughes) **6**:111-12, 119, 121

"One Good Time" (Freeman) **1**:198

"$106,000 Blood Money" (Hammett) **17**:200, 202, 215, 219-220, 222, 224, 230

"One Interne" (Fitzgerald) **6**:47-8

"Oneiric Horror" (Ligotti) **16**:288

"One is a Wanderer" (Thurber) **1**:417, 420, 425, 427, 435

"One Kind of Officer" (Bierce) **9**:52, 61

"One Life Furnished in Early Poverty" (Ellison) **14**:109-10, 115

"One Man, One Boat, One Girl" (O'Faolain) **13**:322

"One Man's Fortune" (Dunbar) **8**:120, 122, 125, 128, 131, 136, 145, 150

"One More Thing" (Carver) **8**:17, 19, 38, 53

"One More Time" (Gordon) **15**:106, 120, 130

"One Night in Turin" (O'Faolain) **13**:288, 320, 322

"One Officer, One Man" (Bierce) **9**:53, 55, 57, 64, 67-8

"One Off the Short List" (Lessing) **6**:197, 199, 200, 203-08, 214, 218

"One of the Chosen" (Calisher) **15**:14

"One of the Family" (Spark) **10**:369

"One of Them" (Powers) **4**:375-76

"One of the Missing" (Bierce) **9**:53, 55-6, 61-2, 65-8, 76-7, 87

"One of Three Others" (Suckow) **18**:394-95, 413-14, 416, 422-23

"One Ordinary Day, with Peanuts" (Jackson) **9**:267

"One Reader Writes" (Hemingway) **1**:211

"One Summer" (Grau) **15**:159, 165

"One Summer" (Lavin) **4**:173, 183

"One Sunday Morning" (Boyle) **5**:64

"The Ones Who Walk Away From Omelas" (Le Guin) **12**:234, 239-41

"One Thousand Dollars" (Henry) **5**:184

"One Trip Abroad" (Fitzgerald) **6**:61, 100, 104

"One True Friend" (O'Faolain) **13**:288

"One Warm Saturday" (Thomas) **3**:394-95, 398, 403, 410-12

"On for the Long Haul" (Boyle) **16**:146

"On Graphology As an Applied Science" (Cortazar)
See "De la grafología como ciencia aplicada"

"On Greenhow Hill" (Kipling) **5**:260

"On His Back under the Night" (Cortazar)
See "La noche boca arriba"

"On His Hands" (O'Hara) **15**:

"Only a Subaltern" (Kipling) **5**:272

"The Only Rose" (Jewett) **6**:169

"An Only Son" (Jewett) **6**:152-53

"Onnagata" (Mishima) **4**:313, 315, 318, 322-23

"On Official Duty" (Chekhov) **2**:128

"On the City Wall" (Kipling) **5**:265

"On the Divide" (Cather) **2**:96-7, 100-01, 105-07

"On the Downhill Side" (Ellison) **14**:115

On the Edge (de la Mare) **14**:70-2, 74, 83, 89

"On the Edge of the Cliff" (Pritchett) **14**:263, 267, 272-73, 291

On the Edge of the Cliff, and Other Stories (Pritchett) **14**:263, 290, 292, 299

"On the Edge of the Plain" (Lawson) **18**:211, 213, 239, 261

"On the Gate" (Kipling) **5**:271, 283

"On the Great Wall" (Kipling) **5**:292

"On the Gulls' Road" (Cather) **2**:99, 104

"On the Makaloa Mat" (London) **4**:266

On the Makaloa Mat (*Island Tales*) (London) **4**:256-57, 266, 270

"On the Quai at Smyrna" (Hemingway) **1**:244

"On the Road" (Hughes) **6**:122, 131-32

"On the Run" (Boyle) **5**:70, 72

"On the Slab" (Ellison) **14**:138

"On the Telephone" (Bulgakov) **18**:89

On the Track and Over the Sliprails (Lawson) **18**:208, 250, 252

"On the Usefulness of Alcoholism" (Bulgakov) **18**:90

"On the Walpole Road" (Freeman) **1**:201

"On the Way Home" (Hughes) **6**:119, 121-23, 132-33

"On the Western Circuit" (Hardy) **2**:206-07, 214, 220, 222-23

"On Time" (O'Hara) **15**:265, 270

"On Writing" (Hemingway) **1**:240, 243

"The Open Boat" (Crane) **7**:100-01, 103-04, 107-13, 116-18, 120, 140, 142-43, 145, 148-49, 151-53

The Open Boat, and Other Tales of Adventure (Crane) **7**:102, 104

Open Door (Valenzuela) **14**:365-66

"Open House" (Gordimer) **17**:157, 160, 186

"The Open Window" (Saki) **12**:315, 318-19, 321, 324

"Orache" (Nabokov) **11**:133

"The Oracle of the Dog" (Chesterton) **1**:133-34, 136

"Oral History" (Gordimer) **17**:163, 191-92

"The Orange Moth" (Aiken) **9**:3-4, 13-14

"The Orchards" (Thomas) **3**:396, 399-402, 407-08

"The Ordeal" (Fitzgerald) **6**:58

"The Ordeal at Mt. Hope" (Dunbar) **8**:118, 120-21, 127, 131, 146

"Order of Illusion" (Ligotti) **16**:276

"Order of Insects" (Gass) **12**:123-4, 133, 139, 152, 156-7

Les oreilles du comte de Chesterfield (Voltaire) **12**:341-43

"The Orgy: An Idyll" (de la Mare) **14**:72, 74, 87-8

"Orientation of Cats" (Cortazar) **7**:69, 71

"The Origin of the Birds" (Calvino) **3**:108-10

"The Origin of the Hatchet Story" (Chesnutt) **7**:14-15

"The Ormolu Clock" (Spark) **10**:353, 361-63

"The Orphanage" (McCullers) **9**:342, 345, 354-55

"The Orphaned Swimming Pool" (Updike) **13**:367

"Orphan's Progress" (Gallant) **5**:138

"Orpheus and His Lute" (O'Connor) **5**:377, 382

Orsinian Tales (Le Guin) **12**:212-19, 222-23, 231, 234, 245-48, 250

"O Russet Witch!" (Fitzgerald) **6**:45, 59, 91-3

"Oscar" (Barnes) **3**:2-4

"Ostatnia ucieczka ojca" ("Father's Last Escape"; "The Last Flight of Father") (Schulz) **13**:328-29, 334

"Otchayanny" ("A Desperate Character") (Turgenev) **7**:324, 337, 362-63

"The Other" (Updike) **13**:402

"The Other Death" (Borges)
See "La otra muerte"

"The Other Gods" (Lovecraft) **3**:274

"The Other Man" (Kipling) **5**:274

The Other One (Colette)
See *La seconde*

"The Other Paris" (Gallant) **5**:125-26, 148

Other People's Ambitions (Suckow) **18**:400-03

"Other People's Stories" (Ozick)
See "Usurpation (Other People's Stories)"

"The Other Rib of Death" (Garcia Marquez)
See "La otra costilla de la muerte"

"Others' Dreams" (Oates) **6**:234

"The Other Side of Death" (Garcia Marquez)
See "La otra costilla de la muerte"

The Other Side of the Sky (Clarke) **3**:125, 131-32

"The Other Two" (Wharton) **6**:421, 424-26

"The Other Way" (Grau) **15**:149, 160

"Other Weapons" (Valenzuela) **14**:353, 355-56, 358

Other Weapons (Valenzuela)
See *Cambio de armas*

"The Other Woman" (Anderson) **1**:42

"Other Women's Households" (O'Hara) **15**:255

"La otra costilla de la muerte" ("The Other Rib of Death"; "The Other Side of Death") (Garcia Marquez) **8**:154-56, 182

"La otra muerte" ("The Other Death") (Borges) **4**:35, 37, 42-4

Otrochestvo (*Boyhood*) (Tolstoy) **9**:375

"El otro cielo" (Cortazar) **7**:55, 57, 59, 61-2

"El otro laberinto" (Bioy Casares) **17**:75-9, 81-2

"The Ottawa Valley" (Munro) **3**:337

Our Ancestors (Calvino)
See *I nostri antenati*

"Our Bovary" (Gordimer) **17**:154

"Our Demeanor at Wakes" (Cortazar)
See "Conducta en los velorios"

"Our English Watering-Place" (Dickens) **17**:124

"Our Exploits at West Poley" (Hardy) **2**:214, 216, 221

"Our Fearful Innocence" (O'Faolain) **13**:292, 312, 322

"Our French Watering-Place" (Dickens) **17**:124

"Our Friend Judith" (Lessing) **6**:201-02, 218-20

"Our Lady of the Easy Death of Alferce" (Oates) **6**:237

"Our Lady of the Massacre" (Carter) **13**:16-19

"Our Oldest Friend" (Pritchett) **14**:255, 298

"Our Pipes" (Lawson) **18**:261

"Our School" (Dickens) **17**:124

"Our Trip (A Diary)" (Bioy Casares) **17**:95

"Our Wall" (Oates) **6**:255

"Our Wife" (Pritchett) **14**:273

"The Outcasts" (O'Flaherty) **6**:262, 264, 284

"The Outcasts of Poker Flat" (Harte) **8**:209-10, 219, 223, 226-27, 232-33, 236, 244, 250-51, 254-55, 257

"The Outing" (Baldwin) **10**:2-4, 6-9

"Out of My Generation" (Updike) **13**:387

"Out of Nowhere into Nothing" (Anderson) **1**:21, 27, 30, 39, 46-7, 53

"Out of Season" (Gordimer) **17**:187

"Out of Season" (Hemingway) **1**:245

"Out of the Deep" ("The Bell") (de la Mare) **14**:65, 68, 80, 86-7, 92

"Out of the Eons" (Lovecraft) **3**:279

"Out of the Sun" (Clarke) **3**:132, 135-36

The Outpost of Progress (Conrad) **9**:143-44, 163

"The Outsider" (Lovecraft) **3**:258, 260, 262, 264, 274

"Outside the Cabinet-Maker's" (Fitzgerald) **6**:51

"Outside the Ministry" (Lessing) **6**:199

"The Outstation" (Maugham) **8**:357, 359, 361, 366-67, 372

"The Oval Portrait" (Poe) **1**:392

"Over" (O'Brien) **10**:330-31, 333

"The Overcoat" ("The Cloak") (Gogol) **4**:82-3, 87-91, 93, 106-08, 110-11, 113-17, 127, 129-30

"The Overcoat II" (Boyle) **16**:143, 145, 151

Overhead in a Balloon: Stories of Paris (Gallant) **5**:147

The Overloaded Man (Ballard) **1**:73-7

Overnight to Many Distant Cities (Barthelme) **2**:50-1, 56

"Over the River and through the Wood" (O'Hara) **15**:252-54, 264-65

"The Overtone" (Lawrence) **4**:238-39

"Overture and Incidental Music for *A Midsummer Night's Dream*" (Carter) **13**:17-18

"Ovsianko the Freeholder" (Turgenev)
See "The Freeholder Ovsyanikov"

"Owen Wingrave" (James) **8**:270

"The Ox" (Bates) **10**:131, 133

"O Yes" (Olsen) **11**:164-66

"O Youth and Beauty!" (Cheever) **1**:90, 110

"Ozème's Holiday" (Chopin) **8**:94, 113

"The Pace of Youth" (Crane) **7**:149

"The Package" (Vonnegut) **8**:437

"The Package Store" (Dixon) **16**:207

"Packed Dirt, Churchgoing, A Dying Cat, A Traded Car" (Updike) **13**:370, 388, 397

"The Pagan Rabbi" (Ozick) **15**:297-98, 300-01, 311-13, 315, 335, 337-39

The Pagan Rabbi, and Other Stories (Ozick) **15**:297-98, 304, 306, 311-12, 314, 328, 331

"The Page" (Atwood) **2**:15, 17

"Page and Monarch" (Pritchett) **14**:296

"Pages from Cold Point" (Bowles) **3**:59, 61-2, 66, 69, 73, 76-7, 85

"A Painful Case" (Joyce) **3**:203, 205, 209-11, 234-35, 246, 249

"Paingod" (Ellison) **14**:106-07, 118

"Pain maudit" (Maupassant) **1**:263

"The Painted Woman" (O'Flaherty) **6**:262, 264

"The Painter" (Hesse) **9**:243

"The Painter's Adventure" (Irving) **2**:262

"A Pair" (Singer) **3**:377, 384

"A Pair of Silk Stockings" (Chopin) **8**:72

"A Pair of Vikings" (Aiken) **9**:7, 13

"La paix du ménage" (Balzac) **5**:5, 29, 31

"La palabra asesino" (Valenzuela) **14**:361-62, 364-65

Pale Horse, Pale Rider (Porter) **4**:327, 329, 331-35, 339-41, 347, 349, 361, 364-65

Pale Horse, Pale Rider: Three Short Novels (Porter) **4**:327-28, 331, 339

"The Pale Pink Roast" (Paley) **8**:389, 397, 414-16

Pal Joey (O'Hara) **15**:263

The Palm-Sized Stories (Kawabata)
See "Tanagokoro no Shōsetsu"

Palomar (*Mr.*; *The Silent Mr. Palomar*) (Calvino) **3**:113-18

Paludes (*Marshlands*) (Gide) **13**:52-3, 56-7, 59, 61-5, 70, 72, 80, 86-9, 91-5, 99, 101

"Pan Apolek" (Babel) **16**:6-7, 26, 28, 30-1, 50, 53, 55, 58-9

"La panchina" (Calvino) **3**:97

"P. & O." (Maugham) **8**:359, 366, 372, 375

"Pandora" (James) **8**:310-12

Pandora (Nerval) **18**:346-48, 350-52, 354, 362, 369-72

"Panel Game" (Coover) **15**:32, 37

"Pantaloon in Black" (Faulkner) **1**:148, 174, 183

"Le papa de Simon" (Maupassant) **1**:261, 271

"The Papers" (James) **8**:321

"Parachutes" (McGahern) **17**:308, 310-15, 318-19, 323

"Paradise" (Lagerkvist) **12**:179, 195

"Paradise" (O'Brien) **10**:330, 341, 343

"The Paradise of Bachelors" (Melville) **17**:359

"The Paradise of Bachelors and the Tartarus of Maids" (Melville) **1**:298, 303-05, 323

The Paradoxes of Mr. Pond (Chesterton) **1**:125, 139

"The Paragon" (O'Connor) **5**:371-72

"Paragraph" (Lish) **18**:286

"Paraguay" (Barthelme) **2**:35, 38, 41

"Le parapluie" (Maupassant) **1**:286

"Pardner" (O'Hara) **15**:250

The Parisian Prowler (Baudelaire)
See *Petits poèmes en prose: Le spleen de Paris*

Paris Spleen (Baudelaire)
See *Petits poèmes en prose: Le spleen de Paris*

"Parker Adderson, Philosopher" (Bierce) **9**:60, 68, 84-5

"Parker's Back" (O'Connor) **1**:344-45, 357, 359, 368-70

"The Parking Lot" (Beattie) **11**:17-18, 20, 22

"The Parrot" (Bowen) **3**:37, 55

"The Parrot" (Singer) **3**:358

"The Parshley Celebration" (Jewett) **6**:156

Parti-colored Stories (Chekhov) **2**:130

"Une partie de campagne" (Maupassant) **1**:260-61

"La partie de trictrac" ("The Game of Backgammon") (Merimee) **7**:280, 283, 287-91

"The Parting" (O'Flaherty) **6**:265, 281, 286, 288

A Part of the Institution (Suckow) **18**:400, 403

"The Partridge Festival" (O'Connor) **1**:356

"The Party" (Barthelme) **2**:39, 55

"The Party" (Chekhov)
See "The Name-Day Party"

"A Party for the Girls" (Bates) **10**:131

"La parure" ("The Diamond Necklace"; "The Necklace") (Maupassant) **1**:273, 278, 280, 284, 286, 288

"El Paso" (Phillips) **16**:326-28, 330, 337

"Los paso en las huellas" (Cortazar) **7**:62

"A Passage in the Life of Mr. John Oakhurst" (Harte) **8**:233

"Passage in the Life of Mr. Watkins Tottle" (Dickens) **17**:110, 138

"A Passage in the Secret History of an Irish Countess" ("Countess"; "The Murdered Cousin") (Le Fanu) **14**:220, 221, 237

"The Passenger" (Calisher) **15**:9

"The Passenger" (Nabokov) **11**:134

"The Passenger's Story" (Twain) **6**:337

"Passer-By" (Clarke) **3**:134

"Passing" (Hughes)
See "Who's Passing for Who?"

"The Passing of Ambrose" (Wodehouse) **2**:356

"The Passing of Black Eagle" (Henry) **5**:158

"The Passing of Enriquez" (Harte) **8**:228

"The Passing of Grandison" (Chesnutt) **7**:16, 19, 22-3, 25-6

"The Passion" (Barnes) **3**:5, 24-7

"Une passion" (Maupassant) **1**:274

"Passion" (O'Faolain) **13**:294-95

"A Passionate Pilgrim" (James) **8**:302

"Une passion dans le désert" ("A Passion in the Desert") (Balzac) **5**:12-14, 31

"A Passion in the Desert" (Balzac)
See "Une passion dans le désert"

"Passions" (Singer) **3**:378

Passions, and Other Stories (Singer) **3**:376-77, 381, 384

"Past Carin'" (Lawson) **18**:210, 225

"Past One at Rooney's" (Henry) **5**:198

"Pastoral" (Anderson) **1**:52

"Pastoral" (Carver) **8**:5, 30, 50

"Pastoral Care" (Gardner) **7**:217, 219-22, 229, 232

The Pastoral Symphony (Gide)
See *La Symphonie pastorale*

"Pastor Dowe at Tacaté" (Bowles) **3**:59, 61-3, 66-7, 69, 79

"The Pastor of Six Mile Bush" (Lavin) **4**:169

The Pastures of Heaven (Steinbeck) **11**:202-03, 206-07, 225, 233, 242, 244, 246

"The Patagonia" (James) **8**:299, 311

"Pat Collins" (O'Hara) **15**:282

"The Patented Gate and the Mean Hamburger" (Warren) **4**:387, 390, 394, 396, 399

"Patent Pending" (Clarke) **3**:133-34

"Pat Hobby's Christmas Wish" (Fitzgerald) **6**:69-70

"The Path of the Moon's Dark Fortnight" (Gordimer) **17**:154

"The Pathways of Desire" (Le Guin) **12**:235

"A Patient Waiter" (Freeman) **4**:201

"The Patriarch" (Grau) **15**:149, 152, 160-61

"The Patriarch" (O'Connor) **5**:393-94

"Patricia, Edith, and Arnold" (Thomas) **3**:402, 405, 410, 412

"Patricide" (Oates) **6**:237

"The Patriot" (O'Faolain) **13**:286, 314, 316

"A Patriotic Short" (Fitzgerald) **6**:70-1

"Patriotism" (Mishima) **4**:313-15, 317-23

"The Patriot Son" (Lavin) **4**:167, 172, 183

The Patriot Son, and Other Stories (Lavin) **4**:165

"The Patron" (Phillips) **16**:330

"La patronne" (Maupassant) **1**:256

"Paul's Case" (Cather) **2**:90-1, 94, 103, 113, 118, 121-22

"The Pavilion on the Links" (Stevenson) **11**:265, 268-69, 280, 296-97, 303, 306

"The Pawnbroker's Shop" (Dickens) **17**:115

"The Pawnbroker's Wife" (Spark) **10**:350, 354, 359, 363

"Payable Gold" (Lawson) **18**:220

"The Peacelike Mongoose" (Thurber) **1**:426

"Peace of Mind" (Boyle) **16**:148, 153, 155

"The Peace of Mowsle Barton" (Saki) **12**:288

"The Peace of Utrecht" (Munro) **3**:321, 326

"Peaches" (McGahern) **17**:298, 303, 309, 319

"The Peaches" (Thomas) **3**:394, 396, 402, 404-05, 410-12

"The Peach-Tree" (Bates) **10**:112

"Peacock" (Carver) **8**:39

"The Pearl" (Dinesen) **7**:165, 167-68, 198

"The Pearl" (Mishima) **4**:313, 317-18, 322

"The Pearl of Love" (Wells) **6**:376

"The Peasant Marey" (Dostoevsky) **2**:166

"Peasants" (Chekhov) **2**:126, 131, 156

"Peasants" (O'Connor) **5**:371, 377-78, 389, 394-95, 398

"Peasant Women" (Chekhov) **2**:155

"Pecheneg" (Chekhov) **2**:155

"The Pedersen Kid" (Gass) **12**:123-24, 126, 129, 131-32, 137, 139, 152-53, 156, 166, 168-73

"A Pedestrian Accident" (Coover) **15**:32

"Pedro Salvadores" (Borges) **4**:14-17

"The Pegnitz Junction" (Gallant) **5**:124, 127, 132-34, 143

The Pegnitz Junction (Gallant) **5**:124, 127, 130-32

"The Pelican" (Wharton) **6**:413, 423, 428-29

"The Pemberton Thrush" (Bates) **10**:121

"The Penance" (Saki) **12**:302

"Pen and Inkstand" (Andersen) **6**:7

"The Pendulum" (Henry) **5**:158-59, 163, 188

"The Pension Beaurepas" (James) **8**:299

The People, and Uncollected Short Stories (Malamud) **15**:234-35

"Un pequeño paraíso" ("A Small Paradise") (Cortazar) **7**:93

"Le père" (Maupassant) **1**:275

"Le père amable" (Maupassant) **1**:259, 284

"Père Raphaël" (Cable) **4**:51, 77-9

"Pereval" (Bunin) **5**:98

"A Perfect Day for Bananafish" (Salinger) **2**:290-93, 295, 297-99, 303, 305, 308, 312, 314, 318

The Perfecting of a Love (Musil)
See "Vollendung der Liebe"

"Perfection" (Nabokov) **11**:123

"The Perfect Life" (Fitzgerald) **6**:47, 49

"The Perfect Murder" (Barnes) **3**:13

"The Perfume Sea" (Laurence) **7**:245, 248-50, 256

"The Peril in the Streets" (Cheever) **1**:99

The Periodic Table (Levi)
See *Il sistema periodico*

"The Perishing of the Pendragons" (Chesterton) **1**:131, 138

"El perjurio de la nieve" (Bioy Casares) **17**:59

"The Perjury of the Snow" (Bioy Casares) **17**:85

"Perlmutter at the East Pole" (Elkin) **12**:94-5, 117-18

"Perpetua" (Barthelme) **2**:55

"Persecution Mania" (O'Faolain) **13**:297

"El Perseguidor" ("The Pursuer") (Cortazar) **7**:50-1, 58, 61, 67-8, 70

Title Index

"Perseid" (Barth) **10**:44, 51, 55-6, 66-9, 71, 91, 93, 101-02, 104
"Pershing or Ten Eyck, Ten Eyck or Pershing" (O'Hara) **15**:253
"The Persistence of Desire" (Updike) **13**:391-92
"Perte d'auréole" (Baudelaire) **18**:35, 49
Pervaya lyubov' (*First Love*) (Turgenev) **7**:321, 323-24, 327-29, 332-34, 337-39, 341, 352
"Pesadillas" ("Nightmares") (Cortazar) **7**:91
"Pesci grossi, pesci piccoli" (Calvino) **3**:96
"Pesn' torzhestruyushchey lyubvi" ("The Love Song of the Conquering Lovers"; "The Song of the Triumphant Love") (Turgenev) **7**:321, 323, 337-38, 362
"Peter" (Cather) **2**:96-7, 100, 105
"Peter and the Wolf" (Carter) **13**:14, 17-18
"Peter Atherley's Ancestors" (Harte) **8**:215
"Peter Goldthwaite's Treasure" (Hawthorne) **3**:183, 185
"La petite danceuse de quatorze ans" (Beattie) **11**:6, 17
"La petite rogue" (Maupassant) **1**:275, 283, 288
"Le petit fût" (Maupassant) **1**:259, 284
"Petition" (Barth) **10**:38, 41-3, 46, 52, 54, 56-7, 59-60, 76, 79, 84, 91, 95, 97
"Petit soldat" (Maupassant) **1**:259
Petits poèmes en prose: Le spleen de Paris (*Little Poems in Prose*; *The Parisian Prowler*; *Paris Spleen*; *Poems in Prose from Charles Baudelaire*; *Prose Poems*; *Short Prose Poems*; *Le spleen de Paris*) (Baudelaire) **18**:3, 6-8, 14-16, 19, 22-5, 27-9, 31-4, 38, 44-8, 50, 52-4, 59, 61-5
"Petlistye ushi" ("Loopy Ears"; "Thieves' Ears") (Bunin) **5**:81, 101-04, 110-13
Petlistye ushi i drugie rasskazy (Bunin) **5**:101
"The Petrified Man" (Welty) **1**:465, 467, 469, 471, 482, 490, 493-95, 497
"The Petrified Woman" (Gordon) **15**:119-20, 123, 139
"The Petrol Dump" (Pritchett) **14**:296
"Petunias" (Walker) **5**:413
"La peur" (Maupassant) **1**:265, 288
Phantasiestüeke in Callots Manier (*Night Pieces after the Manner of Callot*) (Hoffmann) **13**:179, 188-90
"Les Phantasmes de M. Redoux" (Villiers de l'Isle Adam) **14**:397
"The Phantom of the Movie Palace" (Coover) **15**:57, 59, 63, 65
"The Phantom of the Opera's Friend" (Barthelme) **2**:31, 35, 52, 54
"The Phantom 'Rickshaw" (Kipling) **5**:261, 265, 271-75, 297-99
The Phantom 'Rickshaw (Kipling) **5**:272-73
"Phantoms" (Turgenev) **7**:321, 323, 325, 334-35, 338
"The Pheasant" (Carver) **8**:53
"Philip and Margie" (Jewett) **6**:156
"A Philistine in Bohemia" (Henry) **5**:190, 196
"The Philosopher's Stone" (Andersen) **6**:26, 34
Philosophic Studies (Balzac)
   See *Etudes philosophiques*
Philosophie's (Voltaire) **12**:364
"Phosphorus" (Levi) **12**:256
"Physic" (de la Mare) **14**:80, 83
"Piano Fingers" (Mason) **4**:18
"The Piazza" (Melville) **1**:303

The Piazza Tales (Melville) **1**:295-97
"Pickman's Model" (Lovecraft) **3**:261-62
"The Picnic" (de la Mare) **14**:83-4
"Pictor's Metamorphoses" (Hesse) **9**:221, 242, 244-45
Pictor's Metamorphoses, and Other Fantasies (Hesse) **9**:244
"The Picture" (de la Mare) **14**:83-4
A Picture-Book without Pictures (Andersen) **6**:4, 15, 30
"The Picture in the House" (Lovecraft) **3**:262, 275-76, 292-95
"Pictures" (Mansfield) **9**:304, 307, 311
"Pictures of Fidelman" (Malamud) **15**:186-87
Pictures of Fidelman: An Exhibition (Malamud) **15**:178, 181, 184, 190, 192-93, 195, 211, 218, 220, 236, 240-41
"Pictures of the Artist" (Malamud) **15**:185, 193-94
"A Piece of Advice" (Singer) **3**:368
"A Piece of News" (Welty) **1**:468, 478, 487, 496
"A Piece of Steak" (London) **4**:253, 262-63, 291
"A Piece of String" (Maupassant)
   See "La ficelle"
"Pierre Grassou" (Balzac) **5**:18
"Pierre Menard, Author of the *Quixote*" (Borges)
   See "Pierre Menard, autor del *Quixote*"
"Pierre Menard, autor del *Quixote*" ("Pierre Menard, Author of the *Quixote*") (Borges) **4**:15, 26, 30, 34-5
"La pierre qui pousse" ("The Growing Stone") (Camus) **9**:103, 106, 108-110, 118-19, 131-34
"Pierrette" (Balzac) **5**:9
"Pierrot" (Maupassant) **1**:277-78
"The Pig" (Lessing) **6**:196-97, 212-17
"The Pig" (O'Hara) **15**:291
"Pigeon Feathers" (Updike) **13**:370-71, 388, 395, 397, 404, 407
Pigeon Feathers, and Other Stories (Updike) **13**:356, 366, 389-90, 392, 400, 404
"Pig Hoo-o-o-o-ey!" (Wodehouse) **2**:346, 348
"Pigtails, Ltd." (de la Mare) **14**:68, 85, 87
"A Pilgrim and a Stranger" (Suckow) **18**:409, 414
Pilgrim at Sea (Lagerkvist) **12**:188, 191, 194, 198
"Pillar of Salt" (Jackson) **9**:252, 258
"Pillow of Stone" (Grau) **15**:148, 160
"A Pimp's Revenge" (Malamud) **15**:183-84, 192, 194
"A Pinch of Salt" (Jewett) **6**:158
"The Pines" (Bunin) **5**:100
"The Pine Tree" (Andersen) **6**:12, 40-1
Ping (Beckett)
   See *Bing*
"The Pink Corner Man" (Borges)
   See "Hombre de la esquina rosada"
"Pink May" (Bowen) **3**:31-2, 41
"The Pioneer Hep-Cat" (O'Hara) **15**:280
Pipe Night (O'Hara) **15**:248-50, 262, 264-65, 267, 269
"The Pit and the Pendulum" (Poe) **1**:405-06
"The Pitcher" (Dubus) **15**:83, 100
"The Pixy and the Grocer" (Andersen)
   See "The Goblin at the Grocer's"
"A Place in the Heart" (Bates) **10**:119
"The Place of the Gods" (Benet)
   See "By the Waters of Babylon"

"The Place with No Name" (Ellison) **14**:109, 118, 120, 138
"Les plagiaires de la foudre" (Villiers de l'Isle Adam) **14**:397
"Plagiarized Material" (Oates) **6**:237, 242
"The Plague-Cellar" (Stevenson) **11**:304
Plain Tales (Kipling)
   See *Plain Tales from the Hills*
Plain Tales from the Hills (*Plain Tales*) (Kipling) **5**:273-74, 278, 288
"Un plaisant" ("A Joker") (Baudelaire) **18**:17-18, 32, 60
"Planchette" (London) **4**:265, 294-95
Plan de evasion (*A Plan for Escape*) (Bioy Casares) **17**:53-5, 61, 63-4, 94
"The Planets of the Years" (O'Faolain) **13**:291, 318-19
A Plan for Escape (Bioy Casares)
   See *Plan de evasion*
"The Planter of Malata" (Conrad) **9**:147
"Plants and Girls" (Lessing) **6**:217
"The Plattner Story" (Wells) **6**:359, 364-66, 394, 405
The Plattner Story, and Others (Wells) **6**:366-67, 380, 388
The Play, and Other Stories (Dixon) **16**:215
"Playback" (Beattie) **11**:11, 22
Play Days (Jewett) **6**:165-66
"The Playhouse Called Remarkable" (Spark) **10**:359, 361, 370
"Playing With Fire" (Doyle) **12**:64
"Pleasure" (Lessing) **6**:197
"Pleasure" (O'Hara) **15**:248, 265
"The Pleasure-Cruise" (Kipling) **5**:284
"The Pleasures of Solitude" (Cheever) **1**:88
"The Ploughman" (Dinesen) **7**:177
"Plumbing" (Updike) **13**:348
"A Plunge into Real Estate" (Calvino)
   See "La speculazione edilizia"
"Le plus beau dîner du monde" ("The Finest Diner in the World") (Villiers de l'Isle Adam) **14**:377
"Le plus bel amour de Don Juan" ("The Greatest Love of Don Juan") (Barbey d'Aurevilly) **17**:7, 11-14, 19-20, 42-4
"Pocock Passes" (Pritchett) **14**:271, 285-86, 297
Poems in Prose from Charles Baudelaire (Baudelaire)
   See *Petits poèmes en prose: Le spleen de Paris*
"The Poet" (Dinesen) **7**:167-68, 180, 203, 209
"The Poet" (Hesse) **9**:234
The Poet and the Lunatics (Chesterton) **1**:124-26, 132
"The Poet and the Peasant" (Henry) **5**:194
"A Poetics for Bullies" (Elkin) **12**:94-7, 99, 117-18
"A Point at Issue" (Chopin) **8**:70, 73
"A Point of Law" (Faulkner) **1**:177
"Poison" (Mansfield) **9**:310-11
The Poisoned Kiss (Oates) **6**:236, 241-43
"Poker Night" (Updike) **13**:409
"Polar Bears and Others" (Boyle) **5**:54
"Polaris" (Lovecraft) **3**:288
"Polarities" (Atwood) **2**:2-5, 7-8, 10, 13-14
"Poldi" (McCullers) **9**:342, 345, 357
"The Policeman's Ball" (Barthelme) **2**:31, 45
Polikushka (Tolstoy) **9**:376, 389, 393-94, 399, 403
"Political Director of Divine Worship" (Bulgakov) **18**:90
"Pollock and the Porroh Man" (Wells) **6**:388

"Polydore" (Chopin) **8**:93

"Polzunkov" (Dostoevsky) **2**:170, 192-93

"Pomegranate Seed" (Wharton) **6**:426-27, 431-32

"Un pomeriggio Adamo" (Calvino) **3**:97

The Ponder Heart (Welty) **1**:474, 477, 483, 494-95, 497

"The Pool" (du Maurier) **18**:127-28

"The Pool" (Maugham) **8**:369-71

"The Pool of Narcissus" (Calisher) **15**:15, 17

"The Poor Bird" (Andersen) **6**:4

"The Poor Child's Toy" (Baudelaire)
See "Le joujou du pauvre"

"A Poor Girl" (Chopin) **8**:69

"Poor John" (Andersen) **6**:4

"Poor Little Black Fellow" (Hughes) **6**:118, 121-22, 134

"Poor Little Rich Town" (Vonnegut) **8**:436

"Poor Man's Pudding and Rich Man's Crumbs" ("Rich Man's Crumbs") (Melville) **1**:303, 323

"Poor People" (O'Flaherty) **6**:262, 264, 280, 283

"The Poor Thing" (Powers) **4**:368, 372-73

"Poor Thumbling" ("Thumbling") (Andersen) **6**:4, 7

"Pope Zeidlus" (Singer) **3**:364

"Popsy" (King) **17**:295

"Popular Mechanics" (Carver) **8**:14, 18, 26, 30, 44-5

"Porcelain and Pink" (Fitzgerald) **6**:59

"Porcupines at the University" (Barthelme) **2**:56

"Porn" (Walker) **5**:412-14

"Por qué ser así?" (Unamuno) **11**:312

"Le port" (Baudelaire) **18**:6

"Le port" (Maupassant) **1**:264

"Porte cochère" (Taylor) **10**:379, 407

"The Porter's Son" (Andersen) **6**:11-12

"The Portly Gentleman" (O'Hara) **15**:284

"The Portobello Road" (Spark) **10**:350-53, 355, 357-58, 360, 365-66, 368, 370-71

"Portrait" (Boyle) **5**:54

"The Portrait" (Gogol) **9**:102-03, 116, 122, 125

"The Portrait" (Wharton) **6**:414

Portrait of the Artist as a Young Dog (Thomas) **3**:394-97, 399, 402-04, 410-13

"Portraits de maîtresses" (Baudelaire) **18**:18, 25, 37

Die Portugiesin (*The Portuguese Lady*) (Musil) **18**:292-93, 297-303, 322

The Portuguese Lady (Musil)
See *Die Portugiesin*

"Po' Sandy" (Chesnutt) **7**:5-7, 10, 13, 42

"Poseidon and Company" (Carver) **8**:50-1

"Poseshchenie muzeia" (Nabokov)
See "The Visit to the Museum"

"The Possessed" (Clarke) **3**:132, 135, 143-44, 148

"The Possibility of Evil" (Jackson) **9**:256

"Posson Jone'" (Cable) **4**:48, 56, 58, 62, 64-5, 67, 77-80

"The Post" (Chekhov) **2**:130, 156

"The Postcard" (Dixon) **16**:217

"Postcard" (Munro) **3**:322

The Posthumous Writings and Poems of Hermann Lauscher (Hesse)
See *Hinterlassene Schriften und Gedichte von Hermann Lauscher*

"The Post Office" (O'Flaherty)
See "Oifig an Phoist"

"Posy" (Lavin) **4**:166

"Potassium" (Levi) **12**:257

"The Potato Elf" ("Kartofel'nyy el'f") (Nabokov) **11**:117, 137, 139-40

"The Pot-Boiler" (Wharton) **6**:435

"The Pot of Gold" (Cheever) **1**:89, 99

"The Pot of Gold" (O'Flaherty) **6**:271

"Potter" (Gallant) **5**:136-37

Pour finir encour et Autres Foirades (Beckett)
See *Foirades*

"Poverty" (Zoshchenko) **15**:404

"The Powder Blue Dragon" (Vonnegut) **8**:432-33

"The Powder of the Angels and I'm Yours" (Phillips) **16**:325, 328

"Powder-White Faces" (Hughes) **6**:118, 122

"Powerhouse" (Welty) **1**:466, 488, 494

"Powers" (Singer) **3**:360

Prairie Folks (Garland) **18**:144-45, 148, 150, 160, 174-77, 182, 194

"A Prairie Heroine" (Garland) **18**:163, 166, 173

"Pranzo con un pastore" (Calvino) **3**:97

"A Preacher's Love Story" (Garland) **18**:148, 160

"The Precipice" (Oates) **6**:247

"A Predicament" (Poe) **1**:405-06

"Prelude" (Mansfield) **9**:279-80, 282-84, 286, 288-91, 298, 300-01, 303, 305, 307, 309, 311, 313, 316

"A Premature Autobiography" (Oates) **6**:232

"The Premature Burial" (Poe) **1**:407

Premier amour (*First Love*) (Beckett) **16**:73-4, 87-8, 90-1, 97

"The Presence" (Gordon) **15**:116, 121, 131

"The Presence of Grace" (Powers) **4**:370, 381

The Presence of Grace (Powers) **4**:372-73

"A Present for a Good Girl" (Gordimer) **17**:167

"Preservation" (Carver) **8**:26, 32

"The President" (Barthelme) **2**:31

"The President of the Louisiana Live Oak Society" (Gilchrist) **14**:151-52, 155

"Press Clippings" (Cortazar)
See "Recortes de prensa"

"The Pretender" (Gordimer)
See "My First Two Women"

"The Pretender" (O'Connor) **5**:386, 390

"The Pretty Girl" (Dubus) **15**:76, 87-9, 91, 93-4, 96, 101

"Pretty Maggie Moneyeyes" (Ellison) **14**:107-08, 115

"Pretty Mouth and Green My Eyes" (Salinger) **2**:290, 293, 298, 300

"Pretty Poll" (de la Mare) **14**:85

"Previous Condition" (Baldwin) **10**:3, 5, 7, 9-10, 17

"Las previsiones de Sangiácomo" (Bioy Casares) **17**:68-70

"Prey" (O'Flaherty) **6**:281

"The Price of the Harness" (Crane) **7**:104

"Price's Always Open" (O'Hara) **15**:255-56

Pricksongs and Descants (Coover) **15**:34-5, 37-41,43, 45, 47, 49-50, 53, 56, 58, 63

"The Pride of the Cities" (Henry) **5**:159, 194

"The Pride of the Village" (Irving) **2**:240-41, 245, 251

"Priestly Fellowship" (Powers) **4**:376, 381-82

"The Priestly Prerogative" (London) **4**:282

"The Priest of Shiga Temple and His Love" (Mishima) **4**:313, 315-17, 322-23

"Prima Belladonna" (Ballard) **1**:68

"Prime Leaf" (Warren) **4**:387-90, 393, 395, 400

"The Primrose Path" (Lawrence) **4**:234-37

"Un Prince de la Bohème" (Balzac) **5**:31-3

"Prince Hamlet of Shehrigov Province" (Turgenev)
See "A Russian Hamlet"

"Prince of Darkness" (Powers) **4**:370, 383

Prince of Darkness and Other Stories (Powers) **4**:369-71

"The Princess" (Chekhov) **2**:130, 144

"The Princess" (de la Mare) **14**:80

The Princess (Lawrence) **4**:238-40, 242

"The Princess and All the Kingdom" (Lagerkvist) **12**:195

"The Princess and the Pea" ("The Princess on the Pea") (Andersen) **6**:7, 13, 18, 26, 30

"The Princess Baladina—Her Adventure" (Cather) **2**:100

"The Princess Bob and Her Friends" (Harte) **8**:216

Princess Brambilla (Hoffmann)
See *Prinzessin Brambilla: Ein Capriccio nach Jakob Callot*

La princesse de Babylon (Voltaire) **12**:341-42

"The Princess on the Pea" (Andersen)
See "The Princess and the Pea"

"Prinzessin Brambilla" (Hoffmann) **13**:192, 198, 218-19

Prinzessin Brambilla: Ein Capriccio nach Jakob Callot (*Princess Brambilla*) (Hoffmann) **13**:183-84

"Prischepa's Revenge" (Babel) **16**:7, 24-5

"Priscilla" (Calvino) **3**:95-6

"Prishchepa" (Babel) **16**:50

"The Prison" (Malamud) **15**:175

"The Prisoner of the Caucasus" (Tolstoy) **9**:382, 386-87

"Private Lies" (Mason) **4**:19

"The Private Life" (James) **8**:280-81

"The Private Life of Mr. Bidwell" (Thurber) **1**:419

"Private Theatres" (Dickens) **17**:117, 122

"Privilege" (Munro) **3**:334

"The Privy Councilor" (Chekhov) **2**:130

"Problem No. 4" (Cheever) **1**:99

"The Problem of Art" (Gardner) **7**:226

"The Problem of Thor Bridge" (Doyle) **12**:52, 63-4

Problems, and Other Stories (Updike) **13**:383, 385-86, 388

"Problems of Adjustment in Survivors of Natural/Unnatural Disasters" (Oates) **6**:225

"The Procession of Life" (Hawthorne) **3**:181, 190

"The Procession of Life" (O'Connor) **5**:381, 393

"The Prodigal Children" (Benet) **10**:156

"Prodigal Father" (Gallant) **5**:138

"The Prodigal Father" (London) **4**:256

"La prodigiosa tarde de Baltazar" ("Balthazar's Marvelous Afternoon") (Garcia Marquez) **8**:185, 187-91

"The Prodigy" (Singer) **3**:374

"The Prodigy of Dreams" (Ligotti) **16**:277-79, 295, 297

"Professor" (Hughes) **6**:112, 118, 122, 131-32

"Professor Nobody's Little Lectures on Supernatural Horror" (Ligotti) **16**:261, 269, 284-85, 293

"The Professor's Commencement" (Cather)
2:99, 103, 113

"The Professor's Escape" (Aiken) 9:14

"The Profile" (Cather) 2:98, 103-04

"The Progress of Love" (Munro) 3:347, 349

The Progress of Love (Munro) 3:346-48

"Les projets" (Baudelaire) 18:6-7

"Prologue to an Adventure" (Thomas) 3:399, 401

"La prolongada busca de Tai An" (Bioy Casares) 17:70

"Promenade" (Maupassant) 1:260, 274

Prométhée (Gide) 13:52-57, 67

Le Prométhée mal enchaîné (*Prometheus Illbound*; *Prometheus Misbound*) (Gide) 13:59, 61, 65, 72, 79-81, 86

Prometheus Illbound (Gide)
See *Le Prométhée mal enchaîné*

Prometheus Misbound (Gide)
See *Le Prométhée mal enchaîné*

"The Promise" (Steinbeck) 11:209-10, 212-13, 232

"Promise of Rain" (Taylor) 10:417

"The Promoter" (Dunbar) 8:122, 147

"Proof of the Pudding" (Henry) 5:165

"Propavšaja gramotax" ("The Lost Letter") (Gogol) 4:117, 121

"The Properties of Love" (O'Hara) 15:252

"Property" (Singer) 3:374

"The Prophecy" (Schnitzler) 15:343

"The Prophetic Pictures" (Hawthorne) 3:158, 181, 185-86, 190-91

"The Prophet Peter" (Chesnutt) 7:17

"Proprietors of the Olden Time" (Gogol)
See "Starosvetskie Pomeščiki"

Prose Poems (Baudelaire)
See *Petits poèmes en prose: Le spleen de Paris*

Prose Works of Henry Lawson (Lawson) 18:202

A Prospect of the Orchards (Bates) 10:121-22

"A Prospect of the Sea" (Thomas) 3:394, 399, 401, 407-09

"Le protecteur" (Maupassant) 1:280

"A Protégée of Jack Hamlin's" (Harte) 8:249

"Providence and the Guitar" (Stevenson) 11:280

"The Prowler in the City at the End of the War" (Ellison) 14:115

"The Prussian Officer" (Lawrence) 4:197-99, 210, 212, 214-18, 235

The Prussian Officer, and Other Stories (Lawrence) 4:196-98, 202, 230, 235-36

"A Psalm" (Bulgakov) 18:74, 92

"The Psoriasis Diet" (Lish) 18:284

"Psyche" (Andersen) 6:36, 38

"Psyche and the Pskyscraper" (Henry) 5:162

"Psychiatric Services" (Oates) 6:232

"Psychology" (Mansfield) 9:280, 284, 310

"The Psychophant" (Levi) 12:279

"Ptaki" ("Birds") (Schulz) 13:327, 333-34

"The Public Career of Mr. Seymour Harrisburg" (O'Hara) 15:248

"Publicity Campaign" (Clarke) 3:134, 150

"Public Opinion" (O'Connor) 5:374

"Puck of Pook's Hill" (Kipling) 5:271, 273, 292

"Punin and Barbarin" (Turgenev) 7:321, 323-24, 326, 337, 358, 360

"The Pupil" (James) 8:291, 316

The Purcell Papers (Le Fanu) 14:217, 221, 245

"A Purchase of Some Golf Clubs" (O'Hara) 15:270

The Pure and Impure (Colette)
See *Le pur et l'impur*

"Pure as the Driven Snow" (Aiken) 9:6, 14

"The Pure Diamond Man" (Laurence) 7:245

Le pur et l'impur (*The Pure and Impure*) (Colette) 10:262

"The Purloined Letter" (Poe) 1:387-88

"The Purple Hat" (Welty) 1:468-69, 471, 479

"The Purple of the Balkan Kings" (Saki) 12:322

"The Purple Pileus" (Wells) 6:360, 383, 389, 404

"The Purple Wig" (Chesterton) 1:131

A Purse of Coppers (O'Faolain) 13:284, 286, 293, 301-02, 309, 312-13, 316

"The Pursuer" (Cortazar)
See "El Perseguidor"

"A Pursuit Race" (Hemingway) 1:216, 219

"Purun Bhagat" (Kipling)
See "The Miracle of Purun Bhagat"

"Puttermesser and Xanthippe" (Ozick) 15:307-08, 319-23, 325, 327

"Puttermesser: Her Work History, Her Ancestry, Her Afterlife" (Ozick) 15:307, 320, 322, 326

"Put Yourself in My Shoes" (Carver) 8:9, 13, 20, 46, 49

"Pyetushkov" (Turgenev) 7:320

"The Pyrrhon of Elis" (Davenport) 16:198-99

"Pytor Petrovich Karataev" (Turgenev) 7:313

"Quanto scommettiamo" (Calvino) 3:92

"The Quare Gander" (Le Fanu) 14:219-20

"The Quarrel of Two Ivans" (Gogol)
See "The Tale of How Ivan Ivanovich Quarrelled with Ivan Nikiforovich"

"Queen Louisa" (Gardner) 7:233

The Queen of Spain Fritillary (Bates) 10:119

"Queen of the Night" (Oates) 6:246

"The Queen's Twin" (Jewett) 6:152

"Queen Ysabeau" (Villiers de l'Isle Adam)
See "La reine Ysabeau"

"The Queer Feet" (Chesterton) 1:119, 125, 127, 130

"A Queer Heart" (Bowen) 3:33, 41, 43, 49-50

"A Queer Streak" (Munro) 3:347

"Quenby and Ola, Swede and Carl" (Coover) 15:38, 48, 51

Queremos tanto a Glenda (*Glenda*; *We Love Glenda So Much, and Other Tales*) (Cortazar) 1:7:64, 68, 71-2, 79, 90

"que sepa abrir la puerta para ir a jugar" ("May you learn to open the door to go out to play") (Cortazar) 7:95

"The Quest" (Saki) 12:299

"A Question of Re-Entry" (Ballard) 1:68

"The Quest of Iranon" (Lovecraft) 3:274

"Quetzalcoatl Lite" (Boyle) 16:143

"The Quicksand" (Wharton) 6:424

"Quidquid volueris" (Flaubert) 11:71-3, 75-6

"The Quiet City" (Levi) 12:273

The Quiet One (Bates) 10:124

"A Quiet Spot" (Turgenev) 7:328

"The Quince Tree" (Saki) 12:295

"The Quincunx" (de la Mare) 14:84, 91

"Qui sait?" (Maupassant) 1:273

Quite Contrary: The Mary and Newt Story (Dixon) 16:204-05, 210, 214-15

Quite Early One Morning (Thomas) 3:392

"Quitters, Inc" (King) 17:262

"The Rabbi" (Babel) 16:9, 25-6, 28-30

"The Rabbi's Daughter" (Calisher) 15:4, 7, 12, 15, 19

"The Rabbi's Son" (Babel) 16:16, 26, 28, 30-1, 52, 55-6

"The Rabbit" (Barnes) 3:6-7, 22-4

"The Rabbit-Pen" (Anderson) 1:52

"The Rabbits Who Caused All the Trouble" (Thurber) 1:431

I racconti (Calvino) 3:96-7, 116

Racconti e Saggi (*The Mirror Maker*) (Levi) 12:273-78, 280-82

"The Race Question" (Dunbar) 8:122, 147

"Radio" (O'Hara) 15:265, 267-68, 270

"The Raft" (King) 17:274-75

"Rags and Bones" (Gordimer) 17:169, 171

"Rags Martin-Jones and the Pr-nce of W-les" (Fitzgerald) 6:46, 56

"Ragtime" (Nin) 10:299, 301, 303, 305

"The Raid" (Bulgakov) 18:74, 90

"Raid" (Faulkner) 1:170

"The Raid" (Steinbeck) 11:207-08, 225, 232-33, 239-40

"The Raid" (Tolstoy) 9:375

"Railway Accident" (Mann) 5:323-24, 330, 348-50

"The Railway Police" (Calisher) 15:5, 11

The Railway Police (Calisher) 15:5-6, 21-3

"Rain" (Maugham) 8:356-61, 371, 373, 375, 377, 381-84

"The Rain Child" (Laurence) 7:246, 248, 250, 253, 272

"Rain in the Heart" (Taylor) 10:374-76, 385, 387

"Rain in the Sierra" (Pritchett) 14:268, 273, 285

"Rain-Queen" (Gordimer) 17:158

"The Rainy Moon" (Colette)
See "La lune de pluie"

"Rainy Season" (King) 17:295

"The Rainy Station" (Kawabata) 17:251

"Raise High the Roofbeam, Carpenters" (Salinger) 2:291-93, 298, 307, 314

Raise High the Roofbeam, Carpenters. Seymour: An Introduction (Salinger) 2:318

"Ralph Ringwood" (Irving) 2:241

"A Ramble among the Hills" (Irving) 2:266

"Ranocchi Sulla Luna" (Levi) 12:276

"The Ransom of Red Chief" (Henry) 5:193

"Rape Fantasies" (Atwood) 2:3-4, 6-8, 10-12

"Rappaccini's Daughter" (Hawthorne) 3:159, 171, 173-74, 179-80, 189, 191-92

"Rara Avis" (Boyle) 16:146

"Raspberry Spring" (Turgenev) 7:341

"Rasskaz ottsa Aleksaya" ("Father Alexey's Story"; "The Story of Father Alexis") (Turgenev) 7:324, 338, 361-62

"Rat Krespel" ("Councillor Krespel") (Hoffmann) 13:200, 202, 205-06

"Rats" (James) 16:236, 245, 251, 254, 256

"Rats" (Lawson) 18:218, 240-41, 245

"The Rats in the Walls" (Lovecraft) 3:258, 262, 267, 269, 275, 277

"Rattlesnake Creek" (Cather) 2:106

"The Ravages of Spring" (Gardner) 7:214-15, 218, 222, 228-29, 232-33

"The Raven" (Bunin)
See "Voron"

"Rawdon's Roof" (Lawrence) 4:220

"Raw Materials" (Atwood) 2:17-19

"Rayme" (Phillips) 16:336-37, 339

"The Reach" ("Do the Dead Sing?") (King) 17:275

Reach for Tomorrow (Clarke) **3**:124, 129
"Reading a Wave" (Calvino) **3**:113
"A Real Discovery" (Chesterton) **1**:140
"Real Impudence" (Calisher) **15**:9
"Really, *Doesn't* Crime Pay?" (Walker) **5**:401, 405, 408-09, 419
"The Real Thing" (James) **8**:296-98, 302
"The Reaping Race" (O'Flaherty) **6**:264, 281
"A Reasonable Man" (Beattie) **11**:12, 15-17,
"Reassurance" (O'Hara) **15**:281
The Rebecca Notebook and Other Memories (du Maurier) **18**:130
"Recent Photograph" (Bowen) **3**:40
"The Reckoning" (Wharton) **6**:425-26
"A Recluse" (de la Mare) **14**:72-3, 80-1, 83, 85, 88, 90
"A Recollection of Childhood" (Mansfield) **9**:282
"Recollections of a Billiard Marker" (Tolstoy) **9**:375
"The Recollections of Captain Wilkie" (Doyle) **12**:88
"Recollections of Mortality" (Dickens) **17**:123
"Recollections of the Gas Buggy" (Thurber) **1**:431
"The Record of Badalia Herodsfoot" (Kipling) **5**:261
"Recortes de prensa" ("Press Clippings") (Cortazar) **7**:69, 71, 83, 87, 91
"The Recovery" (Chopin) **8**:99
"The Recovery" (Wharton) **6**:414, 420, 423, 428-29
"The Recrudescence of Imray" (Kipling) See "The Return of Imray"
"The Recruiting Officer" (McGahern) **17**:302, 307, 309, 323
"Red" (Maugham) **8**:370
"Red Barbara" (O'Flaherty) **6**:260, 262, 271, 277-78, 285
Red Cavalry (Babel) See *Konarmiia*
"Red Crown" (Bulgakov) **18**:91
"Redemption" (Gardner) **7**:224-27, 235-36, 238, 240-41
"Red-Headed Baby" (Hughes) **6**:109, 118-19, 121, 123-25, 129-30, 141
"Red-Herring Theory" (Updike) **13**:387
"The Red Inn" (Balzac) **5**:18 See *L'auberge rouge*
"Red Leaves" (Faulkner) **1**:147, 162, 168-70, 180
"The Red Moon of Meru" (Chesterton) **1**:129
"The Red Petticoat" (O'Flaherty) **6**:271
The Red Pony (Steinbeck) **11**:204, 207, 209-10, 212-14, 217, 220, 225, 232-33
"The Red Room" (Wells) **6**:366, 383, 388
"The Red Shoes" (Andersen) **6**:4, 7, 34, 37-8
"Red-Stoned Moscow" (Bulgakov) **18**:90
"Reduced" (Bowen) **3**:33
"Reena" (Marshall) **3**:300, 303, 308, 310, 313, 315, 317
Reena, and Other Stories (*Merle: A Novella, and Other Stories*) (Marshall) **3**:313, 315-17
"The Reference" (Barthelme) **2**:55
"Reflections" (Carter) **13**:2, 4
"The Refuge of the Derelicts" (Twain) **6**:339
Reginald (Saki) **12**:286-87, 322, 327-28, 332
Reginald in Russia, and Other Stories (Saki) **12**:287, 322, 328, 331
"Reginald on Besetting Sins" (Saki) **12**:322, 328

"Reginald on House Parties" (Saki) **12**:325, 327, 329
"Reginald on Tariffs" (Saki) **12**:328
"Reginald's Choir Treat" (Saki) **12**:329
"Reginald's Christmas Revel" (Saki) **12**:303, 324
"The Region Between" (Ellison) **14**:146
"Regret" (Chopin) **8**:72-3, 84, 93, 111
"The Rehearsal" (Dixon) **16**:211
"The Reincarnation of Smith" (Harte) **8**:254
"La reine Ysabeau" ("Queen Ysabeau") (Villiers de l'Isle Adam) **14**:378, 382, 396
"Rejuvenation through Joy" (Hughes) **6**:109, 128
"Relato con un fondo de agua" (Cortazar) **7**:58
Los Relatos (Cortazar) **7**:91
"The Reluctant Orchid" (Clarke) **3**:133-34
"The Remarkable Case of Davidson's Eyes" (Wells) **6**:364-66, 376, 393-95, 405
"The Remarkable Rocket" (Wilde) **11**:365, 375-76, 380, 386, 395, 407-09
"The Rembrandt" (Wharton) **6**:414
"Rembrandt's Hat" (Malamud) **15**:187-88, 190, 221
Rembrandt's Hat (Malamud) **15**:188, 190, 197-98, 220
"Reminders of Bouselham" (Bowles) **3**:66
"The Remission" (Gallant) **5**:135-38
"Remnants" (Singer) **3**:385, 387
"The Remount Officer" (Babel) **16**:7, 27, 50, 53
"Le remplacant" (Maupassant) **1**:256
"Rena Walden" (Chesnutt) **7**:19, 21, 33, 35
"Le rendez-vous" (Colette) **10**:274-75
"The Rendezvous" (du Maurier) **18**:136
The Rendezvous and Other Stories (du Maurier) **18**:130, 136
"The Renegade" (Camus) See "Le renégat"
"Renegade" (Jackson) **9**:252, 266
"Le renégat" ("The Renegade") (Camus) **9**:106-07, 109, 116-17, 119, 130-31
"Renner" (Powers) **4**:368, 370, 372-73
"Renters" (Suckow) **18**:396, 398
"Renunciation" (Barnes) **3**:16
"The Repentant Sinner" (Tolstoy) **9**:387
"'Repent, Harlequin!' Said the Ticktockman" (Ellison) **14**:105, 112-15, 117, 124, 134-36
"A Report" (Gallant) **5**:138
"Report from Normalia" (Hesse) **9**:244
"Report on the Barnhouse Effect" (Vonnegut) **8**:428-29
"Report on the Threatened City" (Lessing) **6**:188
"A Report to an Academy" (Kafka) **5**:215-16, 220, 231
Reprinted Pieces (Dickens) **17**:124
"The Reptile Enclosure" (Ballard) **1**:68-9
"Requa" (Olsen) **11**:187-89, 191, 193-97
"The Requiem" (Chekhov) **2**:155
"Requiescat" (Bowen) **3**:40
"Le réquisitionnaire" (Balzac) **5**:16
"De rerum natura" (Boyle) **16**:143
"The Rescue" (Pritchett) **14**:272, 288-89
"Rescue Party" (Clarke) **3**:124-26, 135-36, 148-49
"The Rescuer" (Conrad) **9**:206
"The Rescuer" (Dixon) **16**:216
"Reservations: A Love Story" (Taylor) **10**:417

"The Residence at Whitminster" (James) **16**:230, 232, 234, 237, 246, 255-56
"Residents and Transients" (Mason) **4**:20
Residua (Beckett) **16**:135
"Respectability" (Anderson) **1**:18, 53, 58
"A Respectable Place" (O'Hara) **15**:248, 270
"A Respectable Woman" (Chopin) **8**:72, 96-7, 110, 113
"The Resplendent Quetzal" (Atwood) **2**:3, 5, 7, 10-11, 15-16, 19, 22
"Rest Cure" (Boyle) **5**:55
"Resurrection" (Lish) **18**:280
"The Resurrection" (Suckow) **18**:396, 405, 408, 415
"The Resurrection of Father Brown" (Chesterton) **1**:129, 137-38
"The Reticence of Lady Anne" (Saki) **12**:296, 315
"Retired" (Suckow) **18**:395-97, 409, 414
"The Retired Man" (Schulz) See "Emeryt"
"Le retour" (Maupassant) **1**:285
"Retreat" (Faulkner) **1**:170-71
"The Retreat" (Mason) **4**:21
"Retreat from Earth" (Clarke) **3**:148
"A Retrieved Reformation" (Henry) **5**:158, 170, 193
"The Return" (Anderson) **1**:31, 39, 50
"The Return" (Bowen) **3**:40, 53
"The Return" (Conrad) **9**:151-52
Returning (O'Brien) **10**:334
"The Return of a Private" (Garland) **18**:142, 144, 150, 154, 159, 168, 170, 172, 176, 192
"The Return of Chorb" (Nabokov) **11**:131, 133
"The Return of Imray" ("The Recrudescence of Imray") (Kipling) **5**:262, 273-75, 285
The Return of Sherlock Holmes (Doyle) **12**:51, 60, 62-3
"Return of the Native" (Thurber) **1**:424
"Return Trip Tango" (Cortazar) **7**:69
"Reunion" (Cheever) **1**:100
"Reunion" (Clarke) **3**:133
"The Reunion" (Coover) **15**:35, 43, 45-6
"Reunión" ("The Meeting") (Cortazar) **7**:83, 89-90
"The Reunion" (Nabokov) **11**:133
"Reunión con un círculo rojo" (Cortazar) **7**:85
"Rêve d'enfer" (Flaubert) **11**:71
Le rêve et la vie (Nerval) **18**:328, 330, 337
"Rêveil" (Maupassant) **1**:274
"Revelation" (O'Connor) **1**:341-42, 344
"Revelations" (Mansfield) **9**:313
"A Revenant" (de la Mare) **14**:80, 83, 86-7, 90, 93
"Revenge" (Balzac) See "La vendetta revenge"
"Revenge" (Gilchrist) **14**:150-51, 159
"The Revenge" (Gogol) **4**:85
"Revenge" (O'Hara) **15**:248
"The Revenge of Lard Ass Hogan" (King) **17**:272, 279, 285, 290
"Revenge of Truth" (Dinesen) **7**:177, 180
"Reversal" (Dixon) **16**:208
"The Reversed Man" (Clarke) See "Technical Error"
"The Revolt of 'Mother'" (Freeman) **1**:192, 196-97, 200
"The Revolutionist" (Hemingway) **1**:244
Rewards and Fairies (Kipling) **5**:273, 283, 285, 292

"Rhapsody: A Dream Novel" (Schnitzler)
See *Traumnovelle*
"Rhobert" (Toomer) **1**:445, 450, 458-59
"Rich" (Gilchrist) **14**:151
"The Richard Nixon Freischütz Rag"
(Davenport) **16**:168, 173-74, 177, 191
"The Rich Boy" (Fitzgerald) **6**:46-7, 76, 86-9,
95, 100-03
"Rich in Russia" (Updike) **13**:380
"Rich Man's Crumbs" (Melville)
See "Poor Man's Pudding and Rich Man's
Crumbs"
"The Riddle" (de la Mare) **14**:67, 74, 76-9,
80, 82, 90
The Riddle, and Other Stories (de la Mare)
14:65-7, 90, 92
"Le rideau cramoisi" ("The Crimson Curtain")
(Barbey d'Aurevilly) **17**:7-8, 10-14, 19, 21,
24-6, 40-1, 43-4
"A Ride with Olympy" (Thurber) **1**:431
"Riding Pants" (Malamud) **15**:235
"The Right Eye of the Commander" (Harte)
8:245-46
"Rikki-Tikki-Tavi" (Kipling) **5**:293
"Rinconete y Cortadillo" (Cervantes) **12**:3-4,
6-8, 14, 16, 23, 26-7, 35
"The Ring" (Kawabata) **17**:256-57
"The Ring of Thoth" (Doyle) **12**:85-6
The Ring of Truth (Bates) **10**:124
"El río" ("The River") (Cortazar) **7**:59, 70,
79, 81-3
"Ripe Figs" (Chopin) **8**:93
The Ripening Seed (Colette) **10**:276-77
"Rip Van Winkle" (Irving) **2**:239-51, 253,
256-60, 262-64
"The Rise of Capitalism" (Barthelme) **2**:37,
39, 47
"Rising Wolf—Ghost Dancer" (Garland)
18:178
Rita Hayworth and Shawshank Redemption
(King) **17**:262-65, 271
"Ritter Glück" (Hoffmann) **13**:203, 217-18
"Rituals of Rejection" (Valenzuela)
See "Ceremonias de rechazo"
"The River" (Cortazar)
See "El río"
"The River" (O'Connor) **1**:344-45, 356
"River Rising" (Oates) **6**:227-28, 230, 249-50
A River Runs Through It (Maclean) **13**:260-
63, 265-67, 270-72, 274-76, 278-80
"The R. K. K." (Bulgakov) **18**:89
"The Road" (Babel)
See "Doroga"
"The Road East" (Le Guin) **12**:213, 249-50
"Roads of Destiny" (Henry) **5**:163
"The Roads Round Pisa" (Dinesen) **7**:164,
167-68, 171, 175, 179-80, 182, 187, 198, 208
"The Road to Brody" (Babel) **16**:25, 27, 29,
31, 54-8
"The Road to the Sea" (Clarke) **3**:135-36
Road to Within (Hesse)
See *Weg nach Innen*
The Robber Bridegroom (Welty) **1**:471-72,
483, 489-90, 496
Robert (Gide) **13**:72, 100, 104-05
"Robert Aghion" (Hesse) **9**:231-32, 235
"Robert Kennedy Saved from Drowning"
(Barthelme) **2**:31, 36, 42, 46-7
"The Robin's House" (Barnes) **3**:12
"Robot" (Davenport) **16**:162, 165-66, 170
"The Rock" (Jackson) **9**:254
"Rock, Church" (Hughes) **6**:133

"The Rockfish" (O'Flaherty) **6**:260-61, 267-
69, 280
"Rock God" (Ellison) **14**:118
"The Rocking Chair" (Gilman) **13**:128-30
"The Rocking-Horse Winner" (Lawrence)
4:200-01, 206, 212, 221, 229-30, 233, 238
"The Rockpile" (Baldwin) **10**:4, 7-9, 17
"Roger Malvin's Burial" (Hawthorne) **3**:157,
164, 166-67, 171, 185-86, 189
"Rokovye iaitsa" ("The Fatal Eggs")
(Bulgakov) **18**:69, 72-6, 78, 81-2, 93-9, 105,
108-13
Rolling All the Time (Ballard) **1**:72
"The Romance of a Busy Broker" (Henry)
5:158, 181-82, 194
"The Romance of Madrono Hollow" (Harte)
8:225
The Romance of the Swag (Lawson) **18**:208,
217, 233, 235
"Romance of the Thin Man and the Fat Lady"
(Coover) **15**:32-4, 51
"The Romancers" (Saki) **12**:296
"Roman Fever" (Wharton) **6**:423-24
"Roman Figures" (Bates) **10**:119
Romans et contes philosophiques (*Contes
philosophiques*) (Balzac) **5**:22-3, 31
"The Romantic Adventures of a Milkmaid"
(Hardy) **2**:211, 215-18, 221, 224
"A Romantic Young Lady" (Maugham)
8:380
"Rome" (Gogol) **4**:83
"The Rookers" (Mason) **4**:22
"A Room" (Lessing) **6**:200-01
"The Room in the Dragon Volant" (Le Fanu)
14:214, 216, 225, 237-39, 243
"The Rope" (Baudelaire)
See "La corde"
"Rope" (Porter) **4**:327-28, 339-40, 342
"Rosa" (Ozick) **15**:327
"Rosalie Prudent" (Maupassant) **1**:286
"Rose" (Dubus) **15**:86, 89, 91, 95-6, 101
"The Rose Elf" (Andersen) **6**:12, 30
"A Rose for Emily" (Faulkner) **1**:147-52,
158, 162, 165, 180-81
"The Rose Garden" (James) **16**:229-30, 240,
244, 249, 252-53, 256
A Rose in the Heart (O'Brien) **10**:333, 342,
344
"Roselily" (Walker) **5**:401-02, 405, 408-09
"Rosendo's Tale" (Borges) **4**:18, 20
"The Rose of Dixie" (Henry) **5**:159, 171
"A Rose of Glenbogie" (Harte) **8**:217, 222,
252
"The Rose of Jutland" (Dinesen) **7**:169
"The Rose of New York" (O'Brien) **10**:340
"The Rose of Tuolumne" (Harte) **8**:223, 233
"Le rosier de Madame Husson" (Maupassant)
1:280
"Rothschild's Fiddle" (Chekhov)
See "Rothschild's Violin"
"Rothschild's Violin" ("Rothschild's Fiddle")
(Chekhov) **2**:157-58
"Rouge High" (Hughes) **6**:112, 118
"The Rough Crossing" (Fitzgerald) **6**:61,
100, 103-04
"A Rough Shed" (Lawson) **18**:215
"La rouille" (Maupassant) **1**:256, 272, 274
"Round by Round" (Aiken) **9**:13, 40
"The Round Dozen" (Maugham) **8**:364, 378-
79
*Round the Red Lamp: Being Facts and Fancies
of Medical Life* (Doyle) **12**:88-9

"The Rout of the White Hussars" (Kipling)
5:260
"A Rude Awakening" (Chopin) **8**:88, 103
"The Ruffian" (Dickens) **17**:124
"Las ruinas circulares" ("The Circular Ruins")
(Borges) **4**:5, 10, 18-19, 28-9, 33, 35-6
"The Rule of Names" (Le Guin) **12**:225, 231-
32
"Runaways" (Vonnegut) **8**:433
"Running Dreams" (Beattie) **11**:10, 23
"Rupert Beersley and the Beggar Master of
Sivani-Hotta" (Boyle) **16**:143, 145
"A Rural Community" (Suckow) **18**:395-97,
405, 408
"Rural Life in England" (Irving) **2**:244
"Rusia" ("Rusya") (Bunin) **5**:113
"Rus in Urbe" (Henry) **5**:191
Russia Laughs (Zoshchenko) **15**:387-88
"A Russian Beauty" (Nabokov) **11**:116
A Russian Beauty, and Other Stories (Nabokov)
11:116
"A Russian Doll" (Bioy Casares) **17**:94, 96
A Russian Doll, and Other Stories (Bioy
Casares) **17**:94, 96
"A Russian Hamlet" ("Prince Hamlet of
Shehrigov Province") (Turgenev) **7**:316,
344
"The Russian Who Did Not Believe in
Miracles and Why" (Nin) **10**:306
"Rusya" (Bunin)
See "Rusia"
"Ruthie and Edie" (Paley) **8**:411
"Sabbath in Gehenna" (Singer) **3**:389
"Sabbath in Portugal" (Singer) **3**:376
"The Sack of Lights" (Pritchett) **14**:269, 297
"Sacks" (Carver) **8**:14-15, 18, 20-1, 37-8
"The Sacred Marriage" (Oates) **6**:254
"A Sacrifice Hit" (Henry) **5**:184
"The Sad Horn Blowers" (Anderson) **1**:23,
27, 30
Sadness (Barthelme) **2**:37-40, 46-7, 49
"A Sad Tale's Best for Winter" (Spark)
10:359, 362
"Safe Houses" (Gordimer) **17**:178, 182, 184,
186-87
"Saffercisco" (O'Hara) **15**:253
"Said" (Dixon) **16**:216-17
"The Sailor" (Pritchett) **14**:263, 269, 271,
281, 286, 299, 304-05
"The Sailor and the Steward" (Hughes) **6**:131
"Sailor Ashore" (Hughes) **6**:122, 132
"The Sailor Boy's Tale" (Dinesen) **7**:199
The Sailor, Sense of Humour, and Other Stories
(Pritchett) **14**:256, 267, 271
"The Saint" (Pritchett) **14**:256, 263-64, 267,
269, 271, 292, 298, 305
"The Saint and the Goblin" (Saki) **12**:305
Saint Emmanuel the Good, Martyr (Unamuno)
See *San Manuel Bueno, mártir*
"St. John's Eve" (Gogol)
See "Večer nakanune Ivana Kupala"
"Saint Julien" (Flaubert)
See "La légende de Saint-Julien
l'Hospitalier"
"Saint Katy the Virgin" (Steinbeck) **11**:225-
26, 232-33, 245-46
Saint Katy the Virgin (Steinbeck) **11**:207
St. Mawr (Lawrence) **4**:205, 211-12, 238-29,
241-42
Saints and Strangers (Carter)
See *Black Venus*

"The Salad of Colonel Cray" (Chesterton)
  1:131
"A Sale" (Maupassant)   **1**:262
Salmagundi (Irving)   **2**:241, 250-53
"Salome Müller, the White Slave" (Cable)
  4:49, 59
"Salt" (Babel)   **16**:27-8, 51, 53
"The Salt Garden" (Atwood)   **2**:21
"La salud de los enfermos" (Cortazar)   **7**:61
"Salvatore" (Maugham)   **8**:366
The Same Door (Updike)   **13**:350-52, 354, 356,
  366, 395, 404
"Samson and Delilah" (Lawrence)   **4**:202,
  232-36
"Samuel" (London)   **4**:254-55
"Sanatorium" (Maugham)   **8**:369, 380
Sanatorium pod klepsydra (*Sanatorium under
  the Sign of the Hourglass; Sanatorium under
  the Water Clock*) (Schulz)   **13**:330, 333-38,
  343, 344
Sanatorium under the Sign of the Hourglass
  (Schulz)
  See *Sanatorium pod klepsydra*
Sanatorium under the Water Clock (Schulz)
  13:326, 328
  See *Sanatorium pod klepsydra*
"The Sand Castle" (Lavin)   **4**:178-81
"The Sandman" (Andersen)
  See "Ole Luköie"
"The Sandman" (Barthelme)   **2**:52
"The Sandman" (Hoffmann)
  See "Der Sandmann"
"Der Sandmann" ("The Sandman")
  (Hoffmann)   **13**:179-181, 190, 200, 204-05,
  214-15, 219-20, 223-25, 234-39, 242-47, 250-
  52
"Sandy the Christ" ("Sashka the Christ")
  (Babel)   **16**:25, 29-31, 50, 53, 55
San Manuel Bueno, mártir (*Saint Emmanuel
  the Good, Martyr*) (Unamuno)   **11**:320, 322,
  327, 329-30, 339-44, 351-56, 58
Sans (*Lessness*) (Beckett)   **16**:76-9, 83-6, 88,
  94, 100, 123
"Santa Claus vs. S.P.I.D.E.R." (Ellison)
  14:104, 133
"A Sappho of Green Springs" (Harte)   **8**:247-
  48, 255
"Sarah" (Lavin)   **4**:167, 184
"Saratoga, Hot" (Calisher)   **15**:9
Saratoga, Hot (Calisher)   **15**:9, 23-5, 27
Saratoga, Hot (Calisher)   **15**:
"Saratoga Rain" (Hughes)   **6**:112
"The Sardonic Star of Tom Dooley"
  (Hammett)   **17**:218
Sardonic Tales (Villiers de l'Isle Adam)
  See *Contes cruels*
Sarrasine (Balzac)   **5**:33-4
"The Sartorial Revolution (I)" (Bioy Casares)
  17:74, 86
"Sashka the Christ" (Babel)
  See "Sandy the Christ"
"Satarsa" (Cortazar)   **7**:91
"Satisfaction" (Phillips)   **16**:328
"The Satisfactory" (Pritchett)   **14**:281, 285,
  297
"Saturday" (Gallant)   **5**:141
"Saturday Lunch" (O'Hara)   **15**:288-89
"Saturday Night" (Calisher)   **15**:5
"Saturday Night on the Farm" (Garland)
  18:160, 177
"Saturn, November 11th" (Ellison)   **14**:127
"Saturn Rising" (Clarke)   **3**:132

"Savages" (O'Brien)   **10**:341
"Saved from the Dogs" (Hughes)   **6**:121
"Saviour John" (Lagerkvist)   **12**:179, 196
"The Scandal Detectives" (Fitzgerald)   **6**:49
"A Scandal in Bohemia" (Doyle)   **12**:49, 51-3,
  57-8, 66, 68, 70, 72-3
The Scandal of Father Brown (Chesterton)
  1:128, 139
"A Scandalous Woman" (O'Brien)   **10**:332,
  340-41, 344
A Scandalous Woman, and Other Stories
  (O'Brien)   **10**:330, 332
"The Scapegoat" (Dunbar)   **8**:122, 129, 132,
  137, 141-43
"The Scapegoat" (Pritchett)   **14**:286, 299
"Scarlet Ibis" (Atwood)   **2**:18, 22
Scarmentado (Voltaire)   **12**:340, 342, 357
"An Scáthán" (O'Flaherty)   **6**:289
"Scene for Winter" (Coover)   **15**:36, 58
Scènes de la vie de campagne (*Scenes of
  Country Life*) (Balzac)   **5**:9
Scènes de la vie de province (*Scenes of
  Provincial Life*) (Balzac)   **5**:3, 5, 7-9, 13
Scènes de la vie militaire (Balzac)   **5**:7-9
Scènes de la vie Parisienne (*Scenes of Parisian
  Life*) (Balzac)   **5**:3, 5, 7-9
Scènes de la vie politique (*Scenes of Political
  Life*) (Balzac)   **5**:7-9, 13
Scènes de la vie privée (*Scenes of Private Life*)
  (Balzac)   **5**:3-4, 7, 9, 21-2, 25, 28-31
"Scenes from the Life of a Double Monster"
  (Nabokov)   **11**:110, 113, 128
Scenes of Country Life (Balzac)
  See *Scènes de la vie de campagne*
Scenes of Parisian Life (Balzac)
  See *Scènes de la vie Parisienne*
Scenes of Political Life (Balzac)
  See *Scènes de la vie politique*
Scenes of Private Life (Balzac)
  See *Scènes de la vie privée*
Scenes of Provincial Life (Balzac)
  See *Scènes de la vie de province*
"The Schartz-Metterklume Method" (Saki)
  12:296, 311, 324, 329-30
"Das schicksal des Freiherr von Leisenbohg"
  ("The Fate of the Freiherr von Leisenbohg")
  (Schnitzler)   **15**:346
"The Scholarship" (Mansfield)   **9**:282
"Scholar with a Hole in his Memory"
  (Cortazar)   **7**:59
"The School" (Barthelme)   **2**:53
"School" (O'Hara)   **15**:262
"The School by Night" (Cortazar)
  See "La escuela de noche"
"The School for Witches" (Thomas)   **3**:399,
  408-09
The School for Wives (Gide)
  See *L'école des femmes*
"The Schoolmistress" (Chekhov)   **2**:128
"A School Story" (James)   **16**:233, 245-46,
  256
"Schooner Fairchild's Class" (Benet)   **10**:144,
  152, 154
"Schrödinger's Cat" (Le Guin)   **12**:227-30,
  236, 241
"Schwallinger's Philanthropy" (Dunbar)
  8:122, 132, 137, 147
"The Scorched Face" (Hammett)   **17**:203,
  219, 222-23, 225
"The Scorn of Women" (London)   **4**:286
"The Scorpion" (Bowles)   **3**:59, 61, 68, 70-2,
  79

"The Scoutmaster" (Taylor)   **10**:374-76
"A Scrap and a Sketch" (Chopin)   **8**:98
The Scrapbook of Katherine Mansfield
  (Mansfield)   **9**:281, 309
"The Scream" (Oates)   **6**:248-49
"The Scream on Fifty-Seventh Street"
  (Calisher)   **15**:3
"The Sculptor's Funeral" (Cather)   **2**:90, 94-5,
  98, 100, 103, 105
"Scylla and Charybdis" (Lavin)   **4**:183
"Sea Constables" (Kipling)   **5**:270
"The Sea-Farmer" (London)   **4**:254
The Sea in Being (Hemingway)
  See *The Old Man and the Sea*
"The Seal" (O'Flaherty)   **6**:282
"The Sealed Room" (Doyle)   **12**:65
"The Séance" (Singer)   **3**:369
The Séance, and Other Stories (Singer)   **3**:362,
  369-70, 373
"The Sea of Hesitation" (Barthelme)   **2**:51
"The Sea of Lost Time" (Garcia Marquez)
  See "El mar del tiempo perdido"
"The Sea Raiders" (Wells)   **6**:361, 365, 367,
  389, 393, 406
Searches and Seizures (*Eligible Men*) (Elkin)
  12:92-3, 95, 106-07, 110, 114
"The Searchlight" (Woolf)   **7**:377, 390, 392,
  396
"The Sea's Green Sameness" (Updike)
  13:359-61, 376
"A Seashore Drama" (Balzac)
  See "Un drame au bord de la mer"
"The Seaside Houses" (Cheever)   **1**:100, 105
"The Season of Divorce" (Cheever)   **1**:99
"Season of the Hand" (Cortazar)
  See "Estación de la mano"
"Seaton's Aunt" (de la Mare)   **14**:65-6, 68, 71,
  80-1, 84-5, 87, 89-91
"The Secession" (Bowen)   **3**:40
"The Second" (Schnitzler)
  See "Der sekundant"
"Second Best" (Lawrence)   **4**:197
"Second Dawn" (Clarke)   **3**:131, 135, 144, 150
La seconde (*The Other One*) (Colette)   **10**:254,
  261-62, 267-69, 272
"Second Hand" (Lavin)   **4**:167, 183
"The Second Hut" (Lessing)   **6**:186, 189, 191
The Second Jungle Book (Kipling)   **5**:287, 295
"The Second-Story Angel" (Hammett)   **17**:218
"The Second Swimming" (Boyle)   **16**:143
"Second Time Around" (Cortazar)
  See "Segunda vez"
"Second Trip" (Cortazar)
  See "Segundo viaje"
"The Secret" (Singer)   **3**:385-86
"Le secret de la belle Ardiane" (Villiers de
  l'Isle Adam)   **14**:386
"Le secret de l'ancienne musique" ("Le
  chapeau chinois"; "The Secret of the Old
  Music") (Villiers de l'Isle Adam)   **14**:395
"Le secret de l'échafaud" (Villiers de l'Isle
  Adam)   **14**:389, 397
"The Secret Garden" (Chesterton)   **1**:119,
  134, 137
"The Secret Integration" (Pynchon)   **14**:308,
  315, 320, 322, 332, 335, 340-42, 344-48
"The Secret Life of Walter Mitty" (Thurber)
  1:420, 422, 424, 427, 431-32, 435
"The Secret Miracle" (Borges)
  See "El milagro secreto"
"The Secret Mirror" (Oates)   **6**:237

Title Index

"The Secret of Father Brown" (Chesterton)
1:128, 131

"The Secret of Flambeau" (Chesterton) 1:126

"A Secret of Telegraph Hill" (Harte) 8:233

"The Secret of the Old Music" (Villiers de
l'Isle Adam)
See "Le secret de l'ancienne musique"

"The Secret of the Pyramids" (Mason) 4:23

Secrets and Surprises (Beattie) 11:4-6, 8, 12-
13, 15-16, 22, 27, 29, 32

"Les secrets de la Princesse de Cadignan"
(Balzac) 5:31

"The Secret Sharer" (Conrad) 9:141-45, 147-
51, 156-61, 166, 171-74, 191, 205

"The Secret Sin of Septimus Brope" (Saki)
12:335

"Secret Weapons" (Cortazar)
See "Las armas secretas"

Secret Window, Secret Garden (King) 17:281-
83

"The Sect of the Idiot" (Ligotti) 16:264-65,
267, 276, 282-83, 286-87

"The Security Guard" (Dixon) 16:204

"The Seed of Faith" (Wharton) 6:422

"Seeds" (Anderson) 1:20, 27, 46

"Seen from Afar" (Levi) 12:279

"See the Moon?" (Barthelme) 2:35, 42-3, 53

"Un segno" (Calvino) 3:92

"Segunda vez" ("Second Time Around")
(Cortazar) 7:83-5, 90-1

"Segundo viaje" ("Second Trip") (Cortazar)
7:89

Seis problemas para Don Isidro Parodi (*Six
Problems for Don Isidro Parodi*) (Bioy
Casares) 17:48, 60, 67-8, 71-2, 74

Seis problemas para don Isidro Parodi (*Six
Problems for Don Isidro Parodi*) (Borges)
4:25

Seize the Day (Bellow) 14:3-7, 11, 13-18,
21-3, 26, 32, 34, 46, 49-56, 59

"Der sekundant" ("The Second") (Schnitzler)
15:377

Selected Prose (Bulgakov) 18:86

The Selected Short Stories of John O'Hara
(O'Hara) 15:252

Selected Stories (Debus) 15:94-5, 100-01

Selected Stories (Gordimer) 17:158, 160, 162,
165, 169, 172, 181, 184, 189, 191

Selected Stories (Lavin) 4:163, 186

Selected Stories (Pritchett) 14:260, 272

Selected Works of Djuna Barnes (Barnes) 3:5,
7, 13, 20, 22

The Selected Works of Henry Lawson (Lawson)
18:201

Selected Works of Stephen Vincent Benét
(Benet) 10:143, 156

Selected Writings of Truman Capote (Capote)
2:72, 74

"Selection" (Le Guin) 12:237

"Selections of Lovecraft" (Ligotti) 16:287

"Selections of Poe" (Ligotti) 16:287

"The Selector's Daughter" (Lawson) 18:250

"A Select Party" (Hawthorne) 3:181

"The Selfish Giant" (Wilde) 11:365, 372, 375-
76, 379, 386, 388, 390-93, 396, 401-02, 408

"A Self-Made Man" (Crane) 7:108-09

"Self-Portrait" (Dixon) 16:207, 215

"Selina's Parable" (de la Mare) 14:83

Semeinoe schaste (*Family Happiness*) (Tolstoy)
9:376, 389, 391-92, 403

"Semley's Necklace" (Le Guin) 12:219, 224-
28, 231-32

"Semper Idem" (London) 4:263

"El sencillo don Rafael, cazador y tresillista"
(Unamuno) 11:312-13

"Send Round the Hat" (Lawson) 18:206,
218, 245, 257

"Senility" (Lavin) 4:182

"La Señora Cornelia" ("The Lady Cornelia")
(Cervantes) 12:4-5, 8, 34, 36-7

"Señor Ong and Señor Ha" (Bowles) 3:59,
61, 69, 79

"Sense of Humour" (Pritchett) 14:259, 269,
271, 276, 281, 301-02, 305

"A Sense of Responsibility" (O'Connor)
5:372

"A Sense of Shelter" (Updike) 13:388, 392-94

"The Sensible Thing" (Fitzgerald) 6:46

"The Sentence" (Barthelme) 2:38, 41, 44

"Sentences" (Lish) 18:286

"Sentiment" (Parker) 2:273-74, 280, 285

A Sentimental Education (Oates) 6:246-47

"Sentimentalisme" ("Sentimentality") (Villiers
de l'Isle Adam) 14:378, 381, 384, 396

"Sentimentality" (Villiers de l'Isle Adam)
See "Sentimentalisme"

"The Sentimentality of William Tavener"
(Cather) 2:101

"Sentimental Journey" (Oates) 6:251-52

"A Sentimental Soul" (Chopin) 8:72, 95, 108,
110, 112

Sentimental Tales (Zoshchenko) 15:395, 403

"The Sentinel" (Clarke) 3:124, 127, 135, 145-
46, 149-50

"The Sentry" (O'Connor) 5:369, 372

"Senza colori" (Calvino) 3:92

"Separate Flights" (Dubus) 15:71, 77, 80, 82,
87, 90

Separate Flights (Dubus) 15:69-70, 72, 75-7,
81, 91

"Separating" (Updike) 13:374, 387

"September Dawn" (O'Connor) 5:385, 391-92

"The Seraph and the Zambesi" (Spark)
10:354, 356, 358-359, 361, 366, 370

"The Serapion Brothers" (Hoffmann)
See *Die Serapions Brüder*

Die Serapions Brüder ("The Serapion
Brothers") (Hoffmann) 13:191-92, 195,
202, 217, 228

"Serenade" (Benet) 10:150

"The Sergeant" (Barthelme) 2:53

"Sergeant Carmichael" (Bates) 10:114

"Sergeant Prishibeev" (Chekhov) 2:155

"A Serious Question" (Pritchett) 14:297

"A Serious Talk" (Carver) 8:14, 18-19, 53

Sermons and Soda Water (O'Hara) 15:251,
271

"The Serpent of Fire" (Bunin) 5:87

"The Servant" (Levi) 12:278-79

"A Service of Love" (Henry) 5:171, 185

A Set of Six (Conrad) 9:147, 151, 157, 179

A Set of Variations (O'Connor) 5:373-74, 378

"A Set of Variations on a Borrowed Theme"
(O'Connor) 5:373

"Settling on the Land" (Lawson) 18:201, 215

Sevastopol (Tolstoy)
See *Tales of Sevastopol*

"Sevastopol in August, 1855" (Tolstoy) 9:375

"Sevastopol in December 1854" (Tolstoy)
9:375

"Sevastopol in May, 1855" (Tolstoy) 9:374-
75, 389

"The Seven Bridges" (Mishima) 4:313, 315,
317, 322

Seven by Five: Stories 1926-61 (*The Best of H.
E. Bates*) (Bates) 10:125

Seven Gothic Tales (Dinesen) 7:161, 166, 170,
172, 175, 180, 191, 196-98, 200-03, 208-09

Seven Tales and Alexander (Bates) 10:111

"The Seventh Pullet" (Saki) 12:301

"Seventh Street" (Toomer) 1:443, 450, 458

76 Short Stories (Saki) 12:314

"The Sexes" (Parker) 2:273, 281, 283

"Sex Ex Machina" (Thurber) 1:431

"Seymour: An Introduction" (Salinger)
2:296, 307-09

"Shabbes nakhamu" ("Shabos nahamu")
(Babel) 16:34

"Shabby-Genteel People" (Dickens) 17:111,
116, 133

"Shabos nahamu" (Babel)
See "Shabbes nakhamu"

The Shackle (Colette)
See *L'entrave*

"The Shades of Spring" (Lawrence) 4:197-98,
219

"The Shadow" (Andersen) 6:7, 24, 30, 35, 41

"Shadow, a Parable" (Poe) 1:379

"The Shadow at the Bottom of the World"
(Ligotti) 16:280, 289

"The Shadow Line" (Conrad) 9:151

"The Shadow of a Crib" (Singer) 3:361

"The Shadow of the Glen" (Le Fanu) 14:219-
20

"The Shadow of the Shark" (Chesterton)
1:124

"The Shadow out of Time" (Lovecraft)
3:258-61, 263, 266, 268, 271-72, 274-75, 279,
290

"The Shadow over Innsmouth" (Lovecraft)
3:259. 263, 271-77, 291

"The Shadowy Crown" (Benet) 10:147

"The Shadowy Land" (Grau) 15:155

"The Shadowy Third" (Bowen) 3:54

"The Shaker Bridal" (Hawthorne) 3:185-86

"Shame" (Crane) 7:104

"A Shameful Affair" (Chopin) 8:71, 86

"The Shape of the Sword" (Borges)
See "La forma de la espada"

"The Shape of Things" (Capote) 2:65

"The Sharks" (O'Hara) 15:280

"Shatterday" (Ellison) 14:124

Shatterday (Ellison) 14:125-26

"Shattered Like a Glass Goblin" (Ellison)
14:115

"The Shawl" (Ozick) 15:327

The Shawl (Ozick) 15:327-28

"The Shearing of the Cook's Dog" (Lawson)
18:201, 244

"The She Devil" (Lawson) 18:255

"The Sheep" (Saki) 12:316

"The Shepherdess and the Chimney Sweep"
(Andersen) 6:6, 18, 36

"The Shepherd's Pipe" (Chekhov) 2:130, 156

"The Sheridans" (Mansfield) 9:286-87

"The Sheriff of Kona" (London) 4:269

"The Sheriff's Children" (Chesnutt) 7:13, 16,
18-19, 21-6, 29, 32-5, 37

"She Was Good for Nothing" (Andersen)
See "Good-for-Nothing"

"She Was No Good" (Andersen)
See "Good-for-Nothing"

"The She-Wolf" (Saki) 12:307, 323

"Shifting" (Beattie) 11:4, 7-8, 15, 17

"The Shilling" (O'Flaherty) 6:271

"Shiloh" (Mason) 4:24

Shiloh, and Other Stories (Mason) **4**:29

"Shin Bones" (London) **4**:256, 270

"Shingles for the Lord" (Faulkner) **1**:178

"The Shining Houses" (Munro) **3**:321, 336, 343

"The Shining Ones" (Clarke) **3**:132

"A Ship-Load of Crabs" (Calvino) **3**:116

"The Ship That Found Herself" (Kipling) **5**:279

"The Shipwreck" (Dickens) **17**:123

"The Shipwrecked Buttons" (Jewett) **6**:157

"The Shirt" (Dixon) **16**:211

"The Shirt Collar" (Andersen) **6**:30, 32, 35

"Shisha no Sho" ("The Book of the Dead") (Kawabata) **17**:247

"Shit" (Lish) **18**:275, 282

"The Shocks of Doom" (Henry) **5**:182, 184

"Shock Tactics" (Saki) **12**:303-04, 323, 325

"Shoes: An International Episode" (Bowen) **3**:30, 49

"Shōkonsai Ikkei" ("A View of the Yasukuni Festival") (Kawabata) **17**:248-49

"The Shooting" (Dubus) **15**:73, 88

"The Shooting of the Cabinet Ministers" (Hemingway) **1**:208, 238

"The Shooting Party" (Woolf) **7**:375, 390, 392

"Shoppe Keeper" (Ellison) **14**:126

"Shops and Their Tenants" (Dickens) **17**:117

"The Shore and the Sea" (Thurber) **1**:430

"The Shore House" (Jewett) **6**:150, 157, 167, 170

"Short Feature" (Cortazar)
See "Cortísimo metraje"

"Short Friday" (Singer) **3**:355, 360, 363-64, 383

Short Friday, and Other Stories (Singer) **3**:357, 370, 373, 376

"The Short Happy Life of Francis Macomber" (Hemingway) **1**:217, 230, 232, 234

Short Novels of Colette (Colette) **10**:266-67, 269

Short Prose Poems (Baudelaire)
See *Petits poèmes en prose: Le spleen de Paris*

"The Short-Short Story of Mankind: An Improbable Allegory of Human History Compressed for a Very Small Time Capsule" (Steinbeck) **11**:257-58

Short Stories in Prose and Verse (Lawson) **18**:220, 240, 256, 258

The Short Stories of Conrad Aiken (Aiken) 6, 24, 28

The Short Stories of Saki (Saki) **12**:296, 307, 309

The Short Stories of Thomas Hardy (Hardy) **2**:212

"A Short Trip Home" (Fitzgerald) **6**:47-8, 60, 62

"Shots" (Ozick) **15**:307, 318-19

"Should Wizard Hit Mommy?" (Updike) **13**:400

"A Shower of Gold" (Barthelme) **2**:27-8, 38, 42, 52, 55

"Shower of Gold" (Welty) **1**:483, 485, 493

"The Shrine" (Lavin) **4**:183

The Shrine, and Other Stories (Lavin) **4**:181

"The Shrink Flips" (Pynchon) **14**:308

Shuffle (Michaels) **16**:314, 316-21

"The Shunned House" (Lovecraft) **3**:262, 276, 282

"Shut a Final Door" (Capote) **2**:61-2, 64, 66, 69, 72-6, 83

"Shy Neighbourhoods" (Dickens) **17**:123

The Sibyl (Lagerkvist) **12**:185-92, 194, 198

"A Sick Collier" (Lawrence) **4**:202

"The Sickness of Lone Chief" (London) **4**:287

Siddhartha (Hesse) **9**:211-15, 217, 221-26, 231, 234, 240, 246

Sido (Colette) **10**:278-79, 285

"Sierra Leone" (McGahern) **17**:307, 309, 316-17, 321, 323

"La sierva ajena" (Bioy Casares) **17**:83

"Siestas" (Cortazar) **7**:57

"Sieur George" (Cable) **4**:50, 52, 65-7

"The Sign" (Villiers de l'Isle Adam)
See "L'intersigne"

"Signatures" (Dixon) **16**:207

"Significant Moments in the Life of My Mother" (Atwood) **2**:17, 21-3

"A Sign in Space" (Calvino)
See "Sign of Space"

"Sign of Space" ("A Sign in Space") (Calvino) **3**:104, 109

"The Sign of the Broken Sword" ("Broken Sword") (Chesterton) **1**:127, 136-37, 142

"The Sign of the Potent Pills" (Hammett) **17**:226

"Signor Formica" (Hoffmann) **13**:183

"Signs and Symbols" (Nabokov) **11**:109, 117-18, 120-22, 129, 135-36, 140, 144, 147-48, 150-51, 153, 157-60

"Silas Jackson" (Dunbar) **8**:122, 128, 133, 135, 147

"Silence, a Fable" (Poe) **1**:379

"The Silence of the Valley" (O'Faolain) **13**:288, 293, 297-98, 302, 305, 312, 314, 318

"Silence Please" (Clarke) **3**:133

"The Silences of Mr. Palomar" (Calvino) **3**:113

"The Silent Eaters" (Garland) **18**:147, 177-79, 186, 188-89

"Silent in Gehenna" (Ellison) **14**:102-03

"The Silent Men" (Camus)
See "Les muets"

The Silent Mr. Palomar (Calvino)
See *Palomar*

"Silent Samuel" (Dunbar) **8**:122, 128

"Silent Snow, Secret Snow" (Aiken) **9**:5-7, 9, 12, 20, 22, 30-40, 42-4

"Silver" (Levi) **12**:268

"The Silver Crown" (Malamud) **15**:190, 195, 197-99, 220

"A Silver Dish" (Bellow) **14**:43

"Silver Jemmy" (Benet) **10**:151-52

"The Silver Key" (Lovecraft) **3**:258, 262, 276, 286

"Silver Throat" (Bulgakov)
See "Steel Throat"

"Silvia" (Cortazar) **7**:57

"Sim Burns's Wife" (Garland) **18**:154-55, 160, 176, 184

"Simmering" (Atwood) **2**:19-20

"A Simple Enquiry" (Hemingway) **1**:216

"A Simple Heart" (Flaubert)
See "Un coeur simple"

"Simple Simon" (Andersen) **6**:30

Simple Speaks His Mind (Hughes) **6**:110-11, 113, 137

Simple Stakes a Claim (Hughes) **6**:143

Simple Takes a Wife (Hughes) **6**:113

"Simulacra" (Cortazar)
See "Simulacros"

"Simulacros" ("Simulacra") (Cortazar) **7**:92

"The Sin Eater" (Atwood) **2**:15, 18, 22

"The Singers" (Turgenev) **7**:316

"A Singer's Romance" (Cather) **2**:101

"The Singing Lesson" (Mansfield) **9**:280

"A Single Lady" (Lavin) **4**:166

A Single Lady, and Other Stories (Lavin) **4**:164

"The Sing-Song of Old Man Kangaroo" (Kipling) **5**:287

"The Sinking House" (Boyle) **16**:153, 155

"The Sinner" (O'Flaherty) **6**:277, 280

"Sinners" (O'Faolain) **13**:284, 287-88, 302

"Sins of the Third Age" (Gordimer) **17**:169, 171, 193

"Sir Dominick's Bargain" (Le Fanu) **14**:223, 228

"The Sire de Malétroit's Door" (Stevenson) **11**:269-72, 279, 281, 296-97

"Sir Rabbit" (Welty) **1**:474, 480, 486, 495

"Sis' Becky's Pickaninny" (Chesnutt) **7**:7, 10, 40, 42

Il sistema periodico (*The Periodic Table*) (Levi) **12**:255-57, 259-61, 263-69, 274-76, 279-81

"Sister Imelda" (O'Brien) **10**:334, 341, 345

"Sister Liddy" (Freeman) **1**:199-200

"Sister Peacham's Turn" (Jewett) **6**:156

"The Sisters" (Joyce) **3**:201, 205-06, 208, 211-12, 216-17, 225, 230, 232, 234-35, 237, 244-47, 249

"The Sisters" (O'Connor) **5**:392

"Siwash" (London) **4**:286

Six Feet of the Country (Gordimer) **17**:152-3, 187

"Sixpence" (Mansfield) **9**:282, 310-11

Six Problems for Don Isidro Parodi (Bioy Casares)
See *Seis problemas para Don Isidro Parodi*

Six Problems for Don Isidro Parodi (Borges)
See *Seis problemas para don Isidro Parodi*

Six Stories Written in the First Person Singular (Maugham) **8**:356, 364, 378

"The Sixth Day" (Levi) **12**:279

The Sixth Day, and Other Stories (Levi) **12**:278-81

Six Trees (Freeman) **1**:194

"Sixty Acres" (Carver) **8**:3, 10, 34

Sixty Stories (Barthelme) **2**:46, 51, 56

"Six Years After" (Mansfield) **9**:282

"The Skeleton" (Pritchett) **14**:268, 285, 297, 299, 305

Skeleton Crew (King) **17**:273-76, 290, 294

"Skeletons" (Beattie) **11**:29

"The Skeletons" (O'Hara) **15**:279, 283

The Sketch Book (Irving)
See *The Sketch Book of Geoffrey Crayon, Gent.*

The Sketch Book of Geoffrey Crayon, Gent. (*The Sketch Book*) (Irving) **2**:238-46, 250-55, 257-59, 262, 265, 267

Sketches by Boz of Every-Day Life and Every-Day People (Dickens) **17**:109, 111, 113, 115-17, 120-22, 124-26, 132-34, 139

"Sketches from Memory" (Hawthorne) **3**:157

"A Sketching Trip" (Welty) **1**:480

"Skirmish at Sartoris" (Faulkner) **1**:170-71

"Skull Hunters" (Bulgakov) **18**:89

"Sky Line" (Taylor) **10**:375-76, 385-87

"The Slashers" (Kipling) **5**:277-78

"Slater's Pins Have No Points" (Woolf)
See "Moments of Being: 'Slater's Pins Have No Points'"

"The Slaughterer" (Singer) **3**:358, 384

Title Index

"Slave" (Phillips) **16**:327-28

"Slave on the Block" (Hughes) **6**:119, 121-22, 128, 134

"Sleeping Beauty" (Clarke) **3**:134

"The Sleeping Beauty in the Fridge" (Levi) **12**:278

"Sleeping like Dogs" (Calvino) **3**:112

"Sleepy" (Chekhov) **2**:130, 146-49

"Slice Him Down" (Hughes) **6**:118, 132

"A Slice of Life" (Wodehouse) **2**:347

"A Slight Mistake" ("A Mistake") (Zoshchenko) **15**:388-89, 407-08

"A Slippery Floor" (Nin) **10**:306

"A Slip under the Microscope" (Wells) **6**:360, 381, 384, 393

"A Slip-Up" (McGahern) **17**:309, 317

"Slooter's Vengeance" (Pritchett) **14**:298

"A Sloppy Story" (Dixon) **16**:217

Slow Learner: Early Stories (Pynchon) **14**:333-34, 340-42, 346-49

"Small Avalanches" (Oates) **6**:231

"Small Bear" (Dixon) **16**:206, 211

"A Small Bequest" (Lavin) **4**:167

"A Small, Good Thing" (Carver) **8**:19-26, 30, 39, 56-9

"The Small Lady" (O'Faolain) **13**:314

"A Small Paradise" (Cortazar)
See "Un pequeño paraíso"

"The Small Rain" (Pynchon) **14**:327, 334, 340, 342-43, 347-49

"A Small Star in the East" (Dickens) **17**:123-24

"The Small Town Lovers" (O'Brien) **10**:333

"The Smell of Death and Flowers" (Gordimer) **17**:153, 160

Smert Ivana Ilyicha (*The Death of Ivan Ilych*) (Tolstoy) **9**:368-69, 373-74, 377, 382-83, 394, 396-97

"The Smile" (Ballard) **1**:79

"Smile" (Lawrence) **4**:219

"A Smile of Fortune" (Conrad) **9**:142-43

"The Smile of Winter" (Carter) **13**:2, 4

"The Smilers" (Fitzgerald) **6**:56-7

"Smith and Jones" (Aiken) **9**:4, 12-13

Smog (Calvino)
See *La nuvola di smog*

"Smoke" (Barnes) **3**:18

"Smoke" (Faulkner) **1**:178-80

Smoke, and Other Early Stories (Barnes) **3**:17, 19

Smoke Bellew Tales (London) **4**:289

The Smoking Mountain: Stories of Postwar Germany (Boyle) **5**:56

"The Smuggler" (Singer) **3**:389

"The Snag" (Pritchett) **14**:285

"The Snail and the Rose-Tree" (Andersen) **6**:7

"The Snake" (Steinbeck) **11**:207-08, 225, 233, 237-38

"Snake and Hawk" (Benet) **10**:145-46

"Sneakers" (King) **17**:295

"The Sniff" (Pritchett) **14**:297

"The Sniper" (O'Flaherty) **6**:261, 280

"A Snobbish Story" (Fitzgerald) **6**:50

"Snow" (Beattie) **11**:25-6, 29

"Snow" (Phillips) **16**:330

"Snow Bound at the Eagle's" (Harte) **8**:254

"The Snow Child" (Carter) **13**:9-10, 28

"The Snow Image: A Childish Miracle" (Hawthorne) **3**:159, 177, 183

The Snow Image, and Other Twice-Told Tales (Hawthorne) **3**:184

"Snowing in Greenwich Village" (Updike) **13**:352

"The Snow Queen, a Folk Tale in Seven Parts" (Andersen) **6**:4, 6-8, 13, 18-20, 24-8, 30, 36-7, 40

"The Snows of Kilimanjaro" (Hemingway) **1**:214-15, 217-18, 229, 234

"Snowstorm" (Bulgakov) **18**:86, 88

The Snowstorm (Tolstoy) **9**:382, 389

Sobach'e serdtse (*The Heart of a Dog*) (Bulgakov) **18**:69-71, 73, 75, 82, 86, 93, 96-7, 103-08, 113-22

"The Sobbin' Women" (Benet) **10**:144, 146, 148

"The Sociable at Dudley's" (Garland) **18**:154-55, 160

"Social Cares" (Zoshchenko) **15**:388

"The Social Triangle" (Henry) **5**:198

"A Society" (Woolf) **7**:368, 371, 374, 377, 392-93, 396, 400-02, 404

"Les soeurs Rondoli" (Maupassant) **1**:256, 259, 270, 274, 283, 288

"The Soft Moon" (Calvino) **3**:94, 108-09

"The Soft Voice of the Serpent" (Gordimer) **17**:166-67

The Soft Voice of the Serpent (Gordimer) **17**:151-52, 157, 166, 186

"Der Sohn" ("The Son") (Schnitzler) **15**:351, 371

"Un soir" (Maupassant) **1**:274, 280

"The Sojourner" (McCullers) **9**:323, 332, 341, 345-46, 358

"A Soldier's Embrace" (Gordimer) **17**:163-64

A Soldier's Embrace (Gordimer) **17**:162, 164-65, 181, 191

"Soldier's Home" (Hemingway) **1**:208, 244

"Soldiers of the Republic" (Parker) **2**:276, 281-82

"Soldiers Three" (Kipling) **5**:269

Soldiers Three (Kipling) **5**:259

"Solid Objects" (Woolf) **7**:373, 377, 387, 397

"Solitaire" (Updike) **13**:385

"The Solitary" ("Gregory's Island") (Cable) **4**:50, 72-4

"A Solitary" (Freeman) **1**:197

"La solitude" (Baudelaire) **18**:39

"Solitude" (Maupassant) **1**:262

"Solnechnyy udar" ("Sunstroke") (Bunin) **5**:91, 93, 104-06, 114, 119

"Solo Dance" (Phillips) **16**:330

"Solus Rex" (Nabokov) **11**:117

"So Many Worlds" (Grau) **15**:155

"Sombre récit, conteur plus sombre" ("Sombre Tale, Sombre Teller") (Villiers de l'Isle Adam) **14**:381

"Sombre Tale, Sombre Teller" (Villiers de l'Isle Adam)
See "Sombre récit, conteur plus sombre"

"Some Account of the Latter Days of the Hon. Richard Marston of Dunoran" (Le Fanu) **14**:247

"Some Approaches to the Problem of the Shortage of Time" (Le Guin) **12**:235

"Some Are Born to Sweet Delight" (Gordimer) **17**:178-79, 186, 188, 190-91

"Some Blue Hills at Sundown" (Gilchrist) **14**:161

"Some Day" (Lawson) **18**:239, 248, 250-51, 261

"Some Effects of the Mimer" (Levi) **12**:278

"Some Facts for Understanding the Perkians" (Cortazar)
See "Datos para entender a los perqueos"

"Some Get Wasted" (Marshall) **3**:303

"Some Monday for Sure" (Gordimer) **17**:155, 160, 183

"Someone Has Disturbed the Roses" (Garcia Marquez)
See "Alguien desordena estas rosas"

"Someone to Trust" (O'Hara) **15**:255, 264

"Someone Walking Around" (Cortazar)
See "Alguien que anda por ahí"

Some Others and Myself (Suckow) **18**:393-95, 413, 422-26

Some People, Places, and Things That Will Not Appear in My Next Novel (Cheever) **1**:92, 100

"Some Strange Disturbances in an Old House on Augier Street" ("An Account of Some Strange Disturbances in an Old House on Aungier Street"; "Strange Disturbances on Aungier Street") (Le Fanu) **14**:223-24, 238, 251

Something Childish, and Other Stories (Mansfield)
See *The Little Girl, and Other Stories*

"Something for the Time Being" (Gordimer) **17**:173

Something in Common, and Other Stories (Hughes) **6**:122-23, 127, 133

Something I've Been Meaning to Tell You (Munro) **3**:328, 331, 335, 339, 346

"Something Out There" (Gordimer) **17**:169, 172, 174-76, 185-86, 192

Something Out There (Gordimer) **17**:170, 173, 191

"Something Squishy" (Wodehouse) **2**:355-56

"Something That Happened" (Phillips) **16**:335

Something to Remember Me By (Bellow) **14**:60-1

"Something to Write About" (Andersen) **6**:36

"Sometimes It's OK to Eat Inkwells" (Zoshchenko) **15**:407

"Sometimes They Come Back" (King) **17**:262

"Some Village Cronies" (Garland) **18**:161

"Somewhere Else" (Paley) **8**:420

"Some Words with a Mummy" (Poe) **1**:402

"So Much Water So Close to Home" (Carver) **8**:5, 14-15, 19, 21, 29, 42, 53, 57-60

"The Son" (Bunin) **5**:81, 103-04, 106, 108-10

"The Son" (Schnitzler)
See "Der Sohn"

"Son" ("The Dream") (Turgenev) **7**:321, 325-28, 338, 361

"Son" (Updike) **13**:387

"The Son From America" (Singer) **3**:374

"The Song" (Babel) **16**:27, 31, 52, 54-8

"The Song in the Garden" (Nin) **10**:306

"The Song of Songs" (Gilchrist) **14**:162-63

"The Song of the Flying Fish" (Chesterton) **1**:129, 138

"Song of the Shirt, 1941" (Parker) **2**:277, 280-81, 285-86

"The Song of the Triumphant Love" (Turgenev)
See "Pesn' torzhestvuyushchey lyubvi"

"The Song of the Wren" (Bates) **10**:139

"Songs My Father Sang Me" (Bowen) **3**:41

"Songs My Mother Taught Me" (Calisher) **15**:8

Songs of a Dead Dreamer (Ligotti) **16**:261, 269-70, 279, 282-85, 287, 293, 296

"The Songs of Distant Earth" (Clarke)   3:135-36

"Song without Words" (O'Connor)   5:365, 371, 383, 398

"Sonny's Blues" (Baldwin)   10:2-3, 5-7, 9, 12, 14-17, 21-5

"The Son of God and His Sorrow" (Oates)   6:237

"A Son of the Celestial" (Cather)   2:100, 102

"A Son of the Gods" (Bierce)   9:55-6, 60, 63-4

A Son of the Sun (London)   4:266

"The Son of the Wolf" (London)   4:267

The Son of the Wolf: Tales of the Far North (London)   4:250-52, 258, 264, 278-79, 281-82, 284-87, 290

"The Son's Veto" (Hardy)   2:215-16, 223

"Sophistication" (Anderson)   1:30, 42, 44-5

"The Sorcerer's Apprentice" (O'Connor)   5:371-72

"Sorcières espagnoles" (Merimee)   7:283

"Sorghum" (Mason)   4:25

"Soročinskaja jamarka" ("The Fair at Sorotchintsy") (Gogol)   4:85, 118, 121

Sorok Sorokov (Bulgakov)   18:106-07

"Sorrow" (Chekhov)   2:128

"Sorrow-Acre" (Dinesen)   7:164, 167, 170-71, 174, 177, 185-86, 188-90, 196, 205-08

"Sorrowful Mysteries" (Dubus)   15:83

"The Sorrows of Gin" (Cheever)   1:100

"Sorry Fugh" (Boyle)   16:146, 148-49, 155

"Sorry, Right Number" (King)   17:295

"Sosny" (Bunin)   5:98-9

Sotto il sole giaguro (*Under the Jaguar Sun*) (Calvino)   3:119

Soul Clap Hands and Sing (Marshall)   3:299-304, 307-08, 316-17

"A Soulless Corporation" (Chesnutt)   7:14

"The Soul of Laploshka" (Saki)   12:316

"Souls Belated" (Wharton)   6:423-25

"The Souls in Purgatory" (Merimee)
   See "Les âmes du purgatoire"

"The Sound of the Singing" (Laurence)   7:254, 259-60, 268

"The Sound of Waiting" (Calisher)   15:7, 15, 19

"Sound Sweep" (Ballard)   1:68

"Sound Track" (Calisher)   15:9

"Soup on a Sausage Peg" (Andersen)   6:13-4

"The Source" (Porter)   4:339, 352, 363

"Source of the World" (Bates)   10:121

"The South" (Borges)   4:31

"The Southern Thruway" (Cortazar)
   See "La autopista del sur"

"South of the Slot" (London)   4:254

South Sea Tales (London)   4:266, 283

"Souvenir" (Phillips)   16:326-30

"A Souvenir of Japan" (Carter)   13:4

"Souvenirs occulte" ("Occult Memories") (Villiers de l'Isle Adam)   14:381-82, 389, 393

"The Spanish Bed" (Pritchett)   14:263

"Spanish Blood" (Hughes)   6:118, 132

"The Spanish Lady" (Munro)   3:339

"A Spanish Priest" (Maugham)   8:380

The Spanish Virgin, and Other Stories (Pritchett)   14:268-69, 271

Spanking the Maid (Coover)   15:47, 52-3

"Sparkling Life" (Bulgakov)   18:91

"A Spark Neglected Burns the House" (Tolstoy)   9:388

The Spark (The 'Sixties) (Wharton)   6:439-40

"Speck's Idea" (Gallant)   5:147

"The Spectacles" (Poe)   1:407-08

"The Spectacles in the Drawer" (Ligotti)   16:278-79, 284, 294

"The Spectral Estate" (Ligotti)   16:297

"Spectral Horror" (Ligotti)   16:287

"The Spectre Bridegroom" (Irving)   2:240-41, 246, 251, 255-56

"The Speculation of the Building Constructors" (Calvino)
   See "La speculazione edilizia"

"La speculazione edilizia" ("A Plunge into Real Estate"; "The Speculation of the Building Constructors") (Calvino)   3:91, 111-12, 117-18

"The Speech" (Pritchett)   14:296-98

"Spell Bereavement" (Lish)   18:278, 283

"Spelling" (Munro)   3:339

"The Sphinx without a Secret: An Etching" (Wilde)   11:386, 399, 407

"The Sphynx Apple" (Henry)   5:162

"Spider, Spider" (Aiken)   9:5, 12, 14, 32-3, 42

"Spielerglück" ("Gambler's Luck") (Hoffmann)   13:188

Spiel im Morgengrauen (*Daybreak*) (Schnitzler)   15:345, 367

"Spillway" ("Beyond the End") (Barnes)   3:8-10, 24

Spillway (Barnes)   3:4-5, 12-14, 16, 22

"The Spinoza of Market Street" (Singer)   3:361, 368, 375, 384

The Spinoza of Market Street, and Other Stories (Singer)   3:370

"The Spinster and the Cat" (Suckow)   18:393

"A Spinster's Tale" (Taylor)   10:374-75, 386, 390, 397-98, 406, 409, 412-15, 417

"The Spiral" (Calvino)
   See "La spirale"

"La spirale" ("The Spiral") (Calvino)   3:92, 103-04, 108-09

"Spiritual Séance" (Bulgakov)   18:92

"Spiritus" (Beattie)   11:25, 29

Le spleen de Paris (Baudelaire)
   See *Petits poèmes en prose: Le spleen de Paris*

"The Split Second" (du Maurier)   18:126, 138

"Spoils" (Gordimer)   17:177, 183-84, 187

"The Spooks of Long Gully" (Lawson)   18:232, 234-36

"Sportsmanship" (O'Hara)   15:248, 264-65

"Sport: The Kill" (O'Flaherty)   6:261

"Spotted Horses" (Faulkner)   1:167, 177

"The Spree" (Pritchett)   14:260, 273, 285

"Spring" (Schulz)
   See "Wiosna"

"A Spring Evening" (Bunin)   5:90, 92, 102

Spring Freshets (Turgenev)
   See *Veshnie vody*

"The Spring Hat" (Bates)   10:123

"Spring in Fialta" (Nabokov)   11:112, 114, 128-29

"A Spring Morning" (Pritchett)   14:270, 298

"Spring Rain" (Malamud)   15:235

"A Spring Romance" (Garland)   18:163

"The Spring Running" (Kipling)   5:287

"Spring Song of the Frogs" (Atwood)   2:22

"Spring Sowing" (O'Flaherty)   6:260-62, 264, 269, 271, 273, 281, 283

Spring Sowing (O'Flaherty)   6:261-65, 278, 281, 283

"A Spring Sunday" (Jewett)   6:156-57

Spring-Torrents (Turgenev)
   See *Veshnie vody*

"A Sprinkle of Comedy" (Barnes)   3:18

"Spunk" (Hurston)   4:135-37, 150, 152

Spunk: The Selected Stories of Zora Neale Hurston (Hurston)   4:155

"SQ" (Le Guin)   12:230-31, 241

"Squadron Commander Trunov" (Babel)   16:24, 26, 28-30, 52, 57-8

The Square Egg, and Other Sketches, with Three Plays (Saki)   12:322

"Squire Toby's Will" (Le Fanu)   14:223-24

"Sredni Vashtar" (Saki)   12:287, 293-94, 297, 316-17, 320, 331, 333

"La srta. Cora" (Cortazar)   7:62

"The S.S. *Cow Wheat*" (Babel)   16:22

"The Stage Coach" (Irving)   2:245

"The Stage Tavern" (Jewett)   6:159

"Stalking the Nightmare" (Ellison)   14:126-27

Stalky and Co. (Kipling)   5:277-78, 282

"The Stalled Ox" (Saki)   12:296

"The Stalls of Barchester Cathedral" (James)   16:228-30, 232, 237, 245, 253, 256-57

"The Stampeding of Lady Bastable" (Saki)   12:313, 324

"The Standard of Living" (Parker)   2:278, 281, 283

"Stanley" (Grau)   15:148, 152, 160-61

"The Stanton Coachman" (Dunbar)   8:122

"The Star" (Clarke)   3:125-27, 130, 136-38, 141-42

"The Star" (Wells)   6:360-61, 365, 367, 382, 385-89, 403, 406

"The Star-Child" (Wilde)   11:364, 374, 376, 384, 386, 394-95, 408

"The Stare" (Updike)   13:375

"Starley" (Beattie)   11:15, 17

"The Starlight Express" (Gilchrist)   14:161-62

"Starosvetskie Pomeščiki" ("Old-World Landowners"; "Proprietors of the Olden Time") (Gogol)   4:86, 119-20

"Starry Rash" (Bulgakov)   18:86, 89

"The Stars Below" (Le Guin)   12:223

"The Star That Bids the Shepherd Fold" (O'Connor)   5:383

"A Start in Life" (Suckow)   18:389-91, 396, 398, 410, 418-19, 421

"The Starveling" (Colette)   10:281

"Starye portrety" ("Old Portraits") (Turgenev)   7:327, 362-63

"State Champions" (Mason)   4:26

"The Statement of Randolph Carter" (Lovecraft)   3:258-60, 262, 282

"State of Mind" (Aiken)   9:5, 13-14, 19

"The Station" (Bates)   10:132

"The Station-Master's Cradle" (Bulgakov)   18:89-90

"The Steadfast Tin Soldier" ("The Constant Tin Soldier"; "The Hardy Tin Soldier") (Andersen)   6:7, 16, 18-19, 36, 40-1

"The Steam Excursion" (Dickens)   17:116-17

"Steelman's Pupil" (Lawson)   18:249

"Steel Throat" ("Silver Throat") (Bulgakov)   18:86, 88

"Das Steinerne Herz" (Hoffmann)   13:187

"Stella" (Nin)   10:317, 320

"Stepnoy Korol 'Lir" ("A King Lear of the Steppes"; "A Lear of the Steppes"; "A Village Lear") (Turgenev)   7:318-23, 336, 338, 358, 360-61

"The Steppe" (Chekhov)   2:129-30, 143, 146, 151, 156

"Sterben" ("Dying") (Schnitzler)   15:371

"Sterben" (Schnitzler)   15:371

Title Index

"Sterling Silver" (O'Hara) **15**:280

"The Steward" (Turgenev) **7**:313, 342

"Sticks and Stones" (Michaels) **16**:302-03, 311-12, 321

"Stigmata" (Oates) **6**:224, 226

"Still" (Beckett) **16**:123, 126-27

"Still Life" (Malamud) **15**:171, 174-75, 182-84, 192-94, 222

"Still Life" (Updike) **13**:392

"Still Life with Watermelon" (Mason) **4**:27

"A Still Moment" (Welty) **1**:467-69, 482

"Stillness" (Gardner) **7**:223, 226, 235, 237, 240

"Still of Some Use" (Updike) **13**:403, 409

"Stoat" (McGahern) **17**:299, 309

"The Stolen Bacillus" (Wells) **6**:360, 374-75, 381-83, 395-99, 403

The Stolen Bacillus and Other Incidents (Wells) **6**:364-66, 380, 388, 403

"The Stolen Body" (Wells) **6**:381, 404

"Stolen Pleasures" (Jewett) **6**:156-58

"The Stone" (O'Flaherty) **6**:281

"Stones in My Passway, Hellhound on My Trail" (Boyle) **16**:144

"Stoney Batter" (O'Flaherty) **6**:280-81

"Stop" (Dixon) **16**:207

"A Stop-Over at Tyre" ("A Girl of Modern Tyre") (Garland) **18**:148, 154-55, 161, 163, 166

Storie naturali (*Natural Stories*) (Levi) **12**:274-76, 278-79

Stories (Andersen)
See *Eventyr, fortalte for bøorn*

Stories (Bowen) **3**:39

Stories (Bulgakov) **18**:89, 91

Stories about Lenin (Zoshchenko)
See *Tales of Lenin*

"Stories I Tell Myself" (Cortazar) **7**:69

The Stories of Bernard Malamud (*Collected Stories*) (Malamud) **15**:216, 218

Stories of Five Decades (Hesse) **9**:232-33, 235-36

The Stories of Frank O'Connor (O'Connor) **5**:365

The Stories of F. Scott Fitzgerald (Fitzgerald) **6**:60

The Stories of Henry Lawson (Lawson) **18**:206

The Stories of John Cheever (Cheever) **1**:105-06, 108-09

The Stories of Liam O'Flaherty (O'Flaherty) **6**:260, 265

"Stories of Lough Guir" (Le Fanu) **14**:223

The Stories of Muriel Spark (Spark) **10**:365-66, 368, 370-71

The Stories of Seán O'Faoláin (O'Faolain)
See *Finest Short Stories of Seán O'Faoláin*

Stories of Sinebriukhov (Zoshchenko)
See *The Tales by Nazar Ilyich Sinebriukhov*

Stories of Three Decades (Mann) **5**:308-09, 311

Stories Told for Children (Andersen)
See *Eventyr, fortalte for bøorn*

"The Storm" (Bowen) **3**:38-9

"The Storm" (Chopin) **8**:80, 84, 86, 91, 95

"Storm" (O'Brien) **10**:345-46

"Storm Child" (Garland) **18**:147

"The Storm Ship" (Irving) **2**:254

"The Story about the Anteater" (Benet) **10**:149

Story Book (Hesse) **9**:230-31

"A Story by Angela Poe" (Benet) **10**:142, 144

"The Story fo the Beetle Hunter" (Doyle) **12**:64

"A Story from the Dunes" (Andersen) **6**:18-9, 34

"The Story Hearer" (Paley) **8**:420

"Story in Harlem Slang" (Hurston) **4**:139

"The Story of a Conscience" (Bierce) **9**:64, 67

"The Story of a Disappearance and an Appearance" (James) **16**:230, 232, 237, 245

"The Story of a Horse" (Babel) **16**:25, 28, 50-3

"The Story of a Horse, Continued" (Babel) **16**:27

"The Story of a Lie" (Stevenson) **11**:269, 281

"The Story of a Mine" (Harte) **8**:216

"The Story of a Mother" (Andersen) **6**:6-7, 18-9, 30, 35

"The Story of a Mouse" (Babel)
See "Istoriia moei golubiatni"

"The Story of an Hour" ("The Dream of an Hour") (Chopin) **8**:72-3, 79-80, 84, 87, 99, 102, 108

"The Story of a Non-Marrying Man" (Lessing) **6**:188, 211

"A Story of Beer" (Bulgakov) **18**:90

"The Story of Bras-Coupé" (Cable) **4**:61

"The Story of Father Alexis" (Turgenev)
See "Rasskaz ottsa Aleksaya"

"The Story of Howling Wolf" (Garland) **18**:147, 167, 179-80, 188

"The Story of Jees Uck" (London) **4**:271

"The Story of Keesh" (London) **4**:253

"The Story of Lahcen and Idir" (Bowles) **3**:80

"The Story of Lieutenant Ergunov" (Turgenev)
See "Istoriya leytenanta Ergunova"

"The Story of Muhammad Din" (Kipling) **5**:296

"The Story of My Dovecot" (Babel)
See "Istoriia moei golubiatni"

"The Story of St. Vespaluus" (Saki) **12**:306

"The Story of the Brazilian Cat" (Doyle) **12**:64

"A Story of the Days to Come" (Wells) **6**:389, 390, 403-04, 406-08

The Story of the Gadsbys (*The Gadsbys*) (Kipling) **5**:260, 264-65, 274

"The Story of the Japanned Box" (Doyle) **12**:64

"The Story of the Late Mr. Elvesham" (Wells) **6**:361, 363, 366, 383, 388, 405

"The Story of the Oracle" (Lawson) **18**:250

"A Story of the Stone Age" (Wells) **6**:389-90, 403-04

"Story of the Warrior and the Captive" (Borges)
See "Historia del guerrero y de la cautiva"

"The Story of the Year" (Andersen) **6**:30

"The Story of the Young Italian" ("The Young Italian") (Irving) **2**:260-61, 268

"Story of the Young Man with the Cream Tarts" (Stevenson) **11**:265

"The Story of the Young Robber" ("The Young Robber") (Irving) **2**:255, 257, 262

"The Story of Two Dogs" (Lessing) **6**:198, 200, 203-04, 206, 208

"A Story of Yesterday" (Tolstoy) **9**:374

"The Story-Teller" (Saki) **12**:289, 291, 293, 295, 302

"Storytellers, Liars, and Bores" (Michaels) **16**:306, 309, 311

"A Story with a Pattern" (Lavin) **4**:163, 167-69, 184-85

"A Story without a Title" (Chekhov)
See "An Anonymous Story"

"Story with Spiders" (Cortazar) **7**:69

"The Stout Gentleman" (Irving) **2**:250-51, 254, 259

"La strada di San Giovanni" (Calvino) **3**:97

"Straight Pool" (O'Hara) **15**:248, 264

"Strandhill, the Sea" (McGahern) **17**:302, 308, 318, 320

The Strange Case of Dr. Jekyll and Mr. Hyde (*Doctor Jekyll and Mr. Hyde*) (Stevenson) **11**:262, 264, 276, 279, 290-92, 301-02

"The Strange Child" (Kuhatschek)
See "Das Fremde Kind"

"The Strange Crime of John Boulais" (Chesterton) **1**:138

"The Strange Design of Master Rignolo" (Ligotti) **16**:271, 277, 292, 296

"The Strange Disease" (O'Flaherty) **6**:262

"Strange Disturbances on Aungier Street" (Le Fanu)
See "Some Strange Disturbances in an Old House on Augier Street"

"A Strange Event in the Life of Schalken the Painter" (Le Fanu)
See "A Strange Event in the Life of Schalken the Painter"

"A Strange Event in the Life of Schalken the Painter" ("A Strange Event in the Life of Schalken the Painter") (Le Fanu) **14**:220-21, 224-25, 232-36, 238-39, 252

"The Strange High House in the Mist" (Lovecraft) **3**:262, 277

"Strange Moonlight" (Aiken) **9**:4, 7-8, 13-14, 32-3, 35, 38, 40

"Strange News from Another Star" (Hesse) **9**:235

Strange News from Another Star, and Other Tales (Hesse) **9**:234-35, 244

"The Stranger" (Baudelaire)
See "L'etranger"

"A Stranger" (de la Mare) **14**:80

"The Stranger" (Mansfield) **9**:280, 282-83

"The Stranger" (Schnitzler) **15**:342

"The Strange Ride of Morrowbie Jukes" (Kipling) **5**:262, 265, 273, 278, 299

"Strangers and Pilgrims" (de la Mare) **14**:80, 83, 86, 92

"Strangers in the Night" (Phillips) **16**:325

"Strange Stories by a Nervous Gentleman" (Irving) **2**:251, 261

"A Strange Story" (Turgenev)
See "Strannaya istoriya"

Strange Things Happen Here (Valenzuela) **14**:366-67, 369-70

Strange True Stories of Louisiana (Cable) **4**:49, 51, 53, 58-62, 75

"Strannaya istoriya" ("A Strange Story") (Turgenev) **7**:315, 321, 324, 337, 358-59

"Strašnaja mest" ("A Terrible Vengeance") (Gogol) **4**:103-04, 118-19

"The Strategy of the Were-Wolf Dog" (Cather) **2**:100

"Stratford-on-Avon" (Irving) **2**:245

"Strawberry Spring" (King) **17**:265

"The Stream" (O'Flaherty) **6**:265, 277-78

"The Street" (Lovecraft) **3**:292

"Streetcorner Man" (Borges)
See "Hombre de la esquina rosada"

"Streets" (Dixon) **16**:205

"The Streets—Morning" (Dickens) **17**:116, 134

"The Strength of Gideon" (Dunbar) **8**:128, 136, 141, 144

The Strength of Gideon and Other Stories (Dunbar) **8**:120-21, 124-25, 127, 131, 144-45

"The Strength of God" (Anderson) **1**:18

"The Strength of the Strong" (London) **4**:255

The Strength of the Strong (London) **4**:254-55, 283

Strictly Business (Henry) **5**:171

Strider (Tolstoy) **9**:393

"The String Quartet" (Woolf) **7**:368-69, 374-75, 390, 392, 399

"Strong as Death is Love" (Singer) **3**:386

Strong Hearts (Cable) **4**:50, 62, 75

"Strong Horse Tea" (Walker) **5**:401, 403

"The Struggle" (O'Flaherty) **6**:264, 269

"Stud City" (King) **17**:272, 278-79, 285, 289-90

"The Student" (Chekhov) **2**:158

"The Student of Salamanca" (Irving) **2**:251, 254, 259

"The Student's Wife" (Carver) **8**:11, 46, 50-1, 53

"Studies in Horror" (Ligotti) **16**:287

"The Study of History" (O'Connor) **5**:376

"Stuk...stuk...stuk" ("Knock...Knock...Knock"; "Toc...toc...toc") (Turgenev) **7**:319, 321, 324-25, 338, 358-59

Eine Stunde hinter Mitternacht (*An Hour Beyond Midnight*) (Hesse) **9**:229-31

"The Sub" (Dixon) **16**:207

"A Subject of Childhood" (Paley) **8**:396, 398, 407

"Sublimating" (Updike) **13**:387

"The Subliminal Man" (Ballard) **1**:68-9, 77-8

"Subpoena" (Barthelme) **2**:37, 39

"A Suburban Fairy Tale" (Mansfield) **9**:311

"The Successor" (Bowles) **3**:64-5, 80, 83

"Sucker" (McCullers) **9**:332, 341-42, 344-45, 354-55

"A Sudden Trip Home in the Spring" (Walker) **5**:414

"Suffer the Little Children" (King) **17**:295

The Sugar Crock (Gass) **12**:148

"Sugar for the Horse" (Bates) **10**:117, 131

Sugar for the Horse (Bates) **10**:131

"The Sugawn Chair" (O'Faolain) **13**:314, 320

"Suicide Club" (Doyle) **12**:58

The Suicide Club (Stevenson) **11**:280

"Suicides" (Gilchrist) **14**:150-51

"Suishō Gensō" ("The Crystal Fantasy") (Kawabata) **17**:242

"The Suitcase" (Ozick) **15**:298-300, 311, 314-15, 319, 328-35

Sukhodol (*Dry Valley*) (Bunin) **5**:82-3, 90, 100-01

Sukhodól (Bunin) **5**:81, 87

"Sulfur" (Levi) **12**:264, 268

"Sullivan's Trousers" (O'Faolain) **13**:309, 316

"Summer" (Boyle) **5**:54

"Summer" (Cortazar)
See "Verano"

"The Summer Before" (Steinbeck) **11**:253-54

"Summer Dust" (Gordon) **15**:116, 119, 123, 126, 137, 139

"The Summer Farmer" (Cheever) **1**:99, 106

"A Summer in Maine" (Gilchrist) **14**:163-64

"Summer Night" (Bowen) **3**:39, 41, 46, 51

"Summer People" (Beattie) **11**:25-6, 29

"The Summer People" (Jackson) **9**:258

"Summer's Day" (O'Hara) **15**:248-49, 252-53, 258, 270

"Summer Shore" (Grau) **15**:161, 163-64

"A Summer's Reading" (Malamud) **15**:168, 221

"Summer Theatre" (Cheever) **1**:99

"Summertime on Icarus" (Clarke) **3**:130, 138, 147

"The Summing Up" (Woolf) **7**:376, 381, 390, 392, 411

"Sun" (Lawrence) **4**:238, 240-42

"Sun and Moon" (Mansfield) **9**:282

"The Sun between Their Feet" (Lessing) **6**:198-99, 203, 212

"Sunday Afternoon" (Bowen) **3**:41, 53

"Sunday Afternoon" (Gallant) **5**:141

"Sunday Afternoon" (Munro) **3**:343

"Sunday at Home" (Hawthorne) **3**:189

"Sunday Brings Sunday" (Lavin) **4**:176

"Sunday Evening" (Bowen) **3**:53

"Sunday Morning" (O'Hara) **15**:282, 289

"A Sunday Out of Town" (Dickens) **17**:120-21

"Sunday Teasing" (Updike) **13**:355

"Sunday under Three Heads" (Dickens) **17**:124

"The Sun-Dodgers" (O'Hara) **15**:282

The Sun Dog (King) **17**:282, 284

"The Sun-Dog Trail" (London) **4**:253, 290

"Sunjammer" (Clarke) **3**:132

"Sunlight/Twilight" (Oates) **6**:236-37

"A Sunny Place" (Kawabata) **17**:252

"The Sunrise" (Atwood) **2**:17-18, 21-2

"A Sunrise on the Veld" (Lessing) **6**:186

"The Sun Rises Twice" (Bates) **10**:113

"Sunset" (Faulkner) **1**:177

Sunset (Babel)
See *Zakat*

"Sunshine and Shadow" (Beattie) **11**:10

"Sunstroke" (Bunin)
See "Solnechnyy udar"

A Sunstroke (Bunin) **5**:90

"The Superintendent" (Cheever) **1**:99, 107

"Superiority" (Clarke) **3**:126, 150

"The Superstitious Man's Story" (Hardy) **2**:217

"The Supper at Elsinore" (Dinesen) **7**:168, 177, 186, 190, 203-04

"A Supper by Proxy" (Dunbar) **8**:122, 135, 139

"Suppose a Wedding" (Malamud) **15**:173-75

"Surgery" (Chekhov) **2**:130

Sur l'eau (*Afloat*) (Maupassant) **1**:261-62, 265, 278

"A Surplus Woman" (Gilman) **13**:143

"The Survival of Childhood" (Oates) **6**:224

Survival Techniques (Calisher) **15**:21, 23

"Survivor Type" (King) **17**:274-75

"Susan and the Doctor" (Suckow) **18**:393-94, 409, 416-17

"Susy" (Harte) **8**:222, 251-52

"Suzette" (Chopin) **8**:100

"Svajatye gory" (Bunin) **5**:98

"Swaddling Clothes" (Mishima) **4**:313, 317, 322-23

"Swallows" (McGahern) **17**:299, 304, 308

"The Swan's Nest" (Andersen) **6**:4

"The Sway-Backed House" (Chesnutt) **7**:33

"Sweat" (Hurston) **4**:136-38, 151, 155

"A Sweet Colleen" (O'Faolain) **13**:305

"The Sweethearts" (Andersen) **6**:28, 30, 36

"Sweethearts" (Phillips) **16**:326, 328

Sweethearts (Phillips) **16**:332

"Swept and Garnished" (Kipling) **5**:275, 282

"The Swiftest Runners" (Andersen) **6**:10

"The Swimmer" (Cheever) **1**:94, 100, 102, 106, 108

"The Swineherd" (Andersen) **6**:7, 18, 24, 26, 30-1, 34

"The Swing" (Bunin)
See "Kacheli"

"Sylvesternacht" (Hoffmann) **13**:189

"Sylvia" (Michaels) **16**:314, 317, 320

Sylvia: A Fictional Memoir (Michaels) **16**:317-18

Sylvie: Recollections of Valois (Nerval) **18**:328, 332-35, 337, 343-46, 355, 357, 359-62, 365, 367, 369-70, 376-77, 380, 383

"A s'y méprendre" ("The Very Image") (Villiers de l'Isle Adam) **14**:381, 388, 391

"Sympathy" (Woolf) **7**:409

La Symphonie pastorale (*The Pastoral Symphony*) (Gide) **13**:43, 48-52, 62, 72, 77, 98-9

Symphonies (Gide)
See *Two Symphonies*

"A Symphony in Lavender" (Freeman) **1**:199

"The System of Doctor Tarr and Professor Fether" (Poe) **1**:407

"Tadeo Limardo's Victim" (Bioy Casares)
See "La victima de Tado Limardo"

"Das Tagebuch der Redegonda" (Schnitzler) **15**:346

"Tailors' Dummies " (Schulz)
See "Traktat o manekinach"

"Tails" (Dixon) **16**:211

"Tain't So" (Hughes) **6**:121, 131

"Take Pity" (Malamud) **15**:169, 175, 212, 216-17, 219, 221, 223, 243

"Takes" (Dixon) **16**:218

"The Taking of Lungtungpen" (Kipling) **5**:260, 265

"The Taking of the Redoubt" (Merimee)
See "L'enlèvement de la rédoute"

"Taking the Veil" (Mansfield) **9**:282, 310

"Tale for the Mirror" (Calisher) **15**:3

Tale for the Mirror: A Novella and Other Stories (Calisher) **15**:3-5, 7

"The Tale of Astolpho on the Moon" (Calvino) **3**:101

"Tale of a Vampire" (Hoffmann)
See "Der Vampyrismus"

"The Tale of How Ivan Ivanovich Quarrelled with Ivan Nikiforovich" ("About How Ivan Ivanovič Quarreled with Ivan Nikiforovič"; "The Quarrel of Two Ivans"; "The Tale of Two Ivans"; "The Two Ivans") (Gogol) **4**:82, 84, 86, 105

"A Tale of Jerusalem" (Poe) **1**:407

"The Tale of the Ingrate and His Punishment" (Calvino) **3**:101-02

"A Tale of the Ragged Mountains" (Poe) **1**:400, 402

"A Tale of the White Pyramid" (Cather) **2**:100

"Tale of the Wicker Chair" (Hesse) **9**:242, 244

"The Tale of Tod Lapraik" (Stevenson) **11**:303-06

"The Tale of Two Ivans" (Gogol)
See "The Tale of How Ivan Ivanovich Quarrelled with Ivan Nikiforovich"

"A Tale of Two Liars" (Singer) **3**:375

"A Tale of Two Sisters" (Singer) 3:377
Tales before Midnight (Benet) 10:154, 158-59
Tales by Edgar A. Poe (Poe) 1:388
The Tales by Nazar Ilyich Sinebriukhov (Stories of Sinebriukhov) (Zoshchenko) 15:395
Tales for Children (Tolstoy) 9:382
Tales from Bective Bridge (Lavin) 4:170-72, 185
Tales from the White Hart (Clarke) 3:131, 133
Tales of a Traveller (Irving) 2:241, 244, 246, 250-51, 254-55, 258-62, 268
Tales of Lenin (Stories about Lenin) (Zoshchenko) 15:404, 407, 409
Tales of Men and Ghosts (Wharton) 6:421, 435
Tales of Odessa (Babel)
    See *The Odessa Tales*
Tales of Sevastopol (Sevastopol) (Tolstoy) 9:380
Tales of Soldiers and Civilians (In the Midst of Life) (Bierce) 9:49-50, 55, 59, 65, 75
Tales of Space and Time (Wells) 6:366-67, 380, 389
Tales of Terror and Mystery (Doyle) 12:60, 64
Tales of the Grotesque and Arabesque (Poe) 1:389-90
Tales of the Jazz Age (Fitzgerald) 6:45-6, 56, 58-9, 74, 101
Tales of the Long Bow (Chesterton) 1:133
Tales of Twilight and the Unseen (Doyle) 12:60
"Tales of Two Old Gentlemen" (Dinesen) 7:173
Tales of Unrest (Conrad) 9:151-52
"The Talisman" (de la Mare) 14:83
"A Talk among Leisured People" (Tolstoy) 9:396
"Talking Horse" (Malamud) 15:189, 190, 198, 220, 222
The Talking Trees (O'Faolain) 13:291, 313-14
"The Tall Men" (Faulkner) 1:151, 162
Un tal Lucas (A Certain Lucas) (Cortazar) 7:91-4
"Tamango" (Merimee) 7:280-81, 283, 287-89, 300
"The Taming of the Nightmare" (Chesterton) 1:140
"Tanagokoro no Shōsetsu" (*The Palm-Sized Stories*) (Kawabata) 17:242, 251-58
"Tanhum" (Singer) 3:380
"Tania" ("Tanya") (Bunin) 5:113
"Tante Cat'rinette" (Chopin) 8:94
"Tanya" (Bunin)
    See "Tania"
"An tAonach" (O'Flaherty) 6:287-88
"Tapiama" (Bowles) 3:64-5, 80, 83
Taps at Reveille (Fitzgerald) 6:46-7, 56, 60
"Taras bulba" (Gogol) 4:83, 85-6, 117-19
"Tarquin of Cheapside" (Fitzgerald) 6:58, 60
"A Taste of Honey" (Freeman) 1:196
"Tatlin!" (Davenport) 16:161-62, 165, 167-69, 171, 197
Tatlin! (Davenport) 16:160-61, 163-68, 170-71, 173-77, 183, 185, 187, 195, 197
Le taureau blanc (Voltaire) 12:342
"The Taxidermist" (Cable) 4:50
"Tea" (Gallant)
    See "Thank You for the Lovely Tea"
"Tea" (Saki) 12:313
"The Teacher" (Anderson) 1:18, 45, 52

"The Teacher of Literature" (Chekhov) 2:128, 131-32, 155
"Teacher's Pet" (Thurber) 1:422-23
"Teaching and Story Telling" (Maclean) 13:278-79
"The Teachings of Don B.: A Yankee Way of Knowledge" (Barthelme) 2:40
"Teangabháil" (O'Flaherty) 6:286-89
"Tea on the Mountain" (Bowles) 3:61, 72, 79
"Tears, Idle Tears" (Bowen) 3:33, 41, 47
"Tears—Idle Tears" (O'Connor) 5:371, 395
"The Tears of Ah Kim" (London) 4:257, 270
"Tea with Mrs. Bittell" (Pritchett) 14:272
"Technical Error" ("The Reversed Man") (Clarke) 3:124-25, 129
"A Technical Error" (Henry) 5:165
"Teddy" (Salinger) 2:293, 295, 300-01, 307, 309, 311-12, 316
"Teibele and Her Demon" (Singer) 3:375, 384
"Telemachus, Friend" (Henry) 5:179
"A Telephone Call" (Parker) 2:274, 278, 280, 285
"A Telephone Call on Yom Kippur" (Singer) 3:385-86
"Television" (Beattie) 11:31
"Telling" (Bowen) 3:30, 33, 40
"Telling Mrs. Baker" (Lawson) 18:213, 243, 252, 262
"Tell Me a Riddle" (Olsen) 11:164-68, 171, 174, 176, 178-79, 181, 185, 187, 195, 197
Tell Me a Riddle (Olsen) 11:163, 169, 171, 174, 187-88, 193, 197-98
"Tell Me Yes or No" (Munro) 3:335
"The Tell-Tale Heart" (Poe) 1:384, 393-94, 408
"Tell the Women We're Going" (Carver) 8:14, 30
"Tema del traidor y del héroe" ("The Theme of the Traitor and the Hero") (Borges) 4:10, 23, 30, 39
"The Temperate Zone" (Wharton) 6:428
"Tempests" (Dinesen) 7:171, 197
"The Temple" (Lovecraft) 3:282, 289
"A Temple of the Holy Ghost" (*Woman of the River*) (O'Connor) 1:343
"The Temptation of Jack Orkney" (Lessing) 6:188
The Temptation of Jack Orkney, and Other Stories (Lessing) 6:188
The Temptation of Quiet Veronica (Musil)
    See *Die Versuchung der Stillen Veronika*
"The Temptation of St. Anthony" (Barthelme) 2:37, 54
"The Temptation of St. Ivo" (Gardner) 7:214, 222, 229-30, 232
The Temptation of the Silent Veronika (Musil)
    See *Die Versuchung der Stillen Veronika*
"The Tempter" (Oates) 6:227
"Tenants of the Last Tree-House" (Gordimer) 17:155-56
"The Tender Shoot" (Colette)
    See "Le tendron"
"The Tendrils of the Vine" (Colette) 10:291
"Le tendron" ("The Tender Shoot") (Colette) 10:293-94
"Tennessee's Partner" (Harte) 8:210, 219, 221, 226, 230, 232-33, 236, 244, 255-56, 258-59
"The Ten O'Clock People" (King) 17:294-95
"The Tent" (O'Flaherty) 6:262, 282
The Tent (O'Flaherty) 6:262-65, 278-79, 283

"Les Tentations" (Baudelaire) 18:15, 17, 19, 36, 38, 41
"The Tenth Clew" (Hammett) 17:218, 220, 226
"The Tents of Kedar" (Kipling) 5:261
"Ten Years Dead" (Garland) 18:165
"Teraloyna" (Gordimer) 17:177, 183, 185, 189-90
"La tercera resignación" ("The Third Resignation") (Garcia Marquez) 8:154-55, 169, 182
"Teresa" (O'Faolain) 13:286, 288, 293, 297, 312, 314
"Terminal" (Gordimer) 17:171
"The Terminal Beach" (Ballard) 1:69, 76, 80
The Terminal Beach, and Other Stories (Ballard) 1:68-70, 73
"The Termitary" (Gordimer) 17:181
"Terra incognita" (Nabokov) 11:117, 154
"The Terrible Old Man" (Lovecraft) 3:292
"A Terrible Vengeance" (Gogol)
    See "Strašnaja mest"
"Terror" (Anderson) 1:30
"Terror" (Nabokov) 11:124-25
"The Terrorist" (O'Flaherty) 6:262, 284
"The Terrorists" (Barnes) 3:19
"The Terror of Blue John Gap" (Doyle) 12:61, 80
"El tesoro de la juventud" ("The Treasure of Youth") (Cortazar) 7:95
"Testament of Flood" (Warren) 4:389, 394
"Los testigos" ("The Witnesses") (Cortazar) 7:95
"The Test of Courage" (O'Flaherty) 6:281
"The Test of Elder Pill" (Garland)
    See "Elder Pill, Preacher"
Textes pour rien (Texts for Nothing) (Beckett) 16:71, 75-7, 110-14, 117-23, 130
"Text in a Notebook" (Cortazar) 7:69
Texts for Nothing (Beckett)
    See *Textes pour rien*
"Texturologías" ("Texturologies") (Cortazar) 7:93
"Texturologies" (Cortazar)
    See "Texturologías"
"Thanasphere" (Vonnegut) 8:428
"Thanks for the Ride" (Munro) 3:322, 329, 331, 336, 343
"Thank You" (Kawabata) 17:252-53
"Thank You for the Lovely Tea" ("Tea") (Gallant) 5:138, 142
"That Evening Sun" (Faulkner) 1:147, 162, 181, 183
"That Good May Come" (Wharton) 6:424
"That in Aleppo Once..." (Nabokov) 11:108-09, 111, 113, 129
"That Pretty Girl in the Army" (Lawson) 18:217, 220, 241, 243-44
"That Sophistication" (Anderson) 1:50
"That There Dog o' Mine" (Lawson) 18:244
"That Tree" (Porter) 4:327-28, 330, 339-40, 349
"Thawing Out" (Boyle) 16:146-48, 154
"Theater" (Toomer) 1:441, 443-45, 450, 452, 458, 460-61
"Theatre of War" (Ballard) 1:79, 82
"The Theatrical Young Gentleman" (Dickens) 17:122
"The-Child-Who-Was-Tired" (Mansfield) 9:286, 310, 316
"Theft" (Porter) 4:327, 329, 337-40, 342, 349, 360

A Theft (Bellow) **14**:48-50, 56, 59-61
"Their Losses" (Taylor) **10**:391
"The Theme of the Traitor and the Hero"
    (Borges)
    See "Tema del traidor y del héroe"
"Then It All Came Down" (Capote) **2**:81
"The Theologians" (Borges) **4**:5-6, 25, 28, 30
"There" (Taylor) **10**:397
There and Now (Cortazar)
    See *Ahí y ahora*
"There Are No Thieves in This Town" (Garcia
    Marquez) **8**:185
"There Is No Hope for That" (Cortazar)
    See "Ya no quedan esperanzas de"
"There's a Garden of Eden" (Gilchrist)
    14:152
"There She Is—She Is Taking Her Bath"
    (Anderson) **1**:50
"There's No Future in It" (Bates) **10**:139
There's Something in the Air (Bates) **10**:113-
    15
"There Was a Man Dwelt by a Churchyard"
    (James) **16**:249, 251
"Thermos Bottles" ("Thermos Flasks")
    (Mishima) **4**:313-14, 316-18, 322
"Thermos Flasks" (Mishima)
    See "Thermos Bottles"
Thésée (*Theseus*) (Gide) **13**:43, 48, 52, 54-7,
    62, 71-2, 105-10, 112
Thésée (Gide) **13**:43, 48, 52, 54-57, 71, 72,
    105-110, 112
These Thirteen (Faulkner) **1**:180-81, 184
Theseus (Gide)
    See *Thésée*
"These Walls Are Cold" (Capote) **2**:65
"!!!The!!!Teddy!Crazy!!Show!!!" (Ellison)
    14:128
"They" (Kipling) **5**:266, 271-72, 275, 279-82,
    284
"They Called for More Structure..."
    (Barthelme) **2**:50
"They Called Him 'Ally' for Short" (Lawson)
    18:218
They of the High Trails (Garland) **18**:164
"They're Not Your Husband" (Carver) **8**:9,
    34
"They Wait on the Wharf in Black" (Lawson)
    18:210, 215, 234
"They Way of a Man" (Grau) **15**:158, 165
"They Weren't Going to Die" (Boyle) **5**:63
"The Thief" (O'Connor) **5**:371
"The Thieves" (Grau) **15**:147
"Thieves" (O'Faolain) **13**:292, 316
"Thieves' Ears" (Bunin)
    See "Petlistye ushi"
"The Thimble" (Lawrence) **4**:235, 237
"Thimble, Thimble" (Henry) **5**:159, 171
"A Thing for Nothing" (O'Connor) **5**:365
A Thin Ghost and Others (James) **16**:238,
    251, 255
"A Thing of the Past" (Gordimer) **17**:154
"The Thing on the Doorstep" (Lovecraft)
    3:259, 263, 272, 274-75, 283
"Things" (Lawrence) **4**:219
"Things" (Le Guin) **12**:232
"Things as They Are" (Pritchett) **14**:255, 285
"The Things You Keep" (Grau) **15**:156
"The Thinker" (Anderson) **1**:43-5
"Thin Lips and False Teeth" (Lawson)
    18:249
"The Third Cock-Crow" (Bunin) **5**:82-3
"The Third Ingredient" (Henry) **5**:181-82

"The Third Murder" (Lawson) **18**:217
"The Third Person" (James) **8**:325
"A Third Presence" (Gordimer) **17**:158
"The Third Resignation" (Garcia Marquez)
    See "La tercera resignación"
"The Third Thing that Killed My Father Off"
    (Carver) **8**:14
The Thirteen (Balzac)
    See *Histoire des treize*
Thirteen Ghost-stories by Mr. James (James)
    16:223
Thirteen O'Clock: Stories of Several Worlds
    (Benet) **10**:142, 154, 158
Thirty Stories (Boyle) **5**:56, 63
"The $30,000 Bequest" (Twain) **6**:303, 328-
    30, 343-45
"This Morning, This Evening, So Soon"
    (Baldwin) **10**:5-7, 9
"This Mortal Coil" (O'Connor) **5**:386, 389
"This Son of Mine" (Vonnegut) **8**:432, 438
"Thistledown" (Aiken) **9**:12, 14, 30, 42
This Was the Old Chief's Country (Lessing)
    6:186, 196
"The Thorn in the Flesh" (Lawrence) **4**:197,
    202
"The Thorny Path of Honor" (Andersen)
    6:4, 34
Those Days (Carver) **8**:51
"Thou Art the Man" (Poe) **1**:406
"Thoughts about People" (Dickens) **17**:116,
    132, 136
"A Thousand Deaths" (London) **4**:277
"Thrawn Janet" (Stevenson) **11**:268-69, 279,
    281-82, 304-06
"Three" (Grau) **15**:149, 160
"The Three-Day Blow" (Hemingway) **1**:208,
    219, 244
Three Deaths (Tolstoy)
    See *Tri smerti*
Three Exemplary Novels and a Prologue
    (Unamuno)
    See *Tres novelas ejemplares y un prólogo*
"Three Fantasies in Minor Key" (Bioy
    Casares) **17**:95
"Three Fat Women of Antibes" (Maugham)
    8:379
"The Threefold Destiny" (Hawthorne) **3**:160,
    177-78, 182-83, 189
"The Three Friends" (de la Mare) **14**:68, 83,
    90
"The Three Hermits" (Tolstoy) **9**:373-74, 388
"Three Heroines" (Taylor) **10**:408
"Three Kopeks" (Bulgakov) **18**:89
"Three Lambs" (O'Flaherty) **6**:264, 274
"Three Lindens" (Hesse) **9**:242-43
"Three Meetings" (Turgenev) **7**:314-15, 324-
    25, 328, 335
"The Three Million Yen" (Mishima) **4**:313-
    14, 316-18, 322
"Three Miraculous Soldiers" (Crane) **7**:103,
    106
"Three Partners" (Harte) **8**:216, 222, 248
"Three Pictures" (Woolf) **7**:408, 410-12
"Three Portraits" (Turgenev) **7**:313, 318, 320,
    323
"Three Questions" (Tolstoy) **9**:388
Three Stories and Ten Poems (Hemingway)
    1:206
"The Three Strangers" (Hardy) **2**:202-03,
    205, 208, 212-15, 218, 220, 223, 226-27
Three Tales (Flaubert)

    See *Trois contes: Un coeur simple; La légende
    de Saint-Julien l'hospitalier; Hérodias*
"Three Thousand Years among the Microbes"
    (Twain) **6**:333, 336, 338, 350-53
"Three Tools" (Chesterton) **1**:136
"Three Vagabonds of Trinidad" (Harte)
    8:245, 251
Three Women (Musil)
    See *Drei Frauen*
"Three Years" (Chekhov) **2**:131, 155-57
"Throat of a Black Cat" (Cortazar)
    See "Cuello de gatito negro"
"Through the Gates of the Silver Key"
    (Lovecraft) **3**:262, 267, 272-73, 286, 294
"Through the Looking Glass" (Oates) **6**:228
"Through the Streets of My Own Labyrinth"
    (Nin) **10**:303
"Through the Veil" (Doyle) **12**:80
"Through the Walls" (Levi) **12**:277
"Thrown Away" (Kipling) **5**:261
"Thumbelina" (Andersen) **6**:27-8, 36
"Thumbling" (Andersen)
    See "Poor Thumbling"
The Thurber Carnival (Thurber) **1**:416, 426
"Le Thyrse" ("The Thyrsus") (Baudelaire)
    18:59, 63
"The Thyrsus" (Baudelaire)
    See "Le Thyrse"
La tía Tula (Unamuno) **11**:313-14, 317, 324-
    25, 327, 330, 335, 344-45, 347-48
"Tickets, Please" (Lawrence) **4**:222-23, 226,
    228, 231, 233-35, 242-46
Ti con zero (*Time and the Hunter; t zero*)
    (Calvino) **3**:92, 94-6, 98-9, 107, 117
"The Tide" (O'Flaherty) **6**:262, 279, 285
"Ti Démon" (Chopin) **8**:100
"The Tie" (Kipling) **5**:278
"Ti Frére" (Chopin) **8**:72
"The Tiger's Bride" (Carter) **13**:6, 9, 23, 25,
    27, 30-32
"A Tight Boat" (Chesnutt) **7**:13
"Time and Ebb" (Nabokov) **11**:108, 127, 130
Time and the Hunter (Calvino)
    See *Ti con zero*
"The Time Capsule" (Gilchrist) **14**:161-62
"Time Checkmated" (Levi) **12**:280
"Time Did" (Gordimer) **17**:164, 193
"The Time Element" (O'Hara) **15**:
The Time Element, and Other Stories (O'Hara)
    15:286
"Time Expired" (Bates) **10**:117
"Time, Gentlemen!" (Calisher) **15**:8, 15-17,
    19
"The Time of Death" (Munro) **3**:329-30
"The Time of Friendship" (Bowles) **3**:63-7,
    81-2
The Time of Friendship (Bowles) **3**:63-5, 70,
    79-81, 84
"The Time of Their Lives" (O'Faolain)
    13:320
"Times" (Beattie) **11**:29
*The Times Are Never So Bad: A Novella and
    Eight Short Stories* (Dubus) **15**:76, 81, 83,
    88, 97
"Time's Arrow" (Clarke) **3**:133-34, 142
"The Time the Wolves Ate the Vice-Principal"
    (Steinbeck) **11**:248
"Time to Go" (Dixon) **16**:207-08, 212
Time to Go (Dixon) **16**:206-08, 212-15
"A Tin Can" (O'Flaherty) **6**:276
"The Tinder-Box" (Andersen) **6**:4, 18, 23,
    26-7, 30-2, 36-7

"The Tinkerer" (Coover) **15**:47

"Le tir et le cimetière" (Baudelaire) **18**:3, 18, 35

"Tišina" (Bunin) **5**:98

"Titanium" (Levi) **12**:264, 268

"Titbull's Alms-houses" (Dickens) **17**:123

"Tite Poulette" (Cable) **4**:52, 62, 67-8, 76-7

"Title" (Barth) **10**:42-3, 46-8, 54-5, 61, 63-4, 73-4, 76, 79-81, 85-8, 91, 97-100

"Tlön, Uqbar, Orbis Tertius" (Borges) **4**:6-7, 10-12, 15, 18, 25, 29, 33, 35, 43

"To Be Read at Dusk" (Dickens) **17**:124

"Tobermory" (Saki) **12**:287, 302, 304, 312, 333

"Tobias Mindernickel" (Mann) **5**:322, 334, 336

"To Build a Fire (1902)" (London) **4**:272-74

"To Build a Fire (1908)" (London) **4**:265, 267, 272-76, 278, 280-82, 289-93

"Toc...toc...toc" (Turgenev)
See "Stuk...stuk...stuk"

"To Da-duh, In Memoriam" (Marshall) **3**:301, 303, 307, 313-15, 317

"Today Is Friday" (Hemingway) **1**:228-29

Der Tod in Venedig (*Death in Venice*) (Mann) **5**:307, 309-11, 313-14, 319, 322-27, 331, 338-40, 342-45, 348, 355-56

"Todos los fuegos el fuego" ("All Fires the Fire") (Cortazar) **7**:61, 69

Todos los fuegos el fuego (*All Fires the Fire, and Other Stories*) (Cortazar) **7**:52-4, 60, 62, 64

"Together and Apart" (Woolf) **7**:376, 381, 388

"To Hell with Dying" (Walker) **5**:403, 406, 419, 422

"Told in the Drooling Ward" (London) **4**:255-56, 266

"Told in the Tavern" (Jewett) **6**:159

"The Toll-Gatherer's Day" (Hawthorne) **3**:158

"Les tombales" (Maupassant) **1**:263

"The Tomb of His Ancestors" (Kipling) **5**:266

"The Tommy Crans" (Bowen) **3**:33, 41

"Tommy, the Unsentimental" (Cather) **2**:100, 105

"Tomorrow" (Conrad) **9**:143

"Tomorrow" (Faulkner) **1**:165, 179, 181

"Tomorrow and Tomorrow and So Forth" (Updike) **13**:352

"Tomorrow and Tomorrow and Tomorrow" (Vonnegut) **8**:425, 429-31

"The Tomorrow-Tamer" (Laurence) **7**:249, 261

The Tomorrow-Tamer (Laurence) **7**:245-50, 260-61, 272

"Tom Rivers" (Gordon) **15**:106-07

"Tom's Warm Welcome" (Chesnutt) **7**:14

Tonio Kröger (Mann) **5**:307, 310-11, 316, 318, 324, 331, 342-44, 355

Tonka (Musil) **18**:292-97, 305, 313-17, 322-25

"Tony Kytes, the Arch Deceiver" (Hardy) **2**:206-07

"Too Bad" (Parker) **2**:274, 280, 285

"Too Early Spring" (Benet) **10**:144

Too Far to Go: The Maples Stories (*Your Lover Just Called: Stories of Joan and Richard Maple*) (Updike) **13**:373, 383, 387-88

"The Tooth" (Jackson) **9**:249, 258-60, 266

"A Tooth for Paul Revere" (Benet) **10**:143, 154, 159

"Too Young" (O'Hara) **15**:248, 265, 270

"The Top and the Ball" (Andersen) **6**:18, 32

"Torch Song" (Cheever) **1**:89, 99, 106, 109-10

"Torito" ("Little Bull") (Cortazar) **7**:54, 88-9

"To Room Nineteen" (Lessing) **6**:198, 201-02, 208, 214, 218, 220

"Torpid Smoke" (Nabokov) **11**:117, 154-6

"A Torrent Dammed" (O'Connor) **5**:387

The Torrents of Spring (Turgenev)
See *Veshnie vody*

"La torture par l'espérance" (Villiers de l'Isle Adam) **14**:378, 398

"To Set Our House in Order" (Laurence) **7**:252, 262, 264-65, 269

"Der toten schweigen" ("The Dead Are Silent") (Schnitzler) **15**:345, 376

"To the Man on Trail" (London) **4**:250, 267, 277, 279

"To Thy Chamber Window, Sweet" (Gordon) **15**:106, 120, 129

"The Touch" (O'Flaherty) **6**:265, 285

"A Touch of Autumn in the Air" (O'Faolain) **13**:289, 293-95, 314, 320

"A Touch of Realism" (Saki) **12**:294, 306

The Touchstone (Wharton) **6**:413

"A Tough Tussle" (Bierce) **9**:49, 67

"The Tourist City in the South" (Hesse) **9**:244

"A Tour of the Forest" (Turgenev) **7**:320, 337-38

A Tour on the Prairies (Irving) **2**:244

Le toutounier (Colette) **10**:263

"Toward Evening" (Updike) **13**:355

"Towel with a Rooster" (Bulgakov) **18**:86

"Town and Country Lovers" (Gordimer) **17**:164-65, 193-94

"Town Crier Exclusive, Confessions of a Princess Manque: How Royals Found Me "Unsuitable" to Marry Their Larry" (Elkin) **12**:119-20

"Townies" (Dubus) **15**:77, 79-81, 88, 96

"The Town Poor" (Jewett) **6**:151

"The Toys of Peace" (Saki) **12**:285

The Toys of Peace, and Other Papers (Saki) **12**:285, 289, 322, 328-29

"Traceleen Turns East" (Gilchrist) **14**:162-63

"Track 12" (Ballard) **1**:68

"A Tractate Middoth" (James) **16**:232, 234, 240, 245, 252, 255, 257

"A Tradition of 1804" (Hardy) **2**:215, 220-21

Traffics and Discoveries (Kipling) **5**:266, 272, 283

"A Tragedy" (Lavin) **4**:165, 176, 183

"The Tragedy at Three Corners" (Dunbar)
See "The Tragedy at Three Forks"

"The Tragedy at Three Forks" ("The Tragedy at Three Corners") (Dunbar) **8**:121-22, 125, 136

"Tragedy in a Greek Theatre" (Pritchett) **14**:268-69, 273

"A Tragedy of Error" (James) **8**:302

"A Tragedy of Two Ambitions" (Hardy) **2**:205-06, 214-17, 223

"Tragic" (Hesse) **9**:232, 236

"The Train" (Carver) **8**:25-6, 34

"Train from Rhodesia" (Gordimer) **17**:167, 173, 186

"Training" (Atwood) **2**:3-4, 7-8, 10, 12-13, 16

"The Train Station" (Coover) **15**:48

"The Traitor" (Maugham) **8**:368, 377

"Traitors" (Lessing) **6**:217

"Traktat o manekinach" ("Tailors' Dummies "; "Treatise on Tailors' Dummies") (Schulz) **13**:328-30, 333, 335, 338

La trama celeste (*The Celestial Plot*) (Bioy Casares) **17**:54, 59, 61, 75, 85, 87

"The Tramp" (O'Flaherty) **6**:275, 285

"La transaction" (Balzac) **5**:24

"Transaction" (O'Hara) **15**:257-58

"Transcendent Horror" (Ligotti) **16**:287

"The Transformation of Martin Burney" (Henry) **5**:197

"The Transformation of Vincent Scoville" (Oates) **6**:230

"Transience" (Clarke) **3**:127, 135, 142

"Transients in Arcadia" (Henry) **5**:158, 189

"Transit Bed" (Calvino) **3**:112

"Transit of Earth" (Clarke) **3**:147

The Transposed Heads (Mann)
See *Die vertauschten Köpfe*

"Trapped" (O'Flaherty) **6**:273, 276, 279, 283

"Trastevere" (Lavin) **4**:183, 185

Traumnovelle ("Rhapsody: A Dream Novel") (Schnitzler) **15**:344, 353-54, 366, 372, 374

"Traveller" (Gilchrist) **14**:150-51

Traveller's Samples (O'Connor) **5**:371

"Travelling Abroad" (Dickens) **17**:123

"The Travelling Companion" (Andersen) **6**:18-19, 30-1, 35

"Travel Notes" (Bulgakov) **18**:90

"A Travel Piece" (Atwood) **2**:3-4, 6-7, 10, 12, 15-16

"Treason" (Babel) **16**:27-8, 51

"The Treasure" (Maugham) **8**:380

"Treasure of Abbot Thomas" (James) **16**:225, 228-29, 232-34, 236, 244, 251-53, 255-57

"The Treasure of Franchard" (Stevenson) **11**:268-69, 281, 284

"The Treasure of Youth" (Cortazar)
See "El tesoro de la juventud"

"The Treasure Ship" (Saki) **12**:295, 308, 312

"A Treatise on Housing" (Bulgakov) **18**:92

"Treatise on Tailors' Dummies" (Schulz)
See "Traktat o manekinach"

"The Tree" (de la Mare) **14**:66, 85-6

"The Tree" (Thomas) **3**:399, 402, 408-09

"A Tree. A Rock. A Cloud." (McCullers) **9**:322-23, 327, 329-30, 332, 341, 345-46, 353-54

"The Tree Fort" (Gilchrist) **14**:161-62

"The Tree of Justice" (Kipling) **5**:292

"The Tree of Knowledge" (James) **8**:301

"The Tree of Life" (Kawabata)
See "Inochi no Ki"

"A Tree of Night" (Capote) **2**:61-3, 66, 69, 72-5

A Tree of Night, and Other Stories (Capote) **2**:61-4, 72, 74, 83

"The Trees of Pride" (Chesterton) **1**:122

The Trembling of a Leaf (Maugham) **8**:370-72

Tres novelas ejemplares y un prólogo (*Three Exemplary Novels and a Prologue*) (Unamuno) **11**:313, 317, 323, 331, 345, 348

"Trial by Combat" (Jackson) **9**:250

"The Trial of the Old Watchdog" (Thurber) **1**:426

"The Trial Sermon on Bull-Skin" (Dunbar) **8**:118, 121, 127, 136

Tribulat Bonhomet (Villiers de l'Isle Adam) **14**:378-79

"Tribuneaux rustiques" (Maupassant) **1**:259, 286

"Trick of Nature" (Bulgakov) **18**:90

"A Trillion Feet of Gas" (Updike) **13**:355

"The Trimmed Lamp" (Henry) **5**:171, 185, 198

The Trimmed Lamp (Henry) **5**:155, 192

"The Trinket Box" (Lessing) **6**:196-97, 212-20

"The Trip" (O'Hara) **15**:252, 261, 280-81

"A Trip to Chancellorsville" (Fitzgerald) **6**:47

"A Trip to the Head" (Le Guin) **12**:232-33

Tri smerti (*Three Deaths*) (Tolstoy) **9**:382-83, 389-90

Tristan (Mann) **5**:307-11, 321, 323-24

"The Triumph of Night" (Wharton) **6**:418, 428, 431-32

"The Triumph of the Egg" ("The Egg"; "The Egg") (Anderson) **1**:20, 23, 27, 30, 34, 37-8, 40, 47, 52, 54-5

"The Triumphs of a Taxidermist" (Wells) **6**:380, 384, 388

Trois contes: Un coeur simple; La légende de Saint-Julien l'hospitalier; Hérodias (*Three Tales*) (Flaubert) **11**:37, 52-3, 56-7, 62-6, 70-1, 76-84, 87, 96-9, 101

"Les trois filles de Milton" (Villiers de l'Isle Adam)
See "Les filles de Milton"

The Troll Garden (Cather) **2**:90, 93, 96, 103, 113

"Trotsky's Garden" (Michaels) **16**:307, 309

"The Trouble" (Powers) **4**:368-69, 372

"The Trouble about Sophiny" (Dunbar) **8**:122

"The Trouble of Marcie Flint" (Cheever) **1**:90

"The Troubles of Dr. Thoss" (Ligotti) **16**:261, 263, 271, 274, 278, 283, 289

"The Troublesome Grandfathers" (Zoshchenko) **15**:388

"The Trouble with Stamps" (Bulgakov) **18**:89

"Trouble with the Angels" (Hughes) **6**:112, 118-19, 122, 131

"Trouble with the Natives" (Clarke) **3**:124, 149

"The Trousers" (Dunbar) **8**:122

"The Trout" (O'Faolain) **13**:297

"The Truant" (Irving) **2**:265

"Trucks" (King) **17**:261-62

"True Thomas" (Benet) **10**:148

"The Trumpet" (de la Mare) **14**:88-90, 93

"Trumpeter" (Gardner) **7**:225-26, 233, 235

"Trust" (London) **4**:265

"The Trustfulness of Polly" (Dunbar) **8**:122, 128, 147

Trust Me (Updike) **13**:401-02, 409

"The Truth About Pyecraft" (Wells) **6**:360, 392, 404

"The Tryst" (Oates) **6**:251-52

"The Tryst" (Turgenev) **7**:342-43

"A Tryst at an Ancient Earthwork" (Hardy) **2**:210, 214-15

"The Tsalal" (Ligotti) **16**:292, 295, 297

"Tubal-Cain Forges A Star" (Garcia Marquez)
See "Tubal-Caín forja una estrella"

"Tubal-Caín forja una estrella" ("Tubal-Cain Forges A Star") (Garcia Marquez) **8**:154, 156

"The Tuesday Afternoon Siesta" (Garcia Marquez)
See "Tuesday Siesta"

"Tuesday Night" (Beattie) **11**:14, 16

"Tuesday Siesta" ("The Tuesday Afternoon Siesta") (Garcia Marquez) **8**:183, 185

"Le tueur de cygnes" ("Un mécène") (Villiers de l'Isle Adam) **14**:397

"The Tuggses at Ramsgate" (Dickens) **17**:117, 138

"Tulip" (Hammett) **17**:201, 203, 206, 227, 229

"Tuman" (Bunin) **5**:98

"Tu más profunda piel" ("Your Most Profound Skin") (Cortazar) **7**:95

"A Turkey Hunt" (Chopin) **8**:88

"The Turkey Season" (Munro) **3**:346

"Turned" (Gilman) **13**:126, 141

"The Turn of the Screw" (Oates) **6**:225

The Turn of the Screw (James) **8**:271-76, 283, 291-96, 298, 316, 318, 320, 325-26

"The Turtles of Tasman" (London) **4**:255-56, 266

"Tutto in un punto" (Calvino) **3**:92

"The Twelve Mortal Men" (McCullers) **9**:322, 338

"Twelve O'Clock" (Crane) **7**:108

Twelve Stories and a Dream (Wells) **6**:366-67, 380, 391, 400

Twenty-Five Short Stories by Stephen Vincent Benét (Benet) **10**:143, 156

"Twenty-Four Hours in a Strange Diocese" (Powers) **4**:380

"Twenty-Nine Inventions" (Oates) **6**:225

Twice-Told Tales (Hawthorne) **3**:154-55, 157-61, 180, 184-85, 190

"Twin Beds in Rome" (Updike) **13**:386

"The Twinkle in His Eye" (O'Hara) **15**:287, 291

"The Twins" (Spark) **10**:350, 352, 354, 356, 366

Twixt Land and Sea: Tales (Conrad) **9**:141, 148

"Two" (Singer) **3**:381

"Two Augurs" (Villiers de l'Isle Adam)
See "Deux augures"

"Two Blue Birds" (Lawrence) **4**:220

"Two Boys at Grinder Brothers" (Lawson) **18**:202

"The Two Brothers" (Hesse) **9**:241-43

"The Two Brothers" (Pritchett) **14**:280, 285-86, 298, 305

"Two Colonials" (Calisher) **15**:4, 14

"Two Corpses Go Dancing" (Singer) **3**:370

"Two Doctors" (James) **16**:245, 256

"Two Dogs and a Fence" (Lawson) **18**:233, 244

"Two Families" (Lish) **18**:268

"The Two Flags" (Levi) **12**:276

"Two Friends" (Cather) **2**:100, 109, 115, 117-18

Two Friends (Turgenev) **7**:327

"Two Gallants" (Joyce) **3**:200-01, 205-06, 209, 214, 220-21, 225, 231-34, 237, 246

Two Hussars (Tolstoy) **9**:376, 389

"Two Ivans" (Babel) **16**:50, 56, 58

"The Two Ivans" (Gogol)
See "The Tale of How Ivan Ivanovich Quarrelled with Ivan Nikiforovich"

"The Two Kings and Their Two Labyrinths" (Borges) **4**:28, 30-1, 35

"Two Ladies in Retirement" (Taylor) **10**:379-80, 382, 384, 392, 418

"Two Lovely Beasts" (O'Flaherty) **6**:269-70, 274, 281-82, 285

Two Lovely Beasts, and Other Stories (O'Flaherty) **6**:262-63, 265, 276, 278, 281-83, 285

The Two Magics (James) **8**:296

"The Two Maidens" (Cervantes)
See "Las dos doncelas"

"Two Markets" (Singer) **3**:377

"Two Meditations" (Barth) **10**:42, 54-5, 75, 89-90, 98, 100

Two Memorable Fantasies (Bioy Casares) **17**:48

Two Mothers (Unamuno)
See *Dos madres*

"Two Old Lovers" (Freeman) **1**:197, 200-01

"Two Old Men" (Tolstoy) **9**:377, 387

"Two Old-Timers" (Fitzgerald) **6**:71

"Two Portraits" (Chopin) **8**:72, 87, 98, 110

"Two Potters" (Lessing) **6**:200

"Two Ships" (Boyle) **16**:145-46

"Two Soldiers" (Faulkner) **1**:151

"Two Summers and Two Souls" (Chopin) **8**:99

Two Symphonies (*Symphonies*) (Gide) **13**:42-3

"The Two Temples" (Melville) **1**:303, 323

"Two Thanksgiving Day Gentlemen" (Henry) **5**:187

"Two Views of a Cheap Theatre" (Dickens) **17**:123

"Two White Beans" (Benet) **10**:149

"Two Worlds" (Maclean) **13**:278

"Two Wrongs" (Fitzgerald) **6**:51, 60, 61

Typhoon (Conrad) **9**:141, 143-45, 147, 151-52, 157, 160, 163, 166, 186-88

"The Tyrant" (O'Flaherty) **6**:264

"Tyrants Destroyed" (Nabokov) **11**:126

Tyrants Destroyed, and Other Stories (Nabokov) **11**:122-24

"Le tzar et les grands-ducs" (Villiers de l'Isle Adam) **14**:396

"t zero" (Calvino) **3**:93

t zero (Calvino)
See *Ti con zero*

"The Ugly Duckling" ("The Duckling") (Andersen) **6**:5, 7, 10-11, 18, 30-1, 35, 40

"Uglypuss" (Atwood) **2**:18, 22

"Uisce faoi Dhraíocht" (O'Flaherty) **6**:287-88

"U istoka dnej" (Bunin) **5**:98-9

"Ukridge Sees Her Through" (Wodehouse) **2**:354

"The Ultimate City" (Ballard) **1**:72, 74, 83-4

"The Ultimate Melody" (Clarke) **3**:133-34

"The Ultimate Safari" (Gordimer) **17**:178, 180, 184-85, 188, 191

"Ultima Thule" (Nabokov) **11**:117

Ultimo round (*Last Round*) (Cortazar) **7**:53, 70-1, 80, 91, 94-5

"El último viaje del buque fantasma" ("The Last Voyage of the Ghost Ship") (Garcia Marquez) **8**:154, 160, 167-68, 170-72, 186

Ultimo viene il corvo (Calvino) **3**:106, 116

"Ultor de Lacy" (Le Fanu) **14**:252

"Umney's Last Case" (King) **17**:295

"Unapproved Route" (O'Connor) **5**:371

"Uncertain Flowering" (Laurence) **7**:271-72

"Unclean" (O'Flaherty) **6**:259

"Uncle Anne" (Boyle) **5**:54

"Uncle Jim and Uncle Billy" (Harte) **8**:227, 244

"Uncle Otto's Truck" (King) **17**:274

"Uncle Peter's House" (Chesnutt) **7**:12, 27

"Uncles" (Taylor) **10**:379

"Uncle's Dream" (Dostoevsky) 2:164, 172, 184

"Uncle Simon's Sunday Out" (Dunbar) 8:122, 127, 144

Uncle Tom's Children (Wright) 2:360-61, 363, 365-68, 370-71, 373-75, 379, 381-84, 386-88

"Uncle Valentine" (Cather) 2:98, 113-15

"Uncle Wellington's Wives" (Chesnutt) 7:3, 16, 23, 28-9, 33, 37

"Uncle Wiggily in Connecticut" (Salinger) 2:290, 292, 295, 299, 305-06, 313-14

"Uncle Willy" (Faulkner) 1:151

The Uncollected Short Stories (Jewett) 6:156, 166

The Uncollected Wodehouse (Wodehouse) 2:343

The Uncommercial Traveller (Dickens) 17:123

"The Uncommon Prayer-Book" (James) 16:229-32, 239, 241, 244-45

"The Unconquered" (Maugham) 8:380

"Uncovenanted Mercies" (Kipling) 5:271, 283

"The Undefeated" (Hemingway) 1:209, 216, 218-19, 224, 230, 234

"Under a Glass Bell" (Nin) 10:299, 303-04

Under a Glass Bell (Nin) 10:299-300, 302-06

"Under a Glass Sky" (Bulgakov) 18:90

"Under Glass" (Atwood) 2:3, 6, 10, 13, 16

"The Underground" (Dostoevsky) 2:187

"Undertakers" (Kipling) 5:293

"Under the Boardwalk" (Phillips) 16:328-29

"Under the Deck Awnings" (London) 4:291

Under the Deodars (Kipling) 5:265

"Under the Jaguar Sun" (Calvino) 3:118-19

Under the Jaguar Sun (Calvino)
    See *Sotto il sole giaguro*

"Under the Knife" (Singer) 3:362

"Under the Knife" (Wells) 6:360, 389, 393-94, 405

"Under the Lion's Paw" (Garland) 18:142, 148, 150, 154-55, 159, 163, 167-69, 172, 176, 182-83

"Under the Microscope" (Updike) 13:360, 387

"Under the Rose" (Pynchon) 14:308, 331, 334-38, 341-42, 344, 347-48

"Under the Sky" (Bowles) 3:59, 61-2, 67, 79

"Under the Willow-Tree" (Andersen) 6:4

"Underwater" (Bioy Casares) 17:94, 96

Undiscovered Country: The New Zealand Stories of Katherine Mansfield (Mansfield) 9:281

"The Undismayed Operator" (Bulgakov) 18:89

"Unearthing Suite" (Atwood) 2:17, 22

"The Unexpected" (Chopin) 8:72, 100

"The Unexpected" (London) 4:253, 260-62

"An Unfinished Collection" (Wodehouse) 2:343

"An Unfinished Love Story" (Lawson) 18:201, 248, 250-51

"An Unfinished Story" (Henry) 5:163, 171, 178-79, 182, 185

"The Unfortunate" (Turgenev)
    See "Neschastnaya"

"An Unhappy Girl" (Turgenev)
    See "Neschastnaya"

"Unholy Living and Half Dying" (O'Faolain) 13:301, 305

"The Unicorn in the Garden" (Thurber) 1:427-28, 431

"The Union Buries Its Dead" (Lawson) 18:201-02, 206, 211, 213, 218, 220-21, 233-35, 237-38, 241, 243, 259, 261

Unions (Musil)
    See *Vereinigungen*

A Universal History of Infamy (Borges)
    See *Historia universal de la infamia*

"The Unkindest Blow" (Saki) 12:295-96

"The Unknown Masterpiece" (Balzac)
    See "Le chef d'oeuvre inconnu"

"The Unknown Quantity" (Henry) 5:197

"The Unknown Woman" (Villiers de l'Isle Adam)
    See "L'inconnue"

"The Unknown Woman of the Seine" (Nin) 10:304

"Unlighted Lamps" (Anderson) 1:27, 30, 39, 46-7, 53, 55

"An Unmarried Man's Summer" (Gallant) 5:122, 130-31

"The Unnameable" (Lovecraft) 3:262, 276, 293-94

"The Unnatural Mother" (Gilman) 13:126

"Unpaid Consultant" (Vonnegut) 8:436

"The Unparalleled Adventure of One Hans Pfaall" (Poe) 1:400, 402, 406

"The Unparalleled Invasion" (London) 4:255

"An Unpleasant Predicament" (Dostoevsky) 2:166, 184

"Unprofessional" (Kipling) 5:285

"Unready to Wear" (Vonnegut) 8:434

"The Unrest Cure" (Saki) 12:287, 300, 324, 326

"The Unseen" (Singer) 3:358, 362, 383-84

"Unser Karl" (Harte) 8:220

Unspeakable Practices, Unnatural Acts (Barthelme) 2:29-31, 35, 37-8, 51

"Unstuck" (Updike) 13:404, 409

"Untitled Piece" (McCullers) 9:343, 345, 356-57

"The Untold Lie" (Anderson) 1:21, 34, 39, 41-2, 44, 52

"'Unused'" (Anderson) 1:23, 27, 30, 39-40, 46-7, 53, 55

The Unvanquished (Faulkner) 1:151, 170, 177, 180

"The Unvexed Isles" (Warren) 4:387, 389-90, 395, 400

"Unwelcome Words" (Bowles) 3:85-6

Unwelcome Words: Seven Stories (Bowles) 3:85

"The Unworthy Friend" (Borges) 4:18

"An Unwritten Novel" (Woolf) 7:368, 371-72, 375-76, 378, 382, 388, 392, 397-99, 405, 408-09

"Uomo nei gerbidi" (Calvino) 3:96

"Up, Aloft in the Air" (Barthelme) 2:38

"Up Among the Eagles" ("Where the Eagles Dwell") (Valenzuela) 14:359, 361, 366

Up Among the Eagles (Valenzuela)
    See *Donde viven las águilas*

"Up in Michigan" (Hemingway) 1:207, 219

"Upon the Sweeping Flood" (Oates) 6:224-25

Upon the Sweeping Flood, and Other Stories (Oates) 6:224-25

"Uprooted" (Chekhov) 2:130

"Uprooted" (O'Connor) 5:369, 371, 375-77, 383, 397

"Uprooted" (Suckow) 18:394, 399-400, 405, 407-08, 415

"Up the Bare Stairs" (O'Faolain) 13:300, 302, 304, 306-07

"Up the Coulée" (Garland) 18:142, 144, 148, 150, 154-56, 158-59, 161, 163, 168-70, 172, 175-76, 182, 193

"The Upturned Face" (Crane) 7:109, 143-45

"Uriah's Son" (Benet) 10:146

Urien's Voyage (Gide)
    See *Le voyage d'Urien*

"Das Urteil" ("The Judgment") (Kafka) 5:225-26, 228-29, 232, 240, 243-45, 252-55

"The Used-Boy Raisers" (Paley) 8:399, 406-07

USFS 1919: The Ranger, The Cook and a Hole in the Sky (Maclean) 13:260, 270-71

"Usurpation (Other People's Stories)" ("Other People's Stories") (Ozick) 15:302, 305, 311, 315-17, 326

"Vacation Time" (Boyle) 5:54

The Vagabond (Colette)
    See *La vagabonde*

La vagabonde (*The Vagabond*) (Colette) 10:257, 272-73, 291

"The Valet" (Barnes) 3:22-4

"The Valiant Woman" (Powers) 4:380-81, 383

"The Valley Between" (Marshall) 3:303, 308-09, 312, 315, 317

"The Valley of Childish Things" (Wharton) 6:427

The Valley of the Moon (London) 4:254

"The Valley of the Shadow" (Kipling) 5:261

"The Valley of the Spiders" (Wells) 6:361

"Vampirism" (Hoffmann)
    See "Der Vampyrismus"

"Eine Vampyrgeschichte" (Hoffmann)
    See "Der Vampyrismus"

"Der Vampyrismus" ("Comte Hippolit"; "Cyprian's Narrative"; "Die Hyänen"; "The Hyena"; "Tale of a Vampire"; "Vampirism"; "Eine Vampyrgeschichte") (Hoffmann) 13:186, 215, 228, 230

"Vanadium" (Levi) 12:256, 258, 265-67

"The Vane Sisters" (Nabokov) 11:116, 122-23, 125, 144

"Van Gogh's Room at Arles" (Elkin) 12:119-20

"The Vanishing of Vaudrey" (Chesterton) 1:131

"The Vanishing Prince" (Chesterton) 1:122

"Vanity and Some Sables" (Henry) 5:187

"Vánka" (Chekhov) 2:130

"Vanvild Kava" (Singer) 3:383

"Varieties of Exile" (Gallant) 5:134-35, 143

"Le vase étrusque" (Merimee) 7:278, 280-81, 283, 286-91, 300, 304

"Vastarien" (Ligotti) 16:263-64, 267, 269, 274, 276-80, 283, 285-89, 294

"Vaster than Empires and More Slow" (Le Guin) 12:208-10, 216, 231-33

"The Vats" (de la Mare) 14:66, 82, 90

"Večer nakanune Ivana Kupala" ("St. John's Eve") (Gogol) 4:88, 119-21

Vechera ná khutore bliz Dikanki (*Evenings on a Farm near Dikanka*) (Gogol) 4:85-7, 98, 117

Vechny muzh (*The Eternal Husband*) (Dostoevsky) 2:166-67, 175-77, 184-85

"Velga" (Bunin) 5:98

"Vendée" (Faulkner) 1:171

"Une vendetta" (Maupassant) 1:277

"La vendetta revenge" ("Revenge") (Balzac) 5:4, 22, 29, 31

"The Venerated Bones" (Lagerkvist) 12:195

"La vengeance d'une femme" ("A Woman's Revenge") (Barbey d'Aurevilly) **17**:11, 15, 18-21, 33-4, 36-7, 44
"The Vengeance of 3902090" (Thurber) **1**:419
"The Venturers" (Henry) **5**:159, 190-91
"Venus, Cupid, Folly, and Time" (Taylor) **10**:391, 407, 409, 419
"La Vénus d'Ille" ("The Venus of Ille") (Merimee) **7**:276, 279-80, 283-86, 288, 290, 293-95, 297, 301, 306
"The Venus of Ille" (Merimee)
　See "La Vénus d'Ille"
"Véra" (Villiers de l'Isle Adam) **14**:377, 379, 381-82, 384, 387, 390, 396, 398, 403, 408
"Verano" ("Summer") (Cortazar) **7**:61-3
"The Verdict" (Wharton) **6**:435
El verdugo (Balzac) **5**:21, 31
Vereinigungen (*Unions*) (Musil) **18**:288, 290-93, 317
"Das Verlorene Spiegelbild" ("The Lost Reflection") (Hoffmann) **13**:183, 200
Vermilion Sands (Ballard) **1**:78
"Versamina" (Levi) **12**:278-79
Die Versuchung der Stillen Veronika (*The Enchanted House*; *The Temptation of Quiet Veronica*; *The Temptation of the Silent Veronika*; *Das verzauberte Haus*) (Musil) **18**:288-89, 291-93, 302, 317, 320-22
Die vertauschten Köpfe (*The Transposed Heads*) (Mann) **5**:312-13, 315, 323, 326
Die verwandlung (*The Metamorphosis*) (Kafka) **5**:210-13, 215, 217-20, 224-25, 231, 234, 239-40, 245, 252
Very Far Away from Anywhere Else (*Far Away from Anywhere Else*; *A Very Long Way from Anywhere Else*) (Le Guin) **12**:231, 241
"A Very Fine Fiddle" (Chopin) **8**:88, 103
Very Good, Jeeves (Wodehouse) **2**:346
"The Very Image" (Villiers de l'Isle Adam)
　See "A s'y méprendre"
A Very Long Way from Anywhere Else (Le Guin)
　See *Very Far Away from Anywhere Else*
"The Very Proper Gander" (Thurber) **1**:431
Das verzauberte Haus (Musil)
　See *Die Versuchung der Stillen Veronika*
"Veselyi dvor" (Bunin) **5**:87
Veshnie vody (*Spring Freshets*; *Spring-Torrents*; *The Torrents of Spring*) (Turgenev) **7**:316-17, 320-21, 324-25, 327-29, 334, 336-38, 357-58, 361-62
"The Vessel of Wrath" (Maugham) **8**:375, 378
"Vesti iz rodiny" (Bunin) **5**:98
"A Veteran Falls" (Hughes) **6**:122
"Veteran of the Private Evacuations" (Ballard) **1**:70
"Les veuves" ("Widows") (Baudelaire) **18**:4, 9, 17, 32, 39, 60
"The Vice-Consul" (Pritchett) **14**:273
"La victima de Tado Limardo" ("Tadeo Limardo's Victim") (Bioy Casares) **17**:70, 73
"Victor Blue" (Beattie) **11**:15, 18, 21
"Victoria Kazimirovna" (Zoshchenko) **15**:400-01
"Victory" (Faulkner) **1**:148
"The Victory Burlesk" (Atwood) **2**:19
Victory over Japan (Gilchrist) **14**:152-55, 157-59, 162-63
"La vie boheme" (Gordimer) **17**:167
"The Viennese Opera Ball" (Barthelme) **2**:28

"Le vieux saltimbanque" (Baudelaire) **18**:4-5, 15, 17-18, 27-32
"A View from a Hill" (James) **16**:231, 233, 237, 240, 244
"A View of the Woods" (O'Connor) **1**:342-45, 356
"A View of the Yasukuni Festival" (Kawabata)
　See "Shōkonsai Ikkei"
"Views of My Father Weeping" (Barthelme) **2**:31, 42, 46, 48, 55
"Vigilante" (Steinbeck) **11**:208, 225, 232-33, 241-42, 244
"A Vignette" (James) **16**:251, 254
The Viking Portable Library Dorothy Parker (Parker) **2**:276, 278
"The Village" (Dixon) **16**:217
"A Village Lear" (Turgenev)
　See "Stepnoy Korol 'Lir"
The Village of Stepanchikovo (Dostoevsky)
　See *The Friend of the Family*
"A Village Singer" (Freeman) **1**:197, 200
"The Village That Voted the Earth Was Flat" (Kipling) **5**:277, 280, 282
"Villa Violetta" (Lavin) **4**:183, 185
"The Vindication of Jared Hargot" (Dunbar) **8**:138
"Viney's Free Papers" (Dunbar) **8**:122, 127, 131, 133, 144
"A Vintage Thunderbird" (Beattie) **11**:4-5, 17, 29
Vinter-Eventyr (Dinesen)
　See *Winter's Tales*
"The Virgin and the Gipsy" (Lawrence) **4**:205-06
"Virginia and Paul" (Villiers de l'Isle Adam)
　See "Virginie et Paul"
"Virginie et Paul" ("Virginia and Paul") (Villiers de l'Isle Adam) **14**:379, 381, 384, 386-87, 390, 394, 396
"Virgin Violeta" (Porter) **4**:341, 350
"Virility" (Ozick) **15**:298, 300, 313
"Virtue" (Maugham) **8**:378
"A Virtuoso's Collection" (Hawthorne) **3**:171
"Virus X" (Gallant) **5**:139
Il visconte dimezzato (*The Cloven Viscount*; *The Nonexistent Knight and the Cloven Viscount*) (Calvino) **3**:90-1, 94, 99, 106, 117
Vision de Babouc (Voltaire) **12**:340-1
La vision de Babouc (Voltaire) **12**:342
"La vision de Charles XI" (Merimee) **7**:287, 289
"A Vision of Judgment" (Wells) **6**:360, 391
"The Vision of the Fountain" (Hawthorne) **3**:178, 182
"A Vision of the World" (Cheever) **1**:93-6, 105
"The Vision of Tom Chuff" (Le Fanu) **14**:220, 223
"Visions" (Turgenev) **7**:315
"Una visita al viejo poeta" (Unamuno) **11**:312
"Visitation" (Schulz) **13**:333, 339
"The Visiting of Mother Danbury" (Dunbar) **8**:127
"A Visit Next Door" (Jewett) **6**:158
"A Visit of Charity" (Welty) **1**:470
"A Visit of Condolence" (Lawson) **18**:201
"The Visitor" (Bowen) **3**:40
"The Visitor" (Thomas) **3**:400, 407, 409
"Visitors" (Barthelme) **2**:56
"A Visit to America" (Thomas) **3**:393

"A Visit to Avoyelles" (Chopin) **8**:72, 84
"A Visit to Grandpa's" (Thomas) **3**:397, 402, 405, 410, 412
"A Visit to Newgate" (Dickens) **17**:110, 116-17, 121
"A Visit to the Cemetery" (Lavin) **4**:164-66, 168-69
"The Visit to the Museum" ("Poseshchenie muzeia") (Nabokov) **11**:117, 145, 147, 152
"Vitamins" (Carver) **8**:26, 32
"La viuda de Montiel" (Garcia Marquez) **8**:187-90
"Viva la introyección!" (Unamuno) **11**:312
"Viy" (Gogol) **4**:82, 86, 102-03
"Vizitnye kartochki" ("Calling Cards") (Bunin) **5**:114
"Vlemk the Box-Painter" (Gardner) **7**:223-26, 238-41
"A Vocation and a Voice" (Chopin) **8**:93, 97, 99
"Les vocations" (Baudelaire) **18**:5
"The Voice" (Nin) **10**:300-01, 307-11, 314-15, 317, 322-23
"The Voice" (Pritchett) **14**:271, 286
"The Voice in the Bones" (Ligotti) **16**:271, 274, 280, 288, 296, 297
"The Voice of the City" (Henry) **5**:171, 191, 194
The Voice of the City (Henry) **5**:155, 192
"The Voice of the Turtle" (Maugham) **8**:379
Voices at Play (Spark) **10**:353, 355, 359
"Voices from the Moon" (Dubus) **15**:94, 96, 100-01
Voices From the Moon (Dubus) **15**:81-3, 85-6, 89-96, 98
"Voices Lost in the Snow" (Gallant) **5**:135, 139
"The Voices of Adamo" (Laurence) **7**:245, 249-50
"The Voices of Time" (Ballard) **1**:71, 80
"Vollendung der Liebe" (*The Completion of Love*; *The Perfecting of a Love*) (Musil) **18**:288-93, 317-20
"Von Kempelen and His Discovery" (Poe) **1**:402
"Vor dem gesetz" ("Before the Law") (Kafka) **5**:254
"Voron" ("The Raven") (Bunin) **5**:113
"Vox populi" (Villiers de l'Isle Adam) **14**:381-82, 386, 394-96
"The Voyage" (Mansfield) **9**:278, 282, 303-04
Le voyage d'Urien (*Urien's Voyage*) (Gide) **13**:57-61, 63, 72
Voyage en Orient (Nerval) **18**:328, 334, 336, 346-47, 366
"The Voyage to Rosewood" (Oates) **6**:231
Les vrilles de la vigne (Colette) **10**:261, 263
La vuelta al día en ochenta mundos (*Around the Day in Eighty Worlds*) (Cortazar) **7**:53, 61, 91, 94
"A Wagner Matinée" (Cather) **2**:90-1, 96, 103, 105, 108
"Wahiah—A Spartan Mother" (Garland) **18**:147, 178
"A Waif of the Plains" (Harte) **8**:222, 251
"Wailing Well" (James) **16**:242, 244, 251
"Waiting" (Beattie) **11**:13, 22
"The Waiting" (Borges)
　See "La espera"
"Waiting" (Dubus) **15**:89
"Waiting" (Oates) **6**:232

Waiting for Winter (O'Hara) **15**:276-79, 283-86

"The Waiting Grounds" (Ballard) **1**:68, 76

"The Waiting Supper" (Hardy) **2**:211, 215-16, 219, 223

"Waiting Up" (Updike) **13**:387

"Wakefield" (Hawthorne) **3**:154, 159, 161-62, 178, 189, 191

"Waldemar Daa and His Daughters" (Andersen)
See "The Wind Tells of Valdemar Daae and His Daughters"

"Walker Brothers Cowboy" (Munro) **3**:321, 329, 343, 347

"A Walking Delegate" (Kipling) **5**:279

"Walking on Water" (Munro) **3**:331, 346

"Walking Out" (Beckett) **16**:100

"A Walk in the Dark" (Clarke) **3**:124, 147-49

"A Walk in the Woods" (Bowen) **3**:54

"Die Walkuere" (Mann) **5**:310

"Walled City" (Oates) **6**:251-52

"A Walled Garden" (Taylor) **10**:382, 410

"The Wallet" (Updike) **13**:402

"The Wall of Darkness" (Clarke) **3**:125, 129, 147

"The Walls of Jericho" (Dunbar) **8**:122, 136, 149

"Wally Whistles Dixie" (Beattie) **11**:16, 23, 28

Wälsungenblut ("Blood of the Walsungs") (Mann) **5**:310-11, 321, 323, 344

"Walter Briggs" (Updike) **13**:390, 400

"Walter Kömpff" (Hesse) **9**:235

"Walter T. Carriman" (O'Hara) **15**:264, 269

"The Waltz" (Parker) **2**:274, 281, 283, 285-86

"Wanda's" (Beattie) **11**:16

"Wanderers" (Suckow) **18**:389, 415

"The Wanderers" (Welty) **1**:479, 493

"A Wand'ring Minstrel, I" (Gordimer) **17**:153

"Wan Lee, the Pagan" (Harte) **8**:249

"Wants" (Paley) **8**:397, 399, 416

"Wapping Workhouse" (Dickens) **17**:123

"The Warden" (Gardner) **7**:213-14, 218, 222, 231

"Ward No. Six" (Chekhov) **2**:126, 131-32, 143, 152, 157

"A Ward of Colonel Starbottle's" (Harte) **8**:249

"The Wardrobe" (Mann) **5**:330

"The Warehouse" (Singer) **3**:358, 360

"The Wares in Rio" (Ellison) **14**:146

"The War in the Bathroom" (Atwood) **2**:4, 6-8, 10

"A Warning to the Curious" (James) **16**:232-33, 236-37, 252, 256

A Warning to the Curious (James) **16**:238, 251, 255

"Was" (Faulkner) **1**:148, 173-74, 182

"Wash" (Faulkner) **1**:166, 180

Waste of Timelessness, and Other Early Stories (Nin) **10**:305-06

"The Watch" (Dixon) **16**:200, 211

"The Watch" (Turgenev)
See "Chasy"

"The Watcher" (Le Fanu)
See "The Familiar"

"A Watcher by the Dead" (Bierce) **9**:49

"A Watcher of the Dead" (Gordimer) **17**:151-52

"The Watchers" (Calisher) **15**:5, 17-18

"Watch This Space" (Clarke) **3**:133

"The Water Baby" (London) **4**:270

"The Watercress Girl" (Bates) **10**:120, 131-33

The Watercress Girl, And Other Stories (Bates) **10**:120-21

"The Waterfall" (Gordon) **15**:142

"The Water Hen" (O'Flaherty) **6**:268

The Water Is Wide (Le Guin) **12**:231

"Water-Message" (Barth) **10**:41-3, 46-8, 54, 56, 60, 63, 67, 79, 84, 87, 89, 91, 95, 97-101

"The Water of Izli" (Bowles) **3**:68

"Water Them Geraniums" (Lawson) **18**:202, 204, 220-23, 226-27, 229-30, 232, 234, 262

"The Wave" (O'Flaherty) **6**:261, 264, 268, 285

"The Wave of Osiris" (Lagerkvist) **12**:181

"The Way Back" (Grau) **15**:148

"The Way of a Woman" (Dunbar) **8**:122, 128, 136

"The Way of the Cross" (du Maurier) **18**:129, 137

"The Way of the World" (Cather) **2**:102-03

Wayside Courtships (Garland) **18**:160

"The Wayside Inn" (Turgenev)
See "The Inn"

The Ways of White Folks (Hughes) **6**:109-10, 121-23, 126-29, 131-34, 136-38, 140-42

The Way Some People Live (Cheever) **1**:87-8, 92, 98-100

"The Way to Majorca" (O'Hara) **15**:277, 284

"The Way to the Churchyard" (Mann) **5**:322, 328-29, 334-37

"The Way to the Dairy" (Saki) **12**:314

"A Way You'll Never Be" (Hemingway) **1**:218, 245, 247

"The Weaker Sex" (Kawabata)
See "Yowaki Utsuwa"

"A Weak Heart" (Dostoevsky)
See "A Faint Heart"

"Weak Heart" (Mansfield) **9**:282

"We Are Norsemen" (Boyle) **16**:142-43, 151

"A Weary Hour" (Mann) **5**:330

"The Weaver and the Worm" (Thurber) **1**:428

"The Web of Circumstance" (Chesnutt) **7**:3, 16, 19, 22-3, 29-33, 37

"The Wedding" (Bates) **10**:113

"The Wedding" (O'Flaherty) **6**:260, 265, 277-78, 285

"The Wedding" (Pritchett) **14**:281, 299

"Wedding Day" (Boyle) **5**:54-5, 65, 70-2

Wedding Day, and Other Stories (Boyle) **5**:54

"A Wedding in Brownsville" (Singer) **3**:360, 363, 376

"The Wedding Knell" (Hawthorne) **3**:154

"Wedding Pictures" (Phillips) **16**:325, 328

"Wednesday's Child" (Oates) **6**:225

"We Don't Live Here Anymore" (Dubus) **15**:69-71, 73, 76, 82, 87, 91, 98

We Don't Live Here Anymore (Dubus) **15**:81, 91-3

"We Drink the Wine in France" (Walker) **5**:401

"Weekend" (Beattie) **11**:6-7, 14, 17, 29

"A Week in the Country" (Le Guin) **12**:210, 213, 215-16, 245, 249

"Weekly Serial" (Coover) **15**:39

"Wee Willie Winkie" (Kipling) **5**:269

Weg nach Innen (*Road to Within*) (Hesse) **9**:211

Weird Women (Barbey d'Aurevilly)
See *Les diaboliques*

"Weir of Hermiston" (Stevenson) **11**:296, 299-300

Weir of Hermiston (Stevenson) **11**:268-69, 282, 286

"The Welcome Table" (Walker) **5**:401, 403, 406, 410-11

Welcome to the Monkey House: A Collection of Short Works (Vonnegut) **8**:424-30, 435-36

"We'll Have Fun" (O'Hara) **15**:286

"The Well of Days" (Bunin) **5**:100

"We Love Glenda So Much" (Cortazar) **7**:69

We Love Glenda So Much, and Other Tales (Cortazar)
See *Queremos tanto a Glenda*

"We Often Think of Lenin in The Clothespin Factory" (Davenport) **16**:198

We're Friends Again (O'Hara) **15**:250-51, 272

"The Werewolf" (Carter) **13**:5, 7, 27

Wessex Tales (Hardy) **2**:202-03, 205, 212, 214-15, 220, 223, 225-26, 229

"The Westbound Train" (Cather) **2**:102

"West End" (Aiken) **9**:9, 12, 14

The Western Stories of Stephen Crane (Crane) **7**:153

"A West Indian Slave Insurrection" (Cable) **4**:59, 75

"Westminster Abbey" (Irving) **2**:244-45, 250-51

"Westward" (Levi) **12**:278-79

"A Wet Night" (Beckett) **16**:65, 92-3

"Whacky" (Clarke) **3**:134

"Whales Weep" (Boyle) **16**:146

"The Whale Tooth" (London) **4**:266

"The Wharf" (de la Mare) **14**:80, 82, 88, 90

"What a Misfortune" (Beckett) **16**:69, 92

"What a Thing, to Keep a Wolf in a Cage!" (Calisher) **15**:3

"What Death with Love Should Have to Do" (Oates) **6**:224, 226

"What Do You Do in San Francisco?" (Carver) **8**:32, 34

"What Do You Mean It Was Brillig?" (Thurber) **1**:428

"What Do You See, Madam?" (Barnes) **3**:18

"What Dreams May Come" (de la Mare) **14**:80, 83, 84

"What Father Does is Always Right" (Andersen) **6**:18, 26, 30

"What Goes Up" (Clarke) **3**:134

What I Know So Far (Lish) **18**:266-68, 270, 274, 278, 280, 284

"What I Saw of Shiloh" (Bierce) **9**:98-9

"What Is It?" (Carver) **8**:4, 10, 32

"What Is Left to Link Us" (Lish) **18**:284

"What Kind of Day Did You Have?" (Bellow) **14**:41-2, 50-1, 53-6, 58

"What Men Live By" (Tolstoy) **9**:387

"What's in Alaska?" (Carver) **8**:7, 10-11, 32, 34, 53

"What the Nightingale Sang" (Zoshchenko) **15**:387, 395

"What the Shepherd Saw" (Hardy) **2**:210

"What Was Mine" (Beattie) **11**:30-1

What Was Mine, and Other Stories (Beattie) **11**:30-2,

"What Were You Dreaming?" (Gordimer) **17**:183, 188-89

"What We Talk about When We Talk about Love" (Carver) **8**:15, 17-23, 26, 30, 32, 34, 37-44, 46-8, 51, 56-9

What We Talk about When We Talk about Love (Carver) **8**:13, 15, 17-23, 26, 30, 32, 37-40, 43-4, 46, 48, 56-9

"What You Hear from 'Em?" (Taylor) **10**:379, 396, 399, 401, 407, 411, 415

"What You Want" (Henry) **5**:187

"The Wheelbarrow" (Pritchett) **14**:268, 280, 287

The Wheel of Love, and Other Stories (Oates) **6**:247

"Wheels" (Dixon) **16**:208

"Wheels" (McGahern) **17**:301-02, 307-09, 318, 323-24

"When Alice Told Her Soul" (London) **4**:257, 270

"When Everyone Was Pregnant" (Updike) **13**:358, 387

"When God Laughs" (London) **4**:253

When God Laughs, and Other Stories (London) **4**:253-54

"When It Happens" (Atwood) **2**:4, 6-7, 10, 13, 16

"When I Was a Witch" (Gilman) **13**:125

"When My Girl Comes Home" (Pritchett) **14**:261, 266-67, 301

When My Girl Comes Home (Pritchett) **14**:267, 286

"When the Dead Rise from Their Graves" (Bulgakov) **18**:90

"When the Light Gets Green" (Warren) **4**:389-90, 394, 396, 399, 401

"When the Sun Went Down" (Lawson) **18**:198, 239

"When the Waters Were Up at Jules" (Harte) **8**:214

When the World Screamed (Doyle) **12**:81

"When We Were Nearly Young" (Gallant) **5**:148

"Where Are You Going, Where Have You Been?" (Oates) **6**:238, 244-46

"Where I Lived, and What I Lived For" (Oates) **6**:225, 234-35

"Where I'm Calling From" (Carver) **8**:17, 26-8, 32, 51

Where I'm Calling From: New and Selected Stories (Carver) **8**:41, 45-6, 48-50, 55, 57, 59-61

"Where Is Everyone?" (Carver) **8**:18, 32, 59-60

"Where It Was, There I Must Begin to Be" (Davenport)
See "Wo es war, soll ich werden"

"Where Love Is, God Is" (Tolstoy) **9**:387

"Where Tawe Flows" (Thomas) **3**:397, 406, 411-12

"Where the Cloud Breaks" (Bates) **10**:139

"Where the Eagles Dwell" (Valenzuela)
See "Up Among the Eagles"

"Where the Trail Forks" (London) **4**:258, 286

Where You'll Find Me, and Other Stories (Beattie) **11**:25, 28-9, 32

"Which Is the True One?" (Baudelaire)
See "Laquelle est la vraie?"

"Which New Era Would That Be?" (Gordimer) **17**:153, 161

"Which Was It?" (Twain) **6**:331-34, 337, 350

"Which Was the Dream?" (Twain) **6**:331-34, 337, 340, 350

"While the Auto Waits" (Henry) **5**:158, 189

While the Billy Boils (Lawson) **18**:198; 200, 208, 215, 248-50, 254, 257, 259, 261-62

Whilomville Stories (Crane) **7**:104

"The Whimper of Whipped Dogs" (Ellison) **14**:105, 118

"The Whip-Poor-Will" (Thurber) **1**:422

Whirligigs (Henry) **5**:182

"The Whisperer in Darkness" (Lovecraft) **3**:258-60, 263, 269-71, 274-75, 278-80, 284, 291, 294

"The Whistle" (Welty) **1**:468

"Whistling Dick's Christmas Stocking" (Henry) **5**:161, 170

"The White Cat of Drumgunniol" (Le Fanu) **14**:223

"The White Counterpane" (Dunbar) **8**:127, 134

"White Dump" (Munro) **3**:347-49

"The White Eagle" (Chopin) **8**:99

"The White Flower" (Kawabata) **17**:251

"White Girl, Fine Girl" (Grau) **15**:149, 156

"The White Goddess and the Mealie Question" (Gordimer) **17**:153

"A White Heron" (Jewett) **6**:157, 160, 170-73

A White Heron, and Other Stories (Jewett) **6**:171

"The White Horses of Vienna" (Boyle) **5**:63-4

"The White Man's Way" (London) **4**:253

"White Nights" (Dostoevsky) **2**:171-72

"The White Old Maid" (Hawthorne) **3**:154, 159, 180-81

"The White Pony" (Bates) **10**:132

"The White Quail" (Steinbeck) **11**:207-08, 221, 225, 227-28, 230, 233-36

"The White Rabbit" (Pritchett) **14**:269

"The White Rabbit Caper" (Thurber) **1**:431

"The White Sea" (Kipling) **5**:293

"The White Silence" (London) **4**:250-51, 258, 267, 277, 281-84, 287-88

"White Spot" (Anderson) **1**:52

"The White Stocking" (Lawrence) **4**:198, 202, 230

"Who Am I This Time?" (Vonnegut)
See "My Name is Everyone"

"Who Do You Think You Are?" (Munro) **3**:343

Who Do You Think You Are? (*The Beggar Maid: Stories of Flo and Rose*) (Munro) **3**:333, 335-40, 342-43, 345-47

"Who Do You Wish Was with Us" (Thomas) **3**:395, 398, 403, 406, 411-12

"Whoever Was Using This Bed" (Carver) **8**:43

"Who Has Seen the Wind" (McCullers) 332, 342-44, 347, 354, 360

"Who Is This Tom Scarlett?" (Barnes) **3**:18

"The Whole World Knows" (Welty) **1**:474, 479-80, 483

"Who Made Yellow Roses Yellow?" (Updike) **13**:355

"The Whosis Kid" (Hammett) **17**:219, 221

"Who's Passing for Who?" ("Passing") (Hughes) **6**:132, 141

"Who Stand for the Gods" (Dunbar) **8**:122

"Who's There" (Clarke) **3**:134

"Why Don't You Dance" (Carver) **8**:32, 37, 42-3, 47-8, 51

"Why Heisherik Was Born" (Singer) **3**:385, 387

"Why Honey?" (Carver) **8**:32

"Why I Live at the P. O." (Welty) **1**:465, 468-69, 471, 476-79, 482, 489, 494, 497

"Why I Want to Fuck Ronald Reagan" (Ballard) **1**:70, 75, 82

"Why the Little Frenchman Wears His Arm in a Sling" (Poe) **1**:407

"Why the Waves Have Whitecaps" (Hurston) **4**:140

"Why, You Reckon?" (Hughes) **6**:118, 132

"The Wide Net" (Welty) **1**:467, 469, 471, 494

The Wide Net, and Other Stories (Welty) **1**:466-68, 471, 482, 496

"The Widow" (Babel) **16**:26, 50, 53-4, 58

"The Widow and Her Son" (Irving) **2**:240-41, 251

"The Widower" (Schnitzler)
See "Der wittwer"

"Widows" (Baudelaire)
See "Les veuves"

"The Widow's Might" (Gilman) **13**:126

The Widows of Thornton (Taylor) **10**:388-89, 411, 415

"The Widow's Ordeal" (Irving) **2**:241

"Widow's Walk" (Grau) **15**:163

"The Wife" (Irving) **2**:240-41, 243, 245, 251

"The Wife-Killer" (Singer) **3**:358

"The Wife of a King" (London) **4**:258, 282, 284, 286

"The Wife of Another and the Husband under the Bed" (Dostoevsky) **2**:171, 193

"The Wife of his Youth" (Chesnutt) **7**:2, 15-16, 23, 33-7

The Wife of his Youth, and Other Stories of the Color Line (Chesnutt) **7**:2-3, 15, 19, 21-3, 26, 30, 33, 37-8

"A Wife of Nashville" (Taylor) **10**:415-16

"The Wife of the Autumn Wind" (Kawabata) **17**:252

"The Wife of Usher's Well" (James) **16**:234

"The Wife's Story" (Le Guin) **12**:235

"Wife-Wooing" (Updike) **13**:348-50, 373, 384, 395

"The Wild Goat's Kid" (O'Flaherty) **6**:260, 262, 264, 268-69

"A Wild Irishman" (Lawson) **18**:206

The Wild Palms (Faulkner) **1**:159-61, 167-68

"The Wild Swan" (O'Flaherty) **6**:268

The Wild Swan, and Other Stories (O'Flaherty) **6**:259, 271

"The Wild Swans" (Andersen) **6**:13, 19, 30, 35, 40

"The Will" (Lavin) **4**:165-66

Willa Cather's Collected Short Fiction (Cather) **2**:103, 105

"Will as a Boy" (Dixon) **16**:215

"Willi" (Gallant) **5**:138

"William Bacon's Man" (Garland) **18**:148

"William Reilly and the Fates" (Benet) **10**:160

"William's Wedding" (Jewett) **6**:180

"William the Conqueror" (Kipling) **5**:283

"William Wilson" (Poe) **1**:378, 385-86, 394-97, 407

Willie Masters' Lonesome Wife (Gass) **12**:125, 128, 141-46, 148-50, 152-53

"Willie Winkie" (Andersen) **6**:24

"The Willing Muse" (Cather) **2**:98, 103

"Will o' the Mill" (Stevenson) **11**:268-69, 281

"Willows" (de la Mare) **14**:71

"The Will to Happiness" (Mann) **5**:322-23

"Will You Please Be Quiet, Please?" (Carver) **8**:3-4, 7, 10-11, 18-19, 22, 32

Will You Please Be Quiet, Please? (Carver) **8**:3-6, 17-18, 26, 29, 32, 34, 45, 50, 54

"Will You Tell Me" (Barthelme) **2**:27

"The Wind at Beni Midar" (Bowles) **3**:64, 85

"The Wind Blows" ("Autumn II") (Mansfield) **9**:282, 284, 302, 305

The Wind Blows Over (de la Mare) **14**:89, 92

The Wind Blows Over (de la Mare) **14**:89, 92

"The Windowpane Check" (O'Hara) **15**:283

"The Winds" (Welty) **1**:472

"The Wind Shifting West" (Grau) **15**:148, 152, 150, 164

"The Wind Shifting West" (Grau) **15**:

The Wind Shifting West (Grau) **15**:147-48, 152, 154, 160-61

"The Wind's Tale" (Andersen)
    See "The Wind Tells of Valdemar Daae and His Daughters"

The Wind's Twelve Quarters (Le Guin) **12**:209, 212, 219, 224, 231, 234, 245

"The Wind Tells of Valdemar Daae and His Daughters" ("Waldemar Daa and His Daughters"; "The Wind's Tale"; "The Wind Tells the Story of Valdemar Daa and his Daughters") (Andersen) **6**:12, 15, 18, 24

"The Wind Tells the Story of Valdemar Daa and his Daughters" (Andersen)
    See "The Wind Tells of Valdemar Daae and His Daughters"

"Windy Day at the Reservoir" (Beattie) **11**:30-1, 34

"The Wine Breath" (McGahern) **17**:304, 309, 319, 322

Winesburg, Ohio (Anderson) **1**:17-19, 22, 24-35, 38-46, 48, 51-2, 55, 57-8

Winner Take Nothing (Hemingway) **1**:211, 216-17

"Winter" (Dubus) **15**:96

"Winter" (Gilchrist) **14**:163-64

"Winter: 1978" (Beattie) **11**:9, 23-4

"Winter Cruise" (Maugham) **8**:380

"Winter Dreams" (Fitzgerald) **6**:46, 59, 66, 69, 76, 88, 90-1, 100, 102, 104

"The Winter Father" (Dubus) **15**:75, 82

"Winter in July" (Lessing) **6**:186, 191, 213-14, 217-18

"Winter Night" (Boyle) **5**:55

"The Winter of Artifice" (Nin) **10**:309-12, 314-17, 319-20, 323

The Winter of Artifice (Nin) **10**:300-02, 305-06, 317, 319, 322, 324

"The Winters and the Palmeys" (Hardy) **2**:207, 209

"Winter's King" (Le Guin) **12**:231-32

Winter's Tales (*Vinter-Eventyr*) (Dinesen) **7**:164, 166, 170-71, 175, 180, 193, 195-96, 199-200, 205, 208

"Winter Wind" (Munro) **3**:331

"Wintry Peacock" (Lawrence) **4**:231, 234-35

"Wiosna" ("Spring") (Schulz) **13**:327

"Wireless" (Kipling) **5**:266, 275, 280

The Wisdom of Father Brown (Chesterton) **1**:120-21, 124

"The Wisdom of Silence" (Dunbar) **8**:122, 126, 132, 135, 146

"The Wisdom of the Trail" (London) **4**:282-85, 288

"Wise Guy" (O'Hara) **15**:264

"The Wise Men" (Crane) **7**:101, 126

"Wiser than a God" (Chopin) **8**:69-70, 73, 84, 99

"The Wish House" (Kipling) **5**:275, 280-81

"The Witch" (Jackson) **9**:255-56

"The Witch" (Singer) **3**:377

"The Witch a La Mode" (Lawrence) **4**:220

"Witches Loaves" (Henry) **5**:184

"The Withered Arm" (Hardy) **2**:202-03, 205, 208, 213-14, 217-20, 227-28, 231-34

"With Justifiable Pride" (Cortazar)
    See "Con legítimo orgullo"

"With Old Man Makhno" (Babel) **16**:22

"Without a Hero" (Boyle) **16**:156-57

Without a Hero, and Other Stories (Boyle) **16**:156-57

"Without Benefit of Clergy" (Kipling) **5**:262, 291, 295-97, 299

"Without Colors" (Calvino) **3**:104, 108-09

"With the Night Mail" (Kipling) **5**:268

"The Witness" (Porter) **4**:339-40, 358

"The Witnesses" (Cortazar)
    See "Los testigos"

"The Witnesses" (Updike) **13**:358

"Der wittwer" ("The Widower") (Schnitzler) **15**:345, 376-77

"The Wives of the Dead" (Hawthorne) **3**:159, 164, 186

Wodehouse on Crime (Wodehouse) **2**:352

"Wo es war, soll ich werden" ("Where It Was, There I Must Begin to Be") (Davenport) **16**:199-200

"The Wolf" (Hesse) **9**:230, 235

"Wolf Alice" (Carter) **13**:7, 9, 27-8

"Wolf Dreams" (Beattie) **11**:11, 19-20

"Wolfert's Roost" (Irving) **2**:246

"Wolfert Webber" (Irving) **2**:241, 247, 249, 251-52, 262, 266, 268

"Wolf Lonigan's Death" (O'Flaherty) **6**:261, 276, 280

"The Wolves of Cernogratz" (Saki) **12**:306, 317, 329

"The Woman at the Store" (Mansfield) **9**:281, 284, 302, 305

"The Woman-Hater" (Aiken) **9**:5, 14

"A Woman of Fifty" (Maugham) **8**:380

A Woman of Means (Taylor) **10**:379, 388

Woman of the River (Alegria)
    See "A Temple of the Holy Ghost"

"A Woman on a Roof" (Lessing) **6**:199, 206

"A Woman's Kingdom" (Chekhov) **2**:156-57

"A Woman's Revenge" (Barbey d'Aurevilly)
    See "La vengeance d'une femme"

"The Woman Who Came at Six O'Clock" (Garcia Marquez) **8**:172, 183, 185

The Woman Who Could Not Read, and Other Tales (Zoshchenko) **15**:388, 390

"The Woman Who Had Imagination" (Bates) **10**:130

The Woman Who Had Imagination, and Other Stories (Bates) **10**:112

"The Woman Who Married Clark Gable" (O'Faolain) **13**:293, 322

"The Woman Who Rode Away" (Lawrence) **4**:219, 226, 239

The Woman Who Rode Away, and Other Stories (Lawrence) **4**:230

"The Woman Who Was Everybody" (Calisher) **15**:2, 5

"A Woman with a Past" (Fitzgerald) **6**:50

"A Woman without a Country" (Cheever) **1**:95, 100

"A Woman, Young and Old" (Paley) **8**:388, 390, 396, 398

"Women" (Singer) **3**:358

"The Women of Madison Avenue" (O'Hara) **15**:282

"Women, Politics and Murder" (Hammett) **17**:200

"A Women's Restaurant" (Boyle) **16**:140-42

"The Wonderful Old Gentleman" (Parker) **2**:274, 281, 283

Wonder Stories Told for Children (Andersen)
    See *Eventyr, fortalte for bøorn*

Wonder Tales (Andersen)
    See *Eventyr, fortalte for bøorn*

Wonder Tales for Children (Andersen)
    See *Eventyr, fortalte for bøorn*

"The Wood Duck" (Thurber) **1**:414, 422

"The Wooden Dove of Archytas" (Davenport) **16**:178, 192

"The Woodfelling" (Tolstoy) **9**:375

The Word for World Is Forest (Le Guin) **12**:207-10, 216, 219, 223, 234, 242-43

"The Word of Unbinding" (Le Guin) **12**:231-32

"The Word Processor of the Gods" (King) **17**:276

"Work, Death, and Sickness" (Tolstoy) **9**:388

"The Working Girl" (Beattie) **11**:33

"The Working Party" (Bowen) **3**:30, 40, 49

"The Work on Red Mountain" (Harte) **8**:231, 254

"The World and the Door" (Henry) **5**:182

The World Is Too Much With Us (Bates) **10**:124

"The World of Apples" (Cheever) **1**:112

The World of Apples (Cheever) **1**:97-8, 101

"The World (This One), the Flesh (Mrs. Oedipa Maas), and the Testament of Pierce Inverarity" (Pynchon) **14**:308

"A Worn Path" (Welty) **1**:466, 470, 491-92, 494

"Worship" (Atwood) **2**:20

"The Worst Crime in the World" (Chesterton) **1**:129, 138

"The Worst Thing of All" (Gordimer) **17**:155

Worstward Ho (Beckett) **16**:109, 129-34

"Would You Do It for a Penny?" (Ellison) **14**:126

"The Wounded Cormorant" (O'Flaherty) **6**:260, 262, 268, 282-83

Wounds in the Rain: A Collection of Stories Relating to the Spanish-American War of 1898 (Crane) **7**:104, 108

"Wratislaw" (Saki) **12**:317

"The Wreath" (O'Connor) **5**:372, 389

"Wrens and Starlings" (Powers) **4**:380

"The Wren's Nest" (O'Flaherty) **6**:274, 279

"Wressley of the Foreign Office" (Kipling) **5**:279

"The Wrong House" (Mansfield) **9**:279

"The Wrong Shape" (Chesterton) **1**:121, 129-30, 136

"The Wrong Trousers" (Bulgakov) **18**:90

"Wunderkind" (McCullers) **9**:322, 332, 342-43, 345, 347-48, 350, 354-55

Das Wunderkind (*The Infant Prodigy*) (Mann) **5**:324, 330-31

"Xingu" (Wharton) **6**:418, 422, 428-29, 437

Xingu, and Other Stories (Wharton) **6**:417-19, 421, 435

"Yah! Yah! Yah!" (London) **4**:266

Yakov Pasynkov (*Jacob Pasinkov*) (Turgenev) **7**:314, 320, 324

"The Yankee Fox" (Benet) **10**:150

"Ya no quedan esperanzas de" ("There Is No Hope for That") (Cortazar) **7**:95

"The Yelagin Affair" (Bunin)
    See "The Elaghin Affair"

"Yellow" (Beckett) **16**:70

"The Yellow Beret" (Lavin) **4**:167

"The Yellow Bird" (Chesterton) **1**:124-25, 133

"A Yellow Flower" (Cortazar)
   See "Una flor amarilla"

"The Yellow Gown" (Anderson) **1**:52

"The Yellow Streak" (Maugham) **8**:367, 372

"The Yellow Wallpaper" (Gilman) **13**:118-19, 121-25, 128-41, 145, 147-62, 166, 168, 170-71, 175

"Yentl the Yeshiva Boy" (Singer) **3**:359, 384

"Yermolai and the Miller's Wife" ("Ermolai and the Miller's Wife") (Turgenev) **7**:342

"Les yeux des pauvres" ("The Eyes of the Poor") (Baudelaire) **18**:4, 6, 33, 47-51, 53

"Yostie" (O'Hara) **15**:278, 283

"You Are Not I" (Bowles) **3**:59-61, 66, 68-9, 72, 76-7

"You Can Always Tell Newark" (O'Hara) **15**:251

You Can't Keep a Good Woman Down (Walker) **5**:412-14

"You Have Left Your Lotus Pods on the Bus" (Bowles) **3**:69

"You Know They Got a Hell of a Band" (King) **17**:294-95

"You Know What" (Beattie) **11**:30, 33-4

"You Make Your Own Life" (Pritchett) **14**:269, 271, 297

You Make Your Own Life (Pritchett) **14**:269, 293

"You Must Know Everything" (Babel) **16**:34

You Must Know Everything: Stories, 1915-1937 (Babel) **16**:34

"You Must Remember This" (Coover) **15**:61-2

"You Name It" (Gordimer) **17**:194

"The Young Aunt with the White Hair" (Cable) **4**:49

"The Young Girl" (Mansfield) **9**:279, 310

"The Young Glory of Him" (Hughes) **6**:127

"Young Goodman Brown" (Hawthorne) **3**:164-68, 171-74, 177-78, 180, 182-83, 185-87, 189, 191-93

"The Young Italian" (Irving)
   See "The Story of the Young Italian"

"The Young King" (Wilde) **11**:364, 373, 375-76, 381-82, 384-86, 394-97, 407-09

"Young Lochinvar" (Benet) **10**:150

"The Young Man from Kalgoorlie" (Bates) **10**:113, 139

"The Young Man with the Carnation" (Dinesen) **7**:164, 191-92, 194, 198

Young Men in Spats (Wodehouse) **2**:325, 328

"The Young Robber" (Irving)
   See "The Story of the Young Robber"

"Young Robin Gray" (Harte) **8**:223

"A Young Woman in Green Lace" (Parker) **2**:273, 283

"Your Lover Just Called" (Updike) **13**:387

Your Lover Just Called: Stories of Joan and Richard Maple (Updike)
   See *Too Far to Go: The Maples Stories*

"Your Most Profound Skin" (Cortazar)
   See "Tu más profunda piel"

"Your Obituary, Well Written" (Aiken) **9**:4-5, 7, 12, 14, 30, 34

"You Should Have Seen the Mess" (Spark) **10**:350, 355, 359, 363, 369

"Youth" (Conrad) **9**:140, 143-44, 146-47, 152, 157, 160-66, 171, 175-78

Youth (Tolstoy)
   See *Yunost*

Youth: A Narrative, and Two Other Stories (Conrad) **9**:151

Youth and the Bright Medusa (Cather) **2**:91-2, 94, 98, 103, 111-13

"You Touched Me" (Lawrence) **4**:203-04, 231, 233-36

"You Were Perfectly Fine" (Parker) **2**:272, 278, 281

"You Were Too Trusting, Captain" (Babel) **16**:22

"Yowaki Utsuwa" ("The Weaker Sex") (Kawabata) **17**:247

"Yucca Knolls" (O'Hara) **15**:259

"Yugashima no Omoide" ("Memories of Yugashima") (Kawabata) **17**:249-50

Yunost (*Youth*) (Tolstoy) **9**:375

"Yveline Samoris" (Maupassant) **1**:283

"Yvette" (Maupassant) **1**:263, 275, 283

"Zagrowsky Tells" (Paley) **8**:412

"El Zahir" ("The Zahir") (Borges) **4**:10, 25

"The Zahir" (Borges)
   See "El Zahir"

Zakat (*Sunset*) (Babel) **16**:35

"Zakoldovannoe mesto" ("The Bewitched Spot"; "The Charmed Spot"; "The Enchanted Spot") (Gogol) **4**:117, 121

"Zamostye" (Babel) **16**:27, 54, 57-8

Zapiski iunogo vracha (*A Country Doctor's Notebook*; *The Notes of a Young Doctor*) (Bulgakov) **18**:75, 86, 88-9

Zapiski iz podpol'ya (*Letters from the Underworld*; *Memoirs from Underground*; *Notes from the Underground*) (Dostoevsky) **2**:164-65, 168, 172-73, 178-83, 186, 188-89

Zapiski sumasshedshego ("The Diary of a Madman"; *Memoirs of a Madman*) (Tolstoy) **9**:366-68, 377, 388

"Zeal" (Powers) **4**:370

"Zeitl and Rickel" (Singer) **3**:359

"Zetland: By a Character Witness" (Bellow) **14**:41-2

"Zigzags of Treachery" (Hammett) **17**:200

Zimzum (Lish) **18**:285-86

"Zinc" (Levi) **12**:256-57, 259, 262

"Lo zio acquativo" ("The Aquatic Uncle") (Calvino) **3**:92-3, 109

"Z. Marcas" (Balzac) **5**:27, 31, 33

"Zodiac 2000" (Ballard) **1**:79

"Zone of Terror" (Ballard) **1**:68

"Zooey" (Salinger) **2**:291, 293-94, 296-97, 302-05, 308

Title Index